PRINCIPLES OF MARKETING

third edition

PRINCIPLES OF MARKETING

Dr Frances Brassington

Senior Lecturer
Buckinghamshire Chilterns University College

Dr Stephen Pettitt

Deputy Vice Chancellor
University of Luton

An imprint of Pearson Education
Harlow, England • London • New York • Boston • San Francisco • Toronto
Sydney • Tokyo • Singapore • Hong Kong • Seoul • Taipei • New Delhi
Cape Town • Madrid • Mexico City • Amsterdam • Munich • Paris • Milan

To Adam Stephen Philip,
Brassington and Pettitt's finest edition yet.

Pearson Education Limited
Edinburgh Gate
Harlow
Essex CM20 2JE
England

and Associated Companies throughout the world

Visit us on the World Wide Web at:
www.pearsoneduc.com

First published under the Pitman Publishing imprint 1997
Second edition 2000
Third edition 2003

ISBN 0 273 65791 7

British Library Cataloguing-in-Publication Data
A catalogue record for this book is available from the British Library.

Library of Congress Cataloging-in-Publication Data
A catalog record for this book is available from the Library of Congress.

10 9 8 7 6 5 4 3 2 1
08 07 06 05 04 03

Typeset by 30 in 9.5/11.5 pt ITC Century Book
Printed and bound by Rotolito Lombarda, Italy

brief contents

part one **MARKETING AND ITS ENVIRONMENT** 1

1 Marketing dynamics 3
2 The European marketing environment 44

part two **CUSTOMERS AND MARKETS** 91

3 Consumer behaviour 93
4 B2B buying behaviour 135
5 Segmenting markets 179
6 Marketing information and research 212

part three **PRODUCT** 265

7 Anatomy of a product 267
8 Product management 311
9 New product development 350

part four **PRICE** 389

10 Pricing: contexts and concepts 391
11 Pricing strategies 427

part five **PLACE** 469

12 Marketing channels and logistics 471
13 Retailers and wholesalers 522

part six **PROMOTION** 567

14 Integrated marketing communication 569
15 Advertising 603
16 Sales promotion 652
17 Personal selling and sales management 694
18 Direct marketing and exhibitions 739
19 Public relations and sponsorship 792

part seven **MARKETING MANAGEMENT** 837

20 Strategic marketing 839
21 Marketing planning, management and control 895
22 Services and non-profit marketing 950
23 International marketing 1006
24 E-marketing and new media 1053

contents

Guided tour xii
Preface xv
About the authors xix
Acknowledgements xxi

part one

MARKETING AND ITS ENVIRONMENT

1 Marketing dynamics 3

Learning objectives 3
Introduction 3
Marketing defined 4
The marketing concept in the organisation 20
Marketing management responsibilities 24
Marketing scope 32
Chapter summary 35
Key words and phrases 36
Questions for review 36
Questions for discussion 36
Case study 1.1 *Showing the customer who's Boss* 36
Case study 1.2 *lastminute.com: inspiration and solutions* 39
References 41

2 The European marketing environment 44

Learning objectives 44
Introduction 44
The nature of the European marketing environment 45
The sociocultural environment 48
The technological environment 59
The economic and competitive environment 67
The political and legal environment 76
Chapter summary 85
Key words and phrases 86
Questions for review 86
Questions for discussion 86
Case study 2.1 *Sanpro* 86
Case study 2.2 *A friend in need is a friend indeed* 88
References 89

part two

CUSTOMERS AND MARKETS

3 Consumer behaviour 93

Learning objectives 93
Introduction 93
The decision-making process 95
Buying situations 104
Environmental influences 107
Psychological influences: the individual 109
Sociocultural influences: the group 118
Chapter summary 129
Key words and phrases 129
Questions for review 130
Questions for discussion 130
Case study 3.1 *Reaching the youth market: Euroteens* 130
Case study 3.2 *Breezing out for a night on the tiles* 132
References 133

4 B2B buying behaviour 135

Learning objectives 135
Introduction 135
Defining B2B marketing 136
B2B customers 138
Characteristics of B2B markets 141
Buying decision-making process 151
Roles in the buying process 157
The buying centre 160
Buying criteria 163
The changing nature of supply chains 167
Chapter summary 171
Key words and phrases 172
Questions for review 172
Questions for discussion 172
Case study 4.1 *Alstom China* 172
Case study 4.2 *Fairtrade: playing fair with third-world suppliers* 175
References 177

5 Segmenting markets 179

Learning objectives 179
Introduction 179
The concept of segmentation 180
Segmenting B2B markets 181
Segmenting consumer markets 183
Implementation of segmentation 197
Benefits of segmentation 203
Dangers of segmentation 203
Criteria for successful segmentation 204
Chapter summary 205
Key words and phrases 206
Questions for review 206
Questions for discussion 207
Case study 5.1 *Neu Engineering* 207
Case study 5.2 *The pink pound* 208
References 210

6 Marketing information and research 212

Learning objectives 212
Introduction 212
Marketing research: definition and role 213
Types of research 216
Marketing information systems 221
Decision support systems 225
The marketing research process 226
Secondary research 230
Primary research 232
Ethics in marketing research 256
Chapter summary 258
Key words and phrases 259
Questions for review 259
Questions for discussion 259
Case study 6.1 *Kings Hotel* 260
Case study 6.2 *Gathering information on an up-and-coming market* 261
References 263

part three

PRODUCT

7 Anatomy of a product 267

Learning objectives 267
Introduction 267
Meaning of a product 268
Product classification 270
Understanding the product range 276
Branding 279
Packaging 293
Product design, quality and guarantees 298
Chapter summary 303
Key words and phrases 304
Questions for review 304
Questions for discussion 304
Case study 7.1 *Is small still beautiful second time around?* 305
Case study 7.2 *The market with stiffening competition* 306
References 308

8 Product management 311

Learning objectives 311
Introduction 311
The product lifecycle 312
Market evolution 322
Managing the product mix 328
Customer specified products 337
Product management and organisation 339
European product strategy 340
Chapter summary 342
Key words and phrases 343
Questions for review 343
Questions for discussion 344
Case study 8.1 *Playing the game* 344
Case study 8.2 *Diamonds are no longer a girl's best friend* 346
References 348

9 New product development 350

Learning objectives 350
Introduction 350
The meaning of a new product 351
The importance of new product development 356
The new product development process 358
New product failure 374
Trends in NPD process management 376
Chapter summary 381
Key words and phrases 382
Questions for review 382
Questions for discussion 382
Case study 9.1 *The 3G revolution . . . but not yet* 382
Case study 9.2 *Because we're worth it* 383
References 384

part four

PRICE

10 Pricing: context and concepts 391

Learning objectives 391
Introduction 391
The role and perception of price 392
Pricing contexts 396
External influences on the pricing decision 401
Internal influences on the pricing decision 412
The European influence on pricing 415
Chapter summary 421
Key words and phrases 421
Questions for review 421
Questions for discussion 422
Case study 10.1 *Kitting out the fans* 422
Case study 10.2 *The white stuff* 423
References 425

11 Pricing strategies 427

Learning objectives 427
Introduction 427
Pricing objectives 428
Pricing policies and strategies 435
Setting the price range 443
Pricing tactics and adjustments 453
Issues in pricing 456
Chapter summary 461
Key words and phrases 461
Questions for review 462
Questions for discussion 462
Case study 11.1 *Measuring up to the supplier's expectations* 462
Case study 11.2 *Driving pricing decisions* 463
References 466

part five
PLACE

12 Marketing channels and logistics 471

Learning objectives 471
Introduction 471
Definition of marketing channels 472
Channel strategy 484
Channel structure 490
Behavioural aspects of channels 494
The nature of physical distribution and logistics 500
Customer service concept 509
Chapter summary 514
Key words and phrases 515
Questions for review 515
Questions for discussion 515
Case study 12.1 *Sweet harmony in the distribution channel* 516
Case study 12.2 *French hypermarkets and their smaller suppliers* 518
References 519

13 Retailers and wholesalers 522

Learning objectives 522
Introduction 522
The nature of retailing and wholesaling 523
The structure of the European retail sector 527
Types of retailer 533
Non-store retailing 543
Retailer strategy 545
Wholesalers and distributors 559
Chapter summary 560
Key words and phrases 561
Questions for review 561
Questions for discussion 561
Case study 13.1 *On time every time: the key components of success* 562
Case study 13.2 *Amazon: a pioneering adventurer in e-tailing* 563
References 565

part six
PROMOTION

14 Integrated marketing communication 569

Learning objectives 569
Introduction 569
Communications theory 571
Communications planning model 577
Communications planning model: review 596
Chapter summary 596
Key words and phrases 597
Questions for review 597
Questions for discussion 597
Case study 14.1 *Xbox: the mean green machine* 598
Case study 14.2 *Alliance & Leicester: banking on good communications* 600
References 602

15 Advertising 603

Learning objectives 603
Introduction 603
The role of advertising in the promotional mix 604
Formulating the advertising message 610
Advertising media 621
Using advertising agencies 631
Developing an advertising campaign 634
Chapter summary 643
Key words and phrases 644
Questions for review 645
Questions for discussion 645
Case study 15.1 *Announcing a new arrival* 645
Case study 15.2 *Driving a sober message home* 648
References 650

16 Sales promotion 652

Learning objectives 652
Introduction 652
The role and definition of sales promotion 653
Consumer sales promotion methods (1): money-based 661
Consumer sales promotion methods (2): product-based 665
Consumer sales promotion methods (3): gift, prize, or merchandise based 671
Consumer sales promotion methods (4): store-based 677
Methods of promotion to the retail trade 678
Sales promotion to B2B markets 683
Managing sales promotion 683
Chapter summary 688
Key words and phrases 689
Questions for review 689
Questions for discussion 689
Case study 16.1 *Learning to manage your money* 689
Case study 16.2 *Pennies off the price or points on the plastic?* 691
References 693

17 Personal selling and sales management 694

Learning objectives 694
Introduction 694
The definition and role of personal selling 695
Tasks of the sales representative 699
Forms of personal selling 703

The personal selling process 708
Sales management 720
Chapter summary 732
Key words and phrases 733
Questions for review 733
Questions for discussion 733
Case study 17.1 *Colomer: Spanish leather* 734
Case study 17.2 *Irish Fire Products* 736
References 737

18 Direct marketing and exhibitions 739
Learning objectives 739
Introduction 739
The definition of direct marketing 740
The rise of direct marketing 741
Techniques of direct marketing 744
The role of direct marketing in the promotional mix 769
Managing a direct marketing campaign 770
Database creation and management 775
Trade shows and exhibitions 777
Chapter summary 784
Key words and phrases 785
Questions for review 786
Questions for discussion 786
Case study 18.1 *Camp followers* 786
Case study 18.2 *'The Big Country'* 788
References 790

19 Public relations and sponsorship 792
Learning objectives 792
Introduction 792
The definition of public relations 793
The role of public relations 797
Techniques in public relations 799
Evaluation 806
Corporate reputation 808
Corporate identity 810
Sponsorship 816
Evaluating sponsorship 829
Chapter summary 830
Key words and phrases 831
Questions for review 831
Questions for discussion 831
Case study 19.1 *'A rose by any other name . . .'* 831
Case study 19.2 *Chicken run* 833
References 835

part seven
MARKETING MANAGEMENT

20 Strategic marketing 839
Learning objectives 839
Introduction 839
Definitions and perspectives 841
Strategic marketing analysis 849
Growth strategies for marketing 858
Marketing and competitive strategy 865
Competitive positions and postures 876
Chapter summary 886
Key words and phrases 887
Questions for review 888
Questions for discussion 888
Case study 20.1 *Prudential (A): An evolving competitive strategy* 888
Case study 20.2 *Stopping the bottom falling out of the jeans market* 891
References 892

21 Marketing planning, management and control 895
Learning objectives 895
Introduction 895
Strategic marketing plans and planning 896
The marketing planning process 900
Market potential and sales forecasting 915
Organising marketing activities 924
Controlling marketing activities 928
Marketing planning for the smaller business 931
Chapter summary 941
Key words and phrases 942
Questions for review 942
Questions for discussion 943
Case study 21.1 *Prudential (B): Moving from strategy to action* 943
Case study 21.2 *Chuft Toys and Gifts* 946
References 948

22 Services and non-profit marketing 950
Learning objectives 950
Introduction 950
Perspectives on service markets 951
Services marketing management 961
Franchising 979
Non-profit marketing 992
Chapter summary 999
Key words and phrases 1000
Questions for review 1000
Questions for discussion 1001
Case study 22.1 *Developing a new franchise proposal: budget-priced hostels* 1001
Case study 22.2 *Full Stop* 1002
References 1004

23 International marketing 1006
Learning objectives 1006
Introduction 1006
The meaning of international marketing 1007
Understanding international markets 1015
Market entry methods 1024
International marketing strategy 1034
Chapter summary 1045
Key words and phrases 1046

Questions for review 1046
Questions for discussion 1046
Case study 23.1 *Going international in banking: standardisation or adaptation?* 1046
Case study 23.2 *Wine wars* 1048
References 1050

24 E-marketing and new media 1053

Learning objectives 1053
Introduction 1053
Internet marketing 1055
Marketing and new media 1075
Chapter summary 1091
Key words and phrases 1092
Questions for review 1092
Questions for discussion 1092
Case study 24.1 *'Here's a bit of marketing for you, son'* 1093
Case study 24.2 *From dotcom to dotbomb to dotboom?* 1094
References 1096

Glossary 1099
Index 1111
Index of company names 1129

guided tour

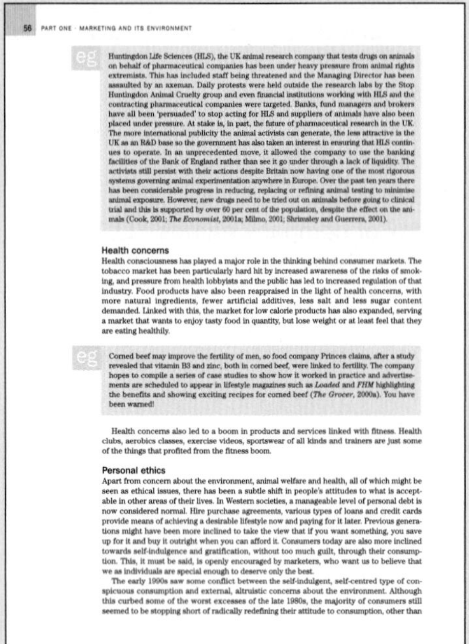

A large number of **examples** are used throughout the text providing engaging illustrations of marketing from a wide variety of industries and countries.

Marketing in action vignettes provide sustained coverage of the practical applications and implications of marketing in the real world.

Corporate social responsibility in action vignettes emphasise the ethical aspects of marketing decisions and practice.

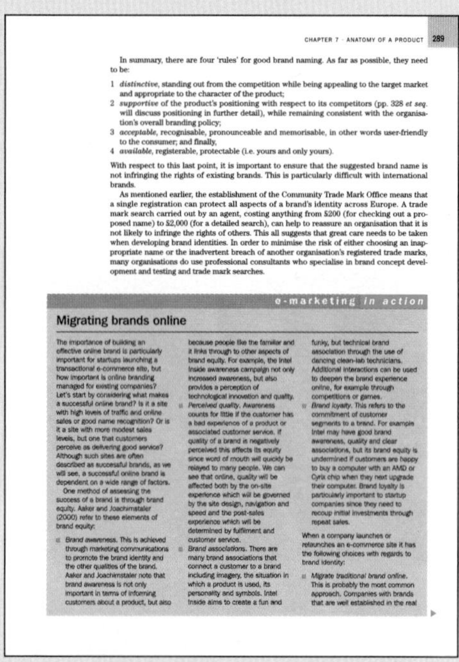

E-marketing in action vignettes provide in-depth coverage of e-marketing and new technology issues.

132 PART TWO · CUSTOMERS AND MARKETS

case study 3.2

Breezing out for a night on the tiles

Since the 1990s, Bacardi-Martini has made a concerted effort to develop new products aimed at a younger market, taking advantage of the growing fashionability and popularity of premium pre-mixed spirit-based drinks among clubbers. In 1995, this sector was worth £20 mn in the UK; by 1999 it had rocketed to £810 mn and estimates for 2000 expected it to break the £1 bn barrier (Mintel, 2000a). The most successful of these pre-packaged spirits (PPS) is Bacardi Breezer, a family of rum and fruit juice drinks (for example lime, lemon, peach, pineapple, watermelon, cranberry). Although launched in 1994, the Breezer brand really became well established in early 1999 when a £5.6 mn advertising campaign targeting 18–24-year-olds assured us 'Bacardi Breezer: there's Latin spirit in everyone.' (Cozens, 1999).

By mid-2000, the advertising spend was £14 mn on what was described as an 'outwardly innocent, inwardly naughty' campaign. James Robinson, account executive on Bacardi at McCann's, was quoted by Brabbs (2000) as saying, 'The ads don't target people – they target a state of mind. Breezer represents a distinctive place in people's night out between beer and spirits – they're neither sober nor wasted on it – and that's what we tried to capture. We were seeking to dramatise the fun and mischievous side that Breezer brings out in you.' The campaign clearly captured the imagination as the brand was worth around £345 mn in 2000, selling nearly one million bottles a day.

In summer 2000, the advertising was further reinforced by the investment of £1.5 mn on the portable *Vivid* tent, 75 ft tall and the length and breadth of a football pitch, for use at events such as music festivals (*Marketing*, 2000). *Vivid* is entered via giant inflatable slides which take consumers to 'pleasure zones' including a glass dance floor made up of TV screens showing tropical fish, a 40 ft helter-skelter, an area with cushions and hammocks, and a games area with table football, air hockey and Quasar. There is also, of course, an ample bar area!

By November 2000, the company estimated that the 'Latin Spirit' campaign had doubled sales volumes of the brand which had become the UK's biggest selling pre-mixed spirit. Its market share by value was almost 40 per cent and it was available in 60 per cent of all UK on-trade outlets (the on-trade sells alcohol for consumption on the premises, for example pubs and clubs, while the off-trade, for example wine shops and supermarkets, sells it for consumption elsewhere) (Mason, 2000). A strong new development was introduced for the run up to Christmas in the character of Tom the cat. Tom lives a normal pampered-puss existence with a sweet little old lady by day, but by night, he's a seasoned cat-about-town clubber, flirting with the girls, hanging round on the bar with the Breezer bottles, and grooving on the dance floor.

Bacardi Breezer also has a dedicated website (http://www.bacardi-breezer.co.uk) which has a strong clubbing theme. The web agency Loudcloud which designed the site said that 'The site will be pretty radical and out there' and that it would provide young adults with 'lunchtime escapism' from the daily routines of work (Chandiramani, 2001).

In a Neilsen report published in March 2001, Bacardi Breezer featured at number 11 in the top twenty best-selling drink brands in pubs in England and Wales. With the exception of Strongbow cider at number nine, the top ten consists of beers and lagers (Young, 2001). The pub and club on-trade is very important to Bacardi Breezer, accounting for 70 per cent of sales volumes. Some 73 per cent of 18–24-year-olds visit a pub or club at least once per week and they are looking for drinks that make fashion and lifestyle statements. Beverage Brands, another key player in the PPS sector said:

> *The highly experimental 18–35-year-olds are seeking more than just a drink, they are constantly looking for a new experience in their drinks repertoire* (as quoted by Mintel, 2000a).

The PPS brands seem to answer well to that need. The use of established 'pedigree' parent brand names such as Bacardi and Smirnoff help to create a quality image which is reinforced by the use of glass packaging. This is also perceived as 'female-friendly'. The brands and the bottles themselves have become fashion statements that drinkers are happy to be 'seen with'. Pubs and clubs like the PPS brands, not only because they are popular, but also because they are

Case studies conclude each chapter, providing an exciting range of material for seminar or private study.

glossary

(Words which are set in *italics* have their own entries in the glossary, where they are further defined.)

4Ps: otherwise known as the *marketing mix*, these are the basic tools of marketing: product, place, price and promotion.

7Ps: an extended *marketing mix* that takes account of the particular characteristics of services markets: product, price, place, promotion, physical evidence, people and processes.

Adaptation: (a) tailoring a product or other aspects of the *marketing mix* to suit the different needs and demands of other markets, usually international; (b) changing production methods or product specifications in a *B2B* market in order to better meet an individual customer's requirements.

Advertising: a paid form of non-personal communication transmitted through a mass medium.

Advertising media: the means through which advertisements are delivered to the target audience. Media include broadcast media, print media, cinema, hoardings and outdoor media.

Advertorial: a form of print *advertising* that is designed to mimic the editorial content, style and *layout* of the publication in which it appears.

Agents and brokers: *intermediaries* who have legal authority to act on behalf of a seller in negotiating sales, but who do not take title to goods themselves.

Alternative currencies: trading stamps, tokens or loyalty scheme points awarded on the basis of the amount spent by the customer that can be accumulated and then exchanged for gifts or discounts.

Ansoff matrix: a framework for considering the relationship between general strategic direction and *marketing strategies*. The four-cell matrix looks at permutations of new/existing products and new/existing markets.

Atmosphere: (a) the elements that come together to make an impact on retail customers' senses as they enter and browse in a store; (b) creating a feeling appropriate to the character of the store and the desired mood of the customers.

Attitude: the stance that individuals take on a subject that predisposes them to act and react in certain ways.

Augmented product: add-on extras that do not form an integral part of the product but which might be used, particularly by retailers, to increase the product's benefits or attractiveness. Includes guarantees, installation, after-sales service, etc.

Awareness: the consciousness that a product or organisation exists.

B2B goods: goods that are sold to organisations for: (a) incorporation into producing other products; or (b) supporting the production of other products directly or indirectly; or (c) resale.

B2B marketing: (also known as industrial marketing or organisational marketing) activities directed towards the *marketing* of goods and services by one organisation to another.

Banner advertising: advertising that appears on a website, usually as a banner across the top of a page that clicks the user through to the advertiser's website.

Behaviour segmentation: grouping consumers in terms of their relationship with the product, for instance their usage rate, the purpose of use, their willingness and readiness to buy, etc.

BIGIF: a form of *product based sales promotion* – buy one get one free also known as BOGOFF.

Boston Box: (also known as the BCG matrix) a tool for analysing a *product portfolio*, plotting relative market share against market growth rate for each product. The resultant matrix classifies products as cash cows, dogs, question marks and stars.

Brand loyalty: occurs when a consumer consistently buys the same brand over a long period.

Branding: the creation of a three-dimensional character for a product, defined in terms of name, packaging, colours, symbols, etc., that helps to differentiate it from its competitors, and helps the customer to develop a relationship with the product.

Breadth of range: the variety of different *product lines* either (a) produced by a manufacturer; or (b) stocked by a retailer.

Breakeven analysis: shows the relationship between total costs and total revenue in order to assess the profitability of different levels of sales volume.

Bulk breaking: buying large quantities of goods and then reselling them in smaller lots, reflecting some of the cost savings made through bulk buying in the resale price. A prime function of *intermediaries*.

Business format franchise: allows a *franchisee* access not only to a product concept, but also to a comprehensive package that allows the product or

An extensive **glossary** provides definitions of key marketing terms.

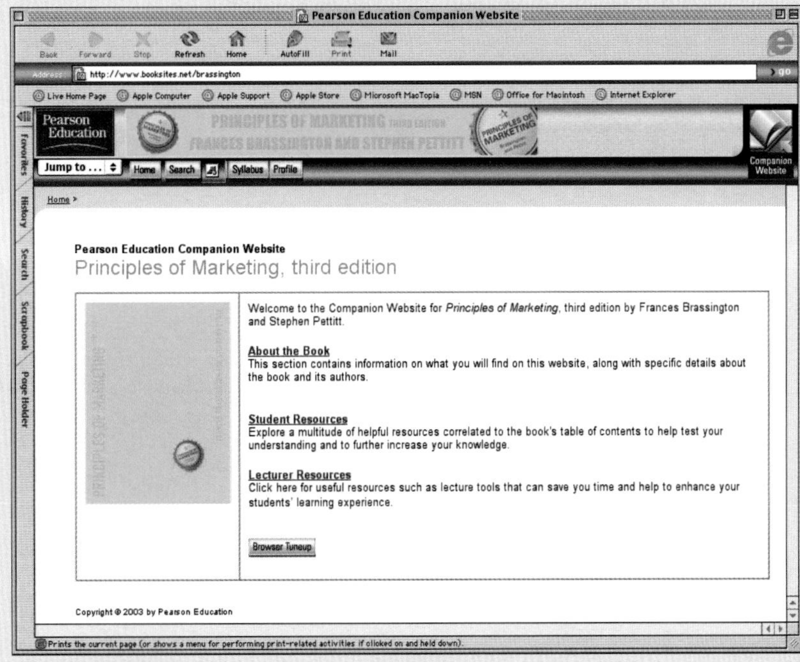

Screenshot reproduced by permission of Microsoft Corporation.

companion website

A Companion website accompanies

PRINCIPLES OF MARKETING

3rd edition

by Brassington and Pettitt

Visit the ***Principles of Marketing*** Companion website at **www.booksites.net/brassington** to find valuable teaching and learning material including:

For students:

- Study material designed to help you improve your results
- 10 multiple choice questions per chapter
- Annotated weblinks for each chapter to articles, company sites, and marketing resources
- Extra case studies

For lecturers:

- A secure, password protected site with teaching material
- An Instructor's Manual
- Answer guidelines for cases and examination quotes
- Supporting PowerPoint presentations for each chapter
- Additional long case studies
- An extra exercise for each chapter which can be set for seminars or homework

Also: This site also features a syllabus manager, search facility, and email results function.

preface

Introduction

The world within which marketing takes place is a dynamic and potentially very exciting one. By its very nature, marketing reflects social and political change, as well as technological and economic trends. All of these things, as well as their own experiences, influence customers' attitudes to organisations and the product packages on offer. Marketers have to understand this if they are going to create offerings that will satisfy, or even delight, their customers. There is something of an element of 'magic' to all this, particularly in consumer markets, as the marketer finds the right blend of ingredients to whet the customer's appetite, to stimulate desire, and to generate a sale. Marketing helps consumers to develop emotional bonds with the products they purchase, and to gain psychological as well as functional satisfaction from their use.

B2B markets too have their own magic. Industrial purchasing might well have a greater element of business-like functionality and cost effectiveness about it, but nevertheless, marketers still have to present the best case to customers, to show them clearly why they should buy from one supplier rather than another. Greater emphasis on long-term buyer–supplier relationships means that the marketer not only has to satisfy the B2B buyer's product needs now, but also has to build trust and reassurance so that cooperation can flourish in the future. In essence, this is not far removed from what the marketer is trying to achieve in a consumer market!

What all this means is that marketing is not a dry, internally focused management function with rigid procedures and sets of rules. It is live, outward looking and interactive. It responds to what is happening both inside and outside the organisation, yet also tries to drive what is happening in order to capitalise on opportunities. This makes marketing fun, but it also makes it dangerous. Marketing creativity and flexibility have to be harnessed within a disciplined and controlled management structure in order to ensure, as far as is possible, that the 'right' things are being done at the 'right' time for the 'right' reasons. Sometimes that means breaking new ground and taking risks.

Marketing is also in the front line of an organisation's attitude to social responsibility and corporate citizenship. Society now expects organisations to ensure that their products are safe and to communicate any risks or problems clearly to the consumer. Organisations are also expected to refrain from selling products in inappropriate ways to vulnerable groups. Marketers have to be able to help the organisation to translate these expectations into practice. Marketers thus have to be creative and flexible, yet disciplined and ethical in everything they do.

In academic terms, the marketing field has reached a sophisticated level of development and is still evolving to incorporate the effects of the changing world. The basic tools of marketing are well established and understood, and theories of consumer and organisational behaviour are becoming increasingly complex. One challenge is to show how all these elements interact with each other in different types of situation, hence the emergence of discrete bodies of literature on international marketing, services marketing, and e-marketing, for example. Another challenge is to explore the impact of emerging issues on both markets and marketers, hence the interest in relationship marketing, 'green' marketing, e-marketing, and marketing ethics.

The job of a good introductory textbook, therefore, is to bring together theory and practice, showing how the two feed from each other. It should cover a wide range of applications, industries and markets, exploring the ways in which marketers are responding to new situations and solving marketing problems creatively. All of this has to be presented within a strong, logical framework that allows the student to develop knowledge and understanding in a structured way. It is also essential, of course, to stimulate the student's interest and curiosity about marketing. Marketing lecturers are privileged in many ways, because their students have already had experience of marketing as consumers. They might be cynical about it, but they have experienced it, and part of the stimulation for the student can be the process of understanding and analysing their own behaviour and responses to marketing activities.

In the light of all this, therefore, this particular textbook aims to be:

- *Comprehensive* in covering a wide range of marketing topics and elements, including the marketing environment, customers and markets, the marketing mix, and specialised applications of marketing such as international marketing and services marketing. There is particularly comprehensive coverage of the promotional mix to reflect the increasingly important role of direct marketing and the sometimes neglected aspects of public relations in the integrated communications mix. The dedication of a chapter to internet marketing and new media brings together many of the themes covered in the rest of the book and reflects the widening application of marketing and the creation of new marketing forms.
- *European* in design and focus. Marketers in most large organisations no longer regard other EU nations as export markets, but as part of one large, single market. This text aims to give students this wider European perspective. While there is a bias towards the UK, cases and examples are drawn from across the EU and from further afield to help demonstrate the underlying principles of marketing in practice. It is important that students learn from, and enjoy, examples from across the EU and beyond, showing the problems arising from operating in markets in transition.
- *Applied.* Marketing cannot be approached as a purely theoretical course of study. It is essential to show how it works in practice, within the context of market conditions and customer behaviour that can be difficult to predict. To that end, not only does each chapter have a full range of examples and vignettes, but also dedicated vignettes covering issues of corporate social responsibility and e-marketing.
- *Wide ranging* in its coverage of markets and organisations. Marketing is not just about fast moving consumer goods operations which employ dedicated marketing specialists. Marketing happens, formally or informally, consciously or unconsciously, on purpose or by accident, in all organisations. It is important, therefore, to present a wide range of different industries and organisational sizes, in both consumer and organisational markets. Examples have thus been drawn from service industries, non-profit organisations, dot-coms and traditional organisations, large and small businesses, operating domestically and/or internationally. Products considered range from lingerie to condoms, from charities to air travel, from car components to the aerospace industry.
- *A good read.* The text has been written with the needs of the first-time marketing student in mind. The combination of theory, examples and commentary is designed to engage readers' attention and interest, and to lead them painlessly through to a substantial understanding of marketing principles and applications. Marketing is a lot of fun and we want to communicate the sense of enjoyment and excitement that can come from working in what is essentially a creative discipline.

Who should use this book

- *Undergraduates* are the prime audience for this text, and the book is intended mainly for use on all-purpose introductory marketing modules. The depth and coverage of some topics, however, such as direct marketing, e-marketing, and marketing communications generally, would make certain chapters useful references for more advanced, specialist modules.
- *Postgraduates* such as MBA or DMS level students will also find in this book a good background text to remind them of basic marketing principles in preparation for more advanced analysis of managerial concepts and case studies. Again, the depth in some of the areas covered would provide useful specialist reading.

Distinctive features of the third edition

The successful features of the first two editions of this text have been retained:

- A clearly written and structured text, including chapter objectives and summary.
- A wide selection of up-to-date vignettes and examples are included in each chapter to illustrate the concepts presented. These are drawn from a range of industries, organisations and countries.
- End of chapter questions give students the opportunity to revise the material presented and to check their understanding of it. Discussion questions, encouraging students to debate issues or to research further into marketing practice can also be used as the basis for seminar work for students working individually or in small groups.
- Each chapter has two case studies, again drawn from a range of industries, organisations and countries. Most have been designed primarily to be discussed within a one hour seminar session and to allow the student to apply the concepts outlined in the text. Some cases are a little longer to allow more detailed consideration of issues.
- The complete range of marketing elements is covered, including direct marketing, as well as a selection of specialist applications, such as services marketing, international marketing, and e-marketing.
- It has been compiled from a European perspective and with a wide European orientation in the examples, vignettes and cases.
- An Instructor's Manual that outlines suggested lecture programmes, presents template OHTs, and guidelines on issues arising from the case studies. The manual also suggests how some of the vignettes can be used as seminar material, and offers ideas for further reading and activities.
- A glossary of key terms is also included, based on the key words highlighted in each chapter.

Some features have been enhanced and some new features introduced:

- The series of 'e-marketing in action' vignettes is an important innovation in this edition, highlighting the rapidly changing development and application of online solutions in marketing.
- Linked with the e-marketing vignettes, we have also paid much more attention throughout this edition to the internet's contribution to marketing strategies and operations, as a service delivery system, a distribution channel, a research tool and as a communications medium. Throughout the book, there are examples, vignettes and cases relevant to e-marketing issues.
- To emphasise the growing importance of e-marketing further, we have added a new Chapter 24 on E-marketing and new media to examine the latest trends and techniques in more depth.
- A series of 'corporate social responsibility in action' vignettes is also an important innovation in this edition. Particularly in the light of recent corporate scandals in the USA, there is increasing pressure on organisations to examine the ethics of what they do and to develop a more critical corporate conscience. Marketers thus have to face up to difficult issues and these vignettes outline some of those conflicts and dilemmas and the ways in which they are handled.
- While some case studies have been updated from the second edition and a few 'old favourites' retained, a significant number have been replaced to maintain a fresh and topical feel, and regular updates on them will be posted on the website. At the time of writing, issues such as the rise and fall of dotcom businesses (Case Study 24.2), strategic management within the financial services industry (Case Studies 20.1 and 21.1), innovation within the computer games console market (Case Study 14.1), and even pricing and distribution conflicts (Case Study 11.1) were still very much in the news and we have thus made as many new cases as possible as up to date as possible.

- Similarly, we have thoroughly overhauled the examples within the chapters and the 'marketing in action' vignettes, including many items that are of current interest. As with the case studies, we feel that it is important to maintain relevance, freshness and topicality. Additionally, we have also made many of the examples and most of the marketing in action vignettes longer and more comprehensive than in the previous edition. These could easily be used as a basis for classroom discussion as an alternative to a case study.
- We have reviewed the photographs and retained a few favourite ones. We have taken care to ensure the relevance of the photographs to the text material so that they add value to the student's reading experience.
- In this edition, a number of cases and vignettes have been compiled from lengthy interviews conducted by the authors. This approach serves a useful purpose in drawing themes together and providing an applied insight into the key concepts covered in the relevant chapter. These managerial perspectives underline the message that marketing concepts have to be integrated into purposeful strategies that have to be implemented in a real and often difficult world.

Supplements

A wide range of supplements are available to support lectures using *Principles of Marketing*. The unprecedented supplements package has been fully updated to reflect the new edition. Many of these are free to those choosing to adopt the book as their main text.

- A comprehensive and easy-to-use Instructor's Manual, designed to help lecturers make full use of the book, which includes:
  - suggested lecture outlines incorporating the OHPs supplied with the text
  - outline answers to the end-of-chapter questions for discussion
  - detailed answers to the case studies within the text, and some supplementary questions and answers
  - a discussion question and outline answer to each of the Marketing in Action vignettes' suggested assignments.
- Numerous colour PowerPoint overheads selected from the book are available on the website.
- Electronic multiple choice question bank contains over 1,000 multiple choice questions, arranged in accordance with the structure of the book. Students answer each question and get immediate feedback in terms of which answer is correct. At the end of the test they are given their total score for that session. The software is from Question Mark, the world leader in software for computerising tests, quizzes and surveys.
- *The Principles of Marketing* companion website is an exciting and involving website which opens up new possibilities for innovative teaching. The website includes material specifically targeted at both students and lecturers, additional cases linked to the chapters within the book and the Instructor's Manual and OHPs that lecturers can download and additional multiple choice questions for students to use as self-assessments via the web. The site is located on *www.booksites.net/brassington*, *see* p. xiv.

about the authors

Stephen Pettitt is Deputy Vice Chancellor at the University of Luton. Previously he was the Pro Vice Chancellor and Dean of Luton Business School and before that, Director of Corporate Affairs at the University of Teesside. He has had, therefore, the opportunity to practise and plan marketing as well as being a marketing educator. He also worked at the University of Limerick in Ireland for four years as a Lecturer in Marketing and was the Managing Director of The Marketing Centre for Small Business, a campus company specialising in research and consultancy for the small business sector.

He worked initially in various sales and marketing management posts for Olivetti, Plessey and SKF before taking up a career in higher education. He holds a bachlor's degree in geography and an MBA and PhD from Cranfield. In addition to a wide experience in marketing education at all levels, he has undertaken numerous in-company training, research and consultancy assignments. He has lectured in marketing and entrepreneurship in France, Poland, Bulgaria, Slovakia, South Africa, Switzerland, the USA and Kenya. He has published over thirty papers and articles along with major studies in tourism innovation strategies, large buyer–small firm seller relationships and small firm development.

Frances Brassington is a Senior Lecturer in Marketing at Buckinghamshire Chilterns University College of High Education. She graduated from the University of Bradford Management Centre with a BSc (Hons) in business studies and a PhD. Her first teaching position was at the University of Teesside where she was also MBA dissertation director and marketing section leader. She has taught marketing at all levels and on a wide range of undergraduate marketing modules and programmes and is currently supervising a number of PhD research students. Her own research interests include retail marketing and the use of project-based learning in marketing education. She has also designed and delivered marketing programmes for managers and academics in Poland and Bulgaria and has given guest lectures in China and South Africa.

acknowledgements

It has taken over a year to prepare this third edition of *Principles of Marketing* and there are many people who have helped, directly and indirectly, in its development. Without them it could not have been done.

Particular thanks are due to Sue Williams for her hard work and resourcefulness in sourcing so many new photographs. It seems that no challenge was too daunting for her and she has given unstintingly of her time and effort. Our most sincere thanks, Sue.

Staff of the University of Luton have also been very supportive. Thanks are due to the library staff for their help on Chapter 6 and Professor Brian Mathews for his continued advice on pricing and on services marketing. All the members of the marketing department within the Business School are thanked for their individual comments and constructive ideas for the book's development.

Colleagues from Buckinghamshire Chilterns University College have been both the sternest critics and the most fervent supporters of this text and have thus made us feel that it was all worthwhile! They have offered constructive insights and feedback on various aspects of the book as well as continuing to supply coffee, comradeship and consolation. Affectionate thanks, therefore, go to Sheena Harland in particular, and to Ruth Hickmott, Sue Matthews and Christine Parsons. Thanks too to Broder Dittschar for undertaking the mammoth task of condensing some of his extensive research findings into Case Study 23.1. Our link with the University of Teesside has also played a role in this project. Thanks to Julie Glover for her friendship and valuable feedback and to Alan 'Smiffy' Smith for his sense of humour as well as for supplying Case Study 24.1 in partnership with Noel Dennis. Heartfelt thanks to them all.

We also thank friends and colleagues from around the world who have contributed to the text and have helped us to deepen our understanding of different markets and cultures. Thanks especially to: Professsor Barra O'Cinneide formerly of the University of Limerick for the inspiration to write case studies and Professor Don Bradley of the University of Central Arkansas for his valuable insights into the impact of the internet in US marketing applications, and Bob Thomas, formerly Managing Director GEC Marconi in China for his fascinating insights into of the practicalities of marketing in China and for introducing us to his business contacts.

We are also grateful to the following for their courage in allowing us access to their brands and businesses for case study material and vignettes, and in some cases giving up so much of their valuable time for in-depth interviews:

- Ian Aizlewood: former Managing Director, Continental Microwave Ltd.
- Geoff Ball: President, Alstom China.
- Lars Becker and Annabel Knight: Flytxt.
- Neil Bradley: Business Development Director – Direct Distribution, Prudential plc.
- David Burton: Marketing Manager, Eidos Interactive Ltd.
- Joan Capdevila: Group Colomer.
- Ian Coomber: former Executive Director, Sales and Marketing, Vauxhall UK.
- Alan Cook: formerly of Prudential plc.
- Phil Cooper: formerly of Chuft Toys and Gifts.
- Jamie Inman, Partners BDDH
- Isabelle Lagerweij, Kimberley-Clark Corporation
- Tony and Duncan Lofthouse: Joint Managing Directors, Lofthouse of Fleetwood Ltd.
- Carl Lyons: Marketing Director, Lastminute.com.
- David Moore: Neu Engineering.
- Amanda Oswald: Corporate Fundraising Manager, RSPCA.
- Richard Pentin and Nina Jasinksi: Partners Andrews Aldridge.
- Tim Pile: former Sales and Marketing Director, Alliance and Leicester.
- David Pugh: Controller, Retail Sales, Vauxhall Motors.
- Rien van Ruremonde: Managing Director, Nedan Zoetwaren BV.
- David Stephens: Wales Tourist Board.
- Gary Stevens and Nik Margolis: Inbox.

We would like to offer general thanks to all those other individuals and organisations who directly and indirectly helped to create the examples, case studies and marketing in action profiles. We are particularly indebted to Dave Chaffey who contributed the 'E-marketing in Action' vignettes.

During the course of this project, we have come to appreciate the excellent journalistic teams who produce *Marketing*, *Marketing Week*, *The Grocer*, *The Financial Times*, *The Economist*, *The Times*, *The Sunday Times*, and the many other publications and websites that keep us all up to date with key developments in marketing across the world.

The Pearson Education team has endured much over the last year, and we would like to thank all those who have helped to bring this third edition to fruition. In particular, we thank Lynn Brandon (former Acquisitions Editor), Tina Cadle-Bowman (Senior Managing Editor), Kay Holman (Senior Project Controller), Colin Reed (Senior Designer), Adam Renvoize (Senior Designer), Bridget Allen (Pre-press Manager), Simon Lake (Product Development Director), and last but certainly not least, Stuart Hay (Textbook Development Manager). Their continuous encouragement, support and occasional nagging have been crucial in getting this edition finished. We also thank the unsung heroes behind the scenes: Robert Chaundy (freelance copy editor), Nigel Johnson (freelance permissions editor), Annette Abel (freelance proof reader), David Barraclough (freelance indexer), Sue Williams (freelance picture researcher) and all of those involved in design, production, marketing, distribution and sales who have made this book the polished, professional package that it is. They've obviously read it!

We were greatly encouraged by the enthusiasm with which the first two editions were received and thank all of you who adopted it and used it. We hope you enjoyed the experience and that you will find the third edition even more stimulating. We have appreciated the reviews and feedback (both formal and informal) that we have had from lecturers and students alike and hope that you will stay in contact with us through our website *http://www.booksites.net/brassington.*

And finally, yet again we offer our deepest apologies to our friends and family for all the neglect they have had to suffer over the last year. We are sure, however, that they have secretly enjoyed the soap opera that has been the book's progress.

We are grateful to the following for permission to reproduce copyright material:

Figure 1.2 adapted from figure on pp. 7–23 from 'The Marketing Concept: Putting Theory into Practice', in *European Journal of Marketing*, Vol. 24, No. 9, 1990, reprinted by kind permission, MCB University Press Ltd, Bradford, (Hooley, G.J et al., 1990); Tables 2.1, 2.2 and 2.3 adapted from Tables 0221, pp. 130–131, 1607, p. 373 and 1103, pp. 269–269, from *European Marketing Data and Statistics* 2001, 36th Edition, Euromonitor plc (2001); Table 2.4 adapted from *Worldwide Corporate Tax Guide* 2002, www.ey.com, Ernst & Young Global Limited, updated as of March 2002; Table 3.1 adapted from 'Consumer Market Beliefs: A Review of the Literature and an Agenda for Further Research', in *Advances in Consumer Research*, Vol. 17, 1990, Association for Consumer Research, (Duncan, C.P., 1990); Table 3.3 reprinted with permission from *Journal of Marketing Research*, published by the American Marketing Association, Wells, W.D., and Gubar, R.G. (1966, Vol. 3, Nov), 'Life Cycle Concepts in Marketing Research', pp. 35–363; Figure 4.2 adapted from *Fashion Design and Product Development*, Blackwell Science, (Carr, H. and Pomeroy, J., 1992); Table 4.2a adapted from 'Single Sourcing: A Management Tool for the Quality Supplier', in *Journal of Purchasing and Materials Management*, Vol. 23, No. 1, 1987, pp. 19–24 (Now the *Journal of Supply Chain Management*), Institute for Supply Management, (Trevelen, Mark, 1987); Table 4.2b adapted from information from pp. 19–28 from 'Sourcing/Contracting Strategy Selection', in *International Journal of Operations and Production Management*, Vol. 10, No. 8, 1990, reprinted by kind permission, MCB University Press Ltd., Bradford, (Ramsey, J., and Wilson, I., 1990); Figure 4.6 adapted from figure from 'Production Technology and the User-Supplier Interaction', in *International Marketing and Purchasing of Industrial Goods: An Interaction Approach*, John Wiley & Sons Ltd., (Johanson, J.; Håkansson, H. (ed.), 1982), copyright © 1982 John Wiley & Sons Limited. Reproduced with permission; Table 4.6 adapted from table on pp. 75–81, '*Strategic Supplier Selection: Understanding Long Term Buyer Relationships*', reprinted with permission from Business Horizons, Vol. 31, No. 4, 1988, Elsevier Science, (Spekman, R.E., 1988), copyright © 1988 by The Trustees at Indiana University, Kelley School of Business; Table 5.3 adapted from 'Reacting Fast', in *Database Marketing*, February 1999, p. 8, and from 'Measuring the Risk', in *Database Marketing*, February 1999, pp. 15–17, Blue Sky Publishing Ltd, (Sleight, P., 1999), copyright © 1999 Peter Sleight, reproduced with kind permission; Figure 6.3 adapted from figure from *Marketing Research: Measurement and Method*, Macmillan, NY, (Tull, D.S., and Hawkins, D.I., 1990), copyright © 1990 Pearson Education, Inc.; Table 6.3 based on Table 10.1, p. 369 from *E-Business and E-Commerce Management: Strategy, Implementation and Practice*, Financial Times Prentice Hall (Pearson Education), (Chaffey, D., 2001); Table 7.1 adapted from data compiled by ACNielsen, a VNU company and leading marketing information company, for 'Biggest Brands, 2001', in *Marketing*, 9 August 2001, pp. 24–34, Haymarket Publishing Services Ltd, (Hiscock, 2001); Figure 7.2 adapted from data from http://www.gsk.com/products/consumerhealthcare.shtml, GlaxoSmithKline Consumer Healthcare, copyright © 2001 GlaxoSmithKline; Table 7.2 based on information from Mintel Market Intelligence (Nov. 1998), Soap, Bath and Shower Additives, copyright © 1998 Mintel International Group Ltd.; Table 7.3 from Brand Quality Ratings 1998, *EquiTrend, Total Research*, (Tel.: 020 8263 5200); Figure 8.3 reprinted and adapted from figure 7–2, p. 262 with the permission of The Free Press, an imprint of Simon & Schuster Adult Publishing Group, from *DIFFUSION OF INNOVATIONS*, Fourth Edition, by Everett M. Rogers. Copyright © 1995 Everett M. Rogers, copyright © 1962, 1971, 1983 by The Free Press; Table 10.1 adapted from table on pp. 16–19 from 'Investing in Capital Assets', in *Purchasing & Supply Management*, March 1995, Chartered Institute of Purchasing & Supply, (Mehta, S., 1995); Table 10.2 based on information from *The Strategy and Tactics of Pricing*, Prentice Hall, (Nagle, T.T., 1987), copyright © 1987, 1995 Pearson Education, Inc.; Table 10.4 adapted from information from www.kitbag.com website, accessed on 30 November 2001, copyright © 2001 Kitbag.com Ltd; Figure 12.11 adapted from Figure 3.2, p. 74 from *The Strategy of Distribution Management*, Heinemann Professional, The Marketing Series, (Christopher, M., 1990), Copyright © 1990 Professor Martin Christopher, reproduced by kind permission; Table 13.6 based on table/ information on p.85 from 'Internationalisation: Interpreting the Motives', in *International Retailing: Trends and Strategies*, Pitman Publishing (Pearson Education), (Alexander, N.; McGoldrick, P.J., and Davies, G. (eds.), 1995). Table 14.2 from table from *The Marketing Communications Process*, McGraw-Hill, (Delozier, M.W., 1975), copyright © 1975 The Estate of the late Professor M. Wayne DeLozier; Table 14.3 adapted from table from *Advertising and Promotion Management*, McGraw-Hill, (Rossiter, J.R., and Percy, L., 1987), copyright © 1987 The McGraw-Hill Companies, Inc.; Figure 14.4 adapted from figure of communications planning flow from Michael L. Rothschild, *Marketing Communications: From Fundamentals to Strategies*, D.C. Heath & Company, copyright © 1987 D.C. Heath and Company, by permission of Houghton Mifflin Company; Tables 15.3, 15.4, 15.6 and 15.7 adapted from Table 12.2, p. 282, Table 12.5, p. 284, Tables 23.7 and 23.8, pp. 437-436, and Table 12.4, p. 283 from *European Marketing Data and Statistics* 2002, 37th Edition, Euromonitor plc (2002); Table 15.5 based on information from Mintel Market Intelligence (15th Nov. 2001), Tea and Herbal Tea, and from Mintel Market Intelligence (1st June 2001), Shampoos and Conditioners, copyright © 2001 Mintel International Group Ltd.; Table 15.8 adapted from table from '*A Guide to Outdoor Advertising – Key Facts*', in http://www.oaa.org.uk/guide.htm, The Outdoor Advertising Association of Great Britain (2002); Tables 16.1 and 16.2 adapted from figures on pp. 7 to 10 from *UK Coupon Market 2000*, NCH Marketing Services Ltd (2001), reproduced with kind permission from NCH Marketing Services Ltd.; Table 16.3 from table on pp. 26–27 from 'Preaching the Loyalty Message', in *Marketing Week*, 1 December 1995, Centaur Communications Ltd. (Mitchell, A., 1995); Table 16.5 from *Guidelines for good sales promotion practice*, Institute for Sales Promotion, reproduced by kind permission of the Institute of Sales Promotion; Table 16.6 adapted from table from *Sales Promotion: How to Create and Implement Campaigns that Really Work*, 3rd Edition, Kogan Page (Cummins, J., 2002); Figure 17.1 adapted from figure on pp. 17-32 from 'Personal Selling & Sales Management in the New Millennium', in *The Journal of Personal Selling and Sales Management*, Vol. 16, No. 4, 1996, (Anderson, R.E., 1996), copyright © 1996 Professor Rolph E. Anderson; Table 18.1 adapted from information from '*UK Direct Mail Volumes*' from website http://www.dmis.co.uk/keystats/keystats.html, Direct Mail Information Service, reproduced by kind permission of the Direct Mail Information Service (DMIS); Table 18.2 adapted from table supplied by Datamonitor from 'Brands Take the Direct Route', in *Marketing Week*, 13 September 2001, pp. 38–39, Centaur Communications Ltd, (Singh & Datamonitor, 2001), reproduced by kind permission of Datamonitor plc; Table 18.3 adapted from table from 'European Direct Mail Data, 2000' from website http://www.dmis.co.uk/keystats/keystats.html, Direct Mail Information Service, reproduced by kind permission of the Direct Mail Information Service (DMIS); Table 18.5 adapted from table on pp.31–32 from 'Talking Business', in *Marketing*, 19 November 1998, Haymarket Publishing Services Ltd. (Cobb, R., 1998), reproduced from *Marketing* magazine with the permission of the copyright owner, Haymarket Business Publications Limited; Table 18.6 adapted from table on pp. 43–44 from 'Call Centres Aim to Encourage Loyalty', in *Marketing*, 28 June 2001, Haymarket Publishing Services Ltd. (Clarke, 2001), reproduced from *Marketing* magazine with the permission of the copyright owner, Haymarket Business Publications Limited; Figure 18.8 from figure of '*Recency, frequency and value model*' from website http://www.talkingnumbers.com/rfvimage.html, Talking Numbers Data Based Solutions Ltd., published with permission of Talking Numbers Data Based Solutions Ltd; Table 18.9 reproduced from *UK Exhibition Facts* Volume 14 (2001), by kind permission of the Exhibition Venues Association (EVA); Table 18.10 reproduced by kind permission of the European Major Exhibition Centres Association (E.M.E.C.A.); Tables 18.11 and 18.12 (UK figures) reproduced by kind permission of the Exhibition Venues Association (EVA); Table 19.1 adapted from an article by Michael Harrison first published in *The Independent* 10/01/2001, p. 18; Table 19.2 adapted from table on p. 25 from 'How to Profit from Sponsoring Sport', in *Marketing*, 16 August 2001, Haymarket Publishing Services Ltd. (Fry, 2001), reproduced from *Marketing* magazine with the permission of the copyright owner, Haymarket Business Publications Limited; Table 20.2 and Figure 20.8 adapted from table and figure from *Strategic Marketing Management: Planning, Implementation and Control*, Butterworth-Heinemann, (Wilson, R.M.S., Gilligan, C., with Pearson, D.J., 1992) reprinted by kind permission of Elsevier Science; Figure 20.6 adapted and reprinted by permission of *Harvard Business Review*, Exhibit I on p. 114 from *Strategies of Diversification* by Ansoff, H.I. Issue No. 25 (5), Sept/Oct 1957, pp. 113–25, copyright © 1957 by the Harvard Business School Publishing Corporation; all rights reserved; Figures 20.11 and 20.12 from figures from 'Marketing Warfare in the 1980s', in *Journal of Business Strategy*, Thomson EC Media Group, (Kotler, P. and Singh, R., 1981), republished with permission – Thomson Media, Eleven Penn Plaza, New York, NY 10001; Table 22.1 from table from *Services Marketing*, 3rd Edition, Prentice-Hall (Pearson Education), Lovelock, C.H., 1996); Table 22.4 adapted from table from *NatWest/British Franchise Association annual survey* conducted by BDRC, http://www.british-franchise.org, copyright © 2002 BDRC; Figure 23.2 adapted from figure from *Cross-cultural Management Communication*, J. Wiley & Sons Limited, (Mead, R.R., 1990), copyright 1990 © John Wiley & Sons Limited. Reproduced with permission; Figure 23.6 adapted from figure from *International Marketing*, 3rd Edition, Financial Times Pitman Publishing (Pearson Education), (Walsh, L.S., 1993). Figure 24.2 from Precision E-mail marketing, in *Direct Marketing*, November 2001, pp. 56–60, Hoke Communications, Inc., (Rizzi, J. 2001), reprinted with permission from Direct Marketing Magazine, November 2001, pp. 56–60, 224, 7th Street, Garden City, NY 11530, tel: +1 (516) 746-6700, e-mail: dmmagazine@aol.com, copyright © 2002 by e-Dialog, Inc.; Figure 24.3 from figure from http://www.flytxt.com/how.html, Flytxt (2002); Table 24.7 adapted from *Integrated Marketing Communications*, Financial Times Prentice-Hall, (Pickton, D. and Broderick, A., 2001), copyright © 2001 David Pickton and Amanda Broderick, reprinted by permission of Pearson Education Limited; Table 24.8 adapted from table from http://epm.netratings.com/uk/web/Nrpublicreports.topadvertisermonthly,

Nielsen//NetRatings (2002); Table 24.9 adapted from excerpts from 'How to develop an effective e-mail creative strategy', in *Target Marketing Magazine*, February 2002, pp. 46–50, North American Publishing Company (Friesen, P., 2002).

Photographs: Age Concern UK p.617; Airbus Industrie p.60; Alstom p.173; Army Recruiting Group/Saatchi & Saatchi p.609; Australian Tourist Commission p.967; Avon Cosmetics p.698; BAE p.149; BAE Systems p.459; B&Q plc p.527; Bass Brewers/BD London p.1054; Benetton UK p.506; Robert Bosch Limited p.302; Botton Village/Camphill Village Trust p.581; Butlins/Biss Lancaster p.316; C&G Mortgages p.97; Cadbury, Trebor Bassett p.914; Cafédirect p.175; Norwich Union Life p.820; Teuscher, Chocolates of Switzerland p.874; Chuft Toys p.947; Circular Distributors Ltd p.667; Club 18–30/JMC Holidays p.83; Colgate Palmolive Ltd p.128; Colgate Palmolive UK Ltd/Starfish p.342; The Colomer Group p.734; Compassion in World Farming p.833; Continental Microwave Limited p.1016; Continental Tyres p.55; Department for Transport, Local Government and the Regions (DTLR) pp.648–50; Diageo p.216; easyjet.com p.760; Electrolux p.353; Euro Food Brands p.474; Experian Ltd. p.189; FBS Cars p.936; Foyles p.15; Flora London Marathon p.818; GlaxoSmithKline p.332, p.378, p.574, p.620; Goodyear p.1033; Gossard Bras p.185; Great Ormond Street Hospital Children's Charity p.994; Greenpeace p.796; Harley-Davidson United Kingdom p.124, p.745; Hayes and Jarvis p.110; Hennes and Mauritz p.1009; Hormel Foods Corporation p.1027; Hugo Boss AG/Modus Publicity p.37; Interbrew p.248; IKEA p.556; Jarvis Hotels/EPC p.975; KEF Audio (UK) Limited p.414; Kimberley-Clark Ltd p.442; Kookaï p.630; Kraft Europe p.1070; Land Lease Europe Ltd. p.548; Lastminute.com p.40; Lever Fabergé p.279; (plus image of Persil in p.608; Linn Products Ltd p.843; L'Oreal Paris/ Advertising Archives p.384; Lofthouse of Fleetwood p.88; Marks & Spencer p.6; Archie Miles p.860; Mindmatics p.1087; Mr Lazenby's Sausages/Northern Profile PR p.432; Mr Lucky Bags Ltd p.200; Nationwide Building Society p.241; Nestlé p.851; Neu International p.208; Odeon Cinemas/ Red Consultancy p.954; Olympus Cameras p.395; Photodisc p.727; Phytopharm p.898; Precious Woods (Schweiz) AG p.54; Princess Yachts International plc p.755; Proctor & Gamble/Good Relations p.669; Reckitt & Benckiser p.292; Red Bull p.352; Reebok/Cake Media p.723; Saga p.49; Scottish Quality Salmon p.1040; Skelair p.490; SKF p.145; Skoda UK p.117; Slendertone p.754; Soleco p.483; T&T Beverages/ Mason Williams PR p.585; Tesco Stores Ltd; p.691; Texaco HACL & Partners p.676; Thomson Holidays p.274; Tibbett & Britten p.502; Toys R Us p.539; Turtle Island, Fiji p.202; UPC Corp. p.1014; Vauxhall Motors p.165; Virgin Money/Harrison Troughton Wunderman p.750; Virgin Trains p.364, p.959; Vision Direct p.411; Wales Tourist Board p.789 (both); Whitbread Hotels p.812; Whitworths Foods p.436; p.1086 http://www.flytext.com; Yomega Corporation Inc. p.322.

In some instances we have been unable to trace the owners of copyright material, and we would appreciate any information that would enable us to do so.

part one

MARKETING AND ITS ENVIRONMENT

1 marketing dynamics

2 the European marketing environment

Ask anybody what marketing is and it is likely that you will get responses such as 'advertising' or 'making people buy things they don't want'. The first chapters of this book should provide you with fuller, more accurate and more useful definitions than these.

Chapter 1 defines and explores marketing as a philosophy of doing business which puts the customer first, and therefore casts the marketing department in the role of 'communicator' between the organisation and the outside world. Marketers have to tackle a surprisingly wide range of tasks on a daily basis to fulfil that function (hence the thickness of this book), and these too are defined.

Communication is, however, a two-way process. The marketing function does not exist only to deliver the organisation's goods and messages, but also to carry information from a dynamic and changing European environment back into the organisation. Chapter 2, therefore, looks at some of the external influences which affect marketing decisions and thus the way in which organisations choose to do business.

After you have read this section, marketing should mean a lot more to you than 'advertising', and you will appreciate that 'making people buy things they don't want' is the one thing that successful marketers do not do.

chapter 1

marketing dynamics

Introduction

LEARNING OBJECTIVES

This chapter will help you to:

1 define what marketing is;

2 trace the development of marketing as a way of doing business and consider the ways in which marketing is changing;

3 appreciate the importance and contribution of marketing as both a business function and an interface between the organisation and its customers; and

4 understand the scope of tasks undertaken in marketing, and the range of different organisational situations in which marketing is applied.

You will have some sort of idea of what marketing is, since you are, after all, exposed to marketing in some form every day. Every time you buy or use a product, go window shopping, see an advertising hoarding, watch an advertisement, listen to friends telling you about a wonderful new product they've tried, or even when you surf the internet to research a market, company or product for an assignment, you are reaping the benefits (or being a victim) of marketing activities. When marketing's outputs are so familiar, it is easy to take it for granted and to judge and define it too narrowly by what you see of it close to home. It is a mistake, however, to dismiss marketing as 'just advertising' or 'just selling' or 'making people buy things they don't really want'.

What this book wants to show you is that marketing does, in fact, cover a very wide range of absolutely essential business activities that bring you the products you *do* want, when you want them, where you want them, but at prices you can afford, and with all the information you need to make informed and satisfying consumer choices. And that's only what marketing does for you! Widen your thinking to include what marketing can similarly do for organisations purchasing goods and services from other organisations, and you can begin to see why it is a mistake to be too cynical about professionally practised marketing. None of this is easy. The outputs of marketing, such as the packaging, the advertisements, the glossy brochures, the all-singing, all-dancing websites, the enticing retail outlets and the incredible bargain value prices, look slick and polished, but a great deal of management planning, analysis and decision-making has gone on behind the scenes in order to bring all this to you. By the time you have finished this book, you should appreciate the whole range of marketing activities, and the difficulties of managing them.

eg

The UK market for breakfast cereal is worth around £1bn and is the largest in Europe. Constant innovation and good marketing have helped Kellogg to achieve 43 per cent market share through a wide range of products targeting different consumer tastes and encouraging consumers to snack on cereals throughout the day. Kellogg's owns six out of the top ten best-selling brands. The strong brand images of Rice Krispies, Frosties and Coco Pops are clearly targeted at the children's market, while Healthwise, All Bran and Optima meet the growing demand for healthy adult breakfasts. Advertising (particularly through characters such as Tony the Tiger) and promotions (such as in-pack gifts) aimed at children helped to differentiate the products, reinforce brand image and build customer loyalty. Children have a huge influence: 60 per cent of housewives with children agreed that they buy the cereals their children like and 20 per cent agree that they buy cereals featuring free gifts or special offers that their children want. Premium prices have also reinforced Kellogg's quality image. Thanks to competitors, however, continuing success is not necessarily guaranteed. Supermarket own-brand products, for instance, positioned close to the market leaders and accounting for about 25 per cent of the market, have made cereals more of a commodity purchase, undermining premium prices and brand images. To stay ahead, Kellogg has had to plan its product management, communications and pricing strategies carefully with a programme of new product launches to keep consumers interested; a high advertising spend to reinforce the Kellogg image; and price cuts and price-based promotional offers to close the pricing gap between Kellogg brands and supermarket own-brands (Brabbs, 2000; Mintel, 1999).

Before launching further into detailed descriptions, explanations and analyses of the operational tasks that make up the marketing function, however, it is important to lay a few foundations about what marketing really is, and to give you a more detailed overview of why it is so essential and precisely what it involves in practice.

This chapter will therefore start by defining what marketing is, by looking at a couple of widely accepted definitions and discussing their implications for organisations. To see how those definitions have emerged, we provide a brief history of marketing and how it has evolved, both as a business function and as a business orientation or philosophy. Building on that, the chapter can then look at the relationship between marketing, the outside world and the rest of the organisation. This will help to establish the role that marketing departments take on, internally and externally, and to define the tools that they use to fulfil those responsibilities. It is important to remember that marketing has a crucial role in helping to set the organisation's overall strategic objectives, and thus we shall discuss the contribution of marketing to defining strategic direction and how the needs of the customer and the needs of the organisation are reconciled.

Finally, to put all of this into context, there will be a practical section discussing the scope of marketing and looking at the variety of marketing applications that exist. To counter the tendency to think of marketing as being relevant only to consumer markets for fast moving physical products, there is a timely reminder of other types of market, such as services, business-to-business (B2B) and non-profit organisations. This section will also outline the influences that are fundamentally changing the way in which academics and managers think about marketing.

Marketing defined

This section is going to explore what **marketing** is and its evolution. First, we shall look at currently accepted definitions of marketing, then at the history behind those definitions. Linked with that history are the various business orientations outlined on pp. 10–15. These show how marketing is as much a philosophy of doing business as a business function in its own right. It is important to get this concept well established before moving on to the next section where we discuss philosophy and function in the context of the organisation.

What marketing means

Here are two popular and widely accepted definitions of marketing. The first is the definition preferred by the UK's Chartered Institute of Marketing (CIM), while the second is that offered by the American Marketing Association (AMA):

> *Marketing is the management process responsible for identifying, anticipating, and satisfying customer requirements profitably.* (CIM, 2001)

> *Marketing is the process of planning and executing the conception, pricing, promotion and distribution of ideas, goods and services to create exchange and satisfy individual and organisational objectives.* (AMA, 1985)

Both definitions make a good attempt at capturing concisely what is actually a wide and complex subject. Although they have a lot in common, each says something important that the other does not emphasise.

Both agree on the following points.

Marketing is a management process

Marketing has just as much legitimacy as any other business function, and involves just as much management skill. It requires planning and analysis, resource allocation, control and investment in terms of money, appropriately skilled people and physical resources. It also, of course, requires implementation, monitoring and evaluation. As with any other management activity, it can be carried out efficiently and successfully – or it can be done poorly, resulting in failure.

Marketing is about giving customers what they want

All marketing activities should be geared towards this. It implies a focus towards the customer or end consumer of the product or service. If 'customer requirements' are not satisfactorily fulfilled, or if customers do not obtain what they want and need, then marketing has failed both the customer and the organisation.

The CIM definition adds a couple of extra insights.

Marketing identifies and anticipates customer requirements

This phrase has a subtle edge to it that does not come through strongly in the AMA definition. It is saying that the marketer creates some sort of offering only after researching the market and pinpointing exactly what the customer will want. The AMA definition is ambiguous because it begins with the 'planning' process, which may or may not be done with reference to the customer.

Marketing fulfils customer requirements profitably

This pragmatic phrase warns the marketer against getting too carried away with the altruism of satisfying the customer! In the real world, an organisation cannot please all of the people all of the time, and sometimes even marketers have to make compromises. The marketer has to work within the resource capabilities of the organisation, and specifically work within the agreed budgets and performance targets set for the marketing function. Nevertheless, profitability can still be questionable. Marketing practice and, in part, marketing thinking, is now accepted within many non-profit organisations, from schools and universities to hospitals, voluntary organisations and activist groups such as Greenpeace and Friends of the Earth. Each must manage its dealings with its various publics and user groups and manage them efficiently and effectively, but not for profit. That important context aside, most commercial companies exist to make profits, and thus profitability is a legitimate concern. Even so, some organisations would occasionally accept the need to make a loss on a particular product or sector of a market in order to achieve wider strategic objectives. As long as those losses are planned and controlled, and in the longer run provide some other benefit to the organisation, then they are bearable. In general terms, however, if an organisation is consistently failing to make profits, then it will not survive, and thus marketing has a responsibility to sustain and increase profits.

The AMA definition goes further.

Marketing offers and exchanges ideas, goods and services

This statement is close to the CIM's 'profitably', but a little more subtle. The idea of marketing as an **exchange process** is an important one, and was first proposed by Alderson (1957). The basic idea is that I've got something you want, you've got something I want, so let's do a deal. For the most part, the exchange is a simple one. The organisation offers a product or service, and the customer offers a sum of money in return for it. Pepsi offers you a can of cola and you offer payment; you sign a contract to offer your services as an employee and the organisation pays you a salary; the hospital offers to provide health care and the individual, through taxes or insurance premiums, offers to fund it. A range of further examples is shown diagramatically in Figure 1.1.

What all these examples have in common is the assumption that both parties value what the other has to offer. If they didn't, they would not be obliged to enter into the bargain. It is up to the marketer to make sure that customers value what the organisation is offering so highly that they are prepared to give the organisation what it wants in return. Whether the marketer is offering a product, a service, or an idea (such as the environmental causes 'sold'

marketing in action

Flower power

Next time you admire a bouquet in a shop or decide to say it with flowers, just think about the marketing decisions that have gone into getting those blooms into the right place at the right time, summer or winter, for you to buy. If you think they come from the nursery down the road you will be mistaken. The bouquet in the store is almost the end point of a series of marketing exchanges that go back to the growers, predominantly in the Netherlands and parts of Africa.

In the UK, it is the supermarkets that have opened up new opportunities for all-year-round cut flowers at reasonable prices, largely at the expense of the independent florists' market share. Over 75 per cent of cut flowers are purchased from a supermarket or large store. The supermarket chains have encouraged changes in their supply chains, as they seek increased shelf-life, daily delivery to replenish stocks, and keen prices to stimulate sales. Sales traditionally peak around key public holidays, especially Easter, Christmas and, of course, St Valentine's Day. In order to spread sales across a wider period, special bouquets are contracted from both domestic and importing packers with the emphasis on flower arranging. Even mail order, the traditional domain of the florists, has been offered by the supermarkets.

Marks & Spencer believes that it is the largest UK fresh florist, offering over 100 varieties of flowers. In one week it sells four million carnations and requires roses all year long from around the world. This type of volume demand has made the UK attractive to both European and international growers. Sierex BV is a major supplier of cut flowers to supermarkets across Europe and claims to be able to distribute at appropriate temperatures and in hydro-packs throughout Europe within 24 hours. It buys from the large auction halls in Holland, where 60 per cent of the world's cut flowers are sold, and also has direct contracts with growers both in the Netherlands and outside Europe. Each year, Sierex assembles 26 million mono and mixed bouquets. The supermarket determines the exact mix to suit its target groups and local tastes. The added value played by Sierex is in careful buying, rapid processing, creative packaging and product display combined with value for money. Chains such as Casino, Promodès and Migros are major customers and the UK is now a prime market for development. In order to meet UK supermarket demand, it has introduced daily deliveries and uses North Sea ferries especially equipped with temperature-controlled facilities.

The growth in year-round cut flower sales in Europe has brought a much needed cash earner for parts of Africa. Zimbabwe and Kenya, for example, can now pick, package, label and price so that products can soon be on the shelves after a twelve-hour flight. For Kenya, cut flowers are now the fourth biggest export earner and it has developed prime markets in Holland, UK, Germany and Switzerland making use of tariff-free exporting for this product category. This market employs over 1 million people in Kenya and brings in $40 mn for the rural economy. Tesco has been instrumental in setting ethical as well as quality and processing standards for the industry through its dealings with the growers' associations. Issues such as above-average wage levels, clothing, nutrition and healthcare for workers are to the fore as well as environmental issues and pest control practices.

The situation in Malawi, however, is more problematic. Despite the high value-added and labour intensive opportunities for cut flowers, part of the sector has been temporarily shut down due to poor management, escalating freight costs (denied by Air Malawi), and high financing costs. Fresh red roses originally for the Netherlands and South Africa remain uncut resulting in a loss of over 700 jobs and $28 mn to the economy. However, the success in other African countries clearly indicates that globalisation of production is now possible even where fast delivery is required. Transport costs of less than 5 per cent of the total cost of the flowers favour companies with a favourable growing environment and to some extent this has been at the expense of European growers. With limited capacity and volumes and higher cost structures, they cannot easily compete nor meet the supermarkets' demand for bulk, year-round supply contracts.

Marks & Spencer offers a range of cut flowers and plants in its stores to encourage its customers to think about 'saying it with flowers'.
Source: **Marks & Spencer plc**

Sources: *The Grocer* (1998); Foottit (2000); *Marketing Week* (2001); Mhone (2000); Van Heck (2000); http://www.sierex.nl.

Figure 1.1 Exchange transactions

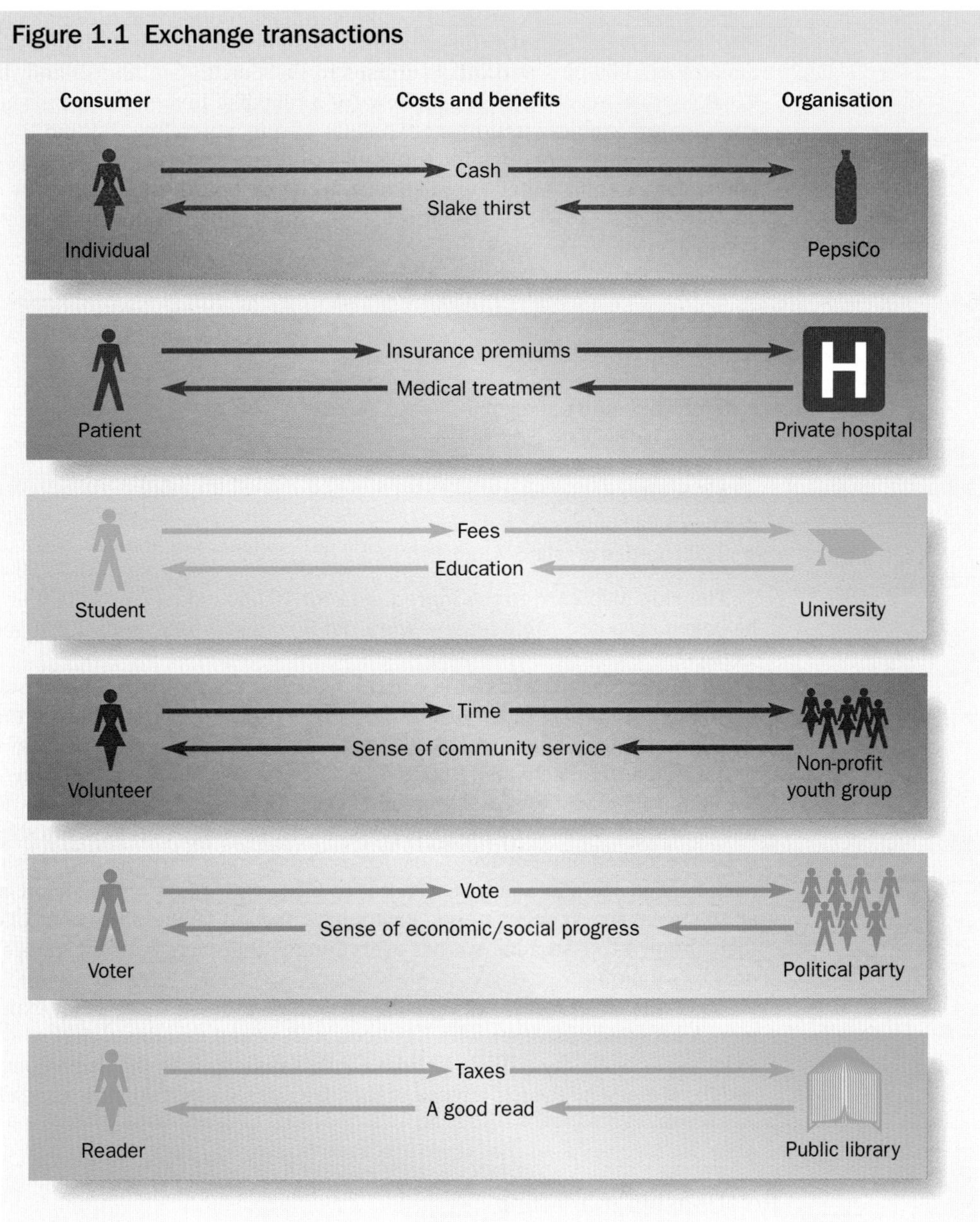

by Greenpeace), the essence of the exchange is mutual value. From mutual value can come satisfaction and possible repeat purchases.

Pricing, promotion and distribution of ideas, goods and services

In saying that marketing involves the conception, pricing, promotion and distribution of ideas, goods and services, the AMA definition is a little more specific in describing the ways in which marketers can stimulate exchanges. It suggests a proactive seller as well as a willing buyer. By designing products, setting sensible, acceptable and justifiable prices, creating awareness and preferences, and ensuring availability and service, the marketer can influence the volume of exchanges. Marketing can be seen, therefore, as a demand management activity on the part of the selling organisation.

Both the CIM and the AMA definitions of marketing, despite their popular usage, are increasingly being criticised as failing to reflect the role and reality of marketing for the twenty-first century. Some criticism concerns the increasing importance of the globalisation of business and the focus on customer retention, relationship building and maintenance that characterises many markets (Christopher *et al.*, 1991; Grönroos, 1997).

eg

P&O cruises, the world's third-biggest cruise operator, mainly targets upmarket holiday-makers aged 50-plus and offers cruises to the Caribbean, Alaska and the Mediterranean. Clearly, cruise passengers are looking for a relaxing, luxury, pampered holiday, and quality and comfort are very important elements of the experience. Behind the scenes, however, this causes huge problems for the cruise operator in terms of planning what food, drink, entertainment and 'hotel' supplies need to be on board or available for any given voyage. Just in terms of food and drink, a 14-day cruise aboard a liner with around 1,200 passengers and crew will require:

- 13 tons of fresh fruit and vegetables
- 4 tons of potatoes
- 4 tons of meat
- 3 tons of fish
- 3 tons of poultry and game
- 14,400 bottles and cans of beer
- 600 bottles of whisky
- 436 bottles of gin, vodka and rum
- Over 1,000 bottles of red wine
- 2,200 bottles of white wine.

The ship also carries the ingredients for 10,000 cakes and 23,000 bread rolls that will be baked on board. We'll let you work out how many toilet rolls 1,200 people would use in 14 days!

All of these supplies have to be in the right place at the right time (the ship can't sail without them!) as well as being of the right quality level to satisfy demanding customers. This takes an almost military approach to logistics as managers can often have only 12 hours to turn a ship around between cruises – 12 hours to disembark the returning passengers, clean the ship, replenish the stores (making sure that not all suppliers try to deliver at the same time!), and get the new holidaymakers on board. On longer cruises, the ships could also need to be re-stocked mid-voyage. Thus, for example, for a Caribbean or world cruise, the company headquarters in Southampton has to liaise with suppliers in Miami, and arrange to get all the necessary supplies to one location, packed in temperature-controlled containers and then shipped to Barbados so that everything is there and waiting when the ship makes its one-day stop-off.

All of this effort to deliver a quality service is essential if customer expectations are to be met. A satisfied customer who has been well wined and dined and who hasn't run out of toilet paper is far more likely to take another holiday with the same company in the future and to recommend the experience to their friends (Rosier, 2001; Varley, 1999).

Relationship marketing

The traditional definitions of marketing tend to reflect a view that the transaction between buyer and seller is primarily seller orientated, that each exchange is totally discrete, and thus lacking any of the personal and emotional overtones that emerge in a long-term relationship made up of a series of exchanges between the same buyer and seller. In B2B markets in particular, each of these exchanges could involve a complex web of interactions between the staff of both organisations, each seeking to work together for their mutual benefit against a history of previous exchanges. Dwyer *et al.* (1987), Gummesson (1987), Turnbull and Valla (1986) particularly highlight the importance of enduring **buyer–seller relationships** as a major influence on decision-making in international B2B markets.

In some circumstances, however, the traditional non-relationship view is perfectly appropriate. A traveller on an unknown road passing through a foreign country may stop at a wayside café, never visited before and never to be visited again. The decision to purchase is thus going to be influenced by the ease of parking, the décor and the ambience rather than by any feeling of trust or commitment to the patron. The decision, in short, is based on the immediate and specific marketing offering. Well-lit signs, a menu in your own language and visibly high hygiene standards will all influence the decision to stop. This scenario describes an approach to marketing where the focus is on a single exchange or transaction between the buyer and the seller and that influences the seller to make the menu look good, the parking available and the décor attractive. The chances of you becoming a regular customer in this instance are, of course, unlikely unless you are a frequent traveller on that route. In contrast, a relationship-focused approach to marketing describes a network of communications and contacts between the buyer and the seller and a series of exchanges over time. Both parties have to be satisfied with the relationship and achieve their respective objectives from it. Marketing, therefore, is part of an interactive process between people, over time, of which relationship creation, building and management are vital cornerstones (Grönroos, 1997; Sheth *et al.*, 1988). Individual exchanges between buyer and seller are important and influenced by previous experiences, good and bad, but any seller that is concerned with the one-off sale and the immediate gain may find that the longer-term interests of both parties are not well served. Companies such as Volvo have supplier relationships that go back fifty years. Unlike the situation with the single exchange or transaction where profits are expected to follow from today's exchanges, in relationship marketing the time perspective can be very long indeed.

Relationship marketing is not just a B2B phenomenon, however. Internet and direct marketing are creating new opportunities for organisations in mass markets to become much closer to their customers. Consumers often stay loyal to familiar brands, retailers and suppliers for many years and with the enormous power of new technology, individual consumers can be identified and profiles developed, whether through loyalty schemes, monitoring internet shopping behaviour or other ways of capturing detailed information (see Chapter 6). It is now possible to track the purchase behaviour of individual shoppers and to create a database for directly targeted communication (see Chapter 18), and with such power it would be a foolish marketer who did not try to maintain customer loyalty and hence improve sales. The UK supermarket chain Tesco, for example, through its Clubcard scheme can track the purchases of individual shoppers, creating a database that allows it to communicate directly and powerfully with consumers. Thus 30-something males who are not buying their fair share of wine should watch out for the promotional mailshot that will soon be on its way!

Wider definition of marketing

So, definitions of marketing are moving away from the single exchange, seller-focused perspective adopted by the CIM and AMA definitions towards more socially relevant and relationship-orientated definitions that are considered to reflect the reality of modern marketing far better. Although relationship marketing over time focuses on customers' needs and attitudes as important points of concern, it can also embrace social and ethical concerns as well as issues more directly related to the series of transactions.

A definition that includes the important elements of both the AMA and CIM definitions, but still embraces the evolving relationship orientation, is offered by Grönroos (1997):

> *Marketing is to establish, maintain and enhance relationships with customers and other partners, at a profit, so that the objectives of the parties involved are met. This is achieved by mutual exchange and fulfillment of promises.*

Such relationships are usually, but not necessarily always, long-term. Some could be little more than a single episode but others could be very enduring. This definition still reflects a managerial orientation towards marketing, but emphasises the mutually active role that both partners in the exchange play. It does not list the activities that marketers undertake, but instead is more concerned with the partnership idea, the concept that marketing is about doing something *with* someone, not doing something *to* them. Of course, not all transactions between buyers and sellers can be considered to be part of a relationship, especially where the purchase does not involve much risk or commitment from the purchaser and thus there is little to gain from entering a relationship (Berry, 1983). This was clearly shown in the wayside café example cited earlier. Overall, however, marketing is increasingly about relationships in both B2B and consumer markets.

The idea of fulfilling promises is also an important one, as marketing is all about making promises to potential buyers. If the buyer decides, after the event, that the seller did not live up to those promises, the chances are that they will never buy again from that seller. If, on the other hand, the buyer decides that the seller has fulfilled their promises, then the seeds of trust are sown, and the buyer may be prepared to begin a long-term relationship with the seller.

Between them, therefore, the three definitions offered say just about everything there is to say about the substance and basic philosophy of marketing. Few would argue with any of that now, but marketing has not always been so readily accepted in that form, as the next two subsections show.

The development of marketing

The basic idea of marketing as an exchange process has its roots in very ancient history, when people began to produce crops or goods surplus to their own requirements and then to barter them for other things they wanted. Elements of marketing, particularly selling and advertising, have been around as long as trade itself, but it took the industrial revolution, the development of mass production techniques and the separation of buyers and sellers to sow the seeds of what we recognise as marketing today.

In the early days, the late nineteenth and early twentieth centuries, goods were sufficiently scarce and competition sufficiently underdeveloped that producers did not really need marketing. They could easily sell whatever they produced ('the production era' in which a 'production orientation' was adopted). As markets and technology developed, competition became more serious and companies began to produce more than they could easily sell. This led to 'the sales era', lasting into the 1950s and 1960s, in which organisations developed increasingly large and increasingly pushy sales forces, and more aggressive advertising approaches (the 'selling orientation').

It was not really until the 1960s and 1970s that marketing generally moved away from a heavy emphasis on post-production selling and advertising to become a more comprehensive and integrated field, earning its place as a major influence on corporate strategy ('**marketing orientation**'). This meant that organisations began to move away from a 'sell what we can make' type of thinking, in which 'marketing' was at best a peripheral activity, towards a 'find out what the customer wants and then we'll make it' type of market driven philosophy. Customers took their rightful place at the centre of the organisation's universe. This finally culminated, in the 1980s, in the wide acceptance of marketing as a strategic concept, and yet there is still room for further development of the **marketing concept**, as new applications and contexts emerge.

Historically, marketing has not developed uniformly across all markets or products. Retailers, along with many consumer goods organisations, have been at the forefront of implementing the marketing concept. Benetton, for instance, developed a strong, unique, international product and retail store image, but within the basic formula is prepared to adapt its merchandising and pricing strategies to suit the demands of different geographic markets. The financial services industry, however, has only very recently truly embraced a marketing orientation, some 10 years or more behind most consumer goods. Knights *et al.* (1994), reviewing the development of a marketing orientation within the UK financial services industry, imply that the transition from a selling to a marketing orientation was 'recent and rapid'. They cite research by Clarke *et al.* (1988) showing that the retail banks were exceptionally early, compared with the rest of the sector, in becoming completely marketing driven. The rest have since followed.

Business orientations

We discuss below the more precise definitions of the alternative approaches to doing business that were outlined above. We then describe the characteristic management thinking behind them, and show how they are used today. Table 1.1 further summarises this information.

marketing *in action*

Marketing myths

The French business magazine *L'Entreprise* gathered together a number of marketing myths to be exploded for the new millennium. One myth relating to consumers and one for each element of the marketing mix have been chosen for discussion.

1 A satisfied consumer is a loyal consumer

Satisfaction helps, but is not necessarily sufficient in itself to guarantee future purchases of a product. After all, satisfaction simply implies that the product has dealt with the problem that the consumer bought it to solve. The next time the consumer is in the market for the same kind of product, other brands offering a better price, a 'new improved' label, more seductive advertising or '20% extra free' might just be more appealing. Marketers have thus to communicate the unique benefits of their products very clearly, constantly monitor changes in customer needs, and try to build relationships with their customers. Loyalty schemes, regular mailshots or magazines relating to the company or brand are examples of tools which help the consumer to feel that something over and above the basic satisfaction of the product is being offered.

2 A strong brand is invincible

A strong brand is an attractive target for aspiring competitors. Supermarket own-label products, for example, packaged and branded in a similar way to the mainstream manufacturer brands, have posed a significant threat to them. The perceived unique benefits of the manufacturer brand are unique no longer. Also, if brand manufacturers become complacent, consumers could become bored with the product or their needs might change. A brand name is thus not sufficient protection against a competitor with a similar or 'better' product (in the eyes of the consumer), nor can it guarantee continued consumer loyalty.

3 A big-name brand can sustain a higher price

Price represents what consumers are prepared to give in exchange for a product. If consumers believe that retailer own-label brands are just as good as manufacturer brands, then they will not pay a premium price for the manufacturer brands. Consumers will only pay 33 pence for a can of Heinz baked beans rather than 21 pence for a can of Tesco own-label or 9 pence for Tesco Value Lines beans if they perceive it to have some unique benefit that they value highly (Superior taste? The kids will actually eat them? You get more beans for your money?). The problem for many brand manufacturers is that they do not want to lower prices for fear that the consumer will think that quality has deteriorated. One way of lowering prices without damaging the brand is to offer a discount on bulk purchases. Heinz, for example, occasionally offers a four-can pack of baked beans for a promotional price of 99 pence (less than 25 pence per can). The consumer recognises that the lower price is due to bulk buying and does not associate it with brand quality. Single cans are still on sale alongside at the regular price.

4 Members of distribution channels do not influence marketing

For consumer products, retailers, especially the supermarket chains, represent an increasingly important influence on manufacturers' marketing efforts, quite apart from the threat of own-label goods. If, for example, supermarkets will not list (i.e. agree to stock) a new grocery product, then its chances of survival are very slim. Products can also get de-listed if they are not performing to the retailer's expectations or demands and, again, that can be fatal for the product. Manufacturers will also have to plan for incentives to encourage retailers to display the product in the prime areas of the store (the ends of aisles and the eye-level shelves) or to feature it in in-store promotions. The bigger retailers can also drive a hard bargain on the price they are prepared to pay for stock, thus reducing the manufacturer's profit margins. More and more, manufacturers are working in partnership with retailers and wholesalers to minimise the potential problems that retailers can cause and to maximise the benefits gained from the retailer's experience and closeness to the consumer. With more expensive consumer goods too, such as electrical goods, the manufacturer is dependent on the retailer's staff to generate sales and needs to offer partnership, training and incentives to protect market share.

5 Advertising always affects sales

Advertising is often used as a long-term image building tool rather than as a short-term sales booster and thus might not have the direct objective of making sales. It is also difficult to measure the exact impact of advertising on sales, especially as most consumers would not admit to being influenced by advertising. Additionally, strong campaigns can continue to affect the consumer long after they have finished and it can be very hard to pinpoint their role in today's purchases. Nevertheless, a manufacturer who wants to spread information quickly to a lot of people about a new product would still find advertising an effective means of generating early sales. Procter & Gamble's Sunny Delight fruit drink was launched in April 1998 with a £9 million European advertising spend and by August 1998 had generated almost £2 million in sales.

Sources: Agède (1998); Bainbridge and Curtis (1998).

Table 1.1 Marketing history and business orientations – a summary

Orientation	*Focus*	*Characteristics and aims*	*Eavesdropping*	*Main era (generalised)*		
				USA	*Western Europe*	*Eastern Europe*
Production	Manufacturing	• Increase production • Cost reduction and control • Make profit through volume	'Any colour you want – as long as it's black'	Up to 1940s	Up to 1950s	Late 1980s
Product	Goods	• Quality is all that matters • Improve quality levels • Make profit through volume	'Just look at the quality of the paintwork'	Up to 1940s	Up to 1960s	Largely omitted
Selling	Selling what's produced – seller's needs	• Aggressive sales and promotion • Profit through quick turnover of high volume	'You're not keen on the black? What if I throw in a free sun-roof?'	1940–1950s	1950–1960s	Early 1990s
Marketing	Defining what customers want – buyer's needs	• Integrated marketing • Defining needs in advance of production • Profit through customer satisfaction and loyalty	'Let's find out if they want it in black, and if they would pay a bit more for it'	1960s onwards	1970s onwards	mid-1990s onwards

Production orientation

The emphasis with a **production orientation** is on making products that are affordable and available, and thus the prime task of management is to ensure that the organisation is as efficient as possible in production and distribution techniques. The main assumption is that the market is completely price sensitive, which means that customers are only interested in price as the differentiating factor between competing products and will buy the cheapest. Customers are thus knowledgeable about relative prices, and if the organisation wants to bring prices down, then it must tightly control costs. This is the philosophy of the production era, and was predominant in Central and Eastern Europe in the early stages of the new market economies. Apart from that, it may be a legitimate approach, in the short term, where demand outstrips supply, and companies can put all their effort into improving production and increasing supply and worry about the niceties of marketing later.

A variation on that situation happens when a product is really too expensive for the market, and therefore the means have to be found to bring costs, and thus prices, down. This decision, however, is as likely to be marketing as production driven, and may involve technologically complex, totally new products that neither the producer nor the customer is sure of. Thus CD players, videos, camcorders and home computers were all launched on to unsuspecting markets with limited supply and high prices, but the manufacturers envisaged that with extensive marketing and the benefits gained from progressing along the production and technology learning curve, high-volume markets could be opened up for lower-priced, more reliable products.

Product orientation

The **product orientation** assumes that consumers are primarily interested in the product itself, and buy on the basis of quality. Since consumers want the highest level of quality for their money, the organisation must work to increase and improve its quality levels. At first glance, this may seem like a reasonable proposition, but the problem is the assumption that consumers *want this product*. Consumers do not want products, they want solutions to problems, and if the organisation's product does not solve a problem, they will not buy it,

A modern form of production orientation can occur when an organisation becomes too focused on pursuing a low cost strategy in order to achieve economies of scale, and loses sight of the real customer need. Tetra Pak, one of the market leaders in carton manufacture ran into problems in the 1990s by concentrating on the interests of its direct customers rather than those of the end user. The focus was on production efficiency, i.e. how many cartons could be filled per hour, rather than on the problems of actually using a carton. Despite making nearly 90 billion cartons each year, the Swedish company did not fully address the problem that some of the cartons were difficult to open and tended to spill their contents rather easily all over the floor. It clearly had the know-how to solve the problem, but in the pursuit of a low-cost operator position, allowed its rival from Norway, Elo Pak to develop a pack with a proper spout and a plastic cap that was more in tune with customer needs. It was also Elo Pak that pioneered the use of plasma technology for barrier coating to improve the range of uses for cartons and the life of the liquids they contained (Mans, 2000). This underlines the need to talk to end users constantly and to be prepared to consider their needs as well as the direct customer, i.e. the carton fillers. Tetra Pak has now realised that consumers want convenient packaging and have redesigned packs to be easier to handle and pour from with more user-friendly openings (http://www.tetrapak.com).

however high the quality level is. An organisation may well produce the best ever record player, but the majority of consumers would rather buy a cheap CD player. In short, customer needs rather than the product should be the focus.

In a review of the history of marketing thinking in China, Deng and Dart (1999) considered the market orientation of traditional state enterprises. From 1949 until economic reform began in 1979, Chinese organisations were part of a very rigid, planned economy. During that time denying marketing was a fundamental part of the political belief system and with a low GDP per capita and widespread scarcity of consumer goods, there was little, if any, incentive for the development of marketing activities (Gordon, 1991). The focus was on manufacturing output and all major marketing decisions such as product range, pricing, and selection of distribution channels were controlled by government. The state set production targets for each enterprise, distributed their products, assigned personnel, allocated supplies and equipment, retained all profit, and covered all losses (Zhuang and Whitehill, 1989; Gordon, 1991). The priority was production and virtually any product would do.

Since the reforms and the opening up of the economy, most enterprises, even if state-owned, have to now make marketing decisions as they are no longer allocated production inputs, nor are their outputs assigned to prearranged buyers. Price controls have been relaxed and distribution lists from the state ended. However, the transition process is not yet complete: many state-owned enterprises are being subsidised to retain employment levels; government power is still great, as the internet café owners recently found when they were shut down overnight; and the distribution infrastructure is still not very efficient. As consumer awareness and purchasing power increase, however, Chinese enterprises will have to become more marketing orientated to survive.

Sales orientation

The basis for the **sales orientation** way of thinking is that consumers are inherently reluctant to purchase, and need every encouragement to purchase sufficient quantities to satisfy the organisation's needs. This leads to a heavy emphasis on personal selling and other sales stimulating devices because products 'are sold, not bought', and thus the organisation puts its effort into building strong sales departments, with the focus very much on the needs of the seller, rather than on those of the buyer. Home improvement organisations, selling, for example, double glazing and cavity wall insulation, have tended to operate like this, as has the timeshare industry.

Schultz and Good (2000) proposed that a sales orientation can also emerge from commission-based reward and remuneration packages for sales people, even though the seller might actually want longer-term customer relationships to be established. When the pressure is on to make a sale and to achieve target sales volumes there is a danger that the sales person will focus on the one-off sale rather than the long-term relationship. There is a tension between the need to spend time on relationships and the urge to move on to the next sale. These issues will be further considered in Chapter 17.

Marketing orientation

The organisation that develops and performs its production and marketing activities with the needs of the buyer driving it all, and with the satisfaction of that buyer as the main aim, is marketing orientated. The motivation is to 'find wants and fill them' rather than 'create products and sell them'. The assumption is that customers are not necessarily price driven, but are looking for the total offering that best fits their needs, and therefore the organisation has to define those needs and develop appropriate offerings. This is not just about the core product itself, but also about pricing, access to information, availability and peripheral benefits and services that add value to the product. Not all customers, however, necessarily want exactly the same things. They can be grouped according to common needs and wants, and the organisation can produce a specifically targeted marketing package that best suits the needs of one group, thus increasing the chances of satisfying that group and retaining its loyalty.

A marketing orientation is far more, however, than simply matching products and services to customers. It has to emerge from an organisational philosophy, an approach to doing business that naturally places customers and their needs at the heart of what the organisation does. Not all organisations do this to the same extent, although many are trying to move towards it. Hooley *et al.* (1990), as a result of an in-depth study of senior marketing executives, suggested that there are different degrees of marketing orientation, as shown in Figure 1.2.

The *marketing philosophers*, the biggest cluster of the four in Figure 1.2, see marketing not only as a function, but as a guiding philosophy of doing business for the whole organisation. In their eyes, marketing is the responsibility of every employee. They also tend to take a more proactive, strategic and planned approach to marketing, and thus have a greater input into corporate strategy.

Sales supporters are the smallest cluster, and they see marketing as restricted to the marketing department, with a focus on sales and promotional support.

Departmental marketers see marketing as restricted to the marketing department but, unlike the sales supporters, they also accept the importance of identifying and meeting customer needs.

Figure 1.2 Marketing approaches

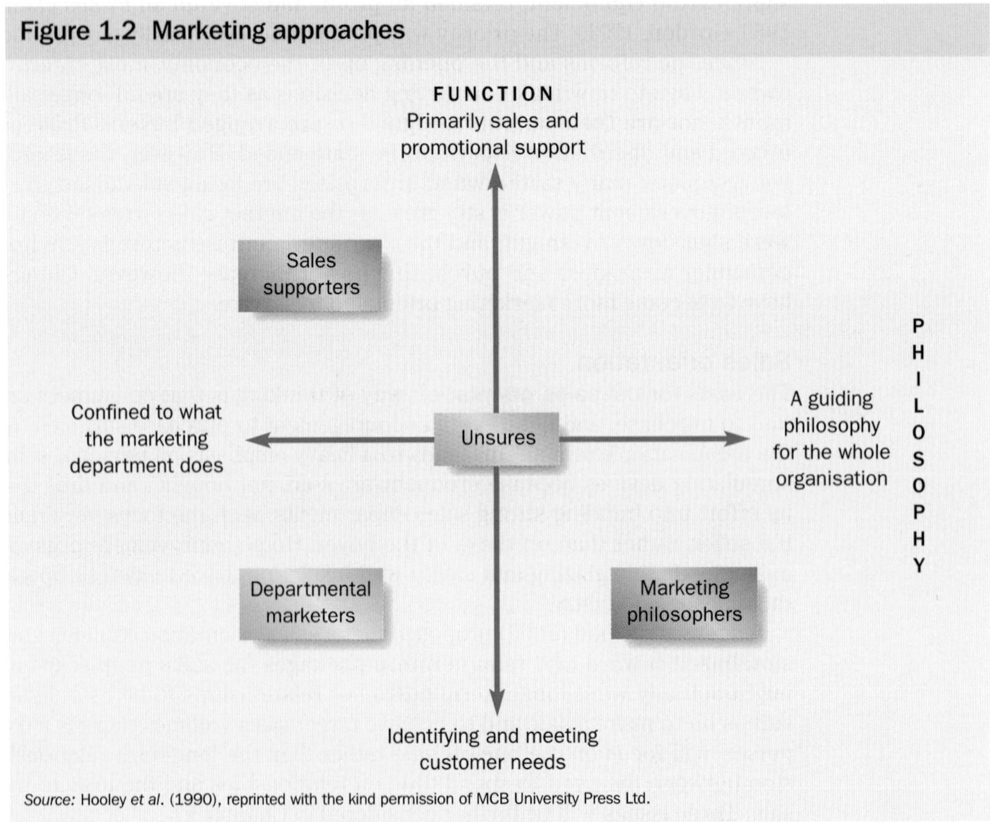

Source: Hooley et *al.* (1990), reprinted with the kind permission of MCB University Press Ltd.

The 'unsures' cannot decide exactly what marketing is for. Their attitude reflects elements of sales support and customer orientation, but they do not see marketing as confined to the marketing department, nor do they see it as an organisational philosophy. Hooley *et al.* suggest that this implies a laissez-faire attitude to marketing rather than any kind of conscious orientation.

Organisations may evolve from sales support to departmental marketing to the guiding philosophy stage, and organisations that reach the philosophy stage may perform better than those which do not.

Henderson (1998), however, urges caution in assuming that a marketing orientation is a guarantee of success in achieving above average performance. There are many internal and external factors at work in determining success, of which effective marketing thinking is but one. If marketing dominates the rest of the organisation it can help to diminish key competencies in other areas such as manufacturing productivity or technological innovation. Furthermore, the marketing department approach to organising the marketing function can isolate marketing from design, production, deliveries, technical service, complaints handling, invoicing and other customer-related activities. As a consequence, the rest of the organisation could be alienated from marketing, making the coordination of customer and market-orientated activities across the organisation more difficult (Piercy, 1992). This underlines the importance of Narver and Slater's (1990) three key factors that help the marketing function to achieve above average performance:

- *Interfunctional orientation* enabling cooperation between the management functions to create superior value;
- *Competitor orientation* to retain an edge; and finally
- *Customer orientation.*

Having established the importance of the marketing concept to an organisation, the chapter now turns to the issue of developing marketing thinking and practice across the organisation.

marketing *in action*

The battle of Charing Cross Road

At 113–119 Charing Cross Road, Foyles, one of the oldest comprehensive bookshops in London, is limbering up after a long, self-imposed rest to take on the 'newcomers' such as Borders (often trading under the *Books* name in the UK), a leading global retailer from the United States, which has a store at 120 Charing Cross Road. It is a battle of retail formats that will also be fought alongside the threat from the increasing number of online booksellers such as Amazon.

Foyles was founded by a book lover at the turn of the twentieth century and became a leading bookstore in London. Before his death in 1963 William Foyle passed the business over to Christina, his daughter, and that is when the rot started. She stubbornly refused to change almost anything. At the time of the changeover, Foyles was *the* bookstore with five floors loaded with books and 30 miles of shelving. It carried a vast stock to cater for most tastes in a relaxed browser-friendly environment. However, other than the titles, little else changed. The philosophy was that a 'good book will sell itself'.

***The shop itself is undergoing a massive £2 million refurbishment programme – with new bookshelves, carpets, lighting & air-conditioning. The in-store signage is being completely overhauled. Source:* Foyles.**

Christina had a passion for books but not for the customers buying them nor staff selling them. Computers and electronic tills were resisted, resulting in customers having to queue twice with dockets just to buy one book. If customers wanted to buy from more than one department, they had to go through separate transactions in each department. The shelves became shabby and the shop in need of some tender loving care. Wages were low and sales staff had no proper employment contracts. The business stood still while others entered the market.

At 120 Charing Cross Road, things were rather different in Borders' new store. The retail marketing formula was applied on a global scale, with the customer at the heart of the business. Starting as a small retailer, the company expanded to over 290 stores in the United States, 32 stores in the UK and outlets in Australia, New Zealand and Singapore. It also has control of Waldenbooks in the US with over 900 stores. It uses category management techniques to build stocks and collections based on customers' needs. One of the seven categories adopted, for example, is children's books. Stores are carefully planned in terms of size and location to exploit fully local market potential, but the range of book titles stocked is largely standardised. The priority at the moment is opening 'superstores', which are much larger than existing stores in the chain. Aisles are wide, stock is clearly laid out, and if shoppers cannot find their desired book on the shelves in the store, by using 'title sleuth' they may find it among the 700,000 titles held at a fulfilment centre. Special order sales have increased by 30 per cent since the introduction of the service in all stores. There is a café operation in all stores along with comfortable chairs so that shoppers can relax and read a little before making a purchase. Relationship marketing through the website and magazine *Inside Borders*, in-store merchandising and retail branding do the rest. Sales are now around $3.3 bn of which about $219 mn comes from the international operation which is the priority for further growth. As sales volume increases, the retailer's buying power also increases and the scope of the retail brand can be extended, for example to include an e-commerce facility co-branded with Amazon.

Meanwhile, under new management after Christina's death, Foyles is enjoying its freedom from the shackles that have held it back since the 1960s. The tills have been computerised, staff (a high percentage of whom are graduates) have been given contracts and provided with customer service training. The dockets and the double queuing have gone. There is now a busy online ordering service. The 33 different departments offering 4 million books across 630,000 titles still remain, however. Sales are already increasing: up 24 per cent in the first four months of 2001 when the market was growing by just 6 per cent, but the new management team knows that there is still a long way to go and it is still a challenge to find the book you really want across so many departments. However, a new information point has been provided on the groundfloor before the customer starts exploring any of the other floors. Foyles still wants to be a bookshop for book lovers and feedback from customers is that it should retain the feel of a 'real' bookshop rather than creating a supermarket-style experience. Finding the balance between modernity and tradition will be a challenge, as Foyles would not wish to lose existing customers in the pursuit of new ones. At least the customer is now coming back into focus, however. Some argue that it is the last proper comprehensive bookshop left in London capable of providing a quality browsing and shopping experience. For book lovers, the hunt and the impulse are both powerful forces.

And who will be the eventual winner? Visit Charing Cross Road and judge for yourself; after all it is your spending power that both are after.

Sources: Davies (2001); http://www.foyles.co.uk; http://www.bordersstores.com.

Emergent marketing philosophies

The marketing concept and the philosophy of a marketing orientation continue to evolve. In increasingly competitive global markets consisting of increasingly demanding customers, organisations are continually striving to find more effective ways of attracting and retaining customers, and sometimes that could mean refining further exactly what marketing means.

Corporate social responsibility: societal and ethical marketing. Interest in ethical issues and a socially responsible approach to marketing has been around for a long time. In the 1970s, for example, Anderson and Cunningham (1972) put forward the idea of the 'socially conscious consumer' while Kinnear *et al.* (1974) focused specifically on the 'ecologically concerned' consumer and what we would now label 'green issues'. Concern with such issues gathered pace through the 1980s and continued into the 1990s as it became clear that business ethics were becoming increasingly important to an increasing number of consumers and that there was thus a link emerging between 'good' ethics, market share and profitability (Mintzberg, 1983; Strong, 1996 for example). In parallel with this, authors have also examined the role of corporate and personal ethics in managerial decision-making as part of the wider field of **corporate social responsibility (CSR)** in a variety of domestic and international business contexts (for example Murphy and Laczniak, 1981; Hunt and Vitell, 1986 and 1993; Allmon *et al.*, 1997).

CSR suggests that organisations should not only consider their customers and their profitability, but also the good of the wider communities, local and global, within which they exist. Dunfee *et al.* (1999), for example, discuss the concept of a 'social contract' between business and society whereby business is permitted to make profit from delivering the goods and services that society wants in return for operating within a moral and ethical framework laid down by society. As Smith and Higgins (2000) put it, consumers now are not only looking for environmentally sensitive and ethically considerate products, but also for businesses to demonstrate a wider set of ethical commitments to society, '[A business] must, as should we all, become a "good citizen"'. Carroll (1999) provides an excellent review of the history and evolution of the CSR concept, but it is his own 1991 paper which provides the basis for the most succinct definition of CSR which will underpin the coverage of CSR in this book:

> *. . . four kinds of social responsibilities constitute total CSR: economic, legal, ethical and philanthropic . . . [B]usiness should not fulfil these in sequential fashion but . . . each is to be fulfilled at all times . . . The CSR firm should strive to make a profit, obey the law, be ethical, and be a good corporate citizen.*
>
> (Carroll, 1991, pp. 40–43, as summarised by Carroll, 1999)

Marketing within a CSR context is concerned with ensuring that organisations handle marketing responsibly, and in a way that contributes to the well-being of society. Consumers have become increasingly aware of the social and ethical issues involved in marketing, such as the ethics of marketing to children, fair trade with third-world suppliers, the ecological impact of business, and the extent of good 'corporate citizenship' displayed by companies, for example. Companies looking to establish a reputable and trustworthy image as a foundation for building long-term relationships with their customers thus need to consider the philosophy of CSR seriously if they are to meet their customers' wider expectations, and create and maintain competitive advantage (Balestrini, 2001). Indeed, some companies, such as Body Shop, have adopted a very proactive approach to societal marketing and have made CSR a central pillar of their whole business philosophy (see Hartman and Beck-Dudley, 1999 for a detailed discussion of marketing ethics within Body Shop International).

The Responsible Century?, a survey published in 2000 by Burson-Marsteller and the Prince of Wales' Business Leaders' Forum, gathered opinions from 100 leading business opinion formers and decision-makers from France, Germany and the UK. Two-thirds 'agreed strongly' that CSR will be important in the future and 89 per cent said that their future decisions would be influenced by CSR (CSR Forum, 2001). Interestingly, the survey points to a shift away from defining CSR purely in terms of hard, quantifiable issues such as environmental performance, charitable donations to an emphasis on softer issues such as treatment of employees, commitment to local communities, and ethical business conduct. Internal as well as external behaviour now matters.

The implications of CSR for marketing is clearly shown by a UK report, *Who Are The Ethical Consumers?*, by journalist Roger Cowe and The Co-operative Bank's head of corporate affairs, Simon Williams (as quoted by Mason, 2000). The report says that 'caring' consumers cross most sociopolitical boundaries, and are not defined by party politics, social class, age or gender. Furthermore, the potential for ethical products and services in the UK could be as high as 30 per cent of consumer markets. This report also researched consumer behaviour with regard to ethical issues. While most consumers had done the obvious things (for example 73 per cent of respondents had recycled materials/waste at least once during the previous 12 months), significant numbers had also done things much closer to the marketer's heart: 52 per cent had recommended companies because of their responsible reputation; 51 per cent had chosen a product or service because of a company's responsible reputation; perhaps more seriously, 44 per cent had avoided a product or service because of a company's behaviour; and 29 per cent had bought primarily for ethical reasons (as reported by Mason, 2000). The ethical bandwagon is gaining momentum.

CSR is rapidly changing from being a 'would like' to a 'must have' feature of business. Although at the time of writing businesses are under no obligation to report on their CSR activities in the UK, many already do – about 80 per cent of the FT-SE 100 companies in the

UK provide information about their environmental and/or social performance (Gray, 2001) – and it is likely that pressure for transparency on CSR will only increase. The latest buzzword in corporate accountability is '360 degree reporting' which acknowledges the need to produce annual reports that take a much more holistic view of a company's activities to meet the information needs of pressure groups, those looking for ethical investments, and the wider audience interested in CSR, rather than just shareholders and traditional bankers. Companies in potentially sensitive sectors such as utilities and transport, have begun to produce separate reports on their CSR performance, for example utility company Kelda Group's *Environment and Community Report* and water company Severn Trent's *Stewardship Report*, and London Transport's *Environmental Performance Report* (Buxton, 2000).

eg

Severn Trent plc, based in the UK midlands, has a turnover of some £1.6 billion and employs over 14,000 people across the UK, US, and Europe. Severn Trent takes CSR very seriously. As an environmental services company, concerned with water treatment, waste disposal and utilities, it has always been focused on 'green' issues, but its commitment to CSR goes much further than that. In its 2001 Stewardship Report 'The environment is our business', Robert Walker, the Group Chief Executive, said, 'Business cannot operate in isolation from society. Our responsibilities are not limited to our customers and shareholders but extend to a wider group of stakeholders, each of whom expects us to be ever more accountable and transparent in the way we do business. . . . Sustainable development encompasses economic and social issues as well as environmental considerations. We wholeheartedly embrace the concept of Corporate Social Responsibility and are playing an active role in the World Business Council for Sustainable Development' (Severn Trent, 2001, p. 1). The Stewardship report thus covers many areas of CSR, not only relating to the Group's approach to the protection of the natural environment, biodiversity, and the efficient use of natural resources within its operations, but also its role within society and local communities, its perceived CSR leadership role among its suppliers and customers in improving the performance of the entire supply chain, and its internal application of ethical principles in its HRM policies, for example. A particularly interesting section of the report is headed 'Governance for Sustainability' which explains how the organisational structure facilitates the integration of CSR throughout the Group and its operations. It also summarises the Group's business principles which include concepts such as 'corporate citizenship', 'integrity', 'respect for local cultures', 'lawfulness', and 'shared values', very much in line with Carroll's (1999) ideas of CSR, mentioned earlier.

Government too is taking an interest in CSR. In March 2001, the UK government launched a website, http:\\www.societyandbusiness.gov.uk, and published a report titled *Business and Society* (DTI, 2001) which aimed to set the agenda for the further development of good CSR practice in British business. The EU is also committed to promoting and reinforcing CSR within European businesses. In 2001 a Green Paper was published with the stated aim:

> *. . .to launch a wide debate on how the European Union could promote corporate social responsibility at both the European and international level, in particular on how to make the most of existing experiences, to encourage the development of innovative practices, to bring greater transparency and to increase the reliability of evaluation and validation.*
>
> (EU, 2001, Executive Summary, paragraph 7, p. 3)

As with the CSR Forum report, the EU definition of CSR incorporates both internal and external elements, thus HRM and health and safety issues are as prominent as environmental concerns and local community involvement. There is also an emphasis on the importance of a holistic approach to CSR, i.e. integrating it into corporate governance and management, reporting and auditing, as seen in the example of Severn Trent above. The message is clear: companies are increasingly being expected to adopt and integrate the CSR concept and those that ignore it risk having it forced upon them eventually either through market forces or through regulation.

Towards 'sustainable marketing'. Inextricably tied in with the concept and best practice of CSR in its widest sense is the idea of sustainable development. Sustainability was defined in the Brundtland Report of 1987 as:

> *development that meets the needs of the present without compromising the ability of future generations to meet their own needs.* (WCED, 1987)

Sustainability is not just concerned with environmental and ecological issues, as important as these are, but also with the social, economic and cultural development of society. The wider 'softer agenda' includes, therefore, the fair distribution of economic benefits, human rights, community involvement and product responsibility. This is taken seriously by business. Echoing the sentiments expressed in the Severn Trent example above, Jurgen Strube, the chairman of BASF, the large German chemical company, said that sustainable development in the areas of the economy, ecology and society will be the key to the success in the twenty-first century (as reported by Challener, 2001). Society cannot continue to enjoy economic growth without reference to the consequences for environmental protection and social stability (*OECD Observer*, 2001).

In the light of the whole CSR/sustainability debate, **sustainable marketing** is likely to become the next stage in the conceptual development of marketing as it focuses on some of the significant long-term challenges facing society in the twenty-first century. The challenge to marketing thinking is to broaden the concept of exchange to incorporate the longer-term needs of society at large rather than the short-term pursuit of individual gratification and consumption. It is not about marketers revising strategies to exploit new societal opportunities, it is about what society can afford to allow marketers to exploit and over what timescale. This sounds very idealistic: in a competitive world in which the customer is free to choose and, moreover, in which business operates on the principle of meeting customers' needs and wants, it sometimes requires courage for a business to change those principles if those changes precede customer concern and government legislation. Consumers within society will have to travel up a learning curve and that process is only just beginning.

We would, therefore, like to define sustainable marketing as:

> *the establishment, maintenance and enhancement of customer relationships so that the objectives of the parties involved are met without compromising the ability of future generations to achieve their own objectives.*

In short, consumers today, whatever the market imperative, cannot be allowed to destroy the opportunities for society tomorrow by taking out more than is being put back in. This not only embraces environmental and ecological issues but also the social and cultural consequences of a consumer society that equates 'more' with 'better'.

Sustainable development in which marketing thinking can play a part may mean that the short-term gain of individual organisations has to be balanced against the consequences for society at large of that gain. There are often pressures to achieve short-term gains in market share or profitability and these pressures do not fit well with time spans of twenty years or more. It follows that governments, often collectively and through agencies and international collaboration, must respond adequately to the challenges of tomorrow if individual enterprises are not able to do so. Progress to date has not been outstanding as too many people live in real poverty and in many places the exploitation of land, water and mineral resources is above critical levels, often just for the sake of supplying developed societies with the products and services they demand.

How does all this impact on the marketing process? The internalisation of costs (making the polluters pay), green taxes, legislation, support for cleaner technology, redesigned products to minimise resources and waste streams, reverse distribution channels to receive products for recycling and consumer education on sustainability are all an essential part of a new marketing agenda for the twenty-first century. To some it is not a choice, but a mandate that cannot be ignored (Fuller, 1999). Ecological and environmental agendas to date have had an impact on marketing strategy, but it has been patchy. The old adage 'reduce, recycle and re-use' has for example influenced the type of packaging materials used to ensure recyclability. Clothing manufacturers have produced plastic outdoor clothing that can be recycled; glue manufacturers have reduced the toxic emissions from their products;

car manufacturers, in accordance with the EU's End-of-Life Vehicle Directive, now have to consider the recycling or other means of disposal of old cars. However, research often indicates that consumers given a free choice are reluctant to pay more for environmentally friendly products such as organic food and many find it hard to establish the link between their individual buying decision and its global impact. It will require a societal balance and adjustment period, but evidence is mounting that if change does not take place, the negative long-term impact on the environment and society could be irreversible.

So in this century, the marketing organisation will have to lead consumer interest and attitude, work with government in that process and only then will its legitimate self-interest be realised. It is important, therefore, that throughout this book, the importance of CSR, sustainable marketing and marketing ethics will be emphasised – look out for the *corporate social responsibility in action* vignettes in each chapter.

The marketing concept in the organisation

What does the philosophy of marketing as a way of doing business mean to a real organisation? In this section we explore the practicalities of implementing the marketing concept, showing just how fundamentally marketing can influence the structure and management of the whole organisation. First, we look at the complexity of the organisational environment, and then think about how marketing can help to manage and make sense of the relationship between the organisation and the outside world. Second, we examine the relationship between marketing and the internal world of the organisation, looking, for example, at the potential conflicts between marketing and other business functions. To bring the external and the internal environments together, this section is summarised by looking at marketing as an interface, i.e. as a linking mechanism between the organisation and various external elements.

The external organisational environment

Figure 1.3 summarises the complexity of the external world in which an organisation has to operate. There are many people, groups, elements and forces that have the power to influence, directly or indirectly, the way in which the organisation conducts its business. The organisational environment includes both the immediate operating environment and the broader issues and trends that affect business in the longer term.

Current and potential customers

Customers are obviously vital to the continued health of the organisation. It is essential, therefore, that it is able to locate customers, find out what they want and then communicate its promises to them. Those promises have to be delivered (i.e. the right product at the right time at the right price in the right place) and followed up to ensure that customers are satisfied.

Competitors

Competitors, however, make the organisation's liaison with customer groups a little more difficult, since by definition they are largely pursuing the same set of customers. Customers will make comparisons between different offerings, and will listen to competitors' messages. The organisation, therefore, has not only to monitor what its competitors are actually doing now, but also to try to anticipate what they will do in the future in order to develop counter-measures in advance. European giants Nestlé and Unilever, for example, compete fiercely with each other in several fast moving consumer goods (**fmcg**) markets.

Intermediaries

Intermediaries often provide invaluable services in getting goods from manufacturers to the end buyer. Without the cooperation of a network of wholesalers and/or retailers, many manufacturers would have immense problems in getting their goods to the end customer at the right time in the right place. The organisation must, therefore, think carefully about how

Figure 1.3 The organisation's environment

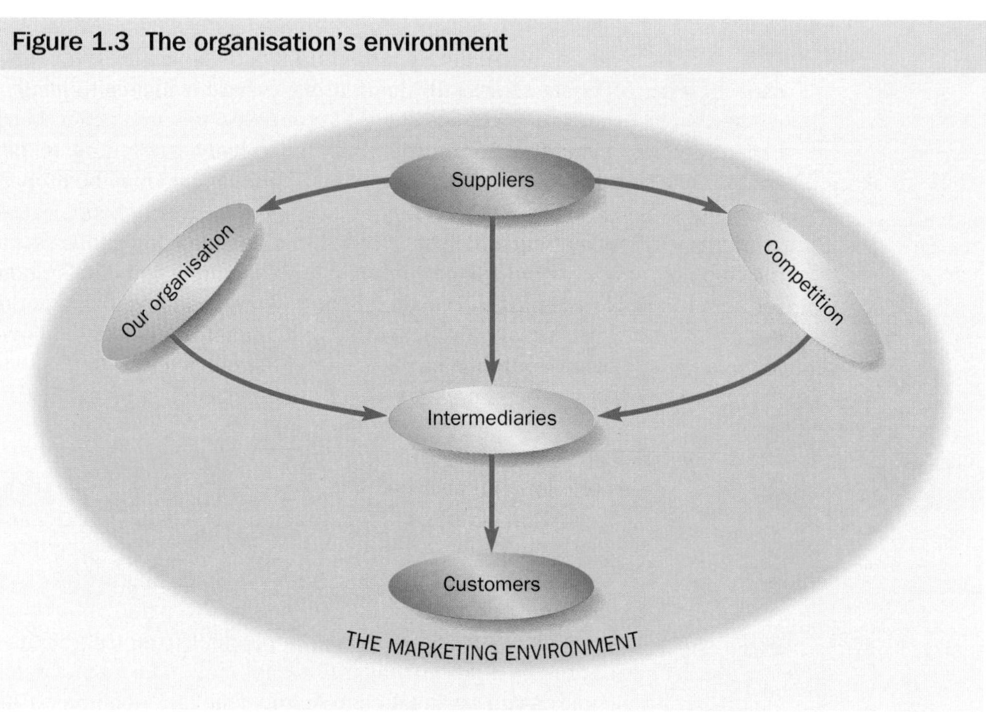

best to distribute goods, and build appropriate relationships with intermediaries. Again, this is an area in which competition can interfere, and organisations cannot always obtain access to the channels of distribution that they want, or trade on the terms that they want.

Suppliers

Another crucial link in the chain is the supplier. Losing a key supplier of components or raw materials can mean that production flow is interrupted, or that a lower-quality or more expensive substitution has to be made. This means that there is a danger that the organisation will fail in its promises to the customer, for example by not providing the right product at the right time at the right price. Choice of suppliers, negotiation of terms and relationship building therefore all become important tasks.

The wider **marketing environment**, which will be discussed in further detail in Chapter 2, covers all the other influences that might provide opportunities or threats to the organisation. These include technological development, legal and regulatory constraints, the economic environment, and sociocultural changes. It is essential for the organisation to keep track of all these factors, and to incorporate them into decision-making as early as possible if it is to keep ahead of the competition.

This overview of the organisation's world has implied that there are many relationships that matter and that need to be managed if the organisation is to conduct its business successfully. The main responsibility for creating and managing these relationships lies with the marketing function.

The internal organisational environment

As well as fostering and maintaining relationships with external groups and forces, the marketing function has to interact with other functions within the organisation. Not all organisations have formal marketing departments, and even if they do they can be set up in different ways, but wherever the responsibility for the planning and implementation of marketing lies, close interaction with other areas of the organisation is essential. Not all business functions, however, operate with the same kind of focus, and sometimes there can be potential conflict where perspectives and concerns do not match up. This subsection looks at just a few other functions typically found in all but the smallest organisations and some of the points of conflict between them and the marketers.

Finance

The finance function, for example, sets budgets, perhaps early in the financial year, and expects other functions to stick to them. It wants hard evidence to justify expenditure, and it usually wants pricing to cover costs and to contribute towards profit. Marketing, on the other hand, tends to want the flexibility to act intuitively, according to fast changing needs. Marketing also takes a longer, strategic view of pricing, and may be prepared to make a short-term financial loss in order to develop the market or to further wider strategic objectives.

In terms of accounting and credit, i.e. where finance comes into contact with customers, the finance function would want pricing and procedures to be as standardised as possible, for administrative ease. An accountant would want to impose tough credit terms and short credit periods, preferably only dealing with customers with proven credit records. Marketing, however, would again want some flexibility to allow credit terms to be used as part of a negotiation procedure, and to use pricing discounts as a marketing tool.

Purchasing

The purchasing function can also become somewhat bureaucratic, with too high a priority given to price. A focus on economical purchase quantities, standardisation and the price of materials, along with the desire to purchase as infrequently as possible, can all reduce the flexibility and responsiveness of the organisation. Marketing prefers to think of the quality of the components and raw materials rather than the price, and to go for non-standard parts, to increase its ability to differentiate its product from that of the competition. To be fair to purchasing, this is a somewhat traditional view. The rise of relationship marketing (pp. 8–9) and the increasing acceptance of just-in-time (JIT) systems (Chapter 12) mean that marketing and purchasing are now working more closely than ever in building long-term, flexible, cooperative relationships with suppliers.

Production

Production has perhaps the greatest potential to clash with marketing. It may be in production's interests to operate long, large production runs with as few variations on the basic product as possible, and with changes to the product as infrequently as possible, at least where mass production is concerned. This also means that production would prefer to deal with standard, rather than customised, orders. If new products are necessary, then the longer the lead time they are given to get production up to speed and running consistently, the better. Marketing has a greater sense of urgency and a greater demand for flexibility. Marketing may look for short production runs of many varied models in order to serve a range of needs in the market. Similarly, changes to the product may be frequent in order to keep the market interested. Marketing, particularly when serving B2B customers, may also be concerned with customisation as a means of better meeting the buyer's needs.

Research and development and engineering

Like production, research and development (R&D) and engineering prefer long lead times. If they are to develop a new product from scratch, then the longer they have to do it, the better. The problem is, however, that marketing will want the new product available as soon as possible, for fear of the competition launching their versions first. Being first into a market can allow the organisation to establish market share and customer loyalty, and to set prices freely, before the effects of competition make customers harder to gain and lead to downward pressure on prices. There is also the danger that R&D and engineering may become focused on the product for the product's sake, and lose sight of what the eventual customer is looking for. Marketing, in contrast, will be concentrating on the benefits and selling points of the product rather than purely on its functionality.

Marketing as an integrative business function

The previous subsection took a pretty negative view, highlighting the potential for conflict and clashes of culture between marketing and other internal functions. It need not necessarily be like that, and this subsection will seek to redress the balance a little, by showing how marketing can work with other functions. Many successful organisations such as Sony,

Nestlé and Unilever ensure that all functions within their organisation are focused on their customers. These organisations have embraced a marketing philosophy that permeates the whole enterprise and places the customer firmly at the centre of their universe.

What must be remembered is that organisations do not exist for their own sake. They exist primarily to serve the needs of the purchasers and users of their goods and services. If they cannot successfully sell their goods and services, if they cannot create and hold customers (or clients, or passengers, or patients or whoever), then they undermine their reason for existing. All functions within an organisation, whether they have direct contact with customers or not, contribute in some way towards that fundamental purpose. Finance, for example, helps the organisation to be more cost effective; personnel helps to recruit appropriate staff and make sure they are properly trained and remunerated so that they are more productive or serve the customer better; R&D provides better products; and production obviously churns out the product to the required quality and quantity specifications to meet market needs.

All of these functions and tasks are interdependent, i.e. none of them can exist without the others, and none of them has any purpose without customers and markets to serve. Marketing can help to supply all of those functions with the information they need to fulfil their specific tasks better, within a market-oriented framework. Those interdependencies, and the role of marketing in bringing functions together and emphasising the customer focus, are summarised in a simplified example in Figure 1.4.

Although the lists of items in the boxes in Figure 1.4 are far from comprehensive, they do show clearly how marketing can act as a kind of buffer or filter, both collecting information

Figure 1.4 Marketing as an interface

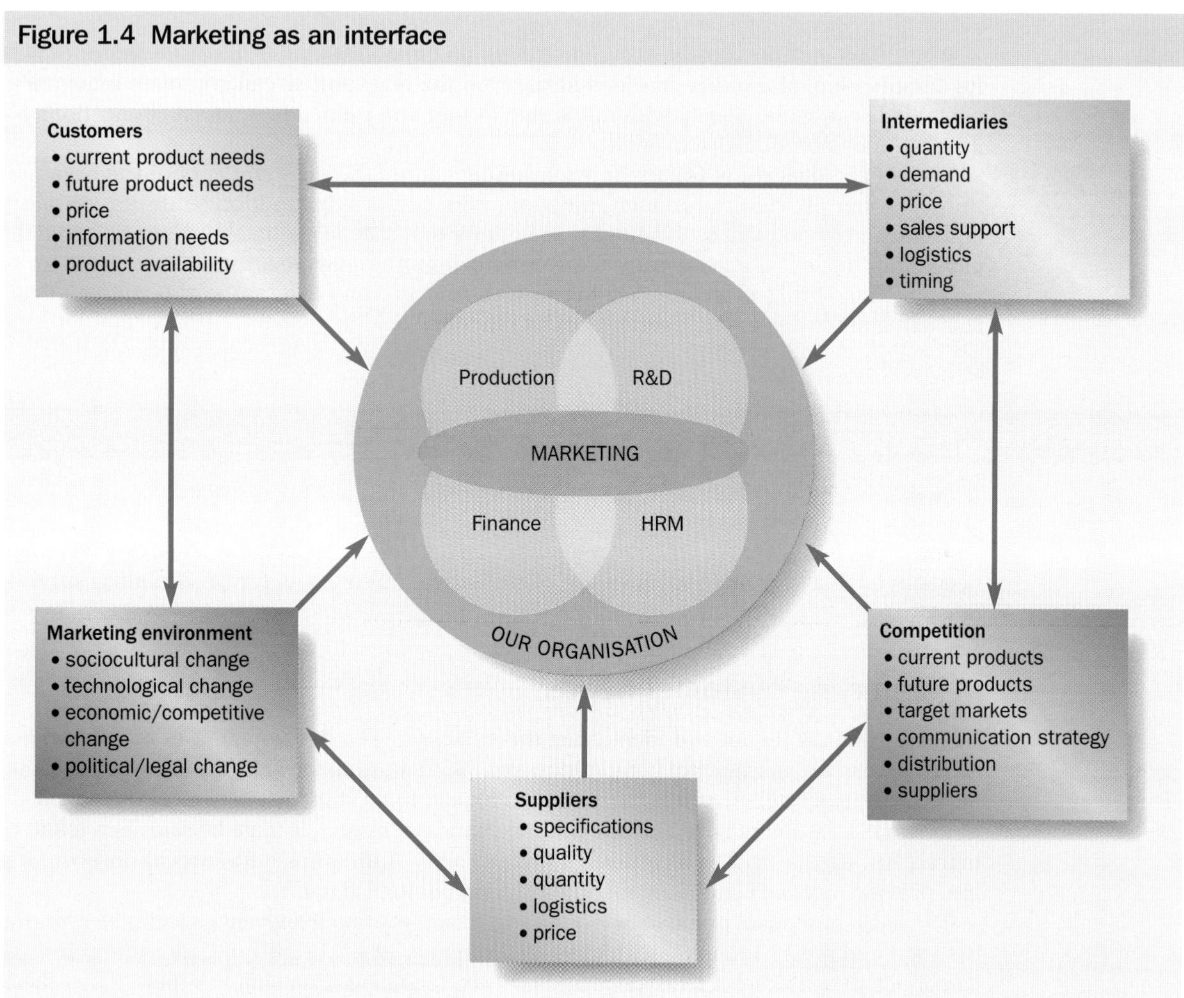

from the outside world then distributing it within the organisation, and presenting the combined efforts of the various internal functions to the external world. Taking, for example, two core issues from the 'customers' box:

Current product needs. To satisfy current needs, production has to know how much is required, when and to what quality specification. Production, perhaps with the help of the purchasing function, has to have access to the right raw materials or components at the right price. Keeping current products within an acceptable price band for the customer involves production, purchasing, finance and perhaps even R&D. A sales function might take orders from customers and make sure that the right quantity of goods is dispatched quickly to the right place. Marketing brings in those customers, monitoring their satisfaction levels, and brings any problems to the attention of the relevant functions as soon as possible so that they can be rectified with the minimum of disruption.

Future needs. Marketing, perhaps with the help of R&D, needs to monitor what is happening now and to try to predict what needs to happen in the future. This can be through talking to customers and finding out how their needs are evolving, or working out how new technology can be commercially exploited, or through monitoring competitors' activities and thinking about how they can be imitated, adapted or improved upon. Inevitably, there is a planning lead time, so marketing needs to bring in ideas early, then work with other functions to turn them into reality at the right time. Finance may have to sanction investment in a new product; R&D might have to refine the product or its technology; production may have to invest in new plant, machinery or manufacturing techniques; purchasing may have to start looking for new suppliers; and personnel may have to recruit new staff to help with the development, manufacture or sales of the new product.

When R&D and marketing do share common goals and objectives, it can be a very powerful combination. Marketing can feed ideas from the market that can stimulate innovation, while R&D can work closely with marketing to find and refine commercial applications for its apparently pointless discoveries.

These examples show briefly how marketing can be the eyes and ears of the organisation, and can provide the inputs and support to help each function to do its job more efficiently. Provided that all employees remember that they are ultimately there to serve the customers' needs, then the truly marketing-orientated organisation has no problem in accepting marketing as an interface between the internal and external worlds, and involving marketing in the day-to-day operation of its functions.

Marketing management responsibilities

This section outlines specifically what marketing does, and identifies where each of the areas is dealt with in this book.

All of marketing's tasks boil down to one of two things: identifying or satisfying customer needs in such a way as to achieve the organisation's objectives for profitability, survival or growth.

Identifying customer needs

Implicit in this is the idea of identifying the customer. The development of mass markets, more aggressive international competition and the increasing sophistication of the customer have taught marketers that it is unrealistic to expect to be able to satisfy all of the people all of the time. Customers have become more demanding, largely, it must be said, as a result of marketers' efforts, and want products that not only fulfil a basic functional purpose, but also provide positive benefits, sometimes of a psychological nature.

The basic functional purpose of a product, in fact, is often irrelevant as a choice criterion between competing brands – all fridges keep food cold, all brands of cola slake thirst, all cars move people from A to B, regardless of which organisation supplies them. The crucial questions for the customer are how does it fulfil its function, and what extra does it do for me in the process? Thus the choice of a BMW over a Lada may be made because the purchaser feels that the BMW is a better designed and engineered car, gets you from A to B in more comfort and with a lot more style, gives you the power and performance to zip aggressively from A to B if you want, and the BMW name is well respected and its status will reflect on the driver, enhancing self-esteem and standing in other people's eyes. The Lada may be preferred by someone who does not want to invest a lot of money in a car, who is happy to potter from A to B steadily without the blaze of glory, who values economy in terms of insurance, running and servicing costs, and who does not feel the need for a car that is an overt status symbol. These profiles of contrasting car buyers point to a mixture of product and psychological benefits, over and above the basic function of the cars, that are influential in the purchasing decision.

This has two enormous implications for the marketer. The first is that if buyers and their motives are so varied, it is important to identify the criteria and variables that distinguish one group of buyers from another. Once that is done, the marketer can then make sure that a product offering is created that matches the needs of one group as closely as possible. If the marketer's organisation does not do this, then someone else's will, and any 'generic' type of product that tries to please most of the people most of the time will sooner or later be pushed out by something better tailored to a narrower group. The second implication is that by grouping customers according to characteristics and benefits sought, the marketer has a better chance of spotting lucrative gaps in the market than if the market is treated as a homogeneous mass.

Identifying customer needs is not, however, just a question of working out what they want now. The marketer has to try to predict what they will want tomorrow, and identify the influences that are changing customer needs. The environmental factors that affect customer needs and wants, as well as the means by which organisations can fulfil them, are discussed further in Chapter 2. The nature of customers, and the motivations and attitudes that affect their buying behaviour, are covered in Chapters 3 (consumers) and 4 (B2B buyers), while the idea of grouping customers according to common characteristics and/or desired product features and benefits is discussed in Chapter 5. The techniques of market research, as a prime means of discovering what customers are thinking and what they want now and in the future, is the subject of Chapter 6.

Satisfying customer needs

Understanding the nature of customers and their needs and wants is only the first step, however. The organisation needs to act on that information, in order to develop and implement marketing activities that actually deliver something of value to the customer. The means by which such ideas are turned into reality is the **marketing mix**. Figure 1.5 summarises the areas of responsibility within each element of the mix.

The concept of the marketing mix as the combination of the major tools of marketing was first developed by Borden in the 1950s (Borden, 1964), and the mnemonic '**4Ps**' (product, price, promotion and place) describing those tools was coined by McCarthy (1960). The marketing mix creates an offering for the customer. The use of the words *mix* and *combination* are important here, because successful marketing relies as much on interaction and synergy between marketing mix elements as it does on good decisions within those elements themselves. Häagen Dazs ice cream, for example, is a perfectly good, quality product, but its phenomenal success only came after an innovative and daring advertising campaign that emphasised certain adult-orientated product benefits. A good product with bad communication will not work, and similarly a bad product with the glossiest advertising will not work either. This is because the elements of the marketing mix all depend on each other, and if they are not consistent with each other in what they are saying about the product, then the customer, who is not stupid, will reject it all.

We now look more closely at each element of the marketing mix.

Product

This area, discussed in Part three (Chapters 7, 8 and 9), covers everything to do with the creation, development and management of products. It is about not only what to make, but when to make it, how to make it, and how to ensure that it has a long and profitable life.

Figure 1.5 The marketing mix

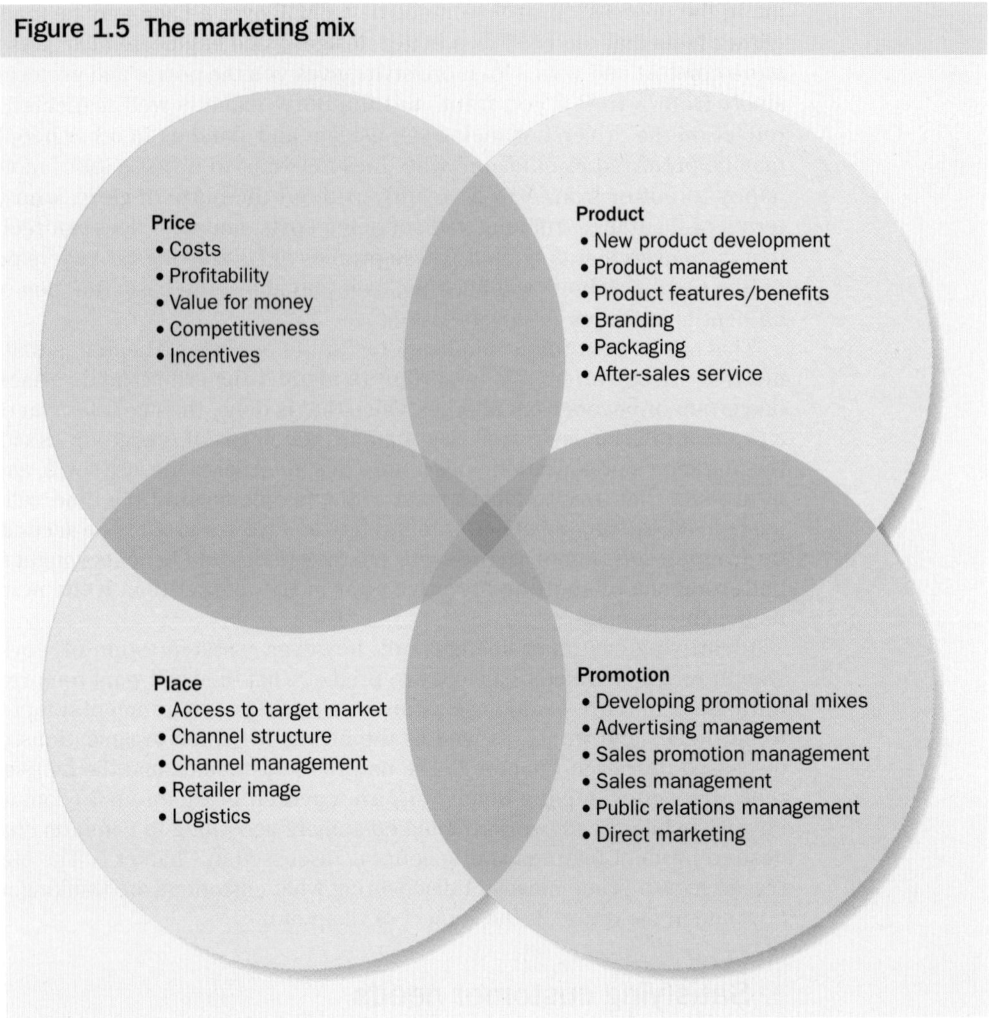

Furthermore, a product is not just a physical thing. In marketing terms, it includes peripheral but important elements, such as after-sales service, guarantees, installation and fitting – anything that helps to distinguish the product from its competition and make the customer more likely to buy it.

Particularly with fast moving consumer goods (fmcg), part of a product's attractiveness is, of course, its brand imagery and its packaging. Both of these are likely to emphasise the psychological benefits offered by the product. With B2B purchases, however, the emphasis is more likely to be on fitness for functional purpose, quality and peripheral services (technical support, delivery, customisation, etc.). As well as featuring in the product chapters, echoes of these concerns will come through strongly in the chapters on buyer behaviour and segmentation (Chapters 3–5).

Although much of the emphasis is on physical products, it must also be remembered that service markets are an increasingly important growth area of many European economies. The product chapters do cover some aspects of services, but the main discussion of the service product is in Chapter 22, which deals with services marketing.

Price

Price is not perhaps as clear cut as it might seem at first glance, since price is not necessarily a straightforward calculation of costs and profit margins. As Part four (Chapters 10 and 11) will show, price has to reflect issues of buyer behaviour, because people judge 'value' in terms of their perceptions of what they are getting for their money, what else they could have had for that money and how much that money meant to them in the first place.

Pricing also has a strategic dimension, in that it gives messages to all sorts of people in the market. Customers, for example, may use price as an indicator of quality and desirability for a particular product, and thus price can reinforce or destroy the work of other elements of the marketing mix. Competitors, on the other hand, may see price as a challenge, because if an organisation prices its products very low it may be signalling its intention to start a price war to the death, whereas very high (premium) prices may signal that there are high profits to be made or that there is room for a competitor to undercut and take market share away.

Overall, price is a very flexible element of the marketing mix, being very easy to tinker with. It is also, however, a dangerous element to play around with, because of its very direct link with revenues and profits, unless management think very carefully and clearly about how they are using it. The focus of the pricing chapters, therefore, is on the factors that influence price setting, the short-term tactical uses of pricing in various kinds of market and the strategic implications of a variety of pricing policies.

Place

Place is a very dynamic and fast moving area of marketing. It covers a wide variety of fascinating topics largely concerned with the movement of goods from A to B and what happens at the point of sale. Part five (Chapters 12 and 13) therefore looks at the structure of channels of distribution, from mail order companies that deal direct with the end consumer, to long and complex chains that involve goods passing between several intermediaries before they get to a retailer. The chapters explore the range of different intermediaries, and the roles they play in getting goods to the right place at the right time for the end buyer, as well as the physical distribution issues involved in making it all happen.

Do not assume, however, that these channels are merely about the movement and transfer of goods. They are also about power, control, manipulation and competitive advantage, and this is a strong theme throughout these chapters.

For consumer goods, the most visible player in the channel of distribution is the retailer. Manufacturers and consumers alike have to put a lot of trust in the retailer to do justice to the product, to maintain stocks, and to provide a satisfying purchasing experience. Retailers face many of the same marketing decisions as other types of organisation, and use the same marketing mix tools, but with a slightly different perspective. They also face unique marketing problems, for example store location, layout and the creation of store image and atmosphere. Retailing has therefore been given its own chapter which explores its particular concerns.

Promotion

The longest section of this book, Part six (Chapters 14–19), is basically about communication, which is often seen as the most glamorous and sexy end of marketing. This does not mean, however, that marketing communication is purely an ‘artistic’ endeavour, or that it can be used to wallpaper over cracks in the rest of the marketing mix. Communication, because it is so pervasive and high profile, can certainly make or break a marketing mix, and thus it needs wise and constant analysis, planning and management.

Chapters 15–19 look at the whole range of marketing communication techniques, not just advertising, but also sales promotions, personal selling, public relations and direct marketing. The activities undertaken within each area, the objectives each can best achieve, their relative strengths and weaknesses, and the kinds of management and planning processes that have to support them are discussed. To put all that into perspective, however, Chapter 14 first looks at the promotional mix as a whole, thinking about the factors that will influence the relative emphasis put on each individual communications area.

That, then, is the traditional 4Ps approach to marketing that has served very well for many years. More recently, however, it has become apparent that the 4Ps as they stand are not always sufficient. In the services sector in particular, they cannot fully describe the marketing activities that are going on, and so an extended marketing mix, the **7Ps**, was proposed by Booms and Bitner (1981), adding people, processes and physical evidence to the traditional 4Ps.

People

Services often depend on people to perform them, creating and delivering the product as the customer waits. A customer's satisfaction with hairdressing and dentistry services, for example, has as much to do with the quality and nature of the interaction between the customer and the service provider as with the end result. If the customer feels comfortable with a particular service provider, trusts them and has a rapport with them, that is a relationship that a competitor would find hard to break into. Even where the service is not quite so personal, sullen assistance in a shop or a fast-food outlet, for example, does not encourage the customer to come back for more. Thus people add value and a dimension to the marketing package way beyond the basic product offering.

Processes

Manufacturing processes, once they are set up, are consistent and predictable and can be left to the production management team, and since they go on out of sight of the customer, any mistakes can be weeded out before distribution. Services, however, are 'manufactured' and consumed live, on the spot, and because they do involve people and the performance of their skills, consistency can be rather more difficult than with normal manufacturing. The marketer, therefore, has to think carefully about how the service is delivered, and what quality controls can be built in so that the customer can be confident that they know what to expect each time they consume the service product. This applies, for example, to banks and other retailers of financial services, fast-food outlets, hairdressers and other personal service providers, and even to professionals such as solicitors and management consultants.

Process can also involve queueing mechanisms, preventing waiting customers from getting so impatient that they leave without purchase; processing customer details and payment; as well as ensuring the high professional quality of whatever service they are buying.

Physical evidence

This final area is of particular relevance to retailers (of any type of product), or those who maintain premises from which a service is sold or delivered. It singles out some of the factors already mentioned when talking about retailers within the place element of the traditional 4Ps approach, such as atmosphere, ambience, image and design of premises. In other service situations, physical evidence would relate to the aircraft in which you fly, the hotel in which you stay, the stadium in which you watch the big match, or the lecture theatre in which you learn.

Other than in the services arena, the 4Ps are still widely accepted as defining the marketing mix. It has never been suggested, however, that the same mix is applicable in all situations or even for the same organisation at different times, so the task of the marketing manager is to review and change the mix to suit emerging circumstances. The marketing mix is simply therefore a set of categories of marketing variables that has become standard in marketing education and is the foundation for the structure of this book. As you read the subsections on the four elements of the marketing mix, look to see where aspects of people, process and physical evidence are being incorporated or implied within that traditional structure. Relationship marketing, in any type of market for any type of product, is increasingly throwing the emphasis on adding value to products through service. Inevitably, the extra 3Ps are going to impinge on that, and will be reflected in discussing applications of the original 4Ps.

The particular combination of the 4Ps used by any one organisation needs to give it **competitive edge**, or **differential advantage**. This means that the marketer is creating something unique, that the potential customer will recognise and value, that distinguishes one organisation's products from another's. In highly competitive, crowded markets, this is absolutely essential for drawing customers towards your product. The edge or advantage may be created mainly through one element of the mix, or through a combination of them. A product may have a combination of high quality and good value (price and product) that a competitor cannot match; an organisation may have established a 24-hour telephone ordering and home delivery service (place) that cannot easily be imitated; an effective and unique communications campaign combined with an excellent product living up to all its promises (promotion and product) can make an organisation's offering stand out above the crowd.

marketing *in action*

Nederman: creating a better workplace

Nederman is not a name that many readers will be familiar with, but it is typical of many engineering companies that have adopted marketing principles in order to build international business in B2B markets. Based in Helsingborg, Sweden, it is a medium-sized company with a turnover of SKr693 mn in 2000. The underlying theme for the company is 'improving your workspace' and it has built a successful international business helping customers to solve their workstation problems. This is achieved by removing air pollution, reducing noise levels, screening out unwanted light, and making a workstation easier to operate in through greater efficiency in providing liquids, power, light, lifting equipment, etc. In short, the company provides a total solution for a workstation environment tailored to meet the customer's requirements.

At the heart of the marketing proposition is the ability to solve customers' problems. Nederman has to listen to the customer then design, manufacture and install solutions either for individual workstations or across a factory area. To be innovative Nederman has to invest in research and development to ensure that its products are at the cutting edge in design and performance. This requires a commitment to R&D and the sourcing of components that meet the specifications required. It is vital that Nederman is then able to listen to its customers and tailor solutions to meet the need. For that reason it must have direct contact both before and after the sale has been made, and if sales agents are used in less important markets, they must be fully trained and skilled in matching customer needs with system solutions. Technical support is available to help in that task, although as in many other B2B markets, the sales person with appropriate technical knowledge and support is at the forefront of the promotional effort. Nederman has eleven sales subsidiaries in its main markets, such as Germany, Spain, the UK and USA, from which the sales teams operate.

The approach to customers is made either by responding to enquiries generated by advertising in trade publications, directory listings, web and print based media, or by participation in trade fairs throughout the main markets. There is always the opportunity for repeat business, thus the importance of satisfied customers. Contact can also be initiated by the sales team, and this is sometimes achieved by offering a free health and safety assessment examining such matters as risk assessment, safety standards, signage, work practice, etc. Experience has indicated that this can often lead to the opportunity to open dialogue about production system improvement. Most of the sales subsidiaries have installed 'working environments' that visitors can inspect to compare with the systems currently used.

An experience with Hamlin Electronics is indicative of the sales and marketing challenge facing Nederman. When Hamlin decided to become involved in developing sensors for air bags destined for the motor industry, it needed new workstations to extract fumes from gluing, printing and varnishing processes. Nederman was approached along with other potential suppliers to consider the specification options prior to a detailed quote. Quotations were prepared on the proposed systems and presentations and site visits to other users were organised so that the buyer could be assured of the benefits of the Nederman offering. Although some time elapsed before the evaluation was complete, Nederman was awarded the contract, but that was not the end of the process, as installing and operationalising the workstations is also an important part of creating a satisfied customer. During all that time and subsequently 'a very good relationship was established with Nederman's contract engineers so that the installation was completed to a high standard. To date we have a maintenance-free system and all the units are popular with the operators who use them on a daily basis,' said the engineer at Hamlin. This forms the basis of further referrals and repeat business.

Source: http://www.nederman.com.

Strategic vision

It is clear that individual marketing activities must be looked at within the context of a coherent and consistent marketing mix, but achieving that mix has to be an outcome of a wider framework of strategic marketing planning, implementation and control. Part seven looks at these wider issues, in Chapters 20 and 21.

Strategy is concerned with looking into the future and developing and implementing the plans that will drive the organisation in the desired direction. Implicit in that is the need for strategy to inform (and be informed by) marketing. Strategic marketing thinking also needs a certain amount of unblinkered creativity, and can only be really successful if the marketer thinks not in terms of product, but rather in terms of benefits or solutions delivered to the customer. The organisation that answers the question 'What business are you in?' with the reply 'We are in the business of making gloss paint' is in danger of becoming too inwardly focused on the product itself and improving its manufacture (the production orientation). A more correct reply would have been: 'We are in the business of helping people to create beautiful rooms' (the identification of customer needs). The cosmetics executive who said that in the factory they made cosmetics but in the chemist's shop they sold hope, and the power tool manufacturer who said that they did not make drills, they made quarter-inch holes, were both underlining a more creative, outward-looking, problem-solving way of marketing thinking. Products are bought by customers to solve problems, and if the product does not solve the problem, or if something else solves it better, then the customer will turn away.

The organisation that cannot see this and defines itself in product rather than market terms could be said to be suffering from *marketing myopia*, a term coined by Levitt (1960). Such an organisation may well be missing out on significant marketing opportunities, and thus may leave itself open to new or more innovative competitors which more closely match customer needs. A classic example of this is slide rule manufacturers. Their definition of the business they were in was 'making slide rules'. Perhaps if they had defined their business as 'taking the pain out of calculation' they would still exist today and be manufacturing electronic calculators. Green (1995) discusses how the pharmaceutical companies are thinking about what business they are in. The realisation that patients are buying 'good health' rather than 'drugs' is broadening the horizons of companies such as Sandoz in Switzerland, GlaxoSmithKline in the UK and Merck in the USA, all of which have diversified into areas of healthcare other than research and development of drugs. GlaxoSmithKline in particular wants to spread its efforts across what it sees as the four core elements of healthcare: prevention, diagnosis, treatment and cure.

Therefore the distinction between the product and the problem it solves matters, because marketing strategy is about managing the organisation's activities within the real world in which it has to survive. In that turbulent and dynamically changing world, a marketing mix that works today may not work tomorrow. If your organisation is too product focused to remember to monitor how customer needs and wants are changing, then it will get left behind by competitors who do have their fingers on the customer's pulse. If your organisation forgets why it is making a particular product and why the consumer buys it, how can it develop marketing strategies that strike a chord with the customers and defend against the competition?

Think about a drill manufacturer that is product focused and invests vast amounts of time and money in developing a better version of the traditional electric drill. How do you think it would feel if a competitor then launched a hand-held, cordless, laser gun that could instantly zap quarter-inch holes (controllably) through any material with no physical effort on the part of the operator, and with no mess because it vaporises the residue? The laser company was thinking ahead, looking at the consumer's problem, looking at the weaknesses in the currently available solutions, and developing a marketing package that would deliver a better solution.

What we are saying here is that it is not enough to formulate a cosy marketing mix that suits the product and is entirely consistent with itself. That marketing mix is only working properly if it has been thought through with due respect to the external environment within which it is to be implemented. As well as justifying the existence of that marketing mix in the light of current internal and external influences, the strategic marketer has to go further by justifying how that mix helps to achieve wider corporate objectives; explaining how it is helping to propel the organisation in its longer-term desired direction, and finally, how it contributes to achieving competitive edge.

Ultimately, competitive edge is the name of the game. If marketers can create and sustain competitive edge, by thinking creatively and strategically about the internal and external marketing environments, then they are well on the way to implementing the marketing concept and fulfilling all the promise of the definitions of marketing with which this chapter began.

corporate social responsibility *in action*

'An untouchable icon'?

Many in Europe and North America consider whale watching to be great fun and worth travelling thousands of miles for. It is a business worth over $1 bn a year. To many Japanese, the whale is more of a luxury item on the menu to be enjoyed at the finest restaurants. The problem is that in 1987 the international community, through the International Whaling Commission (IWC), agreed that the whale was an endangered species that required protection from over-fishing and thus commercial whaling, other than for research purposes, was banned, a decision that still stands. The stage was set for a debate that goes to the core of the sustainable marketing concept: is it appropriate for the wider international community to deny the whale-eating nations of Japan and, to a lesser extent, Norway and Iceland, the right to catch a creature in international waters as a part of their traditional diet?

Japan is a seafood rather than cattle culture and the whale has for thousands of years been used as a source of animal protein. Because of the degree of urbanisation and the limited amount of agricultural land, Japan is only 41 per cent self-sufficient for food, compared with 139 per cent in France and 97 per cent in Germany, so it is natural for the nation to look to the seas. The Japanese Fishery Agency (JFA) feels that sustainable whaling should be allowed, arguing that other fish stocks are being destroyed by an abundance of some species of whales, such as the minke which has recovered in numbers to over 1 million. Indeed, the head of the JFA called the minke whale the 'cockroach of the ocean'. In order to meet customer demand, therefore, the JFA wants a new scheme of conservative quotas and a move from preservation to regulation. There is some support for this position from some other countries who see it as a concession for ensuring greater international cooperation rather than risking alienating a few nations which then pursue other paths.

Meanwhile, the Japanese have still been able to catch whales for 'scientific research' purposes. When one ship returned home with 158 whales caught over three months, seventy more than the previous year and including eight sperm whales, it was almost a hero's welcome. The JFA congratulated the work of the fleet and vowed to protect its activities. Meanwhile, a special dinner of whale meat was organised. In the name of research, Japan still catches around 500 whales each year and it has been estimated that, despite official denial, 2,500 tonnes of whale meat reaches the market each year with a value of £22 mn. According to the JFA, the Japanese culture views wastage as unethical and immoral so it is legitimate for the research by-product (whalemeat) to be distributed. Therefore the research institutes sell to the government to recoup the research subsidies and the meat is then sold on to the local governments who in turn sell to the fish markets. The only local government that does not buy whale meat is in Okinawa, as they prefer dolphins.

There is, however, an alternative view of the whaling industry. Even at consumer level some doubt has been placed on just how important the whale is to the mainstream Japanese diet and there is even some embarrassment over the condemnation of Japan's whaling operations. Greenpeace went further and stated that 'this is a lucrative commercial operation subsidised by the government to sustain the market for whalemeat even though most Japanese are indifferent' (as quoted by http://www.greenpeace.org.uk). A survey conducted by the Japanese Prime Minister's Office found that 77 per cent of Japanese support regulated whaling but a poll by MORI in 1999 found that 61 per cent of those questioned had not eaten whalemeat since childhood and only 1 per cent said they ate whalemeat at least once per month.

Counter-arguments have been presented by such bodies as the International Fund for Animal Welfare (IFAW). They include highlighting how commercial fishing stocks worldwide have been depleted by over-commercialisation rather than by whales, as the Japanese argue, and how Japan has abused the concession for scientific whaling research not only in terms of quantity, but also when some protected whalemeat, such as from the humpback, blue and fin whales, has found its way into the marketplace. IFAW claims that Japan has refused proposals for a DNA monitoring scheme which would enable easier checking of whether catches are within regulations. Meanwhile, a moratorium on commercial whaling is still in force. Some go further and believe on moral grounds that whales should not be killed for any purpose and the regulatory bodies are still not convinced that enough evidence has been accumulated to support the Japanese claim that renewed catching of some species should now be permitted for commercial reasons as stocks have recovered.

To the Japanese, or at least to its fishing industry, whaling has become a symbol of virility and pride that should be respected by the world in the same way that other societies' food culture is respected. They do not wish to have different cultural norms imposed upon them. To many people, however, whaling has become symbolic of the need to protect the environment and many other species in the same way that in the 1970s a focus on whaling led to far greater concern for the oceans, rainforests and wildlife. So, is it satisfied consumers and regulated whalemeat today, and hope that the future will look after itself, or should the IWC continue to take a strong stand?

Sources: *The Economist* (2001a, 2000b); Morishta and O'Regan (2001); Suhre (1999); Watts (2001).

Marketing scope

Marketing plays a part in a wide range of organisations and applications. Some of these are discussed specifically in Part eight and elsewhere in this book, while others are implicit throughout the text.

Consumer goods

The **consumer goods** field, because it involves potentially large and lucrative markets of so many individuals, has embraced marketing wholeheartedly, and indeed has been at the root of the development and testing of many marketing theories and concepts. Consumer goods and markets will be a major focus of this text, but certainly not to the exclusion of anything else. Since we are all consumers, it is easy to relate our own experience to the theories and concepts presented here, but it is equally important to try to understand the wider applications.

e-marketing *in action*

What is e-marketing?

E-marketing can be simply expressed as the use of electronic communications technology to achieve marketing objectives (for example McDonald and Wilson, 2000). The electronic communications technology refers to:

1 The use of internet-based (TCP/IP) network technology for communications within an organisation using an intranet; beyond the organisation to partners such as suppliers, distributors and key account customers using password-based access to extranets and the open internet where information is accessible by all with internet access.
2 The use of web servers or websites to enable informational or financial exchanges as e-commerce transactions.
3 The use of other digital access platforms such as interactive digital TV, wireless or mobile phones and games consoles.
4 The use of electronic mail for managing enquiries (inbound e-mail) and for promotion (outbound e-mail).
5 Integration of the digital access platforms and e-mail with other information technologies such as databases and software for customer relationship management and supply chain management.

To explore some of the many applications of e-marketing, which we will be reviewing as examples in other chapters in this book, is to interpret the relevance of e-marketing using the definition of marketing from the Chartered Institute of Marketing:

> *e-marketing can identify, anticipate and satisfy customer needs efficiently.*

Using the example of the website as a major aspect of e-marketing, consider how a website can fulfil these requirements of marketing. According to Smith and Chaffey (2001) it can help:

- *Identify* needs from customer comments, enquiries, requests and complaints solicited via e-mail and the website's contact facility, bulletin boards, chat rooms, online searches and sales patterns (seeing what's selling and what's not, recorded in the web log which reveals insights into interests determined by pages visited). Online surveys ask how to improve the site or products. Finally, there is a proliferation of online secondary sources of research, many of which provide free in-depth insights into customer needs.
- *Anticipate* customer needs by asking customers questions and engaging them in a dynamic dialogue built on the trust of opt-in e-mail. Collaborative filtering, as used by Amazon helps to identify and anticipate what customers might like given that buyers of similar books have similar interests. Profiling techniques allow many companies to perform data mining to discover and anticipate buyers' needs. Cookie-based profiling allows companies to analyse your interests without even knowing your name – courtesy of a piece of code sent to the visitor's PC. So without knowing your name, your interests are known. It recognises your PC and records which types of sites (interests) you have and can serve adverts and offers based on predicted interests.
- *Satisfy* needs with prompt responses, punctual deliveries, order status updates, helpful reminders, after-sales services and added value services combined with the dynamic dialogue. The dialogue maintains permission to continue communicating and then adds value by delivering useful content in the right context (right time and right amount).
- *Efficiently* means in an automated way (or partially automated) . . . an efficient, yet hopefully not impersonal, way (i.e. it allows tailor-made technology to improve service quality, increase the marketer's memory to help maintain the customer relationship through time).

Sources: Chaffey *et al.* (2003); McDonald and Wilson (1999); Smith and Chaffey (2001).

It is apparent from these applications, that e-marketing extends beyond the website to include all use of digital technology to manage the customer relationship. Databases are increasingly used to manage and record all interactions with customers, whether sales transactions, inbound enquiries via phone or e-mail and outbound communications such as a mailshot or e-mailshot.

An alternative perspective on e-marketing is provided by the term 'internet marketing' which has been described simply as 'the application of the internet and related digital technologies to achieve marketing objectives' (Chaffey *et al.*, 2003). In practice, internet-based marketing will include the use of a company website in conjunction with promotional techniques such as banner advertising, direct e-mail and links or services from other websites to acquire new customers and provide services to existing customers that help develop the customer relationship.

Industrial goods

Industrial or **B2B goods** ultimately end up serving consumers in some way, directly or indirectly. The cleaned wool that the woolcomber sells to the spinner to make into yarn to sell to the weaver to make into cloth eventually ends up in the shops as clothing; the rubber that Dunlop, Goodyear or Firestone buys to make into tyres to sell to car manufacturers ends up being bought by consumers; the girders sold by British Steel to a civil engineering contractor for a new bridge end up serving the needs of individuals. If these organisations are going to continue to feed the voracious appetite of consumer markets successfully (the right product in the right place at the right time at the right price – remember?), then they also have to manage their relationships with other organisations, in a marketing-orientated way. A study by Avlonitis *et al.* (1997) found that companies in B2B markets that had developed a marketing orientation were a lot more successful than those that had not. The buying of goods, raw materials and components by organisations is a crucial influence on what can be promised and offered, especially in terms of price, place and product, to the next buyer down the line. If these inter-organisational relationships fail, then ultimately the consumer, who props up the whole chain, loses out, which is not in the interests of any organisation, however far removed from the end consumer. As Chapter 4 in particular will show, the concerns and emphases in B2B markets are rather different from those of consumer markets, and thus need to be addressed specifically.

Service goods

Service goods, to be discussed in Chapter 22, include personal services (hairdressing, other beauty treatments or medical services, for example) and professional skills (accountancy, management consultancy or legal advice, for example), and are found in all sorts of markets, whether consumer or B2B. As already mentioned on pp. 27–8, services have differentiated themselves somewhat from the traditional approach to marketing because of their particular characteristics. These require an extended marketing mix, and cause different kinds of management headaches from physical products. Many marketing managers concerned with physical products are finding that service elements are becoming increasingly important to augment their products and to differentiate them further from the competition. This means that some of the concepts and concerns of services marketing are spreading far wider than their own relatively narrow field, and this is reflected throughout this book. In between the two extremes of a largely service product (a haircut, for instance) and a largely physical product (a machine tool, for instance), are products that have significant elements of both. A fast-food outlet, for example, is selling physical products, burger, fries and a coke, and that is primarily what the customer is there for. Service elements, such as speed and friendliness of service, atmosphere and ambience, are nevertheless inextricably linked with those physical products to create an overall package of satisfaction (or otherwise) in the customer's mind. This mixture of physical and service products is common throughout the retail trade, and thus services marketing not only features in its own chapter, but also permeates those chapters dealing with distribution (Chapters 12 and 13).

Non-profit marketing

Non-profit marketing is an area that increasingly asserted itself in the economic and political climate of the 1980s and 1990s. Hospitals, schools, universities, the arts and charities are all having to compete within their own sectors to obtain, protect and justify their funding and even their existence. The environment within which such organisations exist is increasingly subject to market forces, and altruism is no longer enough. This means that non-profit organisations need to think not only about efficiency and cost effectiveness, but also about their market orientation – defining what their 'customers' need and want and how they can provide it better than their rivals.

eg

International charity Oxfam (http://www.oxfam.org.uk) believes that it is necessary to boost contributions from its trading operation in order to supplement the funds raised from donations and legacies. In 1999–2000, donations raised nearly £49.7mn – 80 per cent of its income (excluding grants) – and the retail stores added a further £8.8mn contribution after expenses. The first store in the UK was opened in Huddersfield in 1975 as a point for recycling unwanted clothes. In 1985 it opened the first clearance store to sell lines unwanted by other stores and in 1986 launched its first second-hand furniture store. Specialist lines have followed, again around the second-hand theme, including wedding outfits, retro party outfits, toys, electrical goods and books. From 850 stores it sells 27 million items, generating around £43mn in sales. The problem for the stores is tackling the negative public image that it sells second-hand cast-offs of dubious quality. Recent efforts have included using supermodels to emphasise style as well as value for money from the stores but this met with only limited success. In a 2001 trading review it was decided to allow a lot more freedom to the local store managers to build stock and to respond to local conditions. It remains to be seen whether this will enhance the overall image or just reinforce stereotypes. Operating local stores gives market presence and raises marginal income, but it could also have an impact on potential donors if the association with the stores creates an image of Oxfam as a worthwhile, but somewhat downmarket cause. The impression would be very wrong given the range of environmental, human rights and poverty issues it tackles, but a problem for many marketers is that people have the right to believe whatever they want, and that can be positive or negative!

Chapter 22 looks in more detail at the particular marketing problems and situations facing non-profit organisations.

Small business marketing

Small business marketing also creates its own perspectives, as discussed in Chapter 21. Many of the marketing theories and concepts laid out in this book have been developed with the larger organisation, relatively rich in management resources, in mind. Similarly, the implementation of these concepts is often discussed under the assumption that the organisation *does* have the expertise, flexibility and resources available to do whatever the market dictates to a high and idealistic marketing standard. Many small businesses, however, simply cannot live up to this. They often have only one or two managers who have to carry out a variety of managerial functions; such businesses often come into existence as a result of the owner/manager's manufacturing skills, and therefore have a production rather than marketing orientation; the manager/s have enough to do managing the day-to-day operation of the business without getting bogged down in strategic planning; they have very limited financial resources for investment in researching new markets and developing new products ahead of the rest. These are a few of the many constraints and barriers to the full implementation of the whole range of marketing possibilities. Throughout this book we therefore take a closer look at these constraints and consider more pragmatically how marketing theories and practice can be adapted to serve the needs of the small business that wants a long and prosperous future as it develops and grows.

International marketing

International marketing is a well-established field, and with the opening up of Europe as well as the technological improvements that mean it is now easier and cheaper to transfer goods around the world, it has become an increasingly important area of marketing theory and practice. Again, it warrants its own chapter (Chapter 23), not only because of its importance, but also because it creates its own problems. Issues of market entry strategies, whether to adapt marketing mixes for different markets and how, and the logistics of serving geographically dispersed markets all provide an interesting perspective on marketing decision-making.

Chapter summary

- Marketing is about exchange processes, i.e. identifying what potential customers need and want now, or what they are likely to want in the future, and then offering them something that will fulfil those needs and wants. You thus offer them something that they value and, in return, they offer you something that you value, usually money. Most (but not all) organisations are in business to make profits, and so it is important that customers' needs and wants are fulfilled cost effectively, efficiently and profitably. This implies that the marketing function has to be properly planned, managed and controlled.
- Marketing in some shape or form has been around for a very long time, but it was during the course of the twentieth century that it made its most rapid developments and consolidated itself as an important business function and as a philosophy of doing business. By the late 1990s, all types of organisations in the USA and Western Europe had adopted a marketing orientation and were looking for ways to become even more customer focused, for example through relationship marketing.
- The marketing orientation has been a necessary response to an increasingly dynamic and difficult world. Externally, the organisation has to take into account the needs, demands and influences of several different groups such as customers, competitors, suppliers and intermediaries, who all exist within a dynamic business environment. Internally, the organisation has to coordinate the efforts of different functions, acting as an interface between them and the customer. When the whole organisation accepts that the customer is absolutely paramount and that all functions within the organisation contribute towards customer satisfaction, then a marketing philosophy has been adopted.
- Marketing's main tasks, therefore, are centred around identifying and satisfying customers' needs and wants, in order to offer something to the market that has a *competitive edge* or *differential advantage*, making it more attractive than the competing product(s). These tasks are achieved through the use of the *marketing mix*, a combination of elements that actually create the offering. For most physical goods, the marketing mix consists of four elements, product, price, place and promotion. For service based products, the mix can be extended to seven elements with the addition of people, processes and physical evidence. The marketer has to ensure that the marketing mix meets the customer's needs and wants, and that all its elements are consistent with each other, otherwise customers will turn away and competitors will exploit the weakness. Additionally, the marketer has to ensure that the marketing mix fits in with the strategic vision of the organisation, that it is contributing to the achievement of longer-term objectives, or that it is helping to drive the organisation in the desired future direction. These marketing principles are generally applicable to any kind of organisation operating in any kind of market. But whatever the application, the basic philosophy remains: if marketers can deliver the right product in the right place at the right time at the right price, then they are making a crucial contribution towards creating satisfied customers and successful, efficient and profitable organisations.

key words and phrases

B2B goods
Buyer–seller relationships
Competitive edge
Consumer goods
Corporate social responsibility (CSR)
Differential advantage
Exchange process
Fmcg
International marketing
Marketing
Marketing concept
Marketing environment
Marketing mix
Marketing orientation
Non-profit marketing
Product orientation
Production orientation
Relationship marketing
Sales orientation
Service goods
Sustainable marketing
4Ps
7Ps

questions for review

1.1 What is meant by the description of marketing as 'an exchange process'?

1.2 What are the four different types of marketing executive defined by Hooley *et al.* (1990) and how might each manager's approach affect the organisation's attitude to marketing?

1.3 Distinguish between the four main business orientations.

1.4 How do business functions other than marketing contribute towards satisfying customer needs and wants?

1.5 What is competitive edge and why is it so important?

questions for discussion

1.1 Which is the most important element of the marketing mix and why?

1.2 Choose a product that you have purchased recently and show how the elements of the marketing mix came together to create the overall offering.

1.3 Choose three different products within the same market and explain how each one is trying to gain a competitive edge over the others.

1.4 Why is the question, 'What business are we in?' so important? How might

(a) a fast-food retailer,
(b) a national airline,
(c) a car manufacturer, and
(d) a hairdresser

answer that question if they were properly marketing orientated?

1.5 How might the application of the marketing concept differ between a small organisation and a very large multinational?

case study 1.1

Showing the customer who's Boss?

The Hugo Boss brand name covers products such as tailored clothing, sportswear and accessories including fragrances, shoes and other leather items. It has established an international reputation for upmarket 'lifestyle fashion' for those who are prepared to spend to achieve their desired 'look'. Walter Baldessarini, the Chief Executive, is responsible for turning round the fortunes of the company since 1997 and for leading the latest phase of growth for the company. That has only been achieved by becoming less concerned with making fashion statements and more orientated towards understanding what customers actually want from a premium clothing brand.

Hugo Boss, based in Metzingen, Germany, started to go upmarket in the rising affluence of the 1970s, and by the 1980s it was an 'in brand' that signified quality, distinctiveness and the very best of fashion to suit the owner of a Porsche or Ferrari. Sales growth was rapid and most European and North American markets were entered successfully. In the 1990s, however, fashion started to change. Smart gave way to smart–casual and thus extravagance gave way to softer, less bold fashion statements. Hugo Boss failed to spot that trend early and sales growth started to slide, especially in the home market in which sales grew by just 5 per cent in 1997. Hugo Boss suits even started to appear on the clearance rails. This was bad news, as once a clothing brand starts to lose its appeal, it is difficult to reverse its fortunes.

Baldessarini, despite having had no business training, understood the difference between clothes that are designed to make a fashion statement and those that are designed to appeal to target customers. He is quoted as saying 'people are tired of buying ten [suits] at a cheap price. They are buying fewer pieces but at a higher price and spending more overall' (as quoted by Edwards, 2001). Hugo Boss has understood that trend and positioned itself to cater for the expensive suit and the expensive casual clothes segment of the market. There is still a close link between the fashion and brand image, but now customers are part of the product development process rather than just being the eventual recipients of whatever has been designed. Close attention is still given to design and quality to create superior products but only in the context of value for money within the lifestyle philosophy that Hugo Boss now adopts. The appeal now tends to be targeted at the younger, affluent individual who wants quality clothing for a quality lifestyle.

Hugo Boss's timing for a new approach in 1997 fitted with the continued trend towards the smart–casual end of the market and a number of other companies have also succeeded in moving with the trend. Hugo Boss is now made up of three brands, Hugo, Boss and Baldessarini. Boss focuses on smart–casual business and sportswear; Hugo on a 'cool look for an upbeat urban life style'; and Baldessarini is concerned with a luxurious, refined and high quality image. Boss still accounts for over 80 per cent of sales, but the others are growing fast. The branding approach enables collections to be established around different lifestyles but all are united under the company theme of 'innovation, creativity and fashion'. Each collection theme is led by a head designer supported by a creative team which interprets the sketches and assists in fabric and pattern selection. Often Hugo Boss will work with suppliers to modify their fabrics to give the brand names even more distinction, and in total some 80 per cent of materials are exclusive to the company. Selecting the manufacturers is also an important task, as any slippage on quality standards will rebound on Hugo Boss, not the manufacturer directly. This means working closely with chosen suppliers and helping them, where needed, with quality improvements.

The Hugo Boss brand is known all over the world for its variety of quality products from clothes to leather goods, sportswear, shoes and fragrances. Source: **Hugo Boss AG/Modus Publicity**

As part of the recovery plan, both the Hugo and Boss brand names have been extended to include women's collections. In 1998, the Hugo women's collection was launched based on the same formula of brand image, lifestyle fit and creative flair. The phased roll-out, initially in Germany and selected European countries, was later extended to the rest of Europe and North America. Following on from the successful launch of Hugo, the decision was made to launch a Boss women's collection in 1998 aimed at the successful modern woman working in an international world. The collection was formally launched at the Milan fashion show in 2000 and initial orders were taken for December 2001 delivery. Although in the first half of 2001 the ladies' wear ranges were still reporting a loss, there was some confidence that the position would soon be reversed.

Marketing communication plays an important part in developing and maintaining the brand profile for Hugo Boss, although the prime interest for the potential customer is seeing the collections at first hand. Advertising tends to promote the overall brand identity through print media, using specialist magazines, posters and brochures, and a website was recently launched to show the latest collections. Campaigns are normally run around the collections on a seasonal basis and considerable effort is expended to ensure that only top models, photographers and art directors are used, to ensure that the messages and impact are consistent with the brand values. Little use of mass advertising is made: the preference is to ensure that the core identity is communicated by all staff and through all communication channels to create a coherent and consistent image. It is, however, important that the visual impact also reflects the brand personality so brand-orientated PR is also used. Through VIP wardrobing, for example at the premières of new films, reported interviews with designers about style and interpretation, and not least fashion shows, either at the major events such as Milan and Paris or those staged by particular retailers, the brand collections can start to create a 'sensual, real life personality'.

At a corporate level, sponsorship plays a big part in ensuring that the corporate image for Hugo Boss fits with the respective brand images. This ranges from supporting the Guggenheim Museum in New York, to sporting links such as Formula One motor racing, golf, tennis and skiing, which all help to create a corporate brand with a successful, dynamic and international image. For example, the sponsorship of McLaren in Formula One racing is one of the longest lasting partnerships in sport and ensures that the logo features close to the driver's name on the car and appears prominently on clothing. In one season alone, it is expected that Hugo Boss will make 8,500 shirts for McLaren as part of the sponsorship deal. It is believed that the commitment and dedication required to win in motor racing are consistent with the commitment and dedication of Hugo Boss to quality lifestyle fashion. To Baldessarini:

> *McLaren make sexy cars and we make sexy clothes* (as quoted by Edwards, 2001).

Hugo Boss has established a number of directly owned retail shops but also sells through selected speciality and top quality chains. There must be a close fit between the store image and the Hugo Boss brand. The mono brand store is the latest growth area with a store dedicated to all the Hugo Boss brands under one roof. The 5th Avenue 'flagship store' in New York, opened in 2001, shows an extension of that concept, with an internet café, bar and exhibition sharing the 1,400 m^2 selling area with the usual Hugo Boss collections. Considerable attention is paid to ensuring that retailers, and in smaller markets, independent wholesalers, are well trained and understand the Hugo Boss brands and philosophy. Merchandising seminars help provide guidance on making the most of display and point of sale retailing while other courses concentrate on enhancing service levels for a demanding set of customers. To assist in merchandising selection, large trade showrooms have been established so that the collections can be displayed for retailers. Even an extranet is being experimented with so that retailers can directly order and replenish stock from their PCs rather than using the more cumbersome telephone and mail ordering. Face-to-face communication is also important, not only between the company and its retailers via the salesforce, but also between retailers and customers. Retailers, whether directly owned or franchised, stage dinner parties and cocktail events followed by fashion shows to offer a more relaxed and upmarket buying environment to their customers.

Hugo Boss sales are expected to top €1bn in 2001 and are expected to continue to grow at around 20 per cent *per annum*. In the USA, a prime market for expansion, the opening of 23 new stores in shopping malls helped sales to grow by 32 per cent in 1999–2000. In Europe, sales grew in the Netherlands and France by 12 per cent and 19 per cent respectively, although the competitive markets of the UK and Germany only showed single figure sales growth. Overall sales in Germany of DM420mn were not, however, far behind the sales for the rest of Europe at DM593mn and well ahead of the DM288mn in the Americas. It has been the combination of opening new stores (130 over the period 1999–2000), expanding in existing markets and opening up in new countries that has primarily resulted in the spectacular reversal of fortunes in recent years, as virtually all of the growth has been outside the German market. Hugo Boss now sells through 387 shops in 110 different countries.

This case shows that if the product is not right it does not matter how good the rest of your marketing is, you will struggle. If, however, the product is in tune with the needs and lifestyles of at least some of the population, consistent application of marketing thinking and practice throughout the business can lead to success. To Baldessarini:

> *the brands build the company and the company builds the brands* (as quoted by Edwards, 2001).

Sources: Edwards (2001); *Frankfurter Allgemeine Zeitung* (2001); Goldman (2001); Heller (2000); Joachimsthaler and Aaker (1997).

Questions

1 How important has a marketing philosophy been to Hugo Boss? In what ways has it influenced the company's marketing decisions?

2 What new challenges might the introduction of the women's range pose for Hugo Boss' marketing mix?

3 How important a role do you think the New York flagship store plays in Hugo Boss' US marketing strategy?

4 In the light of the discussion earlier in this chapter about sustainable marketing, can the development and marketing of luxury goods be defended?

case study 1.2

lastminute.com: inspiration and solutions

lastminute.com is Europe's number one internet travel website. The company was set up in 1998 with the mission statement:

> *lastminute.com encourages spontaneous, romantic and sometimes adventurous behaviour by offering people the chance to live their dreams at unbeatable prices!*

These dreams do not only concern travel, however. lastminute.com sells three main groups of products and services:

- *Travel*: holidays, flights, hotels, etc.
- *Retail*: gifts (chocolates, gourmet foods, lingerie, adult fun items, etc.) and experiences (e.g. what about a bungee-jumping experience as a gift for your loved one?).
- *Leisure*: tickets for the theatre, concerts or sports events; eating in and eating out (through lastminute.com you can book a restaurant or order a meal to be delivered to your home).

In the early days, there was inevitably something of a product orientation to the company, as it sought to source and sell whatever products it could. As its brand name and reputation have developed, however, it has been possible to develop more of a marketing orientation as partnerships have evolved with suppliers who have come to recognise the potential of lastminute.com as a distribution channel and thus are negotiating more strategically about the most appropriate deals and offerings to place with lastminute.com. The company sees itself as an agent, putting last-minute buyers in touch with last-minute sellers. It is a 'lifestyle' retailer, for cash-rich, time-poor consumers, offering good value rather than being purely a 'bargain basement' store. The focus is on value and service, rather than on price. 'Inspiration and solutions' is a good summary of lastminute.com's core service:

- *Inspiration*: 'It's my friend's birthday. I know that I need a gift, but I don't know what I want'. lastminute.com can offer a variety of suggestions for gifts and experiences.
- *Solutions*: 'I know what I need and what I want: I want an economy class flight from Heathrow to New York next Friday'. lastminute.com can show available flights and prices to allow the customer to choose which they want.

In the view of Carl Lyons, the marketing director,

> *people love the idea of lastminute.com. It evokes a positive image of a shortcut to good times with their friends.*

The product portfolio has evolved over time as the company strives to be able to offer the customer everything for the perfect experience. The latest addition to the product portfolio, for example, is the ability to book a taxi through lastminute.com. Thus the customer planning a special night out with friends can search for, check availability, and make bookings at a theatre and a restaurant, and even take care of transportation too in one easy and convenient transaction. Before a new product or service can be added, however, the company needs to be sure that the customer is ready for it, that it has a clear role within the cohesive set of offerings that lastminute.com makes, that suppliers are willing and able to deliver the promises that lastminute.com makes on their behalf, and that the technical capability is there to allow the transaction and/or the service delivery to take place successfully.

The structure of the company in the UK is similar to that of many others. There are the traditional departments, such as marketing, human resources and finance, as well as departments that reflect the high tech retail focus of the business: a technical department to develop, maintain and manage the internet infrastructure that allows communication and transactions to take place between the company and its customers; three supply managers whose departments source the products and services that lastminute.com sells; and a business development department that manages strategic issues, for example creating and managing partnerships with other companies. Recently, lastminute.com entered into a partnership with Granada Media, for instance in order to generate awareness and traffic from complementary media. The marketing department consists of 13 people who undertake the complete range of well-integrated marketing activities, both online and offline. Although the marketing department can be thought of as being at the hub of the organisation, there is a spirit of mutual support and interdependence between the various departments.

Given the interactivity involved in internet retailing generally, the kinds of products and services that the site is selling, and the 'last minute' focus, it is perhaps not surprising that timing is a key issue in lastminute.com's day-to-day marketing. Advertising

Initially trading on last-minute flights and holidays, lastminute.com now offers a wide variety of products on the internet for those whose time is precious and whose lifestyles require immediate satisfaction. Source: lastminute.com

within the website changes throughout the day to reflect deadlines for products and the customer's changing needs. Thus, for example, in terms of 'eating in' and 'eating out', in the morning the emphasis will be on lunchtime restaurant bookings, whereas in the afternoon, the focus will shift to evening bookings and there will perhaps be more emphasis on family-orientated eating in or out. The marketing department has also recognised that not all customers are willing and/or able to buy through the same platforms all the time. Thus the marketers have worked closely with the technical department to ensure that transactions can be made by phone, through digital interactive television, and via WAP phones as well as over the web from a PC. This is an important element of ensuring that customers can access lastminute.com's services whenever they want and in a way that is most convenient or acceptable to them.

Another very important and dynamic element of lastminute.com's marketing offering is its weekly newsletter distributed via e-mail to over 3.5 million people. The company sees the newsletter, in conjunction with other relationship marketing techniques, as a very cost-effective and quick way of achieving a number of objectives:

- building and maintaining brand awareness and loyalty among customers through frequent communication;
- building and communicating brand personality through the design and 'tone of voice' of the newsletter;
- emphasising the breadth of products and services offered – a customer might, for example, have only purchased a package holiday previously through lastminute.com and thus the newsletter can introduce them to the gifts and broader leisure products and services on offer;
- stimulating demand in terms of both planned and impulse purchases.

The content and distribution of the newsletter is based on the customer database, which allows the company to target individual customers based on their past purchasing history. This is important because it means that the customer is more likely to see some relevance or interest in the newsletter rather than dismissing it as junk e-mail and using anti-spam filtering to prevent it.

The customer database is seen as a powerful weapon for competitive advantage because of its size and sophistication. The database has grown organically over the course of three years (which is a long time in dotcom terms!) and because of the established brand name of lastminute.com, the company finds it relatively easy to continue to recruit new customers to the database. Newer competitors find it more difficult because consumers have become more wary about volunteering personal details to companies they do not know very well. The strong brand name and established reputation of lastminute.com also stimulates less formal, but nevertheless invaluable, marketing benefits such as word-of-mouth recommendation between friends which helps to generate new customers.

Market research is not always easy in the dotcom sector. When lastminute.com was set up, it was something of a pioneer so it was difficult to quantify exactly the market potential. Additionally, there was a lack of established sources of secondary research. In most mature industries, there are good quality, established, standard sources of market information, but in emerging industries, this is not necessarily the case. Now that the market is beginning to mature, research data is starting to be collated. lastminute.com itself, however, undertakes its own ongoing research programme through its continuous 'user monitor' survey. A percentage of visitors to the website are encouraged to fill in an online feedback form giving their views on everything from prices and product offerings to their expectations of what the site should offer. The company is very responsive to the views expressed in this way, and this has contributed to the rapid evolution of the site in terms of both what it offers and how it is offered and delivered.

The company is confident about its future:

> *There has already been a shakeout in this market. The barriers to entry are low, but the barriers to success are high. We have an established customer base; we have good supplier relationships; we have the technical know-how. We have travelled a long way up the learning curve. The key to*

the future will be continuing to serve customers' evolving needs, being quick/first with new offerings, and being consistently true to the brand. Marketing is marketing. It's easy to drape new media in magic but it comes down to whether it's a good business or not.

Sources: with grateful thanks to Carl Lyons, UK Marketing Director, lastminute.com; http://www.lastminute.com; Rosier (2000).

Questions

1 Explain how and why lastminute.com's business orientation has evolved since its launch.

2 Divide lastminute.com's marketing activities into the 4Ps and explain how they fit together to create a consistent marketing mix. How might the other 3Ps of the services marketing mix fit in?

3 From the supplier's point of view, what are the advantages and disadvantages of selling travel and leisure services through an internet-based intermediary such as lastminute.com?

4 'The barriers to entry are low, but the barriers to success are high'. What do you think Carl Lyons meant by this and to what extent and why do you believe it to be true?

References for chapter 1

Agède, P. (1998), 'Le marketing a aussi ses mythes', *L'Entreprise*, 151 (April), pp. 84–9.

Alderson, W. (1957), *Marketing Behaviour and Executive Action: A Functionalist Approach to Marketing*, Homewood, Irwin.

Allmon, D., Chen, H., Pritchett, T. and Forrest, P. (1997), 'A Multicultural Examination of Business Ethics Perceptions', *Journal of Business Ethics*, 16 (2), pp. 183–8.

AMA (1985), 'AMA Board Approves New Marketing Definition', *Marketing News*, 1 March, p. 1.

Anderson, W. and Cunningham, W. (1972), 'The Socially Conscious Consumer', *Journal of Marketing*, 36 (3), pp. 23–31.

Avlonitis, G. *et al.* (1997), 'Marketing Orientation and Company Performance: Industrial vs Consumer Goods Companies', *Industrial Marketing Management*, 26 (5), pp. 385–402.

Bainbridge, J. and Curtis, J. (1998), 'The UK's Biggest Brands, Part 2', *Marketing*, 6 August, pp. 20–1.

Balestrini, P. (2001), 'Amidst the Digital Economy, Philanthropy in Business as a Source of Competitive Advantage', *Journal of International Marketing and Marketing Research*, 26 (1), pp. 13–34.

Berry, L.L. (1983), 'Relationship Marketing', in *Emerging Perspectives of Services Marketing*, L.L. Berry *et al.* (eds), American Marketing Association.

Booms, B.H. and Bitner, M.J. (1981), 'Marketing Strategies and Organisation Structures for Service Firms', in *Marketing of Services*, J. Donnelly and W.R. George (eds), American Marketing Association.

Borden, N. (1964), 'The Concept of the Marketing Mix', *Journal of Advertising Research*, June, pp. 2–7.

Brabbs, C. (2000), 'Kellogg "Luxury" Cereal Targets Career Women', *Marketing*, 14 September, p. 4.

Buxton, P. (2000), 'Companies with a Social Conscience', *Marketing*, 27 April, pp. 33–4.

Carroll, A. (1999), 'Corporate Social Responsibility', *Business and Society*, 38 (3), pp. 268–95.

Carroll, A. (1991), 'The Pyramid of Corporate Social Responsibility: Toward the Moral Management of Organizational Stakeholders', *Business Horizons*, 34 (July/August), pp. 39–48.

Chaffey, D., Mayer, R., Johnston, K. and Ellis-Chadwick, F. (2003), *Internet Marketing: Strategy, Implementation and Practice*. Financial Times/Prentice Hall, Harlow, Essex, UK 2nd edn.

Challener, C. (2001), 'Sustainable Development at a Crossroads', *Chemical Market Reporter*, 16 July, pp. 3–4.

Christopher, M., Payne, A., and Ballantyne, D. (1991), *Relationship Marketing: Bringing Quality, Customer Service and Marketing Together*, London: Butterworth.

CIM (2001), accessed via http://www.cim.co.uk

Clarke, P.D. *et al.* (1988), 'The Genesis of Strategic Marketing Control in British Retail Banking', *International Journal of Bank Marketing*, 6 (2), pp. 5–19.

CSR Forum (2001), 'The Responsible Century?', accessed via http://www.csrforum.com, August 2001.

Davies, J. (2001), 'The Chaos Christina Left Behind', *The Times (2)*, 31 July, pp. 4–5.

Deng, S. and Dart, J. (1999), 'The Market Orientation of Chinese Enterprises During a Time of Transition', *European Journal of Marketing*, 33 (5), pp. 631–54.

DTI (2001), 'Business and Society', accessed via http://www.societyandbusiness.gov.uk, August 2001.

Dunfee, T., Smith, N. and Ross, W. (1999), 'Social Contracts and Marketing Ethics', *Journal of Marketing*, 63 (3), pp. 14–32.

Dwyer, F., Shurr, P. and Oh, S. (1987), 'Developing Buyer and Seller Relationships', *Journal of Marketing*, 51 (2), pp. 11–27.

The Economist (2001a), 'For Watching or Eating?', *The Economist*, 28 July, p. 58.

The Economist (2000b), 'The Politics of Whaling', *The Economist*, 9 September, p. 42.

Edwards, O. (2001), 'Germany's Fashion Genius', *EuroBusiness*, July, pp. 42–5.

EU (2001), 'Green Paper: Promoting a European Framework for Corporate Social Responsibility', accessed via http://europa.eu.int/comm/employment_social/soc-dial/csr/greenpaper_en.pdf, August 2001.

Foottit, C. (2000), 'Kenya: Flower Industry Blooming', *African Business*, July/August, p. 36.

Frankfurter Allgemeine Zeitung (2001). 'Hugo Boss hat volle Auftragsbücher', *Frankfurter Allgemeine Zeitung*, 28 July.

Fuller, D. (1999), *Sustainable Marketing: Managerial-Ecological Issues*, Sage Publications.

Goldman, L. (2001), 'The Boss is Back', *Forbes*, 22 January, pp. 114–5.

Gordon, M. (1991), *Market Socialism in China*, Working Paper, University of Toronto.

Gray, R. (2001), 'Responsibility up the Agenda', *Marketing*, 3 May, p. 39.

Green, D. (1995), 'Healthcare Vies With Research', *Financial Times*, 25 April 1995, p. 34.

The Grocer (1998), 'Dutch Exporter Going Flat out to Grow in Britain', *The Grocer*, 24 January, p. 40.

Grönroos, C. (1997), 'From Marketing Mix to Relationship Marketing – Towards a Paradigm Shift in Marketing', *Management Decision*, 35 (4), pp. 322–39.

Gummesson, E. (1987), 'The New Marketing: Developing Long-term Interactive Relationships', *Long Range Planning*, 20 (4), pp. 10–20.

Hartman, C. and Beck-Dudley, C. (1999), 'Marketing Strategies and the Search for Virtue: A Case Analysis of the Body Shop International', *Journal of Business Ethics*, 20 (3), pp. 249–63.

Heller, R. (2000), 'Making Money in Style', *Forbes*, 18 September, p. 138.

Henderson, S. (1998), 'No Such Thing as Market Orientation – A Call for No More Papers', *Management Decision*, 36 (9), pp. 598–609.

Hooley, G.J. *et al.* (1990), 'The Marketing Concept: Putting Theory into Practice', *European Journal of Marketing*, 24 (9), pp. 7–23.

Hunt, S. and Vitell, S. (1993), 'The General Theory of Marketing Ethics: A Retrospective and Revision', *in* N. Smith and J. Quelch (eds), *Ethics in Marketing*, Richard D. Irwin.

Hunt, S. and Vitell, S. (1986), 'The General Theory of Marketing Ethics', *Journal of Macromarketing*, 6 (Spring), pp. 5–16.

Joachimsthaler, E. and Aaker, D. (1997), 'Building Brands Without Mass Media', *Harvard Business Review*, January/February, pp. 39–50.

Kinnear, T., Taylor, J. and Ahmed, S. (1974), 'Ecologically Concerned Consumers: Who Are They?', *Journal of Marketing*, 38 (2), p. 20.

Knights, D. *et al.* (1994), 'The Consumer Rules? An Examination of the Rhetoric and "Reality" of Marketing in Financial Services', *European Journal of Marketing*, 28 (3), pp. 42–54.

Levitt, T. (1960), 'Marketing Myopia', *Harvard Business Review*, July/August, pp. 45–56.

Mans, J. (2000), 'The European View of Future Packaging', *Dairy Foods*, 101 (6), pp. 42–3.

Marketing Week (2001), 'Fresh Cut Flowers', *Marketing Week*, 22 March, pp. 34–5.

Mason, T. (2000), 'The Importance of Being Ethical', *Marketing*, 26 October, p. 27.

McCarthy, E. (1960), *Basic Marketing*, Homewood: Irwin.

McDonald, M. and Wilson, H. (1999), *e-Marketing: Improving Marketing Effectiveness in a Digital World*. Financial Times Management, Pearson Education, Harlow, UK.

Mhone, C. (2000), 'Malawi: Fading Flowers', *African Business*, December, p. 46.

Mintel (1999), 'Breakfast Cereals, 1/12/99', accessed via http://sinatra2.mintel.com, October 2001.

Mintzberg, H. (1983), 'The Case For Corporate Social Responsibility', *Journal of Business Strategy*, 4 (2), pp. 3–15.

Morishta, J. and O'Regan, F. (2001), 'Whaling: Should Japan be Allowed to Continue?', *The Ecologist*, July/August, pp. 18–21.

Murphy, P. and Laczniak, G. (1981), 'Marketing Ethics: A Review with Implications for Managers, Educators and Researchers', *in* B. Enis and K. Roering (eds), *Review of Marketing 1981*, Chicago: American Marketing Association.

Narver, J. and Slater, S. (1990), 'The Effect of a Market Orientation on Business Profitability', *Journal of Marketing*, 54 (4), pp. 20–35.

OECD Observer (2001), 'Rising to the Global Development Challenges', *OECD Observer*, Issue 226/7 (Summer), p. 41.

Piercy, N. (1992), *Marketing-led Strategic Change*, Oxford: Butterworth-Heinemann.

Rosier, B. (2001), 'P&O Cruises Picks MCBD for £7M Job', *Marketing*, 15 March, p. 4.

Rosier, B. (2000), 'The Long Game', *Marketing*, 31 August, p. 16.

Schultz, R. and Good, D. (2000), 'Impact of the Consideration of Future Sales Consequences and Customer-oriented Selling on Long-term Buyer–Seller Relationships', *The Journal of Business and Industrial Marketing*, 15 (4), pp. 200–15.

Severn Trent (2001), 'Stewardship Report 2001: The Environment is Our Business', accessed via http://www.severn-trent.com/reports/fin/steward2001/pdf/stewardship_report.pdf, August 2001.

Sheth, J., Gardner, D, and Garrett, D. (1988), *Marketing Theory: Evolution and Evaluation*, New York: Wiley.

Smith, P.R. and Chaffey, D. (2001), *eMarketing eXcellence: at the Heart of eBusiness*. Butterworth-Heinemann, Oxford, UK.

Smith, W. and Higgins, M. (2000), 'Cause-related Marketing: Ethics and the Ecstatic', *Business and Society*, 39 (3), pp. 304–22.

Strong, C. (1996), 'Features Contributing to the Growth of Ethical Consumerism – A Preliminary Investigation', *Marketing Intelligence and Planning*, 14 (5), pp. 5–13.

Suhre, S. (1999), 'Misguided Morality: The Repercussions of the International Whaling Commission's Shift From a Policy of Regulation to One of Preservation', *Georgetown International Envoironment Law Review*, 12 (1), pp. 305–29.

Turnbull, P.W. and Valla, J.P. (1986), *Strategies for International Industrial Marketing*, Croom Helm.

Van Heck, E. (2000), 'The Cutting Edge in Auctions', *Harvard Business Review*, March/April, pp. 18–9.

Varley, P. (1999), 'Cruise Control', *Supply Management*, 8 July, pp. 30–2.

Watts, J. (2001), 'Japanese Laud Whaling Haul', *The Guardian*, 8 August.

WCED (1987), *Our Common Future*, Oxford: Oxford University Press.

Zhuang, S. and Whitehill, A. (1989), 'Will China Adopt Western Management Practices?', *Business Horizons*, 32 (2), pp. 58–64.

chapter 2

the european marketing environment

Introduction

LEARNING OBJECTIVES

This chapter will help you to:

1. understand the importance of the external environment to marketing decision-making;
2. assess the role and importance of scanning the environment as a means of early identification of opportunities and threats;
3. appreciate the evolving and diverse nature of the European marketing environment;
4. define the broad categories of factors that affect the marketing environment; and
5. understand the influences at work within each of those categories and their implications for marketing.

Marketing, by its very nature, is an outward-looking discipline. As the interface between the organisation and the outside world, it has to balance internal capabilities and resources with the opportunities offered externally. Chapter 1 has already shown, however, that the outside world can be a complex and difficult place to understand. Although the definition and understanding of the customer's needs and wants are at the heart of the marketing philosophy, there are many factors influencing how those customer needs evolve, and affecting or constraining the organisation's ability to meet those needs in a competitive environment. Thus in order to reach an adequate understanding of the customer's future needs and to develop marketing mixes that will satisfy the customer, the marketer has to be able to analyse the external environment and clarify which influences and their implications are most important.

This chapter will dissect the external environment and look closely at the variety of factors and influences that help to shape the direction of marketing thinking. First, the chapter clarifies the nature of the external environment, underlining why it needs to be understood, and what opportunities that understanding offers to the marketer.

Although the environment consists of a wide variety of factors and influences, it is possible to group them under four broad headings: sociocultural, technological, economic and competitive, and political and legal influences. Each will be examined in turn, discussing the various issues they cover and their implications for marketing decision-making.

eg

Food processors such as Nestlé and Kraft must keep a close watch on trends in the marketing environment if they are to remain competitive and within the law. It is not an easy environment. Over the past few years the consumer has had to cope with the implications of BSE/CJD ('mad cow' disease and its human form), the effect of foot and mouth disease on meat stocks and prices, acceptance of GM (genetically modified) foodstuffs and other scares such as salmonella in eggs and powdered baby milk. All of this starts to raise issues about the integrity of the European food chain and the wisdom of high intensity farming. The paradox is that at a time when most Europeans are spoilt for choice and generally enjoy very high quality foods, there is growing concern over production methods, animal welfare, environmental impact and the impact on public health of chemicals and additives. Whether the European food chain is safe, sustainable and ethical still seems debatable. The Swedish and British attitudes to food processing make an interesting comparison. In Sweden the consumer tends to pay more for food, to cover the higher costs of less intensive farming methods, improved animal welfare and tighter voluntary and legislated welfare controls. It is claimed that consumers are better educated about food and are prepared to pay more for home produced products. In the UK, the market is very price competitive and consumers seek to spend less on food. There are concerns about animal welfare and the intensity of farming, but often the connection is not made with supermarket prices. To many urban dwellers, eggs come from supermarkets, milk from cartons and beefburgers from McDonald's and that is that. Research by Taylor Nelson Sofres suggests that less than 30 per cent of shoppers actually check food labels for the calorie, preservative and additive content, let alone worry about the farming method: as long as it is perceived as 'safe', many don't care. This means that many farmers are now in a trap. The consumer will not pay more for the food; retailers and processors want cheaper supplies, and yet the demand for sustainable and environmentally friendly farming methods grows. At the same time, trade restrictions are being slowly lifted across the EU, and thus cheap supplies are coming in from developing countries with far fewer regulatory and welfare pressures on food processing, which is all very nice for the retailers and the consumers, but not so good for European food producers. And then there is the CAP reform programme . . . but more about that later (*The Grocer*, 2000b; Hunt, 2001).

The nature of the European marketing environment

This section will first define the broad groupings of environmental influences, and then go on to look at the technique of environmental scanning as a means of identifying the threats and opportunities that will affect marketing planning and implementation within the organisation.

Elements of the marketing environment

Figure 2.1 shows the elements of the external environment in relation to the organisation and its immediate surroundings.

Figure 2.1 Elements of the external environment

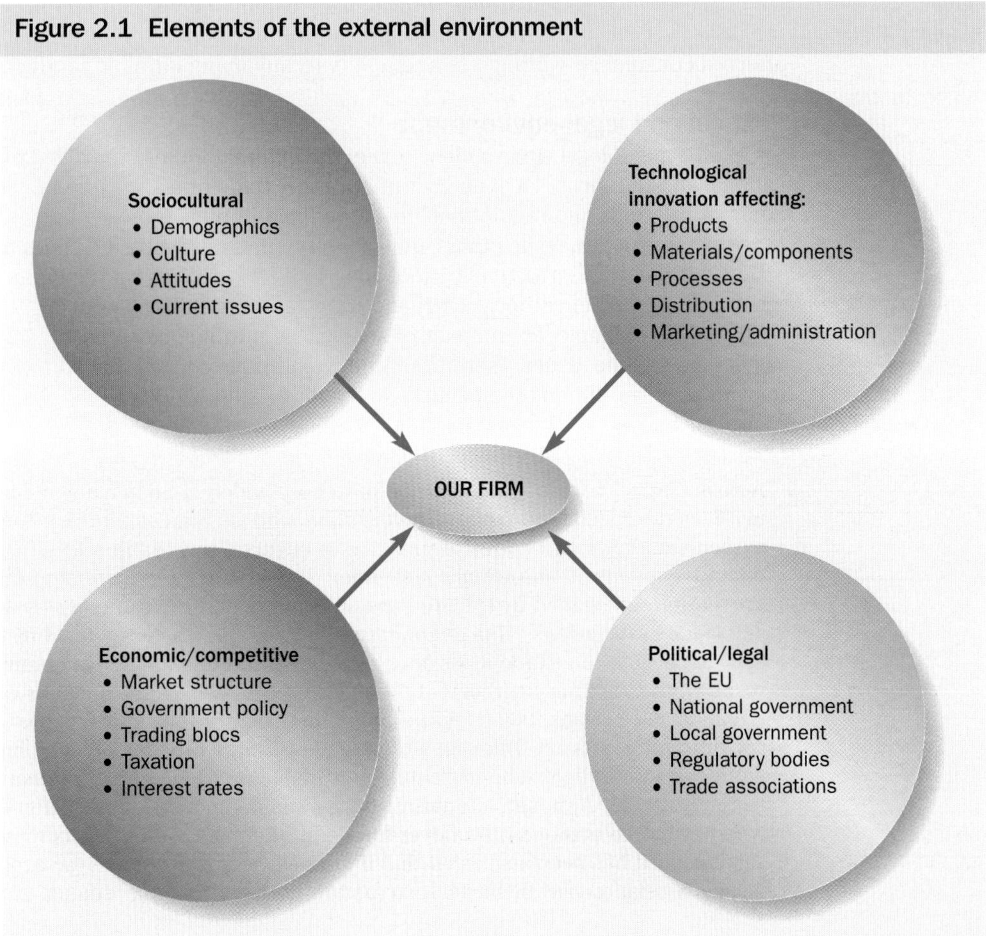

As the figure shows, the elements can be divided into four main groupings, known by the acronym **STEP**: **S**ociocultural, **T**echnological, **E**conomic and competitive, and **P**olitical and legal environments.

Sociocultural environment

The sociocultural environment is of particular concern to marketers as it has a direct effect on their understanding of customers and what drives them. Not only does it address the demographic structure of markets, but it also looks at the way in which attitudes and opinions are being formed and how they are evolving. A general increase in health consciousness, for instance, has stimulated the launch of a wide variety of products with low levels of fat and sugar, fewer artificial ingredients and no additives.

Technological environment

Technological innovation and technological improvement have had a profound effect in all areas of marketing. Computer technology, for instance, has revolutionised product design, quality control, materials and inventory management, the production of advertising and other promotional materials, and the management and analysis of customer information. The rise in direct marketing as a communication technique, discussed in Chapter 18, owes a lot to the availability of cheap and powerful computerised database management. Technology also affects the development of new processes and materials, as well as the invention of completely new products or applications, such as the multimedia home computer, including a CD-ROM drive, or the development of the low calorie sweeteners that have revolutionised the dieting market.

Economic and competitive environment

The economic and competitive environment covers both macro- and micro-economic conditions which affect the structure of competition in a market, the cost and availability of money for marketing investment in stock and new products, for example, and the economic conditions affecting a customer's propensity to buy. The global recession of the late 1990s, for instance, caused a significant increase in unemployment at all social levels, and thus affected consumers' willingness and ability to buy many kinds of products.

Political and legal environment

The political and legal environment covers the external forces controlled by governments, both national and European, local authorities, or other trade or activity orientated regulatory bodies. Some of the rules and regulations developed and implemented by bodies under this heading have the force of law, while others are voluntary, such as advertising codes of practice.

Each of the STEP areas will be looked at in more detail on pp. 48 *et seq*. There is, of course, much interdependence between them. Rules and regulations concerning 'green' aspects of products, for example, are a result of sociocultural influences pressurising the legislators and regulators. Certain issues, therefore, such as international, ethical and green issues, will crop up with slightly different perspectives in the discussion of each STEP element.

eg

Across Europe, voluntary agreements have been widely used in many industrial sectors. This involves the regulators, usually government, and regulatees working together to produce agreed standards and codes of practice to ensure progress in a less formal but more co-operative manner than outright legislation. In Germany the agreement on Global Warming Prevention was signed by the Ministry of Industry and Environment as well as 19 industry and trade associations. This committed members to reduce the level of CO_2 emissions by 2005 according to a trade association target. No targets are set at company level but as a result of the voluntary agreement, no energy taxes were introduced as originally planned. (Delmas and Terlaak, 2001). Sometimes the threat of legislation is designed to prompt a sector to reform its act. Take, for example, the airlines' practice of 'bumping seats' i.e. selling more seats on a flight than are actually available on the expectation that some passengers will not turn up. Although alternative flights and compensation are offered to any travellers who have to be bumped off an over-full flight, the impact on the frustrated traveller can be significant. It has been suggested that if airlines cannot overcome the problem by voluntary means, legislation may be introduced to prevent them from over-selling.

Environmental scanning

Even a brief discussion of the STEP factors begins to show just how important the marketing environment is. No organisation exists in a vacuum, and since marketing is all about looking outwards and meeting the customer's needs and wants, the organisation has to take into account what is happening in the real world. The marketing environment will present many opportunities and threats that can fundamentally affect all elements of the marketing mix, as we saw in the case of the German food processors at the beginning of the chapter. In terms of the product, for example, STEP factors help to define exactly what customers want, what it is possible (and legal) to provide them with, and how it should be packaged and presented. Pricing is also influenced by external factors, such as the competition's pricing policies, government taxation and what consumers can afford. STEP factors also affect promotion, constraining it through regulation, but also inspiring the creativity that develops appropriate messages to capture the mood of the times and the target audience. Finally, the strength of relationships between manufacturers and retailers or other intermediaries is also affected by the external environment. Competitive pressures at all levels of the distribution channel; technology encouraging joint development and commitment in terms of both products and logistics; shifts in where and how people want to buy: all help to shape the quality and direction of inter-organisational relationships.

Thus the marketing mix is very dependent on the external environment, but the problem is that the environment is very dynamic, changing all the time. The organisation therefore has to keep pace with change and even anticipate it. It is not enough to understand what is happening today: by the time the organisation has acted on that information and implemented decisions based on it, it will be too late. The organisation has either to pick up the earliest indicators of change and then act on them very quickly, or try to predict change so that tomorrow's marketing offerings can be appropriately planned.

In order to achieve this successfully, the organisation needs to undertake **environmental scanning**, which is the collection and evaluation of information from the wider marketing environment that might affect the organisation and its strategic marketing activities. Such information may come from a variety of sources, such as experience, personal contacts, published market research studies, government statistics, trade sources or even through specially commissioned market research. Responsibility for collecting and collating the information might lie with individual managers or there could be a committee made up of managers from a range of functions (marketing, R&D, production, etc.) which acts as the environmental eyes and ears of the organisation. It is important, however, to limit the amount of incoming information to a manageable quantity, since there is an infinite amount of potentially relevant material out there and a single organisation cannot handle all of it.

The approach to scanning can vary from being extremely organised and purposeful to being random and informal. As Aguilar (1967) pointed out, formal scanning can be very expensive and time consuming as it has to cast its net very wide to catch all the possible influences that might affect the organisation. The key is knowing what is important and should be acted upon, and what can wait.

There is a great deal of skill and perceptiveness involved in assessing the significance of any piece of information and whether it should be acted upon. Volvo, for example, failed to pick up the early signs indicating the emergence of markets for 'people carriers' and four-wheel drive vehicles, and thus missed out on the growth stages of both markets. Organisations that supply components to the motor industry also have to be alert to changing tastes and trends, in order to plan production. Motor industry analysts predicted that airbags would not be as readily accepted by motorists in Europe as they were in the United States. What actually happened was that motorists quickly warmed to the idea and began to demand airbags as standard. The motor manufacturers were caught somewhat unprepared, and consequently put a lot of pressure on suppliers to fulfil demand immediately.

Environmental scanning is therefore an important task, but often a difficult one, particularly in terms of interpretation and implementation of the information gained. The following looks in more detail at each of the STEP factors, and gives a further indication of the range and complexity of the influences and information that can affect the marketing activities of the organisation.

eg The motor industry is now facing similar decisions over the pace with which to introduce onboard computing into vehicles. Will motorists pay for the electronic wizardry and can it become a competitive advantage? Citroën clearly thinks so. It has been investing in R&D with selected suppliers examining new options in multi-media and in-car communications to enable internet and e-mail access to be offered as standard, as part of a mobile office concept. The C5 model is actively promoted on the basis of its 19 integrated onboard computers covering such features and benefits as computer-assisted parking, low tyre-pressure warning, automatically turning the lights on, and radio volume variation depending upon speed. Voice-recognition technology that can respond to spoken commands and talk back via voice synthesis is predicted to be the next big step forward in this area (http://www.citroen.com).

The sociocultural environment

It is absolutely essential for organisations serving consumer markets, directly or indirectly, to understand the **sociocultural environment**, since these factors fundamentally influence the customer's needs and wants. Despite a 'common market' across Europe, there are still many basic differences in language, culture, cuisine, household size, income levels, spending patterns, women's role in society and perceptions of promotion. These differences must not be overlooked by a marketing manager when planning a European marketing strategy (Jagger, 1998). Many of the factors discussed here will be looked at again in Chapters 3 and 5, and so this is a brief overview of the demographic and sociocultural influences on marketing thinking and activities.

The demographic environment

Demographics is the study of the measurable aspects of population structures and profiles, including factors such as age, size, gender, race, occupation and location. As the birth rate fluctuates and as life expectancy increases, the breakdown of the population changes, creating challenges and opportunities for marketers, particularly if that information is taken in conjunction with data on family structure and income.

If, for example, the birth rate is falling in a particular geographic market, the marketer might interpret it to mean that people are having their children later in life when they are better established economically. This would mean that the parents have much more money to spend per child, and additionally doting grandparents, aunts and uncles might similarly be inclined to spend more. The marketer might therefore come to the conclusion that there is still a lucrative upmarket niche to be served.

At the other end of the scale is what is known as the 'grey market', consisting of the over-55 age group. As Table 2.1 shows, the over-55s represent around one-quarter of the population of most EU countries. Their numbers are increasing, and because of better healthcare and financial planning, a significant proportion are able to indulge in high levels of leisure-orientated consumption, especially as they are likely to have paid off any mortgage or similar long-term debt, and are not likely to have dependent children. 'Generational marketing', for organisations seeking to appeal to this target age group, requires a fundamentally different perspective on the part of advertisers, according to Shannon (1998). Attitudes are changing. For example, research into the over-50s in Germany revealed that rather than thrift and self-denial, the growing emphasis is on enjoyment through consumption. To communicate effectively to this age group, the focus now has to reflect attitude and lifestyle rather than reinforcing an age-based stereotype.

Looking at the oldest segment within the over-55 age groups, we see that the growth in the numbers of the over-80s has serious social implications. In the UK, for example, this group represented only 2.3 per cent of the population in 1971, but by the year 2000 that had risen to nearly 4 per cent. This group depends extensively on health and social service provision, and yet is the poorest of the retired groups. At the other end of the age spectrum, it is

Table 2.1 Population by age group, 50 years and over (% analysis)

Population by age group at 1 January 2000	*55–59*	*60–69*	*70–79*	*80+*	*Total*
Austria	12.4	9.2	7.7	3.5	32.7
Belgium	11.6	10.2	8.2	3.5	33.5
Denmark	13.8	9.0	6.8	3.9	33.5
Finland	13.7	9.4	7.1	3.3	33.5
France	11.4	9.2	7.7	3.6	31.9
Germany	12.2	11.6	7.8	3.5	35.2
Greece	11.7	11.6	8.0	3.5	34.8
Ireland	10.4	7.3	5.3	2.5	25.5
Italy	12.6	11.3	8.6	4.0	36.5
Luxembourg	11.6	9.3	6.8	3.0	30.7
Netherlands	12.6	8.6	6.4	3.2	30.8
Portugal	11.4	10.3	7.6	2.8	32.1
Spain	11.1	10.1	7.9	3.7	32.7
Sweden	13.7	9.2	8.1	5.0	35.8
UK	12.2	9.2	7.3	3.9	32.6

Source: *European Marketing Data and Statistics 2001*, Euromonitor, 36th edition. Extrapolated from Table 0221, pp. 130–1.

eg

Saga Holidays also found that it had to redefine its idea of the most appropriate market to target and its notions of what potential customers want. In the 1990s, Saga shifted its focus from the over-60 to over-50 age group and at the same time diversified from being purely a tour operator to using the brand name to launch publishing and financial services products for the same target market. However, it also found that age alone was not a good indicator of holiday preferences. Over 90 per cent of customers now want holidays abroad compared with 50 per cent ten years ago. They also want anything but two weeks in Benidorm or beach resorts. River rafting, jungle trekking, mountain hiking and elephant safaris are on the agenda as the age group becomes more diverse in outlook and aspirations. In 1996, Saga purchased the cruise ship *Saga Rose*, the only cruise ship exclusively for the over-50s: children and students are definitely not welcome! In a market in which the number of over-60s will grow by 20 per cent in ten years' time, according to Henley Forecasting, and in which the over-50s are generally wealthier and have more leisure time, the future looks promising for Saga, but the formula remains the same: worry-free, well-organised and well-designed services for the 'mature in years, but young at heart' (Chesshyre, 2001; http://www.holidays.saga.co.uk).

The changes in leisure activities and the requirements of customers have led Saga Holidays to offer a greater variety of different holidays for its target audience. The* Saga Rose *shown here arriving in Bora Bora, is a cruise ship owned by Saga and is exclusively for the over 50s.

Source: http://www.holidays.saga.co.uk

now common for an individual's educational career to begin at the age of three and carry on until 23. Again, this has implications not only for the state, but also for educational institutions (public and private) and providers of educational goods and services.

Clearly, the size of a household combined with its income is going to be a fundamental determinant of its needs and wants, and its ability to fulfil them. Table 2.2 gives some basic data on trends in average household size across Europe.

Table 2.2 Average number of occupants per household, 1995–99

Country	*1995*	*1996*	*1997*	*1998*	*1999*
Austria	2.60	2.60	2.50	2.50	2.50
Belgium	2.50	2.50	2.50	2.40	2.40
Denmark	2.30	2.30	2.30	2.30	2.30
Finland	2.40	2.30	2.30	2.30	2.30
France	2.50	2.50	2.50	2.40	2.40
Germany	2.20	2.20	2.20	2.20	2.20
Greece	3.20	3.10	3.10	3.00	3.00
Ireland	3.10	3.10	3.10	3.10	3.00
Italy	2.80	2.80	2.90	2.90	2.90
Luxembourg	2.89	2.86	2.90	2.88	2.89
Netherlands	2.40	2.40	2.40	2.30	2.30
Portugal	3.10	3.10	3.00	3.00	2.90
Spain	3.20	3.20	3.20	3.20	3.20
Sweden	2.30	2.30	2.20	2.20	2.10
UK	2.40	2.40	2.40	2.30	2.30

Source: *European Marketing Data and Statistics 2001*, Euromonitor, 36th edition. Extracted from Table 1607, p. 373.

From Table 2.2, it can be seen that Spain, Greece and Ireland have slightly larger average household sizes than elsewhere in the EU. All of this will have a number of implications for marketers selling into Spain, Greece or Ireland, including perhaps the need for larger pack sizes, and more focus on family-orientated products. However, as Table 2.2 shows, most countries are experiencing a pattern of decline in the average household size. Again, marketers need to be mindful of these changes and to adapt their offerings accordingly. A significant increase in the proportion of single-person households will affect a whole range of marketing offerings, for example solo holidays, smaller apartments, pack sizes and advertising approaches and family stereotypes.

What is also important is the level of disposable income available (i.e. what is left after taxes have been paid), and the choices the household makes about saving and/or spending it. Table 2.3 shows how the spending of disposable income varies across Europe.

Clearly, housing is a fundamental cost, but the proportion of income it takes varies widely across Europe, with the Greeks and Portuguese spending the lowest percentage on housing. Looking at the food column, however, it is in the less affluent economies, such as those of Greece and Portugal, that people are spending relatively more on food as a percentage of their total expenditure. In some of the other categories, the Irish spend a higher proportion than anyone else on tobacco while the Dutch spend more on healthcare; the Germans like their home comforts, with a higher than average spend on household fuels and household goods and services; the Spanish obviously like eating out while the Finns seem to enjoy their alcohol! Of course, patterns of expenditure will be dictated to some extent by national income levels and relative prices.

Such spending patterns are not fixed: they will vary not only because of changes in the demographic and economic structure of the household, but also because of sociocultural influences, discussed in the next subsection. A further factor which cuts across both demographic and sociocultural issues is employment patterns, specifically the number of working women in a community and the rate of unemployment. This influences not only household income, but also shopping and consumption patterns.

Table 2.3 Consumer expenditure by object 1999 (% analysis)

Percentage of total

	Food	*Alcoholic drinks*	*Non-alcoholic drinks*	*Tobacco*	*Clothing*	*Footwear*	*Housing*	*Household fuels*	*Household goods and services*	*Health*	*Transport*	*Communications*	*Leisure/ education*	*Hotels/ restaurants*	*Others*
Austria	12.3	1.5	0.9	1.7	6.0	1.1	16.9	4.1	7.9	6.0	13.3	2.3	8.4	12.0	5.8
Belgium	13.4	2.7	1.2	1.5	5.3	0.6	15.9	3.9	11.4	11.1	11.7	1.1	5.2	6.3	8.7
Denmark	12.2	2.6	1.2	2.3	4.2	1.0	20.4	6.3	6.0	3.0	14.6	1.6	10.7	5.5	8.5
Finland	12.4	3.7	0.8	1.8	3.8	0.7	21.5	4.1	4.6	3.4	13.6	2.6	10.6	7.2	9.1
France	13.7	2.7	0.6	1.5	4.2	1.0	18.9	3.3	6.5	9.8	13.9	1.7	5.9	7.0	9.2
Germany	13.0	1.1	1.4	0.6	3.7	1.0	22.6	6.4	14.2	2.5	13.6	2.0	8.9	5.2	3.8
Greece	19.0	0.4	0.6	2.5	7.8	2.1	8.3	3.5	7.3	7.0	13.1	3.0	7.1	8.9	9.3
Ireland	14.1	2.4	1.2	3.7	5.6	1.0	11.2	3.6	7.3	4.0	12.5	2.0	11.1	11.9	8.4
Italy	14.3	0.8	1.0	1.8	7.4	2.1	16.8	3.4	9.4	3.3	12.8	2.6	7.9	8.7	7.7
Luxembourg	n/a	n/a	n/a	n/a	n/a	n/a	n/a	n/a	n/a	n/a	n/a	n/a	n/a	n/a	n/a
Netherlands	10.7	1.4	0.5	1.4	4.4	0.8	18.5	3.1	7.0	12.5	11.4	2.1	10.1	5.5	10.8
Portugal	23.3	1.9	0.4	1.6	6.5	2.0	8.7	1.9	7.3	5.7	14.8	1.9	8.3	10.3	5.4
Spain	15.6	0.9	0.4	1.6	4.5	2.5	10.7	3.1	6.5	5.5	14.0	1.6	8.2	17.4	7.3
Sweden	12.2	2.4	0.8	1.6	4.3	0.8	26.7	6.0	4.7	2.4	12.9	2.9	9.9	5.0	7.4
UK	10.4	2.3	0.8	2.3	5.3	0.9	15.2	2.8	9.6	1.3	15.1	2.1	11.9	11.5	8.7

Source: *European Marketing Data and Statistics 2001*, Euromonitor, 36th edition. Table 1103, pp. 268–9.

As the data presented here have shown, it is dangerous to generalise about demographic trends across Europe. There are wide variations, particularly between the richer northern and western European states and the poorer southern and eastern states. Thus the marketer needs to understand both the differences and the similarities between nations within Europe, as a means of assessing emerging trends and opportunities.

Sociocultural influences

Demographic information only paints a very broad picture of what is happening. If the marketer wants a really three-dimensional feel, then some analysis of sociocultural factors is essential. These factors involve much more qualitative assessment, can be much harder to measure and interpret than the hard facts of demographics and may be subject to unpredictable change, but the effort is worthwhile for a truly marketing orientated organisation.

One thing that does evolve over time is people's lifestyle expectations. Products that at one time were considered upmarket luxuries, such as televisions and fridges, are now considered to be necessities. Turning a luxury into a necessity obviously broadens the potential market, and widens the marketer's scope for creating a variety of products and offerings to suit a spectrum of income levels and usage needs. Televisions, for example, come in a variety of shapes, sizes and prices, from the pocket-sized portable to the cheap, small set that will do for the children's bedroom, to the very large, technically advanced, state-of-the-art status symbol with flat screen and digital connectivity. This variety has the bonus of encouraging households to own more than one set, further fuelling the volume of the market, particularly as improvements in technology and production processes along with economies of scale further reduce prices.

Broadening tastes and demands are another sociocultural influence, partly fuelled by the marketers themselves, and partly emanating from consumers. Marketers, by constant innovation and through their marketing communications, encourage consumers to become bored with the same old standard, familiar products and thus to demand more convenience, variety and variation.

eg

Deli counter sales are falling all across Europe and in the United States. It has been suggested that the younger generation prefers to pay for pre-packed foods as it is more convenient and there is no need for counter queuing. Time is becoming increasingly precious to many consumers and queuing can be a real turn-off. Madrange, the French cooked meat and charcuterie producer is attempting to address the loss of supermarket sales by introducing 'deli express' which means pre-slicing popular meats and cheeses and wrapping them in deli packaging, branded as 'Ultra fresh' so they can be sold in the 'ready to go' section of the deli counter. It looks like a deli package but has product information, weight and price displayed. It is hoped that the pre-packed option will become attractive to shoppers, combining the deli choice and freshness with the speed and convenience of self-selection. It will also clear some space on the deli counter to offer more exotic premium and regional speciality items which are still popular with shoppers (Hardcastle, 2001).

Consumers want variation and variety not only to stave off boredom, but also as a means of asserting their individuality. Although mass markets are necessary to generate the economies of scale that make products affordable, no consumer wants to think they are identical to their neighbours. They want to feel that their purchasing choices, in everything from their car to the contents of their biscuit tin, create a unique profile that gives them the desired status in others' eyes. Marketers like a certain amount of variety and variation (but not too much or the economies of scale are compromised) because it helps to keep customers loyal (you could use a different variety of one manufacturer's cook-in sauces, if you wanted, every night of the week and still not get bored) and allows scope for the premium-priced niches to emerge.

Fashions and fads are also linked with consumer boredom and a desire for new stimulation. The clothing market in particular has an interest in making consumers sufficiently discontented with the perfectly serviceable clothes already in the wardrobe that they go out to buy new ones every season. For some consumers, it is important for their social integration and their status to be seen to have the latest products and the latest fashions, whether it be in clothing, music or alcoholic drinks. Nevertheless, linking a product with fashion may create marketing problems. Fashions, by definition, are short lived, and as soon as they become widespread, the fashion leaders are moving on to something new and different. Marketers therefore have to reap rewards while they can, or find a means of shifting the product away from its fashionable associations.

More deeply ingrained in society than the fripperies of fashion are underlying attitudes. These change much more slowly than fashion trends and are much more difficult for the marketer to influence. It is more likely, in fact, that the marketer will assess existing or emerging attitudes and then adapt or develop to fit them. As can be seen in Figure 2.2, there are a number of areas in which changes in societal attitudes have influenced marketing approaches. Each is discussed below.

Environmental issues

Environmental issues have been of major concern in recent years, and this area has caused consumers to think more critically about the origins, content and manufacturing processes of the products they buy. Consumers, for example, want products made with the minimum of pollution and are looking for the reassurance, where applicable, that they come of renewable resources. Many paper products now carry notices stating that they are made of wood from managed forests that are replanted after harvesting. In the same spirit, consumers are also demanding that unnecessary packaging is eliminated and that packaging should be recyclable.

Figure 2.2 The impact of societal attitudes on marketing strategy

marketing *in action*

Saving the trees to preserve the woods

Precious Woods Amazon is proud of its record in sustainable logging in tropical regions. The Swiss-owned company was founded in 1994 to show that commercial logging and sustainability could go together. Other loggers have followed, such as Gethal, adopting a planned forest management approach to ensure that rainforest is protected despite commercial interest. Forest management means undertaking proper timber inventories (location, species, measurement), harvesting plans and long harvesting cycles. This is backed up by certification and labelling which clearly communicates to consumers that responsible logging has taken place. The formation of the Forest Stewardship Council (FSC) was regarded even by pressure groups such as Greenpeace as a vital step in making the industry more responsible. Achieving FSC certification means that demanding social, economic and environmental standards have been met. Thus Precious Woods Amazon manages cutting over a 25-year cycle and always seeks to preserve watercourses and to avoid soil erosion. Part of the deal also includes the principles that 85 per cent of the forest should always remain and that no pesticides or chemicals should be used.

The Amazon rainforest is one of the last frontiers on earth. Covering 2.3 million square miles it have been called the earth's lungs as massive amounts of carbon dioxide are absorbed from the atmosphere each year and converted back into oxygen. However, land clearance, often by burning, and indiscriminate logging has meant that 40 per cent of the forest has already been destroyed and the destruction rate is 5,792 square miles of virgin forest destroyed each year. So what has all this to do with marketing and the consumer? It is demand for tropical wood that sets a chain of activities going that can be traced back to the forest. Wood consumption is closely related to per capita income: the higher the income the higher the wood consumption so the more trees get cut.

For Precious Woods Amazon forest management and sustainability are essential factors when it selects logging companies to work with. Here an inventory of the trees is carefully made before decisions are made as to which ones to harvest.

Source: **Precious Woods (Schweiz) AG**

There are two diametrically opposed views over the future of the rainforest. The FSC scheme founded in 1993 enabled the environmentalists to negotiate with, rather than protest against, the commercial loggers. Certification and well-managed forests gave the loggers a way of continuing operations with far less pressure from the WWF, Greenpeace and Friends of the Earth. Ecological management, community involvement and good employment practice are all part of the guidelines. In the past, tropical timber markets in Europe and the US were closed by the boycotting campaigns in the 1990s, but the FSC scheme may allow them to re-open and thus stimulate more cutting in Brazil. The FSC labelling scheme operates worldwide and enables 'ethical buying' to take place, according to the loggers.

The alternative view, expressed by Laschefski and Freris (2001) questions the whole basis of continued logging before the rainforest has recovered from the ravages of the past thirty years. To them, the FSC has given an unwarranted legitimacy to logging under the ecologically sensitive label that allows commercial loggers to continue. At present, 96 per cent of certified forests are owned by either industrial-scale loggers or governments. However, by shifting the ethical buying responsibility to the consumer, it assumes that the buyer in Germany or the UK is conscious of green products, values the FSC scheme and is prepared to pay a little more rather than buy wood that may have been logged outside FSC guidelines. They argue that the FSC marketing certification legitimises logging when the priority should be preservation and re-forestation. Many of these views are strongly contested by Precious Woods.

The issue really comes back to the consumer in developed and developing countries. Pressure will grow in future years for Brazil to export more. The destruction of forests in SE Asia, the emergence of strong timber demand to fuel growth in China, along with the insatiable appetite for quality wood in Europe and North America will create increasing pressure on the loggers to consume more forests even though it would be on a managed basis. Meanwhile, illegal logging still goes on. Forest clearance also continues both for fuel and land as in Brazil 85 per cent of timber is cut for the domestic market that cares little for certification, given how low per capita income is. The WWF, in alliance with the World Bank, aims to increase the number of hectares of certified forest covered by FSC worldwide from 25 million to 200 million by 2005. However, will a marketing solution through the FSC really save the 'lungs of the earth' before it is too late? Should it be allowed to legitimise the continued logging of the rainforest? Will you look for the FSC label the next time you buy wood products?

Sources: Laschefski and Freris (2001); http://www.disasterrelief.org; http://preciouswoods.ch.

Continental Tyres has found that an active approach to environmental issues is taking it into exciting new areas.

Source: Continental.

eg

The car is not really considered to be one of the more environmentally friendly products available, but many component manufacturers are trying to improve the situation. Tyres, for example, are directly and indirectly responsible for a number of environmental problems. They tend to have a short life span, and are difficult to dispose of or to recycle. They can also affect fuel consumption, accounting for up to 16 per cent of a car's average petrol usage, according to industry estimates. Companies such as Pirelli and Continental are therefore working hard to develop more fuel efficient tyres in parallel with looking at ways of improving their durability. Beyond that, they are also thinking about how they can best use tyres that have come to the end of their life. The manufacturers want to develop tyres that can be retreaded more easily and cheaply, and that can be disposed of in a more environmentally friendly way. Goodyear, for example, has launched a more eco-friendly tyre, the GT3, which is made of a rubber mixture based on recyclable materials, including an ingredient derived from maize starch. The new tyre is claimed to consume less energy in production as well as giving the motorist better performance and fuel consumption on the road (*Marketing Week*, 2001; Schmitt, 2001).

All this development activity is spurred not only by an altruistic desire to become 'greener', but also by pressure from motor manufacturers. The motor manufacturers in turn are reflecting consumer concerns and increasing governmental demands for greener motoring.

Animal welfare

The issue of animal welfare is linked with environmental concerns, and shows itself in a number of ways. Product testing on animals has become increasingly unacceptable to a large number of vocal consumers, and thus there has been a proliferation of cosmetics and toiletries, for example, which proclaim that they have not been tested on animals. With some products this may only mean that they are made from ingredients that have been separately animal tested and proved safe in the past, but that the current formulation has not itself been tested. Cosmetics retailer, The Body Shop, has, for example, been at the forefront of positioning itself overtly on this issue, reassuring concerned customers about its own products and publicising the worst excesses of animal testing.

Another area of animal welfare which has captured the public imagination is that of intensive farm production methods. Public outcry against battery egg production, for example, opened new marketing opportunities for free range eggs, since consumers wanted the alternative and were prepared to pay for it. Similarly, outdoor-reared pork and organic beef are starting to appear in supermarkets. Pressure groups are becoming more adept at using advertising and promotional techniques to activate public opinion.

eg

Huntingdon Life Sciences (HLS), the UK animal research company that tests drugs on animals on behalf of pharmaceutical companies has been under heavy pressure from animal rights extremists. This has included staff being threatened and the Managing Director has been assaulted by an axeman. Daily protests were held outside the research labs by the Stop Huntingdon Animal Cruelty group and even financial institutions working with HLS and the contracting pharmaceutical companies were targeted. Banks, fund managers and brokers have all been 'persuaded' to stop acting for HLS and suppliers of animals have also been placed under pressure. At stake is, in part, the future of pharmaceutical research in the UK. The more international publicity the animal activists can generate, the less attractive is the UK as an R&D base so the government has also taken an interest in ensuring that HLS continues to operate. In an unprecedented move, it allowed the company to use the banking facilities of the Bank of England rather than see it go under through a lack of liquidity. The activists still persist with their actions despite Britain now having one of the most rigorous systems governing animal experimentation anywhere in Europe. Over the past ten years there has been considerable progress in reducing, replacing or refining animal testing to minimise animal exposure. However, new drugs need to be tried out on animals before going to clinical trial and this is supported by over 60 per cent of the population, despite the effect on the animals (Cook, 2001; *The Economist*, 2001a; Milmo, 2001; Shrimsley and Guerrera, 2001).

Health concerns

Health consciousness has played a major role in the thinking behind consumer markets. The tobacco market has been particularly hard hit by increased awareness of the risks of smoking, and pressure from health lobbyists and the public has led to increased regulation of that industry. Food products have also been reappraised in the light of health concerns, with more natural ingredients, fewer artificial additives, less salt and less sugar content demanded. Linked with this, the market for low calorie products has also expanded, serving a market that wants to enjoy tasty food in quantity, but lose weight or at least feel that they are eating healthily.

eg

Corned beef may improve the fertility of men, so food company Princes claims, after a study revealed that vitamin B3 and zinc, both in corned beef, were linked to fertility. The company hopes to compile a series of case studies to show how it worked in practice and advertisements are scheduled to appear in lifestyle magazines such as *Loaded* and *FHM* highlighting the benefits and showing exciting recipes for corned beef (*The Grocer*, 2000a). You have been warned!

Health concerns also led to a boom in products and services linked with fitness. Health clubs, aerobics classes, exercise videos, sportswear of all kinds and trainers are just some of the things that profited from the fitness boom.

Personal ethics

Apart from concern about the environment, animal welfare and health, all of which might be seen as ethical issues, there has been a subtle shift in people's attitudes to what is acceptable in other areas of their lives. In Western societies, a manageable level of personal debt is now considered normal. Hire purchase agreements, various types of loans and credit cards provide means of achieving a desirable lifestyle now and paying for it later. Previous generations might have been more inclined to take the view that if you want something, you save up for it and buy it outright when you can afford it. Consumers today are also more inclined towards self-indulgence and gratification, without too much guilt, through their consumption. This, it must be said, is openly encouraged by marketers, who want us to believe that we as individuals are special enough to deserve only the best.

The early 1990s saw some conflict between the self-indulgent, self-centred type of conspicuous consumption and external, altruistic concerns about the environment. Although this curbed some of the worst excesses of the late 1980s, the majority of consumers still seemed to be stopping short of radically redefining their attitude to consumption, other than through economic necessity. A study by Dittmar and Pepper (1994) showed that adolescents, regardless of their own social background, generally formed better impressions of people who own rather than lack expensive possessions. In other words, materialism still seems to play a big part in influencing perceptions and attitudes towards others.

Business ethics

Encouraged by various pressure groups and inquisitive media, consumers now want to see greater levels of corporate responsibility, and more transparency in terms of the openness of companies. Bad publicity about employee relations, environmental records, marketing practices or customer care and welfare now has the potential to move consumers to vote with their pockets and shun an organisation and its products. McDonald's, for example, felt sufficiently concerned about stories circulating about its beef and about its record in the South American rainforests to invest in a considerable marketing communications campaign to re-establish its reputation. The Body Shop again features business ethics strongly in its marketing, emphasising, for example, its 'trade not aid' policy with developing countries and native tribes.

eg

Chocolate manufacturers are generally regarded as upholding high standards of corporate citizenship. Companies such as Nestlé, Cadbury and Hershey buy cocoa in large quantities through the international commodity markets, and so have little contact with the thousands of small farms, especially in West Africa, that grow cocoa beans. It came as a shock, therefore, when accusations were made by UNICEF and Channel 4 in the UK that many migrant workers in West Africa, and the Ivory Coast in particular, were working in conditions not far removed from slavery on some of the one million cocoa and coffee farms. The confectionery industry immediately commissioned the independent Natural Resources Institute (NRI) to investigate and the subsequent findings found little evidence for the allegations but proposed that the wider socioeconomic dimensions of cocoa production should be examined. Given the sheer number of small independent farms involved, it is difficult to police, but just how can the chocolate manufacturers defend themselves against such accusations? The effect of an emotive issue such as child slavery on corporate image could be disastrous. The manufacturers' focus is thus now shifting to *traceability*, which means that the source of particular cocoa or coffee beans can be pinpointed and immediate action taken if any worker abuse is detected. To some, like Anti Slavery International, it is the only way that the confectionery giants can give 100 per cent guarantees to the consumer that offending farms have not been used by them. Up to this point, there had been little interest in tracing the origin of coffee, as much responsibility was delegated to intermediaries, but the NRI argues that true corporate social responsibility means taking a fundamental look at the whole supply chain. Ultimately, traceability will add to costs and that can only be at the expense of the consumer or the chocolate manufacturer (Watson, 2001).

Consumerism and consumer forces

Many of the influences discussed above might never have taken hold and become significant had it not been for the efforts of organised groups. They themselves often use marketing techniques as well as generating publicity through the media, quickly raising awareness of issues and providing a focal point for public opinion to form around and helping it to gather momentum. Figure 2.3, for example, may remind you of some of the campaigns that have been fought in the interests of raising your awareness of ethical and green issues surrounding the clothing industry.

The UK's Consumers' Association has long campaigned for legislation to protect consumers' rights, such as the right to safe products and the right to full and accurate information about the products we buy. As well as lobbying government and organisations about specific issues, the Consumers' Association also provides independent information to consumers, testing and comparing the features, performance and value for money of competing products in various categories. This information is published in *Which?* magazine,

Figure 2.3 Green and ethical issues affecting clothing

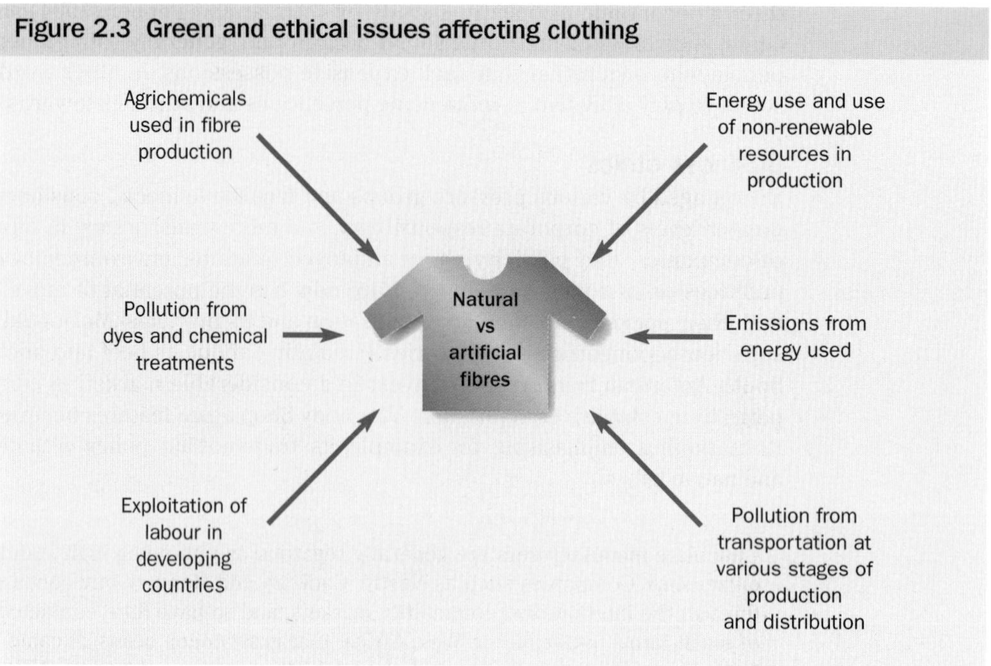

the August 2001 edition of which included reports on answering machines, car reliability, smoking patches and pills, house insurance and stakeholder pensions, for example. In a similar vein, specialist magazines, in fields such as computing and hi-fi, also undertake comparative testing of products of interest to their readership.

eg

Tuna fishing is an activity that has been affected by campaigning leading to the exercise of 'consumer power'. The UK public had been happily buying canned tuna for many years without thinking of anything other than the price, the flavour and the quality of the can's contents. Green pressure groups, with the help of the media, then publicised the fact that the nets that were used to catch tuna also caught dolphins, which could not escape and so died pointlessly. A change in the net design would allow the dolphins to be freed without harm. Public outcry was such that the tuna canners had to take action to preserve sales. The USA-based Earth Island Institute was formed to monitor the harvesting of tuna to ensure that accidental killing of dolphins does not happen. This institute is supported by all the major tuna brands as it provides consumers with the reassurances that they seek, and the registered logo can only be used on cans deriving from approved canners. The canners are in turn monitored to ensure that their supplies are caught only in designated areas and using recommended fishing methods (*The Grocer*, 2001f). The activities of such groups have not only served to change business practices on specific issues, such as tuna fishing, but also accelerated a general cultural change which has awakened the social conscience of organisations (only partly due to the fear of poor publicity and the loss of customers) and has raised the standards of corporate citizenship that consumers expect from business.

High-profile and sometimes militant pressure has been brought to bear on organisations by green groups such as Friends of the Earth and Greenpeace. Although their interest is a wider, altruistic concern with ecology rather than consumer rights, they recognise that corporate practices that are harmful to the environment, wildlife and ecology can be partly discouraged by 'bottom-up' pressure. This means raising awareness, changing attitudes and altering purchasing habits among organisations' core customers.

Consumers have also been encouraged to think about their personal health as well as that of the planet. Sometimes sponsored by government (for example through the UK government's Department of Health) and sometimes through independent groups with a specific interest such as Action on Smoking and Health (ASH) or the British Heart Foundation, the public are urged to change their lifestyles and diets. Once it is generally known and accepted that too much of this, that or the other is unhealthy, food manufacturers are anxious to jump on the bandwagon and provide products to suit the emerging demand.

eg

Awareness that full fat milk is high in cholesterol has been responsible for a significant shift towards semi-skimmed milk which retains most the vitamin and mineral content but cuts down the fat. Sometimes, a health issue does not even need the support of an organised group to capture the public imagination. A flurry of media coverage about research findings which indicated that eating sugar can actually help weight loss had many of us reaching hopefully for the biscuit tin, purely on medical grounds, of course.

The media have already been mentioned several times as an important channel of communication used by pressure groups to ensure that public awareness is triggered. The media are not, however, passive pawns in all this, simply repeating what they are told. They can magnify a story and give it much more credibility and urgency by the amount and quality of coverage given. Debating issues on current affairs programmes or the publication of editorials and opinion columns in the newspapers stimulates interest and provides the necessary perspectives for the audience to judge how they feel about a particular issue. Some sections of the media behave like pressure groups in their own right. Television consumer programmes, such as the BBC's *Watchdog*, investigate and publicise (usually) bad practice or poor service, highlighting product safety issues, unethical selling methods and fraudulent trading. With audiences in millions, these programmes represent quite a power.

Pressure groups and consumer bodies are not just there to criticise organisations, of course. They also encourage and endorse good practice, and such an endorsement can be very valuable to the organisation that earns it. A consumer who is inexperienced in buying a particular type of product, or for whom that purchase represents a substantial investment, may well look for independent expert advice, and thus the manufacturer whose product is cited as *Which?* magazine's best buy in that category has a head start over the competition. Organisations may also commission product tests from independent bodies such as the Consumers' Association or the Good Housekeeping Institute as a means of verifying their product claims and adding the bonus of 'independent expert opinion' to their marketing.

The technological environment

In an increasingly dynamic world, where the creation, launch and maintenance of a new product are more expensive and difficult than ever, no organisation can afford to ignore the **technological environment** and its trends. Even if your organisation does not have the inclination or resources to adopt or adapt new technology, understanding it is important because competitors will exploit it sooner or later, with implications for your product and its marketing.

Technological advance can be generated from two main sources, as far as the marketer is concerned. The first source is external to the organisation and perhaps even external to the market. Thus technology developed for other purposes, academic, medical or military, for example, may have spin-off commercial benefits. In this case, the skill for the commercial organisation is spotting the potential application early enough, negotiating the rights to use or develop the technology further, and successfully developing a marketable product from it before the competition. The second source of technological advance is market driven, by organisations searching for specific solutions to specific marketing problems. The R&D work may be undertaken in-house, or may be contracted out to specialist agencies or university departments. The range of projects involved may vary from very small to very large, and from the refinement of an existing product to the exploration of completely unknown territory.

marketing *in action*

Doing the mile-high breast stroke?

The CEO of Singapore International Airlines (SIA) was anxious to deny rumours that the Airbus 380, the 550-seater superjet for which he had just placed orders, had an onboard gym and swimming pool for weary long-haul passengers. The real reason for the purchase, it was claimed, was to help overcome ground congestion, get more seats on each flight, and make the journey more comfortable and less tedious for passengers. That said, internal configurations are regarded by SIA as a means of competitive advantage so we will have to wait and see just what is offered when the first six planes are delivered in 2006 for the high density routes to Los Angeles, San Francisco and New York (Velloci, 2001).

The A380 will be the world's biggest passenger jet when it takes to the air commercially in 2006. Source: **Airbus Industrie.**

The Airbus A380 is not only going to be the world's biggest passenger jet, but will also be one of the most expensive to develop. The estimated initial investment is expected to be \$11.7 bn, of which \$3 bn has been given in the form of loans from the four governments with jurisdiction over the principal players in Airbus. It has been argued that the Airbus is a great tribute to the new form of technical and business cooperation that is possible within a unified Europe. Aérospatiale Matra, DaimlerChrysler Aerospace (DASA) and Construcciones Aeronauticas all formed an alliance called EADS and this group has an 80 per cent share in Airbus Integrated Company (AIC), with the balance coming from BAe Systems in the UK. It is a group designed to take the bulk of the risks on new projects such as the A380, but in return each company gains directly from any profits made and also through the work allocated in subassemblies. A significant proportion of the production takes place in France, Germany, Spain and the UK.

Central to the decision to develop such a large project, which has been in design since the mid-1990s but will not be commercially available until 2006, is the technical, financial and marketing feasibility. This requires a detailed forecast and analysis of likely changes in the marketing environment in order to establish whether any airlines would be interested in placing orders. The AIC view is that the A380 will be a winner, as it enables airlines to reduce congestion and increase payloads with over 550 passengers being carried on a two-deck, four-engine plane. Trends favour the bigger plane: the long-haul market is expected to grow by around 5 per cent per annum; new slots are difficult to obtain in already congested airports; and there are problems in building new airports or even runways in many countries. Thus the potential for the A380 could be very great, and it is forecast that it will become profitable when the 250th aircraft is delivered, probably nine or ten years after the service entry date in 2006. However, it is a long-term business as it will take nearly twenty years from conception to show a return on investment.

The Airbus view of the market is diametrically opposed to that voiced by the dominant player in the large jet market: Boeing, manufacturer of the 747. Boeing argues that there will be more fragmentation in the marketplace so there will be less need for larger planes. Instead, new routes will be opened that bypass the busy hubs and save time for business travellers by having direct flights, rather than using the high capacity hub-to-hub routes that have dominated air travel. In the same vein therefore, the development effort at Boeing has been put into designing and developing a Mach 0.95 plane, replacing the 767, which would cut an hour off the London – New York route, but will only have 175–250 seats.

Who will be right? Will 'faster' or 'leaner and meaner' be a competitive advantage? These are important questions facing Boeing and Airbus and at stake is the dominance of the long-haul jet market that is expected to require 1,250 planes over the next 20 years. Airbus is aware of Boeing's assessment. There are few secrets in the aircraft manufacturing business. To counter the claims made by Boeing, Airbus argues that there will be fragmentation and consolidation taking place at the same time. There will be a growing market for direct flights, but the airline alliances and limited slots on some routes will still favour high capacity hub-to-hub traffic. Either way, the airlines will no longer have the Boeing 747 as the only choice, so the market will be very competitive over the coming years.

Projects the size and complexity of the A380 need more than market appraisal. Extensive tests and trials are needed to certify airworthiness, satisfying bodies such as the FAA, and to ensure that the aircraft can actually land and take off at airports. Over 80 airports have been surveyed to ensure that they can accommodate the A380 in terms of wing span, weights on bridges, impact on terminal capacity and runway length. Twelve will be ready by 2006 and others will follow shortly after. It must be viable for the airports to invest in any changes, so Airbus has argued that the A380 will reduce congestion and enable more revenues to be earned from landing fees.

Given the scale of the investment, the capital requirements and risks are far too great for just one organisation. In addition to the four stakeholders, each supported by their governments, organisations in the Netherlands, Belgium, Finland, Italy and Sweden have joined the A380 project as risk sharing partners in return for a share of the lucrative subassembly work on the mainframe. This will benefit organisations such as Saab and Belgian Belairbus as up to 40 per cent of the airframe subassemblies will be sourced outside AIC. Attempts were also made to include some Japanese manufacturers in the project but it is alleged that Boeing, which was already in long standing joint ventures with them, effectively discouraged any working with Airbus. Although AIC is the specifier, technical development work still takes place with the component manufacturers. For example, Goodrich in the United States was contracted to supply the landing gear, the largest ever produced.

Governments have a keen interest in the project. If successful the A380 will launch Europe into the superjet league, resulting in significant export sales to help trade balances as well as sustaining 145,000 jobs around Europe. The United States is not keen on the level of government support for the A380, regarding it as anti-competitive because not all the indirect costs are taken into account in specifying the support for the project.

The early signs for the A380 are promising. Over 60 have been ordered and that is expected to grow to 100 one year after the official launch. AIC forecast that it would need to build 4 or 5 per month, so the early orders from Emirates, Virgin, Quantas (12), SIA, Qatar, Fed Ex and Air France will all help to boost confidence. Airlines are concerned with the payback on the planes, the competitive advantage that can be gained and the fit with its customer base. AIC claims that the A380 will cut operating costs by 17 per cent compared with the 747-400, but this claim is hotly disputed by Boeing. Who will be right? What about the swimming pool? Watch this space.

Sources: Arminas (2001); Sparaco (2001); Velloci (2001).

The costs and the risks involved can be very high, since there is no guarantee that an R&D project will be successful in delivering a solution that can be commercially implemented. Nevertheless, organisations feel the need to invest in R&D, recognising that they will get left behind if they do not, and are optimistic that they will come up with something with an unbeatable differential advantage that will make it all worthwhile.

eg

IBM takes R&D very seriously in its desire to be at the head of the innovation curve and to remain competitive. It has learned that lesson the hard way, though. Originally, the world ran on IBM mainframes and databases but the trend towards smaller networked computers meant that competitors took market share away from IBM. In the 1990s IBM sought to regain a dominant position in a fast-moving technologically based industry. The search for technological leadership means developing an understanding of how the market is moving and spotting the areas that are likely to offer opportunities. Although there are many R&D projects running within IBM and the total spend is something like $4,345mn (IBM, 2001a), there are three priority strategic research areas (IBM, 2001b):

- *E-business and online technologies*: this research is examining the human resource and systems implications of the information economy that is developing as a result of the growth of the internet. Such an economy is thought to be based on agents buying, analysing and selling information about the vast number of transactions that will be conducted over the web.
- *Pervasive computing*: with the growth of home-based systems, the research examines the next major wave of product opportunities that will provide interconnected smart devices called 'portable personality'. This will mean that individuals will have the power of a PC in hand-held, credit-card sized devices or in other mobile spaces from watches to cars.
- *Deep computing*: this area is targeting research into marrying computers with human intelligence. By using specialised software, advanced maths and hardware complex problems can be solved to far higher degrees of realism than is now possible.

e-marketing *in action*

Monitoring the European e-commerce environment

Each organisation developing an e-commerce strategy needs to have a good understanding of the adoption of the internet technological environment. In particular, Chaffey (2002) suggests it is important to set an online revenue contribution objective for the e-commerce strategy. This is a measure of the extent to which a company's online presence directly makes an impact on the sales revenue. Online revenue contribution objectives can be specified for different types of products, customer segments and geographic markets. They can also be set for different digital channels such as web, mobile or interactive digital TV as explained in the e-marketing box for Chapter 8, pp. 325–6. Companies that can set a high online revenue contribution objective of say 25 per cent for 2 years' time will need to provide more resource allocation to the internet than those companies who anticipate a contribution of 2.5 per cent. Cisco Systems Inc. (www.cisco.com), maker of computer networking gear, is now selling over three-quarters of its products online amounting to billions of dollars revenue. For other companies such as an fmcg manufacturer or a beverage company, it is unrealistic to expect a high direct online revenue contribution. In this case, an indirect online contribution could be stated. This considers the internet as part of the promotional mix and its role is in influencing a proportion of customers to purchase the product or in building the brand. In this case a company could set an online promotion contribution of 5 per cent of its target market interacting with the brand on the website, other sponsored sites or banner adverts.

To set realistic online strategic objectives for the online revenue contributions e-commerce managers need to analyse the environment to understand the level of customer access and activity in each marketplace. For each geographic market and for each customer segment and for each digital channel such as the internet, interactive digital TV or mobile we need to know the proportion of customers who:

1 Have *access* to the channel.
2 Are *influenced* by using the channel.
3 *Purchase* using the channel.

Current and future demand estimates are informed by market research. One example of such research is provided by DTI (2000). This compares online access, influence and purchasing for businesses within different countries. This data shows, for example, that in 2000 only 22 per cent of micro businesses (organisations with fewer than 10 people) in France had access, but rising to 34 per cent in Italy, 39 per cent in Sweden and 41 per cent in the United Kingdom.

Sources: Chaffey (2002); DTI (2000).

To get the best out of the commercial exploitation of technology, R&D and marketers have to work closely together. R&D can provide the technical know-how, problem-solving skills and creativity, while the marketer can help guide and refine that process through research or knowledge of what the market needs and wants, or through finding ways of creating a market position for a completely innovative product. A lot of this comes back to the question 'What business are we in?' Any organisations holding the attitude that they exist to solve customers' problems and that they have to strive constantly to find better solutions through higher-quality, lower-cost or more user-friendly product packages will be active participants in, and observers of, the technological environment. A striking example of this is the Italian firm Olivetti, which began by making manual typewriters, then moved into computers as it saw the likely takeover of the word processor as a means of producing business documentation.

The technological environment is a fast-changing one, with far-reaching effects on organisations and their products. Technological advances can affect the materials, components and products, the processes by which products are made, administration and distribution systems, product marketing and the interface between the organisation and the customer. Each of these areas will now be looked at briefly, to give just a flavour of the immense impact that technology has had on marketing practice.

Materials, components and products

Consumers tend to take products, and the materials and components that go into them, for granted as long as they work and live up to the marketers' promises. Technology does, however, improve and increase the benefits that consumers derive from products, and raise expectations about what a product should be. Some technological applications are invisible to the consumer, affecting raw materials and components hidden within an existing product, while others create completely new products.

corporate social responsibility *in action*

More leg-room please!

Those of you who have travelled economy class on a long-haul flight will know exactly what it feels like to be cramped into a seat that restricts leg movement, to be unable to eat without your elbow nudging the passenger next to you, and to find that just when you decide to stretch your legs in the cabin, the 'fasten seat belts' sign lights up with a merry little ding! In pursuit of keeping fares down and revenues up, the airlines have long been criticised for cramming as many seats into economy class as possible, which is only comfortable for those passengers of lower than average height and weight. That might now have to change because of DVT (deep vein thrombosis). A thrombosis or blood clot can form in the deep veins of the legs when the body is immobilised for long periods. The symptoms, cramp, shortness of breath and stiffness, could be an early indication of trouble. If the clot breaks free and reaches the lungs it can be fatal. Research from the Nippon Medical School in Japan indicated that 100–125 people were treated for DVT after long-haul flights at Tokyo's Narita airport between 1992 and 2000, of whom 25 died.

Scientific research is, in fact, divided over the link between DVT and long-haul airline travel. A Dutch study of 800 passengers found no link with DVT, whereas a Norwegian study suggested that 1 in 10 suffer. A study conducted at Honolulu International Airport over six years found only 44 cases of DVT of which only seven were not associated with prior risk factors. More extensive research is now under way in Australia into 10,000 medical records as, given Australia's geographical remoteness, Australian travellers have a keener interest than most in the health aspects of long-haul flying. An investigation in the UK conducted by the House of Lords Select Committee on Science and Technology: Air Travel and Health, however, was more definitive and called for major changes in the regulations relating to the health of passengers, including a call for the airlines to take responsibility for providing adequate information to warn passengers of the risks from DVT.

The airlines are in a difficult position. Accept responsibility and a flood of expensive legal claims would follow. The first test case has already been filed in Australia after a passenger died following an Australia to London flight. Central to the case will be whether adequate information and warning was given to passengers before the flight. The lawyer claims that the airlines were aware of the problem five years previously but failed to take action to inform the public. It is further claimed that there are 100 people who have lost relatives or who have themselves suffered from DVT. Virgin, American Airlines and Quantas have all received notice of possible legal action. In addition to legal claims, there would be pressure to redesign cabins to provide more leg room and thus carry fewer passengers at a time when the numbers flying are growing. However, not to accept responsibility and to deny any link could be regarded by some as socially irresponsible, and if a link is proven scientifically, the longer-term legal claims and public condemnation would be very damaging.

There are steps that airlines can take to reduce risks, even though they do not accept that DVT is any greater a problem in air travel than in any other form of transportation. At the very least, passengers can be informed of the need to exercise, drink plenty of water and avoid alcohol on long-haul flights. Already some are giving such advice either in seat pockets or with ticketing, although it is not always easy to undertake exercises on a crowded jet. Singapore Airlines is calling for a more standardised approach by the airlines, rather than each doing their own thing, and for groups of airlines jointly to commission more research (Fiorino, 2001). Emirates has gone further by being first to provide an exercise device, the Airogym, for passengers which allows exercises in a seated position. The product claims are that it increases blood flow through veins by 50 per cent through the use of an inflatable footpad for pumping leg muscles.

Legislation may eventually follow if the link is established. Airlines still claim that the risks are very small for healthy people and, according to some, are in a state of denial. However, if there is stricter control on leg room and seat dimensions, compulsory health warnings and records kept for three months to enable 'traceback' in the event of problems, DVT scares could become a thing of the past. The Federal Air Surgeon's Medical Bulletin in the USA, although stopping short of specifying a direct link is clear about what is now needed:

> *It is only a matter of time before the aviation medical community and the air carriers themselves will be called upon to significantly increase their activity in dealing directly with medical issues associated with air travel and to direct educational efforts on the flying public.* (as quoted by Jordan, 2001)

Unfortunately, one way or the other it is the passenger who will end up paying.

Sources: Asian Business (2001); Durham (2001); Ecklof *et al.* (1996); Fiorino (2001); Jordan (2001); Kite and Bird (2000); *The Times* (2000); Webster (2001).

Low calorie sweeteners

Artificial low calorie sweeteners, for example, are now found in a wide range of foodstuffs. An extremely successful application has been in fizzy drinks, such as colas and lemonades, creating a new segment among diet-conscious adults. Many claim to be able to taste the difference between the regular and diet (or light) versions of the same product, and thus the next stage of the R&D process might be to eliminate this minor discrepancy.

Unleaded petrol

Pressure from those concerned about the environmental and health effects of motor exhaust fumes has led to the development and widespread acceptance of unleaded petrol. The R&D task here was extensive, not only looking at the formulation and quality of the petrol itself, but also requiring adaptation of existing and proposed car engines to be able to take the new fuel with the minimum effect on performance.

Synthetics in clothing

Synthetic fabrics, fibre mixes and dyes have long been research concerns of the clothing industry. Consumers want easy-care clothes that can stand the rigours of machine washing with the minimum of drying and ironing afterwards. They also want their clothes to be hard wearing and for their bright colours to be maintained, despite repeated washing. In this respect, the textile companies can work closely with the detergent manufacturers. More recently, consumer interest has turned back to natural fabrics, such as linen, cotton and silk, and the technological task has been to find ways of treating these fibres to make them easier to care for without compromising their natural characteristics.

Microchips

Microchips are everywhere! Not only are they the heart and soul of our home computers, but they also program our washing machines, CD players and video recorders, among many things. The incorporation of microchips into products has increased their reliability, their efficiency in operation and the range of sophisticated functions that they can perform, all very cost effectively. This in turn has raised consumers' expectations of what products can do, and revised their attitudes towards cost, quality and value for money.

High-tech products

In terms of brand new, innovative high-tech products, the last 15 years or so have opened up a number of new markets, based on invention and the development of commercial processes to allow its exploitation. This is not always an easy or fast process. CD players, videos, camcorders, computers and software have only begun to become common household possessions as technology improves through the manufacturers' learning experiences, as a wider range of products tailored towards definable market segments emerge and as costs come down through economies of scale.

Packaging

Technology is not just about the physical product itself. It can also affect its packaging. Lightweight plastics and glass, recycled and recyclable materials and cans that incorporate a device to give canned beer the character and quality of draught are examples of packaging innovations that have helped to make products more appealing, enhance their image or keep their cost down. Additionally, developments in areas such as lamination and printing techniques have increased the attractiveness and quality of packaging, again helping to enhance the product image.

Production processes

The fulfilment of marketing promises can be helped or hindered by what happens in the production process. More efficient production can, for instance, increase the volume of product available, thus potentially meeting a bigger demand, or it can reduce the cost of the product, thus giving more scope to the pricing decision. Production can also contribute to better and more consistent product quality, again increasing customer satisfaction. Here are some examples where technology has influenced production processes and indirectly affected marketing activities.

Computer aided design systems

Computer aided design (CAD) systems have revolutionised product formulation and testing. In terms of design, technology allows ideas to be visualised, tested and accepted/rejected much more quickly than if paper plans and calculations had to be updated. Anything, from the design of a circuit board, through the arrangement of components inside the product, to the external styling and colourways can be fully explored cheaply and quickly. This means that a certain creative impetus can be generated, because the effects of a 'what if?' exercise can be seen almost instantly, and even the wildest ideas can be given space. Sophisticated software can also simulate how the proposed product design might behave in reality under differing conditions, highlighting the probable weak areas and 'bugs'. The outcome for the customer is that products get to the market more quickly, and in a more refined state, and may be cheaper and more reliable.

Computer aided manufacturing systems

Computer aided manufacturing (CAM) systems help to streamline the production process. Computer controlled robotics and other mechanised systems can undertake tasks faster than human operatives, with more consistency and fewer errors. Robots and computers do not get tired or distracted from their tasks! In the long term, this can cut costs, because the labour input is less and there is less wastage through rejects. Again, the customer gets a more reliable, consistent and potentially cheaper product.

Quality assurance and control

Quality assurance (QA) and quality control (QC) are an important part of manufacturing. Technology has improved not only the methods used for testing samples taken from the production line, but also the capacity to detect faults early during the production process. It has also brought the responsibility for QA closer to the shopfloor operative, who can monitor process levels and outputs as they happen and take corrective action or call for help as soon as it is needed. The implications for the customer are again related to costs and reliability. The fewer rejects that occur and the fewer rejects that slip through to the customer, the better for the manufacturer's reputation and relationship with the customer. This is particularly important in B2B markets where just-in-time (JIT) systems operate (*see* Chapter 4 for more on this). This means that a business buying in supplies from another business wants just the right amount to arrive just at the right time to be fed into the production process. There is no scope for error: if a bad batch is delivered, or if there are too many rejects in it, the consequences can be serious as the buyer has no buffer stocks to fall back on. Thus quality has to be right and the buyer has to be able to rely on that quality.

Materials handling

Materials handling and waste minimisation are both concerns of efficient, cost-effective production management, and are again linked with JIT systems. Stocks of materials need to be closely monitored so that further purchases can be triggered when the level gets low; in a large operation, the location of materials needs to be planned so that they can be accessed quickly and spend the minimum amount of time being transported around the site; the packaging and bundling of materials need to be planned to balance out the sometimes conflicting concerns of adequately protecting and identifying the goods, and making sure that they can be unwrapped and put into the production line quickly. Computerised planning models and advances in packaging technology can both help to increase efficiency in these areas. Waste minimisation is clearly desirable if the manufacturer is going to get the most out of the raw materials. Minimisation through quality control was mentioned earlier, but it can also be achieved through good planning of material usage. A clothing factory, for instance, will use computerised layout planning to work out the best arrangement of the garment components on the cloth before cutting, so that the minimum amount of fabric is discarded.

Benefits to service industries

Even what is essentially a service industry can benefit from technology to improve its ability to serve the customer's needs. The telecommunications industry, for example, has used satellite technology, computerised exchanges and fibre-optic cable, for instance, to extend customers' ability to dial direct to virtually any part of the world, relatively cheaply. On the 'hardware' side of the business, telecommunications now encompasses cordless and mobile phones, answering machines, faxes and modems. Technology has also allowed the industry to extend its range of services, such as linking the domestic telephone to burglar alarms, so that the emergency services are automatically alerted to a problem, or the introduction of text messaging on mobile phones and the ability to access the internet via a mobile.

Administration and distribution

There is little point in using technology to streamline the production of goods if the support systems are inefficient or if distribution causes a bottleneck between factory and customer. Distribution has benefited from technology, as has materials handling, through systems for locating and tracking goods in and out. Integrated ordering and dispatch functions mean theoretically that as soon as an order is entered into the computer, goods availability can be checked and the warehouse can get on with the job of fulfilling it, while the computer handles all the paperwork, printing off packing slips and invoices, for example, and updating customer records. All of this speeds up the sending of orders to customers and reduces labour involvement, costs and risks of errors.

Telecommunications linking into computer systems can extend the administration efficiencies even further. Large retail chains, for example, can be linked with their major suppliers, so that as the retailer's stocks reduce, an order can be sent from computer to computer. Similarly, large organisations with sites and depots spread over a wide geographic area can use such technology to link sites, managing and tracking the flow of goods.

Marketing and customers

Much of the technology discussed above has implied benefits for the customer, in producing the right product at the right time in the right place at the right price. Technology also plays a part in the dialogue between buyer and seller, and thus affects the interface between them.

Market research

Market research has benefited from increased and cheaper computer power, which means that large, complex sets of data can be input and analysed quickly and easily.

Databases

Databases are created not only for market research purposes, but also for selling. Relationship marketing, establishing and maintaining a one-to-one dialogue between buyer and seller, is now possible in mass consumer markets. Organisations such as Heinz see this as an exciting development in consumer marketing, and it is only possible because of database technology that permits the storage, retrieval and maintenance of detailed profiles of many thousands, or even hundreds of thousands, of customers. The technology also allows the creation of tailored, personalised marketing offers to be made to subsets of those customers as appropriate.

Advertising media

The advertising media have improved and proliferated through technology. As well as making use of satellite and cable television channels, advertisers can use teletext pages, videotapes and CDs. Improvements in printing technology have led to better reproduction and thus better-quality print advertisements, for example sharply focused, full-colour advertising is now commonplace in newspapers. Technology has also made its contribution to the creative side of advertising, for example with computer animation or computer manipulation of images to create special effects. In addition, the internet has become an alternative medium for many organisations. It not only allows them to disseminate information about their products, services, news and corporate philosophy, but also to set up interactive dialogue with customers and potential customers. A website can be an exciting communications medium as it can feature sound and video clips and, if the site is well structured, visitors can select the topics that interest them. Also, the information can be updated easily and regularly.

Online ordering

As briefly mentioned earlier, online ordering is a direct link between buyer and seller, allowing for faster reception and processing of orders. Both the internet and interactive digital television allow potential customers to browse through product information, check availability and place an order, all in the comfort of their own armchairs. However, this technology has yet to make a significant impact on consumer markets. The nearest to online ordering that most consumers experience is through telephone shopping, sometimes in direct response to television or print advertising. This is another spin-off from the telecommunications industry, which can now supply sellers with the capacity to handle many hundreds of calls simultaneously.

Sales force support

Another area that can also be enhanced through computer technology is sales force support. Supplying a sales representative with a laptop computer can give access to current information about products, their availability and prices; it can store customer profiles and relevant information; the representative can update records and write reports while the information is still fresh in the mind; and it can store appropriate graphics to enhance a sales presentation. All of this is easily portable and accessible whether the representative is working in Scotland or Greece.

The economic and competitive environment

The effects of the **economic and competitive environment** are felt by organisations and consumers alike, and it has a profound effect on their behaviour. In the next few pages we look first at the macroeconomic environment, which provides the overall backdrop against which marketing activities take place. As well as issues of national interest, such as the effects of government economic policy on commerce, we cover the influence of international trading blocs and trade agreements. All of these things may provide opportunities or threats for an individual organisation. We then turn to the microeconomic environment. This is rather closer to home for the organisation, looking at the extent to which different market structures constrain or widen the organisation's freedom of action in its marketing activities and its ability to influence the nature of the market.

The macroeconomic environment

Figure 2.4 shows the basic economic concept of the circular flow of goods and income that makes a market economy go round. Marketing, as an exchange process and indeed as a force that actively encourages more exchanges, is an essential fuel to keep that flow going. The world is not, however, a closed, self-sustaining loop such as that depicted in Figure 2.4. Its operation is severely affected by the macroeconomic influences generated by government economic policy and by membership of international trading blocs and trade agreements.

Governments can develop and implement policies in relation to several macroeconomic influences, which in turn affect markets, organisations and customers. Just a few of these are discussed below.

Taxation

Taxes may be direct or indirect. Direct taxation, such as income tax and national insurance contributions, reduces the amount of money, or disposable income, that a household has available to spend on the goods and services that organisations provide. Indirect taxation, such as purchase tax or value added tax (VAT), is collected for the government by the seller, who is obliged to add a percentage to the basic price of the product. Thus a PC sold in the UK may be advertised with two prices: a basic price of £999, then £1,174 including VAT.

Some products, such as alcohol, tobacco and petrol, have duty imposed on them, again collected by the seller. Both VAT and duties serve to increase the prices of products for the customer, and marketers need to think about the effect of the tax-inclusive price on the customer's attitude and buying habits. When rates of duty increase, marketers sometimes choose to absorb some of the increase themselves to keep prices competitive, rather than pass on the entire rise to the buyer.

Figure 2.4 Macroeconomic influences on the circular flow of goods and income

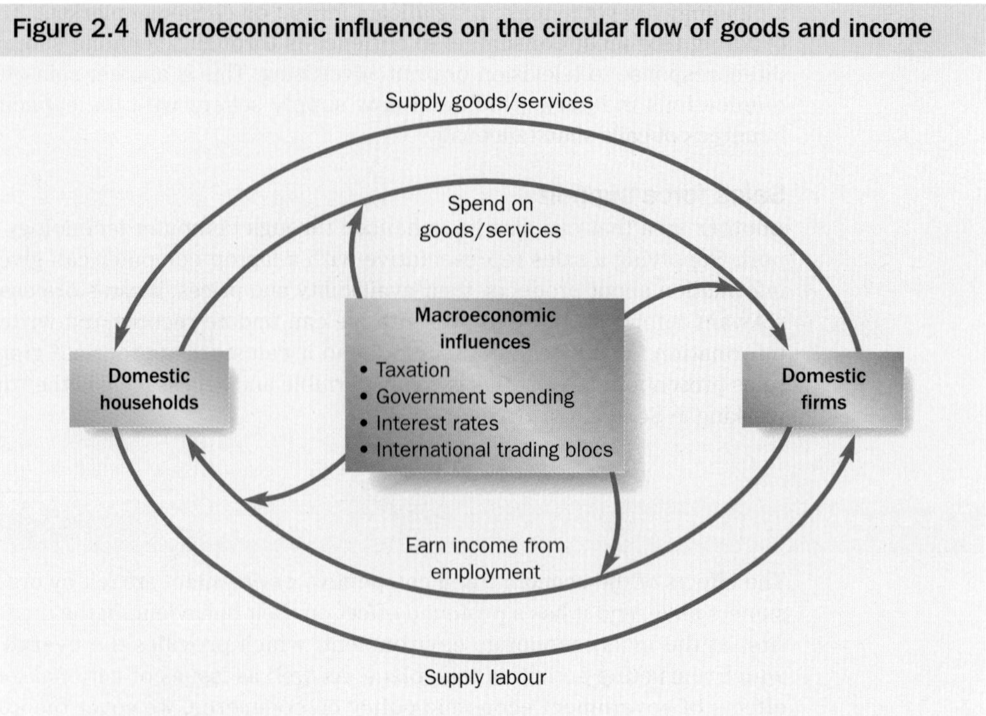

Rates of VAT and duties vary across Europe and despite thirty years of trying, there is still no significant progress in persuading member states to move to a common VAT system based upon harmonised rates and structures (*Business Europe*, 2000). The problems faced by brewers because of the higher excise duties on alcohol and tobacco imposed in the UK compared with France has caused a significant amount of smuggling and reselling. Customs and Excise estimate that 20 per cent of the UK's £84bn annual tobacco turnover is made up of illegal imports, costing the Treasury £3.8bn in lost duty. Similarly, the Brewers and Licensced Retailers Association estimates that a staggering 79 per cent of all beer brought into the UK every day is re-sold illegally (Thornton, 2001). It is one thing to put a crate of wine in the car boot, but quite another to load up a van with alcohol for re-sale with no declaration and no paperwork. The brewers want UK duty reduced so that it is in line with French rates, thus making the 'unofficial' market unprofitable.

The VAT rate on books also varies widely following the European Council of Ministers agreement in 1991 to encourage VAT to be applied. In the UK, however, books are zero rated as the significance of reading to education and culture has been embodied in a refusal to apply taxes that will raise prices (*Business Europe*, 2000). The UK has the largest number of goods exempt from VAT (most foods, newspapers and children's clothing, for example) despite pressures from the EU for closer harmonisation. Table 2.4 shows how VAT rates across Europe varied for consumer goods in January 2000. The European Commission is working towards a narrow band of between 16 and 19 per cent into which all member countries' VAT rates should fall, but a simplified or unified system is still some way off and may become even less achievable as new members join. As VAT is part of the tax revenue system in member states, any move to centralised rates would be regarded as further evidence of federalism.

A further challenge has come from the increased use of e-commerce, as this tends to bypass traditional VAT collection methods for international sales. For example, the UK has vetoed legislation that would have made non-EU competitors e-tailing digitalised products such as music, games and software downloaded from the net to EU consumers, liable for VAT. This would have levelled the playing field with EU marketers who are having to apply VAT. This veto was in line with the US policy of a moratorium on taxation on any goods sold over the net (*International Tax Review*, 2001).

Table 2.4 VAT rates of selected European countries 2001

Standard rate applicable to the majority of consumer goods. Each country applies a lower rate for selected basic commodities, medication and cultural products.

	Rate (%)
Belgium	21
France[1]	19.6
Germany	16
Ireland[2]	21
Italy	20
Netherlands[3]	19
Switzerland[4]	7.6
UK	17.5

Notes: 1 as of April, 2000
2 as of 01 March, 2002
3 as of January, 2001
4 as of 01 January, 2001

Source: *Worldwide Corporate Tax Guide 2002*, Ernst & Young Global Limited, http://www.ey.com, information current as of 01 March, 2002.

Government spending

Governments, like any other organisations, are purchasers of goods and services, but on a grand scale. They invest in defence industries, road building and other civil engineering projects, social and health services and many other areas. Such large purchasing power can be used to stimulate or depress economic development, but if a government decides as a matter of policy to cut back on its spending, industry can be very badly hit. Defence, for example, is an area which many governments are reviewing in the aftermath of the ending of the 'cold war'.

The shipbuilding industry in the UK barely survives and is a shadow of its former glory in days of Empire. When the Ministry of Defence decided to award the £130mn contract for the refit of *HMS Illustrious* to Babcock Rosyth Defence in Fife, it was not only guaranteeing nearly 1,000 jobs for a further 18 months, but also enabling suppliers to benefit from the subcontract work generated. This order, along with a £75mn contract to refit 23 Royal Navy frigates has helped to sustain the yard for the foreseeable future (*Professional Engineering*, 2001).

Interest rates

Government economic policy affects interest rates, which have an impact on both consumers and business. For many consumers, the most serious effect of a rise in interest rates is on their monthly mortgage repayments. Paying £20 or more per month extra to the mortgage lender means that there is that much less cash available for buying other things, and across the country retail sales can be significantly reduced. Interest rate rises can also affect the attractiveness of credit to the consumer, either when buying large expensive items through instalments, or when using credit cards. A consumer thinking about buying a brand new car, for example, may need a loan, and will look at the repayment levels, determined by interest rates, when deciding how expensive a model can be afforded. To try to reduce this potential barrier to purchasing, many car dealers have entered into arrangements with credit companies to offer 0 per cent financing deals to car buyers.

Exchange rates

A country's exchange rate is rather like the price of a share for a company; it is a sign of confidence in the continued prosperity, or otherwise, of an individual nation. Fluctuating exchange rates between different currencies can have a major impact on the prosperity of companies and individual consumers. If a currency is strong, imports become cheaper which is good news for businesses and consumers, but exports become more expensive which is bad news for manufacturers. The strength of sterling in the period after the launch of the euro has been blamed by some for precipitating a manufacturing recession in the UK as prices in the prime continental markets become less competitive.

eg

It is best to book early any planned flight to South Africa from Europe. A shortfall of 4,500 seats a week has been estimated during the peak summer period, largely due to carriers such as Austrian Airlines, Alitalia and Sabena stopping services. In 1997, there were 74 airlines flying to South Africa but by 2001 there were just 52. The reason was the slump in the value of the rand against the US dollar so that a ticket from South Africa to Europe would have become unaffordable to many South Africans, unless the airlines were prepared to absorb some of the currency loss. At a time when the euro has also been weak against the dollar, with a 20 per cent reduction in value, fuel and airport charges transacted in dollars have become even more expensive, so some airlines have given up on the routes. Others have allocated a share of seats for local customers paying in rand, thus making the shortage worse. Demand is being kept artificially high because of the failure to pass on the full costs to the customer. However, the loss to some airlines has meant opportunities for others. BA, KLM, Iberia and Olympic are taking up some of the slots that have become vacant and trust that they can fly through the currency turbulence (Innocenti, 2001).

Exchange rates will be considered again in Chapters 11 and 23, given their important impact on price competitiveness for international trade.

International trading blocs

Governments also negotiate membership of international trading blocs, and the scope, terms and conditions of international trade agreements. Membership of the EU, for example, and particularly the advent of the **single European market (SEM)**, has had a profound effect on the wider commercial dealings of organisations operating within the EU, as well as on the economic and competitive environment. Organisations which exist in countries outside the EU have found it increasingly difficult to sell into the EU, since there are now many more EU-based potential suppliers for purchasers to turn to, and also the logistics of purchasing within the EU are easier.

eg

The EU provides duty-free access to its markets for 48 of the world's poorest and least developed economies. The import of cut flowers from Africa considered in Chapter 1 is part of this arrangement. However, extending the scheme to what are perceived as more sensitive products is causing some concern for the competitiveness of both home producers and their existing suppliers. Particular concern has been expressed over sugar, bananas and rice, for example. France and some of the southern European EU member states are especially concerned on the impact of imports on home produced sugar and rice. It will not be until 2009 that full liberalisation of trade will have occurred on sugar and rice and there is to be a review in 2005 to ensure that non-treaty state produce is not finding its way into the EU market via the poorer nations. Even then, tariff-free quotas will be set based upon normal production to ensure fair play. Currently tariff barriers on this produce keeps prices high and supplies limited. These will be progressively dismantled in the period up to 2009 (*The Grocer*, 2000c; 2001c; 2001e).

A queue of countries are waiting to join the EU. The most likely candidates for joining are the Czech Republic, Poland and Hungary, once all requirements for membership are fulfilled, referenda held and the results ratified by the other member states. There are currently 13 countries at various stages of accession to the EU. If and when they join it will mean that the EU will have 28 member states with a population of 500 million, a very large internal market, and although the overall GDP of all the member states would grow by less than 5 per cent after their inclusion, over time it offers enormous potential for exporters. To qualify for membership, each applicant must meet pre-set criteria such as a having a strong market economy, stable political institutions that can guarantee democracy, the rule of law and a good human rights record. Their laws will have to be fine-tuned to accommodate 35,000 pages of EU legislation, but it is a price worth paying for access to the more prosperous markets in the EU.

The EU is not, however, the only major European international trading bloc. The European Free Trade Association (EFTA) was formed originally in 1959 by Austria, Denmark, Norway, Sweden, Switzerland and the UK, and was later expanded to include Finland, Iceland and Liechtenstein. Its philosophy was simply to make trade between the member states easier. Since several EFTA members subsequently became members of the EU, and as the prospect of the single European market (SEM) raised the perceived barriers to entry to EU markets for non-EU organisations, the remaining EFTA countries (except Switzerland) became involved in the idea of the European Economic Area (EEA), formalised by treaty in 1993. Although not full members of the EU, EEA countries now share some of the benefits of the SEM, and certainly face fewer barriers to trade within the EU than they would otherwise have encountered. Participation in the EEA acted as a stepping stone for Austria and Sweden, who subsequently became full EU members. Similar cooperation and association agreements are in progress with the former communist states of central and eastern Europe, with the immediate aim of helping to stimulate their economics and the longer-term aim of including such countries as the Czech Republic, Poland and Hungary. Others, such as Bulgaria and Slovakia, must wait further reform while still benefiting from EU support. The enlargement of Europe will create new opportunities and problems. The population will grow by 28 per cent, but GDP by only 4 per cent when the new nations are allowed to join. GDP in Hungary and Poland, although growing fast, is still one-third of the average EU level. Each nation will have to meet pre-set criteria and standards for the environment, health and safety and social policy before they will be allowed to enter. All these changes create tremendous opportunities for EU and central European organisations in the run-up to EU enlargement (Barber, 1997).

Beyond the confines of formalised trading blocs, business is often affected by the existence of trade agreements. Some of these are protectionist, in that they are trying to cushion domestic producers from the effects of an influx of imports, while others are trying to liberalise trade between nations. For many years, for example, the UK's textile industry benefited from the multi fibre arrangement (MFA), which protected jobs and businesses by basically restricting the imports of low-priced clothing from various Far Eastern countries. Similarly, Japan agreed to implement voluntary export restraint (VER) with regard to its car industry's sales to Western Europe and the US. This helped to protect domestic car producers and jobs by imposing quotas on Japanese imports. One way of overcoming the restrictions of this VER was international direct investment, i.e. setting up factories within the EU (taking full advantage, by the way, of various EU investment incentives) to produce cars with sufficient local content to be labelled 'European'. Thus those people owning either a Nissan (built in Washington, Tyne and Wear), a Honda (built in Swindon) or a Toyota (built in Derby), for example, are technically driving a British car. From their British manufacturing bases, the companies can legitimately export, without quota constraints, to the rest of the EU under the terms of the SEM.

eg

Earlier, the issue of EU trade agreements was mentioned. Bananas are not grown in Europe, but there is still a quota tariff system in place, largely to serve the interests of the traditional suppliers from the Caribbean where there are many ex-colonial ties and perceived responsibilities. Any system that opens up Europe to all-comers would have a major effect on the banana industry in many Caribbean countries and could result in severe social and economic problems. However, protection for the Caribbean means restrictions for other producers. Chiquita Brands, a US company, is struggling because of the restrictions on the quantity of bananas it can supply the EU. Since 1993, when import controls were introduced, the company's share of EU markets has declined from 40 per cent to 20 per cent. Such controls have been criticised by the WTO for unfairly protecting the EU's own producers and importers and indirectly inflating the price we pay for bananas (*The Grocer*, 2001b; 2001c).

The protectionist stance of agreements like the MFA is, however, being over-shadowed by wider moves towards trade liberalisation, through the General Agreement on Tariffs and Trade (GATT), for example. The broad aim of GATT is to get rid of export subsidies and import tariffs (effectively taxes on imports that push their prices up to make them less competitive compared with the domestically produced equivalent product) to make international trade a great deal fairer. This means that negotiated VERs, which do not depend on tariffs to control imports, are becoming an increasingly important tool.

Despite liberalisation, governments face the problems of unequal economic performance and opportunity in different regions within their sphere of influence. Governments therefore try to overcome the problems of congestion and rising costs in some areas and underused facilities and infrastructure in others through influencing business decision-making with programmes of direct and indirect incentives. In Ireland, for example, the west coast is particularly remote from main European markets, and thus the government offers various tax and capital grant incentives to encourage relocation into the area, indigenous enterprise and business expansion. Similarly, in the Netherlands, a number of assisted areas have been defined to ensure balanced economic growth, including the north-eastern areas of Gronigen, Friesland and Drente, the northern part of Overijssel, and the south-eastern province of Limburg. In these areas, investment premiums are awarded along with cash grants and low-interest loans to encourage R&D investment.

Many of the marketing issues associated with dealing within and with trading blocs, including the SEM, will be considered further in Chapter 23.

The microeconomic environment

The general discussion in Chapter 1 of what marketing is, and its main tools, did not pay particular attention to the structure of markets. It is nevertheless important to think about market structures, because these will influence what sort of competition the organisation is up against, what scope the organisation has to manipulate the 4Ps and how broad an impact the organisation's marketing activities could have on the market as a whole.

Market structures can be defined in four broad categories, based on the number and size of competitors in the market.

Monopoly

Technically, a monopoly exists where one supplier has sole control over a market, and there is no competition. The lack of competition may be because the monopolist is state owned and/or has a statutory right to be the sole supplier to the market. Traditionally in the EU, this applied to public utilities, such as gas, water, electricity, telephone and postal services, and some key industries such as the railways, steel and coal. Government policy in member states over the past twenty years, however, was to privatise and open up some of these industries to competition, with the idea that if they were exposed to market forces and were answerable to shareholders, they would operate more efficiently and cost effectively. By 2000, the OECD reported that over 1 trillion dollars had been transferred worldwide from state to private enterprise. Manufacturing, banking, transportation, energy and public utilities have all been privatised in a significant number of countries. Some countries such as Hungary and Portugal have raised a quarter of GDP from privatisation sales. More recently, the telecommunications industry has the been the focus of attention. In Sweden, for example, the part-sale of shares in Telia, the Swedish telecom company, involved 1 million investors in the largest privatisation in the country. Further activity is expected in Finland now that the government has legislated to relax the requirement that it should hold 34 per cent of telecoms shares. Privatisation in telecoms reflects the changing competitive structure facing the industry that organisations must operate within. With the internationalisation of telecoms, global competitiveness has increased while the pace of technological development requires significant investment to keep up to date. Similarly, state airlines have increasingly become privatised. The sales of Sabena, TAP and Iberia are expected to be completed in 2001 and even the airports themselves have been privatised with private stakes created in Hamburg, Rome and possibly Brussels international airports (*Financial Market Trends*, 2001).

eg

The EU has also taken an interest in some state-owned monopolies. In Sweden, as in other Scandinavian countries, there is a state monopoly for retailing alcohol. The EU rejected the Swedish government's claim that it was better able to control retail sales and thus restrict the potential for Swedes to consume too much liquor. The EU considered that Systembolaget's state monopoly to sell wine, spirits and strong beer was a disproportionate measure for preventing alcohol abuse, and that the protected arrangement contravened the EU ruling on the free flow of goods. The grocery trade, for example, was not able to sell in competition with Systembolaget. In addition, Sweden, as part of its EU accession in 1995, negotiated a special five-year arrangement that restricted the amount of alcohol that could be brought into the country by returning Swedish travellers. The EU is reluctant to renew the agreement. Part of the argument is that the government wants to protect its people from the worst excesses of alcohol by restricting purchases and keeping prices high. There have also been complaints of long queues, poor service and restricted opening times in the state-owned retail alcohol outlets, which further frustrates the consumer. Over 61 per cent of Swedes want the import ban lifted. By comparison, the Germans drink more alcohol per year with no restrictions but the Swedish government wants to hold out as long as possible with over 5 per cent of its tax revenues coming from the monopoly retail chain (*The Economist*, 2000).

In practice, although the privatised companies have restructured themselves internally and revised their business philosophies to suit their new status, they still face limited competition as yet. This is mainly because of the barriers to entry faced by potential competitors, such as the massive capital investment required, or the monopolist's domination of essential resources or infrastructure.

The implication of all this is that a true monopoly is hard to find in a modern market economy, although several near-monopolies are operating. In the UK, a monopoly is deemed to exist where an organisation or a group of collaborating organisations control 25 per cent of a market. Where this occurs, or where a proposed or threatened takeover raises the possibility of its happening, the Competition Commission may undertake an inquiry to establish whether the situation is operating in the public interest and whether there is any unfair competition involved.

eg

In the UK banking sector, when the Lloyds TSB group proposed to purchase Abbey National the Competition Commission found that it would not be in the public interest unless changes were made. The Commission found that the activities of the two organisations overlapped in:

1. markets for financial products sold to personal customers, notably personal current accounts (PCAs), mortgages and savings accounts;
2. markets for financial products sold to small and medium-sized enterprises (SMEs);
3. markets for financial products sold to larger firms; and
4. wholesale banking.

Although areas 3 and 4 were not considered as being against the public interest if the two merged, because of the existence of large global competitors and powerful buyers, 1 and 2 worried the Commission. The market share of the combined company would rise from 22 per cent to 27 per cent in the PCA market and the share of the big four banks, of which Lloyds TSB is one, would rise from 72 per cent to 77 per cent of that market. That kind of increase, it was believed, would impact adversely upon customers by dampening competition. The issues identified included:

- The entrenched position of the big four would be stronger. What little market share the big four have lost through new entrants has been recouped as a result of business acquisitions.
- Customers tend to see switching between banks as a difficult and unrewarding process, and the rate of switching is very low.
- Although telephone and internet-based banks have made some progress, they remain niche players. The great majority of customers continue to bank with multi-service providers which include a national branch network in their range of distribution.

▶

- Branch-based players which have entered in the last ten years, springing from the building society movement, have grown market share only slowly despite their more favourable terms and sustained marketing campaigns.

Abbey National was considered to be one of the few 'new players' that could make some impact on the big four and its loss would result in even less competition. The Commission also believed that the efficiency gains achieved by the merger would not be passed on in lower prices; that customer service could decline if 600 or so branches were closed; and that innovation would not be encouraged in a sector needing more competition. The Commission, therefore, recommended to the Secretary of State that the merger should be prohibited. The findings of the Competition Commission can be challenged by judicial review, but to date that has only happened successfully once, by Interbrew, and that was largely on a procedural point (Competition Commission, 2001; *Financial Times*, 2001).

In theory, monopolists should not need to be particularly bothered about marketing. After all, they have a captive market with no alternative source of supply, so they should be able to price as highly as they want, and not be too concerned about customer service, corporate image, quality, reliability and all the other things that this book covers. In reality, however, monopolies exist with the consent and acquiescence of the government and public opinion, and thus the monopolist is likely to be subject to some kind of control or supervision to make sure that it operates within the public interest. Therefore a strong positive image, good customer service, fair pricing and all the other aspects of marketing soon become essential. Near-monopolies, as we have seen, do face competition, at least in sectors of their businesses, and thus have to be more marketing orientated in their thinking.

This discussion so far has been rather parochial in that it has concentrated on national or regional monopolies. In global markets, however, it is even more difficult, if not impossible, to establish and sustain a monopoly.

As a final thought, the concept of monopoly depends on how 'market' is defined. While it is true that currently SNCF, for example, holds a monopoly on passenger rail travel in France, it does not have a monopoly on moving people from Paris to Lyon. To travellers, rail is only one option, and they might also consider travelling to their destinations by air, by coach or by car. In that sense, the traveller's perception of rail, in terms of its cost, reliability and convenience, is developed in a very competitive context. The UK train operators' advertising over the last few years has indeed sought to acknowledge this, by comparing the benefits of long distance rail travel with the disadvantages of road and air journeys. The opening of the Channel Tunnel in particular has brought the comparison of different modes of travel to the forefront, as leisure and business travellers decide whether to take the plane, the train or the ferry to and from the UK.

Oligopoly

Well-developed market economies are far more likely to see the emergence of oligopolies than monopolies. In an oligopoly, a small number of firms account for a very large share of the market, and a number of the privatised ex-monopolies discussed above are moving into this category. The oligopoly creates a certain amount of interdependence between the key players, each of which is large enough for its actions to have a big impact on the market and on the behaviour of its competitors. This certainly occurs in large-scale, worldwide industrial markets, such as chemicals, oil and pharmaceuticals, because the amount of capital investment required, the levels of production needed to achieve economies of scale and the geographic dispersion of large customers demanding large quantities make this the most efficient way for these markets to be structured.

Other consumer oligopolies are less visible to the casual observer. In the supermarket, the shopper may see a wide variety of brands of clothes-washing detergents, and thus imagine that there is healthy, widespread competition in that sector. Most brands are, however, owned and managed by either Procter & Gamble (P&G) (Ariel, Daz, Bold, etc.) or Unilever (Persil, Radion, Surf, etc.), and the proliferation of brands is more to do with fragmented demand and the creation of discrete segments (*see* Chapter 5) than the fragmentation of

eg

Petrol retailing in the UK has largely been concentrated in the hands of a few companies, such as Shell, BP and Esso. This has periodically given rise to accusations of collusion, specifically in terms of 'price fixing', which would not be allowed in either UK or EU law. In reality, the organisations within the oligopoly watch each other keenly for signals, and when one makes a price move, the others tend to follow very quickly, because this is a price-sensitive market. It may appear to be orchestrated, but the important thing to emphasise is that each organisation makes its decision independently, on the basis of its analysis of what it sees happening in the market. The petrol oligopoly in the UK became somewhat wider after the entry of the supermarket chains into this market. Between 1996 and 1998, 2,600 petrol stations had closed and the supermarket's market share was thought to have reached over 20 per cent by 2000 in volume terms (Patten, 2000). Although the oil companies are fighting back with loyalty schemes and price promotions to match the supermarkets, the damage has been done now that market share has been surrendered.

supply. Again, the supermarkets are the biggest threat to this oligopoly, with their own-brands, such as retailer Sainsbury's own brand Novon.

In marketing terms, it is nevertheless still very difficult for a new brand from a new competitor to enter an oligopolistic market, other than in a small niche. This is because the oligopolists have spent many years and vast amounts of marketing money establishing their brands and shares. In the UK, it was reported that £15mn was spent on advertising Coca-Cola, while £5.2mn was spent advertising rival brand Pepsi (Hiscock, 2001). You can begin to see how such levels of marketing expenditure can act as an effective barrier to entry, and how they can meet any threat from a smaller competitor head-on if they wish.

The supermarket's own-brand threat is more serious because of the retailer's inherent control over a major channel of distribution which neither of the oligopolists can afford to lose. All of this really leaves only very small gaps in the market for the smaller competitor, such as that filled by products such as Ark and Ecover, two detergent brands that positioned themselves as more environmentally friendly than anything else available, appealing to the 'dark green' consumer.

Oligopolists therefore spend their time watching each other, and developing their marketing strategies and tactics on the basis of what the other main players are doing or are likely to do. If, for example, Unilever launches a new brand, or implements a major new marketing communications strategy, P&G would prefer to anticipate it, thus either pre-empting Unilever or at least having a calculated response ready when needed. From P&G's point of view this is essential, even if it is only to maintain the delicate status quo of the two companies' relative market shares.

Monopolistic competition

Good marketing practice and the emphasis on differential advantage have created a market structure that might seem a little paradoxical at first sight: monopolistic competition. The idea is that although there are many competitors in the market (with the emphasis on smaller competitors without enough individual influence to create either an oligopoly or a monopoly, as discussed above), each has a product sufficiently differentiated from the rest to create its own monopoly, because to the customer it is unique, or at least any potential substitutes are considered to be inferior. The concept forms the basis of much of the rest of this book.

Perfect competition

Perfect competition is at the opposite end of the spectrum from monopoly, and is about as likely to be found in practice. It involves many small producers, all supplying identical products that can be directly substituted for each other. No producer has the power to influence or determine price, and the market consists of many small buyers, who similarly cannot influence the market individually. There are no barriers to market entry or exit, and all buyers and sellers have complete information about what is happening in the market. All of this is clearly unrealistic. The influence of marketing concepts on even the smallest organisations, along with the development of powerful buyers and sellers in all kinds of markets, consumer and B2B, mean that these conditions cannot hold, and some kind of monopolistic competition or oligopoly soon emerges.

eg

Farm produce, such as vegetables, is often cited as an example of near perfect competition. While it is true that the market does consist of many small suppliers, i.e. individual farms, the nature of the buyer is more complex, ranging from a family buying a few kilos of carrots from a farm shop, to the fruit and vegetable wholesalers and supermarket chains that buy such quantities that they can influence price and other supply variables. Even the product itself can be differentiated, for example organic and non-organic, or class I and class II quality. The farmer can also differentiate the offering through grading and packaging the produce to suit the retail customer. Even carrots, therefore, can be seen to be moving towards monopolistic competition.

This section has made implicit reference to concepts of supply, demand and pricing. In Chapter 11, which deals with price setting and modification, we go into more detail on the economics of pricing, supply and demand curves and price elasticity.

The political and legal environment

Quite apart from their effect on the economic and competitive environment, governments have a great influence on the character of the general business environment through their policies and the resultant legislation. Organisations have to exist in and operate according to the laws of the societies within which they do business, and thus in addition to the more general laws of contract and commerce, products have to conform to safety laws; manufacturing processes are subject to pollution controls; copyright and patents protect innovation; and retailers' opening hours are restricted in Germany, for example, by the *Ladenschlussgesetz*, and in the UK by the Sunday trading laws. We look below at the role and influence of national governments and the European Parliament in making rules that have a direct effect on the marketing mix.

Regulation is not only defined through legislation from national governments or the European Parliament, however. Organisations are also subject to rules passed by regulatory bodies, some of which have statutory powers delegated to them from government, while others are voluntary groupings, such as trade associations, with codes of practice to which the organisation chooses to adhere. We examine the nature and influence of such bodies on p. 80 *et seq*. Inevitably, governments and other regulatory bodies are influenced in their policy making by other sources, such as lobbyists and pressure groups, and on pp. 84–5 we take a wider view of the influences that drive the legislators and rule makers towards their policies.

Overall, therefore, there are three main forces within the **political and legal environment**, national and local government, the EU, and various regulatory bodies. The degree of relative influence that each force exerts, and the nature of the tensions between them, will vary from country to country and from industry to industry. These forces are important and necessary because the problem with self-regulation is that it creates tension between what is socially desirable and what those in the industry may consider to restrict commerce unduly. Similarly, there is a risk that the interests of the general public, as represented by pressure groups, may also conflict with the needs and desires of commercial organisations, and that too creates tension that the law makers and regulators have to try to resolve.

National and local government

The obvious responsibility of national governments is to determine and maintain the legislative framework within which organisations do business. This will cover areas such as contract law, consumer protection, financial legislation, competition and trading practices, for example. There are variations in approaches across Europe but increasingly, as European integration proceeds and the internal market is fully liberalised, national governments are working within EU guidelines and directives, with the longer-term aim of achieving consistency across member states.

Within the UK, although Parliament passes legislation and puts it on the statute books, the responsibility for implementing and enforcing it is often delegated to specialist bodies, such as the Office of Fair Trading (OFT), Competition Commission, or the Independent Television Commission (ITC). The role of such bodies is discussed further on p. 80 *et seq.*

As well as the legislation they pass that affects the day-to-day business practices of organisations, governments can also have profound effects on the competitive environment. The widespread privatisation of publicly owned utilities and other state-controlled national industries in the 1980s and 1990s, as has already been discussed, presented opportunities for new competitors to enter these markets, as well as profoundly changing the culture and business orientation of the newly privatised companies themselves.

marketing *in action*

Putting a CAP on it: the EU Common Agricultural Policy

Over 46 per cent of the EU's budget goes on subsidising agriculture. The Common Agricultural Policy (CAP) is a system designed to protect farmers in the various member states through guaranteed prices, quotas and subsidies. By protecting farming, rural jobs are protected and rural development made more feasible. However, there is a price: the OECD notes that in 1999 the EU was paying out an average subsidy of $17,000 to every full-time farmer in the EU, compared with an average of $11,000 in countries belonging to the OECD. Such a level of support does not come free, as in order to protect the farmers the average family in the EU pays around $1,200 a year more for food than if they were paying market-based world food prices (*The Economist*, 2001b). In addition, food processors seeking to export are placed at a competitive disadvantage due to higher raw material prices.

As might be expected, the CAP system is increasingly coming under strain. Although progress has been made in cutting subsidies, there is still a long way to go. Ironically, the BSE crisis could be a further cause of more rapid change. The cost of 'emergency measures' to deal with it, through the purchase and slaughter of cattle, has so far been almost €1 bn ($918 mn), out of a total farm budget of €42.8 bn for 2001. If the budget ceiling is fixed, any long-term pressure on beef farmers from foot and mouth disease or BSE could mean reducing subsidies elsewhere. Declining beef sales, as consumers decide to switch to other meats, would only make matters worse because if prices fall, the EU is required to buy beef at up to 60 per cent of the previous EU support price. Environmental issues are also coming to the fore as some politicians believe that subsidies should be used to encourage green rather than wasteful farming. Farmers would have to meet social and ecological criteria before handouts were given.

The 2.2 million olive producers in Europe are typical beneficiaries of the CAP system in practice. The subsidy is based upon production, so the more you produce the more subsidy you receive. The consequences are predictable. In Spain, olive production is booming and even after a belated attempt to restrict the planting of new trees, 2.5 per cent of the entire EU budget now goes on supporting olive growers. With the subsidy based on delivery to the olive mills rather than on the number of trees, the number of olive trees in Spain is expected to increase from 300 to 340 million and there are another 500 million trees around the rest of Europe. Europe is now well on the way to an olive oil lake, as there are only so many olives the EU consumer can eat at one sitting and only so much olive oil that can be used for cooking. Producing more to feed a lake of unwanted oil highlights the worst excesses of CAP and for that reason politicians are coming under increased pressure to undertake significant reform. At least cereal and beef subsidies are unrelated to production or are designed to encourage non-production (*The Economist*, 2001c).

Even in the case of olives, there are environmental issues associated with the subsidy method adopted. Intensive production has led to soil erosion, forest clearance and water shortages. Thus under the environmental protection programme run by the EU, efforts are being funded to combat the impact of intensive farming on the marshland in the Doñana national park in Andalusia. Only the politicians can end the waste. A recent report from the World Wide Fund for Nature suggests linking subsidies to the amount of land under production rather than the amount produced, to take the emphasis away from intensive farming. However, the olive oil farmers from Spain, Greece, Italy and Portugal are a very effective lobbying group in Brussels and with $2 bn a year in handouts there is a strong incentive to retain the status quo. It has been estimated that Spanish olive growers receive half their income from Brussels. With the three-year extension to the current EU's CAP regime, the lake will continue to get bigger (*The Economist*, 2001b).

Perhaps the cynical joke made at the founding of the EU that 'German industry would pay for French farmers' should now be 'European industry would pay for French, Spanish and Greek farmers' as it is closer to the truth, due to a failure to address the underlying issues. The normal rules of supply and demand are effectively discarded under CAP and prices are not allowed to fall to anywhere near the market level. Whether for milk, olives, wheat or beef there is a price that the consumer must pay until EU farm ministers are prepared to contemplate radical reform.

Sources: *The Economist* (2001b; 2001c).

eg

The Danish wind power industry has been heavily supported by government as part of its energy policy. It has also become the world's top producer and exporter of windmills, with Danish companies having 50 per cent of a \$4.5bn global market. In order to get the industry established, the government agreed to pay windmill owners above-market prices for their power as well as subsidising maintenance and investment in new technology. The Danish government pays more than \$300mn to wind generators every year and, in part, that is reflected in some of the highest prices in Europe for electricity. Wind farms may well be the green power for this century, but it is old-fashioned government subsidy in Denmark, not just wind, that ensures the blades keep turning (Echison and Ginsburg, 2001).

Politically driven deregulation has even made its mark on the public sector, particularly in the UK, where hospitals and police forces now find themselves operating in completely new ways as business units. Hospital pathology laboratories, for example, which traditionally were integrated internal departments, are now being asked to compete against external organisations for their own hospital's business, as well as tendering for contracts from other hospitals and the private sector. These are themes that will be pursued further in Chapter 22.

Local government also carries some responsibility for implementing and enforcing laws made at a national level. In Germany, local government has responsibility for implementing pollution and noise control legislation. In the UK, local trading standards officers may well be the first to investigate claims of shady or illegal business practices. Christmas often heralds a flurry of warnings from trading standards officers about dangerous toys, usually cheap imports from the Far East, that do not conform to EU safety standards. Officers can prosecute the retailer and prevent further sales of the offending goods, but by then, significant numbers of the product may already have been sold. Trading Standards offices play an important role in ensuring consumer safety and that fair trading and quality standards are maintained. They are provided by over 200 local authorities in the United Kingdom.

eg

Trading standards officers also look into allegations of short weights and measures. In 1995, for example, they were asked by the angling fraternity in the north-east of England to investigate the practice of selling maggots by the pint. Although officers found that the number and weight of maggots to the pint varied significantly from retailer to retailer, they decided that this was tolerable because of the wriggly nature of the merchandise and, in any case, since this was a long-established method of selling maggots they would not intervene further. It is up to the individual angler to choose a maggot supplier with care! More recently, just what constitutes a pint of beer has been under consideration. It is all about liquid, gas and froth: get the mix wrong and it's a short measure! A pint of beer has been determined to be a pint of liquid which can include the liquid in the head of the froth, but not the gas in the head. Pint pullers must ensure 100 per cent liquid with no measure below 95 per cent. New legislation is being introduced under the Weights and Measures Act and Trading Standards officers will be watching to ensure compliance.

Local authorities in the UK also have responsibility for granting planning permission. For businesses, this means that if they want to build a factory or supermarket, or change the usage of a commercial building, then the local authority has to vet the plans and grant permission before anything can be done. Sometimes this poses no problem at all, and local authorities go out of their way to encourage new industrial and commercial investment in their regions, as it provides jobs and encourages local economic regeneration. Establishing the Nissan car plant in Washington, Tyne and Wear, for example, not only provided new jobs in the factory itself, but also encouraged companies supplying goods and services to Nissan to locate and flourish close to the factory.

In other cases, however, planning permission can sometimes be a major barrier. Local authorities are under pressure from small retailers who are worried about the major shift towards out-of-town superstore shopping. The argument is that town centres and small local businesses are dying because people would rather go to the out-of-town retail park or shopping mall. This means that local authorities are increasingly reluctant to grant planning permission for further out-of-town developments, seriously affecting the growth plans of many large retailers.

eg

In the 1990s, supermarkets were criticised by some for changing the face of the High Street by attracting shoppers to out-of-town hypermarkets, superstores and malls. A number of countries including France and the UK introduced tough planning regimes to limit growth. Now, supermarkets are starting to play a part in urban renewal schemes using brown-field sites largely as a response to the ease and favour given to planning permission for redeveloping sites (Bedington, 2001). The former gas works at Beckton is being transformed by Tesco into a 109,000 ft^2 store. Similarly, the redevelopment of a run-down shopping centre in Seacroft, Leeds and the planned conversion of a derelict railway yard in Leyton by ASDA are all helping to play a leading role in urban regeneration schemes.

Although the EU is making considerable progress towards eliminating national regulations that are contrary to fair and free trade, the scale of the task is great. National environmental laws in Germany and Denmark, for example, have been criticised as favouring local rather than international suppliers. The extent to which regulations affect business, therefore, varies between countries and industries. There is a slow move towards standardisation, which generally means that the advanced industrialised northern European nations are tending to deregulate, whereas the southern nations are tending to tighten up controls. Moves towards deregulation have been accompanied by increased self-regulation within industries.

The European Union

It is unfortunate that the pronouncements from Brussels that make the headlines tend to be the offbeat or trivial ones, such as the proposal to regulate the curve on a cucumber, the redesignation of the carrot as a fruit to allow the Portuguese to carry on their trade in carrot jam, and questions as to whether Cheddar cheese and Swiss rolls can continue to bear those names if they are not made in those places. Despite these delightful eccentricities, the EU works hard towards ensuring free trade and fair competition across member states' boundaries. The development and interpretation of European competition policy has long been an area of debate and controversy. The policy has three main objectives: to create an open and unified European market, to have the 'right' amount of competition in that market and to encourage fair competition unhampered by market abuse and restrictive practices.

The SEM, which officially came into being on 1 January 1993, was the culmination of many years of work in breaking down trade barriers and harmonising legislation across the member states. One area that directly affects marketing is the abolition of frontier controls, so that goods can be transferred from state to state, or carried in transit through states, without lots of paperwork and customs checks. Additionally, road haulage has been freed from restrictions and quotas so that a haulier with a licence to operate in one EU member state can operate in any other. Further European integration is sought through EMU (European Monetary Union) and the introduction of the euro as a replacement for national currencies. This has made cross-border price comparisons a lot easier for customers and created more transparent pan-European competition. The euro has also eliminated problems caused by fluctuating exchange rates, thus reducing the costs of the cross-border movement of goods and encouraging more imports and exports between the countries of the EU. This presents both opportunities and problems to the marketer, which will be discussed further in Chapter 10.

In terms of products themselves, a set of European standards have been implemented through a series of directives, ensuring common criteria for safety, public health and environmental protection. Any product adhering to these directives and to the laws of its own country of origin will be acceptable in any member state. Look for the stylised CE symbol on products as the sign that they do conform to European standards.

In other areas of marketing, harmonisation of regulations and codes of practice across member states has not been so easy. Over the next few years, the EU intends to bring a series of separate legislation together into an overarching EU Communications Act, which would be wide ranging in terms of promotional and media types, including press and TV, direct marketing and sales promotion, online marketing and e-commerce (Simms, 2001). The problem with marketing communications is that the European law makers have to reconcile commercial freedom with consumer protection across 15 different countries, each

eg

Defining just what chocolate actually is or is not has caused controversy in Europe among both politicians and chocolate manufacturers. The argument has been going on for nearly 30 years, since the UK and Ireland joined the EU with chocolate that included cheaper vegetable fats rather than a higher proportion of cocoa fats. The chocolate wars have been fought between an alliance of France and Belgium and a number of others against the UK, Ireland and five other states. An EU directive favouring one side over the other would create an unfair competitive advantage and would be a far cry from a single European market in chocolate. In 1997, the European Parliament ruled in favour of the France–Belgium alliance, overturning a previous compromise EU directive. This meant that the term 'milk chocolate' could not be used by the UK and the other states on its side. That meant that products from the UK and Ireland and some other member states would have to be renamed 'chocolate with milk and non-cocoa vegetable fats' or at least 'milk chocolate with high milk content'. Product labels would also need to show clearly that the product contains vegetable fats. That was not acceptable to the UK chocolate producers and a further compromise was realised in 2000 with directive 2000/36 which agreed to two definitions of chocolate: 'milk chocolate' and 'family milk chocolate', the latter replacing the 'milk chocolate with high milk content' designation for the UK and Irish markets. All this goes to show how a desire to create a common internal market and to establish pan-European rules for the manufacture, composition, labelling and packaging of a product such as chocolate, can run into bureaucratic nightmares (Bremner, 1997; Tucker, 1997; http://www.europa.eu.int).

with its own customs, laws, codes and practices. Sometimes, best practice is followed and harmonisation across all states can be achieved but in other cases, the law of the country in which a transaction originates applies, by mutual recognition. As we shall see in Chapters 14 to 19, there are wide variations in best practice across Europe, so finding a common approach will be difficult. The threats are, however, real for UK advertisers. Sweden, despite an initial rebuff, would still like to see a blanket ban across Europe on television advertising to children and the advertising of alcohol. Other lobbies exist to constrain advertising on 'unhealthy foods', financial services, and even cars (Smith, 2001).

Sales promotion, for example, is regulated in very different ways and with very different attitudes across Europe. The UK is very liberal, in that most sales promotion techniques are permitted and are largely regulated through voluntary codes of practice. In Germany, by contrast, many techniques are banned by law or heavily restricted in the way in which they can operate, for instance free gifts are (generally) banned, while there is a restriction on the value of discounts, vouchers or cash refunds. In the Netherlands, free gifts are permitted, but must not exceed 4 per cent of the value of the item to which they are linked. Even these brief examples give an inkling of the nightmares faced by the European marketer trying to trade across borders, and the pressure on the EU to begin to iron out the inconsistencies.

Advertising too is an area of intense debate within the EU. Issues such as the advertising of tobacco and alcohol, advertising aimed at children, comparative advertising and the regulation and control of advertising media are all under consideration. Again, the aim is to find a way of harmonising codes of practice and legislation that differ widely from member state to member state. Direct marketing is a relatively new area which has great potential for the marketing of goods across Europe, and yet here too, a variety of national codes are in operation. In the UK, for example, 'cold calling' telephone selling (i.e. an organisation phoning a consumer for sales purposes without the consumer's prior permission) is permitted, but in Germany it is almost totally banned. Data protection laws (i.e. what information organisations are permitted to hold on databases and what they are allowed to do with it) and regulations on list broking (i.e. the sale of lists of names and addresses to other organisations) also vary widely across the EU. The relevant EU directives include the Data Protection Directive, the Distance Selling Directive and the Integrated Digital Services Network Directive.

Regulatory bodies

Within the UK, there are many regulatory bodies with greater or lesser powers of regulation over marketing practice. Quasi-governmental bodies such as the Office of Fair Trading (OFT) and the Competition Commission have had statutory duties and powers delegated to them directly by government to ensure the maintenance of free and fair commerce.

The Office of Fair Trading (OFT) in the UK aims to ensure that markets are working effectively. This is achieved by ensuring that competition and consumer protection laws and guidelines are followed in the public interest. It is the OFT that refers mergers, such as the proposed Lloyds TSB–Abbey National merger, to the Competition Commission. Being accountable to Parliament for its performance, it is able to play a powerful role in shaping an organisation's marketing behaviour. Recent activities have included an inquiry into motorway catering facilities, where they found that value for money is generally poor but that it does not arise from anti-competitive practice; a report on the funeral industry (OFT, 2001) which called for better prior information for the bereaved on funeral charges and choices, and the successful achievement of the ability to apply through the courts for 'Stop Now' orders designed to curb the excesses of rogue traders. The latter can be especially important to stop the sale of defective goods and breaches in advertising or credit rules. Further examples can be found on the official website, http://www.oft.gov.uk.

Slightly more remote from central government, quasi-autonomous non-governmental organisations (quangos) have a specific remit and can act much more quickly than a government department. Quangos such as Oftel, Ofgem and Ofwat, for instance, exist to regulate the privatised telephone, gas and electricity, and water industries respectively in the UK. The prime aim for the quangos is to protect consumer interests by ensuring appropriate levels of competition. Ofgem, for example, had six priorities for 2001–2002 which reflect the quango's scope:

- *Social and Environmental Action*: includes an action plan for environmental improvement, sustainable development and ensuring energy efficiency.
- *Regulation of monopoly business*: especially concerned with pricing.
- *Efficient trading in the wholesale electricity and gas markets*: operations, trading arrangements, etc.
- *Managing the move to competitive supply markets*: ensuring service and price levels in the various market groups are in the consumer's interest. Protecting the consumer from misleading sales techniques.
- *Work on industrial structure and competitiveness*: licences, mergers and acquisitions.
- *Work to make Ofgem an efficient regulator.*

The scope of the work of quangos is clearly extensive and offers necessary protection for the consumer in markets that have been privatised. Suppliers in the industry must also consider the likely public and legislative impact of acting outside the public interest in the development of their marketing strategy and its implementation.

Voluntary codes of practice emerge from associations and trade bodies, with which their members agree to comply. The Advertising Standards Authority (ASA), for example, oversees the British Codes of Advertising and Sales Promotion Practice which were merged in 1995 into one comprehensive set of rules covering print, cinema, video, posters and leaflet media. The philosophy of the ASA is that advertisements should be:

- Legal, decent, honest and truthful.
- Prepared with a sense of responsibility to consumers and society.
- In line with the principles of fair competition accepted in business.

The ASA is not a statutory body, and can only *request* an advertiser to amend or withdraw an advertisement that is in breach of the code. Of the 30 million advertisements placed each year, the ASA believes that 97 per cent of print advertisements and 98 per cent of posters adhere to the code. However, if the ASA's Council of 12 people decides that an advertisement contravenes the code, then it does have remedies other than persuasion. It can *request* media owners to refuse to accept or repeat the offending advertisement, generate adverse publicity, and/or *recommend* that the OFT should take proceedings to apply for a legal injunction to prevent publication.

Most advertisers conform to requests from the ASA to withdraw an advertisement and some avoid any possible problems by voluntarily using the pre-publication vetting service. However, the ASA can now ask for vetting for up to two years if a particular advertiser has proven troublesome in the past. Previously, offending campaigns attracted a lot of publicity because of their sensational nature. Then, when the ASA makes a ruling, further publicity is generated, for instance through opinion articles in newspapers discussing advertising standards which include a picture of an offending advertisement so that the readers know what sort of thing they're talking about. Indirectly, therefore, in some cases, ASA involvement rather defeats its own objectives.

With the development of the SEM and transnational advertising campaigns, marketers not only need to consider national laws, self-regulatory rules and systems across the member states. The European Advertising Standards Alliance (EASA) represents the various advertising regulatory bodies, such as the ASA, across Europe. Although it has no direct powers it can intervene on behalf of complainants by asking the various national regulators to act. For example, when a Luxembourgois consumer complained about a French chewing gum manufacturer's health claims, the case was referred back to the French for investigation and action. Table 2.5 lists some advertising regulatory bodies from across Europe.

Table 2.5 European advertising regulatory bodies

France	Bureau de Verification de la Publicité
Germany	Deutscher Werbat (taste and decency)
Netherlands	Stichting Reclame Code
Spain	Asociacion de Autocontrol de la Publicidad (AP)
Sweden	Marknads Etiska Radet (MER)

eg

The ASA takes a close interest in the claims made in advertisements. Danone ran into trouble with the ASA when it claimed that the calcium in a bottle of its Danone Activ was equivalent to the calcium in two glasses of milk. The National Dairy Council took offence at the claim as Danone only used a 250ml glass of liquid which was well below the normal-sized glass. The ASA upheld the claim and Danone was told to use 'commonly accepted glass sizes in future' and to amend its promotional material accordingly (*The Grocer*, 2001g). The ASA is especially mindful of the claims made in the genetically modified (GM) and organic food areas. Iceland also fell foul of the ASA over using misleading and exaggerated claims regarding GM food. The company had for some time taken a strong position on offering organic ranges and non-GM food, but saying in an instore leaflet, for example, that there may have been 'mistakes in genetic engineering', and that a GM bacterium 'may have caused the deaths of 37 people in the US' went too far, according to the ASA (Jardine, 2000). According to the ASA, Iceland had taken the science that was available a little too far, and retailers should avoid using scaremongering tactics to get their message across to consumers.

eg

Club 18–30 in the 1990s and more recently FCUK have become very adept at pushing the frontiers of decency and testing the patience of the ASA in the process. An example of an adjudication by the ASA involved a poster campaign developed by Saatchi & Saatchi for the holiday firm Club 18–30. Copylines such as 'Beaver España', 'Discover Your Erogenous Zones', and 'It's Not Just Sex, Sex, Sex', drew 220 complaints, quite a significant number, which were upheld. The ASA told Club 18–30 to withdraw the advertisements straight away, because they were unacceptable since they had caused widespread offence, and some of them were irresponsible. In more recent years Club 18–30 has toned down its campaign, its reputation established. It is still 'fun in the sun', but within ASA guidelines. An enormous amount of publicity was achieved before the more raunchy posters were withdrawn. To some extent, history is now repeating itself with the continued controversy over the FCUK posters (see pp. 122–3).

By the time the ASA forced the withdrawal of a provocative poster campaign by Club 18–30, the company had already benefited from enormous publicity!

Source: Club 18–30.

The Independent Television Commission (ITC) looks after terrestrial television advertising, while the Radio Authority (RA) supervises radio advertising. These two organisations are statutory bodies and carry a great deal of weight, since they have the power to issue and control broadcasting licences, and compliance with the advertising codes of practice is effectively part of the licence. As with the ASA, the television advertising code ensures that advertisements are not misleading, do not encourage or condone harmful behaviour and do not cause widespread or exceptional offence. The frequency and duration of advertising breaks are restricted and it is the ITC that ensures that there is a distinct break between programmes and advertisements. Pharmaceuticals, alcohol, tobacco and diet products, to name but a few, are subject to tight restrictions under the code of practice and in addition EU directives specify what is and is not allowed. All of this means that although the basic philosophy of the ITC and RA is the same as that of the ASA, their concerns are a little wider, covering the timing of advertisements, making sure that the advertisements are suitably

eg

Thomas Cook was the cause of complaint for 29 viewers when it showed an advertisement with a young Afro-Caribbean man and woman meeting in a supermarket. He asked her how long it had been since they had last met, at the same time noticing that she was heavily pregnant. 'About nine months' she replied. The worried look on the man's face was supported by an end line which said that 'it was time to leave the country', hence the need for Thomas Cook's services. The complainants said that the advertisement was racist and confirmed racial stereotypes of Afro-Caribbean men as irresponsible and promiscuous. The complaints were not upheld, however, and Thomas Cook was allowed to screen the advertisement again as the ITC believed that although some viewers may not appreciate the humour used, it was reflective of a broad stereotype of young men. The Sandals resort was not so fortunate, however, when it showed couples dancing and swimming together and encouraging viewers to send for a brochure. What the advertisement did not say was that only heterosexual couples were welcome and this concerned one single viewer. Advertisements are meant to highlight any important restrictions or qualifications before asking the viewer to invest time and effort in requesting further information. Relying on the reputation of Sandals as a destination for couples and honeymooners was not enough. The holiday company had to cease transmission until the qualification was clearly stated (http://www.itc.org.uk).

differentiated from the programmes, protecting children from unsuitable advertising, prohibiting political advertising and regulating programme sponsorship, among other things.

There are no hard and fast rules about how far an advertiser can go before running foul of regulatory bodies and this becomes even more complex once you start advertising across European boundaries (*see* Chapter 15). A naked couple can kiss in a shower in an advertisement for condoms, but a woman's naked buttocks on a poster are 'unnecessarily shocking' in the words of the ASA. Whether an advertisement causes complaints depends on the medium, the product and the audience likely to see it, so an advertisement that is 'slightly sexist' is fine in men's publications but would be banned in more family orientated media. Posters, because of their size and unrestricted viewing, can be especially difficult. Mentioning religion or race can be a real minefield, especially if the advertisement focuses on a particluar icon or leader. For example, the ASA upheld complaints against an advertisement for the Rey & Co. stationery brand headlined 'Jesus, he loves me', but did not ban a similar advertisement saying, 'Behold! The King of Paper is born'. The direct reference to Jesus made the difference. For Diesel, the 'nuns in jeans' advertisement was banned, not because of the nuns but due to the Virgin Mary featuring in the background (Jardine, 1999).

The Institute of Sales Promotion (ISP), the Institute of Practitioners in Advertising (IPA), the Institute of Public Relations (IPR) and the Direct Marketing Association (DMA) are effectively trade associations. All these areas are, of course, subject to prevailing commercial legislation generally, but, in addition, these particular bodies provide detailed voluntary codes of practice setting industry standards for fair dealing with customers. They are not statutory bodies, and only have jurisdiction over their members, with the ultimate sanction of suspending or expelling organisations that breach the code of practice. All of the bodies mentioned here represent organisations with interests in various areas of marketing communications, but trade associations can exist in any industry with similar objectives of regulating the professional practice of their members. There are, for example, the Fencing Contractors Association, the Glass and Glazing Federation, the Association of British Insurers, the British Association of Landscape Industries, and the National House Builders Confederation, to name but a few! As well as regulating business practice, such bodies can also provide other services for members, such as legal indemnities and representation, training and professional development services, and acting as the voice of the industry to government and the media.

Influences on the political and legal environment

The political and legal environment is clearly influenced by sociocultural factors, and particularly the pressure of public opinion, the media and pressure groups. Greenpeace and Friends of the Earth, for example, have educated consumers to become more aware of the content, origins and after-effects of the products they buy and use, and this led to the phasing out of chlorofluorocarbons (CFCs) as an aerosol propellant and as a refrigerant. The green movement has also spurred the drafting of regulations on the acceptable emissions from car exhausts, which has had a major impact on the product development plans of motor manufacturers for the next few years. Similarly, the consumer movement, through organisations such as the Consumers' Association, has also played an important role in promoting the rights of the consumer and thus in driving the regulators and legislators towards laws and codes of practice regarding product safety, selling techniques and marketing communications, for instance.

Not all pressure on legislators and regulators originates from pressure groups or consumer-based organisations, of course. Trade associations or groupings lobby the legislators to try to influence regulation in their members' favour. Sometimes, the lobbying is designed to slow the pace of change, influence the nature of any planned legislation, and to delay legislation perceived as potentially harmful to the industry's interests. In the case of tobacco, for instance, government must balance public health concerns against the employment and export potential from manufacturers. It is important, therefore, for the marketer to read the changing political environment, within Europe, in export markets and from international organisations such as the WTO and OECD who are influential in guiding change. Most industries face new legislation that affects them one way or another during the course of a year and an early appreciation gives companies more time to exploit an opportunity or to counter a threat. However, it could take between three and five years for legislation to come into effect in Europe, so a longer-term perspective must be taken (Smith, 2001). A failure to get involved early on in lobbying and putting across arguments can have knock-on effects down the line with policies that constrain marketing activity too much without enabling a more open internal market. Some policies could even favour particular member states who have lobbied harder. The Directives on online trading and e-commerce, for example, are topical within the EU, so internet marketers cannot afford to miss out on discussions concerning the legislative framework.

With increasing public concern for sustainability, competitiveness of markets, fair trading, product safety and quality and consumer rights, it is a very brave politician that can ignore the pressures for change. However, lobbying and participating in the legislative discussion can help steer outcomes towards those preferred by an organisation. Organisations such as Greenpeace have become very effective at lobbying key decision makers, but tracking the legislative process can be a long and tortuous process. The Commission in Strasbourg frames EU legislation which is then debated and amended by the European parliament before the legislation is endorsed by the Council of Ministers and then implemented though European Directives. Even then it is not over, as individual member states may have to pass legislation to implement at a local level (Simms, 2001). The greater the understanding of the EU and national political processes, the more an organisation can move with change rather than risk being left behind.

Chapter summary

- This chapter has explored the importance of the external marketing environment as an influence on the way in which organisations do business and make their decisions. Ways in which customers, markets, competitors, technology and regulation are changing are all important pointers to future strategy. Thus failure to understand the environment fully could mean missing out on opportunities or ignoring threats which in turn could lead to lost revenue or, more seriously, loss of competitive advantage.
- Using environmental scanning, a technique for monitoring and evaluating information, organisations can understand their environment more thoroughly, pick up early signs of emerging trends, and thus plan their future activities appropriately. Such information may come from secondary sources, such as trade publications or published research data, or an organisation can commission research to increase their knowledge of the environment. Care must be taken, however, to ensure that all appropriate sources are constantly monitored (but avoiding information overload), and that internal mechanisms exist for disseminating information and acting on it.
- The main framework for the chapter is the categorisation of the marketing environment into STEP factors: sociocultural, technological, economic/competitive and political/legal.
- The first of the STEP factors is the sociocultural environment. This deals with 'hard' information, such as demographic trends, and with less tangible issues, such as changing tastes, attitudes and cultures. Knowledge of demographic trends gives the marketer a basic feel for how broad market segments are likely to change in the future. To gain the fullest picture, however, the marketer needs to combine demographic information with 'softer' data on how attitudes are changing.
- The second STEP factor is technology. An organisation's technological advances may arise from the exploitation of breakthroughs from other organisations, or may be the result of long-term investment in R&D in-house to solve a specific problem. Either way, technology can present the opportunity to create a clear differential advantage that cannot be easily copied by the competition.
- The economic and competitive environment constitutes the third STEP factor, and can be further divided into macro- and microeconomic environments. The macroeconomic environment analyses the effects of the broader economic picture, looking at issues such as taxation, government spending and interest rates. It also takes account of the threats, opportunities and barriers arising from membership of international trading blocs. The microeconomic environment is a little closer to the individual organisation, and is concerned with the structure of the market(s) in which it operates.

- The final STEP factor is the political and legal environment. Laws, regulations and codes of practice emanate from national governments, the EU, local government, statutory bodies and trade associations to affect the way in which organisations do business. Consumer groups and other pressure groups, such as those representing the ecological movement, health issues and animal rights, are active in trying to persuade government to deregulate or legislate, or to influence the scope and content of new legislation.

key words and phrases

Demographics
Economic and competitive environment
Environmental scanning
Political and legal environment
SEM
Sociocultural environment
STEP
Technological environment

questions for review

2.1 What is environmental scanning, why is it important, and what are the potential problems of implementing it?

2.2 What kind of information does the study of demographics cover?

2.3 Summarise the main implications of the SEM for organisations doing business within the EU.

2.4 Differentiate between the macro- and microeconomic environments.

2.5 What are the four main types of market structure?

questions for discussion

2.1 What sources of published demographic data are available in your own university or college library?

2.2 Find and discuss examples of products that are particularly vulnerable to changing consumer tastes.

2.3 To what extent, and why, do you think marketers should be seen to lead the way in addressing 'ethical' issues rather than waiting until consumer concern reaches a level where the organisation is prompted to react?

2.4 What are the differences between the ASA and the ITC? Find and discuss recent examples of adjudications by these two bodies (or equivalent regulatory bodies in your own country). Do you agree with their judgement?

2.5 Using Figure 2.1 as a framework, choose a product and list under each of the STEP factors the relevant influences that have helped to make that product what it is.

case study 2.1

Sanpro

Sanpro or fempro, otherwise known as female sanitary protection (tampons, towels and panty liners) is a massive market, worth some £280 million in the UK, but one that is very difficult for marketers to deal with because of the sensitivities involved.

The balance of the market between tampons (for internal use) and towels (for external use) has changed, partly because of technological development, and partly because of consumer health worries. Advances in the field of superabsorbents has meant that towels can be thinner and more discreet, yet still provide reliability and reassurance. This has made them more acceptable to many women. Added to that, publicity over the risks of toxic shock syndrome (TSS) that can arise from tampon use has put users off these products. This means that in 2000 towels had 62 per cent of the market by value with tampons lagging behind with only 38 per cent (*The Grocer*, 2001d; Mintel, 2001).

The competitive structure of this market has also changed over recent years. In 1997, Procter & Gamble (P&G) took over Tambrands, manufacturer of Tampax.

Although the UK market is now dominated by P&G, which claims over 56 per cent of the tampon sector with Tampax and nearly 48 per cent of the towel sector with Always and Alldays, the threat from supermarket own-brands has increased. Although the growth in own-brands is still slow, the fact that grocery multiples distribute 62 per cent of all products in this market means that the threat must be taken seriously (*The Grocer*, 2001d; Mintel, 2001). One result of all this is to put pressure on the manufacturer brands to maintain a high level of marketing support, yet this is against a backdrop of falling sales value. While sales volumes remained static between 1995 and 2000, because of price pressure from the major supermarkets, sales value actually fell by 13 per cent (Mintel, 2001). This means that manufacturers are particularly keen to ensure that their marketing support is cost-effective and efficient in achieving objectives.

Marketing support in terms of advertising is a very sensitive area. Although press advertising in women's magazines can be quite explicit, many older women in particular are embarrassed about the nature of the product, and do not want to watch television advertisements for tampons, for instance, with other members of the family. Because of this, until 1986 sanpro products could not be advertised on terrestrial television in the UK at all, but gradually the regulatory bodies began to relax the rules. It was only after 1 August 1998, however, that sanpro could be freely advertised around all programmes (except those targeted at children) at any time of day. One of the problems arising from all the restrictions was that the advertisements were often so inoffensive that they did not offer any useful information to women, and clichéd imagery of active young women in tight shorts leading incredibly active and enjoyable lives was felt by many to be patronising. Cinema is seen as a viable alternative to television advertising. According to a survey 79 per cent of all women go to the cinema, nearly 30 per cent more than ten years ago. In the 18- to 34-year-old age group the figure rises to 92 per cent, and 40 per cent go at least once a month (McLuhan, 2000).

Because of the level of competition and sensitivity about the product, sales promotions play an important role. Teenagers are a prime target for the manufacturers, as a high degree of brand loyalty is established in the early years of usage. Promotions such as free tampon containers, discounts for multiple purchases and joint promotions with skin care brands all help to encourage product trial. Investment in education is also important. SCA, owner of the Bodyform brand which holds a 15 per cent share of the external protection market, targets the 9- to 14-year-old age group through educational packages distributed through schools. The company entered into a joint promotion with teenage magazine *Mizz* and in 2000 distributed 500,000 mini-magazines to 3,500 schools. The Mizz-branded magazines contained features appealing to both boys and girls as well as Bodyform samples. SCA also benefited by learning more about the target market through the pupils and teachers who filled in questionnaires or entered competitions in the magazine (Miller, 2000).

The internet too has a lot of potential for reaching the younger target audience. In 2000, P&G launched BeingGirl.com (Neff, 2000), a website targeted at teens with a core focus on facts and advice on menstruation and TSS, along with product information about Tampax, Always and Alldays including a graphic description of 'how to use a tampon' with a downloadable video clip (don't even ask!). The overall character of the site, though, is that of a teen magazine with a chatroom and features on the usual teen preoccupations of boyfriends and zits.

A highly competitive saturated market, at least in the USA and Europe, has also driven new product innovations. SCA, for example, launched a string pantyliner and a string towel. Martin Hodson, the marketing manager said,

> *But around 15 per cent of women now wear G-string underwear and the success of String pantyliners has shown there is still opportunity* (as quoted by *The Grocer*, 2001a).

The launch of the String Towel included not only television advertising, but also cinema, outdoor posters and washroom advertising, postcards in women's health clubs, sampling campaigns, in-store displays, advertisements in retailers' magazines, and posters on retailers' customer toilet doors.

> *We have tried to spread the net to reach women where they actually are. instead of relying on traditional channels* (Martin Hodson, as quoted by McLuhan, 2000).

The Bodyform brand's marketing budget is about £3.2mn (*The Grocer*, 2001a).

Sources: Benady (1997); McLuhan (2000); Miller (2000); Neff (2000); The Grocer (2001a; 2001d); Mintel (2001); http://www.BeingGirl.com.

Questions

1. Outline the ways in which the STEP factors affect this market.
2. Why do you think sales promotions are particularly effective for these products?
3. What do you think might be the potential problems of using interactive websites such as BeingGirl.com to target the teenage groups?
4. In terms of the marketing environment, how does this product category differ from (a) toilet paper and (b) condoms?

case study 2.2

A Friend in need is a Friend indeed

Lofthouse of Fleetwood Ltd is a family-owned company based on the coast in the north-west of England. The company began in 1865 when a Fleetwood pharmacist, James Lofthouse, developed a warming lozenge for trawlermen to suck while at sea. That lozenge, branded as Fisherman's Friend, grew from its small beginnings into what is now a global business. Billions of Fisherman's Friend lozenges are sold every year in over 100 different countries. The main ingredients, including menthol, eucalyptus oil and capsicum tincture, make the lozenge a hot prospect and it is endorsed by medical authorities as an excellent means of clearing bronchial congestion. Although purely medicated confectionery, Fisherman's Friend holds ISO 2002 accreditation.

Because of its heritage, Fisherman's Friend is perceived in the UK as a 'semi-medicated' product, positioned alongside Tunes and Hall's Mentholyptus cough sweets. In overseas markets, however, where the product has no historical roots, Fisherman's Friend is positioned and accepted as 'adult confectionery'. The UK perceptions are reinforced by the retail trade which, in some cases, still sees Fisherman's Friend as a winter product and so does not give it optimum shelf space in the summer months. It is true to say that in past years, sales have experienced peaks and troughs and this is still the case in the UK. In newer markets, where the brand is treated purely as confectionery, there is much less seasonality and the product retains its normal shelf position throughout the year.

Another problem in the UK market for a brand trading on a heritage established over 130 or more years is that many of its loyal customers are from older age groups. The company wants to target a younger market but has found it hard to change the heritage perceptions and create a 'cool' image. The perceptions among the young are still that it is 'the sort of product Granny buys', that 'it'll blow your head off' and that 'I haven't tried it and I know I won't like it'. Despite innovative advertising, those perceptions and the view of Fisherman's Friend being a medicinal product that 'I'll only take as a last resort' still persist. Efforts have been made to get the product sampled by younger consumers. It has been included, for example, in student welcome packs on university and college campuses. Nevertheless, there is still the reaction 'I've tried it once and I didn't like it' to be overcome.

Medicine or sweetie? In any event, brace yourself!

Source: Kelly Weedon Shute Ltd.

To extend the brand, over fifteen years or so from the mid-1980s, variants on the Original Extra Strong Fisherman's Friend brand were introduced. The first was an aniseed flavoured Fisherman's Friend. This has a milder flavour than the original and is targeted at the younger audience which dislikes the strong flavour of the original. A mint flavour was then developed in order to move the brand further towards the mainstream confectionery sector. Other products have been developed to meet the needs of export markets. The Norwegian market, for example, is very health conscious and wanted a sugar-free version. This caused some manufacturing problems for the company, however. The traditional method of making a hard lozenge did not work well with sugar substitutes as they absorbed too much moisture from the air and turned the lozenges very soggy very quickly. Thus a new method was introduced which compresses dry powders into hard tablets. This is very similar to the way in which the pharmaceutical industry makes aspirin tablets, for instance. The investment in the new method proved to be well worthwhile. Original, mint and lemon sugar-free Fisherman's Friends have all proved successful, not only in Scandinavia but also in the UK and other markets.

The company feels that research is an important basis for the strategic thinking that has driven these developments of the brand. Research has shown, for example, that there are different flavour preferences in different countries and the company exploits this information. Fruit flavours are preferred in southern European markets, such as Greece, Italy and Spain, where citrus fruits are grown, while northern Europe and Scandinavia prefer the non-fruit flavours. In France and the Far East, consumers have a milder palate, preferring the newer flavours that are less hot than the original Fisherman's Friend. Focus groups are also used as part of the market research effort to test advertising awareness and recall, and price perceptions. Blind tastings have also provided feedback which has allowed the company to identify the potential of new flavour variants.

In all its markets, including the UK, the company uses independent distributors to sell and distribute the product. Lofthouse of Fleetwood has no sales force of its own. 'Our forte is manufacturing quality products. It's what we enjoy and it's what we do best,' said Duncan Lofthouse, a Director of the company. The company does not consider sales, marketing and logistics to be its strengths, and so it contracts out those activities. Nevertheless, the company still involves itself in the major decision-making. Its in-house technical and planning department designs the packaging, and the company retains control over its own brand. The company tries to keep a consistent brand image in all its markets, but some adaptation to suit local needs is necessary. For humid markets, such as those in the Far East, the brand's packaging has had to be adapted to include a foil lining to preserve the product and prevent it from going soggy. This gives it the same three-year shelf life as the paper packs have in other markets. Otherwise, the packaging is almost identical in all markets. The Fisherman's Friend brand name is in English on the front of all packs, but the back of the pack varies from market to market. The brand name can be represented in the local script (for example, in China, Thailand and Greece) and the local labelling regulations fulfilled.

Lofthouse of Fleetwood liaises closely with the specialist companies it works with. For example, it has worked for 26 years with an independent sales and marketing company, Impex Management Company Ltd which represents only Fisherman's Friend. The relationship involves mutual respect and mutual dependency and works well. Impex and Lofthouse of Fleetwood sit down together to discuss the direction of Fisherman's Friend and the business's objectives and five-year plan.

Source: With grateful thanks to Tony and Duncan Lofthouse.

Questions

1. Summarise the STEP factors that might have affected Lofthouse of Fleetwood's marketing decisions.
2. Why is market research so important to this company?
3. Why should Lofthouse of Fleetwood want to reach a younger market? What is it doing and what more could it do to reach this audience?
4. Lofthouse of Fleetwood contracts its marketing activities to an independent company, Impex, so that it can focus on manufacturing. Does this make Lofthouse of Fleetwood a production or product-orientated company?

References for chapter 2

Aguilar, F.J. (1967), *Scanning the Business Environment*, Macmillan.

Arminas, D. (2001), 'Plans to Hit New Outsourcing Heights', *Supply Management*, 29 March, p. 9.

Asian Business (2001), 'Exercise on Emirates', *Asian Business*, June, p. 34.

Barber, L. (1997), 'Guide to Enlarging the EU Eastwards', *Financial Times*, 8 December, p. 2.

Bedington, E. (2001), 'The Regeneration Game', *The Grocer*, 19 May, pp. 36–8.

Benady, D. (1997), 'P&G Gambles on Tambrands', *Marketing Week*, 17 April, pp. 32–3.

Bremner, C. (1997), 'All Because the Belgians Do Not Like Milk Tray', *The Times*, 24 October, p. 5.

Business Europe (2000), 'A New Strategy on VAT', *Business Europe*, 3 July, p. 7.

Chaffey, D. (2002), *E-business and E-commerce Management: Strategy, Implementation and Practice*. Financial Times-Prentice Hall, Pearson Education, Harlow, UK

Chesshyre, T. (2001), 'Over 50 But Not Up the Creek', *The Times*, 5 May.

Competition Commission (2001), 'Lloyds TSB Group plc and Abbey National plc: A Report on the Proposed Merger'. accessed via http://www.competition-commission.gov.uk.

Cook, S. (2001), 'When the Activists Come to Call', *Management Today*, May, pp. 64–71.

Delmas, M. and Terlaak, A. (2001), 'A Framework for Analyzing Environmental Voluntary Agreements', *California Management Review*, 43 (3), pp. 44–63.

Dittmar, H. and Pepper, L. (1994), 'To Have is to Be: Materialism and Person Perception in Working Class and Middle Class British Adolescents', *Journal of Economic Psychology*, 15 (2), pp. 233–51.

DTI (2000), *Business In The Information Age – International Benchmarking Study 2000*. UK Department of Trade and Industry. Based on 6,000 phone interviews across businesses of all sizes in eight countries. Statistics update: available online at: www.ukonlineforbusiness.gov.uk.

Durham, M. (2001), 'Australia Launches DVT Investigation', *The Independent*, 9 August.

Echison, W. and Ginsburg, J. (2001), 'Denmark Inherits the Wind', *Business Week*, 30 April, pp. 126B–126C.

Ecklof, B. *et al.* (1996), 'Venous Thromboembolism in Association With Prolonged Air Travel', *Dermatol Surg*, 22 (July), pp. 637–41.

The Economist (2001a), 'Britain: Testing Times', *The Economist*, 20 January, p. 50.

The Economist (2001b), 'From Bad to Worse, Down on the Farm', *The Economist*, 3 March, pp. 45–6.

The Economist (2001c), 'Glut, Fraud and Eco-damage', *The Economist*, 30 June, pp. 46–7.

The Economist (2000), 'Europe: Sweden Bottles Up', *The Economist*, 26 February, p. 62.

Financial Market Trends (2001), 'Recent Privatisation Trends', *Financial Market Trends*, June, p. 43.

Financial Times (2001), 'Interbrew's Victory May Speed Reform of UK Competition Procedures', *Financial Times*, 25 June, accessed via http://www.FT.com.

Fiorino, F. (2001), 'Anxious Passengers Seek Answers on DVT Risk', *Aviation Week and Space Technology*, 29 January, pp. 50–1.

The Grocer (2001a), 'Invisible Strings Attached', *The Grocer*, 13 January.

The Grocer (2001b), 'Bananas: Hanging in the Balance', *The Grocer*, 20 January.

The Grocer (2001c), 'US: Chiquita Poised to Slip on Bananas', *The Grocer*, 27 January.

The Grocer (2001d), 'Brandwatch: Mintel Category Report: Sanpro', *The Grocer*, 10 March.

The Grocer (2001e), 'Sugar, Rice, Bananas: New Treaty will Liberate Imports', *The Grocer*, 10 March.

The Grocer (2001f), 'Reassuring Consumers', *The Grocer*, 5 May, p. 23.

The Grocer (2001g), 'Danone: Calcium Claim is Misleading', *The Grocer*, 12 May.

The Grocer (2000a), 'Corned Beef Boosts Your Sperm Count', *The Grocer*, 9 September.

The Grocer (2000b), 'The Food Agenda, Let it Be Real', *The Grocer*, 11 November.

The Grocer (2000c), 'Brussels Report: EU Blocking Trade Tactics, *The Grocer*, 2 December.

Hardcastle, S. (2001), 'Deli and Food to Go', *The Grocer*, 26 May, pp. 49–50.

Hiscock, J. (2001), 'Biggest Brands', *Marketing*, 19 August.

Hunt, J. (2001), 'The Good Life', *The Grocer*, 7 April, pp. 32–4.

IBM (2001a), accessed via http://www.ibm.com/annualreport/2000/, October 2001.

IBM (2001b), accessed via http://www.research.ibm.com, October 2001.

Innocenti, N. (2001), 'Open Skies or Empty Skies for South Africa', *Financial Times*, 6 August, accessed via http://www.FT.com.

International Tax Review (2001), 'UK Delays EU Web Tax Law', *International Tax Review*, June, p. 5.

Jagger, S. (1998), 'State of the European Union', *Marketing Week*, 24 September, pp. 40–1.

Jardine, A. (2000), 'ASA Slams Iceland Over GM Ad Claims', *Marketing*, 11 May, p. 1.

Jardine, A. (1999), 'How Far Can You Go Before an Ad is Banned?', *Marketing*, 8 April, p. 14.

Jordan, J. (2001), 'Medical Risks Associated with Air Travel', accessed via http://www.caami.jccbi.gov, June 2001.

Kite, M. and Bird, S. (2000), 'Airlines Urged to Offer Passengers "Long Leg Class"', *The Times*, 23 November.

Laschefski, K. and Freris, N. (2001), 'Saving the Wood', *The Ecologist*, July/August, pp. 40–3.

Marketing Week (2001), 'Goodyear Treads New Ground Using Maize', *Marketing Week*, 28 June, p. 6.

McLuhan, R. (2000), 'Women Demand a Fresh Perspective', *Marketing*, 25 May, pp. 35–6.

Miller, R. (2000), 'Making the Most of Brand Alliances', *Marketing*, 3 February, pp. 25–6.

Milmo, D. (2001), 'EU Moves on Animal Tested Cosmetics', *Chemical Market Reporter*, 9 April, p. 8.

Mintel (2001), 'Sanitary Protection', *Market Intelligence*, February.

Neff, J. (2000), 'P&G's BeingGirl Mixes Sex Chat and Product Pitch', *Advertising Age*, 31 July, p. 38–9.

OFT (2001), 'A Report of the OFT Enquiry into the Funeral Industry', accessed via http://www.oft.gov.uk, July 2001.

Patten, S. (2000), 'Supermarkets The Catalyst for Fuel Retailing Revolution', *The Times*, 13 September, p. 27.

Professional Engineering (2001), '$160m Orders Shore Up Two Ailing Shipbuilders', *Professional Engineering*, 13 June, p. 4.

Schmitt, W. (2001), 'Green Tire Demand Adds Market Momentum', *Chemical Week*, 7 March, p. 41.

Shannon, J. (1998), 'Seniors Convert to Consumerism', *Marketing Week*, 10 September, p. 22.

Shrimsley, R. and Guerrera, F. (2001), 'Huntingdon Granted Facilities', *Financial Times*, 1 July, accessed via http://www.FT.com.

Simms, J. (2001), 'EU Rules, OK?', *Marketing*, 25 January, pp. 23–5.

Smith, C. (2001), 'Think Long Term or be Left Behind by EU Legislation', *Marketing*, 25 January, p. 19.

Sparaco, P. (2001), 'Airbus Thinks Bigger, Not Faster', *Aviation Week and Space Technology*, 18 June, pp. 106–12.

Thornton, P. (2001), 'Smugglers May Come to Aid of Chancellor's Growth Forecast', *The Independent*, 29 August, p. 11.

The Times (2000), 'Airlines Neglect Passengers' Health', *The Times*, 22 November.

Tucker, E. (1997), 'MEPs Reject Chocolate Compromise', *Financial Times*, 24 October, p. 20.

Velloci, A. (2001), 'Singapore Airlines CEO Sees Mega Transport as "Inevitable"', *Aviation Week and Space Technology*, 16 April, pp. 68–9.

Watson, E. (2001), 'Blind Tasting', *The Grocer*, 9 June, pp. 38–9.

Webster, B. (2001), 'BA Faces Claim For "Failing to Warn" Health Danger', *The Times*, 31 July.

part two

CUSTOMERS AND MARKETS

3 consumer behaviour

4 B2B buying behaviour

5 segmenting markets

6 marketing information and research

Part one emphasised that the customer is the hub of the marketer's universe, so it is only fitting that Part two should give further consideration to this VIP. The dilemma is, however, that each customer is an individual with unique needs and wants, and no organisation can hope to please all of the people all of the time.

Chapter 3 focuses further on the individual as a customer, examining the influences on buying choices and habits, both psychological and social, while looking at the kinds of decision-making processes through which people might or might not go in making a purchase. This is particularly important given the range of cultures to be found across Europe. Chapter 4 explores similar themes, but this time for B2B customers, highlighting the differences between the personal and the corporate shopper.

Additionally, with improvements in distribution and the relaxation of economic barriers, European market potential for many products is unthinkably huge. Organisations therefore have to find ways of breaking markets down into manageably sized segments for each of which essential needs and wants can be defined. This allows a marketing mix to be designed that can at least please a substantial number of people for most of the time. Chapter 5 looks at ways in which this segmentation process can be designed and implemented. The final chapter in this part, Chapter 6, presents an overview of the role of research in defining, monitoring and assessing buyers, markets and marketing activities.

These four chapters are an important foundation for what follows, because context and meaning can only be given to the organisation's decisions on the marketing mix if there are adequate information flows and clear understanding of customers' needs and wants.

chapter 3

consumer behaviour

LEARNING OBJECTIVES

This chapter will help you to:

1. understand the decision-making processes that consumers go through as they make a purchase;
2. appreciate how those processes differ between different buying situations;
3. understand the influences that affect decision-making, whether environmental, psychological or sociocultural; and
4. appreciate the implications of those processes and influences for marketing strategies.

Introduction

In contrast to Chapter 2, which looked at the broad backdrop against which marketers have to do business, this chapter focuses closely on the consumer, who is at the centre of many a marketer's universe. While the consumer is part of the marketing environment, and is shaped to some extent by the influences already discussed in Chapter 2, it is also very important to understand the more personal and specific influences affecting consumers and the nature of the decision-making processes through which they go.

Figure 3.1 offers a deceptively simple model of buyer behaviour that summarises the content of this chapter. The decision-making process itself is presented as a logical flow of activities, working through from problem recognition to purchase to post-purchase evaluation. The next section of this chapter deals with this in depth. It is important, however, to recognise that it is difficult to generalise about purchasing situations, as the nature of the decision-making process is bound to differ according to the kind of product or service that is being considered. Later, therefore (pp. 104 *et seq.*), we discuss how the nature of the product and the situation facing the buyer could change the flow of the decision-making process. Compare, for example, what went into your decision to attend university or college with how you decide whether to visit a Pizza Hut or a nightclub.

You would be very interested in understanding consumer marketing if you made yogurt, a rapidly growing and dynamic product category worth £1.2 bn in the UK. The yogurt market is characterised by a variety of different products meeting different customer needs and usage occasions. It reflects many of the significant lifestyle trends in the food market such as increasing convenience, concern with healthy eating and a desire for value for money. Müller, the leading brand with 36 per cent of the market, has a record of innovation in providing brands to meet these different needs. The core market is met by Corners, the leading yogurt for family consumption. Müllerlight is aimed at the health-conscious by offering a virtually fat-free yogurt that has been actively promoted through sports, health clubs and to women who want to eat more healthily. At the other end of the market are products for those who don't care about the calorie count. The thicker and creamier, the better for self-indulgence. Other sectors include organic yogurts and children's products. Understanding the eating occasion, therefore, and the importance of different consumer preferences has been a powerful influence on product development and promotion in this category (Hardcastle, 2001).

The decision-making process is also affected by a number of other more complex influences, as can be seen in Figure 3.1. Some of these influences relate to the wider marketing environment in which the decision is being made (*see* pp. 107–9). Others, however, relate to the individual purchaser and

Figure 3.1 The consumer buying decision-making process and its influencing factors

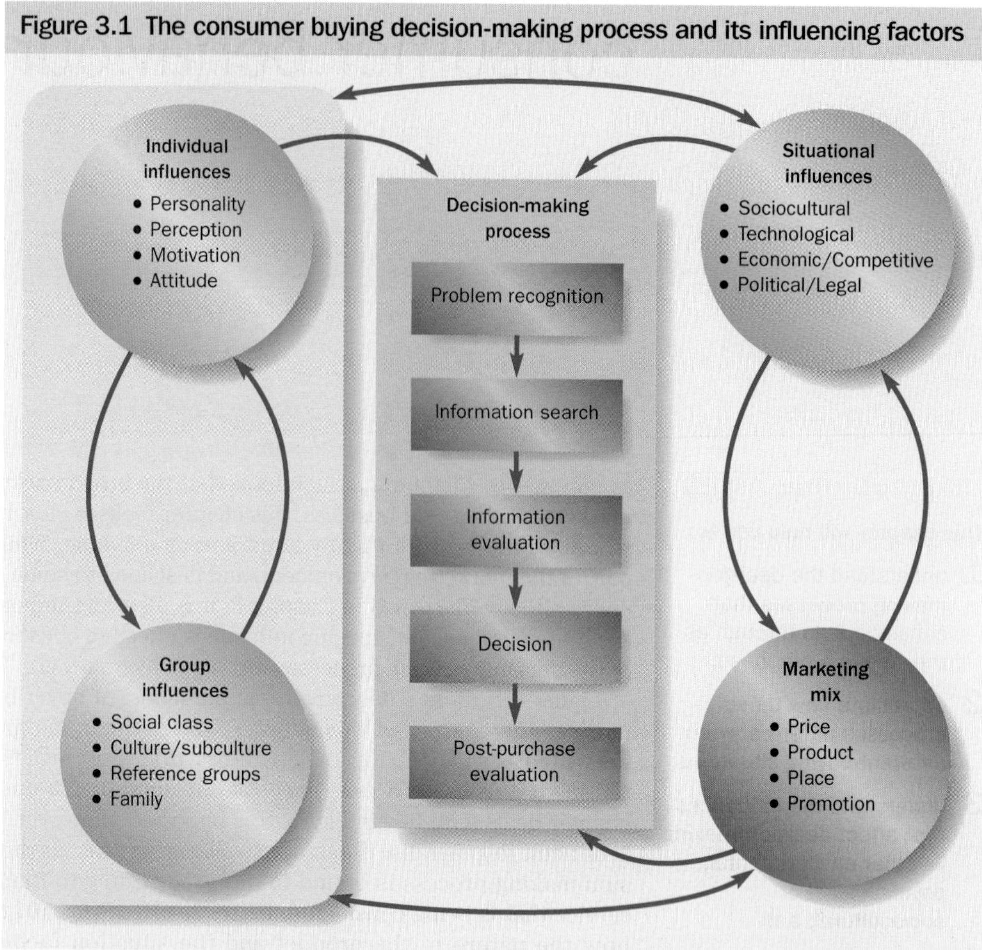

therefore pp. 109–18 will consider those influences emanating from within the individual such as personality, attitudes and learning. Finally, pp. 118–28 will look at how the individuals decisions are affected by their social context, especially family and cultural groupings.

marketing *in action*

'The worst day of my life'

Emma turns to you on screen looking very distressed, with a child in the back seat. Her car has broken down and she should be meeting her boyfriend. She exclaims 'this is the worst day of my life'. Powerful advertising. It plays on the fact, identified by the UK's Automobile Association in 1993, that motorists find the prospect of breaking down very distressing and fear that it can be potentially dangerous if it happens at the wrong time in the wrong place. Emma then goes on to say that she had thought about taking breakdown cover 'but forgot'. Of course, the AA with its 3,500 patrols and even a special joining price is the solution. Of course, most motorists realise the potential danger and inconvenience of breaking down but it is too easy for them to think that it will not happen to them and thus put off signing up. Others, after a year or two of breakdown-free membership, decide to let it lapse. Retention, as well as recruitment, is high on the AA's agenda. The marketing challenge is to get motorists first to appreciate the consequences of a breakdown and the need for fast recovery (hence Emma), and then to take action, not with just any motoring organisation, but with the AA. None of that is easy, especially in a case like this where consumers are expected to buy a service they hope they will never need and the main benefit is 'peace of mind' rather than tangible benefit.

In the mid-1990s a campaign called 'the 4th Emergency Service' was used to cut through the motorist's inertia and to communicate the tangible and intangible benefits. It showed dramatic footage of the emergency services at work, ending with the 4th one, the AA patrolman/rescuer assisting with a roadside 'emergency'. Motorists' respect for the professionalism and essential nature of the emergency services was thus transferred to the AA by association. Over 60 per cent of respondents thought the AA was the 4th emergency service and this had risen to 97 per cent by 1998. Membership soared from 7.5 million to 9.3 million (Clay, 1998). By engendering such a belief, even if it is somewhat mistaken, gave the AA a clear competitive edge in terms of professional rescue over its increasing number of rivals who were competing on price and were communicating 'boring' messages such as their technical capabilities or how fast they could reach a breakdown.

The 4th emergency services positioning has survived, but is no longer the primary focus of communication, hence the Emma campaign (Reynolds, 2001). The new owners of the AA, Centrica, decided to retain the core brand values and the focus on the pre-eminence of roadside repair but wanted to stimulate further recruitment with the messages of reliability, honesty and caring. Emma offered the opportunity for a more direct message appeal emphasising the motorist's predicament and the professionalism of patrols operating at the roadside in difficult circumstances to solve the unwanted problem (Newland, 2000). Although the recall figures did not reach the levels of the 4th emergency service campaign, a 53 per cent figure was achieved.

Sources: Clay (1998); Newland (2000); Reynolds (2001).

The decision-making process

Even thinking about your own experiences as a consumer is enough to help you to appreciate the variety of goods that people purchase, the individuality of each purchasing episode and the complexity of the influences affecting the final decision. Nevertheless, there have been many attempts to create models of **consumer decision-making** of greater or lesser complexity and detail that try to capture the richness of the experience, such as those proposed by Howard and Sheth (1969) and Engel, Kollat and Blackwell (1978). The Engel, Blackwell and Miniard (1990) model presented here, although more concise and simpler in its outline, provides a framework that still allows us to consider, through discussion, many of the more complex elements. It traces the progress of a purchasing event stage by stage from the buyer's point of view, including the definition of likely information needs and a discussion of the level of rationality and analytical behaviour leading to the eventual decision.

We now look at each stage in turn.

Problem recognition

In trying to rationalise the decision-making process, this is a good place to begin. After all, if you are not aware that you have a 'problem', how can you decide to purchase something to solve it? More functional purchases, such as replenishing stocks of washing powder or petrol, may be initiated by a casual glance at current stock levels. Other purchases may be triggered by a definable event. If, for example, the exhaust falls off your car, you will soon become aware of the nature of the problem and the kind of purchase that will provide the remedy.

Those are very practical and straightforward examples, but not all situations are quite so self-explanatory. Where psychological needs are involved, the **problem recognition** may be a slow dawning or may lead to a sudden impulse, when the consumer, realising that the current position or feeling is not the desired one, decides to do something to change it through a purchase (Bruner and Pomazal, 1988). Imagine, for instance, that you are wandering round the supermarket after a tough day at work. You're tired, listless and a bit depressed. You've filled your trolley with the potatoes, bread and milk you intended to buy, but you also slip a bar of chocolate (or worse!) in there on the basis that it will cheer you up as you drive home. The 'problem' here is less definable, based on a vague psychological feeling, and it follows that the solution is also less definable – it could be chocolate, cream buns, wine or clothing, whatever takes the purchaser's fancy.

What the examples given so far do have in common, however, is that the impetus to go into a purchasing decision-making routine comes from the consumer. The consumer identifies or recognises the problem, independently from the marketer, and looks for a solution. As will be seen in the following sections, marketers can then use the marketing mix elements to influence the choice of solution. It is also possible, however, for marketers to trigger the process by using the marketing mix to bring a problem to the consumer's attention. If one was to be cynical, one could accuse them of deliberately creating problems in order to stimulate purchase.

eg

The manufacturers of Radion laundry products ran an advertising campaign in the UK featuring a housewife who suddenly realised that even though the shirt she was ironing had just been washed, there was still a sweaty smell clinging to its armpits. Radion, of course, has the power to eliminate this in the wash. Housewives across the country supposedly became racked with fear and guilt, asking themselves: 'Do I have this problem? Should I switch to Radion?' A problem had been created in the consumer's mind, and a decision-making process initiated, largely through the marketer's efforts.

There is, of course, a significant difference between being aware of a need or problem and being able to do something about it. Many needs are latent and remain unfulfilled, either because consumers decide not to do anything about it now, or because they are unable to do anything. We might all feel the need for a three-week holiday in some exotic part of the world, but we must not only be willing, but also financially able, to disappear over the horizon. Problem recognition, if it is to lead anywhere, therefore requires both the willingness and the ability to fulfil the emerging need.

Whether the problem recognition is stimulated internally (i.e. originates within the consumer) or externally (i.e. is triggered by marketing or other pressures), there are still several stages left in the decision-making process.

Information search

Defining the problem is one thing, but defining and implementing the solution is something else. The questions to be answered include what kind of purchase will solve the problem, where and how it can be obtained, what information is needed to arrive at a decision and where that information is available. In some cases, consumers will actively search out relevant information with a view to using it in making a decision, but they can also acquire information passively, storing it away until it is needed. Thus Bloch *et al.* (1986) distinguish between ongoing search (browsing and storing for future reference) and purposeful search with a particular objective in mind. Daily, consumers are exposed to a wide range of media all designed to influence awareness and recall of particular products and services. Thus they 'know' that Radion eliminates sweaty smells before they get anywhere near a conscious choice of laundry product in the supermarket. When they do get to the point of purchasing, the manufacturers hope that they will recall that knowledge and use it in making the brand choice.

Similarly, the Cheltenham & Gloucester mortgage advertisement is designed to appeal to someone who is already considering house purchase. It is hardly likely to inspire consumers to move house, but it could be useful if consumers are worried about finding the right mortgage for their circumstances before they start looking seriously. In some cases, a consumer might not be planning to move immediately, but the C&G would hope that they will recall the advertisement when the time does come.

The car exhaust example continues to be reasonably straightforward. You need a new exhaust and a supplier must be found. Since consumers usually fall back on their previous experiences and knowledge before undertaking time-consuming research, you may immediately think of a company that you have used before and have been satisfied with, one whose advertising you have seen, or perhaps you ask a close friend to recommend one. Not all external sources of information are controlled by the marketer – don't forget the power of word of mouth as a marketing tool. Friends, family and colleagues, for example, may all give advice, whether based on experience, knowledge or opinion, to the would-be decision maker in this phase. In choosing a university to study at, for example, many overseas students seek advice from friends who have already studied at various universities to narrow down the number of options to consider. Although the type of product and the importance of the purchase may differ, the basic principle is the same. People are more likely to trust information given through word of mouth, because the source is generally assumed to be unbiased and trustworthy, and the information itself often derives from first-hand experience.

In other situations, the consumer might seek out information from the internet, specialist publications, retailers or even from marketing literature. For example, when buying a car,

The information search is made easy with freefone and online access.

Source: C&G.

potential buyers will probably visit competing dealerships to talk to sales staff, look closely at the merchandise and collect brochures. Additionally, they might consult what they consider to be unbiased expert sources of advice such as *What Car?* magazine, and begin to take more notice of car advertisements in all media.

In replacing the car exhaust, of course, you might simply turn to the *Yellow Pages* (either online or the local hard copy directory) and look under 'Exhaust System Dealers'. The impulse buying of chocolate in the supermarket requires even less information searching than that. It is likely to be restricted to seeing what is available within that particular store at that particular time. Think about why this is the case before you get to the later section of this chapter on buying situations (pp. 104–7), where variations in the extent, rationality and formality of the information search in different situations will be discussed.

Hauser *et al.* (1993) emphasise the fact that time pressure can interfere with the information search. They found that consumers spend less time searching for different sources as pressure increases. At the other end of the spectrum, however, **information overload** may cause problems for the potential purchaser. There is evidence to suggest that consumers cannot cope with too much information at product level (Keller and Staelin, 1987). Thus the greater the relevance of the information to consumers, such as the key benefits and applications of the product, the easier it is for them to assimilate and process that information as part of their decision-making. In other words, better and more extensive information may actually lead to poorer buying decisions! Similarly, at brand level Jacoby *et al.* (1974) found on the one hand that more on-pack information tends to make it more difficult for the consumer to select the most appropriate brand, but on the other hand that more information positively affected the consumer's level of certainty and satisfaction regarding the selection. There is clearly a fine balance to be achieved between keeping imagery and messages clean,

e-marketing *in action*

Online searching behaviour

Specific behavioural traits are evident from consumer use of the internet and these have been summarised by Chaffey *et al.* (2002). Studies show that the world wide web is used quite differently by different groups of people. Marketers have to understand these variations in behaviour and provide website content and design consistent with these consumer needs. Lewis and Lewis (1997) identified five different types web users:

- *Directed information seekers*. Looking for product, market or leisure information such as details of their football club's fixtures. This type of user tends to be experienced in using the web and they are proficient in using search facilities.
- *Undirected information seekers*. These are the users usually referred to as surfers, who like to browse and change sites by following hyperlinks. This group tends to be novice users (but not exclusively so) and they may be more likely to click on banner advertisements.
- *Directed buyers*. These buyers are online to purchase specific products. For such users, brokers or cybermediaries who compare product features and prices will be important locations to visit.
- *Bargain hunters*. These users want to use the web to find offers available from sales promotions such as free samples or prizes.
- *Entertainment seekers*. Users looking to interact with the web for enjoyment through entering contests such as quizzes (e.g. You Don't know Jack at www.bezerk.com), puzzles or interactive multi-player games.

Although presented as generic types of users, the characteristics of users can, of course, vary between and within each session when they are logged on, varying for example according to whether they are using the web for work or recreation.

An alternative view of how consumer behaviour in using a website may vary is according to the stage they are in the adoption of a website. Breitenbach and van Doren (1998) make an assessment of how a web user passes through each stage. While such a model may be suitable for some sites which will be visited repeatedly such as a portal such as Yahoo! or MSN, it is less appropriate for a customer visiting a site a single time to make a one-off purchase. Marketers also review how e-marketing, in conjunction with traditional media, can support each of the stages in the buying process. For example:

1 *Generate awareness (of need, product or service)*. Generating awareness of need is conventionally achieved principally through mass media advertising. The internet is not very effective at this since it has a more limited reach than TV, radio or print media.
2 *Position features, benefits and brand*. Once a consumer is aware of a need and is considering what features and benefits they require from a product, then they may turn to the web to find out which suppliers are available or to find the range of features available from a particular type of product. Intermediaries are very important in supplier search and can also help in evaluation through detailed information and reviews.
3 *Lead generation*. Once customers are actively searching for products (the directed information seeker of Lewis and Lewis, 1997), the web provides an excellent medium to help achieve leads by offering incentives such as competitions or access to free information to encourage the user to complete an online form which can be used to profile their interests and find their contact information.
4 *Assist purchase decision*. One of the most powerful features of websites is their facility to carry a large amount of content at relatively low cost. This can be turned to advantage when customers are looking to identify the best product.
5 *Facilitate purchase*. Once a customer has decided to purchase, then a company will not want to lose their custom at this stage! However, some estimates place consumer attrition at 98 per cent of site visitors. The difficulty of placing orders causes consumers to use other sites or channels, so options to place the order by phone or fax should also be included.
6 *Support product use and retain business*. The internet also provides good potential for retaining customers since:
   - value-added services such as free customer support can be provided by the website which encourage repeat visits and provide value-added features;
   - feedback can be provided by customers on products which will indicate to customers that the company is looking to improve its service;
   - e-mail can be used to give regular updates on products and promotions and encourage customers to revisit the site;
   - repeat visits to sites provide opportunities for cross-selling and repeat selling through sales promotions owing to the amount of information that can be displayed on the website.

Sources: Breitenbach and van Doren (1998); Chaffey *et al.* (2002); Lewis and Lewis (1997).

simple and easily understood, and giving consumers enough information to allow them to appreciate the full depth of character of the product and the range of its potential benefits, so that they can develop appropriate expectations and post-purchase evaluative criteria.

Whatever form the information search takes, the data gathered are useless until they are evaluated. However, it is likely that many consumers proceed to evaluation with a minimum of information that furthermore may be too partial, biased or poorly structured for the decision that needs to be made. This is bound to influence the quality of the eventual decision.

Information evaluation

On what criteria do you evaluate the information gathered? An online search could generate over 1,000 entries to sift through and even a typical *Yellow Pages* could provide up to 10 pages of exhaust system dealerships, featuring over 100 potential outlets within reasonable travelling distance. If you have had no previous experience of any of them, then you have to find a means of differentiating between them. You are unlikely to investigate all of them, since that would take too long, and so you may draw up a shortlist on the basis of those with the biggest feature entries in *Yellow Pages*, those whose names pop up first in an internet search, or those who also advertise prominently in the local press or on television. Such advertising may emphasise the advantages of using a particular outlet, pointing out to the consumer what the appropriate evaluative criteria are (speed, friendliness or price, for example). Location may also be an important factor; some outlets are closer to home or work than others. You might telephone three or four of them, dismiss any whose telephone manner is either too surly or too patronising, then compare the rest on the basis of price or their ability to do the job immediately.

Meanwhile, back in the supermarket, your information evaluation is likely to be less time consuming and less systematic. Faced with a set of brands of chocolate that are known and liked, the evaluation is cursory: 'What do I feel like eating?' The nearest to systematic thinking might be (in desperation) the evaluation of which one really represents the most chocolate for the price. Of course, if a new brand has appeared on the chocolate shelf, then that might break the habitual, unconscious grabbing at the familiar wrapper, and make a consumer stop and look closely to evaluate what the new product has to offer in comparison with the old ones.

What has been happening to varying degrees in the above examples is that the consumer has started to narrow down from a wide list of potential options to an **evoked set** (Howard and Sheth, 1969), a final shortlist for serious appraisal. Being a part of the consumer's evoked set, and staying there, is clearly important to the marketer, although it is not always easy. Sutton (1987), for instance, found that it was easier for a new product or brand to enter the evoked set than it was for an existing one that had been considered previously, but rejected.

With the car exhaust, constructing the evoked set means narrowing down to the list of outlets that will be telephoned, whereas with the chocolate purchase, the unconscious visual scan across the shelf may lead to a more deliberate choice between a Snickers, a Mars bar and a Twix. To make a choice from within the evoked set, the consumer needs either a formal or an informal means of selecting from the small number of choices available. This, therefore, implies some definition of evaluative or choice criteria.

Again, marketers will be trying to influence this stage. This can be done, for example, through their communications campaigns (more of this in Chapter 14 and subsequent chapters) which may implant images of products in the consumer's mind so that they seem familiar (and therefore less threatening) at the point of sale. They may also stress particular product attributes, both to increase the importance of that attribute in the consumer's mind, i.e. to make sure that the attribute is number one on the list of evaluative criteria, and to ensure that the consumer believes that a particular brand is unsurpassed in terms of that attribute. Radion and residual armpit smells must be inextricably linked in the consumer's mind, and eradication of armpit smells must be important to the consumer. Point-of-sale material can also reinforce these things, for example through displays, leaflets, the wording on packaging (Chapter 7) and on-pack promotions.

marketing *in action*

Easy Cottages

Easy Cottages from Welcome Holidays from Skipton, Yorkshire, has re-invented itself through the use of an interactive website that frees the consumer from the drudgery of brochure shopping for a cottage to rent for a holiday. The company identified that potential customers often spent hours wading through brochures selecting ideal properties only to be disappointed after a phone call or letter enquiry tells them that the property is already let for the chosen weeks. Selecting a property was also confused by different price bands and various supplements and depending upon the party size and time of year. The Marketing Director of Welcome Holidays described the experience as a 'hardcore sales process'.

The company has 3,500 cottages in the UK, Ireland and France and claims to be the UK's largest and fastest growing independent holiday letting agency, largely achieved by going online with a quality offering and a caring approach to customer service. Over 250,000 people use Easy Cottages each year and 67 per cent of all bookings are made online: all from a marketing budget of just £45,000. The consumer is invited to select an area, specify dates and party size and then they can sit back and let the browser do the rest. Subject to availability, a range of properties are listed, all with photographs. With a further click, further photographs of the property are shown, both internal and external, along with a map and previous visitors' comments. Through a secure server, bookings can be made online or by telephone.

Welcome Holidays believes that it has helped to change the property selection process by making it more thorough and analytical. For those locked into set periods, the whole process used to be a mad scramble for places during the peak periods as soon as the brochure arrived on a Tuesday or Wednesday. Now, Sunday has become the peak booking day, and often later into the night, reflecting the more deliberate and thorough selection process. The consumer may never know what they have missed as an online brochure is constantly updated after new bookings.

Of course, the website is only part of the marketing mix. However, the Marketing Director claims that,

> *The nature of the internet is that it runs to the heart of your business and you have to redesign your business to meet it* (as quoted by *Marketing Week*, 2001).

There are, therefore, implications for customer handling, contact prior to the event and ensuring that promises can be delivered. The company still takes great care to offer only properties that meet its standards and regularly seeks customer feedback to ensure that the experience reality matches the service promise.

Source: *Marketing Week* (2001).

Generally, therefore, what is happening is that without necessarily being conscious of it, the potential buyer is constructing a list of performance criteria, then assessing each supplier or available brand against it. This assessment can be based on objective criteria, related to the attributes of the product and its use (price, specification, service, etc.), or subjective criteria such as status, fit with self-image or trust of the supplier.

To make the decision easier, abstract attributes, such as 'convenience', 'fun' or 'ease of use', are more likely to be used when direct comparison between choices is not easy (Korfman, 1991), for example chocolate vs biscuits, going to the cinema vs going to a nightclub, or even *Shakespeare in Love* vs *Reservoir Dogs* at the video hire shop! Making any decision can be a demanding exercise in terms of time and mental effort, and thus the consumer often adopts mental 'rules of thumb' that cut corners and lead to a faster decision. The consumer is especially prepared to compromise on the quality and thoroughness of assessment when the problem-solving situation is less risky and complicated. Table 3.1, based on the work of Duncan (1990), highlights some of the market beliefs widely held by consumers. These beliefs may not relate directly to the specific **purchasing situation** in hand, but they do act as general decision rules to cut out many of the tedious preliminaries of assessing alternative products. They may focus on brand, store choice, pricing, promotion or packaging, and will serve to limit the size of the evoked set and to eliminate some of the options.

All of this sets the scene for the next stage in the process: the decision.

Decision

The decision may be a natural outcome of the evaluation stage, if one supplier is noticeably more impressive on all the important criteria than the rest. If the choice is not as clear cut as this, the consumer may have to prioritise the criteria further, perhaps deciding that price

Table 3.1 Consumer market beliefs

Products and brands
- The best brands are the ones that sell best
- National brands (manufacturer or retail) are always better than local ones unless you know better
- Generic brands are well-known brand names sold under a different label
- Keep clear of products new to the market until 'bugs' have been ironed out

Store
- You can tell a store by its window display
- Larger stores offer better prices than smaller ones
- Speciality stores are great for learning about product options, but it is best to buy from a discount store
- A store that offers good value on some of its items probably offers it on all its items
- Small stores give better, more personal service than large ones

Price
- Higher prices within a store often mean higher quality
- Sale items can involve seconds and poorer quality merchandise
- Sales are designed to move poor sellers
- Prices will fall soon after the product is launched

Promotion
- When purchasing heavily advertised products you pay for the label and advertising, not higher quality
- The harder the sell, the poorer the product quality
- Free gifts linked to products mean the product may not be up to much

Packaging
- Big containers are always cheaper per unit than smaller sizes
- Environmentally friendly packaging adds cost to the product
- Quality packaging means a quality product

Source: Adapted from Duncan (1990).

or convenience is the one overriding factor. In the car exhaust example, the decision-making is a conscious act, whereas with the impulse purchase of chocolate, the decision may be made almost unconsciously.

In any case, at this stage the consumer must finalise the proposed deal, and this may take place in a retail store, over the telephone, by mail or in the consumer's own home. In the supermarket, finalising the deal may be as simple as putting the bar of chocolate into the trolley with the rest of the shopping and then paying for it at the checkout. With more complex purchases, however, the consumer may have the discretion to negotiate the fine details of cash or credit, any trade-in, order quantity and delivery dates, for example. This negotiation (see Chapter 17 for more on negotiation) may involve further trading of concessions between variables, so that, for instance, you can have your new car within a week as long as you are prepared to accept a red one. If the outcome of the negotiation is not satisfactory, then the consumer may regretfully decide not to go ahead with the purchase after all, or rethink the decision in favour of another supplier – you cannot be certain of your customer until they have either handed over their money or signed the contract!

Suppliers can, of course, make it easy or difficult for potential customers to make their purchases. Lack of sales assistants on the shopfloor, long queues or bureaucratic purchasing procedures may all tax the patience of consumers, giving them time either to decide to shop elsewhere or not to bother buying at all. Even if they do persist and make the purchase (eventually), their impression of the supplier's service and efficiency is going to be damaged and this may influence their repeat purchasing behaviour negatively. A traveller who has to queue for 20 minutes to buy a rail ticket from a cashier may well decide to travel by car next time, whereas one who can purchase a ticket quickly through an automated ticketing machine, such as those found in railway stations and more recently in airports around Europe, will have no negative impressions of service provision.

eg

Vending machines make it easy for the consumer to make a decision and take action almost immediately, as long as they have some loose change in their pockets. Despite the sometimes infuriating ability of machines to gobble up coins faster than they are able to dispense goods, the vending industry in the UK alone is worth £2.5 bn of which £1 bn is generated from refreshment sales. Where impulse purchases are important, such as the confectionery sector in which up to 70 per cent of sales are impulse-led, what is presented, the familiarity of the brand names, and how they are presented can be vital to the sale, thus the growth of chilled and glass-fronted cabinets. New target sectors are being attacked by vending operators to make it easier for you to part with your money whenever and wherever you want. Vending machines for ping-pong balls and swimming hats are popping up in sports centres and you can now buy that desperately needed computer disk from machines in many educational establishments (http://www.ukvending.co.uk).

Even assuming that all these barriers are overcome, the story does not end here. The consumer's involvement with the product does not finish when cash changes hands, nor should the marketer's involvement with the consumer.

Post-purchase evaluation

Whatever the purchase, there is likely to be some level of **post-purchase evaluation** to assess whether the product or its supplier lived up to the expectations raised in the earlier stages of the process. Particularly if the decision process has been difficult, or if the consumer has invested a lot of time, effort and money in it, then there may be doubt as to whether the right decision has actually been made. This is what Festinger (1957) labelled **cognitive dissonance**, meaning that consumers are 'psychologically uncomfortable', trying to balance the choice made against the doubts still held about it. Such dissonance may be aggravated where consumers are exposed to marketing communication that sings the praises of the features and benefits of the rejected alternatives. Generally speaking, the more alternatives that have been rejected, and the more comparatively attractive those alternatives appear to be, the greater the dissonance. Conversely, the more similar to the chosen product the rejected alternatives are, the less the dissonance. It is also likely that dissonance will occur with more significant purchases, such as extended problem-solving items like cars and houses, because the buyer is far more likely to review and assess the decision consciously afterwards.

Clearly, such psychological discomfort is not pleasant and the consumer will work towards reducing it, perhaps by trying to filter out the messages that undermine the choice made (for example advertising for a product that was a rejected alternative) and paying extra attention to supportive messages (for example advertising for the chosen alternative). This all underlines the need for post-purchase reassurance, whether through advertising, after sales follow-up calls and even the tone of an instruction manual ('Congratulations on choosing the Acme Home Nuclear Reactor Kit, we know it will give you many years' faithful service . . .'). Consumers like to be reminded and reassured that they have made a wise choice, that they have made the best choice for them. From the marketer's point of view, as well as offering post-purchase reassurance, they can minimise the risk of dissonance by making sure that potential buyers have a realistic picture of the product, its capabilities and its characteristics. Exaggerated advertising simply raises expectations that cannot possibly be fulfilled in reality, and disappointment and dissonance are almost certain. Another way of making sure that the potential buyer's expectations are rooted in reality is to let them sample the product before purchase, where possible. With fmcg (fast moving consumer goods) products, this is relatively simple to do and allows consumers to pass judgement on product benefits based on experience, rather than simply on what an advertiser tells them (*see* Chapter 16 for more on sampling). With a higher priced, less frequently purchased product such as a car, it is more difficult to offer samples, but at least a long test drive can go some way to creating realistic expectations and emphasising potentially negative points before the customer commits to a purchase.

Thus the post-purchase evaluation stage is important for a number of reasons. Primarily, it will affect whether the consumer ever buys this product again. If expectations have not been met, then the product may not even make the shortlist next time. If, on the other hand, expectations have been met or even exceeded, then a strong possibility of lasting loyalty has been created. The next shortlist may be a shortlist of one! It is important to remember that consumers are not passive, inanimate elements in the marketing process. They do not fade away into insignificance if their relationship with a particular product or supplier ends. According to Smith (1993), dissatisfied customers will tell up to 11 other people about their bad experience, which is two to three times more people than a satisfied customer will talk to. Thus it is important for the marketer to consider how the risks of a poor outcome at the post-purchase phase can best be reduced.

eg

Consumer post-purchase evaluation is personal and subjective and can sometimes even lead to an exaggerated perception of a product's benefits. Household anti-bacterial sprays and germ killers, for example, appear to get things clean, fresh and sparkling. Their advertising and packaging present a confident, no-nonsense image, they promise protection and the total annihilation of dirt and bugs, and their contents often smell strong and powerful. All of these pre- and post-purchase messages, influences and experiences lead some consumers to think that such cleaning products are an adequate substitute for good general kitchen hygiene. Thus 20 per cent of consumers do not change their dishcloths regularly and over 65 per cent do not wash their hands before preparing food. Some experts have criticised manufacturers for lulling them into a false sense of security. Perhaps, the experts say, consumer education should be a much higher priority so that the limits of such products and their proper role within good hygiene practice are better understood (Mintel, 2000b; Norton, 1997).

As has been mentioned already, the marketer can influence the information evaluation that sets up product performance criteria in the consumer's mind. Marketing is about making promises, and the post-purchase evaluation is, to some extent, a measure of how true those promises were. If, therefore, the needs and wants of the consumer have been carefully researched and the marketing mix tailored, balanced and implemented accordingly, then the post-purchase stage should be a happy one for all parties.

Monitoring of post-purchase feelings is an important task of marketing, not only to identify areas in which the product (or its associated marketing mix) falls short of expectations, but also to identify any unexpectedly pleasant surprises the purchaser may have had. The product may, for instance, have strengths that are being undersold. This is a natural part of the cycle of product and service development, improvement and evolution.

To recap on the stages in the decision-making process, look at Figure 3.2. This summarises the general process, and then shows its specific application in the context of (a) the impulse purchase of chocolate, and (b) buying and fitting a car exhaust.

There are some points to note about the process as presented here. First, the consumer may choose to end the process at any stage. Perhaps the information search reveals that there is no obvious acceptable solution to the problem, or the information evaluation demonstrates that the cost of solving the problem is too high. It is, of course, the marketer's job to sustain the consumer's interest throughout this process and to prevent them from opting out of it. Second, the process does not necessarily have to run from stage 1 to stage 5 in an unbroken flow. The consumer may backtrack at any point to an earlier stage and reiterate the process. Even on the verge of a decision, it may be felt necessary to go back and get more information, just to make sure. Finally, the time taken over the process may vary enormously, depending on the nature of the purchase and the nature of the purchaser. Many months of agonising may go into making an expensive, important purchase, while only a few seconds may be invested in choosing a bar of chocolate. The next section looks more closely at this issue.

Figure 3.2 The decision-making processes for chocolate and car exhausts

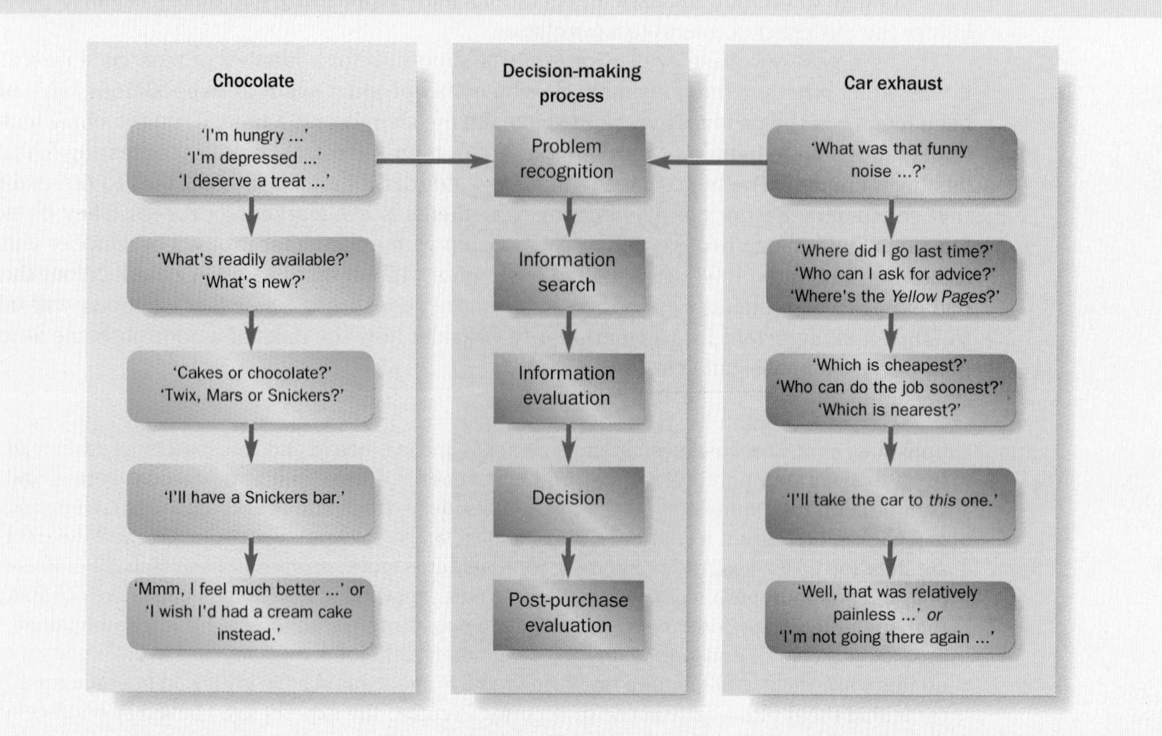

Buying situations

In the discussion of the decision-making process, it has been made clear that both the flow and the formality of the process, and the emphasis that is put on each stage, will vary from situation to situation. Some of these variations are to do with the particular environment relevant to the transaction (*see* p. 107 *et seq.*), while others emanate from the consumer (pp. 109 *et seq.*) or from the consumer's immediate social surroundings (pp. 118 *et seq.*). The current section, however, will look more closely at the effect of the type of *purchasing situation* on the extent and formality of the decision-making process.

Routine problem solving

As the heading of this section implies, a **routine problem solving** purchasing situation is one that the consumer is likely to experience on a regular basis. Most grocery shopping falls into this category, where particular brands are purchased habitually without recourse to any lengthy decision-making process. As with the chocolate-buying example above, there is virtually no information search and evaluation, and the buying decision is made simultaneously with (if not in advance of) the problem recognition stage. This explains why many fmcg manufacturers spend so much time and effort trying to generate such loyalty and why it is so difficult for new products to break into an established market. When the consumer thinks 'We've run out of Colgate' rather than 'We've run out of toothpaste', or when beans really does mean Heinz, then the competition has an uphill marketing task on its hands.

As well as building regular shopping habits, i.e. brand loyalty, the manufacturer is also trying to capitalise on impulse purchasing of many products within this category. While toothpaste and beans can be the objective of a planned shopping trip ('When I go to the supermarket, I need to get . . .'), some other products may be purchased as the result of a sudden impulse. The impulse may be triggered, as mentioned in the previous section, by a realisation of need ('I'm depressed and this chocolate is just what I need to cheer me up'), or by external stimuli, for example eye-catching packaging attracting the shopper's attention. The trigger need not even be inside the store: the smell of coffee or freshly baked bread wafting into the street may draw a customer into a café on impulse, or an attractive shop window display may attract a potential customer into a clothing store that they otherwise had no intention of visiting (even though clothing is not necessarily a routine problem solving purchase). Whatever the trigger, there is no conscious preplanning or information search, but a sudden surge of desire that can only be fulfilled by a purchase that the shopper may or may not later regret.

eg

Elior, the French catering company, has built a solid business on serving routine but last-minute purchases. It runs commercial concession catering operations at airports, motorway service areas, railway stations and even museums, all under contract with the infrastructure providers. In France, it is market leader in many categories and now further expansion is planned in the UK and Spain with the Netherlands, Italy and Belgium also on the agenda for market development. In the UK it has teamed up with Hachette to run multi-service stores on 40 railway station forecourts in the South of England, selling train tickets, food, coffee, snacks, magazines and newspapers (Bruce, 2001). The experience from France and elsewhere is that travellers, having purchased their tickets, are vulnerable to a host of other items if they are effectively displayed and even to the smell of fresh coffee. Research suggests that by raising the quality of ambient stimuli, impulse buying can be stimulated (Matilla and Wirtz, 2001).

The items that fall into the routine problem solving category do tend to be low-risk, low priced, frequently purchased products. The consumer is happy that a particular brand satisfies their requirements, and there is not enough benefit to be gained from switching brands to make the effort of information search and evaluation of alternatives worthwhile. These so-called low involvement purchases simply do not carry enough risk, whether measured in terms of financial loss, personal disappointment or damage to social status, for the consumer to get excited about the importance of 'making the right decision'.

Ehrenberg and Goodhart (1980) proposed a simple three-stage model that covers many routine problem solving purchases. Stage 1 is **awareness** of the brand or product, stage 2 is **trial**, and if the outcome of the trial is satisfactory, stage 3 is **repeat purchase**. Over time, therefore, the repeat purchase becomes habitual, with little or no re-evaluation of the decision. This explains why many manufacturers invest in heavy promotion to generate awareness and trial of new products, as these are necessary foundations for longer-term repeat purchasing behaviour. Later research further supported the relationship between awareness, trial and repeat purchasing, even where consumers indulged in multi-brand and multi-store shopping.

Limited problem solving

Limited problem solving is a little more interesting for the consumer. This is a buying situation that occurs less frequently and probably involves more deliberate decision-making than routine problems do. The goods will be moderately expensive (in the eyes of the individual consumer) and perhaps will be expected to last a long time. Thus the risks inherent in a 'wrong' decision are that much higher. There will, therefore, be some element of information search and evaluation, but this is still unlikely to absorb too much time and effort.

An example of this could be a consumer's purchase of a new piece of hi-fi equipment. If it is some years since they last bought one, they might feel that they need to update their knowledge of who makes what, who sells what, and the price brackets in this market. The information search is likely to include talking to any friends with recent hi-fi buying experience, and a trip round locally accessible electrical goods retailers. To this particular consumer, this is an important decision, but not a crucial one. If they make a 'wrong' choice (as defined in the post-purchase evaluation stage), they will be disappointed, but will feel that they have spent too much money to allow them simply to discard the offending product. Having said that, provided that the hi-fi fulfils its primary function of producing music on demand, they can learn to live with it and the damage is limited.

Some healthcare products might fall into this category of purchase, although they are relatively low-value items. The discomfort caused by minor illnesses can be very stressful for sufferers facing another day at work, and thus it is important to take the best remedy to relieve the symptoms and perhaps effect a cure. In addition, such illnesses are so infrequently suffered that consumers might not be aware of medicines available over the counter (OTC). The purchase thus becomes a limited problem-solving exercise. Retailers and manufacturers do not, however, want consumers to wait until they are ill before making a purchase. They are keen to encourage consumers to stock up on remedies such as Hedex or Andrews Seltzer Extra for common ailments while they are well so that when illness strikes, an appropriate treatment is at hand.

eg

The trend to self-medication for routine ailments helps to relieve the pressure on doctors and creates opportunities for both pharmaceutical companies and retailers. Many of the larger supermarket chains in the UK have now opened pharmacies to process prescriptions, dispense basic advice and generally assist the increasingly health-conscious consumer. ASDA, owned by Wal-Mart is planning to have 94 instore pharmacies by the end of 2001. Some retailers would like to go further and offer online advice and medical supplies, but in the UK, unlike the USA, there are a number of regulatory barriers to overcome. Superdrug, for example, with 700 stores throughout the UK announced in 2000 that it intended to launch a dotcom version as a health resource, but at the time of writing it had still not been opened for business and had been delayed indefinitely (Rosier, 2000). Caution has to be exercised with online pharmacy dispensing as found in the USA where there are over 400 such websites. Not all sites protect customers' interest or confirm the accuracy of the data submitted by the consumer, fitting the mould of 'no prescription, no doctor, no problem'. In one quoted case Viagra was supplied to a six-month-old baby despite the father entering all the correct details for his young son (Rice, 2001)!

The USA's experience provides sobering examples of why retailers need to think through carefully the implications of promoting greater OTC sales. The abolition of retail price maintenance (RPM) for OTC products in the UK in 2001 may well favour the supermarkets if they are able to exploit their economies of scale at the expense of small independent pharmacies (*The Grocer*, 2001). In the USA, consumers have been increasingly turning to supermarkets, not just for medicine and obviously health-related products such as vitamin pills, but also for more general advice on diet, the nutritional value of foods and health implications of other products (aerosols, etc.). Some stores have even organised guided tours of the shelves to tell customers about the nutritional aspects of foods. All of this is in addition to offering in-store health services such as blood and cholesterol testing (Spethmann, 2000). Although the regulatory environments are different, the trend that has started can enable 'the pharmacy' to be used to promote sales across other categories and this could give rise to wider ethical concerns about a conflict of interest. It could happen in the UK too. Research suggests that patients in the UK are already happy to self-medicate for non-acute conditions such as colds and 'flu although most appreciate some advice before purchasing. With busy lifestyles and one-stop shopping, in-store pharmacies, along with lower prices, could play an important role in future healthcare provision.

Limited problem solving is also likely to occur in the choice of service products. In purchasing a holiday or choosing a dentist (word-of-mouth recommendation?) the consumer has one chance to make the right choice. Once you are on the plane or in the dentist's chair, it is too late and the wrong choice could turn out to be expensive and painful. The necessity to get it right first time is thus likely to lead to a conscious and detailed information search, perhaps even going as far as extended problem solving, to which we now turn.

Extended problem solving

Extended problem solving represents a much more serious investment of money, time and effort from the consumer and, consequently, a much higher risk. Purchases of major capital items such as houses or cars fall into this category. These purchases occur extremely infrequently for most people and, given that they often require some kind of a loan, involve a serious long-term commitment. This means that the purchaser is motivated to gather as much information as possible, and to think quite consciously and systematically about what the decision-making criteria should be. That is not to say that the final decision will necessarily be made on purely functional, conscious or rational grounds. If, for example, two different makes of car have similar technical specifications, price, delivery and after-sales service terms, then final differentiation may be in terms of: 'which one will most impress the neighbours?'

The significance of buying situations

So what? Why categorise purchases in this way? After all, one consumer's limited problem-solving situation may be another's extended problem. This matters because it may add another dimension to help marketers develop more efficient and appropriate marketing strategies. If a significant group of potential buyers can be defined who clearly regard the purchase of a hi-fi as a limited problem-solving situation, then that has implications for the manufacturers in terms of both how and what to communicate, and where and how to distribute. If consumers are thought to regard a product as a limited problem-solving purchase, then perhaps the marketer will prefer to distribute it through specialist outlets, where the potential buyer can get expert advice, and can spend time making detailed product comparisons. Communication may contain a lot of factual information about technical specifications and product features (i.e. what the product can do), as well as selling product benefits (i.e. what all that means to you). In contrast, the same product as a routine problem solving exercise may be distributed as widely as possible, to ensure availability, regardless of retailer specialism or expertise, and the communication might centre on product image and benefits, ignoring the detailed information.

Environmental influences

This section is about the wider context in which the decision making is taking place. All of these environmental influences have already been covered in some depth in Chapter 2, so their treatment here will be brief. What is important is to recognise that decision-making is not completely divorced from the environment in which it is happening, whether the consumer is conscious of it or not.

Sociocultural influences

There are many pressures in this category and pp. 118 *et seq.* looks at them more closely. Individuals are influenced both by current trends in society as a whole and by a need to conform with the norms of the various social groups to which they belong, as well as to enhance their status within those groups.

In wider society, for example, there has been a move in recent years towards demanding more environmentally friendly products, and many consumers who are not necessarily 'deep green' have allowed this to influence their decision-making, looking more favourably on CFC-free, recycled or non-animal-tested products. Examples of social group pressures can be seen in children's markets. Many parents feel unfairly pressured into buying particular goods or brands because the children's friends all have them. There is a fear of the child being marginalised or bullied because they don't possess the 'right' things, whether those are trainers, mountain bikes or computer games.

Technological influences

Technology affects many aspects of consumer decision-making. Database technology, for example, as discussed in Chapter 18, allows organisations to create (almost) personal relationships with customers. At its extreme, this means that consumers receive better-tailored personalised offerings, and thus that their expectations are raised in terms of the quality of the product, communication and service.

marketing **in action**

e-woman

The role of women in society and their participation in business and domestic decision-making have changed radically since the 1970s. This is of great interest to marketers as they now find that women have more influence and more spending power. Faith Popcorn is a US futurologist who advises multinational companies on consumer trends and in her view, by 2010, every significant product or service category will be dominated by the companies that succeed in marketing effectively to women. She points to the fact that already in the USA, women make or influence 80 per cent of all consumer, healthcare and vehicle purchases, and more than half of all electronic purchases. Similar things are happening in the UK. More women than ever in the UK are earning more than £25,000 and female unemployment is less than half that of men. Building careers also means that women are having babies later in life and thus in the meantime have more confidence and more disposable income to spend on themselves as well as on their families.

Popcorn also argues that women process information differently, yet this does not seem to feature prominently in companies' marketing strategies. This could explain why marketers are finding the gap between what they think they know and actual buying behaviour getting bigger. One area in which they are starting to understand the female psyche better, however, is in internet marketing. There appear to be distinct differences in the ways in which men and women use the Internet. This is certainly a significant area, well worth understanding: NOP estimates that the UK has nearly eight million female online users while Jupiter MMXI reports that 42 per cent of UK internet users are female. Sun Microsystems has found that, in contrast to men, women tend to visit a limited number of sites but demonstrate a high degree of loyalty. Marketing Director, Louise Proddow said,

> *The average female surfer goes on-line seven times a week for an average of 54 minutes. Thirty per cent will visit only one or two sites; another 30 per cent will visit only three or four. In view of this, the power of the brand is important* (as quoted by Marsh, 2001).

Women also tend to use the internet for practical reasons, so travel, education and shopping sites feature strongly in their surfing habits. The most popular activity, however, is using the internet as a communications tool, so chat rooms and e-mail are also well patronised.

Agency Lowe Digital, which monitors women's online usage has similarly found that women use the internet with a specific purpose in mind, for instance to search for product information. Joy Taylor, Head of e-strategy, said,

> *Women's purchases online will exceed those of men in the next few years but they will only purchase on sites that give them all the information they need and with which they have a comfort level. Important factors in establishing such a comfort level are prompt replies to specific questions, an easy return policy and clear navigation* (as quoted by Marsh, 2001).

iVillage.co.uk is a site designed for women as somewhere they can go to find information and advice. One of the partners behind iVillage.co.uk is Tesco which has promoted the site heavily both on its own tesco.com website and through in-store promotions centred around women's and family issues. The involvement of Tesco, the UK's biggest retailer with a largely female clientèle, is an important element of the site's 'comfort level' and the sense of community created by the chatty and friendly approach helps to create regular repeat visitors. Similarly, handbag.com, another women's portal with which Boots (another female-orientated trusted brand name) is involved, has been able to establish an online community, capitalising successfully on the way women use the internet. Its Marketing Director said,

> *Community is important. Discussion boards are among our most popular areas and the people using them are among the most regular visitors to the site. It seems women put more value on user opinions than on the experts. Our brand awareness campaign has tended to highlight our content whether it be how to find the right car, fashion tips, or getting back on your feet after a break-up* (as quoted by Marsh, 2001).

Given the increasing importance of women's spending power and influence over buying decisions, sites such as iVillage.co.uk and handbag.com represent a real opportunity for advertisers to reach this key audience and communicate with it in a female-friendly environment and in terms that the audience can comfortably relate to. If Faith Popcorn is to be believed, no company that wants to be dominant in its product or service sector can afford to miss out on this opportunity.

Sources: Marsh (2001); Mazur (2000).

In its wider sense, technology applied to product development and innovation has created whole categories of fast evolving, increasingly cheap consumer 'toys' such as videos, hi-fi formats, camcorders and computer games. Many of these products used to be extended problem-solving goods, but they have moved rapidly towards the limited problem-solving area, as discussed above (pp. 105–6). Such shifts occur for two main sets of reasons, which are interdependent. First, as the manufacturer learns more through experience about the product, its technology, its manufacture and its marketing, they are able to reduce their costs, make better quality products and expand the product range to offer a number of different models to suit different kinds of customer. Additionally, over time, competition is likely to increase, again acting as an impetus towards better and cheaper products. Second, as a result of all that, the amount of risk inherent in the purchase reduces for the consumer, who does not, therefore, need to spend quite so much time searching for and evaluating alternative options.

Economic and competitive influences

The 1990s saw recession and economic hardship across Europe and this inevitably affected consumers' attitudes, as well as their ability and willingness to spend. With uncertainty about employment prospects, many consumers postponed purchasing decisions, adjusted their decision-making criteria or cut out certain types of spending altogether. Price, value for money and a conscious assessment of the need to buy become prevalent influences in such circumstances.

Retailers, in turn, had to respond to the slowdown in trade caused by the economic environment. Money-off sales became prevalent in the High Street throughout the year, not just in the traditional post-Christmas period. While this did stimulate sales in the short term, it had one unfortunate effect for retailers. Consumers began to see the lower sale price as 'normal' and resented paying full prices, preferring to wait for the next sale that they were confident would come along soon.

In terms of competition, very few purchases, mainly low-involvement decisions, are made without any consideration of the competition. The definition of what constitutes competition, however, is in the mind of the consumer. The supplier of car exhaust systems can be fairly sure that the competition consists of other exhaust dealers and garages. The supplier of chocolate, however, may be in competition not only with other chocolate suppliers but also with cream buns, biscuits and potato crisps. The consumer's consideration of the competition, however it is defined, may be extensive, formal and time consuming, or it may be a cursory glance across the supermarket shelf, just to check. Competitors are vying for the consumer's attention through their packaging, their promotional mix and their mailshots, as well as trying to influence or interrupt the decision-making process. This proliferation of products and communication can either confuse the consumer, leading to brand switching and even less rational decision-making, or provide the consumer with the information and comparators to allow more discerning decision-making.

Political and legal influences

Political and legal influences, emanating either from the EU or from national bodies, can also affect the consumer. Legislation on minimum levels of product safety and performance, for example, means that the consumer does not need to spend time getting technical information, worrying about analysing it and comparing competing products on those criteria. Legislation and regulation, whether they relate to product descriptions, consumer rights or advertising, also reduce the inherent risks of making a decision. This takes some of the pressure off the customer, leading to better-informed and easier decisions and less risk of post-purchase dissonance.

This discussion of the STEP factors is not exhaustive, but simply acts as a reminder that an individual makes decisions within a wider context, created either by society's own dynamics or by the efforts of the market. Having set that context, it is now appropriate to look more closely at the particular influences, internal and external, that affect the individual's buying behaviour and decision-making.

Psychological influences: the individual

Although marketers try to define groups of potential customers with common attributes or interests, as a useful unit for the formulation of marketing strategies, it should not be forgotten that such groups or market segments are still made up of individuals who are different from each other. This section, therefore, looks at aspects that will affect an individual's perceptions and handling of the decision-making process, such as personality, perception, learning, motivation and the impact of attitudes.

Personality

Personality, consisting of all the features, traits, behaviours and experiences that make each of us distinctive and unique, is a very extensive and deep area of study. Our personalities lie at the heart of all our behaviour as consumers, and thus marketers try to define the particular personality traits or characteristics prevalent among a target group of consumers, which can then be reflected in the product itself and the marketing effort around it. This is beginning to trespass on ground that will be covered later in discussion of psychographic or lifestyle segmentation (pp. 189 *et seq.*), which is hardly surprising as personality helps to establish lifestyle as much as lifestyle affects personality.

In the mid- to late 1980s, advertising in particular was full of images reflecting the personality traits associated with successful lifestyle stereotypes such as the 'yuppie'. Independent, level-headed, ruthless, ambitious, self-centred, materialistic traits were seen as positive characteristics, and thus marketers were anxious to have them associated with users of their products. The 1990s saw a softening of this approach, featuring images orientated more towards caring, concern, family and sharing as the route to self-fulfilment.

With high-involvement products, where there is a strong emotional and psychological link between the product and the consumer, it is relatively easy to see how personality might affect choice and decision-making. In choosing clothing, for instance, an extrovert self-confident achiever with an extravagant streak might select something deliberately *avant garde*, stylishly daring, vibrantly coloured and expensive, as a personality statement. A quiet, insecure character, with underdeveloped social skills, might prefer to wear something more sober, more conservative, with less attention-seeking potential.

Overall, however, the link between personality and purchasing, and thus the ability to predict purchasing patterns from personality traits, is at best tenuous. Kassarjian (1971) probably best summed up the situation in a review of previous studies: some showed a strong relationship between personality and purchasing, the majority showed at best a weak relationship, and a few no relationship at all. Chisnall (1985) takes the more cautious line that personality may influence the decision to buy a certain product type, but not the final brand choice.

Getting away from it all means different things to different people.

Source: Hayes & Jarvis.

Perception

Perception represents the way in which individuals analyse, interpret and make sense of incoming information, and is affected by personality, experience and mood. No two people will interpret the same stimulus (whether it is a product's packaging, taste, smell, texture or its promotional messages) in exactly the same way. Even the same individual might perceive the stimulus differently at different times. For example, seeing an advertisement for food when you are hungry is more likely to produce a positive response than seeing the same advertisement just after a heavy meal. Immediate needs are affecting the interpretation of the message. Alternatively, relaxing at home on a Sunday afternoon, an individual is more likely to spend time reading a detailed and lengthy print advertisement than they would if they were flicking through the same magazine during a short coffee break in the working day. Naturally, marketers hope that their messages reach target audiences when they are relaxed, at leisure and at ease with the world, because then the individual is more likely to place a positive interpretation on the message and is less likely to be distracted by other pressures and needs.

Other pressures and needs do create problems for marketers to overcome. All consumers are bombarded with marketing messages every day, and if they tried to pay equal attention and interpret them all objectively, then they would rapidly go mad. There are, therefore, a number of defence mechanisms to protect the consumer from over-stimulation and to make the interpretation process less stressful.

Selective attention

Consumers do not pay attention to everything that is going on at once. Attention filters allow the unconscious selection of what incoming information to concentrate on. In daily life we filter out the irrelevant background noise: the hum of the computer, the birds in the garden, the cars in the street, the footsteps in the corridor. As consumers we filter out the irrelevant marketing messages. In reading the newspaper, for instance, a split-second glance spots an advertisement, decides that it is irrelevant and allows the eye to read around it.

This means that marketers have to overcome these filters, either by creating messages that we will decide are relevant or by building attention-grabbing devices into the message. A print advertisement, for example, might use its position on the page, intense colour or startling images to draw the eye, and more importantly the brain, to it.

Selective perception

The problems do not stop once the marketer has got the consumer's attention, since people are infinitely creative in interpreting information in ways that suit them. It is less threatening to interpret things so that they fit nicely and consistently with whatever you already think and feel than to cope with the discomfort of clashes and inconsistency.

One way of creating this consistency or harmony is to allow perception to be coloured by previous experience and existing attitudes. A particularly bad experience with an organisation's offering creates a prejudice that may never be overcome. Whatever positive messages that organisation transmits, the consumer will always be thinking 'Yes, but . . .'. Similarly, a negative attitude towards a subject will make the consumer interpret messages differently. For example, someone who is deeply opposed to nuclear power will try to read between the lines of the industry's advertising and PR, looking for cover-ups and counter-arguments. This can distort the intended message and even reinforce the negative feelings. Conversely, a good experience makes it a lot easier to form positive perceptions. The good experience from the past creates a solid foundation from which to look for the best in the new experience.

Selective retention

Not all stimuli that make it through the attention filters and the machinery of perception and understanding are remembered. Many stimuli are only transitory, hence one of the reasons for the repetition of advertising: if you did not notice it or remember it the first time round, you might pick it up on subsequent occasions. Jogging the memory, by repeating messages or by producing familiar stimuli that the consumer can recognise (such as brand names, packaging design, logos or colour schemes), is therefore an important marketing task to reduce the reliance on the consumer's memory.

People have the capacity to remember what they want to remember and to filter out anything else. The reasons for retaining a particular message may be because it touched them emotionally, or it was of immediate relevance, or it was especially entertaining, or it reinforced previously held views. The reasons are many, but the consumer is under no obligation to remember anything.

Learning

Perception and memory are closely linked with **learning**. Marketers want consumers to learn from promotional material, so that they know which product to buy and why, and to learn from experience of the product, so that they will buy it again and pass on the message to others.

Learning has been defined by Hilgard and Marquis (1961) as:

> *. . . the more or less permanent change in behaviour which occurs as a result of practice.*

This implies, from a marketing perspective, that the objective must not only be for the consumer to learn something, but also for them to remember what has been learned and to act on it. Therefore advertising materials, for instance, are carefully designed to maximise the learning opportunity. A 30-second television advertisement selling car insurance over the phone repeats the freephone number four times and has it written across the bottom of the screen so that the viewer is likely to remember it. Demonstrating a product benefit in an advertisement also helps consumers to learn what they are supposed to notice about the product when they use it. The images from Procter & Gamble's advertisement showing the enormous heap of crockery washed by one bottle of Fairy Liquid next to the pathetic heap achieved with a competing product stay in the mind more easily than a simple verbal message would. More generally, showing a product in a particular usage context, or associating it with certain types of people or situations, gives the consumer guidelines about what attitudes to develop towards the product.

Humour, and other methods of provoking an emotional response to an advertisement, can also help a message to stick because the recipient immediately becomes more involved in the process. Similarly, associating a product with something familiar that itself evokes certain emotions can allow those feelings to be transferred to the product. Thus the advertisements for Andrex that feature puppies have helped the British public to learn to think of toilet paper as warm, soft, cuddly and harmless rather than embarrassing.

Motivation

One definition of marketing puts the emphasis on the satisfaction of customers' needs and wants, but what triggers those needs and wants, and what drives consumers towards their fulfilment? Motives for action, the driving forces, are complex and changeable and can be difficult to research, since individuals themselves often cannot define why they act the way they do. An additional problem is that at different times, different **motivations** might take priority and have more influence over the individual's behaviour. Imagine, for example, a traveller driving from Calais to Marseilles. In the early part of the journey, the main priority is to make good time, find somewhere for lunch and provisionally aim to arrive in Lyon in good time to find a reasonable hotel. Long traffic delays on the southbound motorway throw out these plans. It is getting late and the traveller realises that he will not reach Lyon as planned. After seeing a few 'no vacancies' signs, concern starts to mount about the likelihood of finding a room, rather than sleeping in the car. The many hotels passed earlier in the journey were not considered, but now any hotel is likely to be well received. The priority is no longer distance covered but finding the warmth and relaxation of any hotel room. Our traveller's motives, in terms of both content and intensity, have changed during the events of one long-distance car journey. Marketers need to be aware of such influences on patronage motives if they are to market their hotels, restaurants or indeed any business effectively. Think, for example, of the impact on the tired traveller of a well-lit, familiar sign that can be clearly seen from the motorway.

Maslow's (1954) *hierarchy of needs* has long been used as a framework for classifying basic motivations. Five groups of needs, as shown in Figure 3.3, are stacked one on top of another and form a progression. Having achieved satisfaction on the lowest level, the individual can progress to strive to achieve the goals of the next level up. This model does have a certain logic behind it, and the idea, for instance, that true self-actualisation can only grow from solid foundations of security and social acceptance seems reasonable. However, the model was developed in the context of US capitalist culture, where achievement and self-actualisation are often ends in themselves. It is questionable how far these motives can be extended to other cultural contexts.

Examples of consumer behaviour and marketing activity can be found to fit all five levels.

Physiological needs

Basic feelings such as hunger and thirst can be potent driving forces. After a strenuous game of squash, the immediate craving for liquid overrides normal considerations of brand preference. If the sports centre shop only has one type of soft drink in stock, then it will do. Similarly, seasoned shoppers are well aware of the dangers of visiting a supermarket when they are hungry: so much more seems to go into the trolley.

Marketers can capitalise on such feelings. The soft drink manufacturer can ensure that the sports centre stocks that brand and that the product image reflects refreshment and thirst-quenching properties. The food manufacturer can advertise at a time of day when the audience is likely to be feeling hungry so that they are more likely to pay attention to the message and remember it.

Safety needs

Once the individual has taken care of the basic necessities of life, food, drink and warmth, the need for self-protection and long-term survival emerges. In modern Western societies this may be interpreted as the desire for a secure home, protected against intrusion and other dangers (floods and fire, for example). It might also cover the desire for healthcare, insurance services and consumer protection legislation.

Figure 3.3 Maslow's hierarchy of needs

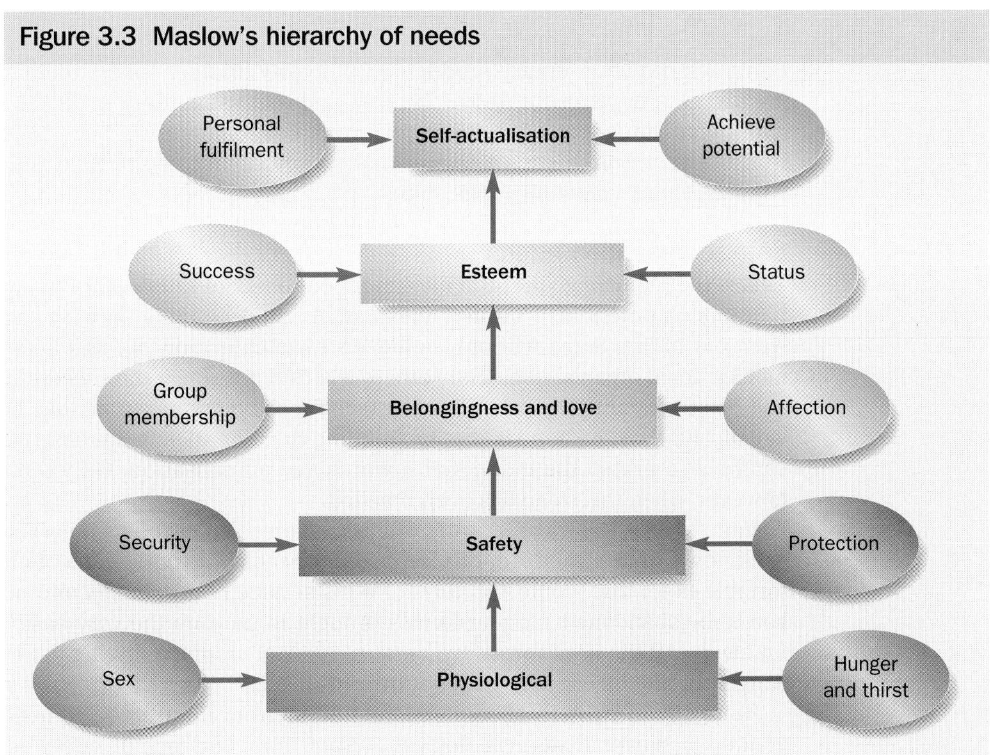

The car market in particular has focused on safety needs as a marketing platform. Driving is an inherently dangerous activity, so the manufacturers try to reassure us that their cars are as safe as possible. Various manufacturers have featured side impact bars, airbags and/or anti-lock braking systems in their advertising, showing how these either protect you or help to prevent accidents.

Safety needs in terms of health protection feature strongly in the marketing strategies of products such as bleaches and toilet cleaners. The kind of approach used often appeals to the mother who takes responsibility for safeguarding the health and well-being of the whole family. The threat from bacteria can be eliminated by choosing the right cleanser.

Belongingness and love needs

This is about emotional security, wanting to feel accepted and valued by those closest to you. Marketers again play on this need through the portrayal of the family in particular. Over many years, advertising told women that they would be better appreciated and loved as wives and mothers if they did their washing in Persil, cooked with Oxo or fed their husbands cornflakes for breakfast.

Fear of loneliness or personal rejection can be a powerful motivator and features strongly in many marketing campaigns. Toiletries such as deodorants, toothpastes and mouthwashes have all advertised on the basis that you will be more lovable if you use these products, and showing the dire consequences of rejection if you don't. Even anti-smoking campaigns aimed at teenagers have tried this approach, implying that the smell of tobacco on your breath will put off prospective boy/girlfriends.

Esteem needs

This extends outwards from the previous stage to cover the individual's need for success, status and good opinion within wider society. This may include professional status and respect, standing within social groups, such as sports clubs and societies, or 'what the neighbours think'.

These needs are reflected in a wide variety of product and services marketing. Most car advertising, for example, contains some kind of message implying that if you drive this car it will somehow enhance your status and gain the respect of others. This even applies to the smaller, less expensive models, where the esteem arises from notions of 'wise choice' or 'a car that reflects the positive elements of my character'. More overtly, esteem can derive from the individual's sheer ability to afford the most expensive and exclusive items. Perfumes and other luxury products play heavily on the implication that you are a discerning and élite buyer, a cut above the rest, and that using these products makes a statement about who you are and the status you hold. Brand names such as Rolls-Royce, Gucci and Rolex have acquired such a cachet that simply saying 'she owns a genuine Rolex' speaks volumes about a person's social status.

Self-actualisation needs

This is the ultimate goal, the achievement of complete satisfaction through successfully fulfilling one's potential. That may mean anything, depending on who you are and what you want out of life. Some will only achieve self-actualisation through becoming the head of a multinational organisation, while others will find it through the successful raising of a happy and healthy family. This is a difficult stage for the marketer to handle, because it is so individual, and thus the hope is that by fulfilling the other needs discussed above, the marketer can help to propel the individual towards self-actualisation. Only the individual can tell, however, when this stage has been reached.

Interestingly, the traveller from Calais to Marseilles introduced earlier seemed to regress back down from higher order to lower order needs! The initial idea of choosing a nice comfortable hotel that would suitably fulfil his service requirements and match his self-image had to be abandoned. Circumstances brought to the fore the very basic physiological need for sleep and the need for safety, both in terms of stopping driving before tiredness made it dangerous and having a secure roof over his head.

Generally in Western economies the fulfilment of the very basic needs can be taken for granted, however. Real physiological hunger, thirst and lack of safety do not exist for most people. Manufacturers of food products, for instance, cannot therefore assume that just because their product alleviates hunger it will be purchased and accepted. Any one of hundreds of food brands can do that, and thus the consumer is looking to see how a particular product can fulfil a higher order need, such as love or esteem. Consequently, foods are often marketed on the basis that your family will enjoy it and love you more for providing it (Oxo, for example) or because your dinner party guests will be impressed (Viennetta or After Eights, for example). The emphasis, therefore, is largely on the higher order needs (belongingness and love, esteem and self-actualisation).

In contrast, emerging market economies are still in the process of moving away from emphasis on the lower order needs (physiological and safety). When the former Communist states began their difficult transition to market economies, the shortages of basic products meant that people were very concerned simply with survival, acquiring enough bread, tea, milk, meat and other staple items to keep themselves going. Whether a particular product helps you to feel better about yourself is rather irrelevant in those circumstances. Now that the transitions are a few years further on, and because of the impact of the marketing efforts of Western organisations entering these markets, higher order needs are increasingly being considered.

Attitudes

As implied at p. 111 above, an **attitude** is a stance that an individual takes on a subject that predisposes them to react in a certain way to that subject. More formally, an attitude has been defined by Hilgard *et al.* (1975) as:

> *. . . an orientation towards or away from some object, concept or situation and a readiness to respond in a predetermined manner to these related objects, concepts or situations.*

Thus in marketing terms, consumers can develop attitudes to any kind of product or service, or indeed to any aspect of the marketing mix, and these attitudes will affect behaviour. All of this implies that attitudes play an important part in influencing consumer judgement, whether through perception, evaluation, information processing or decision-making. Attitudes play a key role in shaping learning and while they are fluid, evolving over time, they are nevertheless often difficult to change.

Williams (1981), in summarising the literature, describes attitudes as having three different components.

Cognitive

Cognitive attitudes relate to beliefs or disbeliefs, thus: 'I believe that margarine is healthier than butter.' This is a component that the marketer can work on through fairly straightforward advertising. Repeating the message that your product is healthy, or that it represents the best value for money, may well establish an initial belief in those qualities.

Affective

Affective attitudes relate to feelings of a positive or negative nature, involving some emotional content, thus: 'I *like* this product' or 'This product makes me *feel* . . .' Again, advertising can help the marketer to signal to the consumer why they should like it, or how they should feel when they use it. For some consumers, of course, affective attitudes can overcome cognitive ones. For example, I may believe that margarine is healthier than butter, but I buy butter because I like the taste better. Similarly, I believe that snacking on chocolate is 'bad', but it cheers me up so I do it anyway.

Conative

Conative attitudes relate to the link with behaviour, thus attitude x is considered likely to lead to behaviour y. This is the hardest one for marketers to predict or control, because so many things can prevent behaviour from taking place, even if the cognitive and affective attitudes are positive: 'I believe that BMWs are excellent quality, reliable cars, and I feel that owning one would enhance my status and provide me with many hours of pleasurable driving, but I simply cannot afford it,' or it may even be that 'Audi made me a better offer'.

It is this last link between attitude and behaviour that is of most interest to marketers. Fishbein (1975) developed a model, a further evolution of his earlier 1967 work, based on the proposition that in order to predict a specific behaviour, such as a brand purchase, it is important to measure the individual's attitude towards performing that behaviour, rather than just the attitude towards the product in question. This fits with the BMW example above, where the most important thing is not the attitude to the car itself, but the attitude towards *purchasing* the car. As long as the attitude to purchasing is negative, the marketer still has work to do. While it is usually accepted that other factors, both personal and situational, also influence behaviour, many writers, such as Lutz (1981) and Foxall (1984), still argue that attitude is a key link in the causal chain between perceptions of product attributes at one end and purchasing intentions and behaviour at the other end. Others, such as Joyce (1967), see a two-way relationship between attitudes and purchasing behaviour, so that experience of the product will also influence, through learning, future behaviour.

Attitudes can thus involve feelings (positive or negative), knowledge (complete or partial) and beliefs. A particular female consumer might believe that she is overweight. She knows that cream cakes are fattening, but she likes them. All these things come together to form her attitude towards cream cakes (wicked, but seductive) and her behaviour when confronted by one (five minutes wrestling with her conscience before giving in completely and buying two, knowing that she will regret it later). An advertising campaign for cream cakes, centred around the slogan 'naughty but nice', capitalised brilliantly on what is a common attitude, almost legitimising the guilt and establishing an empathy with the hopeless addict. The really admirable thing about that campaign was that the advertiser did not even attempt to overturn the attitude.

It is possible, but very difficult, to change attitudes, particularly when they are well established and deeply ingrained. Companies like Lada and Aeroflot have been trying for years with varying degrees of success. The nuclear industry has also been trying to overcome hostile and suspicious attitudes with an integrated campaign of advertising, PR and site visits (http://www.bnfl.co.uk). Many people have indeed been responsive to this openness, and have been prepared to revise attitudes to a greater or lesser extent. There will, however, always be a hard core who will remain entrenched and interpret any 'positive' messages in a negative way.

There is a difference between attitudes that relate to an organisation's philosophy, business ethics or market and those that centre around experience of an organisation's specific product or service. An organisation that has a bad reputation for its employment practices, its environmental record or its dealings with suspect foreign regimes will have created negative attitudes that will be extremely difficult to overturn. Similarly, companies operating in certain markets, such as nuclear power, tobacco and alcohol, will never redeem themselves in the eyes of significant groups of the public. People care too much about such things to be easily persuaded to change their outlook. In contrast, negative feelings about a specific product or brand are more amenable to change through skilful marketing.

eg

Skoda is a remarkable example of how negative attitudes can be tackled head-on with some success. Surely we all remember a few Skoda jokes from over ten years ago, for example, 'why does the Skoda have a heated rear window? To keep your hands warm while you push it'. The communist era in Czechoslovakia meant that the Skoda had become cheap and cheerful but with a terrible reputation matched only by Lada's.

In 1991, VW took over Skoda and after investment in re-tooling, building a quality culture, using components in common with VW brands, and a fresh approach to design, Skoda products improved beyond recognition (Mudd, 2000; Kimberley, 2001). The trouble is that consumers were slow to believe it. In the UK, Skoda found that offering a quality product was not enough and sales development was disappointing. Not to be beaten, rather than adopting a eurobland advertising approach for the new Fabia super mini, with a focus on benefits, styling and features, the UK operation decided to tackle the problem by addressing the negative attitudes head-on. The television advertisements featured a car transporter delivery to a Skoda garage. When the unloading was about to begin, the transporter driver changed his mind and drove off – after all such great cars couldn't be destined for a Skoda dealership (they were!). In a similar vein, an apologetic car worker refuses to accept that the Skoda marque could possibly belong on such a stylish car (it was a Skoda). The overall theme was we've changed the car, now can you change your mind? The self-deprecating humour meant that the advertisement stood out (Simms, 2001).

There is still a long way to go. Negative attitudes are hard to shake off. By the end of the Fabia campaign, however, the number of people who would not buy a Skoda in the UK dropped from 60 per cent to 42 per cent and sales had risen by one-third. In 2001, the campaign was a Marketing Society award winner (*Marketing*, 2001b).

Skoda has used the common negative attitude to its product by turning the joke into a campaign to make the consumer chuckle and take a second look at the new quality cars on offer.

Source: Skoda UK.

As the cream cake example quoted earlier shows, defining attitudes can provide valuable insights into target groups of customers and give a basis for communication with them. Measuring feelings, beliefs and knowledge about an organisation's products and those of its competitors is an essential part of market research (*see* Chapter 6), leading to a more effective and appealing marketing mix. Identifying changes in wider social or cultural attitudes can also provide the marketer with new opportunities, either for products or marketing approaches. In October 2001, a new women's magazine called *New Era* was launched in the UK. It is targeted at those who are either going through or who have just been through a divorce or a relationship break-up, with the slogan 'There is life after marriage'. It combines advice with entertaining lifestyle features and covers a range of topics which are essential reading for its target audience. Its existence is due not only to the fact that there are over 180,000 divorces in the UK every year, but also to more liberal attitudes towards divorce and the problems it creates. This new openness and acceptability of divorce was also evident when VW ran a successful advertisement showing a very happy woman emerging from what the viewer interpreted as a registry office wedding. When she drove away in her VW, however, the slogan painted on the back of the car read 'just divorced'.

In summary, the individual is a complex entity, under pressure to take in, analyse and remember many marketing messages in addition to the other burdens of daily life. Marketers need to understand how individuals think and why they respond in particular ways, if they are going to develop marketing offerings that cut through defence mechanisms and create loyal customers. Individuals' behaviour, however, is not only shaped in accordance with their personalities, abilities, analytical skills, etc., as discussed above, but also affected by wider considerations, such as the sociocultural influences that will be discussed next.

Sociocultural influences: the group

Individuals are influenced, to a greater or lesser extent, by the social and cultural climate in which they live. Individuals have membership of many social groups, whether these are formally recognised social units such as the family, or informal intangible groupings such as reference groups (*see* pp. 123 *et seq.*). Inevitably, purchasing decisions will be affected by group membership, as these sociocultural influences may help the individual to:

1 differentiate between essential and non-essential purchases;
2 prioritise purchases where resources are limited;
3 define the meaning of the product and its benefits in the context of their own lives; and thus to
4 foresee the post-purchase implications of this decision.

All of these things imply that the individual's decision has as much to do with 'What other people will think' and 'How I will look if I buy this' as with the intrinsic benefits of the product itself. Marketers have, of course, capitalised on this natural wish to express oneself and gain social acceptance through one's consumption habits, both as a basis for psychographic or lifestyle segmentation (which will be discussed later on pp. 189 *et seq.*) and for many years as a basis of fear appeals in advertising (*see* Chapter 14 onwards).

The following subsections look more closely at some of these sociocultural influences.

Social class

Social class is a form of stratification that attempts to structure and divide a society. Some argue that egalitarianism has become far more pronounced in the modern Europe, making any attempts at social distinction ill-founded, if not meaningless. Nevertheless, today social class is established largely according to occupation, and for many years, British marketers have used the grading system outlined in Table 3.2. It has been widely used to group consumers, whether for research or for analysing media readership.

Table 3.2 UK socioeconomic groupings

% of population	*Group*	*Social status*	*Occupation of head of household*
3	A	Upper middle	Higher managerial, administrative or professional
14	B	Middle	Intermediate managerial, administrative or professional
27	C1	Lower middle	Supervisory or clerical, junior managerial, administrative or professional
25	C2	Skilled working	Skilled manual workers
19	D	Working	Semi-skilled and unskilled manual workers
12	E	Those at lowest level of subsistence	State pensioners or widows, casual or lowest-grade workers

eg

The growth of the 'middle class' in the UK will probably mean the end of the official six-class structure adopted since 1921, as shown in Table 3.2. Government statistics suggest that half the UK population are now in the middle class and thus the old groupings are too broad and no longer meaningful. The new 'official' social classification introduced in 1998 has 17 categories, based not only on occupation (as in the old system) but also on the size of an individual's employing organisation and the type of contract, fringe benefits and job security that individual enjoys. It also takes into account how much the employer values that individual. These extra factors make a big difference. Looking only at occupation and income, the top social groups earn twice as much as the bottom ones. Accounting for the extra factors, however, makes the top groups seven times more affluent.

This is perhaps a much more realistic way of defining socioeconomic groups. Under the new scheme, those who acquire 'better' status include large-company managers, teachers, policemen and nurses. Those who slide down the scale, however, include shop assistants, plumbers and traffic wardens. For the marketer, the new system creates smaller, more clearly defined and currently relevant groups for targeting purposes. It still does not, however, get into the mind of consumers or explain their buying behaviour. Does all of this matter? Perhaps it does, as long as the top groups are up to seven times more affluent than the bottom ones (Henderson, 1997; Norton, 1998).

Across the EU, different definitions of social class have been used. In the Netherlands, for example, the population is structured into professional and higher managerial, intermediate managerial, clerical and skilled manual, and finally pensioners and the unskilled. In contrast, Germany defines social groups according to monthly household income while France combines the self-employed with senior management and has classes for professional, white-collar and blue-collar employees. However, more fundamental problems can be found in attempting to link consumer behaviour with social class. The usefulness of such systems is limited. They rely on the occupation of the head of the household (more correctly called the main income earner), but fail to put that into the context of the rest of the household. Dual income households are becoming increasingly common, with the second income having a profound effect on the buying behaviour of both parties, yet most of these systems fail to recognise this. They tell very little about the consumption patterns or attitudes that are of such great use to the marketer. The disposable income of a C2 class household may be just as high as that of an A or B household, and they may have certain upmarket tastes in common. Furthermore, two households in the A or B categories could easily behave very differently. One household might consider status symbols to be important and indulge in conspicuous consumption, whereas the other might have rejected materialistic values and be seeking a cleaner, less cluttered lifestyle. These contrasting outlooks on life make an enormous difference to buying behaviour and choices, hence the necessity for psychographic segmentation (*see* pp. 189 *et seq.*) to provide marketers with more meaningful frameworks for grouping customers.

Nevertheless, as Inskip (1995) argues, a deeply rooted sense of class does affect people's perception of the world and their aspirations. In marketing terms, this may mean that middle-class people generally seek out products that will enhance their self-image, self-belief and sense of success. The working class is more firmly rooted in family values, and although they may still aspire to accumulate possessions, they will not change either those values or themselves fundamentally. Inskip claims that marketers do not understand the working class and its needs properly, and thus have either ignored it completely or failed to address it appropriately as they use patronising and stereotypical marketing activities. Since around 46 per cent of the UK population claim to be working class, this is a serious omission. C2 and D consumers do now have money to spend, even if they choose to spend it in areas such as discount retailers or mail order catalogues that marketers do not find particularly trendy or exciting. Part of the problem is that most marketers are themselves middle class. They thus find it easier to relate to middle-class customers, and carry their own prejudices about the working class into their approaches.

Culture and subculture

Culture can be described as the personality of the society within which an individual lives. It manifests itself through the built environment, art, language, literature, music and the products that society consumes, as well as through its prevalent beliefs, value systems and government. As summarised by Chisnall (1985), culture is the total way of life of a society, passed on from generation to generation, deriving from a group of people sharing and transmitting beliefs, values, attitudes and forms of behaviour that are common to that society and considered worthy of retention. Rice (1993, p. 242) similarly defines culture as:

> *The values, attitudes, beliefs, ideas, artefacts and other meaningful symbols represented in the pattern of life adopted by people that help them interpret, evaluate and communicate as members of society.*

Breaking that definition down further, Figure 3.4 shows diagrammatically the influences that create culture.

Cultural differences show themselves in very different ways. Although eating, for example, is a basic natural instinct, what we eat and when is heavily influenced by the culture in which we are brought up. Thus in Spain it is normal to begin lunch at 4 p.m. and then have dinner after 10 p.m., while in Poland most restaurants would be closing down at those times. Similarly, lunch in Central Europe would almost certainly include sauerkraut, but little fish compared with the wide variety offered on a typical Spanish menu. Even the propensity for eating out may be a cultural factor. Riley (1994), for example, argues that eating out is not a major part of the UK's social culture. Thus the restaurateur has the added marketing task in the UK of overcoming the barrier of the consumer's home orientation and persuading them that eating out is an enjoyable social activity.

Of course, culture goes much further in prescribing and describing the values and beliefs of a society. It influences shopping hours, with many Mediterranean supermarkets open for far longer hours in the evening than some of their Northern European counterparts; the beliefs associated with advertising messages and symbols; the lifestyles of the inhabitants; and the products that are more or less acceptable and available in that culture, for example try purchasing an electric kettle in Spain or Italy.

Figure 3.4 Influences on culture

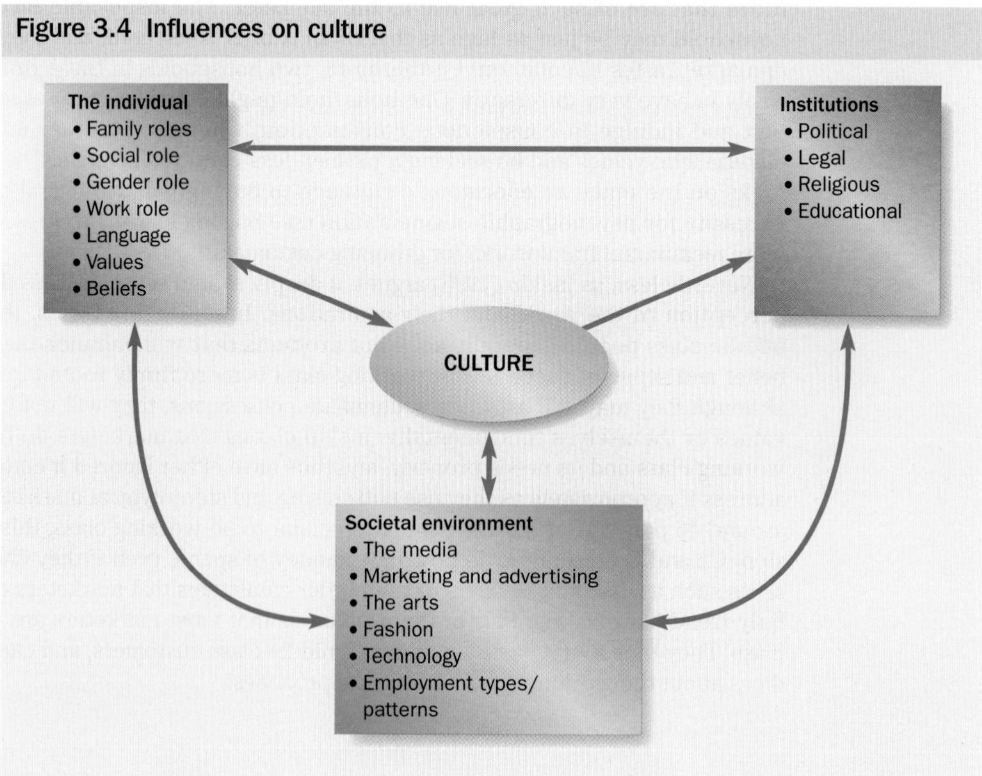

Culture is thus very important for the marketer to understand, first because marketing can only exist within a culture that is prepared to allow it and support it, and second, it has to act within boundaries set by society and culture. Over the past 10 years or so, for example, it has become more and more socially unacceptable in Europe for organisations to use animals for testing cosmetics. Society has informally rewritten one of the rules and marketers have had to respond. Changing attitudes to tobacco, alcohol and marketing to children are also examples of areas within which cultural change is altering organisations' approaches to business. In the UK, for instance, food marketers have been criticised for aiming too much advertising of products such as sweets, soft drinks, sugary cereals, crisps and fast foods at children. These kinds of product are thought to be of dubious nutritional value, if consumed in excess, and are also thought to be contributing to an increase in dental decay among children.

Any culture can be divided into a number of subcultures, each with its own specific characteristics, yet existing within the whole. It depends on the onlooker's perspective just how detailed a division is required. An American exporter might say that Europe represents a culture (as distinct from the US culture), with British, French, German and other national subcultures existing within it. Dealing with the home market, however, a German marketer would define Germany, or increasingly the German-speaking territories of Europe, as the dominant culture, with significant subcultures held within it. These subcultures could be based on ethnic origin (Turkish, Polish, Asian or whatever), religious beliefs, or more lifestyle-orientated groupings, defined by the values and attitudes held. Language may also be an important determinant of subculture. In Switzerland, for example, the three main languages reflect different customs, architecture and even external orientations. The Ticino region (Italian speaking) probably identifies itself more closely with Milan than Zurich or Basle as a point of cultural reference.

eg

It has been argued that companies are ignoring the full potential of ethnic community groups in the UK by not addressing them properly. Ethnic communities account for nearly 5.5 per cent of the UK population and are growing by 2 or 3 per cent per year, yet do not appear to be well targeted by companies. It is an important omission: The Commission for Racial Equality (CRE) estimates that by 2020, ethnic communities will account for 10 per cent of the UK population and their spending power is estimated to be around £15 bn. Research has shown that only 20 per cent of companies think that they target ethnic communities effectively, and 29 per cent are prepared to admit that they to not attempt to reach them at all. Some 25 per cent do not seek feedback from ethnic minorities in focus group research.

Nevertheless, there are advantages to be gained from acknowledging and addressing the specific needs and cultural influences on ethnic groups. It is a complex task. The Asian community, for example, is not in itself homogeneous. There are wide differences in language, religion, country of origin and attitudes. This is reflected in the proliferation of specialist media serving the Asian market. It is targeted by 15 digital TV channels. The four biggest (Zee, Sony, B4U and StarTV) have access to nearly 300,000 Asian households in the UK. There are specialist channels, such as Prime TV, serving the 40,000 households of the Pakistani community and Reminiscent TV, offering a range of channels for its 15,000 subscribers from the Punjabi, Gujarati, Tamil, Bengali, Urdu and Hindu communities. There are five main Asian radio stations, the biggest of which, Sunrise Radio in London, has about 300,000 listeners. There are about 100 Asian press titles, 20 per cent of which are in Asian languages. So the media exist, if companies can come up with the right messages, to reach significant ethnic subgroups directly.

BT is a good example of a company marketing successfully to ethnic communities. It has set up an Asian helpline for non-English speakers to call for information on BT products and services. This is supported by product-specific advertising targeting the Punjabi, Pakistani, Bengali and Gujarati communities using a range of Asian print and radio media. Advertising copy has been written in Gujarati, Urdu, Hindi, Bengali and English. This led to the helpline receiving 1,000 calls per week, twice as many as expected at the launch. BT is also considering launching a similar scheme targeting African and Caribbean communities (Curtis, 2001).

Most European countries, however, have distinct subcultures based on ethnic origin. In the Netherlands there are strong immigrant communities from the Far East, especially Indonesia and Indo-China. In the UK, in cities such as Bradford, Leicester and Birmingham there are strong Asian communities with distinctive lifestyles, retailing and service provision and sense of community. Rafiq (1990) found that Asians have had a significant impact on the structure of UK independent retailing, especially where there is a high proportion of Asian residents. This is driven by the desire for specialist provision to serve the particular product needs of the subculture, and also to provide services that are more in tune with the needs of that community. In support of subcultures, some local development agencies, as well as universities or colleges, now support specialist units to help new entrepreneurs from minority communities to get started.

In many ways, the tension within ethnic-based subcultures is between cultural assimilation into the main, dominant culture and the preservation of cultural diversity in language, dress, food, family behaviour, etc. This tension can be seen even on a European scale, where increased emphasis on travel, rapid communication and pan-European marketing is slowly breaking down barriers at the same time as there is a strong movement towards the preservation of distinct national and regional identities. For example in the West of Ireland, the Gaelic-speaking regions are being heavily supported to prevent relatively small numbers of people from leaving their rural way of life.

As far as the immediate future is concerned, even within a united Europe, people are still celebrating and defending their own cultures and subcultures, and marketers need to recognise and empathise with this. One of the reasons (among many) cited for Disneyland Paris's poor start was that the organisation had underestimated French resistance, in particular, to an undiluted all-American cultural concept in the heart of Europe. Europeans are happy, and indeed eager, to experience Disney on US soil as part of 'the American experience', but cannot accept it, it would appear, within their own culture (http://www.disney.go.com).

Subculture need not only be an ethnic phenomenon, however. The existence of a youth subculture, spanning international boundaries, is widely accepted by marketers, and media such as MTV that reach right across Europe allow marketers to communicate efficiently and cost effectively with that subculture. Brands such as Coca-Cola, Pepsi and Pepe Jeans can create messages that capitalise on the common concerns, interests and attitudes that define this subculture. Pepe Jeans, for example, developed an advertising campaign aimed at the youth market, using MTV, cinema and youth magazines, which featured suicide and alienation from parents as a reflection of youth angst, anxiety and antipathy. Pepe's chief executive was quoted by Steen (1995) as saying:

> *We simply show a world which youth will recognise as being what is around them, one which the older generation may wish wasn't there. It is to be expected that people outside the 12–20 age group may miss the point or be offended.*

The core messages strike at something different from, and perhaps deeper than, national or ethnic culture, and thus may have pan-European currency without necessarily becoming bland in the process. That is not to say that all 16–25 year-olds across Europe should be stereotyped as belonging to a homogeneous 'yoof market'. What it does say is that there are certain attitudes and feelings with which this age group are likely to sympathise, and that these can therefore be used as a foundation for more targeted communication that manages to celebrate both commonalities and differences.

eg

Some advertising agencies deliberately try to appeal to 15–25 year-olds with themes that some seniors could find offensive and shocking. French Connection UK, or FCUK for short, has been an outstanding success in the clothing retail sector at the same time that Marks & Spencer has been under strain. Although the marketing offering has to be right, the full frontal use of the FCUK acronym means any advertising, especially on posters, is likely to get noticed. Since 1997, FCUK has had a few run-ins with the ASA, with some of its advertisements approved and some condemned. Poster themes such as 'fcuk fashion', 'fcuk advertising' met with disapproval, while T-shirts with such themes as 'French Connection me' and 'my place now' along with the FCUK trademark slipped through. To French Connection, it is all meant to be a bit of fun, worth a smile. It could be claimed it was pure coincidence, but the reader is left in no doubt as to the innuendo and FCUK has effectively taken ownership of the f-word (Broadbent, 2001).

The most recent campaign theme, however, met with particular disapproval. Fcukinkybugger.com generated 132 complaints despite being shown on only 13 road sites in London. Of particular concern was the danger of the poster being misread by children. The poster was, therefore, deemed offensive and furthermore, it was decided that for a period of two years, all FCUK posters should be pre-vetted for taste (*Marketing*, 2001a). It will be interesting to see how the 'FCUK America' poster campaign is received in a prudish, less understanding United States (Benady, 2001). Either way, to French Connection it simply reflects the mood of the target audience rather than the attitudes and values of the wider population.

Reference groups

Reference groups are any groups, whether formally or informally constituted, to which an individual either belongs or aspires to belong, for example professional bodies, social or hobby-oriented societies, or informal, vaguely defined lifestyle groups ('I want to be a yuppie'). There are three main types of reference group, each of which affects buying behaviour, and these are discussed in turn below.

Membership groups

These are the groups to which the individual already belongs. These groups provide parameters within which individuals make purchasing decisions, whether they are conscious of it or not. In buying clothing, for example, the purchaser might think about the occasion for which it is going to be worn and consider whether a particular item is 'suitable'. There is great concern here about what other people will think.

Buying clothes for work is severely limited by the norms and expectations imposed by colleagues (a membership group) and bosses (an aspirant group?), as well as by the practicalities of the workplace. Similarly, choosing clothes for a party will be influenced by the predicted impact on the social group who will be present: whether they will be impressed; whether the wearer will fit in; whether the wearer will seem to be overdressed or underdressed; or whether anyone else is likely to turn up in the same outfit.

Thus the influence of membership groups on buying behaviour is to set standards to which individuals can conform, thus consolidating their position as group members. Of course, some individuals with a strong sense of opinion leadership will seek to extend those standards by exceeding them and challenging the norms with the expectation that others will follow.

Aspirant groups

These are the groups to which the individual would like to belong, and some of these aspirations are more realistic than others. An amateur athlete or musician might aspire to professional status in their dreams, even if they have little talent. An independent professional single female might aspire to become a full-time housewife with a husband and three children; the housewife might aspire to the career and independent lifestyle. A young, junior manager might aspire to the middle management ranks.

People's desire for change, development and growth in their lives is natural, and marketers frequently exploit this in the positioning of their products and the subtle promises they make. Bird's Eye frozen meals will not stop you being a bored housewife, but will give you a little more independence to 'be yourself'; buying Nike, Reebok or Adidas sports gear will not make you into Ronaldo, Beckham or Figo, but you can feel a little closer to them.

The existence of aspirant groups, therefore, attracts consumers towards products that are strongly associated with those groups and will either make it appear that the buyer actually belongs to the group or signal the individual's aspirations to the wider world.

eg

The Harley-Davidson brand is all about authority and prestige. It is not a bike for the sports motorcyclist: it seems to attract an awful lot of men in their late thirties and early forties, usually professionals seeking a bit of escapism by cruising the highways. For many of them, ownership of a product that could not be afforded in their dim and distant youth is a symbol of their achievement and success in life. Harley-Davidson dominates the cruiser/touring market, one of four market segments in the motorbike industry. The Harley-Davidson owners' group claims to have 640,000 members with one passion. There are even organised cruising tours so that like-minded individuals can meet. In the US, it has a share of over 60 per cent and it is growing in popularity in Europe. The status is reinforced through clever promotional appeals. In one advertisement, with a church in the background, the headline claims that 'you commit four of the deadly sins just by looking at it'. We will leave the reader to work that one out (Francis, 2000).

Many men, especially as they mature, look at a Harley-Davidson motorbike and dream of the open road, their lost youth and an opportunity to get away from the treadmill of work. The company trades on these aspirations and targets the type of men who have the money to own such a prestige symbol. Source: *Harley-Davidson UK.*

Dissociative groups

These are groups to which the individual does not want to belong or to be seen to belong. A supporter of the England soccer team would not wish to be associated with its notorious hooligan element, for example. Someone who had a violent aversion to 'yuppies' and their values might avoid buying products that are closely associated with them, through fear of being thought to belong to that group. An upmarket shopper might prefer not to be seen in a discount store such as Aldi or Netto just in case anyone thinks they are penny pinching.

Clearly, these dissociations are closely related to the positive influences of both membership and aspirational groups. They are simply the other side of the coin, an attempt to draw closer to the 'desirable' groups, while differentiating oneself from the 'undesirable'.

Family

The family, whether two parent or single parent, nuclear or extended, with or without dependent children, remains a key influence on the buying behaviour of individuals. The needs of the family affect what can be afforded, where the spending priorities lie and how a purchasing decision is made. All of this evolves as the family matures and moves through the various stages of its lifecycle. Over time, the structure of a family changes, for example as children grow older and eventually leave home, or as events break up families or create new ones. This means that a family's resources and needs also change over time, and that the marketer must understand and respond to these changes.

Traditionally, marketers have looked to the **family lifecycle** as proposed by Wells and Gubar (1966), and shown in Table 3.3. Over the years, however, this has become less and less appropriate, as it reflects a path through life that is becoming less common in the West. It does not, for example, allow for single parent families, created either voluntarily or through divorce, or for remarriage after divorce which may create new families with children coming together from previous marriages, and/or second families. Other trends too undermine the assumptions of the traditional model of the family lifecycle. According to Lightfoot and Wavell (1995), estimates from the Office of Population Censuses and Surveys (OPCS) in the UK forecast that 20 per cent of women born in the 1960s, 1970s and 1980s may never have children. Those who do currently elect to have children are tending to leave childbearing until later in their lives, so that they can establish their careers first. OPCS has noted that the birth rate among women in their twenties has dropped, while it has increased rapidly for women in their thirties and forties. At the other end of the spectrum, the number of single, teenage mothers has increased alarmingly in the UK to 3 per cent of girls aged 15–19, the highest figure in the EU. Overall, however, European birth rates are falling, leading to 'ageing populations' throughout the EU as the proportion of children in the population falls.

Table 3.3 The family lifecycle

Stage	*Title*	*Characteristics*
1	Bachelor	Young, single, not living at home
2	Newly married	Young, no children
3	Full nest I	Youngest child under 6
4	Full nest II	Youngest child 6 or over
5	Full nest III	Older, married with dependent children
6	Empty nest I	Older married, no children living at home
7	Empty nest II	Older married, retired, no children living at home
8	Solitary survivor I	In labour force
9	Solitary survivor II	Retired

Source: Wells and Gubar (1966).

All of these trends have major implications for consumers' needs and wants at various stages in their lives, as well as for their disposable incomes, and this will be explored further in Chapter 5. The marketer cannot make trite assumptions based on traditional stereotypes of the nuclear family, and something more complex than the Wells and Gubar model is needed to reflect properly the various routes that people's lives can now take. Figure 3.5 offers a revised family lifecycle for the way people live today.

Regardless of the structure of the family unit, members of a household can participate in each other's purchasing decision-making. In some cases, members may be making decisions that affect the whole family, and thus Figure 3.6 shows how a family can act as a decision-making unit where individual members play different roles in reaching the final decision. The roles that any one member takes on will vary from purchase to purchase, as will the length, complexity and formality of the process. The obvious manifestation of the family decision-making unit is in the ordinary week-to-week grocery shopping. The main shopper is not acting as an individual, pleasing only themselves by their choices, but is

Figure 3.5 A modern family lifecycle model

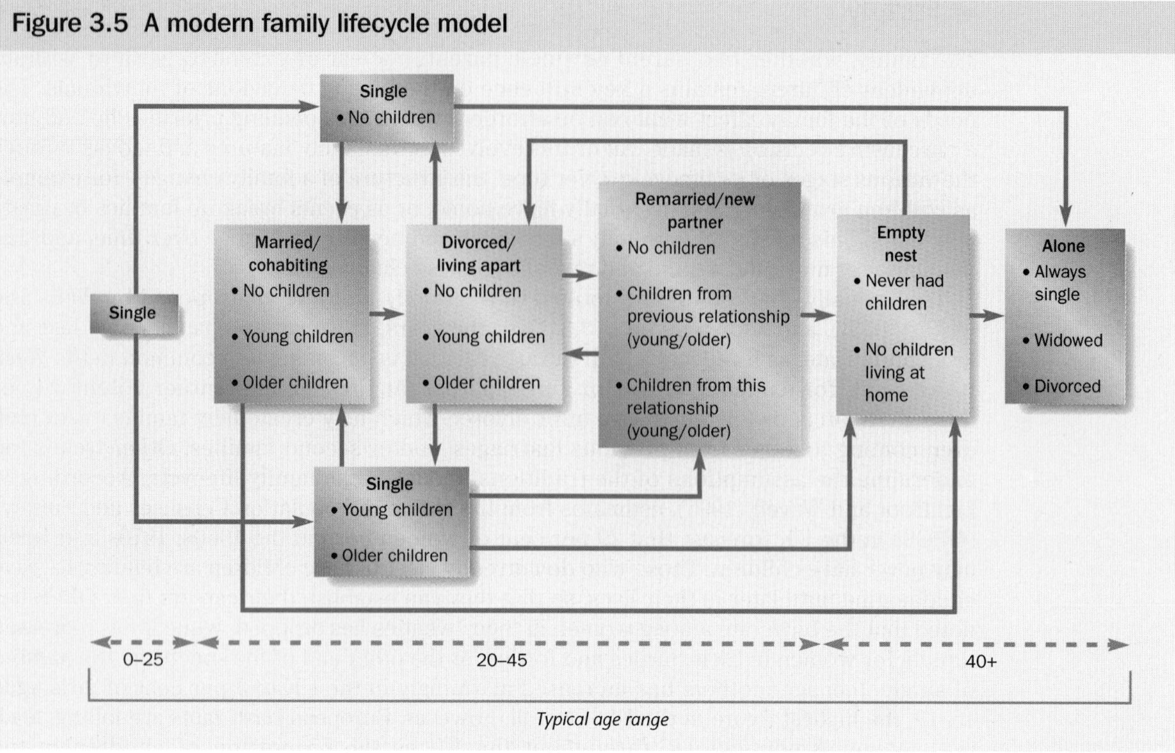

reflecting the tastes and requirements of a group of people. In a stereotypical family, Mother may be the ultimate decider and purchaser in the supermarket, but the rest of the family may have acted as initiators ('When you go shopping, will you get me some . . .?' or 'Do you know that we've run out of . . .?' or 'Can we try that new brand of . . .?') or influencers ('If you buy THAT, don't expect ME to eat it'), either before the shopping trip or at the point of sale.

The buying roles may be undertaken by different family members for different purchases at different times. Thus in the example of purchasing a bicycle, a child may well be the user and influencer, but the parents may be the principal deciders and buyers. Menasco and Curry (1989) suggest that there are two types of decision-making process within a family. The first is *consensual*, where the family agrees on the purchase but needs to agree how it

Figure 3.6 The family as a decision-making unit

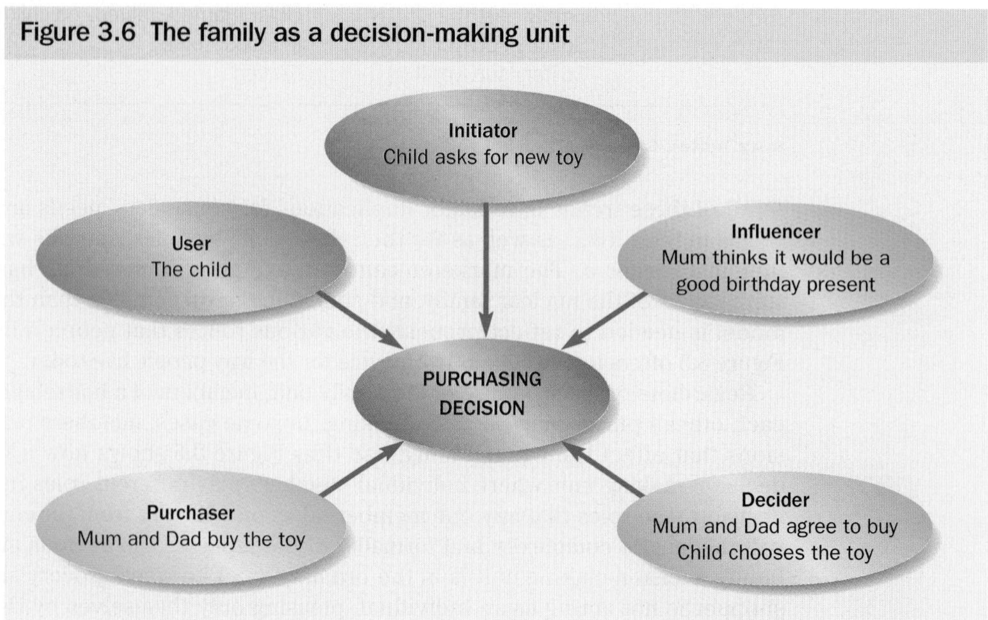

corporate social responsibility *in action*

Pester power: does advertising corrupt our children?

The issue of whether television advertising is a 'bad influence' on children is an ongoing moral and ethical debate with advertisers, legislators and lobby groups often having very different points of view. It is a debate which has become more urgent and more heated, however, as the advertising industry across Europe faces moves to harmonise and standardise regulations across all EU member states in the 2002 Broadcasting Directive. The position in 2001 was very fragmented with member states having a wide variety of rules about advertising to children. Sweden, for example, had banned all domestic television advertising to children under 12; similarly, television advertising aimed at under-12s was illegal in Norway, and heavily restricted in Belgium, Ireland, Holland and Austria. Greece had banned all television advertising for toys before 10 p.m. Italy and Denmark were considering their positions. The UK was not heavily regulated although advertisers were not supposed to encourage children to pester their parents to get them things (but then a clever advertiser can find indirect ways of generating desire . . .). Fear that regulations on children's advertising were going to be tightened considerably were rooted in Sweden's threat to use its 2001 Presidency of the EU to push all member states to opt for a total ban.

The advertising industry is feeling a bit paranoid. Rupert Howell, president of the Institute of Practitioners in Advertising, said,

> *The EU is having more impact on the regulatory environment and is more interventionist than our own government. . . . Advertising is very high profile and an easy target for anyone wanting to score some quick points. We are also up against pressure groups and single issue fanatics. They work hard to attack us, so we have to work even harder to protect our interests. If we don't, we will be hit with more restrictions – it's easy, gesture politics* (as quoted by Curtis, 2000).

Those against a total ban argue on moral grounds, that a ban would curb their right to freedom of speech, and on economic grounds, claiming that if children's advertising was withdrawn, the quality of programming would deteriorate through lack of funding, choice would be restricted, and the price of children's products would go up. In terms of morality versus economics, the cynics argue that while many of the regulations around the EU have been enforced in the name of ethics, in reality, they are simply designed to protect domestic business interests and stifle competition.

The pro-advertising lobby also points to evidence that there is actually little difference in the perceived effects of pester power in Sweden (with a total ban in place) and Spain (without). Research by NOP found that pester power was a bigger problem in Sweden than in Spain. An additional finding, that in-store promotions were seen as more of a problem in Sweden than in Spain gives more ammunition to the pro-advertisers. They argue that if television advertising is banned, then marketers will find other ways of communicating with children, through in-store promotions, for instance, where kids can get their hands on toys and games and be subjected to a much more interactive, hard sell than a 30-second television advertisement could ever hope to achieve. One consultant said,

> *Activity will be more visible, more interactive, more colourful and noisier as brands try to encourage pester power. POP [point of purchase promotions] will have to be more interesting because it will have to sell harder against more competition* (as quoted by Anderson, 1999).

Nevertheless, there are also those who feel that POP activity is actually a more responsible choice because parents are likely to be there as gatekeepers and they can see exactly what the toy is, assess how their child plays with it and then make an informed purchasing decision. This view, perhaps naïvely, does tend to assume that a child will take 'no' for an answer, and fails to take into account the sheer erosion of adult resolve that a determined child can achieve with persistent pester power.

Evidence does exist that television does have a marked effect on pester power. A UK study looking at children's viewing of advertisements for toys and games in the run up to Christmas found that prolonged exposure to adverts in November and December dramatically increased children's demands, as expressed in their letters to Santa Claus. Those who were exposed to the most advertising asked for far more branded toys. A similar study in Sweden, where advertisers are banned from marketing at children under 12, found that they wanted significantly fewer toys than UK children did. There is some good news for UK parents, though: children who watched television with a parent were far less demanding, Watching with a parent seemed to make children less vulnerable because an adult could help to teach them the difference between adverts and programmes. One of the researchers made the point that,

> *A society which exposes young children to many thousands of adverts every year also has a duty to educate those children in consumer literacy and critical viewing* (as quoted by *The Daily Telegraph*, 2001).

The critical role that parents must play is endorsed by Adrian Furnham, Professor of Psychology at University College, London. His extensive studies have concluded that the cause of pester power is not advertising but 'irresponsible parenting'. In his view, parents need to adopt an 'authoritarian' approach, where rules are established, expectations are managed and decisions are explained, all with the child's point of view kept in mind.

Sources: Anderson (1999); Curtis (2000); *The Daily Telegraph* (2001); *Evening Standard* (2000); Oaff (2001).

will be achieved, and thus some problem solving has to be done to enable it to take place. The second type, felt to be more the norm, is *accommodative*, where the family cannot agree and thus bargaining, coercion, power and compromise are used to effect a result.

However, the changing nature of many families, some with two income earners and more participative decision-making, others with single parents on limited incomes, is challenging relatively simple generalisations about buying habits and family influences. Many children, for example, now have (limited) independent financial means, and for various purchases, such as clothes and entertainment, they can be considered as decision makers and buyers in their own right.

The 'pester power' of children on family purchases should not be underestimated. A deep impression was made on one of your authors by the sight of a child, about 10 years old, making a very loud fuss in Sainsbury's one afternoon over a packet of bread rolls. Children are not normally interested in bread rolls, but this particular packet had popular cartoon characters all over it and Mother was not being allowed to move her trolley until the rolls were safely in there. More seriously, parents are often prepared to make great sacrifices in other areas of the family budget and their own individual spending in order to prioritise children's needs and wants, as suggested on p. 125.

Children are an important target group for the marketer, partly because of their ability to pester their parents and influence family purchasing, and partly because of the marketer's desire to create brand loyalty as early as possible in consumers' lives. For instance, Kellogg's gave away 800,000 sample packs of Choco Krispies, while McDonald's provides free meal vouchers to be used as prizes by schools. Not surprisingly, many teachers, parents and consumer groups are concerned that the young and vulnerable may be exposed to unreasonable marketing pressures.

On the other hand a company such as Colgate feels that it serves the community with the material it supplies to primary schools to promote oral hygiene through a range of educational packages. Their altruistic aim is to make children aware of the importance of regular correct brushing of teeth and not early brand loyalty.

Clearly, groups of all kinds have the potential to act as both facilitators and inhibitors of consumer behaviour. An aspiration to join a particular group might make a purchasing decision easier, if the marketing package clearly reflects that aspiration, while membership of an economically interdependent household might mean that, regretfully, a purchase cannot be justified. For each purchase, the individual has to decide which group's influence is the strongest or most important and act accordingly.

Targeting school children, Colgate promotes responsible dental hygiene.

Source: Colgate Palmolive (UK) Ltd.

Chapter summary

This chapter has centred on consumer buying behaviour, in terms of both the processes through which potential buyers pass in deciding whether to make a purchase and which product to choose, and the factors that influence the decision-making itself.

- The decision-making process was presented as a number of stages: problem recognition, information search, information evaluation, decision and, finally, post-purchase evaluation.
- The length of time taken over the process as a whole or over individual stages will vary according to the type of product purchased and the particular consumer concerned. An experienced buyer with past knowledge of the market making a low-risk, low-priced routine purchase will pass through the decision-making process very quickly, almost without realising that it has happened. This is a routine problem solving situation. In contrast, a nervous buyer, lacking knowledge but facing the purchase of a one-off, high-risk, expensive purchase, will prolong the process and consciously seek and analyse information to aid the decision. This is extended problem solving.
- Decision-making is influenced by many factors apart from the type of purchase. Some of these factors are external to the consumer, such as social, economic, legal and technological issues existing within the wider environment. Closer to home, the consumer influences the decision-making process through psychological factors. The type of personality involved; the individual's perceptions of the world and ability to interpret information; the ability to retain and learn from both experience and marketing communication; the driving motivations behind behaviour; and finally the individual's attitudes and beliefs all shape their responses to the marketing offering and ultimately their acceptance or rejection of it. In addition to that, the individual's choices and behaviour are affected by sociocultural influences defined by the groups to which the individual either belongs or wishes to belong. Social class as traditionally defined is of limited help to the marketer, but cultural or subcultural groups provide clearly differentiated groups of potential customers. Other membership groups, formed through work, hobbies and leisure pursuits, provide the individual with norms that act as reference points to aid decision-making. Similarly, aspirations fuel people's needs and wants and marketers can attract customers through reflecting those dreams and promising products that can help fulfil them or at least visibly associate the individual with the aspirant group for a while. One of the strongest group influences comes from the family, affecting decisions on what is purchased, how that decision is made and how the individual feels about that purchase.
- Consumer buying behaviour is a complex area, covering a wide range of concepts, but nevertheless is an important one for marketers to understand because it lies at the heart of all marketing decisions.

key words and phrases

Attitude
Awareness
Cognitive dissonance
Consumer decision making
Culture
Evoked set
Extended problem solving
Family lifecycle
Information overload
Learning
Limited problem solving
Motivations
Perception
Personality
Post-purchase evaluation
Problem recognition
Purchasing situation
Reference groups
Repeat purchase
Routine problem solving
Social class
Trial

questions for review

3.1 Differentiate between the internal and external stimuli that might trigger the consumer buying decision-making process.

3.2 Why is post-purchase evaluation important for:
(a) the consumer; and
(b) the marketer?

3.3 Summarise some of the ways in which marketers can 'help' the consumer at each stage in the decision-making process.

3.4 How and why might the duration of the decision-making process and the extent of information search differ between the three different types of buying situation?

3.5 How do perception, learning and attitudes affect consumer decision-making, and how can the marketer influence these processes?

questions for discussion

3.1 Outline the main sources of information that might be used in purchasing:
(a) a new car; and
(b) a packet of biscuits.

3.2 Think of a purchase that you have made recently. What products or brands made up your evoked set of alternatives, and what choice criteria did you use to differentiate between them to lead to your eventual purchase?

3.3 To what extent do you think that social class is a helpful concept in improving the marketer's understanding of consumer behaviour?

3.4 Define the three main types of reference group. Within each type, think of examples that relate to you as a consumer, and analyse how this might affect your own buying behaviour.

3.5 How might the roles undertaken by various members of a two-parent family vary between the buying decisions for:
(a) a house;
(b) something for tonight's dinner; and
(c) a birthday present for a 10-year-old child?

How would your answer change if it was a one parent family?

case study 3.1

Reaching the youth market: euroteens

The youth market, consisting of teenagers and those in their early twenties, is potentially very lucrative. These consumers have disposable income and are fashion conscious, which means that they are buying often in order to keep up with the latest trends in clothes, music and leisure. Marketers recognise that this group has different needs from older, perhaps more traditional consumers. An increasing number of specialist agencies are now researching young consumers to discover what motivates their purchasing and how they make decisions. Datamonitor's report, *Targeting the Youth Market*, cites four reasons why youth spending power in the USA and Europe is rising (Fry, 2000):

- *parental guilt (a)*: the rising divorce rate means that teenagers can play guilt-ridden parents off against each other;
- *parental guilt (b)*: more affluent parents tend to spend more time socialising away from their children – they see increased pocket money as a means of compensation for their absence, relieving their guilt;
- *more affluent families (a)*: an increase in the number of two-income households can mean more disposable income, some of which can filter down to younger members of the family;
- *more affluent families (b)*: many women are waiting to start a family later in life, after they have established a career which means that the family is established on a sounder economic footing.

Euroquest, a network of market research agencies, produced a survey called *Teenagers Europe*, examining the spending patterns and attitudes of 11–19-year-olds across the UK, France, Germany and Italy. These four countries alone represent a market of 27 million teenagers with £24.8 billion of purchasing power. Their spending priorities are remarkably similar. Clothes are the top priority in Germany, France and Italy, with 'going out' second. In the UK, it is the other way around: 50 per cent of teenagers are fashion conscious and 66 per cent take a lot of care over their appearance; 60 per cent agreed that they could not live without music and thus spending on CDs and related music products is also very high on the list. The average amount of disposable income they have, however, varies from country to country: in the UK it is just over £25 per week, whereas Italy has the lowest figure of around £12. The survey also found that UK teenagers watch television for four or more hours per day, much longer than in any of the other countries, presumably because 75 per cent of UK teenagers have televisions in their bedrooms, again a higher proportion than anywhere else. Perhaps more positively, 90 per cent of UK teenagers use computers, yet again a higher proportion than in any other country. The brand preferences they have in common across all four countries are perhaps as expected: 70 per cent prefer to drink Coke and 60 per cent have visited a McDonald's within the last three months.

GfK carried out a similar survey, *Hopes and Fears: Young European Opinion Leaders* across 16 countries in Western, Eastern and Central Europe and in Scandinavia. This survey found that young people are driven by ambition and are afraid of failure. They want to live life to the full. They are very individualistic and do not want to be 'packaged' or classified. As reported by Croft (1998), they are very suspicious of IT, thinking that it diminishes human interaction and lacks warmth, and the more intellectual individuals 'show no desire for the Global Village or teleworking'. These young people think that they will work longer and harder than any previous generation because the distinction between home and work is no longer clear cut. Girls are less attracted to interaction through the internet than are boys and still prefer the telephone. Mobiles are considered to be too expensive, the fax simply is not popular with this generation and most do not have access to e-mail. The survey also concludes that this generation wants to purchase from companies with a strong sense of social responsibility and an ethical culture. Additionally, this generation is not interested in clichés and is very advertising and marketing literate (although Eastern European youth is not quite as cynical . . . yet). Marketers thus need to keep a respectful distance and communicate carefully. As Croft (1998) puts it, this generation is 'brand aware and brand dismissive . . . nothing is forever'.

These conclusions are echoed by De Parcevaux (1998) in a discussion of French 15–25-year-olds. They are considered to be good at decoding advertising and marketing messages and they have plenty of money to spend on themselves. They conform to the tastes and fashions of their peer group and it is important to them to do so. De Parcevaux suggests that these consumers are:

- *pragmatic and realistic*: they are less receptive to messages of consumption than are older generations and will not be patronised; they like products and messages that do not take themselves too seriously;
- *price sensitive*: 85 per cent of 15–25-year-olds say that a competitive price is an incentive to buy, compared with 60 per cent for environmental issues and 56 per cent for products connected with a humanitarian cause;
- *pleasure seekers*: spending priorities are clothes, going out, hi-fi and video-related products, holidays and leisure; they want anything new, surprising, or aesthetically pleasing, and 75 per cent of them admit to impulse purchasing;
- *keen to assert themselves as individuals*: although they are fashion conscious and peer group influenced, they still want individuality, to differentiate themselves somehow from their friends;
- *flexible in their relationships with brands*: 20–30-year-olds in particular are experienced consumers, have changeable tastes and are prepared to switch brands; for 15–18-year-olds, brands play an important role and they look for 'cult' brands such as cKone;
- *aspiring to universal values*: they want to belong to 'international youth', an identity built from a frontierless culture defined by music and sport;
- *reluctant to do anything that constrains them*: they are not interested in anything hierarchical, organised or too 'packaged' – thus the mobile phone companies' 'pay as you go' schemes are very appealing because there is no contract, no bills and no commitment.

Sources: Croft (1998); De Parcevaux (1998); Fry (2000); Morris (1997); Phillips (1997).

Questions

1. How might the characteristics of French youth, as described by De Parcevaux, affect the marketing mix for (a) clothing, (b) toiletries and (c) soft drinks?
2. How do you think sociocultural influences influence the purchasing decision-making processes of the young people described in these surveys?
3. To what extent is there really a single Euroteen market that is meaningful to marketers?

case study 3.2

Breezing out for a night on the tiles

Since the 1990s, Bacardi-Martini has made a concerted effort to develop new products aimed at a younger market, taking advantage of the growing fashionability and popularity of premium pre-mixed spirit-based drinks among clubbers. In 1995, this sector was worth £20 mn in the UK; by 1999 it had rocketed to £810 mn and estimates for 2000 expected it to break the £1 bn barrier (Mintel, 2000a). The most successful of these pre-packaged spirits (PPS) is Bacardi Breezer, a family of rum and fruit juice drinks (for example lime, lemon, peach, pineapple, watermelon, cranberry). Although launched in 1994, the Breezer brand really became well established in early 1999 when a £5.6 mn advertising campaign targeting 18–24-year-olds assured us 'Bacardi Breezer: there's Latin spirit in everyone.' (Cozens, 1999).

By mid-2000, the advertising spend was £14 mn on what was described as an 'outwardly innocent, inwardly naughty' campaign. James Robinson, account executive on Bacardi at McCann's, was quoted by Brabbs (2000) as saying, 'The ads don't target people – they target a state of mind. Breezer represents a distinctive place in people's night out between beer and spirits – they're neither sober nor wasted on it – and that's what we tried to capture. We were seeking to dramatise the fun and mischievous side that Breezer brings out in you.' The campaign clearly captured the imagination as the brand was worth around £345 mn in 2000, selling nearly one million bottles a day.

In summer 2000, the advertising was further reinforced by the investment of £1.5 mn on the portable *Vivid* tent, 75 ft tall and the length and breadth of a football pitch, for use at events such as music festivals (*Marketing*, 2000). *Vivid* is entered via giant inflatable slides which take consumers to 'pleasure zones' including a glass dance floor made up of TV screens showing tropical fish, a 40 ft helter-skelter, an area with cushions and hammocks, and a games area with table football, air hockey and Quasar. There is also, of course, an ample bar area!

By November 2000, the company estimated that the 'Latin Spirit' campaign had doubled sales volumes of the brand which had become the UK's biggest selling pre-mixed spirit. Its market share by value was almost 40 per cent and it was available in 60 per cent of all UK on-trade outlets (the on-trade sells alcohol for consumption on the premises, for example pubs and clubs, while the off-trade, for example wine shops and supermarkets, sells it for consumption elsewhere) (Mason, 2000). A strong new development was introduced for the run up to Christmas in the character of Tom the cat. Tom lives a normal pampered-puss existence with a sweet little old lady by day, but by night, he's a seasoned cat-about-town clubber, flirting with the girls, hanging round on the bar with the Breezer bottles, and grooving on the dance floor.

Bacardi Breezer also has a dedicated website (http://www.bacardi-breezer.co.uk) which has a strong clubbing theme. The web agency Loudcloud which designed the site said that 'The site will be pretty radical and out there' and that it would provide young adults with 'lunchtime escapism' from the daily routines of work (Chandiramani, 2001).

In a Neilsen report published in March 2001, Bacardi Breezer featured at number 11 in the top twenty best-selling drink brands in pubs in England and Wales. With the exception of Strongbow cider at number nine, the top ten consists of beers and lagers (Young, 2001). The pub and club on-trade is very important to Bacardi Breezer, accounting for 70 per cent of sales volumes. Some 73 per cent of 18–24-year-olds visit a pub or club at least once per week and they are looking for drinks that make fashion and lifestyle statements. Beverage Brands, another key player in the PPS sector said:

> *The highly experimental 18–35-year-olds are seeking more than just a drink, they are constantly looking for a new experience in their drinks repertoire* (as quoted by Mintel, 2000a).

The PPS brands seem to answer well to that need. The use of established 'pedigree' parent brand names such as Bacardi and Smirnoff help to create a quality image which is reinforced by the use of glass packaging. This is also perceived as 'female-friendly'. The brands and the bottles themselves have become fashion statements that drinkers are happy to be 'seen with'. Pubs and clubs like the PPS brands, not only because they are popular, but also because they are quick and easy to serve and they carry a high gross margin of 60–70 per cent, compared with 40 per cent for draught beers (Mintel, 2000a).

Sources: Brabbs (2000); Chandiramani (2001); Cozens (1999); *Marketing* (2000); Mason (2000); Mintel (2000a); Young (2001).

Questions

1 Give an overview of how the buying decision-making process might work for purchasing an alcoholic drink in a pub or club. How might that process differ if the consumer is buying drinks in a supermarket or off-licence?

2 What individual and group influences are likely to affect someone's choice of drink brand?

3 Explain the roles of the various marketing activities described in this case in influencing consumer behaviour.

4 Given the huge range of beers and lagers available and their dominance of the market, why do you think there is still room for products such as Bacardi Breezer?

References for chapter 3

Anderson, P. (1999), 'Child's Play', *Marketing Week*, 9 September, pp. 39–42.

Benady, D. (2001), 'fcuk America', *Marketing Week*, 22 March, pp. 26–9.

Bloch, P. H. et al. (1986), 'Consumer Search: An Extended Framework', *Journal of Consumer Research*, 13 (June), pp. 119–26.

Brabbs, C. (2000), 'Bacardi Parties on with Newest Latin Spirit 'Landlady' Ad', *Marketing*, 15 June, p. 24.

Breitenbach, C. and van Doren, D. (1998), Value-added marketing in the digital domain: enhancing the utility of the Internet. *Journal of Consumer Marketing*. 15(6), 559–575.

Broadbent, G. (2001), 'Design Choice: FCUK', *Marketing*, 10 May, p. 15.

Bruce, A. (2001), 'Connex Stations Set for 40 Stores', *The Grocer*, 11 August, p. 5.

Bruner, G.C. and Pomazal, R.J. (1988), 'Problem Recognition: The Crucial First Stage of the Consumer Decision Process', *Journal of Consumer Marketing*, 5 (1), pp. 53–63.

Chaffey, D., Mayer, R., Johnston, K. and Ellis-Chadwick, F. (2002), *Internet Marketing: Strategy, Implementation and Practice*. Financial Times/Prentice Hall. Harlow, Essex, UK, 2nd edn.

Chandiramani, R. (2001), 'Bacardi Targets Young with Site Revamp', *Marketing*, 28 June, p.13.

Chisnall, P.M. (1985), *Marketing: A Behavioural Analysis*, McGraw-Hill.

Clay, P. (1998), 'Emergency Measures', *Marketing Week*, 14 May, pp. 44–5.

Cozens, C. (1999), 'Latin Spirit Surfaces in Bacardi Breezer Spots', *Campaign*, 9 April, p. 6.

Croft, M. (1998), 'Technology Leaves Teens Cold', *Marketing Week*, 25 June, pp. 38–9.

Curtis, J. (2001), 'Think Ethnic, Act Ethnic', *Marketing*, 5 July, pp. 24–5.

Curtis, J. (2000), 'Should These Ads be Banned?', *Marketing*, 23 March, pp. 28–9.

The Daily Telegraph (2001), 'British Psychological Society: TV Adverts Blamed for Children's Gift Greed', *The Daily Telegraph*, 30 March, p. 13.

De Parcevaux, A.-C. (1998), 'L'art de séduire les 15–25 ans', *L'Entreprise*, No 149, February, pp. 84–8.

Duncan, C.P. (1990), 'Consumer Market Beliefs: A Review of the Literature and an Agenda for Further Research', in G. Marrin *et al.* (eds), *Advances in Consumer Research*, Association for Consumer Research.

Ehrenberg, A.S.C. and Goodhart, G.J. (1980), *How Advertising Works*, JWT/MRCA.

Engel, J.F., Blackwell, R.D. and Miniard, P.W. (1990), *Consumer Behaviour*, Dryden.

Engel, J.F., Kollat, D.T. and Blackwell, R.D. (1978), *Consumer Behaviour*, Dryden.

Evening Standard (2000), 'No Fun For Kids as EU Plans Ads Clampdown', *Evening Standard*, 20 December, p. 31.

Festinger, L. (1957), *A Theory of Cognitive Dissonance*, Stanford University Press.

Fishbein, M. (1967), 'Attitude and Prediction of Behaviour', in M. Fishbein (ed.), *Readings in Attitude Theory and Measurement*, Wiley.

Fishbein, M. (1975), 'Attitude, Attitude Change and Behaviour: A Theoretical Overview', in P. Levine (ed.), *Attitude Research Bridges the Atlantic*, Chicago: American Marketing Association.

Foxall, G. (1984), 'Consumers' Intentions and Behaviour', *Journal of the Market Research Society*, 26, 231–41.

Francis, R. (2000), 'Leaders of the Pack', *Brandweek*, 26 June, pp. 28–38.

Fry, A. (2000), 'Brands Cash in By Targeting Tweens', *Marketing*, 12 October, pp. 39–40.

The Grocer (2001), 'A Bitter Pill or Healthy Competition', Pharmacy Supplement to *The Grocer*, 4 August, pp. 2–3.

Hardcastle, S. (2001), 'Yogurts and Pot Desserts', *The Grocer*, 21 April, pp. 33–6.

Hauser, J. *et al.* (1993), 'How Consumers Allocate Their Time When Searching for Information', *Journal of Marketing Research*, November, pp. 452–66.

Henderson, M. (1997), 'Class Tightens its Grip on Britain', *The Times*, 15 December, p. 7.

Hilgard, E.R. *et al.* (1975), *Introduction to Psychology*, (6th edn) Harcourt Brace Jovanovich.

Hilgard, E.R. and Marquis, D.G. (1961), *Conditioning and Learning*, Appleton Century Crofts.

Howard, J.A. and Sheth, J.N. (1969), *The Theory of Buyer Behaviour*, Wiley.

Inskip, I. (1995), 'Marketers Develop a Class Consciousness', *Marketing Week*, 13 January, p. 23.

Jacoby, J. *et al.* (1974), 'Brand Choice as a Function of Information Load', *Journal of Marketing Research*, 11 (February), pp. 63–9.

Joyce, T. (1967), 'What Do We Know About How Advertising Works?', *Advertising Age*, May/June.

Kassarjian, H.H. (1971), 'Personality and Consumer Behaviour: A Review', *Journal of Marketing Research*, 8 (November), pp. 409–18.

Keller, K.L. and Staelin, R. (1987), 'Effects of Quality and Quantity of Information on Decision Effectiveness', *Journal of Consumer Research*, 14 (September), pp. 200–13.

Kimberley, W. (2001), 'Skoda: An Eastern Europe Success', *Automotive Manufacturing and Production*, June, pp. 26–8.

Korfman, K. (1991), 'Comparability and Comparison Levels Used in Choices among Consumer Products', *Journal of Marketing Research*, August, pp. 368–74.

Lewis, H. and Lewis, R. (1997), 'Give your customers what they want'. *Selling on the Net. Executive book summaries*, 19(3), March.

Lightfoot, L. and Wavell, S. (1995), 'Mum's Not the Word', *Sunday Times*, 16 April.

Lutz, R.J. (1981), 'The Role of Attitude Theory in Marketing', in H.K. Kassarjian and T.S. Robertson (eds), *Perspectives in Consumer Behaviour*, Scott, Foresman.

Marketing (2001a), 'All Outdoor Ads to be Vetted for 'Taste' by CAP', *Marketing*, 5 April, p. 5.

Marketing (2001b), 'Brand Re-vitalisation of the Year', Supplement to *Marketing*, 12 June, p. 12.

Marketing (2000), 'Bacardi Breezer to Lure Clubbers With 'Dance' Tent', *Marketing*, 10 August, p. 4.

Marketing Week (2001), 'New Media Takes Pain out of Cottage Industry', *Marketing Week*, 22 February, p. 55.

Marsh, H. (2001), 'Why Women are Taking to the Net', *Marketing*, 21 June, pp. 33-4.

Maslow, A.H. (1954), *Motivation and Personality*, Harper and Row.

Mason, T. (2000), 'Breezer Unveils £4m Christmas Push', *Marketing*, 9 November, p.7.

Matilla, A. and Wirtz, J. (2001), 'Congruency of Scent and Music as a Driver of In-store Evaluations and Behaviour', *Journal of Retailing*, 77 (2), pp. 273–89.

Mazur, L. (2001), 'Marketeers Need to Find out What We Women Want', *Marketing*, 29 March, p. 18.

Menasco, M.B. and Curry, D.J. (1989), 'Utility and Choice: An Empirical Study of Wife/Husband Decision Making', *Journal of Consumer Research*, 16 (June), pp. 87–97.

Mintel (2000a), 'Alcoholic RTDs', *Market Intelligence*, April.

Mintel (2000b), 'Household Cleaning Products, 25/5/00', accessed via accessed via http://sinatra2.mintel.com, October 2001.

Morris, N. (1997), 'How to Give Youth What They Really, Really Want', *Marketing Week*, 14 August, p. 12.

Mudd, T. (2000), 'The Last Laugh', *Industry Week*, 18 September, p. 38–44.

Newland, F. (2000), 'HHCL Ads Highlight Human Side of AA', *Campaign*, 14 April, p. 4.

Norton, C. (1997), ' 'Dettox Generation' Fails Hygiene Test', *The Sunday Times*, 9 November, p. 10.

Norton, G. (1998), 'Upwardly Mobile Britain Splits into 17 New Classes', *The Sunday Times*, 13 September, p. 1.9.

Oaff, B. (2001), 'The Playground Market', *The Observer*, 29 April, p. 8.

Phillips, A. (1997), 'The Difficulty of Discovering What Makes Euroteens Tick', *Marketing Week*, 11 December, pp. 28–9.

Rafiq, M. (1990), *Are Asians Taking Over British Retailing?*, Paper 1990:12, Loughborough University Management Research Series.

Reynolds, E. (2001), 'AA's Latest Ads Shift Focus from Retention to Recruitment', *Marketing*, 19 April, p. 24.

Rice, B. (2001), 'The Growing Problem with On-line Pharmacies', *Medical Economics*, 4 June, pp. 40–5.

Rice, C. (1993), *Consumer Behaviour: Behavioural Aspects of Marketing*, Butterworth-Heinemann.

Riley, M. (1994), 'Marketing Eating Out: The Influence of Social Culture and Innovation', *British Food Journal*, 96 (10), pp. 15–18.

Rosier, B. (2000), 'Superdrug Set to Unveil E-commerce Services, *Marketing*, 5 October, p. 15.

Simms, J. (2001), 'Think Global, Act Local', *Campaign*, 29 March, pp. 24–5.

Smith, P.R. (1993), *Marketing Communications: An Integrated Approach*, Kogan Page.

Spethmann, B. (2000), 'Strong Medicine', *Supermarket Business*, 15 December.

Steen, J. (1995), 'Now They're Using Suicide to Sell Jeans', *Sunday Express*, 26 March 1995.

Sutton, R.J. (1987), 'Using Empirical Data to Investigate the Likelihood of Brands Being Admitted or Readmitted into an Established Evoked Set', *Journal of the Academy of Marketing Science*, 15 (Fall), p. 82.

Wells, W.D. and Gubar, R.G. (1966), 'Life Cycle Concepts in Marketing Research', *Journal of Marketing Research*, 3 (November), pp. 355–63.

Williams, K.C. (1981), *Behavioural Aspects of Marketing*, Heinemann Professional Publishing.

Young, R. (2001), 'Cider Joins Favourite Pub Drinks', *The Times*, 27 March.

chapter 4

B2B buying behaviour

LEARNING OBJECTIVES

This chapter will help you to:

1. understand the nature and structure of B2B buying;
2. appreciate the differences between B2B and consumer buying;
3. analyse the buying process and the reasons why purchasing varies across different buying situations; and
4. link B2B buying with the development of marketing strategy.

Introduction

The essence of the marketing philosophy was described at the beginning of this book as the satisfaction of customers' needs and wants through the provision of the right products and services, at the right time, in the right place at the right price. This remains true whether that customer is an individual or an organisation. All organisations, whether making products or delivering services, purchase goods and services from a range of suppliers so that they can run their own operations. Consider, for example, a small local garage. It may purchase not only petrol, but also spare parts, tools, supplies, some capital machinery, confectionery, and accountancy services, for instance. Compare that with a large steel producer or car assembly plant and the thousands of suppliers that are dealt with regularly.

There are, therefore, sufficient differences between individuals and organisations in what they purchase and the ways in which they go about their purchasing to make separate consideration worthwhile.

This chapter looks at the special characteristics and problems of B2B markets, beginning with a definition of B2B marketing and a classification of B2B customers. The characteristics of B2B markets are then discussed, and attention is given to the ways in which they differ from consumer markets. The buying decision-making process is analysed, laying the foundations for looking at the roles that individuals and groups play within it. The last two sections examine the criteria, both economic and non-economic, that affect B2B purchasing and the importance of long-lasting buyer–seller relationships.

eg

A purchasing manager for an NHS (National Health Service) Trust in London, responsible for three hospitals, faces a formidable buying challenge. Whether it is equipment for the operating theatres, new beds, ambulances, cleaning or even just catering for the patients and staff, specifications have to be drawn up, suppliers' contracts negotiated, orders placed and operations monitored. Virtually all supplies, other than pharmaceutical products, are handled so it is important that the purchasing function provides professional expertise to the hospitals in the group. This results in an annual spend of £70 mn on 24,000 purchase orders and 125,000 invoices per year. In addition between 20 and 30 major contract tenders have to be prepared each year and, given the size of some of them, they require close attention to ensure that the medical and operational staff get what they want. Part of the purchasing job is routine, and effort is going on to rationalise and streamline ordering where possible, but it is also true to say that purchasing also has to work closely with the wards and clinic staff as new needs and problems emerge. Recently, purchasing was required to source a new type of face mask due to a rise in the number of tuberculosis cases. Any supplier with hospitals in mind clearly needs to understand a lot about how and what hospitals buy if it is to have any chance of doing business (Riley, 2000).

In your wider reading you may come across the terms *organisational marketing* and *industrial marketing*. Generally speaking, these terms are often used interchangeably with 'B2B' or 'business-to-business marketing'. This text, however, uses the term B2B marketing, although we acknowledge that not all organisations that make substantial purchases, for example government departments, universities and hospitals, are in business in the profit-making sense of the word. Thus, as pp. 138 *et seq.* will show, the term B2B marketing covers a wide range of purchasing relationships between a wide range of organisations. First, however, it is important to define more precisely what B2B marketing is.

Defining B2B marketing

B2B marketing is the management process responsible for the facilitation of exchange between producers of goods and services and their organisational customers. This might involve, for example, a clothing manufacturer selling uniforms to the army, a component manufacturer selling microchips to IBM, an advertising agency selling its expertise to Kellogg, Kellogg selling its breakfast cereals to a large supermarket chain, or a university selling short management training courses to local firms. Whatever the type of product or organisation, the focus is the same, centred on the exchange, the flow of goods and services that enable other organisations to operate, produce, add value and/or re-sell. Figure 4.1, even though it only offers a simplified view of this flow, gives an idea of the number and complexity of exchanges involved in getting products to the end user or consumer.

The steel producer, for example, takes raw materials (and we will not even begin to consider the mining, refining and transport processes that go into the production of the iron ore and coke that the steel producer buys) and turns them into steel that is then pressed into

Figure 4.1 Flows within a B2B market

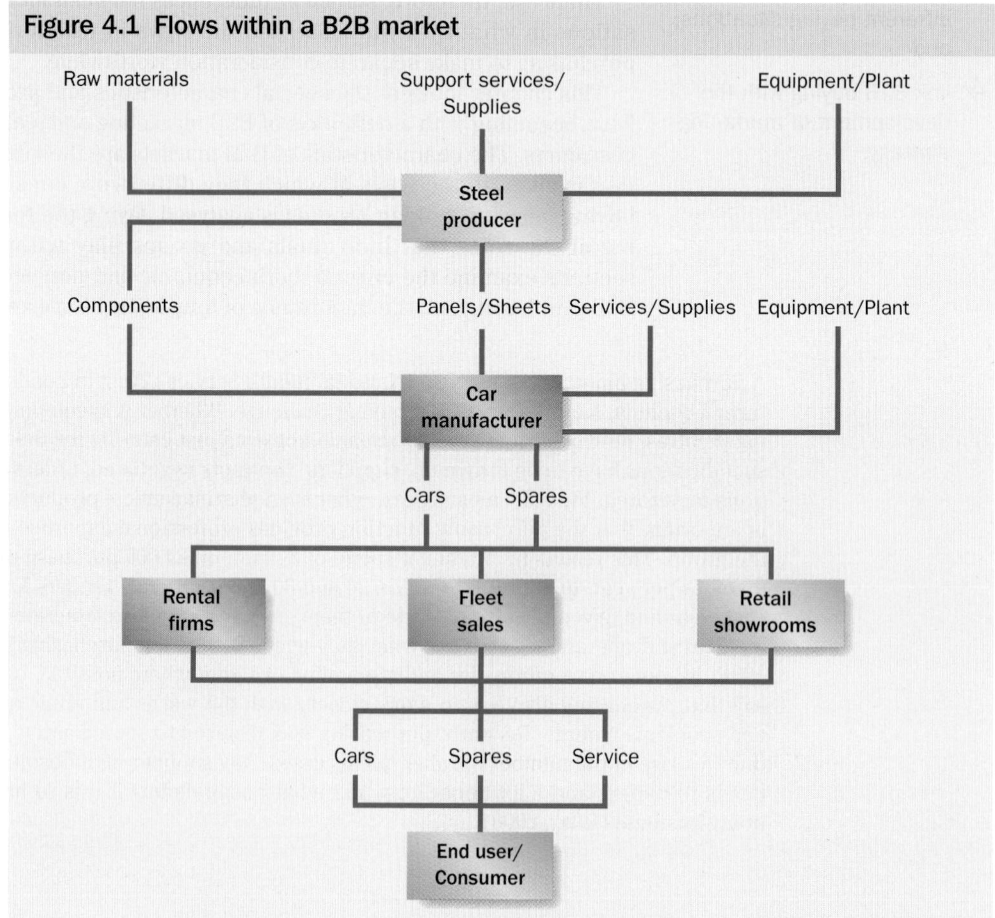

panels or cast into components to sell on. The car producer can then assemble these components, along with others from different sources (glass, plastics, paints, fabrics, tyres, electrics, etc.), with the finished car as the output to be sold on.

Both the steel producer and the car manufacturer use more than just the components and raw materials that make the physical product, however. Both of them also buy in various services and supplies that support the main production without directly providing a physical part of it. For example, proper planned maintenance of plant and machinery is essential for safe and consistent production. The steel producer will perhaps use contract engineering service companies to do this work and would consider it as contributing indirectly to the end product. Similarly, the supplies and services used by the quality control function or the managers and administrators that keep a smooth flow of goods and orders in and out of the organisation support the end product indirectly. Thus an organisation may have to purchase not only raw materials and semi-finished goods, but also financial, technical and management consultancy services.

Once the cars or the spares leave the car manufacturer, the retail showroom, i.e. the car dealership, as a *re-seller*, takes the products and sells them to the general public with little change other than perhaps the addition of number plates and fine tuning of the engine. Most of the *value added* comes from intangible elements of customer service.

Even at the re-seller level, there are also other support services to consider. A car dealership selling to the general public, for instance, would put a lot of thought into the design and ambience of the showroom, the training of its sales and service staff and its advertising and other promotional activities. All these services can be bought in and add to the successful sale of the physical product.

All of this goes to show that B2B marketing and purchasing is a complex and risky business. An organisation may buy many thousands of products and services, costing anything from a few pennies to many millions of pounds per item. The risks are high in these markets where a bad decision, even on a minor component, can bring manufacturing to a halt or cause entire production runs to be scrapped as substandard.

eg

When China decides to buy passenger jets, the world's aircraft manufacturers sit up and listen. The Chinese government has indicated that it will be requiring up to 400 narrow-bodied (Boeing 737s, Airbus 320s, etc.) and wide-bodied (747s, etc.) jets between 2001 and the end of 2005. It can be hardly be said that the Chinese are unfamiliar with the jets on offer, as similar models are currently in service. Nor is the final decision on orders likely to be based solely on functional, performance and cost criteria. Of course, contracts must be negotiated and agreements reached on delivery and various price/lease options, but when dealing with China, the political dimension cannot be ignored. The size of Boeing's share may, in part, be determined by whether Beijing feels that the USA has done sufficient penance for the Hainan island alleged spy-plane incident and how it wishes to use orders for Europe and the USA as a bargaining chip for its WTO membership bid or for negotiating other economic concessions. The government had hoped to split the initial order for 110 narrow-bodied jets three ways, including the purchase of around 30 Tupolev Tu-204s from Russia as a sign of strengthening relations between Beijing and Moscow. However, the country's airlines voiced strong opposition on market and technical grounds. Instead, only about five are expected to be ordered for freight work. Given the broader issues of B2B marketing highlighted in this example it is clear that large orders to countries with strong governmental influence requires lobbying at both the buyer and governmental levels (Doyle, 2001).

There are several differences between B2B and consumer marketing, as Table 4.1 shows. If a consumer goes to the supermarket and finds that their preferred brand of baked beans is not there, then it is disappointing, but not a disaster. The consumer can easily substitute an alternative brand, or go to another supermarket, or the family can have something else for lunch. If, however, a supplier fails to deliver as promised on a component, then the purchasing organisation has a big problem, especially if there are no easily accessible alternative sources of supply, and runs the risk of letting its own customers down with all the commercial damage that implies. Any failure by any link in this chain has a severe impact on the others.

Table 4.1 Differences between B2B and consumer marketing

B2B customers often/usually . . .	*Consumer customers often/usually . . .*
• purchase goods and services that meet specific business needs • need emphasis on economic benefits • use formalised, lengthy purchasing policies and processes • involve large groups in purchasing decisions • buy large quantities and buy infrequently • want a customised product package • experience major problems if supply fails • find switching to another supplier difficult • negotiate on price • purchase direct from suppliers • justify an emphasis on personal selling	• purchase goods and services to meet individual or family needs • need emphasis on psychological benefits • buy on impulse or with minimal processes • purchase as individuals or as a family unit • buy small quantities and buy frequently • are content with a standardised product package targeted at a specific market segment • experience minor irritation if supply fails • find switching to another supplier easy • accept the stated price • purchase from intermediaries • justify an emphasis on mass media communication

Thus the links have to be forged carefully, and relationships *managed* over time to minimise the potential problems or to diagnose them early enough for action to be taken. Policy decisions have to be made about purchasing, for example whether to source from one supplier only (**single sourcing**) or from several suppliers (**multiple sourcing**), or whether to manufacture rather than outsource. In addition, decisions have to be made about how the purchasing process should operate (who is authorised to do what and with what safeguards). All these issues will be addressed later in this chapter.

A final reminder of the volume and variety of B2B buyer–seller relationships is provided in Figure 4.2, which shows in detail the wide range of goods and services essential to a clothing manufacturer. All these goods and services represent relationships that have to be established, maintained and sustained.

B2B customers

So far, only one kind of B2B buying situation has been considered in detail, that of a profit-making organisation involved in transactions with other similarly orientated concerns. There are, however, other kinds of organisation that have different philosophies and approaches to purchasing. Overall, there are three main classes: commercial enterprises, government bodies and institutions, each of which represents a lot of buying power.

Commercial enterprises

Commercial enterprises consist of profit-making organisations that produce and/or re-sell goods and services for a profit. All the members of the flow shown in Figure 4.1 fall into this category, which can be further divided into a number of subgroups.

Users

Users purchase goods and services to facilitate their own production, although the item purchased does not enter directly into the finished product. Examples of this are CAD/CAM systems, office equipment and management consultancy services. Large chemical and steel process manufacturing plants may source a wide range of services from a myriad of local, and often small, suppliers. Plumbers, cleaners, caterers and travel agents thus supply services that are an indirect means to an end rather than a direct influence on production. Although some vetting and inspection may take place before these suppliers are allowed on

Figure 4.2 A clothing manufacturer and its suppliers

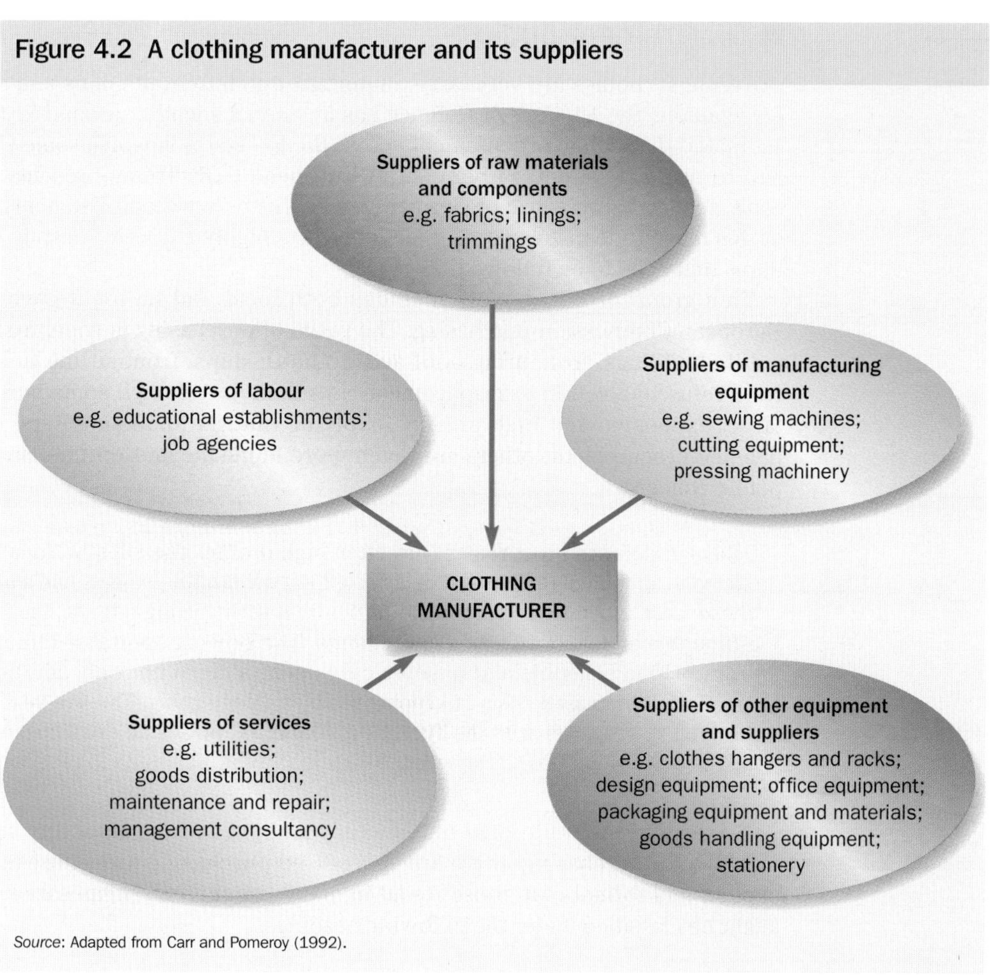

Source: Adapted from Carr and Pomeroy (1992).

to the list of approved suppliers, these procedures are far less rigorous than those imposed on companies wishing to supply goods and materials that do directly enter or support the production process.

Original equipment manufacturers

Original equipment manufacturers (OEMs) incorporate their purchases into their own product, as the car manufacturer does with the electrics, fabrics, plastics, paint, tyres, etc. Some of these components will be recognisable even after the OEM has finished with them, for instance a tyre is a recognisable element of a car and is usually strongly branded by the original supplier, whereas others, such as the paint, are incorporated anonymously. Recognisability is important for the tyre manufacturer as a means of developing links with the end consumer and encouraging brand loyalty when it is time to buy new tyres. OEMs' purchasing is very closely linked with forecast demand for their end products, and needs good buyer–seller coordination as it has to be tied in with production schedules.

Re-sellers

Re-sellers purchase goods for re-sale, usually making no physical changes to them. As mentioned above when discussing the car dealership, the value added stems largely from service elements. A full outline of the role and function of re-sellers can be found in Part five of this book. This group is the closest to the end consumer of the product and should, therefore, be able to feed valuable information back up the chain on what the end market really wants.

Government bodies

Government bodies are very large, important purchasers of goods and services. In the UK, for example, the Ministry of Defence has an annual spend of around £10 bn and it has been estimated that public procurement across the EU states is worth some €720,000 mn, equivalent to between 11 and 14 per cent of European GDP. This represents a potential market equivalent to half the size of Germany's GDP (http://www.europa.eu.int). Purchasing power of this magnitude makes government contracts highly attractive despite the complex procedures that need to be followed.

This group of B2B buyers includes both local and national government, as well as European Commission purchasing. The range of purchasing is wide, from office supplies to public buildings, from army bootlaces to battleships, from airline tickets to motorways, from refuse collection to management consultancy. Although some purchases may be very large, expensive and high profile, involving international suppliers, as is often seen in defence procurement, others are much more mundane and routine, and involve very little public concern.

eg

Delays in defence procurement are often high profile. The UK's National Audit Office concluded in an annual review that delays on 25 of the largest projects had slipped to 28 months. These were attributed to technical difficulties with cutting-edge technology, collaboration difficulties and shifting user requirements. The Bowman portable radio system was eight years behind schedule and in some cases delays mean not only additional project overspends, but increased costs in keeping old technology going. The five-year delay in replacing the Type 42 destroyer with the Type 45, for example, means an extra cost of £565 mn in keeping the older ships afloat (Hayward, 2000).

Because of the traditional bureaucracy and public accountability surrounding government sector purchasing, there are specialised purchasing procedures that are often more explicit and formal than those found in many commercial organisations. Such procedures might be classified under the following headings.

The development of precise specifications for the good or service

For more innovative and large-scale projects, the development of specifications may be done in conjunction with specialist consultants and the potential suppliers' development personnel.

Tendering for the right to supply

Organisations are requested to bid or tender for the right to supply. Some jobs are only open to tender from organisations already on an approved list, while others are open to anyone.

Assessment of tenders

The submitted tenders are assessed and the winning one is chosen.

Tendering is a very competitive process that demands that the suppliers are well tuned into the procedures and are able to find out early what tenders are on offer. Much of this is down to having the right contacts within the purchasing organisation and maintaining good relationships and communication links with them (within ethical boundaries, of course). These issues of buyer–seller relationships are expanded further at p. 150 and pp. 167 *et seq.* It is often too late to establish contact once formal bidding has begun. The contact and reputation building necessary for next year's bids needs to be done this year.

The EU, as part of the single European market (SEM) initiative, issued a Public Services Directive stating that for any of its purchasing needs of €200,000 (€5mn for construction bids) or more, the contract must be advertised openly for tender across all community boundaries. In 1987 some 12,000 tender notices were published in the *EC Official Journal* and this had risen to 90,000 by 1995, although this was estimated to be still a long way from the total number that should have been published. The Public Services Directive aimed to encourage more cross-border trading, especially for smaller companies, but it has been criticised for creating more bureaucracy and actually doing little to help smaller companies to compete across Europe (Nolan, 1997a).

The EU Commission recognises that despite the Directives, much still remains to be achieved in opening up the internal market based upon transparent and competitive purchasing rules. In the harmonisation of standards, for example, only 10 per cent compliance had been achieved in construction by 2001 and even in the important machinery area, just 50 per cent compliance had been achieved (The European Commission, 2001). Unique standards are often a major barrier for suppliers breaking into a new geographic market when they are more familiar with an alternative set of home-based standards. In short, standards can be used to protect domestic suppliers or the very large pan-European operators.

At the core of the problem lies the low rate of response to tenders. The Commission now intends to promote greater use of e-procurement, up to 25 per cent by 2003, and to ensure that all tender notices are internet-based to allow a wider dissemination of opportunities. It also intends to allow some relaxation of the rules concerning dialogue for more complex purchases in the tendering stage itself as this again favours those suppliers who have built up close contact. The problems in achieving open competition are formidable, however. The Commission itself recognises the scale of the task and has concluded that 'from its investigations of complaints, even though the contracting authorities have to establish in descending order the importance attached to the selection criteria, they still enjoy a considerable margin of discretion when awarding contracts' (Proposal for a Directive, 2000.0115). In other words, less tangible considerations can come into play and although the view of the managing director of a radio communications equipment manufacturer that 'the French still want to buy from France, the Germans from Germany and the British from anywhere' may be extreme, it does highlight some of the potential problems when up against strong local suppliers in a B2G situation.

Institutions

This group includes (largely) non-profit making organisations such as universities, churches and independent schools. These institutions may have an element of government funding, but in purchasing terms they are autonomous. They are likely to follow some of the same procedures as government bodies, but with a greater degree of flexibility of choice. A university, for example, has to purchase a wide range of products and services in order to teach and undertake research and consultancy. Large capital projects, such as a new lecture theatre, perhaps part financed by government, may be subject to tendering and closed bidding (i.e. a potential supplier makes a bid without knowing what price anyone else has quoted). Many other supplies are purchased with varying degrees of efficiency and formality from a range of different suppliers. A typical university may deal with over 5,000 suppliers, although the bulk of purchases may come from just a few of them.

Characteristics of B2B markets

The differences between consumer and B2B markets do not lie so much in the products themselves as in the context in which those products are exchanged, that is, the use of the marketing mix and the interaction between buyer and seller. The same model of personal computer, for example, can be bought as a one-off by an individual for private use, or in bulk to equip an entire office. The basic product is identical in specification but the ways in which it is bought and sold will differ.

The following subsections look at some of the characteristics of B2B markets that generate these different approaches.

Nature of demand

Derived demand

All demand in B2B markets is **derived demand** – derived from some kind of consumer demand. So, for example, washing machine manufacturers demand electric motors from an engineering factory, and that is a B2B market. The numbers of electric motors demanded, however, depend on predictions of future consumer demand for washing machines. If, as has happened, there is a recession and consumers stop buying the end product, then demand for the component parts of it will also dry up.

Figure 4.3 represents the links in the chain stretching from forestry to reading material. At each stage in the process, there are different influences on the activities and behaviour of the organisations, yet these have implications both up and down the chain. In northern Europe, for example, between 30 and 40 per cent of the population read newspapers, whereas in southern Europe it is closer to 10 per cent. An increase in that reading rate to bring it closer to the northern level would have a great impact on those supplying paper to the newspaper industry in that region. Similarly, the increase in demand for high-quality, full colour special interest publications (for instance CD review magazines) affects the type, quality and quantity of paper and printing processes demanded.

Another problem with derived demand is that the further up the supply chain an organisation is, the more remote it is from the end consumer and the further ahead it has to look in order to predict demand. In the fashion industry, for example, organisations such as ICI and DuPont that produce dyes and fibres have to be two years ahead of the market. This

Figure 4.3 Influences on a B2B purchasing chain

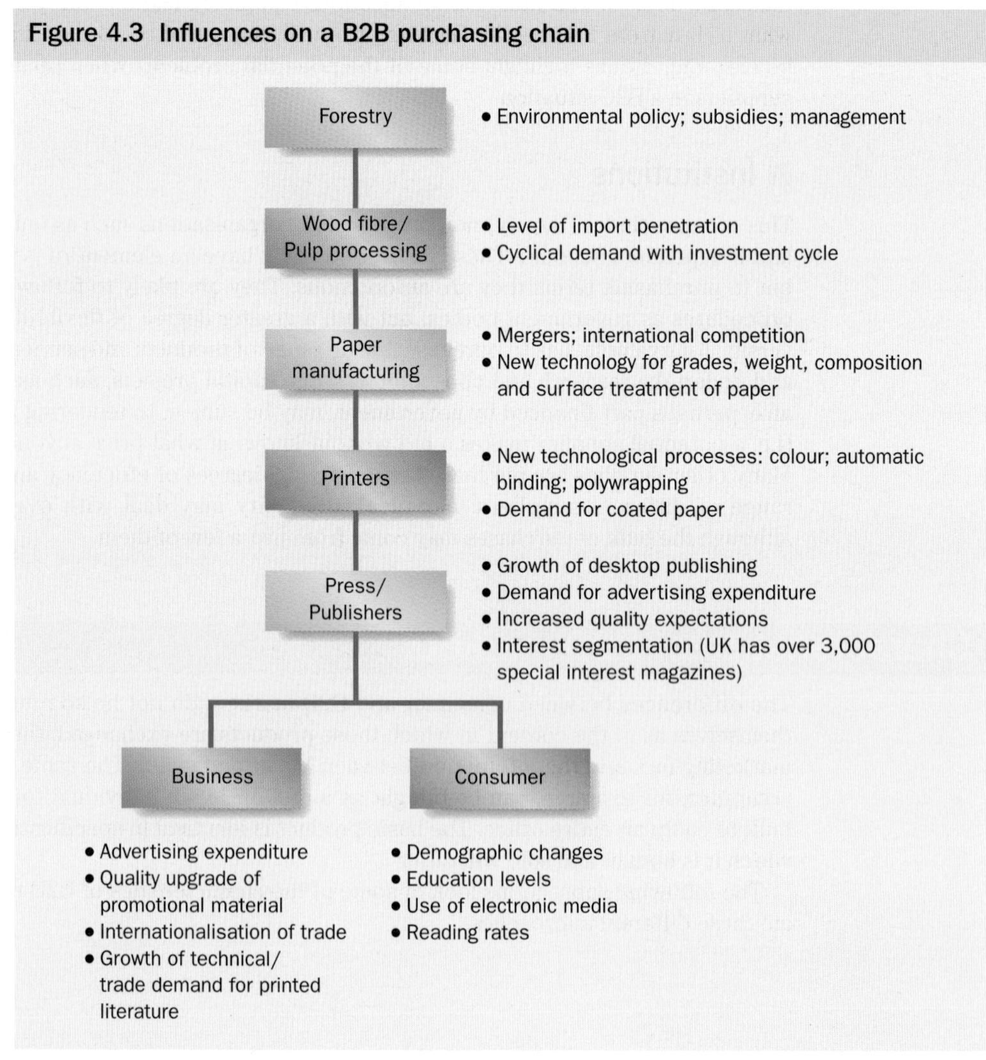

marketing *in action*

Aluminium marketers 'can-do'

Aluminium producers need to keep a close eye on how their customers are using aluminium in their own products if they are to forecast and market effectively. Aluminium has many advantages over traditional steel products: it is more versatile, lighter, does not rust and can be easily recycled, although these benefits usually come at a higher price. In the aerospace industry aluminium's advantages make it a prime choice. The motor industry, however, is only slowly switching to aluminium. At present aluminium can mainly be found in engine blocks and wheels, while steel is preferred for the large tonnage needed for the body panels. Things are changing, however. In the USA, the average quantity of aluminium used to be around 150 lbs per car, but by 2001 it was 250 lbs and it was expected to reach 350 lbs by 2005. Aluminium producers such as Alcan have been working closely with car designers to increase the number of aluminium components in car production, carefully considering cost/performance trade-offs. By substituting aluminium for steel the overall weight of a car can be reduced, leading to better fuel consumption, reduced exhaust omissions, and improved safety with reduced braking distances. Overall, it allows more scope for new features such as air conditioning to be installed. The auto manufacturers need to consider their own competitiveness and customer reaction before deciding to switch.

The canning industry is also another prime market for aluminium although there are significant differences between the USA and Europe in per capita consumption. The average European gets through 70 cans per annum compared with a staggering 370 in the USA. In the USA, aluminium is the canners' first choice, making it the largest market in the world for cans. In Europe, however, around half of the 53 billion cans used each year are made from steel, especially in Germany, although in Finland, Switzerland and Greece almost 100 per cent of cans are aluminium. In this sector, there are also other substitutes. PET (polyethylene terephthalate) is regarded as easier for pack shapes and colour both of which can be important for brand identification and image building, although there is little difference in price compared with aluminium.

Manufacturers, therefore, serve two main industry groupings, dispersed globally. The large commodity markets, such as cans, can be price sensitive and highly competitive. The niche markets tend to involve higher value-added and more product tailoring to meet customer requirements and although still competitive, once the contractual relationship has been made, the relationships tend to be more enduring.

Sources: *Financial Times* (2000); O'Connor (2000); Solman (2000).

means that in spring 2003 they will be deciding what colours and fabrics will be fashionable in spring 2005! Figure 4.4 shows how those two years are used up in the product development process.

Joint demand

It is also important to note that B2B is often **joint demand**. That is, it is often closely linked with demand for other B2B products. For example, demand for casings for computers is linked with the availability of disk drives. If there are problems or delays with the supply of disk drives, then the firm assembling the computer might have to stop buying casings temporarily. This emphasises that there is often a need to plan and coordinate production schedules between the buyer and a number of suppliers, not just one.

Such tight and crucial links are not common in consumer markets. A close example, however, is that demand for carpets can be linked with the level of buying and selling activity in the housing market, but the two things are not as inextricably tied as in the B2B situation above.

Inelastic demand

Elasticity of demand refers to the extent to which the quantity of a product demanded changes when its price changes. Elastic demand, therefore, means that there is a great deal of price sensitivity in the market. A small increase in price will lead to a relatively large decrease in demand. Conversely, inelastic demand means that an increase in price will make no difference to the quantity demanded.

A car battery, for instance, is just one component of a car. A fall in the price of batteries is not going to have an impact on the quantity of cars demanded, and the car manufacturer will demand neither more nor fewer batteries than before the price change. In this context, and indeed in any manufacturing situation where a large number of components are used,

Figure 4.4 Derived demand in the fashion industry

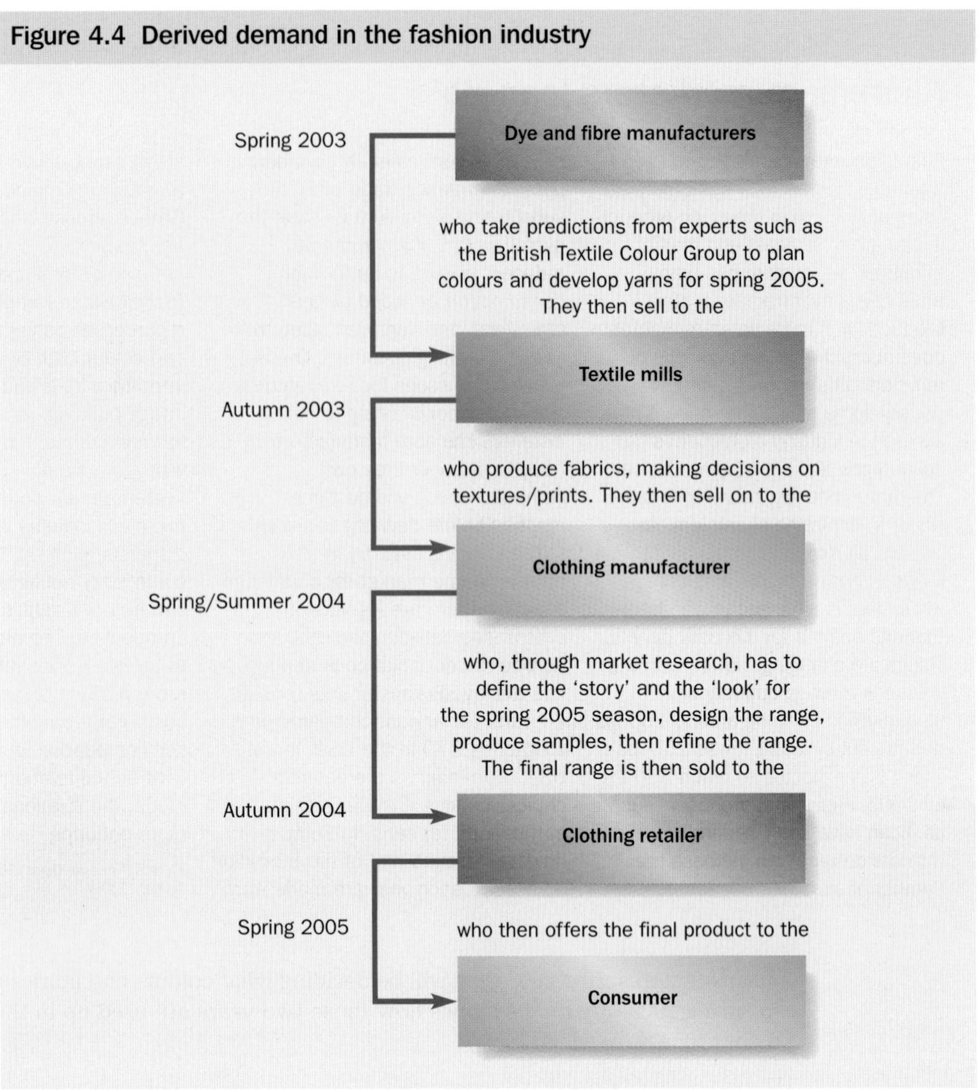

demand is inelastic. Any price changes will be passed on in higher prices charged to the manufacturer's customers or be absorbed into the total costing of the product, or will cause the manufacturer to look for alternative components or cheaper sources of supply (but that takes time and effort and may have implications for production processes, quality and specifications). Whatever happens, demand will not change and in the short term cannot change, since the manufacturer has obligations and orders to fulfil.

Structure of demand

One of the characteristics of consumer markets is that for the most part they comprise many potential buyers spread over a wide geographic area, that is, they are diffuse, mass markets. Think of the market for fast food, for example, which McDonald's has shown to have worldwide appeal to many millions of customers. B2B markets, in contrast, differ in both respects.

Industrial concentration

B2B markets tend to have a small number of easily identifiable customers, so that it is relatively easy to define who is or is not a potential customer. McDonald's can persuade non-customers to try its product and become customers; in that sense, the boundaries of the market are fuzzy and malleable, whereas a manufacturer of kilns to the brick and roofing tile industry would have problems in trying to extend its customer base beyond very specific types of customer.

This kind of concentration opens up all sorts of marketing possibilities in terms of relationship building and personal contact that just would not be feasible in consumer mass markets. It allows more focused targeting and, in some cases, the dedication of specific members of staff to service that relationship, or the establishment of regional offices and/or distribution facilities.

Considerable knowledge, experience and trust can build up between buyers and suppliers. Where there is a finite number of known customers, most organisations in the trade know what the others are doing, and although negotiations may be private, the outcomes are very public. As seen in the Chinese jet purchasing example earlier (*see* p. 137), Airbus and Boeing will be very aware of each other and the strategies they will employ. The number of airlines worldwide with the need for wide-bodied jets, for example, is quite small and the age of the respective fleets, expected retirement dates and the operational problems encountered are widely publicised so there are few secrets or hidden opportunities in the aircraft manufacturing industry.

Geographic concentration

Some industries have a strong geographic bias. Such geographic concentration might develop because of resource availability (both raw materials and labour), available infrastructure or national and EU government incentives. Traditionally, heavy industry and large mass producers, such as shipbuilders, the coal and steel industries and the motor industry, have acted as catalysts for the development of a range of allied suppliers. More recently, airports and seaports have given impetus to organisations concerned with freight storage, movement, insurance and other related services.

eg

Kista, just north of Stockholm, has been described as 'Mobile Valley' because it has the second most important geographic concentration in the world of R&D in mobiles and broadband technology. With a well-educated population and the highest mobile and internet per capita use in the world, the local conditions have been favourable for more modern forms of concentration. International companies such as IBM, Intel, Motorola, Nokia and Siemens have set up competence and research centres in the area which in turn has spawned many smaller niche suppliers and producers. The net effect is a technically highly skilled workforce that favours innovation (Brown-Humes, 2000). Similarly in Germany, the Baden-Württemberg region has developed many science parks and high technology research centres based on what is claimed to be the highest geographic concentration of scientists in Europe. From a traditional manufacturing base, the region now has thriving export businesses, at a rate well above that of many other German länder (Barber, 2000). This new form of geographic concentration provides obvious opportunities for a range of service providers, whether software specialists or marketing consultants!

SKF sells bearings direct to larger OEMs across Europe, especially in the automotive, electrical and mechanical engineering sectors.

Source: SKF.

Concentration can, however, lead to a high degree of mutual dependency. A small, highly specific customer base can leave a supplier very vulnerable if something goes wrong. The closure of a coach works in Shannon, Ireland, resulted in a number of small suppliers also going out of business because they could not find new markets for their skills quickly enough.

Buying process complexity

Consumers purchase primarily for themselves and their families. For the most part, these are relatively low-risk, low-involvement decisions that are made quickly, although there may be some economic and psychological influences affecting or constraining them, as Chapter 3 has shown. In contrast, B2B purchasers are always buying on behalf of other people (i.e. the organisation), which implies certain differences from the consumer situation. These differences give rise to much more complexity in the buying process, and the marketer must appreciate them when designing strategies for encouraging trial and reordering. The various dimensions of complexity are as follows.

B2B purchasing policy

Certain systems and procedures for purchasing are likely to be imposed on the B2B buyer. There may be guidelines on favoured suppliers, or rules on single/multiple sourcing or on the number of quotes required for comparison before a decision can be sanctioned. Often, a purchasing manual is provided for all staff who may be involved in dealing with suppliers. This manual would outline organisational rules and approaches to purchasing, and might list approved suppliers and the procedures to be undertaken for approving a new supplier.

Philips is a global operator in the electronics market with factories all over the world. The company recognises that customer satisfaction depends on the quality of what happens on the production line, which in turn depends on the performance of suppliers. Philips cultivates supplier relationships based on trust and cooperation, and together, Philips and its suppliers develop technology, solve problems, learn from experience and try to avoid errors and misunderstandings. Clearly, Philips cannot develop and maintain deep relationships with every one of its suppliers. Instead, it assesses its suppliers to discover which are the most important in terms of their strategic significance to Philips' business. Philips has three categories of supplier:

1 *Supplier–partners*: these are the most important suppliers and Philips builds intense, involved relationships with them. These suppliers might well have essential knowledge and/or expertise that Philips could not otherwise access or develop for itself. This makes these suppliers extremely significant strategically, as their loss could seriously undermine Philips' current business and future direction.
2 *Preferred suppliers*: these suppliers are less important, but there is still good reason for Philips to work closely with them on issues such as quality, logistics and price to gain mutual benefit.
3 *Commercial suppliers*: these are the least important suppliers and although Philips will encourage better performance in terms of quality, etc., it is unlikely to get involved in helping the supplier to achieve it.

Philips also emphasises the importance of supplier re-evaluation as a basis for improving future performance. A supplier's actual performance is measured against mutually agreed targets in terms of quality, logistics, costs and responsiveness (*European Purchasing and Materials Management*, 1993/94).

An organisation's decision whether to source from a single supplier or from multiple suppliers is another important aspect of **purchasing policy**. With a single source, the purchaser needs to be assured of the continuity and consistency of supply, as well as value for money. Table 4.2 outlines the advantages and disadvantages of alternative sourcing strategies.

It is easy to see how the selection of sourcing policy makes a clear statement to suppliers about value and how the buying company may be willing to play suppliers off against each

Table 4.2 The advantages and disadvantages of alternative sourcing strategies

(a) Single sourcing

Advantages	*Disadvantages*
• Improved communications and understanding between buyer and supplier	• Increased costs through lack of competitive pressure
• Increased responsiveness to buyer's needs	• Increased supply vulnerability
• Shared design of quality control systems	• Reduced market intelligence and thus flexibility
• Elimination of supplier switching costs	• Improved supplier appraisal capacity
• Improvement in product cost effectiveness	
• Reduced prices through larger volumes	
• Reduced prices through reduced supplier costs	
• Enhanced ability to implement JIT systems	

Source: Adapted from Treleven (1987).

(b) Multiple sourcing

Advantages	*Disadvantages*
• Increased competitive pressure	• Perceived lack of commitment
• Improved supply continuity	• Increased costs
• Improved market intelligence	• Less supplier investment
• Improved supplier appraisal effectiveness	• Reduced willingness to adapt
	• Higher operating costs

Source: Adapted from Hahn *et al*. (1986) and Ramsey and Wilson (1990). Reprinted by kind permission of MCB University Press Ltd.

other to obtain the best deal (Zeng, 2000). Other benefits of multiple sourcing include a greater degree of flexibility in technical areas and better protection in the event of supply difficulties from any one supplier (Ansari and Modarress, 1990). The consequences, however, are a large base of suppliers, very short-duration contracts, and the burden of reponsibility for maintaining the necessary technology, expertise, quality, cost and delivery competencies rather than trusting them to suppliers (Render and Heizer, 1997). If building a long-term partnership is not the goal of the buying firm, and if the initial price is more important than longer-term cost efficiencies, then multiple sourcing could well be favoured.

Ramsay and Wilson (1990), in a study of sourcing strategy, challenged the growing belief in Japanese models of long-term single sourcing. They proposed that large, powerful, high-spending organisations might gain more by using competitive pressure to keep a number of suppliers on their toes. This would also reduce the buyer's vulnerability to supply interruption from strikes or breakdowns. Segal (1989) found that the decision whether to adopt single or multiple sourcing was often the result of an overriding organisational attitude to suppliers, arising from whether the buyer wanted close, long-term relationships with suppliers, or an arm's-length, competitive type of atmosphere. Segal does concede, however, that other factors, such as product type, market structure and location, might also influence the decision.

Further restraints might also be imposed relating to how much an individual is allowed to spend under particular budget headings on behalf of the organisation before a second or more senior signature is required. Linking individual spending limits with the most appropriate quotation procedure could give rise to a matrix such as that shown in the hypothetical example in Table 4.3.

This matrix provides clear guidelines on who should be involved, for what amount, and the types and methods of quotation required. However, even in this matrix, much would depend on the nature of the organisation. Clearly, for a car manufacturer placing high volume, repetitive orders, the order value categories would be completely inappropriate.

Table 4.3 Purchasing guidelines

Estimated value of order	*Method of enquiry*	*Type of quote*	*Authorisation*
Below £500	Phone/In person	Oral	Junior manager
£500 – £2000	Written/Catalogues	Non-competitive	Middle manager
£2000 – £20,000	Written	Competitive quotes	Senior manager
Above £20,000	Written	Tenders	Board members

In addition to the formal requirements associated with purchasing, guidelines are often produced on ethical codes of practice. These do not just cover the obvious concerns of remaining within the law and not abusing authority for personal gain, but also address issues such as confidentiality, business gifts and hospitality, fair competition and the declaration of vested interests.

Professional purchasing

The risk and accountability aspects of B2B purchasing mean that it needs to be done professionally. Much negotiation is required where complex customised technical products are concerned and, even for small components used in manufacturing, defining the terms of supply so that they are consistent and compatible with production requirements (for example performance specification, delivery schedules and quality standards) is a significant job. Most consumer purchasing does not involve so great a degree of flexibility: the product is standard and on the shop shelf, with clearly defined price, usage and function; take it or leave it.

Different types of production and operating systems will help to shape an organisation's purchasing task. An inflexible or technology-driven manufacturing organisation, such as a continuous production plant, allows little scope for varying the types of purchases made and needs suppliers who will conform to the standards required for maintaining the system (Sheth, 1977). Furthermore, according to Hallén (1980), if there is no guaranteed economic and stable flow of materials at a consistent quality level, the system will be severely impaired. It is thus critical for the suppliers in such a system to be able to meet the demands of the customer's technology.

Mass production systems are often rigid in the short term, although with careful planning they can be reorganised and modified to accommodate new products. At times of model changes and reorganisation, there may be an opportunity for the supplier to adopt new technical solutions, but often it is the buyer who will determine requirements and dominate the supply situation. This contrasts with unit production, where close discussion and joint development may take place to develop designs and specifications that meet the requirements of the application.

eg

Body Shop wanted some rigid packaging and decided to find a supplier over the internet. So it gave a multi-vendor sourcing site, http://www.webpackaging.com, a try. This site provides contact information for over 1,000 global container suppliers, far more than Body Shop would ever have been able to locate on its own. A sophisticated search mechanism generates contact details and links to appropriate potential suppliers' own websites. From the internet search, a shortlist of suppliers was generated and Body Shop contacted them to request samples. Body Shop ended up with three suppliers, from France, New York and Australia. Although the later stages of negotiation and ordering were conducted offline, the critical research and initial evaluation stage was speeded up considerably by the power of the internet (Barnaby, 2000).

In supplying components for these British built fighter aircraft, suppliers have to be as innovative and as technologically advanced as BAE Systems.

Source: BAE Systems

Group decision-making

The need for full information, adherence to procedures and accountability tends to lead towards groups rather than individuals being responsible for purchasing decisions (Johnson and Bonoma, 1981). A full discussion of the role and structure of groups (*buying centres or decision-making units*) can be found at pp. 160 *et seq*. While there are group influences in consumer buying, for example the family unit, they are likely to be less formally constituted than in the B2B purchasing situation. It is rare, other than in the smallest organisations or for the most minor purchases, to find individuals given absolute autonomy in organisational spending. Mattson (1988) found that product related aspects of the purchase strongly influenced the area of the organisation involved in the purchase, while the size of expenditure influenced the managerial level of those involved.

Purchase significance

The complexity of the process is also dictated by the importance of the purchase and the level of experience the organisation has of that buying situation (Robinson *et al.*, 1967).

For instance, in the case of a **routine re-buy**, the organisation has bought this product before and has already established suppliers. These products may be relatively low-risk, frequently purchased, inexpensive supplies such as office stationery or utilities (water, electricity, gas, etc.). The decision-making process here is likely to involve very few people and be more a matter of paperwork than anything else. Increasingly, these types of purchase form part of computer-based automatic re-ordering systems from approved suppliers. A blanket contract may cover a specific period and a schedule of deliveries over that time is agreed. Bearings for the car and electrical motor industries are sold in this way. The schedule may be regarded as definite and binding for one month ahead, for example, but as provisional for the following three months. Precise dates and quantities can then be adjusted and agreed month by month nearer the time. Increasingly, with JIT systems, schedules may even be day or hour specific!

A **modified re-buy** implies that there is some experience of buying this product, but there is also a need to review current practice. Perhaps there have been significant technological developments since the organisation last purchased this item, or a feeling that the current supplier is not the best, or a desire to renegotiate the parameters of the purchase. An example of this is the purchase of a fleet of cars, where new models and price changes make review necessary, as does the fierce competition between suppliers who will therefore be prepared to negotiate hard for the business. The decision-making here will be a longer, more formal and involved process, but with the benefit of drawing on past experience.

A technical modified re-buy, therefore, is related to changing design and performance specifications, while a commercial modified re-buy involves issues such as price and delivery. The former type may be decided by technical personnel, whereas the latter is more likely to concern the purchasing department.

New task purchasing is the most complex category. The organisation has no previous experience of this kind of purchase, and therefore needs a great deal of information and wide participation in the process, especially where it involves a high-risk or high-cost product. One example of this might be the sourcing of raw materials for a completely new product. This represents a big opportunity for a supplier, as it could lead to regular future business (i.e. routine or modified re-buys). It is a big decision for the purchaser who will want to take the time and effort to make sure it is the right one. Another situation, which happens less frequently in an organisation's life, is the commissioning of new plant or buildings. This too involves a detailed, many-faceted decision-making process with wide involvement from both internal members of staff and external consultants, and high levels of negotiation.

Laws and regulations

As we saw in Chapter 2, regulations affect all areas of business, but in B2B markets, some regulations specifically influence the sourcing of products and services. An obvious example would be the sourcing of goods from nations under various international trade embargoes, such as Iraq in the 1990s. More specifically, governments may seek to regulate sourcing within certain industrial sectors, such as utilities.

eg

When countries forgive each other and trade relations are resumed, the opportunities for B2B can be great. Within two weeks of the fall of Slobodan Milosevic in Serbia a team of industrialists, supported by the UK government, planned to visit the country as part of the re-establishment of trade links that had been banned for many years during the break up of Yugoslavia. A similar mission into Kosovo shortly after peace resulted eventually in orders worth £24 mn and the rebuilding challenge in Serbia offers even greater prospects (*Professional Engineering*, 2000). In some cases, however, the embargoes can go on for a long time. When Iraq invaded Kuwait in 1990 a UN Security Council embargo banned all trade, equating to 44 per cent of the country's GDP. Although some of the conditions have been relaxed on humanitarian grounds, few countries are able to trade legitimately with Iraq over ten years later. In the case of Vietnam it took a lot longer for the Americans to legitimise trade and in the case of Cuba the ban has stretched over many decades (*The Economist*, 2000).

Buyer–seller relationships

Apart from the tangible characteristics of buyer–seller relationships, as formalised in a negotiated, legally drawn-up contract that lays out both parties' responsibilities, obligations and penalty schemes (for late delivery, for instance), there are also less concrete factors shaping the way in which two organisations do business.

Where there is a small number of identifiable customers, then it is possible for the buyer and the seller to build experience, knowledge and trust in each other to an intimate level that consumer marketers can only dream of. Suppliers can tailor their offerings to suit particular buyers, leading to long-term relationships with joint development potential.

One of the problems of such close relationships, however, is dependency. In the short term, the purchaser comes to rely on regular supplies conforming to quality standards, while over a longer period, either party may come to regard the other as essential. For example, a small injection moulding firm found itself selling 80 per cent of its output to a large multinational manufacturer of domestic vacuum cleaners. Since the purchasing organisation also had two alternative suppliers on the sidelines, it was able to exert considerable influence over the small supplier who could not afford to lose the business. These issues are covered more fully at pp. 167 *et seq.*

The result of all the above complex factors working together is to make B2B purchasing a much longer, more formalised process than in consumer markets. B2B buying decisions have to be justified to managers, accountants and shareholders, and are, therefore, likely to be more rationally made, to be based on more solid information and to reflect more collective responsibility than a consumer decision. They are also more likely to lead to long-term, mutually valuable, interdependent relationships between specific buyers and sellers.

Buying decision-making process

It is just as important for marketers to understand the processes that make up the buying decision in B2B markets as it is in consumer markets. The formulation of marketing strategies that will succeed in implementation depends on this understanding. The processes involved are similar to those presented in the model of consumer decision-making described in Chapter 3, in that information search, analysis, choice and post-purchase evaluation also exist here, but the interaction of human and organisational elements makes the B2B model more complex.

There are many models of organisational decision-making behaviour, with different levels of detail, for example Sheth (1973), Webster and Wind (1972) and Robinson *et al.* (1967). How the model is formulated depends on the type of organisations and products involved; the level of their experience in purchasing; organisational purchasing policies; the individuals involved; and the formal and informal influences on marketing. Figure 4.5 shows two models of organisational decision-making and, on the basis of these, the following subsections discuss the constituent stages.

Figure 4.5 Models of organisational buying decision-making

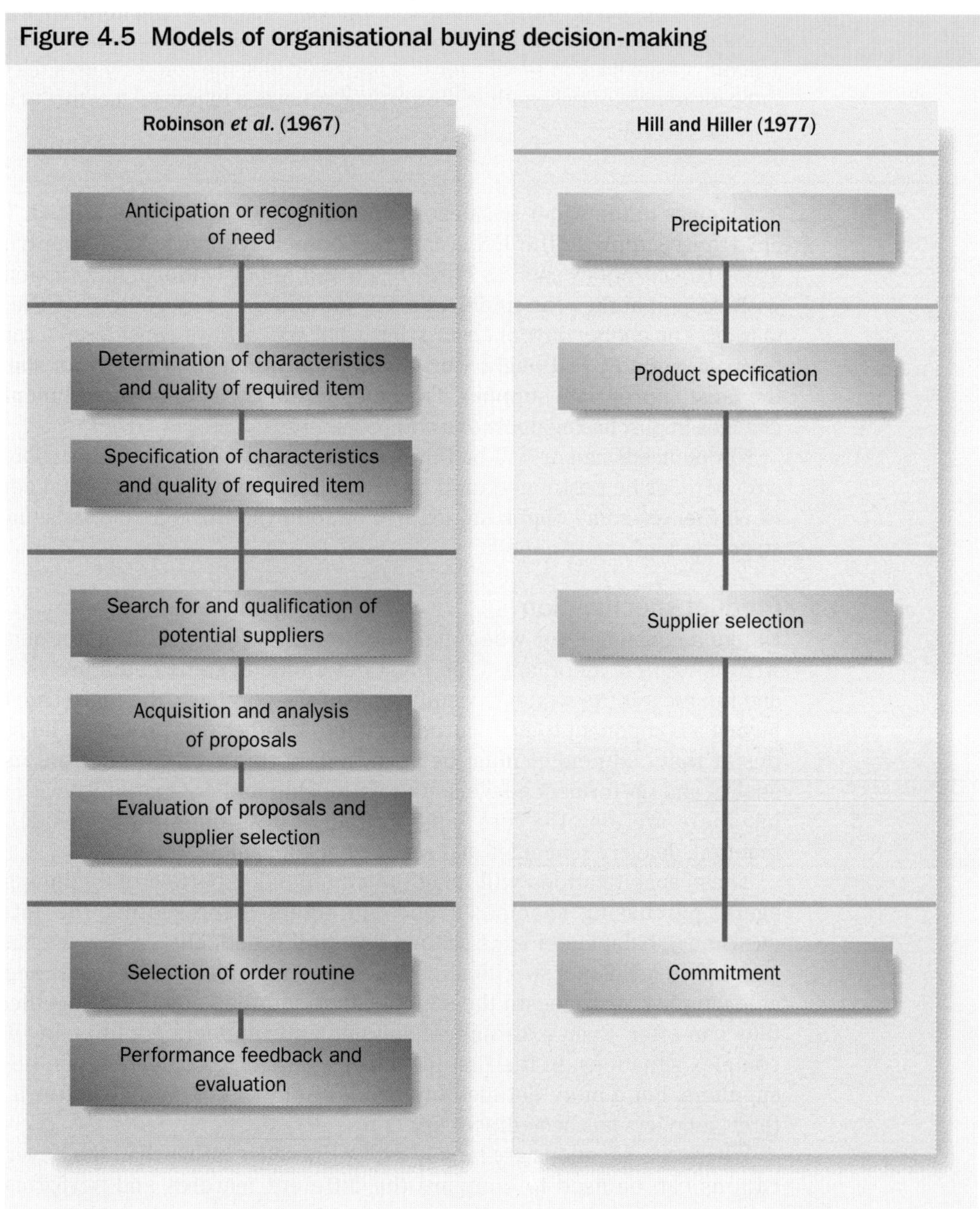

Precipitation

Clearly, the start of the process has to be the realisation that there is a need, a problem that a purchase can solve. The stimulation could be internal and entirely routine: it is the time of year to renew the photocopier maintenance contract. It could be a planned new buy precipitated, for example, by the implementation of expansion plans or the imminent production of a new product. It could also be something more sudden and dramatic than that, such as the failure of a piece of plant or machinery, or a lack of stock.

External influences can also stimulate a need. If the competition has invested in new technology, then other organisations will have to consider their response. Attending trade exhibitions, talking to visiting sales representatives or reading the trade press might also generate awareness of opportunities, whether based on new technology, cost reduction or quality improvements, which would stimulate the buying process.

eg

Potential suppliers may have to help the customer to realise that they have a need. Security Backup Systems, for instance, has to stimulate potential clients to be aware of the importance of storing essential data away from their normal premises, in case of fire or theft. This means exposing potential clients to a problem that they may not have even thought about, and offering a solution that they may not have realised was available. In offering an automatic off-site backup service for PCs and networks, the company uses telemarketing to raise the awareness of risk, outline the cost and arrange a follow-up meeting to discuss the client's needs in detail.

Changes in the wider business environment can also trigger a need. The privatisation of electricity supply in the UK created a competitive market for supplying large industrial users. Organisations such as Ford, Tesco and Abbey National have appointed energy buyers with responsibility for undertaking a modified re-buy review of the electricity supply market. The energy buyers ensure that what was always considered a routine repurchase in the past can now be bought with the most advantageous long-term supply contracts from the most appropriate supplier. Thus changes in the energy environment have precipitated changes in purchasing decisions and processes.

Not all needs can or will be fulfilled and it is possible for the decision-making process to stop here, or be postponed until the organisational or environmental conditions are better. Nevertheless, some opportunities will be followed through and these move on to the next stage, **product specification**.

Product specification

Unlike a consumer, for whom half the fun of shopping is often not quite knowing exactly what is wanted, an organisation must determine in some detail precisely what is required, and the greater the strategic significance of the purchase, the more true this is. Think about buying a component to be incorporated into another end product. The physical characteristics of that component must be specified, in terms of its function, its design, expected quality and performance levels, its relationship and compatibility with other components, but there are also the less tangible but no less important considerations of quantity required, delivery schedules and service backup, among others.

These specifications will need the combined expertise of engineers, production managers, purchasing specialists and marketers (representing the interests of the end customer), balancing ideals against cost and practicality. A key decision early on will be whether to develop a specification based on known particular needs and then locate a suitable supplier, or to locate the supplier first and then adapt the specifications to suit what they can offer. Even external consultants and suppliers could be involved in particularly complex situations. In the first instance, a general specification will be issued to potential suppliers, but a more detailed one would follow later, perhaps after a shortlist of two or three suppliers has been drawn up.

Where specifications are largely set by the seller rather than the buyer, reports and publications can be used to compare the different features and performance of competing products. The publication *What to Buy for Business*, for example, reviews in detail a wide range of business equipment and services, from franking machines to company health insurance. A typical edition reviews such issues as supplier lists, technical data, guidelines on running costs, discounts and after-sales service for various product categories. All of this helps the B2B buyer to make a more informed choice.

A level of fine detail in specifications is understandable in an engineering context, but is not appropriate in all circumstances. An organisation wanting to develop a corporate brochure, for example, might have a certain amount of in-house expertise within its marketing department, but will issue a general brief to a number of external agencies in order to get a fresh perspective in the light of current practice. The brief may specify the number of pages for the brochure, the scope of the content, the target audience and an indication of the price that the organisation is prepared to pay, but the fine detail will be deliberately vague to allow the agency plenty of creative scope. The agency 'interprets' the brief, then makes proposals to the client who can reject or negotiate from there.

It is also worth while at this stage to define the criteria or priorities for choice. It may not necessarily be cost. If a machine has suddenly broken down, then speed of delivery and installation may be of the essence. In the case of new technology, the choice may hinge on compatibility with existing facilities, the future prospects for upgrading it or the service support offered.

marketing *in action*

If you want to stay on board, you have to share the pain of adapting to the tough conditions in the marketplace

The above paraphrased message from Europe's big railway rolling stock manufacturers such as Siemens Bombardier and Alstom sums up the challenge facing component suppliers to these manufacturers: cut prices or else. The whole sector is under pressure from the penultimate customer, the rolling stock buyers. It has been estimated that there has been a 30 per cent fall in prices over the last ten years as buyers have driven efficiency gains and made use of over-capacity in the industry. Furthermore, as manufacturers are increasingly taking responsibility for maintaining the vehicles they supply, the lifecycle cost of components must also be considered. There is little point in saving money today only to have to spend more three years down the line.

It is a sector that is undergoing structural change with fewer rolling stock manufacturers to target yet more operators as state railway companies give way to franchised and regional operators. The manufacturers are undertaking a supplier rationalisation programme, aiming to cut a typical supply base from between 10,000 and 12,000 suppliers down to around half that number. Cultivating a smaller number of strategic supply relationships creates opportunities for closer working and joint problem solving as well as transaction efficiencies.

Siemens Transportation Systems estimates that 70 per cent of its supplies by volume come from just 300 suppliers so there is scope for considerable rationalisation. All suppliers are being ranked on a points system that covers delivery performance, quality consistency as well as unit cost. Companies scoring below 50 per cent face a bleak future unless they are in a strategic supply area in which choices are limited. The remaining suppliers will be required to work even closer with Siemens during the specification and contract negotiation with the rolling stock manufacturers to ensure that more competitive bids can be made.

Valdunes Holding in France, with its roots in the USA, France and Belgium is a strong component supplier to the industry, concentrating on wheels. It is the market leader with 30 per cent of the European market, estimated at 350,000 black forged wheels. Its nearest competitor is Bonatrans with a 24 per cent share, then there is BVV with 16 per cent and a number of other suppliers taking the remaining 30 per cent. There is an expectation that acquisitions and mergers will be necessary for survival, not just within a particular subsector but also leading to greater integration of subsystem suppliers so that larger, completed assemblies can go straight into production, reflecting the desire to assemble rather than manufacture, again a feature of the motor industry.

Alstom operated a 'Stretch 30' programme designed to reduce the cost base by 10 per cent per annum over a three-year period. Although this was achieved, it was not enough and the programme has now been converted into a rolling exercise. The means used are indicative of the dynamics within the sector to which B2B marketers must pay heed:

- Review of supplier performance
- Increased coordination of purchasing across the whole Alstom organisation
- Sourcing from low cost areas such as India, China and eastern Europe
- Design to cost
- Standardisation
- Improved supply chain coordination, including just-in-time (JIT).

▶

It is not all pain for the suppliers, however. Alstom has encouraged existing suppliers to become involved in the design stage of new equipment and this can lead to benefits for all parties concerned. In addition, having a smaller number of suppliers could lead to greater stability for the remaining organisations and even longer-term contracts with performance clauses. Closer working may be especially important as European harmonisation and standardisation become more prevalent. Slowly, national approvals are giving way to European approvals and this in time could lead to longer production runs and greater efficiencies for all the supply chain.

Source: *Modern Railways* (2001).

Supplier selection

The next stage involves the search for a suitable supplier who can best meet all the specified criteria. Sometimes, the inclination to search for potential suppliers can be quite low, and the purchasing department will keep files on who can do what. If existing suppliers can do the job, then they are likely to be favoured. On other occasions, it may be necessary for buyers to be proactive by openly seeking new suppliers and encouraging quotations from those who could meet their requirements. Nevertheless, there is often a bias towards existing suppliers who are known and trusted.

There are some advantages in this approach. Existing suppliers are at least a known quantity, and the purchasing organisation will have experience and a realistic view of their

e-marketing *in action*

Who uses online B2B marketplaces?

Electronic B2B marketplaces are variously known as electronic marketplaces, exchanges and hubs. They are virtual intermediary locations with facilities to enable trading between a large numbers of buyers and sellers. Since most of them are new companies, they are examples of the reintermediation phenomenon of e-commerce. Reintermediation is where new companies that are independent of buyers and suppliers are used to facilitate sales.

An example of a B2B marketplace of European origin is Industry to Industry (www.itoi.com) that was originally a vision of Professor Klaus Schwab, President and Founder of the World Economic Forum that was launched at the WEF's 1999 Annual Meeting in Davos, Switzerland. Industry to Industry has separate spot markets for commodities such as Chemicals, Plastics and Energy. Industry to Industry has partnered with companies who specialise in other aspects of the supply chain, for example SGS and Bureau Veritas handle the inspection of goods, Danzas covers logistics and transportation, and Deloitte Touche Tohmatsu takes care of import/export and taxation issues. It is interesting to note that although it has started as a global exchange it has introduced country specific exchanges such as i2iexchangeitaly (www.i2iexchangeitaly.com) and www.marketplaceitaly.com for small and medium-size enterprises (SMEs). This suggests that even in the global economy localisation of services is necessary for success.

The introduction of the B2B marketplace concept attracted a lot of investment since it provided an opportunity for businesses to change their suppliers more rapidly according to product price and quality criteria. For suppliers they give an opportunity to showcase their products on a global basis in an open competitive marketplace. Research presented by AMR Research at the EmarketplaceWorld Conference in London in February 2002 suggests that business users of eMarketplaces rank their main benefits as:

- ability to share information within trading communities;
- streamlined supply chain operations (obtain supplies more rapidly);
- reduced procurement costs;
- identification of new suppliers;
- support of other business processes.

Despite the promise of B2B marketplaces, the failure of many mirrors the more well known failures of the dotcom e-tailers. However, there are a number of high-profile exchanges created by industry participants including Covisint (automotive), GNX (retail) and Chematch (chemicals) where a large number of transactions are occurring. These are an example of countermediation where existing companies respond with their own intermediaries. PricewaterhouseCoopers reported at the EmarketplaceWorld Conference in London in February 2002 that there are also 30,000 private trading networks currently in development which suggests that the B2B exchange concept is one that is here to stay. Clearly, the challenge for marketers is to ensure they are represented on as many exchanges as appropriate and that they can compete effectively. From an organisational buying perspective, research is required to assess which members of the buying unit use B2B exchanges to select suppliers or purchase supplies online.

Source: Dave Chaffey

capacity to perform. The existing relationship means that there should be better mutual understanding, good working relationships between members of staff within the two organisations and an appreciation of the constraints under which each of them works. Automatically pushing business towards the existing supplier does, however, have its risks. Is the purchasing organisation becoming too dependent on the one supplier? Will this extra business strain the production capacity of the supplier? Is the purchasing organisation missing out on other suppliers with better technology which are anxious to prove themselves? Some exploration of who and what exists beyond the 'usual' supplier makes sense.

Much depends, of course, on the nature of the purchasing task. A low-risk, frequent purchase might not warrant that kind of search effort, and the existing supplier might simply be asked to tender a price for resupply. One or two other known suppliers might also be requested to quote for the job, just as a checking procedure to make sure that the existing supplier is not taking advantage of the established relationship.

In a high-risk, infrequent purchase (i.e. the new task situation), a more serious, lengthy selection procedure is likely to be implemented. There will be complex discussion, negotiation, revision and reiteration at a high level with a number of potential suppliers before a final decision is made. Additional problems may be caused where different suppliers will be expected to work closely together, such as on the building of a new manufacturing plant, for instance. Their compatibility with each other, their reliability and their ability to complete their part within strict time limits dictated by the overall project schedule may all affect the decision-making.

eg

Kruidvat, with over 500 drug stores in the Netherlands and Belgium, wanted to improve its store security and cut wastage by the installation of EAS (Electronic Article Surveillance). This involved detailed discussions with potential suppliers to assess alternative systems and eventually Meto, a leading European supplier based in Germany, was selected. Various systems were compared but the Meto system is expected to reduce pilfering considerably when all 25 million product items are tagged. Of particular importance to Kruidvat was the need to protect small cosmetic items that can come in various shapes. If this could be overcome it would be possible to change the store layout and allow greater use of self-service. The selected supplier had to be able to provide protection for the complete range and meet the specification to provide label and tag formats that could be incorporated into manufacturers' production lines and labelling for cost-effective protection. Linked to the labelling, Meto had to provide a security system to detect theft without causing embarrassment to genuine shoppers. Although there were many months of negotiation, the supply partnerships formed, including the cosmetic suppliers, to allow Kruidvat to strengthen the supply, benefiting all players (http://www.meto.com).

Commitment

The decision has been made, the contract signed, the order and delivery schedules set. The process does not, however, end here. The situation has to be monitored as it unfolds, in case there are problems with the supplier. Is the supplier fulfilling promises? Is the purchased item living up to expectations? Are deliveries turning up on time? The earlier such problems are diagnosed, the more likely it is that remedial action can be taken with the least disruption to production schedules. Commitment, therefore, comes in two parts, the contractual commitment and the review and evaluation process.

The purchasing manager of a large computer assembly plant in Ireland was clear cut in his requirements. He claimed: 'In my experience, 85 per cent of the business is lost or gained on quality and delivery, not on prices. We want what we order when we want it' (Pettitt, 1992, p. 208).

With the introduction of new purchasing strategies, such as JIT, the pressure on suppliers increases. Suppliers have to earn customer commitment through consistency, quality and delivery. Failure to live up to these promises can be very costly for production schedules.

Some buyers adopt formal appraisal procedures for their suppliers, covering key elements of performance. The results of this appraisal will be discussed with the supplier concerned in the interests of improving their performance and allowing the existing buyer–seller relationship to be maintained. New suppliers are sometimes eased into critical supply situations so that their performance can be carefully assessed. Small trial orders can grow into larger batches. This approach is especially used where larger firms are dealing with smaller suppliers.

Other buyers are less tolerant and keep their suppliers under constant threat. A buyer of injection moulded plastic parts, for example, has a policy of withdrawing business from a supplier which fails to meet delivery schedules. Two alternative suppliers are kept in reserve in case this happens. In another company, the buyer of automotive components places the emphasis on quality consistency. If a supplier falls short of quality standards, then again, alternative sources will be activated. Both these examples demonstrate the need for a true marketing orientation among suppliers of fulfilling the customer's needs and wants exactly. These customers are too important to lose, and any complaints have to be handled quickly, efficiently and effectively in order to maintain levels of customer satisfaction.

In a study of the European aircraft industry, Paliwoda and Bonaccorsi (1994) found a trend towards reducing the supplier base to allow closer cooperation and relationships to develop. Airframe manufacturers increasingly expect suppliers to fund development costs from their own resources, and in the avionics and power systems areas, a shift to single (or much reduced) sourcing forms the basis for a preferred supplier system.

In concluding this discussion of the buying process as a whole, we can say that the Hill and Hillier (1977) model has provided a useful framework for discussing the complexities and influences on B2B buying. It is difficult, however, to generalise about such a process, especially where technical and commercial complexity exists. Stages may be compressed or merge into each other, depending on circumstances; the process may end at any stage; there may have to be reiteration: for example if negotiations with a chosen supplier break down at a late stage the search process may have to begin again.

At each stage, a number of decisions have to be made that may well affect the character of the next stage. These various decision factors are summarised in Table 4.4.

Thus if a decision is taken in the specification stage to adopt a certain type of technology, that may then narrow down the choice of potential suppliers. The process will also vary according to whether the purchase is a new task or a re-buy. Remember too that although B2B buying is assumed to be more rational than consumer buying, it still involves the less than predictable human element, and where groups of people are concerned in the buying process there is plenty of scope for its smooth flow to be interrupted. The next section looks in more detail at these human elements.

Table 4.4 Decision problems in the organisational purchasing decision-making process

Stage	*Decision problems*
Precipitation	Do we need to make a purchasing decision or not? What benefits (e.g. cost savings) are we looking for?
Product specification	What quantity are we likely to need? How often? What are the 'must have' attributes? What are the 'would like' attributes? What is our required quantity level? What level of service/support do we want from supplier? What price band are we thinking of?
Supplier selection	Do we want to use existing and/or new suppliers? How do we construct a shortlist of potential suppliers? On what criteria do we select the supplier: price, ability to meet specifications exactly, past experience, solvency, culture? To what extent, and on what features, are we prepared to negotiate?
Commitment	Does the product actually meet our needs? Is the chosen supplier living up to its promises? How do we continue to motivate/evaluate this supplier? How often do we review their status?

Roles in the buying process

A potential supplier attempting to gain an order from a purchasing firm needs to know just who is involved in the decision-making process. As has already been established, B2B purchasing is unlikely to be the result of one person's deliberation and decision. Thus the aspiring supplier wants to know not only who is involved, but at what point in the process each person is most influential and how they all interact with each other. Then, the supplier's marketers can deal most effectively with the situation, utilising both the group and individual dynamics to the best of their advantage, for example tailoring specific communication packages to appeal at the right time to the right people, and getting a range of feedback from within the purchasing organisation to allow a comprehensive product offering to be designed.

Clearly, the amount of time and effort the supplier is prepared to devote to this will vary with the importance and complexity of the order. A routine re-buy may consist of a telephone conversation between two individuals to confirm the availability of the product and the fine detail of the transaction in terms of exact price and delivery. A new task situation, however, with the promise of either a large contract or substantial future business, provides much more scope and incentive for the supplier to research and influence the buying decision.

The rest of this section takes a more focused look at some of the functional areas involved in the decision-making process, detailing their interests and concerns. This lays the foundations for the next section (p. 160) which then examines how these functional areas operate within a group setting.

Purchasing

The role of the purchasing department is to handle relationships with suppliers by, for instance, sourcing suppliers, soliciting tenders, evaluating offers and negotiating or reviewing performance. Purchasing acts as the interface between other internal functions, such as production and finance and external suppliers, and thus has to reflect and represent those internal needs. This means that the function cannot act in isolation, except in the case of very well-established routines.

The role of purchasing will often vary according to the technology being used and the kind of contact needed with suppliers. In Figure 4.6, where unit or small-batch production takes place, such as in building a large gas turbine or specialist vehicles, there may be considerable contact between different departments within the selling and buying organisations. This is because a whole range of specification, quality, design and production issues may have to be discussed before, or even during, the transactions. The role of purchasing in such a situation tends to be less central to the whole process, and is more focused towards offering support in such matters as contracts and supplier suitability etc. In mass production, however, given the need for consistency, reliability and possibly frequent and critical exchanges, the role of purchasing may be enhanced to ensure the free flow of goods into the organisation. The other internal departments may channel their efforts and be coordinated through the purchasing department.

eg

The new purchasing manager at the NSPCC, the UK's leading charity concerned with child protection, decided that changes were needed in purchasing policies and procedures. Charities have to be especially mindful how they spend money as any public criticism could affect fund-raising. Each year, the NSPCC raises £75 mn from donations and legacies and from that, legitimate expenses, such as administration must be deducted. The old system devolved purchasing to all the regional offices and teams resulting in a multitude of contracts and suppliers as often local managers preferred to buy locally. For office stationery alone, it had 160 different suppliers!

The new policies and procedures centralised purchasing to achieve both cost savings and greater efficiency. It was estimated that previously it had cost around £60 to raise an order so any move to reduce the number of suppliers by awarding national contracts was bound to reduce costs. This was just the start. There is now a move to a greater use of e-procurement systems for routine purchasing and the system adopted enables orders with approved suppliers to be both placed and tracked by any of the regional offices. The overall aim is to reduce purchasing costs by 10 per cent and that means a lot more money available for such campaigns as 'Full Stop', considered in Chapter 22 (Riley, 2001).

Figure 4.6 Models of buyer–seller contact in B2B markets

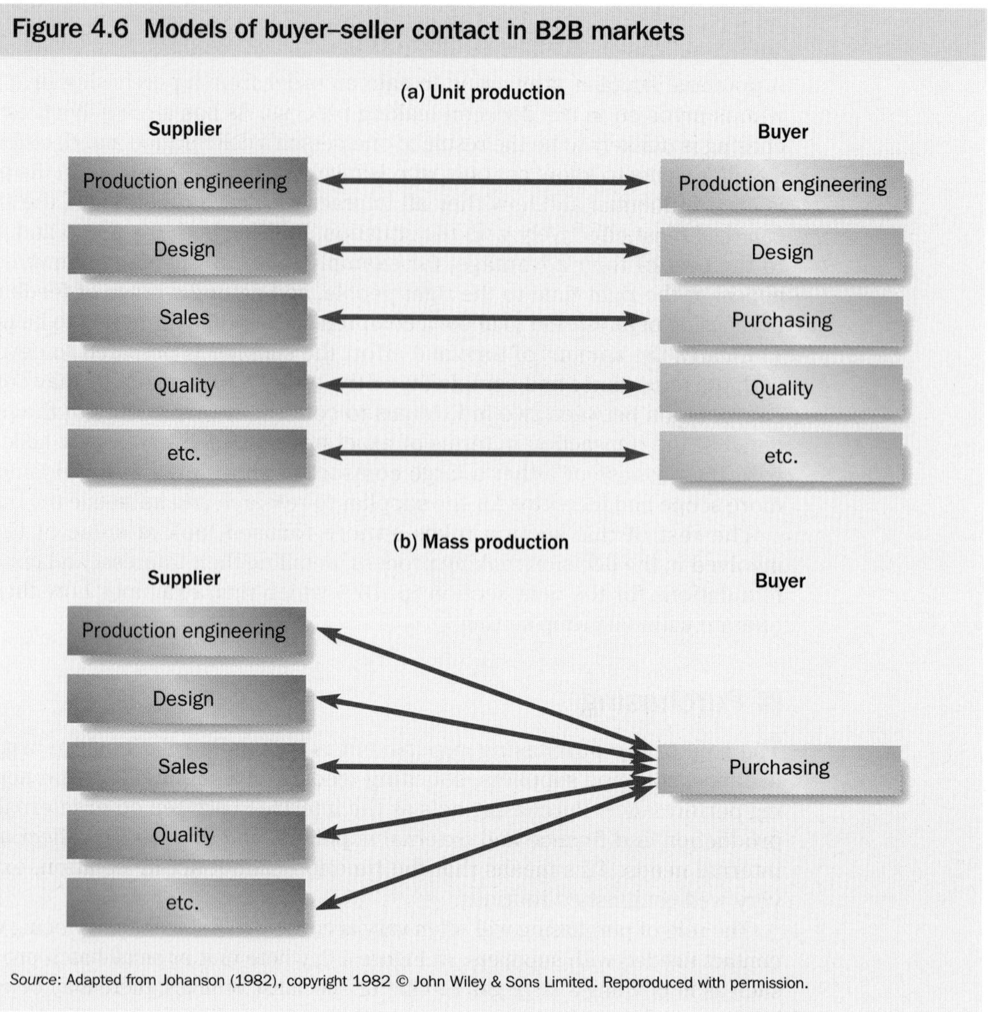

Source: Adapted from Johanson (1982), copyright 1982 © John Wiley & Sons Limited. Reporoduced with permission.

Purchasing rarely initiates the decision-making process, except for routine re-buys or where it acquires information to suggest that a change of policy or supplier could lead to better efficiency. Thus its key role is in the supplier selection and commitment stages, that is, in locating 'good' suppliers, establishing terms and liaising with them.

The main concerns of purchasing are security and consistency of supply, especially where large-scale production schedules are concerned. Lowest cost is, therefore, unlikely to be its prime criterion. The whole area of purchasing is growing in importance as organisations seek cost savings, raised quality levels and better integration with suppliers to strengthen their overall competitiveness in the supply chain. This means developing a clear understanding of the relative significance of individual purchases and of different types of purchases. Figure 4.7 details the various products and services purchased by a university, classified by the security/risk required and the value of the purchases. Strategic cells, SS and SC, suggest long-term supply contracts and careful selection of suppliers. The more tactical areas are divided into *acquisition* (TA), where the priority is minimising effort, and *profit* (TP) where the concern is with savings and improving margins through tendering. With business travel in the TP cell, for example, travel agencies would be required to bid on a regular basis, indicating the service level offered and their discount structures. Such a matrix is a valuable guide to an organisation in selecting those product areas that require special attention.

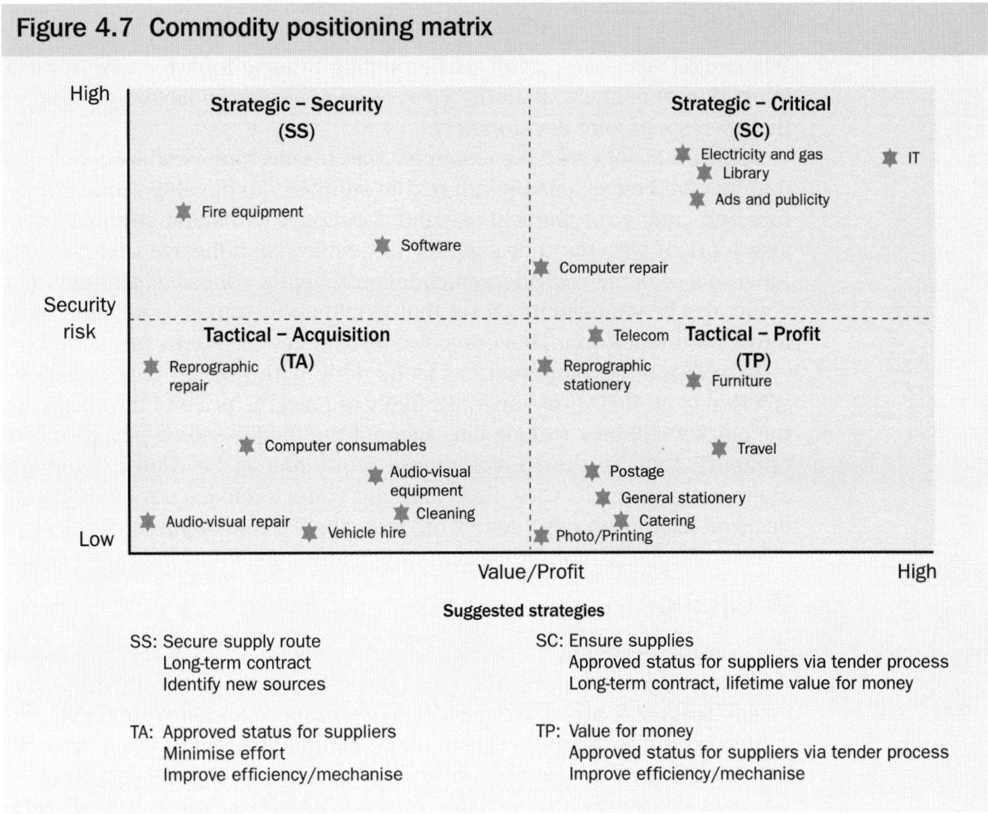

Figure 4.7 Commodity positioning matrix

Production/operations

With prime responsibility for meeting targets for the end product in both quantity and quality terms, the production function also has a great interest in the security and consistency of supply. If a critical component is concerned, then it will be anxious to ensure that the component meets quality and design specifications in order to be entirely compatible with the production flow.

Production staff may, therefore, be mainly involved in the precipitation and specification stages, although if they have an interest as users of the purchased product, they are not going to be entirely absent from the other stages.

In some cases, the production process may have to be adapted to accommodate a particular supplier's technology. This is widespread practice in B2B markets (Johanson and Wootz, 1986; Valla, 1986). While some of these adaptations are driven by logistical concerns alone, issues relating to ease of handling, fit with other organisations' production systems and cost effectiveness may also be considered.

Engineering

Engineering is usually concerned with specification and design, for example when sourcing a component or designing new production facilities, advising production on more efficient methods. Applications engineers may work closely with suppliers to develop solutions to problems, for example pooling their expertise to use CAD systems to design components that both perform to the purchaser's specifications and are feasible, given the supplier's technical capacity and talents. They can also feed specific information back to the supplier to solve a specific end-customer's problem.

R&D

Where R&D has been given a free-ranging brief to look for new, radical solutions to problems, then it is likely, as in the case of engineering, to have close contact with suppliers in the interests of joint development.

Johnson & Johnson, for example, was researching new approaches to wound dressings that involved close liaison with textile suppliers to develop fabrics of the right density, texture and quality for medical use and that could withstand sterilisation. At the same time, it also worked with another supplier to develop an adhesive that not only fulfilled its prime functions of being non-allergenic and sufficiently adhesive (although not too much so), but could also be supplied in a form that would allow it to be easily and efficiently incorporated into a production run. This proved to be a somewhat sticky problem.

In addition, development has to be done within given cost parameters. If the proposed solution to an R&D problem looks likely to push the price of the end product up beyond what the market will bear (taking into account the unique selling points offered by the new development), then further development work has to be done to reduce the costs or find alternatives. In such cases, R&D staff are going to have a strong influence at all stages of the decision-making process, somewhat reducing the role of purchasing to an administrative one.

Finance

For routine production-orientated purchases, it is likely that the finance department will devolve budgets to appropriate managers. Finance will simply take on a monitoring role to ensure that there are no irregularities or variances and provide regular internal information.

It takes a higher-profile role in major capital projects or other large items of expenditure, assessing returns on investments, investigating methods of financing and costing projects, for instance. It may not make the final decision, but it does have an influence in both shaping the feasible options and selecting the most appropriate supplier.

Marketing

The marketing function is primarily concerned with the outputs of the production process, representing the interests of the purchasing organisation's own customers. Marketers' concerns, therefore, are making sure that the implications of whatever is purchased do not compromise the final product offering or its competitive edge. Marketers are likely to approve of options that enhance the offering, perhaps in terms of better quality or improved reliability, thus favouring innovative, reliable suppliers.

Overall, in relation to functional roles in the decision-making process, just who is involved and in what capacity is an amalgam of many factors. The further removed the situation is from routine re-buys, the more people are involved and the more formal and time consuming the process is likely to be. Organisational size, structure and culture will also play a role in defining the process, for instance through the degree of delegation of responsibility and devolved decision-making.

The buying centre

The previous section implied that individuals within the purchasing organisation, as well as having functional roles and concerns, can also play different roles within the decision-making process that cross functional boundaries. This section, therefore, looks at these non-functional roles, and how they interact to form a **buying centre** or **decision-making unit** (DMU).

Table 4.5 compares buying centres in consumer and B2B markets, indicating the membership, the roles they play and the functional areas that may be involved.

Table 4.5 Comparison of DMUs in consumer and B2B markets

Consumer	*Example*	*B2B*	*Example*
Initiator	Child pesters parents for a new bike.	**User**	Machine breaks down; the operator reports it, thus initiating the process. May also be asked to help with specs for replacement.
Influencer	Mother thinks about it and says, 'Well, perhaps he has grown out of the old one.'	**Influencer**	User may influence; may also involve R&D staff, accountants, suppliers, sales reps, external consultants.
Decider	Father agrees and they all go to Toys 'Я' Us where the final decision is the child's, but under restraints imposed by parents' credit card limit.	**Decider**	May be a senior manager with either an active or a passive role in the whole process. May also be the buyer and/or influencer.
Purchaser	Parents pay the bill.	**Buyer**	Handles the search for and negotiations with suppliers.
User	The child.	**Gatekeeper**	Secretarial staff preventing influencers reaching the decision maker; R&D staff withholding information.

Users

Users are the people who will use the end product, for example an operator who will use production machinery, or a secretary who will use a word processor. These people may trigger the purchasing process through reporting a need, and may also be consulted in setting the specifications for whatever is to be bought.

Influencers

Influencers can affect the outcome of the decision-making process through their influence on others. Influence could stem formally from expertise, for example the advice of an accountant on the return on investment from a piece of capital machinery or that of an engineer on a supplier's technical capability, or it could be an informal, personal influence. Their prime role is in specification, information gathering and assessment.

Deciders

Deciders have the formal or informal authority to make the decision. For routine re-buys, this may be the purchasing officer or someone in a functional role, but organisational structures may dictate that the final decision rests with top management, who are fed information and recommendations from below. The decider's role and level of involvement, therefore, will vary widely, depending on individual circumstances.

Buyers

Buyers have the authority to select and negotiate with suppliers. Buyers with different levels of seniority may exist to handle different types of transaction, for example a routine re-buy could be handled by a relatively junior clerical worker, whereas the high-cost, high-risk new buy might require a senior purchasing manager of many years' experience. Where devolved budgeting exists, the buyer may not belong to a formal purchasing department at all, but be someone who also has a functional role such as R&D or marketing.

Gatekeepers

Gatekeepers have some control over the decision-making process, in that they can control the flow of information by denying access to key members of the buying centre. For example, a secretary or purchasing manager may prevent a sales representative from talking directly to an executive, or intercept brochures and mailshots and throw them in the wastepaper basket before they reach the decision maker. Technical staff can also act as gatekeepers in the way in which they choose to gather, present and interpret information to other members of the buying centre.

Bear in mind that the buying centre is not necessarily a fixed entity from transaction to transaction or even within a single transaction. It can be fluid and dynamic, evolving to meet the changing demands of the unfolding situation; it can be either formally constituted (for a major capital project, for instance) or loosely informal (a chance chat over coffee in the canteen between the purchasing manager and an R&D scientist); it can consist of two or three or many people. In other words, it is what it needs to be to do the job in hand.

When analysing the make-up of the buying centre, we should look not only at the allocation of roles between the different functional areas of the organisation, but also at the seniority of the members. Higher expenditure levels or purchases that have a critical impact on the organisation may involve much more senior management. Of course, input from the lower levels of the hierarchy will help to shape the decision, but the eventual authority may rest at board level. Thus, for example, a bank's decision to introduce a new account control system may be taken at a very senior level.

Also, an individual's contribution to it may not be limited to one role. In a small business, the owner/manager may be influencer and buyer as well as decider. Similarly, in a larger organisation, where routine re-buys are concerned, the buyer may also be the decider, with very little call for influencers. Whatever the structure, however fluid the buying centre is, it is still important for the aspiring supplier to attempt to identify the pattern within the target organisation in order to create effective communication links.

Having thus established decision-making structures, the next step is to examine the criteria applied during the process.

marketing ***in action***

Nokia's global sourcing

Nokia is one of the market leaders in mobile phone development and manufacture. It uses 250 million components every day which are purchased from some 400 subcontractors and supply partners. The purchasing challenge for the company is to ensure that supplies can be regularly adjusted to meet growing demand from its production facilities spread across ten countries. It must also be sure that suppliers are capable of producing components that are in line with expected technological advances in a market in which innovation is used to gain competitive advantage.

Given the worldwide scale of production and the need sometimes to adjust product specifications to meet local requirements, purchasing has been divided into two different organisations. First, *local procurement* deals with day-to-day purchasing for the factories. Its primary role is not to source components, but to ensure that adequate supplies of components are available for production. *Global sourcing* is the other organisation. This actually sources materials, negotiates prices and terms, makes delivery arrangements, establishes quality procedures and sets supplier performance standards for appraisal. There is a close link between global sourcing and the R&D and manufacturing experts to ensure that the right technology is available and that it will continue into the future.

Nokia operates on formal contracts with suppliers, specifying prices, quality, quantities, etc. Suppliers are expected to meet these standards and are monitored at a local level to ensure that they comply. By aggregating demand from each of the production units, Nokia is able to get better terms from suppliers because of the scale of the contracts. It insists, however, that a supplier should offer only one collection point in the world from which components can be collected, regardless of where they were produced. It is up to the supplier to handle its own logistics to ensure that the various products arrive in time at that collection point. Nokia then arranges for carriers to handle the transport, customs, etc. to ensure that components arrive on time at Nokia's own plants. This arrangement simplifies the ordering procedures for Nokia's local procurement teams.

Quality monitoring of components is critical so that Nokia can ensure that its own products meet standards. Targets are set for failure rates and robustness, for example, and the company asks each supplier to present its plan for meeting those targets over the lifespan of the contract. Nokia has to be convinced, as it does not inspect goods on arrival. It expects suppliers to take care of testing and to guarantee that they are meeting standards on a consistent basis. When problems do occur, they are normally identified at the local buying points, but it is the global sourcing operation that takes the necessary action with suppliers.

Nokia insists on each supplier nominating an account manager regarded as being responsible for the relationship between the companies on a global basis. The account manager is expected to be senior enough to be credible within Nokia and to carry influence within the supplier's top management if urgent action is required. By establishing clear lines of communication, issues such as annual purchasing agreements to cover forecasting, capacity planning and allocation can be fed through one point. It is then the responsibility of the account manager to link with the rest of the supplier's organisation to ensure that it all happens. It is the supplier's responsibility to adjust its own internal organisation to meet Nokia's requirements.

Although most of the collaboration is on commercial matters, in some areas closer technical cooperation is required. With 'application-specific integrated circuits' (purpose-designed complex microchips), for example, it is necessary for Nokia's engineers to work closely with the supplier's technical staff to create the most appropriate specification. The purchasing function's fear about such arrangements, however, is that it could become locked into a single supplier and this in turn could, it believes, jeopardise supply continuity, especially when the demand for a component is suddenly increased.

Nokia has refined its relationship approach to component suppliers over a number of years. It believes in partnership, openness and trust to ensure that it can plan its capacity and production schedules with a high degree of certainty that suppliers will not let it down. Nokia's faith in its suppliers is perhaps underlined by its stated plan during 2001 to double its outsourcing.

Sources: Kandell (2001); Serant (2001); Taimi (1996).

Buying criteria

In the previous sections, the emphasis in terms of decision-making has largely been on rational, functionally orientated criteria. These task-related or economic criteria are certainly important and reinforce the view of the organisation as a rational thinking entity. It is dangerous, however, to fall into the trap of forgetting that behind every job title lurks an individual whose motives and goals are not necessarily geared towards the greater good of the organisation. Such motives and goals may not form a direct, formally recognised part of the decision-making process, but nevertheless, they can certainly cause friction and influence the outcomes of it.

Economic influences

As has been stressed throughout this chapter so far, it is not always a matter of finding the lowest priced supplier. If the purchasing organisation can make the best use of increased reliability, superior performance, better customer service and other technical or logistical supports from its suppliers, then it can offer a better package to its own customers, with the rewards that brings. This route can also result in lower total costs, since it reduces production delays due to substandard components or delivery failures, and also improves the quality consistency of the purchaser's own end product, thus reducing the costs of handling complaints and replacing goods.

The main criteria have already been discussed in the previous sections of this chapter, so the following are a summary of them.

Appropriate prices

The appropriate price is not necessarily the lowest, but one representing good value for money taking into account the whole service package on offer.

eg

Building a Formula One racing car from scratch is not an easy business. Stewart Grand Prix's three racing cars are each made from 1,400 components sourced from over 1,000 suppliers. The costs per car can be staggering. To design and develop a car can cost £1 mn, a similar amount is spent on tyres, and then some £5 mn of spares are needed every season. The buying criteria are led completely by design and performance technology and the high specification of such cars often means locating special suppliers. Lead times can, however, be short, especially if a re-work is necessary on a component that needs to be upgraded. Because of the high specification, price is nearly always of secondary importance in the buying decision. Instead, good relationships leading to component improvement, reliability, safety and quality are dominant (Nolan, 1997b). After all, who wants to be the buyer who saved a few pence on the component that caused a breakdown during the big race? (http://www.saunalahti.fi)

Product specification

Product specification involves finding the right product to meet the purchaser's specified needs, neither more nor less. There are, of course, various trade-offs between specification and price. The main point is the closeness of the match and the certainty that it will be maintained throughout the order cycle, or that the supplier will be able to meet increasing and changing demands as technology progresses. This is particularly important in areas such as electronics where product lifecycles are getting shorter and shorter.

Quality consistency

It is important to find a supplier with adequate quality controls to minimise defects so that the purchaser can use the product with confidence. This is especially true for JIT systems, where there is little room for failure.

eg

Velden Engineering (UK) manufactures a wide range of component parts and assemblies for various industries and applications, such as medical and aeronautical. In such sensitive areas, it needs to ensure that everything supplied is right first time, as failure can be very expensive indeed. Its customers not only expect compliance with standards such as BS5750 and ISO9002 but also to be supplied with finished components or tested assemblies that can go straight into the production process on a JIT basis. This is a crucial factor in supplier selection.

Supply reliability and continuity

The purchaser needs to be sure that adequate supplies of the product will be available as and when needed, especially where JIT systems are involved. This may mean sacrificing the economies of scale achieved through sourcing from one supplier for the risk-spreading advantages to be had from sourcing smaller amounts from a number of suppliers.

Customer service

Buyers require reassurance that the supplier is prepared to take responsibility for its product by providing fast and flexible backup service in case of problems. This aspect might also include an appraisal of the supplier's longer-term capacity and willingness to become involved in joint development activities. Some customer service is delivered even before the sale is made.

Non-economic influences

Powers (1991) summarises non-economic influences under four main headings: prestige, career security, friendship and social needs, and other personal needs. We look at each of these in turn.

Prestige

Organisations, or more specifically the individuals who make up organisations, hanker after 'status'. They want to be seen to be doing better than their competitors or other divisions within the same organisation. So, for example, they may be prepared to spend a little more when the office accommodation is refurbished on better-quality furnishings, decor and facilities to impress, instil confidence or even intimidate visitors to the site.

Career security

Few people involved in the decision-making process are truly objective about it. They may well be chiefly and genuinely concerned with finding the best solution to the problem, but at the back of the mind there is always the question, 'What does this mean for my job?'

First, there is the risk element. A problem may have two alternative solutions, one which is safe, predictable and unspectacular, and one which is high risk, but promises a high return. If the high-risk decision is made and it all goes wrong, what are the consequences? The individual may not want to be associated with such an outcome and thus will push for the safe route.

Second, there is the awareness of how others are judging the individual's behaviour in the decision-making process: 'Am I prepared to go against the main body of opinion on a particular issue that I feel strongly about or will that brand me as a trouble-maker and jeopardise my promotion prospects?'

Friendship and social needs

Needs such as friendship can be dangerous and can sometimes stray very close to ethical boundaries. It is necessary, however, to value trust, confidence and respect built on a personal level between individuals in the buying and selling organisations. It does help to reduce the perceived risk of the buyer–seller relationship.

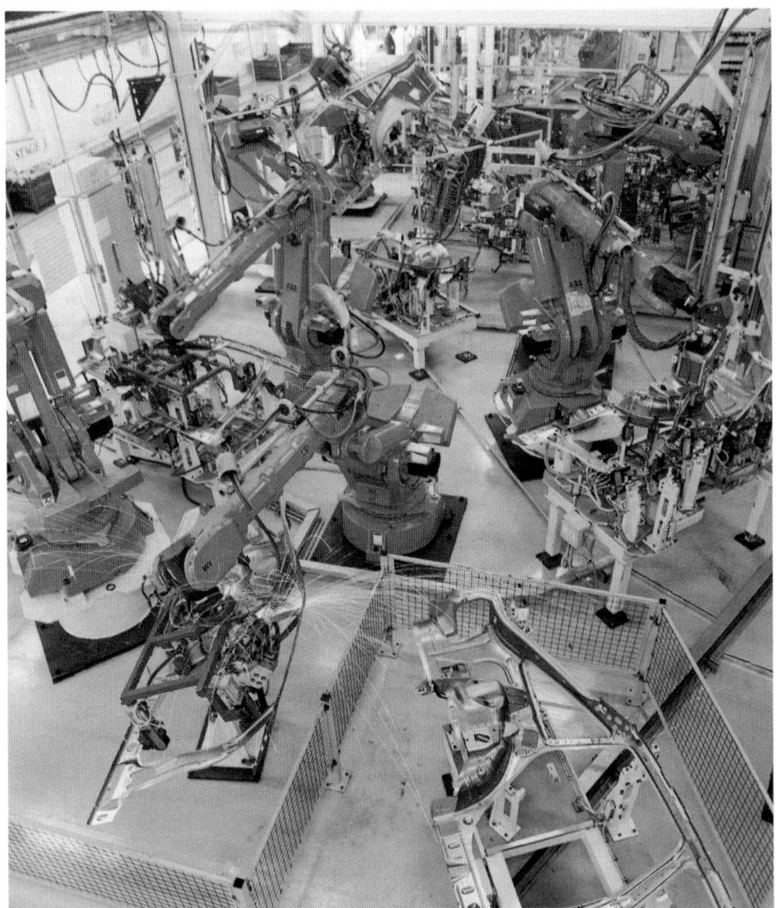

The robot supplier must collaborate with the car manufacturers to develop the right production system.

Source: Vauxhall Motors Ltd.

Other personal factors

The three categories discussed above all provide useful insights into the human elements of organisational behaviour, but their emphasis is still on the relationship between the individual, the job and the organisation. Remember too the individual's personal profile, issues such as demographic characteristics, attitudes and beliefs, discussed in Chapter 3 in the context of consumer behaviour. These, coupled with factors like self-confidence and communication skills, can all shape the extent to which that individual is allowed to participate in and influence the outcome of the decision-making process. A young, recent business graduate with forthright views, for example, may provoke negative reactions in older managers who have progressed through more traditional routes and feel that they have accumulated a wealth of experience, even if the graduate's views are valid.

A further dimension of non-economic forces is trust. Trust is the belief that another organisation will act in such a way that the outcomes will be beneficial to both parties and that it will not act in such a way as to bring about negative effects (Anderson and Narus, 1986). Trust can be built at an organisational level, but can also stem from a series of personal relationships between employees. Lorenz (1988), for example, found from a study of subcontracting in France that personal contacts were a major cause of organisational trust. From that trust can come a whole series of activities that can enhance the relationship, as considered in the following section.

corporate social responsibility *in action*

It takes two to tango

So what would you do? Your flight is about to depart and the queue to get through passport control could take at least an hour when a kind public servant offers to fast-track you for $10. Do you agree? OK, try this one then. For 10 per cent 'commission', a public official will give your company's tender for a new £50 mn construction project favourable consideration. You believe you are offering the best deal anyway and it will guarantee hundreds of jobs back home, not least your own. What would you do? These are the dilemmas of B2B negotiations in some countries. You may not like it, but it is real and depending upon who you listen to, is endemic in some countries.

Hamra (2000) defined bribery as 'an inducement that influences a public official to perform his or her duties in a manner contrary to the course that would otherwise be adopted'. So whether you paid the $10 and/or the 10 per cent commission you have given a bribe and participated in corruption. British and other European nations are not as clean as you might imagine. Lesotho is one of poorest nations in the world and badly needed a new dam to preserve water and assist agriculture. A £5 bn World Bank funded project attracted a lot of interest, not all of it ethical. It has been suggested that the Chief Executive of the company set up to build the project in Lesotho received over £1 mn in bribes for awarding contracts. Three UK firms, Balfour Beatty, Gibb and Kier International have all faced accusations of giving bribes. If a legal ruling goes against them the World Bank has threatened to ban them from future tendering. This is no idle threat: of the 54 companies currently on the World Bank blacklist, 35 are British.

Bribery comes in many forms. A list quoted in Hamra (2000) includes:

- Bribes or kickbacks of cash or expensive gifts, to win contracts that would not otherwise have been awarded to your company.
- Cash or gifts to avoid legal punishment for breaches of the rules.
- Cash to custom officials to avoid import or export duties.
- 'Grease payments' to expedite performance, i.e. paying to jump the queue for licences, permits etc. to custom officials to avoid import or export duties.

The problem is in defining the boundaries, given the economic and competitive pressures. Business customs vary widely across nations and there is no single, universal code of ethics. One country's normal practice of gift giving may be another's bribe. It may be common practice in some countries to allow public officials business dealings to supplement their meagre salaries. Of course, some decide to go further and build personal fortunes. Facilitating payments may also be considered as legitimate, indeed in some countries 'facilitating agents' are widely advertised to help importers find their way through the bureaucracy to progress contracts in a strange country. They make a legitimate charge for their services and at times that might be shared with other officials! The World Bank has estimated that 5 per cent of the value of exports to developing countries is actually spent on one or other form of bribes. That's $50–80 bn. The rate of 'commission' can go as high as 20–30 per cent.

In 1999, the OECD introduced an anti-bribery convention. *The Convention on Combating Bribery of Foreign Public Officials in International Business Transactions* commits all 30 OECD members and four non-members (Argentina, Bulgaria, Chile and Brazil) to adopt common rules to punish companies and individuals found guilty. Most countries involved have taken practical steps to ratify the protocols. This convention also implicates the giver as well as the receiver of bribes, extending good practice from Sweden and the United States. The UK has, however, been slow to prosecute directors responsible for bribery offences, despite the OECD convention, but this is expected to change. B2B marketers will therefore need to take a much more careful approach in future. Hamra (2000) calls for leadership and value statements from senior management, clear policies and guidelines, training and a willingness to undergo external scrutiny as part of an essentially ethical approach to international contracting. However, the OECD convention may be difficult to enforce, despite it being agreed by all members. Where there is a will . . . there are avoidance approaches, such as becoming more covert, or setting up middlemen and agents or offshore accounts. Culture and habits will not change overnight.

Some countries already take a tough stand. In Singapore, five multinationals found guilty of tendering bribes were refused the opportunity to compete for 5 years and the public official went to prison. In China, corrupt public officials can face the death penalty. The new bribery transparency index produced by Transparency International ranks the perceived propensity of different countries to give rather than receive bribes. France and Italy did not make it into the top 20 of countries most likely to give bribes while Germany and the United States, despite the legislation, achieved a middle ranking. China and Korea came out worst, paradoxically, given China's stance on the receipt of bribes. The areas of greatest bribe giving were still public contracts, construction and arms.

So, next time you are offered a free afternoon of corporate hospitality, watch out. It may be at the other end of the spectrum but it is a continuum. There is no such thing as a free lunch, especially now that the OECD acknowledges that it 'takes two to tango'.

Sources: Barnett (2000); Cockroft (1996); Hamra (2000); Moss (1997); OECD (2000); http://www.oecd.org.

The changing nature of supply chains

One matter that has been emphasised repeatedly in this chapter is the potential risks inherent in poor purchasing decisions. The quality of the relationship between the buying organisation and an existing supplier could prove to be a major factor in reducing those risks, and is inevitably going to influence decision-making processes. The history of previous transactions between two organisations leads to understanding, expectations and perhaps an active desire to continue to trade, even at the cost of short-term sacrifice.

There has, therefore, been an increased focus in recent years on the place of buyer–seller relationships in explanations of marketing and decision-making in B2B markets. Porter (1990) goes further in suggesting that an organisation with advantageous relationships with supplier networks has a competitive edge, because of the synergy between them in terms of joint problem solving and information exchange.

This final section of the chapter looks at some of the characteristics of buyer–seller relationships that add a further dimension to the understanding of the decision-making processes already covered.

Durability

Durability refers to the longevity of relationships in B2B markets that might even outlast individuals and managerial generations. Not all exchanges evolve into long-term durable relationships, despite the trend towards relationship marketing. After a first time purchase, the buyer has to decide whether a relationship should be continued (repurchase) or not, and whether it should be enhanced in scope (increased commitment to the supplier) (Selnes, 1998). A decision to continue (repurchase) is different from a decision to enhance or commit to a relationship. Continuity of a relationship is a type of repetitive decision making and may very well continue 'at an arm's length' distance: in a low cost, low risk purchasing situation there may be minimal concern about commitment to the relationship. Paperclips for the office, for example, are a standard product and there is plenty of choice in the market, and thus convenience and possibly low price will be the main concerns.

However, as complexity increases and as it becomes apparent that value can be created by developing a stable, well-tuned relationship, then there may be mutual advantage in continuity. The decision to commit to a relationship is often a strategic one and can involve exchanging confidential strategic information, investing jointly in product development, or the integration of some business functions (Selnes, 1998). The value of building a closer, committed relationship emerges from two dimensions: economic and social.

Economic dimension

Joint development has already been mentioned a few times in this chapter. If a supplier has invested time, effort and money in improving quality or products, or in developing special operating processes or services to suit a particular customer, then the supplier will want the relationship to be sustained so that returns on that investment can be realised. Similarly, the purchaser will not want to start the process from scratch with a new supplier. If the relationship has led to a specialist complex package, then either party may become dependent on the other. In other words, the purchaser cannot easily get the same thing from an alternative supplier and the supplier cannot easily find an alternative customer.

Social dimension

There is a certain security and comfort in dealing with someone you know. There is an existing level of trust, knowledge and friendship to build on. Strengths and weaknesses are known quantities, thereby reducing the risks of taking on a new supplier or customer.

Some relationships can be very long lasting and resistant to change, despite the temptations of competitors' marketing wiles. It is difficult for an outsider to break into such well-developed and managed relationships. A number of studies have been undertaken into the duration of buyer–seller relationships. Over long periods, high degrees of personal and organisational trust can develop. Trust has been defined as 'a willingness to rely on an exchange partner in whom one has confidence' (Moorman *et al.*, 1993). Although trust can create vulnerability, it can still be a very powerful bond: if you believe that the other party will not let you down on expertise, reliability or intentions, the nature of the buyer–seller allocation of roles and responsibilities can change. Decisions to single source, for example, operate a JIT system, or to delegate component building to one supplier, all require a lot of trust, but can deliver significant economic benefits to both parties. To Bistritz *et al.* (1998), trust can provide a key competitive difference.

Approaches to supplier handling

The way in which the purchasing organisation decides to deal with its suppliers can have a fundamental effect on the future of the buyer–seller relationship. According to Spekman (1988), there are two polarised approaches that lead to very different relationships.

Adversarial approach

The purchasing organisation pressurises the supplier to minimise prices and, by insisting on short-term contracts and using multiple sourcing, keeps the supplier alert and sweating. The purchaser is unlikely to be interested in helping the supplier unless there is a direct cost saving to be had. This purchaser will rarely need special products and services and certainly will rarely be prepared to pay for such things. This is a legitimate approach in appropriate circumstances, where there are plenty of alternative sources of supply, the product is fairly standard and price really is the driving criterion.

Collaborative approach

In a collaborative approach, close ties are forged between buyer and seller and there is much interest and value in close cooperation and integration. Such an approach can support valuable work in product design, specification and quality; advanced production processes; flexible scheduling and delivery; and special inventory. There are, however, the risks of becoming too 'cosy', complacent and blinkered, as well as the inherent dangers of mutual dependency.

Collaborative approaches are particularly crucial in JIT environments, as Table 4.6 shows, neatly summarising the reasons that collaboration rather than confrontation should be considered in critical supply situations.

Table 4.6 Collaborative vs adversarial approaches to supplier handling

Adversarial	*Collaborative*
• Multiple suppliers • Regular price quotes • Adversarial negotiations • Sporadic communication • Little cooperation • Quality and time scales to meet lowest threshold • Emphasis on lowest unit price	• Few suppliers • Long-term relationship; mutual investment • Partnerships • Frequent, planned communication • Integrated operations • Quality and time scales 'designed in' • Emphasis on lowest overall cost

Source: Adapted from Spekman (1988), copyright © 1988 by The Trustees at Indiana University, Kelley School of Business.

Supplier relationship portfolio

The focus so far has been on the relationship between one purchaser and one supplier. In reality, a purchaser is likely to maintain a portfolio of suppliers and to develop different levels and intensity of relationship with each, based on need and value.

Some suppliers have the potential to be long-term important partners in joint innovative development, and therefore the purchaser may encourage cooperation in improving both technical capability and quality, while others will be developed as guaranteed, secure, reliable sources of supply. Both of these will deserve a collaborative approach to handling. Others, however, will merit no special consideration, for example where there are plenty of alternative sources readily available, and will be retained at arm's length somewhere nearer the adversarial end of the handling spectrum. It is the job of purchasing to advise on an appropriate portfolio.

Relationship lifecycle

Much emphasis has been put on the potential durability of a buyer–seller relationship, but as with any kind of relationship, it is dynamic, changes its nature over time and is unlikely to last indefinitely. Slater (1997) has argued that maintaining relationships is becoming increasingly difficult in complex and turbulent marketing environments. Baxter and Simon (1993) similarly believe that dynamic environments mean that there have to be more frequent revisions of the nature of the dealings between the parties. Dwyer *et al.* (1987) suggested that buyer–seller relationships evolve over a number of stages over time as both parties gain experience and learn to trust each other. This evolution can be broken down into five stages of the **relationship lifecycle**. The stages are:

Awareness

Awareness occurs as each party learns of each other's existence and potential. This could come about as a result of a sales visit, a trade exhibition or any other means of making an initial contact.

Exploration

Exploration is about discovery and has all the insecurities of adolescent relationships. It is about gaining experience, testing each other out with no real commitment and with high uncertainty over the outcomes. This could mean small trial orders and perhaps even some pre-order assessment.

Expansion

Expansion has the characteristics of romance and the early days of marriage. Partners are working together, valuing the benefits, building orders and mutual trust. There is a rising level of commitment and the partners may even be making special adaptations to suit each other better. The uncertainty is much reduced, and members of staff from the two organisations may be starting to build sound working and social relationships.

Commitment

In the commitment stage, the novelty has worn off, but the partners are comfortable with each other and have built a predictable, stable nest round themselves. There is high mutual trust and respect, well-developed personal networks, and the seller has become a major supplier of special products and services, perhaps to the point where there is a high level of mutual dependency. Most relationships remain in this stage, but a few move on to the next stage.

eg

A good example of the benefits of collaboration is seen in the relationship between the Lawson Mardon Group (LMG), a plastic blow moulder, and Jeyes, a consumer cleaning goods manufacturer. Jeyes needed 200 different types of plastic bottle in a variety of sizes from 250 ml to 5 litre. Seventeen machines were needed to produce the required volume of containers. Jeyes switched from in-house production to buying in from LMG. The risks of thus extending the supply chain were reduced when LMG located its factory next door to Jeyes', with a conveyor belt running between the two for continuous production and supply. Both parties benefited from this arrangement. LMG had a long-term seven-year supply contract with flexibility to allow for changing raw material prices, giving it a secure foundation for building a wider customer base. Jeyes was able to focus on its core business, freed of the responsibility of churning out plastic bottles, yet retaining security and flexibility of supply, delivery reliability, and maintaining quality standards.

Dissolution

This stage is possibly the equivalent to disillusionment and divorce. If stability and satisfaction have been reached in the maturity stage, then the most likely source of danger is complacency. Lack of innovation or service responsiveness on the seller's part, for example, could encourage the purchaser to turn to a younger, more versatile supplier with a good marketing-orientated approach ('I can tell your current supplier doesn't understand you any more. Let me show you my blueprints . . .'). Good and Evans (2001) in an examination of the difficult periods in a relationship, identified a range of behaviours that could be adopted to produce a desired outcome, depending upon whether the parties wanted the relationship to be retained or dissolved. These include:

- Concession making, to give up something of value to show you want to keep the relationship going.
- Contending, to force the other party to yield if one partner believes they are in a dominant position.
- Problem solving, to work together to find a new way of operating in a win-win framework.
- Withdrawal, to allow the relationship to deteriorate towards termination.

Dissolution is a strategic decision and managers should consider carefully its impact and how best to handle it (Giller and Matear, 2001).

eg

Sometimes the dissolution can be carried out with respect and dignity. A small supplier of engineering components, for example, found that its major customer was going to phase out its purchases from that supplier over the next two years. The customer had decided to make the components itself, but acted responsibly by phasing the supplier out over time rather than all at once. Instant termination of the contract would have had a devastating effect on the supplier, which depended on this customer for 60 per cent of its business. At least it now had two years to find alternative customers or to re-organise the business.

The neatness of the stages should not suggest that relationships just happen or are bound to develop in a certain way. As mentioned in Chapter 1, establishing and building successful customer relationships is not just a job for marketing and sales specialists but may also involve other staff such as customer service, engineering or R&D personnel. Within the overall buyer–seller relationship, a complex bundle of individual relationships can flourish to achieve a wide range of necessary tasks (Möller and Wilson, 1995; Narus and Anderson, 1995). The overall relationship usually evolves incrementally (Dwyer *et al.*, 1987) supported by partner-specific adaptations, cooperative behaviour, social and structural bonding and other benefits. All these activities have to be coordinated within a broader range of other relationship management activities to enable the relationship to grow (Gemünden and Ritter, 1997). Walter and Gemünden (2000) proposed that relationship promoters in both the supplier's and buyer's organisations have a significant impact on the extent to which the relationship is focused, coordinated and develops for mutual benefit from an economic and social perspective. This allows satisfaction, trust and commitment to grow and strengthen the durability of the relationship against external challenges. Much remains to be explored in the evolution of buyer–seller relationships. Little is really known about the stages, their underlying determinants and the specific factors that trigger change. However, it is clear that when the relationship between two parties is examined in depth, patterns of evolution do emerge and the key decision points that shape the relationship become apparent. Increasingly, therefore, organisations have to decide which relationships to initiate, develop, and/or continue to invest in, and plan their marketing activities accordingly.

Chapter summary

The focus of this chapter has been B2B buying behaviour and buyer–seller relationships.

- B2B marketing is about exchanges between organisations, whether they are commercial enterprises, government bodies or institutions. B2B markets have a number of distinct characteristics, including the nature of demand (derived, joint and inelastic), the structure of demand (concentrated in size and in geography), the complexity of the buying process and the risks inherent in it.
- The decision-making process that B2B purchasers go through has elements in common with consumer decision-making, but is likely to be formalised, to take longer and to involve more people. B2B buying is likely to involve higher value, less frequently placed orders for products that are more likely to be customised than in consumer markets. Staff with various functional backgrounds, such as purchasing, marketing, accounting, engineering, production and R&D, will be involved in the process and form a buying centre. The membership of the buying centre, the roles played and who takes the lead may vary from transaction to transaction or even from stage to stage within a single process.
- The stages in the decision-making process include: precipitation, product specification, supplier selection, and commitment to a long-term relationship.
- The decision-making process is affected not only by rational, measurable economic criteria (price, specification, quality, service, etc.), but also by non-economic influences (prestige, security, social needs, personality) emanating from the individuals involved.
- The ongoing buyer–seller relationship is increasingly being recognised as a major influencer of B2B marketing strategies. Relationships can be durable and resistant to change, leading to mutual cooperation and the full exploitation of synergy between the two organisations. Other less significant relationships can, however, be kept deliberately superficial. The purchasing organisation has to develop a portfolio of different relationships of varying closeness and depth to suit the whole spectrum of its needs. Organisations also have to recognise that relationships develop over time and pass through a number of developmental stages, until dissolution, perhaps through complacency, or one party's neglect of the other.

key words and phrases

B2B marketing
Buying centre
Decision-making unit (DMU)
Derived demand
Joint demand
Modified re-buy
Multiple sourcing
New task purchasing
Product specification
Purchasing policy
Relationship lifecycle
Routine re-buy
Single sourcing

questions for review

4.1 What are the different categories of B2B customer and how do they differ from each other?

4.2 What are the main differences between B2B and consumer buying behaviour?

4.3 What factors influence the complexity and the amount of time spent on each stage of the organisational decision-making process?

4.4 How might people in different functional roles (for example R&D or marketing) participate in B2B buying?

4.5 Define the main economic and non-economic influences on B2B decision-making.

questions for discussion

4.1 From the supplier's point of view, how might the marketing approaches aimed at a customer making a new task purchase differ from those aimed at a routine re-buy customer?

4.2 How are supplier handling strategies changing as organisations seek to improve their competitiveness?

4.3 What are the stages in the buyer–seller relationship lifecycle, and how is each characterised? What difference might the stages make to the seller's marketing approaches?

4.4 You are the purchasing manager of a large organisation with an enormous annual spend. Most of your contracts are awarded by tender. What would your attitude be to the following offers from potential suppliers, and to what extent would they influence your decision-making:
(a) A bottle of whisky at Christmas?
(b) An invitation to lunch to discuss your requirements?
(c) An offer of the free use of the supplier's managing director's Spanish villa for two weeks?
(d) £1,500?

4.5 What do you think are the advantages and disadvantages of long-term, close buyer–seller relationships?

case study 4.1

Alstom China

Alstom is a France-based global organisation with sales of over €22 bn, employing over 140,000 people in over 70 countries. In the energy field, it has around 20 per cent of the world's installed power generation capacity – that's 650 gigawatts. It is able to combine components, systems and services to design, manufacture and commission power generation infrastructure to customers' specifications, often on a turnkey (ready to run) basis. With that kind of expertise, founded on state-of-the-art research and development and considerable project experience, it is perhaps not surprising that the Chinese authorities have taken a keen interest in accessing Alstom technology.

According to Geoff Ball, President of Alstom China, to be successful in doing business in China one must 'be patient, be local and be prepared to wait five years before gaining a reasonable return on investment'. He should know, as Alstom is now a major supplier of energy and transport infrastructure to China, a position achieved by carefully building a reputation through effective B2B relationships with key decision makers.

The rapid industrial development of China in recent years has been well documented and this is the main driver for the plan to increase the output of electricity generation to 290 gigawatts at a rate of 15,000 megawatts each year at a cost annually of €18.75 bn. With 60 new power stations in various stages of construction that means an awful lot of potential business for Alstom to target. It is already involved in 17 projects, including the Three Gorges hydroelectric power plant, the largest of its kind in the world, the Shanghai Waigaoqiao phase three power plant which provides high steam conditions but reduces the heat and emission rate by 10 per cent, and finally the Daya Bay nuclear power plant.

Alstom is not alone in targeting the market. It has tough competition from Siemens, GE and Mitsubishi, all global players, along with smaller niche manufacturers, as well as an increasing number of local Chinese companies which are often in alliance with the global players. It is important for Alstom to keep a close watch on market developments in China to spot opportunities early. Most power generation purchases are made by the eventual users, the provincial governments, although their role in the buying process is not that great. For effective B2G (business to government) marketing, the various influencers and deciders need to be identified and a communications strategy developed to move from project conception to the final bid acceptance. Geoff Ball outlined the following broad stages in the buying process that his business development staff must be able to influence if they are to succeed.

Project initiation

Each provincial government is responsible for ensuring the economic development of its region within the framework of the state economic and political policy. Energy power planning is a critical part of the industrial infrastructure and with such a dynamic economy, these plans need to be at least five years ahead. It could take anything up to two years before projects are started and a further two to three years before they are finally commissioned. The industrialisation of the western provinces of China and Tibet is currently a major priority for increasing power generation capability, but even the more advanced eastern provinces need to invest in new capacity to support growth and to upgrade or replace coal-fired stations because of tightening pollution controls.

The rapid development of China's industrial infrastructure is a good opportunity for Alstom to further develop its long term business interests there.

Source: Alstom China.

Feasibility study

The state-owned Electrical Design Institute is one of the pivotal organisations that can influence outcomes. Its role is to examine the expected demand for power proposed by the provincial governments, to establish specifications, and to gain formal approval for the project from the state. Within the Institute are the technical specialists capable of advising on various alternative solutions and their cost profiles. Potential suppliers have to be especially active at this stage as it is the major opportunity to influence specifications in directions that will favour your own organisation. For more advanced projects, the technical staff of the Institute may initiate discussions about state-of-the-art alternatives. In reality, however, it is becoming increasingly difficult to differentiate between the global players on quality, efficiency, performance and even bid prices. Although the systems and solutions offered may be different, performance output is often very similar. Maintaining good relations with the technical specialists in the Design Institute is, therefore, critical in ensuring that the technical solutions offered are well understood and, hopefully, favoured. This stage can take between six months and one year and the output is a report to the State Development and Planning Committee (SPDC).

Project decision

The SDPC in Beijing is the formal body that considers economic and political factors before making a decision to proceed. It also decides the type of power generation required, gas, coal, hydro, etc. Issues such as foreign exchange considerations, attracting financial support from the UN or World Bank, whether to seek local or global bids or the political issues associated with dealing with certain countries are all considered. French companies, for example, went through a difficult period for a few months after Thomson supplied satellite technology to Taiwan, and the fortunes of US companies seeking business in China tends to fluctuate with the freeze–thaw in international relations. China tends to use its international ordering as an extension of its international relations policy but any period of 'failed bids' tends to pass quickly if the supplier concerned is commercially reliable.

The localisation of supply contracts can be an important feature at this stage. Global suppliers are primarily used to supply cutting-edge technologies at a time when China does not have the expertise. The trend is clear to see, however: unless the overseas supplier remains ahead in R&D, local companies will eventually be substituted. Contracts for coal-fired power stations up to 6 gigawatts now tend to be awarded only to local companies, so a localisation policy such as that operated by Alstom whereby alliances are formed with Chinese companies can be a sensible way of maintaining an involvement in long-term market development.

Some high-level lobbying is possible at this stage, although access to all the decision makers can be difficult. More subtle PR and indirect communications strategies may be needed. The SPDC has the power to overrule any recommendation from the Design Institute.

Bidding specification approved

At this stage, if the SPDC approves the specifications the formal bidding process can begin subject to any policy restrictions. Normally, the Design Institute's technical proposals are accepted by the SPDC although some reshaping may be required. Once formal bidding is initiated the specifications tend to be rigid. If a supplier cannot meet the requirements at this stage it means disqualification. If, for example, the percentage of localised production or the technical requirements are not met, there is little point in a prospective supplier spending further time on the project. Usually at this stage, pre-quotes are requested as an initial expression of interest. This enables those with a dubious record or an uncompetitive proposal to be weeded out early on, allowing more time to be spent with the preferred bidders. Normally a two or three month timescale is allowed.

Clarification meetings with potential suppliers

After the pre-quotes have been submitted the first 'formal' meeting is held with potential suppliers. This enables questions to be asked and clarification to be sought before initial evaluation. The meetings often involve all the parties involved with the project, local and international, meeting with a large number of experts from the buying committee.

Preliminary evaluation of proposals

At this stage, formal proposal evaluation takes place to reduce the number of bidders down to two or three. A committee of between eight and ten experts shortlists bids on the basis of:

- Specification fit
- Price and cost factors
- Warranty offered
- Performance guarantees
- Reliability record
- Localised supply proposals.

In the experience of Alstom, it is the degree of localisation that is the key factor after technical and cost criteria have been met, for example on the Lanzhou power generation project it was 40 per cent for phase one and 60 per cent for phase two. In addition, serious technology transfer has to be built into the project along with appropriate management development strategies.

Formal tender invitations

The committee, having eliminated many initial bidders, then invites named suppliers to prepare a detailed tender and to enter into formal negotiations. The suppliers know who they are up against and must prepare a winning bid based on the specification and any intelligence as to what the others will be offering. This can be a long process with extensive discussions involving specialists from both sides. Typically it may mean between ten and fifteen people on each side around the negotiation table.

Draft contracts prepared

As part of the tendering stage, draft contracts are often issued so that all the clauses can be considered and discussed before a final selection is made.

Bid evaluation and decision

The committee's final evaluation and decision often revolves around the final contract negotiation, as often the other technical factors have been used to pre-qualify bids. Even when a price has been tendered, it is not unusual for two or three further attempts to be made to reduce it still further. However, these negotiations rarely take place in formal sessions, but are conducted the night before on an informal basis. Sometimes the final decision can be 'political' to ensure that each of the main global competitors retains a continued interest in bidding, so the work will be shared around to some extent. Either at this stage, or earlier in the process, a delegation is formed to visit Alstom in France if it is bidding. This allows the possibility for decision makers to meet a wider range of staff and to look at installations in practice. Some care is taken, however, to ensure that such visits are not regarded as 'jollies' or free holidays.

Best and final offer accepted

Only after all the negotiations are complete and the decision made and ratified by the SPDC are formal and final contracts issued. They are normally signed with the maximum publicity, given the size of the order and its political significance to both parties.

During the whole process, which could take up to two years, suppliers like Alstom have to consider when to lobby and when to enter into normal sales and technical discussions. Lobbying can take place at the most senior level under the guise of invitations and gestures. The meeting of Chairman and CEO of Alstom, Pierre Bilger with Chinese Premier Zhu Rongji, for example, produced a photograph for the corporate literature that 'says a thousand words'. In a risk-avoidance environment, such a high level of contact reduces the personal risks for lower-order decision-makers in selecting the company. Such high-level contact by the Chairman and Geoff Ball's more regular contact with senior officials helps to cultivate more positive attitudes and understanding towards Alstom. The challenge throughout the process, but especially in the early and late stages, is to position the company to make most of the opportunity by demonstrating that the best technical and economic solution lies with them. This means identifying projects early and getting in early to lobby for that position during the negotiation stage, to ensure that the wider decision-making units are contacted and that all the resources of the company are marshalled to prepare and win the bids.

Sources: with grateful thanks to Geoff Ball, President, Alstom, China; Alstom corporate literature.

Questions

1. To what extent and how do the stages in the buying process presented in this case match the more generalised models presented in this chapter?
2. Which stage of the buying process do you think is easiest for Alstom to influence, and why?
3. What are the biggest risks facing the SPDC and what could Alstom do to minimise those risks?
4. How much of a role should 'international politics' play in B2G marketing?

case study 4.2

Fairtrade: playing fair with third-world suppliers

The Fairtrade Foundation was founded in the UK in 1991 by Christian Aid, Oxfam, Traidcraft, CAFOD, the World Development Movement, and The New Consumer and was joined a year later by the National Federation of Women's Institutes. Fairtrade is an alternative to conventional international trade. It is about providing access to markets for farmers of commodity products in developing countries and paying them a fair price. Small farmers with no access to markets have no other option but to sell their crop to local traders who can, and frequently do, exploit them. With nowhere else to sell their crops they often have to accept the price offered to them. Fairtrade, however, covers the cost of production and a little bit more, paying farmers a price that reflects the true value of crops and labour. It also encourages the development of long-term, mutually beneficial partnerships between suppliers and buyers that go beyond purely economic exchanges.

Trading fairly with third-world suppliers and using this as a promotional tool is important for Cafédirect. They use the images of their suppliers to great effect in their advertising and on the product packs.

Source: Cafédirect.

Fairtrade accredited products bear a distinctive logo, known as the Fairtrade Mark, which is an independent guarantee to the consumers that:

- The farmers who produce the product receive a fair price that covers the cost of production and gives them a little bit more. Up to 60 per cent of the value of a shipment is paid in advance to help provide the farmers with working capital.
- The farmers receive a social premium, of 5 US cents per pound of coffee over and above the market price to be used for the benefit of their communities. Some use the premium to build and equip community schools and hospitals, while others use it to build the competitive resources of their community of farmers. In Peru, for instance,

a cooperative decided to use its Fairtrade premiums to buy a new truck which enabled farmers to get their coffee to the town for processing. Previously, farmers would have had to haul coffee down the mountain on their backs, a journey of many hours, or use a donkey if they were fortunate enough to own one. This also meant that the cooperative could compete better with commercial organisations who own their own trucks.

- In the case of coffee, the farmers are guaranteed a minimum Fairtrade price no matter how low the international market price of coffee falls which gives them some security and the confidence to plan ahead. This is very important in a commodity market with volatile prices. According to the ICO, the International Coffee Organisation, coffee prices have fallen by almost 70 per cent since 1980 and in December 2000, coffee prices hit a 30-year low, largely due to oversupply. While demand for coffee has only risen slowly, world production has risen fivefold since 1950.
- The coffee producers are small-scale farmers and manage their own farms by mainly using their own labour.
- The organisation (cooperative or union) that the farmers belong to is democratically elected and responsible to its members for its actions.
- In the case of tea where the majority of producers work on private estates (unlike the small-scale farmers who grow coffee) the Fairtrade Mark is a guarantee that the estate workers are treated fairly and receive the Fairtrade premiums in full.
- To avoid overdependence, no Fairtrade coffee producer sells their entire crop to the Fairtrade market. Even the most active would export no more than about 25 per cent of their entire production to the Fairtrade market and most export considerably less than that. The rest of their production has to be sold to the conventional (non-Fairtrade) market at the prevailing world prices.

There are now some thirty-two Fairtrade accredited product lines available in the UK's major supermarkets, and about fifty more available through other outlets such as Oxfam, Traidcraft and independent stores. According to the Fairtrade Foundation: in 1994 the value of products at the supermarket checkout was £2.75 million and by 2000 it was approaching £22 million. The range of products available includes not only coffees and teas, but also cocoa, chocolate, sugar, fruit and fruit juices.

Cafédirect is a good example of a Fairtrade accredited company. It was formed in 1991 as a joint venture between four organisations: Equal Exchange, Oxfam Trading, Traidcraft, and Twin Trading, and in 1992, Cafédirect became the first Fairtrade accredited coffee to be sold in major supermarkets when the Cooperative Society and then Safeway agreed to stock Cafédirect Medium Roast on a trial basis. Throughout the 1990s, Cafédirect successfully built its portfolio of coffees, including organic and gourmet brands and then in 1998, it launched Teadirect, a blend of black teas from the east African countries of Tanzania and Uganda bought from small-scale tea growers. Of six suppliers in Tanzania and Uganda, four are small-holder tea factories and just two are private estates.

Cafédirect buys its coffee from seventeen producer groups in nine different countries and tea from six producer groups in two different countries. These farmers' groups are organised into unions or central cooperatives. Typically these unions or central cooperatives are made up of a number of different village based co-ops or societies which own it, elect its board and have a say in all democratically made decisions. The size of the farmers' organisations varies considerably, from Bagua Grande in Peru with 100 members, to KDCU in Tanzania with 150,000 members. Cafédirect currently deals with organisations representing over 300,000 farmers. When their families are taken into account it is conservatively estimated that Cafédirect impacts on the lives of 1.23 million people.

Cafédirect has gone beyond the basic requirements of Fairtrade accreditation. For example, it pays the same minimum price for coffee as other Fairtrade buyers but once the market rises above that minimum price, Cafédirect pays a 10 per cent premium rather than the normal 5 US cents premium. It also guaranteed higher minimum prices to producers of organic and gourmet coffee beans to encourage and reward the farmers for the extra work involved in producing these coffees. Cafédirect also runs Producer Support & Development Programmes with its tea and coffee producers. These programmes are not paid for by the Fairtrade premiums, which go directly to the producers, but are funded by Cafédirect itself. The Producer Support & Development teams are made up of full-time staff and consultants with expertise in business, general management, organisational development, agronomics and organic farming. Programmes are tailor-made to address the needs and priorities of each producer organisation, identified through ongoing dialogue and a process of consultation. Current priorities include developing organic production for coffee farmers, improving communication through the provision of e-mail and internet access, the introduction of training and exchange programmes and training producers in price risk management.

An important part of Cafédirect's Producer Support & Development work is helping producers to find new markets for their crop. Development of capacity and skills for the Fairtrade and non-Fairtrade markets helps to strengthen the producers' businesses which indirectly benefits Cafédirect too by reducing dependency. Many of Cafédirect's producers made their very first exports to Cafédirect, but now have the ability and confidence to supply the conventional (non-Fairtrade) market too. In Tanzania, Cafédirect's Producer Support & Development team facilitated an agreement between the Kilimanjaro Native Co-operative Union (KNCU) and ACC, one of the biggest private companies trading in Africa. As a result, in 2000 ACC bought four and a half thousand bags of coffee from KNCU.

Cafédirect now has some 5 per cent of the UK coffee market (Mason, 2000) and although progress in getting Fairtrade accredited products into retail stores has been impressive, there are still other areas for development. The out-of-home market is a very important growth area for Fairtrade. In 2000, Cafédirect's coffee and tea became the first Fairtrade accredited products to be sold by a major high street coffee chain, Costa, from all of its 250 coffee shops. Offices and commercial premises are also switching to Fairtrade teas and coffees in canteens and through Cafédirect-branded Fairtrade vending machines. Many prestigious companies such as Jaguar, John Lewis Partnership, Virgin Megastores, the Co-operative Bank, the Eden Project and the Mayor of London's office are now serving Cafédirect to their staff and clients.

Fairtrade is not purely a UK concept. The Fairtrade Labelling Organisations International (FLO) is an umbrella organisation that coordinates the work of various national Fairtrade initiatives such as the Fairtrade Foundation in the UK, Max Havelaar in Holland and Transfair in Germany and the USA. One of its key aims is to see the introduction of a single worldwide Fairtrade label.

Sources: http://www.cafedirect.co.uk; Mason (2000).

Questions

1 Summarise the reasons why the Fairtrade concept is so important to third-world suppliers.

2 What are the disadvantages to the organisational buyer of purchasing from suppliers through the Fairtrade scheme? Why do buyers continue to trade with these suppliers despite the disadvantages?

3 If you were running a training seminar for small suppliers as part of Cafédirect's Producer Support & Development Programme what key points of advice would you be giving them about establishing and developing relationships with new buyers in different countries?

References for chapter 4

Anderson, J.C. and Narus, J.A. (1984), 'A Model of the Distributor's Perspective of Distributor–Manufacturer Working Relationships', *Journal of Marketing*, 48 (Fall), pp. 62–74.

Anderson, J.C. and Narus, J.A. (1986), 'Towards a Better Understanding of Distribution Channel Working Relationships', in K. Backhaus and D. Wilson (eds), *Industrial Marketing: A German–American Perspective*, Springer-Verlag.

Ansari, A. and Modarress, B. (1990), 'Two Strategies for Regaining US Manufacturing Dominance', *International Journal of Quality and Reliability Management*, 7 (6).

Barber, A. (2000), 'Mittelstand Still the Backbone', *FT Survey: Baden-Württemberg* in *Financial Times*, 28 May.

Barnaby, A. (2000), 'Sourcing Globally, Clicking Locally', *Net Sourcing Magazine*, September, p. 26.

Barnett, A. (2000), 'Time to Pay off the Piper', *Director*, August, p. 29.

Baxter, L. and Simon, E. (1993), 'Relationship Maintenance Strategies and Dialectical Contradictions in Personal Relationships', *Journal of Social and Personal Relationships*, 10, pp. 225–42.

Bistritz, S., Gardner, A. and Klompmaker, J. (1998), 'Selling to Senior Executives Part 2', *Marketing Management*, 7 (3), pp. 18–27.

Brown-Humes, C. (2000), 'Sweden: Sector Enters Sober Times', *Financial Times*, 4 December.

Carr, H. and Pomeroy, J. (1992), *Fashion Design and Product Development*, Blackwell.

Cockcroft, L. (1996), 'Transnational Bribery: Is it Inevitable?', *Business Strategy Review*, 7 (3), pp, 30–9.

Doyle, A. (2001), 'Lobbying Hots up for Beijing Orders', *Flight International*, 6 August, p. 6.

Dwyer, F.R. *et al.* (1987), 'Developing Buyer–Seller Relationships', *Journal of Marketing*, 51 (2), pp. 11–27.

The Economist (2000), 'Iraq and the West: When Sanctions Don't Work', *The Economist*, 8 April, pp. 23–5.

The European Commission (2001), *Single Market Scoreboard*, No. 8, May.

European Purchasing and Materials Management (1993/94), 'Philips Quality', *European Purchasing and Materials Management*, 1993/94 (2), pp. 51–5.

Financial Times (2000), 'Versatile Metal Expands its Horizons', *FT Survey: Aluminium* in *Financial Times*, 25 October.

Gemünden, H. and Ritter, T. (1997), 'Managing Technological Networks: The Concept of Network Competence' in Gemünden, H. and Ritter, T. (eds) *Relationships and Networks in International Markets*, Elsevier.

Giller, C. and Matear, S. (2001), 'The Termination of Interfirm Relationships', *The Journal of Business and Industrial Marketing*, 16 (2), pp. 94–112.

Good, D. and Evans, K. (2001), 'Relationship Unrest – A Strategic Perspective for Business-to-Business Marketers', *European Journal of Marketing*, 35 (5), pp. 549–65.

Hahn, C., Kim, K. and Kim, J. (1986), 'Costs of Competition Implications for Purchasing Strategy', *Journal of Purchasing and Materials Management*, 22 (3), pp. 2–7.

Hallén, L. (1980), 'Stability and Change in Supplier Relationships', in L. Engall and J. Johanson (eds), *Some Aspects of Control in International Business*, Uppsala.

Hamra, W. (2000), 'Bribery in International Business Transactions and the OECD Convention: Benefits and Limitations', *Business Economics*, 35 (4), pp. 33–46.

Hayward, C. (2000), 'Report Slams Lengthening MOD Purchasing Delays', *Supply Management*, 30 November, p. 8.

Hill, R.W. and Hiller, T.J. (1977), *Organisational Buying Behaviour*, Macmillan.

Johanson, J. (1982), 'Production Technology and the User–Supplier Interaction', in H. Håkansson (ed.), *International Marketing and Purchasing of Industrial Goods: An Interaction Approach*, John Wiley and Sons.

Johanson, J. and Wootz, B. (1986), 'The German Approach to Europe', in P.W. Turnbull and J-P. Valla (eds), *Strategies for International Industrial Marketing*, Croom Helm.

Johnson, W.J. and Bonoma, T.V. (1981), 'The Buying Centre: Structure and Interaction Patterns', *Journal of Marketing*, 45 (Summer), pp. 143–56.

Kandell, J. (2001), 'Finland is Now Nokialand', *Institutional Investor*, June, pp. 75–82.

Lorenz, E.H. (1988), 'Neither Friends Nor Strangers: Informal Networks of Subcontracting in French Industry', in D. Gambetta (ed.), *Trust: Making and Breaking Cooperative Relations*, Basil Blackwell.

Mason, T. (2000), 'The Importance of Being Ethical', *Marketing*, 26 October, p. 27.

Mattson, M.R. (1988), 'How to Determine the Composition and Influence of a Buying Centre', *Industrial Marketing Management*, 17 (3), pp. 205–14.

Modern Railways (2001), 'Component Suppliers Must Focus on Quality', *Modern Railways*, June, pp. 53–6.

Möller, K. and Wilson, D. (1995), *Business Marketing: An Interaction and Network Perspective*, Boston: Kluwer.

Moorman, C., Deshpandé, R. and Zaltman, G. (1993), 'Factors Affecting Trust in Market Research Relationships', *Journal of Marketing*, 57 (1), pp. 81–101.

Moss, N. (1997), 'Who Bribes Wins', *The European*, 11 December, pp. 26–7.

Narus, J. and Anderson, J. (1995), 'Using Teams to Manage Collaborative Relationships in Business Markets', *Business-to-Business Marketing*, 2 (3), pp. 17–46.

Nolan, A. (1997a), 'Watching the Directives', *Supply Management*, 27 February, pp. 14–15.

Nolan, A. (1997b), 'Finding the Right Formula', *Supply Management*, 13 March, pp. 14–15.

O'Connor, G. (2000), 'Still Upbeat About the Future', *FT Survey: Aluminium* in *Financial Times*, 25 October.

OECD (2000), 'Transparency International Corruption Index', *OECD Observer*, 7 July.

Paliwoda, S. and Bonaccorsi, A. J. (1994), 'Trends in Procurement Strategies Within the European Aircraft Industry', *Industrial Marketing Management*, 23 (3), pp. 235–44.

Pettitt, S.J. (1992), *Small Firms and Their Major Customers: An Interaction and Relationship Approach*, unpublished PhD Thesis, Cranfield University.

Porter, M.E. (1990), *The Competitive Advantage of Nations*, The Free Press.

Powers, T.L. (1991), *Modern Business Marketing: A Strategic Planning Approach to Business and Industrial Markets*, St Paul MN: West.

Professional Engineering (2000), 'UK Taskforce to Visit Serbia', *Professional Engineering*, 18 October, p. 7.

Ramsay, J. and Wilson, I. (1990), 'Sourcing/Contracting Strategy Selection', *International Journal of Operations and Production Management*, 10 (8), pp. 19–28.

Render, B. and Heizer, J. (1997), *Principles of Operations Management*, Englewood Cliffs: Prentice-Hall.

Riley, H. (2001), 'Buying Better, Helping More', *Supply Management*, 10 May, pp. 32–3.

Riley, H. (2000), 'Life Support', *Supply Management*, 5 July, pp. 28–30.

Robinson, P.J. *et al.* (1967), *Industrial Buying and Creative Marketing*, Allyn and Bacon.

Segal, M. (1989), 'Implications of Single vs Multiple Buying Sources', *Industrial Marketing Management*, 18 (3), pp. 163–78.

Selnes, F. (1998), 'Antecedents and Consequences of Trust and Satisfaction in Buyer–Seller Relationships', *European Journal of Marketing*, 32 (3), pp. 305–22.

Serant, C. (2001), 'SCI Lands Big Deal with Nokia', accessed via http://www.ebonline.com, September 2001.

Sheth, J. (1977), 'Recent Developments in Organisational Buying Behaviour', in A.G. Woodside *et al.* (eds), *Consumer and Industrial Buying Behaviour*, Elsevier.

Sheth, J. (1973), 'A Model of Industrial Buying Behaviour', *Journal of Marketing*, 37 (October), 50–6.

Slater, S. (1997), 'Developing a Customer Value-based Theory of the Firm', *Journal of the Academy of Marketing Science*, 25 (2), pp. 162–7.

Solman, P. (2000), 'European Can Take Up Advances', *FT Survey: Aluminium* in *Financial Times*, 25 October.

Spekman, R.E. (1988), 'Strategic Supplier Selection: Understanding Long-Term Buyer Relationships', *Business Horizons*, 31 (4), pp. 75–81.

Taimi, K. (1996), 'The Face in the Supermarket Window', *European Purchasing and Materials Management*, No. 7, pp. 159–69.

Treleven, M. (1987), 'Single Sourcing: A Management Tool for the Quality Supplier', *Journal of Purchasing and Materials Management*, 23 (1), pp. 19–24.

Valla, J-P. (1986), 'The French Approach to Europe', in P.W. Turnbull and J-P. Valla (eds), *Strategies for International Industrial Marketing*, Croom Helm.

Walter, A. and Gemünden, H. (2000), 'Bridging the Gap Between Suppliers and Customers Through Relationship Promoters: Theoretical Considerations and Empirical Results', *The Journal of Business and Industrial Marketing*, 15 (2), pp. 86–105.

Webster, F.E. and Wind, Y. (1972), *Organisational Buyer Behaviour*, Prentice Hall.

Zeng, A. (2000), 'A Synthetic Study of Sourcing Strategies', *Industrial Management & Data Systems*, 100 (5), pp. 219–26.

chapter 5

segmenting markets

Introduction

LEARNING OBJECTIVES

This chapter will help you to:

1. explain how both B2B and consumer markets can be broken down into smaller, more manageable groups of similar customers;
2. understand the effects on the marketing mix of pursuing specific segments;
3. understand the potential benefits and risks of segmentation; and
4. appreciate the role of segmentation in strategic marketing thinking.

Building on the understanding of buyer behaviour and decision-making processes outlined in Chapters 3 and 4, this chapter concerns a question that should be very close to any true marketer's heart: 'How do we define and profile our customer?' Until an answer is found, no meaningful marketing decisions of any kind can be made. It is not usually enough to define your customer as 'anyone who wants to buy our product' because this implies a product-orientated approach: the product comes first, the customer second. If marketing is everything we have claimed it to be, then the product is only a small part of a total integrated package offered to a customer. Potential customers must, therefore, be defined in terms of what they want, or will accept, in terms of price, what kind of distribution will be most convenient for them and through what communication channels they can best be reached, as well as what they want from the product itself.

Remember too that in a consumer-based society, possession of 'things' can take on a symbolic meaning. A person's possessions and consumption habits make a statement about the kind of person they are, or the kind of person they want you to think they are. The organisation that takes the trouble to understand this and produces a product that not only serves its functional purpose well, but also appears to reflect those less tangible properties of a product in the purchaser's eyes, will gain that purchaser's custom. Thus sport

eg

The business traveller is an important market segment for travel industry operators, such as airlines, hotel chains and car rental companies. Although business travellers expect better service, as frequent travellers they tend to spend more money, more often. This group of customers, therefore, differs significantly from leisure- and economy-class customers. Business travellers sometimes need to book at short notice, travel to tight schedules, travel frequently and could need to change arrangements at the last minute. Airlines have adapted their service provision to meet the needs of this group. Fast check-in facilities, first- or business-class travel options and lounges, special boarding arrangements and loyalty schemes are all important for attracting these customers. Airlines also advertise specifically to the business traveller and keep their pricing competitive within the business flyer segment on competitive routes such as London–Brussels. British Airways (BA) has extended its focus on business travellers beyond just pricing and service. It has introduced the 'flying bed' seating arrangement to enable the business-class traveller to get a good night's sleep as well as more leg room, more shoulder room, seat power, and the freedom to raid the galley whenever the traveller feels peckish. Although the price is higher, around $850 extra on the New York – London route, it is cheap compared with the risks business executives associate with making poor decisions through lack of a comfortable sleep. Already, 40 per cent of the 112 long-haul aircraft have been converted and the rest should be completed by 2003. BA claims to have improved sales by 8 per cent in the first full year of operation of the 'flying bed' service (Evans, 2001).

shoe manufacturers such as Reebok and Nike not only developed shoes for a wide range of specific sports (tennis, soccer, athletics, etc.), but also realised that a significant group of customers would never go near a sports facility and just wanted trainers as fashion statements. This meant that they served three distinctly different groups of customers: the professional/serious sports player, the amateur/casual sports player and the fashion victim. The R&D invested in state-of-the-art quality products, combined with the status connected with the first group and endorsement from leading sports icons, helped these companies to build an upmarket image that allowed them to exploit the fashion market to the full with premium-priced products. This in turn led to the expansion of product ranges to include branded sports and leisure clothing.

All this forms the basis of the concept of segmentation, first developed by Smith (1957). Segmentation can be viewed as the art of discerning and defining meaningful differences between groups of customers to form the foundations of a more focused marketing effort. The following section looks at this concept in a little more depth, while the rest of the chapter will examine how the concept can be implemented and its implications for the organisation.

The concept of segmentation

The introductory section of this chapter has presented the customer-orientated argument for the adoption of the segmentation concept. There is, however, also a practical rationale for adopting it. Mass production, mass communication, increasingly sophisticated technology and increasingly efficient global transportation have all helped in the creation of larger, more temptingly lucrative potential markets. Few organisations, however, have either the resources or the inclination to be a significant force within a loosely defined market. The sensible option, therefore, is to look more closely at the market and find ways of breaking it down into manageable parts, or groups of customers with similar characteristics, and then to concentrate effort on serving the needs of one or two groups really well, rather than trying to be all things to all people. This makes segmentation a proactive part of developing a marketing strategy and involves the application of techniques to identify these segments (Wind, 1978).

It may help you to understand this concept better if you think of an orange. It appears to be a single entity, yet when you peel off the skin you find that it is made up of a number of discrete segments, each of which happily exists within the whole. Eating an orange is much easier (and much less wasteful and messy) if you eat it systematically, segment by segment, rather than by attacking the whole fruit at once. Marketers, being creative folk, have adopted this analogy and thus refer to the separate groups of customers that make up a market as **market segments**.

The analogy is misleading, however, in that each segment of an orange is more or less identical in size, shape and taste, whereas in a market, segments may be very different from each other in terms of size and character. To determine these things, each segment has its own distinct profile, defined in terms of a number of criteria, referred to as *bases* or *variables*, set by the marketer. The choice of appropriate criteria for subdividing the market is very important (Moriarty and Reibstein, 1986) and thus a significant proportion of this chapter is devoted to thinking about the bases by which segments might be defined in both consumer and B2B markets. Leading on from this, there is also the question of influences that might affect an organisation's choice of segmentation variables. Then, once an organisation has defined its market segments, what is it supposed to do with the information? This too is addressed in this chapter.

B2B and consumer markets, in general, tend to be segmented differently and will, therefore, be discussed separately, beginning with B2B markets. If you are unsure of the difference between these two types of market, then revise the content of Chapters 3 and 4 before you go any further.

Segmenting B2B markets

The overall concept of segmentation applies equally to both consumer and B2B markets, but the variables by which they are segmented do differ. One major feature of B2B segmentation is that it can focus on both the organisation and the individual buyers within it. Additionally, there is the need to reflect group buying, that is, the involvement of more than one person in the purchasing decision (Abratt, 1993). All of this can be compared with a family buying situation in a consumer market, but operating on a much larger scale, usually within a more formalised process.

Wind and Cardozo (1974) suggest that segmenting a B2B market can involve two stages:

1 *Identify subgroups* within the whole market that share common general characteristics. These are called **macro segments** and will be discussed further below.
2 *Select target segments* from within the macro segments based on differences in specific buying characteristics. These are called **micro segments** and are discussed at p. 182.

Macro segmentation bases

Macro segments are based on the characteristics of organisations and the broader purchasing context within which they operate. Defining a macro segment assumes that the organisations within it will exhibit similar patterns and needs, which will be reflected in similar buying behaviour and responses to marketing stimuli.

The bases used for macro segmentation tend to be observable or readily obtained from secondary information (i.e. published or existing sources) and can be grouped into two main categories, each of which will now be discussed.

Organisational characteristics

There are three organisational charactistics: size, location and usage rate.

1 *Size*. The size of an organisation will make a difference to the way in which it views its suppliers and goes about its purchasing. A large organisation, for instance, may well have many people involved in decision-making; its decision-making may be very complex and formalised (because of the risks and level of investment involved), and it may require special treatment in terms of service or technical cooperation. In contrast, a small organisation may operate on a more centralised decision-making structure, involving one or two people and with simpler buying routines. The UK clearing banks, for example, tend to segment their business customers by size. Small businesses need sympathetic local support, and the banks target the new start-up segment of the small business market with advice packs and promises of cheap financing along with the support of their own banking adviser.

eg

Similar segmentation strategies are now being employed in the modernising economies of Central Europe. Corporate banking hardly existed in Poland in the 1980s, but following economic reform, the number of companies in Poland has grown from 500,000 in 1990 to over 3 million in 2001. As well as this increase in the potential corporate customer base, the banks have been privatised and many have been taken over or have gone into partnership with Western European and US banks. This has led to a much more marketing-orientated attitude within the Polish banks and has started the process of client segmentation. Small and medium-sized enterprises, defined as those with a turnover of between Zl5-250 have been targeted, initially for savings and loans products, but increasingly with cross-selling of factoring, leasing, trade finance and investment banking. This is changing the role of the banks from being simply lenders and deposit-takers to being financial advisers, and this has far-reaching implications for the type and level of communication required by existing and new customers. The next stage of development, internet banking, is still some way off, however, because of the need to create a stronger and more secure IT infrastructure for Polish businesses (Smorszczewski, 2001).

2 *Location*. Organisations may focus their selling effort according to the geographic concentration of the industries they serve. Such specialisation is, however, slowly breaking down as the old, heavy, geographically based industries, such as shipbuilding, mining and chemical production, become less predominant. Additionally, there is the emergence of smaller more flexible manufacturers, geographically dispersed in new technology parks, industrial estates and enterprise zones. Nevertheless, there are still examples of geographic segmentation, such as that of computer hardware and software sales, or in the financial sector, which is concentrated in London, Frankfurt, Zurich and the major capitals of the world. Organisations providing certain kinds of services might also look to geographic segments. A haulage company might specialise in certain routes and thus look for customers at specific points to make collection, delivery and capacity utilisation as efficient as possible.
3 *Usage rate*. The quantity of product purchased may be a legitimate means of categorising potential customers. A purchasing organisation defined as a 'heavy user' will have different needs from a 'light user', perhaps demanding (and deserving) different treatment in terms of special delivery or prices, for example. A supplier may define a threshold point, so that when a customer's usage rate rises above it, their status changes. The customer's account may be handed over to a more senior manager and the supplier may become more flexible in terms of cooperation, pricing and relationship building. It is generally a better investment to make concessions in order to cultivate a relationship with a single heavy user than to try to attract a number of light users, as implied in Chapter 4.

Product or service application

This second group of segmentation bases acknowledges that the same good can be used in many different ways. This approach looks for customer groupings, either within specific industries as defined by standard industrial classification (SIC) codes, each with its own requirements, or by defining a specific application and grouping customers around that.

The SIC code may help to identify sectors with a greater propensity to use particular products for particular applications. Glass, for example, has many industrial uses, ranging from packaging to architecture to the motor industry. Each of these application sectors behaves differently in terms of price sensitivity, ease of substitution, quality and performance requirements, for instance. Similarly, cash-and-carry wholesalers serve three broad segments: independent grocers, caterers and pubs. Each segment will purchase different types of goods, in different quantities and for different purposes.

The macro level is a useful starting point for defining some broad boundaries to markets and segments, but it is not sufficient in itself, even if such segmentation does happen too often in practice. Further customer-oriented analysis on the micro level is necessary.

Micro segmentation bases

Within a macro segment, a number of smaller micro segments may exist. To focus on these, the organisation needs to have a detailed understanding of individual members of the macro segment, in terms of their management philosophy, decision-making structures, purchasing policies and strategies, as well as their needs and wants. Such information can come from published sources, past experience of the potential buyer, sales force knowledge and experience, word of mouth within the industry, or at first hand from the potential buyer.

Micro segmentation reflects, to some extent, the nested approach to B2B market segmentation suggested by Bonoma and Shapiro (1984). This means starting with broad characteristics, that is, the demographic profile of the customer (understanding the industry, organisational size, etc.) and then developing increasingly fine detail by working through their operating variables (product, technology, quality, etc.), purchasing approach (DMUs, power, buyer–seller relationships, etc.), situational factors (delivery lead times, order size, etc.) and, finally, personal characteristics (the individuals concerned).

An overview of common bases for micro segmentation is given in Table 5.1. If some of the terms given within the table seem a little vague, revise Chapter 4 which goes into them all in much more detail.

Gathering, collating and analysing such depth of information is, of course, a time-consuming and sometimes difficult task, and there is always the question of whether it is either feasible or worthwhile. However, there are benefits in defining such small segments (even segments of one!) if it enables fine tuning of the marketing offering to suit specific

Table 5.1 Bases for micro segmentation in B2B markets

- Product
- Applications
- Technology
- Purchasing policies
- DMU structure
- Decision-making process
- Buyer–seller relationships

needs. Given the volumes of goods and levels of financial investment involved in some B2B markets, the effort is not wasted. An organisation that has a small number of very important customers would almost certainly treat each as a segment of one, particularly in a market such as the supply of organisation-wide computer systems where individual customer needs vary so much. In contrast, in a market such as office stationery, where standard products are sold to perhaps thousands of B2B customers, any segmentation is likely to centre around groups aggregating many tens of customers on the macro level.

Overall, this section has shown that it is useful to be able to segment B2B markets, and that it can be done in a number of ways relating to the nature of both the product sold and the buying organisation. The emphasis here has essentially been a practical one, treating the buying organisation as a rational entity. Chapter 4 (particularly pp. 164 *et seq.*), in looking more deeply at the organisation as the sum of its human parts, demonstrated some of the potential irrationalities that make micro segmentation so fascinating. In consumer markets, rapid progress has also been made towards expanding concepts of segmentation to include what might be termed the less rational influences on purchasing, as the following section shows.

Segmenting consumer markets

Segmenting consumer markets does have some similarities with B2B segmentation, as this section indicates. The main difference is that consumer segments are usually very much larger in terms of the number of potential buyers, and it is much more difficult, therefore, to get close to the individual buyer. Consumer segmentation bases also put more emphasis on the buyer's lifestyle and context, because most consumer purchases fulfil higher-order needs (see, for example, Maslow's hierarchy of needs, discussed at pp. 112 *et seq.*) rather than simply functional ones. The danger is, however, that the more abstract the segments become, the less easily understood they may become by those designing marketing strategies (Wedel and Kamakura, 1999). Each of the commonly used bases is now discussed in turn.

Geographic segmentation

Geographic segmentation defines customers according to their location. This can often be a useful starting point. A small business, for example, particularly in the retail or service sector, operating on limited resources, may look initially for custom within its immediate locale. Even multinationals, such as Heinz, often tend to segment geographically by dividing their global organisation into operating units built around specific geographic markets.

In neither case, however, is this the end of the story. For the small business, simply being there on the High Street is not enough. It has to offer something further that a significant group of customers want, whether it is attractively low prices or a high level of customer service. The multinational organisation segments geographically, partly for the sake of creating a manageable organisational structure, and partly in recognition that on a global scale, geographic boundaries herald other, more significant differences in taste, culture, lifestyle and demand. The Single European Market (SEM) may have created a market of some 400 million potential customers, yet the first thing that most organisations are likely to do is to segment the SEM into its constituent nations.

eg

Take the marketing of an instant hot chocolate drink, made with boiling water. In the UK, virtually every household owns a kettle, and hot chocolate is viewed either as a bedtime drink or as a substitute through the day for tea or coffee. In France, however, kettles are not common, and hot chocolate is most often made with milk as a nourishing children's breakfast. Thus the benefits of speed, convenience and versatility that would impress the UK market would be less applicable in the French market. France would require a very different marketing strategy at best or, at worst, a completely different product.

Geographic segments are at least easy to define and measure, and information is often freely available from public sources. This kind of segmentation also has an operational advantage, particularly in developing efficient systems for distribution and customer contact, for example. However, in a marketing-orientated organisation, this is not sufficient. Douglas and Craig (1983), for example, emphasise the dangers of being too geographically focused and making assumptions about what customers in a region might have in common. Even within a small geographic area, there is a wide variety of needs and wants, and this method on its own tells you nothing about them. Heinz divides its global operation into geographically based subdivisions because it does recognise the effects of cultural diversity and believes in 'local marketing' as the best means of fully understanding and serving its various markets. It is also important to note that any organisation segmenting purely on geographic grounds would be vulnerable to competition coming in with a more customer-focused segmentation strategy.

In summary, therefore, there is limited scope for the application of geographic segmentation on its own. It may be useful for service-based products that require the customer to come to you. For example, hairdressers attract business from a geographic catchment area centred on their salon, but even so, they still segment further on other criteria (for instance sex, age and trendiness). In manufacturing, geographic segmentation may also be useful for organisations operating with very limited resources. By confining its operations to a small geographic area, the organisation can develop a focus that will allow it to expand gradually as business builds up. In the main, however, it is used as a foundation for other, more customer-focused segmentation methods, such as those described below.

Demographic segmentation

Demographic segmentation tells you a little more about the customer and the customer's household on measurable criteria that are largely descriptive, such as age, sex, race, income, occupation, socioeconomic status and family structure.

Demographics might even extend into classifications of body size and shape! It has been suggested that any male with a waist over 102 cm or female with a waist over 88 cm should consider it a warning of obesity. That amounts to an awful lot of people, especially in the UK, Germany and the USA, where the working classes are relatively affluent (Stuttaford, 2001). Over 9 million people in the UK alone are classified as clinically obese and are at risk of weight-related illness. That could be good news for some pharmaceutical and diet food manufacturers, but it presents a challenge to some other business sectors. Clothing retailers such as High and Mighty and Evans primarily target larger men and women respectively. Other retailers have to get their mix of stock sizes right to meet seasonal demand. Marks and Spencer, for example, undertook a survey of 2,500 women and found that the average dress size is now a 14 whereas in 1980 it was a 12. Transport operators such as airlines and railways have even bigger problems. Economy-class seats on many aircraft are around 26 inches wide which is pretty cramped, even for those of us who are not built along the lines of a Sumo wrestler! The increasing size of travellers as well as the bad publicity about deep vein thrombosis being associated with sitting in cramped aircraft on long-haul flights is making airlines rethink their seating arrangements. Train operators are less concerned, however. In a push to cram more passengers into a carriage, modern rolling stock actually offers 6 inches less seat-room for commuters than carriages built in the 1970s (Bale, 2001).

marketing in action

Go for bust: bra wars go high-tech

The British bra and lingerie company Gossard has found that a geographic approach to market segmentation can have some validity. The types of product that sell best in various countries are different, partly for the practical reason that women vary in average size across Europe, and partly because of cultural and lifestyle factors. While the British female figure averages around sizes 12–14, German women tend towards sizes 14–16 and the French towards 10–12. Italian women want to be seductive and thus buy a lot of basques; the Germans are practical and look for support and quality; the French want to be fashionable and impress other women; and the Scandinavians want natural fibres. This is, of course, a grossly generalised survey, but the basic trends are there and give Gossard a basis for developing appropriate new products and strategies for different markets.

Not all bra brands are constrained by geographic markets, however. The Wonderbra was designed to target younger women, aged between 18 and 35, wanting a fashionable, fun, sexy bra that allows them to make the most of their assets. This appeal was reinforced by advertising slogans such as 'Hello, Boys', 'Mind If I Bring a Couple of Friends?' and 'In Your Dreams' alongside scantily clad, beautiful models. It's not all about frills and lace, however. Many new developments aimed at stimulating the bra market are based on technology and engineering. The latest variation on Wonderbra, for example, is a 'variable cleavage' bra, equipped with pulleys to draw the breasts together. Meanwhile, Gossard has launched the Airotic, based on the same principle as a car airbag, which used valves to provide lift. Then there is the Bioform which replaces underwiring with a soft moulded core of plastic around a rigid ring. The Bioform, which starts at size 34C in the UK, is aimed specifically at big women who find normal, underwired bras painful. Another new launch is the Ultimo which has silicone-gel pads sewn into the cups as a safer alternative to implants.

So whatever you are looking for, whether it's frills, thrills, or functionality, the right bra is out there somewhere.

Sources: Broadhead (1995); *The Economist* (2000).

Gossard designs different products for different European markets as both taste and average sizes differ across regional boundaries.

Source: Gossard.

As with the geographic variable, demographics are relatively easy to define and measure, and the necessary information is often freely available from public sources. The main advantage, however, is that demographics offer a clear profile of the customer on criteria that can be worked into marketing strategies. For example, an age profile can provide a foundation for choice of advertising media and creative approach. Magazines, for instance, tend to have readerships that are clearly defined in terms of gender, age bands and socioeconomic groups. The under-35 female reader, for example, is more likely to go for magazines such as *Marie Claire*, *Bella* and *Cosmopolitan* than the over-35s who are more likely to read *Prima*, *Good Housekeeping* and *Family Circle*.

One of the problems facing organisations looking to European markets in particular is that socioeconomic definitions vary widely across different countries, as already shown at p. 119. Efforts are, however, being made to develop a uniform scale, applicable across national boundaries and relevant to the needs of marketers. The outcomes of one such project, reported in Marbeau (1992) and Quatresooz and Vancraeynest (1992) suggest a definition of social grade based on the terminal education age of the main income earner in a household, his or her further education and professional training, and his or her occupation. Additionally, an economic status scale is proposed, based on a household's ownership of 10 carefully chosen consumer durables. This provides a way of comparing different countries without the problems of varying exchange rates, varying purchasing power or income measurement. The extent to which such a system becomes common European currency remains to be seen.

On the negative side, demographics are purely descriptive and, used alone, assume that all people in the same demographic group have similar needs and wants. This is not necessarily true (just think about the variety of people you know within your own age group).

Additionally, as with the geographic method, it is still vulnerable to competition coming in with an even more customer-focused segmentation strategy. It is best used, then, for products that have a clear bias towards a particular demographic group. For instance, cosmetics are initially segmented into male/female; baby products are primarily aimed at females aged between 20 and 35; school fee endowment policies appeal to households within a higher income bracket at a particular stage of the family lifecycle. In most of these cases, however, again as with the geographic method, the main use of demographic segmentation is as a foundation for other more customer-focused segmentation methods.

Geodemographic segmentation

Geodemographics can be defined as 'the analysis of people by where they live' (Sleight, 1997, p. 16) as it combines geographic information with demographic and sometimes even lifestyle data (see below) about neighbourhoods. This helps organisations to understand where their customers are, to develop more detailed profiles of how those customers live, and to locate and target similar potential customers elsewhere. A geodemographic system, therefore, will define types of neighbourhood and types of consumer within a neighbourhood according to their characteristics. Table 5.2 gives an example of how Experian's MOSAIC profiles one of its neighbourhood types. This Group H can be further split into sub-groups: H33 Bedsits and Shop Flats; H34 Studio Singles; H35 Chattering Classes; H36 College and Communal.

A number of specialist companies, including Experian, offer geodemographic databases and some of these are shown in Table 5.3. Most of them are generally applicable to a range of consumer markets, although Residata, for instance, is specifically designed for the insurance industry, and some, like CAMEO have developed variations on the main database to suit different industries or geographic regions. CAMEO Microvision UK is described as 'a flexible lifestage classification system for assessing the geodemographic makeup of a neighbourhood', for instance. CAMEO Financial focuses on assessing credit risk while CAMEO Investor assesses shareholder activity and financial sophistication. There's even CAMEO Ian which predicts the age of an individual by their forename! MOSAIC too has variations. Financial MOSAIC is designed for the financial services industry while Grocery MOSAIC classifies postcodes according to the grocery shopping behaviour of residents.

The databases vary considerably in the sources of data they use, the depth and breadth of coverage, and the number of variables they employ to define and describe neighbourhood types and/or households and/or individuals. CACI claims, for example, that it has a database of 44 million individuals in the UK, compiled from over 11 million lifestyle surveys along

Table 5.2 MOSAIC Group H: stylish singles

- Nearly 1.3 million households, representing 5.4 per cent of all UK households
- 2.8 million people in this group
- Students and young professionals
- First time openers of savings and mortgage accounts
- Frequent visitors to the cinema, concerts and exhibitions
- Like weekend breaks to European capital cities
- Prefer *The Guardian*, *The Independent* and *The Observer*
- Television viewing is light: current affairs and late films preferred
- Shop for food at convenience stores late in the day
- Convenience more important than price
- Prefer the city to the outer suburbs
- Enjoy living in diverse, cosmopolitan, multicultural environment
- Big spenders on mobile phones. CDs, sports equipment, audio and computer equipment

Source: adapted from http://www.uk.experian.com.

with the complete electoral roll and data on over 8 million owners of shares. The client can select and score clusters of individuals on any relevant criterion or criteria, for example credit card usage, size of average telephone bill, or use of computer games. CACI also claims that over 90 per cent of the lifestyle data used is less than two years old (http://www.caci.co.uk).

Geodemographic systems are increasingly becoming available as multimedia packages. MOSAIC is available on CD-ROM, giving the manager access to colour maps, spoken commentary on how to use the system, photographs and text. Experian and other providers are also working on customised geodemographic packages, tailored to suit a particular client's needs.

Table 5.3 Examples of geodemographic classifications

Organisation	*Classification system*	*Examples of data sources used*
ABC Ltd/ISL	Residata	Housing types and structure; risk indices; insurance data; PAF; unemployment statistics; census
CACI	ACORN LifestylesUK People*UK	Census data Lifestyle data; ER; Census; share ownership LIfestyle data; ER; Census; share ownership
Claritas Europe	PRiZM	Lifestyle data; share ownership; company directors; PAF; unemployment statistics; births and deaths
EuroDirect	CAMEO	Census data
Experian	MOSAIC	Census data; credit data; CCJs; PAF; ER; company directors; access to retail centres

Key: CCJs: County Court Judgments: Consumers who have been taken to court for debt recovery
ER: Electoral Register: gives names, addresses and number of adults in 95 per cent of UK households
PAF: Postcode Address File: Royal Mail's database of all addresses in the UK by postcode

Source: Adapted from Sleight (1999a, 1999b), copyright 1999 Peter Sleight, reproduced with kind permission; http://www.caci.co.uk; http://www.uk.experian.com; http;//www.micromarketing-online.com.

e-marketing *in action*

PRiZM: Pan European lifestyle segmentation

PRiZM is an example of Pan European lifestyle segmentation. This and other similar tools such as ACORN and MOSAIC work by characterising each postal unit as containing residents of a particular segment. Claritas, the vendor of PRiZM suggests that PRiZM can be used for these aims by the marketer:

1 To assess market potential or demand for a given area.
2 Develop customer loyalty and value through identifying the most attractive customers.
3 Identify emerging niche markets.
4 Identify and target customers most likely to defect in order to reduce churn.
5 Target telemarketing activity by concentrating on the households with the greatest propensity to purchase.

The type of lifestyle information on which PRiZM is based is indicated by the fields available through the related Prospect Locator database. This data can be purchased for specific purposes. For example, a financial services provider could purchase the data on building insurance renewal month in order to target customers in the period before renewal using a direct mail or e-mail campaign. Examples of data within the Prospect Locator includes:

- Personal information such as age/gender and marital status.
- Household information such as home details, home occupancy, home improvements, building/contents insurance renewal month, MOSAIC and financial MOSAIC.
- Financial information such as mortgage information, investments and savings.
- Assurance information – health, life and pet insurance.
- Charitable concerns – type of charity supported and propensity to make donations.
- Travel – whether self-catering, typical destination, frequency.
- Utility bills – electricity, gas and telephone.
- Hi-tech goods – satellite TV, mobile, home computer and internet access.
- Media – daily, Sunday newspaper, TV viewing, musical interests.
- Motor – annual mileage, car status, spend on next car, insurance.
- Sports interests – what sports participated in.

Source: Claritas Europe claritaseurope@claritaseu.com.

Such systems are invaluable to the marketer across all aspects of consumer marketing, for example in planning sampling areas for major market research studies, or assessing locations for new retail outlets, or finding appropriate areas for a direct mail campaign or door-to-door leaflet drop. O'Malley *et al.* (1995) point out that retailers find geodemographics invaluable. This is because setting up a new retail store location is very capital intensive and represents a long-term commitment. Retailers thus need to monitor a trade area in terms of its catchment, shopper profiles and competitive effects. Geodemographics can help to achieve this.

eg

Door-to-door marketing has evolved still further in its ability to target individual homes. Blanket drops of product samples or sales literature have been used for some time by consumer goods marketers, but the increasing refinement of databases has led to more sophisticated targeting. Circular Distributors, a leading door-to-door drop company, has launched its *Personal Placement* service which can match a purchased or client-provided database with geodemographic neighbourhoods from ACORN and MOSAIC, etc. to identify those areas with a reasonable proportion of target households. Within each neighbourhood postcode there are around 2,500 homes, and there are 8,900 postcodes in the UK. By adopting a micro-targeting system, units as small as 700 households can be identified to reflect differences in housing types even within a neighbourhood. This, matched with mailing lists and databases, enables cost-effective, better targeted door-to-door delivery.

To build a database, a range of criteria can be used, for example how many kids, pets and cars; age profile; ownership of home computer, etc. An organisation, therefore, can target only those who fit a profile, to cut out waste. One client, for example, an ISP, wanted to target households with a CD-ROM and which currently use a PC. A database called *Computer Plan* contained details of 500,000 such users, providing a relevant and low cost means of direct marketing. A further list called *Posh Plan* is being produced to reach the most affluent households in the UK, enabling upmarket products and services to be better targeted. When L'Oréal Elvive wanted to test market a new shampoo in Italy, Circular Distributors targeted householders in the 35–54 age range with more than three adults in the nest. This was then overlaid with supermarket catchment areas to provide an indication of the penetration and acceptance of the dropped samples (Miller, 2001).

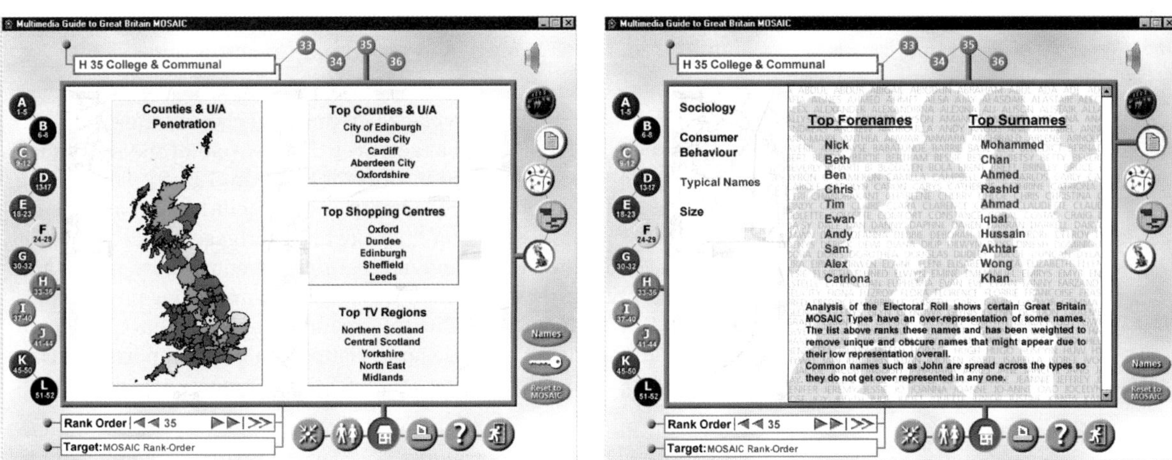

Experian's MOSAIC geodemographic system is available on CD-ROM, thus enhancing its user-friendliness and flexibility.

Source: http://www.experian.com, Experian Ltd.

Psychographic segmentation

Psychographics, or **lifestyle segmentation**, is an altogether more difficult area to define, as it involves intangible variables such as the beliefs, attitudes and opinions of the potential customer. It has evolved in answer to some of the shortcomings of the methods described above as a means of getting further under the skin of the customer as a thinking being. The idea is that defining the lifestyle of the consumer allows the marketer to sell the product not on superficial, functional features, but on benefits that can be seen to enhance that lifestyle on a much more emotional level. The term *lifestyle* is used in its widest sense to cover not only demographic characteristics, but also attitudes to life, beliefs and aspirations.

Plummer (1974) was an early exponent of lifestyle segmentation, breaking it down into four main categories: activities, interests, opinions and demographics.

Activities

The activities category includes all the things people do in the course of their lives. It therefore covers work, shopping, holidays and social life. Within that, the marketer will be interested in people's hobbies and their preferred forms of entertainment, as well as sports interests, club memberships and their activities within the community (voluntary work, for instance).

Interests

Interests refers to what is important to the consumer and where their priorities lie. It may include the things very close to them, such as family, home and work, or their interest and involvement in the wider community. It may also include elements of leisure and recreation, and Plummer particularly mentions areas such as fashion, food and media.

Opinions

The category of opinions comes very close to the individual's innermost thoughts, by probing attitudes and feelings about such things as themselves, social and cultural issues and politics. Opinion may also be sought about other influences on society, such as education, economics and business. Closer to home for the marketer, this category will also investigate opinions about products and the individual's view of the future, indicating how their needs and wants are likely to change.

Demographics

Demographic descriptors have already been extensively covered, and this category includes the kinds of demographic elements you would expect, such as age, education, income and occupation, as well as family size, lifecycle stage and geographic location.

eg

Javalqi and Dion (1999) found that the importance placed on financial choice criteria and the type of financial services for personal banking changed over the lifecycle of the individual. The stages of the family lifecycle were considered in Chapter 3 (*see* pp.125–8). Thus young single people rate such factors as location, service quality, credit facilities and a one-stop approach to banking, newly weds rate the quality of financial and mortgage advice, while for empty nesters, the safety of accumulated funds and interest rates become more important. Although the results are not surprising, there are implications for the marketing programmes of financial service advisors. Given the considerable information that banks have collected on what and how we spend, an underlying lifecycle appreciation can be an important factor in shaping a direct marketing programme to existing and potential customers.

By researching each of these categories thoroughly and carefully, the marketer can build up a very detailed and three-dimensional picture of the consumer. Building such profiles over very large groups of individuals can then allow the marketer to aggregate people with significant similarities in their profiles into named lifestyle segments. As you might expect, because lifestyles are so complex and the number of contributory variables so large, there is no single universally applicable typology of psychographic segments. Indeed, many different typologies have emerged over the years, emphasising different aspects of lifestyle, striving to provide a set of lifestyle segments that are either generally useful or designed for a specific commercial application.

In the USA, for example, advertising agencies have found the Values And Life Style (VALS-2) typology, based on Mitchell (1983), particularly useful. The typology is based on the individual's *resources*, mainly income and education, and *self-orientation*, i.e. attitude towards oneself, one's aspirations and the things one does to communicate and achieve them. The segments that emerge include, for example, *Achievers*, who fall within the category of 'status oriented'. They have abundant resources and are career minded with a social life that revolves around work and family. They mind very much what other people think of them, and particularly crave the good opinion of those who they themselves admire. The implication is that Achievers have largely 'made it' in terms of material success, in contrast to *Strivers* (who are likely to be Achievers in the future) and *Strugglers* (who aspire to be Achievers, but may never make it). Both these segments are also status orientated, but are less well endowed with resources and still have some way to go.

Schoenwald (2001) highlighted some of the dangers in taking psychographic segmentation so far that the relationship between segment characteristics and brand performance becomes lost. Although it may be useful for identifying broad trends, segment boundaries can change as the market changes and some individuals may not fit categories easily or neatly, for example being conservative on financial issues yet highly progressive when it comes to embracing high technology. Schoenwald reminds us that segmentation is a marketing tool for defining markets better and must, therefore, be actionable and not confusing.

eg

The 'grey market' or 'seniors market' is an important segment for travel companies as it represents a potentially affluent group with perhaps more time on their hands. As we saw in Chapter 2 (*see* p. 49), Saga holidays has built a business around the grey market. Shoemaker (2000), in a study of seniors in the USA, found three distinct lifestyle segments among mature holiday makers that marketers could usefully address in different ways, underlining the point that defining a segment purely on age is too broad. Furthermore, he found that these segments were reasonably stable over time. The segments were:

- *Escape and learn*: those who want to visit new places, have new experiences, and may be seeking spiritual and intellectual enrichment through visiting new destinations, historic places and participating in physical activities. The group tends to be in higher income brackets and still employed.
- *Retirees*: this is a less active group that favours a quieter time, often revisiting known and trusted destinations. The visit could be combined with visiting friends and relatives. Most are retired.
- *Active storytellers*: this segment tends to be more sociable, spending time with family and friends or favouring group travel. They enjoy making new friends on a trip and often return enriched but more tired than before they set out. The group enjoy relating their experiences to others upon their return.

With the advent of the SEM, many organisations have been trying to produce lifestyle-based psychographic segment profiles that categorise the whole of Europe. One such study, carried out by Euro Panel and marketed in the UK by AGB Dialogue, was based on an exhaustive 150-page questionnaire administered across the EU, Switzerland and Scandinavia. The main research areas covered included demographic and economic factors, as well as attitudes, activities and feelings. Analysis of the questionnaire data allowed researchers to identify 16 lifestyle segments based on two main axes, innovation/conservatism and idealism/materialism. The results also identified 20 or so key questions that were crucial to matching a respondent with an appropriate segment. These key questions were then put to a further 20,000 respondents, which then allowed the definition of 16 segments, including for example Euro-Citizen, Euro-Gentry, Euro-Moralist, Euro-Vigilante, Euro-Romantic and Euro-Business.

Paitra (1993) similarly defines three Euro-segments under the following headings.

The Moderns. Representing some 30 per cent of Europeans, the Moderns have flexible purchasing power and are open to change, with cosmopolitan tastes and a liking for the exotic and foreign. They have no problem thinking about themselves as European and as nationals of their own country at the same time. They are more likely to be Italian or French than British or German.

The Go-betweens. Representing 40 per cent of Europeans, this group have experienced a change in their attitudes, but not enough to change their buying habits, and thus they are torn between habit and the thrill of the unexpected. They could become Moderns, but are still too tied to their home culture, education and the society within which they live.

Marketing approaches that are obviously pan-European are less likely to influence or affect them than approaches that appear to be rooted in their own culture, etc. This group are more likely to be British or Spanish than French, Italian or German.

The Traditionals. Accounting for the remaining 30 per cent of Europeans, this group holds on tight to local, regional and national traditions. They are very conformist, in that they have a great respect for authority, prefer an ordered existence and resist change, as a bringer of chaos. They are largely unattracted to international or pan-European brands, preferring the very familiar, habitually purchased products that they have always bought. This group is most likely to be German, with some representation in the UK and Italy, and is less likely to be found in France or Spain.

Paitra is convinced, as the above typology shows, that there is no such thing as the generic Euro-consumer. He strongly feels, however, that the Euro-segment that transcends national boundaries does exist, and that international, qualitative studies are going to become increasingly important to marketers in defining and locating such segments.

Despite the extent and depth of research that has gone into defining typologies such as these, they are still of somewhat limited use. When it comes to applying this material in a commercial marketing context, the marketer still needs to understand the underlying national factors that affect the buying decisions for a particular product. These Euro-segments give only a very general flavour of trends and changing attitudes, as part of the sociocultural marketing environment, and are still too simplistic, given the cultural diversity within the EU.

Nevertheless, there are compelling reasons for such methods of segmentation being worth considering and persevering with, despite their difficulties. Primarily, they can open the door to a better-tailored, more subtle offering to the customer on all aspects of the marketing mix. This in turn can create a strong emotional bond between customer and product, making it more difficult for competitors to steal customers. Euro-segmentation adds a further dimension, in that it has the potential to create much larger and more profitable segments, assuming that the logistics of distribution allow geographically dispersed members of the segment to be reached cost effectively, and may thus create pan-European marketing opportunities.

The main problem, however, as we have seen, is that psychographic segments are very difficult and expensive to define and measure. Relevant information is much less likely to exist already in the public domain. It is also very easy to get the implementation wrong. For example, the organisation that tries to portray lifestyle elements within advertisements is depending on the audience's ability to interpret the symbols used in the desired way and to reach the desired conclusions from them. There are no guarantees of this, especially if the message is a complex one (more of this in Chapter 14). Additionally, the user of Euro-segments has to be very clear about allowing for national and cultural differences when trying to communicate on lifestyle elements.

In summary, psychographic segmentation works well in conjunction with demographic variables to refine further the offering to the customer, increasing its relevance and defendability against competition. It is also valuable for products that lean towards psychological rather than functional benefits for the customer, for instance perfumes, cars, clothing retailers, etc. For such a product to succeed, the marketer needs to create an image that convinces consumers that the product can either enhance their current lifestyle or help them to achieve their aspirations. Solomon (1994) summarises the uses of psychographic segmentation as:

1 to define a target market;
2 to create a new view of the market: breaking away from stereotypes;
3 to position the product: making sure product attributes fit with the deeper needs of the customer;
4 to better communicate product attributes: influencing advertising themes and content;

5 to develop overall strategy: identifying opportunities and trends, for instance;
6 to market social and political issues: to home in on groups with basically sympathetic attitudes and beliefs, or to identify those who need more persuasion.

Behaviour segmentation

All the categories of segmentation talked about so far are centred on the customer, leading to as detailed a profile of the individual as possible. Little mention has been made, however, of the individual's relationship with the product. This needs to be addressed, as it is quite possible that people with similar demographic and/or psychographic profiles may yet interact differently with the same product. Segmenting a market in these terms, therefore, is known as **behaviour segmentation**.

End use

What is the product to be used for? The answer to this question has great implications for the whole marketing approach. Think about soup, for instance. This is a very versatile product with a range of potential uses, and a wide variety of brands and product lines have been developed, each of which appeals to a different usage segment. A shopper may well buy two or three different brands of soup, simply because their needs change according to intended use, for example a dinner party or a snack meal. At this point, demographic and psychographic variables may become irrelevant (or at least secondary) if the practicalities of usage are so important to the customer. Table 5.4 defines some of the possible end uses of soup and gives examples of products available on the UK market to serve them.

Table 5.4 Usage segmentation in the soup market

Use	*Brand examples*
Dinner party starter	Baxter's soups; Covent Garden soups
Warming snack	Crosse & Blackwell's soups
Meal replacement	Heinz Wholesoups
Recipe ingredient	Campbell's Condensed soups
Easy office lunch	Batchelor's Cuppa Soups

eg

Even the humble potato has become a victim of usage segmentation. The pre-bagged potatoes sold by some supermarkets are now labelled to indicate suitability for various uses, and thus the shopper can see precisely what is best for baking, roasting, chipping or boiling. Although it is still possible to buy a bag of 'general-purpose' potatoes, the shopper is left with a vague feeling that these are somehow second best for everything!

Benefits sought

This variable can have more of a psychological slant than end usage and can link in very closely with both demographic and psychographic segments. In the case of a car, for example, the benefits sought may range from the practical ('reliable'; 'economic to run'; 'able to accommodate mum, dad, four kids, a granny, a wet dog and the remains of a picnic') to the more psychographically orientated ('environmentally friendly'; 'fast and mean'; 'overt status symbol'). Similarly, the benefits sought from a chilled ready meal might be 'ease of preparation', 'time saving', 'access to dishes I could not make myself', 'a reassuring standby in case I get home late one evening', and for the low-calorie and low-fat versions, 'a tasty and interesting variation on my diet!' It is not difficult to see how defining some of these *benefit segments* can also indicate the kinds of demographic or lifestyle descriptors that apply to people wanting those benefits.

McCain decided to re-brand its oven-ready chips range to fit with the 'surprisingly good for you' slogan. Rather than emphasising speed and convenience, the plan was to educate consumers and make them aware of the 'health benefits' of oven-ready chips. The 'only 5% fat' claim and other facts such as 'the high-fibre option' were designed to exploit growing consumer interest in health matters (*The Grocer*, 1998).

Usage rate

Not everyone who buys a particular product consumes it at the same rate. There will be heavy users, medium users and light users. Figure 5.1 shows the hypothetical categorisation of an organisation's customer base according to usage. In this case, 20 per cent of customers account for 60 per cent of the organisation's sales. This clearly raises questions for marketing strategies, for example should we put all our resources into defending our share of heavy users? Alternatives might be to make light users heavier; to target competitors' heavy users aggressively; or even to develop differentiated products for different usage rates (such as frequent-wash shampoo).

Again, this segmentation variable can best be used in conjunction with others to paint a much more three-dimensional picture of the target customer.

Loyalty

As with usage rate, loyalty could be a useful mechanism, not only for developing detail in the segment profile, but also for developing a better understanding of which segmentation variables are significant. For instance a carefully thought-out market research exercise might help an organisation to profile 'loyal to us', 'loyal to them' and '**switchers**', and then discover what other factors seem to differentiate between each of these groups. More specifically, Wind (1982) identified six loyalty segments as:

1. current loyal users who will continue to purchase the brand;
2. current customers who might switch brands or reduce consumption;
3. occasional users who might be persuaded to increase consumption with the right incentives;
4. occasional users who might decrease consumption because of competitors' offerings;
5. non-users who might buy the brand if it was modified;
6. non-users with strong negative attitudes that are unlikely to change.

Figure 5.1 Consumer product usage categories

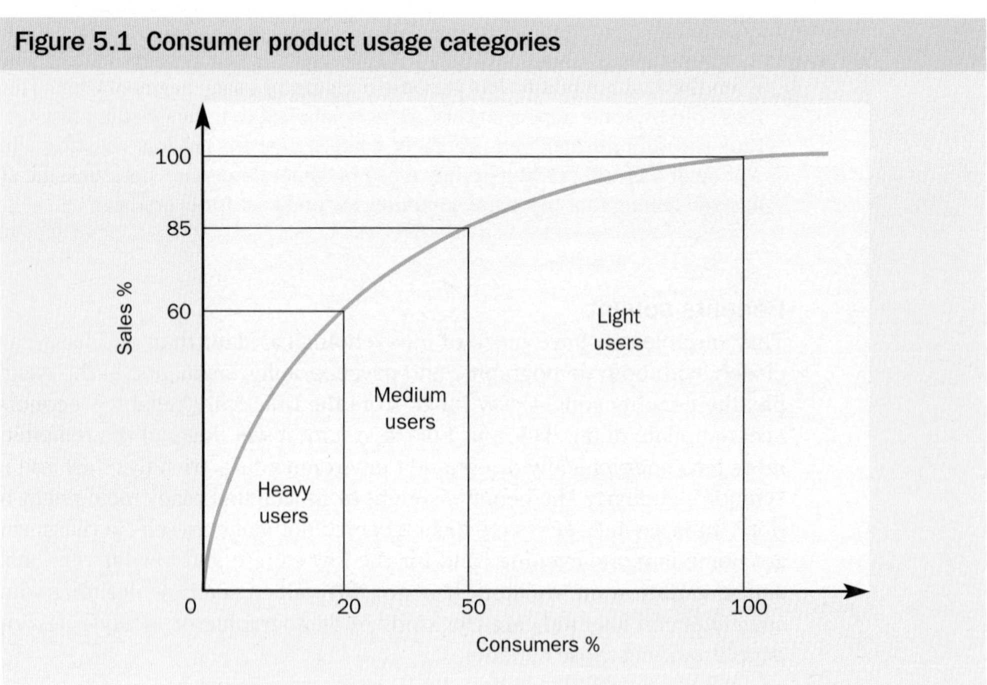

What is certain is that brand loyalty can be a fragile thing, and is under increasing threat. This is partly as a result of the greater number of alternative brands available and incentives or promotions designed by competitors to undermine customer loyalty. The most serious threat in the UK, however, has come from supermarket own-brands, many of which look uncannily like the equivalent manufacturer brands but undercut them on price. Consumers thus believe that the own-brands are just as good, if not identical, and are thus prepared to switch to them and to be more price sensitive. There is more on this issue in Chapter 13.

Assuming that loyalty does exist, even a simple combination of usage rate and loyalty begins to make a difference to the organisation's marketing strategy. If, for example, a large group of heavy users who are also brand switchers was identified, then there is much to be gained from investing resources in a tightly focused marketing mix designed to turn them into heavy users who are loyal to a particular company. Repeat business is important to Burger King. The company has estimated that a single customer can be worth over 100 burgers and fries over a lifetime, amounting to over £3,000. This means that losing a customer through dissatisfaction is an important loss of revenue (Denny, 1998).

Attitude

Again, trespassing on the psychographic area, attitude looks at how the potential customer feels about the product (or the organisation). A set of customers who are already enthusiastic about a product, for example, require very different handling from a group who are downright hostile. A hostile group might need an opportunity to sample the product, along with an advertising campaign that addresses and answers the roots of their hostility. Attitude-based segments may be important in marketing charities or causes, or even in health education. Smokers who are hostile to the 'stop smoking' message will need different approaches from those who are amenable to the message and just need reassurance and practical support to put it into practice. Approaches aimed at the 'hostile' smoker have included fear ('look at these diseased lungs'), altruism ('what about your children?') and vanity (warning young women about the effect on their skin), but with little noticeable effect.

Buyer readiness stage

Buyer readiness can be a very valuable variable, particularly when one is thinking about the promotional mix. How close to purchasing is the potential customer? For example, at a very early stage the customer may not even be aware that the product exists, and therefore to get that customer moving closer to purchase, the organisation needs to generate *awareness* of the product. Then there is a need for information to stimulate *interest* in the product. The customer's ability to understand and interpret that information may lead to *desire* for the product, which in turn stimulates *action*: the purchase itself.

marketing **in action**

Time for a barbie!

On long summer evenings, what could be better than a barbecue? The smell of sausages cooking, beer cans popping, and good company. Introduced from North American and Australian lifestyles, 'the barbie' has become big business in the UK and is expected to be worth £190 mn in 2001. It has become a form of home entertainment. In 2000, not a particularly good year for the weather, it was estimated that 54 million barbecues were held in the UK. A few years ago the pioneers persevered with bangers and burgers covered in tomato ketchup. Now, not only has there been a significant improvement in barbecue facilities, but also the range of foods cooked has become more and more exotic. Steaks often supplement the sausages, and chicken, fish and vegetarian options are often on the menu. Some have suggested that the type of grill used is as much a lifestyle statement as one's choice of car (Levine 1999)!

Although some barbecues are planned, a significant number are held on impulse, perhaps reflecting the unpredictable British weather. In

2000, sales of sauces doubled during the five hottest weekends of the year. It is not, therefore, a price sensitive market. The sausages are often premium, with a range of flavours. Pack sizes have increased to reflect the social nature of the event. New meat flavoured dishes such as Shanghai-style ribs, Moroccan chicken drumsticks and coconut tandoori chicken fillets are all designed to whet our appetites and encourage us to spend more on our barbies. Sauces and marinades have benefited particularly from the new lifestyle activity as tastes have become more adventurous. Jenks, the handler for the Bicks brand of sauces, has produced a dip or marinade '4 in 1 selection' with hamburger, tangy onions, sweetcorn and barbecue flavours.

Point of sale is an important merchandising activity to remind people to stock up, just in case. When different product categories are brought together under the barbecue theme, sales tend to increase. With the exception of meat, Tesco has brought all its barbecue products together under one category in-store in order to promote sales. Sainsbury will experiment with in-store tastings and a barbecue grill in some of its car parks. It does not end with food: there are also the drink suppliers, of course. Research by Interbrew indicated that the barbecue/party is among the ten top drinking occasions each year, accounting for 8 per cent of all the drinking occasions for men. That's an opportunity for well trusted brands, bulk packs and chillers. Similarly, Autan sells more insect repellent and Bryant and May more charcoal briquettes, etc. And all because a new segment has emerged based on behaviour, usage and lifestyle variables.

Sources: Eggleston (2001); *The Grocer* (2001d); Levine (1999).

Figure 5.2 summarises this progression, and Chapter 14 will consider further its influence on the promotional mix.

Behavioural segmentation, therefore, examines closely the relationship between the potential customer and the product, and there are a number of dimensions on which this can be done. Its main achievement is to bring the relationship between customer and product into sharper focus, thus providing greater understanding of the customer's specific needs and wants, leading to a better defined marketing mix. Another advantage of this kind of segmentation approach is that it provides opportunities for tailored marketing strategies to target brand switchers or to increase usage rates. All these benefits do justify the use of behavioural segmentation, as long as it does not lead to the organisation becoming product centred to the neglect of the customer's needs. The customer must still come first.

Multivariable segmentation

As has been hinted throughout the previous sections, it is unlikely that any one segmentation variable will be used absolutely on its own. It is more common for marketers to use a **multivariable segmentation** approach, defining a 'portfolio' of relevant segmentation

Figure 5.2 The AIDA response hierarchy model

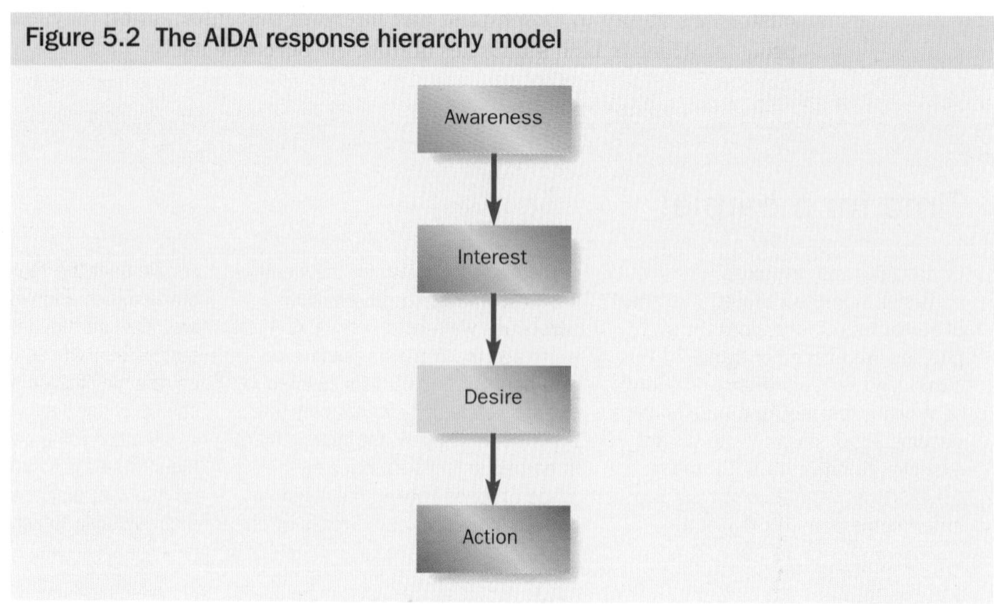

variables, some of which will be prosaic and descriptive while others will tend towards the psychographic, depending on the product and market in question. The market for adult soft drinks includes age segmentation along with some usage considerations (for example as a substitute for wine as a meal accompaniment), some benefit segmentation (healthy, refreshing, relaxing), and lifestyle elements of health consciousness, sophisticated imagery and a desire for exotic ingredients. Similarly, the banking sector is moving from traditional segmentation based upon corporate and retail customers to approaches aimed at creating segments based upon combinations of customer attitudes towards bank services and expected benefits. Simply grouping customers according to demographic criteria failed to reflect their attitudes towards technology and their readiness to use it, which could be strategically important as internet banking develops further (Machauer and Morgner, 2001).

The emergence of geodemographics in recent years, as discussed at pp. 186 *et seq.* above, is an indicator of the way in which segmentation is moving, that is, towards multi-variable systems incorporating psychographics, demographics and geographics. These things are now possible and affordable, as Chapter 6 will show, because of increasingly sophisticated data collection mechanisms, developments in database creation and maintenance (*see* Chapter 18) and cheaper, more accessible computing facilities. A properly managed database allows the marketer to go even further and to incorporate behavioural variables as the purchaser develops a trading history with a supplier. Thus the marketers are creeping ever closer to the individual consumer. The UK supermarkets that have developed and launched store loyalty cards that are swiped through the checkout so that the customer can accumulate points towards discounts, for example, are collecting incredibly detailed information about each individual shopper's profile. It tells them when we shop, how often, which branches of the store we tend to use, how much we spend per visit, the range of goods we buy, and the choices we make between own brands and manufacturer brands. The supermarkets can use this information to help them define meaningful segments for their own customer base, to further develop and improve their overall marketing mix or to make individually tailored offers to specific customers.

Implementation of segmentation

This chapter so far has very freely used the phrase 'segmenting the market', but before segmentation can take place, there has to be some definition of the boundaries of that market. Any such definition really has to look at the world through the consumer's eyes, because the consumer makes decisions based on the evaluation of alternatives and substitutes. Thus a margarine manufacturer cannot restrict itself to thinking in terms of 'the margarine market', but has to take a wider view of 'the spreading-fats market' which will include butter and vegetable oil based products alongside margarine. This is because, generally speaking, all three of these product groups are contending for the same place on the nation's bread, and the consumer will develop attitudes and feelings towards a selection of brands across all three groups, perhaps through comparing price and product attributes (for example taste, spreadability, cooking versatility and health claims). This opens up a much wider competitive scene, as well as making the margarine manufacturer think more seriously about product positioning and about how and why consumers buy it. Similarly, the adult soft drinks market cannot be too restrictive in its market definition. It is still competing to a certain extent with the more traditional soft drinks (both the fizzy ones such as colas and lemonades and the still fruit juices) and alcoholic drinks, as a substitute. The key to its continued growth and success lies in pulling it away further from the wider, mainstream beverages markets (alcoholic and non-alcoholic), through clear differentiation in terms of all elements of the marketing mix, to reduce the 'substitute' effect. The various manufacturers involved can then concentrate more on competition and further segmentation within the adult market.

This whole issue of market definition and its implications for segmentation comes back, yet again, to what should now be the familiar question of 'What business are we in?' It is a timely reminder that consumers basically buy solutions to problems, not products, and thus in defining market segments, the marketer should take into account any type of product that will provide a solution. Hence we are not in 'the margarine market', but in the 'lubricating bread' market, which brings us back full circle to the inclusion of butter and vegetable oil based spreads as direct competitors.

It is still not enough to have gone through the interesting exercise of segmenting a market, however it is defined. How is that information going to be used by the organisation to develop marketing strategies? One decision that must be made is how many segments within the market the organisation intends to target. We look first at **targeting**.

Targeting

There are three broad approaches available, summarised in Figure 5.3, and discussed in detail below.

Concentrated

The concentrated approach is the most focused approach of the three, and involves specialising in serving one specific segment. This can lead to very detailed knowledge of the target segment's needs and wants, with the added benefit that the organisation is seen as a specialist, giving it an advantage over its more mass-market competitors. This, however, carries a risk of complacency, leaving the organisation vulnerable to competitive entry into the segment.

In terms of management, concentration is attractive because costs are kept down, as there is only one marketing mix to manage, and there is still the potential for economies of scale. Strategically, the concentration of resources into one segment may lead to a stronger, more defendable position than that achievable by competitors which are spreading their effort more thinly. However, being a niche specialist may make it more difficult for an organisation to diversify into other segments, whether through lack of experience and knowledge, or through problems of acceptance arising from being identified with the original niche.

The benefits also need to be weighed against the other potential risks. First, all the organisation's eggs are in one basket, and if that segment fails, then there is no fallback position. The second risk is that if competitors see a rival establishing and clearly succeeding in a segment like this, then they may try to take some of it.

Figure 5.3 Segmentation targeting strategies

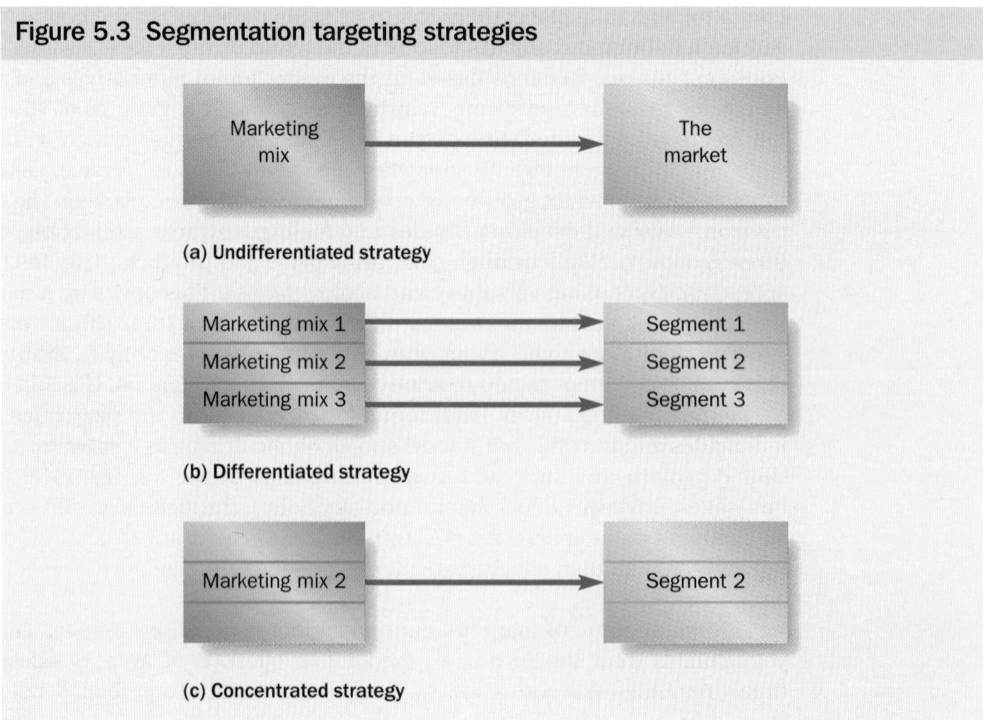

Differentiated

As Figure 5.3 implies, a differentiated strategy involves the development of a number of individual marketing mixes, each of which serves a different segment. For example, Ford manufactures a range of cars, covering a number of different segments, from the Focus at the bottom end of the price range, generally intended for the younger female driver, to the Scorpio in the higher price bracket, intended for the status seeking executive.

As with the concentrated strategy, this approach does allow the organisation to tailor its offerings to suit the individual segments, thus maintaining satisfaction. It also overcomes one of the problems of concentration by spreading risk across the market, so that if one segment declines, the organisation still has revenue from others.

To be implemented properly, this approach requires a detailed overview of the market and how it is developing, perhaps leading to the early detection of new opportunities or emerging segments. This knowledge is valuable for an organisation with a healthy curiosity about its environment, but is acquired at a cost (in terms of both finance and managerial time). It also leads to increased costs in trying to manage the marketing mixes for a number of products, with possible diseconomies of scale.

Overall, a differentiated strategy dilutes the organisation's efforts through the thin spreading of resources. The organisation must, therefore, be very careful not to overreach itself in the number of segments it attempts to cover. Nevertheless, it can help an organisation to survive in highly competitive markets.

marketing *in action*

Sweet profits

The British spend more than £5.5 bn each year on confectionery which suggests one of the sweetest tastes in Europe, after Switzerland. That equates to a bar of Cadbury's chocolate nearly every day for the typical consumer. There are many strong traditional brands in the market from suppliers such as Mars, Nestlé-Rowntree, and Cadbury Trebor Bassett (CTB), with a combined market share of around 68 per cent, alongside a host of smaller, specialised brands occupying various niches. Outside the more innovative children's sector, the main trends have been heritage, tradition and quality in a fairly stable market.

A closer examination of two suppliers reveals different approaches to target marketing. Cadbury Trebor Bassett has undertaken a significant amount of research on market segments. This has been used to guide its own marketing strategy as well as helping retailers to decide what to stock and how to merchandise different brands. It has identified five main market segments based upon the purpose of spend. These segments are:

- *Immediate eat*: typical products are Wispa (CTB), Mars Bar, and Kit Kat (Nestlé Rowntree – remember the 'have a break, have a Kit Kat' campaign?). This segment represents about 34 per cent of the market.
- *Home stock*: bought as part of the weekly shop but to eat later. Rather than impulse buying, it is a planned spend. Typical products include Dairy Milk (CTB), and large bags of Maltesers (Mars). This segment represents about 25 per cent of the market.
- *Kids*: purchases for or by children for such occasions as after school, parties, treats, etc. Typical products include Cadbury's Buttons (CTB) and Nestlé's Milky Bar. This segment is worth about 17 per cent of the market.
- *Seasonal*: this segment consists of Easter eggs, seasonal boxes for Christmas, etc. and is worth about 9 per cent of the market.
- *Gift*: chocolate purchased as a token of appreciation, as a gesture, for a special celebration or for after dinner consumption. Typical products are Roses (CTB) and Quality Street (Nestlé-Rowntree). This segment represents about 15 per cent of the market.

With 28 per cent of the confectionery market, CTB can claim the greatest variety of tastes, textures and flavours from a full product portfolio. It operates a differentiated approach to the market, i.e. each segment is serviced by at least one brand and each brand is marketed in a different way. Although some activities aim to promote the corporate brand name, each brand has its own marketing campaign. CTB invests heavily in the brands to build and maintain consumer awareness as a means to drive sales, for example the launch of Cadbury's Miniature Heroes cost £4.8 mn for an integrated marketing communications campaign.

Mr Lucky Bags operates a concentrated targeting approach from its headquarters in Stoke on Trent. It has targeted the children's segment since its foundation in 1991 with a formula that puts high quality sweets with small toys, stickers, games, books and other collectables into an opaque bag. It

Mr Lucky Bags targets its marketing on children by highlighting the fun and value of the product as well as using recognisable licensed characters to encourage children to buy the product or persuade their parents to buy it.

Source: Mr Lucky Bags Ltd.

does not sell to any other segments in the confectionery market but prefers to concentrate all its innovative and management effort into adding fun, value and sophistication for children, something which the managing director believes has been lost by the larger players.

Lucky Bags have a been a great hit, helped not least by linking up with such entertainment companies as Warner and Cartoon Network for character licensing and merchandising. Bags are themed around such icons as Noddy, Tom and Jerry, Barbie, Rugrats and Action Man. Although 50 per cent of sales are to children, the balance is sales to adults as gifts to children. Of course, the company recognises that there will be no repeat purchase if the child is not satisfied with the contents after the fun of searching and discovery in the bag. In an effectively stagnant market it has achieved a 10 per cent year on year growth and now exports to nearly 30 countries. Effectively Mr Lucky Bags has created its own market and although share has dropped down to 70 per cent as other competitors jump on the bandwagon, new ideas, new characters and a readiness to innovate has sustained a dominant market position.

Sources: The Grocer (2001a; 2001b; 2001c).

Undifferentiated

The undifferentiated approach is the least demanding of the three approaches, in that it assumes that the market is one great homogeneous unit, with no significant differences between individuals within that market. Thus a single marketing mix is required that serves the needs of the entire market. The emphasis is likely, therefore, to be on developing mass communication, mass distribution and as wide an appeal as possible.

An undifferentiated approach does have some apparent advantages. It involves relatively low costs, as there is only one marketing mix that does not require the depth of research, fine tuning and updating that a concentrated or differentiated strategy would entail. It could also lead to the possible maximisation of economies of scale, because of having a single product in a potentially large market.

It is naive to hope that you can please everyone. What is likely to happen in reality is that some people will like your product offering more than others, and thus a segment (not of your own definition) will emerge by default. Because your product has not been tailored to that segment, it is unlikely to be exactly what that segment wants, and therefore any competitor who does target the segment more closely will attract those customers. This is similar to what is happening in the potato example cited at p. 193 above, where the 'general-purpose' product is becoming overshadowed and pushed into a perceived 'second-best' position by usage specific varieties.

eg

Through processes taking place beyond the farm gate, many food manufacturers can introduce more differentiation in what could easily be a homogeneous market. Olive oil producers are a good example. The olive picked from the tree can be processed and packaged in many different ways and thus differentiation is created through the processing, cleaning, pressing and filtering of the olives and the suggested end use of the oil. The problem in the UK is that many consumers are not particularly familiar with olive oil use and do not always understand the differences between, for instance, virgin oil and refined grades. Instead, they tend to regard olive oil in terms of its country of origin. The challenge is thus to educate consumers so that they can select the right olive oil for different uses (Crosskey, 1997).

If an undifferentiated approach is possible at all, then it might best be suited for products with little psychological appeal. For example, petrol is essentially a very ordinary product that many of us purchase regularly but never even see (unless we are not very adept with a self-service pump). It makes the car go, regardless of whether it is a Rolls-Royce or a Lada and, traditionally, the only discriminating factor between brands has been price. Petrol retailers have now begun to create market segments, through the petrol itself (as with unleaded and petrols with extra additives); through the extended product (providing car washes, mini-supermarkets, etc.); and also through strong corporate images that create brands and engender loyalty. All of this is moving the petrol retailers away from undifferentiated strategies.

Quite apart from the advantages and disadvantages connected with each of the alternative approaches above, there are a number of factors influencing the choice of targeting strategy.

Marketing theory may well point to a particular strategy as being ideal, but if an organisation's resources cannot support and sustain that strategy, then an alternative must be found. A smaller organisation may, for example, need to adopt a concentrated strategy (perhaps based on a geographic segment in a consumer market, or on a specialist niche in a B2B market) to generate the growth required to allow a wider coverage of the market.

It is also important to make the choice of strategy in the context of the product itself. As has already been indicated, certain types of product lend themselves more readily to certain approaches, for example a product with many potential variations that involve a high level of psychological relationship with the customer (such as clothing or cosmetics) is better suited to a differentiated or concentrated approach. Other products with a more functional bias can be treated in a more undifferentiated way.

It must be reiterated, though, that undifferentiated approaches are becoming increasingly rare. Salt used to be held up to marketing students as the prime example of a commodity product sold in an undifferentiated way. Table 5.5 demonstrates how all that has changed.

Table 5.5 Differentiation in the salt market

- Table salt
- Cooking salt
- Sea salt
- Rock salt
- Alpine rock salt
- Iodised salt
- Low-sodium salt
- Garlic salt
- Celery salt

et cetera!

The product's lifecycle stage (*see* Chapter 8 for a full definition of this concept) might also affect the choice of strategy. For example, an innovative new product, of which neither the industry nor the consumer has past experience, may first be marketed with an undifferentiated strategy in order to gain practical knowledge of the market's behaviour and reactions. It is very difficult to undertake meaningful market research in advance of launching such a new product, because the market may have problems conceptualising the product or putting it into context. It will be in the growth and maturity stages of the lifecycle that differentiated strategies will emerge as competitors enter the market and organisations learn from experience.

That last comment is a reminder that strategic decisions cannot be taken in isolation from the activities of the competition. If competitors are clearly implementing differentiated strategies, then it is dangerous for you to adopt a more dilute, undifferentiated approach. It may make more sense to identify the segments within which the competition is strong and then to assess whether it would be possible to attack them head-on in those segments or to find a different niche and make that your own. Thus competition is affecting not only the choice of approach, but the actual choice of segment(s) to target.

corporate social responsibility *in action*

'As close to paradise as can be found'

Turtle Island represents for some the perfect holiday destination. The remote Fijian island in the Yasawa chain was purchased by Harvard graduate Richard Evanson in 1972 as a place to get away from it all, but also as the basis for a business so that his paradise could be shared. Development was needed before business was possible. A circular road was sympathetically built around the island, guest paths were established, Honduras mahogany trees were planted (some 300,000 trees over 26 years), to supplement the local species, and to encourage ecological diversity, stop soil erosion, create wind breaks and add to natural beauty. A three-acre organic vegetable garden was planted, extensive composting and recycling facilities were developed, and solar panel water heating installed to reflect a concern for ecology and the development of sustainable tourism.

The mission and values of the owner are to ensure that the marketing strategies fit with the culture and heritage to create sustainable tourism. Too many of the 'wrong' kind of tourists can soon degrade the local culture and environment. Turtle Island is at the opposite end of the spectrum from Benidorm or Blackpool. The capacity is just 14 rooms on a private 500-acre estate and there are no plans to change that. Guests wanting to lie on the beach drinking all day, or sleeping all day and clubbing all night are certainly not welcome. Turtle Island is designed to appeal to English speaking couples who can communicate and enjoy each other's company and humour. It's first name terms as soon as you arrive and a key part of the experience is the interaction with staff and other guests.

The island resort is positioned as the nearest thing to paradise, and clearly to the targeted segment it is just that, as occupancy is high and many bookings cannot be fulfilled for the required dates. The climate, lush vegetation, activity programme ranging from snorkelling to mountain biking, the all-inclusive pricing policy, and the opportunity to 'get away from it all' appear highly attractive. The price structure is designed to keep the resort exclusive. Excluding airfares (you need a small seaplane to get to the island) the charge is over $1,000 per couple per night and the minimum permitted booking is six nights to provide plenty of opportunity to unwind.

What is important about Turtle Island is that the environmental responsibility and commitment demonstrated by the owner has been good for business and good for the island and its 2,600 inhabitants. The concern with ecology, the deliberate attempt to restrict the number of tourists, the use of local materials (guests stay in traditional wood bures), the provision of medical facilities to the locals and a concern for monitoring, controlling and minimising the unfortunate impact of tourism, such as sewage, reef damage and social pollution have given rise to international acclaim. Developed from an overgrazed and abused island with most of its trees cut down, the Turtle Island resort has won international recognition including a BA Environmental award. The package of experiences and the ecological orientation have proved to have a strong appeal to a specific market segment and the owner deliberately sought to reflect that when designing the tourist package.

The island has not been without controversy, however. *The Lonely Planet 1997* guide suggested that the island was distinctly unfriendly to gays given its exclusive nature and priority to social mixing between the guests. This was strongly denied, countering that the island had been taking 'any sort of couple' for at least five years. The comments in subsequent editions of *Lonely Planet* were modified, but it goes to show that near perfection on one dimension of CSR can still leave a company open to accusations, however unfounded, on another. Bookings do not appear to have been affected, however, and the careful segmentation and positioning strategy continues to bring success.

Sources: http://www.turtlefiji.com; Chesshyre (2000); Evanson (1999).

Targeting the desire for the perfect holiday on a desert island but with all the facilities and service that the consumer needs to have a relaxing, carefree holiday, The Turtle Island resort more than satisfies the customers willing to pay for the privilege.

Source: http://www.turtlefiji.com.

Benefits of segmentation

The previous sections of this chapter should at least have served to show that market segmentation is a complex and dangerous activity, in the sense that the process of choosing variables, their measurement and their implementation leaves plenty of scope for poor management and disappointment. Nevertheless, there are few, if any, markets in which segmentation has no role to play, and it is important to remember the potential benefits to be gained, whether looking at the customer, the marketing mix or the competition.

The customer

The obvious gain to customers is that they can find products that seem to fit more closely with what they want. These needs and wants, remember, are not only related to product function, but also to psychological fulfilment. Customers may feel that a particular supplier is more sympathetic towards them, or is speaking more directly to them, and therefore they will be more responsive and eventually more loyal to that supplier. The organisation that fails to segment deeply enough on significant criteria will lose custom to competitors that do.

The marketing mix

This is a timely reminder that the marketing mix should itself be a product of understanding the customer. Market segmentation helps the organisation to target its marketing mix more closely on the potential customer, and thus to meet the customer's needs and wants more exactly. Segmentation helps to define shopping habits (in terms of place, frequency and volume), price sensitivity, required product benefits and features, as well as laying the foundations for advertising and promotional decisions. The customer is at the core of all decisions relating to the 4Ps, and those decisions will be both easier to make and more consistent with each other if a clear and detailed definition of the target segments exists.

In the same vein, segmentation can also help the organisation to allocate its resources more efficiently. If a segment is well defined, then the organisation will have sufficient understanding to develop very precise marketing objectives and an accompanying strategy to achieve them, with a minimum of wastage. The organisation is doing neither more nor less than it needs to do in order to satisfy the customer's needs and wants.

This level of understanding of segments that exist in the market also forms a very sound foundation for strategic decisions. The organisation can prioritise across segments in line with its resources, objectives and desired position within the market.

The competition

Finally, the use of segmentation will help the organisation to achieve a better understanding of itself and the environment within which it exists. By looking outwards, to the customer, the organisation has to ask itself some very difficult questions about its capacity to serve that customer better than the competition. Also, by analysing the competitors' offerings in the context of the customer, the organisation should begin to appreciate the competition's real strengths and weaknesses, as well as identifying gaps in the market.

Dangers of segmentation

The benefits of segmentation need to be balanced against the dangers inherent in it. Some of these, such as the risks of poor definition and implementation of psychographic segmentation, have already been mentioned.

Jenkins and McDonald (1997) raise more fundamental concerns with market segementation processes that are not grounded in the capabilities of the organisation. To them, there needs to be more focus on how organisations should segment their markets rather than a focus on how to segment using the range of variables mentioned earlier in this chapter. To decide on the 'should' means having an understanding of the organisation, its culture, its operating processes and structure which all influence the view of the market and how it could be segmented (Piercy and Morgan, 1993).

Other dangers are connected with the essence of segmentation: breaking markets down into ever smaller segments. Where should it stop? Catering for the differing needs of a large number of segments can lead to fragmentation of the market, with additional problems arising from the loss of economies of scale (through shorter production runs or loss of bulk purchasing discounts on raw materials, for instance), as mentioned at p. 199 above. Detail needs to be balanced against viability.

Within the market as a whole, if there are a number of organisations in direct competition for a number of segments, then the potential proliferation of brands may simply serve to confuse the customer. Imagine five competitors each trying to compete in five market segments. That gives the customer 25 brands to sort out. Even if customers can find their way through the maze of brands, the administration and marketing difficulties involved in getting those brands on to the supermarket shelves can be very costly.

As Chapter 4 showed, such problems are less likely to occur in B2B markets. Where an organisation has a very small number of high spending customers, each one can legitimately be treated as a separate segment with its own marketing mix tailored to it.

Criteria for successful segmentation

Cutting through the detail of how to segment, and regardless of the complexities of segmentation in different types of market, are four absolute requirements for any successful segmentation exercise. Unless these four conditions prevail, the exercise will either look good on paper but be impossible to implement, or fail to deliver any marked strategic advantage.

Distinctiveness

Any segment defined has to be *distinctive*, that is, significantly different from any other segment. The basis of that difference depends on the type of product or the circumstances prevailing in the market at the time. It may be rooted in any of the segmentation variables discussed above, whether geographic, demographic or psychographic. Note too the use of the word *significant*. The choice of segmentation variables has to be relevant to the product in question.

Without a significant difference, segment boundaries become too blurred, and there is a risk that an organisation's offerings will not be sufficiently well tailored to attract the required customers.

Tangibility

It must be remembered that distinctiveness can be taken too far. Too much detail in segmentation, without sound commercial reasoning behind it, leads to fragmentation of effort and inefficiency. A defined segment must, therefore, be of a sufficient *size* to make its pursuit worthwhile. Again, the notion of size here is somewhat vague. For fmcg goods, viable size may entail many thousands of customers purchasing many tens of thousands of units, but in a B2B market, it may entail a handful of customers purchasing a handful of units.

Proving that a segment actually exists is also important. Analysis of a market may indicate that there is a gap that existing products do not appear to fill, whether defined in terms of the product itself or the customer profile. The next stage is to ask why that gap is there. Is it because no organisation has yet got round to filling it, or because the segment in that gap is too small to be commercially viable? Does that segment even exist, or are you segmenting in too much detail and creating opportunities on paper that will not work in practice?

Accessibility

As well as existing, a defined segment has to be *accessible*. The first aspect of this is connected with distribution. An organisation has to be able to find the means of delivering its goods and services to the customer, but this may not be so easy, for example, for a small organisation targeting a geographically spread segment with a low-priced infrequently purchased product. Issues of access may then become an extension of the segment profile, perhaps limiting the segment to those customers within a defined catchment area, or those who are prepared to order direct through particular media. Whatever the solution to problems of access, it does mean that the potential size of the segment has to be re-assessed.

The second aspect of access is communication. Certain customers may be very difficult to make contact with, and if the promotional message cannot be communicated, then the chances of capturing those customers are much slimmer. Again, the segment profile may have to be extended to cover the media most likely to access those customers, and again, this will lead to a smaller segment.

Defendability

In talking about targeting strategies at pp. 198 *et seq.* above, one of the recurrent themes was that of the competition. Even with a concentrated strategy, targeting only one segment, there is a risk of competitors poaching customers. In defining and choosing segments, therefore, it is important to consider whether the organisation can develop a sufficiently strong differential advantage to defend its presence in that segment against competitive incursions.

B2B markets

Most of the above discussion has centred on consumer markets. With specific reference to B2B markets, Hlavacek and Ames (1986) propose a similar set of criteria for good segmentation practice. They suggest, for example, that each segment should be characterised by a common set of customer requirements, and that customer requirements and characteristics should be measurable. Segments should have identifiable competition, but be small enough to allow the supplier to reduce the competitive threat, or to build a defendable position against competition. In strategic terms, Hlavacek and Ames also propose that the members of a segment should have some logistical characteristic in common, for example that they are served by the same kind of distribution channel, or the same kind of sales effort. Finally, the critical success factors for each segment should be defined, and the supplier should ensure that it has the skills, assets and capabilities to meet the segment's needs, and to sustain that in the future.

Chapter summary

This chapter has focused on the complexities and methods involved in dividing markets into relevant, manageable and targetable segments in order to allow better-tailored offerings to be developed.

- In B2B markets, segmentation techniques are divided into macro and micro variables or bases. Macro variables include both organisational characteristics, such as size, location and purchasing patterns, and product or service applications, defining the ways in which the product or service is used by the buyer. Micro segmentation variables lead to the definition, in some cases, of segments of one customer, and focus on the buyer's management philosophy, decision-making structures, purchasing policies and strategies, as well as needs and wants.
- In consumer markets, five main categories of segmentation are defined: geographic, demographic, geodemographic, psychographic and behaviour based. Between them, they cover a full range of characteristics, whether descriptive, measurable, tangible or intangible,

relating to the buyer, the buyer's lifestyle and the buyer's relationship with the product. In practice, a multivariable approach to segmentation is likely to be implemented, defining a portfolio of relevant characteristics from all categories to suit the market under consideration.

- The implications of segmentation are wide reaching. It forms the basis for strategic thinking, in terms of the choice of segment(s) to target in order to achieve internal and competitive objectives. The possibilities range from a niche strategy, specialising in only one segment, to a differentiated strategy, targeting two or more segments with different marketing mixes. The undifferentiated strategy, hoping to cover the whole market with only one marketing mix, is becoming increasingly less appropriate as consumers become more demanding, and although it does appear to ease the managerial burden, it is very vulnerable to focused competition.
- Segmentation offers a number of benefits to both the consumer and the organisation. Consumers get an offering that is better tailored to their specific needs, as well as the satisfaction of feeling that the market is offering them a wider range of products to choose from. The organisation is more likely to engender customer loyalty because of the tailored offering, as well as the benefits of more efficient resource allocation and improved knowledge of the market. The organisation can also use its segmentation as a basis for building a strong competitive edge, by understanding its customers on a deeper psychological level and reflecting that in its marketing mix(es). This forms bonds between organisation/product and customer that are very difficult for competition to break. There are, however, dangers in segmentation, if it is not done well. Poor definition of segments, inappropriate choice of key variables or poor analysis and implementation of the outcomes of a segmentation exercise can all be disastrous. There is also the danger that if competing marketers become too enthusiastic in trying to 'outsegment' each other, the market will fragment to an unviable extent and consumers will become confused by the variety of choice open to them.
- On balance, segmentation is a good and necessary activity in any market, whether it is a mass fmcg market of international proportions, or a select B2B market involving two or three well-known customers. In either case, any segment defined has to be distinctive (i.e. features at least one characteristic pulling it away from the rest that can be used to create a focused marketing mix); tangible (i.e. commercially viable); accessible (i.e. both the product and the promotional mix can reach it) and finally, defendable (i.e. against competition).

key words and phrases

Behaviour segmentation
Brand loyalty
Buyer readiness
Demographic segmentation
Geodemographics
Geographic segmentation
Lifestyle segmentation
Macro segments
Market segments
Micro segments
Multivariable segmentation
Psychographics
Switchers
Targeting

questions for review

5.1 What is the difference between macro and micro segmentation in B2B markets?

5.2 What are the main demographic variables used in consumer markets?

5.3 What is psychographic segmentation and why is it so difficult and so risky to do?

5.4 In what major way does behavioural segmentation differ from the other methods? Outline the variables that can be used in behavioural segmentation.

5.5 What are the three approaches to targeting and what factors might affect the marketer's choice of targeting strategy?

questions *for discussion*

5.1 How might the market for personal computers, sold to B2B markets, be segmented?

5.2 Find examples of products that depend strongly on demographic segmentation, making sure that you find at least one example for each of the main demographic variables.

5.3 Choose a consumer market and discuss how it might be segmented in terms of benefits sought.

5.4 For each targeting strategy, find examples of organisations that use it. Discuss why you think they have chosen this strategy and how they implement it.

5.5 How can market segmentation influence decisions about the marketing mix?

case study 5.1

Neu Engineering

Neu Engineering is a project management company which designs, builds (with the help of subcontractors), installs and maintains industrial plant for a wide variety of customers. It specialises in pneumatic conveying, that is, moving powders, granules and other dry products around a factory or other industrial site. The conveying systems usually move the materials by either blowing them or sucking them through pipelines. There is more to the system than just pipelines, however, as the company also incorporates silo storage, mixing, weighing, drying or cooling equipment into the system. The industrial buyer is offered a complete, customised package. Thus a food processing company might need to store sugar under suitably cool and dry conditions, then move it from the silo in weighed batches to a mixing vat along with other ingredients, such as flour or milk powder that have travelled through their own section of the conveying system. Neu Engineering also takes a serious and innovative approach to safety and environmental issues. Many powders are potentially explosive; sugar and milk powder, for example, and an explosion in a custard powder factory (which did not have a Neu Engineering system installed) demolished the side of the building. Systems have to be able to prevent or contain any such incident safely. It is also important to protect workers from any dust emissions or leakages by ensuring that the system has appropriate exhaust and/or ventilation built in.

The majority of Neu Engineering's business comes from clients in three main industries.

1 *Pharmaceuticals*: customers in this market include Johnson & Johnson, GlaxoSmithKline, Nycomed and Zeneca. Customers such as these value the fact that Neu Engineering has the expertise to build a system to standards demanded by the FDA (the Food and Drug Administration, the US regulatory and licensing body). They are also concerned with protecting their materials from contamination, preventing any leakage into the working environment, appropriate controlled storage, and absolute accuracy in weighing and mixing. Thus Neu designs and installs 'automatic dispensaries' for tablet production in Zeneca's factories in Macclesfield and Reims which deliver all those benefits, as well as giving the computerised recordability, traceability and repeatability required by FDA regulations. Neu Engineering is a leader in this market because it entered the market early and is recognised as a specialist.

2 *The food industry*: customers such as Cadbury, Tate and Lyle, Birds Eye, Heinz, Kellogg and Nestlé also require fully contained, temperature-controlled and hygienic systems in storing and conveying a wide variety of solid ingredients for their food products. Flour, sugar, chocolate granules, coffee beans, peas, and barley are among the materials that travel successfully around factories in Neu Engineering systems. The company built a system to intake, convey, batch, weigh and mix the spices for Birds Eye's 'Steakhouse' production line, for example. This replaced manual materials handling, improving efficiency and accuracy. Neu Engineering also won a contract to build ten cereal plants in Russia. There is even something of a second-hand market. Sweden's leading confectionery manufacturer, Marabou, sold a storage, conveying and weighing system to another company, Kungsornen, which dismantled it then moved it 100 miles and rebuilt it!

3 *Plastics*: customers in this industry include ICI, BP, Amoco, Kellogg and Samsung. This industry is a

large user of pneumatic conveying systems and, compared with pharmaceuticals, requires heavy-duty systems that can move anything up to 60 tonnes per hour over 500 m. This is one of the most competitive of the three main markets that Neu Engineering is in and, although the jobs tend to be big, profit margins are almost half those that can be gained in the other markets. It is also a more cyclical industry than the others. Every five years or so, when the industry is in a boom phase, all the plastics manufacturers expand fast and there are plenty of opportunities for companies such as Neu Engineering. When it is in a slump, however, the manufacturers have too much capacity and there is no expansion and thus no new contracts. It is therefore dangerous to be too dependent on such an industry. Nevertheless, as in other industries, innovation wins business. Neu Engineering spent over £100,000 developing an innovative high-pressure, low-velocity conveying system which has been installed at plants in Spain, the Netherlands, Malaysia and Argentina.

Sometimes it is not easy to win customers; it took Neu Engineering five years to 'get into' Kellogg, but once successful, the inherent quality of the product ensures that up to 80 per cent of its business is repeat business. Neu Engineering would ideally like to focus in the future on key regular customers. It firmly believes that only by being a market driven company will it be able to tackle the challenges of the new millennium. A strategy for the future is a strategy for success.

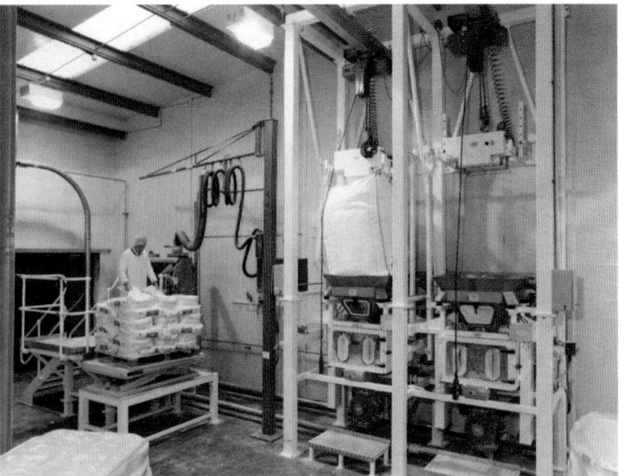

Dry ingredients are handled and processed using Neu International systems

Source: Neu International.

Questions

1. What macro and micro segmentation bases are in evidence in this case?
2. What, if anything, do those segmentation bases have in common with those used in consumer markets?
3. Why do you think Neu Engineering gains such a high proportion of repeat business?
4. What kind of targeting strategy is Neu Engineering using now, and what strategy is it moving towards? To what extent do you think this move is a good idea?

case study 5.2

The pink pound

It is very difficult to estimate the size of the gay market in the UK. Although gay culture has increasingly become part of the mainstream, with many more openly gay celebrities and gay themes and characters featuring regularly in television dramas and comedies, Mintel (2000a; 2000b) has found that the gay market is largely a hidden population. Estimates of the size of the gay population vary between 3 per cent and 15 per cent of the total population but in Mintel's view it is likely to be towards the lower end of the scale overall with a higher concentration in urban areas. Estimates of its spending power also vary between £6 bn and £8 bn per annum.

There is some consensus on the characteristics of the gay market, however. Gay consumers are perceived to have a higher than average income, and almost 60 per cent of gay men are either single or not cohabiting. Those who are cohabiting are likely to be in dual-income households. In terms of spending patterns, therefore, the lack of dependants and responsibilities gives gay consumers more opportunities for lifestyle spending with a strong focus on leisure and socialising. *The Gay Times* has found that 80 per cent of its readership comes from the ABC1 socioeconomic groups, compared with 43 per cent of the general population.

There is plenty of opportunity for reaching the gay market. Mintel's (2000b) survey found that 77 per cent had internet access at home and/or at work which is much higher than the national average of 26 per cent. The internet is important in that it allows gay people to build a stronger sense of community and it gives marketers a chance to locate and target the gay market efficiently and discreetly. The average household income of the gay internet user is $42,500. There are many ISPs and portals set up specifically for online gays (see for example http://uk.gay.com, http://www.rainbownetwork.com or http://www.pinklinks.co.uk). These sites attract mainstream advertisers, such as Tesco Direct, Marks and Spencer Financial, Virgin, British Airways, First Direct and IBM as well as companies specifically targeting the gay community.

There are also print media. In the UK, Chronos Publishing produces four national gay publications: *Boyz* (a free weekly magazine aimed at the younger end of the gay market), *The Pink Paper* (weekly newspaper sold via mainstream newsagents), *Fluid Magazine* (monthly style and listings magazine), and *Homosex* (free monthly glossy magazine focusing on sex and relationships). The other major media owner is the Millivres-Prowler Group which owns *The Gay Times* as well as a number of gay shops called Prowler. *The Gay Times* is a monthly, glossy publication which is one of Europe's best-selling gay magazines. Newsagent WH Smith classifies *The Gay Times* as a Tier One magazine, i.e. it must be stocked in every branch. Although the circulation figures for gay publications are not as high as those of mainstream media – *The Gay Times*, for example, has a circulation of around 70,000 – they do deliver a high quality affluent audience.

Many mainstream companies have still not realised the potential of the gay market. Market research has found that 86 per cent of companies have not communicated specifically with gay audiences. Many companies say that they target all groups, not just niche markets, and besides that, they can reach the same audience through mainstream media. In their view, many gays' purchasing decisions are made using the same criteria as heterosexual consumers. Companies could, however, be missing out. A phenomenal 92 per cent of gay consumers surveyed said that they were more likely to favour companies that acknowledge and support gay people, and 88 per cent said that it is important to them that a company is gay-friendly.

There are some product and service sectors in which gay consumers are explicitly targeted. The development of 'gay villages', particularly in London, Brighton and Manchester, has in turn led to many overtly gay pubs, bars, restaurants, clubs and shops opening close to each other. This creates a focal point for gay communities and indeed, gay pubs and clubs are important social venues. Mintel (2000b) found that 90 per cent of gay respondents were pub visitors (compared with 69 per cent of the general population) and 81 per cent had visited a club (compared with less than 30 per cent of the general population). Interestingly, club visiting does not decline with age among the gay community as dramatically as it does among the general population.

According to Mintel (2000b), the five most important factors which contribute towards enjoyment of a gay venue were cited as:

- type of music (77 per cent)
- not intense or intimidating (75 per cent)
- have been before and liked it (68 per cent)
- spacious with seating areas (62 per cent)
- cheaper drinks and special offers (56 per cent).

The majority of gay bars and pubs are run by independents, although some mainstream breweries have committed themselves to the gay market. Bass, for example, runs 28 gay pubs across the UK while Scottish & Newcastle runs a number of gay pubs, mainly in London (6 outlets) but with two in Manchester, purely due to their location on Canal Street at the heart of the 'gay village'. Some operators focus purely on the gay sector, such as the Manto Group (centred on Manchester) and Kudos Group (centred on London).

The holiday market too lends itself to gay targeting by both mainstream and specialised companies. There are many specialised gay tour operators and travel agents, although the majority of gay holidaymakers still use mainstream travel suppliers as long as they appear to be gay-friendly. Some companies and destinations are, however, perceived as homophobic, and these tend to be avoided. Sandals, for example, explicitly advertises its resorts as being for heterosexual couples only.

According to Mintel (2000a), respondents in its survey took an average of 2.07 holidays each per year, and 72 per cent of them had taken at least one holiday lasting a week or longer within the previous year. *The Gay Times* found that 41 per cent of its readership took two or more holidays per year. The beach/resort holiday destination is almost as popular with the gay community as with anyone else but gay holidaymakers are more likely to take city-based holidays (23 per cent of Mintel's respondents) than the general population (9 per cent). Mintel (2000a) points out that cities are more likely to have some form of gay infrastructure, in the form of bars and clubs, that would add value to a holiday.

Surprisingly, only 4 per cent of Mintel's respondents had been on a gay-themed holiday and only 3 per cent had booked their holiday using a gay travel agent or tour operator. Around 11 per cent had actually booked holidays over the internet which is much higher than among the general population in which less than 2 per cent of holidays are booked on the internet. Via the gay websites mentioned earlier, it is easy to find gay-orientated travel agencies. http://www.throb.co.uk, for example, offers holidays to popular gay or gay-friendly resorts in Spain and offers incentives to encourage booking over the internet.

In summary, Mintel (2001a) says that gay holiday-makers want a more diverse array of gay travel products, targeting them with 'quality gay-friendly holidays, rather than gay-themed holidays'.

Sources: Fry (1998, 2000); Mintel (2000a, 2000b).

Questions

1. To what extent does the gay segment conform to the criteria for successful segmentation?
2. What segmentation bases are relevant to the gay pub/club and holiday markets?
3. What are the risks and rewards for a mainstream company targeting the gay segment?

References for chapter 5

Abratt, R. (1993), 'Market Segmentation Practices of Industrial Marketers', *Industrial Marketing Management*, 22, pp. 79–84.

Bale, J. (2001), 'Seats Built for Those that Travel Light', *The Times*, 15 February.

Bonoma, T.V. and Shapiro, B.P. (1984), 'How to Segment Industrial Markets', *Harvard Business Review*, May/June, pp. 104–10.

Broadhead, S. (1995), 'European Cup Winners', *Sunday Express*, 7 May, p. 31.

Chesshyre, T. (2000), 'Gay Can Be Green in Fiji', *The Times*, 19 February.

Crosskey, P. (1997), 'Sales Press Forward', *The Grocer*, 3 May, pp. 41–2.

Denny, N. (1998), 'Listening to Your Customers is Vital', *Marketing*, 19 November, p. 18.

Douglas, S.P. and Craig, C.S. (1983), *International Marketing Research*, Prentice-Hall.

The Economist (2000), 'Bra Wars', *The Economist*, 2 December, p. 64.

Eggleston, S. (2001), 'Barbecue and Beer', *The Grocer*, 24 March, pp. 49–53.

Evans, R. (2001), 'Luxury Liners', *Barrons*, 9 April, pp. 25–6.

Evanson, R. (1999), 'A Global Icon in Sustainable Tourism', Paper presented at the *2nd Annual Samoan Tourism Convention*, 24–25 February 1999.

Fry, A. (2000), 'Profits in the Pink', *Marketing*, 23 November, pp. 41–2.

Fry, A. (1998), 'Reaching the Pink Pound', *Marketing*, 4 September, pp. 23–6.

The Grocer, (2001a), 'A Little Luxury Goes a Long Way', *Advertising Supplement* to *The Grocer*, 24 March, pp. 2–3.

The Grocer, (2001b), 'Sweet and Powerful', *Advertising Supplement* to *The Grocer*, 24 March, p. 8.

The Grocer, (2001c), 'Time to Get Lucky!', *Advertising Supplement* to *The Grocer*, 24 March, p. 26.

The Grocer (2001d), 'BBQ Week: Bigger and Better', *The Grocer*, 24 March, p. 59.

The Grocer (1998), 'Taking the Guilt out of Eating Chips', *The Grocer*, 24 October, p. 73.

Hlavacek, J.D. and Ames, B.C. (1986), 'Segmenting Industrial and High Tech Markets', *Journal of Business Strategy*, 7 (2), pp. 39–50.

Javalqi, R. and Dion, P. (1999), 'A Life-cycle Segmentation Approach to Marketing Financial Products and Services', *The Service Industries Journal*, 19 (3), pp. 74–96.

Jenkins, M. and McDonald, M. (1997), 'Market Segmentation: Organizational Archetypes and Research Agendas', *European Journal of Marketing*, 31 (1), pp. 17–32.

Levine, E. (1999), 'When Barbecue is Serious Business', *Business Week*, 31 May, p. 174.

Machauer, A. and Morgner, S. (2001), 'Segmentation of Bank Customers by Expected Benefits and Attitudes', *The International Journal of Bank Marketing*, 19 (1), pp. 6–18.

Marbeau, Y. (1992), 'Harmonisation of Demographics in Europe 1991: The State of the Art. Part 1: Eurodemographics? Nearly There!' *Marketing and Research Today*, 20 (1), pp. 33–40.

Miller, R. (2001), 'Marketers Pinpoint Their Targets', *Marketing*, 18 January, pp. 40–1.

Mintel (2000a), 'The Gay Holiday Market, 8/11/00', accessed via http://sinatra2/mintel.com, October 2001.

Mintel (2000b), 'The Gay Entertainment Market, 12/12/00', accessed via http://sinatra2/mintel.com, October, 2001.

Mitchell, A. (1983), *The Nine American Lifestyles: Who Are We and Where Are We Going?*, Macmillan.

Moriarty, R. and Reibstein, D. (1986), 'Benefit Segmentation in Industrial Markets', *Journal of Business Research*, 14 (6), pp. 463–86.

O'Malley, L. *et al.* (1995), 'Retailing Applications of Geodemographics: A Preliminary Investigation', *Marketing Intelligence and Planning*, 13 (2), pp. 29–35.

Paitra, J. (1993), 'The Euro-consumer: Myth or Reality?', in C. Halliburton and R. Hunerberg (eds), *European Marketing: Readings and Cases*, Addison-Wesley.

Piercy, N. and Morgan, N. (1993), 'Strategic and Operational Market Segmentation: A Managerial Analysis', *Journal of Strategic Marketing*, 1, pp. 123–40.

Plummer, J.T. (1974), 'The Concept and Application of Lifestyle Segmentation', *Journal of Marketing*, 38 (Jan), pp. 33–7.

Quatresooz, J. and Vancraeynest, D. (1992), 'Harmonisation of Demographics in Europe 1991: The State of the Art. Part 2: Using the ESOMAR Harmonised Demographics: External and Internal Validation of the EUROBAROMETER Test', *Marketing and Research Today*, 20 (1), pp. 41–50.

Schoenwald, M. (2001), 'Psychographic Segementation: Used or Abused', *Brandweek*, 22 January, pp. 34–8.

Shoemaker, S. (2000), 'Segmenting the Travel Market: Ten Years Later', *Journal of Travel Research*, 39 (1), pp. 11–26.

Sleight, P. (1997), *Targeting Customers: How to Use Geodemographic and Lifestyle Data in Your Business*, 2nd edn, NTC Publications.

Sleight, P. (1999a), 'Reacting Fast', *Database Marketing*, February, p. 8.

Sleight, P. (1999b), 'Measuring the Risk', *Database Marketing*, February, pp. 15–17.

Smith, W.R. (1957), 'Product Differentiation and Market Segmentation as Alternative Marketing Strategies', *Journal of Marketing*, 21 (July).

Smorszczewski, C. (2001), 'Corporate Banking', *Euromoney: The 2001 Guide to Poland*, May, pp. 4–5.

Solomon, M.R. (1994), *Consumer Behaviour*, 2nd edn, Allyn and Bacon.

Stuttaford, T. (2001), 'The Heart Bears the Ulitimate Burden', *The Times*, 15 February.

Wedel, M. and Kamakura, W. (1999), *Market Segmentation: Conceptual and Methodological Foundations*, Dordrecht: Kluwer Academic Publishers.

Wind, Y. (1982), *Product Policy and Concepts, Methods and Strategy*, Addison-Wesley.

Wind, Y. (1978), 'Issues and Advances in Segmentation Research', *Journal of Marketing Research*, 15 (3), pp. 317–37.

Wind, Y. and Cardozo, R. (1974), 'Industrial Marketing Segmentation', *Industrial Marketing Management*, 3 (March), pp. 153–66.

chapter 6
marketing information and research

LEARNING OBJECTIVES

This chapter will help you to:

1 recognise the importance of information to an organisation and the role information plays in effective marketing decision-making;

2 understand the role of a marketing information system and a decision support system, and develop an awareness of the various types of information available;

3 become familiar with the various steps involved in the marketing research process;

4 outline the sources of secondary and primary data, understand their role and the issues involved in their collection and analysis; and

5 appreciate some of the ethical concerns surrounding marketing research.

Introduction

The nature and role of market research in Europe have seen significant changes in recent years, as organisations increasingly look to do business in a wider range of EU markets. To be effective in penetrating these markets requires specialised and sophisticated approaches to identifying, assessing and satisfying market demands in a competitive environment. In a community with 15 member states, each with subtly different needs and market characteristics, effective information on the markets that are of interest is essential to help the organisation to make a better decision on the most appropriate market entry and competitive strategies. To support all this, the organisation also needs a properly designed and managed information system to enable timely and appropriate information to be available for the marketing decision maker. In the UK alone, organisations spend over £1 bn a year on research and conduct over 15 million consumer interviews in the search for the 'right' answers (Forestier-Walker, 2000).

Every aspect of marketing considered in this book, including the definition of markets and market segments, the formulation of an integrated strategy based on the 4Ps and planning and control mechanisms, requires the collection and analysis of information. The better the planning, data collection, information management and analysis, the more reliable and useful the outputs become, and thus marketers are able to make decisions that are more likely to satisfy the needs and wants of selected market segments. The organisation that is prepared to contemplate making a significant change to its marketing effort, without first assessing likely market reaction, is running a very high risk of failure.

In general, gathering information on the actual or potential marketplace not only allows the organisation to monitor trends and issues concerning its current customers, but also helps it to identify and profile potential customers and new markets, and to keep track of its competition, their strategies, tactics and future plans. In this context, market research and information handling offer the organisation a foundation from which it can adjust to the changing environment in which it operates.

eg

Barclaycard became one of the biggest spenders in the sponsorship industry when it agreed to pay £48 mn for the right to have its name associated with the English Premier League. Effectively, it was buying the right to reach millions of football fans in a subtle way rather than through 'in your face' advertising, and as the Premiership is broadcast to over 142 countries worldwide, Barclaycard would also benefit from international exposure. Nevertheless, as we shall see in Chapter 19, despite the enormous brand or corporate name coverage from sponsorship, it is still essential that its objectives are clear and capable of measurement so that the sponsor can be sure that sponsorship is actually delivering its full promotional potential. Barclaycard had to think carefully about how to use market research to ensure that it was getting value for money.

Of particular significance was the need to change the approach to brand tracking to ensure that the message was getting across and that more positive attitudes were being generated. Ipsos UK, a market research agency was awarded the contract to research awareness and brand impact as the sponsorship developed. The agency already ran a syndicated sponsorship awareness study *Sponsortest*, and had therefore built up a lot of market information and experience of sponsorship research. Other agencies also undertake more in-depth research with a cross-section of the target consumers and evaluate the relative impact of the different media covered by the sponsorship deal. Barclaycard is, however, an exception from a number of other sponsoring organisations which often undertake little measurement research, as it has realised that effective market research underpins most marketing decision-making (Smith, 2001).

Marketing information and research principles and practice are often similar across a wide range of situations in consumer and B2B market contexts, although they may, of course, become market specific in terms of their focus. Thus assessing the market for machine tools in Germany and Spain, for example, may differ in terms of the sources of data and information used, but the need for the careful selection of key information sources and the design of a user survey of key potential buyers may well follow similar lines.

This chapter first considers the role of marketing research and discusses the structure of the marketing information system (MIS) as a means of collecting, analysing and disseminating timely, accurate and relevant data and information throughout the organisation. It then looks at the marketing research planning framework. The stages in designing and implementing a marketing research project are considered, from defining the problem to writing a brief and then executing the project and disseminating the findings. The chapter also looks in detail at sourcing and collecting secondary (or desk) research, from existing or published sources, and primary (or field research) derived from scratch through surveys, observation or experimentation for a specific purpose. The important aspects of designing samples and data collection instruments are explored in some depth, since however well managed the rest of the research process is, asking the wrong questions in the wrong way to the wrong people is a recipe for poor quality marketing information.

Finally, because marketing research is potentially such a complex process, with so much riding on its findings, and because organisations often delegate it to agencies, it is important that it is carried out professionally and ethically. There is, therefore, a section on ethical issues involved in marketing research at pp. 256 *et seq*.

Throughout this chapter, the terms *client* and *researchers* have been used. Client means the organisation that has commissioned the marketing research, whether from an external agency or from an in-house department. Researchers mean the individual or the team responsible for actually undertaking the research task, regardless of whether they are internal or external to the client organisation.

Marketing research: definition and role

Marketing research is at the heart of marketing decision-making and it is important to understand what it involves and its place within the organisation. This section thus discusses the meaning of marketing research and the role that it plays in helping managers to understand new or changing markets, competition, customers' and potential customers' needs and wants.

Defining marketing research

Marketing research is a critical input into marketing decisions and can be defined as:

> *Marketing research is the function which links the consumer, customer, and public to the marketer through information – information used to identify and define marketing opportunities and problems; generate, refine, and evaluate*

> *marketing actions; monitor marketing performance; and improve understanding of marketing as a process. Marketing research specifies the information required to address those issues; designs the method for collecting information; manages and implements the data collection process; analyses the results; and communicates the findings and their implications.*
>
> (AMA definition as quoted by McDaniel and Gates, 1996)

Marketing research links the organisation with the environment in which it is operating and involves specifying the problem, gathering data then analysing and interpreting those data to facilitate the decision-making process. Marketing research is an essential link between the outside world and the marketer through the information used to identify and define marketing opportunities and problems, generate, refine and evaluate marketing actions, monitor marketing performance and improve understanding of marketing as a process. Marketing research thus specifies the information required to address these issues and designs the methods for collecting the necessary data. It implements the research plan and then analyses and interprets the collected data. After that, the findings and their implications can be communicated.

The role of marketing research

The role of marketing research in consumer markets has become well established across the EU. It is particularly important for manufacturers, because of the way in which retailers and other intermediaries act as a buffer between manufacturers and their end consumers. If the manufacturer is not to become isolated from market trends and changing preferences, it is important that an accurate, reliable flow of information reaches the marketing decision maker. It might be very limiting if only feedback from the trade were used in making new product and marketing mix decisions.

Another factor facing the consumer goods marketer is the size of the customer base. With such a potentially large number of users and potential users, the onus is on the organisation to make sure that it generates a backward flow of communication from those customers. The potential size of consumer markets also opens up the prospect of adapting products and the general marketing offering to suit different target groups. Decisions on product range, packaging, pricing and promotion will all arise from a well-understood profile of the different types of need in the market. Think back to Chapter 5, where the links between market segments and marketing mixes were discussed in more detail. Marketing research is essential for ensuring that segments exist and that they are viable, and for establishing what they want and how to reach them. As markets become increasingly European and global in their scope, marketing research plays an even more crucial role in helping the organisation to Europeanise its marketing effort, and to decide when to standardise and when to vary its approaches as new markets are opened up.

marketing *in action*

Understanding you

If you are a recent graduate or if you are about to graduate, then the market researchers are interested in you. The Abbey National, a financial services company, wanted to understand better the aspirations and lifestyles of a target group of customers that, if attracted early, could become long-term important customers. Through a research agency, Future Foundation, it surveyed 800 students in four UK universities and the results were compared with the actual life experiences of students who had graduated ten years previously.

Students' dreams at graduation soon changed with reality. Out went the single, *Friends*-type lifestyle, with the aim of living in London, Sydney or New York, and in came the desire for a permanent relationship, probably one child and living close to one's home town. After ten years, just 10 per cent were living the single lifestyle, over 70 per cent had become domesticated and most preferred to be in their home area. The urban lifestyle was still preferred to rural living, however, and the home-ownership vision, although strong, extended to purpose-built flats or semi-detached houses only. Immediately after graduation, over half of the former students found themselves living at their parents' home after being faced with the economic reality of student loans and the cost of housing, and 40 per cent did not want to pay for the privilege and couldn't wait to move out again. Most, especially males, tended to outstay their welcome.

Overall, the results confirm that students' ideals and lifestyle aspirations soon transform, turning them into more steady, family-oriented employees. According to Abbey National's research, facing so many significant life changes in a short period of time, graduates wanted a bank that could grow and change with them, rather than abandon them if the going got tough. This was becoming increasingly important as the graduates sought to repay their student debt. From such generalised research, Abbey National is better able to understand the lifestyle pressures facing the age group and the aspirations and motivations that could result in the need for financial services.

Source: http://www.futurefoundation.net.

In B2B markets, the role of marketing research is still very similar to that in consumer markets, in that it helps the organisation to understand the marketing environment better and to make better informed decisions about marketing strategies. Where the two types of market may differ is in the actual design and implementation of marketing research, because of some of the underlying factors peculiar to B2B markets, such as the smaller number of customers and the closer buyer–seller relationships, as introduced in Chapter 4. Despite any differences, the role of marketing research is still to provide an essential insight into opportunities, markets and customers.

An organisation can collect its data in different ways. Data can come from secondary sources (published data, discussed at pp. 230 *et seq.*) or primary sources (data collected for a particular research project, discussed at pp. 232 *et seq.*). Primary data might be collected by commercial market research agencies, which will undertake specific, commissioned projects for clients. These agencies can vary considerably in size and specialisation, depending on whether they are large multinationals or small operations. Some will offer the full range of services, but others will choose to specialise in particular areas of marketing research, such as large-scale field surveys.

However, marketing research can also be undertaken by the organisation's own marketing research department, if it has one, and secondary data can be obtained from a range of commercial and government-sponsored bodies. If it is decided to undertake the research internally, the organisation has to be sure that the range of expertise exists to cope with the problem in hand. The problem is that the greater the in-house expertise available, the more expensive and difficult it is to keep it employed throughout the year.

A larger organisation, such as KLM, tends to be better equipped for formal marketing research, as it recognises that it can become remote from customers, whereas a smaller organisation has more day-to-day contact with its customers, although that can lead to a narrow view, being oblivious to new ideas and opportunities. Whatever its situation, an organisation must be confident that it is sufficiently well informed to be able to make marketing decisions with the support of timely and accurate information. Trevaskis (2000) reported that UK businesses were trying to get closer to consumers rather than become too remote. Spending more time with real people doing real things, closer involvement in research agency projects, and involving consumers in business decisions, are all being used to help bridge the divide.

Marketing research can take many forms, from being a highly specialised project requiring expert knowledge and considerable expense, to being quite informal and inexpensive. The amount of time and cost to allow for each project will, of course, vary considerably. An organisation with a proper respect for marketing research and the support it offers to decision makers will allow a project to take as long as it needs, and to cost as much as it needs, to solve the defined problem, without getting lost in irrelevant fine detail.

The need for marketing research sometimes arises because the organisation needs specific details about a target market, which is a well-defined, straightforward descriptive research task. Sometimes, though, the research need arises from a much broader question, such as why a new product is not achieving expected market share. The organisation may have a theory about the nature of the problem, but it is up to marketing research to establish whether any assumptions are correct and to check out other possibilities. In practice, most marketing researchers spend a fair proportion of their time on informal projects, undertaken in reaction to specific requests for marketing information. Often these projects

eg

Bailey's Irish Cream is often drunk at home by a loyal band of drinkers. Bailey's wanted the liqueur brand to have wider appeal, however, especially outside the home and among younger consumers. It decided to use market research to provide better insights into attitudes towards and perceptions of the brand. In one study, a group of consumers aged between 18 and 30 were asked to keep a record of their reactions to drinking Bailey's in situations when it would not normally be considered. These included drinking it at Sunday breakfast after a night out, at a funeral, and as a pick-me-up, and the reactions to each situation were recorded. A quantitative research questionnaire was also used, asking multiple choice questions on respondents' brand perceptions. Four group sessions with around six people in each were held and participants were asked what products they associated with Bailey's. The results of the research were perhaps somewhat sobering for the company: Bailey's is valued as part of a home-based, comfortable, relaxing experience rather than a social drink for a night out. It was thus going to be tough to re-position the product (Clarke, 2001).

In order to appeal to a wider group of drinkers, particularly the 18–30 age group, the makers of Bailey's Irish Cream have promoted it as a constituent in alternative cocktails and recipes for ice cream. The website www.baileys.com is also called the Pleasuredome and appeals to drinkers seeking some additional pleasures.

Source: Diageo.

lack the scientific rigour associated with the more formal definition of market research. However, problems of a more innovative and complex nature have to be solved through major, formal pieces of market research, simply because of the risks involved in going ahead without the fullest possible insights.

Types of research

So far, the discussion of marketing research has been very general and has not distinguished between different types of research. There are, however, three main types of research, each suitable as an approach to different kinds of problem.

Exploratory research

Exploratory research is often undertaken in order to collect preliminary data to help clarify or identify a problem, rather than for generating problem solutions. Before preparing a major proposal, some exploratory work may be undertaken to establish the critical areas to be highlighted in the main body of the research.

An American manufacturer of high-pressure fire-fighting hose nozzles wanted to enter the European market with its most recent innovative design. Before it made a serious commitment to detailed market research across Europe to establish customer reaction and the market entry strategy, some exploratory research was undertaken. This made use of secondary data to establish who the competition would be, what the safety and product standards across Europe were and, not least, what the trends and profile of purchasing by the different fire-fighting authorities were. In addition, a small number of key interviews were held with purchasing bodies in Germany, France and the UK to establish the procedures for trial and adoption in those markets.

This provided a valuable insight into the characteristics of European markets and revealed that significant differences existed in what had been believed to be a relatively homogeneous market. In this case, exploratory research helped to identify the areas that the main survey would consider in more depth and ensured that the company's original assessments and expectations were tested before detailed surveys were designed.

Exploratory research can be conducted through a number of different techniques. Secondary sources of information may be enough (*see* pp. 230 *et seq.*), or the organisation may wish to undertake small-scale qualitative research such as surveys of knowledgeable persons or small group discussions (*see* p. 236). In some circumstances, the organisation may even choose to use observational research (*see* pp. 240 *et seq.*) for its exploratory data. However, whatever the method chosen, in each case the purpose is to make an initial assessment of the nature of a marketing problem, so that more detailed research work can be planned appropriately.

Descriptive research

Descriptive research aims to provide the marketer with a better understanding of a particular issue or problem. Descriptive research can range from quite specific briefs, for example profiling the consumers of a particular brand, assessing the actual purchase and repurchase behaviour associated with that brand and the reasons behind the behaviour exhibited. Most research in this category tends to be of a large-scale survey type, designed to provide a means of better understanding of marketing problems through the presentation of both quantitative and qualitative data (*see* below).

The Campaign for Real Ale (CAMRA) used descriptive research to understand better who does and does not drink real ale. Some 487 men were surveyed to reveal consumption habits. Over 62 per cent do not drink real ale but 8 per cent get through around ten pints a week and 1 per cent consume 30 pints (assuming they were sober enough to give accurate responses). Social status is not a good indicator of preferences, with 56 per cent of As and Bs and 58 per cent of Ds and Es keeping off real ale. All this information will help CAMRA to develop strategies to face the challenge of increasing real ale consumption (Mason, 2001).

Causal or predictive research

This type of research is undertaken to test a cause-and-effect relationship so that reasonably accurate predictions about the probable outcome of particular actions can be made. The difficulty with this kind of research for the marketing manager is that to be confident that more of x does cause more of y, all the other variables that influence y must be held constant. The real-world laboratory is rarely so obliging, with competitors, retailers and other intermedieries, and the marketing environment generally, all acting independently, doing things that will change the background conditions. Thus researchers trying to establish, for instance, whether or not a promotional 10 per cent price reduction would increase sales volume by 15 per cent during a specified period are faced with the problem of ensuring that all the other variables that might influence sales volume are held constant during the research. Random sampling may help in this process, so that the 10 per cent offer would only be made in a random selection of stores, with the other stores offering normal terms. Any difference in the performance of the product in the two groups of stores is likely to have been caused by the special promotion, since both the 'normal' and the 'promotional' product have been subjected to identical environmental factors, impacting on all the stores, during the same period.

The origins of research data

There are two main types of data, which are generated by fundamentally different research approaches.

Qualitative research

Qualitative research involves the collection of data that are open to interpretation, for example people's opinions, where there is no intention of establishing statistical validity. This type of research is especially useful for investigating motivation, attitudes, beliefs and intentions, rather than utilising probability-based samples. With this approach, many of the methods used to generate data are grounded in the behavioural sciences. They are often based on very small-scale samples and, as a result, cannot be generalised in numerical terms. Although the results are often subjective, tentative and impressionistic, they can reflect the complexity that underlies consumer decision-making, capturing the richness and depth of how and why consumers act in the way they do. Most marketing research is about helping marketers to understand what consumers will do next and what they will buy in the future, so quantitative surveys on buying intentions or on past buying decisions might not be reliable. According to Forestier-Walker (2000):

> *Marketers need to reframe their perceptions of the research industry away from the myth of objectivity and embrace the value of subjectivity.*

Quantitative techniques, despite their statistical rigour, are rarely able to capture the full complexity and the wealth of interrelationships associated with marketing activity. The real value in qualitative research, therefore, lies in helping marketers to understand not what people say, but what they mean (or think they mean), and a range of techniques have been developed to assist in that task such as:

- survey research/questionnaires
- focus groups
- in-depth interviews
- observational techniques
- experimentation.

All of these are discussed further at pp. 232 *et seq.*

Quantitative research

Quantitative research involves the collection of information that is quantifiable and is not open to the same level of interpretation as qualitative research. It includes data such as sales figures, market share, market size, consumer product returns or complaints, and demographic information (*see* pp. 184 *et seq.*) and can be collected through primary research, such as questionnaire-based surveys and interviews, and through secondary sources, including published data.

Quantitative research usually involves larger-scale surveys or research that enable a factual base to be developed with sufficient strength to allow statistically rigorous analysis. Most of us have been on the receiving end of quantitative research at some time or another, having been collared by an interviewer armed with a clipboard interviewing respondents in the street. The success of quantitative research depends in part on establishing a representative sample that is large enough to allow researchers to be confident that the results can be generalised to apply to the wider population. It is then possible to specify that 'Forty-five per cent of the market think that . . . whereas 29 per cent believe . . .' The research can be undertaken through telephone interviews, face-to-face interviews, or mail questionnaires (*see* pp. 238 *et seq.*), and can also utilise secondary data sources (*see* pp. 230 *et seq.*).

The internet is now starting to revolutionise quantitative research. The early emphasis was on gaining cooperation online and structuring questions, but now the techniques used are becoming more sophisticated, interactive, usable over time and more directly linked to systems to integrate all data sources whether online or offline (James, 2001).

Continuous research

A large number of research projects are developed specifically to better understand and to overcome marketing problems as they are identified. At pp. 226 *et seq.* we trace the development of such projects from inception through to final evaluation. Some research, however, is conducted on a continuous basis. **Continuous research** is available on an ongoing basis for a subscription or agreement to purchase the updated findings. Usually offered by market research agencies, syndicated research provides much useful data on an ongoing basis. In the UK, retail purchases by consumers are tracked by A C Nielsen, while Target Group Index (TGI), produced by BMRB, plots the fortunes of some 5,000 brands. Similar services are available in all the main European markets. The quality of such research is very high, but the important advantage is shared cost, since Nielsen data, for example, are essential to any large multiple retailer or brand manufacturer and they will all buy the data. The price for each organisation is still far, far less than the cost of doing or commissioning the research individually. The big disadvantage, of course, is that competitors also have access to exactly the same information.

There are a number of different approaches to generating continuous data.

Consumer panels

Market research companies recruit large numbers of households which are prepared to provide information on their actual buying and consumption patterns on a regular basis. The panel may be constituted to provide as wide a coverage of the population as possible, or it may be defined to home in on a particular segment. The make-up of a consumer panel can be quite specific. The Pre- and Post-Natal Survey (PNS), operated in the UK, runs a regular survey of 700 pregnant women and 600 mothers with babies up to six months old. For manufacturers of baby foods, nappies, toiletries and infant medicines, such inside information can be invaluable. Taylor Nelson Sofres Superpanel is the UK's leading continuous consumer panel and provides purchasing information on all main grocery markets. The panel was launched in 1991 and now consists of 15,000 households which are demographically and regionally balanced to offer a representative picture of the various sub-markets. Data is collected twice weekly through electronic terminals in the home, with purchases being recorded via home-scanning technology (http://www.tnsofres.com).

Data can be extracted from consumer panels in two main ways: home audits and omnibus surveys.

Home audits. The consumer is expected to throw nothing away, and that includes cans, wrappers and all other forms of packaging. Refuse is placed in a special container that is checked at regular intervals by an independent auditor, who also checks the food cupboard and fridge/freezer. Sometimes additional questions are asked to supplement the survey. Increasingly, electronic terminals are installed in homes to allow regular tracking of brand usage. A C Nielsen Homescan has 126,000 households globally in 18 countries linked to in-home bar scanners that record grocery purchases as well as collect answers to survey questions (http://www.acnielsen.com). Information is simply downloaded to the research company on a regular basis using a modem. This method is increasingly replacing the old-style consumer diary, which recorded the same kind of information but using pen and paper technology!

Television viewership panels are very similar, in that they involve the recruitment of households and the installation of in-home monitoring equipment. This time, the objective is to use the equipment to enable minute-by-minute recording of audience viewing by channel. From these data, organisations such as AGB and RSMB are able to provide detailed ratings for programmes and viewing patterns during commercial breaks, a critical factor in the sale of advertising time.

Consumer panels enable buying profiles to be built up over time and provide much useful information for brand managers. Panel data are particularly useful for assessing consumer loyalty, brand switching and the frequency and quantities purchased.

Omnibus surveys. An omnibus survey, as the term suggests, enables an organisation to participate in an existing research programme whenever it is felt appropriate. When an organisation wants to take part, it can add a few extra questions to the next round of questionnaires sent to the large number of respondents who are regularly contacted. The big advantage is cost, although normally the number of questions that can be asked on behalf of a specific organisation is very small. The speed with which answers are received is also an important factor.

There are three types of omnibus survey: those carried out face-to-face during an interviewer visit to the home, telephone surveys and finally internet interviews. Face-to-face omnibuses tend to offer a larger sample size, often around 2,000 adults, and allow support material to be used. They are also better for exploring more complex or sensitive issues (for example health or finance related questioning) than the other two methods. Telephone omnibuses offer a faster turnaround time (about 4 to 5 days quicker than a face-to-face survey) but the sample sizes tend to be smaller and the scope of questioning is more limited. Internet omnibuses are new and are now spreading after their introduction in the United States. They are all based on self-completion of questionnaires and the sample must be carefully controlled to avoid unwanted respondents. It is, however, a very quick way of accessing the views of the internet population.

To speed up the collection and input of data, many research companies use **CATI** (computer aided telephone interviewing) and **CAPI** (computer aided personal interviewing) (see p. 252 *et seq.*). These techniques enable larger panels to be formed and the data to be processed much quicker. Each interview lasts no longer than 30 minutes to avoid interviewee fatigue. Taylor Nelson Sofres Consumer Omnibus has a number of options:

- *Capibus* is the UK's largest weekly omnibus offering a sample of 2,000 adults, interviewed face-to-face with full results within ten days. Questions can be targeted and considerable information on the individual and household is collected.
- *PhoneBus* is run twice-weekly providing data from 2,000 UK adults. It offers a four-day turnaround so if the questions are submitted by 10 a.m. on Tuesday, responses in full tables are available by Friday lunchtime. Most of the fieldwork is undertaken by CATI and random digit dialling is used to make the sample more representative by including ex-directory telephone users.
- *Ncompass* is Taylor Nelson Sofres' international omnibus, compiled through data collected by offices in over 80 countries. Results can be available within two weeks and if the Speedline is used, that can be reduced to just six days in the main European markets from a sample of 1,000 adults per country.
- *Autobus* focuses on motoring samples with over 1,000 motorists contacted each week of the year. Such specialist omnibus services are especially useful for the fast gathering of information on specific sectors.

Other companies such as Access Ominbus Surveys and RSGB Omnibus also offer regular omnibus surveys in a similar manner allowing considerable choice in selecting the most appropriate survey for the target audience.

The internet is now starting to have a bigger impact on consumer panel research. Nielsen, for example, has a 9,000-strong panel of internet users in the UK and 90,000 worldwide and this is growing at a rapid rate as part of audience measurement research (Gray, 2000b). Every time a page is visited, specialised software installed in participants' computers records the information for Nielsen. French-owned NetValue is working with Taylor Nelson Sofres to develop high quality internet panels across Europe to provide reliable usage estimates and sampling standards. To be of value, a panel must be representative of each national population as a whole. NetValue measures internet usage in a number of countries including the UK, France, Germany and the US. Some caution must, however, be exercised in the use of internet research. MORI, after using e-mail in an IT survey panel dropped it because of falling response rates and reverted to telephone interviews. Although the online panel was a lower cost to clients, this had to be related to its effectiveness in actually generating data (http://www.researchlive.com).

Retail audits

The retail audit concept is perhaps the easiest to implement, as it relies on trained auditors visiting selected retail stores and undertaking regular stock checks. Increasingly, the use of barcode scanning is providing even more up-to-date information on what is sold where and when. Changes in stock, both on the shelf and in the warehouse, indicate an accurate figure for actual sales to consumers by pack size. This information is especially useful for assessing brand shares, response to sales promotions and the amount of stock being held within the retail trade. Along with information on price levels, the brand manager has much useful information with which to make revised marketing mix decisions.

Marketing information systems

In order to serve the information needs of the organisation and to support decision-making, marketers need to focus not only on collecting data and information, but also on how to handle and manage issues of storage, access and dissemination (McLuhan, 2001b). A research report is no use to anyone if nobody knows where it is or that it exists, or if the people who need it do not have the authority or means to access it. Thus it is vital to develop a system of organising and structuring information into a meaningful form to provide timely flows to managers, whether on an *ad hoc* or a continuous basis. The complexity of managing a continuous flow of information into the organisation demands a well thought-out information gathering, storage and retrieval system. There is little point in having a highly complex information system that cannot readily deliver what managers want, when they want it and how they want it. Any system must be responsive to the needs of the users.

A marketing information system (**MIS**) has been defined as:

> *an organised set of procedures and methods by which pertinent, timely and accurate information is continually gathered, sorted, analysed, evaluated, stored and distributed for use by marketing decision makers.*
>
> (Zikmund and d'Amico, 1993, p. 108)

Nowadays, most of these systems are data based and use high-powered computers. System requirements need to coordinate data collection and decision support, as shown in Figure 6.1. The MIS should be tailored to the specific requirements of the organisation. These will be influenced by the size of the organisation and the resources available as well as the specific needs of decision makers. While these needs are likely to be broadly similar between organisations, they will not be exactly the same and therefore the design of the systems and their sophistication will vary. What is important is that the information is managed in a way that facilitates the decision-making process, rather than just being a collection of data gathering dust.

Haburi.com established an MIS to improve its tracking of web customers across Europe. The system was designed to identify 'value' customers, the group that buys most frequently, prefers premium brands, and makes the fewest returns. At the other end of the spectrum, another group of customers tends to shop for bargains only, seeks low-priced lines, and often returns goods. By tracking the former group, Haburi.com was able to maximise sales to customers within the group, improve conversion rates and service levels, and keep in touch with them better, using the software provided by SAS and Delano to analyse its transactional database (McLuhan, 2001b).

It can be seen from Figure 6.1 that an MIS provides a comprehensive framework for managing information. Information comes in a variety of forms and from a range of sources, any of which can be of critical importance to any organisation, whether large or small, profit or non-profit orientated, government or private, local, national or multinational. In the current fast changing, information-rich, technological environment, organisations tend to be overwhelmed with information. Along with generating huge amounts of data about their

Figure 6.1 The marketing information system

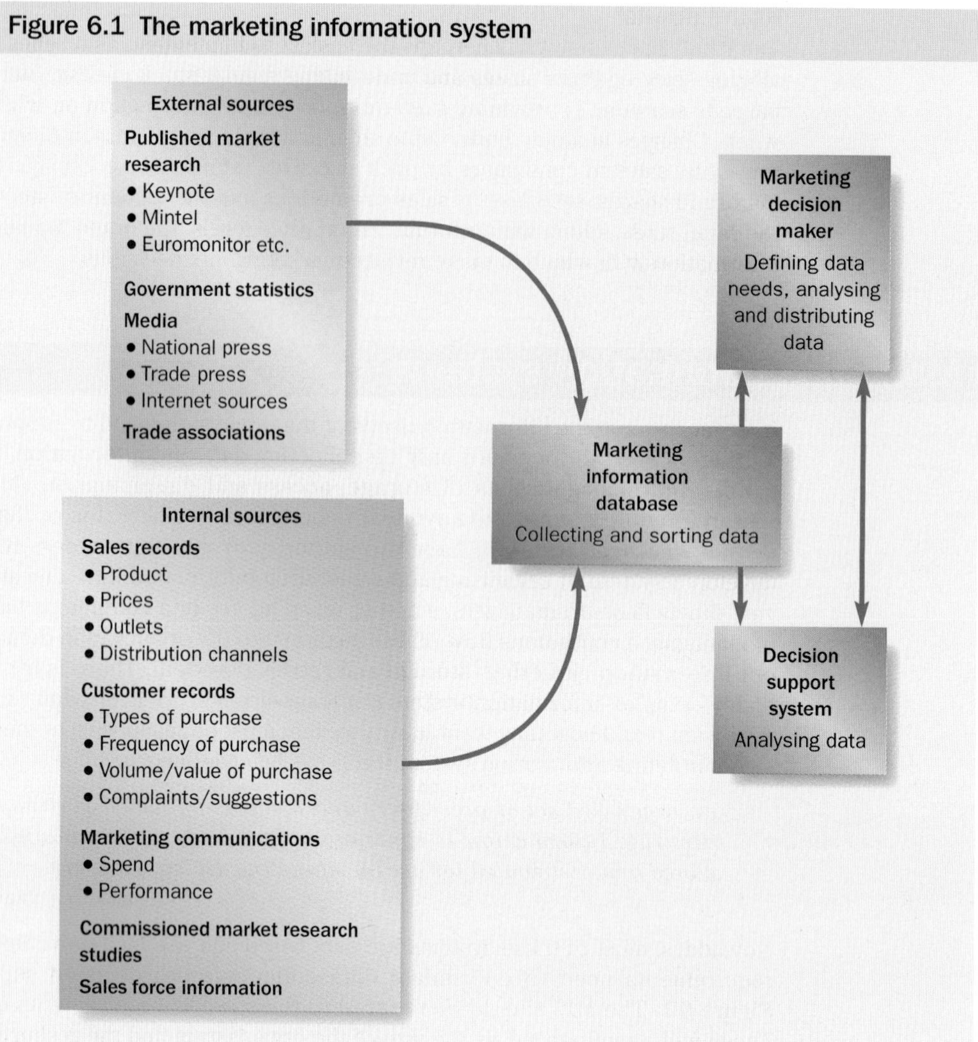

day-to-day activities (sales, customer details, incoming and outgoing orders, transactions, service requirements, etc.), organisations are usually in various stages of gathering other data about competitors, new product tests, improved service requirements and changing regulations, for example. The problem often becomes not how to get the data but what to do with them, and how they should be managed to turn them into useful information. This is where the MIS comes in, to provide a means of managing information, even for small or medium-sized organisations. Unless the organisation has a system that can collect, evaluate, analyse and distribute this information, providing it in a form that is useful, the organisation is not getting the maximum benefit from what it has. Timeliness of information, whether it be for short- or long-term decision-making, is also of importance, as the provision of immediate feedback or projected trend details to decision makers can provide a competitive advantage in the marketplace.

The other requirement of information is that it should be appropriate to the needs of those using it. Just as you may have difficulty identifying the information you need to make decisions about a range of options facing you, such as whether to update your computer, buy the new software version of your word processing package, go on an overseas holiday, or even look for a new job, organisations encounter the same problems, but usually on a much larger scale. They have to manage the information they have, identify what information they need, and present it in the form that the various decision makers require. Not all information that the organisation has is necessarily appropriate for all marketing decision makers. It is therefore important to identify the various needs of those decision makers and to ensure they are supplied with only the information that meets their needs. This facilitates decision-making and helps to avoid information overload. The questions in Table 6.1 help to identify information requirements by getting managers to answer a range of questions relating to their own individual needs.

Table 6.1 Defining information requirements

- What decisions do you make on a regular basis?
- What types of information do you need to make these decisions?
- What types of information do you regularly receive?
- What types of information do you need but do not currently get?
- What types of specific information are you likely to request?
- What is the time frame in which you would like to receive the information (daily, weekly, fortnightly, monthly, half-yearly etc.)?
- What are your areas of specific interest?
- What are your likely sources of that information (internal reports, trade magazines, etc.)?
- What are your data analysis requirements?
- What formats for the information (summary, table, graphs, print, computer disk/file, etc.) are most appropriate for you?

The growth of Customer Relationship Management (CRM) has challenged MIS systems to provide timely and focused data on different customer groups. Marketing consultants Claritas divide the client's database into sections: those who spend a lot with both the company and the market, those who spend little with either the company or the market, and those who spend with just one. Marketing actions are then determined by the characteristics of each group. If, for example, good customers tend to switch frequently to other suppliers, the focus for any marketing effort tends to be on retention and loyalty building offers. Lapsed customers require a different approach. This is only possible due to the building and maintenance of an effective database (McLuhan, 2001b).

marketing *in action*

Keeping an eye on mother

Lifestyle changes can be a good predictor of when consumers will be interested in certain goods and services. One company, Bounty, offers a worldwide target marketing service to help organisations seeking to market to such 'changers' exploit their opportunities. Pregnancy and birth is one such lifestyle change that represents enormous potential for marketers. Initial contact is made when the woman visits the obstetrician to confirm a pregnancy and she receives a pregnancy information pack containing a Bounty Pregnancy Guide. This way, Bounty reaches 92 per cent of expectant mothers. A questionnaire card inside the pack asking for the recipient's name, address and the expected date of the baby's birth can then be redeemed at any Mothercare retail store for a free Mother-to-Be gift pack, containing sample products and money-off vouchers. Johnson & Johnson and Procter & Gamble are both among the companies providing products in the pack. With a redemption rate of 80 per cent, a large database of expectant mothers is created.

After the birth, Bounty's *New Mother* programme kicks in. Within 72 hours of giving birth, 92 per cent of new mothers will be visited by one of the 280 Bounty ladies in the UK. Again a gift pack incentive is used, but during the bedside visit the mother's name and address is verified, further details recorded on other children and their ages, and the new mother is asked for her agreement to receive further mail samples and direct mail offers. The data collected at the time of the birth are used to update and enhance the pre-natal data that Bounty collected several months previously. In this way, a more complete profile of the consumer and the samples received can be built up on the database. Research indicates that new mothers often stay with the products they receive in hospital, so baby product suppliers are keen to

▶

work with Bounty in making the gift packs attractive and effective.

Bounty also seeks to maintain its relationship with the new mother. A card in the Bounty Young Family Guide within the gift pack asks for the mother's name and address, and the name and age of her new child, acting as another data capture mechanism. Completed cards can then be redeemed for a Progress pack within six months of the birth at Boots, the UK multiple retailer. Seventy per cent elect to trade the information card for the pack. Bounty, therefore, has at least three opportunities to capture data to expand, enhance and update its database.

Of course, all of this is not just done for the sake of gathering information. Bounty makes its mother-to-be and new mother lists available for rent to UK marketers, although it does seek to control usage to avoid claims of exploitation and damage to its relationships with doctors and hospitals. Before Bounty rents a list to a prospective mailer, it approves the mailing and checks the credentials of the mailer.

Source: Yorgey (2000).

Sources of marketing information

As indicated at the outset of this chapter and in Figure 6.1, there are two main sources of information for an MIS system, internal and external:

External sources

External sources are either *ad hoc* studies using secondary and primary research, or continuous data provided by the various syndicated and omnibus studies mentioned earlier. Information comes from sources external to the organisation, such as customers, suppliers, channels of distribution, strategic alliance partners, independent third parties, commercial agencies, industry associations, CSO, Eurostat, etc., and external sources like the internet. These are increasingly being recognised by the business community as a potential means of keeping up with developments in research and a range of other business-related areas, as well as providing a computer link with many millions of computer users, both individual and B2B. The challenge for the marketing manager is to integrate these findings into the organisation to effect change. Much will depend on the purpose of the research. Some may be specifically designed to support decisions of a tactical nature that need to be addressed as a matter of some urgency, others are part of a longer-term strategic development process indicating trends and opportunities.

Internal sources

Information also comes from internal sources within the organisation. These include the internal record keeping system (production, accounting, sales records, purchase details, etc.), marketing research, sales representatives' field reports, call details, customer enquiries and complaints, product returns etc. All of this information, again, must be managed appropriately and distributed in a timely fashion if it is going to be used effectively to assist decision-making.

The development of Electronic Point of Sale (EPOS) technology has revolutionised the flow of information within retail operations, providing a base for fast and reliable information on emerging trends. Either by using a laser barcode scanner or by keying in a six-figure code, retailers can be right up to date in what is moving, where and what the immediate impact will be on stock levels. Retail managers can monitor movement on different product lines on a daily basis and adjust stock, orders and even in-store promotions, based on information either from individual stores or across all the branches. Tesco, with its Clubcard loyalty scheme, can track and record the purchasing and shopping habits of millions of individual customers, and tailor its marketing offerings, both locally and nationally, based on solid, internally generated information. Direct response marketing, as will be discussed further in Chapter 18, similarly allows a wide range of organisations to build databases of information about individual customers.

The flow of sales force information into an MIS provides access to up-to-date profiles on customers' expectations, account problems and competitive activity. The key is to structure the data entry at sales representative level so that there is as little delay as possible in the flow. Gathered as part of the sales representative's daily reporting routine, information on calls made, orders, new accounts plus other interesting snippets all enable a closer link between sales and marketing decision-making. Clegg (2001) emphasised the importance not just of collecting externally generated marketing data but also of ensuring that there is effective communication within the organisation so that customer contact personnel in particular can contribute fully to building market research knowledge. If the marketing database is seen as being owned by the research department rather than being a knowledge reservoir for the whole organisation, it may not be so well informed of the experiences of customer-facing staff.

Organisations thus get everyday information, often as a matter of course, from a variety of sources that can influence their decision-making, but *intelligence* means developing a perspective on the information that provides a competitive edge, perhaps in new product opportunities or the opening up of a new market segment.

The main difficulty is information overload (Smith and Fletcher, 1999) where there is too much information and not enough intelligence. One study suggested that 49 per cent of managers surveyed cannot cope with the information they receive and another that organisations use as little as 20 per cent of their knowledge (Von Krogh *et al.*, 2000), meaning that a lot of perhaps useful intelligence is locked away or not evident to the decision maker. Collecting marketing information should not, therefore, be an end in itself but should be part of a valuable and usable knowledge management source that can be accessed upon demand in a meaningful and digestable form. As organisations become flatter and increased empowerment allows more local decision-making, the pressure to create more powerful, yet usable online information databases will increase (Smith and Culkin, 2001)

Sometimes environmental scanning can provide useful insights. By deliberately looking at the various influences on product markets, an organisation may spot early warning signs before the competitors are aware of them. This will help in the forward planning process and will be especially useful as an input to strategic development decisions.

Decision support systems

The availability and use of a range of computer-based decision support systems (**DSS**) are changing the way information is used and presented to decision makers, and the way in which they interpret it (Duan and Burrell, 1997). While an MIS organises and presents information, the DSS actually aids decision-making by allowing the marketer to manipulate information and explore 'What if . . .' type questions. A DSS usually comprises a software package designed for a personal computer, including statistical analysis tools, spreadsheets, databases and other programs that assist in gathering, analysing and interpreting information to facilitate marketing decision-making. By having the DSS connected to the MIS, marketers further enhance their ability to use the information available. Effectively, this brings the MIS to the desktop, and even to the personal laptop, with the appropriate connections, servers and modems. This can encourage wide use of information, although there may be some problems about restricting access to more sensitive areas and ensuring that the complexity can be handled from a systems perspective.

The use of simple spreadsheets and databases, for example, allows an organisation to keep track of customers' ordering details, payments, returns and product complaints on an individual basis. From this information, marketers can project future sales, keep track of complaints, identify who their regular customers are, what quantities they are buying, as well as patterns of purchase etc. One of your authors failed to visit her local supermarket as frequently as the retailer would have liked, despite having a store loyalty card. This resulted in a very polite letter reminding her of the benefits of buying at that store rather than elsewhere and telling her about a few promotional offers that might be of interest. Thus overall the DSS can be used with statistical analysis to try to identify significant patterns and trends, in both sales and customer behaviour, as well as for predicting the future course of those trends and the impact of marketing decisions on them. A DSS was developed to help decide the launch price of a new pharmaceutical product. The system enabled various marketing, sales force and pricing actions to be assessed to find the best price to charge. The system simulated market conditions as closely as possible to assess the impact of price on sales, share and profits over time (Rao, 2000).

The MIS or DSS will never replace decision makers, only help them. Marketing decisions still need the imagination and flair that can interpret 'hard' information and turn it into implementable tactics and strategies that will maintain competitive edge.

The marketing research process

When an organisation has decided to undertake a research project, it is important to make sure that it is planned and executed systematically and logically, so that the 'right' objectives are defined and achieved as quickly, efficiently and cost effectively as possible. A general model of the marketing research process is presented here, which can be applied to a wide range of real situations with minor adaptations. The broad stages, and the decisions and problems associated with them, from the initiation of the research through to the final review of the outcomes, should be common to most research exercises. The model is shown in Figure 6.2, and although it may suggest a logic and neatness that is rarely found in practice, it does at the very least offer a framework that can be tailored to meet different clients, situations and resources. Each stage in the process will now be discussed in turn.

Problem definition

Problem definition is the first and one of the most important stages in the research process, because it defines exactly what the project is about and as such influences how the subsequent stages are conducted, and ultimately the success of the project itself. The organisation sponsoring the research, whether it intends to use in-house researchers or an

Figure 6.2 The market research process

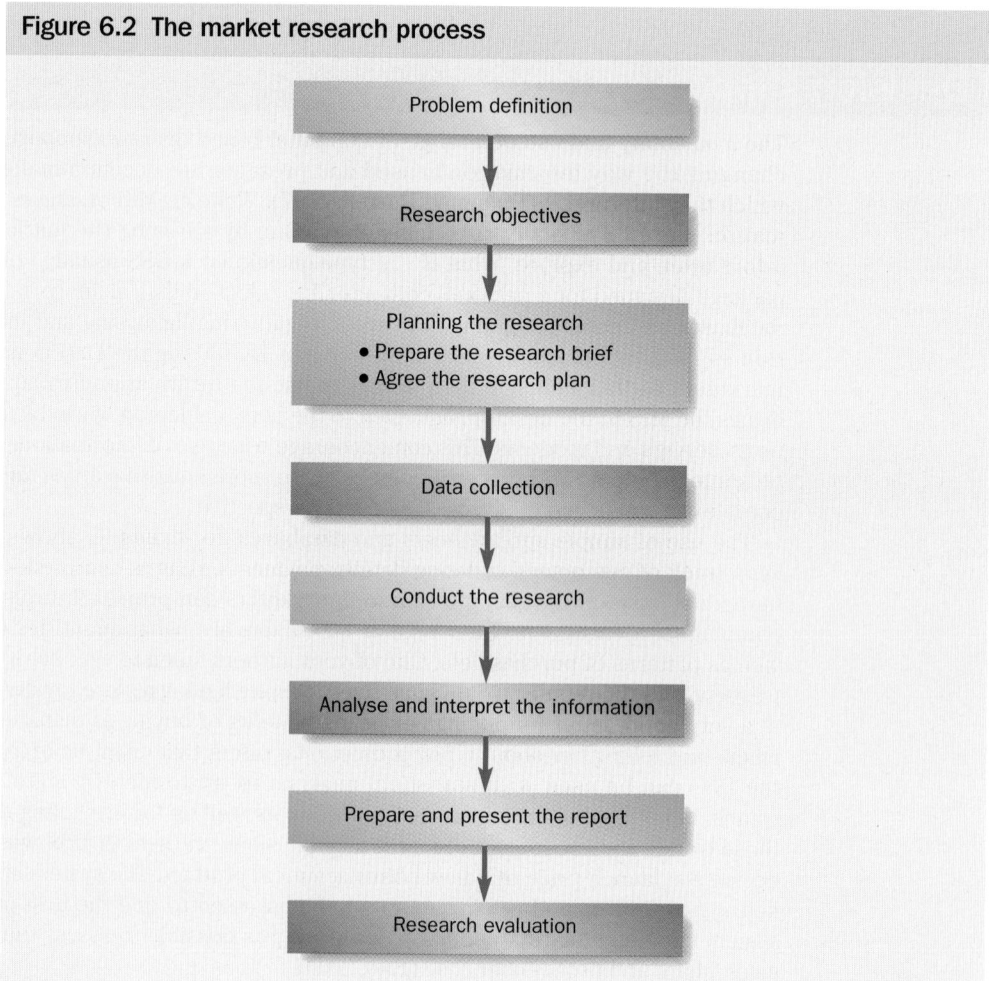

agency, needs to define precisely what the problem is and how that translates into research objectives. This may also lead to the identification of other concerns or problems that need to be included in the project. For example, if the fundamental problem has been defined as 'People are not buying our product', the organisation may feel that it should not only explore people's attitudes to the product itself, but also look at how they rate the product on other aspects of the marketing mix in comparison with the competition.

Once the broad nature of the problem has been established, the next stage involves more precise definition of objectives.

Research objectives

The tight specification of research objectives is important to ensure that the project is developed along the right lines. Usually, primary objectives need to be distinguished from secondary objectives. The primary objective for an electric components manufacturer seeking to enter the French market, for example, might be to establish the market potential for the products specified and to indicate appropriate market entry strategies. The secondary objectives tend to be more specific and comprehensive. For the components manufacturer they might include:

- defining market trends and competitive structure over the past five years
- profiling the existing main suppliers in terms of strengths and weaknesses (products, prices, distribution, branding, service, etc.)
- identifying the main buyers of electrical components
- identifying the main buying criteria when purchasing
- surveying potential trade and end users for willingness to switch supply source.

The list above is not exhaustive, but the main point is that objectives clearly drive the whole research process, and should provide the necessary foundations for whatever management decisions will have to be taken at the end. In all cases, the research objectives need to be clearly and concisely stated in writing to ensure that the research brief can be adequately prepared.

eg

BT Cellnet wanted to know how families used mobile phones to stay in touch. The objective was specified as finding out the nature and purpose of the day-to-day interaction taking place over the phone between family, friends and work colleagues. The overall purpose was to enable better forecasts to be made of how new mobile communication forms are likely to be received. The study ran for over a year and involved an extensive survey of daily communications behaviour, including a one-day diary completed by 1,500 people covering communications activity at home and at work. The survey revealed the magnitude of both inbound and outbound communication in the morning and the practices adopted to cope, including a steady switch from telephone to e-mail for communication at work (http://www.futurefoundation.com).

The skill at this stage lies in being sufficiently broad minded and flexible to avoid being misled by assumptions and prejudices that may not be valid, yet being focused enough to allow the project a strong sense of direction and a chance of being achieved within time and cost constraints. To be successful at this stage, the project team needs good communication and a solid understanding of the issues involved. This is where exploratory research may be useful, in eliminating some of the possibilities or filling some basic gaps in knowledge and understanding. This could involve some preliminary discussions with distributors, experts or customers. The information collected, including any secondary data, can then be used to prepare the research brief for the formal commissioning of work.

Planning the research

The planning stage falls into two main parts: first, the preparation of the research brief, and second, agreeing the research plan. This applies equally whether the research is conducted in-house or not.

Prepare the research brief

The research brief originates from the client. Its quality and precision can vary widely. In some cases, the client has a vague idea of what the problem is, but is not sure what the underlying causes or dynamics are. They thus rely heavily on researchers to specify the problem and then decide on the best research design, effectively asking them to undertake the first two stages of the research process. In many ways, the development of this kind of brief is rather like consultancy and may be part of that kind of overall process.

In other cases, however, the brief may be highly specified for researchers. The organisation has already undertaken the first two stages of the research process and thus has made a detailed analysis of the current situation, identified the problem that needs to be addressed and formulated its exact requirements. The brief can then be handed over complete to either a marketing research agency or the in-house department.

The main points of the research brief (adapted from Hague, 1992) will be:

- a definition of the problem, including its history
- a description of the product to be researched
- a description of the market to be researched
- specific research objectives
- time and financial budget
- reporting requirements.

This brief may be the subject of modification and negotiation during the meetings.

Agree the research plan

On the basis of the brief, a research plan needs to be agreed before the project begins. Not only is this important for cost and timing considerations, but it also ensures that the data generated will enable management decisions to be resolved without the need for further analysis. There is nothing worse than completing a major research project only to find that the results are at best of only partial use to managers!

The details of the research plan will vary according to the project. Many of the points that will be covered in the subsequent stages of the research process need to be outlined in the plan. This will help the clients to appreciate the specification they are contracting for, and indeed open any debate about the time and cost constraints early enough to negotiate changes. The research plan ideally should contain:

- background information for the research
- research objectives (based on decisions that need to be made and the criteria to be used)
- research methods (secondary and/or primary)
- type of analysis to be employed
- degree of client involvement
- data ownership
- details of subcontractors (if any)
- level and timing of ongoing reporting
- format of final report
- timing and cost of research.

An organisation with a major research project may well ask a number of research agencies to tender for the business. Each agency will obviously propose different research plans. These need to be evaluated alongside the organisation's more usual buying criteria. The final decision by the clients should be based on confidence that the chosen agency can best meet its information needs through the research plan proposed, but within any constraints imposed.

Data collection

The first requirement in preparing the research plan is to identify clearly what additional data are needed and then to establish how they are to be collected. This may involve collecting both primary and secondary data, or just primary data.

Secondary research

Sometimes also referred to as *desk research*, **secondary research** consists of data and information that already exist and can be accessed by an organisation. Thus, for example, it would include published government statistics and published market research reports. All of the data included in the tables in Chapter 2, for example, come from secondary sources. The advantage of secondary research is that it can be much cheaper and quicker to access, and may provide information that the organisation would not otherwise have the time, resources or inclination to gather. The organisation does, however, need to be careful that secondary data are current and that they are appropriate and applicable to the problem in hand. We will look in detail at secondary research below.

eg

Sports Marketing Surveys was commissioned to assess the feasibility of building a new golf course in Surrey. Most of the research was drawn from existing data such as the population profile within a 30-minute drive time, a listing of existing and new courses planned, and a profile of potential competitors such as their green fees, joining fees and the length of course and waiting lists. From the secondary research, a demand model, and market analysis, a sensible financial analysis could be made dealing with different scenarios. Recommendations were also made on the level of fees and services expected (http://www.sportsmarketingsurveys.com). The Early Learning Centre also uses secondary data when considering a new retail location. By using a GIS, birth data, father's occupation and mother's age, it can find appropriate locations near more affluent parents (Hayward, 2001).

Clearly, if secondary research is available that answers the question or solves the problem, then that is the quickest and most efficient way of gathering the necessary data. In many cases, however, secondary data may not be directly applicable, or may only give half the picture. This means that a market research project will often incorporate both primary and secondary research, each complementing the other.

Primary research

Sometimes also called *field* research, **primary research** is undertaken by, or commissioned by, an organisation for a specific purpose. The required information does not already exist in any available form and so the research has to be undertaken from scratch.

eg

MRSL concentrates on undertaking regular research in the travel industry for airports and related service providers. It runs specialist teams at most of the UK's main airports focusing on issues such as:

- travel industry related issues, e.g. satisfaction with travel agents, evaluation of potential new services, monitoring attitudes to companies/facilities/major events
- traveller related issues, e.g. goods or services needed during stay, clarity and usefulness of information provision, activity patterns during stay
- airport related issues, e.g. upmarket retailing, catering, new facility development
- airline related issues, e.g. advertising, passenger satisfaction
- service related issues, e.g. speed of connection, quality of handling.

Source: http://www.mrsl.co.uk.

The advantage of primary research is that it is exactly tailored to the problem in hand, but it can be expensive and time consuming to undertake. We will look in detail at methods of primary research at pp. 232 *et seq*.

Once the researchers have recognised that information is needed that is not currently available, they must decide from what source they can most effectively get that information. It is well worth checking secondary data sources first to see what has already been done. The pursuit of secondary data should be exhaustive, as secondary data are usually far more cost effective and quicker to collect than primary data. However, because secondary data were collected for another purpose they are not always in a form that is useful or appropriate, and thus they often have to be re-analysed to convert them into a form that can be used for a particular project. Even if secondary data are available, or can be converted, they may still not be sufficient to meet all the researchers' needs, and thus a primary research study may still have to be developed to fill the gaps or further explore the issues. If there are no appropriate secondary data commercially available, then a primary research study will have to be developed from scratch.

Secondary research

There is little point in commissioning expensive primary research if the data needed have already been obtained by other organisations, either on a commercial basis or as part of their normal information-gathering and dissemination activity. Secondary data can be either internal or external to the organisation. The former is considered to be part of the normal MIS (marketing information system), as outlined at pp. 221 *et seq*. External secondary data offer valuable information to researchers, once sourced. There is a wide variety of sources to consider, such as government departments and agencies, university libraries, higher education research organisations, other libraries, industry associations, trade and professional bodies, commercial information sold to industry or published in magazines or newspapers or online, to name but a few. Of course, as already mentioned, the major drawback with secondary data is that the information has been collected for purposes other than this particular research project, and may not be in a suitable or usable form.

Secondary data can nevertheless play a variety of roles in the research process. Its main role is probably in providing background information on industries and markets, in terms of trends, dynamics and structure. Some of this information may be useful in its own right in informing management decision-making, although it is more likely to provide pointers for further primary research. It can also provide useful information that may assist in sample selection for surveys by indicating the main competitor and customer groups.

Sources of secondary data

It would be impossible to list all potential sources of data, as the number of sources is vast and much will depend on the type of research project in question. A discussion with a business librarian will soon reveal how extensive such a list can be! However, a number of the more commonly used sources are listed in Table 6.2.

Using secondary data

Secondary data vary widely in terms of relevance and quality. Boyd *et al.* (1977) suggest four criteria for evaluating secondary data sources:

1 pertinency of the data;
2 who collects the data and why;
3 method of collecting data;
4 evidence of careful work.

Although secondary sources of data are widely used, as they tend to be low cost and usually easily obtainable once a source has been identified, the criteria above do suggest some potential problem areas. Often the data fail to get down to the micro level necessary to support management decisions. The focus is often at industry level rather than the sector or segment of particular interest, perhaps within a defined geographical area. Some data may have been collected to promote the well-being of the industry, rather than to provide wholly accurate figures, and sometimes they are not always accurate because of their source, their age or the way they were collected. However, for most surveys the sorting, sifting and analysis of secondary data are useful for purposes ranging from developing sample frames (*see* pp. 244 *et seq.*) to providing comprehensive insights into market size, structure and trends.

Table 6.2 Sources of secondary data

EU sources		
from Eurostat, the EU's statistical office	*European Economy*	Economic trends in member states
	Panorama of EC Industry	Trends in 100+ product groups
These and other publications are available	*CRONOS*	Economic and social trends in member countries
from Euro-info centres and European	*REGIO*	Demographic database
Documentation Centres	*COMEXT*	Intra-EU trade and extra-EU trade data
UK government sources		
from the Central Statistical Office	*Annual Abstract of Statistics*	
	Regional Trends	
Other European Government	*Social Trends*	
Statistics Offices:	*Monthly Digest of Statistics*	
INSEE (France)	*Census of Production*	Manufacturing industry statistics
Instituto National Estadistica (Spain)	*Census of Distribution*	Retail and wholesale statistics
Central Bureau voor de Statistiek (Netherlands)	*Business Monitor*	Product market information
	Digest of Tourist Statistics	Statistics on the tourism industry
	Guide to Official Statistics	A list of all available UK government publications
Chambers of Commerce		Local information and business contacts
Trade associations		Specialist reports and/or libraries for members
Commercial publications		
Published by Dun & Bradstreet	*Dun's Europa*	Information on top European enterprises
	Who Owns Whom	Information on which companies own other companies and brand names
	Key British Enterprises	Top British enterprises; similar publications available country by country
	Datastar	Online database of international companies
Published by Euromonitor	*Retail Monitor International*	Monthly report on retail trends and statistics
	European Directory of Retailers and Wholesalers	Information on 3,000 distribution companies across Europe
	European Marketing Data and Statistics	
	International Marketing Data and Statistics	
	World Marketing Data and Statistics	
	Retail Trade International	
	Consumer Europe	Statistics on 250 consumer products across Europe
	The Book of European Forecasts	Data on lifestyles and trends across Europe
	Market Research Europe	Monthly Journal
	Market Research International	Monthly Journal
Published by Mintel	*Mintel Market Intelligence*	Monthly market research reports on various consumer goods
	European Lifestyles	Data about consumers in EU countries
Published by NTC Publications	*European Marketing Pocket Book*	Data and statistics about European consumer markets
	Retail Pocket Book	Data and statistics on UK retail industry
	British Shopper	Data and statistics on UK consumer shopping habits
Published by Keynote Reports	*Market Sector Overviews*	Research reports on consumer goods
	Industry Trends and Forecasts	Research reports on industries
Published by Newman Books	*Directory of European Retailers*	4,000 retailers
Published by Graham and Trotmans	*The Major Companies of Europe*	8,000 companies
Published by Pricewaterhouse Coopers	*Guide to European Companies*	
Published by ELC International	*Europe's 15,000 Largest Companies*	
Published by CBB Research	*Directory of European Industrial and Trade Associations*	
Published by Manor House Press	*Store Buyer International*	9,000 retail buyers
From other publishers	*Kompass*	Information on who manufactures what; various European editions
	Yellow Pages	
Other useful organisations	*Economist Intelligence Unit*	
	Financial Times Management	
Online sources	*http://www.dis.strath.ac.uk*	Summary of sites with business information
	http://www.europages.com	European business directory
	http://www.eiv.com	Country reports and news
	http://www.dti.gov.uk	Overseas trade and market information

Online databases

Up until the 1990s most secondary data was print-based. Directories, both specialist and general, were essential tools for the market researcher. Although most directories are still in hard copy, most have been supplemented by CR-ROMs and by direct internet access via websites such as yell.com. They tend to appeal to different audiences. Hard copies are normally found in libraries while businesses have shifted over to CD-ROMs, and those wanting regular updates tend to use online versions (Whiteling, 2002). The key to the internet is offering an effective search engine so that the drudgery can be taken out of searching for and sourcing information. In internet versions, it is the relevance of the data to the task that is making them ever more attractive (Wilson, 2001). The more sophisticated the search engine, the more powerful the directory in making it easy to search for and access suitable or appropriate data.

Other market research databases are also going online. Euromonitor, through its Market Research Monitor, offers an online database available on subscription to cover 1,300 consumer market and retail briefings. It covers consumer market analysis from 52 countries, and market profiles from four major industrialised countries: the UK, France, Germany and the US (Marshall, 2000; http://www.euromonitor.com). It pays, therefore, to explore thoroughly what is currently available before going out and generating more information at a far higher cost.

Primary research

Once the decision to use primary research has been made, researchers have to define what data need to be collected and how. This section looks specifically at 'how'. First, there is an overview of primary research methods. For example, the data needed may be drawn from personal interviews, telephone or mail surveys, involving customers, non-customers, suppliers, retailers or any other group of interest. These are not, however, the only methods of data collection and thus the section also looks at observational and experimental research methods.

Whatever method is chosen as most appropriate to the client's information needs, researchers then have to think about defining a sample of individuals or organisations from the total population of interest (defined as a market segment or an industry, for instance). This topic is covered in some depth at pp. 244 *et seq.* Finally, of particular interest to those conducting surveys, pp. 247 *et seq.* look specifically at questionnaires.

Research methods

The three most commonly used methods for collecting primary data are interviews and surveys, observation and experiments.

Interviews and surveys

Interviews and surveys involve the collection of data directly from individuals. This may be by direct face-to-face personal interview, either individually or in a group, by telephone or by a mail questionnaire. Each of these techniques, considered in turn below, has its own set of advantages and disadvantages, which are summarised in Table 6.4.

e-marketing *in action*

Inside the mind of the website visitor

Online market research data is used to reveal profiles of customers and their opinion of the online experience. The website offers several novel methods for collecting primary data. These are compared in Table 6.3, based on Chaffey (2002).

Table 6.3 A comparison of different on-line metrics collection methods

Technique	*Strengths*	*Weaknesses*
1.Server-based log file analysis of site activity. The log file is added to every time a user requests a piece of information from the web server (a hit). It is analysed using a separate log file analyser which indicates the number of unique visitors, sessions, page viewed and their sequence (clickstream).	• Directly records customer behaviour on site plus where they were referred from • Low cost	• Not based around marketing outcomes such as leads, sales • Size, even summaries may be over 50 pages long • Doesn't directly record channel satisfaction • Undercounting and overcounting • Misleading unless interpreted carefully
2. Browser-based site activity data. Similar data is collected to the log file analysis method, except here the data is recorded on a separate (remote) server by the activation of program code each time a user opens a page.	• Greater accuracy than server-based analysis • Counts all users cf. panel approach	• Relatively expensive method • Similar weaknesses to server-based technique apart from accuracy • Limited demographic information
3. Panel activity and demographic data. Internet panel data is collected in a similar way to home-based TV panels. Panel members, who are selected to be representative of the demographics of the user population, agree to have software installed on their PC that sends data that is collected by the monitoring organisation. Similar data can also be collected by internet service providers (ISPs).	• Provides competitor comparisons • Gives demographic profiling • Avoid undercounting and overcounting	• Depends on extrapolation from limited sample that may not be representative
4. Outcome data, e.g. enquiries, customer service e-mails. These are recorded by other information systems such as the e-commerce server.	• Records marketing outcomes	• Difficulty of integrating data with other methods of data collection when collected manually or in other information systems
5. Online questionnaires. Customers are prompted randomly – every *n*th customer or after customer activity or by e-mail	• Can record customer satisfaction and profiles • Relatively cheap to create and analyse	• Difficulty of recruiting respondents who answer completely accurately • Sample bias – tend to be advocates or disgruntled customers who complete
6. Online focus groups. Comments are typed into a bulletin board or chat room in response to a moderator's questions and comments by other group members.	• Relatively cheap to create	• Difficult to moderate and coordinate • No visual cues as from offline focus groups
7. Mystery shoppers. Sample customers are recruited to evaluate a site by finding products, placing orders and making support enquiries by e-mail and phone and then recording their experience by filling in a web-based form.	• Structured tests give detailed feedback • Also tests integration with other channels such as e-mail and phone	• Relatively expensive • Sample must be representative

Source: Chaffey (2002).

Table 6.4 Comparative performance of interview and survey techniques

	Personal interviews	*Group interviews*	*Telephone survey*	*Mail survey*
Cost per response	High	Fairly high	Low	Very low
Speed of data collection	Fast	Fast	Very fast	Slow
Quantity of data collectable	Large	Large	Moderate	Moderate
Ability to reach dispersed population	Low	Low	High	High
Likely response rate	High	Very high	Fairly high	Low
Potential for interviewer bias	High	Very high	Fairly high	None
Ability to probe	High	High	Fairly high	None
Ability to use visual aids	High	High	None	Fairly high
Flexibility of questioning	High	Very high	Fairly high	None
Ability to ask complex questions	High	High	Fairly high	Low
Ability to get truth on sensitive questions	Fairly low	Fairly high	Fairly high	High
Respondent anonymity	Possible	Fairly possible	None	None
Likely respondent cooperation	Good	Very good	Good	Poor
Potential for respondent misunderstanding	Low	Low	Fairly low	High

Personal interviews. A personal interview is a face-to-face meeting between an interviewer and a respondent. It may take place in the home, the office, the street, a shopping mall, or at any prearranged venue. In one extreme case, a holiday company decided to interview respondents who were at leisure on the beach. One can imagine the varied responses!

There are three broad types of personal interview:

(a) the in-depth, largely **unstructured interview**, taking almost a conversational form;
(b) the **structured interview**, which allows the interviewer far less flexibility to explore responses further and results in a more programmed, almost superficial interview;
(c) a combination of these, the **semi-structured interview**, which is based around a programmed script, but the inclusion of some open-ended questions gives the interviewer scope to pursue certain issues more flexibly.

The unstructured interview can be used for collecting quantitative data, but is rather more useful for exploring attitudinal and motivational issues. Although a standard set of questions may be used as a guide, there is often considerable scope for the interviewer to explore some topics in more depth if additional unforeseen themes emerge in the interview. Generally, the questions are more of a checklist than a rigid format to follow. Given that an unstructured interview may provide one or two hours of intense exploration, it is important that the interviewer is properly briefed, can judge whether the respondent is starting to go off at a tangent or raising new issues of real relevance, and can adjust to the changing pattern of the interview. Often high-level interviewing skills are needed, along with a sound knowledge of the product-market concept being examined. These interviewing skills must also include the ability to record the interview accurately if a tape recorder or video recorder is not being used. Further problems that can emerge in the data analysis stage will be considered below.

marketing **in action**

Category management

Category management (CM) is a partnership between a supplier or a small number of suppliers and a retailer. A category is a group of brands that have something in common that makes them complement each other, compete directly or act as substitutes for each other. Examples of categories might include breakfast cereals, dairy products, bagged snacks or hot beverages. It is not just fmcg products that have adopted category management techniques. Borders (see pp. 15–16) re-organised to emphasise category management for specialised categories of books, children's products, multimedia, gifts, stationery and the café (Mutter, 2001). Each category has its own sales and marketing team and different merchandising activities. The objective of CM is to streamline the number of brands offered in the store in a category and to manage logistics, space allocation on the shelf, pricing and promotions for the category as a whole to enhance sales and profits for both the retailer and the supplier. CM has not, however, been without its critics (Basuroy *et al.*, 2001). It has been suggested that both consumers and brand owners lose out despite the fact that CM is claimed as a win-win situation as it eliminates the cost of inefficiency for all. They claimed that retailers win at the expense of the other two parties; the consumer pays higher prices and the supplier gets lower prices. Either way, the process is information hungry, as the whole business has to start to be managed by a good understanding of consumer impact and by facts rather than intuition in the supplier–retailer–consumer chain (Marsden, 2001).

Market research has a big role to play in developing and implementing CM effectively, but according to Reed (1998) it is a very different, more complex kind of research because it has to examine all the levels in the partnership. Before CM, retailers and major manufacturers tended to stick to their own areas and confine their research problem to those areas. Retailers thus mainly worried about how customers shop and manufacturers mainly worried about consumer behaviour connected with brands and brand image. Under CM, both sets of concerns come together and add a further dimension relating to how brands fit together and interact with each other within a category. Certainly, market research objectives that are to influence CM decisions have an impact on what kind of research is done. More research, for example, is likely to be carried out in the retail environment itself and researchers will be looking for representative samples of category users rather than representative households (Reed, 1998). For market research companies, all this means bigger, more complex research studies, and the need to ensure that objectives are well defined and that findings are clearly communicated.

The Harris Research Centre undertook research for brand manufacturer Van den Bergh Foods to discover in detail how shoppers in store buy 'yellow fats' as part of a category management exercise. To answer the client's questions, this complex research involved (Qureshi and Baker, 1998):

- *36 hours of shopper observation using remote control video equipment*. This allowed researchers to see how shoppers naturally behaved at the fixture: how long they spent, how they reacted to point of sale material, what products they picked up, what they selected, etc.
- *1,200 entrance/exit interviews*. Entrance interviews establish what intentions shoppers have when starting the shopping trip, including whether they intend to buy a specific brand of yellow fat or just any brand, or whether they have no intention of buying at all. Exit interviews of the same consumers then record what actually happened, whether they bought what they planned or switched brands, or impulse purchased something that they had not intended to buy on entering the store.
- *1,300 shopper interviews at the fixture*. This allows researchers to probe the reasons that shoppers think they are behaving as they are, as it is happening. Thus the researcher can ask about price awareness, influences on selection, reasons for final selection, etc.
- *200 in-store, in-depth interviews*. This helps researchers to check out shopping routes around the store and to gain deeper insights into how shoppers behave in the store as a whole.
- *72 accompanied shopping interviews*. A researcher visits the shopper at home before a shopping trip and investigates pre-shopping behaviour and decisions. Then the researcher accompanies the shopper around the store and gathers information about issues connected with the retailer (e.g. branding of the store, colour schemes, layout, queueing, parking, fixtures, service, etc.), but putting the emphasis on their relationship with the category and how the shopper buys that category.

The results of all these primary research methods give Van den Bergh a detailed and three-dimensional view of not only how its brands fit into the consumer's life at home, but also their role and impact on the shopping trip, how its brands and the competitors' brands affect the consumer's decisions and behaviour at the fixture, and how those brands fit into the retailer's store.

The main advantage of the unstructured interview is the depth that can be explored and the ability to push the respondent on meaning and accuracy. However, the time taken to complete an interview, and the cost of each interview, make large-scale surveys of this nature prohibitively expensive. In B2B markets, they are often used on a small-scale basis to fill gaps left by other approaches such as mail or telephone surveys.

The structured personal interview adopts a standard questionnaire in wording, layout and order that the interviewer must follow strictly. Little use is made of open-ended questions and the questionnaire is carefully designed for ease of recording information and progress through the interview. This may be especially important if the questionnaire is being administered in the street, thus interrupting a respondent's planned shopping trip. The use of a standardised questionnaire means that the responses from a large number of individuals can be handled with considerable ease, as there is no need for further interpretation and analysis. Furthermore, the interviewer retains control over the completion of the

Primary data collection is a familiar sight in the majority of High Streets and shopping centres. The interviewer relies on interviewees being amenable and giving up some time.

questionnaire. This approach is used by opinion pollsters and organisations seeking to quantify responses to predetermined questions. As less skilled interviewers are needed, the whole process can be completed more quickly than the unstructured interview, in terms of both field work and data processing. The limitations stem mainly from the need to design and pilot the questionnaire very carefully to ensure that it meets the specification expected of it. We look more closely at some of these questionnaire issues at pp. 247 *et seq*.

Group interviews and focus groups. Group interviews are used to produce qualitative data that are not capable of generalisation to the wider population, but do provide useful insights into underlying attitudes and behaviours relevant to the marketer. A group interview normally involves between six and eight respondents considered to be representative of the target group being examined. The role of the interviewer is to introduce topics, encourage and clarify responses and generally guide proceedings in a manner that is effective without being intrusive (Witthaus, 1999).

An increasingly popular type of group interview is the consumer workshop, taking over from the **focus group**. They are still face-to-face encounters, but involve the marketers and the public meeting under the control of trained researchers. These workshops can help decision makers to understand buyer attitudes and behaviour, as they are also part of the workshop process. This can shorten development timetables as a series of focus groups may have to be spread over several weeks and reports then have to be written. The consumer workshop allows immediate reflection and quick decisions to be made by the professional marketers who are part of the process. Birds Eye used the workshops to understand better why some consumers buy ready prepared potatoes and others buy fresh ones. The decision makers went away with a group of consumers, each one paid a fee, along with a brand development consultancy to discuss the humble potato. There are, of course, risks in the approach. Relying too much on direct responses from a small number of consumers can present an inaccurate picture and some see it as part of being customer focused rather than as a serious approach to market research due to its vulnerability to delivering 'what you want to hear' (Gofton, 2000).

In this kind of group situation, individuals can express their views either in response to directed questions or, preferably, in response to general discussion on the themes that have been introduced. Often, the interaction and dialogue between respondents are more revealing of opinions. So that participants will relax enough to open out like this, it is often helpful to select the group concerned to include people of a similar status. For example, a manufacturer of an innovative protective gum shield for sports persons organised different group interviews for sports players (users) and dentists (specifiers). Further subdivision could have been possible by type of sport, or to distinguish the casual player from the professional.

Group interviews are especially useful where budgets are limited or if the research topic is not yet fully understood. If secondary data have clearly indicated in quantitative terms that there is a gap in the market, group interviews may be useful in providing some initial insights into why that gap exists, whether customers are willing to see it filled and with what. This could then provide the basis for more detailed and structured investigation. There are of course dangers in generalisation, but if between four and six different discussion groups have been held, some patterns may begin to emerge. For the smaller business with limited funds, group interviews may provide a useful alternative to more costly field techniques.

Telephone interviews. Telephone interviews are primarily used in B2B markets in Europe as a means of reaching a large number of respondents relatively quickly and directly. Whereas there is variation across Europe in home telephone ownership, virtually every business is connected and so a ready-made network exists to reach targeted respondent groups. It is far more difficult to ignore a telephone call than a mail survey, although the amount and complexity of information that can be gathered are often limited. In the absence of any visual prompts and with a maximum attention span of probably no more than 10 minutes, the design of the questionnaire needs to be given great care and piloting is essential to ensure that the information required is obtainable.

The range of applications is wide but the telephone is especially useful for usage and purchase surveys where market size, trends and competitive share are to be assessed. Other applications include assessing advertising and promotional impact, customer satisfaction studies and establishing a response to a very specific phenomenon, such as the launch of a new export assistance scheme. Kwik Fit Exhausts telephones its recent customers to establish the degree of satisfaction with their recent purchase.

The interviewing process itself is highly demanding. Being able to generate interest and keep the attention of the respondent is critical, yet at the same time the information required must be collected in an effective and unbiased manner. The use of software packages can enable the interviewer to record the findings more effectively and formally and to steer through the questionnaire, using loops and routing through, depending on the nature of the response. With the demand for such surveys, a number of agencies specialise in telephone research techniques.

eg

Telder, based in Utrecht in the Netherlands, offers a full range of market research services including telephone research. Although not a large company, it nevertheless has 70 interviewers per shift using CATI. Quality control is maintained by careful training and by listening to and observing interviews via the computer system as they are happening. This enables helpful feedback to be given to the interviewer (http://www.telder.com). Hermelin Research in Scandinavia has over 230 computerised interviewing stations at its CATI centres in Norrköping, Halden, Pori and Copenhagen. To the company the design of the computer support system is crucial in reflecting the aims of the research and giving clear guidelines to the interviewers. In the CATI forms, recording sounds for music surveys is possible, for example. Careful design also helps the structuring of the data once captured to provide the client with the insights required. The interviewers are again central to Hermelin. They need a basic knowledge of computers and are selected for different kinds of surveys in different areas depending on their level of education, age and experience for the project (http://www.hermelin.swe).

Mail questionnaires. This popular form of research involves sending a questionnaire through the post to the respondent for self-completion and return to the researchers. Questionnaires can, of course, also be handed out at the point of sale, or included in product packaging, for buyers to fill in at their own convenience and then post back to the researchers. Hotels and airlines assess their service provision through this special kind of mail survey, and many electrical goods manufacturers use them to investigate purchasing decisions.

While the mail survey has the advantage of wide coverage, the lack of control over response poses a major problem. Researchers cannot control who responds and when and the level of non-response can create difficulties. Response rates can drop to less than 10 per cent in some surveys, although the more pertinent the research topic to the respondent, and the more 'user friendly' the questionnaire, the higher the response rate. The variable cost of a 1,000 questionnaire postal survey is between £600 and £800. That excludes the cost of buying a mailing list or investment in specialised mail handling equipment. It is not the cost of the mailing that counts, however, but the cost per response gained when response rates can vary between 5 per cent and 50 per cent (http://www.b2binternational.com). Offering a special incentive can also work (Brennan *et al.*, 1991). In a survey of Irish hotel and guest house owners, the offer of free tickets to a local entertainment facility proved an attractive incentive. Other larger-scale consumer surveys promise to enter all respondents into a draw for a substantial prize.

There are other obvious things that can be done to ensure higher response rates. A clear, spacious and user-friendly layout, gentle reminders and follow-up approaches to non-respondents and a supportive, persuasive covering letter all assist in increasing the responses. However, the non-respondents in themselves may pose a problem. It is important to assess whether the respondents, as a group, may be different from the late and non-respondents. Those who think more strongly about a topic, for example, are more likely to respond than those with a more marginal interest, perhaps representing casual or light users.

Mail surveys are especially prevalent in B2B markets, where target respondents can be more easily identified from contacts or mailing lists. The process of mailing can also be readily implemented and controlled using the organisation's normal administrative and mailing infrastructure already set up for response logging, address label generation, folding and franking, etc. One way of trying to improve response rates for B2B mail surveys is to warn or notify the desired respondent in advance that the survey is on its way. Haggett and Mitchell (1994), reviewing the literature on pre-notification, found that overall it increases response rates by around 6 per cent and on average reduces by one the number of days taken to respond. The telephone shows the best results, increasing responses by 16 per cent, while postcards only manage a 2.5 per cent improvement. There is, however, no evidence to suggest that the quality of the response is also improved.

There is no one best method to select from the group discussed above. Much will depend on the nature of the research brief, especially in the light of the resources available and the quality and quantity of information required for decision-making. A direct face-to-face interview, for example, allows for deeper exploration by the interviewer, an evaluation of body language and generally higher response rates, but it has the disadvantages of possible misinterpretation, distortion or bias in the interviewer's report, especially if the interviewer is inexperienced, poorly trained or poorly supervised. There is also a chance that the interviewee will give what they feel to be more acceptable responses, rather than their genuine belief about a particular question. All of these factors, including the type of questions asked and the structure of the interview, have the potential to influence and distort the results of the survey.

The other factor that has become of significant concern is the cost of the research survey. Face-to-face interviews, especially if conducted on an in-depth basis, tend to be the most costly and time consuming, thus making this form of survey less attractive. Other survey techniques, such as group interviews, telephone surveys and mail questionnaires, all provide alternative, cheaper ways of gathering data. Each of them, however, also has its own set of limitations. Ultimately, the decision on choice of technique has to put aside absolute cost considerations and think in terms of finding the most cost-effective way of collecting those vital data.

Internet research

The growth in the use of the internet is having a big impact on the market research industry. Business opportunities have been created by the significant increase in the number of dotcoms, clicks and mortar companies, ISPs, and online advertisers, all of them using market research to guide decision-making. Online research is, however, now also being increasingly used in preference to other research methods. Billings (2001) reported that electronic market research revenues in the US in 2000 were \$179 mn, up from \$23 mn in 1998. In Europe the market is worth \$31 mn (compared with \$3 mn in 1998), but that figure was expected to double within two years. The UK electronic market research sector is estimated to be worth in the region of \$8 mn, which is still only about 1 per cent of UK market research. By 2004, according to Poynter (2000a), around 50 per cent of market research will be conduced over the internet.

Internet usage rates will determine the speed and scope of internet market research. In the UK, the figure is 45 per cent compared to 60 per cent in the US, so obtaining a representative sample of the population is still highly problematic. It's fine if you want to research internet users, but for more targeted or representative samples it has severe limitations. A range of techniques is being employed, however, including online focus groups, questionnaires, pop-up surveys and extended e-mail groups. Table 6.5 highlights the advantages and disadvantages of online research, but as internet usage expands, technology improves and research industry experience and techniques grow, many of the disadvantages should be overcome. The big attractions are the significantly reduced data collection costs and the speed of setting up and implementing research activities. As with any research technique, however, it is important to ensure that what comes back is reliable and useful. There is always a risk that 'cheap' will mean devaluing the quality of the research.

The market research company, Future Foundation, has used the internet for qualitative research, including week long e-mail groups, online moderated groups with panels and offline groups (Cornish, 2001; http://www.futurefoundation.net). Others are making full use of the power of the internet to present media such as sounds, images and video clips or to use complex question routings that are incompatible with the printed page or interview (Bolden *et al.*, 2000).

Table 6.5 Advantages and disadvantages of internet research

	Type of online research	
	Quantitative	**Qualitative**
Benefits	Inexpensive compared with traditional research methodologies Fast turnaround Automated data collection Can show graphics, sometimes video No interviewer bias in data Data quality (logic checks and in-depth open-ended answers) Seamless international coordination	Slightly faster and cheaper than traditional focus groups Avoids dominance by 'loud' personalities More client control Can show concepts or websites Easier to recruit respondents Can be coordinated internationally and allows for mixed nationalities
Limitations	Respondent 'universe' Sampling issues: narrow target audience; difficult to identify; understanding the sample Often self-completion based, therefore potentially self-selecting Technical problems	Lose non-verbal elements of traditional focus groups Less useful for emotive issues Online moderation requires new skills Some respondents can be hampered by slow typing speeds Technical problems Sampling issues: narrow target audience can be tricky to identify; can be difficult to understand the sample

Source: Alex Johnston, Technology and Communications Director for New Media Research International, as reported by Gray (2000b).

The law on data collection over the internet is tightening. The UK's Data Protection Act prohibits the collection of data without consent, or for purposes not disclosed at the time. This means that the consumer must be made aware of any recording of websites browsed or online purchases in advance, allowing them to opt out if they want (Anstead, 2000). This also applies to online research. In order to undertake a survey prior permission has to be obtained from respondents before a potentially unwanted e-mail is sent. It is not enough that a customer's name is on a list: it is essential that people agree in advance to their e-mail addresses being used for that purpose. Obtaining e-mail addresses and ensuring that the consumer is happy to be sent information is one thing, but persuading people to e-mail back to verify their identity and signify their willingness to participate – a process known as closed-loop verification – is another (Billings, 2001). This is bad news from the researcher's point of view, because if a significant proportion of potential respondents opts out, it will reduce the representativeness of online research.

Some organisations have, however, used e-mail focus groups successfully (Adriaenssens, 1999). In a study assessing the potential for a new financial services brand, selected respondents from a consumer panel who had agreed to the release of their e-mail addresses were formed into nationwide virtual focus groups. The mechanism adopted was the moderated e-mail group (MEG) in which a facilitator e-mails questions to respondents who then return their responses within an agreed time frame. The process is repeated as if in a one-to-one interview. After each phase of research, a summary document is produced by the moderator which is then sent to each respondent for comment. This enables the respondents to see what other respondents are thinking which could change the direction of their own thoughts, just like a 'real' focus group. This can be an ongoing, interactive process as the moderator can collate responses as the survey unfolds and can quickly produce interim documents for perusal by the respondent group.

Mobile phone research is also becoming more widely used in specific projects. It is an instant medium and therefore has potential use in behavioural and attitudinal studies (Billings, 2001). WAP interviews can take place immediately after an event or experience if spontaneous feedback is wanted, such as after a TV show or sports event. Until WAP technology has become more widely accepted, however, its use as a reliable research tool is limited.

The internet will increasingly become a useful way of researching customer behaviour, especially for online purchasing. It is also emerging as a complementary tool for collecting consumer research data alongside traditional methods. Although it may not replace these methods, its advantages of higher response rates, spontaneity, multimedia application and personalisation will help to improve the targeting of those harder-to-find groups. Some pundits go further. Poynter (2000b) proposed that by 2005:

- Around 80 per cent of research in the EU will be via people/lists who have 'opted in' to a database.
- 95 per cent of this research will be conducted via the internet.
- More people will be accessing the internet via WAP technology than via PCs.
- Analogue television will be in the process of being phased out while digital television with internet access will be growing fast.
- More people will be accessing the internet via game stations.
- Sales of PCs for the home will start to fall.
- Several aspects of research will have all but disappeared including:
  - Interviewers
  - Customer satisfaction research
  - Store audit research.

In short, watch this space!

Observational research

This method involves, as its name implies, the observation by trained observers of particular individuals or groups, whether they are staff, consumers, potential consumers, members of the general public, children or whoever. It is used not just by market researchers, but by advertising agencies, direct marketing agencies, design consultancies and even companies with their own research deprtments. The intention is to understand some aspect of their behaviour that will provide an insight into the problem that has been identified by the marketing research plan. For example, trials are often conducted with new products in which consumers are asked to use a particular product and are observed while they do so, thus giving information about design, utility, durability and other aspects, such as ease of use by different age groups, and whether people naturally use it in the intended way. This provides an opportunity to test the product and observe how it is used first hand.

eg

The Nationwide Building Society has built a 'Usability Centre' in Swindon so that it can invite consumers to read its literature and test its cash machines in a simulated atmosphere. The centre has a fully working branch and a lounge with a television and sofa to help recreate the customer's experience of the places in which they come into contact with information and equipment. This helps Nationwide to understand better the actual interaction between consumers and the Society's branches and messages (Moeng, 2001). Tennents Caledonian Breweries preferred to observe the real thing in an attempt to understand how consumers behave in a bar towards premium draught beer. Researchers observed consumer behaviour in real bars, then introduced themselves and asked consumers why they had behaved that way (Miles, 2000).

By simulating the customer's experiences of their services in their usability centre, Nationwide can better understand the interaction between customers and staff and improve them where necessary.

Source: Nationwide Building Society.

Another form of observational research that deliberately seeks feedback on employee performance is *mystery shopping*. This allows a researcher to go through the same experience as a normal customer, whether in a store, restaurant, plane or showroom. As far as the employees are concerned, they are just dealing with another customer and they are not aware that they are being closely observed. The 'shopper' is trained to ask certain questions and to measure performance on such things as service time, customer handling and question answering. The more objective the measures, the more valuable they are to marketing managers in ensuring that certain benchmark standards are being achieved. Mystery shopping is widely used by the larger retailers and service organisations. When first introduced it was designed to identify sloppy service staff so that they could be removed when the report was received by management. Now, it is part of a more comprehensive assessment of the service and shopping experience that real consumers enjoy or endure. It supports staff training and helps the organisation to understand the customer–service provider interface (Bromage, 2000).

The potential problems that can be experienced with interviews are also likely with observation where human observers are used. That is, the training and supervision of observers are of great importance and, since it is more subjective, the likelihood of misinterpretation is higher. On the other hand, mechanical observation tools may be used to

marketing *in action*

In bed with the consumer?

Culture Lab, a behavioural research company, has taken the art of observational research to its limits with Project Keyhole, in which researchers live with a family for a number of days (but not the nights!) and record everything. The big advantage is that the researcher can see not only what is bought, but also how it is used in the home environment. The researcher can also observe the quirkier aspects of behaviour, for example how it changes according to time of day or mood, etc. Culture Lab's clients get a customised piece of very detailed qualitative research; each client is allocated its own group of households and can research whatever it wants within them.

The main difference between this technique and more traditional forms of observational research is the way the research gets so close to the consumer. Because researchers stay with consumers for several days in their own homes, the presence of the researchers is eventually ignored and the behaviour observed is natural as well as taking place in the right context. An important advantage of the approach is that it picks up inconsistencies between what people say they do and what they actually do, for so long a problem of conventional market research. Observed habits appeared to change due to random factors such as mood, time of day and even the weather. It is also true to say, however, that this can be expensive and time-consuming research. It does produce a mass of data that can be very difficult to interpret, especially as those data have to be interpreted to suit the needs of a single client. There is a risk that researchers get involved in too much detailed observation that ends up giving the client no more than a less intensive exercise would have done. It is also important to remember that all this detailed information is related to a very limited number of households and individuals. The original Culture Lab experiment covered just 12 households. Can the conclusions be generalised over an entire mass-market customer base?

Some care has to be taken when using such intrusive methods, even with the consent of the individuals or families. It can easily go wrong as the founder of Culture Lab reported: on one assignment, the man went out and his partner went upstairs to do her homework (she was a student) under the duvet, duly followed by the male researcher. Now there's a situation that could have been misinterpreted! Researchers now tend to work in pairs, and women shadow women. As clearer sets of guidelines emerge to protect all parties, observational research is likely to continue to grow as a technique. The Data Protection Act covers all film, video and studio recordings and the Market Research Society Code of Conduct states, among other things, that nobody should be adversely affected or embarrassed through participation. Recordings can only be used for research purposes and all privacy must be respected when requested.

Sources: Curtis (1998); Miles (2000).

overcome bias problems, such as supermarket scanners monitoring the purchases of particular consumers or groups of consumers, and the Nielsen people meters, used to monitor the viewing and listening habits of television watchers and radio listeners.

Other devices can be used to observe or monitor closely the physiological responses of individuals, such as their pupil dilation (using a tachistoscope) when watching advertisements, to indicate degree of interest. A galvanometer, which measures minute changes in perspiration, can also help to gauge a subject's interest in advertisements.

eg

Specialised software is now available to enable real-time recording of consumer behaviour in a retail environment. A system developed by DMP DDB, Noldus and Tracksys created an improved method to introduce speed and rigour into the observational process. First, a store map is scanned into the PC and the relevant aisles, checkouts and other zones of interest are specified by the researcher. This map is then displayed during data collection on a mini-notebook PC with a touch screen. When an 'interesting' consumer enters the store, the researcher must first request permission to observe him/her as they are followed by camera through the store using the screen. Behavioral variables can also be recorded according to pre-selected categories, for example what products the consumer is looking at, picking up, placing in their basket, or returning to the shelf. Data files collected during the day can be e-mailed to a central database where detailed analyses of the data can be carried out. This includes the time spent in different areas of the store, the frequency of movement between the various zones of interest, and the number of times shoppers engaged in different behaviours, e.g. browsing, picking products up, talking to co-shoppers, asking for assistance, etc. This data can be calculated per individual or across different groups of customers according to age, sex or other independent variables. By reducing the long and tedious hours of observing the observers' videos, conclusions can be drawn more quickly and effectively (http://www.noldus.com).

In some ways, observation is a more reliable predictor of behaviour than verbal assertions or intentions. Where interaction is not needed with the respondent, or where the respondent may be unable to recall the minutiae of their own behaviour, direct observation may be a valuable additional tool in the researcher's armoury. It is particularly informative when people are not aware that they are being observed and are thus acting totally naturally, rather than changing their behaviour or framing responses to suit what they think researchers want to see or hear. Observation can be relevant in both consumer and industrial markets. In the latter, observation at exhibitions and shows can provide useful insights into behaviour. Also, the actual tracking of buyer decisions and experiences as they work through the system (i.e. order processing, packaging, delivery, invoicing, after-sales service, etc.) can reveal much about operating procedures for usage, buying and logistics in a way that would be difficult to discover and fully understand through post-purchase questioning.

Experimentation

The third method through which primary data can be collected is by conducting an experiment. This may involve the use of a laboratory (or other artificial environment), or the experiment may be set in its real-world situation, for example test marketing a product (more on that in Chapter 9). In the experimental situation, researchers manipulate the independent variable(s), for example price, promotions or product position on a store shelf, and monitor the impact on the dependent variable, for example sales, to try to determine if any change in the dependent variable occurs. The important aspect of an experiment is to hold most of the independent variables constant (as well as other potentially confounding factors) while manipulating one independent variable and monitoring its impact on the dependent variable. This is usually possible in a laboratory, where control of the environment is within the power of researchers, but far less possible in a real-world situation where a myriad of external complications can occur that can confuse the results.

eg

Love it or hate it, the *Pop Idol 2002* competition won by Will Young, who beat 9,999 other contestants to win a recording contract was a great success for Thames Television. It was also an excellent piece of market research, as elimination of finalists one by one over ten weeks according to votes cast in a viewers' telephone poll identified just which singers were most likely to capture the public imagination and thus could be the greatest success for the show's financial backers from the music industry. Effectively, the record company not only persuaded the public to participate willingly in the market research on a grand scale (over 8.5 million votes were cast in the final show of the series) but also to pay for the privilege, with each call costing 10p. It was weekly test marketing and the voting arrangements gave virtually instant feedback. In an industry dominated by almost built-in obsolescence and with few long-term performers, experimenting under real-time conditions with different music styles provided valuable insights for the record label BMG on the type of tracks to record and likely attractiveness of different performers in the public's perception (Woods, 2002).

For example, a manufacturer may want to find out whether new packaging will increase sales of an existing product, before going to the expense of changing over to the new packaging. The manufacturer could conduct an experiment in a laboratory, perhaps by setting up a mock supermarket aisle, inviting consumers in and then observing whether their eyes were drawn to the new packaging, whether they picked it up, how long they looked at it and whether they eventually chose it in preference to the competition. The problem with this, however, is that it is still a very artificial situation, with no guarantees that it can replicate what would have happened in real life. Alternatively, therefore, the manufacturer could set up a field experiment, trialling the new packaging in real stores in one or more geographic regions and/or specific market segments and then monitoring the results.

Not all experimental research designs need to be highly structured, formal or set up for statistical validation purposes. For example, side-by-side experiments where shop A offers a different range or mix from shop B, which in all other respects is identical to shop A, can still reveal interesting insights into marketing problems, even though the rigour of more formal experimental designs is not present.

Sampling

Particularly in mass consumer markets, time and cost constraints mean that it is impractical to include every single target customer in whatever data gathering method has been chosen. It is not necessary even to begin to try to do this, because a carefully chosen representative sample of the whole population (usually a target market) will be enough to give the researchers confidence that they are getting a true picture that can be generalised. In most cases, researchers are able to draw conclusions about the whole population (i.e. the group or target market) based on the study of a sample. The skill, therefore, lies in making sure that the selected sample is indeed representative. If it is not, then the results of the research may not give an accurate picture of the relevant population and decisions made are likely to be wrong. While it is true that a sample is never absolutely identical to the population that it is supposed to represent, if selected correctly it will tend to have the same characteristics as that population and conclusions drawn about the sample should reflect those of the population. In other words, the reliability of the results from the sample is high and decisions can be based on those results with confidence.

Figure 6.3, based on Tull and Hawkins (1990), shows the main stages in the **sampling process**. Each will be considered briefly in turn:

Population definition

The population to be surveyed will derive from the overall research objectives. Often this will be based on a target market or segment, but even then further definition based on markets, products or behaviours is unlikely to be necessary to create a tightly defined population. In consumer markets, the population may be defined by any of the variables considered in Chapter 5, provided that researchers can use them operationally. In B2B markets the population is usually defined in terms of organisational characteristics and industries.

Sampling frame

The sampling frame is the means of access to the population to be surveyed. It is basically a list from which individual names can be drawn. Registers of electors or lists of organisations compiled from directories such as *Kompass* and *Dun and Bradstreet* are examples of possible sampling frames. Internal customer records may also provide a sampling frame, although researchers need to be very sure that such records give a complete picture, and that there is no doubt that this is the required population for the study, rather than just a cheap, quick and easy way of generating an extensive list of names.

Figure 6.3 Stages in the sampling process

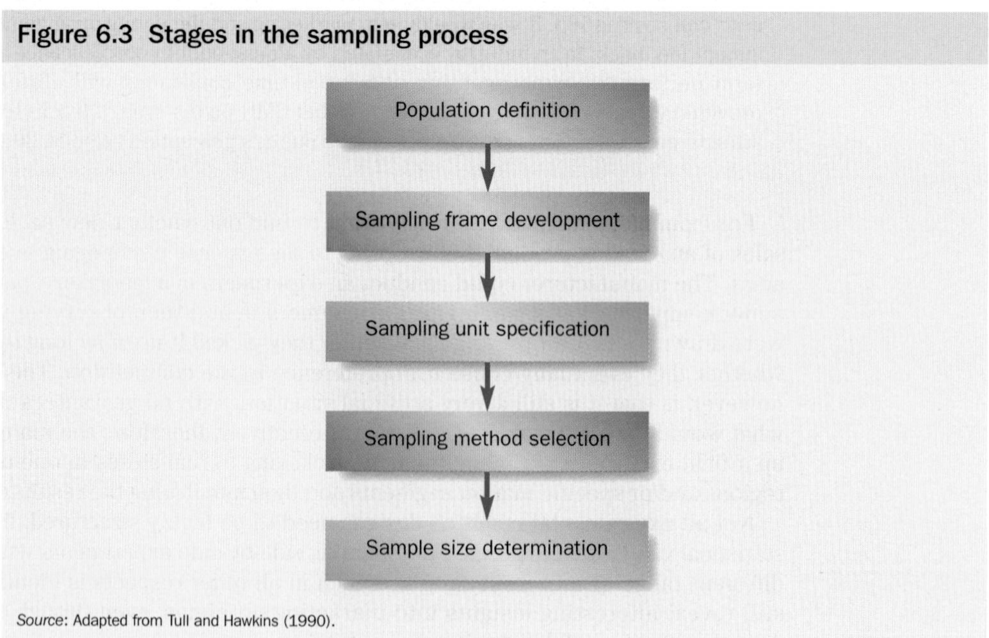

Source: Adapted from Tull and Hawkins (1990).

Sampling unit

The sampling unit is the actual individual from whom researchers want a response. In consumer markets, the sampling unit is usually the name attached to the address in the sampling frame. In B2B markets, however, this stage can be complex because, as we saw in Chapter 4, organisations have a number of individuals concerned with decision-making. So if an organisation wanted to survey builders' merchants across Germany, a two-stage process might have to be used. First, the sample unit might be represented by the individual firm selected, and then a secondary stage might focus the individual within that organisation who should be the subject of attention (the sampling element). It is very important to identify the right individual, as the responses of the purchasing manager in this case may be different from those of the managing director.

Sampling method selection

The next step in the process is to select the sample method, which is the means by which individual sample units and elements are selected from the larger sampling frame. The main and early decision is whether to use probability or non-probability sampling methods.

Probability sampling. Random, or *probability sampling*, where each member of the population has an equal or known chance of being selected for the sample, offers specified levels of confidence about the limits of accuracy of the results. So if a retailer wanted to do a survey to establish satisfaction levels with checkout services, it might decide to interview every thirtieth customer coming through the checkouts during research sessions held at different times of the week. At the end of the process, the retailer might be able to conclude that the findings were correct to the 95 per cent level of confidence – in other words there was only a one in 20 chance that the sample was biased or unrepresentative.

Stratified sampling is an important method of probability sampling, which involves the division of the sampling frame into defined strata or groups that are mutually exclusive. Random probability samples are then drawn independently from each group. This method is widely used in B2B markets, as they naturally divide into discrete layers or bands, reflecting for example company size, geographic location, market shares or purchase volumes. Researchers could decide, therefore, to take a 100 per cent sample (census) of all the larger firms (defined perhaps by turnover or number of employees) and then use random sampling with the rest. By effectively restructuring the sample frame in a manner best suited to the project, greater confidence can be enjoyed that the sample closely reflects the population in question.

An alternative form of stratified sampling is *area sampling*. Returning to our survey of German builders' merchants, the first stage would be to divide Germany into regions and then randomly select a small number of those regions as the basis for the sample. Within each chosen region, researchers randomly select the organisations for the sample. They may end up studying merchants in the Leipzig, Karlsruhe and Hannover areas, rather than a sample from across Germany that would involve considerable time and expense to follow up.

With a random sampling method, it is important for researchers to ensure that the sampling frame used does enable each member to have an equal chance of being selected. Furthermore, actually obtaining responses from the selected sample can be quite difficult. What if the thirtieth customer through the checkout doesn't want to stop? What if there's nobody at home when the interviewer calls round or phones? What if the sampling frame is out of date and the selected consumer has moved house or died? Any of these circumstances violates the ideal of the random sample.

Non-random sampling. *Non-random samples* are much easier to identify than random samples because they are not based on the same strict selection requirements and allow researchers a little more flexibility. The results from these samples are not representative of the population being studied and may lack the statistical rigour generated by random sampling, but they are still often of considerable use to researchers. Two main non-random sampling methods may be used:

1 *Judgemental sampling*. This method is widely used in B2B market research. Sample units are selected deliberately by researchers, because they are felt to represent better sources of the required information. Given the concentrated nature of many industries, if a contracting company for pipework cleaning wanted to enter a new geographical market, for

example, it would probably make sense to survey the larger users if that was the target segment of interest, rather than draw at random from all users, large and small. Of course, no inference could be drawn about the wider population from such a sample method.

2 *Quota sampling*. Quota samples are formed when researchers decide that a certain proportion of the total sample should be made up of respondents conforming to certain characteristics. It may be decided, for example, that for a particular study, the sample should consist of 400 non-working women aged between 25 and 35, 250 full-time working and 350 part-time working women in the same age group. This breakdown may reflect the actual structure of the market under consideration. Each interviewer is then told how many completed questionnaires to bring back within each quota category. The choice of respondents is not random, since the interviewer is actively looking for people who fulfil the quota definitions and, once the quota is full, will reject any further respondents in that category. The criteria for defining quotas often use geographic or demographic factors, for example age bands, employment, the structure of the family unit, location, car owners, etc., whatever is felt to reflect the structure of the market.

The advantage of quota sampling is that it is quicker and cheaper to do than a full random sample would be, as no sample frame has to be devised and researchers do not have to worry whether the sampling frame is up to date or not. Furthermore, interviewers are not committed to following up specific respondents. Under a quota sample, if a particular respondent does not want to cooperate, then that's fine – the interviewer will look for another one.

Sample size

A final yet very important consideration in the sampling process is sample size. While it may be true that the larger the sample, the greater the confidence that it truly represents the population of interest, there is no point in spending more time and money pursuing any bigger sample than you have to. With random sampling based on statistical analysis, researchers can have confidence within prescribed limits that the sample elements are representative of the population being studied. It is not so much the size of the sample selected that matters, as the tolerated risk of sampling error that researchers are prepared to accept and the cost that is incurred in adding to the number of sampling elements.

eg

Golf research programmes have been conducted in both Europe and Australia in recent years by the specialist agency, Sports Marketing Surveys. During the 2001 Australian survey, 4,000 golfers were interviewed face to face, split by state and type of golf course to give a representative cross-section of the golfing population. The data included the demographics of the golfer:

86 per cent male
81 per cent 35 years or older
11 per cent single figure handicap
75 per cent 10–36 handicap
14 per cent no handicap
95 per cent had played for 2 years of more.

To what extent and why do you think that this is a representative sample, and could the findings be generalised to a European context (http://www.sportsmarketingsurveys.com)?

As one would expect, the higher the levels of confidence required, the greater the size of the sample needed. In Europe, surveys of consumer buying habits are often around 2,000 units, which would typically yield a 95 per cent confidence level that the sample reflects the characteristics of the population. In B2B markets, sample sizes of between 300 and 1,000 can be used to produce high levels of confidence. This would be especially true when suppliers operate within limited geographical areas (such as plumbers, or van hire firms), the value of sales is usually small (motor factors), and the buying organisations are also small (http://www.b2b international.com). With stratified samples, provided that the strata have been carefully defined according to relevant characteristics, even smaller sample sizes may be permissible, especially if they are supported by a full census of some of the more critical groups, such as the leading buying organisations dominating purchases in a market. Sometimes, two-stage research can be useful to break down a market. The first stage would involve sampling smaller establishments, perhaps by telephone interview, and then the second stage would use a judgement sample to examine the known larger purchasers in more detail.

Questionnaire design

The questionnaire is a commonly used research instrument for gathering and recording information from interviews, whether face-to-face, mail or telephone surveys, as described earlier. Researchers soon learn that the best planned surveys soon fall apart if the questionnaire is poorly designed and fails to gather the data originally anticipated. Even the most professional researchers can still make mistakes that only come to light when the responses come back, i.e. when it is too late. To minimise the risk of disappointment, however, there are several dimensions to consider in questionnaire design.

Objectives

The aim of a questionnaire is closely linked with the overall purpose of the research. It is tailormade to meet the information requirements of the study and therefore lies at the heart of the research process. If the questionnaire is to fulfil its role properly as a means of data collection, then there are several areas that need to be analysed, as outlined in Table 6.6.

Some thought also needs to be given to ensuring that the questionnaire will retain the interest of the respondent, so that full completion takes place. It is easy with self-administered questionnaires for the respondent to give up if the questionnaire becomes tedious,

Table 6.6 The objectives of a questionnaire

Objective	*Suggestions*
To suit the nature of the target population	Pitch the questions in a way they can understand; ask questions they can be expected to be able to answer given their knowledge and experience.
To suit the research methods	For example, a telephone survey cannot use the kind of visual aids that a face-to-face interview can; a postal survey is less likely to get responses if it is lengthy or if it is probing feelings/attitudes.
To suit the research objectives	It must be designed appropriately to gather the right information for answering the research questions – no more, no less.
To collect the right kind of data	The quality and completeness of responses are important for a successful survey. There must also be the right depth of data, whether it is factual or probing attitudes, beliefs, opinions, motivations or feelings.
To aid data analysis	Ensure that it is as easy as possible to take the raw data from the questionnaires and input them accurately into any analytical framework/software package being used.
To minimise error and bias	Ensure that the questionnaire is 'tight' enough to allow it to be administered by any interviewer, to any respondent, at any time, in any location with consistency. Also ensure that questions cannot be misinterpreted or misunderstood.
To encourage accurate and full responses	Avoid leading or judgemental questions; ensure clarity in the way questions are asked; ensure that respondents feel at ease rather than threatened or intimidated by the questions.

seems to be poorly explained, or is too long or complex. When an interviewer is involved, the motivation can still be lost, despite the best efforts of the interviewer, although it takes more courage for a respondent to terminate a face-to-face interview in mid flow than simply to put a pen down.

It is thus important to make sure that the questionnaire takes as little time as possible to complete. Research in the US found that 20 per cent of consumers thought that questionnaires in general, including 30-minute telephone surveys, were too long (McDaniel *et al.*, 1985). According to Gander (1998), the 30-minute survey is still common, making the interviewer's job much more difficult.

Types of questions

There are two main types of question that can be asked in a questionnaire: **open-ended questions** and **closed questions**. The category of open-ended questions has many significant style variations within it, but they all allow considerable scope for the respondent to express views on the selected theme (and in some cases, on other themes!). Closed questions force the respondent to choose one or more responses from a number of possible replies provided in the questionnaire.

eg

As part of an exercise to reassess both new product development and brand positioning Scottish Courage, owned of brands such as John Smith's and Foster's, decided to use questionnaire research. It used nine 'Killer Questions' to address the research problem. These included 'What are our market essentials?', 'What is our core usage occasion?' and 'What are the key visual and verbal symbols for this brand?'. Few respondents would be equipped to answer these questions directly, so they were broken down into more easily answered questions that could be used in a face-to-face survey of 600 beer drinkers in their homes using a 45-minute questionnaire (Shields, 2001).

I've filled in your survey; now you fill my glass!

Source: Whitbread.

Open-ended questions. Questions such as 'In the buying of garden furniture, what factors do you find important?' or 'What do you think of the trend towards out-of-town shopping centres?' are open ended because they do not give a range of potential answers for the respondent to choose from. In both cases, interviewers could be faced with as many different answers as there are respondents. Using such questions can, therefore, be rewarding, because of the rich insights given in a relatively unrestrained manner. The difficulties, however, emerge in recording and analysing the responses, given their potential length and wide variations. Nevertheless, it has been argued that using open-ended questions can help to build the goodwill of the respondent through allowing an unrestricted response (Chisnall, 1986).

Closed questions. Closed questions fall into two broad groups, dichotomous and multiple-choice questions. *Dichotomous questions* allow only two choices, such as 'yes or no' or 'good or bad'. These questions are easy to ask and easy to answer.

With careful pre-coding, it is also relatively easy to analyse responses and to use them for cross-tabulation with another variable, for example to find out whether those who say that they do use a product pay more attention to product-specific advertising than those who say that they do not use it. The problem with dichotomous questions is that it can take very many questions to obtain a relatively small amount of information. This can be critical where the length of the questionnaire needs to be constrained.

Multiple-choice questions are a more sophisticated form of closed question, because they can present a list of possible answers for the respondent to choose from. This could be, for example, a list of alternative factors that might influence a purchasing decision (price, quality, availability, etc.), or it could reflect alternative levels of strength of feeling, degree of importance or other shades of variation in response to the variable under consideration. Figure 6.4 gives examples of different types of multiple-choice question.

These questions need to be designed carefully, to incorporate and group as wide a range of answers as possible, since restraining the amount of choice available creates a potential source of bias. The alternative responses need to reflect the likely range, without overlap or duplication, since this too may create bias. By offering an 'other, please specify' category, these questions provide some opportunity to collect responses that were not originally conceived (but that should have been identified in the pilot stage) or responses that do not fit neatly into the imposed structure. However, the advantage of multiple-choice questions is that again they are relatively straightforward to analyse, if pre-coding has been used.

Multiple choices can also be used to overcome some respondent sensitivities. If asked 'How old are you?' or 'What do you earn?' as open questions, many people may refuse to answer because the questions are too specific and personal. Phrasing the question as 'To which of these age groups do you belong, 17 or under, 18–24, 25–34, 35–44, 45 or over?' allows respondents to feel that they have not given quite so much away. It is unlikely in any case that knowing a respondent's exact age would be of any greater use to researchers. The bands need to be defined to reflect the likely scope of responses from the target respondents, and to be easy for them to relate to. Professionals, for example, will be more likely to relate to bands based on annual salary than manual workers, who are more likely to know what their weekly wage is. The scope of responses will also vary between these two groups. The bottom band in a survey aimed at ABC1 socioeconomic groups may be 'less than £15,000', whereas the equivalent of this figure in weekly wage terms may provide the top band for a C2DE-orientated survey.

Figure 6.4 Examples of multiple-choice questions

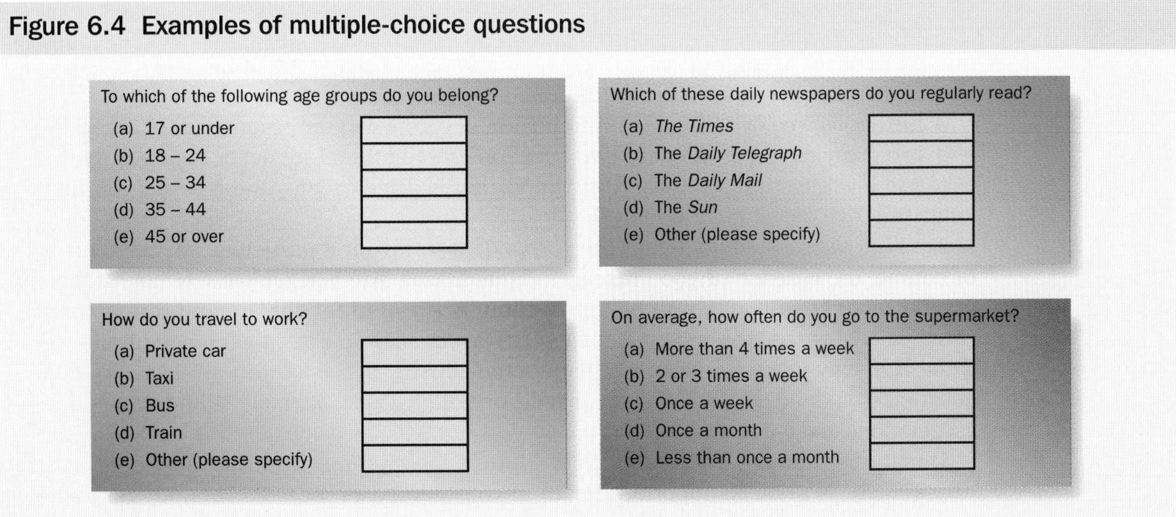

Rating scales are a form of multiple-choice question, widely used in attitude measurement, motivational research and in situations where a number of complex, interacting factors are likely to influence a situation. There are a number of scaling methods, including:

1 *Likert summated ratings.* A large number of statements, relevant to the research study, are built up from preliminary research and piloting. These statements are then given to respondents who are asked to respond on a five- or seven-point scale, for example 'strongly agree', 'agree', 'neither agree nor disagree', 'disagree' and 'strongly disagree'. The responses are scored from 5 (strongly agree) down to 1 (strongly disagree). The average score across all respondents can then be used to establish the general strength of attitude towards the variable under consideration. An examination of the pattern of individual responses may also reveal issues of interest to the marketer.

   Likert scales are very popular with researchers because of their relative ease of implementation. The statements must, however, be carefully derived and relevant to the phenomena being studied. The scale itself must accurately reflect the range of respondents' views.

2 *Semantic differential scales.* These scales were developed to measure differences in the meaning of words or concepts. This method involves a bipolar five- or seven-point rating scale, with each extreme defined by carefully selected adjectives representing opposite extremes of feeling. A study of retail store atmosphere might offer a series of scales including 'warm – cold', 'friendly – unfriendly', or 'fashionable – unfashionable', for example. Once the scales have been defined, the product (or whatever) is rated on each of them to reveal a profile of the respondent's opinion. Such scales can also be used for measuring corporate image or advertising image and for comparing different brands. In the latter case, if two products are plotted at the same time on the same scales, significant differences may emerge, and help the marketer to understand better the relative positioning of products in consumers' minds.

Examples of both types of rating scale can be found in Figure 6.5.

The wording of questions. The success or failure of a questionnaire lies as much in the detail as in the grand scheme and design. This includes the detailed wording of questions so that the respondent fully understands what is required and accurate responses are encouraged. The next few paragraphs raise a number of pertinent issues.

It is always important to ensure that the *meaning of words and phrases* is fully understood by the respondent. Particular effort should be made to avoid the use of jargon and technical language that may be unfamiliar to the respondent. Additional complications arise from surveys that are intended for pan-European implementation, as commonly used phrases may not translate well into different cultures.

Ambiguity can lead to misunderstandings and thus poor or inaccurate responses. A question such as 'Do you buy this product frequently, sometimes, seldom or never?' seems to be clear and unambiguous, but think about it for a minute. What does 'frequently' mean? To one respondent it might mean weekly, to another it might mean monthly. Researchers should therefore be as specific as possible.

A further source of ambiguity or confusion occurs when the respondent is asked to cope with too many concepts at once. Two questions should therefore never be *piggy backed*, i.e. asked in one question, such as: 'How important is price to you, and how do you think we could improve on value for money?'

Leading questions may tempt the respondent to favour a particular answer. This is not, of course, the essence of good research. Thus asking 'Are you, or are you not, in favour of capital punishment?' is more balanced than 'Are you in favour of capital punishment?', which is edging the respondent towards 'Yes' as an answer. Even the choice of one word in a question may be seen as leading. 'Should the UK stay in the EU or not?' is a very different question from 'Should the UK leave the EU or not', because each question triggers different associations and emotions.

Questions that are *too closed* are a kind of leading question that may also frustrate researchers. 'Is price an important factor in your purchase?' begs the answer 'Yes', but even if it was a balanced question, the responses tell very little. It does not indicate how impor-

Figure 6.5 Examples of rating scales

Likert scale

	Strongly agree	Agree	Neither agree nor disagree	Disagree	Strongly disagree
Safeway's prices are generally lower than those of other supermarkets					
Safeway's offers the widest range of groceries					
Safeway's staff are always friendly and helpful					
I never have to queue too long at the checkout					
Supermarket own-brands are just as good as manufacturers' brands					
Low prices are important to me in choosing a supermarket					
Supermarkets should provide more personal services					

Semantic differential scale

	1	2	3	4	5	6	7	
Modern								Old-fashioned
Friendly								Unfriendly
Attractive								Unattractive
Spacious								Crowded
High quality goods								Low quality goods
Wide choice of goods								Limited choice of goods
Convenient opening hours								Inconvenient opening hours
Tidy								Untidy
Short queues								Long queues
Low prices								High prices

tant price is to the respondent or what other factors influence the purchase. An open-ended or multiple-choice question might tell much more.

Researchers need to be sympathetic to people's *sensitivity*. Some areas are highly personal, so building up slowly may be important and 'soft' rather than 'hard' words should be used, for example 'financial difficulties' rather than 'debt'. Of course, the more sensitive the information, the more likely the respondent is to refuse to answer, lie or even terminate the interview.

Coding and rules. It is more important to obtain accurate and pertinent information than to design a questionnaire that embraces everything but rarely gets completed. Hague (1992) proposes an *ideal length* for three different types of questionnaire:

- telephone interviews: 5 to 30 minutes;
- visit interviews: 30 minutes to two hours;
- self-completion: four sides of A4, 20–30 questions.

A street interview would need to be very much shorter than 30 minutes to retain interest and prevent irritation.

The *layout* of the questionnaire is especially important for self-administered questionnaires. A cramped page looks unappealing, as well as making it difficult to respond. Where an interviewer is in control of the questionnaire, the layout should assist the recording and coding of responses and ease of flow through the interview to maintain momentum. Most questionnaires are now designed with *data coding* and ease of analysis in mind. This means that all responses to closed questions and multiple choices need to be categorised before the questionnaire is released, and that the layout must also be user friendly for whoever has to transfer the data from the completed questionnaire into a database.

The *order of the questions* is important for respondents, as the more confusing the flow and the more jumping around they have to do, the less likely they are to see it through to completion. Similarly, to assist the interviewer, the more routing and skipping that are built into the questionnaire, the easier it is to administer.

Support materials and explanation can be very important. For a mail survey a covering letter can be reassuring and persuasive while, at an interview, the interviewer needs to gain the respondent's attention and interest in participation. Visual aids, such as packaging or stills from advertising, can also get respondents more involved, as well as prompting their memories.

Piloting

Whatever care has been taken in the design of the questionnaire, problems usually emerge as soon as the questionnaire is tried on innocent respondents. Piloting a questionnaire on a small-scale sample can help to iron out any 'bugs', so that it can be refined before the full survey goes ahead. Initially, a fresh eye from colleagues can eliminate the worst howlers, but for most projects, it is best to set aside time for a full field pilot. This would mean testing the questionnaire on a small sub-sample (who will usually not then participate in the main survey) to check its meaning, layout and structure and, furthermore, to check whether it yields the required data and whether it can be analysed in the intended manner.

Conduct the research

Once the research plan has been developed and the methods of collection and proposed analysis identified, it is necessary to go about conducting the research itself. This stage will vary according to the type of research. The demands of a consumer survey involving perhaps thousands of respondents over a wide geographic area are very different from those of a select number of interviews in depth.

Particularly in primary research, it is this part of the process that often presents the biggest problem, because the collection of the data should not be left to poorly trained or badly briefed field researchers. Using people who do not recognise the importance of their role may cause them to take less care, allow bias to be introduced into the process or, at the extreme, to cheat in some way so that they can ostensibly fulfil their obligations, but with the minimum effort and with no regard for truth or accuracy. Over the past ten years, however, considerable progress has been made in professionalising research interviewers, moving away from the rather clichéd image of housewives earning extra cash. Training is now widespread and more male interviewers have been recruited both to enable access to previously no-go areas, such as high-crime housing estates and to handle situations where gender may matter during the interview (Gray, 2000a).

During the development of the research plan those involved, who are usually well qualified and trained, are at pains to ensure the accuracy of data collection, realising that important decisions may be made on the results. They are therefore very careful in what they do and how they go about structuring the research. On the other hand, those who will be responsible for actually collecting the data, field workers, interviewers and even their supervisors are more removed from the design and development process and less aware of the implications of data quality (or lack of it). Furthermore, they may not be adequately prepared in terms of training (poor interviewing skills or data-recording techniques), they may not be motivated (often being poorly paid and employed on a part-time basis) or they may not be appropriately or adequately supervised (such as when conducting research over a wide geographic area). Each of these shortfalls has the potential to distort the results of the research itself. It must be said, however, that the research industry is well aware of these problems and has developed quality control standards, especially with regard to interviews and contact with the general public, with which reputable suppliers of marketing research comply.

eg

Recruiting market research interviewers is not an easy job. Staff have to be prepared to work afternoons and evenings to make sure that they get representative samples of all kinds of workers. They also have to be well organised and good at managing themselves and their time, especially if they are working out in the field rather than in a telephone interview call centre, for example. All researchers need a strong sense of responsibility and have to be prepared to take an ethical approach to what they do. Field researchers have to be tough, to cope with less cooperative interviewees or to deal with the stranger kinds of people one meets when spending a lot of time hanging around city streets with a clipboard.

Research companies take a great deal of care in recruiting and training researchers. Some companies undertake lengthy initial telephone screening, partly to give applicants a better idea of what the job entails and partly to help develop a profile of the candidate. Many companies then insist on a face-to-face interview to check a candidate's appearance (especially for field researchers), their interaction skills and their ability to deal with situations. This is important because staff are effectively representing the research company and its clients and they have to be able to develop a rapport with interviewees quickly, reassure them and hold their attention, often through a fairly long and detailed survey.

Research company Gallup maintains that only 1 out of 16 candidates makes it through its selection procedures, a clear indication that the company sees the quality of its staff as an important asset. Those recruiting interviewers for telephone research call centres are less concerned about the appearance of their staff but more concerned about their telephone voice and ability to establish rapport without the face-to-face contact. Some companies even recruit people with certain regional accents to help this process (Gander, 1998).

There are a number of areas, in any kind of face-to-face research, where careful attention to detail can pay dividends. The prime purpose of the interviewer is to deliver the questions in an orderly, structured and accurate manner, where appropriate asking secondary questions, and finally accurately recording the responses of the respondent in line with the measurement instruments selected. The greater the need for the interviewer to depart from a carefully prepared script and *modus operandi*, the greater the skill involved and the higher the cost of the interview. This is particularly emphasised in the implementation role of the interviewer who conducts a group discussion or an in-depth interview. The dangers of interview bias are always present where the interviewer records what they think has been said or meant, not what has actually been said in response to a question. This sort of bias can be particularly pronounced where open-ended questions are being used. There are some situations where conducting field research is especially challenging, such as when particular targets or subjects need to be covered. The extremely affluent or poor, ethnic minorities, youth and corporate executives are often harder to reach than many target groups in the UK (Gray, 2000a). Community intermediaries are often used, for example, to reach target groups such as older Asian women and the Jamaican community and persuade them to participate in research. Researchers wishing to investigate the pink pound would find it difficult to knock on doors finding respondents. Therefore a lot of research is undertaken in places where gay people hang out, such as in clubs. That in itself does not necessarily deliver a representative sample of gay men, and sometimes respondents are asked to refer their friends.

New technology is making a big impact in the implementation of field research by assisting in the questioning and recording process. Computer aided telephone interviewing (**CATI**) and computer aided personal interviewing (**CAPI**) have revolutionised data collection techniques and are now widely used after their introduction in the UK in 1992. CAPI means that each interviewer is provided with a laptop computer which has the questionnaire displayed on screen. The interviewer can then read out text from the screen and key in the responses. The pre-programmed questionnaire will automatically route the interviewer to different parts of the questionnaire as appropriate (e.g. those who have/have not purchased in the previous three months) and will prompt the interviewer to clarify any illogical answers. It helps quality control by creating greater consistency in interviewer questioning and the recording of answers and furthermore allows the interviewer to concentrate on building a rapport with the respondent to help prevent fatigue and loss of interest in more complex questionnaires. CATI provides similar technology for telephone interviewing and again allows for greater consistency in interviewing and the recording of information. The additional advantage of both methods is the ability to download data quickly for analysis thus offering clients a faster turn-around time on their data requests.

Analyse and interpret the information

While the quality of the research data is essential, it is the analysis of the data, i.e. turning raw data into useful information, that provides the most value to the organisation. It is on the basis of the reports prepared from the data analysis that significant managerial decisions are likely to be made. Few surveys are undertaken without a detailed consideration of how to code, enter and classify the data generated. The use of sophisticated computer hardware and software packages provides a powerful means of processing large quantities of data relatively easily. CAPI, CATI, scanners that can read completed questionnaires, complex statistical analysis and data manipulation have improved the speed, accuracy and depth of the analysis itself. However, it is still the human element, the researcher's expertise in identifying a trend or relationship or some other nugget hidden within the results, that provides the key component for decision makers and transforms the data and techniques used into valuable information.

eg

Speed of analysis is often just as important as the depth of analysis in some situations. Some clients want information within days of starting a campaign rather than waiting until three weeks after it has finished. With time-sensitive products, such as video/DVD and CD releases, the sales data from the first few days is a good indicator of the success of the campaign. If adjustments have to be made to the campaign, they often have to happen in the first week (McLuhan, 2001a).

Researchers need to be conversant with such statistical techniques as correlation analysis, regression analysis, multivariate analysis, factor analysis, cluster analysis and the repertoire of significance tests. These techniques fall into either the descriptive category or relational, ranging from simple cross-tabulations through to highly sophisticated multivariate analysis. With more sophisticated segmentation and targeting of markets, market researchers need to be able to handle data analysis more flexibly to cross-relate trends and to identify emerging subtle differences between customer groups.

Some care needs to be exercised in the interpretation of quantitative data. Outputs of calculations should never overrule sound common sense in assessing the significance and relevance of the data generated. There is sometimes the danger of analysis paralysis, where the use of highly sophisticated techniques almost becomes an end in itself, rather than simply a means of identifying new relationships and providing significant new insights for management. While the old saying that trends, differences or relationships are only meaningful if they are obvious to even the untrained statistical eye may be going too far, it does highlight the danger of misinterpreting cause and effect and the differences between groups of consumers, arising from over-reliance on finely balanced statistics pursued by researchers.

Not all data are quantitative, of course. Qualitative data arising from in-depth interviews or group discussions pose a different kind of challenge to researchers. Whereas quantitative data have to prove their reliability when compared with the wider population, qualitative data can never be claimed to be representative of what a wider sample of respondents might indicate. The main task of qualitative data, therefore, is to present attitudes, feelings and motivations in some depth, whether or not they are representative of the wider population.

To handle qualitative data analysis, great care must be taken in the recording of information. Video or taped interviews are thus helpful in enabling classification and categorisation of the main points to be checked and explored in depth. Similarly, issue or content analysis enables particular themes to be explored across a range of interviews. For example, if researchers wanted to identify the barriers to exporting in small firms, they might define such themes as market entry, market knowledge, finance or using agents as indicative of the main barriers to be assessed. The data analysis might be supported by a range of quotations from the interviews. Because of the richness and complexity of this kind of data, skilled psychologists are often used to explore and explain much of what is said and, indeed, not said.

So although the risks of bias are great in qualitative analysis, both in data selection and analysis, and although the results can, in untrained hands, be rather subjective and conjectural, the advantage arises from the fresh insights and perspectives that more rigorous statistical techniques would simply not generate.

Prepare and present report

The information provided by researchers must be in a form that is useful to decision makers. Too often, research reports are written in highly technical language or research jargon that, to a layperson, is confusing or meaningless. Marketers who want to use these reports to make decisions need them to be easily understandable. A report that is too complex is all but useless. The language and the use of visual aids, such as graphs and charts, become critical elements in the presentation and interpretation of research reports. Various software packages, such as Microsoft's Powerpoint, greatly assist presentation through incorporating graphs, pie charts, histograms and other illustrations, in full colour. All of this helps the marketing decision maker to understand the main points of the research findings. That is why the formal presentation of the report, whether written or verbal (which allows the client to ask questions and seek clarification of points made), should be given as much thought, care and attention as any previous stage in the research process. It also allows the results to be personalised for the receiving organisation which can improve the perceived credibility of the findings and thus increase willingness to take action (Schmalensee, 2001).

Although a verbal presentation can play an important part in sharing understanding, it is the report itself that has the power to influence thinking significantly. Arguments can be carefully presented, with data used appropriately in their support, and the detail surrounding the main findings can be displayed to increase the client's confidence that the research was well executed to plan. There are no standard report formats, as much will depend on the nature of the research task undertaken.

The main areas covered, which closely follow the issues discussed in this section, are summarised in Table 6.7.

Table 6.7 The report

Title page	Contains, for example, report title; client; research company; date
Contents	Shows clearly the structure and content of the report and where in the report to find it
Preface	Sets the background to the report defining the marketing problem; summarises the researchers' interpretation of the original brief
Executive summary	Summarises the main points of the report, including conclusions and recommendations
Research methods	Explains how the research was done and why, with respect to the objectives of the research
Findings	Presents and collates the data collected
Conclusions	Interprets the data; draws out the key points
Recommendations	Identifies action and priorities arising from the conclusions and examines their implications
Appendices	Contain the fine detail that is not needed for the main body of the report or that would clutter up the report too much, e.g. a copy of a questionnaire, raw data or peripheral background information

Research evaluation

Research projects rarely go completely to plan. Although greater care in conducting pilot studies and exploratory research will make it more likely that the actual outcomes will match those planned, problems may still emerge that will require careful consideration in weighing up the value of the project. Thoughtful analysis of the planning, conduct and outcomes of the project will also teach valuable lessons for the future to both clients and researchers.

This stage can involve a review of all aspects of the research plan described above. Any deviations need to be understood, both in terms of the current results and for designing future research. With regard to the research project undertaken, the most important point is whether the research actually provided a sufficient quality and quantity of information to assist management decision-making. Sometimes, the research objectives may have been ambiguous or poorly framed in the context of the marketing problem being addressed. Ultimately, it is the marketing manager who must take responsibility for ensuring that the objectives and research plan were compatible and reflected the requirements, although researchers can help in this task.

eg

Perhaps the ultimate test for the value of the research is what action or decisions were made as a result of it. A small manufacturer of made-to-order fabricated metal cabinets had seen sales and profitability decline over several years. Market research identified changes in customer buying preferences away from the specifications offered by the firm, and profiled a more competitive climate, caused by new entrants. This study led to a fundamental rethink of the quality of the products being offered and the need to open up new markets.

Far too often, research is undertaken but the findings are only partially accepted, or at worst ignored, as not conforming to preconceived notions and prejudices. To be fair, it is difficult for managers to assess whether the findings are believable. Given the eclectic mixture of information and the tendency of managers to factor in management or marketing 'intuition', it is relatively easily either to accept too readily what you want to know or to dismiss that which is uncomfortable (Johnson and Mathews, 1997; Smith and Culkin, 2001). Although poorly designed and executed research is best ignored, and researchers have the responsibility for presenting the findings of the research accurately and persuasively, the true value of the project lies in the extent to which it offers added power to the manager for making better decisions. This kind of evaluation helps the client to understand better when research was a 'good buy' or a 'bad buy' and how to improve things next time around.

Ethics in marketing research

The ethical concerns surrounding market research have been the subject of an ongoing debate in the industry for a long time. Because much consumer research involves specific groups of consumers, including children and other groups that might be considered vulnerable, it is essential that the researchers' credibility is maintained and that the highest standards of professional practice are demonstrated. This is vital if researchers are to maintain the confidence of their clients, as well as that of the general public and the government, and so the industry has established a set of professional ethical guidelines. Members are expected to comply with these guidelines, although there is still some debate about their interpretation. The market research guidelines include such matters as protecting the confidentiality of respondents or clients, not distorting or misrepresenting research findings (for example, two major newspapers could both claim to be the market leader by using readership figures gathered over different time spans and failing to mention the time period), using tricks to gain information from respondents, conducting an experiment and not telling those being studied, and using research as a guise for selling and sales lead building.

The European Society for Opinion and Marketing Research (ESOMAR), a leading marketing research association, is actively trying to encourage members to stamp out the practice of 'sugging' (selling under the guise of market research) through an agreed code of practice.

corporate social responsibility *in action*

Finding out what kids are up to

When market researchers have to investigate children's behaviour and motivation as consumers, they have to proceed with extreme caution. It is very easy to step over both the legal line and industry codes designed to protect children and young people from predatory practices. Nevertheless, marketers cannot afford to ignore the needs of a segment estimated to be worth £300 bn. Market research is especially important among these 5 to 16 year-olds because they can change their minds and preferences frequently and not always with reason, and there is a real risk that today's best selling product is tomorrow's uncool fad from the past. Thus implementing carefully designed research that generates reliable insights and data ethically and with due respect to both children and their parents is well worth the effort.

The Market Research Society (MRS) has issued strict guidelines for researchers. Measures such as obtaining parental consent for interviews with under 16s in the home and preventing interviewer and child being alone together help to protect the rights of children and ensure that they are not exploited. The MRS Code of Conduct also seeks to reassure parents and protect the researcher from unfortunate claims (Cowlett, 2001).

Researchers also have a responsibility to prepare valid reports for their clients. Children are not easy to engage in research unless considerable care is taken in selecting research methods, location, group and interviewer dynamics, and response mechanisms. Children are often eager to please, may be intimidated by adult interviewers and may not understand the concepts and language used in research. Creative ways of engaging children often have to be employed, using pictures, toys, play and multimedia stimuli.

An interactive website (http://www.yorg.com) conducts online research through a network of schools. The website claims that the surveys are completed in school classes by 21,000 children aged between 6 and16 over the course of the year. The children respond intuitively to specialist software with full teacher approval as part of an IT session, each child playing on a multimedia workstation. They researchers go on to say, 'We don't bore them with books of multiple choice answers that are worse than homework. Our research programme involves them completely by using technology they love and understand. These kids respond live, on screen and with their peers. They interact with our software online so that the data gets to you fast, making your planning work in kid's time, not past times. You experience the honesty of today's kids as they have fun learning about themselves. Enrol your brand and learn fast what kids are really saying when the adults get out of their way.' (www.yorg.com).

Throughout the process, there is not a researcher in sight. Profiles are then developed for different children's segments so that eager marketers can understand the target market better. Boys aged between 10 and12, for example, are described as 'Money Mercenaries' with the following sample descriptors:

- Turned on by money and the prospect of making money.
- Prime target for financial institutions – savings/earnings schemes rule!
- Explosive energy – often boisterous and impulse driven.
- Bicycles, blades and music accessories are status objects prized by peers.
- Sports and computer interests intensified. Computer magazines avidly read.
- Violent TV and videos rule! Combat sports are essential viewing. Schwarznegger remains a hero. Soaps keenly watched. Collections are in the decline. Entertained by TV advertising but sceptical of hard sell.
- Big brand (global) preferences, particularly sports brands, which translate into fashion statements.
- Mothers still important as clothes suppliers, footwear excepted!
- Girls kept at some distance – tolerated.
- Risk takers with tobacco, alcohol, drugs (including solvent abuse) and gambling.

Such profiles are no doubt read avidly by marketers keen to keep up with events and to tap into the potential. It does, however, raise perhaps another more serious social question: to what extent do we want today's youth to be exposed to better informed and targeted marketing effort? Who should decide what is acceptable? Is it right to target sports and music-related merchandise at this age group? Is the marketing of violent television programmes and video games or overt appeals to materialism in the child's best interests? High degrees of professionalism and ethical standards are adopted by most market research companies and brand suppliers when children are involved, but that does not take away the need to question the societal impact of excessive exposure to naked commercialism. Does the profile above simply lead branded-goods thinking, or is it a product of previous marketing exposure?

Sources: Cowlett (2001); Flack (1999).

There is a conflict of interest between selling and research. Selling requires clear, persuasive communication outwards from the organisation, while research needs to preserve neutrality if the respondent is to open up fully. Research can certainly inform the selling process, helping the marketer to make better, more effective decisions, but if the two become confused or merged with each other then neither functions particularly well. For example, a new small business entrepreneur organised interviews with potential customers for 'market research purposes'. However, although the session began with a face-to-face in-depth interview based around a questionnaire, the respondent started to 'freeze' half-way through, as the 'researcher' started to enthuse about the benefits of the new manufacturing service planned. That respondent would not take kindly to being manipulated into listening to a sales pitch when he thought that he was doing a new business a favour by participating in research. Any goodwill (or potential sales) will almost certainly have been destroyed.

Codes of conduct are therefore especially useful in influencing the behaviour of the more responsible organisations within the industry. Within the UK, the Market Research Society has an extensive code of conduct covering such areas as professional ethics, sampling conditions and practice and the presentation of findings. ESOMAR has developed a similar, internationally based code of practice to augment local specifications. The growth of online research is creating demands for more regulation and tailored codes of conduct rather than allowing ethical conflicts to develop (DeLorme *et al.*, 2001).

BMRA, the British Market Research Association, is a trade association representing the interests of market research companies and helping to regulate them. It requries its members to subscribe to a code of conduct and insists that its larger members are accredited by the Market Research Quality Standards Association (BMRA, 1998). Of course, not all providers of market research are committed to compliance and not all bad practice can be eliminated, but considerable progress is being made across Europe.

Chapter summary

- Marketing managers find it impossible to make decisions effectively without a constant flow of information on every aspect of marketing. Everything, from defining target markets to developing marketing mixes to making long-term strategic plans, has to be supported with appropriate information.
- The organisation needs to coordinate its information, collected from a variety of sources, into an MIS. A formal MIS brings everything together under one umbrella and provides timely and comprehensive information to aid managers in decision-making. DSS build on the MIS, also to help decision-making. The DSS uses a variety of computer tools and packages to allow a manager to manipulate information, to explore possible outcomes of courses of action and to experiment in a risk-free environment. There are three different types of market research, exploratory, descriptive and causal, each one serving different purposes. Depending on the nature of the problem under investigation, any of the three types of market research may use qualitative or quantitative data. Rather than individually pursuing a series of marketing research studies, an organisation can participate in *continuous research*, undertaken by a market research agency on an ongoing basis and usually syndicated.
- There is a general framework for the conduct of a marketing research project that can be applied to almost any kind of market or situation. It consists of eight stages: problem definition, research objectives, planning the research, data collection, research implementation, data analysis, reporting findings and research evaluation.
- *Secondary research* provides a means of sourcing marketing information that already exists in some form, whether internal or external to the organisation. Gaps in secondary data can be filled through *primary research*. The main methods of primary research are interviews and surveys, observation and experiments. *Sampling* is a crucial area for successful market research. There is no need to survey an entire population in order to find answers to questions. As long as a representative sample is drawn, answers can be generalised to apply to the whole population. *Questionnaires* are often used as a means of collecting data from the sample selected, and they must reflect the purpose of the research, collect the appropriate data accurately and efficiently, and facilitate the analysis of data.
- Ethical issues in market research are very important. Researchers have to comply with codes of practice to protect vulnerable groups in society from exploitation. They also have to ensure that repondents recruited for market research studies are fully aware of what they are committing themselves to and that they are not misled at any stage in the research process.

key words and phrases

CAPI (computer aided personal interviewing)
CATI (computer aided telephone interviewing)
Closed questions
Continuous research
DSS (decision support system)
Focus groups
Marketing research
MIS (marketing information system)
Open-ended questions
Primary research
Qualitative research
Quantitative research
Rating scales
Sampling process
Secondary research
Semi-structured interview
Structured interview
Unstructured interview

questions for review

6.1 Why is *market research* an essential tool for the marketing manager?

6.2 What kinds of marketing problems might be addressed through:
(a) *exploratory*;
(b) *descriptive*; and
(c) *causal* research projects?

6.3 What are the main stages in the *sampling process* and what does each involve?

6.4 Define the stages of the *market research process* and outline what each one involves.

6.5 Discuss the role and content of an *MIS* and how it might relate to a *DSS*.

questions for discussion

6.1 Without looking back at pp. 230–2, how many *sources of secondary data* can you list? Check your list against pp. 230–2 and then investigate what your library has to offer.

6.2 Evaluate the appropriateness of each of the different *interview and survey-based primary research methods* for:
(a) investigating the buying criteria used by B2B purchasers;
(b) defining the attitudes of a target market towards a brand of breakfast cereal;
(c) profiling purchasers of small electrical goods; and
(d) measuring levels of post-purchase satisfaction among customers.

Clearly define any assumptions you make about each of the situations.

6.3 Design a questionnaire. It should contain about 20 questions and you should use as many of the different types of question as possible. Pay particular attention to the concerns discussed at pp. 247–52 of the chapter. The objective is to investigate respondents' attitudes to music CDs and their purchasing habits. Pilot your questionnaire on 12 to 15 people (but preferably not people on the same course as you), analyse the results and then make any adjustments. Within your seminar group, be prepared to discuss the rationale behind your questionnaire, the outcome of the pilot and any data analysis problems.

6.4 Why is an ethical approach to marketing research important and what are the main areas of concern?

6.5 Why is a sound *research brief* important, what should it contain and how does it influence each of the subsequent stages in the process?

case study 6.1

Kings Hotel

As a rough guide, assume that £1 = 25 Polish zloty (zl).

The Kings Hotel is situated on the inner ring-road, some ten minutes walk from the historic centre of the Polish city of Kraków. It is near the Wavel castle, the ancient Polish Royal Palace which is a major tourist attraction. The Kings Hotel is the second oldest hotel in Kraków. Only recently, a refurbishment programme started in some of the rooms covering redecoration, provision of modern, if standard furniture, furnishings and bathroomware. Not least, some improvement was made to the public areas. Direct dial telephones were installed in each room and the manager was delighted to open a Business Centre offering a fax, PCs and internet connections. The hotel is split into four operating units.

1 A three-star hotel (the front part), with 72 beds. The price of a double room is 1,200 zl per night, and that price remains the same all year.
2 A two-star hotel (the rear part), with a mix of bedrooms sleeping up to four per room, and a total capacity of 78. The price is 600 zl per night for a double room, and again the price is constant all year round.

   (As a comparison, prices at the nearby Hotel Majestic, one of the best in Kraków, are 1,455 zl in low season and 2,190 zl in high season.)
3 A disco bar with a street entrance. This is rented out privately, but infrequently.
4 A restaurant at the front of the hotel at groundfloor level, primarily serving hotel guests.

The hotel management has avoided tour bookings wherever possible. It did deal with the Polish airline LOT a few years ago for block bookings, but found that more profitable business from independent travellers had reached a sufficient level to reduce the need for such trade. Prices are already comparatively low, and no discounts are offered to private individuals or groups. Most of the customers in the summer season are tourists and outside that period they tend to be business travellers, especially visiting university staff and local government officers.

Little promotion is undertaken, but a multi-language brochure has been designed. Good relations are maintained with the Kraków tourist office, which finds accommodation for travellers, and the hotel advertises in tourist board publications. The hotel also advertises on a poster site at the local airport. The real concern is that most other hotels have already been modernised to achieve Western European standards. An independent traveller had found the Kings Hotel room plain and a little shabby, but spacious and clean. It did have a television and an en-suite bathroom with a shower, but no drinking water. The hotel itself looked somewhat 'tired' and lacked extra facilities, such as room service, porters and direct dial international telephone facilities. To receive breakfast, the guest had to get a voucher from reception and then walk out of the hotel, round the corner into the hotel's restaurant.

The manager decided that further development of the hotel was necessary to get it up to major city centre standards, especially if the business and independent traveller segment was to be expanded. He hoped that a questionnaire for independent guests would provide a valuable insight into the type of customers visiting the hotel and the sort of facilities they would like to see.

The manager has two sons, Bogdan and Adam, both on a tourism management course at the local university. He asked them how he should go about market research to find out more about his guests and what independent and business travellers wanted during a short stay. Bogdan proposed that he should prepare a questionnaire to be given to guests as they check in at the hotel along with a letter explaining the purpose of the exercise. A box should be provided at reception for the completed questionnaires and guests would be reminded of the need to deposit it before they left. Bogdan had learned that a prize draw, perhaps with a number of free nights stay at the hotel offered as a prize, could act as an incentive to generate a good response rate. He even designed a series of questions that could be asked to get things moving:

Questionnaire

1 Are you male or female?

2 How old are you? ____ years ____ months

3 How did you travel to the hotel?

Car ____

Airline ____

Train ____

Coach/bus ____

Other ____

4 How long do you normally stay in a hotel?

1 week ____

2 week ____

More than 2 weeks ____

5 Have you been to this hotel before?

6 If you had to choose between the following, which do you think are the most important for the hotel to provide?

A larger car park _____, bath in every room _____, airport pick-up service _____, bar _____, shop _____, computerised booking _____, 24-hour room service _____, internet connection in every room _____, don't know _____

Thank you for helping with this questionnaire, which when completed should be put in the box at the reception desk.

Adam was not so sure about the approach suggested by his brother. He had just studied an internet marketing module and thought that e-mail research could be very useful if guests' business cards could be obtained. He was also aware that specialist lists could be bought from which samples of business travellers could be selected. This could help to develop a more general picture of business travellers' needs and wants, regardless of whether they had ever stayed at the Kings Hotel or not. For the independent traveller, Adam proposed organising some focus groups during the guests' stay at the hotel, to which he could invite groups of up to six guests for wine, snacks and with some in-depth discussion of prior expectations and the actual level of service experienced. Father was just confused about whether to offend just one of his sons, or to offend both of them by rejecting both their proposals. He tended to favour questionnaires as he had seen them widely used in other hotels, but he recognised that perhaps he needed a more scientific approach.

Source: Adapted from a case prepared by Pat Badmin.

Questions

1 To what extent and why do you feel that the research method employed is appropriate for gathering the information needed?

2 Criticise the questionnaire outlined in the case in terms of the choice of questions, their wording and their response mechanism.

3 What marketing problem is this research trying to help solve? What information do you think the hotel manager would actually need in order to investigate this problem?

4 Design your own questionnaire of up to 20 questions to address the manager's problem. Explain your choice of questions and the response mechanism, and discuss when and how you would undertake the survey.

case study 6.2

Gathering information on an up-and-coming market

The condom market can be viewed as a bit of a laugh, as a bit of an embarrassment, as a moral outrage, or as deadly serious, given the risks of sexually transmitted diseases or unwanted pregnancy. To condom manufacturers, however, it is a commercial business just like any other which must be based, as with any company, on sound marketing information about consumers and their buying behaviour.

Condom purchases vary between planned and impulse buys. An NOP Health Monitor survey found that travelling abroad either for business or pleasure often led to planned purchases before the trip. The report found that 81 per cent of people thought a holiday to be the most likely occasion for casual sex, while in the 48–55 age group, 18 per cent thought a business trip more likely. Although men were the larger group of pre-holiday purchasers, 58 per cent of women expecting a sexual experience on holiday travelled with condoms purchased at home. Such planned purchases are actively encouraged by condom manufacturers, as the customer can be assured of a quality product and a familiar brand by buying at home.

Impulse or reminder purchases represent the second group, where availability is essential for continued sales. The policy of Durex is to suggest to retailers that condoms should be easy to find, self-selected, preferably from special displays, and clearly priced to avoid any interaction with sales staff or at the checkout. This reflects the changes taking place in distribution patterns. Condoms are no longer sold exclusively in pharmacies or barbers' shops (Boots sells nearly 30 per cent of condoms in the UK by value, while pharmacies and other chemist chains hold a 25 per cent share) but also in supermarkets (23 per cent share) as a toiletry alongside razors and shampoos. This exposes the product to both men and women, and encourages customers to treat condoms as a normal part of the regular shopping routine. ASDA believes that women represent the largest purchase group in its stores. A variety of different types of outlet have been targeted to accommodate the change in purchase patterns, such as late night grocery stores and vending machines (10 per cent share) in 'strategic places' such as discos, pubs and student social facilities. New outlets such as off-licences and record shops began putting condoms on self-service display, while 24-hour stores cater for the distress and impulse segment. Pack sizes tend to be larger in the grocery store, reflecting planned purchases. Although internet selling only accounts for 5 per cent of the market, it is nevertheless becoming more popular as it allows consumers to buy condoms and have them delivered discreetly to their home without face-to-face contact with sales staff. Despite all these changes, however, it has been estimated that 30 per cent of consumers still have some reservations about purchasing condoms.

In parallel with changes in distribution patterns, condoms have experienced considerable expansion in the range of products available. In recent years, they have become stronger, more sensitive and more reliable. Variations in strength, size, colour, texture and flavour have all been offered to the market. The major suppliers to the UK market are:

- *SSL International*. SSL owns the Durex brand which holds 75 per cent of the UK market by value. Variants on the core Durex brand include Extra Safe, Avanti, Fetherlite and Select (including coloured and flavoured condoms – strawberry, banana, orange and mint).
- *Mates Healthcare*. The Mates brand is Durex's major UK competitor with its Original, Variety, Ribbed and Conform variants.
- *Condomania*. Condomania claims to be the first UK brand selling direct to customers via the internet (http://www.condomania.co.uk), offering a large variety of condoms and related products. Condomania also entered a licensing deal to produce Condomania South Park Condoms in 1999, targeting the 16- to 25-year-old group, and distributing via stores such as Virgin Megastores, Top Man, and Our Price.
- *Condomi* claims to be Europe's largest manufacturer of condoms, making over 300 million a year. Condomi sells its Stimulation, Sensation, Premium and Supersafe variants in the UK through Boots, Superdrug and other chemists. It also targets the younger end of the market with its slogan, 'you don't have to carry the brand your Dad used'. Its website, available in five languages, includes online shopping, but also has pinups, news and magazine elements making it more of a lifestyle site than just a place to shop.

Government health campaign advertising worked well for the manufacturers in creating generic demand for the product. In 1984, only 31 per cent of males and 35 per cent of females said that they would use a condom the first time they had sex with someone, but by 2001, 87 per cent of people said they would not have sex with a new partner without using a condom (this figure falls to 70 per cent among the 16–20-year-old group, however). It is also easier now for manufacturers to advertise directly and more explicitly, although they still have to be careful not to offend people too much or else they will not listen to the message. All the major manufacturers link themselves with various safer sex organisations, government sponsored health education programmes, and events. Durex supports National Condom Week in the UK, just one example of its global involvement in AIDS education and healthcare issues. Condomania too has sponsored World Aids Day 2000 in conjunction with the Terrence Higgins Trust and donated 10 per cent of its December internet sales to the Trust. Mates Healthcare contributed £1 mn to the Virgin Healthcare Foundation and gave a grant of £21,000 to the Institute of Population Studies at Exeter University for a study into condom shapes.

Overall, however, developing new products in this market and getting the approach right is not always easy. Durex claims that it bases its product development on in-depth research into people's sexual habits and attitudes, developing brands to meet different consumer needs and preferences. Durex failed, however, with a new brand called Assure, targeted at young women. It was packaged in a pastel coloured unbranded box, to keep in a handbag. The target market turned out to be confident enough to buy the brand that suited them best, regardless of the discretion, or lack of it, in the packaging design. In contrast to the Durex approach, Mates focuses on size and comfort, supporting its range of different sized condoms with a 'size does matter' advertising campaign. The company claims that a pilot study indicated that men can tell the difference between shapes and sizes and that choosing the right condom makes a difference.

Sources: Bray (1997); Mintel (2001); http://www.durex.co.uk.

Questions

1 Briefly outline the types of market research information that might be useful to a condom manufacturer.

2 What are the problems of undertaking primary consumer research for a product like this? How can these problems be overcome?

3 Thirty per cent of buyers still have some reservations about purchasing condoms. Suggest a programme of primary research that might tell the manufacturers why this is.

4 To what extent do you think it would be ethical for condom manufacturers to undertake a survey of 14–16-year-olds?

References for chapter 6

Adriaenssens, C. and Cadman, L. (1999), 'An Adaptation of Moderated e-mail Focus Groups to Assess the Potential for a New Online (Internet) Financial Services Offer in the UK', *Journal of the Market Research Society*, 41 (4), pp. 417 ff.

Anstead, M. (2000), 'Taking a Tough Line on Privacy', *Marketing*, 13 April, p. 31.

Basuroy, S., Mantrala, M. and Walters, R. (2001), 'The Impact of Category Management on Retailer Prices and Performance: Theory and Evidence', *Journal of Marketing*, 65 (4), pp. 16–32.

Billings, C. (2001), 'Researchers Try Electronic Route', *Marketing*, 29 March, pp. 27–8.

Boyd, H.W. *et al.* (1977), *Marketing Research*, 4th edn, Irwin.

BMRA (1998), 'BMRA – What Does BMRA Stand For?', advertisement in *Marketing Week*, 25 June, p. 50.

Bolden, R., Moscarola, J. and Baulac, Y. (2000), 'Interactive Research: How Internet Technology Could Revolutionise the Survey and Analysis Process', paper presented at *The Honeymoon is Over! Survey Research on the Internet* Conference, Imperial College, London, September 2000.

Bray, L. (1997), 'Focus on Condoms', *The Grocer*, 15 February, pp. 49–50.

Brennan, M. *et al.* (1991), 'The Effects of Monetary Incentives on the Response Rate and Cost Effectiveness of a Mail Survey', *Journal of the Market Research Society*, 33(3), pp. 229–41.

Bromage, N. (2000), 'Mystery Shopping', *Management Accounting*, April, p. 30.

Chaffey, D. (2002), *E-business and E-commerce Management: Strategy, Implementation and Practice*, Financial Times Prentice Hall.

Chisnall, P.M. (1986), *Marketing Research*, 3rd edn, McGraw-Hill.

Clarke, A. (2001), 'Research Takes an Inventive Approach', *Marketing*, 13 September, pp. 25–6.

Clegg, A. (2001), 'Talk Among Yourselves', *Marketing Week*, 6 December, pp. 41–2.

Cornish, C. (2001), 'Experiences of Qualitative Research on the Internet', in Westlake, A., Sykes, W., Manners, T. and Rigg, M. (eds), *The Challenge of the Internet*, proceedings of the second ASC International Conference on Survey Research Methods.

Cowlett, M. (2001), 'Research Can be Child's Play', *Marketing*; 10 May p. 35.

Curtis, J. (1998), 'Keeping Up with the Jones's', *Marketing*, 19 November, pp. 28–9.

DeLorme, D., Zinkhan, G. and French, W. (2001), 'Ethics and the Internet: Issues Associated with Qualitative Research', *Journal of Business Ethics*, 33 (4), pp. 271–86.

Duan, Y. and Burrell, P. (1997), 'Some Issues in Developing Expert Marketing Systems', *Journal of Business and Industrial Marketing*, 12 (2), pp. 149–62.

Flack, J. (1999), 'Child Minding', *Marketing Week*, 8 July, pp. 41–4.

Forestier-Walker, M. (2001), 'Research is Not a Substitute for Talent and Skills', *Marketing*, 29 November, p. 22.

Gander, P. (1998), 'Just the Job', *Marketing Week*, 25 June, pp. 51–4.

Gofton, K. (2000), 'Consult the Consumers', *Marketing*, 24 August, p. 33.

Gray, R. (2000a), 'How Research Has Narrowed Targets', *Marketing*, 10 February, pp. 31–2.

Gray, R. (2000b), 'The Relentless Rise of Online Research', *Marketing*, 18 May, p. 41.

Haggett, S. and Mitchell, V.W. (1994), 'Effect of Industrial Prenotification on Response Rate, Speed, Quality, Bias and Cost', *Industrial Marketing Management*, 23(2), pp. 101–10.

Hague, P. (1992), *The Industrial Market Research Handbook*, 3rd edn, Kogan Page.

Hayward, C. (2001), 'The Child-catchers', *Marketing Week*, 18 October, pp. 45–6.

James, D. (2001), 'Quantitative Research', *Marketing News*, 1 January, p. 13.

Johnson, C. and Mathews, B. (1997), 'The Influence of Experience on Service Expectations', *International Journal of Service Industry Management*, 8 (4), pp. 290–305.

Marsden, A. (2001), 'Why Categories Can Breathe Life into Marketing', *Marketing*, 6 September, p. 22.

Marshall, J. (2000), 'Monitoring Market Research Online', *Information World Review*, October, p. 31.

Mason, T. (2001), 'Two-thirds Don't Drink Ale or Beer in an Average Week', *Marketing*; 4 October, p. 5.

McDaniel, C. and Gates, R. (1996), *Contemporary Marketing Research*, 3rd edn, West.

McDaniel, S. *et al.* (1985), 'The Threats to Marketing Research: an Empirical Reappraisal', *Journal of Marketing Research*, 22 (February), pp. 74–80.

McLuhan, R. (2001a), 'How to Aid Clients Using Technology', *Marketing*, 30 August, p. 48.

McLuhan, R. (2001b), 'How Data Can Help Target Customers', *Marketing*, 27 September, p. 25.

Miles, L. (2000), 'A Watchful Eye on Consumer Habits', *Marketing*, 20 April, p. 35.

Mintel (2001), 'Contraceptives', 1 August, accessed via http://www.mintel.com.

Moeng, S. (2001), 'At Home with Big Brother', *Financial World*, September, pp. 42–3.

Mutter, J. (2001), 'Borders Adopts Category Management', *Publishers Weekly*, 5 February, p. 10.

Poynter, R. (2000a), 'Keynote: A Guide to Best Practice in Online Quantitative Research', paper presented at *The Honeymoon is Over! Survey Research on the Internet* Conference, Imperial College, London, September 2000.

Poynter, R. (2000b), 'We've Got Five Years', paper presented at *The Honeymoon is Over! Survey Research on the Internet* Conference, Imperial College, London, September 2000.

Qureshi, B. and Baker, J. (1998), 'Category Management and Efficient Consumer Response: the Role of Market Research', *Marketing and Research Today*, 26(1), pp. 23–31.

Rao, S. (2000), 'A Marketing Decision Support System for Pricing New Pharmaceutical Products', *Marketing Research*, 12 (4), pp. 22–9.

Reed, D. (1998), 'Categorical Truths', *Marketing Week*, 25 June, pp. 45–9.

Schmalensee, D. (2001), 'Rules of Thumb for B2B Research', *Marketing Research*, 13 (3), pp. 28–33.

Shields, G. (2001), 'Meeting the Need for Actionable Consumer Insight – The Scottish Courage Perspective', paper presented to the MRS conference, March.

Smith, C. (2001), 'Is Barclaycard on the Way to Glory in the Premiership?', *Marketing*, 16 August, p. 17.

Smith, D. and Culkin, N. (2001), 'Making Sense of Information: A New Role for the Market Researcher?', *Marketing Intelligence and Planning*, 19 (4), pp. 263–71.

Smith, D. and Fletcher, J. (1999), 'Fitting Market and Competitive Intelligence into the Knowledge Management Jigsaw', *Marketing and Research Today*, 28 (3), pp. 128–37.

Trevaskis, H. (2000), "You Had to Be There": Why Marketers are Increasingly Experiencing Consumers for Themselves and the Impact of this on the Role and Remit of Consumer Professionals', *International Journal of Market Research*, 42 (2), pp. 207–17.

Tull, D.S. and Hawkins, D.T. (1990), *Marketing Research: Measurement and Method*, Macmillan.

Von Krogh, G., Ichijo, K. and Nonaka, I. (2000), *Enabling Knowledge Creation: How to Unlock the Mystery of Tacit Knowledge and Release the Power of Innovation*, New York: OUP.

Whiteling, I. (2002), 'Sibling Rivalry', *Marketing Week*, 24 January, pp. 39–40.

Wilson, R. (2001), 'Search Engines', *Marketing Week*, 5 July, pp. 53–4.

Witthaus, M. (1999), 'Group Therapy', *Marketing Week*, 28 January, pp. 43–7.

Woods, R. (2002), 'Pop Idol or Puppet?', *Sunday Times*, 10 February, p. 12.

Yorgey, L. (2000), 'Reaching Expectant and New Mums', *Target Marketing*, March, pp. 60–3.

Zikmund, W. G. and D'Amico, M. (1993), *Marketing*, West.

part three

PRODUCT

7 anatomy of a product

8 product management

9 new product development

Chapter 7 poses a very simple question, 'What is a product?', and finds that the answer is somewhat less simple. It is related to what the buyer really wants from the product, whether that consists of practical performance, psychological benefits or both, and the ways in which marketers choose to communicate that through the product via branding, packaging, design and quality.

Following an analysis of this complex anatomy of the product, Chapter 8 can then look critically at more detailed product management issues, such as the product lifecycle and its influence on marketing decision-making, the importance of developing a balanced portfolio of products and brand management. It also opens the debate about the advantages or otherwise of pan-European branding.

One of the lessons to be learned from the product lifecycle theory is that most products have a finite life span. As a product matures, therefore, decisions have to be made about what to do next. Chapter 8 examines some possibilities, such as relaunching an improved version of the product, while Chapter 9 takes the route of new product development, that is, allowing the product to die and replacing it with something new. The processes and problems of new product development are fully explored.

chapter 7

anatomy of a product

Introduction

LEARNING OBJECTIVES

This chapter will help you to:

1. define and classify products and the key terms associated with them;
2. understand the nature, benefits and implementation of branding;
3. appreciate the functional and psychological roles of packaging;
4. understand the broad issues relating to product design and quality and their contribution to marketing.

The product is at the heart of the marketing exchange. If the product does not deliver the benefits the customer wanted or if it does not live up to the expectations created by the other elements of the marketing mix, then the whole exercise has been in vain. Remember that customers buy products to solve problems or to enhance their lives and thus the marketer has to ensure that the product can fully satisfy the customer, not just in functional terms, but also in psychological terms. The product is important, therefore, because it is the ultimate test of whether the organisation has understood its customer's needs.

The example below raises a number of interesting questions about what makes a product and the importance of brand image and customer perceptions of it. Clearly, marketers have to understand the nature of these questions and base strategic decisions about the development and management of product offerings on the answers. To start the process of thinking about these issues, therefore, this chapter examines some fundamental concepts. The definition of product and ways of classifying products lead to some basic definitions of product ranges. Then, the underlying concepts that give the product its character and essential appeal to the buyer will be examined. These include branding, packaging and labelling, design, style and quality, and the role of peripheral areas such as guarantees in enhancing the product offering. The wider issues of product management and new product development will then be discussed in the following two chapters. The first task for this chapter, meanwhile, is to define the meaning of the term *product*.

eg

Perhaps the best known product and brand name in the world is Coca-Cola. First trademarked in 1887, everything about the product such as the bottle shape, the colours and packaging design, and the logo design that has been developed from the word Coca-Cola, is instantly recognisable, distinctive, and familiar to almost everyone globally. As one of its advertising campaigns of the 1990s put it, 'If you don't know what it is, Welcome to Planet Earth' (Pavitt, 2001). In blind tasting, Coca-Cola may not score significantly better than its rivals in terms of taste and quality, but the strength of the brand name and the brand image have certainly helped it to maintain its market dominance. Product and branding concepts are not just linked with inanimate physical products, however. The pop music industry is very sophisticated in its use of marketing techniques to create products and brands out of artists and bands. Morgan (2001) claims that over a seventeen-year career, pop icon Madonna 'has achieved what every brand strives for: an enduring, unique, meaningful and relevant place in consumers' hearts and minds'. She goes on to suggest that Madonna's brand is expressed through three core values: provocativeness (demanding attention and generating positive and/or negative reactions to her messages), innovation (taking risks to allow the 'brand' to evolve) and reality ('Striving for perfection but acknowledging imperfection').

Meaning of a product

The product is one half of the exchange that interests marketers (price is the other half; see Chapters 10 and 11). A formal definition of product may be that:

> *a product is a physical good, service, idea, person or place that is capable of offering tangible and intangible attributes that individuals or organisations regard as so necessary, worthwhile or satisfying that they are prepared to exchange money, patronage or some other unit of value in order to acquire it.*

A product is, therefore, a powerful and varied thing. The definition includes tangible products (tins of baked beans, aircraft engines), intangible products (services such as hairdressing or management consultancy) and ideas (public health messages, for instance). It even includes trade in people. For example, the creation and hard selling of pop groups and idols are less about music than about the promotion of a personality to which the target audience can relate. Does a Madonna fan buy her latest album for its intrinsic musical qualities or because of the Madonna name on the sleeve? Politicians too try to sell themselves as people with caring personalities in exchange for your vote at election time. Places are also saleable products. Holiday resorts and capital cities, for example, have long exploited their natural geographic or cultural advantages, building service industries that in some cases become essential to the local economy.

Whatever the product is, whether tangible, intangible or Madonna, it can always be broken down into bundles of benefits that mean different things to different buyers. Figure 7.1 shows the basic anatomy of a product as a series of four concentric rings representing the **core product**, the **tangible product**, the **augmented product** and finally the **potential product**.

The *core product* represents the heart of the product, the main reason for its existence and purchase. The core benefit of any product may be functional or psychological and its definition must provide something for the marketer to work on to develop a differential advantage. Any make of car will get the purchaser from A to B, but add on to that the required benefits of spaciousness, or fuel economy or status enhancement, and a definition of a core product to which a market segment will relate begins to emerge. The core benefit of a holiday could be to lie in the sun doing absolutely nothing, being pampered for two weeks, at one end of the spectrum or, at the other end, to escape from the world by seeking adventure and danger in unknown terrain. Although it might be argued that a Club 18–30

Figure 7.1 The anatomy of a product

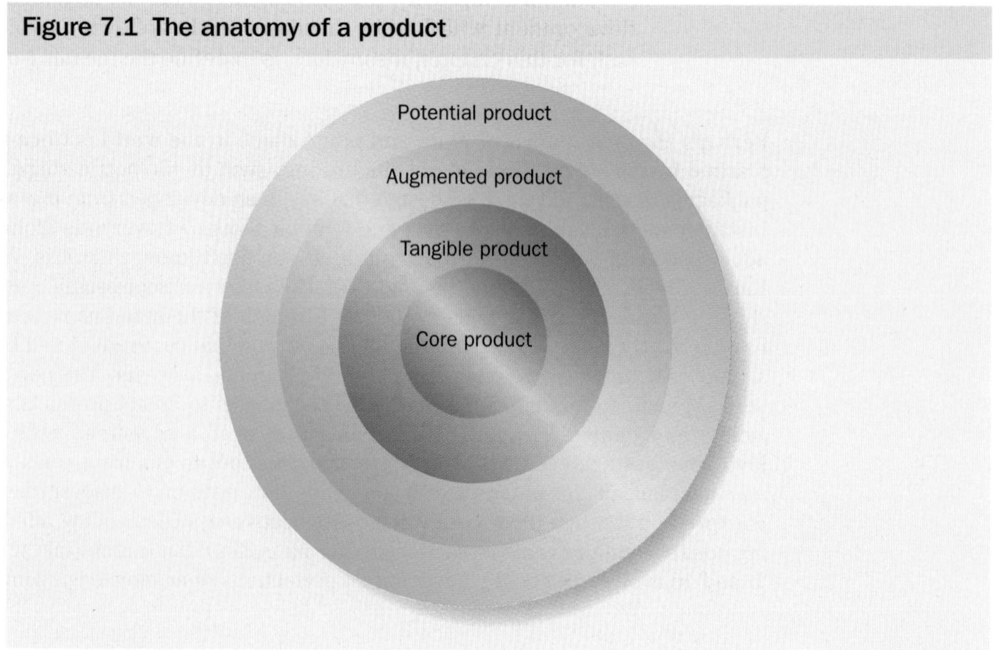

holiday could satisfy both those core benefit requirements, generally speaking very different packages will emerge to meet those needs.

The definition of the core benefit is important because it influences the next layer, the *tangible product*. The tangible product is essentially the means by which the marketer puts flesh on the core product, making it a real product that clearly represents and communicates the offer of the core benefit. The tools used to create the product include design specification, product features, quality level, branding and packaging. A car that embodies the core benefit of 'fast and mean status symbol', for example, is likely to have a larger engine, sexy design, leather upholstery, lots of electric gadgets, built-in CD player, definitely be available in black or red metallic paint (among other choices) and certainly carry a marque such as BMW rather than Lada.

The *augmented product* represents add-on extras that do not themselves form an intrinsic element of the product, but may be used by producers or retailers to increase the product's benefits or attractiveness. A computer manufacturer may offer installation, user training and after-sales service, for instance, to enhance the attractiveness of the product package. None of this affects the actual computer system itself, but will affect the satisfaction and benefits that the buyer gets from the exchange. Retailers also offer augmented products. An electrical retailer selling national and widely available brands such as Hoover, Zanussi, Indesit or Hotpoint needs to make its own mark on each transaction so that the buyer will want to shop there again in the future. Augmenting the product through extra guarantees, cheap financing, delivery and breakdown insurance is more likely to provide memorable, competitively defendable and relatively inexpensive mechanisms for creating a relationship with the consumer than is price competition.

eg

London Design agency Pearlfisher has used experts from around the world to identify potential luxury goods, foods and services for the future, especially for the very rich (Hiscott, 2001). It wanted to create visions of the future that could guide innovation and creativity. Ideas such as 'first class sky cruising' in aircraft equipped with casinos, ballrooms and gourmet chefs to create pleasure in the journey rather than the destination; designer cars serving individual needs; functional foods matched with individual DNA profiles, and designer everything are key elements of the future products. There could even be computer-based cooking for the lazy eater (BBC News, 2001c). Fanciful? Maybe, but some ultra-luxury products do see the light of day. Since February 2000 project work has been undertaken on a designer Bentley for the Queen to use on state occasions. When delivered in 2002, it will have a rear door design that will enable her to stand up straight before stepping to the ground, flexible opaque panels for extra privacy, folding rear-facing chairs, and unique upholstery and carpets. (Peek, 2001). On top of that there is armour plate, bulletproof glass, anti-mine cladding and run-flat tyres and satellite telecommunications. The price is a mere £10 mn, compared with a standard Bentley price of £250,000, but the company decided to present the car as a free gift to the Queen for her Golden Jubilee.

Finally, the *potential product* layer acknowledges the dynamic and strategic nature of the product. The first three layers have described the product as it is now, but the marketer also needs to think about what the product could be and should be in the future. The potential product can be defined in terms of its possible evolution, for example new ways of differentiating itself from the competition.

Doyle (1998), however, takes a slightly different view. He considers that the potential product reflects such high levels of added value and differentiation that the product is better protected against competitors and substitutes. Achieving this kind of potential has been one of the foundations of success for such organisations as French Connection, Red Bull, Kellogg and Levi over many years. Thus Kotler is saying that potential simply reflects what might be done with the product in the future, whereas Doyle is saying that it provides a strategic focus in itself.

In summary, all four layers of product contribute to the buyer's satisfaction, but the outer two depend on the definition of core product to determine how they are realised. The core itself may be functionally based, in terms of what the product is supposed to do, or it may be benefit or promise based, in terms of how this product will make you feel. It is, however, in the outer layers, the tangible and augmented product, that most of the overt marketing competition takes place (Parasuraman, 1997). The challenge for the marketer is to find out just want customers think is added value, real or subjective (Piercy and Morgan, 1997). Research suggests that it means different things to different people so it is likely to vary across segments (de Chernatony *et al.*, 2000; Wikström and Normann, 1994), across cultures for the international marketer (Assael, 1995) and even for the same customer over time (Jaworski and Kohli, 1993).

Product classification

To bring order to a wide and complex area of marketing, it is useful to be able to define groups of products that either have similar characteristics or generate similar buying behaviour within a market. Such classification schemes allow some generalisations to be made about appropriate marketing strategies for each group.

Product-based classification

A product-based classification groups together products that have similar characteristics, although they may serve very different purposes and markets. There are three main categories: **durable products**, **non-durable products** and **service products**.

Durable products

Durable products last for many uses and over a long period before having to be replaced. Products such as domestic electrical goods, cars and capital machinery fall into this group.

Non-durable products

Non-durable products can only be used once or a few times before they have to be replaced. Food and other fmcg goods fall into this category, as do office consumables such as stationery and computer printer cartridges.

Service products

Services represent intangible products comprising activities, benefits or satisfactions that are not embodied in physical products. Items such as financial services, holidays, travel and personal services create problems for marketers, because of their intangibility and inherent perishability. Services are so different that they warrant their own chapter in this book (Chapter 22).

The nature and implementation of the marketing mix are likely to be very different for each of these categories of product. A durable is likely to be an infrequently purchased, relatively expensive good. It may require selective distribution through specialist channels and a communications approach that is primarily centred on information and function rather than psychological benefits. In contrast, a non-durable is likely to be a frequently purchased, relatively low-priced item requiring mass distribution through as wide a variety of outlets as possible and mass communication centred on psychological benefits. Services have to find ways of either bringing the service to the consumer or persuading the consumer to come to the service delivery point. Communication has to develop both functional and psychological benefit themes as well as reassuring the potential customer of the quality and consistency of the service offered.

These outlines are, of course, broad generalisations of limited use and it is not difficult to think of exceptions within each category (compare cars and washing machines in the durable group, for instance). Although these classifications are ostensibly based on product characteristics, it has proved to be impossible to talk about them without some reference to buyer behaviour, so perhaps it is time to make this dimension more explicit and instead to think about user-based classifications of products.

The following subsections deal in turn with consumer markets (goods purchased for personal or family consumption – *see* Chapter 3) and B2B markets (goods purchased for business or institutional use – *see* Chapter 4). Although both groups look for satisfaction from their purchases, the kinds of products they buy and the buying influences and behaviour that predominate are very different, thus meriting separate treatment. It is important to note that even the same product can be marketed very differently, depending on whether it is aimed at a consumer or a B2B purchaser, as will be shown, for example, at p. 274 *et seq.*

User-based classifications: consumer goods and services

The contents of this section are very closely linked with the content of pp. 104 *et seq.*, where differences in buyer behaviour were based on whether the purchase was a routine response situation (i.e. a familiar, low-risk and frequently encountered situation), a limited problem solving situation (some unfamiliarity, medium risk, less frequently encountered) or an extended problem solving situation (no experience, very infrequent, high-risk purchase). If we begin with these behavioural categories, it is possible to identify parallel groups of goods and services that fit into those situations, giving a very powerful combination of buyer and product characteristics for outlining the basic shape of the marketing mix.

Convenience goods

Convenience goods correspond to the routine response buying situation. They are relatively inexpensive, frequent purchases. The buyer puts little effort into the purchasing decision and convenience often takes priority over brand loyalty. This is especially true of supermarket-based shopping. If the desired brand of breakfast cereal is inexplicably unavailable within the store that the shopper is visiting, they will probably buy an alternative brand or do without rather than take the trouble to go to another shop.

The marketing implications of such a product definition are similar to those outlined for the non-durable on p. 270 above. Wide distribution needs to be assured to make it as likely as possible that the product will be under the consumer's nose. Communication needs to be aimed directly at consumers to get them as involved as possible with the product through the creation of brand image to offset brand-switching indifference. Packaging and brand imagery need to be as attention grabbing and as memorable as possible to facilitate recognition and positive brand choice at the point of sale. The market may well be price sensitive and thus the producer and retailer should be prepared to accept low margins and to seek profit through volume.

eg

The growth in petrol station forecourt retailing was very high during the 1990s. No longer content with just selling petrol, a number of oil companies either run their own forecourt shops selling convenience foods or have entered into arrangements with specialist retailers. By the end of the decade, Esso and BP/Mobil each had nearly 2,000 retail outlets offering an ever increasing range of services, including food, alcoholic drinks, and cash dispensers as well as auto services. The next phase of development by Texaco is to include tie-ins to Dunkin' Donuts, Pizza Hut, Burger King, Upper Crust and McDonald's in order to offer branded fast food. Interestingly, in the USA, the focus is increasingly on convenience stores that sell petrol (rather than the other way round) with nearly 80 per cent of petrol sold through such stores. In 2000, 96 per cent of all new convenience stores opened sold petrol. In the UK, with a steady contraction in the number of petrol stations, often it is non-petrol sales that enable some stations to remain open. The formula is the same: convenient access, long opening hours, fast service and one-stop shopping. Things have moved on from simply seeking to capture the odd impulse buy. In time, the petrol station in the UK could become the focal point of community retailing in the same way as the Post Office used to be (Linnell, 1998; *National Petroleum News*, 2001).

The types of goods involved may be staple items, such as groceries, but could also include impulse or emergency purchases. For example, a consumer browsing through a bookshop with no particular intention to buy may be caught suddenly by a particular title, jacket design or author's name and make an immediate decision to buy. In an emergency, such as dealing with a burst water pipe in the home, convenience takes on a less lazy definition. The need for a solution to the consumer's problem develops an urgency that precludes extensive shopping around. In both the impulse and the emergency situations, the key to making a sale is essentially the same: be in the right place at the right time with the right product and be ready to ambush the unsuspecting customer.

Shopping goods

Linked with limited problem solving behaviour, **shopping goods** represent something more of a risk and an adventure to consumers, who are thus more willing to shop around and plan their purchases and even to enjoy the shopping process. Comparison through advertisements and visits to retail outlets may be supplemented by information from easily accessible sources, such as consumer organisations' published reports, word of mouth from family and friends and brochures, as well as advice from sales assistants in the retail setting. A moderately rational assessment of the alternative products based on function, features, service promises and guarantees will lead to a decision.

The effort required by this process is worth it if the purchase is significant or if the consumer will have to live for a long time with the consequences of the decision (see the hi-fi example at p. 105). Whether a purchase falls into this category depends on the individual consumer's perceptions of the importance and complexity of the purchase, as well as their previous experience within the market concerned. One consumer's shopping good is another's convenience or speciality good. Within the shopping goods classification, there may be brand and/or store loyalty involved, or no loyalty at all. There may also be a pre-existing short list of preferred brands within which the detailed comparison and final choice will be made.

The implications of all this for the marketer affect all aspects of the marketing mix, not just product. The mass distribution strategies of the convenience good may no longer be appropriate. The consumer is more likely to seek out certain specialist retailers and see what they have available than to purchase impulsively from a supermarket shelf, because of the nature of the product and the buying behaviour it invokes. This makes the careful targeting of key retailers essential. A toaster manufacturer needs a presence in Curry's, Comet and Argos, and even in some of the grocery hypermarkets because those are the places the consumer will go to seek market information. Toasters are in fact a grey area, in the sense that for a significant number of consumers they are closer to convenience items than shopping goods. That might not, however, be the case for Dualit toasters.

eg

Forget the £20 version of a toaster. If you want a Dualit toaster, they start at over £100 and go can go up to over £200. Each one is hand-built and they are made in limited quantities, despite increasing demand. The toaster does not pop up; it stops cooking when the timer tells it to and then keeps the toast warm until you throw a lever to get it out. It is designed to last, with cast aluminium ends, stainless steel bodywork and patented heating elements that can produce two, three, four or six variations. Although old fashioned production methods are used, it offers state-of-the-art performance. You would have to shop around to find one, however. You have little chance of finding one in the High Street electrical stores, but you might strike lucky in selected stores such as John Lewis. Dualit prides itself in offering a 'shopping good' (Pearman, 2001; http://www.dualit.co.uk).

The volume of goods sold will be lower than for a convenience item, but the margin on each unit will be much higher. Price sensitivity could go either way with these products. A consumer who is confused by the amount of information to be analysed and is having difficulty comparing competing products on the basis of performance and features may resort to price as the deciding factor. A more expensive one may be purchased on the basis that it must be a better quality product, or a cheaper one may be bought on the basis that it will do the job and there's no point spending more on fancy frills.

Communication might also take two directions. Establishing a strong corporate name is important, so that when the consumer enters the market the name either springs to mind as an obvious choice or at least seems very familiar, and therefore comforting, when it is encountered. Organisations such as Ariston, Zanussi and Hotpoint have used mass advertising in this way, so that even consumers who are not currently interested in buying kitchen appliances are aware that they exist and have some perception of what the company name stands for. The hope is that these perceptions will be transferred to the actual products at the appropriate time.

The other direction for communication is that of working closely with the retail trade. If a consumer seeks information at the point of sale to guide product choice, then obviously any manufacturer wants its product to be the one with the strongest retailer backing. Providing training or incentives (*see* Chapter 16 on trade sales promotion) to retailers or individual sales assistants, as well as help with point-of-sale displays and provision for joint promotion (*see* Chapter 16), all help to forge stronger links between producer and retailer with a view to developing a competitive edge.

Speciality goods

Speciality goods equate with the consumer's extensive problem-solving situation. The high-risk, expensive, very infrequently purchased products in this category evoke the most rational consumer response that a manufacturer could hope to find. It is not entirely rational, however. The psychological and emotive pull of a brand name like Porsche could still override objective assessment of information, leading to a biased, but happy, decision for the consumer. If you allow the inclusion in this category of products like designer perfumes, those that cost several hundred pounds for 50 ml and would be a once (or never) in a lifetime purchase for most consumers, then rationality goes right out of the window and the purchase is made entirely on the basis of the dream and the imagery woven around the product.

The products in this category need very specialist retailing that will provide a high level of augmented product services, both before and after the sale. Limiting distribution to a small number of exclusive and well-monitored outlets not only protects the product from abuse (for example inappropriate display or sales advice), but also helps to enhance the product's special image and the status of the buyer.

eg

Choosing where to go on an annual holiday is a high-risk decision for many households. After saving up all year, the last thing you want is building sites, cockroaches, airport delays and food poisoning. Thomson Holidays is the UK's number one tour operator but it faces stiff competition from the likes of JMC, etc. It uses its advertising campaigns to differentiate its holidays by focusing on range, quality, and peace of mind. One campaign featured a 50-second television advertisement incorporating the line, 'Would you risk the love of this fine woman for the price of a *curry*?' as Roland Rivron berated a fellow passenger for seeking a cut price deal. The £5 mn 'Fanny and Daversham' campaign run in 2001 was created in the style of a nineteenth-century costume drama where the characters fantasised about a future world where they could book a trouble free experience with Thomson. Both of these campaigns were designed to build brand quality, integrity and honesty rather than focusing on sun, sand, sea, sex and price discounting. To succeed, Thomson needs to focus consumer attention on the full range of factors that customers consider when evaluating alternative holidays, rather than a simple orientation towards the package price (Arnold, 2001; McLuhan, 1999). As Thomson sees it,

> *We see our task as trying to stop the downward price spiral. A holiday is one of the most important purchases you make during the year; if you were buying a car you wouldn't make an instant decision if one were cheaper by £20.*
>
> (as quoted by McLuhan, 1999)

The (relatively) very low volumes sold of these products are compensated for through their high profit margins. Prices are high not only to reward the producer and retailer for their care for the product and its buyer, but also because the buyer is likely to perceive a high price as a positive benefit (*see* Chapter 11 on the pricing of luxury goods and on psychological pricing), enhancing the status of the purchase.

Communication will be a more extreme version of the shopping goods scenario, with much emphasis on name and image building. This is likely to focus more on the psychological benefits of choosing that manufacturer or that product rather than on the functional benefits as such. At these price levels, function and quality can almost be taken for granted: it is the extra intangible psychological 'something' that differentiates between competing

The 'Fanny and Daversham' campaign drew the audience's attention to the many different components that go into making a good holiday, and the difficulties that choosing a holiday can cause. Here the message is that Thomson Holidays offers a trouble free experience.

Source: Thomson Holidays/The Advertising Archives.

products. There is also going to be even closer cooperation between manufacturer and retailer, who will take care that any joint promotional efforts do not compromise the product's quality or status level.

Unsought goods

Within the **unsought goods** category, there are two types of situation. The first is the sudden emergency, such as the burst water pipe or the flat tyre. The organisation's job here is to ensure that the consumer either thinks of its name first or that it is the most accessible provider of the solution to the problem.

The second unsought situation arises with the kinds of products that people would not normally buy without aggressive hard-selling techniques, such as timeshare properties and some home improvements.

User-based classifications: B2B goods and services

This type of classification of B2B goods and services is linked closely with the discussion at pp. 149 *et seq.*, where the spectrum of buying situations from routine re-buy to new task purchasing was discussed. The novelty of the purchase influences the time, effort and human resources put into the purchasing decision. If that is then combined with the role and importance of the purchase within the production environment, it is possible to develop a classification system that is both widely applicable and indicative of particular marketing approaches.

Capital goods

Capital equipment consists of all the buildings and fixed equipment that have to be in place for production to happen. Such items tend to be infrequently purchased and, given that they are expected to support production over a long lifetime and that they can represent a substantial investment, they are usually regarded as a high-risk decision in the new task category. This category might also include government-funded capital projects such as the building of motorways, bridges, housing and public buildings like hospitals and theatres.

The purchasing organisation will therefore use extensive decision-making, involving a wide range of personnel from all levels of the organisation and perhaps independent external consultants as well. The seller will also have to be prepared to spend a great deal of time and effort researching the buying organisation and cultivating a relationship with its key personnel during the decision-making process. In some cases, the seller might have to become involved in developing a tailormade product for the buyer. Such purchasing is likely to centre on rational criteria, so the seller will have to bid for the contract, communicating the quantifiable benefits of the product, in competition with a number of alternative suppliers.

Accessory goods

Accessory goods are items that give peripheral support to the production process without direct involvement. Included in this group, therefore, will be items such as hand tools, fork-lift trucks, storage bins and any other portable or light equipment. Office equipment is also included here, such as wordprocessors, desks, chairs and filing cabinets.

Generally speaking, these items are not quite as expensive or as infrequently purchased as the capital goods. The risk factor is also lower. Buying the 'wrong' desk will not jeopardise the organisation in the same way as would buying the 'wrong' production machinery. An unreliable fork-lift truck can disrupt production, but even so, it is relatively quick and simple to replace. All of this indicates that the length of and the degree of involvement in the purchasing process will be scaled down accordingly into something closer to the modified re-buy situation.

The seller's main task, therefore, would appear to be to ensure that the prospective purchaser has all the relevant up-to-date information to hand. The purchase of office equipment, for example, might be delegated to the office manager without reference to more senior management, within an overall budget. The office equipment supplier then needs to maintain regular contact, making sure that the latest catalogue is in the office manager's hands, so that when a purchasing decision is due, that is the catalogue that is used. Regular visits from a sales representative can help to communicate or negotiate special offers and deals, as well as providing a human point of contact for the office manager.

Raw materials

Raw materials arrive more or less in their natural state, having been processed only sufficiently to ensure their safe and economical transport to the factory. Thus iron ore is delivered to Corus; fish arrives at the Findus fish-finger factory; beans and tomatoes are delivered to Heinz; and fleeces arrive at the textile mill. The raw materials then go on to further processing within the purchaser's own production line. The challenge for the supplier of raw materials is how to distinguish its product from the competition's, given that there may be few specification differences between them. Often, the differentiating factors in the purchaser's mind relate to non-product features, such as service, handling convenience, trust and terms of payment, for example.

Semi-finished goods

Unlike raw materials, semi-finished goods have already been subject to a significant level of processing before arriving at the purchaser's factory. They still, however, need further processing before incorporation into the ultimate product. A clothing manufacturer, therefore, will purchase cloth (i.e. the product of spinning, weaving and dyeing processes), which still needs to be cut and sewn to create the ultimate product.

Components and parts

Components and parts are finished goods in their own right, which simply have to be incorporated into the assembly of the final product with no further processing. Car manufacturers, for example, buy in headlamp units, alarm systems and microchips as complete components or parts and then fit them to the cars on the assembly line.

There is an important distinction to be drawn here between products specified by the supplier and those specified by the buyer. If the components are buyer-specified, then the sales representative's main responsibility is to make sure that the right people are talking to each other. This might mean, for instance, coordinating the efforts of applications engineering personnel within the selling organisation with the engineering and specifying staff within the buying organisation. Even when the product has been agreed, there is still a need to maintain the relationship. This would be particularly critical if specific capital investments have been made by either party. Buyer specified products will be discussed further at pp. 337 *et seq.*

In contrast, supplier specified products demand clear appreciation of customer needs, carefully designed and priced products and effective selling and promotion to exploit the opportunities identified by market research. Often, the competitive edge comes from designing unique parts for targeted applications, which can be delivered to a standard and consistent quality level to meet customer requirements.

Supplies and services

Finally, there are several categories of minor consumable items (as distinct from the accessory goods discussed above) and services that facilitate production and the smooth running of the organisation without any direct input.

Operating supplies. Operating supplies are frequently-purchased consumable items that do not end up in the finished product. On the factory floor, these will include things like the lubrication oils for the production machinery. In the office, this group mainly includes stationery items such as pens, paper and envelopes, as well as computer consumables such as printer toner or ink cartridges and floppy disks.

Maintenance and repair. Maintenance and repair services ensure that all the capital and accessory goods continue to operate smoothly and efficiently. Maintenance and repair may take place on a planned basis, regularly servicing and checking equipment. They may also be called in on a trouble-shooter basis, when an actual problem develops. Remember, though, that maintenance and repair are not just about looking after equipment, but also about looking after the working environment, from mending the roof to emptying the office wastepaper baskets. This category can also include minor consumable items, such as cleaning materials, which assist in providing this service.

Business services. Business services may well be a major category of purchases for an organisation, involving a great deal of expenditure and decision-making effort, since they involve the purchase of services like management consultancy, accounting and legal advice and advertising agency expertise. This takes the discussion back to new task purchasing and its associated problems of involvement and risk.

Understanding the product range

Very few organisations are single-product companies. Most offer a variety of different products and perhaps a number of variations of each individual product, designed to meet the needs of different market segments. Car companies clearly do this, producing different models of car to suit different price expectations, different power and performance requirements and different usage conditions, from the long-distance sales representative to the family wanting a car largely for short journeys in a busy suburban area. The same happens in B2B markets. Ingersoll-Rand, for example, has developed a whole range of portable compressors for use on construction sites. These range from small units that will run a single tool to high-capacity, high-pressure specialist units. A construction or engineering contractor can choose the appropriate unit to do the job in hand most cost effectively and most efficiently. Service companies also vary their products to suit different customer groups. A business school will offer undergraduate and postgraduate courses; post-experience courses for practising managers; full-time and part-time courses; tailored training packages for industry; and consultancy.

To understand any product fully, it is essential to appreciate its position in the wider family of the organisation's products. The marketing literature uses a number of terms when talking about the product family that are easy to confuse because of their similarity. Here are some definitions that sort out the confusion and offer some insight into the complexity of the product family. Figure 7.2 shows how all of these terms apply to the products produced within the Consumer Healthcare division of GlaxoSmithKline.

Product mix

The **product mix** is the total sum of all the products and variants offered by an organisation. A small company serving a specialist need in a B2B market may have a very small, tightly focused product mix.

Specialist companies also exist in consumer markets, of course. Van Dyck Belgian Chocolates, for example, offers boxed chocolates, chocolate bars, liqueur chocolates, fruit-flavoured chocolate, nut chocolates, etc. A large multinational supplier of fmcg goods, such as Nestlé, has a very large and varied product mix, from confectionery to coffee to canned goods.

Product line

To impose some order on to the product mix, it can be divided into a number of **product lines**. A product line is a group of products that are closely related to each other. This relationship may be production orientated, in that the products have similar production requirements or problems. Alternatively, the relationship may be market orientated, in that the products fulfil similar needs, or are sold to the same customer group or have similar product management requirements. A company such as Minolta may define three of its product lines as still cameras, video cameras and photocopiers. These labels make sense because those three groups involve different technologies, and also because they sell to very different customers and markets.

Figure 7.2 GlaxoSmithKline consumer healthcare product mix (as at 13 April 2001)

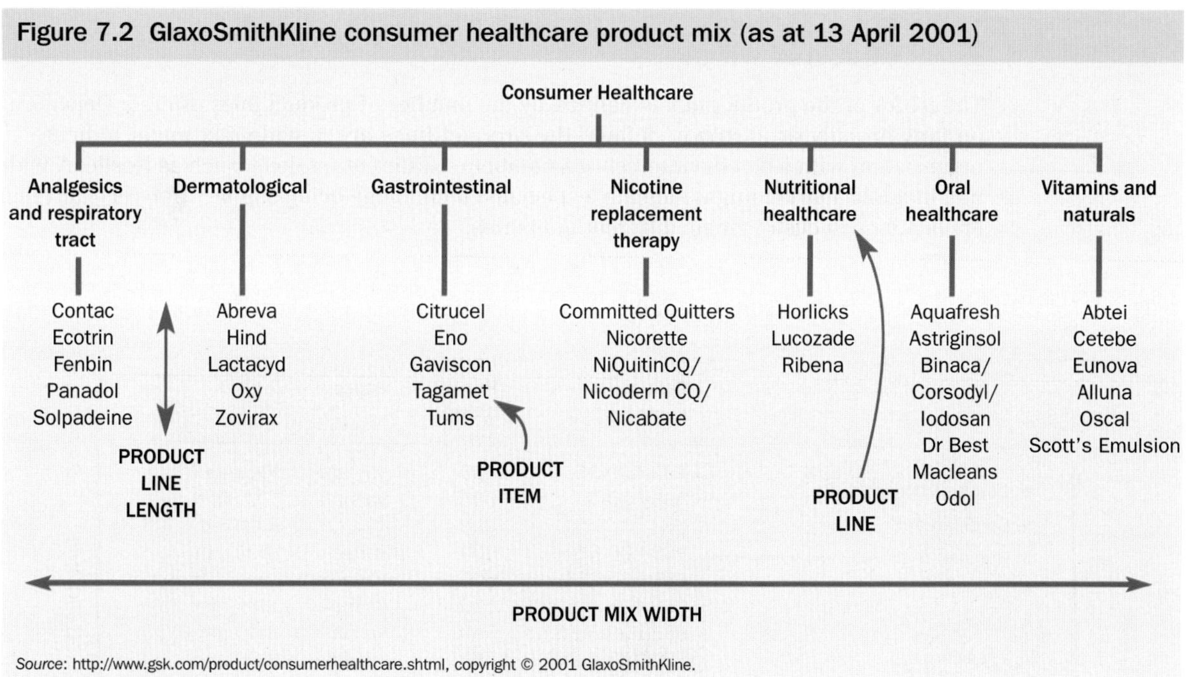

Source: http://www.gsk.com/product/consumerhealthcare.shtml, copyright © 2001 GlaxoSmithKline.

Product item

A product line consists of a number of **product items**. These are the individual products or brands, each with its own features, benefits, price, etc. In the fmcg area, therefore, if Heinz had a product line called table sauces, the product items within it might be tomato ketchup, salad cream, mayonnaise, reduced calorie mayonnaise, etc.

Product line length

The total number of items within the product line is the **product line length**. Bosch, for example, might have a product line of DIY power tools, as shown in Figure 7.3. Its equivalent industrial range of power tools would probably be even longer.

Product line depth

The number of different variants of each item within a product line defines its *depth*. A deep product line has many item variants. A deep line may be indicative of a differentiated market coverage strategy where a number of different segments are being served with tailored products. If we look again at the Bosch example in Figure 7.3, we can break hammer drills down into a number of variants, giving a depth of ten, each of which has different performance and application capabilities, as well as fitting into different price segments ranging from under £50 to over £120.

Similarly, in an fmcg market, the Lynx brand (known as Axe outside the UK) produced by Lever Fabergé offers great product line depth in male toiletries. Under the Lynx umbrella, aftershave, shaving gel, shower gel, body spray, deodorant (in stick, roll-on and spray forms), shampoo, and conditioner are offered in a variety of fragrances with suitably exotic and macho names such as Voodoo, Gravity, Africa, Phoenix, Apollo and Atlantis. This depth does not aim to cover different market segments, but does offer sufficient variation and choice to keep the target segment interested and loyal. The line includes all the basic male toiletry products so that the customer does not need to purchase anything from outside the line, and the variety of fragrances, with a new one introduced every year to keep the line fresh and interesting, allows the customer to experiment and have a change from time to time!

Product mix width

The *width* of the product mix is defined by the number of product lines offered. Depending on how broadly or narrowly defined the product lines are, a wide mix might indicate an organisation with a diverse interest in a number of different markets, such as Nestlé. A wide mix in a B2B market might indicate a specialist technology being supplied for very different applications to customers in different industries.

Figure 7.3 Bosch DIY power tools product line

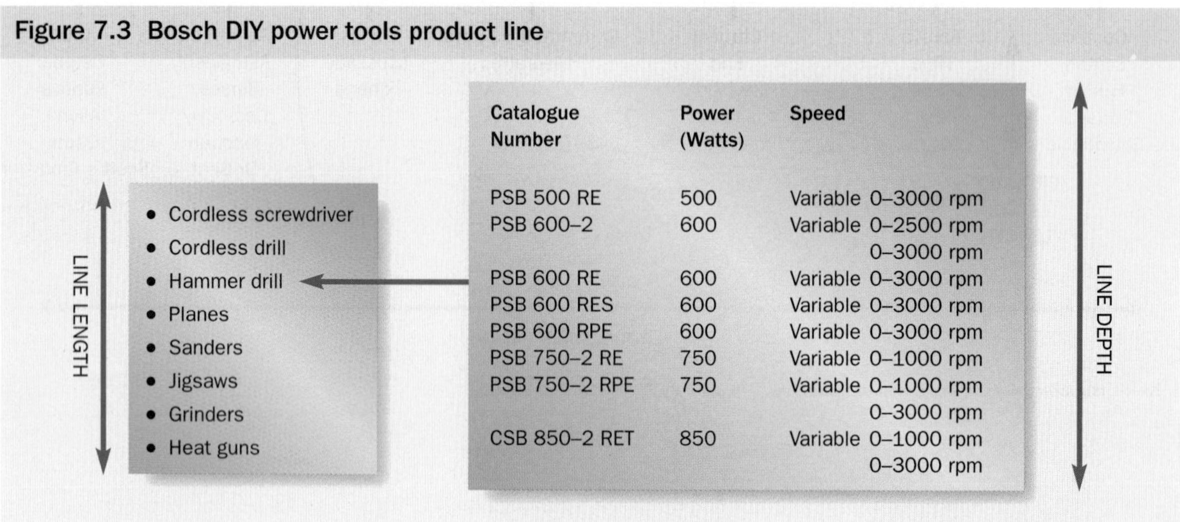

By continually adding alternative fragrances to the Lynx range, the male buyer tends to remain loyal to the overall brand and not look elsewhere for something new or different.

Source: The Advertising Archives/Lever Fabergé.

These definitions will be important for the next chapter's discussion of managing the product mix.

Branding

Branding is an important element of the tangible product and, particularly in consumer markets, is a means of linking items within a product line or emphasising the individuality of product items. It must never be forgotten, however, that a 'good' product and service is needed to enable effective communication to build the brand (Marconi, 2001). Branding can also help in the development of a new product by facilitating the extension of a product line or mix, through building on the consumer's perceptions of the values and character represented by the brand name. This points to the most important function of branding: the creation and communication of a three-dimensional character for a product that is not easily copied or damaged by competitors' efforts. The prosaic definition of brand, accepted by most marketers, is that it consists of any name, design, style, words or symbols, singly or in any combination that distinguish one product from another in the eyes of the customer. Brands are used by people to establish their status far more than religion or political party. We are often judged by the brands we select, the football teams we support, the television programmes we watch, the clothes we buy, the car marque we drive, where we eat and even what we eat. All of these are cues that others use to classify an individual. It is, therefore, perhaps of no great surprise that brands are often not about physical attributes but a set of values, a philosophy that can be matched with the consumer's own values and philosophy. Orange represents a bright future, Nike is about achievement ('just do it') and Avantis about life (Bunting, 2001).

Branding is a thus very important activity in consumer markets. *Marketing*'s annual survey of Britain's biggest brands shows how much business a brand can bring to its owner

Table 7.1 The UK's top 10 brands, 2001

Brand	*Owner*	*Sales (£mn)*	*Ad. spend (£mn)*
Coca-Cola	Coca-Cola	665–670	15.66
Walker's crisps	PepsiCo	480–485	7.95
Nescafé coffee	Nestlé	315–320	14.25
Stella Artois lager	Interbrew	310–315	6.47
Müller	Müller	285–290	9.26
Persil laundry products	Lever Bros	230–235	17.00
Andrex toilet tissue	Kimberly-Clark	200–205	5.00
Robinsons	Britvic Soft Drinks	180–185	5.39
Kit Kat	Nestlé Rowntree	170–175	8.63
Pepsi	PepsiCo	170–175	5.24

Source: adapted from data compiled by AC Nielsen, a VNU company, Hiscock (2001).

and the level of advertising support that brands can command. Table 7.1 gives details of the top 10 brands from the 2001 survey.

An organisation's approach to branding depends on its overall product mix and individual line strategy, as will be shown at pp. 290 *et seq*. First, however, it is necessary to look a little more closely at the meaning of branding, beyond the raw definition already presented.

The meaning of branding

The definition of brand provided above offered a variety of mechanisms through which branding could be developed, the most obvious of which are the name and the logo. As with the product mix jargon discussed in the previous section, you are likely to meet a number of terms in the course of your reading and it is important to differentiate between them.

marketing *in action*

Is Barbie starting to feel her age?

Most women in their forties start to worry about spreading waistlines, a few wrinkles and the first sign of grey hairs, but not Barbie. Born in 1959 to Mattel, she has not only kept her figure and youthful looks but she continues to give unending pleasure to millions of children around the world. At one time it was estimated that three Barbie dolls were being sold worldwide every second. Barbie as a brand is not about dolls and clothes, it is about young girls allowing their imaginations to create a desirable lifestyle; it is about escapism, make-believe, control and self-expression. Mattel has understood that by progressively refining the doll as technology has improved over the years and allowing 'sister' dolls to emerge with clothes and features reflecting emerging consumer tastes and attitudes. Christie, for example, an Afro-Caribbean doll was introduced in 1968 and a wheelchair-bound doll was launched in 1997. Over 150 new Barbies are released each year on a worldwide basis.

The evolution of the brand has sought to reflect the changing role of women in society. The 1959 Barbie had heavy make-up. This was replaced by a more natural look in 1967, and then a happier looking Barbie followed in 1977. The focus now is on creating the more intelligent and sophisticated appearance befitting a career Barbie. The latest concept is the 'I Can Be' Barbie, offering 80 different careers with appropriate clothes, accessories and career information sheets, thus Dr Barbie comes complete with uniform, examination table and medical accessories (purely for the doll's use, of course). Keeping up with the times, the careers are also featured on the Barbie (http://www.Barbie.com) website. New dolls keep arriving. The launch of the first feature-length video, Nutcracker, saw the debut of Clara, a new look doll ballet star, accompanied, of course, by a full range of related merchandise, clothes and accessories. Attempts are also being made to encourage older girls to keep an interest in Barbie. The career packs help but so too do branded Barbie products, clothing, backpacks and instant cameras. It remains to seen whether teenage girls wish to be associated with the Barbie image.

So the brand essence is allowing outfits and experiences to be created for Barbie and her friends, male or female. They are then free to participate in everyday life situations wearing whatever captures the imagination and playing whatever role is required. The bimbo image might well have gone (except for her bust!), but the fictional world in which Barbie undertakes every kind of career going, keeps Ken hanging on and owns an improbably extensive wardrobe still enthrals.

Sources: Baar (2001); Hussey (1998); *Marketing Week* (2001); Moorhead (2001).

Brand name

A brand name is any word or illustration that clearly distinguishes one seller's goods from another. It can take the form of words, such as Weetabix and Ferrero Rocher, or initials, such as AA. Numbers can be used to create an effective brand name, such as 7-Up. A browse through the telephone directory of any British town is likely to reveal a small company called A1 Taxis. The A1 name is popular with small operators partly because it has connotations of quality, but mainly because the quirks of alphabetical order mean that it comes very early in the telephone book listing and is thus more likely to attract a potential customer's attention. Brand names can also be enhanced by the use of an associated logo, such as the one used by Apple computers, to reinforce the name, or through the particular style in which the name is presented. The classic example of this is the Coca-Cola brand name, where the visual impact of the written name is so strong that the onlooker recognises the design rather than reads the words. Thus Coca-Cola is instantly identifiable whether the name is written in English, Russian, Chinese or Arabic because it always somehow *looks* the same.

The strategic issues surrounding the choice and use of brand name are examined further at p. 288.

Trade name

The trade name is the legal name of an organisation, which may or may not relate directly to the branding of its products.

eg

Cadbury's (http://www.cadbury.ac.uk), as an organisation, has deliberately developed a strong image for the Cadbury corporate name to act as an umbrella for all its product brands. Hence its products benefit both from the affection that consumers hold for the corporate name and from the individual character developed for Cadbury's Flake, Cadbury's Dairy Milk, Cadbury's Drinking Chocolate and all its other products.

Some companies prefer to let the brands speak for themselves and do not give any prominence to the product's parentage. Washing powder brands produced by either Unilever or Procter & Gamble do not prominently display the company name, although it is shown on the back or side of the pack. Few consumers would realise that Persil, Surf and Radion come from the same stable. Similarly, RHM produces brands such as Paxo that have no obvious corporate identity.

There is more on the strategic implications of the degree of corporate branding used at pp. 290 *et seq.*

Trade mark

A trade mark is a brand name, symbol or logo, which is registered and protected for the owner's sole use. To bring the UK into line with EU legislation, the Trades Marks Act, 1994 allowed organisations to register smells, sounds, product shapes and packaging, as well as brand names and logos (Olsen, 2000). This means that the Coca-Cola bottle, the Toblerone bar and Heinz's tomato ketchup bottle are as protectable as their respective brand names. Advertising slogans, jingles and even movements or gestures associated with a brand can also be registered as trade marks. The Act prevents competitors from legally using any of these things in a way that may confuse or mislead buyers, and also makes the registration process and action over infringement much easier. By 1996 it was also possible to register trade marks for the whole of Europe by filing a single application to the Community Trade Mark Office in Alicante, Spain, rather than having to apply for registration country by country. Dutch company Senta secured the first EU-wide trade mark for the 'smell of cut grass' to attach to its tennis balls. After having the smell rejected at the first attempt in 1998, the Office of Harmonization in the Internal Market upheld the appeal and the scented tennis balls 'Scenter Court' could go into production. This is a test case for companies wanting to trademark smells. At present, perfume companies can trademark logos and names but not smells. So be prepared for the whiff of almost anything in the coming years (Bird, 2000).

Trade marks are valuable properties, as organisations invest much time and money in creating them and educating consumers about what they stand for. This means that there is also value in trade that capitalises on the illegal use of brand names. Companies such as

Nike and Reebok have put a great deal of effort into trying to stem the flow on to the market of counterfeit, low-cost copies of their brands. These counterfeits, allegedly sourced from the Far East, are poor-quality goods that damage the company name and image if purchased as 'originals'. Even B2B markets are not immune to this trend, which has been seen in the markets for motor spare parts and aircraft parts, among others. There are mixed messages regarding the impact of counterfeiting. A study by Nia and Zaichkowsky (2000) suggested that 70 per cent of those surveyed felt that the value, satisfaction and status of the luxury brand was not decreased by the availability of counterfeits. Stipp (1996) found that the suppliers of counterfeit goods argued that they were simply allowing other consumers, who cannot have the genuine product, to realise their dreams at a lower price. That view is not, however, shared by legislators and most brand manufacturers who believe that counterfeiting is sheer deception and must be stopped.

eg

There has been a long dispute between Arsenal FC and Matthew Reed, an Arsenal supporter who also sells Arsenal memorabilia such as scarves and hats from a stall in the front garden of a house near the ground. The merchandise was not just red and white, but bore the words 'Arsenal' and 'Gunners' as well as the distinctive badge. As far as Arsenal FC was concerned these were registered trade marks so it took Reed to court on the basis of trade mark infringement. It argued that purchasers might think that the merchandise sold by Reed was officially licensed. The stall, however, displayed a prominent disclaimer saying that the goods were not endorsed by Arsenal FC. Reed had also been selling from the site for 31 years so the judge ruled, surprisingly, that customer confusion was not likely and that badges were merely signs of support and loyalty, and so Reed could continue trading. Experts still believe, however, that it is a direct abuse of the legitimate Arsenal trade mark, since by using the trade mark Reed gained an advantage that he otherwise would not have had. The matter may now go to the European court as a test case (Rose, 2001).

Brand mark

The brand mark is specifically the element of the visual brand identity that does not consist of words, but of design and symbols. This would include things like McDonald's golden arches, Apple's computer symbol, or Audi's interlocking circles. These things are also protectable, as discussed under trade marks above.

The benefits of branding

Branding carries benefits for all parties involved in the exchange process and in theory at least makes it easier to buy or sell products. This section, summarised in Figure 7.4, looks at the benefits of branding from different perspectives, beginning with that of the buyer.

Consumer perspective

Branding is of particular value to the buyer in a complex and crowded marketplace. In a supermarket, for example, brand names and visual images make it easier to locate and identify required products. This is expecially important as it has been estimated that the average consumer inspects just 1.2 brands per purchase on average (Kahn, 1998). Strong branding can speak volumes about the function and character of the product and help consumers to judge whether it is their sort of product, delivering the functional and psychological benefits sought. This is especially true for a new, untried product. The branding can at least help the evaluation of product suitability, and if there is an element of corporate branding (as discussed with Cadbury's above) it can also offer reassurance about the product's quality pedigree.

This all aids in the shopping process and reduces some of its risks, but it goes further. Giving a product what amounts to a three-dimensional personality makes it easier for consumers to form attitudes and feelings about the product. It gets them sufficiently interested to want to be bothered to do that. This has the double effect of creating brand loyalty (the product as a trusted friend) and of creating something special in the consumer's mind that the competition would find difficult to touch.

Figure 7.4 The benefits of branding

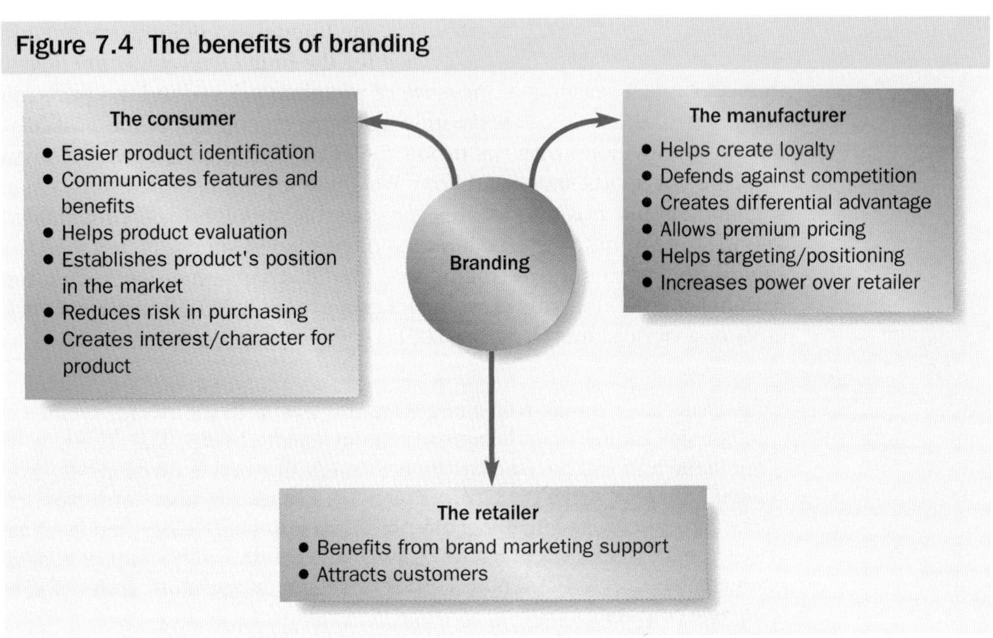

It is especially important for companies to build trust when they are asking consumers to become involved with them in life-transforming tasks, such as taking out a pension or other significant personal finance package. It is then necessary to establish a real relationship rather than an arm's length, 'take the money and run' transaction. This relationship manifests itself not only through the product or service consumption, but also through the brand's values, which are essential for building trust and winning affection (Mitchell, 1999).

This has led to brands being regarded as 'packaged meanings' that shoppers can identify with and that organisations are happy to engender. Being able to humanise products with characteristics such as being honest, friendly, trustworthy, fun or *avant garde* all helps to build stronger customer relationships and makes the product attributes almost secondary. With 'passion brands' such as football club Manchester United (*see also* case study 10.1, p. 422), religions, pressure groups, political parties, etc., rationality almost goes altogether. Such brands reflect the 'buyer's' inner belief in values and create very strong emotions. They do not have 'consumers' and 'targeted products'; they have followers, who buy into what the brand stands for and who feel part of a community. Whatever the weather, the distance to be travelled or the team's results, bands of fans go through the turnstiles and many more participate from the armchair by watching television and buying from the shop. Manchester United, commercially the most successful club in Europe, is happy to work with these emotions. Club websites, merchandise, media products and memorabilia all help to generate significant amounts of extra revenue (Mitchell, 1998).

There are critics, however, who claim that the consumer is being manipulated and that brands are becoming ever more intrusive into modern lives. One of the demands made during the anti-capitalism riots in Seattle was 'give us back our brains'. Bunting (2001) captured the essence of the debate by claiming,

> *Brands have become a powerful social force, building up a near unassailable position in people's hearts and minds through ideologies which are impossible to challenge, given the vast huge sums invested on promoting them. And there's the rub – we have handed over ideology and our most effective form of connecting people in a fragmented, multi-cultural society to a bunch of clever brand consultants who sit in funky designed offices with exquisite flower displays.*

Manufacturer perspective

The manufacturer benefits, of course, from the relationship of the buyer with branding. The ease of identification of the product at the point of sale, the connotations of quality and familiarity and the creation of a three-dimensional product personality all help the manufacturer.

The manufacturer's key interest is in the building of defendable brand loyalty to the point where the trust, liking and preference for the brand overcome any lingering price sensitivity, thus allowing a reasonable measure of premium pricing and the prevention of brand switching. Some of the best known brands that have emerged over the past fifty years have become almost synonymous with the product sector: Kelloggs for cereal, Hoover for vacuum cleaners, Nike for sports shoes and Sony Walkman for the personal stereo market. Achieving such a 'generic brand' position creates considerable strength for the manufacturer in shaping marketing strategy, but it is no guarantee of continued success – ask Levi's or Marks & Spencer. In addition, with a more fragmented media environment (see Chapter 15) and increased national competition, it is now much harder for new brands such as Egg, Orange and Virgin to achieve generic status (Brierley, 2001).

eg

Preussag, the German-based largest tour operator in the world, decided to change its name to become the first pan-European holiday master brand, TUI. The new logo incorporates a red smile and will be used by the previously distinctive divisions of Thomson Travel, Lunn Poly, Britannia Airways, JetAir, Nouvelles Frontières, and Fritdresor, as well as Preussag. The separate logos will all become subsidiary to the TUI logo and it remains to be seen how long the individual brand names will actually continue to feature. Preussag owns 3,660 travel agencies, 88 aircraft, 270 hotels and dozens of tour operators, so few will escape the new distinctive corporate smile.

Developing pan-European branding is not easy in the holiday business. The intention is more about pooling and streamlining back-office resources rather than literally ensuring that different nationalities exchange pleasantries around the swimming pool, unless that is what they want. The typical British holidaymaker does not mix well with other nationalities, whereas the Germans tend to be less insular but have very different tastes, none of which is supportive of customer mixing. The focus of the name change will therefore be on corporate branding to ensure that at all points of contact with the brand there will be a unifying message. Another contender for the name was Thomson, but that could have caused confusion with the French electrical firm so TUI was chosen. In case you are wondering, TUI stands for Touristik Union International – not the sexiest or most memorable of brand names (Clark, 2001; Rogers, 2001a, 2001b)!

Other more subtle advantages of branding for the manufacturer are linked with segmentation and competitive positioning strategies. In a study of consumer assessment of six brands of sports shoes in Spain, Belén del Río *et al.* (2001) found that consumers observed greater differences between the branded shoes than was merited by the actual product differences. This result suggests that the brand name can be a key factor in competitive strategy.

Different brands can be used by one organisation to target different segments. Because the different brands have clearly defined individual characteristics, the consumer does not necessarily link them and thus does not become confused about what the organisation stands for. Even where there is a strong corporate element to the branding, as with Ford cars, the individual models within the range are clearly seen as separate products, serving different market needs, with price differences justified in terms of design and technical specification. Consumers view this wide range of brands positively, as a way of offering as tailored a choice as possible within the confines of a mass market.

Strong branding is also important for providing competitive advantage, not just in terms of generating consumer loyalty, but also as a means of competing head-on, competing generally across the whole market in an almost undifferentiated way or finding a niche in which to dominate. Research published by the European Brands Association supports the 'virtuous circle' of brand investment: heavy *advertising* creates *brands* which *grow market share* to enjoy greater *economies of scale* in advertising and promotion, which enables *higher R&D* and *advertising spend* to *introduce more innovation* and branded products (Lightfoot, 1998). Brand imagery can help to define the extent of competition or exaggerate the differentiating features that pull it away from the competition. Table 7.2 examines the toilet soap market, identifying the different levels of competitive activity in different market segments, as represented by available brands. Despite the power of branding and brand imagery, some are now questioning whether the move towards global brands is both

Table 7.2 The UK's toilet soap market, 2002 (selected brands)

Manufacturer	*Family segment*	*Luxury/beauty*	*Skincare*	*Cosmetic*	*Deodorant*
Lever Fabergé		Lux		Dove	Shield
Cusson's	Imperial Leather	Pearl		Cusson's Mild Cream	
Procter & Gamble	Fairy	Camay		Olay Conditioning Bar	Zest
Colgate Palmolive	Palmolive				
Beiersdorf UK				Nivea Creme	
Accantia Health and Beauty			Simple		
Own label			The Body Shop Boots Natural		

inevitable and desirable (MacKenzie, 2001). The danger is that local and national identity can be lost with global branding and some regard the global brand as a cultural takeover. This is starting to result in global brands being allowed some local variation, within the context of an overall brand identity, for example there are variations in the menus at some McDonald's restaurants across Europe. It could, however, also encourage a shift to what are perceived as truly local brands rather than brands regarded as blandly international. The Nestlé approach is to have a strong corporate brand underpinning localised smaller scale brands that are fine-tuned to individual markets rather than adopting a purely monolithic approach. If a trend towards local brands does develop, the priority will be to provide greater local autonomy, more marketing discretion on promotion, and possible joint ventures for local production. It could end up being more expensive, but at least it will enable the global players to remain dominant (Bunting, 2001).

Retailer perspective

The retailer benefits from branding to a certain extent. Branded products are well supported by advertising and other marketing activities, and so the retailer has some assurance that they will sell. Branded products do draw customers into the store, but the disadvantage is that if a brand is unavailable in one store, then the shopper is likely to patronise another instead. The retailer may prefer the shopper to be less brand loyal and more store loyal! Supermarkets have always recognised the value and necessity of manufacturer-branded goods, but they have also looked for ways of reducing the power that this gives the brand owner. This issue will be looked at in detail in the next subsection.

marketing *in action*

The true value of a brand?

A brand asset has been defined as,

> *a name and/or symbol used to uniquely identify the goods and services of a seller from those of its competitors, with a view to obtaining wealth in excess of that obtainable without a brand' (Tollington, 1998).*

To have a meaningful brand asset requires identification and quantification. Brand valuation emerged through the 1990s as an important measure for brand owners assessing the effectiveness of their brand marketing strategies, their long-term advertising and even the overall worth of the company. Brands represent a financial value to a company reflected through the goodwill component of a balance sheet. The physical assets of a company often now only represent a small part of the value of that company: it is reputation that is worth paying for, as it can bring you loyal customers and committed staff. When Ford bought Jaguar it was estimated that the physical assets were just 16 per cent of the value of the company and when Vodafone bought Orange, physical assets were just 10 per cent of the value (Bunting, 2001). This reflects the real value of strong brand names.

Interbrand Newell & Sorrell, in research for trade magazine *Marketing Week*, plotted the growth in brand values for top US and UK companies between 1988 and 1998. Brand value was calculated by comparing market capitalisation with net tangible or physical assets. The difference between these two figures shows the goodwill gap, i.e. the extent to which potential investors value a company over and above its tangible assets such as plant and machinery. Although these differences can be accounted for by a range of factors, such as management ability, patents and distribution strength, research has found that a significant part of the difference can be accounted for by the worth of the brands. In the case of Coca-Cola the figure is 4,000 per cent of the tangible assets, Cadbury Schweppes is 33 per cent or £1.5 bn and Scottish & Newcastle Breweries is 158 per cent.

A similar study by Interbrand and Citibank examining stock market performance found that those companies that were heavily branded tended to outperform the rest of companies in the FT–SE 350 index by between 15 and 20 per cent over a 15-year period. Brand value clearly makes a difference to companies.

The history of brand valuation can be traced back to 1988 when Rank Hovis McDougall (RHM) successfully defended against a hostile takeover by including the value of its brands in its balance sheet. Since then, organisations such as Burmah Castrol, Cadbury Schweppes, ICI and Disney have all used brand-valuation techniques for management and acquisition purposes. The value of brands to many companies has now become so important that it has been argued that the chief executive should ultimately be the brand manager and that all staff need to realise that they are in the front line of brand delivery. Such an approach is clearly demonstrated by Richard Branson at Virgin, where the strength of the Virgin brand name has successfully carried it into many sectors.

The recognition of brands as assets is likely to become more emphasised in future as finance directors and accountants increasingly use brand-valuation techniques in balance sheets. In December 1998, the UK Accounting Standards Board recommended through Standards 10 and 11 that the value of acquired brands should be included in company accounts. Most brand valuations are, however, excluded from published balance sheets and are often only considered during mergers and acquisitions when they can be used to increase the asset base and force up the bidding price (Tollington, 2001). However, because of issues of the subjectivity and reliability of valuation measurement, the accounting profession still treats brand valuation with some caution.

Sources: Baird (1998); Bunting (2001); Butterfield (1998); Butterfield and Haigh (1998); Tollington (1998, 2001).

Lest this discussion should seem too enthusiastic about branding, we now turn to some of the disadvantages. Echoing one of the risks of segmentation (discussed in Chapter 5, pp. 203–4), there is the danger of proliferation if brands are created to serve every possible market niche. Retailers are under pressure to stock increasing numbers of lines within a product area, which means in turn that either less shelf space is devoted to each brand or retailers refuse to stock some brands. Both options are unpleasant for the manufacturer. The consumer may also begin to see too much choice and, at some point, there is a risk that the differences between brands become imperceptible to the consumer and confusion sets in.

Types of brands

The discussion so far has centred on the brands created and marketed by manufacturers and sold through retail outlets. An area of growing importance, however, is the brand created by a wholesaler or retailer for that organisation's sole use. This development has taken place partly because of conflicts and power struggles between manufacturers and retailers (*see* Chapter 12), and partly because the retailers also need to generate store loyalty (*see* Chapter 13) in a highly competitive retail sector.

This section, therefore, distinguishes between the brands emanating from different types of organisation.

Manufacturer brands

Most manufacturers, particularly in the fmcg sector, are at arm's length from the end buyer and consumer of their product. The retail sector is in between and can make the difference between a product's success and failure through the way the product is displayed or made available to the public. The manufacturer can attempt to impose some control over this through trade promotions, but the manufacturer's best weapon is direct communication with the end buyer. Planting brand names and recognition of brand imagery in the consumer's mind through advertising or sales promotion gives the manufacturer a fighting chance of recognition and selection at the point of sale. Furthermore, the creation of a strong brand that has hard-core loyalty can tip the balance of power back in favour of the manufacturer, because any retailer not stocking that brand runs the risk of losing custom to its competitors.

The creation and management of a **manufacturer brand** generate many responsibilities and costs in terms of promotion, distribution, quality control and product development, but if the process is managed effectively, then it does represent a valuable asset, both financially and strategically.

Retailer and wholesaler brands

The growth of **own-label brands** (i.e. those bearing the retailer's name) or own-brands has become a major factor in retailing. Supermarkets and clothing stores, in particular, have been very active in creating physical products exclusive to the store, reflecting the retailer's name. The responsibility for the development and maintenance of the brand falls on the retailer. The retailer may or may not manufacture the products directly, but either way, the product will not admit its provenance. 'Manufactured in the UK for J Sainsbury PLC' is the nearest you are likely to get.

Why do it? One possible problem a retailer has is that if a consumer is buying a recognised manufacturer's brand, then the source of that purchase is less relevant. A can of Heinz baked beans represents the same values whether it is purchased from a corner shop or from Harrod's. Retailers can differentiate from each other on the basis of price or service, but they are looking for more than that. The existence of a range of exclusive retailer brands that the consumer comes to value creates a physical reason for visiting that retailer and no other. These brands also serve the purpose of giving the consumer 'the retailer in a tin', where the product in the kitchen cupboard is a constant reminder of the retailer and embodies the retailer's values in a more tangible form, reinforcing loyalty and positive attitudes.

Other reasons include the fact that the retailer can earn a better margin on an own-brand and still sell it more cheaply than a manufacturer's brand. This is because it does not face the product development, brand creation and marketing costs that the manufacturers incur. The retailer's own-brand is sold on the back of the retailer's normal marketing activity and not with the massive advertising, promotion and selling costs that each manufacturer's brand has to bear. Even the comparatively small production runs involved with retailers' brands need not increase costs too much, if the own-brand is either the manufacturer's brand with a different label or a slight variation.

The use of own-brand varies across different retailers. Some retailers, such as Kwik Save, use their own label to create a no-nonsense, no-frills, value-for-money, generic range. Others, such as Marks & Spencer, Sainsbury's and the Albert Heijn chain in the Netherlands, have created own-brands that are actually perceived as superior in quality to the manufacturer's offerings.

It is apparent that some supermarkets are using own-brand products increasingly as a central pivot around which to cluster a select but small number of manufacturer brands. Given that own-label products seem to put so much power into the hands of the retailers, why do manufacturers cooperate in their production? For a manufacturer of second string brands (i.e. not the biggest names in the market), it might be a good way of developing closer links with a retailer and earning some sort of protection for the manufacturer's brands. In return for the supply, at attractive prices, of own-brand products, the retailer might undertake to display the manufacturer's brands more favourably, or promise not to delist them, for example. The extra volume provides some predictability for the manufacturer and it also could help to achieve economies of scale of benefit to both parties.

The danger, of course, is that of the manufacturer becoming too dependent on the retailer's own-brand business. The supplier–buyer relationship needs to be carefully monitored and handled (*see* pp. 150 *et seq.*). Some retailers, such as Marks & Spencer and the Irish retailer Dunne's, demand a high level of influence over the operations of their own-label suppliers, to the point of expecting to take a significant proportion of the supplier's output, yet retaining the right to drop a supplier which fails to live up to expectations. The smaller, more vulnerable organisation in particular needs to develop an active policy of diversification to offset the strategic risks of over-dependency.

A final twist in the evolution of the own-brand scene over the past few years has been an increasing consumer cynicism, giving credence to the view that retailers' own-brands are only the manufacturers' brands with different labels, but much cheaper. To counter this, some big manufacturers have made it explicit that they do not operate in the own-brand market. Nescafé and Procter & Gamble have advertised on this basis and Kellogg's packaging actually states, 'We don't make cereals for anyone else'. Their fear is understandable. Why continue to spend more on manufacturer brands when you can get the same goods cheaper with an ASDA label on them?

The battle between own-label and manufacturer brands is expected to intensify in the coming years, especially as own-labels confront the manufacturers' claims of better quality head-on by also positioning themselves on quality as much as on price (Kahn, 1998).

■ Branding strategy

This chapter has already hinted at a number of important dimensions to be considered in developing and maintaining a branding strategy. Each one will now be treated separately.

Selecting a brand name

If all the benefits to the buyer mentioned at pp. 282 *et seq*. are going to be achieved through branding, then the name becomes a crucial choice. It must be memorable, easy to pronounce and meaningful (whether in real or emotional terms). As manufacturers look increasingly towards wider European and international markets, there is a much greater need to check that a proposed name does not lead to unintended ridicule in a foreign language. Neither the French breakfast cereal Plopsies (chocolate-flavoured puffed rice) nor the gloriously evocative Slovakian pasta brand Kuk & Fuk are serious contenders for launch into an English-speaking market. From a linguistic point of view, care must be taken to avoid certain combinations of letters that are difficult to pronounce in some languages. The combination 'th' is fine in English but not in French, while the combination 'cz' poses no problem to a Polish speaker but challenges most of western Europe. The danger is, of course, that by trying to avoid challenging anyone linguistically, imagination is lost and the Eurobrand becomes the Eurobland. Some brand names such as Adidas, Findus, Mars and Lego have nevertheless managed to avoid the pitfalls. Birds Eye, while retaining the bearded sea captain and pack design for its fish products, becomes Iglo in Germany and Captain in France (Ensor, 1997).

Language problems apart, the ability of a brand name to communicate something about the product's character or functional benefits could be important. Blackett (1985) suggests that approaches to this can vary, falling within a spectrum ranging from freestanding names, through associative names, to names that are baldly descriptive. This spectrum is shown with examples of actual brand names in Figure 7.5. Names that are totally freestanding are completely abstract and bear no relation to the product or its character. Kodak is a classic example of such a name. *Associative* names suggest some characteristic, image or benefit of the product, but often in an indirect way. Pledge (furniture polish), Elvive (shampoo) and Impulse (body spray) are all names that make some kind of statement about the product's positioning through the consumer's understanding of the word(s) used in the name. The extremely prosaic end of the spectrum is represented by descriptive names. Names such as Chocolate Orange, Shredded Wheat and Cling Film certainly tell you about what the product is, but they are neither imaginative nor easy to protect. Bitter Lemon, for example, began as a brand name and was so apt that it soon became a generic title for any old bottle of lemon-flavoured mixer. Somewhere between associative and descriptive names come a group with names that are descriptive, but with a distinctive twist. Ex-Lax (laxative), Lucozade (fizzy glucose drink) and Bacofoil (aluminium cooking foil) are names that manage to describe without losing the individuality of the brand.

Figure 7.5 The brand name spectrum

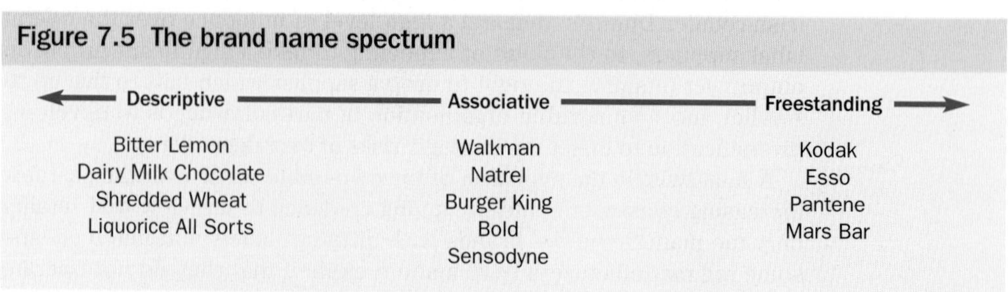

In summary, there are four 'rules' for good brand naming. As far as possible, they need to be:

1 *distinctive*, standing out from the competition while being appealing to the target market and appropriate to the character of the product;
2 *supportive* of the product's positioning with respect to its competitors (pp. 328 *et seq.* will discuss positioning in further detail), while remaining consistent with the organisation's overall branding policy;
3 *acceptable*, recognisable, pronounceable and memorisable, in other words user-friendly to the consumer; and finally,
4 *available*, registerable, protectable (i.e. yours and only yours).

With respect to this last point, it is important to ensure that the suggested brand name is not infringing the rights of existing brands. This is particularly difficult with international brands.

As mentioned earlier, the establishment of the Community Trade Mark Office means that a single registration can protect all aspects of a brand's identity across Europe. A trade mark search carried out by an agent, costing anything from £200 (for checking out a proposed name) to £2,000 (for a detailed search), can help to reassure an organisation that it is not likely to infringe the rights of others. This all suggests that great care needs to be taken when developing brand identities. In order to minimise the risk of either choosing an inappropriate name or the inadvertent breach of another organisation's registered trade marks, many organisations do use professional consultants who specialise in brand concept development and testing and trade mark searches.

e-marketing *in action*

Migrating brands online

The importance of building an effective online brand is particularly important for startups launching a transactional e-commerce site, but how important is online branding managed for existing companies? Let's start by considering what makes a successful online brand? Is it a site with high levels of traffic and online sales or good name recognition? Or is it a site with more modest sales levels, but one that customers perceive as delivering good service? Although such sites are often described as successful brands, as we will see, a successful online brand is dependent on a wide range of factors.

One method of assessing the success of a brand is through brand equity. Aaker and Joachimstaler (2000) refer to these elements of brand equity:

- *Brand awareness*. This is achieved through marketing communications to promote the brand identity and the other qualities of the brand. Aaker and Joachimstaler note that brand awareness is not only important in terms of informing customers about a product, but also because people like the familiar and it links through to other aspects of brand equity. For example, the Intel Inside awareness campaign not only increased awareness, but also provides a perception of technological innovation and quality.
- *Perceived quality*. Awareness counts for little if the customer has a bad experience of a product or associated customer service. If quality of a brand is negatively perceived this affects its equity since word of mouth will quickly be relayed to many people. We can see that online, quality will be affected both by the on-site experience which will be governed by the site design, navigation and speed and the post-sales experience which will be determined by fulfilment and customer service.
- *Brand associations*. There are many brand associations that connect a customer to a brand including imagery, the situation in which a product is used, its personality and symbols. Intel Inside aims to create a fun and funky, but technical brand association through the use of dancing clean-lab technicians. Additional interactions can be used to deepen the brand experience online, for example through competitions or games.
- *Brand loyalty*. This refers to the commitment of customer segments to a brand. For example Intel may have good brand awareness, quality and clear associations, but its brand equity is undermined if customers are happy to buy a computer with an AMD or Cyrix chip when they next upgrade their computer. Brand loyalty is particularly important to startup companies since they need to recoup initial investments through repeat sales.

When a company launches or relaunches an e-commerce site it has the following choices with regards to brand identity:

- *Migrate traditional brand online*. This is probably the most common approach. Companies with brands that are well established in the real world can build on the brand by duplicating it online. Sites from companies such as Ford, Orange and Disney all have identical brand identities and values that would be expected from experience of their offline brands. The risk of migrating existing brands online are that the brand equity may be reduced if the site is of poor quality in terms of performance, structure or information content.

- *Extend traditional brand: variant.* Some companies decide to create a slightly different version of their brand when they create their website. The DHL site (http://www.dhl.co.uk) is based on an online brand 'Red Planet' which is based on a spaceship concept. Users order couriers and track using controls on a spaceship console. Through using this approach, the advantages of a brand variant are illustrated well. The company is able to differentiate itself from similar competing services and this can be used in online and offline promotion to distinguish the site from its rivals. The use of an online brand variant helps raise the profile of the web services and helps the customer think of the site in association with the company.
- *Partner with existing digital brand.* It may be that a company can best promote its products in association with a strong existing digital or internet brand such as Yahoo! or Freeserve. For example, the shopping options for music and book sales on Freeserve are branded as Freeserve although they are actually based on sites from other companies such as record seller Audiostreet.com. Freeserve is given brand prominence since this is to the advantage of both companies.
- *Create a new digital brand.* It may be necessary to create an entirely new digital brand if the existing offline brand has negative connotations or is too traditional for the new medium. An example of a new digital brand is the Egg banking service which is part of Prudential, a well established company. Egg can take new approaches without damaging Prudential's brand, and at the same time, not being inhibited by the Prudential brand. Some of the characteristics of a successful brand name are that it should be simple, distinctive, meaningful, and compatible with the product. These principles can be readily applied to web-based brands. Examples of brands that fulfil most of these characteristics are CDNow, CarPoint, BUY.COM and e-STEEL. Others suggesting that distinctiveness is most important are Amazon, Yahoo!, Expedia, Quokka.com (extreme sports), E*Trade, and FireandWater (Harper and Collins) books.

Sources: Aaker and Joachimstaler (2000); Chaffey (2002).

Product range brand policy

For most fmcg organisations, the decision on whether to brand the product range or not is an easy one. Branding is essential for most products in these markets. Difficulty arises with some homogeneous products because in theory the customer does not perceive sufficient difference between competing products to make branding feasible. As suggested at p. 200 in the discussion on undifferentiated products, however, there are fewer and fewer truly homogeneous products to be found. Petrol brands, for example, have now been created that differentiate on the basis of service factors and the use of sales promotions as an integral part of the offering.

Branding is of even less significance when supplying B2B markets, because of the differences in buyer behaviour. There is, however, increasing interest in branding in some sectors. Computer systems are heavily branded for instance and, at the other end of the purchasing spectrum, organisations supplying consumables are turning to branding as a means of trying to engender customer loyalty. Stationery companies, such as Arjo Wiggins fine papers with its Conqueror, Connoisseur and Keay Kolour brands, are branding paper and other office goods.

Once the decision to brand has been made, there are still a number of choices, one of which is the degree of independence that the brand is to be given in terms of its relationship with both other brands and the originating organisation.

Generic brands represent one extreme, where a single brand image covers a wide range of different products. This is mainly found in supermarkets, where a range of very low-priced, basic staple products are packaged with the minimum of frills and often the minimum permissible information on the packaging, such as Tesco's Value Lines. This is still a form of branding, in the sense that it is creating a distinctive character for a set of products.

At the opposite extreme, individual products are given entirely separate individual brand identities. There is thus no obvious relationship between different products produced by the same organisation. This is known as *discreet branding*. It is a useful policy to adopt if the intention is to compete in a number of different segments because it reduces the risk of one product's positioning affecting the consumer's perception of another product. It also means that if one product gets into trouble, perhaps through a product-tampering scare or through production problems causing variable quality, the other products are better insulated against the bad reputation rubbing off onto them too. The big disadvantage of the discreet approach to branding, however, is that each brand has to be set up from scratch, with all the expense and marketing problems associated with it. The new brand cannot benefit from the established reputation of any other brand.

One way of allowing brands to support each other is by using a *monolithic* approach to branding, which uses a family name (usually linked with the corporate name) with a single brand identity for the whole product range.

eg

Heinz (http://www.heinz.com) is a prime example of the monolithic approach. The Heinz brand is well respected and very strong, but individual Heinz products have little identity of their own. Brand names are descriptive and always include the word Heinz to link them, such as Heinz Cream of Tomato Soup, Heinz Baked Beans, Heinz Low Calorie Mayonnaise etc. Even the label design of each product shows that it clearly belongs to the Heinz family, further drawing the products together. Such family unity creates a strong overall image and allows new products easy entry into the existing product lines (although it might take consumers a while to notice a new flavour of soup in among the rest). It is also possible to achieve economies of scale in communication, if desired, and distribution, through treating the family as a unit rather than as a number of independent products. The danger is, however, that if one product fails or gains a bad reputation, the rest may suffer with it.

A compromise between monolithic and discreet branding is an approach that allows individual brand images, but uses a corporate or family name as a prominent umbrella to endorse the product. Some organisations, such as Ford and Kellogg, use a *fixed endorsed* approach. Here, there is a rigid relationship between the company name and the brand, with a high degree of consistency between the presentation of different brands (but not as extreme as the Heinz approach). A *flexible endorsed* approach, such as that practised by Cadbury's, gives the brand more latitude to express its individuality. The company name may be more or less prominent, depending on how much independence the organisation wants the brand to have. These products seem to enjoy the best of both worlds. The family name gives the products and any new products a measure of credibility, yet the individuality of the products allows variety, imagination and creativity without being too stifled by the 'house style'. Marketing costs are, however, going to be higher because of the need to develop and launch individual identities for products and then to communicate both the family image and the individual brand images.

Developing a brand extension policy

A kind of flexible endorsement that does not involve the corporate name is where a brand name is developed to cover a limited number of products within a product line. Consumers may be more favourably inclined towards brands that are associated with known and trusted products (DelVecchio, 2000).

eg

Reckitt and Benckiser, the Anglo-Dutch household group, established the Dettol brand name in 1933. The name was extended to include a whole range of clearly related products, such as Dettox, Dettol antibacterial soap, foam bath, antiseptic cream, pain relief spray and handwash in a mini-family, again capitalising on the established reputation of the 'parent' product.

Reckitt and Benckiser brands have gained worldwide sales so that few kitchen and bathroom cabinets are without at least one. Most of its brands, such as Lemsip, Disprin, Mr Sheen and Finish, are strong and thus a high proportion of sales come from products that are either number one or two in their categories. After the merger between Reckitt and Colman and Benckiser in 1999, the priority for the new group was to focus on five core categories: surface care, home care, dishwashing, health, and fabric care, and then to invest heavily in the family brand range in each category to retain a strong position. The review of branding policy that took place meant that Dettox was renamed to become a more direct member of the Dettol family, as the step from disinfectant to cleaning fluids is not that great.

Traditionally, Dettox was for things and Dettol was for people, so the success of the name change will depend on how consumer perceptions adapt. If consumers cannot relate to Dettol rather than Dettox, even though the product itself remains the same, they will switch to competing brands. Dettol has already been extended into many areas and some argue that this could be one extension too many (Singh, 2001; Trefgarne, 2001).

This example raises the issue of *brand extension*. Dettol has been very successful in launching variants or new products. Such a policy is cost efficient in that it saves the cost of developing totally new images and promoting and building them up from nothing: for example, easyJet is actively extending its brand name into 'easyEverything'. The launch of cyber cafés is the first such move using a formula similar to the one that made easyJet so successful. The cafés offer low-cost internet access to the public with easyJet's trademark no-frills service. It has been argued, however, that the introduction of additional products to the brand family can dilute the strength of the brand (John *et al.*, 1998). As the number of products affiliated to a brand name increases, the original brand beliefs may become less focused and start to be fuzzier in consumers' minds. To some extent, Virgin has suffered from this. Extending the brand name from a successful airline to the more problematic rail service could damage the core brand reputation. Consideration of brand extension also begins to highlight some of the marketing issues involved in branding that will be discussed further in the next chapter on product management.

In summary, any individual organisation is faced with a range of decisions including whether or not to brand, the character of its brands and the degree of independence each brand is given. A smaller organisation with limited resources and a limited number of products may take a monolithic approach, whereas a larger organisation may be better able to create discreet brands if it chooses. Whatever the situation, however, the branding and brand management decisions have to be made in the context of market segments, positioning and the competitive environment. Branding can be a strain on resources if the brand identity is not well established or if it is under threat.

An organisation that uses branding effectively, whether creating a monolithic brand family, a fixed or flexible endorsed set of brands or taking a discreet branding approach, is in a powerful position with the retail trade in gaining shelf space and cooperation. It can also be in a better position to engender consumer loyalty, whether to an individual product

The strength of the Dettol brand has allowed numerous extensions.

Source: Reckitt & Benckiser.

or to a range (which would allow product switching within the variety offered in the range, without the loss of overall sales). All of this helps to make branding a very active and strategically important area in marketing.

Packaging

Packaging is an important part of the product that not only serves a functional purpose, but also acts as a means of communicating product information and brand character. The packaging is often the consumer's first point of contact with the actual product and so it is essential to make it attractive and appropriate for both the product's and the customer's needs.

eg

McVitie's (http://www.unitedbiscuits.co.uk) has managed to differentiate its Jaffa Cakes (http://www.jaffacakes.co.uk) brand from supermarket 'look-alike' own brands by producing innovative packaging for mini-Jaffa Cakes. The pack consists of six individually sealed plastic segments, joined by perforations, which can be easily separated. The pack is bright orange, with the texture of orange peel to emphasise the nature of the product. Each segment provides a portion of Jaffa Cakes and can be packed into a lunch box or just used as a convenient snack. Meanwhile, the other five segments remain sealed and therefore stay fresh until required.

Packaging is any container or wrapping in which the product is offered for sale and can consist of a variety of materials such as glass, paper, metal or plastic, depending on what is to be contained. The choice of materials and the design of the packaging may have to take account of the texture, appearance and viscosity of the product, as well as its perishability. Dangerous products such as medicines or corrosive household cleaners need special attention. Other design issues might include the role of the packaging in keeping the product ready for use, the means of dispensing the product and the graphic design, presenting the brand imagery and the statutory and desired on-pack information.

eg

Heinz (http://www.heinz.com) undertook a re-packaging exercise to bring greater coherence to the appearance of its soups, pasta meals and beans. For convenience foods, packaging design has to be clear and distinctive to attract busy shoppers moving through supermarkets. Research had indicated to Heinz that shoppers were moving more quickly through aisles and spending less time on shopping. Although the traditional packaging colours for tomato soups and beans were retained, colour was used to emphasise the distinctiveness of other ranges. 'Big Soup' labels were, therefore, presented with a dark green background rather than red. Similarly, 'Chef's Specials' pasta meals, such as ravioli and macaroni cheese, appeared with a yellow background including the traditional Heinz keystone design, rather than in their original orange and bright green respectively (Smith, 1998).

Naturally, there is a cost involved in all of this and thus the organisation needs to be reassured that a particular solution to its packaging needs and problems will either serve a functional purpose or enhance the product's image and competitive standing in the market. Equally, trying to save money by skimping on packaging could be a false economy. If the packaging does not work (literally or metaphorically), then the customer is likely to reject the whole product. Although it can cost £100,000 to create a packaging design for an fmcg product, it seems a very reasonable sum compared with the £3 million or more that will be spent on the advertising to launch that same product. McKenzie (1997) found that the packaging design was becoming a vital element in developing a brand proposition to the consumer both in advertising and point-of-sale promotion. This could be the case both for a new product launch and for relaunching existing products that might be starting to look tired.

With the rise of the self-service ethos in consumer markets, packaging has indeed grown in importance. It has to communicate product information to help the consumer make a choice, to communicate brand image and positioning and, mostly, to attract attention at the point of sale and invite the consumer to explore the product further (Pieters and Warlops, 1999). Even in B2B markets, packaging is important. To serve B2B customers' needs, suppliers have to think about how best to bundle quantities of product together for ease of handling for fast-moving products, how best to protect products that will be held for a time in storage or how to make it as easy as possible for a customer to unpack and introduce a component or product into a production line.

Thus packaging is an important part of the overall product offering and has a number of marketing and technical dimensions, some of which are discussed below.

Functions of packaging

Functional

First among the functions of packaging are the practicalities. Packaging must be *functional*: it must protect the product in storage, in shipment and often in use. Packaging may consist of a number of layers, each serving a different purpose. A packet of frozen beefburgers, for example, may have an outer cardboard box. This protects the product in transit and handling, creating units of a standard size that can easily be packaged together for delivery to the retailer. The outer box also allows the retail display to be attractive and tidy, presenting necessary product information, cooking instructions and selling points to the consumer. Within the box, the burgers may be sealed in groups of six inside clear plastic wrapping. This prevents them from suffering 'freezer burn', a natural process of deterioration in unprotected frozen food. The individual burgers are finally separated from each other with a single sheet of film to prevent them from sticking together.

Frozen food is not the only area in which it is necessary to preserve freshness. Jars of coffee and cans of dried milk, such as Marvel, have an inner seal that serves the double purpose of keeping the product fresh until it is opened and reassuring the customer that the product has not been tampered with before purchase.

Other packaging functions centre on convenience for the consumer, both in terms of ease of access and ease of use. The ring-pull tins now used for canned sardines, for example, have made the sweat and (usually) bloodshed associated with the old-style key-operated tins a thing of the past (corned beef canners take note!). An example of packaging that also helps the usage of the product is shower gel. The lid of the pack, incorporating a hook, is removed and clipped to the bottom of the pack to allow it to be hung in the shower. A self-sealing mechanism in some packs means that the contents do not drip out unless the pack is purposefully squeezed. In the convenience food sector, ease of use has come with the development of packaging that can be placed straight inside a microwave oven and thus serves as a cooking utensil. These last examples also underline the necessity for packaging materials, design and technology to develop in parallel with markets and emerging market needs. The Co-op launched Braille on its own-label medicine packaging to help the UK's one million blind and partially sighted people who need to tell the difference between medicines. To achieve this breakthrough, the Co-op had to work with packaging suppliers to develop different techniques for printing cartons and labels (*The Grocer*, 2001). Consumer pressure for fewer preservatives and additives in food products has also encouraged the development of packaging that better preserves pack content. Conversely, advances in packaging technology can themselves lead to the opening up of new opportunities. The development of the 'widget', a device incorporated into beer cans, has opened up the market for canned beer that behaves and tastes like draught.

A less positive driving force behind packaging development was the sad spate of attempts at corporate blackmail through product-tampering scares and from unscrupulous traders diluting products or even refilling bottles of water from the tap and selling them as new. Many jars or packages now have at least a visually prominent seal on the outer pack with the verbal warning that the product should not be used if the seal is damaged.

Promotional

In addition to offering functional information about product identity and use, packaging also serves a *promotional* purpose. It needs to grab and hold the consumer's attention and involve them with the product. This means that the packaging is actually adding value to the brand; this can be achieved through the combination of materials, shape, graphics and colour. It has been suggested that packaging may be the biggest medium of communication for three reasons (Peters, 1994):

1 its extensive reach to nearly all purchasers of the category;
2 its presence at the crucial moment when the purchase decision is made; and
3 the high level of involvement of users who will actively scan packaging for information.

This involvement of the user makes the packaging an essential element in branding, both in the communication of brand values and as an essential part of the brand identity (Connolly and Davidson, 1996).

Finally, packaging can literally be used for promotional purposes. It gives the manufacturer a powerful medium of communication. It can be used, for example, as a means of distributing coupons, for advertising other related products, announcing new products, presenting on-pack offers or distributing samples and gifts. A special can was developed for Lucozade Sport, for example, that allowed 'instant win' vouchers to be sealed into the packaging, separate from the liquid. There is more on all of this in Chapter 16 on sales promotion.

eg

The added psychological value of the packaging is an absolutely essential part of some products. Perfumes, for example, rely heavily on their packaging to endorse the qualities of luxury, expense, exclusivity, mystery and self-indulgence that they try to represent. Champagne, a perfume by Yves St Laurent, comes in a crimson-lined gold box, which opens out like a kind of casket to reveal an elegant bottle representing a champagne cork, complete with gold wire. It is estimated that the packaging for such a product actually costs about three times as much as the content of the bottle itself. Closer to the mass market, Easter eggs are also an example of the packaging outshining the content. Novelty carton shapes, bright graphics, ribbons and bows are central to the purchasing decision and dull any natural inclination to compare the price with the actual chocolate content.

Packaging in the marketing mix

Packaging plays an important part in the marketing mix. This chapter has already outlined its functional importance, its communication possibilities and its crucial role as a first point of physical contact between the buyer and the product. Effective and thoughtful packaging is recognised as a means of increasing sales.

Even the choice of the range of pack sizes to offer the market can reinforce the objectives of the marketing mix. Trial-size packs, clearly labelled as such, help with new product launch (*see also* Chapter 16) by encouraging low-risk product trial. Small-sized packs of an established product may reinforce a commitment to a market segment comprising single-person households or infrequent users. Larger packs target family usage, heavy users generally or the cost-conscious segment who see the large pack as better value for money. The increase in out-of-town shopping by car means that consumers are far better able than ever before to buy large, bulky items. This trend has developed further into the demand for multiple packs. When the US warehouse club Costco first opened in the UK, it only sold in bulk quantities such as gallon jars of HP Sauce, 10-kilo packs of dishwashing powder and 4-kilo packs of minced beef. These sizes were, however, later found to be somewhat larger than the customer really wanted, even when buying in bulk. Pack sizes may also be closely linked with end-use segmentation (*see* p. 193). Ice cream can be packaged as either an individual treat, a family block or a party-sized tub. The consumer selects the appropriate size depending on the end use, but the choice must be there or else the consumer will turn to another brand.

Any organisation needs to appreciate the different packaging demands of different markets. Ensor (1997) examined differences in packaging preferences across Europe. Cans are more popular in France and Spain than card or foil because of the small size and lower prevalence of refrigerators and microwaves, yet soup is traditionally sold in packets. Germans prefer their cake wrapped in foil as they believe it means a fresher product, while the French like a cellophane window so that they can inspect the cake. In France and Spain, packaging has to work hard in the hypermarkets because of the wide range of products stocked in each category and thus colour, shape, type and size of pack all have an impact on the shelf. Retailer Albert Heijn, with over 650 stores in the Netherlands, some of them small, prefers smaller pack sizes. All of this means careful research in European countries so that the most appropriate package can be developed.

In developing a new product or planning a product relaunch, an organisation thus needs to think carefully about all aspects of packaging and its integration into the overall marketing mix of the product. Although only a small number of brands can be supported by heavy national advertising, for the rest, packaging represents the investment priority for communicating the brand message (Underwood *et al.*, 2001). The technical and design

corporate social responsibility *in action*

Burying it, burning it, recycling it and the flowerpot men

A visit to your local household refuse dump will quickly reveal the extent of the waste disposal problem facing European society. Add industrial waste and the problem is magnified significantly. It is perhaps not surprising, therefore, that in 1994 the framework for the European and Packaging Waste Directive was introduced and this has, through national regulations, had a significant impact on how packaging and packaging waste is handled. The Directive required that at least half of all waste packaging should be recovered. Increasingly, therefore, the emphasis is on recycling rather than burying or incinerating waste.

The UK is well below European averages on recycling waste. Switzerland, Germany and Austria have already reached the 50 per cent recycling level, while the UK had notched up just 11 per cent by 2000 (Brown, 2001). The preference in the UK has been to dump waste in landfill sites, a short-term cheap option. Even if the latest estimates that 33 per cent of waste will be recycled by 2025 are realised, the UK will still be well behind the rest of Europe. Part of the problem has been the infrastructure for the processing of materials that could be recycled. Some newspapers collected for recycling, for example, have later been dumped in landfills because there were no plants available to take them, even as free raw material for newsprint. In comparison with Germany, where substantial levies are imposed to fund a now almost viable recycling network, the UK infrastructure is underdeveloped.

The EU Directives and national legislation such as the Producer Responsible Obligations (PRO) in the UK have had a major impact on organisations. It links the packaging chain from the manufacturers of raw materials through to retailers so that each financially contributes to the cost of waste recovery. Retailers are expected to pick up the tab for nearly 50 per cent of packaging waste recovery in the UK, the packers and fillers 37 per cent and the raw material producers just 10 per cent. All companies with an annual turnover of £2 mn or more and handling over 50 tonnes of packaging a year are obliged to comply. However, the tough approaches being adopted are not without critics. Bickerstaffe (1999) argued that the cost of implementing the regulations was out of proportion to the environmental benefits. Food, for example, often has a value of 10 times the cost of the packaging, so better packaging and larger packs could reduce waste. Others have argued that the recycling targets are not achievable because there is no real market for the end product (Gander, 2001).

The battle over plastic flowerpots is indicative of the pervasiveness of current and probable future legislation. In 2000, Hillier Nurseries, of Romsey, was charged with failing to register under the PRO regulations in 1998 and therefore was accused of not taking reasonable steps to recover and recycle packaging waste, i.e. plastic flowerpots. Although a local magistrate argued that 'without the pot there will be no plant. If the pot is "packaging" the plant must be the almost unique, if not unique, product to be produced within its own packaging as opposed to other products which are produced and then put into packaging' (as quoted by Brown, 2000). In other words, it was argued that the plant would not grow without the pot. The High Court did not agree, however, and ruled that the case should be sent back to the magistrates' court for a conviction and penalty. So plastic flowerpots are packaging and, therefore, must be recycled. This has placed an obligation on all garden nurseries, above the threshold, to contribute to the recycling of potted plants.

And now the paradox. Retailers and manufacturers feel under attack from increasingly complex and costly legislation imposed by EU and national government agencies determined to enforce it to protect the environment (albeit at different rates across Europe). We, as consumers, however, continue to demand ever more exciting and interesting packaging that can chill, preserve, reseal and make more convenient the presentation and consumption of our food products. The level of concern among consumers for what happens to the discarded bottle or flowerpot is still relatively low.

Sources: Bickerstaffe (1999); Branigan (2001), Brown, D. (2000); Brown, P. (2001); Gander (2001).

considerations, along with the likely trade and consumer reactions, need to be assessed. Consumers in particular can become very attached to packaging. It can be as recognisable and as cherished as a friend's face and consumers may not, therefore, take kindly to plastic surgery! Sudden packaging changes may lead to a suspicion that other things about the product have also changed for the worse. All of this goes to show that, as with any aspect of marketing, packaging design and concepts need careful research and testing, using where possible one of the growing number of professional consultancies in the field.

Labelling

Labelling is a particular area within the packaging field that represents the outermost layer of the product. Labels have a strong functional dimension, in that they include warnings and instructions, as well as information required by law or best industry practice. Labels state, at the very least, the weight or volume of the product (often including a stylised letter 'e', which means that the variation in weight or volume between packs is within certain tolerances laid down by the EU), a barcode and the name and contact address of the producer. Consumer demand has also led to the inclusion of far more product information, such as ingredients, nutritional information and the environmental friendliness of the product. Unfortunately research indicates that EU customers still find nutrition labelling difficult to understand (Wandel, 1999) and many want clearer labelling to help them make dietary descisons (Shine *et al.*, 1997).

The European Commission is struggling to develop common standards for product labelling across Europe based on successful schemes such as Germany's Blue Angel and the Scandinavian Nordic Swan. The Ecolabel, based on the well-established Blue Angel scheme, gives a consumer reassurance that the products displaying it conform to EU environmental standards. A number of washing machines carry the Ecolabel, reflecting standards in energy, water and detergent consumption. Food labelling about additives and nutritional values has also received attention and this is likely to evolve further with public concern about the identification of genetically modified foods. There has, however, been some concern expressed that the information is too complex and confusing to the consumer and there may be a need to show information in a more graphical way. Despite the potential problems, the EU Parliament has proposed an elaboration of the Ecolabel logo, with additional information, and its extension to retail and service providers (*European Policy Analyst*, 1998a).

The prominence and detail of health and safety instructions are also becoming increasingly important, as organisations seek to protect themselves against prosecution or civil liability should the product be misused. These instructions range from general warnings to keep a product out of the reach of children, to prohibitions on inhaling solvent-based products, through to detailed instructions about the use of protective clothing. Appropriate labelling of medicines is essential if patients' lives are not to be put at risk. If errors are to be reduced, the drugs need to be clearly differentiated and the descriptions sufficiently detailed while being easy to understand. Although problems are not all down to labelling issues (look alike and sound alike trade marks can also cause confusion), there is still a need for idiot-proof instructions. With over 2 million prescriptions written each day in the UK, the challenge for pharmacists and prescribers is to ensure safety in use, as just one error that could have been prevented by better labelling is one too many (Meikle, 2001).

Clear labelling in terms of the matters discussed in this section is important and necessary. The information may be incorporated into the outer packaging as a whole or there may be a distinctive and separate label. Many B2B products, for example, may be plainly wrapped and bear a very functional label, serving to identify only the product and its use.

Product design, quality and guarantees

Design

The preceding discussion of packaging has already mentioned one aspect of design. But there is far more to design than just pretty logos, graphics and attractive packaging. Design is an integral part of the product itself, affecting not only its overall aesthetic qualities but also its ergonomic properties (i.e. the ease and comfort with which it can be used) and even its components and materials. All of this together can enhance the product's visual appeal, its ability to fulfil its function and its reliability and life span.

eg

Video Net, a video on demand system, wanted an electric plug that could fit through a letterbox so that it could send its modem, complete with plug, through the post. It needed either a smaller plug or expensive couriers. The solution was a folding plug, designed by Rutland Gilts that met both the strict British Standard 1363 and Vision Net's requirements. The design process took two years to fine-tune the nine parts of the plug/adapter. Market research revealed that although people would not be prepared to pay any extra for the plug on its own, manufacturers of mobile phones, laptops, travel accessories were all very interested. The new European and UK plug is now being developed which will provide even more flexibility in use, and all because a company wanted to save on delivery costs! (Design Council, 2001a).

Industrial designers have to tread a fine line between innovativeness and customer expectations. Microsoft, for example, has designed an ergonomic computer keyboard that allows the wrists and hands to maintain a much more natural position while typing, reducing the risk of strain and making the typist more relaxed. The new keyboard looks good too, with gentle curves replacing the familiar boxy shape of traditional keyboards. The benefits are unquestionable, yet people are so used to the old design that despite the discomforts, they are slow to make the change. Innovative design can, nevertheless, be the making of a product.

eg

Viewers of the hit film *Gladiator* will recall how much the splendours of ancient Rome and the crowded Coliseum views added to the atmosphere of the film. Sadly it was not real, but the product of computer graphic design combined with live film elements. Just 50 real actors were used to create the entire Coliseum scene, and although the tigers were real, they were added post-production thanks to Mill Film in Soho where most of the elements were blended for Dreamworks Studio. Its skills in 2D and 3D computer graphics were recognised with an Oscar for Best Visual Effects in 2000, and subsequent films it has worked on have included *Harry Potter*, *Tomb Raider*, *Cats and Dogs*, and *Hannibal*. This all goes to show that design is not just about physical products but can involve a whole range of imagery to create appeal and value to customers (Design Council, 2001b).

Design is increasingly being recognised as being more than just the shape and colour of new products. it also involves the process by which new products and service are produced to meet customer needs and bring creative ideas to reality (Design Council, 2001c). Research by the UK Design Council, however, has indicated that smaller companies are often far less design-orientated than larger ones and in some companies, design still plays only a small role in the marketing and product development process. One of the difficulties in assessing the real contribution of design to business performance has been the difficulty of measuring 'good design' beyond impressionistic and descriptive criteria. Hertenstein and Platt (2001) examined the effect of design on the financial performance of 51 firms. They found that firms having a reputation for good design were stronger on virtually all financial measures. Although design effectiveness was still assessed by a panel of experts, after considering the individual design activities, they found for example that sales growth was 23 per cent higher in the effective design group than the industry average and 36 per cent below average for the less effective design group. The authors recognise, however, that good design is no substitute for good management and the successful firms may score well on many other criteria such as marketing and manufacturing. Over all, the message is clear:

design effectiveness can be an important part of business effectiveness and the more good ideas that a company can bring to fruition, the more new products it can roll out. Governments have, however, recognised the importance of design in helping industry to gain a sustainable competitive edge in global markets. Bodies such as the UK's Design Council, the Netherlands Design Institute and the French Agence pour la Promotion de la Création Industrielle promote and support good design practice. The EU also encourages design with initiatives such as the biannual European Community Design Prize aimed at small and medium-sized businesses.

Quality

Unlike design, quality is a very well-understood concept among managers. Many organisations now recognise the importance of quality and have adopted the philosophy of total quality management (TQM), which means that all employees take responsibility for building quality into whatever they do. TQM affects all aspects of the organisation's work, from materials handling to the production process, from the product itself to the administrative procedures that provide customer service. Marketers, of course, have a vested interest in all these manifestations of quality, because creating and holding on to customers means not only providing the quality of product that they want (and providing it consistently), but also supporting the product with quality administrative, technical and after-sales service.

marketing *in action*

Three thousand four hundred reasons to rethink?

That's how many people were killed on the roads in the UK in 2000, and a further 40,000 were injured. The human cost is tragic and the government wants to cut the number of deaths and serious injuries by 40 per cent by 2010. Excessive speed can kill, so anything that keeps motorists from speeding can only be good for society. It is claimed that where speed cameras have been operating, for example, the number of people killed has been reduced by 18 per cent. Better still, the fines collected from speeding motorists can be used to speed up the installation of more cameras, thereby generating more revenue.

But for every measure there is a counter-measure. Have you ever been caught for speeding? If so, you might well appreciate the value of a radar detector which gives you early warning of police radar guns and speed cameras, allowing you to slow down before you pass them. Should motorists be allowed to buy them? The government says 'no', on the basis that the only reason you fit one is to allow you to exceed speed limits in the knowledge that you can slow down when you have to. If you planned to comply with the law, you would not want one in the first place.

Until January 1998, operating in-car radar detection devices was against the law, on the basis that you needed a licence for the receiver. A judge then ruled, however, that as no signal was being emitted from radar guns or speed cameras, no licence was needed as detectors were not 'receiving devices'. This paved the way for a £10 mn business in car accessories costing between £140 and £800 each. For the very sophisticated, the Geodesy warning system, made by Morpheos, a British company, uses a satellite Global Positioning System (GPS) to locate all 4,300 fixed speed cameras in Britain and flashes when the driver approaches a speed camera. Some have gone even further. The Snooper SLD 920 Laser Blinder claims to offer motorists protection against all UK laser speed guns by temporarily stopping them from obtaining a reading. Websites have sprung up offering devices and one, http://www.SpeedCamerasUK.com lists over 500 speed cameras around the country with practical tips on how not to get caught by the well-concealed devices.

The typical owner of radar detection equipment is not the 'boy racer', but tends to be over 40, have a higher income, covers high mileages, and generally is a middle class law abiding citizen with no penalty points on his licence. The problem is convincing others of your reasons for having one if you are so law abiding. The Advertising Standards Authority has banned advertisements from companies selling the devices as the offer implicitly condones the breaking of speed limits. For the time being, the police have accepted that detection devices are here to stay until further legislation can be introduced which could wipe out the detection industry overnight. The situation is currently under review. Evidence from the US suggests that detection devices actually make motorists more aware of speed and reduce the number of accidents.

Of course there is an easy, free way of avoiding prosecution: don't break the speed limit in the first place.

Sources: Foxall (2001); *The Guardian* (2001); Roberts (2001); Young (2001).

In judging the quality of the product itself, a number of dimensions may be considered, as shown in Figure 7.6.

Performance

Performance is about what the product can actually *do*. Thus with the Bosch hammer drills mentioned earlier (*see* Figure 7.3), a customer might perceive the more expensive model with a variable speed of 3,000 rpm as being of 'better quality' than a more basic lower-powered drill. The customer might have more difficulty judging between competing products, however. Black & Decker, for example, produces a range of hammer drills that are very similar to the Bosch ones, with minor variations in specification and price levels. If both the Bosch model and the equivalent Black & Decker model offer the same functions, features, benefits and pricing levels, the customer might have problems differentiating between them in terms of performance and will have to judge on other characteristics.

Durability

Some products are expected to have a longer life span than others and some customers are prepared to pay more for what they perceive to be a better-quality, more *durable* product. Thus the quality level built into the product needs to be suited to its expected life and projected usage. Thus a child's digital watch fitted into a plastic strap featuring a licensed character such as Barbie or Batman, retailing at around £5, is not expected to have the same durability or quality level as a Swiss Tissot retailing at £125. Disposable products in particular, such as razors, biros and cigarette lighters, need to be manufactured to a quality level that is high enough to allow them to perform the required function for the required number of uses or for the required time span, yet low enough to keep the price down to a level where the customer accepts the concept of frequent replacement.

eg

Quality and durability are high priorities for Northrup Grumman Space Systems which produces satellite sensors and smart weapons. If you are producing the software to guide smart bombs or the sensors that keep satellites working there can be no tolerance for error or poor performance. This has implications for the total design, tooling, manufacturing and testing processes. It really is rocket science for Northrup (Bartholomew, 2001).

Reliability and maintenance

Many customers are concerned about the probability of a product breaking down or otherwise failing, and about the ease and economy of repairs. As with durability, some customers will pay a price premium for what are perceived to be more *reliable* products or for the peace of mind offered by comprehensive after-sales support. These days most makes of car,

Figure 7.6 Product quality dimensions

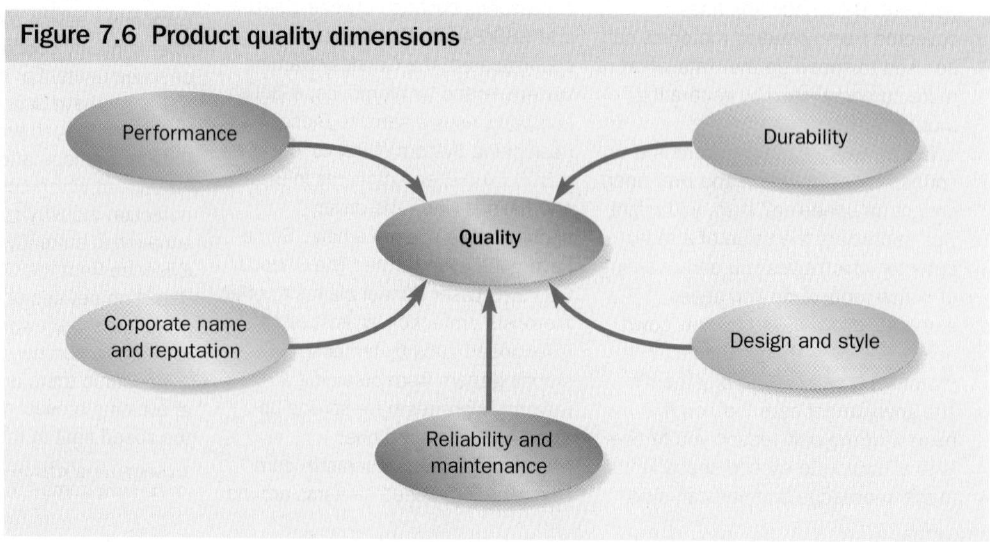

for example, are pretty reliable if they are properly maintained and so car buyers may differentiate on the basis of the cost and ease of servicing and the cost and availability of spare parts. For example, among the appealing features of the Trabant are its durability, its reliability and a mechanical simplicity that allows many repairs to be done by the owner.

Design and style

As mentioned earlier, the visual and ergonomic appeal of a product may influence perceptions of its quality. The sleek, stylish, aerodynamic lines of the Lambourghini contrast sharply with the functional boxiness of the Lada. Packaging design can also enhance quality perceptions.

eg

The Haberman Anywayup Cup is a prized possession to stop a toddler dripping juice all over you or, worse still, your neighbour's carpet. It used innovation in design, with a slit valve to control the flow of liquid, and yet still matched the alternatives for style. Designed by a mother who had suffered from more traditional cups, the non-spill cup was named as a Design Council Millennium Product; it won the Gold Medal at the Salon International des Inventions in Geneva; and it received two honours at the 2000 Design Effectiveness Awards. Its superior design has led to sales of over £10 mn in over 70 countries since its launch in 1995 (Haberman, 2001).

England's Fly Fishers also used innovation in design and style to carve out a new market niche. The company designed an inflatable fishing jacket that not only matched those already on the market for style, but also had the added advantage of a life-saving device that gives automatic self-inflation and is self-righting. This means that the jacket will inflate even if the wearer is unconscious or unable to inflate an orthodox lifejacket and that the head will be kept above water. Just the thing for the unfortunate fisherman taking a premature dip, and not bad for sales either, as the company exports its goods throughout Europe and the Americas (Warman, 1997).

Corporate name and reputation

If, after all that, customers are still uncertain about the relative quality offerings of the alternative products under consideration, they may fall back on their *perceptions of the organisation*. Some may feel that Black & Decker is a well-established, familiar name, and if they have had other Black & Decker products that have served well in the past, then that might swing the quality decision in Black & Decker's favour. Others may decide in favour of Bosch because of its associations with high-quality German engineering.

Marketers recognise that quality in the marketplace is a matter of perception rather than technical specification. This is particularly true in consumer markets, where the potential customer may not have the expertise to judge quality objectively and will use all sorts of cues, such as price, packaging or comparison with competitors, to form an opinion about quality level. A survey by Total Research, called EquiTrend, measured brand quality perception among consumers of over 170 brands in some 30 product and service categories. Table 7.3 shows the top 10 brands from the 1998 EquiTrend and their overall quality ratings out of a maximum possible score of 10. Incidentally, Bosch power tools came 12th in the list and Black & Decker power tools came 19th.

Even in B2B markets, the quality agenda is still set by the customer, who will soon let the manufacturer know if its product is unacceptably inconsistent or if its response to complaints or queries is too slow or inadequate. If the manufacturer is lucky, the customer will give it warning of their discontent and give it a chance to do something about it, but if the manufacturer is unlucky, the customer will simply stop buying from it. This further underlines the need for some kind of constant dialogue with customers to ensure that the warning signs are picked up early. In general, investment in quality is good for business, creating satisfied and loyal customers.

The variety of different power tools that Bosch offers the consumer give them the possibility of choosing the right power tool that suits them when they undertake DIY jobs around the home.

Source: Robert Bosch Limited.

Table 7.3 Brand quality ratings, 1998

Rank	*Brand*	*Perceived quality*
1	Mercedes-Benz Cars	8.46
2	BMW Cars	8.31
3	Disney World, Florida	8.01
4	Cadbury's Dairy Milk Chocolate Bars	7.96
5	Lego Toys	7.95
6	Duracell Batteries	7.95
7	Sony Televisions	7.89
8	Fisher-Price Toys	7.80
9	Kodak Photographic Film	7.78
10	Kellogg's Corn Flakes Cereal	7.68

Source: EquiTrend, Total Research, London. Reprinted with kind permission.

Guarantees

One way in which an organisation can emphasise its commitment to quality and its confidence in its own products and procedures is through the *guarantees* it offers. Although customers are protected under national and EU laws against misleading product claims and goods that are not fit for their intended purpose, many organisations choose to extend their responsibility beyond the legal minimum. Some will offer extended warranties. Double-glazing companies, for example, routinely offer 10- or 15-year guarantees on their windows, which is fine as long as the company is still in existence in 10 or 15 years' time! Others are less ambitious and simply offer 'no questions asked' refunds or replacements if the customer is unhappy with a product for any reason at all. Retailer Marks & Spencer has operated such a policy for many years and, although this can be abused, it is generally highly valued by customers. Such schemes not only reflect the organisation's confidence in its product and its commitment to customer service, but also reduce the risk to the customer in trying the product. The guarantee is therefore a signal that manufacturers use to indicate product quality when consumers cannot gauge what to expect in advance of purchase (George, 1996).

A new EC Directive has been introduced to bring more harmonisation to guarantee protection and practice across member states (Directive 1999/44/EC). Its main purpose is to create more clarity and transparency across the EU without introducing burdensome legal rules that could lead to lengthy wrangles about interpretation. In the drafting of the Directive, which member states then have to reflect in local legislation, guarantees are

eg

The growth of internet shopping has highlighted the importance of guarantees. As you cannot feel, touch or see the product in advance, a full refund satisfaction guarantee can be a powerful part of the offer. It has been estimated that such a guarantee can increase catalogue response or web conversion by between 5 and 15 per cent (Baird, 2001). As a rule of thumb, cancellation rates under such schemes should be no higher than 7 per cent of gross sales, so estimates can be made of the cost of satisfaction guarantees against the expected returns. Lands' End, the clothing catalogue shopping firm offered its German customers an unconditional, unlimited guarantee. The German courts, based on a 1932 statue, ruled that such a practice created unfair competition as it was not common practice in Germany. Lands' End turned it to its advantage in a European marketing campaign, however (Girard, 2000). In Germany, the advertisements featured black strokes over the wording of the guarantee with the words 'advertising not allowed by German courts'. In the UK, the advertisements called the guarantee 'so good, the Germans banned it'.

recognised as playing an important part in the competitive offering. The substance of the guarantee, beyond minimum standards such as it being stated clearly and being easily understood, should be left to the guarantor. Extended warranties are not covered in the Directive. The Directive has been criticised by some for avoiding some contentious areas and for not being sufficiently clearly drafted in others to be of significant value (Twigg-Flesner, 2000).

It may also be possible for the organisation to use its guarantees to create a differential advantage over its competitors. The danger is, however, that promises can be copied. The largest UK supermarket chains, for example, trying to shift the emphasis away from price competition to quality of service, are all now offering very similar packages, including refund and replacement schemes on any product that fails to satisfy. Perhaps the real differentiator will be the speed, efficiency and courtesy with which those promises are fulfilled. In strategic terms, the biggest potential problem is that once similar guarantees have become widespread within a particular market or industry, they start to be seen as a normal part of the product package and their impact may be lost as customers look for other differentiating factors.

Chapter summary

- Product is defined as covering a wide variety of goods, services and ideas that can be the subject of a marketing exchange. The product itself is layered, consisting of the core product, the tangible product and, finally, the augmented product. Using the tangible and augmented product, manufacturers, service providers and retailers can create differential advantage. Products can be classified according to either their own characteristics (durable, non-durable or service) or buyer-orientated characteristics. In consumer markets, these are linked with the frequency of purchase and the length and depth of the information search. In B2B markets, they are more likely to relate to the final use of the product. An organisation's product mix, made up of individual product items, can be divided into product lines. These are groups of items that have some common link, either operational or marketing based. Product mix width is established by the number of product lines, while product line depth is defined according to the number of individual items within a line.
- Branding is an important way of creating differentiated tangible products. It helps the manufacturer to establish loyalty through the three-dimensional character imposed on the product, as well as deflecting consumer attention away from price. Branding is carried out not only by manufacturers, but also by retailers who want to create a more tangible character for themselves, as well as wanting consumers consciously to prefer to shop at their outlets. Branding issues concerning manufacturers include the choice of brand name and the choice of product range brand policy.
- Packaging is another important element of the tangible product which serves not only to protect and preserve the product, but also to inform the consumer and to help them readily identify the brand. Labelling, as a specific area of packaging, covers the legally

necessary information to be included on the pack as well as the additional information the consumer demands.

- Product design is an important but often under-estimated function, as it can help to create differential advantage, by building in new useful features or benefits and emphasising the way in which the product differs. In many organisations, however, design is not given the priority, resources or consideration that it deserves, partly because of its traditionally lowly status and partly because it does not feature strongly in the kinds of strategic planning frameworks that managers commonly use. Quality is also an important concept, but its contribution, unlike that of design, has been fully recognised and through TQM programmes it has been integrated into all aspects of organisational performance. Guarantees reflect the organisation's confidence in its products and its procedures and reduce the perceived risk to the potential customer in trying a product. These guarantees or manufacturers' warranties are over and above any legal protection to which the customer is entitled. Guarantees can create a differential advantage, provided that the competition cannot copy them, or they might be necessary simply to keep pace with competitors who implemented them first.

key words and phrases

Augmented product	Non-durable products	Product mix
Branding	Own-label brands	Service products
Convenience goods	Potential product	Shopping goods
Core product	Product items	Speciality goods
Durable products	Product line length	Tangible product
Manufacturer brands	Product lines	Unsought goods

questions for *review*

7.1 What is the *augmented product* and why might it be important?

7.2 What is a *speciality product* and how might its marketing mix and the kind of buying behaviour associated with it differ from those found with other products?

7.3 What are the six different categories within the *user-based product classification system* for B2B products?

7.4 What are the advantages and disadvantages of *monolithic* branding compared with *discreet* branding?

7.5 How can design contribute to the success of a new product?

questions for *discussion*

7.1 Choose three different brands of shampoo that you think incorporate different *core products*.
(a) Define the *core product* for each brand.
(b) How does the *tangible product* for each brand reflect the *core product*?

7.2 Adapt Figure 7.1 to suit the specific example of a personal computer:
(a) for family use; and
(b) for the use of a small business.

How do your two diagrams differ from each other, and why?

7.3 Choose a manufacturer of consumer products and list all the brands it sells. How might these brands be grouped into product lines and why? (You might find Figure 7.2 helpful.)

7.4 List as many functions of packaging as you can.

7.5 Develop a weighted set of five or six criteria for 'good' labelling. Collect a number of competing brands of the same product and rate each of them against your criteria. Which brand comes out best? As a result of this exercise, would you adjust your weightings or change the criteria included?

case study 7.1

Is small still beautiful second time around?

The original Mini became an icon for the sixties generation, a triumph of its time for innovative style and mechanical engineering. Its owners included The Beatles, Mick Jagger, Peter Sellers and Twiggy and it played a star role with Michael Caine in the movie *The Italian Job*. As an aside, it also won the Monte Carlo rally three times. At its launch in 1959, however, its creators had no such pretensions or ambitions for the car. It was simply a response to the possibility of petrol rationing. Its fuel economy and a competitive price tag of £497 set it aside from the rest, and it became almost a generic name for small cars.

Although The Beatles' music and Mick Jagger all survived well beyond the swinging '60s, by 1972 fashions had changed and the Mini brand was in decline. It increasingly became a small volume, niche car with a cult following re-living earlier times. An influx of competitive small cars, a shift in consumer preference for more space and comfort, and changing design appreciation meant that the Mini became stuck with being a likeable, but dated brand. Although the Mini was kept in production, the then owner BL (British Leyland) was looking for a replacement. Its efforts were not an unqualified success, however. The Mini Metro launched in the 1980s, again an economical, low-priced brand, was again soon left behind by later entrants in terms of quality, design and performance. To succeed in the small car segment requires production efficiency and volume sales along with some distinguishing features. The Metro did not survive the Mini and is best remembered as the car people learned to drive in after the British School of Motoring adopted the brand for its fleet in the 1980s.

In the 1990s, the Mini passed into BMW's hands and plans were laid for a new Mini. The brand name was considered so strong and evocative that it was capable of a renaissance. The challenge was to create a car that was readily identified with the old Mini and handled like a Mini, yet had twenty-first century quality and comforts. It was described as a baby BMW at £10,300 for the entry-level Mini One and £11,600 for the sporty Mini Cooper. The new Mini retained its sense of fun, both in its looks and its heart. The Cooper S version had a 1.6-litre engine offering 130 bhp for those seeking the on-road experience of the original. BMW avoided making the same mistake as VW, however. When VW launched the new Beetle in 1999 it was priced at £15,000, well beyond the target market's price limit, especially for a two-car household. BMW had originally planned to launch the Mini at £14,000, but changed it to the more competitive £10,000, just a little higher than some of the popular alternatives.

So will the new or 'retro' Mini sell? The initial target markets are past Mini drivers and BMW owners seeking a second vehicle. The appeal could then broaden if the Mini becomes established as a powerful competitor to mass market cars such as the Renault Clio, Audi A2 and Mercedes A-class. The production target for 2001 was a modest 20,000 but in a full year, 100,000 will be nearer the expected number leaving the production line in Oxford. At the UK launch, it already had 6,000 advance orders, 2,500 in Britain alone, and prospective buyers soon had to join a six-month waiting list. Registrations in the first eight weeks were claimed to be double those of the Ford Puma in 1997 and more than ten times the number of new VW Beetles sold over the equivalent two-month launch period in 1999. To meet demand, a rolling launch was planned with the rest of Europe two months behind the UK launch and the USA and Japan targeted for 2002.

Some critics believe, however, that BMW could be underestimating both the competition and how much more fickle consumers are now compared with the 1960s. The small car market is already crowded and as a 'fashion vehicle' the Mini's shelf life in the showroom could be short, without regular freshening up. Often, car models are given a facelift every three years, not the seven years planned by BMW for the Mini. There is also a question as to whether BMW will make money out of the Mini. The problem with small cars with small price tags is small profits, if they make any profit at all. Golding (2001) suggests that 250,000 a year is the minimum realistic volume and even then, the contribution to profitability is usually judged more by the degree to which the small cars raise the purchase volumes of the components they have in common with larger cars in the range. Even with worldwide sales, there is little prospect of the Mini approaching the 250,000 level. The nearest car to the Mini in the BMW range is the 3 series compact until the I series is launched in 2004, so the Mini stands alone in the range and may not be well positioned to encourage drivers to trade up.

BMW does tend to take a long-term view on its investments, which is probably a good thing as the

Mini required a new production line, cost one-third more to develop than had been budgeted, and was late to market. There could also be difficulties with the UK staying out of the euro, as BMW prefers to buy parts and components in euros rather than risk exchange rate fluctuations. Additionally, UK-based manufacture also means that BMW incurs production costs in sterling yet must price for most EU markets in euros. However, the attraction of the Mini is that it allows BMW, a marque more associated with quality and seriousness in the luxury car market, to market a brand that, in its new guise, captures the fun and style of small car motoring.

Sources: Barrett (2001); Chittenden (2001); Edwards (2001); Golding (2001); Lister (2001).

Questions

1 What is the core product that the Mini offers compared with the mainstream BMW range?

2 How could the Mini's core product be translated into tangible, augmented and potential products as represented in Figure 7.1?

3 What are the advantages and disadvantages of using an existing brand name for this new product launch?

4 In general in the car market, why do many manufacturers place almost equal emphasis on the corporate name and the individual model name, e.g. the Ford Focus, the Renault Clio, etc. What kind of branding strategy is this?

case study 7.2

The market with stiffening competition

Viagra was something of an accidental discovery. Scientists testing an angina drug found that as a side effect it seemed to cure impotence in many patients. It did not take long for its manufacturer, Pfizer (http://www.pfizer.com), to decide to focus on its unexpected benefit and to develop the product further as an anti-impotence drug. The drug was licensed by the US FDA (Food and Drugs Administration) and launched in the US in April 1998, amidst a huge fanfare of serious and not so serious media hype. In the first month, 570,000 new prescriptions for Viagra were issued, generating $100 mn in revenue.

At the launch, the priority for Pfizer was to retain control over the brand image, ensuring that it was positioned as Pfizer wanted it to be and that accurate information was given to the public. A campaign estimated to be costing tens of millions of dollars on consumer-orientated advertising in popular magazines such as *Time*, *Life* and *Newsweek* was undertaken. The enormous level of pre-launch publicity that Viagra had generated was not necessarily a good thing. The publicity was out of Pfizer's control, meaning that it could be inaccurate and/or damaging to the brand image. The thousands of jokes made about the brand could well have had a negative effect, making patients embarrassed about owning up to an impotence problem and asking for the drug. Pfizer waited until the worst of the publicity had died down before launching its campaign to make sure that its message was heard properly and that the drug was taken more seriously. This, along with all the media hype, had led to a rapid take-up after its introduction.

Sales continued to grow as the product was progressively launched on worldwide markets. In 1998 total sales had reached $776 mn, $1,016 mn by 1999 and $1,344 mn by 2000, representing over 5 per cent of human drug sales for Pfizer. The 2000 Annual Report proclaimed that more than 300 million Viagra tablets have been prescribed for more than 10 million men in more than 100 countries: Viagra had become a worldwide brand in a very short period of time.

Pfizer also faced other problems with Viagra. The hype about the drug was such that a lot of people wanted it and a lot of people wanted to supply it. There was a proliferation of websites offering it, such as http://www.xtra-med.com offering Viagra for anything from $6 per dose, posted to you in a plain package. Because the internet is a global network with no central regulatory control, however, it is difficult for Pfizer to do much about this. Both Pfizer and the American Medical Association are adamant that prospective Viagra patients should undergo a full physical examination before a prescription is given. Websites, however, only take prospective patients through a series of questions about their medical history that are evaluated by a doctor, who then approves or fails to approve the prescription. If a buyer really wants the drug, it can be relatively easy to work out the 'right' questionnaire answers to ensure that the doctor approves the prescription. Anyone who is prepared to lie like that is hardly likely to be put off by website disclaimers and warnings about the folly of supplying false information.

All the US publicity was heard in Europe and made the European market a little more difficult to enter. When Viagra was eventually licensed in Europe late in 1998, the UK health minister pronounced that Viagra would not be made available on the National Health Service (NHS). This had a lot to do with NHS priorities: impotence is not high on the list, apparently, and there were fears about the cost to the NHS if all the hype produced the same sort of level of demand as in the US. There were fears that it would cost the NHS £1bn per year if it was available on demand. Although some relaxation has subsequently taken place, and doctors are allowed more say in prescribing the drug, it is still not readily available on prescription. Impotence in itself is not enough for free treatment – it must be caused by specific medical conditions such as diabetes.

There have been more serious setbacks, however. Early on, there were reports of a number of deaths from cardiac problems, allegedly exacerbated by the drug. In January 1999, after around 130 deaths, *Medical Marketing and Media* reported that the FDA was requiring Pfizer to change the label on Viagra to draw the user's attention to the risk of death, heart attacks and hypertension, among other effects noticed after the drug had been launched. Subsequent research has, however, been more positive. Pfizer claimed in its 2000 Annual Report that an analysis of 82 separate studies involving 4,497 patients taking Viagra found no increased risk of heart attack or death. In a UK study, the Drug Safety Research Unit at Southampton published a study in the British Medical Journal (BMJ) which showed no evidence of a higher risk of either fatal heart attack or heart disease after taking the distinctive little blue Viagra pill. Nevertheless, scares still flare up from time to time. In 2001, Germany's Health Minister indicated that she would examine prescription guidelines for Viagra after reports of hundreds of fatalities, but cautioned against blaming the deaths on the drug.

The greatest challenge yet to the new brand came when Pfizer lost some patent protection. The main ingredient in Viagra is sildenafil, and potential competitors Eli Lilly and Icos Corporation challenged the legitimacy of the original patent issued in 1993. A judge ruled that the knowledge on which it had been based was already in the public domain in 1993 and that the patent was now restricting research by other companies. Although the molecular structure of Viagra was still protected, therefore, the main active ingredient was then open to competitors. The first serious challenge came from Uprima after it received its European licence in 2001. Its makers, Abbott Laboratories, claimed it worked more quickly than Viagra, with fewer side-effects and cost less than £5 for both low and high dosage tablets. Quick action can help spontaneity, unlike Viagra which has to be taken at least an hour before sex.

Competition is thus becoming much stiffer. GlaxoSmithKline and Bayer plan to launch Vardenfil as an alternative male erectile deficiency solution for the US market. Palatin Technologies adopted a different approach in developing PT-141, a 'sniff and sex' aerosol. Under tests, a single whiff made male rats 'interested' for an hour and made female rats actively seek sexual contact with males. Full-scale human trials are now planned. Unlike Viagra, PT-141 is a chemical copy of a hormone and acts directly on the brain, and a small trial on men suffering from ED showed that the spray was 80 per cent effective. Pfizer and others are also searching for cures for the low libido attributed to female sexual arousal disorder, with which Viagra has not had any great success, but that will be another story.

Sources: BBC News (2000a, 2000b, 2001a, 2001b); *Business and Health* (1998); Gopal (1998); Greenhalgh (1999); Gribben (2001); Hawkes (2001); Le Fanu (2001); *Medical Marketing and Media* (1999); *The Observer* (2001); West (1998).

Questions

1. What issues do you think a pharmaceutical company like Pfizer has to take into account when deciding on a brand name for a new drug?
2. How would you classify Viagra as a consumer product?
3. To what extent do you think the packaging considerations are the same for Viagra and a mainstream fmcg product?
4. Assess the threat posed to Viagra by new entrants to the market.

References for chapter 7

Aaker, D. and Joachimstaler, E. (2000), *Brand Leadership*, New York: Free Press.

Arnold, M., (2001), 'Will Thomson's Tactics Help it to be Distinctive?', *Marketing*, 21 June, p. 15.

Assael, H. (1995), *Consumer Behavior and Marketing Action*, Cincinnati: South-Western College Publishing, 5th edn.

BBC News (2001a), 'Viagra Alternative Arrives in UK', 30 May, 2001, accessed via http://www.news.bbc.co.uk.

BBC News (2001b), 'Viagra: "No increased heart attack risk", 16 March 2001, accessed via http://www.news.bbc.co.uk.

BBC News (2001c), 'Dishing Up "Food" for the Future', 12 June, accessed via http://www.news.bbc.co.uk.

BBC News (2000a), 'Pfizer Lost its Exclusive Patent Friday', 28 April 2000, accessed via http://www.news.bbc.co.uk.

BBC News (2000b), 'Pfizer Loses Viagra Patent', 8 November 2000, accessed via http://www.news.bbc.co.uk.

Baar, A. (2001), 'PMH Ages Barbie', *Adweek*, 27 August, p. 10.

Baird, B. (2001), 'Satisfaction Guaranteed', *Target Marketing*, June, p. 12.

Baird, R. (1998), 'Asset Tests', *Marketing Week*, 1 October, pp. 28–31.

Barrett, L. (2001), 'The Baby Beamer', *Marketing Week*, 21 June, pp. 24–5.

Bartholomew, D. (2001), 'Targeting Quality', *Industry Week*, October, pp. 49–50.

Belén del Río, A., Vázquez, R. and Iglesias, V. (2001), 'The Role of the Brand Name in Obtaining Differential Advantages', *Journal of Product and Brand Management*, 10 (7), pp. 452–65.

Bickerstaffe, J. (1999), 'We're Really Snowed Under', *The Grocer*, 27 March, p. 46.

Bird, S. (2000), 'Game, Scent and Match for Grassy Tennis Balls', *The Times*, 25 May, p. 1.

Blackett, T. (1985), 'Brand Name Research – Getting it Right', *Marketing and Research Today*, May, pp. 89–93.

Branigan, T. (2001), 'Judges Endorse Europe's View of Plastic Flowerpots', *The Guardian*, 30 January, p. 1.7.

Brierley, S. (2001), 'Powerful Brands Aren't as Strong as they Used to Be', *Marketing Week*, 9 August, p. 27.

Brown, D. (2000), 'Garden Centre Defeats EU in Battle of the Plant Pots', *The Daily Telegraph*, 12 June, p. 8.

Brown, P. (2001), 'Britain at Bottom of Recycling League', *The Guardian*, 6 June, p. 1.9.

Bunting, M. (2001), 'The New Gods', *The Guardian*, 8 July, p. 2.4.

Business and Health (1998), 'Virtual Viagra', *Business and Health*, December, p. 11.

Butterfield, L. (1998), 'Brands Become the Biggest Assets of All', *Sunday Times*, 20 September, p. 3.8.

Butterfield, L. and Haigh, D. (1998), *Understanding the Financial Value of Brands*, The Institute of Practitioners in Advertising.

Chaffey, D. (2002), *E-business and E-commerce Management: Strategy, Implementation and Practice*, Harlow: Financial Times Prentice Hall.

Chittenden, M. (2001), 'Mini Comes Back as a Trendy Teuton', *Sunday Times*, 8 July, p. 8.

Clark, A. (2001), 'Uniting Europe with a Smile: How Preussag is Redesigning the Package Holiday', *The Guardian*, 24 August, p. 1.28.

Connolly, A. and Davidson, L. (1996), 'How Does Design Affect Decisions at the Point of Sale?', *Journal of Brand Management*, 4 (2), pp. 100–7.

de Chernatony, L., Harris, F. and Dall'Olmo Riley, F. (2000), 'Added Value: Its Nature, Roles and Sustainability', *European Journal of Marketing*, 34 (1/2), pp. 39–56.

DelVecchio, D. (2000), 'Moving Beyond Fit: The Role of Brand Portfolio Characteristics in Consumer Evaluations of Brand Reliability', *Journal of Product and Brand Management*, 9 (7), pp. 457–71.

Design Council (2001a), 'Folding Plug Fits Through the Letterbox', accessed via http://www.designcouncil.org.uk.

Design Council (2001b), 'Soho Company Brings Rome to Life', accessed via http://www.designcouncil.org.uk.

Design Council (2001c), *Design in Britain 2001/2002*, London: Design Council.

Directive 1999/44/EC, Directive 1999/44/EC of the European Parliament and of the Council of 25 May 1999 on Certain Aspects Of The Sale Of Consumer Goods And Associated Guarantees (1999) O.J. L 17 I71/12 of 7 July 1999.

Doyle, P. (1998), *Marketing Management and Strategy*, 2nd edn, Prentice-Hall Europe.

Edwards, O. (2001), 'The Big Hydrogen Gamble', *Eurobusiness*, September, pp. 36–40.

Ensor, J. (1997), 'Interpreting the European Market', *The Grocer*, 15 March, p. 67.

European Policy Analyst (1998), 'Environment Report', *European Policy Analyst*, 3rd quarter, p. 67.

Foxall, J. (2001), 'Blind Justice', *The Daily Telegraph*, 24 February, p. 1.

Gander, P. (2001), 'Packaging', *The Grocer*, 31 March, pp. 45–8.

George, D. (1996), 'The Price – Quality Relationship Under Monopoly and Competition, *Scottish Journal of Political Economy*, 43, pp. 99–112.

Girard, P. (2000), 'Lands' End Winks at German Ruling', *Catalog Age*, January, p. 6.

Golding, R. (2001), 'The Mini is Back but What's the Return?', *The Independent*; 2 May, p. 4.

Gopal, K. (1998), 'Please Pass the Viagra', *Pharmaceutical Executive*, October, pp. 28–30.

Greenhalgh, T. (1999), 'On the Pill', *Accountancy*, January, p. 58.

Gribben, R. (2001), 'Glaxo Targets Viagra Market', *The Daily Telegraph*, 15 November, p. 36.

The Grocer (2001), 'There's Bags of Enlightenment', *Focus on Packaging* supplement to *The Grocer*, 31 March, p. 51.

The Guardian (2001), 'Saving Lives on the Roads: It is Simple and Doesn't Cost Much Money', *The Guardian*, 14 August, p. 1.5.

Haberman, M. (2001), 'A Mother of Invention', *Director*, June, p. 68.

Hawkes, N. (2001), 'Improved Sex Life Not to be Sniffed At', *The Times*, 27 October, p. 1.

Hertenstein, J. and Platt, M. (2001), 'Valuing Design: Enhancing Corporate Performance Through Design Effectiveness', *Design Management Journal*, 12 (3), pp. 10–9.

Hiscock, J. (2001), 'Biggest Brands 2001', *Marketing*, 9 August, pp. 24–34.

Hiscott, G. (2001), 'Future Lifestyles of the Rich are in Blueprint', *Western Mail*, 28 November, p. 7.

Hussey, M. (1998), 'Seriously, It's Barbie', *The Express*, 26 January, p. 19.

Jaworski, B. and Kohli, A. (1993), 'Market Orientation: Antecedents and Consequences', *Journal of Marketing*, 57, pp. 53–70.

John, D., Loken, B. and Joiner, C. (1998), 'The Negative Impact of Extensions: Can Flagship Products be Diluted?', *Journal of Marketing*, 62 (1), pp. 19–32.

Kahn, B. (1998), 'Mastering Marketing: Part Four Brand Strategy', *Financial Times Supplement*, pp. 4–6.

Le Fanu, J. (2001), 'Why Viagra Keeps Flowers Fresh for Weeks', *The Sunday Telegraph*, 2 September, p. 4.

Lightfoot, W. (1998), 'Never Mind the Low Prices, Feel the Quality', *The European*, 5–11 October, p. 22.

Linnell, M. (1998), 'Prime Time at the Pumps', *The Grocer*, 6 February, pp. 34–6.

Lister, S. (2001), 'Sixties Throwback is Instant 21st-century Hit', *The Times*, 12 July, p. 11.

Lorenz, C. (1994), 'Skin-deep Styling is Not Enough', *Financial Times*, 13 June, p. 17.

MacKenzie, D. (2001), 'Brands Have to Meet Customers' "Local" Demands', *Marketing*, 30 August, p. 18.

McKenzie, S. (1997), 'Package Deal', *Marketing Week*, 11 September, pp. 67–9.

McLuhan, R. (1999), 'Thomson Ads Go For Service', *Marketing*, 28 January, p. 21.

Marconi, J. (2001), 'The Brand Marketing Book: Creating, Managing, and Extending the Value of Your Brand', *Journal of Consumer Marketing*, 18 (1), pp. 75–83.

Marketing Week (2001), 'Mattel to Introduce "Career" Barbie Range', *Marketing Week*, 15 November, p. 8.

Medical Marketing and Media (1999), 'New Viagra Labelling Warns of Deaths', *Medical Marketing and Media*, 34(1), p. 32.

Meikle, J. (2001), 'Labelling for Drugs to be Reviewed', *The Guardian*, 21 April, p. 1.6.

Mitchell, A. (1998), 'Sky's the Limit for New Breed of Passion Brands', *Marketing Week*, 17 September, pp. 44–5.

Mitchell, A. (1999), 'How Brands Touch the Parts Others Can't Reach', *Marketing Week*, 18 March, pp. 22–3.

Moorhead, J. (2001), 'At 42, is Barbie Past It?', *The Guardian*, 8 May, p. 2.10.

Morgan, M. (2001), 'Branding the Madonna Way', *Brandweek*, 24 September, p. 22.

National Petroleum News (2001), 'Convenience-store Fill-ups Continue to Rise', *National Petroleum News*, October, p. 43.

Nia, A. and Zaichkowsky, J. (2000), 'Do Counterfeits Devalue the Ownership of Luxury Brands?', *Journal of Product and Brand Management*, 9 (7), pp. 485–97.

The Observer (2001), 'German Minister Links Viagra to Spate of Deaths', *The Observer*, 9 September, p. 16.

Olsen, J. (2000), 'Disharmony in Europe Puts Brand Owners at Risk', *Managing Intellectual Property*, Dec/Jan, pp. 52–63.

Parasuraman, A. (1997), 'Reflections on Gaining Competitive Advantage Through Customer Value', *Journal of the Academy of Marketing Science*, 25 (2), pp. 154–61.

Pavitt, J. (2001), 'Branded: A Brief History of Brands 1: Coca-Cola', *The Guardian*, 9 July, p. 2.4.

Pearman, H. (2001), 'Dualit Toaster', *Sunday Times*, 4 November, p. 6.

Peters, M. (1994), 'Good Packaging Gets Through to the Fickle Buyer', *Marketing*, 20 January, p. 10.

Peek, L. (2001), 'Jubilee Bentley Gift for the Queen', *The Times*, 20 December, p. 8.

Piercy, N. and Morgan, N. (1997), 'The Impact of Lean Thinking and the Lean Enterprise on Marketing: Threat or Synergy?', *Journal of Marketing Management*, 13, pp. 679–93.

Pieters, R. and Warlops, L. (1999), 'Visual Attention During Brand Choice: The Impact of Time Pressure and Task Motivation', *International Journal of Research in Marketing*, 16, pp. 1–16.

Roberts, R. (2001), 'Road Accidents Costing UK plc £2.7 bn a Year', *Western Mail*, 21 November, p. 19.

Rogers, D. (2001a), 'Is Thomson Losing its Identity?', *Marketing*, 30 August, p. 15.

Rogers, D. (2001b), 'Preussag Travel Group Set for TUI Rebranding', *Marketing*, 30 August, p. 42.

Rose, D. (2001), 'Trademark Trouble', *The Times*, 24 April, Law p. 5.

Shine, A., O'Reilly, S. and O'Sullivan, K. (1997), 'Consumer Use of Nutrition Labelling', *British Food Journal*, 99 (6), pp. 290–6.

Singh, S. (2001), 'Brand Clean Up Starts with Axing of Dettox', *Marketing Week*, 29 November, p. 19.

Smith, A. (1998), 'Heinz Soups up its Old Image', *Financial Times*, 2 October, p. 13.

Stipp, D. (1996), 'Farewell My Logo', *Fortune*, 27 May, pp. 128–40.

Tollington, T. (2001), 'The Role of "Separability" in the Accounting Disclosure of Brand Assets in the UK', Middlesex University Business School, *Accounting and Finance Discussion Paper Series*, No. 19, September.

Tollington, T. (1998), 'Brands: The Asset Definition and Recognition Test', *Journal of Product and Brand Management*, 7 (3), pp. 180–92.

Trefgarne, G. (2001), 'Reckitt Dishes Up Some Bright Prospects', *The Daily Telegraph*, 1 March, p. 36.

Twigg-Flesner, C. (2000), 'New Rules for Guarantees: For Better or Worse?', *Consumer Policy Review*, May/Jun 2000, pp. 10–5.

Underwood, R., Klein, N. and Burke, R. (2001), 'Packaging Communication: Attentional Effects of Product Imagery', *Journal of Product and Brand Management*, 10 (7), pp. 403–22.

Wandel, M. (1999), 'Food Labelling from a Consumer Perspective', *British Food Journal*, 99 (6), pp. 212–9.

Warman, C. (1997), 'Happy Landings for Anglers Who Cast off', *The Times*, 20 October, p. 40.

West, D. (1998), 'On-line Prescriptions Have Adverse Reactions', *Pharmaceutical Executive*, November, p. DTC28.

Wikström, S. and Normann, R. (1994), *Knowledge and Value*, London: Routledge.

Young, R. (2001), 'How Motorists Can Evade the Devices', *The Times*, 14 August, p. 6.

chapter 8

product management

LEARNING OBJECTIVES

This chapter will help you to:

1 understand the product lifecycle concept, its influence on marketing strategies and its limitations;

2 appreciate the importance of product positioning and how it both affects and is affected by marketing strategies;

3 understand the scope and implications of the various decisions that management can take with regard to product ranges, including deletion;

4 define the role and responsibilities of the product or brand manager; and

5 outline the issues surrounding pan-European branding.

Introduction

The previous chapter defined what a product is and some of the terms that are used in talking about products within organisations and markets. Even that general overview raised a number of strategic issues relating to how an organisation is supposed to manage such an important resource as its product range. This chapter addresses those issues.

Products need managing throughout their working lives. Someone has to decide what products should be created and when is the best time to launch them. Someone has to help the product to capitalise on its strengths and iron out its weaknesses. Someone has to decide whether an older product, past its prime, should have its life extended through modification or marketing strategy or whether it should be allowed to die peacefully. Such decisions are critical to an organisation's strategy, since after all the product range is at the heart of the supplier–buyer relationship. Product management, therefore, requires clear lines of authority and effective and efficient organisation. In consumer markets, many product management decisions are made by the marketing manager, but in B2B markets, responsibility is shared across a range of functional areas, including research and development (R&D), engineering and after-sales service personnel.

This chapter is concerned with the strategic concepts and tools that help those managers, whether marketers or engineers, to make the best decisions about their products. The first concept presented is that of the product lifecycle. This traces the life story of the product, helping managers to understand the pressures and opportunities affecting products as they mature. The important area of new product development is considered in the next chapter, but the difficulties of supporting a product in its early stages are addressed here as being crucial to the future well-being of the product. Within a product range, some products can live very long and profitable lives, such as Smarties, Dettol, Bovril, Mars Bar and, of course, Coca-Cola.

eg

Brand consultancy *Future Brand* undertook a pan-European survey of 448 consumers to establish the brands most likely and least likely to survive until 2015. Those considered most likely to survive included Coca-Cola, Microsoft, Heinz, Sony and Nestlé to name but a few. According to the survey, however, the likes of Marks & Spencer, Daewoo and Apple had better watch out, as it is believed they will disappear without trace. There are, of course, methodological problems in predicting terminal decline or everlasting success on the basis of such a limited survey so far ahead of possible corrective management action, but nevertheless, it is an interesting indication of how brands are perceived today. Speculative nonsense? Maybe, but it is a sobering reminder that no brand, large or small has a special right to survive and that managing products, from birth to perhaps eventual withdrawal is a significant challenge for marketers (Singh and Hedberg, 2001).

To create and sustain long-lived brands such as those listed above, the product range needs to be managed in sympathy with changes in the customer and competitive environment through the concept of product positioning and repositioning. This may involve changes in marketing strategies, including promotion, packaging, design or even in the target market profile. In the 1960s, for example, Coca-Cola introduced the can of Coke for the first time in addition to the traditional bottle. This changed the way in which the product was purchased and consumed and thus its image. Every product has to be assessed and managed according to how the consumer perceives it in relation to the competition. This is a natural extension of the targeting decision discussed at p. 198 *et seq.*

The natural processes of product maturity and decline lead to the discussion of product deletion issues. No product has an infinite life span and deciding the best time either to refresh and relaunch a product or to withdraw it altogether is difficult. It requires a critical review of the product's market performance, an analysis of its past (and potential future) contribution to overall profitability and a sound grasp of what is happening in the market.

Finally, this chapter returns to the practical problems of managing these processes, presenting a brief overview of product management structures as a foretaste of the more detailed review in Chapter 21.

The product lifecycle

The **product lifecycle** (PLC) concept reflects the theory that products, like people, live a life. They are born, they grow up, they mature and, eventually, they die. During its life, a product goes through many different experiences, achieving varying levels of success in the market. This naturally means that the product's marketing support needs also vary, depending on what is necessary both to secure the present and to work towards the future. Figure 8.1 shows the theoretical progress of a PLC, indicating the pattern of sales and profits earned. The diagram may be applied either to an individual product or brand (for example Kellogg's Cornflakes) or to a product class (breakfast cereals).

The PLC concept offers no hard and fast rules for product management, but it can act as a useful guide for thinking about what a product has achieved and where it is heading in the future. There are, however, some reservations about the usefulness of this concept (Dhalla and Yuspeh, 1976). As you read the rest of this section, think about what those reservations might be, then compare your thoughts with the critical appraisal of the concept at pp. 318 *et seq.* First, it is important to describe in some detail the stages of the PLC. Figure 8.1 indicates that there are four main stages, introduction, growth, maturity and decline, and these are now discussed in turn along with their implications for marketing strategy.

Figure 8.1 The product lifecycle

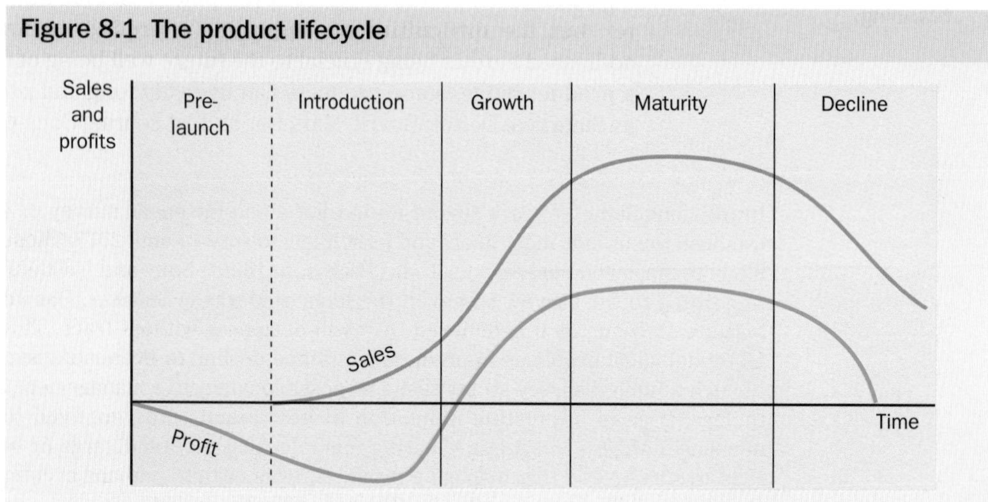

Stage 1: introduction

At the very start of the product's life as it enters the market, sales will begin to build slowly and profit may be small (even negative). A slow build-up of sales reflects the lead time required for marketing efforts to take effect and for people to hear about the product and try it. Low profits are partly an effect of the low initial sales and partly a reflection of the possible need to recoup development and launch costs.

The marketer's main priority at this stage is to generate widespread awareness of the product among the target segment and to stimulate trial. If the product is truly innovative, there may be no competitors yet and so there is the added problem of building primary demand (i.e. demand for the class of product rather than simply demand for a specific brand) as a background to the actual brand choice.

In most cases, the new product is an addition to an existing market and will either be targeted at a different segment or be offering additional features and benefits. There are a number of problems facing the marketer. First, there is a need to gain distribution. With new fmcg goods, the retail trade may be hard to convince unless the product has a real USP (unique selling point), because of the pressure on shelf space and the proliferation of available brands. In parallel with that, there is still the task of generating awareness among consumers and moving them through towards a purchase. The decision on the product's price, whether to price high or low or whether to offer an introductory trial price, could be an important element in achieving that first purchase.

eg

Microsoft's new operating system, Windows XP, was, according to the company, a highly successful launch, with 7 million licences shipped in the first two weeks after the official launch. Early retail sales were double those of any previous Windows version. Several trade pundits, however, believed that sustained sales would be slow as there was no 'killer' application for the new system, so consumers would wait until they purchased new machines before they bothered with XP (Darrow, 2001). It is one thing to be interested, but another to develop the motivation to buy. Despite a $136 mn advertising spend in the USA, retail sales of XP dropped from 400,000 in the first month after launch to 250,000 in the second month whereas Windows 98 had sold 350,000 in its second month. Most copies of operating systems are sold as part of a new computer sale and 2001 was a sluggish market (Ayres, 2001).

Given the failure rate of new products and the importance of giving a product the best possible start in life, the introduction stage is likely to make heavy demands on marketing resources. This can be especially draining for a smaller organisation, but nevertheless is necessary if the product is to survive into the next stage: growth.

Stage 2: growth

In the growth stage, there is rapid increase in sales. One reason for this might be that word is getting around about the product and the rate of recruitment of new triers accelerates. Another reason is that the effects of repeat purchases are starting to be seen. There is some urgency at this stage to build as much brand preference and loyalty as possible. Competitors will now have had time to assess the product, its potential and its effect on the overall market, and will thus have decided their response. They may be modifying or improving their existing products or entering a new product of their own to the market. Whatever they do, they will deflect interest and attention away from the product and there is a risk that this will flatten the growth curve prematurely unless the company takes defensive steps.

Figure 8.1 shows that profits start to rise rapidly in this stage. This too might be affected by competitive pressure, if other organisations choose to compete on price, forcing margins down. Again, repeat purchases that build brand loyalty are the best defence in these circumstances.

Even though the product might seem to be still very young and only just starting to deliver its potential, towards the close of the growth stage might be a good time to think about product modifications or improvements, either to reinforce existing segments or to open up new ones. This is about keeping one step ahead of the competition. If the initial

eg

The UK internet market grew rapidly in 2001, but not all internet service providers gained from that growth by any means. Freeserve, formerly owned by retailer Dixon's and now by the French company Wanadoo, had 2.03 million subscribers in August 2001 compared with 2.05 million at the same stage of the previous year. During the same time the number of UK households with internet access grew from 6 million to 10 million, indicating how far Freeserve had fallen behind in the race for share (Lambeth, 2001b). Unlike AOL, which offers flat-rate access to the BT network, at considerable cost to the company (so it is claimed), Freeserve has not sought what it regards as loss-making business. It does, however, intend to switch to a new BT service that allows ISPs flat-rate access to the national network. At the same time, the number of AOL users grew from 1 million to around 1.5 million as a result of heavy media advertising and flat-rate monthly charging, so that it could eventually challenge the Freeserve's number 1 position in the market. AOL appears to be planning to build a loyal user base during the growth phase of the market, which it can hold onto when the market flattens out.

novelty of your product has worn off, buyers might be vulnerable to competitors' new products. This might also threaten the security of your distribution channels, as heavy competition for shelf space squeezes out weaker products perceived as heading nowhere. This all reinforces, yet again, the need for constant attention to brand building and the generation of consumer loyalty, as well as the necessity for the cultivation of good relationships with distributors.

Another good reason for considering modifying the product is that by now you have real experience of producing and marketing it. The more innovative the product (whether innovative for your organisation or innovative within the market), the more likely it is that experience will have highlighted unforeseen strengths and weaknesses in the product and its marketing. This is the time to learn from that experience and fine tune the whole offering or extend the product range to attract new segments.

eg

DVD recorders have now replaced mobile phones as one of the major growth product areas. Offering far better picture and sound quality than VHS video, which is now over twenty years old, consumers are increasingly switching systems. Over the three years after their introduction in 1998, three million players were sold, 2 million of which were sold in 2000 alone (Poulter, 2001b). Prices tumbled, in some cases to below £100 and sales were expected to double in 2002 (Arthur, 2001). DVD brands are now entering the growth stage with everything to play for. At the start of 2002, while 90 per cent of UK homes had a video recorder, only 10 per cent already had DVD. As recordability becomes cheaper and as consumers become more willing to switch formats and dump their video collections, DVD will continue to grow. In 2001, however, 4 million video players were still sold which suggests that the changeover period could take several years yet, but as long as the growth continues, the consumer electronics companies will not complain.

This is not to imply that an organisation should advocate change for the sake of change. Any changes must be the result of detailed analysis of what is happening in the market and projections of what is likely to happen in the event of various developments taking place. It is strategic change, it is planned change, it is purposeful change in the best interests of the organisation, the product and the customer.

At some point, the growth period comes to an end as the product begins to reach its peak and enters the next stage: maturity.

Stage 3: maturity

During the maturity stage, the product achieves as much as it is going to. The accelerated growth levels off, as everyone who is likely to be interested in the product should have tried it by now and a stable set of loyal repeat buyers should have emerged. The mobile phone market, for example, had achieved 70 per cent penetration in the UK by the end of 2001 and sales levelled off to upgrading and replacement rather than converting those harder-to-win customers. This is not a cause for complacency, however. There are few new customers available and even the laggards have purchased by now. This means that there is a high degree of customer understanding of the product and possibly of the market. They know what they want, and if your product starts to look dated or becomes unexciting compared with newer offerings from the competition, then they might well switch brands. Certainly, the smaller or more poorly positioned brands are going to be squeezed out. In these circumstances, the best hope is to consolidate the hard-core loyal buyers, encouraging heavier consumption from them. It may also be possible to convert some brand switchers into loyal customers through the use of sales promotions and advertising.

At this stage, there is likely to be heavy price competition and increased marketing expenditure from all competitors in order to retain brand loyalty. Much of this expenditure will be focused on marketing communication, but some may be channelled into minor product improvements to refresh the brand. Distribution channels may also need careful handling at this stage. Unless the product remains a steady seller, the retailer may be looking to delist it to make room on the shelves for younger products.

The sales curve has reached a plateau, as the market is saturated and largely stable. Any short-term gains will be offset by similar losses and profits may start to decline because of price competition pressure. It is thus very important to try, at least, to retain existing buyers. Sooner or later, however, the stability of the maturity phase will break, either through competitive pressure (they are better at poaching your customers than you are at poaching theirs) or through new developments in the market that make your product increasingly inappropriate, pushing the product into the decline stage.

eg

It is possible for the marketer to take action to extend the maturity stage or even to stimulate new growth in the market. Scotch whisky is a mature product (in all senses of the phrase) in its biggest markets, the UK and France. This is partly because of the high level of competition in the market, over 2,000 brands, and partly because of the image of whisky as 'something your parents drink'. The potential to inject new life into the market has come from the trend in countries such as Portugal, Spain and Greece, where whisky is commonly drunk with water, ice or cola by the under-30 age group. If whisky manufacturers can successfully give their brands a more youthful emphasis and a more consistent European image, then they may be able to extend the lifecycle still further.

Berenson and Mohr-Jackson (1994) suggest that organisations often turn to new products rather than rejuvenating existing ones to extend their lifecycles. Consider, for example, how some brands have been revitalised, through changes in size (introducing smaller or larger sized packs), strength (for instance extra strong tissues), ingredients ('new improved'), form (stick, roll-on, powder, and spray deodorants), flavour (for instance flavoured cough drops), colour or quality. If rejuvenation is a better option, the organisation should consider a number of issues:

1 Why the product is going into decline.
2 Whether the marketing environment is right for a rejuvenation strategy.
3 What the product name communicates to the market.
4 Whether there is still a potential segment worth reaching.
5 Whether there is any possibility of creating value for customers.

These questions can help the organisation to assess the relative advantages of rejuvenation over a full new product launch.

Stage 4: decline

Once a product goes into decline for market-based reasons, it is almost impossible to stop it. The rate of decline can be controlled to some extent, but inevitably sales and profits will fall regardless of marketing effort.

marketing in action

Happy campers

Butlins holiday camps (http://www.butlins.co.uk) grew rapidly in the 1950s as the C2, D and E socioeconomic groups in particular had more leisure time and more disposable income for family holidays. However, by the 1970s, trends in the marketing environment were working against the established Butlins concept. Holidaymakers found cheaper and sunnier alternatives in Spain, rejected the highly regimented and enclosed atmosphere of the holiday camp and came to expect much higher standards of facilities and entertainment. Knobbly knees competitions and beauty contests are strictly yesterday's entertainment. The number of centres has been rationalised to just three: Minehead, Bognor Regis and Skegness, and the investment has been considerable with Rank, which bought the company from Sir Billy in 1972, spending £150 mn since 1997 on upgrades. Gone are the tiny wooden chalets not much larger than garden sheds, replaced by more spacious and better equipped family apartments. Now, it's indoor whirlpools, wave machines and multi-sport centres. A vast pavilion forms the centrepiece of all Butlins' Resorts, creating an undercover area of shops, bars and amusements.

The Splash water world is the central feature of the revamped Butlins holiday camp at Skegness where customers can enjoy a holiday all year round.

Source: Butlins/Biss Lancaster.

Butlins has been positioned as a year-round resort with all day entertainment to attract more couples. Special event and short break packages for drama and dance workshops, kit building, circus skills and art tuition have been introduced. Butlins still, however, wanted to retain its core target market of families with young children during the high season. The problem is that customer attitudes and beliefs change slowly and Butlins has never quite shaken off the 'Good morning campers', 'Hi-di-Hi' 1960s holiday camp image lovingly portrayed in the long-running television comedy series. As described by Middleton (2001), although the activities may be more middle class, you wouldn't mistake the customers at the Butlins' Burger King outlet for guests at a Henley Regatta picnic and there's still a lot of cropped stubble heads, replica football shirts and union jack shorts on the men, and gold jewellery in the ears or elsewhere on the girls from two years of age upwards.

That's the heart of the problem: a Butlins holiday is still cheap and perhaps the locations are wrong, as none of the resorts are in the UK top ten seaside destinations and the bar attracts more than its fair share of attention. Perhaps some of the other statistics say it all: at the Skegness centre the guests consume 20,000 hamburgers and two tons of chips per week. The facilities may have been upgraded but so too have the alternatives and the core appeal still appears to be the same despite the attempts at repositioning. Rank ran out of patience with the losses incurred at Butlins and sold it to Bourne leisure along with some other holiday operations such as Warner and Oasis. Somebody soon may decide that it's time for the redcoats to lead the last waltz.

Sources: Arnold (2001); Ezard (2001); Heptinstall (2001); Middleton (2001); Power (2001).

Decline can often be environment related rather than a result of poor management decisions. Technological developments or changes in consumer tastes, for example, can lead to the demise of the best-managed product. New technologies are increasingly becoming a powerful force that can destroy an established market in a few years. Polaroid built a market around instant photos, but digital cameras offer the same facility with a lot more flexibility. Cravens *et al.* (2000) highlighted the danger of becoming obsessed with improving and extending products in the mature or decline stages and not recognising more fundamental changes to the market. A similar pattern could be experienced in the future as MP3 and MP4 formats with download facilities render conventional CD formats obsolete.

eg

The nappy market still has not bottomed out. The market is contracting through no fault of the brand manufacturers. The birth rate and population trends have declined in the UK by 11 per cent since 1999 and further decline is projected to 2004. There may be fewer babies, but mothers are, however, often economically better off, older and prepared to spend more, especially on age-specific nappies. Since 1997, the disposable nappy market has slipped from maturity into decline, falling by 17 per cent since 1995 (Mintel, 2000). At brand level, the fortunes vary. Pampers Baby Dry declined by nearly 12 per cent in value in 2001 from 2000 and Kleenex Huggies by over 50 per cent after the introduction of Huggies Freedom as a replacement, indicating that product innovation can play a role even in markets under stress (*The Grocer*, 2001c).

eg

Whatever the fashion in new cars, in India there are some models that still sell well despite having been around since the 1950s and having to compete with many modern marques. The Ambassador, based on the Morris Oxford, has created a niche market due to its reliable, rugged reputation and good fuel economy. Ideally suited to Indian roads of variable quality, around 40 per cent of the Ambassador's sales are to taxi operators. Despite being the oldest model still in production in India, around 23,000 of them are sold per year. The influx of cars from Europe and Japan has resulted in a decline in the traditional consumer segment, but the model still survives. New versions are still being introduced. In 2000, the Ambassador 2000 DSL was launched with a 5-speed gear-box, better seating, overdrive and servo-assisted brakes, all within a 1950s exterior (Jagannathan, 2000)!

Some products are deliberately sacrificed on the altar of consumer demand. Fashion products with a naturally short lifecycle capitalise on shifting consumer tastes and the rise and fall of popular icons, and are managed with the expectation of a short maturity and a quick decline.

Faced with a product in decline, the marketer has a difficult decision of whether to try slowing down the decline with some marketing expenditure, or to milk the product by withdrawing support and making as much profit out of it as possible as it heads towards a natural death. In the latter case, the withdrawing of marketing support aimed at distributors in particular is quite likely to speed up the delisting process.

The problem with a declining product is that it can absorb a great deal of management time for relatively little reward. Decisive action is called for so that management effort can go into the newer products that need it. There are a number of possible options for dealing with declining products. The option of complete deletion is considered separately at pp. 336 *et seq.*

Milking or harvesting

The strategy of milking or harvesting centres around the idea of allowing nature to run its course with little or no marketing support. The product is allowed to fade away naturally while the profits are reaped. After all, if a product has had a long and useful life and has built up a good solid core of loyal users, it is not going to die overnight and the organisation might as well extract the last little bit of return on the investment it has made in the product over the years. Let the buyers drift away gradually and let the product die when it is no longer economic to produce it or when the retailers drop it.

This strategy has the advantage of maximising the useful life of the product, as well as generating the cash and the time to help establish new products. The slow decline of the product gives the organisation adjustment time to get used to the declining cash flow and to find other means of generating revenue. It is also less of a shock to the consumer (and other interested parties in the market) than the sudden disappearance of what might still be a popular product, with all the resentment that would cause.

Phased withdrawal

The milking strategy has a certain amount of drift attached to it. The product can continue indefinitely, as long as there is a purchaser out there. With a phased withdrawal, however, the ultimate cut-off date for the product is set, along with a number of interim staging posts. The interim stages might involve pulling the product gradually from different channels of distribution, or might focus on withdrawal from geographic areas.

The planned withdrawal does have some certainty about it. The organisation knows in advance what is going to happen to the product and can take that into account when planning its marketing strategies. It also allows time to plan replacement products (with the possibility of phasing them in as the old product is phased out) and does not prematurely cut off the income from the declining product. For the customer, however, there is an element of unpleasant surprise if the product disappears suddenly from their favourite retailer or from their area.

Car manufacturers normally operate on a phased withdrawal basis, so that both dealers and the public are well aware of when new models will be launched.

Contracting out or selling

A way of keeping loyal users of the product happy is to sell the brand to a niche operator or to subcontract its marketing and/or production. To a smaller, perhaps more flexible firm, the remains of the product's market might represent a manageable challenge that could earn what seems to it to be a satisfactory return. This way, the originating organisation is rid of a product it no longer wants, consumers do not lose a product that they do want, and the subcontractor or buyer gains access to, and experience with, a brand that they could probably never have built for themselves. Quaker, for example, bought the US soft drink brand Snapple for $1.7 bn. Although the brand was declining at the time of its purchase, Quaker felt that it had the management and marketing skills to make it successful.

Once the decision is made and the implementation plans drawn up, the process can be allowed to run its course with the minimum of managerial interference.

Facets of the PLC

The PLC is more of a guide to what could happen rather than a prescription of what will happen. At its best, it does provide some useful indications at each stage of some of the marketing problems and issues that could arise. It is, after all, a form of collective wisdom based on the history of many brands.

In reality, however, it is too general and superficial a concept to stand alone. Mercer (1993) emphasises that in many markets the product or brand lifecycle is longer than the planning cycle of the organisation, especially for very mature products. This can lead to short-term rather than long-term thinking about how a brand should develop. Before applying the concept in practice, it is necessary to dig deeper and think about a number of issues before the PLC becomes a really useful tool.

Length of PLC

How long is a piece of string? It is very difficult to predict how long it will take a product to move through its life. The length of the PLC varies not only from market to market, but also from brand to brand within a market. Some board games, for example, such as Monopoly, Scrabble and more recently Trivial Pursuit, are well-established, long-term sellers, whereas other games, particularly those linked with television shows (remember Countdown, Blockbusters and Neighbours board games?) have much shorter spans.

It is even more difficult to predict when the key transition periods from one stage to the next will happen, yet this is critical information for planning strategy changes. The problem is that the length of the PLC is affected by so many things. It is not only the pace of change in the external environment, but also the organisation's handling of the product throughout its life. The organisation's willingness and ability to communicate effectively and efficiently with both the trade and the consumer, its policy of supporting the product in the critical early period and its approach to defending and refreshing its products will all affect how the PLC develops.

Self-fulfilling prophecy

Linked with the previous point, there is a real danger that the PLC can become a self-fulfilling prophecy (Wood, 1990). A marketing manager might, for example, imagine that a product is about to move from growth into maturity. Theory may suggest appropriate marketing strategies for this transition and, if these are implemented, the product will start to behave as though it is mature, whether it was really ready for it or not. This demonstrates a basic marketing dilemma: should the PLC drive marketing strategies, or should the PLC be defined as an outcome of strategies derived through other means?

The shape of the PLC

The shape of the PLC offered in Figure 8.1 is necessarily a generalisation. Products that get into marketing problems at any PLC stage will certainly not follow this pattern. Products that spend relatively longer in one stage than another will also have distorted PLC curves. A product that has a long and stable maturity, for instance, will show a long flat plateau in maturity rather than Figure 8.1's gentle hillock. Different market circumstances could also distort this hypothetical curve. Five different scenarios, the innovative product, the imitative product, the fashion product, the product failure and the revitalisation, each with its own PLC shape, are shown in Figure 8.2.

Innovative product. The innovative product is breaking totally new ground and cannot really utilise consumers' previous experience as a short cut to acceptance. The marketer will have to overcome ignorance, suspicion and scepticism, thus extending the introduction stage. People feel that they have managed perfectly well without this product in the past, so why do they need it now? This is a question that both microwave oven producers and 3M, the manufacturer of Post-It Notes, have managed to answer to the customer's satisfaction. Having to educate the market from scratch is neither easy nor cheap. Sony, in introducing the Walkman, had to undertake this task and, of course, it not only laid the foundations for its own product, but also broke the ground for 'me too' subsequent imitative entrants.

As stated at p. 313, the introductory stage does hinge on creating awareness, encouraging trial of the product and winning over the retail trade. In the case of innovative products, this is an even more crucial, but much longer process.

Figure 8.2 PLC Variations on a theme

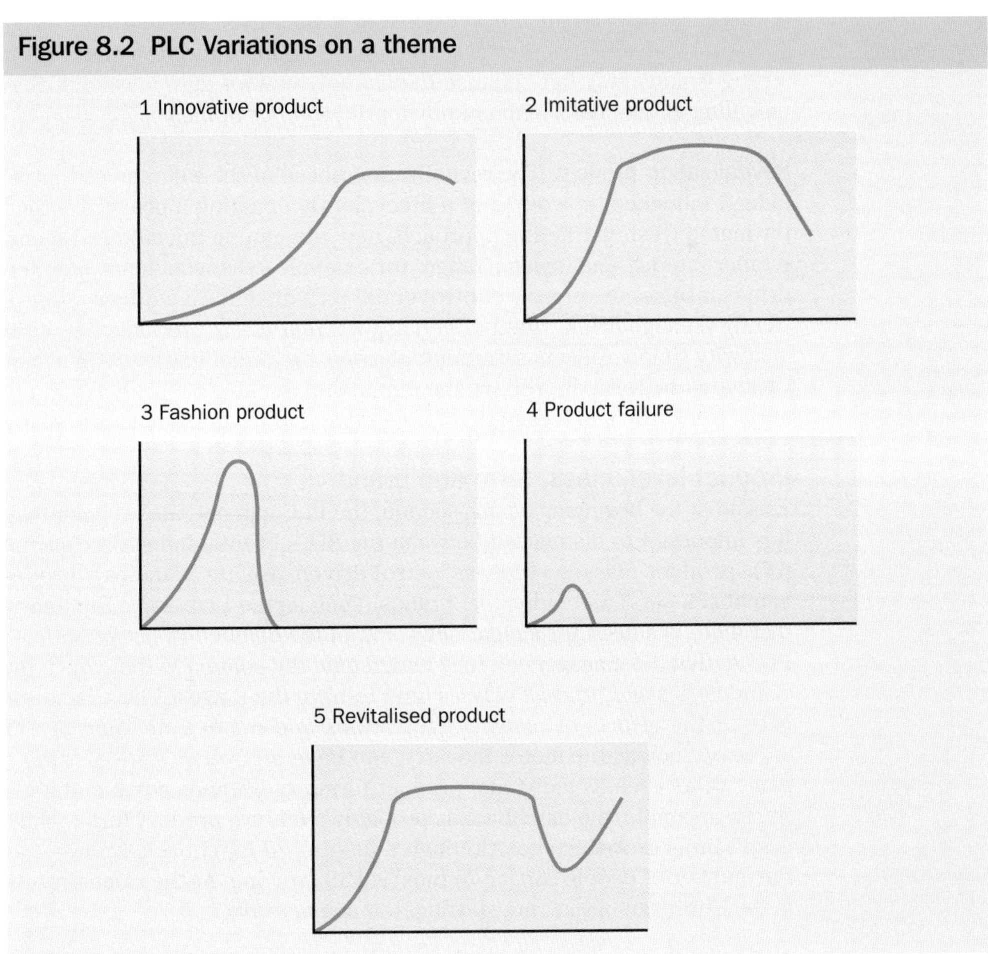

Imitative product. Imitative products, such as new confectionery brands or the first non-Sony personal stereo, do not require as much spadework as the innovative product. They take advantage of the established market and the buyer's existing knowledge and past experience, and thus will move into the growth stage very quickly. The main considerations for the imitative marketer are establishing clear, differentiated positioning of the product against existing brands, encouraging trial and making repeat purchase as easy as possible.

Fashion product. Fashion products have a naturally short PLC. Fads are an extreme form of fashion product, accentuating the rapid sales increase followed by the rapid decline. The timing of entry into the market is critical and those who succeed in making a quick return in these markets are those who spot the trend early. There is little opportunity for late entrants. It is interesting to note that some fads retain a hard core of enthusiasts, for example skateboarding.

eg

Not all fashion items have as short an existence as a clothing fad. Up until September 11th, 2001, the Swiss Army knife was essentially regarded as a fashion item rather than a mobile tool box. The product had been in maturity for many years, but the terror attacks on the USA changed all that. Penknife sales generally slumped by between 40 and 60 per cent as people could no longer take them on planes and they could be interpreted as offensive weapons (Hall, 2001). This prompted new strategies, such as the introduction of a pocket tool kit with no blades and the development of a consumer education programme to encourage travellers to carry their knives in checked-in baggage. It remains to be seen whether the decline is temporary or part of a long-term change in preference.

Product failure. Some products never even achieve a growth stage: they fail. This may be because the product itself is badly thought through or because it never gained awareness or distribution. New food products from small manufacturers without the resources to create strong brands may fail because they simply cannot gain mass distribution from retailers unwilling to take risks with unknown producers or brands.

Revitalisation product. The revitalisation phase of the PLC shows that marketing effort can indeed influence the course of a lifecycle. By updating a product, either through design or through a fresh marketing approach, new life can be injected to regenerate customer and retailer interest and loyalty. Tango, for example, was a standard, uninteresting fizzy orange drink until some surreal, controversial and imaginative advertising repositioned it as a trendy teenage drink. Hiam (1990) argued that many products can be revitalised and that 'maturity simply reflects saturation of a specific target market with a specific product form'. Changing the form of product and expanding the target market could help new growth creation. Generally it is argued that 'it is a myth that products have a predetermined life span'.

Product level, class, form and brand

As said at the beginning of this section, the PLC can operate on a number of different levels. It is important to distinguish between the PLCs of total industries (such as the motor industry), product classes (such as petrol-driven private vehicles), product forms (such as hatchback cars) and individual brands (such as the Fiat Uno). Rink and Swan (1979) argue that there is a need for a clear definition of the distinction between these four categories of PLC so that the manager can fully understand the context within which the brand is evolving.

Industries and product classes tend to have the longest PLCs, because they are an aggregate of the efforts of many organisations and many individual products over time. An industry, such as the motor industry, can be in an overall state of fairly steady maturity for many years even as individual product forms and brands come and go. In the motor industry, for example, the hatchback is probably a mature product form, while the people carrier is still in its growth stage. Although a number of hatchback 'brands' have come and gone, the number of people carrier 'brands' is still growing. At the same time, the earliest entrants in the European market are starting to reach maturity.

eg

The pet food market is a mature market given the nation's love affair with pets. A restaurant in Chelsea even offers a dog menu with lamb steak at £6.95. A mature market does not, however, mean stagnant brand marketing strategies. There is a shift towards premium products; products targeted at different stages of a pet's life; and products offering increased convenience. Although wet food still dominates the market, the dry food sector has seen significant growth as it is no longer sold as a lazy way to serve a pet meal, but as a healthy alternative. Dry pet food can be bought in bigger sizes and remains fresher longer. Although overall pet food sales have remained fairly static, dry cat food for example grew by 17 per cent from 2000 to 2001 despite a significant price premium. At the same time, the canned sector declined by 12 per cent. With over 400 pet food suppliers in Europe, individual brands grow and decline within the context of the broader market trends, highlighting the necessity of considering the levels of the PLC concept (*The Grocer*, 2001d; Watkins, 2001).

Focusing down further to the individual brand level, it can be even more difficult to judge the nature of the PLC because there are so many competitive factors to take into consideration. Each factor, for example a competitor's pricing or promotional approach, has an influence on the strategies formulated for the brand and a direct effect on its success or failure. A brand's growth phase may not be as rapid as hoped or may not achieve as high a level of share as planned if a major competitor can find a way of distracting the market's attention during the critical launch period. To some extent, a predictable range of likely competitor actions and their outcomes can be foreseen and contingencies can be built into product planning to account for them. Nevertheless, it is still very difficult to forecast sales, to define the best strategies for each stage, the duration of each stage and the overall curve dynamic. The PLC concept provides no guarantees, despite its neatness. There are too many unpredictable factors influencing a product's life and too much depends on the quality of the care, commitment and imagination with which the product is managed.

Despite these weaknesses, the PLC is a well-used concept. Product marketing strategies should, however, take into account other considerations as well as the PLC, as the next section shows.

marketing *in action*

The yo-yo craze: the fad that bounces back

Fads and crazes are especially challenging to marketers as it is very hard to predict whether they will take off, how fast and for how long they will last. If the predictions and timing are wrong, then the marketer risks either being too slow to benefit before the craze passes or being left with unsold stock. The trouble with fad products, however, is that traditional marketing rules do not apply. There is no point in building for the long term if there is not going to be one and thus being flexible enough to capitalise quickly on a craze is critical.

Fad products often crop up in the toy market which, in the UK alone, is worth around £800 mn per year. The yo-yo is a craze toy with a different kind of product lifecycle because it keeps coming back! Popular for short periods in the 1960s, 1970s and 1980s, sales suddenly burst into life yet again in 1998. In 1997, the UK's largest independent toy retail chain, The Entertainer Group, hardly sold a yo-yo. In the first quarter of 1998, however, sales went up to between 3,000 and 4,000 yo-yos per week. By the end of the year the sales level had reached between 15,000 and 18,000 per week. The British Association of Toy Retailers estimated that sales nationally were approaching 150,000 per week and the yo-yo become the top-selling toy for pre-teen children. In an era of sophisticated computer games and in a market faced with an ever-increasing array of tempting toys, it was not a bad performance for a simple wheely thing on a piece of string.

So why did the yo-yo make a comeback? Some argue that the craze was fuelled by parents who saw it as a wholesome and nostalgic alternative to letting their kids gaze at a computer screen all day. A more likely explanation, however, is that marketers made the yo-yo a more acceptable play alternative by careful product development and a marketing campaign selling the yo-yo's benefits as an outdoor toy, emphasising its street credibility. Product improvements encouraged ease of use, for example the 'centrifugal clutch system' makes it easier to perform tricks, even for beginners. To encourage children to practise their skills and to reinforce brand awareness, yo-yo company Yomega started a reward programme

The Rolls-Royce of yo-yos!

Source: Yomega Corporation Inc.

called 'Tricknology'. If children bought the yo-yos from accredited stores they could be tested to earn certificates at bronze, silver, gold and platinum levels.

Skills development was not the only attraction. Through design and colour, the yo-yos became fashion accessories rather than just toys and some kids even began collecting them! Although yo-yos can be purchased for as little as £1, the average sale value was between £8 and £15, with premium products costing up to £100. Children became brand conscious, looking for the 'coolest' names such as Yomega X-Brain and Pro Yo III, and perhaps the fact that some schools banned yo-yos from playgrounds only served to enhance the 'cool' factor.

By the new millennium the craze was over. The shortages reported a few years previously were things of the past and the yo-yo had again become a niche product. Yomega still offers a wide selection on its website of both classic and fashion accessory yo-yos. Yo-yo events are still held around the world but they are a shadow of the 1998 event in Japan, attended by 41,000 people. Membership is still promoted for the Yomega Yo-Yo Association where like-minded people can meet. Products are still available in some specialist retail stores, but the queues to buy them have gone. Roll on 2007. The product is mature, yet appears to reinvent itself on a cyclical basis before it slips into decline. As yo-yo means 'come back' in the Tagalog dialect of the Philippines, even though the late 1990s craze ended, the yo-yo is almost guaranteed to make another reappearance – eventually!

Sources: Gray (1998); Rigby (1998); Wright (1998), http://www.yomega.com.

Market evolution

The marketing manager needs to understand how markets develop over time, in order better to plan and manage products, their lifecycles and their marketing strategies. Three components are involved in market evolution: the way in which customers adopt new products, the evolution and acceptance of technology and, finally, the impact of competition.

The diffusion of innovation

The product lifecycle is clearly driven by changes in consumer behaviour as the new product becomes established. The rate at which the growth stage develops is linked in particular to the speed with which customers can be led through from awareness of the product to trial and eventual adoption of the product, in other words how fast the AIDA model (*see* Figure 5.2 on p. 196) works. The problem is, however, that not all customers move through it with equal speed and eagerness and some will adopt innovation more quickly than others. This has led to the concept of the **diffusion of innovation** (Rogers, 1962), which looks at the rate at which innovation spreads across a market as a whole. Effectively, it allows the grouping or classification of customers depending on their speed of adoption into one of five adopter categories, as shown in Figure 8.3.

Innovators

Innovators are important in the early stages of a product's lifecycle to help get the product off the ground and start the process of gaining acceptance. They form only a small group, but they buy early and are prepared to take a risk. In consumer markets, innovators tend to be younger, better educated, more affluent and confident. In B2B markets, innovators are likely to be profitable and, again, willing to take risks in return for the potential benefits to be gained from being first.

Innovators may be category specific. A consumer who is an innovator in the hi-fi market, for example, may be a laggard when it comes to small kitchen appliances or photographic equipment. It depends on the individual's interests and inclinations and to some extent on what kinds of product they think are important in establishing their status in other people's

Figure 8.3 Diffusion of innovation: adopter categories

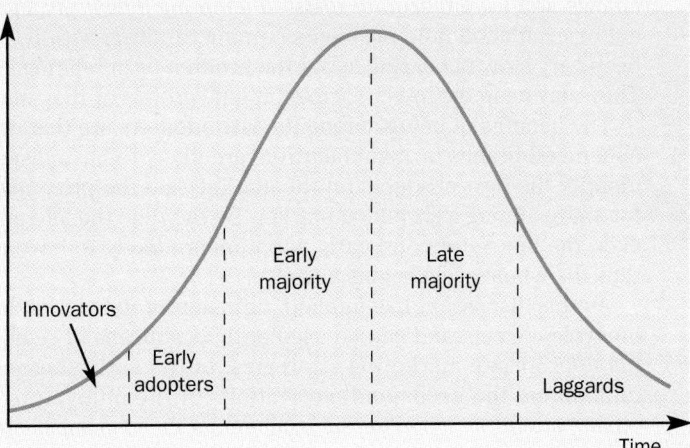

Source: Based on Rogers (1962). Reprinted and adapted from figure 7–2, p. 262 with the permission of The Free Press, an imprint of Simon & Schuster Adult Publishing Group, from *Diffusion of Innovations*, Fourth Edition, by Everett M. Rogers. Copyright © 1995 Everett M. Rogers, Copyright © 1962, 1971, 1983 by The Free Press.

eyes. Within a particular product category, the innovator may continue to show innovative tendencies over time, wanting to be the first with a series of new products. Thus those who were the first to adopt car phones may also be the first to adopt in-car computerised navigation systems.

Early adopters

Early adopters enter the market early, but are content to let the innovators take the real pioneering risks with a new product. They do, however, soon follow the lead of the innovators and are always alert to new developments in markets of interest to them. Once the early adopters begin to enter the market, the growth stage of a PLC can then develop.

Both innovators and early adopters tend to be opinion leaders and thus it is important for the promoter of a new product to target them and win them over. The mass market, however, looks particularly to the early adopters for a lead, as they are more of a mainstream group than the innovators. The early adopters are thus critical for making a product generally acceptable and for spreading word-of-mouth recommendations about the product's value and benefits.

Early majority

With the *early majority* the mass market starts to build up, as more and more people enter it. The early majority are more risk averse than previous groups and want some reassurance that the product is tried and tested before they will commit themselves to it. This group may be relatively well educated, with above-average incomes, but that may depend on the nature of the product concerned. Digital cameras, for example, have entered this stage, but many consumers may be holding back until the price comes down. When a product does reach the early majority, social pressure may begin to build: 'You really must get yourself an ice-cream maker – you can't possibly manage without one.' This begins to move the product towards the late majority.

Late majority

The *late majority* customers are perhaps less interested or bothered about the product category, or are content to wait until they see how the market develops. They are a little behind the early majority and want even more reassurance about the product's benefits and worth. It could be argued that DVD players have entered this stage. The late majority may have more choice of alternative products in the market, as competition builds, and will certainly have the benefit of the accumulated knowledge and experience of the previous groups. Once the late majority has been converted, the product is likely to be reaching its mature stage, a steady plateau of repeat purchases, with very few new customers left to enter the market.

Late adopters or laggards

The last remaining converts are the *late adopters* or *laggards*. They may be very averse to change and have therefore resisted adopting a new product, or they may have had attitudinal or even economic problems coming to terms with it. Alternatively, they may just have been very slow in hearing about the product or in relating its benefits to their own lifestyles. They may be in the lower socioeconomic groups or they may be older consumers.

The benefits of being among the late adopters are that others have taken all the risks; the ephemeral brands or manufacturers are likely to have disappeared; it may thus be easier to identify the best products on the market; and the price may be falling as competitors fight for share among a shrinking market. By the time the late adopters get into the market, however, the innovators and early adopters are likely to have moved on to something else and thus the whole cycle begins again!

As this discussion has implied, diffusion of innovation has strong links with the product lifecycle concept and can be used both as a means of segmenting a market and for suggesting appropriate marketing strategies. In the early stages, for example, it is important to understand the needs and motivations of the innovators and early adopters and then to attract attention and generate trial among these groups. Other than knowing that they have innovative tendencies, however, it can be difficult to profile the groups using more concrete demographic or psychographic variables. In that case, it is important for the marketer to think in product terms. Perhaps hi-fi innovators and early adopters may be reached through specialist magazines that review new products, for example.

According to Gatignon and Robertson (1985), building on the work of Rogers (1962), six main factors affect the rate of product adoption:

1 *Relative advantage*: additional benefits and value added compared with alternatives.
2 *Compatibility*: fit with consumer tastes, needs, attitudes, etc.
3 *Complexity*: the less complex the product or the more user friendly it is, the quicker the rate of adoption.
4 *Divisibility*: whether it can be tried on a limited basis to reduce the risk of trial, e.g. computer software demonstration disks.
5 *Communicability*: ease of communicating benefits.
6 *Perceived risk*: what it will cost the buyer in terms of both money and pride if the purchase turns out to be a 'wrong' decision.

The marketer can consider these factors when developing products and their marketing mixes. Market research can help to define compatibility and to determine the most attractive relative advantage. Risk can be reduced through warranties, free samples, trial prices and pack sizes or 'satisfaction or your money back' promotions. Communication can be helped through product demonstrations or samples.

corporate social responsibility *in action*

Why turkeys don't vote for Christmas

It has been estimated that the British consume around 6 million turkeys around Christmas time very year. No traditional Christmas dinner can be without a suitably stuffed turkey with all the trimmings. A turkey is not just for Christmas, however. Year-round sales have opened up new market sectors, such as turkey burgers, through processing. This means that a more planned approach to turkey rearing as a mass market industrially farmed product. The supermarkets have also taken particular care to ensure that the supply chain, right back to the turkey factory farm, provides supply consistency to the standards expected. There is another side to the supply chain, however, that could depress or change consumer preferences. Let's just spare a thought for the poor old turkey.

Animal welfare campaigners claim that turkeys are often reared in appalling conditions, cramped, thoroughly miserable and packed with injured and dying birds. The conditions do vary, but at worst, the sheds, which can contain up to 25,000 birds, are not cleaned so the floor is coated with urine and dung. Additionally, the birds often develop weak legs because of the cramped conditions and rapid weight gain they are expected to achieve. Unless they are de-beaked, a process involving slicing off the beak with a red-hot blade, distressed factory farmed birds can attack each other. The official loss before slaughter from all causes is 15 per cent, sometimes higher (Poulter, 2001a).

Some of the worst farms are thought to supply the major supermarket chains, so these miserable birds could well end up on your plate. The supermarkets are, however, sensitive to such claims, regarding animal welfare as a priority, and they have the purchasing power to enforce change. Most have strict codes of conduct on animal welfare for all suppliers to prevent injury and distress, so that in-store claims of 'farm fresh', 'welfare assured' and 'prime quality' produce actually have some meaning. The key, of course, is how frequent and rigorous the inspection process is during the rearing cycle.

Whatever the rearing conditions, there is still the issue of slaughter. The natural life span of a turkey is up to ten years, but farmed birds rarely survive beyond 12 to 26 weeks. Even the slaughter process lacks dignity. Birds are unpacked from crates, hung upside down from shackles and left for several minutes before the line moves the turkeys through a bath of electrified water which is meant to cause unconsciousness before their throats are cut. A small percentage of birds, still struggling, miss the water and are alive for the throat cutting and the final pre-rendering in the feather-loosening tank (*The Ecologist*, 2001/2002).

In selecting turkeys, the attributes that consumers tend to look for are freshness and size, but they pay little attention to rearing conditions. They tend to rely on the trustworthiness and reputation of the retailers to create an ethical supply chain that ensures good animal welfare during rearing and processing (if that is not a contradiction). Campaigns and claims such as those highlighted in this text could change that consumer perception and in time it may force both retailers and farmers to go to even greater lengths to ensure that turkey products are positioned to reflect the highest animal welfare standards rather than relying on an unquestioning consumer. It could lead to a greater emphasis on free-range turkeys . . . if the consumer is prepared to pay the price premium.

Now you know why turkeys really don't vote for Christmas. Perhaps it is better that we consumers don't visit turkey farms, don't ask questions, and just worry about the indigestion. Then again, you could try a cruelty-free Christmas recipe as proposed by Compassion in World Farming (http://www.ciwf.co.uk).

Sources: The Ecologist (2001/2002); Poulter (2001a).

Technological impact

Technology also evolves over time. Sometimes this evolution is gradual, allowing the product to develop incrementally through new models and upgrades, but with no major shocks to the customer. Sometimes, however, technical breakthroughs occur that radically alter the expectations of the market and its competitive structure. Such technological discontinuities tend to create a period of intense change and disturbance to the *status quo* as new products emerge that capitalise on the breakthrough. Whole industries can be wiped out by these changes if adaptation does not take place (Tushman and Anderson, 1986). The demand for black and white televisions, steam locomotives and mechanical cash registers changed dramatically as a result of technological discontinuity. Fortunately for many organisations, such radical changes are rare and take some time to work through to the market.

Technological innovation can thus be used to extend the product lifecycle, by helping to refresh and update the product, but it can also shorten a lifecycle by rendering a product obsolete.

e-marketing *in action*

Diffusion of digital innovation

One of the great challenges of managing e-marketing is to be able to assess accurately how new technological innovations can be applied to give competitive advantage. For example, those companies such as Dell and Cisco which foresaw the importance of the internet as a sales channel were able to adjust their strategy to take best advantage of this new medium. The current and future usage levels of other technology platforms must also be assessed. For example, when the technology was developed to access the Internet through mobile phones using WAP (wireless application protocol), in the late 1990s, companies had to decide whether to invest in providing this access platform for their customers.

A bank, for example, may have taken the decision to offer web-based internet banking, but would also need to consider whether to offer banking using WAP phones or interactive digital TV services. This decision had to be taken against a background of rapid increase adoption of PC-based internet access so much hype was generated by the manufacturers through the media. Companies who based their decision on hype alone would typically have not realised a satisfactory turn on investment since the users of WAP-based services were much lower than expected. A similar situation is also faced by marketers considering the introduction of the GPRS (General Packet Radio Service) or so-called 2.5G technology which offers up to 10 times the speed of WAP and an always-on connection to the internet. The future offers the 3G technology of the UMTS standard which entered trial in Tokyo in late 2001. This offers performance sufficient to transmit full-colour images and video and could offer many new applications.

Clearly, market research is necessary to assess the future potential of these technologies. Market researchers such as E-Mori (http://www.e-mori.co.uk), NOP (http://www.nopres.co.uk) and technology analysts such as Datamonitor (http://www.datamonitor.com), Forrester (http://www.forrester.com), Gartner (http://www.gartner.com) and IDC (http://www.idc.com) conduct the research and provide the data to marketers to assist in making these decisions. The diffusion of innovation concept can be used to assess the current stage of adoption – for example in many Western European countries PC-based web access is now at the late majority stage of adoption whereas WAP usage is still at the innovator/early adopter stage.

Of course, taking the decision to offer a new access platform to customers is only a small part of the role of the marketer. Once a company decides to introduce a new technology platform it has to carefully assess the barriers and facilitators of customer adoption and then develop the marketing strategies to encourage adoption. For example, some banks offered free WAP handsets to customers who decided to adopt online banking.

Source: Dave Chaffey.

Competitor entry timing

In the same way that consumers can be classified according to their willingness and ability to adopt innovation, competitors can be classified according to their timing in entering a market. In any specific product market, competitors can be categorised in five main groups:

Pioneers

Pioneers are the innovative organisations that create new markets or are the first to get to the market. They may invest heavily in R&D and marketing to keep the new ideas flowing and to commercialise them. This group might include organisations such as Sony, 3M and Philips.

Early imitators

Organisations that are *early imitators* see what the pioneers have done, recognise the market's potential and then copy them. An early imitator's product is likely to be a 'me too' product, with very little to differentiate it from the pioneer. Any differentiation is likely to arise from elements of the marketing mix other than product. The entry of early imitators may coincide with the growth stage of the lifecycle when there is enough demand and enthusiasm to support a number of very similar competing products.

Early differentiators

An organisation that takes the basic product and improves it or adds new features is an *early differentiator*. The early differentiator's product does, therefore, offer distinct features and benefits, but builds on the pioneer's original product concept. The entry of such competitors is likely to happen during the growth stage.

eg

Microsoft was a relatively late entrant into the video games market when it launched the X-Box console in 2001. This was part of a strategy to move from the office into the living room. Microsoft has, however, to compete against established players such as Sony and Nintendo and their daunting reputations and market shares if it wants to achieve its target of a 40 per cent share of the $20 bn market. Much depends on Microsoft's claims of product superiority, although with just 15 to 20 X-Box games available compared with 144 for the PlayStation 2, users might just decide whether there is a real play advantage to be had, whatever the technology (Hamm and Greene, 2001).

Early nichers

As a market moves towards saturation and maturity, the level of general competition becomes intense and any new entrant is likely to look for a specific *niche* segment. This segmentation could be based on any of the variables examined in Chapter 5, such as product benefits, price sensitivity or psychographics.

Late entrants

In an established mature market, it will be difficult for a new entrant to compete unless it has some means of clear differential advantage. This could be in terms of price, distribution or promotional weight. A *late imitator* is unlikely to be able to achieve these things without the strong financial backing provided by its other products in other markets, or by acquiring an established product in the market, as with Quaker's acquisition of Snapple mentioned earlier. For a small organisation without such backing, entering a market at this stage could be a high-risk, unfeasible strategy. Clearly, these categorisations are somewhat generalised, but they do add another dimension to the PLC. They help in understanding how a market's PLC might evolve and what kinds of marketing strategies are appropriate at each stage given the competitive environment. Many of these issues will be further explored in Chapter 20.

Managerial responses

By using the PLC together with analysis of customers, technology and competitors, as outlined above, the marketing manager can begin to paint a detailed picture of the factors that are likely to influence the shape of the PLC, its duration and the strategies that might be appropriate at each stage. Table 8.1 summarises this approach from the point of view of a pioneer organisation, looking at the projected PLC of a radically new consumer product. As

Table 8.1 PLC Stages: Characteristics and strategies

	Introduction	*Growth*	*Maturity*	*Decline*
Market characteristics				
Type of customer entering market	*Innovators*	*Early adopters* *Early majority*	*Late majority*	*Late adopters*
Type of competitor entering market	*Pioneer*	*Early imitators* *Early differentiators* *Early nichers*	*Late entrants*	
Number of products on the market	*One*	*Few*	*Many*	*Declining*
Technological development	*Discontinuity – radically new concept*	*Incremental – fine tuning – differentiation*	*Incremental – possibility of interruption by discontinuity?*	*None or minor*
Financial characteristics				
Sales	*Low*	*Growing rapidly*	*Growing slowly*	*Declining*
Costs per customer	*High*	*Average*	*Low*	*Low*
Cash flow	*Negative*	*Acceptable*	*High*	*Acceptable*
Profit	*Negative*	*Rising rapidly*	*High*	*Declining*
Main marketing objectives				
Re consumer	*Gain awareness* *Generate trial*	*Widen acceptance* *Generate trial/repeat sales*	*Remind/reinforce* *Encourage loyalty*	*Milk last sales*
Re competition	*Establish premier position*	*Defend*	*Compete*	
Re distribution	*Gain acceptance* *Increase shelf space*	*Widen distribution*	*Maintain shelf space*	*Keep product available*
Re product	*Establish*	*Fine tune*	*Refresh/relaunch/vary* *Maintain*	*Drop/sell*
Marketing mix				
Product range	*Basic* *Brand building*	*Enhanced*	*Extension/variety* *Brand image reinforcement*	*Rationalisation*
Price	*Skimming* *– capitalise on early entry*	*Lower* *Penetration*	*Low* *Match/beat competition*	*Steady*
Channels of distribution	*Limited*	*Increasing*	*Maximum*	*Declining*
Consumer promotion focus				
• *Advertising*	*High: Awareness*	*High: Image building*	*Moderate: Remind/reinforce*	*Minimal: Remind*
• *Sales promotion*	*High: Trial*	*High: Repeat purchase*	*Moderate: Short-term share gain*	*Low: Reward loyalty*
Trade promotion				
• *Ads/promotions*	*High: Awareness/acceptance*	*Minimal: Reinforce/defend*	*Moderate: Defend/relaunch*	*Minimal: Remind*
• *Personal selling*	*High: Awareness/acceptance*	*Lower: Repeat orders*	*Moderate: Reinforce/relaunch*	*Minimal: Repeat orders*

the PLC's externally generated characteristics unfold, the organisation's strategies also develop, as a means of either minimising threats or maximising opportunities. However, the manager needs to exercise caution in assuming that the future will unfold neatly according to plan. In a marketing environment that is witnessing reduced new product development cycle times, customer-driven product development and increasing global competition, there is less certainty than ever. Models that appear to be conceptually very simple and predictive then become very dangerous managerial tools.

Managing the product mix

In a dynamic marketing environment, the product mix is not static. The effects of changing technology, evolving competition and changes in customer needs mean that it is most important for an organisation to find ways of keeping its product ranges fresh and interesting. This opens up a number of management problems, requiring planned procedures and strategies in order to:

1 retain and maintain existing products so that they continue to meet their objectives;
2 modify and adapt existing products to take advantage of new technology, emerging opportunities or changing market conditions;
3 delete old products that are close to the end of their working lives and no longer serve their purpose; and finally,
4 introduce a flow of new products to maintain or improve sales and profit levels and to form a firm foundation for tomorrow's markets. This latter point will be dealt with separately in Chapter 9.

An organisation, therefore, needs a balanced **product portfolio**, capable of sustaining it satisfactorily over its planning horizons. Note that the portfolio ideally must be *balanced*, containing neither too many new nor too many declining products. Too many new products could put an organisation at risk, as product launch is resource intensive with no guarantee of success. At the other extreme, too many declining products could threaten the future of the business, as sales and profits start to fall. Even if replacement or diversification plans are in place, unless they are implemented over a longer period, the organisation could find itself coping with too much change and new product risk. In an ideal world, mature but still strong products can provide the stable cash flow against which a planned programme of new product establishment and declining product deletion can take place.

Positioning products

A crucial decision, which could affect the length of a product's life and its resilience in a market over time, concerns the product's positioning. **Product positioning** means thinking about a product in the context of the competitive space it occupies in its market, defined in terms of attributes that matter to the target market. The important criterion is how close to the ideal on each of those attributes, compared with competing products, your product is judged to be by the target market. Harrod's, for example, is positioned as a high-quality, exclusive departmental store. In order to reinforce this positioning with its target market, Harrod's (http://www.harrods.com) makes sure that its product ranges, its staff expertise, its displays and overall store ambience are of equally high quality.

It is the target customer's definition of important attributes and their perception of how your product compares on them that matter. Marketing managers have to stand back from their own feelings and must ensure that the attributes selected are those that are critical to the customer, not those that marketing managers would like to be critical. The range of attributes judged to be important will vary according to the particular market segments under consideration. Chapter 5 offered further insights into the relationship between segmentation and product characteristics.

Further need for managerial objectivity arises when a positioning exercise is carried out. While managers may take steps to create a product and marketing package that they think will fill a previously defined position, they still need to ensure that they closely monitor the target market's opinions to make certain that the required image and message are being conveyed.

The concept of product positioning is clearly focused on a customer-based perspective, but it still has serious implications for product design and development. The decision about positioning is made during the product's development and will be reflected in a whole range of the product's characteristics, including brand image, packaging and quality, as well as in the pricing and communication elements of the marketing mix.

Defining and selecting an appropriate position for a product involves three stages.

Stage 1

Detailed market research needs to be carried out during the first stage in order to establish what attributes are important to any given market segment and their order of preference. This background research will centre on a class of products rather than on individual brands within the class. Thus a particular segment, for example, might regard softness, absorbency and a high number of sheets on the roll as the three most important attributes of toilet tissue, in that order of preference.

Stage 2

Having identified the important attributes, in the second stage further research now short-lists the existing products that offer those attributes. Brands such as Kleenex Velvet and Andrex might be seen as fulfilling the needs of the toilet tissue segment mentioned above.

Stage 3

In the third stage, it is necessary to find out:

(a) what the target market considers to be the ideal level for each of the defined attributes; and

(b) how they rate each brand's attributes in relation to the ideal and to each other.

The conclusions from this hypothetical research may be, for instance, that while Andrex has more sheets per roll than Kleenex (thus apparently achieving a better rating for Andrex on an important attribute), in relation to the ideal Andrex is perceived to have too many (too bulky for the roll holder), whereas Kleenex might be perceived to have too few (runs out too quickly). Both products could thus improve their offering.

Once the positioning process has been completed for all the relevant attributes, it is useful to be able to visualise the complete picture graphically, by creating a perceptual map of the market. Figure 8.4 shows such a hypothetical map of the toilet tissue market, using price and softness as two dimensions that might represent important attributes. This shows

Figure 8.4 Perceptual map of the toilet tissue market

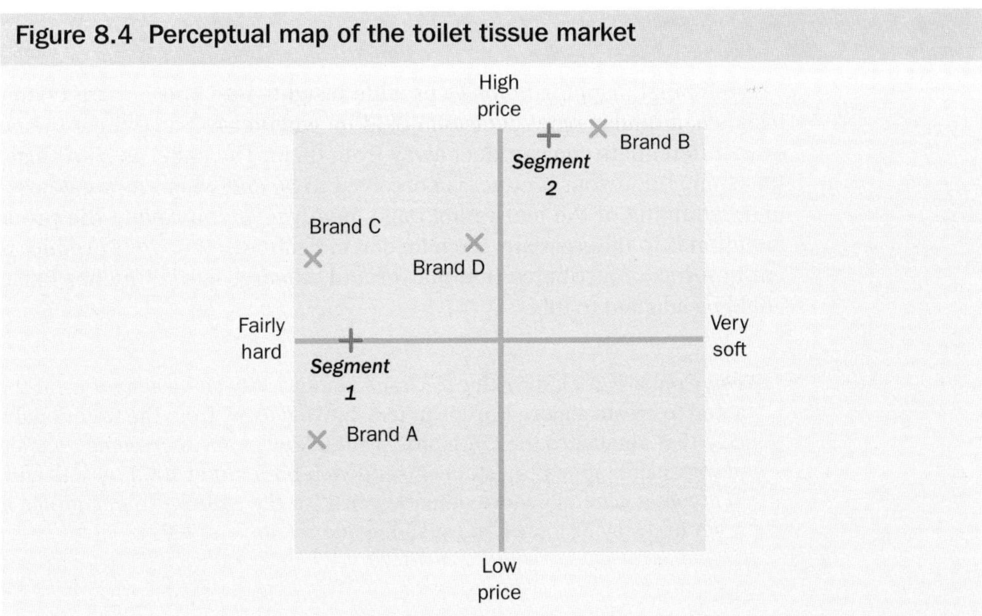

that Brand A is serving the bottom end of the market in Segment 1, offering a cheap, purely functional product, whereas Brand B is aimed at the discerning customer in Segment 2 who is prepared to pay a little more for a gentler experience. Brand C seems to be closer to Segment 1 than Segment 2, but is overpriced compared with Brand A for a similar quality of product. Brand D is floating between the two segments, with nothing to offer that is particularly appealing to either.

In some cases, of course, two dimensions are insufficient to represent the complexities of target market opinion. Although this creates a far more difficult mapping task, any number of further dimensions can be included using multidimensional scaling techniques (Green and Carmone, 1970). Figure 8.5 expands the mapping of the toilet tissue example to include additional dimensions. In such a case, the map is an invaluable aid to understanding complex product relationships, almost at a glance, saving many pages of confusing verbal description.

As can be seen from Figure 8.5, Segment 1 wants high performance and Brand E is well positioned to serve its needs. Segment 2 is fairly concerned about performance characteristics, but also thinks that the aesthetics of the tissue are important, so that it coordinates with bathroom decor and fittings. Brand E might be able to serve this segment better by expanding its colour range, without alienating Segment 1. Segment 3 is the value-conscious economy segment that wants the largest number of sheets per roll for the least amount of money. Segment 4 has more of an environmental conscience than the others and Brand G is well positioned for them. Brand F, however, is poorly positioned to serve any of the existing segments and its managers need to think carefully about which direction to take with it.

Figure 8.5 Multidimensional perceptual map of the toilet tissue market

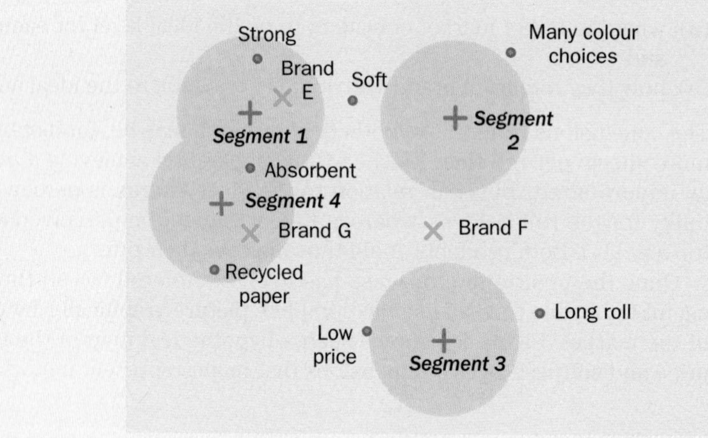

Perceptual mapping helps to provide insights into appropriate competitive actions. For instance, a fundamental decision could be whether to try to meet the competition head-on or to differentiate your product away from them. The map can show just how far away from the competition your product is perceived to be and where its weaknesses lie, leading to an understanding of the marketing tasks involved in improving the product offering. If the intention is to differentiate, the map can indicate whether your product is sufficiently different in terms of attributes that matter and whether market niches exist that your product could be adapted to fill.

eg

When Compass took over the 28 Granada motorway service stations in the UK, it decided it wanted to create a more European feel, moving away from the traditional UK service station image that dominates the UK motorist's thinking, while increasing revenue. The re-branding and expansion aimed to establish sandwich bars, other food outlets and clothes retailers, and create a generally more upmarket feel for the stations to encourage a transient captive market into staying longer and spending more (Bowers, 2001).

All of this implies that assessing and defining meaningful product positioning is an important early step in marketing management. This process can bring to light opportunities, it can highlight potential dangers of cannibalising one's own products and it can help to define competitive pressures, strengths and weaknesses. It is also a step in making the decision to modify a current product range by repositioning selected products.

Repositioning and modifying products

Positioning might have to be adjusted for many reasons as both the product and its market mature. Developing technology, evolving competition, changing customer needs and wants all mean that products have to be constantly appraised and reviewed. Nevertheless, a major **product repositioning** exercise can be very costly and risky (alienating or confusing existing buyers and failing to attract new ones, for instance). This means that the marketing manager needs to be sure that the changes will be perceptible and relevant to the target market, that the market is willing to accept change and that the repositioning will produce measurable benefits.

It is important to distinguish here between a fundamental repositioning exercise and minor product refreshment. The latter is a natural part of the PLC, when small changes that suggest progress and improvement are implemented to prevent the product image from becoming stale. Car manufacturers, for instance, will change their colour ranges and redesign various accessories each year, but the market does not interpret these as anywhere nearly as radical as a repositioning would be. Fine tuning the product itself can be done without seeking to reposition and, conversely, repositioning can take place through pricing, promotion or distribution without any change to the product. Kellogg, for example, used advertising to reposition its Cornflakes brand as an adult snack that can be eaten at any time of day rather than as a basic and rather boring children's breakfast. The slogan 'Have you forgotten how good they taste?' implies a long-established brand heritage, with connotations of familiarity, reassurance and quality.

Repositioning has a number of serious implications. It might involve redefining or enlarging segments and it may well involve redesigning an entire marketing strategy. Such a fundamental revamp of a product is most likely to take place in the maturity stage of the PLC, when the product is beginning to fade a little.

There are three main areas for repositioning and product improvement.

Quality

As discussed at pp. 299 *et seq.*, quality has a number of dimensions. With physical products, quality can be defined in terms of reliability, durability and dependability, which are generally applicable across most products. There are, however, product-specific quality dimensions that the target market could use as indicators of a quality product, such as speed, taste, colour, materials, ingredients and even price and packaging (*see* Chapter 11 and pp. 293 *et seq.*).

marketing *in action*

Repositioning gives the brand a sporting chance

Lucozade (http://www.lucozade.com) used to be positioned as an invalid's drink, with the slogan 'Lucozade aids recovery'. Its advertising in the 1960s used to show a poorly child being tended by a caring mother who gave him Lucozade. As general health and living conditions have improved, however, this became too much of a niche position. If people only bought Lucozade when there was sickness in the household, the purchase frequency and volume would be very low, especially when compared with other more mainstream fizzy drinks. In the 1980s, therefore, Lucozade was repositioned to capitalise on the growing health boom. Instead of being a semi-medicinal 'illness' drink, with all the negative connotations that implies, it became a specially formulated, glucose-rich, sports energy drink for active and busy people, and this positioning has been endorsed by the sponsorship of sports teams, for example sponsoring the Lions' 2001 Australian tour, making sure that each member of the team consumed two litres of Lucozade Sport per day during the tour. It still

As a sports drink Lucozade has lost its image as something to be drunk when you are ill, and replaced it with the idea that it gives you the energy to keep up with your active lifestyle.

Source: GlaxoSmithKline.

retains its premium price and quality image, but has created much more positive connotations and a rationale for more frequent purchase and consumption. The repositioning was achieved partly through packaging, for instance in a 'one-shot' bottle (no longer just the large size bottle), selling alongside other soft drinks (colas, etc.), and partly through powerful celebrity advertising featuring current sports heroes.

Although Lucozade was the pioneer in opening up a new sector through repositioning, as the market grew, the sector split into 'sports' and 'functional'. The functional sector concentrated on energy drinks, with brands such as Red Bull dominating (see p. 352). Meanwhile, the focus for sports drinks is replenishing carbohydrates and electrolytes quickly, and rehydrating the body after exercise. This subsector is still dominated by Lucozade Sport with £34 mn in sales in 2000, but Coca-Cola intends to relaunch its Powerade brand to capture a significant share, using 'Get Up, Stay Up' as its campaign theme. Powerade is packaged in a sports cap bottle with flavours such as the blue coloured Ice Storm Berry that was so successful on its US launch. Lucozade will, however, be defending its position with new flavours and an increased marketing spend planned for 2002.

The website, http://www.lucozadesport.com lists the research reports linking sports drink with exercise; however, not all experts agree as to the real value. A study of many energy 'sports drinks' has resulted in concerns about the validity of some of the claims being made. Despite being positioned as 'healthy', many drinks had high sugar content, with one brand dishing up 19 level teaspoons of sugar in one serving, and some had caffeine levels three times higher than those of traditional colas. As the public becomes more informed, discerning and wary of marketing claims, brand personalities and values will have to evolve too. But then again, if it tastes good and you enjoy it, perhaps that is enough!

Sources: Hawkes (1997); Johnson (2001), Newnham (2001).

eg

The Jaguar brand name (http://www.jaguarcars.com) has such strong associations with quality in the luxury car market that the company decided to extend the brand into aircraft. Jaguar linked up with Raytheon in the US to produce the Beech King Air Jaguar special edition. Jaguar quality manifests itself through the interior fittings and furnishings, leather seats, Jaguar green carpeting, special colours and liveries and even walnut cabins. All the aircraft registrations will end with XJ to emphasise the Jaguar link. The Jaguar XJ8 car costs over $50,000 in the USA and the Jaguar special edition plane over $2.6 mn, some $66,000 more than the same aircraft without the special edition interior (Brennan, 1997).

Quality for service products tends to arise from the customer's perceptions of the physical support mechanisms and the infrastructure that help to create an appropriate interactive environment. An efficient appointments system, friendly reception and provision of coffee and magazines in a pleasant waiting area, for example, all add to the perceived quality of a service operation in the minds of customers. Naturally, this must be reinforced by consistent, reliable and satisfactory delivery of the service itself.

In changing the quality of a product, the movement can be towards either relatively higher quality or relatively lower quality. Lowering the quality is likely to lose existing customers, but at the same time could open up an expanded market if it brings the product into a more affordable price range. Lowering the quality does not necessarily mean making actual changes to the product; it can be an act of omission. An organisation could make a conscious decision to withhold any further development and modification resources from a product, despite seeing competing products improve. This means that the organisation's product quality is declining relative to the rest and may indicate that the product is being phased out and that resources are being saved for investment in future products.

Raising the quality of a physical product could be achieved perhaps through better components or refined manufacturing. For a service product, it could mean major refurbishment for the premises or developing the way in which the experience is packaged. Whatever the product or the means employed, raising the quality offers the prospect of charging higher prices and increasing profit margins. It might, however, lead to increased competition from other organisations greedy for a share of that prosperity. The other point to consider carefully is whether the target market will either recognise or value the newly raised quality.

eg

The football experience for domestic competitions could eventually be repackaged to serve the interests of the top clubs. Although the UEFA Champions League has been a great success for the football clubs involved, the G14, the top clubs in Europe, have held talks with agencies about developing a collective brand identity that could move them closer to forming a breakaway European Super League. Football brands are big business, with Manchester United, Real Madrid and Bayern Munich, the three most commercially successful clubs in Europe, leading the pack. The emergence of the G14 from being a lobbying group to one with a commercial presence would strengthen the hand of the big clubs on and off the football pitch. It would go beyond just influencing the allocation of broadcasting and commercial revenues from European club competitions and speed up the introduction of a repositioned Super League offering pan-European league football of the highest quality. While this would be financially lucrative for the G14 clubs and exciting for the spectator, it could also eventually mean the end of money-spinning visits from the top clubs to such places as Ipswich Town or Charlton Athletic in domestic competitions (Kleinman, 2001a).

Design

Thinking in an aesthetic rather than an engineering context, design affects the impact of the product on the senses. This concept can be difficult to handle, as it covers areas such as the appearance, texture, taste, smell, feel or sound of the product, all of which involve the customer in some very subjective assessments. These areas do, however, provide many combinations of variables that could offer the opportunity for change. If the objective is to reposition a product, just changing its visual appearance or its packaging (probably with 'new improved . . .' splashed across it) could give customers sufficient cues and justification for revising their opinions of it.

eg

Design is clearly an important factor in fashion clothing markets. Brand names become closely associated with certain characteristics or a certain 'look' that helps to position them in the 1990s. Jaeger, for example, was closely associated with traditional, classic looks, but the organisation felt that it needed to be more fashionable and stylish as the brand's growth had slowed compared with its competitors. The solution was to retain a core classic range, so as not to alienate loyal customers, but to supplement it with capsule collections of more fashionable merchandise. This signalled a subtle rather than radical shift in Jaeger's positioning to widen and refresh its appeal.

It must be stressed that any design changes are a waste of time and resources unless they matter to the market, can be communicated to that market and are implemented to achieve defined objectives.

Performance

Like design, performance relies on the customer's initial, rather impressionistic assessment. A more concrete appreciation of performance may only come after product use. The kind of factors under consideration here include convenience, safety, ease of handling, efficiency, effectiveness and adaptability to different situations. A car's performance, for instance, can be measured in terms of its acceleration, braking ability or fuel economy, depending on what is important to the buyer. Improving the fuel economy at the expense of acceleration might change the character of the car, making it less appealing to a 'boy racer' type of segment, but positioning it more firmly and more positively in the 'heavy urban usage' segment. Even the fuel itself has been repositioned in terms of its performance-enhancing capabilities, with some brands promising to be more engine friendly or to improve engine performance.

Quality, design and performance are often inextricably interlinked. Proposed changes under one heading have implications for the others. Improving a car's fuel economy may involve better-quality components under the bonnet as well as a more aerodynamic body design.

It does not really matter whether a proposed change is classified as relating to quality, design or performance, or all three. What does matter is that as part of the product management process, all the relevant options are assessed to make sure that the product continues to achieve its maximum potential, either within its existing segment(s) or through repositioning into a new one. Quality, design and performance all provide possibilities for the major or minor changes that will ensure this.

Product range management

The discussion above concentrated on the adjustment and adaptation of existing products and their marketing mixes to reposition the offering in the customer's mind. Taking this concept a step further, the organisation may wish to leave existing products as they are and use the assessment of positioning to identify opportunities for new products to fill or extend the current range. This approach to new product development may use existing products as a basis, rather than the more radical departures envisaged in the next chapter. These decisions are all part of the ongoing product audit, constantly checking to make sure that product offerings continue to serve the market's needs and wants. A major advantage is that all the positive attitudes and perceptions of the original brand's customers can be transferred to the new product that evolves (Aaker and Keller, 1990).

Two broad options are available: extending the product line and filling the product range.

Extending the product line length and depth

Extending the product line involves looking at the current range and deciding whether to extend it upwards, downwards or in both directions. An upwards extension might involve introducing a higher-priced, higher-quality, more exclusive product, while a downwards extension might require a basic, no-frills product at a rock-bottom, mass-market price.

In thinking about such an extension, the marketer needs to be sure that the gaps thus filled are worth filling. Will sufficient customers emerge to take up the new product? Will the trade accept it? Is it a significant profit opportunity? Will it simply cannibalise existing products? This last issue is particularly important; there is no point in extending a product range downwards if the main effect is to pull customers away from an existing mid-range product.

Extending upwards. Extending upwards has a number of attractions, assuming that the organisation has the ability to produce a suitably attractive and consistently high-quality product offering. An upwards extension could create a product with higher margins (*see* Chapter 11) as well as enhancing the organisation's image. It also helps to build a kind of staircase for the customer to climb. As the customer becomes more affluent or as their needs and wants become more sophisticated, they can trade up to the next product in the range and still maintain their loyalty to one organisation. A business school, for example, with established post-experience management programmes at certificate and diploma levels, might extend its product range upwards to include an MBA. The intention would be that students should work their way through all three qualifications in the course of their management careers. Similarly, a bank might create a new savings scheme offering higher rates of interest for balances over £10,000 to prevent a customer with such funds from taking their money elsewhere.

eg

Pringle, a Scottish knitwear firm best known for its sweaters and golf sponsorship, tried to extend upwards into luxury goods, such as high-quality luggage and accessories. At the same time, it was also expanding sideways into non-knitwear clothing and its own retail outlets. This combination of upwards and sideways expansion did not work well. The Pringle brand name was appearing on too many items that were too far removed from its core image. This diluted the impact and exclusivity of the name and meant that customers did not perceive the luxury goods as being suitably classy or élite.

Extending downwards. The downwards extension can be used to attack competitors operating at the volume end of the market. It can build a larger base of sales if a lower-priced product broadens the number of potential customers. Then, by introducing people to the bottom of the range product and forming some kind of relationship with them, it may be possible to get them to trade up, thus assisting sales of the mid-range product. This would be the ideal situation, but do remember the risks of cannibalisation if the bottom of the range product acts as a magnet to existing mid-range customers. There can be a risk of undermining brand equity by extensions at the bottom of the range. This can cause an overall loss of equity to the whole range that is greater than the incremental sales of the new products (Reibstein *et al.*, 1998).

Careful thought also needs to be given to the logistic implications of extending downwards if it opens up bigger markets. This might mean shifting higher volumes of goods to more outlets, as well as increased commitment to mass communication in order to reach the greater number of potential buyers. Hi-fi manufacturers, for instance, make sure that they extend their ranges downwards, partly to catch the mass market with cheap and cheerful, value for money music systems, and partly to try to encourage brand loyalty in the younger buyers who will eventually trade up the range. Similarly, Heinz has managed to extend downwards in the beans market by undertaking own-label manufacture for retailers. This has allowed it to gain a position at the price sensitive, discount end of the market without damaging the overall brand image.

Both kinds of range extension clearly have benefits and risks that need to be assessed before a decision can be made. The biggest danger, perhaps, is that of stretching scarce management and cash resources so thinly that current products suffer from neglect and new extensions to the range never have a real chance of becoming established on a firm foundation.

Filling the product range

The option of **filling the product range** involves a very close examination of the current range, then creating new products to fill in any gaps between existing products. This could be a relatively low-cost option, as it would be likely that existing distribution and promotional activity could be applied to the new products. As implied in the previous section, the range extension option is opening new ground, thus requiring a possible review of distribution and promotional activity.

One way of filling out the range could be to increase the number of variants available. The product remains the same, but it has a range of different presentations. Thus a food product might be available in single-serving packs, family-sized packs or catering-sized freezer packs. Tomato ketchup is available in squeezy bottles as well as in glass ones.

eg

Heinz has been very active in new product development in recent years, offering alternative packaging and new varieties around the traditional soup, baked beans and tomato sauce recipes. Chunky and Weightwatchers soups cater for very different usage segments from the standard soups and have proved to be highly successful. Heinz soup bars are now being evaluated, microwaveable soups are on offer, and the next stage could be soup from vending machines on garage forecourts. Best of all, green ketchup caught the buyer's imagination in the USA and should now be available in Europe. It tastes just the same as the red version, but offers a highly squeezable bottle and creates new fun opportunities for the under-12s (*The Grocer*, 2001a; 2001b).

Manufacturers of laundry detergents have long used range filling as a means of keeping consumer interest and persuading them to buy different products for different uses. This means that when the UK supermarket Safeway launched its own brand of laundry products, Cyclon, it had to provide a wide range of variants in order to compete with the established brands in the market. Thus the range included biological, biological with fabric conditioner, non-biological and coloureds washing products. All of these are available as powder or liquid, standard or concentrated, in boxes and bottles or in refill bags and pouches, and in different sizes. Excluding different pack sizes, this provided the shopper with over 30 different choices!

Filling the range can be a useful strategy for keeping the competition out, by offering the consumer some novelty and a more detailed range of products closer to their needs, and to add incrementally to profits at relatively low risk. The danger, however, is the risk of adding to costs, but with no overall increase in sales. This is the risk of cannibalisation, of fragmenting existing market share across too many similar products. There is the added irony that the consumer might well be indifferent to these variants, being perfectly satisfied with the original range.

Deleting products

The final stages of a product's life are often the hardest for management to contemplate. The decision to eliminate a poor seller that may be generating low or even negative profits is a tough one to make. The economic rationale for being ruthless is clear. A product making poor returns absorbs management time and can quickly drain resources if it is being kept alive by aggressive selling and promotion. Such a product may also have a marginal competitive position and be unlikely to recover any significant share in the market. As the product's sales volumes inevitably decline, its unit costs start to increase (*see* Chapter 11) and the product becomes a burden.

There is, however, often a reluctance to take action. There are various reasons for this, some of which are purely personal or political. Managers often form emotional attachments to the products they have looked after: 'I introduced this product, I backed it and built my career on it.' If the offending product was launched more recently, then its deletion might be seen as an admission of failure on the part of its managers. They would, therefore, prefer to try just once more to turn the product round and to retain their reputations intact.

eg

It eventually happens to the best of them – deletion. The Renault Safrane was a big car that not enough people wanted to buy. It may well have been a sofa on wheels, with soft seats, supple suspension and loaded with gadgets, but it failed to make a big impact after its launch in 1992. It faced particular problems in the European market because of the strength of German big cars, especially BMW, Mercedes and Audi. It developed a reputation for being boring and attracted poor resale values. Although it just about survived into the new millennium, a face-lift in 1996 actually made little impact, advertising was withdrawn in the UK, and a replacement, the VelSatis, was designed to take its place (Dron, 2001; Simister, 1999).

Other reasons for being reluctant to delete a product are based on a desire to offer as wide a range as possible, regardless of the additional costs incurred. While there is still some demand (however small) for a particular product, the organisation feels obliged to continue to provide it, as a service to its customers. Suddenly deleting that product might result in negative feelings for some customers. Car owners in particular become attached to certain models and react badly when a manufacturer decides to withdraw them from the available range.

Managers may also find it difficult to calculate the full product cost. Where costs are shared between several different products, for example, there may be a number of justifiable ways of splitting those costs, depending on what you want to prove. Coming to an agreement that a product is covering its variable costs and making at least a contribution to fixed costs and overheads is useful, but it is only a beginning. Opportunity costs also have to be considered, which means defining what else could be done with the resources (manufacturing, financial, labour and management) that are being invested in this product. If those resources could be employed more profitably on something else within the strategic context of the business, then the product in question may be less secure.

All of this means that there is a need for a regular systematic review to identify the more marginal products, to assess their current contribution and to decide how they fit with future plans.

If new life can be injected into a product, then all well and good, but if not, then there are three broad options.

Phase out

Phasing out means allowing a gradual decline of the product with little change during the year, as long as it is making some contribution. There will then be a review at the end of the year to decide whether to continue with the product any longer or not.

Run out

Running out entails a deliberate effort to sell more in the product's main markets, but without heavy marketing expenditure. Self-financing promotions may be the most that the organisation will allow. In this situation, the organisation expects to lose sales, but will make a greater return on each sale because of the lack of investment in marketing support.

Drop or sell

In the worst case, the organisation finds that it can no longer sustain a product that is making little or no contribution. Major customers may be notified in advance to allow them adjustment, stocking or re-sourcing time. With fair warning of the product's demise, customers are less likely to be caught by surprise and thus less likely to feel angry that they have not been informed. They may not like the decision, but at least they have time to discuss it and get used to it.

Colman's French Mustard is no more. This was not strictly a commercial decision, as it was based on a ruling from the European Union. When the parent company, Unilever, bought a competitor, Amora Maille, in 2000, the EU ruled that Unilever had too high a market share and so Colman's French Mustard was deleted to reduce the alleged monopoly position. From now on, it will have to be mustard from Dijon or Bordeaux rather than Norwich. Unilever chose, however, not to sell the brand, contrary to the EU view, as it could have been a threat in the hands of a strong competitor. Instead, Unilever discontinued it to focus on better developing the Amora Maille brand name (Bridgett, 2001).

As a general rule, many companies have not introduced regular deletion procedures (Avlonitis, 1985; Greenley and Bayus, 1994). The price of this failure is long and sometimes unprofitable product ranges, which serve the needs of neither the customer nor the manufacturer.

Customer specified products

So far, the assumption has been made that the manufacturer or the service provider specifies the product. Particularly in B2B markets, this is not always the case, as a specific customer might have such unique requirements that standard product offerings will not suffice. The supplier's skill lies in designing and developing a standard specification that can be used as a basis for fine tuning and compromise in accordance with individual customer needs.

To provide customised products, the supplier needs to develop technical capabilities. This might mean investment in capital goods, machinery and plant to allow customer specifications to be met. A heavy haulage company, for example, will have to be able to load large items on to trailers but may only have the ability to handle items up to 500 tonnes. Any heavier object that a customer may want to have transported is beyond the haulier's technical capability. As well as technical capability, a supplier might have to be able and willing to be responsive in the design, production and delivery of the product or service. In the case of the haulier, extensive negotiation will be necessary on the collection, movement and installation of any load, although what is possible is restricted by the haulier's available technology. If suppliers claim to be prepared to be responsive to special requirements, they must be sure that their own suppliers can be equally responsive if necessary.

In some B2B markets, a supplier might have to adapt facilities or even invest in new facilities, just to serve the needs of one or two customers. Small manufacturing subcontractors often invest in new machinery to service one or two major customers in the hope that further business may then be found, given their expanded capabilities and capacity. In this case, the supplier's investment in its ability to meet customised needs can give it a means of generating customer loyalty. However, if those customers can still easily source the same goods from elsewhere, then such specific investment might be dangerous (Blois, 1980). Nevertheless, preparedness to adapt and invest for a specific customer is widespread in B2B markets. Sometimes it is instigated by the customer and sometimes by the supplier as a means of winning orders (Cunningham, 1986; Turnbull and Valla, 1986). Often, however, a smaller supplier does not have the luxury of choice and is expected to adapt itself as a sign of commitment to a larger customer. In return, the supplier perhaps gets slightly longer-term contracts and other forms of cooperation from the customer.

eg

The Joint Strike Fighter (JSF) programme has been described as the largest single defence procurement contract ever, with a $24 bn development phase and a projected production target of 3,000 aircraft. The prime contractor, Lockheed Martin, is required to build a network of suppliers around the world to provide an integrated programme for components and the subassemblies needed for the aircraft. The main user, the US armed services, and others from around the world approved by the US, worked with Lockheed and principal suppliers such as BAe and Pratt and Whitney to develop a product concept and performance specification. Four levels of suppliers were identified and at each level the ability to meet delivery and technical specification was paramount. The levels were:

Level 1: Suppliers of major subassemblies such as engines.
Level 2: Key-critical suppliers providing common products, such as fuel systems, for all three F 35 variants.
Level 3: Component-specific suppliers.
Level 4: Suppliers offering materials to other direct F35 suppliers at an agreed price.

In each case the supplier has to adapt the product offered and extend production capability to ensure that the customer and eventual user requirements are met (Lewis *et al.*, 2001).

This example highlights the amount of time and effort that a buyer might have to put into sourcing a customised product successfully. It also explains why some buyers may be prepared to sacrifice precision of specification and make do with a standardised product instead, where possible. To develop a specification, and then find and assess suppliers who are willing and able to meet it may be too time consuming and expensive to be justified. In some cases, however, it cannot be avoided. A crucial component of a larger system, such as a unique printed circuit board (PCB) for a machine-tool operating system, will have to be customised.

Interestingly, there are suppliers of PCBs who specialise in the low-volume, prototype, customised end of the market. They provide fast service and technical responsiveness and then as soon as the PCB moves out of the development stage and into full-scale mass production, the contract is handed over to other high-volume, low-unit-cost manufacturers.

Even if a supplier has the capability to produce to customer specifications, the job still has to be done efficiently and within a cost structure that leads to an acceptable price from both parties' perspectives. The trade-off between price and specification will depend on many factors, such as how critical the product is to the buyer, whether high prices can be passed on to the buyer's ultimate customer and the nature of the market niche occupied by the buyer. In some situations, the product is not completely customer specified, but is a compromise between customer needs and suppliers' technical capabilities. This means that there has to be 'give and take' in the advice and design stage to produce a valued and cost-effective package. This is especially true where physical products are purchased that do not actually enter into the buyer's own product, but help the buyer to enhance its service or production capability offering to its own customers.

Even consumer markets may be able to offer customer specified products, within limits. Fitted furniture has to be supplied to fit room dimensions, although the customer is likely to choose from a range of prefabricated types of unit which will then undergo minor adjustments to make them fit. Clothes can be tailormade to fit an individual, although again, the range of styles and fabrics within which that can be done may be predetermined and limited. In Pizza Hut, customers have plenty of flexibility to design their own pizzas, but within a range of toppings specified by the organisation. This strikes a successful yet delicate balance between cost-effective production and the personal touch so valued and so difficult to achieve in mass markets.

Product management and organisation

There is a range of management structures for marketing, depending on the tasks required and the environmental opportunities and threats. A traditional functional organisation that emphasises sales and distribution lacks the holistic approach to marketing so necessary for successful brand development. Also, in some organisations, the number of products to be managed may be large. This means that some kind of focus is needed to ensure that each product gets appropriate management support and attention, as well as to exploit the synergies between products and between their marketing strategies.

Products are extremely important as revenue earners and so they need careful management. Product-centred management structures can help to ensure that they do get the care they deserve. A product or brand manager handles part of a range or even an individual brand if it is very critical. **Product managers** operate across all functional areas, especially marketing, but also liaise with R&D, production and logistics to ensure the best opportunities and treatment for their product(s). Their job is to manage the product throughout its lifecycle, from launch, through any modifications, to its eventual demise. It can often be a total commitment and may include commissioning research, liaising with distribution and even handling sales with major account negotiations. The product manager will also be involved in planning advertising approaches, media selection and packaging. This model has been popular ever since it was first pioneered by Procter and Gamble in 1931. The structure is very hierarchical, with vertical linkages to coordinate activities between the bottom and top layers of the company (Low and Fullerton, 1994).

Product managers clearly cannot undertake all this alone. They play a key role in a project team, taking the product through from idea to commercialisation. These teams are always multifunctional, because of the need to consider project viability from all angles. If the launch is successful, then the day-to-day management of the product will be turned over to the product manager, with less input from the initial team.

In terms of planning, controlling and monitoring product performance, the product manager is likely to have to produce an annual product plan, specifying actions, resources and strategies for the coming trading period. This helps the manager to justify the investment of resources in the product and also allows early recognition of problems with the product and proposed corrective action.

This kind of product management structure is used in larger fmcg organisations in particular, where there is significant emphasis on new product development and major mass-market brands. It may also be applicable in some B2B markets, but as Davis (1984) suggests, the structure and complexity of some B2B markets mean that other options may also have to be considered. If, for example, the same product or component is sold to a range of different end users, then it may be better to divide management responsibility by end user (or segment) rather than by product. A car component, for example, may be sold to car manufacturers, servicing and repair workshops or specialist retailers. Each of these customer groups needs different handling and the component manufacturer may prefer to have specialist marketing managers for each one. A different approach is to divide marketing management responsibility on a geographic basis, particularly where international marketing is the norm. The logic is the same as for the end-user focus: each territory has a unique profile and very different demands and handling needs, requiring a specialist manager. Both of these alternatives, allocating responsibility by end user or geographic area take account of the day-to-day marketing needs of the organisation's products, but potentially leave an unfilled gap for a 'product champion'. The last thing the organisation wants is for managers to develop the attitude that they only sell the product and that its wider strategic development is 'somebody else's problem'. In more recent years, flatter more horizontal structures have been employed to allow for more fexibility and speed of response in dynamic, fast-changing environments (Muzyka *et al.*, 1995). Management layers have been reduced and product managers tend to manage more brands (Hankinson and Hankinson, 1998). Flatter structures enable faster internal communication, more team working and easier cross-functional cooperation when making product range decisions.

European product strategy

Creating a brand that can be established across Europe, a **Eurobrand**, is neither easy nor cheap, as the motor industry has found in striving to create a 'world car' that can suit all tastes internationally. Many smaller companies feel that they have a sufficiently difficult job on their hands creating and maintaining a presence in their own local national market without worrying about the rest of Europe. Even some of the bigger household name organisations, such as Nestlé, have consolidated their European presence as much through the acquisition of companies in each local market as through establishing pan-European brands.

Lynch (1994) is uncompromisingly blunt in defining the criteria essential for Eurobrand building:

1 *Resources*: Lynch estimates that a marketing communications budget of no less than $60 million is needed for three years to establish the brand, unless, of course, a much longer-term phased introduction is planned.
2 *Quality*: The need for consistent quality in both the product itself and the production, logistical and administrative procedures that support it should not be underestimated. Operating on a pan-European basis is more difficult than operating within a national market.
3 *Timing*: According to Lynch, it will take at least five years to establish a Eurobrand and short-term returns on investment should not be expected.

These three criteria alone put Eurobranding out of the reach of most organisations. There are also practical considerations, for example culture and language. These can affect everything from the brand name (remember Plopsies and Kuk & Fuk; not to mention other gems from non-English speaking markets, such as Fanny, Spunk, Bum and Crap?), to the imagery associated with the brand, to the advertising. The marketer has to decide whether to use an identical approach in all corners of the European market, or whether to make adaptations, perhaps to the advertising or the packaging, for particular local or cultural conditions. (More detailed discussion on these issues will be found in Chapter 23 on international marketing.) English is the main second language for most continental Europeans which means that packaging could become more multilingual with English alongside a number of different language versions, but most markets are a very long way from using just one common language.

When Mars decided to relaunch its Pedigree Advance, a specialist veterinary brand, it decided to adopt a pan-European approach. The product, which strengthens dogs' immune systems, is only available through the pet trade and vets. A new visual identity and packaging was designed to appeal to a common segment across Europe rather than being modified for individual markets (Kleinman, 2001b). Similarly, Scott Worldwide, manufacturers of the Baby Fresh brand of baby wipes also moved to a European brand image to cover pack size, pack colour and imagery, all of which were standardised with the use of animal icons to signify product variants. Some local promotional message variation is, however, permitted.

Halliburton and Hunerberg (1987) found that strategic variables such as positioning and product range transferred more readily across borders than pricing, which needs to reflect local conditions. Advertising and distribution tended to vary between standardised and differentiated approaches. It is, however, difficult to generalise. Nescafé, while giving the impression of being a standardised international brand, actually varies in blend, flavour and product description to suit local taste (Rijkens, 1992). This highlights the difference between the concept and the brand in terms of standardisation. For Nescafé, there is often considerable conformity across Europe on packaging, labelling and basic communications mix strategies, whereas specific message design and pricing are subject to more local control. Bolz (1992) also found more of a standardised, pan-European approach in the areas of product specification, brand name, design and packaging than in pricing and promotion. The decision to standardise is also influenced by external factors, such as the homogenisation of demand, the existence of global segments, economies of scale and global competition in the sector. Factors such as retail structure and the legal and technological environments, however, tend to create barriers to standardisation.

All of this assumes that there is a pan-European market for the product, demanding volumes that justify the investment. Despite the potential problems, however, there are many pan-European brands (some of which are also global brands). The car manufacturers successfully sell the same model across Europe, while Procter & Gamble, Johnson & Johnson, Colgate Palmolive, Heinz and Nestlé all maintain pan-European fmcg brands. Although many of those brands have been around for many years, it is still possible to launch a new brand on a pan-European basis. Gillette's Natrel deodorant was launched with heavy marketing support across the EU, using not only identical product and brand imagery in all countries, but also identical packaging and advertising.

eg

Tiscali, the Italian ISP, decided to concentrate on one single European brand 'Tiscali Anytime' and 'Tiscali Classic' rather than retaining a host of local brand names such as LineOne, World Online and Libertysurf in the UK. This has the benefit of simplifying database management so that the total of 4 million customers could more easily be targeted with further internet offers as well as the Tiscali branded mobile phone service (Lambeth, 2001a).

All of this not only increases production and administrative efficiency, and provides a sales force better tailored to the market's needs, but also allows the organisation to use its European size to compete effectively against national competitors in each country. In B2B markets, as Chapters 4 and 7 have already indicated, there is a far higher propensity to adapt product offerings to suit individual customers, regardless of geographic boundaries. The nature and significance of these product adaptations will vary according to market structure, technological forces and the importance of the buyer–seller relationship. However, Europroducts have been developed in some B2B markets such as software, computers, trucks and machine tools, where any adaptations tend to be minor, for example trucks for the UK market need to be right-hand drive!

eg

Despite the tendency towards pan-European marketing approaches, power often resides in local markets, as that is where local marketing budgets exist. Although overall marketing strategy and pressure for brand consistency may be promoted at a European level, individual brand marketing often still takes place at a national level (Mazur, 2001). Canon, specialists in cameras and printers, has struggled to achieve European consistency and has had to centralise its marketing budget to build strength supported by budget muscle. McDonald's also has to be careful in balancing the needs of individual franchisees across Europe against the requirement for brand development. This is reflected in variations in menus and pricing across different geographic markets. Moving to a managed pan-European approach, although becoming more common, has been slow to progress for a number of companies (*Marketing Week*, 2001).

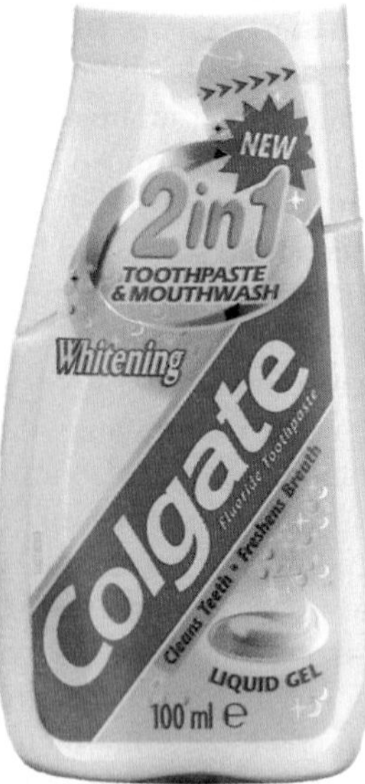

Whatever the language that appears on the packaging, the customer can recognise Colgate toothpaste and stay faithful to the brand wherever they are in Europe.

Source: Colgate Palmolive/Starfish.

In summary, the advantages of pan-European branding are:

- defining segments across borders, increasing the size of the potential market;
- achieving economies of scale in production, administration, marketing and sales effort;
- gaining competitive advantage over nationally orientated competition.

The potential dangers of pan-European branding are:

- a segment too geographically spread to be served efficiently;
- presenting a bland product through trying to be all things to all people and trying to avoid cultural or linguistic problems;
- high investment and long lead times, stretching resources and patience to breaking point;
- making so many concessions to local differences that you end up with a series of loosely related products rather than a single pan-European brand.

As more Eurobrands evolve, it has been argued, there will be fewer new brands introduced at a national level and more that are targeted across wider European markets to appeal to Eurosegments, using common brand names, packaging and positioning (Guido, 1991). In support of this view, Doyle (1998) considers that the focus should be on appealing to a particular segment rather than focusing on standardisation or adaptation issues. Thus there may be a wide diversity of products, appealing to segments that are free of geographic boundaries.

Chapter summary

- The product lifecycle (PLC) concept is the foundation for the idea that products move through stages in their lives and that they may, therefore, have different marketing needs over time. The PLC suggests four stages: introduction, growth, maturity and decline. Inevitably, the PLC is a very general concept, perhaps too general to be of real use, and there are many practical problems in using it. For an organisation, product management is important not only for making sure that existing products live profitable and efficient lives, and that they are deleted at the most appropriate time, but also to enable it to plan for the future and the flow of new products, taking advantage of new technologies and other opportunities. This implies the need for a balanced portfolio of products: some still in development, some in the early stages of their lives, some more mature and some heading for decline.

- One way of ensuring that products get the most out of their lifecycles is to think about how they are positioned. This means defining what attributes or benefits are important to the market, then researching how your product, its competitors and a hypothetical ideal product are rated against those criteria, then analysing each brand's position in relation to the others and to the ideal. Perceptual mapping, using two or more dimensions, can help to visualise the state of the market. All of this can stimulate debate as to whether a product needs to be further differentiated from its competitors or brought closer to the market segment's ideal.
- Rather than repositioning existing products, an organisation may choose to introduce new products, based on existing ones, to fill perceived gaps. Current ranges may be extended up market, down market or in both directions. The organisation needs to make sure, however, that any such extensions are acceptable to the trade and to customers, do not stretch resources too thinly and will not compromise or cannibalise existing products. A further option is to fill out an existing product range, without moving up or down market, perhaps by increasing the number of variants available, for example in terms of pack sizes or packaging formats. The decision to delete a product can be a difficult one. Emotional attachment to products, a reluctance to admit defeat or difficulty in proving that a product is making a loss may all delay deletion. When a product is to be deleted, there are several options. Phasing out allows gradual decline; running out means a deliberate selling effort in main markets but without heavy support; drop or sell means deleting the product completely. Customer specified products cause their own marketing difficulties for manufacturers, as the product has to be produced efficiently, to specification and within cost constraints. The manufacturer may have to adapt facilities in order to make what the customer wants. Sometimes products are not totally customer specified, but involve a compromise between manufacturer and buyer.
- In fmcg companies in particular, product or brand managers may be given the responsibility of looking after a particular product or group of products. Although a similar product management structure may be found in B2B markets, alternative options may be considered. Management responsibility may be divided by end user or on a geographic basis, again because the needs of different regions may differ. In either case, the organisation can develop managers with depth of expertise relating to a specific group of end users or a particular geographic market.
- The creation of the SEM opened up opportunities for pan-European branding. For many smaller organisations, however, this is not a serious issue and they do not have the resources or the real desire to move beyond their own national boundaries. Organisations interested in pan-European branding need abundant resources, to be sure that they can deliver consistent quality in all aspects of the operations and marketing and that they are prepared to support the brand through a long lead time before the product begins to make a return on its investment.

key words and phrases

Diffusion of innovation
Eurobrand
Extending the product line
Filling the product range
Product lifecycle (PLC)
Product manager
Product portfolio
Product positioning
Product repositioning

questions *for review*

8.1 Define the four stages of the *product lifecycle*.

8.2 What are the alternative ways of allocating *product management* responsibility in B2B markets?

8.3 Discuss the relationship between *product adopter categories* and the *stages of the PLC*. What are the implications for the marketer?

8.4 Define *product positioning* and summarise the reasons why it is important.

8.5 Outline the alternative *product deletion methods* available and the advantages and disadvantages of each.

questions for discussion

8.1 In what ways might *customer specified products* complicate the product management task?

8.2 Why is *product management* essential?

8.3 Choose a consumer product area (be very specific – for example, choose shampoo rather than haircare products) and list as many brands available within it as you can.
(a) What stage in the *PLC* has each product reached?
(b) What stage has the *product class* or *form* reached?
(c) Does any one organisation own several of the brands and, if so, how are these brands distributed across the different *PLC stages*?

8.4 What circumstances might lead an organisation towards *pan-European branding*?

8.5 Find an example of:
(a) a successful *pan-European brand*; and
(b) an unsuccessful *pan-European brand*.

What do you think has contributed to the success/failure?

case study 8.1

Playing the game

Eidos, a global publisher and developer of 'entertainment software', is perhaps best known for its series of *Tomb Raider* games featuring heroine Lara Croft. In the fast moving games market, Eidos is committed to constant new product development. It indirectly employs over 500 development staff and launches 20 or more games every year.

It takes two very expensive years to develop a game. The normal sequence of events is that the game development team gets a game idea, a game is developed and extensively tested and then Eidos works out how to sell it. It is thus essentially a product-led process and mainly internally orientated. The company also looks to take advantage of opportunities arising from the marketplace, however. Eidos gained the licence to produce the computer game version of the hit television quiz show *Who Wants to be a Millionaire?* at the height of its popularity. Eidos sold two million units of its first Millionaire game when it was released in Britain and Germany in 2000 but the second edition in 2001 was thought to have sold only 1.2 million, even though it was introduced in eight countries. After that unexpected downturn in performance, the company is unlikely to release a third edition. The poor performance was felt to be partly due to the fading novelty of Millionaire and partly due to gamers turning to new games, such as the one based on the Harry Potter books (produced by Eidos' competitor Electronic Arts):

> *There is only a finite amount of dollars in the marketplace and when a phenomenon like [Harry Potter] comes along it takes away from games like Millionaire.* (Mike McGarvey, Eidos' chief executive, as quoted by Cassy, 2001)

There are risks. A game can be delayed for a year, for example, because new technology comes in and the whole thing has to be upgraded. Early adopters buy the new upgraded hardware and so games have to be upgraded too, sometimes even before launch. Delays are not always Eidos's fault, however. The launch of three games had to be delayed in 2000 because Sony was late in launching its PlayStation 2.

There is a strong relationship between the software and the hardware. The hardware companies need big games or else their consoles will not sell. They are looking at the price and quality of the games. They do not contribute to game development costs although they will supply the hardware for the development process. Eidos is always looking at new hardware and technology to take advantage of, but waits until it is sure that it has achieved penetration into a critical mass of homes before adopting it. By the end of 2001, Eidos had already produced *Mad Dash Racing*, its first game for the Microsoft X-Box (due to be launched in the UK in March 2002).

The marketing run-in starts ahead of the launch and 95 per cent of the marketing effort for the product is put into the pre-launch and launch stages. Once a game is out, the media interest wanes and using chart-track reports Eidos knows within two weeks whether a game is a retail winner or not. Launch costs vary, running as high as £1 mn for a UK campaign. The two main communications spending areas are on cooperative advertising with the trade and then specialist print and television media. PR, both internal and external is also very important. Within broad parameters, the launch budget is determined on a percentage of predicted sales or forecast revenue. It is difficult to forecast because lots of games are being launched all the time. Much depends on what else is being launched at the same time as a product, particularly rival games of the same genre. The success of a game also depends on what is happening in the wider entertainment field. Games are competing for a mind share of the consumer's leisure time. Thus if a good film has just been released, that can have a negative effect on time spent gaming, whereas if the weather is bad during the summer, that can have a positive effect.

The retail shelf life of a PC or console game can be as short as 90 days and most profit is made within this period. Given the potential brevity of the product lifecycle, lead times between ordering and production are very short, a matter of days. Stock outs are rare but short-lived, and are most likely to occur around the Christmas rush. The lifecycle can be extended by re-releasing repackaged games, for instance under the Eidos 'Premier' brand name at a budget value-for-money price level. This catches the new users or laggards. Compilations, i.e. packaging a couple of previously released titles together also works. Games are sold at a standard trade price and it is up to the retailer to set a retail price from there. There are standard benchmarks for pricing in different markets, though there are no huge pricing differences between them, particularly as Eidos does not want to encourage 'grey imports' and upset its retail customers!

In terms of distribution channels, once upon a time specialist independent retailers were the largest buying group, but the entry of retailers like Virgin, Game and HMV in recent years means that most sales now come from High Street multiples. Internationally, exclusive distributorships are sometimes awarded in a particular country. The biggest European markets are Germany, France, Italy, Spain and Scandinavia. Eidos has been one of the last companies to get into direct sales over the internet. The UK does, however, supply mail order and online sales companies.

Every new product is a gamble and success cannot be guaranteed. One of Eidos' biggest successes, however, has been *Tomb Raider*. Eidos wanted a different action-character and so went for a sexy female, Lara Croft. The game's enormous popularity took the company by surprise. Eidos believe that while many factors contributed, a major factor may be that male fans have developed an emotional bond with Lara; an element of protectiveness, 'caring for her', in the player's mind. Interestingly, Lara also appeals to female players; 20 per cent of *Tomb Raider* sales are made to women, the largest segment for any game.

As well as the product benefits of entertainment, excitement and testing problem-solving skills, there were several other factors in the success of *Tomb Raider*:

- its superior technology which it has managed to retain from *Tomb Raider 1* through to *Tomb Raider 4*, thus keeping ahead of the competition;
- the Lara appeal: this has led to an urban myth that there are secret codes built into the program relating to sex. It's not true!
- its launch coinciding with the emergence of the 'girl power' zeitgeist;
- *Tomb Raider* appeals to a wider family market that might, for instance, only be buying a game or two at Christmas and its income facilitates other new product developments. Paramount's *Tomb Raider* film was felt to have had a positive impact on the brand, stimulating awareness and interest in the games.

For the future, emerging technologies are opening up new possibilities, such as games downloaded from the internet, games downloaded and played through interactive television gaming channels, and games played on mobile phones, but Eidos believes that there will always be a market for boxed console-based games because it represents a tangible product and is more 'real' (cf. real books vs on screen text). Nevertheless, the size of the user base for televisions and mobile phones far exceeds the size of the console market. Market analysts have predicted that the wireless gaming market could be worth $4 bn by 2005. Communications companies and game developers alike (including Eidos) are thus taking this emerging sector seriously:

> *We are not trying to take on hard-core gamers but there are a load of people who would like to get Tomb Raider without having to pay for a console. There is a large base of people not interested in PCs and if they can get the internet and games on their TV they would be interested.* (David Harby, Commercial Manager, Nokia Home Communications, as quoted by Quicke, 2001)

The interactive entertainment industry is still in its infancy, and Eidos itself is a young firm which feels that the industry has a bright future: the interactive experience has very few limits, its appeal will never go away.

Sources: Cassy (2001); Cope (2001); Quicke (2001), and with grateful thanks to David Burton, Marketing Manager of Eidos Interactive Ltd.

Questions

1. Draw the product lifecycle for (a) the Lara Croft series of games, (b) the Millionaire game and (c) the console-based games market as a whole, explaining your reasoning. What types of lifecycle have you drawn (see Figure 8.2)?
2. To what extent and how does Eidos' approach to product launches reflect what you would expect from product lifecycle theory?
3. To what extent and why do you think that the product lifecycle concept could be a useful tool for a market like this?
4. What is the emerging new technology likely to do to the shape of the traditional console-based boxed game product lifecycle? What should companies like Eidos do?

case study 8.2

Diamonds are no longer a girl's best friend

The 1990s were difficult for the diamond industry. Demand from South East Asia and Japan declined dramatically because of economic recession and although the US still remained a lucrative market, there was so much over-supply that producers could not maintain profitable prices. The world trade in rough or uncut diamonds is dominated by De Beers from South Africa, with around 70 per cent market share. De Beers' sales of rough diamonds struggled in the adverse market conditions and even by 2001, it forecast that it would fall far short of its \$4.8 bn target. Although De Beers only mines just under half of world production, through its Diamond Trading Company (DTC) (formerly called the Central Selling Organisation (CSO) until 2001) based in London, it manages the distribution of up to 80 per cent of all uncut diamonds, either by entering into distribution contracts with other mining companies or by buying diamonds on the open market. It was a system that had survived, in a modified form, since its introduction in the nineteenth century.

De Beers considered that the CSO was a 'benevolent monopoly' that had served the industry well for many years by protecting consumers' investments in diamonds and maintaining suppliers' price levels. Thus in the past, De Beers could influence world prices for diamonds by adjusting supply to meet fluctuations in demand. If prices started to fall because of weak demand, it could cut supply and sustain prices by producing diamonds to keep in reserve as 'buffer stocks' rather than for the open market. This was an expensive option, however, as it meant carrying uncut diamond stock worth up to \$5 bn. The CSO, now DTC, purchased the production of the 13 mines owned or co-owned by De Beers in South Africa, Botswana, Namibia and Tanzania, equivalent to 44 per cent of the world's output. It also bought \$120 mn from Canada's Ekati mine and \$1.5 bn from Russia, adding a further 25 per cent of the \$6.8 bn annual diamond production. In the CSO era, the diamonds were separated into 14,000 categories and then divided into 'boxes' for 'sighting' by its 125 'partners', powerful cutters, in the diamond trade. De Beers set the prices and quantity in advance and both were non-negotiable. The partners then released the diamonds for processing for consumer or industrial use.

Things started to go wrong in the 1990s, however. The Soviet Union, the world's second largest producer (by value) of diamonds had an agreement to sell all its diamonds to the CSO. The collapse of the Soviet Union in 1991 and the disintegration of communism made it difficult for Russia to protect this agreement, however. Now, an increasing percentage of diamonds are sold outside the CSO/DTC. In 1996 the cartel was undermined again when Australia's Argyle diamond mine became the first major producer to terminate its contract with De Beers. Argyle produces more diamonds, by volume, than any other mine in the world. Although the diamonds are not of good quality, they are useful for jewellery at the lower end of the market. If that was not bad enough for De Beers, a new diamond superpower was emerging: Canada. The discovery in the 1990s of several rich diamond deposits in the Northwest Territories further eroded De Beers' monopoly as it could not dominate supply even though it had a stake in some of the companies. With the emergence of all these producers prepared to trade on the open market, De Beers, in an effort to keep prices high, was forced both to hold back a large portion of its diamonds and to purchase much of the excess supply of its new competitors, often at inflated prices. Its stockpile soared from \$2.5 billion to \$5 billion, tying up much of the company's cash.

A second major force for change was that De Beers' monopoly position was increasingly being questioned. In the US in particular, the antitrust regulators had been investigating De Beers for years and still have an outstanding indictment against the company from a 1994 price-fixing case. As a result, De Beers could not deal directly with its largest market, and its directors could not even visit the US for fear of arrest. Its American customers were required to visit London to trade. There were also growing fears that ever-tightening legislation in the EU could make the prime trading base of De Beers difficult to operate within.

So, that's the background: an increasingly adverse and competitive marketing environment and a monopoly position under threat. De Beers' response marked a radical change from tradition, at least in theory, as it sought to change its image from 'diamond cartel' to 'supplier of choice' in 2001. The shift marked an increased focus on demand stimulation rather than supply.

De Beers had already spent over 100 years building a glittering image for diamonds. Slogans such as 'diamonds are for ever' and 'diamonds are a girl's best friend' helped consumers to attribute 'luxury', 'special', 'mystique' and 'romantic' characteristics to diamonds and also made De Beers a very wealthy organisation. De Beers also invented 'occasions' products, such as the 10th wedding anniversary diamond eternity ring ('show her you would marry her all over again'), the 25th anniversary necklace and the 'sweet 16' pendant. De Beers' annual promotional spend on generic advertisements for diamonds was typically between $150 and $200 mn, which benefited the whole market, rather than specifically promoting its own name. It could afford to do so when it controlled 80 per cent of the market.

However, it was clear that consumers, other than a small core of wealthy middle-aged women, no longer thought of diamonds in the way they used to. The whole ritual of engagement, marriage and eternity rings has gone somewhat out of fashion. Lifestyles and attitudes have also changed: the number of occasions on which expensive jewellery can be worn has diminished; jewels cannot be worn in the street for fear of mugging; and they don't quite go with tracksuits and trainers. Some would not wish to make such overt displays of luxury, even if they could afford to do so. It's no longer 'cool' to flaunt it. Diamonds, in whatever form, still make a welcome gift, of course, but many couples would now rather go to Africa or Alaska for the experience rather than spend the money on a piece of rock mined there.

The 'supplier of choice' strategy is concerned less with trying to control all of the world supply than on adding value to the diamonds De Beers does control through a series of marketing and branding initiatives. De Beers began to focus on differentiating its own output to make them the buyer's first choice and to attract better prices. Rather than treating diamonds as a commodity, branding is intended to highlight the distinctiveness of a De Beers controlled diamond. *Forevermark* became De Beers' hallmark for guaranteeing the integrity of its diamonds. De Beers also renamed itself when it formed a new company, for marketing purposes, in partnership with French conglomerate LVMH Moët Hennessy Louis Vuitton, to develop a retail strategy for the De Beers brand. The *Forevermark* will now signify a distinct brand of diamond. The aim of all brand advertising is to build belief in the value of the brand above all others. It will be a challenge to get the message across and establish a significant market share: unlike in the perfume industry in which the top 15 perfume brands dominate 80 per cent of the market, the top 15 jewellery brands hold just 15 per cent. There have, however, been examples of successful branding. Rothman, a US diamond wholesaler, launched 'Hearts of Fire' in 1995, spending 8 per cent of sales on marketing (compared with the industry average of just 1 per cent). The brand came from nowhere to make $40 mn sales by 2000. The differentiation came from the cut, exhibiting perfectly symmetrical patterns on the diamond. It is that type of approach that De Beers will have to use if it is to move away from generic branding.

Some critics think that De Beers still wants it both ways, however. As long as it controls a large percentage of the market, a significant proportion of sales will work their way back to the DTC. The partnership with LVMH even allows *Forevermark* branded diamonds and 'De Beers' jewellery boutiques in Europe, the US and Japan to compete directly with some of its DTC 'sighted' customers. De Beers has tried to downplay this conflict by emphasising that the new company will be independent from De Beers and will have to purchase its diamonds like any other retailer and not directly from De Beers. The EU Commission claims, however, that De Beers could favour its own jewellery retailing business at the expense of other jewellers, even though any party would be free to buy from any source. This questions whether De Beers has really changed at all. Are the new initiatives still designed to retain a dominant grasp on the market, albeit in a more subtle form?

So the future of the diamond industry is uncertain. In the first six months of 2001, De Beers' sales of uncut diamonds were 25 per cent down as demand struggled to recover in the US where nearly 50 per cent of world diamond purchases are made. The branding exercise and partnership with LVMH could work, as could the liberation of the supply to the diamond trade. This could make De Beers what *The Economist* (1998–99) calls the Coca-Cola of luxury goods, facing competition but with the marketing and distribution skills to be successful. A director of De Beers claimed at that time that he understood the task ahead:

> *We must now compete for the consumer's discretionary dollar – not just against other jewellery, but against weekends in Paris, Dior dresses and luxury cars.* (*The Economist*, 1998–99)

But will diamonds continue to be a girl's best friend? The success of the brand will ultimately be based on the premium value associated with diamonds. If that is challenged as society moves on, the changes in the industry may just be too little, too late.

Sources: Armstrong (2001); Ashworth (2001); Bedell (2001); Cochrane (2001); Doran (2001); *The Economist* (1997–98, 1998–99); Gooding (1998); Hawkes (2001); Morrison (1998); Newland (1998), Rubin (2001); Stein (2001); Tully and Ross (2001); http://ww.edata.co.za; http://www.adiamondisforever.com.

Questions

1 To what extent is it in a marketing manager's interests to restrict supply of a product and maintain high prices?

2 If diamonds are in the same market as weekends in Paris, Dior dresses and luxury cars, what are the implications for the way they might be marketed?

3 Was De Beers right in committing itself to developing its own brand? What are the potential risks of doing this?

4 How do you think that the market for diamonds is likely to change in the future as new producers further develop their independence from De Beers as an intermediary?

References for chapter 8

Aaker, D.A. and Keller, K.L. (1990), 'Consumer Evaluation of Brand Extensions', *Journal of Marketing*, 54 (June), pp. 27–41.

Armstrong, P. (2001), 'De Beers Attacks Brussels on Retail Inquiry', *The Times*, 20 April, p. 30.

Arnold, M. (2001), 'Butlins Takes on Warner Holidays Chief', *Marketing*, 4 October, p. 2.

Arthur, C. (2001), 'Rocketing DVD Sales Indicate Demise of the Video', *The Independent*, 21 December, p. 9.

Ashworth, J. (2001), 'De Beers Hit by American Slowdown', *The Times*, 24 August, p. 25.

Avlonitis, G.J. (1985), 'Product Elimination Decision Making: Does Formality Matter?', *Journal of Marketing*, 49, pp. 41–52.

Ayres, C. (2001), 'Microsoft Hit By Poor Sales of Windows XP', *The Times*, 20 December, p. 28.

Bedell, G. (2001), 'Diamonds are for Never in the Modern World', *The Independent*, 20 June, p. 4.

Berenson, C. and Mohr-Jackson, I. (1994), 'Product Rejuvenation: A Less Risky Alternative to Product Innovation', *Business Horizons*, 37(6), pp. 51–7.

Blois, K.J. (1980), 'Quasi-integration as a Mechanism for Controlling External Dependencies', *Management Decision*, 18(1), pp. 55–63.

Bolz, J. (1992), *Wettbewerbsorientierte Standardisierung der Internationalen Marktbearbeitung*, Darmstadt.

Bowers, S. (2001), 'European Touch for M-way Services', *The Guardian*, 7 May.

Brennan, S. (1997), 'Jaguar Gets its Claws into a Luxury Plane', *Times*, 28 February, p. 47.

Bridgett, D. (2001), 'Now Europe Forces Colman's to Cut the French Mustard', *Mail on Sunday*, 15 April, p. 41.

Cassy, J. (2001), 'Millions No Longer Attract Gamers to Eidos', *The Guardian*, 13 December.

Cochrane, L. (2001), 'They're Still A Girl's Best Friend', *Sunday Times*, 2 December.

Cope, N. (2001), 'Waning Popularity of "Millionaire" Hits Sales of Eidos Computer Game', *The Independent*, 13 December.

Cravens, D., Piercy, N. and Prentice, A. (2000), 'Developing Market-driven Product Strategies', *Journal of Product and Brand Management*, 9 (6), pp. 369–88.

Cunningham, M.T. (1986), 'The British Approach to Europe', in P.W. Turnbull and J.P. Valla (eds), *Strategies for International Industrial Marketing*, Croom Helm.

Darrow, B. (2001), 'Lack of Innovation Hinders Adoption of XP, Partners Say', *CRN*, 19 November, p. 76.

Davis, E.J. (1984), 'Managing Marketing', in N.A. Hart (ed.), *The Marketing of Industrial Products*, McGraw-Hill.

Dhalla, N.K. and Yuspeh, S. (1976), 'Forget the Product Life Cycle Concept', *Harvard Business Review*, Jan–Feb, pp. 102–12.

Doran, J. (2001), 'EU Warning for De Beers', *The Times*, 26 July, p. 30.

Doyle, P. (1998), *Marketing Management and Strategy*, 2nd edn, Prentice-Hall Europe.

Dron, P. (2001), 'Renault Ready for Top Brand', *The Daily Telegraph*, 30 June, p. 5.

The Ecologist (2001/2002), 'Christmas is Coming', *The Ecologist*, December 2001/January 2002, p. 17.

The Economist (1997–98), 'Glass with Attitude', *The Economist*, 20 December–2 January, pp. 89–90.

The Economist (1998–99), 'De Beers is It', *The Economist*, 19 December–1 January, pp. 89–90.

Ezard, J. (2001), 'Skegness', *The Guardian*, 31 July, p. 2.

Gatignon, H. and Robertson, T.S. (1985), 'A Propositional Inventory for New Diffusion Research', *Journal of Consumer Research*, 11 (March), pp. 849–67.

Gooding, K. (1998), 'Diamond Industry between a Rock and a Hard Place', *Financial Times*, 29 October, p. 36.

Gray, R. (1998), 'How the Yo-yo Bounced Back', *Marketing Week*, 22 October, p. 21.

Green, P. E. and Carmone, F. J. (1970), *Multidimensional Scaling and Related Techniques in Marketing Analysis*, Allyn and Bacon.

Greenley, G.E. and Bayus, B.L. (1994), 'A Comparative Study of Product Launch and Elimination Decisions in UK and US Companies', *European Journal of Marketing*, 28(2), pp. 5–29.

The Grocer (2001a), 'Profile: Heinz', *The Grocer*, 3 February.

The Grocer (2001b), 'Heinz: Told You So – Green Sauce is on its Way', *The Grocer*, 23 June, p. 5.

The Grocer (2001c), 'The Grocer Top Products Survey', *The Grocer*, 15 December, p. 83.

The Grocer (2001d), 'The Grocer Top Products Survey', *The Grocer*, 15 December, p. 85.

Guido, G. (1991), 'Implementing a Pan-European Marketing Strategy', *Long Range Planning*, 24(5), pp. 23–33.

Hall, A. (2001), 'Swiss Army has Need of Cutting Edge as Knife Sales Blunted', *Evening Standard*, 6 November, p. 35.

Halliburton, C. and Hunerberg, R. (1987), 'The Globalisation Dispute in Marketing', *European Management Journal*, 4 (Winter), pp. 243–9.

Hamm, S. and Greene, J. (2001), 'In This Game, Microsoft Is More David Than Goliath', *Business Week*, 19 November, p. 46.

Hankinson, P. and Hankinson, G. (1998), 'The Role of Organisational Structure in Successful Global Brand Management: A Case Study of the Pierre Smirnoff Company', *Journal of Brand Management*, 6 (1), pp. 29–43.

Hawkes, N. (1997), 'The 'Sporting' Drink with 19 Spoons of Sugar', *The Times*, 21 October, p. 5.

Hawkes, S. (2001), 'Slump in Demand for Diamonds Hits Profits', *Western Mail*, 8 September, p. 32.

Heptinstall, S. (2001), 'That Camp Mentality Left in the Cold by a Weekend at the New-look Butlins', *Mail on Sunday*, 15 April, p. 100.

Hiam, A. (1990), 'Exposing Four Myths of Strategic Planning', *The Journal of Business Strategy*, Sept/Oct, pp. 23–8.

Jagannathan, V. (2000), 'Turning Around Hindustan Motors', 3 November, accessed via http://www.domain-b.com.

Johnson, B. (2001), 'Coca-Cola Muscles in on the Sports Sector', *Marketing Week*, 22 November, p. 22.

Kleinman, M. (2001a), 'G14 Football Clubs Seek United Brand', *Marketing*, 26 April, p. 1.

Kleinman, M. (2001b), 'Pedigree Advance Set for Pan-Euro Relaunch', *Marketing*, 17 May, p. 3.

Lambeth, J. (2001a), 'Tiscali Rebrands as . . . Tiscali', *The Daily Telegraph*, 30 August, p. 1.

Lambeth, J. (2001b), 'Freeserve Crawls in Soaring Market', *The Daily Telegraph*, 13 September, p. 1.

Lewis, P., Warwick, G., Norris, G. and Penney, S. (2001), 'F-35: All Aboard', *Flight International*, 11–17 December, pp. 26–32.

Low, C. and Fullerton, R. (1994), 'Brands, Brand Management and the Brand Management System,' A Critical-historical Evaluation', *Journal of Market Research*, 31, pp. 173–90.

Lynch, R. (1994), *European Business Strategies: The European and Global Strategies of Europe's Top Companies*, Kogan Page.

Marketing Week (2001), 'Breaking Down National Barriers', *Marketing Week*, 14 June, p. 3.

Mazur, L. (2001), 'Brands Return to a Pan-European Marketing Style', *Marketing*, 14 June, p. 20.

Mercer, D. (1993), 'Death of the Product Life Cycle', *Admap*, September, pp. 15–9.

Middleton, C. (2001), 'Knobbly Knees Get the Elbow', *The Daily Telegraph*, 29 September, p. 7.

Mintel (2000), 'Nappies and Baby Wipes', 27 April, accessed via http://www.mintel.com.

Morrison, S. (1998), 'Ekati Mine Opens in Canada', *Financial Times*, 14 October, p. 36.

Muzyka, D., De Konig, A. and Churchill, N. (1995), 'On Transformation and Adaptation: Building the Entrepreneurial Organisation', *European Management Journal*, 13 (4), pp. 346–61.

Newland, F. (1998), 'On the Rocks', *Marketing Week*, 16 July, pp. 34–7.

Newnham, D. (2001), 'A Hard Act to Swallow', *The Guardian*, 1 July, p. 18.

Poulter, S. (2001a), 'Crippled, Cramped, Dying. Is This the Truth About Your Christmas Turkey?', *Daily Mail*, 12 December, p. 14.

Poulter, S. (2001b), 'DVD', *Daily Mail*, 21 December, p. 13.

Power, B. (2001), 'Rank Says Goodbye to Redcoats in £700m Sale', *The Independent*, 28 September, p. 19.

Quicke, S. (2001), 'Tough Times Ahead for Game Boys', *The Independent*, 14 March.

Reibstein *et al.* (1998), 'Mastering Marketing Part Four: Brand Strategy', *Financial Times Supplement*, pp. 7–8.

Rigby, R. (1998), 'Craze Management', *Management Today*, June, pp. 58–62.

Rijkens, R. (1992), *European Advertising Strategies: The Profiles and Policies of Multinational Companies Operating in Europe*, Cassell.

Rink, D.R. and Swan, J.E. (1979), 'Product Life Cycle Research: A Literature Review', *Journal of Business Research*, 78 (September), pp. 219–42.

Rogers, E.M. (1962), *Diffusion of Innovation*, The Free Press.

Rubin, D. (2001), 'Diamonds Are Becoming Canadian Arctic's Best Friend', *ENR*, 5 March, p. 14.

Simister, J. (1999), 'Why Doesn't Anyone Buy The . . . Renault Safrane?', *The Independent*, 11 December, p. 8.

Singh, S. and Hedberg, A. (2001), 'Endurance Test for Tomorrow's Brands', *Marketing Week*, 8 November, pp. 21–2.

Stein, N. (2001), 'The De Beers Story: A New Cut on an Old Monopoly', *Fortune*, 19 February, pp. 186–206.

Tully, K. and Ross, P. (2001), 'The Private Face of De Beers', *Corporate Finance*, November.

Turnbull, P. and Valla, J.P. (1986), 'The Strategic Role of Industrial Marketing Management' in P.W. Turnbull and J.P. Valla (eds), *Strategies for International Industrial Marketing*, Croom Helm.

Tushman, M.L. and Anderson, P. (1986), 'Technological Discontinuities and Organisational Environments', *Administrative Science Quarterly*, Winter, pp. 439–65.

Watkins, S. (2001), '1.8 bn Fortune for the Pet Food Fat Cats', *Mail on Sunday*, 15 July, p. 3.

Wood, L. (1990), 'The End of the Product Life Cycle? Education Says Goodbye to an Old Friend', *Journal of Marketing Management*, 6 (2), pp. 145–55.

Wright, R. (1998), 'Craze for Yo-yos Comes Full Circle to Boost Sales', *Financial Times*, 7 October, p. 1.

chapter 9

new product development

Introduction

LEARNING OBJECTIVES

This chapter will help you to:

1 define the various types of product 'newness' and the marketing implications of each;

2 understand the reasons for new product development;

3 analyse the eight stages in the new product development process;

4 appreciate the reasons for new product failure; and

5 outline some current trends in R&D management.

Chapter 8 considered issues of product development, modification and deletion within the context of an existing product portfolio. Sometimes, however, to satisfy strategic objectives it is not enough just to manipulate existing products. Organisations need a flow of new products to keep their portfolios fresh, their customers interested and their sales growing. This chapter, therefore, is devoted entirely to **new product development** (NPD).

Obviously, the pace of NPD will vary depending on the pressures to change and the scale of change required. Complex, technology-based products, such as new drugs, may be launched and then continue as stable products for a number of years, with any further development effort focusing on minor changes and improvements. In fmcg markets, however, there is more likely to be a rapid rate of NPD. Despite the promising hopes held for some of these new products, it is a stark fact that most, up to 90 per cent, will fail to achieve their potential and will not survive. This is a sobering thought, given the time, resources and money that often go into developing a new product.

The fact is that nobody can give any guarantees that any new product will succeed and the more radical the new product idea, the more true this becomes. NPD is not just about *invention*, it is also about *innovation.* Invention is about the creation of ideas and physical products, but innovation is about finding appropriate applications and commercialising those ideas and products. It is something of a cliché, but the British are generally thought to be good at invention but very poor at innovation, whereas the Japanese are astute when it comes to defining and exploiting the commercial possibilities of an idea or product.

eg

When Fiat launched the new Stilo model in September 2001 the stakes were high. Not only was it a €900 mn (£570 mn) investment, it also aimed to take on strong competitors such as the Volkswagen Golf, GM's Astra, and the Ford Focus in the tough mid-market 'C' segment of the European car market. The Stilo is a deliberate attempt to reduce Fiat's dependency on the Punto, its best-selling small car. The Stilo's targets were ambitious: 350,000 sales in 2002 and 400,000 in 2003 out of a total segment of 4 million cars per year. To assist with market penetration, features such as radar cruise control, satellite navigation, in-car e-mail access, and an 'easy-go' transponder which allows the driver to unlock the car and switch on the engine remotely, were all available. This approach is consistent with Fiat's position in offering value-for-money cars with built-in design extras and Italian design flair. The launch also coincided, however, with deteriorating market conditions. Fiat does not have large cash reserves to ride any downturn, so the stakes have become even higher (Lofthouse, 2001). There is no guarantee that the new model, as with so many other new product launches, will achieve all that is expected of it.

It is, however, possible to assess or minimise the risks of NPD through effective and efficient planning and management of the NPD process. This chapter will later outline a framework, identifying the stages of NPD and the relevant questions that should be asked of any NPD project. First, however, it is necessary to discuss in more detail the definition of 'new products', as it is always important to clarify the context within which NPD is being undertaken. We consider also the rationale for pursuing an active programme of planned new product launches and point out that in some circumstances, organisations could be failing strategically through their inaction and reluctance to commit themselves to NPD.

The particular emphasis of this chapter is on the introduction of the framework to guide NPD from initiation through to commercialisation. It can be argued that such a procedure can reduce but not eliminate the risks associated with new product launch. An examination of the causes of new product failure reveals that many failures could be avoided with better analysis and research in the development stage. In reality, not all new products are manufacturer initiated and driven. In some B2B markets, the NPD approach may be customer led or a joint effort between buyer and supplier. The final section in this chapter, therefore, examines the underlying approach and rationale for various types of cooperative new product development.

The meaning of a new product

This section looks at precisely what a new product is, exploring definitions of 'new' from the organisation's point of view and then discussing the problem from the buyer's perspective.

Types of newness

The term 'new product' appears to be pretty clear cut. There are, however, differing degrees of newness that can make a significant difference to the way in which an organisation handles that product. The risks, opportunities and strategies associated with that product will partly depend on the type of newness in question. At one extreme, newness could simply involve a new pack size or colour, while at the other extreme, the product could represent a radical, mould-breaking innovation. There are, of course, many options between these two extremes.

A number of these options are of particular interest and will now be discussed in turn.

New to the company, new to the market

The most exciting option is the product that is new to the company and new to the market; it represents a completely new idea that has never been offered before. Technological breakthroughs often provide the basis for such radical new products. It is not so long since the invention and commercialisation of the home video recorder, the CD player and the personal computer (to name but three) created vast new markets and made a huge impact on the lifestyles of many individuals.

One problem with this category of new product is that potential buyers might be suspicious of a totally new concept – will it be reliable, will it be superseded, will I look a fool in two years' time for having bought it? The second problem is in persuading potential buyers that they actually need this product. After all, if one had lived one's life without a video recorder, why get excited about its invention? Marketers have to address both these problems. The key to them both, perhaps, lies in targeting a segment of innovators and opinion leaders (*see* pp. 322 *et seq.*). If they accept the product, then maybe the suspicion of the rest of the market will be reduced because they can see that other people have bought it. Furthermore, when the rest of the market sees that people they look up to (opinion leaders) have embraced the new product, desire for the product becomes a social need for its intangible status benefits rather than a real need for its core function. Generally, the whole marketing mix needs to be handled with care. If the market has no experience of anything quite like this, there is no clear reference point against which to develop a market-oriented marketing mix.

If the risks and marketing problems are so great, then why engage in this kind of innovation? If it works, then there is the respect and reputation gained from being first, not only

marketing **in action**

'The Drink That Gives You Wings'

Red Bull is one of the biggest soft drink successes over the past ten years. The slim blue-silver can has developed a following among those who claim that it helps them with virtually everything – to work better, play better and even perform better in the bedroom. Red Bull was launched in the UK in the mid-1990s of Austrian parentage. Initially in the UK, it was positioned as an energy drink, but after two years that was changed to a 'stimulation' claim, and sales have grown considerably, capitalising on the rapid growth of the functional energy drink sector. In 2001, it was the UK's third biggest soft drink by value, behind Coca-Cola and Pepsi-Cola according to a Zenith International 2001 survey. In the energy and sports drink sector, estimated to be worth £750mn, it had an 86 per cent brand share by 2000, more than double the combined sales of Lucozade's energy and sports brands (see pp. 331–2).

Introduced in 1987 in Austria, the brand has taken each of its markets by storm, even though the soft drink sector is saturated with existing and new entrant brands. The key has been the identification of high growth, low cost niches, such as sports and energy. Research in 1980 by the Japanese concluded that taurine, the active ingredient in many energy drinks, could help cardiovascular functioning. Dietrich Mateschitz, the founder of Red Bull, identified possibilities for marketing energy-orientated drinks in a society where many people work longer hours yet still want to play hard. Energy drinks containing taurine, glucuronolactone, caffeine and important vitamins and carbohydrates are claimed to help with physical endurance, improved reaction, speed and concentration and a feeling of well-being. Unlike sports drinks, the ingredients in the new generation of functional drinks that Red Bull leads enhance performance rather than replace energy or the fluid lost in exercise as originally conceived in sports drinks. Enhancers are intended for use in times of increased stress or strain rather than during exercise and fit well with modern lifestyles.

Red Bull has also developed 'psychological' properties that have helped it to become a 'cool' drink, capturing the target market lifestyle, culture and even language. It has become associated with clubbing and staying up all night, and is perceived as a pick-me-up for the morning after. It has proved to be a particular success in Student Union bars. It created, according to Hein (2001), mystique, a belief in the product that goes far beyond the original concept of the brand back in 1987.

This drink, along with others in the energy sector, is not without its critics. Ian Tokelove of the Food Commission, a UK organisation that represents consumer interests, is quoted as saying (Newnham, 2000):

> *You're buying into the image. You're paying a lot of money for something you could make at home incredibly cheaply – for pence. But then you wouldn't get that lovely can and you wouldn't get the sexy marketing. But to any average member of the public, these drinks are going to have no effect on so-called performance. These drinks are crammed-packed full of sugar. People don't realise that when these drinks make the energy claim, what they are in fact saying is that this product is full of sugar and is therefore not necessarily good for the health. It can affect the way you behave. You will get a sugar rush – get jittery, and so on. It's basically the body trying to cope with the extra sugar.*

Many of the drinks also contain caffeine, which can encourage repeat purchasing and even withdrawal symptoms, if caffeine intake from all sources is suddenly reduced. The recommendation from the authorities was that it should not be mixed with alcohol or drunk after exercise because too much caffeine could lead to thickening of the arteries in susceptible people, despite Red Bull being only the equivalent of a cup of filters coffee.

In today's culture where working hard and playing hard too are seen as the norm, Red Bull is promoted as a drink which will replace your energy and allow you to push the margins further.

Source: Red Bull.

Red Bull, despite its critics, demonstrates that successful new product launches often combine product functionality (taurine, caffeine, etc.) with psychological attributes, and together they can effectively create a new niche in an otherwise crowded market. The concept of the soft drink can hardly be described as new, but energy drinks, led by Red Bull have created a new sub-market of considerable interest to many other energy claiming brands. Often, however, it is the early entrants that attract the most powerful market position, as Red Bull demonstrates. Although it is relatively highly priced, at around £1.20 per can, it has created a loyal and believing customer base.

Sources: Bee (2001); Brabbs (2001); Croft (1998a); Hein (2001); Newnham (2000).

with the market, but also with shareholders, potential investors and even potential employees (visibly successful organisations attract the brightest candidates). In marketing terms, there is the opportunity to establish a strong, prime position in the market before the real competition starts. Against this, the innovative organisation is bearing the costs and risks of development and market creation and has to face the prospect of competitors coming in later with cheaper imitative products (*see* pp. 326 *et seq.*), unless it pursues proactive further development to stay ahead.

New to the company, a significant innovation for the market

Where a product represents a significant innovation for the market, the core product concept itself is familiar, but there is a new twist to it that makes it innovative and exciting. Examples of this might be the first combined washer-dryer, the first fax machine to operate with ordinary paper or the first car fitted with a catalytic converter.

The marketing task is perhaps a little easier here, because the basic product concept is a familiar one. The main job is one of communicating the nature of the innovation and the added benefits it confers on the product. The consumer can compare the new product with the old from their own experience and thus reach an opinion as to the value of the innovation. A family that has had to live with the inconvenience of the space taken up by a washing machine and a tumble dryer in a small house would not need much persuading about the benefits of a combined machine.

eg

The world's first automatic vacuum cleaner could be the answer to many a household's prayers. Electrolux's Trilobite was launched in Sweden in 2001 and is to be 'rolled out' across Europe. It has the capacity to navigate its way around a room with the use of sonar electronics and can recharge itself when the batteries are running low. Although the Trilobite cannot yet go up stairs or empty its own dust, Electrolux believes that between 4 and 5 per cent of the vacuum-cleaning public would pay £1,000 for the privilege of letting a machine do the work. The target market in the first instance is the young, rich, urban male, but Electrolux believes that the Trilobite will soon catch on more widely. The Trilobite is, however, only just ahead of the pack, as Dyson, with 50 per cent of the UK market, will launch its own automatic cleaner, the DC06, in 2002 which is to be priced at £2,000 to reflect its extra sucking power and versatility (Charles, 2001). A more traditional push-along vacuum cleaner will set you back around £125, but if you have £1,000 or more to spend, the Trilobite could be the answer. Then again, at that price, perhaps a manual clean is not so bad after all! (Only a man could have written that sentence!).

The Electrolux Trilobite cleaner is the first automatic vacuum cleaner. It uses sonar in the same way a bat does to navigate around a room and to avoid objects such as the dog.

Source: Electrolux.

New to the company, a minor innovation for the market

A product that represents only a minor innovation for the market is less exciting than the previous option from the market's point of view, as the product offered is not particularly different from what already exists. The challenge and the burden of newness rest much more heavily on the organisation than on the market. An organisation might, for example, enter the existing video recorder market for the first time with a machine that is easier to program than any competitor's product. While this is a worthwhile feature that will attract interest, it is not sufficiently innovative to turn the market upside down.

eg

The refillable tissue box from Georgia Pacific, rather unimaginatively called 'Le Box' was a flop the first time it was offered in the UK. Originally launched in September 2000, the company thought that the innovative concept would capture between 7 and 12 per cent of the market value in the first year. Unfortunately, due to problems with pricing, pack design and merchandising, its share reached a high of just 1.8 per cent of the tissue market. Consumers preferred the traditional disposable box approach. The price differential of over 50p more than premium tissues appeared to be too high even for a product that was meant to augment home design through colour coding (Carmichael, 2001b).

In this situation, there should not be too much risk involved in the product concept itself, as that is largely established, tried and tested. The risks and problems arise from trying to gain distribution and break into an established market that may consist of a number of powerful competitors who will use marketing counter-measures to prevent the successful entry of a new product.

New to the company, no innovation for the market

An organisation offering a product that represents no innovation is offering a completely imitative product, based on a competitor's approach and technology, and the market perceives little difference between them. Many organisations consciously decide to take this 'me too' approach to NPD (*see* pp. 356 *et seq.*). For a smaller organisation with limited resources, it makes sense to let the bigger competitor spend the time, effort and money developing the radical new concepts (as with products that are either new to the market or significant innovations), then when the market is established and known, it can launch a slightly cheaper imitation and get a foothold in the lower end of the market. The imitator may be able to achieve a cost advantage, if it has learned from the experience of the innovator. Sony suffered from this with the Walkman. It invented the concept, developed it into a viable commercial proposition, created the market and launched the first product, yet within a couple of years, it was facing stiff competition from a whole range of cheaper 'me too' imitations offering no significant new features. *See also* pp. 326 *et seq.* for further discussion about imitative products.

Overall, Booz-Allen, Hamilton Inc. (1982) estimated, based on a longitudinal study, that only 10 per cent of new products were truly innovative to the market. Most fell into the other categories listed above, especially that of being new to the company but offering little innovation to the market. Perhaps it is not surprising that the majority of new products fail. Rudolph (1995), in a study of over 8,000 new products launched in the US, found that between 80 and 90 per cent failed within a year.

■ Customer-orientated perspectives

As implied in the previous section, it is the customers' view of newness and their reaction to that newness that count. This section looks more specifically at the buyer's degree of learning and adjustment to the new product as reflected in their buying behaviour and their use of the product or service, linking all of this with the supplier's perspective discussed above.

The buyer's approach to dealing with new products has to be put into the context of the level of innovation within a market, which can be categorised in three ways, **continuous innovation**, **dynamically continuous innovation** and **discontinuous innovation**, as shown in Figure 9.1.

Figure 9.1 The innovation continuum

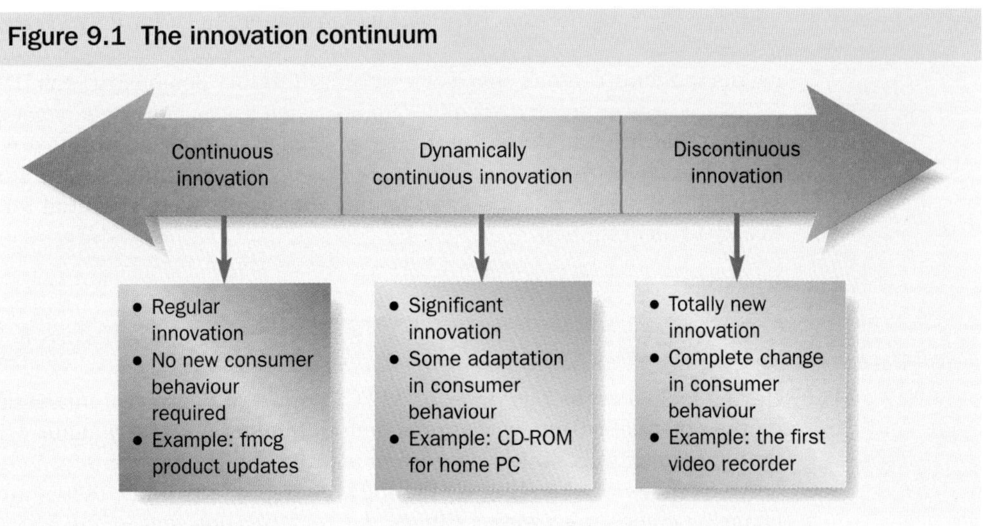

Continuous innovation

In a market characterised by continuous innovation, new product introductions are regular occurrences. No new behaviour is really required of the consumer, who is used to sizing up new products regularly and includes that activity as a matter of course in the decision-making process. It imposes a small amount of low-risk, limited decision-making on what would normally be a routine response situation (*see* pp. 104 and 271 *et seq.*).

Fmcg markets, such as that for laundry detergents, often see new product launches, usually with minor or no innovation incorporated in them. 'Now washes even whiter', 'Washes cleaner at even lower temperatures', 'More concentrated cleaning power than ever', 'With added stain digesters' are the types of phrase that appear on laundry products to signify some level of continuous innovation. Consumers may see them in the supermarket, look at them, then make a decision as to whether to try them or remain loyal to their existing brand. This emphasises that the key task for the marketer with such new products is to generate awareness and gain distribution.

Dynamically continuous innovation

A market characterised by dynamically continuous innovation tends to involve new products with a degree of significant innovation. Because the innovation represents a big change in a familiar product, it is likely to require some change in buying behaviour. While the buyer has a familiar frame of reference for the product, the new features and benefits have to be understood and integrated into that familiar picture. The introduction of the electric toothbrush, for instance, might have caused problems for some consumers. The function would be well understood, but what are the advantages of an electric one over a manual brush? How do I know that it's safe? This is related to limited problem solving situations (*see* pp. 105–6) and thus emphasises the need for the marketer to provide information and to explain the new benefits to the prospective purchaser. In selling a fax machine that does not require special paper in order to receive incoming messages, marketers do not need to explain the function and benefits of the fax itself, which are very well established, but they do need to show how the plain paper feature differentiates the machine from the competition and how it saves money and time, etc.

Discontinuous innovation

Discontinuous innovation represents the biggest upheaval for the potential customer and relates most closely to extended problem solving (*see* pp. 106–7). It requires a whole new learning experience for the customer, with new patterns of consumption behaviour. The consumer has to understand the underlying concept of the product and then relate it to their own life, visualising how it will fit in. This process is linked to the issues of suspicion and acceptance raised in the discussion of the marketing problems of products new to both the market and the organisation. Customers need hard information about what the product is and what it does, but they also need guidance on its benefits and what that means to them. There is also a role here for product demonstrations. The microwave oven, for example, was greeted with incredulity when it was launched, because it was difficult to believe that it could do all the things promised without compromising the quality of the food. The advertisements could achieve a certain amount, but 'seeing is believing', and seeing the machine in action and tasting the results were essential for proving that it did live up to its promises.

The importance of new product development

Having looked at the outcomes of NPD, in terms of degrees of innovation and their impact on the potential customer, it is now time to think more clearly about why NPD is so important. Organisations do not operate in a static environment, but are constantly facing the consequences of changing technology, changing customer tastes and preferences and changing competitor product ranges. Any organisation that is positively managing its product portfolio will recognise that its existing products are in different stages of their lifecycles and can be modified to maximise their potential, but, inevitably, new products will be needed to replace the mature and declining ones.

Although it is an important part of product strategy, NPD can be a very risky business. The commercial and financial risks can be very high, with many new products failing. In the fmcg sector, new product failure is commonplace, with only one in ten new products surviving the first year and often only those with large marketing budgets have any hope of lift-off (Carmichael, 2001a). This is paradoxical, given that consumers seem to be demanding more of everything: more taste, greater convenience, more novelty, and greater variety. Nevertheless, failure rates are very high, and yet organisations are increasingly driven to NPD as a means of gaining competitive edge. In 2001, Mars took the brand equity of Bounty and launched the brand's first extension since 1989: Bounty Calapuno (Dempsey, 2001). It was given a £9 mn budget and achieved £3 mn in sales in the first three months. Mars claimed it as a great success in its efforts to strengthen its position in the year-round boxed chocolate market. In contrast, Olivio with butter struggled in its first year despite being an extension of the original, very successful Olivio brand. Unilever Bestfoods recognised early on that it was not doing well and plans were prepared to wield the axe rather than incur more marketing support costs. The investment in NPD can be very substantial in some industries. According to Elliott and Beavis (1994), for example, the UK pharmaceutical industry invests 12 per cent of its sales revenue in R&D, compared with the UK average of 1.6 per cent.

The organisation, therefore, needs a new product strategy that is linked with the overall strategic plan of the business. It is essential to look ahead and assess how much sales or profit will have to be generated from today's or tomorrow's new products in three or five years' time. Our discussion of the product lifecycle (*see* pp. 312 *et seq.*), pointed out that it takes time to get a new product established, and the one that is intended to be the big revenue earner in five years' time might have to be launched now and therefore should already have spent some time in development.

The approach to NPD can be either reactive or proactive.

Reactive approach

The *reactive* approach is taken by the organisation that is happy to respond to what others do, rather than seeking to outmanoeuvre its competitors. This organisation is happy to let others take risks and face the problems of breaking new ground, then it will enter the market when it is clear that further opportunities exist. The organisation may be late into the market, but may have the production or marketing muscle to capitalise on the situation. This organisation avoids costly launch errors and can even eventually use that experience to extend the technology.

The reactive organisation is most likely to have its emphasis on application and design engineering. As said earlier, however, the imitative market entrant does have the problems of breaking into an established market in which others may already have built reputation and market share. With the Walkman market, Sony had the established lead and the quality reputation, so the imitators concentrated on getting manufacturing costs down to allow them to produce cheaper, lower-quality products to create a new segment at the bottom end of the market.

Proactive approach

The *proactive* organisation deliberately sets out to find new ideas and seeks to commercialise them early before the competition step in. This approach requires a strong commitment to R&D, consumer research and market awareness. It also needs willingness to take risks and the kind of organisational culture that encourages enterprise. Such an organisation may deliberately scan the environment for opportunities and then develop products to fit the perceived gap in the market. If the organisation, however, has insufficient resources to develop an idea from scratch, it may then seek or initiate joint ventures or licences.

Proactive NPD is far from easy and there are a number of considerations to be taken into account when thinking about this approach. First, such an investment in NPD is expensive and time consuming, with no guarantees of success. This commitment, therefore, really needs to take place against a backdrop of an existing portfolio comprising steady profit-earning products, in order to keep the organisation and the NPD process ticking over. Furthermore, a new product in the early days after its launch may continue to consume more resources than it generates, so the organisation needs to be sure of its short-term cash flow. Finally, fast-moving changes in the marketing environment mean that there is an increasing tendency for lifecycles to shorten, with the result that organisations are under pressure to produce successful new products more often, yet with shorter payback periods (*see* Chapter 11).

eg

Sony, one of the best known names in consumer electronics, has a consistent record of outstanding and constant product innovation. Its success stories include the Walkman personal stereo, the 3.5" floppy disc, the Compact Disc, the Sony PlayStation, and the MiniDisc. It is now at the forefront of a new wave of innovation as the consumer electronics market continues to evolve rapidly with digitalisation. Audio-visual and information technology have effectively merged with the rise of digital technology to create opportunities for a further new generation of products. Sony remains proactive in R&D to fuel innovation. It has seven main laboratory research facilities to generate new product ideas (http://www.sony.co.jp/en):

- Internet Laboratories (networking technology)
- Frontier Science Laboratories (material and device technology)
- A^3 Research Center (signal processing technology)
- Digital Creatures Laboratory (robotic technology)
- Wireless Telecommunication Laboratory (wireless telecommunication technology)
- Cyber Technology Laboratory (frameworks for data processing technology)
- Fusion Domain Laboratory (fusion of device and nanometer technologies)

Overall, around 6 per cent of sales are ploughed back annually into R&D. In the electronics business, around 70 per cent of expenditure is on the development of prototypes of new products and less than 30 per cent on mid- to longer-term technologies (*Marketing*, 2001).

Either way, perhaps one of the main motivating forces for NPD is a justifiable paranoia: if our organisation does not invest in NPD, the competition certainly will and that will place us at a longer-term disadvantage. It is important, however, to manage the NPD process appropriately within the organisational context and structure.

Cooper and Kleinschmidt (1987) compared product successes and failures against various factors that might affect the likelihood of success. The most important factor was having a good-quality, well-managed NPD process. This was closely followed by a need for the new product to offer a clear competitive advantage. Other important factors included synergy between the new product and the organisation's technological and marketing strengths; the quality and thoroughness of the early stages of the NPD process; the effectiveness of the technological and marketing inputs into the NPD process; and, of course, having top management support. This, then, emphasises the importance of the NPD framework, the subject of the next section.

The new product development process

This section develops an eight-stage framework that can guide the NPD process. Shown in Figure 9.2, it is presented as a logical sequence, narrowing down from a broad spread of potential general ideas in the first stage to the commercialisation of a single, highly developed concept in the final stage. Clearly, the implementation of the process will vary according to the particular organisation involved and the market context within which it is operating. Some stages may be truncated, others may be extended, according to circumstance. In a complex, high-technology market, the process may be extremely formal and take many years to complete, while in a fast-moving fashion market, the process may be reiterated three or four times a year, for each new season. Nevertheless, despite the variations, it is still important to recognise that such a framework or process brings a degree of rigour to NPD that can help to reduce the risks and problems of failure (Booz-Allen, Hamilton Inc., 1982).

Each stage in the NPD process will now be discussed in turn.

Figure 9.2 The new product development process

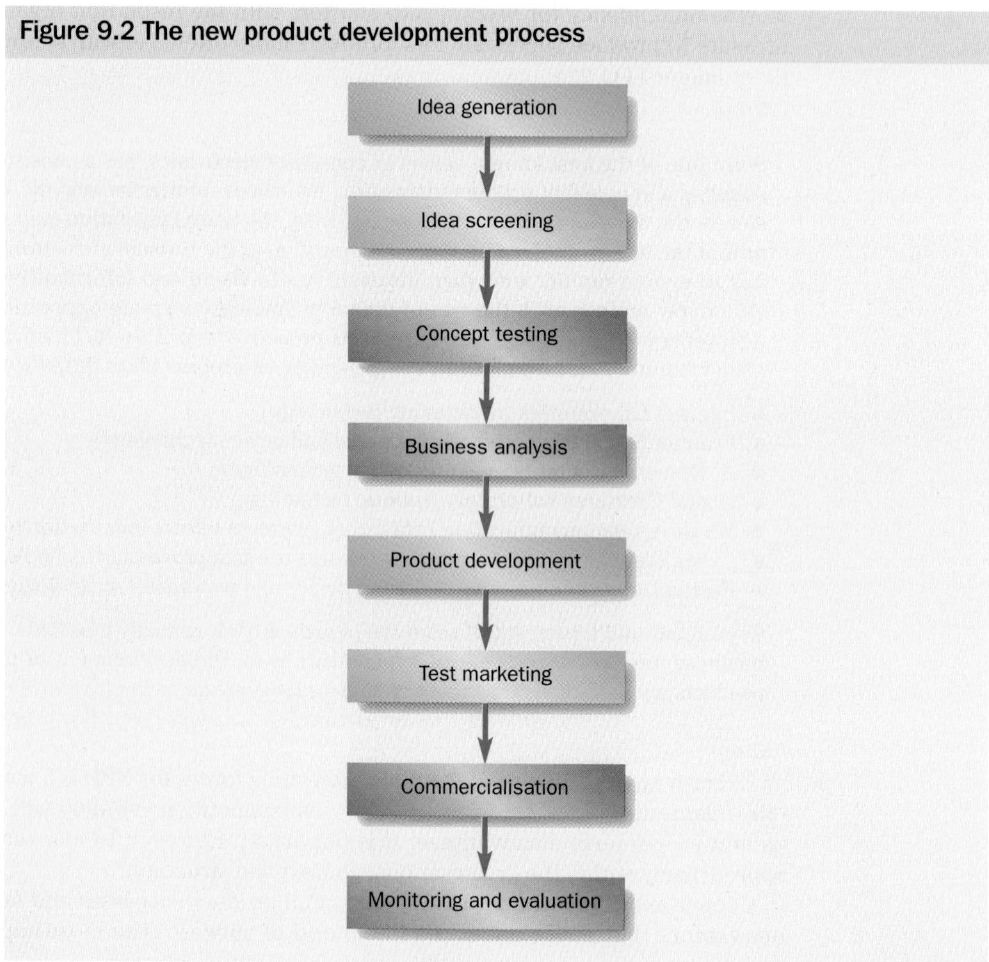

Idea generation

Any new product has to start somewhere as the germ of an idea. In view of the investment and commitment that will be given to this process, it is important in the early stages to let the corporate imagination range as freely as possible, just to make sure that all the options have been thought of. There is a need for an ongoing flow of new ideas. It does not matter how ridiculous some of them might sound; at this stage anything goes and you never know what potential an idea might have. Ideas can always be abandoned at the next stage if serious appraisal shows them to be inappropriate. Rarely do these ideas emerge out of nowhere, however. Some ideas develop from a combination of recognising emerging market needs and exploring technical feasibility. Thus ideas may be either problem or opportunity driven. Whatever the source of ideas, however, some kind of formal mechanism is usually needed to generate and collect them. There are, however, dangers in becoming formulaic in idea generation. The director of the design consultancy Elmwood suggested that many UK organisations stifle creativity rather than create a culture for the free flow of creative ideas from staff within the organisation (Croft, 1998b). Many ideas are simply ignored rather than being welcomed.

There are a number of main sources of new product ideas, discussed under the following headings.

Research and development

R&D is the obvious source of new product ideas. After all, that is what an organisation's R&D staff are paid to do. In some organisations, the R&D department can be given a very tight brief ('Develop something that conforms to these specifications'); in others, they can be given freedom to range widely ('Do what you want, as long as you deliver something we consider commercially viable'). The first approach has the advantage of making sure that R&D activity and expenditure are controlled, since it is problem or project driven and has defined aims and objectives. The second approach, however, allows R&D scientists full creative scope to do what they are good at, and it does throw up products that otherwise would never have been conceived.

eg

Batteries have a habit of running low just when you need them most. Although some brands, such as Duracell promote long life, NEC is working on fuel cells that can turn methanol directly into electricity and could have many times the capacity of current lithium-ion batteries. It is working closely with Japan Science and Technology Corporation and the Institute of Research and Innovation to provide cells that can offer ten times more power than lithium-ion at a comparable price. This would mean that mobiles and laptops could have weeks rather than hours or days of operation before re-charging was necessary. The interest from manufacturers wanting to exploit any breakthrough quickly in their own product designs is, therefore, considerable. Commercialisation is not, however, expected until between 2003 and 2005 (Carbone, 2001).

R&D work can also vary from being completely self-sufficient, working only within the company environment, to collaborative research with other organisations, external institutes or universities. This latter approach allows the organisation to draw on a much wider pool of expertise on a particular project than they could ever reasonably hope to employ for themselves, but has the drawback of placing the work in a more public arena where the competition might detect it. There is more on this at pp. 376 *et seq.*

Generating and developing ideas through R&D can involve fairly long time-scales, with far from certain reward. Maintaining an R&D department is thus expensive, yet essential for a proactive organisation. Sometimes, external inventors approach an organisation with their own ideas. They might wish to sell the idea to the organisation or to enter into a collaborative development deal, splitting the profits. The Black & Decker Workmate began life as such an idea.

Competitors

There are two categories of competitor to consider here: actual and potential. Actual competitors are those who operate in your existing market and have products there already. Looking in detail at the products themselves and assessing the marketing strategies around them can lead to an understanding of the concept's strengths and weaknesses and thus how it can be improved. This analysis can form the basis of a new improved version, albeit a potential 'me too' product, with a more focused marketing strategy.

Potential competitors operate in areas from which others are currently absent. If the organisation's strategic plan suggests a need to redefine the market, then potential competitors may become actual competitors. This could, for example, apply to export markets. An organisation thinking of entering a foreign market would need to assess existing coverage of that market and develop its own product and marketing offering accordingly.

In some situations, there may be no intention of entering into direct competition with the potential competitors studied, but every intention of lifting ideas from them. A study of tourism innovation in Ireland found that a common source of new products was visits by entrepreneurs to other countries, where they picked up new ideas. Also in Ireland, efforts have been made by the Irish Development Authority and the Irish Goods Council to build up an ideas bank from looking at import substitution possibilities. This involved identifying product sectors such as foodstuffs and electronics where home producers could be given help to develop products and thus enter the market.

eg

Entrepreneurs may also identify a specific gap in a market and use that as the basis for establishing a business. A couple designed a carrying case for their daughter's ballet tutu, because there was nothing on the market other than bin liners that could hold a tutu without damaging it! In its first year of trading by direct selling to consumers, that small company expected a turnover of £300,000 and was beginning to receive enquiries from dancewear shops wanting to stock the product, and even football clubs wanting bags made up in their team colours.

Employees

Employees can be encouraged to suggest new product ideas through suggestion boxes and competitions. Organisations such as Toyota, Kodak and General Motors operate such schemes. Employees may be able to think of improved ways of producing the product or new features to incorporate. It is very easy to underestimate the vested interest of the workforce in the organisation's products and their knowledge. After all, they work with the organisation's products on a daily basis and their jobs depend on continued progress and development within the market. A number of methods of generating new ideas from employees have been proposed (Croft, 1998b). These include awards, allowing time and space for new ideas, forming cross-functional teams, training staff in creative thinking and always adopting a positive attitude to new ideas, however wild they may be. Often, appointing a 'director of change, creativity and growth' can act as a focal point for the fostering of ideas.

Employees who have regular contact with customers and the trade should be given special attention. Service engineers and sales representatives, for example, come into contact with customer problems as a normal part of their working day and may thus generate potential ideas that can offer product opportunities. It is important, therefore, to make sure that such employees are encouraged to have discussions with customers and that the reporting mechanisms are in place to capture and collate the information arising from them.

Customers

The organisation is in business to serve the customer's needs and wants and so it is crucial to be in touch with customers, not only on the informal basis discussed above, but also through formal research techniques. Monitoring changing customer attitudes and feelings about products and markets and their usage patterns provides fertile ground for new ideas. Whether this research is regularly purchased secondary data or opportunity-driven commissioned research, it may reveal important gaps early enough to allow the organisation to gain competitive advantage in its NPD programme.

eg

Have you ever been sea sick? It can be a rough experience but it soon passes. If you are on a US Navy landing craft, however, you (and your stomach!) would be expected to train on a regular basis to survive all types of weather, fit to fight. R&D is, therefore, taking place to produce a simulator that creates the motions of a ship in rough weather, including 10ft seas. This would enable year-round training, regardless of the real weather conditions. To develop the software, Artis LLC and a spatial orientation lab are working on a 30-month project with the US Navy to respond to a project that will ultimately improve operational effectiveness (Sharke, 2001).

In B2B markets, customers are a particularly important source of product improvement and innovation ideas. Von Hippel (1978), looking at scientific instrument markets, found that 82 per cent of major improvements and 70 per cent of minor improvements in four different instruments arose from customer suggestions. Some organisations go as far as to identify lead users, those customers whose needs are evolving ahead of the market in general. Working with lead users, organisations can develop their innovative ideas and products early and then adapt them for the wider market (Von Hippel, 1986). Similarly, Bonaccorsi and Lipparini (1994) found that a leading Italian firm derived significant improvements in NPD through close, cooperative partnerships with innovative suppliers.

Licensing

Licensing can be a useful way of getting access to new products without the time and expense of full-scale NPD. Licensing is a contractual relationship in which a manufacturer (licensor) who owns trade mark or patent rights over a product or technology allows another organisation (licensee) to manufacture and market that product in return for royalties or other payments. Licences are often used as a means of entering international markets without direct investment, and are further considered in that context in Chapter 23. A small US manufacturer of orthopaedic aids and specialist hospital equipment, for example, had neither the resources nor the know-how to get into the European market. It thus searched for an English-speaking organisation based in Europe that would act as a licensee for the products. Grolsch, a Dutch brewer, decided to expand the number of licensing agreements for its premium brands as part of its efforts to reduce costs and to better penetrate western markets. In the UK, the beer is brewed by Bass and an expansion to Australia was expected. In the US, no licensing agreements were to be sought as only imported beers attract premium prices there (Cramb, 1999).

marketing *in action*

Developing safer aircraft tyres

The tragedy of the Paris Concorde crash provided a new product opportunity for Michelin which had never before supplied either Air France or British Airways with tyres. The crash was caused by debris on the runway shredding a tyre which then ruptured a fuel tank and caused a fatal fire. Although much of the focus was on strengthening the fuel tanks, Michelin also carried out research to see whether a tyre it was developing for conventional jets could also be used by Concorde. The Paris accident was not the first time that Concorde tyres had burst; there had been 57 incidents over 25 years. This accident, however, its fatal consequences, and the grounding of all Concordes increased the stakes for the airlines to find a comprehensive, and publicly reassuring solution.

The new product called Near Zero Growth had a reinforced radial tyre that stretched 80 per cent less under typical pressures than previous designs, reducing the risk of a rupture. Use of more supple materials, that have now been patented, also ensured that any blow-out would produce much smaller and lighter debris. The solution took just seven months to find rather than the expected three years of R&D and testing. The result, a tyre that does not explode, means safer air travel not just for Concorde passengers, but all travellers, and if it had been available at the time of the crash Concorde could still have been one of the few aircraft that had never suffered a fatal crash. It took, however, such a shocking event to stimulate a process of customer usage focused new product development.

Sources: Marston (2001); Webster (2001).

A licensing agreement may cover the use of patents, manufacturing expertise or technical services, but a major issue is often whether or not the licensor's trade mark will be used. Nevertheless, a cooperative agreement between licensor and licensee can generate benefits in terms of new technology and ideas for both parties. The licensing route is attractive for smaller organisations with limited resources, either as an exporting strategy (as a licensor) or as a means of product range development (as a licensee).

Organised creativity

A number of techniques for encouraging staff to develop new ideas exist. Majaro (1991) suggests brainstorming, synectics, attribute listing, forced relationships and morphological analysis.

Brainstorming. Brainstorming involves a group of 6 to 10 people in an intensive session focusing on a specific problem. The purpose is to generate as many ideas as possible, however wild they are. The benefit of the group session is that one person's idea may spark off other ideas from the rest of the group. In discussing brainstorming, Osborn (1963) suggests that there should be no negative comments about any idea during the sessions; that outlandish ideas should be accepted; that the more ideas generated, the better; and that ideas can be combined to create better ones.

Synectics. Synectics is a group technique similar to brainstorming, but less problem specific. This frees the group from any mental straitjacket and allows it to enter into more exploratory thinking.

Attribute listing. Attribute listing means listing all the attributes of a product and then changing each one in search of a new combination. Osborn (1963) suggests thinking in terms of other uses, adaptation, rearrangement, reversal, magnifying or minimising attributes, combination or substitution.

Forced relationships. Forced relationships as a technique considers products in relation to each other. Manufacturers of telephones, computers and hi-fi equipment, for example, may generate new product ideas by thinking of their products in relation to, say, a car and considering the technology involved, the design and styling and how the product would fit into the car's cockpit fascia.

Morphological analysis. Morphological analysis means looking at a problem and its components and then finding connections and solutions. Thus thinking about a golf buggy might lead to consideration of options relating to fuel source, power transmission, body shape and surface contact.

Agencies and consultants

Many agencies and consultancies specialise in providing information to organisations to assist in the generation of new product ideas. In the fashion industry, for example, agencies exist to predict colour and fabric trends so that designers and manufacturers can develop appropriate ranges for future seasons.

General intelligence

Apart from the specific sources already mentioned, there is also a range of external sources, most of which are not specific to the organisation. These sources provide very general information that can be interpreted by the organisation to reveal possible new ideas. Such sources include trade magazines, exhibitions, distributor comments, government agencies, libraries and general research publications.

Despite the range of sources of new ideas, only a few ideas are likely to amount to anything. A large and regular supply is therefore needed. If an organisation really wants a successful NPD programme, it must ensure a systematic and ongoing effort.

Once the pool of ideas has been collected, it is time to move on to the next stage, idea screening.

Screening ideas

This second stage of NPD is where a preliminary scan of the ideas is conducted, in order to eliminate those that are unlikely to prove appropriate or successful. This means undertaking an assessment of an idea's potential, using information that is already available within the organisation. If the idea does not seem to fit within what is already known, or if nobody seems prepared to make out a case for following it through, there is little point in investing in more serious and costly external research and testing. It is best to drop bad ideas (after a fair hearing) as soon as possible, partly to allow concentration on the better ideas and partly to prevent a bad idea gaining unjustified management momentum as time goes on.

The objective of this stage is thus to assess whether the idea fits with the broad strategic plans and development directions of the organisation. It is also important to establish whether the idea's implementation is technically feasible. Usually, the idea and its preliminary screening analysis are presented to management as a proposal. This will describe the product arising from the idea, outline how it complements existing products, analyse its market segments, define and analyse the competition, and forecast its likely margin and its sales profile over time so that recommendations can be made whether or not to proceed.

Many organisations use a semi-formal weighting procedure to establish the relative importance of various screening criteria. This produces a score for each idea, allowing them to be compared with each other. Table 9.1 shows an example, suggesting the main criteria that might be applied for screening assessment purposes. In this case, Idea 1 scores significantly better than the other two.

Table 9.1 Idea screening criteria

Criterion	*Weighting*	*Idea 1*		*Idea 2*		*Idea 3*	
		Raw score	*Weighted score*	*Raw score*	*Weighted score*	*Raw score*	*Weighted score*
Fit with corporate strategic goals	15	8	1.20	3	0.45	5	0.75
Fit with marketing strategic goals	15	7	1.05	3	0.45	5	0.75
Market growth	5	9	0.45	9	0.45	3	0.15
Size of target market	10	6	0.60	8	0.80	9	0.9
Access to market	10	4	0.40	9	0.90	7	0.7
Differential advantage offered	10	9	0.90	5	0.50	7	0.7
Profitability potential	10	7	0.70	7	0.70	4	0.4
Timing	5	8	0.40	7	0.35	9	0.45
Synergy with existing products	5	7	0.35	3	0.15	6	0.3
Synergy with existing technology	5	7	0.35	3	0.15	2	0.1
Synergy with existing distribution channels	5	3	0.15	8	0.40	8	0.4
Synergy with existing skills and assets	5	6	0.30	4	0.20	5	0.25
Total	100	81	6.85	69	5.50	70	5.85

Note: Raw score = marks out of 10; Weighted score = (raw score × weighting)/100.

It can be seen that each specific factor assumes a different weighting, according to its overall importance in a successful launch. In some cases, management has a maximum of 100 points to divide between all the relevant criteria. Having such a limited number of points to distribute means that there is likely to be an overt, critical discussion on why particular criteria have been included and why certain criteria deserve more points than others. This in itself is a useful process, forcing managers to think hard about how their market ticks.

Some care clearly needs to be taken in assessing ideas on such criteria. Ideas at the extreme ends of the spectrum (the excellent or the complete non-starters) pass through this process very easily, but the ones in the middle, on the borderline between 'accept' and 'reject', could be more difficult to assess. The numerical score itself has a spurious certainty about it and, in reality, for a borderline idea, it should be possible to override the score and argue about its strengths and weaknesses on a more qualitative level. Remember that the assessment criteria and their weightings are in themselves management judgements, based on perceptions of previous experience, and thus there is always room for doubt or argument.

Concept testing

Once an idea has been accepted in principle at the internal screening stage, it needs to have some external endorsement. This, then, is the third stage of NPD: **concept testing**, which can be defined as:

> *A printed or filmed representation of a product or service. It is simply a device to communicate the subject's benefits, strengths and reasons for being.*
>
> (Schwartz, 1987)

Concept testing starts to describe, profile and visualise the product in a way that potential customers would understand. What is presented to potential buyers at this stage may still only be sketchy concepts, in the form of working statements, drawings or storyboards, or it may go as far as models and mock-up packaging. There are two main types of concept statement: core ideas and positioning statements. Core ideas consist of short, general statements of what the product can do. There is no attempt to sell, as such, and all this type of statement is doing is testing whether the basic idea is acceptable or attractive. Positioning statements may comprise several paragraphs, focusing on main and secondary benefits, as well as outlining aspects of the product's marketing mix. Here, the researcher is trying to get as close as possible to assessing a realistic package that the potential customer might encounter in the marketplace.

eg

The Virgin Voyager train was launched in 2001 in a blaze of publicity. It had to be impressive so that Virgin could make an impact on its potential passengers. It was manufactured by Bombardier and in the pre-production stage, extensive consultation and approval was needed for the design concept. Without such approval, expensive mistakes can occur. A cab simulator, for example, was built in France and Virgin train drivers and the trade unions were invited to be involved in the cab design. After the early experiences, it was suggested that the drivers would prefer a traditional cooling fan in the cab rather than air conditioning, so this was done. Similarly, various mock-ups of the carriages were provided to enable extensive customer and client feedback to be gained (Cordner, 2001).

Virgin's thorough testing of its new locomotives and redesigned rolling stock ensures that they have a successful reception by the general public when they are in normal use.

Source: Virgin Trains.

The overall objective, then, is to assess the relative attractiveness of each idea to the people whom the organisation hopes will eventually buy the product. The kinds of questions asked are included in Table 9.2. Such an assessment provides management with further information about the strengths and weaknesses of each idea and a rating on a scale from 'definitely would buy' to 'definitely would not buy'.

Table 9.2 Concept testing

Hypothetical concept statement for a self-chilling beer can

A can of beer that cools itself, whatever the outside temperature. When the sealed can is opened by pulling a tab, the pressure releases a special capsule that can chill a can from a room temperature of 23°C down to 5°C in thirty seconds. The taste of the beer is unaltered and it will feel as if it has come straight from the fridge. The can will still be fully recyclable and requires no special storage. The price of the drink may rise by around 5%.

A group of consumers may then be asked the following questions to establish such factors as need, perceived value, the impact on trial, how to communicate benefits and likely usage rates:

- What problems do you find with the temperature of beer served from a can?
- Do you understand the benefits of the new can?
- Do you believe in the benefits offered?
- Will these benefits be important to you?
- Would you require any more evidence to support the claims made?
- Do you think that the new price of the beer is fair for the value offered?
- Would you certainly/probably/not sure/probably not/certainly not buy beer in these cans?
- Would the new can increase your total purchases of beer or would they remain the same?

This stage of the process sometimes produces surprises (there would be no point doing it if it did not). Management's favourite ideas can be rejected by the consumer, while apparently weak or borderline ideas emerge with hidden appeal. Whatever the outcomes, management should now have a fuller picture of each idea and may, therefore, reject a few more and carry a small number through to the next stage, a thorough business analysis.

Business analysis

The fourth stage of NPD requires the product concept to be specified in greater detail so that production, marketing and financial projections can be made. It may involve, for example, forecasting new product sales and the rate of repeat purchase. Some of the issues addressed at this stage may well be the same as those included in the preliminary screening earlier, but here, the organisation is looking for more depth, more rigour and more evidence. Beyond this stage, it can become very expensive to drop an idea because of the capital investment and management time involved in developing and creating prototypes of both the product and its marketing strategy. It is important, therefore, that this stage should be thorough and that management is fully convinced and committed to any idea carried beyond it.

There are three main dimensions to consider: marketing, finance and production.

Marketing strategy

It is particularly important to show evidence of the nature of the *market*, its shape, size, dynamics, competitors and likely competitor reaction, along with any customer feedback gained so far. Further research may be undertaken at this point to clarify or further explore specific areas of concern. All of that activity looks at the external picture. It is also essential to demonstrate the internal strategic benefits to be gained and the demands that will be made on marketing resources by continuing with a particular product idea. Thus the product's relationship with the existing product portfolio, its distribution, sales and promotional needs all have to be addressed in some detail. None of those considerations, however, can make sense without some kind of outline of the marketing programme envisaged for launching and sustaining the product, considering all elements of the marketing mix.

All of these elements have to be fully costed and linked with a range of alternative sales and profit projections that are realistic and both optimistic and pessimistic.

Production

Satisfactory marketing of the product is not enough. The organisation has to be able to *produce* it as well. Detailed analysis, therefore, is needed on all aspects of manufacturing, such as material and component sourcing and storage, factory space, labour and machinery requirements. Thought also needs to be given to whether introducing this product will affect other production lines and schedules. Again, all this needs to be costed in the context of various possible levels of production. Only then can the sales and profit projections be appreciated. The sales figures projected may look healthy in themselves, but may actually be below the threshold for economies of scale to operate on the production side. This might mean that the product can only just break even at best, unless its production costs can be brought down, or its marketing strategy is revised radically to open up a bigger market at a higher price.

If the costs of production are thought to be too high, or if the disruption to current activities is too great, then it might be decided that it would be better to subcontract manufacture to another organisation, in which case an extremely careful and detailed analysis of the risks and benefits would have to be undertaken, along with a detailed search for potential suppliers.

Financial analysis

Both of the areas discussed so far, marketing and production, have cost implications. These need to be fed into detailed calculations of the costs associated with different volumes and a breakeven analysis. Decisions also need to be made on the level of fixed costs and overheads that would need to be apportioned to the product. The financial analysis would also have to decide how to treat the R&D and development costs associated with the product, in terms of the amount to be charged to the product and over how many years it should be recovered.

The objective of the financial analysis is to provide information about the return on the investment in development, the likely payback period and the product's profit sensitivity should its market share develop in various ways, both good and bad. Chapter 11, on pricing, will develop these concepts further and look at how they might have an impact on the pricing decision.

Competitive response

One of the most difficult things to gauge in all of this is competitive reaction. That is why all of these analyses have to include an element of 'what if?' about them and take account of good, average and poor sales performance. Patent protection or heavy branding may help to protect against the competition launching a 'me too' product too quickly, but if a product launch threatens the competition's existing market shares, then the organisation concerned will have to be prepared for swift and damaging competitive response. That will reflect not only on its sales, but also on its marketing costs if, for example, an advertising or price war results.

Product development

The business analysis has brought through one or two ideas with real potential. Now, it is time to commit significant investment to produce the actual product. Everything that can be done theoretically has been done. Any further analysis requires a *real* product in order to allow demonstration, product trials, performance assessment and usage testing.

Just how problematic this fifth stage of NPD is depends on how innovative the new product is. The process may be more straightforward if the product utilises known technology. With a new shape of potato crisp, for example, more of the risk will lie in the organisation's ability to create a market presence than in its ability to produce a consistent quality product. With new engineering products (such as components), capital investment items (such as production machinery) or even new food types (such as microwavable frozen chips), extensive development work will be required before production reaches an acceptable level of efficiency, quality and consistency.

eg

Following on from the Virgin Voyager example on page 364, train testing was also an important part of the development process. Prior to 'field' tests, maintainers, testing and commissioning staff were sent to Belgium to ensure that adequate training could take place. A £3 mn 'off running line test' facility was also built near Wakefield, including track and buildings for the test trains. All of this enabled a smoother transition to actual trials on the East Coast mainline when the train was put through its paces before entering revenue earning services. Meanwhile, the famous tilting mechanism cannot yet be tried in the UK so it is being tested in France before the launch of the Super Voyager in a few years' time in the UK (Cordner, 2001).

The staff involved at this stage will depend on the nature of the technology concerned. Design engineers, development engineers, R&D scientists, manufacturing and tooling experts may all play a part with an engineering or capital product. With foodstuffs, extensive laboratory testing, along with initial taste trials, may be required. The organisation will call on any type of expertise, whether available internally or consulted externally, in order to get it right. In any case, a sound appreciation of product specification and legal requirements (touching on safety, health or performance, for example) is necessary.

It is impossible to specify a length of time for this development process. An aircraft takes many years to develop and involves many different areas of expertise, from interior design to micro-electronics. A fashion product may take a matter of weeks, by necessity. However long it takes, the objective is to answer questions on whether the product can be made cost effectively, within business plan guidelines, and whether it is capable of performing consistently under realistic conditions.

Towards the end of the development phase, if the product is looking good, plans can be made for market and customer testing. In fmcg markets, this means developing brand identity, packaging, labelling, promotion, pricing and launch strategy, etc. When Churnton, a new cheese, was launched in the UK it was subjected to trial tasting sessions in Safeway supermarkets. This allowed the manufacturer to gauge the likely repeat purchase rates (80 per cent) and to refine its promotional pitch. In B2B markets, this stage is more likely to involve the development of appropriate support manuals and associated training or installation guides so that a realistic test can go ahead.

corporate social responsibility *in action*

Hidden waves

The rapid growth of mobile telephone use has created a dilemma. On the one hand, the UK government, among others, has gained £22.5 bn in revenue from licences for the new 3G networks (see Case Study 9.1) and the mobile communications sector is geared up for a significant breakthrough in technology that will create even more mobile traffic. On the other hand, however, research is suggesting that there may be a link between the excessive use of mobile phones and brain tumours (epithelial neuroma) at the periphery of the brain at the spot closest to where mobiles are held. In addition, children are more even susceptible to the effects of mobile phone radiation because they have thinner skulls.

There are around 40 million mobile phones in use in the UK. A survey by the watchdog Powerwatch found that 85 per cent of children aged between 10 and 15 in Britain have mobile phones. Research carried out at Orebro University in Sweden compared over 1,500 people surviving brain tumours with healthy people. The conclusion was that those people who had used mobile phones for five years or more were 26 per cent more likely to develop a tumour. This figure rose to 77 per cent for people using mobiles for ten years or more, and tumours were 2.5 times more likely to occur on the side of the head against which the phone was held. A further study in the USA by the General Accounting Office, however, concluded that 'given the long-term nature of much of the research being conducted . . . it will likely be many more years before a definitive conclusion can be reached on whether mobile phone emissions pose any risk to human health' (as quoted by Brewin, 2001). In short, we don't really know. Similar scares took place around twenty years ago when microwave ovens became popular, yet mobiles are twenty times more powerful than other domestic appliances. Industry funded studies tend to play down the side effects of mobile use and government funded studies in the UK and USA will take several years to complete. The ever sceptical UK public tends to have little confidence in official studies anyway after the BSE 'debates' in the 1990s.

Given such a lack of clarity in the findings, should society take the risk, especially of children excessively using mobiles, until the research evidence clearly proves or disproves the link between mobile use and health? What should mobile phone retailers and manufacturers do? Are mobile advertisements aimed at children irresponsible? Should premium pricing plans be introduced for children to deter adoption? Should parents be better educated on the potential risks? Rather like cigarettes, should mobiles carry a potential health warning statement? Should mobiles carry a radiation absorbtion rating to indicate the amount of thermal energy that enters the brain by using the appliance?

Perhaps the US legal system will help us all decide. There is to be a test case by brain tumour victims against Verizon Wireless which has a 45 per cent stake in Vodafone. The claim alleges suppression of research findings, negligent design of phones, inadequate warnings, and misrepresentation of health hazard information, among others. In the meantime, perhaps e-mails and letter writing have their attractions after all.

Sources: Brewin (2001); Coghill (2001); Edwards (2001); Hawkes and Henderson (2001); Pitcher (2001).

Test marketing

Particularly in consumer markets, before the decision is made to proceed with a full launch, the potential product can be offered on a limited basis in a defined geographic area, under conditions that are as realistic as possible. Within the UK, this geographic area is likely to correspond with a regional TV area to allow advertising to run only within the boundaries of the test market. This enables an assessment to be made of the likely outcomes of a full national launch.

Test marketing, the sixth NPD stage, answers a number of critical questions about the product. It gives an indication of whether the target market will actually buy the product and whether they will repeat the purchase or not. It shows the trade response to the product and how it performs in reality against the competition. Conducting market research to monitor the progress and outcomes of the test market can assess trade and consumer response to elements of the marketing mix, identifying which aspects are successful and which might need revision, and it can also offer valuable information on how the market rates the various product attributes and benefits. Again, this can identify where product improvements need to be made before the full launch.

eg

Dairy Crest decided to trial its two pint milk pouch system before a full-scale launch. Three UK counties were selected: Hampshire, Oxfordshire and Somerset, and the bag was on offer at selected supermarkets and for doorstep delivery. The pouches can be frozen and are sold with a plastic container into which to pour the milk once it has been opened. Such an innovation is good news for the environment as millions of plastic milk bottles are thrown away each year without being recycled and the pouch will mean fewer plastic bottles in the first place. Although new to the UK, the concept has already been well accepted in Canada and Switzerland. This could all be part of a revolution that has seen glass bottles replaced by poly-bottles and cartons, and now perhaps the pouch (Keating, 2001).

Test marketing is not an extension of the development stage. Much of the product testing should already have been undertaken and the obvious bugs ironed out. This stage may be seen as a trial run for the major launch, in which all the elements of the planned marketing offering are assessed.

In summary, test marketing offers a number of benefits:

1 it is a real test in a real environment;
2 it offers a last chance for fine tuning;
3 it gives the opportunity to vary some of the mix variables. For example, a test market might take place in two geographically different (but demographically similar) regions, each of which has a different advertising approach, with all other elements of the market-

ing mix held constant. This might help to decide which advertising approach is the more effective in terms of generating sales or creating the right product image;

4 it allows the assessment of things that are difficult to predict on paper, such as awareness generated, propensity for repeat buying, etc.

All of this allows the adjustment of the overall business plan and the launch strategy. It is especially important as a guide for the fine detail, such as how much to produce initially, where to supply, whether to run more or less advertising, etc.

Test marketing seems like a good idea, but there are a number of areas that need careful consideration before a decision is made on whether to test market or go straight into a national launch.

Test area selection

If the results of the test market are going to be scaled up to give a picture of the total market, then the organisation needs to be absolutely sure that the test market is indeed representative of the overall target market. The criteria for selection will vary from product to product, taking into account factors such as distribution structure, media availability, competitor activity and the detailed breakdown of the target market profile.

Competitive response

Even within an area selected as being as typical as possible, there are risks that the test marketing may go wrong. Competitors will not sit back passively and let another organisation proceed with test marketing. If they find out that test marketing is to be conducted in a particular region, they may at least try to distort the results. They could do this quite simply by running sales promotions, either aimed at the trade, so that the retailers stock up with competitors' products and will be less willing to take on large quantities of the test-marketed product, or aimed at consumers to divert their attention from the test product.

A potentially more serious problem of test marketing is that it gives the competition a great deal of warning and much detail about what is planned. This might just give them enough lead time to bring forward their own plans and launch their own version of the product with full knowledge of the test marketers' position. This is especially easy if the basis for the new product lies in relatively superficial aspects such as packaging or branding rather than in fundamental product attributes or technicalities.

Timing and duration

Other problems relate to the timing and the duration of the test market. The organisation needs to ensure that any seasonal factors affecting sales are taken into account when planning and evaluating the test market. Also, the duration of the test market needs to be carefully considered. If it goes on for too long, then all that happens is that the organisation stops learning anything useful or new and this unduly delays the big launch. A prolonged test market means that the competition is being given a longer lead time to think of a response to the national launch. Too short a test market period, however, might mean that important effects are missed. Enough time must be allowed to enable the target market to become aware of the product, try it, then settle down into a regular purchasing pattern. It may also take some time for advertising and other promotional efforts to reach their full potential.

All three of the areas discussed above must be taken into account when planning and evaluating the effects of a test marketing exercise. In particular, the typicality of the test area and the possible effects of untypical behaviour or spoiling tactics from the competition need to temper the way in which the results are scaled up to reflect the national picture.

If the risks of test marketing are too great, especially with the delay and the danger of competitors' alternatives coming on to the market, then there are a number of alternatives.

1 *Simulated test market*. This is a much reduced version of the full test market discussed above and involves the introduction of a brand to a number of selected stores. Free samples might be distributed and consumers questioned about their buying habits and brand preferences. These consumers are then tracked through their product usage, questioned on their assessment of the product's attributes and repurchasing behaviour.

2 *Controlled distribution minimarkets.* Again, this technique is often store specific. Purchase of the new product is monitored electronically and, if possible, repurchases are also tracked.

Both of these methods lower the costs of test marketing, as well as being quicker to produce results. Most importantly, however, they make a less public impact, allowing the organisation to keep elements of its product launch plans away from the competition's direct scrutiny.

Overall, provided it is carried through with thought and sufficient time is available to do it properly, test marketing can be a very valuable step in the launch process, especially for products that eventually pass through mass distribution channels.

Its role is less clear cut, however, with services and B2B products.

Test marketing for services

Cowell (1984) points out that test marketing for services is not always possible. Large service providers, such as airlines or banks, who produce mass-market services can test a new service package on an individual route or in an individual region. This will help them to answer the question of whether they have developed a product that is really attractive to the people it was designed for and whether they are selling it effectively. There will then be an opportunity for refining the service itself and its delivery, and perhaps its marketing strategy, before offering the product from all the organisation's service outlets.

Many small service providers, however, are geographically centred anyway and thus the test market is the entire real market! In this case it may be less a matter of test marketing and more a matter of pacing the development of the business. Thus the market may be tested initially with a compact range of core services and then the organisation can open out to a greater range of services when viability has been established.

Test marketing for B2B products

According to Moore and Pessemier (1993), there are several reasons for test marketing not being appropriate for B2B products:

1 *Market structure.* The market may consist of a small number of potential customers in total, or a very small number of customers may account for a large proportion of sales in this market. Either way, a test market would become tantamount to a full launch.
2 *Buyer–seller relationships and customisation.* In many B2B markets, close and durable working relationships develop, which in turn lead to joint product development. This means that the potential buyer is involved in NPD from the start, with an implied commitment to purchase what is effectively a customised product at the end of it. Since the buyer is involved in prototype testing as part of the joint development process, and since issues such as price and availability are also negotiated as part of the development, test marketing as such is a rather redundant concept.
3 *The product's life span and purchase frequency.* Some B2B products, such as capital equipment for example, have very long life spans and are thus purchased very infrequently. This means that although there may be many potential customers in total, at the time that an organisation with a new product is ready to test market it, there may actually be very few potential customers ready to consider the product now. Again, this effectively means, therefore, that the test market would consist of all potential customers who are able and willing to buy.

Clearly, much depends on the type of product. Low-cost, low-risk, relatively frequently purchased goods that are applicable across a range of business customers lend themselves to consumer-type test marketing. On the other hand, test marketing is less applicable to customer specified or high-cost, high-risk capital items (which tend to be developed with the cooperation of the customer anyway) with a very limited number of customers in the whole market. Where test marketing is appropriate, Hart (1993) suggests that it can be done geographically, in a particular region or in a small foreign market, or that it can be tested in a particular industry or market segment. Moore and Pessemier (1993) advocate the use of trade shows and exhibitions (of which more in Chapter 19) as a means of exposing new products or prototypes to a range of 'expert' scrutiny to get feedback on what amendments might have to be made before full commercialisation. The problem with this, of course, is that the ideas are exposed to competitors as well as to potential customers.

Commercialisation

By the seventh stage, commercialisation, everything that can be done to ensure the successful launch of the new product has been done. The surviving product is now ready for its full launch.

Any significant changes to the product after the test marketing stage can be very expensive, not just in terms of direct costs, but also in opportunity cost terms if a competitor gets in sooner. This is especially true with products that have a short lifecycle, such as high technology consumer products. It is also true that significant changes after the test market effectively take the whole NPD process back a stage or two, if the changes fundamentally alter the concept so that further business analysis, product development and test marketing have to take place.

Assuming, however, that no significant changes happen, the product is now ready to launch. Many of the topics covered in this book as a whole apply to the details of the marketing programme for the product launch. Areas such as positioning (pp. 328 *et seq.*), strategies for the introduction stage of the product lifecycle (p. 313), price setting (Chapter 11) and the initial promotional programme (all the chapters in Part Six) are of particular relevance to new product launch.

In terms of how to go about launching the product, there are two main alternatives at this stage.

Immediate national or international launch (the sprinkler strategy)

Making the product available in all target markets at the same time achieves two things. First, it makes a big impact, providing a single focus for a large PR, advertising and promotional blitz. Second, it allows little scope for the competition to sneak in, either with a launch of its own to eclipse yours or with a loud promotional voice to distract the market from your new product. If you are investing considerable promotional resources in making a big issue out of the national launch, it will be difficult and expensive for the competition to shout louder than you.

The risk of a national launch, however, is that it leaves the organisation open to teething troubles. A test market can reduce those risks, but it cannot guarantee against them. Working in a carefully managed test market is different from day-to-day operation on a national scale. Production routines that work well on the sort of quantities required for a test region may not scale up as well or as efficiently as planned, for example. Both consumers and the trade have long memories, and early problems with supply or quality will taint an organisation's and a brand's reputations.

eg

Nestlé ran into trouble when it sought to trial its ready-to-drink cans of Nescafé. Although its 'hot when you want' tins were on trial, they nevertheless managed to find their way into a growing number of retail outlets throughout the UK. Such was the interest in the new concept, that the trial in the Midlands in the summer of 2001 led to cash and carries supplying outside the specified region and long before the 2002 planned national launch date. The 300 ml cans use a quicklime and water reaction at the touch of a button to heat 210 ml of white coffee with sugar, thus allowing hot coffee to be consumed anywhere. It would appear that the early success of the product could mean an earlier launch than originally planned if there is not to be some discontent within the retail trade (*The Grocer*, 2001b).

Rolling launch (the waterfall strategy)

A rolling launch or waterfall strategy is an alternative to the high impact approach (Kalish *et al.*, 1995). It involves building towards full national coverage by starting with one or two recognised distribution areas, then gradually adding new regions to those already served as experience and success accumulate. This means that the organisation can concentrate on getting the logistics of distribution and production right and can also fine-tune marketing strategies in the light of experience.

Whether to use this approach depends a great deal on the resources available. A smaller or less well-established company could have difficulty in financing and managing a full national launch, yet could make an effective impact within a limited region. Success within that limited region would then finance the addition of further areas to the new product's distribution. The decision might also depend on the organisation's experience in NPD and any similarity between the new product and existing ones. If the new product is part of a family of related brands, then it might make sense to go for the national launch through the same distribution channels and with similar marketing strategies as are used for the other brands. Even if the brand is free standing, i.e. unrelated to existing products, if it makes use of the same sales or distribution channels, then again, a national launch might be feasible.

In some cases, rolling out can have an international dimension. In Ireland, with a small domestic market, organisations can start with that home base as almost a test market, but to achieve significant volume sales, they then have to roll out to attack the UK and other European markets as they gain experience.

Kalish *et al.* (1995) argued that the expected lifecycle of the product, the difficulty or familiarity of foreign markets and the state of competition in those markets are all important determinants of whether a 'sprinkler' or 'waterfall' approach is appropriate.

Monitoring and evaluation

As with any marketing activity, the story does not end just because all the practical tasks within a particular framework have been completed. There always has to be time given over to reflection on how well the process itself has been implemented and how successful or otherwise the outcomes have been. NPD, as a particularly difficult activity to manage and get right, deserves that kind of review more than most.

Part of this final NPD stage will relate to the *process* and part to the *performance* of the product itself after launch. The process may be reviewed in terms of whether each stage was given due consideration, whether the right kinds of people were involved in it, whether it needed more time or resources, whether it took more time and resources than it need have done or whether the quality of the information, analysis and decision-making was as high as the organisation would wish. Taking time to address such issues might at least lead to a better and more efficient NPD exercise on the next occasion.

No matter how good the management and implementation of the NPD process, the real measure of its success is the product to which it gave rise. Before the product is launched, performance criteria will be set for it. These criteria might include volume or value sales targets, market share relative to competition, trade take-up of the product or promotion objectives linked with awareness generation, product trial or attitude formation. Setting such criteria allows the forecast performance to be compared with actual performance. Any mismatch between the two needs to be carefully analysed to find out whether it arose from poor management decision-making, lack of information, poor forecasting or unforeseen market conditions. In any event, lessons need to be learned for the future. Some further insights into the problems of evaluating new product failure are given at p. 374 *et seq*.

The entire NPD process presented here follows a logical pattern of stages, from initial idea generation through to commercialisation and evaluation. As each stage progresses, the number of ideas being followed through reduces and the investment of money and time becomes greater and more serious. At any stage, it is possible for the organisation to terminate the process or to backtrack to an earlier stage. If, for example, business analysis shows that the favoured idea is not feasible for whatever reason, then the idea generation stage may be run again to find something on a slightly different track. In any case, the NPD process should not be regarded as a linear model with strictly sequential stages. In some cases consideration of one stage may not necessarily await the completion of the previous one and thus there can be overlap and a number of parallel events taking place (Fuller, 1994). Although the longer the process goes on, the more expensive it gets, it is still cheaper to drop a new product just before it is launched than to face the public embarrassment and the massive costs of a market failure. The aim of the whole NPD process is to reduce the considerable risks of failure, but each stage is sufficiently complex to leave plenty of scope for an organisation to get it wrong.

Mistakes in managing the NPD process can lead to two types of wrong outcome, broadly speaking. The first is a decision to launch when the product should not have been allowed out (a *go error*) and this is discussed in the following section. The second is a decision not to launch a new product that eventually could be successful (a *drop error*).

All the time, the organisation is having to balance the risk of rushing the NPD process and making either of those two types of error against the costs of prolonging it. MacFie (1994) found that with food products a totally new product can easily take a year to launch, although the average is just 28 weeks. In a dynamic market environment characterised by almost continuous development of new technologies and products, and increasing costs of new product development, the pressure is on to achieve faster times to market (Hardaker *et al.*, 1998). Under market conditions of 20 per cent growth rate, 12 per cent price erosion, and a five-year product life, a six-month delay in entry to the market could, according to Dumaine (1989), cost up to one-third of total lifetime after-tax profit of the product. The more comprehensive the approach to considering NPD, however, the greater the chance of success (Booz-Allen, Hamilton Inc., 1982). That must be weighed against the competitive advantage of getting to the market early (Gehani, 1992). For that reason parallel processing with the overlapping stages highlighted above and greater use of cross-functional teams are compromises that can encourage speed while retaining rigour (Cooper and Kleinschmidt, 1994; Hart *et al.*, 1999; Wind and Mahajan, 1997).

The organisation also has to decide how much commercial risk it is prepared to take. If it is too risk averse, then there is a greater danger of a drop error, while if it is too daring, there is a greater risk of a go error.

e-marketing *in action*

Using the internet to inform NPD

The interactivity possible through a company website lends itself to creating a dialogue with customers about their future product requirements. This dialogue can be direct or indirect. With the direct approach, a company can directly ask its customers about their requirement in future products – a form of online focus groups or questionnaires. Care must be taken that this data is not available to competitors, so such discussions will usually take place on a password-protected extranet.

In addition to direct use of the internet as a market research tool, it can be also be indirectly used to understand customers' requirements by reviewing feedback from different stages of the buying decision. For example, Epson (http://www.epson.com) has a product selection tool to help users select complex products. These tools enable users to select different criteria such as cost, number of colours, speed and paper size, when purchasing a printer and the tool then suggests the most suitable model. The data collected from such a tool could be used to assess the requirements of different types of users. After purchase has been made, further information is available from post-sales support. A diagnostic support tool helps users fix problems without the need to call a help desk. Different questions are asked about the problem and then appropriate suggestions are made. This tool records country of purchase, operating system, model and the type of problem, so it can be used to identify common user configurations and common design problems which can be resolved in future versions of the printers.

A further indirect method of collecting customer input to new product development is to provide tools where customers can design their ideal product. For example, Barbie.com provides a tool for children to select their ideal doll and accessories. Such feedback could then be incorporated into future toys. For older consumers, car manufacturers use a similar tool. BMW, prior to launch of its Z3 roadster set up an interactive website where users could design their own dream roadster. The information was stored automatically in a database and could be combined with information on the profile of site users. This could be used to give an indication of which combinations were the most sought after and should therefore be put into production. This is the idea of the Prosumer which can be taken to mean the proactive consumer. The Prosumer concept was introduced in 1980 by futurist Alvin Toffler in his book *The Third Wave*. According to Toffler, the future would once again combine production with consumption. In *The Third Wave*, Toffler saw a world where interconnected users would collaboratively 'create' products. Note that he foresaw this over 10 years before the web was invented!

Alternative notions of the prosumer, all of which are applicable to e-marketing are catalogued at Logophilia WordSpy (http://www.logophilia.com/WordSpy):

- 'A consumer who is an amateur in a particular field, but who is knowledgeable enough to require equipment that has some professional features ("professional" + "consumer")'.
- 'A person who helps to design or customize the products they purchase ("producer" + "consumer").'

- 'A person who creates goods for their own use and also possibly to sell ("producing" + "consumer").'
- 'A person who takes steps to correct difficulties with consumer companies or markets and to anticipate future problems ("proactive" + "consumer")'

Source: Dave Chaffey.

New product failure

New product failure is a very real and very common phenomenon. The introduction to this chapter stated that something like 90 per cent of new products fail. Failure can also be very expensive. While a larger organisation can carry a certain level of loss from a failure (although that does not mean that it either encourages or enjoys it), a small, newly formed organisation may go out of business completely if its one and only project fails.

Failure is sometimes a difficult thing for managers to cope with, especially if they think that it will reflect badly on either their status or their career prospects. Failure is, therefore, sometimes rationalised or hidden. It might be justified, by saying that the failed product was not really not part of the organisation's objectives or that it did not really fit with the organisation's capabilities. Poor top management support or lack of development resources are commonly cited as reasons for failure. Deeper analysis often reveals many other reasons.

Failure defined

Even the term 'failure' needs to be more precisely defined, as it can carry shades of meaning.

Outright failure – lost money

A product may be a failure because it is not covering its variable costs and it is not making any contribution to fixed costs and profit (*see* Chapter 11). Such failures could arise either because the sales volumes are too low (*see* below) or because there was a major miscalculation of unit production or distribution costs.

Outright failure – major negative market response

Another type of outright failure occurs when the market has rejected the product outright. It has not come anywhere near its sales targets and therefore is likely to be either losing money or not earning as much as the organisation forecast.

Partial failure – failure to make contribution to fixed costs and profit

A partial failure occurs when the product has been accepted by the market, but for some reason is not living up to financial expectation. Again, this may be a result of the miscalculation of costs. This is only a partial failure, because the product's standing in the market seems to be satisfactory and while that is the case, and while the product is managing to cover its variable costs at least, it might be redeemable with a certain amount of effort.

Partial failure – failure to achieve its set objectives

When a product fails to achieve its set objectives, the issues involved are similar to those discussed above in relation to monitoring and evaluation. Failure is a relative term and thus a product can superficially seem to be performing well in the market and making a comfortable contribution to fixed costs and profit, yet still be labelled a failure because it is performing below expectations. The question is, of course, whether those expectations were realistic in the first place.

Partial failure – no longer fits organisational strategy

A product cannot be blamed for failing to fit in with organisational strategy. Particularly if the NPD process has been long and difficult, by the time the product is launched the organisation might have moved on strategically. This may mean that the product no longer fits easily into the desired product portfolio, or that the management views it as out of keeping with the kind of image it now wishes to project. At this point, the organisation faces a number of options such as repositioning (*see* pp. 331 *et seq.*) or deletion (*see* pp. 336 *et seq.*).

There are many reasons for products failing, and some of the more frequently quoted include:

1 Too small a target market, which is too specialised for the volumes originally planned or those needed for breakeven.
2 Insufficient differentiation from existing offerings, leading to another 'me too' imitative product.
3 Poor or inconsistent product quality.
4 No access to the market, because the organisation is unable to get trade distribution and does not have sufficient resources to sell direct.
5 Poor timing in terms of the industry lifecycle. Launching too early (before the market is fully formed and ready) or too late (after the peak has passed) has an impact both on the resources needed for a successful launch and on the investment pay-back period.
6 Poor marketing, through either an insufficient spend or a badly allocated spend. It may be that not enough attention was paid to the main competitive alternatives, leading to a marketing strategy that was unable to cut through competitors' activities.

In an ideal world, every one of these reasons for failure is avoidable. Within the NPD framework presented, all these issues of competitive activity, state of the market, market size and production capability should be addressed and the organisation should not be caught out by such failures after launch. In the real world, however, time is short, managers are under pressure to make decisions within very tight deadlines, information is expensive and incomplete, corners are cut, assumptions are made, risks are taken and, sometimes, a product launch simply does not work out. Woodcock *et al.* (2000), in a study of smaller UK businesses found that many of these issues were compounded by the low levels of available resources, and that as a result businesses were too late in chasing new product opportunities. The challenge for all new product launches is to ensure both speed and quality of decision making (Crick and Jones, 1999).

There can be little doubt that new product development is expensive, risky and time consuming. The rewards, however, both financially and in terms of organisational kudos can be very great and that is what continues to fuel interest. In fmcg growth categories it is often essential to keep up the pace of NPD to remain competitive and that often means that the time from idea to market has to be much reduced, thus creating the risk of shortcuts and incomplete research. Being first to market does not, however, guarantee success either. Mars Celebrations and Pot Noodle, despite their innovative concepts, both lost leadership positions to later entrants. Clear strategies, therefore, have to be drawn up to ensure that new and improved products actually meet customer needs and expectations. To help achieve a successful launch, an integrated approach towards marketing communications needs to be taken (*see* Chapter 14) because if potential customers are not aware of the new product proposition or fail to understand it, they can hardly be expected to buy it.

A study of 2,250 fmcg product launches concluded that only one in seven met the success criteria of £1 mn sales or a 2 per cent category share in the first year after launch (Morley, 1999). Brand extensions or brands using existing names such as Aero or Mars, generally have twice the success of new names and any product has double the chance of success when it is promoted within the first few weeks of launch (Dowding, 2001). For groceries, successful new brands peak in the 13–24 week period compared with 25–52 weeks for eventually unsuccessful brands. Often it is de-listing by the supermarkets that marks the beginning of the end for an unsuccessful brand. Failed products also appeared to suffer from insufficent market research and over-exaggerated promotional claims that could not be fulfilled. Interestingly, successful products tended to be priced above average for the sector and were launched with the retailers' objectives in mind (Morley, 1999).

It also needs to be emphasised that although the process presented in this chapter is a cool, rational approach to the NPD problem, it has to be implemented by people who often have their own agendas. (Refer back to pp. 164 *et seq.* to remind yourself of the issues involved.) Managers become emotionally attached to their own pet projects and will sometimes take the risk of seeing a product through to launch come what may, rationalising away any warning signs. Some may see the new product as their big career break or as a means of differentiating themselves from their colleagues in the eyes of senior management. Some may take a gamble on a borderline project for the personal rewards and status that success would bring. Such human interest might well drive a difficult launch to success but, equally, it might drive it to an inevitable failure.

Trends in NPD process management

The main message from this chapter should be that NPD is a necessary, costly and risky process. It requires adequate levels of investment and management commitment if it is going to succeed in ensuring that tomorrow's products are ready when needed (Brown and Eisenhart, 1995). It also requires time, however, which perhaps is the scarcest commodity of all. As competitive pressures increase and as the lifecycles of products become shorter, the temptation is to push a new product out on to the market as quickly as possible. This sense of urgency is further heightened by financial pressure, particularly in periods of recession, where the emphasis is on keeping development costs as low as possible and putting a new product out to begin to recoup its development costs as soon as possible. In fmcg markets, for example, the NPD time has been reduced from around two years to between three and six months in some cases (Matthews, 1995). Clearly, there is a great risk here of launching an under-developed, under-researched, second-rate product, which may well fail before the marketers can fine tune the offering after launch.

Research and development

Reducing the NPD time does not necessarily mean compromising the effectiveness of the process. Renault has managed to cut both the costs and time taken in NPD through changes in its management structure. By opening a Technocentre in 1995, the whole process of NPD from conception through prototyping and final development was cut from just over eight years to just over three. Previously the stages had been sequential and geographically dispersed, but the new centre enabled better coordination and project management. It also cut the cost of developing and launching a new car model by anything from 10 to 25 per cent.

Maintaining a strong commitment to R&D is essential in many sectors if a company wants to be first or early to market with new products. Such a strategy does, however, require a significant and ongoing investment of funds for sometimes uncertain returns. As with any new product activity, it is a challenge at the R&D stage to select those breakthroughs that will become market winners and generate acceptable return on the investment. British companies have been criticised for investing less in R&D than their international counterparts (Brown, 2001). The overall UK company R&D intensity (R&D as a percentage of sales) is 2.1 per cent compared with the international average of 4.2 per cent (http://www.innovation.gov.uk). In the same study, undertaken by the Department of Trade and Industry (DTI), it was found that aerospace, a traditional British manufacturing strength, was the only sector in which R&D spending was significantly above average. Food processing and pharmaceuticals were slightly above average. All six other sectors investigated revealed a significantly lower ratio of R&D to sales, varying from about 20 per cent less in the automotive sector to between 30 per cent and 60 per cent less than the international average for chemicals and construction.

Industry in the UK is not alone in being the subject of criticism for underfunding R&D. A report found that although the Netherlands had high quality scientific research, the supply of R&D was behind a number of other EU countries when international companies were considered (*Het Financieele Dagblad*, 2001). The eleventh annual R&D scoreboard published by the DTI in the UK indicates the scale of R&D in large UK and international companies. Since 1996, the R&D investment in these companies has grown at a compound rate of 10 per cent (Cookson, 2001). Table 9.3 shows the leading companies in a number of industrial sectors by their R&D investment as a percentage of sales. The rates vary considerably from less than 4 per cent of sales in engineering to over 14 per cent in software and IT.

Table 9.3 R&D Scoreboard: R&D investment by selected sectors

Sector	*Average R&D (% of sales)*	*Company*	*Largest total R&D investment (% of sales)*	*Company*	*Highest R&D investment (% of sales)*
Aerospace	4.6	BAe Systems	10.2	Snecma (France)	14.40
Auto and parts	4.0	Ford	4.0	Denso (Japan)	8.50
Chemicals	4.7	Bayer	7.7	Bayer	7.70
Electrical	5.9	Siemens	7.1	Novellus Systems	15.20
Engineering	3.7	Mitsubishi	4.5	H'berger Druckmaschinen	7.80
Health	9.5	Abbots Labs. USA	9.8	Guidant USA	13.90
IT hardware	8.2	IBM	5.5	PMC Sierra, USA	25.70
Media and photo	4.4	Eastman Kodak	5.6	Reuters	9.00
Personal care	3.4	Procter & Gamble	4.8	Procter & Gamble, USA	4.80
Pharmaceuticals	12.8	Pfizer	15.0	Millennium Pharmaceuticals	137.10
Software and IT	14.7	Microsoft	16.4	Electronic Arts, USA	29.40

Source: DTI International scoreboard 2000. Based on the amount of R&D that is funded by the company anywhere in the world. R&D paid for by governments and other external sources is excluded.

The report concluded that those companies that cut R&D spend during a downturn often found it more difficult to protect market share and added value during an upturn. Furthermore, there appears to be a positive correlation between R&D intensity (R&D as a percentage of sales) and sales growth.

Research and Development (R&D) is not just the preserve of industrial goods companies. Tulip, the Danish meat processor, built a DKr21 mn (£1.7 mn) new product development centre at Vejle, Denmark to provide production and presentation facilities and a full-scale kitchen where products can be developed and demonstrated to customers. This enables potential new products to be prepared in the kitchen, tested and even moved to pilot production before full commercialisation without disrupting the production processes of the company's standard lines (*The Grocer*, 2001a).

The complexity and cost of developing truly innovative and breakthrough products often means that the organisation does not have all the advanced technologies at its disposal. Strategic R&D alliances have, therefore, been formed and R&D consortia forged such as the one between General Motors and Toyota (Wind and Mahajan, 1997). Other organisations wishing to tap into as wide a range of innovative technology as possible are increasingly turning to **outsourcing R&D**, i.e. contracting out R&D to other organisations such as commercial or government laboratories, consultants and universities. There is indeed little point in an organisation's trying to re-invent or develop a technology for itself if there is another organisation that can do that work better and whose expertise can be bought. Thompson (2001) argued that to sustain growth in innovation-driven industries, companies are having to create partnerships with external firms to provide quick, flexible and affordable access to new capabilities and technologies. 'Innovation access' can enable an organisation to acquire sufficient capacity to keep up with new opportunities through a network of suppliers and partnerships for the benefit of the whole value chain.

There are, however, a number of potential problems arising from outsourcing. The contracting organisation may not ultimately have total control of what might become a critical technology for its business and, furthermore, may run a higher risk of details of that technology being leaked to competitors than if the R&D were totally in-house. Time lags might also be a problem, since it takes time for an organisation to realise it has a problem that is worth outsourcing; to locate a suitable contractor; to brief them on the background to the organisation and its R&D needs; then to discuss and refine the terms and conditions of the required work. The internal implications of outsourcing also need to be carefully thought through. The organisation may lose its internal R&D impetus altogether, becoming rather too dependent on external bodies for its innovation. Where internal R&D and outsourcing do exist in parallel, the organisation will also have to be careful to avoid attitude problems towards the external ideas (for example, internally sourced ideas might be given priority in terms of implementation, time and resources).

Half-way between outsourcing and the Renault approach is the idea of partnership, or **collaborative R&D** (Houlder, 1995). This means that two or more organisations pool their resources and their expertise to undertake a specific project that will benefit both/all of them.

As with outsourcing, collaboration is a way of sharing costs and tapping into a wider field of expertise, but unlike outsourcing, both the risks and the potential commercial benefits are also shared. Before matters reach this stage, however, a big problem with collaboration can be finding an appropriate partner in the first place. In industries where there is close buyer–supplier cooperation, collaborative R&D partnerships can emerge naturally within the supply chain. Microprocessor manufacturer Intel, for example, entered into a joint development venture with Hewlett Packard.

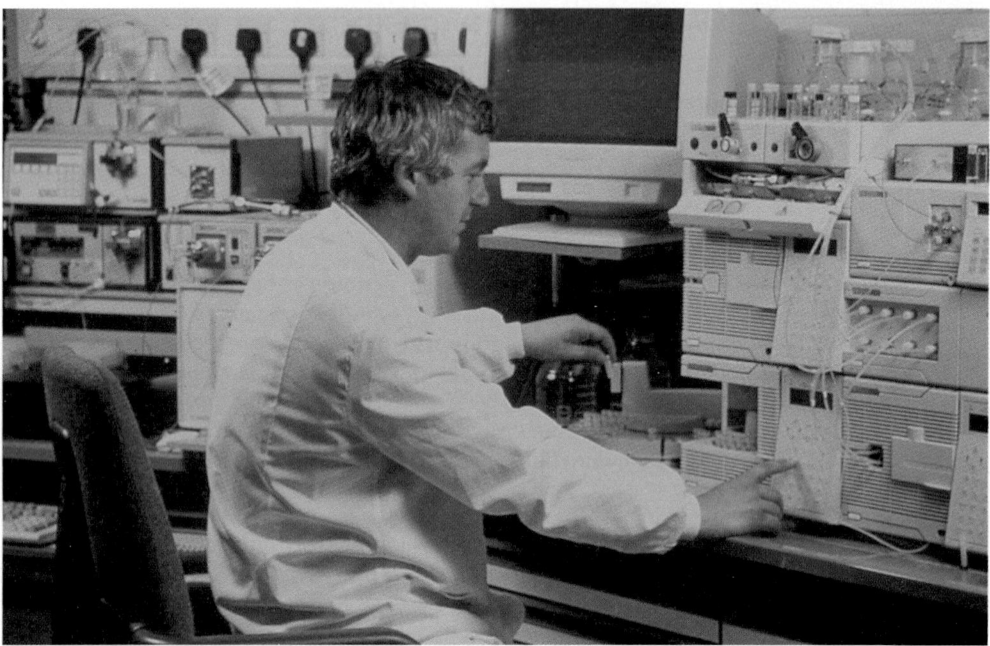

Rapid analysis of new chemical entities using the very latest advances in chromatography and mass spectrometry to reveal their structure and likely properties.

Source: GlaxoSmith Kline.

With the exception of companies whose circumstances are similar to those described above, most smaller, low profile companies do not find collaborators easily, particularly where the nature of the R&D concerned may cut across industries or scientific disciplines. This all, however, further assumes that organisations know precisely what kind of partner they are looking for and for what purpose or objective. Some ideas for collaboration only emerge after organisations have come together and talked to each other about their respective problems and areas of expertise. With this in mind, national governments, the EU, universities and other bodies with an interest in promoting innovation have promoted conferences, forums and clubs (e.g. the European Industrial Research Managers' Association) to allow dialogue between organisations that otherwise might never even think of talking to each other. It was at such a forum organised by the government-backed Centre for the Exploitation of Science and Technology that Yorkshire Water and Siemens came together to develop a sensor for monitoring toxic waste.

marketing in action

When size really is everything

Nanotechnology, the study and manufacture of structures and devices about the size of a molecule, could lead to further significant advancement in many industries and applications, just as the microchip did a few years ago. A nanometre is just a millionth of a millimetre, or one-thousandth of the thickness of a human hair. The obvious applications are in micro-electronics, enabling the increased miniaturisation of everything. It can go much further, however. Gesellschaft für Diamantprodukte (GFD), a company based in Ulm, Germany, for instance, is working on a surgical scalpel based on a nanostructured diamond that would enable cataracts to be removed far more effectively from eyes. Meanwhile, scientists at Cornell University have created a cluster of nanoscopic machines that can spin propellers at 480 revolutions per minute opening up the prospect of machines operating within the body to repair damaged cells, making *Star Trek*-style medical technology a reality.

Some products that have benefited from nanoscience will soon hit the market, such as nanomaterials to make sunscreens transparent, aerosol cans non-clogging, floor waxes harder and longer-lasting, and glasses scratch-resistant. The real impact, however, has yet to happen, as most development activity is in the pre-product phase. That is likely to change over the next five to ten years, and so leading-edge companies cannot afford to ignore nanoresearch and development, either in terms of developing new concepts or in improved commercial applications. Computers, medicine, biotechnology, aerospace, toys, agriculture and energy are just a few of the areas that could benefit from nanoadvances in how things are made and in the products that are sold. Computers the size of one of the fibres in a shirt would make laptops a thing of the past, and hard disks with 100 times the capacity of most of today's may not be far away thus making floppy disks obsolete. At present much of the research is taking place in universities, funded by industry and government or in the laboratories of large multinationals such as IBM, who want to be in the market early with the next generation of products. In the USA, government funding for research quadrupled from 1997 to 2001 to $519 mn per annum and similar effort is taking place across Europe, a recognition of the potential impact on future competitiveness.

It is up to individual organisations to decide whether they want to be at the forefront of a new technology that consumes significant funds in basic research, or whether they feel flexible enough to emulate the technology of others after the breakthrough has been announced. In either case, the timing of the breakthrough is hard to predict for the manufacturers concerned. It is one thing to have the nano of an idea, but another to convert that to leading product designs and successful applications.

Sources: *The Economist* (2001b); Fong (2001); Rombel (2001); *Scientific American* (2001).

Finally, as a form of summary of this section, Table 9.4 brings together the advantages and disadvantages of using the three types of R&D approach discussed: in-house, outsourcing and collaboration.

Organisation for NPD

As this chapter has made clear throughout, NPD is a serious and necessary business and accordingly needs the right kind of management support and organisational structures if it is to flourish and produce results. This section looks in further detail at the kinds of teams and individuals who might be involved in NPD.

Product or brand manager

A product or brand manager has responsibility for a single product or brand family, and thus has developed extensive knowledge of a specific market. The brand manager may be able to spot new opportunities in that market or ways of stretching or filling product lines. The risk, of course, is that the brand manager is too involved in managing the current product, or is too emotionally attached to it to threaten its future with a new product. Quite apart from that, an individual who is a good brand manager may not necessarily be equally good at developing and appraising new product opportunities. Thus although the brand manager has a valuable role to play, the NPD process is likely to involve others.

Market manager

A market manager has responsibility for a particular market, which may be defined in terms of customer type or product type. An organisation manufacturing and selling motor spares

Table 9.4 Advantages and disadvantages of various ways of organising R&D

	Advantages	*Disadvantages*
Outsourcing	Reduced costs Access to wider technology Access to a wide pool of R&D talent Use only when needed Solves specifically defined problems Access to facilities	Information leaks Requires trust Lose in-house R&D impetus Time lags Lack of control/motivation Lack of control over critical technologies Good communication needed
Collaboration	Shared costs Access to wider technology Access to wider facilities Access to a wide pool of R&D talent Shared risks Multi-industry/cross-disciplinary synergy possible Involvement/development of in-house R&D function	Shared benefits Needs trust Danger of domination by one partner Danger of unequal benefits Locating a suitable partner
In-house	Secrecy Total control over process Total control over critical technology Industry/company/product knowledge among researchers Quick response/always available Reap all the rewards	Cost Limited expertise Limited facilities May be too close to the problem Permanent resource to be funded and maintained

may define its markets as independent garages, franchised car dealerships, multiple chains such as Kwik Fit and mass retailers such as Halfords. Market managers develop deep knowledge of the customer needs and wants within their own markets, but as with the brand managers, their expertise is best deployed as part of a wider team.

New product manager

A new product manager is employed specifically to seek out new product opportunities and is likely to be found in a consumer market where the emphasis is on marketing rather than technical innovation. The existence of such a post formalises commitment to new products and ensures that the NPD process is in the hands of someone who understands how it works and will take responsibility for implementing it. Nevertheless, the new product manager may need to draw on the expertise of others within the organisation.

Venture team

The Renault approach discussed above is an example of the venture team. This is a group of selected individuals from various functional areas who are given the freedom to work solely on NPD, unhindered by other responsibilities and relatively independent of the rest of the organisation. In the Renault case, this went as far as providing a separate, purpose-built site for the team to work in. Such an approach clearly signals a long-term, serious investment and commitment to NPD.

New product committee

A new product committee may take responsibility for defining the organisation's new product policies, aims and objectives and may also make the ultimate decision about which new products to launch. Such a committee is likely to consist of senior managers from a range of functional areas, thus not only coordinating NPD strategy and effort throughout the organisation, but also visibly endorsing commitment to NPD at the top level.

Cross-functional team

The cross-functional team comprises all areas of the organisation that need to work together to bring an idea to market. Typically, it would include individuals from a variety of functional areas, such as marketing, R&D, manufacturing, and purchasing. The priority is for team working, group rather than hierachical decision-making and empowerment to speed up the whole NPD process. Close coordination is considered vital for successful NPD (Wind and Mahajan, 1997). Unlike members of a venture team, however, the cross-functional team members may have to cope with their involvement in NPD in addition to their normal duties, although in some cases they may be temporarily seconded to the cross-functional team full time. Once the NPD problem is solved, the cross-functional team disbands.

Clearly, the number of individuals concerned and the range of functional areas involved in an NPD exercise will vary according to the size of organisation and the nature of the NPD task in hand. Thus within a single organisation, a variety of flexible NPD approaches may be employed to suit different conditions.

Chapter summary

- There are different degrees of product 'newness'. A product might be completely *new to the market*. Such products are totally innovative and can emerge from technological advances. Alternatively, a product might be a *significant innovation for the market*, where the basic product concept is familiar, but there is a new twist to it. The other two options represent *minor* or *no* innovation to the market. These are products that either offer little change (of minor but not fundamental interest to the market) or are purely imitative. The buyer's attitude to new products may also be influenced by the rate at which new products are introduced into the market. In fmcg markets, for instance, there is *continuous innovation*, where new product launches are fairly common and it is difficult (and expensive) to get the consumer deeply excited about any single launch.
- New product development is important to organisations for many reasons, including the need to maintain competitive advantage through innovation and better serving the customer's changing needs and wants. There are two types of approach to NPD. The first is to be *reactive*, to wait and see what others do and then follow or imitate, and the second is to be *proactive*, to set the pace and standard and be the one whom others follow or imitate. Whatever the approach, NPD is not an easy activity and there are many potential problems that can arise. In order to minimise the risks, therefore, the NPD process needs careful and skilful management.
- An eight-stage framework, building from the initial idea generation through to actual product development, test marketing and launch, helps to define the necessary NPD activities and shows how they fit together in a logical sequence.
- Even with a well-planned, resourced and managed NPD framework, things can go wrong. An organisation may decide to launch a product that should have been rejected (a *go error*) or to dump a product that could have succeeded (a *drop error*). Such errors reflect the delicate balancing act that NPD represents: risk vs safety, investment vs uncertain rewards, speed to market vs taking enough time to make a considered and well-researched decision, proactiveness vs reactiveness. Many new products do fail, for a variety of reasons. It should be emphasised, however, that many common reasons for failure, such as too small a target market, insufficient differentiation, poor quality, poor distribution, poor timing or poor marketing, are entirely avoidable if the NPD process is researched and handled correctly. The reality is, however, that many organisations are under pressure and do not feel that they have the time and resources to do things as thoroughly as they should.
- It is possible to cut the time spent on the NPD process by more effective and efficient management, although this requires long-term commitment and investment. Other organisations have attempted to reduce the costs of NPD by outsourcing their R&D, that is, by using external bodies to undertake work on their behalf. While this allows the organisation to tap into wider technology and expertise, it may compromise commercial secrecy, increase the time taken for the NPD process and remove much control from the organisation. Another trend is that of collaborative R&D, where organisations enter into complementary partnerships to achieve specific R&D goals. Both partners benefit from shared risks and from synergy between their respective skills and industrial experience.

key words and phrases

Collaborative R&D
Continuous innovation
Concept testing
Discontinuous innovation
Dynamically continuous innovation
New product development (NPD)
Outsourcing R&D
Rolling launch
Test marketing

questions for review

9.1 What is the difference between *dynamically continuous innovation and discontinuous innovation*?

9.2 What are the eight stages of the NPD process?

9.3 What is *concept testing* and why is it a crucial stage in the NPD process?

9.4 How are marketing, production and financial concerns brought together at the *business analysis* stage?

9.5 What is the difference between *outsourced* and *collaborative* R&D?

questions for discussion

9.1 Find an example of a new product for each of the *types of newness* categories discussed at pp. 351 *et seq*. What particular marketing problems do you think the organisations launching each of those products might have had?

9.2 What are the potential benefits and pitfalls of using a screening approach based on rating ideas against weighted criteria?

9.3 How might the *product development* stage differ for:
(a) an fmcg product; and
(b) an B2B product?

9.4 To what extent do you think that *test marketing* is a good idea?

9.5 Find examples of two recently launched fmcg products, one of which was given a *full national launch* and the other of which was *rolled out* gradually. Why do you think the particular approach chosen was appropriate for each product?

case study 9.1

The 3G revolution . . . but not yet

Third generation (3G) mobile phones are about to revolutionise how we use mobiles. The problem for the mobile operators is to know when they will be launched and how successful they will be in replacing traditional phones. 3G will provide multimedia applications from the mobile, including pager facilities, high-speed internet access and digital voice reproduction and full motion video combined, thereby offering a significant advance on current technology. It will be far more advanced than WAP which uses standard GSM (Global System for Mobile Communication) networks.

By the end of 2000 there were nearly 400 million GSM users in 158 countries, and that number is expected to grow rapidly to 500 million by 2005 and over 1 billion by 2010. According to the International Telecommunications Union (ITU), China already has the world's second largest mobile subscriber base with 85 million subscribers, and in 2002 it is expected to surpass the US as the world's largest cellular market. In northern Europe, Germany leads with 48 million mobile subscribers, while the UK has 40 million and France has 29 million.

Currently, the world mainly uses 2G technology since the launch of the improved 2.5G in 2001. The latter enables data to be handled more easily but still not as fast or as flexibly as 3G. Speed is not, however, essential for the majority of mobile users and some service operators such as the Netherlands-based KPN Mobile, believe that the new 2.5G services would boost revenues per subscriber by 35 per cent and take some of the edge off the eventual 3G launch. With the anticipated success of 2.5G systems in both Europe and the United States, the pressure to deploy 3G systems rapidly is being alleviated. There will be only limited 3G deployment in 2002, and it is not expected to emerge significantly in the prime US market until 2004 or even later. One2One, the mobile phone operator owned by Deutsche Telekom, does not plan to launch its 3G phone service until the second half of 2003.

For a successful launch, the infrastructure has to be in place, but current bandwidths are not sufficient for high-speed data transmissions to mobiles. This means that new mobile masts and systems support will have to be developed to enable the technology to operate. Because mobiles use the airwaves, governments are entitled to charge mobile operators a licence fee. In 1983 when A&TT sought a licence, it was free, but not now that governments have realised the extent of the revenue generating possibilities. Companies have no choice but to pay up: no licence, no entry to the market. It has been estimated that $105 billion has already been spent on 3G licences across Europe (the highest being the $46 million spent in Germany) so the start-up costs for the operators such as the UK's Vodafone and Germany's T-Mobile and France Telecom are clear to see. The licences are sold by auction, and some say that too high a financial burden has been put on the operators long before the first 3G phone has actually been sold. In Sweden and Finland, however, the governments took a different approach, awarding the licences for a nominal fee to the operators judged to be best placed to drive the industry forward. In Norway, network operator Sonera handed back its Norwegian 3G licence rather than sustain the costs over an extended period.

If licence fees were not enough, a further $125 bn of investment is needed for masts and the infrastructure even before marketing and administrative costs are considered. The situation varies across Europe. In Sweden, operators can share masts, but in the Netherlands, each operator must build its own. In Germany, a controlled sharing model has been adopted. All these up-front costs must be set against the potential market of €1.2 trillion by 2010, unless of course there is a 4G.

The real problems only begin for the operators, however, as they seek to bring 3G to market as fast as they can to get a return on investment. There have been a number of delays. Getting handset technology right to cope with the multiple functions has proved difficult. Generally the systems themselves are ready but there must be handsets to interface with the systems. They are also very costly, between $300 and $500, or about twice as much as conventional GSM phones. Prices will drop with volume, but high initial prices must either be absorbed or passed on and may therefore dampen sales. This is taking place at a time when the mobile sector is depressed as penetration levels are now high in most EU countries, and with the high costs of 3G licences and investment in the infrastructure, a number of operators such as KPN and France Telecom are reporting heavy losses.

The ultimate success of 3G will be customer take-up rates. Will mobile users switch from 2G or 2.5G to 3G for the additional benefits? Market trials are now being undertaken to assess both technology feasibility and consumer reaction. The most comprehensive trial is in Japan. A fledgling 3G network is being deployed by NTT DoCoMo in Tokyo, six months later than originally planned. A small pilot project, limited to 4,500 customers who were given free handsets and no monthly charge, was undertaken in Tokyo. As a result, a number of technical problems were addressed, such as handsets freezing; the fact that only 50 per cent of attempts to connect to the network were successful; and batteries that lasted less than a day. Many of the technical bugs were resolved and the world's first 3G service called Foma was launched on 1 October 2001. One user was quoted as saying, 'there's nothing new on the service that I really feel I must have.' If that were repeated it would be a very worrying message to telecom companies around the world, hoping for a 'must have technology'. Advantages were, of course, recorded: faster data services meant a more pleasant online experience, and that meant that customers were inclined to spend more time online, but to be fair many of the benefits such as video and music on demand were not available during the trial. The Isle of Man was the first major trial in Europe when BT launched MM02. Initial results supported the Japanese experience, that take-up will be determined in part by the range of applications that are available. Generally, information was downloaded faster than using modems, a useful feature for video and audio streaming and downloading, and this was especially powerful when the phone was connected to a laptop. When the phone was handheld, however, there was more difficulty with picture continuity.

The benefits of mobile commerce are still some way off. Reviewing bank accounts on screen, mobile sales presentations, location-based devices that flash up on screen messages as consumers approach a restaurant or shop, examining tourist attractions or hotels on the move, will all be possible once the infrastructure and services are fully in place, but will they be well enough targeted and available soon enough to appeal to users? So what will be the take-up of 3G? On the answer to that question rests the fortunes of the European mobile industry. Interestingly, when AT&T launched a mobile service in 1983 it predicted that the market would grow to 900,000 US subscribers by 2000. In actual fact, it had grown to 100 million by 1999, quite apart from worldwide sales. Delia MacMillan, of Gartner Dataquest, was quoted in April 2000 as saying, 'technology succeeds when it makes an application faster, easier or cheaper'. 3G does that, but the first operators will be the ones who discover all the problems, especially for user applications. Billing approaches, multiple handsets, mobile commerce will all require users and providers alike to travel rapidly along a steep learning curve. Consumer applications will be the first priority, followed by personal area networks that will allow organisations to deal with customers in a more personalised way. When all these services are rolled out, operators will have to make sure that 3G really does make lives more flexible and time efficient and that it complements lifestyles. Consumers will demand more, but will want to pay relatively less, whatever the technology.

Sources: Bickers (2001); Dunn (2001); *The Economist* (2001a); Hadden (2001); Lavacks (2001); Reinhardt *et al.* (2001); Rosen (2001); Siber (2001); Turner (2000); Vaughan-Adams (2001); Wray (2001a, 2001b).

Questions

1. Summarise the major areas of cost and investment to the operators in developing and launching 3G technology. Why would any company in this market be prepared to spend such a large amount of money on 3G?
2. What factors are likely to influence the rate of acceptance and subscription to 3G phones among consumers?
3. At what stage in the new product development process are the trials in Japan and the Isle of Man likely to have taken place? Why do you think these trials were important?
4. To what extent is the introduction of 3G a response to consumer demand?

case study 9.2

Because we're worth it

French company L'Oréal generates a turnover of over $8 bn from its worldwide interests in cosmetics, skincare and haircare markets. Two of its operating divisions within consumer markets are L'Oréal Paris (which owns brands including Elnett, Elvive, Recital, Plénitude and various cosmetics lines) and Laboratoires Garnier (Ambre Solaire, Fructis, Maybelline New York, Belle Color, Nutralia and Synergie, among others). To achieve and maintain its number one position in markets that are moving fast in terms of both technology and fashion, L'Oréal has had to invest heavily in innovation. The company employs more than 2,500 chemists, biologists and pharmacists and spends about 3 per cent of turnover on R&D. Unilever and Procter & Gamble, L'Oréal's main competitors, spend only 1.5 per cent and 1.7 per cent respectively of their cosmetics turnover (which is 20 per cent lower than that of L'Oréal in any case). The aim of L'Oréal's R&D is to deliver 2,000 new formulae to the marketers, who can then launch 2,000 new products every year. Nicolas Rosselli, assistant head of haircare products, said:

> *Innovation is our driving force. In the salons of our customers who are professional hairdressers, one sees that there is a marked demand for differentiation. Each customer wants to be able to offer consumers something that the others do not have.*

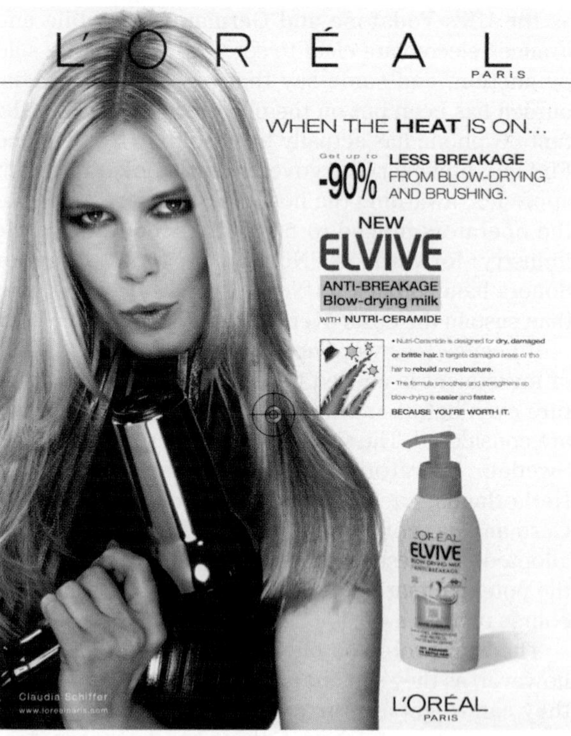

Using recognisable stars to promote its products, L'Oréal emphasises the fact that its customers are equally valued and 'worth it'.

Source: The Advertising Archives/L'Oréal Paris.

This means that L'Oréal always has to be at the forefront of fashion and has to have new products and services ready to offer when the market wants them. New products are part of a strategy to build a dozen or so megabrands that are rooted in a local culture's sense of beauty, but can also appeal to different segments of a global market. The company is adept at continuously bringing innovation to the marketplace and maximising the use of established brand names with new products targeted at these subsegments and niches. It supports its products with an annual marketing spend alleged to be over 30 per cent of sales on its 12 core brands. It streamlines packaging, bulk buys advertising, and gains economies of scale in the aggressive management of these top performing brands which helps provide the resources to plough back into further R&D.

Some new product ideas are initiated by marketing and R&D then has to be responsive in coming up with a formula. Marketers had noticed, for instance, that young Japanese people were fed up with having black hair but had found that hair colourings used in the West gave very poor results on their hair. R&D took the problem and developed a product that began by bleaching the hair to prepare it to take the desired colour. The resulting Féria range was an instant success. There is not always a quick response, however. Marketers wanted a natural fruit-based shampoo range for the European market but it took R&D 10 years to come up with the formulae for the Fructis range! As well as working on ideas initiated by marketing, it is important for the scientists to have some freedom to work on their own long-term ideas and projects, even if there is no immediately obvious commercial application, which can then be patented to protect them from the competition. Much of the work on sun skincare protection brands was the result of laboratory research that found and tested new formulae, including a variant for children. L'Oréal owns the patents for around 110 molecules and applied for over 400 patents of all types in 2000.

There is a delicate balance to be struck between 'creative' R&D, promising long-term solutions, and 'marketing led' R&D, maintaining the impetus to keep launching new commercially viable products, which L'Oréal has tried to find through a three-level structure:

1 *Advanced research*: this is the 'creative' level taking the longer-term view. It is critical for advancing knowledge in the skin, hair and nails areas relevant to L'Oréal; for developing new ingredients; for better understanding and improving the effectiveness of new ingredients and products; and for better understanding their toxicological effects.
2 *Applied research*: this level takes over ideas from both L'Oréal's own advanced research and from what has been done outside the company to refine new raw materials and to put new technology into practice. Although it does not take very long to develop and synthesise a molecule, it takes a lot longer to evaluate its effectiveness, mix it with other ingredients to create a usable product, find the means of making it on a commercial scale and get it accepted by the regulatory bodies. It is important that every new L'Oréal product is exciting, offers a new and clear benefit and proves itself acceptable in use. It took three full years to develop and launch Ambre Solaire Children's Sun Lotion due to the need to come up with a formula that offered maximum protection to children's delicate skin while being water- and sand-resistant. In addition, it had to be easy to apply and give confidence to parents applying the protection. All of this makes globalisation very complicated, because of diverse regulations, consumers and cultures. Another job for applied research is to watch the competition, examining in detail the world's press, surfing the web and getting hold of other companies' new products. About 1,000 arrive every year, and between 700 and 800 of them are examined in minute detail by about 20 people who do nothing else.
3 *Product development*: at this level, formulae are further refined and the products, including the packaging, actually created. Development is especially important as the interface with marketing, and development staff and marketers work closely together.

Underlying the development work is a clear focus on the product, thanks to continual exchanges between R&D and marketing. It is important that researchers do not lose sight of industrial reality, especially at the applied research and product development levels. Informal contacts are encouraged and it is not unusual to see scientists participating in product launch activities. But there are also more formal contacts. At Lancôme, for example, formal meetings include:

- one day per month to discuss the progress of current projects;
- monthly themed meetings to discuss specific topics, for example wrinkles or greasy skin;
- two or three meetings per year for the scientists to reveal their new goodies to the marketers;
- product launch meetings to agree the scientific and marketing platform for each product;
- an annual strategy meeting with board-level managers to look at plans for the next three to five years.

The reward for all this effort can be very high. The Fructis range, for example, took 10 years to develop and when the tests showed spectacular results on the quality of hair, it was launched in France in July 1996. Within the first six months alone, it had sold nearly 5 million units and since then it has helped L'Oréal capture 28 per cent of the European shampoo market by being rolled out into international markets, not only in western Europe but also in Scandinavia, Russia and Chile.

Sources: Alexandre (1998); Edmondson et al. (1999); Hendarwan (2001); L'Oréal (1998), Morais (2000); Shamoon (2001); http://www.loreal.com.

Questions

1 Why is new product development so important for a company like L'Oréal?

2 What are the potential risks of launching up to 2,000 products a year into global markets?

3 What do you think are the problems of managing the R&D–marketing interface? Do you think that L'Oréal has solved those problems?

4 To what extent does L'Oréal follow the new product development process outlined in Figure 9.2?

References for chapter 9

Alexandre, R. (1998), 'L'Arme Secrète de L'Oréal', *L'Essentiel du Management*, May, pp. 15–22.

Bee, P. (2001), 'So How Safe are These Instant Energy Drinks?', *Daily Mail*, 17 July, p. 43.

Bickers, C. (2001), 'Mixed Signals on 3G Phones', *Far Eastern Economic Review*, 27 September, pp. 36–7.

Bonaccorsi, A. and Lipparini, A. (1994), 'Strategic Partnerships in New Product Development', *Journal of Product Innovation Management*, 11(2), pp. 134–45.

Booz-Allen, Hamilton Inc. (1982), *New Product Management for the 1980s*, Booz-Allen, Hamilton Inc.

Brabbs, C. (2001), 'Red Bull Soars into Top Three Soft Drinks', *Marketing*, 8 February, p. 2.

Brewin, B. (2001), 'Report on Health Risks From Cell Phones Inconclusive', *Computerworld*, 28 May, p. 7.

Brown, K. (2001), 'British Industry Falling Behind on Investment, Says Government Study', *Special Report on R&D* in *Financial Times*, 10 December.

Brown, S. and Eisenhart, K. (1995), 'Product Development: Past Research, Present Findings, and Future Directions', *Academy of Management Review*, 20(2), pp. 343–78.

Carbone, J. (2001), 'New Cells Would Boost Run Time of Portable Equipment', *Purchasing*, 18 October, p. 59.

Carmichael, M. (2001a), 'Marriages of Convenience', *The Grocer*, 25 August, pp. 32–3.

Carmichael, M. (2001b), 'Georgia Pacific Relaunches Le Box with Neater, Cheaper Parent Pack', *The Grocer*, 24 November, p. 53.

Charles, G. (2001), 'Does Electrolux's Robotic Vac Suck?', *Marketing Week*, 22 November, pp. 21–2.

Coghill, R. (2001), 'Inappropriate Measures', *The Ecologist*, October, pp. 28–9.

Cookson, C. (2001), 'Survey – R & D Scoreboard', *Financial Times*, 27 September.

Cooper, R. and Kleinschmidt, E. (1994), 'Determinants of Timeliness in Product Development', *Journal of Product Innovation Management*, 11 (5), pp. 381–96.

Cooper, R.G. and Kleinschmidt, E.J. (1987), 'New Products: What Separates Winners From Losers?', *Journal of Product Innovation Management*, 5 (September), pp. 169–84.

Cordner, K. (2001), 'Voyager Sails Through Acceptance', *Modern Railways*, December, pp. 46–8.

Cowell, D. (1984), *The Marketing of Services*, Butterworth-Heinemann.

Cramb, C. (1999), 'Grolsch Targets Mature Markets', *Financial Times*, 10 February, p. 35.

Crick, D. and Jones, M. (1999), 'Design and Innovation within "Successful" High-tech Firms', *Marketing Intelligence and Planning*, 16 (6), pp. 21–30.

Croft, M. (1998a), 'Energy Drinks Gain Impetus', *Marketing Week*, 9 July, p. 21.

Croft, M. (1998b), 'Time to Nurture Creativity', *Marketing Week*, 12 November, pp. 40–1.

Dempsey, K. (2001), 'The Right Stuff', *The Grocer*, 7 July, p. 60.

Dowding, S. (2001), 'New Product Development Must Yield Staying Power', *The Grocer*, 12 May, p. 61.

Dumaine, B. (1989), 'How Managers Can Succeed Through Speed', *Fortune*, 13 February, pp. 53–9.

Dunn, D. (2001), 'Silicon Suppliers Undeterred By Stalled 3G Market', *EBN*, 8 October, p. 1.

The Economist (2001a), 'Business: Think Thin and Crispy', *The Economist*, 9 June, p. 64.

The Economist (2001b), 'Survey: The Smaller the Better', *The Economist*, 23 June, pp. 5–8.

Edmondson, G, Neuborne, E., Kazmin, A. Thornton, E. and Anhalt, K. (1999), 'The Beauty of Global Branding', *Business Week*, 28 June, pp. 70–5.

Edwards, D. (2001), 'Hold That Call', *The Ecologist*, October, pp. 26–8.

Elliott, L. and Beavis, S. (1994), 'Feeling Frail After 15 Year Slimdown', *The Guardian*, 8 November, p. 14.

Fong, P. (2001), 'One Tiny Step Forward for Nanomedicine', *Business Week*, 5 February, p. 110B.

Fuller, W. (1994), *New Food Product Development: From Concept to the Market Place*, Boca: CRC Press.

Gehani, R. (1992), 'Concurrent Product Development for Fast-track Corporations', *Long Range Planning*, 25 (6), pp. 40–7.

The Grocer (2001a), 'Focus on Denmark: State of the Art NPD Centre', *The Grocer*, 16 June.

The Grocer (2001b), 'Hot When You Want, But Not Right Now', *The Grocer*, 1 December, p. 8.

Hadden, A. (2001), 'Great Expectations for 3G', *Telecommunications*, July, pp. 47–51.

Hardaker, G., Ahmed, P. and Graham, G. (1998), 'An Integrated Response Towards the Pursuit of Fast Time to Market of NPD in European Manufacturing Organisations', *European Business Review*, 98 (3), pp. 172–7.

Hart, N.A. (1993), *Industrial Marketing Communications*, Kogan Page.

Hart, S., Tzokas, N. and Saren, M. (1999), 'The Effectiveness of Market Information in Enhancing New Product Success Rates', *European Journal of Innovation Management*, 2 (1), pp. 20–35.

Hawkes, N. and Henderson, M. (2001), 'Study Highlights Tumour Risk of Mobile Phones', *The Times*, 5 September, p. 6.

Hein, K. (2001), 'Red Bull Charging Ahead', *Brandweek*, 15 October, p. 38.

Hendarwan, E. (2001), 'Europe au naturel', *Global Cosmetic Industry*, August, p. 60.

Het Financieele Dagblad (2001), 'R&D-aanbod in Nederland blijft achter', *Het Financieele Dagblad*, 4 December.

Houlder, V. (1995), 'Partners in Innovation', *Financial Times*, 24 March, p. 16.

Kalish, S. *et al.* (1995), 'Waterfall and Sprinkler New Product Strategies in Competitive Global Markets', *International Journal of Research in Marketing*, 12, pp. 105–19.

Keating, M. (2001), 'Milk in a Bag Knocks Old-time Bottles Off the Doorstep', *The Guardian*, 14 August, p. 1.5.

L'Oréal (1998), advertising supplement to *The Grocer*, 10 October.

Lavacks, P. (2001), 'The Great Northern European 3G Gamble', *Strategic Direct Investor*, September/October, pp. 36–41.

Lofthouse, R. (2001), 'Which Way to Go?', *Eurobusiness*, December, pp. 58–60.

MacFie, H. (1994), 'Computer Assisted Product Development', *World of Ingredients*, pp. 44–9.

Majaro, S. (1991), *The Creative Process*, Allen & Unwin.

Marketing (2001), 'Outstanding Marketing Achievement', *The Marketing Society Awards 2001* supplement to *Marketing*, 14 June, pp. 6–7.

Marston, P. (2001), 'New Tyre Speeded Return of Supersonic Aircraft', *The Daily Telegraph*, 8 November, p. 3.

Matthews, V. (1995), 'Innovators Out to Beat the Odds', *Financial Times*, 9 February, p. 19.

Milner, M. (2001), 'Euro 900m Gamble on Fiat's New Model', *The Guardian*, 5 September, p. 1.20

Moore, W.L. and Pessmier, E.A. (1993), *Product Planning and Management: Designing and Delivering Value*, McGraw-Hill.

Morais, R. (2000), 'The Color of Beauty', *Forbes*, 27 November, pp. 170–6.

Morley, C. (1999), 'Set For a Splash', *The Grocer*, 3 April, pp. 28–9.

Newnham, D. (2000), 'A Hard Act to Swallow', *The Guardian*, 1 July, p. 18.

Osborn, A.F. (1963), *Applied Imagination*, 3rd edn, Schreiber.

Pitcher, G. (2001), 'Smart Move to Protect the Brain From Damage', *Marketing Week*, 14 June, p. 33.

Reinhardt, A., Baker, S. and Echikson, W. (2001), 'All That Money on 3G – And For What?', *Business Week*, 26 March, p. 60.

Rombel, A. (2001), 'Nanotechnology: The Next Big Thing is Very Small', *Global Finance*, February, pp. 20–3.

Rosen, E. (2001), 'The Great Global 3G Challenge', *Network World*, 6 August, pp. 36–8.

Rudolph, M. (1995), 'The Food Production Development Process', *British Food Journal*, 97 (3), p. 3.

Schwartz, D. (1987), *Concept Testing: How to Test New Product Ideas Before You Go to Market*, American Marketing Association.

Scientific American (2001), 'Megabucks for Nanotech', *Scientific American*, September, p. 8.

Shamoon, S. (2001), 'Because You Know L'Oréal is Worth it', *The Times*, 30 June, p. 6.

Sharke, P. (2001), 'Seasick Simulator', *Mechanical Engineering*, October, p. 18.

Siber, R. (2001), 'The Wireless Web: Do You Get It?', *Chief Executive*, February.

Thompson, D. (2001), 'Get Big Enough (But Not Too Big) to Source Innovation', *Research Technology Management*, November/December, p. 22.

Turner, A. (2000), 'Is Your Mobile Set About to Become Obsolete?', *The Times*, 2 November, p. 2.

Vaughan-Adams, L. (2001), 'One2One Delays 3G Phone Launch Until Second Half of 2003', *The Independent*, 23 November, p. 18.

Von Hippel, E. (1978), 'Successful Industrial Products from Customers' Ideas', *Journal of Marketing*, 42 (January), pp. 39–49.

Von Hippel, E. (1986), 'Lead users: A Source of Novel New Product Concepts', *Management Science*, 32 (July), pp. 791–805.

Webster, B. (2001), 'BA Concordes to be Fitted With Tough New Tyres', *The Times*, 8 June, p. 12.

Wind, J. and Mahajan, V. (1997), 'Issues and Opportunities in New Product Development: An Introduction to the Special Issue', *Journal of Marketing Research*, 34 (1), pp. 1–12.

Woodcock, D., Mosey, S. and Wood, T. (2000), 'New Product Development in British SMEs', *European Journal of Innovation Management*, 3 (4), pp. 212–22.

Wray, R. (2001a), 'One2One Cuts 900 Jobs in UK', *The Guardian*, 22 November, p. 1.27.

Wray, R. (2001b), 'Online: And Next Year . . .', *The Guardian*, 6 December, p. 5.

part four

PRICE

10 pricing: context and concepts

11 pricing strategies

It is natural to assume that the price of a product is very closely related to the cost of producing it. Since the purpose of marketing is to create and hold a customer at a profit, pricing policies have to reflect a reward to the organisation for its efforts. Manufacturing costs, however, are only the beginning of the story. Chapter 10 looks into a number of influences on pricing decisions, such as distribution channels, long-term marketing and corporate objectives, competitor pricing and customer expectations, and finds that it is far from being a simple arithmetic 'cost plus' calculation.

Price is an important indicator of the positioning of the product for potential customers who sometimes have too little experience of the product or the market to judge it by other factors. Price is often equated with quality or used as a means of comparing competing products. For some products, such as motor insurance, price can even be the primary criterion for choice with wide implications for the organisation. A price-sensitive market means that the organisation might have to find ways of cutting costs or increasing volume to maintain profits or it might be able to use creative marketing to reposition into less sensitive segments.

Linking with this, Chapter 11 examines the rationale behind a number of pricing strategies open to organisations, from deliberately setting high prices through to aggressive low-price strategies. Pricing can also be used as a short-term tactical tool, as a means of diverting customers' attention away from competitive products, for example, and trying to influence their behaviour. Whatever is done, however, pricing must be consistent with the message generated by the other elements of the marketing mix or else the buyer may become confused or suspicious.

chapter 10

pricing: context and concepts

LEARNING OBJECTIVES

This chapter will help you to:

1. define the meaning of price;
2. understand the different roles price can play for buyers and sellers and in different kinds of market;
3. appreciate the nature of the external factors that influence pricing decisions;
4. explore the internal organisational forces that influence pricing decisions;
5. understand the impact of the single European market and the euro on pricing.

Introduction

At first glance, **price** might seem to be the least complicated and perhaps the least interesting element of the marketing mix, not having the tangibility of the product, the glamour of advertising or the atmosphere of retailing. It does, however, play a very important role in the lives of both marketers and customers, and deserves as much strategic consideration as any other marketing tool. Price not only directly generates the revenues that allow organisations to create and retain customers at a profit (in accordance with one of the definitions of marketing in Chapter 1), but can also be used as a communicator, as a bargaining tool and as a competitive weapon. The customer can use price as a means of comparing products, judging relative value for money or judging product quality.

Ultimately, the customer is being asked to accept the product offering and (usually) to hand money over in exchange for it. If the product has been carefully thought out with the customer's needs in mind, if the distribution channels chosen are convenient and appropriate to that customer, if the promotional mix has been sufficiently seductive, then there is a good chance that the customer will be willing to hand over some amount of money for the pleasure of owning that product. But even then, the price that is placed on the product is crucial: set too high a price, and the customer will reject the offering and all the good work done with the rest of the marketing mix is wasted; too low, and the customer is suspicious ('too good to be true'). What constitutes 'a high price' or 'a low price' depends on the buyer, and has to be put into the context of their perceptions of themselves, of the entire marketing package and of the competitors' offerings. Pricing has a spurious certainty

eg

You would think that in the rosy glow of satisfaction and pride at taking delivery of your nice new shiny car, the registration plate would be the last thing you would think about. You would also think that the registration plate itself would be a minimal part of the total cost of the car. For some people, however, a personalised registration plate is the ultimate status symbol, and it is worth paying a considerable sum of money to get the plate they want. Since 1989, the UK's Driver and Vehicle Licensing Agency (DVLA) has been developing a profitable business in personalised plates as a spin-off from its formal governmental licensing role.

Dealers have also sprung up, offering second-hand plates. The car buyer can, of course, just select from the limited range of registration numbers available from the car dealer at the time of the purchase as part of the purchase price of the car, but a designer registration from the DVLA will cost at least £499. Some particularly attractive registrations due for release in 2001 include MU51CAL, DE51RES and DE51GNS and these are expected to sell for up to £30,000 each at auction – nearly three times more expensive than the average family car. This all goes to show that from a consumer perspective, it is not the cost that matters, but the perceived value, and that is the first important lesson for marketers when setting prices (Arnold, 2001).

about it because it involves numbers, but do not be misled by this; it is as emotive and as open to misinterpretation as any other marketing activity.

It is thus important for the marketer to understand the meaning of price from the customer's point of view, and to price products in accordance with the 'value' that the customer places on the benefits offered.

This chapter expands on these initial concepts of price. It will look further at what price is, and what it means to marketers and customers in various contexts. It will also examine more closely the role of price in the marketing mix, and how it interacts with other marketing activities. This sets the scene for a focus on some of the internal factors and external pressures that influence pricing thinking within an organisation. The final section of the chapter tackles some of the issues affecting pricing on a Europe-wide basis.

The role and perception of price

Price is the **value** that is placed on something. What is someone prepared to give in order to gain something else? Usually, price is measured in money, as a convenient medium of exchange that allows prices to be set quite precisely. This is not necessarily always the case, however. Goods and services may be bartered ('I will help you with the marketing plan for your car repair business if you service my car for me'), or there may be circumstances where monetary exchange is not appropriate, for example at election time when politicians make promises in return for your vote. Any such transactions, even if they do not directly involve money, are exchange processes and thus can use marketing principles (go back to Chapter 1 for the discussion of marketing as an exchange process). Price is any common currency of value to both buyer and seller.

Even money-based pricing comes under many names, depending on the circumstances of its use: solicitors charge fees; landlords charge rent; bankers charge interest; railways charge fares; hotels charge a room rate; consultants charge retainers; agents charge commission; insurance companies charge premiums; and over bridges or through tunnels, tolls may be charged. Whatever the label, it is still a price for a good or a service, and the same principles apply.

Price does not necessarily mean the same things to different people, just because it is usually expressed as a number. You have to look beyond the price, at what it represents to both the buyer and the seller if you want to grasp its significance in any transaction. Buyer and seller may well have different perspectives on what price means. We now turn to that of the buyer.

The customer's perspective

From the buyer's perspective, price represents the value they attach to whatever is being exchanged. Up to the point of purchase, the marketer has been making promises to the potential buyer about what this product is and what it can do for that customer. The customer is going to weigh up those promises against the price and decide whether it is worth paying (Zeithaml, 1988).

In assessing price, the customer is looking specifically at the expected benefits of the product, as shown in Figure 10.1.

Functional

Functional benefits relate to the design of the product and its ability to fulfil its desired function. For example, a washing machine's price might be judged on whether or not it can handle different washing temperatures, operate economically and dry as well as wash.

Quality

The customer may expect price to reflect the quality level of the product (Erickson and Johansson, 1985). Thus a customer may be prepared to pay more for leather upholstery in a car, or for solid wood furniture rather than veneer, or for hand-made Belgian chocolates

Figure 10.1 Factors influencing customers' price assessments

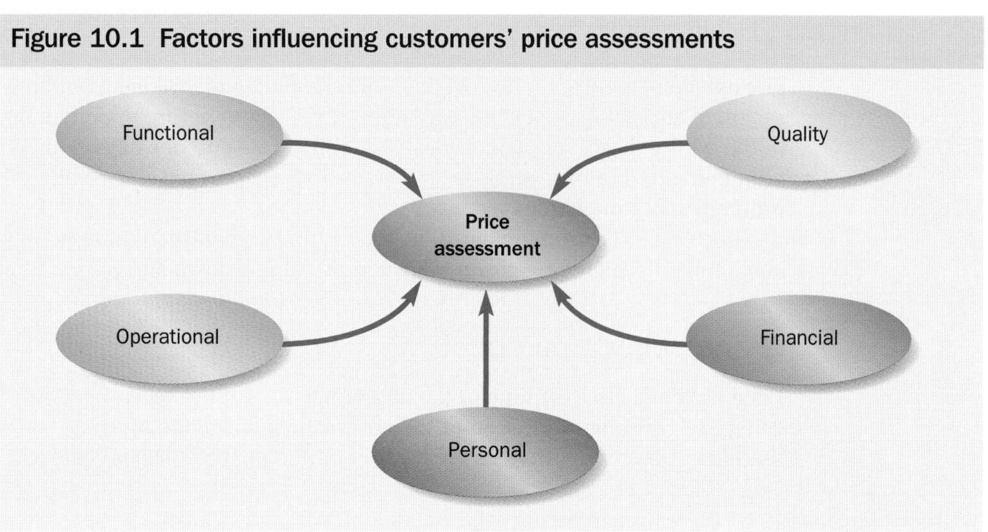

rather than mass produced. Quality perceptions may be to do with the materials or components used in the product, as in these examples, or with the labour involved in making it. Quality may also, however, be a less tangible judgement made on the basis of corporate image. BMW, Heinz and Cadbury's are perceived as quality companies, and therefore they are perceived as producing quality products. The consumer can thus accept that those organisations might charge higher prices.

Operational

In B2B markets, price may be judged in relation to the product's ability to influence the production process. For example, a new piece of machinery might be assessed on its ability to increase productivity, make the production line more efficient or reduce the labour content of the finished goods. Even in a consumer market, operational issues might be considered. For instance, the purchase of a microwave oven increases the operational efficiency of the kitchen, both making it easier to cater for the staggered mealtimes resulting from the modern family's fragmented lifestyle, and giving the chief cook more time to pursue other interests.

Financial

Particularly in B2B markets, many purchases are seen as investments, and therefore the expected return on that investment is important in judging whether the price is worthwhile or not. New machinery, for example, is expected to pay for itself over time in terms of increased efficiency, output, labour saving, etc. Note that this judgement is made not only in terms of production outputs, but also in terms of long-term cost savings, efficiency gains and productivity improvements.

Personal

Personal benefit is a difficult category for the marketer to gauge, as it attempts to measure price against intangible, individual, psychological benefits such as status, comfort, self-image (Chapter 3 reminded you about these benefits), etc. Some high-involvement products, such as perfumes, use high pricing deliberately as a means of amplifying the upmarket, sophisticated, exclusive images portrayed in their packaging, distribution and advertising strategies, thus increasing the status enhancement and 'feel good' factor of the purchase. Chapter 11 will examine aspects of psychological factors in price setting further.

Remember too that B2B markets are not immune from the effects of personal factors. Purchasing can be influenced by the individual motivations of people involved (as discussed at pp. 164 *et seq.*), and even by a desire to enhance a corporate self-image.

The problem is, of course, that different buyers put different values on different benefits. This endorses the need for market segmentation (*see* Chapter 5), which can begin to sort out groupings of like-minded customers so that appropriately tailored marketing mixes (including price) can be developed.

So far, it has been assumed that **price perception** and judgements of value are constant in the mind of the potential buyer. They are, however, variable according to circumstances. For example, a householder thinking of replacing water pipes would probably be very price sensitive and get quotes from a number of plumbers before making a decision. A burst pipe in the winter, however, would have that same householder paying almost any price to get a plumber round immediately. In any such distress purchase, the value placed on immediate problem solution justifies paying a **premium price**.

Another factor influencing price perception is scarcity. Where supply is severely limited and demand is high, prices can take on a life of their own and begin to spiral.

The seller's perspective

Price is a distinctive element of the marketing mix for the *seller*, because it is the only one that generates revenue. All the other elements represent outgoing costs. Price is also important, therefore, because it provides the basis of both recovering those costs and creating profit.

eg

Camera manufacturers produce wide ranges of products, priced differently to cater for different segments' needs. Even when focusing on the relatively new technology of digital cameras, manufacturers recognise that at the bottom end of the market is the customer who sees a camera as a means to an end. This customer wants to capture the moment and may not be concerned with the number of pixels, connectivity or the media card options. They just want to point and shoot, and let the camera do the rest. Some products at this end of the market may be less than £100.

The serious amateur, on the other hand, might be interested in the process of taking the picture and will, therefore, take far greater interest in the technical specifications and the quality and flexibility of any output. Aspects such as zoom capability, back-lighting and flash modes could all be important and as a result prices can range from £250 to over £1,000, as customers are prepared to trade features and benefits for price. Finally, the professional photographer might be prepared to go straight to the top of the range to maximise the quality of output. Specifications will thus often be closely studied and add-on items considered. To get the right package, the professional photographer could well be prepared to pay several thousand pounds.

Profit = Total revenue – Total cost

where total revenue is the quantity sold multiplied by the unit price, and total cost represents the costs of producing, marketing and selling the product. Quantity sold is itself dependent on price as well as on the other marketing mix elements. The motor industry has suggested that although a car dealership selling a large number of cars every year could well generate 80 per cent of its turnover from car sales, it is generating only just over one-third of its total profits from those sales. In comparison, the workshop might only generate 5 per cent of turnover, but 25 per cent of profit. This reflects the fact that for some products, competitive pressures may keep margins tight. To increase profit in such areas, therefore, the organisation may have to find a way of either reducing the costs involved, or justifying higher prices.

The seller, however, must always take care to think about price from the perspective of the customer. In pure economic terms, it would be assumed that reducing a price would lead to higher sales because more people could then afford and want the product. As the introduction to this chapter suggested, however, a low price may be interpreted as making a negative statement about the product's quality, and a sudden reduction in price of an established product may be taken to mean that the product's quality has been compromised in some way. Even petrol, the stereotypical homogeneous product, has been a victim of this.

Similarly, a high price may not always be a bad thing for a seller. If buyers equate price with quality (and in the absence of information or knowledge of the market, it may be the only indicator they pick up), then a higher price might actually attract customers. Part of the psychological benefit of the purchase for the customer might well be derived from its expense, for example in purchasing gifts where one feels obliged to spend a certain amount on the recipient either to fulfil social expectations or to signal affection. The higher the

The customer is paying both for the brand and the quality that promises success when buying the Olympus E-20P – a top of the range digital SLR camera.

Source: Olympus Cameras.

price, the more exclusive the market segment able to afford the product or service. Many more rail travellers, for example, choose to travel second class than in the higher-priced first-class accommodation.

The seller also needs to remember that sometimes the cost to the customer of purchasing a product can be much greater than its price. These broader considerations might have an inhibiting effect on purchase. A consumer buying a DVD player for the first time, for example, will not only look at the ticket price of the machine, but also weigh up the costs of replacing favourite video cassettes with discs. A business buying a new computer system has to consider the costs of transferring records, staff training and the initial decrease in productivity as they learn to find their way around the new system and the costs of installation (and of removing the old equipment). The whole marketing strategy for a product has to recognise the real cost to the customer of accepting the offering and work to overcome such objections, whether through pricing, a better-tailored product offering or effective communication and persuasion.

eg

The roller towel had been replaced by hot-air dryers and paper towels in many organisations' washrooms on the basis that these were cheaper, easier to service and more hygienic. The cotton towel industry has fought back, however, demonstrating that when consumables, transport, labour, dispenser costs and disposal are taken into account, the roller towel system can be up to 58 per cent cheaper to operate per month. Added to that, the industry has improved the design of roller dispenser cabinets and the laundering standards to overcome the poor hygiene image, and has proved that cotton is much more efficient and consistent at drying. In industries such as food processing, catering and pharmaceuticals where hygiene standards are becoming increasingly stringent, and in a world where environmental friendliness is a serious concern, it is not surprising that the combination of cost advantage and performance benefits found in cotton roller towels is irresistible!

Whatever type of market an organisation is in, whatever market segments it seeks to serve, it must always be aware that price can never stand apart from the other elements of the marketing mix. It interacts with those elements and must, therefore, give out signals consistent with those given by the product itself, place and promotion. Price is often quoted as a reason for not purchasing a product, but this reflects a tendency to use price as a scapegoat for other failings in the marketing mix. Price is a highly visible factor and at the point of purchase it hits the buyer where it hurts – in the pocket. As has been said before in this chapter, if the rest of the marketing mix has worked well up to the point of sale, then the price should not be too great an issue, because the buyer will have been convinced that the benefits supplied are commensurate with the price asked. Price is seen here as a natural, integrated element in harmony with the rest of the offering. It could be argued that a buyer who is wavering and uses price as the ultimate determinant of whether to purchase is either shopping in the wrong market segment or being ill-served by sloppy marketing.

Pricing contexts

This section summarises the impact on pricing of the issues and characteristics prevailing in various kinds of market. It highlights the fact that pricing is not just a cost-driven exercise, but a skill that requires knowledge and understanding of both the customer and the external environment.

Consumer markets

There is much competition for *consumers*' disposable income. This is reflected in both the range of different product markets available for them to spend in and the variety of products competing in any one market. Consumers also have a great deal of discretion over whether they spend or not. There are very few real necessities and, on many occasions, consumers buy because they want to, rather than because they need to.

Also, as a result of the fact that consumers are largely buying to please themselves, their assessment of competing products in most markets is often informal, irrational or even non-existent. As discussed in Chapter 3, psychological factors can play a much greater role than analytical skills. Even where hard product information is provided, the consumer does not necessarily make the effort to digest it properly or retain it. It may simply be used selectively as support for a decision that has already been made. Price too, as has already been pointed out, may be interpreted variously, depending on the individual customer. If you want the product badly enough, then you will justify the expense somehow.

All of this makes it very difficult to identify scope for **price negotiation** and, indeed, in most consumer markets, the unit price of the goods is so low that there is no need for such a tool. The price is on the product; take it or leave it. There are some exceptions, however. Consumers expect to negotiate the price of a new car with the dealer, and the dealer recognises this and sets the opening price at a level where he can afford to be beaten down 10 or 15 per cent. This has almost taken on the aura of a ritual and, in many cases, it actually adds to the psychological benefits of car buying because consumers feel that they have been astute enough to drive a hard bargain, which enhances their self-image.

Nevertheless, price is still an important element of the consumer product's marketing mix. **Price banding** can be a useful addition to a market segmentation exercise, as a segment that is prepared to spend £10 to £20 on a product needs to be served differently from a segment prepared to pay £30 to £40. In making planned purchases of clothes, for example, consumers will sometimes decide to buy a certain item and set the price band within which they are prepared to shop. They then seek out the item within the band that offers the best value in terms of colour, fabric, style, etc. If they cannot find anything satisfactory within that band, only then will they consider shifting to another price band.

eg

Being able to customise price to suit individual customers can offer considerable potential to the marketer. Simon and Butscher (2001) propose a number of strategies for price customisation so that each customer is charged the amount they are prepared to pay. The problem, however, is to group customers into manageable segments according to the perceived value of the product or service to them, as most organisations cannot act like internet auctions or made-to-measure tailors, where each product or service is always priced individually. Market research on the perceived value of product attributes (see Case Study 11.2, p. 463, on pricing Vauxhall cars), price bundling and multiple product strategies all help to achieve price customisation.

A consumer for whom price is the primary consideration in comparing competing offerings is said to be **price sensitive**. In dealing with such consumers, marketers have to be particularly careful to get the price right because customers are less likely to be seduced by non-price factors into moving outside their preconceived price band. Price sensitivity can, therefore, be a meaningful way of differentiating between groups of customers.

Retail and wholesale markets

Retail and wholesale markets take a far more rational approach to price interpretation than do consumer groups. As intermediaries, they have to look in two directions, at both the manufacturer and the consumer. They have to be realistic about what price they themselves can charge for a product to their customers, and this in turn establishes what kind of price they are looking to pay to the manufacturer, if they are to maintain a reasonable profit margin. This price also needs to reflect the services in respect of selling the product that the intermediary has to perform.

Looking in the opposite direction at the consumer, retailers and wholesalers will also expect pricing structures to reflect demand. For example, if a product is going to have mass-market appeal and will sell in high volumes, then the intermediaries will need to be able to sell it at a competitive price, especially if it is a new brand entering an established market.

Price discipline is also expected, in the sense that manufacturers should not be seen to be selling direct to the public at lower prices than the retailers could set. Price discipline sometimes goes further than this, and retailers become upset if they think that manufacturers are selling to other retailers at lower prices. The major UK supermarket chains, for example, were incensed when they thought that manufacturers were selling branded lines to warehouse clubs such as Costco more cheaply than to themselves. The manufacturers justified any lower prices on the basis of the quantities ordered. Manufacturers also expect price discipline from retailers, however. Kellogg's decision to stop supplying a discount chain because it was selling Kellogg's products at below cost was upheld in the courts.

Intermediaries are also knowledgeable about alternative product offerings and will therefore use price as a bargaining weapon where they can. Manufacturers in turn may well be willing to make price concessions in order to gain distribution through a powerful retail chain. Another means by which the retailer can keep prices lower is by offering own-brand goods. These compete directly with the manufacturers' brands, but tend to be sold at lower prices. Where a market is under severe price pressure, manufacturers may have to rethink their product policies. Chapters 12 and 13 explore many of these points in more detail, looking closely at the often complex relationships between manufacturers, intermediaries and consumers.

Service markets

Services, as Chapter 22 will show, are different from tangible goods. Because a service is intangible, it is very difficult to assess its quality before purchasing it. Often, **price comparison** is the nearest a potential buyer can get to working out the relative quality of similar competing offerings. A hungry traveller stopping in a strange town may be faced with two restaurants on opposite sides of the road. Both have similar menus, both look to be equally clean, attractive and well patronised. The traveller may then look at their relative prices and decide that the more expensive of the two might give bigger portions, use better ingredients or offer better service.

Another peculiar feature of services is that they are perishable, in that they happen at a particular time and place and, if there is no customer there, the 'product' is lost. A service is not like a packet of cornflakes that can sit on a supermarket shelf until it is sold. If, for example, there are empty seats on a flight from Amsterdam to Berlin, then those unsold tickets represent wasted product and therefore lost revenue because that same flight can

marketing *in action*

A cheap and cheerful bed for the night

Since the late 1980s, the UK hotel market has been revolutionised by the growth of the budget sector, characterised by Travel Inn, Ibis, and Express by Holiday Inn. Between 1999 and 2001 alone, there was an increase in the number of budget hotel rooms from 39,000 to 60,000, and between 1995 and 2000, the number of budget hotels increased by an average of 15 per cent per annum to over 800.

The original budget hotels tended to be fairly basic but operated to a consistent standard, often operated by chains to a flat-rate pricing structure. There were often no service frills, no restaurants within the hotel itself and minimal extra facilities in the rooms, such as telephones and mini-bars. Instead, hotels in this sector offered an alternative to higher priced hotels with wider services and bed and breakfast/guest houses that were of variable standard. To the weary traveller, the possibility of booking in advance via a centralised reservation system, getting a guaranteed level of service, and the convenience of arriving and departing to the guest's schedule rather than fitting into the landlady's schedule offered an attractive advantage. Prices were set to fall below the typical full-service hotel but above the typical bed and breakfast. Furthermore, customers paid per room, not per person, so a family could stay for the same price as an individual, subject to maximum room occupancy, of course.

More recent developments have tended to add back some of the service. Six-foot-wide beds, secure parking, 24-hour reception, and an adjacent, on-site bar and restaurant are now standard features. The new Sleep Inn at Cambridge, for example, offers internet access, direct-dial telephones, clothes presses, hairdryers and even a TV with a PlayStation in the rooms, but still only costs £49.95 on weeknights. Express by Holiday Inn offers free breakfast to guests at the adjacent restaurant and although each bedroom has a work area, dataport, and telephone, guests can still book a meeting room, which also has fax and photocopying facilities.

Price structures have also changed. Rather than pricing by season or individual location, tiered pricing now tends to operate according to the general location and day of the week. Thus prices may vary depending on whether a hotel is in a city centre or not, with London as the most expensive. Express by Holiday Inn usually operates different prices for weekdays and weekends. In short, the early emphasis on price competition is being replaced with a value for money approach when service levels and delivery are of a consistent standard. The success of budget hotels, especially with business travellers has led to a decline in middle market hotels and B&Bs.

As evidence of consistency, branding has played an important role in building occupancy. Although only 30 per cent of the UK hotel market is served by branded chains, compared with 70 per cent in the USA, many of these brands are in the budget segment. As competition increases, however, there may be pressure to develop more facilities rather than to cut prices. Interestingly, in many of the US budget chains extras such as continental breakfast and swimming pools are regularly used to differentiate, often with only a small price premium. In the UK, the Malmaison hotels in the North of England and Scotland often use architecturally interesting buildings and each room has a CD player while there is a small gym, a brasserie and café on the ground floor. That perhaps is the irony: in time the real budget hotel concept, as typified by Formula 1, will become only a niche in a more sophisticated budget-priced sector.

Sources: Singh (2001), Upton (2001).

never take place again. Pricing, however, can help to ensure that these losses are minimised. Reducing the cost of a ticket as the flight time gets closer may encourage someone to purchase it. The airline may not make as much profit on that ticket as it would like, but as long as it is covering its variable costs and making a contribution to fixed costs and profit, then that is better than no sale at all.

An airline represents service marketing on a very large scale, with many skilled employees able to deliver consistent quality service to many customers simultaneously. Many service businesses, particularly in the field of personal services such as hairdressing or dentistry, are reliant on the skills of one or two individual service providers. In such cases, price may be used as a means of restricting demand, by excluding those who cannot afford the price (or those who do not place sufficient value on that service).

Non-profit markets

Non-profit organisations, discussed further in Chapter 22, differ in that they see themselves as existing and operating for the benefit of the public rather than for the creation of profits. Their objectives, therefore, are to encourage people to use their services or products, or to participate in their activities. Pricing can have a major role in achieving that, if goods and services are sold at cost or subsidised to a point where they are visibly below market rates. Some activities, such as minority interest arts events, could not be produced on a commercial basis unless ticket prices were astronomically high, and therefore public subsidy or sponsorship is essential to keep prices down to an affordable and accessible level.

Public benefit need not always be about increasing and encouraging demand. Environmental awareness means that many pressure groups are concerned about the impact of visitor numbers on popular beauty spots. The provision of access, facilities and amenities, along with the erosion of footpaths, has a devastating effect on the place. This has led to consideration of using entry fees or high car-parking fees as a means of discouraging visitors. Similarly, in the years before it pedestrianised the city centre, the City of Oxford implemented very high car parking charges to deter shoppers from bringing their cars into a congested city centre and to encourage the use of 'park and ride' public transport. Zermatt has gone one step further and has banned all vehicles unless they have a special permit. This is to protect the local environment and the ambience of the town, in view of the large number of tourists who visit the area every year.

Unlike the practice in most ordinary consumer markets, where the price is directly exchanged between buyer and seller, in the non-profit sector price sometimes passes through a third party. When this happens it can blunt the consumer's price sensitivity. Where medical services are paid for through an insurance policy, for example, the consumer can begin to think that the visit to the doctor is 'free' and the connection between the service and its price is lost. Such disconnection can lead to overuse of a 'free' service, causing pricing problems for the service provider. Next year's insurance premiums rise to compensate and consumers grumble about it, becoming even more determined to get their money's worth.

In public services, paid for through taxation, moves have been made to reduce the disconnection between price and service by imposing direct charges that contribute towards the cost of maintaining and improving service provision. Prescription charges made under the UK's National Health Service do not in most cases cover the full cost of the drugs supplied, but contribute towards it and remind the user that the service is not 'free'. In some cases, the charges levied do not even recoup the costs of collecting them, such as the tolls on the Humber Bridge. Raising these charges to a more economic level would potentially cause both political difficulties and public outcry, as happened when the tolls were set on the newly opened Skye bridge. In France, however, the tolls on the Loire bridge between St Nazaire and St Brevin have been abolished to encourage economic regeneration in the region. The private consortium that built the bridge still had 16 years left of its rights to collect tolls, but the two local authorities concerned bought up those rights, thus giving them the freedom to drop the toll.

B2B markets

In B2B markets, the difference between price and real cost is particularly marked. As mentioned above at pp. 394–5, the costs of installation, training, scrap, financing, etc. are all used to put the price of major purchases into perspective. Add to this the costs and risks incurred if it turns out that a bad purchasing decision has been made, and you can begin to appreciate why B2B buyers spend so much time and effort analysing potential purchases from all angles. It is rarely the case that the lowest price on paper wins the order. Deeper analysis may reveal that the lowest price actually incurs the highest cost. Mehta (1995), for example, in discussing capital investments, suggests 12 points that affect the total cost and that should form part of the buying centre's evaluation criteria. These points refer to technological and commercial factors, and are listed in Table 10.1.

An organisation's sensitivity to price may well vary according to the type of item being purchased. More time will be spent considering the price of a component (such as an aircraft engine) that represents a high percentage of the cost of the finished product than on one that represents a fraction of 1 per cent (such as the rivets that hold the engine on the aircraft).

Table 10.1 Technological and commercial factors affecting the total cost of a capital investment

1	Cost of necessary accessories to achieve full capacity	Transport; installation; commissioning costs; manuals
2	Cost and need for spares	Cost of spares including sourcing; importing; delivery time/cost
3	Actual performance of same equipment in other companies	Assess reliability; running costs; operator problems; maintenance
4	Demonstration and guarantees	Supplier's ability to 'prove' what the equipment can do; promises on spares availability; servicing
5	Eco-friendliness	Dust, noise, smoke, fumes and other pollutant outputs; cost of safe effluent disposal
6	Safety	Safety of operators and others; long- and short-term effects on health
7	Cost of providing special operating conditions	Provision of new facilities, e.g. air conditioning or pressurised chamber
8	Any supplier's costs associated with installation/trials	Travel and accommodation costs incurred while supplier sets up equipment and runs tests. Is the buyer responsible for this?
9	Training costs	Training operators; costs incurred until they become efficient and achieve output/quality level required
10	Other service costs	Other service needed during installation
11	After-sales service costs	Repairs; maintenance; downtime while awaiting repair
12	Cost of preventive maintenance	Frequency of servicing required; complexity and time needed for scheduled maintenance; cost of downtime and staffing

Source: adapted from Mehta (1995).

Many organisations try to eliminate unnecessary cost and waste by using **value management**. Value management involves teams who look very closely at processes and products to analyse where the greatest costs are being incurred, and where the greatest value is added. This focuses attention on the critical areas of the production process where cost savings in terms of bought-in components, production methods or systems will yield the greatest benefits. Value management teams are likely to include members from all the different organisational functions, as well as possibly representatives of suppliers' companies. Once priority areas for cost saving have been identified, the supplier can be instrumental in helping to find solutions, perhaps by looking critically at its own cost profile or by working cooperatively with the buyer to develop new, more efficient components. It has been claimed that value management can achieve savings of between 20 per cent and 30 per cent of the cost of bought-in parts (*Purchasing and Supply Management*, 1995).

It is also characteristic of B2B markets that many prices are negotiated, particularly with critical components, custom-made goods, or high-volume bulk purchases. It is common to find that purchases are put out to tender, putting the onus on the seller to design an acceptable offering at a good value price. Both of these areas are considered in Chapters 11 and 4.

All of this highlights one of the distinctions between consumer and B2B markets: consumer markets tend towards fixed prices set and controlled by the seller, whereas B2B markets tend to operate more flexibly, with the buyer having a lot more bargaining power.

e-marketing *in action*

Online B2B auctions drive down prices

Although online auctions are best known for the billions of dollars worth of items traded through business-to-consumer exchanges such as eBay, online business-to-business auctions have also become significant. Healthcare company GlaxoSmithKline started using online reverse auctions in 2000 to drive down the price of its supplies. For example, it bought supplies of a basic solvent for a price 15 per cent lower than the day's spot price in the commodity market and Queree (2000) reported that on other purchases of highly specified solvents and chemicals, GlaxoSmithKline is regularly beating its own historic pricing by between 7 and 25 per cent. FreeMarkets, the company that manages the SmithKline Beecham auctions, quotes examples of savings achieved by other clients in these virtual marketplaces: 42 per cent on orders for printed circuit boards, 41 per cent on labels, 24 per cent on commercial machinings and so on.

The reverse auction process starts with a particularly detailed Request for Proposals (RFP) from which suppliers ask to take part and then selected suppliers are invited to take part in the auction. Once the bidding starts, the participants see every bid, but not the names of the bidders. In the final stages of the auction, each last bid extends the bidding time by one more minute. One auction scheduled for two hours ran for four hours and 20 minutes and attracted more than 700 bids!

Sources: Chaffey (2002); Queree (2000).

External influences on the pricing decision

The previous sections of this chapter have shown that there is more to pricing than meets the eye. It is not a precise science because of the complexities of the marketing environment and the human perceptions of the parties involved in the marketing exchange. There will always be some uncertainty over the effect of a pricing decision, whether on distribution channels, competitors or the customer. Nevertheless, to reduce that uncertainty, it is important to analyse the range of issues affecting pricing decisions. Some of these are internal to the selling organisation, and are thus perhaps more predictable, but others arise from external pressures, and are therefore more difficult to define precisely. There is also some variation in the extent to which the organisation can control or influence these issues. Figure 10.2 summarises the main areas of *external influence*, while this section of the chapter defines them and gives an overview of their impact on the pricing decision, in preparation for the more detailed scrutiny of price setting and strategies in Chapter 11.

Figure 10.2 External influences on the pricing decision

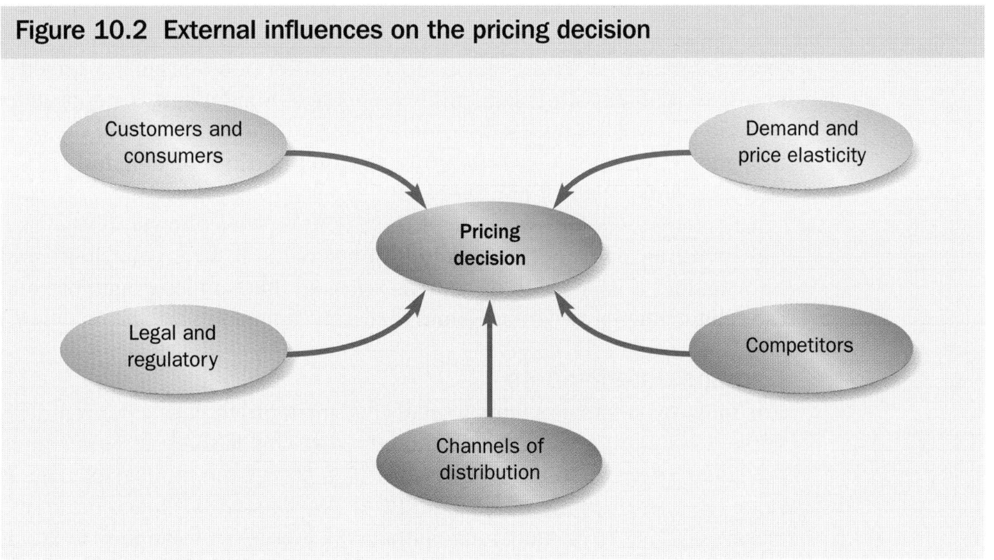

Customers and consumers

As pp. 392 *et seq.* and 396 *et seq.* showed, pricing cannot be considered without taking into account the feelings and sensitivities of the *end buyer*. Different market segments react to price levels and price changes differently depending on the nature of the product, its desirability and the level of product loyalty established.

eg

The discerning coffee drinker who likes the taste of Nescafé and always buys that brand may not notice when the price rises, but even if they do spot the price rise, they might still continue to purchase Nescafé because they value the brand's benefits so highly. A segment that perceives coffee as a commodity and does not mind what it tastes like as long as it is hot and wet might be more inclined to be price sensitive. They might have been buying the same brand on a regular basis, but if its price rises then they certainly will notice and switch to something cheaper.

The marketer has to be careful to set prices within an area bounded at the bottom end by costs and at the top end by what the market will tolerate. The bigger that area, the more discretion the marketer has in setting price. The organisation can increase its pricing discretion either by reducing costs (thereby lowering the bottom boundary) or by raising the consumers' threshold (by better-targeted communication or by improving the product offering).

The consumers' upper threshold is difficult to define as it is linked closely with perceptions of the product and its competitive standing. A product perceived as better than the competition will have a higher upper threshold than one perceived as poor value. In the latter case, the upper limit on price may be very close to cost. Similarly, a product with strong brand loyalty attached to it can push its upper limit higher because the product's desirability blunts any price sensitivity, enabling a price premium to be achieved. By basing a price on the perceived value of the offer, a close match can be found with what the customer is prepared to pay (Nimer, 1975; Thompson and Coe, 1997).

Demand and price elasticity

Customers' attitudes towards price and their responsiveness to it are reflected to some extent in economic theories of *demand*. Marketers' pricing objectives and the estimation of demand are thus very closely linked (Montgomery, 1988). As pricing objectives change, for example if there is a decision to move upmarket into a premium-priced segment, the nature and size of potential demand will also change. Similarly, it is important for the marketer to be able to estimate demand for new product. The definition of demand is flexible here; it may mean demand across an entire product market, or demand within a specific market segment, or be organisation specific.

Chapter 21 will look at some of the techniques used to establish sales and market potential in terms of usage or product sales with different market conditions. Using this information, it is possible to address an issue that has long been of concern to economists: the relationship between price and demand.

Demand determinants

For most products, it seems logical that if the price goes up, then demand falls and, conversely, if the price falls, then demand rises. This is the basic premise behind the standard demand curve shown in Figure 10.3, which shows the number of units sold (Q1) at a given price (P1). As price increases from P1 to P2, demand is expected to fall from Q1 to Q2. This classic demand curve may relate either to a market or to an individual product. As an example, if the dollar is weak against other currencies, Americans generally find foreign holidays more expensive and thus do not travel. Similarly, the Asian financial crisis reduced the number of Japanese tourists.

Figure 10.3 The classic demand curve

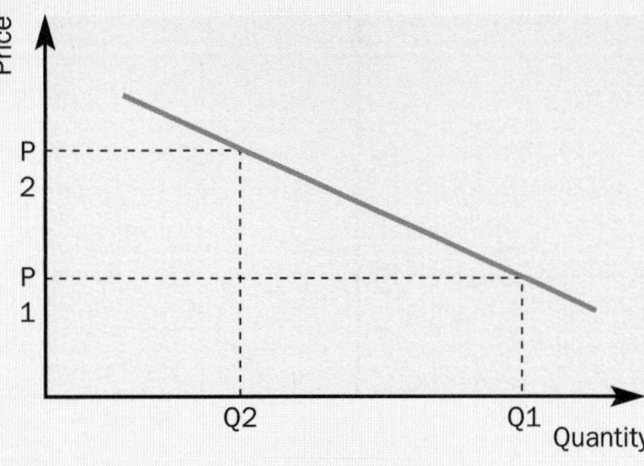

The shape of the demand curve, however, will be influenced by a range of factors other than price. Changing consumer tastes and needs, for example, might make a product more or less desirable regardless of the price. The economic ability to pay is still there, but the willingness to buy is not. Fluctuations in real disposable income could similarly affect demand, particularly for what could be considered luxury items. In a recession, for instance, consumers may cut back on demand for foreign holidays or new cars. In this case, the willingness exists, but the means to pay do not. The availability and pricing of close substitute products will also change the responsiveness of demand. For example, the introduction of the CD player into the mass market had a disastrous effect on demand for record players.

eg

The price of canned mackerel remained stable for five years. But in 2001, quayside prices when the mackerel were landed in Norway were 50 per cent up on previous years. Similarly, the retail price for the canned fish rose up by 20 per cent. This was not caused by a shortage of mackerel but by increased demand from Russia and the Ukraine where economic progress is driving consumer demand for fish. At the same time, the Japanese found a new use for mackerel in sushi recipes, so with stable supply the price of mackerel increased significantly, even though in the traditional European markets mackerel's appeal to younger consumers as a healthy eating option had changed little (*The Grocer*, 2001a).

All of these factors are demand determinants that the marketer must understand in order to inject meaning into the demand curve. As Diamantopoulos and Mathews (1995) emphasise, however, demand curves are very subjective in nature. They depend very much on managerial judgements of the likely impact of price changes on demand, since most organisations do not have the kind of sophisticated information systems that would allow a more objective calculation. In reality, then, it is a *perceived* demand curve that drives managerial decisions rather than a 'real' one.

Not all products conform to the classic demand curve shown in Figure 10.3. Some products with a deep psychological relationship with the consumer, perhaps with a high status dimension, can show a reverse price–demand curve where the higher the price is the higher the demand. As Figure 10.4 shows, as the price goes down from P1 to P2 and demand falls from Q1 to Q2, the product loses its mystique and demand falls. There is, however, still an upper threshold beyond which the good becomes too expensive for even a status-conscious market. Then as the price rises higher, beyond P3, a more normal relationship holds true in which higher price leads to lower demand. This creates a boomerang-shaped demand curve. Knowing at what point the curve begins to turn back on itself could be useful for a marketer wishing to skim the market. Price too high and you could have turned the corner, becoming too exclusive.

Another dimension of the demand curve is that marketers can themselves seek to influence its shape. Figure 10.5 shows how the demand curve can be shifted upwards through marketing efforts. If the marketer can offer better value to the customer or change the

Figure 10.4 The boomerang demand curve

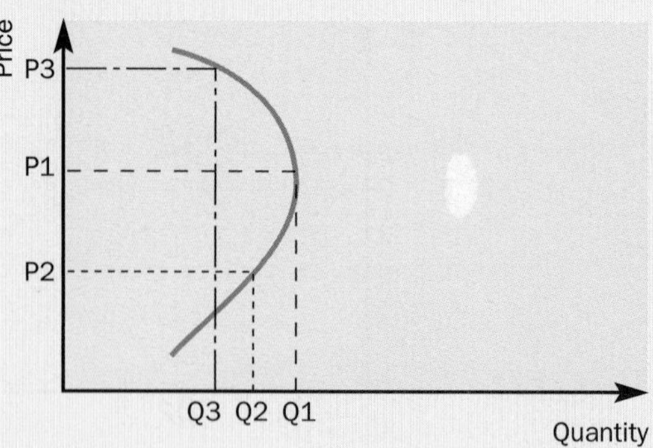

eg

Fine fragrances, especially those with designer names, might fall into this category of demand curve. The fragrance houses have been careful to price them sufficiently highly to position them well away from ordinary toiletries. This means that fine fragrances appeal not only to a well-to-do segment who can easily afford this sort of product on a regular basis, but also to those who aspire to be part of this élite and are prepared to splash out what seems to them to be a large sum of money occasionally to bring themselves closer to a world of luxury and sophistication. In either case, the high price is part of the appeal and the excitement of the product. The higher the price, the bigger the thrill. If the price became too high, however, the aspiring segment would probably fall away and live out their fantasies with something more affordable. They might find £30 to £80 acceptable, but £70 to £120 might be perceived as too extravagant. Even the élite segment might have its upper threshold. If the price of designer-label fine fragrances becomes too high, then they might as well buy the designer's clothes instead if they want to flaunt their wealth and status!

customer's perceptions of the product, then a higher quantity will be demanded without any reduction in the price. It is valuable for the marketer to be able to find ways of using non-price-based mechanisms of responding to a competitor's price cut or seeking to improve demand, to avoid the kind of mutually damaging price wars that erode margins and profits. This may create a new demand curve, parallel to the old one, so that demand can be increased from Q1 to Q2 while retaining the price at P1.

Price elasticity of demand

It is also important for the marketer to have some understanding of the sensitivity of demand to price changes. This is shown by the steepness of the demand curve. A very steep demand curve shows a great deal of price sensitivity, in that a small change in price, all

Figure 10.5 The parallel demand curve

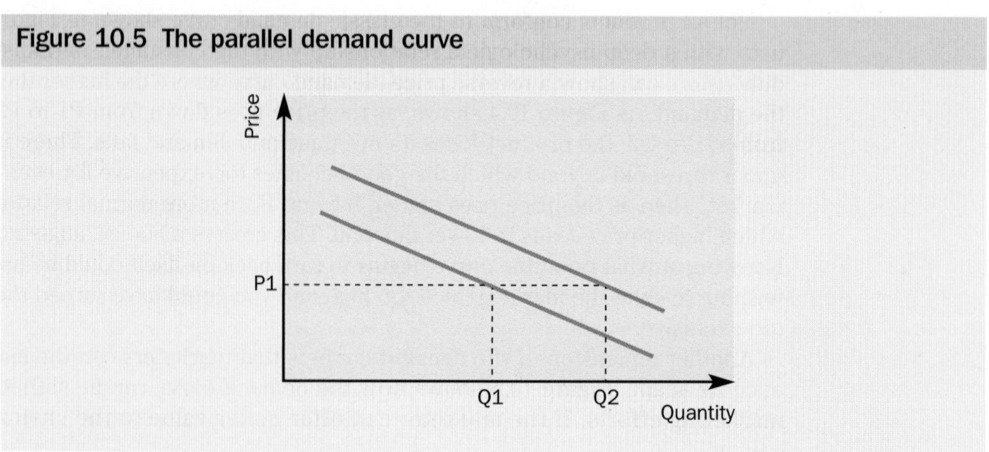

other things remaining equal, leads to a big change in demand. For some essential products, such as electricity, the demand curve is much more shallow; changes in price do not lead to big changes in demand. In this case, demand is said to be inelastic because it does not stretch a lot if pulled either way by price. The term **price elasticity of demand** thus refers to the ratio of percentage change in quantity over percentage change in price:

$$\text{Price elasticity} = \frac{\%\ \text{change in quantity demanded}}{\%\ \text{change in price}}$$

Thus the higher the price elasticity of demand, the more sensitive the market. Goods like electricity will have a price elasticity much closer to zero than do goods like convenience foods. For most goods, as the quantity demanded usually falls if the price rises, price elasticity is often negative, but by convention, the minus sign is usually ignored. To summarise, there are three possible forms of elasticity.

Elastic demand. Where demand is elastic, a small percentage increase in price (from P1 to P2) produces a large percentage decrease in quantity demanded (from Q1 to Q2), as shown in Figure 10.6. The price elasticity is greater than one (ignoring the minus sign). The effect on total revenue is that a rise in price leads to a reduction in revenue, because the extra income from the price rise does not fully compensate for the fall in demand. Conversely, a fall in price increases demand to the point where total revenue rises, because the income from the new customers more than compensates for the decrease in revenue from existing ones.

Figure 10.6 The elastic demand curve

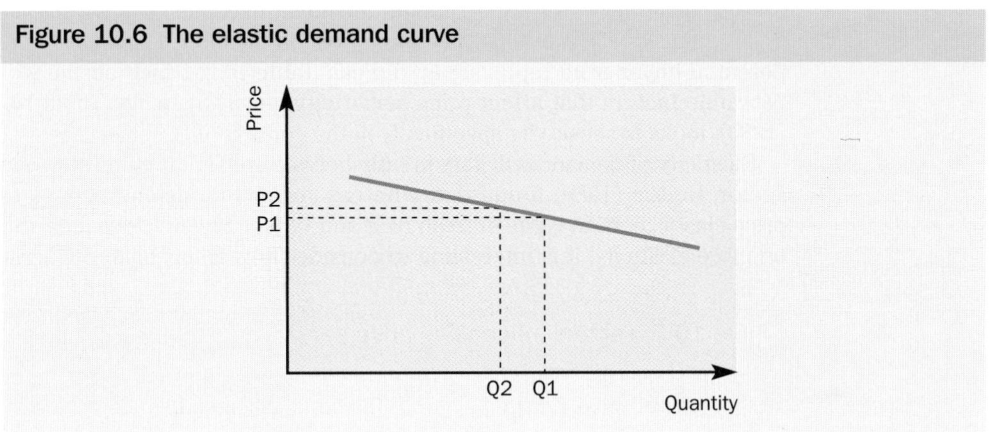

Inelastic demand. Where demand is inelastic, a small percentage increase in price (from P1 to P2) produces a very small percentage change in quantity demanded (from Q1 to Q2), as shown in Figure 10.7. The price elasticity will be between zero and one. In total revenue terms, income increases as the price increases, and falls as the price falls. The change in demand is not sufficient to compensate, as it is with elastic situations.

Figure 10.7 The inelastic demand curve

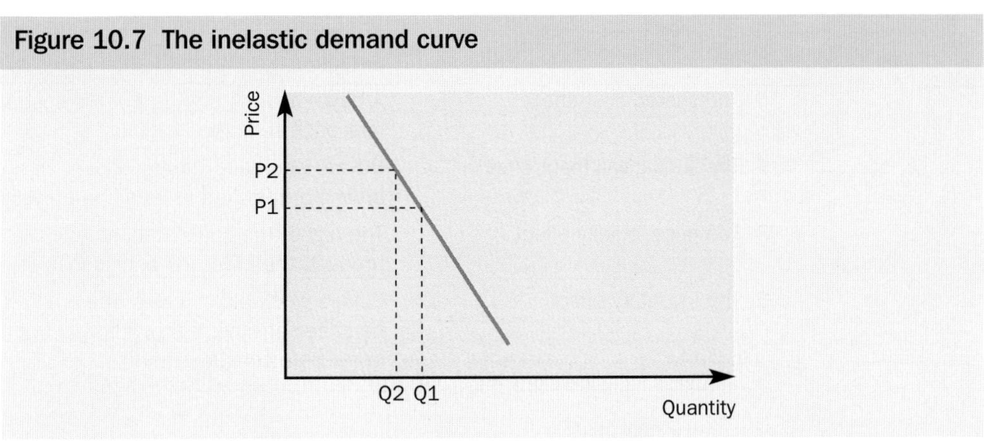

Unitary demand. An unlikely, but theoretically possible, situation is that where the percentage change in price leads to an identical percentage change in quantity demanded. The price elasticity is exactly one, and total revenue will remain the same.

It is important for the marketer to understand price elasticity and its causes, whether for an organisation's brand or within the market as a whole, as a basis for marketing mix decisions. There are a number of factors that will influence the price sensitivity (i.e. the price elasticity of demand) of customers. According to economic theory, the emergence of more, or closer, substitutes for a product will increase its price elasticity as buyers have the option of switching to the substitute as the price of the original product rises. From a marketing perspective, however, it does not seem quite so simple. The emergence of vegetable-based spreadable fats, for example, has offered consumers an alternative to butter and thus something with which to compare the price of butter. Further than that, however, it has completely changed the character of butter's demand curve from that of a necessity (a fairly flat straight line) to that of a luxury (more of a boomerang shape). Those who now choose to buy butter because of its superior taste or because of the status it bestows on the contents of the buyer's fridge will be no more price sensitive now than they ever were and, indeed, may even be less so.

As well as looking at the influence of substitutes on the shape and steepness of demand curves, it is also interesting to consider the relative importance of the purchase to the buyer. A purchase involving a relatively large cash outlay compared with the buyer's income will make that buyer more price sensitive. As discussed in Chapter 3, the more risky and infrequent the purchase, the more rational the buyer becomes, and more important the value for money aspects of the offering become. A rise in the price of cars, for example, might deter a potential buyer from replacing an old car. Table 10.2, based on the work of Nagle (1987), lists nine factors that affect price sensitivity generally, while Table 10.3, based on Porter (1980), looks at sensitivity specifically in the context of B2B markets.

Elasticity of demand will vary greatly between different types of product. Within the food sector, Bolton (1989) found that whereas coffee brands and convenience foods are very price elastic, certain types of fresh fruit and vegetables are price inelastic. As a final thought on price elasticity, it is interesting to consider how it has been deliberately manipulated in

Table 10.2 Factors influencing price sensitivity

1 The unique value effect	The better differentiated the product, the lower the price sensitivity
2 The substitute awareness effect	The greater the number of substitutes available, the greater the price sensitivity
3 The difficult comparison effect	The more difficult it is to make a direct comparison between different products, the lower the price sensitivity
4 The total expenditure effect	The smaller the proportion of total spend this product represents, the lower the price sensitivity
5 The end benefit effect	The greater and more valued the end benefit of the product, the lower the price sensitivity
6 The shared cost effect	A buyer bearing only part of the cost of a product will be less price sensitive
7 The sunk investment effect	Buyers who have already bought complementary products or who are 'locked in' to a system will be price sensitive
8 The price–quality effect	The higher the quality and the prestige image of the product, the lower the price sensitivity
9 The inventory effect	Buyers who hold stocks of the product are more likely to be price sensitive than are those who purchase for immediate consumption

Source: Based on Nagle (1987).

Table 10.3 Factors influencing price sensitivity in B2B markets

1 The total expenditure effect	The smaller the proportion of the total spend this product represents, the lower the price sensitivity
2 The penalty for failure effect	The greater the cost of failure if the wrong choice is made, the lower the price sensitivity
3 The overall saving effect	The greater the overall savings or improvement in performance the product makes, the lower the price sensitivity
4 The contribution to quality effect	The higher the quality of the buyer's own product, the lower their price sensitivity
5 The degree of customisation effect	The more customised or differentiated the product, the lower the price sensitivity
6 The end customer sensitivity	The more price sensitive the buyer's own customer, the more price sensitive the buyer becomes
7 The buyer's ability to absorb costs	The more profitable the buyer and the better able to absorb costs, the lower the price sensitivity
8 The buyer's ignorance effect	The less the buyer knows and the looser their purchasing specifications, the lower their price sensitivity
9 The decision maker's motivation effect	The less motivated the decision maker in terms of cost minimisation, the lower the price sensitivity

Source: Based on Porter (1980).

the case of tobacco products. The UK government has pursued a consistent policy over the years of imposing increasingly punitive taxes on tobacco as a social welfare issue. Basically, the aim has been to push tobacco prices up to the point where price elasticity comes into operation and smokers give up the habit because it is too expensive. This point has not yet been reached, as addicts are proving to be remarkably resilient in absorbing the price rises and maintaining their inelasticity.

Channels of distribution

An organisation's approach to pricing has also to take into account the needs and expectations of the other members of the *distribution chain*. Each of them will have a desired level of profit margin and a requirement to cover the costs associated with handling and reselling the product, such as transport, warehousing, insurance and retail display, for example. Even with a service product, such as insurance or a holiday, distributing through agents who claim commission on sales to cover premises, staffing, administration and profit has an impact on the price of the service.

All of this tends to erode the manufacturer's pricing discretion, because effectively it adds to the producer's costs and takes the total much nearer to the consumer's upper limit. How much erosion there is will depend on the balance of power between manufacturer and intermediaries.

Competitors

The point has been made several times during the course of this chapter that pricing decisions have to be made in a *competitive* context. The level and intensity of competition and the pricing decisions that other organisations make in the market will influence any producer's own pricing. It is not just about relative positioning ('If the budget version is £10 and the premium quality version is £70, then if we want to signal a mid-range product we have to charge £45'). It also concerns strategic decisions about the extent to which the organisation wishes to use price as an aggressive competitive weapon. Price and non-price competition will be discussed further in Chapter 11.

The influence of competition on price will depend on the nature of the product and the number and size of competitors within the market.

Monopoly

Few monopoly situations, where there is only one supplier serving the whole market, exist. Traditionally, monopolies have been large state-owned enterprises providing public services such as utilities, telecommunications and mail, or operating economically crucial industries such as steel and coal. Legislation protected the monopoly from competition. In theory, monopolists have no competitive framework for pricing and can, therefore, set whatever prices they like as the customer has no choice but to source from them. In practice, however, governments and independent watchdog bodies have imposed regulations and pressurised monopolists into keeping prices within socially acceptable limits. Even if that was not enough, the growth of international competition and the availability of alternatives also have an impact. The price and availability of fuel, oil, gas or nuclear power, for instance, all affect the price and demand for coal.

The last 15 years or so have seen UK government policy moving towards privatising state-owned organisations and creating conditions that will allow free-market competition to emerge. This is already evident in the telecommunications market, where the emergence of new competition changed the way in which British Telecommunications develops its service and pricing policies.

Oligopoly

The UK's deregulated telecommunications market is an oligopoly, where a small number of powerful providers dominate the market between them. Each player in the market is very conscious of the rest and makes no move without due consideration of the likely competitive response. Pricing is a particularly sensitive issue in such markets and, where oligopolists choose to price very closely with each other, accusations of collusion are bound to arise. Sudden changes in price by one organisation might be construed as a threat by the rest, but prior and public notification of price rises, as will be discussed at Chapter 11, can be used to defuse suspicion.

These developments are not surprising, as a price war between oligopolists is something that all parties involved would prefer to avoid. Since oligopolists are likely to be fairly evenly matched, it is difficult for any one of them to be sure that it can win. While the war goes on, the consumer may be happy, but the oligopolists are simply eroding their profit margins to dangerously thin levels, not gaining any competitive ground, and causing themselves much stress about the eventual outcome.

marketing *in action*

Never mind the poverty, count the profit

How much is a cup of coffee? Well, we can all make an educated guess. A lovely latte or a foamy cappuccino might set you back around 90p in the university canteen or up to £2.70 in a trendy coffee house. And how much of that finds its way back to the coffee growers in places like Africa and Latin America? Not a lot.

While sophisticated consumers in 2001 were paying highly sophisticated prices for their mochas, lattes, and chocolate brownie frappuccinos, the growers would be lucky to get $0.40 per pound for the beans they supply – less than half of what they were paid in 1999. At that price, it means real hardship and unemployment in the countryside, especially in Latin America, as the cost of production is double the selling price. In contrast, the trendy coffee houses such as Starbucks, Costa Coffee, Coffee Republic, etc. and companies such as Nestlé, the world's largest coffee roaster, are reporting rapidly growing profits. Starbucks' profits, for example, tripled over a five-year period while Nestlé's profits from coffee in 2001 were around $1 bn. Of course, the intermediaries between the grower and the end consumer, i.e. the roasters, retailers and coffee houses, add value to the beans in terms of processing and service delivered and they are entitled to be rewarded for that. Nevertheless, it is not in their interests to see growers going out of business.

The growers' problems arise from a number of related factors. The key issue is one of over-production. Demand is rising by only 1.5 per cent per annum, while supply is expanding by 3.5 per cent. This is compounded by rising productivity – the International Coffee Organisation (ICO) estimated that 2000/01 world production was the highest since

1964/65 – and the entry into the market of Vietnam, a new producer. Up until the 1990s, the market was regulated by export quotas, but since their abolition, coffee exports have increased hugely while export revenues are lower than they were 20 years ago. There is a vicious circle here: as prices fall, producers export more to try to compensate, flooding the market and depressing prices even further.

The immediate outlook is not good. The World Bank estimates that it could take until 2010 for coffee prices to regain the same price levels as in 1997/98. Why should any of this matter? About 70 per cent of the world's coffee is produced on farms of less than five hectares and thus an estimated 20 million households in some of the poorest parts of the world depend on income from coffee to pay for food, clothing and education. As Watkins (2001) puts it, 'Price data cannot capture the scale of the human tragedy unfolding across the developing world. The livelihoods of these households are collapsing, with devastating consequences for poverty and the environment.' Aid agencies such as Oxfam are very concerned that if low prices are sustained, not only could the livelihood of millions be destroyed in the short term, but there could also be a shortage of investment in future expansion leading to longer-term economic damage in less developed countries.

Some countries support the idea of a coffee retention plan, under which exporters withhold 20 per cent of their production to restrict supply and boost prices back to something near $1 per pound. Quite apart from the fact that not all countries are prepared to go along with this idea, it is likely that it would only succeed in adding to stocks without tackling the fundamental problem of over-supply. A more radical idea is a one-off programme of destroying about 1 mn tonnes of low-grade coffee and paying $250 mn in compensation to growers, partly financed by a windfall tax on coffee roasters such as Nestlé and Kraft Foods.

Oxfam is also very supportive of fairtrade schemes (see Case Study 4.2), which guarantee to pay producers higher prices than the market rate. Partnership between fairtrader Cafédirect and Costa Coffee means that consumers can enjoy their favourite tipple and still feel that the grower is getting a good deal. But more can still be done, and here is a sobering thought to end with: if only a halfpenny extra went from every cup of coffee to the coffee producers, the situation would be transformed.

Sources: Ahmed (2001); Crawshaw (2001); *The Economist* (2001); Mathiason (2001); Watkins (2001).

Monopolistic competition

Most markets fall into the category of monopolistic competition where there are many competitors, but each has a product differentiated from the rest. Price is not necessarily a key factor in these markets, as product features and benefits serve to differentiate a product and diffuse the competitive effect. The emphasis in these markets is on branding or adding value so that the customer is prepared to accept a different price from its competitors. Miele, a German manufacturer of kitchen and laundry appliances, for example, has developed a reputation for selling very high-quality goods at a price premium. It can thus price its products substantially higher than those of its competitors, because Miele's customers believe that they are getting good value for money in terms of quality, durability and service.

Perfect competition

As with its direct opposite, the monopoly, perfect competition is hard to find. It implies that there are very many sellers in the market with products that are indistinguishable from each other in the eyes of the buyer. There is, therefore, little flexibility on price, because no one seller has either enough power to lead the rest or the ability to differentiate the product sufficiently to justify a different price. If one seller increases the price, either the rest will follow suit or customers will change suppliers, bringing the aberrant supplier back into line. One supplier's reduction in price will attract custom until such time as other suppliers follow suit.

To avoid this kind of powerless stalemate, most markets have evolved into offering differentiated products, even with the most uninteresting commodities (*see* the example at p. 201 on salt, for instance). Nor does the equality of suppliers last for long in most markets. One or two more astute or powerful suppliers usually emerge to lead the market into monopolistic competition.

eg

A visit to the local fruit and vegetable market demonstrates a near perfect market at work. Products are clearly priced, the merchandise is usually visible for comparison and competing suppliers are contained within a defined area. Depending on the season, many prices are set at similar levels. If any differentiation does take place, it could be with a smile, the free provision of a carrying box, or a discount for buying particular goods in quantity (if carrots, for instance, are priced on every stall at 18p per kg, one might differentiate by offering 2 kg for 30p).

Legal and regulatory framework

European marketers increasingly need to understand the national and European *legal and regulatory framework* when setting and adjusting prices. Aspects of this were discussed at pp. 76 *et seq.* Some organisations, such as public utilities, tend to have their pricing policies carefully scrutinised by the government to make sure that they are in the public interest, especially where a near-monopoly is operating. Even after privatisation, such organisations are not entirely free to price as they wish. As mentioned in Chapter 2, for example, the privatised water, gas, telephone and electricity companies in the UK are answerable to quasi non-governmental organisations (QUANGOs), watchdog bodies set up by the government. Even the National Lottery has its pricing, distribution of funds and profits overseen by a QUANGO, Oflot.

These are high-profile cases involving large and important organisations whose activities fundamentally affect the whole population and the economy. For the most part, however, Europe subscribes to the idea that a free market should determine prices without governmental interference. Authorities, whether national or EU based, will nevertheless become involved in pricing issues where they feel that unfair competition or price fixing is taking place. In the UK, for example, the Office of Fair Trading (OFT) is the first port of call for complaints about pricing and if the OFT cannot resolve the problem, it may refer the case to the Competition Commission (MMC). It in turn may refer a case to the EC.

eg

Both domestic and European regulatory watchdogs have far-reaching powers to investigate what they consider to be anti-competitive practices. In July 2001, nine mobile phone companies in the UK and Germany were 'visited' as part of an investigation on overcharging for using mobile phones abroad (Osborne and Wray, 2001). So-called 'roaming prices' are often not clear to consumers and are unrelated to the cost of a call. Consumers in the UK and some other EU countries often pay 63p a minute for calls which is more than 10 times what a US consumer would pay for the same service. The Commission became suspicious when it found that the costs of calls were surprisingly similar, resulting in little price competition. If an organisation is found guilty of price fixing it can be fined up to 10 per cent of its turnover.

In the UK, resale price maintenance, that is, the power of manufacturers to determine what the retail price of their products should be, was abolished in the early 1960s. Although it was retained in a few selected product areas, over the years it has been gradually dropped. The latest area in which resale price maintenance has been abolished is vitamins, minerals and dietary supplements. The idea behind this price maintenance was to protect small, neighbourhood pharmacies by ensuring that the bigger High Street chains had no price advantage over them. Some bigger retailers resented this, however. The supermarket chain ASDA cut up to 20 per cent off the prices of brands in those categories, forcing the manufacturers to take ASDA to court to uphold their right to dictate the price. The case went against ASDA, which then had to increase prices again and await the outcome of an OFT review of the situation. In the meantime, all the major supermarkets pointedly and heavily discounted their own-label vitamins, minerals and supplements, as they were perfectly entitled to do. The price maintenance on this category of products was finally abolished in 2001.

corporate social responsibility *in action*

Caught in the act!

Both Roche and BASF fell foul of the European Commission when the latter found that there had been a nine-year conspiracy to control prices in the vitamins market (Guerrera and Jennen, 2001). Both parties, along with a number of other companies, were accused of working together to ensure that prices of vitamin products were kept artificially high and that there was no excessive price competition to bring them down. The cartel was exposed in 1999 and investigation by the Commission resulted in fines of €462 mn for Roche, as leader of the cartel (*Le Temps*, 2001), and €296 mn for BASF (Court, 2001). Both organisations were expected to appeal. The scale of the fines was more than double the previous record of ECU 270 mn imposed on a shipping cartel, due to the extent of the price fixing, the length of time it had been operating and its being in a health-related market.

A similar probe took place in the United States where antitrust legislation tends to be tougher. Not only was Roche fined $500 mn, but a former executive was jailed for four months and fined $100,000 for playing an active part in the cartel's operation. The EU Commission is coming under increased pressure to take ever stronger measures against uncompetitive practices, regardless of the previous reputation of the organisations being investigated. Both Roche and BASF are amongst Europe's largest and oldest drug companies. Aventis, the French drug company, escaped fines, however, as it 'co-operated with the enquiries and the Commission are keen to encourage whistleblowers so that other cartels can be exposed' (Court, 2001). In order to avoid a repeat of such incidents, Roche and a number of other companies now conduct training programmes for their staff on anti-competitive behaviour and have strengthened the internal audit function to root out such reputation-damaging practices.

Sources: Court (2001); Guerrera and Jennen (2001); *Le Temps* (2001)

Within the EU, some industries have negotiated selective distribution agreements that effectively allow them to control prices by having the right to decide who should or should not be allowed to sell their products.

Finally, at a more mundane level, manufacturers and retailers may be obliged by law to include duty or tax as part of their pricing. Alcohol and tobacco in particular are targeted by many governments for high rates of duty, partly as a public health measure (keep the prices high to discourage over-consumption), and partly as an excellent revenue earner. In the UK, petrol is also subject to high rates of duty (with a higher rate on leaded petrol than on unleaded or diesel). Excise duties and VAT account for 80 per cent of the cost of a litre of unleaded petrol and the actual cost of the fuel is only around 8p per litre.

As mentioned at p. 68, varying rates of VAT are charged on various categories of products across the EU. When the UK government decided to impose VAT on domestic fuel, the gas and electric companies had no choice but to add it to their customers' bills, thus increasing the overall price of these utilities.

marketing **in action**

Seeing light at the end of the High Street

Sometimes, in order to maintain higher prices and margins, retailers can put pressure on manufacturers to refuse to supply other retailers who might be prepared to discount. Has this happened in the retail market for contact lenses?

The contact lens retail market in the UK industry is dominated by a few big chains such as Boots and Dollond & Aitcheson, which account between them for about 70 per cent of the market of 2.5 million users. The independent retailers have struggled to maintain share against these strong multiples.

There have been a number of battles in the contact lens sector. In 1984, opticians lost their monopoly position for supplying contact lenses and as a result new competitors such as Vision Direct emerged, offering lower priced mail-order alternatives. Vision Direct complained to the OFT that contact lens manufacturers were being put under pressure by the High Street opticians to withdraw supplies from it. The opticians argued that under the 1989 Opticians Act, contact lenses can only be supplied if the sale is effected by a registered doctor or optician. The mail-order companies had, however, found what they considered to be legitimate ways around the Act. It could be argued that the High Street opticians objected because they knew that they could not compete on price because they needed more expensive High Street locations and testing and diagnostic services. Despite its lower prices, Vision Direct still claimed to be making a 20 per cent margin on its contact lenses (Nuki, 1997).

Vision Direct used competitive pricing as a differentiator.

Source: Vision Direct.

The opticians won the first round of the battle because in 1999, Vision Direct was successfully prosecuted in the UK for flouting the rules on prescription established by the profession's regulator, the General Optical Council. These rules state that contact lenses can only be supplied with a proper prescription (specification) and by a registered optician or qualified general practitioner. That has not, however, deterred others. Postoptics has now emerged as the UK's largest independent retailer of lenses in just three years through mail-order and internet ordering, offering, it claims, prices on average one-third lower than High Street prices. The formula is similar to that of Vision Direct in that it sells the lenses offered by all the main manufacturers but does not offer the healthcare provided by High Street opticians. The High Street opticians claim that it is easy to cut prices when you do not offer the vital eye-care support. Postoptics has, however, sought to get round the legislation by adopting a strict protocol of prescription verification and cross-checking, for example only accepting prescriptions less than one year old as the specification guide for the lenses.

Many independent opticians may not be able to compete on price as effectively as the larger operators. A number refuse to supply specifications when patients reveal they are planning to buy from Postoptics or from other mail-order and internet rivals. Postoptics' brochure, therefore, lists those opticians who are willing to provide lens specifications. Unlike Vision Direct, however, the company has faced no pressure from the manufacturers, which have continued to supply the business. They consider that with the development of e-commerce, new distribution methods are inevitable.

Will Postoptics survive where Vision Direct failed? Although Postoptics has 90 per cent of the mail-order contact lens market, the General Optical Council wants new rules to cover the new forms of outlet such as Postoptics, by specifying prescription use and allowing the High Street operators to show the eye-care element separate from the cost of the contact lenses. The profession believes that this will show that many High Street operators are in fact more competitive than mail-order suppliers and it could also encourage the High Street retailers to open up internet business operations where they can use the power of their brand names. The real threat (and opportunity) for both opticians and Postoptics may not, however, come from price competition, but from the quality of the customer relationship. It could be argued that opticians have been slow to learn the value of managing relationships and keeping loyal customers through personal service. That will pose a further challenge to Postoptics, but other organisations such as Amazon have shown how CRM techniques can be used over the internet, and with Postoptics showing a margin of only around 10 per cent, any move away from price may actually be a benefit to it.

Sources: Renton (2001); Trapp (2000); http://www.postoptics.co.uk.

Internal influences on the pricing decision

Pricing is, of course, also influenced by various *internal factors*. Pricing needs to reflect both corporate and marketing objectives, for example, as well as being consistent with the rest of the marketing mix. It is also important to remember, however, that pricing may also be related to costs, if the organisation is looking to generate an acceptable margin of profit. Figure 10.8 summarises the internal influences on price, and the rest of this section discusses each of them in further detail.

Figure 10.8 Internal influences on the pricing decision

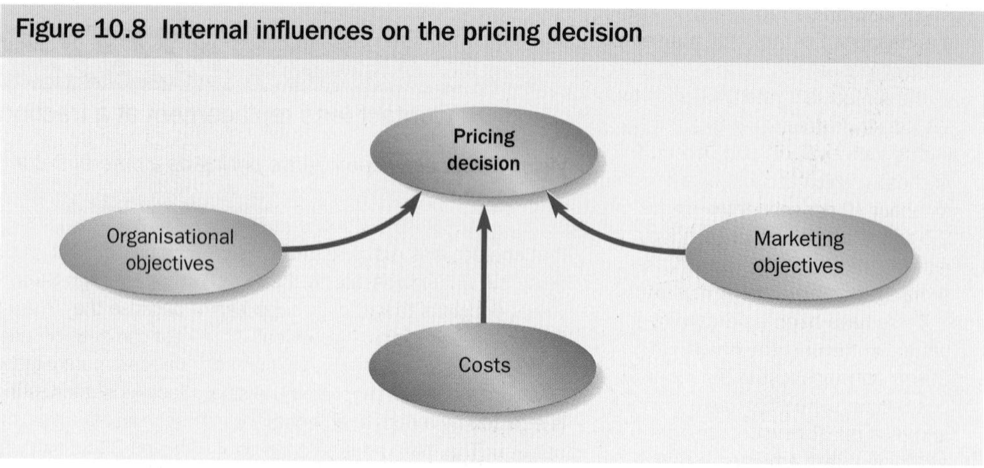

Organisational objectives

The area of *organisational objectives* is an internal influence, linked with corporate strategy. Marketing plans and objectives have to be set not only best to satisfy the customer's needs and wants, but also to reflect the aspirations of the organisation. These two aims should not be incompatible! Organisational objectives such as target volume sales, target value sales, target growth in various market segments and target profit figures can all be made more or less attainable through the deployment of the marketing mix and particularly through price.

Corporate strategy is not simply concerned with quantifiable target setting. It is also concerned with the organisation's relative position in the market compared with the competition. Pricing may be used to help either to signal a desire for leadership (whether in terms of lowest cost or price, or superior quality) or to establish a clearly differentiated niche, which can then be emphasised and consolidated through the other elements of the marketing mix. In launching the *Midnight Sun* brand of butter on to the UK market, the Finnish company Valio used high-quality silver packaging as well as pricing the product to match the market leader, Lurpak, to communicate an upmarket image to the customer.

At the other end of the pricing spectrum, discount supermarket chains, such as Netto, Aldi, Lidl and Kwik Save, are trying to achieve objectives relating to price leadership in the market. Obviously, low pricing within their stores is their primary tool, but this can only be achieved through cost reduction (hence the minimalist retail environment and low levels of customer service) and accepting lower profit margins (1 per cent, compared with the industry average of between 5 per cent and 8 per cent). Achieving all of this is also dependent on attracting many more customers through the doors to generate the higher volume of sales needed to make a reasonable profit. The higher volumes also give the discount retailer scope for negotiating more favourable terms with the manufacturers for bulk buying.

Organisational objectives can change over time as the organisation and its markets evolve. A new business, or a new entrant into a market, faces initial problems of survival. There is a need to generate orders to use excess capacity and to establish a foothold in the market. Relatively low pricing (at the sacrifice of profit margins rather than quality) is just one possible way of doing that. Once established, the organisation can begin to think in terms of target profits and building a competitive position, which may involve a revised approach to pricing. Using price as part of an integrated marketing mix, the organisation can aim to achieve market leadership in terms of whatever criteria are important. Once leadership is achieved, objectives have to be redefined to maintain and defend that leadership, thus keeping competition at arm's length.

Corporate objectives can also have both short- and long-term dimensions to them. In the short term, for example, a small business on the verge of collapse might use low price as a survival tactic to keep it afloat, even if its longer-term ambitions include quality leadership at a higher price.

Marketing objectives

As the previous subsection has implied, marketing and organisational objectives are very closely interrelated and influence each other to a great extent. The distinction, though, is that while organisational objectives relate primarily to the operation, the well-being and the personality of the organisation as a whole, *marketing objectives* are more closely focused on specific target markets and the position desired within them.

Marketing objectives are achieved through the use of the whole marketing mix, not just the price element, emphasising again the need for an integrated and harmonious marketing mix. An organisation may have a portfolio of products (*see* pp. 328 *et seq.*) serving different segments, each of which requires a different approach to pricing. Such a differentiated strategy can be seen in telecommunications, with British Telecommunications developing a range of tariffs for both domestic and business users to suit different needs and priorities.

eg

The manufacturer of KEF Audio (UK) (http://www.kef.com) Ltd has a range of 40 products in its range (hi-fi stereo pairs and home theatre multi-speaker systems), plus sixteen custom installation loudspeakers (for building into room walls and use outside). Prices start at £99.99 per pair for the entry level Cresta 1 hi-fi pair, rising to £8,999.99 for the flagship Reference 207 hi-fi pair. As long as the market recognises the functional and quality differences between the models in such a range, the wide spread of prices need not cause confusion or conflict as to what the organisation stands for.

In that sense, it is no different from a car manufacturer making a cheap and cheerful £8,000 run-about model at one end of the range and a sleek, executive £40,000 status machine at the other. The key is to use the other elements of the marketing mix to support the price or to provide a rationale for it. The concept of the product portfolio and the management issues surrounding it are fully covered in Chapter 20.

Another product concept that might influence the pricing of a particular product over a period of time is the product lifecycle (*see* pp. 312 *et seq.*). In the introductory stage, a lower price might be necessary as part of a marketing strategy to encourage trial. Advertising this as 'an introductory trial price' would be one way of preventing 'low price = low quality' judgements. As the product becomes established through the growth and early maturity stages, and gains loyal buyers, the organisation may feel confident enough to raise the price. As indicated earlier, this has to be done with due reference to the competitive situation and the desired positioning for both product and organisation. In late maturity and decline, it is possible that price reductions could be used to squeeze the last breath out of the dying product.

The top end of the KEF Loudspeaker range – the new 270.

Source: KEF Audio (UK) Limited.

Costs

From a marketing perspective, price is primarily related to what the customer will be prepared to pay for a particular product offering. The actual *cost* of providing that offering cannot, however, be completely ignored. Marketing is about creating and holding a customer at a profit, and if an organisation cannot produce the product for less than it can sell it for, then its presence in that market is questionable.

The cost of producing the product, therefore, represents a floor below which the product cannot be sold profitably. However, defining cost may not be so straightforward. In a hotel, for example, the majority of its costs are fixed in the short term (staffing, facilities provision, maintenance, etc.) and are incurred regardless of the room occupancy. The variable costs associated with an actual guest (such as laundry and consumables) are relatively low. In setting the price of a room, therefore, the organisation has to reflect both the estimated variable costs and an element of contribution towards fixed costs and profit based on predicted levels of business, so that in the long run all costs are met and an acceptable level of profit made.

In the short term, however, it may not be possible to adhere strictly to a cost-recovery formula. The price has to stand in a competitive and unpredictable environment, and may have to be flexible enough to be used as a competitive weapon or as a promotional tool to maintain volume of sales. Thus a hotel may be prepared to let a room at a discount of anything up to 40 per cent of the normal rate at a quiet time of the year when the supply of hotel rooms far exceeds the demand. This is acceptable as long as the price covers the variable costs of letting that room and makes some contribution towards fixed costs and profit. Similarly, at busy times when rooms are hard to find, the hotels can afford to stand by their published rates.

Another important dimension of cost is the concept of joint or shared costs that are divided between a number of products produced by one organisation. Central provision of, for example, R&D facilities, maintenance, quality assurance and administrative costs has to be paid for through revenue generated and therefore has to be reflected in prices. Often the rules for allocating these costs across product lines are arbitrary, and not necessarily closely linked with predicted sales and the market's price sensitivity.

It is therefore clear that costs do play an important role in price setting. They will be further discussed in Chapter 11.

The European influence on pricing

Much of the general discussion on pricing in this chapter and the next is applicable to any organisation, whether it is trading solely within its own national boundary or on a Europe-wide basis. The impact of increasing European integration, however, culminating in the launch of the common hard currency in twelve member states from 1 January 2002 has created fresh challenges for pricing decision makers. This applies not only to organisations operating within the 'eurozone', but also to the other member states that have chosen to operate outside the zone for the time being. The impact of one pricing zone with 300 million people and covering one-fifth of world trade is a powerful force for change for those in and out of the zone.

The impact of the SEM

The creation of the Single European Market (SEM) meant the removal of fiscal, physical and technical barriers to trade, and an increase in the number of organisations operating in more than one country. In marketing terms, as discussed in earlier chapters, the SEM opened up the possibility of pan-European products, or at least of products that are largely standardised across Europe but with adaptations to suit local tastes, preferences or marketing environments. Price may be the element of the marketing mix that is most likely to be adapted for local conditions, as incomes, spending patterns and price sensitivities vary widely across the EU. Price is also a very flexible tool, far easier to adapt than a product!

The implications of the SEM on pricing were predicted by Quelch and Buzzell (1989), who suggested at that time that prices would be forced downwards because of:

1 *decreased costs* through higher-volume sales with more common packaging (and other marketing elements) across the EU and cheaper logistics (since technically there are no import/export regulations and paperwork to fulfil) that also tend towards uniformity;
2 *the opening up of public procurement contracts* to broader competition from across the EU, hence leading to keener prices;
3 *foreign investment*, raising production capacity;
4 *the rigorous enforcement of competition policy*, fewer trade restrictions, less opportunity for building monopolies;
5 *a general increase in competitive activity*, forcing prices down.

Smith (1998) questioned whether the SEM had really achieved all the benefits originally expected, especially when a single currency was not available to support a single market. An Institute of Directors survey found that 38 per cent of UK firms actually found that costs increased as a result of the SEM. Another survey by the European Commission found that just 12 per cent of Portuguese, 17 per cent of Dutch and 20 per cent of French firms surveyed believed that the SEM had worked for them. The two areas of particular concern were state aid that made fair foreign competition more difficult and in public procurement, where 90 per cent of contracts are awarded within the domestic market. Both of these barriers prevented the realisation of the full benefits of price competition.

The launch of the euro is the logical extension of the SEM and together they are expected to create a series of opportunities and challenges that organisations will have to adjust to. These include:

1 *Greater price transparency across member states*

Price variations across Europe can be very large. A report by Lehman Bros on 53 products across Europe found that prices varied on average by 24 per cent after the effects of VAT and other taxes were removed (Smith, 1999). The relative price of the same product can vary considerably, for example. In the Netherlands, the 'Alg' mirror retails for the same price as the 'Krabb' mirror. In Germany, the Alg mirror sells for less than half the Krabb's price (Giles, 2001). These price differences reflect pricing strategies that exploit differing price sensitivities and the amount of local competition in member state markets. The introduction of the euro makes price comparisons much easier and allows consumers to buy products across borders more easily. It is unlikely that German shoppers are going to make many journeys just to buy products from Greece, but if they start hopping over the border to the Netherlands on a regular basis, it could cause problems for local traders. The advent of the euro does not necessarily mean that prices will become identical across Europe, but it does mean that prices are open to more detailed comparison. This is especially true in B2B markets, where buyers can more readily access information on suppliers from other member states.

2 *More opportunity for Eurobrand building with a common positioning*

The euro could lead to increased Europe-wide branding activity (Philips, 1998). As the prices for a particular brand become similar across Europe, there is more reason for positioning that product in the same way across all countries. If manufacturers do want to vary the positioning of a Eurobrand, however, then it will have to be done through brand image rather than pricing. Iced tea, for example, is very popular in mainland Europe, but not in the UK. Now that the product is priced in euros, it would be difficult to sell it more cheaply in the UK, if it was a eurozone member, in an effort to stimulate demand, because consumers in other European markets might notice and resent it. The manufacturers would thus have to try more subtle approaches to the UK market.

3 *No exchange rate fluctuations and currency hedging*

The euro eliminates exchange-rate uncertainty for members and thus could lead to more stable trading conditions within the zone. Eurozone organisations no longer have to set foreign prices to include a buffer in case of adverse shifts in exchange rates, nor do they have to incur the cost and management time involved in hedging international transactions

(Whyman, 2001). Of course, such uncertainty still exists for EU members outside the zone and while the UK and the Scandinavian countries remain as outsiders only partial benefits may be realised. More controversially, it has been argued that the convergence of interest rates will lead to more stable economic environments. Such an argument assumes, however, that the pressures and economic conditions in individual member states are such that convergence is a benefit rather than a liability by removing national flexibility. It is too early to state whether these benefits are being realised, although the ability to quote prices in euros and to deliver at that price is a significant improvement for suppliers. They do not have to make allowances for any unforeseen exchange rate fluctuations or exchange costs. Without the need to create a contingency for fluctuations, there is the possibility that transaction costs could be reduced and some of the benefit passed on to customers. The European Commission estimated that transaction cost savings could amount to 0.4 per cent of total EU GDP per year (European Commission, 1990).

But there are also potential problems:

1 *The risk of brand positioning confusion during changes*
There are fears that the euro will disturb established price perceptions and consumer brand values in member state markets (Shannon, 1998; Whyman, 2001). If consumers do become confused about prices, it could disturb markets, especially for national brand leaders. The demand side of the eurozone is still operating at a national level, shaped by language, cultural factors and historical patterns of distribution and relative pricing (Martin, 2001). Such differences in cultures will remain rather than diminish, despite convergence, and marketers therefore need to understand the real impact on actual rather than theoretical consumer behaviour (Shannon, 2001).

Already, there are issues surrounding new price levels resulting from the introduction of the euro. For example, a straight conversion from local curriences to the euro could spoil psychological pricing effects. In the UK, for example, many prices end with 99 pence, so that the price seems lower to the consumer, i.e. £9.99 'feels' a lot cheaper than £10.00. In Germany, the key psychological price points were DM1.49, which accounted for 20 per cent of groceries, and DM2.99 and DM0.99, which accounted for 80 per cent. These figures do not convert easily into attractive and familiar euro numbers, for example DM1.49 is now €0.76. Even the effort involved in employing mental arithmetic to convert prices varies. Germans simply halve DM prices to get a rough estimate of the euro price, but Austrians have to divide their schilling prices by 13 to get a euro equivalent.

There have also been allegations that some manufacturers have used the introduction of the euro to force through price rises. It has been reported that 'eurorounding' in France has led to an increase of 7.2 per cent in bread prices, 7.5 per cent in butter prices, and 22 per cent in washing powder prices. A further French study highlighted above-average price increases on 20,000 products (Orton-Jones, 2002). SuperQuinn and Tesco in Ireland, however, announced price freezes for the changeover period so that consumers would be able to compare prices easily before the euro becomes the sole currency (*The Grocer*, 2001b).

2 *Lack of harmonisation of VAT and other sales taxes across Europe will still create differences*
This problem is considered in more detail in the following section. Sometimes it is difficult for the consumer, as in the case of price differentials in euro car pricing, to differentiate between the tax effects and deliberate attempts to create different pricing levels. Some price disparity is caused by differing cost bases in the different countries (Seddon, 2000). Property costs are at least 30–40 per cent higher in the UK than in France and Germany. Distribution costs are higher in the UK partly because of fuel tax differentials and partly because of poorer economies of scale: the typical continental food retailing outlet is an 80,000 sq. ft. hypermarket, which is twice the size of a UK supermarket, restricted in size by planning authorities. Across Europe, retail markets are different; products are rarely identical; buyers have imperfect information about prices in different locations; tastes vary around the world; and the costs of local inputs, including taxation, differ. All of this makes price referencing and convergence difficult to realise (Giles, 2001).

3 *Difficulties for those European countries not in the first wave of EMU*
The first twelve countries in the eurozone – Austria, Belgium, Finland, France, Germany, Greece, Ireland, Italy, Luxembourg, the Netherlands, Portugal and Spain – practised dual pricing for several years up to January 2002 so that consumers could become more familiar with the new currency. In those countries not in the first wave, such as Sweden and the UK, decisions have had to be taken as to how to deal with the new arrangements with their trading partners. Some retail stores even list euro prices and are prepared to take the hard euro currency. Effectively, quotations in the domestic, non-euro currency are becoming fewer and fewer, especially for organisations active across Europe.

Marsh (1998) identified two types of British companies that are concerned with the euro. First, those with direct exports to the eurozone effectively operate as eurozone members as they are given little choice by their customers. Euro bank accounts and trading facilities are used by such organisations. The second group are suppliers to those domestic customers who in turn are further down a supply chain that ends in the eurozone. Increasingly, this second group is trading and pricing in euros due to supply chain pressure and the need to minimise the fluctuation risks for the whole supply chain. Complex and extensive Europe-wide supply chains are driving euro usage for all EU members, regardless of decisions taken by national politicians.

It is the smaller organisations that may be less well prepared for the eurozone. A UK government sponsored survey in 1998 revealed that 95 per cent of small and medium-sized enterprises (fewer than 250 employees) had at that time made no preparations for the impact of the euro and perhaps more suprising, some 65 per cent considered that no preparations were necessary (Simon, 2000). The euro may create more intensive competition across Europe forcing down prices in the UK, especially for those smaller firms that do not have market dominance. There will be greater opportunities for companies to break into foreign markets but that also means a threat of market share erosion in the domestic market. This process would be more intensive for smaller UK companies if entry into the eurozone was accepted.

4 *Prices could rise if non-EU competition is stifled*
The effect of creating the eurozone could be to create a much more closed economy than previously experienced by the individual countries comprising the EU. Euroland will become comparable with the USA, which generates 11.5 per cent of its GDP from international trade, compared with 8 per cent in Japan. The average in Europe is 13 per cent, although it is 20.9 per cent in Germany and 23.6 per cent in Britain (Lightfoot, 1998). If the closer integration of Europe has the effect of making it more difficult for outsiders to compete, there is a danger that in some areas, especially where industries experience some protection, prices may not fall but rise. From the perspective of the UK, the impact may be more mixed. Inter-EU trade is a much smaller proportion of the UK's total international trade than for most member states, and the dollar–sterling rate is more critical than the euro–sterling exchange rate.

It is too early to understand fully the effects of the launch of the eurozone. Healey (2000) concluded that while the benefits are significant, cumulative over time and reasonably uncontroversial, the associated costs are more uncertain, exaggerated and are likely to diminish over time. The cost, for example, of actually changing accounting and financial systems to the hard currency will have been absorbed after a few years. Overall, the shift to euro use for all member states is compelling for B2B organisations, but in consumer goods markets there may be less pressure towards standardisation if there are sound reasons, based in distribution or marketing, for the differences. Price is, after all, just one component of the full value and cost of a product to the consumer.

The growth of European travel and Europe-wide media, however, will both act as a force for consistent pricing. The impact will be far greater in B2B markets and it is probably this factor that will eventually persuade the non-euro nations to join, in order to retain national competitiveness in key employment sectors despite the political fallout and economic uncertainty associated with the perceived loss of sovereignty.

Price differentials

As the euro grows in popularity and becomes an accepted hard currency, **price differentials** across Europe are more likely to follow differing tax rates rather than marketing strategy considerations (Kelly, 1998). As mentioned in Chapter 2, VAT and excise rates do vary considerably across the EU, and moves towards harmonisation still have some way to go, with the result that countries such as Denmark with its 25 per cent VAT rate are still well above the average of 15 per cent. Until such time as EMU is fully implemented and tax rates are harmonised, however, the capacity for price differentials remains and the reasons for those differentials are not always clear.

Price differentials might also arise according to consumers' willingness and ability to pay. The price of tea and coffee in Swiss cafés is something of a shock to the foreign traveller, but is widely accepted by the Swiss themselves who are willing and able to pay such prices. Implicit in all this is the necessity for the marketer to understand the pricing context of the local market, and to see it through the consumer's eyes.

eg

The media are often keen to compare the cost of typical shopping basket between countries, and in the UK, comparisons are usually made with France. Diamond (2000) claimed that a Christmas shop in France cost a grand total of £799.31, compared with £1,304.15 in typical British stores, saving £504.84. A typical comparison was made in *The Observer* in the run up to Christmas 2000, when prices at Auchan, in Cité Europe at Calais were compared with the equivalent UK supermarket prices (Livingston, 2000). Comparisons were made between such items as aluminium foil (£2.09 in UK, £1.34 in France) and 4.5 kg Persil (£6.30 in the UK, £4.88 in France). These price comparisons exclude the much publicised savings on French wines and Belgian beers, thus encouraging British shoppers to invade Calais. Cité Europe is well prepared. It offers 200 stores and is close to the Eurotunnel exit. At Carrefour in Cité Europe, English is widely spoken, the signs are bilingual and in-store tasting sessions are widely used to extend the British palate. Real price comparisons are, of course, difficult to make if exchange rate fluctuations and the effects of bulk buying are taken into account, but the pleasures of the day out and a full shopping basket are proving to be extremely attractive to Brits from all over the country.

It is necessary to understand the consumer's living standards, lifestyle, aspirations and purchasing patterns, as well as the alternatives open to that consumer in terms of competitors and substitutes. The organisation might also have a brand-building job to do to establish credibility in the European consumer's eyes. A brand that has been carefully nurtured over the years in its home market to achieve a position where it can command a handsome price premium may mean nothing to the consumer in another European country. The organisation might even have to price low to get into that market against strong local competition, and then begin to build reputation.

There are still wide differentials between car prices in different parts of Europe. The reality is that it costs far more to buy an identical model in some European countries than in others. A report by the European Commission which compared prices across Europe of the 81 best-selling models produced by the world's 25 largest car companies found that, as of 1 May 2001, Britain was the most expensive country in the EU in which to buy 52 out of the 81 models (Osborn, 2001). What is surprising is that such differences still existed after many years of warnings by the Commission that the manufacturers should not discriminate against the British consumer. Even government intervention, public campaigning and the transparency of the internet failed to make significant inroads into relative prices. Effectively, the UK has been a cash cow for the motor industry and has been referred to as the 'Treasure Island' by US car-makers, due to the high profit margins that can be generated (Seddon, 2000).

The Commission report revealed, for example, that a Fiat Marea was on sale in Britain for £9,197 before tax in May compared with a price of £5,583 in Denmark, a difference of 58.3 per cent. Fiat generally, Nissan and Renault were among the manufacturers listed as charging UK consumers far more than their continental counterparts. In their defence, the manufacturers claim that providing right-hand drive vehicles, higher purchase tax elsewhere and better promotional offers in the UK along with the pound being strong against the euro, makes differentials inevitable. However, at the premium end of the market, the differences were very small for BMW, Mercedes and Audi models.

Other competitive pressures are also continuing to build. Virgin Cars, the biggest online car dealer in the UK, offers an average discount of 18 per cent on cars sourced from mainland Europe. Slowly, the arguments against the manufacturers are taking ground. The Commission is alleged to have indicated that it costs the same to make a left-hand drive vehicle as a right-hand drive one, and the sterling arguments have been dismissed as prices have remained relatively high whatever the exchange rate. One of the central causes has been identified as the Block exemption which allows car manufacturers to dictate prices through selected and licensed distributors which has created less price competitiveness. The Block exemption scheme is to be reviewed in 2002 (Evans-Pritchard, 2001).

Parallel trading

Parallel trading takes place when products sold in one country find their way into another country, where they are resold at higher prices. Such trading can even apply to services. Some passengers have found it cheaper to phone Calais to buy a UK–France ticket for Le Shuttle than to buy it in the UK.

Parallel trading is increasingly difficult to avoid, especially as retailers source more widely, looking for price bargains across Europe and beyond. Consumers too may be tempted by parallel trading, for example as they notice the car price differentials already outlined, or if they value the differences in alcohol and tobacco prices. Pressure is building for some national governments to set up legislative barriers to make parallel trading less attractive, despite the fact that this might go against the spirit of the SEM. Such barriers might include the payment of local VAT rates when bringing back into the country goods that command high prices at home but that are available more cheaply in neighbouring countries. Denmark, for instance, is concerned about cross-border parallel imports from Germany.

eg

The parallel trading of prescription medicines is widely practised across the EU even though the drug manufacturers are keen to stop the practice. Distributors buy medicines from pharmaceutical wholesalers in countries where they are cheaper and then sell them into countries where they are more expensive. This results in competition between the 'official supplier' and the parallel importer selling to wholesalers and pharmacies (Macarthur, 2001). The practice is only possible because of differential pricing across Europe arising from individual member states adopting different polices on drug pricing. Bayer recently successfully appealed to the European Court against a ECU 3 mn fine levied by the European Commission in 1996 when it accused Bayer of trying to limit deliveries to wholesalers who were parallel trading a new heart drug, Adalat, into the UK. Article 81 of the Treaty of Rome prohibits agreements that result in the restriction of competition by imposing supply quotas to segment the market on national boundaries, so the case will now be considered by the European Court of Justice. If the ruling is upheld and Bayer wins, the opportunities for parallel trading will be much diminished for drugs. In the UK alone the NHS is believed to save around £80 mn a year through being able to buy cheaper, parallel imports. The total direct losses to the drugs companies from parallel trade across Europe has been estimated at €500 mn (Meikle, 2001).

Chapter summary

- Pricing is a broad area, defined as covering anything of value that is given in exchange for something else. 'Price' is a blanket term to cover a variety of labels and is a key element in the marketing exchange. Price is usually measured in money, but can also involve the bartering of goods and services.
- Price serves a number of purposes. It is a measure against which buyers can assess the product's promised features and benefits and then decide whether the functional, operational, financial or personal advantages of purchase are worthwhile or not. The seller faces the difficult job of setting the price in the context of the buyers' price perceptions and sensitivities. In a price-sensitive market, finding exactly the right price is essential if customers are to be attracted and retained. The seller also needs to remember that price may involve the buyer in more than the handing over of a sum of money. Associated costs of installation, training and disposal of old equipment, for example, are taken into account in assessing the price of a B2B purchase. The relationship between buyer and price differs according to the type of customer and the type of market. Consumers are likely to be more influenced by non-price factors in making their personal purchasing decisions within preconceived price bands while wholesalers and retailers are more pragmatic about price. They know what the consumer is willing to pay and thus seek prices from manufacturers that allow them to sell competitively to the public, yet still cover their costs and an acceptable profit margin. In service markets, price may be used as a means of regulating the demand pattern, either dropping the price to ensure the fullest take-up of the service, or increasing the price to limit the number of customers to a level that the service provider can cope with. B2B markets represent the situation where both buyer and seller are likely to take as rational a view of price as possible.
- The external influences influencing the pricing decision include customers, channels of distribution, competition and legal and regulatory constraints.
- Corporate and marketing objectives set the internal agenda in terms of what pricing is expected to achieve, both for the organisation as a whole and for the specific product. The organisation's costs relating to the development, manufacture and marketing of the product will also affect price.
- The creation of the SEM opened up new opportunities for pan-European marketing, with lower costs, but also with more price competition. Currently, price differentials can be quite wide in some product sectors across Europe. This might be because of differing local market conditions or because of differing tax rates. Tax harmonisation has not yet been achieved in the EU. Price differentials might also arise from different consumer profiles, knowledge and attitudes to brands and products. The introduction of the euro, however, should mean more price transparency and consistency.

key words and phrases

Premium price
Price
Price banding
Price comparison
Price differentials
Price discipline
Price elasticity of demand
Price negotiation
Price perception
Price sensitivity
Value
Value management

questions for *review*

10.1 What factors affect the customer's interpretation of price?

10.2 How can a seller distract the customer's attention from a high price?

10.3 List the internal and external influences on pricing decisions.

10.4 Define price elasticity. Why is this an important concept for the marketer?

10.5 To what extent and why do you think that costs should influence pricing?

questions for discussion

10.1 Choose a manufacturer that produces a range of products serving different price segments in a consumer market. How does the manufacturer 'justify' the different prices?

10.2 Find an example of a price-sensitive consumer market. Why do you think this market is price sensitive and is there anything that the manufacturers or retailers could do to make it less so?

10.3 Compare consumer and B2B attitudes to price, explaining how and why they differ.

10.4 To what extent do you think the classic demand curve as shown in Figure 10.3 is a useful guide for the marketing manager in practice?

10.5 Choose a consumer product and explain the role that pricing plays in its marketing mix and market positioning.

case study 10.1

Kitting out the fans

Love it or hate it, Manchester United is big business. It is a worldwide brand name that generates a loyalty and affinity that enables the soccer club, like many others, to develop merchandise, media products and alliances with service providers on a scale not thought possible in the era before the English Premier League was established. Merchandising sales have been helped as soccer has repositioned itself from a working-class game, sometimes dominated by violent youth, to a family entertainment dominated by middle and higher earners. For many clubs, what happens on the pitch or terrace is just a small part of a powerful marketing organisation.

Manchester United can be considered a typical 'passion brand', characterised by a sometimes fanatical following and a strong sense of belonging that is far removed from the discerning and rational consumer. Its following spreads far wider than its Old Trafford ground and many supporters have never seen a live game. Even passion brands are not immune from criticism, however, and there is a risk of over-commercialisation, which can undermine the special relationship between the club and the consumer.

A major source of revenue is the sale of replica kit. The market for replica shirts alone is worth about £210 mn per annum. Manchester United sells around 500,000 per year, Arsenal 350,000, and Tottenham Hotspur 250,000. Between 1993 and 2001, Manchester United introduced something around 20 new kits, and at around £40 per shirt, that represents a major investment for its keenest fans. One really dedicated fan even paid £4,600 for a second-hand Manchester United shirt, although admittedly it was the one worn by Ole Gunnar Solskjaer when he scored the injury-time winner against Bayern Munich in the 1999 Champion's League Final in Barcelona. The incentive for clubs to change kits is clear and does not necessarily relate to fashion or sponsorship: the absence of a new Manchester United strip in the 1997–98 season, however, meant a drop in merchandise sales of 16 per cent on the previous year's level.

Fans have long been grumbling about the high prices of replica kit and allegations of price-fixing have been rife. In 1999, the Football Association, the Premier League and the Scottish Football Association agreed to try to stop price-fixing for replica football kits, for instance stopping practices such as shops being threatened with not receiving supplies if they slash prices. Prices had been expected to drop by up to one-third – but it didn't happen. Table 10.4 shows 2001 prices for an adult replica shirt:

Table 10.4 Replica kit: adult shirt prices 2001

Selected Premiership clubs

Club	*Price*
Arsenal	£39.99
Chelsea	£39.99
Derby County	£39.99
Leeds United	£39.99
Manchester United	£48.00
Newcastle	£40.00
West Ham United	£39.99

Sources: online club shops and http://www.kitbag.com, accessed 30 November 2001.

According to Arkell (2001), the biggest winners are the manufacturers rather than the football clubs. If a shirt costs £40, about £20 goes to the manufacturer (yet it allegedly only costs about £7 to make one), about £13 goes to the retailer and £7 on tax, leaving a minimal amount for the club. The clubs gain from selling licences to the manufacturers in the first place and from royalties on each kit sold. The clubs also obviously earn more by cutting out the middleman and selling kit via their own retail stores and mail-order operations.

Nevertheless, as a result of years of criticism from fans that top clubs had been financially exploiting them, a charter, incorporated into the Premiership rules, came into force in the 2000–2001 season covering a range of issues such as ticket prices, complaints handling and replica kit. In terms of replica kit, the charter states that they will have a minimum lifespan of two years and carry a sticker on them stating the launch date. Premiership clubs could, therefore, be fined for changing their kits too regularly or for failing to conduct research among fans on the design and number of new strips. The charter does not, however, deal with the issue of pricing replica kit.

In addition, the Competition Act came into force in 2000 which allows fines of up to 10 per cent of turnover to be imposed on companies proved to have been involved in price-fixing. In September 2001, OFT officials raided the British offices of sportswear retailers and manufacturers, including JJB Sports, Nike and Umbro, as part of a probe into price-fixing of replica sports kits. The OFT made it clear, however, that 'No assumption should be made at this stage that there has been an infringement of competition law. We will not be in a position to decide that until we have all the facts' (as quoted by Arkell, 2001).

It would appear that the worm has turned at last. Sales of replica football kits are falling, partly because of changing fashions (hardly a consideration for the die-hard fans, surely) and partly because of parents rebelling against the cost. A Mintel survey showed that 43 per cent of respondents with families felt that football clothing was too expensive. It is interesting to note that Manchester United has found that replica kit sales through its own outlets are holding up well, but sales through other retailers are declining.

As Fresco (2001) points out, many clubs are trying to protect their revenue by diversifying their range of merchandise. Now that we've told you about them, can you continue to live without Niall Quinn's Disco Pants CD (courtesy of Sunderland) or Norwich City knickers?

Sources: Arkell (2001); Chaudhary (2000); Farrell (1998); Fresco (2001); Mintel (2000b); Mitchell (1998); Narain (2001).

Questions

1 Why is merchandise so important to a Premier League soccer club? Why do clubs go into retailing and mail-order when their core business is football?

2 What do you think are the internal factors influencing a club like Manchester United's pricing decision for replica kit?

3 What kind of factors are consumers taking into account when assessing the retail price of replica kit? Do you think they are sensitive to price or to the number of new kits that come out?

4 Why do you think the kit prices listed in the table above are so similar from club to club?

case study 10.2

The white stuff

Most consumers in the UK have two main choices when it comes to buying milk. They can either have it delivered daily to their doorsteps, in traditional one pint bottles, priced at about 48p per pint, or they can buy in cartons or plastic bottles from the supermarket, priced between 21p and 28p per pint, depending on the size of the container. The average price differential between doorstep and supermarket milk is around 15p. The price of the doorstep pint partly reflects the cost and value of the service provided, and partly the higher operating costs of a relatively inefficient distribution system. Doorstep delivery companies have to run and maintain fleets of milk floats or vans and employ people to make the deliveries, pick up the empty bottles, and collect the money from individual households. At the end of the 1990s, there were still some 15,000 milkmen doing their rounds. In contrast, supermarkets are buying in bulk and having deliveries made in bulk to regional depots, which is much more cost effective.

The basic price of milk used to be controlled by the Milk Marketing Board, which had a monopoly over supply. In 1994, however, the milk market was deregulated, opening the market up to free competition. The immediate effect was an increase of between 8 per cent and 11 per cent in milk prices. Most dairy farmers in England and Wales joined a cooperative called Milk Marque which, with control over 65 per cent of supplies, could easily push for higher prices in the interests of its members. The farmers have nevertheless not found life easy. Between 1997/98 and 2000/01 DEFRA figures indicate that the average net margin per cow fell from £220 to £46 and many producers found that the prices that they were receiving for their milk was below the cost of production. Even so, a report from the Competition Commission, published in July 1999, found Milk Marque guilty of monopoly practice controlling price and supply. Milk Marque thus voluntarily agreed to split itself into three wholly separate regional cooperatives as from 1 April 2000 and Milk Marque itself ceased to exist on 1 April 2001.

First Milk is one of Milk Marque's successors. It has more than 4,000 producer members and sells milk to dairy processors across the UK. The processors then turn the milk into the full range of dairy products, including fresh milk, cheese, yogurt, desserts, butter and bulk food ingredients. There are four main processors in the UK supplying liquid milk to the retail trade and for doorstep delivery: Express Dairies with about 30 per cent market share; Dairy Crest (25 per cent); MD Foods (12 per cent) and Robert Wiseman (12 per cent). As well as supplying supermarket own-label liquid milk, the processors have also developed premium liquid milk brands of their own. Dairy Crest, for example, owns Frijj, a range of flavoured milks (retailing at between £1.50 and £1.70 per litre) including limited edition promotions such as the Comic Relief custard flavoured milkshake and the Jaffa Cake flavoured product. MD Foods has launched Cravendale PurFiltre which stays fresh in the fridge for seven days after it is opened and for almost three weeks unopened. It is, however, more expensive than 'normal' milk, at around 59p a litre.

Farmers too have been looking at ways to improve their revenues through value-added. In 1999, when farmers were receiving very low prices for their milk, many decided to 'go organic'. They had been assured by government and by the retail trade that rapid growth in consumer demand would continue and that prices would hold up. It takes two years and many thousands of pounds to convert to organic status, and in addition, the ongoing production costs (e.g. in terms of organic animal feed, etc.) are significantly higher than conventional milk production. A glut of organic milk, therefore, hit the market in 2001, as did the realisation that demand had been badly overestimated, and that consumers were somewhat price-sensitive and not prepared to pay too high a premium for the organic product. This has led to a collapse in producer prices for organic milk, and much of the milk being sold as conventional (and being traded at conventional prices) is actually organic.

Customer price-sensitivity has been encouraged by the supermarkets who see milk as a valuable loss leader, bringing customers into the store and reinforcing 'value for money' images. In January 2002, a six pint bottle cost £1.37, just over 22p per pint. The supermarkets still watch each other's milk prices carefully, and try to match them. If one breaks ranks, the others soon follow. A result of this is that the supermarkets are barely breaking even on milk. They are often making as little as 2p gross margin per pint, which is not sufficient even to cover the cost of the chilled storage.

One other major reason for milk still being so cheap, despite the best efforts of Milk Marque and the companies supplying milk to the supermarkets, is to do with changing consumer habits and lifestyles. There has been a decline in milk consumption generally, and it is perceived as having a boring, commodity image, particularly among young people. In addition, the more milk consumers buy from supermarkets, the greater the supermarkets' economies of scale and price negotiation power. Partly because of the convenience of 'one stop' shopping and partly because of the price, the supermarkets' share of the milk market has risen rapidly (*see* Table 10.5).

Table 10.5 Shares of the milk market

	Supermarket % market share	*Doorstep delivery % market share*
1980	10	90
1990	38	62
1995	55	45
1997	62	38
2001	77	23

Mintel also suggests that smaller households have more erratic milk consumption patterns, and thus buying from the supermarket makes more sense. Some industry pessimists estimated that eventually the supermarkets would capture 85 per cent of the market.

Nevertheless, many consumers find that purchasing milk from the supermarket is actually more convenient than a doorstep delivery. Improvements in milk quality and its processing means that its shelf life has increased, so that consumers can buy enough milk in bulk to last up to 10 days. The four and six pint bottles take up less room in the fridge than the equivalent number of glass bottles would, and consumers can buy as much as they want whenever they want rather than being tied to a certain number of pints per day. The customer does not have to worry about being at home either to take the milk in every day, or to pay the delivery person weekly (and check the bill, of course).

If consumers do not want or appreciate the service offered by the doorstep delivery, they will not be prepared to pay a premium for it. Also, as the gap between doorstep and supermarket prices widens, the bigger that premium becomes and the smaller the number of consumers who will pay it.

Sources: Brooke (2001); Maitland (1996a, 1996b); Mintel (2000a); Morgan (2002); Murphy (1997); Murray West (2001); Pickard (2001); Vidal (2002); *Western Mail* (2002).

Questions

1. Draw a flow chart showing the distribution chain for liquid milk from the cow to the consumer. At each stage (excluding the cow!) summarise the key internal and external factors influencing the price.
2. What kind of pricing strategy do you think the supermarkets are using for milk and why?
3. What difference is the splitting up of Milk Marque likely to make to the marketplace?

References for chapter 10

Ahmed, R, (2001), 'Coffee Prices Plummet', *African Business*, Jul/Aug, pp. 23–4.

Arkell, H. (2001), 'Raid on Replica Soccer Kit Companies as "Price-Fixing" is Probed', *Evening Standard*, 6 September, p. 18.

Arnold, M. (2001), 'Will New Licence Plates Push Sales?', *Marketing*, 6 September, p. 19.

Bolton, R.N. (1989), 'The Robustness of Retail Level Price Elasticity Estimates', *Journal of Retailing*, Summer, pp. 193–219.

Brooke, C. (2001), 'Milk that Stays Fresh for Three Weeks', *Daily Mail*, 20 January, p. 19.

Chaffey, D. (2002), *E-business and E-commerce Management: Strategy, Implementation and Practice*, Harlow: Financial Times Prentice Hall.

Chaudhary, V. (2000), 'Greedy Clubs are Called to Account: Premier Fans Promised New Deal Over Ticket Prices and Replica Kits', *The Guardian*, 17 August, p. 1.32.

Court, M. (2001), 'EU Fines Vitamin Cartel £530m', *Financial Times*, 22 November.

Crawshaw, P. (2001), 'Coffee Prices are Slumping', *The Independent*, 17 May, p. 3.

Diamantopoulos, A. and Mathews, B. (1995), *Making Pricing Decisions: A Study of Managerial Practice*, Chapman & Hall.

Diamond, A. (2000), 'I Did My Christmas Shopping Across the Channel', *Daily Mail*, 14 December, p. 54.

The Economist (2001), 'Drowning in Cheap Coffee', *The Economist*, 29 September, pp. 67–8.

Erickson, G.M. and Johansson, J.K. (1985), 'The Role of Price in Multi-attribute Product Evaluations', *Journal of Consumer Research*, 12, pp. 195–9.

European Commission (1990), 'One Money, One Market', *European Economy*, 44, Luxembourg: Office for the Official Publications of the European Communities.

Evans-Pritchard, A. (2001), 'Car Buyers in Britain "Still Being Ripped-off"', *The Daily Telegraph*, 20 February, p. 5.

Farrell, S. (1998), 'Clubs Accused of Fixing Replica Soccer Kit Prices', *The Times*, 24 February, p. 6.

Fresco, A. (2001), 'Football Club Profits Hit as Fans Rip Off Replica Shirts', *The Times*, 3 April, p. 9.

Giles, C. (2001), 'Price of Variety', *Financial Times*, 21 November, p. 18.

The Grocer (2001a), 'Mackerel Price Up', *The Grocer*, 8 September, p. 27.

The Grocer (2001b), 'Tesco and Superquinn Vow to Freeze Prices for Euro Arrival', *The Grocer*, 15 December, p. 6.

Guerrera, F. and Jennen, B. (2001), 'Vitamins Cartel Faces Euros 850m EU Fine', *Financial Times*, 21 November, p. 1.

Healey, N. (2000), 'The Case for European Monetary Union', in M. Baimbridge, B. Burkitt, and P. Whyman (eds), *A Single Currency for Europe?*, London: Macmillan.

Kelly, J. (1998), 'Disharmony Ahead on Value Added Tax', *Financial Times*, 3 December, p. 39.

Le Temps (2001), 'Amende recorde pour le cartel des vitamines, dirige par Roche', *Le Temps*, 22 November.

Lightfoot, W. (1998), 'Will the Euro be Strong and Stable?', *The European*, 14–20 December, p. 36.

Livingston, S. (2000), 'Escape Pull-out Guide to Christmas Bargains in Calais', *The Observer*, 12 November, p. 9.

Macarthur, D. (2001), 'Parallel Trading of Medicines: The Case for a Fair Deal', *Consumer Policy Review*, Jan/Feb, pp. 6–10.

Maitland, A. (1996a), 'Price Rise Prompts Fresh Outcry Over Milk Marque', *Financial Times*, 16 January, p. 7.

Maitland, A. (1996b), 'Surge in Supermarket Milk Price Eases Squeeze on Processors', *Financial Times*, 28 February, p. 9.

Marsh, P. (1998), 'Acceptance of the Inevitable Gains Currency', *Financial Times*, 15 October, p. 21.

Martin, P. (2001), 'Japanese Lessons on the Euro', *Financial Times*, 8 November, p. 17.

Mathiason, N. (2001), 'A Satisfying Blend', *The Observer*, 8 July, p. 12.

Mehta, S. (1995), 'Investing in Capital Assets', *Purchasing and Supply Management*, March, pp. 16–19.

Meikle, J. (2001), 'Drug Company's Legal Battle Puts Price Savings at Risk', *The Guardian*, 19 February, p. 1.6.

Mintel (2000a), 'Milk and Cream', 28 March, accessed via http://www.mintel.com.

Mintel (2000b), 'The Football Business', 8 November, accessed via http://www.mintel.com.

Mitchell, A. (1998), 'Sky's the Limit for New Breed of Passion Brands', *Marketing Week*, 17 September, pp. 44–5.

Montgomery, S.L. (1988), *Profitable Pricing Strategies*, McGraw-Hill.

Morgan, T. (2002), 'Farmgate Milk Prices in the New Year', *Western Mail*, 5 January, p. 8.

Murphy, C. (1997), 'Is Delivery Coming Home?', *Marketing*, 9 January, p. 13.

Murray West, R. (2001), 'Desperation on Doorstep Delivery', *The Daily Telegraph*, 5 October, p. 38.

Nagle, T.T. (1987), *The Strategy and Tactics of Pricing*, Prentice Hall.

Narain, J. (2001), 'United are Beaten at Home by Tesco Bonanza for Families as Supermarket Sells Replica Kit at Half Price', *Daily Mail*, 30 April, p. 23.

Nimer, D. (1975), 'Pricing the Profitable Sale Has a Lot to Do with Perception', *Sales Management*, 114 (19), pp. 13–4.

Nuki, P. (1997), 'Contact Lens 'Cartel' Can Cost Customers £100', *Sunday Times*, 26 October, p. 1.10.

Orton-Jones, C. (2002), 'Are You Ready Europe?', *Eurobusiness*, January, pp. 120–2.

Osborn, A. (2001), 'British Motorists Still Caught in Car Price Rip-off, Says EC', *The Observer*, 22 July, p. 1.

Osborne, A. and Wray, R. (2001), 'EC Raids Mobile Phone Firms', *The Guardian*, 12 July, p. 1.21.

Philips, G. (1998), 'Staking a Claim on the Future', *The Times*, 21 October, p. 33.

Pickard, J. (2001), 'Glut Reduces Prices Paid to Organic Dairy Farms', *Financial Times*, 18 December, p. 5.

Porter, M.E. (1980), *Competitive Strategy*, Free Press.

Purchasing and Supply Management (1995), 'Value In, Cost Out', *Purchasing and Supply Management*, June, p. 29.

Quelch, J.A. and Buzzell, R.D. (1989), 'Marketing Moves Through EC Crossroads', *Sloan Management Review*, 31(1), pp. 63–74.

Queree, A. (2000), Technology Supplement to *Financial Times*, 1 March.

Renton, J. (2001), 'Internet Contact Lens Retailer Pokes Opticians in the Eye', *Sunday Times*, 14 January, p. 11.

Seddon, E. (2000), 'Come on Down: The Price is Wrong', *Marketing*, 2 November, pp. 36–7.

Shannon, J. (2001), 'Same Currency Different Culture', *Marketing Week*, 19 April, p. 32.

Shannon, J. (1998), 'Euro Puts a Tax on Brand Values', *Marketing Week*, 26 February, p. 27.

Simon, H. and Butscher, S. (2001), 'Individualized Pricing: Boosting Profitability with the Higher Art of Power Pricing', *European Management Journal*, 19 (2), pp. 109–14.

Simon, Lord D. (2000), 'EMU and the Opportunities for British Business', in M. Baimbridge, B. Burkitt, and P. Whyman (eds), *A Single Currency for Europe?*, London: Macmillan.

Singh, S. (2001), 'The Move to Cheaper Sleeping', *Marketing Week*, 14 June, pp. 38-9.

Smith, D. (1998), 'How Single Is the Single Market?', *Management Today*, January, pp. 55–8.

Smith, D. (1999), 'Life with the Euro', *Sunday Times*, 3 January, p. 3.5.

Thompson, K. and Coe, B. (1997), 'Gaining Sustainable Competitive Advantage Through Strategic Pricing: Selecting a Perceived Value Price', *Pricing Strategy and Practice*, 5 (2), pp. 70–9.

Trapp, R. (2000), 'The Visionary Service is for Your Eyes Only', *The Independent*, 10 December.

Upton, G. (2001), 'Budget Hotels, But They Have All the Frills', *Evening Standard*, 19 February, p. 72.

Vidal, J. (2002), 'Treachery on the Shelves', *The Guardian*, 24 January, p. 19.

Watkins, K. (2001), 'Spilling the Beans', *The Guardian*, 16 May, p. 9.

Western Mail (2002), 'First Milk Stops Supplies to Express Dairies', *Western Mail*, 15 January, p. 4

Whyman, P. (2001), 'The Impact of Economic and Monetary Union on British Business', *European Business Journal*, 13 (1), pp. 28–36.

Zeithaml, V.A. (1988), 'Consumer Perceptions of Price, Quality and Value', *Journal of Marketing*, 52 (July), pp. 2–22.

chapter 11

pricing strategies

LEARNING OBJECTIVES

This chapter will help you to:

1 understand the managerial process that leads to price setting and the influences that affect its outcomes;

2 appreciate the multiple and sometimes conflicting objectives impacting on pricing decisions;

3 define a range of available pricing strategies and their application in different market and competitive situations;

4 understand the available pricing methods and tactics, and their most appropriate use; and

5 appreciate some of the special issues affecting pricing in B2B markets.

Introduction

Economists' models of pricing tend to be based on costs and simplified models of demand structures without taking into account the reality of the marketing situation. It is rare to find that pricing can be achieved through the simple application of a formula, since the actions of marketers and competitors, as well as the perceptions and behaviour of consumers all have an influence on the pricing decision. Chapter 10 outlined many of these internal and external influences. The reality of pricing is that organisations do not have perfect information, as the economists assume, nor are consumers and competitors passive players in the process. Thus a certain amount of skill is required to assess how both consumers and competitors will respond to a particular pricing decision in the context of a particular marketing mix. The pricing decision is only simple for an organisation that consciously follows the rest of the market rather than tries to lead it.

Building on the foundations of price influences laid down in Chapter 10, this chapter examines the stages that organisations go through to establish the price range and to set the final prices for their products. Figure 11.1 gives an overview of the process. Setting price objectives, stage 1, ensures that the corporate and marketing objectives of the organisation are taken into consideration in the pricing decision. Stage 2, estimating demand, assesses likely market potential and consumer reaction to different price levels, and was covered at pp. 402 *et seq*. Within this structure, marketing managers can then begin to define pricing policy in stage 3. This is the guiding philosophical framework within which pricing strategies and decisions are determined.

eg

Research by the Henley Centre suggested that different groups of consumers value time differently. 'Cash rich' but 'time poor' customers might be prepared to pay more for their products and services if they can access the service more quickly and conveniently than if they waste time queueing. This has led to some supermarkets considering the introduction of a fast-moving checkout line in which customers pay more for the benefit of moving through the line more quickly. One problem is avoiding offence to the majority of customers who want good service but are not prepared to pay a premium. There could also be problems if the majority of customers elect to take the fast lane. Research has suggested that one in four full-time workers would be interested in using such a system.

Another way of using price to manage retail and service traffic is 'off-peak discounts'. B&Q, for example, offered a 10 per cent discount to pensioners if they used the store on a Wednesday. Restaurants use 'happy hours' to encourage early evening customers and cinemas offer, like B&Q, pensioner matinees at low entrance prices. It is possible to vary price effectively by time of day, week, month or year as long as the marketer understands the impact on existing and potential customers, communicates the conditions of the offer clearly, and makes sure that the customer base accepts the validity of the basis for the price discrimination.

Figure 11.1 Determining a price range – overview

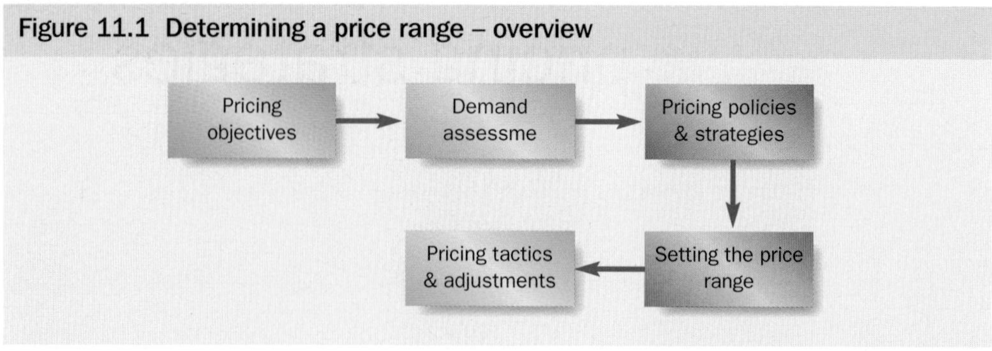

Pricing strategies deal with the long-term issues of positioning within the market and the achievement of corporate and marketing objectives. Establishing cost–volume–profit relationships at stage 4 checks that the estimated sales of the product can generate acceptable levels of income at any given price in order to cover costs and make an adequate profit. Implicit in all of this is the fact that pricing has to take place in a competitive environment, and thus the marketing manager must assess how competitors will react to various possible prices, and the extent to which the proposed price reflects the desired competitive positioning of the organisation and its products.

These first four stages culminate in stage 5, pricing tactics and final adjustments that focus on the practical application of pricing in the marketing mix and in the context of the market segments to be served. Pricing procedures set the method by which prices are calculated in the light of strategies to arrive at the final figure. Tactics, however, allow those prices to be varied on a planned, structured basis or in the shorter term on a one-off or irregular basis, perhaps to take advantage of sudden market opportunities or to overcome unforeseen difficulties.

Although Figure 11.1 presents a neat, logical flow, in reality the pricing decision is likely to involve many reiterations and merging of stages. Some stages may be omitted, others may be extended to take into account special conditions within a market. There may also be conflict, for example between corporate level pressure to maximise profit and competitive assessment that indicates a market that is already well served at the higher-priced end. Such conflicts need to be resolved to avoid the risks of inconsistent pricing within a poorly defined marketing mix. It is also difficult to generalise about the price-setting process, not only because it operates uniquely in every organisation, but also because it will vary greatly between different types of product and market depending on the dynamics and maturity of the specific situation.

Finally, this chapter reviews some of the special considerations connected with price setting in B2B markets, such as negotiation, tendering and the setting of internally derived transfer prices between different departments or divisions of an organisation.

First, however, we discuss the general stages of the pricing process outlined in Figure 11.1, beginning with pricing objectives.

Pricing objectives

Any planned approach needs to be founded on what has to be achieved, and that applies as much to pricing as to anything else. Its role in the marketing mix as well as its role as the generator of revenue and profit has to be defined. In that sense, price is a delicate balance between serving the customer's needs and wants and serving the need of the organisation to recoup its costs of manufacturing and marketing and to make a profit.

Price objectives, therefore, should be closely linked with organisational and marketing objectives (Baumol, 1965). Some of these may be financially based, whereas others may be related to volume of sales. Pricing objectives thus have implications for many functional areas of the business, such as finance, production and distribution, as well as for marketing.

Those other functional areas may also influence pricing. If in the short term, for example, finance detects a cash flow problem, marketers may be pressurised into dropping prices to convert products into cash quickly. In the longer term, the corporate strategists may see the organisation's only means of survival to be the defeat of a major competitor, and price may be a key weapon in that. This also underlines the fact that objectives need not be absolutely fixed; they can vary in the short or long term to meet changing needs and pressures.

eg

Preferences in the £600 mn pizza market are changing. Frozen pizza sales through supermarkets have been declining while fresh chilled pizza is growing in popularity as it is associated with better quality, taste and freshness. ASDA has deliberately positioned itself to take advantage of that shift. As market prices for chilled pizza generally increased, ASDA deliberately reduced its prices so that a standard chilled pizza cost £1.59 in ASDA compared with the market average of £1.98. Despite rises in raw material prices, ASDA has sought to retain permanent savings as part of its 'every day low pricing' (EDLP) strategy. ASDA claims that EDLP aims to reinforce its overall competitive position by offering 10–15 per cent better value than its competitors (*The Grocer*, 2001c; Hardcastle, 2001; Mintel 2001b).

Inevitably, where there are so many objectives relating to so many functional areas, conflicts will arise. In that case, management must work to ensure that compromises and decisions are made, and priorities set in the best interests of the organisation and its customers.

As with objectives in any area of management, pricing objectives must be clearly defined, detailed, time specific and never inconsistent with each other (Diamantopoulos and Mathews, 1995). Clearly, these ideals are easier to achieve in an organisation dealing with a small number of large transactions or a few products. The complexity increases, however, for an organisation dealing in a number of markets, with a large number of customers, or with a number of products. Many Japanese companies tend to take a longer-term view of pricing and consider the profit not from individual product lines alone, but from the whole portfolio of products (Howard and Herbig, 1996). By taking a long-term view, price is considered in the context of the value of the relationship over the longer term, rather than as a short-term opportunity to increase profits. Rather than letting costs dictate prices, the tendency among Japanese companies is to set the price on long-term market considerations and then to work backwards to get costs into line.

In summary, Figure 11.2 shows the basis of conflicting objectives between different functional areas of the organisation, and each of these will be further discussed below, starting with financial objectives.

Figure 11.2 Conflicting price objectives

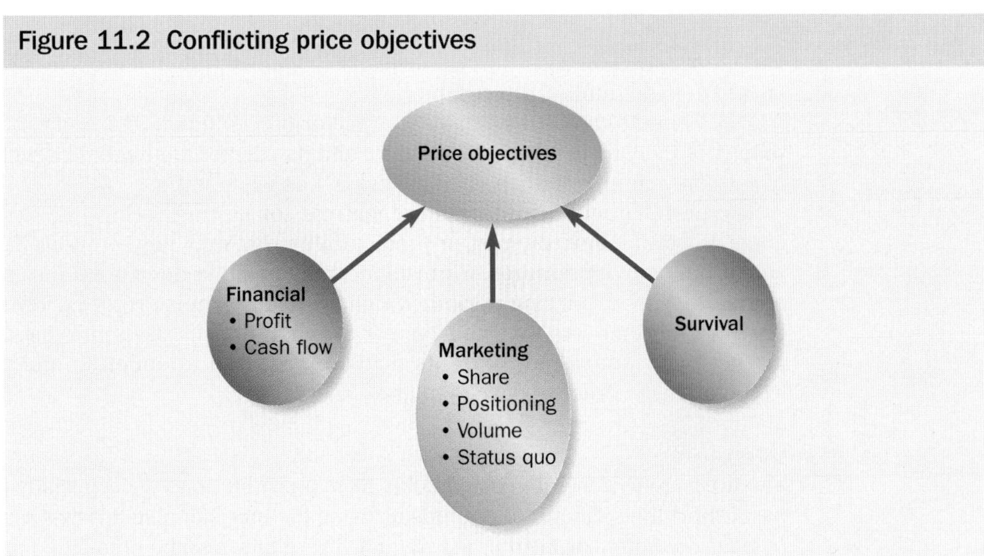

Financial objectives

Financial objectives can have both short- and long-term dimensions. For instance, the necessity to generate sufficient cash flow to fund the day-to-day operation of the organisation is a short-term objective, whereas the need to generate funds to allow reinvestment in research and development is a longer-term goal. Long-term objectives ultimately provide the means of satisfying shareholder expectations and generating the means of investing in sound foundations for the future.

Most financial objectives centre on either profit or cash flow. We look at profit-based objectives first.

Profit

Return on investment. Pricing is used in the context of return on investment as the means of achieving a specified rate of return on the investment made in the product. One of the interesting questions relating to return on investment (ROI) is the length of time it should take to recoup that investment and begin generating clear profit. If a long-term ROI is acceptable, that gives the marketer the opportunity to build the product strategically, creating and protecting market share through planned market penetration with strong marketing support. It means that the product can be allowed to develop at its own pace with less risk of its existence or position being threatened by management looking for a quick, clear profit.

Short-term ROI implies more of a performance orientation. The product is under pressure to generate large amounts of cash to pay for itself and make a clear profit quickly. The danger is that these pressures can lead to inappropriate marketing strategies, for example setting too high a price or attempting to make a niche product into a mass-market item to generate volume sales in order to bring in revenue. This lack of patience can, therefore, jeopardise the product's success and thus severely reduce the eventual return on the organisation's investment.

There is a skill involved in setting target ROI, not only because it assumes a degree of knowledge of revenue and cost behaviour that may not be possessed, but also because it has to balance the short-term pressure to bring money in against the possible longer-term strategic desire to build market position slowly but thoroughly. The more volatile and the less predictable the market environment into which the product is being launched, the more problematic becomes the ROI decision.

Profit maximisation. Economics texts often talk of profit maximisation as an organisation's ultimate goal. In reality, an organisation may actually settle for profit satisfaction based on whatever targets have been negotiated through the short- and long-term business plan. Maximisation is an impossible ideal, as it implies perfect knowledge of the cost and demand function beyond the organisation's previous experience. It is particularly impracticable, for example, in a smaller organisation where the owners may not have the time or the inclination, let alone the expertise, to build a maximisation model. Satisfaction based on knowledge of the market and previous experience, however imperfect, may be the main objective to be fulfilled through pricing.

Profit targets can be measured in actual or percentage terms, and can be based on expectations of the way in which the product and its market are likely to develop or expectations of year-on-year growth, namely that past trends will continue.

The problem with profit-based objectives for pricing is that they encourage a sense of control over the environment or predictability that may not be either justifiable or sustainable. Competitive pressures, for instance, may create a downward pull on prices during the course of the accounting period, which will compromise target profits. Alternatively, an organisation that sets its profit targets too high may create a pricing structure within the market that attracts new entrants who are prepared to undercut and accept lower profit expectations in order to develop market share.

Cash flow

The pressure to generate cash quickly from a product may be especially great if the product has a short lifecycle, such as goods utilising the merchandising rights associated with a film (e.g. *Harry Potter* or *Lord of the Rings*). There may also be pressure if a producer feels that there is only a short lead time available to capitalise on a new product before heavy competition enters the market.

Cash flow considerations are also strong where an organisation has high operating costs and/or fluctuating or seasonal demand. A retailer who stocks lawnmowers, for example, may be prepared to sell the machines at a lower price at the end of the summer in order to turn the stock into hard cash, to avoid the costs of keeping the stock over the winter and to clear the warehouse in preparation for the latest models to be introduced next spring. All of this is worth the reduced margins on the mowers sold cheaply.

Sales and marketing objectives

Clearly, sales and marketing objectives are important influencers of the pricing decision. Target market share, relative position within the market and target volume sales can all be affected through pricing choices.

Market share and positioning

An organisation's marketing objectives may relate to either maintaining or increasing market share. The implications of this for pricing need to be carefully considered. Maintenance of market share in a highly competitive market may mean that prices cannot be increased for the next trading period, or even that they have to be reduced to face competitors who undercut. Increasing market share may mean aggressively low pricing to attract switchers from competing products. Alternatively, high prices might help to establish a high-quality position that appeals to more discerning customers.

The interaction between price and quality, and the need for consistency between them, are shown in Figure 11.3. Where price and quality are equal, or where quality level exceeds price, the consumer certainly benefits and thus the seller may have established a useful position. If the price exceeds the quality, however, to the bottom left of the matrix, the offering represents bad value for money and the seller is likely to lose customers unless something is done to remedy the inconsistency.

Obviously, price is not the only factor affecting performance. Astute use of advertising, for example, may help to achieve market share objectives without giving way so much on price. Using price this way as a competitive weapon may be less effective than hoped, since price moves are too easily copied by other organisations.

Volume sales

Seeking volume sales may well be related to market share objectives, but arises more from an operational focus on capacity. In different kinds of production activity, pricing may be used as a means of maintaining the operational smooth running of the organisation. With continuous production, involving the mass production of identical products, there is the ability to pile up stocks of the finished product until it is sold. At some point, however, the

Figure 11.3 Price–quality matrix

Price		Product quality: *Low*	Product quality: *Medium*	Product quality: *High*
	Low	Economy position	Value position	Excellent value strategy Underpriced?
	Medium	Poor value position Overpriced?	Medium value position	Value position Underpriced?
	High	Poor value strategy Overpriced?	Poor value position Unsupported price premium	Premium positioning

marketing in action

Putting the sizzle back into the sausage market

Lazenby's (http://www.lazenbys.co.uk) has helped to create a premium-priced, upmarket niche within a sausage market that was dominated by mass-produced products sold on low price. The company has become the market leader in the premium sausage niche market, a move that has proved highly profitable for a relatively small firm in the market. The business started in 1983 with just one Dicker-filler, a hand-operated sausage machine. At that time, UK supermarket sausage prices were between 49p and 69p per pack. Lazenby's positioned itself at around the £1 mark, a price that meant that it took five years before the first supermarket contract was won. Meanwhile, the brand image developed, centred on a traditional image of a smiling butcher, Mr Lazenby, suitably attired in a clean, white butcher's apron.

By 2001, sales of fresh, frozen and loose sausages were worth around £430 mn, with over £100 mn sold at the premium end of the market. During 2001, although the market overall grew by 3 per cent, the premium sector grew by 7 per cent as consumers continued to trade-up to better quality products. Many manufacturers had developed premium brands and in the constant search for differentiation had introduced products made from more and more exotic meats (venison, wild boar, ostrich and kangaroo, for example), herbs, spices and added ingredients (such as beer, cranberry and mushroom). O'Hagan is one such competitor who claims to be making Britain's best sausages. He claims that his recipes have been copied for years and in an effort to regain control, has launched a branding and licensing operation for O'Hagan sausage shops for sales through pubs and restaurants. The small company makes 130 different varieties of sausage each week and claims more than 2,000 recipes. Each is a premium sausage, with a high meat content, minimal fat and salt, and no artificial ingredients (Davies, 2001).

Mr Lazenby has had to be as innovative as the rest and has been very active in new product development to sustain the premium price position. Over the past few years, the Mr Lazenby brand has been extended to include a crispy coated sausage in 'hot and spicy' and 'Chinese' flavours to appeal to the youth market. Special occasions also provide sausage opportunities. The exotic Mr Lazenby sausage containing oysters, pork and ginger was a one-off concoction targeted, perhaps not surprisingly, at all those lovers around St Valentine's Day. Each year it plans to launch a few new sausage flavours to allow loyal customers to experiment a little more.

The quality theme extends throughout the raw material and production process. The combination is simple: 100 per cent pork, natural skins and real flavourings. Price tends to be used by consumers as a quality indicator in the sausage market, although in reality, higher-priced products do not always use higher-quality ingredients. In 2001, Mr Lazenby was one of the first sausage manufacturers to introduce a new quality inspection mark scheme policed by the independent European Food Safety Inspection Service (EFSIS).

Despite occupying a premium position, Lazenby's still had some tough negotiating to do with the larger supermarket chains as it expanded its distribution. Richard Lazenby, the owner, claimed:

> *I know for a fact that one major UK supermarket chain is making margins of 45 per cent on our products and 90 per cent of that is profit – but it's always the supplier who ends up having to carry the can.*

Love is ...

Source: Mr Lazenby's Sausages/Northern Profile.

Pressures on margins and the need to reinvest in new equipment to retain the leadership position in a growth market means that premium prices are an essential part of the overall strategy.

Sources: Darwent (1996); Davies (2001); *The Grocer* (2001b); Mintel (2001a).

stockpiles may become unacceptably large, leading to pressure to sell at a discount to clear them. In a recession, for instance, many car manufacturers face this problem if they keep their production lines running at more or less normal capacity in the hope that the market will pick up soon.

Batch or unit production, involving the production of small numbers (even down to one-off jobs) of different goods at a time, is more concerned with keeping the business afloat than with the running of a particular line. Shipbuilding operates in this way; while one job is being carried out, management are looking to fill the order book for the future, whether with large multimillion-pound projects or with small maintenance jobs just to keep the workforce occupied and make a contribution to overheads. Pricing is used very aggressively in such markets to win the contract that will secure the short- or long-term future of the organisation.

In a service industry, because of the inherent perishability of the product, price becomes more important as the deadline for service delivery approaches. In a hotel, for example, if it means the difference between letting a room tonight and not letting it, then price may become negotiable for an eleventh-hour potential guest. Pricing is also used extensively in service situations as a means of evening out fluctuating demand. Again, in the hotel industry, weekend or midweek special deals help to direct demand to the quieter parts of the week, allowing the hotelier to maintain occupancy rates while still recouping the variable costs of so doing.

Status quo

Linked closely with maintaining market share, the objective of preserving the *status quo* implies an organisation that is happy for things to continue as they are and does not want the market's boat to be rocked. Even a market leader may be happy simply to retain share rather than seek even more, and may prefer not to challenge a smaller, lower-priced competitor for fear of damaging its own position in the process.

eg

Icelandair's (http://www.icelandair.is) average fare to the USA is 35 per cent lower than that of bigger airlines such as SAS, and it carries more Norwegians and Swedes to Florida than any other airline. The other airlines are happy for Icelandair to do this, however, since the airline is not perceived as a serious threat because of the small scale of its operations. In 2001, it operated just twelve Boeing 737 and 757 aircraft, which as narrow-bodied jets are not ideally suited to transatlantic travel. Use of such planes also means a landing or change at Reykjavik, a choice that many travellers might pay extra to avoid, especially in winter!

One of the problems of using pricing as a means of gaining share is indeed the risk of a price war. One organisation reduces its prices and then all the others start a downward spiral of undercutting. The ultimate outcome of this is that margins become increasingly small, the weakest organisations fall by the wayside, relative market shares are unlikely to change, and nobody wins other than the consumer. This is a very expensive way of maintaining the *status quo*. Even a smaller supplier may elect to maintain the *status quo* by matching rather than challenging competitors' prices. According to Perks (1993), to win a price war, an organisation should only target weaker competitors, fight from a position of strength and extend the war over a long period to wear down the competition.

An organisation may, of course, choose to match prices in some product areas, but not in others. Even the upmarket UK supermarkets, for example, are seen to compete aggressively on price on a select number of basic product lines, yet quietly make up for this by charging price premiums on others.

Price as a stabiliser can, therefore, be a very powerful force. It also strengthens the arguments for a philosophy of profit satisfaction rather than maximisation, as discussed at p. 430 above, through the trade-off between the perceived gains and losses of failing to follow on price.

Price matching rather than undercutting may well maintain the *status quo*, but it also opens the door for non-price competition, where the focus is on the other elements of the marketing mix. An organisation that can demonstrate that it offers a better product (by whatever criteria matter to the target market) can neutralise, to some extent, the market's sensitivity to price. This is difficult to do, but it does mean that it is easier to build and retain loyalty, thus defending against competitive erosion of both market share and margins. The more price sensitive the customers, the less loyal they are.

corporate social responsibility *in action*

Money going up in smoke

The price of a packet of cigarettes is a complicated and contentious issue. The price is influenced not only by the usual business-orientated considerations, but also by the imposition of significant levels of duty by governments. While smokers and tobacco companies feel that levels of duty are too high, the anti-smoking lobby want to see increased duty forcing prices high enough to deter people from smoking. For governments, however, tobacco contributes a lot to the exchequer and they have to tread a fine line when setting duty between raising revenues and promoting a healthier society. Just before the budget statement in Ireland in 2001, the Office of Tobacco Control called for the price of a packet of 20 cigarettes to be doubled to deter young people from starting to smoke, as with growing affluence, cigarettes had come within the purchasing power of children. In the event, the Irish smoker breathed a sigh (or more likely a cough) of relief as price increases averaged just 10 pence as the government was more concerned with the effect price rises on inflation.

This example typifies the debate over cigarette prices that leaves the cigarette manufacturers constantly under pressure to justify their existence. Dr John Garner, chairman of the British Medical Association's Scottish Council is quoted as saying that 'tobacco duty saves lives; taxes are never going to be popular, but quite simply, higher prices make people stop smoking and encouraging those who smoke to quit' (as quoted by Starrs, 2001). Currently in the UK around 80 per cent of the cost of a packet of cigarettes is duty. The manufacturers get around 12 per cent and the wholesale and retail trade the remaining 8 per cent. With such high rates of duty, it is profitable for smugglers to bring cigarettes into the UK from France and Belgium, where lower duties can mean savings of around £2 per packet of 20. It has been estimated that up to one-third of cigarettes in the UK are smuggled and that the government loses between £3 bn and £4 bn in duty per annum. If people are buying cheap cigarettes from a dodgy bloke in the pub, it is also bad news for the retail trade. Often tobacco sales can represent up to 25 per cent of turnover, but in order to remain even remotely competitive, margins are often less than 10 per cent. In addition, cigarettes, like newspapers, are traffic builders for independent retailers, drawing people into the shop where they are then likely to make other impulse purchases.

Gallaher, with brands such as Benson & Hedges and Silk Cut dominates the premium end of the cigarette market, operating in a challenging environment in which government, consumer groups and smugglers all have a major impact on sales. The company has, however, sought to take a responsible approach to cigarette manufacturing, claiming to sell its products only to informed adult smokers, people who have a right and have exercised their right to smoke. It operates a corporate website to encourage a sensible debate on smoking and health (http://www.gallaher-group.com). It is also proud of its record in promoting debate on the risks associated with smoking. As a defence against being priced out of the market or from cigarettes being banned altogether, it espouses a number of principles to demonstrate its approach to corporate social responsibility:

1 It must be clear to all that a real health risk exists. People who choose to smoke are more likely to contract certain diseases than those who do not smoke. Indeed, for many years, Gallaher has proceeded on the basis that some smokers are more likely to contract certain diseases, such as lung cancer, heart disease and certain other circulatory and respiratory diseases, than non-smokers.
2 Gallaher recognises the rights and responsibilities of governments around the world to regulate the manufacture, distribution and marketing of tobacco products. However, regulation does need to be balanced and demonstrably correct in the pursuit of public health policy objectives.
3 Gallaher remains committed to making product changes that are capable of reducing the risks associated with smoking while recognising that there is no conclusive consensus of approach to what is a safer cigarette.
4 Gallaher has successfully pursued a policy of lowering tar yields and continues this today. This policy of gradual reduction was adopted by Gallaher and subsequently endorsed by the UK Government.
5 Gallaher acknowledges that, in today's language, smoking is regarded as addictive. Gallaher believes that although smoking is a habit, and for some a very strong habit, people can give up smoking and do so.
6 Gallaher acknowledges that there are those in the public health community who believe that environmental tobacco smoke poses a health risk to non-smokers. But, whilst readily accepting that environmental tobacco smoke can be a source of considerable annoyance to non-smokers, the conclusions reached by those in the public health community appear to be based upon weak and inconclusive science.

7 Gallaher recognises the role of governments around the world to set the tax levels for the sale of tobacco products. The company believes that taxes should be set at a fair level; smokers should not be punished financially for the pleasure of being smokers.
8 Gallaher believes that only informed adults should smoke; children should not smoke. The company has supported a number of initiatives over the years addressed at reducing the incidence of smoking by children, the most recent being a commitment to print the message 'For adult use only' on all packs of the company's cigarettes sold around the world.
9 Gallaher believes that the prime responsibility for communicating health messages to the public about smoking is that of government. It would be inappropriate for the company to do anything that would in any way undermine or challenge such health communications. However, the company does additionally accept its own responsibility to communicate a reminder to smokers, each and every time they pick up a pack of a tobacco product, that there is a health risk associated with smoking.
(Extracted and adapted from http://www.gallaher-group.com).

So where does this leave the pricing debate? If tobacco companies are prepared to accept their social responsibility, should the price of a packet of cigarettes be allowed to reflect market conditions and compete with the smugglers or should it be kept artificially high to reflect public health objectives?

Sources: Bedington (2001); *The Grocer* (2001a, 2001d, 2001e); Starrs (2001); http://www.gallaher-group.com.

Survival

In difficult economic circumstances, survival can become the only motivating objective for an organisation. Long-term strategic objectives have no currency if you are likely to be out of business tomorrow. Imagine a small company that has found that its market does not have the potential it originally predicted. Price is a very obvious and flexible marketing mix element to change in order to keep goods flowing out and cash flowing in. As discussed at p. 433 above, even a larger firm, such as a shipbuilder, may be prepared to suffer short-term losses to keep the operation intact, even though this cannot be sustained indefinitely without reducing the size of the operation in some way.

Pricing policies and strategies

Pricing policies and strategies guide and inform the pricing decision, providing a framework within which decisions can be made with consistency and with the approval of the organisation as a whole. Policies and strategies help to specify the role of pricing and its use in context of the marketing mix (Nagle, 1987). Such frameworks are especially important in larger organisations where pricing decisions may be delegated with some discretion to line managers or sales representatives. They need sufficient rules to maintain a consistent corporate image in front of the market without being unduly restricted.

There are many situations in which a sales representative, for instance, may need policy guidance. Imagine a sales representative visiting a customer who tells him that a competitor is offering a similar product more cheaply. Company policy will help the representative to decide whether or not to get involved in undercutting or whether to sell the product benefits harder.

Other situations where policy and strategy guidelines may be of use include responding to a competitive price threat in a mass market, setting prices for new or relaunched products, modifying price in accordance with prevailing environmental conditions, using price with other marketing mix elements and, finally, using price across the product range to achieve overall revenue and profit targets. Some of these situations are discussed in more detail below. In any situation, guidelines can provide the basis for more detailed pricing strategies designed to achieve price objectives. These guidelines should be founded on sound pricing research that encompasses competitors' strategies and customers' views of value, as well as internal costs (Monroe and Cox, 2001).

New product pricing strategies

In addition to all the other pressures and risks inherent in new product development, as discussed in Chapter 9, it is important to get the launch price right as it can be difficult to change it later. It can be easy and tempting to set a low price to attract customers to a new launch, but this can establish attitudes and perceptions of the quality and positioning of the brand that would be difficult to overturn. A subsequent price rise might be viewed with some hostility by the customer. The safest route to low price entry with an option of raising it later is to make the price a promotional issue. Clearly signalling the low price as an introductory offer, a short-term trial price both attracts attention and encourages trial of the new product, and when the price does rise to its 'normal' level, there is no confusion or suspicion in the customer's mind.

eg

When Whitworths launched 'Sunny Raisin' targeted as a healthy alternative snack for kids, it decided to offer a special introductory price of 99p instead of the normal £1.49 for 18 snack packs. This promotion was designed to encourage trial and attract kids to the supporting website (http://www.sunnyraisin.co.uk) which builds Californian Cool characters such as the Unraisinable Brothers and Rockin Robbie using trendy words such as 'dig' and 'dork'.

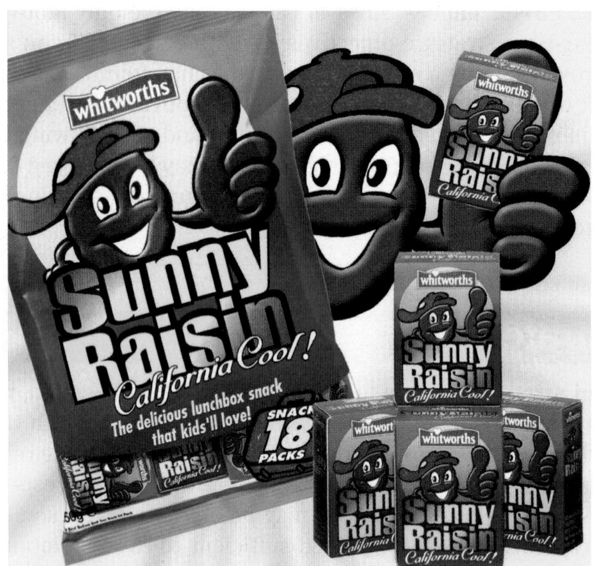

Sunny Raisins are sold in handy-sized boxes for children to take in their lunchboxes or schoolbags as a high energy snack or as an alternative to crisps or chocolate.

Source: Whitworths Foods.

Another aspect of the high or low price setting decision is the likely impact on the competition. A high price might encourage them to enter the market too, as they see potentially high profit margins. The organisation launching the new product may not, however, have too much choice. Internal pressure to recoup development costs quickly, as discussed at p. 430, may force a high price, or alternatively a price-sensitive market might simply reject a high price and force prices lower.

According to Monroe and Della Bitta (1978), much depends on how innovative the new product is. A new brand in a crowded market can be precise with its price positioning as there are many competitors to compare with, and both the price setter and the consumer can 'read' the price signals clearly. A completely unknown product, such as the very first domestic video recorder, has no such frame of reference. The price setter can work on three things. First, the prices of other domestic electrical goods might give clues as to the sort of prices consumers expect to pay. This is a tenuous link because this new product is so obviously different it may not be comparable, especially in the mind of an opinion-leading consumer. Second, market research may have been carried out to discover how enthusiastic consumers are about the new idea, and hypothetically what they would pay to possess it. Again, this may be misleading because the consumers have no experience of this product and may not themselves be able to foresee in theory how they would respond in practice.

Third, the price setter can work on internal factors such as costs, breakeven analysis and return on investment. This serves as a starting point and experience and emerging competition will allow a more realistic price structure to evolve. It is a dangerous route, however. If that cost-based price turns out to be inappropriate, rescuing the product could be almost impossible, particularly if astute competitors are learning from your mistakes and launching realistically priced products themselves.

With all this in mind, the high or low entry price decision boils down to two alternative strategies, **skimming** or **penetration**, first proposed by Dean (1950).

Price skimming

In order to skim, prices are set high to attract the least price-sensitive market segments. Such pricing might appeal, for instance, to opinion leaders who want to be seen to be first with any new product regardless of the price, or to those who seek status and see high price as the mark of an exclusive product.

Skimming has a number of advantages. It allows the organisation to establish a quality brand image that could serve as a stepping stone to future development of lower-priced, more mass-market versions. If the product in question is a difficult one to produce, then pricing to keep the market small and exclusive can also give breathing space to gain learning experience on lower volumes while still marketing the product in a real market. The risk here, of course, is that high price raises high expectations, and if that learning experience does not go well, then the market will think that the product quality is too poor or inconsistent to justify the price, a bad reputation will stick and the future of the product becomes questionable. Finally, it is easier to reduce price than to raise it. If an initial high price does not generate the required response, it can be slowly lowered until an appropriate level is found.

eg

High definition digital television sets were priced high when they were first launched but prices are now starting to drop in the USA and Europe. In 1998, a 60 inch projection unit would have cost around $8,000, but by 2001 it could be bought for around $3,000. The dramatic drop in price could be due to economies of scale, as the volume of sales has risen with consumers' growing appreciation of high definition picture quality for DVD usage. It could also be an outcome of the manufacturer's journey along a learning curve: as cumulative sales volumes build, the manufacturer gets more efficient at making the televisions and the manufacturing cost per unit falls. Finally, increasing competition could also have something to do with it, as potential buyers start to have more choice and can make price comparisons. Whatever the causes, the pioneering manufacturers are now able to lower prices and this in itself helps support further expansion in demand as more price-sensitive segments for home entertainment can be targeted (Heller, 2001).

Penetration pricing

In an attempt to gain as big a market share as possible in the shortest possible time, an organisation may price aggressively below existing competition, deliberately paring its margins for the sake of volume. This is *penetration pricing*. It may be a necessary strategy if cost structures are such that a very large volume of sales is required to break even or to achieve economies of scale in production or marketing terms. It is a risky strategy because it could establish a poor-quality brand image and also, if it does not work, it would be very difficult to raise the price.

It is, nevertheless, a legitimate strategy to seek to deny the competition volume share within the market. Penetration pricing of a new product, particularly in a market where product differentiation is difficult, reduces the attractiveness of market entry to competitors unless they can be sure that they can produce and market much more efficiently and on a tighter cost base. Penetration pricing is also useful in elastic demand situations where price is a critical factor for the buyer.

As emphasised above, the choice of launch price should take into account future plans for the pricing and positioning of the product. Some products can enter a market with a skimming price and retain it, particularly luxury goods that are well differentiated from each other and have an element of uniqueness about them. The Swiss company Bueche Girod, for example, advertised a 9 carat gold and diamond ladies' watch for £1,675 with a matching necklace for a further £2,975. In markets where a new product has a high level of technological innovation and customers have no benchmark against which to compare prices, the introductory price may skim, but this will give way to something more competitive as rival products enter the market, economies of scale are achieved and costs reduce with the learning curve. In contrast, penetration pricing at launch sets an aggressive, value for money stance that the manufacturer would find hard to break away from, regardless of what the competition do. This product will always have to be priced competitively.

Product mix pricing strategies

A product that is part of a product range cannot be priced in isolation from the rest of the range. The range has to be viewed as an entity, and different products serve different purposes that come together to benefit the whole. In seeking to serve the needs of a number of market segments and build a strong competitive defence across the market, one product may be allowed to earn a relatively low return while another is skimming.

Within an individual product line (*see* pp. 276 *et seq.* for the distinction between range and line), such as SLR cameras, each product within the line offers additional features and their pricing needs to be spaced out accordingly. Customers see the set of products within the line and relate the price steps with additional features, benefits or quality. This may also encourage consumers to trade up to a more expensive model in the line as they begin to indulge in a type of marginal analysis: 'For an extra £20 I can have a zoom facility as well. Seems like a better deal . . .'. The process may not be so rational. As discussed at p. 394, price may be used as an indicator of quality in the absence of other knowledge or indicators. Thus a buyer may find a model within the product line at (or slightly beyond) the preconceived spending limit and feel that the best possible quality purchase has been made, regardless of whether the product benefits and features are useful or appropriate.

Rather than presenting a predetermined collection of standard products with standard prices, some organisations prefer to offer a basic-priced product to which the consumer can then add extras, each of which adds to the overall price. The beauty of this is that the basic price seems very reasonable and affordable, and thus the consumer can easily get to the stage of wanting the product. Once that stage is reached, the odd few pounds here and there for extra features seems insignificant, even though the final total price may be somewhat higher than the consumer would have been comfortable with in the first place. At least the customer is getting a personally tailored purchase.

eg

Holiday packages prominently feature low prices on their brochures to attract attention and make themselves seem eminently affordable. Two weeks in the sun for only £99 per person soon increases to something closer to £300 when airport transfers and taxes are added, along with the supplements for a local departure, insurance, better-quality accommodation with a sea view, full board, and an August rather than May holiday. Buying a car is also a minefield of extras. Delivery charges, taxes, registration plates, metallic paint, sunroof, alarm system, central locking are among the items that may not necessarily be quoted in the advertised price.

The problem with any such approach is knowing what to leave out and what to include in the basic price. A basic price that does not include non-optional items such as tax is likely to lead to an unimpressed customer. There is also the danger that a competitor who comes in with an all-inclusive price may be seen as attractive by customers who feel that they have been deceived by overpriced extras that are actually essentials. In the USA, both General Motors and Ford led the car market in offering *one-price selling* or *value pricing*, where they offered vehicles with a fixed set of options at a fixed, non-negotiable price. Such moves take away the uncertainty about what the real price will be and what is or is not included in the price, as well as relieving the buyer of the ordeal of having to haggle over price (Moskal, 1994).

This discussion has raised issues of the psychology of pricing, which will be further discussed at pp. 450 *et seq.*

Managing price changes

Prices are rarely static for long periods. Competitive pressures may force prices down, either temporarily or permanently, or new market opportunities might increase the price premium on a product. The pressure of cost inflation means that the marketing manager has to decide whether to pass these cost increases on to customers through prices charged, and when. However, changing prices can have a serious effect on profit margins and on market stability. If the changes are too significant, whether on transatlantic air fares or the price of vegetables in the local market, it is almost inevitable that competitors will respond in some way. Price changes not only cause ripples through the market, but also have an impact on sales volume. Normally, it is likely that a price cut will increase volume, and it is sometimes a very fine calculation to predict whether the profit margin earned on the extra volume gained more than compensates for the lost margin caused by the price cut. At various times, an organisation might be faced with the prospect of initiating price changes, or of responding to competitors' price changes.

Initiating price cuts

Initiating price cuts can be a very dangerous activity. Any organisation considering such a move needs to think through carefully the likely impact of any changes on both customers and competitors. Table 11.1 shows how much extra volume needs to be sold to make up for the lost margin on any given price cut. It can be seen that if the initial gross profit margin was 30 per cent and a price cut of 10 per cent was introduced, unit sales would need to increase by 50 per cent just to maintain the original profit level. For even the best of organisations, assessing the likely impact of such a price cut on the market is a tough challenge.

Table 11.1 The impact of price reductions on sales volume

If you cut your price by: %	*If your gross profit margin is (%)* 5	10	15	20	25	30	40
	you need an increase in unit sales of (%):						
1	25.0	11.1	7.1	5.3	4.2	3.4	2.6
2	66.7	25.0	15.4	11.1	8.7	7.1	5.3
3	150.0	42.9	25.0	17.6	13.6	11.1	8.1
4		66.7	36.4	25.0	19.0	15.4	11.1
5		100.0	50.0	33.3	25.0	20.0	14.3
6		150.0	66.7	42.9	31.6	25.0	17.6
7		233.3	87.5	53.8	38.9	30.4	21.2
8			114.3	66.7	47.1	36.4	25.0
9			150.0	81.8	56.3	42.9	29.0
10			200.0	100.0	66.7	50.0	33.3
11			275.5	122.2	78.6	57.9	37.9
12			400.0	150.0	92.3	66.7	42.9
13				185.7	108.3	76.5	48.1
14				233.3	127.3	87.5	53.8
15				300.0	150.0	100.0	60.0
16				400.0	177.8	114.3	66.7
17				566.7	212.5	130.8	73.9
18					275.1	150.0	81.8
19					316.7	172.7	90.5
20					400.0	200.0	100.0
21					525.0	233.3	110.5
22					733.3	275.0	122.2
23						328.6	135.3
24						400.0	150.0
25						500.0	166.7

Nevertheless, organisations still do cut prices from time to time. They may do so for short-term tactical reasons, such as clearing excess stock, or as part of a more fundamental strategic 'value for money' repositioning creating extra savings for consumers (Dodds *et al.*, 1991). Much depends on whether the organisation sees itself as a price leader or follower in the market. A leader may wish to make the first move, leaving competitors with the problem of whether to respond, and how. There are a number of reasons for cutting price, including the following.

Capacity utilisation. Where excess production capacity is found in a market, there is a temptation to lower prices to levels that do not cover full costs, but at least cover the variable cost and make some contribution towards fixed overheads, just to keep the production lines busy. Such price cutting cannot carry on indefinitely, but might serve a useful purpose in the short term until either recovery or shakeout.

eg

The events of 11 September 2001 had major implications for international tourism. London, so often a magnet for foreign tourists, suffered as potential visitors stayed at home. For the hotel sector, room yields, the average amount spent per night per room, dropped by one-third in October 2001 (Bird, 2001). West End audiences were down by 15 per cent over the same period. Although in the long term the visitors are expected to return, in the short term a lot of capacity remains unfilled.

One hotel closed temporarily, but many cut their room rates by up to two-thirds in a bid to attract guests, even though many were UK resident rather than high spending international tourists. One journalist undertook some first-hand research and found that up to four different prices were available depending upon the method of contact (Chesshyre, 2001). At the London Hilton the published rate was £382 for a double room mid-week. £200 was offered on the telephone, which was reduced to £176 after a bit of haggling. Buying through Superbreaks reduced the rate to £136 on a bed and breakfast basis. Similar savings could be found at Claridges and Jury's Kensington. However, as soon as the tourists return and capacity increases, rates will once again move closer to the published levels.

Market dominance. If an organisation enjoys a strong price and cost leadership position and is not likely to fall foul of competition legislation, it may pay to seek an even more dominant position through selective or across the board price cuts. Such action could help to eliminate or at least squeeze some competitors, but an organisation following this strategy also runs the risk of making customers more price sensitive.

Market defence. If a market segment is under attack or if demand is weak compared with other alternatives, it may pay an organisation to defend its position by lowering prices to minimise the impact of the threat. This could be a dangerous strategy in the long term, but by creating short-term difficulties for the attacker, it may help the organisation to retain share.

A sudden unsignalled price cut might be seen by competitors as the first move in a price war. An organisation needs to be sure that it can win and be sure of what it is going to achieve by such an aggressive act. An advance warning of a price increase is less likely to be viewed with hostility. It gives the competition time to reflect on its implications and to make a considered response, which does not necessarily mean a panic descent into further undercutting. It also allows good customers to stock up at the old prices or enables further negotiation time in B2B markets. Many annual subscriptions to magazines are offered to readers at the existing rate, with a clear indication that the subscription rate will rise in the near future. This is an incentive to 'act now'. An early notification of price increases, often associated with the introduction of new and revised products, gives a short-term flurry of excitement to the market as customers aim to beat the deadline.

Responding to competitors' price cuts

When a competitor initiates price cuts, whether selective or across the board, a very careful response needs to be planned. Much again will depend on how and why the change has taken place. Is it overt and threatening, covert and threatening or clearly signalled with some attempt at justification, for example spare capacity?

The response to a competitor's price cut can take three broad forms: ignoring the decrease, responding head-on by matching or undercutting the competitor or deflecting the decrease, by emphasising added value rather than price.

Ignoring the decrease. This can be a high-risk strategy if the price cut is significant and clearly related to an aggressive campaign to gain market share. Once share is lost it is very difficult to win it back. The brand equity built up may be sufficient to retain loyalty. The value of the brand may actually decrease when consumers relate price to product quality and use price as a proxy for the quality. If consumers think that a lower price means lower quality, it may be best to ignore the price cut, at least in the short term (Yoo *et al.*, 2000).

eg

Many years ago, Bic (http://www.bicworld.com) created turmoil in the pen industry with low pricing, disposability and heavy promotion through mass distribution. Many traditional suppliers failed to spot the threat emerging across Europe quickly enough and lost substantial market share by not responding. The desirability of matching a price cut may depend on whether it is perceived to be a short-term or long-term measure. If it is longer term, there may be a case for introducing an economy brand and repositioning the threatened product slightly more upmarket. This is effectively what happened in the pen industry, as suppliers introduced higher-quality, well-differentiated pens, while seeking to match the lower Bic prices through new cheap alternatives based on a similar competitive formula.

Undercutting. Responding by *undercutting the competitor* might easily lead to a flurry of price cuts, stimulating a price war in which the consumer may well be the only winner. Sectors such as petrol, transatlantic air fares, supermarkets and cross-channel travel have all experienced price wars in recent years. Price war threats are especially prevalent in oligopolistic markets, but many organisations seek to avoid them for the kind of reasons discussed on p. 433 (Lambin, 1993).

Deflecting the cut. *Deflecting the price cut* may be an appropriate option if the cut is not very severe and sufficient brand loyalty and differentiation have reduced customers' price sensitivities (Yoo *et al.*, 2000). Various options can be used to add value to the product at existing prices. This could include larger pack sizes, more features, more services, better packaging or promoting the product quality and benefits more aggressively. In extreme circumstances, of course, the only commercially sensible option may be to concede defeat and move on.

eg

Andrex® brand toilet tissue pricing strategy. Andrex® toilet tissue is consistently priced higher than average UK market, either in terms of everyday shelf price, promotional price or through roll sheet count. Its pricing strategy is directly tied to its product quality and high level of brand equity; in other words, it is based on trust. The Andrex® brand is able to command a higher price due to its exceptional brand equity and by having gained consumers' trust through consistently offering high quality products. The brand has been around for 60 years, has held the UK market's no. 1 position for 40 years, and can proudly claim to have the longest consistent advertising campaign in the country, with its puppy icon. Sustained investments in product innovation and marketing efforts and consistency in marketing strategy and plan implementation have been key to the brand's success. Through premium pricing, the brand is able to drive category value and able to continuously re-invest cash back in the brand to stay relevant to consumers.

Conditions in the market place during 2001, combined with product innovation capabilities, led Andrex® to reduce the number of sheets on a roll, proportionally reduce its pack price in line with sheet reduction, and improve product performance. By holding its price per sheet, Andrex® delivered a better product at proportionally the same price per sheet, hence maintaining its historical premium priced and equity positioning. This launch, along side a campaign of 'Andrex® at a price you'll love', helped to defend and grow market share into 2002, whilst maintaining brand health and brand equity.

® Andrex and the Andrex Puppy are registered trademarks of Kimberly-Clark Ltd.

The main difficulty with responding to price increases is that decisions often have to be made quickly in order to protect short-term volumes and there might be too little time for detailed 'what if . . . ?' planning. Thus the surprise of a sudden price cut from a competitor and the speed of response needed can lead to poor decisions in the long run. The nature of

The cute puppy in this ad emphasises the soft yet strong qualities which Andrex highlights for its toilet tissue.

Source: Kimberley-Clark Ltd.

the response will, in part, reflect the organisation's strategic plans and the importance of the product under threat. If it is central to future development, then careful but decisive action may be needed. If it is a marginal product, perhaps in the later stages of its lifecycle, there may be less sense of urgency.

e-marketing *in action*

Online price comparison puts customers in control

The application of the internet for online supplier selection and trading has created new challenges in creating pricing strategies. Prices are under pressure through the trend towards commoditisation. Once price becomes the major criterion on which purchase is determined, the internet facilitates the selection of the lowest price option. This increases competition which enhances the downwards direction on price. Different approaches to online buying resulting in lower prices are described in Smith and Chaffey (2001), for example:

- Price transparency in supplier selection: as prices are published on the web, buyer comparison of prices is more rapid than ever before.
- Storing prices digitally in databases also enables shopping 'bots' (short for robots) (http://www.shoppingbots.com) and robot shoppers (http://www.searchbots.com) that find the best price. Services such as Kelkoo (http://www.kelkoo.com) enable the user to specify the book or music they wish to purchase and then a database search suggests the lowest cost source. An example of the effect of this on suppliers following a premium pricing strategy is provided by that reported in a dispute between Abbey National and financial comparison site Moneysupermarket.com, *Revolution, October 2000*. The bank had reportedly requested that several comparison sites not list them, but the comparison sites refused to do this and were taken to court.
- Once buyers can (a) specify exactly what they want and (b) identify suppliers – they can run reverse auctions as described in the previous chapter for GlaxoSmithKline. Qualified bidders undercut each other – for both business and consumer products. For example, at MedicineOn-line.com elective procedures such as laser eye corrections or plastic surgery required by a particular customer are fought over by rival practices.
- Aggregated buying or customer unions as introduced by LetsBuyit (http://www.letsbuyit.com) reduce the cost to consumers since a group of say 100 buyers purchase a similar product at a volume buying discount.
- Name your price services such as Priceline (http://www.priceline.com) also lead to increased price competition with the market they operate in – here hotels and air tickets.
- New intermediaries that can sell products without the cost of a retail network also drive down prices, since online cost savings are passed on to customers. Take the car market; at launch several new online car retailers such as Virgin Cars (http://www.virgincars.com) and Jamjar (http://www.jamjar.com) promised 30 per cent savings.
- A final consideration is the move from fixed prices to rental, and leasing prices. Cars, computers, flight simulators and now even music can be hired or leased.

It is likely that as software 'bots' become more sophisticated, more of the pricing selection and negotiation strategy will be performed automatically. A prototype next generation e-commerce server from the University of Washington uses gaming strategies to decide when to bargain even harder during the negotiation of complex contracts.

Source: Smith and Chaffey (2001).

Initiating price increases

Not all price changes involve cuts. Price increases may also be initiated, whether because of cost pressures or for legitimate strategic reasons. As with initiating price cuts, however, any move to raise prices needs to be considered very carefully, to assess customer and competitor response. The likelihood of customer acceptance of the price increase can be estimated from previous experience and from known sensitivity within price ranges. Much, however, will ultimately depend on whether competitors choose to ignore the increase or to follow suit. This assessment need not be based entirely on guesswork. Previous experience, actual and anticipated market conditions, demand stability or volatility and not least an estimation of production capacity within the industry might all influence the likely reaction. Sometimes cost pressures, perhaps arising from increases in wage rates or in raw material prices, affect all competitors in the market, making a general price increase more likely.

Cost pressures. Manufacturers can no longer assume that higher raw material prices can be passed on automatically to customers through higher prices. However, depending in part on the relative bargaining positions, reduced costs might not necessarily be reflected in lower prices to the customer. In the 12 months to June 1998, for instance, food manufacturing prices fell by 1.4 per cent and raw material costs by 7.9 per cent, whereas food retail prices rose by 0.5 per cent.

Curbing demand. Not all price increases are cost driven. In situations where demand is buoyant and shortages are starting to emerge, the supplier can use price to curb demand or to capitalise on the profit opportunity. This can be achieved in several ways other than through a straight price rise. One method is to withdraw concessions or discounts. Thus, for example, the number of cheap seats available on a particular flight often reflects the likely level of overall demand. This emphasises the flexibility and responsiveness of pricing as a marketing tool, since thanks to online booking systems, the airline can adjust its discounts in accordance with sales levels. An indirect way of raising prices is to 'unbundle' the product or service so that elements that were originally included in the price are now charged as extras. What used to be an all-inclusive price for a restaurant meal, for instance, may suddenly no longer include drinks or a service charge. Similarly, installation and training might begin to be charged to the purchaser as an additional cost on a new office word-processing network.

Responding to competitors' price increases

When an organisation is faced with a competitor's price rise, it has to decide whether and how to respond. There are three possible responses: respond in kind by matching the competitor's move; maintain price levels, but differentiate the product by emphasising how much better value it now represents; or refuse to respond at all. Responding in kind is perhaps the safest option from a market stability perspective. Many organisations prefer to follow others in implementing price rises, rather than taking the leadership risks. Smaller firms may use the leader's price as a reference point, follow the price and continue to compete on non-price factors such as location, service and adaptability. Promoting further differentiation may be the best option for defending a niche.

Even if the price increase is replicated, the higher margins can be ploughed back into adding value. This could mean offering more product per sale, or including services that were originally charged for or increasing promotional activity to develop stronger product loyalty. Not responding at all is perhaps the highest-risk option, if it is perceived as an aggressive response designed to gain market share. Smaller firms may have more flexibility in their response, as their actions are likely to have only a marginal impact. For example, larger airlines are unlikely to care whether or not Icelandair follows their price increases.

The specific response selected will primarily depend on how much the other organisations in the market want market stability and to shelter under the price umbrella created by the price leader.

Setting the price range

Once the strategic direction of the pricing decision has been specified, a price range needs to be set within which the final detail of price can be established. A **pricing method** is needed that can generate purposeful and sound prices throughout the year. The method and its rigidity will obviously vary depending on whether the organisation is setting one-off prices for a few products or many prices for a large product range or is in a fast-moving retailing environment.

There are three main pricing methods, which take into account some of the key pricing issues already discussed. They are cost based, demand based and competition based. The organisation may adopt one main method of operation or use a flexible combination depending on circumstance. Each method will be discussed in turn, once the general principles of cost–volume–profit relationships have been established.

The cost–volume–profit relationship

The demand patterns discussed at pp. 402 *et seq.*, although established and understood in their own right, also need to be understood in the context of their relationship with costs, volume of production and profit. The marketer needs to understand how the organisation's costs behave under different conditions, internally and externally generated, in order to appreciate fully the implications of marketing decisions on the operation of the organisation. The marketer should understand the different types of costs and their contribution to the pricing decision. The four most important cost concepts are fixed costs, variable costs, marginal cost and total cost. These are now defined.

Definitions of costs

Fixed costs. Fixed costs are those that do not vary with output in the short term. This category thus includes management salaries, insurance, rent, buildings and machine maintenance, etc. Once output passes a certain threshold, however, extra production facilities might have to be brought on stream and so fixed costs will then show a step-like increase.

Variable costs. Variable costs are those that vary according to the quantity produced. These costs are incurred through raw materials, components, and direct labour used for assembly or manufacture. Variable costs can be expressed as a total or on a per unit basis.

Marginal cost. The change that occurs to total cost if one more unit is added to the production total is the marginal cost.

Total cost. Total cost is all the cost incurred by an organisation in manufacturing, marketing, administering and delivering the product to the customer. Total cost thus adds the fixed costs and the variable costs together.

To reiterate what was said in Chapter 10, costs may not be the only factor involved in setting prices, but they are an important one. No organisation would wish to operate for very long at a level where its selling price was not completely recovering its costs and making some contribution towards profit.

There are two main approaches to examining the cost–volume–profit relationship: marginal analysis and breakeven analysis.

Marginal analysis

Marginal analysis is concerned with what happens to a business when production or sales changes by just one unit. The focus is, therefore, on what is happening to costs and revenues at the very edge or margin of operations. Thus the marginal cost is the additional cost incurred by the production of one more unit and, similarly, the marginal revenue is the extra income derived from selling one extra unit.

Figure 11.4 shows a situation where the marginal cost is high at low-quantity production levels. As production levels increase, marginal cost then decreases because of both production and marketing economies. Then, however, a point is reached where the organisation is overstretching its production capacity, and inefficiencies arising from overworked labour and machinery send the marginal cost upwards again.

Meanwhile, the marginal revenue curve in the same figure shows how each additional unit sale affects total revenue. The pressure to expand sales, thus broadening the market, leads to lower prices, to make the product more affordable, and therefore to lower revenue.

Figure 11.4 Marginal cost and revenue

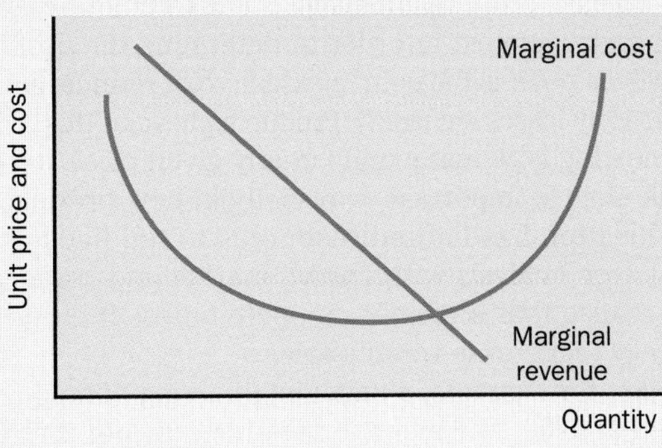

Thus marginal revenue usually shows a downward slope. The message is simple: each additional unit sale, at least theoretically, generates less revenue than the previous unit sold because the price is falling.

At the heart of marginal analysis lies the search for the point where marginal revenue is equal to marginal cost. Up to that point, each additional unit sale generates more revenue than it incurs costs, and therefore it is worth producing and selling that unit. Beyond that point, however, the situation is different. Each additional unit begins to incur more cost than it can earn in revenue. Thus it becomes increasingly uneconomic to carry on producing extra units. This is all summarised in Figure 11.5, which shows the relationship between profit and price, total revenue, and total cost.

All of this may seem to be somewhat theoretical and far removed from the realities of pricing in real markets. Emerging strategic opportunities or changing competitive situations may be more urgent motivators of pricing decisions than whether producing one more unit is economic or not. No organisation can operate without due consideration of competitors' actions and price threats, which can soon change the best-laid revenue analysis.

The model can have some bearing in more stable, less dynamic markets, where there is reasonable and predictable knowledge of cost schedules and demand sensitivity. Marginal analysis can at least demonstrate the folly of chasing sales for the sake of sales. In most new product situations where information is scarce or incomplete, or where a competitive market is very volatile, however, such analysis becomes rather more academic.

Figure 11.5 Profit maximisation

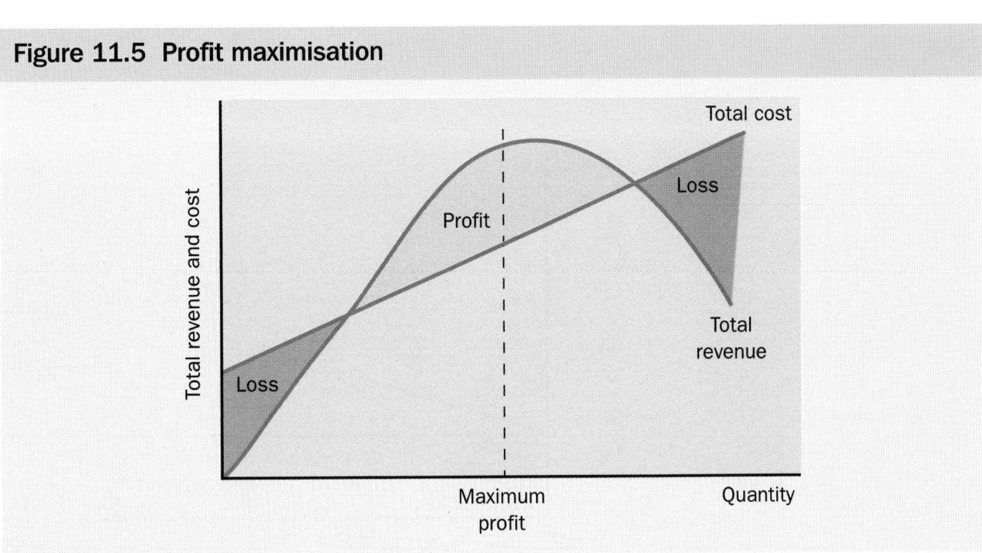

Breakeven analysis

Breakeven analysis offers a simpler, more convenient approach to examining the cost–volume–profit relationship. It is a technique that shows the relationship between total revenue and total cost in order to determine the profitability of different levels of output. The **breakeven** point is the point at which total revenue and total cost are equal (i.e. no profit is made, nor are any losses incurred). Producing beyond this point generates increasing levels of profit.

Knowing how many units at any given price would have to be made and sold in order to break even is important, especially in new product and small business situations where an organisation has limited resources to fall back on if losses are incurred. Combining the breakeven analysis with known market and competitive conditions may make an organisation realise that it cannot compete unless it either reduces costs or develops a marketing strategy to increase volume sales.

Take, for example, a small engineering company wishing to produce a component to be priced at £200. The average variable cost per unit is £100, while the total fixed costs to be recovered are £200,000 per year.

$$\textbf{The breakeven point} = \frac{\textbf{total fixed costs}}{\textbf{unit price} - \textbf{variable costs}}$$

$$= \frac{£200\ 000}{£200 - £100}$$

$$= 2000 \text{ units per year}$$

Figure 11.6 shows this information in a breakeven chart.

Breakeven analysis helps to show the impact on contribution to fixed costs and profit of alternative price levels. It is mechanically very simple to calculate, provided that costs are known, and any spreadsheet package can be used to set up a model to test the impact of different prices or cost structures. Breakeven is particularly useful in situations where fixed costs represent a high proportion of total costs. Once the breakeven point is reached, the fixed costs are all covered and any sales beyond that are mostly profit (because the variable cost component is so low). If this is a price-competitive market, therefore, it is useful to know where the breakeven point is so that prices can be set as low as possible, but without crossing the breakeven point into loss.

The problem with the approach is that it focuses internally on cost structures and externally on a potentially simplistic relationship between price and sales. It must always be tempered by an appreciation of realistic market and competitive conditions, and put into the context of how the organisation can use other marketing techniques to bolster or develop demand to achieve sales more effectively.

Figure 11.6 Breakeven chart

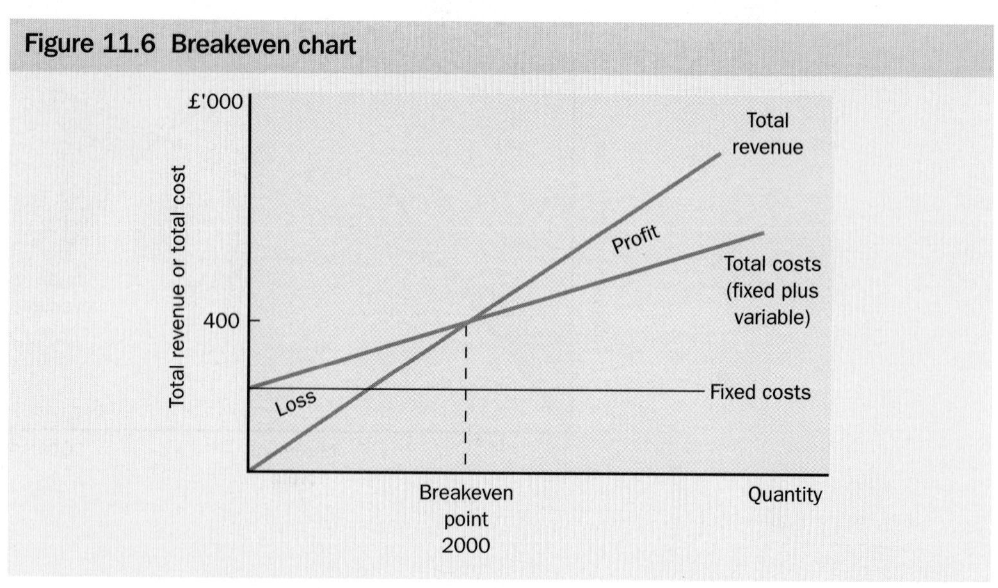

Cost-based methods

The emphasis in *cost-based* pricing methods is on the organisation's production and marketing costs. Analysis of these costs leads to an attempt to set a price that generates a sufficient profit. The obvious disadvantage is the lack of focus on the external situation. An organisation implementing such a method would need to be very sure of the market's response. It is, however, a simple method to use, drawing the sort of direct parallels between cost and price that make accountants very happy. There are some variations in cost-based pricing.

Mark-up

Especially in the retail sector, where it can be difficult to estimate demand patterns for each product line, percentage **mark-up** is used as a means of price setting. This means that the retailer starts with the price paid to the supplier for the goods and then adds a percentage to reach the retail price to the customer. In fmcg high-volume markets this can be as low as 8 per cent, whereas in low-volume fashion clothing markets it can be 200 per cent or more. Mark-ups may be standard across all retailers in a particular sector, although the smaller business may have to accept a lower mark-up to compete with the retail prices of bigger operators who can negotiate better cost prices from suppliers. A retailer such as Costco that deliberately violates the mark-up traditions of its sector can be seen as initiating an all-out price war.

Mark-up can be expressed as a percentage of cost or as a percentage of the retail selling price. If a French wine merchant, for instance, buys a bottle of wine from a vineyard for €3 and adds €2 as the mark-up, thus achieving a retail price of €5, then the mark-up as a percentage of the cost is:

$$\textbf{mark-up/cost price} \times \textbf{100}$$

That is:

$$2/3 \times 100 = 66\%$$

Expressed as a percentage of retail price the mark-up is:

$$\textbf{(retail price – cost price)/retail price} \times \textbf{100}$$

This gives:

$$2/5 \times 100 = 40\%$$

It is thus important to be clear which kind of mark-up is being considered. The latter type, percentage of retail price, may be more relevant in a situation where a market is price sensitive and the retailer knows at what price the product must be sold. Using the retail price and the cost of the good from the supplier, the mark-up achieved can be calculated and the retailer can decide whether this is sufficient to cover selling costs and profit.

Mark-ups must work hard. As well as covering profit, they have to cover the retailer's operating costs. Figure 11.7 shows how mark-ups operate through the distribution chain. Sometimes the mark-ups become bigger the closer one is to the end consumer because of all the services the retailer is expected to supply, such as personal selling and attractive product displays. Each mark-up down the chain may be considered a reward for services rendered. The wholesaler's mark-up, for instance, recognises the efficiency brought to the market by the wholesaler, in providing a central meeting point for manufacturers and retailers (there is more on the role of the wholesaler in Chapter 12). The wholesaler's mark-up poses an added difficulty for the small retailer. In paying for the services rendered by the wholesaler, the small retailer sacrifices some of its own mark-up if it still wishes to sell at a price close to that of the big operator who buys direct from the manufacturer.

Although this is basically a cost-based pricing method, it does not operate in isolation from external events. Retailers will be wary of implementing a mark-up that leads to a retail price way out of line with the competition, or that violates the consumer's expectations. This is particularly evident in the comments on the small retailer in the preceding paragraphs.

Figure 11.7 Mark-up in the distribution chain

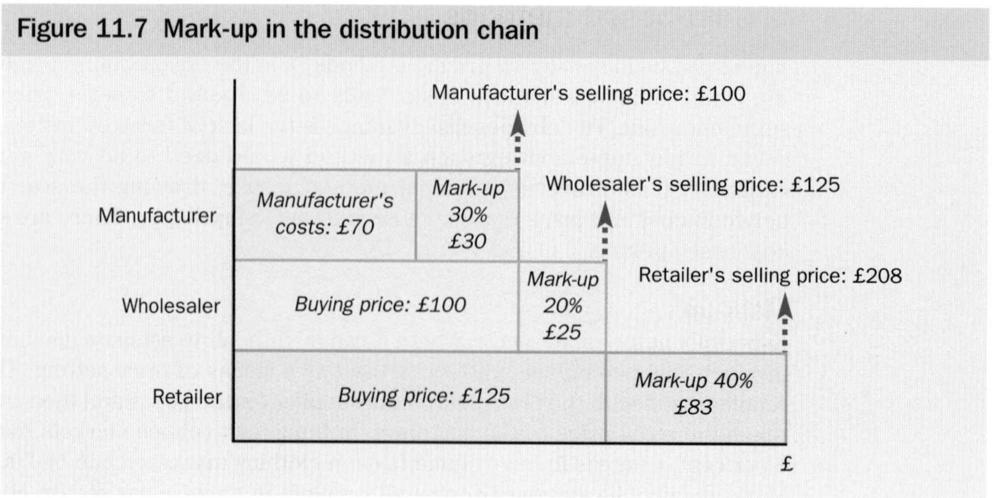

Cost-plus pricing

Cost-plus pricing involves adding a fixed percentage to production or construction costs. It is mainly used on large projects or for custom-built items where it is difficult to estimate costs in advance. The percentage will be agreed between buyer and seller in advance, and then just before, or after, the project's completion, buyer and seller agree the admissible costs and calculate the final price. It sounds straightforward enough, but in large, complex construction projects, it is not so easy to pin down precise costs. Problems arise where the seller is inflating prices, perhaps through the use of transfer pricing (*see* p. 459), and it can take some time for buyer and seller to negotiate a final settlement.

An industry operating on this kind of pricing method, using a standard percentage, is oriented less towards price competition, and more towards achieving competitiveness through cost efficiency.

Experience curve pricing

Over time, and as an organisation produces more units, its experience and learning lead to more efficiency. This can also apply in service situations (Chambers and Johnston, 2000). Cost savings of between 10 per cent and 30 per cent per unit can be achieved each time the organisation doubles its experience, as shown in Figure 11.8. In Figure 11.8(a), an aggressive pricing strategy is being adopted, as prices are being set in anticipation of future cost savings to be derived from increased experience. Schroeder (1993) argues that the steeper

Figure 11.8 Experience curve pricing strategies

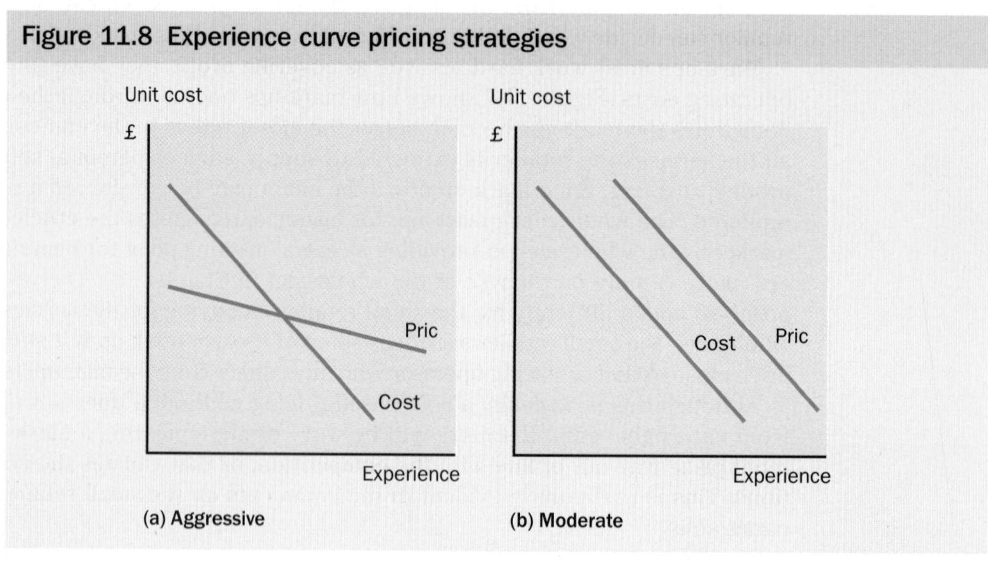

learning curve can be effective in keeping out potential competitiors. In Figure 11.8(b), however, a more moderate approach is being adopted, in which prices fall with cost savings as they are achieved.

Some organisations use this learning curve, essentially predicting how costs are going to change over time, as part of the price-planning process. Such planning means not only that the organisation is under pressure to build the volume in order to gain the experience benefits, but also that if it can gain a high market share early on in the product's life, it can achieve a strong competitive position because it gains the cost savings from learning sooner (Schmenner, 1990). It can thus withstand price competition.

Although the savings are made mainly in production, there is still a close link with the volume share and price-dominating strategies discussed earlier. Scanners and WAP phones are examples of products that are reducing their relative prices, partly because of the experience curve effect.

The problem with cost-based methods is that they are too internally focused. The price determined has to survive in a marketplace where customers and competitors have their own views of what pricing should be. An organisation's price may thus make perfect sense in cost terms and generate a respectable profit contribution, but be perceived as far too high or far too low by customers in comparison with the features and benefits offered. The price may also be way out of line compared with a competitor with a different kind of cost base.

Demand-based pricing

Demand-based pricing looks outwards from the production line and focuses on customers and their responsiveness to different price levels. Even this approach may not be enough on its own, but when it is linked with an appreciation of competition-based pricing, it provides a powerful market-orientated perspective that cost-based methods just do not provide.

At its simplest, demand-based pricing indicates that when demand is strong, the price goes up, and when it is weak, the price goes down. This can be seen in some service industries, for example, where demand fluctuates depending on time. Package holidays taken during school holidays at Christmas, Easter or in the summer when demand is high are more expensive than those taken at other times of the year when it is more difficult for families to get away. Similarly, holidays taken when weather conditions at the destination are less predictable or less pleasant are cheaper because there is less demand. Even within the course of a single day, travel prices can vary according to demand. Tickets on shuttle flights between Heathrow and UK regional airports vary in price depending on when the peak times for business travellers occur.

marketing *in action*

'A flight from Dublin to London? That will be £10, including tax'

At a time when over 100,000 jobs have been lost in the US airline industry and European airlines are suffering from changed travel patterns after 11 September 2001, the budget airlines such as Ryanair and easyJet have experienced a boom in ticket sales. British Airways and KLM have cut staff, Swissair has gone bankrupt and Sabena has filed for bankruptcy, routes have been cut, planes grounded and some other national airlines are teetering on the edge. The air passenger market is in turmoil and the winners so far have been the low cost, low price operators.

Rather than cut capacity and staff, the low cost airlines cut their fares even further to keep passengers flying. In one week alone in October 2001, Ryanair sold half a million tickets, double its previous best month and easyJet sales rose 27 per cent in September 2001 compared with the previous year. The low cost airlines better understood the psychology of potential travellers in the aftermath of September 11th. People just didn't want to fly unless they had to, for example as business travellers. But as the price came down to unimaginably low levels, the temptation to go away for a long weekend or on a trip increases, especially if it is to what is perceived as a relatively safe destination. Having taken the decision to fly once, there is a good chance that they will fly again, thereby sustaining the loyalty and allowing new routes and services to be offered (Binyon, 2001). The budget airlines realised this early on and intensified price competition rather than pursuing the other options.

Admittedly, it is difficult for the big airlines to follow suit. They traditionally make their money from business class and transatlantic travel. Cutting prices

▶

in the former may have little impact as it is companies that pay for the tickets, while the loss of the profitable transatlantic trade has had a serious impact on already fragile margins. Lowering economy class fares would perhaps make the larger airlines too vulnerable. However, September 11th probably only served to exaggerate and accelerate the effect of underlying problems in the industry that would have had to have been dealt with sooner or later anyway. The speed with which capacities were cut and redundancy programmes announced suggests that the industry had been in trouble for some time. For many years, the national airlines had been protected, subsidised and allowed to control key routes and key slots at the major airports. Many would have fallen by the wayside had free competition been allowed to operate, but national pride would have meant such bankruptcies or mergers were unthinkable.

Sources: Arnold (2001); Binyon (2001).

There is an underlying assumption that an organisation operating such a flexible pricing policy has a good understanding of the nature and elasticity of demand in its market, as already outlined at pp. 402 *et seq*.

There are a number of interesting and more subtle forms of demand-based pricing.

Psychological pricing

Psychological pricing is very much a customer-based pricing method, relying as it does on the consumer's emotive responses, subjective assessments and feelings towards specific purchases. Clearly, this is particularly applicable to products with a higher involvement focus, i.e. those that appeal more to psychological than to practical motives for purchase. All the following are examples of psychological pricing.

Prestige pricing. Prestige pricing is used by the consumer as a means of assessing quality, as discussed at pp. 392 *et seq*. The high price attracts the status-conscious consumer, the discerning customer for whom price is no object. Luxury goods such as fine jewellery, designer clothing and porcelain all need to be priced at high-prestige levels. A lower price would deter that group of customers from buying.

Odd-even pricing. Odd-even pricing is the technique of ending a price with certain numbers, usually odd ones, for example £4.99. It is a widely practised method, which seems to have an effect on the buying public. The research on the subject is far from conclusive, but Blattberg and Neslin (1990), among others, found that an increase in sales could be achieved simply by ending the price of the goods with a 9 rather than any other digit. It would appear that consumers view prices ending in 9 as lower prices and think that retailers offering such prices are better value. Further, when consumers were asked to recall the prices later, the prices ending with 9 were recalled as lower than they really were. In some situations, retailers can strive for the opposite effect. If £4.99 is a bargain, then £5.00 emanates quality. This is all far from being proved conclusively, however.

eg

A study by Gendall *et al.* (1997) found that odd pricing produces greater demand than a slightly higher price, and thus a kink in the downward-sloping demand curve. With products such as low-priced grocery items, however, there is no difference between .99 and .95 price endings in terms of demand.

Price lining. Price lining is a technique that is favoured in a product mix strategy in which a number of products are sold at specific price points. Sometimes an organisation will work back from these price points regardless of the cost differences between the products in the line. For example, a clothing retailer might sell ladies' skirts at £25, £40 and £55, capitalising on customers' ideas of price banding (*see* p. 396). At one extreme, the skirts at each of these prices might all be purchased from the supplier at the same price, but they are marked up to price points on the basis of style, colour and the expected response of the typical customer.

Too many price points may confuse customers and may prevent differentiation. Three or four price points are better than trying to operate eight or nine. Figure 11.9 shows a stepped demand curve where demand is inelastic within particular price bands represented by dif-

Figure 11.9 The stepped demand curve

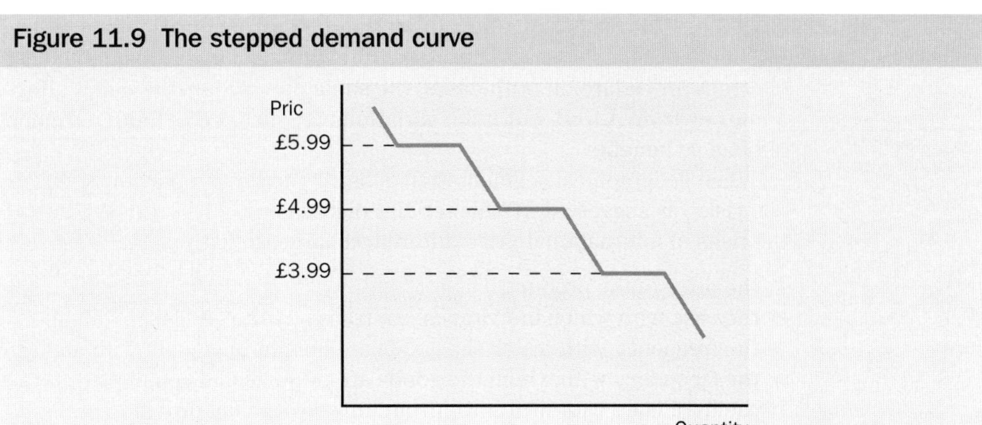

ferent price points. Price lining works because it makes it easier for the customer to choose. As the price is held constant within the band, choice can be made on other, perhaps aesthetic, grounds such as fabric, style or colour.

Bundle pricing. Bundle pricing involves assembling a number of products in a single package to save the consumer the trouble of searching out and buying each one separately (Ansari *et al.*, 1996). It makes it easier to buy, attracting the shopper who is short of time or is risk averse. Personal computers are often sold in this way, with all the hardware, software and peripherals bundled as a package that will enable the user to start some serious computing within minutes. Bundling has a psychological benefit, but it also has an economic rationale, perhaps leading to a lower overall price to the consumer or lower marketing costs for the supplier. Herrmann *et al.* (1997) found that five component bundles generated the most interest while three or seven component bundles had less appeal as being not attractive enough (three) or too complex to evaluate (seven). It was also helpful to have the elements closely related, such as product insurance with the product.

Promotional pricing. Promotional pricing is closely linked with the discussion in Chapter 16 on sales promotion. It can be used to stimulate a market or to reinforce perceptions of value in the short term. Selecting a limited number of lines for a price promotion, as practised in the retail sector for example, attracts consumers' attention, draws them into the store and makes them feel as though they are benefiting from a bargain. The retailer hopes that the costs of providing a number of such price leaders are recouped by the sales of full-priced items, either to new customers or to existing customers spending the money they saved on the bargains (sales that would not otherwise have been made).

Time-specific mark-downs. End of season sales, one-day sales, sales of the type 'sale ends Saturday' are common in the retail sector. A greater level of psychological excitement can be created among customers by providing a limited number of cut-price goods on a first-come first-served basis. Those who do not get the bargain of their choice still spend in the store and enjoy the thrill of the chase. More sedately, retailers and manufacturers use price promotions based on rewards for spending over a certain amount, or coupons rewarding repeat purchase as a means of offering the customer that little something extra.

Whether intended to stimulate demand, to encourage product trial, to take the risk out of purchase or to reward consistent and loyal behaviour, all these price promotion techniques show the flexible use of price as a tactical weapon in the marketing mix, supporting and supported by the other mix elements.

Price differentiation. Price differentiation involves the use of different prices for different segments. The same basic product is offered, but the associated services differ. A drink from a vending machine, for example, is more expensive than one from a supermarket because of the convenience, the machinery and its maintenance and the refrigeration. First-class travel on an aircraft costs much more than economy class not because it gets travellers to their destination any more quickly, but because of the extra comfort and easier check-in procedure. In both cases, the same core product is being offered, a can of Coke or a journey from A to B, but price variations are justified by both peripheral services and psychological benefits.

When geographical segmentation is being used to support price differences there are special risks, as suggested in Chapter 10's discussion of the euro. Wildner (1998) proposed that the risks of international price differences increase with:

- the price of the product;
- the ease with which individuals can transport the goods;
- the frequency with which the goods are bought by people with higher incomes;
- the frequency with which the goods are purchased through the internet;
- the frequency with which goods are offered by mail order.

Overall, demand-orientated pricing, regardless of how it is implemented, can be very powerful in achieving a strong, defendable market position. It can also lead to higher profit levels. The problem, however, lies in the difficulty of estimating demand response.

Competition-based pricing

This chapter has frequently warned of the danger of setting prices without knowing what is happening in the market, particularly with respect to one's competitors. According to Lambin (1993), there are two aspects of competition that influence an organisation's pricing. The first is the *structure of the market*. Generally speaking, the greater the number of competitors, i.e. the closer to perfect competition the market comes, the less autonomy the organisation has in price setting. The second competitive factor is the product's *perceived value* in the market. In other words, the more differentiated an organisation's product is from the competition, the more autonomy the organisation has in pricing it, because buyers come to value its unique benefits.

eg

Internet service providers (ISPs) have adopted competition-based pricing. Most ISPs in the USA tend to adopt flat rate plans which means that users pay the same amount regardless of usage. In Europe and Asia, the main form of competition-based pricing is the price per minute plan, where users pay according to the time they spend connected to the internet. Although this is gradually changing towards the US model, pioneered by global operators such as AOL, variable rates do still apply. Despite aggressive competition for users, most competitors in Europe tend to try to offer the lowest price within a pricing plan rather than trying to offer more customised plans to suit the needs of different user groups (Altmann and Chu, 2001).

Most markets are becoming increasingly competitive, and a focus on competitive strategy in business planning emphasises the importance of understanding the role of price as a means of competing. An organisation that decides to become a cost leader in its market and to take a price-oriented approach to maintaining its position needs an especially efficient intelligence system to monitor its competitors. Levy (1994) looks at organisations that offer price guarantees in B2B markets. Any supplier promising to match the lowest price offered by any of its rivals needs to know as much as possible about those rivals and their cost and pricing structures in order to assess the likely cost of such a promise.

In consumer markets, market research can certainly help to provide intelligence, whether this means shopping audits to monitor the comparative retail prices of goods, or consumer surveys or focus groups to monitor price perceptions and evolving sensitivity relative to the rest of the marketing mix. Data gathering and analysis can be more difficult in B2B markets, because of the flexibility of pricing and the degree of customisation of marketing packages to an individual customer's needs in these markets. There is a heavy reliance on sales representatives' reports, information gained through informal networks within the industry and qualitative assessment of all those data.

Competitive analysis can focus on a number of levels, at one end of the spectrum involving a general overview of the market, and at the other end focusing on individual product lines or items. Whatever the market, whatever the focus of competitive analysis, the same decision has to be made: whether to price at the same level as the competition, or above or below them.

An organisation that has decided to be a price follower must, by definition, look to the market for guidance. The decision to position at the same level as the competition, or above or below them, requires information about what is happening in the market. This is pricing based on the 'going rate' for the product. Conventional pricing behaviour in the market is used as a reference point for comparing what is offered, and the price is varied from that. Each supplier to the market is thus acting as a marker for the others, taking into account relative positioning and relative offering. Effectively, pricing is based on collective wisdom, and certainly for the smaller business it is easier to do what everyone else does rather than pay for market research to prove what the price ought to be, and run the risk of getting it wrong. In a seaside resort, for example, a small bed and breakfast hotel is unlikely to price itself differently from the one next door, unless it can justify doing so by offering significantly better services. Within an accepted price range, however, any one organisation's move may not be seen as either significant or threatening by the rest.

The dangers of excessive price competition, both in terms of the cost to the competitors and the risk to a product's reputation, thus attracting the 'wrong' kind of customer, have already been indicated. But if neither the organisation nor the product has a particularly high reputation, or if the product has few differentiating features, then price competition may be the only avenue open unless there is a commitment to working on the product and the marketing mix as a whole. An extreme form of competitive pricing is practised through tendering, which is discussed at p. 458.

Pricing tactics and adjustments

Pricing tactics and adjustments are concerned with the last steps towards arriving at the final price. There is no such thing as a fixed price; price can be varied to reflect specific customer needs, the market position within the channel of distribution or the economic aspects of the deal.

Price structures

Particularly in B2B markets, *price structures* give guidelines to the sales representative to help in negotiating a final price with the customer. The concern is not only to avoid overcharging or inconsistent charging, but to set up a framework for pricing discretion that is linked with the significance of the customer or the purchase situation.

eg

At one extreme, price structure may involve a take it or leave it, single price policy such as IKEA operates. It offers no trade discount for organisational purchasers, seeing itself largely as a consumer-orientated retailer. Compare this with some industrial distributorships, which offer different levels of discount to different customers. Most try to find a middle ground, between consistent pricing and flexibility for certain key customers.

Special adjustments

A variation on price structures, *special adjustments* to list or quoted prices can be made either for short-term promotional purposes or as part of a regular deal to reward a trade customer for services rendered. Figure 11.10 shows the range of discounts and other incentives that can mean that the price paid for an item (for example home appliances) is significantly less than the list price.

Figure 11.10 From list price to actual price

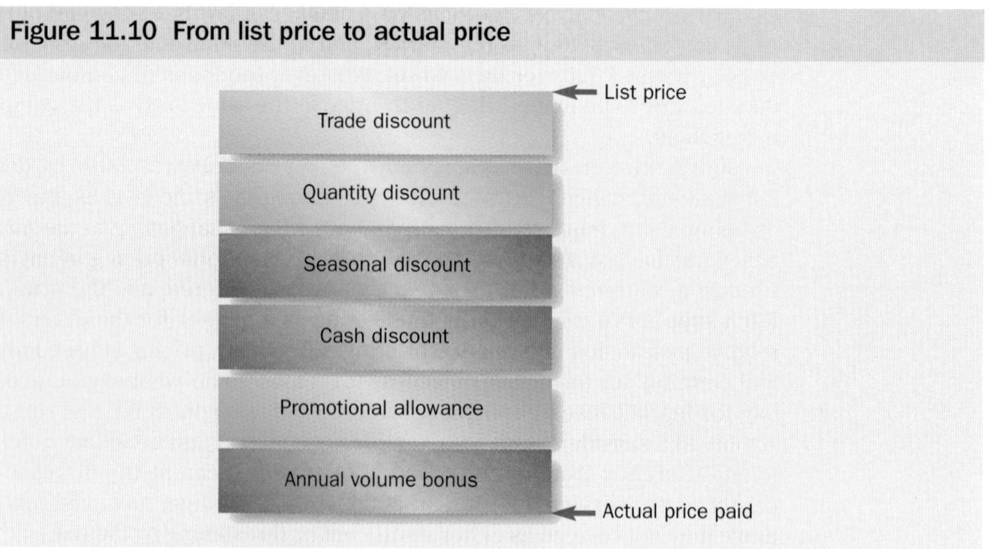

As the channel of distribution becomes deeper or wider, there is a need for more structure and careful planning of special adjustments to price structures. There are three main types of special adjustment, which are not mutually exclusive.

Discounts

Discounts consist of reductions from the normal or list price as a reward for bulk purchases or the range of distribution services offered. The level and frequency of discounts will vary according to individual circumstances. Blois (1994) points out that most organisations offer discounts from list prices and that these discounts form an important part of pricing strategies. There are also different types of discount.

Trade discounts. Trade discounts, sometimes called functional discounts, are based on the services that the buyer (a retailer or wholesaler) is expected to perform in the future in reselling the goods. They are normally well understood between buyer and seller, and may be agreed as part of an annual negotiation. The value of the discounts depends on the services to be performed and the location of the buyer in the distribution channel. The closer the buyer is to the end consumer, the higher the service charges and the greater the discount. Different markets have their own traditional discount structures established, but of course any member may seek to violate tradition for competitive reasons.

Quantity discounts. Quantity discounts encourage bulk purchases. Bulk discounts come into force if a single order exceeds a certain volume or value level. Cumulative discounts build up over time. At the end of a trading period, the quantity purchased is totalled and a percentage rebate given back to the buyer. Both types of discount encourage larger purchase quantities, and the cumulative discount also encourages loyalty over time.

There are examples of both types of discount in consumer and B2B markets. The promotional technique of 'buy two and get the third free' is effectively a bulk discount and is found on many products in many supermarkets. Similarly, a promotion that requires a consumer to collect tokens then send them off for a cash rebate is a form of cumulative discount. In B2B markets, a retailer may be offered a twelfth case of a product free if 11 are initially purchased (quantity discount), or a rebate on the number of cases of a product sold by the end of the trading period (cumulative discount).

Seasonal discounts. Seasonal discounts are usually offered to offset cash flow difficulties, as discussed earlier at p. 431, or to overcome the problems of utilising capacity in quieter periods. Examples are discounts for buying heating fuel in the summer, retailers being offered discounts for stocking up on seasonal merchandise earlier, or car hire tariff reductions over weekends. Such discounts could be seen as a form of reward to the purchaser for taking on the risks of an early purchase.

Cash discounts. Cash discounts encourage prompt payment in a form that is easiest and cheapest for the seller to handle. They can operate at all levels of all types of market. A small retailer, buying supplies from a wholesaler, may be offered a better price per case of a product if immediate payment is made than if a 30-day invoice has to be sent. A small retailer, for example, might purchase goods to the value of £1,000 and the bill might specify: '£1,000, 2/10 net 30'. This means that if the bill is paid within 10 days, the customer can have a 2 per cent discount on the total of £1,000; otherwise the £1,000 is payable in full within 30 days of the invoice date. In some cases interest may be charged if the bill is not settled after 30 days.

It can sometimes be difficult to make the rules stick. If, for instance, a customer takes the discount but pays after the 10-day deadline, there is the potential for a dispute. From the customer's perspective, the discount for prompt payment may not always be particularly attractive when compared with the short-term cash flow implications of losing the use of that money. Sometimes in consumer markets a cash discount will even be given to consumers who use cash or cheques rather than credit cards, reflecting the extra cost to the retailer of processing credit card transactions.

Allowances

Allowances are similar to discounts, but usually require the buyer to perform some additional service. Trade-in, for example, makes a transaction more complicated because it involves the exchange of a good as well as money for whatever is being purchased. It is a common practice in the car market, where consumers trade in their old cars as part exchange for a new one. The qualitative judgement of the value of the trade-in disguises the discount offered, and it is further complicated by the attitudes of the respective parties. A car that is an unreliable liability to the owner may have potential to a dealer with a particular customer in mind or a good eye for scrap. The owner thinks they are getting a good deal on the old car, while the dealer thinks they can actually recoup the trade-in value and make a bit more besides.

Promotional allowances, often used as trade incentives, mean that a retailer can be rewarded for participating in point-of-sale promotions, or joint advertising, through cheaper or free goods. The retailer also reaps the added benefit of the synergy gained from being associated with the promotional activities of leading brands.

Geographic adjustments

Geographic adjustments are those made, especially in B2B markets, to reflect the costs of transport and insurance involved in getting the goods from buyer to seller. In consumer markets, they can be seen in the case of mail-order goods, which carry an extra charge for postage and packing.

In B2B markets, the terms of delivery and what is or is not included in the price need to be established in advance as part of the negotiated contract. An ex-works price does not include any delivery costs; effectively, the buyer collects. A price quoted as FOB (free on board) means that the seller is obliged to deliver the goods to some agreed point, be that an airport, a railhead, a goods depot or whatever, and then the buyer bears the charges from there. A price quoted as CIF (cargo, insurance, freight) generally means that the seller incurs all costs to the buyer's door.

Zoned pricing relates price to the geographic distance between buyer and seller. A DIY warehouse, for example, might add a £5 delivery charge to any destination within five miles, £7.50 for up to 10 miles, £10 for up to 15 miles and so on, reflecting the extra time and petrol involved in delivering to more distant locations. Operating a single zone means that the delivery price is the same regardless of distance, as is the case with the domestic postal service, which charges on the weight of letters rather than the destination. The international mail service does, however, operate on a multiple-zone basis, dividing the world up into areas and pricing to reflect different transport costs.

From a marketing perspective, the key decision is the extent to which freight costs can be absorbed, and how far they can be used as a negotiating tool with customers. This is an especially critical question for a smaller organisation as it begins to develop business outside its home market.

Issues in pricing

There are several issues connected with pricing that should be considered in the setting and managing of prices in B2B markets.

Negotiating prices

In B2B markets and even in some consumer situations where high-value purchases such as cars are involved, *negotiation* usually takes place. This determines the final price agreed between the parties and the nature of the offer package that will be provided for that price. Negotiation is therefore concerned with the communication processes that take place between the two parties to arrive at a mutually acceptable bargain. Lysons (1993, p. 215) defined negotiation as:

> *any form of verbal communication in which the participants seek to exploit the relative strengths of their bargaining positions to achieve explicit or implicit objectives within the overall purpose of seeking to resolve the identified areas of disagreement.*

Many negotiations revolve around price and/or cost trade-offs with the rest of the commercial package offered. Thus a buyer may agree to pay a slightly higher price than it had intended if the seller agrees to deliver more quickly than originally suggested.

Baily (1987) identified four main situations where negotiation may be used:

1 an established supplier wants to increase the price or to change the offer package;
2 the buyer wants an established supplier to reduce the price or to change the offer package;
3 a potential supplier wants to oust the existing supplier;
4 there is no regular supplier and it is a new task purchase.

On a slightly smaller scale, hotel managers regularly have to negotiate deals with organisations for conference and banqueting contracts. Issues such as accommodation, menus, local transport, facilities and the overall price all have to be agreed and offer considerable scope for discussion.

Increasingly, negotiation is part of the continual exchange process that characterises a long-term business relationship. In these situations both parties may seek cooperative nego-

marketing *in action*

A baa-gain offer ewe can't refuse

Caledonian MacBrayne (http://www.calmac.co.uk), a ferry owner operating the Hebrides to Scottish mainland service, ran into trouble when trying to segment the market for travel by price. The company was anxious to encourage more island farmers to use the ferries to take their sheep to the market on the mainland. The farmers on the remote island communities of Uist, Barra, Mull and Colonsay need to take their sheep to the markets in Oban in the western Highlands. The normal prices for the five-hour sailing between Barra and Oban were £104 return for a car and £29 per passenger, but under the sheep discount scheme, the price was just £2.35 per sheep, with no charges for car or passenger.

It did not take long for the canny farmers to work out how to use the system. Some cars were packed with sheep, but others just had one woolly passenger along with suitcases and passports. The farmers were using the scheme to take a holiday on the mainland and beyond. It was even more perplexing when a few weeks later the cars returned with tanned drivers and sheep still on board. This did not mean a flood of sheep sunning themselves on the Costa Del Sol; they were being left with friendly farmers on the mainland, so even the sheep had a holiday. They certainly rarely made it to the market!

Caledonian MacBrayne sheepishly admitted that it had got into a mess with an initiative designed to help the local economy and its own profits without fleecing customers. A councillor for the Western Isles Council was quoted as saying that: 'We do know that there has been some serious evasion of fares and certain people's sheep seem to have become quite well travelled recently.' Was this woolly scheme one baa-gain offer too many?

Sources: Coles (1998); Harris (1998).

tiation. This is where a win–win deal, with both parties getting something that they want, is the best outcome, as it is in the interests of both parties for the relationship to continue. There is little point in one party obtaining a short-term advantage that might lead to longer-term mistrust and poor supply from the other. If, for example, a buyer who purchases a large proportion of the total output of a small firm drives prices down to a level that is uneconomic for the small supplier, supply problems and even discontinuities might start to occur. Such problems might arise because the small supplier compromises on quality or processes in order to meet the new, tighter cost targets.

eg

When aircraft manufacturers negotiate with carriers, the negotiations can be long and complex concerning not just the aircraft, but also the servicing, financing and support arrangements. When Boeing and Airbus go head-to-head, however, the going can get tough and the stakes are high. Recently, Boeing extended the tradition of buy-back to include not just aircraft nearing the end of their economic life, but also nearly new planes and in one case for Singapore Airlines, the deal covered 15 modern A340-300s and a further two still in production (Doyle, 2001). Effectively, such a practice could be regarded as buying market share for the Boeing 777 family. It also invites a competitive response from Airbus, as it suggests that the Airbus A340 is somehow an inferior product. To Boeing, it is a fair business practice to be considered during a negotiation. Airbus is considering how it will respond.

In other situations, there may be competitive negotiation, where neither party has any real intention of creating a long-term relationship. These deals can easily become win–lose deals, where one or other party gains at the expense of the other. For example, an organisation purchasing a second-hand piece of capital machinery cannot expect the seller to be concerned with the long-term reliability of that equipment. It is up to the buyer to check out and assess the state of that machinery. Sometimes, competitive negotiations break down completely and neither party gains anything. The seller fails to sell and the buyer fails to buy, and effectively this is a lose–lose arrangement!

There are many potential areas of the offer that might have to be negotiated, and Figure 11.11 highlights typical areas of concern. Of course, these will vary from situation to situation. The key skill in effective negotiation is the ability to negotiate elements of the package in terms of a trade-off. Thus the trade-in allowance may be increased if payment is made in total up front, or a discount may be increased if the customer collects the item at its own expense. Not all elements of negotiation will involve price, but virtually all of them will involve cost. A good negotiator will concede on areas that cost little, but are highly valued by the other party. An organisation selling a photocopier might agree to send out an engi-

Figure 11.11 Negotiation variables

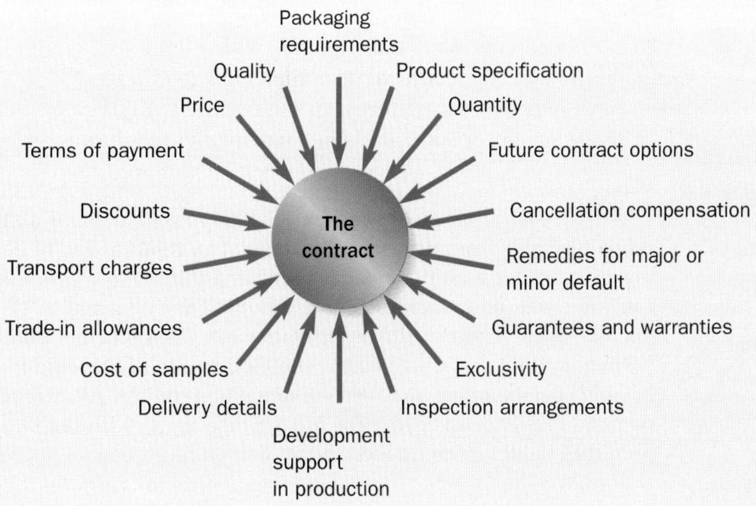

neer within two hours of any repair call, in order to secure a higher price for the machine. The buyer gets the peace of mind of knowing that it will not be left with a broken-down photocopier for too long and will feel that the slightly higher purchase price is thus justified, while the seller will be confident that the machine is so reliable that the agreement will never, or rarely, be put to the test!

Generally, the more the buyer is locked in to the supplier's specification, the more limited the alternative sources and the greater the urgency of demand. This tends to enhance the negotiating position of the supplier. There is more on negotiation, and the relative power balance between the negotiating parties, in Chapter 17.

Tendering and bidding

Tendering is another feature of pricing in B2B markets. Tenders are offers made by suppliers concerning the price, terms and conditions of supply. The successful supplier's tender may then form the basis of detailed negotiation to finalise the terms of the deal, but with the clear understanding that it will be awarded the contract. Tendering is widely used in capital goods purchasing where large sums are involved. Many services ranging from training contracts and management consultancy to cleaning and plumbing can also be purchased through tenders. Some invitations to tender are restricted to approved or selected suppliers, while others are open to any organisation that wants to bid. A large organisation, for example, may encourage a wide range of smaller businesses to bid for its catering or cleaning services, although fairly strict criteria may be applied to eliminate the weaker bids. Tenders are often advertised in the relevant trade press. *Construction News*, for example, contains details of private and public tenders called for, in the UK, EU and worldwide. Thus invitations to tender can range from applications for pre-qualification for the design and construction of the Bhairab Bridge in Bangladesh to the dredging of Scalloway harbour for the Shetland Islands Council.

eg

Tenders (http://www.tenders.co.uk) is a powerful database of all European Public Procurement Contracts and Contract Award Notices derived from the Office for Official Publications of the European Union. It contains 450,000 documents with, it is claimed, between 500 and 800 new entries each day. Such a service is useful for the B2B marketer as it can identify new opportunities when all tenders for public works, service and supply contracts above a certain threshold must be advertised across the EU. This can represent €500 bn euros in contracts.

The first phase of the tendering process is normally an initial expression of interest. The buyer will let it be known, perhaps through advertisements in relevant trade publications, that they are about to begin a particular purchasing process, and will invite potential suppliers to express an interest in submitting a tender. This is effectively a pre-qualification stage, as the buyer can weed out potential suppliers with a dubious reputation or those who are unlikely to be able to meet the technical or commercial requirements. The remaining potential suppliers who have expressed an interest in the contract can then be invited to prepare and submit a formal tender, a process that in itself can involve much time, effort and expense.

eg

When the UK's Ministry of Defence decided to seek bids for a £1 bn support vehicle contract, it received bids from two main consortia. The vehicles had to be able to cope with earthmoving, construction and specialist plant in addition to more specialist applications such as runway repair and amphibious operations. They also had to be all-weather vehicles, able to operate in the Arctic or the desert with ease. The two consortia, ALC (Amey-Lex) and Fastex (Brown & Root and Caterpillar), combined large organisations capable of meeting the challenging specifications and field service requirements. After receiving the two bids, the MOD plans to take at least a year for further discussion with the two potential suppliers before a preferred bidder is announced (http://www.tenders.co.uk).

It is not always the lowest tender that wins, however. A buyer might consider a certain bid too low, and might doubt the bidder's ability to deliver what they promised at an acceptable quality level. Sometimes, therefore, a buyer might feel that a higher price is worth paying to be more certain of the outcome and to cut down the risk of potential problems as the project unfolds.

eg

As China's economic system has adopted more 'free-market' characteristics, the government has moved to more open bidding procedures rather than awarding contracts to 'preferred suppliers' without tendering being opened up to others. The Yantai municipal government in Shandong province claims to have saved 675,000 Yuan ($81,000) when it purchased 180 computers. Forty bids were received and five passed through to the final decision phase. This method of procurement is new in China and has already been used for such items as vehicles, photocopiers, air conditioners and medical appliances (Chuanjiang Ju, 1999).

The tendering might end, as in many of the examples quoted above, with further negotiation to finalise the fine detail of the contract. However, it is also possible, usually where smaller jobs are involved, for the buyer to ask for sealed bids. This means that the winning supplier is selected with a minimum of contact, and thus there is no further negotiation of terms. The buyer either takes or leaves the supplier's original offer. In these cases, potential suppliers seek to influence the tendering process well before the formal invitations to tender are issued. By building contacts, influencing specifications and raising its reputation, a supplier may feel that its total offering, not just its price, might receive a more sympathetic hearing from the buyer when it comes to analysing the formal tenders. This, of course, raises issues of what constitutes fair and ethical practice, as discussed in Chapter 4.

Transfer pricing

In larger organisations, there is often a considerable amount of internal trading between different divisions of the company and across national boundaries. A typical car manufacturer may concentrate production of engines, body parts and transmission systems in different divisions and in different locations. Fiat and SKF both have transfer price arrangements for 'selling' parts and finished products respectively to other parts of their own organisations.

Purchasing aircraft is a complicated process involving negotiations with various manufacturers.

Source: BAE Systems.

Transfer pricing is thus used to cover the movement of goods or services across organisational boundaries. These prices may be set at commercial rates, based on full overhead recovery and profit criteria, or at a reduced rate agreed within the group. Where transfer prices cover the movement of goods across national or trading bloc boundaries, there is clearly scope to use them creatively as a means of shifting funds around the world with the maximum tax advantages. With different rates of corporation tax in different countries, prices can be adjusted to minimise the organisation's total tax liability.

According to Livesey (1976), there are three different types of transfer prices as follows.

Negotiated prices

With *negotiated prices*, business units or divisions are encouraged to act in a semi-commercial manner in determining transfer prices to other business units. This means negotiation between the two parties, but there are dangers in this approach. If one buying unit decides that it can get a better deal elsewhere, another part of its own organisation may be left with idle capacity, with the result that overall profits suffer. The organisation may avoid this problem by making it compulsory to source internally. This, however, distorts the negotiating position by creating a captive buyer and a captive seller, both of whom know that they will have to reach some kind of agreement.

Market prices

External (*market*) prices are used as a guide to what the buying unit should be prepared to pay. They are commonly used in organisations where business units act as profit centres and therefore cannot afford to give away their outputs too cheaply to other business units. Unfortunately, as this and the last chapter have shown, there may be some debate as to what exactly constitutes a representative price, given the various trade-offs that are possible. List prices or average prices rarely reflect market reality.

Cost-based systems

The previous methods of transfer pricing have taken the line that the transfer price should reflect what the component concerned is worth either to the buying unit of the organisation or to the end customer. In contrast, the *cost-based systems* approach looks simply at what it cost to produce the component. There are many options within this approach, based on marginal cost, full cost or marginal cost plus a percentage for overhead recovery. The problem with this approach is that it does not reflect market changes or lower cost structures elsewhere. It also does not reflect the opportunity cost of the production capacity used, especially where limits are being reached. In other words, the business unit supplying the component might have external customers clamouring to buy more at much higher commercial prices than the internal cost-based market pays. If the supplying unit cannot expand its capacity or divert sales from the internal to the external market, then it might be losing out severely on a profit opportunity. With a cost-based pricing method, it cannot make up for any of that lost external business through higher internal prices. Despite these weaknesses, this approach is the most popular of all those on offer.

Given all these complications and the lack of any ideal method of transfer pricing, some organisations are happy to allow business units to purchase from the best source, whether internal or external to the organisation. Across Europe, different nations have different policies towards intra-organisational transactions. In the Netherlands, for example, special provisions for determining taxable profit can eliminate distortions caused by transfer pricing so that, for tax purposes, the terms and conditions are comparable to those imposed on transactions between unrelated parties. If there is a doubt, therefore, market prices can be used to ascertain appropriate prices for tax purposes. Similar principles apply in Germany and controls can be stringent. If a German subsidiary company is burdened with costs and expenses that do not reflect the market situation or conditions that could reasonably be imposed on third parties, then the tax authorities can become involved.

Multinational organisations are, however, coming under closer scrutiny to ensure that the methods of transfer are consistent with good accounting practice. The introduction of the euro has increased exposure as there is now greater price transparency to the national tax authorities. The main international principle guiding transfer pricing is the 'arm's length principle'. A transaction is considered to be compliant when the conditions imposed and prices paid are comparable to those imposed and paid by independent enterprises in comparable circumstances (Felgran and Yamada, 2001).

Chapter summary

- The first stage in price setting is the consideration of the organisation's pricing objectives, whether they relate to *financial targets* or *sales targets*. Financial targets can centre on either profit or cash flow. Sales objectives can relate to desired market share and the organisation's position within the market, or to volume sales targets. Other influences on pricing objectives involve strategic assessment of the market and the organisation's position within it, and analysis of competitors' likely responses to price decisions. For organisations in trouble, the possibility of dropping prices as a temporary survival mechanism might be a means of keeping the business intact.
- The second stage is demand assessment. Estimates of demand have to be put into the context of what the individual organisation can be expected to achieve. *Marginal analysis* is one method of finding an optimum level of production that covers costs and makes a profit. A simpler, more realistic approach to looking at the relationship between costs, profit and production volume is *breakeven analysis*. This calculates the volume of sales required, at a given price, to cover costs and begin to make a profit. It is then up to the organisation to work out whether it can produce (at least) that volume and whether it has the marketing skills to sell so much.
- This information, along with an evaluation of competitors' activities, can guide the organisation towards the third stage: determining appropriate pricing policies and strategies. *Skimming* (high, premium pricing signalling a quality good) and *penetration* (pricing low to gain large market share quickly) are examples of possible strategies for launching new products on to the market. Pricing an individual product also has to take the context of the rest of the *product mix* into account, as well as the pricing moves made by *competitors* within the market.
- The fourth stage is setting the price range which can be cost based (operationally centred), demand based (customer centred), or competition based (copying or differentiating from the rest). In practice, some consideration is given to all three methods as all these elements are central to successful marketing strategy.
- The final stage, pricing tactics and adjustments, allows the organisation to take advantage of short-term or unique opportunities by manipulating price to offer discounts, allowances or geographic adjustments to individual customers or groups of customers.
- In most B2B markets and in some consumer purchasing situations, *negotiation* may be necessary to arrive at a final price. Negotiation tends to trade off price against other elements of the total offering, in that the seller is trying to obtain the highest price possible in return for features, benefits or services that are valuable to the buyer, but cost little to the seller. Potential suppliers are sometimes asked to *tender* or bid for a contract. This means that the supplier offers a price along with details of what the buyer can expect for that price, and the buyer decides which supplier should get the contract. Very large companies with a number of different operating divisions or with multinational subsidiaries might also become involved in *transfer pricing*. Transfer prices may be used as a means of moving money from one country to another, or from one profit centre to another, and thus do not necessarily relate closely to open market prices.

key words and phrases

Breakeven
Discounts
Mark-up
Penetration
Price objectives
Pricing method
Pricing policies and strategies
Pricing tactics
Psychological pricing
Skimming
Tendering
Transfer pricing

questions for review

11.1 Define the various stages involved in *setting prices*.

11.2 How can pricing help to achieve *marketing* and *sales objectives*?

11.3 What factors might prompt an organisation to initiate either a *price cut* or a *price rise*?

11.4 What are the advantages and disadvantages of *cost-based pricing methods*?

11.5 Define *transfer pricing* and summarise the various available methods of calculating a transfer price.

questions for discussion

11.1 Define *penetration pricing* and find an example of an organisation that has used it for one of its products.

11.2 How can organisations justify charging *different prices* for different products within their product ranges?

11.3 Define three methods of *psychological pricing*, then find and discuss examples of each one in practice.

11.4 To what extent and why do you think that a marketing manager's pricing decision should be influenced by the competition's pricing?

11.5 Develop a checklist of five important points that you would like a sales representative to bear in mind when trying to achieve a favourable outcome from price negotiation with a potential customer.

case study 11.1

Measuring up to the supplier's expectations

For many years, the owners of high-quality brands have maintained tight control over where and how their goods are sold through selective distribution strategies. In 1997, however, the UK supermarkets started to take an interest in perfume, clothing, sportswear and electrical goods brand names and wanted to stock and sell them at a discount. Surprisingly, the supermarkets did not find this to be a straightforward task. Tesco, for example, had approached companies directly, but had been refused supplies on 'image criteria'. Levi Strauss said that it would supply Tesco if it met its distribution criteria relating to location, affinity with the target consumer, other brands stocked, presentation and staff training. The problem is that a supermarket is unlikely to meet the high standards demanded on such criteria.

The manufacturers have always argued that they have spent a great deal of time and money building exclusive, quality brands (Levi's has spent $6 bn over ten years) and that supermarkets do not provide the right kind of selling ambience because they give the impression of a commodity type of routine purchase. The manufacturers also claim that supermarkets cannot give the kind of personal service and expertise that their customers expect and demand. ASDA, however, takes the view that,

> *Brands argue that they have created an attitude and an ambience for their products – but we don't believe this is consistent with the location of purchase. . . . How can perfume brands say that environment devalues the brand when consumers can buy these products off a trolley in the gangway of an aircraft?* (as quoted by Jardine, 2001)

The supermarkets thus turned to other sources of supply from the grey market, which consists of importers, wholesalers and distributors with surplus stock that they are prepared to sell. This is not necessarily a satisfactory source as it cannot guarantee regular supplies, it might not have the latest designs or models, and it might not have the full product range. The margins on grey-market products are not necessarily attractive. It has been estimated that Tesco bought Levi jeans from Mexico for £26 per pair and was selling them at £30 (compared with a High Street price of £55). Nevertheless, the grey market is better than nothing, and Tesco, along with other supermarket chains, has successfully sourced and sold millions of pounds worth of designer gear at up to half the normal High Street price.

Levi Strauss was incensed and took Tesco to court on the grounds that re-selling goods sourced from outside the EU or the EEA (European Economic

Area) without Levi's consent infringed Levi's trademark registration. Levi's view is that the argument is about protecting its whole brand, not just the price:

> *It is about us trying to differentiate our brand. We are trying to sell to people who think that Levi's is more than just a pair of jeans. Tesco customers only think they are getting a bargain because of the brand image. But the very fact that Tesco sells them undermines the image.* (as quoted by Ryle, 2001a)

The fear is that by turning the brand into a price-orientated commodity, the damage will be such that nobody will want them, even at Tesco prices. Nearly five years of wrangling in the national and European courts culminated in November 2001 in a final ruling from the European Court of Justice (ECJ) in favour of Levi Strauss. The ruling means that importers will have to prove that they have the brand-owner's consent when re-selling goods sourced from outside the EEA, instead of the brand-owner having to prove that it had not consented. At the time of the ruling, Tesco had already bought £150 mn of designer merchandise from within the EEA which it could still legally re-sell, but a consignment of cheap Levi's jeans from the US had to be redirected to Tesco's Eastern European stores. Tesco, ASDA and Safeway all said that they would continue to sell discounted designer goods.

As things stand in December 2001, Tesco is about to go back to the High Court in London to argue that the European Trademark Directive is a breach of its human rights, in the hope that the case will be referred back to the ECJ. It is also likely that the debate over the Trademark Directive will be taken up at EU level through political lobbying by the UK government. The UK government is broadly supportive of Tesco in that there is a perception that the UK consumer is being 'ripped-off' by having to pay prices for designer goods that can be up to 40 per cent higher than in other EU countries. The EC, however, is more in favour of the brand-owners, with the view that parallel imports inhibit investment in new brands and may make trademark-holders withdraw products from the market. An EU study showed that the effect on reducing prices is only less than 2 per cent while the real benefit lies in the transfer of up to 35 per cent of profits from manufacturers to retailers. Nevertheless, consumer perception is that the supermarkets are offering a much better deal: 88 per cent of UK adults said they would rather buy discounted Levi's from a supermarket than full-price at a Levi's store. Only 8 per cent said they were prepared to pay the extra.

In a somewhat bizarre twist, given that it has spent several years arguing for its right to protect the premium price of its brands, Levi Strauss announced that it was going to reduce clothing prices in its own 15 discount outlets. Jeans prices are expected to be set at between £20 and £30 rather than matching the High Street £40 to £50. As Smith (2001b) puts it,

> *To constrain Tesco's ability to sell cheap jeans looks indefensible if Levi's then broadens the range of discount stock available through its … Factory Outlets.*

It seems that the whole issue of luxury goods pricing is entering a new phase.

Sources: Castle and Beard (2001); Jardine (2001); Patten (2001); Patten and Elliott (2001); Poulter (2001); Ryle (2001a, 2001b); Smith (2001a, 2001b); Tsang (2001).

Questions

1. Why do the manufacturers seems to want to maintain high prices for their goods? What sort of pricing strategy are they implementing?
2. How are external factors affecting Tesco's pricing strategy for products like Levi's?
3. Discuss the advantages and disadvantages of allowing supermarket retailers unrestricted access to 'first-hand' supplies of branded products like these and the freedom to set whatever retail price levels they want, from (a) the manufacturer's, (b) the retailer's and (c) the consumer's points of view.

case study 11.2

Driving pricing decisions

Vauxhall Motors UK is owned by General Motors and is a sister company of Opel. It sells cars in the UK that have been manufactured either in the UK or Europe and holds some 15 per cent UK market share. The pricing decision for a car evolves with the new product development process, resulting in a six-stage model of price setting:

1 Product positioning

The pricing decision for a new model is broadly based on the planned product positioning of the car. Rarely is a new model in the motor industry completely unique and so it is usually possible to identify direct competition and use their prices as a reference point. This in itself is not enough, of course. The business plan is a crucial document that indicates how price will vary over the life of the model and how returns on investment will vary with different price assumptions within the context of the business environment. The plan has to consider, for example, what manufacturer allowances and discounts will be offered during the model's lifecycle and whether any changes in list price are planned from the outset. All of this is covered at this stage with alternative cost–volume production options presented to guide decision making. Setting a broad price level early also helps to guide the designers so that they can develop sensible specifications within reasonable cost levels.

Management judgement is needed to assess whether the market will buy the proposed model in sufficient volume at the price point agreed and whether the initial concept stacks up against the competition, both in terms of what is currently offered and any forthcoming new models. Market analysis and research can provide a broad indication of general acceptability, but more detailed further research is necessary.

The outcome of this stage is the decision whether to go ahead with the development of the proposed model or not. If a commitment is made, then even now it is considered too late to change or reposition the concept.

2 Determining the specification options

The objective of this stage is to determine the various accessory/specification packages throughout the planned model's range compared with the defined competitors', and then to determine how much the customer is willing to pay. To achieve this, there is heavy emphasis on pricing research. Small groups of customers are confronted with a fibreglass model and a mock-up interior of the vehicle. Different specification options relating to styling, space, safety or comfort features for example can be added or taken away from the model. The research then plots the responses of the groups to the various option changes to test their willingness to trade off between price and purchase preference.

The method can be summarised as:

- Car A (Vauxhall) offers the first price and specification set to be tested.
- Car B (a vehicle from the competitor set) has a different price and specification.

The customer selects their preferred car and then the price or the specification of the other is varied to find the point at which the customer will switch. This enables Vauxhall to assess the value of the specification to the potential customer. After this has been repeated enough times, a profile emerges as to which specification combination and price level is most competitive for the new model.

'We don't use cost plus pricing at all at this stage; it really is market based. It concerns the perception of value according to different specification bundles. The analysis of the trade-offs really is useful as, for example, we can find out what air conditioning or heated seats are worth to real potential customers.'

3 Price modelling

Now, the company is in a position to determine the impact of different specification options on sales and market share. By establishing the specification options Vauxhall can better predict the profitability impact beyond the cruder cost–volume–profit measures used in the initial assessment. Vauxhall is not looking to be the cheapest in the segment, but to select a list price based upon comparative specification options.

The impact of special promotions and allowances can also be introduced in more detail at this stage, before a final decision on the list price. A report is then made to a committee comprising senior management from Vauxhall Europe and General Motors Europe. The committee can make recommendations on the list price position based on the general market data, the findings of the group research analysis and the wider pan-European marketing positioning, though the final decision is always made locally. Judgement is also necessary as sometimes new entrants and their impact on the planned sales development have to be considered.

Thus competitive benchmarking is crucial in arriving at the list price of a model, but then the focus has to shift to encouraging potential customers to 'walk up the range' from basic to high specification models.

4 List price structure

This is an important area for marketing as often the perceived value to the customer of the extra specifications gained from walking up the range is far greater than the cost of providing them. The further the customer can be moved from the basic model, the greater the opportunity for higher margins and profitability. All of this is planned from the outset using the results from the pricing research to establish the detailed price points within the range and the size of the price gaps.

Sometimes, the manufacturer's pricing objective is actually to limit demand to match the available supply, however. During the first year or so of a model's life, when teething problems in production are likely to occur, demand can be deliberately restricted by charging a premium or by not offering any special allowances or discounts. Where there is an opportunity to charge a premium, Vauxhall does consider doing so. Because diesel engines, for example, are more expensive to produce, Vauxhall always seeks a higher price to reflect increased costs.

Nevertheless, normally cost is just one determinant of the price and at the time the final list price is determined, cost plays only a minor role compared with perceived value relationships.

5 Price variations

Even though Vauxhall goes to great lengths to get the list prices right, allowances also have to be built into the pricing structure to allow flexibility for sales promotions. List prices for cars tend to be fairly stable as the trade does not like frequent changes which can lead to uncertainty or confusion for customers. Extra support through increased allowances is the typical way of gaining short-term sales with the benefit that they add value in the consumer's mind rather than focusing on the model's price. Free car insurance, extended warranties, low cost credit, free servicing, etc. are all powerful ways of adding value and their introduction and withdrawal are forms of price re-alignment. In addition, Vauxhall's buying power means it can often obtain these kinds of benefits cheaply thereby offering the customer a better deal.

In the old days dealers were given a 17 per cent discount and through hard bargaining a consumer could knock the dealer's retail price down. The emphasis was on price negotiation and the margin lay with the dealer, thus the manufacturer had less scope to add value through sales promotion. Now, the dealer discount is down to 10 per cent which means that dealers have less scope for reducing prices and manufacturers can now introduce allowances for anything between 3 per cent and 7 per cent depending upon market circumstances. Early on, few allowances are offered in order to restrict demand, but later, once all the production problems have been resolved, allowances are used more heavily. These allowances are usually built into the business plan and are especially useful for extending the life of the product or for boosting sales of an old model before the introduction of a new one.

All these allowances are heavily researched to establish their perceived value to the customer and the impact of changes on sales. The difficulty with allowances is that they can be difficult to take away and customers may come to expect them as a norm.

6 Dealer pricing

As indicated earlier, the standard approach in the motor trade is to offer the dealer a discount on list prices, usually around 10 per cent. They then take possession of the stock and take responsibility for storage, financing and service. There is often not much margin left these days for serious price discounting, but that is welcomed in the industry. It has been found that the greater the scope for discounts, the greater the price competition and channel instability.

Additional allowances are given, based on dealer performance, usually on a quantity of sales basis or customer satisfaction basis. Sometimes extra bonuses are given to promote a particular model or features, if Vauxhall is trying to move stock or combat a potential competitor threat.

Overall, this system has evolved over many years and Vauxhall has developed considerable experience in examining pricing options and integrating market-based, value-based and cost-based data to make list price and allowance decisions. There is still scope for management judgement, but research plays a major role in informing decision-making.

Source: With grateful thanks to Ian Coomber, former Executive Director Sales and Marketing, Vauxhall Motors UK.

Questions

1. To what extent and how does the Vauxhall six-stage process of price setting conform with the five-stage model presented in Figure 11.1 of this chapter?
2. What are the advantages and disadvantages of using competition-based pricing in a market like this?
3. Assess the importance of market research in Vauxhall's price setting process.
4. If Vauxhall was considering selling cars direct via the internet, what impact might it have on the pricing decision?

References for chapter 11

Altmann, J. and Chu, K. (2001), 'How to Charge for Network Services – Flat-rate or Usage-based?', *Computer Networks*, August, pp. 519–31.

Ansari, A., Siddarth, S. and Weinberg, C. (1996), 'Price a Bundle of Products or Services: The Case of Non-profits', *Journal of Marketing Research*, 33, pp. 86–93.

Arnold, M. (2001), 'Airlines Fight to Survive Crisis', *Marketing*, 27 September, p. 27.

Baily, P.J.H. (1987), *Purchasing and Supply Management* (5th edn), Chapman & Hall.

Baumol, W.J. (1965), *Economic Theory and Operations Analysis*, Prentice Hall.

Bedington, E. (2001), 'In Need of a Quick Fix', *The Grocer*, 15 September, pp. 36–7.

Binyon, M. (2001), 'Airlines Must Cut Prices Not Jobs or Routes', *The Times*, 6 October, p. 22.

Bird, L. (2001), 'London Calling at Cut-price Rates', *The Times*, 20 November, p. 5.

Blattberg, R.C. and Neslin, S.A. (1990), *Sales Promotion: Concepts, Methods and Strategies*, Prentice Hall.

Blois, K. (1994), 'Discounts in Business Marketing Management', *Industrial Marketing Management*, 23(2), pp. 93–100.

Castle, S. and Beard, M. (2001), 'Supermarkets to Defy Bar on Cheap Designer Goods', *The Independent*, 21 November, p. 10.

Chambers, S. and Johnston, R. (2000), 'Experience Curves in Services: Macro and Micro Level Approaches', *International Journal of Operations & Production Management*, 20 (7), pp. 842–59.

Chesshyre, T. (2001), 'Five-star Luxury Going for a Song', *The Times*, 20 November, p. 5.

Chuanjiang Ju (1999), 'Government Benefits from Open Bidding System', *China Daily*, 7 April, p. 3.

Coles, J. (1998), 'Sheep Day Return', *The Express*, 13 October, p. 16.

Darwent, C. (1996), 'Bangers and Cash', *Management Today*, June, pp. 72–4.

Davies, K. (2001), 'Sausage King Launches Franchise Operation', *The Grocer*, 15 December, p. 20.

Dean, J. (1950), 'Pricing Policies for New Products', *Harvard Business Review*, 28 (November), pp. 45–53.

Diamantopoulos, A. and Mathews, B. (1995), *Making Pricing Decisions: A Study of Managerial Practice*, Chapman & Hall.

Dodds, W., Monroe, K. and Grewal, D. (1991), 'Effects of Price, Brand, and Store Information on Buyers' Product Evaluation', *Journal of Marketing Research*, 28 (August), pp. 307–19.

Doyle, A. (2001), 'Boeing Deals Fast But Loose', *Flight International*, 11–17 September, p. 36.

Felgran, S. and Yamada, M. (2001), 'Transfer Pricing: A Truly Global Concern', *Financial Executive*, November, p. 21.

Gendall, P. *et al.* (1997), 'The Effect of Odd Pricing on Demand', *European Journal of Marketing*, 31(11/12), pp. 790–813.

The Grocer (2001a), 'Lifting the Smoke Screen', *Guide to Tobacco* supplement to *The Grocer*, 5 May, p. 4.

The Grocer (2001b), 'Manufacturers Urged to Sign up as Sausages Get the Quality Mark', *The Grocer*, 27 October, p. 14.

The Grocer (2001c), 'See it in Store Says Asda: We Are 15% Better Value', *The Grocer*, 3 November, p. 6.

The Grocer (2001d), 'Irish Government Urged to Double Cigarette Prices', *The Grocer*, 1 December, p. 8.

The Grocer (2001e), 'Just 10p More for Cigarettes', *The Grocer*, 8 December, p. 10.

Hardcastle, S. (2001), 'Grocer Focus: Pizza', *The Grocer*, 17 November, pp. 49–52.

Harris, G. (1998), 'Islanders Discover Sheep-day Return', *The Times*, 13 October, p. 3.

Heller, L. (2001), 'Better pricing, DVD Growth Keep HDTV Sales on the Rise', *DSN Retailing Today*, 5 November, p. 35.

Herrman, A., Huber, F. and Higie, R. (1997), 'Product and Service Bundling Decisions and their Effects on Purchase Intention', *Pricing Strategy and Practice*, 5 (3), pp. 99–107.

Howard, C. and Herbig, P. (1996), 'Japanese Pricing Policies', *Journal of Consumer Marketing*, 13 (4), pp. 5–17.

Jardine, A. (2001), 'The Right to Grey Goods?', *Marketing*, 19 July, p. 26.

Lambin, J.J. (1993), *Strategic Marketing:* A European Approach, McGraw-Hill.

Levy, D.T. (1994), 'Guaranteed Pricing in Industrial Purchases: Making Use of Markets in Contractual Relations', *Industrial Marketing Management*, 23(4), pp. 307–13.

Livesey, F. (1976), *Pricing*, Macmillan.

Lysons, C.K. (1993), Purchasing, *M&E Handbooks* (3rd edn), Pitman Publishing.

Marketing Week (2001), 'Andrex Ads to Focus on Price Cuts', *Marketing Week*, 9 August, p. 7.

Mintel (2001a), 'Sausages and Meat Pies', 28 March, accessed via http://www.mintel.com.

Mintel (2001b), 'Pizza', 1 August, accessed via http://www.mintel.com.

Monroe, K. and Cox, J. (2001), 'Pricing Practices that Endanger Profits', *Marketing Management*, September/October, pp. 42–6.

Monroe, K. and Della Bitta, A. (1978), 'Models for Pricing Decisions', *Journal of Marketing Research*, 15 (August.), pp. 413–28.

Moskal, B. (1994), 'Consumer Age Begets Value Pricing', *Industry Week*, 21 February, pp. 36–40.

Nagle, T.T. (1987), *The Strategies and Tactics of Pricing*, Prentice Hall.

Patten, S. (2001), 'Tesco Battles on in Levi's Case', *The Times*, 18 December, p. 20.

Patten, S. and Elliott, V. (2001), 'Tesco Seeks Law Change After Ruling', *The Times*, 21 November, p. 25.

Perks, R. (1993), 'How to Win a Price War', *Investor's Chronicle*, 22 October, pp. 14–15.

Poulter, S. (2001), 'Tesco Loses Fight to Sell "Bargain" Designer Jeans', *Daily Mail*, 21 November, p. 17.

Ryle, S. (2001a), 'Is Levi's Heading for Checkout?', *The Observer*, 8 April, p. 5.

Ryle, S. (2001b), 'Levi Stitches up Cut-price Jeans', *The Observer*, 25 November, p. 1.

Schmenner, R. (1990), *Production/Operations Management*, New York: Macmillan.

Schroeder, R. (1993), *Operations Management*, New York: McGraw-Hill.

Singh, S. (2001), 'Paper Cuts', *Marketing Week*, 9 August, pp. 22-5.

Smith, C. (2001a), 'Tesco's Low Prices Fail to Credit Levi's Brand Investment', *Marketing*, 21 April, p. 19.

Smith, C. (2001b), 'Levi's Loses Out as Discounts Put on a Mixed Message', *Marketing*, 29 November, p. 21.

Smith, P.R. and Chaffey, D. (2001), *eMarketing eXcellence: At the Heart of eBusiness*, Oxford: Butterworth-Heinemann.

Starrs, C. (2001), 'Tobacco Industry Left Fuming Over Price Increase', *The Electronic Herald*, 22 March.

Tsang, L. (2001), 'Levi's Wins Battle Against Cut-price Clothes', *The Times*, 27 November, p. 9.

Wildner, R. (1998), 'The Importance of Understanding Consumer Reactions', *Marketing and Research Today*, 27(4), pp. 141–7.

Yoo, B., Donthu, N. and Lee, S. (2000), 'An Examination of Selected Marketing Mix Elements and Brand Equity', *Journal of the Academy of Marketing Science*, 28 (2), pp. 195–211.

part five

PLACE

12 marketing channels and logistics

13 retailers and wholesalers

Place, or distribution, can become the element of the marketing mix that causes the biggest headache to a manufacturer. The other three mix elements remain under the manufacturer's control, but once the product is out of the factory gate, it is at the mercy of the intermediaries within the distribution channel. Chapter 12 defines the main types of distribution channel available to manufacturers and discusses the advantages or otherwise of each. It also focuses on both the importance of cultivating good relationships within distribution channels and, where possible, ways of gaining and maintaining control over channel members. The final part of Chapter 12 looks at the logistics function, and how goods are moved cost effectively from the manufacturer through the distribution channel to the end customer.

Chapter 13, in contrast, centres on the retailer as the main interface between manufacturer and end consumer. Retailers face particular problems, such as choice of location, merchandising and image development, which are all discussed in this chapter. Many of these problems are, at heart, centred on making decisions on elements of the marketing mix, but the application in retailing gives them a different and interesting angle. This chapter also looks at the rapidly emerging field of internet retailing.

chapter 12

marketing channels and logistics

LEARNING OBJECTIVES

This chapter will help you to:

1 define what a channel of distribution is and understand its contribution to efficient and effective marketing effort;

2 differentiate between types of intermediary and their roles;

3 appreciate the factors influencing channel design, structure and strategy and the effect of conflict and cooperation within channels;

4 define logistics, appreciating the importance of customer service and its implementation within logistics;

5 identify the functions involved in logistics and the decisions contributing to their management.

Introduction

Part of the responsibility of a marketing-orientated organisation is to get the product to the customer in the right place at the right time. This has led to the development of extremely efficient and sophisticated distribution systems. Imagine what life would be like for a consumer without those familiar distribution systems. The onus would be on us as consumers to find out what is being supplied, when and where. Without the backup of a customer orientation, issues of supply, location, timing, quantity and assortment would all be resolved to suit the supplier's, not the customer's, abilities and preferences. This is fine, as long as demand outstrips supply and consumers are prepared to invest considerable time and even money in sourcing goods. Such a scenario is not impossible. Before the changes in eastern Europe, a consumer's first activity after finishing work was often to join the queues for essential items of food such as bread.

This indicates the importance of a sound distribution infrastructure, both in the structure of a modern economy and as a tool in the marketing mix, and provides the main theme of this chapter. This topic is often referred to as 'place' to cover the decisions and strategies that enable the product to flow to the consumer, whether from the market, direct to the home, via a wholesaler or from a retail outlet.

The chapter begins with a definition of channels of distribution, highlighting the role played by different types of intermediaries, and looks at the relative merits of using intermediaries compared with direct selling. Attention then turns to the strategic decision making necessary to design and implement a channel strategy. While the main emphasis will be on the manufacturer selecting a channel structure and strategy to achieve market coverage and marketing objectives, the power of the intermediary should not be forgotten. In many countries, the power of negotiation rests with the intermediary, who may select or deselect manufacturers' products. Such action has a major impact on the manufacturer, but little impact on the intermediary.

eg

Mitsubishi is one of the largest global producers of cars. In Europe, it manufactures 120,000 cars in the Netherlands and along with 180,000 cars from worldwide production, distributes them to 24 European distributors, some of which are company owned. They in turn pass them on to over 2,000 dealers across Europe. To back up the new car distribution, a 26,000 m^3 warehouse stocks over 110,000 different parts. This distribution chain has to compete with those of other manufacturers, and that means advertising, dealer and distributor training, special promotions and keeping both new cars and parts moving. Above all, it has to ensure that the right vehicle (or part) is in the right place at the right time. A major objective for Mitsubishi is to draw dealers and distributors closer to its priorities and plans through closer working and excellent support. A new IBM system was installed to provide a faster, more efficient integrated order-processing and parts distribution service to distributors and dealers. With the new system, the distributor can access the central warehouse inventory to check stock items, stock levels, delivery date, status updates, shipping information and much more. Integration of the parts ordering-process has enabled Mitsubishi to reduce three warehouses to one, and to reduce stocking levels, while providing a greatly improved parts service. The dealers now stock almost no parts, knowing that they can be supplied quickly from the central warehouse. This is an example of how distribution and customer service levels can be enhanced by carefully designed contractual and physical distribution systems and policies that benefit the whole distribution chain (http://www.ibm.com; http://www.mitsubishi-motors-euro.com).

Although channels of distribution are important economic structures, they are also social systems involving individuals and organisations. This chapter, therefore, also considers issues associated with the general conduct of the relationship. Such relationships may be characterised by conflict, cooperation, trust or a climate of mutual hostility and discontent, despite the economic pragmatism that binds both parties together.

This chapter also examines the processes of physical distribution that enable products to flow from manufacturer to consumer. After an initial review of some of the key concepts, the difficulty of balancing customer service against distribution costs is considered in terms of the total logistics system, which highlights the need for adopting a 'total' approach to distribution management. The various functions and management decisions are then examined in the context of the main choices that lead to different distribution cost and service profiles. These include transportation modes, storage and materials handling.

Of course, in service situations there is no product movement or storage because production and consumption are normally simultaneous. In that case, the channel of distribution is primarily concerned with providing access to the booking and reservation system and in handling the sales and negotiating process associated with such access (*see* Chapter 22). The emphasis in this chapter, therefore, will be the movement of physical goods.

Definition of marketing channels

A **marketing channel** can be defined as the structure linking a group of individuals or organisations through which a product or service is made available to the consumer or industrial user. The degree of formality in the relationships between the channel members can vary significantly, from the highly organised arrangements in the distribution of fmcg products through supermarkets, to the more speculative and transient position of roadside sellers of fruit and vegetables.

eg

When Carrefour decided to expand into China, it found that a number of factors influencing its retail and distribution strategy differed from those it experienced in its domestic market, France. Although the Chinese market is huge, with potentially 1.3 billion consumers, it is widely dispersed and the distances between major population centres can be vast. Given the poor transportation infrastructure, the notion of national buying and local distribution is not as feasible in China as it is in France. For some goods, Carrefour has had to select three different suppliers to provide the same product to its 27 hypermarkets spread across 15 Chinese cities. Even then, lorries are often delayed due to road congestion and at times some lorries have been 'lost' altogether. While a typical store in France might receive 8 to 10 lorries per day from a regional distribution centre, a Chinese branch might receive up to 300 deliveries per day direct from suppliers (although some deliveries are made by bicycle!).

Carrefour also found wide differences in income levels, local customs, food tastes, local bureaucracy and consumer demands between Chinese regions. In the larger cities such as Shanghai and Beijing, consumer tastes are adapting and becoming much more sensitive to western food retail formats, which is not surprising, given that there are 25 hypermarkets in Shanghai alone. In some of the 34 provinces, however, the experience is much more limited.

There is still a preference, for example, for fresh produce bought from street markets and as many households do not have freezers, it is rare to find demand for a wide range of frozen food. Unlike in France, the product assortment offered tends to vary by region and according to local circumstances. Despite the differences, Carrefour turns over $33.6 mn a year from a typical store in China, about 60 per cent of the turnover of a similar sized store in France and despite the average spend being four times lower (Goldman, 2001; Hunt, 2001).

There are several different types of **intermediary**, each with a slightly different role. These will now be defined, and then we shall look at the ways in which these intermediaries come together to create different kinds of distribution channels between manufacturer and consumer. As a means of summarising all of this, this section will finally consider the rationale for using intermediaries at all.

Types of intermediary

Many marketing channels involve the physical movement of goods and the transfer of legal title to the goods, although the physical movement may be separate from the change of title, especially if external transport carriers are used. As the goods pass from hand to hand, each intermediary adds a *margin* to the price of the goods, which may or may not reflect the value added. Various functions are performed by the various types of intermediary in return for their margins. Some purchase an assortment of products from various suppliers and then add value by storing, breaking bulk, and then adding services (e.g. credit, delivery) during the resale process. In some situations product transformation may take place, especially in packaging and in the image of the product, which may be enhanced by instore promotion.

However, not all intermediaries between the manufacturer and consumer necessarily take legal title to the goods, or even physical possession of them, as the following descriptions show.

Wholesalers

Wholesalers do not normally deal with the end consumer but with other intermediaries, usually retailers. However, in some situations sales are made directly to the end user, especially in B2B markets, with no further resale taking place. An organisation may purchase its catering or cleaning supplies from a local cash and carry business that serves the retail trade. A wholesaler does take legal title to the goods as well as taking physical possession of them.

Retailers

Retailers sell direct to the consumer and may either purchase direct from the manufacturer or deal with a wholesaler, depending on purchasing power and volume. Retailers come in many different formats, sizes and locations as we shall see in Chapter 13.

Distributors and dealers

Distributors and dealers are intermediaries who add value through special services associated with stocking or selling inventory, credit and after-sales service. Although these intermediaries are often used in B2B markets, they can also be found in direct dealing with consumers, for example computer or motor dealers. The term usually signifies a more structured and closer tie between the manufacturer and intermediary in order that the product may be delivered efficiently and with the appropriate level of expertise. Clearly, some retail outlets are also closely associated with dealerships and the distinction between them may be somewhat blurred.

Franchisees

A **franchisee** holds a contract to supply and market a product or service to the design or blueprint of the franchisor (the owner or originator of the product or service). The franchise agreement covers not only the precise specification of the product or service, but also the selling and marketing aspects of the business. The uniformity of different branches of

McDonald's is an indication of the level of detail covered by a franchise agreement. There are many products and services currently offered through franchise arrangements, especially in the retail and home services sector, considered in Chapter 22.

Agents and brokers

Agents and brokers are intermediaries who have the legal authority to act on behalf of the manufacturer, although they do not take legal title to the goods or indeed handle the product directly in any way. They do, however, make the product more accessible to the customer and in some cases provide appropriate add-on benefits. Their prime function is to bring buyer and seller together. Universities often use agents to recruit students in overseas markets.

eg

Euro Food Brands acts as a broker for a small number of continental European brand manufacturers that want to develop in the UK, but have neither the resources or the expertise to act independently. It mainly represents brands that are well established in their own domestic markets, such as Barilla (pasta and pasta sauces from Italy) and illy Caffe. illy Caffe is a family-owned business that concentrates on top quality coffee, and although it sells in over sixty countries worldwide, it often prefers to work through brokers such as Euro Food brands. Similarly, Covinor, a French manufacturer of mustard, vinegar and sauces, supplies 90 per cent of food retailers in France, but again prefers to work through brokers in the UK. The key benefit that the broker can offer is the contact list and the expertise of the sales force in getting products onto the retailers' shelves (http://www.eurofoodbrands.co.uk).

The specific role of each channel member will vary depending on a range of market and strategy issues. The next subsection looks at how these intermediaries relate to each other, and discusses further the specific roles that each plays in getting goods to end users.

Channel structure

The route selected to move a product to market through different intermediaries is known as the *channel structure*. The chosen route varies according to whether the organisation is dealing with consumer or B2B goods. Even within these broad sectors, different products might require different distribution channels.

This company distributes specialist European brands throughout the UK market.

Source: Euro Food Brands.

Consumer goods

The four most common channel structures in consumer markets are shown in Figure 12.1. As can be seen, each alternative involves a different number of intermediaries, and each is appropriate to different kinds of markets or selling situations. Each will now be discussed in turn.

Producer–consumer (direct supply). In the producer–consumer direct supply channel, the manufacturer and consumer deal directly with each other. There are many variants on this theme. It could be a factory shop or a pick-your-own fruit farm. Some manufacturers sell direct to the public through mail order. The increasing cheapness and ease of setting up customer databases (to be discussed in detail in Chapter 18) mean that direct selling by telephone or mail order is becoming a more attractive distribution option. Alternatively, goods may be sold through a network of sales offices. Door-to-door selling, such as that practised by double-glazing companies, and party plan selling, such as Tupperware and Ann Summers parties, are all attempts by producers to eliminate intermediaries. Clearly, this route has the advantage of control and simplicity, but this must be weighed against the cost and resource efficiency of directly building a company-owned sales and distribution force. The internet is now becoming an established direct distribution channel for some suppliers. Information on products, prices and delivery can be placed on the internet at relatively low cost. To complete the sales cycle, such companies can align with express delivery services to get orders to customers fast. The internet is also a complete distribution channel for some operators, such as those in the travel and bookselling sector.

Producer–retailer–consumer (short channel). The producer–retailer–consumer route is the most popular with the larger retailers, since they can buy in large quantities, obtaining special prices and often with tailormade stock-handling and delivery arrangements. This route is typically used by large supermarket chains and is most appropriate for large manufacturers and large retailers who deal in such huge quantities that a direct relationship is efficient.

Figure 12.2 shows a highly simplified form of the goods and information flow between a manufacturer and a retailer. The fast capture and processing of information are critical for the efficient and effective functioning of such systems. Tesco, for example, has automated its business chain to such a degree that orders, invoicing and payments are all triggered by shoppers passing through the checkouts.

In the car trade, a local dealer usually deals directly with the manufacturer, because, unlike fmcg products, there is a need for significant support in the supply infrastructure and expertise in the sales and service process. This is an example of the grey area between retailing and distributorships, discussed at p. 473.

Producer–wholesaler–retailer–consumer (long channel). The advantage of adding a wholesaler level can be significant where small manufacturers and/or small retailers are involved. A small manufacturing organisation does not necessarily have the skills or resources to

Figure 12.1 Channel structures for consumer goods

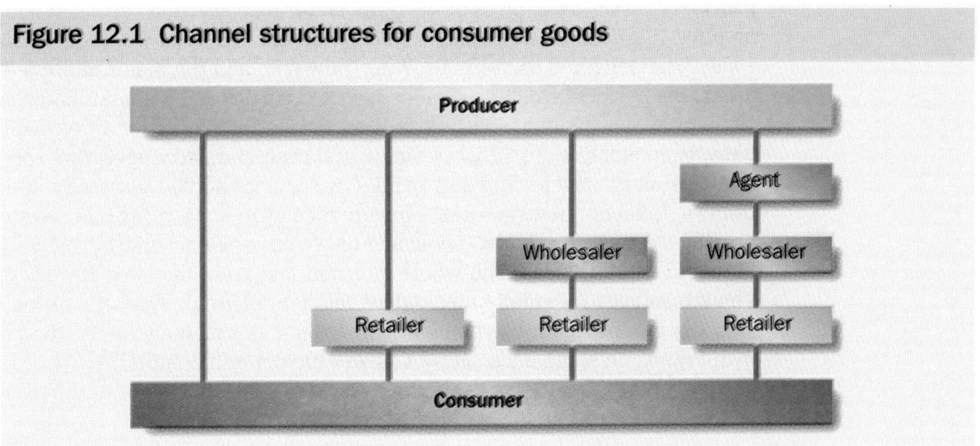

Figure 12.2 The flow of products and information between a large manufacturer and a large retailer

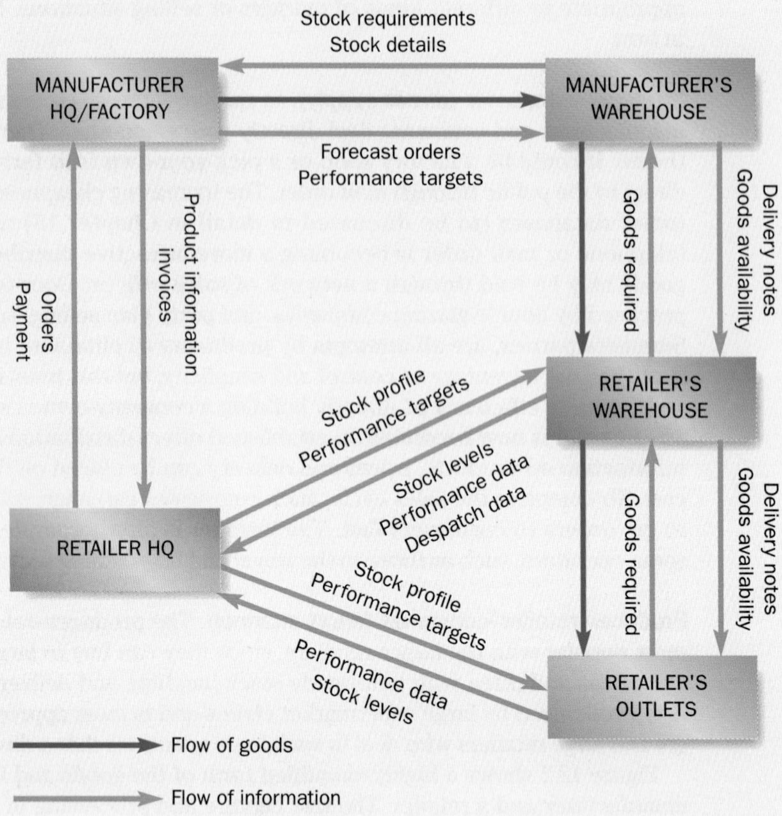

reach a wide range of retail customers and, similarly, the small corner shop does not have the resources to source relatively small quantities direct from many manufactures. The wholesaler can provide a focal point for both sides, by buying in bulk from manufacturers, then splitting that bulk into manageable quantities for small retailers; bringing a wider assortment of goods together for the retailer under one roof; providing access to a wider range of retail customers for the small manufacturer; and similarly providing access to a wider range of manufacturers' goods for the small retailer. Effectively, the wholesaler is marketing on behalf of the manufacturer.

eg

The independent grocery sector is serviced by a number of wholesalers and cash and carry providers. Nearly two-thirds of the trade is through cash and carries in which the retailer can be offered greater choice or more items than the delivered wholesaler handles (*The Grocer*, 1999). The delivered sector is growing, however, and the major multiple depot wholesalers are taking business from the smaller cash and carries and the unaffiliated groups.

Sugro UK, a Nantwich-based wholesale group that is part of a German-based parent company, is an amalgam of 79 wholesalers and cash and carry operators specialising mainly in confectionery, snacks and soft drinks. It services 43,000 outlets including CTN (confectionery, tobacco, news) stores, convenience stores, petrol forecourt stores and pubs. To provide the service, it has 350 field and telesales personnel and 450 delivery vehicles to negotiate and support sales. The whole international group handles 250,000 different products. The advantages for small independent retailers sourcing from the group are mainly linked with the group's centralised bulk buying from major manufacturers, the availability of Sugro own-brands on some lines, as well as an efficient and comprehensive stocking and delivery service. To be competitive itself, Sugro aims to provide a 'point of difference' for the retailer so that a win–win situation is created (http://www.sugro.co.uk).

The wholesaler can also act on behalf of relatively large manufacturers trying to sell large volumes of frequently reordered products to a wide retail network. Daily national newspapers, for example, are delivered from the presses to the wholesalers, which can then break bulk and assemble tailormade orders involving many different titles for their own retail customers. This is far more efficient than each newspaper producer trying to deal direct with each small corner shop newsagent.

Producer–agent–wholesaler–retailer–consumer. This is the longest and most indirect channel. It might be used, for example, where a manufacturer is trying to enter a relatively unknown export market. The agent will be chosen because of local knowledge, contacts and expertise in selling into that country, and will earn commission on sales made. The problem is, however, that the manufacturer is totally dependent and has to trust the quality of the agent's knowledge, commitment and selling ability. Nevertheless, this method is widely used by smaller organisations trying to develop in remote markets, where their ability to establish a strong presence is constrained by lack of time, resources or knowledge.

B2B goods

As highlighted in Chapter 4, B2B products often involve close technical and commercial dialogue between buyer and seller, during which the product and its attributes are matched to the customer's specific requirements. The type and frequency of purchase, the quantity purchased and the importance of the product to the buyer all affect the type of channel structure commonly found in B2B markets. Office stationery, for example, is not a crucial purchase from the point of view of keeping production lines going and, as a routine repurchase, it is more likely to be distributed through specialist distributors or retailers such as Staples, Office World or Rymans. In contrast, crucial components that have to be integrated into a production line are likely to be delivered direct from supplier to buyer to specific deadlines. The variety of B2B distribution channels can be seen in Figure 12.3. Each type will now be discussed in turn.

Manufacturer–user. The direct channel is most appropriate where the goods being sold have a high unit cost and perhaps a high technical content. There is likely to be a small number of buyers who are perhaps confined to clearly defined geographical areas. To operate such a channel, the manufacturer must be prepared to build and manage a sales and distribution force that can negotiate sales, provide service and administer customer needs. In some cases, the sales representative will both sell and install the product, as happens with computer software applications.

Manufacturers may also operate their own sales branches or offices. These organisations are owned and operated by the manufacturer, but fulfil many of the functions and roles of a wholesale operation. They allow the manufacturer to retain more control over the way in which the distribution channel works, and can increase the effectiveness and efficiency of the links between manufacturers and their customers, but they may also be a necessity if the manufacturer needs wholesale services that are not available on the open market.

Figure 12.3 Channel structures for B2B goods

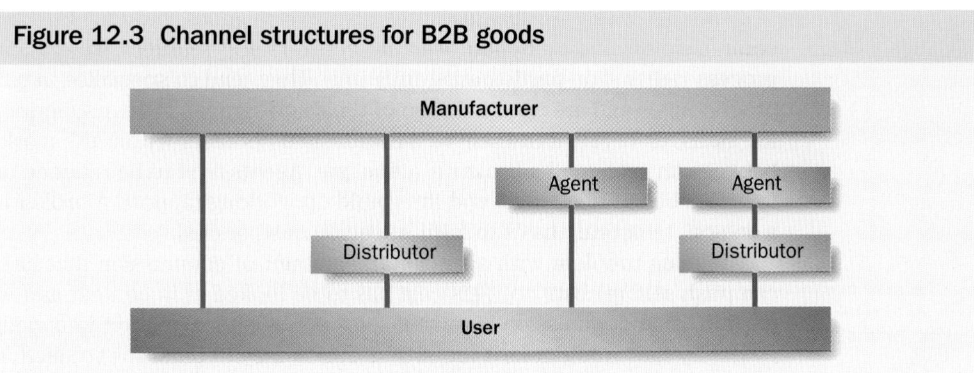

eg

AB Konstruktions-Bakelit, one of Sweden's largest manufacturers of industrial plastic components, deals directly with customers such as Volvo, Saab and Alfa Laval. This is because of the need for considerable dialogue during the design and development stage to ensure a close fit between the customer's specification and components that are made to order. There would be a very high risk of misunderstanding if a third party were introduced.

Sales branches tend to be situated away from the manufacturer's head office in areas where demand is particularly high. They are a conveniently situated focal point for the area's sales force, providing them with products and support services so that they in turn can better meet their customers' needs more quickly. Sales branches may also sell products themselves directly to small retailers or wholesalers.

Sales offices do not carry stock, so, although they might take orders from local customers, they are only acting as agents and will pass the order on to head office. Again, they provide a locally convenient focus in busy areas.

Manufacturer–distributor–user. Less direct channels tend to be adopted as the number of customers grows, the size of customers reduces, and the number of intermediary functions also increases. Building materials, for example, are often sold to builders' merchants, who then sell to the building trade based on lower order quantities, and consequently with a greater range of stock availability but greater proximity to local need. The philosophy is similar to that of the short channel of distribution discussed in the consumer context on page 475.

eg

This less direct type of structure can also apply to software products. Moser GmbH is one of the leading software houses in Germany and specialises in selling to trade and handicraft organisations. Although it had over 10,000 software installations in Germany and the Netherlands, it decided to seek expansion elsewhere in Europe. This was done by selling through other software and system houses which already had the sales and technical appreciation to generate sales for Moser.

Manufacturer–agent–user. Sometimes an agent is introduced to act on behalf of a group of manufacturers in dealing with users in situations where it would not be economically viable to create a direct selling effort, but where there is a need for selling expertise to generate and complete transactions.

eg

Teijo Pesukoneet from Nakkila in Finland specialises in technically advanced cleaning machines for metal components in enclosed cabinets. Although it has its own sales offices in Sweden and Norway, it operates through agents in other main European markets such as the UK and Germany. Agents are trained to handle technical queries and sales enquiries but relay orders to Finland for direct delivery.

Generally speaking, agents do not take title to goods, but may buy and sell, usually on a commission basis, on behalf of manufacturers and retailers. They facilitate an exchange process rather than participating fully in it. They tend to specialise in particular markets or product lines and are used because of their knowledge, or their superior purchasing or selling skills, or because of their well-established contacts within the market. The distinction between an agent and a broker is a fine one. Agents tend to be retained on a long-term basis to act on behalf of a client, and thus build up working rapport. A broker tends to be used on a one-off, temporary basis to fulfil a specific need or deal.

The main problem with agents is the amount of commission that has to be paid, as this can push selling costs up. This cost has to be looked at in context and with a sense of proportion. That commission is buying sales performance, market knowledge and a degree of flexibility that would take a lot of time and money to build for yourself, even if you wanted to do it. The alternative to using agents, therefore, may not be so effective or cost efficient.

marketing *in action*

South African oranges

The next time you tuck into a South African orange, stop to think of the many stages in the distribution channel through which the product has moved, from the South African orange growers to the local supermarket. Each year South Africa exports some 50 million cartons of oranges, with western Europe consuming over 50 per cent of them. The industry is made up of 200 private farmers and 1,200 growers in cooperatives. Many growers and cooperatives pool their output for marketing and distribution purposes under the Capespan International selling operation (50 per cent owned by Fyffes). The challenge for Capespan has been to align its distribution strategy with increased international competition, greater customer sophistication and the demands of ever-powerful supermarket chains. Product freshness, variety, quality and supply must all meet customer demand and the product must move smoothly through the supply chain from grower to buyer.

The oranges move from the growers to the fruit-handling facilities run by Capespan near the major ports such as Durban, Cape Town and Port Elizabeth. Capespan purchases the oranges and then adds handling and transportation costs and a profit margin. The services provided include some initial de-greening, environmental control, labelling and packing, all before shipment. It also arranges shipment, increasingly in large bulk bins for ease of handling, from the ports. At this stage, data is collected on the fruit, size, type, quality grade, treatment and origin. Another service that Capespan undertakes is to move the oranges to cold storage before they depart for Europe. Most of these processes are provided by Capespan subsidiaries: Fresh Produce Terminals provides cold storage and warehousing facilities, Cape Reefers provides shipping coordination and CSS Logistics, the clearing and forwarding documentation.

European ports such as Flushing, Sheerness and Tilbury have been selected as destinations. A partnership approach between Capespan and the port authorities has resulted in a specialist infrastructure for handling and storing palletised or binned oranges. In order to ensure that the right oranges arrive at the right EU port, data is sent to Capespan planners in Europe, who then decide which fruit should be unloaded at which port to meet local demand. On arrival, Capespan re-inspects the produce. Where necessary, the cartons are labelled and quality control checks undertaken to ensure that the fruit is consistent with specific buyers' expectations. This all helps to preserve the reputation of the Capespan brand name, Outspan. There are plans to add more valuable services such as pre-packing, size grading and fruit preparation for fresh fruit salad. After processing, the oranges are ready either to enter the UK domestic distribution chain or to go for further storage. Because an electronic data system has been used, fruit that has ripened during transit is ready to leave port quickly in 'table-fresh' condition.

Shipment can be to external pre-packers contracted by the supermarkets or straight to the wholesale and supermarket distribution systems at regional or central warehouse collection points. These shipments fulfil orders placed either direct by the supermarkets or through selling agents dealing with Capespan in the UK. Some oranges go into the fruit and vegetable distribution chain and end up being sold in markets and through wholesalers dealing with specialist fruit and vegetable stores.

Capespan relies heavily on timely information produced at every step of the supply chain to manage the procurement, distribution, marketing and sales processes. Customised information systems and pallet tracking systems such as Paltrack are used for pallet tracking and stock control. Using data provided by the order and shipments, a decision support infrastructure ensures that information is generated to support Capespan's key decisions, such as destination priorities, and that information is also provided in the most useful form to suppliers. Capespan also uses web technology throughout the supply chain, such as its extranet (http://www.ourgrowers.co.za) which links Capespan with its growers/suppliers, allowing access to critical market information in real time from marketplaces around the world. Other internet sites provide an encyclopaedia of information to customers and support grower/customer interaction.

Sources: Shapley (1998); http://www.capespan.com; http://www.networking.ibm.com.

Manufacturer–agent–distributor–user. A model comprising manufacturer–agent–distributor–user links is particularly useful in fast-moving export markets. The sales agent coordinates sales in a specified market, while the distributors provide inventory and fast restocking facilities close to the point of customer need. The comments on the longest channel of distribution in the consumer context (*see* p. 477) are also applicable here.

Increasingly, using multiple channels of distribution is becoming the rule rather than the exception (Frazier, 1999). Where there is choice, the retailer could have a virtual, web-based store as well as physical retail outlets. In global markets stronger branded manufacturers could adopt different methods to reach customers, depending upon local distribution structures. Dutta *et al.* (1995) found that augmenting an indirect channel with a direct channel improves the manufacturer's ability to manage the indirect channel. Using multiple channels enables more market segments to be reached and can increase penetration levels, but this must be weighed against lower levels of support from trade members who find themselves facing high degrees of intra-channel competition.

The type of structure adopted in a particular sector, whether industrial or consumer, will ultimately depend on the product and market characteristics that produce differing cost and servicing profiles. These issues will be further explored in the context of the main justification for using marketing intermediaries, described next.

e-marketing *in action*

How the internet impacts on channel structures

Chaffey *et al.* (2003) summarise the two alternative, but contradictory implications of channels becoming electronically mediated networks:

1 *Ephemeral relationship impact*. Here relationships are short-term and driven primarily by the price of commodities. A buyer seeking to purchase will typically obtain a product after assessing the offerings of different suppliers at an intermediary. For example, an evaluator intermediary such as e-STEEL provides a spot-market for large volume steel purchases. The increased use of new intermediaries is referred to as reintermediation.

2 *Lock-in relationship impact*. Here, a hierarchical network develops with a well-defined structure in which the value-chain does not change. A buyer seeking to purchase will typically obtain a product from a pre-determined supplier since there is an established relationship based on particular technology links and well established quality levels. Cambridge-based Chivers Hartley, a leading UK manufacturer of preserves, jellies and sauces provides an example of the second situation.

Since 85 per cent of Chivers Hartley's business is conducted with supermarkets, who dictate that their customers must trade electronically with them for receiving orders and invoicing, electronic data interchange (EDI) accounts for over 90 per cent of Chivers Hartley's business transactions. Chivers Hartley has also opened up its intranet to share business intelligence with other supply chain partners by allowing them direct access to its production and logistics information. The intranet is an especially valuable tool for the company's national account managers. They can now access key production information in order to provide accurate delivery dates when in discussion with buyers at the major multiples. The system is growing in its use at Chivers Hartley – currently it is used in sales and marketing, accounts and purchasing departments.

Source: Chaffey *et al.* (2003).

Rationale for using intermediaries

Every transaction between a buyer and a seller costs money. There are delivery costs, order picking and packing costs, marketing costs, and almost certainly administrative costs associated with processing an order and receiving or making payment. The role of the intermediary is to increase the efficiency and reduce the costs of individual transactions. This can be clearly seen in Figure 12.4.

Figure 12.4 The role of intermediaries

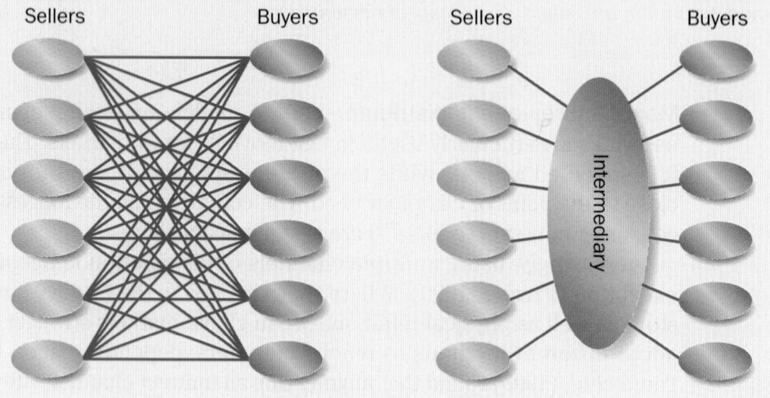

If six manufacturers wished to deal with six buyers, a total of 36 links would be necessary. All of these transaction links cost time and money to service, and require a certain level of administrative and marketing expertise. If volumes and profit margins are sufficient, then this may be a viable proposition. However, in many situations this would add considerably to the cost of the product. By using an intermediary, the number of links falls to just 12, and each buyer and each seller only needs to maintain and service one link. If this makes sense when considering only six potential buyers, just imagine how much more sensible it is with fmcg goods where there are millions of potential buyers! On economic grounds alone, the rationale for intermediaries in creating transaction efficiency is demonstrated.

However, there are other reasons for using intermediaries, because they add value for the manufacturer and customer alike. These value added services fall into three main groups (Webster, 1979), as shown in Figure 12.5.

Transactional value

The role of intermediaries in assisting transaction efficiency has already been highlighted. To perform this role adequately, the intermediary, as an interconnected but separate entity, must decide on its own strategic position in the marketplace, and therefore assemble products that it believes its own desired customers need and then market them effectively. The selection is extremely important, and requires careful purchasing in terms of type, quantity and cost to fit the intermediary's own product strategy.

The *risks* move to the intermediary, who takes *title* to the goods and, as legal owner, is responsible for their resale. Of course, it is in the manufacturer's interest to see the product moving through the distribution system in order to achieve sales and profit objectives. However, the risk of being lumbered with obsolete, damaged or slow-moving stock rests with the intermediary, not the manufacturer. This is a valuable service to that manufacturer.

With the transfer of title and risk, the need to *market effectively* increases. Intermediaries may recruit and train their own sales forces to resell the products that they have assembled. This is another valuable service to the manufacturer, as it means that the product may have a greater chance of being brought to the attention of the prospective customer, especially in B2B markets. An intermediary can use the full range of promotional weapons available, including advertising, point-of-sale promotion and direct mail (*see* Chapters 15, 16 and 18). An industrial distributor may have a sales counter or a telephone sales operation, or it may have an external field sales force to sell the product in question (Anderson and Narus, 1986). The intermediary may take sole responsibility for this function, or carry it out in cooperation with the manufacturer, sharing the decisions and the expenses.

Logistical value

A critical role for the intermediary is the assembly of an *assortment of products* from different sources that is compatible with the needs of the intermediary's own customers. This assortment can operate at product or brand level. A drinks wholesaler, for example, may

Figure 12.5 Value added services provided by intermediaries

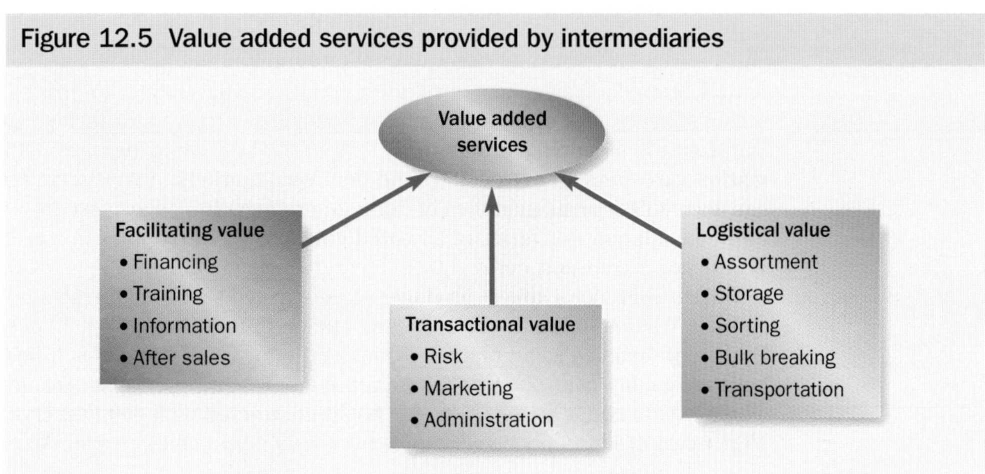

eg

Dexion Ltd, a member of Constructor Dexion Group, is a leading storage equipment manufacturer, handling everything from small orders from independent retailers through to fitting out large automated warehouses. It can provide up to 14,000 different products for office, commercial and industrial applications. For the larger contracts Dexion has its own sales force to deal with the complexity of agreeing the design and installation, the price and building a long-term relationship. One system installed with British Central Electrical, part of the OTRA NV electrical wholesaling group, had to be specially designed to handle 25,000 items with 24-hour turnaround. The small user market, however, is served by 50 UK Dexion distributors. This mixed channel system has enabled Dexion to expand to over 100 countries and become a market leader (http://www.dexion.com). The emphasis is on fast ex-stock supply and local sales and marketing based on sound knowledge. With over 33 sales offices in 24 countries and 180 distributors in 70 countries it is well placed to be able to create value through a range of applications.

offer a full range of merchandise from beer to cognac, but with in each category considerable brand choice may also be offered. The benefit to the customer is the wide choice available from one source, supported perhaps by a competitive and comprehensive pre- and post-sales service. However, for other intermediaries the choice may be more limited. If one manufacturer occupies a dominant position, the choice of competing brands may be severely restricted to just complementary products. In many car dealerships, for example, only one manufacturer's new cars can be sold, although there might be more flexibility over second-hand cars.

Assortment strategy is a critical variable in a retailer's marketing strategy. The key is to build an assortment to reflect the needs of the target market.

eg

Assortment strategy can be clearly seen in the music business. Some stores specialise only in classical or rock and associated sheet music. Others aim to provide a little of everything, but primarily concentrate on the bestsellers in CD and tape. A further group aim to provide depth of range by covering many older, slower moving titles.

In any of these strategies there are risks in misjudging changes in customer fads or tastes. This is particularly noticeable in high fashion areas where even the sale rails do not move assortments that have been left behind. The trend, however, in a society where disposable incomes are increasing, is for deeper choice within more specialised assortments, whether the all-Japanese store in North London or cuckoo-clock shops in Berne.

A further dimension of logistical value is the *accumulation and storing of products* at locations that are appropriate and convenient to the customer. The small manufacturer can make one large delivery of output to the wholesaler's warehouse, where it can be stored until a retailer wants it, and broken down into smaller lots as necessary. The hassles of transporting small quantities to many different locations, finding storage space and insuring the goods are taken away from the manufacturer.

eg

A walk around a market in a developing country reveals row upon row of sellers with small tables offering piles of undifferentiated home-grown carrots or turnips and little else, a far cry from town centre markets in the UK or France. By using intermediaries, farmers or market gardeners do not need to find their own markets. A fruit and vegetable wholesaler can accumulate small quantities of different products from specialist growers, sort them, and then make larger deliveries of assorted goods to the next point in the chain, thus gaining economies in transport costs.

Soleco is France's largest producer of pre-packed salads and fresh stir-fry and snack vegetables. Trading under the Florette and Manon brands, it enjoys a 42 per cent share of the French pre-packed salad market. To make the business a success, it had to invest in high levels of quality control, strict temperature control and specialist preparation machinery. It also needed regular supply. Not only has it contracted with 450 French growers, but about 15 per cent of its supply needs comes from Italy, Spain and Portugal. All crops are allocated batch numbers as part of an ISO 9001 system. Through such transparency, Soleco can assure the trade that the 'use by' date will never exceed seven days after processing, fewer on more fragile items such as lettuce. Soleco knows the field of origin, the variety, the date of harvesting, and the date and place of packaging to ensure that even when distribution lines are extended, freshness of the produce can be guaranteed (http://www.soleco.co.uk). All of this enables the consumer to enjoy top quality, fresh produce.

Appealing to the customer as a convenience product, Florette sells pre-packed salad leaves which come from a variety of suppliers.

Source: Florette.

Sorting is a very basic step in the logistical process, and means grouping many diverse products into more uniform, homogeneous groups. These groups may be based on product class and further subdivided by such factors as size, shape, weight and colour. This process may also add value by *grading*, which means inspecting, testing or judging products so that they can be placed into more homogeneous quality grades. These standards may be based on intermediary or industry pre-determined standards. Large supermarket chains, for example, are particularly demanding about the standardisation of the fruit and vegetables that they retail. If you look at a carton of apples in a supermarket, you will see that they are all of a standard size, colour and quality. Mother Nature hasn't quite worked out how to ensure such uniformity, so the producers and wholesalers have to put effort into sorting out and grading the top quality produce for the High Street. The second-class produce ends up in less choosy retail outlets, while the most irregular specimens end up in soup, fruit juices and ready meals.

A further important role for the intermediary, as already implied, is **bulk breaking**, the division of large units into the smaller, more manageable quantities required by the next step in the chain. Whereas a builder's merchant may purchase sand by the lorry load, the small builder may purchase by the bagged pallet load, and the individual consumer by the individual bag. The value of bulk breaking is clear to the DIY enthusiast, who certainly would not wish to purchase by the pallet load. There is, of course, a price to pay for this convenience, and the consumer would expect to pay a higher price per bag purchased individually than the builder would pay per bag purchased by the pallet load.

A final role is in actually *transporting the product* to the next point in the chain. Lorry loads may be made up of deliveries to several customers in the same area, thus maximising the payload, and with careful siting of warehouse facilities, minimising the distances the products have to travel. Again, this is more efficient than having each manufacturer sending out delivery vans to every customer throughout the country.

Facilitating value

The intermediary also offers a range of other value added services either to the manufacturer or to the customer. Not only do intermediaries share the risks, as outlined above, they also provide a valuable *financing* benefit. The manufacturer only has to manage a small number of accounts (for example with two or three wholesalers rather than with 200 or more individual retailers) and can keep tighter control over credit periods, thus improving cash flow. As part of the service to the consumer, retailers may offer credit or other financial services such as credit card acceptance, easy payment terms and insurance. Manufacturers selling direct would not necessarily be interested in such financial services.

Other activities also add value. Local demonstrations and consumer *training* provided by intermediaries enable the manufacturer to avoid costly labour inputs. Market *information* and *feedback* are precious commodities, as we saw in Chapter 6. The intermediary is much closer to the marketplace, and therefore alert to changes in consumer needs and competitive conditions. Passing on this information up the channel of distribution can enable manufacturers to modify their marketing strategies for the benefit of all parties. While there is no replacement for systematic, organised market research, information derived from sales contacts and meetings with intermediaries provides specific, often relevant intelligence. For the small manufacturer, with very limited market research resources, this can be particularly invaluable.

All the above functions need to be performed at some point within the marketing channel. The key decision concerns which member undertakes what role. This decision may be reached by *negotiation*, where the power in the channel is reasonably balanced, or by *imposition*, when either manufacturer or retailer dominates. Whatever the outcome, the compensation system in terms of margins needs to be designed to reflect the added value role performed.

An appreciation of added value dispels the commonly held belief that involving intermediaries simply increases the price of goods to the consumer. It also dispels the view of some small business marketers that they cannot afford to pay a margin to the intermediary, and so must deal direct. Clearly if intermediaries, especially wholesalers, were eliminated, the services provided would still need to be performed and, in many cases, this would be done somewhat less efficiently. The result could be a rise in prices or a severe limitation on the availability of less popular products, or perhaps even to put smaller manufacturers out of business. If, for example, wine distributors were eliminated, retailers then would have to create trading relationships with individual wineries worldwide, and might never find out about new, specialist wines. At the same time, immense problems would be created for wine producers in finding retail outlets, organising delivery and absorbing distribution costs.

Ultimately, the existence of intermediaries gives everyone a fighting chance of concentrating on what they are best at doing, whether that is producing, selling or consuming.

Channel strategy

With the various added-value roles implicit in the marketing channel, decisions need to be taken about the allocation and performance of these roles, the basis of remuneration within the system and the effectiveness of alternative configurations in enabling market penetration to be achieved competitively and efficiently. This is **channel strategy**. As indicated earlier, these decisions do not necessarily revolve around the manufacturer, despite the origins of the product.

Channel structures

The basic forms of channel design were outlined in Figures 12.1 and 12.3. These are known as conventional channels, in which the various channel activities are agreed by negotiation and compromise, recognising that both sides need each other. The particular structure adopted should reflect the market and product characteristics, taking into consideration such factors as **market coverage**, value, quantity sold, margin available etc. (Sharma and Dominguez, 1992). The structure can be described by the number of levels utilised, ranging from the simplest (two layers) through to the most complex (five or more layers).

Where a manufacturer needs to reach distinct target markets, a dual or multiple distribution approach may be adopted, which means that each target market may be reached by two or more different routes. For example, IBM will sell direct to large users and organisations, but will go through the retail trade to reach the consumer segment. This pattern works well, provided that discreteness is maintained and as long as the arrangement reflects the various buyers' differing pre- and post-purchase servicing needs. However, problems can emerge if the same product is sold to the same target market through different channels. A book publisher, for example, may create some friction with the book trade if it actively encourages direct ordering and other subscription services at lower prices than the retail trade can manage. This potential for conflict may well increase as direct marketing and home shopping gain in popularity.

Market coverage

One way of thinking about which types of channel are appropriate is to start at the end and work backwards. The sort of questions to ask relate not only to the identity of the end customer, but also to their expectations, demand patterns, frequency of ordering, degree of comparison shopping, degree of convenience and the associated services required. All of these elements influence the added value created by place, and the density and type of intermediaries to be used, whether at wholesaler or distributor or retail level. Market coverage, therefore, is about reaching the end customer as cost effectively and as efficiently as possible, while maximising customer satisfaction. To achieve this, three alternative models of distribution intensity can be adopted, as shown in Table 12.1, each of which reflects different product and customer requirements from place (Stern *et al.*, 1996). They are discussed below, in turn.

Table 12.1 Alternative distribution intensities: general characteristics

	Intensive	*Selective*	*Exclusive*
Total number of outlets covered	Maximum	Possibly many	Relatively few
Number of outlets per region	As many as possible	A small number	One or very few
Distribution focus	Maximum availability	Some specialist retailer knowledge	Close retailer/ consumer relationship
Type of consumer product	Convenience	Shopping	Speciality
Number of potential purchasers	High	Medium	Low
Purchase frequency	Often	Occasionally	Seldom
Level of planned purchasing by consumers	Low	Medium	High
Typical price	Low	Medium	High

Intensive distribution

Intensive distribution occurs where the product or service is placed in as many outlets as possible, and no interested intermediary is barred from stocking the product. Typical products include bread, newspapers and confectionery, but more generally, most convenience goods (*see* p. 271) fall into this category. The advantage to the consumer is that convenience and availability may be just around the corner, and they can invest a minimum of time and effort in the purchasing process. Using this kind of market coverage also assumes that availability is more important than the type of store selling the product, hence the growth of non-petrol products on sale in garages. However, if a product is on sale in every corner shop, it can be difficult for the manufacturer to ensure that the product is being maintained to the desired standard. This may not be a problem with canned or packaged goods, but with more perishable refrigerated or frozen foods, for example, the manufacturer's quality standards may be seriously compromised by poor handling. Even minor irritations can affect the consumer's attitude and satisfaction. In many less well-development retail markets, for example, many small shops do not have the refrigeration facilities to allow them to sell ice-cold cans of Coke.

Intensive distribution usually involves a long chain of distribution (manufacturer–wholesaler–retailer–consumer). It is an efficient means of getting the product as widely available as possible, but total distribution costs may be high, especially where small retailers are concerned and unit orders are low.

Selective distribution

As the term suggests, a more selective approach is designed to use a small number of carefully chosen outlets within a defined geographic area. These are often found with shopping products (again, *see* p. 272) where the consumer may be more willing to search for the most appropriate product and then to undertake a detailed comparison of alternatives. Unlike intensively distributed goods, which can virtually be put on a shop shelf to sell themselves, selectively distributed products might need a little more help from the intermediary, perhaps because they have a higher technical content that needs to be demonstrated, for instance. Manufacturers may also need to invest more in the distribution infrastructure, point-of-sale materials and after-sales service. It may thus pay to select a smaller number of intermediaries, where support such as training and joint promotions can be offered and controlled.

eg

The major fine fragrance manufacturers have long adopted a selective distribution strategy. Their rationale for this is that they are selling a luxury, upmarket product that needs to have an appropriate level of personal selling support and the right kind of retail ambience to reinforce and enhance the product's expensive image. In the early 1990s, they repeatedly refused to supply discount chemist chains such as Superdrug in the UK, who wanted to undercut the prices charged by upmarket department stores and other existing fragrance retailers. Pressure from Superdrug and other discount retailers which obtained unofficial but perfectly legal supplies from third parties has thus led to wider availability of fragrances and a significant focus on price competition from all but the most upmarket retailers.

The selective distribution approach is not unique to consumer goods. An Irish distributor of tractor seats for a UK organisation was required to carry local stocks and to fit the replacement seats to conform with European safety standards. Such regulation and control are only possible if a manageable number of outlets are allowed to handle the product. The Irish distributor, therefore, had major territorial rights across the west and south-west of Ireland. It was meant to handle all replacement sales by building up relationships with farmers, farm equipment repair shops and service agents.

Exclusive distribution

Exclusive distribution is the opposite of intensive distribution, and means that only one outlet covers a relatively large geographic area. This type of distribution may reflect very large infrastructure investments, a scattered low density of demand or infrequently purchased products. In B2B markets, the impact on the customer may not be particularly significant if a sales force and customer service network are in place. However, in consumer markets there may be some inconvenience to the customer, who may have to travel some distance to source the product and may effectively have no choice about who to purchase from.

eg

In consumer markets, the obvious example of exclusive distribution is new cars. A particular dealership will have the right to sell brand new Ford cars, for example, within a defined geographic area. Ford goes even further, in that it will not consider any multi-franchise proposal. This means that the dealer cannot sell Ford cars and Fiat cars, for example, from the same premises. Similarly, Ford will not give permission for any of its dealers to operate any motor-related business within 50 km of the Ford franchise. If consumers do not like that dealership for some reason, then they will have to travel some distance to find the next Ford dealer, or else buy a Renault locally instead.

Such an exclusive approach may even fit in with the product's own exclusivity. It would also be appropriate where high degrees of cooperation in inventory management, service standards and selling effort are required between manufacturer and intermediary (Frazier and Lassar, 1996).

eg

When Mustang, an American-based manufacturer of small four-wheeled construction vehicles, wanted to build a presence in the UK market, it appointed a sole distributor offering a sales force experienced in selling small equipment into the building trade.

Influences on channel strategy

There are several alternative channel design decisions facing the manufacturer who has a choice, but there are also several factors that may constrain these choices. These factors are outlined below, and are shown in Figure 12.6. While it may be desirable to adopt an optimal design in terms of marketing effectiveness and efficiency, rarely do organisations have the luxury of a clean sheet of paper. More often, they inherit the consequences of previous decisions, and the risks of changing design midstream need to be carefully considered before any planned improvement.

Organisational objectives, capabilities and resources

The channel strategy selected needs to fit in with the organisation's objectives, capabilities and resources. If the objective is to generate mass appeal and rapid market penetration, then an intensive distribution approach would be necessary. This would have to be supported, however, with an equally intense investment in other marketing activities such as promotion. If the focus was on repositioning upmarket into a more exclusive niche, then a selective or even an exclusive distribution approach would be called for.

An organisation that wishes to control marketing activities, and is well endowed with resources, may assume many of the channel functions directly. A small organisation with a small market share may have little choice but to concentrate on manufacture and direct dealing with an intermediary. A lack of resources and a lack of expertise and contacts may leave no option.

Objectives may change over time as environmental circumstances evolve. For example, demands for an improved delivery service or increased geographic coverage may require new distributors, more distributors or incorporating better service levels in the service structure of existing distributors.

Market size, dispersion and remoteness

No channel strategy decision can ignore the impact of the market. If a manufacturer wishes to penetrate a market some distance from its base, it may lack the contacts, market knowledge or distribution infrastructure to deal directly. There may be little choice but to deal with intermediaries. Similarly, a small organisation might lack the resources necessary for building sales contacts and maintaining customer service, especially if resources are limited and there is a need to develop sales volume quickly.

When demand is more highly concentrated, or where there are a few, readily identifiable customers, it may be possible to build a direct operation, keep full control and eliminate intermediaries. Efficiency may be obtained in negotiation, delivery and support services. By way of contrast, a large, dispersed market, such as that for magazines, may require a well-structured, efficient chain of intermediaries.

Figure 12.6 Factors influencing channel strategy

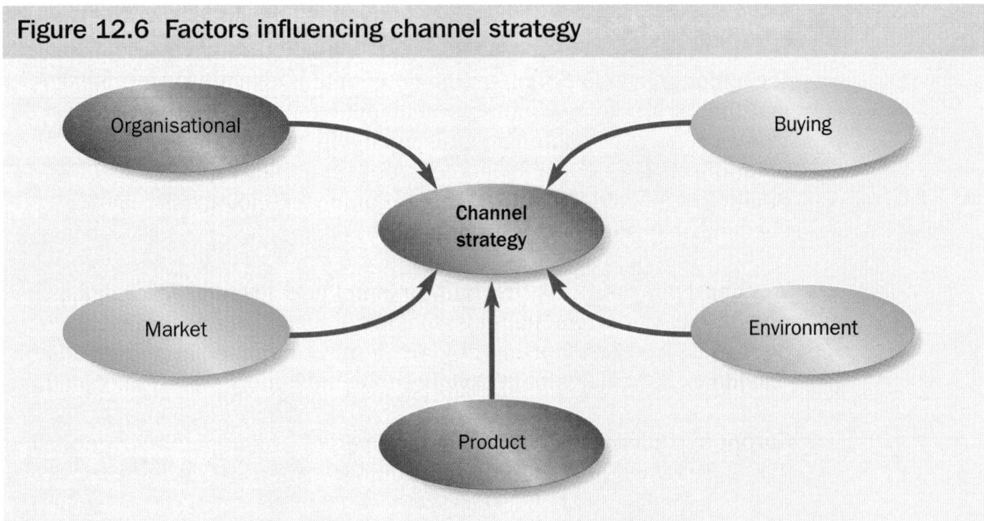

Buying complexity and behaviour

Understanding customer needs and buying criteria goes to the heart of effective marketing and has a major influence on channel selection (Butaney and Wortzel, 1988). Questions such as who buys, where they buy and how frequently they buy all indicate the kind of intermediary best suited to reach target customers. Matching the intermediary with customer needs, buyer expectations and product position is a challenging task. The move to out-of-town shopping, with its advantages of easy parking, convenience and large assortments under one roof, has meant a refocusing of effort by some manufacturers to ensure that they are well represented. Similarly, if a product occupies a specialist position, there is little point in dealing with a wholesaler that is primarily concerned with mass distribution.

Understanding the product classifications presented in Chapter 7 is also likely to influence design. Convenience, routine decisions may require much more widespread distribution than shopping goods where a more systematic evaluation of the selection criteria may suggest the type of intermediary required in terms of service, range, display and demonstration, etc.

Product characteristics

Products that are complex to purchase, install or operate, products that are of high unit value and products that are customer specific tend to be distributed directly to the customer or through highly specialised intermediaries. This reflects the need for close dialogue during the pre- and post-sale situations that may be lost if additional parties are involved. By way of contrast, fairly standard, routinely purchased, low-unit-value products tend to be distributed intensively through intermediaries.

McQuillan Engineering Industries (MEI) is a supplier of a wide assortment of components for aircraft interiors, such as overhead bins, galleys, sink units and even nuts and bolts. However, although considerable stocks are held, everything is manufactured to customer designs and specifications, and when demanded they can be assembled on site. Customers include Boeing, Saab and Airbus. With a specialism in batch or prototype production, the distribution and sales method is direct because of the complexity of individual customer orders. This contrasts with replacement parts for domestic electrical equipment, which are standardised by model and are widely stocked either in manufacturers' warehouses or through intermediaries such as repairers.

Other product factors may also have an impact. Highly perishable products need short distribution channels to maintain product quality or to assist in rapid turnover. Items that are non-standard or difficult to handle or items that have the potential to create transport problems may be less attractive to intermediaries (Rosenbloom, 1987).

Changing environment

The changing business environment, discussed in Chapter 2, creates new problems and opportunities for channel design. Three issues demonstrate the effect.

Technology. Technology offers the potential for closer integration between the manufacturer and the intermediary. Online systems may enable direct access to stock availability, electronic ordering and automated dispatch with the minimum of negotiation, if any. Electronic point-of-sale (EPOS) data can facilitate very rapid responses within the distribution system. Smaller organisations still relying on older technology such as the telephone and manual checking may soon become marginalised.

Working patterns. The growth in the number of women working has had a profound effect on some distribution channels, making some channels more difficult to operate, such as door-to-door selling during the daytime, while home shopping and convenience shopping outside usual trading hours have become much more widely accepted.

European Union regulations. Generally speaking, manufacturers have the right to decide which intermediaries should or should not distribute their products. Both national and European regulatory bodies start to become interested, however, where exclusion of certain intermediaries might be seen as a deliberate attempt to distort competition or to achieve price fixing. See, for example, Case Study 11.1 (at p. 462) and the legal debate over Levi Strauss' refusal to supply supermarket chains with jeans. The debate hinged on whether the refusal to supply was based on a legitimate concern over trademark protection and the quality of the retail premises and staff, or whether it was simply an attempt to prevent retail prices falling.

Manufacturers also need to be careful over the restrictions that they try to impose on intermediaries as part of a contract. They might, for example, insist that an intermediary does not carry competing products. This is usually permissible, depending on the market structure, the definition of what constitutes competition and whether there is any direct alternative available to an intermediary who does not wish to accept such a clause.

Selecting a channel member

The final phase of the channel design strategy is the selection of specific intermediaries. There may be a number of reasons that a selection decision needs to be made, some of which are not part of a new strategic formulation or realignment. Typical examples would be:

- to add more intermediaries to increase market penetration;
- to replace existing intermediaries because of poor performance or contract termination;
- to add new intermediaries to service a new product range;
- to create a network of intermediaries for market entry.

Whatever the reason, the selection decision should be compatible with the overall channel strategy. The selection decision tends to become more critical as the intensity of distribution itself becomes more selective or exclusive. In mass-distribution decisions, such as those concerning products like confectionery, any willing outlet will be considered. However, where a selective distribution approach is adopted, great care must be taken over the final selection of intermediary, as a poor decision may lead to strategic failure. For example, the selection of a wholesaler to allow entry into a new European market may be critical to the degree and speed of penetration achieved.

eg

Klemm is part of the Ingersoll-Rand group and specialises in a range of German-built piling and drilling rigs for construction sites. Its channel approach is often to appoint sole distributors in target countries. Thus in the UK, Skelair handles all sales, while in the Netherlands, Drilcon has exclusive rights. Klemm seeks to develop a close and effective relationship with its distributors. Although individual domestic markets may be relatively small, the selling task is complex in defining machines for applications and good after-sales service is also crucial. This demands close technical support and a level of trust and confidence between manufacturer and distributor (http://www.klemm-bt.com).

In situations where organisations need to select intermediaries on a fairly frequent basis, it would be useful to select on the basis of pre-determined criteria. Table 12.2 highlights a range of issues that should be examined as part of an appraisal process.

Table 12.2 Selection criteria for intermediaries

Strategic	*Operational*
• Expansion plans	• Local market knowledge
• Resource building	• Adequate premises/equipment
• Management quality/competence	• Stockholding policy
• Market coverage	• Customer convenience
• Partnership willingness	• Product knowledge
• Loyalty/cooperation	• Realistic credit/payment terms
	• Sales force capability
	• Efficient customer service

The relative importance of the various criteria will vary from sector to sector and indeed over time. Inevitably, there is still a need for management judgement and a trading off of pros and cons, as the 'ideal' distributor that is both willing and able to proceed will rarely be found.

Reverse selection

Not all manufacturers have the power or ability to design their channel strategy and to select the ideal members. Effectively, the intermediaries have the choice of whether or not they will sell the products offered. This luxury of choice is not just restricted to supermarkets and large multiple retailers. Travel agents can only stock a limited number of holidays, and are very careful about offering new packages from smaller tour operators. In some industrial distribution channels, the intermediary can decide whether or not to stock ancillary products around the main products that it sells on a dealership basis.

Reverse selection also suggests that intermediaries are proactive in looking for new manufacturers to complement their supply sources, or at a minimum that they are considering whether to extend the assortment being offered. In many B2B situations it is the buyer that initiates the contact process with suppliers.

Klemm used the drilling rig expertise of its UK distributor, Skelair International, to develop sales in the UK.

Source: Skelair International.

Channel structure

The traditional view of channels of distribution suggests a group of independent manufacturers and intermediaries working together within negotiated guidelines and operating functions to exploit a market opportunity. This does reflect the situation in many cases, where mutual benefit forces consensus rather than competitive behaviour between channel members.

However, a growing number of channels are being effectively led and managed by one channel member who can control the policies, strategies, actions and returns of the other members. These are called **vertical marketing systems** (VMS), and represent an advanced form of channel integration. Such integration may improve supply consistency, lower costs and lead to more effective marketing. Before we examine in more detail the various forms of channel integration, we now provide a brief review of the types of competition that may be experienced in channels. This review forms the basis for an appraisal of the benefits of integration.

Competition in channels

Not all competition in channels comes from traditionally expected direct sources, as we see from Figure 12.7. Sometimes, internal channel competition can reduce the efficiency of the whole channel system. Each of the four types of competition identified by Palamountain (1955) is considered in turn below.

Horizontal competition

Horizontal competition, as can be seen in Figure 12.7, is competition between intermediaries of the same type. This type of competition, for example between supermarkets, is readily visible. Each one develops marketing and product range strategies to gain competitive advantage over the others.

Intertype competition

Intertype competition refers to competition at the same level in the channel but between different types of outlet. Thus, for example, the battle between the department stores, the High Street electrical retailers and large out of town warehouse operations to sell hi-fi

Figure 12.7 Competition in channels

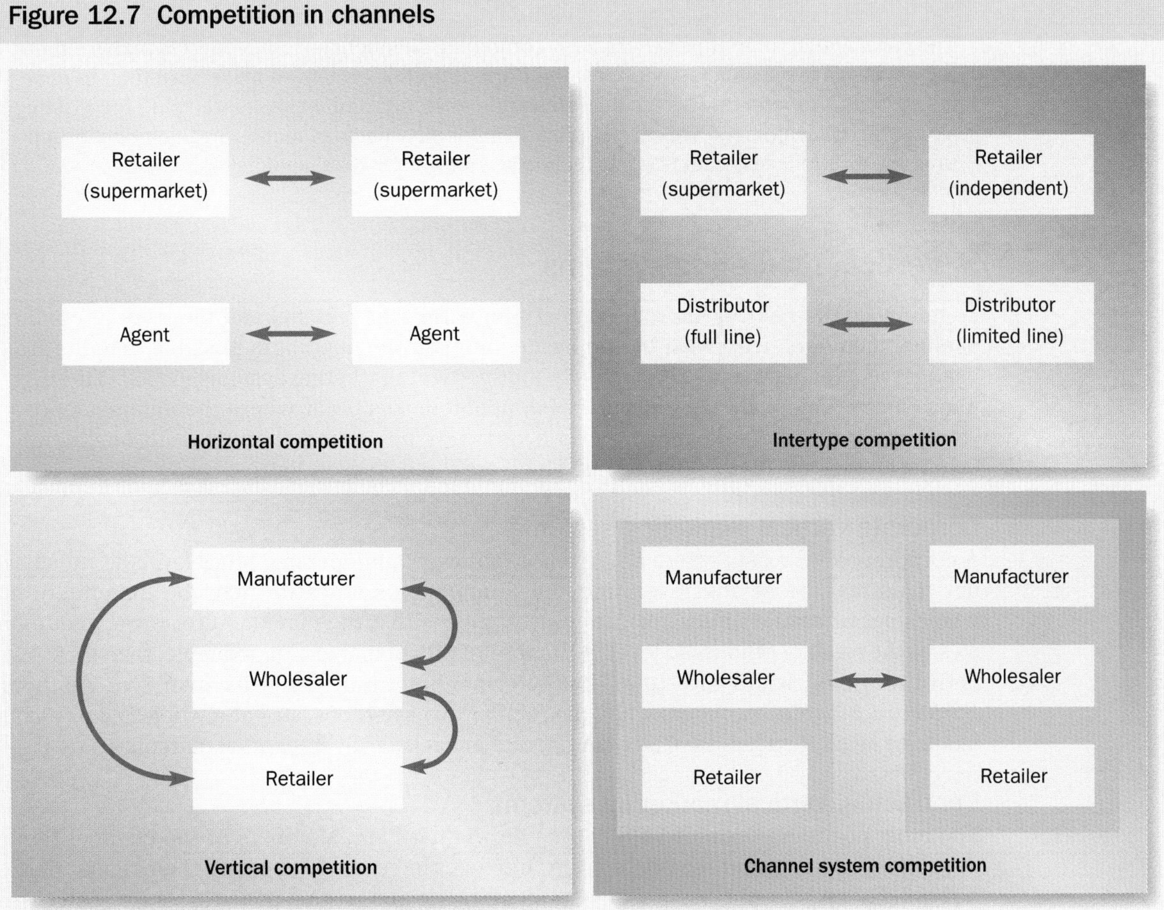

equipment to the same customer base is a form of intertype competition. The manufacturer that has a choice may need to develop different approaches to handle each retailer type. Of course, there are dangers if a manufacturer is seen to give unwarranted preference to one type over another, given the intense rivalries that can develop. This may start to lead to dysfunctional channel behaviour.

The supermarket chains, for instance, were dismayed by the fact that the big brand manufacturers agreed to supply Costco, the warehouse club open to the general public, when it first set up in the UK. The argument was that the manufacturers were supplying Costco at lower prices than those offered to the supermarkets, and thus Costco could further undercut them. The supermarkets threatened to delist brands if the manufacturer did not even out the price differentials, but in the end did not carry out the threat. Even the strongest supermarket chain cannot risk being without certain key brands.

Vertical competition

Vertical competition can soon become a serious threat to the integrity and effectiveness of a channel. Here, the competition is between different levels in the channel, such as wholesaler and retailer, or even retailer and manufacturer. This type of competition can soon lead to internal rivalry, where the focus shifts from cooperative market penetration, focused outwards, to mutual cannibalism, focused inwards.

Channel system competition

The last form of channel competition is where a particular channel is in competition with different, parallel channels. The focus for the operator, therefore, is on ensuring that its system is more efficient and competitive than the others. The emphasis is on total channel efficiency, which may, however, involve some suboptimisation in the interests of a more effective chain.

eg

The car manufacturers operate through competing channel systems, especially where there are exclusive arrangements with dealers. Ford, therefore, wants to make sure that its channel system is functioning better than Renault's or Honda's to create extra value for existing and potential customers. This has implications for all aspects of marketing, including promotion, distribution, customer service, technical support and product development.

Vertical marketing systems

To minimise the risks of internal competition within the channel and the risks of conflict, channel members, who wish to cooperate and gain the maximum possible benefits from channel membership, may form closely knit vertical marketing systems (VMS). These systems can become highly organised and dominated, to a point where the independence of some of the members disappears into a vertically integrated channel, with one member owning all or some of the other levels. There are three types of VMS.

Corporate vertical marketing systems

A corporate VMS exists where an organisation owns and operates other levels in the channel. This may be at any level, and the dominant organisation may be manufacturer, wholesaler or retailer. *Forward integration* means that the manufacturer owns and operates at the retail or wholesale level. A number of oil companies, for example, own their own petrol stations, while Firestone, the tyre manufacturer, owns its own tyre retailers. *Backward integration* occurs when the retailer owns and operates at a wholesale or manufacturing level. Retailers such as C&A operate in backwardly integrated markets.

Contractual vertical marketing systems

The most prevalent form of VMS is the contractual VMS. Members of the channel retain their independence, but negotiate contractual agreements that specify their rights, duties and obligations, covering issues such as stock levels and pricing policies, for example. This

eg

The corporate VMS has the advantage of creating a channel that is tailormade for the owner's product and marketing objectives. Furthermore, those objectives are shared throughout the channel. The owner also has ultimate control over the activities of the channel and its members. In Chapter 7 (*see* p. 284), we introduced Preussag, the German tour operator. Preussag operates a VMS so that it can tailor its holiday packages to client needs and ensure that these objectives are shared throughout the channel, as it has the ultimate control of its members' activities. The VMS includes travel agents selling the packages, airlines taking customers to holiday destinations, and the hotels looking after them, all packaged by owned, branded tour operators. In these situations, care must be taken to allay public fears that such close arrangements could restrict customer choice and result in biased advice from travel agents supporting one tour operator at the expense of others.

prevents unnecessary internal conflict and suboptimal behaviour. Three types of contractual system are commonly found.

Retail cooperatives. A retail cooperative exists where groups of retailers agree to work together and to combine and increase their purchasing power by supporting their own wholesaling operation. This sort of agreement helps the small independent retailers who are members of the cooperative with greater range, access to promotion and more competitive pricing.

Wholesaler voluntary chains. A wholesaler voluntary chain is one where a wholesaler promotes a contractual relationship with independent retailers, whereby the latter agree to coordinated purchasing, inventory and merchandising programmes. The coordination enables some of the benefits of bulk buying and group promotion to be realised by smaller operators. Mace and the Independent Grocers' Alliance are UK examples.

Franchise systems. Franchising is fast becoming a major model of contractual arrangement across Europe. Franchising is an ongoing contractual relationship between a franchisor who owns the product concept and a franchisee who is allowed to operate a business, within an agreed territory, in line with the methods, procedures and overall blueprint provided by the franchisor. Managerial support, training, merchandising and access to finance are effectively exchanged for conformity and a specified fee and/or royalties on sales. Franchising will be considered again in Chapter 22.

Administered vertical marketing systems

Coordination and control are achieved in an administered VMS through the power of one of the channel members. It is, in reality, a conventional channel within which a dominant force has emerged. Therefore, although each member is autonomous, there is a willingness to agree to interorganisational management by one of its members. Contracts may or may not be used to govern the parameters of behaviour.

eg

Marks & Spencer uses an administered VMS to forge very close links with its suppliers, and to dominate decisions about what is supplied, how it is manufactured, quality levels and pricing. Suppliers accept this dominance because they regard M&S as a prestigious and trustworthy customer, and respect its experience of the market. Similarly, Ahold, the Dutch retailer, offers leadership within its distribution channels in terms of product development, manufacturing and purchasing.

The emergence of these integrated forms of channel system is increasingly questioning the traditional approach to channel management. They also provide a context within which behavioural aspects of channel relationships can be examined.

Behavioural aspects of channels

Most of this chapter so far has concentrated largely on economic issues involved in channel decisions. However, all channel decisions are ultimately made between people in organisations. There is, therefore, always the potential for disagreement over the many decisions needed to ensure that the system operates effectively. Issues such as expected roles, allocation of effort, reward structures, product and marketing strategies are among those that deserve close attention. A channel is an interorganisational social system comprising members who are tied together by a belief that by working together (for the time being at least), they can improve the individual benefits gained. The channel also offers the potential for one member to have a significant impact on the position of another member, for example the appointment by a manufacturer of a competing retailer in a town.

It is necessary, therefore, to examine the behavioural processes at work and how they are influenced by, and exert influence on, channel decision-making.

Cooperation and partnerships

A climate of cooperation is perhaps the most desirable within a channel system. It does not just happen, but needs to be worked on and cultivated with positive cooperation signs and signals. Cooperation can be defined as:

> *Similar or complementary co-ordinated action taken by a firm in interdependent relationships to achieve mutual outcomes or singular outcomes with expected reciprocation over time.* (Anderson and Narus, 1990)

In other words, you scratch my back and I'll scratch yours, and we shall both be better off. Boyd and Walker (1990), for example, suggest a variety of ways in which the functional performance of channel members in terms of quantities purchased, selling and promotional effort and after-sales service levels can be enhanced by incentives.

Some view conflict and cooperation as being at opposite ends of a continuum, while others view them as distinct concepts. Whatever the view, strong cooperation can lead to a feeling of satisfaction and partnership, one of give and take. Cooperation may lead to strong personal and organisational ties that are difficult for outsiders to break. However, not all cooperation need be voluntary. A weaker channel member may think it best to cooperate and comply with the wishes of a more powerful member, rather than risk retribution.

There are many areas of potential cooperation, and Table 12.3 lists some of them.

Table 12.3 Areas of cooperation

• Advertising allowance	• Training staff
• Payment for retailer displays	• Support for new store openings
• Contests/competitions	• Joint advertising
• Merchandisers	• Joint selling
• Demonstrators	• Joint mailings
• Samples/bonus goods	• Delivery costs
• Local market research	• Sales promotions
• Special packaging/displays	• Own-label supply
• Automatic reordering	• Support with store fixtures
• Returns allowance	• Price promotions

It is best to assess cooperation in terms of who does what, an approach that requires a clear view of expected roles and functions. An overall agreed package or programme may guide the way in which channel members work together for their common benefit. This programme should be based on obtaining competitive advantage for the whole system, as well as benefiting particular links (Jaworski and Kohli, 1993). The whole approach embodies the notion of partnership rather than competitive relationships. After all, the system is pointless unless it leads to synergies, that is, unless the members feel that they are gaining more by membership than they could achieve alone or by membership of a different system.

Good communication, in terms of amount, direction, medium and content, is also essential for closer cooperation in a channel (Mohr and Nevin, 1990). In a study of computer dealers, Mohr *et al.* (1999) found that effective communication led to greater satisfaction, stronger commitment and better coordination. The development of electronic sharing of data and intelligence is stregthening many channel relationships as technology helps all members to make better decisions in times of market uncertainty as well as reducing selling and coordination costs (Huber, 1990).

Conflict

Conflict is a natural part of any social system. A definition of conflict is:

> *Tensions between two or more social entities (individuals, groups or larger organisations) which arise from incompatibility of actual or desired responses.*
>
> (Raven and Kruglanski, 1970)

Conflict may exist where, for example, one channel member feels that another member is not dealing fairly with it, or that the system is not working sufficiently in its favour. The key to dealing with conflict is not to allow it to continue until it reduces channel efficiency or effectiveness, or even results in legal problems. Channel conflict may be issue specific, such as discontent related to changes in margins, or may involve general confrontation on a range of issues. Clark's shoes, for instance, needs to be aware of the potential for conflict as it operates a parallel distribution system. It distributes partly through its own shops, and partly through other shoe retailers. It must support both channels equally.

There are two different types of conflict, each capable of generating varying degrees of intensity in dysfunctional behaviour:

1 *Manifest conflict*, which is overt between channel members and may block goal achievement.
2 *Underlying conflict*, which, although not overt, is capable of developing into manifest conflict, but can still shape willingness to cooperate.

There are numerous possible causes of conflict, some arising from poor understanding, others from a fundamental difference of opinion that goes to the heart of the relationship. The kinds of operational problems either caused by conflict or triggering conflict are shown in Table 12.4. These problems may, however, be symptomatic of deeper pressures, which can be broadly categorised into five areas, described below.

Incompatible goals

Different channel members want different things. One, for example, may be seeking growth, while another is looking towards consolidation and stability. Their goals are incompatible.

Role conflict

Where there is disagreement about who should do what, role conflict may arise. A manufacturer, for example, may feel that a wholesaler is not putting enough promotional effort into

Table 12.4 Areas of conflict

• Manufacturer/retailer brands	• Delivery arrangements/schedules
• Prices/margins/discounts	• Product exclusivity
• Quality	• Contract flexibility
• Special services	• Display/promotion prominence
• Territory exclusivity	• General compliance
• Market information	• Listing money
• Direct sales	

reselling a particular product, while the wholesaler may feel that it is the manufacturer's responsibility to promote the product overtly to the retail trade.

Members of a channel need to ensure that conflict does not get out of hand and become dysfunctional, as that could lead to reduced channel performance. The contract used to regulate the relationships, although usually varying in length, detail and restrictiveness, tends to outline the mechanisms for resolving conflicts when they break out (Lusch and Brown, 1996).

Decision domain conflict

This is disagreement about who is in the best position to make marketing decisions. Retailers may feel that because they are closer to the end consumer than the manufacturer, they are better positioned to know what kind of point-of-sale material would perform well, whereas manufacturers, closer to the product, may feel that they should dictate what should be done.

Perceptions of reality

Different channel members may interpret the same phenomena in different ways and may have different perceptions of reality. The Costco example (pp. 492 *et seq.*), for instance, shows how the brand manufacturers saw Costco as a beneficial influence in expanding their intensive distribution and better serving the consumer, while the retailers saw it as a threat to their margins and well-being. This certainly caused channel conflict.

Expectations

Different channel members may have different expectations about what should happen in the future. Such conflict may include definition of the best outcomes from a situation, how to overcome resource scarcity, how to allocate resources better, or how profit margins should change in the light of a changing business environment.

eg

The danger of conflict in a channel is ever present. Sometimes disputes can become public and embarrassing to both sides. Landmark, a leading buying group in the UK, criticised drinks suppliers for not being supportive during a benzene contamination scare. Many of the suppliers, it was argued, were not prepared to cope with product recalls and gave poor and ineffective advice. With potentially 52 million cans to be removed from the shelves, it was a major headache for retailers to identify which products could have been affected (Dearden, 1998). Also in the grocery trade, cash and carry operator Bestway claimed that some suppliers were giving better terms and conditions to multiples and delivered wholesalers rather than cash and carry operators. It considered such prices to be discriminatory and alleged that this made it more difficult to give its own retailers the best prices. The suppliers rejected this accusation and stated that it was caused by a confusion between normal and promotional prices (*The Grocer*, 1998).

The response to conflict can even worsen the situation. The exercise of power can be a great source of conflict (Stern and Gorman, 1969), for instance where the strongest member of the channel seeks to impose a solution against the wishes of the others. In contrast, unexercised power could be seen as benevolent restraint and a sign of willingness to cooperate (Frazier, 1983), thus reducing the tensions.

Conflicts can vary in frequency, intensity, duration, content and impact (Magrath and Hardy, 1988). Some conflict can be a powerful reforming pressure, resulting in a stronger, more efficient channel, but too much becomes dysfunctional. This may involve a refusal to cooperate.

Conflict needs to be spotted early and dealt with before it becomes too overt. This can be helped by regular meetings, frequent communication, and ensuring that all parties emerge satisfied from negotiations. It is critical that each channel member should fully understand their role and what is expected of them, and that this is agreed in advance. If conflict does become overt, communication, formation of channel committees, a fast arbitration service and top management commitment to resolution are all essential to prevent an irrevocable breakdown of the channel.

In any channel, there are likely to be periods of manifest conflict and periods of calm and cooperation. Similarly, there may be conflict in one area, for example profit-margin split, but cooperation in others, for example promotion.

corporate social responsibility *in action*

Buy local

The UK's Prince Charles warned supermarkets and consumers that the countryside's natural beauty could be at risk if shoppers fail to support local producers by buying more regional food and drink. If the agrifood sector could expand, then the sustainability of rural life could be enhanced and there would be less risk of rural areas disappearing under housing developments. Sustainable local foods, such as speciality farmhouse cheeses, distinctive apple varieties, and locally reared meat, can help reconnect consumers with farmers and give the public real choices about the food they eat, the way it is produced and its impact on the countryside, says the CPRE. This view is reflected in the Countryside Agency's *Local Products Programme* which aims to improve environmentally sound land management and to support rural communities. Its 'Eat the View' slogan was designed to increase consumers' awareness and strengthen their links with the economic vitality of the countryside. This means creating stronger consumer demand for certain products, and helping small and specialist producers to find markets in the face of increasing globalisation and the powerful forces of large retailers.

To be successful, any programme has to encourage more farmers, supermarkets, independent retailers and manufacturers to work together in a flexible, win–win manner. Altruism is not enough for supply chain cooperation: all parties need to achieve an outcome that is both sustainable and meets commercial criteria. The problem is that farmers and processors are often good at growing and processing but unskilled, badly informed and naïve about downstream supply chain issues such as branding, marketing and service consistency. At the other end of the chain, there is also the problem of what can be done to encourage retailers, especially the large multiples, to operate on a local scale when their own systems are geared around national buying and national distribution systems and volume.

In fact, the supermarket chains have already realised the benefits of 'localness' by allowing some local produce from small suppliers onto their shelves. There is a perception among food shoppers that local food is more trustworthy and of better quality. Sainsbury's, for example, has a dedicated regional sourcing team to select locally produced foods from all parts of the UK. It stocks 2,480 regional lines in the areas of their origins and these are sourced from around 375, often small, regional suppliers. Somerfield works with 600 small businesses, generating £10 mn of sales in 600 stores. It is also planning to hold roadshows to link retail buyers with local farmers.

There are strategic issues associated with how the multiples treat smaller suppliers, especially on pricing and supply continuity, and these are highlighted in Case Study 12.2. More practical adjustments also need to be made. Getting delivery of produce from a small producer to a supermarket regional distribution depot can be a problem and supermarkets sometimes have to make special allowances by, for example, accepting shipment direct to stores. Cobblewood Mushrooms in Selby, Yorkshire, for example, provides fresh mushrooms to its local Safeway store every day. Often, however, the retailers prefer shipment to distribution centres, not the stores. Some suppliers have complained that the multiples are passing on the extra costs of distribution to producers by opening more depots and then expecting supply to each. Usually, retailers will not allow suppliers to recoup these costs through higher prices. Tesco has introduced a scheme where empty lorries returning from making deliveries to stores collect goods from some smaller suppliers to ease their problems of delivering to distribution centres.

Supermarkets dominate the grocery market, so any business needs to weigh the risks and problems of dealing with them against the restriction to potential by not doing so. A Code of Conduct is currently being considered by the food industry to improve and guide relationships between local suppliers and the supermarkets following a critical Competition Commission report. Should the supermarkets go further with supporting training, brand development and business improvement on the basis that stronger, committed local suppliers can mean better opportunities for local produce in the stores?

Sources: Bedall (2001a, 2001b); Bedington (2001); Competition Commission (2000); CPRE (2002); MLC Industry Strategy Ltd. (2001); http://www.countryside.org.uk.

Power–dependency

Power has received considerable attention in the behavioural science literature as a basis for explaining the interaction between two individuals or organisations. It was defined by El-Ansary and Stern (1972) as follows:

> *The power of a buyer or seller is his ability to control the decision variables in the marketing or purchasing strategy of another member in the supply chain. For this control to qualify as power, it should be different from the influenced member's original level of control over his marketing or purchasing strategy.*

This means that one channel member might wield considerable power over other members, and might clearly be able to exercise that power to the cost of the others, yet can choose not to use that power. Power can be possessed to influence events without it actually being used (Bacharach and Lawler, 1980). Marks & Spencer possesses a great deal of power over its suppliers, but although pursuing rigorous standards and tough bargaining, it values the building of longer-term relationships that do not depend on aggressive or hostile acts. The existence of power in a channel need not be a bad thing. Although some argue that the use of power is indicative of a sick and dysfuntional relationship when compared with demonstrable trust and commitment (Morgan and Hunt, 1994).

In a distribution channel, any member might seek to use power-based strategies to influence the others. Power can derive from many sources, real or perceived. A very popular classification comes from French and Raven (1959).

Reward power

Reward power is based on B's perception that A has the ability to provide rewards for B. Such rewards might include volume of business, higher margins or sales and promotional support. As mentioned earlier, a small supplier might feel that a large retailer such as Marks & Spencer has reward power. If the supplier complies exactly with the M&S way of doing things, then that will bring it increased or at least repeat M&S business next season.

Coercive power

Coercive power is based on B's perception that A has the ability to mediate punishments for B. The withdrawal of many of the above mentioned rewards by A could constitute the use of coercive power, for instance the threat of delisting a particular product line. The Costco example given earlier might again be relevant here. The retailers' threats to boycott the brands of certain manufacturers who were also supplying Costco could be interpreted as an attempted exercise of coercive power.

Legitimate power

Legitimate power is based on B's perception that A has the legitimate right to prescribe behaviour for B. This legitimacy could arise from the existence of clauses in formal contracts, or less clearly through the norms or expectations of either party. A contractual VMS, or franchise, often gives one member legitimate power. A franchisee expects the franchisor to specify how the business should be set up and run, since that is part of what the franchisee is investing in.

Referent power

Referent power is based on B's identification with A. In other words, B respects A and might wish to be associated with A to reap reputational and other spin-off effects. A's power might also arise from B's acceptance that both parties are inextricably linked, so that they must succeed or fail together. This kind of power calls for a high degree of empathy and shared communication.

Expert power

Expert power is based on B's perception that A has some special knowledge or expertise, perhaps in market insights, product development or promotion, which gives A influence over B's actions. A small manufacturer or a small retailer might regard an experienced wholesaler as having expert power.

In any channel situation, there may be several different power sources operating, and they may not all be in the hands of the same channel member. When combined, they could provide a basis for an administered VMS, as described earlier. In some situations, one source of power could be cancelled out or counterbalanced by another source wielded by a different channel member. In other cases, high joint power could lead to strong trust and commitment, because of the common interests, attention, and support found in such channel relationships (Kumar *et al.*, 1995; Lusch and Brown, 1996). As relationship marketing approaches become more widely used, Weitz and Jap (1995) found that organisations are relying less and less on power as a coordination and control mechanism and only when there is a clear difference in dependency, such as between a large supermarket and small supplier, does it tend to be more evident in influencing the conduct of relationships.

eg

A classic example of the exercise of power is the relationship between the large supermarket chains and the major brand manufacturers. Over the years, each side has tried to exploit power over the other, to the point where the balance of power between them is now a delicate see-saw, tipping slightly in favour of one and then the other. The brand manufacturers have, through brand building, made sure that their products are indispensable to the consumer and thus essential to the retailer, while the retailers have tried to exploit their intensive coverage of the market, making them indispensable to the brand manufacturers. In almost every European country, a small number of distributors account for a very large proportion of business, and this concentration is increasing as retailers join forces, entering into international strategic alliances for purchasing and distribution.

Each party has tried to reduce the power of the other at various times. The manufacturers, for example, have tried to limit their dependence on the big supermarkets by cooperating with the emergent discount chains (Costco springs to mind again), while the retailers have tried to wean consumers off the big brands on to good quality own-brand products (*see* pp. 287 *et seq.*). The uneasy balance, however, remains.

This last scenario raises another concept, *dependency*, that is very closely linked to the development and exercise of power. This is where one party becomes highly dependent for its well-being on the actions of the other party. What is actually happening between the manufacturers and the retailers is that in reality neither can manage without the other, and there is a mutual dependency that limits what each dare do.

Dependency might also be derived from the relative importance of the transactions to the parties involved. If a retailer takes a large share of one supplier's output (say 80 per cent), yet that only represents a small proportion of the retailer's overall needs (say 5 per cent), then that supplier is extremely dependent on the retailer, who immediately has the basis for coercive power at least. If the supplier does not comply, the retailer can easily drop the supplier with relatively little inconvenience to themselves, but with devastating consequences for the supplier.

Finally, B might become dependent on A because there is no obvious alternative, or because the costs and time involved in switching would be too great. As A occupies such a specialist niche in its own market, A may well possess expert or referent power, and the dependency might tempt A to try to exercise coercive power over B. If A pushes this too far, however, B might rebel and decide that locating or developing an alternative partner would now be worthwhile.

All of these tensions and influencing strategies tend to encourage the emergence of channel leaders who regulate and control events. In Europe in the grocery sector, retailers have progressively taken over marketing channels since the 1960s. Their control is now almost complete in some countries, such as the UK and France, or well on its way in others such as Spain and Italy (Bell *et al.*, 1997; Paché, 1998). Some wholesale systems, such as those matching up small manufacturers and small retailers, develop leadership at that level rather than at the retail level. Car manufacturers still provide leadership within the automotive trade, because exclusive dealerships and selective distribution mean that the dealers have a great deal to lose if a manufacturer decides not to deal with them any more.

Atmosphere

The tendency towards power–dependency relationships, conflict–cooperation and the general level of trust in the relationships within a channel are important variables affecting the overall climate that governs ongoing relationships and decision making. The way in which all these elements come together sets the scene for the channel either to flourish for the benefit of all parties, or to be plagued by internal strife and inefficiency.

The atmosphere reflects the history of the relationship between the channel members. It is the accumulation of all the positive and negative feelings that have developed during the exchange and operation of the contracts. The atmosphere is, therefore, an outcome of a relationship, and plays a part in influencing future events (Håkansson, 1982). A climate of hard bargaining may well lead to defensive behaviour if one party feels hard done by. In another situation, problems may be solved not so much by confrontation as by discussion and compromise.

At the heart of the relationships between channel members is trust, defined as:

> *The firm's belief that another company will perform actions that will result in positive outcomes for the firm, as well as not take unexpected actions that would result in negative outcomes for the firm.* (Anderson and Narus, 1986)

The level of trust existing within a channel can vary from a complete absence to very high degree of completeness. It can also be very long-lasting and set the scene for the conduct of the relationship. Trust can lead to cooperation, good communication and an ability to resolve differences speedily and effectively. Trust is, therefore, an essential requirement for the implementation of relationship marketing within a channel, which in turn should lead to better synergy between channel members. There is a need to understand more fully the role of trust and expectations in channel behaviour in order to explain why some relationships are remarkably well adjusted and others are almost a continual battle between buyer and seller.

The nature of physical distribution and logistics

Broadly speaking, **physical distribution** is about the handling and movement of outbound goods from an organisation to its customers. Distribution might be direct, using company-owned transport, or indirect, using external agencies and the kinds of channel structures considered at pp. 474 *et seq.* **Logistics** has a wider brief, since it is concerned with inbound raw materials and other supplies and their movement through the plant as well as with the outbound goods. It also concerns itself with strategic issues such as warehouse location, the management of materials and stock levels and information systems.

The next two subsections look in a little more detail at each of the two areas.

Physical distribution management

Physical distribution management (PDM) is concerned with the organisation and management of the storage and movement of goods from the end of the production line (finished goods) to the end customer. The range of functions undertaken includes receiving and processing orders, picking and packing (materials handling), managing the infrastructure such as warehouses, managing stock and the selection of transportation methods, either direct to the end customer or to a point where bulk will be broken prior to shipment to the individual customer. Physical distribution has been transformed in the past two decades by advances in technology and related processes. Computers, electronic data interchange (EDI), satellite communication systems, handheld scanners and barcode label equipment, and the internet, are among the technologies that have helped this transformation (Frazier, 1999). Each has contributed to improved service levels and operational effectiveness. PDM is now fundamental to the marketing concept (Mentzer *et al.*, 1989).

In supermarkets, distribution costs take up 3 per cent of sales revenues and in convenience stores the figure goes up to 7 per cent (Rowe, 1998). In order to keep these costs to a minimum, it is important that members in the supply chain work with others to share information, develop responsive stock management and control, and run efficient transport systems. Warehousing and transportation are obvious areas of concern where greater efficiencies can be sought. Companies are moving towards a pan-European approach, but often internal distribution systems are replicated in different countries rather than being considered as part of a Europe-wide system.

Taking an overview of PDM as it relates to a particular channel of distribution, it is important to note that the structure of the *physical* distribution channel may not coincide exactly with that presented earlier in this chapter, unless one or more members decide to undertake those roles directly. Figure 12.8 compares the two structures, showing the increased level of detail needed to describe physical distribution from manufacturer to consumer.

Figure 12.8 Channel management and physical distribution management

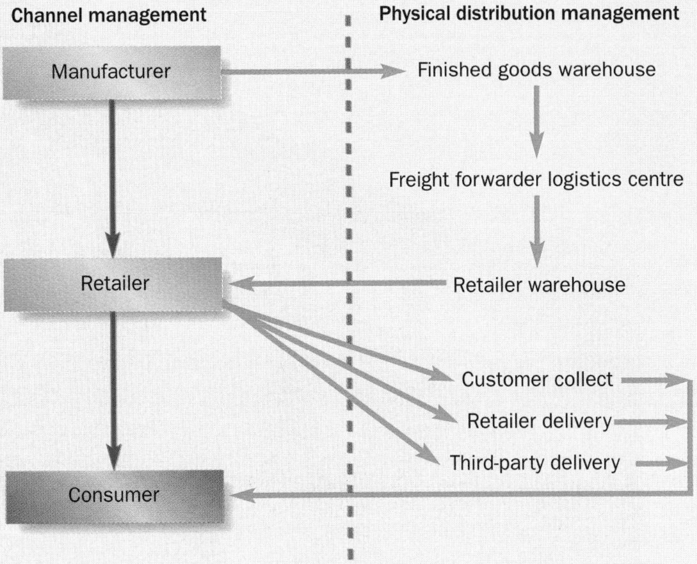

eg

Tibbett & Britten, a British-based international logistics specialist, has over 320 depots in 33 countries, 11,000 commercial vehicles and employs over 33,000 people worldwide. Its turnover in 2000 was over £1.5 bn and it handles £60 bn-worth of goods for clients. Most of its business is based on long-term relationships with customers and often, a dedicated infrastructure is part of the contract. In the automotive industry, for example, Tibbett & Britten can undertake pre-delivery inspection, preparation and enhancement as well the normal services of storage, trucking, documentation, import handling and onward delivery. Within the clothing market, it handles hanging garments for multiples and independent retailers.

When things go wrong, however, the significance of the logistics partnerships that T&B create is soon highlighted. When it won the distribution contract for Mothercare, early teething troubles meant severe stock disruption in stores as products were misplaced in the Northamptonshire warehouse and distribution could not be implemented to fulfil replenishment needs. Mothercare asked some suppliers to ship directly to stores and it rented temporary warehouse space while Tibbett & Britten sorted out the problems.

Despite its being a big player in international logistics, you will rarely see a lorry in the Tibbett & Britten livery, as that of the clients is often used (Goodley, 2001; *The Independent*, 2001; http://www.tbg.co.uk).

The extra intermediaries in a physical distribution channel do not take title to the goods, or take any direct part in their own right in transformation, adding product value or promotion. Such intermediaries are called **facilitators**, as their main function is to undertake the storage and movement of goods to ensure a free flow, and to help the main members of the distribution channel to achieve their objective of having the right goods in the right place at the right time, as cost effectively as possible. Typically, these intermediaries include transportation companies, those who rent out warehouse space and insurance and administration agents.

Although these facilitators might not add product value through transformation, they do add it through creating availability and service.

PDM has emerged as an important variable in the marketing mix in recent years. The links with customer service are obvious. A fast, reliable, timely level of service where and when customers want it can be an important way of adding value, enhancing customer satisfaction and strengthening relationships (Mentzer *et al.*, 1989). However, there are other

Tibbett & Britten's vehicles normally carry the logo of the company for which it is handling the logistics.

Source: Tibbett & Britten.

implications arising from increasingly global and competitive markets. Some stem from retailers managing inventory levels more effectively in order to increase stock turnover. By stocking less and relying on fast, frequent delivery, they have increasingly passed the burden of storage backwards to the manufacturer and wholesaler, so that they are responsible for coping with fluctuations in demand. With the aid of computer technology, many items can be controlled at a level of sophistication not possible a few years ago. Such changes have cost implications that demand careful assessment by the manufacturer or wholesaler.

An additional pressure is that holding stock represents locking up cash, which in turn is likely to increase an organisation's borrowing requirement, leaving it vulnerable to fluctuating interest rates. This is a burden that each channel member would prefer someone else to bear, but the further back up the chain it passes, the fewer options there are for passing it on. The best solution, therefore, is to use management skills and technology to minimise the burden throughout the chain and to evaluate what integration and rationalisation can take place within that chain (Cooper, 1994).

Other areas of PDM have experienced cost pressures. Transportation has been hit by rising fuel costs, the requirement for high levels of safety and pressures to reduce damage to the environment through pollution. Similarly, as organisations internationalise their trading, by definition PDM costs will increase in real terms to cover the additional costs of crossing boundaries. These costs may be direct, for example import duties and extra insurance cover, or indirect, such as time lost through waiting at customs posts (it can take days for commercial vehicles to get across some eastern European borders, for instance).

Given all these pressures, the cost dimension cannot be ignored. The challenge is to find the balance between cost and added value. In some situations there may be little choice. Who wants to be the manufacturer who cannot supply a small replacement part for a capital plant breakdown that is holding up a car assembly line? In other situations, costs will have to be carefully monitored against the achievement of agreed customer service objectives. There is often a trade-off between cost and customer service, offering many possibilities for the marketing manager (Christopher, 1990).

Logistics management

There are limitations to the distribution concept described above, as it fails to reflect the inward flow of materials and parts that also have an impact on the costs and the quality of customer service provided. While it is not argued that marketing should control these inbound logistics, marketers need to be involved in their design and planning to ensure an integrative approach. A definition of *logistics*, amended from Bowersox (1978), is:

> *The process of strategically managing the movement and storage of materials, parts and finished inventory from suppliers, through the firm and on to customers.*

Logistics, therefore, is an all-embracing concept that focuses on the physical movement and transformation of goods all the way from the source of supply to the point of consumption. The shift from a PDM to a logistics perspective has led to significant benefits, including improved customer service, stock minimisation at all levels in the distribution chain, no costly stockouts and, finally, a lower total cost for all members (Mentzer and Williams, 2001).

Companies are increasingly using logistics to lower costs, yet raise the standards of service to customers. Computers can be customised at the last minute, to match new orders or the market they are supplying, while in book distribution external logistic centres enable rapid selection, packing, transport, invoicing and collection using one provider. In the car industry and for some fmcg products, the results of effective supply chain management are becoming even more important in lowering costs. Some companies are now experimenting with international stock-free delivery chains, the ultimate form of JIT. This means that products from Belgium, for example, are delivered straight on to a production line in Germany with no supporting buffer stock. Similarly, fmcg suppliers may be required to deliver to a distribution warehouse on a cross-docking basis just as a load is being consolidated to send to a particular supermarket. With such pressures to eliminate stockholding costs, suppliers need fault-free supply chains to remain competitive.

The difference between logistics management and PDM can be seen in Figure 12.9, which shows the all-embracing role of logistics compared with the narrower remit of PDM. Byrne and Markham (1993) highlighted the vital linkage between logistics management and customer service. That linkage is further emphasised through the following scenario. A retailer blames the wholesaler or manufacturer for a delayed part (a physical distribution problem), when it is actually the supplier of the castings to the manufacturer who is the ultimate cause (a logistics problem). Customers may care little; all they know is that they have a service problem, but the marketing manager in the manufacturing organisation needs to look backwards as well as forwards in finding a solution to that problem.

eg

Wincanton, a large logistics operator, runs a 284,000 ft^2, fully-automated National Distribution Centre (NDC) for Littlewood's, a leading UK multiple retailer. Littlewood's wanted a system that allowed daily replenishment direct to shelf for its 112 stores, reduced lead times, removal of store stockrooms and a distribution operation that could deliver to individual stores in a package-free way. The NDC provides a maximum 48 hours from sale to replacement on the store floor. The ordering system developed ensures that requests for even just one garment are processed as quickly and as efficiently as those for much larger amounts. A cross-docking system is in operation, capable of handling 28,000 flat (boxed) and 18,000 hanging garments in single units per hour. This minimises the time that stock is in the warehouse as 150 suppliers often deliver on a daily basis. All this enables the retailer's costs to be minimised while still offering high service levels and full range offerings to its customers (http://www.wincanton.co.uk).

Figure 12.9 Physical distribution management and logistics

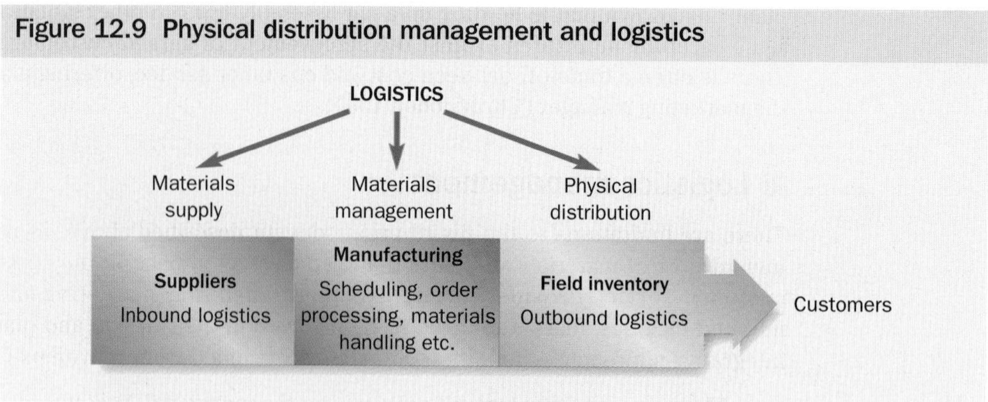

This example shows the integrative nature of logistics and the difficulty of managing it, as it cuts across different functions within a business as well as across different businesses, linking supply sources with demand. It is primarily a framework for guiding forecasting, planning and strategies rather than just another self-contained business function (Smith, 1997). It is therefore important that regular and reliable information is allowed to flow between all the connected parts and that no one part, whether internal or external to the organisation, is allowed to have an undue or negative impact on the others. The supplier who fails on the delivery of castings may subsequently, albeit indirectly, affect the relationship between the manufacturer who uses those castings and its customers, and so on down the line to the end consumer.

The logistics system will, of course, vary from organisation to organisation. In a bank or financial services operation, most of the inward-bound materials are money and supplies. Logistics, in terms of movement and storage activities, may not be a significant part of the product cost. This contrasts with producers such as Apple, Volvo or BMW, who purchase both raw materials and components from many different sources, and then move finished goods to geographically spread markets and customers. Logistical costs will still vary widely, however, depending on the kind of manufacturer or market concerned. The key variables that will influence the scale and complexity of the logistics process are shown in Figure 12.10.

Within a channel of distribution, logistical costs will vary from member to member, reflecting the roles undertaken (Paché and des Garets, 1997). Whether at this macro level (i.e. the combined logistics of the whole channel of distribution), or at a micro level (i.e. the logistical concerns of one channel member), it is important to focus on the total cost rather than to

Figure 12.10 Influences on the logistics process

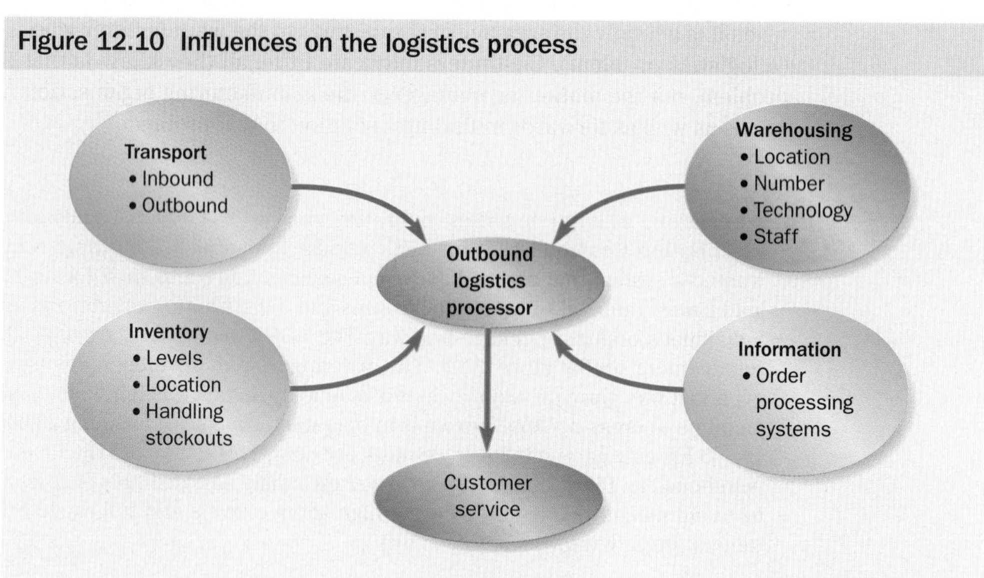

marketing *in action*

Benetton

Benetton presents an excellent example of how a global logistics concept can be put into operation in a situation where over 5,000 stores in more than 120 countries need a regular supply of garments responsive to changing tastes and fashions. At the heart of the operation is an integrated 190,000m^2 distribution centre and three production facilities at Castrette in Italy. Although garment design is undertaken inhouse, manufacturing can also be subcontracted to organisations working to Benetton's tightly specified standards. The production system is pan-European with facilities in Hungary, Croatia, the Iberian peninsula and Tunisia. The facilities at Castrette can manage up to 120 million garments per year operating on an IT-controlled production–warehousing–distribution cycle. By using IT, Benetton can delay the final production schedule until the last minute. Orders are taken three times a day and processed during the night to ensure that they can be produced the following day.

After production, the goods enter a sophisticated packaging system. The Robostore 2000 system can divide deliveries by geographic area and then by individual retailer's packaging requirements. Linked with the fully automated distribution centre, garments are received ready for order assembly into vehicles. This highly automated distribution system can handle over 40,000 incoming and outgoing boxes per day but employs just 19 staff. There is also storage space for 400,000 boxes, although the intention is for minimal stocks to be held centrally. The restocking period for European shops is now down to eight days from order and that for the USA to just 12 days. Reductions in re-ordering periods result in lower stock costs for the retailer and less risk of a reduced price rail (http://www.benetton.com).

Shipment is then made direct to the retailers without any use of distributors, wholesalers or regional warehouses. Benetton also went into a joint venture in freight forwarding, as a direct result of the international orientation of its business, to manage and smooth the paperwork flow as carriers cross national boundaries. Various cost trade-offs have been made in this system, not least the decision to have one highly efficient warehouse rather than a number of less automated centres, with a knock-on effect on stockholding. Similarly, order processing costs per garment have been reduced through automation, although transport costs may be somewhat higher. Another main trade-off derives from the decision not to use intermediaries but to supply direct. Effectively, that channel decision influences the rest of the logistics agenda.

pursue blinkered strategies that lower costs in one area, only to raise them in another. A decision to close local depots, for example, might increase transportation costs and even inventory costs if the level of goods in transit increases. The effectiveness of this approach, particularly when other organisations are involved, will depend on the nature of the contractual relationships, ranging from informal through to highly prescribed and controlled, and the willingness to work as a system rather than as discrete elements. Many of the issues discussed in Chapter 4 regarding buyer–seller relationships will influence the nature of the supply chain and the sharing of logistical costs. These will be considered further in the next section.

Total logistics cost concept

Implicit within a logistics perspective is the notion that decision-making concerning the movement and storage of materials should be done as a whole rather than in discrete parts (Sussams, 1991). There are a number of cost areas that should be considered as part of the logistics and distribution system. These cost areas are often interdependent, because as costs decrease in one area, the costs in another may increase. For example, as the number of stockholding points increases, the cost of holding inventory will also rise, but the cost of transportation may fall as not only are fewer goods moved, but they are moved shorter distances to the end user.

That example may apply at either the macro or the micro level. A channel of distribution consisting of a number of cooperative and integrated members may take an overview of warehousing or distribution depots relevant to the whole channel, and make logistical decisions that may increase the costs of one member, but will decrease the costs and increase the overall efficiency of the entire channel. The member bearing the increased direct costs may be rewarded in other ways, by increased business or increased profit margins to offset the increased operating costs, for example. At the micro level, an organisation may simply look at its own internal cost effectiveness. The trade-off principle can be seen in the

Set in the heart of the countryside, this Benetton distribution centre uses robotics to provide an efficient service to its retail outlets.

Source: Benetton UK.

hypothetical example shown in Figure 12.11. The ideal number of distribution outlets is three, when transportation costs are considered alongside inventory costs. Although neither cost in itself is at a minimum, the total logistics cost is minimised for the system as a whole.

A full understanding of the impact of logistics costs often demands a considerable quantity of accounting data and the use of decision support systems to consider the full range of

Figure 12.11 Total logistics costs: trade-offs

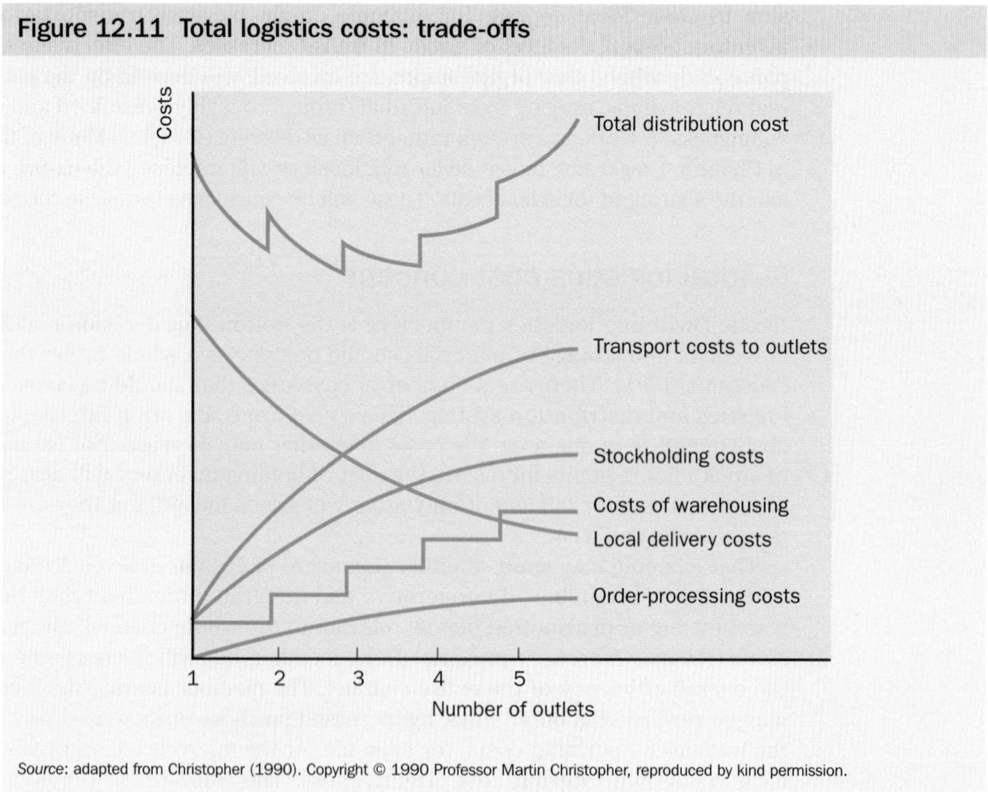

Source: adapted from Christopher (1990). Copyright © 1990 Professor Martin Christopher, reproduced by kind permission.

variables and the effect of 'what if?' scenarios. The use of IT has opened up considerable potential for logistics operations.

However, the principle remains the same: it is the system cost rather than the individual functional cost that is critical. A number of the main cost areas are briefly considered below.

Order processing and administration

Order processing and administration are the areas associated with writing, receiving, acknowledging and processing an order, through to invoicing and confirmation, statements as well as credit checking. They run in parallel with the physical distribution flow but are closely related to it.

These various stages are outlined in Figure 12.12. In some cases, the whole process may be almost instantaneous. An order placed at Argos, the retail catalogue shopping business, is processed simultaneously with payment as soon as stock availability has been verified. Instructions are issued online to the stockroom behind the scenes, and the goods are brought forward for immediate collection by the customer. The whole order processing cycle may take less than five minutes. Large retail chains, their regional distribution depots and their suppliers are increasingly linked, to make the order processing cycle a much faster and more efficient operation. All of this has been made possible by the use of computer-based systems that can handle order processing, transport planning, production planning, inventory levels and account management as part of an integrated system. Such integration is becoming increasingly essential where high-volume transactions are involved.

Inventory

Inventory is often a significant feature of an organisation's assets. Inventory can be in transit or in storage, represented by work-in-progress. Typical costs include financing (the cost of money tied up in stock, storing work-in-progress, insurance, etc.), write-offs (depreciation, wastage, etc.) and other losses.

Inventory management is central to the problem of how to balance customer service against physical distribution costs. Too much stock, although it will permit a high level of product availability – which may please customers – will result in high carrying and obsolescence costs. Too low a level of stock may result in frustrated customers, brand switching and eventually lost market share. Inventory management can also generate internal conflict between the marketing department, which wishes to maximise choice and availability, the production department, where longer or continuous runs assist lower unit costs but do not necessarily produce the range required in a timely manner, and the finance department, which is seeking to keep costs down through lower inventory levels.

Figure 12.12 Stages in order processing

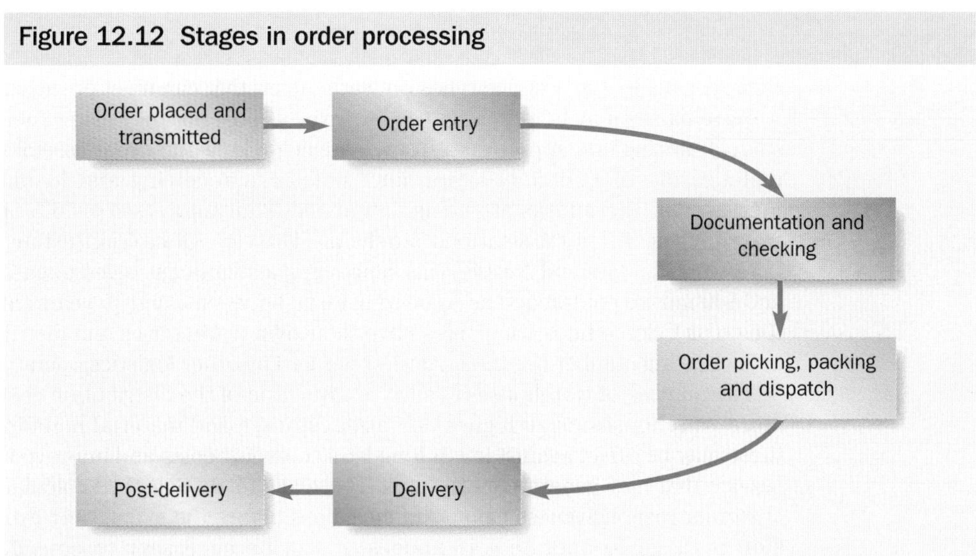

Transport

Transportation is central to any logistics system, moving goods in time and place, thus providing the means to service urgent replacement or maintain inventory levels within a channel system. The selection of alternative modes of transport has different cost and service outcomes that can be used creatively by the marketer. The availability of many perishable foods out of season is a tribute to conscious decisions to use air freight, with the premium price involved. Some market segments are happy to pay premium prices for the benefits of all year round tomatoes or early new potatoes.

There are five main modes of transport that can be considered for product movement. These are rail, road, air, pipeline and water transport. Intermodal transport, where more than one mode of transport is used provides a sixth option. The selection of a mode needs to be made with both company and customer needs in mind. Each mode offers advantages and disadvantages that normally require some trade-off between sometimes conflicting criteria such as speed and cost.

Transport can be either *trunk*, representing bulk movement over a distance between manufacturer and customer or between manufacturer and distribution point, or *local*, representing relatively small shipments to the final user. An example is the postal system. Bulk mailing is undertaken by lorry, rail or air, while delivery to the doorstep is by small van or even on foot.

Outlet

Outlet costs are the capital and operating costs incurred in maintaining facilities to store and handle products.

Warehousing. Warehousing is an important link in the physical distribution chain. It enables goods to be stored and subsequently moved according to customer demand. The type and role of the warehouse will vary according to the demands of the product.

However, the main role of the warehouse is to help provide the level of customer service agreed in the marketing plan by enabling a rapid supply or resupply of products from locations considered appropriate for responding to that demand.

The main decision facing manufacturers and intermediaries is whether a warehouse is needed at all and, if so, what kind of warehouse it should be. The growth of JIT systems has reduced the need for the level of investment in warehousing that was necessary when safety stocks had to be held. In an ideal situation, JIT removes the need for warehousing, but the reality is that even retailers cannot function reliably or efficiently without any warehousing function at all. Warehouses play an important role in smoothing out the imbalances between supply and demand. Take, for example, apples. In the absence of adequate temperature-controlled storage, the market would be awash with local apples in the autumn, yet they would be in scarce supply in the spring unless expensive imported alternatives were introduced. Of course, the storage of goods can be taken to extremes as, for example, where EU intervention has created wine lakes, butter mountains, etc. in an effort to regulate the market. However, again, the practice relies on warehouses that can meet preservation needs.

Warehouses may be primarily used to store goods, but they also enable further handling, such as sorting into appropriate storage areas, picking and order assembly, further packing, palletisation or containerisation and, not least, receiving and loading transportation. Increasingly, these tasks are being automated. Wincanton (*see* p. 503) operates automated warehouses for organisations such as Britvic, GlaxoSmithKline, Lever Fabergé, Littlewood's, Mars and Nestlé. This represents a significant investment of between £20 mn and £40 mn, so contracts tend to be long-term, between 5 and 15 years (http://www.wincanton.co.uk). Sometimes companies have their own warehouses and distribution centres, but an increasing number use the facilities operated by other logistics operators.

The number of warehouses needed is a function of the distribution cost–service trade-off. More warehouses mean higher operating, storage and material handling costs. However, these may be offset against lower long-haul transport costs and improved levels of customer service that may generate more sales. These are finely balanced calculations, especially as customer responsiveness cannot be measured before the event, only estimated. If the decision is taken to operate warehouses, it will be necessary to consider the location of

eg

Salvesen Masters Fresh Foods is one of the largest food logistics companies in Europe. In the UK, it operates regional distribution centres for major supermarket chains and works closely with food producers such as Danone and Chiquita bananas. It has its own refrigerated warehouses and manages others for its customers. It recently invested £2.4 mn in a new distribution centre in Evesham. During the night, fresh produce from southern England is brought to this new facility, where Salvesen takes care of handling and commissioning, and is then distributed to supermarkets in Scotland. Innovative IT systems, a private fleet of lorries and modern warehouses ensure fast availability to maximise the time that the fresh produce can displayed in the store (Trepins, 2001a).

customers and acceptable order cycle times. The location decision will also reflect the accessibility of motorways or other transport modes, such as airports, for both inbound and outbound distribution. London Heathrow is Europe's second largest cargo airport. It handled 1.4 million tons of cargo in 2000 and over a five-year period, over £960 mn was invested in cargo facilities. The Netherlands, however, remains the logistics capital of Europe, especially for US companies. Nearly 57 per cent of American distribution centres in Europe, such as Reebok's, are located in the Netherlands. Most of these companies have established operations in and around the port of Rotterdam and Schipol airport. Both locations have again made heavy investments in their port and logistics infrastructures during the last few years. These centres not only serve the European continent, offering all four modes of transport, but also as a transhipment point into the United Kingdom, Scandinavia, and Mediterranean markets (Trepins, 2001a; 2001b).

Warehouse costs relate to the purchase and rental of space and the associated infrastructure for picking and packing stock efficiently. The increasing use of computer systems to guide picking has allowed greater use of random storage systems, as companies seek to increase space utilisation. Goods can be stored wherever there is room, and the computer system can quickly identify where they are, thus reducing the need for the more disciplined and orderly storage that a manual system would dictate.

Materials handling. *Materials handling* is essentially an internal operation concerned with moving products into, around and out of the warehouse or manufacturing operation. Materials handling is an integral part of a warehouse operation. The complexity of handling thousands of lines, with increasingly high labour costs, means that mechanisation is playing an ever more significant role. This typically includes automatic picking equipment, mobile platforms, cranes, conveyors and fork-lift trucks. Some automated warehouses can handle large volumes of goods using robotic equipment and a computerised control centre. In some *retail* warehouses, such as Ikea, some of the picking and handling responsibility for all but the heaviest items has been transferred to the consumer. Given the labour costs inherent in materials handling, the capital infrastructure and the costs of lost or damaged stock, materials handling needs careful planning.

Costs concerned with the materials handling system are concerned with the physical processing of orders into economic shipment sizes in line with customer service expectations and functionally sound protection for movement. This includes palletisation and loading.

Customer service concept

The output of logistics and physical distribution is the level of service that the customer receives (Lambert and Stock, 1997). This can be defined in many ways, according to the specifics of the product-market situation. The challenge is to match the level of **customer service** provided with the need to constrain costs within planned levels. Too high a level of service could lead to excessively high costs that cannot be covered through pricing. Too low a level of service may enable a close control of costs but little positive response from potential customers. The key is to find the balance through careful research, planning and experimentation.

Customer service can be defined as the interaction of all the factors that affect the process of making products and services available to the buyer. These factors, although situation specific, cover such areas as inventory levels, delivery frequency, consistency and reliability of delivery, ease of order administration and the time taken from order placement through to satisfactory installation or consumption. From a study of customer service practices, LaLonde and Zinzer (1976) concluded that customer service variables could be categorised into three areas: pre-transactional, transactional and post-transactional.

Pre-transactional variables

Pre-transactional service activities relate to the corporate policies and procedures that establish the frameworks and administrative systems to achieve the desired levels of customer service. Implicit in this is the setting of customer service standards that can act as a benchmark for measuring achievement. Typical standards cover such areas as reliability, consistency, time, stockouts and accuracy. In practical terms, they might be translated into goals such as:

- 99 per cent of orders fulfilled satisfactorily;
- all refunds made within one week of goods receipt;
- all orders processed to dispatch within 24 hours;
- all orders delivered within 48 hours;
- all lunches served within 10 minutes of order.

These standards derive from the competitive position planned and the expectations of the target customers. Different market segments will respond to customer service provision in different ways. Part of the standard setting process, therefore, must be the assessment of the costs of provision and whether the additional costs can be recovered from that market segment. The standards set for customer service thus need to be linked with the strategic marketing plan to provide a cost-effective market impact. This will require effective integration of all the activities that are undertaken from order entry through to delivery, to avoid suboptimisation and weak links. It is critical that these standards are clearly communicated to staff to ensure compliance.

Transactional variables

Transactional service activities are the main dimensions of the implementation phase that actually creates customer service. The concern with physical distribution and administration provides performance measures against the pre-determined standards.

marketing *in action*

Efficient consumer response

Efficient Consumer Response (ECR) is the process through which retailers and suppliers work together to reduce inefficiencies in the supply chain for the benefit of all parties. Born in 1993 in the United States, it means working more cooperatively than has been the tradition to ensure that change is implemented and ultimately benefits the consumer. Better-managed supply chains could be in the interests of both manufacturer and consumer. According to an ECR Europe report (2002), ECR consists of four strategies of supplier–retailer cooperation that help to create superior value for the consumer at a lower cost. These strategies are:

- **Efficient replenishment** which links the consumer, retail store, retailer distribution centre, and supplier into an integrated system. Accurate information flows quickly through EDI linkages between trading partners, while products flow with less handling and fewer stockouts from the supplier's production line into the consumer's basket.
- **Efficient promotion** which refocuses suppliers' promotional activities away from retailer-sponsoring to selling through to the consumer. A key aspect of efficient promotion is better matching the promotional product flow to consumer demand, thus reducing the amount of inventory in the system. Another aspect is developing the best mix of consumer-oriented promotions within product categories.
- **Efficient store assortment** which is about offering the right

assortment of products to the target consumers. This provides the essential starting point for optimum use of store and shelf space. Adopting an effective assortment management approach improves turnover and profit returns per unit of space (m^2). The ultimate goal of efficient assortment is to find the best assortment that both satisfies the consumer and enhances retailers' and suppliers' business results.

- **Efficient product introduction** addresses the processes of developing and introducing new products that offer a solution to unfulfilled or partially fulfilled consumer needs. The goal is for suppliers and retailers to develop more consumer-orientated products at lower costs through more cooperative effort.

Thus although the prime focus of ECR has been logistics, it also extends to promotions, assortment, category management and product development. According to Coopers and Lybrand (1997), ECR principles could generate savings of $33 bn for European supply chains, the equivalent of 7 per cent off consumer prices, 4.8 per cent off operating costs and 0.9 per cent off inventory costs.

Tesco has enjoyed benefits from adopting ECR. Its distribution task is challenging, with over 800 stores ranging from the petrol forecourt convenience shop to High Street stores and out-of-town hypermarkets. With the need to lower distribution costs and to reduce the average order time to delivery to within 48 hours, close cooperation with the supply chain has been necessary. Tesco has placed particular emphasis on talking with the chain to agree common standards and operating practices that will lead to customer benefits in price or quality. The Supply Chain Development Director, Graham Booth, described the Tesco approach to ECR as:

> *an evolutionary process that requires wide and continuing education to install in today's and tomorrow's managers that underlying philosophy of cooperation between buyer and supplier in order to remove non essential costs from every part of the supply chain* (as quoted by Varley, 1999).

Despite the claims made for its ability to revolutionise supply chains, progress in ECR thinking has been patchy. For Tesco, the prime focus is on information sharing to help make better supply chain decisions. One of the stumbling blocks, however, appears to be the notion that ECR is something you do to the supply chain rather than with it, in a truly cooperative manner. It is not about leading channel decisions, but sharing channel decisions. The Competition Commission (2000) report clearly indicates the dominant role of supermarkets in that process. Category management, for example, is essential for demand management at the point of sale in fmcg markets. While larger suppliers work closely with the supermarkets, almost as category advisors, many smaller suppliers often do not have the resources to participate fully, nor is it particularly encouraged. To be successful implies a degree of trust between the parties and this is sometimes lacking. The greatest success has been in efficient, heavily IT-based replenishment systems, the logistics component of ECR.

Three aspects of efficient replenishment systems have been piloted in Europe:

1. *Continuous replenishment* means that suppliers generate their orders using inventory data supplied by the retailer in order to provide continuous supply rather than batch delivery. Service levels have improved as a result of the system and inventory and warehouse space costs have lowered.
2. *Cross-docking* is used with fresh produce in particular. At distribution centres, stocks are coordinated through the IT system to ensure that the arrival of inbound trucks from suppliers and the departure of retailers' trucks are so close that goods can move from one to the other without going into stock. This means that stock can move easily within the distribution centre. Although trials have shown a loss of transport efficiency, operating costs overall can fall and the shelf life of fresh goods can be increased by up to three days.

   Wavin Trepak, a logistics operator from the Netherlands dealing in fresh produce, developed a standardised crate that is fully stackable and can be handled by robots. This system is important for its dealings with Albert Heijn, one of the leading Dutch retailers, as the crates can be rolled straight from the lorry on to the sales floor. This system is also easier for cross-docking.
3. *Roll-cage sequencing* enables products to be stored in the distribution centre by category. This enables easier handling in the distribution centre and results in better packed pallets that are easier for the retail store to deal with. In trials, 200 extra labour hours were incurred in the distribution centre, but this was offset by a saving of 700 hours in stores.

ECR Europe, the joint industry and trade body for ECR, proposes that the essence of ECR is still the most effective way of delivering the right products to consumers at the right price. It suggests, however, that this implies a dramatic change in current business practices. ECR is about redesigning the processes, altering paradigms and changing attitudes. For all the claims made for ECR, the reality so far suggests that supply chains still have a long way to go and the priority to date has been streamlining order planning and fulfillment. True collaborative planning, extending right through to the supermarket shelf and embracing consumer buying behaviour, merchandising schedules, order methods, promotions and pricing will require more comprehensive redesign of processes. A lot will depend on how committed the powerful retailers really are to such a process.

Sources: Coopers and Lybrand (1997); Competition Commission (2000); ECR Europe (2002); Edmunds (2001); Mitchell (1997); Varley (1999); Williams (1999).

The main elements, shown in Figure 12.13, are discussed below.

Order cycle time

Time is an important measure in physical distribution. The order cycle time relates to the total time between placing an order and satisfactory receipt of the product. The lower the cycle time, the faster stock can be replenished and the lower the inventory levels that need to be held by the customer. Included in order cycle time is the whole process of administration, delivery and installation, where appropriate.

Consistency and reliability of delivery

Delivery must be on time, orders must be filled accurately and goods received in prime condition. In some situations, it is better to have a slightly longer delivery period that is guaranteed, rather than one that may be quicker but could be vulnerable to delays.

Inventory availability

The availability of inventory refers to the range and depth of stock normally held that provides the essential input to delivery. The balance is between stocking in depth on the faster moving, volume products and retaining a sufficient level of stock of, or at least fast access to, slower moving items. Finding parts for obsolete products is always a challenge if their supply is erratic.

Order size constraints

Some companies implement a minimum order policy. This can penalise light users, but reflects the high administrative and delivery costs on small order sizes.

Ordering convenience

Different customers want different convenience standards. These could relate to opening hours, the use of non-cash alternatives or ease of booking.

Delivery times and flexibility

The issues of delivery times and flexibility highlight whether the delivery is on the customer's or the supplier's terms. Customers operating just-in-time (JIT) systems clearly need

Figure 12.13 Consumer service and transactional variables

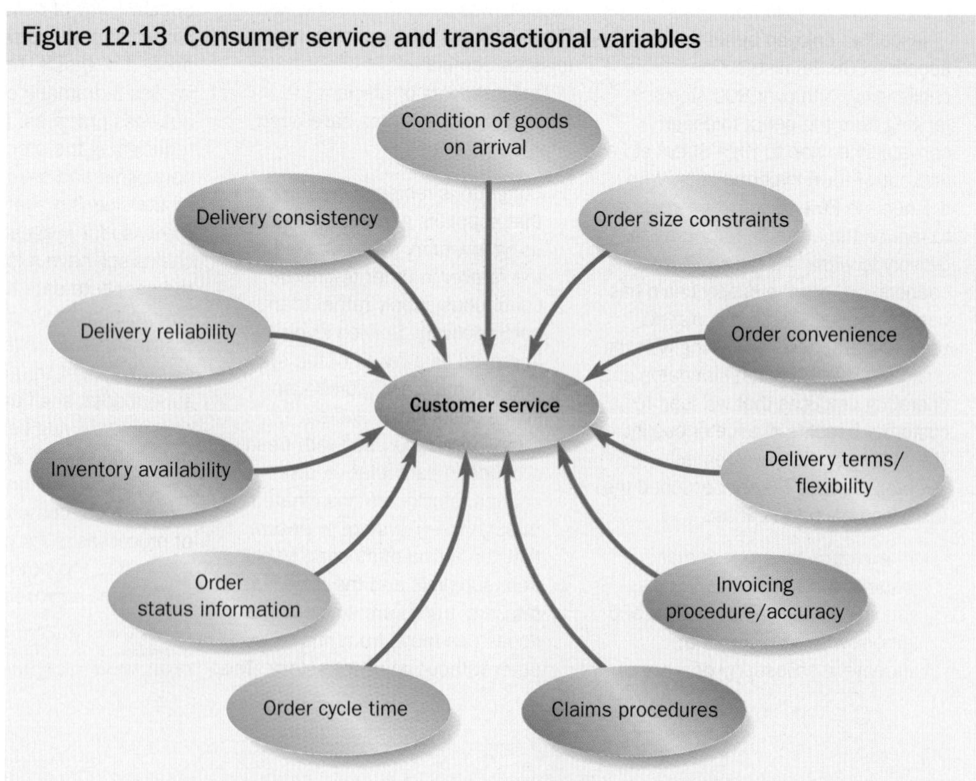

to be able to specify their delivery requirements. On smaller, less crucial orders, however, it may be necessary for the customer to accept the standard delivery schedule with no guaranteed time of arrival.

Invoicing procedures and accuracy

Customers can be extremely irritated by administrative errors and inaccuracy in such areas as invoicing, as it takes time and effort on their part to point out and help resolve the problem. The kinds of problem that may occur are receiving the same goods twice, inaccurate invoices and poor recording of financial statements.

Claims procedure

A 'no questions asked' approach to alleged shortfalls or damaged stock is critical for customer confidence. In consumer markets, this is an accepted part of customer service for many retailers. Marks & Spencer and WH Smith offer full refunds or exchange for goods, whatever the reason for their return. Other retailers are slightly less generous, offering only credit notes for items returned for reasons other than product faults.

Condition of goods on arrival

Quality checking and sensible, functional packaging are vital to service provision. For want of a missing dowel or screw, for example, a customer may need to incur the time and expense of returning to the DIY superstore before they can assemble their flat-pack bookcase.

Order status information

The ease with which shipments may be traced, whether standard or not, and quick identification of where they are delayed or lost, are important means by which to reassure the customer of the management effectiveness of the whole process.

Post-transactional variables

Post-transactional service activities relate to the support given to the product while it is in use. Typical areas include product guarantees, installation support, replacement parts and servicing and the efficient handling of complaints. The sale does not end with delivery. If the buyer cannot use the product properly or if there are delays when something goes wrong, it can be a great source of frustration and dissatisfaction. This is especially important when the purchase represents an essential input into the buyer's own product.

The above elements constitute the cost areas that arise from providing a level of service. Costs, or the margin required, set the parameters within which service levels can be planned. As service levels move towards 100 per cent standards, the costs of provision increase disproportionately, as shown in Figure 12.14. At very high service levels, the stockholding levels and transport urgency increase dramatically, without necessarily increasing the customer's willingness to respond by paying higher prices. Figure 12.15 shows that customer sensitivity to high levels of service does not necessarily translate into sales, although it may well enhance loyalty levels. Customers themselves may be prepared to trade service off against cost considerations within agreed parameters. Overall, organisations are expected to experience considerable change over the next decade in how they manage logistics within the EU. Skjoett-Larsen (2000) identified seven trends to watch out for:

- Closer cooperation and longer-term supply chain management relationships.
- Specialisation and globalisation in the supply chain with more value-added activities undertaken externally, especially in Eastern Europe.
- More strategic partnerships and alliances with key suppliers.
- More virtual enterprises utilising the benefits of internet applications rather than physical logistics.
- The growth in e-business throughout the supply chain, including EDI and direct sales.
- Greening the supply chain in product usage, transportation and disposal.
- Relationship management methods will dominate all aspects of the supply chain.

These trends could create both opportunities and threats for the marketing manager seeking to use logistics for sustainable competitive advantage.

Figure 12.14 The cost of customer service

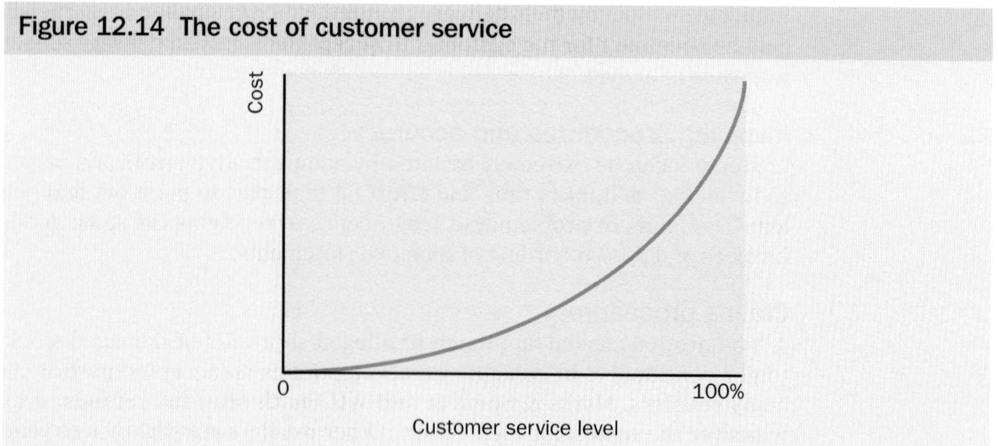

Figure 12.15 Customer sensitivity to service

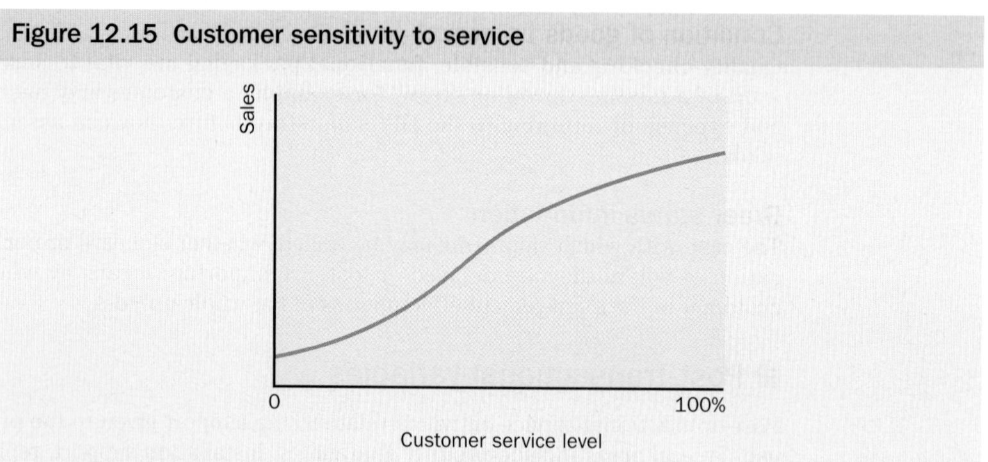

Chapter summary

- The channel of distribution is the means through which products are moved from the manufacturer to the end consumer. The structure of channels can vary considerably depending on the type of market, the needs of the end customer and the type of product. Consumer goods might be supplied direct, but in mass markets for convenience goods, however, this might not be feasible and longer channels might be used. B2B markets are far more likely to involve direct supply from manufacturer to B2B buyer. Some B2B purchases, however, particularly routine repurchases of non-critical items such as office stationery, might be distributed in ways that are similar to those used in consumer markets, with various intermediaries involved.
- Intermediaries play an important role in increasing efficiency and reducing costs, reduce the manufacturer's risk, gather, store, sort and transport a wide range of goods, and ease cash flow for manufacturers and for customers. These functions are not all necessarily performed by the same member of the distribution channel and the decision as to who does what may be made by consensus or by the use of power in the channel.
- Manufacturers are not restricted to using only one channel. There are three broad levels of intensity of distribution, each implying a different set of channels and different types of intermediary: intensive distribution, selective distribution and exclusive distribution. Channel design will be influenced by a number of factors, including organisational objectives, capabilities and resources. Market size might also constrain the choice of channel, as might the buying complexity associated with the product and the buying behaviour of the target market. The changing environment can also influence the choice of channel. Selecting specific intermediaries to join a channel can be difficult but this choice can be a critical success factor since, for example, the speed of entry and the degree of penetration into a new market can depend on the right choice of intermediary. Sometimes,

however, the intermediary has the power to reject a manufacturer or a specific product. Vertical marketing systems (VMS) have evolved to create a channel that is more efficient and effective for all parties, ideally working towards the common good in a long-term relationship. Clearly, voluntary cooperation is the best way of achieving an effective and efficient channel. However, conflict might arise and, if it is not dealt with promptly and sensitively, might lead, sooner or later, to the dissolution of that channel.

- Physical distribution is about the handling, storage and movement of outbound goods, including order processing and transportation. The channels of distribution may include facilitators such as transportation and warehousing specialists. Logistics includes the handling of inbound materials and components, as well as managing outbound inventory, effectively linking supply sources with demand. The design of the logistics system will vary depending on the type and size of the organisation, and thus its costs will also vary widely. The overall aim of logistics and PDM is to provide customer service, but this has to be balanced against the cost. Thus the organisation or the members of the distribution channel must be careful to match the level of service with actual customer needs, avoiding unnecessary costs.

key words and phrases

Agents and brokers
Bulk breaking
Channel strategy
Customer service
Direct supply
Distributors and dealers
Facilitators
Franchisee
Intermediary
Inventory management
Logistics
Market coverage
Marketing channel
Physical distribution
Physical distribution management
Retailers
Vertical marketing systems
Wholesalers

questions *for review*

12.1 What are the different types of *intermediary* that might be found in a distribution channel?

12.2 In what ways can intermediaries make a channel of distribution more *cost efficient*?

12.3 What are the five factors influencing *channel strategy*?

12.4 What are the relative advantages and disadvantages of an *administered VMS* compared with the other two types?

12.5 What are the three groups into which customer service variables can be categorised and what kinds of service does each group cover?

questions *for discussion*

12.1 To what extent and why do you think that the creation of a VMS can improve the performance of a channel and its members?

12.2 What kind of market coverage strategy might be appropriate for:
(a) a bar of chocolate;
(b) a toothbrush;
(c) a home computer;
(d) a marketing textbook;

and why?

12.3 Using Table 12.2 as a starting point, develop lists of criteria that a manufacturer might use in defining:
(a) 'good' retailers; and
(b) 'good' wholesalers to recruit for consumer market channels.

12.4 To what extent and why do you think that warehousing can contribute to effective and efficient PDM?

12.5 Discuss how a power–dependency relationship might work between:
(a) a large brand manufacturer and a large supermarket chain;
(b) a small manufacturer and a large supermarket chain;
(c) a multinational manufacturer of hi-fi equipment and a UK-based High Street electrical goods retailer; and
(d) a small manufacturer of high technology, specialised components and an export agent.

case study 12.1

Sweet harmony in the distribution channel

Lofthouse of Fleetwood manufactures the confectionery/medicinal sweet Fisherman's Friend (*see* Case Study 2.2), but contracts out its marketing to an independent company, Impex, and its distribution to independent distributors. Impex is heavily involved in appointing distributors. It selects and interviews up to six candidate distributor companies, undertaking detailed SWOT analyses on their potential, and it then makes a recommendation to Lofthouse of Fleetwood about which one would be the ideal partner in a particular market. The quality of those recommendations is reflected in the fact that over 25 years, only 5 out of 100 distributors have had to be changed. Among the criteria for selecting a distributor, Lofthouse of Fleetwood includes the following:

- *The products it handles*: a distributor should be selling complementary lines and have experience and suitable contacts in relevant product markets.
- *Its relationship with the competition*: a distributor should not be handling direct competitors' products (and if it was, there would probably be a clause in its contract preventing it from handling Fisherman's Friend); Lofthouse of Fleetwood wants exclusivity.
- *Its structure*: the number of sales representatives and their coverage of the market.
- *Its size*: Lofthouse wants a distributor to be small enough for Fisherman's Friend to have an important role and an adequate share of the distributor's management time and attention. The company prefers to be a big fish in a smaller pool. This needs to be balanced, however, against the need to have a distributor big enough to have the right contacts and to achieve the objectives of the product in its market.
- *Its financial status*: the distributor needs to be financially stable and secure and Lofthouse of Fleetwood is looking for a long-term relationship.
- *Its culture*: because Lofthouse of Fleetwood is looking for a long-term relationship, it is important that a distributor has a similar culture and ethos. The company often finds that because it is a family business, it works well with distributors that are also family businesses.

One distributor that has had a long-standing and successful relationship with Lofthouse of Fleetwood is its Dutch distributor, Nedan Zoetwaren BV. Its profile certainly fits the criteria above. The company is privately owned and has been in business for over 40 years. It distributes confectionery into the Dutch market and started with Stimorol chewing gum, imported from Denmark. Fisherman's Friend was taken into the portfolio in 1974. The company employs 45 people, 24 of whom are involved on a day-to-day basis in sales. Four people are involved in account management, and then there are two well-established sales forces; 11 people work in the sales force covering impulse outlets (for example petrol stations and convenience stores) and 9 in the sales force covering the grocery trade. The company acts as a distributor representing Wrigley's chewing gum and Cadbury's chocolate as well as Fisherman's Friend, but it also manufactures confectionery products of its own based on liquorice and wine gums, under Nedan's Autodrop brand name.

Nedan sells around 750,000 boxes, each with 24 packs of Fisherman's Friend, every year. That amounts to 18 million packages for a population of 15 million, some 20 per cent above the POPPPPY (packets of product per person per year) target, which puts the Netherlands fifth in the POPPPPY league table, behind Norway, Singapore, Germany and Switzerland. Nedan has only had one year when Fisherman's Friend sales fell, otherwise it has been steady upward progress. The sales force still has to work hard, though, to maintain the success. Some 42 per cent of Fisherman's Friend sales are generated from the impulse sector, tobacconists and petrol stations, and that position has to be defended hard in a very competitive market.

Communication is an important part of the strategy and advertising plays a vital role. Lofthouse of Fleetwood decided on an umbrella advertising campaign across Europe via satellite television to create a consistent image through one concentrated message. In addition to this, all the regional distributors do their own advertising, within set guidelines, via terrestrial television. A manual, available on CD-Rom, shows distributors how the product and brand should be presented. In the Netherlands, advertising is commissioned and controlled by Nedan in consultation with Lofthouse of Fleetwood and Impex. There is an advertising allowance from the manufacturer, but Nedan spends more than that as a means of developing and defending its own market.

In terms of pricing, Lofthouse of Fleetwood cannot dictate resale and retail prices. There is one consistent list price for all distributors, although bulk discounts can be negotiated. Distributors are free, however, to set resale prices according to conditions in their own local markets, although the company will advise a distributor if its prices seem to be too far out of line with those of other distributors. Retail buyers and buying groups, such as Carrefour, Ahold and Tesco, and particularly those operating right across Europe, know very well what prices are like in different European countries and will place their orders in the cheapest market. The advent of the euro, however, means greater price transparency, although there are still variations in VAT and sales tax rates in different countries which will cloud the issue somewhat. It is true to say, however, that the general increase in and ease of pan-European trade are encouraging more pricing consistency between European distributors who cannot work in total isolation from each other. Although they do have their own defined territories, any decisions distributors make on pricing, for instance, take into account what is happening in neighbouring and other markets. Nedan is confident that its pricing is comparable with that of other European distributors, however, and does not feel that its major customers, such as Ahold, could gain any advantage from shopping around. Pricing in euros emphasises the consistency.

As part of their contracts, distributors are expected to carry about one month's stock. In general terms, once a market is established, demand is fairly predictable, unless there is a 'flu epidemic or some other unpredictable effect. Nedan has never had any serious problems in replenishing its stocks from the UK. Nedan, in turn, receives orders electronically from its own customers and undertakes to deliver within 24 hours.

Although the Netherlands – UK ordering routine is very well established, occasional meetings, either in the UK or in the Netherlands, offer an opportunity to discuss any real or potential concerns at a senior level and help to cement the relationship further. Distributors are also encouraged to network with each other and exchange information so that they are more likely to work collaboratively than competitively and Nedan finds this a positive and useful experience. Distributors exchange ideas on how to make cost savings and achieve economies of scale, for example. Lofthouse of Fleetwood facilitates this networking by organising two conferences per year, one in Europe and one in the Far East, so that distributors can meet with each other and with the company to discuss tactics.

The relationship between Lofthouse of Fleetwood and Nedan is built on mutual trust, cooperation and communication. Nedan feels that Lofthouse of Fleetwood strikes about the right balance between creating and maintaining a consistent brand image across its global markets while allowing local distributors sufficient autonomy to distribute and market the brand appropriately for their own environments. Lofthouse of Fleetwood brings its manufacturing expertise and strategic vision for the brand to the relationship as well as coordinating the cohesive network of distributors that allows best practice to be disseminated. The distributors themselves bring their local knowledge and contacts and their operational expertise in marketing and growing the brand to the benefit of all parties.

Sources: Adapted from interviews with Rien van Ruremonde, Managing Director of Nedan Zoetwaren BV and with Duncan and Tony Lofthouse, Joint Managing Directors of Lofthouse of Fleetwood Ltd. Our grateful thanks to all of them.

Questions

1. Summarise the reasons why Lofthouse of Fleetwood chooses to use distributors rather than dealing direct with the retail trade itself.
2. What kind of market coverage strategy would you expect to find in the confectionery market and why? What evidence is there in the case that Lofthouse of Fleetwood/Nedan conform to that strategy?
3. Outline the different issues and problems you think Nedan might face in dealing with large multiple supermarket chains and small convenience stores.
4. Why are trust and cooperation so critical in the relationship between Lofthouse of Fleetwood and Nedan? In what ways are trust and cooperation built and expressed in this relationship?

case study 12.2

French hypermarkets and their smaller suppliers

Many French small and medium-sized enterprises (SMEs) which manufacture consumer goods see the hypermarkets as an appropriate and easy way of reaching a mass market. It is not so easy, however, to get a product accepted by the hypermarkets in the first place, nor is it always easy to survive the pressure of dealing with powerful retailers. The hypermarkets put increasing pressure on suppliers to cut prices and to provide more support services, and many smaller companies, especially those which depend too much on a small number of large retailers, cannot survive.

Duarig, for example, was a manufacturer of sports equipment that was forced out of business completely because of the pressure on its profit margins. Over 80 per cent of its output was sold to the hypermarkets. Cipem, a supplier of artificial flowers, realised that it was too small to resist the pressure from the hypermarkets or to negotiate better terms for itself. The hypermarkets demanded more and more services from Cipem, which eventually got to the point where it could no longer deliver. Others found that the only way to survive when dealing with hypermarkets was to make fundamental, and not necessarily welcome, changes in their operations. Lewinger, for example, a manufacturer of knitwear, found that to maintain profit margins, it had to begin to manufacture in low-cost countries such as Poland and Vietnam. Palladium (shoes) tried to maintain control by supplying its goods in limited quantities to the hypermarkets, so that it could get the benefits of mass-market distribution without the risk of compromising its exclusive image. The hypermarkets responded by producing copies of Palladium's canvas shoes, which meant that Palladium then had to get involved in litigation about the alleged 'counterfeiting'.

Not all SMEs have bad experiences with hypermarkets, however. SMEs serve a useful role in injecting novelty and diversity into the retailer's assortment through the regional products they produce which are popular among consumers and contribute to local development. Furthermore, they are the ideal partners for own-brand products since their know-how, flexibility, responsiveness and openness to change are key elements in such partnerships. Eighty per cent of Auchan's products are produced by SMEs. Auchan has formalised its commitment to SMEs via rules covering all parties' undertakings and obligations. These rules go beyond the usual legal or regulatory frameworks. Many stores also sign agreements with SMEs in the form of a charter aimed at creating local networks and improving quality. These charters tend to favour local products and enshrine commercial procedures which are transparent to one and all. Such partnerships serve to promote at a national level all those SMEs which have performed well locally. The group's international presence enables SMEs producing Auchan products to gain a foothold in new markets. Auchan is not just committed to French SMEs: eight partnership agreements have been signed in Portugal with SMEs for fruit, vegetables and meat. These are linked to guaranteed annual volumes. The aim is to sign 170 contracts by 2005.

SMEs which work closely with retailers can use the relationship as a means of strategic development. Routin, for example, began by supplying own-brand fruit concentrates and juices to Carrefour. As the managing director said, it allowed the company to show what it could do and to demonstrate the quality of its goods. It now also supplies other major hypermarket chains, such as Systême U, Auchan and Continent. The success of the own-label products gave Routin the experience and the retail contacts to launch a manufacturer brand, Fruiss, a range of fruit syrups. Fruiss was accepted by the hypermarkets for a number of reasons, and not just because it came from a tried and trusted supplier. Fruiss was carefully positioned so that it did not directly compete with any of the own-label products that Routin already supplied. It was thus not seen as a threat. In case there were any residual doubts in the retailers' minds, Routin ensured that the hypermarkets could make a healthy profit margin on the brand. As a final inducement, Routin also developed and installed imaginative point-of-sale display material to reassure the retailers that the product would be noticed by consumers and would be attractive to them.

Acting as an own-label manufacturer, therefore, can be a good way for an SME to develop and grow, and indirectly to become an important force in its product market. Carrefour has signed up a small company with 70 employees to provide all its own-label gherkins! The hypermarkets seem happy enough to deal with small enterprises and to be an influence on their growth. Carrefour claims to have direct relationships with some 25,000 SMEs, although in some product areas supply is quite concentrated. Carrefour, for example, sources seven million pairs of socks from eight suppliers, and five million items of underwear from seven other suppliers.

To be successful, any SME has to appreciate how the hypermarkets work in terms of purchasing, and what both the hypermarkets and their customers want. To have a fighting chance of survival, the SME has to try to divert negotiation away from price. Concessions on delivery, quantity, promotion or point-of-sale material, for example, might be easier for the SME to maintain than wafer-thin margins, which can then be put under further pressure later. None of this is easy. A survey of manufacturers, consumers and retailers (*see* Table 12.5) found that each group had different ideas about what factors were most important in the success of a new product.

Metronic, a manufacturer of television aerials, satellite dishes and related products, overcame the focus on price by offering the hypermarkets more in the way of service. To make life easier for the retailer, Metronic offered a complete product-line management package, as well as taking responsibility for product display in the stores and giving the retailer regular data on the market and the competition.

Sources: Competition Commission (2000); Declairieux (1995).

Questions

1. What kind of power do the hypermarkets tend to exert over their small suppliers?
2. What are a small supplier's risks and rewards in dealing with a hypermarket?
3. How can own-label products provide an opportunity for the small manufacturer?
4. Other than going down the own-label route, what can a small supplier do to improve its chances of getting its products listed by the hypermarkets? Are there any potential problems with the strategies that you are suggesting?

Table 12.5 Factors in the success of a new product

	Consumers	*Retailers*	*Manufacturers*
Attractive price	1	1	6
Quality/performance	2	5	1
Ease of use	3	6	3
Known brand name	4	3	5
Technological innovation	5	4	2
Promotional support	6	2	4

Ranked in order of importance where 1 = most important.

References for chapter 12

Anderson, J. and Narus, J. (1986), 'Towards a Better Understanding of Distribution Channel Working Relationships' in K. Backhaus and D. Wilson (eds), *Industrial Marketing: A German–American Perspective*, Springer-Verlag.

Anderson, J. and Narus, J. (1990), 'A Model of Distributor Firm and Manufacturer Firm Working Partnerships', *Journal of Marketing*, 54 (January), pp. 42–58.

Bacharach, S. and Lawler, E. (1980), *Power and Politics in Organisations*, Jossey-Bass Inc.

Bedall, C. (2001a), 'Charles: Rural Beauty at Risk', *The Grocer*, 13 May, p. 10.

Bedall, C. (2001b), 'Charles Pushes Local Sourcing', *The Grocer*, 28 July, p. 13.

Bedington, E. (2001), 'Little and Large', *The Grocer*, 24 March, pp. 38–40.

Bell, R., Davies, R. and Howard, E. (1997), 'The Changing Structure of Food Retailing in Europe: The Implications for Strategy', *Long Range Planning*, 30 (6), pp. 853–61.

Bowersox, D. (1978), *Logistics Management*, Macmillan.

Boyd, H. and Walker, O. (1990), *Marketing Management: A Strategic Approach*, Irwin.

Butaney, G. and Wortzel, L. (1988), 'Distribution Power Versus Manufacturer Power: The Customer Role', *Journal of Marketing*, 52 (January), pp. 52–63.

Byrne, P. and Markham, N. (1993), 'Only 10% of Companies Satisfy Customers', *Transport and Distribution*, December, pp. 41–5.

Chaffey, D., Mayer, R., Johnston, K. and Ellis-Chadwick, F. (2003), *Internet Marketing: Strategy, Implementation and Practice*, Financial Times Prentice Hall (2nd edn).

Christopher, M. (1990), *The Strategy of Distribution Management*, Heinemann.

Competition Commission (2000), *Supermarkets: A Report on the Supply of Groceries from Multiple Stores in the United Kingdom*, Competition Commission.

Cooper, J. (1994), 'Jeux Sans Frontieres', *Purchasing and Supply Management*, March, p. 4.

Coopers and Lybrand (1997), *European Value Chain Analysis Study*, Coopers and Lybrand.

CPRE (2002), 'Sustainable Local Foods: Reconnecting Consumers, Farmers, Communities and the Countryside', accessed via http://www.cpre.org.uk.

Dearden, A. (1998), 'Landmark Hits out at Suppliers', *The Grocer*, 6 June, p. 11.

Declairieux, B. (1995), 'Comment se faire reférences', *L'Enterprise*, No. 119, Septembre, pp. 26–40.

Dutta, S., Heide, J. and John, G. (1995), 'Understanding Dual Distribution: The Case of Reps and House Accounts', *Journal of Law, Economics and Organization*, 11 (April), pp. 189–204.

ECR Europe (2002), 'Category Management Best Practice Report', The Partnering Group/Roland Berger and Partners, accessed via http://www.ecrnet.org.

Edmunds, K. (2001), 'ECR: Ready for Action', *Beverage World*, 15 March.

El-Ansary, A.I. and Stern, L.W. (1972), 'Power Measurement in Distribution Channels', *Journal of Marketing Research*, 9 (February), pp. 47–52.

Frazier, G. (1999), 'Organizing and Managing Channels of Distribution', *Journal of the Academy of Marketing Science*, 27 (2), pp. 226–40.

Frazier, G. and Lassar, W. (1996), 'Determinants of Distribution Intensity', *Journal of Marketing*, 60 (October), pp. 39–51.

Frazier, G. (1983), 'On the Measurement of Interfirm Power in Channels of Distribution', *Journal of Marketing Research*, 20 (May), pp. 158–66.

French, J. and Raven, B. (1959), 'The Bases of Social Power' in D. Cartwright (ed.), *Studies in Social Power*, Ann Arbor, University of Michigan Press.

Goldman, A. (2001), 'The Transfer of Retail Formats into Developing Economies: The Example of China', *Journal of Retailing*, 77 (2), pp. 221–42.

Goodley, S. (2001), 'Delivery Difficulties Belabour Mothercare', *The Daily Telegraph*, 17 November, p. 29.

The Grocer, (1998), 'Pervez Attacks Discriminatory Pricing', *The Grocer*, 1 August, p. 8.

The Grocer, (1999), 'Difficult Future Forecast for Cash and Carry Firms', *The Grocer*, 9 January, p. 12.

Gundlach, G. and Cadotte, E. (1994), 'Exchange Interdependence and Interfirm Interaction: Research in a Simulated Channel Setting', *Journal of Marketing Research*, 31 (November), pp. 516–32.

Håkansson, H. (1982), 'An Interaction Approach' in H. Håkansson (ed.), *International Marketing and Purchasing of Industrial Goods: An Interaction Approach*, John Wiley & Sons.

Huber, G. (1990), 'A Theory of the Effects of Advanced Information Technologies on Organizational Design, Intelligence, and Decision Making', *Academy of Management Review*, 15 (1), pp. 47–72.

Hunt, J. (2001), 'Orient Express', *The Grocer*, 12 May, pp. 36–7.

The Independent (2001), 'The Investment Column: Tibbett & Britten', *The Independent*, 19 December, p. 19.

Jaworski, B. and Kohli, A. (1993), 'Market Orientation: Antecedents and Consequences', *Journal of Marketing*, 57 (3), pp. 53–70.

Kumar, N., Scheer, L. and Steenkamp, J-B. (1995), 'The Effects of Perceived Interdependence on Dealer Attitudes', *Journal of Marketing Research*, 32 (August): 248–56.

LaLonde, B. and Zinzer, P. (1976), *Customer Service: Meaning and Measurement*, National Council of Physical Distribution Management.

Lambert, D. and Stock, J. (1997), *Strategic Logistics Management*, Irwin.

Lusch, R. and Brown, J. (1996), 'Interdependency, Contracting, and Relational Behavior in Marketing Channels', *Journal of Marketing*, 60 (October), pp. 19–38.

Magrath, A. and Hardy, K. (1988), 'Ten Ways for Manufacturers to Improve Distribution Management', *Business Horizons*, November/December, p. 68.

Mentzer, J., Gomes, R. and Krapfel, R. (1989), 'Physical Distribution Service: A Fundamental Marketing Concept?', *Journal of the Academy of Marketing Science*, 17 (Winter), pp. 53–62.

Mentzer, J. and Williams, L. (2001), 'The Role of Logistics Leverage in Marketing Strategy', *Journal of Marketing Channels*, 8 (3/4), pp. 29–48.

Mitchell, A. (1997), *Efficient Consumer Response: a New Paradigm for the European FMCG Sector*, Financial Times Retail and Consumer Publishing.

MLC Industry Strategy Ltd (2001), *Setting Up Initiatives for the Collaborative Marketing of Local/Regional Products: Best Practice Procedures*, MLC Industry Strategy Ltd.

Mohr, J. and Nevin, J. (1990), 'Communication Strategies in Marketing Channels: A Theoretical Perspective', *Journal of Marketing*, 54 (October), pp. 36–51.

Mohr, J., Fisher, R. and Nevin, J. (1999), 'Communicating for Better Channel Relationships', *Marketing Management*, 8 (2), pp. 38–45.

Morgan, R. and Hunt, S. (1994), 'The Commitment – Trust Theory of Relationship Marketing', *Journal of Marketing*, 58 (July), pp. 20–38.

Paché, G. (1998), 'Logistics Outsourcing in Grocery Distribution: A European Perspective', Logistics Information Management, 11 (5), pp. 301–8.

Paché, G. and des Garets, V. (1997), 'Relations inter-organisationelles dans les canaux de distribution: les dimensions logistiques', *Recherche et Applications en Marketing*, 12 (2), pp. 61–82.

Palamountain, J.C. (1955), *The Politics of Distribution*, Harvard University Press.

Raven, B.H. and Kruglanski, A.W. (1970), 'Conflict and Power' in P. Swingle (ed.), *The Structure of Conflict*, Academic Press.

Rosenbloom, B. (1987), *Marketing Channels: A Management View*, Dryden.

Rowe, J. (1998), 'Multiples Must Learn to Adjust', *The Grocer*, 1 August, p. 9.

Shapley, D. (1998), 'The Cape Crusaders', *The Grocer*, 20 June, pp. 59–63.

Sharma, A. and Dominguez, L. (1992), 'Channel Evolution: A Framework for Analysis', *Journal of the Academy of Marketing Science*, 20 (Winter), pp. 1–16.

Skjoett-Larsen, T. (2000), 'European Logistics Beyond 2000', *International Journal of Physical Distribution and Logistics Management*, 30 (5), pp. 377–87.

Smith, K. (1997), 'Right to Reply', *Supply Management*, 27 November, pp. 24–9.

Stern, L., El-Ansary, A. and Coughlan, A. (1996), *Marketing Channels*, Prentice Hall, 5th edn.

Stern, L. and Gorman, R. (1969), *Marketing Channels* (2nd edn), Prentice Hall.

Sussams, J. (1991), 'The Impact of Logistics on Retailing and Physical Distribution', *International Journal of Retail and Distribution Management*, 19(7), pp. 4–9.

Trepins, D. (2001a), '3PLs Invest Heavily in UK Logistics Centers', *Logistics Management and Distribution Report*, November, p. E9.

Trepins, D. (2001b), 'The Dutch Haven't Lost their Touch', *Logistics Management and Distribution Report*, November, p. E13.

Varley, P. (1999), 'Trend Spotter', *Supply Management*, 4 March, pp. 34–6.

Webster, F.E. (1979), *Industrial Marketing Strategy*, John Wiley & Sons.

Weitz, B. and Jap, S. (1995), 'Relationship Marketing and Distribution Channels', *Journal of the Academy of Marketing Science*, 23 (Fall), pp. 305–20.

Williams, S. (1999), 'Collaborative Planning, Forecasting, and Replenishment', *Hospital Material Management Quarterly*, November, pp. 44–51.

chapter 13

retailers and wholesalers

Introduction

LEARNING OBJECTIVES

This chapter will help you to:

1 understand the role and importance of retailers and wholesalers within the distribution channel;

2 classify retailers according to a number of different organisational and operating dimensions;

3 differentiate between types of retailer, appreciating their individual contribution to the retailing scene and their problems;

4 analyse the particular strategic and operational marketing concerns of retailers; and

5 understand the role played by different types of wholesaler.

Shopaholics of the world unite! Retailing is one of the highest-profile areas of marketing and, like advertising, has had a tremendous impact on society, culture and lifestyles. To some, shopping is an essential social and leisure activity, while to others, it is a chore. It offers some a chance to dream and, for most of us, an opportunity at some time or other to indulge ourselves. We often take for granted the availability of wide ranges of goods and know that if we search hard enough, we will find just what we are looking for. Some people, indeed, find that half the fun is in the searching rather than the ultimate purchase.

Although to us as consumers retailing means fun, excitement and the opportunity to splash out vast quantities of cash (thanks to plastic cards!), it is a very serious business for the managers and organisations that make it happen. It is often the last stage in the channel of distribution before consumption, which means that there is an important role for the retailer in being so close to the final consumer. Not only do retailers have to buy, sort, store and promote goods, they also have to take the risk of being left with poorly selling and loss-making product lines. To avoid this, retailers have to ensure a close match between their capabilities and the merchandise offered, which in turn arises from a clear understanding of their own market appeal, reflected in such areas as store location, merchandise selection, customer service and general ambience and image. Compare the shopping experience provided by, for example, a large hypermarket and a small clothes boutique. One is large, cheap, cheerful, convenient, busy and impersonal, while the other is small, relatively expensive, cosy and places a distinct emphasis on personal service. These differences are the result of careful retailer strategy decisions focused on developing their individual competitive strengths.

eg

Safeway in the UK and Dutch retailer Ahold are both keen to change the nature of the shopping experience and to encourage shoppers to spend a little longer in store. At the first Safeway hypermarket in Plymstock, Devon, the idea of a 'hub' was created at the centre of the store. It is a café-style seating area where, with the fresh food counter on one side and the books and CDs displays on the other, shoppers can meet and relax and of course contemplate what extra little treats to buy. The idea is not new to supermarkets. Some of the Albert Heijn branches operated by Ahold feature 'circle stores' with a market area in the centre featuring a coffee shop, bakery, cooking school and freshly prepared food snacks. The ring of convenience products leads the shopper down 'themed streets' of other grocery products. Supermarkets are keen to encourage new ways of presenting themselves uniquely, other than on price. The greater the quality of the experience, the longer the stay for some shoppers and perhaps the greater the spend. This message has certainly been learnt by some book retailers who offer comfortable armchairs and free coffee to maximise browsing (Bedington, 2001b; *The Grocer*, 2001g; Hunt, 1998, 1999).

This emphasis on the retailer's strategic thinking in terms of merchandise sourcing reinforces the point made in the previous chapter, that the choice of outlet may not be a completely free decision for the manufacturer. This is because the power balance has progressively swung towards the retailers, given their concentration of purchasing power.

Wholesalers are less evident to the general public, yet they play a vital role in servicing both retail outlets and industrial users, as discussed in Chapter 12. The key to successful wholesaling is to have a clear focus on which target customers are to be served, and then to become highly responsive in terms of stock, service and buying and selling efficiency. For many manufacturers, wholesalers and agents are essential intermediaries, as access to the retail or industrial user could become highly expensive and difficult without their services.

However, the role of retailers and wholesalers is not just restricted to the forward movement and promotion of goods. They also send information back up the distribution channel by providing feedback to the manufacturer about market changes, customer preferences and opportunity areas. Sometimes this feedback can be implicit in a retailer's actions, for instance refusing to re-order, or through established sales patterns. More systematic research and information gathering, however, as described in Chapter 6, may provide especially rich explicit insights sooner and in more depth.

This chapter starts with a review of the importance of retailing and wholesaling in the distribution channel. It then examines in some detail the different forms of retail outlet. Non-store retailing is also considered, as what we are seeing now in this area may lead to significant new developments and fundamental structural change in the retailing world over the next 10 years or so. Finally within the retail sector, current trends and their impact on the main strategy dimensions are considered, with particular regard to such areas as location, merchandising and competitive positioning. The chapter concludes with a more detailed look at wholesaling. Particular attention is paid to the different types of wholesaler and their potential for taking up an effective role within the channel of distribution.

The nature of retailing and wholesaling

Retailing and wholesaling are both about buying and selling for a profit. Of course, that is a gross simplification of the very important roles that both play in bridging the gap between producers and consumers. Both receive goods from a wide range of different sources and then (often) redistribute them to convenient locations along with a marketing package that is valued by their customers or the final consumer. Usually, these locations are shops and warehouses but, increasingly, other forms of non-store retailing are becoming evident, as will be seen later. The main distinction between the wholesaler and retailer is that the wholesaler is primarily focused on other resellers or B2B users, whereas the retailer is focused primarily on the much larger, but highly differentiated, consumer market.

Retailing and wholesaling can best be defined in terms of the main functions that both perform.

Assembling a range of goods

The main function of a retailer is to *assemble a range of products and services* that complement its own strengths and match the needs of the target market. Within a particular product area or market, variety is ensured, as retailers seek to differentiate their offerings from those of their competitors, although increasingly this is becoming more difficult.

eg

Think about the variations between music stores in the High Street, for instance. Some retailers specialise in a particular style of music, going for depth without breadth, while others go for breadth of coverage without the depth, stocking the bestselling popular items from a variety of music styles, but not much more. Others have heavily diversified into videos and computer games. HMV in the UK, however, has chosen to maintain a tight focus on music, claiming that customers should be able to find any current recording that they want, at least within the largest of its 521 stores. Its computerised stock-control system means that HMV can assess demand and track the availability of the 270,000 releases current in the UK at any one time.

HMV also has an online selling operation which allows customers to search for an album in various music categories, see a listing of tracks, check availability and in some cases listen to a sample track. This enables a wider group of customers to be reached and reduces the pressure on some of the smaller local stores where the range carried may be more limited (Finch, 2001b).

Thus by assembling goods, retailers provide both *place utility* and *time utility*. Place utility means that the goods are at a convenient location that reduces the effort that the customer has to make in finding and purchasing a desired range of goods. It may take place either through providing mail order facilities or home delivery or through providing handy retail premises to receive visiting customers. In the case of home shopping, the catalogue, website or television channel provides the 'showroom' so that customers, from the comfort of their own armchairs, can order by mail, telephone or e-mail for home delivery. This must be the ultimate in place utility. Time utility similarly means reducing the amount of time that the customer has to invest in the purchasing process, and is linked with place utility.

Wholesalers can play a major role in providing the wide assortment of goods required. While some retailers deal directly with manufacturers, others, particularly smaller stores, may prefer the convenience and accessibility of the wholesaler, especially where fast, responsive supply is assured. In the book trade, for example, it is difficult for a retailer to offer anything like the total number of titles available. Instead, the retailer acts as an order conduit, so that either the wholesaler or the publisher can service individual orders that have been consolidated into economic shipment sizes. The wholesaler can maintain a much wider range of products than is possible in all but the largest retail groups, and can provide efficient support activities for rapid stock replenishment.

Providing storage and transportation

The provision of *storage and transportation* has become increasingly important with the widening distance, in terms of both geography and the length of distribution channels, between producer and consumer. Purchasing patterns increasingly include products sourced from wherever the best deal can be offered, whether local or international. As production becomes more concentrated into a relatively small number of larger operations, the need to move products over large distances increases. The distance can be even greater in the foodstuffs area, with the demand for exotic and fresh foods from elsewhere in Europe and well beyond. The availability of Chilean grapes in the UK supermarket in winter, for example, is the end point of a long series of distribution decisions including a number of intermediaries.

Retailers and wholesalers, by allowing larger shipments to be made and then breaking bulk, play an important role in establishing economies of scale in channels of physical distribution. Some wholesalers are themselves heavily involved in performing physical distribution roles such as inventory planning, packing, transportation and order processing in line with customer service objectives. This assists the manufacturer as well as the retailer. Often the wholesaler will incur costs in inward-bound transportation, maintain a safety stock buffer and absorb associated inventory and material handling expenses, all of which represent savings for the manufacturer.

Giving advice and information

Both retailers and wholesalers are part of the forward *information flow* that advises customers and persuades them to buy. Although in the supermarket environment the role of personal advice is minimal, many retailers, especially those in product lines such as clothing, hobbies, electrical goods and cars, are expected to assist the consumer directly in making a purchase decision and to advise on subsequent use. These are the kinds of goods that require limited or extended decision-making behaviour, as discussed at pp. 105–7 earlier.

marketing **in action**

Home delivery or 'drive thru' grocery shopping?

Not every shopper enjoys the 'fun' of shopping, especially when it involves a trip to the supermarket. It is this group, those who cannot, or prefer not to visit the supermarket, but who must buy, that has been the target of several attempts to develop home ordering and home delivery grocery services. The latest estimates, however, suggest that home shopping still only accounts for around 1 per cent of UK grocery sales.

The reasons why home shopping should be popular are clear: increasingly busy lives with extended working hours; the increasing number of people at work, especially women; the feeling that people have better things to do with their free time such as 'real' leisure pursuits; and growing acceptance of home delivery in a range of sectors such as books, pizza, flowers, etc. All of this, combined with the increasing use of the internet, sets the scene for significant growth in home grocery shopping. The trouble is that the supermarket chains that have experimented with online grocery shopping have had variable results. Somerfield and Budgens closed down their home delivery operations in 2000 due to poor take-up. In contrast to that, Tesco and Sainsbury are often quoted as the two most successful operators. The Sainsbury's 'To You' online home delivery business, however, is thought to have lost £29 mn in just six months in 2001 and is thought to have cost £200 mn overall in getting it launched. Its original idea was to follow US practice, with central warehouses serving the online orders rather than adopting the Tesco model of picking from local store shelves. Sainsbury's now offers store picking alongside the central warehouse and has 40 stores offering the service, a number that is likely to expand.

Tesco.com has persevered with home shopping for five years and is starting to see results. Although the level of profit that has been made from this venture is unknown, its turnover has grown to over £300 mn and it has 750,000 registered customers of whom 70,000 shop regularly. Tesco claims that it has opened up new market segments and attracted business away from Waitrose in the south and Sainsbury's in the north of the UK. Customers do not just order groceries; CDs, DVDs and wine are also popular. Perhaps what is more important is that while the typical shopper at Tesco spends under £25 per visit, the online shopper spends over £80 (presumably on the basis that if you are going to pay a £5 delivery fee, you might as well make it worthwhile). Tesco offers 40,000 products online and operates a fleet of 800 vans to ensure prompt delivery.

At present, the future is far from clear, however. Forrester Research has suggested that home shopping will account for 2 per cent of grocery turnover by the end of 2002 and Dresdner Kleinwort Benson has estimated that by 2008, 10 per cent of the UK food market sales with a value of £14 bn will be delivered to the home. This supports Tesco's belief that online shopping could be the biggest revolution in supermarket shopping since self-service was introduced. Independent research is less encouraging, however. An Institute of Grocery and Distribution survey has suggested that most consumers have little interest in buying groceries over the internet: they prefer to choose food in-store, don't like paying online and enjoy the spontaneity and exploration of shopping. The level of understanding is also low, as they think that the product range will be limited with shorter shelf life and that they will lose out by having fewer price promotions.

Other retailers such as Waitrose and ASDA are thought to be considering expanding operations, despite the existing operators' variable results. Interestingly, in the USA, where home shopping began, a new scheme called 'On the Go' run by Shaw's, a Sainsbury subsidiary, proposes a hybrid model that offers the benefits of convenience without the prohibitive cost that faces most retailers trying to plan deliveries on a low delivery charge rate. For a flat rate fee of $4.95, customers can order from 20,000 lines on the multiple's website, pay by credit card and collect the assembled order from the store, rather like a 'drive-thru' arrangement at a fast food restaurant, without ever leaving the car. Now there's a thought.

Sources: Finch (2001a); *The Grocer* (2002a; 2001d, 2001f); Ryle (2001).

Wholesalers are also important sources of advice for some retailers and users. The more specialised a wholesaler, the greater the opportunity for developing an in-depth market understanding, tracking new or declining products, analysing competitive actions, defining promotions needed and advising on best buys. This role may be especially valuable to the smaller retailer who has less direct access to quality information on broader trends in a specific market. Similarly, an industrial distributor may be expected to advise customers on applications and to assist in low-level technical problem solving.

Transferring title

Both wholesalers and retailers (but not agents) take title to goods and services. Within the context of warranty restrictions, the intermediary accepts legal responsibility for the product, including its storage, security and resale. This has a direct bearing on the pricing,

eg

IKEA, despite having had a €10.4 bn turnover and 255 million customer visits in 2000, has been criticised over the level of customer service and advice it offers. It has achieved high degrees of consistency worldwide in its operations, with self-assembly, self-service, high-design merchandise that is affordable, especially for the first-time homeowner. The problem, however, can be seen (and experienced) by anyone visiting an IKEA store on a busy Saturday. Parking can be difficult, the availability of instore advice variable, the checkout queues long and there is an overall impression that the retailer is seemingly reluctant to make the shopper's burden easier. The solutions are straightforward, but have not yet been implemented. Opening more stores would help, but primarily it is about staffing levels, so hiring more in-store staff, installing more checkouts, and finding promotional methods to spread shopper visits more evenly over the week could all help. Making the website transactional would also help a lot. Currently, it is claimed by IKEA that its strategies are 'geared towards generating customers into stores where they can actually sit on and touch products' (as quoted by Stewart-Allen, 2001). IKEA is, however, piloting an online ordering system as well as an e-mail customer enquiry line. Other retailers have provided an adequate shopping experience online and few people nowadays want to spend a whole or half day battling for a parking space, searching for trolleys and queueing at checkouts. IKEA's challenge is to improve customer service satisfaction to match the high levels of merchandise satisfaction it achieves.

display and control of the products offered, the processing of cash and/or credit transactions, and the implementation of materials handling into and around the showroom and, if necessary, out to the customer. Some of these functions can be passed on to the customer. In IKEA, for instance, the customer can see display products in a showroom and then pick the required products unassisted from warehouse storage racks before going on to the checkout.

When the wholesaler takes title to goods, there are direct financial and other benefits to the producer, for which the wholesaler is rewarded through a profit margin. These benefits include lower distribution and logistics costs, credit and cash flow benefits, reduced selling and administration costs as a result of dealing with a relatively small number of customers, and a valuable information flow back to the manufacturer.

Providing an appropriate environment

Both wholesalers and retailers receive customers in their premises. The wholesaler in the grocery trade will probably operate like an overgrown supermarket, allowing selected and vetted trade customers to choose and even collect goods during their visit. In other situations, such as a builder's merchant, a mixed operation may exist. Some high-value, low-bulk products will be sold by counter service only, rather than on a self-service basis.

In most retail situations, the consumer enters a carefully planned and controlled environment designed to create a retail environment that helps to establish and reinforce the ambience and image desired. In some, this may be a low-cost minimalist approach that reinforces a no-frills, value for money philosophy, with simple picking from racks and pallets or drums. In others, music, decor and display are all subtly developed and designed around themes to create a more upmarket, higher-quality shopping experience. The whole area of retail atmosphere will be readdressed at p. 552 *et seq.*

The retail environment can also include a range of additional services. Convenient parking is a critical issue where customers are buying in bulk, or want fast takeaway services (the 'drive-thru' fast food operator has found the logical solution to this one!). Additional services in the form of credit, delivery, returns and purchasing assistance can help to differentiate a retailer.

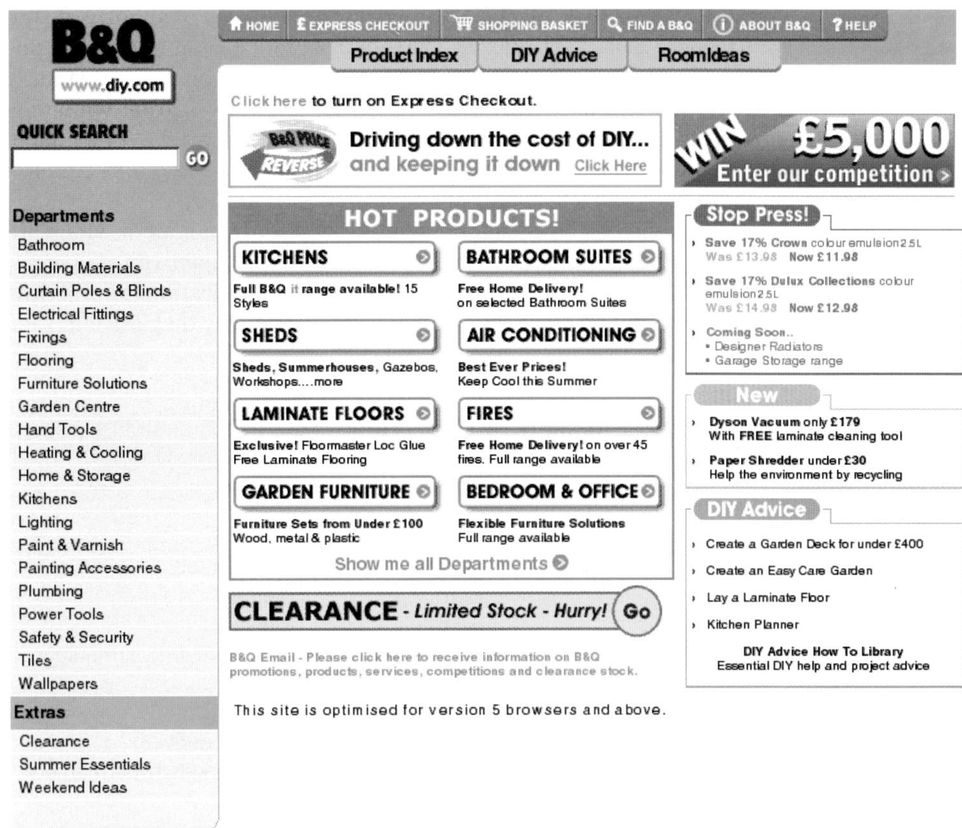

B&Q uses e-commerce as a new way of offering customers advice and guidance on its products.

Source: http://www.diy.com, B&Q plc.

eg

Many retailers are embracing e-commerce as a means of providing additional services to their customers. A website can provide information for customers in their own homes, perhaps on product availability, pricing, special offers or new products. The website can also educate customers, not only by establishing the company's policies on the environment or employee relations issues, for example, but also by giving them ideas about how to use products or about other products in the company's range. Online ordering then makes it very easy for customers to place an order, which can then be delivered to their homes. DIY chain B&Q's website (http://www.diy.com) incorporates an online ordering service aimed at the amateur DIY enthusiast. B&Q feels that with over 300 UK stores, its online service is not so much about extending its geographic reach as adding value for its customers through convenience, service and information.

The structure of the european retail sector

Retailing across Europe is big business. Total retail sales across the EU in 1999 amounted to some $1,934,059 mn, with Germany, France, the UK and Italy as the leading nations, accounting for almost 77 per cent of the total between them (Euromonitor, 2001).

Table 13.1 shows the top 20 west European retailers, ranked by global sales. While only eight of them are clearly defined as being in grocery-related sectors, it is interesting to note that at least eight more, particularly from the 'diverse' sector, do also have significant interests in grocery retailing. In geographic terms, the list is dominated by German, French and UK organisations. Table 13.1 looks at global sales, but a list based purely on European sales would feature most of the same names albeit in a slightly different order (*Retail Intelligence*, 2000; IGD, 2002a). Carrefour would remain at number one, but Tesco would leap to the number two spot because despite its international standing, it only generates about 10 per cent of its turnover outside its domestic market while many of the other big name retailers do a lot more business outside Europe. Ahold, for example, generates only 33 per cent of its turnover from Europe, 60 per cent from North America, 7 per cent from South America and less than 1 per cent from the Far East.

Retailers can be classified on a number of criteria, not all of which are immediately obvious to the average shopper. A later section of this chapter (pp. 533 *et seq.*) will concentrate on store types, but this section discusses other classification criteria, which will also help to shed further light on what retailers actually do and why they are important to both manufacturer and consumer.

Table 13.1 Europe's 20 largest retailers by global turnover, 2000

European rank	*World rank*	*Company*	*Home market*	*Retail sector*	*Global sales $mn*
1	2	Carrefour	France	Hypermarket	55,302
2	3	Metro	Germany	Diverse	46,633
3	8	Rewe Gruppe	Germany	Diverse	36,561
4	10	Ahold	Netherlands	Supermarket/hypermarkets	35,775
5	11	ITM Enterprises (inc. Spar)	France	Diverse	35,218
6	13	Edeka Gruppe	Germany	Diverse	31,788
7	14	Aldi Gruppe	Germany	Food/discount	31,570
8	16	Tesco	UK	Supermarkets/hypermarkets	30,401
9	17	Tengelmann Gruppe	Germany	Diverse	29,501
10	20	J Sainsbury	UK	Supermarkets/hypermarkets/DIY	25,835
11	21	Leclerc	France	Diverse	23,532
12	22	Auchan	France	Hypermarkets/diverse	23,449
13	23	Otto Versand	Germany	Mail order	22,066
14	28	Kingfisher	UK	Diverse	17,442
15	30	Lidl & Schwarz Gruppe	Germany	General merchandise/discount	16,874
16	31	Casino	France	Supermarkets/hypermarkets	16,122
17	33	Karstadt Quelle Gruppe	Germany	Department stores/mail order	15,801
18	34	Delhaize Le Lion	Belgium	Supermarkets	15,234
19	41	Marks & Spencer	UK	Variety stores/general merchandise	12,668
20	46	Migros	Switzerland	Diverse	12,438

Source: Extracted and adapted from *The World's 100 Largest Retailers* accessed via http://www.chainstoreage.com.

Form of ownership

Retailing was for many years the realm of the small-independent business. Some grew by adding more branches and some grew by acquisition, but it is only since the 1950s that the retail structure of the High Street has evolved significantly, favouring the larger organisation. Nevertheless, there are still several predominant forms of ownership to be found.

Independent

Still the most common form of ownership in terms of number of retail outlets is independent, with over 62 per cent of UK outlets falling into this category. In sales volume terms, however, this group accounts for less than 30 per cent. Marked variances exist between retail categories, with a significant role for the small independent in the drinks sector and in CTN (confectionery, tobacco and news) retailing. Similar patterns exist across Europe, especially in France, Spain and the Benelux countries, which have above average densities of small retailers. Typically, the **independent retail outlet** is managed by a sole trader or a family business. For the consumer, the main benefits are the personalised attention and flexibility that can be offered. These operations can be highly individualistic in terms of the variety and quality of merchandise stocked, ranging from very upmarket to bargain basement.

Although it may not be possible for the small independent to compete on price and breadth of range offered, the key is to complement the big multiples rather than to try to compete head-on. Howe (1992) is clear about forces that work against the small retailer, such as changing population patterns, the drift towards out of town shopping, supply and resource problems and the sheer scale and professionalism of the large multiple chains. To combat this, the small retailer thus needs to look for niches, specialised merchandise, flexible opening hours and special services and to make more effective use of suppliers. This boils down to sound management and marketing thinking.

eg

Small village grocery shops are becoming an endangered species. Estimates have suggested that 300 close every year and that around one-third of all villages now have no local store. Turnover varies widely. Some smaller stores are hard pushed to generate £20,000 per week, but more favoured locations can easily double that. The Rural Shops Alliance estimates that there are only about 12,000 rural shops left; the rest have become victims of increased consumer mobility and the attraction of the supermarkets, some of which actually run weekly free bus services to their stores. The key to survival is diversification. Having the local Post Office franchise can be a big help, as it attracts people into the store, but it is also about offering fax and photocopying facilities, internet access, lottery access, cash points, video hire, flexible opening hours and fresh local produce. Although shopping for convenience items or those forgotten on the main shopping trip provides basic turnover for the village store, what is really needed to increase the value and loyalty of customers is a change in the retailer's attitude and the creation of a service-orientated multi-activity centre appealing to the cross-section of the community that could create a captive audience (Gregory, 2001a; 2001b).

Corporate chain

A corporate chain has multiple outlets under common ownership. The operation of the chain will reflect corporate strategy, and many will centralise decisions where economies of scale can be gained. The most obvious activity to be centralised is purchasing, so that volume discounts and greater power over suppliers can be gained. There are, of course, other benefits to be derived from a regional, national or even international presence in terms of image and brand building. Typical examples include Next and C&A. Some chains do allow a degree of discretion at a local level to reflect different operating environments, in terms of opening hours, merchandise or services provided, but the main strength comes from unity rather than diversity.

Contractual system

The linking of members of distribution channels through formal agreements rather than ownership (i.e. a contractual system) was included in the discussion of vertical marketing systems in Chapter 12. For retail or wholesale sponsored cooperatives or franchises, the main benefit is the ability to draw from collective strength, whether in management, marketing or operational procedures. In some cases, the collective strength, as with franchises, can provide a valuable tool for promoting customer awareness and familiarity, leading in turn to retail loyalty. The trade-off for the franchisee is some loss of discretion, both operationally and strategically, but this may be countered by the benefits of unity. **Franchising** might also pass on the retailing risk to the franchisee. When Benetton's performance was poor in the US market, 300 stores closed, with all the losses borne by the franchisees rather than by Benetton (Davidson, 1993).

If the independent retailer wants to avoid the risks of franchising (*see* Chapter 22 for a more detailed discussion of franchising), yet wants to benefit from collective power, then affiliation to either a buying group or a voluntary chain might be the answer. Buying groups are usually found in food retailing and their purpose is to centralise the purchasing function and to achieve economies of scale on behalf of their members.

Level of service

The range and quality of services offered vary considerably from retailer to retailer. Some, such as department stores, offer gift-wrapping services, and some DIY stores offer home delivery, but in others most of the obligation for picking, assessing and taking the product home rests with the customer.

Three types of service level highlight the main options.

Full service

Stores such as Harrods provide the full range of customer services. This includes close personal attention on the shopfloor, a full range of account and delivery services, and a clear objective to treat each customer as a valued individual. Such high levels of service are reflected in the premium pricing policy adopted.

Limited service

The number of customers handled and the competitive prices that need to be charged prevent the implementation of the full range of services, but the services that are offered make purchasing easier. Credit, no-quibble returns, telephone orders and home delivery may be offered. This is a question of deciding what the target market 'must have' rather than what it 'would like', or defining what is essential for competitive edge. A retailer, such as Next, which claims to sell quality clothing at competitive prices, cannot offer too many extra services because that would increase the retailer's costs. They do, however, have to offer a limited range of services in order to remain competitive with similar retailers.

Self-service

In self-service stores, the customer performs many of the instore functions, including picking goods, queueing at the checkout, paying by cash or perhaps credit card, and then struggling to the car park with a loaded trolley. Some food and discount stores operate in this mode, but the trend is towards offering more service to ease bottleneck points that are particularly frustrating to the customer. This could include the provision of more staff at the delicatessen counter, more checkouts to guarantee short queues, and assistance with packing.

Merchandise lines

Retailers can be distinguished by the merchandise they carry, assessed in terms of the breadth and depth of range.

Breadth of range

The **breadth of range** represents the variety of different product lines stocked. A department store (*see* pp. 533 *et seq.* for a fuller discussion) will carry a wide variety of product lines, perhaps including electrical goods, household goods, designer clothing, hairdressing and even holidays.

Depth of range

The **depth of range** defines the amount of choice or assortment within a product line, on whatever dimensions are relevant to that kind of product. A music store stocking CDs, tapes, minidiscs and vinyl records could be said to have depth in its range. Similarly, a clothing store that stocks cashmere jumpers might be said to have a shallow range if the jumpers are available only in one style, or a deep range if they are available in five different styles. Introducing further assortment criteria, such as size range and colour, creates a very complex definition of depth. A specialty or niche retailer (*see* pp. 539 *et seq.*), such as Tie Rack would be expected to provide depth in its product lines on a number of assortment criteria.

Figure 13.1 shows the difference between these two terms. It is easy to see, in this figure, how tensions can arise between breadth and depth. Since retailers have limited resources and limited space at their disposal, there is a basic choice to be made between breadth and depth. If they go for breadth, they can provide a wide variety of different kinds of goods, but

eg

Hennes and Mauritz (H&M) is Sweden's fifth largest company and operates around 730 stores in 14 countries. It is still expanding in the UK, USA, Germany and Austria. It owns over a dozen own-labels covering men's, women's and children's clothing, casual and classic wear, and underwear and outerwear. These labels are targeted at specific segments in the 18–45 age range, for example Clothes is very trend conscious, Hennes is classic fashion and Mama is the maternity range. The assortment is, however, varied by region to suit local demographics and tastes. Although it is a speciality retailer, concentrating on fashion, it provides a broad but shallow range, compared with other fashion retailers which specialise in just women's wear or jeans (narrow and deep). H&M is happy to offer low prices, reasonable quality and a wide range of fashionable clothing. To keep customers interested in its stores and to broaden the width of range further, new products designed by 70 in-house staff are introduced every day and no product is kept in the stores for longer than one month. That means some stores receive between two and four deliveries each day, and slower moving items soon hit the mark-down racks. It also means an extensive logistics operation involving regional warehouses, with half supplied from within Europe and the rest from Asia. Most other fashion retailers tend to change ranges only two to four times a year (Scardino, 2001; Teather, 2001).

Figure 13.1 Breadth vs depth

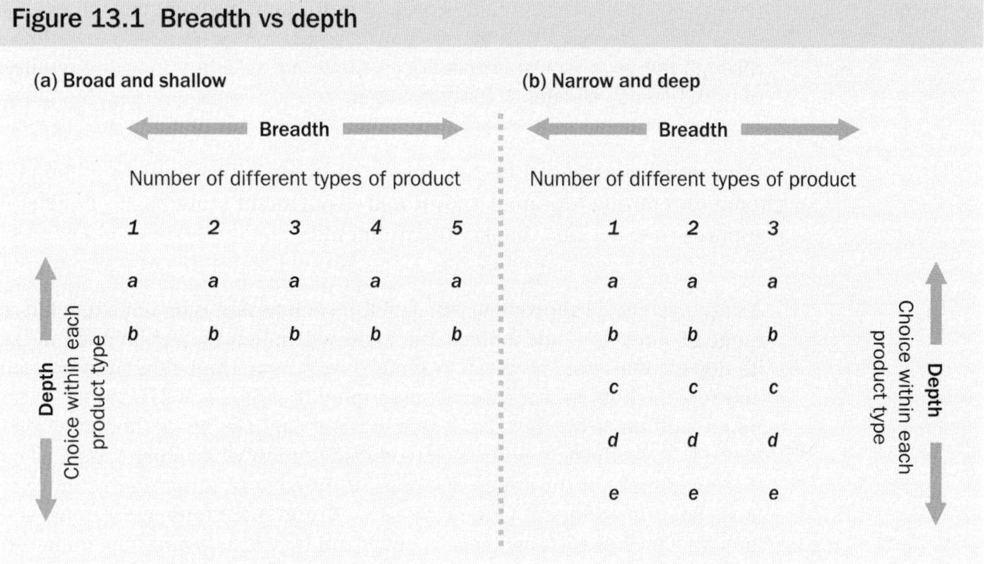

probably would not be able to stock those products in significant depth. Limits may be placed on the number of different brands, or the range of styles, sizes or colours available within a product area. Sacrificing breadth for depth means that the retailer can satisfy demand for a whole variety of different brands, sizes, colours or styles, but only within a very narrowly defined range of goods.

In many cases, customers are happy to accept a polarised choice, patronising department stores when depth of range does not really matter to them, or where the level of customer service they know they will get from the store matters more. Speciality retailers attract custom from those who do want the depth of choice, perhaps because they are engaged in extended problem solving and want access to as many alternatives as possible, or because they want an unusual combination of size, colour and style, for example, that only a specialist stockist would keep. The speciality retailer might also be seen as more knowledgeable and committed to the product area, and this might reduce the risk inherent in the purchase in the customer's mind.

As Figure 13.2 shows, some retailers do try to compromise by offering a mixed approach. Some products, perhaps popular, fast moving lines, will be stocked in depth.

Figure 13.2 The mixed approach

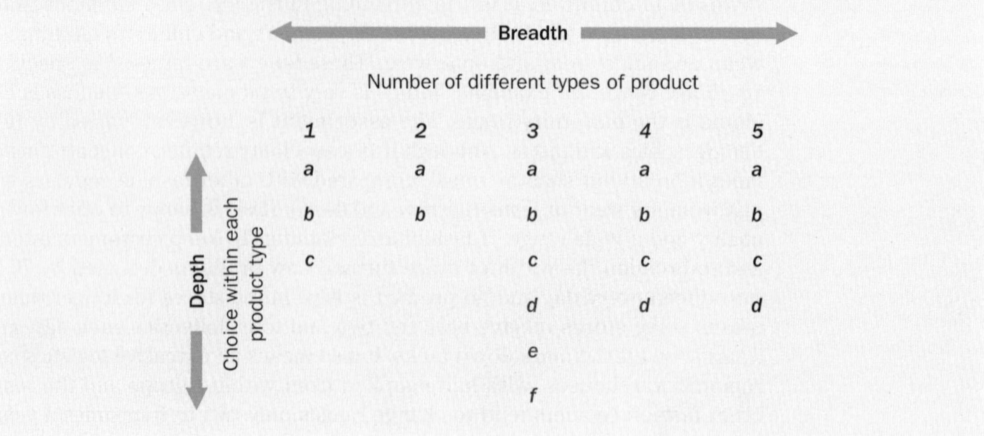

Breadth

Number of different types of product

Depth

Choice within each product type

1	2	3	4	5
a	*a*	*a*	*a*	*a*
b	*b*	*b*	*b*	*b*
c		c	c	c
		d	*d*	*d*
		e		
		f		

eg

A clothing store might stock a much wider range of colours and sizes for a classic, polo-neck jumper selling at a competitive price than for an extremely fashionable (and therefore short shelf life) velvet jacket selling at a premium price. Breadth and depth might also vary through the year. At Christmas, for instance, most ladies' clothing retailers expand in terms of both breadth and depth for party wear.

The problems caused by the choice of breadth or depth can also be reduced by careful choice of retailing format. A traditional department store has to restrict itself because of the pressures of space and display requirements.

eg

A catalogue retail showroom (*see* p. 543), such as Argos, is not expected to display its whole range of stock 'live' and is thus able to provide much greater breadth and depth of range than its department store rivals. It is limited only by its logistical systems and ability to update and replenish its in-store warehouses quickly. Argos has 475 stores. Despite the breadth of range it offers, it was felt that Argos was not capitalising on the increased demand for home-based PCs, so the new line was introduced at most of its stores. Also, as a means of reducing the complexity of the Argos offering for customers, a number of more focused catalogues have been introduced. One of these is Argos Additions, a clothing and home catalogue including brands such as Reebok, Levi's and Gossard. In addition, online shopping and ordering has been introduced that can involve secure payment, home delivery or showroom collection. The main problem for Argos is its image. Its stores look tired and a little down-market; many people buy well-known brands from them, but few admit to it, although its shopping catalogue has massive penetration and sales have consistently grown. Argos has remained true to its strengths, providing convenience, availability and choice at low prices (Jardine, 2001; Kleinman, 2001).

Operating methods

The area of operating methods has seen significant change, with the recent growth of alternatives to the traditional approach. Traditional store retailing, which itself includes a wide number of types of retailer, still predominates. These various types are considered in the next section. Non-store retailing, however, where the customer does not physically travel to visit the retailer, has become increasingly popular. This is partly because of changing customer attitudes, partly because of the drive upmarket made by the mail-order companies in particular, and partly because of technological advances in logistics. The whole area of non-store shopping will be further discussed at p. 543 *et seq.*

Types of retailer

A walk down any High Street or a drive around the outskirts of any large town reveals a wide range of approaches to selling us things. There are retailers of all shapes and sizes, enticing us in with what they hope are clearly differentiated marketing mixes. Taking into account the large number of small independents, there are many thousands of retailers in the UK alone, and yet in the UK, the top three retailers, Tesco, Sainsbury's and ASDA between them hold well over 50 per cent share of retail turnover.

The following discussion groups retailers according to the type of retail operation that they run. Each type will be defined, and the role it plays within the retail sector will be discussed. This should help to clarify why it is important for the health of the retail sector to support the diversity of shapes and sizes of retailer, and why the small corner shop is just as valuable in its way as the top 10 retailers.

Department stores

Department stores usually occupy a prominent prime position within a town centre or a large out of town shopping mall. Most towns have one and some centres, such as London's Oxford Street, support several.

Examples of department stores are:

- UK: Debenham's, House of Fraser, John Lewis
- France: Printemps, Galeries Lafayette
- Germany: Karstadt
- Netherlands: Vendex
- Switzerland: Manor

Department stores are large and are organised into discrete departments consisting of related product lines, such as sports, ladies' fashions, toys, electrical goods, etc.

eg

Royal Vendex KBB is the main non-food retail company in the Netherlands, with a portfolio of department stores and speciality stores. The company operates 27 well known formats across more than 2,500 outlets in seven countries and generates total net sales of €4.6 bn. Its department stores have three formats, Vroom & Dressman, Hema, and Bijenkorf, each acting as separate business units, with different positioning strategies and customer profiles. The stores have own label women's, babies' and children's clothing, personal care products, spectacles, shoes, home and interior decoration products, consumer and household electronics including computers, books, in-store catering services, external restaurants, bakery, internet shopping services, and photo service. Although the combined sales of these stores is €990 mn, operating margins are between 4 and 6 per cent, reflecting the competitive markets in which department stores operate (http://www.vendexkbb.com).

To support the concept of providing everything that the customer could possibly want, department stores extend themselves into services as well as physical products, operating hairdressing and beauty parlours, restaurants and travel agencies. In some stores, individual departments are treated as business units in their own right. Taking that concept a little further, it is not surprising that **concessions** or 'stores within a store' have become common. With these, a manufacturer or another retail name purchases space within a department store, paying either a fixed rental per square metre or a percentage commission on turnover, to set up and operate a distinct trading area of its own. Jaeger, a classic fashion manufacturer and retailer, operates a number of its own stores throughout the UK, but also generates over one-third of its turnover from concessions within department stores such as House of Fraser.

There are sound reasons on both sides for the operation of concessions.

eg

Both Manchester Utd and High Street pharmacy and beauty store Boots have used concessions to spread their distribution coverage, but have chosen a multiple retailer and a supermarket chain respectively. Six trial Boots stores were opened as mini-stores within branches of Sainsbury's supermarkets and if successful, the idea will be rolled out to all Sainsbury's large, out-of-town stores. Each mini-store will stock double the number of health and beauty products that a typical Sainsbury's store carries, and thus while Boots gains access to supermarket shoppers in new locations, Sainsbury's gets to offer a wider range of products within its own premises. Similarly, Manchester Utd, following a successful pilot scheme with sports retailer Allsports, is planning to have 22 Allsports outlets selling Manchester Utd merchandise as part of a concession arrangement, in addition to a similar trial at 20 Woolworth's stores. Again Manchester Utd is gaining fast, low risk access to prime sites and the retailers can offer an additional reason why shoppers should visit the stores. This is part of a drive to make Manchester Utd the first £1 bn soccer brand, and already, it earns more than four times the merchandising revenue of any other UK club (Crace, 2001; *The Grocer*, 2001e; Snoddy, 2000).

The department store perspective. A concession brings a bit of extra variety and life to a store, and may bring in customers who would not otherwise have patronised that department store. A concession might also trade in a product that the department store owners themselves would not want to take a risk on. Given the uncertainties facing the retail sector, concessions take up what might otherwise be excess floor capacity, and provide a steady income per square metre. Overall, because concessions are clearly distinct from the rest of the store, they are a good way of extending the variety and scope of the store without necessarily compromising its core image.

The manufacturer's perspective. There are two broad reasons that a manufacturer might wish to operate a concession within a department store. The first is a general desire to reduce the influence of the intermediaries and thus have a High Street presence, but without going through the lengthy and expensive rigmarole of setting up a retail operation from scratch. One deal, head office to head office, gives the manufacturer a stake in a number of prime sites across the country, as well as giving them access to the department store's facilities and support systems if required. More specifically, the second reason for taking out a concession is that a manufacturer might wish to have tighter control over the way in which its product is displayed and sold. There is always a risk that if your product is only one of many hundreds that a department store sells, it will not get the handling, display or personal selling attention that you think it deserves.

Another retail name's perspective. Why should a department store allow another established High Street retailer to have space on its premises? Often, it is because they are both owned by the same parent company. In general terms, there are several possible reasons for this kind of cohabitation:

1 *Encouraging cross-selling*: customers who go into the department store specifically to visit the concession might get drawn into browsing in the wider store (and vice versa).
2 *Lack of suitable sites*: in a particular town, there may not be a suitable property available for opening a new branch. Taking a concession at least establishes a presence in that town until something more appropriate can be found. It also reduces the risk of rushing into a less than desirable property for the sake of it.
3 *Shortage of space*: even if the retailer does have a branch in the town, the shop might not be big enough to display the full range of merchandise. If the original branch cannot be extended, then a concession in the department store in the same town gives some expansion of trading space, although it is a far from optimal solution.
4 *Corporate rationalisation*: High Street shops are expensive to operate and maintain. A corporate decision might be made, therefore, to cut back on the number of 'free-standing' branches by closing some down and relocating them in local department stores as concessions. Similarly, if the department store is having a rough time, putting concessions into it might increase its turnover and performance as well as mopping up excess capacity.

The department store is not without problems. In the UK, it is under threat from out-of-town shopping and the general growth of specialist retailers. There are also difficulties with the high cost of city centre location and operation. The department stores' answer to these threats has been a concerted effort to improve their purchasing policies, to update their image and provide a higher-quality ambience through refurbishment of existing stores, and to locate new stores in out-of-town retail parks. John Lewis, for example, at the Bluewater shopping centre (see Marketing in Action on p. 549), boasts half-a-million product lines, 2,500 different types of furnishing fabric, 75 different ranges of carpet, 80 models of televisions, and for the connoisseur, over 150 types of lightbulb.

Variety stores

Variety stores are smaller than department stores, and they stock a more limited number of ranges in greater depth. Stores such as BHS and Marks & Spencer in the UK, and Monoprix in France provide a great deal of choice within that limited definition, covering ladies' wear, menswear, children's clothing, sportswear, lingerie, etc. Most, however, carry additional ranges. BhS, for example, offers housewares and lighting while Marks & Spencer offers shoes, greeting cards, plants, and extensive and successful food halls within its stores.

Like department stores, the major variety stores such as Monoprix in France and Kaufhalle in Germany operate as national chains, maintaining a consistent image across the country and some also operate internationally. Whatever the geographical coverage of the variety store chain, given the size of the stores, they need volume traffic (i.e. lots of customers) and thus to develop a mass-market appeal, offering quality merchandise at no more than mid-range price points. Variety stores tend to offer limited additional services, with a tendency towards self-service, and centralised cashier points. In that sense, they are something between a department store and a supermarket.

Supermarkets

Over the last few years, the **supermarket** has been accused of being the main culprit in changing the face of the High Street. The first generation of supermarkets, some 30 years ago, were relatively small, town centre operations. As they expanded and cut their costs through self-service, bulk buying and heavy merchandising, they began to replace the small, traditional independent grocer. They expanded on to out-of-town sites, with easy free parking, and took the customers with them, thus (allegedly) threatening the health of the High Street.

The wheel then turned full circle. As planning regulations in the UK tightened, making it more difficult to develop new out-of-town superstores, retailers began looking at town centre sites again. They developed new formats, such as Tesco Metro and Sainsbury's Local, for small stores carrying ready meals, basic staple grocery goods such as bread and milk, and lunchtime snacks aimed at shoppers and office workers.

eg

Generally, supermarkets are large, self-service stores, carrying a comprehensive range of fmcg products, sometimes including in-store bakeries, delicatessens and fishmongers. A typical supermarket is clearly zoned by product group, but always has central checkout facilities. Branches often also stock some convenience items, such as pharmaceuticals, newspapers, hardware, etc. The larger branches of retailers such as Auchan, Carrefour or Tesco may carry clothes, small DIY items, electrical goods, etc. Others, such as Sainsbury's, have developed parallel chains (Sainsbury's Homebase) to deal specifically with the less frequently purchased hardware, DIY and gardening goods. Similarly, Auchan has diversified into DIY (Leroy Merlin), sport (Decathlon), electrical goods (Boulanger) and many other areas.

The dominance of supermarkets is hardly surprising, because their size and operating structures mean that their labour costs can be 10–20 per cent lower than those of independent grocers, and their buying advantage 15 per cent better. This means that they can offer a significant price advantage. Additionally, they have made efficiency gains and increased their cost effectiveness through their commitment to developing and implementing new technology in the areas of EPOS, shelf allocation models, forecasting and physical distribution management systems. The effective management of retail logistics has, therefore, become a major source of sustainable competitive advantage (Paché, 1998). Most supermarkets, however, work on high turnover and low operating margins. Table 13.2 shows the operating margins of the leading European grocery retailers. Interestingly, the UK supermarkets lead the pack, reflecting greater purchasing power, a less price-sensitive and more service- and quality-sensitive market, and a market that is less influenced by the heavy discounters than in mainland Europe.

Table 13.2 The operating profit margins of leading European grocery retailers, 2001–02

Company	*Home market*	*Operating margin %*
Tesco	UK	5.8
Morrisons	UK	5.4
Safeway	UK	5.0
Ahold	Netherlands	4.3
Delhaize Le Lion	Belgium	4.1
Carrefour	France	3.7
J Sainsbury	UK	3.4
Casino	France	3.3
Metro	Germany	2.2
Somerfield	UK	–0.1

Source: HSBC Securities, as quoted in the IGD's *Grocery Retailing Financial Analysis* report accessed via http://www.igd.org.uk.

marketing *in action*

When the heavy discounters hit town

Discount grocery retailers are characterised by limited product ranges that generally do not include brand leaders, low-cost 'no-frills' stores and low-priced goods. As they rely on selling high volumes of products to generate profit, they have expanded across Europe in search of greater volumes and economies of scale. Netto started in Denmark, and Aldi and Lidl both originated in Germany, which has a strong discount retail culture, unlike the UK and other parts of Europe. In Germany the discounters have a 25 per cent market share, while in the UK it is only 2.5 per cent. Each of them is a powerful force in its home market and the discount retail formula has been transferred successfully to many other European countries, including Poland. The stores tend to be between 500 and 1,000 m^2 and are mainly situated in highly populated residential areas. Continental shoppers still tend to value buying from independent butchers, grocers and fishmongers to supplement discount grocery purchases, whereas in the UK, as in the USA, consumers prefer a one-stop shop with everything under the one roof (Howard, 2000). Hogarth-Scott and Parkinson (1994) researched the effect of a discounter opening a store close to an established supermarket in the UK. They found that although 57 per cent of shoppers had tried the discounter once, only 4 per cent of customers had been lost to the discounter, representing 4.7 per cent of turnover.

Little has changed since that research was done. Although Aldi, Lidl and Netto now have 611 stores, up from 566 in 2000, they still account for just 2 per cent of the UK grocery market even after a ten-year presence. In its *Grocery Retailing 2001* Report, the IGD has suggested that the three chains faced similar problems: the competitive strength of the large multiples and difficulty in finding suitable sites. Even though the sales space has been increasing, it has not had the effect of attracting market share away from the multiples.

So why are the discounters having such a tough time in the UK, compared with the rest of northern Europe? Aldi, Lidl and Netto have all found the UK market difficult because the mainstream UK grocery multiples, such as Tesco, ASDA, Sainsbury's and Safeway, have defended their market share vigorously. The UK shopper has been 'trained' not to be price sensitive and to value the service, the ambience, the choice of 30,000 product lines and quality own-label products offered by the multiples (Table 13.3 compares the two types of retailer). While the multiples attract shoppers mainly from the ABC1 social groups who spend over £20 on average per visit, the discounters

Table 13.3 A comparison between discount and mainstream grocery retailers

Discounters	*Multiples*
Emphasis on low prices	High, medium and low-priced products offered
Small number of product lines (c. 1000)	High number of product lines (20,000–30,000)
Focus on fast moving, high-volume products	Focus on providing choice and complete ranges
Unknown brands stocked	Premium brands stocked
Products on sale change as stock is sometimes bought opportunistically on price	Consistent offering from week to week
Price-orientated own-label goods	Both price-orientated and quality-orientated own-label ranges
Mainly operating from small, edge-of-town sites	Emphasis on out-of-town superstores/hypermarkets
Minimal services	Extra services developed and emphasised as differentiating features
Minimum staffing	More cashiers, service desk staff, shelf fillers, customers' bag packers
Minimal, low-maintenance, 'no-frills' layout and display	Layout and displays used to entice shoppers, enhance goods and contribute to image and atmosphere
Customer loyalty based on price competitiveness	Customer loyalty based on convenience, service, range, own-brand preference, etc.

attract over 70 per cent of their clientele from the C2DE groups and they spend just over £12 per visit. Analysts have predicted that the discounters will start to move more upmarket to try to capture more affluent shoppers and to improve margins. Most of the discounters' stores in the UK, for instance, are relatively small and located on edge-of-town sites to attract non-car-borne shoppers. Acquiring premises on out-of-town sites and retail parks is not easy and the larger multiples tend to get first choice if they are prepared to cooperate on the broader site development issues such as access, car parking, etc. Lidl, for example, is broadening its site selection criteria in the face of difficulties in finding new sites for its expansion programme and the problems of gaining planning consent at the local level. Out-of-town sites attract the affluent shoppers and the parking provision means that they can buy more per trip without worrying about how they are going to carry it all home.

Sources: *The Grocer* (2002b; 2001c); Hogarth-Scott and Parkinson (1994); Howard (2000); IGD (2001); Robinson (1999).

Hypermarkets

The hypermarket is a natural extension of the supermarket. While the average supermarket covers up to 2,500 m^2, a superstore is between 2,500 and 5,000 m^2 and a hypermarket is anything over 5,000 m^2 (URPI, 1988). It provides even more choice and depth of range, but usually centres mainly around groceries. Examples of hypermarket operators are Intermarché and Carrefour in France, Tengelmann in Germany and ASDA in the UK. Because of their size, hypermarkets tend to occupy new sites on **out-of-town** retail parks. They need easy access and a large amount of space for parking, not only because of the volume of customers they have to attract, but also because their size means that customers will buy a great deal and will therefore need to be able to bring the car close to the store.

The hypermarket format is particularly strong in France, the UK, Portugal and Spain. In Ireland, however, hypermarkets are not so strong and only account for 11 per cent of grocery turnover. Obtaining planning permission is becoming increasingly difficult for new hypermarket locations anywhere in Europe, however. Nevertheless, a small number of developments are still taking place as part of new out-of-town shopping centres, with the hypermarket, such as Auchan playing a central role. The new 'hypermarket for better living' in Val d'Europe, Marne-la-Vallée (Paris region, France), is a further example of continued

eg

Auchan plans to be one of the top three retailers in the world through growth and acquisition. It operates both supermarkets and hypermarkets and aims to open 50 hypermarkets annually up to 2004 and to double supermarket sales within 5 to 7 years. It currently has 261 hypermarkets in 14 countries and 566 supermarkets in France (Atac), Spain (Sabeco), Italy (SMA, Colmark), and Poland (Billa). The main characteristics of hypermarkets compared with supermarkets from Auchan's perspective are shown in Table 13.4.

Table 13.4 A comparison of the characteristics of hypermarkets and supermarkets in the Auchan chain

	Hypermarket	*Supermarket*
Sales area	3,000 to 18,000 m^2	4,000 to 8,000 m^2
Staff	200 to 900	40 to 200
Customers per day	5,000 to 30,000	1,000 to 5,000
Number of product lines	30,000 to 100,000	7,000 to 10,000
Number of checkouts	20 to 90	5 to 20
Petrol station	Auchan managed	Varies
Parking	1,000 to 5,000 cars	50 to 400 cars
Foodstuffs	up to 80 per cent of sales	up to 90 per cent of sales

Auchan offers both own-brand and discounted products from other manufacturers. There are currently more than 5,000 Auchan own-brand products, most clearly marked with an A. Exceptions are made in some sectors such as textiles, sport, car accessories, home decoration, wines and spirits, and children's goods. Individual brand names are used for these such as *In Extenso* for textiles, *Cup's* for sport and *Genium* for car accessories, together with the Auchan logo.

Despite the spread and range of outlets, there is some variability according to the economic and physical environment, the climate, consumer habits, competition and the population mix faced by individual locations. The core value remains, however: offering an extensive range of low priced products in one retail format that offers convenience and speed (http://www.auchan.com).

development. The extended range of services include a beauty salon, a nursery, computers for use by customers, the possibility of watching DVD trailers and listening to the CDs on offer, and an optician. The Irish planning authorities have looked at the effects of hypermarket and superstore developments in other EU countries and concluded that they damage town centres, leading to the closure of small shops, and cause traffic congestion. As a result of this, the Irish government decided to introduce new planning guidelines designed to prevent further development of superstores and hypermarkets. The new guidelines mean that supermarket developments within the Dublin area will be limited to no more than 3,500 m^2 and, outside Dublin, no more than 3,000 m^2 (*The Grocer*, 1999a).

The impact on the environment and town planning is, therefore, a far more important consideration than in the past in granting planning permission. Arrangements for the recycling of packaging, store architecture which blends in with surroundings, access arrangements, and the impact on retail diversity are now to the fore. The situation across Europe is little different from in the UK and Ireland. Spanish law favours small local stores with a surface area of below 300m^2, and in Poland before planning permission is granted, the impact of the hypermarket on the employment structure in an area has to be specified (Auchan, 2001). In France, the birthplace of European hypermarkets, planning regulations have become more stringent in recent years for any developments over 1,000m^2. This has slowed down the domestic expansion of hypermarkets and encouraged the likes of Auchan and Carrefour to expand internationally.

Out-of-town speciality stores

An out-of-town **speciality store** tends to specialise in one broad product group, for example furniture, carpets, DIY or electrical. It tends to operate on an out-of-town site, which is cheaper than a town-centre site and also offers good parking and general accessibility. It concentrates on discounted prices and promotional lines, thus emphasising price and value for money. A product sold in an out-of-town speciality store is likely to be cheaper than the same item sold through a town centre speciality or department store.

The store itself can be single storey, with no windows. Some care is taken, however, over the attractiveness of the instore displays and the layout. Depending on the kind of product area involved, the store may be self-service, or it may need to provide knowledgeable staff to help customers with choice and ordering processes. Recent years have seen efforts to improve the ambience of such stores and even greater care over their design.

Toys ' Я' Us in particular has become known as a *category killer* because it offers so much choice and such low prices that other retailers cannot compete. Its large out-of-town sites mean that it is efficient in terms of its operating costs, and its global bulk buying means that it can source extremely cheaply. Shoppers wanting to buy a particular toy know that Toys ' Я' Us will probably have it in stock, and shoppers who are unsure about what they want have a wonderful browsing opportunity. Additionally, the out-of-town sites are easily accessible and make transporting bulky items much easier. The small, independent toy retailer, in contrast, cannot match buying power, cost control, accessibility or choice and is likely to be driven out of business.

eg

Even category killers are not immune from the need to change, however. Toys 'Я' Us is currently going through a 'turnaround strategy' to strengthen the retailer after a few years of depressing results. There will be more attention paid to branding, sourcing exclusive merchandise, improving customer service, linking the toys format with Kids 'Я' Us, and revamping the stores to attract parents and kids back there (Boyes, 2001; English, 2001; Prior, 2001).

Toys 'Я' Us makes shopping easy for customers with its out-of-town sites with free parking.

Source: Toys 'Я' Us.

Town centre speciality stores

Table 13.5 below highlights some of the UK's leading speciality stores, although some, for example Dixon's, operate from both town centre and out-of-town locations. Like out-of-town speciality stores, town centre speciality stores concentrate on a narrow product group as a means of building a differentiated offering. They are smaller than the out-of-town speciality stores, averaging about 250 m^2. Within this sector, however, there are retailers such as florists, lingerie retailers, bakeries and confectioners that operate in much smaller premises. Well-known names such as H&M (*see* p. 531), Superdrug, Thorntons, Next and HMV all fit into this category.

Table 13.5 UK leading speciality retailers, 2001

Group name	*Store names*	*Turnover (2001) £mn*
Arcadia Group	Burton Dorothy Perkins Evans Miss Selfridge Principles Topman Topshop Wallis	£1,889.8
The Boots Company	Boots The Chemist Boots Opticians Halfords	£5,220.9
Dixon's Group plc	Dixon's Curry's PC World The Link Stores	£4,688.2
Kingfisher	B&Q Comet MVC Castorama* Darty* Wegert*	£12,134.2
Next	Next	£1,588.5
WH Smith Group	WH Smith	£2,735.0

* Not UK-based retail chains

Source: IGD *UK Non Food Retailing Fact Sheet*, accessed via http://www.igd.org.uk.

Other examples of products sold through town centre speciality stores are footwear, toys, books and clothing (although often segmented by sex, age, lifestyle or even size). Most are comparison products, for which the fact of being displayed alongside similar items can be an advantage, as the customer wants to be able to examine and deliberate over a wider choice of alternatives before making a purchase decision. Given their central locations, and the need to build consumer traffic with competitive merchandise, the sector has seen the growth of multiple chains, serving clearly defined target market segments with clearly defined product mixes, such as most of the High Street fashion stores. To reinforce the concept of specialisation and differentiation, some, especially the clothing multiples, have developed their own-label brands.

eg

A visit to Thorntons is strictly about self-indulgence or buying gifts. Its slogan, 'Chocolate Heaven Since 1911' captures the core values of the brand. It now has 500 company-owned or franchised confectionery shops throughout the UK and also sells by catalogue and online. The format is always the same, only the range stocked expands or contracts depending on the size and profile of each shop. It aims to be the finest sweetshop in town. Although the locations do vary from shopping malls to airports and railway stations, the retail formula normally specifies the products to promote by season, the required selling area, the type of window displays, and the serving arrangements (O'Grady, 2001; http://www.thorntons.co.uk).

Town centre speciality stores are usually a mixture of browsing and self-service, but with personnel available to help if required. The creation of a retail atmosphere or ambience appropriate to the target market is very important, including for instance the use of window display and store layout. This allows the town centre speciality store to feed off consumer traffic generated by larger stores, since passing shoppers are attracted in on impulse by what they see in the window or through the door. The multiples can use uniform formulae to replicate success over a wide area, but because of their buying power and expertise, they have taken a great deal of business away from small independents.

Convenience stores

Despite the decline of the small, independent grocer in the UK, there is still a niche that can be filled by **convenience stores**. Operating mainly in the groceries, drink and CTN sectors, they open long hours, not just 9 a.m. until 6 p.m. The typical CTN is still the small, independent corner shop that serves a local community with basic groceries, newspapers, confectionery and cigarettes, but the range has expanded to include books, stationery, video hire, and greetings cards.

They fill a gap left by the supermarkets, which are fine for the weekly or monthly shopping trip, if the consumer can be bothered to drive out to one. The convenience stores, however, satisfy needs that arise in the meantime. If the consumer has run out of something, forgotten to get something at the supermarket, wants freshness, or finds six unexpected guests on the doorstep who want feeding, the local convenience store is invaluable. If the emergency happens outside normal shopping times, then the advantages of a local, late-night shop become obvious. Such benefits, however, do tend to come at a price premium. To try to become more price competitive, some 'open-all-hours' convenience stores operate as voluntary chains, such as Spar, Londis, Today's and Mace, in which the retailers retain their independence but benefit from bulk purchasing and centralised marketing activities. The priority for many CTNs is to keep trying new services and lines that might sell in the local community. A large number now have off-licences, fax facilities, and the provision of other outsourced services, including dry cleaning and shoe repairs. The National Lottery ticket terminals have provided a boost to income, while even sales of travel cards and phone cards have generated new streams of revenue.

Two more recent developments in convenience retailing are forecourt shops at petrol stations and computerised kiosks. Many petrol retailers, such as Jet and Shell, have developed their non-petrol retailing areas into attractive mini-supermarkets that pull in custom in their own right. In some cases, they are even attracting customers who go in to buy milk or bread and end up purchasing petrol as an afterthought. The total market in 1999 was estimated at around £25 bn, an increase of 25 per cent since 1995, showing just how fast convenience store retailing on the forecourt has grown and what an important revenue earner it has become. The next stage of development could be more cash dispensers installed at forecourt sites, and eventually internet access. Forecourts could also become pick-up locations for home shopping orders. Offering a diversified portfolio of services can be a critical factor in the survival of some rural petrol stations and fuel sales are expected to drop below 20 per cent of sales, on average, over the next few years.

Meanwhile, computerised kiosks might be able to augment the services that a convenience store can provide. Such kiosks, networked, can provide opportunities to purchase a wide range of merchandise not normally carried in the store, such as novelty cakes, or allow tickets to be purchased, flowers to be ordered, barbecues and hardware to be bought, paid for and either home-delivered or delivered to the shop. Moneybox is currently piloting the Smart Shopper kiosk and if successful, it could be rolled out by convenience chains such as Spar (Bedington, 2001a).

Discount clubs

Discount clubs are rather like cash and carries for the general public, where they can buy in bulk at extremely competitive prices. Discount clubs do, however, have membership requirements, related to occupation and income.

eg

Costco is a form of discount club for both traders and individual members. Operating from 13 UK warehouses and 360 more across seven countries, the principle is to stock a wide range of merchandise for small business owners. Products are packaged, displayed, and sold in bulk quantities in a no-frills, warehouse atmosphere on the original shipping pallets. The warehouses are self-service and the member's purchases are packed into empty product boxes. By stripping out the service and merchandising, the prices can be kept low. Individual members must meet certain qualifying criteria based on current or former occupation such as working in education or local government (*The Grocer*, 2001b; http://www.costco.co.uk).

The discount clubs achieve their low prices and competitive edge through minimal service and the negotiation of keen bulk deals with the major manufacturers, beyond anything offered to the established supermarkets. Added to this, they pare their margins to the bone, relying on volume turnover, and they purchase speculatively. For instance, they may purchase a one-off consignment of a manufacturer's surplus stock at a very low price, or they may buy stock cheaply from a bankrupt company. While this allows them to offer incredible bargains, they cannot guarantee consistency of supply, thus they may have a heap of televisions one week but once these have been sold, that is it, there are no more. The following week the same space in the store may be occupied by hi-fis. At least such a policy keeps customers coming back to see what new bargains there are.

The main problem for consumers is that unless they have large families, or a very spacious garage for storage, the minimum purchase quantities for any single item are intimidating. One solution is to form an informal cooperative with a number of like-minded friends and, acting as a mini-wholesaler, break bulk and resell to them. Most consumers, however, would probably not be interested in the management and administration involved, and would prefer to pay the slightly higher prices for the convenience of the local supermarket.

Markets

Most towns have markets, as a last link with an ancient form of retailing. There are now different types of market, not only those selling different kinds of products but street markets, held on certain days only; permanent markets occupying dedicated sites under cover or in the open; and Sunday markets for more specialised products.

Typical market products include fresh food, clothing and housewares. Some goods are downmarket, but others are simply unusual, for example a craftsman or craftswoman selling items that they have made themselves.

eg

The value of the market stall as a first step on the retailing ladder is well understood. The management of the Gateshead Metro Centre, for example, not only rents out permanent retail space, but also hires out a number of mobile barrows, situated throughout the shopping centre, at relatively low rents. This gives a more lively, market type of character to the public areas, but, more importantly, gives an opening for small traders, or individuals with little cash but a lot of entrepreneurial flair, to test a retail concept and to begin developing a business. Many barrow retailers then build up sufficient confidence and resources to take on a permanent shop unit.

Catalogue showrooms

A fairly recent development, **catalogue showrooms** try to combine the benefits of a High Street presence with the best in logistics technology and physical distribution management. The central focus of the showroom is the catalogue, and many copies are displayed around the store as well as being available for the customer to take home for browsing. Some items are on live display, but this is by no means the whole product range. The consumer selects from the catalogue, then goes to a checkout where an assistant inputs the order into the central computer. If the item is immediately available, the cashier takes payment. The consumer then joins a queue at a collection point, while the purchased product is brought round from the warehouse behind the scenes, usually very quickly.

A prime example of this type of operation is Argos, which carries a very wide range of household, electrical and leisure goods. It offers relatively competitive prices through bulk purchasing, and savings on operating costs, damage and pilfering (because of the limited displays).

Non-store retailing

A growing amount of selling to individual consumers is now taking place outside the traditional retailing structures. Non-store selling may involve personal selling (to be dealt with in Chapter 17), selling to the consumer at home through television, internet or telephone links or, most impersonally, selling through vending machines. Some of these areas clearly have strong roots in direct marketing, which is the subject of Chapter 18, but they will be briefly introduced here.

In-home selling

The longest-established means of selling to the consumer at home is through door-to-door selling, where the representative calls at the house either trying to sell from a suitcase (brushes, for example), or trying to do some preliminary selling to pave the way for a more concerted effort later (with higher-cost items such as double glazing, burglar alarms and other home improvements). Cold calling (i.e. turning up unexpectedly and unannounced) is not a particularly efficient use of the representative's time, nor is it likely to evoke a positive response from the customer. Organisations are more likely now to qualify leads in advance, thus sending representives out to people who have already expressed an interest, for example by returning a 'more information please' coupon from an advertisement, or using the cheaper method of telephone selling to arrange an initial interview.

A more acceptable method of in-home selling that has really taken off is the party plan. Here, the organisation recruits ordinary consumers to act as agents and do the selling for them in a relaxed, sociable atmosphere. The agent, or a willing friend, will host a party at a house and provide light refreshments. Guests are invited to attend and during the course of the evening, when everyone is relaxed, the agent will demonstrate the goods and take orders.

Since the pioneering days of the Tupperware party, many other products have used the same sort of technique. Ann Summers, for instance, is an organisation that sells erotic lingerie and sex aids and toys through parties. The majority of the customers are women who would otherwise never dream of going into 'that kind of shop', let alone buying 'that kind of merchandise'. A party is an ideal way of selling those products to that particular target market, because the atmosphere is relaxed, the customer is among friends, and purchases can be made without embarrassment amidst lots of giggling. One of the best features of party selling is the ability to show and demonstrate the product. This kind of hands-on, interactive approach is a powerful way of involving the potential customer and thus getting them interested and in a mood to buy.

The main problem with party selling, however, is that it can be difficult to recruit agents, and their quality and selling abilities will be variable. Supporting and motivating a pyramid of agents and paying their commission can make selling costs very high.

e-marketing *in action*

Whither the online mall?

A virtual or electronic mall is a website which brings together different electronic retailers at a single virtual (online) location. This contrasts with a fixed location infrastructure – the traditional arrangement where retail organisations operate from retail stores situated in fixed locations such as real-world shopping malls. However, potential customers could view the product assortment of retailers located anywhere in the world from their workstations and laptops without the need to travel and so the advantages for the consumer of retailers in one destination were lost. Another facility to emerge was Speciality Malls, which were designed to facilitate comparison shopping as all participating retailers had a similar product range. This approach was less than successful as the individual retailers were not able to derive any competitive advantage and as a result many electronic malls ceased to exist. Retailers, however, continued to develop their own web presence through the 1990s in the form of *destination* websites in a similar way to the development of a fixed location destination store. We will now examine the online fortunes of one virtual mall – BarclaySquare as described by Chaffey *et al*. (2003).

In 1995 Barclays Merchant Services began to promote BarclaySquare as '. . . the UK's most exciting shopping centre development' (Barclays Merchant Services promotional literature, 1995). The new retail development would have: a potential customer base of 35 million people with an expected growth rate of 10 per cent per month, unlimited *virtual* development space for expansion, opportunities for participating retailers to make substantial savings on fixed costs compared with a fixed location operation in the real world and a target audience of cash rich, time poor intelligent adults. The service provided the convenience of all-year-round shopping for consumers from their office or the comfort of home.

BarclaySquare eventually offered a good mix of core tenants including: Argos, Blackwells and Victoria Wine and with the support of Barclays Merchant Services should have given the customers confidence to use the innovative service. This was an excellent example of visionary management commitment to online retailing but was it ahead of its time?

Source: Chaffey *et al*. (2003).

Mail order and teleshopping

Both mail order and teleshopping will be explored further in Chapter 18. This section, therefore, gives a brief introduction in order to acknowledge their place as alternative forms of selling or retailing to consumers. **Mail order** has a long history and traditionally consists of a printed catalogue from which customers select goods that are then delivered to the home, either through the postal service or via couriers. This form of selling has, however, developed and diversified over the years. Offers are now made through magazine or newspaper advertisements, as well as through the traditional catalogue, and database marketing now means that specially tailored offers can be made to individual customers. Orders no longer have to be mailed in by the customer, but can be telephoned, with payment being made immediately by credit card. The strength of mail order varies across Europe, but is generally stronger in northern Europe than in the south. It is strong in Germany through companies such as Otto Versand, Quelle and Nekermann.

Teleshopping represents a much wider range of activities. It includes shopping by telephone in response to television advertisements, whether on cable, satellite or terrestrial channels. Some cable and satellite operators run home-shopping channels, such as QVC, where the primary objective is to sell goods to viewers. Teleshopping also covers interactive shopping by computer, using mechanisms such as the French Minitel system or the internet. The internet in particular offers interesting opportunities to a variety of sellers, including established retailers. Many, such as Toys 'Я' Us and Blackwell's Bookshop, have set up 'virtual' stores on internet sites, so that a potential customer can browse through the merchandise, select items, pay by credit card and then wait for the goods to be delivered.

Through the development of video catalogues and 'specialogues', and through further exploitation of other direct marketing techniques such as telephone ordering and selling via the internet, mail order and related forms of non-store retailing could have an interesting future, complementing High Street retailing in the eyes of the shopper. There will be a further discussion of internet shopping in Chapter 24.

Vending

Vending machines account for a very small percentage of retail sales, less than 1 per cent. They are mainly based in workplaces and public locations, for example offices, factories, staffrooms, bus and rail stations, etc. They are best used for small, standard, low-priced, repeat purchase products, such as hot and cold drinks, cans of drink, chocolate and snacks, bank cash dispensers and postage stamps. They have the advantage of allowing customers to purchase at highly convenient locations, at any time of the day or night. Vending machines can also help to deliver the product in prime condition for consumption, for example the refrigerated machines that deliver a can of ice-cold Coke. A human retailer cannot always maintain those conditions.

In the workplace, vending machines can be a valuable complement to normal catering services. If the machine is situated near to the shopfloor or working area, then employees do not have to waste time trekking across to a remote part of the site to get a drink, for instance. Similarly, the vending machine can help to save time and reduce queues in the canteen by dealing with employees' minor purchases, leaving the canteen staff to handle larger purchases.

Although vending machines take up little space and do not require staff in constant attendance, they do need regular and frequent servicing, whether to replenish stocks or empty the cash box or simply for preventive maintenance to ensure that the service is sustained. Overall, the UK market is very buoyant and is valued at £3.1 bn. With the pressure on increased convenience and 24-hour access to products, the use of vending machines is expected to grow over the next few years, both in terms of what can be vended and the locations such as schools, hospitals, transport facilities and sports and leisure facilities (Keynote, 2000).

eg

Consumers are used to vending machines selling snacks, drinks, stamps and parking tickets, but could they get used to buying books in this way? One company, Travelman, has developed the idea of producing short stories on single sheets of paper folded like maps, which would take about 40 minutes to read. This would make them ideal for commuters or travellers. Although it also sells online, offering choices ranging from mysteries to classic titles, the ability to vend opened up a significant new distribution channel to reach the impulse rather than planned purchase market. In 2001, the first of a planned chain of green and white vending machines for short stories was introduced at South Kensington tube station. Selling at £1 each, it is claimed that the titles are an easy read on a cramped tube train. The owner of the business is clear about the profile of the typical buyer, as he claimed on BBC Radio 5 that 90 per cent of us are too stupid to appreciate good literature, and the success of the business, launched in 1998, would lie with the remaining 10 per cent. Perhaps we should all stick to reading the ads or looking out for Mornington Crescent (Sutcliffe, 2001).

Retailer strategy

This section looks more closely at some of the strategic issues and decisions facing retailers, including location, product mix, competitive positioning, store image and atmosphere, merchandising, the use of technology and, finally, strategic alliances. All these areas could be critical to the marketing success of retailers (Davies, 1992).

Location

Location is a very important area for decision, since if the wrong location is chosen for a store (or, worse, a series of wrong locations for a chain of stores), the retailer can lose a great deal of business by failing to reach or attract the right kind of customer to generate a viable level of trade (Anderson, 1993). In addition to lost business, there is also the waste of the money invested in acquiring the site or premises and building and/or shopfitting. A supermarket chain such as Tesco or Sainsbury's can spend more than £20 million per new store, including site-acquisition costs.

Choice of location is linked to social and demographic changes. For example, increasing rates of car ownership and the rising number of working women with too little time to shop for their families have helped the rise of the out-of-town superstore site. But there are other, more general factors that also affect the location decision. Some of these are considered in turn.

Catchment

For a given location, the retailer needs to know the size of the population on which the store can draw and, more specifically, what proportion of that population matches the desired market segment profile. Some estimate also needs to be made of the likely average expenditure per customer to see if the store will generate sufficient turnover, given the likely competitive response to the store's opening. Further work may also be undertaken to assess the market's response to the retailer's presence and promotional activity (Davies and Rogers, 1984; Wrigley, 1988). Catchment is not only about the resident population, but about the location's accessibility and proximity to other attractions, such as railway or bus stations, that will generate passing consumer traffic.

Type of goods

Different locations suit different kinds of goods and shopping needs or habits. Think about the difference between convenience and shopping goods, for instance (defined at pp. 271–3). Convenience goods need to be readily available, geographically close so people can buy almost at whim, whereas shopping goods involve a more deliberate purchasing decision and the consumer is more prepared to travel and invest time and money. Convenience goods, therefore, favour locations with a nearby, dense catchment area or at least a lot of passing, impulse-buying traffic, and shopping goods can be a little more remote, providing that there is the space to present an extensive range of goods for the customer to compare and choose from.

McGoldrick (1990) classifies the factors affecting location decisions as population, accessibility, competition and costs. Figure 13.3 gives examples of some of the factors that might be considered within each category. This figure also outlines the three main stages in an ideal retail location strategy (Bowlby *et al.*, 1984).

Figure 13.3 Factors influencing the location decision-making process

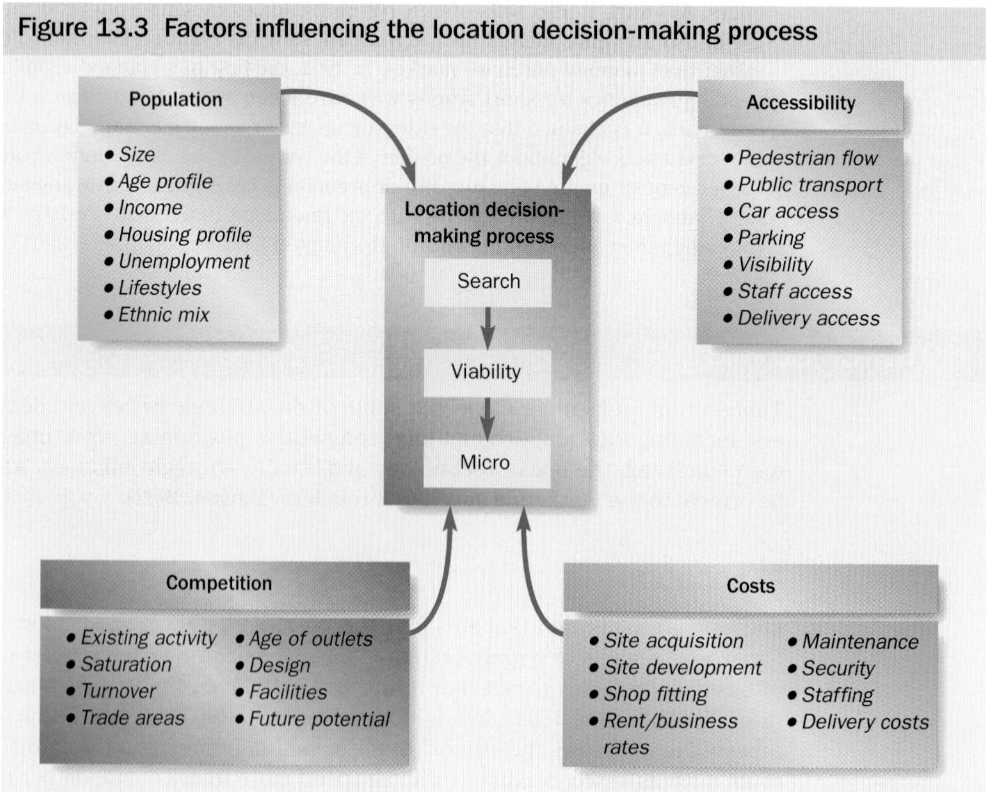

Location decision-making process

The location decision-making process consists of three stages.

Search for good locations. At the broadest level, the retailer has to decide which regions, cities or towns to locate in. *Spatial marketing* helps to profile defined geographic areas by socioeconomic categories. It can also establish retail spend potential, thus linking in to minimum threshold requirements, that is, the lowest forecast spend level that makes further investigation worthwhile.

eg

Many retailers now use GIS (geographic information systems) to assess potential locations. A GIS includes maps and geodemographic data (*see* pp. 185 *et seq.*) from other commercial databases. The retailer can add any data of its own about its stores, customers and competitors. Companies like Vauxhall Motors can then use it to evaluate catchment areas (for instance the neighbourhood profile of customers, the size of the catchment area to see how dealerships are spread, and to plan new outlets). The GIS can thus profile a geographic area to assess a potential new store location by predicting turnover, profitability and even the amount of store traffic that it would take from existing stores. Supermarket chain Safeway spent around £500,000 developing a GIS that includes loyalty-card data, store data, competitor data and the National Shoppers' Survey data as well as the MOSAIC geodemographic package. This helps Safeway to build up profiles of various customer types and their shopping habits, and to assess the proportion of local grocery spend that a new store would attract, taking into account drive times (i.e. how long shoppers are prepared to take travelling to and from supermarkets), its own existing stores and those of its competitors. It also assesses the attractiveness of local stores in terms of the fascia, store format, parking provision, whether there is a petrol station, in-store café or dry cleaner, etc. Once a store is up and running, the GIS can help answer questions such as 'What if the competitor builds a new store nearby?' or 'How much more turnover would we generate if we extended our existing store?' (Bowie and Wilcox, 1999).

Assessment of viability. Narrowing down a little, the retailer focuses on the *viability* of a specific site. At this stage, store turnover forecasting using multiple regression techniques may be implemented. This will take into account determinants of sales levels and it is especially important where location is seen as a particularly critical factor. It focuses on the type of customers, public transport and proximity to competitors, among many other things. Being close to competitors may be a good or a bad thing. Generally, for convenience goods it is not good, but with a shopping product, the closeness may encourage consumers to visit both stores and make comparisons and the 'better' retailer will win.

Assessment of micro factors. At the most detailed level, the retailer fine tunes by looking at the impact of micro factors, such as pedestrian flows, the profile of local shops, the proximity of other key retailers (such as Marks & Spencer, which always generates plenty of passing consumer traffic), nearness of car parks and the ease of parking, and the site's overall appearance. As well as factors that are related to the environment around the site in question, the retailer will consider micro factors relating to the site itself, such as ease of access for loading and unloading, the length and terms of the lease or ownership conditions, and any planning permission needed. The challenge is to establish which micro factors are the most important.

Given the level of investment involved, and the high costs of failure or poor decisions, the larger retail chains use sophisticated, often tailormade, computerised planning models rather than rules of thumb or hunches. At the very least, the smaller retailer can gain access to material such as the CACI database that profiles shopping centres.

Classification of locations

In general terms, available locations can be classified into three broad areas.

City centre. In the centre of a town or city, the focus is on offices, shopping and public transport termini. There are usually designated retailing zones within such centres. Famous shopping areas in Europe include Oxford Street in London, the Kurfurstendamm in Berlin and Grafton Street in Dublin. City centres attract the largest stores, and often feature shopping malls and pedestrian precincts, covered or open. The presence of a number of big-name retailers does generate extra consumer traffic, thus they act as magnets for smaller retailers. Such sites are, however, expensive to occupy and maintain, and are dominated by products such as clothing, footwear, jewellery and financial services.

Suburban. In suburban locations, neighbourhood corner shops or small shopping parades are often found at road intersections or on the edges of large housing estates. They largely serve local needs for convenience goods and, to a lesser extent, shopping goods, through shops of about 200 m^2. Some shopping parades are owned and operated by local authorities which rent the shops to the retailers, others are owned by property companies.

Out-of-town. First developed in the UK in the 1970s, out-of-town sites are located at the edges of towns and cities, often next to major roads or at the intersections of major trunk routes. A site can either be dedicated to one massive superstore, such as a supermarket, or be home to a small range of purpose-built stores (say up to 10). The kinds of products sold on out-of-town sites are typically groceries, furniture, electrical goods and DIY, retailed through well-known supermarkets and discount multiples. The sites are easily accessible and, compared with city centre stores, have lower rents and local authority rates. Most large towns and cities now have them.

The 1980s saw the logical extension of out-of-town sites into retail parks, with much larger numbers of free-standing stores of 2,500 m^2 or more. Under cover, retail parks have developed along the US model into very large complexes indeed. Out-of-town shopping malls, such as the Metro Centre at Gateshead and Meadowhall, just off the M1 near Sheffield, have taken the traditional mix and range of stores out of the city centre, and reproduced it on a much bigger scale on a purpose-built site with easy access. The Metro Centre, for example, on two storeys, provides nearly 150,000 m^2 of retail space, with the additional bonus of 10,000 car parking spaces (which can all be occupied at peak times near Christmas) and a whole range of leisure activities, such as a multiscreen cinema and a bowling alley.

Bluewater is offered to the customer as the modern total leisure experience which also includes retail therapy.

Source: Photo courtesy of Lend Lease, photographer Adrian Brooks.

marketing in action

Bluewater sees shoppers dive in

Bluewater is Europe's largest retail development, with 1.5 million ft^2 of selling space and some 330 stores. It has a strategically chosen location, 40 km from the centre of London, close to the M25 with easy access for major roads and railway links. Costing £350 mn to build, it opened in March 1999. It is more than just a shopping mall, however. Its main target is upmarket, ABC1 consumers who are 'shopping centre averse', and thus they are called guests rather than customers and are being offered an 'experience' rather than a 'shopping trip'. The 'experience' focus is emphasised by the provision of 200,000 ft^2 of leisure and catering as well as 1.5 million ft^2 of retail space. The development has 50 acres of parkland featuring seven lakes (some with boating and fishing), over 50 restaurants, cafés and bars, entertainment areas, a 12-screen cinema and a 200-child crèche. The designers and owners have also tried to build in ways and facilities for making the shopper's visit less stressful. They paid careful attention to the road system and layout, created 13,000 parking spaces that are 25 per cent bigger than normal for ease and convenience, and built welcome lounges at the entrances.

In terms of the retail space, anchor stores were considered important to this development and the developers made particular efforts to persuade John Lewis, Marks & Spencer (M&S) and House of Fraser to open 'power branches', i.e. those with a large amount of investment and innovation. M&S, for example, opened a 146,000 ft^2 store (its largest purpose-built store) with glass elevators and marble floors. A 20,000 ft^2 food hall has 90 employees and 8 ft wide pathways with designer shelving and lighting. The store also has a 140-seater café overlooking the lakes. The retail part of Bluewater is triangular and the anchor stores are situated at the corners of the triangle to encourage shoppers to explore as much of the shopping centre as possible.

In its first year of operation, Bluewater attracted 25 million people (its eventual target is 30 million) who between them spent £660 mn. The average spend was over £121 per shopping trip. In the second year, 26 million people spent £753 mn there. It had been expected that most visitors would come from within a one-hour drive-time radius of Bluewater, and indeed, only 20 per cent of guests were found to have travelled for over an hour to get there. The attention to detail in designing Bluewater as a leisure destination rather than as just another shopping mall clearly paid off. Surveys have shown that nearly 90 per cent of people who visited Bluewater purchased something; 98 per cent of guests said that their visit was highly enjoyable or enjoyable; and almost 90 per cent of guests visiting Bluewater for the first time said they would return. Considering the 'shopping centre averse' nature of the target market, these are remarkably positive results.

Sources: Buxton (1999); Gannaway (1999); http://www.bluewater.co.uk.

Product range

Breadth and depth of product range stocked were mentioned earlier (*see* p. 530) as a means of classifying retailers. Speciality stores and niche retailers, such as Tie Rack, concentrate on a few product lines, stocked in considerable depth. Supermarkets and department stores carry a wide product mix. Migros, for example, a Swiss cooperative group, not only retails food but stocks some 22,000 non-food items. Migros is also into travel, printing, publishing, oil, insurance and many other products and services. It is difficult, however, to keep a broad-ranging product mix and substantial product line depth without investing in large quantities of stock and all the associated costs that go with that.

corporate social responsibility in action

Should bras support dictators?

Marks & Spencer, along with a number of other leading European retailers, has adopted an ethical global sourcing policy. It cannot afford the public outcry and media backlash of being associated with bad labour management practices or with regimes that are corrupt or abuse human rights. M&S acts as a beacon of good practice and its approach to business ethics and social responsibility is embodied within its Global Sourcing Principles. The main dimensions of the policy are clear statements relating to:

- Offering high quality and value to consumers without exploiting the people who work for its suppliers.
- Making regular visits to suppliers to monitor standards on child labour, safety, pay, terms of employment, and working hours as part of an 'ethical audit'. Reference is made to groups representing government, business, trade unions and human rights.

▶

- Insisting on decent working conditions and fair rates of pay.
- Operating a policy of continual improvement with suppliers, enforced by strict sanctions when standards are not met. (Direct suppliers are meant to operate similar checks and controls further down the supply chain.)

Together with each supplier, M&S establishes a set of standards, which includes specifications appropriate to the industries and countries producing the goods. It is the supplier's responsibility to achieve and maintain these standards.

There is a special section within the principles dedicated to workforce rights, an issue of special importance to suppliers in some developing countries:

> *The people working for our suppliers are to be treated with respect, and their health, safety and basic human rights are to be protected and promoted. Each supplier must, as a minimum, fully comply with all relevant local and national laws and regulations, particularly with regard to: working hours and conditions, rates of pay and terms of employment, minimum age of employment. Moreover, whatever the local regulations, workers should normally be at least 15 years old; as a norm, they should be free to join lawful trade unions or worker's associations* (quoted from http//www2.marksandspencer.com).

According to some lobby groups and the media, not all organisations have adopted such a principled approach, and there is a real issue for retailers as to how far they should the question the supply chains beyond the immediate supplier. There may well be satisfaction with the manufacturer's production and workforce practices, but what happens when they in turn are supplied by smaller manufacturers from around the world? That is where Burma comes in. According to lobby groups, there are 400 garment manufacturers in Burma, attracted by the low pay and the military junta's prohibition of unions. Working hours can be up to 60 hours per week and the wages are some of the lowest in the world. A BBC *Newsnight* documentary reported that armed soldiers would appear if there was any protest over working conditions. According to a lobby group, Burma Campaign UK, members of the public could unwittingly be playing a part in the chain of complicity as the garments often end up on the UK High Street. The reason that companies buy from Burma, they claim, is because it provides cheaper clothes that are much in demand in the High Street. It also means, of course, higher profits compared with sourcing from within the EU.

Triumph International is the latest company to come into the firing line. The German multinational is one of Europe's leading suppliers of lingerie. In 1996, Triumph International established a company in Burma called Myanmar Triumph International. It opened a factory there in 1997 which exports almost 100 per cent of its lingerie production to the international market. The factory employs 845 Burmese workers who, according to Triumph, work a 48-hour week for US$1.00 per day. Various accusations are made by the campaigners including:

- Triumph's landlord UMEH is a military controlled institution. Members of its board are all linked to the military regime. Burma's Defence Ministry's Directorate of Procurement (responsible for weapons procurement) is a 40 per cent shareholder and largely directs UMEH operations. The remaining 60 per cent of share capital is reserved for active and retired military officers, army-owned business enterprises and friendship societies including veteran groups.
- Almost 100 per cent of Triumph's Burma production is for export. Therefore, in addition to rental payments to UMEH, the company will also pay a 5 per cent tax to Burma's authorities on all production for export.
- As a member of the European Apparel and Textile Organisation (EURATEX) Triumph subscribes to the Code of Conduct negotiated with the European Trade Union Federation of Textiles, Clothing and Leather (ETUC: TCL), which includes the ILO forced labour convention. The Code also affirms the right for workers to form and join a trade union and to negotiate freely – a right denied to workers in Burma.

Triumph does not accept the claims and one of the directors is reported as saying 'The people in Burma do not pay taxes, this is not possible in that country. So if the government has to construct a road or an airport or something else, how could they do it differently?' Triumph has consistently refused to close down its production site, arguing that a withdrawal would mean the dismissal of 845 employees in a country where 13 million people live below subsistence levels and 40 per cent of children suffer from malnutrition. The campaign according to Triumph is political and is inappropriately directed at a private company.

Ultimately the consumer is at the end of the chain that leads back to Burma. We ask few questions (sometimes) and rely on retailers to act in a socially responsible manner on our behalf. According to the Clean Clothes Campaign, the consumer should take an interest as not all retailers act in as responsible a manner as M&S. That gives you the power to send a message back to the dictatorship in Burma.

Sources: Saner and Nathan (2001); http://www2.marksandspencer.com; http://www.cleanclothes.org.

Product assortment

Most retailers, therefore, will have to compromise, considering product assortment in terms of purpose, status and completeness. *Purpose* means the fit between customer needs and the retailer's revenue requirements. *Status* refers to the relative importance of different products or depths of line. Thus the retailer will define the prime product and then those that are accessories or add-ons to that. The prime product in a petrol station, for example, is obviously petrol, while food and snacks are desirable, but of secondary importance. That last example links into *completeness*, which is the need to meet customer expectations. Thus motorists expect to be able to buy sweets or cigarettes in a petrol station, and feel that they are receiving inferior service if those kinds of goods are not available.

Product type

The type of products stocked is also important. The retailer may wish to fill only a particular quality niche, or may select a range of products covering different quality levels and price points to fulfil the needs of a wider range of customers. Whether to occupy a niche or to develop a wider specialism is an important decision. If the niche is tightly defined with a very deep assortment, then the retailer will have to hold a large quantity of slow moving stock, tying up working capital and storage space. Going for a broader, shallower mix might help things to move a little more quickly. Figure 13.4 summarises various influences on product assortment strategy.

Some retailers do not specialise at all, but take a scrambled merchandising approach, by buying in fast moving items that sell in volume but are not necessarily related. This achieves a number of things:

1 *It assists impulse purchases.* As with discount clubs (mentioned at p. 542), consumers come in to see what there is and buy while it is still available.
2 *It can generate more sales and profit.* A careful selection of seasonal items for Christmas that are outside the normal product mix in a convenience store can lead to extra sales.
3 *It can improve convenience.* The petrol stations, for example, through developing the range of merchandise and services offered in the forecourt shop, have effectively created one-stop shops that can meet most impulse needs of the motorist and those who live close to the garage.
4 *It assists traffic generation.* A wider mix of merchandise attracts a wider mix of customer, certainly for convenience goods.

The retailer does, however, run the risk of losing its distinct image in the mind of the customer. It is also possible to get it wrong, since widening the product mix can project the retailer into unrelated, unknown areas away from its core business, for example a decision to stock CDs in garage forecourt shops, or the newsagent that stocks Christmas trees.

Walters and White (1987) argue that a wide range of issues should be allowed to influence assortment policy. These include careful research, planning and links with corporate strategy. All of this should be focused towards meeting the needs of the target market and is just as important as merchandise style and service.

Figure 13.4 Factors influencing product assortment strategy

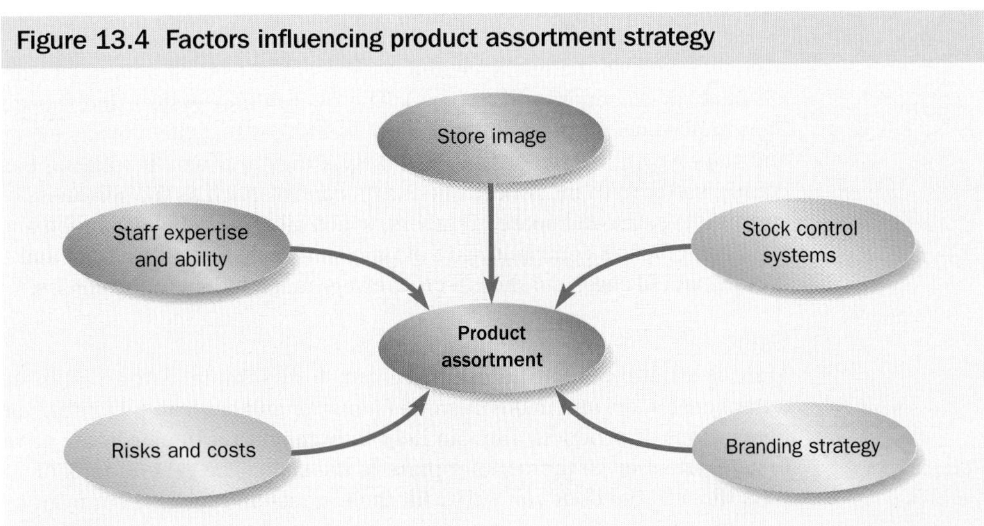

Category management

Product-related decisions, particularly in the grocery sector, are also influenced by category management. According to the Institute of Grocery Distribution (IGD), category management is:

> . . . *the strategic management of product groups through trade partnerships, which aims to maximise sales and profit by satisfying consumer needs*
>
> (http://www.igd.org.uk)

Category management takes the retailer–supplier relationship beyond simple buying and selling into a long-term partnership in which the longer-term strategic health of a whole product group (or category) is developed. Thus the retailer and the supplier share data and information so that they can understand better how consumers define a category and make their buying decisions within it. This can help the retailer to assess how many brands should be offered within the category and to define clearly the role that each one plays in serving customer needs and wants. Suppliers benefit because the streamlining of the number of brands within a category can reduce direct competition and the positioning of the remaining brand(s) can be strengthened as the supplier knows more about why and how it is purchased. Retailers and suppliers can also work together to develop new products to fill gaps in a category, as well as planning pricing and promotional strategies, and point of sale displays (see also the Marketing in Action vignette on pp. 234–5).

Retail competitive positioning

Retailers do not operate in a vacuum and they have to consider how they shape up against their perceived competitors, and how well they differentiate their offering. This clearly means looking at the market, especially at other retailers, in terms of the criteria that distinguish one retailer from another in the customer's mind. This analysis reflects the totality of the offer, in terms of merchandising, brand image, products, pricing, atmosphere and image, and service quality. An independent clothing retailer specialising in designer labels, for example, will position itself as an exclusive, refined, high-priced outlet, with a high level of personal service. In contrast, a High Street multiple targeting the teenage market might position itself as a value for money, lively, vibrant outlet that keeps up with fashion trends. In general, the kind of philosophy applied to product positioning, discussed at pp. 328 *et seq.*, applies equally to retail positioning, although the contributing factors will differ.

Store image and atmosphere

The image and atmosphere of a store are the sum of the physical elements of interior and exterior design, and the layout and displays that create an environment and ambience that consumers find attractive.

Exterior factors that influence perceptions of **store image** include the shop front itself, window displays, the entrance and perhaps even ease of access (traffic congestion in the car park, or closeness to car park). The overall impression that these make is especially important to new customers, who may feel either that the store is exciting and welcoming and thus worth a visit, or that it is dirty, dingy and worth walking past. A store may, of course, suffer from influences outside its control, such as the seediness or cleanliness of the surrounding area and nearby retailers, which all affect a buyer's mood and perception.

Interior factors contributing to **atmosphere** include lighting, wall and floor coverings and fixtures and fittings, and the effects are very much linked to the senses.

Sight

Sight is stimulated by the use of colour, for example. For a restaurant, red and yellow attract customers and make them feel hungrier and eat faster. Lighting too affects mood and perceptions of products and can help to highlight particular items or ranges or draw customers' attention to the remoter parts of the shop. The general look of a store as customers walk through the door can either lift their spirits and make them want to go in and browse, or underwhelm them to the point where they walk straight out again or only focus functionally on a specific item of interest.

Sound

Total silence is all too rare in retail settings. Most have some sort of music playing, even if the customer does not consciously notice it. Whether it is pop, middle of the road, classical or muzak will depend on the retailer's assessment of the preferences of the target market and the image that is to be projected. Soft music may relax shoppers and make them stay in the store longer, while loud music can reinforce a stimulating, vibrant atmosphere that deliberately sets out to excite the customer.

Scent

Smells are very important. Supermarkets make sure that the cooking smells from the instore bakery are filtered back into the store so that customers can enjoy the smell of fresh bread, start feeling hungry and buy more food. Department stores often site the cosmetics counters near the main entrance so that the customer is hit with an exotic blend of upmarket perfume smells. This can be very pleasant, but they need to be careful that the smell isn't so overpowering that it overloads the senses and makes customers feel nauseous! Some smells communicate cleanliness (pine, for example), some communicate luxury (wood or leather, for example), while others are pleasantly stimulating (coffee and bread, for example). All, however, can be used to create and fix a particular impression in the consumer's mind.

Other sensory experiences

As well as the factors already mentioned, the consumer does have other, largely tactile, experiences in the retail setting. The feeling of walking on carpet rather than lino, the look and feel of natural wood fittings and the texture and feel of fabrics around the store, for example, again enhance or detract from the perceived image of the store. Finally, the retailer must bear in mind the comfort of the customer and how that is affected by the temperature of the store. If it is too hot or too cold, the customer will not feel at ease and will leave the premises more quickly.

It is hard to separate any of these factors, since the consumer tends to experience them as an integrated whole. The consumer will, however, certainly notice if one factor is out of keeping with the rest. The atmosphere thus created can be enhanced by the customer's feeling of the 'user friendliness' of the store. The provision of spacious, cool changing rooms with adequate lighting and mirrors for trying on clothes, easy access for disabled people, enough room to move between the displays without feeling cramped or lost, displays that make it easy to see the goods properly and to their best advantage, and fast, efficient packing and payment handling all help to make the customer feel more relaxed, and thus willing to spend more time, and money, in the store.

Other shoppers

A less controllable factor that can have a profound effect on a customer's behaviour is the degree of crowding in a store. Shoppers walking past an upmarket fashion boutique might be tempted to go in but, if there is no other customer inside, may feel self-conscious, not wanting to be the focus of the sales assistants' attention. Similarly, an empty restaurant might put potential customers off, either because they feel self-conscious about going in, or because they think that the emptiness is a reflection of the quality of the food. The only kind of store that might possibly benefit from lack of crowds is a supermarket, because of its more impersonal atmosphere. There is something inherently satisfying about having a branch of Sainsbury's virtually to yourself and experiencing hassle-free shopping! At the other extreme, overcrowding is no more attractive. Customers cannot move freely or examine the merchandise properly and the queues at the checkouts get longer.

It is not only the number of other shoppers that matters. In some situations, the types of other shoppers affect the consumer. Some people would feel very awkward about going into a fashion store if they felt that they were very different from the shoppers already in there.

Similarly, if a shopper was trying to decide whether to buy a particular item of clothing and saw someone old enough to be their grandmother and four sizes bigger choosing the same item, it could make them feel differently about the garment.

As a final thought, remember that store image is not simply a function of the atmosphere factors discussed in this section. It is also affected by additional services offered, merchandise, location, advertising and promotion, brands stocked and pricing. In other words, store atmosphere and store image are simply elements deep inside a detailed marketing mix that must hang together and be linked in with a strategically defined competitive position, as well as meeting the expectations of target customers.

Merchandising strategies

Store image and atmosphere are also affected by the retailer's approach to *layout* and *display*, which can influence both the customer's behaviour within the store and their perception of the retailer's positioning. They affect how people move around the store, which items attract their attention and their propensity to interact with the merchandise. Retailers might, however, be restrained in what they can do with layout and display by the kind of factors shown in Figure 13.5.

Store layout

McGoldrick (1990) suggests that most store layouts conform to one of three broad types, or combine elements of them. The alternative layouts are shown in Figure 13.6.

Grid pattern. The grid pattern is the kind of layout adopted by most supermarkets, with systematically arranged aisles. These tend to lead the shopper around the retail space along a largely predictable route that covers most of the store. Supermarkets try to prevent the shopper from taking short cuts by making sure that staple items, such as sugar, bread, milk, etc., are placed well apart from each other and scattered around the store. Thus the shopper who only wants a few basic things still has to pass lots of tempting items that might just lead to a few extra, impulse purchases. Routine-response staple items are also piled high to reduce the frequency of shelf refilling, and are placed in narrow aisles to keep shoppers moving, since they do not need to browse around these goods. In contrast, wider aisles are used for the more exotic, less frequently purchased premium goods, such as ready meals, so that shoppers can move more slowly, have their attention captured and browse comfortably.

Figure 13.5 Factors influencing layout and display

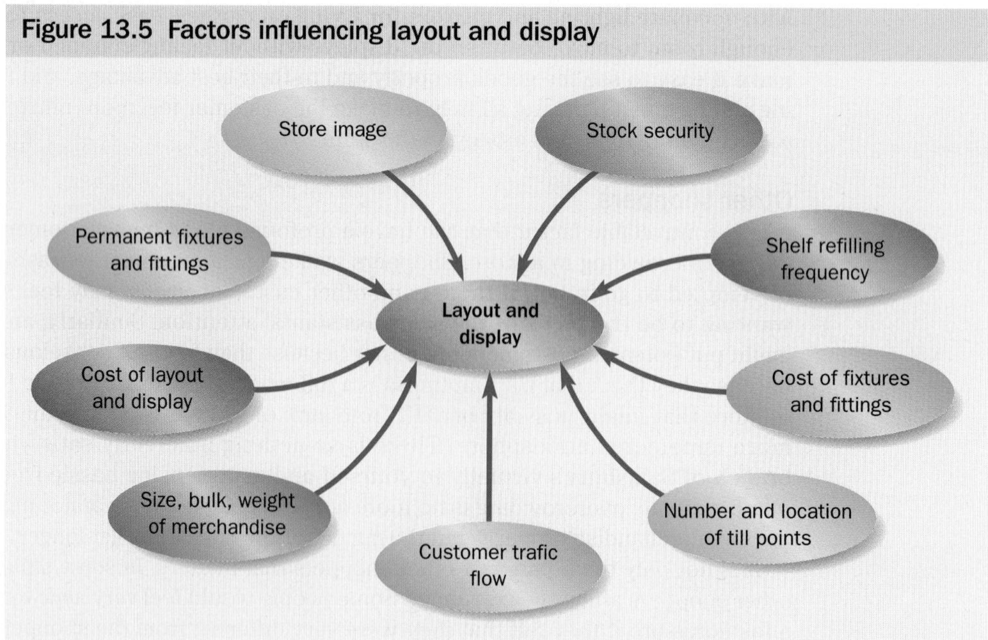

Figure 13.6 Alternative approaches to layout

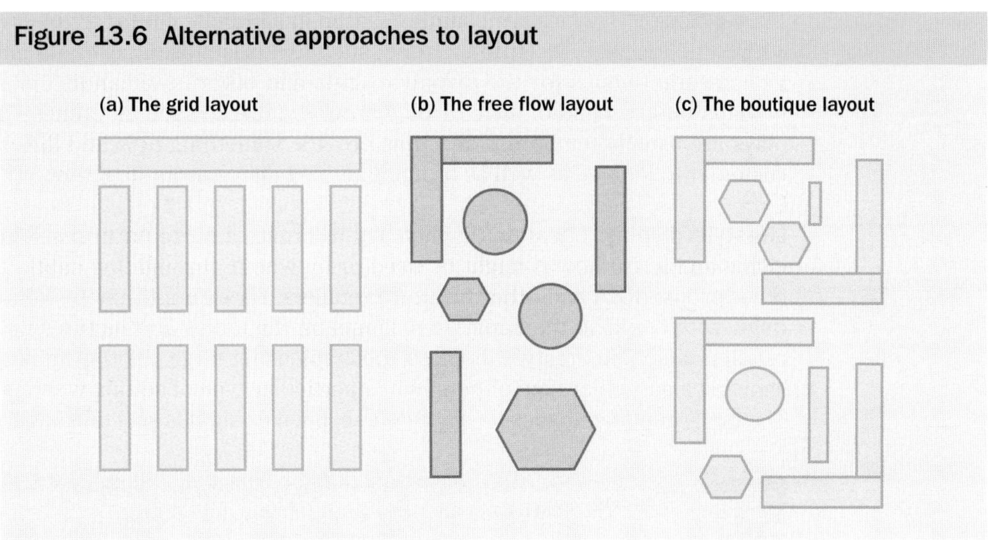

Grid layouts do make sure that the shopper covers as much of the store as possible, and they are easy and cheap to install and maintain. They can, however, be rather boring and regimental, giving the impression of 'functional' shopping. The shopper might also be inclined to associate them with 'pile it high and sell it cheap' discount approaches to retailing, although the fixtures and fittings and the lighting used by some supermarket chains do give a better-quality feel.

Free flow. The free flow pattern is more irregular, involving a variety of different sizes, shapes and heights of fixtures and fittings. Shoppers are free to take any route around the store, and can thus either browse around everything in any order they choose, or cut through directly to one display at the back of the store if they prefer. Fashion retailers and others trying to achieve a strong visual 'look' that stimulates customers but encourages them to take their time browsing use this kind of layout. It can, however, be expensive to set up and maintain, and it does not use the available floor space as efficiently as a grid layout.

Boutique. Whereas in a free flow layout the customer perceives the selling area as essentially a single space, in a boutique layout the perception is of a number of discrete, separate spaces. This might be particularly useful in a large selling space, such as a department store, where very different departments and concessionaires want to create their own unique and more intimate character.

Many stores combine elements of the three types of layout. A superstore might well use a grid layout for its groceries and other fast moving lines, but use a free flow approach for clothing, books or videos, for example. Similarly, a variety store such as Boots will vary its approach. Boots uses a supermarket-style grid layout for fast-moving, staple items such as tights, shampoos, soaps and sticking plasters, but a free flow approach for gift-orientated toiletries, toys and household goods. In some larger stores, the gift department, for example, might even be a boutique layout.

Display

Whatever the type of layout adopted, the retailer also has to think about the way in which merchandise is displayed within it. Rosenbloom (1981) suggests five alternatives.

Open display. Open displays make the merchandise easily accessible to shoppers and encourage them to pick up and examine goods closely. Fashion stores in particular like to encourage such involvement, so that customers can feel the texture and quality of the fabric, can hold a garment up in front of themselves to check its length or whether it suits them, or can be encouraged to try it on.

Theme display. Themes are commonly used in all kinds of retailers to create a focal point to attract a customer's attention. Events such as Christmas, Easter and Mother's Day all provide natural themes for the display of gifts and other merchandise. A supermarket might perhaps build an end-of-aisle display around a theme such as Chinese cookery. These displays are usually temporary and thus provide something new and different for the regular customer to look at, as well as bringing related merchandise together.

Lifestyle display. Lifestyle displays try to create a more natural setting for the product, giving an idea of how it might be used or by whom, through the subtle use of pictures and other props. IKEA and other furniture retailers, for example, show their goods in room settings, with books in the bookcases, lamps on the tables and pictures on the walls. Fashion retailers also use lifestyle displays, perhaps using large photographs at the point of sale showing a particular type of person in a particular type of setting wearing a particular outfit. The mail-order catalogues have, of course, been doing this sort of thing for years.

Ikea shows its products in room settings so that customers can match their lifestyle aspirations to what is on offer.

Source: IKEA Ltd.

Coordinated display. A coordinated display is similar to lifestyle and themed displays in that it brings together related goods. In a coordinated display, goods that are usually sold or used together are displayed together. Thus a women's clothing store might display coordinating jackets, skirts and trousers together, or include accessories in a clothing display. Even supermarkets might use coordination, for example by displaying marzipan, icing sugar, ready made icing, food colourings and edible cake decorations together near the flour, dried fruit and other home baking goods.

Classification dominance display. The aim of a classification dominance display is to suggest specialisation and expertise within a particular product group through the sheer choice of goods displayed. Thus a branch of WH Smith, for instance, might have a display of biros and fountain pens covering a wide range of prices, colours, designs and brands. Displays like this are meant to give the customer the impression that *this* is the only place to shop for these kinds of goods.

Technology

Technological advances have allowed retailers to improve the services that they offer their customers and to increase their productivity for a better competitive edge.

Barcode scanning not only helps to get customers through the checkout more quickly, but also streamlines stock management. Electronic point-of-sale (**EPOS**) systems can monitor exactly what products are being sold and how fast, and can trigger reordering or shelf replenishment through direct links, often to centrally located warehouses.

eg

Electrical retailer Curry's delivers small goods to stores in line with EPOS data. Orders for less frequently purchased, larger goods can be sent from the store to a central depot via computer, and then the goods are delivered direct to the customer. Such systems can cost upwards of £50,000, but are essential for giving the customers what they want and expect. Some supermarkets are currently experimenting with self-scanning systems, whereby the customer scans goods as they are put into the trolley. This means that when the customer gets to the checkout, the bill has already been calculated and thus just needs to be paid. This saves on both time and staffing costs.

More strategically, the information gained through EPOS about spending patterns, by brand and by retailer branch, can be used for negotiation with manufacturers or suppliers, or for planning store promotion.

Technology has also fundamentally changed the way in which consumers pay for their purchases. EFTPOS (electronic funds transfer at point of sale) systems have made the use of debit and credit cards very much easier and more acceptable to the retailer and customer alike. Sweeping a card through a reader and letting the till print out the cheque or voucher is much faster and much less prone to error than the old manual systems. For the retailer, it means shorter checkout queues and also faster cash flow, because the day's financial data are downloaded to the bank's computer overnight, instead of the retailer having to pay cheques and credit card slips into the bank manually and then waiting for them to go through the three-day clearing system.

Retailer own-brands

There is a fine balance of negotiating power between retailers and suppliers. There are some manufacturer brands that the retailers cannot afford to miss out on, and some retail chains that the manufacturer brands cannot afford to be absent from. One tactic that the retailers have used to tip the balance in their favour a little more is the own-label. Over the last few years, certain supermarkets have been proactive in developing good quality, value for money, own-label products across all the main lines they carry. Own-label products represent around 40 per cent of grocery sales on average. For some retailers it is higher, for example 95 per cent of Aldi's products are own-labels while Lidl has 80 per cent, Tesco 40 per cent and Carrefour 33 per cent (Stanley, 2002). Own-label penetration also varies by product sector, with over 80 per cent for some bakery products, down to less than 20 per cent in confectionery. An extensive pan-European survey showed that shoppers from the Netherlands buy most own-label products (55 per cent of purchases), followed closely by the UK (52 per cent), with Italy down at the bottom end of the league with 14 per cent. This is not surprising given that 57 per cent of UK shoppers think that own-labels are as good as the manufacturers' brands, compared with only 32 per cent of Italians. The most important criteria for judging own-labels were freshness, value for money and quality. Although almost 75 per cent of European shoppers think that own-labels represent equal or better value than manufacturer brands, 34 per cent of UK shoppers feel that increased value for money would make own-labels more attractive to them (*The Grocer*, 1999b).

Own-label brands are not unique to the grocery trade. Over the counter medicines, clothing brands such as Next, The Gap and Benetton, footwear, DIY products (B&Q), and electrical appliances have all been own-branded. Although when own-labels were first introduced they tended to suggest poorer quality, reinforced by the supermarkets' generic value lines, there is now a growing number of own-labels at the premium end of the market, such as Tesco's *Finest* range with widespread appeal (Smith, 2001). The base of own-label development has now stalled as category management approaches tend to favour a broader consideration of choice in a category to maximise category performance, rather than an over concentration on own-labels. In some cases local supply can enhance the diversity feel on the shelf (*see* CSR in Action, p. 497).

Europeanisation and strategic alliances

Many retailers see international activity as an important part of their businesses and for some it represents a significant proportion of their total turnover. IKEA, for instance, generates 88 per cent of its sales outside Sweden, and both Dutch retailer Ahold and Delhaize Le Lion, a Belgian food retailer, similarly generate around 80 per cent of their turnover from international retailing. The reasons for internationalisation are many and varied. Some are 'push' factors, arising from conditions within the domestic marketing environment that leave the retailer little choice but to internationalise, while others are 'pull' factors, favourable conditions within foreign markets that make them attractive to the retailer. Alexander (1995) neatly summarises the push and pull factors, as shown in Table 13.6.

Table 13.6 Push and pull factors influencing retail internationalisation

Push factors	*Pull factors*
Economic instability	Economic stability
Low market growth	High market growth
High operating costs	Underdeveloped retail structure
Poor operating environment	Favourable operating environment
Need for economies of scale	Large market
Hostile competition	Innovative retail culture
Mature domestic market	Investment potential
Small domestic market	Niche opportunities
Format saturation	Company-owned facilities/operations
Restrictive regulatory environment	Relaxed regulatory environment
Consumer credit restrictions	Positive social environment
Political instability	Political stability

Source: Based on table on p. 85 from '*Internationalisation: Interpreting the Motives*', in *International Retailing: Trends and Strategies*, Pitman Publishing (Pearson Education), (Alexander, N., McGoldrick, P.J., and Davies, G. (eds.), 1995).

As mentioned earlier, retailers also form looser international alliances, based on contracts and agreements rather than on degrees of total or co-ownership. These are often geared towards the streamlining of purchasing and logistics rather than direct involvement or interference in each other's retailing operations.

Buckley (1994) raises a few potential problems with alliances that do not involve ownership. While joint buying power may achieve lower prices, that power cannot be used most effectively unless the retailers can threaten the supplier with delisting in *all* the alliance members' stores. Such unanimity might be difficult to achieve. There might also be cultural differences. Products that might be popular and acceptable in one country might not be wanted in another, thus limiting the buying scope of the alliance. Finally, Buckley points out that membership of an alliance might hinder a retailer's ability to expand into its partners' domestic markets, or eventually to take over a partner. A fuller discussion of these strategies and the methods employed to enter new markets will be considered in Chapter 23.

Wholesalers and distributors

The emphasis of the chapter now shifts up the distribution channel, away from the retailer to the wholesaler. As consumers, we already know a great deal about the structure of retailing and the variety of retailers that exist to serve our needs. We know much less, however, about the organisations that make sure that the retailers have access to the goods we want to buy. Wholesaling is just as complex a world as that of retailing, with as much variety in the sizes, structures and roles undertaken by its organisations. This section, therefore, will define the range of different types of wholesaler.

Full service wholesalers

As the name implies, full service wholesalers offer the fullest range of wholesaling services, from sourcing and bulk breaking to transportation to marketing and management advice. They are of particular value to the smaller manufacturer or retailer that does not have the necessary expertise to do many of these things for itself. Häagen Dazs, for example, used to deliver ice cream direct to independent retailers, but found that the minimum order quantity, or *drop*, required to make this viable was far too high for many small independents. It switched, therefore, to distribution through specialist frozen-food wholesalers so that shopkeepers could buy only one case at a time if they wanted. Most of the delivered wholesalers operate large depot-based systems to hold and manage stock. Whereas the cash and carry operators considered below tend to be local, the catchment area of delivered wholesalers can be as high as 100 miles. The majority of customers are grocery retailers and profit margins tend to be very slender, just 1 per cent on some items. A number of buying or symbol groups are also run by delivered wholesale companies for indepenent retailers. The retailers join the voluntary chain, which entitles them to trade under the name and fascia of the group, for instance Mace, Spar, Londis, Nisa Today, and Landmark. Typical services of a symbol group would be the provision of own-label brands, promotions, advice and support, and negotiation with larger manufacturers. Londis offers 600 own-label brands priced at 10 per cent lower than the category leaders. These brands account for 20 per cent of wholesaler turnover and 35 per cent of retailer sales. Over 40 per cent of wines, spirits and cider are own-label sales. Membership of a buying group can allow the retailer to benefit from economies of scale and access to unique product lines via own-labels without losing the right to independent ownership.

Full service wholesale merchants may carry a wide range of product lines, or they might choose to focus on a few lines in depth, or they might be speciality wholesalers, such as the frozen-food specialists mentioned above. All of them, however, sell mainly to retailers. Full service wholesalers that sell to manufacturers or non-retailing organisations are called industrial distributors. Again, they might choose to carry a range of products or to specialise.

Limited service wholesalers

In contrast to the full service operators, limited service wholesalers only undertake clearly defined services, as a means of keeping their costs down. They may, for example, choose not to provide transport services or not to stock large quantities of products.

A typical kind of limited service wholesaler, commonly found across Europe, is the *cash and carry*. These outlets accounted for £9.2 bn sales or 60 per cent of the UK grocery wholesale trade in 2000 and are served by wholesalers such as Booker-Iceland, Makro and Bestways (Howard, 2001). These wholesalers serve the needs of the very small retailer, which uses them rather as an individual consumer would use a supermarket. The retailer goes to the cash and carry, browses and selects the required goods, organises payment (either cash or on account), then takes the goods away with whatever transport they have organised for themselves. It is an efficient way for a small retailer to get access to a wide range of branded and other goods at reasonable prices. The cash and carry buys in bulk and then passes on some of the savings to its customers so that they can also make a return or keep their prices lower. Even so, it is still difficult for the small, independent retailer to compete with supermarkets that can sell items to the public at lower prices than the independent can even purchase them at. To try to help with this, many cash-and-carry operators produce own-brand goods, such as Bestway's 'Best-in' range and Nurdin and Peacock's 'Happy Shopper' label, and generic lines, such as Bestway's 'Save-on' products, that allow the small retailer to offer low prices while retaining its margins.

eg

Metro/Makro from Germany is a major force in worldwide cash-and-carry operations. The C&C division has 365 depots in 20 countries trading as either Metro or Makro, a broad and deep food assortment with special emphasis on fresh produce, and a broad non-food assortment. It is targeted at smaller enterprises, retail, catering or professional as well as institutional bulk buyers. The idea is to offer wide choice under one roof (*The Grocer*, 2001a).

The distinction between full, delivered and limited service cash and carry wholesalers is becoming increasingly blurred in the grocery sector. The days of small independent retailers turning up with a van at a cash and carry to order and collect are numbered. Intense competition in the marketplace and the emergence of convenience-oriented multiple retailers, such as petrol forecourt stores, are leading to more and more services being offered by cash-and-carry operators. Some are multiple depot operators such as Makro, offering a delivered service, others are buying group wholesalers such as Nurdin and Peacock and Bestways offering value lines and again a delivered service, and finally there are the traditional unaffiliated operators, often in a single depot catering for only a small percentage of wholesaler sales. Many of the larger wholesaler operations have focused on added value, improved distribution systems, IT and e-commerce. Nowadays, independent retailers are just as likely to order online as visit the cash and carry to order (IGD, 2002b; 2002c).

Chapter summary

- Both retailers and wholesalers bridge the gap between manufacturer and end consumer, but whereas retailers tend to deal directly with end consumers, wholesalers tend to deal with retailers and other B2B buyers. Nevertheless, both can perform broadly similar functions and provide suitable premises for the sale of goods. Suitability can relate to the ambience of the place, services and the facilities provided for customers, as well as the synergy between different manufacturers' products.
- Retailers can be classified according to a number of criteria: form of ownership (independents, corporate chains or contractual systems), level of service (full or limited), merchandise lines (breadth and depth) and operating methods (type of store, whether department store, supermarket, variety store or other). Non-store retailing, closely linked with direct marketing, has also become increasingly popular and widespread. It includes in-home selling, parties, mail-order operations, teleshopping and vending machines.
- Retailers have particular strategic and operational marketing decisions to make on location, product range, positioning, etc. Store image and atmosphere create the character of the store and are important in influencing the customer's perception of it. Both exterior factors (frontage, site, window displays, etc.) and interior factors (affecting sight, sound, scent and other tactile experiences) make a contribution. The aim is to stimulate the customer, yet make them relaxed enough to want to stay in the store, browsing and buying. Layout and display can further affect the customer's behaviour. Technology also plays a significant role in the retailer's ability to service customers and to supply them with what they want when they want it. Retailer own brands can help to enhance the image of the store as well as giving the retailer extra bargaining power over suppliers. In addition, some larger retailers have begun to internationalise their operations in various ways. Some have acquired foreign retailers, some have entered into joint ventures and others have entered into looser contractual alliances, usually geared towards pooling purchasing power and offering mutual marketing support.

- There are two broad types of wholesaler. Full service wholesalers offer a full range of services, including bulk breaking, transportation, delivery and management advice. Limited service wholesalers keep their costs down by providing only a few, clearly defined services for their customers. They will not usually, for example, undertake deliveries. Cash and carries are the commonest form, serving the needs of small retailers which use the cash and carry just as a consumer uses a supermarket. The wholesaler can buy in bulk and pass on some of the cost savings to the small retailer. Cash and carries also sell own-label goods to give the smaller retailer an opportunity to sell price-competitive goods and to give them a point of differentiation from the large supermarket chains.

key words and phrases

Atmosphere	**Depth of range**	**Out-of-town**
Catalogue showrooms	**Discount clubs**	**Speciality stores**
Breadth of range	**EPOS**	**Store image**
Concessions	**Franchising**	**Supermarkets**
Convenience stores	**Hypermarkets**	**Teleshopping**
Corporate chain	**Independent retail outlet**	**Variety stores**
Department stores	**Mail order**	

questions *for review*

13.1 Summarise the main functions of *wholesalers* and *retailers*.

13.2 What factors might be considered in providing an appropriate *selling environment*? How might the importance and the decisions made about these factors differ between retailers and wholesalers?

13.3 What are the predominant forms of retail ownership, and what are the main problems facing each of them?

13.4 What advantages does *out-of-town retailing* offer to a speciality retailer and its customers?

13.5 What factors influence the *assortment* of goods stocked by a retailer?

questions *for discussion*

13.1 Find examples of:
(a) full service;
(b) limited service; and
(c) self-service stores in the same retail sector.

What contribution does the level of service make to each store's marketing approaches?

13.2 What is a *category killer* and how might its activities affect other retailers? Give examples.

13.3 In what ways and to what extent do you think that *non-store retailing* poses a threat to conventional retailers?

13.4 Choose a retailer and analyse how its store atmosphere is made up.

13.5 Find examples of retailers that use:
(a) grid layout;
(b) free flow layout; and
(c) boutique layout.

Explain how each layout seems to affect shoppers' behaviour within those stores and what contribution it makes to the overall image and atmosphere of the stores.

case study 13.1

On time every time: the key components of success

The challenge for RS Components, an industrial distributor, is handling a large amount of orders and stock every day. With over 1.5 million customers worldwide and a claim that every ten seconds an engineer somewhere in the world calls one of the distribution points, the operation has to be highly effective, if high levels of stock availability, fast and efficient order processing and a quality delivery service are to be consistently achieved. In the UK, RS Components buys over 130,000 products, including electrical, electronic, industrial, health and safety and information technology components and equipment, from over 3,000 suppliers. It has a call centre, a trade counter and direct mail activities which help to fulfil the 60,000 order lines it receives each day. Goods are then shipped according to customer wishes, using a flexible delivery service to allow the method to fit the customer's requirements. Orders are normally despatched for next day delivery free of charge to account holders, but if a guaranteed delivery service is needed then a charge is levied. RS Components is, therefore, typical of many wholesalers or distributors that support other businesses, whether they are manufacturing, retail or service-based businesses, and it makes its living by efficient bulk buying, added value service, and effective selling.

Having been in business since 1937, RS Components has acquired considerable knowledge about customer requirements and ordering patterns. It has used IBM technology to help it to record order information to enable a proactive approach to buying and selling. It moved from data recording to data mining which means that historical order patterns from customers are analysed in detail so that the sales team can 'inform' customers of products they may wish to purchase in addition to their main order. This is called 'opportunity selling'. Some product combinations are rather obvious, such as soldering irons and solder, but more technical combinations are less easily spotted yet do provide the opportunity for additional sales.

In practice, customers do not consider the product suggestions as an unwarranted intrusion, but as an enhancement of service levels. RS Components claims that it has led to increased sales, higher customer satisfaction and fewer minimum orders, which ultimately increases the efficiency of the entire material handling, packaging, and shipping operation. When the average order size is only around £80, decreasing the number of separate orders is a big help in achieving an efficient operation.

Another IT system for 'Warehouse Product Allocation' was also initiated in 1995. The company had set up a warehouse in the midlands in addition to the main warehouse in Corby and products had to be efficiently shipped between these locations. To undertake this task, it was essential that RS Components knew in advance what products should be allocated to which warehouse. This would avoid the need for split order handling and delivery. The IT system allowed the inter-site parcel traffic to be reduced from 17 per cent to just 6 per cent meaning a direct saving on delivery cost. The system also supports twelve other trade counters located around the UK, each stocking over 50,000 products tailored to meet the needs of local businesses. It also has one cash and carry warehouse.

Both these IT innovations demonstrate the importance of distributors keeping track of historical ordering patterns as the foundation for stock planning, sales and service provision. When handling a large number of customer orders, it is essential to design a database that can provide detailed insights into customer buying patterns and product sales profiles. RS Components makes sure that orders find their way into the historical database for re-use, regardless of whether they are made by telephone, mail order, online or in person.

Providing information on 130,000 products is an important part of the distributor's role. Effectively RS Components is making the customer's life simpler and more efficient by gathering together information from many different manufacturers. Up until recently, the printed catalogue was central to this task. Updated every six months, it comprises six books totalling 5,500 pages with products grouped according to known selling combinations. Over one million catalogues were distributed worldwide to all customers on the mailing list. The free catalogue is a popular reference point for product solutions and has been a critical part of the selling operation for over 50 years. Prices are listed and these are honoured for the life of the catalogue. The catalogue did most of RS Components' selling!

The catalogue is, however, expected to be phased out as the website is now attracting greater use (http://www.rs.com). The website details the same information as the catalogue, but enables live information, such as special offers, to be displayed and provides for integrated ordering and transaction monitoring. This, in turn, is expected to lead to faster order turnaround, greater accuracy, and, not least, increased order efficiency to reduce costs. It is a sales and marketing tool as much as an ordering channel. Despite costing £2 mn, the elimination of a lot of paperwork brings considerable benefit to both buyer and seller. Under the manual ordering regime, RS Components found that the total cost to its customers was between £60 and £120 per order, but by internet transactions that figure is expected to fall to around £10, resulting in significant customer savings. In addition, the customer can see the order history on screen, and orders received before 8 p.m. can be delivered the next day.

As a marketing tool it plays a major part in helping RS Components to manage its customer relationships, despite the large customer base. The site can even be customised for the individuals who use it, as well as their companies, by analysing the needs of more than 250,000 registered users, offering them self-checking ordering and new product updates. The system also records past online orders to facilitate re-ordering and enquiries for that customer. In some companies, up to 100 people could use the catalogue, so the website makes company internal communication and buying easier. To RS Components, customer relationship management therefore means giving customers access to relevant online product information, a database of more than 25,000 technical documents, a full online catalogue with search facilities, and transaction management. It aims to save them money and make their lives a little easier.

The formula used so successfully in the UK has been used elsewhere in Europe and beyond, but the UK still represents 50 per cent of RS Components' £824 mn turnover. Depots are operated in most European countries and as many common products are offered as possible, but local variations mean that 130,000 products can grow to 700,000 listings. Promotions and customer service are also tailored to suit the local market. The introduction of the e-commerce facility has made information dissemination far more flexible and manageable. Nine sites have been rolled out across Europe, often country-specific, and in seven languages. All still offer the same customer benefits as the UK although local competition can be stronger. RS Components now operates in 22 countries and exports to a further 160 worldwide.

RS Components is, therefore, a successful industrial distributor that has utilised IT advances to achieve competitiveness by helping customers to make their operations more straightforward. It is all part of the declared strategy to lead the high service segment of every distribution market in which it operates. Speed, immediate availability, convenience and reliability are the determining factors for many customers in their choice of supplier, not price, according to RS Components. That is reflected in gross margins of about 50 per cent for RS Components that fund additional IT investment and international growth. This can be contrasted with the large order values and lower gross margins of high-volume wholesalers and distributors, who do not always offer the level of service provided by RS Components.

Sources: Hoare (2001); *Marketing Week* (2001); http://www.rs.com; http://www.ibm.com.

Questions

1. Summarise the factors that have led to RS Components' success in its marketplace.
2. What role do marketing and IT play in RS Components' business and how are they integrated?
3. In what ways might the customer profile and buying behaviour faced by RS Components differ from what a major supermarket chain faces? How are those differences reflected in terms of marketing and operations?

case study 13.2

Amazon: a pioneering adventurer in e-tailing

Amazon, with its motto 'Work Hard, Have Fun and Make History', was set up in 1994 in Seattle as an online retailer (or e-tailer) specialising in selling books at up to 40 per cent discount from its http://www.amazon.com site. In April 1998, Amazon set up its UK operation, http://www.amazon.co.uk to make it quicker and easier for UK customers to order and receive their books. To ensure parity with amazon.com, which UK customers can still access, of course, the idea is that UK book buyers should be paying the same sort of prices as their US counterparts after delivery costs have been accounted for. US customers benefit too. A link between amazon.co.uk and amazon.com means that American customers can access 200,000 UK titles that they could not get in the USA. A similar site serving German speaking customers, http://www.amazon.de, was also developed in 1998, while French and Japanese sites followed in 2000 and 2001 respectively. These non-US sites between them contributed 22 per cent of Amazon's sales in 2001, but it is hoped that this will rise to 50 per cent eventually.

From the start, Amazon pursued a hybrid strategy, focusing on the one hand on customer service relationship management and on the other hand on the distribution systems and infrastructure. It is clear about the need to have fully integrated and computerised systems. It is linked with its suppliers so that it can deal smoothly and efficiently with its customers' orders. It also has systems designed for dealing with small, occasional orders from millions of customers. Amazon works with book distributors to dispatch goods quickly without holding large stocks itself. Anything that is not held in stock is delivered to Amazon by the distributor within 24 hours and then repackaged along with the rest of the customer's order and sent out again as soon as possible.

Since its launch, Amazon has sold to over 35 million customers from 220 countries and has seen its business expand rapidly in line with the general growth in internet usage and shopping. Amazon has itself made a significant contribution to furthering the cause of online shopping. In 1999, 20 per cent of UK households were online, by 2001 it was 35 per cent and by 2005 it has been estimated that it will be 51 per cent. It is a similar story in Germany, Amazon's other key European market, where some 47 per cent of households are expected to be online by 2005. Internet shopping has also seen phenomenal growth: in 1999, around 25 per cent of UK online users bought something over the internet (compared with 20 per cent of German online users). That had risen to 38 per cent in 2001 (34 per cent in Germany) and is expected to hit 58 per cent by 2005 (54 per cent in Germany). E-tailing is attractive not just because of the growth potential, but also because the internet attracts high earning shoppers who can make impulse purchases from their home computers and from the systems at their place of work.

Amazon is in the right sort of market for internet retailing. According to the Boston Consulting Group, the internet is best suited for low weight, high value products that can be delivered through the post, such as CDs, videos and books. Shoppers seem to appreciate this. In 2000, the $350 mn spent online on books, music and videos accounted for nearly 13.5 per cent of all online expenditure by UK shoppers, and in Germany, it was nearer 17 per cent. It is likely that shoppers know what it is they want to buy, whether it is a CD by a favourite artist or a book for mum's birthday, or at least can get a good idea from the website blurb (and many websites operate a generous returns policy, just in case). As Steve Johnson of Andersen Consulting said, 'You've read the review, you want it, you don't need to try it on' (as reported by Kuchinskas, 1998). With over 1.5 million titles on offer, the chances are that Amazon will certainly have anything the customer wants. Amazon argues that the reader reviews, author interviews and browsing system help customers locate what they want, even if they are not sure quite what it is, and more than compensate for the lack of personal selling.

Although Amazon has pioneered internet bookselling, it does face fierce competition from the likes of barnesandnoble.com, borders.com and BOL.com. As a means of reinforcing its pre-eminence, it has introduced an associates programme, now with 500,000 members, to increase its presence across the entire web. Associates agree to put Amazon's logo and a link on their own websites and then earn commission on sales from customers 'entering' Amazon through those sites.

Perhaps because of tough competition, Amazon has also diversified into different e-tail sectors. As well as selling CDs, gifts, toys, cameras, phones, electrical goods, software, and videos/DVDs, Amazon runs internet auctions. Any of its registered auction customers can buy from and sell to each other. Amazon is acting as an 'infomediary' to link its customers together, effectively creating a horizontal distribution channel. The potential is also there for an infomediary to act as a gatekeeper, representing its customers' interests. If a significant number of its customers wanted to buy a specific product, the infomediary could ask suppliers to bid for the business or undertake a supplier search, getting a better price through bulk buying. It can also sell access to targeted groups of its customers to interested suppliers.

Some diversification has also come from forming partnership deals with other companies in areas where Amazon does not feel that it has the necessary inhouse expertise. Thus amazon.co.uk sells wines in partnership with Virgin Wines; travel in partnership with expedia.co.uk; and phones in partnership with The Carphone Warehouse.

Sources: Barker (2001); Euromonitor (2001); *Harvard Business Review* (1999); Kuchinskas (1998); McKegney (2000); Milliot (1999); Sutcliffe (2002); http://www.amazon.co.uk; http://www.amazon.com.

Questions

1. What are the differences, from the shopper's point of view, between shopping at Amazon and shopping at a real bookshop?
2. To what extent are image, atmosphere and layout appropriate concepts for an online bookshop?
3. Can a High Street retailer successfully offer online selling in parallel with its more traditional retailing? What factors would have to be considered in setting up the online operation?

References for chapter 13

A.C. Nielsen (1999), *The Retail Pocket Book 1999*, NTC Publications.

Alexander, N. (1995), 'Internationalisation: Interpreting the Motives', in P. McGoldrick and G. Davies (eds), *International Retailing: Trends and Strategies*, Pitman Publishing.

Anderson, C.H. (1993), *Retailing*, West.

Auchan (2001), 'Hypermarkets Won't Be Built Without Prior Employment Forecast', *Polish News Bulletin*, 14 December, accessed via http://www.auchan.com.

Barker, T (2001), 'Amazon Sees Break-even in UK and Germany', *Financial Times*, 25 October, p. 26.

Bedington, E. (2001a), 'A Gateway in C-space', *The Grocer*, 11 August.

Bedington, E. (2001b), 'Living Up to the Hype', *The Grocer*, 15 December, pp. 36–8.

Bowie, S. and Wilcox, I. (1999), 'Location, Location, Location', *Database Marketing*, February, pp. 38–41.

Bowlby, S. *et al.* (1984), 'Store Location: Problems and Methods 1', *Retail and Distribution Management*, 12(5), pp. 31–3.

Boyes, S. (2001), 'Reinventing Toys 'R' Us', *Corporate Finance*, September, pp. 27–8.

Buckley, N. (1994), 'Baked Beans Across Europe', *Financial Times*, 14 April, p. 19.

Buxton, P. (1999), 'Bluewater Experience', *Marketing Week*, 11 February, pp. 34–5.

Chaffey, D., Mayer, R., Johnston, K. and Ellis-Chadwick, F. (2003), *Internet Marketing: Strategy, Implementation and Practice*, Financial Times Prentice Hall, 2nd edn.

Crace, J. (2001), 'Manchester United plc', *The Guardian*, 1 May, p. 68.

Davidson, H. (1993), 'Bubbling Benetton Beats Recession', *Sunday Times*, 4 April, pp. 3–11.

Davies, G. (1992), 'Positioning, Image and the Marketing of Multiple Retailers', *International Review of Retail Distribution and Consumer Research*, 2(1), p. 13.

Davies, R.L. and Rogers, D.S. (1984), *Store Location and Store Assessment Research*, John Wiley.

The Economist (1998), 'Knickers to the Market', *The Economist*, 28 February, pp. 68–9.

English, S. (2001), 'It's Not All Fun and Games as "Kid's Recession" Hits Toys 'R' Us Hard', *The Daily Telegraph*, 14 July, p. 27.

Euromonitor (2001), *European Marketing Data and Statistics 2001*, Euromonitor, 36th edn.

Finch, J. (2001a), 'Sainsbury Hits a 10-year Sales High', *The Guardian*, 22 November, p. 1.24.

Finch, J. (2001b), 'Sweet Music: Tills Start to Jingle at HMV', *The Guardian*, 8 December, p. 24.

Gannaway, B. (1999), 'Bluewater Horizons', *The Grocer*, 24 April, pp. 40–3.

Gregory, H. (2001a), 'Country Ways', *The Grocer*, 31 March, pp. 36–8.

Gregory, H. (2001b), 'What it Takes', *The Grocer*, 24 November, pp. 26–8.

The Grocer (2002a), 'Asda Ditches Depots in Online Arm Restructure', *The Grocer*, 5 January, p. 5.

The Grocer (2002b), 'Lidl Squeezed by Planners', *The Grocer*, 5 January, p. 6.

The Grocer (2001a), 'C&C Bolsters Sales Growth', *The Grocer*, 4 August, p. 14.

The Grocer (2001b), 'Costco Total is Now 13', *The Grocer*, 1 September, p. 8.

The Grocer (2001c), 'Discounters Struggle to Boost Share in the UK', *The Grocer*, 15 September, p. 14.

The Grocer (2001d), 'Consumers Fight Shy of On-line Groceries', *The Grocer*, 22 September, p. 12.

The Grocer (2001e), 'Boots Ahead of Schedule', *The Grocer*, 20 October, p. 14.

The Grocer (2001f), 'Shaw's Decides to Trial 'More Viable' Net Shopping Service', *The Grocer*, 17 November, p. 16.

The Grocer (2001g), 'Safeway Creates Instore Theatre in the Round', *The Grocer*, 24 November, p. 6.

The Grocer (1999a), 'Irish Plan Crackdown on Major Superstores', *The Grocer*, 24 April, p. 11.

The Grocer (1999b), 'The Bigger Picture', *The Grocer*, 24 April, p. 53.

Harvard Business Review (1999), 'Whither Amazon.com?', *Harvard Business Review*, March/April, p. 141.

Hoare, S. (2001), 'Streamline Ordering, Eliminate Paperwork', *ECRM* supplement to *The Times*, 11 April, p. 5.

Hogarth-Scott, S. and Parkinson, S.P. (1994), 'The New Food Discounters: Are They a Threat to the Major Multiples?', *International Journal of Retail and Distribution Management*, 22(1), pp. 20–8.

Howard, J (2001), *Cash and Carry Outlets*, KeyNote Report N51021, June.

Howard, J (2000), *Discount Retailing*, KeyNote Report 52170, November.

Howe, W.S. (1992), *Retailing Management*, Macmillan.

Hunt, J. (1998), 'Heijn Works to Fix New Concept', *The Grocer*, 12 September, p. 15.

Hunt, J. (1999), 'Going into Orbit', *The Grocer*, 9 January, p. 32.

IGD (2002a), 'Who's Really Who in Global Grocery Retailing?', accessed via http://www.igd.org.uk.

IGD (2002b), 'Cash and Carry Grocery Wholesaling', accessed via http://www.igd.org.uk.

IGD (2002c), 'Delivered Trade Grocery Wholesaling', accessed via http://www.igd.org.uk.

IGD (2001), 'Grocery Retailing, 2001', accessed via http://www.igd.org.uk.

Jardine, A. (2001), 'Argos Diversifies to Update Image', *Marketing*, 5 August, p. 4.

Keynote (2000), *Automatic Vending*, December, KeyNote Report KN29040.

Kleinman, M. (2001), 'Can Argos Hold on to a Position of Strength?', *Marketing*, 27 September, p. 13.

Kuchinskas, S. (1998), 'The E-commerce Cometh', *Mediaweek*, 21 September, pp. IQ8–IQ12.

Marketing Week (2001), 'From Trading Platform to Marketing Tool', *Marketing Week*, 25 October, p. 47.

McGoldrick, P. (1990), *Retail Marketing*, McGraw-Hill.

McKegney, M. (2000), 'Amazon Blazes Trail in Europe', *Advertising Age*, 18 September, p. 78.

Milliot, J. (1999), 'Amazon.com Eyeing Distribution Improvements', *Publishers Weekly*, March 22, p. 12.

O'Grady, S. (2001), 'Sweet Smell May Be Thornton's Success', *The Independent*, 8 December, p. 5.

Paché, G. (1998), 'Logistics Outsourcing in Grocery Distribution: A European Perspective', *Logistics Information Management*, 11 (5), pp. 301–8.

Prior, M. (2001), 'TRU's Eyler Touts sound Growth Plan', *DSN Retailing Today*, 18 June, p. 3.46.

Retail Intelligence (2000), 'Europe's Top 20 Retailers', accessed via http://www.retailindustry.about.com.

Robinson, P. (1999), 'Economical with the Facts', *The Grocer*, 16 January, pp. 32–4.

Rosenbloom, B. (1981), *Retail Marketing*, Random House.

Ryle, S. (2001), '@business: Delivering the Goods Brings Net Success', *The Observer*, 12 August, p. 6.

Saner, E. and Nathan, A. (2001), 'Bra Firm Caught in Burmese Row', *The Times*, 23 December, p. 9.

Scardino. E. (2001), 'H&M: Can it Adapt to America's Landscape?', *DSN Retailing Today*, 17 September, pp. A10–A11.

Smith, J. (2001), 'Closing the Gap', *The Grocer*, 19 May, pp. 56–7.

Snoddy, R. (2000), 'Man Utd to Kick Off Expansion with 45 Outlets', *The Times*, 29 March.

Stanley, J. (2002), 'Brands versus Private Labels', accessed via http://www.retailindustry.about.com.

Stewart-Allen, A. (2001), 'Ikea Service Worst in its Own Backyard', *Marketing News*, 23 April, p. 11.

Sutcliffe, T. (2002), 'Journey to the Source of the Amazon', *The Independent*, 7 February, p. 7.

Sutcliffe, T. (2001), 'Read All About It – Tube to Get Old-time Vending Machines that Sell You a Story', *The Independent*, 16 January.

Teather, D. (2001), 'H&M Plans to Open 50 Fashion Stores', *The Guardian*, 22 June, p. 1.23.

URPI (1988), *List of UK Hypermarkets and Superstores*, Unit for Retail Planning Information.

Walters, D. and White, D. (1987), *Retail Marketing Management*, Macmillan.

Wrigley, N. (1988), *Store Choice, Store Location and Market Analysis*, Routledge.

part six

PROMOTION

14 integrated marketing communication

15 advertising

16 sales promotion

17 personal selling and sales management

18 direct marketing and exhibitions

19 public relations and sponsorship

What is marketing if it isn't communication? The philosophy of marketing (discussed in Chapter 1) as the interface between an organisation and the outside world, particularly its customers, implies that all marketing activities are destined to communicate something to someone, somewhere. This communication may be direct and tangible, an advertisement for example, but it may also be indirect and intangible: think about the ways in which price communicates with a potential buyer, for instance.

There is certainly synergy between direct and indirect communication. Advertising messages centred on product quality can be reinforced by tacit communication though price and packaging, or a sales representative's credibility can be enhanced by what is implicitly communicated by the product's performance. In practice, the direct and indirect elements of communication are inseparable, but in the following six chapters, the emphasis is on the overt means by which organisations communicate.

Chapter 14 introduces the concept of integrated marketing communication and its application in marketing and also looks at some of the factors influencing an organisation's choice of promotional mix elements. Each of these elements is then explored in more detail in Chapters 15 to 17, which look at advertising, sales promotion and personal selling, defining the tools and techniques used within each area, their appropriate use and the problems of implementation. Chapter 18 examines direct marketing, an increasingly important means of injecting a personal touch back into mass markets. Finally, Chapter 19 explores public relations, sponsorship and exhibitions – all of which are now recognised as valuable marketing communication techniques. Although examples of the use of e-communications and new media such as SMS text messaging can be found throughout these chapters, Chapter 24 will deal more specifically with these issues later.

chapter 14

integrated marketing communication

LEARNING OBJECTIVES

This chapter will help you to:

1 understand the importance of planned, integrated communication in a marketing context;

2 appreciate the variety and scope of marketing communication objectives;

3 explain the use of promotional tools in the communication process;

4 identify the factors and constraints influencing the mix of communications tools that an organisation uses; and

5 define the main methods by which communications budgets are set.

Introduction

The promotional mix is the direct way in which an organisation attempts to communicate with various target audiences. It consists of five main elements, as shown in Figure 14.1. Advertising represents non-personal, mass communication; personal selling is at the other extreme, covering face-to-face, personally tailored messages. Sales promotion involves tactical, short-term incentives that encourage a target audience to behave in a certain way. Public relations is about creating and maintaining good-quality relationships with many interested groups (for example the media, shareholders and trade unions), not just with customers. Finally, direct marketing involves creating one-to-one relationships with individual customers, often in mass markets, and might involve mailings, telephone selling or electronic media. Some might classify direct marketing activities as forms of advertising, sales promotion or even personal selling, but this text treats direct marketing as a separate element of the promotional mix while acknowledging that it 'borrows' from the other elements.

Ideally, the marketer would like to invest extensively in every element of the mix. In a world of finite resources, however, choices have to be made about which activities are going to work together most cost effectively with the maximum synergy to achieve the communications objectives of the organisation within a defined budget. Budgets obviously vary widely between different organisations, and depending on the type of product involved and the communications task in hand.

This chapter, along with the five that follow it, will aim to explain why such choices are made.

Figure 14.1 The elements of the promotional mix

eg

Amazon.co.uk uses different elements of the promotional mix to communicate different messages to different audiences and to achieve different objectives. It often uses e-mail to communicate with its regular customers. Sometimes, it will send a personal message to tell the recipient about a new book or other merchandise that is relevant to them in the light of their past purchases. The message contains a hyperlink so that the recipient can easily visit the site to find out more and to pre-order the book before publication. E-mail is also used to offer or advertise incentives to customers. Virtual vouchers offering 'money off your next order' are sent to encourage customers to re-visit the site and buy more merchandise. Personal messages are also used to inform the customer about a special offer that they can find on the site, for example three best-sellers for £10. Sometimes, though, Amazon wants to reach a wider audience, perhaps with the objective of attracting non-users to visit the site for the first time. Banner advertising on other websites generates awareness of Amazon, and its partnership with search engines, so that you can click on the Amazon logo to get details of books relevant to your search, also leads potential customers to the site. Mainstream media are used too. In March 2002, for example, Amazon placed an advertisement in *The Times* newspaper offering 3 CDs for £20 to entice people to visit the site to see what was on offer and perhaps to buy.

Each element of the promotional mix has its own chapter, which discusses in some detail the element's strengths and weaknesses and its appropriate use. This chapter, therefore, provides a more general strategic overview by focusing on the integrated marketing communications planning process. Pickton and Broderick (2001, p. 67) define integrated marketing communication as

> *... a process which involves the management and organisation of all agents in the analysis, planning, implementation and control of all marketing communications contacts, media, messages and promotional tools focused at selected target audiences in such a way as to derive the greatest economy, efficiency, effectiveness, enhancement and coherence of marketing communications effort in achieving predetermined product and corporate marketing communications objectives.*

This definition emphasises the need to plan and manage the integrated marketing communications function carefully and strategically within the market context and using the full range of communications tools effectively and efficiently. This chapter, therefore, looks at some of the influences that shape an appropriate blend within the promotional mix, allowing the marketer to allocate communication resources most effectively.

Communication, even mass market advertising, begins and ends with people, which means that it has plenty of scope for going wrong. The first part of this chapter, therefore, takes a look at communications theory from first principles, building up a simple model of communication. This is then applied in a marketing context to highlight the danger areas where marketing communication efforts can fail. These concepts may appear to be very abstract or theoretical, but they nevertheless form an important foundation for applied decision making and may make the difference between success and failure.

On the basis of these concepts, the main focus of the chapter is on developing a planning framework within which managerial decisions on communication activity can be made. Each of the elements of the simple communication model is incorporated into this framework, whether implicitly or explicitly, with a view to minimising the danger of misunderstanding and failure. Each stage in the planning flow is discussed in turn, with particular emphasis being given to relevant issues and the kind of integrated promotional mix that might subsequently be appropriate. It is becoming increasingly important for organisations to design and implement effective integrated marketing communications strategies as they expand their interests beyond their known domestic markets.

Communications theory

Schramm (1955) offers a seminal definition of communication that serves as a sound basis for developing a model of communication:

> *The process of establishing a commonness or oneness of thought between a sender and a receiver.*

Communication model

Superficially, communication is a very simple process that we all perform a lot of the time, and take for granted. It would seem from the definition above that all you need is for someone to send a message and someone to receive it, as shown in Figure 14.2.

However, even the three apparently simple elements of Figure 14.2 raise a number of questions that Figure 14.2 does not address.

Encoding the message

Put yourself in the position of having to tell a professor that an assignment will not be handed in on time. The intent of the message is clear enough, but *what* precisely are you going to say and *how* exactly are you going to say it? Here are some alternatives. (This situation is, of course, purely hypothetical. The authors do not hold themselves responsible for the consequences of your using any of these approaches in reality!)

- 'I can't hand in my assignment on time. I'll deliver it on Friday.' (assertive/assumptive)
- 'I'm sorry, but I haven't quite finished my assignment yet. Please can I hand it in on Friday?' (apologetic/appealing)
- 'I've done it, honestly, but the dog ate it, so I need to print it out again – would Friday be all right?' (possibly honest . . .)

There are many, many more alternatives. The point is that, as the sender, you would assess each of these alternative approaches in order to predict their likely effect on the receiver of the message. Naturally, you would choose the one most likely to achieve the desired outcome. This relies on your perceptions of the receiver's attitudes, character and state of mind. The third excuse might be appropriate for a professor with a soft-hearted, sympathetic (or gullible) streak, whereas the second excuse would appeal to an honest, straightforward, no-nonsense type. The first excuse guarantees you a 'fail' from any self-respecting academic. In other words, you make a choice as to how you encode the message, first so that it will be understood by the receiver and second to increase the chances of achieving the objectives of the communication.

Communication channel

A further complication arises when you consider the means by which the message is relayed to the receiver, that is, the choice of channel of communication. Will you deliver the message yourself, verbally, or will you leave a note and run away? The choice of channel might affect the success of the communication. The verbal method allows you to assess the response to your initial message, giving you the flexibility to try again with a different approach, if at first you don't succeed. It also gives you the opportunity to employ non-

Figure 14.2 The basic elements of communication

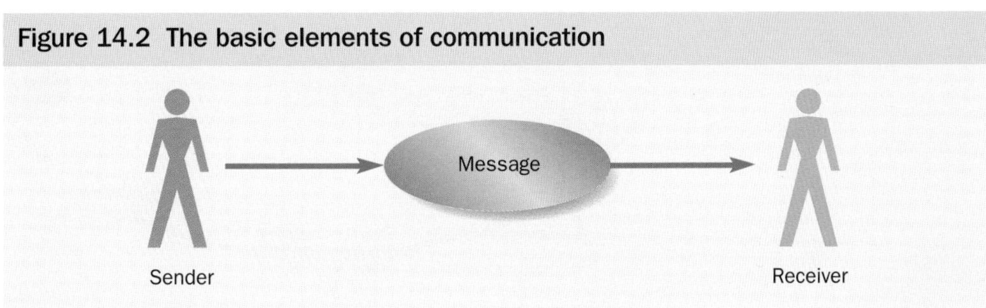

verbal communication to reinforce the message. The tone of voice used (assumptive, quietly polite or pleading), the look in the eyes (hostile, guilty or pleading) all communicate in their own right, and need to be consistent with the verbal message. The written message, on the other hand, is moderated by its legibility (typewritten or handwritten), and perhaps the physical characteristics of the paper. It does not offer the quick flexibility of message and response of the verbal method.

Decoding

Figure 14.3 extends the initial communication model to include the concepts of 'encoding' and 'channel', and also includes a new element, **decoding**, on the receiver's side of the model. The receiver is not a passive subordinate in the communication process, but is a dynamic influence and partner. It is not enough that you have delivered the message to the receiver's eyes or ears; it has to be understood and interpreted. Your message may well be a sequence of simple words, but the receiver is unlikely to take them at face value. The receiver interprets those words according to their own personality, their mood, how they feel about the sender of the message, how they react to the way in which the message has been sent or worded, and their own needs and wants. So if, for example, you try to use the second excuse – 'I'm sorry, but I haven't quite finished my assignment yet. Please can I hand it in on Friday?' – it might be decoded as:

- 'I am a lazy student and I never hand work in on time – here I go again.'
- 'I am normally a conscientious student, but I genuinely have a problem and I am trying my best to solve it as soon as possible with the least inconvenience to you.'
- 'I'm being honest with you, so do me a favour.'

The decoding depends entirely on the receiver's perceptions, and whether the receiver is willing to accept a verbal request or would prefer formal written contact. All this in turn can have a profound effect on the *response* offered. The first decoding option might lead to a flat and unequivocal refusal to comply with the request; the second to a more sympathetic 'Yes, certainly, Friday will do, and do you want to tell me what the problem is?', while the third might elicit a more cynical 'Just this once, but you'd better be on time with the next one'.

Feedback

Whatever the response, it provides **feedback** to the sender on whether the message has been received, understood, interpreted as desired and acted on appropriately. Satisfactory feedback may close this communication episode, whereas unsatisfactory or ambiguous feedback may cause the sender to want to communicate further, going round the model again.

Figure 14.3 A simple communication model

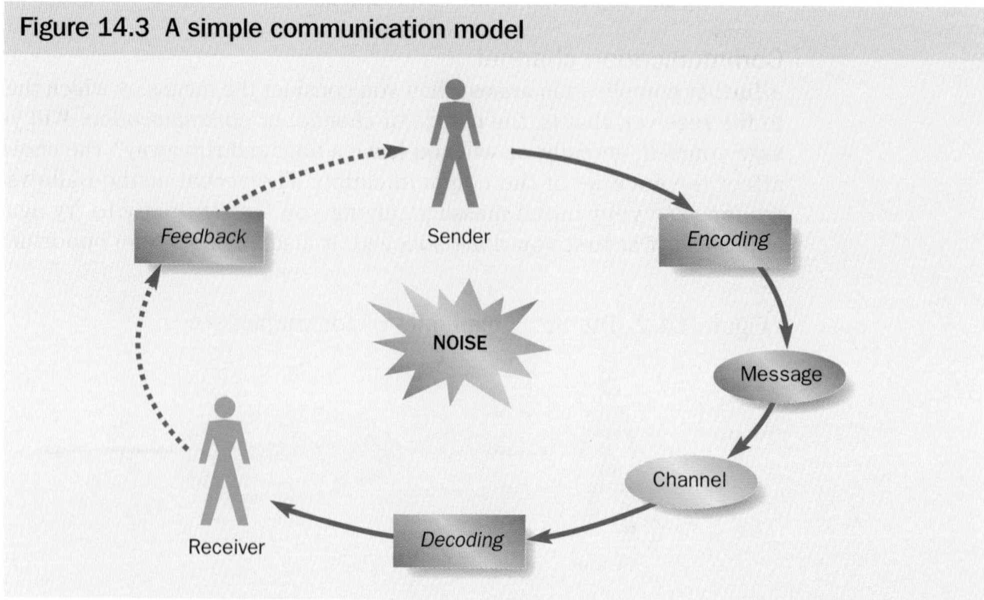

Noise

The final element of the model is **noise**. This consists of all extraneous activity and influences that might interfere and distort information at any point in the communication process. There could literally be physical noise – crackles on a telephone line, other people talking, traffic, background noise etc. – which could blot out or distort part of the intended message. There are, however, other less obvious sources of 'noise' that nevertheless have the same sort of interfering effect, such as the paper running out or crumpling up in a fax machine (thereby distorting or obscuring the message), or perhaps other events distracting the sender's or receiver's attention ('I'll read this message later. I have a train to catch').

Shared meaning

To return to the definition of communication offered at the beginning of this section, the model developed here demonstrates that the process of achieving 'commonness or oneness of thought', or shared meaning between sender and receiver, is not quite as easy and straightforward as it might appear. 'Shared meaning' is more than the successful transmission of words from one party to another, but requires sound mutual understanding of each other, and the active participation of both sender and receiver.

So what has all this to do with marketing? 'Shared meaning' has everything to do with marketing, since an organisation must understand what its market wants, and a market must understand what an organisation is offering and how that will fulfil their needs and wants. There must be two-way communication between buyer and seller if that is to be accomplished. Even a brief attempt to apply the simple communication model in a marketing context highlights some important lessons for the marketer. We look at each of the main components in turn:

Sender

The sender of a marketing message may be the organisation, perhaps in conjunction with an advertising agency, which wants to communicate a message to a defined audience.

Receiver

The receiver of a marketing message may be the individuals within that audience. A pharmaceutical company, for example, might target doctors or pharmacists, whereas a holiday company such as Saga would target the over-50 age group.

Message

The message is what the sender wants the audience to know or understand as a result of receiving the communication. This might be: 'Buy one of our holidays because we understand your needs', or 'This is our new product', or 'Don't drink and drive'.

eg

Research undertaken by GlaxoSmithKline, maker of the Ribena range of concentrated blackcurrant juice, showed that consumers tended to use more squash if they kept it ready-diluted in the fridge. The company wanted, therefore, to find a way of persuading mums to make up bulk quantities of Ribena and store it in the fridge. A sales promotion was run in which a free jug was attached to 2 litre bottles of Ribena. The jug would fit either onto a shelf or into a fridge door compartment. The promotion was run over July and August in the major supermarket chains and over 1 million jugs were given away. The impact on brand sales was significant: a 37 per cent increase over the equivalent period in the previous year (http://www.spca.org.uk).

Encoding

Encoding is where the sender's understanding of the receiver pays dividends. Does the target market only need information? Does it want to be entertained? Persuaded? Threatened? What kind of imagery appeals to this target segment? Artistic? Abstruse? Amusing? What choice of music or voice-over will best enhance the effect of the message in

To encourage greater use of Ribena concentrated blackcurrant juice, the company offered a jug which would allow larger quantities of diluted juice to be kept in the fridge.

Source: GlaxoSmithKline.

the mind of the target? There are many difficult questions relating to what to say and how to say it that can only be answered through clear knowledge of the target market.

The potential Saga holidaymaker might respond to relaxing scenes, such as almost deserted sunny beaches or gentle activities like rambling, rather than the frenzied disco scene more reminiscent of a Club 18–30 holiday. The core message in each case is actually the same, 'Buy one of our holidays because we understand your needs', but the encoding is appealing to different perceptions of what makes a good holiday.

Channel

The channel is the means by which the encoded message is passed on to the receiver. There are many different choices, for example television, print, electronic or personal contact. Again, what is most appropriate can only be established through knowledge of the target market.

Decoding

The decoding phase is a difficult one for the marketer, who can only trust that the right message, encoding and channel decisions have been made in order to increase the chances of the message being interpreted as desired. This becomes particularly problematic where there are mass markets and subtle, sophisticated messages. The more marketers aggregate and generalise behaviour, the less predictable becomes the response of the individual, and

eg

The ITC received 125 complaints about a television advertisement for Pampers Total Care nappies. The advertisement claimed that the product could not only 'handle pee but also soft poo'. Complainants found these words rather offensive and furthermore felt that the graphics used to demonstrate the product in action had put them off their food! In its judgement, the ITC felt that the words simply represented the way the many mothers describe babies' bodily functions and thus were not offensive and that the graphics were innocuous. The complaints were not, therefore, upheld. Seventeen complaints against Curry's, the electrical goods retailer were, however, upheld. The retailer had advertised a sale featuring a number of specific products with the words 'Tomorrow only. Limited stock' superimposed. Complainants had found, however, that when they went to the store, they found that 'limited stock' meant that only the first ten customers purchasing each featured item were actually offered the advertised sale price. Everyone else was expected to pay the full retail price. The ITC's decision hinged on the interpretation of the term 'limited stock' and the view that most people would think it meant the absolute number of items available rather than just the (rather more limited) number available at the reduced price. The ITC decided that the advertising had been misleading and ordered it not to be re-shown (http://www.itc.org.uk).

the more complex the message, the less likely it is that it will be interpreted by each individual exactly as desired.

As mentioned at pp. 109 *et seq.*, individuals tend to interpret incoming messages very differently, depending on their personalities, experience, interest and knowledge, among other things. Selective perception, for example, means that people will hear what they want to hear, or what is of specific interest at that time, and disregard the rest of the communication. With television advertising in particular, people are exposed to so much of it, so often, that they have learned to screen it out or ignore it. This means that there is greater pressure on the sender to develop messages that are encoded in such a way that they can break through those defences and be interpreted appropriately.

Feedback

Feedback is how the recipient of the message responds to it. This might mean overt action, such as purchasing a product or requesting more information, but it might also be less overt, involving the generation of awareness and the development of attitudes. A great disadvantage of any kind of mass communication, such as television advertising, is that feedback can be slow and painful to collect. This contrasts with face-to-face communication where feedback can be assessed immediately. Even if the intent of the message was to sell the product, sales figures only tell part of the story and more detailed investigation is required to try to establish the role of advertising in those sales and the effectiveness of the message. Meaningful feedback is itself the result of a planned communication effort to collect it on behalf of the organisation.

Since marketing communication is an expensive activity, it is important to monitor the outcomes of what is done and, if necessary, modify or change some aspect(s) of the communication process. Even before mass communication takes place, organisations often test their advertising messages with a limited audience to see whether they achieve what was intended.

e-marketing *in action*

How well does the Schramm model apply online?

The classic communications model of Schramm (1955) can still be used to help understand the effectiveness of marketing communication using the internet. With internet marketing the communications channel is typically the website. We can consider how different elements of the model constrain the effectiveness of internet marketing. Actions can then be taken to overcome these constraints:

- Encoding can be considered to be the design and development of the site content or e-mail which aims to convey the message of the company and is dependent on understanding of the target audience.
- Noise is the external influences that affect the quality of the message. In an internet context this can be slow download times, the use of plug-ins that the user cannot use or confusion caused by too much information on screen. Alternatively it could be other distractions in the user's environment – literally noise.
- Decoding is the process of interpreting the message and is dependent on the cognitive ability of the receiver which is partly influenced by the length of time they have used the internet.

The model can also be used to consider how feedback occurs online. The ease of capturing online feedback is one of the key advantages of the internet. For example, if a user clicks on a banner advert, this is recorded immediately on a database. Real time analysis can occur – if it is found that one type of banner advert is more effective than another, then it can be replaced immediately.

Website visitor activity data records the number of visitors on the site and the paths or clickstreams they take through the site as they visit different content. Such data gives detailed information on content and services accessed by e-commerce site visitors. Traditionally this information has been collected using log file analysis. The server-based log file is added to every time a user downloads a piece of information such as a web page or graphic (a hit) and is analysed using a log file analyser. Examples of transactions within the log file are:

Yoursite.com - - [05/Oct/2002:00:00:49 -000] "GET /index.html HTTP/1.0" 200 33362
Yoursite.com - - [05/Oct/2002:00:00:49 -000] "GET /logo.gif HTTP/1.0" 200 54342

A log file analyser is a separate program such as Webtrends that is used to summarise the information on customer activity in a log file. Hits are not useful measures of website effectiveness since if a page consists of 10 graphics, plus text, this is recorded as 11 hits. Page impressions and site visits are better measures of site activity. Other feedback is not automatic, but is collected when a user completes an online feedback form or customer satisfaction survey.

Now consider the weaknesses in applying the communications model of Schramm (1955). These include:

1 The model involves only two main participants – the sender of the message and the recipient. On many websites there is interaction with other users through communities such as discussion groups, chat rooms or knowledge bases, for example of software support. This can be considered as another form of 'noise' online.

2 The web-based channel is arguably more complex than other channels, for example a user may be downloading more than one web page simultaneously while writing a report and also listening to music at the same time. This again can be considered an example of noise.

3 The decoding process may differ according to how the user has set up their PC. For example how many colours can it display, at which resolution, with which plug-ins and what version of the web browser is being used. This is very different from a television or print ad whether everyone sees the same format of message.

Source: Dave Chaffey.

Noise

Noise covers any factors that interfere with any aspect of the communication process between sender and receiver. An obvious interference in the receipt of an advertising message, for example, is if the intended receiver is not watching the television when the advertisement is broadcast! Many people regard the commercial breaks as opportunities to make a cup of coffee, or to 'channel hop'. Such behaviour poses a big problem for advertisers. There are no easy answers to this, other than scheduling the advertisement at the beginning or end of a commercial break and starting it with some incredible attention-grabbing device. Other 'noise' includes the clutter of other advertising messages, particularly for competing products, which the receiver is trying to process. The impact of a message may be reduced if it is surrounded by equally stimulating and exciting messages, and there is even the risk of messages becoming confused with each other in the receiver's mind. Noise thus either causes the message to be distorted in the receiver's mind or to fail to reach the receiver's attention at all (Mallen, 1977).

The lessons from this application of the model are fundamental to successful and cost effective marketing communication: know your target market inside out, define exactly what response you would like from the target market and invest in the mechanisms to monitor and evaluate the actual response you receive. This all indicates the need for thorough and logical planning of the organisation's communications activities. The following sections take up this theme, and offer a framework within which integrated marketing communications decisions can be developed and justified.

eg

Interactive television (iTV) can help to reduce the noise surrounding the message. With the average viewer being exposed to 290 commercials per week and a barrage of alternative brands in the stores, interactive television can make the advertiser stand out. The technology means that the product is exposed to the potential customer in real time and a transaction, whether a purchase or a request for more information, can be completed before a competitor gets a chance to present an alternative. That is especially important when over 40 per cent of the advertisements to which we are exposed are forgotten within one week (Turznski, 1999). Dedicated home shopping, banking and holiday channels can be ready for consumer action at the touch of a button. As Knight (2002) points out, companies are starting to use iTV to generate quality sales leads, provide further information and to generate customer feedback. Nissan, for example, used iTV to allow interested consumers to see a video of the vehicle, order brochures and/or request a test drive. The company claimed that a large number of brochures and test drives were generated and that the quality of sales leads generated was very high. Procter and Gamble too has found iTV a good medium for developing closer relationships with its customers. Using the Sky digital channels, during Pampers advertisements, consumers could access the Pampers iTV Baby World Service offering advice and information for mothers, a newsletter and a baby picture gallery so that you could upload a photo of your little darling and see him on the telly (*Marketing*, 2001). With the continued growth of digital television and the further development of the technology, and as targeting becomes ever more sophisticated, iTV looks set to become a mainstream part of integrated communications strategies.

Communications planning model

Figure 14.4, adapted from Rothschild's (1987) communications decision sequence framework, includes all the main elements of marketing communications decision-making and links closely with the theory of communications discussed above. Given the complexity of communication and the immense possibilities for getting some element of it wrong, a thorough and systematic planning process is crucial for minimising the risks. No organisation can afford either the financial or reputational damage caused by poorly planned or implemented communications campaigns.

Each element and its implications for the balancing of the promotional mix will now be defined and analysed in turn. The first element is the situation analysis, which has been split into three subsections: the target market, the product and the environment. Bear in mind, however, that in reality it is difficult to 'pigeon hole' things quite so neatly as this might imply, and there will, therefore, be a lot of cross-referencing.

Situation analysis (1): the target market

B2B or consumer market

The *target market* decision most likely to have an impact on the balancing of the overall promotional mix is whether the market is a consumer market or a B2B market. Recalling the comparison made in Chapter 4 between consumer and B2B markets, Table 14.1 summarises the impact of the main distinguishing features on the choice of promotional mix. The picture that emerges from this is that B2B markets are very much more dependent on the personal selling element, with advertising and sales promotion playing a strong supporting role.

The converse is generally true in consumer markets. A large number of customers each making relatively low value, frequent purchases can be most efficiently contacted using mass media. Advertising, therefore, comes to the fore, with sales promotion a close second, while personal selling is almost redundant. Figure 14.5 shows this polarisation of B2B and consumer promotional mixes. This does, of course, represent sweeping generalisations about the nature of these markets, which need to be qualified. The product itself, for instance, will influence the shape of the mix, as will the nature of competitive and other environmental pressures. These will be addressed later (pp. 583 *et seq.* and 587 *et seq.*).

Figure 14.4 The communications planning flow

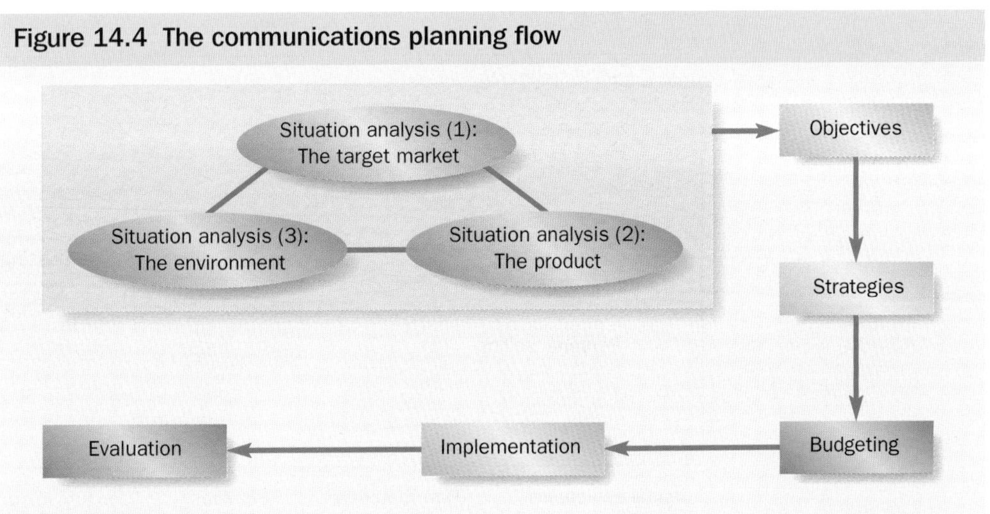

Source: Adapted from figure in Michael L. Rothschild, *Marketing Communications: From Fundamentals to Strategies*, copyright © 1987 D.C. Heath and Company. By permission of Houghton Mifflin Company.

Table 14.1 B2B vs consumer marketing communications: characteristics and implications

B2B	Consumer
Fewer, often identifiable customers • *Personal and personalised communication feasible*	Usually mass, aggregated markets • *Mass communication, e.g. television advertising, most efficient and cost effective*
Complex products, often tailored to individual customer specification • *Need for lengthy buyer–seller dialogue via personal selling*	Standardised products with little scope for negotiation and customisation • *Impersonal channels of communication convey standard message*
High value, high-risk, infrequent purchases • *Need for much information through literature and personal representation, with emphasis on product performance and financial criteria*	Low value, low-risk, frequent purchases • *Less technical emphasis; status and other intangible benefits often stressed; incentives needed to build or break buying habits*
Rational decision-making process over time, with a buying centre taking responsibility • *Need to understand who plays what role and try to influence whole buying centre*	Short time scale, often impulse purchasing by an individual or family buying unit • *Need to understand who plays what role and to try to influence family*

Push or pull strategy

Remember, however, that even consumer goods marketers are likely to have to consider B2B markets in dealing with channels of distribution. Figure 14.6 offers two strategies, push and pull, which emphasise different lines of communication (Oliver and Farris, 1989). With a **push strategy**, the manufacturer chooses to concentrate communications activity on the member of the distribution channel immediately below. This means that the wholesaler, in this example, has a warehouse full of product and thus an incentive to use communication

Figure 14.5 B2B vs consumer promotional mix

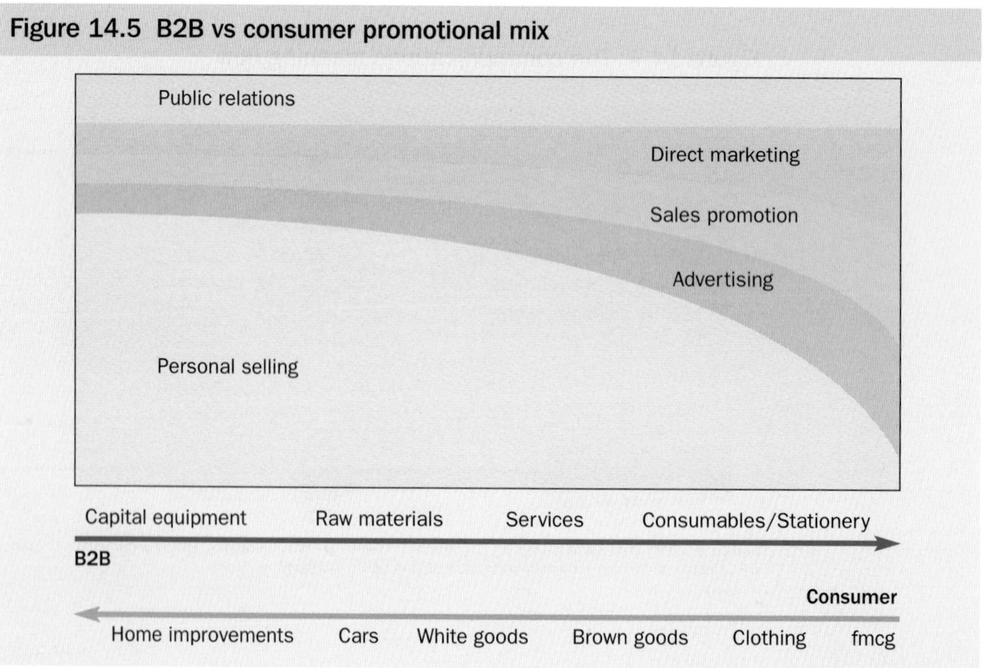

Figure 14.6 Push–pull strategy

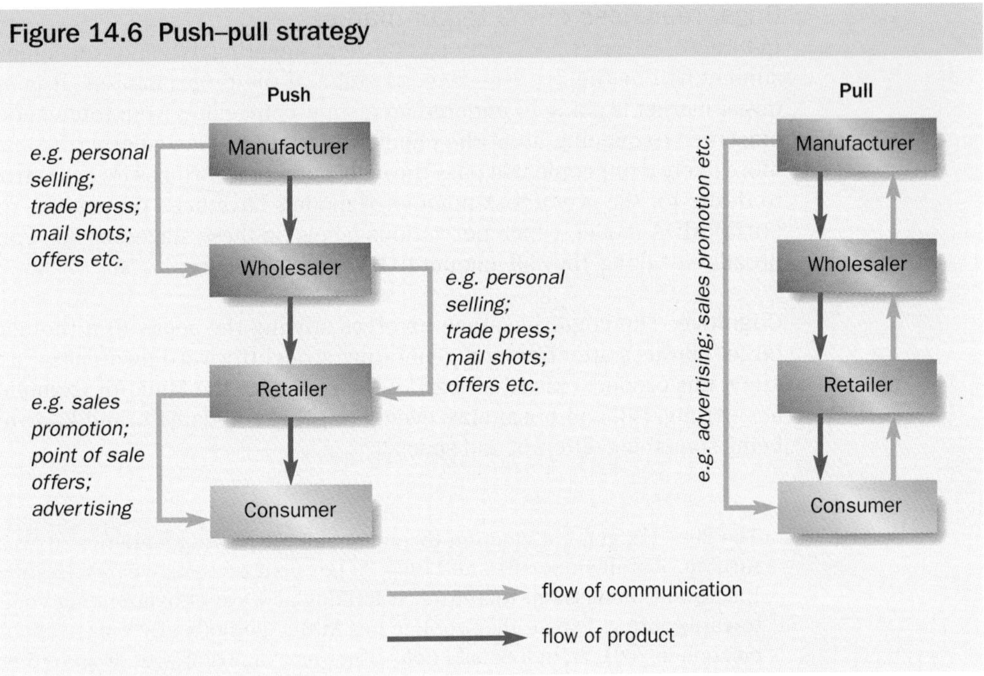

to make a special effort to sell it quickly on to the retailer, who in turn promotes it to the end consumer. The product is thereby pushed down the distribution channel, with communication flowing from member to member in parallel with the product. There is little or no communication between manufacturer and consumer in this case.

In contrast, the **pull strategy** requires the manufacturer to create demand for the product through direct communication with the consumer. The retailers will perceive this demand and, in the interests of serving their customers' needs, will demand the product from their wholesaler, who will demand it from the manufacturer. This bottom-up approach pulls the product down the distribution channel, with communication flowing in the opposite direction from the product!

The reality is, of course, that manufacturers take a middle course, with some pull and some push to create more impetus for the product.

eg

Pharmaceutical companies have to be very careful how they market prescription drugs. Although consumers are the end users of their products, it is doctors who do the prescribing and who are, therefore, the key decision makers. Companies effectively have to use push strategies to ensure that their products make it down the chain as far as the patient. There are, however, restrictions in the UK on what drugs companies can ethically do. Under government rules, companies dealing with the NHS can only offset a maximum of 7 per cent of their sales against marketing and promotion. Furthermore, promotional freebies given to individual doctors cannot be worth more than £5, thus branded pens, notepads and calendars are probably OK, but a meal out in a top restaurant with a sales representative isn't. In addition to advertising in medical journals, direct marketing and visits from sales representatives, an effective means of targeting doctors is through medical conferences and many pharmaceutical companies spend a lot of money sponsoring conferences, exhibiting at them, and entertaining doctors. This is acceptable as long as the conference has clear educational content and any hospitality is 'secondary to the meeting, . . . appropriate and not out of proportion to the occasion'. Educational meetings focused on particular areas of medicine are very useful to the marketers as they help doctors to understand the relative performance of different drugs, and they hear it in detail from reputable colleagues rather than just from a sales representative making a quick visit to the surgery (Benady, D., 2002).

Buyer readiness of the target market

In terms of message formulation, a further tempering influence on communication with consumers will be the **buyer readiness** stage of the target market. It is most unlikely that a target market is going to undergo an instant conversion from total ignorance of a product's existence to queuing up at the checkout to buy it. Particularly in consumer markets, it is more likely that people will pass through a number of stages *en route* from initial awareness to desire for the product. A number of models have been proposed – for example Strong's (1925) AIDA model, which put various labels on these stages, as shown in Figure 14.7 – but broadly speaking, they all amount to the same sequence:

Cognitive. The cognitive stage involves sowing the seeds of a thought, i.e. catching the target market's attention and generating straightforward awareness of the product: 'Yes, I know this product exists.' As part of the launch of the Mini, for example, BMW used media advertising, PR, and hospitality events to get the updated brand known and understood as being something different and special.

eg

The 2001 UK general election threw up some worrying statistics. It was the lowest voter turnout overall since 1918 and only 39 per cent of 18–24-year-olds bothered to vote. The Electoral Commission, therefore, is looking at ways of overcoming young people's apathy towards voting. Part of the problem lies in the methods of voting available. For the general election in 2001, an individual could either have a postal vote or go to their local polling station to write a cross on a ballot paper. It seems as though that was just too much like hard work for many potential voters. More than half of 18–24-year-olds are in favour of telephone or internet voting instead of the traditional methods. The other part of the problem is an education and communications issue. Young people are not interested in politics and don't see the point of voting. The Electoral Commission and the politicians are thus faced with the task of convincing young people that their votes can make a difference on the issues that matter to them.

Changing attitudes will begin in schools as social studies, including voting processes and the creation of legislation as part of the syllabus, becomes part of the national curriculum for 11–16-year-olds. For the current group of 18–24-year-olds, however, the May 2002 local elections were heralded by a radio and poster campaign on the theme of 'Votes are Power' to encourage them to turn out to vote. Overcoming such deep-seated apathy, however, is going to be a long-term task which will need all the tools and skills of the professional marketing communicators (Thurtle, 2002).

Figure 14.7 Response hierarchy models

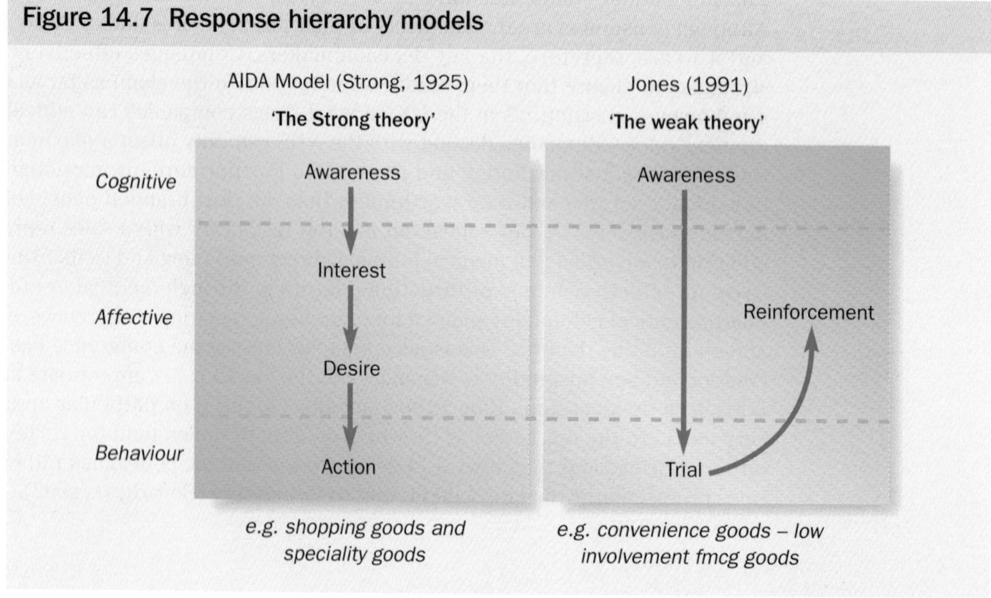

Affective. The affective stage involves creating or changing an attitude, i.e. giving the consumer sufficient information (whether factual or image based) to pass judgement on the product and to develop positive feelings towards it: 'I understand what this product can do for me, and I like the idea of it.'

Behaviour. The behaviour stage involves precipitating action, i.e. where the strength of the positive attitudes generated in the affective stage leads the consumer to desire the product and to do something about acquiring it: 'I want this product and I'm going to go and buy it.' Many press advertisements incorporating a mail order facility are operating at this level.

marketing *in action*

Botton Village

Botton Village, one of eight communities comprising the Camphill Village Trust, is described as a very special place where 160 people with special needs can live in a family community setting that utilises their skills in various craft and agricultural activities. There are five farms and ten workshops on the site selling goods such as hand-crafted toys and organically grown farm produce. Situated in the North Yorkshire Moors national park, the community needs to raise sufficient funds from donors to supplement its income from the state and from its trading activities.

Fund raising is essential for supporting new projects and supplementing income. Open days and fairs are held during the year and a distribution system enables some of the produce, such as foods and toys, to be sold both through local retailers and internationally. It has a regular net surplus income of around £2.0 mn per year raised largely through highly professional and targeted direct marketing. A single mailing can generate between £5,200 and £9,400 per thousand donors mailed in one segment. As a smaller charity, it is not easy for Botton Village to stand out against the better-known charities seeking donations. It has a very small marketing budget, no full- or part-time fund raisers and it needs external professional advice in developing campaigns.

The main problem facing any charity is the danger of donation fatigue or overload. Sometimes mailing lists are shared and special appeals can divert funds, an important obstacle if the donor has a finite limit to spend with charities. It has been estimated that a charity donor can receive up to 12 appeals during a year. The Botton Village approach to mailing its 76,000 active donors is to maintain communication and nurture the relationship throughout the year, not just during a special appeal. After the first donation, a thank-you letter is sent within 48 hours, regardless of the size of donation. An early response is considered important for building the relationship and has been found to affect future giving. Donors also have a wide choice of options, including donation through Gift Aid legacies, and a regular payment plan.

Photograph showing the activities at Botton which appears in promotional material gives donors an insight into the work they are supporting.

Source: Botton Village/Camphill Village Trust.

Four mailings per year are sent out, linked with a newsletter that focuses on the people helped within the community and outlines key activities and future events. It encourages donors to feel involved and to see tangible effects from their giving. The mailing letters are all personalised and vary in appeal depending on the donor plan adopted. All donations are logged on the database and if no further donations are received during the following year, the donor is sent a reminder. If further contact produces no results, the donor is placed in the group that receives only a Christmas card, before finally being dropped after a further two years. Botton is concerned not to be seen as intrusive in its mailings and so donors can opt out of regular communication at any time. Even though some switch to Christmas contact only, donations still run at a high level from this group.

The direct marketing group has been very successful and is now supported by the website. Botton can receive as high as a 50 per cent response rate from some mailings, whereas typical figures are 15 per cent for 'warm' mailings and less than 1 per cent for 'cold' mailings. Even when it shares lists with other charities, it can achieve response rates of around 5 per cent rather than the norm of 1 per cent. The first mailing is crucial and the specially developed pack focuses on the work of the community, its ideals and the lives of those that it is designed to help. By adopting a sensitive and caring approach along with professional marketing, Botton has achieved many of its targets for fund raising.

Sources: Marketing Week (1999); http://www.ukonline.co.uk/botton.village.

The speed with which a target market passes through these stages depends on the kind of product, the target market involved and the marketing strategies adopted by the organisation. Nevertheless, each stage becomes increasingly more difficult to implement, since more is being asked of the consumer. Generating awareness, the first stage, is relatively easy as it involves little risk or commitment from the consumer, and may even operate unconsciously. The second stage needs some effort from consumers if it is to be successful, because they are being asked to assimilate information, process it and form an opinion. The third and final stage requires the most involvement – actually getting up and doing something, which is likely to involve paying out money!

The **Strong (1925) theory of communication** proposed these stages as forming a logical flow of events driven by marketing communication. Advertising, for example, creates the initial awareness, stimulates the interest and then the desire for the product, and only then does trial take place. In other words, the attitude and opinion are formed before the consumer ever gets near the product. There is, however, another school of thought that maintains that it does not always happen like that. The **weak theory of communication** (Jones, 1991) accepts that marketing communication can generate the awareness, but then the consumer might well try the product without having formed any particular attitude or opinion of it. Only then, after the purchase and product trial, does the marketing communication begin to contribute to attitude and opinion working alongside consumer experience of the product. This would make sense for low-involvement products, the frequently purchased boring goods about which it is difficult to get emotional, such as washing powder.

eg

A consumer might see a television advertisement for a new brand of washing powder and then forget about it until the next trip to the supermarket. The consumer sees that new brand on the shelf and thinks, 'Oh yes, I saw an ad for that – I'll give it a try' and buys a packet. Having tried the product, the consumer might decide that it is quite good and then start to pay more attention to the advertising content as a way of legitimising and reinforcing that opinion.

Whatever the route through the response hierarchy, the unique characteristics of each stage imply that differing promotional mixes may be called for to maximise the creative benefits and cost effectiveness of the different promotional tools. Figure 14.8 suggests that advertising is most appropriate at the earliest stage, given its capacity to reach large numbers of people relatively cheaply and quickly with a simple message. Sales promotions can also bring a product name to the fore and help in the affective stage: using a sample that has

Figure 14.8 Buyer readiness stages and the promotional mix

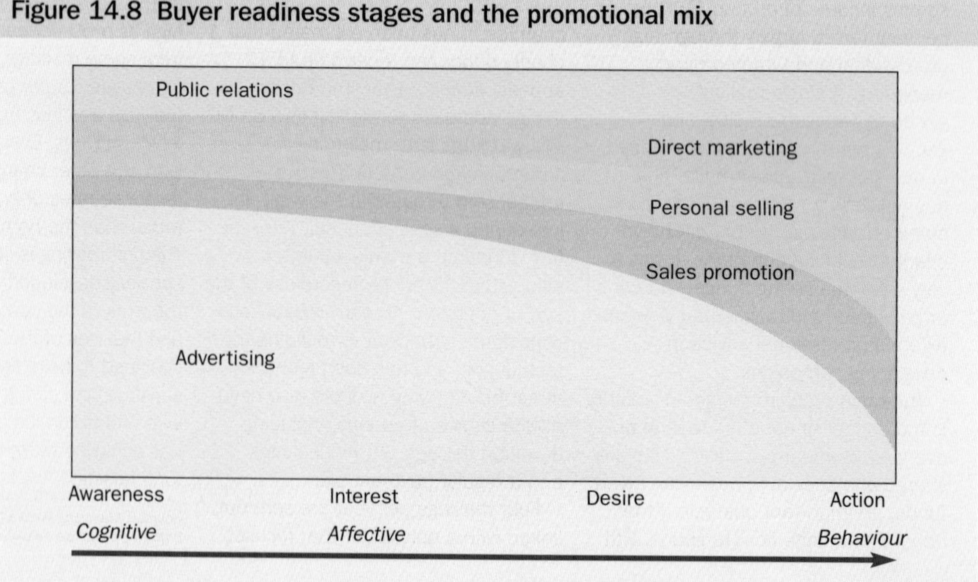

been delivered to the door certainly generates awareness and aids judgement and recognition of a product. Adding a coupon to the sample's packaging is also an incentive to move into the behaviour stage, buying a full-sized package.

Notice that in Figure 14.8 the role of advertising diminishes as the behaviour stage moves closer and personal selling comes to the fore. Advertising can only reiterate and reinforce what consumers already know about the product, and if this wasn't enough to stimulate action the last time they saw/heard it, it may not be so this time either. At this point, potential buyers may just need a last bit of persuasion to tip them over the edge into buying, and that last kick may be best delivered by a sales representative who can reiterate the product benefits, tailoring communication to suit the particular customer's needs and doubts in a two-way dialogue. With many fmcg products sold in supermarkets, however, this is not a feasible option, and the manufacturer relies on the packaging and, to some extent, the sales promotions to do the selling at the point of sale without human intervention. Many fmcg products, therefore, strive for distinctively-coloured packaging that stands out on the supermarket shelf, commanding attention. This issue will be readdressed in the following subsection.

In reality, individuals within the target market may pass through the stages at different times or may take longer to pass from one stage to the next. This means that it may be necessary to develop an integrated promotional mix recognising that the various elements are appealing to sub-segments at different readiness stages, with imagery and content tailored accordingly. The implementation of the various elements may be almost simultaneous, with some fine tuning of the campaign over the longer term.

Knowledge of the target market is an important foundation stone for all of the communication decisions that you are going to make. The more you know about the people you want to talk to, the more likely you are to create successful communication. This does not only mean having a clear demographic profile of the target market, but also having as much detail as possible about their attitudes, beliefs and aspirations, and about their shopping, viewing and reading habits. In addition it is important to understand their relationship with your product and their perceptions of it. This will be explained in relation to communication objectives at pp. 589 *et seq.*

This is a good time for you to look back at Chapter 5 and revise some of the methods of segmenting markets, whether consumer or B2B, since the criteria by which the target market is defined (including product-orientated criteria) may well have a strong influence not only on the broad issue of balancing the promotional mix, but also on the finer detail of media choice and creative content.

Situation analysis (2): the product

Inextricably linked with consideration of the target market is consideration of the *product* involved. This section will look again at the area of B2B and consumer products in the light of the influence of other product characteristics, and then explore the specific influence of the product lifecycle on the promotional mix.

B2B and consumer products

It is simplistic in the extreme to define a product either as a B2B purchase, personal selling being the best way to sell it, or as a consumer product, which must be advertised. Other product characteristics or the buying habits associated with the product may make such a distinction meaningless.

eg

An illustration of this 'grey area' is the sale of double glazing to domestic householders. Strictly speaking, this is a consumer market, in that the product is being purchased by individuals or families for private consumption. There are, however, a number of features suggesting that this particular product has more in common with typical B2B purchases than with other consumer goods. It is an expensive, infrequent purchase with a high level of technical personalisation required to match the product exactly with the customer's needs. It involves a fairly rational decision-making process that takes place over time, and there is a high demand for product information and negotiation before commitment to purchase is made. To the buyer, it is a high-risk purchase that may well involve several members of the family (effectively acting as a buying centre) and will almost certainly involve a great deal of persuasion, reassurance and dialogue from a sales representative.

All these product and customer-orientated characteristics completely override the superficial definition of a consumer product and point to a different kind of promotional mix. Advertising, along with website content, play a role in generating awareness of a double glazing company's existence and in laying the foundations for corporate and product image building. They also prepare the way for the sales representative, since a potential customer who has seen an advertisement for a sales representative's company or has read the information on the website will have an impression of what kind of company this is, and will feel less uneasy about the sales representative's credibility and trustworthiness. The personal selling element is, however, the most important and effective element of this mix because of the need for information, product tailoring and negotiation in the affective and behaviour stages. It is also cost effective in relation to the likely value of a single order.

At one end of the consumer product spectrum, a frequently purchased, low-involvement, low unit price bar of chocolate would not, of course, warrant such an investment in personal selling to millions of end consumers, even if such an exercise were logistically possible. The marketing would be more likely to conform to the standard mix, emphasising mass communication through advertising.

eg

Another example chosen to illustrate the grey area between consumer and B2B markets is that of day-to-day consumable office supplies, such as pencils, pens and paperclips, for small businesses. This has more in common with the chocolate bar than the double glazing, although technically it is a B2B product, in that it is used to support the production of goods for resale. Compared with most B2B purchases, it is a routine re-buy, a low-priced, low-risk, low involvement purchase, probably delegated to an individual who goes out to the nearest stationer's or office supplies retailer at lunchtime with the contents of the petty cash tin. It is simply not cost effective to use personal selling of such a range of products to that buyer who belongs to a large and ill-defined target market (there are thousands of small businesses, in every kind of activity and market, and geographically widespread) and who makes such small-value purchases. At best, personal selling should be targeted at the stationer's or the office supplies retailer.

The two examples above serve as a warning that some B2B products behave more like consumer products and vice versa.

The product lifecycle stage

One further product characteristic that may affect the approach to communication is the *product lifecycle stage* reached (*see* pp. 312 *et seq.*). Since the overall marketing objectives tend to change as the product moves through each stage, it is likely that the specific communications objectives will also change. Different tasks need to be fulfilled and thus the balance of the promotional mix will alter.

Introduction. With the launch of a new consumer product, it is likely that there will be high initial expenditure on the promotional mix. Advertising will ensure that the product name and benefits become known and spread quickly among the target market, while sales promotions, perhaps based on coupons and sampling, help to generate trial of the product. Sales promotions will also be used in conjunction with intense personal selling effort to gain retailer acceptance of the product.

Growth. Communications activity is likely to be a little less intense as the product begins to find its own impetus and both retailers and consumers make repeat purchases. There might

eg

In launching T&T, a new fruit juice-based carbonated soft drink brand, in the UK the manufacturers wanted to gain retail support and to target the brand at teenagers, not only creating awareness of the brand, but taking the consumer right through to desire and action. A campaign was developed which centred on sponsoring the *Popstars* television show, a 13-week talent search which culminated in the creation of the band Hear'Say. Advertising featuring the T&T band (consisting of four different-flavoured cans of T&T) was screened around the programme to reinforce the brand message. This was supported by a website, http://www.ttbeverages.com, featuring games, an instant-win promotion with *Popstars* related prizes, a mail-in promotion offering a *Popstars* CD holder in exchange for six tokens, and a free draw with concert tickets as prizes (http://www.spca.org.uk). Following the initial success of the brand, in January 2002 a further promotion was launched auctioning tickets for the 2002 Brit Awards ceremony among other prizes. Consumers had to collect on-pack tokens and make an online bid for prizes. March 2002 saw the £2 mn 'Keep it Real' campaign launched, centred around youth icon Ali G and linked with the release of his film *Ali G 'Indahouse'*. The T&T website featured an Ali G section with downloadable clips from the movies, games and competitions. By early 2002, two years after the product's launch, the company claimed a 1.5 per cent share of the carbonated drinks market in the UK (not a bad performance, considering that the market is dominated by Coke and Pepsi) and was forecasting a 3 per cent share by the end of 2002, thanks to Ali G (http://www.mason-williams.presscentre.com). Respec.

By linking its T&T drink to the Popstars television show, the manufacturer caught the interest and enthusiasm of the teenage audience it was targeting.

Source: Mason Williams/T&T.

also be less emphasis on awareness generation and information giving, and more on long-term image and loyalty building. As competitors launch similar products, it is important to ensure that differential advantage is maintained, and that customers know exactly why they should continue to buy the original product rather than switching over to a competitor. This could mean a shift towards advertising as a prime means of image creation that works over a longer period.

Maturity. The maturity stage is likely to be a defensive or holding operation, since competitors with younger products may be threatening to take custom away from the product. Most people know about the product, most people (apart from a few laggards) who are likely to try it already have done so. Thus the role of communication is reminding (about the brand image and values) and reassurance (about having chosen the right product), probably through mass advertising. In B2B markets, this stage is likely to be about further developing and consolidating relationships with customers in preparation for newer products in your portfolio.

Decline. Marketing communication is not going to rescue a product that is clearly on its way out; it can only stave off the inevitable for a while. The majority of consumers and, for that matter, distributors, will have already moved on to other products, leaving only a few laggards. A certain level of reminder advertising and sales promotion might keep them in the market for this product for a while, but eventually even they will drift off. There is little point in diverting resources that could be better used on the next new product.

eg

Sunny Delight was launched in the UK market in 1998. Within two years, it had become a firm favourite with £150 mn of sales, second only to Coca-Cola in the UK soft drinks market. It was marketed as 'The great stuff kids love' and the label on the bottle presented it as a 'vitamin-enriched citrus drink'. Parents believed that somehow because it was a fruit-based drink it was healthier for their kids and therefore didn't mind how much of it they drank. During 2000, however, the brand began to attract adverse publicity as parents and food lobby groups cottoned on to the fact that Sunny Delight was only 5 per cent fruit juice and actually contained just as much sugar as Cola drinks. In the year to October 2001, sales fell by 38 per cent. In spring 2002, therefore, Procter and Gamble, Sunny Delight's owner, relaunched a reformulated Sunny Delight brand. New flavours, such as apple, blackcurrant and kiwi, were introduced and the amount of sugar has been cut by 84 per cent. The packaging has also been re-designed to make it look less like a fruit juice. The Original Sunny Delight is still sold alongside the new products. The total investment in the revitalisation of the brand is thought to be some £20 mn, including a £5 mn advertising campaign and £7 mn in direct marketing and sales promotion (Dignam, 2002; Poulter, 2002; Rogers, 2002).

The above analysis assumes that a product takes an unexceptional course through the classical stages of the lifecycle. Many consumer goods, however, are revamped at some time during the maturity stage to extend their lifecycle. In such a case, there is every reason to rethink the communications package and treat the process more like a new product launch. There is much to communicate both to the trade and to the consumer about the 'new improved' brand, the increased value for money, the enhanced performance, more stylish looks or whatever aspects are being emphasised. In a sense, this stage is even more difficult than the new product launch, as the marketer has to tread a fine line between overturning old preconceptions about the product, convincing the market that there is something new to consider and confusing and alienating existing users who might think that the familiar, comforting brand values have been thrown out.

The lifecycle concept, as discussed at pp. 318 *et seq.* does have its problems, and in the context of marketing communication, its unthinking, rigid application as a primary basis for communications planning is dangerous. If a product is assumed to be mature/declining, then the application of a communications package appropriate to that stage may well hasten its demise. There are other, more relevant factors, both internal and external, which should have a far greater bearing on the planning process. Some of the external factors will now be discussed.

eg

Coca-Cola is a very mature, universally known brand which makes repositioning quite difficult. Coke wanted, however, to target 16–24-year-olds and reposition itself among that group as an exciting and relevant teen brand. To involve teenagers, which Coke describes as a difficult-to-target, brand aware and often cynical group, Coke picked up on the idea that while youngsters are happy to buy on the internet, many of them do not have credit cards with which to do it. Thus an auction website was set up (http://www.cokeauction.co.uk) using ring-pulls and labels as an alternative currency. The consumer had to log on to the website, register and open an online account which would be credited with 500 free 'Coke Credits' as a starter. Ring-pulls and labels could then be converted into more credits (10 ring-pulls = 1,000 credits). Using the credits, consumers could then bid for items such as fashion goods, shopping sprees, and a trip to Las Vegas, in auctions. You could even bid to have your face featured on the Coke advertisement in Piccadilly Circus and even for £25,000 towards

University fees and living expenses. The campaign ran for 15 weeks and over 1.1 million visits were made to the site and over 80,000 items were auctioned. Nearly 80 per cent of users were under 29 years old (Brooks, 2000; Gofton, 2000; *The Guardian* (2000); http://www.spca.org.uk).

Situation analysis (3): the environment

Again, some revision of an earlier chapter might stand you in good stead here. Chapter 2 analysed the marketing environment in some detail. This section will, therefore, only look at ways in which environmental elements specifically affect communications.

Social and *cultural* aspects of the environment will mostly have an impact on the message element of communication. What is said about the product and the scenario within which it is depicted in advertisements will reflect what is socially acceptable and culturally familiar to the target market. There must be something that they can recognise, identify with and/or wish to aspire to, if they are going to remember the message, and particularly if they are expected to act on it. This reinforces what was said at p. 577 *et seq.* about the necessity of knowing the target market well.

Organisations are particularly keen to spot changes and shifts in social mores and then to capitalise on them, often creating a bandwagon effect. The 'green' issue is a good example of this. Many companies perceived that there was pressure on them to produce environmentally friendlier products, but rather than lose time in developing really new alternatives (and risk lagging behind their competitors), a few simply created new advertising messages and emphasised green-orientated product claims on their packaging to create the desired image. However, questionable approaches have been widely publicised, such as labelling washing-up liquid 'phosphate free', when that kind of product doesn't ever contain phosphate anyway, and emphasising that packaging can be recycled when the recycling facilities do not exist, leading to confusion and suspicion in the consumer's mind about all green claims. Peattie (1992) offers a concise but thorough review of green marketing communication and how it should be done.

eg

During the 1990s the safety of silicone breast implants was publicly questioned on several occasions. Activated by anti-implant groups such as Silicone Support and Survivors of Silicone, stories in television documentaries and in the press linked the implants with silicone poisoning and sometimes deformity caused by poor surgery. The Conservatives (twice) and the Labour party both instigated reviews in the UK that could have resulted in the banning or severe restriction of implant use. That would have been bad news for McGhan breast implants from the market leader Inner Medical. A successful PR campaign was mounted by McGhan to remind journalists, politicians and the wider public that breast implants were used not just for cosmetic reasons, but also for reconstruction after a mastectomy (*PR Week*, 1999).

The most recent governmental review was set up in 1997 and concluded on scientific grounds that silicone was as safe as any other material used in implants, although there were grounds for improving the information available to women so that they could make informed choices. The Independent Review Group consists of people with no vested interests in the subject, and its first report was published by the Chief Medical Officer in May 1998. The sources included implanted women, doctors, lawyers, women's support groups and Members of Parliament capable of studying the scientific evidence from the USA (http://www.silicone-review.gov.uk). Although the industry had a direct opportunity to put its case to the review group, the PR campaign helped to ensure that an alternative view was presented to a public that was starting to believe the negative publicity about implants.

The controversy continues, however. The European Commission is considering tightening up the rules on breast implants which would mean that implants would only be available for those aged 18 or over; there would have to be independent counselling before and after surgery; and there would be compulsory national registers of every implant operation carried out (Castle, 2001). For the manufacturers of silicone implants, this is still better than an outright ban, although that has not been ruled out as studies into their long-term safety are ongoing.

A more general criticism of advertisers' influence in the social and cultural area is about their alleged use and reinforcement of stereotypes. The advertisers argue that they simply reflect society as it is, and that it is not their business to change it – they *respond* to the customer's changing attitudes and lifestyle. Should there, however, be concern that if people see stereotypes being constantly presented through advertising as the norm, and even as states to be aspired to, then maybe the impetus to question their validity and to break them will be less urgent? This is a complex 'chicken and egg' debate that you may want to pursue for yourself outside these pages. There are no easy answers.

To be fair to the advertisers, the whole area of stereotypes does perhaps present one of the great insoluble dilemmas of mass communication. In moving away from one stereotype, it is too easy to replace it with another. Because the advertiser is trying to appeal to a relatively large number of individuals (even in a niche market), it is impossible to create an image that reflects every member of the target market in detail. What emerges, therefore, is a superficial sketch of the essential characteristics of that group and its aspirations, i.e. a stereotype! Thus the stereotypical housewife who lives in the kitchen and is fulfilled through the quality of her cooking has been usurped at the opposite extreme by the equally unrealistic power dressing, independent dragon of the board room with the slightest whiff of Chanel and femininity. It seems that the advertisers cannot win.

eg

Stereotypes can provide a rich seam of humour in advertising. In a television advertisement for Bounty kitchen roll, two big, hairy, unshaven labourers dressed in pretty print frocks and dire wigs, 'Barbara' and 'Maureen', race each other to see whose kitchen roll can clean 'her' hob without disintegrating. It offers an ironic, self-depreciating twist on the well-established and well-understood housewife stereotype that appeals to the modern woman for whom cleaning a hob is not the single most satisfying experience in life. It has to be said too that the formula works: the message that Bounty is stronger and better is clearly stated and demonstrated by the advertisement and perhaps is made all the more memorable by the jokey execution. Another jokey execution ran into trouble over stereotyping, however. Retailer WH Smith ran a series of advertisements featuring a middle-class family from the south of England visiting their rather unsophisticated relatives in Newcastle-upon-Tyne who were all portrayed as extremely overweight and speaking in broad Geordie accents. All the characters were played by popular actor Nicholas Lyndhurst. The ITC received 129 complaints from people who saw the advertisements as offensive stereotypes of Newcastle people and/or overweight people. The ITC decided that the portrayal of overweight people was exaggerated and unreal and that it was just sufficient to reduce the risk of causing distress or harm. The Geordie stereotyping was felt to have remained within the boundaries of acceptable humour and was unlikely to have caused much offence. The complaints were not, therefore, upheld (http://www.itc.org.uk).

No communications plan can be shaped without some reference to what *competitors* are doing or are likely to do, given the necessity of emphasising the differential advantage and positioning of the product in relation to theirs. This could affect every stage of the planning, from the definition of objectives, through the creative strategy, to the setting of budgets. These themes will be taken up under the appropriate headings later in this chapter, and will also feature in the chapters on the individual tools of the promotional mix.

Another important factor to take into account is the *legal/regulatory* environment, as discussed in Chapter 2. Some products are restricted as to where and when they can be advertised. In the UK, for instance, cigarette advertising is not permitted on television. Restrictions may also exist about what can or must be said or shown in relation to the product. Toy advertising cannot imply a social disadvantage through not owning a product, and must also indicate the price of the toy. More generally, advertising aimed at children cannot encourage them to pester their parents to purchase (not that they normally need encouragement). Some regulations are enshrined in law, while others are imposed and applied through monitoring watchdog bodies such as the Advertising Standards Authority. Professional bodies, such as the UK's Institute of Sales Promotion or the Direct Marketing Association, often develop codes of practice to which their members undertake to adhere. As yet, no unified codes have been developed that apply across Europe.

corporate social responsibility *in action*

Don't drink and advertise!

The advertising and promotion of certain product categories such as alcohol are very closely regulated in the UK. The ASA (Advertising Standards Authority) regulates print, cinema, outdoor and electronic media and sales promotions while the ITC (Independent Television Commission) and the RA (Radio Authority) regulate broadcast media, although the ASA and ITC codes on alcoholic drinks are very similar. The ASA code, *British Codes of Advertising and Sales Promotion*, allows humour in advertising, but says that advertisements should not lead people towards unwise drinking habits. They should be socially responsible and not encourage excessive drinking. The code also states that advertisements should not in any way target the under-18s in terms of their content, imagery or their use of real or fictional characters, nor should advertisements appear in any medium if more than 25 per cent of its audience is under 18. People in advertisements shown drinking alcohol cannot appear to be under 25 years old.

Advertisers also have to be careful of the claims they make for their products: they can give factual information about the strength of the drink, but cannot make strength or the drink's capacity to get you drunk the major theme of the advertisement; they cannot claim that the drink will make you more popular, more sexy, or more successful; and they cannot claim that people who drink are brave, tough or daring for doing so. Advertisements cannot show alcohol being consumed in situations in which it would be dangerous or in which concentration is essential, for example driving or operating machinery.

These rules inevitably lead to complaints to the ITC and the ASA as advertisers strive to understand where the boundaries of acceptability lie, and as consumers put their own interpretations on messages (the invisible penis – see below – being a prime example of an advertiser being criticised for something that isn't actually in the advertisement at all!). In 2000, complaints were made to the ASA over a poster campaign for the brand Red Square. One poster featured the boxer Lennox Lewis and the words 'energising Red Square and Lennox Lewis – a winning combination'. The ASA felt that the association between sport and alcohol implied that alcohol was healthy, and furthermore, that the use of the word 'energising' could encourage people to consume the product before sport or exercise. 'Energising' was also criticised as misleading because alcohol is essentially a depressant. Nor did the ASA like the use of 'winning combination' as it suggests a link between alcohol and sporting achievement. The company was asked to drop the energising claim altogether and to change its overall approach in future.

Posters for Smirnoff Vodka have also been the subject of ASA scrutiny. One poster showed a naked man (and complainants believed that his penis was actually visible) sliding down a banister with a large round finial at the bottom. The slogan was 'If Smirnoff made painkillers'. While the advertiser made it clear that the man had actually been wearing flesh-coloured pants, the ASA felt that the public belief that there was a visible penis in the picture was sufficient to render the poster offensive and therefore that complaint was upheld. Not so much above-the-line as below-the-belt advertising. Perhaps more seriously, the ASA also decided that although the poster was clearly meant to be humourous and surreal, it did depict drunken activity and could encourage excessive drinking, and therefore the advertiser should change the approach in future.

By no means are all complaints upheld. The ITC looked into complaints that a television advertisement for Miller Genuine Draft condoned and encouraged drinking and driving. The advertisement showed members of the rock band Fun Lovin' Criminals getting bored in a traffic jam, drinking their Miller Genuine Draft and then performing an impromptu concert at the side of the road. The complaints were not upheld because, the ITC felt, the band were clearly shown only as passengers in a stationary car. There was no implication that any of those seen drinking were or had been doing any driving.

Sources: http://www.asa.org.uk; http://www.itc.org.uk.

Objectives

Now that the background is in place and there exists a detailed profile of the customer, the product and the environment, it is possible to define detailed objectives for the communications campaign.

Table 14.2, based on the work of DeLozier (1975), summarises and categorises possible communications objectives. The first group relates to awareness, information and attitude generation, while the second group is about affecting behaviour. The final group consists of corporate objectives, a timely reminder that marketing communications planning is not only about achieving the goals of brand managers or marketing managers, but also about the contribution of marketing activity to the wider strategic good of the organisation.

What Table 14.2 does not do is to distinguish between short-, medium- and long-term objectives. Obviously, the short-term activities are the most pressing and are going to demand more detailed planning, but there does still need to be an appreciation of what happens next. The nature and character of medium- and longer-term objectives will inevitably

Table 14.2 Possible communications objectives

Area	*Objective*
Cognitive	Clarify customer needs Increase brand awareness Increase product knowledge
Affective	Improve brand image Improve company image Increase brand preference
Behaviour	Stimulate search behaviour Increase trial purchases Increase repurchase rate Increase word-of-mouth recommendation
Corporate	Improved financial position Increase flexibility of corporate image Increase cooperation from the trade Enhance reputation with key publics Build up management ego

Source: Copyright © 1975 The Estate of the late Professor M. Wayne DeLozier.

be shaped by short-term activity (and its degree of success), but it is also true that short-term activity can only be fully justified when it is put into the context of the wider picture.

Finally, Table 14.2 also stresses the importance of precision, practicality and measurability in setting objectives. Vague, open objectives such as 'to increase awareness of the product' are insufficient. Who do you want to become aware of the product: the retail trade, the general public, or a specific target segment? How much awareness are you aiming to generate within the defined group and within what time scale? A more useful objective might therefore be 'to generate 75 per cent awareness of the product within three months among A, B and C1 home-owners aged between 25 and 40 with incomes in excess of £25,000 per annum who are interested in opera and the environment'.

Until such precise definitions of objectives have been made, the rest of the planning process cannot really go ahead – how can decisions be made if you don't really know what it is you are aiming for? Precise objectives also provide the foundation for monitoring, feedback and assessment of the success of the communications mix. There is at least something against which to measure actual performance.

Strategies

Having defined objectives, it is now necessary to devise strategies for achieving them. The analysis done so far may already have established the broad balance of the promotional mix, but there is still the task of developing the fine detail of what the actual message is to be, how best to frame it and what medium or media can be used to communicate it most efficiently and effectively.

eg

Cadbury's Txt'n'Win was an interesting interactive sales promotion using text messaging. The promotion primarily targeted 16–24-year-olds, who are well used to texting as a means of communication. Codes were printed inside Cadbury's chocolate bar wrappers which the consumer had to text to a given telephone number to find out whether or not they had won. The promotion was supported by radio advertising and internet activity. In eight weeks, 2.3 million entries had been received, representing about 3.5 per cent of consumers and almost twice the response of previous comparable promotions, allowing Cadbury's to capture detailed customer data that can be used in more targeted campaigns in the future (http://www.spca.org.uk).

Designing the message content, structure and format poses questions for managing any element of the promotional mix. Message content is about what the sender wants to say, while message structure is about how to say it in terms of propositions and arguments. The message format depends on the choice of media used for transmitting or transferring the message. This will determine whether sight, sound, colour or other stimuli can be used effectively. These are important themes, which will be further addressed in the context of each element of the promotional mix in the following five chapters. A money-off sales promotion, for example, is certainly appropriate for stimulating short-term sales of a product, but will it cheapen the product's quality image in the eyes of the target market? Is the target market likely to respond to a cash saving, or would they be more appreciative of a charity tie-in where a donation is made to a specific charity for every unit sold? The latter suggestion has the added benefit of enhancing corporate as well as brand image, and is also less easy for the competition to copy.

With advertising in particular, the organisation might use a character or a celebrity to communicate a message on its behalf to give it **source credibility**. The audience will see the spokesperson as the source of the message and thus might pay more attention to it or interpret it as having more credibility (Hirschman, 1987).

marketing ***in action***

Would you buy anything from these people?

Using celebrities in advertising can make a big impact. The charity Respect for Animals made a 60-second film called *Fur and Against*, attacking the use of fur in the fashion industry to coincide with the 2002 London Fashion Week. The film featured actors Jude Law and Sadie Frost, singers Sir Paul McCartney, George Michael, Moby, Chrissy Hynde and Mel C., fashion designer Stella McCartney and model Helena Christensen. The advertising agency that made the film argued that 'The use of celebrity works on three levels: to create a powerful anti-fur message to the general public; as a celebrity-to-celebrity message to the fashion industry; and on a craft level' (as quoted by Benady, A., 2002). There is also a view, however, that the use of celebrities can be dangerous, especially for a charity, because it could trivialise the message or even sabotage it. There should be a clear link between the celebrity and the cause. Thus Michael J. Fox makes sense as a spokesperson for Parkinson's disease, but David Ginola and landmines is a more problematic linkage. Sabotage may be inadvertent: the use of Geri Halliwell in a breast cancer campaign created concern among younger women rather than raising awareness among the real at-risk target group of older women.

There is also a risk that celebrities will fail to live up to the high ethical standards they endorse. Naomi Campbell appeared in a PR stunt on behalf of PETA, 'I'd rather go naked than wear fur', yet not long afterwards was back on the catwalk . . . modelling fur.

Even for mainstream fmcg goods, experts constantly stress the need to achieve a good fit between the celebrity and the product. Coca-Cola is endorsed by teen pop star Christina Aguilera, while Britney Spears represents Pepsi. She fits the young profile of customers that Pepsi is trying to attract and as she grows up from 'kid star to broad based pop star', as Pepsi puts it, Pepsi's marketing will evolve accordingly. Her contract with Pepsi is estimated to be worth around $2 mn per year. Once a celebrity has been associated with a product, their every appearance in the media acts as a reminder. And yet, 'Success depends on the personality of the celebrity and how well they fit with the brand and the advertising idea. Spurious celebrity campaigns don't work', said one agency. A series of John Cleese advertisements for Sainsbury's failed partly because the agency assumed that his Basil Fawlty character *per se* would sell the product and forgot the core advertising skills of engaging the audience and creating a believable scenario and claims for the product. 'Where a celebrity is used for celebrity's sake they rarely have the power to motivate consumption and purchase. When they are used in a way that's relevant to the product advertised, in an engaging, believable manner, then the ad has a lot of power.' (Don Dillon, European Regional Director, McCann Erickson as quoted by Cowen, 2000).

There is a need, therefore, to find a celebrity who sums up the values that you want to associate with the product and then spend a lot of time and money building up the association between celebrity and product. There is a risk of 'promiscuous' celebrities diluting the effect of the association by endorsing so many products that nobody knows what they really stand for. There is also a risk that a celebrity will 'misbehave', courting bad publicity, or that they will be caught doing something that questions their endorsement of the brand. In October 2001, for example, Pepsi's Britney Spears was caught drinking Coke by an Australian newspaper. Oops I did it again, as the diva herself might say.

While not quite in the same league as Britney, Gary Lineker, ex-England football captain turned television presenter, signed a £1.5 mn five-year deal with Walker's Crisps in 2000.

His contract also has an exclusivity clause preventing him from endorsing any other product during that time to avoid any confusion about what brand Lineker represents. Walker's is running a bit of a risk, however. It has been using Lineker since 1994 and over the years, the brand has become almost inseparable from Lineker, thus the size of the new contract's fee is perhaps not so surprising. If this five-year association with Lineker is equally successful, what will it cost Walker's to renew it again? Meanwhile, in the run up to the 2002 World Cup, England captain David Beckham signed a (reportedly) £100,000 deal to promote Golden Wonder snack brands, including Wotsits Goalden Balls. This could cause some interesting debate in the Beckham household, as David's wife Victoria 'Posh' Beckham is endorsing Walker's upmarket crisps, Sensations.

The actual cost of using a celebrity can vary widely. According to Hampton (2001), it can cost anything up to £3 mn to get a celebrity to endorse a product; £100,000 or more if they are to star in a television advertisement; and up to £50,000 for a voice-over in a television advertisement. Is the cost justified, however? Bashford (2001) cites research showing that 91 per cent of UK consumers say that celebrity endorsement makes no difference to whether or not they purchase a product, and 4 per cent said that it would make them less likely to buy. The 16–24-year-olds, however, are more likely to be swayed: 13 per cent of them said that celebrity endorsement would make them more likely to buy.

Sources: Bashford (2001); Benady, A. (2002); Bruss (2001); Conlan (2002); Cowen (2000); Hampton (2001); Kleinman (2002).

Whether the spokesperson, or presenter of the message, is a well-known celebrity or an invented character, it is important to link their characteristics with the communication objectives, as seen in Table 14.3.

Table 14.3 The VisCAP model of presenter characteristics and communication objectives

Presenter characteristics	*Communication objectives*
Visibility • How well known the presenter is	Brand awareness
Credibility	
(i) Expertise • *Knowledge about the product category*	Information and attitude building • *Both low and high involvement products*
(ii) Objectivity • *Reputation for honesty and sincerity*	Information and attitude building • *High-involvement products*
Attraction	
(i) Likeability • *Attractive appearance and personality*	Changing attitudes towards the brand • *Low involvement products*
(ii) Similarity • *To target audience members*	Changing attitudes towards the brand • *High involvement products*
Power • *Authoritative occupation or personality*	Create intention to purchase

Source: Based on table from *Advertising and Promotion Management*, McGraw-Hill, (Rossiter, J.R., and Percy, L., 1987), Copyright © 1987 The McGraw-Hill Companies. Inc.

The marketing manager might also have to decide whether or not to use personal or impersonal media. Table 14.4 compares the marketing advantages and disadvantages of a range of media, from informal word-of-mouth contact such as friends recommending products to each other through to a formal professional face-to-face pitch from a sales representative.

Whichever element of the communications mix is being used, the important consideration is to match the message and media with both the target audience and the defined objectives. These issues are covered in further detail for each element of the mix in the following chapters.

Table 14.4 Comparison of personal and impersonal media for communications

	Word of mouth	Sales representative	Personalised mail shot	Mass media advertising
Accuracy and consistency of delivery	Questionable	Good	Excellent	Excellent
Likely completeness of message	Questionable	Good	Excellent	Excellent
Controllability of content	None	Good	Excellent	Excellent
Ability to convey complexity	Questionable	Excellent	Good	Relatively poor
Flexibility and tailoring of message	Good	Excellent	Good	None
Ability to target	None	Excellent	Good	Relatively poor
Reach	Patchy	Relatively poor	Excellent	Excellent
Feedback collection	None	Excellent – immediate	Possible – depends on response mechanism	Difficult – costly and time consuming
	Personal ←			→ **Impersonal**

Budgeting

Controlled communication is rarely free. The marketer has to develop campaigns within (often) tight budgets, or fight for a larger share of available resources. It is important, therefore, to develop a budgeting method that produces a realistic figure for the marketer to work with in order to achieve objectives. Even in the same sector, the spend on advertising can vary considerably. In the chicken and burger fast food sector, for example, in 2000, McDonald's spent around £42.3 mn on advertising, while its biggest-spending rivals, KFC and Burger King, spent £12.9 mn and £11.3 mn respectively (Mintel, 2002b). Similarly, in laundry products, Lever Fabergé spent £20 mn advertising Persil, while Procter and Gamble (P&G) spent only £8.5 mn advertising the Ariel brand in 2000. The 2001 figures look very different, however: in the first ten months of 2001, P&G spent £16.7 mn on Ariel while Lever Fabergé spent £17.4 mn on Persil (Mintel, 2002a).

There are six main methods of budget setting, some of which are better suited to predictable, static markets, rather than dynamic, fast-changing situations.

Judgemental budget setting

The first group of methods of determining budgets are called **judgemental budget** setting because they all involve some degree of guesswork.

Arbitrary budgets. Arbitrary budgets are based on what has always been spent in the past or, for a new product, on what is usually spent on that kind of thing.

Affordable method. The affordable budget, closely linked to the arbitrary budget, is one which, as its name implies, imposes a limit based either on what is left over after other more important expenses have been met or on what the company accountant feels to be the maximum allowable. Hooley and Lynch (1985) suggest that this method is used in product-led rather than in marketing-led organisations because it is not actually linked with what is to be achieved in the marketplace.

Percentage of past sales method. The percentage of past sales method is at least better, in that it acknowledges some link between communication and sales, even though the link is illogical. The chief assumptions here are that sales precede communication, and that future activities should be entirely dependent on past performance. Taken to its extreme, it is easy to imagine a situation in which a product has a bad year, therefore its communication budget is cut, causing it to perform even more poorly, continuing in a downward spiral until it dies completely. The judgemental element here is deciding what percentage to apply. There are industry norms for various markets; for example in the pharmaceutical industry, 10 to 20 per cent is a typical advertising/sales ratio, but this drops to less than 1 per cent in clothing and footwear. For industrial equipment the advertising/sales ratio is often lower than 1 per cent although the sales force cost/sales ratio is often considerably higher in such industries. However, this is only part of the picture. The industrial equipment manufacturer might well invest much more in its sales force. Such percentages might simply be the cumulative habits of many organisations and thus might be questionable when considered in the context of the organisation's own position and ambitions within the market.

Percentage of future sales method. None of the budgeting methods so far considered takes any account of the future needs of the product itself. However, the percentage of future sales method is an improvement, in that communication and sales are in the right order, but again there is the question of what percentage to apply. There is also an underlying assumption about there being a direct relationship between next year's expenditure and next year's sales.

Data-based budget setting

None of the methods examined so far has taken account of communications objectives – a reminder/reinforcement operation is much cheaper than a major attitude change exercise – or indeed of the quality or cost effectiveness of the communication activities undertaken. There is a grave risk that the money allocated will be insufficient to achieve any real progress, in which case it will have been wasted. This then paves the way for the second group of techniques, called **data-based budget setting** methods, which eliminate the worst of the judgemental aspects of budgeting.

Competitive parity. The competitive parity method involves discovering what the competition is spending and then matching or exceeding it. It has some logic, in that if you are shouting as loudly as someone else, then you have a better chance of being heard than if you are whispering. In marketing, however, it is not necessarily the volume of noise so much as the quality of noise that determines whether the message gets across and is acted on.

If it is to have any credibility at all, then the competitive parity method must take into account competitors' own communications objectives, how they compare with yours and how efficiently and effectively they are spending their money. For all you know, the competitors have set their budgets by looking at how much you spent last year, which takes you all back into a stalemate similar to that of the arbitrary budget method.

Objective and task budgeting. The final method of budgeting, arguably the best, is objective and task budgeting. This is naturally the most difficult to implement successfully. It does, however, solve many of the dilemmas posed so far and makes most commercial sense. It requires the organisation to work backwards. First define the communications objectives, then work out exactly what has to be done to achieve them. This can be costed to provide a budget that is directly linked to the product's needs and is neither more nor less than that required. A new product, for example, will need substantial investment in integrated marketing communication in order to gain acceptance within distribution channels, and then to generate awareness and trial among consumers. A mature product, in contrast, might need only 'maintenance' support, which will clearly cost much less. The only danger with objective and task budgeting, however, is that ambition overtakes common sense, leading to a budget that simply will not be accepted.

The art of making this technique work lies in refining the objectives and the ensuing budget in the light of what the organisation can bear. It may mean taking a little longer than you would like to establish the product, or finding cheaper, more creative ways of achieving objectives, but at least the problems to be faced will be known in advance and can be strategically managed.

eg

The European Central Bank (ECB) was faced with a huge challenge in planning a large pan-European campaign to launch the euro on 1 January 2002. A mix of PR, direct marketing and above the line advertising was required to inform individuals and organisations about the changeover arrangements in the Eurozone countries as well as ensuring that the look, feel, size, denominations and security features of the new currency would be recognisable to everyone. A PR campaign running throughout 2001 constantly disseminated information through the media, while a mass media campaign with broadcast and print advertising began in September 2001 along with a public information leaflet drop to 300 million Europeans. The mass media campaign centred around the slogan 'The Euro. Our Money', and a single campaign was translated into 11 languages rather than trying to develop a different campaign for each country. Publicis was the agency which developed the campaign in liaison with the ECB, national central banks, government finance ministries and other bodies. The agency had 70 staff working on the project, including 30 at a specially-opened 'Euro Buro' office near the ECB headquarters coordinating teams at other Publicis offices across Europe. The objectives of this integrated campaign were non-negotiable and had to be achieved if the euro launch was going to run smoothly. The campaign was designed around those objectives, and the cost is reported to have been between £50 and £80 mn (*Financial Times*, 2001; Garrett, 1999; http://www.euro.ecb.int).

Mitchell (1993), as reported by Fill (2002), suggested that 40 per cent of companies use the objective and task method, while 27 per cent use a percentage of future sales, 8 per cent use a percentage of past sales, and 19 per cent use their own methods. Overall, across the whole promotional mix, organisations are likely to use some kind of composite method that includes elements of judgemental and data-based techniques (Fill, 2002).

Positioning the budgeting element so late in the planning flow does imply that the objective and task method is the preferred one. To reiterate, there is no point in throwing more money at the communication problem than is strictly necessary or justifiable in terms of future aims, and equally, spending too little to make an impact is just as wasteful.

Implementation and evaluation

The aim of planning is *not* to create an impressive, aesthetically pleasing document that promptly gets locked in a filing cabinet for a year. It is too easy for the planning process to become an isolated activity, undertaken as an end in itself with too little thought about the realities of the world and the practical problems of making things happen as you want them to. Throughout the planning stages, there must be due consideration given to 'what if . . .' scenarios and due respect given to what is practicable and manageable. That is not to say that an organisation should be timid in what it aims to achieve, but rather that risks should be well calculated.

Planning also helps to establish priorities, allocate responsibilities and ensure a fully integrated, consistent approach, maximising the benefits gained from all elements of the communications mix. In reality, budgets are never big enough to do everything, and something has to be sacrificed. Inevitably, different activities will be championed by different managers and these tensions have to be resolved within the planning framework. For example, many organisations are reappraising the cost effectiveness of personal selling in the light of developments in the field of direct marketing.

An equally important activity is collecting feedback. You have been communicating with a purpose and you need to know at least whether that purpose is being fulfilled. Monitoring during the campaign helps to assess early on whether or not the objectives are being met as expected. If it is really necessary, corrective action can thus be taken before too much time and money is wasted or, even worse, before too much damage is done to the product's image.

It is not enough, however, to say that the promotional mix was designed to generate sales and we have sold this much product, and therefore it was a success. The analysis needs to be deeper than this – after all, a great deal of time and money has been invested in this communication programme. What aspects of the promotional mix worked best and most cost effectively? Was there sufficient synergy between them? Do we have the right balance within each element of the mix, for example choice of advertising media? Are consumers' attitudes and beliefs about our product the ones we expected and wanted them to develop? Have we generated the required long-term loyalty to the product?

It is only through persistent and painstaking research effort that these sorts of question are going to be answered. Such answers not only help to analyse how perceptive past planning efforts were, but also provide the basis for future planning activity. They begin to shape the nature and objectives of the continued communication task ahead and, through helping managers to learn from successes and mistakes, lead to a more efficient use of skills and resources. The following chapters will discuss some of the techniques and problems of collecting feedback on specific elements of the promotional mix, and Chapter 6 is also relevant in a more general sense.

Communications planning model: review

Rothschild's (1987) model of the communications planning process (see Figure 14.4) is an invaluable framework, as it includes all the main issues to be considered in balancing the promotional mix. In reality, however, the process cannot be as clear cut or neatly divided as the model suggests. Planning has to be an iterative and dynamic process, producing plans that are sufficiently flexible and open to allow adaptation in the light of emerging experience, opportunities and threats.

It is also easy, when presented with a flow-chart type of model like this one, to make assumptions about cause and effect. There is a great deal of logic and sense in the sequencing of decisions indicated by this model – definition of target market defines objectives; objectives determine strategies; strategies determine budgets and so on – but in reality there have to be feedback loops between the later and earlier elements of the model. Budgets, for instance, are likely to become a limiting factor that may cause revision of strategies and/or objectives and/or target market detail. Objective and task is the preferred approach to budget setting, but it still has to be operated within the framework of the resources that the organisation can reasonably and justifiably be expected to marshal, as discussed earlier.

The concluding messages are, therefore, that the planning process:

1 is very important for achieving commercial objectives effectively and efficiently;
2 should not be viewed as a series of discrete steps in a rigid sequence;
3 should not be an end in itself, but should be regarded as only a beginning;
4 should produce plans that are open to review and revision as appropriate;
5 should be undertaken in the light of what is reasonably achievable and practicable for the organisation;
6 should be assessed with the benefit of hindsight and feedback so that next year it will work even better.

Chapter 21 looks at marketing planning more generally, and will further discuss the techniques and problems of implementing plans within the organisational culture.

Chapter summary

- Communications theory indicates that a number of dynamic elements are involved in a piece of communication, each of which has the potential to make the process break down. In a marketing context, these risks have to be understood and minimised, given the importance of effective communication to the success of products and given the level of investment often required for integrated marketing communication activity. The main stages in the planning flow include analysing the situation, defining objectives, defining strategies, setting budgets and implementation and evaluation.

- Communications objectives must be precise, practical and measurable. They can be cognitive (e.g. creating awareness and disseminating knowledge), affective (e.g. creating and manipulating brand images); behavioural (e.g. stimulating the consumer to purchase action) or corporate (e.g. building and enhancing corporate image).
- Different promotional tools are effective for different types of objective. While advertising might be more appropriate for cognitive objectives, personal selling and sales promotions could be better for behavioural objectives, for example. Direct marketing can be very useful in creating and enhancing longer-term relationships with customers.
- Communications budgets can be set in a number of ways. Judgemental methods involve a degree of guesswork, for example being set arbitrarily or on the basis of what can be afforded. They can also be set on the basis of expected future sales, or made dependent on historical sales figures. Data-based methods are more closely related to what is actually happening in the marketplace and include competitive parity and the objective and task method.

key words and phrases

Buyer readiness
Channel of communication
Communication
Data-based budget setting
Decoding
Encoding
Feedback
Judgemental budget setting
Noise
Pull strategy
Push strategy
Source credibility
Strong theory of communication
Weak theory of communication

questions *for review*

14.1 What are the five main elements of the *promotional mix*?

14.2 What are the stages in the *marketing communications planning flow*?

14.3 What are the three broad stages of *buyer readiness*, and how might the balance of the promotional mix vary between them?

14.4 What are the main categories of *marketing communication objectives*?

14.5 What are the six main methods of *budget setting*?

questions *for discussion*

14.1 Within a marketing communication model, give three specific examples of noise, outlining how it might disrupt the communication process.

14.2 How and why might the balance of the promotional mix differ between:
(a) the sale of a car to a private individual; and
(b) the sale of a fleet of cars to an organisation for its sales representatives?

14.3 For each of the STEP factors of the marketing environment, give three examples of influences on the promotional mix.

14.4 What are the main advantages and disadvantages of *objective and task* budget setting compared with the other methods?

14.5 To what extent do you think that the advantages of using a systematic planning process for integrated marketing communication outweigh the disadvantages?

case study 14.1

Xbox: the mean green machine

'I don't think the gaming industry has ever had as much energy as it has now. We're entering the golden age of gaming. Whatever happens, there will be better games on every platform because Microsoft have come in and set a new standard and, when Sony or Nintendo release their next machines, they're going to be completely different. Why? Because of Xbox.' (Richard Teversham, Xbox's Head of UK Marketing as quoted on http://www.gamesradar.com)

So what is the Xbox? It is Microsoft's first foray into the fast-moving world of computer games consoles. It's a highly competitive world too, dominated by Sony (PlayStation2) and Nintendo (Gameboy Advance), but a lucrative one. The global video game market is said to be worth \$20 bn and analysts estimate that by 2005, the annual market for games consoles alone will be worth £28 bn. In the UK alone, it is forecast that the computer games market in 2002 will be worth £2 bn, up from £1.6 bn in 2001. Microsoft itself believes that while 30 per cent of UK households currently have a games console, in the future, they'll be as common as video recorders are now. It is hardly surprising, therefore, that Microsoft has been tempted to enter this market.

Having decided to enter, Microsoft moved fast, taking only 18 months from initial brainstorming to product launch, and from 20 people working on the project to 2,000. The Xbox is different from its competitors and has been described as being more like a cheap PC with a powerful graphics chip rather than a traditional console. It is currently the only console with built-in broadband capability so that eventually gamers will be able to download new levels, characters, and games, and online multiplayer gaming is due to start in the summer of 2002 in the Japanese market.

The Xbox was launched first in the US on 15 November 2001, followed in Japan in February 2002 and Europe in March 2002 with a \$500 mn worldwide advertising campaign. Its global target was to sell between 4.5 and 6 million Xbox consoles by June 2002. In the US alone, Microsoft had sold 1.4 million consoles by the end of 2001. The Japanese launch was a little less promising, however. In the first week after its launch, Xbox had sold only 150,000 units (although 250,000 units had been shipped to Japan). In comparison, when Sony launched the PlayStation2 in Japan in 2000, it sold 720,000 within three days and 1 million within a week. There was also a technical problem that caused some bad publicity: nearly 600 complaints were received about the consoles damaging DVD and CD games. Microsoft's response to these complaints was said to be hesitant – it took nearly two weeks. This alienated early buyers and tarnished its image. Three Japanese retailers suspended sales of the Xbox for two weeks until Microsoft confirmed that it would replace or repair offending consoles. Sandy Duncan, Microsoft's Vice-president of Xbox Europe, blamed adverse publicity that turned a few technical glitches into 'Xbox ate my DVD' headlines. In Microsoft's opinion it was a very minor problem that certainly hadn't been an issue in the US market.

Meanwhile, the simultaneous launch in 16 European countries was scheduled for 14 March 2002 and a lot of preparation went into it. 'Europe as a console market is as important as the US in terms of volume – if we are going to be successful we have to be successful over here' said Sandy Duncan, Microsoft's Vice-president of Xbox Europe. Microsoft invited the top two retailers from each country to an Xbox event in Milan in 2001, and in October 2001, Xbox hosted the X01 event experience ('more than a press conference or trade show') in Cannes providing details on the European price, availability and shipment quantities (1.5 million consoles for the first three months to the end of June). X01 ran over two days and around 1,000 journalists and representatives of the video games industry attended. There was as much emphasis on the games and future development plans for games as on the hardware.

Advertising broke in the games and consumer press on 7 February 2002 followed by a television campaign nearer to the launch date. Retailers also had an important role to play and 7,000 pre-launch demo units were installed in European retail outlets. The weekend of 9–11 March was the final opportunity to pre-order an Xbox in the UK before the official launch. Sony wasn't prepared to let Microsoft have it all its own way, however, and chose that same weekend to promote the launch of *Metal Gear Solid 2: Sons of Liberty*, what Sony describes as 'the biggest games launch the industry has ever seen'. That game had taken 550,000 pre-orders and was expected to turnover £9 mn in its first weekend on sale.

Around 300 stores across the UK started selling the machines at midnight on 13 March. Electronics Boutique opened 168 of its 330 UK stores at midnight and this retailer claimed to have received 'tens of thousands' of pre-orders. Virgin Megastores (official retail partner for the launch) had all-night parties running in London, Birmingham, Glasgow and Manchester, themed as Xmas Eve – mince pies, prezzies from Santa (including Xbox merchandise), entertainment and a gaming area where punters could play on demo machines. Thus several hundred people were in the queue for the launch at the Virgin Megastore in Oxford Street. A student who bought his console just after midnight said, 'I love my PlayStation 2 but the Xbox is even better. The games are more advanced and more exciting. Besides, it's something to spend my student loan on' (ever heard of books, mate?). To heighten the excitement, the person at the head of the queue in London to buy his Xbox after midnight was whisked home in a limo with an escort of six motorbikes. A poll of 3,000 people who pre-ordered Xbox from Amazon found that 75 per cent of them intended to take a day off work to play with their new toy. The desirable status of the Xbox was perhaps finally confirmed not long after midnight when the first one had been stolen from someone waiting for a bus home!

The launch itself was not the end of the campaign, however. From the 29 March to 1 April, Xbox was at Multiplay UK's i10 event, the UK's largest LAN gaming event. A thousand UK gamers attended and the Xbox Experience featured 8 networked Xboxes to allow 16 people to compete at Halo all at the same time. Other demo machines were also available. Also, once customers have bought Xbox games, they can be entered into a customer database, built through registration cards distributed in the game boxes and through http://www.playmore.com, Xbox's 'brand experience' website.

Xbox is also supported by http://www.xbox.com which has information about the Xbox and its games, news updates, competitions, and a chat room. Visitors can also sign up to receive a newsletter or take out an Xbox magazine subscription. The site also features Xbox TV: 'the place to take a sneaky look at games before you buy 'em'. It shows video clips of the games so you can see the graphics, hear the sound effects and see the action, and also get background information on how the games were created. The quality and desirability of the games are obviously important influences in selling the console. The Xbox launched with 20 games, costing about £45 each (claimed to be the strongest portfolio of games ever for a console launch) but 60 are planned by the end of June. Halo is one of only a handful of games to get a 10 out of 10 rating from Edge, an influential European games magazine. The hardware and software are extensively covered and reviewed in games magazines and on gaming websites such as: http://www.gamesdomain.com, http://www.gamespot.co.uk, http://www.gamesradar.com; and http://www.computerandvideogames.com.

Sales of games are also important financially as Microsoft earns approximately 30 per cent royalty on every game sold for the Xbox. In the US, nearly 4 games are being sold with every Xbox while early indications show that on average 2.5 games are sold with a European Xbox. This is especially important as analysts' estimates suggest that Microsoft could be losing as much as $125 on each console sold and will not break even for five years, despite the royalties earned on games. As it is, the Xbox console cost around £300 at its launch, compared with around £200 for a PlayStation2.

According to http://www.computerandvideogames.com (20 March 2002), Xbox sold 48,000 units in its first three days in the UK market. Trade speculation is that Microsoft shipped 80,000 units for the launch (cf. PlayStation2 selling c. 70,000 in the UK in two days), although Microsoft claims that Xbox was 'a near sell-out' on its first day. In the longer term, competitor Nintendo's GameCube is due for its European launch on 3 May 2002 with a £60 mn launch budget and a target of selling 1 million consoles by July. Analysts forecast that by 2006, PlayStation will have sold between 90 and 110 million consoles with Xbox and GameCube selling between 25 and 35 million each. Then gamers will be looking to the next generation of consoles.

Sources: Abrahams (2002); Chandiramani (2002); Cope (2002); *Daily Post* (2002); *Daily Record* (2002); Grande (2002); Harney (2002); Islam (2002); Lambeth (2002); Nakamoto (2002a, 2002b); Rowan (2002); Uhlig (2002); Wray (2002); http://www.computerandvideogames.com; http://www.gamesradar.com; http://www.xbox.com.

Questions

1. Categorise the various communications activities mentioned in the case according to whether they represent push or pull tools.
2. To what extent do you feel that the negative publicity received in the Japanese market is likely to have been a problem?
3. Why do you think advertising alone was not considered sufficient for the European launch?
4. Analyse the likely role of xbox.com in the future marketing communications strategy of Xbox.

case study 14.2

Alliance & Leicester: banking on good communications

The Alliance & Leicester is a leading financial services organisation in the UK with a product range including personal loans, insurance, mortgages, current and savings accounts and credit cards (all of which are transacted through the retail branches), ATMs, call centres and internet banking. Tim Pile, former Sales and Marketing Director, discussed the role of marketing communication within the company.

Within Alliance & Leicester, the Sales and Marketing Director has control of all aspects of marketing strategy, including product development, pricing, branch offices and branding, and not just the advertising and promotion mix. An important role, therefore, is to integrate all marketing activities in the context of the overall strategic plan and direction. Marketing communications are not treated as comprising different elements that work in isolation. The various tools and methods are integrated to achieve the desired marketing communications objectives, including increased customer attention, attraction, retention and satisfaction. To achieve that with multiple products selling into different market segments, Alliance & Leicester focuses on the 'interconnectedness of all communication activities' to create the necessary impact in the competitive markets in which it operates.

The aim of marketing communication is to sell products while building the corporate brand. The two must be consistent and interconnected. For that reason, the company has adopted a strong corporate branding framework for its media advertising and product literature. 'All our product literature is consistent in terms of its imagery, style, use of colour, use of logo and the type of language. Only the text varies according to the product claims and benefits.'

Tim believes that in financial services the distribution channel is an integral part of the marketing communications strategy as it helps shape how the customer is spoken to and the nature of that contact. For example, one of its competitors, MBNA, has a direct marketing operation with no branches. He stated that 'it thinks nothing of a mail drop of 15 million to promote a product such as credit cards, whereas the NatWest has an extensive branch network and tends to rely more on direct mailings to support local sales staff with leads for new business. So to us, marketing communications can be a means of distribution for financial services products and this is why we have all been so active in moving to direct marketing approaches'.

Understanding the involvement and interaction between the customer and the product is also important. For example, Alliance & Leicester finds that 90 per cent of personal loans can be handled by post or telephone, but that most saving investment decisions usually involve a visit to the branch. People want the reassurance of a personal contact and to ensure that their trust is well placed. The branch sales staff are trained to handle these situations otherwise it would undermine the achievements of other promotional activities in generating enquiries and interest.

Commenting upon the changes in the promotional mix during the 1990s, Tim highlighted a radical shift from mass marketing to mass customisation. 'Direct marketing has enabled one-to-one communication, mass customisation if you like, rather than mass marketing which implied large-scale media advertising. This means that we can treat each customer as unique and target different financial products at them at different times depending upon our assessment of their needs. We still use television from time to time, but at nowhere near the level of a few years ago. The trend will continue as the media fragments into smaller and smaller audiences.'

Alliance & Leicester has developed a highly sophisticated direct marketing organisation to service its existing 5.7 million customers and also to attract new customers based on the customer profile most likely to respond to a particular mailing. Its data warehouse enables it to prepare response propensity models so that it has a good idea what financial products customers are likely to be interested in at different times. It tracks response rates by each customer cell, products, month, location, customer type, campaign etc. It also tracks the 'cost to acquire' a customer and constantly experiments with different mixes to lower cost and improve effectiveness.

Of course, there is no point in developing a highly professional and sophisticated direct marketing system if the customer contact lets the organisation down. It now has an advanced customer call centres that can handle up to 250,000 calls per month for fulfilment and 2 million customer service calls. It uses different freefone contact numbers to route calls to specialists as it offers such a wide range of financial products. Operators have to be able to offer advice and screen customers to direct them to the most suitable products. All its customer contact staff are trained to high standards in customer handling as well as in the products.

However, Tim is less sure about the future impact of the internet, questioning some of the claims about the future impact on consumers. 'Never has so much hype been given to a new medium and too few people are taking a critical view of its impact. Of course, the internet has changed and will continue to change financial services marketing and we have invested heavily in our award winning site (http://www.alliance-leicester.com). On our website we display brochures, provide application facilities and have hyperlinks to other related pages within the product range. We also intend to be at the forefront of internet banking but I do not think that in the short term it will replace the branch offices. There will still be an important role for other communication tools in general and our branch offices in particular. For example, the branches will support the internet to become like a convenience store where products and services can be assessed, discussed and purchased. They will become advice centres and points where personal interaction is possible. In short they will work alongside the internet, not be replaced by it.

'In my view, as internet usage increases, it will be direct mail usage that will decline. The power to link the profile of the internet user to target advertising messages precisely would benefit financial products. However, the profile of internet users is not developing as fast as some would like. Interestingly, it is the older market that is becoming the heavier users as they have the time to learn and surf the web. The young professional, an important segment for us, is often too busy to spend hours surfing. I suspect much will also depend upon how quickly legislation catches up with direct marketing; given the power of the web, inevitably controls will be introduced.'

Because of Alliance & Leicester's umbrella approach to product development and management, the challenge is to ensure that the one brand, Alliance & Leicester, is able to meet a plethora of customer needs through the various products within the portfolio. Most of its direct marketing and media advertising is aimed at promoting products, whereas the umbrella brand must be established to make the reception for those products more favourable. PR and to a lesser extent sponsorship are the main tools for directly building the corporate umbrella brand. The PR team and agency work closely with the marketing staff to develop stories and messages that build the image and reputation of the brand. They are closely involved in the marketing planning process. The reluctance to use sponsorship, however, reflects the difficulty in being able to justify the expenditure when evaluation is so difficult.

There is one final dimension to the umbrella brand: staff. The service they provide, the quality of the interaction with the customer is considered crucial for reinforcing the umbrella brand image and reputation and extends far wider than perhaps the product being discussed. 'Total brand communication' requires an integrated marketing communications strategy, blending the different elements of the promotional mix together to create an impact and then ensuring that staff can live up to the expectations and claims for the brand. 'We always launch our new products to staff first and we always train, incentivise, communicate and reward staff at the branches due to the critical role they play in supporting the Alliance & Leicester brand. It would all come to nothing if our branch sales staff were not performing in converting product interest into sales and in retaining our customer loyalty. I cannot see internet marketing changing that. Supporting it, yes, but not changing it.'

Source: with thanks to Tim Pile, former Sales and Marketing Director, Alliance & Leicester.

Questions

1 What does integrated marketing communications mean to Alliance & Leicester?

2 What do you think are the particular marketing communications problems for financial services products? How can the various elements of the promotional mix be best used to overcome them?

3 What impact do you think market research and information gathering might have on Alliance & Leicester's communications planning?

4 With particular reference to marketing communications issues, to what extent and why do you agree with Tim Pile's view that traditional bank branches 'will work alongside the internet, not be replaced by it'?

References for chapter 14

Abrahams, P. (2002), 'Microsoft Urged to Play by the Rules', *Financial Times*, 13 March, p. 20.

Bashford, S. (2001), 'A Famous Face is Not Sufficient to Lure Customers', *Marketing*, 12 July, p. 5.

Benady, A. (2002), 'For and Against Celebrity Endorsement', *The Times*, 22 February, p. 21.

Benady, D. (2002), 'Sugar the Pill', *Marketing Week*, 14 February, pp. 37–41.

Brooks, H. (2000), 'Cyber Pocket Money', *The Guardian*, 10 August, p. 10.

Bruss, J. (2001), 'Star Power', *Beverage Industry*, November, p. 34.

Castle, S. (2001), 'Europe Planning Tough Rules for Breast Implants', *The Independent*, 16 November, p. 11.

Chandiramani, R. (2002), 'Microsoft's Xbox Adopts "Positive" Brand Positioning', *Marketing*, 24 January, p. 1.

Conlan, T. (2002), 'Posh v Becks: In the Battle of the His 'n' Hers Crisps', *Daily Mail*, 7 March, p. 11.

Cope, N. (2002), 'All-American Game Boy Wins Through in War of the Consoles', *The Independent*, 4 March, p. 15.

Cowen, M. (2000), '£1.5 m Buys a Lot More of Mr Nice Guy', *The Independent*, 10 December, p. 19.

Daily Post (2002), 'New Xbox Stolen Within Hours', *Daily Post*, 15 March, p. 2.

Daily Record (2002), 'Gamers' Midnight Rush for the Xbox', *Daily Record*, 14 March, p. 3.

DeLozier, M.W. (1975), *The Marketing Communications Process*, McGraw-Hill.

Dignam, C. (2002), 'The Comeback of Sunny Delight', *The Times*, 27 February, p. 32.

Fill, C. (2002), *Marketing Communications: Contexts, Strategies and Applications*, 3rd edn, Financial Times Prentice Hall.

Financial Times (2001), 'The Euro Campaign', *Financial Times*, 19 June, p. 8.

Garrett, J. (1999), 'Agencies Contest £80mn "Euro" Brief', *Campaign*, 30 April, p. 1.

Gofton, K. (2000), 'Promoters Adapt to Dotcom Needs', *Marketing*, 5 October, pp. 57–8.

Grande, C. (2002), 'Plug and Play Broadband Gaming Promises Valuable New Revenue Streams', *Financial Times*, 26 March, p. 4.

The Guardian (2000), 'Cashpoints', *The Guardian*, 26 August, p. 8.

Hampton, N. (2001), 'How Stars Earn Those Astronomical Fees', *Evening Standard*, 18 June, p. 6.

Harney, A. (2002), 'Microsoft Fired Up for Console Wars', *Financial Times*, 7 February, p. 28.

Hirschman, E. (1987), 'People as Products: Analysis of a Complex Marketing Exchange', *Journal of Marketing*, 51(1), pp. 98–108.

Hooley, G. and Lynch, J. (1985), 'How UK Advertisers Set Budgets', *International Journal of Advertising*, 3, pp. 223–31.

Islam, F. (2002), 'Gates' Baby Plays Catch-up', *The Observer*, 17 March, p. 6.

Jones, J. (1991), 'Over Promise and Under Delivery', *Marketing and Research Today*, 19 (November), pp. 195–203.

Kleinman, M. (2002), 'Beckhams Go Head-to-head in Snacks Ad Drive', *Marketing*, 7 March, p. 1.

Knight, P. (2002), 'Let's Not Miss a Chance to Make iTV a Big Winner', *Marketing*, 21 February, p. 20.

Lambeth, J. (2002), 'Microsoft's Black Box Squares Up to its Rivals', *The Daily Telegraph*, 12 March, p. 33.

Mallen, B. (1977), *Principles of Marketing Channel Management*, Lexington Books.

Marketing (2001), 'Best Use of Interactive TV', *The Marketing Awards: Connections 2001* supplement to Marketing, November, p. 20.

Marketing Week (1999), 'IDM Silver Award Winner', *Marketing Week*, 20 May, p. 62.

Mintel (2002a), *Clothes Washing Detergents and Laundry Aids*, 29 January, accessed via http://www.mintel.com.

Mintel (2002b), *Chicken and Burger Bars*, 13 March, accessed via http://www.mintel.com.

Mitchell, L. (1993), 'An Examination of Methods of Setting Advertising Budgets: Practice and Literature', *European Journal of Advertising*, 27 (5), pp. 5–21.

Nakamoto, M. (2002a), 'Xbox Flaw Blights Microsoft in Japan', *Financial Times*, 8 March, p. 21.

Nakamoto, M. (2002b), 'Microsoft Shows Slow Reactions', *Financial Times*, 12 March, p. 22.

Oliver, J. and Farris, P. (1989), 'Push and Pull: A One-Two Punch for Packaged Products', *Sloan Management Review*, 31 (Fall), pp. 53–61.

PR Week (1999), 'Breast Implants', *PR Week*, 4 December, p. 11.

Peattie, K. (1992), *Green Marketing*, Pitman Publishing.

Pickton, D. and Broderick, A. (2001), *Integrated Marketing Communications*, Financial Times Prentice Hall.

Poulter, S. (2002), '£12mn "Healthy" Makeover for Sunny Delight', *Daily Mail*, 21 February, p. 39.

Rogers, D. (2002), 'P&G in £12mn Relaunch of Sunny Delight', *Marketing*, 14 February, p. 2.

Rossiter, J. and Percy, L. (1987), *Advertising and Promotion Management*, McGraw-Hill.

Rothschild, M. (1987), *Marketing Communications: From Fundamentals to Strategies*, Heath.

Rowan, D. (2002), 'Video Game Giants Roll Out Big Guns for Marketing War', *The Times*, 9 March, p. 9.

Schramm, W. (1955), *Process Effects of Mass Communication*, University of Illinois Press.

Strong, E. (1925), *The Psychology of Selling*, McGraw-Hill.

Thurtle, G. (2002), 'Balloting Blair's Babies', *Marketing Week*, 28 February, pp. 25–7.

Turznski, G. (1999), 'Will Interactive Media Bring Advertisers Relief?, *Marketing Week*, 10 June, p. 16.

Uhlig, R. (2002), 'Games Fans Lured by the X-factor', *The Daily Telegraph*, 15 March, p. 3.

Wray, R. (2002), Xboxed Up and Nowhere to Go', *The Guardian*, 12 March, p. 21.

chapter 15

advertising

Introduction

LEARNING OBJECTIVES

This chapter will help you to:

1 define advertising and its role within the promotional mix;

2 appreciate the complexities of formulating advertising messages and how they are presented for both print and broadcast media;

3 differentiate between types of advertising media and understand their relative strengths and weaknesses;

4 appreciate the role played by advertising agencies and the importance of cultivating good agency–client relationships; and

5 understand the stages in the management process of managing advertising activities.

The average European is bombarded daily with an ever increasing number of advertising messages, whether on television, radio, print or posters. Branded goods, machine tools, restaurants, AIDS prevention and thousands of other goods, services and messages are all promoted through advertising. The battle is to attract and hold attention so that the advertising has the opportunity to generate the desired effects. Rarely can this be achieved by one advertisement.

Regardless of the type of organisation, and whatever the mix of media used, any promises made must be consistent between different advertisements and must be delivered when the customer demands them. This implies a high level of integration between advertising decisions and their implementation and the rest of the marketing mix elements.

This chapter examines the role of advertising in the promotional mix and the important aspects of message design and media selection in the development of successful campaigns. The stages in developing an advertising campaign are then presented, along with the main management decisions at each stage. Sometimes these decisions are made in conjunction with the support of an external advertising agency, while in other organisations the campaign process is controlled almost exclusively in-house. The decision to use an agency and the importance of the client–agency relationship are thus also considered within the chapter.

In 2001, Orange, a subsidiary of France Telecom, was confirmed as the UK's number one mobile phone operator, with a customer base that had grown by 65 per cent over the first half of the year. By the end of 2001 it had 12.4 million subscribers. Advertising had a large part to play in that success, but becoming number one does not mean that the company can sit back and slacken off on the communications front. Orange has continued to use high profile advertising campaigns to maintain its hard-won status. Orange used television advertising in its £4 mn campaign in January 2002, for instance, to promote text messaging among 'light users'. The advertisement showed how text messaging could play an important emotional role in staying in touch with friends and loved ones. Then, in March 2002, Orange UK launched a multimedia campaign to persuade high-value customers from other networks to switch to Orange. The campaign included radio, TV, outdoor and online media. Orange's advertising spend in 2001 amounted to just over £51 mn, with £18 mn spent on television advertising; £12.4 mn on press advertising; £3.5 mn on cinema advertising; £2.5 mn on outdoor media; and the rest on direct mail. Clearly, with this level of budget, it is vitally important to make the right strategic decisions not only about the campaign objectives, but also about the message itself, the media to be used and the creative approach. It is also important to monitor carefully and evaluate the impact and cost-effectiveness of campaigns (Cowen, 2001; Grant, 2002; *Marketing*, 2002; White, 2002).

The role of advertising in the promotional mix

Advertising can be defined as any paid form of non-personal promotion transmitted through a mass medium. The sponsor should be clearly identified and the advertisement may relate to an organisation, a product or a service. The key difference, therefore, between advertising and other forms of promotion is that it is impersonal and communicates with large numbers of people through paid media channels. Although the term 'mass media' is often used, it has to be interpreted carefully. The proliferation of satellite and cable television channels, along with the increasing number of more tightly targeted special interest magazines and the use of the internet, means that on the one hand advertising audiences are generally smaller, but on the other the audiences are 'better quality'. This implies that they are far more likely to be interested in the subject matter of the advertising carried by their chosen medium. A publication such as *Classic FM Magazine*, for example, carries advertising from a wide range of recording companies, both large and small, who see this medium as a cost effective way of reaching a much larger concentrated group from their target market than any other medium, even television, could generate.

Advertising normally conforms to one of two basic types: product orientated or institutional (Berkowitz *et al.*, 1992), as shown in Figure 15.1. A product-orientated advertisement focuses, as the term suggests, on the product or service being offered, whether for profit or not. Its prime task is to support the product in achieving its marketing goals.

Product-orientated advertising can itself take one of three alternative forms, **pioneering**, **competitive**, or **reminder and reinforcement** advertising.

Pioneering advertising

Pioneering advertising is used in the early stages of the lifecycle when it is necessary to explain just what the product will do and the benefits it can offer. The more innovative, technically complex and expensive the product is, the more essential this explanation becomes. Depending on the product's newness, the prime emphasis might well be on stimulating basic generic demand rather than attempting to beat competition.

eg

Advertising for Holsten UK's fruit-flavoured beer is likely to be pioneering. Scheduled for a May 2002 launch, the new brand, likely to be named Holsten Fusion, was developed to fill a gap in the market for a refreshing drink that is sweeter than normal beers but less sweet than existing FABs (flavoured alcoholic beverages) targeted at 18–27-year-olds. Although the FAB market is established, and worth over £280 mn per year in the UK, the products within it are based on spirits, such as vodka and rum, rather than beers. Holsten is, therefore, going to have to pioneer a new sector in the FAB market and explain to the target audience the features and benefits of 'alcopop lager' and how it is different from other FABs (Addelman, 2002).

Figure 15.1 Types of advertising

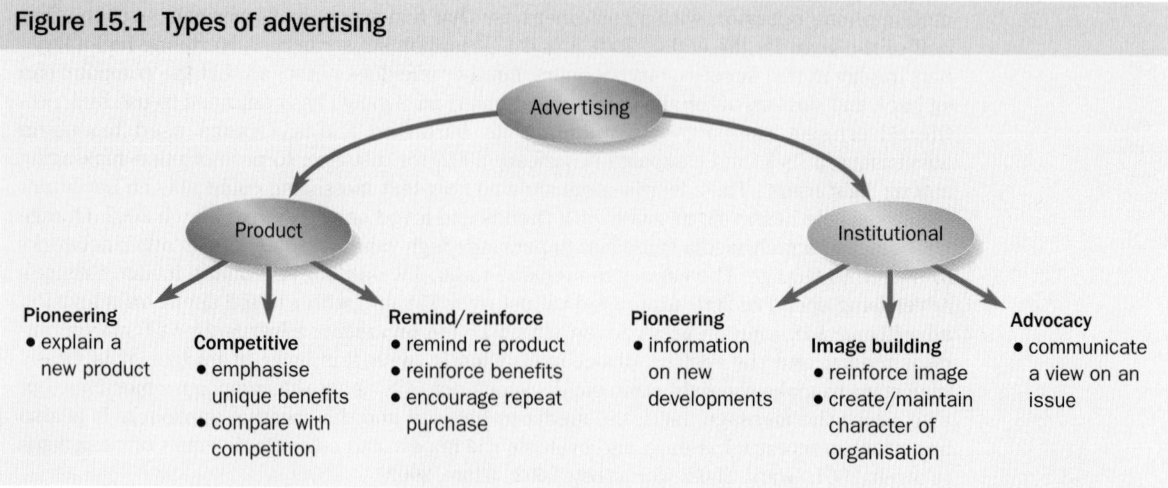

In these cases, the prime emphasis in the advertising is to provide enough information to allow potential buyers to see how this product might relate to them, and thus to stimulate enough interest to encourage further investigation and possibly trial. Further aspects of this use of promotion were considered in Chapter 8.

Competitive advertising

Competitive advertising is concerned with emphasising the special features of the product or brand as a means of outselling the competition. Usually the seller seeks to communicate the unique benefits, real or imaginary, that distinguish the product and give it its competitive edge. Given that most markets are mature and often crowded, this type of advertising is very common and very important.

eg

The ale sector within the UK beer market is struggling to maintain its share, given the aggressive competition it faces from lagers and pre-packaged spirits, such as Bacardi Breezers, in particular. Advertising thus plays an important role in establishing distinctive brand images and trying to create differential advantage. Boddingtons 'Cream Of Manchester' campaign during the 1990s, starring sexy model Melanie Sykes, really put the brand on the map, in more ways than one, as a down-to-earth northern product with a sense of humour. This was reinforced by the subsequent 'Chilled Cream' campaign featuring cartoon character Graham the Cow who represented the brand for over two years. The £4 mn 2002 campaign, however, dropped the cream theme and returned to sexy female models using the slogan 'It's a bit gorgeous'. In one advertisement, for example, an actress finds her co-star such a turn-off that she has to pretend he's a pint of Boddingtons in order to produce a convincing screen kiss. Smith (2002) does, however, raise the concern that dropping the creaminess means dropping an essential differentiating characteristic of the brand which was at the heart of its positioning. As Smith's article puts it, 'There are any number of merely "gorgeous" beers out there', so what is there to distinguish Boddingtons from its direct competitors in the ale sector and from the strongly-positioned lager brands?

At least with beers consumers can try the different brands and then decide which one they like.

This underlines one of the critical features of good and effective advertising: it must have truth at its core. Advertising simply cannot be used to create a false image, because as soon as consumers try the product or service for themselves, they will compare the reality against the advertising promises and pass judgement.

Comparative advertising

A form of competitive advertising that has grown in significance in recent years is **comparative advertising**. This means making a direct comparison between one product and another, showing the advertiser's product in a much more favourable light, of course (Muehling *et al.*, 1990). Alternatively, the comparison may be more subtle, referring to 'other leading brands' and leaving it up to the target audience to decide which rival product is intended. Initially, it was thought unwise to use a direct comparison approach as it gave a free mention to competitors and was likely to bring about a 'knocking copy' reaction. However, advertisers have now realised that in a competitive world even if they do make a comparison with a market leader with already high awareness levels, the effect need not be negative.

Through careful selection of the benefits and judgement criteria to be emphasised, a comparative advertisement might encourage a perception of relative superiority, despite the selectivity used. The advertiser must be careful with this approach to avoid abusing the competition or presenting false comparisons. Thus any comparative product appeal must be made with care from a legal perspective. Any claims must be clearly sustainable.

A competitor might well see all this as a challenge and run its own comparative advertising to redress the balance. In extreme cases, ill-considered comparative advertising might lead to claims of unfair practice and to legal action.

marketing *in action*

Shall I compare thee to a summer's day? No, just to your major competitor

The EC Directive on Comparative Advertising has legitimised comparative advertising as being in the interests of competition and public information. In some countries, such as Germany, this has opened up the opportunity to use comparative advertising for the first time. This prompted Berndt Michael, deputy chairman of agency Grey Europe, to develop guidelines for advertisers thinking of using the technique (Shannon, 1999). These points are also endorsed and reinforced by other experts (see, for example, Gray, 2001; Mason J., 2000; and Staheli, 2000).

Do not use comparative advertising:

- If your product has no significantly different advantage over the rest that is meaningful to the target market.
- If you are a market leader. Why draw attention to the products that are challenging you? Why tempt competitors to respond by knocking down the claims you have carefully set up or by emphasising your weaknesses?
- If you are trying to build long-term sustainable image. Comparative advertising is a short-term, aggressive tool that risks damaging your image if it is seen as 'knocking copy' (i.e. as gratuitous insults to other products). A knocking war between you and your main competitors benefits nobody in the long term as it simply alienates customers. Research in the UK has shown that 62 per cent of consumers think that it is unacceptable for brands to criticise each other in advertising. Similarly, comparative advertising can be good at pointing out provable factual differences between products, which is fine if consumers tend to make their purchasing decisions on factual, rational criteria, but it is harder for it to create an emotional bond with the customer and that too is not helping long-term image.
- Unless you are careful about the way in which you communicate direct comparisons. Comparisons can make customers feel uncomfortable, as they are effectively being told that they made the wrong choice when they purchased the competitor's product. To deal with the resulting cognitive dissonance, they are likely to think of reasons for the competitor's product being actually better than yours, despite what your advertising says, and persuade themselves that they did make the right choice. Humour can help to soften the blow, however, without losing the essential point of the comparison. ITV Digital wanted to get across the message that it broadcast more live football than Sky. One advertisement featured a woman saying that Michael Owen is her favourite footballer because 'he really knows how to wear a pair of shorts'. The advertisement's conclusion, therefore, was 'ITV Digital: More Live Men in Shorts Than Sky!' delivered by a loud voice-over.

Not all companies appreciate being the subject of unfavourable comparisons. British Airways (BA) sued Ryanair over an advertisement comparing prices headed 'Expensive Ba....ds. Despite describing the headline as 'mere vulgar abuse', the High Court judge ruled in favour of Ryanair on the basis that the core claim within the advertisement, that BA's prices were higher than Ryanair's, was substantially true. The advertisement had actually been withdrawn anyway after the ASA ruled that it was likely to cause serious or widespread offence. Nevertheless, the judge called BA 'immature' for bringing the action in the first place.

Sources: Brabbs (2001); Gray (2001); Mason J. (2000); Shannon (1999); Staheli (2000).

Reminder and reinforcement advertising

Reminder and reinforcement advertising tends to operate after purchase. It reminds customers that the product still exists and that it has certain positive properties and benefits. This increases the chances of repurchase and sometimes might even persuade consumers to buy larger quantities. The main emphasis is not on creating new knowledge or behaviour but on reinforcing previous purchasing behaviour, and reassuring consumers that they made the right choice in the first place.

Such advertising alongside product usage does help the consumer's learning experience. Frequent exposure to advertising that emphasises just how long a bottle of Fairy Liquid lasts makes the washer-up look at the bottle in their own kitchen and think, 'Yes, it has actually been there a while . . ..' Complete victory to the advertiser.

This kind of advertising clearly relates to established products in the mature stage of the product lifecycle where the emphasis is on maintaining market share at a time of major competition. It is also important if the weak theory of advertising, outlined at p. 582, is accepted. That would mean that post-purchase reminder, image building and reinforcement advertising actually create the attitudes and preferences that lead to further purchases.

eg

Kellogg, the breakfast cereal manufacturer, has a very well-established corporate brand name in the UK market. In the late 1990s, however, it found that it was losing sales to supermarket own-brand products. This was happening because the own-brand ranges had a directly equivalent, but cheaper, product for each of the main Kellogg brands. In Tesco, for instance, Kellogg's Cornflakes were competing against Tesco Cornflakes; Frosties against Frosted Flakes; Rice Krispies against Rice Snaps and Coco Pops against Choco Snaps etc. Kellogg responded to this by targeting lapsed buyers and users of its Cornflakes with a reminder advertising campaign designed subtly to reinforce the brand heritage and quality. Most adults are aware of the existence of Kellogg's Cornflakes and what they are, and so do not need information, just a gentle reminder. The slogan 'Remember How Good They Taste?' took adults back to the last time they tried Kellogg's Cornflakes, encouraging them to recall their own experience of the brand and how much they liked it. A small price cut, prominently marked on the box, also helped to encourage re-trial.

Consumers might be vaguely aware of a brand name because they have seen advertisements although they do not consciously remember them. This might be enough to make them pick up that product in the supermarket, almost as an impulse purchase, and try it. Then, they begin to take more notice of the advertisements and learn about the product benefits, relating them to their own usage, as in the Fairy Liquid example mentioned above.

Institutional advertising

In contrast, **institutional advertising** is not product specific. It aims to build a sound reputation and image for the whole organisation to achieve a wide range of objectives with different target audiences. These could include the community, financial stakeholders, government and customers, to name but a few. A number of these issues are picked up in Chapter 19 as they form an important part of a public relations campaign.

Institutional advertising may be undertaken for many reasons, as shown in Figure 15.1, for example pioneering, in the sense of presenting new developments within the organisation, image building, or advocacy in the sense of presenting the organisation's point of view on an issue. Some institutional advertising might be linked with presenting the organisation as a caring, responsible and progressive company. These advertisements are designed to inform or reinforce positive images with target audiences. Others may adopt an advocacy perspective, indicating the organisation's view on a particular issue for political, social responsibility or self-interest reasons. There will be more on this in Chapter 19, on PR.

Advertising within the marketing mix

The above categorisation of product and institutional advertising broadly describes the direct uses of advertising. Within the marketing mix, advertising also plays a less direct but equally important role in supporting other areas of marketing activity. In B2B markets, advertising often directly supports the selling efforts of the sales team by generating leads, providing information on new developments to a wider audience more quickly and creating a generally more receptive climate prior to the sales visit.

Similarly, with sales promotion, a short-term incentive offer may be actively advertised to encourage increased traffic. For example, airlines offering 'two for one' deals or a free ticket competition frequently support their promotions with media advertising. Furniture stores also make frequent use of television and press advertising to inform the public of short-term promotional price cuts or low/no interest financing deals to stimulate interest in furnishing and to draw people into stores that they might not otherwise have thought of visiting at that particular time.

More strategically, advertising may be used to reposition a product for defensive or aggressive reasons in order to improve its competitive position. This may be achieved by demonstrating new uses for the product or to open up new segments, either geographically or benefit based.

corporate social responsibility in action

Laughing all the way to a successful CRM partnership

Cause-related marketing (CRM), a promotional link-up between a brand and a cause or charity, can provide an interesting focus for an advertising campaign, as well as generating publicity. Lever Fabergé's Persil brand, for example, was associated with Comic Relief's Red Nose Day 2001, raising money to fund programmes helping disadvantaged people both in the UK and in Africa. Comic Relief's 2001 theme, 'Say Pants to Poverty', was a perfect match for a laundry brand and Persil's packs were temporarily and prominently emblazoned with all kinds of underwear reflecting the theme. A donation was made to Comic Relief for each pack sold and the packs effectively used their space to advertise Comic Relief, with fundraising ideas and information. Persil's own advertising also reflected the 'Pants' theme. Television, print, poster and other outdoor media were all used to display images of white boxer shorts with a nice red nose print and the slogan, 'Saying Nice Clean Bright Pants to Poverty'. Over six weeks, Persil raised over £300,000.

Manor Bakeries' Mr Kipling brand, which produces 'exceedingly good cakes' also joined in with the fun. Mr Kipling's cherry bakewell became the official Red Nose Cake with a donation made for each pack sold, and again, this featured heavily in television advertising. The cakes raised over £50,000.

Lever Fabergé's Persil washing powder brand, used in many UK households and thus given wide exposure, has been associated with the Comic Relief campaign in recent years.

Source: Reproduced with kind permission of Lever Fabergé.

For both companies, the incorporation of advertising into the CRM effort served a number of purposes. beyond the normal objectives of promoting their brands. Obviously, the advertising helped to emphasise the companies' involvement with Comic Relief, reinforcing their other PR and promotional efforts on behalf of the charity, and this in turn could contribute to that elusive but desirable goal of generating 'emotional engagement' among consumers. The CRM link reinforces the integrity of the brand and its manufacturer, adding another dimension to the brand proposition. Comic Relief in particular is quite a powerful CRM linkage, as a lot of excitement is generated through PR and other marketing communications efforts in the build up to Red Nose Day, and a lot of individuals get involved in fundraising events. Seeing a big name advertiser also 'doing its bit' gives the company a more human face and reinforces a sense of the company pulling with the wider community for a common, altruistic motive. Comic Relief benefits, of course, not only from the donations from the packs sold, but also from the free exposure it gets through the prime advertising slots and sites purchased by its CRM partners.

Sources: Arnold (2001a); http://www.bitc.org.uk; http://www.comicrelief.com; http://www.elida.co.uk.

In other situations, advertising may support other marketing mix activities to spread demand or to reduce sales fluctuations. The problems of seasonality are well known in the services field, whether in relation to holidays, restaurants or cinemas. Combined with pricing, advertising may seek to spread or even out demand patterns, saving the service provider from having to accept periods of marked under-utilisation of capacity. The various cross-channel ferry companies, for example, advertise low-priced deals to France during the winter to boost passenger numbers.

Overall, advertising's role within an organisation depends on a range of contexts, environments and competitive challenges, and may even change within the same organisation over time. The detailed role of advertising will be specified in the marketing plan, which will clearly specify objectives, resources, activities and results expected. These issues will be revisited at pp. 634 *et seq.*, where the stages in developing an advertising campaign are considered.

eg

Although one might expect the British Army to be a defensive advertiser, its 'Be the Best' campaign was definitely on the offensive. The objective was to improve recruitment, not only by raising awareness of army careers, but also by showing that ordinary people can use army training to cope with difficult situations and make life or death decisions. The army was particularly targeting 14–21-year-olds, including graduates. To draw viewers into the television advertisements and get them involved, the advertisements set a problem and invited the audience to solve it. An advertisement at the beginning of a commercial break, for example, showed an army team and its vehicle stuck in heavy snow at night with no cold weather gear and just one blanket between them. 'Who gets the blanket? You have two minutes to decide.' Then, at the end of the commercial break, one wrong answer and a reason for it would be presented and the audience invited to think again. The advertisements were run over the course of two weeks and then towards the end of the run the right answer was given: wrap the blanket around the vehicle's engine or nobody will be going anywhere the next morning. Every advertisement in the series featured a hotline number and this proved to be very successful. The army claims that 1 in 3 callers was converted to an application to join up. This campaign was backed up by radio advertising, which reaches 85 per cent of men aged under 25, and the army's website, which generates about 1,000 applications per month (Cozens, 1999; McLuhan, 1999).

Ten – SHUN! grabbing advertising?

Source: Saatchi & Saatchi/Army Recruiting Group.

Formulating the advertising message

The essence of communication, as outlined in the previous chapter, is to decide what to say, to whom, by what means and with what results. This section centres on the very demanding decision area of designing an appropriate message, with the emphasis on the message content, its tone and how it can then be presented for either print or broadcast communication.

Message

Before producing an advertisement, you need to know who the target audience is and give careful consideration to what you want to say to them. This requires a sound understanding of the targets, their interests, needs, motivations, lifestyles etc. In addition, there needs to be an honest appraisal of the product or service to determine the differential characteristics or benefits that are worth highlighting to achieve the desired results. Table 15.1 presents a short quiz to test how well you have retained advertising messages over the years.

Table 15.1 Test your slogan recall

If you are familiar with the UK advertising scene, then try this test to see just how well you can remember which brands have said what to you. Some of these slogans go back to the 1960s, but have survived and are still remembered.

Write the name of the product in the 'Brand' column then check your answers against those given in Table 15.10 on page 644.

Slogan	*Brand*
Beenz Meenz ???	
??? refreshes the parts other beers cannot reach	
Just do it	
??? puts a tiger in your tank	
Happiness is a cigar called ???	
A ??? a day helps you work, rest and play	
And all because the lady loves ???	
The car in front is a ???	
The mint with the hole	
P-p-p-pick up a ???	
It's good to talk	
I bet he drinks ???	
The world's favourite airline	
The web's favourite airline	
Because life's complicated enough	
The future's bright, the future's ???	
The art of performance	
Feeling is everything	
You can do it when you ??? it	
Top breeders recommend ???	

Message formulation

Clearly, marketing and promotional objectives are at the heart of message formulation. If the prime objective is to generate awareness, then the message must offer clear information to alert the audience to what is on offer. If the objective is to stimulate enquiries, then the focus would need to be on moving the customer through to action, making sure that the response mechanism is clear and easy to use (more of this in Chapter 18). There also needs to be consistency between the product positioning (*see* pp. 328 *et seq.*) desired and the content and style of the advertisement.

The main aim in message design and execution is to prepare an informative and persuasive message in terms of words, symbols and illustrations that will not only attract attention but retain interest through its presentation so that the target audience responds as desired. Grabbing and holding attention may mean making someone watch an entire 30-second television advertisement, read a long, wordy print advertisement, or simply dwell long enough on a non-verbal graphic image to start thinking about what it means. Whatever the medium or the style of communication, it is therefore essential that the message is understandable and relevant to the audience.

Themes

Sometimes the message may be sent out through both broadcast and print media using the same theme. In other cases, a number of different messages may be communicated in different ways over the length of the campaign.

The formation of the SEM created new opportunities for the adoption of pan-European messages. Some organisations such as Coca-Cola, Martini and Benetton have, for many years, standardised their basic advertising messages throughout Europe. Their view is that their products appeal to market segments, based on factors other than geography, which exist across the whole of Europe. These segments are based on age, lifestyle, beliefs and attitudes. Such transnational lifestyle segments tend to be the exception rather than the rule, however. It is very difficult in practice to develop pan-European messages that can appeal to the variety of different national cultures and attitudes that still exist across Europe.

eg

As Murphy (1999) points out, 'Strong advertising may help, drive the product, but the retail environment is where the purchasing decision is actually made'. He argues that it makes sense to extend the themes and images developed in advertising campaigns into other marketing activities such as point-of-purchase (POP) materials. This reminds customers of the advertising messages when and where they are making serious purchasing decisions and provides an opportunity to influence that decision. John Smith's Extra Smooth Bitter, for example, is represented by the six-feet-tall cardboard cut-out 'No Nonsense Man', both in pubs and in broadcast advertising. He looks like a typical young casual drinker with a glass of beer in his hand and a tee-shirt saying 'John Smith's doesn't need any nonsense to help sell it (that's why I'm here)'. A similar cut-out of Lara Croft appeared in and around retail outlets to advertise Lucozade, although one poor Lara outside a certain campus shop had been artistically defaced in the tee-shirt department with a marker pen to make her look like a convincing Miss Wet Tee-shirt 2002 candidate!

POP is very much a tool of integrated marketing communications. In 2001, for example, Shell developed a sales promotion across nine European markets to increase customer loyalty. Customers picked up a game card and then were given a sticker with a letter on it with every subsequent petrol purchase. The objective was to collect the right stickers to spell out 'Shell' to win a prize. The success of the promotion depended on the support of radio and outdoor media advertising to raise awareness, and perhaps to encourage drivers to seek out Shell stations specifically so that they could participate, and also good POP advertising to remind them about it at the point of sale and to reinforce excitement about the potential prizes (Middleton, 2002).

Message execution

The execution of the message can also be a problem. Research has shown that British advertising shows a sophisticated humour and is high on emotional content. German advertising, in contrast, has much less humour and is more straightforward and informative (Munzinger, 1988). Language barriers can also prevent the effective translation of sophisticated messages from one culture to another. Nevertheless, this can be avoided by largely visual advertising, which completely avoids complicated dialogue. One other solution is to develop fairly bland, inoffensive advertising that can easily be understood and adapted. The same images will be used in different countries, with any verbal elements translated into the local language.

eg

Television advertising for Ricola cough sweets from Switzerland, for instance, showed simple, stereotypical images of Switzerland (the Matterhorn, men in ethnic costume blowing long horns, mountain pasture etc.) then cut to an English voice-over describing the product's 13 herbal ingredients. The Ricola advertisement deliberately played on its Swiss heritage and could be used across Europe, because other Europeans could relate in similar ways to the Swiss stereotype shown.

Other organisations go to the opposite extreme and use universal images, familiar in any Western culture, that cannot be associated with any particular country. This brings us back to advertisers such as Benetton and Martini, as well as US companies such as Coca-Cola, IBM and 3M.

The attraction of having a single pan-European approach is the cost savings in development and production of advertising, but this has to be balanced against the potential loss of creativity. It also makes the dangerous assumption that advertising objectives are the same across different countries. Many of these issues are equally applicable to wider international marketing and will thus be discussed further in Chapter 23.

Creative appeals

After the marketing issues of message content have been considered, the creative task can proceed. It is here that agencies can play a particularly major role in the conceptualisation and design of messages that appeal effectively. Two broad dimensions of **creative appeal** guide advertisement production. One dimension is rational or emotive appeals, and the other is whether the advertisement is product or customer focused.

Rational appeals centre on some kind of logical argument persuading the consumer to think or act in a certain way. However, often it is not just a case of *what* is said, but also *how* it is said. The bald logic in itself may not be enough to grab and hold the consumers' attention sufficiently to make the message stick. How it is said can introduce an *emotional appeal* into the advertisement to reinforce the underlying logic of the message. The concern here is not just with facts but also with the customer's feelings and emotions towards what is on offer. It is often the emotional element that gives the advertisement an extra appeal.

eg

Many advertisements that feature scientists in white coats have rational appeals at their core. Your toilet is full of germs, but our laboratory tests (enter white-coated bespectacled boffin clutching test tube) have shown that our product kills more germs more quickly with longer-lasting effect than our rival's product (split screen shot: on left sparkling white spotless porcelain, on right dubious-looking, murky, streaky porcelain), so buy our product (end with reassuring contented smile from boffin clutching pack). A nice twist on the boffin theme was used when Henkel launched Glist 3-in-1 automatic dishwashing tablets in the UK. The £6 mn campaign featured actress Julie Walters extolling the virtues of Glist surrounded by white-coated boffins. Her view is that if the boffins from the Good Housekeeping Institute say the product is good, then it must be because 'you can't beat a good boffin' (Arnold, 2001b).

Fear is not, of course, the only kind of emotional appeal. Positive emotions can be equally effective in creating memorable and persuasive messages, which do not necessarily need any solid rational basis in order to be effective. Humour and sex are particularly powerful tools for the advertiser, particularly in appealing to people's needs for escapism and fantasy. A few examples of positive emotional appeals are shown in Table 15.2. Emotional appeals are especially useful when it is difficult to create a meaningful difference and superiority over more rational appeals.

Table 15.2 Positive emotional appeals

Company or brand	*Slogan*
Acuvue (contact lenses)	**Do wonderful things with your eyes**
Ariel (laundry products)	**That's another load off your mind**
Clarins (cosmetics)	**Life's more beautiful**
Ford Fiesta	**Get out more**
L'Oréal (cosmetics and haircare)	**Because I'm worth it**
MG cars	**Life's too short not to**
Nike	**Just do it**
Philips (electrical goods)	**Let's make things better**

To capitalise on fear, the toilet cleaner advertisement introduces elements that arouse fear of the health consequences of having a dirty toilet, while the shampoo advertisement subtly hints that having dandruff makes you a social embarrassment. Fear provides an ideal mechanism for advertisements wishing to show a 'problem and solution' or 'before and after' type of scenario. The fear is generated and then dispelled through using the product, and they all live happily ever after.

It may be argued that television is better at creating emotional appeals, as it is more lifelike, with sight, sound and motion to aid the presentation, whereas print is better for more rational, factually based appeals.

Product-orientated appeals

Product-orientated appeals centre on product features or attributes and seek to emphasise their importance to the target audience. The appeals may be based on product specification (airbags or side impact protection bars in cars, for example), price (actual price level, payment terms or extras), service (availability) or any part of the offering that creates a potential competitive edge in the eyes of the target market. Taken to its extreme, this might lead to comparative advertising, as discussed at pp. 605–6.

With a product-orientated appeal, there are several options for specific message design strategy. These include the following.

How to solve a problem. As already discussed, solving a problem can be tied in with an emotional appeal, perhaps with fear of the consequences of not tackling a problem such as body odour or bad breath, for example. The product-orientated element of the advertisement shows how the product provides the solution. In a less emotional way, B2B advertising can also focus very effectively on problem solution.

ADtranz provides rolling stock to train operators of all kinds all over the world. To highlight the reliability of its products and the back-up support it offers its customers, advertisements (for example that appearing in *Modern Railways*, October 2000, p. 13) have used a problem-solving approach. The advertisement, headed 'Keeping the network running like clockwork' emphasises the pressures that train operators are under to keep services running consistently and reliably to performance targets. The body text of the advertisement then goes on to tell us about ADtranz's network of customer support service centres and reassures potential customers that 'Train operators can rely on our commitment to help them deliver passengers to their destinations on time, all of the time'.

Product comparison. Product comparison forcefully emphasises the product's superiority when compared either directly with a competing brand or generally with other products in the same class. Such an approach was discussed earlier in the Marketing in Action vignette on p. 606.

Slice of life. Slice of life advertisements demonstrate how the product fits into a lifestyle that either approximates that of the target market or is one with which they can identify or to which they can aspire.

eg

Since 2000, grocery retailer Sainsbury's has very successfully used a slice of aspirational celebrity life in its advertising. Jamie Oliver, known as 'The Naked Chef' is a popular, down-to-earth, cheeky young Essex guy without any of the pretensions often associated with top chefs. The series of television advertisements show him in a whirl of activity throwing meals together from Sainsbury's ingredients in his home for visiting friends and family. One advertisement shows Jamie sneaking off to his mum's house and begging for a curry, complaining that his wife, Jules, is into 'all that low fat malarkey'. While he lounges on the sofa, the viewer sees his mum make a curry – out of low fat ingredients – which he then wolfs down. After he has gone, the advertisement ends with mum on the telephone to Jules telling her that Jamie never suspected a thing. The slice of life theme was nearly jeopardised, however, when Jules hit the headlines after being photographed coming out of rival supermarket, Waitrose, with a huge amount of grocery shopping. A few weeks later, she made sure she was photographed with lots of Sainsbury's shopping instead (Adamson, 2002; Watson, 2001)!

Nevertheless, research has shown that his character really appeals to the target audience of female 30-something shoppers and his first two years with Sainsbury's were so successful in increasing sales that he was given a four-year extension to his contract, at a cost of about £500,000 per year (Beard, 2002).

News, facts and testimonials. News, facts and testimonials offer hard information about the product or proof through 'satisfied customers' that the product is all it is claimed to be. Such approaches tend towards the rational, and may be endorsed by a celebrity or by supporting explanation and examples. Magazine advertisements trying to sell goods that the target market might perceive to be more expensive, or goods that sound too good to be true, or goods that a customer would normally want to see or try before purchase, often use testimonials from satisfied customers. These might help to alleviate some of the doubt or risk and encourage the reader to respond to the advertisement.

eg

When Johnson and Johnson launched Benecol, a range of margarine, yoghurt, cheese, milk and snack bars, it used testimonial-based advertising to get across the message that the products reduce cholesterol levels. Targeted at women aged over 45, the advertisements used Carol Vorderman, the nation's favourite girl-next-door brainbox, to chat with ordinary users who had measurably reduced their cholesterol levels after a few weeks using Benecol products. They emphasised how much better they felt and how good the products tasted. Similarly, in 2000 Van den Bergh launched Flora pro.activ cholesterol-reducing spread on the UK market with a £10 mn advertising campaign of which £2.4 mn was spent on television advertising. It capitalised on the brand's success in other markets by using Australian consumers to speak on behalf of the product.

In B2B markets, testimonials are a particularly good way of demonstrating how well you deliver your product and service, and how highly your clients think of you, as well as showing off the quality of your client base. Testimonials have even become bargaining tools. In the US particularly, some companies agree to feature in testimonials (not only advertising, but interviews, sales calls, events and briefings as well) as a contractual clause in exchange for discounts. Digital Paper Corp., for example, has negotiated testimonial agreements with Boeing, Kodak, General Motors, and Volvo, among others (Bawden, 2002; Frook, 2001; Mason T., 2000).

Advertorials. In magazines and trade publications, news and fact-based approaches can also take the form of **advertorials**. These are designed to fit in with the style, tone and presentation of the publication so that the reader tends to think of them as extensions to the magazine rather than advertisements.

The overall objective is that the reader's attention should be able to flow naturally from the magazine's normal editorial content into and through the advertorial and out the other side, maintaining interest and retention. This is particularly effective where the advertorial is short.

Print media advertorials are very popular. Research by magazine publisher Emap showed that advertorials work just as well as normal advertising in moving the reader through from awareness to interest, but are a lot better for getting information across and feeling as if they are part of the publication. Because of the association with the editorial style of the publication and the effectiveness of advertorials, media owners tend to charge more for the space, sometimes up to 20 per cent more than if exactly the same space in the same issue was used for ordinary advertising. Research has also shown that readers understand the difference between advertorial and editorial and do not feel 'conned' into reading advertorial. In fact, readers trust advertorials more because of the implied link between them and the publication itself. As long as there is interestingly presented information and no hard sell, readers actually enjoy advertorials (*Marketing*, 1999a).

Advertorials can appear in newspapers as well as magazines, of course. NFU Mutual, an insurance company specialising in rural areas, for example, occasionally runs advertorials in *The Western Mail*, a regional newspaper based in Cardiff. One of its advertorials contained two pieces, one focused on the potential hazards of country driving, and the other on pension planning. In a journalistic style, the 'article' on road safety gave a lot of practical tips to help motorists drive more safely (and presumably, therefore, make fewer insurance claims!) and the format meant that the points could be expanded in detail and there was no sense of any selling going on. At the end of the piece is a single sentence pointing out the main benefit offered by NFU Mutual motor insurance. In a similar vein, a later advertorial covered the topic of rural crime against farms with lots of suitably scary statistics (NFU Mutual 2001, 2002).

Even the biggest companies can find a place for advertorials in their advertising campaigns. When Microsoft launched its XP operating system, it ran advertorial supplements in *The Daily Telegraph* for three consecutive Saturdays looking at the XP system itself and at home entertainment and communications. One of the advertorials also included a CD-ROM giving demonstrations and tips. According to *Marketing Week* (2001), the cost to Microsoft of these advertorials was rumoured to be 'a six-figure sum'.

Customer-orientated appeals

Customer-orientated appeals are focused on what the consumer personally gains through using this product. Such appeals encourage the consumer by association to think about the benefits that may be realisable through the rational or emotional content of the advertisement. Typically, they include the following.

Saving or making money. Bold 2-in-1, for example, could sell itself simply on the product-orientated appeal that it incorporates both a washing powder and fabric conditioner in its formulation. In fact, its advertising takes the argument further into a customer-orientated appeal, demonstrating how this two-in-one product is cheaper than buying the two components separately, thus putting money back in the purchaser's pocket.

This is also a strong appeal in cost conscious B2B markets. British Telecommunications ran an advertisement (*Marketing Week*, 4 April 2002, p. 14), for instance, emphasising cost saving as the major benefit of its B2B services. The advertisement featured a mini-case study showing how a particular client had saved £200,000 in one year.

Fear avoidance. The use of fear avoidance appeals is a powerful one in message generation and has been extensively used in public, non-profit-making promotions, for example AIDS prevention, anti-drinking and driving, anti-smoking and other health-awareness programmes. Getting the right level of fear is a challenge: too high and it will be regarded as too threatening and thus be screened out, too low and it will not be considered compelling enough to act on.

Security enhancement. A wide range of insurance products aimed at the over-50s are advertised not only on the rational basis that they are a sensible financial investment, but also on the emotional basis that they provide peace of mind. This is a customer-orientated appeal in that it works on self-interest and a craving for security. Stairlifts are also sold on the basis of security enhancement, with the implication that they make going up and down stairs easier for the elderly. The advertisements also suggest that with a stairlift, the elderly will be able to retain their independence and remain in their own homes longer, a great concern to many older people.

Self-esteem and image. Sometimes, when it is difficult to differentiate between competing products on a functional basis, consumers may choose the one that they think will best improve their self-esteem or enhance their image among social or peer groups. Advertisers recognise this and can produce advertisements in which the product and its function play a very secondary role to the portrayal of these psychological and social benefits. Perfumes, cosmetics and toiletries clearly exploit this, but even an expensive technical product such as a car can focus on self-esteem and image.

Alfa Romeo (http://www.alfaromeo.com) advertises its Alfa 156 model to French executives with macho promises in the headline of 'Power and mastery at your fingertips'. The body copy of the print advertisements starts by emphasising the Formula 1 technology in the car, then goes on to talk about cornering and overtaking abilities and finally implies a certain relaxed superiority, whatever the traffic or road conditions. All of this clearly appeals to a male ego that likes to have its status and dominance reflected in its choice of car and driving style, rather than just being one of the crowd.

Usage benefits – time, effort, accuracy etc. An approach stressing usage benefits is very similar to a rational, product-orientated appeal, but shows how the consumer benefits from saving time, or gains the satisfaction of producing consistently good results through using this product. Such savings or satisfactions are often translated into emotional benefits such as spending more time with the family or winning other people's admiration. They even work in B2B advertising.

Gulfstream sells its executive jets to companies, not on sexiness or status, but on usage benefits. Its advertisements in trade and business publications (for example that appearing in *EuroBusiness*, March 2002, p. 93) emphasise comfort, quality, performance and reliability as well as customer service and after-sales product support. Similarly, Executive Airlines, a private-flight airline, offers executives flexibility, privacy and fewer delays: 'our company makes travel time-productive' (*EuroBusiness*, March 2002, p. 88).

Execution of consumer-orientated appeals

The execution of consumer-orientated appeals, particularly those with a high emotional content, provides more scope for creative imagination. Approaches may include:

Humour. The series of advertisements centred around the slogan 'I bet he drinks Carling Black Label' showed people (and once a squirrel) performing comically impossible feats to the admiration of a couple of onlookers. Underlying the genuinely funny and entertaining structure of the advertisements, however, was the implication that the Carling Black Label drinker is confident, resourceful, witty and admired, which may well have appealed to the aspirations of its young male target market.

Sex. Although it is rare these days to see the overtly offensive sexual portrayal of women in advertising, more subtle sexuality is still rife. As long as people are interested in sex, and as long as they feel insecure about their ability to be successful in relationships, then advertisers will find a role for sex in selling products.

An advertiser may hint that using a particular brand of deodorant, skin cleanser, aftershave or toothpaste will increase your attractiveness. Alternatively, the effect might be more subtly erotic, such as in the series which ran for many years of Cadbury's Flake advertisements that implied a fantasy-based, self-indulgent pleasure that could be interpreted as bordering on the sexual (it is important to note, however, that this interpretation is strictly in the mind of the beholder and is not explicitly presented on the screen).

It is also interesting to see that after many years of being criticised for exploiting women, advertisers are redressing the balance and becoming increasingly willing to exploit men. The 'himbo' is becoming almost as common an image as the 'bimbo' used to be. An example of this is the series of Diet Coke television advertisements, showing females drooling and fantasising over rather handsome blokes.

eg

Even the charity Age Concern has attempted to grab attention using sexual imagery. As part of its remit to break down negative stereotypes of older people and to become more relevant to the 40- and 50-something generation, it used a poster campaign which echoed the imagery and style of the Wonderbra series of advertisements. The poster showed an attractive 56-year-old model wearing a black bra with the heading 'The first thing some people notice is her age' (Chandiramani, 2001).

Breaking stereotypes, Age Concern used an older model unexpectedly wearing a black bra to catch the attention of the public.

Source: Age Concern UK.

Animation. Cartoons have an almost universal appeal. As well as using well-known celebrities such as Bugs Bunny or Tom and Jerry to endorse products, advertisers can create exclusive animated characters which can inhabit invented worlds and do impossible things.

eg

The adventures of Kellogg's Tony the Tiger, who advertises Frosties, have entertained for over 30 years. Tony also offers the brand a strong, readily identifiable character that can be used both for advertising and as a platform for sales promotion activities. Cartoon characters also have the advantage that while they do not age, they are nevertheless adaptable as the tastes and demands of the target audience mature. Tony's appearance and character are not the same as they originally were.

Music, visual atmosphere. Any emotional effect can be enhanced or reinforced by careful choice of music and/or visual setting. Maxell cassette tapes, for example, used a parody of the song *The Israelites*, entitled *Me Ears Are Alight*, to demonstrate the clarity of the product. The humour and the point of the message, however, depended on the audience's ability to identify the original song. Classical pieces have also been successfully used to create moods in advertisements. British Airways adopted the 'Flower Duet' from *Lakmé* as its theme, while in British minds, Dvořák's *New World Symphony* will forever conjure up images of Hovis bread. Music and strong visual imaging can, of course, serve a useful purpose in international markets by conveying emotion and mood without language problems (Appelbaum and Halliburton, 1993).

marketing *in action*

It's music to the advertiser's ears

Using pop tracks in advertisements can benefit both the advertiser and the artist. The choice of track helps to grab attention and to signal to the target audience that this is likely to be their sort of product. It also helps to create emotion and atmosphere in the advertisement itself. Since 1985, Levi Strauss has successfully developed a striking series of jeans advertisements featuring classic pop tracks. Twelve songs used by Levi's, for instance Marvin Gaye's *Heard it through the grapevine*, have subsequently made it into the UK top 10 for a second time. The artist also benefits from what is effectively a mini pop video, often with extremely high production values. Where the track and the visual imagery are well matched, the synergy between them can make a big impact on an audience. Fun Lovin' Criminals didn't even bother with a pop video for their single *Loco* – they just let it feature in a Miller beer advertisement instead.

Through advertising, many older recordings and artists find a new cult lease of life. Lenny Kravitz, whose career had stagnated somewhat, allowed his track *Fly away* to be used in a Peugeot advertisement. It was released as a single afterwards and also made it to the top of the charts. Many other tracks by various artists have achieved better sales on re-release after featuring in an advertisement than they did originally, such as The Clash's *Should I stay or should I go?*. Some artists are thus very happy to have their material used by advertisers. Moby agreed to lease every track from his 1999 album *Play* to sell over 600 different products. Some, however, see it as literally selling-out. Chumbawumba turned down a $1 mn offer from Nike to use their single *Tubthumping* in a campaign. Singer Alice Nutter said, 'It depresses us that a piece of music becomes nothing more than a piece of music to flog a lifestyle. I loved that Moby album until it became one big car advert' (as quoted by Cox, 2001). Ouch.

Nevertheless, the advertisers have become so adept at promoting artists and tracks, that the music industry is becoming very proactive in bringing its wares to their attention. Music publishers appointed executives with the sole aim of getting tracks into advertisements and 'selling' bands to the advertising industry. When Guinness made its surfing horses advertisement, it asked the music publisher Chrysalis if it had any suitable music. It was offered a track from the band Leftfield's album *Rhythm and Stealth* before it was even released, and the advertisement became a key part of the album's own marketing strategy.

Sources: Cox (2001); Edwards (2000); Wilson (1999).

Once the decisions on message design and execution styles have been made, the framework exists for more detailed consideration of message presentation. We now turn, therefore, to presentation for print media, and then to broadcast media.

Print presentation

The final design of the words, illustrations, symbols and layout completes the message design and execution stage. Whatever the design selected, readers must be attracted to the message and their interest retained for sufficient time to enable them to reach a conclusion. Print is passive, and so it must, by its creativity, create an active and involved reader, whether using a directory, newspaper, magazine or sales literature.

Copywriting

Copywriting is the creative task of putting together the verbal elements of the message. This includes the headlines, any subheadings, body copy and captions. The headline is the main means of attracting attention to the page and is often the first thing read. At its least subtle, the headline aims to communicate a benefit to the reader as an incentive to read on. Where the basic message is very straightforward and rational, the headline might follow suit. 'PC Price Madness' and '50% Off Sale!' are both headlines signalling the type of advertisement that shows lots of different products along with slashed prices.

However, headlines are often a little less direct in their execution, particularly where the appeal is more subtle or emotionally based. 'Live the difference' (the headline for a Renault VelSatis advertisement), for instance, sets the mood for the advertisement and seeks to raise curiosity. The incentive to read on emerges from the desire to find out what on earth this is all about. Headlines are not, however, presented in isolation. They can link with an illustration or body copy to stimulate further involvement.

The body copy is the main part of the text in the advertisement. It should flow from the headlines and build on the propositions that need to be made. The length will vary and in some cases will be minimal or completely absent. Assuming that the advertisement has not been deliberately designed to work with just a headline and/or a strong illustration alone, the body copy has to retain the interest of the reader through to the conclusion. A large percentage of readers will not get past the headline, but for the small percentage that do, the copy has a persuasive and informative job to do. Good copy should:

- *Sell the benefits*: copy should sell the benefits to the reader, whether product-orientated or emotional.
- *Communicate with the individual*: copy should communicate with an individual, not to a mass audience. The message should suggest to readers that the copy has been especially prepared for them. This means using examples and language relevant to the target audience because they will stop reading it as soon as they get bored or decide that it's not really talking to them.
- *Be credible*: copy must be credible, as this encourages the reader to accept the essence of the sales arguments presented, whether or not they are in the market at that time.
- *Reflect a simple, clear and concise message*: it may not be necessary to cover all the issues in one advertisement. Selectivity and a clearly focused attempt to explain may be sufficient to get the basic message across. This does not mean that the advertising has to be boring. People expect advertising to tell them what they need to know in a digestible, but nevertheless entertaining form. Dull copywriting, however worthy the content, will not retain interest.

The copy must flow from point to point and end in a clear call for action, whether to reflect, enquire or buy. The specific copy generated will depend also on the overall style. It may be straight copy, but often involves some combination with pictures, artwork and illustrations, and thus the synergy between all the separate elements needs to be carefully thought through. If the advertisement is designed to generate a direct response from the reader, then the prominence of phone numbers or the design of a reply coupon should be carefully considered. Chapter 18 on direct marketing takes up some of these issues further.

Layout

The **layout** refers not just to the words but also all the artwork, including photography, drawings and logos. The layout shows how the copy and illustration(s) hang together from a rough concept stage through to the final agreed advertisement. This format enables a number of creative ideas to be explored before a final, irrevocable decision is made. The illustrations can sometimes be even more powerful than the headline, as they can communicate more symbolism to the reader than words.

Illustrations can be photographs, tables and charts, line drawings and graphs, or indeed any type of non-copy content, including free attachments, such as the scented cards included in perfume advertisements.

Finally, the overall design of the advertisement must be attractive and must encourage the reader to follow through. To achieve this requires, apart from an understanding of what makes the reader tick, a sound understanding of print production processes and the aesthetics of the layout proposed. The aesthetics include the balance between the advertisement elements, the focal point of attention, the eye movement for the reader, the relative proportions of the elements and the unity of style and moods generated.

Broadcast presentation

Broadcast presentation includes television and radio commercials. In contrast to print production, broadcast presentation has no layout, but a script to guide the dialogue, narration, sound effects and music. This ultimately includes the production details to cover camera work etc. where appropriate. The script enables discussion between the creative and marketing staff before the expensive commitment to shooting or recording. Once agreed, the script is developed into a **storyboard**, which has three components: the main scenes and actions, the written description of what occurs and the audio effects. Although at this stage it is still a static format, not using sight, sound or motion, it is a pragmatic response to the problem of incurring production costs at an exploratory stage.

After the initial agreement, the storyboard goes through further stages of refinement prior to final shooting. A number of formats are possible with television commercials. Some advertisements adopt a documentary kind of style, with either an announcer or an expert telling the audience authoritatively about the product on offer. Similarly, demonstrating the product in use gives rational credibility to its claims, especially when its performance is compared with that of rival products. Moving towards a more emotionally based format, some advertisements use a testimonial approach, in which a 'satisfied customer' or a celebrity swears that the product is wonderful. The kind of advertisement that begins with statements like 'I used to have dandruff until I discovered Head and Shoulders' or ends with things like 'So, Mrs Bloggs, you definitely won't swap your one box of new improved Daz for two boxes of your old powder?' falls into this category.

Animation (discussed at p. 617 above) clearly lends itself to television advertising, and can be used to inform, to entertain, or to create product image, just as using live people can. Much television advertising, though, uses a **slice-of-life** type of approach to demonstrate the product in context, with strong inputs of emotion and humour to increase the audience's involvement and entertainment impact.

Now you know the secret of her energy

Source: GlaxoSmithKline.

Advertising for most branded products is trying to pre-sell the goods, so the advertisement has to be sufficiently impressive for its impact still to be felt some time later when consumers actually get to the supermarket.

eg

A particularly interesting slice of animated cyberlife showing a product in an appropriate context was Lucozade's television campaign starring Tomb Raider action heroine Lara Croft which ran for over three years. In the advertisements, Lara did her normal job of confronting ravening wolves and generally escaping from tight situations. When she needed an energy boost, she selected the Lucozade glucose drink from her ration pack, then sprang back into action again. Lara was a good choice for the campaign, partly because she lives an extreme form of the energetic lifestyle in which Lucozade is positioned, and partly because of her appeal and cult status among the under-25 target audience. Further impact was made when the Tomb Raider film was released in the UK in 2001. The product was temporarily renamed Larazade and 40 million special edition bottles were produced. A £5 mn campaign using television, cinema and outdoor media helped Lucozade to benefit from Lara's new-found movie star status and the hype surrounding the film (Cavanagh, 2001).

Guidelines for broadcast presentation

There are a number of guidelines to assist in the commercial writing process. Clearly, whatever is shown must attract and hold viewers. It is important that the story is told in an entertaining yet relevant manner. This means using interesting ways of showing people interacting with the product.

In addition, the first few seconds of the commercial need to gain attention, in the same way as the headline in print must. This may be by a direct challenge or an unusual or evocative scene or music. There is, however, sometimes a conflict between aesthetic values and selling in advertising. An advertisement might use stunning special effects, broadcast images that remain in the mind, or create a minor masterpiece of cinematic art, but if viewers cannot understand the commercial message or cannot match the correct product or service with the advertisement, then it has failed.

Advertisers do face problems if they want to avoid clichés or what might be seen as stereotypical advertisements for the sort of product involved. Car advertisements, for example, are typically about speed, performance, status or safety.

eg

When Peugeot launched its new 406 model, it wanted to get out of that rut. Peugeot felt that consumers, saturated with technical data, saw most competing cars within a particular class as very similar in terms of performance and specification etc. To stand out from the crowd, therefore, the Peugeot 406 advertisement used powerful and emotional imagery in which the car itself played an almost incidental role. The television advertisement was shot in black and white, although some shots featured a little girl in a red coat (a reference to the film *Schindler's List*) and focused on the passing thoughts of the Peugeot driver. The impact came from images such as the girl in the path of a skidding lorry, a man giving a kiss (or possibly the kiss of life – it was deliberately ambiguous) to another man, and a protester in front of a tank. The purpose was to focus on drivers as individuals, making them feel special. This is consistent with Peugeot's slogans, 'The Drive of Your Life' and 'There Is No Such Thing as an Average Person'. To maximise the impact, the initial advertisement was three minutes long and shown simultaneously on every commercial terrestrial and satellite station serving the UK.

Overall, with television the objective is to create 30- or 60-second dramas, vignettes or jokes that are as heavily loaded with emotional connotations as with product benefits. The big advantage of television is that it does enable feelings to be attached to the product. The more lively the imagery and believable the advertisement, the greater the effect may be. In a similar way, radio has the benefit of creating lively images in the mind.

Advertising media

Advertising media are called on to perform the task of delivering the message to the consumer. The advertiser needs, therefore, to select the medium or media most appropriate to the task in hand, given their relative effectiveness and the budget available. Table 15.3 shows the percentage of total advertising spend by medium in different European countries in 2000. It is interesting to note that print takes a higher percentage than television in many countries. This is a stark reminder that most organisations either cannot afford expensive television advertising or find it inappropriate. Print media, such as local and national newspapers, special interest magazines and trade publications, have thus become the primary focus for most organisations' advertising efforts.

This section will look further at each advertising medium's relative merits, strengths and weaknesses, but first defines some of the terms commonly used in connection with advertising media.

Table 15.3 Advertising expenditure by medium 2000 (% analysis)

	Television	*Radio*	*Print*	*Cinema*	*Outdoor*
Austria	24.3	8.7	60.0	0.5	6.5
Belgium	44.0	9.0	36.9	1.5	8.6
Denmark	17.8	1.8	54.7	0.5	
Finland	19.9	3.1	73.7	0.2	3.0
France	28.7	7.2	51.7	0.9	11.5
Germany	23.3	4.1	67.7	0.9	4.1
Greece	33.8	5.3	42.4	5.2	13.4
Ireland	31.6	8.1	50.3	0.9	9.1
Italy	52.2	5.5	37.7	0.6	4.0
Luxembourg	10.1	14.9	70.9	1.9	
Netherlands	16.8	5.7	74.0	0.4	3.1
Portugal	57.7	6.8	26.3		9.2
Spain	42.2	9.4	43.3	0.8	4.2
Sweden	23.0	3.4	68.9	0.4	4.3
UK	32.6	4.2	57.0	1.2	5.0

Source: Euromonitor (2002), extracted from Table 12.2, p. 282.

Some definitions

Before we proceed to examine the advertising media, several basic terms need to be defined, based on Fill (2002).

Reach

Reach is the percentage of the target market that is exposed to the message at least once during the relevant period. If the advertisement is estimated to reach 65 per cent of the target market, then that would be classified as 65. Note that reach is not concerned with the entire population, but only with a clearly defined target audience. Reach can be measured by newspaper or magazine circulation figures, television viewing statistics or analysis of flows past advertising boarding sites, and is normally measured over a four-week period.

Ratings

Ratings, otherwise known as TVRs, measure the percentage of all households owning a television that are viewing at a particular time. Ratings are a prime determinant of the fees charged for the various advertising slots on television.

eg

The most expensive regular advertising slots in UK television occur during the soap opera *Coronation Street* which is screened four times per week. A 30-second slot can cost around £100,000. Some one-off television advertising opportunities can cost even more: a 30-second slot during the England vs Portugal match during the Euro 2000 tournament cost £340,000 (http://www.ipa.co.uk).

Frequency

Frequency is the average number of times that a member of the target audience will have been exposed to a media vehicle during the specified time period. Poster advertising space, for example, can be bought in packages that deliver specified reach and frequency objectives for a target audience.

Opportunity to see

Opportunity to see (OTS) describes how many times a member of the target audience will have an opportunity to see the advertisement. Thus, for example, a magazine might be said to offer 75 per cent coverage with an average OTS of three. This means that within a given time period, the magazine will reach 75 per cent of the target market, each of whom will have three opportunities to see the advertisement. According to White (1988), it is generally accepted that an OTS of two-and-a-half to three is average for a television advertising campaign, whereas a press campaign needs five or more. As Fill (2002) points out, an OTS figure of 10 is probably a waste of money, as the extra OTSs are not likely to improve reach by very much and might even risk alienating the audience with overkill!

Ideally, advertisers set targets to be achieved on both **reach** and **frequency**. Sometimes, however, because of financial constraints, they have to compromise. They can either spend on achieving breadth of coverage, that is, have a high reach figure, or go for depth, that is, have a high level of frequency, but they cannot afford both. Whether reach or frequency is better depends entirely on what the advertisement's objectives are. Where awareness generation is the prime objective, then the focus may be on reach, getting a basic message to as many of the target market as possible at least once. If, however, the objective is to communicate complex information or to affect attitudes, then frequency may be more appropriate. An advertiser trying to encourage brand switching, for example, in an fmcg market may find that it takes several exposures to the advertisement before the idea of trying a different brand takes root in the consumer's mind.

Of course, when measuring reach, the wider the range of media used, the greater the chances of overlap. If, for instance, a campaign uses both television and magazine advertising, some members of the target market will see neither, some will see only the television advertisement, some will see only the print advertisement, but some will see both. Although the overall reach is actually likely to be greater than if just one medium was used, the degree of overlap must enter into the calculation, since as a campaign develops the tendency is towards duplicated reach.

Television

Television's impact can be high, as it not only intrudes into the consumer's home but also offers a combination of sound, colour, motion and entertainment that has a strong chance of grabbing attention and getting a message across. Provided that the television is actually switched on, the message in vision or at least sound is being delivered. That does not, however, necessarily mean that anyone is there watching or listening. One of the perennial problems in television advertising is the 'empty armchair' syndrome – the tendency of people to go to the bathroom, make a cup of coffee or do a thousand and one other things while the advertisements are on. Even if they stay in the same room, they might be chatting or otherwise making their own entertainment, distracting them from the advertising.

Nevertheless, television advertising does present a tremendous communication opportunity. Television enables a seller to communicate to a broad range of potentially large audiences. This means that television has a relatively low cost per thousand (the cost of reaching a thousand viewers) and that it has a high reach, but to largely undifferentiated audiences. Some differentiation is possible, depending on the audience profile of the programmes broadcast, and thus an advertiser can select spots to reach specific audiences, for example during sports broadcasts, but the advertising is still far from being narrowly targeted.

The problem, therefore, with television is that its wide coverage means high wastage. The cost per thousand may be low, and the number of thousands reached may be very high, but the relevance and quality of those contacts must be questioned. Television advertising time can be very expensive, especially if the advertisement is networked nationally. Actual costs

eg

A new product launch in the fmcg sector is almost guaranteed to be an expensive undertaking. When Kellogg launched its cereal bars in the UK, for example, it spent £8.6 mn, including £3.3 mn on outdoor media and £3.9 mn on television advertising. Companies and brand managers not only have to think of media costs but also of production costs for advertisements. Guinness's 'surfer' ad, featuring surfers riding huge waves with giant white horses leaping out of them, cost £1 mn just for production and took a year to make. Although using a celebrity in an advertisement might cause fewer production problems than creating white horse effects, it still costs a lot of money (*see* p. 591–2).

will vary according to such factors as the time of day, the predicted audience profile and size, the geographic area to be covered, the length of time and number of slots purchased and the timing of negotiation. All of this means that very large bills are soon incurred.

Quite apart from the cost involved, television is a low involvement medium. This means that although the senders control the message content and broadcasting, they cannot check the receiver's level of attention and understanding, because the receiver is a passive participant in what is essentially one-way communication. There is no guarantee that the receiver is following the message, learning from it and remembering it positively. Retention rates tend to be low, and therefore repetition is needed, which in turn means high costs.

Furthermore, the amount of time allowed for advertising is usually strictly controlled, which tends to force up the rates for prime time advertising and increase the competition for the best slots. The prime slots in the UK and Germany, for example, are often booked over six months ahead, and yet in Spain, advance booking does not extend beyond a few weeks.

The growth of internationally broadcast cable and satellite television channels is changing the shape of television advertising by creating pan-European segment interest groups. MTV, for example, has opened up communication with a huge youth market linked by a common music culture.

Nevertheless, there are still problems with cable and satellite. The levels of penetration differ across Europe. For example cable penetration is high in Belgium, Denmark, Ireland and the Netherlands, as can be seen in Table 15.4, but is still relatively low in Greece, Italy, Spain, and the UK. Satellite is also only just taking off and is best established in Austria, Denmark, France and Germany. Through the advent of digital television and the marketing efforts of its providers, however, it is likely that both cable and satellite will grow significantly by 2005. Also, demand is still weak for true pan-European programmes, and there is not always the flexibility to concentrate on specific geographic markets through these channels. Thus you advertise to the whole of Europe or none of it. Last, but not least, there is the language problem. Whether the channel broadcasts in English, German or French, it is automatically going to exclude a large number of people throughout Europe who do not understand the language, although the capability does exist for broadcasters to feed different things into different regions. Cartoon Network, for example, is available in 40 million homes in 35 countries. It offers tailored packages in different countries, for example broadcasting in Polish in Poland and in Dutch in the Netherlands. On the Netherlands' national Herring Day holiday, Dutch viewers were treated to a feast of Popeye cartoons (Fry, 1999).

Table 15.4 Cable and direct-to-home satellite television 2000

	Television households (TVHH) ('000)	*Cable households ('000)*	*Cable households (% of TVHH)*	*Satellite households ('000)*	*Satellite households (% of TVHH)*
Austria	3178	1115	35.1	1220	38.4
Belgium	4196	3784	90.2	174	4.2
Denmark	2172	1395	64.2	1324	61.0
Finland	2234	966	43.2	343	15.3
France	23553	3839	16.3	14022	59.5
Germany	36411	19768	54.3	13 271	36.4
Greece	3244	30	0.9		
Ireland	1243	971	78.1	179	14.4
Italy	19125	288	1.5	1048	5.5
Netherlands	6749	6007	89.0	314	4.7
Portugal	3365	958	28.5	354	10.5
Spain	12328	480	3.9	1473	12.0
Sweden	4084	2088	51.1	829	20.3
UK	25259	3997	15.4	6045	23.9

Source: Euromonitor (2002), extracted from Table 12.5, p. 284.

Radio

Radio has always provided an important means of broadcast communication for smaller companies operating within a restricted geographic area. It is now, however, beginning to emerge as a valuable national medium in the UK because of the growth in the number of local commercial radio stations and the creation of national commercial stations such as Classic FM, Virgin Radio and talkSPORT.

While still not as important as television and print, in general terms radio can play a valuable supportive role in extending reach and increasing frequency. Despite being restricted to sound only, radio still offers wide creative and imaginative advertising possibilities and, like television, can deliver fairly specific target audiences. Narrow segments can be attractive for specialist products or services.

eg

Classic FM, with its programming of classical music, has created a new radio-listening segment of older, affluent, potential customers who otherwise would be difficult and expensive to contact as a group. Advertisers of financial products, home furnishings and other 'exclusive' products have found a very cost effective medium.

Compared with television, radio normally offers a low cost per time slot. However, as a low involvement medium, it is often not closely attended to, being used just as background rather than for detailed listening. More attention might be paid, however, to the car radio during the morning and evening journey to and from work. Nevertheless, learning often only takes place slowly, again requiring a high level of repetition, carrying with it the danger of counter productive audience irritation at hearing the same advertisements again and again. Radio is, therefore, a high frequency medium. Television for the same budget will provide more reach, but far less frequency. The choice between them depends on objectives, and brings us back to the earlier 'reach vs frequency' discussion. Large advertisers can, however, use the two media in conjunction with each other, with radio as a means of reminding listeners of the television advertisements and reinforcing that message.

Table 15.5 shows the way in which total advertising spend was split between different media in 2000 in two different consumer product markets. Although it can be seen that television and the press are the dominant media, taking surprisingly similar shares in both markets, radio still has a supporting, albeit small, role to play. It is perhaps not surprising that radio plays a much smaller role in the shampoo market, as visual imagery is very important in demonstrating the product benefits of glossy, healthy, glamorous hair!

Table 15.5 A comparison of the media outlets used to advertise tea and shampoo and conditioners, 2000

Medium	*Tea*		*Shampoo and conditioner*	
	£mn	*%*	*£mn*	*%*
Television	15.2	68.8	36.8	68.9
Press	4.1	18.5	9.5	17.8
Outdoor	1.0	4.6	3.5	6.6
Cinema	0.7	3.1	3.0	5.6
Radio	1.1	5.0	0.6	1.1

Sources: Mintel (2001a; 2001b).

One of the main problems with radio is still that there are many commercial stations. Furthermore, the advertising slots tend to be grouped together, creating clutter, and it is difficult to build reach and make an impact. Nevertheless, the costs of production can be low, comprising scriptwriting and delivery. This, combined with the potential of a local orientation, means that radio is still accessible and attractive to the small business advertiser.

Cinema

Cinema is not a major medium, but can be used to reach selected audiences, especially younger and male. In the UK, for example, nearly 80 per cent of cinema goers are in the 15–34 age group. The improvement in the quality of cinema facilities through the development and marketing of multiplexes has led to something of a resurgence in cinema audiences over the last 10 years or so. The popularity of cinema going and the kind of audiences delivered to advertisers are shown in Table 15.6.

Table 15.6 Cinema screens and attendances 2000

	Screens (number)	*Attendances (millions)*
Austria	486	16
Belgium	463	22
Denmark	322	11
Finland	346	8
France	4694	166
Germany		153
Greece	368	14
Ireland	219	15
Italy	4819	108
Luxembourg		1
Netherlands	502	22
Portugal	380	16
Spain	4896	135
Sweden	1168	17
UK	2152	143

Source: Euromonitor (2002), extracted from Tables 23.7 and 23.8, pp. 435–6.

Cinema goers are a captive audience, sitting there with the intention of being entertained. Thus the advertiser has an increased chance of gaining the audience's attention. The quality and impact of cinema advertising can be much greater than that of television, because of the size of the screen and the quality of the sound system. Cinema is often used as a secondary medium rather than as a main medium in an advertising campaign. It can also screen advertisements, rated consistently with the film's classification, that would not necessarily be allowed on television.

Magazines

The main advantage of a printed medium is that information can be presented and then examined selectively at the reader's leisure. A copy of a magazine tends to be passed around among a number of people and kept for quite a long time. Add to that the fact that magazines can be very closely targeted to a tightly defined audience, and the attraction of print media starts to become clear. Advertisers also have an enormous range of types and titles to choose from.

There are several different types of magazine carrying advertising.

General and news-based magazines

With publications such as *Time*, *The Economist* and *Reader's Digest*, an advertiser needs to ensure that the readership profile matches closely with the target segment, given the general orientation of these magazines. Further selectivity may be possible through regional or country editions.

Special interest magazines

There exists an enormous number of special-interest magazines, each tailored to a specific segment. As well as broad segmentation, by sex (*Freundin* for women in Germany; *Playboy* for men anywhere), age (*J-17* and *Mizz* for teenage girls; *The Oldie* for the over-50s in the UK) and geography (*The Dalesman* for Yorkshire and its expatriates), there are many narrower criteria applied. These usually relate to lifestyle, hobbies and leisure pursuits, and enable a specialist advertiser to achieve a very high reach within those segments.

Trade and technical journals

Trade and technical journals are targeted at specific occupations, professions or industries. *Industrial Equipment News*, *The Farmer*, *Accountancy Age* and *Chemistry in Britain* each provide a very cost effective means of communication with groups of people who have very little in common other than their jobs.

Whatever the type of publication, the key is its ability to reach the specific target audience. New technology has created this diversity of magazines to suit a very wide range of targets.

Magazines have other benefits. Some may have a long life, especially special-interest magazines that may be collected for many years, although the advertising may lose relevance. Normally, though, an edition usually lasts as long as the timing between issues. The regular publication and the stable readership can allow advertisers to build up a campaign with a series of sequential advertisements over time to reinforce the message. An advertiser may also choose to take the same slot – for example the back page, which is a prime spot – to build familiarity. The advertiser may even buy several pages in the same issue, to gain a short burst of intense frequency to reinforce a message, or to present a more complex, detailed informational campaign that a single- or double-page spread could not achieve.

eg

There has been an interesting growth in international rather than purely national magazines. *Vogue*, for instance, is a recognised name across the world, yet produces different editions to suit the different tastes of various geographic regions. Airlines also have to cater for international readerships with their in-flight magazines. BA issues *Business Life* to frequent flyers, *High Life* on certain routes and *Sinbad* for Middle Eastern routes. These magazines carry advertising not only for the airline, but also for hotels, car rentals, computers and business services etc. Long-haul flight magazines also include direct response advertising (*see* Chapter 18), capitalising on the bored captive audience. Although these in-flight magazines conform to high standards in production, their circulation and readership can obviously vary considerably.

Magazines also have one potentially powerful advantage over broadcast media, which is that the mood of the reader is likely to be more receptive. People often save a magazine until they have time to look at it properly, and because they are inherently interested in the magazine's editorial content, they do pay attention and absorb what they read. This has a knock-on effect on the advertising content too. People also tend to keep magazines for reference purposes. Thus the advertising may not prompt immediate action, but if readers suddenly come back into the market, then they know where to look for suppliers.

Improvements in print and paper technology have enabled high quality advertising to be produced, which is especially important if the product is to be shown at its best. Advertisements for food, clothing, holidays or cosmetics, for instance, are all looking to provoke a strong positive emotional desire ('Oooh, that looks nice') through the stimulus provided by the graphic image. Some magazine advertising is almost an art form.

The specific cost of a magazine advertising slot will vary according to a number of factors. These include its circulation and readership profile, the page chosen and the position on the page, the size of the advertisement, the number of agreed insertions, the use of colour and bleed (whether the colour runs to the edge of the page or not), and any other special requirements.

The growth of truly international magazines is partly restricted by language. English language publications are clearly fine for US and UK markets, and to some extent for business segments in Europe, but the proportion speaking English in Europe is widely variable.

Figures quoted by de Mooij (1994) suggest that 72 per cent of people in the Netherlands understand English, 44 per cent in Germany and just 12 per cent in Spain. Balkanair, the Bulgarian national airline, compromises by printing all its in-flight magazine articles in both Bulgarian and English on facing pages (presumably either halving the content or doubling the cost in the process).

Newspapers

The main role of newspapers for advertisers is to communicate quickly and flexibly to a large audience. National daily papers, national Sunday papers and local daily or weekly papers between them offer a wide range of advertising opportunities and audiences. Table 15.7 shows the number of newspapers available in various European countries in 2000.

Table 15.7 Number of newspapers 2000

Country	*Number*	*Country*	*Number*
Austria	174	Italy	543
Denmark	40	Netherlands	86
Finland	218	Portugal	944
Greece	60	Sweden	195
		UK	576

Source: Euromonitor (2002), extracted from Table 12.4, p. 283.

Classified advertisements are usually small, factual and often grouped under such headings as furniture, home and garden, lonely hearts etc. This is the kind of advertising used by individuals selling their personal property, or by very small businesses (for example a one-woman home hairdressing service). Such advertisements are a major feature of local and regional newspapers. *Display advertising* has wider variations in size, shape and location within the newspaper, and uses a range of graphics, copy and photography. Display advertisements may be grouped under special features and pages: for instance, if a local newspaper runs a weddings feature it brings together advertisers providing the various goods and services that the bride-to-be would be interested in. Such groupings offer the individual advertisers a degree of synergy. Local newspapers are an important advertising medium, not only for small businesses, but for national chains of retailers supporting local stores and car manufacturers supporting local dealerships. In 2000, regional press had a 19.6 per cent share of total UK advertising revenue of £13,267 mn, second only to television's 28 per cent. National newspapers had a share only of 16 per cent (http://www.newspapersoc.org.uk).

During the daily scan for news, readers may notice advertisements and with repetition they may eventually remember them. When a reader is actively seeking information then the newspaper, especially the classified section of a local paper, may be a prime source of products or services.

The main problem with newspaper advertising is related to its cost efficiency – if the advertiser wants to be more selective in targeting. Wastage rates can be high, as newspapers can appeal to very broad segments of the population. Furthermore, compared with magazines, newspapers have a much shorter life span and can have problems with the quality of reproduction possible. Although colour and photographic reproduction quality in newspapers is rapidly improving, it is still inferior to that offered by magazines, and can be inconsistent. The same advertisement, for instance, published in different newspapers or on different days can take on varying colour values and intensities, and be more or less grainy or focused.

Advertising hoardings, ambient and outdoor media

The last group of advertising media includes posters and hoardings, ambient media (such as advertising on bus tickets, toilet walls and store floors) as well as transport-orientated advertising media (advertising in and on buses, taxis and trains and in stations). It can be very cost effective. According to Ray (2002), it can cost £30 to reach 1,000 through television but only £2.80 through outdoor media. Table 15.8 shows the number of outdoor advertising sites in the UK in 2002.

Table 15.8 Number of outdoor advertising sites in the UK 2002

	Site	*Number*
Roadside	6 sheet (1.2m × 1.8m)	75 000
	48 sheet (10 ft × 20 ft)	35 000
	96 sheet (10 ft × 40 ft)	4 500
	Other	20 000
	TOTAL	**134 500**
Transport	Rail	11 000
	Number of buses	37 000
	London Underground	151 000
	Taxis	36 000
	TOTAL	**235 000**

Source: http://www.oaa.org.uk

Whatever the type of outdoor medium used, the purpose is generally the same: to provide quickly digestible messages to passers-by or to provide something for a bored passenger to look at. As with any medium, the advertising may be a one-off, or it may be part of a multimedia campaign. An advertisement at an airport for a nearby hotel would be a one-off but long-term campaign with a very focused purpose, whereas a hoarding advertising a car would probably be only one element tied into a campaign with a theme extending across television, print and direct marketing as well.

Advertising posters range from small home-made advertisements placed on a noticeboard to those for giant hoardings. This section concentrates on the latter group. Hoarding sites are normally sold by the month. Being in a static location, they may easily be seen 20–40 times in a month by people on their way to and from work or school etc. In the UK, over one-third of poster sites are taken by car or drink advertisers. The reach may be small, but the frequency can be quite intense. They can, however, be affected by some unpredictable elements, out of the control of the advertiser. Bad weather means that people will spend less time out of doors, and are certainly not going to be positively receptive to outdoor advertising. Hoardings and posters are also vulnerable to the attentions of those who think they can improve on the existing message with some graffiti or fly posting.

Nevertheless, hoardings offer an exciting medium with great deal of creative scope, capitalising on their size and location. Backlighting, for example, can give a clearer, sharper image, while the potential of video hoardings to create moving, changing messages opens up many possibilities. The latter is especially valuable for attracting passers-by to a restaurant or leisure facility, for example. It pays, however, to be careful in the location of such ultra-creative billboards, since to be the cause of multiple pile-ups by distracting drivers' attention is not desirable PR!

Size is one of the greatest assets of the advertising hoarding, creating impact. Over 80 per cent of hoarding space in the UK is taken by 4-, 6- or 48-sheet sites (a 48-sheet hoarding is 10 feet by 20 feet). Also, sites can be selected, if available, according to the match between traffic flows and target audience. However, in appealing to a mobile audience, the message needs to be simple and thus usually links with other elements of a wider campaign, either for generating initial awareness or on a reminder and reinforcement basis.

marketing *in action*

The great outdoors

Almost anything can be used as an advertising medium: bus tickets, tube tickets, hot air balloons, airships, supermarket trolleys, shops' floors, airline meal trays, sandwich bags, even cows and toilet walls. Campaigns using these 'ambient media' can be very creative and their value to the advertiser is reflected in the fact that around £90 mn is spent every year on this kind of advertising.

Some campaigns are particularly memorable. Cows were recruited to wear coats advertising vegetarian cookery courses, for instance. Toyota used petrol pumps to advertise its fuel-efficient Prius model. This targeted motorists at a time when they are thinking about how much it costs to fill up their cars, and when they have nothing better to do than read and consider the advertisement on the pump. Toyota's commercial director said, 'You're never going to mass-market a product with ambient, but it's a valuable filler'. Similarly, an online recruitment company advertised on sandwich bags to target people when they were taking time out during the working day and likely to be thinking about how lousy their current jobs are. The bags might even be taken back to the office and left lying around for other people to see.

High flying advertisers might like the idea of doing business with bmi media which sells all kinds of advertising associated with bmi British Midland aircraft. 350,000 passengers per month can be targeted through the in-flight magazine, cards placed on meal trays, advertisements on seat backs, and through advertising in airport business lounges. A more down-to-earth form of ambient medium is the taxi cab. Taxi Media is a company selling advertising space in and out of taxi cabs in London and across the UK. Taxis can be branded both inside and out and drivers can participate by handing out freebies or advertising messages. Similarly, PhoneSites sells advertising space on and in telephone boxes. Research suggests that 30 per cent of the UK population uses a payphone every month and that increases to 73 per cent of 16–24-year-olds. PhoneSites also offers to set up 'hot buttons', automatic direct dialling through to the advertiser. Research has shown that this generates 40 per cent higher response rates than just printing a full telephone number for the consumer to dial.

It's a lot more fun than waxing.
Source: Kookaï.

Even traditional outdoor media such as posters can also attract attention through controversy. A poster by French fashion retailer Kookaï showing a tiny man pushing a lawnmower down a woman's bikini line ran on French poster sites and in women's magazines with no problems. Kookaï then wanted to use the same image in a £100,000 campaign in the UK featuring the advertisement on buses in Manchester, London and Leeds. Just before it was due to be launched in London, however, TDI, the agency responsible for selling London Transport bus advertising space, decided to ban the ad as being in poor taste. Kookaï's response was to develop a new advertisement showing a portion of the original advertisement with 'censored' slashed across it. The new caption read, 'They say our ad is too risqué . . . we don't'. The new advertisement duly appeared on the buses.

Sources: Croft (2001); *Marketing* (1999b); Ray (2001); Woolgar (1999).

Finally, there are the *transport-orientated media*. These include advertisements in rail or bus stations, which capture and occupy the attention of waiting passengers who have nothing better to do for a while than read the advertisements. Similarly, advertising inside trains, taxis and buses has a captive audience for as long as the journey takes. Advertising on the outside of vehicles, perhaps even going so as far as to repaint an entire bus with an advertisement, extends the reach of the advertisement to anyone who happens to be around the vehicle's route.

Using advertising agencies

It is not surprising, given the complexity and expense involved, that many organisations employ an agency to handle the development and implementation of advertising programmes. It is important, however, to select the right kind of agency, not only in terms of its practical ability to do what needs to be done and to solve the problems that need to be solved, but also in terms of its creativity, its culture and its ability to empathise with the product and its target market. In this section, therefore, we will examine briefly the different types of advertising agency, then discuss criteria for selecting an agency, and finally, there will be a few thoughts on client–agency relationships.

Full service agencies

Full service agencies provide a full range of services, including research, creative work, artwork, media buying etc. Larger agencies might also have the capacity, or at least have subsidiaries or sister companies in the sales promotion, PR and direct marketing fields, in order to offer a full 'through-the-line' integrated marketing communications service. If a client's account is not large, the agency may bill separately for creative work. With large accounts, some discount can be achieved through the 15 per cent agency commission earned for media buying. Using a full service agency does not mean that the client abdicates all responsibility, but that the advertising is developed jointly. The advantages are that specialist skills can be drawn on as needed; new, different perspectives on the communication problem may be gained; and the client can change agencies if not satisfied. Using a full service agency is also easier to manage and control, and there is less risk of sensitive information leaking out, because everything is self-contained (Smith and Taylor, 2002). As with any buyer–supplier liaison, however, the quality of the relationship, trust and understanding are all very important.

Limited service agencies

Limited service agencies tend to specialise in one or a small number of parts of the total process. Creative shops or 'hot shops' specialise in creative work while media independents specialise in the planning, scheduling, buying and monitoring of media, for example. Agencies specialising in 'new media' such as the internet and SMS advertising are also emerging. Limited service agencies may bid on a speculative basis, receiving a fee only for the proposals selected. The advantage of the limited service agency is that it enables the client to select the best talent to suit their various needs on an *à la carte* basis. It does, however, mean more work for the brand manager in coordinating the effort involved, and there is a risk of information leaks as more different organisations become involved (Fill, 2002; Pickton and Broderick, 2001; Smith and Taylor, 2002).

A few very large organisations might prefer to develop their own expertise in-house, with dedicated staff to manage the campaign. The in-house department may provide the full range of services or supplement skills from external sources such as limited service agencies with particular specialisms. At the opposite extreme, there are special difficulties for smaller businesses, as they do not have the expertise or the amount of money to spend to attract significant agency interest. In such a business the owner or the individual responsible for all marketing may handle media and campaign development.

Working in-house gives the advertiser more control and there is no risk of over-dependency on an outside agency. It may even save money, although an in-house department may not have the same media purchasing power as an agency. The organisation will, however, have to be sensitive to potential gaps in its expertise, as well as the risk of becoming too blinkered in its approach to its own advertising. Using outside agencies does at least bring fresh and objective minds to the problem.

Selecting an agency

Clearly, selecting an agency is very important since its work can potentially make or break a product. Different writers suggest different checklists against which to measure the appropriateness of any given agency. The following list has been compiled from the work of Fill (2002), Pickton and Broderick (2001), Smith and Taylor (2002), and White (1988), and is also shown in Figure 15.2.

Relative size of agency and client

As already mentioned, it might be useful to try to match the relative sizes of the client and the agency, certainly in terms of the proposed advertising spend. This is to ensure the right level of mutual respect, attention and importance. The client might also want to think ahead strategically, and choose an agency that will either grow with the client or be able to meet increased future needs. This might mean coping with a bigger account, coping with integrated communications, or coping with international advertising.

Location and accessibility

A smaller business with a limited geographic market might prefer to work with a small agency that has deep local knowledge and understanding. A larger business, wishing to keep a close eye on what the agency is doing and thus wanting frequent face-to-face meetings with the account team, might also find it more convenient to use an agency located nearby.

Type of help required

Clearly, a client wants an agency that can supply the kinds of services and expertise required. The client might want a full service agency, or just specialised help in media buying, for example. The client might also want an integrated service, covering a wide range of communications techniques, not just advertising. Any prospective agency thus needs to be measured against its ability to deliver an appropriate package.

Specialism

Some agencies have a reputation for specialising in particular products or services, for example higher education advertising or financial services advertising. Some clients might find this attractive on the basis that they can be sure that the agency has detailed knowledge of the relevant marketing and competitive environments. Others, however, might find it off-putting. They might feel that the agency works for the client's competitors or that

Figure 15.2 Criteria for selecting an advertising agency

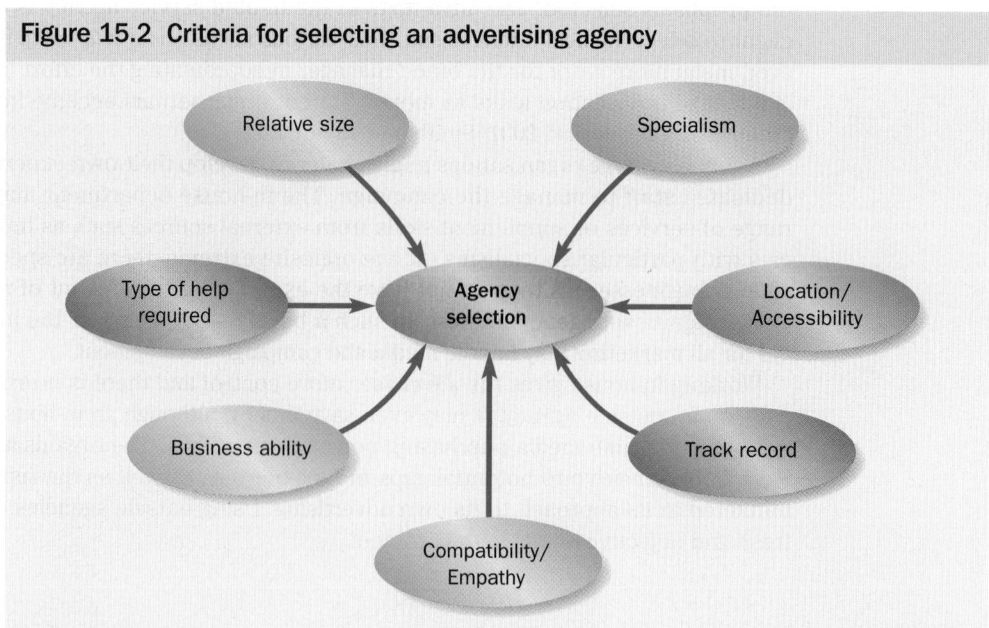

they are 'stale' from doing too much work in one field. Nevertheless, a degree of relevant experience in some related area might be a good indicator of an agency's ability to handle this new account.

Track record

Regardless of whether the agency specialises in particular types of advertising or not, a new client is going to be interested in its track record. How has the agency grown? Who is on its client list? How creative is its work? How effective is its work? Does it seem able to retain its clients, generate repeat business from them and build strong relationships?

Compatibility, empathy and personal chemistry

Compatibility and empathy are about corporate culture and outlook and about individual personalities. Clearly, a client wants an agency that is sympathetic to what the client is trying to achieve and can find the right way of talking to the target audience. A great deal of this depends on client–agency communication and the ability of the agency personnel who will be working on the account to get on well with the individuals from the client company with whom they will be liaising. It is quite legitimate, therefore, for the client to ask just who will be working on the account.

Business ability

Advertising is extremely expensive and so a client wants to be reassured that the agency can work within budget, cost effectively, efficiently and within deadlines. This might, therefore, mean looking at their research and planning capabilities. Furthermore, a client should make sure that they understand the basis on which they will be charged by the agency and precisely what is and is not included.

The client–agency relationship

Whatever the type of agency used, a good relationship is essential. With sound briefing, mutual understanding, and an agreed system of remuneration, the agency becomes an extension of the organisation's own marketing team. Cooperation may depend on mutual importance. For instance, a large client working with a large agency is fine, but a small client dealing with a large agency may become lost. There may be other constraints affecting agency choice. If an agency deals with a competitor, for example, then the conflict of interest needs to be avoided.

Research undertaken at the Marketing Forum by Richmond Events Ltd among both agencies and clients looked at the factors most likely to cause a breakdown in client–agency relationships, and those most likely to promote a positive relationship. The top ten factors cited in each category are shown in Table 15.9.

Table 15.9 Advertising agency–client relationships

Ten factors likely to cause relationship breakdown	*Respondents citing factor (%)*	*Ten factors likely to promote a positive relationship*	*Respondents citing factor (%)*
Lack of personal chemistry	47	Understanding the brand	52
Unreliable delivery	44	Mutual trust	47
Poor creative performance	38	Creative excellence	41
Lack of proactive thinking	30	Long-term partnership	33
Poor communication	23	Proactive thinking	32
Lack of strategic input	22	Planning effectiveness	18
Poor business results	19	Working within budget	14
Inability to learn from experience	18	Continuous improvement	14
Going over budget	17	Respect for deadlines	12
Overpriced production	13	Senior management contact	10

Source: Richmond Events, *The Marketing Forum* 1999. Reprinted with kind permission.

It is clear that the ability to deliver the goods, in terms of timing, creative content and within budget, is crucial to success. Communication and developing deeper mutual understanding and trust are also important if the agency is going to diagnose, understand and solve the client's advertising problem. If these points are taken out of the advertising agency context, they can be seen to be the fundamental criteria for any good buyer–supplier relationship.

Developing an advertising campaign

It is almost impossible that one free-standing advertisement in the press or on television would be sufficient to achieve the results expected, in terms of the impact on the target audience. Normally, advertisers think about a campaign that involves a pre-determined theme but is communicated through a series of messages placed in selected media chosen for their expected cumulative impact on the specified target audience. The elements of the campaign are expected to integrate synergistically so that each advertisement placed both supports and is supported by the others. Campaigns can run for varying lengths of time, for a few weeks, for a season, or for many years with little change in formulation. The annual drink–drive campaigns (*see* Case Study 15.2, page 647 *et seq.*), for example, change their approach and message slightly every year, although the broad thrust is always consistent. They also tend to focus mainly on the few weeks around Christmas and New Year.

There are a number of stages in the development of an advertising campaign. Although the emphasis will vary from situation to situation, each stage at least acknowledges a need for careful management assessment and decision-making. The stages are shown in Figure 15.3 and are discussed in turn below.

Figure 15.3 Stages in developing an advertising campaign

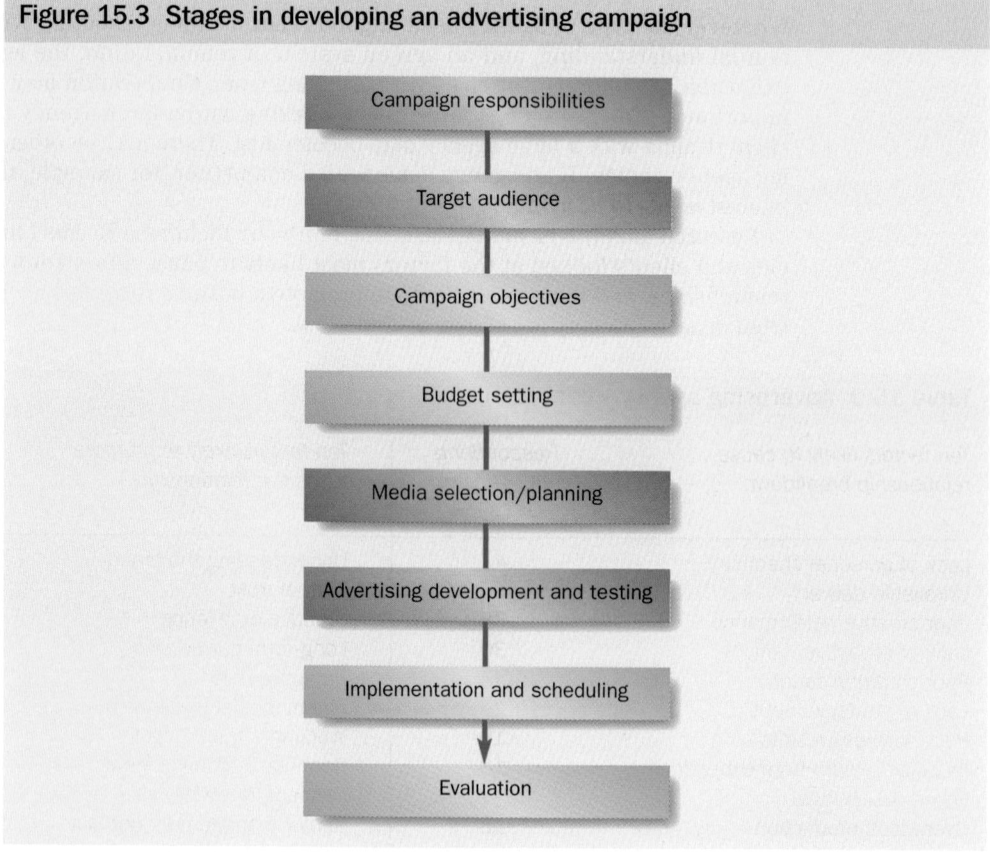

Deciding on campaign responsibilities

This is an important question of organisational structure and 'ownership' of the campaign. If management is devolved on a product basis, then overall responsibility may rest with the brand or product manager. This certainly helps to ensure that the campaign integrates with sales promotion, selling, production planning etc., since the brand manager is very well versed in all aspects of the product's life. If, however, management is devolved on a functional basis, then the responsibility for an advertising campaign will lie with the advertising and promotion manager. This means that the campaign benefits from depth of advertising expertise, but lacks the involvement with the product that a brand manager would supply. Whatever the arrangement, it is essential to define who is ultimately responsible for what tasks and what elements of the budget.

Selecting the target audience

As discussed at pp. 577 *et seq.*, knowing who you are talking to is the foundation of good communication. Based on segmentation strategy, the target audience represents the group at whom the communication is aimed within the market. In some cases, the segment and the target audience may be one and the same. Sometimes, however, the target audience may be a subdivision of the segment. If, for instance, an organisation served a particular hobby segment, different approaches to advertising would be taken depending on whether they wanted to talk to serious, casual, high spenders, low spenders, general-interest or specific-interest subgroups. This underlines the need to understand the market and the range of target audiences within it.

A profile of the target audience increases the chances of successful promotion and communication. Any details, such as location, media viewing (or listening or reading) habits, geodemographics, attitudes and values, can be used to shape the propositions contained within the campaign or to direct the creative approach and media choice.

eg

An advertising agency thinking about advertising a brand of watches in different European countries found from research that in general, Italians treat watches like fashion accessories and might own several to coordinate with different outfits. In contrast, Germans assess watches according to the sophistication of their technology and the number of different functions built in, whereas the British just want a functional and reliable way of telling the time. Clearly, these differences in target market attitudes towards watches will lead to fundamentally different advertising approaches for the brand in those countries.

In B2B markets, the focus is likely to be on understanding the decision-making processes and buying centre membership (*see* Chapter 4), to help create an industry-based segmentation and communication approach.

Whatever the type of product, if the assessment of the target audience is incomplete or woolly, there may be problems in directing campaign efforts later.

Campaign objectives

Communication objectives were considered at pp. 589 *et seq.*, and provide a clear view of what the advertising should accomplish. These objectives need to be specific, measurable and time related. They must also indicate the level of change sought, defining a specific outcome from the advertising task. If there are no measurable objectives, how can achievements be recognised and success or failure judged?

Most advertising is focused on some stage of a response hierarchy model, such as those presented in Figure 14.7 (p. 580). These models highlight the stages in the process of consumer decision-making from initial exposure and awareness through to post-purchase review. Issues such as liking, awareness or knowledge, preference and conviction are important parts of that process, and advertising can aim to influence any one of them. These can thus be translated into advertising objectives with measurable targets for awareness generation, product trial and/or repurchase, attitude creation or shifts, or positioning or preferences in comparison with the competition.

These objectives should be driven by the agreed marketing strategy and plan. Note the difference between marketing and advertising objectives. Sales and market share targets are legitimate marketing objectives as they represent the outcomes of a range of marketing mix decisions. Advertising, however, is just one element contributing to that process, and is designed to achieve specific tasks, but not necessarily exclusively sales.

Campaign budgets

Developing a communication budget was considered at pp. 593 *et seq*. Look back to these pages to refresh your memory on the methods of budget setting. Remember that there is no one right or wrong sum to allocate to a campaign, and often a combination of the methods proposed earlier acts as a guide.

Often the setting of budgets is an iterative process, developing and being modified as the campaign takes shape. There is a direct link between budgets and objectives such that a modification in one area is almost certainly likely to have an impact in the other. Even if the underlying philosophy of the budget is the 'objective and task' approach, practicality still means that most budgets are constrained in some way by the cash available. This forces managers to plan carefully and to consider a range of options in order to be as cost effective as possible in the achievement of the specified objectives.

The first job is to link marketing objectives with the tasks expected of advertising and promotion. Targets may be set, for example, in relation to awareness levels, trial and repeat purchases. Not all these targets would be achieved by advertising alone. Sales promotion, and of course product formulation, may play a big part in repeat purchase behaviour.

Increasingly, computerised models are being introduced to relate objectives and budgets more closely. However, there is still room for managerial judgement and common sense, operating from experience and knowledge of what makes customers and competitors tick. It has been argued that establishing the budget for advertising and marketing is as much a political process as a management task (Piercy, 1987).

Media selection and planning

The various media options were considered individually at pp. 621 *et seq*. The large range of alternative media needs to be reduced down to manageable options and then scheduling (discussed at p. 639) planned to achieve the desired results. The resultant media plan must be detailed and specific. Actual media vehicles must be specified, as well as when, where, how much and how often. This means planning bookings by date, time and space. The plan is the means by which exposure and awareness levels can be achieved. The important aim is to ensure a reasonable fit between the media vehicles considered and the target audience so that sufficient reach and frequency are achieved to allow the real objectives of the advertising a fighting chance of success. This is becoming more difficult as audience profiles and markets change (Mueller-Heumann, 1992).

There are two main approaches to reaching the target audience. The first is a 'shotgun' approach that aims to reach a large number of people across all segments, whether targets or not, accepting that there will be considerable waste. Much television advertising falls into this category. The second approach aims to achieve a close match between the target audience and the advertising media, such as would be the case with a hobby or specific interest group. This approach assumes that the advertiser has a good understanding of the segments and that the media exist for reaching them.

The profile of activity is specified in the media plan, which summarises the choices made regarding medium, vehicle and scheduling. The plan has an important role to play in integrating the campaign effort into the rest of the marketing plan and in communicating requirements clearly to any support agencies.

A number of considerations guide the selection of media, as shown in Figure 15.4. These are discussed briefly below.

eg

Brand awareness of Rennie, an indigestion remedy, was already high, but the company wanted to convert this into increased sales over the Christmas period. The advertising agency felt, however, that television advertising had had a limited effect in previous years, and thus a different approach was needed. The agency negotiated a package with ITV to sponsor a Christmas 'viewing experience'. Rather than linking the brand with just one programme, a package of 29 programmes broadcast between 16 and 30 December 2000 was selected with Rennie receiving 186 credits overall including pack shots. The programmes were selected according to audience levels, timing and scheduling, and included a number of 'Christmas Specials' to reinforce the link between Rennie and people's habit of sitting in front of the television eating and drinking too much! The strategy worked: sales figures showed a significant improvement over the previous year's performance (http://www.mediacomuk.com).

Figure 15.4 Factors influencing media selection

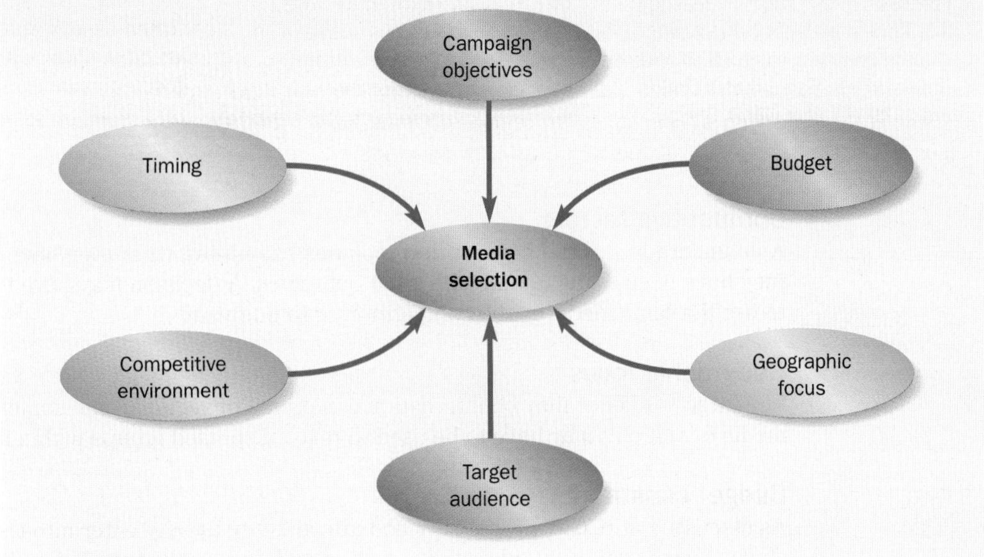

Campaign objectives

The media selected must ensure consistency with the overall objectives for the campaign in terms of awareness, reach etc.

Target audience

The target audience is critical to guiding the detailed media selection. As close a fit as possible is required between medium and audience.

e-marketing *in action*

The rise and fall of banner advertising

Banner advertising is often thought of simply in terms of driving traffic to a website. There are, however, several outcomes that a marketing manager may be looking to achieve through a banner advertising campaign. Cartellieri *et al.* (1997) identify the following objectives:

- *Delivering content*. This is the typical case where a clickthrough on a banner advertisement leads through to a corporate site giving more detailed information on an offer. This is where a direct response is sought.
- *Enabling transactions*. If a clickthrough leads through to a merchant such as a travel site or an online bookstore the advert is placed to lead directly to a sale. A direct response is also sought here.
- *Shaping attitudes*. An advertisement that is consistent with a company brand can help build brand awareness.

▶

- *Soliciting responses*. An advertisement may be intended to identify new leads or as a start for two-way communication. In these cases an interactive advertisement may encourage a user to type in an e-mail address.
- *Encouraging retention*. The advertisement may be placed as a reminder about the company and its service.

The death of banner advertisements has been forecast since their first use, but the global value of banner advertising has increased year on year. By 1999 it had only reached $3.3 billion or 1 per cent of total global advertising value, but Forrester Research estimated that it could reach 10 per cent within 5 years.

The main argument for why banner advertising will decline in importance is that there is currently a 'novelty value' in banner advertisements. New internet users of which there are millions each month, may click on banners out of curiosity or ignorance. More experienced users tend to filter out banner adverts concentrating mainly on the text content of the site where the advertising placement is. Data at e-marketer (www.emarketer.com) shows a dramatic decline in average clickthrough rate from over 2 per cent in the mid-1990s to less than 0.2 per cent in 2001. Much advertising inventory also remains unsold suggesting that supply outstrips demand and has been the death knell for many portals such as Excite that rely on advertising revenue as a significant component of their revenue model.

Despite these figures, innovative online advertising techniques that increase the prominence of adverts on websites mean that online advertising is here to stay, particularly since it is required to pay for much free content on the web. New innovations include skyscraper advertising (long columns), interstitials that appear between pages, superstitials or pop-ups that appear in a new window, interactive advertisements that can be typed into to perform a search and overts which can roam anywhere on the screen – the Reebok belly that was attacking couch potatoes being a good example.

Sources: Cartellieri *et al.* (1997); Chaffey *et al.* (2003).

Competitive factors

A consideration of the competition includes examining what they have been doing, where they have been doing it, and with what outcomes. A decision may have to be made whether to use the same media as the competition or to innovate.

Geographic focus

The target audience may be international, national or regional, and sometimes a selection of media or vehicles may have to be used to reach dispersed groups within the target audience.

Budget constraints

As discussed at p. 636, practicality and affordability usually enter into the planning at some stage. A proposal of 20 prime-time slots on television might well give the chief accountant apoplexy and have to be replaced with a more modest print campaign that makes its impact through stunning creativity.

Timing

The plan needs to take into account any lead-in or build-up time, particularly if the product's sales have a strong element of seasonality. Perfumes and aftershaves, for example, look to Christmas as a strong selling period. Advertisers of these products use glossy magazine advertising all year round, but in the weeks up to Christmas, add intensive and expensive television campaigns (it's a good job we don't have smellyvision yet) to coincide with consumers' decision-making for gifts. Similarly, timing is important in launching a new product, to make sure that the right level of awareness, understanding and desire have been generated by the time the product is actually available.

As with any plan, it should provide the reader with a clear justification of the rationale behind the decisions, and should act as a guide as to how it integrates with other marketing activities.

Advertising development and testing

At this stage, the advertisements themselves are designed and made, ready for broadcasting or printing. The creative issues involved have already been covered elsewhere within this chapter. As the advertisement evolves, **pre-testing** is often used to check that the content, message and impact are as expected. This is particularly important with television advertising, which is relatively expensive to produce and broadcast, and also would represent an extremely public embarrassment if it failed.

Tests are, therefore, built in at various stages of the advertisement's development. Initial concepts and storyboards can be discussed with a sample of members of the target audience to see if they can understand the message and relate to the scenario or images in the proposed advertisement. Slightly further on in the process, a rough video of the advertisement (not the full production – just enough to give a flavour of the finished piece) can also be tested. This allows final adjustments to be made before the finished advertisement is produced. Even then, further testing can reassure the agency and the client that the advertisement is absolutely ready for release. Print advertisements can similarly be tested at various stages of their development, using rough sketches, mock-ups and then the finished advertisement.

White (1988) suggests a number of questions that pre-testing advertisements might answer, and these are summarised in Figure 15.5.

Pre-testing is a valuable exercise, but its outcomes should be approached with some caution. The testing conditions are rather artificial, by necessity, and audiences (assuming even that the testers can assemble a truly representative audience) who react in certain ways to seeing an advertisement in a theatre or church hall might respond very differently if they saw that same advertisement in their own homes under 'normal' viewing conditions.

Implementation and scheduling

In the implementation phase, a number of professional experts may be needed to develop and deliver the advertising campaign. These will include graphic designers, photographers, commercial artists, copywriters, research specialists and, not least, media and production companies. The role of the advertising manager is to coordinate and select these professionals within a budget to achieve the planned objectives.

A key part of the implementation phase is the scheduling of the campaign. This describes the frequency and intensity of effort and guides all production decisions. There are many different scheduling patterns (Sissors and Bumba, 1989). Sometimes, advertising takes place in *bursts*, as shown in Figure 15.6. This means short-term, intense advertising activity, such as that often found with new product launches. Most organisations do not have the resources (or the inclination) to keep up such intense advertising activity indefinitely, and thus the bursts are few and far between. The alternative is to spread the advertising budget out more evenly, by advertising in *drips*, also shown in Figure 15.6. The advertising activity is less intense, but more persistent. Reminder advertising for a frequently purchased mature product might take place in drips rather than bursts.

Figure 15.5 Information gained from pre-testing advertisements

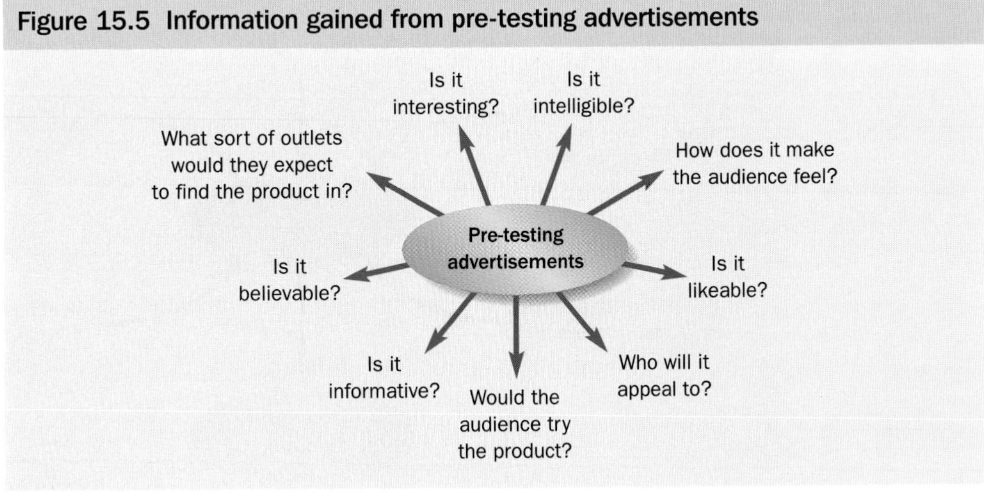

Figure 15.6 Advertising expenditure strategies; 'bursts' and 'drips'

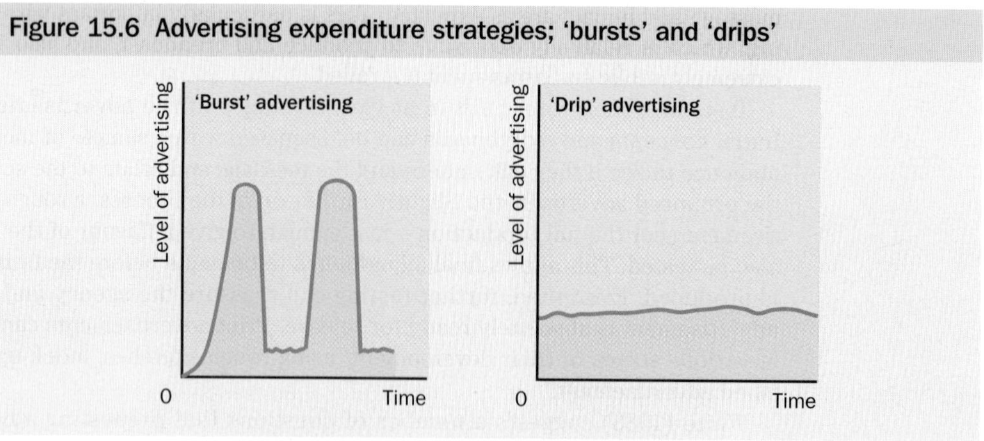

A number of factors will help to determine the overall schedule, as shown in Figure 15.7. These are briefly discussed in turn below.

Marketing factors

Marketing factors might influence the speed of the impact required. An organisation launching a new product or responding to a competitor's comparative advertising might want to make a quick impact, for example.

The turnover of customers in the market

If turnover of customers is high, then there is a need to advertise more frequently to keep the message available for new entrants into the market.

Purchase frequency and volatility

If demand is highly seasonal or perishable, then the scheduling might provide for a short period of high-frequency advertising. The peak time for advertising perfumes and toys, for example, is in the run up to Christmas. Similarly, various chocolate products peak at Easter or Mother's Day, for example. Alternatively, there may be a link with brand loyalty. Higher loyalty may need less frequency, provided that the product is not under competitive attack. This is, however, a dangerous assumption.

Figure 15.7 Factors influencing advertising schedules

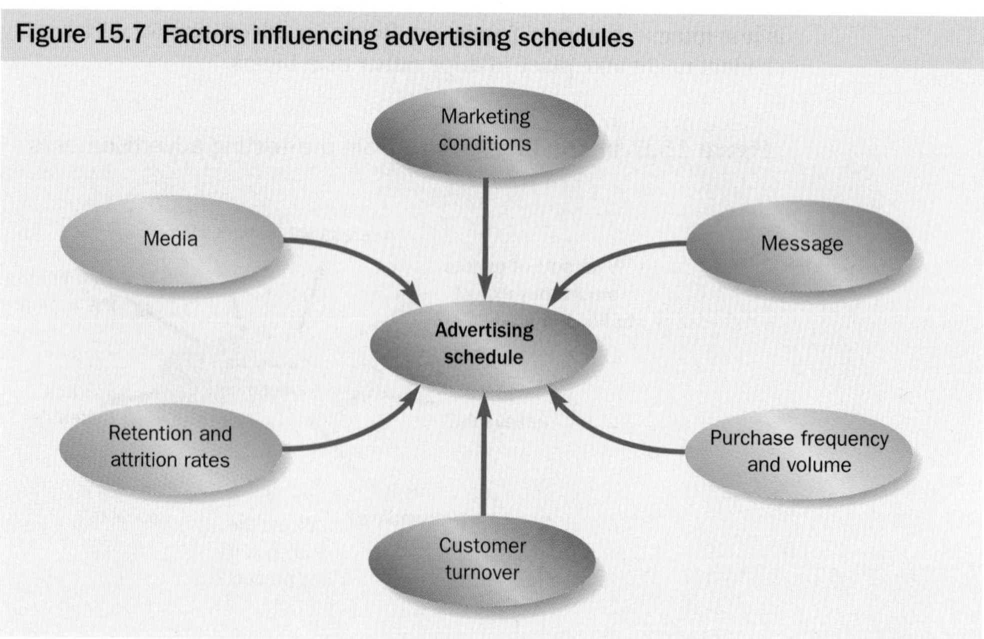

Retention and attrition rates

If the danger of forgetting is high, then the advertiser is likely to need a more active campaign implemented at regular intervals. Different groups learn and forget at different rates. Therefore these retention and attrition rates of the target audience are yet another assessment that needs to be made.

Message factors

A campaign for a new product may need more repetition than one for an established product, because of the newness of the message. More generally, simple messages or those that stand out from the crowd demand less repetition. Similarly, smaller advertisements or those placed in less noticeable spots within a print medium may need more frequency to make sure they are seen.

In broadcast media, however, there is some debate over the relative effectiveness of 10-, 30- and 60-second slots. It seems that longer is not always better. Ten seconds may be sufficient to generate awareness, through a short, sharp impact. Two 30-second slots may be more powerful than one of 60 seconds. However, such a general debate is rather meaningless, since so much depends on the context of the advertising. If there are many other messages (and particularly if they are direct competitors' messages) in the pool, then a much greater impact will have to be made just to create awareness. Finally, impact is not just an issue of how many seconds you buy, it is about what you do with them. A 10-second blast of something stunningly novel and memorable is going to achieve far more than 60 seconds of an advertisement that is a rehash of things that we have all seen before. Research has indeed shown that 10-second advertisements score nearly as highly on recall (34 per cent) as 30-second advertisements (42 per cent) while a 50-second slot scored 58 per cent recall. Nevertheless, the study also showed that 65 per cent of the audience either left the room or did other things while the advertisements were on. Interestingly, it was also found that advertising recall depended on the type of programme being watched, with dramas leading to higher recall than soap operas, and that the more involved with the programme the viewer was, the greater the chances of them actually watching the advertisements (*Marketing Week*, 1999).

It is important for the advertiser to remember that advertisements and ideas 'wear out', that is, as the audience becomes familiar with them, they are less likely to notice or remember them. This is an effect of selective perception, boredom or irritation (Petty and Cacioppo, 1979).

Media factors

With print media in particular, the better the fit between the advertisement and the surrounding editorial or news content, the fewer opportunities to see (OTS) are needed. This is because the reader is more likely to be interested in the advertisements or to read them as part of the publication, as discussed earlier in connection with advertorials, rather than mentally filtering them out. Similarly, the longer the reader's attention span, whether this stems from interest in the publication, or because the reader is concentrating on the whole content rather than skimming it, the fewer the number of OTSs needed.

The fewer media or advertising vehicles in the plan, the fewer OTSs are likely to be needed. This smaller limit may be important for a smaller business with a limited budget or for a major business seeking to dominate a particular medium by means of monopolising the best slots or positions. Such dominance increases the repetition to those in the target audience. The more congested the medium, the more OTSs there need to be, to cut through the background 'noise'.

Forgetting is part of our daily lives, and so any campaign must seek to minimise forgetting. Time is an important factor, and without reminder advertising or other promotional support, the tendency is to forget. There are exceptions, however. For a consumer durable product, for example, the high involvement necessary may assist in decreasing the rate of forgetting because the purchaser has put a great deal of time and conscious effort into making the decision, as discussed in Chapter 3.

None of this makes one media plan better than another. It depends on objectives and the particular market circumstances prevailing. If the product is new or seasonal, a more intensive effort may be appropriate. The scheduling plan may, of course, evolve over time. During the introduction stage of the product lifecycle an intensive burst of advertising will launch the product, and this may then be followed by a more spread-out campaign as the growth stage finishes. Creating awareness in the first place is expensive, but critical to a product's success.

Campaign evaluation

The evaluation is perhaps the most critical part of the whole campaign process. This stage exists not only to assess the effectiveness of the campaign mounted, but also to provide valuable learning for the future.

There are two stages in evaluation. *Interim evaluation* enables a campaign to be revised and adjusted before completion to improve its effectiveness. It enables a closer match to be achieved between advertising objectives and the emerging campaign results.

Alternatively or additionally, *exit evaluation* is undertaken at the end of the campaign. A number of **post-tests** are possible, and some of them are defined below.

Aided (prompted) recall

In aided (prompted) recall, pictures of advertisements are shown to a sample audience. Questions are asked about whether they have noticed these advertisements on television, the radio or in print. The research may go further to investigate level of comprehension.

Unaided (spontaneous) recall

In sponteneous or unaided recall, questions are asked about what advertisements the respondent has noticed recently. No clues are given, so this exercise is much harder for the respondent to do. Sometimes, however, the exercise may be focused on a specific product area, but it is still up to the respondent to remember what advertising they have seen or heard.

Attitude tests

Questions are formulated to measure the respondent's attitude to a product. An attitude test may take place both before and after the advertising campaign so that the level of attitude change effected by the advertising can be measured.

Enquiry tests

The success of the advertising is measured by the number of requests for product information, premiums or sales visits generated. The enquiry test is a simple measure, and is especially useful for small businesses with small budgets, who need to make sure that their advertising works harder. Early in a new campaign, a direct response mechanism (*see* Chapter 18) may be deliberately built in to see what interest is being generated. This gives feedback before the campaign is expanded.

Sales tests

Sales tests are a form of controlled experiment in which an advertising campaign may be run in one area, but not in another. Although it is difficult to keep all other things equal, the running of such a test does give some indication of the impact of the advertising on retail sales etc.

The method of evaluation selected will depend on the original objectives. If these are related to awareness or attitude change, then recognition, recall tests or attitude change tests are appropriate. If the purpose is to influence sales or market share, then the number of enquiries received or sales tests may be used, although neither of these may be a fair assessment, because advertising is only one of many factors contributing to sales. It must be remembered that just because a product's advertisement is recognised or its details are recalled, purchase does not necessarily follow. The consumer might not be able to find anywhere convenient that sells the product, or they might find the price a little too high, or they might be well disposed towards the product, but have even stronger feelings about the competition. These constraints emphasise the need for a fully integrated marketing mix with all its elements working in harmony with each other.

eg

World Books, a book club, was worried about falling response rates to its door-to-door and direct mail campaigns. In certain television regions, therefore, an advertising campaign was developed to tell people that a mailshot or door drop was on its way, and encouraging them to respond to it. Analysis showed that response rates increased by over 25 per cent in areas where the advertising was shown and that the 6,000 extra responses generated virtually paid for the television advertising (http://www.mediacomuk.com).

Chapter summary

- Advertising is a non-personal form of communication with an identified sponsor, using any form of mass media. Advertising can help to create awareness, build image and attitudes and then reinforce those attitudes through reminders. It is an invaluable support for other elements of the promotional mix, for example by creating awareness and positive attitudes towards an organisation in preparation for a sales team, or by communicating sales promotions. Advertising also has strategic uses within the wider marketing mix. It can contribute to product positioning, thus supporting a premium price, or it could help to even out seasonal fluctuations in demand.
- The advertising message is extremely important. It has to be informative, persuasive and attention grabbing. It has to be appropriate for the target audience and thus speak to them in terms to which they can relate. There are several types of creative appeal that advertisers can use: rational, emotional and product centred. Once the message and its appeal have been decided, the advertisement has to be prepared for print or broadcasting. In either case, the advertisement has to be relevant to the target audience, making a sufficient impact to get the desired message across and to get the audience to act on it.
- The advertiser has a wide choice of media. Television has a wide reach across the whole population, but it can be difficult to target a specific market segment precisely. Radio can deliver fairly specific target audiences, and is an attractive medium for smaller companies operating in a defined geographic area covered by a local radio station. Cinema is a relatively minor medium delivering captive, well-profiled audiences. It can make a big impact on the audience because of the quality of the sound and the size of the screen. Print media broadly consist of magazines and newspapers. Magazines tend to have well-defined readerships who are receptive to the content of advertisements relevant to the magazine's theme. Newspapers, on the other hand, have a very short life span and are often skimmed rather than read properly. A reader is unlikely to read through the same copy more than once. Outdoor media includes advertising hoardings, posters, ambient and transport-related media. They can provide easily digested messages that attract the attention of bored passengers or passers-by. They can generate high frequency as people tend to pass the same sites regularly, but can be spoiled by the weather and the ambience of their location.
- Advertising agencies are often used to provide expertise. Choosing an agency is an important task, and an organisation needs to think carefully about the relevant criteria for choice. Once the client has signed up an agency, it is then important to continue to communicate and to build a strong mutual understanding, with both sides contributing according to expectations.
- Managing advertising within an organisation involves a number of stages. First, campaign responsibilities need to be decided so that the process and the budget are kept under proper control. Once the target market and their broad communication needs have been defined, specific campaign objectives can be developed. Next, the budget can be set in the light of the desired objectives. Media choices, based on the habits of the target audience, the requirements of the planned message and the desired reach and frequency, can then be made. Meanwhile, the advertisements themselves are developed. Testing can be built in at various stages of this development to ensure that the right message is getting across in the right kind of way with the right kind of effect. Once the advertising has been fully developed, it can be implemented. Both during and after the campaign, managers will assess the advertising's effectiveness, using aided or unaided recall, enquiry tests or sales tests, depending on the original objectives.

Table 15.10 Test your slogan recall: answers

Here are the answers to the quiz in Table 15.1 on p. 610

Score 1 point for each correct answer:
15–20: congratulations – you are an advertiser's dream target!
10–14: you are an alert and advertising-literate consumer
6–9: you need to pay a bit more attention to those advertising messages
5 or less: oh dear. Have you ever seen or heard *any* advertising?

Slogan	*Brand*
Beenz Meenz ???	**Heinz**
??? refreshes the parts other beers cannot reach	**Heineken**
Just do it	**Nike**
??? puts a tiger in your tank	**Esso**
Happiness is a cigar called ???	**Hamlet**
A ??? a day helps you work, rest and play	**Mars**
And all because the lady loves ???	**Milk Tray**
The car in front is a ???	**Toyota**
The mint with the hole	**Polo**
P-p-p-pick up a ???	**Penguin**
It's good to talk	**BT**
I bet he drinks ???	**Carling Black Label**
The world's favourite airline	**British Airways**
The web's favourite airline	**easyJet**
Because life's complicated enough	**Abbey National**
The future's bright, the future's ???	**Orange**
The art of performance	**Jaguar**
Feeling is everything	**Durex**
You can do it when you ??? it	**B&Q**
Top breeders recommend ???	**Pedigree Chum**

key words and phrases

Advertising
Advertising media
Advertorial
Comparative advertising
Competitive advertising
Copywriting
Creative appeal
Frequency
Full service agencies
Institutional advertising
Layout
Limited service agencies
Pioneering advertising
Post-testing
Pre-testing
Reach
Reminder and reinforcement advertising
Slice-of-life
Storyboard

questions for review

15.1 In what ways can advertising support the other elements of the promotional mix?

15.2 What are the different ways in which *product-orientated* appeals can be used?

15.3 Define *reach* and *frequency*. Why might there be a conflict between them in practice?

15.4 What advantages might *cinema advertising* have over *television*?

15.5 Describe the *stages* in developing an advertising campaign.

questions for discussion

15.1 Find examples of advertising that uses:
(a) a rational appeal; and
(b) a fear appeal.

Why do you think the advertisers have chosen these approaches?

15.2 What are the guidelines for good copy for a print advertisement? Find a print advertisement and discuss the extent to which it conforms with those guidelines.

15.3 Find a current advertising campaign that uses both television and print media. Why do you think both media are being used? To what extent is each medium contributing something different to the overall message?

15.4 Find out the cost of:
(a) a 30-second advertising slot on your regional commercial television channel at 8 p.m. on a weekday evening;
(b) a 30-second slot at the same time on your local commercial radio station;
(c) a full-page advertisement in your local newspaper; and
(d) a full-page advertisement in a national daily newspaper.

15.5 Develop a checklist of criteria against which a prospective client could assess advertising agencies. Which criterion would you say is the most important, and why?

case study 15.1

Accouncing a new arrival

bmi british midland (hereafter bmi) is the UK's second largest full service airline and operates over 2,000 flights per week. In 2001 it carried over 6.5 million passengers. Its main operational base is at Heathrow where it holds 14 per cent of all take off and landing slots. Through its membership of Star Alliance, a grouping of 14 airlines offering seamless travel worldwide, it is also able to offer an international network reaching all areas of the globe.

bmi had been thinking for a while about launching a low-cost airline subsidiary to compete with easyJet, Go, Ryanair and Buzz, but Go's decision to start operating from East Midlands Airport, where bmi has a major presence, increased the stakes in putting these plans into action. Because it was a new business, when bmi's marketing department approached advertising agency Partners BDDH to work on the launch strategy, there was still a lot of strategic brand development to be done before the advertising plan could be considered. In one sense, this is a fairly unusual case in that the agency was faced with a completely clean sheet – no brand name, no brand image to work with. Normally, products and services come to advertising agencies with a lot of baggage in terms of their brand image and the echoes of old campaigns. Here, however, Partners BDDH was fully involved in helping bmi decide that the branding and positioning should reflect a low cost approach but particularly emphasise bmi's reputation for friendliness. This had to be embodied in a strong brand image that would clearly differentiate this airline from its longer-established and very well recognised competitors. This was also thought to be important because forecasts suggested that while the low cost airline market was currently still growing, within 2 or 3 years, it would start to reach saturation, prices would have levelled off, and potential passengers spoilt for choice would start to take their prejudices and attitudes towards the various airlines into account when making a choice. Thus non-price differentiation looks set to become more important in the future.

After a lot of consideration, therefore, the name 'bmibaby' was chosen because it:

- maintains a link with its bmi parent company name giving the reassurance that it was a 'proper' airline
- conveys the caring positioning through the baby connotations
- has personality – it is not a bland descriptive name
- has staying power – it is different but not so 'off the wall' that it will look dated in a year or two.

Having convinced the client that bmibaby was the right name, the next stage was to find the right spokesperson to personify the brand. In the absence of a publicly well known charismatic founder (such as easyJet's Stelios Haji-Ioannou or Virgin's Richard Branson) it was decided to invent a character: Tiny the cartoon baby. Partners BDDH felt that Tiny could be used very flexibly in all kinds of advertising media and other marketing activities to establish and sell the bmibaby brand. Partners BDDH worked closely with design consultancy Landor to design Tiny.

In parallel with this, advertising and marketing plans were evolving. bmi was making decisions on routes and budgets, and ensuring that the new brand name and image were clearly incorporated into the website, tailfin design, staff uniforms etc., while PhD, bmi's media buying agency, was starting to work on the media plan for the launch campaign. As bmibaby was a new brand, the initial objectives were to build up awareness quickly and loudly and to establish the brand personality strongly. As the airline would only be operating from East Midlands airport initially, the target audience was geographically concentrated within a 1 or 2 hour drive of the airport but otherwise had quite a wide profile consisting of ABC1 people with sufficient disposable income and the inclination to take short-break holidays. Taking all of this into account, it was decided that the full range of media should be used, including television, radio, print, outdoor and ambient media. bmi was initially tentative about using television, as this is not commonly used by low cost airlines, but Partners BDDH and PhD persuaded them of its strategic value in generating widespread awareness quickly and in building brand image. This first campaign was virtually all concentrated on the East Midlands catchment area, although a very small percentage was spent on advertising in destination cities such as Dublin. Ambient media were included in the mix, as bmi was keen to explore what ambient media could achieve. Thus passengers at East Midlands Airport found themselves following trails of baby-sized footprints featuring information about bmibaby destinations around the concourse floor!

In terms of budgeting, bmi initially set out with an overall budget figure of £5 mn that had to cover all the marketing costs associated with setting up the new airline. While this might be thought large for what was effectively a regional campaign, it was necessary because the objectives of creating awareness and brand image quickly pointed towards making a lot of noise within a short space of time to get bmibaby noticed. Creatively, the brief was quite straightforward: to announce the birth of the airline, inform the audience which destinations would be covered and to advertise the prices. The message had to delivered clearly but with as much personality as possible. The first advertisements designed took clarity and simplicity to an extreme. They were designed in black and white, presented the factual information, and only featured Tiny, the baby, unobtrusively in the corner as a logo. Partners BDDH decided that this execution did not communicate enough personality and so gave Tiny a bit more to do. Thus the advertisements presented to, and accepted by, the client featured Tiny prominently, carrying a suitcase with the relevant information displayed on it, for example.

In addition, the agency was liaising closely with bmi to develop scripts and voices for Tiny's television and radio appearances. It was decided that Tiny should have the voice of an adult male and have a mischievous side to his character. Having explored a few candidates, actor Matt Lucas (also known as George Dawes from *Shooting Stars*) was chosen to provide Tiny's voice. Choice of music was also very important as that too adds character to the brand and acts as an instantly recognisable reminder, especially for the radio advertising which cannot rely on the visual image. A strong link with a particular piece of music also acts as a consistent thread that can link different media, executions and campaigns together. Initially, the song *Be My Baby*, originally recorded by the Ronettes, was selected. There were problems negotiating the rights with Motown, however, and in any case on reflection it was concluded that the song was just too famous – it might overpower the brand and lead to a situation where everyone remembers the song but not the brand with which it is associated! Instead, the 1930s song *Everybody Loves My Baby* was suggested, and as it was jaunty, fresh and unexpected, it was enthusiastically adopted. Instead of using the original recording, a new version, arranged to fit a 30-second advertising slot, was recorded.

In general terms, the typical timescales and stages involved in planning and implementing an advertising campaign are:

- The client briefs the agency on what is required. The agency then takes between 2 and 4 weeks to turn that into a creative brief that is acceptable to the client
- The creatives are briefed and then take between 3 and 4 weeks to come up with appropriate ideas which are presented to the client for feedback
- A further 2 to 4 weeks are spent reviewing/refining/reworking ideas on an iterative basis until the client is satisfied
- Time taken in the production process varies according to the medium used. For a television advertisement, it can take between 10 and 18 weeks to source the production company; sort out actors, costumes, props, locations etc.; shoot the advertisement; and then do the post-production editing. Radio, print and poster advertising can be developed in a much shorter time span.

While all this is going on, the media buyer is also involved in making decisions about reach, frequency, OTSs, and scheduling. This is not necessarily all formulaic, as judgements about the quality and impact of the creative execution, the synergy between different media and the complexity of the message will affect these decisions. Some of these decisions also have to made quite early on in the planning process, as outdoor media tend to get booked up fairly quickly and there are penalties if television advertising slots are booked after a specified advanced booking date, and so the client sometimes has to be prepared to make an early firm commitment to specific media and timings.

The impact of the bmibaby campaign was very positive and there was a good response to the brand name. As a service product, the impact of the chosen branding on staff is an important consideration. While some staff had early reservations about the bmibaby name and branding, it did not take long for them to embrace it wholeheartedly, and senior managers have noted that there seems to be a positive, relaxed and optimistic attitude among staff who now see the brand/company as fun and interesting to be associated with. At the time of writing, formal campaign evaluation is still in its early stages. Tracking studies are monitoring basic awareness levels of the brand and some basic attitudinal research is taking place to assess whether the target audience has assimilated the message. More in-depth qualitative research on the impact of the creative approach is still to be done and is likely to happen after the campaign has been running for a full year. Meanwhile, one positive sign is that sales targets for the first three months' trading were exceeded by two-thirds.

Thus encouraged, bmi made the decision to go ahead with a plan to introduce bmibaby flights from a second base, Cardiff Airport. Thus as well as maintaining the impetus of the original launch in the East Midlands, Partners BDDH also had to handle the Welsh launch. Since the original launch had been so successful it was decided to replicate that campaign, with minor adjustments to suit local needs better, in Wales. In August 2002, within a week of the announcement that bmibaby flights from Cardiff would start in late October 2002, tickets were already selling well.

As bmibaby has developed, the range of marketing communications activities has also started to evolve. Sponsorship deals have been agreed, for example with Cardiff Rugby Club, Derby County FC and Nottingham Forest FC. Although Partners BDDH was not involved in setting up these deals, it has been involved in designing and producing associated signage and advertising materials. Away from sports, bmibaby also sponsors the weather updates on Central television.

By September 2002, things were looking good. bmibaby had acquired its own sales and marketing manager; the decision had been made to transfer all of bmi's services operating out of East Midlands Airport to the bmibaby brand; and the possibility of operations from a third airport from 2003 were being evaluated.

Source: with grateful thanks to Jamie Inman, Partners BDDH; http://www.bmibaby.com.

Questions

1. In general, what were the main marketing communications objectives for the new airline? To what extent is advertising the most appropriate means of achieving them and what can each medium contribute?
2. Summarise the role of the advertising agency in bmibaby's launch. What are the advantages and disadvantages of using an external agency for these tasks?
3. Outline the methods that could be used and the potential problems that Partners BDDH could face in evaluating the effectiveness of its advertising campaign for bmibaby.
4. bmibaby's new sales and marketing manager has been appointed from outside bmi. If you were Partners BDDH's account manager what issues and/or concerns might you like to see discussed or clarified in the course of your first few meetings with her?

case study 15.2

Driving a sober message home

Every year around Christmas, the UK government sponsors an advertising campaign to prevent drinking and driving. Over the years, the messages, based around fear of the consequences of drinking and driving, succeeded in raising public awareness generally but were not making the desired impact on the core target audience of young males. The problem was that the audience felt that for such horrible things to happen, the driver had to be absolutely blind drunk, and since they themselves were never in that state, the message did not apply to them. From 1992 onwards, therefore, the tone of the fear campaign was altered.

The 1994 campaign, for example, pointed out that 'even great blokes can kill', featuring a driver who had only 'had a quick one' and then been responsible for killing the parents of two young children. In 1995, the campaign changed direction slightly by showing the damage that 'a quick one' can do to the driver himself. The television advertisement showed a young man, clearly paralysed and brain damaged, being spoon-fed liquidised food by his worn-out mother. With each spoonful, she is encouraging him with 'Come on, Dave, just one more'. In the background as a ghostly echo, pub noises can be heard, specifically a group of lads having a good time and encouraging each other with 'Come on, Dave, just one more'. The message made all the more impact by focusing on what could happen to me (i.e. a largely selfish concern) rather than on what I could do to an unknown third party (i.e. appealing to a sense of responsibility or duty).

1995 drink/drive campaign

Source: Department of Transport Local Government and the Regions.

The 1998 campaign changed direction again. The series of 15 advertisements reconstructed police videos of real fatal accidents with police radio messages talking of dead bodies smelling of alcohol. There was no voice-over, allowing the reality of the video and the messages and conversations between members of the emergency services to speak for themselves. The end shot is of a black screen with the message 'Don't drink and drive' fading to 'Don't drink and die'. Although no bodies are actually seen, some of the advertisements were still graphic enough to have to be shown only after 9 p.m.

Accident scenes featured strongly again in the 2000 campaign. The £1.9 mn campaign used television, radio, outdoor media and point-of-sale media (posters and postcards) in pubs and clubs on the theme of 'Drinking and driving is one Christmas tradition we can all do without. THINK'. The television advertisements showed real accident scenes accompanied by favourite Christmas songs, *Silent Night*, *Mistletoe and Wine*, and *I wish it could be Christmas every day* but no voice-over. The radio advertisements featured extracts from pop tracks with verbal endorsements of the anti-drink-drive message from the artists. In 2001, £1 mn was spent on repeating the same television campaign, but supported by new radio advertisements.

All these campaigns have made an impact and raised awareness, but the difficulty lies in actually challenging and changing people's attitudes and behaviour without seeming t preach or lecture at them. The Department of Transport, Local Government and the Regions (DTLR) says, 'We want people to sit up and take notice, whatever approach we take, whether hard-hitting or more subtle. We are constantly looking at new ways of making advertising work and keeping a freshness to it so people don't look at the ad and think "oh no not again"' (as quoted by Hedberg, 2001).

Government research seems to suggest that while it has been a slow process, the series of campaigns since 1976 have succeeded in changing attitudes to drink driving. Research among men who drive and who also drink outside the home has shown that the percentage who had driven after drinking on at least one occasion in the previous week had fallen from 51 per cent in 1979 to 23 per cent in 1997. The percentage claiming to 'leave the car at home' when going drinking had risen from 54 per cent in 1979 to 79 per cent in 1997. Social attitudes also seem to have changed for the better: the percentage agreeing with the statement 'it is difficult to avoid drinking and driving in the social context' had fallen from 61 per cent in 1979 to a mere 19 per cent in 1997. Nevertheless, as Clarke (2000) says, 'It's one thing to say your behaviour has changed, another to change your behaviour, and still another to measure that change.' The measurable statistics look promising, however. In 1979, the number of fatalities in collisions in which one or more driver was over the legal drink–drive limit was 1640. By 2000 that had fallen to 520, and over the same period, the percentage of drivers killed who were over the legal limit dropped from 32 per cent to 19 per cent.

The correlation between the advertising and the falling death rate may not be as clear as it seems, however. Shock-tactic drink–drive advertising that left absolutely nothing to the imagination was used in the state of Victoria, Australia, between 1990 and 1997. The number of alcohol-related road deaths halved, but as Clarke (2000) points out, that was as much to do with a police crackdown on enforcing the relevant laws as with advertising. Experts interviewed by Roberts (2001) also take the view that the only real way to cut the carnage is zero-tolerance of drink-driving and heavy penalties. Ireland has used similar shock advertising, but there has been no appreciable change in the numbers of fatalities. Similarly, in New Zealand where shock advertising was not supported by other activities, the change in the death rate was minimal. A 1998 study in New Zealand found little evidence to suggest that the advertising had had any effect on the behaviour of drivers who drink. Australian research found that the more graphic the gory scenes in an advertisement, the more likely it is that the viewer will attribute the crash to non-drink related causes beyond the driver's control.

There are also concerns that 17–24-year-old men are over-represented in terms of both the number of positive breath tests and the casualty figures, probably because young drivers overestimate their own abilities and tend to be less responsible than older

2001 drink/drive campaign

Source: Department of Transport Local Government and the Regions.

1998 drink/drive campaign

Source: Department of Transport Local Government and the Regions.

Gradually campaigns to encourage people to not mix drinking and driving have become more hard hitting, showing the reality of the death and destruction it causes.

Source: Department of Transport Local Government and the Regions.

ones. This poses a particularly tough communications task because of the well-entrenched role that alcohol seems to play in young people's lives, even by the age of 17. A study into adolescent drinking behaviour by MacKintosh *et al.* (1997) found that for 14- and 15-year-olds, drinking is a 'normal' part of their social lives and drinking to excess for the sake of getting drunk is quite common. While 16- and 17-year-olds drink more in total than the younger age group, they are more mature in their attitudes.

> *Although this age group may still drink to get drunk, they are learning their own limits and are more likely to see drinking as enhancing their social activities rather than as being their social activity. They enjoy both the process and outcome of drinking . . . Alcohol was a 'social lubricant' for most and they talked about its ability to relax them, to increase their confidence and to lower their inhibitions* (MacKintosh *et al.*, 1997).

Given these social attitudes, and in the face of a drinks industry that spends some £227 mn per year on advertising to tell young people in the sexiest ways permissible that alcohol is sophisticated, fun, enjoyable and an essential 'social lubricant', can the DTLR really win with its essentially gloomy messages?

Sources: *Campaign* (1998); Clarke (2000); DMB&B (1995); Hedberg (2001); MacKintosh *et al.* (1997); Roberts (2001); http://www.alcoholconcern.org.uk; http://www.dtlr.gov.uk.

Questions

1. Why is this kind of campaign much more difficult to design in advertising terms than a 'normal' fmcg campaign?
2. What types of appeal have been used in the campaigns outlined in this case? To what extent and why do you think they might have worked?
3. What are the advantages and disadvantages of the different main types of advertising media for a campaign like this?
4. The Government has pinpointed 17–24-year-old males as a particularly vulnerable group. How could this group be targeted better?

References for chapter 15

Adamson, C. (2002), 'Jules Back On Message at the Shops', *Evening Standard*, 22 February, p. 18.

Addelman, M. (2002), 'Holsten Launches Hybrid Fruit-flavoured Lager in the UK', *Marketing Week*, 7 March, p. 6.

Appelbaum, U. and Halliburton, C. (1993), 'How to Develop International Advertising Campaigns that Work: The Example of the European Food and Beverage Sector', *International Journal of Advertising*, 12(3), 223–241.

Arnold, M. (2001a), 'CRM Shows its Winning Ways', *Marketing*, 19 July, p. 19.

Arnold, M. (2001b), 'Bringing Henkel Home', *Marketing*, 11 October, p. 4.

Bawden, T. (2002), 'A Functional Food Served With Hunour', *The Times*, 27 February, p. 32.

Beard, M. (2002), 'Sainsbury Signs Jamie Oliver in £2mn Deal', *The Independent*, 17 January, p. 11.

Berkowitz, E. N. *et al.* (1992), *Marketing*, Irwin.

Brabbs, C. (2001), 'Two-thirds Find Comparative Ads "Unacceptable"', *Marketing*, 20 September, p. 4.

Campaign (1998), 'AMV Unveils Graphic Anti-drink-drive Xmas Campaign', *Campaign*, 4 December, p. 2.

Cartellieri, C., Parsons, A., Rao, V. and Zeisser, M. (1997), 'The Real Impact of Internet Advertising', *The McKinsey Quarterly*, 3, pp. 44–63.

Cavanagh, R. (2001), 'Lucozade to Rebrand for Lara Croft Film', *Marketing Week*, 19 April, p. 5.

Chaffey, D., Mayer, R., Johnston, K. and Ellis-Chadwick, F. (2003), *Internet Marketing: Strategy, Implementation and Practice*, 2nd edn, Financial Times Prentice Hall.

Chandiramani, R. (2001), 'Is Age Concern Wise to Target Younger Market?', *Marketing*, 20 September, p. 15.

Clarke, M. (2000), 'Advertising with Plenty of Body', *Sunday Times*, 17 December, p. 28.

Cowen, M. (2001), 'Cowen on...Orange', *Campaign*, 12 October, p. 19.

Cox, T. (2001), 'Just Another Rock 'n' Roll Brand', *The Observer*, 1 April, p. 6.

Cozens, C. (1999), 'Saatchis Creates New Army Recruiting Drive', *Campaign*, 23 April, p. 7.

Croft, M. (2001), 'A Flash in the Pan', *Marketing Week*, 16 August, pp. 37–9.

De Mooij, M. (1994), *Advertising Worldwide: Concepts, Theories and Practice Of International, Multinational and Global Advertising*, 2nd edn, Prentice Hall.

DMB&B (1995), *A DMB&B Case Study: Drink–Drive*, DMB&B.

Edwards, M. (2000), 'Brand on the Run', *Sunday Times*, 10 December, p. 14.

Euromonitor (2002), *European Marketing Data and Statistics 2002*, Euromonitor, 37th edn.

Fill, C. (2002), *Marketing Communications: Contexts, Strategies and Applications*, 3rd edn, Financial Times Prentice Hall.

Frook, J. (2001), 'Companies Swop Good Deals for Testimonials', *B to B*, 10 December, p. 1.

Fry, A. (1999), 'Euro TV Builds on Decade's Growth', *Marketing*, 13 May, pp. 43–4.

Grant, J. (2002), 'Orange Ad Highlights Emotional Value of Text Messages', *Marketing*, 17 January, p. 20.

Gray, R. (2001), 'Fighting Talk', *Marketing*, 20 September, pp. 26–7.

Hedberg, A. (2001), 'Government Exchanges Preaching for Teaching', *Marketing Week*, 13 December, p. 20.

MacKintosh, A., Hastings, G., Hughes, K., Wheeler, C., Watson, J. and Inglis, J. (1997), 'Adolescent Drinking: The Role of Designer Drinks', *Health Education*, 97 (6), pp. 213–24.

Marketing (2002), 'Company CV: Orange', *Marketing*, 7 March, p. 50.

Marketing (1999a), 'Reading Between the Lines', *Marketing*, 21 January, pp. 21–2.

Marketing (1999b), 'Hair Today, Gone Tomorrow', *Marketing*, 21 April, p. 80.

Marketing Week (2001), 'Microsoft to Promote Windows XP in Daily Telegraph Supplement Deal', *Marketing Week*, 12 October, p. 12.

Marketing Week (1999), 'Commercials Should Break With Tradition', *Marketing Week*, 21 January, p. 12.

Mason, J. (2000), 'Judge Throws Out BA Attack on Ryanair', *Financial Times*, 6 December, p. 4.

Mason, T. (2000), 'Flora Canvasses Aussies in £2.4m UK pro.activ Ads', *Marketing*, 31 August, p. 4.

McLuhan, R. (1999), 'Success for Army's Initiative-testing Recruitment Drive', *Marketing*, 27 May, p. 26.

Middleton, T. (2002), 'Global POP', *Marketing Week*, 11 April, pp. 36–7.

Mintel (2001a), *Tea and Herbal Tea*, 15 November, accessed via http://www.mintel.com.

Mintel (2001b), *Shampoos and Conditioners*, 1 June, accessed via http://www.mintel.com.

Muehling, D. *et al.* (1990), 'The Impact of Comparative Advertising on Levels of Message Involvement', *Journal of Advertising*, 19(4), pp. 41–50.

Mueller-Heumann, G. (1992), 'Markets and Technology Shifts in the 1990s: Market Fragmentation and Mass Customisation', *Journal of Marketing Management*, 8(4), pp. 303–14.

Munzinger, U. (1988), 'Ad*Vantage/AC-T International Advertising Research Case Studies', *ESOMAR Seminar on International Marketing Research*, 16–18 November.

Murphy, D. (1999), 'Taking Your Ads In-store', *Marketing*, 18 March, pp. 35–6.

NFU Mutual (2002), 'Hidden Hazards of the Country Road', *Western Mail*, 5 January, p. 21.

NFU Mutual (2001), 'Time to Check Out Your Security Measures', *Western Mail*, 13 October, p. 21.

Petty, R.E. and Cacioppo, J.T. (1979), 'Effects of Message Repetition and Position on Cognitive Responses, Recall and Persuasion', *Journal of Personality and Social Psychology*, 37 (January), pp. 97–109.

Pickton, D. and Broderick, A. (2001), *Integrated Marketing Communications*, Financial Times Prentice Hall.

Piercy, N. (1987), 'The Marketing Budgeting Process: Marketing Management Implications', *Journal of Marketing*, 51(4), pp. 45–59.

Ray, A. (2002), 'Using Outdoor to Target the Young', *Marketing*, 31 January, p. 25.

Ray, A. (2001), 'Ambient Enters the Mainstream Arena', *Marketing*, 21 June, p. 31.

Roberts, R. (2001), 'Get Tough on Drink-drivers', *Western Mail*, 7 December, p. 2.

Shannon, J. (1999), 'Comparative Ads Call for Prudence', *Marketing Week*, 6 May, p. 32.

Sissors, J. and Bumba, L. (1989), *Advertising Media Planning*, 3rd edn, NTC Business Books.

Smith, P. and Taylor, J. (2002), *Marketing Communications: An Integrated Approach*, 3rd edn, Kogan Page.

Smith, R. (2002), 'Boddingtons Braves Cream-free Strategy', *Marketing*, 28 February, p. 15.

Staheli, P. (2000), 'We're the Best But We're Not Allowed to Tell You', *Evening Standard*, 26 April, p. 59.

Watson, S. (2001), 'Posh and Becks Modelling for M&S?', *The Guardian*, 16 November, p. 2.12.

White, J. (2002), 'Lowe Unveils Orange Ads Targeting Users From Rival Networks', *Campaign*, 1 March, p. 6.

White, R. (1988), *Advertising: What It Is and How To Do It*, McGraw-Hill.

Wilson, R. (1999), 'Commercial Sounds', *Marketing Week*, 6 May, pp. 47–52.

Woolgar, T. (1999), 'Outdoor Answers Back', *Campaign*, 16 April, p. 29.

chapter 16

sales promotion

LEARNING OBJECTIVES

This chapter will help you to:

1 define sales promotion and appreciate its role in the communications mix through the objectives it can achieve;

2 understand the range of available methods of sales promotion in consumer markets and their objectives;

3 understand the range and objectives of sales promotion methods used by manufacturers to stimulate retailers; and

4 gain an overview of the issues involved in the sales promotion planning process and their implications for the application and practice of sales promotion methods.

Introduction

Traditionally the poor cousin of advertising, sales promotion actually covers a fascinating range of short-term tactical tools that can play a vital complementary role in long-term promotional strategy. Its aim is to add extra value to the product or service, over and above the normal product offering, thus creating an extra inducement to buy or try it. Although individual sales promotions are usually regarded as short-term tactical measures, sales promotion generally, as an element of the promotional mix, is increasingly being recognised as a valid strategic tool, working alongside and supporting other promotional elements.

This chapter will define more clearly what sales promotion is and what strategic role it can play within the promotional mix. It considers in detail the various methods associated with consumer, B2B and trade promotions, discussing what each can contribute towards given marketing objectives. If new products are planned, for example, a number of sales promotions may be designed to encourage product trial. If competitive activity is increasing, then sales promotion efforts may be directed at retaining customer loyalty and generating repeat purchases. The chapter will not, however, only look at the implementation issues, but also consider the management concerns that lie behind sales promotion. To be effective, sales promotion programmes must be carefully planned and managed. The key management issues will be considered from a campaign development perspective.

eg

Extra excitement can be added to sales promotions by linking them with current events. The 2002 World Cup, for example, generated a lot of linked promotional activity as brands sought to exploit public interest. Nestlé's 'Know your football, know your chocolate' campaign, fronted by Terry Venables, for example, ran across five different Nestlé confectionery brands. The promotion featured on 55 million product wrappers and included an instant win element, with thousands of £10 prizes at stake, while ten winning wrappers gave consumers the chance to win up to £10,000. The ten winners were telephoned by Terry Venables, who asked them two easy questions, one on football and one on chocolate. Each question answered correctly won £5,000. The promotion was integrated with television, radio and print advertising, which informed consumers about the promotion and generated interest and excitement around it.

Planning and executing a promotion like this is no easy matter, however. First of all, with five different brands involved, Nestlé had to ensure that all the relevant brand managers were happy with the concept and that the promotion fitted well with the individual brand strategies. A lot of market research then went into deciding the fine details of the promotion and ensuring that it would stand out in what is a very competitive market. Eight focus groups were held involving both men and women aged between 16 and 34, and including people with varying levels of interest in football. The results of the research helped to determine the prize structure, the POS support for the promotion, the way in which the promotion was delivered, and the scripts of the advertisements, as well as the choice of Terry Venables. The research showed that cash delivered through instant wins would be the most effective motivator (Kleinman, 2002; Pemble, 2002).

Nestlé clearly takes its promotions seriously, and rightly. Promotion has an important role to play in the integrated marketing communications mix and can generate interest and excitement around a brand, as well as giving consumers a real reason to try it and buy it.

The role and definition of sales promotion

According to the Institute of Sales Promotion, **sales promotion** is:

> ... *a range of tactical marketing techniques designed within a strategic marketing framework to add value to a product or service in order to achieve specific sales and marketing objectives.*

The word 'tactical' implies a short, sharp burst of activity that is expected to be effective as soon as it is implemented. The fact that this activity is *designed within a strategic marketing framework* means, however, that it is not a panic measure, not just something to wheel out when you do not know what else to do. On the contrary, sales promotion should be planned into an integrated communications mix, to make the most of its ability to complement other areas such as advertising and its unique capacity to achieve certain objectives, mostly tactical, but sometimes strategic (Davies, 1992).

The key element of this definition, however, is that the sales promotion should *add value to a product or service*. This is something over and above the normal product offering that might make buyers stop and think about whether to change their usual buying behaviour, or revise their buying criteria. As the rest of this chapter will show, this takes the form of something tangible that is of value to the buyer, whether it is extra product free, money, a gift or the opportunity to win a prize, that under normal circumstances they would not get.

Perhaps the main problem with the definition is that the area of sales promotion has almost developed beyond it. The idea of the short-term tactical shock to the market is very well established and understood, and will be seen to be at the heart of many of the specific techniques outlined in this chapter. With the development of relationship marketing, that is, the necessity for building long-term buyer–seller relationships, marketers have been looking for ways of developing the scope of traditional sales promotion to encourage long-term customer loyalty and repeat purchasing behaviour. Loyalty schemes, such as frequent flyer programmes or the Shell smart card, are sales promotions in the sense that they offer added value over and above the normal product offering, but they are certainly not short-term tactical measures – quite the opposite. Wilmshurst (1993) clearly states that creatively designed sales promotions can be just as effective as advertising in affecting consumers' attitudes to brands. This means, perhaps, that the definition of sales promotion needs to be revised to account for those strategic, franchise-building promotional techniques:

> ... *a range of marketing techniques designed within a strategic marketing framework to add extra value to a product or service over and above the 'normal' offering in order to achieve specific sales and marketing objectives. This extra value may be of a short-term tactical nature or it may be part of a longer-term franchise-building programme.*

The rest of this section will focus on the objectives that sales promotion can achieve. Sales promotion objectives are best discussed in the context of the relationship within which they are happening, as shown in Figure 16.1. The techniques linked with these objectives will be discussed in much more detail in later sections of the chapter.

Figure 16.1 Communication links through sales promotion

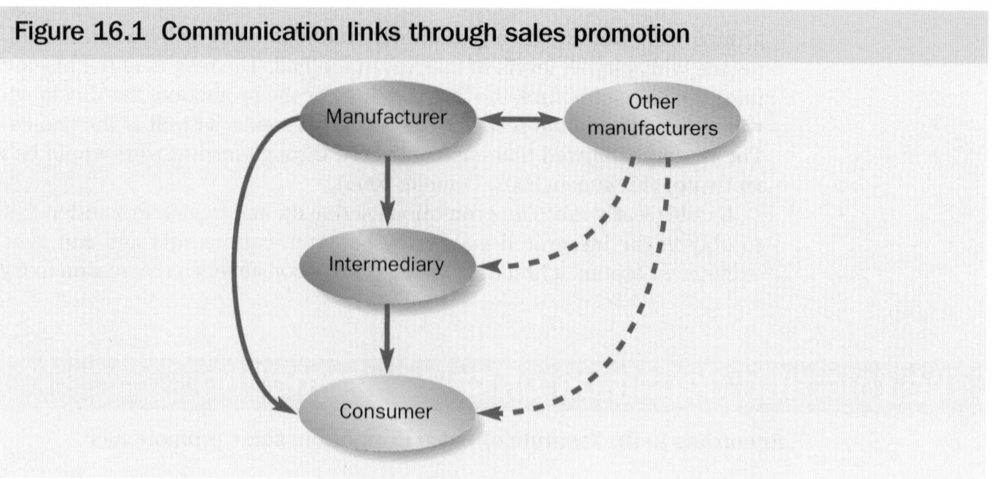

Manufacturer–intermediary (trade promotion)

The intermediary provides a vital service for the manufacturer in displaying goods to their best advantage and making them easily available to the consumer. Any individual intermediary, however, performs this function for a number of manufacturers, and so a manufacturer might wish to use sales promotion techniques to encourage the intermediary to take a particular interest in particular products for various purposes. However, depending on the balance of power between manufacturer and intermediary, the manufacturer might have little choice in the matter. Intermediaries might expect or insist on sales promotions before they will cooperate with what the manufacturer wants.

As shown in Figure 16.2, and discussed below, trade promotions revolve around gaining more product penetration, more display and more intermediary promotional effort. As Fill (2002) points out, however, this might cause conflict between the manufacturer and the intermediary, since the intermediary's prime objective is to increase store traffic. The level of incentive might thus have to be extremely attractive!

Figure 16.2 Manufacturer–intermediary sales promotion objectives

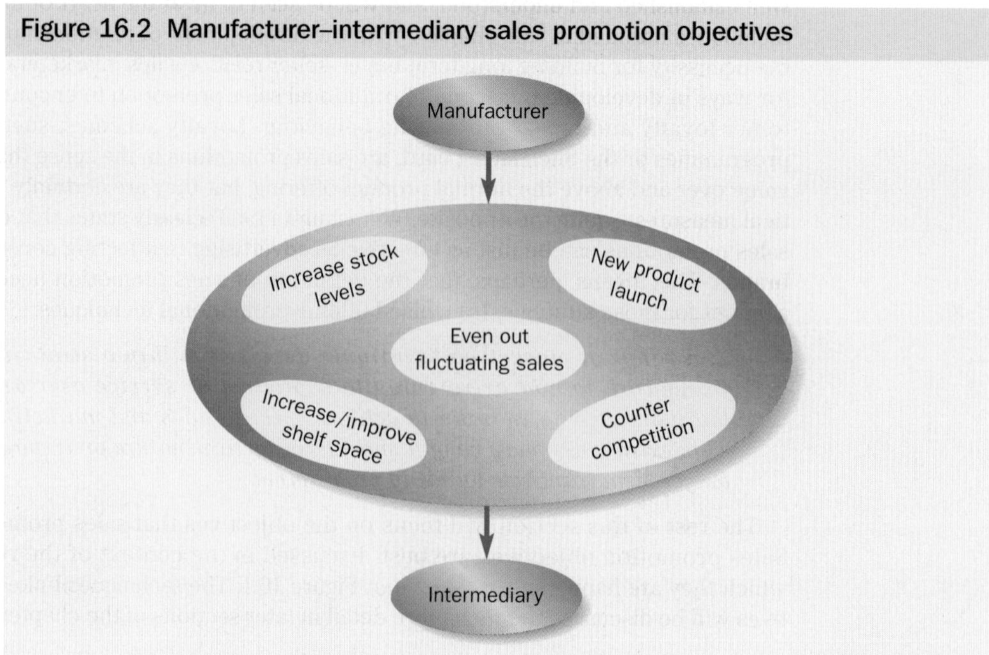

Increase stock levels

The more stock of a particular product that an intermediary holds, the more committed they will be to put effort into selling it quickly. Furthermore, intermediaries have limited stock-holding space, so the more space that your product takes up, the less room there is for the competition. Money-based or extra-product-based incentives might encourage intermediaries to increase their orders, although the effect might be short lived and in the longer term might even reduce orders as intermediaries work through the extra stock they acquired during the promotion.

Gain more and better shelf space

There is intense competition between manufacturers to secure shelf space within retail outlets. Demand for shelf space far outstrips supply. Intermediaries are, therefore, willing to accept incentives to help them to allocate this scarce resource to particular products or manufacturers. Again, this may link with money- or product-based trade promotions, but could also be part of a joint promotion agreement or a point-of-sale promotion, for instance. The quality of the shelf space acquired is also important. If a product is to capture the consumer's attention, then it needs to be prominent. This means that it must be displayed either at the customer's eye level or at the end of the aisles in a supermarket where the customer is turning the corner and all the trolley traffic jams occur. There is keen competition for these highly desirable display sites, also called *golden zones*, and again, intermediary-orientated sales promotion may help a manufacturer to make its case more strongly.

New product launch

The launch period is a delicate time in any new product's life, and if the distribution aspects of the marketing strategy are weak, then it could be fatal. A new product needs to be accepted by the appropriate intermediaries so that it is available for all those consumers eager to try it. To the trade, however, a new product is a potential risk. What if it doesn't sell? Trade promotions (particularly with a push strategy – *see* pp. 578 *et seq.*) can reduce some of that risk. Money-based promotions reduce the potential financial losses of a product failure, while '**sale or return**' promotions remove the fear of being left with unsaleable stock. Sales force support, meanwhile, can reassure the intermediary that staff are ready, willing and able to sell the product and fully understand its features and benefits. This is particularly appropriate with more complex, infrequently purchased items, such as electrical goods.

Even out fluctuating sales

Some products, such as lawnmowers, ice-cream and holidays, suffer from seasonality. While the design of the product offering or the pricing policies adopted can help to overcome these problems, sales promotion can also play a part. If manufacturers are able to encourage intermediaries to take on more stock or to push the product harder during the 'quieter' periods, sales can be spread a little more evenly throughout the year. This process can also be enhanced by a related consumer-orientated promotion, so that the manufacturer is gaining extra synergy through simultaneous push and pull activity.

Counter the competition

It has already been indicated that a manufacturer is competing with every other manufacturer for an intermediary's attention. Sales promotions, therefore, make very useful tactical weapons to spoil or dilute the effects of a competitor's actions. If, for instance, you are aware that the competition is about to launch a new product, you might use a trade sales promotion to load up a key intermediary with your related products, so that at best they will be reluctant to take on the competition's goods, or at worst, they will drive a much harder bargain with the competitor.

Retailer–consumer (retailer promotions)

In the same way that manufacturers compete among themselves for the intermediary's attention, retailers compete for the consumer's patronage. Store-specific sales promotions, whether jointly prepared with a manufacturer or originating solely from the retailer, can help differentiate one store from another, and entice the public in. Retailers also try to use sales promotions in a longer-term strategic way to create store loyalty, for example through card schemes that allow the shopper to collect points over time that can be redeemed for gifts or money-off vouchers. Retailers use sales promotion for many reasons and these are summarised in Figure 16.3.

Increase store traffic

A prime objective for a retailer is to get the public in through the shop door. Any kind of retailer-specific sales promotion has a chance of doing that. Money-off coupons delivered from door to door or printed in the local newspaper, for example, might bring in people who do not usually shop in a particular store. Such promotions might also encourage retail substitution, giving shoppers an incentive to patronise one retailer rather than another. An electrical retailer might advertise a one-day sale with a few carefully chosen items offered on promotion at rock-bottom prices. This bait brings potential customers to the store, and even if the real bargains have gone early, they will still look at other goods.

Increase frequency and amount of purchases

Even if a customer already shops at one retailer's outlets, the retailer would prefer them to shop there more often and to spend more.

eg

Short-term promotions are often used by retailers to increase store traffic. Supermarket chain Safeway, for instance, uses price-based offers to draw shoppers into its stores. By advertising rock-bottom bargains on a selected number of big-name brands in the local press and through door-to-door leafleting within a store's catchment area, shoppers are tempted to pay a visit. The range of offers changes week by week, thus keeping the shopper's interest fresh. The hope is that the shopper will keep returning every week and that once in the store, they will buy far more than just a limited range of discounted brands.

Increase store loyalty

Supermarkets in particular use sales promotion as a means of generating store loyalty. The kinds of activities outlined in relation to increasing the frequency and amount of purchases help towards this, as does a rolling programme of couponing and money-off offers. The problem with this type of promotion, however, is that it risks creating a 'deal-prone' promiscuous customer who will switch to whichever retailer is currently offering the best package

Figure 16.3 Retailer–consumer sales promotion objectives

In the UK, Tesco was the first with its Clubcard, and Sainsbury's followed with its Reward card. Shoppers have an incentive to shop regularly at a particular retailer in order to accumulate points. Using the customer database, coupons and money-off vouchers can be regularly issued and delivered to the customer's own home, thus creating a stronger, more personal retailer–customer link (*see also* Case Study 16.2, pp. 691–2).

of short-term promotions. To counteract this, some retailers have introduced loyalty schemes using swipe cards.

Increase own-brand sales

As discussed at pp. 287 *et seq.* and p. 557 *et seq.*, retailers are increasingly investing in their own-brand ranges. These are, therefore, legitimate subjects for a whole range of consumer-orientated promotions. These promotions do not have to be overtly price or product based.

In-store free recipe cards can help to promote the store's fresh foods or own-label products by giving the shopper meal ideas and encouraging them to buy the ingredients. This can be linked with other promotions so that, for instance, one of the own-label ingredients could feature a price reduction to encourage purchase further. The magazines sent out with loyalty card statements and vouchers can also promote own-label goods, again through recipes, through editorial copy explaining how products can be used and their benefits, or through the more obvious mechanism of extra money-off vouchers.

Even out busy periods

In the same way that manufacturers face seasonal demand for some products, retailers have to cope with fluctuations between the very busy periods of the week or year, and the very quiet times. Offering sales promotions that apply only on certain days or within certain trading hours might divert some customers away from the busier periods.

A one-day sale on a Wednesday or Thursday can be a good way for a retailer to divert shoppers away from the busier weekend, especially if it is well advertised in the local area. One DIY retailer also instituted Wednesday afternoon discounts for senior citizens, presumably because that is an easily defined group who can change their shopping day because they are not likely to be working. Supermarkets in particular find the wide variation in the number of people shopping each day very difficult from the point of view of both making sure that there is adequate staff cover available and keeping the shelves full for shoppers. They are thus considering price-based promotion to reward those who shop at a quieter times and penalise those who are 'cash rich, time poor'.

Manufacturer–consumer (manufacturer promotion)

While it is obviously important for manufacturers to have the distribution channels working in their favour, there is still much work to be done with the consumer to help ensure continued product success. After all, if consumer demand for a product is buoyant, that in itself acts as an incentive to the retail trade to stock it, effectively acting as a pull strategy. There are many reasons for manufacturers to use sales promotions to woo the consumer, and some of these are outlined below and summarised in Figure 16.4.

Encourage trial

The rationale in encouraging trial is similar to that discussed earlier in relation to the intermediary and new product launches. New products face the problem of being unknown, and therefore consumers may need incentives to encourage trial of the product. Samples help consumers to judge a product for themselves, while coupons, money off and gifts reduce the financial penalty of a 'wrong' purchase. Sales promotions thus play an important role in the early stages of a product's life.

Figure 16.4 Manufacturer–consumer sales promotion objectives

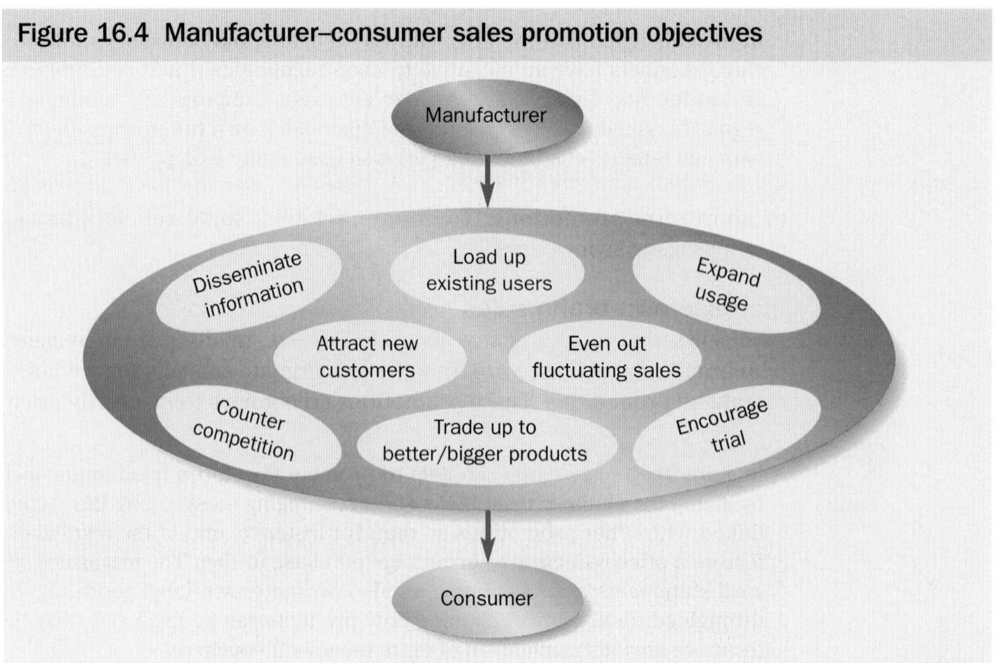

Expand usage

Expanding usage involves using sales promotion to encourage people to find different ways of using more of the product so that, of course, they purchase more.

eg

Mayonnaise brand Hellmann's offered consumers a free recipe book when they purchased jars of its various mayonnaise products. The book, with 12 recipes, could be obtained by calling a telephone number on the label. The jars themselves carry special edition labels with pictures encouraging consumers to use Hellmann's in different ways (*Promotions and Incentives*, 2002). This promotion integrates well with the theme of Hellmann's television advertising which also shows imaginative ways of using the product with a broad range of different foods and meal occasions.

Disseminate information

Sales promotions can be used effectively as a means of getting information across to consumers. Even a small sample pack distributed door to door, for example, not only lets the consumer experience the product, but also gives the manufacturer a chance to tell that consumer quite a lot about the product's features and benefits, where to buy it, and related products in the range. While advertising can do the same sort of information dissemination, it is easily ignored. If the consumer is tempted to try the sample, then they may take more notice of the information with it, and only then pay attention to the advertising.

Attracting new customers

An established product may be striving to acquire new customers, either by converting non-users or by turning irregular customers or brand switchers into regular buyers. Advertising can only go so far in creating a positive image of the product, and sales promotion may be necessary to generate that first trial, or that repeat purchase. The kind of promotion that depends on collecting tokens over time to qualify for a mail-in offer might be sufficient, if it is backed up with strong advertising, to set up regular purchasing habits and brand preference.

Trade up

There are two facets to **trading up**. One is getting the consumer to trade up to a bigger size, and the other is to get them to trade up to the more expensive products further up the range. Trading up to bigger sizes is particularly useful where the manufacturer feels that the customer is vulnerable to aggressive competition. The bigger size will last longer and, therefore, that consumer is going to be exposed less frequently to competitive temptation at the point of sale. Any promotional effort that applies only to the bigger size rather than the smaller one might achieve that kind of trade-up objective. Persuading consumers to trade up to a product higher up the range benefits the manufacturer because such products are likely to earn higher margins. Car dealers and manufacturers often try to do this. Again, using promotions that are specific to one model or product in the range, or using increasingly valuable and attractive promotions as the range goes up, can help to focus the customer's mind on higher things. Price-based promotions are probably not a good idea in this case, because of the risk of cheapening the product's image.

Load up

Loading up is partly a defensive mechanism to protect your customers from the efforts of the competition. A customer who is collecting tokens or labels towards a mail-in offer with a tight deadline, or who finds a cut price offer particularly seductive, might end up with far greater quantities of the product than can be used immediately. Effectively, that customer is now out of the market until those stocks are used up. This is a two-edged sword: the advantage is that they are less likely to listen to the competition; the disadvantage is that you will not be selling them any more for a while either, as you have effectively brought your sales to that customer forward. Of course, if that customer was originally a brand switcher, or a non-user, then you have gained considerably from loading them up.

Even out fluctuating sales

Evening out fluctuating sales links with the comments made above in relation to manufacturer–intermediary sales promotions. If seasonality is a problem, then sales promotion aimed at the consumer could help to even out the peaks and troughs a little.

Countering the competition

Again, the concept of countering or spoiling competitors' activities was introduced in the discussion of manufacturer–intermediary sales promotions. Diverting the consumer's attention through your own promotion can dampen the effects of the competitors' efforts, particularly if what they are doing is not particularly creative in its own right. Also, as discussed at p. 368, a well-chosen, regionally based sales promotion can seriously distort or introduce an element of doubt into the results of a competitor's test marketing.

Manufacturer–manufacturer (business promotion)

The relationship between manufacturers in the area of business promotion is less clear-cut than any of the other relationships studied so far. When we look at the negotiation of large contracts between organisations, we see that many of the activities that in other circumstances have been classed as sales promotions, such as discounts, added extras and time-limited offers, tend to be included in personal selling as part of the negotiation process leading to the final deal. Manufacturer–manufacturer sales promotions are also tightly linked to trade exhibition attendance, which will be considered in detail in Chapter 19.

Even the freebies, such as calendars, corporate neckwear, and golfing holidays do not class as sales promotions, as they do not link directly with specific products for sale. They are part of the wider area of relationship building between organisational buyers and sellers.

Sales promotion objectives: overview

The previous subsections have looked at sales promotion objectives within specific commercial relationships. They covered a wide variety of objectives, all of which fall into three broad categories as shown in Figure 16.5: communication, incentive and invitation. These are discussed in turn below.

Figure 16.5 Sales promotion objectives: overview

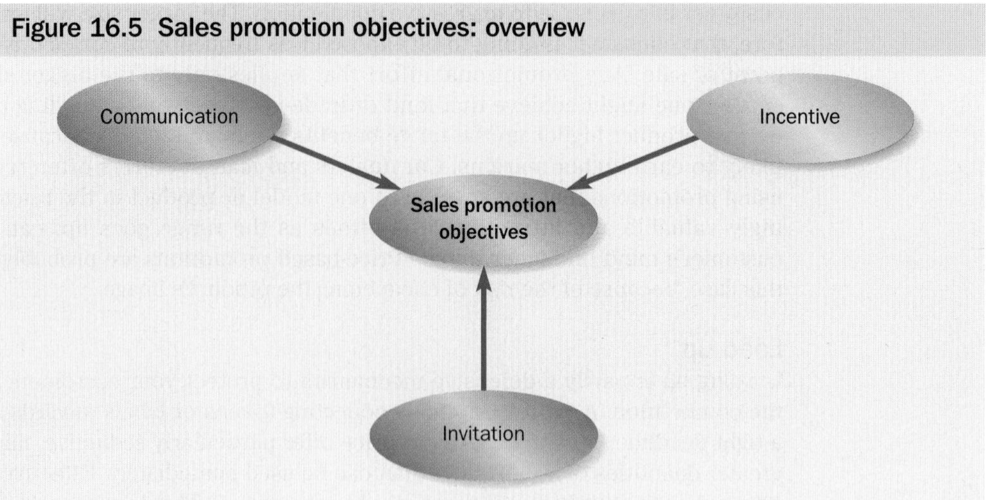

Communication

Sales promotion has a capacity to communicate with the buyer in ways that advertising would find hard to emulate. Advertising can tell people that a product is 'new, improved', or that it offers certain features and benefits, but this is conceptual information, which people may not fully understand or accept. Sales promotion can, for instance, put product samples into people's hands so that they can judge for themselves whether the claims are true. Learning by one's own experience is so much more powerful and convincing than taking the advertiser's word for it.

As Chapter 14 made clear, grabbing attention is an important starting point for any communication. Thus an on-pack sales promotion, for instance, particularly one that prominently features the word 'FREE', draws the product to the shopper's attention and perhaps makes them receptive to the product's underlying message.

Incentive

The incentive is usually the central pillar of a sales promotion campaign. The potential buyer has to be given encouragement to behave in certain ways, through an agreed bargain between seller and buyer: if you do this, then I will *reward* you with that.

With consumers, the aim may be to encourage brand switching or to fortify wavering existing customers by providing additional rewards and increased value to those who try or repeat buy. If extra benefits are provided, the price conscious or premium conscious customer may be attracted. Similarly, the objective may be to reward those customers who are normally loyal to the brand or producer, but perhaps are the target of competitive action. Occasional rewards for the more frequent purchaser, or those who purchase in larger quantities, can help to maintain their loyalty and goodwill.

eg

In common with many airlines, SAS operates a loyalty scheme whereby travellers earn points for each flight they take with the number of points awarded varying according to the length of the flight. Points can be exchanged for free flights or other rewards. In March 2001, however, the Swedish Competition Authority decided that SAS's EuroBonus scheme distorted competition and banned SAS from awarding points that can be used for free flights on domestic routes where there is a competitor. According to the Authority, many scheme members are regular business travellers, and thus their companies pay for their flights, but the individuals get the points and the resulting free flights for their personal use. Individuals naturally tend to join the scheme of the airline that offers the most flights, and with a 70 per cent share of the domestic market, that puts SAS in a very strong position. All of this means that choice of airline for a domestic flight is more likely to be made on the attractiveness of its benefits package rather than on price or service quality, and in the Authority's view, this leads to unfair competition and higher prices. The Authority claims that 10 per cent of the price of an SAS ticket goes towards the cost of the EuroBonus scheme, although SAS dispute this and say that it is only 1 per cent (Nicholas, 2001).

The intermediary also needs incentives as encouragement to stock the product in quantity and to sell it enthusiastically to the end buyer. Like consumers, intermediaries may be price or premium conscious, and incentives help them to swing towards particular brands or manufacturers.

Invitation

The promoted product is saying, 'Buy ME, and buy me NOW'. The promotion is, therefore, an invitation to consider this product, to think about your buying decision, and to do it quickly. The ephemeral nature of most sales promotions reinforces the urgency of taking up the invitation immediately. It prevents the buyer from putting off trial of the product, because the 'extra something' will not be around for long. For the consumer, in particular, the point of sale represents the crucial decision-making time. A product that is jumping up and down, shouting 'Hey, look at me!' through its sales promotion is offering the clearest possible invitation to do business.

Communication, incentive and invitation are all linked together. Elements of all three are present in the objectives of most sales promotions, but their mix and emphasis may change, depending on target audiences and circumstances. Peattie and Peattie (1995) highlighted how sales promotion is not only strong in the fmcg area but can be applied to services marketing, especially through the use of competitions and loyalty schemes.

Within the three main categories of sales promotion discussed earlier in this section (consumer, retail trade and organisation-orientated sales promotions), there are a number of possible techniques for achieving defined objectives. The techniques in each area are not mutually exclusive; ideas can be drawn from any one area and applied in another. The techniques selected will not only depend on the objectives and target audience of the sales promotion campaign, but also be influenced by a range of factors. These typically are market characteristics, competitive levels and activities, promotional objectives and the relevance of each technique to the product and its cost profile.

The following sections outline a number of sales promotion methods, classified by target audience. These methods will be defined and linked with objectives, and then specific examples of applications will be discussed. The list of methods described is not necessarily exhaustive. Sales promotion is an inherently creative area, subject to development as new ideas are introduced. Nevertheless, the following sections do cover the core methods, both established and emerging.

Consumer sales promotion methods (1): money-based

Money-based sales promotions are a very popular group of techniques used by manufacturers or intermediaries. Sometimes they work on a 'cash-back' basis (*see* p. 664), but more often they are immediate price reductions, implemented in various ways, designed as a short-term measure either to gain competitive advantage or to defend against competitive actions. Such price reductions must be seen to be temporary or else the consumer will not view them as incentives. Furthermore, if money-based methods are used too often, consumers will begin to think of the promotional price as being the real price. They will then think of the product as being cheaper than it really is, and adjust their perceptions of positioning and quality accordingly (Gupta and Cooper, 1992).

Another drawback of this group of sales promotions is that because money-based sales promotions are so common among consumer goods, it is very difficult to raise much enthusiasm about them in the market. The main problem is the lack of creativity that usually accompanies these methods. It is also far too easy for a competitor to copy or match a money-based promotion, and thus any competitive advantage may be short lived.

It is also important to remember that money-based promotion can be an expensive way of putting money back in the pockets of people who would have bought the product anyway. If an organisation offers 10p off a product, then that costs the organisation 10p per unit sold in addition to the overhead costs of implementing the offer. In other words, in most cases money-based sales promotions cost the organisation their full cash value, unlike many of the merchandise offers, yet the long-term effect (especially if the technique is overused) may be to cheapen the value of the product in the consumer's eyes (Jones, 1990). Effectively, this is a form of indirect price competition, and as discussed in Chapter 11, any price reduction needs to be balanced by volume increases in sales and against the product's reputation. Generally speaking, with money-based sales promotions, the short-term increase in sales needs to offset the extra marketing, distribution and handling costs associated with the promotion, as well as the lost revenue from those who would have purchased anyway (i.e. if you use a 20p coupon against a £1 product that you would have purchased anyway, then for the manufacturer that is 20p lost revenue rather than 80p extra revenue).

In their favour, however, money-based promotions are relatively easy to implement, they can be developed and mobilised quickly, and they are readily understood by the consumer. They appeal to many consumers' basic instincts about saving money, and the value of 10p off a price, or £1 cash back, is easy for the consumer to assess. If the objective of the exercise is to attract price-sensitive brand switchers, or to make a quick and easy response to a competitor's recent or imminent actions, then this group of methods has a part to play. The range of money-based methods is summarised in Figure 16.6.

Reduced price offers (1): shelf

Retailers frequently implement reduced price offers at the point of sale of the product. Although nothing appears on the product itself, the consumer is drawn to the surrounding notices or leaflets advertising the offer.

Such offers do have a sense of urgency about them, because consumers cannot be sure that the same offer will be available next time they visit that outlet, so they must take advantage of it immediately. They are very simple and quick to implement, costing only what it takes to notify the customers about the offer and the amount given back to the consumer through the reduced price. Local press advertising might be used to communicate a whole range of such offers, available this week only, to help increase store traffic.

eg

The major supermarket chains are keen to give the impression that they offer better value for money than their competitors and short-term reduced price promotions are one way of reinforcing this stance. All the major chains have their generic ranges (*see* pp. 290 *et seq.*) at the bottom of the price range and occasionally these are used to make attention-grabbing price statements. Thus at various times shoppers have found washing-up liquid at 7p per bottle, tins of beans at 3p per can and other products selling at approximately 10 per cent of the price of their premium branded competitors. These are in addition to a day-to-day selection of less drastic short-term price cuts on other own-label and premium brands. The voluntary chains too need to develop their own price cutting strategies in order to compete with the major multiples. Spar, for instance, has its ongoing X-tra Value initiative which offers three weekly promotions covering all product categories within store (http://www.spar.co.uk).

Figure 16.6 Money-based sales promotion methods

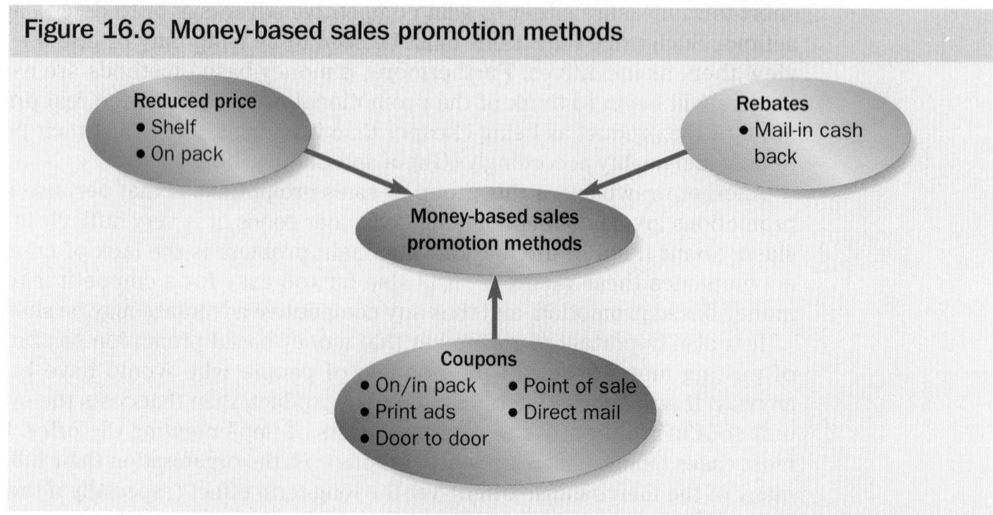

Reduced price offers (2): on-pack

The second type of reduced price offer features on the product pack itself. The offer is likely to originate from the manufacturer, but sometimes takes the form of a joint promotion between the manufacturer and one particular retailer. Greater expenditure and a longer lead time is required here, as the packaging has to be printed specially for the offer. Again, it is a simple kind of sales promotion, with a sense of urgency, as is a shelf-based offer. Sometimes, reduced price is presented to the customer as a **trial price** when a product is being launched, as discussed at p. 436.

Coupons

Coupons are a more complex form of money-based sales promotion. They are printed vouchers that the consumer takes to a retail outlet and uses to claim a set amount of money off a product. Their use is widespread and flexible, and Table 16.1 shows the extent of coupon use in the UK. A manufacturer can issue coupons applicable to one specific product or a range of products, redeemable at any retail outlet stocking the product. Nearly 4 billion manufacturer coupons were issued in 2000. Retailers issue coupons redeemable only in their stores against specific products, as outputs from their loyalty schemes, or on any basket of shopping totalling more than a stated sum. Over 1 billion retailer coupons were issued in 2000. Joint coupons, specifying both retail outlet and manufacturer's product, are also used.

Table 16.1 Coupon distribution and redemption, 2000

Coupon distribution (billions)	5.1
Coupon redemption (millions)	531.0
Total value of coupons redeemed (£mn)	244.3
Coupons' average face value (pence)	72.0

Source: *UK Coupon Market 2000*, reproduced by kind permission from NCH Marketing Services Ltd.

Coupons are distributed using a variety of means. They are printed within advertisements, on leaflets delivered from door to door, on inserts within magazines and newspapers, through direct mail, at the point of sale and on packs. Table 16.2 shows what proportion of redeemed coupons were distributed through each medium and the proportion of redeemed coupons originating from those media. It is interesting to see that of all coupons redeemed, just under 24 per cent were distributed in- or on-pack, despite the fact that this method of distribution accounts for less than 10 per cent of all coupons issued. This presumably is because the coupons will be reaching many people who already like and use the product and will therefore be motivated to buy it again, using the coupon. Effectively, this is a reward for current users. In contrast, coupons distributed through mass media perform less well. Although newspapers and magazines between them account for over 40 per cent of all coupons distributed, they only account for 7 per cent of redemptions. There is much wastage with these media because many readers will not be even remotely interested in the coupon's product and those who are interested have to remember to keep the magazine, cut the coupon out, take it to the shops and use it.

The technology is also now available to allow retailers to issue coupons at the checkout, as an integral part of the bill issued to the customer. Checkouts that use laser scanning equipment can analyse the purchasing profile of the current customer, and issue coupons against the next purchase of something that has already been bought, or against a related product, or even against the retailer's own-brand equivalent of a purchased manufacturer's brand.

Manufacturers issue coupons with a number of reasons in mind. They act as a kind of pull strategy, creating an upturn in consumer demand for the product, thus encouraging retailers to stock and prominently display the brand. By telling them what is available and by reducing the financial risks of purchase, coupons can help the consumer get round to

Table 16.2 Coupon distribution and redemption by medium, 2000

	Share of redeemed distribution (%)	*Average redemption rates by medium (%)*
By application	*	43.0
Consumer events	*	8.0
In/on pack	23.7	26.5
Direct mail	33.3	20.9
Door to door	3.4	3.0
Other	6.2	17.0
In-store	24.7	16.2
Magazines	4.5	1.7
Newspapers	4.2	4.0

* Too small to measure

Source: *UK Coupon Market 2000*, reproduced by kind permission from NCH Marketing Services Ltd.

trying a product, making a subsequent purchase, or trading up, either to larger sizes or to products further up the range. The main problem for manufacturers is misredemption. Some supermarkets, overtly or covertly, will accept any coupon at the checkout, regardless of whether the consumer has actually bought the coupon's product or not. Preventing this from happening is difficult.

Retailer-specific coupons aim to bring consumers into those outlets and to keep them coming back. Like manufacturer coupons, retailer coupons can also have product-based aims. These may include encouraging consumers to try own-brand products, to repurchase or to trade up. As a part of the supermarkets' loyalty schemes, retailer-specific coupons are distributed through direct mail to scheme members.

For whoever issues the coupon, redemption rates are crucial and can vary from just over 1 per cent with coupons in magazines to over 25 per cent with coupons appearing on or in packs. Not surprisingly, it has been found that the higher the coupon value, the greater the interest and redemption. According to NCH's analysis of the UK coupon market, it has also been found that using personalised coupons can improve redemption rates by between 3 and 6 percentage points. Personalised coupons also allow the issuer to track exactly who is responding, when and where, which is useful data for planning future campaigns.

Overall, the UK is following the lead of the USA where couponing has become one of the main forms of sales promotion because of its flexibility and its direct application to the brand.

Coupons are subtly different from the other money-based promotions already discussed. With shelf and on-pack price cuts, the offer is open to all purchasers, and there is a very direct link between the price cut and the product that may cheapen the brand. A coupon does not look like a price cut, mainly because the price quoted at the shelf or on the product remains intact. The coupon is also a little more selective, in that only those who collect a coupon and remember to redeem it qualify for the discount.

However, to counter that, coupons are very common, and consumers are over-exposed to them. Unless a coupon carries a significant discount on the product, or applies to something intrinsically new and exciting, it is difficult as a consumer to be enthusiastic about them. Increasingly, coupons are being used by people who would have purchased anyway, so the rate of favourable brand switching or recruitment of new users might not be as high as the manufacturers hope. If coupons are being applied to mature products and being redeemed mainly by existing buyers, then all the manufacturer is doing is reducing profits (*see* p. 439).

Rebates

A **cash rebate** or 'cash-back' scheme involves a little more work and loyalty from the consumer. Tokens or labels have to be collected from packaging, involving a number of purchasing episodes, and then mailed in to qualify for either hard cash or a substantial coupon (retailer or product specific). This is similar to gift-based schemes, but involves cash rather than gifts or merchandise. In this case, the 'prize' is widely accepted and valued, and handling costs are considerably reduced.

However, if the amounts of money are small, the customer may not develop much interest and may not bother to redeem the offer. It has even been argued (Fill, 2002) that rebates can sometimes be viewed negatively by the customer, who might see them as inconvenient and too much trouble to claim. To some consumers, rebates might even suggest low-quality products that need special help to sell them. For an established product that is well known in terms of image and quality, however, a rebate scheme might achieve a number of things. It is not seen as a direct price cut to all purchasers, and therefore is less likely to taint the image than other methods so far discussed. The customer is working for the rebate through repeat purchases and the effort of collecting and mailing the tokens, and thus the rebate will be valued when it comes. Depending on the time limit put on the sales promotion and the number of tokens required to qualify for the rebate, it may be possible to increase the number and frequency of purchases, even if it is only existing buyers who take advantage of the offer. Because it is a mail-in offer, the manufacturer gets the added benefit of customer names and addresses, offering future potential of direct marketing (more of this in Chapter 18).

eg

When Persil did a rebate offer, it not only asked for labels, but also for till receipts showing the product purchases. If consumers responded to this on a large scale, there is potentially a lot of rich information to be had out of this. Most supermarkets now issue itemised till receipts, so the manufacturer can see what other products consumers buy with their Persil, where they purchased (always the same outlet or a variety?), how frequently they purchased, when they purchased (even down to the time of day), the total number of items purchased and the amount spent on each shopping trip. This may not constitute scientifically rigorous market research, but it certainly gives a quick-and-dirty feel for shopping habits, and might indicate directions for future promotional activities with a more specific focus.

Rebates do not only apply to manufacturer products. Look back to p. 656, where retailer cash rebate schemes aimed at increasing the value and frequency of purchasing were discussed.

Consumer sales promotion methods (2): product-based

One of the risks of money-based promotions that was constantly reiterated in the previous section was the ease with which consumers could relate the promotion to price cutting, and thus the image of the product could, in their eyes, be cheapened. One way of overcoming that problem is to opt for a promotion centred on the product itself. The first method discussed in this section, extra product, demonstrates how this works. The second method, sampling, shows how a product-centred technique can achieve a much greater range of difficult objectives than any money-based activity. Figure 16.7 summarises **product-based sales promotion** methods.

Extra product

There are two main alternatives for the 'extra product' technique.

Extra free

The 'extra free' technique involves offers such as an own-label can of tomatoes with '20% extra free'. Just in case the customer has problems understanding what 20 per cent looks like, the can would have a prominent band around the top of the label in a different colour from the usual packaging giving a rough idea of which part of the contents is free. Similarly, a pack of own-label kitchen roll was offering three rolls for the price of two and had a large red flash down the side of the pack proclaiming 'ONE ROLL EXTRA FREE'.

Obviously, such offers require changes in the packaging graphics to communicate the offer, and may even involve major changes in the physical size of the package to accommodate

Figure 16.7 Product-based sales promotion methods

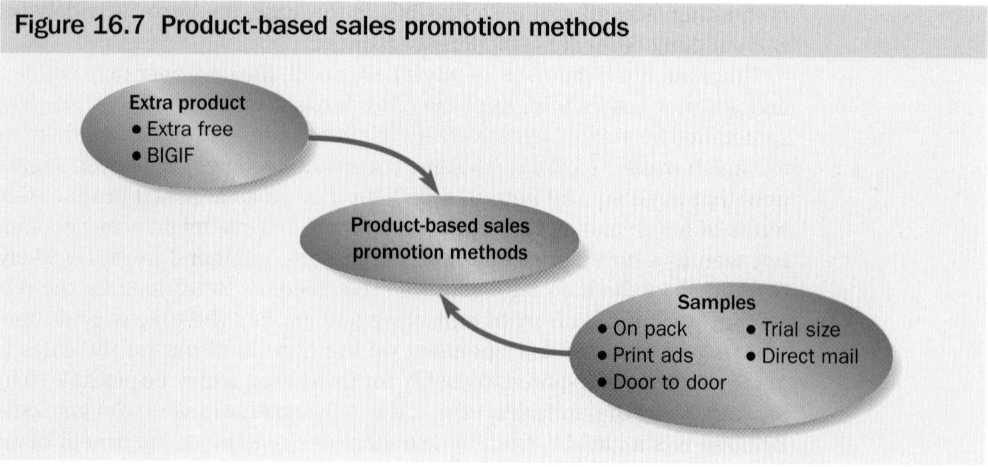

the extra product. If own-label tomatoes are normally sold in 400 gram cans, then producing a 480 gram can will require planned production changes.

A money-based promotion might put 20p back in the consumer's hand; a product-based promotion might give them 20p's worth of extra product free. To the manufacturer, either option rewards the buyer with 20p, but the buyer's perceptions of the two are very different. 20p in the hand is 'giving something back', whereas extra product free is clearly 'giving something in addition' and in the consumer's mind, might be valued at a good deal more than 20p. These product-based promotions, therefore, break the link between promotion and price. This method may be especially attractive as a response to a competitor's price attack, as it can shape the value image of a product without a direct price war.

BIGIF or BOGOFF

In contrast to offering extra free product within a single package, the **BIGIF** (Buy 1 Get 1 Free) or the BOGOFF (Buy One Get One For Free) offers centre on bigger rewards, and are aimed primarily at loading up the customer. Effectively, the offer is saying '100% EXTRA FREE'. As discussed at p. 659, manufacturers may have a particular interest in making sure that the consumer has a kitchen full of their brands, as a means of making them less sensitive to the competition and getting them used to having that product around.

e-marketing *in action*

Integrated online sales promotions

For transactional e-commerce sites, the internet can be used to deliver sales promotions in a conventional manner as described in this chapter. For example, reduced price offers or a BIGIF/BOGOF approach can equally be used in any online store. The online environment has the advantage that it is more responsive. If, for instance, an airline has capacity underutilisation, i.e. spare seats, it can instantly change its prices on a particular flight or offer them to customers via an online auction.

However, the online presence also offers the opportunity for sales promotions where a product is not purchased online. One example of this would be an on-pack promotion where the consumer has to visit the website to gain a further benefit which can be available online or delivered through the post when contact details are provided. Kinder eggs and Marmite both used this technique to achieve site visits (in separate campaigns). The benefit of this form of sales promotion is that firstly it reduces the cost of administering the sales promotions – it is a customer self-service approach where they type their details into an online form which is then added to a database for actioning. Secondly, it gives further opportunities for a consumer to interact with the brand while they are on the website – to provided added-value information or offer further promotions. A further example of an integrated online sales promotion is offering a discount via a website. The customer prints a coupon and redeems it in a real-world shop. This approach has been used by Carphone Warehouse.

Source: Dave Chaffey.

Retailers are increasingly using a variation on this method, based around bulk purchasing, making the offer, 'Buy two and get a third one free' (B2G3F? – it doesn't quite have the same ring as BOGOFF, does it?).

eg

Procter and Gamble launched Ariel Futur Alpine by offering a 1 litre refill free with every 1.5 litre bottle bought. The two packs were presented together in a cardboard box with the word FREE prominently displayed in red on a yellow background. The promotional boxes were also placed in an end of aisle 'golden zone' in Tesco, for example, and extra loyalty card points offered with them. All of this made the new Alpine variant attractive to the consumer, not only to generate awareness and trial, but also to load up customers to protect them from the competition. Supermarkets also regularly offer discounts for bulk purchases with varying conditions, anything from 'buy one get one free' to 'buy six get a seventh free'. Sometimes bulk purchases are encouraged by packaging products together, as in the Ariel example. Tesco offered three cans of red kidney beans banded together in a cardboard sleeve with £1.19 printed prominently on it, representing a saving on three separate cans.

These offers may need shorter lead times than the 20 per cent extra free type, because they do not involve significant changes to the packaging. Two ordinary packs can be banded together away from the main production line if necessary. In the case of the retailers' B2G3F offers, no banding is needed at all. The offer is made through notices at the shelf, and the computerised checkout is programmed to make the discount automatically when the required number of items have been scanned through.

marketing *in action*

Bringing the product to consumers – wherever they are

Sampling is a powerful promotional tool: a survey showed that over 70 per cent of consumers believed that free samples received through door-to-door distribution were 'very useful', and even people who claim they do not like unaddressed mail still welcome samples, coupons and special offers. Using the sophisticated techniques offered by geodemographic profiling systems (see pp. 186 *et seq.*) it is now possible to target door-to-door sampling and other drops to specific households. As one agency put it, 'Client companies know exactly who they want to target from their databases and they only want to deliver their message to those people. All the tools are there. We now have the potential to understand every postcode in the country' (as quoted by Miller, 2001). Door-to-door specialists, Circular Distributors, launched Personal Placement in 2000, a door-to-door service that delivers targeted messages to selected households, i.e. it only delivers to households that match specified profiles. According to Circular Distributors, 'We can deliver to specific households based on a range of criteria – everything from whether they own a cat or have a home computer or have children between the ages of five and 16'. This cuts out wastage and reduces the cost of a door-to-door sampling exercise. One client was a large ISP that wanted to distribute CD-ROMs to households with a PC. Circular Distributors was able to deliver to 500,000 computer-owning addresses. 'It is a precise and low-cost method of placing a tangible item directly into the hands of this hard-to-reach, but very valuable, audience'.

Even with this precision, door-to-door sampling has to work hard to grab attention and to ensure safe delivery of the sample, however. When Philips wanted to tell consumers about its Softone light bulbs, it dropped a bag through the door with a brochure about the product and a money-off voucher. If the consumer was interested, they left the bag outside the door the next day after ticking a box to say which colour bulb they wanted and the sample was left in the bag for them. This allowed the company to deliver a fragile object safely and allowed consumers to opt out of the sampling exercise if they wanted to, thus making it more cost effective and better targeted.

A bright idea for distributing light bulb samples

Source: Circular Distributors Ltd.

Home is not the only place where marketers can offer samples to consumers. An airport delivers a captive audience, often with time to kill while waiting for a flight, often in a spending frame of mind, and often looking to airport stores for new experiences. Nestlé offered samples of its Polo Supermints to travellers at Gatwick airport and then directed them to the shops where they were on sale. Similarly, samples of alcoholic drinks can be offered just a short distance away from the duty-free stores that sell those brands. World Duty Free offers drink, cosmetic and fragrance samples in both departure and arrivals areas at airports near to its retail stores. The company has found that sampling is much more effective than money-off vouchers or gifts in stimulating sales.

Ferry terminals and railway station concourses can also be good places to carry out a sampling exercise. Concourse Initiatives, a company that markets and manages concourse space, claims that rail commuters tend to be affluent ABC1s aged under 45, and that 70 per cent of them are primary grocery buyers, in broad terms an attractive target group for many manufacturers. Around 2.4 million people pass through London Liverpool Street station every week, and outside London, stations in Birmingham, Leeds, and Glasgow can deliver 0.5 million passengers or more per week. Given that passengers have, on average, 7 minutes of 'dwell time' to kill while waiting for trains, stations offer a wonderful sampling opportunity. For one client, a walk-in freezer was built on a concourse and 25,000 ice-cream samples per day handed out. Over three years, Häagen Dazs handed out over 1 million samples in this way. Similarly, samples of draught Guinness have been handed out on a concourse, with a follow-up leaflet giving the consumer money off a Guinness four-pack as well as the opportunity to phone in for a free Guinness glass. Interestingly, alcohol sampling is allowed in small measures on concourses but the drink cannot be handed out in bottles or in large quantities. It cannot be given to station staff or consumers aged under 18 and a security guard must be present at all times.

For many manufacturers, the numbers of consumers that concourses deliver are attractive, but there are potential problems. First, size isn't everything. It might be a large audience, but it is a broad one and it is difficult to identify and select a more specific sub-group out of it. Second, consumers on concourses, especially commuters, are often rushing to be somewhere else and, unless they have time to kill waiting for a train, are not likely to be receptive to messages, especially if they are stressed. Nevertheless, leaflets can be handed out quickly for consumers to look at later (on the train?) and incorporating competitions on them is a good way of generating responses and thus leads.

Sources: Fletcher (1999); Gray (1999); McLuhan (2000); Miller (2001); Wilson (2001); http://www.initgroup.com.

Samples

Where the main objective is to persuade people to try a product, sampling is often used. People can experience the product for themselves at little or no financial risk and decide on their own evidence whether to adopt the product and buy the full-sized pack or not. **Samples** are thus popular and effective. Seventy per cent of households claim to use the free samples that come through the letterbox. The added bonus, particularly with those samples distributed away from the point of sale, is that the sample's packaging can teach the consumer about the product's benefits, and through graphics that relate directly to the full sized pack, aid brand recognition in the store.

The costs of sampling can be very high. The packaging has to be specially designed and produced, and then there are the costs of distribution. The aim is the future generation of sales, and if it takes a sample to convert a 'possibly would buy' into a 'definitely will buy', then it is a justifiable expense.

In the area of traditional sampling, a one-use or one-portion sample is usually sufficient, and there are a number of ways in which it can be distributed. These are discussed below.

eg

In November 2001, Pantene Pro-V (Procter and Gamble) undertook an extensive mystery sampling campaign to create excitement and drive trial of the shampoo and conditioners in the range. With absolute confidence in product performance, Pantene Pro-V launched a campaign, encouraging women around the UK to trial an unbranded mystery shampoo and conditioner and decide for themselves: 'You Try It'. You Decide'. The campaign was supported by extensive television and radio advertising, targeted sampling in health clubs, and in health and beauty trade shows. In addition, Pantene Pro-V worked with a series of leading women's magazines, offering readers the chance to trail the mystery products, fill in a diary of their experiences and win the chance to appear in their favourite magazine.

With holistic images and the recognisable selling line, 'What's The Secret of Beautiful Hair?', the Pantene Pro-V mystery sampling campaign led to at least 2.8 million women in the UK trailling the products. As part of this, free samples were distributed through Boots stores nationwide, and a website was set up (http://www.youtryyoudecide.co.uk) which took visitors through a questionnaire on the products and then offered the chance to win £250 of hair and beauty treatments (*Marketing Week*, 2002b).

The targeted sampling, holistic messaging and the distinctive website thus helped to bring the Pantene Pro-V products directly to the right audience and encouraged excitement and trial. An advertising campaign alone would not have had the same impact. By the next hair-care purchasing occasion, the consumer might have forgotton the advertising, and thus would not look for this product. Then the routine purchase of the old brand would be made as usual. If the consumer has tried the sample, however, at the point of sale they will remember the product benefit/memorable product experience and there is a strong chance that the routine purchasing habit can be broken.

On-pack

If a manufacturer is launching a new product in a range, then samples could be given away with existing products. The objective is to inform existing customers of the new product and to allow them to try it. The problem is that this type of promotion is limited to those who buy the existing product. If new customers are required, then usually other mechanisms must be used.

eg

When Cussons launched its Carex Family Soft Wipes, a portable pack of wipes for hand cleaning outside the home, sampling was used in addition to advertising. A free pack of 15 wipes was given away with bottles of Carex handwashing liquid, and packs were also included within 350,000 Bounty Toddler Packs, given away free to new mothers (*The Grocer*, 2002a).

Trial sizes

To recoup some of the costs of producing the samples, **trial sizes** can be sold in retail outlets at a minimal price. Sold as products in their own right, they may attract a wider audience than simply those who already purchase the same manufacturer's existing brands. The small cost is insignificant to the consumer, who still sees it as a relatively risk-free way of trying something different. As with on-pack distributions, it is a good mechanism for introducing new products, or new colours or flavours within an existing product line.

Customers were teased by a mystery sample and then the identity of the product was finally revealed. Having tried the sample, customers were more likely to purchase the relaunched product.

Source: Proctor and Gamble/Good Relations

Print media

Because print media allow the targeting of fairly narrowly profiled audiences, this can be an efficient way of distributing samples to potential buyers. Cosmetics and toiletries, for example, are often sampled through women's magazines. Some samples associated with print media have become very significant in their own right. Computer magazines give away demonstration disks featuring various types of software.

eg

In the highly competitive hobby and lifestyle magazine sector, on-magazine gifts are often used to attract and retain readers. *Red*, a monthly glossy women's magazine, gave away a novel, which is a little different from the cosmetics and beauty bags more commonly associated with such publications. Sometimes, a publication itself can become the sample to be given away. *Red* offered mini-sized versions of the magazine given away with Olay skincare purchases from Superdrug. As the magazine's editor out it, 'The mini-edition of *Red* is designed to be a real treat for Olay purchasers and provides the perfect opportunity to communicate the magazine's core values to women who may have heard of it, but not yet tried it' (as quoted by Mason, 2001).

Some magazines, however, carry free gifts that have become part of their normal offering. *Classic CD*, a monthly magazine specialising in classical music, gives away a full-length (around 70 minutes) CD with every issue, every month, featuring tracks from recent releases. Free CDs regularly feature material from EMI, Philips, RCA, Deutsche Grammophon, Sony and Hyperion, among others. For the record companies, this is an unbeatable way of whetting the appetite of potential buyers, and for consumers, the CD makes excellent listening, and acts as an audible shop window, reassuring them that they will like particular recordings. This is sampling at a very sophisticated level.

Direct mail

Samples that are small, light and non-perishable can be distributed by direct mail, either to people already on a mailing list, or to those who respond to an offer made in an advertisement.

eg

The Pantene product relaunch samples (see p. 668) were mainly distributed through retailer Boots. It was also possible, however, to get hold of samples in the mail by requesting them on the website http://www.youtryyoudecide.co.uk. The consumer fills in an online form and the site promises that a sample will be received within 10 days. Using a more traditional direct response mechanism, Twinings tea samples were offered in *Red* magazine. A full-page advertisement outlined the benefits of Twinings Chai brand and gave an address to which readers could write to get a sample pack. In both these cases, the consumer takes the initiative to request a sample. Other companies use established databases to send out samples to existing customers or previous enquirers. When a new mother signs up to get her free Bounty pack of baby product samples, she finds herself on all sorts of mailing lists. Pampers, for example, sends out samples of its new products, and because the database records the child's date of birth, so the nappy sample sent can be the right size for that baby's stage of development.

Door to door

Door-to-door distribution is a popular but expensive way of distributing samples. Delivering the sample to the house means that you are not dependent on particular existing purchasing patterns (in terms of either store or brand preference), you are not depending on the consumer to notice the sample in-store, nor are you asking them to pay towards the sample. Effectively, you are putting the sample directly into their hands in an environment where it is likely to be remembered and used. Some targeting is possible, using geodemographic segmentation to prioritise distribution areas (*see* pp. 186 *et seq.*), but generally this is mass sample distribution.

Samples might be distributed through the letterbox, or more expensively through a personal call. Personal calls make sure that samples only go to those households that will use them and can also be used for more extensive market research data collection. They also ensure that the sample is put into the hands of a responsible adult rather than being eaten on the doormat by the dog or abducted by the children!

eg

When Philips did its door-to-door sampling exercise with the Softone light bulb (*see* p. 667), a sample bulb was left for the customer on request. The free bulb only had a life span of 10 hours, which was clearly marked on the packaging (Fletcher, 1999). This was long enough to make the consumer think that they were getting good value from the sample and to let them get used to the effect of the Softone bulb, but not so long that they forgot where the bulb came from or what brand it was. Philips would also have been hoping that the consumer would already have used the accompanying money-off voucher and have a replacement bulb handy by the time the sample bulb blew, or that they would still have the voucher and use it on the next shopping trip after the sample was finished with.

Consumer sales promotion methods (3): gift, prize or merchandise based

A wide range of activities depend on the offer of prizes, low-cost goods or free gifts to stimulate the consumer's buying behaviour. Holidays, brand-related cookery books, mugs or clothing featuring product logos and small plastic novelty toys are among the vast range of incentives used to complement the main product sale.

There are many ways in which these incentives can be offered, each with a different impact and its own objectives, as summarised in Figure 16.8.

Figure 16.8 Gift-, prize- or merchandise-based sales promotion methods

eg

As an incentive to persuade parents to enquire about children's saving plans, Aberdeen Asset Management offered a free Thomas the Tank Engine video. The company was somewhat taken aback, however, when it received over 40,000 enquiries in one month. Things got even worse when the company then offered a second video to customers who actually invested in the plans. Staff found that the warehouse, which normally deals with fund managers' reports, was suddenly crammed with thousands of videos. The number of warehouse staff had to be doubled and, in the words of the warehouse director, 'Everyone is mucking in to stuff envelopes and make sure the videos get out. The staff have got right into it and now know all the characters off by heart' (Dow, 2001).

Self-liquidating offers

Self-liquidating offers invite the consumer to pay a small amount of money, and usually to submit specified proofs of purchase, in return for goods that are not necessarily directly related to the main product purchase. The money paid is usually just enough to cover the cost price of the goods and a contribution to postage and handling, and thus these promotions become self-financing if the expected number of customers takes them up.

Often, such a promotion is used to reinforce the brand name and identity of the products featuring the scheme.

eg

A link-up between Disney and Britvic showed good synergy between the partners in the promotion, the premium offered and the target market. A promotion featured on bottles of Robinsons fruit juice concentrates offered a *Monsters, Inc.* alarm clock with a detachable cuddly Sully character. The 12-week promotion was timed to coincide with the build-up to the release of the film in February 2002 and the period immediately after its release. To get the clock, consumers had to send in four bottle caps and £6.99. The number of caps required gives at least short-term brand loyalty, while the £6.99 covers the basic costs of providing the clock and administering the offer. The tie-in with the film ensures extra consumer excitement about the promotion as it benefits from synergy with the film's own marketing efforts. As well as featuring prominently on the packs, the promotion was supported with a £2 mn advertising campaign on children's television and in the press (*The Grocer*, 2002c). In the first month of the campaign the brand achieved its highest ever four-weekly volume share of 49 per cent, and highest ever household penetration of 54 per cent (Derrick, 2002).

The problem with most self-liquidating promotions is that response levels tend to be low, as consumers have to be prepared to spend money and make an effort to benefit from the offer. Furthermore, the premium itself has to be very interesting and different to get a good response. Plain mugs can easily be purchased cheaply from discount stores, but brand-specific ones that can only be sourced through the promotion have something more attractive about them. They are 'exclusive', and they are only available for a limited time, hence the incentive value.

Free mail-in

In the case of a free mail-in, the consumer can claim a gift, free of charge, in return for proofs of purchase and perhaps the actual cost of postage (but not handling charges or the cost of the gift itself).

eg

Kitchen Devils, a kitchen knives brand, offered a free chopping board in return for the barcode from one of its products, a till receipt showing its purchase, and 52p in stamps to contribute to postage. As kitchen knives are by no means frequently purchased, inexpensive fmcg goods, asking for only the one proof of purchase in return for a substantial premium is reasonable. In contrast, fmcg brands such as breakfast cereals are more demanding.

Free mail-ins have increased in popularity in recent years. The free goods attract the consumer and encourage a higher response rate, and the responses potentially provide the organisation with direct marketing opportunities. The main aim, however, in sales promotion terms is to encourage the consumer to make enough additional purchases to collect the necessary proofs of purchase within a carefully assessed time period. The frustration of not quite managing to collect enough to meet an offer deadline, or of feeling coerced into buying unreasonably large quantities of goods in a short space of time, might turn consumers against a brand.

Of course, the promotion is only free to the consumer. The promoter has to consider carefully the merchandise costs, postage, packing, processing and even VAT. All of this has to be put into the context of the likely response rate, so that the total cost of the promotion can be forecast and an appropriate quantity of merchandise can be ordered and available when the promotion begins.

Free inside or on-pack

Offering free gifts contained inside or banded on to the outside of the pack can make a big impact at the point of sale because the reward is instant, and the purchaser does not have to make any special effort to claim it. One-off gifts are designed to bring the consumer's attention to a product and to encourage them to try it. The offer might shake them out of a routine response purchase and make them think about trying a different brand.

In-pack promotions

In-pack promotions are often used in child-orientated breakfast cereals and, to stimulate repeat purchase, the gifts often form part of a related series.

The costs of in-pack gifts can be high, especially when offered with food products. There may be limitations on size, materials, toxicity, protection and smell in order to conform to hygiene standards. These costs, as well as the direct promotion costs, must be considered.

eg

Breakfast cereals often run in-pack promotions, sometimes linked with films, such as Nestlé's Cheerios tie-in with Disney's *Monsters, Inc.* which offered six different movin' monster cards, one in each pack, to collect. Similarly, Kellogg's linked with the film *Jimmy Neutron, Boy Genius* and offered a series of gadget spoons based on characters from the movie in packs of its children-orientated cereals. Both these promotions not only offer the immediate incentive of a free gift, but the idea of collecting the whole set ensures that the kids keep pestering mum to carry on buying those brands while the promotion is available.

Kellogg's World Cup 2002 promotional gift wouldn't fit into the pack! A free cereal bowl, designed to look like half a football was offered when the consumer bought two large packs of certain Kellogg's brands. Prominent end-of-aisle displays with clear signage featured piles of the bowls and packs of the relevant products, making it easy for the consumer to grasp the point of the promotion quickly and pick up two packs and a bowl.

On-pack promotions

Gifts attached to the outside of the pack are less constrained and, again, provide an immediate reward for purchase. They may even be more attractive than in-pack gifts, as the purchaser can actually see and evaluate the gift in advance.

eg

Rather than offering a separate free gift, the packaging itself can be used as an incentive. Twinings tea, for example, offered a free tea caddy with its 50-teabag packs of Earl Grey and English Breakfast teas. The bags were packed inside metal caddies replicating the Twinings logo and packaging images (*The Grocer*, 2002d). Similarly, Oxo stock cubes have been sold (with no increase in price) in attractive tins, plastic money boxes and pencil cases instead of the usual cardboard box. All of these items are kept for a long time and are heavily branded, thus providing the constant reminder. Obviously the costs of such sales promotions are high in terms of product and handling, but the rewards are often very recognisable and tempting to the consumer at the point of sale, as the consumer's attention is attracted to the fact that there is clearly something different about the packs.

Free with product

'Free with product' is similar to an on-pack offer, except that the gift is not attached to the product but has to be claimed at the checkout. The forerunner of current practice was the plastic daffodil free with soap powder in the 1950s. There are often logistical and practical difficulties for high volume supermarkets in using this method, so its use has declined somewhat. Laser scanning checkouts, however, do allow supermarkets to run their own versions of this kind of offer. The consumer, for example, might be invited at the point of sale to buy a jar of coffee and claim a free packet of biscuits. The computerised checkout can tell whether the conditions of the promotion have been met and automatically deducts the price of the biscuits from the final total.

Customer loyalty schemes

Given the increasingly high cost of creating new customers, organisations have turned their attention to ways of retaining the loyalty of current customers. Major international airlines have their frequent flyer schemes, many different retail and service organisations give away air miles with purchases, and petrol stations and supermarkets issue swipe cards through which customers can accumulate points as mentioned earlier. All of these schemes are designed to encourage repeat buying, especially where switching is easy and generic brand loyalty is low. Brian Woolf, an American database marketing expert, proposes eleven rules for getting the best out of a loyalty scheme. These are outlined in Table 16.3.

Table 16.3 The 11 Ps of loyalty marketing

1	**Pricing**	Be customer specific – reward the best
2	**Purchases**	Make product-specific offers
3	**Point flexibility**	Occasionally offer double points, for example
4	**Partners**	Develop alliances with other retailers
5	**Prizes**	Weekly prize draw for cardholders, for example
6	**Pro-bono**	Allow customers to convert points into charity donations
7	**Personalisation**	Direct mail, specifically targeted at customer
8	**Privileges**	Invite cardholders to special events, for example
9	**Participation**	Invite best customers to take part in new variations of scheme
10	**Pronto**	Generate offers at the point of sale
11	**Proactive**	Use information to predict/pre-empt customer behaviour

Source: Woolf, as quoted by Mitchell (1995).

Price promotions can be dangerous in that they encourage consumers to become price sensitive, and are easily copied by competitors. Tokens, points and stamps that can be traded in for other goods are all ways of adding value to a product, while avoiding costly price competition. They are thus known as **alternative currencies**.

Trading stamps

Trading stamps are a long-established example of alternative currency. The number of stamps awarded at the point of sale is directly proportional to the value of purchases made. The stamps can be redeemed at the customer's convenience for gifts. Supermarkets and petrol stations widely participated in these schemes until the 1970s. The problem with stamps was that they tended to drive prices upwards at a time when straight price discounting was a more attractive alternative for the consumer.

Points and tokens

In place of trading stamps, new variants have emerged. Loyalty cards allow points to be accumulated electronically, for example.

One of the problems with loyalty schemes, however, is the sheer number of them. When every airline has a frequent flyer scheme and when every supermarket has a loyalty club, then the competitive edge is lost. Furthermore, there is evidence that the loyalty generated by such schemes is questionable, as will be seen in Case Study 16.2 (*see* pp. 691–2). Nevertheless, loyalty schemes are fast becoming an established part of the marketing scene. The next logical progression is to think about pan-European schemes. There are both cultural and legislative difficulties with this, however. Those in the industry feel that pan-European schemes can at present be built around a broad strategy, but need to incorporate sufficient tailored flexibility to allow for different countries' cultures and legislation covering promotional activities.

eg

The Coke and T&T auctions mentioned in Chapter 14 effectively utilised a form of alternative currency. Labels and ring-pulls could be exchanged for electronic points to be 'spent' via the internet. The second wave of the Coke Auction online promotion, called 'Real Coke Rush' offered consumers the chance to buy experiences that will give them a 'rush', such as white water rafting, by collecting labels and ring-pulls to exchange for online credits (Brabbs, 2001). Similarly, promotions such as Tesco's Computers for Schools (*see* pp. 827 *et seq.*) offer vouchers that can be collected and exchanged for computer equipment.

Contests and sweepstakes

Gifts given free to all purchasers of a product necessarily are limited to relatively cheap and cheerful items. As Hoover found out, giving away expensive freebies to all purchasers is uneconomic. **Contests and sweepstakes**, therefore, allow organisations to offer very attractive and valuable incentives, such as cars, holidays and large amounts of cash, to very small numbers of purchasers who happen to be lucky enough to win. Such promotions might be seen as rather boring by consumers, unless there is something really special about them.

corporate social responsibility *in action*

Ensuring free and fair competition

A legal ruling in 1999 cast doubt on whether prize draws and instant-win promotions linked with brands are actually legal. A law was already established requiring draw promoters to state clearly that no purchase is necessary in order to enter, otherwise the draw becomes an illegal lottery. A High Court judgement, however, deemed one such draw illegal because it was too difficult for consumers to participate without making a purchase. In this specific case, a retailer had supplied scratchcards to customers, but the majority of those cards were tied to a purchase. A solicitor suggested that in the light of the ruling, promoters should use advertising and point-of-sale communication to encourage consumers to take the 'free entry' route and that they should ensure that at least 15 per cent of entrants to such a draw come from that route. By 2002, however, there was no visible evidence that this advice was being followed.

The sales promotion industry was further rocked by the launch of the 'Must Win Club'. Consumers pay a subscription and the club guarantees two prizes in six months or less from free prize draws and instant-win promotions. By making bulk applications on behalf of its members, the club is exploiting the 'no purchase necessary' free entry route which, as the legal ruling above emphasised, must be genuine, realistic and unlimited. The club's activities are perfectly legal, but the sales promotion industry, facing an extra 50,000 entries to its prize draws and instant wins, clearly feels that the club is not playing fair in terms of the spirit of the promotions. The advice of the Institute of Sales Promotion is that as long as the terms and conditions of the promotion clearly state that 'You can enter by sending your name and address by post on a plain piece of paper to ... Entries must not be sent through agents or third parties. Any such entries will be invalid' then the promoter can legitimately exclude the club's bulk entries. A quick scan of a range of on-pack prize draws shows that promoters are indeed taking this advice, but there is clearly a fine line between maintaining the spirit of the promotions and risking tarnishing the company's reputation for social responsibility by building in exclusions.

In the current climate, it will be interesting to see just how long the club can continue to fulfil its guarantee of prizes to its members, and what the next legal challenge to the promotions industry will be.

Sources: Darby (1999); *Marketing Week* (1999); http://www.isp.org.uk.

Contests

Contests have to involve a demonstration of knowledge, or of analytical or creative skills to produce a winner. Setting a number of multiple choice questions, or requiring the competitor to uncover three matching symbols on a scratch card, or asking them to create a slogan, are all legitimate contest activities.

eg

'Get there before the moles do' was the advertising slogan used by petrol company Texaco to support its Treasure Hunt sales promotion. The company buried five Mercedes SLK convertibles in secret locations across the UK, then gave out clues to their locations on cards given away with petrol purchases. Each site was marked with a Texaco hub cap under which was a spade, instructions and a flag. A hotline was also set up so that treasure hunters could check that they had indeed found the right site before they put in any digging effort. One vehicle was dug up in Kelso, Scotland, but the three people who found it said that they wouldn't be able to drive it because they couldn't afford the insurance! Around 3.6 million people took part in the hunt and 400,000 people called the hotline. The promotion was supported by broadcast, print, POS and poster advertising, and the PR coverage generated was estimated to be worth £3 mn (Brabbs, 2000; *Daily Record*, 2000; Middleton, 2002).

Texaco customers were teased with clues as to the location of a buried car when they bought fuel. Large numbers were encouraged to choose Texaco for their next refuel in the hope of a further clue.

Source: Texaco HACL & Partners.

Sweepstakes

Sweepstakes do not involve skill, but offer every entrant an equal chance of winning through the luck of the draw. Additionally, they must ensure that entry is open to anyone, regardless of whether they have purchased a product or not. Thus *Reader's Digest* prize draws have to be equally open to those not taking up the organisation's kind offer of a subscription.

Such activities are popular with both consumers and organisations. The consumer gets the chance to win something really worthwhile, and the organisation can hope to generate many extra sales for a fixed outlay. With price or gift-based promotions, the more you sell, the more successful the promotion, the more it costs you because you have to pay out on every sale. With competitions and sweepstakes, the more successful the activity, the more entries it attracts, yet the prizes remain fixed. The only losers with a popular contest or sweepstake are the consumers, whose chances of winning become slimmer! However, at some stage consumers may become bored with such activities, especially if they do not think they have any reasonable chance of winning. At that point, a more immediate but less valuable incentive might be more appropriate.

All contests and sweepstakes are strictly controlled in the UK under the Lotteries and Amusements Act 1976, and a code of sales promotion practice guides the presentation and administration of such schemes. It is essential for an organisation to seek professional legal and expert advice to avoid any allegation of illegal or questionable practice that could backfire on the promoter. Despite the problems and the need for caution, contests and sweepstakes can, however, provide a lift to flagging product interest and generate additional awareness. Table 16.4 summarises some of the issues on which decisions need to be made before such promotions can be implemented.

Table 16.4 Contests and sweepstakes: issues for decision

- Communicating the promotion – on/in-pack? leaflet? print media? etc.
- Prize structure and description
- Prize limits
- Entry conditions
- Proof of purchase requirements
- Eligibility and geographic restrictions
- Supplementary rule availability
- Entry method – mail? phone?
- Closing date
- Selection criteria for winner
- Tie breaker
- Notification of results

Consumer sales promotion methods (4): store based

This section looks more generally at what can be done within a retail outlet to stimulate consumer interest in products, leading perhaps to trial or purchase.

Point-of-sale displays

Sales promotion at the point of sale (**POS**) is critical in situations where the customer enters the store undecided or is prepared to switch brands fairly readily. Many different POS materials and methods can be used. These include posters, displays, dispensers, dump bins and other containers to display products. New technology has further changed POS promotion with flashing signs, videos, message screens and other such attention-seeking display material. Interactive POS systems can help customers to select the most appropriate offering for their needs, or can direct them to other promotional offers.

Thomas Cook, the travel agent, for example, uses a system that helps customers to select holidays, while Daewoo uses interactive screens to help consumers 'design' the car they want.

The main objectives of POS promotion are to inform the customer and to persuade them to try or retry the product. In some areas it has been suggested that up to 55 per cent of purchasing decisions are made in-store. This means that the manufacturer has to ensure that the product 'talks from the shelf' to attract attention.

However, as seen in Chapter 13, retailers are increasingly dominating the shelves in their own stores. It is they who decide on the coordinated image for the store and strictly control the use of manufacturer-inspired POS material. They want impact, but do not want their stores to look like a loose collection of POS jumble, nor do they want too many flimsy, tacky-looking cardboard displays.

Demonstrations

In-store demonstrations are a very powerful means of gaining interest and trial. Food product cooking demonstrations and tasters are used by retailer and manufacturer alike, especially if the product is a little unusual and would benefit from exposure (i.e. new cheeses, meats, drinks etc.). Other demonstrations include cosmetic preparation and application, electrical appliances, especially if they are new and unusual, and cars. These demonstrations may take place within the retail environment, but the growth of shopping centre display areas provides a more flexible means for direct selling via a demonstration.

Organisations sometimes use **field marketing agencies** to handle in-store demonstrations and other promotional activities. The agency may well hand out samples and demonstrate products, but it also makes sure that products are properly displayed and checks where they are positioned on the shelf, particularly in relation to the competition.

eg

Linking back to sampling, Birds Eye Wall's believes that providing potential customers with cooked samples of product at the point of sale is extremely effective for stimulating sales. Using a mobile kitchen, 10,000 cooked samples a day can be produced in a supermarket car park. In 2001, Sainsbury's had 250 mobile sampling units set up in its car parks, available for any advertiser to use. In 2002, it decided to use 12 of them for itself, to promote its 'Be Good to Yourself' healthy-eating product range (*Marketing Week*, 2002a). If shoppers sample and like the products then they are more likely to go to look for them in the store and buy them.

Methods of promotion to the retail trade

Manufacturers of consumer goods are dependent on the retail trade to sell their product for them. Just as consumers sometimes need that extra incentive to try a product or to become committed to it, retailers too need encouragement to push a particular product into the distribution system and to facilitate its movement to the customer. Of course, many of the consumer-orientated activities considered in previous sections help that process through pull strategies.

eg

Powerade is an isotonic sports drink owned by Coca-Cola. When three new flavours were launched early in 2002, trade advertising was undertaken to convince retailers that they should stock the product. The advertising highlighted the £7 mn allocated as brand support for the launch period and during 2002, as well as reiterating the product benefits. A trade-orientated promotion consisting of '12 bottles for the price of 9' through participating wholesalers was prominently featured in the advertisements. A hotline telephone number was also given so that retailers could call to request a point-of-sale promotional pack.

Some trade promotions are tightly linked with consumer promotions to create a synergy between push and pull strategies.

The main push promotions are variations on price promotions and direct assistance with selling to the final customer. These will now be looked at in turn.

Allowances and discounts

Allowances and discounts aim to maintain or increase the volume of stock moving through the channel of distribution. The first priority is to get the stock into the retailer, and then to influence ordering patterns by the offer of a price advantage. All of the offers discussed here encourage retailers to increase the amount of stock held over a period, and thus might also encourage them to sell the product more aggressively. This may be especially important where there is severe competition between manufacturers' brands.

Individual case bonuses

The most popular form of trade price promotion is the one whereby a retailer or distributor is offered a price reduction on each unit or case purchased (for a limited period only). The advantage of this method is that it is very flexible to introduce and drop, especially with the widespread use of direct ordering systems by phone, fax or computer.

Volume allowances

An allowance or discount could depend on the retailer fulfilling a condition relating to volume purchased. The allowance may take several forms. It could, for instance, be a fixed amount per case provided that an agreed number of cases is purchased. Thus a retailer buying a minimum of 20 cases of a product, for instance, might qualify for a 2 per cent discount on the order total that is not offered to the retailer who only buys 19 cases. Alternatively, the allowance might only apply to those cases purchased over and above the minimum order threshold. Thus the retailer gets no discount on the first 20, but does get a 2 per cent discount on the 21st and subsequent cases. Allowances might also operate on smaller quantities quoted in units.

Discount overriders

Discount overriders are longer-term, retrospective discounts, awarded on a quarterly or annual basis, depending on the achievement of agreed volumes or sales targets. These may be applicable to an industrial distributor selling components as a retail outlet. Although the additional discount may be low, perhaps 0.5 per cent, on a turnover of £500,000 this would still be an attractive £2,500.

Count and recount

Count and recount is also a retrospective method in that it offers a rebate for each case (or whatever the stock unit is) sold during a specified period. Thus on the first day of the period, all existing stock is counted and any inward shipments received during the period are added to that total. At the end of the period, all remaining unsold cases are deducted. The difference represents the amount of stock actually shifted, forming the basis on which a rebate is paid. Figure 16.9 shows an example of the calculations involved. This method is not easy to administer and is, of course, potentially time consuming to operate.

Figure 16.9 Count and recount rebate

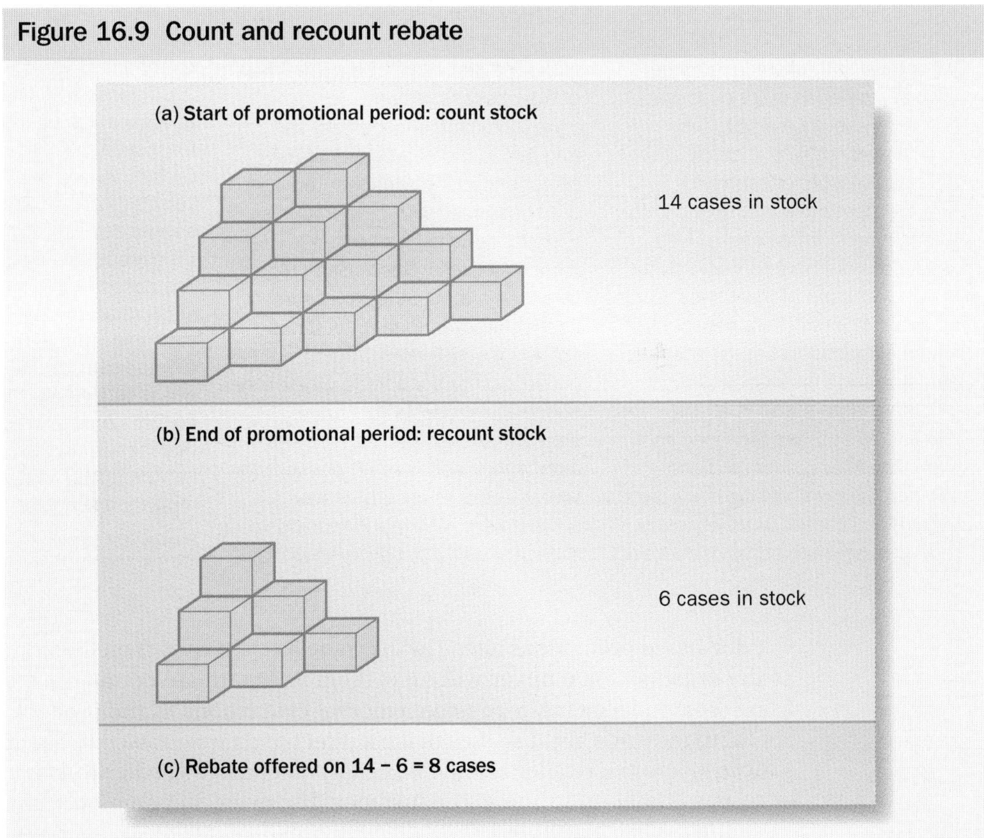

Free merchandise

The equivalent of the consumers' BIGIF (see p. 666 *et seq.*) but on a larger scale, this method involves the offer of free merchandise in return for an agreed level of purchases, for instance buy 10 cases and get another two free. Indirectly, this is a price-based promotion in the retailer's eyes, as it effectively reduces the average cost of all the cases purchased of that brand. The free merchandise need not necessarily be the product itself.

Bendicks offered a free merchandise promotion to smaller retailers through special cases bought from selected wholesalers and cash and carries. The cases contained rolls of Werther's Original and Campino sweets and offered 120 rolls for the price of 98. The 22 free rolls, the equivalent of a 20 per cent discount on the price of the merchandise, were worth £6.60 at the recommended retail price, thus giving the retailer £6.60 extra profit. In addition, the case converted to a display unit to be put on the store's counter. The retailer had the choice of offering a further consumer-orientated promotion of 'buy any two for 49p' to encourage brisk sales, or could sell the rolls at the usual price of 30p each (*The Grocer*, 2002b).

marketing *in action*

Trade promotions

Calypso Cups and Kwenchy Kups are fruit flavoured soft drinks sold in plastic cups with a straw and targeted at children. They are advertised by the manufacturer, Calypso Soft Drinks Ltd, to retailers in the trade magazine, *The Grocer*. One advertisement, as well as emphasising the fact that Calypso is 'The UK's number 1 cup drink. Stock up or miss out', offered a summer special promotion of 24 cups per carton for the price of 20. This encouraged retailers to stock up for the peak season, effectively by offering them more profit per carton through the four free drinks. Free stock does not have to mean giving the retailer more of the same, however. To introduce a new product line, manufacturers can bundle it as free stock with an existing product with which the retailer is already familiar. When Swan launched its extra slim filter tips for smokers, it bundled them with its cigarette papers in cash and carries. Thus when the retailer bought two boxes of packs of cigarette papers, a box of 18 packs of filter tips was also given free. Since each pack retails at 49p, this represents a clear profit to the retailer of £8.82. An offer like this encourages the retailer to consider the new product, stock up with it, and generate awareness and sales with customers, which in turn helps to make the new product a normal part of the retailer's offering.

New product launches are very frequent in the health and beauty sector and this means that retailers are bombarded with new products vying for the shelf space that is vital to product success. Successful products, those generating at least £1 mn annual turnover, tend to be those achieving a high level of retail penetration through trade promotions. Successful products had trade promotions over the first four weeks after launch and over 70 per cent for twelve weeks to ensure retailer commitment. Where the manufacturer is dealing with a large national chain, such as the major supermarket groups, the trade promotions will happen directly between the manufacturer and the retailer. With smaller retailers, as seen in the Swan example above, a promotion can be delivered through a wholesaler or cash and carry using methods very similar to those common in consumer promotions.

Confectionery manufacturer Haribo advertised its 'Best Ever Cashback Promotion 2002' to retailers in *The Grocer*. Tokens were included in selected cartons and drums of the sweets and Haribo promised to send a £5 cheque in exchange for 25 tokens. The special packs were available to small retailers via wholesalers and cash and carries. Haribo also operates a 'retail club' through its website which entitles members to information on forthcoming promotions, merchandising gifts, and samples of new products, as well as advice and marketing support.

Sources: Croft (1999); http://www.haribo.com/uk/retailclub.

Price-based promotions aimed at the trade are less risky than those aimed at consumers, as the organisational buyer will view them as legitimate competitive tactics rather than using them judgementally to make emotive evaluations of the product. Price promotions appeal to the trade because they make a direct and measurable impact on the retailer's cost structure, and the retailer has the flexibility to choose whether to keep those cost savings or to pass them on to the end consumer. However, in common with price promotions

Who said that trade advertising had to be dull?

Source: Calypso Soft Drinks Ltd.

offered to the consumer, trade-orientated price promotions do have the disadvantage of being quickly and easily copied by the competition, leading to the risk of mutually destructive price wars.

Selling and marketing assistance

A number of manufacturer-supported sales and marketing activities assist the re-seller by means of promotion at both local and national level.

Cooperative advertising

In cooperative advertising a manufacturer agrees to fund a percentage of a retailer's local advertising, as long as the manufacturer's products are featured in at least part of the advertisement. Normally, the support is limited to media buying rather than creative costs, and is usually set in proportion to the value of product purchased by the retailer from the manufacturer. However, in some cases, standard broadcasting messages or advertising designs, which can be adapted by agreement, are made available to the re-seller.

Cooperative advertising support can be very costly, and thus the manufacturer needs to think very carefully before offering it, as it can potentially put far greater pressure on the manufacturer's own promotional budget than some of the methods previously discussed. A further problem arises from the sometimes uncoordinated advertising programme that may develop. In some regions there may be overlap, but in others the retailer may have little interest in media advertising, resulting in incomplete coverage.

Although in theory manufacturer support may result in better advertising, attempts by resellers to crowd a print advertisement with products, often with price promotions, tend to undermine the position and value of some goods – fmcg brands in particular. Rather than leaving the control of the advertisement in the hands of an individual re-seller, therefore, some manufacturers prefer to develop dealer listings. These are advertisements, controlled by the manufacturer, which feature the product and then list those re-sellers from whom it can be purchased. These are particularly common with cars, higher value household appliances, and top of the range designer clothing, for example.

Merchandising allowances

Using money to provide merchandising allowances rather than for funding advertising may have a more direct benefit to the manufacturer. Payment is made to the retailer for special promotional efforts in terms of displays and in-store promotions such as sampling or demonstrations. This is especially attractive if the product moves quickly and can sustain additional promotional costs.

Sales-force support: consumer markets

A manufacturer may wish to offer training or support for a retailer's sales representatives who deal directly with the public. Such assistance is most likely to be found in connection with higher-priced products of some complexity, for which the purchaser needs considerable assistance at the point of sale. Cars, hi-fi equipment and bigger kitchen appliances are obvious examples of products with substantial technical qualities that need to be explained. With perfumes and fine fragrances, on the other hand, personal service at the point of sale is seen as an important reinforcement of the luxury of the purchase. Manufacturers of such products need retail sales assistants to be well versed in the features and benefits of the products, to be aware of how to match those features and benefits with each customer's needs and, not least, to be enthusiastic about selling the products.

Free training

Free training helps to forge a closer relationship between manufacturer and both retailers and their staff, as well as fulfilling the objective of giving the sales assistants the necessary knowledge base. Even so, such training may not be enough to instil enthusiasm for selling the product and so, to gain an extra selling edge, further incentives aimed at the retailer's sales team might be necessary.

Sales contests

Various prizes, such as cash, goods or holidays, may be used in sales contests to raise the profile of a product and create a short-term incentive. Unfortunately, the prizes often need to be significant and clearly within the reach of all sales assistants if they are to make any real difference to the selling effort. This is especially true when other competitors may adopt similar methods.

Premium money

Other more direct incentives than those already mentioned are also possible. Additional bonuses, i.e. premium money, may be made available to sales assistants who achieve targets. These are useful where personal selling effort may make all the difference to whether or not a sale is made. However, the manufacturer needs to be sure that the cost is outweighed by the additional sales revenues generated.

Sales promotion to B2B markets

As the introduction to this chapter made clear, sales promotion in its strictest sense is inappropriate to many B2B markets. The role of discounts and incentives in B2B selling is dealt with in other parts of this book, most notably Chapters 4, 11, and 17. Discounts and incentives are applicable in situations where the buyer and seller are in direct contact and there is room for negotiation of supply conditions. Of course, where B2B marketing starts to resemble consumer marketing, for example in the case of a small business buying a range of standard supplies from a wholesaler, much of what has already been said about manufacturer–consumer or retailer–consumer sales promotions applies with a little adaptation.

The issue of sales force support for retailers selling on to consumers was discussed at p. 682. This same issue will now be looked at from the point of view of a B2B market, as an example of how the same basic techniques and philosophies behind sales promotion can be subtly adapted to a different kind of market.

eg

JCB decided that it needed to give a boost to its sales of earthmoving and construction machines so it invited a group of 200 or more UK distributors and their top customers to the Torrequebrada Hotel in Malaga. The event was not only a sales conference, but also a forum in which to demonstrate over 30 different machines that were either being introduced for the first time or part of a relaunch. Similar events were held for distributors from France, Italy, Germany and Spain. In total, some 1,500 delegates were involved in a series of back-to-back conferences, the cost of which was claimed to be into six figures.

The sales promotion event was seen as an important part of relationship building with dealers and customers, as well as an opportunity to demonstrate products. Although national events could have been organised, or promotions centred around individual distributorships, an event like this generates a much greater impact, as well as giving JCB a captive audience undistracted by the pressures of day-to-day business. Taking northern Europeans to Spain during a temperate March could also have been an attractive feature of the event!

In industrial distribution situations, it is even more important than in consumer markets for the distributor's sales representatives to have full product knowledge and commitment. As the distributor is likely to carry many product lines, the sales representative is unlikely to be knowledgeable about all products and applications, and thus training through manuals and briefings funded by the manufacturer are likely to assist in selling to the end customer. That takes care of the knowledge base, but even that might not be enough, and the provision of sales aids and a formal sales training programme might need to be introduced for the distributor's sales force. As well as providing detailed training, the manufacturer's own sales force may undertake joint visits with the distributor's representatives to raise the profile of the product in selected areas. Not only does this directly support the selling effort and provide valuable feedback on customer problems, it also enables informal advice to be given on the best methods of presenting the product and service.

Managing sales promotion

When we look at the range of objectives (*see* pp. 653–6) achievable through sales promotion, we see that the flexibility and directness of many of the methods described are particularly valuable to the marketing manager as part of a coordinated promotional programme. Whereas advertising can produce longer-term results, sales promotion can complement that by providing an immediate POS impact that is very important in attracting and keeping loyalty, especially in retail situations.

This statement should not, however, be taken as in any way undermining the strategic role that sales promotion can also play in the promotional mix. In building and maintaining a brand identity, sales promotion (particularly when the techniques used are not price-based) can play a role in adding value to the brand, supporting and enhancing its character. Although the specific objectives and themes of sales promotion may alter during the life of the brand, that invaluable support role will not, and thus even if sales promotions only have a short-term impact, they should, in aggregate, contribute towards the long-term objectives of the product.

All of this implies that sales promotions have to be carefully thought through, and properly designed to fit in with wider market efforts, both corporate and brand specific. Sales promotion thus has to be planned and managed, and the various stages in this process are outlined in Figure 16.10 and discussed below.

Figure 16.10 The sales promotion management process

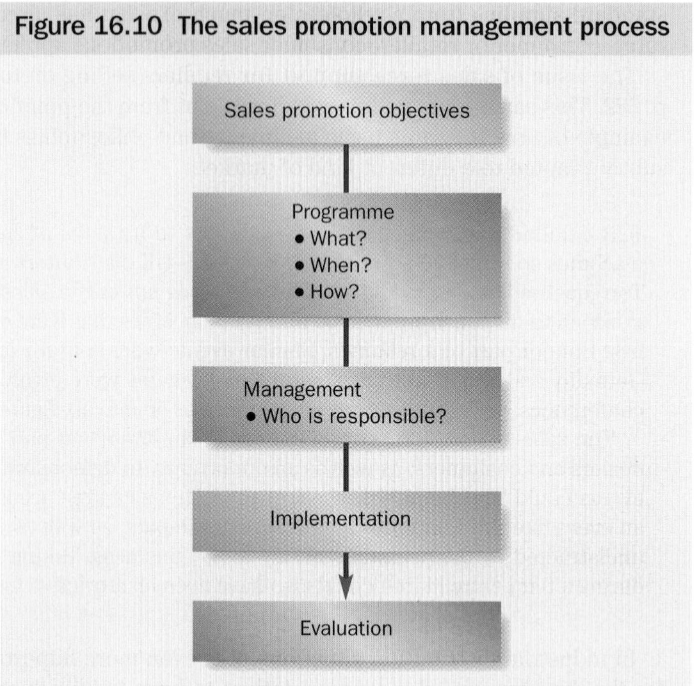

Objectives

As the earlier sections of this chapter have shown, many different sales promotion techniques exist to address a wide range of objectives. The definition of appropriate sales promotion objectives should emerge from a much wider strategic integrated marketing communication plan. Any sales promotion programme undertaken has to fit harmoniously with other activities within the promotional mix, as well as making a positive contribution to achieving the overall objectives of the product's marketing mix.

The actual sales promotion techniques employed will themselves depend on the objectives defined and the context within which the sales promotion will take place.

The choice between price and non-price sales promotions may be crucial as the product's lifecycle runs its course. In the early stages, when trial by consumers and retail trade acceptance are vital, the focus may be on samples, coupons and introductory price cuts. Clearly communicating such price cuts as 'trial' or 'introductory' helps to avoid the danger of cheapening the brand's quality.

As the brand develops, so the focus of sales promotion objectives may shift to reminders of the product and retaining loyalty, especially if competing brands are also coming on to the scene. This may be an appropriate point at which to begin to build additional brand value with gifts and competitions. In the mature stage of the lifecycle, price competition may become more intense and so special bonuses and price promotions may predominate.

Programme

In the development of a sales promotion campaign, as with any other promotional activity, there must be a clear link between the activity, its objectives and the target audience.

Target market

The earlier parts of this chapter distinguished between consumer, trade and B2B sales promotions, but even within those broad categories, the specific needs of different *market segments* need to be considered. A number of breakfast cereal sales promotions, for instance, were mentioned earlier in this chapter, some of which are targeted at children (as users and influencers) and some of which are targeted at adults (as purchasers and users). Similarly, consumers vary in their degree of sensitivity to price and coupon offers. Market segmentation, therefore, can help to determine what kind of sales promotion might be most appropriate, and can also be a major guide to the likelihood of a sales promotion's achieving its objectives.

Campaigns and costs

After the definition of the target audience and sales promotion objectives, a shortlist of alternative *campaigns* can be developed according to the budget available. Unlike a media budget, the sales promotion budget can have far-reaching impact across the organisation, which if not carefully assessed can lead to a resource-intensive campaign. This problem is compounded in that the final cost of the campaign may not be known until it is over. Coupon redemption rates, gift take-up and cash-backs, for instance, are difficult to estimate in advance.

There are two main types of cost category in sales promotion.

Communication cost. Communication cost relates to all the costs incurred in bringing the sales promotion to the target groups. These typically include artwork, print costs (including special packaging), media support and distribution.

Fulfilment cost. Fulfilment cost relates to the cost of handling the campaign and financing the programme offers, whether rebates, prizes, merchandise or discounts. As we saw earlier, even free gifts incur postage and packaging costs. Forecasting redemption rates, and therefore fulfilment cost, is notoriously difficult and depends on both internal and external factors, such as trade support, competitive activity and the effectiveness of the rest of the promotional mix. It is often useful to develop a scenario of likely outcomes for budget outline purposes.

Implementation

As with any communication programme, the duration, intensity, coverage and timing of the campaign need to be finalised according to the tasks in hand. Although an individual offer may be short term to gain impact and retain interest, it may itself be a part of a planned series of developing promotional activity, and thus has to be slotted into its appropriate place. Many child-orientated breakfast cereals, for example, permanently feature sales promotions, beginning a new one as soon as the old one ends. These promotions are varied, appealing to different age groups, and utilising different techniques. If the current sales promotion is a free in-pack gift, the next is more likely to be a longer-term mail-in offer. These cereal brands have got to the point where the sales promotion is an expected part of the product offering; it is a shock not to find an offer on the back of a cereal pack!

Guidelines

A number of principles need to be followed to ensure good practice, as outlined by the UK Institute of Sales Promotion and shown in Table 16.5.

Pan-European guidelines on ethical practice and harmonisation of laws and regulations have not yet been achieved. This means that different countries allow different types of promotion or restrict activities in different ways.

Table 16.5 Guidelines for good sales promotion practice

Legality	Check any statutory controls/restrictions, e.g. on contests/sweepstakes
Code of practice	What you do should reflect the spirit as well as the letter of the law
Consumer's interests	Deal fairly with the consumer and do not exploit them
Consumer satisfaction	Do not disappoint consumers by raising unrealistic expectations
Fairness	Treat all individuals and participating groups equally
Truthfulness	Do not mislead or deliberately confuse the consumer
Limitations	Exclusions and limitations should be clearly communicated
Suitability	Ensure that the promotion is inaccessible to inappropriate groups where necessary, e.g. children
Administration	Handle consumer queries and responses quickly and efficiently
Responsibility	Prime responsibility lies with the promoter!

Source: Reproduced by kind permission of the Institute of Sales Promotion.

eg

The development of harmonised sales promotion rules across the EU is a tricky issue. National rules vary widely, with the UK at one extreme taking a very liberal view and Germany at the other, taking a very restrictive view of what should be allowed. There is some argument within the EC about harmonisation proposals, and the UK sales promotion industry is afraid that objections from the more restrictive states such as Germany, France, Greece and Italy will lead to much tighter regulation than it would like. The European Promotional Marketing Alliance (EPMA), the body through which the Institute of Sales Promotion (ISP) and the British Promotional Merchandising Association (BPMA) are campaigning, is supportive of a more liberal approach based on the UK model. The ISP is anxious: 'It could finish promotional marketing in this country if it goes the wrong way' (ISP director general Edwin Mutton, as quoted by Gray, 2002). In the worst case scenario, promotions such as free gifts and instant wins might be banned, denying brands important marketing tools as well as inflicting real damage on sales promotion agencies and promotional merchandising specialists (Gray, 2002; http://www.isp.org.uk). The arguments rumble on …

Management

The responsibility for sales promotion will depend partly on the company's policies on the use of external agencies, and partly on the use and demands of sales promotion campaigns.

Using an outside agency brings greater flexibility and fresh ideas into sales promotion campaigns. For the smaller organisation, there may be little choice but to use outside help as an extension of the in-house marketing expertise. However, the agency will need to be clearly briefed and at times managed to ensure that an appropriate type and standard of service are achieved. This is especially true if ongoing assistance is needed to decide on campaign modifications and review. These will often be costed on a time basis.

In-house provision will depend on the structure of the organisation's marketing department. Responsibility may rest with the product manager, marketing services manager, marketing manager or promotions manager. The important points are that there should be direct accountability for sales promotion decisions, and that they are properly integrated and managed within the context of the marketing plan. Clearly, creating in-house sales promotion facilities enables the acquisition and development of skills that can reinforce subsequent campaigns.

Evaluation

Given the range of sales promotion methods available and the increasing spend on such techniques, it is important to assess thoroughly the effectiveness of the programmes developed. This assessment should cover whether the objectives have been met and whether the results were achieved cost effectively. A number of sources can be used:

1 *Sales force feedback*. Being in the front line, the sales force can quickly get a feel for how a programme is being received by the trade.
2 *Sales data*. Although sales data are a crude measure, early indications of increased shipments may show that a sales promotion is beginning to take off.
3 *Retail audits*. Audits such as Nielson will track changes in distribution, stock levels and market share during and immediately after the campaign.
4 *Consumer audits*. These will indicate changes in customer behaviour, especially that concerned with trial and repeat purchase during the promotion period.
5 *Redemptions*. These are a direct measure of the campaign, such as the number of coupons returned, free gifts claimed, numbers entering the contest, etc. These should not be viewed in isolation, but within the context of the campaign and its overall objectives.

However, as with any promotional evaluation, the results cannot be looked at in isolation. Other elements of the mix and the relative level of competitor activity will all play a part in shaping overall results. Only by commissioning pre- and post-campaign research can the underlying influences be identified, and the impact on users and non-users of the product assessed.

Joint promotions

Sometimes, the risks and costs of sales promotion can be shared with other organisations by entering into **joint promotions**. If the two products or services have synergy, if they appeal to a similar target audience, or if the two organisations operate on a similar philosophy, then a joint promotion can make a big impact, benefiting both organisations and their customers.

eg

Clover, the margarine brand, ran a joint promotion with the Lego company. If the consumer found a 'lucky disc' inside their promotional pack of Clover, they won either one of ten family breaks to Legoland Windsor, or one of hundreds of Lego Jack Stone sets. Every promotional pack also contained a voucher, worth up to £19, giving free entry for one child to Legoland Windsor. If consumers didn't fancy their chances at an instant-win promotion, they could buy two 500g tubs of Clover with a limited edition gift attached to them for £2.99. The gift packs contained one of three different Lego Racers cars and offered free membership of the Lego club. According to Paul Davies, group product manager for Clover, the primary objective of the promotion was not just to increase sales: 'it is a branding exercise to highlight our family positioning. We were looking for an instantly recognisable brand that would make Clover stand out in the five seconds it takes the average shopper to choose a yellow fat, and Lego really stood out' (as quoted by Hunt, 2002).

If a joint promotion is to be successful in all respects, then not only must the right partners be working together, but they must also be clear about what each is bringing to the promotion and how the costs are to be allocated. Joint promotions are not an excuse to try to get someone else to pick up the bill. In many cases, each partner might even pay as much as they would have done for a solo campaign in order to achieve the benefits of reaching a larger audience with a better proposition. Cummins (1989) suggests six factors that help to create successful joint promotions, and these are summarised in Table 16.6.

Table 16.6 Factors influencing successful joint promotions

Factor	*How to implement*
Involve everyone	Include senior management from both parties
Make realistic promises	Only promise what you can deliver
Avoid unplanned changes	Make sure you know at the start what you are committed to
Build in good liaison	Maintain communication and develop problem-solving processes
Bargain realistically	Maximise **mutual** benefit at **reasonable** and **fairly shared** cost
Be proactive	Do not sit back and expect the other party to do everything!

Source: Adapted from Cummins (1989).

Chapter summary

- Sales promotion is part of a planned integrated marketing communications strategy that is mainly used in a short-term tactical sense, but can also contribute something to longer-term strategic and image building objectives. Sales promotions offer something over and above the normal product offering that can act as an incentive to stimulate the target audience into behaving in a certain way. Manufacturers use promotions to stimulate intermediaries and their sales staff, both manufacturers and retailers use them to stimulate individual consumers and manufacturers might use them to stimulate other manufacturers.
- The methods of sales promotion are many and varied. In consumer markets they can be classed as either money-based (for example, money off), product-based (for example, buy one get one free), or gift-, prize- or merchandise-based (for example, a free toy inside a box of cereal). Customer loyalty schemes in particular have become increasingly popular in the retail trade and in service industries. The problem with them is, however, that as they become more common, they lose their competitive edge and consumers become as disloyal as they were ever inclined to be. Given the high costs of setting up and running such schemes, their cost effectiveness might be questionable.
- Manufacturers stimulate retailers and other intermediaries by offering money back, discounts, free goods and 'sale or return' schemes, among other methods. They also offer sales force incentives to encourage a more committed selling effort from the intermediary's staff.
- Any sales promotion programme has to be planned, implemented and managed. The first stage is to be clear on its objectives, and how those fit into the wider marketing strategy. Then, within the design of the actual programme, the manager must be clear about who the target audience is, what the most appropriate methods of sales promotion are for reaching that audience given the stated objectives, and how much all that will cost. The manager also has to determine the operational issues, such as the timing, duration, intensity and coverage of the promotion, as well as defining any qualifying criteria. All this should be done within current laws and guidelines. The organisation has to decide whether to handle the promotion in-house or to use an agency. Either way, there should be a clear definition of who is responsible for what. Once the sales promotion has run its course, its performance should be assessed and analysed in order to learn from its successes and mistakes. A final issue of sales promotion management is whether to enter into joint promotions with other organisations. Where there is natural synergy between the partners, and a clear division of costs and responsibilities, joint promotions can be very successful. Both organisations can reach a wider audience with a far better proposition than they could have afforded working alone.

key words and phrases

Alternative currencies	Discount overriders	Sale or return
BIGIF	Field marketing agencies	Sales promotion
Cash rebate	Joint promotion	Samples
Contests and sweepstakes	Loading up	Self-liquidating offers
Cooperative advertising	Money-based sales promotions	Trading up
Count and recount	POS	Trial price
Coupons	Product-based sales promotions	Trial sizes

questions for review

16.1 What is *sales promotion* and in what ways does it differ from advertising?

16.2 How do the objectives of *retailer–consumer* sales promotions differ from those of *manufacturer–consumer* sales promotions?

16.3 How do *self-liquidating offers* differ from *free mail-in offers*, and in what circumstances might each be appropriate?

16.4 What is *count and recount*? Why might a retailer prefer it to a *buying allowance*?

16.5 Outline the key stages in the *sales promotion management process*.

questions for discussion

16.1 Research a recent new product launch by a manufacturer in a consumer market. What role did sales promotions play in that launch?

16.2 Choose an fmcg product area (breakfast cereals or hot chocolate drinks, for example) and analyse the sales promotions currently offered on the range of available brands in terms of the methods used, duration, size of reward etc.

16.3 To what extent are the sales promotion methods used in consumer markets equally applicable in B2B markets?

16.4 What kinds of sales promotion are:
(a) '20% extra free';
(b) 'send in £9.99 plus five proofs of purchase to get a branded sweatshirt'; and
(c) 'when you open the product packaging, look to see if there is a cheque for £5,000 inside'?
Why might manufacturers use them?

16.5 Find three examples of joint sales promotions and discuss the benefits for the organisations concerned and their customers.

case study 16.1

Learning to manage your money

A prime target market for UK bankers is the student segment. When young people go to college or university, they usually gain greater financial independence and have to learn the art of careful cash management. They thus need bank accounts. There is a lot of competition for this segment, despite the fact that it is not particularly profitable for the banks. The real attraction of the student segment for banks is their longer-term above average earning potential. Customer loyalty to banks can often be high, so once a consumer has decided which bank to use, it can be difficult to encourage them to switch allegiance. At the early stage of the bank–customer relationship, therefore, the banks put up with incurring the costs of providing the full range of facilities that students need, without earning much in return through overdraft charges, as student overdrafts are generally charged at lower preferential rates. The banks also feel that they have a social responsibility not to allow young people to get into so much debt that they cannot cope financially.

In the UK, with the ending of student grants and the introduction of tuition fees for all students except those from low income families, the emphasis has switched to student loans and parental support. Although loans are readily available, it does mean that a student will incur debt which must be repaid as soon as subsequent income reaches a threshold level. It is thus perhaps not surprising that an increasing number of students undertake part-time employment while studying and some, especially mature students, decide either to study part time or not to bother at all. According to the National Union of Students (NUS), 41 per cent of full-time undergraduates undertake paid work during periods of study. On average, students work 13 hours per week for £4.53 per hour in paid employment. NUS calculations for the academic year 2001–2002 suggest that outside London, after the maximum student loan has been accounted for, a student still needs a further £4,200 to cover basic living costs and expenses. Within London, the shortfall is nearer £5,000.

In the UK, however, in contrast with the USA, the tradition is to keep any employment to a minimum, reinforced by sometimes rigid course structures, heavy emphasis on independent study and peer and parental expectation that the student should take three or four years to complete a degree. In the USA, many students take far longer to complete their degrees and select a pace to suit their work demands, maximising the use of flexible credit accumulation models. In the USA, courses are timetabled to meet peaks in demand; for example the same course can be offered day-time and evening. Some universities have gone even further, as has Kettering University in Detroit, by offering degrees that are employer sponsored and in which students spend six-month blocks alternating between work and study. With the relative inflexibility of the UK system, despite the introduction of modular schemes, student debt is likely to mount from student loans, tuition fees and any overdraft or bank loan facility topping up the shortfall. A typical student could leave university, in the absence of any parental support or employment income, with as much as £25,000 worth of debt.

Barclay's Bank has emerged as a market leader in the student segment, despite a history of problems in the 1960s and 1970s when students were urged to boycott Barclay's in protest against the company's South African interests. In some instances, Barclay's was prevented from coming on to campuses during freshers' weeks and other forums for meeting new students. Since then, Barclay's has successfully used a series of promotional campaigns to attract students. Locating branches or cash dispensers on campuses, offering subsidised banking and making presentations to student groups are all part of its marketing armoury. A timely talk on 'managing your budget' during induction week, for example, can act as a soft sell, even though the bank's products or services are not overtly promoted.

Barclay's has been especially strong in using sales promotion to attract new accounts. This approach was considered important as students often could not differentiate between the core offerings of the major banks. In the late 1980s and early 1990s incentives such as gift vouchers, Filofaxes, clothes and CDs all played a part in building a strong market position. As the 1990s progressed, however, the focus switched to service and the various financial products that students might need during their course of study.

Barclay's, along with many other banks, offers an interest-free credit overdraft of up to £1,250. It also provides a number of extra incentives to attract students. Within the overdraft there is a special £200 buffer to cover special short-term circumstances. A further £1,750 can be added to the overdraft at a preferential interest rate. As an extra incentive, successful applicants for a student account with a Barclaycard are given £30 of gift vouchers that can be spent in Waterstone's or HMV on books, videos or CDs: £20 when they open the account and £10 when they first use the Barclaycard. Other discount vouchers, holiday discounts and deals on books are made available during the year, designed to build loyalty and goodwill between the bank and student. Furthermore, for the academic year 2001–2002, students were offered 3 per cent cashback on all purchases made on the Barclaycard until 1 January 2002, then 1 per cent thereafter until graduation. Additionally, Barclay's provides free student access to online banking.

Of course, Barclay's, along with the other banks in this segment, has to balance social responsibility against competitiveness. Special student business officers aim to build a trusting relationship with the student in order to identify problems early. Unfortunately, despite all these careful measures, most universities are full of horror stories of how some individuals become seriously burdened with debt due to overspending and abuse of the credit facilities offered.

In general, though, most students manage their finances sensibly and the banks are eager to get their business. Most promotions are heavily displayed at the point of sale, especially in branches close to campuses. The literature provides application details or serves as a guide to further discussion. There is, however, still further scope for imaginative incentive campaigns. One year, Barclay's offered a 'Rent Free' promotion as an incentive for students to visit their local branch and to open an account. The scratchcard-based promotion enabled a student to win £2,500, at that time a year's rent. The promotion, supported by media advertising, was successful in generating branch traffic. There were seven winners nationwide. With a share of around 30 per cent in the student segment, it is essential for Barclay's to maintain its innovative promotional edge.

Sources: Course handbook, Kettering University; http://www.nus.org.uk; http://www.personal.barclays.co.uk

Questions

1. What kinds of sales promotions do the banks use in the student segment and what are they trying to achieve?
2. Why do you think the banks have tended to move away from gift-based promotions to money-based offers?
3. What are the problems of using sales promotions in such a highly competitive, concentrated market?
4. How might the use of sales promotion methods differ for a financial services product compared with an fmcg product?

case study 16.2

Pennies off the price or points on the plastic?

The major UK supermarket multiples have long competed with each other using sales promotion techniques, such as price offers, BIGIFs and free recipe cards available in-store. One or two also used promotions designed to encourage longer-term loyalty and regular shopping habits. These tended to take the form of issuing cards that were stamped at the checkout every time the customer spent more than a certain amount. When the card was full, the customer qualified for a discount. These 'mini-loyalty schemes' were only used infrequently and did not allow the retailer to track individual shoppers or to analyse their buying patterns and preferences.

Permanent loyalty schemes that allow the retailer to capture and analyse customer data on an ongoing basis began to emerge in the UK supermarket sector in 1995. The technology to handle the massive amounts of data about customers and the minutiae of their daily shopping habits existed, and Tesco, the first of the major multiples to develop such a scheme, decided that the time was right to do it. To participate, customers have to register, filling in a short form giving details about themselves and their domestic situation. They then receive a 'Clubcard' that is swiped through the checkout every time they shop so that points are accumulated electronically, with one point awarded for each pound spent. Every quarter, the customer receives a statement showing how many points have been collected, and turning them into money-off vouchers on the basis of one penny for each point collected.

Since its launch, Tesco's scheme has expanded and developed further. In June 1996, for example, Tesco launched Clubcard Plus. This is a combined loyalty and credit card, in that holders pay a fixed sum every month into their Clubcard Plus account and then can use the card to do their shopping and even to withdraw cash at the checkout. A credit facility, up to the same sum as the usual monthly payment, is also available on the card. Whenever the customer's Clubcard Plus account is in credit, however, interest is paid on the balance.

Ways of redeeming points have also evolved to try to keep the Clubcard scheme interesting and fresh for customers. The vouchers can be used in-store to get discounts against shopping, but they can also be used to 'buy' Air Miles or for Clubcard Deals. The Clubcard Deals are goods and services, such as family days out at visitor attractions, cinema tickets and even speciality weddings. According to Tesco, in 2001, Clubcard was the biggest loyalty scheme in the UK with 12 million members; over 1.7 billion points were earned, enough for £170 mn in money-off vouchers; and the use of Clubcard Deals helped Tesco customers to

The Tesco Clubcard is offered to all customers and they are encouraged to present it each time they shop. They benefit from targeted mailings, offers, vouchers and the possibility of saving for Air Miles.

Source: Tesco Stores Ltd.

save over £25 mn on a wide range of offers. One in three UK households has a Clubcard and they play a part in 8 out of 10 sales. In May 2002, Tesco entered into an agreement to allow jewellery chain H. Samuel to award Clubcard points. As in the Tesco stores, one point is given for every £1 spent and accumulated points can be redeemed for Tesco vouchers, Air Miles, or Clubcard Deals. It is likely that other partnerships with other retailers will soon follow.

More interesting partnerships with suppliers are also on the cards. Tesco is looking to exploit the links between its Clubcard and its home shopping service, Tesco.com. Using Clubcard data, Tesco can develop lists of customers to be targeted with personalised e-mails jointly with a particular supplier. It could, for example, develop a list of customers who buy a rival brand and then e-mail an incentive to switch including a link back to the Tesco.com site. Unilever was the first supplier to participate.

It is also true that questions have been raised about the ability of such schemes to influence loyalty. A MORI poll showed that over half of UK shoppers hold one or more loyalty cards. Nearly 70 per cent of cardholders claimed that the cards did not influence their choice of where to shop. The problem is that many people hold cards for more than one retailer and therefore the card itself is not likely to be the prime store choice criterion. Nearly 90 per cent said that they were more concerned with getting lower prices than points. More than 25 per cent said that they rarely or never redeem the points they collect. Nevertheless, an NOP poll showed that 73 per cent of card holders use them as often as possible to save money, and 73 per cent prefer saving money on their shopping bills rather than using points for Air Miles or for buying or gaining discounts on other goods and services such as Clubcard Deals.

Because of findings like these, not all retailers are convinced about the value of a loyalty card scheme, and some have had their fingers burned. Safeway discontinued its ABC card in May 2000 after five years of operation and a £250 mn investment because it was felt that the scheme was not paying for itself through increased sales or increased customer value. ASDA spent £32 mn and five years testing a scheme in the mid 1990s but abandoned it soon after the Wal-Mart takeover. Both ASDA and Safeway are now EDLP-orientated (every day low price). It is interesting to note that the two supermarkets with the most loyal customers are ASDA and Morrison's, neither of which has a loyalty card scheme.

Thus Tesco and Sainsbury's, the two market leaders, have been left in head-to-head competition in loyalty card terms. The schemes provide a flexible mechanism through which other promotional activities can take place. The retailer can, for instance, link with a brand and offer a double or treble points promotion very quickly. Through the Tesco Clubcard magazine, mailed out regularly to customers along with their vouchers, tailored offers relevant to the recipient's shopping habits can be made. Thus money-off coupons relating to specific brands or product categories can be used to reinforce brand loyalty or to increase the volume or frequency of purchase.

The biggest advantage of a loyalty card, however, is the quantity and quality of data it generates on customer purchasing preferences and habits thus providing the basis for measuring the response to various types of promotional offer so that better targeted and better designed promotions can be developed in the future. The use of data is starting to go further than that, however, and what started off as a humble promotional tool is starting to play a pivotal role in retail strategy, and even in manufacturer strategy. Tesco is using its Clubcard data to determine the layout and product assortment carried by individual stores. The company sees this as a 'pull' strategy with customers essentially driving decisions. Tesco is extending this 'pull' up the distribution channel to manufacturers by sharing its knowledge with them, collaborating on promotional deals, and selling advertising space to them in its Clubcard magazine mailings. Such is the value of these services that Procter and Gamble decided to launch its new hair care brand, Physique, exclusively through Tesco stores and advertising exclusively through Tesco media. As Mitchell (2002) puts it, 'Loyalty cards (and the internet) make mass "bottom up" signalling from consumers economically viable – for the first time. ... The Tesco experience ... shows that when marketing initiatives are shaped by signals coming from the consumer ... then targeting costs plummet and responses soar'.

Whatever fancy plans they have for their loyalty schemes, retailers would perhaps do well to remind themselves of a fundamental marketing truth: 'The best way to establish loyalty is to give people what they want at a price they are prepared to pay' (Brian Roberts, senior European retail analyst for Mintel as quoted by Thurtle, 2001). ASDA, Safeway and Morrison's already have this at the core of their offering, and only time will tell whether Tesco's pull strategy will succeed in implementing it in the most powerful way yet.

Sources: Goodman (2002); *The Grocer* (2002e); Hemsley (2002); Mitchell (2002); Swengley (2001); Tesco (2002a; 2002b); Thurtle (2001); Tomlinson (2001); Williams (2001).

Questions

1. What factors have led the supermarkets towards these kinds of loyalty scheme and what do they hope to achieve from them?
2. What are the practical problems of setting up, managing and maintaining a promotion like this?
3. In what ways do you think suppliers could benefit from loyalty card schemes?
4. In the longer term, do you think that retailers such as Safeway, ASDA and Morrison's are right to reject the loyalty card concept?

References for chapter 16

Brabbs, C. (2001), 'Coke Steps Up Local Activity in UK', *Marketing*, 22 February, p. 7.

Brabbs, C. (2000), 'Texaco Entombs Cars for Treasure Hunt Promotion', *Marketing*, 6 July, p. 4.

Croft, M. (1999), 'It's Looking Good for Beauty', *Marketing Week*, 18 March, pp. 38–9.

Cummins, J. (1989), *Sales Promotion: How to Create and Implement Campaigns That Really Work*, Kogan Page.

Daily Record (2000), 'Buried Merc Found by Trio', *Daily Record*, 18 July, p. 13.

Darby, I. (1999), 'Court Verdict Threatens Scratchcard Promotion', *Marketing*, 1 July, p. 8.

Davies, M. (1992), 'Sales Promotion as a Competitive Strategy', *Management Decision*, 30(7), pp. 5–10.

Derrick, S. (2002), 'Making Money From Movies', accessed via http://www.pandionline.com.

Dow, B. (2001), 'Tanks a Lot, Boss', *Daily Record*, 3 December, p. 7.

Fill, C. (2002), *Marketing Communications: Contexts, Strategies and Applications*, 3rd edn, Financial Times Prentice Hall.

Fletcher, K. (1999), 'Getting the Most out of Mailshots', *Marketing*, 13 May, pp. 38–9.

Goodman, M. (2002), 'Supermarket Cards Fail to Keep Shoppers Loyal', *Sunday Times*, 3 February, p. 3.

Gray, R. (2002), 'Sales Promotions Battle for Survival', *Marketing*, 14 March, p. 27.

Gray, R. (1999), 'Targeting Results', *Marketing*, 13 May, p. 37.

The Grocer (2002a), 'Cussons Splashes Out £4m to Help its Refreshed Carex Range Clean Up', *The Grocer*, 12 January, p. 53.

The Grocer (2002b), 'Bendicks Offers Savings to Retailers', *The Grocer*, 19 January, p. 65.

The Grocer (2002c), 'Robinsons Aims to Clock Up Monster Sales with Disney', *The Grocer*, 26 January, p. 64.

The Grocer (2002d), 'Twinings Aims to Stimulate Sales with Caddy Offer', *The Grocer*, 26 January, p. 64.

The Grocer (2002e), 'Tesco Link with Suppliers for Personalised Online Appeal', *The Grocer*, 16 February, p. 4.

Gupta, S. and Cooper, L. (1992), 'The Discounting of Discount and Promotion Brands', *Journal of Consumer Research*, 19 (December), pp. 401–11.

Hemsley, S. (2002), 'Loyalty in the Aisles', *Promotions and Incentives* supplement to *Marketing Week*, 21 February, pp. 9–10.

Hunt, K. (2002), 'Clover Links Up With Lego To Build Brand', accessed via http://www.pandionline.com.

Jones, P. (1990), 'The Double Jeopardy of Sales Promotions', *Harvard Business Review*, September/October, pp. 141–52.

Kleinman, M. (2002), 'Venables to Front Nestlé World Cup Work', *Marketing*, 4 April, p. 2.

Marketing Week (2002a), 'Sainsbury's Promotes Own Brand with TMV', *Marketing Week*, 24 January, p. 8.

Marketing Week (2002b), 'Pantene Unveils "Mystery" Sample Promotion as Part of £9m Revamp', *Marketing Week*, 28 February, p. 6.

Marketing Week (1999), '"Illegal" Threat to Prize Draws', *Marketing Week*, 1 July, p. 9.

Mason, T. (2001), 'Red Teams up with Olay and Superdrug', *Marketing*, 3 May, p. 7.

McLuhan, R. (2000), 'Promoting Sales in Departure Lounges', *Marketing*, 7 December, pp. 39–40.

Middleton, T. (2002), 'A Winning Formula', *Promotions and Incentives* supplement to *Marketing Week*, 21 February, pp. 3–6.

Miller, R. (2001), 'Marketers Pinpoint their Targets', *Marketing*, 18 January, pp. 40–1.

Mitchell, A. (2002), 'Consumer Power is on the Cards in Tesco's Plan', *Marketing Week*, 2 May, pp. 30–1.

Mitchell, A. (1995), 'Preaching the Loyalty Message', *Marketing Week*, 1 December, pp. 26–7.

Nicholas, G. (2001), 'Swedes Miss the Points as Free Flights are Grounded', *Financial Times*, 20 March, p. 18.

Peattie, K. and Peattie, S. (1995), 'Sales Promotion – A Missed Opportunity For Services Marketers?', *International Journal of Service Industry Management*, 6(1), pp. 22–39.

Pemble, A. (2002), 'Nestlé Targets Football Fans With Cash Quiz', accessed via http://www.pandionline.com.

Promotions and Incentives (2002), 'Hellmann's Runs Free Cook Book Recipe Incentive', accessed via http://www.pandionline.com.

Swengley, N. (2001), 'Shop Loyalty Cards Buy Cupboard Love', *Evening Standard*, 22 May, p. 5.

Tesco (2002a), 'Air Travel Set to Soar as Tesco Team Up with Air Miles', press release dated 15 March, accessed via http://www.tesco.com.

Tesco (2002b), 'H Samuel Joins Clubcard Scheme', press release dated 29 April, accessed via http://www.tesco.com.

Thurtle, G. (2001), 'M&S Card Will Need a Strong Hand', *Marketing Week*, 13 December, pp. 19–20.

Tomlinson, H. (2001), 'Yes, I Do Have a Card, But is There a Loo?', *The Independent*, 25 March, p. 5.

Williams, C. (2001), 'A Revolution in the Way We Shop', *Western Mail*, 14 September, p. 18.

Wilmshurst, J. (1993), *Below The Line Promotion*, Butterworth-Heinemann.

Wilson, R. (2001), 'Tried and Tested', *Promotions and Incentives* supplement to *Marketing Week*, 6 September, pp. 15–8.

chapter 17

personal selling and sales management

Introduction

LEARNING OBJECTIVES

This chapter will help you to:

1. appreciate the role that personal selling plays in the overall marketing effort of the organisation;
2. define the tasks undertaken by sales representatives;
3. differentiate between types of sales representative;
4. analyse the stages involved in the personal selling process and understand how each one contributes towards creating sales and developing long-term customer relationships;
5. appreciate the issues, responsibilities and problems involved in sales management.

Many organisations employ sales forces to help in the promotional process. Whether that sales force takes a primary role in creating customers and then servicing their needs, or whether it simply receives orders at the point of sale, will vary according to the type of product, the type of customer and the type of organisation. As Chapter 14 suggested, personal selling will probably play a much bigger role in the promotional mix of a high-priced, infrequently purchased industrial good, for example, than in that of a routinely purchased consumer product.

Nevertheless, personal selling is important in some consumer markets. Car manufacturers spend many millions on advertising, but the purchase decision is made and the final deal negotiated at the showroom. The sales assistants thus play a very important role, particularly in guiding, persuading and converting the wavering customer without being too pushy. To do this, the sales assistant not only needs to know the product well, but also needs to be trained to judge the state of mind and the motivations of the potential customer so that a sale is made rather than lost. In the car industry, failure at this stage lets the whole glossy marketing process down. The sales representative selling assembly robots to a car manufacturer faces a slightly different situation. The task is still to try to encourage the buyer to make a decision to buy and then a decision to buy from you. In this case, however, the selling process will involve extensive discussion with operational and financial staff, and might include coordination between the seller's own staff and the buyer's decision-making unit, in such areas as technical specification, trials and installation. This is a high level, demanding job, but still needs sound product and sales training and an understanding of customer psychology. Many of these issues were discussed in Chapter 4. In some situations, product differences might be very small and the fit between the buyer's needs and the seller's offering be very close for several competing packages. The sales representative may then make the difference through the way in which the process is handled and the degree of trust and respect generated.

Regardless of whether the sales force is selling capital machinery into manufacturing businesses, fmcg products into the retail trade or financial services to individual consumers, the principles behind personal selling remain largely the same. This chapter will address those principles and show how they apply in different types of selling situation.

eg

Nucare is a intermediary between over 1,200 independent UK pharmacies and the main pharmaceutical suppliers. It organises its sales force by region and these Territory Business Managers report to a National Field Sales Manager. The territories tend to be large, such as Wales and West of England, and as a result the total national sales force is fewer than ten. An important part of the selling role is new business generation, i.e. signing up pharmacies to buy both generic and branded products, but in parallel with that, the sales force also has to increase the value of existing customers by selling more to them. In a highly competitive sector dominated by High Street pharmacy superstores, the role requires an understanding of in-store marketing, branding and merchandising, and niche products as well as the more obvious customer handling skills to build and maintain sales. For that reason, the company requires both pharmacy sector understanding as well as account management and selling skills (http://www.nucare.co.uk).

As a foundation for discussing the deeper issues concerning personal selling, it is important first of all to establish a definition of what personal selling is, and to look at the different roles it can play and the objectives it can achieve. This can then be put into the context of the wider promotional mix to show how personal selling differentiates itself from the other elements and how it complements them. From this, the chapter moves on to look at some of the skills and techniques involved in selling, using a framework that traces the selling process through from identifying likely prospects to making the sale and following it up. Having looked at selling from such a practical point of view, it is important to round off the picture by considering some of the managerial issues surrounding personal selling. These include the problems of selecting sales representatives, their training, deployment, compensation and evaluation.

The definition and role of personal selling

According to Fill (2002, p. 16), **personal selling** can be defined as:

> *An interpersonal communication tool which involves face to face activities undertaken by individuals, often representing an organisation, in order to inform, persuade or remind an individual or group to take appropriate action, as required by the sponsor's representative.*

As a basic definition, this does capture the essence of personal selling. *Interpersonal communication* implies a live, two-way, interactive dialogue between buyer and seller (which none of the other promotional mix elements can achieve); *with an individual or group* implies a small, select audience (again, more targeted than with the other elements); *to inform, persuade or remind ... to take appropriate action* implies a planned activity with a specific purpose.

Note that the definition does not imply that personal selling is only about making sales. It may well ultimately be about making a sale, but that is not its only function. It can contribute considerably to the organisation both before and, indeed, after a sale has been made. As a means of making sales, personal selling is about finding, informing, persuading and at times servicing customers through the personal, two-way communication that is its strength. It means helping customers to articulate their needs, tailoring persuasive selling messages to answer those needs, and then handling customers' responses or concerns in order to arrive at a mutually valued exchange. As a background to that, personal selling is also a crucial element in ensuring customers' post-purchase satisfaction, and in building profitable long-term buyer–seller relationships built on trust and understanding (Miller and Heinman, 1991).

One final thought on the definition: personal selling need not be a face-to-face activity. Think of it more as a voice-to-ear activity! Recent years have seen a big growth in telephone selling techniques and teleconferencing as cost-effective alternatives (Smith, 1993). Remember too that although personal selling depends primarily on the spoken word, audio-visual aids and demonstrations are often used to enhance that, providing a much more stimulating experience for the potential buyer.

eg

Avon, the cosmetics company, employs over 160,000 representatives in the UK (3 million worldwide) and 500 area sales managers for its direct selling operation, which is the largest in the world. The representatives have a key role in providing advice, demonstrating products, allowing sampling and relationship-building in their territories. Changes are starting to happen, however. Although the catalogue and door-to-door approach is still used, in the US e-representatives are an alternative type of service provider. In the UK, IT is helping the company to manage the sales process better. The area managers are increasingly being provided with PCs so that orders can be placed online and monitored. It will be interesting to see whether this is the start of a process that could eventually change the whole nature of selling within Avon as internet usage develops (Ashworth, 2001; http://www.avon.com).

Having thus defined the broad essence of personal selling, it is now appropriate to discuss where and how it fits in to the overall promotional mix.

Chapter 14 has already offered some insights into where personal selling fits best into the promotional mix. We discussed how personal selling is more appropriate in B2B than consumer markets at p. 577, while pp. 583 *et seq.* looked at its advantages in promoting and selling high-cost, complex products. The discussion at p. 582 also notes that personal selling operates most effectively when customers are on the verge of making a final decision and committing themselves, but still need that last little bit of tailored persuasion.

All of that discussion in Chapter 14 is relevant here for putting personal selling into context, but there is more to be said. By looking at the main characteristics of personal selling, it is possible to compare it in more detail with the other elements of the promotional mix, highlighting its complementary strengths and weaknesses. The characteristics to be examined are impact, precision, cultivation and cost.

Impact

If you do not like the look of a TV advertisement, you can turn it off, or ignore it. If a glance at a print advertisement fails to capture your further attention, you can turn the page. If an envelope on the doormat looks like a mailshot, you can put it in the bin unopened. If a sales representative appears on your doorstep or in your office, it is a little more difficult to switch off. A person has to be dealt with in some way, and since most of us subscribe to the common rules of politeness, we will at least listen to what the person wants before shepherding them out of the door. The sales representative, therefore, has a much greater chance of engaging your initial attention than an advertisement does.

It is also true, of course, that an advertisement has no means of knowing or caring that you have ignored it. Sales representatives, on the other hand, have the ability to respond to the situations in which they find themselves, and can take steps to prevent themselves from being shut off completely. This could be, for instance, by pressing for another appointment at a more convenient time, or by at least leaving sales literature for the potential customer to read and think about at their leisure. Overall, you are far more likely to remember a person you have met or spoken to (and to respond to what they said) than you are to remember an advertisement. In that respect, personal selling is very powerful indeed, particularly if it capitalises on the elements of precision and cultivation (*see* below) as well.

Precision

Precision represents one of the great advantages of personal selling over any of the other promotional mix elements, and explains why it is so effective at the customer's point of decision-making. There are two facets of precision that should be acknowledged: targeting precision and message precision.

Targeting precision

Targeting precision arises from the fact that personal selling is not a mass medium. Advertising can be targeted within broad parameters, but even so, there will still be many wasted contacts (people who are not even in the target market; people who are not currently interested in the product; people who have recently purchased already; people who cannot currently afford to purchase etc.). Advertising hits those contacts anyway with its full message, and each of those wasted contacts costs money. Personal selling can weed out the inappropriate contacts early on, and concentrate its efforts on those who offer a real prospect of making a sale.

Take a simple B2B situation, for instance. A brochure sent to a potential industrial buyer through the post may be addressed to an inappropriate person in the organisation and be put in the bin, the purchasing director's secretary may open the mail and decide not to pass it on, or it may be addressed to someone who is no longer employed within that organisation. In contrast, personal contact with the organisation can establish the identity of the best person to talk to and whether the organisation is even remotely interested in doing business. Both of those issues can be followed through with persistence until satisfactory answers are received. Thus the personal selling effort can then begin properly with a fighting chance of achieving something.

Message precision

Message precision arises from the interactive two-way dialogue that personal selling encourages. An advertisement cannot tell what impact it is having on you. It cannot discern whether you are paying attention to it, whether you understand it or whether you think it is relevant to you. Furthermore, once the advertisement has been presented to you, that is it. It is a fixed, inflexible message, and if you did not understand it, or if you felt that it did not tell you what you wanted to know, then you have no opportunity to do anything about it other than wait for another advertisement to come along that might clarify these things. Because personal selling involves live interaction, however, these problems should not occur. The sales representative can tell, for example, that your attention is wandering, and therefore can change track, exploring other avenues until something seems to capture you again. The representative can also make sure that you understand what you are being told and go over it again from a different angle if you are having difficulty with the first approach. Similarly, the representative can see if something has particularly caught your imagination and tailor the message to emphasise that feature or benefit. Thus, by listening and watching, the sales representative should be able to create a unique approach that exactly matches the mood and the needs of each prospective customer. This too is a very potent capability.

Cultivation

As Chapter 4 implied, the creation of long-term, mutually beneficial buyer–seller relationships is now recognised as extremely important to the health and profitability of organisations in many industries. The sales force has a crucial role to play in both creating and maintaining such relationships. Sales representatives are often the public face of an organisation, and their ability to carry the organisation's message professionally and confidently can affect judgement of that organisation and what it stands for. When Avon, the cosmetics company decided to target the teenage beauty business, they realised that to build and maintain customer relationships it had to reconsider whether the direct sales force employed was suitable for the different customer group. The new range 'exclusively for teens' is to be launched globally in 2003, but instead of using an army of 'Avon ladies', the company intends to recruit teenagers who are better placed to demonstrate and promote the products to that audience (Singh, 2001).

Sales representatives can also do something that advertising cannot: they can develop personal relationships with people in client organisations. Turnbull (1990) highlighted the information exchange capability and the technical and commercial roles played by sales representatives. These help to reduce the social and cultural distance between buyer and seller. Such relationships can smooth the way to easier inter-organisational negotiation, and they can also make information gathering much easier. A sales representative can potentially find out a great deal more about an organisation's purchasing philosophy by having a friendly chat over a drink with his friend, the purchasing manager from XYZ & Co., than any formal inquiry or survey. Accepting the contention (*see* pp. 164 *et seq.*) that organisational decision-making can be affected by less rational human motivations means that the interpersonal bonds between organisations must be fully encouraged and exploited (Cunningham and Homse, 1986).

Selling cosmetics and toiletries to friends and neighbours in the comfort of your own home is the way in which Avon works very successfully.

Source: Avon Cosmetics.

Cost

All the advantages and benefits discussed above come at a very high cost, as personal selling is extremely labour intensive. In addition, costs of travel (and time spent travelling), accommodation and other expenses have to be accounted for. It can cost well over £50,000 to keep a sales representative on the road, and for the more demanding roles, a cost in excess of £100,000 can be expected. Generally, the salary paid is only around 50 per cent of the total cost of keeping a sales representative mobile and connected. The actual time spent selling to a customer can vary considerably, and estimates of 50 per cent of time spent on travelling, 20 per cent on administration, 20 per cent on call planning and 10 per cent on actual face-to-face contact are not uncommon (McDonald, 1984; Abberton Associates, 1997). IBM found that whereas telemarketing sellers could handle 50 calls in a day, the typical sales representative is often hard pressed to manage 5 sales calls per day (Blackwood, 1995). This means that the cost of a typical call could be as high as £200 for capital equipment, but just £27 for consumer goods, where more frequent sales calls are undertaken (Abberton Associates, 1997). An e-mail could cost less than 30 pence. This emphasises the importance of call effectiveness and achieving better personal interrelationships, as only then can the high cost of personal selling be justified.

Many organisations spend more on this element of the promotional mix than on any other, particularly in B2B markets. Estimates vary, but it is suggested that the number of sales representatives employed in various capacities is very large indeed. In the UK it has been estimated that there are around 470,000 people in selling roles costing over £19 bn per annum, well ahead of the spend on media advertising (Abberton Associates, 1997).

Changing roles

The role of personal selling in the promotional mix is changing, and that in turn is changing the demands on both sales staff and sales managers. A number of behavioural, technological and managerial influences are creating the need for smaller sales forces consisting of

Figure 17.1 Influences changing the selling role

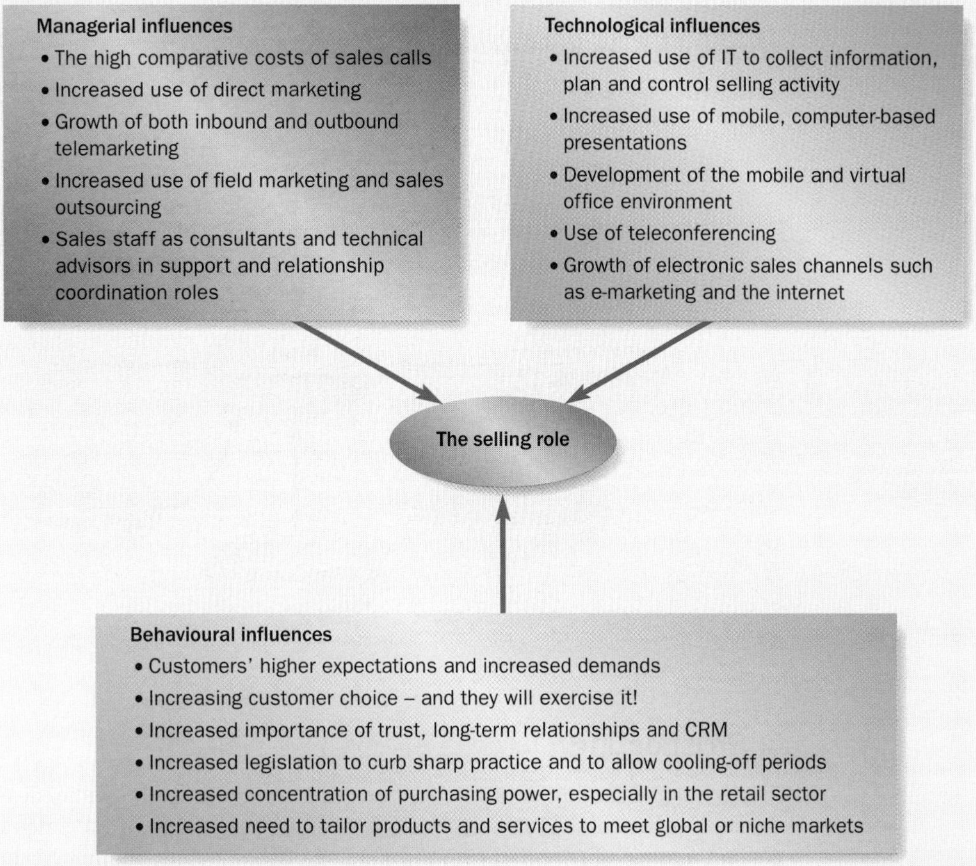

Managerial influences
- The high comparative costs of sales calls
- Increased use of direct marketing
- Growth of both inbound and outbound telemarketing
- Increased use of field marketing and sales outsourcing
- Sales staff as consultants and technical advisors in support and relationship coordination roles

Technological influences
- Increased use of IT to collect information, plan and control selling activity
- Increased use of mobile, computer-based presentations
- Development of the mobile and virtual office environment
- Use of teleconferencing
- Growth of electronic sales channels such as e-marketing and the internet

The selling role

Behavioural influences
- Customers' higher expectations and increased demands
- Increasing customer choice – and they will exercise it!
- Increased importance of trust, long-term relationships and CRM
- Increased legislation to curb sharp practice and to allow cooling-off periods
- Increased concentration of purchasing power, especially in the retail sector
- Increased need to tailor products and services to meet global or niche markets

Source: adapted from Anderson (1996), reproduced by kind permission of Professor Rolph E. Anderson.

well-qualified sales people who are capable of developing long-term relationships, increasing value added, and generating mutually profitable outcomes for all parties (Anderson, 1996). Figure 17.1 shows these influences.

Tasks of the sales representative

There is a tendency to think of the sales representative in a one-off selling situation. What the discussion in the previous sections has shown is that in reality, the representative is likely to be handling a relationship with any specific customer over a long period of time. The representative will be looking to build up close personal ties because much depends on repeat sales. In some cases, the representative might even be involved in helping to negotiate and handle joint product development. All of this suggests a range of tasks beyond the straight selling situation.

Clearly, the nature of the selling task and the range of activities with which the sales representative becomes involved will vary according to many factors. The more complex, technical or expensive the product, the more time the representative will have to spend in clarifying what is required, working with the customer to select the right product offering for the situation and ensuring satisfactory post-purchase performance. With routine, low priced, frequent purchases, the sales representative's role becomes much more administrative, just filling in the order forms. In a dynamic, fast-changing market, the representative may be briefed to take on an information-gathering role, finding out through personal contacts who is saying what to whom, and what moves are likely to be planned.

Figure 17.2 summarises the range of typical tasks of the sales representative, each of which is defined below.

Figure 17.2 Typical tasks of the sales representative

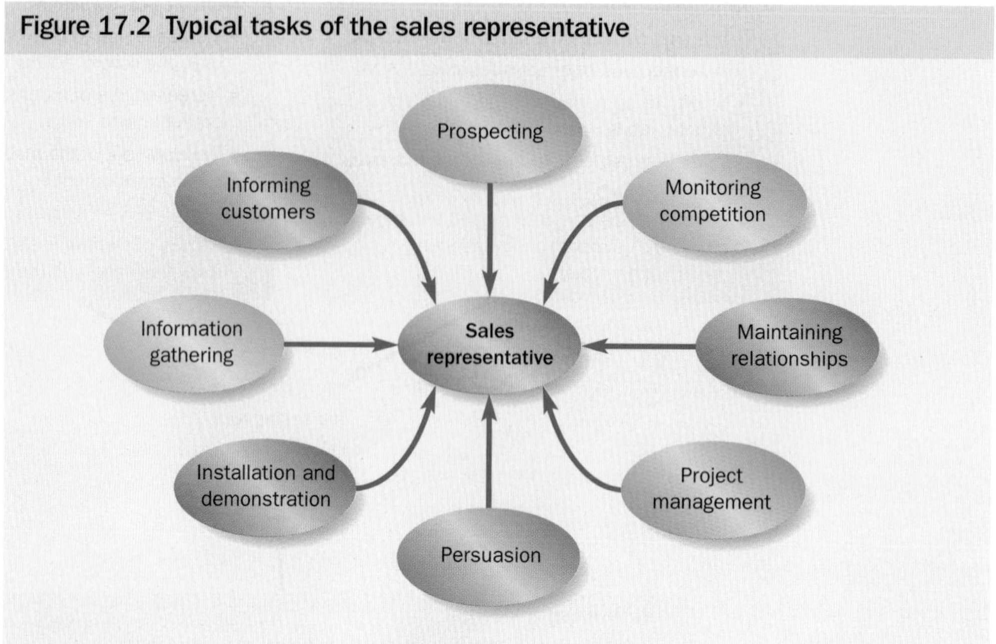

Prospecting

Prospecting is finding new potential customers who have the willingness and ability to purchase. For Rentokil Tropical Plants, for example, the role of the sales representative is to contact a range of potential clients including offices, hotels, shopping centres and restaurants to design and recommend individual displays of tropical plants on a supply and maintenance basis. Prospecting is an important task, particularly for organisations entering a new market segment or for those offering a new product line with no established customer base.

eg

When Pennine Telecom was appointed as a major Dolphin Telecommunications service provider, it had to employ a sales team to launch a new communications technology for businesses. The new communication system offered two-way radio, cellular phone, paging and large volume data transfer within one system. Most of the early work of the sales team was to find potential customers through cold calling and by appointment and then to convince them of the usage benefits of the system compared with its existing one.

Informing

Informing is giving prospective customers adequate, detailed and relevant information about products and services on offer. In B2B markets, once contact has been made with prospects, the sales representative needs to stimulate sufficient information exchange to ensure a technical and commercial match that is better than the competition.

Persuading

Persuading is helping the prospective customer to analyse the information provided, in the light of their needs, in order to come to the conclusion that the product being offered is the best solution to their problem. Sometimes, presenting the main product benefits is sufficient to convince the buyer of the wisdom of selecting that supplier. On other occasions, especially with purchases that are technically or commercially more complex, the persuasion might have to be very subtle and varied, according to the concerns of the different members of the buying team.

Installing and demonstrating

Particularly with technical, B2B purchases, the buyer may need considerable support and help to get the equipment installed and to train staff in its use. The sales representative may join a wider team of support personnel to ensure that all this takes place according to whatever was agreed and to the customer's satisfaction. The representative's continued presence acts as a link between pre- and post-purchase events, and implies that the representative has not stopped caring about the customer just because the sale has been made.

This role is also relevant for organisations supplying the retail and wholesale sectors. Area merchandisers for DeLonghi household appliances, for example, are required to support the selling effort with in-store merchandising, training retail staff and making product presentations in store.

Coordinating within their own organisation

The role of the sales representative is not just about forward communication with the buyer. It is also concerned with 'representing' the customer's interests within the selling organisation. Whether concerned with financial, technical or logistical issues, the sales representative must coordinate and sometimes organise internal activities on a project basis to ensure that the customer's needs are met. At Duracell, the UK market leader in batteries, a national account manager is responsible for all aspects of the relationship with the large grocery chains. This includes external roles of display, distribution and promotional planning as well as internal coordination of logistics and product category management. Similarly in SKF, an account manager for high volume users would be expected to coordinate technical problem solving, supply schedules, logistics and contractual matters.

marketing *in action*

Let the buyer beware

Personal selling is not always a popular career option with graduates, as people tend to think in terms of stereotypes such as 'Swiss Tony' from *The Fast Show* or 'Del Boy' from *Only Fools and Horses*. The truth is a long way from this. Sales staff play a critical role in enabling commerce to be conducted globally, but still, the sales representative is often regarded as someone not to be trusted and out to serve their own needs rather than their customers'. This perception is often reinforced by the media with accounts of how consumers were tricked into buying things they did not want at grossly inflated prices. It is conveniently forgotten that without sales staff, many legitimate organisations could not function and many consumers would not have access to the range of products and services they want. Nevertheless, the following three examples demonstrate the seamy side of selling that the public is often exposed to.

The deregulation of the gas and electricity industries in the UK led to a large number of complaints over the sales tactics employed by representatives to encourage consumers to switch supplier. Most of the effort was door-to-door selling targeting residential users, but representatives could even be found touting for business in shopping centres and motorway service areas. Some of the practices employed, however, such as creating confusion over the contract to be signed, pressure selling and feeding misleading information, took their toll on the reputation of the energy companies and eventually led to regulation by the government watchdog, Ofgem. The conditions required appropriate selection and training of sales staff; sales agent identification; audits of all doorstep or telesales; cancelling contracts when requested; and providing complaint handling procedures, including compensation arrangements. All of this was designed to reduce the number of complaints and start to regain public trust and belief that companies are offering genuine opportunities for consumers to find a more appropriate energy supply scheme.

Then there is rising damp. According to a report by the *Sunday Times*, when moving house, many buyers are told that they have a rising damp problem in their new property that can only be cured by damp

▶

proofing treatment costing anything up to £5,000. Mortgage valuation surveys tend to be rather conservative and cautious and so statements such as 'recommend further specialist investigation of dampness' are often found in the report. That is where the damp proofing companies come in. Some of these companies call their sales representatives 'surveyors' and armed with an electrical meter that they place on the wall, serious dampcourse problems are invariably found. But are they real problems? Cynically, the more dampcourse treatment required, the more commission the sales representatives earn. According to some industry experts, however, in the majority of cases treatment is not required and in any case the meters are designed for timber, not plaster and brick. Often the problem is poor heating and ventilation and defective guttering, not damp proofing in need of repair. So even if the consumer finds peace of mind in having the work done, it could well be money that need not have been spent.

Admission tutors in universities also perform a selling role, and it is an increasingly important role. The number of places is expanding far faster than the number of students to fill them. At times, however, just who is buying and who is selling becomes unclear. At Oxford University, course quotas are set to attract the most able students. Apply too late or be judged to fall short of the required standards and a rejection letter follows. An undercover *Sunday Times* reporter, posing as a wealthy banker, approached two Fellows from Pembroke College, Oxford in order to secure a place for his son on a programme that was already full. The offer of a £300,000 donation to the cash-strapped college to increase the quota was well received and the deal was done by the tutors with no reference to the university management. Unfortunately for the tutors it had all been recorded on tape, including the statement that it had happened before and that 'if the story gets out, we'd all be blown away'. Swift action was taken by the university and the Fellows left, but the fallout from the ensuing PR nightmare, the perception that privilege can be purchased ... at a price, is likely to remain for a long time.

The financial services sector is perhaps the greatest source of concern about sales methods, but that will be considered in more detail in the *CSR in Action* vignette later in this chapter (see p. 729). Once again it must be emphasised, however, that the above examples are not really representative of the selling profession as a whole and many sellers are held in great esteem by buyers in long-term B2B relationships. Sharp practice and pressure selling would soon be rejected and are entirely inappropriate, if long-term win-win situations are being established or maintained.

Sources: Howell (2002); Lister (2002); Mesure (2001); Ofgem (2000).

Maintaining relationships

Once an initial sale has been made, it might be the start of an ongoing relationship. In many cases, a single sale is just one of a stream of transactions and thus cannot be considered in isolation from the total relationship. An important role for the sales representative is to manage the relationship rather than just the specifics of a particular sale. This means that in many organisations, more substantial and critical relationships have a 'relationship manager' to handle the various facets of the buyer–seller evolution (Turnbull and Cunningham, 1981). In some cases, the sales representative might have only one relationship to manage, but in others, the representative might have to manage a network based in a particular sector.

eg

The prime responsibility of an account manager at Colgate-Palmolive is to maintain and develop business relationships with major multiple retailer accounts. These relationships in some cases go back over many years. In order to achieve this, the emphasis is on cooperation and customer development through working together in such areas as category management, logistics and merchandising. There is a need to ensure a close fit between retail requirements and Colgate-Palmolive's brand strategies. This means that the account manager must be able to analyse brand and category information in order to develop plans that will help sales of Colgate's personal and household care products. Any account manager who sought short-term sales gains at the expense of customer trust and goodwill would not benefit Colgate-Palmolive's long-term plans for the account.

Information and feedback gathering

The gathering of information and the provision of feedback emphasises the need for representatives to keep their eyes and ears open, and to indulge in two-way communication with the customers they deal with. 'Grapevine' gossip about what is happening in the industry might, for example, give valuable early warning about big planned purchases in the future, or about potential customers who are dissatisfied with their current supplier. Both of these situations would offer opportunities to the organisation that heard about them early enough to make strategic plans about how to capitalise on them. In terms of relationships with existing customers, sales representatives are more likely than anyone to hear about the things that the customer is unhappy about. The representative is in an ideal position, therefore, to make sure something is done to reassure the customer or to put the defect right before the customer's dissatisfaction gets out of hand. It is well worthwhile for the representative to report back even minor problems to give central management as detailed a picture as possible about reaction to products and offerings.

This feedback role is even more important when developing business in export markets, where the base of accumulated knowledge might not be very strong. Personal contacts can help to add to that knowledge over time (Johanson and Vahlne, 1977).

Monitoring competitor action

The representative works out in the field, meeting customers and, in all probability, competitors. As well as picking up snippets about what competitors are planning and who they are doing business with, the representative can provide valuable information about how his or her organisation's products compare with those of the competition in the eyes of the purchasers. During the course of sales presentations, prospective customers can be subtly probed to find out what they think are the relative strengths and weaknesses of competing products, what they consider to be the important features and benefits in that kind of product, and how the available offerings score relative to each other (Lambert *et al.*, 1990).

Thus while selling remains the central activity for a sales representative, the roles of prospecting for new customers, maintaining communication links with customers, servicing customers' needs before and after sale and information gathering are no less important in enhancing the selling process and maximising the investment in such a labour-intensive promotional element.

Forms of personal selling

It has already been suggested that different market situations and different product and customer types will vary the demands made on a sales force. These variations relate to the amount of selling effort that needs to be done and the degree of selling skill required to identify and satisfy customer needs. It is important to identify the level of selling required, because the more an organisation demands of its sales force in terms of expertise or skill in handling important long-term customer relationships, the more it has to pay them. There is simply no point in employing a high quality group of professional sales people who can undertake all the roles defined in the previous section if all you want them to do is sit by the phone and fill in order forms. That is an inefficient waste of resources.

Accepting, then, that not all sales representatives will be required to fulfil all those roles, it is possible to define three broad categories of sales representative: the **order taker**, the **order maker** and **sales support** (Moncrief, 1988).

Order takers

As the title implies, order takers tend to have a somewhat administrative role. They either have a regular set pattern of customer contact, or wait for customers to contact them or to come to them. Generally, they are only concerned with routine or low involvement purchasing. This category can be further divided into two subgroups.

External order takers

External order takers are mainly concerned with processing orders where initial contracts have been agreed. The buyer–supplier relationship already exists, and most of the concern is with re-ordering and stocking up. In such cases, the important details of the transaction are already known (pricing, discounts, product offering) and so the representative's role is simply to note details of quantity required and make sure the order is duly processed. In selling to major retailers it is usual for the initial contact to be handled by other, more senior sales people.

The external order taker is typical in selling to retailers, and may have perhaps one or two added functions. A junior sales representative with a confectionery manufacturer, for example, might be given responsibility for visiting garage forecourt shops not only to replenish stock, but also to check displays to make sure that the organisation's products are being given adequate space relative to the competition. The job involves a minimal amount of new selling. The external order taker may also be involved in arranging in-store displays, or in helping the customer to implement special promotions.

Where a steady routine of order taking has been established, the customer may become dependent on the predictability of the representative's visit to keep their own shelves stocked and thus their own business running smoothly. The importance of the external order taker, therefore, as representing the familiar, friendly and reliable face of the supplier should not be underestimated.

eg

Aico Ltd manufactures smoke, heat and carbon monoxide alarms. The company mainly deals through the electrical wholesale trade, so the role of the sales representative is to call frequently on existing accounts within a defined geographic area. The sales representative would not only be expected to take orders, but would also ensure that merchandising, stocking and promotions are being used to the full as a means of selling goods on to retailers and the electrical trade. Also in the electrical trade, Pact (http://www.pact-int.co.uk) employs merchandising representatives to manage in-store displays and to take repeat orders from established customers. This is achieved in part by examining stock and sales patterns in a customer's account to ensure that adequate stock levels are being held.

Inside order takers

Inside order takers remain within the confines of the employing organisation and wait for customers to come to them. Again, they can commonly be found in retailing and distribution. A retailer might telephone a manufacturer requesting an urgent delivery of stock. The inside order taker will receive and process that request. A sales assistant working within a retail store waiting for a customer to come through the door is also an inside order taker.

The role of inside order takers may vary. Some will need to be able to answer simple questions, take orders, check delivery and complete transactions. At the other extreme, all that is needed is a telephone sales clerk to handle all incoming calls and to take orders with the minimum of customer contact. An inside order taker of the latter type is likely to be employed either with well-understood products in a straight re-buy situation, or where the buying situation is not at all complex. For example, mail order catalogue companies now use inside order takers to handle telephone sales. The consumer phones up, gives their personal details and the product order to the telephonist, who inputs the data into a computer and can thus immediately tell the customer whether the goods are still available and confirm the order. With the growth of online ordering and with direct links into order processing systems, the more routine the order taking task, the more likely it is that the role could be either automated or further de-skilled.

Although order taking may seem to be a low level activity, it is nevertheless an important sales function. It is true that order takers do rely on other sales staff or the general marketing effort for contacts, but they represent an efficient means of processing and servicing large numbers of customers properly.

The essence of order taking is not to get involved in detailed explanation, negotiation or new selling. Where the sales representative's role does extend to include those things, or incorporates product demonstration, such as trying to sell a car to a consumer, then the sales representative moves into the next category, order makers.

Order makers

The order maker is what most people understand by the term 'sales representative'. The order maker has to find prospective customers, identify customer-specific problems and needs, sell the appropriate product, then assist with installation and training. In other words, the order maker has to take on most of the roles outlined at Figure 17.2 above.

The order maker therefore needs a good understanding of each prospective customer's situation and how the product or service being sold can match with that. Order making demands a high level of creativity, the ability to explain and persuade, and the ability and willingness to build relationships with customers. These requirements clearly have implications for the kinds of skills needed and training needed to develop a truly professional approach to the job.

There are two broad facets of order making. One is the generation of new business, requiring an ability to identify and make initial contact. The second is a focus on enhancing the long-term relationship with an existing customer, not just by keeping them topped up with supplies of the current product they already purchase, but by extending the range of products they buy. If they buy more of the same, that is order taking; if they buy products that they have never bought before, that is order making. This means a very close relationship with customers and an in-depth appreciation of their situation and problems.

Attracting new customers can be very demanding. Potential buyers are approached by sales representatives from many organisations, so why should they listen to you or treat you any more kindly than any of the others? Furthermore, when economic times are hard, there is much buyer inertia, meaning that they will put off buying for as long as possible, and then only buy what they really need. The representative has to find a way of cutting through this inertia. Even if the buyer does listen and is willing in principle to purchase, the time taken between the initial contact and the first significant order places great strain on the sales representative, especially in a market where there may be many alternative products.

eg

Microgen is a leading company in the storage, retrieval and processing of information services for business. The sales representative in the company must always be seeking new business solutions to improve customer operational efficiency. This is often taking place with new clients and so high-level relationship building skills are required. The salesperson has to take the client from first meeting through to a decision to ordering, and often beyond. Although the challenges are great, so too are the rewards, with on-target earnings of up to £100,000 per annum (http://www.microgen.co.uk). Small companies can also be creative in making sales. A coach company from Nottingham shifted the business from local trips to continental holidays. This provided an opportunity for the coach drivers to become multi-skilled as drivers, safety experts, and guides but also as sales representatives. Given the time spent with customers and the rapport built up, the drivers were well placed to sell further holiday ideas, especially towards the end of a customer's current holiday. Sales increased by 5 per cent after drivers were thus used (O'Donnell, 2001).

Maintaining existing customers can also be very demanding. The representative must not only protect those customers from the competition, but also ensure that the ongoing purchase pattern is maintained and even improved with new applications and technology. The representative has also to be alert to opportunities arising from existing customers – don't forget that customers can be a great source of new ideas.

Although order making can be very effective in creating the new customers that keep an organisation moving forward and growing, it is nevertheless a costly part of promotion. The organisation needs to reserve the order making effort for worthwhile prospects and high profile customers, and not waste it on routine follow-up work.

There are risks in classifying selling roles into the three broad groups mentioned above, as it may be a poor guide to selecting the most appropriate selling skills and characteristics. The 1990s saw the emergence of two powerful forces that have had a major impact on selling. First, relationship management and maintaining the long-term trust and confidence of customers has shifted the emphasis to high-level selling activities. Second, order taking is progressively being replaced by telemarketing and field merchandising, both of which will be discussed in Chapter 18. To Sujan *et al.* (1994) it is the difference between effort quality (i.e. working to improve the conversion rate) and effort quantity (i.e. order taking). Darmone (1998) also highlighted the problems of adopting the three categories in dynamic sales environments and proposed that the focus should shift to the amount and processing complexity of information, along with the demands of time management and allocating priorities across a set of customers. The more demanding each becomes, the higher the level of selling skills required.

Sales support

Sales support is a broad term encompassing a variety of staff whose role is to augment the efforts of the mainstream sales force. Sales support staff could, for example, take on the burden of locating and initially screening potential new customers, passing that information on to the sales force so that the real selling process can begin. They may also provide sales training, provide technical support or take care of after-sales service.

There are two interesting categories of support staff worth mentioning.

marketing *in action*

The sales rep: on the endangered list?

A sales representative is an expensive asset for an organisation to maintain. Representatives need cars, computers, mobile phones, samples, presentation equipment and administrative support. They also run up bills for hotel accommodation and entertaining clients. When economic times are hard, therefore, many organisations cut their sales forces or rationalise them to save on costs. Other factors have also led to a reduction in the number of sales representatives. In consumer goods markets, for instance, there has been a reduction in the number of small independent retailers and a corresponding increase in the share of business taken by the big multiples. The bigger retailers tend to have computerised stock control systems with online ordering, so that there is no need for a representative to visit individual branches so often (if at all). HP Foods, for example, had between 70 and 100 sales representatives in the 1970s. By the millennium, the number had been slimmed down to 12 business development executives who each manage a portfolio of national and regional accounts. The largest proportion of HP's orders, however, comes in via computers or the telephone.

There is, of course, still a role for the representative in consumer goods markets in visiting smaller retailers, both to take orders and to help with promotional events or point-of-sale displays. Many organisations, however, find it cheaper and more efficient to use contract sales staff from field marketing agencies for such tasks. When Mars launched Celebrations, for example, a field marketing agency was used rather than Mars' own sales force to work with cash and carry and other wholesalers to provide free samples, provide product information and to negotiate special point-of-sale displays. The benefit of contract staff is that the organisation only has to pay for them when they want them, and can have as large or small a 'sales force' as a particular task or project requires. Contract sales staff tend to work in small territories and thus have established close relationships with the retailers and other customers that they regularly visit.

Field marketing (FM) has grown in popularity over the last ten years as an effective substitute for client-owned sales forces where the emphasis is on the more routine tasks of order taking and in-store demonstrations. FM has been defined as 'the business of creating, directing and managing full-time merchandising, sales and training teams to influence change at the point of purchase' (Gary MacManus, Aspen Field Marketing, as quoted by Middleton, 2001). The main activities are sales, i.e. acting as a client's sales team or supplementing the activities of the client's sales team or meeting specific coverage or time requirements; merchandising; auditing; and mystery shopping. As a sector it is expanding fast, with growth rates in 1999 and 2000 of between 30 and 35 per cent in sales.

Some organisations might worry, however, that because contract sales staff are not employed by them full time, there might be questions about their loyalty and motivation. Agencies are well aware of this and try to overcome it by setting up quality control systems to monitor the performance of their staff in the field, and ensuring that staff are fully and properly briefed at the start of an assignment. To try to engender 'loyalty' to the task in hand, the agency will also ensure that a member of staff is only working for one client in a particular product market at a time. Because of the amount of time contract staff spend in the field and because of the wide range of customers and product types they deal with, these agencies can amass a wealth of data about what is going on in the market that a company's own sales force would not have either the time or the resources to collect. Agencies can thus feed information back to clients, providing an additional benefit to their service.

As field marketing has grown in popularity, so its role has expanded from just being point-of-sale merchandising. The contract sellers' sales forces are becoming better trained, more IT literate and skilled in providing useful market information back to the contracting company. There are two broad areas in which contract sales staff are currently used: in fmcg, dealing with retailers, and in door-to-door selling, covering a wide range of products and services including cable television, utilities and financial services. High pressure selling and mis-selling were exposed in the utilities sector, where untrained and unscrupulous sales people made a wide range of promises that could not be honoured to encourage consumers to change energy suppliers (see Marketing in Action vignette, p. 701). Most reputable field marketing agencies seek to avoid such problems through careful recruitment, appropriate training and local control. For example, it has been suggested that the ratio of sales representatives to managers should be 10:1 in fmcg and 6:1 in door-to-door selling.

Thus, although the grocery trade still dominates the use of FM agencies, other sectors have now started to realise the benefits of more flexible sales force arrangements. The major credit card companies recruit new card holders through direct selling using agencies and car manufacturers such as Honda, BMW and Volvo use FM to encourage sampling and test drives. Some smaller companies have found that using FM agencies can provide them with a dedicated sales team they could never previously have afforded. The next stage of development is likely to be closer integration of FM into pan-European promotional campaigns. According to field marketing agency CPM, however, few truly pan-European FM campaigns are being run, with companies such as Mars and Disney preferring to run separate country-by-country FM campaigns. Some larger companies are seeking to find one agency to handle all their different campaigns across Europe. So Momentum, with 33 offices across Europe has organised a test drive campaign for Saab in six European countries and P&G has operated similar activities in eleven EU states. The need to address local market situations and culture will for some time act as a brake on genuine pan-European FM campaigns.

So, the sales representative might not be about to become extinct. What is certain is that organisations are rethinking how they manage and organise their sales forces and their selling processes. Thus the role and the tasks of representatives will change, and how they are employed might change, but they will always be needed in some capacity.

Sources: Gofton (2002); McLuhan (2001a, 2001b); Middleton (2001); Miles (1998); http://www.ukfm.co.uk.

Missionary sales representatives

Missionary sales representatives focus on a particular market segment or product to give enquiries and sales an initial lift. They do not generally work with the selling organisation's customers, but with the customer's own customers. Pharmaceutical companies, for instance, use missionaries to persuade general practitioners to prescribe new drugs for their patients. The actual sales of the drugs, however, are made by the conventional sales force to pharmacists or wholesalers. The missionary is effectively implementing a *pull strategy* (as defined at pp. 578 *et seq.*), by communicating with groups a couple of stages further down the distribution chain than their own organisation or its direct customers. Figure 17.3 summarises how the missionary approach works.

Figure 17.3 The role of the missionary

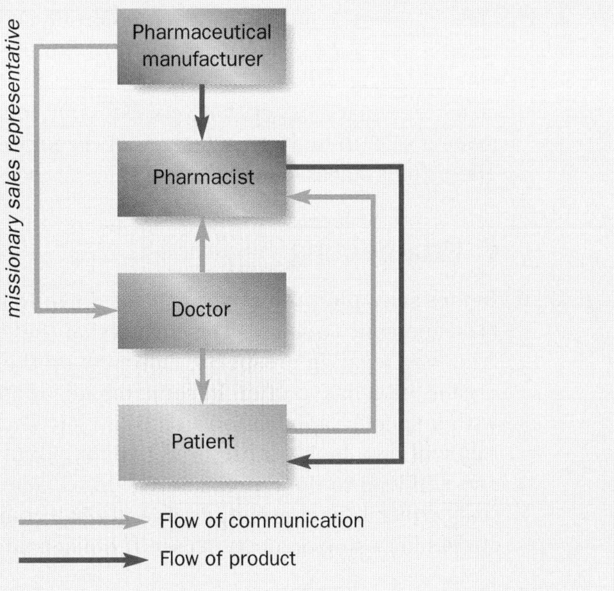

Sales engineers

Sales engineers, on the other hand, are directly concerned with the organisation's customers and the end users of its products. Their concern is with the technical or application problems of the product. They could be called in at any stage of the sales process. Particularly with a complex B2B product, in the early stages of the selling process they may have to advise on systems design. Later in the process, they might help with installation, training or even maintenance.

Often, these support staff can pick up early warning of problems and emerging opportunities, so they need to have good links with the main sales force, and the organisation needs to have mechanisms in place to make sure that the knowledge they pick up in the field is shared and used.

The personal selling process

Many textbooks, videos and gurus claim to offer the secret to successful sales presentations. In reality, there is no one approach that is right for all situations, nor is there any one approach that is right for all types of sales representative. This is hardly surprising, because the essential strength of personal selling is the human contact, and the infinite flexibility of the sales representative to create a unique and tailored approach for each prospective customer. At the heart of the sales process is the sales representative's ability to build a relationship with the buyer that is sufficiently strong to achieve a deal that benefits both parties. As shown in Chapter 4, organisations need to buy if they are to achieve their objectives. In many situations the main decision relates to *supplier choice* rather than whether or not to buy. The sales representative's role is to highlight the attractions of the specification, support, service and commercial package on offer. Differences between products, markets, organisational philosophies and even individuals will all have a bearing on the style and effectiveness of the selling activity.

Although it has just been suggested that personal selling does not lend itself to a prescribed formula, it is possible to define a number of broad stages through which most selling episodes will pass (Russell *et al.*, 1977). Depending on the product, the market, the organisations and individuals involved, the length of time spent in any one of the stages will vary, as will the way in which each stage is implemented (Pedersen *et al.*, 1986). Nevertheless, the generalised analysis offered here provides a useful basis for beginning to understand what contributes to successful personal selling.

Figure 17.4 shows the flow of stages through a personal selling process. It does not begin with meeting the customer; that itself is the outcome of an earlier pre-contact stage in which the prospective customer has to be identified. The actual selling stages themselves end with closing the sale, but the model also proposes the extra, necessary stage of following up to ensure a satisfied customer in the post-purchase period. Clearly, at any stage of such a complex human activity things can, and often do, go wrong. Although **conversion rates** between enquiries and real orders vary considerably, it is always useful, if the process ends in failure to make a sale, to look at each stage of the process to establish just where things went wrong. The various stages in the personal selling process are discussed in full below.

Prospecting

Before sales representatives can get down to the real job of selling something, they have to have someone to sell to. This means that there has to be some sort of mechanism for identifying and locating prospects, matching up the prospects' likely needs with what the selling organisation has to offer. In some organisations, perhaps those selling an industrial product with a specific application to a relatively small number of easily defined B2B customers, this will be a highly structured activity, involving sales representatives and support staff, and will lead to the representative going out on a call knowing that the prospect is potentially fruitful. In contrast, double glazing companies often employ canvassers to walk the streets knocking on doors to see if householders are likely prospects. This is not a particu-

Figure 17.4 The personal selling process

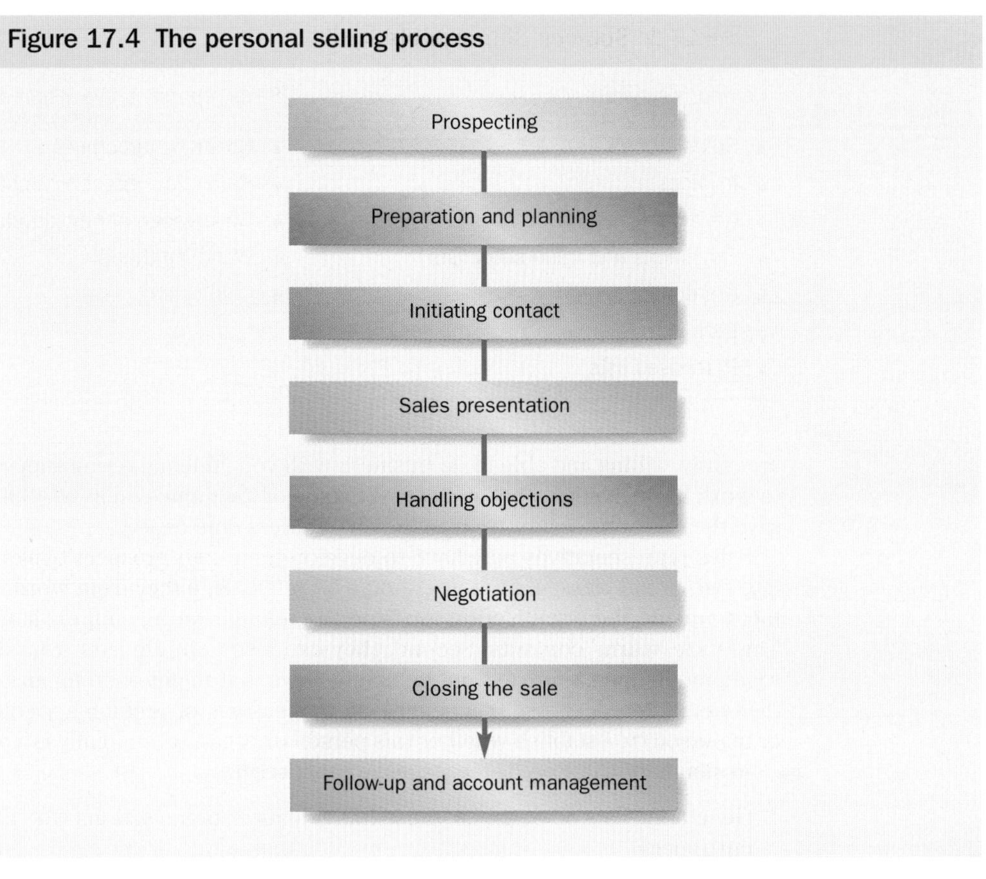

larly efficient use of the representatives' time, as most people will say that they are not interested, but in promoting an infrequently purchased, high-priced product, yet in a mass market, it is difficult to see what else in the way of prospecting they can do. Consumers seeing advertising for double glazing might get as far as thinking, 'I must get round to doing something about that bathroom window', but because of the expense and the mess involved, it is too easy to put it off and not respond. More direct stimulation, such as that provided by personal selling, is needed to turn that lethargy into 'I will do something'.

The latter example also shows that prospecting is especially difficult with one-time purchases where there is a constant need to replenish contacts. Once a household has bought double glazing, it is not going to repeat the purchase for many years, and so the organisation is constantly starting from scratch, putting considerable resources and efforts into prospecting. In a market where there is the potential for large repeat sales, prospecting may be a smaller part of the selling role, confined to replacing declining or lost customers.

In a B2B rather than a consumer market, the sales representative needs a prospect bank, a pool of potential customers to be drawn on as appropriate. This bank is often a combination of company-inspired and self-researched names and details of prospects. Table 17.1 identifies the wide range of sources of prospects.

Company-inspired prospects are taken from a wide range of sources that can be categorised into three types. First, there are potential customers who have made enquiries or responded to advertising, but not been followed up already. Second, there are those who have already been approached in an exploratory way, for example through telemarketing, and look promising enough to deserve further encouragement. Third, and most problematic, are the lists of names. These lists might be purchased from a list broker or be compiled from a trade directory or a list of organisations attending a particular trade exhibition. While these lists will conform to broad criteria relating to the types of organisations or people on them, so that they are generally relevant to the seller, they are still 'colder' than the first two categories outlined above. This is because there is no means of telling whether those on the list are even in the market for your sort of product, never mind whether they

Table 17.1 Sources of prospects

Company inspired	*Sales representative inspired*
• Sales records	• Scanning directories
• Invoices	• Referrals – direct or via sales support staff
• Advertising responses	• Observation of new developments
• Exhibitions and trade show lists	• Watching the media
• General enquiries	• Cold calling
• Lists from telemarketing campaigns	
• Purchased lists	

are ready, willing and able to do business with you. Telemarketing support staff may be able to work through such a list and convert some of the names on it into the second category to save the sales representative from much pointless **cold calling**.

Sales representatives may have to develop their own prospect banks. Their activity falls into two broad classes. First, there may be referrals, either from word of mouth from contacts outside the organisation, or from the telemarketing support staff discussed above. These are 'warm' contacts. Second, they can also compile lists from directories, or from scanning the media for relevant company news that might open up an opportunity. As with the telemarketers above, this might lead to a session of preliminary cold calling (by phone or in person) to establish whether this person or organisation really is a viable prospect.

In summary, there are three stages in prospecting:

1 Generating lists of **leads**, i.e. those individuals or organisations who could be prospective customers.
2 An initial assessment of whether each lead can be developed into a **prospect**, i.e. somebody who is likely to want and can afford to buy the product. This screening is often done prior to a visit.
3 This third stage often only comes after initial contact has confirmed that there is a need (whether the prospect realises that there is a need or not) and that the prospect has the ability, if so motivated, to purchase. This is a **qualified prospect**.

The outcome of this stage of the selling process is a qualified prospect list from which more targeted selling effort can proceed.

Preparation and planning

Identifying a qualified prospect is only the beginning of the process. Before the real selling begins, it is very important to obtain further information on the prospect in order to prepare the best and most relevant sales approach and to plan tactics.

In selling to a B2B customer, this may mean scanning a number of company reports, assessing the norms for that industry in relation to likely buying criteria and needs. Analysing the prospect's company report might promise indications of the strategic direction in which it is moving, as well as revealing its financial situation. It is also necessary to think about the kind of purchasing structures that the representative is going to have to work through, identifying the most likely influencers and decision makers. In B2B situations, for example, a key question may be whether to target the engineering staff early on to get their technical support for the product, encouraging them to re-specify their needs in your favour, or whether to try to motivate the formal buyers to consider alternative sources (i.e. you). Look back at pp. 160 *et seq.* to remind yourself about the structure and importance of the buying centre in B2B purchasing behaviour. In addition to finding out who to concentrate on, it is also useful to find out as much as possible about the application of the product and the features and benefits required. This allows the representative to construct a **sales presentation** that will be relevant to the buyer and thus will have more chance of engaging their attention and being persuasive.

Sales representatives in B2B markets are fortunate that sufficient information exists about their buyers to allow them to prepare so well in advance. In consumer markets, it is more likely that representatives have to think on their feet, analysing customers while they are face to face with them. If a couple walk into a car showroom, the sales representative has to work out how serious they are about buying, what alternatives they are considering, what their decision-making criteria are, how price sensitive they are, who the main user will be, and who has the ultimate decision-making responsibility. As if that wasn't enough, there is also the problem of working out the best product offering and deal to match those needs and that profile. If, in the course of a 10- or 20-minute encounter, the sales representative makes any misjudgement about that couple and their needs, then in all likelihood the sale is lost.

Where it is possible, therefore, doing the homework is essential, and it often needs to be very thorough, especially in situations involving large, complex projects with stiff competition. Also, if the competition is already well entrenched in doing business with a prospect, it is even more important to find out as much as possible in advance, since getting that customer to switch supplier will probably be an uphill task unless you can find the right approach with the right people.

Initiating contact

Making the first contact with the prospect is a delicate operation. There are two ways of approaching this stage. First, the initial telephone call that qualifies the prospect may be used to solicit an appointment. Failure to achieve that means that the selling process cannot begin. The phone call should not, however, be allowed to draw the sales representative into detailed discussion, as it is unlikely that serious and fruitful dialogue can take place without the use of sales aids and direct contact. Before the telephone call, an introductory letter may be sent to introduce the sales representative and the organisation so that the phone call does not come as a total surprise, but there still remains the important objective of making an appointment.

The second approach is to use cold calling. This means turning up on the doorstep in the hope that someone will see you, as the double glazing sales representative does. This can be very wasteful in terms of time and travel. There is no guarantee that the representative will get access to the key people, who probably would not in any case be able to spare time without a prior appointment. Even if the representative does get access, it is unlikely that a properly tailored sales presentation will have been prepared if there has not been preliminary contact with the prospect. Cold callers are often seen as time wasters, and do not do themselves or their organisations any favours in the eyes of the prospects.

eg

Whether it is double glazing, paved drives, kitchens, insurance or fresh fish, the cold calling, door-to-door sales representative is often seen as an unwelcome, intrusive time-waster. Although the door can always be slammed, elderly people in particular often become flustered and are vulnerable to predatory or persistent callers. The reputable sellers, however, obviously do not like having their image tainted by the activities of fly-by-night builders and con artists. The Direct Selling Association (DSA) has thus sought to encourage self-regulation in the UK through the introduction of a code of conduct. Sales staff from its 60 members must carry clear identification and make it clear that there is a 14-day cooling-off period to cancel products and services. Otherwise, it is a case of 'buyer beware' as disreputable companies tend not to subscribe to trade associations and exploit legal loop holes that bypass the Office of Fair Trading rights and leave the consumer vulnerable to over-charging and poor quality and service (Stewart, 2002).

Once an approach has been made and an appointment secured, the next stage is the initial call. This helps the representative to discover whether the initial assessment of the customer's likely need is borne out in practice. In these early meetings, it is important to build up rapport, mutual respect and trust between buyer and seller before the more serious business discussion gets under way. The time spent in establishing this relationship is well spent. It helps to build a solid foundation for the later stages of discussion.

The challenge at this point is to demonstrate to the prospect that it is worthwhile to talk about their needs, and to entertain the idea of revising their product purchasing specifications or their current practices. The danger here is of allowing the meeting to develop into a detailed product discussion before the prospect's real needs have been fully explored. In some cases, establishing these needs may mean undertaking a more detailed survey of current usage or application before a more formal sales presentation takes place. Remember that customers do not buy products, they buy solutions to problems. The product should be presented to the prospect within the context of how that product is a solution to an agreed problem, not as the sole and abstract object of the discussion.

Again, it must be stressed that it is not easy to generalise. Different products, applications, competitive states, organisational and even individual characteristics are all likely to have an impact on the length and depth of the exploration of customer needs.

The sales presentation

At last, the representative has enough insight and information to allow the preparation of the sales presentation itself that lies at the heart of the selling process. The ease of its preparation and its effectiveness in practice owe a great deal to the thoroughness and quality of the work done in the earlier stages. The objective of the sales presentation is to show how the product offering and the customer's needs match. The presentation must not be product orientated, but be concerned with what the product can do for that particular customer. In other words, do not sell the features, sell the benefits.

Three approaches are possible, although there is a tendency to rely mainly on the third one.

Stimulus–response

The stimulus–response approach works on the simple assumption that given the right stimulus, the customer will respond in the right way. It is most appropriate in consumer markets where people are buying low-risk, low involvement products. In McDonald's, for example, the sales staff will always suggest a drink or french fries if you only ask for a burger. The stimulus is the suggestion of a drink, and that is meant to prompt you into making an instant decision and saying yes to something that otherwise you might not have asked for. Similarly, although buying a pair of shoes can be more of a limited decision-making process (in that they cost a bit more than a burger, and are purchased less frequently), the stimulus–response technique is also used to prompt the purchase of the less expensive extras such as laces and polish.

Formula selling

Formula selling involves training representatives in a standard approach so that they can follow a rigid set of rules as the 'ideal method' to cover the relevant (and irrelevant!) points and achieve results. Formula selling is becoming increasingly less common. One reason for its decline is that customers are wise to it. Another is that it is relatively ineffective and inefficient as it does not feed off an essential strength of personal selling, namely tailoring the message to the customer.

This approach, therefore, usually means that the representative imparts a standard bundle of information to a set pattern, regardless of circumstances and needs. Its last bastions are in door-to-door selling and telemarketing. Its biggest problem is that it does not allow spontaneity and feedback from the customer, nor does it encourage interaction between buyer and seller. The customer feels that the representative has a set speech to get through, come what may, and begins to resent that they are not being consulted, yet are expected to provide a passive audience to listen to material of doubtful relevance.

Need satisfaction

The most widely used approach, and probably the most effective, is need satisfaction, even though it is more difficult to implement. It involves listening to the customer, asking questions to identify needs, assessing their reactions and tailoring the presentation to suit the circumstance. It is a problem-solving approach.

In B2B markets, the need satisfaction technique should be well under way by the selling stage if the preparation has been done properly. The customer's reaction to the sales presentation should concern matters of fine detail, to be explored and resolved. It should not throw up surprises about needs and wants for the representative to have to deal with. In contrast, in a consumer market, selling cars for example, the representative is on more of a knife edge, and the listening and questioning at this stage are incredibly important to establish the customer profile and needs. Clearly, such an approach would not be appropriate in a McDonald's retailing situation where a large number of customers choosing from a very limited range of low-risk product options need to be handled quickly.

In some B2B selling situations, it could even be suggested that the sales representative is acting in a consultative role, using a wider knowledge of the customer's industry to propose informed solutions to the customer's problems. Some advertising agencies, such as Barker's, specialise in advertising for the higher education sector. By building up sound experience of the advertising needs of universities and colleges, especially when recruiting students, they are able to demonstrate a wide and detailed appreciation of the market. Of course, the limiting factor is that some universities would prefer not to use the same agency as their primary competitors (*see* p. 623).

Whatever the broad approach taken, there may be some practicalities to be handled as part of the presentation. The representative may have to demonstrate the product, for example. The product or sample used must look right, and will need to be explained, not in technical terms, necessarily, but in terms of how it offers particular benefits and solutions. A demonstration is a powerful element of a sales presentation, because it gets the prospect involved and encourages conversation and questions. It provides a focus that can dispel any lingering awkwardness between buyer and seller. Also, in getting their hands on the product itself, or a sample, the prospect is brought very close to the reality of the product and can begin to see for themselves what it can do for them. Even in a consumer market, this is important. The car dealer takes prospective buyers out for a test drive so that they can experience the 'feel' of the car, and better imagine themselves owning it. The buyers feel that they are judging the car for themselves, and not just taking the sales representative's word for it. The test drive tells most prospective car buyers much more about the character of the vehicle than half an hour of peering under the bonnet listening to detailed technical specifications from the dealer.

eg

When a 61-year-old man enquired about a £5,000 spa bath at a Merlin Timber Products showroom, it allegedly led to his death. Although the prospective customer just wanted a brochure, the keen salesman invited him and his wife to witness a demonstration of the water turbulence created by high powered air pumps, blowers and jets. Unfortunately, as the customer was invited to feel the therapeutic turbulence, the jets of air also sprayed the unsuspecting customer with a fine mist. Two days later he complained of 'flu-like symptoms and just seventeen days later died of multiple organ failure from legionnaire's disease. Samples taken from the water confirmed that the bacteria were present three weeks after the incident. The Surrey Health Council, under whose environmental responsibility the showroom came, found that the ozoneator was not working properly and if it had been, the bacteria would have been killed. The Council also found that sales staff had not been properly trained about the health risks associated with demonstrating spa baths, so the accident that happened was, to some, entirely predictable. The coroner recorded a verdict of accidental death on the poor customer (Payne, 2002).

Even where it may be difficult to demonstrate the product, other involvement devices may be used. In B2B markets particularly, it may be possible to visit existing customers who have purchased similar products or systems. This gives the opportunity to see the product in application, and to talk to someone who is reasonably unbiased not only about the product, but also about their experience of the seller's after-sales service and ability to honour their promises.

If none of that is possible, then at least the presentation should incorporate plenty of audio-visual aids to keep the attention of the prospect and to prevent any danger of monotony creeping in. Involving members of the sales support team may also help to provide a more detailed and interesting picture for the prospect, and help to answer any of the wider questions or needs that might arise.

Handling objections

It is indeed a rare and skilful sales representative who can complete an entire sales presentation without the prospect coming out with words to the effect of 'that's all very well, but …'. At any stage in the selling process that involves the customer, objections can and probably will be made. These may arise for various reasons: lack of understanding; lack of interest; misinformation; a need for reassurance; or genuine concern. The sales representative must be prepared to overcome objections where possible, as otherwise the sale is likely to be lost completely. If the customer is concerned enough to raise an objection, then the representative must have the courtesy to answer it in some way. Homespun wisdom among seasoned sales representatives argues that the real selling does not begin until the customer raises an objection.

Table 17.2 summarises typical objections that occur time after time, regardless of the specific selling situation. Some objections are so predictable that it should be possible to anticipate them and answer them even before the customer gets around to raising them! It is important to develop counter-arguments. For example, many customers in many different types of market will raise an objection to the effect that the whole thing is too expensive for them. Whether this is a real concern or a last-ditch attempt to provoke the representative into price concessions is irrelevant. The representative must have an answer to it, perhaps using it as an opening to discuss credit or leasing terms, or to reiterate the savings made by switching to this product or investing in it.

Table 17.2 Typical objections

- Your company
- Your product
- Your service
- Your pricing
- You
- You are not competitive enough
- Delivery delay
- I can't afford it
- I don't need it

Organisations that do not subscribe to the formula approach to selling often do train their sales staff to handle specific objections that commonly arise in their field in a set way. The following are a selection of objection handling techniques commonly used in personal selling. Each is appropriate for a different kind of objection.

Ask the objection back

If the prospect comes out with something vague, then it is appropriate for the representative to ask for further elaboration, either to define the objection better, or to find out whether the objection is real or a stalling excuse. Exploring the objection also allows the representative and the customer to define whether the objection is fundamental or peripheral.

If a buyer says 'I think your product is not as good as product x', the sales representative should explore what is meant by the use of the word 'good'. This could cover a whole range of different areas in the competitive offering. The representative's response may therefore be designed to explore in more detail the underlying problem by asking 'In what way is it not as good?'

Agree and counter

Agreeing with the objection and countering it is often called the 'yes, but' technique. Where the objection is founded in fact, all the representative can legitimately do is agree with the substance of it, then find a compensating factor to outweigh it. Thus if the prospect argues that the product being sold is more expensive than the competition's, the representative can reply with 'Yes, I agree that value for money is important. Although our product is more expensive initially, you will find that the day-to-day running costs and the annual maintenance add up to a lot less …'. Such a technique avoids creating excessive tension and argument, because the customer feels that their objection has been acknowledged and satisfactorily answered.

Boomerang

A variation on the previous technique involves turning the objection into a reason for buying. Thus if the prospect says something like 'This model's getting a bit old; I think I'd be better going for the new generation', then the sales representative might reply with 'This model's technology has been around for a number of years, and that's the very reason why you should buy it. It's tried and trusted – our customers have five million of these components in service and the failure rate is less than 0.5 per cent. The new generation model is twice the price and yet to be proved in practice.'

Feel, felt, found

The previous techniques have all answered rational objections, based on some aspect of the product or the deal. If the prospect retreats from rationality, and appears to be making fairly inarticulate, emotional objections, perhaps demonstrating a lack of confidence in their decision-making ability, then this is the appropriate technique to use. Thus the prospect says, 'Well, I accept what you say, but I just don't feel certain about this'. To this the representative replies, 'I understand how you feel. Many other people have felt like that, but they've found that buying this product was actually the best decision'. In other words, the representative is offering the empathy, sympathy and reassurance that will bolster the prospect's confidence in the purchasing decision.

Denial

Denial is a dangerous technique to use unless you are very sure of your ground and your prospect. All the previous techniques have been careful not to contradict the prospect, but all have demonstrated diplomacy and sympathy with the prospect's point of view. Denial, on the other hand, involves telling the prospect that they are wrong. To reduce the risk of antagonising the prospect, any denial must be accompanied by proof of why the objection is wrong or misinformed. Even with proof, the prospect might still be offended that the representative has dared to contradict them, or might feel that somehow they have been made to look foolish, and they therefore decide to take their business elsewhere.

An indirect denial might take some of the edge off the situation. If, for example, the prospect says 'I've heard that you failed to fulfil your delivery promises to Bloggs & Co'., the representative, rather than using the direct denial of 'No, that's not true', which is defensive and potentially antagonistic, might initially ask the objection back with a reply such as 'Where have you heard that, then?' The dialogue that follows this might allow the representative to discredit the source of the rumour or to set the facts straight without overtly telling the prospect that they are wrong. If the situation is handled well, the prospect may conclude that they were wrong, and the representative is saved from awkwardness.

All in all, handling objections requires a very careful response from representatives. They must not see objections as a call for them to say just anything to clinch the sale, since doing so will only lead to legal or relationship problems later. The representative must assess the situation, the type of objection and the mood of the customer and then choose the most appropriate style of response, without overstepping any ethical boundaries in terms of content. It is critical that winning the argument used to overcome the objection does not lead to a lost sale. Objections may interrupt the flow of the sales process either temporarily or permanently, and unless they are overcome, the final stages of the selling process cannot be achieved.

Negotiation

Some aspects of negotiation have already been covered at pp. 456 *et seq.*, since the trade-off between price and the package offered does tend to be the main subject of most negotiation. To put negotiation in its proper context within the selling process, this subsection broadens the view of negotiation, emphasising the effect of the relative balance of power between the two parties on their negotiating positions.

Once the main body of the sales presentation is drawing to a close, with all the prospect's questions and objections answered for the time being, the selling process may move into a negotiation phase. Negotiation is a 'give and take' activity in which both parties try to shape a deal that satisfies both of them. Negotiation assumes a basic willingness to trade, but does not necessarily lead to a final deal. The danger for the sales representative, of course, is that a deadlocked or delayed negotiation phase may allow a competitor to enter the fray.

There are two types of negotiation:

1 *The cooperative or win–win negotiation.* This assumes that by trading concessions, a better deal can result for both parties. Concessions need not centre on price alone. They can take in issues like delivery schedules, delivery or insurance costs, product specifications, trade-ins or credit terms. For example, the buyer may agree to pay the delivery charges, in return for the seller's agreement to offer an extended warranty. The technique is to trade something that is relatively cheap for you, but is valuable to the other party. Thus an extended warranty costs little to the seller in reality, but means peace of mind and potential repair cost savings to the buyer.

   This type of negotiation is especially prevalent when longer-term relationships are being built up. The seller might consider it worth giving away major concessions on a first deal in order to ensure future business from that buyer. There is little point, as a seller, in driving a hard bargain for short-term gain if the long-term relationship flounders as a result.
2 *The competitive negotiation.* The hard bargain focused on short-term gain is appropriate and typical in one-off situations. Rather than seeking a better deal for both parties, the emphasis is on gaining as much advantage as possible over the other party. It still may mean some trading of concessions, especially those that cost you little but are of value to the other party.

Despite the fact that deals are becoming more complex, sales staff are still expected to be able to negotiate. If they are going to be given the power to negotiate on behalf of the organisation, then they need clear guidelines on how far they are permitted to go in terms of concessions, and what the implications of those concessions would be. An extra month's credit, for example, could be quite expensive, particularly for an organisation with short-term cash flow problems, unless it is traded for another prized concession. This effectively means that the sales representative needs financial as well as behavioural training in order to handle complex and sometimes lengthy negotiations.

There are some matters that the representative can consider that might help to establish a successful negotiating position.

The obvious judgement to make concerns the *relative power balance* between buyer and seller. If the buyer has many alternative options, and does not appear to be particularly eager to have that representative's product specifically, then that representative might have to be prepared to give away a considerable amount of ground in order to make a sale. The activities of the competition might also affect what goes on between this buyer and this seller. If the competition have been very aggressive and have already made attractive offers to the buyer, then this seller might feel obliged to make a better offer, depending on how badly the sale is wanted. The only means of saving this situation is if the seller is astute enough not to get locked into purely price-based comparisons with the competition. The representative should, if possible, define the 'better offer' in terms of features, benefits and peripherals other than price, in order to create an offering that is less easy for the competition to copy or undercut, and to blur the distinction between competing products somewhat.

It is, of course, possible that the balance of power lies in the hands of the selling organisation, if it has a unique product, service or expertise to offer that would be difficult to source elsewhere. If that is the case, the seller can afford to be a little less accommodating in terms of concessions.

Another important consideration is the sales representative's assessment of the *limits* within which each party is negotiating. Both parties will enter the negotiation with some idea of their minimum and maximum boundaries in terms of what they want to get and what they are prepared to give way on. The buyer, for example, has minimum performance criteria to which the product must conform, and a maximum price that the organisation is prepared to pay for it. At the same time, the buyer will also have an upper price limit in mind, along with an idea of the extras desired, whether these relate to the product specifications or to peripheral service offerings, the provision of which would justify moving up closer to that limit. The selling organisation too will have defined minimum requirements, in terms of the rock-bottom price they are prepared to go down to, and the maximum they are prepared to give away in concessions. It is a delicate judgement, but if the seller can work out when the buyer is close to their absolute limit, it can make all the difference between a sale and a lost sale. Attempting to push the buyer beyond their threshold means that there is a real risk that they will withdraw from the process.

As a final point, it must be said that negotiation need not be a separate and discrete stage of the selling process. Negotiation may emerge implicitly during the process of handling objections, or may be an integral part of the next stage to be discussed, closing the sale.

Closing the sale

The closing stage of the personal selling process is concerned with reaching the point where the customer agrees to purchase. In most cases, it is the sales representative's responsibility to **close the sale**, to ask for the order. If the sales presentation has been well prepared, if the customer's questions and objections have been satisfactorily handled and if the negotiation issues have been largely resolved, then closure should flow quite naturally with no problems.

Where the representative is less sure of the prospect's state of mind, or where the prospect still seems to have doubts, the timing of the closure and the way in which it is done could affect whether a sale is made. Try to close the sale too soon, and the buyer might be frightened off; leave it too long, and the buyer might become irritated by the prolonged process and all the good work done earlier in the sales presentation will start to dissipate.

Watching the buyer's behaviour and listening to what they are saying might indicate that closure is near. The buyer's questions, for example, may become very trivial or the objections might dry up. The buyer might go quiet and start examining the product intently, waiting for the representative to make a move. The buyer's comments or questions might begin to relate to the post-purchase period, with a strong assumption that the deal has already been done.

A representative who thinks that the time to close is near, but is uncertain, might have to test the buyer's readiness to commit to a purchase. Also, if the prospect seems to be teetering on the edge of making a decision, then the representative might have to use a mechanism to give the buyer a gentle nudge in the direction of closure.

There are many ways of closing the sale (Jacoby and Craig, 1984), and a number are considered below.

Alternative close

The representative may offer the buyer a number of alternatives, each of which implies an agreement to purchase. The buyer's response gives an insight into how ready they are to commit themselves. Thus if the representative says, 'Would you like delivery to each of your stores or to the central distribution point?', there are two ways in which the buyer might respond. One way would be to choose one of the alternatives offered, in which case the sale must be very close, since the buyer is willing to get down to such fine detail. The other response would be something like, 'Wait a minute, before we get down to that, what about ...', showing that the buyer has not yet heard enough and may still have objections to be answered.

Assumptive close

In the assumptive close the sales representative assumes that the customer will buy and carries on into the details of the transaction. The representative will say, 'I'll arrange for delivery within two weeks then', to which the buyer can agree without argument; agree, but argue for one-week delivery time; or disagree and pull the dialogue back into the negotiation or objection handling stages.

Time pressure close

A buyer who is clearly on the edge of a decision may be triggered into action by being offered a limited response time. Thus a suggestion that this is the last item in stock and that if the buyer does not agree to purchase it now, the seller might not be able to source another, could be a powerful incentive to act. Threats of imminent price rises, stockouts, or of the type 'sale ends Saturday' can all increase the sense of urgency, but do run the risk of being challenged by the buyer. The representative needs to be sure that the time pressure can be justified.

The ease of bringing the sale to a close, and the type of closing problems that might arise, will depend on the commercial complexity of the transaction. Sometimes, negotiating a trial order or agreeing to 'sale or return' on goods may reduce the risks of purchase sufficiently to bring the sale to some kind of close. In some situations, the initial commitment to purchase may itself trigger a range of complex negotiations to finalise the deal.

Follow-up and account management

The sales representative's responsibility does not end once a sale has been agreed. As implied earlier at pp. **000** *et seq.*, the sales representative, as the customer's key contact point with the selling organisation, needs to ensure that the product is delivered on time and in good condition, that any installation or training promises are fulfilled and that the customer is absolutely satisfied with the purchase and is getting the best out of it.

e-marketing *in action*

Sales force automation (SFA)

What are the implications of digital technologies for personal selling? Firstly it can be used as a support tool. O'Connor and Galvin (1999) identify three separate generations of sales force automation (SFA) tools. These are:

- **Generation 1: personal information and contact management.** The first generation of SFA tools included products such as ACT!, Goldmine and Maximizer. These were designed to help sales representatives to manage contacts and time and increase their selling effectiveness. Such powerful time and contact management tools had not existed previously and were accepted quickly and enthusiastically. Note that such tools are still in use in smaller organisations.
- **Generation 2: networked contact management.** The second generation of tools were essentially networked versions of the first, connecting the contact-tracking database and personal productivity tools of the sales force with the corporate network, contact and prospect database. Sales representatives were equipped with laptop computers that they synchronised or 'replicated' with the corporate network each day.
- **Generation 3: technology-enabled selling.** The third generation of SFA has its primary focus on making the sales force effective where it matters most: in front of the customer. The new generation of tools allows sales representatives to configure products, prepare proposals, give illustrations and quotes and track orders, using their laptops.

It can be suggested that there is now a fourth generation of SFA system. Here the SFA system is part of a larger customer relationship management (CRM) system such as Siebel (www.siebel.com). The CRM system gives the sales representative a much more detailed picture of the customer. All interactions or 'moments of truth' between a company and a customer will be recorded including responses to direct marketing campaigns and complaints and details of the customer's profile recorded online through the website and through conventional sales representatives' visits.

Furthermore it can be suggested that the website can be used to support the sales representatives when they are meeting customers on site. Consider, for example, the sales representative who visits lecturers to encourage them to adopt textbooks. They may refer lecturers to a website such as www.booksites.net to help explain the benefits of a textbook and to highlight added-value tools such as multi-choice question banks, PowerPoint slides and additional case studies. However, in addition to supporting the sales representatives, the website also presents a threat. With the internet providing detailed information, the need for sales representatives to explain the benefits of products or to assist in the selection process may no longer be necessary. Witness the reduction in sales representatives used for doorstep selling of cosmetics and encyclopaedias. This is one of the classic channel conflicts the internet introduces that must be managed in order that sales representatives remain effective – is it in their interest to mention their organisation's website as a detailed source of information that could replace them?!

Source: O'Connor and Galvin (1999); Dave Chaffey.

At a more general level, the relationship with the customer still needs to be cultivated and managed. In a B2B market, contacts made with the range of staff involved in the buyer's decision-making unit need to be nurtured. Where the sale has resulted in an ongoing supply situation, this may mean ensuring continued satisfaction with quality and service levels. Even with infrequently purchased items, ongoing positive contact helps to ensure that when new business develops, that supplier will be well placed. In the case of the consumer buying a car, the sales representative will make sure in the early stages that the customer is happy with the car, and work to resolve any problems quickly and efficiently. In the longer term, direct responsibility usually passes from the representative to a customer care manager who will ensure that the buyer is regularly sent product information and things like invitations to new product launches in the showrooms.

In the B2B market, an important role for the sales representative is to manage the customer's account internally within the selling organisation, ensuring that appropriate support is available as needed. Thus the representative is continuing to liaise between the customer and the accounts department, engineering, R&D, service and anyone else with whom the customer needs to deal.

Turnbull (1990) highlighted six important ways in which personal contact can help to maintain effective relationships with customers. These are shown in Figure 17.5 and discussed briefly in turn below. At various times in the selling process the buyer and seller may perform different activities in support of each of the following aspects of personal contact.

Figure 17.5 The role of personal contact in maintaining good customer relationships

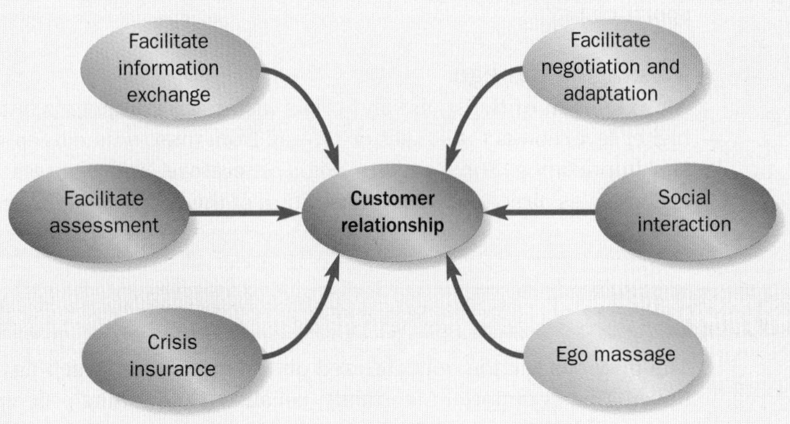

eg

Incyte is at the cutting edge of bio-informatics, trading in genomic information-based tools that help with an understanding of the molecular basis of disease. The key account managers control a small number of accounts in the pharmaceutical and biotechnology industries across Europe and each one can generate many millions of pounds of sales. They work closely with each customer throughout the buying process and beyond and in some cases several projects can be running in parallel. It is often difficult to know where one project ends and a new one begins. Most of the key account managers have PhDs in life sciences and are at least bilingual. In contrast, a national account manager for Jeyes is primarily concerned with wholesale and cash and carry customers. ECR (*see* pp. 510 *et seq.*) and category management principles along with a good understanding of branding and own-label are considered vital for developing business. This enables account managers to build the confidence of their customers and to implement an agreed plan.

Facilitating information exchange

Facilitating information exchange goes beyond hard data concerning the product, and relates to relatively confidential information that can lead to a deeper assessment. Such sensitive information will only be exchanged, however, where experience, trust and respect have been built up through a history of personal contact.

Facilitating assessment

Personal contact, coupled with the free exchange of information, enables the buyer to assess the product and commercial offering in order to make a decision on selecting a supplier.

Facilitating negotiation and adaptation

Facilitating negotiation and adaptation will vary from relatively simple commercial negotiation through to complex technical and commercial discussion to find a fit between the buyer's and seller's respective needs. These discussions could include ways of adapting a product, manufacturing processes and delivery systems.

Crisis insurance

Some personal contacts might only be activated at a time of difficulty and thus could be said to amount to crisis insurance. A supplier to a large buyer, for example, might only plan to meet with the buyer's managing director once a year, out of courtesy. However, if difficulties do arise in the meantime, that contact may be activated as a form of security or insurance, with a direct appeal to intervene.

Non-commercial social interaction

Although most buyer–seller interpersonal interaction takes place within an organisational context, there might also be some private social interaction that will affect the commercial relationship. This might include membership of other social groups, such as a church or sports clubs.

Massaging the ego

An extension of the social and crisis insurance contacts is 'massaging the ego', whereby higher level contact is sought or offered from time to time to enhance one party's feelings of self-importance. Some buyers might, therefore, appreciate a visit once a year from the seller's sales director as a demonstration of the value of their account.

Sales management

The previous section concentrated on the mechanics of selling something to a prospective buyer. That is important, certainly, because if the selling process does not work well, then there will be no sales and no revenue. Somebody has to show the customer the benefits of dealing with that particular seller. No matter how good the product or the other promotional elements are, they have to be sold.

Equally important, however, is the management of the sales force. Whether in a multinational organisation or a small company, the selling effort needs to be planned and managed. In a very small business, the owner, perhaps with some assistance, may undertake most of the selling and manage it by default. In a larger organisation, a sales manager will be assigned the tasks of achieving sales results through formal management of a sales force. Whatever the size or the character of a business, sales management provides an essential link between the organisation's strategic marketing plans and the achievement of sales objectives by the representatives in the field. Sales management ensures that the selling effort fits with the overall tasks specified in the marketing plan and strategy. It is perhaps surprising, therefore, that many sales managers receive little formal sales management training when they are promoted from the sales force (Anderson *et al.*, 1996).

Again, it is difficult to generalise about the specific tasks of sales management, as they will obviously vary between different organisations and different markets. A number of areas commonly found are, however, examined in this section. These include establishing a sales plan and strategy; specifying and recruiting sales representatives; training and developing staff; motivation and compensation policies; and, finally, controlling and evaluating the selling effort.

eg

Procter and Gamble decided to reorganise its sales force away from a retail focused strategy to more specific brand selling activities. Although the large retailers would still be serviced by account teams, each individual sales representative was to be given a more specific remit. Instead of having responsibility for the whole paper category from nappies to toilet rolls, for example, under the new structure an individual representative would take responsibility for a specific area within the category such as paper tissues. Through the reorganisation, it is expected that higher levels of expertise will be developed in advising retailers on merchandising and in-store marketing activities (Bittar, 2001).

Sales planning and strategy

The sales plan outlines the objectives for the selling effort and the details of how the plan should be implemented. This plan itself arises from, and must fit closely with, the marketing objectives set for products and market share, etc. In designing and implementing the sales plan, there are three interrelated decisions to be made.

Specifying the sales objectives

There are two types of sales objective to be specified. The first is the general sales targets to be achieved by the sales force as a whole. The second is the definition of sales targets specific to individuals or groups within the sales force.

Setting sales objectives provides an essential yardstick against which to measure progress and to motivate and influence the selling effort. Normally, quantitative measures are used to specify exactly what is required. At the level of the total sales force, the targets will be in terms of sales value and/or volume. Setting objectives in sales and profit terms is often necessary either to avoid the dangers of chasing low profit sales or to lessen the temptation to reduce margins to generate more sales volume but less gross profit (*see also* Chapters 10 and 11).

Using market share as a basis for sales targets, rather than sales value or volume, carries its own risks. The reasons are similar to those outlined at p. 635 in the discussion of advertising objectives. Although the sales force's efforts are very important for achieving sales, the effectiveness of that selling effort is also affected by other factors. These include such matters as price levels, company image, product specification and the support of other promotional techniques. While measures of product sales compared with the nearest competitor and year-on-year market share changes are useful indicators of selling performance, they must not be seen in isolation.

For the individual sales representative, many of the same measures still apply. Often, at this level, the sales objectives are called **sales quotas**, and again they are defined in sales value or volume terms. However, it is often useful to clarify these objectives further, perhaps by breaking them down into a number of targets relating to specific product ranges. Where a wide variety of products is offered, there may be weaker ones that need to be highlighted in the setting of objectives, either to boost their sales by setting ambitious targets, or to direct the sales force's attention away from them by setting low targets.

Targets for individual sales representatives need not only relate to selling quantities of products. Performance targets might be agreed in terms of the number of sales calls, the number of new accounts recruited, the call frequency, call conversion rates (i.e. turning prospects into buyers) or selling expenses.

Detailing the sales organisation

Decisions have to be made about organising the sales force. Flexibility in this area depends on whether the organisation already has a sales force or whether one has to be created.

A newly appointed sales manager would normally inherit an existing sales force. One priority for the new manager would be to review the current structure and establish whether it could be modified. Obviously, in a new organisation there are more options available, as the manager does not have to think about the costs of dismantling any existing structure.

For a new organisation, a more fundamental question may be raised about whether a direct sales force is required at all. An organisation may decide to sell through an independent agent (*see* p. 474) to increase coverage, for example. To do this the organisation must be sure that the agent has the necessary expertise and selling effort. There is little point in losing one's own sales force or opting out of ever setting one up, if the only gain is poorer performance, whatever the savings in salaries and expenses.

Assuming that the selling effort is to be managed internally, the sales manager has four broad choices for organising the sales force: geography, product, customer type, customer importance. Each of these will now be discussed in turn.

Geographic structure. In a European context, a geographic structure normally means dividing Europe up into its individual nations, then subdividing each nation by region, then, if necessary, further dividing each region into sales territories. Thus France, for example, would be a national sales area, Alsace would be a regional division within it, and Strasbourg would be a final subdivision with its own sales representative. Sales representatives are assigned to each geographic territory according to a formula described later (*see* Figure 17.6), and represent all or a specified number of company products within that territory.

Figure 17.6 Calculating the size of a sales force

The inputs

C = Number of customers
F = Average call frequency per customer per year
L = Average number of calls per representative per day
N = Average number of selling days per representative per year

The calculations

Stage 1 T = C × F	= Total number of calls per year
Stage 2 D = T/L	= Total number of selling days required per year
Stage 3 S = D/N	= Number of sales representatives required

Example

If: C = 300 (number of customers)
F = 4 (average call frequency per customer per year)
L = 3 (average number of calls per representative per day)
N = 133 (average number of selling days per representative per year)

Then: T = 300 × 4	= 1200	= Calls per year
D = 1200/3	= 400	= Selling days required and
S = 400/133	= 3.01	

Thus 3 sales representatives are needed

eg

Reebok employs sales people on a geographic basis, so the sales representative in Scotland, for example, would cover all products for his/her customers and have sole responsibility for sales within that territory. By operating on a geographical basis the sales representative can build a stronger relationship with the retailers and help them to plan their merchandise arrangements to suit local market differences. Having a sole representative means that the channel of communication for that customer with the supplier is clear and unambiguous.

The focus on one area has the advantage of minimising travel costs and avoids the danger of call duplication that exists in the other methods discussed later. In addition, having representatives familiar with the local economy encourages a more knowledgeable approach for identifying and exploiting new opportunities. This could be an advantage in situations where the product or service is sold to a wide range of different customers who are geographically scattered, for example financial services. However, if the organisation operates in a specialised, geographically concentrated industry, or if detailed technical product knowledge is needed, then the geographic option has more limited appeal.

Product-based structure. As an alternative to the geographic approach, a product-based structure means that individual sales representatives specialise in selling only a limited number of

An enticing window display of a known brand will encourage the passing consumer to enter and possibly purchase the product.

Source: Reebok/Cake Media.

products from the organisation's total range. This kind of structure allows the organisation to develop experts in particular product technologies who can act as consultants or problem solvers as well as sales representatives. A product-based structure may also be appropriate where the organisation offers a wide range of very diverse products in its portfolio.

eg

Philips (http://www.philips.com) has structured its selling effort around the main divisions of the company. Therefore the consumer electronics division sales force is responsible for sales of such products as DVD players, digital televisions and CD players to retailers. In contrast, the business electronics division would handle such items as digital transmission systems and sell direct to business users. Similar sales teams have been organised around other divisions such as lighting and medical. However, although the company is organised around distinct product types, geographic territories are still used to allocate the defined areas to sales staff.

This approach enables the organisation to recruit more selectively and to develop expertise within its sales force that could give a competitive edge. The disadvantages mirror the advantages of the geographic option. Travel costs increase, as a single representative may have to service customers across Europe. This also has implications for travelling time (and the more time spent travelling, the less time spent selling). Furthermore, the representative may have to acquire a much wider range of knowledge about local conditions and culture relating to the various customers visited. Finally, duplication of calls may increase, because if one customer wants to purchase a wide range of the seller's products, two or three different representatives with different product responsibilities may have to call.

Customer-based structure. A customer-based structure, in contrast, is designed to reflect the needs of different types of customers, rather than being product centred. This might mean dividing customers by industry, so that one representative deals with the automotive trade, while another deals with aerospace. This has an attractive logic, as organisations within a particular industry may well have similar needs, similar applications and similar problems. The representative can develop detailed industry knowledge and form long-term personal relationships with customers. Another way of classifying customers is by the nature of their business, that is, whether they are manufacturers or re-sellers. Each category would require a very different selling approach, because there are fundamental differences in their buying motives.

Whatever the classification system used, the customer-based approach does ensure a better match between the support and expertise needed by the customer and the skills of the sales representative. However, although call duplication may be low, the potential for geographically spread customers means higher travelling and customer servicing costs.

Customer importance. Finally, a variant of the customer-based approach is a structure based on the size or importance of the customer. The Pareto effect (discussed at p. 194) will identify the important strategic role played by a small number of important customers. If 20 per cent of our customers account for 80 per cent of our business, then that 20 per cent deserves the best care and attention we can offer them. If the major accounts are selected for special attention, the better sales representatives can focus on improving buyer–seller relationships, selling in depth, and coordinating the efforts of all the selling organisation's personnel to achieve a high service level for those customers. Those representatives become advanced forms of customer specialists and, where there are very large accounts, may represent only one account.

Research by Pardo (1997) that examined major accounts from the customers' perspectives found that as long as the seller's focused attention gave real added value, not just more frequent, high powered selling visits, there was much to gain for the customer's organisation. It especially enabled problem-solving tasks to be handed over to an external organisation that was trusted and competent to advise, thus emphasising the consultancy role and strategic thinking role, as found by Holley (1999) in the computer industry.

eg

Reebok also employs National Account Managers to handle the larger retail accounts. Given the size and importance of these accounts to the company, a manager may have just one account to handle. Nevertheless, the role requires very close and in-depth working relationships to be formed with the customer at both head office and store level as well as the ability to negotiate contracts at the highest level. An important part of the role is taking responsibility for developing a strategic plan to guide Reebok's development with that customer. This requires an ability to handle category management and to undertake brand development and marketing support to ensure that Reebok products easily move to and through the retail channel despite intense competition.

Even in a small business, the owner may choose to retain and maintain a personal relationship with the more important customers, delegating the other accounts to the sales representative(s).

There is clearly no one universally applicable and appropriate organisational structure. Sometimes a mixed structure may be best, combining geographic and major customer specialisation. Johnson & Johnson, for example, employs regionally based territory sales managers for its UK consumer products, but with specific responsibility for certain types of customer, such as independent pharmacies and wholesale cash and carries. This allows the organisation to benefit from the advantages of both types of allocation, while reducing the effect of their disadvantages. The chosen structure will be the right one as long as it reflects the objectives and marketing strategy of the firm. Increasingly, the internationalisation of organisations is causing a reconsideration of the way in which sales are structured across national and EU borders (Hill and Still, 1990). The important point is not to see the sales structure as fixed, but regularly to assess its relevance and its ability to achieve its objectives. If the structure appears to be failing in any way, then questions must be asked and answered, and management may have to be prepared to modify its approach.

Establishing sales coverage and deployment

A further decision has to be made on the ideal size of the sales force. A number of factors need to be considered, such as the calling frequency required for each customer, the number of calls possible each day, and the relative division of the representative's time between administration, selling and repeat calls (Cravens and LaForge, 1983). All these matters will have an impact on the ability of the sales force to achieve the expected sales results from the number of accounts served. For a smaller business, the issue may be further constrained by just how many representatives can be afforded!

Figure 17.6 (*see* p. 722) shows a formula commonly used to assess the size of a sales force. Within the formula, there are several underlying deployment and coverage issues. For example, call frequency will vary according to the size of the decision-making unit within the buying organisation and the frequency of purchase. It may be possible to vary the call frequency depending on the customer's potential and careful use of non-personal communication, such as mailshots etc.

eg

Increasingly IT is being used to determine sales territory size and sales force deployment. CABC offers *Territory Master* which creates sales territories, organises accounts and allocates leads. Using postcode data and customer databases, the software creates a set of territory schemes according to call frequency and coverage required. Two standard reports are possible: the territory report which identifies what is in each territory, and a postcode report which identifies the postcodes within a territory. By using the software, integrated selling and direct marketing campaigns are possible (http://www.cabc.co.uk).

Closely linked with the issue of sales force size is the problem of dividing the whole sales area into individual territories. The size, shape and sales potential may well vary between territories, and these need to be considered when setting sales targets and coverage policies.

The size and deployment of the sales force are not fixed, but must be varied according to emerging opportunities and analysis of resource efficiency. The growth of telemarketing along with the increasingly high cost per personal sales call have made some organisations think much more carefully about where, when and how to employ the sales team.

Recruitment and selection

As with any recruitment exercise, it is important to begin by developing a profile of who the organisation is looking for. A detailed analysis of the selling tasks should lead to a list of the ideal skills and characteristics of the representative to be recruited. As mentioned at pp. 703–6, there are significant differences between order takers and order makers, so the recruiter must at least know where the recruit is to fit in and what tasks they will be undertaking.

Many researchers have attempted to identify the ideal mix of traits that go to make up the super sales representative (Mayer and Greenberg, 1964; Lockman and Hallaq, 1982). The lists of traits rarely agree, contain a huge range of characteristics, and furthermore centre on matters that are difficult to discern and measure in an individual. The challenge for the sales manager is to relate those lists to the specific needs of the recruiting organisation. This means understanding the market, understanding what customers want from representatives, defining selling requirements, and analysing why certain existing representatives appear to be more successful than others. Table 17.3 lists the attributes of sales representatives typically appreciated by buyers.

A common dilemma is whether previous experience is an essential requirement. Some organisations prefer to take on recruits new to selling, then train them in their own methods rather than recruit experienced representatives who come with bad habits and other organisations' weaknesses. Others, especially smaller organisations, may deliberately seek experienced staff, wishing to benefit from training programmes that they themselves could not afford to provide. The eventual choice will depend on the organisation's decision on what it requires in terms of such factors as age, background, experience, qualifications, etc. A supplier of greeting cards, personalised stationery and postcards considered the most important factors to be experience in sales, a background in retail greeting cards and direct experience of selling into similar outlets. A large car dealer when seeking a new car sales representative demanded two years' new car sales experience as a minimum, although a parallel trainee position highlighted the need for someone who was articulate, with an outgoing personality. The Chally Group (1998) proposed a number of important pointers for sales managers when recruiting and developing sales personnel including the need to find people who can learn and adapt, and be team players rather than solo players, and to tailor recruitment and selection to the selling roles. Training should also be available as a continuous process with easy-access resources. This means paying particular attention to the professional intellect of the selling function and making sure it is refined to a high standard.

Table 17.3 Sales representative attributes typically appreciated by buyers

- Thoroughness and follow-up
- Knowledge of seller's products
- Representing the buyer's interests within the selling organisation
- Market knowledge
- Understanding the buyer's problems
- Knowledge of the buyer's product and markets
- Diplomacy and tact
- Good preparation before sales calls
- Regular sales calls
- Technical education

eg

Pearl Assurance has over 3.5 million customers who are serviced through a network of area managers and agents. For both types of selling roles, no previous experience in the financial services sector is needed. For the agents there is not even a requirement for sales experience, although some exposure to a customer service background is favoured. Their main role is to follow up domestic and small business sales leads and to deal with basic policies in motor and household insurance. Candidates for the area manager positions are judged more on their stability and interpersonal skills than knowledge of the financial services sector. This fits with the need for sales staff that can be trusted by the prospective customer before they are prepared to commit to a more complex personal pension or life assurance policy.

The actual selection process needs to be designed to draw out evidence of the ability of each candidate to perform the specified tasks, so that an informed choice can be made. The cost of a poor selection can be very high, not just in terms of recruitment costs and salary, but also, and perhaps more seriously, in terms of lost sales opportunities or damage to the organisation's reputation. In view of the importance of making the right choice, in addition to normal interview and reference procedures, a number of firms employ psychological tests to assess personality and some will not confirm the appointment until the successful completion of the initial training period.

Training

The recruitment process generally only provides the raw material. Although the new recruit might already have appropriate skills and a good attitudinal profile, training will help to sharpen both areas so that better performance within the sales philosophy of the employing organisation can be developed. Sales force training applies not just to new recruits, however. Both new and existing staff, even well-established staff, may need skills refinement and upgrading.

Today's sales representative has to be IT literate.

Source: Photodisc.

Training may be formal or informal. Some organisations invest in and develop their own high quality training facilities and run a regular series of introductory and refresher courses in-house. This has the advantage of ensuring that the training is relevant to the organisation and its business, as well as signifying an ongoing commitment to staff development.

Other organisations adopt a more *ad hoc* approach, using outside specialists as required. This means that the organisation only pays for what it uses, but the approach carries two serious risks. The first problem is that the training may be too generalised and thus insufficiently tailored to the organisation's needs. The second problem is that it is too easy for the organisation to put off training or, even worse, to delete it altogether in times of financial stringency.

Finally, a third group uses informal or semi-formal 'sitting with Nelly', on the job coaching. This involves the trainee observing other representatives in the field, and then being observed themselves by experienced sales representatives and/or the sales manager. There is nothing quite like seeing the job being done, but with this approach the organisation needs to take great care to deal with a number of points. One concern is to ensure that such training is comprehensive, covering all aspects of the job. Another is to ensure that bad habits or questionable techniques are not passed on. The main problem with this kind of on-the-job training is that the training is not usually done by professional trainers. Therefore the quality can be variable, and there is no opportunity for fresh ideas to be introduced to the sales force.

eg

BT Retail employs over 4,500 telemarketing sales staff to deal with its domestic and small business users. One of the difficulties it faced was in introducing new products successfully by telesales. The sales advisors were thought to lack confidence when discussing new products, deals were not closed and sometimes inconsistent messages actually harmed the brand's integrity. Accenture, a HR development company, recommended a shift away from classroom-based to web-based training programmes. Through a web-based sales situation simulator, the trainee can be taken through a number of different conversations with customers thus providing an almost real-life exercise in which mistakes can be made with no harm to the sale. It also allowed the telemarketers to become familiar with the products as they were asked questions during the conversation, and they also gained useful insights into how the products could be sold. It is claimed that sales shot up for the products selected for training and the cost of web-based training was half that of classroom situations. It also meant that the whole of the sales force could be trained within a four-week period (Wray, 2002).

There are a number of dimensions that can be covered by training programmes, depending on the training needs identified by the organisation. Programmes may need to cover the organisation's products (and those of the competition), company information (relating to their own organisation, its competitors and their key customers), applications, market information and, not least, developing greater competency in selling and negotiation skills and techniques. It is the job of the sales manager to determine the relative emphasis in the training, its location, who participates, the length of a programme and the overall fit between the training budget, training outcomes and sales objectives.

Whereas larger organisations such as IBM and Xerox will have comprehensive training programmes, smaller organisations and re-sellers might have only limited facilities and rely on recruiting experienced staff. With re-sellers, for example, there is a need not only for product knowledge but also for sales skills, yet it could be too expensive to provide sales training for a small number of staff. Thus it could be necessary to group a number of smaller dealers together for sales training to make it worthwhile. Rasmusson (1999) highlighted the potential for industry-related seminars in computing and found that training directly helped encourage incremental sales and customer retention.

Motivation and compensation

Any sales effort needs well-motivated sales people. Apart from the fact that enthusiastic and motivated representatives will sell better, effective sales people are often in high demand by other employers. Often the success of the selling effort is linked to the acceptance and effectiveness of the sales compensation programme (*Business Wire*, 2002).

An organisation will not only want to motivate new recruits to join its sales force, but also have an interest in making sure that they are sufficiently well rewarded for their achievements that they will not easily be poached by the competition (Cron *et al.*, 1988). There are many ways in which the sales team can be motivated to achieve outstanding results and rewarded, but they are not all financially based.

eg

Rentokil Initial with interests in hygiene, tropical plants, office solutions and medical services offers a package of financial and non-financial benefits to attract and retain staff. Part of the compensation comes in the form of benefits for a mobile phone, pension scheme, company car, regular training and promotion prospects. The salary package includes a basic salary and monthly commission potentially leading to on-target earnings of £29,000–£35,000 (with top earners on £50,000), and an incentive scheme based on quarterly and annual performance. This comprehensive range of benefits is part of a culture that values the sales force and believes that there is a direct link between motivated sales representatives and additional sales.

Even a sense of belonging to a team can be important. Selling can be a lonely activity. Imagine spending your working life out on the road, with mostly only telephone contact with the sales manager, enhanced by the occasional meeting. It is not easy to maintain enthusiasm for the job, or to feel that your work is valued under such conditions. Bringing representatives back to HQ regularly for team meetings, seminars and briefings may help to foster team spirit. It provides an opportunity for the team to share views and experiences, and allows clear two-way communication regarding achievements and expectations. Training programmes can also play a part in reassuring employees that they are valued, and in bringing teams back together again.

By involving the representatives in managerial activities such as developing their own territory sales plan, the organisation gains in two ways. First, it can plan with the benefit of the representative's knowledge and experience of the territory, and second, it gives employees a greater sense of control over their own working as well as a feeling that there is open and cooperative management. Providing representatives with mechanisms for regularly feeding back updated intelligence into the organisation, through a direct data link, makes them feel that they are offering more than just selling expertise and can thus assist in developing positive motivation.

corporate social responsibility *in action*

Risking your future prosperity

Mis-selling is a new word in the marketing lexicon popularised by some high profile examples of the sale of financial services products. Mis-selling is a type of selling activity that is so focused on the needs of the seller, that the best interests of the buyer are not considered. This has resulted in poor advice, dubious claims and downright lies at times in order to close the sale. Winterthur Life, for example, owned by the Credit Suisse Group was fined £500,000 by the financial services regulator and had to put aside £10 mn against possible compensation payments to 10,000 homebuyers after mis-selling endowment mortgages. Sales staff had incorrectly confirmed that the mortgage amount would definitely be covered when the endowment policy matured.

Mis-selling can be found in many situations, for instance sales representatives persuading people to give up good occupational pension schemes to join inadequate private ones; selling endowment policies that were unlikely to cover the linked mortgage at maturity; selling overpriced insurance for loan repayments; and savings plans with hidden charges that soon offset any gains. Sometimes it can be many years before the unwitting individual finds out that the financial product purchased does not live up to expectations. In an era of whistle blowing, regulation and media investigation, however, some cases of poor practice come to light sooner rather than later and can be dealt with. After the industry regulator became involved in the pensions mis-selling scandal, for example, it is thought to have cost companies £14 bn to pay the required compensation to the victims.

The reason for such sales practices goes back to a basic rule of sales staff remuneration: the sales representative can make more money by selling than by not selling, i.e. the greater the sales, the greater the commission. For many years, field sales staff in the financial services sector were paid on a commission-only basis or were promised large bonuses for on-target performance. Equitable, one of the companies accused of mis-selling, did not have a commission scheme for individual sales, but did have an attractive bonus scheme based on the overall income generated. In those circumstances, a fat bonus is a powerful incentive to sell at all costs.

Although many people are more wary about pension sellers now, other areas are still vulnerable to abuse. According to Cooper (2002), mortgage cover insurance can be overpriced and is not always needed, but it is a commission-earning opportunity. Although many sellers, therefore, may offer the traditional monthly premium, some offer the 'advantage' of a single five year premium. While the former might cost about £5 for every £100 of cover, the single premium could cost £8.50 per £100, and as it is paid as a one-off lump sum, the sales representative could get £3,000 commission compared with only around £500 on a monthly contract. To make matters worse, some policies are sold to self-employed people or contract workers who are actually ineligible to make a claim when they are out of work.

Some companies are, however, taking a firmer line on alleviating some of the causes of mis-selling. St James Palace ordered its 1,100 sales representatives to stop what is called 'churning', i.e. persuading customers to stop some existing policies in favour of the new ones offered. Churning has even taken place when sales representatives change companies and try and take their old customer base with them by ditching previously sold policies for new ones! It is the customer who often loses out in exit penalties and lost terminal bonuses. Others, such as Winterthur, decided to compensate policyholders where there was evidence of mis-selling.

The Financial Services Authority (FSA) is the regulatory body that investigates complaints and sets the standard for the industry. As a result of its previous investigations, some companies have been advised to change their selling practices and to improve sales representative training so that they can give better advice. However, it is the motivation and compensation packages being offered that are the prime cause of the problem, human nature being what it is. In some cases, if sales targets are not achieved then a sacking may not be far behind. One sales representative has been quoted as saying, 'We have a £7,000 target every month. I would have to sell 140 stakeholder pensions to meet the target, but I would need to sell only 14 endowments. What do you think salesmen do in this situation? I do not want to get rich, I just want to keep my job' (as quoted by Gardner and Cooper, 2001).

The FSA is now investigating the commission payment arrangements for a number of product areas in which mis-selling is suspected. Its position is that commission should never bias sales because, under its rules, sales representatives must give the best advice for the client and not be influenced by remuneration. The pressure to meet increasingly challenging sales targets, however, both for sales representatives and High Street financial services outlets, means that it really is a case of 'caveat emptor'.

Sources: Cooper (2002); Cowie (2001); Gardner and Cooper (2001); Levene (2002); Wheatcroft (2002); http://www.fsa.gov.uk.

Sometimes, sales managers can create an element of healthy rivalry among sales representatives through sales contests. If the rewards are seen as valuable and achievable, contests can renew a representative's interest in doing a good job. Household goods, holidays or cash bonuses, for example, are tangible and attractive motivators. These contests

taken on call policy, training or motivation, or even that problems may lie not with the sales force, but with the product or its marketing strategies.

Developments in IT are making the task of communicating with and receiving information from the field sales force more effective. This means that trends can be identified sooner, and corrective action planned and implemented more quickly and with more authority. Baldauf *et al.* (2001) argue that the increased emphasis on relationship management means that sales managers are putting more emphasis on longer-term outcomes rather than short-term performance and this in turn is having a major impact on developing coaching schemes to improve performance rather than excessively focusing on results with that attendant 'hire-and-fire' mentality.

Table 17.5 Calculating sales performance

Quantitative measure	*Means of measuring*
Productivity	
Calls per day	Number of calls/number of days worked
Calls per account	Number of calls/number of accounts
Orders per call	Number of orders/total number of calls
Account development and servicing	
Account penetration	Accounts sold to/total number of accounts available
Sales per account	Total sales value/total number of accounts
Average order size	Total sales value/total number of orders
Expenses	
Sales expenses	Expenses/sales made
Cost per call	Total costs/total number of calls made

Chapter summary

- Although personal selling can be an expensive and labour-intensive marketing communication activity, it has a number of advantages over other forms of communication. It makes an *impact*, because it involves face-to-face contact and is less likely to be ignored; it can deliver a *precise and tailored* message to a target customer who has already been checked out to ensure that they fit the right profile; it helps in the *cultivation* of long-term buyer–seller relationships.
- The roles undertaken by sales representatives are many and varied. They *prospect* for new customers; they provide customers with relevant and detailed *information*; they *persuade* customers to buy; they help to *demonstrate and install* products; they *represent the customer's interests* within the selling organisation; they help to *maintain good buyer–seller relationships* over time; they *collect information and feedback* from the field, and they *monitor* what the competition are doing in the field and how customers feel about the competition.
- Some sales representatives will be order takers, for example taking repeat orders from customers or recording and processing inbound orders. Some will be order makers, for example going out prospecting for new business, and some will act in a support role.
- The personal selling process can be a long and complicated marketing activity to implement. The process starts with the identification of prospective customers, and then the representative has to do as much background work on the prospect as possible in order to prepare an initial approach and a relevant sales presentation. Initial contact breaks the ice between buyer and seller, allowing an appointment to be made for the real selling to begin.

The sales presentation will give the representative the opportunity to present the product in the best possible light, using a variety of samples and audio-visual aids, while allowing the customer to ask questions and to raise any objections they may have. Negotiating the fine details of the deal may lead naturally to closing the sale, and then all that remains is for the representative to ensure the customer's post-purchase satisfaction and work towards building a long-term relationship leading to repeat business and further purchases.

- Sales management is an important area of marketing, and involves a number of issues. *Sales planning and strategy* means making decisions about sales objectives, both for the organisation as a whole and for individual sales representatives or teams. *Recruitment* and *training* are also both important aspects of sales management, and *training* too concerns the sales manager. Apart from benefiting from training programmes, sales representatives have to be properly *motivated and compensated* for their efforts. This means not only designing an appropriate and attractive package of pay and other benefits, but also making sure that representatives are fully involved in the life of the organisation generally and, more specifically, in any decisions involving themselves. A natural part of all this is *performance evaluation*. Sales managers need to ensure that representatives are achieving their targets and, if not, why not.

key words and phrases

Closing the sale
Cold calling
Commission
Conversion rates
Leads
Order maker
Order taker
Personal selling
Prospecting
Prospects
Qualified prospects
Sales presentation
Sales quotas
Sales support

questions for review

17.1 What are the major *advantages* of personal selling and what can they contribute to the marketing effort?

17.2 What are the typical tasks of a *sales representative*?

17.3 Why might a sales representative's role include coordination within the selling organisation?

17.4 What are the stages in the personal selling process?

17.5 What are the main issues that the sales manager must consider as far as sales *planning* and *strategy* are concerned?

questions for discussion

17.1 Give examples of three different kinds of sales support staff and analyse their contribution to the personal selling effort.

17.2 In what ways do you think a sales representative could make the sales presentation more relevant and interesting for the prospective customer?

17.3 What techniques might a sales representative use to counter the following objections:
(a) 'Your competitor's product is a lot cheaper ...'
(b) 'I don't think my wife would like it if I bought this ...'
(c) 'I've heard that your service engineers are very inefficient.'

17.4 Summarise the relative advantages of allocating sales responsibilities on the basis of:
(a) geographic regions;
(b) product-based criteria; and
(c) customer-based criteria.

17.5 Find 20 job advertisements for sales representatives and summarise the range of characteristics and skills sought. Which are the most commonly required and to what extent do you think that they are essential for a successful sales representative?

case study 17.1

Colomer: Spanish leather

The Colomer Group, based in Vic, Spain, produces high quality leather products for clothing, footwear and gloves. Clothing products represent 85 per cent of sales. It is a world leader in lamb skin, goat skin and pigskin tanning and finishing. Its customers include many of the top design and manufacturing names in Europe.

Raw skins are a by-product of meat production, so the supply of raw material is in no way related to the demand for leather goods. Prices can, however, fluctuate considerably, depending on the availability and quality of skins. Although leather goods are still regarded by many as high-priced luxuries, there are marked differences between the average price levels for leather from some of the developing countries and those from producers such as Colomer. Typical price levels per square foot vary from €1.25 to €6.50. Colomer tends to sell in the €5.00 or more price range. Linked with price variations, quality can also vary depending on the consistency and purity of the raw skin. Colomer, for example, only uses skin from the best small sheep such as entrefino, merino and lambs. Careful skin inspection and buying is essential for retaining a premium position. Although the leather industry has been around for many years, in order to retain a competitive edge Colomer has invested heavily in product development, innovation and the use of new technology to enable better, high quality finishes to be achieved. It is in the fashion business and must identify trends and new opportunities early enough to be prepared for a season up to two years ahead.

Colomer has around 800 customers worldwide, but 600 of them are based in Europe. The company mainly deals with either independent designers or, more normally, designers contracted to clothing manufacturers. Many of the customers are thus small, requiring a sales visit only once or twice a year. The larger manufacturers demand closer attention. The Italian market is of major importance because of the presence of many top designer labels, and currently around 35 per cent of European sales go to this market.

In Europe, Colomer operates through a combination of direct sales and sales agents. Most of the sales staff have had many years in the leather industry and understand the product from a technical perspective. Such knowledge is considered important as the sales people need to help the designers and buyers develop the most appropriate specification for the finished leather. Factors such as regularity, durability and comfort, waterproofing, washability, dry-cleaning capability and perspiration fastness may all have to be considered as part of the sales process. Other issues include whether nappas, sueded leather or shearling finishings are to be selected and the range of colours available. Increasingly, ecological considerations must be taken into account, both in production processes and in the materials used.

The commercial aspects also have to be negotiated. Because volumes tend to be large, margins tend to be small, with limited scope for giving discounts. Although Colomer is the market leader in a range of leathers, there are more specialised niche producers that provide tough competition, even though the range of finishings they offer is limited. The leather manufacturers from developing countries tend to sell on price, but delivery can be erratic, their quality variable and their product ranges narrower. Some markets, such as in the UK, tend to offer more fertile ground for these producers, but premium branded clothing manufacturers across Europe tend to deal only with top quality leather that will be delivered to agreed schedules. Given the fashion seasons, any delay could result in lost sales opportunities, as over 60 per cent of sales are made over the summer period when the trade stocks up for the main winter season. The collection for a season is often developed two years ahead of delivery.

The 15-strong worldwide sales force is organised by product and on geographical lines. In clothing

Colomer supplies the leather for chic designer goods.

Source: Colomer.

leather, there are three sales staff across Europe while footwear and gloves have one representative each for Europe. The sales director is based in Vic. The role of the sales representatives is to work through designated national agents and to deal directly with some of the larger accounts as well as supporting the agents with technical and sales advice. Because there is a fair amount of travel involved, the company feels that men are better able to be away from home for frequent periods without problems arising from family commitments. Female staff have been employed in sales roles but in the company's view it was not a great success.

Most members of the sales team have been with the company for many years and few have any formal academic qualifications. Although they understand the leather industry well, there is still an annual sales meeting where new designs and materials are introduced, as well as classes run in sales techniques, delivered by university staff from Barcelona. Around 20 days per year are dedicated to all aspects of training. Most of the sales team are Spanish nationals but they are also proficient in English. Further support in language training is given by the local university. Some of the team can speak Italian and French.

The sales agents comprise an important part of the promotional activity. Normally one agent is selected for each country and is given the responsibility for acting as the day-to-day interface with the customer as the Colomer sales representative is likely to be elsewhere in Europe. Italy is an exception, given the importance of the market. There is a full-time sales representative based there as well as three agents with defined territories. Physical shipments go direct to the customer and the agent is notified of dispatch. In the UK, the agent is based in London, close to the main UK customers, many of whom are small Asian-owned businesses. The UK is regarded as a very price sensitive market and the dominance of the large retail chains has restricted the potential for premium leather products. A high proportion of the leather for the multiple retailers comes from cheaper sources in India and the Far East.

The agents tend to be experts in the country market with good trade contacts, but they are not usually technical experts. As part of the induction process, however, the agents spend frequent periods at the manufacturing plant and also receive close support from the sales representatives. Agents are not allowed to sell competitors' lines, but the selling of non-competing lines is allowed, such as car leather. Colomer prefers an exclusive agency agreement to ensure that it receives the dedication and commitment necessary. Most agents are appointed on a one-year trial basis after which a longer-term contract may be negotiated. Colomer is confident that it can assess the value and capability of an agent within one year. The agency commission rates are around 3 per cent of sales, reflecting the low margins earned within the sector. Colomer considers that this rate is high for the sector and encourages more dedicated effort to their products. However, some are considered to be less efficient as repeat sales can be relatively straightforward and coordination can be difficult when the direct sales teams are also involved.

Most members of the sales force are on a high basic salary with a low commission. Given the agency support and problem-solving role, a high basic salary was considered appropriate as too much reliance on commission could result in shorter-term sales thinking rather than building longer-term relationships based on quality and trust. Commission is linked to achievement of overall sales targets not the profitability of individual orders. With profit margins of only around 10 per cent and the tendency to sell from published list prices, the sales representatives have the discretion only to give up to 5 per cent discount, and even then it has to be an exceptionally large order.

Source: With grateful thanks to Joan Capdevila, Colomer.

Questions

1. What do you think are the ideal characteristics for a successful sales representative working for a company like Colomer in the leather trade? How might these characteristics differ for a representative working for one of the competitors selling mainly on price?
2. What are the advantages and disadvantages to Colomer of giving a high basic salary to the sales representatives?
3. What problems might arise from a mixed selling approach which uses both sales representatives and agents?
4. Can an operation using both geographic and product based sales organisation work? Why does Colomer do it this way rather than using other customer based methods of sales organisation?

case study 17.2

Irish Fire Products

Irish Fire Products (IFP), based in the west of Ireland, is a distributor for a range of fire extinguishers, fire blankets, sprinkler systems and other fire-prevention accessories such as alarms, signage and doors. Most of the products sold are of relatively low value compared with an integrated fire-prevention system designed to a customer's specific requirements for protecting commercial premises. Despite the low technology used, IFP, a small business, has prospered for over 20 years, competing with other distributors across Ireland as well as with the direct sales forces of companies such as Nu-Swift and Chubb. The market is mature, with most growth coming from the demands of new legislation. More recently, some customers have been increasingly looking for more sophisticated systems that IFP does not provide.

The company employs around 25 staff. Half are based in the headquarters and warehouse in administrative and logistics functions, and the rest are sales staff and support engineers. A wide range of stock is carried, including many different brands of extinguisher designed to combat different types of chemical and material fires. Goods are normally despatched within a few days of the receipt of an order, and often the sales representative will undertake delivery and installation. Overall, customer service and prices are considered comparable with what competitors are doing, although IFP is concerned about some new entrants to the market who do not give good advice to customers and often sell on price. IFP's owner, Mike Dalton, considers these 'cowboys' to be a threat because they have low overheads that he cannot match. The costs of entering the market are low, and sometimes former salespeople start their own businesses with minimal stock and sales support. In replacement situations, he has found that an increasing number of customers are prepared to buy on price rather than on the pre- and post-sales service offered. Although sales are just about holding up, margins are increasingly being pressurised.

Most organisations need some form of fire-prevention and fire-control systems. Legislation and safety regulations determine the exact specification demanded. The selling process itself differs, depending on whether it is repeat or new business. Regular customers tend to repeat buy with minimal shopping around, unless the value of the item is high. In some cases the sales representative makes additional sales by comparing current equipment against changing fire regulations and changes in material risks. Recommendations are then made to the customer. Customers can vary from a small restaurant or shop to industrial premises, universities and large organisations. Many purchasing decisions cannot be deferred for long because of the insurance and legal implications of being caught out by fire inspectors.

Even where IFP had not supplied a particular prospect before, if a gap in provision was identified, there was a good chance of converting the sale. This also works in reverse from time to time, when other sellers gain sales on the basis of price, once the need has been established. If the sale cannot be closed quickly, there is always the risk of a customer going elsewhere. In new business situations, especially with building extensions and new premises, the demands on the sales representative are sometimes greater because of having to sell through architects and technical experts, as well as having to quote against competition and negotiate the final deal. These customers are often as much concerned with specification match, overall fire system effectiveness and after-sales service as they are with taking the lowest price.

Mike Dalton decided early on that the key to his business was an aggressive and motivated sales force. There is a range of brochures, often supplied by the manufacturer, and directories are used, but otherwise, little advertising and few other promotional methods are employed. By 2000, IFP had 10 sales representatives, a national sales manager, a field sales manager based in Dublin, and two sales support engineers who could be used for diagnosis or installation. The national and field sales managers are also expected to handle the major accounts, along with Mike Dalton, leaving the rest of the 10,000 or so potential accounts to the sales team.

For the first three months after appointment, each sales representative is paid a low salary plus commission, but after that it is commission only, although an average sales representative can gross between €3,500 and €4,000 per month plus personal use of company van or car. Mike Dalton feels that the system employed is right because it keeps the sales team on their toes. With up to 1,000 potential accounts per territory and many more unknown prospects, the financial motivation to encourage more cold calling is thought to be essential. Most of the sales team are happy with the arrangement and, even if a bad patch is hit after the trial period, the owner will often provide short-term advances on commission. It is never a long-term problem, as poor performance is normally dealt with by the termination of the representative's contract. The sales managers are paid by part commission and part salary and they are responsible for mentoring the sales team and dealing with any problems.

Although most of the sales team had some previous sales experience, most needed product training in fire prevention and control equipment before starting to sell. This training is normally done by the owner or the sales manager on the premises for two weeks before the representative takes over a territory. No formal sales training system is in place, although from time to time one- or two-day courses are run by staff from the local university. These courses cover general sales topics and tend to be seen as part of the annual sales meeting rather than part of a comprehensive skills development programme. Overall, most of the sales team tend to adjust to the uncertainty of commission-only sales and some have been in their jobs for several years. The sales managers have both worked their way through the ranks as super salespeople and so are well versed in giving advice to less experienced colleagues in the job. The managers are particularly concerned with keeping call rates up – at least 10 per day is a minimum expectation – as well as encouraging high standards of product presentation. Over a two-year period, the turnover of sales staff has been around 25 per cent, a figure with which the owner is comfortable.

It is against this background that Mike Dalton contemplated the most appropriate actions for maintaining market position and countering the growing competitive threat.

Source: Lightly adapted from an actual company.

Questions

1 What kind of remuneration package is used with the sales representatives? What are the problems with it?

2 IFP wants to encourage sales representatives to do more cold calling. Is the company going the right way about achieving this? What else can be done?

3 Is the training programme adequate? What should go into a formal sales training programme?

4 How can Mike Dalton fight the pressure from the more sophisticated integrated systems at one end of the market and the cowboys at the other? What are the implications for the sales force?

References for chapter 17

Abberton Associates (1997), *Balancing the Selling Equation: Revisited*, accessed via http://www.cpm-int.com.

Anderson, R. (1996), 'Personal Selling and Sales Management in the New Millennium', *The Journal of Personal Selling & Sales Management*, 16 (4), pp. 17–32.

Anderson, R., Mehta, R. and Strong, J. (1996), 'An Empirical Investigation of Sales Management Training', *Working Paper No. 96–1*, Department of Marketing, Drexel University.

Ashworth, J. (2001), 'The Avon Lady Takes High-tech to Doorsteps', *The Times*, 24 September, p. 22.

Baldauf, A., Cravens, D. and Piercy, N. (2001), 'Examining the Consequences of Sales Management Control Strategies in European Field Sales Organizations', *International Marketing Review*, 18 (5), pp. 474–508.

Bittar, C. (2001), 'P&G Eyes Sales Force Revamp Amid Slump', *Brandweek*, 1 October, p. 32.

Blackwood, F. (1995), 'Did You Sell $5 Million Last Year?', *Selling* , October, p. 47.

Business Wire (2002), 'Gartner Dataquest Says IT Services Companies Need to Change Service Sales Compensation Programs', 11 February, accessed via http://www.businesswire.co.uk.

Chaffin, J. (2002), 'Commissions Culture Drove EES Offshoot', *Financial Times*, 7 February, p. 27.

Chally Group (1998), *The Customer-Selected World Class Sales Excellence Research Report*, Dayton, Ohio.

Churchill, G., Ford, N., Walker, O., Johnston, M. and Tanner, J. (2000), *Sales Force Management*, 6 edn., Richard D. Irwin Inc.

Cooper, K. (2002), 'Whistleblower Warns of Fresh Misselling Scandal', *Sunday Times*, 10 March, p. 1.

Cowie, I. (2001), 'Winterthur May Pay £10m for Mis-selling', *The Daily Telegraph*, 26 September, p. 31.

Cravens, D. and LaForge, R. (1983), 'Salesforce Deployment Analysis', *Industrial Marketing Management*, July, pp. 179–92.

Cron, W. *et al.* (1988), 'The Influence of Career Stages on Components of Salesperson Motivation', *Journal of Marketing*, 52 (July), pp. 179–92.

Cunningham, M. and Homse, E. (1986), 'Controlling the Marketing – Purchasing Interface: Resource Development and Organisational Implications', *Industrial Marketing and Purchasing*, 1(2), pp. 3–27.

Darmone, R. (1998), 'A Conceptual Scheme and Procedure for Classifying Sales Positions', *Journal of Personal Selling and Sales Management*, 18(3), pp. 31–46.

Fill, C. (2002), *Marketing Communications: Contexts, Strategies and Applications*, 3rd edn, Financial Times Prentice Hall.

Gardner, N. and Cooper, K. (2001), 'Mis-selling Risk as Firms 'Bully' Salesmen', *Sunday Times*, 4 November, p. 1.

Gofton, K. (2002), 'Field Marketing Grows Up', *Campaign*, 25 January, p. 22.

Good, D. and Stone, R. (1991), 'How Sales Quotas are Developed', *Industrial Marketing Management*, 20(1), pp. 51–6.

Hill, J. and Still, R. (1990), 'Organising the Overseas Salesforce: How Multinationals Do It', *Journal of Personal Selling and Sales Management*, 10 (Spring), pp. 57–66.

Holley, R. (1999), 'Major Account Management: Not Just Another Job', *Computer Reseller News*, 3 May, p. 125.

Howell, J. (2002), 'Beware the Great Rising Damp Scam, Miss Jones', *Mail on Sunday*, 17 February, p. 21.

Jacoby, J. and Craig, S. (1984), *Personal Selling*, Heath.

Johanson, J. and Vahlne, J. (1977), 'The Internationalisation Process of the Firm: A Model of Knowledge Development and Increasing Foreign Market Commitment', *Journal of International Business Studies*, 8 (1), pp. 23–32.

Lambert, D. *et al.* (1990), 'Industrial Salespeople as a Source of Market Information', *Industrial Marketing Management*, 19, pp. 141–5.

Levene, T. (2002), 'Insurer Orders Churning Freeze', *The Guardian*, 9 February, p. 5.

Lister, S. (2002), 'Academics Resign Over "Bribe" for Oxford Place', *The Times*, 25 March, p. 9.

Lockman, B. and Hallaq, J. (1982), 'Who Are Your Successful Salespeople?', *Journal of the Academy of Marketing Science*, 10 (Fall).

Mayer, M. and Greenberg, H. (1964), 'What Makes a Good Salesman', *Harvard Business Review*, 42 (July/August), pp. 119–25.

McDonald, M. (1984), *Marketing Plans*, Butterworth-Heinemann.

McLuhan, R. (2001a), 'Food Remains Top for Field Activities', *Marketing*, 30 August, p. 37.

McLuhan, R. (2001b), 'UK Agencies Focus on European Arena', *Marketing*, 30 August, p. 42.

Mesure, S. (2001), 'Npower's Doorstep Salesmen Slated by Regulator', *The Independent*, 3 October, p. 17.

Middleton, T. (2001), 'Field Questions', *Marketing Week*, 22 November, pp. 51–3.

Miles, L. (1998), 'Discipline on the Doorstep', *Marketing*, 19 November, pp. 37–40.

Miller, R. and Heinman, S. (1991), *Successful Large Account Management*, Holt.

Moncrief, W. (1988), 'Five Types of Industrial Sales Jobs', *Industrial Marketing Management*, 17, pp. 161–7.

O'Connor, J. and Galvin, E. (1999), *Marketing & Information Technology*, 2nd edn, Financial Times Pitman Publishing.

O'Donnell, J. (2001), 'Tricks of the Trade that Boost Sales', *Sunday Times*, 25 November, p. 12.

Ofgem (2000), 'Confidence Boost for Customers', news release dated 21/06/2000, accessed via http://www.ofgem.gov.uk.

Pardo, C. (1997), 'Key Account Management in the Business to Business Field: the Key Account's Point of View', *Journal of Personal Selling and Sales Management*, 17(4), pp. 17–26.

Payne, S. (2002), 'Shopper at Garden Centre Died After Testing Spa Bath', *The Daily Telegraph*, 15 February, p. 8.

Pedersen, C. *et al.* (1986), *Selling: Principles and Methods*, Irwin.

Rasmusson, E. (1999), 'Training Resellers to Sell', *Sales and Marketing Management*, May, p. 65.

Russell, F. *et al.* (1977), *Textbook of Salesmanship*, 10th edn, McGraw-Hill.

Singh, S. (2001), 'Avon Plans Global Teen Assault', *Marketing Week*, 16 August, p. 5.

Smith, P. (1993), *Marketing Communications*, Kogan Page.

Stewart, C. (2002), 'Cold Comfort for those Cold Callers', *The Times*, 26 January, p. 8.

Sujan, H. *et al.* (1994), 'Effort Quantity and Effort Quality: Learning Orientations, Working Smart and Effective Selling', *Journal of Marketing*, 58 (July), pp. 39–52.

Turnbull, P. (1990), 'Roles of Personal Contacts in Industrial Export Marketing' in D. Ford (ed.), *Understanding Business Markets: Interaction, Relationships and Networks*, Academic Press.

Turnbull, P. and Cunningham, M. (1981), *International Marketing and Purchasing: A Survey Among Marketing and Purchasing Executives in Five European Countries*, Macmillan.

Wheatcroft, P. (2002), 'Equitable Investors Could – and Should – Have Looked Before They Leapt', *The Times*, 29 January, p. 14.

Wray, R. (2002), 'MCA Awards 2002: HR/Organisational Development', *The Guardian*, 7 February, p. 5.

chapter 18

direct marketing and exhibitions

LEARNING OBJECTIVES

This chapter will help you to:

1 understand what direct marketing is and why it has risen in importance in recent years;

2 review the various methods used in direct marketing, appreciating their relative strengths and problems in implementation;

3 analyse direct marketing's contribution to achieving marketing communication objectives, and how direct marketing can integrate with other elements of the promotional mix;

4 appreciate the broad issues involved in managing a direct marketing campaign;

5 appreciate the importance of creating and maintaining a database of customers and understand the importance of using the database as a direct marketing tool; and

6 appreciate the contribution that exhibitions can make to achieving marketing objectives and how to exploit them to the full.

Introduction

Over the past decade, direct marketing has grown to become a significant element of the communications mix, emerging from relatively specialised beginnings in traditional mail order and what is derisively labelled 'junk mail'. It can now play an important supporting role, adding an extra dimension to the other elements of the promotional mix. Look at the increasing number of television and print advertisements, for example, which offer some kind of direct response mechanism (phone or mail) to encourage direct dialogue between supplier and customer, over and above the 'normal' objectives of the advertisement. Direct marketing can also be used as a central strategy in its own right as a means of attracting and retaining customers.

As the Harley-Davidson vignette later in this chapter implies, direct marketing is more than just 'junk mail'. It encompasses a wide range of commonly used techniques, not only direct mail but also telemarketing, direct response mechanisms, mail order, and internet marketing. The chapter will look at each of those areas, although internet and new media issues will be covered in more detail later in Chapter 24. The main aspects of managing direct marketing campaigns will be explored, starting with the need for careful targeting and working through the construction and maintenance of customer databases. A number of legislative issues will be discussed, as European governments and the EU seek to regulate the excesses of direct marketing.

eg

Saab is positioned in the tough premium sector of the car market in which sales have been declining in recent years. The difficulty for Saab was that although advertising and direct marketing had succeeded in raising awareness levels from 5 to 29 per cent, only 17 per cent of those responding to the campaign had requested a test drive. Experience has taught most motor manufacturers that the test drive is an important stage in the buying process and provides a great opportunity to showcase the product and to close the sale afterwards. Saab had found that the conversion rate was 1 in 4 after test drives. In 2000, therefore, Saab decided on a direct marketing campaign to make test drives more appealing by offering a 24-hour test drive (without the car salesperson!), the first such offer in the sector.

The mailing list was difficult to assemble, as any list can soon become dated. Response data from the 1999 promotional activity was updated using models that took into account the individual's capability to buy a Saab. A mailshot developed around the creative theme of 'Letting Go' supported by the promise that 'after 24 hours you won't want to give it back' was sent to cold and warm potential customers, supported by mail and online response mechanisms. Further campaigns, using the same theme on various products were run throughout the year, supported by outdoor posters and press advertising. Most of the promotions had different incentives such as prize draws and Swiss army penknives to provide an extra incentive to respond. The campaign increased the number of leads from 3,469 in 1999 to 19,744 in 2000 and response rates rose to 3.1 per cent, well above the previous 0.6 per cent. Despite falling sales, Saab improved its market share and found that the increased response rates helped to reduce the cost of each response to just £39. Saab was the worthy gold award winner of the annual IDM awards in 2001 for a campaign that was effective due to its single-minded call to action, yet achieved it on a modest budget by motor industry standards (*Marketing Week*, 2001a).

The final section of the chapter looks at trade shows and exhibitions, a useful part of the B2B communications mix in particular. We examine their role and value to organisations, not least their ability to generate qualified sales leads and to reinforce the organisation's presence and image in the marketplace as a basis for future direct marketing campaigns.

First, however, the chapter will begin by defining exactly what direct marketing is, and then examine its role in the marketing plan.

The definition of direct marketing

The US Direct Marketing Association has defined **direct marketing** as:

> *An interactive system of marketing which uses one or more advertising media to effect a measurable response at any location.*

This is quite a broad definition which does, however, capture some basic characteristics of direct marketing. **Interactive** implies two-way communication between buyer and seller, while *effect a measurable response* implies quantifiable objectives for the exercise. *At any location* implies the flexibility and pervasiveness of direct marketing, in that it is not inextricably linked with any one medium of communication, but can utilise anything (mail, phone, broadcast or print media) to reach anyone anywhere. What this definition does not do, however, is to emphasise the potential of direct marketing as a primary means of building and sustaining long-term buyer–seller relationships.

It is, therefore, proposed to extend this definition to form the basis of the content of the rest of the chapter:

> *An interactive system of marketing which uses one or more advertising media to effect a measurable response at any location, forming a basis for creating and further developing an ongoing direct relationship between an organisation and its customers.*

The key added value of this definition is the phrase *ongoing direct relationship*, which implies continuity and seems to contradict the impersonal approach traditionally offered by mass media advertising. Is it really possible to use mass media in a mass market to create a relationship with a single customer? Is it really possible to capitalise on the advantages of personal selling that arise from one-to-one dialogue to build and sustain that relationship without the need for face-to-face contact?

If the answer to those two questions is to be 'yes', then the problem becomes one of information gathering and management. To create and sustain *quality* relationships with hundreds, thousands or even millions of individual customers, an organisation needs to know as much as possible about each one, and needs to be able to access, manipulate and analyse that information. The database, therefore, is crucial to the process of building the relationship. We will look in some detail at the issues of creating, maintaining and exploiting the database at pp. 775 *et seq*.

The definition given above and the comments made about it apply as much to internet marketing as to the more traditional forms of direct marketing. Indeed, it could be argued that internet marketing is the ultimate in interactive media. Wherever the customer is in the world, the same messages can be accessed, perhaps even in different languages, thus giving them an enviable consistency and locational flexibility. Measurability and the ability to begin and maintain relationships with enquirers and customers are easily built into website design. Linking data captured from a website with a centralised database is a natural step for an organisation looking to improve its customer knowledge and customer service provision cost effectively. We thus look in detail at this emerging, powerful marketing tool at pp. 765 *et seq.*, particularly at its capacity to play a role in marketing research and planning, distribution and selling and, of course, communication.

Direct marketing is being used increasingly across a wide range of both consumer and B2B markets. In particular, in consumer markets, it has always been a central feature of the marketing strategies of book clubs, which have seen phenomenal growth over the past few years and are now expanding into CDs, videos and computer software. Even in the relatively conservative financial services industry, there has been a marked increase in the direct selling and direct marketing of a wide range of banking facilities and insurance. The next section of this chapter looks more closely at the characteristics and conditions that have led to both the enthusiastic adoption of direct marketing by organisations and its acceptance by their customers.

The rise of direct marketing

There are a number of reasons for the rapid growth of direct marketing, connected with the changing nature of the customer, the marketing environment and, in particular, technological development. The major growth influences are shown in Figure 18.1.

Figure 18.1 Reasons for the growth in direct marketing

Push factors

Changing demographics and lifestyles

In practical terms, many more women are now working, and therefore have less time for shopping, preferring to use what little spare time they have for other leisure activities. Direct marketing, therefore, offers the convenience of shopping by phone, mail or internet with a minimum of effort, particularly if it is possible to use a credit card for easy payment.

Increasing competition

Direct marketing offers organisations the opportunity to create loyal customers. If customers have entered into dialogue with an organisation, and have had their needs and wants met through a series of tailored offerings, then it is going to be quite difficult for the competition to poach those customers. Furthermore, using techniques such as direct mail, an organisation can communicate at length and in depth with its customers personally and relatively privately. In contrast, a television or print advertisement is limited in its scope, has to appeal to a much broader segment, and is seen by the competition (who can then work to counter its effects immediately) as soon as it is screened or published.

Media fragmentation

The increasing number of advertising media available, particularly for organisations looking towards pan-European markets, presents both problems and opportunities. It is a problem because the reduced reach per medium makes advertising less attractive for general mass communication. It is an opportunity for direct marketing because audiences are fragmenting into better-profiled groups. The growth of specialist magazines and reading patterns, along with more specialist satellite TV channels, such as MTV, and the internet, make it easier to locate a defined segment. It also makes it more cost effective to build in direct response mechanisms, because a higher proportion of the audience reached will be interested, and thus a relatively high response rate might be expected.

Increasing media and sales costs

Communication is becoming very expensive. Personal selling is too slow and involves a high cost per call, and is inappropriate for most consumer markets. With traditional advertising, it can be difficult to make the kind of impact that actually leads to action, and thus the outcomes and cost effectiveness of an advertising campaign can be difficult to define. Direct response advertising, followed up by direct mail activity, prompts the customer into action, providing measurable results that allow the cost effectiveness of targeting pre-determined receptive audiences to be properly judged.

Pull factors

Increased customer confidence

The big benefit of using direct marketing to build an ongoing relationship with an individual customer is that as time goes on, the customer's trust and confidence in the organisation build up. The hardest job is to get the initial purchase, but once customers have had one successful and satisfactory experience, they will be much more receptive and willing to try again. A shrewd direct marketer can capitalise on this by analysing a customer's purchasing habits in order to tailor future offerings to fit that customer's profile, and by gently nudging the customer upmarket into more expensive purchases.

A further aspect to consider is the customer's self-confidence. Some customers prefer to have a discreet direct relationship with organisations, and to make their purchases by mail order. Adult incontinence products, for example, are widely available through pharmacists, yet many customers purchase by mail to avoid what they see as the embarrassment of having to ask for the products or being seen to purchase them.

New distribution channels

Many of the types of direct marketing that have been mentioned not only affect approaches to communication, but also have an impact on the use of distribution channels. Until recently, one of the big drawbacks of mail order was the length of time that a customer had to wait for the delivery of goods. Improvements in the management of logistics (*see* Chapter 12) and increasing competition among carriers means that delivery times have been cut from the old-style 'allow 28 days' to 48 (or even 24) hours, with increased reliability and reduced costs. Combining all that with the convenience factor, cutting out the time and hassle of crowded shopping centres, and the potential of increased merchandise selection, we can begin to see why direct distribution is increasingly becoming acceptable.

Contact and relationship building

The ways in which organisations relate to their customers have evolved extensively in recent years. An essential part of customer relationship management is understanding customers, keeping them informed and creating a positive reason for them to continue to do business with you. Direct marketing helps this task very cost effectively. Contrary to popular opinion, committed customers often do welcome regular contact, preferably by mail or increasingly e-mail, but even at times by telephone. A 'thank you' call or 'how are you getting on' can be useful ways of showing you care for recent buyers of high involvement goods. Personalised mail from the supermarket, based on loyalty card data, outlining the latest offers and promotions can be useful information for the shopper. Direct marketing is also well placed to support the intitiation of contact in B2B markets and for maintaining contact in both B2B and B2C markets.

More precise targeting

A feature of direct marketing is that it can be used for precision targeting, whether by geography, demographics, usage or previous enquiry/response patterns. This links with the discussion on segmentation in Chapter 5. It also brings specialist goods within the reach of consumers. Someone with a particular interest in railways, for example, might find that their local bookshop has a very limited range of titles, and that it takes time (and money) to travel to a place with an appropriate bookshop. Joining a railway, industrial history or general history book club solves many of those problems by bringing the specialist range into the customer's own home.

Cross-selling opportunities

Cross-selling is a deliberate attempt to encourage an existing customer to purchase other items from the range. Although some care should be taken when cross-selling, as it can cause some resentment, it is valuable because it enables an organisation to sell the full range of goods and/or services it offers and helps to maximise the value of individual customers. This was seen in the case of the AA (at p. 94), where the link between the AA breakdown service and its financial services has been successfully managed using the membership database. Telephone call centres can handle both outbound sales calls and respond to inbound enquiries from other response mechanisms.

Facilitating factors

Database technology advances

It is now realistic for even the smallest company to develop and manage some kind of customer database relatively cheaply. The costs (and size) of the hardware have reduced dramatically, while the power and quality of both hardware and software have increased. Thus it is now possible to hold a vast amount of detail on each individual customer, and it is relatively quick and simple to update and analyse the data held to create better marketing strategies for both existing and future customers.

Impact of new communications technology

There is little point in making any effort to elicit a direct response unless the capability exists to handle the volume of responses generated. With telephone response, for example, it is now possible using automated systems to handle many hundreds of calls simultaneously, reducing the risk of losing potential respondents through the frustration of failing to get through quickly. It is also necessary to keep the costs of response as low as possible for both the organisation and its customers. Freephone numbers and freepost addresses represent the most attractive option for the customer. Both BT and the Post Office are aware of the opportunities that direct marketing offers them as 'middlemen' (or facilitators), and will work with organisations to agree a package that represents the most efficient and cost effective use of their services.

New links with online marketing

Online marketing is rapidly changing the way in which organisations handle direct marketing. As internet penetration across Europe continues to rise, the potential for integrated campaigns becomes much greater through the power of a website to inform and entice customers, display products, and process orders. Organisations that innovated with freephone numbers and call centres a few years ago are now focusing their attention on online transactions. The same is true of mail order catalogue selling which is going through a renaissance supported by consumers' ability to shop online from the catalogue (at p. 765 *et seq.*).

Many of the issues mentioned in this section are interrelated. Consumer attitudes to direct marketing have, for example, mellowed as technology has allowed organisations to target personalised mailshots more appropriately, so that what is received through the letter box is less likely to be dismissed outright as 'junk'. The pioneering work of organisations such as the *Next Directory* in developing upmarket, high-quality merchandise, and successfully developing the logistics to fulfil a promise of 48-hour delivery, have also revolutionised UK attitudes to mail order. This has in itself provided the impetus for greater commitment and investment in direct marketing by a wide range of organisations.

The discussion so far has talked generally about the concept of direct marketing, with passing reference to specific areas such as direct mail and direct response, among others. The next section looks more closely at each of these areas and their individual characteristics. Figure 18.2 gives an overview of the range of direct marketing areas.

Figure 18.2 The range of direct marketing techniques

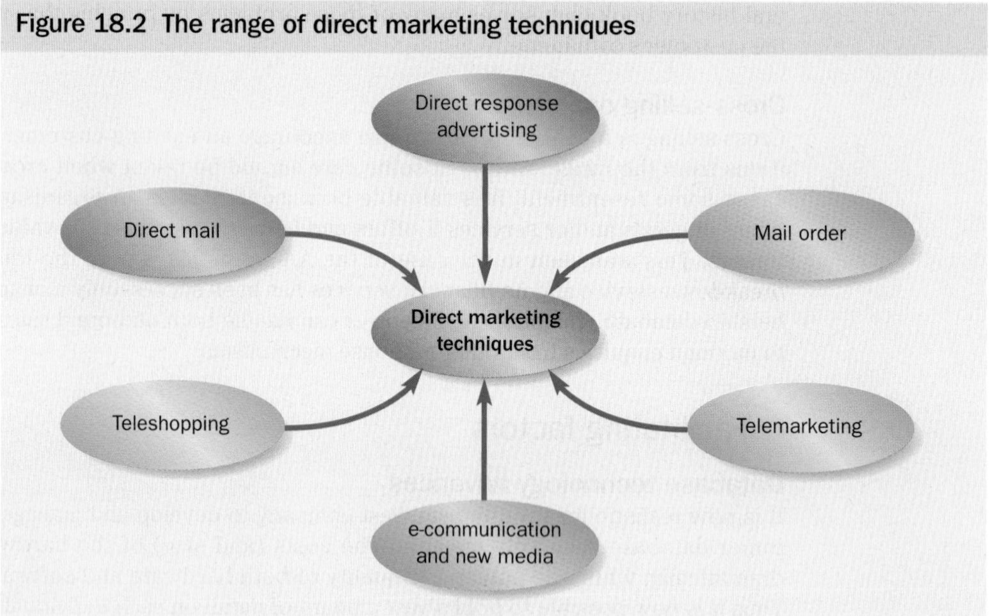

Techniques of direct marketing

The scope of direct marketing is very wide. It utilises what might be called the more traditional means of marketing communication, such as print and broadcast advertising media, but it has also developed its own media, through mail, telecommunications and modem. Each of the main techniques in direct marketing will now be considered in turn.

Direct mail

Direct mail is material distributed through the postal service to the recipients' home or business address to promote a product or service. What is mailed can vary from a simple letter introducing a company or product through to a comprehensive catalogue or sample. Many mailshots incorporate involvement devices to increase the chances of their being opened and read, through stimulating curiosity.

marketing **in action**

The open road to success

For many, a Harley-Davidson is *the* motorcycle. It has wide appeal, from those seeking the Rolls-Royce of motorbikes to those seeking to relive their lost youth on two wheels. The focus is on status and Harley's marketing data suggests that the average age of an owner is 44 and the median income is $80,000 in the USA and £30,000 in the UK. The Harley-Davidson has an almost cult following and owners congregate each year for rallies held around the country, such as Sturgis, South Dakota. Building on its success in the USA, Harley-Davidson wanted to develop the UK market.

Research in the UK indicated that there were some different brand perceptions compared with the US and these had to be tackled if the aggressive sales targets were to be realised. Although overall the majority of motorbike owners aspired to ride a Harley, there were some concerns over poor reliability, performance and high costs. A pan-European advertising campaign was developed by Partners BDDH and the brand direct response strategy in the UK was assigned to Partners Andrews Aldridge. The prime campaign objectives were to activate the desire to ride a Harley and to generate leads and enquiries for test rides. The test ride is crucial as it is an opportunity to create the 'experience' and to reinforce the brand's authority as well as providing an opportunity for the dealers' sales teams to address any unfounded concerns. Since 1999, three campaigns have been designed and executed by Andrews Aldridge: the 'Dream Ride' campaign; 'New Generation' campaign; and the 'Questions' campaign. Each is now considered briefly in turn.

Harley-Davidson

Source: Harley-Davidson.

The 1999 Dream Ride campaign used direct mail for the first time on a large scale, partly to encourage existing customers to upgrade and partly to tempt potential customers to seek a test ride. Mailing lists were derived both from in-house prospect lists of people who had had previous contact with Harley, and from cold lists of those with a motorbike licence and a similar profile to the older, more affluent Harley rider. Direct response was also encouraged from advertising in specialist magazines such as *Motorcycle News*, *Ride* and *Bike*. Mailings went to 16,000 targeted individuals and included a unique test ride invitation. It appeared to be a video giving the recipients a Harley test ride from the comfort of their armchair. Since there is no substitute for actually riding a Harley, the video box was empty apart from a leaflet inside that said 'Don't be ridiculous' and invited them to test ride the real thing and enter the 'dream ride' promotion. After all, 'nothing can create the Harley experience short of the open road'. The campaign was linked with the opportunity to visit a dealer in order to enter a competition. All the recipient had to do was to describe their ideal experience on a Harley so that the dream could come true. The winner had a trip from New Orleans to the Florida keys on a Harley 'Fat Boy'. The promotion coincided with the dealers' busiest months and succeeded in pulling customers into the showrooms. Dealers often received more leads in a day than they usually received in a month.

To keep the campaigns fresh and original, although the 2000 New Generation campaign had the same objective, to encourage test rides, there was also an additional task: to motivate consumers to re-appraise the brand in the light of recent product modifications. Again, both cold and warm mailing lists were used drawn from readership and lifestyle profiles.

The creative theme evolved around a man on the street admiring a Harley as it rides past with the headline 'Some things will never change', but inside the reader is introduced to the recent improvements along with the line 'Some things already have', detailing the modifications to the bike's handling and performance. The dream ride competition was repeated and Harley leather jackets were given to ten runners-up. Over 140,000 mailshots were sent out in October 2000 and as a result, over 25 per cent of all the calls to the call centre were generated by the campaign.

Finally, the Questions campaign was run in May 2001 with the objective of targeting 16,000 recent enquirers and those who had responded to previous media campaigns but had not yet purchased a bike. Rather than using general lists, however, the focus was on the best prospects from biker event registrations and previous enquirers. The mailing carried the headline, 'If you haven't got a Harley yet, you need to ask yourself a few questions' and the focus was on offering a test drive to convince the waverers. As each recipient had originally initiated contact with Harley, the message could be hard hitting and be more benefit-orientated. A short incentivised questionnaire was also included, seeking feedback for the reasons for non-purchase so that any subsequent communication could be even better targeted. The incentive this time, aimed at non-users, was the offer of five free courses at Rider's Edge, the Harley riding school. The response rate was 8.7 per cent and the cost of each response was just £15. It has been estimated that the campaign generated a return on the promotional investment of 18.1 per cent, showing the potential impact of sustained direct mailing campaigns. At the dealer front line, there usually was a significant uplift in enquiries as Harley began to understand better the customer's buying needs and how to address any purchase barriers.

Sources: Kleinman (2001a); Harley-Davidson (2002); and with grateful thanks to Richard Pentin, Partners Andrews Aldridge.

Most direct mail is unsolicited. Organisations compile or buy lists of names and addresses, and then send out the mailshot. The **mailing list** used may be cold, that is, where there has been no previous contact between the organisation and the addressee, or may reflect various selection criteria based on data held about previous or existing customers.

Direct mail is widely used in both consumer and B2B markets. The financial services sector, for example, sends out mailshots to encourage people to apply for credit cards, mortgages, loans and insurance quotes. The pharmaceutical and medical supplies companies send out mailshots to doctors, pharmacists and dentists, partly to make them aware of what is available, and partly to pave the way for a later call from the sales representative. Consultants, contractors and suppliers similarly target organisational buyers and decision makers. Sometimes, different members of the distribution channel can work together.

Direct mail has the problem that it has suffered from bad PR. All of us as consumers can probably think of a couple of examples of direct mail we have received that have been completely inappropriate, and misconceptions about direct mail's effectiveness are often based on such personal experiences of receiving 'junk'. Historically, this has arisen partly from the lack of flexibility and detail within databases, and partly from poor marketing thinking. In the earlier days of direct mail, marketers were obsessed with the power of databases to generate vast numbers of contacts and to process personalised mailshots at high speed. This created a false bonus in going for volume rather than concentrating on more carefully targeted use, since it was as easy to send 100,000 mailshots as 10,000. If the organisation was looking for a pre-determined response rate, then there was an advantage in mailing larger numbers of mailshots, even though the majority were wasted. This then led to resentment among those receiving vast quantities of inappropriate material, and the labelling of direct mail as ineffective junk (Miles, 2001a). Increasingly, though, marketers are using the information at their disposal more intelligently, and mailing smaller groups of well-defined prospective customers, using better-designed creative material. They are also keeping their databases more current, and so a household should not receive direct mail addressed to people who moved away or died over a year ago. In theory, then, an individual should be receiving less direct mail, but what they do receive should be of prime relevance and interest. Making sure that the mailings hit the target is, therefore, becoming an issue for many mailers, although a large number are still content to send out mailings without checking postal addresses and with outdated information. With a business decay rate of 37 per cent, it is important that data is cleaned on a regular basis. In consumer markets it is even more imperative, for example mailings sent to people that have recently died are the largest source of complaints to the Data Protection Registrar. The ReaD Group runs a Bereavement

Register to avoid causing distress but only 1,000 companies actually use the data to clean their lists. Clearly, if regular major cleaning of data does not take place, the effectiveness of mailings and the response rate will suffer (Miles, 2001a).

Although the information in Table 18.1 is heartening, it may not be enough. Think about the hierarchy of effects models shown in Figure 14.7, and how direct mail fits into those. Using the AIDA model as an example, opening the envelope begins the *awareness* stage, reading the content generates *interest* and *desire* and, finally, the mailshot clearly defines what subsequent *action* is expected. The main objective is to move the recipient quickly through all the stages from awareness to action. The key is not simply the opening of the envelope, but whether the content can pull the reader right through to the completion of action. As a consolation prize, if the recipient reads the content but chooses not to respond, there may still be an awareness or interest effect that may 'soften up' the customer for subsequent mailings or, in B2B markets, a sales visit.

Table 18.1 Some facts about direct mail in the UK

1	The average UK household receives 13.1 items of direct mail every four weeks (17 for the AB socioeconomic group)
2	Business managers are sent an average of 14 direct mail items per week
3	4,939 million items of direct mail were sent out in 2001. These were split: 75 per cent B2C mailing and 25 per cent B2B mailings
4	Direct mail volume has increased by over 100 per cent in the last 10 years
5	In 2001, £2,228 mn was spent on direct mail advertising compared with £895 mn in 1991
6	On average, 68 per cent of B2C direct mail is opened and 43 per cent read. The lowest is household insurance (16 per cent) and the highest is travel (81 per cent)
7	Response rates overall average 10 per cent. They range from 3.5 per cent for credit cards to over 22 per cent for brown goods (TVs, hi-fis, etc.)
8	38 per cent of consumers find direct mail intrusive compared with 81 per cent for telesales
9	In B2B markets opinion on the value of direct mail is almost equally divided between 'useful' and 'not useful'
10	Business managers open 83 per cent of their direct mail, 9 per cent is re-directed to a colleague and 16 per cent is filed or responded to
11	The average consumer spends £514 per year on average through direct mail
12	More than £23.4 billion of consumer business is generated every year by the direct mail industry

Source: adapted from http://www.dmis.co.uk reproduced by kind permission of Direct Mail Information Service (DMIS).

Advantages of using direct mail

Direct mail accounted for 12.4 per cent of promotional expenditure (non-sales force spend) in 2001 and its biggest users were mail order retailers, financial services companies, retailers and charities (http://www.royalmail.co.uk). There are a number of advantages of using direct mail.

Targeting. Using the post code system, targeted campaigns can be developed based on geodemographic criteria. Combine that with the depth of knowledge held about existing customers, and even more detailed targeting can be achieved (McLuhan, 2002a). Similarly, with B2B lists, targeted efforts at specific, named individuals within organisations is possible. Even purchased lists can be used for clearly targeted campaigns. The London Herb and Spice Company wanted to create awareness of its fruit teas and so used a mailshot aimed at 90,000 users of competitive products.

e-marketing *in action*

Permission marketing

The concept of permission marketing has been a driving force for recent investment in online marketing and customer relationship management. Permission marketing is a term coined by Seth Godin. Godin (1999) notes that while research used to show we were bombarded by 500 marketing messages a day, with the advent of the web and digital TV this has now increased to over 3,000 a day! From an organisation's viewpoint, this leads to a dilution in the effectiveness of the messages – how can the communications of any one company stand out? From the customer's viewpoint, time is seemingly in ever-shorter supply, customers are losing patience and expect reward for their attention, time and information. Godin refers to the traditional approach as interruption marketing. Permission marketing is about seeking the customer's permission before engaging them in a relationship and providing something in exchange. The classic exchange is based on information or entertainment – a B2B site can offer a free report in exchange for a customer sharing their e-mail address which will be used to maintain a dialogue, a B2C site can offer a screensaver in exchange. Think what the logical conclusion of this is. Companies will pay customers to view ads. This has already happened with www.alladvantage.com offering targeted customers payment in exchange for viewing ads from high end auto brands.

From an e-commerce perspective, we can think of a customer agreeing to engage in a relationship when they agree by checking a box on a web form to indicate that they agree to receive further communications from a company. This is referred to as *opt-in*. This is preferable to *opt-out*, the situation where a customer has to consciously agree not to receive further information.

The importance of incentivisation in permission marketing has been emphasised by Seth Godin who likens the process of acquisition and retention to dating someone. Godin (1999) suggests that dating the customer involves:

- offering the prospect an *incentive* to volunteer;
- using the attention offered by the prospect, offer a curriculum over time, teaching the consumer about your product or service;
- reinforce the *incentive* to guarantee that the prospect maintains the permission;
- offer additional *incentives* to get even more permission from the consumer;
- over time, leverage the permission to change consumer behaviour towards profits.

Opt-in e-mail is vital in communicating the retention offers either through regular e-mail communications such as a newsletter or higher impact irregular e-mail communications such as details of a product launch. Remember that e-mail has the power of traditional push communication. It enables a targeted message to be pushed out to a customer to inform and remind and they are certain to view it within their e-mail inbox; even if it is only deleted, it cannot be ignored. Contrast this with the web – a pull medium where customers will only visit your site if there is a reason or a prompt to do this. The database is vital in recording the customer's profile, interests and recording all interactions that are part of the ongoing relationship.

Once an e-mail address has been collected, managers must plan the frequency of e-mail communications. Options include:

- *Regular newsletter*. For example, once a day, once a week, once a month. It is best if customers are given choice about the frequency.
- *Event-related*. These tend to be less regular and are sent out perhaps every three or six months when there is news of a new product launch or an exceptional offer.
- *E-mail sequence (multi-stage e-mail)*. Software can be purchased to send out a series of e-mails. For example, after subscription to a trial version of an online magazine, e-mails will be sent out at 3, 10, 25 and 28 days to encourage a subscription before the trial lapses.

Sources: Chaffey (2002); Godin (1999).

When operating on a European basis, however, it must be remembered that regulations on list broking vary from country to country. Laws are more lenient in the Netherlands and France than in the UK and Germany. In the UK, list broking is allowed as long as the individuals on the list know and consent to the practice. Effectively, there has to be an opt-in clause for further contact from company A, with which the individual already has contact, and a separate opt-in clause to have the details sold to company B with which the individual may never had had any contact. The 1998 Data Protection Act is a significant step towards protecting consumers from an invasion of unwanted mailings, provided they read the opt-in clauses carefully (Coad, 2001). Both data holders and data processors have to be far more alert to their responsibilities under the Act.

eg

Boots ran into trouble with the Advertising Standards Authority (ASA) for sending mailings to customers who had specifically asked not to be contacted. The letter said 'When you joined the Advantage card scheme, you expressed a preference not to receive mail from us.

However, we thought you might like to know that you are missing out on…'. Unfortunately for Boots, some of its cardholders did not want to know and the one complaint was upheld by the ASA. Under the Data Protection Act of 1998, which came into force in 2001, it is illegal to mail consumers with further offers if they have opted out. In this case, Boots apologised and indicated that it would refrain from further mailings (Brabbs, 2001).

Personalisation. With new technology in ink-jet imaging, laser printing and electronic processing, large numbers of personalised mailings can be undertaken regularly. Although the novelty of receiving mailshots that begin 'Dear Mrs Shufflebottom, You will be the envy of Railway Terrace, Heckmondwike, if you take advantage of our wonderful offer ...' has worn off, there is still an undeniable intimacy about personalisation that other advertising media cannot achieve.

eg

Marketing Week's subscription department has ensured that both the envelope and letter are personalised in such a way as to assume a close and ongoing relationship. The envelope appears to have been handwritten and carries a first-class stamp, with no franking machine to blow its cover. It appears to be personal mail and, therefore, attracts more immediate attention. Inside, the subscription reminder is again personalised along with an invoice and free business reply service.

Response rates. Depending on the quality of the database and the selection criteria underpinning the mailing list, the response rate for direct mailing can be high. This has already been seen in the examples mentioned earlier. All of this is a product of the personal, confidential, selective and flexible nature of direct mail. Some sectors are struggling to achieve response rates of even around 1 per cent. In the financial services area, although the average response rate is just 1.3 per cent, warm prospects are six times more likely to respond than cold ones and mortgage providers generally enjoy higher response rates than credit card companies (*Marketing*, 2001).

Flexibility. The creative scope of what can be included in a mailshot is very flexible, allowing varied and interesting campaigns, which can even be phased if required. This flexibility extends to frequency, size, colour, length, copy, layout and quality, as well as the inclusion of videos, CDs, gifts or samples.

Attention seeking. Even if only for a brief moment, the mailing holds the attention of the reader far more exclusively than advertising. An involvement device that requires the recipient to do something (a competition scratch card; something that needs careful unfolding; a video to play) reduces the chances of the mailing being discarded unread.

eg

Virgin Money from the outset has sought to make financial services jargon-free, flexible and appropriate to the customer. A mailing selling its credit card services contained all that, but with a difference. Rather than a standard letter, the integrated message was enclosed inside a card 'envelope' which was shaped and designed to look like a credit card, but bigger, easy to slip through a letterbox, but too big for a wallet. The teaser headline was 'Virgin has plans to change the world of credit cards' on the address side while the reverse looked just like the real plastic card. Inside, using a blueprint image to follow through the 'plan' concept, Virgin detailed a credit card plan tailored to the recipient on six criteria such as annual fee, balance transfer offer etc., along with a summary of the benefits and an application form. The same mailing could be returned post-paid and, of course, Richard Branson included a personal note of invitation. Virgin used creativity both to gain attention and to carry the theme right through the application process, provided you wanted another credit card of course!

Developing a direct mail campaign

It must, however, be stressed that a mailshot is only as good as the data underpinning it. If, for example the mailing list contains many small firms that frequently change their address, or an area of high turnover in residential property, then its quality and its ability to deliver a satisfactory response rate are questionable.

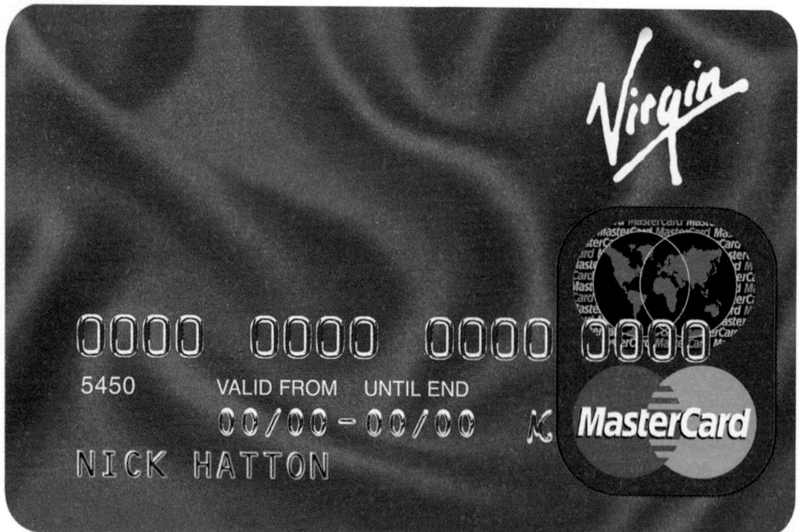

Being such a well-known brand, Virgin chose to use an inventive way to catch the eye of the consumer – a mailshot looking like a credit card.

Source: Campaign created by Harrison Troughton Wunderman for Virgin Money, 2002.

The mailing list is the first of a number of specific areas in developing a direct mail campaign that need to be examined.

Mailing list management. A list is a collection of names and addresses of individuals or companies grouped together on pre-determined criteria. Getting the list right (i.e. fit for its purpose) is a major challenge. Direct mail must have accurate targeting, drawing on the same concepts as market segmentation, discussed in Chapter 5.

Lists are either internal or purchased. Internal lists can be compiled from a variety of sources, including past and present customers, enquirers, prospects or compilations from published sources, for example through a systematic scan of trade directories, telephone books etc. Great Ormond Street Children's Hospital (http://www.gt-ormond-st-hospital.org.uk) is concerned with fund raising to support its development priorities in research, equipment and treatment. With over 22,000 inpatients and 78,000 outpatients each year, half of whom are under the age of two, there is always a need for more cash. Although there is a comprehensive programme of fund-raising activities from active donors, including sponsored websites, corporate sponsorship and employee giving, the hospital is also concerned not to lose lapsed donors. It can target its database of lapsed donors with special mail campaigns to attract them back. In one campaign, it achieved 6,000 responses from the 22,000 lapsed donors at that time. Lists can also be purchased from other organisations which maintain customer databases and wish to trade information.

eg

When Pharmacia wanted to run a campaign for its Nicorette nicotine replacement products it had to make sure that its mailing list was confined to people trying to give up smoking. It runs a Fresh Start programme to help smokers kick the habit, and those registering either by mail or online were used as the basis for the mailing list. The campaign itself had to be carefully designed and timed. According to Pharmacia, research indicates that the challenge is great:

- 70–90 per cent of smokers want to quit, but only 1 in 3 will be successful.
- 40 per cent of smokers who have had a heart attack resume smoking within days of leaving hospital.
- 50 per cent of smokers who have had laryngectomies continue to smoke.
- More than 50 per cent of heroin and cocaine users and alcoholics declare that cigarettes are more difficult to give up than their other addiction.

Pharmacia sent advent calendars to registered Fresh Start participants and the mailing offered daily tips on how to overcome the continued craving to smoke. The timing of the campaign was perfect, just right to fit with New Year's resolutions. It was recognised, however, that the success rate would be small, but in health matters every life saved is a small victory. An online version was also provided (Kleinman, 2001c; http://www.nicorette.co.uk).

Lists purchased from external sources need to be carefully checked to make sure that they are relevant and up to date. Next time you fill in a reply coupon, look to see if it has small print at the bottom to the effect that: 'We may wish to pass your details on to other carefully selected companies'. Unless you tick the box stating that you would rather deny the company this privilege, your details are liable to be sold on to another company. Organisations also exist specialising in consumer research and list compilation.

marketing in action

A list for everything ...

... At least that's the way it seems. There is a large number of list providers and the marketer must ensure that any list offered reflects the required target audience, as well as asking the more obvious questions about the age, source and accuracy of the mailing data being offered.

HLB provides more than 10 million names each year to over 150 clients. It works on managing over 65 consumer databases that allow interrogation and tailoring depending upon whether a mass mailing or niche campaign is required. Of particular importance are the subscription databases. So if you want a list of 15,000 *Wisden Cricket Monthly* readers, 53,200 *Christian Holidays* subscribers or 120,000 consumers that use fcuk by mail, HLB can provide it. One of the larger databases is the combined list of magazine subscribers to BBC magazines and 'Reader Offer' buyers, a database of over 1 million active and lapsed subscribers. Such a list allows high volume mailings as well as more targeted mailings to readers of, for instance, *BBC Gardeners' World* or *BBC Top Gear* magazines. The profile for each list is detailed by age, gender, income, lifestyle interests and propensity to purchase.

Dun & Bradstreet, meanwhile, operates on an international scale with a range of datasets that offer access to consumer names, addresses and attributes in many countries. The datasets have also been screened for individuals who have opted out through the MPS and TPS (Mailing and telephone preference services, respectively) and the Gone Away Suppression Service. Lists can be acquired on a one-off rental basis or on a long-term lease with updating.

Dun & Bradstreet cooperates with the Data Exchange, a data sharing club, a list of 40 million independently generated and shared consumer records built from individual data covering insights into lifestyle, life stage, personal attributes, leisure interests, financial characteristics, shopping preferences, etc. Similarly the Roll Call Data software is built on the electoral roll, a universe of 45 million individuals and 26 million households, which are described by geodemographic characteristics. Dun & Bradstreet will help with analysing and modelling from these lists. Like HLB, it also offers standard subscription lists.

Finally, Wyvern Direct Response specialises in highly targeted lists, especially those based around occupational groups. By working with publishers, it has been able to assemble a comprehensive selection of names that are very suitable, if particular groups are being targeted. Its lists cover, for example, 95 per cent of all UK subscribers to healthcare publications, including 41,000 GPs, 37,000 hospital doctors, 23,000 practice nurses and 15,000 health visitors. Similarly, by working with the Jane's Aerospace and Defence Directories, an international list of relevant specialists is available, including 8,000 in the UK, 13,000 in the rest of Europe and 15,000 in the United States. This list, totalling 50,000 names, is ideal not only for defence manufacturers, but for travel, IT, exhibition and training product and service providers.

So, every time you subscribe to something or become a customer, the process of recording and analysing begins. They are watching you reading about them!

Sources: http://www.wyverncrest.co.uk; http://www.hlb-lists.co.uk; http://www.dnb.com.

In the UK, the Royal Mail offers a postcode address file (PAF) containing over 1.6 million postcodes and nearly 27 million delivery possibilities. The file is regularly updated and is the most complete address database in the UK. The linked Postzone files contain the grid references, local authority ward codes and NHS codes for all postcodes in the UK. These files can be matched with existing or purchased data using specialised software that can run on a PC. These data must be checked and cleaned at regular intervals to ensure that names and addresses are correct. Often this work is handled by a specialist external agency, but there is a threshold of 10,000 records beyond which it becomes more economical to develop in-house capability, especially if the data are complex in their construction and are for specialist mailings and use. No system is 100 per cent accurate and often even the larger companies send their data out for extensive checking and cleansing.

Once established, the PAF can be used with a mainframe to enable easy selection of geographically based mailing lists, although additional information would be necessary to introduce lifestyle or purchasing behaviour variables.

There is a note of caution, however, as a lot of mail still finds it way back as 'return to sender', as people and businesses move on. Miles (2001a) estimated that business data could decay at the rate of 37 per cent per year and that £126 mn of marketing budgets are wasted through poor mailing. If a company sends out a mailing of 200,000 items with a five per cent error (duplications, moved, undeliverable, etc.) it could cost £100,000 a year. The Royal Mail MailMax online calculator enables a more accurate cost to be established for inefficient address management. Ultimately lists are only as good as the cleansing and updating that is carried out as a mater of routine. If an organisation does not wish to invest directly in that activity it may be better for it to contract the management to an outside list specialist. Some organisations argue against the purchase of lists, as it indicates that customer information is not being collected appropriately within the organisation. Sometimes it may be worth partnering with another non-competitive organisation to share lists for a complementary product or service.

There are some simple rules that can be followed in database list management that many mailers would be advised to follow (Miles, 2001a).

- Always gain a customer's permission before additional information is sent.
- Have well developed tools to manage and filter data on an ongoing basis.
- Make the 'unsubscribe' options obvious and simple to use.
- Be consistent in data capture between media.
- Protect the data captured.

Creative implementation. Designing the content of a mailshot is the realm of a well-briefed copywriter. It is certainly not simply an extension of letter writing. The prime objective of most mailshots is to generate a response, which really means that the recipient's attention and interest have to be engaged quickly, if a rapport is to be established. Even if the recipient starts to read, there is still the danger of distraction and rejection. The role of direct mail is still evolving, according to Kemp (2001), and it is now being used to promote the brand and to reinforce the relationship rather than being just a response-orientated medium. This is enabling greater use of creativity in the design of the content, covering initial impact, personalisation, involvement, benefit orientation and flow to move the reader through to a conclusion. Personalisation, involvement devices, benefit orientation and flow are therefore critical to holding the reader.

eg

Cadbury Trebor Bassett ran a major direct marketing campaign just before Christmas to link confectionery with the season's festivities. It wanted to capture the mood of the season and to provide creative solutions to encourage brand recall and provide purchase reminders. The mailing featured a self-assembly tabletop Christmas tree designed to hold Cadbury's Roses and Miniature Heroes sweets; a Christmas countdown calendar to help families plan the run-in to the big day; gift ideas that could be purchased by telephone or online; and a competition to win £250 towards the Christmas shopping. The mailing was sent to 550,000 people profiled from the Jigsaw database (Kleinman, 2001b).

The envelope or packaging can also be part of the creative appeal. Placing a message on the outside of the envelope might increase the chances of its being opened, as well as building some sense of anticipation. Teaser messages, coloured envelopes, windows to show a glimpse of an incentive, whether it is a gift or a prize draw, all assist in this process. Thus one of the Great Ormond Street Hospital's lapsed donor mailshot campaigns had the words 'Link up with them this Christmas' on the outside of the envelope, with the 'Link up' presented as a logo written in paper chains.

It should be noted, however, that some organisations take an opposite view. Some consumers will dump an envelope, unopened, straight into the bin, if it is obviously a piece of direct mail. The strategy, therefore, is to make the envelope as innocuous and unobtrusive as possible, so that the recipient has to open it to make sure that it isn't something important. Once the envelope is opened, there is a greater chance that the content will be read. One Amex mailshot was sent in a plain white envelope with just the Amex logo on it. The existing card holders at whom the mailshot was targeted would have assumed that it was something to do with their account.

Table 18.2 Europe's expenditure on direct marketing per person, 2000

Country	*Expenditure per capita ($)*
France	111.6
Germany	118.3
Italy	26.6
Netherlands	152.2
Spain	61.4
Sweden	88.2
UK	71.6
Europe	86.0

Source: *Datamonitor*, as quoted by Singh (2001), reproduced by kind permission of Datamonitor.

Table 18.3 Volume of direct mail by country, 2000

Country	*Volume of direct mail (millions of items)*
Germany	6567
UK	4664
France	4501
Switzerland	1535
Netherlands	1532
Spain	796
Norway	374
Denmark	237
Portugal	196

Note: data not available for Belgium, Finland, Italy, Sweden and Ireland.

Source: http://www.dmis.co.uk, reproduced by kind permission of Direct Mail Information Service (DMIS).

The response mechanism is also important, especially for B2B direct mail where the main objective is often to generate leads rather than sales *per se*. Response cards not only assist the ease of reply, but also the initial qualification of leads. They can be used to gain additional information on the buyer prior to contact, to assess whether the contact is worth following up, and what kind of follow-up is most appropriate. Reply paid cards should not be an add-on, but a well thought out means of improving the quality of leads generated.

Table 18.2 shows the per capita expenditure on direct marketing in a number of European countries in 2000. Across Europe there are some marked differences. The lowest spend is in Italy where developing effective lists has been difficult and manufacturers have not actively pursued direct marketing techniques. The Netherlands, France and Germany are the three biggest users, although Table 18.3 indicates that when direct mail only is examined, the UK is second in the volume of mailings. Direct mail still dominates direct marketing expenditure, although telemarketing and direct response advertising are growing, especially in the UK. Far from being a mature medium, direct mail has also experienced growth as part of an integrated campaign, especially for organisations seeking to move recipients to their websites. To put things in proportion, however, it must be noted that US expenditure on direct mail and telemarketing is five times higher than Europe's (Singh, 2001).

Direct response advertising

Direct response advertising appears in the standard broadcast and print media. It differs from 'normal' advertising because it is designed to generate a direct response, whether an order, an enquiry for further information or a personal visit. The response mechanism

eg

Slendertone UK became the market leader in the body-toning market within three years of its launch and much of this was attributed to its successful use of direct response media. Market share grew from 6 to 49 per cent. While sales went up sixteenfold, the cost per sale reduced by 40 per cent in just two years. How do they do it? After building a profile of target customers, the company is able to match it with the reader and viewer profiles of different media. The full range of direct response media are used, including television, press and radio as well as direct mail, catalogues and point-of-sale materials in selected retail outlets. Over 40 titles are used and each is tracked for the number and nature of responses. The campaigns are well integrated with the emphasis on creating impact. Potentially the world's largest bottom featured on a billboard advertisement with the headline 'Does my bum look big in this?' at the junction of Oxford Street and Tottenham Court Road to announce the launch of the Slendertone Flex Bottom and Thigh System. Worth a trip to London to see it? (http://www.slendertone.com).

By using an eye-catching large bottom and making the viewer think of the common question 'Does my bum look big in this', Slendertone managed to attract the attention of passers by.

Source: Slendertone.

may be a coupon to cut out in a print advertisement, or a phone number in any type of advertisement. This area has grown in popularity in recent years as advertisers seek to get their increasingly expensive advertising to work harder for them.

By using advertising media, direct response advertising's initial targeting, unlike that of some of the other forms of direct marketing, relies much more on an assessment of the medium's reader or viewer profile than on a pre-prepared mailing list. Responses to such advertising, however, can then be used as a database for other forms of direct marketing in the future.

eg

The response levels achieved on ITV's *Pop Idol*, when over 8.5 million people voted on the last night of the show indicate the power of DRTV. Even on less high profile television game shows and in other successful campaigns involving charities or products, an average of 100,000 calls can be received, the bulk of which occur within 20 minutes of the announcement. That is a big challenge to the telephone answering system and there is nothing worse than a frustrated caller who keeps getting an engaged tone. There are some who still think that Will Young only won *Pop Idol* because many Gareth Gates supporters could not get through! For the *Who Wants to Be a Millionaire* show around 100,000 calls per show are generated. Initial calls are handled automatically with callers answering a simple question. From those who answer correctly the list is reduced by randomly selecting 100. The National Canine Defence League also used DRTV but because it only used cable and satellite channels, the level of response was more manageable. As callers were making donations by credit card, if the calls could not be answered personally, a call-back mechanism was employed, and 90 per cent of callers were happy with that (McLuhan, 2002b).

Types of direct response advertising

There is a range of types of direct response mechanisms that can be used in advertising. Advertisers can provide an address to write to, a coupon to fill in and send off for more information, telephone numbers or website addresses. Either the advertiser or the customer can pay for any postal or telephone charges. Throughout the rest of this discussion, the costs are considered from the consumer's perspective, i.e. 'freepost' means postal response that is free to the respondent and 'pay post' means that the respondent has to pay normal postage rates.

Freepost (coupon) and freephone

Scottish Widows (http://www.scottishwidows.co.uk) supported its television advertising campaign for ISAs with press advertising that involved freepost, freephone and internet options for obtaining further information. The coupon was primarily concerned with collecting the enquirer's name and address, but the date of birth and postcode were included to reveal useful background information. A request for daytime and evening telephone details left the enquirer in no doubt what the follow-up approach was going to be!

Franklin Mint, a company specialising in moderately expensive collectibles, regularly advertises to sell straight off the page. An American bald eagle pocket watch was offered for £59 payable by monthly instalments and with a full 30-day money-back guarantee. The advertisement claimed that the watch incorporated the 'original art of the world-renowned wildlife artist [Ted Blaylock] into the design of a precision timepiece'. Although no money had to be sent with the order, an invoice of £29.50 plus £2.95 would be issued on delivery and a further invoice for the final payment the following month. Response could either be by coupon or freephone.

Pay post (coupon) and pay phone

Neville Johnson designs and manufactures exclusive fitted furniture for the home. It uses the Sunday colour supplement magazines to generate enquiries from advertisements showing how loft and sloping roof space can be used as an office with fitted furniture. The coupon asks the customer to provide basic information and a contact telephone number. Interested consumers can either mail the coupon at their expense or can use the telephone, again at their own expense.

Pay post (no coupon) and pay phone

If the discerning shopper is tempted by a Princess yacht after seeing the advertising, the onus is on them to telephone, fax or write to either the distributor or the main office, at their own expense. Then again, if you can't afford the telephone call, you can't afford the yacht. If you do, however, decide to take the plunge for 'Power, Precision and Passion' you would be in distinguished company, with David Coulthard having recently taken delivery of a new Princess V42. Contact through the website (http://www.princess-yachts.com) is the most likely response mechanism, and on that site, the stunning photographs and detailed technical data would keep even the most casual observer interested.

Freepost and pay phone

Bonusprint, a photo developing company, glued a freepost envelope to its full-page advertisement to make it as easy as possible for readers to order photographic prints at special

Princess Yachts are aimed at a high-spending public who want quality and value as well as excitement when they purchase this boat.

Source: Princess Yachts International plc.

reduced prices, and claim their free photo album. The loosely attached envelope attracts attention to the advertisement, because it changes the weight and the feel of the page, thus making it difficult to ignore, while the free album offer further encourages response. The envelope has all the necessary information about prices etc. on it so that if it became detached from the advertisement, it could still be used. Given the nature of the response sought in this case, getting people to put their films in the envelope and post them, the lack of a freephone response mechanism is entirely understandable.

Pay post (coupon) and freephone

In contrast to Neville Johnson above, Conquest Fitted Furniture uses direct response advertising in quality magazines to promote interest in its fitted office furniture. It uses a freephone 0800 number, provides a fax number and a coupon to send off to receive a brochure or arrange for a designer to call. It requests no more than the customer's name, address and telephone number for subsequent follow-up.

Freephone only

Although many companies are linking freephone numbers and websites, Mountfield ran a press advertising campaign using only a freephone telephone number through which readers could locate their nearest stockist or request a brochure on Mountfield lawn tractors. With a purchase price approaching £2,000 for its products, Mountfield thought that interested customers would be prepared to invest a little more time in the information gathering stage of the buying process. Similarly, David Wilson Homes offered no address but a free phone number and website address for seekers of more information.

Internet

With the growth of internet use, web response mechanisms even for standard media advertising are evolving rapidly and the main aim of some advertisements is to direct readers to a website. When Champion spark plugs, for instance, advertised in a Formula 1 supplement in a monthly magazine, the prime focus was a product picture and the only response mechanism was via the website (http://www.championeon.com). Palm Computing followed a similar approach when it advertised its Palm V model in France; it provided just an 0800 number and the website details (http://www.palm-europe.com), a pattern repeated by Siemens Computer Systems (http://www.sni.fr). The website provides access to far more detailed content and visual imagery than could ever be delivered by traditional advertisements, as can be seen by the Princess yacht example above.

Approaches to direct response advertising

As all these examples show, some organisations approach direct response much more seriously than others. The ones who expect the consumer to pay for a phone call or postage, or who expect the consumer to compose a letter rather than filling in a coupon, are immediately putting up barriers to response. Why should consumers make any undue effort, or even pay directly, to give an organisation the privilege of trying to sell them something? In the light of that view, organisations either need to have incredibly compelling direct response advertising that makes any effort or cost worthwhile or, more realistically, they need to minimise the effort and cost to the potential customer. Schofield (1994) confirms that certainly in B2B markets, response should be as easy as possible. The easier the response, the greater the number of enquiries and the greater the conversion rate and revenue per enquiry.

Direct response advertising on television

The use of direct response advertising on television (DRTV) is beginning to grow. Some products are marketed on satellite channels across Europe using toll-free telephone support. CDs and tapes, for example, are actively promoted on the music channels. Holiday companies use a toll-free line to receive requests for brochures, while the insurance industry is starting to appreciate the value of direct response television advertising to generate requests for quotes. If the advertisement is being used to sell off the screen (as opposed to simply generating enquiries) and hard cash is wanted, the risk limit is around £10–£15 and the product must be easily demonstrated and explained.

eg

Sight Savers International, the international blindness charity, uses DRTV to recruit more donors so that it can continue its work in the developing nations. The two main areas of its marketing budget are DRTV and direct mail. The advantage of television is the powerful images that can be presented, such as a young mother in Malawi suffering from trachoma, with the camera seeing through her eyes. The television can communicate not only the misery of those who are suffering, but also the immense relief and joy that comes as a result of treatment funded by SSI. It has used fragmented media to its advantage by targeting niche segments through satellite and cable, whereas terrestrial advertising costs would have been prohibitive (Kleinman, 2000).

Different media and more creative approaches encourage direct response. Book Club Associates (http://www.bca.co.uk) relies primarily on inserts in magazines relevant to specialist areas such as ancient and mediaeval history, the arts, fantasy and sci-fi and railways to sell membership to its range of clubs. Normally, very low priced introductory offers are designed to stimulate trial. It has also used door drops and television advertising to generate further enquiries.

eg

Even the phone number used can help generate responses, especially with radio advertising where the listener might have to remember a number after only hearing it rather than seeing it. Forte hotels, for example, uses the number 40 40 40, of course, while some previous classics included the insurance company with the owl in its logo, Guardian Direct, using 28 28 20 (too-whit, too-whit, too-woo) and BUPA's Dental Cover service with the number 230 230 (tooth hurty, tooth hurty).

Since Forte introduced the 40 40 40 line as part of a programme to centralise its telephone reservation system, it claimed to have improved its conversion of enquiries into sales from 25 per cent to 40 per cent. Some numbers are memorable in their own right, without strong links to the company or brand. Disney has 000000, for example, Yell's Talking Pages 0800 600 900 and BT 0800 800 800, while others have a memorable flow to them such as Fidelity Investments with 0800 414142, Renault with 0800 525150, Life Search for insurance policies with 0800 316 3166 and Tourism Ireland with 0800 917 2002, the direct line for its 2002 brochures.

Direct response has only been possible because of allied developments in the widespread use of credit cards that make remote ordering easier, the use of freephone numbers, and improvements in response handling techniques and technology. However, the principles of advertising described in Chapter 15 still have to be applied when the specific elements of direct response messages and media are considered. McAlevey (2001) identified a number of principles to follow to enable more effective direct response. Although generated in a North Amercian cultural context, a number of them are relevant to European DR users seeking greater impact and higher response rates. The principles are:

- the focus should always be on what sells;
- don't always reinvent the wheel when designing campaigns;
- make the 'offer' the central theme of the creative execution;
- long copy can sell if the reader is engaged;
- select creativity that sells, not that which just looks good;
- always test and measure response;
- select and retain media not on their ratings, but on their ability to sell for you;
- always ask for the order or for further action. It must be loud, clear, easy to understand and easy to execute.

The important point about direct response is that it should not just be advertising with an 0800 number or coupon tacked on. In developing the campaign, the creative execution and planning should be driven by the premise that the more effective the message and delivery mechanism, the greater the sales response. The focus then is always on measurable outputs; i.e. sales. To McAlevey, success is 40 per cent the offer, 40 per cent the media/lists used and 20 per cent the message creativity. Perhaps that is why some of the hard-hitting direct response television adsvertisements for double glazing (no names!) are such a turn off.

Telemarketing

While direct response advertising and direct mail both imply the use of an impersonal initial approach through some kind of written or visual material, **telemarketing** makes a direct personal, verbal approach to the potential customer. However, although this brings benefits from direct and interactive communication, it is seen by some as extremely intrusive. If the telephone rings, people feel obliged to answer it there and then, and tend to feel annoyed and disappointed if it turns out to be a sales pitch rather than a friend wanting a good gossip. The Henley Centre found that only 16 per cent of consumers actually welcome calls and the rest are basically not interested (McLuhan, 2001). Techniques are being employed by telemarketers to overcome this, including grabbing attention early on by using accents to link with the brand. One company, for example, employs New Zealanders and South Africans to link off-road vehicles with rugged voices! Further stereotypes are also exploited: a Northern or Irish accent is often felt to be friendly, while a Scottish or Yorkshire voice might be associated with people who are careful with money, an especially useful attribute if the product is financial services. If the brand is aimed at children then someone with a young voice might be preferred. Ultimately, consumers want the caller to be nice and to know what they are talking about rather than reading from a script. Not least, they want callers to be as fast as possible (Murphy, 2001). Despite that, it can be very difficult to curtail a telemarketing call without resorting to rudeness, and many people feel awkward about doing that. At least a piece of direct mail can be dismissed and put in the bin quickly and without leaving a feeling that someone has been offended in some way.

Telemarketing, therefore, can be defined as any planned and controlled activity that creates and exploits a direct relationship between customer and seller, using the telephone.

eg

Hertz Lease is a leading vehicle leasing and management service provider in the UK and European B2B markets. Rather than the sales force using cold calling and prospecting techniques, Hertz Lease decided that it would prefer them to use their time more effectively by following up qualified sales leads. For over five years HSM, a telemarketing company, has been assigned to generate around 200 sales appointments per month for the sales force to follow up. As part of the exercise, HSM was contracted to build a database on company and fleet information for research purposes and to guide telemarketing campaign planning. Over time, the role of telemarketing has changed and as the internal staff have become better trained and sufficiently experienced to take dialogue further with senior staff in the buying organisation, now all inbound enquiries are handled by the HSM team.

There have been a number of benefits from the relationship between Hertz Lease and HSM, not only by generating sales leads and databases, but also helping to improve the productivity of the sales force. They can now concentrate on the hottest clients, with whom their higher-level sales and negotiation skills can be used to best advantage. In addition, regular contact can be maintained with the target prospect base using direct mail, telemarketing and e-mail marketing contact. This enables a more timely response, should a customer seriously consider changing or developing its vehicle management system. The sales team could not maintain such a presence cost effectively (http://www.hsm.co.uk).

Hertz Lease is an example of **outbound telemarketing**, where the organisation contacts the potential customer. **Inbound telemarketing**, where the potential customer is encouraged to contact the organisation, is also popular. This is used not only in direct response advertising, but also for customer care lines, competitions and other sales promotions.

eg

Prolog offers a range of telemarketing and order fulfilment services. One of its clients, Screenshop, demands a 24 × 7 × 52 service, as it is a 24-hour shopping channel operating on satellite television. Screenshop operates in a fast-moving environment with the accent on selling high volumes of a variety of products from kitchenware to music collections. It sells via DRTV, over the web and through catalogues. Prolog offers an integrated service with telephone order taking, customer service, high volume pick and pack, order processing and banking. This leaves Screenshop to concentrate on purchasing, merchandising and marketing.

Screenshop selects its 'TV infomercials' according to the products to be offered and the viewing habits of its target audience. The schedules selected are provided to Prolog in advance so that it can adjust the staffing levels to give a timely response. Engaged lines can mean lost business. Technology is also employed to ensure that calls are routed to available agents and that additional agents can be brought in if demand exceeds expectation (http://www.prolog.uk.com; http://www.screenshop.co.uk).

Scope for telemarketing

Telephone rental or ownership is high across Europe, averaging over 80 per cent of households, and thus if an appropriate role can be defined for telemarketing within the planned promotional mix, it represents a powerful communication tool. As with personal selling (*see* pp. 695 *et seq.*), there is direct contact and so dialogue problems can be addressed. Similarly, the customer's state of readiness to commit themselves to a course of action can be assessed and improved through personal persuasion, and efforts made to move towards a positive outcome. Telemarketing can also be used to support customer service initiatives. A carefully designed and managed inbound telemarketing operation can provide an important, sometimes 24-hour, point of contact for customers. This is an important part of maintaining an ongoing relationship with the customer.

eg

Abbey National Direct has a system that recognises the telephone number from which an inbound call originates and can route the call to the staff member who dealt with that customer last time they called. This clearly allows the customer to develop a more personal relationship with the organisation as well as providing consistency. As the one-to-one relationship develops, it also becomes easier for the staff member to try to sell other financial services products to that customer.

Nevertheless, outbound telemarketing in particular is still not widely accepted by consumers and is often seen as intrusive. Where customers have an existing relationship with an organisation, however, and where the purpose of the call is not hard selling, they are less suspicious. Research by Datamonitor, reported by Bird (1998), found that 75 per cent of respondents like receiving calls that check their satisfaction with the product or service or that simply thank them for their custom. The figure drops to less than half if the call is linked to information gathering and a sales pitch. If the outbound calls are badly handled, research by Outbound Teleculture has indicated that 70 per cent of customers become annoyed and in some cases this damages the reputation and prospects for future business for that company.

Marketing tasks. It would be misleading, however, to imply that telemarketing is only about high pressure selling. As a form of personal selling, it certainly lends itself to that kind of application, but there is a whole range of marketing tasks that can be performed using telemarketing methods. As Table 18.4 shows, telemarketing has a clear role at an operational level, not only making sales, but also improving distribution, customer service, technical support, information gathering and credit control. A particular challenge is to integrate it creatively into the rest of the promotional mix.

Table 18.4 Applications of telemarketing

- Generate leads
- Screen leads before follow-up
- Arrange appointments for representatives
- Direct sales
- Encourage cross/up selling
- Dealer support
- Account servicing
- Market research
- Test marketing

eg

When easyJet was launched in 1995, most of its bookings were made through the easyland telephone reservation centre at Luton. It was almost exclusively a telemarketing reservation system, as travel agents were not used. The website was launched in 1997 but online bookings were not possible until the following year. Since that date, however, the transformation has been virtually 100 per cent. A new online booking policy was introduced so that seats booked more than two months in advance of a departure date could only be purchased online. This did not deter passengers, as by September 2000 over 4 million seats were sold online, 85 per cent of total seat sales and by July 2001 over 10 million seats were sold online as the airline continued to expand. The early forecast for online booking was just 30 per cent of total sales!

The reasons for the shift reflect increased internet usage, the incentives offered by easyJet to book online, and its desire to keep costs low. Whereas the internet can handle six or seven e-mail bookings per second, the call centre struggled during peak periods, especially if there was an unexpected upsurge in demand. Internet bookings are cheaper for easyJet to process and therefore any move to end telephone booking completely would be consistent with the low cost airline position (Wootliff, 2001). In comparison Ryanair, another low cost airline, takes about 65 per cent of its bookings online. The interesting question is whether the internet will eventually take over inbound booking and reservation services in most sectors in which the levels of advice and information are routine or low.

easyJet planes whether on the ground or in the air are instantly recognisable with their bright orange logo.

Source: easyJet.com.

Although the percentage of marketing budgets allocated to telemarketing is still low, in some sectors it is above 10 per cent of all spend (Cobb, 1998). The main uses of telemarketing in organisations are shown in Table 18.5.

Inbound telemarketing

Customer service and care lines are an important growth area within inbound telemarketing. Ideally these are set up to allow customers to make direct contact with an organisation to ask questions or to pass comment on products and their use. Some centres can also take

Table 18.5 The use of telemarketing

New business lead generation	28%
Customer care	26%
Customer service	26%
Brand loyalty	14%
Crisis management	6%

Source: Cobb (1998), reproduced from *Marketing* magazine with the permission of the copyright owner, Haymarket Business Publications Limited.

direct orders. Many companies use call centres and customer service centres. Sitel, for example, (http://www.sitel.com) has as it clients Mitsubishi. British Gas, Nokia and Renault to name but a few. Renault outsourced its call centre to Sitel in Spain and from that an integrated electronic solution was developed, initially in Spain and now across Europe, whereby Sitel would manage electronic and customer service support. This included the dealer network, information requests for new model launches, warranty and insurance services, bad debt recovery, leasing enquiries, lead generation, sales of accessories and database verification. All electronic media are used: telephone, e-mail, fax, and internet offering five different languages for use in many European countries. This example is typical of integrated solutions that are tailored to the requirements of the client and are staffed by dedicated and trained professionals employed by Sitel. Sitel also works in the B2B arena, for example offering technical support and customer help desks, warranty support and account management programmes for computer hardware and software suppliers.

Care line numbers are sometimes included in advertisements and on packaging to assist consumer response. Kellogg provides an 0800 number for comments and enquiries through a customer care line open from 8 a.m. to 6 p.m. Monday to Friday.

eg

PPP Healthcare uses inbound telemarketing to improve standards of customer care to its members. Initially the concept started as a customer helpline that was staffed by qualified professionals such as pharmacists, midwives and nurses who could dispense advice to the worried caller. The service was not just for those wishing to make a claim, but could handle even routine calls from policy holders such as how to treat an upset stomach or sunburn. Staff at its health information service, Health at Hand, have access to a large electronic library to provide members with the latest information on health topics. The service has evolved to provide advice not just on medical issues but on the organisations that can help, health scares, and where to locate mobile doctors, late-night chemists and other out of hours support. PPP, however, goes to some lengths to advise callers that Health at Hand is no substitute for a GP, that it will not provide a diagnosis and that the information it provides either verbally or via fact sheets should not be used for self-diagnosis (http://www.ppphealthcare.co.uk). The service has been so successful that some pharmaceutical companies have contracted the service to provide healthcare advice to their own clients, as part of raising their service levels. Pharmaceutical companies have an interest in ensuring compliance with the instructions on medicines to effect a cure and to reinforce brand loyalty as well as avoiding litigation. By printing helpline numbers on bottles or packs, the customer is free to call in and sort out usage problems such as side effects and drug combinations.

There is an added advantage in operating a customer care and service line as it enables the organisation to build a database of enquirers, their concerns and profiles and even buying patterns. When Boots set up a care line for hayfever sufferers it received over 100,000 calls, an ideal database for building a subsequent promotional campaign offering remedies.

Outbound telemarketing

Outbound telemarketing has also grown in recent years, reflecting the increasing cost of a salesperson's time and a greater acceptance of the telephone, especially in repeat business situations. Productivity can be high from these centres and the calls can be carefully targeted to reach the right audience. The latter is especially true as databases become more sophisticated and various loyalty schemes make a more receptive audience. There is a world of difference between receiving a sales call for double glazing two years after having it installed by a competitor and a call from an insurance company advising you to enhance your cover and take advantage of a special offer. B2B outbound has been in use for some time, and is regarded as an important means of making appointments or taking repeat business, although the latter is now being strongly challenged by direct IT links. The growth area in this sector is in low-value orders for small businesses that may not merit frequent direct calling. Some companies are still reluctant, however, to use outbound telemarketing in consumer markets because of its perceived intrusiveness. Clarke (2001) suggests a number of do's and don'ts of telemarketing, as shown in Table 18.6.

Table 18.6 Do's and don'ts of telemarketing

Do:

- ✓ Make sure phone agents know your brand and what you're seeking to achieve
- ✓ Opt for centres that have flexible technology so updating and upgrading it are a simple process
- ✓ Look for a wide technology base including reliable hardware, reporting and predictive dialling
- ✓ Maximise opportunities – ensure operators are trained and aware enough to turn complaint calls into sales
- ✓ Make sure your automated call handling has no loops and is simple to use
- ✓ Give the caller the chance to talk to a live operator at any time
- ✓ Use a medium that's relevant to both customers and products, and give customers immediate service
- ✓ Ensure your callers receive a service that matches your brand in tone and handling

Don't:

- ✗ Be tempted by cutting-edge technology that may prove difficult to use
- ✗ Waste your time and resources: customers are more likely to accept outbound calls from companies that have a good reputation, which sell products relevant to them and with which they have an existing relationship
- ✗ Keep valued customers waiting on the line for too long: try to give them an honest estimated waiting time

Source: Clarke (2001), reproduced from *Marketing* magazine with the permission of the copyright owner, Haymarket Business Publications Limied.

eg

Seeboard sells energy to approximately 2 million households and businesses in the UK, mainly selling gas and electricity in the Kent, Sussex and Surrey areas. Although it had a strong brand awareness and customer base within its home territory, when it decided to expand beyond that to elsewhere in the UK it was faced with trying to reach a potentially large number of consumers with a limited marketing infrastructure, little existing brand awareness, and heavy competition. It contracted Telegen to provide an outbound telemarketing service to target the residential and business sectors outside its home patch. Telegen established a dedicated outbound call centre to include dialling technology, digital call recording capability and tailored telesales training modules dedicated to Seeboard's requirements. Using prepared IT technology, the operators had access to scripts, tariffs and payment mechanisms to help with a smooth conversion.

Despite it being a tough marketing challenge, the operation has, according to Telegen, exceeded Seeboard's expected telesales performance, including improved hourly agent performance, acquisition cost reduction and shorter than expected lead-in times for system development and set up. Within a 6-month period Telegen has expanded the Seeboard team to over 100 full-time staff, suggesting that conversion effectiveness is moving in the right direction (http://www.seeboard.com; http://www.telegenuk.com).

Many of the techniques used in selling, considered in the previous chapter, can be applied to outbound telephone calls. Building trust, conversational styles, empathising with the customer and understanding and being able to communicate with confidence the product benefits relevant to the listener are all crucial. This can be a challenge if the call centre staff are not well trained or if there is a high turnover of staff so that relationship building becomes more difficult. Perhaps even more important is that the marketer should understand when outbound telemarketing has a role to play, and when it is best to focus on generating enquiries to follow up with a personal visit. Call centres are becoming more sophisticated in both storing and using information as well as offering multi-media, e-mail or SMS as well as traditional telemarketing. By using the knowledge base developed, a centre can become more effective in working with clients when designing its services. Telemarketers are especially keen to take relationship marketing roles away from the host organisation along the lines of the Renault example on p. 761 (Miles, 2001c).

Limitations of telemarketing

In addition, and again in common with personal selling, there are limitations on the practical application of telemarketing, and a number of operational and regulatory issues have to be considered.

Operational issues. For inbound calls in particular, the organisation has to ensure that the system is designed to cope with the expected volume of calls and can handle them speedily and efficiently. Potential customers who cannot get through at all, or who are kept waiting, are likely to give up trying. The problem is made worse by the fact that 80 per cent of responses to a direct response television advertisement, for example, will be made within 10 minutes of the advertisement being screened. After 12 minutes, the response rate is likely to be negligible. Although large volumes of calls are not common within such timescales, a call centre needs flexibility as many organisations set call response time standards, such as '85 per cent of calls to be answered within 20 seconds', and in some cases the target may be as low as 10 seconds. That can be a challenge, such as when the unexpectedly early announcement of the Norwich Union demutualisation generated 9,000 calls in 30 minutes (Curtis, 1998)!

Another issue, partly operational and partly strategic, concerns the kind of line to use. Providers such as BT offer a number of options to the marketer, some of which are free or cheap to the caller, others of which carry a premium rate charge.

Clearly, freephone numbers are most attractive to the customer, but do incur costs for the organisation providing the service. These costs have to be balanced against the enhanced service level effectiveness provided by freephone numbers. In 1998, BT reported a 140 per cent increase in customer use of 0345 numbers and a doubling in use of 0800 numbers to 2.7 million minutes. Most customers recognise 0800 as being freephone, but the understanding of the other numbers drops to around 57 per cent for 0345 and just 23 per cent for 0990 numbers. Organisations now use 0800 numbers as an integral part of their promotional strategy, such as Renault and Tourism Ireland, mentioned earlier. Marketers need to find the code and tariff system that works best for their business and then ensure that the supporting infrastructure and service are in place to handle customer expectations.

eg

Directory and information service providers such as Scoot use telephone response mechanisms to support the online information request service. Scoot was formed in 1995, originally as Freepages, and initially relied on freephone numbers such as 0800 192192 in the UK for caller enquiries. Now Scoot UK provides information on almost two million businesses, services and cinemas throughout the UK, 24 hours a day, 365 days a year. Its main service is to put buyers in touch with sellers, enabling them to connect via the telephone, Vodafone 333, the internet at http://www.scoot.co.uk, WAP and digital TV. It provides a choice of local suppliers along with enough information for the customer to make an initial choice. With mixed media contact, especially with the growth of online data searching, a new telephone number was introduced, 0900 2 192192 that was no longer free, but charged 50p per minute to use the call centre in Telford. The centre handles over 2 million calls per month, including the non-emergency 999 calls for eight police forces. A similar charging system was also introduced in the Netherlands with a 0900 0700 number (http://www.scoot.com).

Outbound telemarketing has its own set of problems. As already mentioned, cold calling for sales purposes is not popular with the public, and has increasingly become the subject of regulation and restriction. In Germany most cold calling is banned whereas in the UK it is permitted, although organisations are not allowed to use automatic dialling systems that play prerecorded sales messages. Outbound customer service calls are useful, however. These might be used as an after-sales follow-up to check that customers are satisfied with their purchases. They might also be integrated into a longer-term relationship marketing strategy.

eg

Next Directory, for example, tried an experiment with 'welcome calls', made to new customers just after receipt of their first order. After six months, it was found that 92 per cent of those customers who had been 'welcomed' were still active, against only 86 per cent of those who had not received a welcome call. Furthermore, the welcomed customers were spending about 30 per cent more.

Whatever the purpose of outbound telemarketing, it is important to ensure that the operators making the calls are well trained, knowledgeable and courteous. Well-targeted and carefully prepared lists of numbers to call can help to reduce the irritation factor to those called, although pre-screening can be difficult. It can be especially annoying or upsetting to get calls for people who have died or who have moved away. Technology can help to deal with the volume and efficiency of outgoing calls. A central computer dials a number and routes the call to an operator when a reply is detected. If the number called is engaged, or if an answering machine is reached, the computer terminates the call and puts that number to the back of the queue to try again later. The increasing use of technology will help to expand and improve the operational capability of call centres. In most cases customers will think that they are talking direct to the company, so if it goes wrong it is the company, not the call centre, that is blamed and risks damaging its image.

Regulatory issues. Pan-European telemarketing is not easy, partly because of language and cultural differences, and partly because of the variation in what is and what is not allowed in different countries. The EU has developed the Distance Selling Directive, an attempt to harmonise regulations to make cross-border direct marketing easier. The original proposals would have meant a complete ban on cold calling by telephone and on unsolicited e-mail. Lobbying by the direct marketing industry, however, managed to get these bans dropped from the proposals. Instead, e-mail can still be used in unsolicited approaches, but prior consent is needed for telephone cold calling. Under the 1999 Telecommunications Regulations, therefore, telephone calls can only be made if solicited, so the target customer has to either agree in advance that calls can be made or the list must be cleansed using the **telephone preference service** (TPS) (Coad, 2001).

The TPS is designed to protect consumers from unwanted communication. In the UK, for example, consumers can register with a central agency if they do not wish to receive cold calls. The problem is, however, that currently not all organisations are members of the voluntary scheme, and thus consumers will continue to get calls from non-subscribing businesses. The scheme also excludes calls to business numbers, market research calls and customer service calls. Similar schemes exist in parts of Europe, for instance in the Netherlands, and the EU is looking to impose preference schemes on all member states eventually. All of this is part of a legislative process to stop list information being used irresponsibly and without the individual's consent. Effectively, it is giving power back to the consumer.

E-communication and new media

The rapidly growing area of e-communications and new media will be considered in depth in Chapter 24. It is probably too early to appreciate the full potential impact of some of the recent developments, but the growth of web and online marketing, texting and e-marketing gives marketers the ability to reach large audiences cost effectively while retaining the targeting power of direct marketing. The challenge for planning an integrated marketing communications programme is to understand the potential of these relatively new and fast-changing areas, consider how they will fit into the mix, and execute them effectively. Whether it is web, WAP, SMS (and increasingly EMS), or e-mail communication, each information delivery gateway needs to be considered and exploited to its full advantage. In the previous sections of this chapter we have seen how some of these vehicles are already being used. At present, they are largely supplementing other communication elements, but as in the easyJet example, substitution over time is inevitable. What is certain, however, is that as bandwidth speeds improve dramatically, 3G generation technology becomes widely accepted (*see* pp. 382 *et seq.*), and users become fully adapted to new media, there will be many more creative opportunities open to the marketer.

Mail order

Mail order, as the name suggests, involves the purchase of products featured in advertising or selected from a catalogue. The goods are not examined before ordering, and thus the advertisement or the catalogue has to do a good sales job. Mail order companies promote themselves through any media, and receive orders through the mail, by telephone or via an agent. Direct selling through one-off, product-specific advertisements (such as the Franklin Mint operation) has largely been covered at pp. 753 *et seq.* under direct response advertising. This section will therefore concentrate on the mail order catalogue sector.

In the 1960s, the mail order catalogue in the UK was a very heavy and comprehensive document, selling absolutely everything a household could possibly need from clothes, through to toys and power tools, on extended credit. Catalogues were mainly aimed at the poorer sections of society who could not afford to buy things for cash when they wanted them. Mail order catalogues ran on an agency system in which the agent sold to friends and earned commission on sales. The agent was responsible for collecting the owed money weekly. The main strengths of the traditional catalogue were as shown in Figure 18.3.

Weaknesses of traditional catalogues

Traditional catalogues did, however, have their weaknesses, and these are discussed below.

Figure 18.3 The traditional strengths of mail order

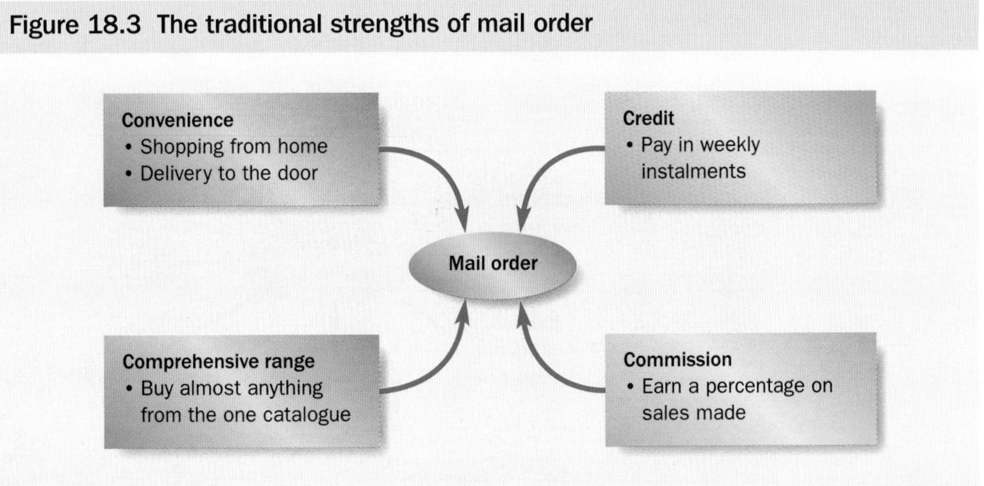

Lack of speed. Catalogues asked customers to allow 28 days for delivery, and it often did take as long as that for orders to be processed and deliveries made. That lead time was in addition to the time taken for an order to pass through the postal system and be delivered to the organisation. It also took a long time before customers would be informed that an item was out of stock, and then they would have to go through the whole ordering process again.

Downmarket image. The range and quality of merchandise, the emphasis on credit and the presentation of the catalogues meant that mail order was seen very much as a preserve of the C2, D and E socioeconomic groupings.

Lack of targeting. Although the general image was downmarket, there was historically little effort to target catalogue offers closely to customer needs. Catalogues were generalists, so each customer was offered everything. This meant that a great deal of what was offered, including mid-season promotions, was irrelevant to many customers.

The agency system. Many customers just did not want the bother of running an agency. The paperwork and the debt collection involved made it unattractive, even when commission was being earned. Customers wanted to be able to purchase for themselves and their immediate families, with as little administrative responsibility as possible.

Modern mail order catalogues

The home shopping market is now going through a period of rapid growth, as much as 20 per cent per year according to Smith (2001), and it is now worth £15 bn in the UK. Although that figure covers all forms of home shopping, including online purchasing, it is dominated by mail order catalogue sellers. Modern mail order catalogues have abandoned the large, comprehensive catalogues and are now more varied, better quality, and niche targeted. Some of the reasons why catalogues have become popular again are shown in Figure 18.4. A key factor in the change has been the Europeans catching up by learning from the US experience. Developments in database building techniques, customer acquisition, promotion, fulfilment, postal services and logistics have all helped the shift towards speciality catalogue selling. An average specialty catalogue in the UK might have a listing of around 1 million names, compared with only 150,000 nine years ago. Germany boasts even bigger list universes, while the French list market is similar in size to the UK's, and Scandinavia's is not far behind (Metcalfe, 2000). Now, approximately one in ten households in Europe receives one or more shopping catalogues each year.

Figure 18.4 How modern catalogues overcame mail order's weaknesses

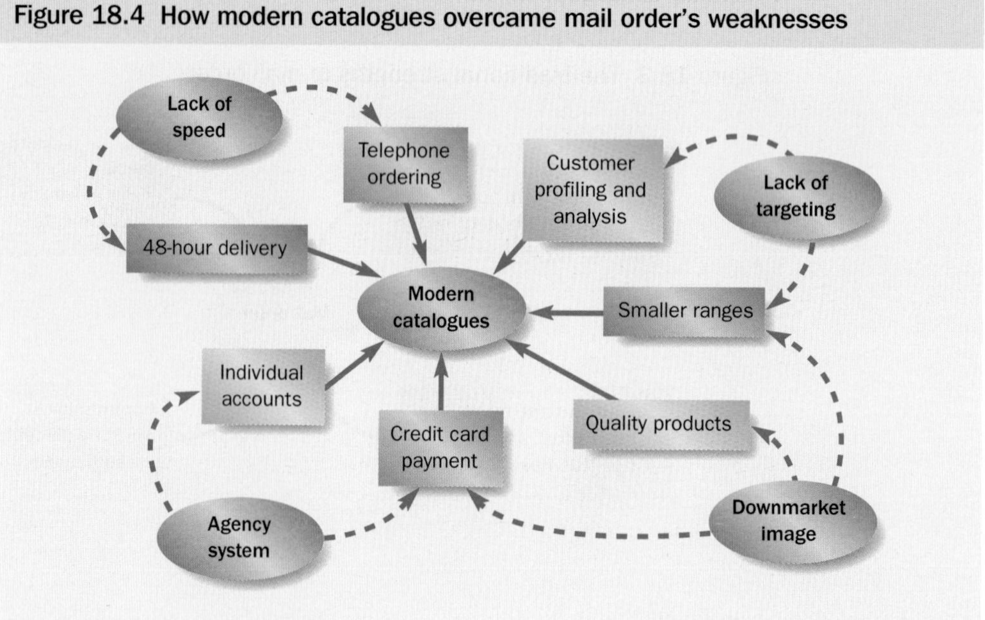

eg

The *Next Directory* pioneered the renaissance of the mail order catalogue in the UK, first by trading on its well-established, respected and upmarket High Street name. It also speeded up the ordering process and the delivery logistics, through improved technology and distribution systems, to allow telephone ordering and guaranteeing 48-hour delivery. This was the first really high quality catalogue in terms of graphics, photography and the inclusion of fabric swatches. Most importantly, Next Directory targeted the young, trendy end of the market with high disposable income; 40 per cent of its customers were in the A and B socio-economic groups.

The *Next Directory* broke the mould in terms of attitudes towards mail order, and opened the way for others to move upmarket. The traditional generalist catalogues still exist, albeit much slimmer than in the past, but there is now a wide range of specialist mail order publications, covering goods from garden plants to toys, books and clothing. Even the generalist catalogues now have the technology to analyse their customers' profiles and buying habits and can, therefore, make tailored, relevant individual offers. Payment systems are much more flexible, allowing cash payment, credit if customers want it, or the use of credit cards if they prefer, while the agency system has been pushed into the background.

There are now two main types of catalogue.

Non-store catalogues. Non-store catalogues are catalogues that do not have links with High-Street retail outlets. The catalogue is the sole 'shop window'. Traditionally, catalogues carrying the full range of household and fashion goods have been seen as downmarket, and they have found it difficult to move upmarket in the consumer's eyes.

Following Next's example, a number of new smaller catalogues of specialist clothing, such as Lands' End and Racing Green, aimed at a more upmarket audience, have emerged. Other catalogues in DIY, B2B goods, computers and many other sectors also now exist, and there is greater acceptance among more affluent segments of buying from smaller, more targeted catalogues rather than the larger, more traditional blockbusters.

eg

Lands' End is an international mail order catalogue seller. Although it does have sixteen stores in the US, two factory stores in the UK and a store in Japan, the bulk of its business is mail order and online selling. In 2001 in the US, it distributed 269 million catalogues and on its website it claims that it gets between 40,000 and 50,000 calls on a typical day, but during the Christmas period this can rise to 100,000 calls a day on 1,100 phone lines. Eight catalogues are available, although in Europe the catalogue choice is more limited. It has 6.7 million customers who have made at least one purchase in the previous year. Its US mailing list has 31 million names.

The catalogue came to the UK in 1991 and with a 24 × 7 × 52 operation, carefully selected merchandise, a full guarantee that merchandise can be returned at any time for any reason, the operation has grown to make Lands' End one of the dominant players in the mail order market. Although telephone ordering still predominates, the online ordering facility is rapidly growing in popularity. In addition, with the wider acceptance of websites, it is becoming much easier to enter markets than in the era when everything depended upon the catalogue.

The website increases the speed with which a database can be developed in a new market. From registrations on the web, it is far easier now to ensure that the catalogues reach people who are interested rather than having to rent a list of names. When Lands' End entered the French market, it used only PR and some limited media advertising to attract customers to its website. As the list builds, it plans to introduce a paper catalogue (Sliwa, 2001; http://www.landsend.co.uk).

This kind of catalogue is really a form of distribution channel, in that the operator performs the tasks of merchandise assembly, marketing and customer service. The important thing is to find the selection of merchandise appropriate to the market niche served, and to design an appealing kind of service package (in terms of ordering mechanisms, delivery, returns, etc.).

eg

A number of niche companies use mail order to expand their customer base. James Meade offers timeless classic clothes through five targeted mail order catalogues, two retail stores in Bath and Salisbury and more recently an online ordering site. Robert Humm sells old and out of print railway and waterway books to an international customer base. Again it has a shop and a website, but the catalogue released two or three times a year often contains collections not offered elsewhere and, therefore, customers are charged for the privilege of receiving it. Finally, Orvis specialises in fishing merchandise, primarily through catalogue selling but since 1998, the online catalogue has been taking an increasing percentage of sales. All three companies have been successful in developing mail order databases from customer and enquirer lists and have used them to target their activities through specialised publications, increasingly well supported by online ordering facilities (http://www.orvis.co.uk; http://www.jamesmeade.com; http://www.roberthumm.co.uk).

Store catalogues. As a response to the increasing interest in the non-store sector, some retailers are producing their own catalogues clearly linked with their High Street operations. Such catalogues support retail sales by extending the shop window into the customer's home. They also expand coverage, reaching people who might otherwise find it difficult to get to a store, and trade on the retailer's reputation, building on its buying expertise.

eg

Laura Ashley decided to re-enter the mail order clothing catalogue sector in 2001 in order to compete with its main rival, Next. A trial was undertaken of a 28-page clothing catalogue distributed in its stores along with its home furnishings counterpart. The results were encouraging, and it was decided that the new catalogue should be launched on a quarterly basis, as part of the objective of becoming a multi-channel seller with retail stores, an online shop, and catalogues (*Marketing Week*, 2001b). Other retailers, such as Argos in the UK and IKEA, have gone as far as designing their entire retail concept around a catalogue. The shopper can browse through the catalogue at home, select goods and then go into a High Street 'showroom' to examine and purchase goods on the spot. This seems to combine the best elements of both the catalogue and the retail outlet.

Advantages and disadvantages of mail order

Regardless of the type of operation, the basis of the mail order business is the catalogue. As a major selling tool, a great deal of thought and effort is required to get it right and tailor it to the target market. The main advantages of mail order to the consumer are convenience and efficiency and, for some, easy credit. This is especially valuable in areas remote from larger city centres where regular shopping trips are difficult. For the organisation, by avoiding expensive High Street locations and the associated display and personal selling costs, the opportunity is provided for a wider variety of lower cost offerings. However, unless catalogues are updated regularly, and unless shoppers are happy not to experience the 'fun' of trial and shopping around for speciality items, the catalogue range may still not suit the more discerning shopper. Table 18.7 shows the perceived advantages and disadvantages of mail order over retailing from the consumer's perspective.

Teleshopping

Developments in communications technology in telephone, cable and satellite television are enabling significant growth in home-based shopping or **teleshopping** (*see* pp. 544 *et seq.*), even before the impact of the internet is considered. Direct marketing through these media can vary from fairly standard one-off advertisements screened during a normal commercial break, to slots featured in dedicated home shopping programmes or channels, usually involving product demonstration, often to a live audience. The main problem with developments in this area is not the capability of the technology, but the willingness of consumers to participate. Much depends, of course, on the number of homes connected to either satellite or cable systems, and there are variances across Europe, as we saw in Table 15.4 earlier. Digital television has, however, opened up further sales channels for companies such as QVC, which specialises

Table 18.7 Typical advantages of mail order over retail outlets

Advantages of shops over mail order	*Advantages of mail order over shops*
Can see/touch goods	Delay payment
Can try on/test goods	Choose at leisure
No delay in acquiring purchases	Choose at convenience
Easy to return goods	Easy to return goods
Easy to compare prices	Saves time
Cheaper	No pestering
Shopping is enjoyable	Shopping is not enjoyable
Advice/service available	Home delivery of purchases

in selling via the television and has 10,000 products on offer, There are also new opportunities for travel agencies and other retailers, a trend that is likely to continue.

The role of direct marketing in the promotional mix

The previous sections have defined the nature of direct marketing, and some of the tools and techniques involved. This section draws all that together to look at how direct marketing fits in with the other elements of the promotional mix. Although, as previous sections have shown, direct marketing can overlap with advertising, the key distinction between direct marketing and the other elements of the promotional mix is the personalised direct approach that relies on another communication channel, such as a telephone, mail or computer link. At the centre of the activity is a direct response from the customer. For example, a successful mail campaign depends on accurate personalised targeting and a response mechanism that can prompt further contact. It requires action by the customer to generate a measurable response to the promotional effort.

Objectives of direct marketing

There are a number of tasks that direct marketing can perform, depending on whether it is used for direct selling or supporting product promotion. The tasks may be related to ongoing transactions and relationships with customers. At its most basic, therefore, direct marketing can fulfil the following objectives.

Direct ordering

Direct marketing aims to enable direct ordering, whether by telephone, mail or, increasingly, by direct computer linkage. The use of credit cards, passwords and specific account numbers makes this possible. All kinds of direct marketing techniques can be used to achieve this, but the example of online ordering of CDs, mentioned earlier, is particularly interesting because sellers can both take the order and deliver the product immediately.

Under the EU's Distance Selling Directive, however, customers will have the right to change their minds within seven working days and withdraw from the contract. It will be the supplier's responsibility to make sure that customers have details of how to annul the transaction and to make any refund within 30 days.

Information giving

Direct marketing aims to open a channel of communication to enable potential customers to ask for further information. Information may be given verbally by a sales person, or through printed literature. Again, many techniques can achieve this objective, including customer care lines, as seen in the examples of PPP and Boots.

Visit generation

Direct marketing aims to invite a potential customer to call in and visit a store, show or event with or without prior notification. Nissan, for example, used direct mailshots targeted at fleet buyers to encourage them to visit the Nissan stand at the UK Motor Show.

Trial generation

Direct marketing aims to enable a potential customer to request a demonstration or product trial in the home, office or factory.

Achieving the objectives of direct marketing

These objectives can be achieved through a variety of means. They can be regarded as stages in the selling process from making the initial contact to creating a loyal customer. In some cases, the selling company may directly seek business, perhaps by using the telephone to contact lost or former customers, or by introducing a direct online ordering system for regular volume customers, such as dealers and distributors. In other cases, the response may come from the customer as a result of other promotional efforts, such as advertising or sales promotion campaigns.

How and when to use direct marketing

Initiation

An important decision in direct marketing is how best to use it at various stages of the relationship with the customer. The earliest stage, *initiation*, can be very difficult, as it involves creating the initial contact and making the first sale. A combination of appealing advertising and sales promotion techniques may be used, for example, to overcome the potential customer's initial apprehension and risk aversion. Thus in its introductory offer, a book club may reduce the customer's perceived risk through drastic price reductions on the first order (any four books for 99p each), and further specifying a period within which the books may be returned and membership cancelled without obligation. Alternatively, a sale on credit or even a free trial may ease the customer's initial fears, despite the high administration costs. Any of these methods makes it easier for customers to part with their cash on the first order, thus opening the opportunity for a longer-term relationship.

Relationship building

Most direct marketing is in fact aimed at the *relationship stage* customer. This is when the seller has started to build a buying profile, supported by more widely available non-purchase specific data. This enables a steady flow of offers to be made, whether by telephone, mailshot or catalogue update. Customers are also likely to be more responsive at this stage, as they have established confidence in product quality and service performance.

Combination selling

Finally, combination selling results from using contacts gained from one medium, such as a trade exhibition, for regular contact by direct marketing means. This could be the mailing of special offers, price lists, catalogues or telephone calls to gain a face-to-face meeting etc. The direct marketing activity is therefore used in combination with other methods. As mentioned earlier, Boots used the contacts generated by its pollen count care line to provide a mailing list for material on hayfever remedies and other related products.

Managing a direct marketing campaign

If direct marketing is going to create, build and maintain relationships with new and existing customers, then it needs to be carefully targeted and managed. A failure in any one of the main areas may result in inappropriate messages directed at the wrong targets. The main stages in the development of a direct marketing campaign are outlined in Figure 18.5 and considered in turn below.

Figure 18.5 Managing a direct marketing campaign

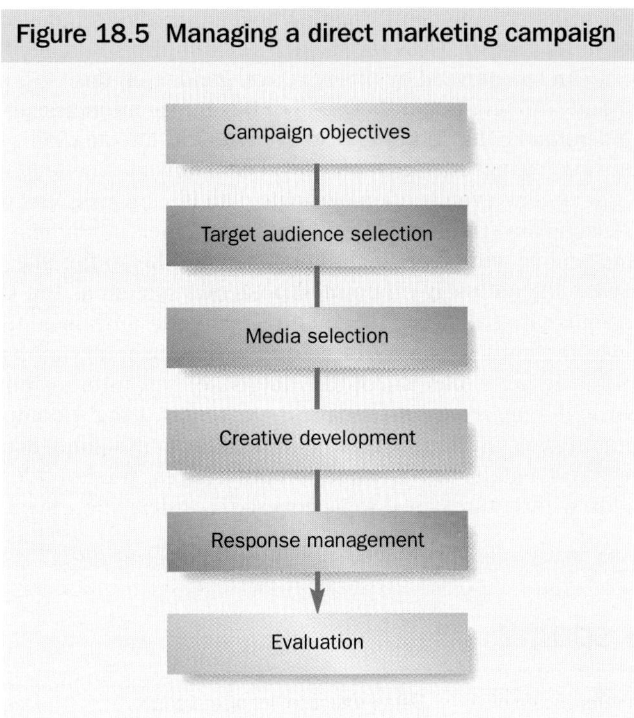

Campaign objectives

As with all marketing activities, the definition of objectives provides an important foundation, guiding subsequent management decisions. Direct marketing objectives must be linked with wider marketing and promotional objectives, and their definition must relate to target audiences and measurable results. Desired outcomes may be expressed in terms of market awareness, number of responses sought or conversion of enquiries into sales. Lloyds TSB tested telemarketing as a method of generating leads for its commercial finance division. A target of 110 good prospects in six weeks was set for the telemarketing agency, but the actual figure achieved was 300 in six weeks (http://www.listening.co.uk).

Prospects and target selection

Prospects can be in a number of states:

1 *Possible prospects*: a broad pool of potential customers about whom little is known.
2 *Probable prospects*: a list selected through qualification on some pre-determined criterion.
3 *Unconverted enquiries*: those who have had previous contact with the organisation, showing an interest in its products, but who have not yet committed themselves.
4 *Former or lost customers*: those who have purchased in the past, but not recently.
5 *Existing customers*: those with an established pattern of custom who are still actively purchasing.

Generally, the nearer the top of that list a prospect falls, the higher the cost per sale. Existing customers will need much less persuasion and incentive to buy than a completely unknown, 'cold' prospect. Note too that information held on present customers can always assist in the targeting of new customers. By identifying the key characteristics of the most valued existing customers, such as demographic, geodemographic and psychographic details (look back to Chapter 5 to brush up on the definitions of these terms), media preferences, products purchased and response profiles, qualification criteria can be defined for screening out the best new prospects, along with an offer that is most likely to appeal to them.

As pp. 750 *et seq.* indicated, commercial market research data agencies can provide lists of qualified prospects. The European Direct Marketing Association, for example, provides an international list search service and can also provide details of European list brokers.

The sheer volume of information held is surprising and also gives some cause for concern in terms of privacy. CCN database, for example, holds information on 43 million consumers that can be analysed by lifestyle, age, gender, creditworthiness, postcode, purchasing habits or any combination of these. All of this information assists in profiling and helps not only to understand behaviour, but also to predict it. Information systems are slowly, but inexorably, moving from geodemographic level data down to the individual household level.

Accessing even geodemographic data is, however, less easy in some European countries. Census data (the foundation of most commercial databases) and standards vary in format and timing, and postcode systems may not be so flexible. For example, Germany does not have such a closely pinpointed postcode system as the UK. In Germany, whole cities are often treated as homogeneous for postcode purposes, therefore undermining one of the main methods for direct targeting. Variations in systems mean that we are still some way from having a pan-European database, but international lists are becoming available through conference attendance, car rental, freight companies, hotels and publishers. In practical terms, there are some difficulties in designing pan-European software for database management. Issues of salutation differences, gender, titles, use of first names and different address structures need to be covered. Locally produced software may not easily adapt.

corporate social responsibility *in action*

Anyone for spam?

No, not the much revered Spam of Monty Python, school dinners and spam fritters fame, but the modern version that is fast becoming the most irritating side of direct marketing. Spam is the unsolicited e-mail messages sent to consumers from listings acquired without the receiver's permission. Although the EU Council of Ministers wants spam e-mail to be banned, with a preference for an opt-in scheme, the European Parliament has taken the position that spam should be outlawed only according to the wishes of individual member states (Boyarski *et al.*, 2002). The opt-in scheme already exists in Germany, Austria, Italy, Denmark and Sweden and others are likely to follow soon. In the case of Germany, where consumer protection is especially tough, sending unsolicited e-mails, although not illegal, does violate the country's competition laws. The direct marketing industry favours an opt-out approach, so if you forget to tick the box you can expect a flood of unwanted mail (Meller, 2001).

Although relevant laws and directives are in place, for example a 1999 privacy directive issued by the EU requiring marketers to tell consumers what data they will collect and retain, exactly how it will be used in the future, and then giving them the option of opting in or out of the process, spam e-mails and even some junk mail is still being sent that flouts the law (Dirskovski, 2001; Bertagnoli, 2001). In the UK, the 1998 Data Protection Act also prohibits spamming. Although junk mail has been progressively legislated against, through tighter controls on the resale of mailing lists and the obligation on direct marketers to allow consumers to opt-in for additional mailings, it is not the same for direct e-mail campaigns in which everything from financial services to 'herbal Viagra' and outright pornography has been promoted on an unsolicited basis. If a reply is made, even to tell them to get lost, your existence is confirmed and another batch of e-mails will soon arrive, some of which may contain viruses. It is also a problem if you want to let children near the computer.

There are some interesting variants to spamming. In the UK, viral campaigns are regarded as entirely legitimate, where you can relay a web page and message on to a friend in return for a small incentive. Handbag.com, for example, a London-based women's portal covering relationships, health, careers and beauty, has a list of 150,000 users and logged a 48 per cent response rate with a recent viral campaign (Bertagnoli, 2001). By sending on messages, the list is expanded without significant effort from the marketer.

Unlike junk mail, it is much harder to legislate against spamming because junk e-mail originating from Russia or the Far East is not under local jurisdiction and it is difficult for the ISPs to track down and stop it. Spammers have little regard for the law or the impact on the DM industry as a whole and will move their operations to places whence it is not illegal to send spam e-mail. The annual cost of handling this number one source of customer complaints has been estimated at £17 mn (Otley, 2002). Although filtering software can help by picking up key words and phrases such as sex, Viagra and 'xxx action', the only real solution is never to reply to any spammed e-mails and never to give out your e-mail address. Word screening can be especially difficult if you are in the erection business, whether in steel or concrete! All of this unwanted activity could have a knock-on effect on other areas of direct marketing such as direct mail and telemarketing, if consumers become more resentful of unwanted intrusion. It will also affect legitimate direct marketing organisations, as the opt-in approach will reduce the power of listings. Spam is not synonymous with direct marketing, and indeed it is not good practice for many organisations as it does not involve accurate targeting. It is, however, giving the industry a bad name and it will, if not stopped, make legitimate e-mail marketing campaigns such as those considered in Chapter 24, more difficult.

Sources: Bertagnoli (2001); Boyarski *et al.* (2002); Dirskovski (2001); Meller (2001); Otley (2002).

Media selection

After the initial selection of the target customer group, the most appropriate media need to be selected to generate the planned response. The full range of media discussed in Chapters 14 and 15 are available, but their use will be influenced by the size and profile of audience reached, availability, the predicted cost per sale, and their general cost effectiveness for implementing a multimedia or single-medium campaign. In terms of cost, for example, Fill (1999) estimates that to reach a decision maker in an organisation, telephone selling would cost about £10, direct mail about £1.50 and a personal sales call about £175. Although these figures are very generalised, they do underline the importance of cost effectiveness and the need to justify media choices in terms of objectives and expected benefits.

The choice of medium will also depend on what stage in the buying process the prospective customers have reached. Three main stages can be identified.

1 *Response initiation*. The initial contact, generating an expression of interest, can be achieved through almost any medium, for example broadcast and print advertising, magazine inserts, mailshots, or door-to-door leaflet drops. We have already looked at the various response mechanisms (freephone, freepost, etc.), and discussed their role in generating the desired outcome (*see* pp. 753 et seq.).
2 *Information and action*. Responding to the customer's request for more information and, where necessary, fulfilling the order and delivery process involves more direct contact from seller to buyer. Appropriate media include direct mail, telephone, point-of-sale information and the sales force (particularly in B2B markets).
3 *After-sales*. Once customers have been created, it is important to keep in touch with them and promote new offers from time to time. Again, the seller needs to be proactive through media such as direct mail, telemarketing and the sales force.

Experience with direct marketing suggests the importance of an integrated multimedia campaign. This means ensuring that the best combination of techniques is used to move the potential customer through to a sale. The Harley-Davidson vignette on p. 745 highlighted the importance of an integrated campaign in which direct marketing can play an important part.

Creative development

Depending on the nature of the direct marketing campaign, a brief may be developed for either internal specialists or external consultants. This brief is similar to that used in advertising and sales promotion, and relates the target customers' needs with marketing objectives and product benefits on offer. There are a number of areas that need to be addressed, as shown in Figure 18.6. These are discussed in somewhat more detail below.

Figure 18.6 Issues influencing creative development

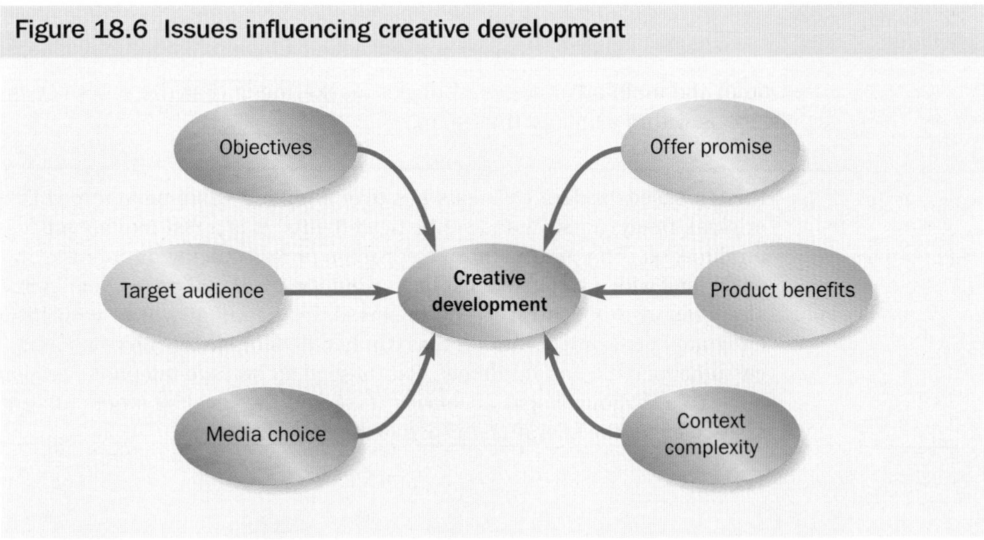

1 *Objectives.* These indicate what the campaign is expected to achieve and defines the required response targets.
2 *Product benefits.* These describe the key features and relate them to the potential benefits that can be promoted.
3 *Target audience.* This profiles the audience to provide a sound 'feel' for the typical customer.
4 *Offer promise.* This encompasses the key benefits to offer and how they can be supported.
5 *Tone of communication.* The tone will be influenced by the media selected. The formality and communication style need to be specified.
6 *Layout, graphics, scripts.* The physical look of the offer is important for attracting and retaining attention, especially if the campaign is likely to be given only a short period to make an impact. The offer must end by encouraging action relating to the campaign objectives. At a very practical level, it must also be remembered that advertisements used in a campaign may require more space in different countries because of language differences. Compared with English, languages such as Italian and Spanish require 20–25 per cent more space, and German and the Scandinavian languages need 25–30 per cent more. This is quite apart from the normal concerns about translating words and phrases literally from one language to another.
7 *Positioning.* This concerns relating the offer to the many other competitor efforts in the customer's mind.
8 *Restrictions.* Any legal and corporate restrictions need to be identified and complied with.
9 *Action.* As the key to direct marketing is action, the mechanism and ease of responding need to be carefully considered.

eg

Red Cat helps catalogue sellers with design and production. It has rejected what it considers the 'bland' approach to catalogue design, where it becomes difficult to differentiate one offering from another. The test of a good catalogue, Red Cat considers, is whether it sells the product or not, whether it sells more than the last one or not. This puts the emphasis on creativity and innovation in design, photography and producing copy with an 'editorial feel' (Miles, 2001b).

The Early Learning Centre uses catalogues to support product sales and to improve the positioning of its products among a wider audience. It also helps it to keep in touch with its customers. By adding an emotional appeal through design and photography, the catalogue makes more impact on the reader and encourages purchase action. With a print run of 2 million and 100 pages, produced twice a year, the catalogue has become a useful support to retail and online sales, as well as a selling vehicle in its own right (http://www.elc.co.uk).

Response management

One of the main advantages of direct marketing is that the response is direct and usually happens within a limited time span.

eg

French-based Modern Originals has over 2 million customers across Europe for its novel, original, funny, unusual and sophisticated gifts. It is a fast-moving business in terms of the products on offer and the need to process orders quickly. It operates in five EU countries online and with a catalogue that has a print run of 20 million per year. Achieving fast and reliable response is central to the business. In the UK it works with Prolog to provide an integrated mail order solution that can handle storage, enquiry handling, order processing, customer service and fulfilment. Ratios such as average telephone response time, achievement to a 72-hour dispatch service level and the level of stockouts are all useful in the assessment of the operation (http://www.prolog.uk.com).

A number of ratios can be developed to analyse responses to help increase effectiveness. These ratios include:

- cost per enquiry;
- cost per order;
- response rate;
- conversion rate from enquiry to order;
- average order value;
- renewal or repeat order rate.

With direct marketing campaigns a unique code can be given to distinguish specific advertisements or promotions. This enables patterns and trends to be identified and these can be used to predict further responses based on customer profiles.

Database creation and management

Any organisation with a serious intention of utilising direct marketing needs to think very carefully about how best to store, analyse and use the data captured about its customers. This means developing a **database** with as detailed a profile as possible about each customer in terms of geodemographics, lifestyle, purchase frequency and spend patterns. In B2B markets, information might also be held about decision makers and buying centres. Whatever the kind of market, the deeper the understanding of the customer, the easier it is to create effective messages and products. However, if database usage goes wrong, it can cause some unfortunate errors, for example offering maternity wear or prams to pensioners. When the database works well, it can help to offer products that will appeal to the target audience and generate a response, enabling relationships to build and prosper.

This section looks at some of the issues connected with database creation and management, as summarised in Figure 18.7. Note that the end of the first cycle, customer recruitment and retention, is the start of a stronger second cycle, based on better, recorded information and subsequent targeting.

Customer information

Although internally developed databases are nearly always more appropriate than those available externally, they do take time to develop and maintain. External lists can be

Figure 18.7 Database creation and management

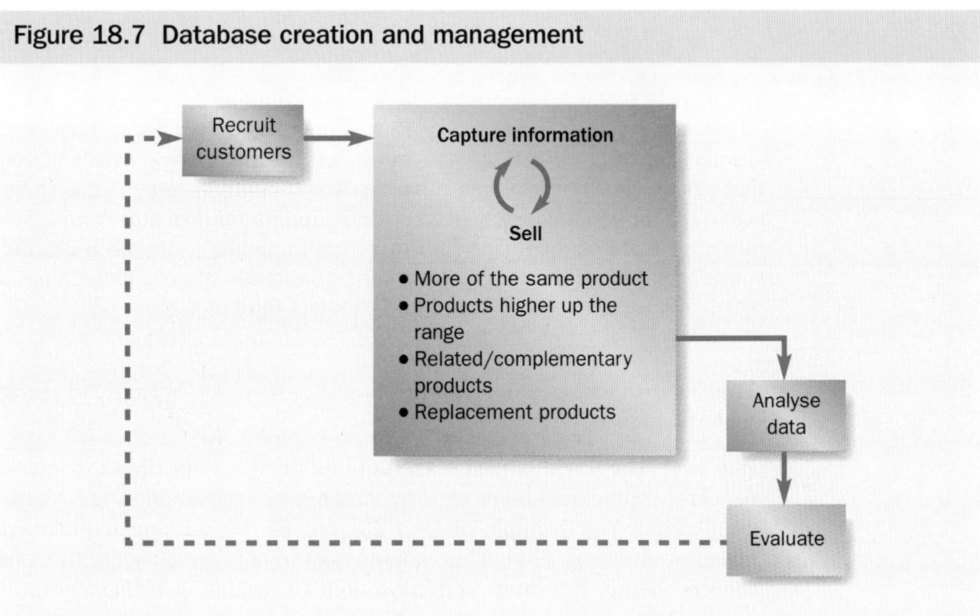

Table 18.8 Customer information for database building

- Contact name
- Company name (if applicable)
- Type of company (if applicable)
- Address
- Geodemographic profile
- Psychographic profile

- Previous contacts
- Previous responses
- Purchases actually made
- Frequency of purchases
- Value of purchases
- Types of purchase
- Media responsiveness
- Promotional responsiveness

purchased, with over 4,000 being available in the UK and some 20,000 in Europe. The selection of the most appropriate list depends on purpose and selection criteria. Geodemographic profiles, such as ACORN and Mosaic, highlight the areas offering the highest probability for identifying the best targets, based on a combination of neighbourhood and demographic detail such as family, education, occupation, etc.

The customer and sales database is a most valuable source of information for relationship management and campaign planning. Having the software to edit, sort, filter and retrieve data is essential (Lewis, 1999). Typical information contained in a database describes customer profiles. Through analysis and model building, its predictive potential can be exploited. The first part of Table 18.8 summarises the kind of information that helps to create a rich profile of existing customers, and the second part tracks the developing buyer–seller relationship.

Keeping customers and re-selling to them

As with any marketing effort, the continuation of exchanges will depend on how well needs have been satisfied, service provided and value offered. However, the real challenge for direct marketing is to continue to communicate actively with the customer and win further orders after the initial contact has been made. This can be achieved by keeping in regular contact and developing a range of initiatives to encourage further orders. These could be further sales of the same product, sales of new offers, or cross-selling into related product areas to maximise the returns from established contacts.

Classifying the customer list to reflect loyalty, purchase activity, susceptibility to future offers and age of listing can help to determine the best way of approaching future communication and offers. For example, individual car owners tend to change cars every two or three years, and therefore it might be appropriate to identify customers who are coming to the end of their second year and implement an intensive campaign of sending them financing and product information with a view to getting them into the showroom.

It is always more cost effective to retain customers than to win new ones, so careful use of direct marketing can assist the overall promotional programme. The maintenance and updating of the database provide good means of tracking customer needs, wants and satisfaction, helping to make marketing decisions that maximise the chances of retaining a loyal customer base.

eg

The British Airways Executive Club has been running for over ten years and has 2.5 million members. It wanted to integrate off- and online activity into its customer relationship programme but had to obtain updated customer information and e-mail addresses. It considered that e-mail would be an effective vehicle for keeping members informed of promotions and news. It sent incentivised mail to request updated information and a few personal profile questions that could be useful for targeting particular promotions at different groups. As a reward for filling out the questionnaire, respondents were given a list of destinations to which 500 business class flights could be won (Miles, 2001a).

There are five stages in a retention and customer development programme. These are considered in turn.

1 *Welcome.* The obvious first stage applies shortly after the customer has become active. An early contact can be reassuring, and assists in engendering receptivity to further communication. The example of *Next Directory's* 'welcoming' experiment has already been mentioned (*see* p. 764). That scheme led to significantly greater numbers of new customers being retained and also led to their spending 30 per cent more than 'non-welcomed' customers.

2 *Selling up*. Apart from normal repeat business, such as occurs with customers of a book club, organisations should encourage the customer to adopt a better or higher valued model. This approach would be appropriate for a wide range of products and services including cars, cameras and credit cards. American Express, for example, used direct mail to encourage green Amex cardholders to trade up to gold card status. The timing of contact will depend on the expected replacement period for the product.
3 *Selling across*. The selling across or cross-selling stage is where an organisation tries to sell a wider range of products than those in the area originally selected. A customer who purchases car insurance from a particular company might subsequently receive mailings about house insurance or private health cover, for example.
4 *Renewal*. With products that involve annual or regular renewal, such as motor insurance, the timing of appropriate and personalised communication around the renewal date can reinforce repeat purchases.
5 *Lapsed customers*. Customers may be temporarily dormant or permanently lost. A continuation of communication may be appropriate for a period of time so as not to lose contact, especially if reorder frequencies are high.

Review and recycle

As implied above, once a database is up and running it should be monitored, reviewed and evaluated periodically to make sure that it is working well and achieving its full potential. This is not just about 'cleaning' the database (i.e. making sure that it is up to date and that any individuals who have disappeared without trace are deleted from it), but also about data analysis. As part of the strategic planning process, the organisation can look for opportunities to cross-sell to existing customers or to get them to trade up, for instance. Managers can also review whether the nature and frequency of contact are sufficient to achieve full customer potential. Perhaps more importantly, they can assess whether they have recruited the kind of customer expected and whether targets have been met.

All of this analysis can be used to plan the continuation of database building. Although the organisation will be trying primarily to hold on to the customers it already has, there will inevitably be some wastage as customers lose interest, or as their tastes and aspirations change, or as they move house without telling anybody. That wastage, as well as the organisation's own growth aspirations, means that new customers will have to be sought. Learning from the first implementation of the cycle, managers can assess whether the 'right' kind of media were used to attract the 'right' kind of desired customer. They can refine their profiling and targeting in order to improve response rates and perhaps attract even more lucrative customers. They can review which promotional offers or which kinds of approach were most successful and repeat those with new customers, or try similar activities again.

Ideally, as the organisation builds its relationship with customers over time, and as it repeats the cycle of recruitment and retention with increasing numbers of customers, it should learn and become better at serving its customers' needs. This can only happen, however, within a framework of tight planning, management, analysis and control.

Trade shows and exhibitions

Both B2B and consumer sellers may introduce **trade shows and exhibitions** into their promotional mixes. Such events range from small-scale local involvement, for example a specialist bookseller taking a stall at a model railway exhibition, to an annual national trade show serving a specific industry, such as the DIY and Home Improvement Show, or Pakex for the packaging industry. In either case, the exhibition may become an important element of the year's marketing activities, as this section will show. Even those who specialise in organising and supporting exhibitions have their own exhibitions!

Allison Transmissions, a subsidiary of General Motors, has successfully used exhibitions to re-establish itself in the European market. As a supplier of automatic transmissions for commercial vehicles, it was having difficulty in getting specified by the vehicle manufacturers. To do so meant a two-pronged approach, influencing users as well as the manufacturers. Unlike in the USA, automatic transmission is not widely used across Europe so part of the job was to convince users that it could be better than manual transmission.

Exhibitions were used to present a unified corporate image and message across Europe. Through product demonstrations, including 'ride and drive', it was possible to show potential customers the benefits of specifying automatic when renewing the vehicle fleet. The company particularly targeted uses where the vehicle is constantly stopping and starting, such as refuse vehicles, buses and fire engines. The national truck and bus exhibitions were targeted, such as the IAA (Hanover) in Germany. Despite having relatively few customers, the power of the exhibition is in the face-to-face contact and high visual impact. Allison now spends 30 per cent of its marketing budget on exhibitions, more than on any other element in the promotional mix (Rines, 1999).

Benefits of attending and participating in exhibitions

Benefits for the small business

Exhibitions and shows can be of particular importance to the smaller business that may not have the resources to fund an expensive marketing communications programme. The exhibition can be used as a cost effective means of building more 'presence' and reputation with the trade, and to generate potential sales leads. Small businesses in the UK, however, seem less inclined to use exhibitions than those from other European countries. According to Hall (1995), in 1994 UK small businesses spent about 10 per cent of their marketing budgets on exhibiting, whereas the French spent 20 per cent and the Italians 30 per cent.

Benefits of international exhibitions

International exhibitions can be particularly valuable because they bring together participants from all over the world who might otherwise never meet, and can thus lead to export deals.

The London Book Fair has grown from its humble UK-orientated beginnings in 1971 when it was a small booksellers' fair into a major international event. By 2001, it had over 1,500 companies exhibiting, attracting over 12,000 visitors, 7,000 of whom were in the exhibition hall at Olympia on one single day. One-third of the visitors were from outside the UK, attracted by the opportunity to meet international publishing companies, organised by groupings such as children's, academic and technical publishing along with remainder sellers and retailing and publishing solution providers. The typical audience is booksellers/retailers, literary agents, librarians, authors, teachers and publishers. It has become an ideal place to keep up with new developments, to meet the trade and to plan future purchases (Zaleski, 2001; http://www.libf.co.uk).

Trade exhibitions and shows

Although some exhibitions, such as the Motor Show, the Ideal Home Exhibition and Clothes Show Live, are open to the general public for part or all of their duration, the serious business of exhibiting takes place in B2B markets. The National Menswear Exhibition may be less well known to the consumer than Clothes Show Live, but it is of far greater importance to manufacturers and retailers in making sure that the right goods reach the right shops at the right time.

The Nürnberg International Toy Fair has been running for 50 years. It represents an opportunity for the trade to present new products to retail buyers from across Europe. New product launches are often planned to coincide with the fair to maximise both the impact to visitors and the subsequent coverage in the trade and hobby press. The main European model railway magazines such as *Continental Modeller* and *Eisenbahn Journal* carry extensive reports on new releases from such manufacturers as Fleischmann, Marklin and Rivarossi.

For the manufacturer, attending exhibitions provides a formal opportunity to display the product range and to discuss applications and needs with prospective customers in a neutral environment. Depending on the type of show and the care that an organisation puts into planning its presence there, an exhibition provides a powerful and cost effective way of getting the message across and making new contacts that may subsequently turn into sales.

Comparison of the benefits of exhibitions and personal selling

Despite the increasing cost of attending shows, a number of benefits can be gained from attendance, which will be compared with what can be achieved through personal selling, the main alternative in B2B marketing.

Product launch and demonstration

An exhibition, as well as providing an organisation with an opportunity to launch or test market new products, enables it to set up working demonstrations of products. Blythe (1999) found that most visitors to exhibitions are interested in new products and gathering information rather than being directly sold to. Demonstrations give potential customers the chance to have hands-on experience of the product and can act as a focal point for discussing applications with individuals or small groups. With a product that is bulky or difficult to set up, a sales representative cannot always provide such demonstrations when visiting potential customers.

eg

Sharwoods, the Indian, Thai and Chinese food manufacturer, sells into both retail and wholesale channels and uses exhibitions as an integral part of its strategy. For each show, it sets specific, measurable targets and the main priority is to encourage tasting for retail and consumers, an experience that is difficult to achieve through any other medium. The chef demonstrations are very powerful for attracting visitors to the stand, as is free tasting. It attends fine food and ethnic food fairs as well as consumer events, with the aim of showcasing new products and generating new sales from the new trade contacts made (http://www.exhibitionswork.co.uk).

Learning experience

The event allows the exhibitor to be present alongside major competitors, learning of new developments and trends and even making comparisons. Taking time to visit other exhibitors' stands can provide a wealth of information that sales representatives would not necessarily pick up in their day-to-day operations.

Lead generation

A valuable aspect of an exhibition is that it concentrates many potential new customers in one place over a short period. A small company with a limited sales force simply does not have the time or resources to generate and follow up large numbers of geographically dispersed leads from scratch. At an exhibition, potential buyers come to you because they are interested, and an initial face-to-face meeting can take place. Even if that meeting does not directly generate a sale, the ice has been broken, the lead has been qualified, and the relationship can be further developed by the sales force after the exhibition. The advantage of an exhibition as a lead generator becomes even more obvious with international events. For a UK company, the cost of attending an exhibition in Frankfurt might be higher than that of one held in London, but the time and effort saved, not to mention the uncertainty involved in trying to locate and follow up foreign leads, should more than compensate. Attendance at a foreign exhibition can be an excellent way for an inexperienced organisation to find its first export customers.

Sunny Delight is one of the best selling drinks in the UK. When it was launched, the brand owner Procter and Gamble (P&G) decided that an exhibition presence was necessary to encourage retailers to stock the product. The stand itself was colourful and exciting in order to attract visitors to an unknown brand. An island site was chosen so that visitors could access it from all sides. P&G was particularly keen to establish a database of independent retailers for follow-up contact. With plenty of free samples, television monitors showing the brand advertising and stands to explain the trade and consumer promotions, the short-term series of exhibitions was a great success. Whereas a typical stand at a retail exhibition attracts between 10 and 15 per cent of visitors, P&G attracted 35–40 per cent and 2,106 visitor contacts were made at the Birmingham Convenience Retailing Show (http://www.exhibitionswork.co.uk).

Relationship building

Even with existing customers, goodwill and relationship building can be furthered if customers are invited to the exhibition stand. Hospitality is an equally important element of the exhibition, and many organisations host parties or receptions for key customers, suppliers or the trade press to foster good relationships. There are also informal, personal networks to develop, renew and refresh.

The Vitafoods exhibition held annually in Geneva provides OTC pharmaceutical, nutraceutical, vitamin, dietary supplement, botanical, cosmetics and functional food manufacturers and marketers an opportunity to meet and conduct business with leading suppliers of raw materials and ingredients and other related services. It is an international exhibition with 3,500 representatives from over 80 countries present. The 300 exhibitors include Roche Vitamins Europe, Béghin-Meiji and Nichimen Europe. These companies have invested substantially in the nutraceuticals industry and attract an audience of the top multinational food and pharmaceutical manufacturers from around the globe (http://www.vitafoods.co.uk). It is typical of specialist exhibitions that allow retail and wholesale buyers to meet with manufacturers to find out what is new and what is worth ordering.

As discussed in Chapter 4, personal relationships between people who work for different organisations within an industry can help to spread information around as well as improving the commercial relationship between their firms.

Visitors' sense of purpose and absorption in the atmosphere

An exhibition takes place in a neutral location over a clearly defined period of time. It is important enough to draw in decision makers and people within an industry who might otherwise be difficult to see. People are there because they want to be, and for the purposes of gathering information and making contacts. The atmosphere can be vibrant, busy and fun, heightening the excitement and stimulation. All of this adds to the visitor's sense of enjoyment and fulfilment. The sales representative, on the other hand, could be calling on someone, in their own workplace, who is extremely busy and reluctant to be seen. The representative might have problems attracting and retaining attention and interest, because the phone never stops ringing, or the manager has made it clear that time is precious and there is a problem on the production line that really must be sorted out immediately.

Brand building

An exhibition can be used to make brand statements very powerfully to customers. This leads to brand-led stand design, which conveys clear messages about the company and what it stands for (Goddard, 1999). These should be in line with the desired brand positioning. Through a combination of colour, giant product replicas, furnishings and other imagery, the customer is provided with an insight into what the company is about. For those selling intangible products such as telecommunications, the stand is actually as close as the customer is likely to get to the technology that provides the service.

Market presence

A reasonable objective, particularly for a small company or a new entrant into an industry, is to build awareness, both of the organisation and of the products offered. The larger multi-product company commonly finds that, although the company and its main products are known, there may be several 'blind spots' in the range and thus the exhibition can be used to display them. By comparison, there is a limit to what the sales representative can achieve in this respect. The representative can certainly try to display the full product range to a customer or potential customer, but in terms of raising the organisation's profile within the industry, it would take a long-term determined effort by the entire sales force to achieve as much as a single three-day exhibition could. It does not necessarily follow, however, that the bigger the brand the bigger the exhibition stand must be, if there is no story to tell and no coherence to what is on offer (Foley, 2001).

eg

Although the biennial motor show held at Birmingham's National Exhibition Centre is a feature in most motor manufacturers' calendars, some of the other shows have run into trouble. The London Motor Show planned for November 2001 was cancelled after a number of manufacturers decided not to exhibit. MG Rover, Mercedes-Benz and Volkswagen group's Audi, Seat, Skoda and VW brands initially indicated that they were not planning to attend the show and others decided to follow. Although the shows are useful for PR purposes and for promoting new models, they have become very expensive in recent years and as soon as some manufacturers declare their intentions, others are prone to follow. Ironically, at a time when the main London shows are in difficulty, a targeted exhibition at Docklands Canary Wharf drew 20 manufacturers and more than 150 cars including Mercedes-Benz, Aston Martin, Jaguar and Porsche. The expectation was that although the visitor numbers would be smaller than the main shows, a higher percentage would be in a position to buy (Griffiths, 2000; 2001a; 2001b).

PR spin-offs

As the high point in an industry's year, the major national or international exhibition will receive a great deal of publicity within the trade press at least. An organisation with a particularly creative stand or with something exciting to unveil at the show should be able to generate substantial coverage. Some shows generate much more widespread publicity. The Motor Show in the UK, for example, usually has a whole BBC programme devoted to it on a Sunday afternoon when the exhibition is on. This gives valuable airtime to a wide variety of exhibitors, presenting their stands and products to a mass audience.

The hospitality aspects discussed earlier are also a part of the PR effort, whether they centre around customers and suppliers, or cultivating trade press relations.

Corporate boost

Although working at an exhibition can be exhausting, it is different from the day-to-day jobs that most people do. Even for sales representatives, it provides an opportunity to work with colleagues rather than alone, and to meet customers without the slog of travelling. Participating in an exciting event, benefiting from the hospitality, and getting together with old acquaintances all help to boost morale, especially if the exhibition has been a commercial success too.

Importance of exhibitions to organisations

Given these potential benefits it is perhaps surprising that exhibitions do not take a more prominent role in organisations' marketing plans. The overall figures for UK business generally are no more impressive than those for small businesses (quoted earlier). Exhibitions only take up about 8 per cent of the marketing budget of UK organisations, whereas the figures for other countries are: France, 17 per cent, Germany, 21 per cent, Japan, 25 per cent and the USA, 26 per cent (John, 1996). Nevertheless, the exhibition sector in the UK is quite healthy, as shown in Table 18.9, which demonstrates how the number of exhibitions and visitors in the UK evolved between 1993 and 2000.

Table 18.9 The number of UK exhibitions and visitors, 1993–2001

	1993	*1994*	*1995*	*1996*	*1997*	*1998*	*1999*	*2000*	*2001*
Exhibitions	671	691	733	710	841	843	817	868	823
Visitors	9.5	10.3	9.7	10.4	10.7	11.0	10.1	11.1	9.1

Source: Reproduced by kind permission of the Exhibition Venues Association (EVA).

In a comparison of international exhibition venues, the UK's main sites, the NEC in Birmingham and Earls Court in London, compare very favourably with the other 12 members of the European Major Exhibition Centres Association, as can be seen in Table 18.10.

Table 18.10 International exhibition venues, 1999

	Number of exhibitions	*Number of exhibitors*	*Number of visitors (millions)*	*Exhibition area rented (million m^2)*
Barcelona	63	11115	3.0	1.4
Basel	36	11779	1.2	0.8
Birmingham	179	42286	2.6	2.3
Bologna	23	20409	2.7	1.8
Brussels	52	10218	1.9	1.0
Düsseldorf	40	29419	1.7	2.4
Frankfurt	49	37129	2.2	2.4
Leipzig	29	12361	1.0	0.9
London	147	32340	3.1	1.5
Lyon	33	11981	1.4	1.1
Madrid	57	14307	2.3	1.6
Milan	71	29475	4.2	3.1
Munich	74	31701	2.0	2.3
Nürnberg	59	19245	1.1	1.6
Paris	108	37059	6.3	2.6
Paris-Nord	40	25296	1.5	1.9
Utrecht	81	23860	2.2	1.9
Valencia	32	6940	1.1	1.0
Verona	29	13041	1.0	1.0

Source: Reproduced by kind permission of the European Major Exhibition Centres Association (E.M.C.A).

According to the Exhibition Venues Association (EVA) the total number of exhibitions in the UK over 2,000 m^2 in 2000 was 868, the highest figure since records began in 1988. The number of exhibitions over 20,000 m^2 was 14 and there were 64 over 20,000 m^2. London hosts 35 per cent of all exhibitions, the West Midlands 25 per cent and Scotland 9 per cent. Lifestyle and giftware account for 12 per cent of all exhibitions and arts, services and hobbies 20 per cent. Visitor attendance in 2001 topped 11 million. Most trade sectors have at least one exhibition per year. Although international visitors were only a small percentage of total visitors to UK exhibitions, the importance of over 280,000 international buyers for generating leads and sales is well recognised by export-led companies. Table 18.11 looks more closely at the results of a survey undertaken by the EVA, showing outcomes and attitudes to exhibitions by sector.

Reasons for attending exhibitions

The EVA also looked at the reasons for organisations attending exhibitions. These are shown in Table 18.12 alongside the remarkably similar results of a US survey reported by

Table 18.11 Exhibition statistics by sector

	Engineering	*Computing*	*Food*
Cost per contact (£)	41	35	62
Cost per sale (£)	215	161	182
Average annual budget (£'000)	25.0	44.8	20.3
Spend per exhibition (£'000)	7.4	n/a	3.0
How worthwhile (%)			
Exceptionally	2	3	7
Very	33	35	48
Fairly	40	38	31
Marginally	19	17	14
Not	2	4	0
Under review	3	3	2

Source: Reproduced by kind permission of the Exhibition Venues Association (EVA).

Hart (1993). There has to be more of a reason to attend the show than 'our competitors do' or 'we always go'. Nevertheless, the cost of exhibiting needs to be considered in comparison with alternative ways, if indeed there are any, of achieving the same objectives.

Table 18.12 Why organisations use exhibitions

UK survey	*Per cent*	*US survey*	*Per cent*
Sales leads	83	Gain qualified leads	71
Presence in the market	70	Maintain image	63
Launch new products	35	Intensify awareness	60
Direct selling	25	Presence in the market	56
		Launch new products	31
		Direct selling	25

Sources: UK survey: Reproduced by kind permission of the Exhibition Venues Association (EVA), US survey: Hart (1993).

There are many factors to consider before deciding to attend an exhibition. Some of the more important criteria are (Wilmshurst, 1993):

- type of visitors and previous attendance patterns;
- participation by main competitors;
- advice from agents, trade and local representatives;
- exhibition organiser's and independent assessment of previous events;
- the promotion and organisation of the event;
- the expected costs to be incurred and the objectives to be realised from the event.

In another survey of exhibition users, EVA found that nearly three-quarters of visitors to exhibitions are in the organisational buying unit, that 29 per cent did not normally see supplier representatives, 11 per cent were expecting to actually buy at an exhibition and most interestingly, exhibitions were rated above catalogues, publications, the internet, sales representatives and direct mail as a means of assisting purchasing decisions among exhibition goers (http://www.exhibitionvenues.com).

Importance of planning for exhibitors

These reasons for attendance are put into sharp perspective by an examination of the reasons for poor exhibition performance (Dudley, 1990), as shown in Table 18.13. These areas of potential disappointment clearly demonstrate that central to any exhibition decision is

Table 18.13 Reasons for poor exhibition performance

- Inadequate statement of objectives
- Poor-quality visitors
- Bad location of the stand
- Ineffective stand quality/design
- Poor personnel performance
- Lack of follow-up of leads/enquiries
- Ignoring the competition: they get the visitors
- Poor recognition of company by buyers
- Poor corporate identity leading to low recall
- Poor organisation/control of exhibition logistics
- Inadequate staffing arrangements
- Inadequate budget/cost controls

Source: Dudley (1990).

the willingness to plan fully, well in advance of the event, including making sure that all participating personnel are comprehensively briefed to handle the event for its duration (Donald, 2001). Inadequate preparation, even down to poor stand lighting and decor or a shortage of support material, is going to detract from the performance and pull at the event. If added to that there is a parsimonious approach that tries to cut costs through poor-quality space, displays and too few staff, it is easy to see how disappointment might arise.

Preparation might also mean coordinating the exhibition with the selling effort, making sure that sales representatives invite customers to visit the stand, for example, or with advertising, by featuring participation in the exhibition in advertisements. In all cases, accurate records need to be kept of the visitors to the stand so that the sales force can follow up leads within a short period to take full advantage of the contacts. An exhibition should not be seen as an opportunity for the sales force to get away and have a good time, although enjoyment is not precluded! A sobering thought for those inclined to treat exhibition attendance as a holiday is that the average company spend on exhibiting was £10,500 in 1997. Nevertheless, the EVA has estimated that a sales representative on the road only spends about 180 hours a year on face-to-face selling. How many customers does that represent? At an exhibition, in contrast, a sales team can be contacting up to 50 prospects per hour, a much more efficient use of their time.

Finally, more flexible mobile exhibitions, whether taking the form of a specially fitted caravan or a shopping centre display or a display set up in a hotel room, provide many of the advantages of meeting potential customers without the costs associated with high profile, national exhibitions.

Field marketing can help with mobile exhibitions (*see* p. 706). It enables car brands to be taken out to meet customers rather than waiting for enquiries and visits to showrooms. By going to shopping centres, cinemas and events, field marketing can provide the opportunity for prospective customers to see, feel and even drive a car they otherwise might not have considered. For example, 80 per cent of Alfa Romeo customers are male, so field marketing was used to try to encourage women to consider an Alfa. It also teamed up with David Lloyd health clubs for test driving roadshows on its 147 model. Posters advertised a free test driving roadshow one month before the weekend in question, and members were encouraged to book a test drive in one of five cars, or at least to remember to bring their driving licences on the day. By showing the vehicle, it creates interest, makes a brand impression and generates word-of-mouth comment (Gannaway, 2001). The key elements of success for any roadshow are location, duration and timing. The better the venue in line with the target audience the more chance there is for the show to have an impact (Gannaway, 2002). Thus an exhibition does not have to be a high profile international event, it could also be one vehicle displayed in your local supermarket. The job of the marketing manager is to find the right exhibition mix in line with the broader promotional objectives.

Chapter summary

- Direct marketing has become more important in recent years for several reasons, including changing consumer lifestyles, competitive pressure, technological advances and the general move towards relationship marketing.
- There are several approaches to direct marketing that an organisation might consider. Direct mail can be very effective in stimulating responses from tightly defined target audiences made up either of existing customers or of new ones. Direct response advertising uses broadcast and print media with the aim of stimulating some kind of response

from the target audience. Telemarketing specifically covers the use of the telephone as a means of creating a direct link between organisation and customer. The telephone provides a quick, easy and cost effective response mechanism, and can be used both to increase the impact and creativity of advertising and sales promotion, and to provide a human character for the organisation. Mail order catalogues now target their customers with 'specialogues', providing narrow selections of better quality goods that suit the customer's profile. Some catalogues are solely mail order operations, while others are developed by retailers as a means of extending their established High Street business. The most recent development is the catalogue showroom, such as Argos. Part of mail order's appeal is its use of the telephone to speed up transactions. The caller can find out if a particular item is in stock and, if required, make payment immediately by credit card. This principle has been further developed to open up the teleshopping industry. Satellite channels sell the same goods across Europe in this way, and there are whole channels on cable and satellite devoted to home shopping.

- Direct marketing thus takes a variety of forms and can achieve a wide range of objectives. As well as direct ordering of goods, direct marketing can support the sales effort with information campaigns and after-sales customer care initiatives. It can also pave the way towards sales by inviting potential customers to try out products or to make appointments to see sales representatives.
- To achieve all this, however, the direct marketing campaign should be well planned, designed and executed. The campaign objectives should be clearly laid out and measurable. The target audience should also be clearly defined. This in turn leads to the selection of the most appropriate media and message. Media choice is also influenced by the campaign's objectives. Once the advertisement or other material has been developed, the organisation has to ensure that all the likely responses can be handled quickly and efficiently. The planning process should also allow for the response to the campaign to be measured and evaluated so that lessons can be learned for the future. Organisations reap the best benefits from direct marketing when they use responses to build databases so that any one campaign or offer becomes just one of a series of relationship building dialogues.
- It is important, however, to create and maintain a database that can cope with a detailed profile of each customer and their purchasing habits and history.
- Exhibitions and trade shows vary from small local events to major national or international shows. They bring together a wide range of key personnel in one place at one time, and can thus generate a great many potential sales leads cost effectively. For exhibition attendance to be successful, however, the organisation should ensure that it is a planned element of the overall marketing mix and that it has clear objectives and purposes. It is important to invest adequate funds to make a suitable impact on the show's visitors and to prepare staff carefully so that they make the most of the opportunities offered at the exhibition. After the exhibition, it is crucial that any leads generated are followed up quickly, before the visitors have the chance to forget the good impressions made by the organisation.

key words and phrases

Database	Interactive	Telemarketing
Direct mail	Internet marketing	Telephone preference services
Direct marketing	Mailing list	Teleshopping
Direct response advertising	Mail order	Trade shows and exhibitions
Inbound telemarketing	Outbound telemarketing	

questions for review

18.1 What general issues have led to the rise in popularity of *direct marketing*?

18.2 Summarise what you consider to be the key success factors for a *direct mail campaign*.

18.3 In what ways can *telemarketing* support and enhance the other elements of the promotional mix?

18.4 Explain the role that direct marketing can play in both creating and retaining customers.

18.5 What factors might contribute to successful *exhibition attendance*?

questions for discussion

18.1 Collect three pieces of direct mail and for each one assess:
(a) what you think it is trying to achieve;
(b) how that message has been communicated;
(c) what involvement devices have been used to encourage the recipient to read the mailshot; and
(d) how easy it is for the recipient to respond in the required way.

18.2 Carry out your own analysis of the advertising in a magazine. Discuss examples of good and bad direct response advertising from that magazine. What overall conclusions can you draw?

18.3 To what extent, and why, do you think that outbound telemarketing should be controlled by legislation or codes of practice?

18.4 For each of the techniques of direct marketing outlined in Figure 18.1, assess their relevance to:
(a) consumer markets; and
(b) B2B markets.

18.5 Imagine that you are a customer of a mail order CD club. Specify what information about yourself the club's database should ideally hold. Which parts of that information would be of greatest use to the organisation in designing an appropriate offer for you?

case study 18.1

Camp followers

Eurocamp, part of the Holiday Break organisation, is a market leader in European camping and mobile home holidays. It is particularly attractive to families with children looking for relatively inexpensive beach and lakeside holiday locations. Eurocamp has 187 sites in 8 countries and attracts holidaymakers from across Europe. Most of the sites are in France (111) and Italy (51) and it is the market leader for organised campsite holidays in the UK, Ireland, Germany and the Netherlands. Group sales were £103 mn from all its sites which trade under several brand names, and 53 per cent of sales are generated under the Eurocamp brand itself. As most customers book early, and as the company holds optional pitches on campsite contracts, it can achieve profitable levels of occupancy on the campsites, although the challenge facing Eurocamp, as well as many other holiday operators, is how to extend the season beyond the traditional peaks in July and August. Occupancy during the 'shoulder months' of May, June, September and, in warmer southern climates, October, outside the school holiday period, can make all the difference to overall profitability. These are important months in which to undertake promotional efforts to extend the season and for that Eurocamp uses direct marketing.

Research has indicated to Eurocamp that its customers do not buy on price and that there is a high degree of satisfaction among past holidaymakers. Eurocamp, like many other holiday operators, has the advantage of being able to build a detailed customer database from enquiries and actual bookings. Family size, car type, postcode information, frequency of booking, site facility information, preferred destinations and even attitudinal data are all available for analysis from routine operations. Generally, the previous year's customers are the best prospects and they normally form the prime target for communication.

Advertising in a range of magazines and newspapers helps to generate enquiries, using freephone or coupon response. This triggers the sending of a brochure as the main selling tool. A multimedia CD-ROM has also been developed to provide a more novel way for consumers to assess a particular holiday camp destination. The website provides extensive information on the various

Figure 18.8 Recency, frequency and value model

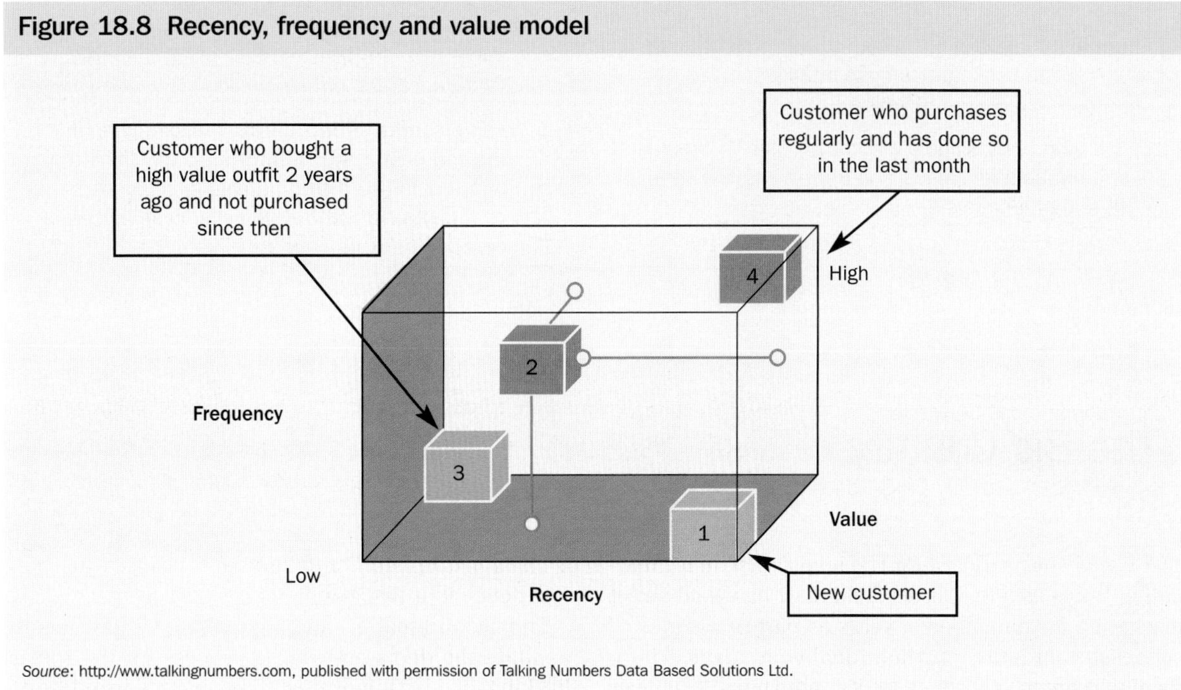

Source: http://www.talkingnumbers.com, published with permission of Talking Numbers Data Based Solutions Ltd.

locations, describes packages and special offers and provides a mechanism for customer feedback and brochure requests. The overall key to the promotional campaign, however, is the building of an effective database. Initially, Eurocamp analysed RFV data (recency, frequency and value) relating to the previous five years' bookings. RFV analysis traces the relationship with individual customers over time, how it is changing and provides guidelines for direct promotional activity. From the analysis of such data a three-dimensional model, as shown in Figure 18.8, can be constructed. For Eurocamp, the RFV data were also considered in terms of family lifecycle and income level information, which could be obtained from the booking forms.

As Eurocamp was able to sell its peak season holidays many times over, it concentrated on the shoulder month customer profiles. Using standard SPSS software, it undertook data cross-tabulation to highlight the loyal and high value customers contained in the data. Customers were grouped into 15 categories ranging from low value spenders who last visited five years ago to those taking a holiday twice a year with Eurocamp and spending an above-average amount. This enabled the priority value customers to be identified. The relationship with RFV and family lifecycle also proved interesting. Families travelling in June were found to be completely different from those taking a holiday in the peak season. They sought quieter campsites, less busy roads, yet still wanted good weather for the outdoor life associated with camping. All of this analysis resulted in a reshaped database that could be used by the marketing department for special direct promotions.

The refined database was then used to identify those customers more likely to participate in a shoulder month holiday. In particular, families with pre-school children and retired, empty nest couples were identified and the mailshots reflect the needs of these different groups. The pre-school families receive literature showing many happy children enjoying an almost adult-free zone, except for, of course, the relaxed mum and dad. Mention is made of on-site sports and games, children's couriers and children's discos. The empty nesters would find it hard to see a child in the literature they receive. The focus for them is on healthy walking, bicycling, companionship and a generally peaceful environment. In both cases, the accompanying, personalised letter reminds the reader of last year's holiday in the hope of rekindling happy memories.

Further work is being undertaken to match the main target customers for the shoulder months with the magazines and papers that are used for advertising. Research has already revealed that broadsheet readers (i.e. *The Times*, *The Independent*) tend to spend more on each holiday but travel less frequently, while tabloid readers spend less but travel more frequently. Responses by postcode are also being examined to establish whether some neighbourhood areas have a greater propensity to take holidays during the shoulder season. This helps guide decisions on the need for targeted mailings. Mailshots are now sent to the priority and targeted customers three or four times a year. Eurocamp's approach to relationship marketing is based on its success in database establishment and subsequent data mining to profile customers to guide marketing decision-making.

Sources: Lawson (1999); http://www.talkingnumbers.com; http://eurocamp.com.

Questions

1 Why do you think Eurocamp is putting such an emphasis on direct marketing?

2 What kind of data could a company like Eurocamp capture about its visitors and how might this be of use to its marketers?

3 Eurocamp has identified groups of higher spending and lower spending visitors. How might the direct marketing approach differ between these two groups?

4 Eurocamp seems to be focusing exclusively on its existing and past customers. How do you think the company could use direct marketing to approach potential customers who have never experienced Eurocamp or perhaps have never even heard of it?

case study 18.2

'The Big Country'

The Wales Tourist Board (WTB) is responsible for marketing Wales as a tourist destination. It has used direct marketing for a number of years as part of a series of successful integrated promotional campaigns. There were two broad objectives for its campaigns, whatever the creative execution. First, it had to generate awareness and initial interest in Wales as a holiday destination through image-building television and print advertising. Research had indicated that even in the UK, the brand image of Wales was outdated and based on stereotypical images of rugby, coalmines and castles and of the people not always being friendly and welcoming to tourists. The challenge over the past ten years has been to develop the image of Wales as an attractive, fun-seeking place and a friendly holiday destination that is close to the main UK centres of population but can offer a very different holiday from one in England. It was also essential to tackle head-on some potential tourists' negative perceptions based upon memories of windswept caravan parks, poor hotel standards and language barriers in some parts of the country. All of these were out of date, but had to be addressed if the product was to be perceived as relevant to the target market.

The bulk of the image-building used by the WTB has been based on high quality film footage and photographs of traditional themes such as mountains, castles and beaches, although more recently tourists participating in casual walks on the beach, cycling and other outdoor pursuits have featured. It is, however, becoming more difficult to create a distinctive theme based on the product alone (sand, scenery and buildings) as many more tourist boards are starting to focus on the tourist experience, i.e. tourists actually enjoying the product. The Irish Tourist Board, for example, has focused on individuals enjoying leisure pursuits with captions such as 'Francesa from Milan took a hack along a Sligo beach', while New Zealand offered dramatic scenery to capitalise on the success of *The Lord of the Rings* movie, inviting tourists to experience it at first hand.

The second major campaign objective has been to facilitate the decision-making process for the tourist thinking of visiting Wales. That meant providing a response mechanism to make it easy to acquire a brochure, to access more information and even to get direct help in booking a holiday. The latter is important, as any campaign will be judged by the trade on the number of visitors rather than the number of direct responses to an advertisement.

WTB tends to develop campaigns to last for three of four years. In the mid-1990s the theme was 'Land of Inspiration' which featured well known stars who were born in Wales and the campaign focused on scenery and heritage. This was replaced by a direct response campaign in 1998 that was a great success and achieved national awards. The 'Two Hours and a Million Miles Away' campaign demonstrated the contrast between the stress of the city and the wide open spaces of Wales. As part of the campaign, a dirty van toured London and Birmingham looking out especially for slow moving traffic. In the dirt on the back of the van was scribbled (painted) 'Clean air is just two hours away' with a subheading linked to the overall 'million miles' theme. The freephone number

Welsh Tourist Board.

Source: The Wales Tourist Board.

Dusty, but effective direct response advertising.

Source: The Wales Tourist Board.

was an important part of the campaign. Around 200,000 enquiries per annum were generated resulting in requests for 500,000 brochures for the twelve regions within Wales. The actual number of visitors, however, fluctuated each year, and the foot-and-mouth disease outbreak in 2001 hit the industry hard.

Tourism is important to the economy in Wales. The WTB claimed that the direct marketing campaign generated £68 mn in revenue and earned £30 for every £1 spent on marketing in the UK to justify the spending. These figures were estimated from following up enquiries to establish if a holiday in Wales had materialised. The average spend per tourist was known so the conversion rate from enquiry to visit enabled tourist spending to be estimated. However, the overall promotional challenge remained; to encourage more second holidays and short breaks, especially outside the school holiday period (occupancy already approached capacity anyway during the peak holiday periods).

The campaign for 2002 changed to promote 'a new and challenging identity for Wales' as 'The Big Country' inspired by the people and the landscape. The WTB wanted to evolve the message and the brand identity for its tourism product. It decided to adopt a theme based upon the film *Big Country*, which although now dated, remains a classic and the association highlights Wales as having people with big emotions and passion, albeit with mountains somewhat smaller than the Rockies. To help the advertisements make an impact, the music from *Big Country* was recorded by the BBC National Orchestra of Wales. It is, in part, a tongue-in-cheek overselling campaign that relies on subtle humour. One of the advertisements, for example, made the statement that Wales is 'bigger than Texas if you flattened out all the hills', which although not true does get people thinking. The emphasis was on big emotion, fun and lots of things to do, a million miles from the wind-swept caravans! From the initial advertising research, the spontaneous recall figures for the Big Country theme were claimed to be at record highs and the aim of being different and distinctive appeared to be succeeding.

A media spend of £10 mn over three years is planned to cover television, radio, press and again direct marketing. There is a new call centre and a website, http://www.visitwales.com, to help potential visitors request brochures and to book holidays via a new Destination Management System. The television advertisements are targeted at the large UK metropolitan areas covered by the Granada, Midlands, Wales and West and London television regions. All the UK will be covered by satellite. Four different commercials have been shot, but each is in line with the new campaign theme and each includes a direct response mechanism.

The direct marketing campaign will include regular mailings to a database of 1 million previous enquirers considered good prospects and the overall campaign is expected to generate 300,000 responses, similar to the levels achieved on the previous campaign which had been running for nearly five years. By April 2002, around 150,000 responses had already been received and further promotion was planned for the late spring and autumn. Generally the campaigns are becoming year-round with bursts of activity supported by direct marketing around January, the late spring and autumn. Normally, response rates to the database mailings hover around 15 per cent on campaigns, although with updated lists it can be as high as 25 per cent. The increased use of online searching is making it more difficult to keep lists up to date as the viewer does not have to leave contact details. WTB do know that there have been over 60,000 hits on the UK website in the current campaign (it has different sites for different countries) and this figure is expected to grow still further as the online booking service becomes fully operational.

Around 7 million trips are made to Wales each year by UK holiday makers, either as a main holiday or for short breaks, amounting to a spend of £895 mn. Tourism is thus an important source of revenue for the small nation, representing 7 per cent of its GDP and providing 10 per cent of all its jobs. Direct marketing plays an important part in attracting that tourism income.

Sources: http://www.wtbonline.gov.uk; and with grateful thanks to David Stephens of the WTB.

Questions

1 What were the strengths of the 'Two Hours and a Million Miles Away' campaign?

2 Given the success of the 'Two Hours and a Million Miles Away' campaign, why do you think the WTB felt it necessary to change to 'Big Country'? Was this a good decision?

3 How do you think a direct marketing campaign targeting 'previous enquirers considered good prospects' might differ from a campaign targeting 'cold' prospects?

4 To what extent and how does the WTB integrate its marketing communications programme? Assess the importance of direct marketing in that programme and discuss whether that role is likely to become more or less important over the next few years.

References for chapter 18

Bertagnoli, L. (2001), 'E-marketing Tricky in Europe', *Marketing News*, 16 July, p. 19.

Bird, J. (1998), 'Dial 0 for Opportunity', *Marketing*, 29 October, pp. 31–3.

Blythe, J. (1999), 'Visitor and Exhibitor Expectations and Outcomes at Trade Exhibitions', *Marketing Intelligence and Planning*, 17 (2), pp. 100–10.

Booth, E. (1999), 'Will the Web Replace the Phones?', *Marketing*, 4 February, pp. 25–6.

Boyarski, J., Fishman, R., Josephberg, K. and Linn, J. (2002), 'European Authorities Consider "Cookies" and "Spam"', *Intellectual Property & Technology Law Journal*, 14 (3), p. 31.

Brabbs, C. (2001), 'ASA Slams Boots for Unsolicited Customer Mailing', *Marketing*, 20 September, p. 3.

Chaffey, D. (2002), *E-business and E-commerce Management: Strategy, Implementation and Practice*, Financial Times Prentice Hall.

Clarke, A. (2001), 'Call Centres Aim to Encourage Loyalty', *Marketing*, 28 June, pp. 43–4.

Coad, T. (2001), 'Don't Drop Me a Line', *Marketing Week*, 1 November, pp. 39–41.

Cobb, R. (1998), 'Talking Business', *Marketing*, 19 November, pp. 31–2.

Curtis, J. (1998), 'Life on the Floor', *Marketing*, 3 December, p. 35.

Dirskovski, R. (2001), 'EU Cannot Hope to Halt Spam Via the Statute Book', *Marketing Week*, 6 December, p. 14.

Donald, H. (2001), 'Effective Events', *Marketing Week*, 26 July, pp. 39–41.

Dudley, J. (1990), *Successful Exhibiting*, Kogan Page.

Fill, C. (1999), *Marketing Communications: Frameworks, Theories and Applications*, 2nd edn, Prentice-Hall.

Foley, T. (2001), 'Taking a Stand', *Marketing Week*, 17 May, p. 63.

Gannaway, B. (2001), 'How Field Work Can Attract Car Buyers', *Marketing*, 15 November, p. 33.

Gannaway, B. (2002), 'How to Maximise a Roadshow's Reach', *Marketing*, 4 January.

Goddard, C. (1999), 'Brands Make a Stand', *Marketing*, 14 January, pp. 25–6.

Godin, S. (1999), *Permission Marketing*, Simon & Schuster.

Griffiths, J. (2001a), 'Carmakers Opt to Join Targeted Motor Show', *Financial Times*, 18 April, p. 6.

Griffiths, J. (2001b), 'Threat to Motor Show Denied', *Financial Times*, 24 November, p. 2.

Griffiths, J. (2000), 'London Motor Show "Will Go Ahead Regardless" of Defections by Carmakers', *Financial Times*, 22 November.

Hall, C. (1995), 'Get a Fair Share Abroad', *Daily Express*, 26 June, p. 39.

Harley-Davidson (2002), *Developing A Brand Response Strategy For Harley-Davidson: Direct Marketing Campaign Summary 1999 – 2001*, Partners Andrews Aldridge.

Hart, N. (1993), *Industrial Marketing Communications*, Kogan Page.

John, R. (1996), 'How To Steal the Show', *Marketing*, 4 January, pp. 19–23.

Kemp, G. (2001), 'Direct Mail Faces Creative Overhaul', *Marketing*, 27 September, pp. 27–8.

Kleinman, M. (2001a), 'Harley Pushes Brand Prestige', *Marketing*, 17 May , p. 16.

Kleinman, M. (2001b), 'Cadbury Plans Christmas Drive', *Marketing*, 15 November, p. 13.

Kleinman, M. (2001c), 'Nicorette in "Quit Smoking" DM', *Marketing*, 20 December, p. 11.

Kleinman, M. (2000), 'Sight Savers Builds with DRTV', *Marketing*, 7 December, p. 16.

Lawson, J. (1999), 'Happy Campers', *Database Marketing*, March, pp. 36–8.

Lewis, M. (1999), 'Counting On It', *Database Marketing*, May, pp. 34–7.

Marketing (2001), 'Financial Brands Record Less Than 1% Response Rate', *Marketing*, 29 March, p. 12.

Marketing (1999a), 'The Client Perspective', *Marketing*, 11 March, p. 54.

Marketing Week (2001a), 'IDM Gold Award Winner', *Marketing Week*, 17 May, p. 47.

Marketing Week (2001b), 'Laura Ashley Set to Roll out Ladies Mail-order Catalogue', *Marketing Week*, 27 September, p. 9.

McAlevey, T. (2001), 'The Principles of Effective Direct Response', *Direct Marketing*, April, pp. 44–7.

McLuhan, R. (2002a), 'How to Adapt Mail to Boost Response', *Marketing*, 10 January, p. 23.

McLuhan, R. (2002b), 'How to Deliver on a DRTV Campaign', *Marketing*, 31 January, p. 27.

McLuhan, R. (2001), 'How DM Can Build Consumer Loyalty', *Marketing*, 3 May, pp. 45–6.

Meller, P. (2001), 'DM Industry Welcomes EU Spam Decision', *Marketing Week*, 15 November, p. 8.

Metcalf, J. (2000), 'The New European Market', *Catalog Age*, February, pp. 51–3.

Miles, L. (2001a), 'Should DM Still be Missing its Mark?', *Marketing*, 14 June, pp. 29–31.

Miles, L. (2001b), 'Red Cat Sells Off the Page', *Marketing*, 28 June, p. 19.

Miles, L. (2001c), 'Call Centres Exploit Technology Growth', *Marketing*, 18 October, pp. 35–6.

Murphy, D. (2001), 'Getting Personal in Telemarketing', *Marketing*, 2 August, pp. 33–4.

Otley, T. (2002), 'Flooded Out by Junk e-mails', *The Times*, 1 March, p. 2.5.

Rines, S. (1999), 'Point of Contact', *Marketing Week*, 25 February, pp. 63–4.

Schofield, A. (1994), 'Alternative Reply Vehicles in Direct Response Advertising', *Journal of Advertising Research*, 34(5), pp. 28–34.

Singh, S. (2001), 'Brands Take the Direct Route', *Marketing Week*, 13 September, pp. 38–9.

Sliwa, C. (2001), 'Clothing Retailer Finds Worldwide Business on the Web', *Computerworld*, 30 April, p. 40.

Smith, P. (2001), *Keynote Report: Home Shopping*, May.

Wilmshurst, J. (1993), *Below-the-Line Promotion*, Butterworth-Heinemann.

Wootliff, B. (2001), 'easyJet to Ground Telephone Service', *The Daily Telegraph*, 8 February, p. 36.

Zaleski, J. (2001), 'London Book Fair 2001: A Royal Success', *Publishers Weekly*, 9 April, p. 9.

chapter 19

public relations and sponsorship

Introduction

LEARNING OBJECTIVES

This chapter will help you to:

1 define PR and the areas of marketing activities it covers;

2 understand its role in supporting the organisation's activities and in reaching various groups, or publics, with differing interests and information needs;

3 outline the techniques of PR, their appropriateness for different kinds of public, and how they might be evaluated;

4 appreciate the importance of corporate identity, why organisations might wish to change identity, and the processes involved in change; and

5 understand the role of sponsorship in the marketing communications mix and the benefits and problems of different types of sponsorship.

Looking back to Chapter 2 and the discussion there on the marketing environment, it is clear that organisations need to be concerned about much more than just their trading relationships with their target markets. Customers are important, but a business as a whole cannot function effectively without the support and cooperation of its financial backers, its employees and trades unions, its suppliers, the legal and regulatory bodies to which it is answerable, interested pressure groups, the media, and many more groups or 'publics' which have the ability to affect the way in which the organisation does business. There is no direct trading relationship between the organisation and many of the publics listed above, which means that the objectives of whatever communication takes place are centred more on explaining what the organisation stands for, and creating a strong, positive corporate image than on a hard sell. Public relations (PR) is the area of marketing communications that specifically deals with the quality and nature of the relationship between an organisation and its publics. Its prime concern is to generate a sound, effective and understandable flow of communication between the organisation and these groups so that shared understanding is possible.

eg

Some organisations have drawn very heavily on managed public relations to minimise the impact of adverse circumstances, such as Union Carbide, the US company operating the Bhopal plant in India where 2,600 people died after a toxic leak; Exxon Corporation whose tanker caused a major oil spill in Alaska; Babcock and Wilcox whose nuclear reactor failed at Three Mile Island; and closer to home, Shell's disposal of the Brent Spar oil drilling platform; the UK's Railtrack facing a persistent barrage from the media over the state of the nation's rail infrastructure; and in Einschende, Netherlands when an explosion caused by the accidental detonation of 100 tons of fireworks stored at a private warehouse occurred in a residential neighborhood.

With the growth of environmental pressure groups, increased intolerance of environmental abuse, and the need to keep up with a rapidly changing eco-agenda, some larger organisations have taken the shrewd move of employing former prominent environmentalists to advise them on 'green' policy formulation and development. Lord Melchett, for example, the former director general of Greenpeace UK joined a major corporate public relations firm, Burton-Marsteller, which specialises in minimising PR damage and includes both Exxon and Union Carbide as former clients. The role of the activist turned consultant is to advise companies on corporate social responsibility. From a positive perspective, this could be seen as a commitment to corporate awareness and cooperation, on the basis that prevention is better than cure.

The cynics, however, argue that it could be used to mitigate against eco-campaigns through well informed counter-measures from seasoned lobbyists and speakers who are regarded as having 'moral authority' on green issues. Most eco-campaigns depend upon gaining the support of the media, the public and eventually government, if an individual organisation is reluctant to change its ways, so any effective counter-measures to dampen down the publicity could reduce the impact of ongoing campaigns such as GM foods, low sulphur petrol, and sustainable forestry, to name but a few (Milmo, 2002).

As the range of publics implies, PR has a broad brief and a difficult objective to achieve. While publicity or press relations can make a significant contribution, PR utilises a much wider range of activities, which this chapter will cover. First, however, it is important to discuss in more detail exactly what PR is, why it is so important, and what is involved in its management. Then the chapter will go on to look in more detail at some specialist areas of PR, including corporate identity and sponsorship. Through this, the chapter will show how PR interacts with other areas of the promotional mix to create synergy, and how it can sometimes draw on techniques such as advertising in achieving its objectives.

The definition of public relations

First, we discuss some formal definitions of PR and the activities covered by it, and then we proceed to a more focused overview of the various publics that might be of interest to an organisation.

Public relations defined

Stanley (1982, p. 40) defined **public relations** as:

> *A management function that determines the attitudes and opinions of the organisation's publics, identifies its policies with the interests of its publics, and formulates and executes a programme of action to earn the understanding and goodwill of its publics.*

The Institute of Public Relations (IPR) is rather more succinct in its definition:

> *The deliberate, planned and sustained effort to institute and maintain mutual understanding between an organisation and its publics.*

The latter is, nevertheless, a more useful definition that gets close to the core concern of PR, which is *mutual understanding*. The implication is that the organisation needs to understand how it is perceived in the wider world, and then work hard to make sure, through PR, that those perceptions match its desired image. Two-way communication is essential to this process. Another interesting element of this definition is the specific use of the word publics. Advertising, in its commonest usage, is usually about talking to customers or potential customers. Public relations defines a much broader range of target audiences, some of whom have no direct trading relationship with the organisation, and thus PR encompasses a wide variety of communication needs and objectives not necessarily geared towards an eventual sale. Advertising can certainly be used as a tool of PR, but as this chapter will show, it is not the best communication method for many publics or objectives. Finally, the definition emphasises that PR is *deliberate, planned and sustained*. This is important for two reasons. First, it implies that PR is just as much of a strategically thought out, long-term commitment as any other marketing activity, and second, it counters any preconceptions about PR simply being the *ad hoc* seizing of any free publicity opportunity that happens to come along.

The essence of PR, as stated in the introduction, is to look after the nature and quality of the relationships between the organisation and its various publics. This means that PR covers the management of a range of activities that create and maintain the character and status of the organisation in the eyes of those who matter. It includes, therefore, activities such as:

- the creation and maintenance of corporate identity and image;
- the enhancement of the organisation's standing as a corporate citizen, through activities such as arts and sports sponsorship, charitable involvement and community initiatives;
- the communication of the organisation's philosophy and purpose, through activities such as open days, visitor centres and corporate advertising;
- media relations, both for the dissemination of good news stories and for crisis management, including damage limitation.

All of these activities will be discussed in this chapter, but before we do that, it is important the look in more detail at just who the various publics are.

Publics defined

A **public** is any group, with some common characteristic, with which an organisation needs to communicate. Each public poses a different communication problem, as each has different information needs and a different kind of relationship with the organisation, and may start with different perceptions of what the organisation stands for (Marston, 1979).

eg

A university has to develop relationships with a wide range of publics. Obviously, there are the students and potential students and the schools and colleges that provide them, both nationally and internationally. The university also has to consider, however, its staff and the wider academic community. Then there are the sources of funding, such as local authorities, the government, the EU and research bodies. Industry might also be a potential source of research funds, as well as commissioning training courses and providing jobs for graduates. It is also important for a university to foster good press relations. Local media help to establish the university as a part of its immediate community, national media help to publicise its wider status, while specialist publications such as the *Times Higher Education Supplement* reach those with a specific interest and perhaps even the decision makers within the sector.

A number of different publics, which relate generally to any kind of organisation, are shown in Figure 19.1 and discussed below. It is, however, important to remember that any individual may be a member of more than one public. This means that although the slant

Figure 19.1 Publics

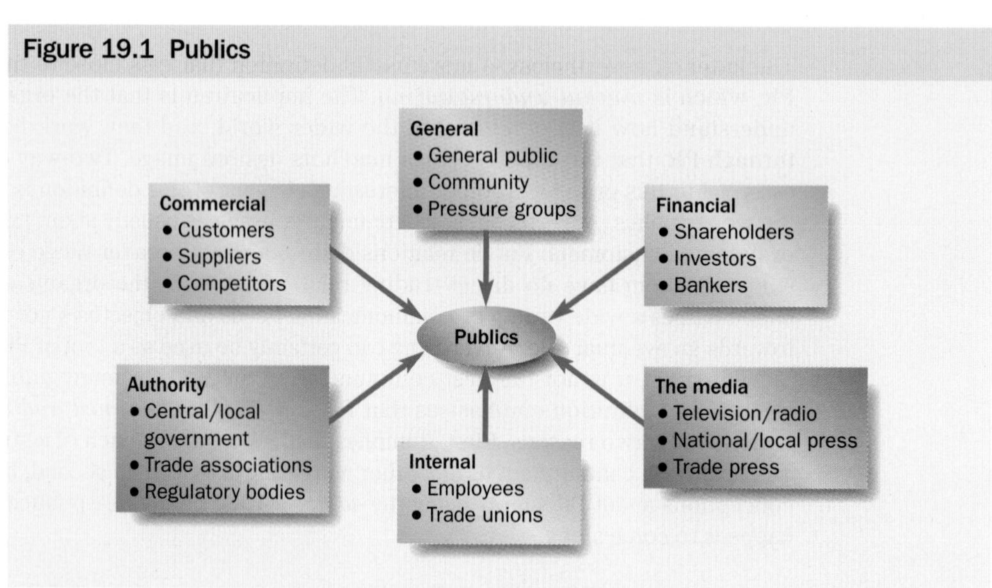

and emphasis of messages may differ from public to public, the essential content and philosophy should be consistent. Appropriate techniques within PR for communicating with a range of different publics will be looked at later (*see* pp. 799 *et seq.*).

Commercial

The commercial group includes anyone who has some kind of trading relationship with the organisation, or those who trade in competition with them. It obviously includes, therefore, customers, suppliers and competitors. The main role of PR in relation to this group is to act in synergy with other sales-orientated marketing communication, such as advertising and personal selling. Public relations can be used to convey product information, through editorial coverage in trade magazines, for example, to reinforce attitudes and opinions, or to offer reassurance about product choice, as well as providing a wider umbrella of positive corporate image.

Internal

The internal group consists of those who work within the organisation, and support organisations represented within the workplace. It therefore covers management, administrative staff, production operatives and trade unions. Internal PR is important for keeping employees informed about what the organisation is doing, for boosting morale, engendering a sense of belonging, and helping to reinforce the desired corporate culture.

Financial

Members of this group have some kind of financial interest in the organisation. The group therefore consists of shareholders, potential investors, bankers and the wider financial community. Public relations contributes towards instilling confidence in the organisation, which means that current investors are less likely to pull out, potential investors are more likely to invest and bankers will be more flexible. It goes without saying, however, that PR cannot be used to disguise a basically unsound business, but it might help to buy a little tolerance or flexibility from creditors or backers. Public relations also comes into its own during takeover battles and when mergers are proposed.

Authority

'Authority' is a loose label that covers those who have the power, whether statutory or voluntarily given, to influence the way in which an organisation conducts itself. Central and local government, trade associations and regulatory bodies are all included. Maintaining good relationships with these groups might give the organisation a louder voice in consultation on drafting proposed rules or legislation, or at least give sufficient advance warning of what is in the pipeline to allow them to prepare fully for its implementation or to lobby against it. Greenpeace has become expert at lobbying and using other methods of generating media attention to exert pressure on both governments and organisations to change, as seen in the Amazon rainforest example at p. 54.

eg

Monsanto has to work hard to convince governments and regulatory agencies to allow genetically modified (GM) crops to be grown. Rarely is the dialogue and lobbying reported in the press, but behind the scenes a lot of work goes into creating persuasive arguments to change policy. India lifted a four-year ban on the growing of GM crops to allow the production of three bio-engineered types of cotton and also indicated that it would reconsider its stance on soya and corn. Similarly in Brazil, the commission on GM foods recommended an overturn of a ban on GM crops and food, to the benefit of Monsanto with its pesticide resistant soya. In Europe, however, where environmentalists have succeeded in making consumers wary of GM food, and Monsanto's attempts to influence government policy have made less progress than in some of the developing nations (Lean and Branford, 2002).

The media

The media are an important group because most members of the other publics listed here will take notice of what they are saying. The media, including television, radio, national and local press and trade and professional press, constitute both a public in their own right and a tool of

Greenpeace uses PR astutely in its quest to raise public awareness of environment issues and to prompt companies and governments into action. The MV Artic Sunrise on route to Belem to check on illegal logging in the Amazonian rainforests.

Source: © 2001 Greenpeace/Daniel Beltra

PR. Good media relationships are essential, whether the organisation wants to feed 'good news' stories to other publics or to minimise the risk of very hostile media reaction in a crisis.

eg

There is a fine line between journalism and public relations. The journalist is charged with writing newsworthy stories for the target audience, whether on cars, DVD players or medical equipment, and the PR organisation is responsible for ensuring a flow of positive messages to the same audience. Both parties need each other and sometimes the corporate hospitality in the beer tent, at an overseas conference or at a sports fixture can result, perhaps, in a less than critical report. Paton (2001), however, reported that in some cases, especially in health journalism, freelance journalists were being provided with all expenses paid trips to international conferences and site visits to write, for a fee, an article on the experience or newsworthy item studied. In addition to the writing, there have been reports of the fee also being linked to selling the article to targeted commissioning editors without revealing the nature of the fee transaction. This completely compromises the neutrality of the journalist, it is argued, as it breaches the journalist's independence. If the relationship is declared, it puts the journalist's reputation at risk, unless it is handled as in the travel industry, where articles clearly state that there were free flights, hotels, etc. If the relationship is not declared, then it breaches an unwritten convention within journalism.

Customers or potential customers are influenced by the non-advertising messages they see or hear in the media, whether on the news, in consumer programmes or as features, and may well change their attitudes and purchasing habits as a result. Celebrity chefs, it would appear, set an example to us all. Whether it is Delia Smith, Gary Rhodes or Ainsley Harriott, on the television and in the press they extol the virtues of fresh, hygienically prepared, scrumptious home-cooked meals. The reality for an increasing number of people, however, is that they struggle to cook even the most basic food properly and often prefer to patronise the local takeaway or reach for convenience food, and this is especially true for those with busy lifestyles and households in which both partners are working. To allow these consumers to fulfil the expectations that the celebrity chefs raise, therefore, the convenience food manufacturers have expanded their ranges to include interesting and healthy meals and exotic sauces and toppings. At least this creates the illusion of an exotic, well-prepared culinary experience, keeping the consumer interested through variety and quality (Davies and Phillips, 1999).

Sometimes negative events are linked with particular organisations. Product-tampering scares (such as glass in baby food), product faults (such as washing powder damaging clothes) or what are perceived to be unethical practices are seen as newsworthy items that could seriously damage an organisation's standing if the coverage were allowed to run on unchecked. The organisation needs to have a mechanism for putting its own side of the story and limiting the damage. Similarly, on the positive side, an organisation with good news to tell, such as job creation, winning a large contract or the launch of an innovative new product, will crave media attention to spread the story far more widely than an advertising budget could, and to give it more credibility.

General

The final group covers the general public at large. This includes the local community, special interest groups and in particular, opinion formers and leaders. It is now accepted that organisations need to be seen as good corporate citizens and have to play a part in the communities in which they are based. Public relations can help this process by, for example, making sure that a company's sponsorship of a local young athlete, environmental project or community group is adequately and positively publicised. It is also clear that organisational activities are under increased public scrutiny from pressure groups who are prepared to publicise and lobby against what they see as unacceptable practices. The clash between Monsanto and the environmentalists over influencing consumer perception and government policy on GM food was considered above. Opinion leaders and pressure groups alike have the power to influence public opinion which, in turn, can seriously affect sales or lead to pressure on 'authority' to regulate, legislate or restrict operations.

Not all publics will be regarded by an organisation as having equal importance. Some will be seen as critical, and be given priority in targeting PR activities, while others will just be left ticking over for the time being. As the organisation's situation changes, the priority given to each of the publics will have to be reassessed (Wilmshurst, 1993).

Even in the quietest and most stable of industries, the membership of each public will change over time, and their needs and priorities will also evolve. This process of change emphasises the need to monitor attitudes and opinions constantly, and thus to identify current and future pressure points early enough to be able to defuse or control them.

The role of public relations

As with any marketing activity, managers must be sure that PR integrates with the rest of the organisation's promotional efforts, and that it is clearly related to wider company objectives. Cutlip *et al.* (1985) distinguish between **marketing PR** and **corporate PR**. Although the two are not mutually exclusive, there may be differences in their scope and objectives.

Marketing PR

Marketing PR may be used for long-term strategic image building, developing credibility and raising the organisation's profile, to enhance other marketing activities. When used in this way, it becomes a planned element of the wider promotional mix, working in synergy with the others. A new product launch, or the introduction of a big new innovative advertising campaign, for instance, might benefit from planned PR aimed at specific audiences through specific media to generate interest and awareness.

eg

Canestan, produced by Bayer, is a market leader for the treatment of dermatological and gynaecological fungal infections. A marketing problem identified from market research was that both men and women often felt embarrassed about discussing the condition and seeking treatment for such problems as sweat rash, athlete's foot, 'jock itch' and thrush. To counter these barriers to further market development, Bayer decided to hit the issue head-on and ran a PR campaign with the headline 'Embarrassment is becoming a health hazard'. This attracted considerable media coverage and prompted demand for special information booklets produced by Bayer, one targeted at the general public and another at health professionals. The main purpose of such marketing PR is to reinforce brand awareness, to create and strengthen relationships and to highlight readily available solutions to problems. This campaign was one of a number run by the company for Canestan, such as publishing research findings at specialist seminars and conferences. The 5th World Congress of Prenatal Medicine held in Barcelona in 2001 had more than 3,000 medical experts from over 60 countries present. Such product-specific PR is widely used in many sectors as part of an integrated approach to marketing communications (*Marketing*, 2001; http://www.bayer.com).

Corporate PR

It is possible to use corporate PR as part of a long-term relationship building strategy with various publics or as a short-term tactical response to an unforeseen crisis. By definition, short-term circumstances are somewhat unpredictable, and therefore any organisation needs to have contingency plans ready so that a well-rehearsed crisis management team can swing into action as soon as disaster strikes. This means, for example, that everyone should know who will be responsible for collating information and feeding it to the media, and that senior management will be properly briefed and trained to face media interrogation. Such measures result in the organisation being seen to handle the crisis capably and efficiently, and also reduce the chances of different spokespersons innocently contradicting each other, or of the media being kept short of information because everyone thinks that someone else is dealing with that aspect. Although the duration of the crisis may be short, and thus the actual implementation of PR activities is technically a short-term tactic to tide the organisation over the emergency, the contingency planning behind it involves long-term management thinking. Longer term, corporate PR plays a useful role in generating goodwill and positive associations with key audiences, some of whom may one day be customers.

eg

Following on from the Canestan example above, Bayer also operates an extensive range of activities designed to reinforce a positive, caring, responsible image among the wider public. In its home town of Leverkusen, it offers free cinema entry on selected dates for different audiences under the BayKomm heading. It also operates a Communications Centre for primary and secondary schools as part of a tour of the production facilities. It is claimed that the Centre does not advertise products, but illustrates the opportunities and problems presented by modern chemicals and pharmaceuticals. With over 200 exhibits, models, video clips, pictures and charts the multi-media tour is designed to stimulate children rather than to explain the finer points of the industry. So answers to questions such as 'Our pet has got fleas – what can we do?', 'How do worms gets into apples?', and 'How do Bayer plastics get into toys?' are all revealed.

Given the many potential uses of corporate PR, it is important that there is clear thinking as to what is expected with different audiences and how best to approach each target group. Without such a rationale for action, it is difficult to assess what outcomes and achievements have been realised (Stone, 1991).

marketing in action

ConvaTec: nursing relationships

ConvaTec, part of Bristol Myers Squibb, is the world leader in colostomy, ileostomy and urostomy bags and associated products. These are used by patients who have undergone major surgery to have parts of their bowel removed, often to prevent the spread of cancer, and thus have an artificial opening to remove body waste. ConvaTec products mean little to consumers who usually have no awareness and understanding of stoma care, unless they themselves become patients. Then stoma bags become essential for the rest of the patient's life and patients have to learn rapidly about the technology and products used. The number of stoma patients in the UK is around 100,000. Around 350 specialist nurses play a significant role in helping patients to adjust to the use of stoma products, and in advising them what to purchase, how frequently, and how to dispose of the bodily waste. The nurse, therefore, plays a key role in influencing the patient's usage and in directing customer loyalty towards particular brands. The market is a competitive one, with several players competing with ConvaTec for market leadership.

The patient might well be the end user of the product, but actually takes little part in the choice of a stoma case system. Stoma care starts in hospital, but stoma nurses can reinforce product loyalty, because they continue to maintain relationships with patients after they have gone home. The hospital is thus the key for the stoma system marketers as, unless significant problems emerge, once a brand has been recommended by the nurse, the GP tends to issue repeat prescriptions without question, and there is little incentive or reason for patients to consider or initiate brand switching. It is, therefore, essential that patients are exposed to ConvaTec products early on to build and retain market share. Other manufacturers are also aware of the importance of that first brand choice and the nurses' influence over it. Around 25 per cent of nurses are sponsored by other manufacturers, which might influence the recommendations they make to patients. This sponsorship also might help the hospital pharmacists and accountants to appreciate the cost effectiveness of stocking certain systems.

Some nurses, however, feel under pressure working for commercial sponsors, as they are vulnerable to contract re-negotiation and even withdrawal if the funding conditions are not met. One senior nurse is quoted as saying that 'undue influence on dispensing methods is sometimes exerted on sponsored stoma care nurses'. ConvaTec has thus chosen not to pursue the route of building its own nurse base through sponsorship. The marketing approach adopted aims to build a direct relationship with the patient, at the same time as helping the independent nurse to keep up to date with new methods and products in the stoma area. The programme with nurses includes regular symposia where nurses are encouraged to give feedback on their experiences; provision of educational materials, sometimes linked with training; a quarterly journal, *Eurostoma*, to present information on current issues and research; and a resource centre available for stoma nurses to use. This approach is far less direct than that of other manufacturers as the nurses, although clearly being influenced by the various promotional methods, are encouraged to remain independent; and indeed, that is presented as being of benefit to both nurses and patients.

Patients are also encouraged to make direct contact with ConvaTec should they be experiencing difficulties or if they have ideas for product improvement. A confidential advisory helpline has been set up and a website (http://www.convatec.com) provides online brochures and educational services to customers. For example, in the pages on ostomy in teens, considerable effort is taken to convince worried readers that a near-normal life can continue after an ostomy operation. The site goes on to describe in some detail stoma care with reference to the products supplied by ConvaTec. Practical tips are given on diet, clothing and even how to handle sexual relationships. The important point is that a one-to-one relationship is being forged with the user. This all helps to foster product use satisfaction and to reinforce brand loyalty.

Sources: *Management Today* (1996); McCartney (1997); http://www.nursing-standard co.uk; http://www.convatec.com; with thanks to Dr Dick Foskett.

Techniques in public relations

The PR manager has a range of techniques and activities to draw on, limited only by imagination. The first area to look at is that of **publicity** and **press relations**, a major concern within the PR remit. Other external communications and internal PR will then be discussed. While considering techniques, it is important to relate them to the target publics and the PR objectives for which each is appropriate. The range of techniques is summarised in Figure 19.2.

Figure 19.2 Techniques in public relations

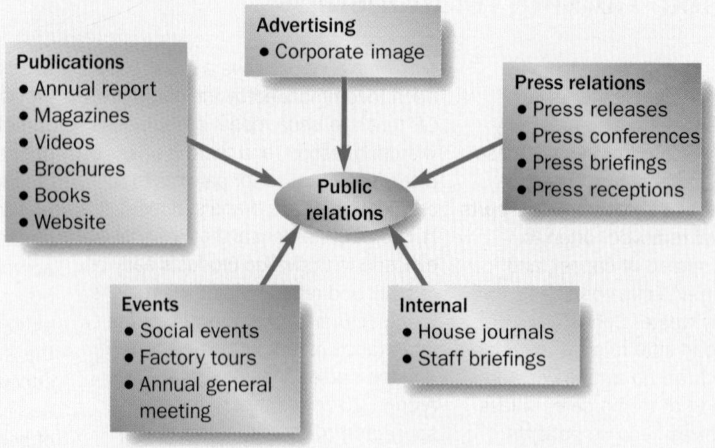

Advertising
- Corporate image

Publications
- Annual report
- Magazines
- Videos
- Brochures
- Books
- Website

Press relations
- Press releases
- Press conferences
- Press briefings
- Press receptions

Public relations

Events
- Social events
- Factory tours
- Annual general meeting

Internal
- House journals
- Staff briefings

Publicity and press relations

Public relations and 'publicity' are often mistakenly used as interchangeable terms. Publicity is, however, simply one of the tools available for achieving the overall PR objective of creating and maintaining good relationships with various publics. Publicity is thus a subset of PR, focused on generating media coverage at minimal cost to the organisation. In other words, publicity happens when the media voluntarily decide to talk about the organisation and its commercial activities.

Wolverhampton University is proud of its achievements in providing access to higher education for working class students. Although it is by no means alone among universities in that regard, it stole a march on the others by facilitating a story in *The Guardian* about its achievements after a good league table ranking. It worked on the old adage 'if you've got it, flaunt it'. The article praised the university's achievements in attracting over 43 per cent of its students from social classes C2, D and E at a time when changes in student funding in the UK made it far more difficult for students to study if they did not wish to run up big debts (*see* Case Study 16.1). The article also covered the views of some of the students, providing the university with a platform to demonstrate its value as an education provider and the positive actions it was taking to improve the life chances of its students (Arnot, 2001).

All areas of the mass media can be used for publicity purposes. Within the broadcast media, apart from news and current affairs programmes, a great deal of publicity is disseminated through chat shows (authors plugging their latest books, for instance), consumer shows (featuring dangerous products or publicising companies' questionable personal selling practices, for instance) and special interest programmes (motoring, books, clothing, etc.). Print media also offer wide scope for publicity. National and local newspapers cover general interest stories, but there are many special interest, trade and professional publications that give extensive coverage to stories of specific interest to particular publics. It must also be remembered that sections of the media feed each other. National newspapers and television stations may pick up stories from local media or the specialist media and present them to a much greater mass audience.

Generating good publicity

Publicity may be unsought, as when the media get the smell of scandal or malpractice and decide to publicise matters which perhaps the organisation would rather not have publicised. To reduce the risk of bad publicity, however, most organisations cultivate good press relations, and try to feed the media's voracious appetite with 'good news' stories that will benefit the organisation. This can be done through a number of mechanisms.

Press releases. Traditionally, press releases consist of a one-page, brief outline of the essential facts behind a story, with a contact name and number being provided for those who wish to obtain more information. It is also common practice to back up a press release with photographic and video material to encourage the media to take up a story.

Many organisations have created snippets of video material that are made available to television news agencies, for example. These snippets feature fairly bland shots, such as the production line or exteriors of the factory or head office, appropriate for backing a wide range of stories about the organisation. Thus a news story about BA's latest wage agreements or restructuring will be backed by footage, provided by the company some time previously, showing onboard views, check-in desks or a BA aircraft taking off. The availability of such material means that the organisation's story is more attractive to the news agency and it may give it more air time because it has the pictures to fill out the news item without having to go to a lot of trouble. The news agency can either use the material as it is or edit their own interviews or other coverage into this footage.

Unfortunately, the majority of press releases end up in the news editor's bin. This is partly because organisations produce far too many of them, often covering pretty mundane events, and partly because they are often produced with little imagination. The news editor needs an 'angle' that captures the imagination and might provide the focus for an interesting story.

Press conferences. One of the problems with press releases is that they are used so frequently and it is difficult to make yours stand out from all the others that land on an editor's desk every day. This might make organisations look for more personal contact with the media to make a bigger impression.

e-marketing *in action*

Exploiting PR and sponsorship online

A website can be used to support traditional print-based PR by enabling journalists to register their e-mail address so that they can be sent new releases immediately and an archive of press releases can be maintained online. The website itself can act as a PR tool. The airline easyJet is active in using the web as a PR tool: easyJet aircraft, for example, were emblazoned with oversize 'www.easyjet.com' logos to promote the website; easyJet ran an online competition to guess the losses of rival airline Go and received 65,000 entrants and also enhanced press coverage; owner Stelios Haji-Ioannou has a 'personal views' page with a 'message from Stelios'. His staff uses its immediacy to keep newspapers informed about new promotions and offers by phoning and e-mailing journalists and referring them to the website rather than faxing.

Online newsletter *WhatNextOn-line* (http://whatsnextonline.com/wno/current.html) reports that it is more difficult to control online communications. In addition to information published on the website and passed on in a conventional manner through press releases to magazines and their online equivalents there are now a variety of sources for what they refer to as 'unstoppable communications'. These unstoppable communications follow a many-to-many communications model rather than the traditional one-to-many. Journalists and customers increasingly read these sources which include blogs (short for web logs – an online diary produced by industry insiders), online newsletters, e-zines, chat rooms, news groups and other discussion forums. The implication for marketers is that they should monitor these.

Existing sponsorship deals can be transferred to the web. These can enable a greater frequency and depth of interaction with the sponsoring brand. For example, sponsors of football leagues will gain exposure from football fans visiting their website. Paid for sponsorship of another website, or part of it, especially a portal, for an extended period is a good way to generate traffic for an online presence. Co-branding is a lower cost method of sponsorship and can exploit synergies between different companies. For example, Internet Service Provider Freeserve (www.freeserve.com) has a partnership arrangement with Streetson-line, a books and music e-tailer, to promote its products online. Clearlybusiness (www.clearlybusiness.com) is a joint venture between Barclays and Freeserve with 130,000 registered users which is positioned as an independent. It has discussion forums at http://community.clearlybusiness.com/forums/ which are an example of the online PR sources referred to in the previous section.

Source: Dave Chaffey.

A *news conference* could be used where there is a major story to announce or where a crisis has erupted and there is a need to update the media from the organisation's point of view. Journalists gather to receive information and to ask questions so that they can then go away and write up the material quickly.

A *press briefing* has slightly less urgency about it, and will be used to clarify or explain details about a story. Government departments often use daily press briefings to talk about the background to policy and about ongoing activities. This material will then be sourced as contextual material when something really newsworthy happens.

A *press reception* is even more relaxed. This is part of maintaining good press relations and involves inviting chosen members of the press, whether national or trade media, to some kind of party to mingle with executives from the organisation and to chat informally. An organisation might hold a press reception, for instance, as part of a wider PR campaign to allow the media to meet a newly appointed managing director.

Involving the media. Press releases and the other methods of feeding information to the press do work well, but sometimes more can be gained by going a little further and getting the media more involved in what is happening.

eg

When P. J. Holloway became the sole UK distributor for fans made by the German firm Rosenberg Ventilation, if it had simply issued a press release, it might have gained limited coverage in the trade press. Instead, it invited key journalists to visit Rosenberg's manufacturing facility in Germany. As a result of this extra investment in press relations, it found that its coverage was considerable and many more complimentary comments than they could otherwise have expected were made about the product benefits.

Advantages of publicity over advertising

The media are obviously very powerful, not only as a public in their own right, but also as a third-party channel of communication with other publics. It may be argued that advertising can do just as good a communication job, in spreading good news to mass audiences, but publicity has a few advantages.

Credibility. Advertising is paid for, and therefore publics have a certain cynicism about the bias within the message. Publicity, on the other hand, is seen as free, coming from a neutral third party, and therefore has more credibility. An advertisement can tell you that a particular make of car has especially good roadholding capacity and you may or may not choose to believe it, but if a newspaper's motoring correspondent or the BBC's *Top Gear* programme concludes that the car demonstrates good roadholding, then that constitutes neutral expert opinion and thus carries more weight. As part of its re-positioning, Skoda (*see* pp. 116–17) worked hard with the motoring media and business press to encourage them to use their authoritative voices to state that the brand was different and better, and that old consumer perceptions were no longer valid. Although Skoda met the challenge head-on in its own advertising, the third-party endorsement was critical to the brand's recovery.

Reach. To make sure that the widest possible audience is reached with advertising would involve a multimedia strategy that would be extremely expensive to implement. A good PR story that captures the imagination so that it gets wide coverage across both print and broadcast media can achieve an incredible level of reach (*see* p. 622) at a fraction of the cost, and might even make an impact on sections of the audience who wouldn't normally see or absorb advertising.

Excitement. Publicity, by definition, is about news. Whatever is being publicised is of current and topical concern and therefore generates its own excitement. Once a story starts rolling, it can gather its own momentum as the media start vying with each other to generate the most coverage or to find a new angle on the story. Extensive media coverage of the concern over so-called alcopops (alcoholic lemonades and colas) is one such example.

Disadvantage of publicity over advertising

These advantages do, however, need to be balanced against the big disadvantage, *uncontrollability*. Whereas advertising gives the advertiser complete control over what is said, when it is said, how it is said and where it is said, the control of publicity is in the hands of the media. The organisation can feed material to the media, but cannot guarantee that the media will adopt the story or influence how they will present it (Fill, 2002). The outcome of this might be, at worst, no coverage at all, or patchy coverage that might not reach the desired target publics. Another potential risk is distortion of the story.

When BA unveiled its new colour scheme and tail designs for its aircraft in 1997, it was praised for its innovative, ethnic designs, reflecting the various nations that BA serves. Others, however, were less kind, including a very public admonishment when Baroness Thatcher covered up a model with a handkerchief in full view of the national media. Despite the fact that the new designs had cost £60 mn, the decision was made in 1999 to return to the British flag for all new planes and to repaint at least half the fleet. This followed a market research report suggesting that in BA's core market, the UK, the ethnic tail fins were extremely unpopular with some customers, who even switched to other airlines in protest (Parsley, 1999).

It is not true to say that there is no such thing as bad publicity. The risks of negative coverage can, however, be minimised by the maintenance of ongoing, good press relations, and by setting up a crisis management plan so that if disaster strikes, the damage from bad publicity can be limited and even turned to advantage.

Other external communication

Other forms of external communication are also used for PR.

Advertising

Advertising can be used as a tool of PR, although it is something of a grey area. The kind of advertising to which we are referring here is not the selling or promoting of a specific product or range of products, but the type that concentrates on the organisation's name and characteristics. As previously suggested, although this sort of advertising lacks the impartiality of publicity, it makes up for it in terms of controllability. As a means of helping to establish and reinforce corporate image, it is certainly effective, and as a mass medium will reach members of most publics.

Philips, for example, felt that it needed to refresh its corporate image because its brand was seen as 'too technical'. Mass media advertising, therefore, was used to reach opinion leaders in consumer markets to generate a more user-friendly image.

Events

An organisation can host or participate in various events for PR purposes. As well as press conferences, mentioned above, the organisation may host other social events. If it has just opened a new factory, for instance, it may hold a party on the premises for key shareholders, employees, customers and suppliers. Such one-off events will also, of course, create media interest.

An important public is the one with a financial interest in the organisation. The organisation's annual general meeting is an important forum for both shareholders and the financial media. Efficient administration and confident presentation can help to increase credibility (although none of that can disguise a poor financial position).

Companies within the motor industry have become masters at organising events for PR purposes. When Saab launched the 9-5 [sic] range of cars in 2001, it invited journalists from around the world to the Royal Danish School of Art and Architecture in Copenhagen. This building was chosen specifically for its minimalist, functional design which was thought to link well with the brand's identity. Saab also took its guests to vehicle testing events at a disused military airbase to demonstrate the link between Saab and aircraft manufacturing.

Daimler-Chrysler, in launching its SMART car in the UK went for an extravaganza, hiring a specialist event company to perform a world premiere of Phat Red Arrows, a display team of expert drivers driving SMART cars with appropriate red, white and blue smoke trails to please the audience invited to the Wembley arena (Cowlett, 2002).

Publications

An organisation can commission a wide range of print and video material to support its PR efforts. Videos can be used, as already mentioned, to support press coverage, or can be sent to potential customers or clients to give them a flavour of how the organisation operates. Most universities, for example, will have a recruitment video to send out to schools and colleges to give a more three-dimensional feel for the place than the prospectus alone can manage. At the other end of the university education process, university careers offices stock corporate videos and brochures of organisations looking to recruit graduates.

Annual reports. An important publication is the organisation's annual report, distributed primarily to shareholders and the financial media, but often sent out to anyone who expresses an interest in the organisation. Like the annual general meeting, it is an opportunity to present the organisation in the best possible positive light and to make public statements about the organisation's achievements and its future directions. With the growth in website usage, reports are often available in both print and acrobat reader file form to capture photographs and layout. PR specialists and external writers are often used to ensure that the message is both appropriate and well presented to an increasingly informed and discerning audience.

Company histories. As a one-off exercise, organisations may decide to publish their 'autobiography' either for limited or general circulation. Although the appeal may be limited to those with contact with the organisation concerned, company histories provide a rich perspective on the trials and tribulations associated with long-term survival.

eg

Richard Perceval Graves produced a commissioned book '*The Story of Castrol*' to mark the company's centenary in 1999, although the circulation was only internal. Pencorp specialises in writing and helping organisations reflect on where they have been in their history so they can learn from the experiences. Its book on Slough Estates, one of the pioneering industrial parks in the UK, was distributed to 6,000 employees, major shareholders and company contacts. The book also went on sale locally and a leather bound version was available to VIP visitors to the estate (http://www.pencorp.co.uk; http://www.richardgraves.org).

Lobbying

Lobbying is a very specialised area, designed to develop and influence relationships with 'authority', particularly national and EU governmental bodies. Lobbying is a way of getting an organisation's views known to the decision makers, and trying to influence the development and implementation of policy.

Internal communication

Although employees and other internal publics are exposed to much of the PR that is directed to the external world, they do need their own dedicated communication so that they know what is going on in more detail, and they know it before it hits the wider media (Bailey, 1991). This emphasis on keeping people informed rather than in the dark reflects quite a major change in employers' attitudes towards their employees. It is important for motivation, as well as being a means of preparing people for change and strengthening corporate culture. Two main areas of communication are considered overleaf.

corporate social responsibility *in action*

Negative PR meltdown

The headline 'Terror attack on Sellafield "would wipe out the north" (Brown and Norton-Taylor, 2002) was a clear message, if one was needed, that British Nuclear Fuels Ltd (BNFL) was really up against it in PR terms. The claim by a scientist increased fears that a September 11 type of attack on the Sellafield nuclear plant in Cumbria would, depending on the wind direction, wipe out Newcastle, Edinburgh or Leeds. If the wind was easterly then Dublin in Ireland would have just half an hour to prepare. This claim comes on top of long-term sustained pressure from the Irish government for Sellafield's closure on health and environmental grounds because of its radioactive waste. BNFL's reputation has not been helped by its admission that one of its staff falsified some of the quality records.

Taking on a foreign government is a big challenge for BNFL. The coast of Ireland is not far from Cumbria and any environmental threat is shared between both countries. The Irish government took out a full page advertisement in *The Times* costing £20,000, backed by 100 members of the Fianna Fail party to try to stop a new reprocessing plant being built at Sellafield and urging its complete closure. The advertisement stated that the site had contaminated the Irish Sea and Ireland for more than 40 years and that the new MOX plant (to manufacture fuel made from mixed oxides, hence MOX, of plutonium and uranium using material recovered from old, spent fuel rods) has no economic or environmental justification. Campaigners in the east of Ireland have already claimed that higher than average cancer rates are linked to Sellafield.

Not content with seeking to gain public support for the cause, Ireland is seeking guarantees that there will be no movement of radioactive material through Ireland's waters and it plans to take its case to the European court. It stated that it would 'raise [Sellafield] at every possible level and get support from other countries' (Colgan and Sheehan, 2001). It is also pursuing diplomatic avenues by lobbying other European governments, especially Norway and the Netherlands. The Norwegian PM used a television broadcast to urge citizens onto the streets of Bergen during an international conference on the protection of the North Sea to protest against the UK's continuation of nuclear discharges from Sellafield. The British government has consistently maintained that all radioactive discharges are stringently regulated to rigorous standards and that already emissions have been cut by 99 per cent, and thus the Irish and Norwegian governments were overstating the problem. However, at the Bergen conference the Environment Minister slipped up when he said that people were right to be concerned about radioactive waste from Sellafield. He also conceded that although the risk to health was minimal, it was having an effect on the fishing industry in Norway.

The two major environmental pressure groups, Greenpeace and Friends of the Earth have also been unsuccessfully campaigning. Both highlight the dangers of the plant itself and the movement of fuels for reprocessing at the plant. Greenpeace constantly lobbies the British government and BNFL to change policies and it has become skilled at exploiting the media opportunities arising from good press relations. By highlighting details such as the progress of ships carrying the waste, it encourages others to take action. During a shipment of MOX fuel to Japan through the Tasman Sea in 2001, a flotilla of small yachts sailed from Australia and New Zealand to oppose the shipment. The flotilla protest was supported by the New Zealand Government. Under international law, no shipment of MOX can go ahead unless it is authorised by the US government, so that too is subject to lobbying. Greenpeace maintains a section of its website on the issues associated with BNFL and there are links to another website, http://www.shutsellafield.com, which has an active public campaigning focus, including information for schools.

As BNFL is a state-owned company, governmental resources can be used to present the legal and confidence-building counter-arguments. There were, however, five separate public consultation exercises, beginning in February 1997, before the Government finally approved the start of operations at the Sellafield MOX Plant. The MOX fuel will initially be manufactured for the export market and will be dispatched on armed ships or perhaps even by aircraft direct from Sellafield in Cumbria. The risks come from transportation, from residual processing waste and the storage of long-lived low level hazardous waste. Higher level radioactive waste is returned to BNFL's international customers.

BNFL also has to keep the confidence of its customers for nuclear waste processing. The Japanese were shocked over the falsification of quality data on reprocessed fuel from Sellafield and immediately suspended contracts (Connor, 2000). As part of the counter-offensive, the management of BNFL is keen to highlight the benefits of nuclear energy and to allay fears about nuclear safety and environmental impact. The Chief Executive plays a major role in leading the PR effort. He is quoted as saying 'We must be bold enough to ensure that the facts of what we do conquer the fear of what we are thought to do' (as quoted by Gow, 2001). For the general public, the Sellafield visitor centre is ideal for finding out about the mysterious atom. The centre attracts 150,000 visitors per year making it one of West Cumbria's largest attractions, and rarely does it attract opposition. Cameras and binoculars are not always welcome, however, on the plant tour buses. In addition, a PR firm is helping BNFL to retain public confidence, for example by encouraging individual briefings with selected journalists known to be sympathetic to the nuclear industry.

Sources: Brown (2002); Brown and Norton-Taylor (2002); Bunyan (2000); Colgan and Sheehan (2001); Connor (2000); Cowan (2001); Gow (2001); Greenpeace (2002; 2001); Kite (2002); http://www.greenpeace.org.uk; http://www.shutsellafield.com.

House journals and newsletters

Presented in the style of newspapers or magazines, these are a vital form of communication. Not only can they cover the important trivia of workplace gossip (Maureen from purchasing is getting married on Saturday; marketing beat accounts at five-a-side soccer last weekend; Albert from maintenance will be retiring next month after 50 years' service) which keeps the place vibrant and alive, but they can also be used for crucial managerial communication. Few people would want to read a long working paper written by the managing director on quality management or production targets, but most would at least glance at a well-illustrated, short, clearly written summary of the important points presented in journalistic style. The **house journal** can help to draw disparate parts of an organisation together, renewing a sense of belonging, as well as providing information. This can be particularly important in large organisations, such as retailers and large multinationals, whose staff work in geographically dispersed branches. Shell UK, for example, runs a quarterly inhouse magazine called *Shell Focus* covering many topical issues concerning the organisation, including a company-orientated update on the various public debates over Shell's environmental record and its activities in Nigeria.

Briefings

Briefings provide a good mechanism for face-to-face contact between management and staff, and for increasing staff involvement and empowerment. Frequent, regular departmental or section meetings can be used to thrash out operational problems and to pass communication downwards through the organisation. Less frequently, once a year perhaps, more senior management can address staff, presenting results and strategic plans, and directly answering questions. Internal staff briefings are also likely to feature in a crisis management plan. If staff are hearing disaster and scare stories in the media, then they need to be reassured and given full and accurate information about what is being done. After all, their jobs may be at stake.

Evaluation

Any PR programme should have begun with specific objectives relating to specific publics and, in order to learn from the experience, needs to end with an evaluation of success or failure (Palin, 1982). Haywood (1984) suggests seven commonly used measures of results, some of them qualitative, others less so. They are summarised in Figure 19.3, and discussed below.

Not all of these measures will be appropriate for all PR campaigns. The choice of method depends on the defined objective of the PR programme and the target publics involved. In all PR campaigns, however, it is important to define objectives at the start and to define the means by which outcomes will be measured. It is also important to ensure that those measures adequately identify the contribution of PR against the competing background of other marketing techniques.

Budget

This is a straightforward assessment of whether the planned activity has been completed within the given budget and timescale. This seems fine as a measure of management planning and control, but it does not say much about the quality of the activity or whether it actually made any appreciable difference to anything. Thus it provides no measure of the activity's cost effectiveness.

Awareness

Using standard market research techniques (*see* Chapter 6), an organisation can try to establish whether there has been any increase in awareness of the organisation among the target publics. Care must be taken, however, to try to differentiate between the effects of PR and those of other marketing activities, and also to establish where the synergies between them lie.

Figure 19.3 Evaluating public relations

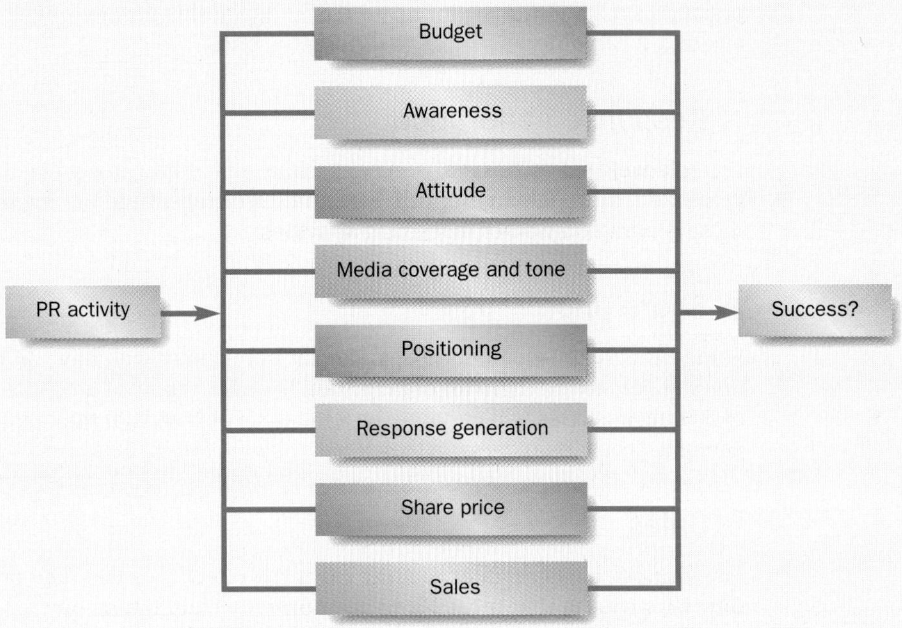

PR activity
Budget
Awareness
Attitude
Media coverage and tone
Positioning
Response generation
Share price
Sales
Success?

Attitude

Building on the identification of changes in awareness, research can establish not only the levels of awareness and knowledge, but also how target publics now feel about the organisation, and to what extent the PR has affected this. Ideally, this post-PR research should be compared with the pre-PR position to give a clearer picture of how far and how deeply the PR has penetrated attitudes.

Media coverage and tone

There are two facets to media evaluation in relation to a PR programme. The first is simply finding out how much media coverage the PR generated. This can be measured in air time or column inches, for instance. It is, however, dangerous to be unduly impressed by the sheer *quantity* of coverage; getting the message into the right medium for the target public is much more important.

The second, and harder part, is assessing the *tone* of the coverage, whether it emphasised the right aspects of the story, whether it was generally favourable, and whether the coverage was suitably prominent. There are many subjective elements within such an assessment, and it might best be combined with the attitude research, to look at coverage from the point of view of its effects rather than its quantity.

eg

When Coca-Cola launched its Coke Auction site (*see* pp. 586–7), it offered 'must have' items and 'must experience' opportunities in return for ring-pulls and labels. It used a series of 'newsworthy prizes' to attract attention, including a free university education and a chance to have a white Christmas by having your house covered in real snow. The promotion was covered in most of the national and regional titles with a combined audience of 150 million, and attracting space that would have cost £1.3 mn to purchase for advertising. All of this information was invaluable to Coca-Cola in assessing the value of the PR campaign (*Marketing*, 2001).

Positioning

Evaluating position means assessing how the PR activity has affected the positioning of the organisation in relation to its competitors. Again, this may be linked with attitude research, and may mean different things to different publics.

Response generation

It is relatively easy to quantify response, in terms of how many enquiries or leads have been generated, although, again, it is essential to differentiate between the results of PR and those generated by other marketing activities.

Share price

Some PR activities aimed at the financial public may well have an effect on the organisation's share price. Where an organisation is under threat of a hostile takeover bid, the level of dealing in shares will certainly be a measure of how well the organisation has used PR to persuade its shareholders not to sell out.

Sales

The ultimate measure in evaluating PR is the effect on sales. The problem with measuring this, however, is that most PR is not normally orientated towards affecting sales. As so many other matters have a much greater influence on sales, it might be impossible to state with any certainty what the contribution of PR has been. In an unusual situation, however, such as a product-tampering scare, when the story hits the media there will inevitably be a sharp drop in sales, and any slowing or reversal of that decline is likely to be an outcome of the quality of the PR response to the crisis. In such a case, direct attribution is possible with some confidence.

Corporate reputation

In recent years, corporate reputation management has emerged as a distinct driving philosophy behind corporate PR (Hutton *et al.*, 2001). Corporate reputation is concerned with:

> *...how people feel about a company based on whatever information (or misinformation) they have on, company activities, workplace, past performance and future prospects.* (Fombrun, 2000)

A company's reputation is, therefore, a fundamental factor in the effectiveness of its communications and transactions with both internal and external publics. The problem for organisations is that it is the perception of a company, rather than the reality, that those publics adopt (*Business Europe*, 2002). That perception is made up of a bundle of value judgments about an organisation's attributes that often have evolved over a considerable period of time. Compare, for example, your perception of the reputations of Microsoft vs Macintosh, Volvo vs Seat, or MFI vs IKEA, and why you think that way.

The increased attention paid to corporate reputation and, in part, corporate identity, the visible face of the organisation, reflects the emergence of more demanding stakeholders and thus a link between reputation and trust which can in turn lead to a powerful form of competitive advantage. Consumers, for example, are demanding higher standards of ethical behaviour from organisations and increasingly will consider a company's track record on issues such as the environment and human rights before making purchase decisions. In Denmark, it has been suggested that as many as 50 per cent of all consumers will decide not to purchase a product on ethical/environmental grounds and that these consumers tend to be better educated, wealthier and more critical than the average Danish consumer (Pruzen, 2001). Similarly, the reputation of the organisation plays a key role in encouraging and reassuring investors and retaining good employees.

eg

Before being placed into administration by the UK government, Railtrack struggled unsuccessfully to regain its reputation and the trust of the rail regulator, investors, train operators, the travelling public and the government. The Paddington rail accident followed by the de-railment at Hatfield were significant blows to the confidence placed in Railtrack and the barrage of press coverage following these accidents helped to undermine any recovery. The company became embroiled in crisis PR from which it could not recover. Saying 'sorry' was not enough to regain confidence against claims of complacency and ineffective management, and its reputation sank so low that the government was faced with little choice but to step in (Arnold, 2001).

Reputation management is not just about the PR department; it is a cross-functional concept (O'Connor, 2001). The stakeholder may be positive about the products sold and the information provided on the website, but could think that the after-sales care or servicing is far from convincing. A major task for corporate PR is to make sure that the communications strategies and messages that are directed at its various publics are consistent with the overall planned positioning of the organisation. That requires a firm understanding of how the publics perceive the organisation. Fombrun (2000) suggested that people justify their feelings about companies around six broad categories, as shown in Figure 19.4.

Figure 19.4 Perceived corporate reputation: what the stakeholder thinks

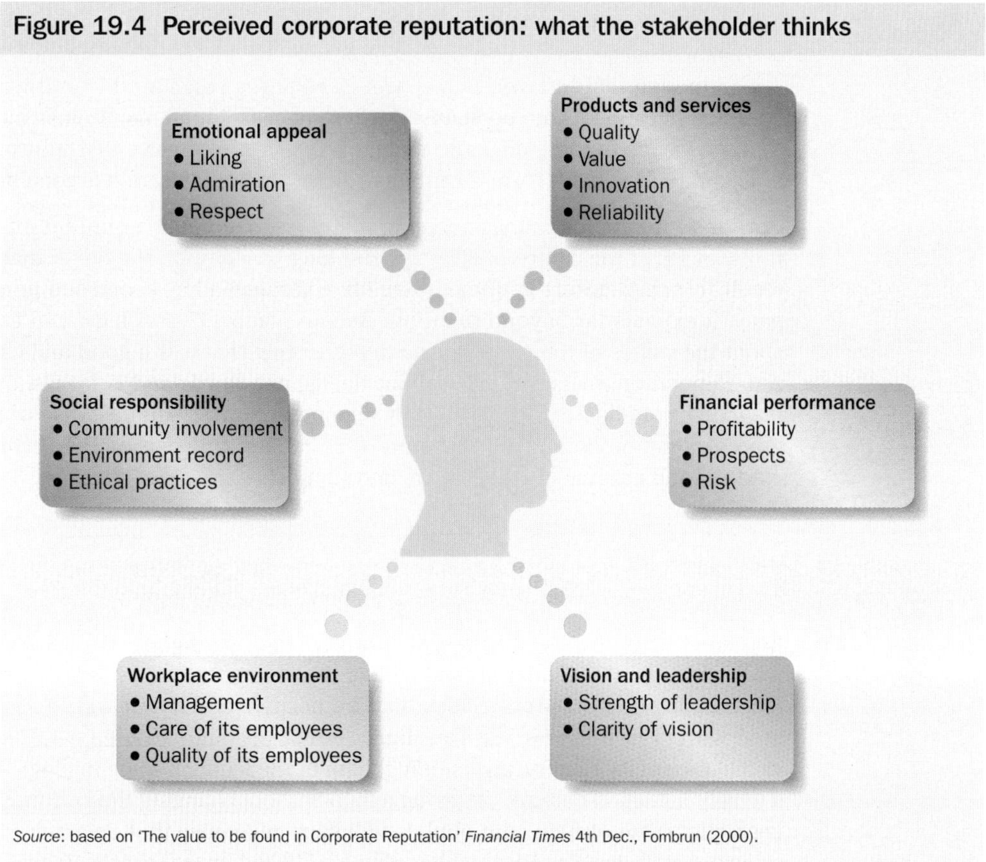

Source: based on 'The value to be found in Corporate Reputation' *Financial Times* 4th Dec., Fombrun (2000).

An important role of PR is to help reinforce positive feelings on these six dimensions using the range of techniques described in this chapter. This means working across the organisation to ensure that the best is made of all its positive attributes, but sometimes campaigns may also have to be developed to try to alter negative perceptions.

Perceptions and values do vary across national boundaries, as they can sometimes be culturally specific. Cowlett (2001) highlighted the differences between US and European organisations: those in Europe put more emphasis on the 'softer' side of business values than those in the US, seeking to project an image of being friendly and caring. There are differences between European countries, too. Although values associated with customer service, quality and innovation are paramount across Europe, compared with Iberian companies, those from Scandinavia and the UK particularly emphasise integrity, reliability, competence, value and friendliness in their corporate communications.

Fombrun (2000) has identified five principles to guide the management of corporate reputation, drawing upon segmentation, targeting and branding concepts:

- *Distinctiveness.* Strong reputations result when companies occupy a distinctive position in the minds of stakeholders and when companies move into an empty niche such as Body Shop did a number of years ago with its reputation for 'green' cosmetics.
- *Focus.* Reputations are often enhanced when companies focus on a core theme. Johnson & Johnson has spent many years building a reputation for trustworthiness with a core focus on nurturing and caring. It is no accident that babies feature highly in its corporate communications, despite baby products accounting for less than 10 per cent of its product portfolio.
- *Consistency.*: A company should be consistent in all its actions and communications with its publics. A reputation can be weakened if a company tries to maintain compartmentalised relationships with different stakeholders with different, unrelated themes.
- *Identity.* Strong reputations are built on companies being genuine. In the long run, trying to manipulate external images by relying on advertising and public relations will fail if it is disconnected from the company's identity and reality.
- *Transparency.* Strong corporate reputations develop when companies are transparent in conducting their affairs. Transparency requires considerable and well thought through communication. Often companies with stronger reputations disclose more information, are more visible in the media and make every effort to ensure that information is timely and accurate. This helps form the impression that the organisation is genuine and credible.

Corporate reputation management is, therefore, becoming an important part of PR activity. It places PR at the centre of strategic thinking based upon the belief that strong reputations result from generating genuine, distinctive values and a recognised personality for a company. It extends far beyond the more limited perspective of legal and ethical conduct. It is about the values of the organisation and ensuring that it is a good and caring corporate citizen. Reputation management is about deeds, not words and is far removed from the much maligned 'spin-doctoring'. It is about openness, honesty and a sense of purpose in an integrated communications programme that makes full use of PR techniques to improve external and internal understanding and support.

Corporate identity

Corporate identity refers to the way in which an organisation chooses to present itself to the world. Ideally the identity should reflect the character and philosophy of the organisation, emphasising those characteristics that are positive and that it would most like to be associated with (Van Riel and Van Den Ban, 2001). Although an organisation's logo is the most visible face of its identity, this is only the tip of the iceberg, since the logo should emerge from a deeply ingrained culture. Changing a logo without changing the culture correspondingly is a cosmetic waste of time, and publics will soon recognise that under the fresh veneer lie the same old attitudes. Van Riel and Van Den Ban (2001) argue that the degree to which the organisation has a strong set of positive or negative associations and a high familiarity will have an impact on the nature of the perceptions people attach to the identity or logo.

The creation of new companies or the decision to signal a change in company culture and mission is often accompanied by name changes and new logos. Table 19.1 indicates some recent changes and their rationale. One of the most controversial changes of all in recent years was the change of name of the Post Office Group to Consignia which is considered in this case study at the end of this chapter.

Table 19.1 Nice names, shame about the reasons ...

New name	*Old name*	*Date of change*	*Rationale*
Arriva	Cowie	January 1998	The bus company decided Arriva was 'more continental'. 'Derived from the verb 'to arrive', the new name reflected the core benefit provided by any passenger services company', it said.
Carillion	Tarmac Construction Services	August 1999	Derived from 'carillion', meaning 'peal of bells', after demerging from Tarmac. 'It struck a chord', said a spokesman. 'It summed up the new culture and it was mould-breaking.'
Thus	Scottish Telecom	October 1999	'We repositioned ourselves as a United Kingdom-wide data and internet provider', the company explained. 'The name is an empty vessel that we can build a reputation on.'

Source: adapted from Harrison (2001).

Reasons for changing identity

The 1980s and 1990s saw a boom in the corporate identity business, as organisations both large and small became aware of the importance of presenting a sharp image to their various publics. They realised that they needed to manage and plan their identities rather than letting an image evolve by accident. There are many reasons that organisations eventually decide to develop or change their corporate image, as shown in Figure 19.5 and discussed below.

Figure 19.5 Reasons for changing corporate identity

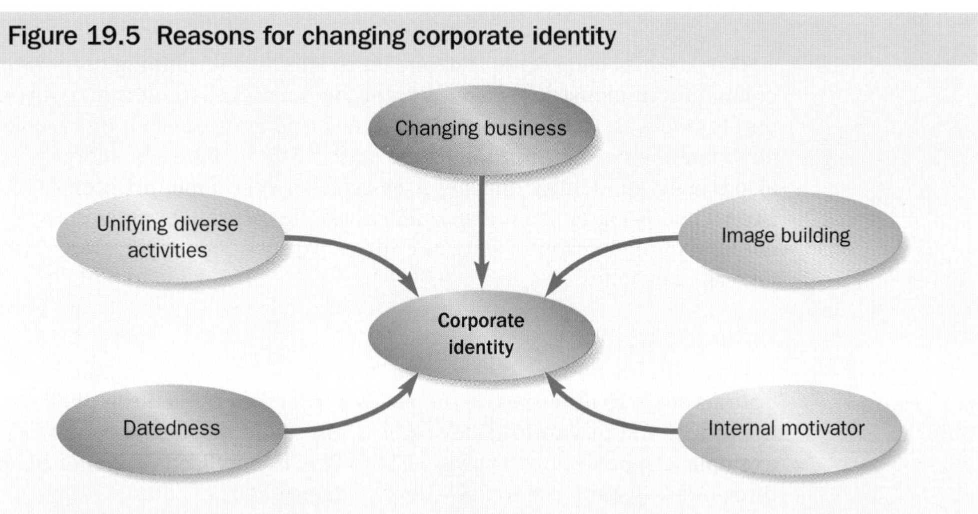

Datedness

An existing identity may come to look old fashioned and it may be considered to be having an adverse effect on publics who see it as a sign of an organisation that is being left behind.

eg

Whitbread found that the image of its 200+ budget hotels in the Travel Inn chain had become somewhat dated and so decided on a revamp. Part of this was updating the logo, a rather tired-looking logo with white lettering on a blue background with a small green bed sign, to a new identity featuring a half moon with a human face at rest, in modern colours (see illustration below). This was part of a £300 mn investment up to 2004 to upgrade and add bed capacity along with a revitalised advertising campaign. The change in identity was regarded as an important signal to the market of something different (Rogers, 1999).

Before and after: giving a more human face to Travel Inn.

Source: Whitbread Plc.

Changing or developing business

Some organisations find that their existing identities are no longer appropriate because of the way their business has evolved.

In the UK, a Home Office report concluded that the police needed to develop a recognisable and familiar national logo to help reduce the public's fear of crime. By adopting an old blue lamp (reminding older people at least of the 'Dixon of Dock Green' friendly neighbourhood bobby on the beat) or a design based on the distinctive policeman's helmet, for example, a clearer identity could be created for the police force and it might reassure people that the reality of crime is not as bad as the fear. The report stated that although crime had fallen by 43 per cent in the eight-year period to 2002, the fear of crime had actually grown. By adopting a national rather than local brand but with the use of PR activities at local force level, a flow of positive stories and messages could help to rebuild public confidence (Travis, 2001).

Privatisation can create a strong motivation for rethinking corporate identity. Privatised companies in industries such as water and electricity took the opportunity for radical corporate redesign to emphasise their new found status and to disassociate themselves from any lingering poor reputation of the state owned industries. Mergers or acquisitions might also trigger an identity change. A merger between Smit, a Dutch offshore contractor, and Brown and Root, an American underwater engineering company, created an entirely different kind of organisation from either of its parents. This was reflected in its new identity and logo as Rockwater.

Differentiation

Linked with the previous point is the fact that, as markets become more competitive, organisations strive to differentiate themselves from the competition. While this is obviously done at product and promotional levels, it is also done through corporate identity. Consider, for example, the power of the swoosh for Nike, the stylised propeller blade for BMW, and the three-pointed star for Mercedes-Benz (Glancey, 2001).

Unifying diverse activities

Large organisations engaged in a wide variety of activities have a particularly fine balancing act to achieve. On the one hand, they want each operating division or subsidiary company to have a certain degree of autonomy and to be seen as a specialist in its own field, yet on the other hand, they still want the divisions or subsidiaries to be seen to have the backing of the wider organisation and to benefit from its standing and reputation. An umbrella style of corporate identity can allow the divisions or subsidiaries to retain their own names and character, but visibly draws them all together under a unified house style that marks them as being related to each other.

When organisations formally merge there is a pressing need to develop a new, unified identity that makes a statement to the financial community, shareholders, customers and employees alike about the equality within the merger and the character of the new organisation. When Price Waterhouse merged with Coopers and Lybrand in 1998, the new name became PricewaterhouseCoopers (http://www.pwcglobal.com). Although Lybrand was dropped, the new organisation had a clear link with the values and strength of the past. Even the name itself was displayed with a bolder C to highlight the link between the two originally separate names. Despite the merger, a clear identity was retained that would still be familiar to the customer. When the former British Steel amalgamated with Hoogovens of the Netherlands the title Corus was successfully launched to move away from what was considered an outdated market image, although the old problems of excess market capacity still plagued the new company.

Image building

Clearly, a prime motivation for working on corporate image is to communicate the desired image. Careful thought about the elements of the image and the impression they convey can lead to an effective change in attitudes. This can be reinforced by using effective PR and advertising to explain the meaning of the new identity when it is launched.

Pizza Hut has more than 7,000 restaurants worldwide, so any change in logo design has to be approached with care. Although the original logo had served well for over 20 years, Pizza Hut wanted to reflect its healthier eating approach and the wider selection of vegetarian food available. Landor (http://www.landor.com) created a logo based on a roof image and used a freehand typography to convey a more casual and enjoyable eating experience, adding vibrant green and yellow colours to convey freshness and fun. It also created a palette of secondary veggie icons to provide a toolbox of elements with which to build a cohesive new brand. The changes were planned to help Pizza Hut upgrade its image and to demonstrate its relevance to changing tastes and eating habits.

Internal motivator

Finally, a corporate identity exercise, if managed properly, can be a useful means of effecting internal changes in attitudes. The process of thinking about identity, as discussed below, makes the organisation as a whole look at where it is and where it is going, and what it means to work for that organisation. Launching a new identity can represent a fresh start, or a renewed sense of purpose and direction.

The change process

There are many good reasons for going ahead with a change in corporate identity, but the exercise is only as good as its implementation. It is a sufficiently specialised area to warrant the involvement of professional corporate identity consultants who will oversee the whole process. This subsection deals with the change process.

Figure 19.6 outlines the broad stages involved in the change process, each of which is discussed below.

Research

Before the identity change process can begin, it is essential to carry out research both internally and externally, with a variety of important publics, to establish exactly how the organisation is currently viewed, and what kind of organisation those publics would ideally like to see. Until this is done, the extent and direction of change required will be uncertain.

Setting objectives and criteria for the new identity

A formal statement sets out what the identity is to achieve and what characteristics it is to reflect. This will be based on the research undertaken, and will balance the needs of the

Figure 19.6 Stages in the corporate identity change process

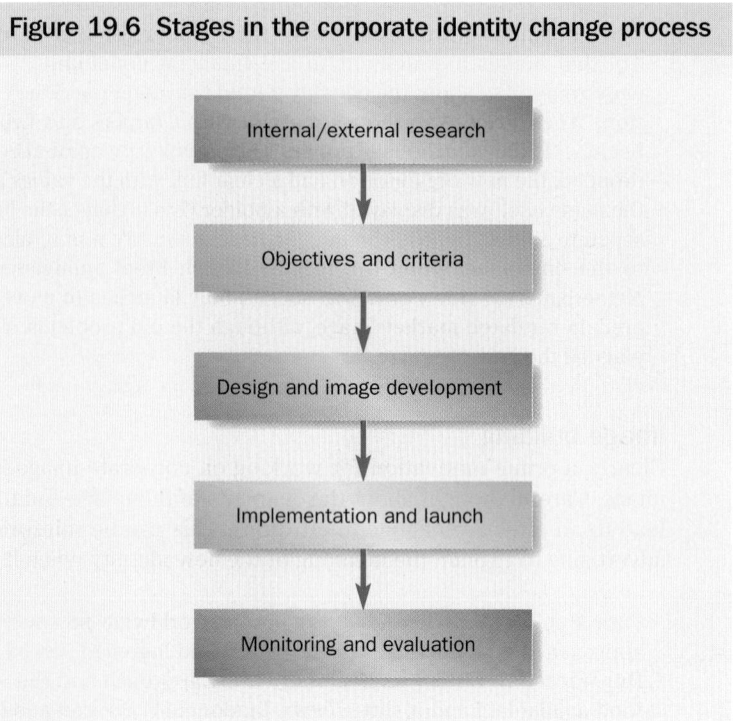

various external publics consulted with the organisation's internal mission statement and future direction.

Design and development of the new image

It is in the design and development stage that the words and concepts are translated into a visual image. The design team may come up with a number of alternative design solutions, which may have to be tested with focus groups to see whether they evoke the right responses and which one is liked most. In practical terms too the identity has to be sufficiently flexible to be used in a variety of contexts, such as on stationery, vehicles, uniforms and products, for example. It also has to work in a range of media, in both colour and monochrome, and the logo itself has to work in a variety of sizes. This stage may take some time and involve a lot of reiteration, but it is worth it to get the design elements right. An organisation expects to have to live with a new identity for a long time. Pizza Hut, for example, had to apply its new image to the exterior of buildings, interior signs, menus, stationery, souvenir merchandise, uniforms and much more, while Travel Inn, in moving from a blue to a purple theme had to coordinate the colour changes throughout the motels, including carpets, decor and all promotional literature.

Implementation and launch

Much work is involved at the implementation and launch stage – in making sure that the new identity is properly installed and utilised throughout the organisation and that it is recognised and understood by internal and external publics. Staff briefing sessions are needed in order to explain the new identity and how it is to be applied and used, and then there are the practical problems of, to name but a few, replacing all the organisation's stationery stocks, repainting the fleet of delivery vans and informing all the interested publics about the new identity. The sheer scale of this task may mean that it is impossible to unveil the new identity overnight and thus a gradual roll-out during a transition period may have to be adopted.

Even if there has been a gradual roll-out, there is still likely to be an official launch date when the new identity is properly recognised and takes over from the old one. This is a good excuse for extensive advertising and a whole range of PR activities to inform publics and to reassure them that the good things they valued about the organisation have not been lost.

Monitoring and evaluation

Finally, it is important to monitor the implementation and evaluate the effects of the new identity as it settles down. This means ensuring that everyone in the organisation is applying the identity correctly and consistently, and that they are adhering to the guidelines laid down for its use (part of the design process will be the production of a manual showing exactly how the identity should be applied on different items and in different contexts). It also means carrying out research to assess how well recognised and accepted the identity has become among various publics, and what connotations are attached to it. The outcomes of this may mean going back to the design team for some fine tuning.

Problems with the change process

Even the brief description of the change process presented here shows that it is a long and potentially difficult task to redesign a corporate identity. There are several pitfalls that can make that task even more difficult, if not downright impossible, and these are summarised in Figure 19.7. It is essential, for example, for the whole process to have the full commitment of top management. If they are not prepared to drive and legitimise the exercise then there is no reason to expect anyone else in the organisation to take it seriously, or for it to take on anything other than the character of a cosmetic exercise.

Figure 19.7 Reasons for the failure of an identity change

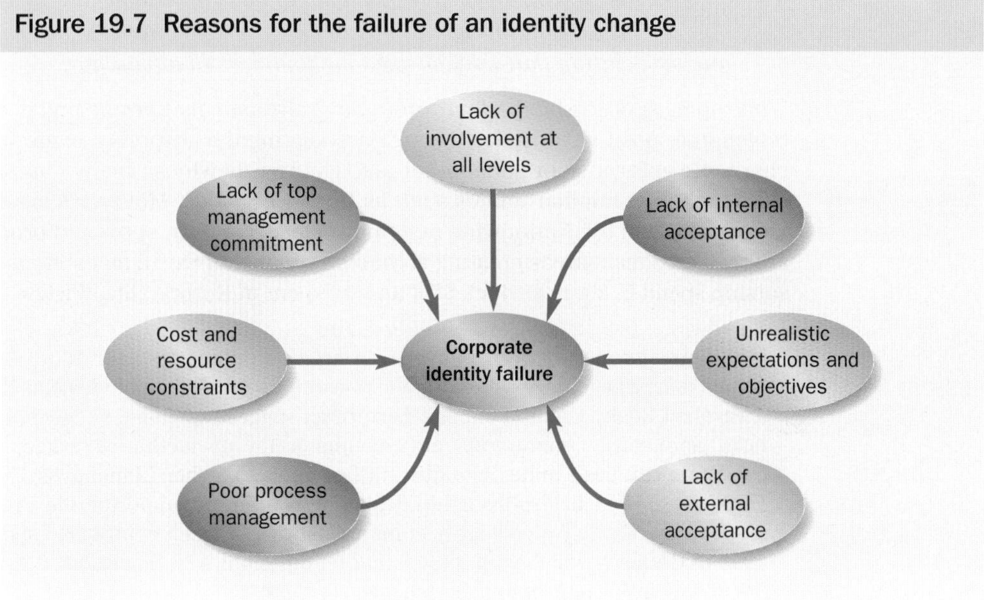

It is not enough, however, just to have the commitment of top management. Staff at all levels of the organisation need to know what is going on and where possible to participate in the process, even if only at the research stage. Creating a shared interest and ownership of the new identity is essential for its eventual acceptance. If a new identity is not accepted, then it has to be the fault of some element of the management process. Perhaps the preparatory research was badly carried out (or not carried out at all) or misinterpreted. The design stage may have been skimped so that an identity was hurriedly chosen and implemented without enough thought or staff involvement. Another danger area is implementation and launch. Perhaps staff were not given adequate briefing about the new identity or perhaps PR and other communication aimed at external publics was inadequate.

To be successful, corporate identity change needs to have, as well as top management commitment to the philosophy of change, the right person managing it on a day-to-day basis. This is an important project and should not be given to a junior trainee as something to do between making cups of tea for the office manager. The person in charge needs to have sufficient authority and managerial skills to make it all happen and to win over the doubters. Entrusting the project to a suitably experienced manager reduces the risk of the exercise falling apart because of inadequate research, poor planning, poor control or a lack of attention to detail.

Given the ideals of commitment, thoroughness and participation already suggested, it is clear that this kind of exercise cannot be done cheaply. It is an expensive investment in the organisation's future and well-being. If management starts putting unrealistic cost constraints on the work, then it is likely that corners will be cut and the outcomes will be poor and disappointing. There is a danger that management will view an identity change as a cheap way of avoiding facing up to more fundamental organisational problems. It cannot be emphasised enough, however, that corporate identity should not be used as a cosmetic means of papering over cracks. Changing identity does not compensate for bad management, inadequate or inappropriate products or a poor attitude to customer service. If an organisation has problems of this type, then it needs to do something rather more radical than simply changing the name and/or the logo. If the organisation is unrealistic about what corporate identity can do for it, then the exercise will be a failure.

Sponsorship

Sponsorship is defined by BDS Sponsorship (http://www.sponsorship.co.uk) as:

> *... a business relationship between a provider of funds, resources or services and an individual, event or organisation which offers in return some rights and association that may be used for commercial advantage.*

While some sponsorship certainly does have altruistic motives behind it, its main purpose is to generate positive attitudes through associating the corporate name with sport, the arts, charitable enterprise or some other activity. That is why so many companies use sponsorship, including familiar names such as Coca-Cola, JVC, McEwan's lager, Carlsberg, Opel, Lloyds TSB and the Nationwide building society. The arts, sport and broadcast sponsorship are the three main areas creating an industry that was worth an estimated $24.6 bn in sponsorship spend in 2001 of which $7.4 bn was spent in Europe (http://www.sponsorship.com).

eg

Mobile telephone operators have been active in using sponsorship to carry their brand names to large audiences. Vodafone's sponsorship portfolio includes Manchester United, the Australian Rugby Union team and Ferrari, all suggesting global excellence through association. Sponsoring champions also means a lot of media coverage, nationally, on a pan-European basis and sometimes further afield, as when Manchester United toured Asia. Vodafone approaches sponsorship deals not as a fan or supporter, but in terms of what the association can do for corporate communications. It has a centralised sponsorship strategy team in Germany which guides local market decisions and ensures that all the spin-off benefits arising from sponsorship are realised (Fry, 2001).

Vizzavi, the internet portal owned by Vodafone and Vivendi, took a chance when it agreed to sponsor the 2002 Pop Idol Contest to the tune of some £2 mn. It could not have known what an outstanding success the show would become with a sponsorship package which included on-air credits, online support and promotional and merchandising rights. The peak time exposure before, during and after every commercial break would have cost Vizzavi far more in advertising expenditure and probably would have made a lot less impact (Brech, 2001a).

Sponsorship grew in popularity during the 1980s, partly because of its attractiveness as a supporting element in the promotional mix, and partly because of the growing cost of media advertising compared with the potentially greater coverage of various sports and arts activities (Meenaghan, 1998). Sponsorship has also become more global and has fitted well with the increased trend towards brand globalisation (Grimes and Meenaghan, 1998). Its growth was also helped by the tobacco companies using it as a means of achieving exposure in spite of the ban on television advertising.

There is a clear distinction between sponsorship and charitable donations (Fill, 2002). Patronage is the giving of gifts in whatever form, with no intention of influencing the commercial success of the company. Examples might include supporting a local hospital, or allowing company sports facilities to be used by outside groups. Sponsorship does seek a return, however indirect it may be, on the investment, although it is mainly about image building rather than selling the product as such. Despite this business orientation, sponsorship may involve only indirect influence on the target audience. The name of the sponsor may only be incidental to the proceedings, for instance the Orange–British Academy Film awards (http://www.bafta.org.com) or Le Crédit Agricole's sponsorship of the Tour de France, and there may be no mention at all of products or services. This creates a challenge for the marketing manager, as the effects of sponsorship tend to be long term and, although sponsorship may reinforce a company name, it need not support any understanding of the product ranges on offer. The effect on sales, therefore, is often unclear unless the sponsorship is supported by a promotional campaign or a series of events is planned during a concentrated period.

Types of sponsorship

Four main areas of sponsorship have attracted most interest: sport, broadcast sponsorship, the arts and cause related marketing.

Sport

With the widespread appeal of sport across all ages, areas and lifestyles, it is perhaps not surprising that sports sponsorship has grown in popularity. This is especially true when it is linked to the televising of the events. The mass audiences possible through television, even for some minority sports, enable the widespread showing of the sponsor's name.

eg

Flora has been sponsoring the London Marathon since the mid-1990s, as part of its commitment to a healthier Britain, as it claims. There is a clear link between the brand values and the nature of the event. As a bonus, television viewing figures often exceed six million, there is a website which clearly links the event to Flora and it has resulted in spontaneous awareness increasing to above 50 per cent. It now even has an international dimension, with the Flora Sydney marathon in 2002 (http://www.london-marathon.co.uk).

Many sports attract heavy television coverage and so although the typical sponsoring costs may be high, in comparison with the cost of direct television advertising, such sponsorship can actually be very cost effective. Table 19.2 shows the main sports sponsors in the UK in 2002 and the sums being spent on major events and leagues.

Table 19.2 Value of sports sponsorship

Sponsor	*Property*	*Price*
Orange	Arrows F1 team	£70 mn over 3 years
Barclaycard	Premier League	£48 mn over 3 years
Coca-Cola	Premier League highlights on ITV	£50 mn over 3 years
Vodafone	Manchester United	£30 mn over 4 years
Axa	FA Cup	£25 mn over 4 years
Mastercard	World Cup 2002	£20–£30 mn
Zurich	Rugby Union	£15 mn over 3 years
Nationwide	Football League	£12 mn over 3 years
Npower	English Test Cricket	£11 mn over 3 years
Norwich Union	UK Athletics	£10 mn over 4 years
The Guardian	Manchester Evening News Commonwealth Games	£2 mn
NTL	British Lions in Australia	£1 mn
Norwich Union	BT Global Challenge	£500,000

Source: Fry (2001), reproduced from *Marketing* magazine with the permission of the copyright holder, Haymarket Business Publications Limtied.

Paula Radcliffe crossing the finishing line to win the 2002 Flora London Marathon.

Source: Flora London Marathon

eg

In 2001, Ellen MacArthur took second place in the Vendee Global solo round the world yachting race and became the fastest woman and youngest person to circumnavigate the world in a single-handed race. That has become a very attractive sponsorship association for Kingfisher, her official sponsor, with a deal thought to be worth between £3–£5 mn over a five-year period. Her achievements were broadcast around the world and hit the headlines in both broadcast and print media. Kingfisher is associated with MacArthur's determination, skill, professionalism, courage and success, not bad attributes in support of its own corporate reputation. Other sponsors were anxious to come on board after the success, but Kingfisher and MacArthur valued the long-term relationship implied by the five-year deal. The fortunes of sports people can fluctuate and the longer-term contract can provide the extra security. After all, the next Route du Rhum may not be all plain sailing (Wheatley, 2002).

Sponsorship of sport has the added benefit that although people may ignore commercial breaks, they do pay attention when a 'real' programme is on, and therefore may be more likely to absorb the sponsor's name.

Soccer has been one of the major sports to attract sponsorship because of its large-scale media coverage in all kinds of media. This has attracted sponsors at player, club, national league and international levels throughout the world.

Arsenal has a range of sponsors associated with the club. The official kit sponsor is Nike, a deal worth £40 mn over seven years, but the club sponsor is Sega, which replaced an 18-year link between JVC and the club. Sega has the pride of place on the shirts and thus can benefit most from television coverage of matches in the UK and the European Champions League competition. Citroën is the official car supplier (the French connection!) and Carling is the commercial partner. The Sega deal was worth £10 mn over four years, a bargain compared with the £30 mn paid by Vodafone to Manchester United for the same period.

Barcelona felt that it could afford to reject an £8 mn per year deal for its shirts, believing that its following of over 60 per cent of Spanish men aged between 15 and 69 and a further 7 million fans across Europe is worth a higher price (Sharkey, 2002).

At league level, Barclaycard committed £48 mn to be the English Premier League sponsor for the 2001–2004 period, taking over from Carling which sponsored the league for nine years. It sought to follow an integrated approach by using sponsorship alongside its television advertising campaign; it planned a football related credit card; and will invest a further £4 mn on a grass-roots football programme. An additional attraction was the opportunity to feature in named broadcasts to 142 countries with a cumulative audience over the sponsorship period of 500 million people in the UK alone (White, 2001). Even for that price, it still did not get complete soccer coverage, however. Coca-Cola also supports the ITV highlights programme (*see* p. 821) and Ford is supporting Sky's live coverage, all of whom will be competing for the public's 'sponsor awareness' (Smith, 2001).

International soccer sponsorship is often too big a challenge for individual organisations, however large they are. For the World Cup in France 1998 there were 12 official sponsors paying as much as £250 mn each to FIFA for the privilege. Mastercard has been a major main sponsor of the World Cup since 1990, and although no official disclosure has been made on the sums involved, it is thought to be in excess of $20 mn per cup. The 2002 tournament was especially attractive in terms of global reach and appeal to advertisers as it was being held in for the first time in the Asian market (Matthew, 2001).

eg

Sponsorship is not just for the big national teams, the global brand names and the big retailers, however. A small menswear retailer, Rodier, struck a deal to dress the players and management of the Perpignan rugby club in its merchandise. The deal cost FF100,000, a large sum for a company with a turnover of only FF1.8 mn. It did pay off, however. One Saturday, a signing session was organised in the local store featuring Raphaël Ibanez, a Perpignan player who is also in the French national side. The store saw three times as many customers as usual that day and increased its sales by 30 per cent (Guerin and Mahout, 1999).

If the sponsorship of tournaments does not appeal, then there is always the option of sponsoring individual athletes or players, or of sponsoring teams or leagues. Some sportsmen and women come at a high price. An Olympic medal winner should be able to net around £1 mn in sports endorsements and sponsorship. Tim Henman, with his clean cut British image, wears the logos of Adidas and Mercedes-Benz and has been seen on Kellogg's cereal boxes and Flora margarine packaging, despite his main sponsor being HSBC. Tiger Woods is believed to have the biggest sponsorship support of all time for an individual: American Express is believed to have paid £25 mn and Nike a further £65 mn over five years. That must be matched, however, with the television exposure, and Nike estimated that on the final day of the 2001 Masters tournament the camera featured his cap (and Nike's logo) for nine minutes and six seconds and the shirt for one minute and 23 seconds. Such exposure on US television alone would cost around £3 mn (Burleigh, 2001). Overall, individual personalities are thought to account for £1.5 mn of sponsorship spend, but the challenge for sponsoring organisations is either to catch rising stars before they hit a peak, or to ensure that the spin-off benefits are maximised.

eg

Cricket has had mixed fortunes in attracting sponsorship, especially in England where the national team has struggled to match some of its international competitors. Additionally, the sport had a declining audience and an ageing customer base. It also experienced major changes as Channel 4 replaced the BBC as the live test match broadcaster, although this has helped to attract younger, more ethnically diverse viewers to help freshen up the sport's image for sponsors. Cornhill, after 23 years sponsoring UK-based test cricket gave up the sponsorship rights in 2000, claiming that its diverse brands were not adequately covered by a single sponsorship. Utilities provider Npower took over the sponsorship of home-based test series for the ECB as part of a three-year deal thought to be worth £11 mn. The sponsorship meant that matches were referred to as 'The Npower Test Series', and were considered useful to Npower as it extended its product portfolio from electricity and gas to insurance services and, in due course, telecoms. The company believed that sponsoring cricket would help with the insurance extension where familiarity and trust were important in choice decisions. Despite the fluctuating fortunes of test cricket sponsorship, in 1999 CGU Life entered into a 4 year deal, worth about £6 mn, to sponsor the National Cricket League, the largest deal of its kind for a domestic one-day league. The sponsorship provided CGU with a stake in every game, the title rights to the league and major perimeter advertising at all first class grounds (Harverson, 2000; http://www.sportsworld.co.uk).

The bails may be flying but CGU scored a six with its sponsorship.

Source: CGU Life Services Limited.

On a more limited basis, companies can sponsor match programmes, balls or even the corner flags. Smaller or non-league clubs are appealing for local businesses who want to reinforce their role in the community, and even large organisations can value this.

eg

The Elms operates five-a-side football leagues in the London area. It claims a captive audience of 5,000 males aged between 18 and 40 coming from the largest names in British industry. Seventy-five per cent of the 400 participating teams are corporate teams, organised into 35 leagues. Its website claims to have 13,000 dedicated users each month. Media coverage is via local radio, such as Capital Gold, and there are other print and promotion opportunities from a very specialised and targeted sponsorship opportunity. A league sponsorship varies between £875 and £1,225 for one ten-week league playing one evening per week. Sponsors include Sabre, Fleetdrive and Minerva (http://www.the-elms.co.uk).

All of this works well as long as the sport and the individual clubs continue to maintain a 'clean' image. A riot in the stands or a punch-up on the pitch generates the kind of publicity and media coverage of the type 'What kind of depths has the game sunk to?' that sponsors will not want to be associated with. Every time a player is sent off for violent conduct with the sponsor's name on his chest, an F1 vehicle breaks down, a player becomes embroiled in a scandal in his or her personal life, there is a risk to the sponsoring organisation. It has also been suggested that sponsors are becoming concerned over the commercial risks associated with ethical problems such as the drug testing that has featured in some high profile cases (O'Sullivan, 2001). Overall, however, the main advantage of sports sponsorship remains the ability to reach large, often global audiences and sometimes to communicate with audiences that normal advertising would find difficult to reach. Tennis, golf, yachting and rugby, for example, tend to appeal to A and B socioeconomic groups. The quadrennial Rugby World Cup tournament offers 2,500 hours of television coverage to a global audience of 3.1 billion people in 209 countries, making it very attractive to sponsors. Minority sports can have their attractions too. The UK women's gold medal in curling in the 2002 winter Olympics will attract far more income into the sport than the £15,000 it had generated in the pervious year. Perhaps that sport will leave its roots and attract a wider audience, backed by sponsors, of course (Corrigan, 2002).

marketing in action

M&S goes formal for the Olympics

Marks & Spencer decided to kit out the British Olympic team with formal wear for the 2000 games held in Sydney. This included the outfits needed for the opening ceremony which was broadcast throughout the world. Although it was the retailer's first significant venture into sports sponsorship, it considered that the link would generate a positive association with quality and achievement as well as making a statement about M&S as a British fashion brand. The £3 mn sponsorship of the formal wear was thus regarded as a natural link with its own core business. By sponsoring the team, M&S became one of the 'gold sponsors' of the games which enabled it to work alongside brands such as Adidas, British Airways, Lloyds TSB and Kellogg's. It also gave M&S the opportunity to use the Olympic rings logo on its carrier bags, vans and marketing communications.

By the end of 2001, however, M&S decided that after one year it was no longer commercially viable to continue sponsoring the team. It decided not to bid for the 2002 Winter Olympics or the 2004 Athens summer games. The Marketing Director concluded from the sponsorship experience that to obtain full benefit, there had to be many more appropriate opportunities to exploit the connection, through related marketing activities. The Marketing Director was quoted as saying, 'Sponsorship can be a great marketing tool, but only for certain brands at certain stages in their life cycles' (as quoted by Kleinman, 2001b). The focus thereafter was to be on community projects rather than high profile sports sponsorship. In 2000/2001 the value of M&S's contribution to the community was £7.1 mn.

Sources: Jardine, (2000); Kleinman, (2001b); http://www.marksandspencer.com.

Broadcast sponsorship

Broadcast sponsorship, sponsoring programmes or series on television or the radio, is a relatively new area in the UK. Television sponsorship forms the largest part of broadcast sponsorship, but it still comprises a minor proportion of a channel's commercial income compared with advertising revenue.

eg

Domino's Pizza uses broadcast sponsorship as it wants us to watch more television. Research indicated that we are more likely to order a home-delivered pizza if we are glued to our favourite programme. Domino's sponsored *The Simpsons* on BSkyB, believing that the programme's viewers reflected its target customers, as well as, of course, its sponsorship being entirely appropriate given Homer Simpson's special relationship with pizza (Mmmm, pizza). Through television credits, special promotions and hyperlinks from the Sky and Simpson's web pages to the Domino's site, brand share has risen from 15 to 19 per cent and sales of Domino's Pizza increased by 29 per cent in 1998 (*Marketing Week*, 1999).

Television broadcasters have started to exploit the potential of gaining sponsorship for major sports coverage such as the soccer World Cup, league action and other major events. The broadcasters gain much needed additional revenue and the sponsors are clearly linked to the show in all screenings and associated promotional coverage. It has not been without problems, however.

eg

Sponsoring soccer broadcasting was difficult for a number of companies in the 2001–2002 season. First, Coca-Cola had to reconsider the value of the sponsorship of ITV's Premiership highlights programme, originally scheduled for prime-time viewing on a Saturday night. The £50 mn three-year deal provided a useful inflow of funds to help offset the £183 mn that ITV had paid to win the right from the BBC to show recorded highlights. ITV claimed that the early evening prime-time slot would attract an audience of young males and family-orientated viewing, a segment of interest to Coca-Cola as well as advertisers of beer, financial services and cars. Unfortunately, the audiences were not forthcoming, and with ratings hovering below five million, ITV decided to make an embarrassing shift to a 10.30 p.m. slot, the original time of BBC's *Match of the Day*. As a comparison, *Blind Date* regularly attracted eight million viewers in the prime-time Saturday evening slot. Coca-Cola was forced to reconsider the value of the deal, as the price for the sponsorship was related to the size and quality of the audience delivered. In addition, the viewing profile changed with the shift to late-night viewing. From the outset, however, Coca-Cola had been aware of the potential of a fall-back schedule and negotiated accordingly (Brech, 2001b; Cassy, 2001; Wilkinson, 2001).

The problem is that although many sports clubs and organisers are keen to exploit the potential of sponsorship to cover their own rising costs, the viewing public is becoming more selective as to how it spends its time. Sponsors are, however, becoming aware that potential audiences may not materialise.

In other parts of Europe, the level of sponsorship is much higher than in the UK. Some in the industry claim that the restrictions imposed by the Independent Television Commission (ITC) are too tight. The ITC rules say, for example, that an organisation cannot sponsor programmes directly relating to its products (but a 'good match' is acceptable).

Thus, Lego's sponsorship of *Tots TV* was acceptable, but PPP (a private medical insurance company) was asked to terminate its sponsorship of *Peak Practice*, a medical drama, because of a potential conflict of interest.

Furthermore, a sponsor's products cannot feature in the show, nor can sponsors have any editorial control over the programme's content. Satellite has a little more flexibility and is allowed to incorporate the sponsor's name into the programme title and to have up to two minutes of sponsor's credits. The ITC rules are taken from an EU Directive and are thus the same as those imposed in other parts of Europe, although they may be enforced more rigorously in the UK.

Even within the current regulatory framework, broadcast sponsorship still has much to offer. As with advertising, of course, it is reaching potentially large audiences and creating product awareness. Further than that, however, it also has the potential to help enhance the product's image and message by association. *London's Burning*, a drama series about fire fighters, for example, was sponsored by Commercial Union, an insurance company. To get the best out of broadcast sponsorship, however, it should be integrated into a wider package of marketing and promotional activities. This might mean using characters or themes from the programme in promotional materials.

Cadbury's decision to sponsor the popular television soap *Coronation Street* with £10 mn allowed it to access the characters from the programme in other marketing activities. In addition, of course, the company is able to reach a large audience of over 15 millon households four times a week with an opportunity to stand out in the crowded confectionery market. The sponsorship does not just cover the Cadbury's brand name, but also features individual brands such as Creme Eggs, Roses, Time Out, Crunchie, Wispa and others from time to time. According to Granada it is claimed that 'there is a perfect match between the integrity of the programme and the commercial expectations of the advertisers' (http://www.cadbury.co.uk). The association has become so successful that the chocolate animations topping and tailing the show are now regarded by many viewers as an integral part of it and Cadbury's has run a number of well-subscribed sales promotions integrated with the *Coronation Street* credits.

The opportunity to reach such a large audience with such frequency and positive association reveals the power of broadcast sponsorship compared with straightforward television advertising. Some broadcasters, however, fear that advertising revenues could fall if broadcast sponsorship grows significantly in popularity.

One of the fears that broadcasters have, particularly when thinking of large deals such as Cadbury's and *Coronation Street*, is that advertising revenues will fall. If Cadbury's spends £10 million on sponsorship, will it then spend £10 million less on standard advertising? Perhaps one of the potential advantages for broadcasters is that sponsorship allows them to build better relationships with advertisers, and thus they might be able to negotiate sponsorship packages that guarantee a certain level of advertising spend too.

Broadcasting targeted at the youth market is becoming more popular for sponsorship as the audience can be difficult to reach via conventional media. MTV Network Europe organised a European Music Awards event in Frankfurt. Carlsberg's, Intel's and Ericsson's sponsorship along with the sale of lucrative advertising slots around the broadcasts improved MTV's revenue by 24 per cent over the year. The coverage to 1 billion homes, including those in the US, proved highly successful with the only criticism coming from those who thought that the music was Anglo-Amercian dominated (Koranteng, 2001). Similarly, VK Vodka supported the UK version of *Temptation Island*, shown on Sky One. The reality TV series features otherwise faithful couples thrown into the company of other men and women to see if they will succumb to temptation. The £300,000 campaign featured a brand appearance on the credits and VK branding on all promotional activity. The show originated in the US and there some advertisers such as Sears and Quaker Oats withdrew support due to what they perceived as the show's objectionable content (Mason, 2001).

The arts

Arts sponsorship is a growing area, second only to sport in terms of its value in the UK where in 2000 it was worth around £150 mn, more than double what it was worth five years before (National Campaign for the Arts, 2002). Over half of the money, however, went on projects in London. The art forms covered range widely from music, including rock, classical and opera, to festivals, theatre, film and literature.

eg

Barbie featured in her own movie in 2001, displaying her prowess as a ballet dancer. It was therefore an obvious link for Mattel, the owner of the Barbie brand name, to sponsor the English National Ballet's Christmas run of *The Nutcracker.* The £85,000 sponsorship was important for the ENB, struggling with a large deficit, and fitted the needs of Mattel. The ENB's chief executive was quoted as saying, 'Ballet is all about fantasy and taking people into an imaginary world. So is Barbie. The deal will also help us get new people into the theatre to see the production'. Other sponsors of the ENB have included Herbert Smith and Harrods. Herbert Smith is an international law firm and was a major sponsor of ENB in 2001, providing support for *Double Concerto*, a new ballet by the talented young choreographer Christopher Hampson. This was the only new production the Company was able to present during the financial year 2001–2002, largely due to the sponsorship. Herbert Smith benefited from the programme of national activities by having corporate entertainment facilities, both at the World Première and the London Première of its sponsored production. It also received recognition through branding and joint publicity campaigns to enhance its corporate profile and raise awareness of its support of the arts in Britain (Branigan, 2001; http://www.ballet.org.uk).

Although dance, drama and music have been especially attractive to sponsors, new areas are now being opened up. For example Fay Weldon produced a novel commissioned and originally privately printed by the upmarket jewellery firm Bulgari. Although some purists regarded the notion of sponsored novels as a 'moral corruption', it does reflect a process that has been going on for over a hundred years since Pear's Soap purchased the painting *Bubbles* to be used in its own promotional material. There is a risk, of course, that if readers do not like the context and the commercial link they may resist the purchase, but so far there is little evidence to suggest that this is the case. On a larger scale for literature, the British Library regularly seeks sponsorship for specific events, such as the £60,000 required to mount an exhibition to mark the four hundredth anniversary of the East India Company (Kennedy, 2001; http://www.portico.bl.uk).

To arts organisations, at a time of declining state funding, private sponsorship has become critical for survival. The state subsidy of the Berlin Philharmonic Orchestra, for example, reduced from 57 per cent of its budget in 1997 to 48.4 per cent in 2000, while that of the Teatro alla Scala in Milan has been cut from well over 50 per cent to 44.3 per cent (*The Economist*, 2001). The theatres, opera houses, orchestras and galleries are not, however, able to sit back and wait for the sponsorship income to roll in. They have to be proactive and approach potential sponsors and donors for money. In the US, there has been a strong tradition of the arts being privately funded and a culture of philanthropy has developed both at corporate and personal levels. Trustees of arts organisations are not only expected to donate money but also to encourage others to do so. The European approach is a little more reticent and corporate sponsorship is preferred, such as Ernst and Young's sponsorship of art exhibitions, including works by Picasso, Monet and Bonnard, that have bought considerable acclaim and an opportunity for private viewings for its clients.

There is a difference between marketing-driven sponsorships, sometimes more cynically interpreted as 'philanthropy aligned with profit motives', and giving donations, which do not place the same obligations on the parties or give access to the wider benefits associated with a more commercial relationship (Meenaghan, 1998; Varadarajan and Menon, 1988). In some cases, donors might even wish to remain anonomyous. Governments can also help with tax breaks for donors. In recent years, there has been some relaxation of tax laws to encourage long-term contracts with companies, such as in Italy where La Scala in Milan, having been awarded private foundation status, has been seeking new sponsorship arrangements with local firms.

What all of these companies have in common is that they are trying to reach an audience that is often older, more affluent, and more highly educated than the typical sports audience, but is also a lot smaller. A wider, if perhaps somewhat less discerning, youth audience can be reached through rock music. Youth audiences are notoriously difficult to reach and to communicate with because of their cynicism about advertising. Various companies have become involved with sponsoring rock and pop events. A number of companies have sought to appear target-audience-friendly by sponsoring events for individual artists, such as the Lloyds TSB Live Tour of The Corrs and the Celine Dion tour sponsored by Avon Cosmetics. Safeway agreed to sponsor a pop concert in 2002 called World Favourites. A London venue was chosen to attract major international acts and the objective was to tie the event in with the launch of Safeway's own-label Mediterranean, oriental and other ethnic food ranges to ensure that the promotional effect could be maximised. Meanwhile, Carling switched from the soccer Premiership to sponsoring two big music tours a year through a promoter that could attract artists such as Rod Stewart, U2 and Madonna. The sponsorship is thought to be worth £20 mn over three years and in addition to the joint badging, will give Carling exclusive 'pouring rights' at the venues (Finch, 2002; Kleinman, 2002).

The important consideration for marketers in deciding whether to sponsor these events is understanding the link between the product and the music. To gain maximum value, it is necessary to ensure that the event features in all aspects of the communications mix, including packaging, advertising and sales promotion. This means exploiting the association before, during and after the music event.

Sponsoring festivals can be particularly useful in boosting unprompted awareness among the target group. The benefit of association between the brand and the event is often enough to justify involvement, but where that can be extended it can add further value to the sponsorship. Sometimes, this can be achieved by a spin-off recording that is released soon after the event.

With arts sponsorship there are a number of opportunities to present the sponsoring organisation, including on stage, in programmes, through associated merchandise including videos and CDs, around venues, and even on tickets. There are also advantages in hosting key customers and suppliers at high profile events, by offering the best seats and perhaps hosting a reception during the interval or after the show.

The popularity of the arts has grown in recent years. While the attractiveness of highbrow cultural activities to A, B and C socioeconomic groups is evident, their ever-widening appeal has created new opportunities to reach different target groups in a quality way.

eg

Orange has been one of the most active sponsors of the arts for a number of years, giving around £500,000 per year. Its support for the Orange Prize for Fiction, given annually for the best novel written by a woman, places it in a very positive light with professional women in the 25–50 age range, a group that has appeared to be more reluctant to embrace mobile phones. Despite its sizeable investment in arts sponsorship, Orange believes that in return its media coverage is the equivalent of £4 mn in advertising alone, thereby enabling increased brand awareness. After five years, Orange is anxious to make sure that the sponsorship does not become stale, so each year it looks for new PR angles such as an all male jury alongside an all female jury (*Financial Times*, 2001).

Despite this, however, the arts cannot be complacent about their importance to corporate sponsors. During difficult trading times, organisations have been known to cut their arts budgets substantially. There has also been a change in corporate thinking, with a shift in emphasis towards supporting charities and 'good causes' with more immediate public appeal rather than the arts, which might be perceived as élitist. There are also difficulties in assessing the marketing benefits of arts sponsorship, and the fact that it is easier and cheaper to purchase tailormade corporate hospitality packages than to sponsor one's own event. Nevertheless, there are some positive signs. Sponsorship from large, London-based organisations may be falling, but there is growth in the sponsorship of regional and local arts groups from smaller, provincial based organisations.

Cause related marketing

Linkages between organisations and charities benefit both parties. If, for example, a company runs a sales promotion along the lines of 'We'll donate 10p to this charity for every token you send in', the charity gains from the cash raised and from an increased public profile. Consumers feel that their purchase has greater significance than simple self-gratification and feel good about having 'given', while the company benefits from the increased sales generated by the promotion and from the extra goodwill created from associating its brands with a good cause. Murphy (1999) argues that companies are taking a longer-term view of cause related marketing because of the positive image associated with a good and caring cause.

eg

J&B Rare Scotch Whisky associated itself with raising money to help endangered species such as the black rhino by making a donation for each promotional bottle sold. The impact of such activities is greater if there is a clear synergy between the brand and the charity, or at least if the charity has a particular appeal to the same target audience as the brand. A scheme to save rare plant and animal species through sponsorship support was not well subscribed. Tesco did support the skylark with £100,000 and the water vole raised £150,000 from Norsk Hydro, a Norwegian chemical and oil company. Even the dung beetle raised a few thousand pounds and Glaxo Wellcome decided to back a medicinal leech with £18,000. However, around 100 species that still need saving have no backers, including the red squirrel. The issue for a potential sponsor is that there is little direct link between the brands and the animals and the audiences are very specialised, so the only real benefit is a feeling of good citizenship (Nuttall, 1998).

Not all **cause related marketing** is linked with sales promotions, however. Many large organisations set up charitable foundations or donate cash directly to community or charitable causes. Others might pay for advertising space for charities, whether on television, radio, press or posters. This is important at a time when consumers are becoming more conscious of the ethical and 'corporate citizenship' records of the companies they patronise.

eg

While most sponsorship activities are usually related to the wider integrated marketing mix, cause related activities often tend to be part of the PR activity of an organisation and may be treated as free-standing. Thus although Nationwide has paid large sums for sponsoring the football league, it also supports a number of community projects and causes that it considers to be appropriate and worthy of support. Its flagship charity is the Macmillan Cancer Trust to which it has donated £2 mn since 1993. In part, the support has been financial but it also involves Nationwide's staff as, for example, in the 'World's Biggest Coffee Morning' allowing staff at the branch level to raise further funds. Over £3 mn has been raised for the cause in this way (*Marketing Week*, 2002; http://www.nationwide.co.uk).

Organisations clearly do not just take an altruistic view of their charity involvement. As with any other marketing activity, it should be planned with clear objectives and expected outcomes. Kodak-Eastman (http://www.kodak.com) has clear policies for selecting which causes and events it will sponsor on a worldwide basis. Criteria such as the scale of the impact, the opportunity for spin-off on-site sales, the fit with the core business, target customers and values and the link with the wider media are used. It is also one of a growing number of organisations using the internet to describe its sponsorship portfolio and to assist potential recipients in approaching the organisation through a structured checklist, although it is mainly orientated towards the USA. The application process also asks the proposer not only to describe the proposed sponsorship but also to indicate the benefits to Kodak on the criteria listed above. One of these schemes is the support given to *National Geographic* to allow it to transfer the last 108 years of its high quality magazines onto CD-Rom. The fit with the target customers and values in producing photographic imagery is clear. At a local level in the UK, Kodak has undertaken community relations programmes around its four main sites in Harrow, Hemel Hempstead, Annesley and Kirby. Support has included supported fun runs, cameras and films for raffles, and sponsored photographic projects in schools (http://www.kodak.co.uk).

The Woodsy Owl scheme in the USA, linked with the Forestry Service, aims to promote environmental awareness in young children. As part of the scheme, Kodak participates in numerous events held around the USA. The company organises workshops at these events covering picture taking techniques, displays, etc. On an international scale, for the Cannes International Film Festival Kodak organises or hosts a series of high-profile events such as being the joint sponsor of the Camera D'Or award, hosting the Women in Film Association and organising the book signing by Henri Alekan on his latest work on cinematographic history. In the Kodak pavilion, the company hosts many opportunities for guests to meet those in the film industry and runs special events for guests from particular countries. This clearly shows the close link between event sponsorship and corporate hospitality and relationship building.

The role of sponsorship

Despite the connotations of charity, community support, entertainment and fun, sponsorship is still a serious commercial tool for the marketing manager. As with any other promotional activity, it is important to specify clearly the objectives of pursuing a sponsorship campaign and to plan the activities carefully to ensure that they are relevant and that they are achieved. Evaluation, however, can be a problem with sponsorship, as it is often used in support of other promotional activities, and thus isolating the sponsorship effect may be difficult.

Sponsorship offers the potential to support the broader PR strategy, both directly and indirectly. Directly, it can provide a venue for meeting key customers or suppliers in an informal setting, or more generally improve awareness and attitudes towards the sponsoring company or individual brands (Meenaghan, 1998). Indirectly, it can support employee, government and community relations through emphasising the sponsor's enlightened sense of social responsibility and good corporate citizenship. Furthermore, it can support wider marketing objectives through increasing product awareness and even enhancing product and corporate image. Schools have become the latest type of organisation to become alert to the possibilities of local fund raising and sponsorship. With budgets tight, finding organisational and private donors is becoming a valuable way of providing the extra facilities and resources that would otherwise not be invested in. Buile School in Salford organised a Valentine's Ball with tickets at £50 per head. The purpose was to raise enough funds to support a bid to government to enable the school to specialise in art, highly appropriate given its location in Lowry country. The head of Benton Park, a secondary school in Leeds, advertised in *Private Eye* for a 'sugar daddy' to give some cash. Despite being a beacon school, its bid for specialist technology status had been turned down. After the controversial advertisement and the associated publicity, ten offers of sponsorship came forward to support the project. Although for some such antics are not regarded as mainstream to the work of a head teacher, the opportunities for small-scale sponsorship from local organisations are potentially great if they are approached in the right way on projects that capture the imagination and offer a spin-off benefit to the sponsor (Smithers, 2002).

marketing *in action*

Computers for schools

When supermarket chain Tesco decided to undertake a cause related community sponsorship programme, it wanted an idea that would give it a high profile and a uniqueness that were not readily available from many traditional community-based sponsorship activities. The outcome, the Tesco Computers for Schools annual event, has now been running very successfully since 1992 and has even attracted its own sponsors, such as Nestlé Ice Cream, Coca-Cola and Pringles with the brands linked to the promotion. In 2001, over 4,000 computers and 66,000 other items of equipment were given to the schools, making the grand total of new computers since the scheme was launched in excess of 40,000 and the total equipment worth over £70 mn.

The scheme allows shoppers to collect vouchers, normally over a 10-week period, with one voucher given for every £10 spent in a Tesco store. Programme sponsors, such as Coca-Cola, might fund an extra voucher for the purchase of their brands. The local schools collect the vouchers from willing donor shoppers to cash them in for computer equipment and software from a special 50-page catalogue. The initiative is especially valuable to schools as it provides much needed access to equipment that may not otherwise be available from their hard-pressed budgets. Over 60 per cent of UK schools now take part in the scheme.

Tesco has worked hard to ensure that it receives considerable public relations benefit from the scheme. Not only does it generate increased store traffic, it also enhances Tesco's reputation as a good corporate citizen that is responsible and caring in its community. The chief executive of Tesco stated, 'Education remains a high priority at Tesco. Tesco believes that one of the most important contributions it can make to the community is to help equip schools with resources that will give children the skills they need for the future.' In order to emphasise the community orientation, regionally based launches, alongside the national launch each year, provide an excellent media opportunity. The local launches often feature schoolchildren, Tesco staff and local celebrities and dignitaries. In 2001, spin-off events were undertaken to raise the profile of the scheme. Stores cut and shared a Tesco Computer for Schools birthday cake with local schools and celebrities. On other occasions balloons have been let loose at stores to create additional photo opportunities. The awards events themselves have become 'must attend' high profile events for local MPs, MSPs and other local politicians and dignitaries.

Tesco has now become the leading schools-based promotion organisation. The coordinated approach between stores, schools and the media has been highly effective. In order to maintain its position, Tesco has extended its involvement in education. It now sponsors three other awards:

- **The Every Little Helps Award:** to recognise the special contribution to school or community life by an individual who is a help to others and makes a difference.
- **The Working Together Award:** for a group of young people who have worked as a team to improve their school or community.
- **The Young Scientist Award:** for young people who have used their knowledge of science to explore new ideas in an innovative way.

Tesco is also a co-sponsor of the Green Code Programme for Schools, a £1 mn computer-based programme to encourage children to explore environmental issues and the importance of sustainability. All of these sponsored activities work closely in the communities surrounding the growing number of Tesco stores and are designed to demonstrate its commitment to the enhancement of education as part of its wider values, described as, 'treating people how we like to be treated. As such, we recognise our responsibilities to communities and to the environment, wherever we operate. Our philosophy of "Every Little Helps" underpins these wide-ranging responsibilities' (http://www.tesco.co.uk).

Although other companies have also become involved with school-based promotions, the Tesco scheme remains the one to emulate. It creates a lot of goodwill where it matters – in the community. That, of course, is no bad thing as an appeal to shoppers and also for the planning authorities as finding new sites becomes increasingly problematic.

Sources: Tesco *Computers for Schools* press information, kindly provided by Bell-Pottinger.

A number of factors need to be considered before a sponsorship decision is made, as summarised in Figure 19.8.

The first consideration is *relevance*, which is perhaps the most important factor. There needs to be a match between the chosen sponsorship and the target audience that the organisation is seeking to influence. Sports sponsorship can attract global broadcast coverage and has the flexibility to reach niche or multi-segment audiences with specific demographic or psychographic profiles (Meenaghan, 1991). Whether mass or local audiences are delivered depends on the nature of both the sponsorship and the event itself. Sports sponsorship is especially useful for delivering young male audiences that are otherwise difficult to reach or resistant to other marketing communication methods.

While sports sponsorship is now widely used by sponsors to build corporate image and brand prominence globally, arts sponsorship is still usually too exclusive to attract mass

Figure 19.8 Factors influencing sponsorship choice

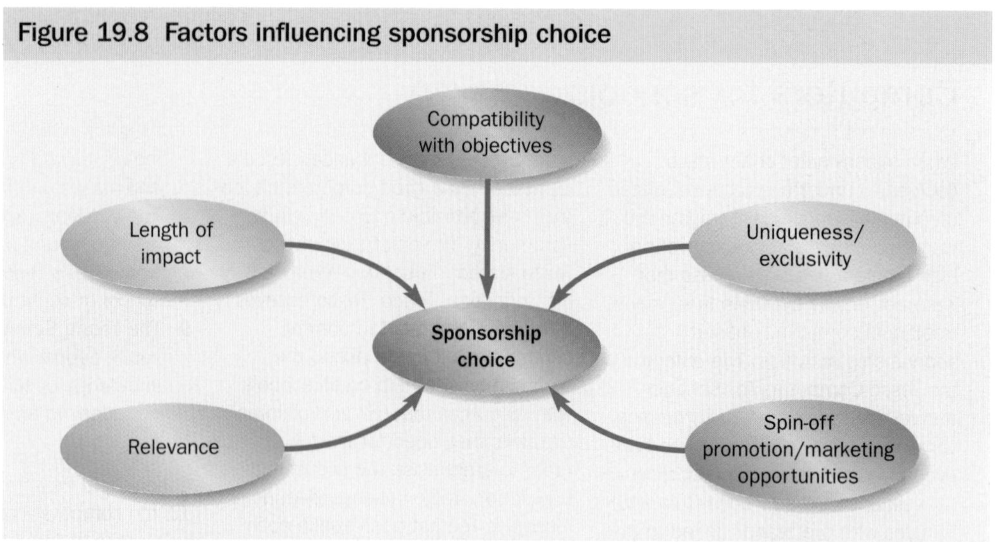

audiences (Marshall and Cook, 1992). The arts have a less public profile and thus a much smaller share of sponsorship spend. Some sponsors still consider it a specialist vehicle for attracting a particular niche. Often, community relations and hospitality are important objectives for arts sponsorship as part of a PR programme (Witcher *et al.*, 1991), but sports sponsorship is often more central to marketing strategy, with the focus on audience reach, brand and product awareness and not least, media exposure (Sparks, 1995).

The *length of impact* made may also be a consideration. One-off events, unless they are very high profile such as a major concert or the World Cup, tend not to have the capacity to build the continuity or establish the name familiarity that sponsoring a sports league or series of events would bring. For that reason, many sponsorship deals tend to last for three years with an option to renew. Stipp and Schiavone (1996) suggest that high-status events, even only a one-off, create marketing opportunities for sponsors because the audience has such a high regard for the event. There are situations, however, in which a limited length of impact can still be useful if it is part of an integrated campaign. Rover, as part of its launch strategy for the Rover 75, linked up with Classic FM to present two summer concerts featuring Lesley Garrett and the Mediæval Bæbes respectively. The aim was to help generate awareness of the new model with what Rover hoped would be a sympathetic target audience (http://www.classicfm.com). Bainsfair (2000) considers that sponsoring sportsmen or sportswomen can actually bring a quicker awareness to a brand, provided that the person features in a planned follow-up marketing campaign to exploit the opportunity.

Uniqueness might be desirable, but as already mentioned, it is not always possible to be a sole sponsor, especially for large international events or where the costs are very high. Although sports sponsorship has worked well for Zurich in Rugby Union, Stella Artois in tennis, Energiser in international athletics and NatWest in cricket, football and F1, the market is becoming cluttered. Different sponsors of leagues, cups, broadcasting, shirts and clubs makes for confusion in the mind of the soccer target audience, for example, and only by heavy investment can a breakthrough be achieved (Fry, 2001). Compare soccer's clutter with the clarity of Flora's sponsorship of the London Marathon mentioned earlier, by which it has achieved some degree of uniqueness as the main sponsor associated with the run for a number of years.

It is also important to consider the potential for *spin-off promotion* and other marketing activities from the sponsorship. Goddard (1999) emphasised the importance of spending more money on advertising and promotion to maximise the impact of the actual sponsorship. Therefore Rover supported both radio and press advertising to ensure that the concerts to celebrate the launch of the Rover 75 were successful. Although Flora spent £1 mn on sponsoring the London Marathon, it spent a further £10.5 mn on extra brand support, often featuring the sponsorship deal. Sporting and cultural events provide a focus for corporate hospitality, as well as an opportunity for sales promotion themes. A company sponsoring the Olympics, for example, might run an on-pack competition to win a trip to the games. Thus Kodak's involvement with the Cannes International Film Festival is extensively used for networking and meeting events with a wide range of either influencers or customer groups. Similarly, major sports events provide valuable tickets to the sponsors for relationship building.

Wella, the haircare company, decided to sponsor F1 through a deal with Toyota. The television coverage was a big attraction as it could help generate awareness of Wella's global hair, cosmetic and perfume brands at a time of intense competition with Proctor and Gamble and Unilever. The intention was to exploit the link, not just at the events and on the cars, but also in its wider marketing campaigns (Kleinmann, 2001c).

Finally, it is always important to ensure that the activity is *compatible* with the sponsor's overall promotional objectives. The fit between the sponsor and the sponsored event does seem to be a crucial element of sponsorship (Crimmins and Horn, 1996). The better the fit, the more responsive the audience may be to the sponsor's messages on the basis that they are serious about the event and share the passion. In the same vein, sponsoring too many events may actually produce a worse response than being associated with just one or two high profile activities (Speed and Thompson, 2000). It is easy to get involved with sponsorship because the MD loves soccer or fancies a guaranteed box at the opera for the season. This will cloud judgement over the real fit with the commercial objectives, and call the cost effectiveness of the sponsorship into question. In this sense, sponsorship decisions should be as calculated and unemotional as any other advertising decision.

Evaluating sponsorship

Whatever type or method of sponsorship is used, however, it is important to establish the most appropriate means of evaluating results. A number of methods are possible.

1 *Media exposure measurement.* Establishing how much air time on television or radio, or how many column inches in the print media, were given to the event is one measure. The problem is, however, that this measurement takes place after the event, and at best can help to decide whether to continue with future involvement.
2 *Assessing communication results.* Pre- and post-tests on awareness, image, etc. can be undertaken to assess whether the sponsorship was noticed and what improvement is made to awareness levels, attitudes and opinions about the sponsor.
3 *Measuring sales results.* Given the indirect nature of sponsorship amid the more powerful impact of other marketing activities, it is unlikely that measuring sales results would yield significant findings proving a causal link between sponsorship and sales.
4 *Feedback from participating groups.* Measurement by obtaining feedback is perhaps easiest to implement where the sponsorship is targeting a small well-defined audience, for example those invited to attend a sponsored concert and its associated hospitality.

Sponsorship can, therefore, be a very powerful means of generating awareness and brand recognition, but like any other promotional variable it must be planned, resourced and managed. Fry (2001) identified a number of reasons why some sponsorship programmes are not considered successful:

- failure to establish objectives at the outset;
- choosing the wrong property;
- failing to integrate the property into the overall marketing programme;
- not setting aside a big enough budget to exploit title rights effectively; and
- failing to take account of what the competition is already doing.

To work well sponsorship has to be regarded as a creative platform that can influence PR, design, sales promotion, above-the-line advertising, online marketing and hospitality. Although sponsorship's role does vary, for example Witcher *et al.* (1991) found that arts sponsorship tends to be managed by the PR department and sports sponsorship by marketing, both benefit from being an integral part of a marketing communications effort. There are also risks, however. Speed and Thompson (2000) suggested that the perceived sincerity of the sponsor may be at risk if excessive leveraging or publicity highlights the commercial objectives of the sponsor. Although audiences know why sponsorship takes place, they appear to have some resistance to their sport or pastime being invaded by exploitative commercialism.

Chapter summary

- Public relations is about the quality and nature of an organisation's relationships with various interested publics. These might well include customers and suppliers, but also include shareholders, trade unions, the media, government and other regulatory bodies and pressure groups, among many others.
- Public relations performs an important supporting role, providing a platform of goodwill and credibility from which other marketing activities can develop and be enhanced. Public relations becomes particularly important in limiting the damage and repairing credibility when a crisis strikes an organisation.
- Publicity and press relations are important areas of PR. The media can be valuable in communicating messages to all kinds of publics and even in influencing opinion. Publicity, 'free' media coverage, has the added bonus of being seen as objective and therefore more credible. Organisations are therefore anxious to foster good press relations so that they might be treated less critically should they suffer a 'bad news' crisis. Press releases and press conferences are commonly used ways of getting information to the media, as well as means of fostering personal relationships with key journalists. There are, however, more controllable methods of PR. Advertising can be used to build corporate image and attitudes, and special events and publications can also target key publics. Given the variety of PR methods available, however, it can be very difficult to evaluate PR's success.
- Corporate identity is an important consideration for any organisation. Its identity communicates its values and its character, and thus should be strong, clear and distinctive. A desire to change an identity may arise for a number of reasons, but it is not just a cosmetic issue of designing a pretty new logo. It needs extensive research to find out why the old identity was not working and to establish the criteria for the new one. The development of the new image ideally needs to be done in consultation with employees at all levels and, where appropriate, in all divisions of the organisation to make sure that it will be suitable and acceptable from all perspectives. The implementation and launch also need meticulous planning to ensure that all the practical and perhaps even emotional problems of the change are avoided. Finally, the new image should be monitored and evaluated once it has been launched to ensure that it is recognised, properly understood and accepted. Where the change process is not properly planned and managed, problems can occur. Identity change thus needs top management commitment and support and cannot be hurried.
- Sponsorship is used by many organisations as a means of generating PR and enhancing both their image and their other marketing communications activities. Sponsorship might mean involvement with sport, the arts, broadcast media or charities or other good causes. Both parties should gain. The sponsor benefits from the PR spin-offs from the activities and the public profile of the organisations and/or events it supports, while those receiving the sponsorship benefit from cash or benefits in kind. Sponsorship might be corporate or brand specific, and the sponsor's involvement might be plainly obvious or quite discreet. Evaluating sponsorship is not easy, but there are a few guidelines for avoiding disappointment. These include the match between the parties concerned, the expected outcomes, potential spin-offs and compatibility with the sponsor's wider marketing objectives.

key words and phrases

Cause related marketing	Marketing PR	Public relations
Corporate identity	Press relations	Sponsorship
Corporate PR	Public	
House journal	Publicity	

questions for review

19.1 What is *PR* and in what ways does it differ from other elements of the promotional mix?

19.2 List the advantages and disadvantages of *publicity*.

19.3 Outline the potential benefits of developing a *house journal*, such as those discussed at p. 806.

19.4 Briefly describe the stages an organisation should go through in changing corporate identity, explaining why each is important.

19.5 What can sponsorship offer that media advertising cannot?

questions for discussion

19.1 At p. 794 a range of different publics are mentioned with which a university might have to create and maintain relationships. Draw up a similar list for your own university or college and:
(a) briefly outline what aspects of the institution's activities might be of particular interest to each of those publics; and
(b) suggest appropriate PR methods for each of them.

19.2 Find a corporate story that has made the news recently. It might be a 'crisis', a takeover battle, job losses or creation, new products or big contracts, for instance. Collect reports and press cuttings from a range of media on this story and compare the content. To what extent do you think that:
(a) the media have used material provided by the organisation itself?; and
(b) the story has developed beyond the control of the organisation?
(c) Imagine yourself to be the organisation's PR manager. Write a brief report to the managing director outlining what you feel to be the benefits and disadvantages of the coverage your organisation has received, and what you think should be done next regarding this story.

19.3 Find out as much as you can about three different arts sponsorship projects. What role do you think the sponsorship plays in the sponsor's marketing strategy and what benefits do you think they derive from it?

19.4 What are the dangers of sponsorship from the recipient's perspective?

19.5 Draw up a table outlining alternative methods for evaluating PR, sponsorship and exhibitions, and the potential pitfalls of those methods.

case study 19.1

'A rose by any other name ...'

When the Post Office was awarded greater commercial freedom by the UK government, it decided to signify the new status with a change of name to Consignia. Although for domestic purposes the familiar names of Royal Mail and Parcelforce would be retained on uniforms, shop fronts and vehicles, for corporate and international customers the new name Consignia would apply. With ownership of nearly twenty companies internationally, the term Consignia was regarded as being more modern, meaningful and neutral following the traditions established by Diageo, Invensys and Elementis. Some of its international competitors use 'Royal' in their titles, so Consignia thought it should become a little more distinctive. Research had also indicated that the terms British Post Office and UK Post would not be that attractive to overseas customers. In addition, with interests in financial services, home shopping, marketing and telecommunications, the rationale for a new name appeared strong. The cost of the name change was thought to be in the region of £2 mn.

Although the Directors of the Post Office thought the new title was 'modern and meaningful' and had focus group research to support it, some critics thought otherwise. The trades unions considered the change 'rushed and ill-conceived' while Utley (2001) argued that it was more ancient than modern and had overtones of Latin, making the name Consignia 'ancient and meaningless'. The reality is that Consignia does not appear in any dictionary, Latin or English, and attempts to link it with the verb 'to consign' also ran into trouble as cynics similarly began to deconstruct the name in terms of the words 'con' and 'insignia'. Perhaps the mood amongst those who cared at the time was summed up by Utley (2001) when he reported that:

> *Companies such as these would inspire a great deal more trust if they had the honesty to trade under the names by which they have become known. So what if the Post Office is no longer concerned solely with the post? A company's name does not have to tell us everything about it but 'Consignia' tells us precisely nothing.*

The following year was fraught with difficulty for the new company. The Royal Mail in the UK faced direct competition for the first time and it found that the new regulatory system meant that price increases could not be made simply to offset revenues lost elsewhere. What was really required was for Consignia to become more market driven by providing more flexibility in delivery, for example, enabling commuters to collect their mail from the railway station, and ensuring on-time delivery services for next day post. New competition would speed up that process. Reform was unavoidable anyway, as the embryonic liberalisation of European postal industries would allow consumers more choice in who should deliver their mail.

Losses mounted and as part of its recovery programme, by early 2002 there were fears that around 40,000 jobs would have to be lost over the three years in order to contain costs. Losses were running at £1.5 mn per day. Parcelforce had been particularly badly hit by express delivery parcel firms and lost £200 mn in 2002. Consignia appeared to be caught between its public service obligations and its commercial ambitions. It was not free of the former, as it still had to deliver mail to isolated communities in the Scottish Islands, yet found it hard to innovate and compete with private operators in the prime markets in the large metropolitan areas. As a large bureaucratic organisation that had not previously had to compete to survive, generating innovation was a challenge at a time when flexibility was needed.

The media generally took a critical line on Consignia, and although not quite generating the same amount of vitriolic coverage as Railtrack, the term 'Mailtrack' was used from time to time. Stories covered the closure of branches, threatened redundancies, dropping second-class mail, charging customers for delivery and portrayed a service that was struggling to cope. It was difficult for Consignia to generate success stories in a climate of suspicion and lack of trust in its ability to manage its way out of its problems. According to the Director of Corporate Affairs the constant barrage of criticism was becoming a confidence issue:

> *We are now an issue. We are now fighting for the hearts and minds of our customers more than we had to before. At dinner parties, everyone wants to tell you their horror stories.*
> (as quoted by Beckett, 2002)

Slipped into the announcements early in 2002 was the suggestion that the name Consignia was under review and that it might return to its former title, whatever the original logic for the change in the first place. That was not the first time such a possibility had been mentioned. A senior executive, under a barrage of questions on BBC's *Today* programme admitted that there was a better name for Consignia: The Royal Mail! To some, the Post Office had become a 'Marks & Spencer', having lost touch with a changing customer base yet having a brand name and assets that could, with good management, allow a recovery. The issue was whether a name change reversal should be part of that strategy. The old name had come to represent a set of values and meaning to stakeholders and according to some, only by changing back could a signal be given that the service was being relaunched, not just with customers but also the staff. As a 'people business', low morale had to be improved to encourage productivity and change.

In mid-June 2002, the inevitable happened, and just 16 months after the Consignia name was adopted, it was dropped in favour of 'Royal Mail Group plc'. According to Harrison (2002), Consignia considered the Royal Mail name more appropriate, as it had decided to abandon its overseas expansion plans to allow it concentrate on its UK business which lost £1.1bn in 2001. This latest name change is reported to have cost £1 mn.

Sources: Beckett (2002); Gibbs (2002); Harrison (2002); Kleinman (2001a); Pike (2001); Scouller (2002); Utley (2001); Wray (2002); http://www.consignia.com.

Questions

1 Why did The Post Office Group change its name to Consignia?

2 How valid is it to have one name for the general public and another for business and corporate customers?

3 To what extent do you think the problems facing Consignia are related to the name change?

4 Was Consignia right to decide to re-name itself Royal Mail? What do you think might have been the implications of doing this?

case study 19.2

Chicken run

To Compassion in World Farming (CIWF), the thirty-year fight to ban battery hen farming was well worthwhile. On 15 June 1999, the EU Council of Agricultural Ministers voted effectively to put an end to the practice by 2012, with a number of interim measures to be introduced in the meantime to improve the lot of the birds and the conscience of the consumer. The CIWF long argued that battery farming was cruel and detrimental to the health of hens. In the old system, each hen was confined to a floor space of 450 cm^2, roughly the size of an A4 sheet of paper, in a windowless shed with 90,000 other hens. In the cages the birds could not stretch, flap their wings, dust-bathe, scratch or nest. Relief only came at about 72 weeks when they were sold to food processors for pies, soups or pet foods.

The EU Directive stated that from 2002 there must be 750cm^2 of space per hen, a nest, perches and litter for pecking and scratching. By 2007, the area has to have better perches and nests and all perchery systems must move from the current 25 birds per m^2 to 9 per m^2, a significant gain for freer movement. Also, by 2004 eggs have to be labelled according to their method of production. The combination of changes proposed in the Directive will strongly tip the balance towards controlled free-range and barn-egg production. This is the culmination of 30 years of campaigning to end a practice that CIWF argued was cruel and detrimental to the health of the hens. Right up to the day of the decision, CIWF fought a campaign using advertising, fund-raising events, video, demonstrations and lobbying to secure change. Even though it knew it had a great chance of being successful, it was still setting up information stands and demonstrating about the need for change right to the last. Even after the directive the campaign goes on, albeit on a reduced scale to end battery farming completely, long before the 2012 deadline. Attention has also turned to non-EU countries where the ban does not apply.

CIWF was up against stiff competition from intensive farming groups, some of which are well represented by those in influential positions. It had to use a variety of promotional methods to secure change and the lobbying of influencers and decision makers was particularly critical. Although UK-based, CIWF has branches in France and Ireland and offices in Italy and the Netherlands, and all of them approached their local MEPs to present the case for change. Any change had to be Europe-wide. Face-to-face meetings, the production of scientific research refuting claims that the economic cost of banning battery farming would be prohibitive and videos were all used to get the message across. Official bodies condemned the practice, including the European Commission's Scientific Veterinary Committee (1992 and 1996) and the House of Commons Agricultural Committee (1981), but despite these endorsements for change, battery farming persisted.

CIWF, therefore, also had to convince the general public in order to put further pressure on decision makers. As early as 1991, it was found that an overwhelming percentage of the British public thought that battery hen farming caused suffering. An NOP poll in 1997 found that 89 per cent of respondents thought it cruel to keep hens in battery cages. Hetty the Hen was a stroke of genius, as she made the issue tangible for many people. She was a 6ft tall, bald, debeaked hen that made guest appearances at events to create photo opportunities to draw public attention to the campaign. In order to overcome any concern that free-range alternatives would be at a prohibitive price, an argument propagated by its

Politicians shouldn't mess with this chick!

Source: CWIF.

opponents, CIWF was able to present evidence to the public that free-range egg production would only add 1.5p per egg to the price. With increasing public support, its campaign, supported by other animal welfare charities such as the RSPCA, started to have a more significant impact on politicians.

Even after MEPs had accepted the need for change, CIWF found that it was important to keep getting the message across to gain further conviction for action sooner rather than later. The objective was a complete Europe-wide ban on battery hen farming. When the MEPs on the agricultural committee met to consider the proposal for change, CIWF went to Strasbourg and set up an exhibition in the main parliamentary building to show the cruelty of intensive methods and the benefits of free-range farming. The incessant pressure, typified on the CIWF website, meant that when the bill to ban factory farm systems was presented to the full parliament in January 1999, the MEPs voted for a full ban from 2009, clearing the way for the Council of Ministers' decision in June. However, recommendations and good intentions do not always lead to legislation and further action to reinforce the importance of change and to secure a final ban meant that the campaign continued.

In the six months between January and June 1999, CIWF continued to lobby the agriculture ministers to ensure that the Directive was finally ratified. Further large demonstrations were held for the benefit of ministers in Brussels and Paris. Numerous local events and trade fair demonstrations were organised. In the UK, indoor public events were held, usually screening previously unseen video footage of battery hens suffering, followed by an outdoor demonstration the same or the next day at the regional Ministry of Agriculture offices. A giant 750,000-signature petition was submitted to the UK Minister in March and campaigners came along to give vocal support. The banners proclaimed, 'Minister, we are banking on you to ban battery cages'.

CIWF also commissioned NOP to survey over 1,000 people on their attitudes to battery farming in the UK and in May 1999 found that 86 per cent were in favour of a complete ban and that 96 per cent would pay a few more pence to have free-range eggs. Hetty turned up at numerous events, such as the National Pig and Poultry Fair in Warwickshire, along with her retinue of campaigners. Another survey was released in May reporting the findings from nine major supermarket chains. This challenged the myth put out, it was claimed, by opponents, that only 14 per cent of retail eggs sold were from free-range systems. The report found that the average was 30 per cent and in Safeway and Waitrose it was 52 and 65 per cent respectively. Marks & Spencer had gone even further by stocking only free-range eggs. All these findings were sent to the UK's Ministry of Agriculture in good time for the final EU decision. The Campaign Director for CIWF stated, 'The British public were clearly using the power of their purse to show their disgust at the cruel battery cage' (http://www.CIWF. co.uk). The success of the campaign was largely due to effective lobbying. Its website contains a step by step guide on how to influence EU decision-making. The advice suggests, for example, that any argument should be based on science and not emotion, communication should be kept short and clear, and petitions and postcard campaigns to Ministers and parliamentarians should be used. The legislative and parliamentary approval process is explained and the key influencing points highlighted. The CIWF should know what it is talking about, given its success with many campaigns. Food processors may not be keen when faced with potentially larger production costs, but the hens will soon be very grateful.

Sources: *PR Week* (1999); http://www.CIWF.co.uk.

Questions

1. Define the various publics targeted by CIWF.
2. To what extent do you think that Hetty has been useful in CIWF's campaign?
3. Why is PR so important and so prominent in a campaign like this?
4. What PR lessons do you think other campaigners for reform could learn from CIWF's experience?

References for chapter 19

Arnold, M. (2001), 'Can Railtrack Ever Win Back the Public's Trust?', *Marketing*, 28 June, p. 1.

Arnot, C. (2001), 'Wolves Make Good', *The Guardian*, 30 October.

Bailey, J. N. (1991), 'Employee Publications' in P. Lesly (ed.), *The Handbook of Public Relations and Communication*, (4th edn), McGraw-Hill.

Bainsfair, P. (2000), 'Bainsfair on ... Sports Sponsorship', *Campaign*, 28 July, p. 27.

Beckett, A. (2002), 'Out of Sorts', *The Guardian*, 23 January, p. 2.2.

Branigan, T. (2001), 'Barbie to Support the Ballet', *The Guardian*, 10 September, p. 1.4.

Brech, P. (2001a), 'Vizzavi Ties with Pop Idols in £2m Sponsorship First', *Marketing*, 26 July, p. 1.

Brech, P. (2001b), 'Coca-Cola Reconsiders ITV Premiership Value', *Marketing*, 25 October, p. 3.

Brown, P. (2002), 'Norwegian PM Backs Protest Over Sellafield', *The Guardian*, 21 March, p. 8.

Brown, P. and Norton-Taylor, R. (2002), 'Terror Attack on Sellafield "Would Wipe Out The North"', *The Guardian*, 10 January, p. 1.7.

Bunyan, N. (2000), 'Bad Day for the Mighty Atom', *The Daily Telegraph*, 19 February, p. 4.

Burleigh, J. (2001), 'Why They Just Do It', *Evening Standard*, 12 June, p. 8.

Business Europe (2002), 'The Reputation Effect', *Business Europe*, 20 February, pp. 1–2.

Cassy, J. (2001), 'Coke Sponsors Football for £50m', *The Guardian*, 7 June, p. 1.28.

Colgan, P. and Sheehan, M. (2001), 'Ahern Seeks European Allies in Sellafield Battle', *Sunday Times*, 25 November, p. 30.

Connor, S. (2000), 'Shake-up as BNFL Responds to Criticism', *The Independent*, 18 April, p. 7.

Corrigan, P. (2002), 'Winter Olympics: Leave No Stone Uncurled for the Grass Roots', *The Independent*, 24 February, p. 15.

Cowan, R. (2001), 'Irish PM's Sellafield Plea to Britons: Dublin Places Full-page Advert in Fight Against Nuclear Plant', *The Guardian*, 24 November, p. 13.

Cowlett, M. (2002), 'How Innovative PR Benefits Marques', *Marketing*, 17 January, p. 25.

Cowlett, M. (2001), 'Understanding PR Practice in Europe', *Marketing*, 18 October, p. 29.

Crimmins, J. and Horn, M. (1996), 'Sponsorship: From Managerial Ego Trip to Marketing Success', *Journal of Advertising Research*, 36 (4), pp. 11–21.

Cutlip, S. *et al.* (1985), *Effective Public Relations*: Prentice Hall.

Davies, K. and Phillips, R. (1999), 'Farewell Mrs Beeton', *The Grocer*, 29 May, pp. 34–6.

The Economist (2001), 'Hands in Their Pockets – Private Money for the Arts', *The Economist*, 18 August, pp. 67–9.

Fill, C. (2002), *Marketing Communications: Contexts, Strategies and Applications*, 3rd edn, Financial Times Prentice Hall.

Financial Times (2001), 'Eyes on the Prize for Generosity', *Financial Times*, 9 November, p. 16.

Finch, J. (2002), 'Trade off: Carling Takes its Brand to the Music Industry', *The Guardian*, 9 January, p. 1.20

Fombrun, C. (2000), 'The Value to be Found in Corporate Reputation', *Financial Times*, 4 December, p. 2.

Fry, A. (2001), 'How to Profit From Sponsoring Sport', *Marketing*, 16 August, pp. 25-6.

Gibbs, G. (2002), 'Consignia Consigned to the Bin', *The Guardian*, 14 June, p. 28.

Glancey, J. (2001), 'How Well Do You Know Your Logos?', *The Guardian*, 9 July, p. 2.16.

Goddard, L. (1999), 'Making the Most out of Being a Sponsor', *PR Week*, 30 April, pp. 15–16.

Gow, D. (2001), 'Interview: Hugh Collum, Chairman, BNFL: The Nuclear Ghostbuster', *The Guardian*, 3 November, p. 1.28.

Greenpeace (2002), *BNFL Sets Nuclear Timebomb Ticking on the Anniversary of the Chernobyl Disaster*, Greenpeace press release, 26 April, accessed via http://www.greenpeace.org.uk.

Greenpeace (2001), *Leaked Documents Reveal BNFL in Crisis with Dissatisfied Customers who are Threatening Legal Action*, Greenpeace Press Release, 10th October, accessed via http://www.greenpeace.org.uk.

Grimes, E. and Meenaghan, T. (1998), 'Focusing Commercial Sponsorship on the Internal Corporate Audience', *International Journal of Advertising*, 17 (1), pp. 51–74.

Guerin, J-Y. and Mahout, C. (1999), 'Les Bons (et Mauvais) Coups du Sponsoring', *L'essentiel du Management*, 52, June, pp. 6–8.

Harrison, M. (2001), 'Post Office Under Attack as it Turns into Consignia', *The Independent*, 10 January, p. 18.

Harrison, M. (2002), 'Humbled Consignia Reinvented as Royal Mail plc', *The Independent*, 23 May, p. 20.

Harverson, P. (2000), 'Likely Backers Fail to Declare Interest', *Financial Times*, 1 September, p. 13.

Haywood, R. (1984), *All About PR*, McGraw-Hill.

Hutton, J., Goodman, M., Alexander, J. and Genest, C. (2001), 'Reputation Management: The New Face of Corporate Public Relations?', *Public Relations Review*, 27 (3), pp. 247–61.

Jardine, A. (2000), 'M&S to Dress Olympic Team', *Marketing*, 17 February, p. 3.

Kennedy, M. (2001), 'And Now, A Few Words From Our Sponsor', *The Guardian*, 4 September; p. 1.3.

Kite, M. (2002), 'Minister Accepts Sellafield Fears are Legitimate', *The Times*, 22 March, p. 16.

Kleinman, M. (2002), 'Safeway in Major Pop Concert Tie-up', *Marketing*, 31 January, p. 3.

Kleinman, M. (2001a), 'Consignia's Survival Strategy', *Marketing*, 15 November, pp. 24–5.

Kleinman, M. (2001b), 'M&S Drops Link to GB Olympic Team', *Marketing*, 22 November, p. 2.

Kleinman, M. (2001c), 'Wella to Sponsor Toyota's F1 Team', *Marketing*, 20 December, p. 2.

Koranteng, J. (2001), 'Sponsorships Should Pay Off For MTV Network Europe', *Amusement Business*, 26 November, p. 9.

Lean, G. and Branford, S. (2002), 'GM-free Nations Fall To', *The Independent*, 31 March, p. 8.

Management Today (1996), 'Management Today/Unisys Service Exellence Awards'.

Marketing (2001), 'Public Relations Agency of the Year: Cohn & Wolfe', *Marketing*, 13 December, pp. 17–8.

Marketing Week (2002), 'Hollis Sponsorship Awards: Charity and Community Sponsorship', *Marketing Week*, 25 April, p. 45.

Marketing Week (1999), 'Brand Sponsorship', *Marketing Week*, 15 April, p. 57.

Marshall, D. and Cook, G. (1992), 'The Corporate (Sports) Sponsor', *International Journal of Advertising*, 11 (4), pp. 307–24.

Marston, J. (1979), *Modern Public Relations*, McGraw-Hill.

Mason, T. (2001), 'VK Vodka Kick to Back UK's Temptation Island', *Marketing*, 27 September, p. 7.

Matthew, G. (2001), 'Sponsor Hopes to Score at World Cup', *Financial Times*, 3 December, p. 10.

McCartney, I. (1997), 'No Strings Attached', *Nursing Standard*, 14 May.

Meenaghan, T. (1998), 'Current Developments and Future Directions in Sponsorship', *International Journal of Advertising*, 17(1), pp. 3–28.

Meenaghan, T. (1991), 'The Role of Sponsorship in the Marketing Communications Mix', *International Journal of Advertising*, 10, pp. 35–47.

Milmo, C. (2002), 'Eco Campaigners Go Corporate as Global Firms Set Out to Prove They Really are Green – Awaretics as We Know It?', *The Independent*, 14 January, p. 3.

Murphy, C. (1999), 'Brand Values Can Build on Charity Ties', *Marketing*, 25 March, p. 41.

National Campaign for the Arts (2002), *Arts and Business 1999/2000 Survey*, accessed via http://artscampaign.org.uk.

Nuttall, N. (1998), 'Big Business Shuns Call of Wild in Animal Rescue Flop', *The Times*, 6 January, p. 5.

O'Connor, J. (2001), 'UK Corporate Reputation Management: The Role of Public Relations Planning, Research and Evaluation in a New Framework of Company Reporting', *Journal of Communication Management*, September, p. 53.

O'Sullivan, T. (2001), 'A Leap in the Dark for Sponsors Facing Drugs Tests', *Marketing Week*, 30 August, p. 25.

PR Week (1999), 'Bald Bird Beats Battery Barons', *PR Week*, 12 February, p. 8.

Palin, R. (1982), 'Operational PR', in W. Howard (ed.), *The Practice of Public Relations*, Butterworth-Heinemann.

Parsley, D. (1999), 'BA to Fly the Flag Again and Ditch Ethnic Tailfins', *The Sunday Times*, 6 June, p. 1.28.

Paton, N. (2001), 'When is a Story Not a Story?', *The Guardian*, 22 October, p. 8.

Pike, A. (2001), 'Post Office Marks New Status with Name Change', *Financial Times*, 10 January, p. 5.

Pruzan, P. (2001), 'Corporate Reputation: Image and Identity', *Corporate Reputation Review*, 4 (1), pp. 50–64.

Rogers, D. (1999), 'Travel Inn Updates Corporate Image', *Marketing*, 29 April, p. 4.

Scouller, T. (2002), 'Could a Change of Name Boost the Morale of Consignia Staff?', *Marketing*, 28 February, p. 18.

Sharkey, P. (2002), 'Barca Can Afford to Reject £8m Shirt Sponsorship – Not Premier Clubs', *Western Mail*, 23 March, p. 11.

Smith, C. (2001), 'Is Barclaycard on the Way to Glory in the Premiership?', *Marketing*, 16 August, p. 17.

Smithers, R. (2002), 'Special Pleading', *The Guardian*, 22 January.

Sparks, R. (1995), 'Rethinking Media Evaluation: Tobacco Sponsorship, Airship Messages and Narrative Conventions in Motorsports Telecasts', *Proceedings of the 7th Bi-Annual World Marketing Congress*, Melbourne.

Speed, R. and Thompson, P. (2000), 'Determinants of Sports Sponsorship Response', *Journal of the Academy of Marketing Science*, 28 (2), pp. 226–38.

Stanley, R. E. (1982), *Promotion: Advertising, Publicity, Personal Selling, Sales Promotion*, Prentice Hall.

Stipp, H. and Schiavone, N. (1996), 'Modeling the Impact of Olympic Sponsorship on Corporate Image', *Journal of Advertising Research*, 36 (4), pp. 22–8.

Stone, N. (1991), *How to Manage Public Relations*, McGraw-Hill.

Travis, A. (2001), 'Police "Need Logo and Spin Doctors"', *The Guardian*, 7 December, p. 1.10

Utley, T. (2001), 'The Accent is on Change for the Sake of Change', *The Daily Telegraph*, 10 January, p. 29.

Van Riel, C. and Van Den Ban, A. (2001), 'The Added Value of Corporate Logos: An Empirical Study', *European Journal of Marketing*, 35 (3/4), pp. 428–40.

Varadarajan, P. and Menon, A. (1988), 'Cause Related Marketing: A Coalignment of Marketing Strategy and Corporate Philanthropy', *Journal of Marketing*, 25 (3), pp. 58–74.

Wheatley, K. (2002), 'MacArthur on Speed Mission', *Financial Times*, 4 January, p. 11.

White, D. (2001), 'Big-name Signings For All Seasons', *The Daily Telegraph*, 4 October, p. 65.

Wilkinson, A. (2001), 'Coke to Slash the Value of Premiership Sponsorship', *Marketing Week*, 25 October, p. 12.

Wilmshurst, J. (1993), *Below-the-Line Promotion*, Butterworth-Heinemann.

Witcher, B., Craigen, G., Culligan, D. and Harvey, A. (1991), 'The Links Between Objectives and Function in Organisational Sponsorship', *International Journal of Advertising*, 10 (1), pp. 13–33.

Wray, R. (2002), '40,000 Postal Jobs Face Axe', *The Guardian*, 25 March, p. 2.

part seven

MARKETING MANAGEMENT

20 strategic marketing

21 marketing planning, management and control

22 services and non-profit marketing

23 international marketing

24 e-marketing and new media

In offering you a detailed and comprehensive introduction to the important elements of marketing, this book has had to take a 'pigeon hole' approach, treating each element as a separate entity. Throughout the text, however, it has been made clear that all these elements are interdependent and must be integrated into a consistent and coherent overall strategy.

This section, therefore, serves two purposes. First, in Chapter 20, issues of strategic marketing and competitive strategy are addressed. Increasingly, marketing managers are expected to play an additional role in supporting the corporate planning process by focusing on the important areas of product market strategy and marketing resource allocation as well as the more traditional mix of management perspectives. Chapter 20, therefore, also outlines the interface between corporate and marketing planning frameworks, and how each influences and is influenced by the other. Second, Chapter 21 examines the marketing planning process, and the role it plays in providing a structured framework within which marketing actions can be undertaken. Chapter 21 also looks at the importance of planning in smaller businesses and how its role changes as the business evolves. The importance of planning, based on sound assessment of the organisation's present position, both internal and external, as stressed in Chapter 14 on integrated marketing communication, cannot be understated.

Chapters 22 and 23 have been included because it is recognised that a broad introduction to a subject such as marketing has to generalise. In some respects this is a strength – it is hoped that the variety of industries, products and experience illustrating this text has been both entertaining and informative for you. This breadth and variety do, however, make it more difficult to envisage how all the elements of the marketing mix mesh together in specific practical applications. Chapters 20 and 21 begin the integration process, but Chapters 22 and 23 take it further, in looking at specific situations and types of organisation.

As many of the examples cited in the text so far have related to physical products, Chapter 22 centres on services marketing, such as banking, travel and tourism, and personal services. Marketing tends to be thought of as belonging in large, profit-making businesses. To redress this, Chapter 22 also looks at the non-profit sector, where organisations such as charities, the police, medical and other public services are increasingly adopting a marketing orientation and marketing strategies. Chapter 23 looks at the problems, pitfalls and rewards of international marketing, both within Europe and further afield. The chapter examines the reasons why organisations internationalise and the impact of the international marketing environment on their decisions. Different ways of entering foreign markets are discussed, along with the debate on whether organisations should standardise or adapt their products and marketing offerings in international markets.

Finally, Chapter 24 looks at the role and applications of e-marketing and new media. While these emerging themes have certainly found their way into all the previous chapters, it is nevertheless important to take the time to consider them in their own right and to assess their increasing impact on marketing strategy and the ways in which the marketer communicates with customers and services their needs and wants.

chapter 20

strategic marketing

LEARNING OBJECTIVES

This chapter will help you to:

1 define marketing strategy and the internal and external influences affecting it;

2 understand the various types of portfolio model used to develop a strategic view of the organisation and the competitive context within which it operates;

3 outline different strategies for achieving growth and their appropriate use;

4 differentiate between types of competitors, appreciate the perspectives from which they can be analysed, and start to define appropriate strategies for dealing with them; and

5 understand the concept of competitive positioning and the range of strategies and tactical actions broadly appropriate for achieving and maintaining a position.

Introduction

So far, this book has looked at the practical aspects of marketing, from identifying consumer needs and wants through to designing and delivering a product package that aims to meet those needs and wants, and maintains customer loyalty despite the efforts of the competition. The tools that make up the marketing mix are, of course, critical for implementing the marketing concept. Each one adds value to the overall offering, contributing towards a competitive edge that will attract the target market. What exactly constitutes the best mix to adopt varies from situation to situation and must be the subject of research, experimentation and management judgement. So far, the focus on the marketing mix elements has largely been operational and orientated to the short term. Managers must, however, think of their operational marketing mixes in the context of wider, more strategic questions, such as:

- Which markets should we be in?
- What does our organisation have that will give it a competitive edge? (This need not necessarily come directly from marketing.)
- Do we have the resources, skills and assets within the organisation to enable planned objectives to be achieved?
- Where do we want to be in five or even 25 years' time?
- What will our competitors be doing in three or five years' time?
- Can we assume that our current *modus operandi* will be good enough for the future?

These concerns are strategic, not operational, in that they affect the whole organisation and provide a framework for subsequent operational decisions. The focus is on the future, aligning the whole organisation to new opportunities and challenges within the changing marketing environment, as discussed in Chapter 2. The questions suggested above seem deceptively simple, but finding answers to them is, in fact, a highly skilled and demanding task. The future welfare of the whole organisation depends on finding the 'right' answers. As Chapter 2 showed, trends within the marketing environment can be difficult to spot, and even if the organisation does see them, their implications can still be unclear and contradictory. This is particularly true where competitors are concerned. Even the best-laid plans can be severely disrupted by competitive action, especially when the competition refuses to act predictably or to play by 'the rules' as you define them. Thus there is a constant need for information gathering, updating and analysis as a fundamental part of strategic planning in the first place, and then as a part of monitoring and controlling the implementation of those plans.

Gaining an understanding of the external environment is not enough in itself. The organisation also has to take a long hard look at its internal resources, assets and skills to assess whether the organisation is sufficiently well equipped to meet the challenges of the external environment. Strategic marketing planning thus might have long-term implications for the direction and shape of the whole organisation rather than just affecting the operational management of the marketing mix elements themselves. The strategic marketer is, therefore, a catalyst for change through highlighting the need to create a better fit between the market's needs and the capabilities and resources of the organisation. The stakes are high, for the organisation that gets it wrong can face very serious consequences, particularly if long-term investments in plant, machinery or product development have been made on the basis of a particular interpretation of the marketing environment.

eg

Despite the dominance of many large manufacturer and supermarket fmcg brands, smaller companies' brands still survive, and some have a strong market share. Italian brand Filippo Berio Olive Oil has established an international reputation for quality. It has even established itself as the UK market leader with between 25 and 30 per cent market share, although it is up against a new entrant, Unilever's Bertolli brand, which is being supported by a £6 mn marketing campaign, including £2.8 mn of media advertising. Compare this with the total of £2 mn spent by Berio in 2001, of which £436,000 was spent on advertising. If Berio had sought to go head-to-head on advertising during Bertolli's one-month intensive campaign run, it would have spent all its annual budget. Instead, Berio played on its heritage and quality strengths by focusing on specialist food magazines and trade magazines, communicating to those who recognised quality olive oil and were already converted. To date, the strategy appears to have been working and it was rumoured that the Unilever brand was failing to make a significant impact (Charles, 2002b).

Similarly, Kettle Chips has been able develop a successful niche alongside the high profile crisp giant Walkers (as endorsed by Gary Lineker, Victoria Beckham, etc. – *see* pp. 591–2) by sticking to direct marketing, internet marketing and the use of strong public relations. It refuses to advertise. Launched in the US in 1978, it has established a reputation as a premium crisp, free of artificial flavours and as a bonus the crisps are Kosher, GM-free and suitable for vegetarians (Bateman, 2001). It has a reputation for innovation, most recently introducing crisps using organically grown potatoes and upmarket flavours such as Sea Salt and Balsamic Vinegar. It sells just 750,000 bags of Kettle Chips a week in the UK, compared with Walkers' 8 million packets a day, but it still has a profitable business.

These examples demonstrate how brands from smaller companies can survive and prosper, not by replicating the mass advertising spends made by the likes of Unilever and Walkers, but by concentrating on point-of-sale and focused promotion. It is also important to note, however, that the products offered are different and positioned well apart from those of the larger competitor (Charles, 2002c).

This chapter first introduces strategic marketing issues by defining some of the commonly used terms and showing how they fit together. Some, however, will not be considered in depth until the next chapter. A number of techniques have been developed for analysing strategic marketing problems, especially those concerned with the interface between the products offered and the dynamics and structure of the related markets. Product portfolio and market attractiveness models are therefore considered at pp. 849 *et seq.* There then follows a review of a variety of strategic options that are closely related to marketing issues. These include growth directions, developing and maintaining a competitive position and deciding on how to compete, ranging from direct attacks to almost independent decision-making regardless of competition. Competitive strategies and their impact on marketing are then explored. This area has grown in importance in recent years, reflecting the increased level of competition in many markets, often on an international scale. Chapter 21 will then build further on this chapter by examining the implementation of strategic and operational marketing through the planning process.

Definitions and perspectives

Marketing strategy cannot be formulated in isolation. It has to reflect the objectives of the organisation and be compatible with the strategies pursued elsewhere in the organisation. This means that marketers must refer back to corporate goals and objectives before formulating their own strategy, to ensure consistency, coherence and relevance.

It would be inappropriate to imply, however, that marketing strategy is always subservient to corporate strategy. Many aspects of marketing actually influence corporate strategy. In a marketing-orientated organisation, the needs of customers and the maintenance of competitive edge are important ingredients in formulating corporate strategic direction and priorities. Furthermore, the product is at the heart of the business and thus marketers' product decisions, for instance deletion, modification or range extension, are likely to have a major impact on the organisation as a whole. In this context, the strategic aspects of marketing are likely to have a major (but not exclusive) impact on the formulation of corporate strategy, as seen in the Linn vignette on p. 843. The two-way process between marketing and corporate strategy is shown in Figure 20.1.

To help to clarify the two-way interaction, the rest of this section is divided into two. First, we provide an overview of some of the different, and often overlapping, internal strategic perspectives, both corporate and marketing specific, that marketers have to consider in their strategic thinking. We then examine some of the broader factors that affect the formulation of marketing strategy in practice.

Strategic marketing frameworks

This subsection outlines some of the strategic perspectives of the organisation, starting with the broad picture required by corporate strategy, then gradually focusing down towards the very specific detail of marketing programmes.

Corporate strategy

Corporate strategy concerns the allocation of resources within the organisation to achieve the business direction and scope specified within corporate objectives. Although the marketing department is primarily responsible for responding to perceived marketing opportunities and favourable competitive environments, it cannot act without the involvement of all other areas of the organisation too. Corporate strategy, therefore, helps to control and coordinate the different areas of the organisation, finance, marketing, production, R&D etc., to ensure that they are all working towards the same objectives, and that those objectives are consistent with the desired direction of the business as a whole.

Although the techniques for corporate planning may vary between different sizes and types of organisation, the objective is always the same: to match targeted opportunities with resources, focused activity and strategies. Typical issues of concern to corporate planners might thus be market expansion, product development priorities, acquisition, divestment, diversification and maintaining a competitive edge. In a smaller firm the planning process

Figure 20.1 The two-way interaction between marketing and corporate strategy

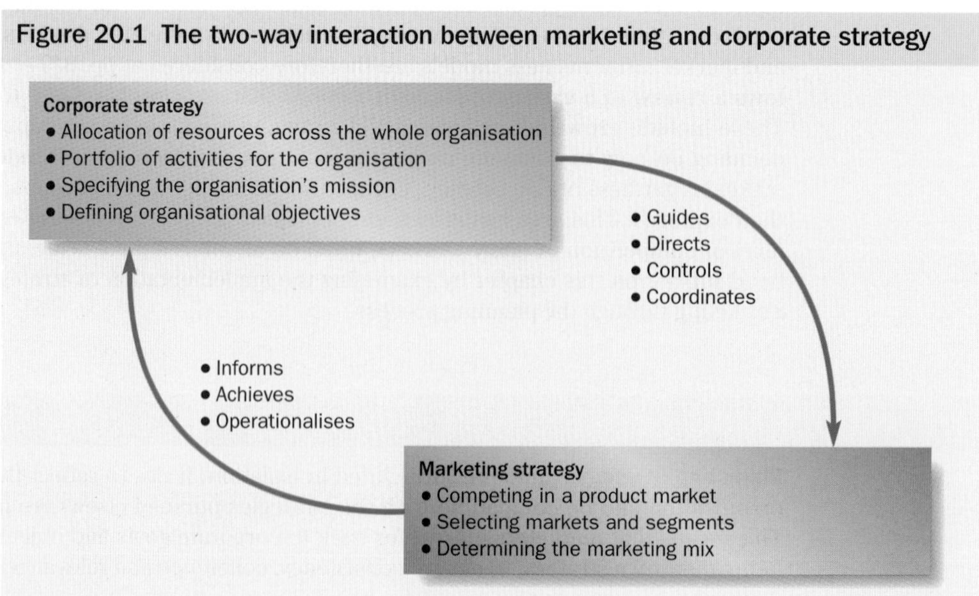

marketing *in action*

A sound strategy

Linn Products is a Scottish manufacturer of high quality hi-fi equipment that targets the high-performance, top end of the European market. It made its mark with its first product in 1972, the Linn Sondek LP12, a transcription turntable that became the benchmark against which all the others are judged. The company applied the same standards and positioning to Linn speakers and the first solid state pitch accurate amplifiers. Linn now has over 50 products including CD players, tuners, amplifiers, and speakers that it sells in 30 countries. In just under 30 years, Linn has become a world leader in sound technology, innovative design and precision engineering. It operates a policy of continuous improvement to ensure that it stays at the cutting edge of its niche.

More recently, Linn diversified into the home theatre market, a growing sector at the top end of the hi-fi market. In 1994 the Knekt system was launched, an advanced multi-room sound distribution and control system. It is powerful stuff. A 16-source system, for example, could distribute to 128 rooms. This was followed in 1995 by entry into the digital multi-channel sound market with the Linn AV51, a new home cinema and multimedia high-fidelity sound system. This means that buyers can have a designed-in system in a number of rooms and, because it is multi-channel, they can both watch a movie and listen to audio in the same room from the same entertainment system. People are now taking for granted that they can access all their entertainment needs throughout the home and the Knekt system allows this kind of multi-use. It attracts attention at the top end of the market. When Harrods' furniture department decided to design a new display area, it featured Linn custom-installed home entertainment products. Linn was also selected to design a new audio system for the Aston Martin V12 Vanquish, one of the most technologically advanced Aston Martins ever built. Linn products were considered ideal for its discriminating and demanding customers and the products enhanced the exclusive image of the car.

Linn's mission is 'to thrill customers who want the most out of life from music, information and entertainment systems that benefit from quality sound by working together to supply them what they want when they want it'. Each product has the signature of the product builder. One product builder is responsible for the assembly, testing and packaging of an item. An old fashioned attention to detail does not mean old fashioned inefficient production processes, however. Linn claims to have one of the smallest plants in the world with automated materials handling right up to the assembly point. Within that, 'real-time' manufacturing is practised, meaning that each day's production is made to order for specific customers. The product designers too are close to the customer and are committed to continuous improvement.

Linn's customer care philosophy extends from the manufacturing process through to the distribution channel. The company is selective about appointing dealers because it sees the key to selling its products as the expertise and product demonstration offered by the retailer. Linn is looking for those retailers that are the best in their area and have a quality reputation that fits with Linn's own. It wants retailers that want to sell quality products and are prepared to spend time with customers demonstrating and installing them. Retailers should be able to:

- work with customers to discover what kind of musical expectations and sound needs they have
- appreciate the cost–value relationship inherent in Linn systems, if necessary comparing them with the competition
- show customers how best to use and accommodate equipment
- help customers consider system expandability.

Linn is very reluctant to supply retailers that are not trained or are unable or unwilling to stock the range for demonstration purposes.

Overall, Linn is an excellent example of how the vision and values of the leader of a business are translated into marketing strategy. Although one might expect the customer to be at the heart of a business from which a compact disc player could set you back £12,000 and to which a rock star paid £200,000 for a sound system for each room of his house, Mr Tiefenbrun, the owner, is controversially quoted as saying, 'the customer comes third, the supplier comes first and the employee second. It was only by working with suppliers that the company got the components that worked in the way that customers wanted. Satisfied customers follow on from satisfied suppliers and employees' (as quoted by Murden, 2001).

Sources: Murden (2001); http://www.linn.co.uk.

Linn speakers are quality products sold to customers by knowledgeable retailers with time to discuss individual needs.

Source: Linn Products Ltd.

could be fairly straightforward, but for a larger firm with distinct business areas this planning might mean making tough decisions about resource allocation and strategic priorities, which might create a degree of internal conflict.

To help to make the corporate planning process more manageable, larger organisations often divide their activities into **strategic business units** (SBUs). An SBU is a part of the organisation that has become sufficiently significant to allow it to develop its own strategies and plans, although still within the context of the overall corporate picture. SBUs can be based on products, markets or operating divisions that are profit centres in their own right. Each SBU might face very different marketing environments, achievement targets, strategies and competitors. Given that SBUs might have different growth and financial profiles, it is important at corporate level to assess both the current performance and future potential of each SBU and then decide overall priorities and resource allocation.

Competitive strategy

Competitive strategy determines how an organisation chooses to compete within a market, with particular regard to the relative positioning of competitors. Unless an organisation can create and maintain a competitive advantage, it is unlikely to achieve a strong market position. In any market, there tend to be those who dominate or lead, followed by a number of progressively smaller players, some of whom might be close enough to mount a serious challenge. Others, however, are content to follow or niche themselves (i.e. dominate a small, specialist corner of the market). As we show later (*see* p. 865), there are many ways of competing, and the choice of competitive strategy guides subsequent detailed corporate and marketing strategy decisions.

Marketing strategy

The marketing strategy defines target markets, what direction needs to be taken and what needs to be done in broad terms to create a defensible competitive position compatible with overall corporate strategy within those markets. It is, therefore, concerned with many of the aspects considered in buyer behaviour (Chapters 3 and 4), as well as the decision to target particular market segments (Chapter 5). Marketing mix programmes can then be designed to best match organisational capabilities with target market opportunities. Many of the cases and examples highlighted in Chapters 7–19 show how various marketing mix strategies are used to achieve marketing objectives. Although chosen strategies vary, depending on the context, they all share the same marketing-orientated philosophy.

Marketing plan

It is in the marketing plan that the operational detail, turning strategies into implementable actions, is developed. The **marketing plan** is a detailed, written statement specifying target markets, marketing programmes, responsibilities, time-scales and resources to be used, within defined budgets. Most marketing plans are annual, but their number and focus will vary with the type of organisation. The plan might be geographically based, product based, business unit based, or orientated towards specific segments. An overall corporate marketing plan in a large organisation might, therefore, bring together and integrate a number of plans specific to individual SBUs. Planning at SBU level and then consolidating all the plans ensures that the corporate picture has enough detail, and allows overall implementation and control to be managed.

Marketing programmes

Marketing programmes are actions, often of a tactical nature, involving the use of the marketing mix variables to gain an advantage within the target market. These programmes are normally detailed in the annual marketing plan, and are the means of implementing the chosen marketing strategy. Linn hi-fi systems, mentioned earlier in this chapter, found that an advertising campaign of £250,000 using quality journals, a direct mail programme, an annual brochure and a bi-annual magazine was appropriate for stimulating trial and maintaining customer relationships. Programmes provide clear guidelines, schedules and budgets for the range of actions proposed for achieving the overall objectives. These are determined within the framework of the overall marketing plan to ensure that activities are properly integrated and that appropriate resources are allocated to them.

Influences on marketing strategy

Figure 20.2 outlines the various influences on an organisation's marketing strategy, each of which is now discussed in turn.

Organisational objectives and resources

Marketing strategists need to be guided by what the organisation as a whole is striving for – what its objectives are and what resources it has to implement them. Some organisations might have very ambitious growth plans, while others might be content with fairly steady growth or even no growth at all, that is, consolidation. Clearly, each of these alternatives implies different approaches to marketing.

eg

ISS from Denmark has declared its aspiration to 'advance the Facility Support Services Industry and to lead it globally'. This provides a clear sense of direction for supporting marketing and management strategies. ISS provides a comprehensive range of services to industry within custom-designed facilities management programmes that can cover cleaning, maintenance and catering. It has also targeted customer segments in the aviation, automotive, hospital, and care provision industries, as well as clean-room services for computer facilities, etc. It operates in 36 countries, has 75,000 business customers and employs 265,000 people worldwide, the majority in the delivery of front line services. Given that complex mix of products, markets and priorities it is essential that all parts of the organisation are aware of the company's direction and the rate of change.

To help the organisation achieve its aspiration, a 'Create 2005' programme has been developed to guide development for six specific strategic initiatives:

- ***Carve out and conceptualise.*** Reinforce the roles of the business units in serving international market segments by moving away from a country-by-country approach to a more international perspective.
- ***Redefine and rebrand.*** To signify the shift from multi-services to facility services. This needs new branding and corporate identity, thereby creating the new ISS. The new logo, introduced in 2000, embraced the communication of quality, friendliness and dynamism that is now to be reinforced.
- ***Encentivise staff*** [sic]. Through training, empowerment and incentive, recognise that employees are the organisation's most valuable asset.
- ***Add new businesses fast.*** By being creative and using ISS's strong market position to achieve mergers, acquisitions and/or partnerships.
- ***Transform and consolidate.*** The transformation of ISS will keep the facility services country organisations focused while new businesses are built fast. ISS will continue its consolidation of the industry and leverage the institutional skills of the group: management of people, entrepreneurship, concept development, and mergers and acquisitions.
- ***Exit and spin-out if beneficial.*** ISS will enter partnerships if it facilitates growth. Exiting can happen when requirements are not met, when a leading position cannot be obtained, when external value exceeds internal value or when it is necessary to realise value. (http://www.iss-group.com).

These broad organisational objectives and statements of strengths act as a guide to more detailed marketing strategy formulation. The Create 2005 programme also specified a number of specific goals to be reached and these will be considered further in the next chapter (*see* p. 902).

Resources are not only financial. They also include skills and expertise, in other words any area of the organisation that can help to add value and give a competitive edge. The exploitation, through marketing, of things that the organisation does well, such as manufacturing, technical innovation, product development or customer service, might help to create non-financial assets such as reputation and image, which are difficult for competitors to copy.

Figure 20.2 Influences on marketing strategy

eg

Swiss Company Holcim, formerly Holderbank, is one of the world's largest suppliers of cement, aggregates and concrete with sales of CHF 13.6 bn in 2001. For any company of this nature to survive, there have to be economies of scale in production, consistent supplies of raw material and low transport costs. Holcim has established three fundamental strategic principles to guide its competitive position: cost leadership in its many overseas markets, market leadership to achieve volume sales, and strong vision and firm control over central strategy yet still allowing local autonomy.

To achieve cost leadership, Holcim invests heavily in technology to reduce unit costs and often locates plants either near to raw materials or near to customers. Through a process of acquisition and new plant openings, it now has interests in cement plants in 70 countries, giving the company over 630 ready-mix concrete plants, many of which operate under different names. Wherever Holcim decides to expand, largely driven by construction opportunities because of demographic development or infrastructure renewal, the formula is the same: large volumes, efficient operations and local service. The strategic risk is spread by its involvement in many different markets, each at different stages of growth, decline and maturity, and this allows it to concentrate on its core business, to the point of divesting more marginal activities. Although Europe is still its strongest market, Latin America is a high priority. Most of its investment is now in emerging markets, but it is facing increasing international competition from France's Lafarge and Mexico's Cemex and the change of name to Holcim was part of a strategy to start building a global brand. That may also help with pricing. In Thailand more than 40 per cent of cement is bought over the internet, and brand names are considered important in achieving premium prices. In any case, in Asia generally the 'better' the brand name the higher the prices (*Financial Times*, 2001).

As the cases of ISS and Holcim show, marketing strategies do need to be compatible with corporate objectives and to capitalise on available resources.

Attitude to change and risk

The corporate view on change and risk often depends on the approach of top management. Risk tolerance varies widely from individual to individual, and from management team to management team. Managers will also, of course, be guided by the nature of the organisation and their interpretation of its business environment. The managing director of a small business may not want to take on high risk projects, feeling that the firm's size makes it more vulnerable to failure through its lack of resources. A larger firm might be able to absorb any losses, and therefore feel that the risk is worth taking.

The Performance Group (1999) in its studies of corporate innovation has found that enterprise depends on a willingness to accept mistakes rather than punish them, and that this stance, along with a tolerance of risk and innovation, is essential for a culture that welcomes change and significant development. Henry McKinnell, chairman of Pfizer, is often quoted as saying that the pharmacautical industry has a 99 per cent failure rate. The organi-

eg

In the pharmaceutical and biotech sectors particularly, some small businesses take a very positive approach to risk. The biotech sector is experiencing rapid growth through a steady stream of technological breakthroughs, many coming from smaller companies. Being a smaller organisation can help to create a culture that encourages flexibility and inventiveness, as long as there is sufficient capital to see it through the leaner start-up period. Venture capitalists do absorb some of that risk on the promise of future returns. Specialist bioinformatics companies such as Lion Biosciences of Germany, GeneData of Switzerland, and NetGenics of the US, for example, have all been supported that way (Cookson, 2001). Due in part to its well developed science park network, the UK has five of the top ten European biotech companies and has twice as many products in clinical or pre-clinical trials as the rest of Europe put together (Swann, 2002). Often, just one new product breakthrough can generate multi-million pound revenues, transforming the prospects of a small company. The challenge is then to move on to spread the risk by becoming a multi-product organisation. Amgen has managed that transition with three medicines on the market; its first has been out for 12 years and the second for 10, yet it still maintains a 20 per cent annual growth rate (Taylor, 2001).

The giant pharmaceutical companies, by contrast, invest far more heavily, perhaps two or three times the level of smaller biotech companies as they need to record global product sales in the billions rather than millions to sustain growth. This can sometimes increase the development period and stifle some inventions that do not meet that criterion. Often, the large pharmaceutical companies could learn from the enterprise and drive of the smaller biotech companies, while the smaller companies could learn from the expertise of the big manufacturers in achieving success in getting ideas to the marketplace. These differences have led some to suggest that the pharmaceutical and biotech sectors are working closer together, with one, biotech, almost becoming the breeding ground for new ideas which are then capitalised upon by the pharmaceutical companies through alliances and takeovers (Dyer, 2001).

sation that creates a culture for failure avoidance may often fail a lot quicker, because innovation is necessary in most sectors to remain competitive, as can be seen from many of the examples in this book. The organisation that can encourage change, ideas and innovation may be better able to exploit emergent product and market opportunities as they arise.

Market structure and opportunities

Markets vary considerably in their structure and dynamics. Some are fairly stable and not a great deal happens in them unless one of the major players decides to become aggressive and seeks to improve its competitive position. Some markets are simply too complacent. A good example would be the Dutch agriculture sector, which has been criticised for failing to keep up with market changes and increased levels of European competitiveness. Although competitiveness has been maintained in cut flowers and seeds, ground has been lost in the dairy, vegetable and pork sectors. The real problem has arisen from changes in the marketing environment, as consumers have sought a wider variety of products and higher product specifications, and European supermarket buyers have sought greater efficiency.

eg

Mothercare (http://www.mothercare.com) is a retailer of specialist accessories and clothing for babies and children up to eight years old. In the UK, it is claimed that over 90 per cent of pregnant women visit one of its 245 stores before giving birth, generating a turnover of over £300 mn. From its launch in 1961, Mothercare worked hard to establish a reputation for quality, own-label brands, an attractive retail environment and a comprehensive range including maternity wear. Since 1984, export sales have been developed through direct retail outlets and franchises, resulting in operations in over 30 countries.

Despite its strong market presence, in recent years its performance has not lived up to expectations and market share has been lost. Particular difficulties have been experienced in the 4-to-8 year-old segment because children are developing fashion-consciousness from an earlier age, but even apart from that, Mothercare has been under attack in all segments. Pregnancy is no longer an excuse for the removal of fashion clothing from the wardrobe, and Mothercare has had some difficulty in providing an acceptable variety of fashionable maternity clothing compared with more fashion-orientated stores. The trendier end of the children's clothing has been driven by the likes of Baby Gap and Higswa Junior, while the value end of the market has been hit hard by ASDA, Tesco and Hennes & Mauritz. Even the more upmarket niches have been targeted by retailers such as Gap, Next, and Tom and Daisy (Bashford, 2002; Kleinman, 2002). Boots has moved aggressively into the babywear segment, so in all areas the fight is on.

The challenge for Mothercare, therefore, is to plot its future corporate and marketing strategy. Should it concentrate on pregnancy and babies and toddlers, where margins tend to be higher and there is still a strong awareness and market penetration, rather than including the 4-to-8 year-old segment? Mothercare is still a respected and valued brand, but some of its clothes have failed to make an impact in a society where children have become a fashion statement. Even though the new Mothercare World format (stores above 10,000 ft^2) are replacing smaller stores that can hold only limited ranges, the brand is caught in the structural changes in the market. Interestingly, Mothercare's dot.com business is growing rapidly and provides information, convenience and an opportunity to examine a catalogue online. This relatively new channel may yet have a big impact on re-shaping the market again, favouring leading brands such as Mothercare. Even smaller stores can be made bigger with access to online ordering in store.

The impact of the increasing internationalisation of organisations is that previously dormant markets can be suddenly transformed into dynamic competitive arenas by the entry of a new, foreign competitor. This can be seen in the UK construction industry. Companies suffered badly in the 1990s, partly because of the depressed state of the construction market generally, but also because of increasing difficulties in competing with European, Japanese and American rivals entering the UK market. For many years, contracting was often a national and sometimes even a regional business with a large number of smaller firms. With the arrival of international competitors, most of whom are much larger, smaller firms were finding it harder to win contracts and to do battle in European markets.

Often, such turbulence only happens over a limited period until a new *status quo* is reached through a new market structure that redefines relative market shares. In the case of construction, that could mean considerable rationalisation within the UK industry. Sometimes, the turbulence is created by innovation and new product technology that again has the potential to redefine how players actually compete. In some growth markets, turbulence can be high until the market stabilises and competitors become more entrenched, leaving fewer opportunities for new entrants.

eg

Ribena, the blackcurrant drink, dates back to the 1930s and has become a well established brand. In recent years, however, it has experienced the need for change to keep up with increased turbulence in the marketplace. For nearly a decade, the soft drinks market has grown significantly, fuelled by new flavours, ingredients, formats, packaging, and usage occasions backed by increased marketing budgets (Hardcastle, 2002c). Ribena is number four of all soft drinks in the UK, but the sector is still being squeezed by new areas such as energy and sports drinks. Ribena is up against Proctor & Gamble's Sunny Delight and Britvic's Robinsons brands all of which have equally powerful marketing support. In recent years, after a period of growth in the late nineties, Ribena's sales have started to slip and in an effort to retain its position, Ribena's owner Glaxo SmithKline has had to revitalise its marketing effort. It introduced a number of new variants such as 'Ribena Light', but not all have been successful. The launch of 'RibenaToothkind' led to controversy when Ribena had to withdraw its claim that the drink did not lead to tooth decay after an ASA ruling (Johnson, 2002). Sales for the brand range were estimated to have dropped by around 10 per cent during that period because of the negative publicity.

To reverse the trend, the relaunch will cost £27 mn and will include new packaging, a focus on taste, and a doubling of advertising spend to £10 mn, as well as sponsorship of the FA Premier League (Arnold, 2002). The brand is, at its core, a good one. It is distinctive, has taste, and generates a feeling, like Lucozade, that it is a healthy drink. Although it is a difficult product to challenge head-on, the markets it sells into are highly competitive and not so secure. The target market is mothers with children, including the competitive children's lunchbox sector, but Ribena has resisted calls to reposition itself towards an older audience capitalising on brand loyalty that goes back to adults' own dim and distant lunchbox days! Nevertheless, Ribena is now having to find ways of dealing with far more market turbulence than ever before.

Competitor strategies

The competitive structure in different product markets will vary to create conditions of strong or weak competition. In markets such as computer chips, the dominant competitor has a major influence over the level and nature of competition. Challenges can still arise, but nevertheless, within constraints set by governmental competition policy and public pressure, a dominant competitor is effectively able to decide when and how to compete. The dominant competitor is likely to be confident that it has sufficient strength through its market position, volume sales, and thus perhaps through its cost base to fight any serious challenger successfully.

eg

Computer chip manufacturer Intel dominates its markets through size and speed. It dominates world manufacturing capacity and has geared up its R&D to shorten the development time for new generations of chips. Through its dominant strength, Intel has developed a strong capacity in motherboards and chip sets for PCs, regardless of the individual brand name of the final computer sold. This has created a situation that competitors find increasingly difficult to overcome.

Achieving such dominance provides a strong basis for competitive advantage as it makes building, sustaining and defending a market position relatively easier. The strategies that lead to this will be explored in the next section.

Stategic marketing analysis

Strategic marketing planning makes use of a number of analytical models that help to develop a strategic view of the business, and thus can be used as decision-making aids. The various models outlined below can be applied either to SBUs or to individual products, and thus the use of the word 'product' throughout the discussion should be taken to mean either. The fundamental concept of many of these models is that although products may be managed as individual entities on an operational basis, strategically they should be viewed as a **product portfolio**, that is, a set of products, each of which makes a unique contribution to the corporate picture. The strategist needs to look at that corporate picture and decide whether, for example, there are enough strong products to support the weak ones, whether the weak ones have development potential or whether there are appropriate new products in development to take over from declining ones. The product portfolio at corporate and product range level can be clearly identified in the Nestlé vignette (at p. 850).

Managing SBUs or a product portfolio means that management has to consider products *relative* to each other and ensure that each is fulfilling its allotted strategic role and that the overall balance is right. Management might decide, for example, that the strategic role of a mature product is to generate revenues to provide the stability and investment needed for a risky new product. The new product's role, on the other hand, might be to become sufficiently well established within the next three years to take over from the mature product as it declines.

Product portfolio analysis: the Boston Box

Sometimes referred to as the **Boston Box**, or the BCG matrix, the Boston Consulting Group (BCG) market growth–relative market share model, shown in Figure 20.3, assesses products on two dimensions. The first dimension looks at the general level of growth in the product's market, while the second measures the product's market share relative to the largest competitor in the industry. This type of analysis provides a useful insight into the likely opportunities and problems associated with a particular product.

marketing *in action*

Feeding the world

Nestlé is the world's largest food company, with 479 factories, 225,000 employees and sales in excess of CHF71,000 mn. The company plans globally by product groups, within each of which is a portfolio of brands. Nestlé's challenge is to manage the portfolio of activity at product group level while allowing individual regions or countries to operate at a devolved divisional level. Six of its worldwide corporate brands generate 70 per cent of its sales: Nestlé, Nescafé, Nestea, Maggi, Buitoni, and Friskies. Nestlé itself generates 40 per cent of sales on its own. In any market segment it aims to have at least one-third more market share than its nearest rival. There are specific brands dedicated to national or regional markets, although this is tending to consolidate towards fewer, more global brands (Betts and Hall, 2002). It is still largely a food and drink company with plans to dominate globally in sectors such as coffee, water, pet foods and ice cream. This priority influences many aspects of strategic marketing planning between the headquarters in Switzerland and the respective divisions around the world.

Nestlé does not just focus on growth for existing brands and product groups. It is very active in acquiring and divesting brands to ensure a close and sensible fit within the overall brand portfolio. The strategy is to build strength in long-term priority areas and to divest in areas with limited potential and strategic fit.

Two product groups will now be briefly considered in turn to demonstrate the issues of portfolio management at both company and brand levels.

Beverages

This division contains the world's leading coffee brand, Nescafé, which generates significant cash for the business. Launched in 1938, the brand has grown to market leadership and claims that over 3,900 cups are drunk per second across 120 countries. Despite its age, it still achieves double digit growth in SE Asia and Europe, in part due to brand extensions into, for example, Nescafé Cappuccino and the relaunch of Nescafé Original. Nestlé also has world leadership in chocolate and malt-based drinks such as Nesquik, Milo and Nescau. Other products in the group include roasted coffee, teas, fruit juices and cereal drinks.

In order to retain the lead position for Nescafé, Nestlé still supports the brand with marketing and new product variants. In recent years the priority has been to innovate with new speciality tastes and to improve the distribution channels for corporate sales. In this group, the strategic attention tends to be on global development rather than focusing on individual countries. Within the product portfolio new products are also introduced or new markets attacked on a rolling launch basis to safeguard the longer-term viability of the portfolio. In 1998, ready-to-drink Nescafé in a can was launched in Thailand and liquid concentrate for iced coffee was introduced to Japan.

The mineral water division is a significant growth market for Nestlé. Formed by the acquisition of Perrier in 1992, it now has the strong brands of Perrier, Vittel and Contrex to enable a strong competitive position to be realised. Investment is still taking place in this product group. Dar Natury, a market leader in Poland was purchased in 2001 to secure dominance of that market, and the purchase of Al Manhal in Saudi Arabia has created a strong position in the Middle East for Nestlé owned brands. Nestlé Aquarel, natural spring water, has been launched in six European countries and it is planned to make it the first pan-European bottled water brand by 2010, as it is launched on a rolling basis. In addition, as part of a global branding initiative, the Perrier Vittel name is to disappear to be replaced by Nestlé Water to consolidate a world market share of around 16 per cent. Within this product group, trading profit is around 17 per cent, reflecting the strong market position of some of the brands.

Chocolate and confectionery

Nestlé is also a world leader in chocolate and confectionery, with such international brands as KitKat, Smarties, Lion and After Eight. Other brands such as Femina and Baby Ruth are specific to certain geographic regions. Acquisition has been used in the past, most notably in the UK with the purchase of Rowntree. Both sales and profit have been under pressure in this group. New product development has been active, however, with the successful launch of KitKat Chunky, Aero Honeycomb and After Eight biscuits. Smarties has also undergone considerable brand extensions in recent years, with Smarties eggs and mini Smarties. Local brands that do not fit, such as Fox (famous for its Glacier Mints) in the UK, have been sold to release resources for the major brands and for further innovation.

Within this product group, trading profit is just 11 per cent because of the tough times the sugar confectionery market has been experiencing, but that is still higher than many others in the industry.

Other product groups include ice cream and dairy products, prepared foods and cooking aids, and pharmaceuticals. With all these distinct product areas, Nestlé must plan its portfolio if it is to achieve its target of 4 per cent real internal growth per annum. The organisational structure is still primarily national rather than regional and this has had an effect on the slower development of worldwide marketing, in advertising and brand development. In the UK market it has been suggested that its image is poorer than many other areas and consumers are not aware of the extent of Nestlé brand ownership (Tungate, 1999). However, with such a large portfolio covering over 120 countries, it is a challenge to achieve any type of focused image. The recent wave of acquisitions and divestments is not only being resourced by the more successful brands in each product area, but also by targeted investment across the portfolio to enable more resource intensive options to be pursued. This may in time result in less discretion for national divisions in strategic marketing decision-making.

The sales of Nestlé's different brands can be revitalised by the introduction of a familiar product with a different form, such as the KitKat Chunky.

Source: Nestlé UK.

Source: Betts and Hall (2002); Tungate (1999); http://www.nestle.com.

Market growth reflects opportunities and buoyancy in different markets. It also indicates the likely competitive atmosphere, because in high growth markets there is plenty of room for expansion and all players can make gains, while in low growth markets competition will be more intense, since growth can only be achieved by taking share away from the competition. The model assumes a range of between zero (or decline) and 25 per cent growth (or more, if relevant to a particular industry). Some fine tuning is possible to reflect market circumstances.

Market share position is measured on a logarithmic scale against the product's largest competitor. Thus a relative share figure of 0.2 means that the product only achieves 20 per cent of the market leader's sales volume, a potentially weak competitive position. Similarly, a share figure of 2 would mean that the product has twice the market share of its nearest rival. A share figure of 1 means roughly equal shares, and therefore joint leadership.

Figure 20.3(a) gives an example of the resultant matrix after all the products of an organisation have been thus analysed. The next stage is to plot the products within a simpler four-cell matrix that reflects the differing competitive positions, as shown in Fig. 20.3(b).

Figure 20.3 BCG matrix

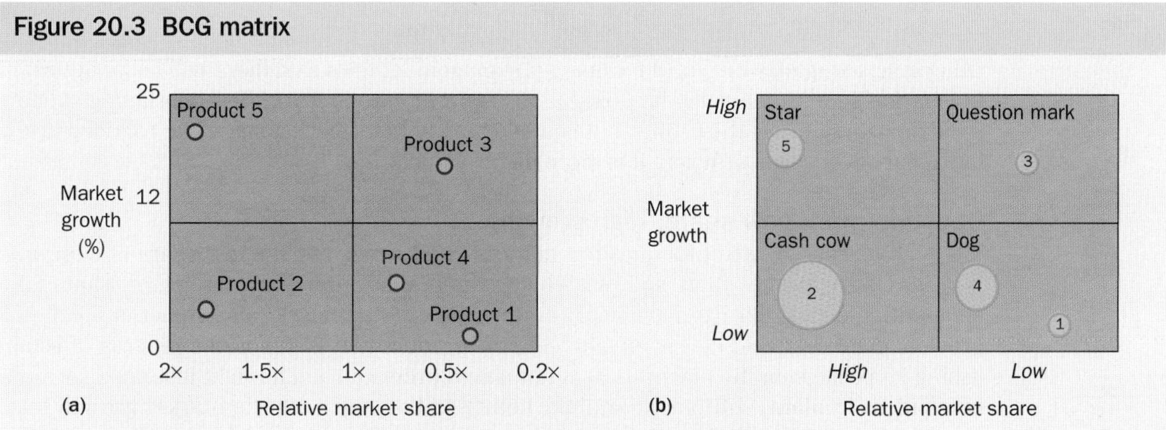

Plotting each product's position within the matrix

Each cell offers different types of business opportunities and imposes different resource demands. The general labelling of the cells as 'high' and 'low' gives an instant and sufficient feel for each product's situation, and the circle that represents each SBU's contribution to the organisation's total sales volume provides a further indication of the relative importance of different products. In Figure 20.3(b), for example, Product 2 can be seen to be the biggest contributor to overall sales volume, whereas Product 1 contributes very little.

This model provides a guide to the most appropriate corporate investment and divestment options. The 'ideal' model is one where the portfolio is reasonably balanced between existing strength and emerging opportunity. The great advantage of the model is that it forces managers to reflect on current and projected performance, and to ask important questions about the continued viability of products, their strategic role and the potential for performance improvement.

We now look in turn at each cell of the matrix.

Dog (low share, low growth)

A dog holds a weak market share in a low growth market, and is likely to be making a loss, or a low profit at best. It is unlikely that its share can be increased at a reasonable cost, because of the low market growth. A dog can be a drain on management time and resources.

eg

Liptonice, a cold, fizzy, canned lemon tea, and other products like it had proved to be successful in continental Europe and its owners were confident that it could succeed in the UK market too. What they had not taken into account, however, was the nature of the British consumer's love affair with tea and the perception of it among younger consumers. In the British mind, tea should be drunk hot and milky – even drinking it hot and black with lemon is considered a bit risqué. The ritual of making tea 'properly' is also deeply culturally ingrained. Add to that the young person's view that tea is for grannies, and the prospects for canned, cold, fizzy lemon tea start to look less promising. A £6 mn product launch and later a £4 mn relaunch failed between them to achieve the product's target of £20 mn sales per year and the product quietly disappeared from UK stores. The initial failure has not, however, deterred further attempts. In 2002, Lipton Ice Tea was relaunched with a £5 mn marketing campaign in the growing cold soft drinks market. Initial trials suggested that the drink was especially popular with students and an extensive outdoor sampling campaign is planned to persuade the British consumer to acquire a European taste. Sixty students have been hired as student brand managers to develop brand credibility and a merchandising campaign for 5,000 retail outlets. Time will tell whether the relaunched drink will become an outright dog or at least enable a breakthrough in encouraging consumers to try a new soft drink product and maybe even adopt it (*The Grocer*, 2002b; *Marketing*, 2002).

The question, therefore, is whether or not to shoot the dog, that is, withdraw the product. Much depends on the strategic role that the dog is fulfilling and its future prospects. It may, for example, be blocking a competitor (a guard dog?), or it may be complementing the company's own activities, for example creating customers at the bottom of the range who will then trade up to one of the organisation's better products (a guide dog, or a sheep dog?). Otherwise, a dog may be worth retaining if management feels that there will be an upturn in the market soon. It may also be possible to retain the product with less marketing support (which might improve the profits, but is unlikely to help its market share), or to reposition it into a narrower segment where it is more highly valued.

Question mark (low share, high growth)

The high market growth of a question mark is good news, but the low share is worrying. Why is relative market share so low? What is the organisation doing wrong, or what is the competition doing right? It may simply be that the question mark (also sometimes called a problem child or a wild cat) is a relatively new product that is still in the process of establishing its position in the market. If it is not a new product, then it might just need far more investment in plant, equipment and marketing to keep up with the market growth rate. There is also a risk, however, that a question mark with problems might absorb a great deal of cash just to retain its position.

eg

The suncare market is growing at a rapid rate as health warnings about the dangers of excessive exposure at last start to make an impact on consumers. In the UK, the market is worth around £140 mn and grew by around 20 per cent in 2001. It is dominated by brands such as Ambre Solaire, Malibu, and Nivea. Each has a variety of products within the range, such as high factor sun protection, self-tanning products, after-sun and coloured products. The children's niche in particular grew by 46 per cent, much of which is accounted for by factor 30 and above sun protection products. Against that background, Faulding Consumer from Australia entered the UK market with Banta, targeted at the youth market. It offers non-greasy sun lotions and gels that have been highly successful in Australia, where the brand established a 13 per cent share in just two years. The question is whether such a late entrant into the market can also build share against strong and innovative competitors (Hardcastle, 2002b).

Some of the alternatives for question marks, such as dropping or repositioning, are the same as for the dogs, but there are some more creative options. If the product is felt to have potential, then management might commit significant investment towards building market share, as mentioned above. Alternatively, if the organisation is cash rich, it might seek to take over competitors to strengthen its market position, effectively buying market share.

Star (high share, high growth)

A star product is a market leader in a growth market. It needs a great deal of cash to retain its position, to support further growth and to maintain its lead. It does, however, also generate cash, because of its strength, and so it is likely to be self-sufficient. Stars could be the cash cows of the future.

eg

As mentioned in Chapter 15 (*see* p. 604), Holsten is considering entering the growing FAB (flavoured alcoholic beverage) market with Holsten Fusion, a lager with added fruit flavour. The challenge will be to establish a 'star' position, capitalising on the FAB market largely created by the success of Bacardi Breezer and Smirnoff Ice as well as fuelling the market growth further by offering different choices. Research has shown that a few pints of lager can sometimes leave a bitter taste in the mouth so a sweeter drink (but not as sweet as the spirit-based FABs) could counter that effect, thus creating the opportunity for Fusion. Nothing can be taken for granted. When Strongbow launched new flavours for cider, sales fell far short of expected levels. Fruit beers have been in the UK for nearly twenty years and have remained a niche product. The question, therefore, is whether Fusion can become a star in a sector that it can help to kick-start, or a dog in a niche market going nowhere (Addelman, 2002).

Cash cow (high share, low growth)

As market growth starts to tail off, stars can become cash cows. These products no longer need the same level of support as before since there are no new customers to be had, and there is less competitive pressure. Cash cows enjoy a dominant position generated from economies of scale, given their relative market share.

eg

Kodak is in the fortunate position of having a cash cow in a consumer film business that is at best mature, but more likely to be declining, given the impact of digital photography. In 2001, Kodak generated $1 bn in free cash flow, a considerable percentage from consumer film. Such large cash flows are enabling Kodak to generate new business sectors such as the health imaging unit, new digital imaging and screen technologies. Kodak cannot be complacent, however. Fuji and others are trying to get a bigger share of the profitable consumer film business, and digital photography has the potential to change the storage and display of traditional photographs. Why bother to print when digital storage and retrieval is so straightforward? Sales of digital cameras reached 30 per cent of all camera sales in 2001 and although Kodak makes digital cameras, it is not yet a profitable business unit and every sale takes a customer away from the high margin film business. Margins on high quality paper and digital processing are considerably lower than on film. Cash cows don't live for ever – get the picture (Carter, 2002; Serwer, 2002)?

The management focus here is on retention and maintenance, rather than on seeking growth. Management might be looking to keep price leadership, and any investment will be geared towards lowering costs rather than increasing volumes. Any excess cash can be diverted to new areas needing support, perhaps helping to develop dogs and question marks into stars.

Two further categories were proposed by Barksdale and Harris (1982) as follows.

War horses (high share, negative growth)

War horses are market leaders, but their cash generating position is under threat because of negative market growth. Management options depend on whether the decline is terminal or temporary. If it is terminal, then the strategy should be to harvest for as long as possible, offering minimal marketing support, as most volume comes from repeat sales based on loyalty. Any investment, whether in promotion or plant, should look for a swift payback. If the decline is temporary, it is probably worth riding the storm, maintaining support to enable cash generation to continue.

eg

The household cleaning market has been growing in recent years, largely due to premium product development. Few of us like household cleaning chores and anything that does the job quicker and better is likely to be a winner. In 2001, the market grew by 12 per cent and a number of new formats such as window wipes have made a big impact, helping to double sales in the window cleaning sector in the same period. These chemically impregnated single-use disposable cloths have also been developed for cleaning floors, carpets and toilet seats. This has been bad news, however, for other brands offering liquid, spray, and scouring pad formats. The Fairy brand of sponges, scourers and cloths was sold by Procter & Gamble to EGL Homecare, an own-label cleaning and personal care product company when P&G decided that the brand had no future. Other scouring brands are also being squeezed. Scouring powders do what they say they do, and scour a surface away, thus potentially damaging the surfaces of baths, enamel basins and pans. Consumers are prepared to shift to equally effective but less damaging alternatives (Hardcastle, 2002a; http://ww.www.unilever.com).

Dodos (low share, negative growth)

As the name implies, the dodo product is almost certain to become extinct, as low share of a declining market means that sales volumes are dwindling away. Management needs to undertake regular reviews of returns generated, adopting a contribution-based approach to such a product. As soon as the product's contribution becomes negative, it is a candidate for early termination.

Once the BCG matrix has been developed for an organisation, it can be used to assess the strength of the company and its product portfolio. Ideally, a strong mix of cash cows and stars is desirable, although there may be embryonic stars among the dogs and question marks. The situation and the portfolio become unbalanced where there are too many dogs and question marks and not enough cash cows to fund new developments to allow them to break out of those cells. There is also a risk dimension to all this. The organisation as a whole is vulnerable if there are too many products with an uncertain future (question marks).

Four main assumptions underpin the BCG model:

1 gains in market share are made by investing in a competitive package, especially through marketing investment;
2 market share gains have the potential to generate cash surpluses as a result of economies of scale and the learning curve;
3 cash surpluses are more likely to be generated when products are in the maturity stage of the lifecycle;
4 the best opportunities to build a strong position occur during a market's growth period.

Abell and Hammond (1979), however, identified a number of weaknesses in the BCG model and its assumptions, for instance that cash flow and cash richness are influenced by far more than market share and industry growth, and that return on investment (ROI) is a more widely used yardstick of investment attractiveness than cash flow. Although it is conceptually neat, the BCG matrix does not adequately assess alternative investment opportunities when there is competition for funds, as for example when it is necessary to decide whether it is better to support a star or a question mark.

Market attractiveness model: the GE matrix

Developed first by General Electric (GE), the market attractiveness–business position portfolio assessment model was designed to overcome some of the problems of models such as the BCG matrix.

The **GE matrix** adds more variables to aid investment decision appraisal. It uses two principal dimensions, as seen in Figure 20.4: *industry attractiveness* (the vertical axis) and *business strengths* (the horizontal axis). Within the matrix, the circle size represents the size of the market and the shaded part the share of the market held by the SBU.

The first dimension, industry attractiveness, is a composite index determined by market size, rate of growth, degree of competition, pace of technological change, new legislation and profit margins achieved, among others. The second dimension, business position, is another composite index, comprising a range of factors that help to build stronger relative market share, such as relative product quality and performance, brand image, distribution strength, price competition, loyalty, production efficiency, etc. Both dimensions need to work positively together, since there is little point in having a strong position in an unattractive market, or a weak position in a strong market.

Within the matrix, there are three zones, each implying a different marketing and management strategy:

1 *Zone 1 (high attractiveness, strong position)*. The strategy here should be investment for further growth.
2 *Zone 2 (medium attractiveness)*. Because there is a weakness on one dimension, the strategy here should be one of selective investment, without over-committing.
3 *Zone 3 (least attractive)*. Either make short-term gains or proceed to pull out.

The main areas of concern with this model are linked to methodology and the lack of clear guidelines for implementing strategies.

Figure 20.4 GE matrix

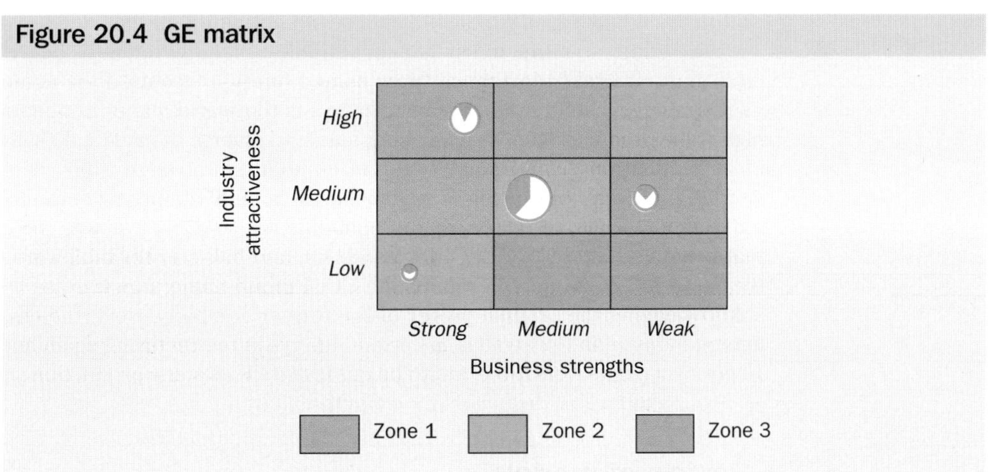

Shell's directional policy matrix

Shown in Figure 20.5, the **Shell directional policy matrix** has two dimensions, competitive capabilities and prospects for sector profitability. The nine cells of the matrix offer different opportunities and challenges, so that placing each product in an appropriate cell provides a guide to its strategic development.

Figure 20.5 Shell directional policy matrix

Competitive capabilities	Unattractive	Average	Attractive
Weak	Disinvest?	Gradual withdrawal?	Take a risk?
Average	Gradual withdrawal?	Maintain or look for growth?	Try harder!
Strong	Cash generator!	Look for growth?	Maintain leadership!

Prospects for sector profitability

eg

Visitors to Cornwall may remember seeing giant white slagheaps from china clay workings. The mining company that generated these 'white mountains', English China Clays (ECCI), fought a hard battle to retain its independence through a series of restructuring efforts to establish a strong market position in attractive and core markets.

ECCI, from its origins in the nineteenth century, became a major international player in industrial minerals and white pigments, especially kaolin and calcium carbonates along with speciality chemicals. These are widely used in the paper, board, plastics and paints industries. ECCI is the world leader in speciality minerals, supplying 7 million tonnes across five continents. By 1999, sales had reached €2 bn, largely achieved through a programme of divestment and investment. Early in the 1990s, ECCI found that funds were too limited to build world-class businesses in areas of strength, so those activities offering relatively poor potential or which did not fit well with the core business were divested. The building materials division, for example, worth about £350 mn and the second largest operation in the group, was sold (Lorenz, 1995). The funds released enabled ECCI to build in the more attractive areas of industrial and speciality chemicals, which were considered to be higher value added but required considerable R&D to keep pace with user industry needs. Investment was also needed to fund expansion in the competitive US market.

These efforts to retain independence were in vain, however, as in 1999 an even larger minerals giant, Imetal from France (now named Imerys), acquired the company as part of its own strategy to build market power. Imerys is the world leader in mineral processing with high value products, such as china clay, sold into diverse industries. ECCI was considered an ideal acquisition given its newly found competitive strength. Imerys' activities are now divided into four core businesses with facilities in 20 countries: ceramics and specialities; building materials; refractories; and pigments and additives. It was the ceramics business that generated interest in ECCI for its kaolin, and ball clay for tableware, sanitaryware and tile sectors. The group still retains the ECCI brand name, however, as a link with the past acknowledging the original power of the former company. Nevertheless, the future of the mining industry in Cornwall is uncertain. Imerys is restructuring again and around 300 jobs, 10 per cent of the workforce, are to be cut in the UK as some production shifts to Brazil.

Review of models

Portfolio models have been criticised, but they have, nevertheless, been useful in forcing managers, especially in large complex organisations, to think more strategically. They can certainly be used as diagnostic tools to give an overview of the current position and to stimulate debate on what could happen if direction is not changed. These models do not, however, give solutions about what strategies should be adopted, and they need to be supported by clear action plans. The main problem with them is the rather simplistic use of variables that contributes to the axes and the decision rules sought from the models. The preoccupation with market share is of particular concern, since it might be just as valid to consolidate and perform better as to pursue high growth, high share business. The models also fail to consider the synergies between businesses, where one may support another.

In some situations, it might be more appropriate to focus on a small number of areas and perform really well in these than to over-extend in the pursuit of market share or market growth. In many markets, a set of businesses survive with little reference to market share as niche operators. They might, therefore, develop attractive returns without necessarily seeking market share for its own sake or incurring the costs and risks associated with the pursuit of relative sales volume. This is also true in situations where technological change and obsolescence can quickly erode any significant advantage gained.

Some methodological weaknesses emerge when the models are implemented in practice:

1 how to weight the variables for a composite index such as that which the GE model uses. Different managers could have different opinions about how to weight variables, leading to very different-looking matrices for the same organisation;
2 the guidelines used to distinguish zones or cells are open to some debate. Different rules may apply in different situations;
3 the measures used on each matrix also need careful examination. Often, the preoccupation with market share, SBUs and production suggests a bias away from the smaller business and the service business. In a small business, share may be of minimal importance compared with dependable niches. The service business has very different operational concerns from a manufacturing organisation, given the focus on service performers and facilities rather than production lines.

Although these models are commonly described in textbooks, they are not so widely used in practice. They are conceptually easy to design, but very difficult to implement effectively. They require considerable management skill and judgement, because of their focus on the identification of variables, weighting decisions and future changes, rather than just on present, tangible, measurable factors.

eg

Nestlé is having to decide whether its innovative 'Hot When You Want' brand of self-heating coffee cans is likely to be a star of the future or a premature war horse. The cans that enable hot coffee to be served at the press of a button on the can were launched on a test market basis in 2001. Although initial reaction was positive, it did not lead to significant sales at the test outlets and so a decision has to be made whether to drop the idea or to risk rolling out for a national launch (Mowbray, 2002b). Dr Oetker, the large German food company was more confident that it could soon gain a leadership position in the declining UK frozen pizza market. Consumer taste is switching towards chilled pizzas and the frozen sector declined by 3 per cent in 2001. The 10 inch frozen pizza, thin and crispy, will initially come in Mozzarella, Speciale, Funghi and Hawaiian varieties, retailing at £1.99 each. A £5 mn advertising budget has been allocated to support the brand. To gain the top spot, it will have to overcome market leaders Schwan and McCain and some experts believe that far from creating a cash cow, Dr Oetker could be dealing with a dodo within a few months of launch (*The Grocer*, 2002a; Mowbray, 2002a).

Overall then, although portfolio models can be useful planning tools, company-specific and pragmatic approaches used by organisations such as Unilever could be more appropriate. Where they are used at all, there is often a tendency to use them as diagnostic tools rather than as predictive tools. Their real advantage is their focus on corporate objectives, and the contribution that marketing decision-making makes to that process. Above all, however, it must be remembered that they are tools to assist decision-making, not a series of rules that lead to inevitable conclusions and decisions.

Growth strategies for marketing

The previous section looked at the corporate perspective on strategic planning, presenting a number of models that can guide marketing strategy development. This section examines a number of different strategies that organisations might adopt if their priority is growth. It is important to remember, however, that growth is not always a priority. In many small firms, for example, survival or sustaining the *status quo* might be the main objective. In other situations, standing still might be the right strategy if the market is starting to tighten up. The preoccupation with growth, therefore, should not be assumed to be relevant to all organisations all the time.

Managing growth is not without problems, because of the demands it imposes on management time and resources, and not least because of the additional risks created. For those who are facing growth opportunities, and who have the capabilities to exploit them, a number of options are available. The product–market matrix proposed by Ansoff (1957) provides a useful framework for considering the relationship between strategic direction and marketing strategy. The four-cell matrix shown in Figure 20.6 considers various combinations of product–market options. Each cell in the **Ansoff matrix** presents distinct opportunities, threats, resource requirements, returns and risks, and will be discussed in the next two subsections.

Figure 20.6 Ansoff's growth matrix

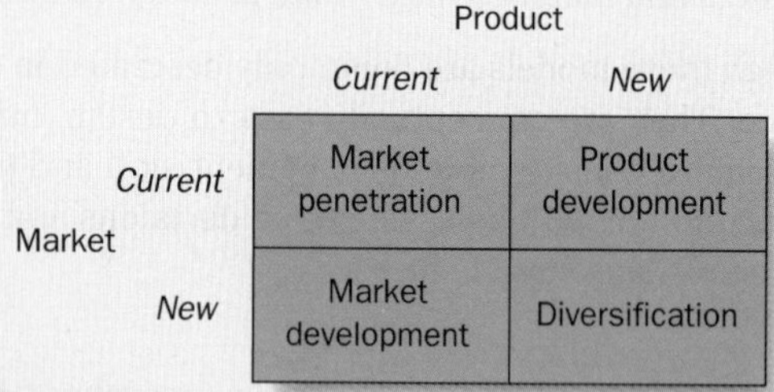

Source: Ansoff (1957). Adapted and reprinted by permission of Harvard Business Review. Exhibit 1 on p. 114 from *'Strategies of Diversification'* by Ansoff, H.I. Issue No. 25 (5), Sept/Oct 1957, pp. 113–25, Copyright © 1957 the Harvard Business School Publishing Corporation; all rights reserved.

marketing **in action**

Unilever goes for growth

Unilever, the large fmcg multinational is going for growth. Under the heading 'Path to Growth' it has been fundamentally reviewing and changing its product portfolio to achieve sales growth of between 5 and 6 per cent overall on a turnover of €53.4 bn. It has been carefully managing its product portfolio in recent years to guide investment and divestment decisions. In the late nineties it classified its brands into categories A and B (Campbell, 1999). At that time it had around 1,800 brands in its portfolio and believed that it could not achieve category dominance with such a large range and thus pruning was needed to release resources to support growth. Category A brands such as Dove, Lynx, Lipton, Hellmann's, Magnum, Omo and Cif were deemed central to future plans whereas category B brands such as Pears Shampoo, Timotei and Brut were up for review. The criteria used to differentiate the brands were based on the planning models presented in this chapter, adapted to the Unilever context and environment. The criteria were:

- Size of the brand: volume share, value share, number of customers
- Loyalty: strength of loyalty
- Potential: new market segments, brand extension, etc.
- Trends: at market and product levels.

The overall aim was to reduce the portfolio to 400 leading brands which would then become the focus of product innovation, brand extension and increased marketing support. There would also be associated benefits in logistics and service levels with less variety and higher volumes on the remaining brands. The change could not happen overnight, but the expectation was that by 2004 the leading brands would account for 95 per cent of Unilever's turnover, compared with 84 per cent in 2002 and 75 per cent at the start of the programme in 1999. By 2002, around 97 per cent of all advertising expenditure was concentrated on the top 400 brands.

In the analysis, Unilever did not take a country by country view but considered the global competition in its main markets and the position of its global brands in each. In some cases, product development was used to strengthen its position, for example the Dove range of soaps has experienced considerable extension into shampoo, deodorant and skincare products in all regions as well as being rolled out to new regions such as Asia. As part of the renewed effort, Dove sales increased by 29 per cent in 2001. Pro Activ, Cuilese and Brunch spreads have been launched in Europe as well as new formats for Cornetto. Cornetto sales grew by 21 per cent during 2001.

When it considers that a faster track can be employed through acquisition, which of course is also a means of removing a potential competitor, Unilever has been very active. In 2000 it made 20 acquisitions to the value of €30.5 mn including:

- Bestfoods: foods (international)
- Amora Maille: culinary products (France)
- Ben & Jerry's: ice cream (primarily in the United States)
- Codepar/SPCD: home and personal care (Tunisia)
- Cressida: foods, home and personal care (Central America)
- Jaboneria: foods, home and personal care (Ecuador)
- Slim Fast: nutritional bars and beverage products (United States).

The Bestfoods acquisition was especially challenging as it had a large portfolio of brands and employed 33,000 people in 63 countries in 120 factories. The priority was thus on rationalisation and integration. This involved selling off some duplicate or poor fit brands such as Campbell, combining the sales forces, grouping media buying and ensuring a unified effort in segments in which one was stronger than the other. It gave Unilever control, however, over strong brands in adjacent categories such as Hellman's and Knorr which it could build on a global scale. Unilever has already been able to achieve global leadership in tea, ice cream and spreads as a result of the Bestfoods takeover.

At the same time, however, the disposal programme has also been very active, some for strategic reasons and others as part of any competition agreements associated with an acquisition. Over 50 brands have already been divested. Minor brands and those with no long-term future or fit have gone already: Elizabeth Arden fragrances was sold for €244 mn; its Unilever's North American sea food business was sold to Nippon Suisan; its refinery business at Unimills in the Netherlands was sold, and so was Johnson Wax professional, to name but a few. At the same time, other brands have been harvested prior to disposal or termination.

To help the focus, Unilever concentrated its brands into two global divisions: Unilever Bestfoods, and Home and Personal Care. Both divisions have an executive board, responsible for divisional strategy and for implementation across the world. This has helped to overcome one of the main difficulties often facing organisations when disposing of products, i.e. local management who are resistant to terminating 'their' brands and who prefer to argue that repositioning will rejuvenate sales. In Unilever, the clear sense of purpose and strategy right through the organisation enables an almost ruthless approach to product portfolio management that regards acquiring and building brands as the other side of the disposal coin.

Sources: Campbell (1999); http://www.unilever.com.

Intensive growth

Three cells of the Ansoff matrix offer opportunity for sustained growth, although each one has different potential according to the market situation.

Market penetration

The aim of **market penetration** is to increase sales volume in current markets, usually by more aggressive marketing. This means using the full range of the marketing mix to achieve greater leverage.

eg

A number of continental European brands have significantly penetrated the UK market. Müller has established a 40 per cent share of the yoghurt market and has become the second largest food brand in the country since its 1987 UK launch. The German company swept aside UK competitors, St Ivel, part of Unigate, and Eden Vale which have both fallen back from their comfortable 1987 market shares of 40 per cent each. Müller has achieved this dramatic turnaround through strong product development and by using price to out-compete the local rivals. Its main advantage was the split-pot yoghurt, with plain yoghurt in one half and fruit in the other allowing consumers to choose how they mix and eat their yoghurt. Prices were set low to achieve economies of scale and an annual £10 mn advertising budget is normally allocated to the brand. The UK competitors did not think that a split-pot format would catch on, and by the time they found out that it had succeeded, it was too late and they were unable to claw market share back. The combination of regular innovation, value for money promotions, widespread distribution and national advertising has been a powerful force for building and retaining Müller's market lead. The 'three for 99p' type of offer characterises Müller and between 80 and 85 per cent of sales are made that way (Carmichael, 2002; Hardcastle, 2001; Urry, 2001).

Market development

Market development means selling more of the existing product to new markets, which could be based on new geographic segments or could be created by opening up other new segments (based, for example, on age, product usage, lifestyle or any other segmentation variable). Danish firms control nearly half of the world's market for wind turbine machines. Companies such as Vestas Wind Systems and Nordtank Energy Systems depend heavily on achieving growth by developing new markets.

eg

The prime objective of these companies is to grow by opening up new markets around the world. Vestas Wind Systems (http://www.vestas.com) is the world's leading manufacturer of wind turbines. The world market for wind turbine systems is expected to continue growing over the next ten years due to greater energy consumption, more environmental awareness and greater efficiency as technology continues to lower unit costs. From its origins in Scandinavia, Vestas now has a 24 per cent share of the global market for wind power, which itself grew by over 50 per cent in 2001. European markets have been opened up, especially in Germany and Spain, and other markets being developed include Japan, the USA, China and Australia. In 2000, it agreed a new dealership in Japan to form Vestech Japan Corporation, which is owned by a number of large Japanese corporations including Toyota and Kawasaki. This has enabled a fast entry into an otherwise difficult market. Additionally, contracts were signed for the first time in Costa Rica and Iran while the less well cultivated markets in Poland and Portugal showed positive signs. By opening up new markets, Vestas is able to retain and build its global position.

Part of the market development strategy is to establish local production facilities through acquisition or direct investment. In addition to Denmark, factories exist in Germany, Spain and India and sales offices are also being opened to support the development of a market, as it may take some time to achieve regulatory approval and to negotiate with power providers. Despite the international coverage, the success of Vestas has been built on the platform of product development, occupying 9 per cent of the workforce, quality, pre- and post-sales service, efficient production and competitive pricing. Although still primarily a wind turbine producer, Vestas' sales had grown from DK2830 mn in 1996 to DK9521 mn by 2001, helped by a market that continues to grow.

Wind power at work in Wales.

Photographer: Archie Miles.

Product development

Product development, as covered in Chapter 9, means selling completely new or improved products into existing markets.

Bloomsbury Publishing is one of Europe's leading independent publishing houses and it requires a steady flow of new authors and desirable titles to grow. Formed in 1986, its core competence is its ability to identify new authors and then use its marketing skills to ensure that the books are launched successfully. Its authors include Michael Ondaatje (*The English Patient*), David Guterson (*Snow Falling on Cedars*) and not least J. K. Rowling. In 2001, six of its books were in the *Daily Telegraph* top ten list and although the Harry Potter *Goblet of Fire* went straight to the number one position in paperback, the number of top ten successes indicates the wider strength of having an active approach to new product development either by author or title. Few would have predicted the success of the Harry Potter series at its launch. The initial print run was 1.5 million copies, but worldwide sales now far exceed 100 million. The series takes over 19 per cent of the £140 mn children's book market, with the next nearest series taking just 3.9 per cent. In addition, clever merchandising and the sale of film rights opens up even more profitable opportunities for author and publisher. Even the Harry Potter website receives 15 million hits per month. With further books planned in the series, Bloomsbury is thus well placed to reap further benefit from its ability to spot winners from the hundreds of manuscripts and proposals it receives (*Marketing Week/CIM*, 2001; http://www.bloomsbury.co.uk).

Diversified and integrative growth

Growth through **diversification** takes place outside the value chain, for example developing new products and new markets, whereas growth through integration takes place within the chain, for example making components yourself rather than buying them in.

Specialist Computer Holdings (SCH) achieved very rapid growth in its computer sales and service group by moving into mail order computer sales and through the Byte chain of computer stores. This integrative growth was partly organic and partly through acquisition. By developing in unfamiliar but related technology areas (diversification growth), it was able to increase its turnover rapidly.

Both diversification and integration might involve radical new departures into unknown technical, managerial or marketing areas.

Growth through diversification

Diversification, the final cell in the Ansoff Matrix, happens when an organisation decides to move beyond its current boundaries to exploit new opportunities. It means entering unfamiliar territory in both product and market terms. One of the main attractions of this option is that it spreads risk, moving the organisation away from being too reliant on one product or one market. It also allows expertise and resources to be allocated synergistically, for example theme parks diversifying into hotel accommodation, or airlines diversifying into tour packages. Calori and Harvatopoulos (1988), in a study of diversification in France, found both offensive and defensive reasons for diversification, with outcomes such as a stronger financial position or greater synergy with existing operations. The danger is, of course, that the organisation spreads its effort too widely into areas of low expertise, and tries to position itself against more specialist providers.

There are two main types of growth through diversification as follows.

Concentric diversification. Concentric diversification happens where there is a link, either technological or commercial, between the old and the new sets of activities. The benefit is, therefore, gained from a synergy with current activities. An organisation could, for example, add new, unrelated product lines to its portfolio, but still use the same sales and distribution network.

eg

Video distributor Contender established a successful £6.8 mn video distribution business from scratch. That is still small, however, by industry standards. The UK market for videos is dominated by large US distributors such as Warner, Universal, Buena Vista and 20th Century Fox, between them accounting for 65 per cent of the market. Contender holds a share of less than 1 per cent. As an intermediary, it buys the rights to a programme, typically for around £100,000, and then sells it on to retail outlets. Contender found its niche by distributing programmes with adult appeal such as the TV series *The Avengers* and *Bad Girls*. A typical title will sell between 25,000 and 50,000 copies over 12 months with profit of around £3 per sale. The key to success is buying the right programme rights and then being able to sell them on. That is getting harder as the larger organisations have increasing power over the production as well as the distribution of videos.

Contender decided, therefore, to diversify into video production and publishing, using the core competencies and industry appreciation acquired in the original business. The fragmentation of media and new television channels increasingly allows for specialist and more personalised video material. It typically costs £100,000 to produce a relatively low budget programme such as the Helen Adams Dance Workout video, a series looking at British waterways or children's videos. Original programmes now account for around 15 per cent of Contender's sales and a further 10 per cent is expected to come from spin-off merchandising and books, especially in the children's programmes area. Although the company has the industry skills and market contacts necessary to expand into video production, mistakes are made with programmes that simply fail, and then the up-front costs invested before any sales revenue is generated cannot be recouped. This eventually could lead to a loss of independence because when video production companies get to a certain size, around £15 mn sales, they become attractive acquisition targets for larger, better capitalised industry players (Sumner-Smith, 2002).

Conglomerate diversification. The conglomerate diversification route is taken when an organisation undertakes new activities in markets that are also new. This involves risks in both the product development area and gaining acceptance in the marketplace.

eg

American Express decided to become a multi-product business, building on its image and experience with certain lifestyle segments gained through its credit cards. Not only was direct banking piloted in Germany, but consideration was also given to mobile phone services, travel products and private health care. The common thread for the diversification was the use of the Amex name.

Growth through integration

Meanwhile, integrative growth means staying within the same value chain but entering new roles or processes, either to ensure greater control of the overall process or to gain expansion. There are a number of options.

Backward integration. The focus in backward integration is on guaranteeing the quantity and quality of supply within acceptable cost guidelines. This could mean looking closely at raw materials, semi-processed materials, components or services supplied. A large manufacturer of vehicle refrigeration units in Ireland, for example, acquired the capacity to produce one of the components. This meant that these components were now made in-house, thus effectively terminating supply arrangements with some local small suppliers. Marks & Spencer, in contrast, does not seek formal ownership of its suppliers, but firmly controls their operations through tight specifications, prices, quantities and exclusivity agreements.

Backward integration might not be undertaken by choice. Suppliers may not be able to meet the buyer's specifications, or the buyers might want access to the supplier's technology to allow them to redesign and control the specification, for example.

Forward integration. Forward integration occurs where the organisation sets up or acquires dealers, distributors, wholesalers or retailers in order to control the distribution process in terms of physical supply, inventory, selling effort, etc. This could also include controlling the major customers for your product.

Cockerill Sambre (http://www.cockerillsambregroup.com), the major Belgium-based steel producer, has set up companies further down the distribution channel, primarily through acquisition, to process its products to meet specific applications, such as coatings and galvanising. In addition, it has established a dense network of steel service centres to cover a number of European markets. For example, Disteel in Belgium, Dikema & Chabot in the Netherlands and Scandinavia, the PMU Group, France's leading steel distributor, and in the UK ASK McGowan all provide the local technical expertise and ready machined stock close to users. These centres sell 4.5 mn tonnes of steel per annum, of which 50 per cent comes from Cockerill's steel division, thus helping to retain overall competitive strength in main markets such as the automotive, packaging, agricultural and construction industries.

Horizontal integration. The objective of horizontal integration is to absorb competitors, to strengthen either market coverage or market position. This route might result in cost savings if, for example, product distribution overlap can be eliminated and a common distribution network used. Within the greeting card industry, for example, larger producers tend to acquire the more successful smaller operators who find it difficult to break out of confined niches as they lack the distribution and merchandising strengths to deal with the larger retailers. In other horizontal acquisitions, the partners may be complementary rather than direct competition.

eg

Holcim's strategy, considered at p. 846, is primarily achieving growth through horizontal acquisition. It is sometimes a race against its main rivals who are pursuing a similar strategy (Hall, 2002). The Portuguese cement group Cimpor, the seventh largest in Europe, found itself in the centre of the wider battle for the global domination of the cement industry. In 2000, Holcim purchased 6 per cent of Cimpor's shares, and then rival Lafarge bought 10 per cent so that the two were locked in a battle to dominate not just the Portuguese market, but also to gain access to Cimpor's overseas markets (Wise, 2001b). Over 50 per cent of the Portuguese company's sales were from the 17 plants in seven countries (Wise, 2001a). Cimpor's interests extended to Mozambique, Morocco, Tunisia, Egypt and the most strategically important, Brazil. Meanwhile, Holcim was even prepared to transfer 24 million tonnes of cement production capacity in Spain, Latin America and Africa to Cimpor in return for acquiring a stake of less than 50 per cent. It has been left to the Portuguese law courts to decide Cimpor's fate. This battle clearly demonstrates how seriously some players approach the achievement of market dominance by absorbing competitors.

Each of the alternative growth strategies is summarised in Table 20.1. As has been seen in the Nestlé vignettes (pp. 850–1), acquisition is still used as a growth strategy, but increasingly organisations are finding that a wide, diversified portfolio might well spread risk, but does little to help achieve a dominant position in the market. Nestlé tended to acquire companies only in areas that were compatible with its aim of leadership in certain food and beverage sectors and divested where the fit was poor, as shown by the plans for the sale of Fox.

Table 20.1 Alternative growth strategies

Intensive growth
- Market penetration
- Market development
- Product development

Diversified growth
- Concentric diversification
- Conglomerate diversification

Integrative growth
- Backward integration
- Forward integration
- Horizontal integration

e-marketing *in action*

Internet growth strategies for SMEs

Chaffey (2002) reviews the application of the Ansoff matrix as a means for marketing managers to discuss market and product development using electronic technologies. Options to be considered in an e-commerce context are:

- *Market penetration*. Digital channels can be used to sell more existing products into existing markets. Online channels can help to consolidate or increase market share by providing additional promotion and customer service facilities among customers in an existing market. The internet can also be used for customer retention management. This is a relatively conservative use of the internet. A risk is cannibalisation of existing customers from other channels which may lead to reduced profit margins compared with other channels.
- *Market development*. Here, online channels are used to sell into new markets, taking advantage of the low cost of advertising internationally without the necessity for a supporting sales infrastructure in the customer's country. This is a relatively conservative use of the internet, but is a great opportunity for SMEs to increase exports at a low cost. It does, however, mean overcoming the barriers to exporting as described in the e-marketing vignette in Chapter 23.

  A less evident benefit of the internet is that as well as selling into new geographic markets, products can also be sold to new market segments or different types of customers. This may happen simply as a by-product of having a website. For example, RS Components (see Case Study 13.1) a supplier of a range of MRO items, found that 10 per cent of the web-based sales were to individual consumers rather than traditional business customers. The UK retailer Argos found the opposite was true with 10 per cent of website sales from businesses, when their traditional market was consumer-based. The internet could offer further opportunities for selling to market sub-segments that have not been previously targeted. For example, a product sold to large businesses may also appeal to SMEs, or a product targeted at young people could also appeal to some members of an older audience.
- *Product development*. New digital products or services can be developed that can be delivered by the internet. These are typically information products, for example online trade magazine *Construction Weekly* has diversified to a B2B portal *Construction Plus* (http://www.constructionplus.com) which has new revenue streams. This is innovative use of the internet.
- *Diversification*. In this sector, new products are developed which are sold into new markets. For example *Construction Plus* is now international while formerly it had a UK customer-base.

The benefits and risks of adopting a market and product development approach are highlighted by the creation of Smile (http://www.smile.co.uk) an internet-specific banking subsidiary of the Co-operative Bank in the UK. Smile opened for business in October 1999 and in its first year added 200,000 customers at a rate of 20,000 per month. Significantly, 80 per cent of these customers represented market development in the context of the parent, since they were not existing Co-op customers and typically belonged to a higher income segment. As well as the new online banking products available from Smile, a secure shopping zone has been developed which is a new revenue model since each purchase made from the site will provide affiliate revenue (a small percentage of the sales price is paid by the retailer to Smile). Retailers also pay Smile for placing advertisements and promotions within the shopping zone. The risks of the new approach are highlighted by the costs of these innovations. It is estimated that in its first year, costs of creation and promotion of Smile increased overall costs of the Co-op bank by 5 per cent. However, overheads are relatively low since Smile only employs 130 people and it is targeted for profit 3 years from launch.

Source: Chaffey (2002).

Other 'no growth' options

Not all strategies have to be growth-orientated. *Harvesting* is a deliberate strategy of not seeking growth, but looking for the best returns from the product, even if the action taken may actually speed up any decline or reinforce the no growth situation. The objective is, however, to make short-term profit while it is possible. Typically, products subjected to harvesting are likely to be cash cows in the mature stage of their lifecycles (*see* pp. 312 *et seq.*), in a market that is stable or declining, as considered at pp. 849 *et seq*. Harvesting strategies could involve minimal promotional expenditure, premium pricing strategies where possible, reducing product variability and controlling costs rigidly. Implementing such strategies helps to ensure that maximum returns are made over a short period, despite the potential loss of longer-term future sales. Effectively, the company is relying on the short-term loyalty of customers to cushion the effect of declining sales.

In more extreme cases, where prospects really are poor or bleak, *entrenchment* or *withdrawal* might be the only option. A timetable for withdrawal or closure would be developed and every effort made to maximise returns on the remaining output, in the full knowledge that harm will be done to sales volume in the short term. Some care should, however, be exercised when considering withdrawal, as highlighted in our discussion of dogs (see p. 852). Although the profit potential may be poor and the costs of turnaround prohibitive, the loss of a product in a range may affect other parts of the range adversely. Thus entrenchment, protecting the product's position as best you can without wasting too many resources on it, might be the most appropriate course of action.

eg

Unilever decided to sell its woollen-care detergent brand, Stergene, after a significant loss in market share, reported as over 70 per cent, between 1999 and 2001. The brand's share of the market was just 0.5 per cent by 2001 and for Unilever, seeking to be market leader in its prime product sectors, it was a choice between heavy marketing investment for an uncertain future, or disposal as part of its 'path to growth' strategy considered at pp. 858–9 (Singh, 2002).

Sometimes brands might be allowed to die slowly rather than be subjected to a firm decision to terminate.

Marketing and competitive strategy

No organisation operates in isolation. The organisation is not free to develop a business and marketing strategy without reference to the competitive environment. In recent years, the analysis and development of competitive strategy has become a major area of concern in many markets, reflecting the changing economic environment, and especially the internationalisation of trade. Competitors are an important factor that will influence the eventual success or failure of a business in any market. Ignore competition, and the likelihood of being taken by surprise or of being caught out by a strong new product or a major attack on a loyal customer base is very great and can create severe problems. That is why it is important to consider systematically a number of aspects of competitive behaviour.

Competitor analysis

Competitor analysis is a systematic attempt to identify and understand the key elements of a competitor's strategy, in terms of objectives, strategies, resource allocation and implementation through the marketing mix. A sound understanding of these areas enables stronger defences to be built and sustainable competitive advantage to be created and, not least, provides a foundation for outmanoeuvring the competition to gain share or market position.

At the macro level, Porter (1979) in his Five Forces Model defined the competitive forces that operate in an industry. They are:

- the bargaining power of suppliers
- the bargaining power of customers
- the threat of new entrants
- the threat of substitute products and services
- the rivalry among current competitors.

Porter's five forces form a useful starting point for undertaking a competitive analysis, in particular because they encourage a very wide definition of competition. Competition is not just about established, direct competitors at end-product level, but also about indirect and future competitors and about competition for suppliers. Before the development of the Channel Tunnel, the cross-channel ferry companies felt little need to compete aggressively with each other. Once the concept of the tunnel became a reality, however, they were shaken into action because of the perceived competitive threat.

The Porter model gives a sound foundation, but there are still several areas that should be analysed, if there is to be a full appreciation of competitors.

Competitor identification

As the Porter model implies, the identification of competitors is often broader than it first appears. The exercise should look at potential competitors, focus on the extent to which market needs are being satisfied and look at the needs that are emerging, as well as evaluating the activities and capabilities of the obvious competition. Latent or new competitors can take a market by surprise.

There are several types of competitors:

- *similar specific* – same product, technology, and target market, for example Sega vs Nintendo
- *similar general* – same product area, but serving different segments, for example Häagen Dazs vs Wall's ice cream
- *different specific* – same need satisfied by very different means, for example Eurostar vs British Airways between London and Paris
- *different general* – competing for discretionary spend, for example a holiday vs a new car.

An organisation needs to decide with whom it is really competing, and from which category of competition the main threats are emerging. A market leader might base its marketing strategy on the overall stimulation of demand (i.e. tackle the *different general* competitors, on the basis that it will pick up the largest share of any new business created), while a minor player might be more concerned with taking share from *similar specific* competition.

Any organisation should take a wide view of who it is competing with. Small local shops discovered the hard way that they were competing with the supermarket multiples. The process can, however, work the other way round: it is possible for what appears to be a small niche operator to shake up a market. Häagen Dazs, for example, entered the UK by opening up a whole new 'adult indulgence' segment in the ice-cream market which grew so fast that it caused existing players to rethink their marketing strategies.

Competitive clusters

Once competitors are identified, it might be possible to group them into clusters, depending on their focus and strategy. Figure 20.7 shows how advertising agencies can be clustered.

The vertical axis in Figure 20.7 covers a geographic spectrum. At one end are the purely local, typically small operators, perhaps based in a town or city. Then come regional agencies, for example based in Lyon or Leeds, that may have some national accounts. These are followed by national agencies that operate throughout the country, and are often based in

Figure 20.7 Strategic groupings: advertising agencies

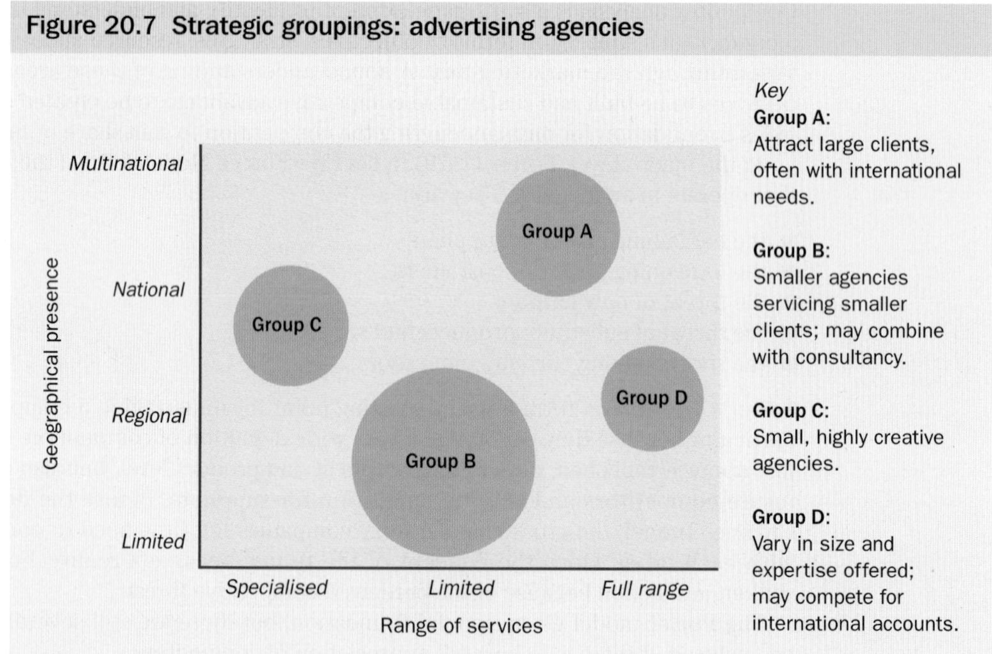

the capital. European agencies handle European accounts, working through a network of offices in other capitals, while at the far end of the spectrum are the international agencies, operating from major world capitals. The horizontal axis covers the range of services, beginning with the specialists (handling for example only one task, such as media buying or one type of advertising, such as direct response). Limited service agencies handle mostly advertising work, but not research or wider aspects of marketing, while full range agencies offer most services directly or by affiliation. Finally, diversified agencies offer all marketing services on a 'one-stop shop' basis.

Once the clusters have been identified, the strong and weak competitors in each group can then be considered, and strategic opportunities defined. It is clearly easier to enter the market as a local, specialised or limited service agency than as a major international player, but subsequent evolution may be possible. It is important to remember, however, that there might still be competition between different clusters. A local agency could bid for a national contract, for example, but might find it difficult to convince a potential customer that they have the expertise, resources and track record.

There are a number of different characteristics that can be used for identifying strategic clusters, as shown in Figure 20.8. This can provide a useful framework for identifying opportunities, but remember that in order to implement the technique, the organisation needs detailed competitor information, not just on financial performance but also on segments served and marketing strategies etc.

corporate social responsibility *in action*

Watch out, the rubbish spies are about

If you think that espionage and intelligence gathering are largely the preserve of state security departments or dirty politics you are mistaken. Corporate intelligence gathering (not corporate espionage) has become a business in its own right, even though it does sometimes operate right up to the boundaries of business ethics and legality. The Society of Competitive Intelligence Professionals represents 6,000 organisations in 45 countries, many specialising in particular branches of work such as computing and database investigation (Edgecliffe-Johnson, 2001a). Computer scientists and librarians rub shoulders with those who have formerly worked on covert government projects.

The growth of international competition in which market entry timing and speed of competitive response can be vital, has made quality intelligence a desirable commodity. Corporate intelligence gathering does not imply breaking the law. Most operators are entirely legal, and do not pose as suppliers, customers or journalists, but simply make use of the wealth of information that is publicly available on the internet and from other open information sources. A significant source of information is also employees who talk too much on their mobiles over lunch, or in airport lounges or at interviews. Others do not shred sensitive information but put it in a waste bin from which it can later be retrieved. Trade fairs and receptions are particularly satisfying places for intelligence seekers. Some companies even employ professional sitters to hang around places where corporate executives might gather and reveal secrets (Edgecliffe-Johnson, 2001b).

Proctor & Gamble ran into trouble for hiring corporate intelligence agents to sift the rubbish bins outside Unilever's new product headquarters in Chicago. P&G was keen to understand better Unilever's plans for the haircare market and resorted to somewhat unconventional means to gain an inside track. An operation was run by a number of subcontractors to gather intelligence on the haircare business, but part of it involved trespassing on the Unilever headquarters (Serwer, 2001) to rifle through the bins. It is thought that over 80 documents were sourced (Edgecliffe-Johnson and Jones, 2001). The operation was eventually exposed by a whistleblower, but the damage had been done (Neff, 2001). Although the spying took place without the knowledge of P&G's senior executives and none of the information was used for commercial purposes, it did considerable harm to P&G's reputation. P&G senior executives stopped the operation as soon as they found out about it, fired the executives involved in the project and apologised to Unilever, but the PR repercussions spread around the globe. It is one thing to gather information, but quite another to go beyond the boundaries of accepted ethical and fair behaviour.

It is believed that P&G had acquired considerable insight into Unilever's brands, new product plans, margins, promotional campaigns and much more. Although P&G insists that it broke no laws, it openly admitted that the practice violated strict guidelines regarding its business policies (Serwer, 2001). Once the matter was in the public domain, an apology was not enough for Unilever, however. It has been suggested that an undisclosed settlement was made for about \$10 mn, the documents were returned and P&G was forced to reveal its own plans for the haircare market for the coming three years. P&G also promised not to use any of the information gained. It has also been suggested that P&G had to forego the right to launch certain new products before the end of 2003 to ensure that none of the information acquired was used commercially (Serwer, 2001). While the sums of money are not that great in the global multi-billion dollar haircare market, they represent a symbolic statement about how seriously both companies have taken the matter. John Pepper, P&G's chairman, in an effort to rebuild confidence and steady shareholder nerves said, 'I have been personally involved in ensuring that none of the information has been or will be used in any P&G plans. This agreement will have no impact on the effectiveness of our product or marketing plans and will not inhibit fair and vigorous competition in the marketplace' (as quoted by Edgecliffe-Johnson and Jones, 2001).

Unilever and P&G have been head-to-head in the past and the latest episode might not have attracted so much attention in other markets with less of a history of confrontation. P&G likes to dominate markets and reacts aggressively to any serious competitive threat. It is not frightened to use its considerable advertising spend, distribution power and marketing muscle to sweep aside competitors. The corporate intelligence gathering exercise reflected a concern that Unilever might thwart P&G's plans by launching an assault on the haircare market in which P&G is dominant. Unilever plans to extend the highly successful soap and skincare brand Dove into shampoo, building on high brand loyalty levels. In the US market, P&G has 31 per cent of the market compared with Unilever's 20 per cent, so any progress is likely to be at the expense of the other. Dove, with a £35 mn advertising plan in 2002 as part of the 'path to growth' strategy considered earlier (see pp. 858–9) could be the product that will enable a challenge to succeed. At such a time, if P&G is having to reveal its own plans and counter-strategies in the sector for the next three years, any information it originally gleaned from the bins may turn out to have been very costly trash.

The law on intelligence-gathering does not help a great deal. Clearly, bugging and breaking and entering are off limits, but there is no international law on rifling through rubbish bins. If rubbish is considered 'abandoned property' then it is fair game, but if it is on private property or in a company bin that is another matter. Most companies do have business intelligence staff and set strict guidelines and standards that must be followed. In P&G's case, these standards appear to have been breached by over-zealous 'rubbish archæologists'. The real danger if an organisation is caught, is the loss of reputation as British Airways found in the 1990s when Virgin accused it of dirty tricks in accessing confidential files and as P&G has now found in rubbish sifting. So the next time you discuss a deal nearing completion on your mobile in a busy place, throw away a confidential photocopy page because it is off centre, or tear a report in two rather than shred it, be careful!

Sources: Benady (2001); Edgecliffe-Johnson (2001a, 2001b); Edgecliffe-Johnson and Jones (2001); Neff (2001); Serwer (2001).

Figure 20.8 Characteristics that define strategic groups

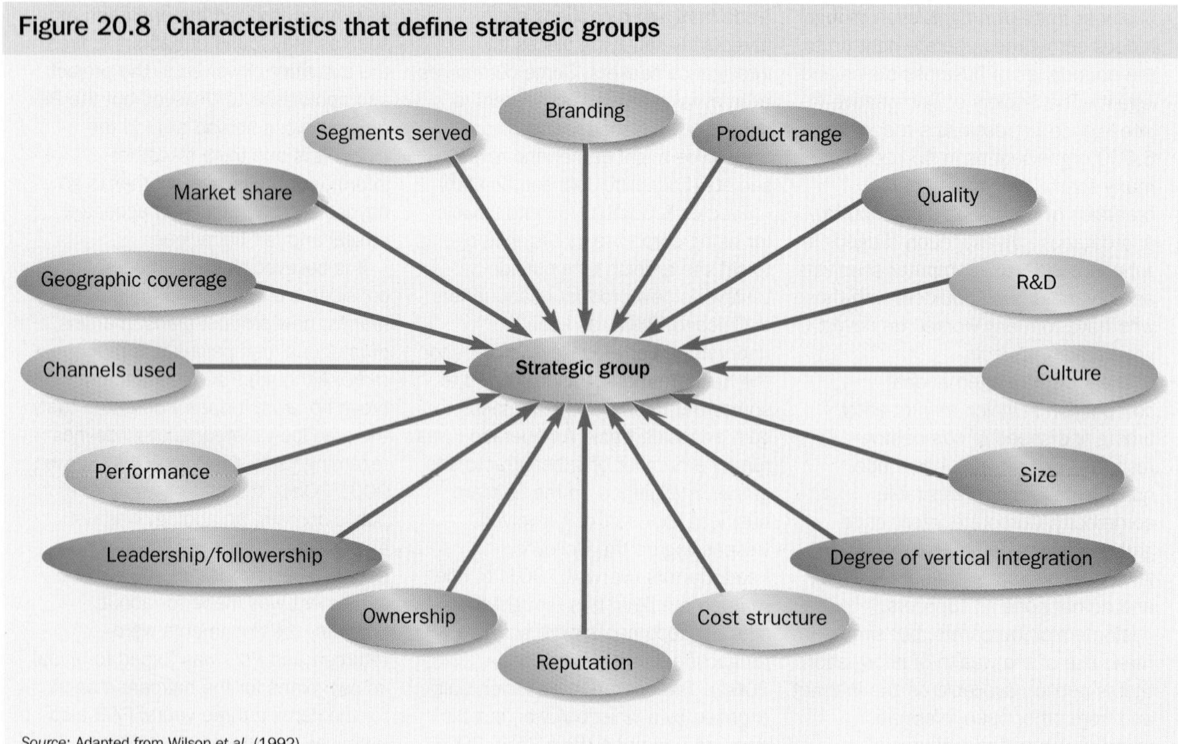

Source: Adapted from Wilson *et al*. (1992).

Competitive strengths and weaknesses

Examining a competitor's strengths and weaknesses provides a valuable insight into its strategic thinking and actions. A full range of areas should be examined, for example manufacturing, technical and financial strengths, relationships with suppliers and customers and markets and segments served, as well as the usual gamut of marketing activity. It is particularly worth undertaking a detailed review of the product range, identifying where volume, profits and cash come from, where the competitor is the market leader, where it is weak and where it seems to be heading.

Of course, the required information may not all be readily available. Shared customers or suppliers can be a useful source of information, but the organisation might also have to make use of secondary data, especially sales reports, exhibitions and press cuttings, etc. The analysis of this information should be considered in the context of *critical success factors*. These are the factors or attributes that are essential if an organisation is to have any chance of success in a particular industry. Often, they evolve around technology, image, finance, service, quality, distribution, management or the skills of the workforce. Each competitor can be rated on each factor to assess their strong and vulnerable points. This information can be used later to plan and launch an attack.

eg

India has developed a strong IT sector concentrating on designing and repairing software for international organisations, especially in the United States, the destination of two-thirds of the exports. Labour costs tend to be lower and the infrastructure has benefited from supportive governmental economic policies. Most of the companies are, however, low value, high volume maintenance operators which have not been able to compete in high value-added areas. Some are, however, now considering moving into software products for which marketing expertise is needed and capital required to invest in product development well ahead of any sales revenue. To succeed, Indian companies would have to compete in crowded markets in which global competitors are well established; develop a strong understanding of user applications; and establish a presence through sales and support teams. Some Indian companies have already made the transition. I-Flex from Bangalore was set up by Citibank in the US to develop software products on a dedicated basis. The expertise thus gained enabled it to develop other financial software products for clients in south-east Asia and Europe. It has, however, had to spend 12 per cent of its revenue on marketing compared with 1 per cent for the typical software service company in India (Merchant, 2002).

Competitors' objectives and strategies

It is important to understand what drives competitors, what makes them act as they do. Most firms have multiple objectives beyond the simple notion of profit. Objectives could relate to cash generation, market share, technological leadership, quality recognition or a host of other things. Sometimes developing an understanding of a competitor's product portfolio provides a valuable insight into likely competitive objectives. Once you understand their objectives, you have strong clues about how their strategy is likely to unfold in terms of their positioning, marketing mix and vulnerable points for attack, or your best means of

eg

Airbus and Boeing are global rivals for the passenger aircraft market (*see* pp. 60–1). As rivals for virtually every major contract from national airlines, each has a detailed insight into the strengths and weaknesses of the other. Of critical importance is getting the basic aircraft design right in the first place and each has taken a radically different view of future air passenger demand. Airbus is planning the A380, the world's biggest airliner with 555 seats and due for a maiden flight in 2004, whereas Boeing is going for the sonic cruiser, with 250 seats, in an aircraft built to travel at 98 per cent of the speed of sound. One is built for volume hub-to-hub traffic, the other for fast point-to-point services. These polarised alternatives reflect radically different views on the future of passenger demand over the next twenty years. There might, however, be no loser, as both could serve different niches with neither dominating the global market. What will be clear, however, is that both will know exactly how to argue against the other when trying to close a deal (*The Economist*, 2002).

defence. Furthermore, if you can assess the relative importance of their objectives, you can go further in assessing their likely future plans and their reaction to market or competitive events. Competitive retaliation, for example, is likely to be more intense if the competitor has a strong vested interest in the market, such as profit contribution, growth, opportunities, etc.

Competitive reaction

It is very important to be able to assess competitors' responses to general changes in the marketing environment and to moves in major battles within the market. These responses could range from matching a price cut or an increase in promotional spend, through to ignoring events or shifting the ground completely. An organisation can learn from experience how competitors are likely to behave. Some will always react swiftly and decisively to what is seen as a threat, others may be more selective depending on the perceived magnitude of the threat.

eg

The cereal market in the UK is both static and highly competitive. Although the market is led by Kellogg's, Weetabix, Nestlé and Quaker also feature in the top ten ready-to-eat brands. With such powerful players, any product innovation advantage rarely lasts for long. When Kellogg's launched Special K Red Berries, for example, Jordan launched the same fruit in its Oat Sensations range and Quaker added new flavours to its Harvest Crunch range. Most brands also attract heavy promotional budgets with an emphasis on developing a distinct brand identity, often using icons such as the Honey Monster for Quaker's Sugar Puffs or through distinctive positioning such Weetabix's Alpen and Ennis Foods' Breakfastables. Most of the manufacturers watch closely what the others are doing and the secrecy behind planned product launches and sales promotions is designed to give a short-term lead through surprising the competition (Eggleston, 2002).

It is not always easy to predict competitive reaction, as it is likely to be influenced by a range of factors, including cost structures, relative market positions and the stage reached in the industry or product lifecycle.

Competitive information system

The above discussion of competitor analysis demonstrates the need for a well-organised and comprehensive competitor information system. This would be part of the MIS discussed in Chapter 6. Often, data need to be deliberately sourced on an ongoing basis, collated, analysed, disseminated and discussed. Then, management at all levels can learn what is happening. They may dispute the findings or the data may provide a basis for seeking further insights. It is impossible to provide a complete checklist of areas that need to be considered, but Wilson *et al.* (1992) provide useful guidelines, as shown in Table 20.2.

Clearly, information is the key to outmanoeuvring and limiting the threats of competition, and should be gathered and analysed on both an individual competitor and competitive cluster basis.

Table 20.2 Useful information about competitors

- Sales
- Customers
- Products
- Advertising and promotion
- Distribution and sales force
- Pricing
- Finance
- Management
- Anything else ...

Source: Wilson *et al*. (1992).

Alternative competitive strategies

It has been argued that organisations should select a generic strategy that provides the direction for subsequent operational decisions, including marketing (Porter, 1980). Three **generic strategies** are proposed, as shown in Figure 20.9. Each one imposes different pressures on the organisation to ensure that resources and capabilities are consistent with the requirements of the strategic alternative selected. The expectation is, however, that the vigorous pursuit of the chosen strategy will create a *sustainable competitive advantage*. The three alternatives are cost leadership, differentiation and focus. Each one is now considered in turn.

Cost leadership

Through the strategy of cost leadership, the organisation seeks a cost advantage over its competitors. This might involve efficiency drives, tight cost controls or a preoccupation with low-cost production. It almost certainly means a ruthless attack on waste, in the drive to gain cost advantage. It might mean investment in production to achieve productivity gains, or it might mean investment in marketing to ensure that adequate sales volumes are achieved.

eg

In the earlier example of Holcim SA (*see* p. 846), the main element of its competitive strategy was to ensure consistent and appropriate quality and the lowest unit of cost. To achieve a cost leadership position there had to be careful plant location decisions and investment in production technology to ensure that it always kept one step ahead of the competition. Large volumes also required large orders, so contracts were pursued aggressively using a direct sales force.

In the above example, the low-cost position was designed not so much to cut prices as a market leader, but to maintain and build its market dominance. The problem with cost leadership is, however, that it tends to put undue emphasis on price. A cost leader can entertain a price war and, with a more efficient cost base, can contemplate winning. Cost leadership can also give a defensive cushion. A competitive supply market might, for example, encourage a powerful buyer to demand yet lower prices. The cost leader can deliver on those prices and perhaps still retain a small advantage. Such a focus on costs and price can also have the advantage of making it less attractive for new entrants to come into the market.

In short, the firm with cost leadership will feel the pinch last. There are two main sources of cost leadership, productivity and linkage effectiveness.

Figure 20.9 Generic strategies

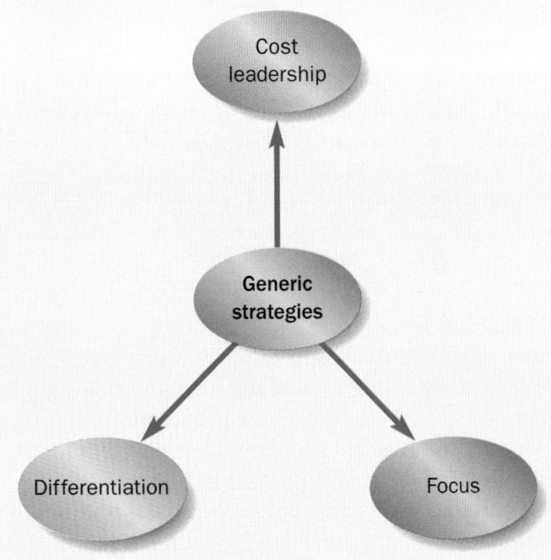

Productivity. There are a number of ways within a manufacturing environment to reduce and maintain low or lower average unit costs compared with the competition. *Economies of scale* suggest that as production volume increases, unit costs decrease. Plant and equipment might be more efficient or be able to cope with additional volume without a proportional increase in overheads and support services. A 20 per cent increase in production volume does not mean a 20 per cent increase in staffing, R&D or supplies management costs. The increased production gives more volume over which to spread fixed costs, thus lowering the average unit cost.

Such economies of scale may be linked with higher overall annual volumes, or an ability to better utilise capacity to the full over the course of the year if the overall capacity is fixed. Many service providers, including airlines and hotels, face problems in how to fill off-peak capacity. Often it is the ability to solve this problem that will determine overall success.

The *experience curve* is another means of building a low cost base. This concept suggests that as cumulative volume increases, so does experience in manufacture, which might mean less wastage or higher productivity, and thus have a beneficial influence on cost. In other words, the more you do something, the more proficient you become at it. That benefit will only be achieved, however, if management responds to the opportunity for cost reduction created. Thus as electronics companies have become more experienced in the mass production of DVD players, their manufacturing efficiency has risen and costs decreased accordingly.

This means that through learning to produce, specialise and innovate in process design, improving the performance of production equipment and redesigning or standardising production, the operation becomes more efficient and the opportunities for cost reduction increase. The Boston Consulting Group estimated that as cumulative output doubles, average cost is reduced by 15–20 per cent. This favours those firms aggressively seeking market share gains, as they can further enhance their competitive position.

Of course, there are limits to how far cost efficiencies can be gained through economies of scale and learning. Economies of scale arise from the size of operation and volume produced compared with competitors. There may come a point where the economies of scale turn to diseconomies, as a result of unmanageable size and complexity. Learning curve effects arise from cumulative effects over time, regardless of operational scale. The benefits of learning might lead to further scale effects as the market position of the cost leader increases. In many ways, the efficient organisation will be chasing ever smaller gains in average unit costs. The biggest gains are often to be had during the launch and early stages of a new product, not during the maturity phase.

Linkage effectiveness. Not all gains come from production itself, whether the operation is a factory or a hotel. Some can derive from linkages with other areas of the organisation, the supply network and customer and channel interfaces. Large production volumes need successful marketing and logistics to ensure their efficient throughput to customers. In particular, pricing and distribution strategies and promotional approaches need to generate a sufficient flow of trade. Mass production requires mass distribution to keep goods flowing. One of the reasons that Wal-Mart's prices are something like 17 per cent lower than those of its US competitors is that despite the volumes of goods handled, it has a very efficient logistics systems that minimises the amount of stock held while ensuring availability on the shelves.

eg

HMV is the UK's market leader for CDs, with a 21 per cent share. It has 135 stores in the UK and a further 190 in eight other countries. It operates by building scale to offer maximum choice, maintaining high stock levels and providing a pleasant environment for browsing. Most of its retail stores are larger than those of its local competitors to enable it to exploit its strengths and they are serviced by an efficient logistics and merchandising system to support volume sales. To maintain its strength, a further 65 stores in the UK are planned over the next three to five years, and overseas the number of stores in Japan will increase from 34 to 100 and in Canada from 98 to 140 stores (Shah, 2002).

Working closely with suppliers to ensure timely and competitive component and materials supply can be a source of cost saving. The need to reduce inventories both before and after the production line emphasises the role of 'just in time' systems, supplier partnerships, efficient physical distribution and the right dealer network or channel. All of these are essential if the cost advantages created in production are actually to reach the marketplace. Some organisations go further and integrate supply lines either horizontally (thus sharing costs in some areas, for instance physical distribution) or vertically, by controlling suppliers and the distribution network. Not all control and gains from integration have to be based on legal ownership. Managed supply chains based on supplier dependency, such as those created by large retail multiples, can achieve many of the same results without the problems of ownership.

Problems of cost leadership. There are, however, several problems with a cost leadership position:

1 The focus is on cost as a competitive weapon rather than on the range of other factors that customers might find important. Some customers will be prepared to pay more for added value or a stronger brand image.
2 The focus is purely on product cost, not the total cost of purchase to the customer, including after-sales costs, change costs and usage costs.
3 As we saw in Chapters 10 and 11, price is the easiest of the marketing mix variables to replicate in the short term, and price wars are rarely beneficial to all suppliers in the long run.
4 The cost leader may become more resistant to change, becoming locked into obsolete or less relevant production technology. New technology can erode both the scale effect and the benefits of learning. The benefits of the technological efficiency gained might thus become the cause of inertia and eventual demise.

Differentiation

The second generic strategy is differentiation. In order to succeed, an organisation must offer something to the buyer that the buyer values, and that is different from the rest. This differentiation is usually defined in terms of better performance, better design or a better fit with the customer's needs. The tradition within Germany's long-established piano manufacturers is to seek high quality and excellent design in the face of stiff competition from the Far East. Manufacturers such as Bechstein in Berlin, Steinway in Hamburg and Bluthner in Leipzig have all resisted the temptation to go downmarket, and although the market is relatively small the industry has survived. The value added must be sufficient to command a price premium, but that in no way means that the organisation can forget about costs. The offering still needs to be competitive, and the organisation must justify the price–value relationship.

The aim is to create an edge over rivals and to have a differentiation package that is sustainable over time. In marketing, this can be 'real' (e.g. a product design feature) or 'imaginary' (a strong brand image or advertising campaign). People really do have to believe that there is a difference. Remember, though, that this approach might not achieve market leadership, even if the product is regarded as superior. Buyers might still be prepared to accept second best at a lower price.

eg

Teuscher (http://www.teuscher.com) truffle shops claim to offer a fairytale experience to all their visitors. Top quality chocolate surrounded by elaborate design in over 25 stores worldwide helps Teuscher to stand out from the crowd. The designs are deliberately themed and changed simultaneously in all shops four or five times per year. Examples have included autumn pheasants, pink flamingos and bears, to name but a few, all set amid plants and flowers. Attention to detail also extends to the products themselves. The raw material is carefully selected couverture that has been specially tempered and has a high cocoa content and low melting point. Such delights as champagne truffles, chewy florentines, candied orange slices, hearts and fish shapes, golf balls, trains and pianos are all offered – in chocolate, of course. This attention to detail, a high level of creativity and an emphasis on premier class make Teuscher shops very special places (Style, 1999).

Teuscher chocolates offer the customer many different varieties of their truffles aimed at chocolate connoisseurs.

Source: Teuscher Chocolates of Switzerland.

The main advantage of a differentiation strategy is that it takes the focus away from price, and therefore might lead to the possibility of charging a price premium. It might also generate buyer loyalty, reducing their tendencies towards substitution or switching. The organisation does, however, have to think through the marketing activity that supports this strategy very carefully, and must plough back any price premium into sustaining its position.

The sources of differentiation can emerge from any area of the market offering:

- *product*: branding; innovation; quality; specification; design; image; patents;
- *price*: price positions; price–value combinations;
- *place*: intensive distribution, exclusive distribution; back-up, service support;
- *promotion*: creativity; spend;
- *service:* strong trusting relationships with customers; adaptation; transaction-specific investments.

The difficulties with this approach stem from environmental changes. More experienced consumers may see through 'imaginary' differences, and even question the value offered for the price premium. As the market matures, imitators might reduce margins, and it becomes more difficult to retain the level of marketing investment required. New types of competitors might also disturb the *status quo*, for example telephone banking or chains of opticians offering 'your glasses in one hour or less'.

Focus

An organisation adopting a focus strategy is deliberately selective, focusing on a narrow group of customers, rather than on the whole market. There are many ways of selecting appropriate segments, but the organisation building a long-term strategy needs to ensure that they are durable. The philosophy here is to do a little thing thoroughly and well by

eg

Wolfking (http://www.wolfking.com) is a Danish manufacturer of specialist machinery for the food processing industry. The company has always focused its operations on narrow areas and then sought to be the best in those areas. From its early origins in mink farming equipment, then in stainless steel meat processing machines in the 1970s, it has expanded into computer control systems and pet foods, but has always been associated with meat processing. With an overall objective to be a leading global manufacturer and supplier of machinery and advanced processing lines for minced meat and raw materials, Wolfking has established a market leadership position through direct operations and acquisition. For example, when it wanted to get into the allied processing of cured and marinated meat sector it purchased Belam BV in the Netherlands in 1992 and Scanio in Denmark in 1998.

To help achieve the focused strategy there has had to be heavy investment in new technology, product development and new systems that can offer tailor-made complete solutions, if necessary, to the meat trade, retail and processors. The other critical element of the strategy is expanded market coverage. It sells through distributors and sales offices in most major markets and operates sales and service companies in China, the USA, the UK, Germany and Brazil.

meeting the needs of a clearly defined group far better than anyone else. Focus in itself might not be enough, however, and the organisation might have to combine it with cost leadership or differentiation to build advantage.

If a focus strategy is to succeed, the organisation must understand segments thoroughly, how their needs are changing and what range to offer. If you are not serving a segment more effectively than your competitors, then you are in a poor position. To some extent, the scope for focus strategies has been opened up by the advent of the SEM. It is easier now for organisations to adopt a European market segmentation approach. Similar segments may exist in different countries, and thus although the segment may be small in each country, aggregated across Europe, it becomes an attractive option. Imagine, for example, the pan-European segments for premium brands of designer clothes, sports cars, fragrances and jewellery. An organisation operating in one of these segments might adjust its offering slightly to reflect local differences, but the key is the focus on a pan-European segment. It could be possible to define subsegments, perhaps based on natural clusters, for example Nordic, German or Iberian markets, but the danger here is that the segmentation becomes purely geographic rather than behavioural.

The risk with this segmentation approach is that the segments identified might not be sustainable long term, or might be undermined locally by competition. Although there is pressure on larger organisations to take a fairly standardised approach across Europe, with minor implementation variances, there is still room for the smaller business to compete. Many small organisations, perhaps with a local or regional orientation, survive alongside larger suppliers because of their local presence, local service and responsiveness and differentiation to reflect specific local characteristics, for example food taste or the need for personalised attention.

Choice of generic strategy

The actual choice of generic strategy depends on three criteria:

- the fit between the demands of the strategy and the organisation's capabilities and resources
- the main competitors' abilities on similar criteria
- the key criteria for success in the market and their match with the organisation's capabilities.

Once these criteria have been assessed, the organisation can select the best strategy to build a strong position. In some cases an organisation might not have a free hand, since the nature of the marketing environment and the competitive stances already taken by other firms might force a particular strategic direction.

Assuming, however, that an organisation does have a free choice, it should take into account its potential sources of advantage and how they might best be used to exploit each alternative strategy. These sources of advantage might be:

1 *Skills*. The question of skills concerns the hiring, training and development of key staff, who could be in R&D, selling, quality assurance or any area that could help to implement a particular strategy.
2 *Resources*. The issue of resources refers both to the level and deployment of resources, for example promotional spend, R&D investment, financial reserves, production facilities and market coverage, and to brand strength.
3 *Relationships*. The quality and long-term stability of supplier–customer relationships provide an asset that is durable in the face of many of the short-term pressures that are created by new entrants and competitors. Such relationships might tend to favour a focus strategy, for example.

Whichever strategy an organisation chooses, there must be ruthless commitment to it. Half-hearted implementation will mean that the strategy is ineffective and the organisation will be vulnerable to attack. Trying to implement parts of all three strategies in some kind of hybrid is equally dangerous. The organisation might then have to deal with the worst of all worlds: having no cost advantage, poor differentiation and an inappropriate or fuzzy focus. Nevertheless, there is some interrelationship between the three strategies. Although differentiation is the opposite of a cost leadership strategy, because differentiation incurs costs, a dominant position achieved through differentiation may itself help to achieve volume economies in manufacturing and distribution.

Furthermore, even if the commitment to the chosen strategy is strong in theory, it can still be difficult to stick to it in practice. If cost leadership is the chosen strategy, then beware of the customer requesting special modifications. Although flexible manufacturing methods are enabling more scope for variation during the assembly process, such customising needs to be within defined cost parameters. Despite the fact that Cummins produces a specified range of diesel engines, for example, it is also able, through flexible manufacturing, to accommodate some variability for customer specification, including colour, features and even packaging. However, Cummins would not be in the business, within a mass production system, of building prototypes and limited batch-produced lines. Similarly, if differentiation is the chosen strategy, there are risks in the pursuit of the low price option. If the focus strategy is to be implemented on a pan-European basis, then decisions have to be taken on how much adaptation can be allowed for local needs in different countries.

Competitive positions and postures

A final stage in the determination of a competitive strategy is to decide how to compete, given the market realities, and how to either defend or disturb that position. This means that the organisation has to consider its own behaviour in the context of how competitors are behaving, and select the most appropriate strategy that will enable overall objectives to be achieved. Two aspects need to be considered, **competitive position** and competitive posture. Competitive position refers to the impact of the organisation's market position on marketing strategies, whereas **competitive postures** are the strategies implemented by organisations in different positions who want to disturb the *status quo*.

Competitive positions

An organisation's competitive position usually falls into one of four categories, according to its relative market share. The four categories, and the kinds of marketing strategies that go with them, are shown in Figure 20.10 and are now considered in turn.

Market leader

In many industries, one organisation is recognised as being ahead of the rest in terms of market share. Its share might only be 20–25 per cent, but that could still give it a dominant position. The market leader tends to determine the pace and ways of competing in the

Figure 20.10 Competitive position and strategy

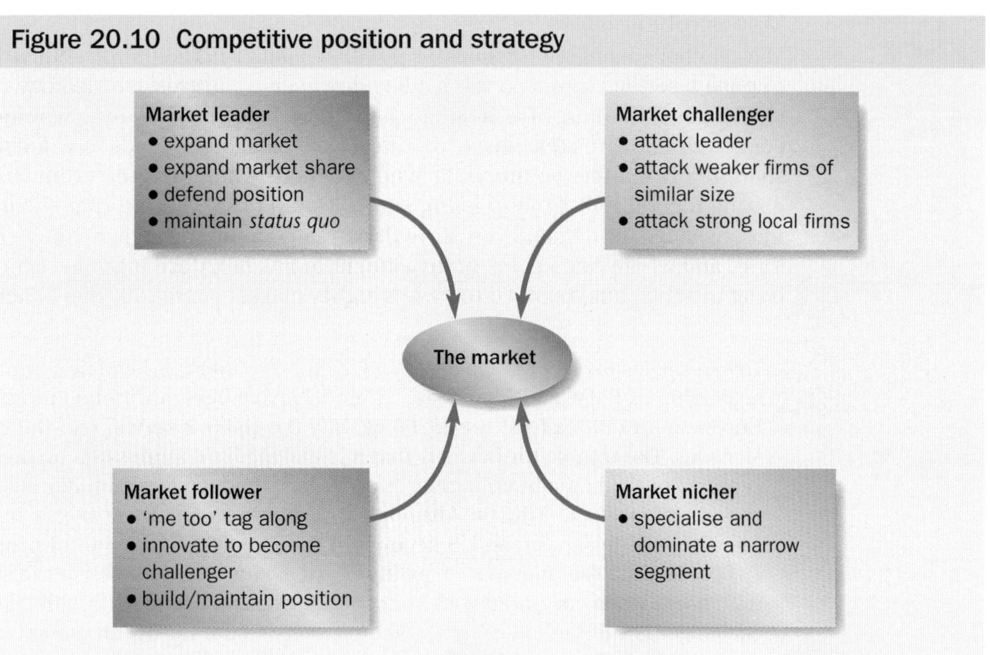

market. It sets the price standard, the promotional intensity, the rate of product change and the quality and quantity of the distribution effort. Effectively, the market leader provides a benchmark for others to follow or emulate.

eg

Wrigley has a 50 per cent share of the global chewing gum market, but that rises to almost 100 per cent in the UK. Covering 140 countries, it is a dominant player by any standards. It has, however, resisted product diversification and brand extension strategies and prefers to concentrate on its core business. It still pursues new product innovation, however, with launches of X-cite, a mint chewing gum hybrid, and Eclipse, a strongly flavoured mint pellet gum. Over 75 per cent of its sales in the UK are generated by brands that did not exist 15 years ago and some launches actually help grow the overall market. Despite its dominant position, Wrigley is still nevertheless attacked by competitors with new products targeting particular sectors, such as dental gums. Colgate is keen to take a bigger share of the UK gum market, although as yet its target is still just 7 per cent of the market, a long way short of Wrigley (Charles, 2002a).

Market leadership can be at company, product group or brand level. Hellmans claims over 50 per cent of the UK mayonnaise market, just ahead of a series of own-brand products. Chivers Hartley is the market leader in jams and marmalades, and Otto Versand is Germany's market leader in mail order. In each case there are a number of rivals, so the power associated with being a leader might not necessarily be very great, especially if markets are defined from a European rather than a domestic perspective.

Market leadership lends itself to a number of strategic alternatives, none of which is mutually exclusive:

- *expand total market* by creating new uses, new users, or more intense use;
- *expand market share* via the marketing mix. This assumes that share and profit are related;
- *defend position* against challengers, through continuous innovation, or through expanding the range to get more shelf space. This strategy has been seen in many high-profile marketing battles between leaders and challengers, such as Coca-Cola vs Pepsi, Avis vs Hertz, Unilever vs Procter & Gamble;
- *seek stability* and retention of customer base, as have organisations such as Kodak, Benetton, Nestlé and L'Oréal.

Market challengers

Market challengers are organisations with a smaller market share, but who are close enough to pose a serious threat to the leader. However, an aggressive strategy can be costly, if the challenger is thinking of attacking where there is uncertainty over winning. Before making a concerted effort to steal share, therefore, the challenger needs to ask itself whether market share really matters so much, or whether there would be greater benefit from working on getting a good ROI from existing share. Dolan (1981) found that rivalry is greater where there is stagnant demand (i.e. growth can only come through stealing share from competitors), and where fixed costs or investment in inventory are high (i.e. economies of scale can bring benefits, but you need to have a higher market share to achieve them).

eg

Toyota's plans for its prestige car brand, Lexus, are taking it head first into a challenge to the leadership of BMW and Mercedes. Its models have been positioned against the established European brand leaders: the IS200 against the BMW 3 series, and the GS430 against the Mecedes. The trouble for Lexus is that it is making little impression on the strong brand perceptions of the home-built brands. Many regard the Lexus as simply a smartened up, higher spec version of the Toyota. Although worldwide sales of the Lexus range in 2000 were 243,000 outside Japan, the US accounted for 211,000 of those and Europe for fewer than 19,000. Despite the undisputed quality of the Lexus and its better performance and engine refinement when compared with Mercedes, for example, and even with a lower price tag, the challenger is still finding it hard going to penetrate the European market sufficiently to generate the desired level of 75,000 sales per annum by 2008–2010 (Lofthouse, 2001).

Assuming that the decision is made to attack, there are two key questions: where to attack, and what the likely reaction will be. There are several options:

- attack the market leader;
- attack weaker firms of a similar size;
- attack firms who are strong but very local.

It is never easy to attack leaders, who tend to retaliate through cutting prices or by investing in heavy promotion etc. It is, therefore, a high-risk but high return route. The challenger needs a clear competitive advantage to exploit to be able to neutralise the leader. When Quaker Petfoods challenged Pedigree Petfood's Whiskas' dominance of the catfood market, for instance, it did it by product improvement to create a high-quality brand with premium packaging, supported by appealing press and television advertising. Despite Whiskas' £10 mn spend (compared with Felix's £3 mn), its market share fell within three years from 50 to 35 per cent. The challenger might also have to be prepared to absorb short-term losses as a result of defending against the leader's retaliation. Again, Felix had to increase its advertising spend considerably to attack the leader. The moral of this story is not to enter the fight unless you are really convinced that you can win and are prepared to invest in the battle. The difficulty in some markets is spotting the market challengers of tomorrow. Whereas BMW can track the progress of Lexus, a new competitor that could radically change the shape of marketing must also be considered.

eg

Fogdog (http://www.fogdog.com) may not be a name that readily springs to mind in the sporting goods market, but it was launched with the objective of challenging traditional sports retailers in the same way that Amazon challenged traditional bookselling. In the USA, it quickly established a reputation as a source of any sporting and outdoor equipment that could be bought online. It stocked over 250 brand names including Nike and Reebok, represented by 15,000 products and over 60,000 stocking units, a vast choice. The site had around 200,000 hits per month and the US product range would fit into four shops the size of Harrods! Even without trying, Fogdog made 15 per cent of its sales in Europe and with a sports market estimated to be worth in excess of £3 bn in the UK alone, it decided to open a UK office to service Europe. It failed, however, to grow internet traffic levels on its site significantly and mounting problems back in the US meant that the office was closed quickly. At least the traditional sports retailers can now breathe a little easier for a while (Evans, 2001; Hunt, 2000).

Market followers

Given the resources needed, the threat of retaliation and the uncertainty of winning, many organisations favour a far less aggressive stance, acting as market followers. There are two types of follower. First, there are those who lack the resources to mount a serious challenge and prefer to remain innovative and forward thinking, without disturbing the overall competitive structure in the market by encouraging open warfare. Often, any lead from the market leader is willingly followed. This might mean adopting a 'me too' strategy, thus avoiding direct confrontation and competition.

eg

BMI British Midland is the UK's second biggest scheduled airline and as a result has to fight on two fronts: against the market leader, British Airways, for the scheduled market, and against the low-cost airlines such as Ryanair and easyJet. When British Airways announced discounts on domestic flights, BMI had little option but to follow suit, as it competes on many of the same routes, especially into Heathrow. It has 14 per cent of all landing slots at congested Heathrow and operates over 2,000 flights a week, so any loss of passenger loading would have serious consequences. In addition to price cutting, it sought to make its tickets more flexible, for example, by removing the requirement to stay over a Saturday night. Given a freer hand, BMI might not have made these moves as it is also competing with the low-cost airlines and has had to invest in an offshoot, bmibaby, to compete head-on with the low-cost operators, primarily from its East Midlands and London bases. Any price war is likely to make a difficult financial position worse, but it cannot afford to widen the gap with BA if it wishes to retain its market position (Harrison, 2002).

The second type of follower is the organisation that is simply not capable of challenging and is content just to survive, offering little competitive advantage. Often, smaller car rental firms operate in this category by being prepared to offer a lower price, but not offering the same standard of rental vehicle or even peace of mind should things go wrong. A recession can easily eliminate the weaker members of this category.

Hammermesch *et al.* (1978) and Saunders (1987) found that some market followers seek deliberately to build and maintain that position through a range of strategies, which include careful and narrow segmentation, highly selective R&D and a focus on quality, differentiation and profitability rather than on cost and share gains.

Market nichers

Some organisations, often small, specialise in areas of the market that are too small, too costly or too vulnerable for the larger organisation to contemplate. Niching is not exclusively a small organisation strategy, as some larger firms may have divisions that specialise. The key to niching is the close matching between the needs of the market and the capabilities and strengths of the company. The specialisation offered can relate to product type, customer group, geographic area or any aspect of product/service differentiation.

eg

Dwr y Cwm sells bottled water from the heart of Snowdonia in Wales. Using natural water from underground sources, a supply of 5,500 gallons per hour can be achieved, enough to meet the expected demand for the new business. Rather than competing head-on with the national brands in the retail sector, Dwr y Cwm will be concentrating on hotels, restaurants and conference venues for distribution throughout the UK. The brand trades on the purity and freshness qualities of natural water from Snowdonia, and by concentrating on a niche that has received less attention it hopes to build a defendable position (Jones, 2001). Askey's from Buckinghamshire has also established a niche business and is a market leader with its range of wafers, cones and toppings for ice-cream manufacturers. It occupies a niche that other larger manufacturers would not find profitable to develop (http://www.askeys.com).

Niching often takes place in more technologically advanced markets too. Oxley is a private company with sales of around £12 mn that specialises in taking novel ideas and turning them into products, from miniature metal devices to instrument display panels, often with military applications. Defence contractors account for 70 per cent of its sales. Its key skill in technical ingenuity has enabled it to build a niche and defend against competitor attack.

Around 20 per cent of its staff are employed in R&D from specialisms in materials science, electronics design, chemistry, manufacturing and test engineering, optics and software to ensure that it can stay at the cutting edge. Although it is able to respond to customer design problems, it also has established a product range from its inventions and the high margins from these products generates cash for investment elsewhere. These products include optical filters and identification lights for aircraft such as the Tornado fighter. They enable pilots to use infrared night goggles without being blinded by their own aircraft's lighting. It also makes millions of tiny gold-plated spheres that fit into telecoms base stations sold by Ericsson and Motorola, the two biggest forces in the mobile phone industry. In this area it has developed a worldwide niche for precision and originality (Marsh, 2001).

The main problem for market nichers is the challenges created if the niche starts to disappear due to innovation and change. One of the problems faced by Sock Shop, the niche hosiery retailer, for example, was that larger retailers such as Marks & Spencer encroached on its niche by providing equally wide and deep hosiery assortments at competitive prices, thus eroding the differential advantage of the niche operator.

Competitive postures

The previous section considered the underlying rationale for defending, attacking or ignoring what is going on in the market from the point of view of an organisation's relative market position. This section examines *how to attack* or *how to defend* a position. A number of analogies from texts on warfare have been used (*see* e.g. Kotler and Singh, 1981) to describe the various options and the difficulties associated with them. Four broad postures are considered here, although the final two owe their roots to diplomacy rather than warfare.

Aggressive strategies

Aggressive strategies are implemented when one or more players in a market decide to challenge the *status quo*. Again, the question of who to attack, when to attack and where to attack all need to be answered carefully in the context of the resources needed, the competitive reaction and the returns to be gained at what cost. Even in warfare, head-on assaults can be costly and do not always succeed. Five broad aggressive strategies can be contemplated, as shown in Figure 20.11.

Frontal attacks. A challenger contemplating a head-on attack in marketing terms needs to be very well resourced relative to the market leader. A full-scale attack means matching and winning on all the competitive variables such as price, mass distribution, product features and the rest. A more limited frontal attack may pick off some customer groups who could be more vulnerable to a new offering, for example those who are more service conscious. BMI, mentioned earlier at p. 879, could no longer afford to see its market share eroded by the low-cost airlines and so decided to meet the threat head-on. In 2000, both easyJet and Ryanair overtook BMI in terms of passenger volumes on domestic and European routes. It entered the low-cost airline segment with a frontal assault through its own offshoot, bmibaby. It replicated the package of no frills and low prices but it was backed by a strong service support infrastructure at its base at East Midlands airport (Odell, 2002; http://www.flybmi.com).

Flank attack. Many successful attacks occur because the enemy has been outflanked and its strategy has been disrupted. By attacking particular segments, product weakness areas or poor distribution facilities, progress can be made despite the overall strength of the competition. Such tactics are called technological flanking and segmental flanking.

Flank attacks can lead to encirclement if the poorly defended segment is used by the challenger to build an image and reputation in the market in preparation for a further attack in an area of direct concern to the leader.

Figure 20.11 Attack strategies

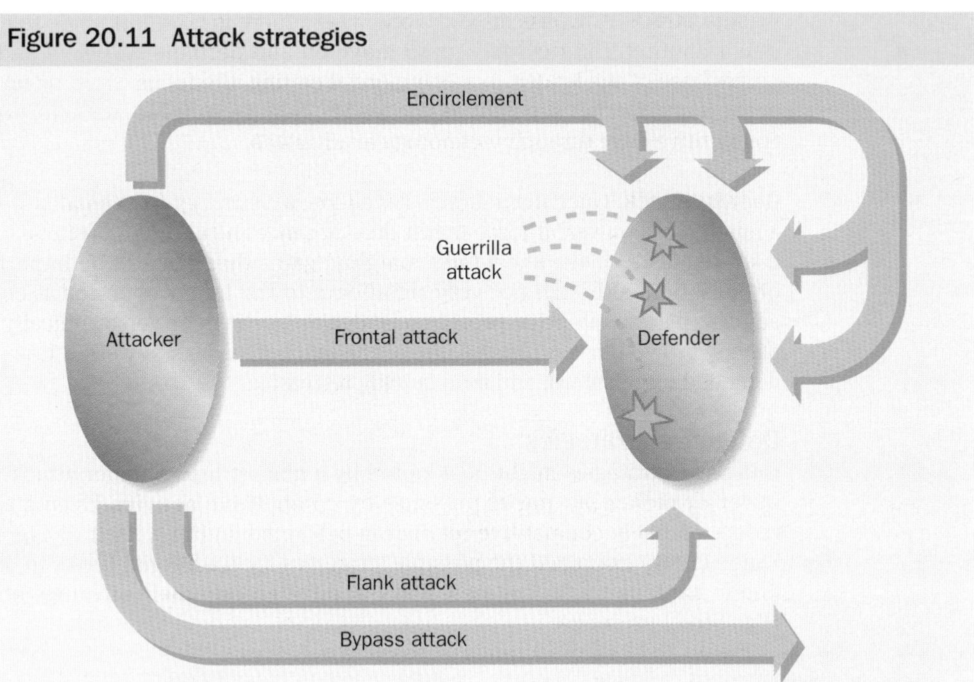

Source: Kotler and Singh (1981). Reproduced with permission of Thomson Media, Eleven Penn Plaza, New York, NY 10001

eg

The wet shaving market has seen many upheavals since Bic (http://www.bic.fr) took the market by storm in the 1960s with the disposable razor. The Bic attack was full frontal, offering convenience, low prices and ease of repurchase supported by heavy advertising and mass distribution. Gillette and Wilkinson Sword retaliated within three years with their own versions, but a third of the market had already been lost. Since then there have been many other shaver wars as one party seeks to gain a product or market advantage over the other. In the early 1990s, for example, innovation took place in the premium wet shaving sector with the launch of the Sensor and Protector close shave systems. In 1999, the battle continued as Wilkinson Sword launched a high-tech response, the FX Diamond, to the Gillette Mach 3 triple-blade razor.

This razor enabled it to capture 69 per cent of the razor market, well ahead of the number two, Wilkinson Sword with just 15 per cent. The battle has continued into the new millennium and has been joined by a potentially powerful third brand. Unilever, with its Lynx brand, hopes to exploit the established brand name through extending into the shaving market with a youth-orientated product that also has a triple blade. Despite Unilever's £5 mn television advertising spend, however, the power of Gillette in that market will still present a tough challenge for Lynx's flank attack (Oldfield, 2000). Furthermore, Gillette responded by launching its own upgraded Mach 3 Turbo version in 2002 using 'antifriction blade technology'. The launch was to be supported by a £140 mn worldwide advertising campaign. To avoid any replication by competitors, it is covered by 35 different patents (Mazur, 2002; Singh, 2001).

Encirclement attack. Encirclement means launching an attack on many fronts with rapidity and force so as to spread panic and overwhelm the opposition. It is difficult to defend a position with enough concentrated force and effect when faced with an all-out attack on all sides. Although short-term losses may be experienced by the challenger, the outcome might eventually be significant advances in market share. This could be achieved by the pure breadth of range, such as that offered by Seiko watches, aggressive pricing at consumer and retail levels, heavy pull promotion, and a relentless drive to attack segments either on a sequential or a parallel basis.

Bypass attack. A bypass attack is one where there is no effort made to engage the enemy in direct conflict, but the tactic is to move on and perhaps surround and slowly reduce the power base of the leader. In a commercial setting, the focus could be on unrelated products in the same market segment as the leader, new geographic markets, and always seeking a competitive edge through technological advances.

Guerilla attack. Guerrilla action is a well-known strategy for a small group operating against a much more powerful force that it dare not meet head-on. In business, the purpose of such a strategy is to make short-term marginal gains that can still be important for the smaller organisation, although not very significant to the larger operator. It could mean bursts of activity, perhaps in price promotions, dealer loadings or geographically concentrated campaigns, or even in recruiting some of the market leader's key staff. It is about hitting poorly defended targets hard, and then quickly retreating.

Defensive strategies

Defensive strategies might be adopted by a market leader under attack, or by a market follower or nicher put under pressure by competitive activity. Even a challenger needs to reflect on likely competitive retaliation before committing itself to aggressive acts. Van der Zande (2001) examined the possible strategies for traditional banks to counter the threat of online banking by finding new ways to differentiate their offerings other than through a High Street presence.

Figure 20.12 shows a range of possible defences.

Fixed position defence. One option is to sit tight and defend the current position. This can be risky, in that such defences might then be bypassed rather than attacked directly. In commercial terms, the organisation that seeks to hold position without adopting fresh ideas can run into trouble.

Mobile defence. Rather than defending existing products, the focus in mobile defence turns to broadening the market appeal and even diversifying away from that market, as the ciga-

Figure 20.12 Defence strategies

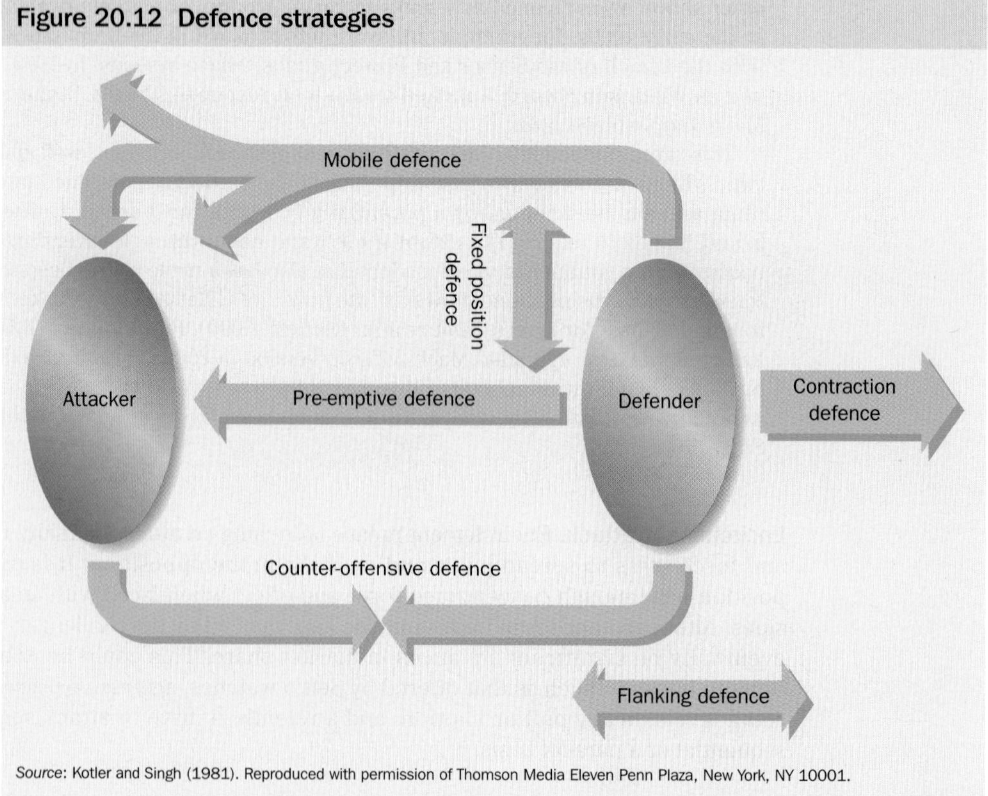

Source: Kotler and Singh (1981). Reproduced with permission of Thomson Media Eleven Penn Plaza, New York, NY 10001.

Travel agents have been accused of being too complacent about the threat of direct links between supplier and customer that are made possible by the internet. Although the power of the internet is recognised, travel agents tend to believe that it is an alternative distribution channel, not a force that could radically reshape the industry. This has allowed the online travel agency sector to grow at a rapid rate alongside the websites of airlines offering direct bookings. For the High Street travel agent, both are eating into the traditional travel booking business. GetThere, a computer reservations system company, found that 800 of its large corporate clients used online booking services for 13.5 per cent of all travel in 2001, nearly double the previous year. Barclaycard reported that 71 per cent of business travellers had booked via the internet in the past year and even more intended to do so in the future (Bray, 2002). It is becoming easier and more usual to book direct, so the trend is likely to continue.

In the US, where only 26 per cent still use a travel agent for personal travel, specialist online booking agencies accounted for 45 per cent of all online bookings in 2001 and direct booking through travel operators for another 25 per cent of sales. Although the travel agents still play an important role in airline bookings, recently in the US some of the airlines have become less concerned about upsetting the travel agents (Nairn, 2002) and have eliminated travel agency commissions to make online ticketing more attractive (Maselli, 2002). The airlines are still negotiating performance based commissions with high-volume travel agencies, but smaller agencies are being squeezed out of the market. Ignoring these trends could be dangerous for UK travel agents, who have argued that customers prefer direct contact with sales staff and value the expertise of travel agents in finding the best deals.

rette companies have done. This means, however, that an organisation must be prepared to redefine its priorities and the type of business it is in, and keep an open mind. It does not mean a retreat, but it does reduce vulnerability and opens up new segments, for example developing bicycles into an item for the health and leisure segments.

Flanking defence. In military situations, the rear or flank is often seen as a weak area. If it is attacked, this can turn the course of a battle.

Internet auction sites are increasingly taking a share of business by offering better service, flexibility and better commission deals than the traditional auction houses such as Sotheby's and Christie's. The main advantage of internet auctions is convenience, instantaneous participation, and even entertainment, although some of that must be tempered with occasional fraud, tax implications and problems with the sale of regulated goods. eBay, from the US, generated £63 mn in sales through its UK site in 2001. Globally, it generates $15 bn worth of business and is a unique company in that it has almost no cost of goods, no stock, minimal marketing costs, and no large capital expenditure beyond its website infrastructure. It provides a service that does not need premises and employs a minimal number of staff. The challenge now is to continue to move beyond stamps, books, old records and figurines to higher value items such as cars, computers, holiday homes and antiques. A Gulfstream corporate jet was sold via eBay for $4.9 mn and at the other end of the scale a book is sold every 4 seconds. Now, even the traditional auction houses are having to move towards greater use of websites if they are not to be completely outflanked (Abrahams and Barker, 2002; Barker, 2002).

A flanking defence therefore means paying attention to the market to ensure that any weak spots are identified and defended before a competitor becomes too powerful. The marketing history books are full of examples of poor flank defending. Smiths Crisps, for example, used to dominate the potato crisp market until Golden Wonder entered the fray. Smiths was considered to be an adult snack, with one flavour option only, and to be purchased in pubs. The Golden Wonder market entry was based on a children's snack, sold through shops and supermarkets. The rest is history. The flank was not defended by Smiths and it lost its market dominance position.

Contraction defence. In contraction defence, rather than risk the threat of being overwhelmed in one major defensive position, an organisation undertakes a selective withdrawal, to delay or even offset the attacking force. In commercial terms, that could mean withdrawing from marginal segments and areas where the presence is small and cannot be defended. This might mean that in areas where strengths do exist a better, more concentrated fight can take place. When under threat, the core business must be defended at all costs. It has been rumoured that BMI is considering withdrawing from or rationalising its US routes due to the decline in the transatlantic market since September 11th, 2001 (Odell, 2002). Normally, US routes can be very profitable, but reduced passenger volumes and some discounting generated losses at a time when BMI is also having to battle in its other segments, as seen on pp. 879 and 880 (*Financial Times*, 2002).

Pre-emptive defence. The phrase 'the best form of defence is to attack' is now a recognised business strategy. If an organisation feels that it might soon be under attack, rather than wait for that to happen it takes deliberate aggressive actions. This might mean a particular marketing mix emphasis, for example advertising, dealer loaders or new products. Alternatively, signals can be sent that any attack would be vigorously defended. Following on with the BMI example mentioned earlier at p. 879, BMI accused Go of announcing new, unspecific promises of phantom services to be introduced at East Midlands airport to thwart or deter BMI from launching its own low-cost airline. Go did not succeed, however, as the existence of bmibaby testifies (Harrison, 2002).

Counter-offensive defence. Once hostilities have begun, a number of counter-offensive measures can be taken in defence. Many of these actions are aggressive, but retaliatory. Three responses are possible. First, *head-to-head confrontation* means matching action with action. This, incidentally, is how price wars start. It does not just centre on price moves, however: it might also mean investing as much in advertising as the competition or launching a similar new product. It shows that no competitive advantage can be gained. The second possible response is to *outflank and attack*, which means finding the competitor's weak spots, in terms of product areas, market segments, marketing methods, for example, and ruthlessly attacking them so that it hurts deeply and quickly. The final response is to *hit where it hurts most*, which means attacking the cash cow or resource base of the attacker. The attacker will make efforts to defend the cash cow, and in this way the attentions of the attacker can be deflected.

eg

The games console market, considered in Case Study 14.1, has experienced a round of price cutting as Nintendo (GameCube) and Microsoft (Xbox) vie for second spot in the market behind Sony (PlayStation 2). For both companies, Europe is an important market as part of building a strong global position. Xbox first announced a 38 per cent cut in its European game console prices to enable a more aggressive stance to be taken against the PlayStation 2. Nintendo's launch plans were then also revised to lower the GameCube's launch price from the planned €250 to €199, almost matching the Xbox's new European price of €200. Sony was considering whether it could ignore the round of price cutting (Nakamoto, 2002).

Cooperative and independent

It would be incorrect to assume that all competitive behaviour is challenging and confrontational. Many situations are characterised by peaceful co-existence and at times by cooperative alliances between competitors. In independent situations, a firm may neither know nor care about competition. That does not mean to say that competition does not exist. Competitive threats could be overlooked. You might, for example, own the only bee farm in an area, but you will still be competing for the time, attention and interest of the day tripper with many other local attractions, albeit very different from your own. Alternatively, an organisation may see others as operating in ill-defined but parallel segments. One fencing contractor might specialise in farming/industrial jobs and another in consumer markets. They might advertise accordingly, and while not turning any work away, peacefully work alongside each other. In these cases, aggressive marketing behaviour is unlikely to be provoked unless a major new competitor disturbs the *status quo*.

In markets dominated by a handful of competitors, perhaps on a global scale, ignoring the competition can, however, be folly if a significant new threat or oportunity is overlooked. That could apply equally to the multinational seeking to expand coverage and to the small independent video rental store overlooking the trend towards DVD and online, direct-to-screen rentals.

Strategic alliances were briefly covered in Chapter 13 (pp. 558 *et seq.*) in the context of retailing. Strategic alliances occur when organisations seek to work together on projects, pooling expertise and resources. This could include R&D, joint ventures or licensing arrangements, sometimes on a worldwide scale. Many large construction projects demand that different firms work together to provide a turnkey package. The alliance can be general, on many fronts or specific to a certain project (Gulati, 1998).

eg

Philips forged a strategic alliance with Dell to bring about collaboration on a range of electronics projects, including computer monitors. The arrangement includes cross-supply of components to be incorporated into each other's products, sharing knowledge and building joint computing architecture, for example for Philips' medical systems division. The deal also allowed Philips products to appear on the Dell website in the US, a market it had had trouble developing. The deal was anticipated to be worth $5 bn over five years (Cramb, 2002). Meanwhile, Hino Motors, the Japanese lorry manufacturer and Scania, the Swedish equivalent, also decided to form a strategic business alliance. Scania would provide heavy trucks for Hino to sell in Japan under its own brand name and dealer network. It was not an equity deal, but based on contractual agreement. In return, Hino would provide light and medium trucks to Scania. This enables both companies to enter markets that otherwise would be very difficult in terms of establishing brand awareness and dealer networks (Burt and Ibison, 2002).

Not all alliances and joint ventures work out as expected. It had been planned that Coca-Cola's non-fizzy drinks brands and Procter & Gamble's snacks brands would be moved into a joint venture company. Within six months the deal was off, however, even before the competition authorities had had their say, probably because the deal had not been fully thought through from a commercial and synergy perspective. According to one academic quoted in Benady, D. (2002), many alliances and joint ventures do not have long life spans in any case, not because they fail, but because they succeed. By allowing rapid learning in a new market sector, enhanced business opportunities and a chance to understand the other party, the alliance may break up because both or one party feels it can now go it alone or it could lead to a merger, as shown in the example below.

eg

The joint venture proposed between Bayer AG and Aventis SA for the blood plasma business involves forming a new entity that combines Bayer's biological products business group with the Aventis subsidiary, Aventis Behring. Bayer would have the substantial majority interest with an option to acquire the remainder. It is, therefore, intended as a more enduring arrangement than a time-specific joint venture. The intention was to form a stronger health care business in the strategically important biological products area. The benefits were claimed to be better economies of scale in the collection of blood and a broader geographic reach. It would also allow the combined market share to put rival Baxters into second position. In the longer term, however, it is expected that Aventis will sell the remainder of its interest to concentrate on the ethical drug business (*Chemical Market Reporter*, 2002).

There are many forms of alliance that can be created for mutual benefit. A number of non-competing organisations in the consumer goods area are forming marketing alliances to reduce costs and improve market impact. Coca-Cola uses marketing alliances to dominate the non-carbonated juice beverage market. It is working with Walt Disney to market its Minute Maid juices under the Disney brand, using containers featuring Mickey Mouse and Winnie the Pooh etc. The alliance was expected to generate $200 mn over 4 years (Liu, 2001). Hilton, the hotel group, has also formed a marketing alliance with Saga, the holiday company (*see* p. 49) so that Saga customers could stay at Hilton hotels at the lowest available rate.

Such a deal helps the Hilton to attract visitors from a market segment with plenty of leisure time, a good level of disposable income, and with an inclination for better standards. It also enables Saga to extend the range of services offered to its customers at minimal extra cost (*Sunday Times*, 2001). BP went further and formed a marketing alliance with the Red Cross as part of its social responsibility programme. The arrangement allows customers to donate money to the Red Cross at petrol stations across Europe and is backed by above the line, direct and online marketing (Kleinman, 2001). Alliances targeted at complementary market sectors, such as the Hilton–Saga alliance, are often best positioned to maximise impact and exploit any category management potential. The toy company Fisher Price teamed up with P&G's Pampers brand, for instance, to share information, perform joint direct marketing, sampling and in-store promotions.

Joint ventures and alliances are also widely used in international marketing as a means of market entry and development. These will be considered on pp. 1031 *et seq.* when international marketing strategies are discussed.

Finally, *collusion* is where firms come to an 'understanding' about how to compete in the market. Legislation prevents this from extending to deliberate price fixing: neither retailers nor manufacturers can openly collude to set retail or supply prices between them, although they can, of course, watch each other's pricing policies carefully and choose to match them if they wish.

eg

The European Commission accused the great auction houses of Sotheby's and Christie's of operating an illegal price fixing cartel in the UK and Europe. If this is true, the costs could be high. Fines could be imposed of up to 10 per cent of turnover and legal challenges could be made by aggrieved customers claiming that they have been overcharged as a result of any price fixing. The specific allegations relate to the decision by the two auction houses to change from a flat-rate seller's commission to a sliding scale in 1995. Other aspects, such as advances paid to sellers, guarantees given for auction results and payment conditions have also come under scrutiny.

These two auction houses account for 90 per cent of the international auction market, allowing them considerable power to increase prices. The alternative 'competitive model' would mean severe competition especially in market downturns which would advantage buyers. Both companies claim that price fixing is a thing of the past and corrective action has been taken to stop collusion. The damage to their reputation has already been done, however. A similar case proven in the US led to Sotheby's and Christie's being forced to pay $512 mn in compensation to customers to settle claims, as well as Sotheby's facing a $45 mn fine (Ringshaw, 2002).

Although collusion is the unacceptable side of cooperation, the scale of investment and rate of change in technology, accompanied by increasingly global markets is likely to generate more alliances and ventures in future.

Chapter summary

- This chapter has been concerned with marketing strategies, the longer-term consideration of where the organisation wants to be and how it can get there using its products and its marketing mixes. The organisation has to decide how it wants to position itself relative to the competition, whether it wants to be perceived as a leader, a follower or a niche operator, and how it wants to deal with competition. Marketing strategy thus creates, maintains and reinforces corporate positioning and how it is perceived, by using the elements of the marketing mix to capitalise on strengths, overcome weaknesses, defend against threats and exploit opportunities within the business environment. Outcomes of this analysis are the marketing plan that specifies the overall direction of the organisation and marketing programmes that spell out the operational tasks to be undertaken in order to implement the plan.

- Strategic marketing planning often revolves around analysis of the organisation's product portfolio. The Boston Box provides a diagnostic tool that can act as a basic foundation for strategic decisions. The Boston Box does, however, have its critics because of its emphasis on the desirability of market growth and high market share. Other portfolio models, such as the GE matrix and the Shell directional policy matrix, have therefore been developed to try to overcome some of the Boston Box's weaknesses by redefining the axes in more detail, increasing the number of cells, and thus trying to be more specific about associated courses of action.
- Where growth opportunities are identified, there are a number of alternative strategies available, as defined, for example, by the Ansoff matrix. Not all strategies revolve around the concept of growth. Harvesting, associated with cash cows, means reaping the benefits of a product without actively seeking growth for it. Entrenchment, protecting a current position, might be appropriate for a dog deemed essential to the overall portfolio, while withdrawal might be considered for a completely useless dog.
- Central to the marketing plan is as deep an understanding of competitors as possible. Models such as Porter's five forces can help to analyse competitive structures systematically and provide a starting point for building strategies. In designing marketing strategies, it is also important to understand how competitors are likely to react and the implications of that reaction for the successful implementation of the strategies. In terms of the strategies themselves, there are broadly three generic options. The first is cost leadership, seeking to gain a cost advantage over the competition. An alternative is to seek differentiation, offering something different, better or more valued by the customer than that offered by the competition. The third generic strategy, a focus strategy, means concentrating on one specific segment of the market and serving it thoroughly. The actual choice of generic strategy depends on the organisation's capabilities and resources, the nature of the competition faced and the key factors for success in that market. In practice, it might be difficult to stick rigidly to one of these strategies alone and there might have to be some flexibility.
- An organisation also needs to consider competitive position and competitive posture. Competitive position defines an organisation as a market leader, a market challenger, a market follower or a market nicher. Competitive posture is about how to attack or defend a position. This covers aggressive strategies for attacking competitors in different ways, and defensive strategies to be used when the competition attacks. Competition need not always involve confrontation, however. It is possible to work cooperatively with competitors or other organisations. Strategic alliances or joint ventures have become increasingly appreciated as ways of exploiting synergies between organisations and opening up new opportunities that neither party would have the resources to pursue alone.

key words and phrases

Ansoff matrix
Boston Box
Competitive position
Competitive posture
Competitive strategy
Diversification
GE matrix
Generic strategies
Market development
Market penetration
Marketing plan
Marketing programmes
Marketing strategy
Porter's five forces
Product development
Product portfolio
Shell directional policy matrix
Strategic business units

questions for review

20.1 Define the main factors influencing organisations' *marketing strategy*.

20.2 What is a *product portfolio* and what are the problems of implementing portfolio models in practice?

20.3 Which three cells of the Ansoff matrix offer *growth opportunities*?

20.4 What issues might an organisation take into account when undertaking *competitive analysis*?

20.5 Define the four different types of *competitive position*.

questions for discussion

20.1 To what extent do the cells of the Boston Box reflect the stages of the product lifecycle (PLC)? What does the Boston Box offer as an analytical tool that the PLC does not?

20.2 For each cell of the Ansoff matrix, find and discuss an example of an organisation that seems to have implemented that particular growth strategy.

20.3 Choose an organisation and apply Porter's five forces to its industry or market. What are the implications of your findings for your chosen organisation's strategic development?

20.4 To what extent do you think that market leadership is the best competitive position to aspire to?

20.5 Discuss the relative merits and appropriate use of each of the competitive postures described in this chapter.

case study 20.1

Prudential (A): An evolving competitive strategy

Prudential, 'The Pru', is one of the UK's leading insurance and pension providers. It offers a wide range of financial products including annuities, corporate and individual pensions, with-profits bonds, and investment products to over 6 million customers. Under the corporate umbrella are brands such as The Pru itself, Egg and M&G. This case study traces The Pru's competitive strategy over the past ten to fifteen years, while Case Study 21.1 follows on by examining influences on marketing planning. Neither case considers the allied brands such as Egg and M&G or the overseas operations.

The Pru's products were all marketed and sold through its own financial consultants; through independent financial advisors (IFAs); by direct marketing (telephone, internet and mail); via the workplace to corporate pension customers; and via affinity and banks' IFAs. Central to The Pru's purpose is the need to maximise the return for its customers as well as its shareholders through well-designed and attractive financial products that are trusted and provide the required level of security. Relationships with customers tend to be long term, reflecting the length of time over which a policy would run, and a particular challenge is to encourage customers for one financial service to trade up or across to other products. In marketing terms, The Pru has to overcome many customers' low level of understanding and knowledge of financial products. It also has to ensure that the most suitable products are sold to customers, within an increasingly stringent regulatory framework and avoiding allegations of either misselling (*see* p. 729) or dissatisfaction.

The Pru's success was built on the direct sales force (DSF) concept which provided widespread geographic coverage and direct contact with millions of people putting aside a small amount in savings each week. In the late 1980s, the DSF includes around 9,000 agents doing a mixture of collecting cash door-to-door and small amount of face-to-face selling. They were organised into about 12 divisions served by 400 district offices. In addition there were also three or four specialist sales people in each district office, for example specialising in pensions or life insurance. The sales force compensation structure was complex. They would get a small basic salary (c. 20 per cent of remuneration) plus advance commission which was then adjusted in hindsight according to actual commission. Commission did not just depend on last week's sales, however, it depended on the ongoing status of old policies too, as it was important to keep policies from lapsing.

As far as the public was concerned, the image of The Pru at this time revolved around two themes:

- the man from The Pru – the local personal contact; and
- the 'Mighty Pru' – the big, secure, reliable institution.

These themes formed the basis of its competitive advantage. In the late 1980s, however, The Pru realised that this system of agents and sales specialists was becoming outdated and very expensive to maintain. Added to that, the 1986 Financial Services Act and various consumer protection acts meant that companies had to be more rigorous in training staff to recognised qualification standards, and monitoring and controlling their performance.

So in the late 1980s/early 1990s, despite a traditional internal culture that was resistant to change, a review was initiated to explore how The Pru should revise and develop its strategy, given a marketing environment that was markedly different from that of the 1950s, when the system was in its heyday. Bank accounts and credit cards had become widespread, for example; consumers were more confident in managing their financial affairs; disposable incomes were a lot higher. The outcome of the strategic review was a decision to streamline the DSF operation and redefine the roles within it. Thus two distinct types of sales representative were created:

- financial consultants (the biggest proportion) who advise customers and sell financial services products (similar to order makers – *see* pp. 705–6);
- customer service representatives who collect money, administer maturity claims etc. (similar to order takers – *see* pp. 703–4).

This broke the traditional mould and allowed The Pru to be more flexible and responsive to regulatory and market changes. The 9,000 salesforce began to reduce, largely by attrition. As the door-to-door business began to reduce over time, the number of customer service representatives could also be reduced, leading to further staffing and cost reductions. Additionally, the number of regions was reduced to 5 from 12 and the number of district offices halved to 200 or so, also reducing costs. Although still part of the differentiation of the company, the DSF strategy was undergoing major change with an inevitable impact on The Pru's strategic marketing capability.

By 1994, The Pru had stopped selling new policies involving door-to-door cash collection, the first large insurer to do so, because it was just not cost effective for the customer. The cost of collecting cash door-to-door is high. Something like one-thirteenth of the premiums on such a policy go towards covering the cost of collection. This means that less of the customer's cash is actually available for investment and therefore the returns on the policy are lower. Besides that, more customers were now prepared to use direct debits and other remote forms of payment.

By 1995, the door-to-door business had run down to the point where the customer service representative model was not working well. Contracts were changed and representatives given the options of becoming cash collectors, retraining to become financial consultants, or accepting redundancy. About 1,000 became cash collectors and somewhat fewer retrained as financial consultants (many of those who had really wanted to do that had already done it). Eventually, the remaining 1,400 'Pru Traditionalist' cash collectors had their employment contracts taken over by another company when the cash collection business was outsourced. The door-to-door cash collection era for The Pru was over, but had the competitive advantage gone with it?

Turning its back on the door-to-door business was a major risk. Around 4 per cent of the UK population are classified as 'hardened cash payers' who either don't like or don't have bank accounts, so The Pru had effectively decided that this business could be put at risk and the competitive advantage surrendered in an effort to concentrate its resources on the wider market, exploiting its market dominance and brand reputation. Clearly new segments had to be opened up or expanded through the use of direct marketing and the financial consultants.

The next stage of reorganising the business began in 1997 with the *Concerto* strategic review. One of the things *Concerto* reviewed was the economics of the DSF which was still a sales-driven organisation. While the DSF had given The Pru an edge over competitors, this operation consisted of some 5,000 people and was not economic as the cost of distribution was higher in some cases than the revenues being generated. Concern over margins was growing. A sales representative is expensive, earning on average £25,000–£30,000, then national insurance and pension contributions etc. add a further 25 per cent on top of that, and then there's the car and the laptop. By this time, The Pru had changed the pay shcemes so that a much larger proportion of pay was fixed and there was now commission on specific product sales. Margins had to be high to cover such expenses, yet competition was actually forcing margins down. The focus started to shift to encourage the sales team to improve productivity which could be driven up either by volume (sell more products) or value (sell more valuable products with higher premiums). In the latter case, a move towards targeting more upmarket customers would be necessary, but this would require a better integrated promotional campaign.

In 1999/2000, product margins continued to decline, especially now that online and direct marketing were becoming increasingly popular with customers, particularly for low margin ISAs. The popularity of stakeholder pensions was also growing, but again offered limited margins. The IFAs operating in niche markets could handle it, but serving a mass market via a DSF was no longer feasible as the productivity levels could not respond to compensate for the tighter margins. With stakeholder pensions, for instance, the legislation allows only a 1 per cent administration charge to be levied, which tends to assume that the products are bought rather than sold/advised upon.

Competitors were also making a serious impact on The Pru's thinking. Some competitors were moving to direct selling, but only in certain commoditised product areas such as Direct Line's development of the general insurance market. The more complex the product, however, the smaller the proportion of people who are willing to deal remotely with the seller. For instance in buying a pension, people want face-to-face contact and advice. The Pru did investigate whether people would be prepared to pay for advice. Initial market research showed that they would, but further probing on just how much they would be prepared to pay suggested that consumers thought that up to £50 was about right. The actual cost of advising on a product such as a stakeholder pension however, is more like £200. There is a segment of the IFA market that is fee-based, so there are consumers out there willing to pay a realistic market rate, but these are not The Pru's traditional customers.

Against this background, in early 2001 The Pru decided that the best strategy was to break finally with the DSF tradition and thus The Pru was faced with the need to generate new business from sources other than the DSF. The scene was now set for switching strategic effort into D2C (direct to consumer) relationship marketing and this is now a major role for the new Direct to Consumer division. With a DSF, you do have some flexibility. If a product is complex, for example, the representative can explain it and tailor it to customer requirements. Without a DSF, that task has to be undertaken by direct marketing, whether through a mailing, a website or a call centre. Research has indicated that around 60 per cent of consumers prefer face-to-face interaction for financial products such as life assurance and pensions, but this drops to around 40 per cent for credit cards and home insurance. With little face-to-face selling, products have to be less complex and easier to understand yet still contain a powerful enough proposition to move the potential customer to action. Whatever is communicated through direct marketing has to be capable of being understood and giving the recipient sufficient confidence to act. This will become easier as more people become more used to D2C and on-line approaches. Although the D2C channel within the financial services industry has grown in recent years, it still makes up less than 5 per cent of the total Association of British Insurers' market: IFAs still dominate with around 60 per cent share. Overall, financial products sales are growing as disposable income increases and the direct market is expected to continue growing in the medium to long term.

Overall, market growth is very product dependent, driven by new financial products becoming available. There have also been economic and demographic changes as well as distribution changes driven by the regulators and consumer groups. Changes to products are also driven by changes in taxation and legislation, for instance removing tax relief on life insurance premiums or making PEPs tax-free or gaining tax relief on pension payments. One of the problems for The Pru is differentiating itself on products which are easily copied by competitors. The sales force contact was originally the main differentiation point, but that has now gone. Differentiation can also be achieved through charges and returns, but now other important factors have become the overall corporate brand reputation and financial strength. The Pru's promotional focus on trust, reliability and security has not changed for over twenty years. A relaunch of The Pru brand is planned for late 2002 and the two themes of the brand image, contact/trust and strong/big/secure, will be retained, but given a more modern interpretation of those core values.

Source. With grateful thanks to Neil Bradley, Business Development Director – Direct Distribution, Prudential.

Questions

1 What were the key factors leading to the demise of the DSF?

2 In terms of the Ansoff matrix, how would you classify the decision to adopt a D2C strategy and why?

3 From The Pru's point of view, how might the business strengths required for successful D2C marketing differ from those required for a DSF-focused approach?

4 To what extent do you think portfolio analysis could have played a role in the decision to phase out and eventually drop the DSF?

case study 20.2

Stopping the bottom falling out of the jeans market

The lifecycle of the denim jeans market shows a series of peaks and troughs as jeans go in and out of fashion. In 1999 the market was definitely in a trough, with sales volumes falling at about 11 per cent per year, for a number of reasons. As denim moves through the fashion cycle and becomes 'uncool' again, other products take over. This time it was combat pants. Combat, cargo and carpenter pants became popular because opinion formers such as the band All Saints and clubbers wore them, and this style filtered through to the youth market generally which was bored with denims and the obvious marketing efforts that went with them. Combats were practical and, initially at least, unbranded and unmarketed. Some companies spotted the trend early and responded accordingly. Both The Gap and Wrangler, for instance, introduced combat ranges relatively early on, before companies like Levi's had probably even noticed that there was a trend to spot! The problem was summed up by Damian Mould, chief executive of integrated youth marketing agency Slice thus:

> *The consumer market was once one where the tradition that Levi's relies on mattered. But it has become more aspirational and youth-focused. This meant that other denim brands, unencumbered by history, could quickly and easily define themselves within the new cultural currency and move in on the lucrative youth market* (as quoted by Grant, 2002).

Certain brands in the jeans market were not just losing out to the combat cult, however. Middle-of-the-road jeans, such as Levi's 501s, also found themselves stranded between the designer brands at the top end of the market and retailer own-brands, such as The Gap, at the mass market end, both taking sales away from them. Demographic factors have also made life a lot tougher. The core market, 18- to 25-year-olds, is declining in numbers in Europe as well as turning away from jeans as 'something dad wears'. In the UK, jeans sales overall fell by 14.3 per cent in 1998. In the UK and Europe Levi's suffered particularly badly, being so dependent on one brand, the 501s. Through the late 1980s and early 1990s, the 501s brand had shown rapid and satisfying growth and, unlike its competitors, Levi's had seen no reason to innovate or to spread its risk. It was so sure of its customers that it forgot to check how their needs and wants were changing as the market matured and to see how the competition was better meeting those needs and wants. Effectively, Levi's was a one-product company offering no new or different 'looks' to its customers. In the UK market, Levi's further alienated some customers by refusing to supply 'non-approved' retailers such as supermarket chain Tesco with jeans. When Tesco started selling Levi's sourced on the grey market (*see* Case Study 11.1) at reduced prices, this focused the consumer's attention on price and value for money.

In such a difficult environment, companies have to be alert to changes in the market and have strategies in place for dealing with them and even for survival. Part of Levi's problem was that it was not responsive enough. It was rather internally focused on 'doing very well what has always been done' (Heller, 1999). The US company, for instance, spent two years and $850 mn reducing the time it took to get new products to the market from 15 months to 3 months and retail stock replenishment time down from three weeks to a target level of three days. The problem was that not only had nobody thought through the cost implications of offering that kind of service, but more fundamentally, while this systems development was going on, the company failed to pay due attention to the marketplace and sales just evaporated.

Once Levi's had identified its problems, it began to act, first with a restructuring. The post of UK marketing director was abolished and replaced with a regional marketing and development director for Northern Europe (including the UK, Benelux countries, Norway and Sweden). In the UK, market research showed that lack of innovation was the key issue among the core 18- to 25-year-old market and furthermore that new products would bring back young customers.

Thus Levi Strauss began to take a more segmented approach. It introduced high-fashion hand-crafted jeans at the top end of the market to compete with the designer labels, retailing for about €300. In the middle of the market, innovations such as its 'Red Tab', 'Twisted' and 'Engineered' product ranges were designed to rekindle interest among fashionable youth. Early signs were promising. Grant (2002) reported that the Engineered range, as worn by opinion-leader Britney Spears, and the sponsorship of live music events had helped the brand to regain some street cred. At the bottom end of the market, it was planning to launch a low-priced product range retailing for about €45 (c. £27) in Europe, i.e. about 60 per cent of the price of the mainstream Levi's products, competing on price with competitors such as Lee and Wrangler. It might just bring back those customers who were buying the cut-price, grey market jeans from supermarkets. James Hobbs, account director at Taylor Nelson Sofres Fashion Trak thinks that:

> *It's a smart move. Currently, sales of jeans at £45-plus account for only 8.5 per cent of the market, whereas £30-plus accounts for 24 per cent. So it triples their potential sales* (as quoted by Benady, A., 2002).

Overall, Levi Strauss hopes that by 2003 the combined effects of these moves will at least stabilise sales. It is a tall order: by June 2002, things were still looking gloomy. Over the previous 12 months, factory closures and job losses had continued in the interests of streamlining operations and cutting costs; the company had announced losses of some $80 mn; and worldwide sales had fallen by a further 12 per cent. Whether it is doing enough still remains to be seen.

Sources: Barrett (1998); Benady, A. (2002); Buckley (2002); Grant (2002); Heller (1999); Jardine (1999); Lee (1999); Munk (1999).

Questions

1. Into which cells of the Shell directional policy matrix would you place (a) Levi's 501s, (b) Levi's high-fashion hand-crafted jeans, and (c) The Gap's range of own-brand jeans? Justify your answer, stating clearly any assumptions that you are making.
2. What kind of aggressive or defensive strategy do you think the introduction of the low-priced €45 product range is? Why? What are the risks of this particular strategy?
3. What are the advantages and potential problems of replacing the UK marketing director with a regional marketing brand development director for Northern Europe?
4. What can Levi's learn from its experiences and what impact might those lessons have on its future marketing strategies?

References for chapter 20

Abell, D. and Hammond, J. (1979), *Strategic Market Planning*, Prentice Hall.

Abrahams, P. and Barker, T. (2002), 'Ebay: The Flea Market that Spanned the Globe', *Financial Times*, 11 January, p. 24.

Addelman, M. (2002), 'Fresh Fruit or a Rotten Idea from Holsten?', *Marketing Week*, 14 March, p. 22.

Ansoff, H. (1957), 'Strategies for Diversification', *Harvard Business Review*, 25(5), pp. 113–25.

Arnold, M. (2002), 'Is Taste the Weapon to See Off Ribena's Rivals?', *Marketing*, 21 March, p. 13.

Barker, T. (2002), 'Ebay Figures Dwarf QXL', *Financial Times*, 19 April, p. 26.

Barksdale, H. and Harris, C. (1982), 'Portfolio Analysis and the PLC', *Long Range Planning*, 15(6), pp. 74–83.

Barrett, L. (1998), 'Hard-hit Levi's Cuts Top UK Role', *Marketing*, 22 October, p. 1.

Bashford, S. (2002), 'Why Are Modern Mums Deserting Mothercare?', *Marketing*, 24 January, p. 11.

Bateman, M. (2001), 'A Chip Off the New Block', *The Independent*, 2 September, pp. 33–4.

Benady, A. (2002), 'Jeans Group Unveils its Third Leg', *Financial Times*, 5 February, p. 18.

Benady, D. (2002), 'Joint Ventures that Lead to Mixed Results', *Marketing Week*, 11 April, p. 21.

Benady, D. (2001), 'Burst Bubbles', *Marketing Week*, 22 November, pp. 24–7.

Betts, P. and Hall, W. (2002), 'Swiss Cash Cow in Search of Richer Pastures', *Financial Times*, 8 April, p. 12.

Bray, R. (2002), 'Internet Booking on the Increase', *Financial Times*, 12 February, p. 17.

Buckley, N. (2002), 'Levi Reports Loss of $80.9m', *Financial Times*, 21 June, p. 17.

Burt, T. and Ibison, D. (2002), 'Hino Motors Set for Alliance with Sweden's Scania', *Financial Times*, 19 March, p. 17.

Calori, R. and Harvatopoulos, Y. (1988), 'Diversification: Les règales de conduite', *Harvard – L'Expansion*, 48 (Spring), pp. 48–59.

Campbell, L. (1999), 'Why Unilever B Brands Must be Cast Aside', *Marketing*, 10 June, p. 13.

Carmichael, M. (2002), 'Move Over Britannia', *The Grocer*, 13 April, pp. 38–9.

Carter, A. (2002), 'Kodak's Promising Developments', *Money*; February, p. 39.

Ceramic Industry (2000), 'Supplier Profile: From Imetal to Imerys', *Ceramic Industry*, April, p. 21.

Chaffey, D. (2002), *E-business and E-commerce Management. Strategy, Implementation and Practice*, Financial Times Prentice-Hall.

Charles, G. (2002a), 'Wrigley Prospers by Sticking With Gum', *Marketing Week*, 7 February, p. 18.

Charles, G. (2002b), 'Unilever Bertolli Olive Oil Launch in Trouble', *Marketing Week*, 11 April, p. 5.

Charles, G. (2002c), 'Dwarves, Standing on the Toes of Giants', *Marketing Week*, 18 April, p. 20.

Chemical Market Reporter (2002), 'Bayer and Aventis Pool Blood Businesses', *Chemical Market Reporter*, 25 February, p. 2.26.

Cookson, C. (2001), 'Bioinformatics and Big Biology', *Financial Times*, 27 November, p. 2.

Cramb, G. (2002), 'Philips and Dell Agree on Global Alliance', *Financial Times*, 28 March, p. 32.

Dolan, R. (1981), 'Models of Competition: A Review of Theory and Empirical Evidence', in B. Enis and K. Roering (eds), *Review of Marketing*, American Marketing Association.

Dyer, G. (2001), 'The Power Shifts to Industry's Wunderkinds', *Financial Times*, 27 November, p. 5.

The Economist (2002), 'Towards the Wild Blue Yonder', *The Economist*, 27 April, pp. 75–7.

Edgecliffe-Johnson, A. (2001a), 'Boom Time for "Dumpster Divers"', *Financial Times*, 4 September, p. 29.

Edgecliffe-Johnson, A. (2001b), 'Tricks of the Corporate Spying Trade', *Financial Times*, 1 September, p. 9.

Edgecliffe-Johnson, A. and Jones, A. (2001), 'P&G to Pay $10m for Spying on Unilever', *Financial Times*, 7 September, p. 1.

Eggleston, S. (2002), 'Cereals', *The Grocer*, 9 February, pp. 39–42.

Evans, L. (2001), 'Dot-com Survivor', *Sporting Goods Business*, 23 February, p. 12.

Financial Times (2002), 'BMI Losses Threaten US Flights', *Financial Times*, 18 February, p. 1.

Financial Times (2001), 'Holderbank Lays New Foundations', *Financial Times*, 30 March, p. 20.

Grant, J. (2002), 'Can Levi's Engineer a Reversal of Fortunes?', *Marketing*, 18 April, p. 13.

The Grocer (2002a), 'Dr Oetker is Confident of Seizing Number One Spot in Frozen Pizza', *The Grocer*, 23 March, p. 8.

The Grocer (2002b), 'An Ice Cuppa Tea is Tickling the Tastebuds of the Iced Beverage Sector', *The Grocer*, 4 May, p. 64.

Gulati, R. (1998), 'Alliances and Networks', *Strategic Management Journal*, 19 (4), pp. 293–317.

Hall, W. (2002), 'Profits at Holcim Drop by 8%', *Financial Times*, 5 April, p. 25.

Hammermesch, R. *et al.* (1978), 'Strategies for Low Market Share Business', *Harvard Business Review*, 56 (May–June), pp. 95–102.

Hardcastle, S. (2002a), 'Household Cleaning and Paper Goods', *The Grocer*, 16 February, pp. 47–50.

Hardcastle, S. (2002b), 'Suncare: It's A Hot Topic', *The Grocer*, 27 April, p. 46.

Hardcastle, S. (2002c), 'Soft Drinks', *The Grocer*, 4 May, pp. 47–50.

Hardcastle, S. (2001), 'Yogurt and Pot Desserts', *The Grocer*, 21 April, pp. 33–6.

Harrison, M. (2002), 'BMI Joins Price War by Cutting Domestic Fares', *The Independent*, 17 April, p. 23.

Heller, R. (1999), 'When Goliaths Start Wobbling', *Management Today*, June, p. 34.

Hunt, J. (2000), 'Can the Yanks Still Pull it Off?', *The Guardian*, 28 September, p. 14.

Jardine, A. (1999), 'Life for Denim in Combat Era', *Marketing*, 4 March, p. 19.

Johnson, B. (2002), 'Ribena Fighting for Hearts and Mums', *Marketing Week*, 21 March, pp. 19–20.

Jones, D. (2001), 'Family-run Snowdon Water Scheme Will Create 30 Jobs', *Daily Post*, 21 November, p. 2.

Kleinman, M. (2002), 'Mothercare Aims for Warmer Look in Stores Revamp', *Marketing*, 4 April, p. 1.

Kleinman, M. (2001), 'BP Set to Partner Red Cross Cause in European Deal', *Marketing*, 20 September, p. 1.

Kotler, P. and Singh, R. (1981), 'Marketing Warfare in the 1980s', *Journal of Business Strategy*, 2 (Winter), pp. 30–41.

Lee, J. (1999), 'Can Levi's ever Be Cool Again?', *Marketing*, 15 April, pp. 28–9.

Liu, B. (2001), 'Coca-Cola and Disney Plan Drinks Venture', *Financial Times*, 1 March, p. 30.

Lofthouse, R. (2001), 'Lexing Europe', *EuroBusiness*, August, pp. 44–6.

Lorenz, A. (1995), 'English China Clays' New Chemistry', *Management Today*, October, pp. 48–52.

Marketing (2002), 'Unilever Aims to Revamp Lipton Ice Tea for UK Market', *Marketing*, 14 March, p. 3.

Marketing Week/CIM (2001), 'Harry Potter', *Marketing Week/CIM Effectiveness Awards 2001*, pp. 6–7.

Marsh, P. (2001), 'Step by Step into New Market Niches', *Financial Times*, 20 January, p. 17.

Maselli, J. (2002), 'E-ticketing Threatens Travel Agents', *Informationweek*, 25 March, p. 28.

Mazur, L. (2002), 'Innovation and Branding Make a Powerful Mix', *Marketing*, 28 March, p. 16.

Merchant, K. (2002), 'New Approaches Needed as Pressures Begin to Bite', *Financial Times India Survey*, 5 March.

Mowbray, S. (2002a), 'Dr Oetker Determined to be a Major UK Player', *The Grocer*, 9 March, p. 6.

Mowbray, S. (2002b), 'Hot When You Want Production Pauses', *The Grocer*, 20 April, p. 5.

Munk, N. (1999), 'How Levi's Trashed a Great American Brand', *Fortune*, 12 April, pp. 82–90.

Murden, T. (2001), 'Hi-fi Boss Who Strikes a Very Different Note', *Sunday Times*, 17 June, p. 7.

Nairn, G. (2002), 'A Challenge From Online Agencies', *Financial Times*, 13 March, p. 11.

Nakamoto, N. (2002), 'Nintendo Cuts GameCube Price in Europe', *Financial Times*, 23 April, p. 30.

Neff, J. (2001), 'P&G: Spy Skids', *Advertising Age*, 3 September, p. 3.23.

Odell, M. (2002), 'BMI Takes the Fight Back into the Skies', *Financial Times*, 2 April, p. 21.

Oldfield, C. (2000), 'Unilever Goes For a Cut of Razor Market', *Sunday Times*, 10 September, p. 2.

Performance Group (1999), *Breakthrough Performance through People*, The Performance Group, Oslo, Norway.

Pickard, J. (2002), 'Imerys Cuts 300 Mining Jobs', *Financial Times*, 8 March, p. 2.

Porter, M. (1979), 'How Competitive Forces Shape Strategy', *Harvard Business Review*, 57(2), pp. 137–45.

Porter, M. (1980), *Competitive Strategy*, Free Press.

Ringshaw, G. (2002), 'Hammered', *The Sunday Telegraph*, 21 April, p. 5.

Saunders, J. (1987), 'Marketing and Competitive Success', in M. Baker (ed.), *The Marketing Book*, Macmillan.

Serwer, A. (2002), 'Kodak: In the Noose', *Fortune*, 4 February, pp. 147–8.

Serwer, A. (2001), 'P&G's Covert Operation', *Fortune*, 17 September, pp. 42–4.

Shah, S. (2002), 'HMV Takes Advantage of Retail Boom to Unveil £1bn Flotation', *The Independent*, 12 April, p. 21.

Singh, S. (2002), 'Unilever Sells Flagging Stergene', *Marketing Week*, 14 March, p. 8.

Singh, S. (2001), 'Gillette in $200m Mach3 Successor Launch', *Marketing Week*, 1 November, p. 5.

Style, S. (1999), 'Step Right in here for the Chocoholic's Dream Shop', *Greater Zurich supplement to Financial Times*, 29 June, p. IV.

Sumner-Smith, D. (2002), 'Video Minnow Must Take on the Industry Giants to Grow', *Sunday Times*, 17 February, p. 12.

Sunday Times (2001), 'Hilton Sign Marketing Alliance with Saga', *Sunday Times*, 16 December, p. 2.

Swann, C. (2002), 'Incubators Help Britain Keep Ahead', *Financial Times*, 1 May, p. 2.

Taylor, P. (2001), 'Two Cultures are Merging', *Financial Times*, 27 November, p. 5.

Tungate, M. (1999), 'Nestlé Makes Moves to Befriend the British', *Marketing*, 20 May, p. 15.

Urry, M. (2001), 'Brand That Cornered the Market in Yoghurts', *Financial Times*, 13 October, p. 8.

Van Der Zande, D. (2001), 'Strategic Renewal From an Industry Perspective', *Long Range Planning*, 34 (2), pp. 259–261.

Wilson, R., Gilligan, C. and Pearson, D. (1992), *Strategic Marketing Management*, Butterworth-Heinemann.

Wise, P. (2001a), 'Cementing its Overseas Standing', *Financial Times*, 29 June, p. 2.

Wise, P. (2001b), 'Cement Group is a Vital Ingredient in the Global Mix', *Financial Times*, 21 August, p. 22.

chapter 21

marketing planning, management and control

LEARNING OBJECTIVES

This chapter will help you to:

1 understand the different types of plan found within organisations and the importance of formal planning processes;

2 define the stages in the marketing planning process and their contribution to sound, integrated plans;

3 appreciate the various methods of estimating or forecasting both market and sales potential;

4 outline alternative ways of structuring a marketing department and their advantages and disadvantages;

5 understand the need for evaluation and control of marketing plans and their implementation, and the ways in which this can be achieved;

6 understand the special characteristics of a small business and how marketing helps small businesses from their start-up to maturity.

Introduction

Much of this text so far has been concerned with the development of competitive advantage through the careful design and implementation of an appropriate and integrated marketing mix. After selecting the most appropriate target markets, the organisation can create an offering that is of value to the chosen market segment(s) through a tailored package of pre-sale, consumption and post-sale benefits. This is a dynamic process because the marketing environment changes, competitive actions change and, not least, customer needs and preferences are also liable to change. This process of matching between the organisation and all aspects of the environment cannot be left to chance since it requires careful planning and management. Marketing, at both strategic and operational levels, plays an important part in that process.

The previous chapter looked at marketing planning's contribution to the process of matching organisational capability strategically to the environment. The products offered, the markets targeted and the basis of competitive advantage all have a significant impact on company success and the operational plans of the various functions within the organisation. Marketing planning, alongside other areas such as financial and production planning, are part of the functional planning that takes place at divisional, business unit or individual company level. Its aim is to ensure that marketing activities are appropriate to the achievement of corporate objectives, can be implemented within resource limits and are capable of creating and sustaining a competitive position.

The first part of this chapter examines some of the issues associated with designing a planning system for marketing and how it fits into the organisational planning process. Then, the various stages of the marketing planning process are discussed in detail. Although the implementation of the planning process may vary from situation to situation, the outline given here at least demonstrates the interrelated nature of many planning decisions. Attention then turns to the important role of forecasting, which is sometimes neglected, but is nevertheless a fundamental part of the planning process. Poor forecasting increases the likelihood of formulating inappropriate plans, whether at a strategic or operational level.

The chapter then moves on to examine other managerial issues associated with managing marketing. Making sure that the organisational structure of the marketing function is appropriate, for example, is essential to the achievement of the tasks specified in the plans. Within any kind of structure, the degree of specialisation, motivation, responsiveness and expertise of staff will be a major factor in determining how well and how successfully those tasks are performed and completed. Issues of marketing control and analysis are considered because without adequate and timely control systems, even

eg

Marketing planning is important to car rental companies if they are to remain competitive in a market dominated by global organisations such as Hertz, Budget and Avis. A company like Holiday Autos (http://www.holidayautos.co.uk) has created and defended a niche, as the name suggests, targeting holidaymakers. It does not actually rent the cars out, leaving that to the experts, but it acts as an intermediary, agreeing bulk prices with the rental companies and then aggressively marketing and passing on some of the discounts. It has, therefore, access to 750,000 cars, ranging from budget cars to luxury and off-road vehicles, in 4,000 locations.

The marketing plan and strategy is carefully developed. It seeks to play to its strengths, i.e. no insurance excess charged; the wide choice of vehicles offered; the number of locations; straightforward booking through its call centre and online; discounted prices; and even a travel information section on the web covering route planners, health advice and other useful information (Wall, 2001). Because of its intermediary role, innovation has revolved around the service package featuring no-nonsense benefits such as no insurance excess, fully inclusive prices and late deal offers. Before the launch of Holiday Autos, it was always wise to check for the hidden and not-so-hidden extras, and with some car rental companies that is still the case.

It is a fast moving business and an MIS is employed to give daily feedback on prices and sales so that rapid adjustments can be made in any of the 40 countries in which it operates. Close monitoring takes place during any promotional campaigns or where special discounts are being offered direct or through tour companies. It also watches what the demand generators, such as low-cost airlines and holiday companies are doing. Holiday Autos realised, for instance, that as the low-cost airlines started to increase promotion and gain sales after September 11th 2001, it would be an opportunity for Holiday Autos itself to increase its promotional spend similarly when others were cutting back (Hoare, 2002).

To achieve a nimble response in the market, a management structure that enables quick and effective decisions is needed. To remain just ahead of the market curve requires managers to be empowered but well coordinated within the framework of an agreed strategy and plan. The company may have longer-term aims and objectives, but the priority is making the most of the opportunities presenting themselves in the present.

the best-laid plans may be blown off course without managers realising the seriousness of the situation until it is too late to do anything about it. Finally, the chapter looks at the particular problems of managing marketing and planning for smaller businesses.

Strategic marketing plans and planning

Planning can be defined as a systematic process of forecasting the future business environment, and then deciding on the most appropriate goals, objectives and positions for best exploiting that environment. Organisational and functional strategies and plans provide the means by which the organisation can set out to achieve all that. All organisations need to plan, otherwise both strategic and operational activities would at best be uncoordinated, badly focused and poorly executed. At worst, the organisation would muddle through from crisis to crisis with little sense of purpose, until eventually competition would gain such an advantage and demand reach such a low level that continuation would just not be viable.

Planning is therefore an activity, a process in business that provides a systematic structure and framework for considering the future, appraising options and opportunities, and then selecting and implementing the necessary activities for achieving the stated objectives efficiently and effectively. The marketing plan provides a clear and unambiguous statement concerning what strategies and actions will be implemented, by whom, when and with what outcomes. Andersen (2000), however, questions excessive reliance on strategic planning compared with the need for management autonomy and organisational learning in an era where adaptability and flexibility are necessary to cope with the rapid rate of environmental change.

It is important to distinguish between *plans*, the outcomes of the planning process, and *planning*, the process from which plans are derived. While the process of planning is fairly standard and can be transferred across functions and organisations, there are often wide variations in the actual use of plans to guide strategy and operations. This is partly because there are several different types of plan that can emerge from a planning process. The next subsection looks in detail at some of them.

Types of plan

Plans can be developed to cover many different aspects of an organisation. In some cases, they may be designed and developed as part of an integrated corporate system of long-term planning, encompassing the whole organisation, while in others, they may be used to address specific short-term issues of concern. Plans may be differentiated in terms of a number of features. These are as follows.

Organisational level

Managers are involved with planning at all levels of an organisation. The concerns of managers, however, change at higher levels of the organisation, and the complexities affecting planning also change. The more senior the manager, the more long term and strategic becomes the focus. At the highest level, the concern is for the whole organisation and how to allocate resources across its various functions or units. At lower levels, the focus is on implementation within a shorter-term horizon, and on operating within clearly specified parameters. The marketing director may thus have a particular concern with developing new innovative products and opening new segments, while the sales representative may have to focus on sales territory planning to achieve pre-determined sales and call objectives.

Timescale

Plans may be short-, medium- or long-term in focus. *Short-term* normally means the shortest period of time appropriate to the operations of the organisation. Normally this is one year, or in some industries, such as fashion, one season. Such plans are usually about implementation, the achievement of specified objectives and allocating clearly defined responsibilities. *Medium-term plans* are more likely to cover a one to three year period. The focus is not so much on day-to-day operations and detailed tactical achievement as on renewal. This involves the redesign and redefinition of activities to create, maintain and exploit competitive advantage. This could include the opening up of a new market, a new product innovation, or a strategic alliance to improve market position, for example. *Long-term* plans can be anything from 3 to 20 years, with the timescale often dictated by capital investment periods. If it takes 10 years to commission, build and earn a payback on a major capital project, such as a new manufacturing plant or new machinery, then the planning horizon will have to be extended to take into account the various influences that could affect the feasibility of the project. Long-term plans are nearly always strategic in focus and concerned with resource allocation and return.

Regularity

Most longer-term plans have annual reviews to monitor progress. Shorter-term plans are often part of a hierarchy linking strategy with operations. Some plans, however, are not produced regularly as part of an annual cycle, but are campaign, project or situation specific. A *campaign plan*, for example, might have a limited duration to achieve defined objectives. As seen in Chapter 15, advertising is normally linked to a theme built into an integrated campaign covering perhaps media advertising, sales promotion, selling, distribution and pricing. *Project plans* are specific to particular activities, perhaps a new product launch, a change in distribution channels, or a new packaging innovation. These activities are of fixed duration and are not necessarily repeated.

Contingency plans are efforts to cater for the 'what if?' questions that emerge in more turbulent environments. Planned responses to any possible scenarios that might occur are prepared. A major new competitor entering the market, a supply shortage or a radical product innovation from a competitor could all affect the best-laid plans. By thinking through the implications and alternatives before the crisis arises, a number of options can be identified to support management if the scenario really materialises.

Focus

Plans will vary in their focus across the organisation. *Corporate plans* refer to the longer-term plans of the organisation, specifying the type of business scope desired and the strategies for achieving it across all areas of the business. The focus is on the technology, products, markets and resources that define the framework within which the individual parts of the organisation can develop more detailed strategies and plans. *Functional or operational plans* are, therefore, developed within the context of the organisational corporate plan but focus on the implementation of day-to-day or annual activities within the various parts of the organisation.

Organisational focus

Plans will vary according to the nature of the organisation itself. A number of alternative ways of organising marketing are considered later (*see* pp. 924 *et seq.*). If the organisational focus is on products, then plans will also take that focus, while if markets or functional areas are emphasised, plans will reflect that structure. For example, a functional organisational marketing plan will have distinct elements of pricing, advertising, distribution, etc. If SBUs are formed, then there is immediately a requirement for a two-tier planning structure: (a) considering the portfolio of SBUs at a corporate level, and (b) for each SBU, looking at the more detailed organisational design. Similarly divisional, regional, branch or company plans may all be used in different circumstances.

marketing ***in action***

Taking a long-term view: the right strategic medicine?

Pharmaceutical companies must take a long-term planning view if they are to enhance their product portfolios with innovations which are hopefully miracle cures that mean mega-profits. Although the planning horizon may be very long from invention through to pre-clinical testing, clinical trial and eventual commercialisation, as soon as a drug is ready for launch a number of short-term operational plans must come into effect to ensure that a market leadership position can be achieved and/or a return gained from the many years of investment. As considered in the case of Pfizer's Viagra (see pp. 306 *et seq.*), competitive products, some of which claim to offer additional benefits, are now coming onto the market thus reducing the return on the R&D investment associated with the drug.

As the first botanical pharmaceutical company Phytopharm's mission is to research and develop innovative medicines to treat chronic and poorly understood diseases.

Source: Phytopharm.

The challenge for the pharmaceutical companies is to spot the potential winners early. Neurological diseases such as Parkinson's and Alzheimer's are particularly distressing for families and a guaranteed market is there for any company getting new drugs to the market early. Worldwide, there are around 12 million Alzheimer's sufferers and with an ageing population, that figure is expected to grow to 22 million by 2025. Phytopharm, a small company based in Cambridgeshire, believes that it has a remedy for Alzheimer's, delaying its advance by regenerating the nerve cell receptors that allow the disease to develop. Although still on trial, its P58 and P63 could revolutionise treatment and, if successful, create a multi-million pound market.

Phytopharm's work on P58 and P63 is part of its business strategy to focus on drug discovery from plant extracts, taking them to the point of successful clinical trials and then seeking partners for commercialisation on an agreed royalty basis. This keeps Phytopharm's focus on its strengths rather than extending it into manufacturing, sales and marketing. It also enables it to focus on the poorly understood and difficult-to-treat diseases for which successful new drugs could revolutionise healthcare. Normally, Phytopharm has about ten products from four drug discovery platforms under development at any one time: for example it is currently working on eczema cures (P55) and with a population of 60 million sufferers in Europe and the US and an anticipated market size in excess of $3 bn, the returns could be high. Similarly P54, an extract from two tropical plant species, addresses inflammatory bowel disorders and is in now in clinical trials.

Although at the cutting edge of research, the company is not yet in profit. In 2001 its income was £1.5 mn and its expenses £5 mn, £4 mn of which went on research and development expenditure. While investors eventually hope to earn a return on investment, much depends on Phytopharm's ability to be first to find a cure, to negotiate licensing deals, and to ensure that a balance is achieved between R&D expenditure and eventual income. The organisational focus may well be on research, but eventually some of the cures must generate the levels of royalties that could transform the organisation from cash-starved to cash-rich.

Sources: Grosvenor (2001); http://www.phytopharm.co.uk.

Planning: benefits and problems

There are several benefits to be gained from taking a more organised approach to planning marketing activity. In summary, the benefits can be classified as relating to the development, coordination or control of marketing activity, as shown in Figure 21.1.

Despite the obvious benefits, we cannot assume that all organisations practise planning, and even those that do might not achieve all the results they expect. Planning in itself does not guarantee success. Much depends on the quality of the planning, its acceptance as a fundamental driving force within the organisation, and the perceived relevance of the resulting plans. There are thus many ways in which the process can go wrong.

One major pitfall is a tendency to become technique-oriented, losing sight of what planning is actually for. The production of big, complex, multicoloured BCG or GE matrices becomes an end in itself, and too little time and attention is devoted to working out what they mean and their implications for strategic decision-making and planning. There is also a risk that because techniques produce clear, pretty pictures, with things neatly pigeonholed, managers take them too literally and look for formulaic solutions. 'This product is a dog, therefore *we must* do THIS or THIS.' Such attitudes stifle creativity and ignore the true

Figure 21.1 Benefits of planning

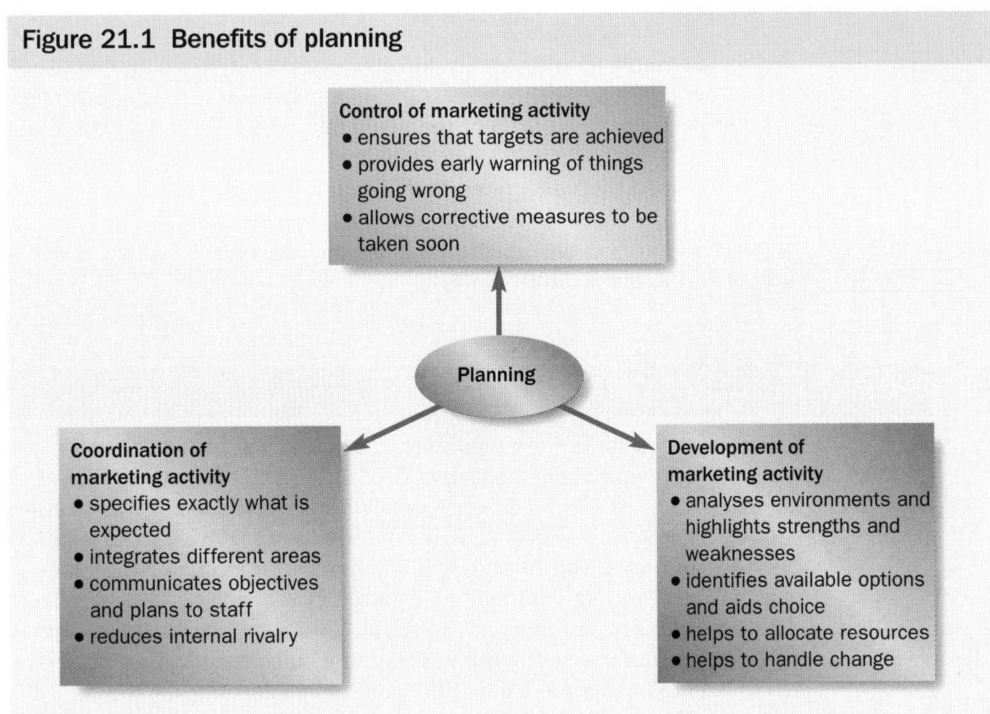

complexity of the world. Techniques such as the BCG matrix were never meant to be used in this way; they act as guides, they stimulate debate, but they do not offer pat solutions.

Finally, managers can become very fond of certain techniques. This is dangerous because any one technique only gives a partial insight, and occasionally looking at things from a new perspective can add new dimensions. That is not to suggest, of course, that the organisation should go to the opposite extreme of concentrating too much on the planning process itself. Too many techniques may just confuse the real issues, creating a fog around the whole process. A complementary portfolio of carefully chosen techniques needs to be defined, and regularly reviewed for appropriateness.

Another potential problem arises perhaps from embracing planning rather too eagerly. The urge to set up dedicated planning departments can divorce the professional planner from the managers who have to live with the resulting plans and implement them. Differentiating so clearly between the planner and the manager is far more likely to lead to plans that are not valued and end up locked in a filing cabinet, unused. The way to reduce this risk and to overcome such problems is to make sure that managers are still wholly involved in the process so that they feel some ownership of the plans. Clear and regular communication is absolutely crucial.

eg

In Chapter 20, Nestlé's long-term strategies to build market dominance in selected product sectors were discussed. This involved a regular re-appraisal of the contribution of different product areas and the portfolios contained within them. The longer-term strategic marketing plans would, therefore, have defined the desired position and outlined the strategies to achieve it, such as innovation, joint ventures and acquisition/divestment. The operational marketing plans would, however, be more focused, concentrating on particular products and indicating actions and responsibilities. So, for example, Buitoni, Unilever's market-leading pasta brand, is being attacked by Barilla, the number four brand, largely through product development and heavy promotion. Thus Buitoni's annual marketing plan in the UK is likely to include a number of counter-measures including sales promotion, new recipes and media advertising to retain the high consumer awareness and loyalty to the brand (Hardcastle, 2001).

In practical terms, marketing planning can fall down simply because of unreliable marketing information. As Chapter 6 made clear, accurate and timely information is essential if the planning process is going to mean anything at all. Good information is only part of the story, however. Planning is about using that information to forecast trends in the market and its environment, then to develop strategies and budgets in response to it, in an iterative and integrated way. Some organisations are good at the forecasting part, while some are good at the budgeting part, but too many fail to bring all this together in an analytical planning process, centred on strategic thinking.

In summary, there is a need for full integration between the **planning process** and the resulting plans. There is no room for a weak link in the chain, since the plans are only as good as the process that generated them, and the process is pointless if it does not result in acceptable, implementable plans.

The marketing planning process

The process of marketing planning in an organisation will vary, depending on whether a strategic or operational perspective is adopted. The **strategic marketing plan** differs from an **operational marketing plan** on two key dimensions, according to Abell (1982). First, the strategic marketing plan deals with the total strategy in a market linking customers, competitors and organisational capability. Operational marketing plans, on the other hand, normally deal with the marketing mix strategy that will be used to gain leverage in a market. The strategic marketing plan, therefore, guides all planning and activities at a functional level, not just in marketing but across the whole organisation. Second, strategic marketing plans tend to be prepared at an SBU or company level, while the operational marketing plan is more often concerned with products and market segments.

eg

Pilkington Glass, one of the world's largest manufacturers of glass and glazing products, developed long-term corporate strategies aiming to make it the number one or number two supplier in selected geographic markets. Essential to achieving this was a detailed review and restructuring of its marketing positioning and activities. The strategic plan, therefore, identified three sectors in which leadership was to be sought and retained: building, automotive and related technical markets. It also outlined the strategies for getting there, including product development and improving market coverage, while the operational marketing plans focused on any price promotions/changes, plans to improve service by online ordering in the automotive sector and developing the market in Brazil, thus providing a guide to local managers on how to put the strategy into practice.

The role of any operational marketing plan is important when an organisation employs over 27,000 people worldwide with manufacturing in 25 countries and sales in 130 countries. During tough economic conditions, when the housing, construction and car markets are not bouyant on a global scale, uncoordinated local actions outside the overall policy and direction of the company, for example price cutting or positioning the products in an inappropriate manner, could have effects across the company (Foley, 2002). It is also important to take a unified approach to new product development. Pilkington is a market leader in 'added value', such as self-cleaning double glazing, and when it launches a new product, it rarely does it on a country-by-country basis, but in groups of countries in one go.

The previous chapter dealt with many of the issues associated with the strategic marketing plan and its contribution to the overall strategic management process in an organisation. In the corporate planning process, marketing acts as a critical link between customers, competitors and the strategic direction and objectives of the organisation. Thus appraising opportunities, market attractiveness, competitive positioning and portfolio management are important tools in the corporate planning process. The marketing plan, however, although well subsumed in the strategic planning process, still operates as a means of integrating activities, scheduling resources, specifying responsibilities and providing benchmarks for measuring progress.

The purpose of marketing planning has been defined as:

> *to find a systematic way of identifying a range of options, to choose one or more of them, then to schedule and cost out what has to be done to achieve the objectives.*
>
> (McDonald, 1989, p. 13)

If this definition is to work in practice, an organisational structure is needed to ensure that the process is properly managed. Without such a structure, there is a danger that key stages may be omitted, or given insufficient attention. Although the structure will vary according to the complexity and variability of the organisation, and the emphasis may vary according to the turbulence in the environment and the resultant challenges facing the organisation, a number of broad phases in the planning process are likely to operate in any case. The main stages in the planning process are shown in Figure 21.2 and each stage is considered in turn. The early stages of this planning process form part of strategic marketing planning.

Corporate objectives and values

Corporate objectives are at the heart of the planning process, since they describe the direction, priorities and relative position of the organisation in its market(s). These objectives help to create guidelines for marketing plans, since the output of the corporate planning process acts as an input into the marketing planning process.

Objectives are normally presented in terms of different kinds of targets.

Quantitative targets

Quantitative financial targets are items such as market share (by value), sales, profit and ROI, over a set time period. These could be broken down into specific targets for each of the various organisational units. Therefore within a university, the student number targets (the equivalent of sales targets) could be allocated across different faculties, and these will

Figure 21.2 Stages in the planning process

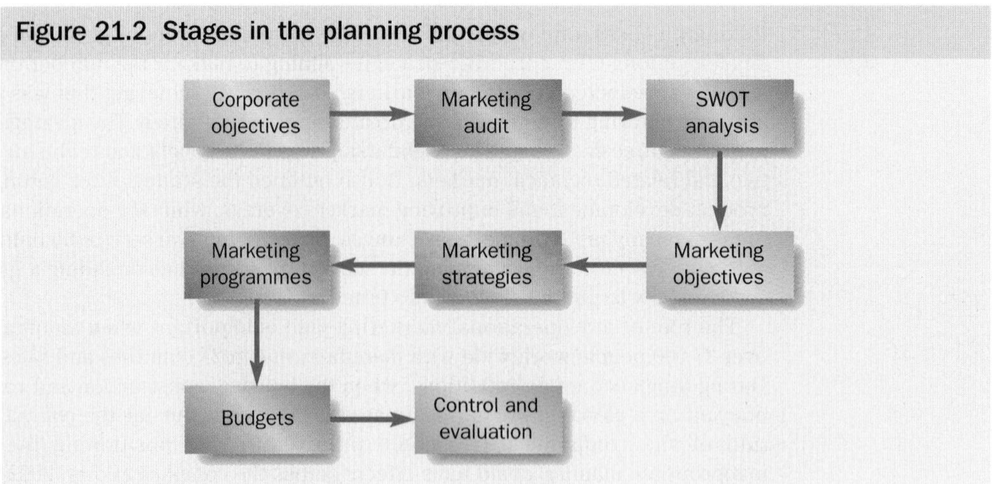

in turn determine the financial allocations. ISS (considered at pp. 845–6) has set targets as part of its 'Create 2005' programme that are all capable of measurement on an interim and terminal basis. The targets are:

Financial

- To double earnings per share
- To double operating profits.

Operating:

- To achieve at least 6 per cent organic growth on average (as opposed to acquisition growth)
- To make at least a 6 per cent margin in business units.

These targets will clearly guide the direction of the business over the next few years and evidence as to their achievement (or not) will be available for all stakeholders and the public to witness.

Philosophical targets

Philosophical targets, often called vision and values statements, have grown in popularity in recent years as a more enduring and all-embracing perspective of where an organisation seeks to journey and how it intends to conduct itself on the way. McDonald's has the vision of providing the world's best quick service restaurant experience and to achieve that, it seeks to provide a level quality, good service, cleanliness and value that makes every customer in a restaurant smile. In contrast, Vivendi, the entertainment company, has the vision of being the world's preferred creator and provider of entertainment, education and personalised service to consumers anywhere, at any time and across all distribution platforms.

Value statements are now becoming more popular as a guide to how the organisation will conduct itself. Vivendi, for example, concentrates on seven main areas in its public statements:

- Consumer focus
- Recognise and value cultural diversity
- Value creation for the benefit of stakeholders
- Encourage creativity and innovation
- Importance of teamwork
- Observe strict ethical standards
- Social responsibility and responsiveness fully endorsed.

Clearly, the fine words are easy, but the challenge is to put them into practice. Most organisations embrace the shortlist above, although some highlight additional areas. UBS, the Swiss banking organisation, for example, also highlights 'progressive partnerships' based on trust and shared vision, reflecting perhaps the nature of the client–bank relationship in financial servcies.

The vision and values statement is often linked to a mission statement, which is sometimes separate and sometimes incorporated within the vision statement. A mission statement represents where the organisation is today and where it wants to be in the future. Often they are less enduring than vision statements, which may last for generations. Mission statements are intended to guide functional and business unit areas in their strategic development. Some organisations, such as Boeing, have become so large and complex that a number of the operating divisions have subsidiary mission statements that fit ultimately into the over-riding theme. Mission statements should encompass segments served, the needs to be fulfilled in the market, and the technological or service character of the organisation (Abell, 1982). It should encapsulate the distinctive and principal values of the organisation, but from a market rather than a product orientation.

Day (1990) identified four characteristics of a well-thought-through mission statement:

- *Future orientated*: linking the future with its impact on the business.
- *Reflecting the values and orientation of the leader*: providing support and clear guidelines to staff.
- *Stating strategic purpose*: indicating the direction and strategy to be followed, the targets and competitors to beat.
- *Enabling*: providing clear guidelines to managers lower down the organisation in their preparation of SBU or functional plans.

To Wensley (1987), mission statements should be 'short on numbers and long on rhetoric but remaining succinct'. The mission statement provides the essential guidelines for managers in making their day-to-day decisions and when preparing operational plans. Nevertheless, the corporate mission statement needs to be supported by quantitative and qualitative targets that reflect this mission.

Qualitative targets

Qualitative targets include items such as service levels, innovation and scope. These rarely have just one objective, but are often found in a mixture with defined priorities. Drucker (1955) highlighted eight areas, as shown in Figure 21.3.

marketing **in action**

Companies with a mission

Mission statements are increasingly being developed to indicate the priorities facing the organisation for the forseeable future. Pilkington Glass has market dominance in mind with its mission statement of seeking to be 'a dynamic, market driven, global provider of glass products, judged best in class by our customers, our people and our shareholders'. The fit with the strategy described at p. 901 is therefore well founded. Siemens has gone further and proposes a mission statement associated with its CSR practice: 'our knowledge and our solutions are helping to create a better world. We have a responsibility to the wider community and we are committed to environmental protection'.

Boeing (http://www.boeing.com), meanwhile, specifies its mission statement through a vision and core competencies approach. The vision is for 'people working together as one global company for aerospace leadership'. Three core competencies relate to internal and external focus around closeness and understanding of customer needs, large-scale systems integration and efficient, cost effective design and production. These statements are then followed by an extensive list of values.

Subway (http://www.subway.com), a sandwich retail chain, has adopted a core values and philosophies approach to describe its philosophical targets. They are:

- commitment to customer satisfaction through high-quality food with exceptional service and good value;
- taking pride in serving customers and community;
- valuing a sense of urgency, to emphasise innovative and entrepreneurial behaviour;
- to ensure fairness, mutual respect and teamwork.

Finally, Avis (http://www.avis.com) aims to provide 'a stress free rental experience by providing safe, dependable vehicles and special services to win the customer's loyalty'. The vision is to become the world's leading car rental company.

The above examples demonstrate the range of approaches used by organisations to capture their values and purpose. Although most do tend to be very generalised, they provide a sense of direction to guide more detailed planning and strategy formulation.

Figure 21.3 Qualitative targets

Whatever the type of objective, they all must be realistic, achievable within a specific timescale, and cited in order of priority. This will lead to a hierarchy of interlinking objectives. In any case, objectives should reflect the competitive and market positions considered in Chapter 20. In practice, however, defining objectives is often a case of managing trade-offs, such as those suggested by Weinberg (1969) in Table 21.1.

The outcome of this stage should be a clear statement of what is expected of the functional units within the organisation and their plans.

Table 21.1 Trade-offs in setting objectives

- Short-term profit vs long-term growth
- Profit margin vs market positioning
- Direct sales effort vs market development
- Penetrating existing markets vs developing new ones
- Profit vs non-profit goals
- Growth vs stability
- Change vs stability
- Low-risk vs high-risk environments

Source: Weinberg (1969).

corporate social responsibility *in action*

Cadbury Schweppes: walking the CSR talk

Cadbury has developed from a small family business established on Quaker values into an international company that still upholds the importance of taking a socially responsible approach to all facets of its work, despite being a commercial enterprise. Quakers have strong beliefs that are carried through into campaigns for justice, equality and social reform, reflected in Cadbury's original ideal of helping to end poverty and deprivation in Victorian Britain. The foundations for a corporately socially responsible organisation were, therefore, laid over 100 years ago and have endured and been embodied in the social responsibility programme of today, despite the tremendous change, diversification and internationalisation that has happened in the company.

The over-riding policy statement highlights the central importance of CSR to business strategy:

Good ethics and good business go together naturally. We firmly believe that our responsibility and reputation as a good corporate citizen plays an important role in our ability to achieve our objective of growing value for our shareowners.

Keeping a watch over all aspects of the company's activities is a Corporate and Social Responsibility Committee at board level and chaired by a high profile non-executive director, Baroness Wilcox, a former head of the National Consumer Council.

The CSR policy at Cadbury Schweppes breaks down into five areas: corporate governance; human rights; community and social investment; environment; and employment practices. Not all these areas are examined in detail in this book, but each, individually and collectively has helped to build a strong reputation, confidence and a record of achievement that could be considered a model. Each area is considered briefly in turn:

- *Corporate governance*: A corporate governance policy embraces the broad principles of business dealings and conduct with all Cadbury's publics in terms of ethics, openness and honesty. These reflect the enduring values inherited from the past. It also has a code of conduct approved by the board to which all employees are expected to adhere. This code embraces more practical issues for example, legal and compliance issues, handling of conflicts of interests, gifts, dealing with competition, whistleblowing, confidentiality and political contributions. Each employee is provided with their own copy of the code and compliance to the code is enforced through the management process. To Cadbury, good ethics and good business go together.
- *Human rights*: Cadbury is particularly sensitive to the dangers of operating in cultures where different norms and practices may apply. The reports of slave child labour in the cocoa industry in West Africa were of particular concern (see p. 57). Although the allegations were made about the Ivory Coast where Cadbury does not buy, it is playing a full part in the industry, along with governments and NGOs to ensure that such practices are stamped out. It fully contributes to surveys of child labour practices, independent monitoring and the certification of cocoa to ensure that all conditions have been met. Closer to home, the company has also published its own human rights and ethical trading policy covering labour rights, dignity at work, health and safety, fair remuneration, diversity, a respect for differences and the need for personal development. Progress measurement in each of these areas is assessed by a working group reporting to the CSR Committee. This will increasingly also apply to the supply chains feeding into the company. A programme of education and implementation is now under way in all its businesses around the world.
- *Community and social investment*: Cadbury also recognises the role and responsibilities it has in the communities in which it operates. The policy is not about handouts and high profile gift giving but takes a longer-term integrated approach as part of a 'managing for Community value' programme. This means carefully selecting the initiatives to encourage and taking on a longer-term approach to achieving agreed objectives. It has a Foundation that makes grants to projects and partner organisations, especially in the fields of education and employment, focusing on social exclusion and deprivation in places such as Birmingham, Sheffield, Bristol and London.
- *Environment*. Sustainability is central to the policies in this area. The 'Environmental Report' outlines the programmes the company has undertaken in developing long-term sustainability, protecting the environment and assessing the environmental impact of its prime activities. The policy itself is still evolving to include transportation, supply chain management and raw material sourcing. The report also considers a number of areas such as waste management, water conservation and energy use to demonstrate the company's efforts to improve the environment. The beverages plant in Carcagente in Spain, for example, recycles all of its organic waste. Packaging is more problematic, but the PET, glass bottles and aluminium cans can all be reprocessed in-house or with specialist recyclers. Even broken pallets are repaired and re-used. Between 1997 and 1999, the percentage of waste that was recycled improved from 75 per cent to 82 per cent.
- *Employment practices*. This area of CSR covers a variety of human resource issues such as personal development, the working environment and equal opportunities, all of which are beyond the scope of this text.

By adopting such a comprehensive approach to CSR, the values embodied within Cadbury and the business principles espoused are put into practice. Care has to be taken, however. One attempt to undertake cause-related marketing in Kenya led to a blurring of objectives. When sponsoring the Mediae Trust which produces radio programmes for rural communities focusing on social and environmental themes such as animal husbandry and child abuse, the distinction between education and advertising became confused. Cadbury paid for the air time for Mediae broadcasts in return for some advertising space, so although it helped product sales, it also contributed to broader rural social development policies. However, one audience member is quoted as saying, 'I like the show because it educates us, like what to do if your child is mistreated, it also teaches us how useful Cadbury's is; that it builds healthy bodies' (as quoted by Turner, 2002). Overall, though, Cadbury has 'walked the talk' and presents a good example to other companies.

Sources: Turner (2002); http://www.cadburyschweppes.com.

The marketing audit

Audit is a term more commonly used in financial management to describe the process of taking stock of an organisation's financial strengths, weaknesses and health, through checking and analysing changes in its assets and transactions over a given period. The philosophy of the **marketing audit** is very similar, in that it systematically takes stock of an organisation's marketing health, as the formal definition implies:

> *[The audit] is the means by which a company can understand how it relates to the environment in which it operates. It is the means by which a company can identify its own strengths and weaknesses as they relate to external opportunities and threats. It is thus a way of helping management to select a position in that environment based on known factors.*
>
> (McDonald, 1989, p. 21)

The marketing audit is really the launching pad for the marketing plan, as it encourages management to reflect systematically on the environment and the organisation's ability to respond, given its actual and planned capabilities. The marketing audit, just like its financial counterpart, is first and foremost about developing a shared, agreed and objective understanding of the organisation. It thus concerns such questions as:

1 What is happening in the environment? Does it pose threats or opportunities?
2 What are our relative strengths and weaknesses for handling and exploiting the environment?
3 How effective are we in implementing marketing activity?

In order to answer such questions, managers have to look at both environmental variables (i.e. an external audit) and operational variables (i.e. an internal audit).

The **external audit** systematically looks at the kinds of issues covered extensively in Chapter 2 as the STEP factors. Sociocultural changes, such as in the demographic make-up of a market or in public concerns or attitudes, may well influence the future strategic direction of an organisation. The early identification of technological change might also change strategic direction, as the organisation plans ways of exploiting it to make cheaper, better or different products ahead of the competition. Economic and competitive factors are both, of course, very important. Low disposable incomes among target customers may force the organisation towards more rigorous cost control or into changing its product mix, while high interest rates on organisational borrowing might delay diversification or other expansion plans. Competition also has to be analysed very carefully on all aspects of its marketing activities, including its response to STEP factors and its choice of target markets. Finally, the external audit should note what is happening in terms of the legal and regulatory frameworks, whether national or European, that bind the organisation.

eg

National Car Parks (NCP) is Europe's largest car park operator with around 530 car parks and it also provides management services for municipally owned car parks (Batchelor, 2001). Since the 1950s, it has evolved from organising parking on reclaimed bomb sites to property-led parking and finally to being a service company offering complete town centre parking services. Increasingly, through its current owners Cendant, it works to pursue combined property development and parking solutions for places such as Soho, Ipswich, Leeds and Liverpool (Jameson, 2002). Once built, car parks are essentially cash businesses. There are opportunities for added-value services such as tyre checks, car valeting and servicing, fleet services and associated ticket sales through the car park office. If it were to undertake an external audit, it might raise the following issues, among others:

1 *Competition.* A number of rivals from mainland Europe and the USA have entered the UK market.
2 *Negotiating for sites.* Increased competition means that acquiring new sites or even renewing the leases on existing ones is more difficult. On the other hand, competitors who are struggling provide an opportunity for NCP to pick up sites and contracts.
3 *Management contracts.* Many site owners (local authorities, airports, hotels, shopping centres etc.) now prefer to award management contracts to car park operators, rather

than giving them complete autonomy over the car park operation. NCP's traditional approach has been one of autonomy, and its competitors have been faster to accept management contracts.

4 *Service*. Direct parking is now available from operators such as Interlink (http://www.webworld.co.uk/mall/inter-link). These competitors offer lower prices and collect customers from their hotels.

5 *Government policy for transport*. The government's drive to get cars off the road could have an adverse effect on demand for parking. On the other hand, city centre traffic restrictions and proposed tolls to get into centres could lead to an increase in demand for 'park and ride' schemes and thus edge-of-town parking. Any move to invest in light rail options such as those running in Manchester, Birmingham, London Docklands and Croydon could depress city centre demand for regular parkers and season ticket holders, especially given the UK Government's aim to double the use of trams by 2010 (Harper, 2000). In the first six weeks of light rail operation, the demand for car parking in the centre of Croydon dropped by nearly 10 per cent.

6 *Security*. Both the general public and the police are pressurising car park operators to install increasingly sophisticated security systems.

7 *Shopping habits*. The rise of out-of-town shopping with ample free parking not only pulls shoppers away from town centres, NCP's traditional territory, but also highlights the high cost of town centre parking. 'Park and ride' schemes operated from edge-of-town sites into the centres might provide an opportunity for NCP in cooperation with local authorities.

8 *Property development opportunities*. These opportunities might become available on a partnership basis.

Sources: Batchelor (2001); Foster (1996); Jameson (2002); Harper (2000); http://www.ncp.co.uk.

The **internal audit** focuses on many of the decision areas discussed in Chapters 3–19 and their effectiveness in achieving their specified objectives. It is not just, however, a *post mortem* on the 4Ps. Auditors will also be interested in how smoothly and synergistically the 4Ps fit together, and whether the marketing actions, organisation and allocated resources are appropriate to the environmental opportunities and constraints.

Table 21.2 summarises the issues that a marketing audit should consider.

Table 21.2 Marketing audit issues

- Macro environment: STEP factors (see Chapter 2)
- Task environment: *competition, channels, customers* (see Chapters 3–5)
- Markets (see Chapter 20)
- Strategic issues: *segmentation, positioning, competitive advantage* (see Chapters 5 and 20)
- Marketing mix (see Chapters 7–19)
- Marketing organisational structure and organisation (see Chapter 21)

The audit should be undertaken as part of the planning cycle, usually on an annual basis, rather than as a desperate response to a problem. The audit is a systematic attempt to assess the performance of the marketing effort, looking from the present backwards, although when it is done thoroughly it can be a time-consuming activity. To help the audit process, it is critical to have a sound marketing information system covering the marketing environment, customers, competitors, etc., as well as detail on all areas of the organisational marketing effort, as outlined in Chapter 20.

The main risk in undertaking the marketing audit is a lack of objectivity. This may arise from being too close to the situation to see it clearly, or from a fear that if the audit is too objective, a manager's past decision-making might be criticised. The use of external consultants could overcome these problems, but nevertheless, going through the process itself internally can be a valuable experience for managers.

Marketing analysis

The marketing audit is a major exercise which ranges widely over all the internal and external factors influencing an organisation's marketing activity. It generates, therefore, a huge amount of material that has to be analysed and summarised to sift out the critical issues that will drive the marketing plan forward.

SWOT analysis

The commonest mechanism for structuring audit information to provide a critical analysis is the **SWOT analysis** (strengths, weaknesses, opportunities, threats).

Strengths and weaknesses. Strengths and weaknesses tend to focus on the present and past, and on internally controlled factors, such as the 4Ps and the overall marketing package (including customer service) offered to the target market. The external environment is not totally ignored, however, and many strengths and weaknesses can only be defined as such in a competitive context. Thus, for example, our low prices may be seen as a strength if we are pricing well below our nearest competitor in a price sensitive market. Low prices may, however, be a weakness if we have been forced into them by a price war and cannot really sustain them, or if the market is less price sensitive and our price is associated with inferior quality when compared with higher-priced competitors in the minds of the target market.

Opportunities and threats. Opportunities and threats tend to focus on the present and the future, taking a more outward-looking, strategic view of likely developments and options. Thus the organisation that is the price leader in a price sensitive market might see the opportunity to get its costs down even further as a means of maintaining its position and pressurising any challengers. The challenger's SWOT analysis would define that same scenario as a threat, but might see an opportunity in opening up a new, non-price-sensitive segment. Many opportunities and threats emerge from the marketing environment, when shifts in demographic and cultural factors are taken into account; when developments in emerging markets, such as eastern Europe, are analysed; when, in fact, the implications of anything included in Chapter 2's STEP factors is considered.

eg

WH Smith has become an international player in the book and stationery retail market, with around 530 stores in the UK and a further 575 in the US, Australia and Asia. If it were doing a SWOT analysis, it might identify the rise in online commerce and learning as both a threat and an opportunity. It is a threat in the sense that it has generated new competitors such as http://www.amazon.co.uk focusing on the UK as well as making it relatively easy for UK consumers to buy from the USA or anywhere else. The threat is intensified with the evidence that there is a significant shift towards online book buying.

Related opportunities for a High Street retailer could be that the online market is young enough to support more providers and a retailer could open a parallel distribution channel to sell online to compete directly with the likes of Amazon. WH Smith has, in fact used its strengths as an established retail name and as a distributor to open its own e-commerce website, but it has not yet made a significant impact. WH Smith has also identified a trend in consumer preferences, accelerated by the online revolution and the associated fragmentation of mass markets, towards more focused retailers rather than generalists. One way that WH Smith has tried to capitalise on this is by acquiring Hodder Headline, which is involved in children's and educational publishing. This backward integration could improve WH Smith's expertise and focus in those areas as well as strengthening any online offer (Hollinger and Rawsthorn, 1999). WH Smith must not, however, lose sight of its core retailing business and will have to pay greater attention to making its retail stores more amenable, to encourage browsing and impulse buying as well as giving people a reason to visit 'real' shops rather than online ones (Hirst, 2001).

With the recognised strengths of the WH Smith brand name and its High Street coverage, a number of further strategic options and imperatives arise from the environmental changes:

- Reposition stores to become 'retail entertainment' sites capitalising on new technology. 'Project Touch' will, for example, enable consumers to get information in-store on cooking, cinema times, music charts, etc. Internet terminals and refreshment areas are also being considered (Kleinman, 2001; 2002).
- Develop speciality and targeted own-brand publications through Hodder Headline in areas such as cookery, travel, children's fiction and home education.
- WH Smith already has 60 per cent of the home education market in the UK, so by using another acquisition, Helicon, it could expand into the growing online learning market (Doran, 2001).
- In time, publishing and online book retailing could become even closer and WH Smith would be well placed in both marketing and technological terms to move with the emerging opportunities.

By assessing each of these options in detail in the light of the SWOT findings, the company is better placed to plan its future priorities and positioning.

Understanding the SWOT analysis

The SWOT analysis, therefore, helps to sort information systematically and to classify it, but still needs further creative analysis to make sense of it. The magnitude of opportunities and threats, and the feasibility of the potential courses of action implied by them, can only really be understood in terms of the organisation's strengths and weaknesses. If strengths and weaknesses represent 'where we are now' and opportunities and threats represent 'where we want (or don't want) to be' or 'where we could be', then the gap, representing 'what we have to do to get there', has to be filled by managerial imagination, as justified and formalised in the body of the marketing plan.

eg

West Coast Fish Products is a small fish processing company in Ireland, which smokes salmon, trout and mackerel, using a special blend of woods, herbs and spices to achieve a distinctive flavour. Although its main market is in Ireland, it is looking towards European markets, especially Germany and Switzerland. Even though it is a small company, it uses a formal approach to marketing planning, identifying priorities for marketing strategy development. Its SWOT analysis revealed the following issues:

1 *Strengths*
   (a) reputation for quality in raw materials and processes;
   (b) value added products using herbs;
   (c) knowledge of the market and contacts in Germany, France and Switzerland;
   (d) good location for accessing raw materials.

2 *Weaknesses*
   (a) no formal organisation for marketing;
   (b) emphasis on quality and production rather than on systematic market development;
   (c) buyers tend to initiate contact – company not sufficiently proactive;
   (d) limited resources for intensive market development;
   (e) most competitors have larger market share;
   (f) remote European location means higher transport costs and reduces shelf life of products by up to seven days;
   (g) retail and catering trade dominated by a few large customers.

3 *Opportunities*
   (a) increasing European consumption of smoked salmon;
   (b) fish seen as a healthy product, low in fat and cholesterol;
   (c) contract catering sector relatively underdeveloped;
   (d) the rural, green image of Ireland reflects positively on Irish food products;
   (e) government aid programmes for small businesses in exporting, marketing, etc.;
   (f) new potential in US and Japanese markets.

4 *Threats*
   (a) seasonal demand, peaking at Christmas;
   (b) domestic Irish market relatively small;
   (c) smoked salmon regarded in Ireland as luxury speciality food;
   (d) pressure on prices in domestic market from retail and catering buyers;
   (e) low levels of supplier loyalty;
   (f) highly competitive European market (80 competitors in Ireland alone) with strong competition from Norway and Denmark in particular;
   (g) market pressure to raise quality standards, especially with smoked salmon;
   (h) business vulnerable to impact of disease and pollution in fish stocks;
   (i) tougher European legislation affecting processing, additives, handling, marketing etc.;
   (j) variety of tastes and demands (colour, saltiness, dryness, etc.) across different European markets.

From this profile, marketing objectives could then begin to be formulated.

Marketing objectives

As the previous subsection implied, the desire to exploit strengths and opportunities, and to overcome weaknesses and threats, gives a foundation for the definition of marketing objectives. Objectives are essential for clearly defining what must be achieved through the marketing strategies implemented, and also provide a benchmark against which to measure the extent of their success. **Marketing objectives** do, however, have to be wide ranging as well as precise, as they have to link closely with corporate objectives on a higher level but also descend to the fine detail of products, segments, etc. They must, therefore, be *consistent*, with each other and with corporate goals, *attainable*, in that they can be achieved in practice and their progress can be measured, and *compatible* with both the internal and external environments in which they are to be implemented. These criteria are generally applicable, despite the fact that marketing objectives can vary over time and between organisations.

e-marketing *in action*

easyJet and the 5Ss

Smith and Chaffey (2001) highlight some of the objectives of e-marketing using the mnemonic of the '5Ss'. The 5Ss of e-marketing objectives are Sell, Serve, Speak, Save and Sizzle. An organisation may set objectives as part of the marketing planning process in some or all of these categories. Here we take the example of low cost airline easyJet (http://www.easyjet.com) to illustrate the 5Ss:

- *Sell*. To grow sales through wider distribution, promotion and sales. easyJet was founded by Stelios Haji-Ioannou, the son of a Greek shipping tycoon who reputedly used to 'hate the internet'. In the mid-90s Haji-Ioannou reportedly denounced the internet as something 'for nerds', and swore that it wouldn't do anything for his business. However, he decided to experiment with a prototype site, and sat up and took notice when sales started to flow from the site. Based on early successes, easyJet decided to invest in the new channel and proactively to convert customers to using it. To help achieve this, an initial target of selling 30 per cent of seats online by the year 2000 was set. By August 2000, the site accounted for 38 per cent of ticket sales and by 2001 it had risen to over 90 per cent of seats. Of course, this success is based on the relative ease of converting direct telephone-sale customers to online customers.
- *Serve*. To add value by giving customers extra benefits online. When easyJet customers have a query, the easyJet contact strategy is to minimise voice calls through providing carefully structured Frequently Asked Questions (FAQ) and e-mail forms to encourage online communication.
- *Speak*. Get closer to customers by tracking them, asking them questions, creating a dialogue, and learning about them. easyJet is active in using the web as a PR tool, for example:
  - easyJet aircraft are emblazoned with oversize 'www.easyjet.com' logos;
  - easyJet ran a competition to guess the losses of rival airline Go and received 65,000 entries and also enhanced press coverage;
  - owner Stelios Haji-Ioannou has a personal views 'message from Stelios' page; and
  - standard press release pages are regularly updated.

- *Save*. Save costs (of service, sales transactions and administration, print and post). The internet is important to easyJet as it helps it to reduce running costs, which is important for a company where each passenger generates only a small profit. Part of the decision to increase the use of the internet for sales was to save on the building of a £10 mn call centre which would have been necessary to sustain sales growth if the internet was not used as a sales channel. As an example, a 1999 sales promotion offered 50,000 seats to readers of *The Times*. The scalability of the internet helped deal with demand since everyone was directed to the website rather than the company needing to employ an extra 250 telephone operators.
- *Sizzle*: extend the brand online. Reinforce brand values in a totally new medium. easyJet.com has gradually become an important part of the easyJet brand. The site is visually designed to support offline communications about the brand and all communications on-site reinforce offline communications and the character of the brand.

Source: Smith and Chaffey (2001).

Guiltinan and Paul (1988) identified four fundamental areas within which marketing objectives may be defined:

1 achieving market share growth or maintenance;
2 the maintenance or improvement of profitability;
3 establishing an opening marketing position;
4 maximising cash flow, harvesting.

eg

Ryanair, the Ireland-based low-cost airline, continued to expand despite the problems that the major scheduled airlines faced after September 11th 2001. The core theme underlying its marketing objectives is to offer a no-frills, price-orientated proposition that few other airlines can match. Expansion has been progressive since the company started in 1985. Initially, it broke the high price levels operated by British Airways and Aer Lingus on the Dublin–London route by offering fares at half their rates. New aircraft were bought and new services established by the early 1990s, and services were expanded from Dublin to Glasgow, Birmingham, Manchester and Gatwick. By 1995, Ryanair was carrying over 1.5 million passengers, double the figure for 1989. At that stage, prices were reduced further, with some fares as low as €30 (Edwards, 2001).

The service package has to be worked out backwards from the low price and expected capacity on each flight. Onboard services such as meals cost extra, online booking cuts out commission to travel agents; and lowest cost airport services are used. Sometimes, for example, the gates used are well away from the main terminal and even the choice of airport has led to some criticism. For instance, Copenhagen was the advertised destination, but Malmo (Sweden) was the destination airport, some 45 minutes' bus ride away. Similarly, the Frankfürt Hahn destination airport is actually 60 miles west of the commercial centre (Peachey, 2002). These less popular airports not only make it easier to get take-off and landing slots, but also mean lower landing charges. Price is always the main feature in any advertising and it is normally compared directly with the main scheduled carriers' prices.

Even as Ryanair expands and develops its hubs at Stanstead and Hahn, the marketing formula remains with tactics designed to beat off the competition. The Hahn expansion takes Ryanair head-to-head with Lufthansa with the declared intention to 'break its high fares monopoly in the German market' (as quoted by Done, 2001), as it did to Aer Lingus nearly twenty years ago. Ryanair might not have it all its own way, however, as Lufthansa is planning to launch its own low-cost airline (Harnischfeger, 2002).

Whatever the basis of the objectives, they cannot be left at such a descriptive level. It is not enough to say that our objective is to increase our market share. That leaves too many questions unanswered, such as:

- Volume (i.e. focus on quantity) or value (i.e. focus on revenue) share?
- How much more share?
- For which products?
- In which segment(s)?
- At which competitor's expense?

It is essential to quantify and make explicit precisely what is intended. Even when those questions have been answered, the objective is still quite general, and a number of detailed subobjectives, which will perhaps relate to constraints or parameters within which the main objective is to be achieved, should also be defined. The main objective of increasing market share, for example, may have subobjectives relating to pricing. Thus the marketing manager might have to find a way of increasing market share without compromising the organisation's premium price position.

eg

For West Coast Fish Products, introduced earlier, the primary broad marketing objective might be to improve its profitability in the domestic Irish market through more effective and efficient marketing. It might also strive to improve its marketing position in selected European markets. With limited resources, however, this can only be done if there is a disciplined approach to developing one or two markets in depth rather than seeking orders from a wide geographic area. Detailed marketing objectives would then have to be defined that outline quantified targets relating specific products to specific markets.

Marketing strategies

A marketing strategy is the means by which an organisation sets out to achieve its marketing objectives. The main areas of focus are the definition of the target market and the marketing mix employed. They are not only described in qualitative terms, but are also specified in terms of the resources required and the structure and allocation of responsibility for implementation.

In terms of the target market, the planner needs to ensure that the right group has been selected, matching with the conclusions drawn from the SWOT analysis. The organisation should, of course, be able to make an attractive offering to that segment, and have the expertise to create and sustain differential advantage, whether it is looking for defendable niches or to compete head-on in a crowded mass market segment. Chapter 5 looked more closely at segmentation bases and target market selection. The choice of target segment will be influenced by the competitive structure of the market, and thus by the organisation's choice of competitor against whom it wants to compete, and how. This in turn links with generic competitive strategies and the concept of competitive positioning, as outlined in Chapter 20 (pp. 871 *et seq.*).

In reality, an organisation will be presented with a range of strategic options, relating to its defined objectives. Some will be related to increasing volume (as in Ansoff's product and market matrix presented in Figure 20.6), while others relate to improving profitability and holding on to what the organisation already has (reducing costs, increasing prices, changing the product mix, streamlining operations, etc.).

Within each area examples of actions might be to:

1 *Reposition the product.* The Mars bar was born in 1932 and by 1999 sales had reached two billion bars. A downturn in the chocolate market and a drop in UK sales of 11 per cent in 2001 was, however, enough to make the brand manager decide that it was time to kick some life back into the brand. Mars believed that the positioning was wrong. Chocolate is no longer central to healthy snacking, and the energy claim captured by the 'helps you to work, rest and play' slogan was outdated. The new position will thus be based around 'indulgent treat' and 'pleasure you can't measure' themes with new packaging and a below-the-line promotional push. It is not easy to change consumer attitudes to well established brands, however, and the multi-million pound campaign will have to work very hard if it is to succeed (Mowbray, 2002).

2 *Improve product packaging.* The Smartie cardboard tube could soon be a thing of the past if a new packaging idea works for Nestlé. The Smarties plastic 'can' contains 65 standard-sized Smarties in a re-sealable ring-pull container. Although the cardboard tubes also have a re-sealable lid, rarely do the sweets stay in the tube long enough for it to be useful! (*The Grocer*, 2002).

3 *Alter prices*. Although the battery market is growing in volume, fuelled by consumer desire for mobility, it is falling in value as price promotions, such as Duracell's '3 for the price of 2' and Energizer's 'buy 1 get 1 free' offers, bring prices down. Do the manufacturers have the courage, however, to move away from price promotions and spend more on promotion and point-of-sale for what for many people is either a 'distress' or impulse purchase (O'Brien, 2001)?

4 *Improve productivity*. When Unilever took over Bestfoods (*see* p. 858), the first priority was to increase marketing productivity by merging sales teams, distribution channels and marketing campaign planning as a means of lowering the cost profile and improving sales volumes.

5 *Standardise*. Jungheinrich is a leading manufacturer of lift trucks (for example fork-lift trucks and other loading and unloading machinery). It uses a common chassis for a range of different lift trucks. By standardising the component, the organisation can achieve cost efficiency in both logistics and manufacturing, yet can still offer a wide range of trucks to meet different customer needs.

6 *Change sales or customer mix*. Sellotape still derives over half its sales from its original product launched in the 1930s, but it has gradually developed a more segmented approach, to change both the product and customer mix. There are products for DIY, children, gift wrapping and general home stationery, as well as a brand aimed at the small office.

For West Coast Fish Products, the strategy might be to occupy a narrow niche with high quality, clearly differentiated, unique products. Within the domestic Irish market, this would mean increasing the promotional effort targeted at top class restaurants and hotels, and opening up a new segment of high-class catering services. This is not just a question of promotional activity, of course, but also needs to be carried through to product appearance, packaging, delivery and order processing, etc. Prices, however, are under pressure from competitive forces, so it might be difficult to accompany any push upmarket with a corresponding price increase. In the international market, the priority is to fine tune the marketing mix strategy to meet the needs of selected European wholesale and retail markets.

Marketing programmes

Whereas the previous stage was about designing marketing strategies, this one is about their detailed implementation. The marketing programme will precisely specify actions, responsibilities and timescales. It is the detailed statement that managers have to follow if strategies are to be put into operation, as it outlines required actions by market segment, product and functional area. Within the marketing programme, each mix element is considered individually, covering all the decision areas outlined in Chapters 7 to 19. This is in contrast to the marketing strategy itself, which stresses the interdependency between elements of the mix for achieving the best synergy between them. Now, the individual strands that make up that

West Coast Fish Products drew up a series of planned actions for the main segments served. In the domestic Irish market, for example, the programme aimed at the trade segment might entail:

- sales visits to the top 25 hotels and restaurants;
- sales visits to 30 large catering companies;
- attendance at relevant trade shows and fairs;
- improving design, labelling and durability of packaging;
- improving logistics to reduce order processing and delivery times;
- launching a new line of fresh eels;
- encouraging bigger average order size to improve sales volume and efficiency.

In each case, responsibility will have to be allocated, resources specified, schedules drawn up and activities described in much more detail. For this company, it might well mean that the directors have to spend time meeting customers and developing new business rather than concentrating on the manufacturing processes.

strategy can be picked out, and for each functional area, such as pricing, managers can go through planning processes, audits, objectives, strategies, programmes and controls.

On the basis of the overall marketing strategy, managers can emphasise those areas of comparative strength where a competitive edge can be gained, strengthen those areas where the organisation is comparable with its competition, and work to develop further or overcome those where the organisation is more vulnerable. The key challenge at the end of it all, however, is to ensure that the marketing mix is affordable, implementable and appropriate for the target segment. With that in mind, and given the dynamic nature of most markets, managers will also have to review the mix on a regular basis to make sure that it is still fresh and still serving the purposes intended.

Marketing budgets

The marketing plan must specify and schedule all financial and other resource requirements, otherwise managers might not be able to accomplish the tasks set. This is partly about costs, such as those of the sales force which include their associated expenditures, advertising campaigns, dealer support, market research, etc., and partly about forecasting expected revenues from products and markets. In determining budgets, managers need to balance precision against flexibility. A budget should be precise and detailed enough to justify the resources requested and to permit detailed control and evaluation of the cost effectiveness of various marketing activities, yet it also needs the flexibility to cope with changing circumstances.

eg

When Cadbury Schweppes introduced its Managing For Value (MFV) programmes, it had far-reaching effects on marketing planning and budgeting. The underlying concept of MFV is that all existing and proposed products have to be profitable to survive. This means assessing a brand's impact, not just in terms of marketing returns, but also in terms of the total capital investment, such as in production machinery and logistics. To assess the return, marketing managers were expected to consider a variety of cost equations and schedules on different marketing and production options. The MFV also focused more attention on the effectiveness of the marketing budget and its contribution to market share, volume and earnings growth. The sponsorship of *Coronation Street* (*see* p. 822) was an outcome of the MFV drive, as it enabled a stronger focus on the master brand. It also allowed advertising expenditure on some individual brands to be reduced or redirected away from media advertising, although this was subsequently modified to allow individual brands also to be featured in the sponsorship (Murphy, 1999). Cadbury has a total marketing expenditure of over £1.1 bn, representing nearly 20 per cent of sales revenue, which is steadily increasing year-on-year. The marketing plan must thus ensure that spend follows the various brands' strategic priorities and focuses appropriately on markets highlighted for development.

Even the best-established brands in a market will have to work hard to justify their marketing budgets.

Source: Cadbury Trebor Bassett

We discussed budget setting, and some of the issues surrounding it, in Chapter 14 in a marketing communications context (*see* pp. 593 *et seq.*). Many of the points made there are more widely applicable, particularly the relative strengths and weaknesses of objective and task budgeting compared with methods based on historical performance (for example basing this year's budget on last year's with an arbitrary 5 per cent added on).

Marketing controls and evaluation

Control and evaluation are both essential if managers are to ensure that the plans are being implemented properly and that the outcomes are those expected. As part of the planning process, therefore, managers will have to specify what will be measured, when, how and by whom. Although the defined marketing objectives provide the ultimate goals against which performance and success can be measured, waiting until the end of the planning period to assess whether they have been achieved is risky. Instead, managers should evaluate progress regularly throughout the period against a series of benchmarks reflecting expected performance to date. If, for example, the overall objective is a 20 per cent increase in volume sales over 12 months, managers might expect after three months to see at least a 5 per cent improvement on the equivalent figure for the previous year, as strategies begin to take effect and gather momentum. At that three-month staging post, managers can then decide whether their strategies appear to be well on target for achieving objectives as planned or whether the deviation from expected performance is so great that alternative actions are called for.

Control and evaluation can take either a short- or a longer-term perspective. In the short term, control can be monitored on a daily basis through reviewing orders received, sales, stockturn or cash flow, for example. Longer-term strategic control focuses on monitoring wider issues, such as the emergence of trends and ambiguities in the marketing environment. This has strong links with the marketing audit, assessing the extent to which the organisation has matched its capabilities with the environment and indeed the extent to which it has correctly 'read' the environment.

This whole area of control and evaluation will be considered in greater detail at pp. 928 *et seq.*

Market potential and sales forecasting

The extent to which plans can be successfully implemented depends not only on managers' abilities in setting and implementing strategies, but more fundamentally on their ability to predict the market accurately. This means two things: first, assessing the market potential, that is, working out how big the total cake is, and second, forecasting sales, that is, calculating how big a slice of that cake our organisation can get for itself. The following subsections will look at both of these areas, especially the factors influencing their calculation and the methods used.

Market and sales potential

The concept of **market potential** is very simple, but in practice it is very difficult to estimate. Market potential is the maximum level of demand available within the total market over a given period, assuming a certain level of competitive marketing activity and certain conditions and trends in the marketing environment. This definition immediately raises problems in calculating a figure for market potential, as it involves many assumptions about competitors and the environment, needs a precise definition of 'the market' and requires methods of quantifying the variables concerned.

Market potential

We now look more closely at some of the difficulties in estimating market potential.

Maximum level of demand. The calculation of maximum level of demand should be product or service specific, and means calculating the demand if all possible buyers were to purchase to their fullest realistic extent in terms of volume and frequency. It is an idealised concept that is difficult to measure, for many reasons. For example, any individual's decision about whether to purchase, how much and how often is, in practice, influenced by many factors. One factor is marketing activity, such as campaigns encouraging product substitution or increased consumption. If market potential is partially dependent on marketing effort, then a range of alternative 'maximum levels of demand' become immediately possible.

Total market. The potential total market is really a question of boundaries. In the same way that calculation of profit can vary according to the way in which an accountant interprets the rules, total market size can vary according to the definitions used to mark market boundaries.

Level of competitive activity and trends in the marketing environment. As we showed in Chapter 2, the marketing environment is a very dynamic and complex phenomenon that has a fundamental impact on the organisation. A change in any aspect of the marketing environment can, therefore, have a corresponding effect on market potential. Competitors can also implement strategies that change the nature of the market as a whole, either by opening up new segments, increasing demand through marketing communication efforts, or by launching new products that effectively create a new market.

eg

There is a well known story of the shoe sales representative arriving in a remote Amazon jungle community to find that none of the locals are wearing shoes. Is this a hopeless market with no potential, or a prime market for development? A similar problem faced Kooshies Baby Products from Canada when it sought to launch non-disposable nappies onto the Chinese market as part of a joint venture with a flannel cotton products company in China. Unlike Kooshies' other international markets, China was not used to non-disposable, flannel nappies, and has a preference for brushed cotton. Flannel is considered inferior and the Chinese are less interested in the environmental aspects of nappy use. Just 20 Kooshies non-disposable nappies can replace up to 7,000 disposable ones. Other product adaptations were necessary: white waistbands were associated with funerals and animal patterns on nappies were not appreciated. So, just what is the Chinese market potential? Twenty million babies are born in China each year, but how many of those can be considered as representing real market potential given the environment described? What is the sales potential for Kooshies and is it worth the risk and the investment required to develop it (Gamble, 2001)?

Over time, market potential will change, depending on the forces at work. All of these forces are beyond the organisation's control, yet the organisation has to try to predict them. It is also important when looking at the environment to be clear about the time period being considered, the stage of growth reached by the market, and the rate of change, especially in technology that is likely to affect the environment. Clearly, the further ahead the organisation is looking, the greater the uncertainty in predictions.

Sales potential

Even after the potential has been estimated for the market as a whole, an organisation will then need to determine its own **sales potential**, that is, the share of the market that it could reasonably expect to capture. Obviously, sales potential is partly a result of the organisation's marketing effort and its success in attracting and holding customers. Although the level of total market potential will create a ceiling for an organisation's individual sales potential, in reality sales potential should be based on a clear understanding of the relative success of individual organisations' marketing efforts. The decision to launch a new range or to increase promotional expenditure could help to raise the level of sales potential. As already mentioned, in some situations the actions of an individual organisation can increase the potential for all competitors by expanding the market potential as a whole. Thus if a

The Gambia Tourist Authority believes that there is considerable sales potential for the Gambia as a tourist destination and has a target of attracting 1 million tourists to the country by 2020. Measuring potential is not easy, although there is considerable data on tourism trends worldwide. It is known that 100,000 tourists visit the Gambia each year, but an increase in the Gambia's share can only come from a combination of favourable trends in international demand and the competitiveness of the Gambia's offering. Forecasts suggest that tourism to Africa will grow from 28 million visitors in 2000 to 77 million by 2020, and worldwide tourism demand will grow to 1.6 billion tourists. On that basis, 1 million may appear modest but it still means ensuring that the mix of facilities, attractions and overall tourist products and services is sufficient to realise the potential. It is still regarded as a relatively unknown destination but it is competitively priced compared with other packages from Europe (Sonko, 2002).

major player in the market or a number of competitors increase their promotional spends, that might stimulate the market for all competitors, not just those undertaking the marketing effort.

Having a clear idea of market and sales potential provides a useful input to the marketing planning process. It is especially important for planning selling efforts and allocating resources. The allocation of sales force effort, and the establishment of distribution points and service support centres, for example, can reflect sales potential rather than actual sales, thus allowing scope for expansion. Similarly, sales potential can also be used to plan sales territories, quotas, sales force compensation and targets for prospecting.

Estimating market and sales potential

The methods used for estimating sales and market potential will vary, depending on just how new or innovative the product or service is, and how mature the market is. The two main groups of methods discussed here are *breakdown*, that is, working from the aggregate level of the whole market down to the segment of interest, and *build-up*, that is, starting with individual customers then aggregating up to industry or market totals.

Breakdown methods

Breakdown methods fall into two main groups: those based on total market measurement and those based on statistical series analysis.

Total market measurement. The total market measurement method begins with any total industry or market data that may be available from secondary research, and then breaks that information down to market segment level and thence to the organisation's own sales potential. This method relies heavily on the availability of a long series of data on industry sales volume and consumption by segments within that market, but rarely are such complete and detailed data available. Potential is thus often estimated from what data are available and then adjusted to take account of the current marketing environment. Once market and segment potentials have been established, sales potential can be derived by estimating competitors' relative market shares and then calculating how those might change as a result of expected actions, for example a new product launch.

Statistical series analysis. Statistical series analysis is a means of calculating potential for market segments. It is based on developing a statistical relationship, correlating sales and key factors influencing them. The success of this method depends on identifying the right factor or combination of factors (i.e. statistical series) to use in the analysis. Cox (1979), for example, quotes the case of a company trying to establish potential for production machinery. The analysis was based on a single factor, the number of production employees within each industry using that kind of equipment. Several other statistical series, such as expenditure on new equipment and value of products shipped, had been tested but discarded. In some industries, the appropriate factor to use is fairly obvious. The potential for building material sales in a region, for example, is closely related, as one might expect, to the number of building contracts and the size of their floor area. The calculation might be further influenced by weightings reflecting managerial judgements on the relative importance of segments and the likely effect of other environmental factors on the future development of those segments. Thus knowledge that the authorities in a certain region are about to invest in an extensive campaign to attract new industry into its neighbourhood might make the building materials company weight that region more highly than a similar region with lower future growth prospects.

Build-up methods

There are three main methods for aggregating data to produce reliable market and sales potential figures: census, survey and secondary data.

Census. The census method is based on a detailed consideration of every buyer and potential buyer in a market. This may be difficult, if not impossible, in mass consumer markets, but is more feasible in industrial situations, where demand might be concentrated and orders infrequent but of high value. With large capital plant, such as turbine generators or aircraft engines, for instance, a census could provide a good indication of market and sales potential as the customer base is very small. The market potential is effectively the sum of all the potentials estimated for individual purchasers.

Survey. The survey method is more widely used in consumer markets where a representative sample (look back at Chapter 6) of consumers are asked about their purchase intentions. This information can then be used as a basis for calculating total market or sales potential. The main problem, however, is that respondents might lie about their intentions, or fail to follow them through in the future. Consumers might well be genuine in saying that yes, they do intend to replace their car within the next 12 months, but an unexpected redundancy, repairs to the roof of the house, or the allure of an exotic holiday might cause them to revise their intentions. Even more problematic is establishing intent to purchase a particular brand. A consumer might genuinely intend to replace their car with a Ford, but if at the time of the actual purchase Renault or Volvo are running a particularly attractive promotion, then . . . who knows?

Secondary data. Finally, secondary data can be used to establish sales and market potential. Internal sales records can be used to predict individual customers' purchasing on the basis of past behaviour. In this approach, the sales potentials are produced first and the market potential is then derived from those figures.

eg

The headline claims that 'African cactus could help fight obesity'. If that can be substantiated, the market potential can be clearly defined, as the number of people classified as obese can be determined from secondary sources. A considerable percentage may be prepared to do something about it, so the potential could be estimated using various impact scenarios. Phytopharm, a UK biotechnology firm, is faced with assessing potential as it has isolated the important active ingredient of the cactus and is now undertaking safety tests and clinical trials. The current estimates for sales potential, around $4 mn a year may well turn out to be conservative, if the 'cure' is proven (Firn, 2001).

Market and sales forecasting

Marketing often plays a central role in preparing and disseminating **forecasts**. This is perhaps one of its most important functions, as the sales and market forecasts provided are the basis of all subsequent planning and decision-making within most areas of the organisation. Whether the organisation is a car manufacturer forecasting the demand for each model, a tour operator forecasting demand for specific destinations, or a university forecasting numbers of full-time, part-time and overseas students by programme area, the forecast is the starting point for all subsequent decisions. Get it wrong and the whole organisation can be caught out by major capacity or cash flow problems. In fashion markets, for example, it can

In the previous chapter (*see* p. 869), we considered the rivalry for global dominance of the skies between Airbus and Boeing. Both companies accept the view that the market for air travel will triple over the next 20 years, but they disagree on the structure of that demand. Boeing believes that the total demand will be for 18,120 new aircraft, of which only one-third will be large Jumbo-type models. Airbus, however, believes that the market will only be for 14,670 aircraft, but around half of those will be large variants such as the A380. With such a different view of the market, it is perhaps not surprising that each company is pushing forward different design options (*The Economist*, 2002). The differences are based on the assumptions that underpin the models for demand forecasting. The world's airline fleet was about 20,500 in 2001, but short-term changes are hard to predict, especially given the impact of September 11th 2001. In terms of world fleets, Boeing has over 10,000 planes flying (51.7 per cent) and Airbus around 2,550 (12.5 per cent) (Kingsley-Jones and Duffy, 2001).

be very difficult to forecast what styles are going to sell in what quantities, hence the popularity of 'end of season' sales as retailers try to sell off surplus stock. Holiday companies also find forecasting difficult, and again find themselves selling off surplus holidays at a discount right up to departure dates.

Forecasting and planning are, however, different functions. Forecasting attempts to indicate what will happen in a given environmental situation if a specific set of decisions and actions is implemented with no subsequent changes. Planning assumes that the environmental situation, especially that relating to the competitive arena, can be influenced, or at least better dealt with, by changing management decisions and actions. The focus of planning is, therefore, on alternatives and outcomes. Of course, there needs to be interaction between planning and forecasting, so that forecasts can be revised to take account of the new conditions likely to be created by the implementation of proposed plans.

There is no such thing as a rigid or absolute forecast. Different forecasters using different forecasting methods are almost certain to come up with different results. Forecasts should, however, share some common characteristics, as suggested by Wheelwright and Makridakis (1977). They should:

- be based on historical information from which a projection can be made;
- look forward over a specific, clearly defined time period;
- make clearly specified assumptions, since uncertainty characterises the future.

Forecasts often evolve from the general to the specific through a process of information assessment, sharing and iteration between senior staff, professional planners and line managers. This evolution allows managers to arrive eventually at a forecast based on an agreed set of assumptions regarding the industry and market environment, and compatible with planned effort at a corporate level. The process of reconciliation between the 'specialists' and line managers in sales and marketing is important for generating commitment and a sense of responsibility for the forecasts agreed. Genna (1997) in a study of purchasing managers found that only 59 per cent of them believed that the sales forecasts they received from sales and marketing areas were only 'somewhat accurate'. This calls into question the usefulness of those forecasts in guiding production planning. Another study by Mentzer and Bienstock (1998) found that 55 per cent of forecasters do not access market information when developing sales forecasts, so the problems of inaccurate and unrealistic forecasting are perhaps not surprising.

If forecasts are to be operationally relevant, they should progress through four levels of detail, so that formulating assumptions, identifying key trends, and operational planning and decision making can all be included. These four stages, proposed by Wolfe (1966), are shown in Figure 21.4.

Each stage clearly builds on the previous one, and thus the impact of changes can be traced throughout the process. A range of methods can be used for forecasting, depending on the stage being undertaken. Each method differs in its cost profile, complexity in preparation, rigour and ability to generate the range of projections needed to plan the next stage. The following subsection looks at a number of forecasting methods.

Figure 21.4 Four-stage approach to forecasting

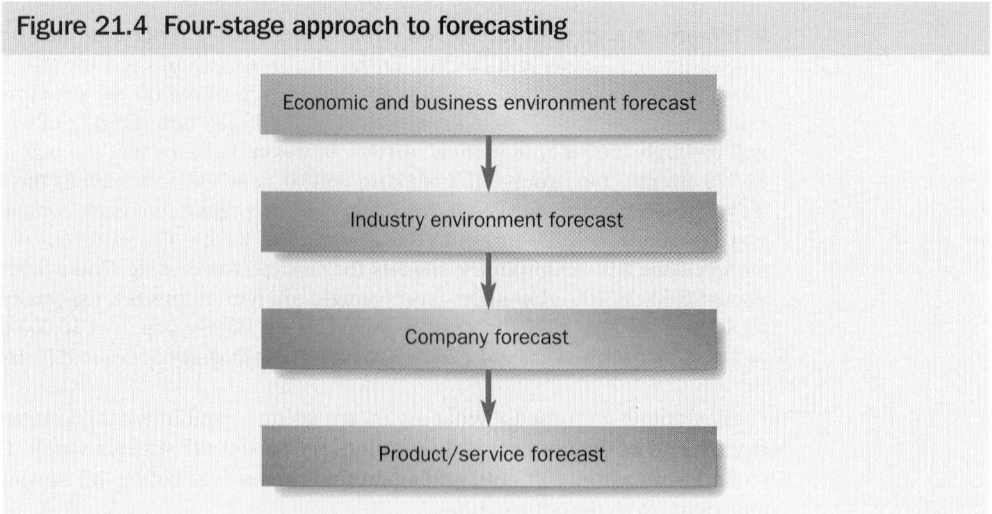

Forecasting methods

Forecasting methods fall into two main groups. *Qualitative techniques* are often used in the earlier stages of forecasting to describe the likely changes and to help define more precisely the assumptions used. *Quantitative techniques* tend to be used in the later stages, when production schedules and financial planning require hard numbers on which to make plans. All these techniques are shown in Figure 21.5.

Qualitative methods

Qualitative methods do not rely on hard, statistical data, but centre on 'soft' data based on expertise, knowledge and judgement. There are several methods of qualitative forecasting.

Management judgement. Management judgement is perhaps the riskiest source, as it relies on the people at the top or on experts within the organisation to predict what will happen. While the people involved may have a wealth of expertise and knowledge between them, there is a risk that they are too close to the organisation, its way of doing things and its markets to be truly objective. Their assumptions and prejudices may lead to an incomplete or inaccurate picture (Bunn and Taylor, 2001). Although management judgement does not lead to rigorous forecasts, it does at least encourage the systematic analysis and justification of available data and management attitudes.

Figure 21.5 Forecasting methods

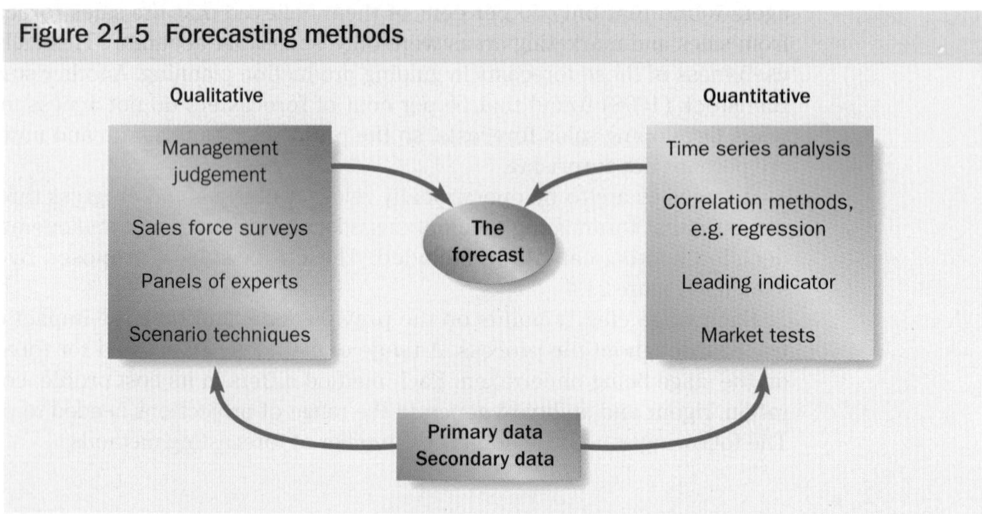

eg

Just how many viewers would a new BBC3 digital channel for young adults attract and what impact would it have on the other channels, especially Channel 4? These are important questions for the service providers and for the government which has to approve the plans. Channel 4 claims that it would attract millions of viewers and thus Channel 4 would lose substantial advertising revenue. In the longer term, that could strengthen still further the power of the BBC in broadcasting. The BBC claims, however, that it needs a channel like BBC3 to win back lost audiences. At the heart of the question is the nature and quality of the assumptions behind management judgements as to the likely level of viewer switching and new viewer attraction. Although forecasting models can be built to demonstrate interactions under various assumptions, it will still come down to executive and political judgement as to which forecast should be accepted (Douglas, 2002).

Sales force surveys. Sales force surveys can provide a wealth of information. Such surveys involve asking sales representatives to provide forecasts on customers, dealers, accounts etc. The sales force is a valuable source of expert opinion, since representatives are very close to customers on a daily basis, and will learn of likely changes in purchasing intentions early. As with a primary research survey, however, any forecast derived from this method should be treated with caution. In addition to any bias introduced by the customer, the representatives might also influence the forecast, either through naïvety or through consideration of their own agendas. A naïve representative, for example, underestimating barriers and constraints, might assume that when our new product is launched, sales to certain customers will boom. More insecure representatives might prefer to underestimate future demand and overestimate the barriers so that their own performance will look better. The cynical representative, on the other hand, might underestimate future demand because sales targets and bonus arrangements depend on it. Thus the more pessimistic the forecast, the lower the sales target and the sooner the bonuses start to accrue.

eg

Siebel Systems, a software company from silicon valley, uses its sales force judgement on progress with customers as a basis for sales forecasting. Sales representatives are expected to forecast future prospects with customers as well as indicating the number of sales that can be closed in the immediate future. This requires the sales staff to have a good understanding of what customers are likely to do and in part sales commissions are paid on accurate forecasting. By being able to rely on the sales force forecasts, judgements on new promotional campaigns, capacity planning and other marketing changes can be made ahead of competitors. It also enables better planning of the work of the sales support teams so that they can provide backup for individual sales staff at critical times (Kerstetter, 2001).

Representatives might thus be over-optimistic or pessimistic, or protective of their own position and interests, but rarely realistic. Management do, of course, recognise these biases, and try to make allowances for representatives' involvement, motivation and realism. Nevertheless, the sales force survey is still an attractive technique, as it slots into the existing structure of the organisation and can easily provide forecasts for individual customer groups, sales territories, areas, operating divisions or products.

Panels of experts. Panels of experts consisting of specially chosen eminent industrialists, economists, management consultants or academics, for example, may be asked for their opinions. These individuals are chosen for their sound knowledge and opinions of a market or its environment, and the membership of the panel will be balanced to represent a range of areas of expertise. The panel will be presented with forecasts and views of the future, and then asked to comment. The quality of the results will depend on the quality and commitment of the experts used, but even the best experts get it wrong sometimes.

Scenario techniques. Scenario techniques aim to provide a complete picture of trends and events to create a more integrated and complete view of alternative situations. Although a panel of experts can be used for such a purpose, the main method used tends to be the

Delphi technique. The *Delphi method* pools expert opinion, on the assumption that group opinion is better than that of an individual. It is especially useful for very long-range forecasting and technological forecasting. The experts used are not brought together, and they do not know who else is involved. Each one is questioned on issues and trends, then the collective responses are distributed to all members of the team with a further, more detailed questionnaire. This process is repeated until a rounded profile is obtained, the median of the group response. The main problem is potential bias, as members are influenced by feedback from the collective responses. For short-term, organisation-specific forecasts, the same approach can be used involving the sales team and managers.

Quantitative methods

The majority of quantitative techniques are concerned with the analysis of historical data to establish trends and make projections for the future based on a time series. More sophisticated models have also been developed, however, that aim to reflect the complex interactions between variables that help explain cause and effect, thus enabling the organisation to be better prepared for an uncertain future.

Time series analysis. Time series analysis is a means of using historical data to predict the future. Analysis of historic data can reveal patterns in the organisation's sales figures. These patterns include the following.

1 *Trends.* Extrapolation of data on a straight or curved line basis can give a broad view of the general direction in which sales are moving.
2 *Cycles.* These reflect periodic changes in patterns over a period of time. It is important to analyse the reasons for cycles. Some may be caused by external factors, such as fluctuations in the economy leading to upturns and downturns in business, while other short-term fluctuations could reflect the outcomes of successful marketing activities. Cycles may last years or months, and tend to recur. The UK's construction industry is used to 'boom and bust' cycles linked with the state of the UK economy. When the economy is depressed, nobody wants to build new offices, factories, supermarkets or other retail space. Furthermore, a long-term depression in the housing market means that there is little building work in that sector either. Normally, when the economy recovers, the construction industry follows close behind.
3 *Seasonality.* This covers shorter-term fluctuations around an overall trend, and may even be observed on a daily or weekly basis, if the organisation wants to get down to that level. Obviously, some markets are naturally highly seasonal, such as summer holidays, toys as Christmas gifts and gardening products, and any forecasting is going to produce pronounced seasonal effects.
4 *Random factors.* These are very difficult to predict, but nevertheless, any forecast is going to have to make allowances for the effects of strikes, riots, civil commotion and acts of God, as the insurance industry would put it.

At the end of this detailed analysis of trends and patterns, managers are better able to estimate the sales forecast for the coming period, perhaps giving pessimistic, optimistic and expected figures. Time series analysis builds on long-term trends and short-term fluctuations, and can be smoothed exponentially, placing more emphasis on recent data. The problem with time series analysis, as with any technique based on historical data, is that it assumes that things will carry on steadily into the future without any major deviation. This might be a reasonable assumption if the market concerned is stable and predictable, but a highly dangerous assumption in unstable, fluctuating markets.

Correlation method. If time series analysis is felt to be inappropriate, the forecaster might prefer to use a correlation method (or statistical demand analysis). Techniques such as multiple regression are, like time series analysis, based on historical data but instead of assuming that sales are simply a function of time, they try to identify other factors that influence sales. Thus, for example, sales of domestic conservatories might be expressed as a function of a number of other variables:

$$Q = f(x_1, x_2, x_3)$$

where Q is the quantity of conservatories demanded,
x_1 is disposable income,
x_2 is the cost of borrowing, and
x_3 is the number of households with gardens, but without conservatories.

By analysing statistically a series of historic data relating to Q and x_1 to x_3, an equation can be developed which gives the best explanation of the quantitative relationship between sales and the other variables involved. Thus analysis might reveal that

$$\text{Sales} = c + 3(x_1) + 50(x_2) - 0.05(x_3)$$

It would then be possible to forecast future sales by inserting estimated future values of x_1 to x_3 into this equation, or to forecast sales in a different region, for example by inserting known values of x_1 to x_3 from that region.

This type of method can be difficult to implement, since it needs an extensive historic data bank to work with if the best possible equation is to be devised. Managers still need to exercise a certain degree of caution when using such equations. The forecast is never going to be 100 per cent accurate, and there is still the underlying assumption that the relationship between all the variables is going to continue into the future in the same way as it has in the past. The main problem with using an equation like this for forecasting, however, is the estimation of future values of x_1 to x_3. Any unforeseen swings in their behaviour might render the whole forecast meaningless.

Leading indicators. Leading indicators are useful for shorter-term forecasting. These indicators give advance warning of trends and changes in the marketing environment so that the organisation can adjust or plan accordingly. The definition of the key indicators will vary from industry to industry. A carpet manufacturer, for example, might look at the rate of new business start-ups or the amount of new office space being developed (on the basis that new businesses might want to carpet their new offices). In consumer markets, the leading indicators might be house sales, the rate of new house building, or even trends in average disposable income or unemployment levels. These all affect consumers' willingness and ability to buy new carpets, and will have an impact on the type, quality and price of carpets that the manufacturer produces.

Market tests. Market tests, as discussed at pp. 368 *et seq.* give an insight into real behaviour rather than focusing on intentions. They are very useful as a part of new product development and launch programmes, and can help to forecast likely future performance. Managers need to be sure, however, that the structure of the test and the area in which it takes place are as truly representative of the target market and the planned marketing mix as possible.

Overall, the more cross-checking of forecasts that takes place using different techniques, the more tailor-made the techniques to suit the industry, the organisation's product and its target market's purchasing characteristics, the better and more reliable the forecast will be.

Primary research. Primary research looks outside the organisation by surveying customers. In a B2B market, key customers could be asked their opinions of trends and how their own consumption patterns are likely to change. In consumer markets, a sample of consumers within a segment could similarly be surveyed, although this is more likely to be part of a bigger quantitative survey. In either case, it is essential that the research is sufficiently deep to allow the assumptions underlying the respondent's opinion to be thoroughly understood. Respondents are not always willing, however, to give information or may simply not know much about the issues raised. There is also a risk that B2B customers may feel that they are being asked to reveal commercially sensitive information that might be used against them in future negotiations. This may lead to non-response or to lies! Respondents may even be over-optimistic about their own intentions so that when customer intentions to purchase are aggregated, the resulting forecast is far too high.

Secondary data. Some secondary data can also be used to help create a general picture. Organisations can make use of published research data (*see* pp. 230 *et seq.*), such as those published by *Euromonitor*, to validate their own understanding of the way the market is moving, to raise new issues, and to act as a basis for further detailed investigation. Similarly, publications by various banks and government bodies provide the kind of background information on economic and industrial trends, demographics and social trends that can lead to a deeper understanding of the marketing environment.

Organising marketing activities

Effective marketing management does not happen by itself. It has to have the right kind of infrastructure and place within the organisation in order to develop and work efficiently and effectively. First, therefore, we discuss the role and place of the marketing department within the organisation as a whole. That is followed by an overview of different ways of structuring a marketing department, and finally we consider issues surrounding the implementation of marketing plans.

Organisational location of marketing

Central to the marketing philosophy is a focus on customer needs. As discussed in the early chapters of this book, marketers act as an interface between customers and other functions within the organisation. By understanding markets, customers' needs and wants and the ways in which they are changing and why, the marketer is providing essential information for planning corporate direction and the activities of other functions within the organisation. The production department, for example, needs to know what products will be demanded, with what variations, to what specifications, in what quantities and when, so that they can plan to produce them. Most, if not all, of these decisions will be marketing driven.

So that marketing can fulfil its role effectively, therefore, and be taken seriously, marketing managers should be equal in status to senior managers from other functional areas. They also need to work closely with other managers, not just for information exchange but also on joint projects, for example new product planning and development, inventory management, physical distribution or logistics management.

It is important, however, to distinguish between a functional marketing department and marketing orientation as a management philosophy. A small organisation might not have a marketing department as such, but it can still practise a marketing orientation very effectively through the closeness of its relationships with its customers and its responsiveness to their needs. In contrast, any organisation can have a marketing department, yet not be truly marketing-orientated. If that marketing department is isolated from other functional areas, if it is just there to 'do advertising', then its potential is wasted. Marketing orientation permeates the whole organisation and *requires* marketing's involvement in all areas of the organisation.

Whether or not there is a marketing department, and how it is structured, depends on a number of factors. These might include the size of the organisation, the size and complexity of the markets served, the product and process technology and the rate of change in the marketing environment. There are several ways of incorporating and structuring marketing within the organisation, and these are discussed below.

Organisational alternatives

In thinking about how marketing might be organised, it is important to be clear about the tasks involved in marketing. Marketers have to research and analyse markets and customers. They have to forecast sales and then plan, develop, implement and manage elements of the marketing mix. They also have a wider corporate role in supporting the organisation's strategic development, interfacing with other functions. The marketer's focus is not just on today, but on the future as well. These tasks open up a number of choices for organising staff, delegating authority and responsibility and specifying line management relationships. The purpose is to clarify who makes what decisions and who is responsible for their implementation, and to ensure that all this is done at an appropriately senior level with proper monitoring and control.

There are four main choices for structuring marketing management within a department, focusing on function, products, regions or segments. The marketing department might also choose to develop a matrix structure, allowing an equal focus on both function and products, for example. These are all shown in Figure 21.6. The organisation might, of course, choose not to have a formal marketing department at all. Each of these choices is discussed below.

Functional organisation

A functional department is structured along the lines of specific marketing activities. This means there are very specialised roles and responsibilities, and that individual managers have to build expertise. Such a department might have, for example, a market research manager, an advertising and promotions manager and a new product development manager, each of whom will report to the organisation's marketing director.

This system works well in organisations where the various business functions are centralised, but problems can arise where they are decentralised. Then, functional marketing tasks have to be coordinated across diverse areas, with greater or lesser degrees of cooperation and acceptance.

eg

Many university marketing departments are organised on functional lines. A number of specialised roles concerned with public relations, print and prospectuses, advertising, schools liaison and market research can often be found reporting to a marketing manager. Product development issues and fees tend to be the domain of the faculties and departments rather than the marketing department due to the significance of academic quality control, curriculum design and delivery, often within a regulated setting.

Figure 21.6 Forms of marketing organisation

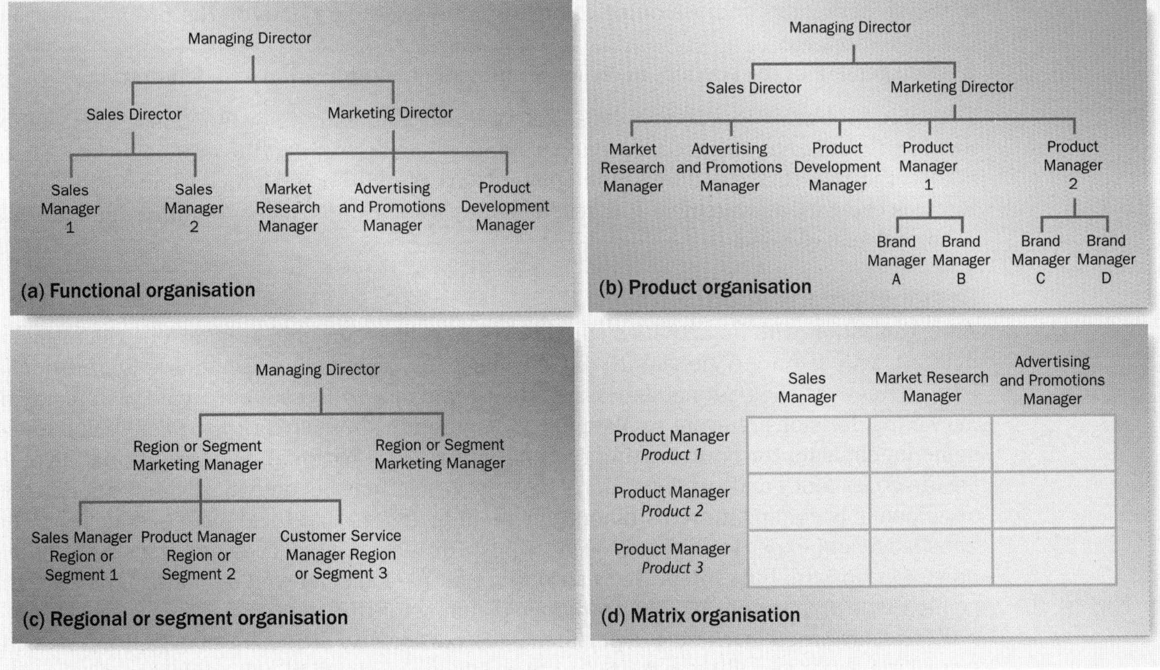

Product organisation

Giving managers responsibility for specific products, brands or categories of product might suit a larger company with major brands or with diverse and very different product interests. The manager, reporting to a product group manager or a marketing director, builds expertise around the product, and is responsible for all aspects of its development, its strategic and marketing mix planning and its day-to-day welfare. Other specialist staff, such as market researchers, might be involved as necessary to help the product manager.

eg

Cadbury Schweppes organises its marketing effort around its leading brands. Titles such as assistant product manager, product manager, senior product manager and group product manager are all used to signify different responsibility levels within the marketing department. The product managers are responsible for the brands and marketing mix planning for such products as Flake, Crunchie, Wisp and Twirl. Ultimately, all these positions report through to a marketing director at board level (http://www.cadburyschweppes.com). Siemens organises itself around its business portfolio, Information and Communications, Automation and Control, Power, Transportation, Medical, and Lighting. The individual groups are responsible for their own worldwide marketing plans and strategies, usually with the various regional or national units expected to support the activities with localised, but integrated, marketing plans. It is also important to ensure, however, that there is a lot of cross-group and cross-regional cooperation to maximise any market opportunities. Marketing staff are, therefore, attached to divisions but have functional and in some cases regional responsibilities (http://www.siemens.com).

The product, brand or category management approach is very popular in fmcg markets. It gives clear lines of management responsibility, but there is still a need for a central function to coordinate the overall portfolio. As mentioned at pp. 339 *et seq.*, there are potential problems with internal rivalry as managers seek to champion their own brands. A little healthy rivalry is not necessarily a bad thing, but it must not be allowed to get out of hand or to cloud management judgement.

The typical tasks of a product or brand manager include:

- the development of competitive strategies and plans consistent with corporate objectives
- the production of annual marketing plans, forecasts and budgets
- the design and development of support strategies for the sales and distribution team
- the gathering or commissioning of primary and secondary data on the product, market, competitors etc.
- management of the product in terms of innovation, modification and deletion.

The main problem with product organisation is working with other functions, such as production, finance, etc. to get the resources, attention and effort that the product needs. There is also the risk that too many management layers will be introduced, hence the move towards category management (i.e. responsibility for a group of brands) rather than individual brand management.

Regional organisation

An organisation with its activities spread over a wide geographic area, or one operating in markets with distinct regional differences, might find regionally based marketing responsibility attractive. The regional marketing manager, along with a support team, will make all marketing decisions relevant to planning and operations in that territory. There will then be some mechanism for coordinating regional efforts at a national or international level to ensure consistency and strategic fit. As larger organisations become more international, this approach is becoming more common. The main benefit is that local managers develop the knowledge and expertise to know what is best for their region. They can then develop the most appropriate, fully integrated marketing mix package, as well as contributing intelligently to the organisation's overall strategic planning for that region.

Regionally based marketing departments are particularly attractive to organisations with a great emphasis on selling in the field, where close coordination and control are necessary.

eg

Procter & Gamble (http://www.pg.com) approaches its organisational structuring on the basis of 'Think Globally and Act Locally'. The Global Business Units (GBUs) have worldwide responsibility for a defined set of brands. These GBUs cover the four main areas of the business: baby, feminine and family care; fabric and home care; food and beverage; and health and beauty care. The brand team is responsible for building the range and brand values and plotting competitive position in key markets. Ideally, a new product launch will be almost simultaneous globally, carrying a unified message. The team is responsible for the broad aspects of the marketing campaign and for specifying the production and packaging requirements.

P&G also has Market Development Organisations (MDOs) allocated in seven different regions. For example, the European headquarters are in Geneva. Some local modification of campaigns is possible to address local markets, for example in terms of pack sizes or distribution channels, and the MDO would specify how adjustment should be made. The MDOs would also have responsibility for the sales team and local sales promotions.

Every marketing employee fits into either a GBU or MDO team, although a small number comprise a corporate team. Most marketing expenditure is controlled by the GBUs and 80 per cent of market research is also undertaken by those teams. PR is, however, split 50:50 between the MDOs and the corporate team reflecting the distinction between PR supporting local marketing effort and corporate PR, as considered in Chapter 19.

It is also appropriate for service industries, such as hospitality, where local conditions may differ and where, again, close control and coordination of service delivery are required.

Segmental organisation

An organisation that serves diverse groups of customers with very different needs might choose to develop marketing teams dedicated to each of those groups. This is because the marketing decision-making and the marketing mixes have to be tailored to the individual needs of segments in which the competitive threats may be very different.

A brewery, for example, will market to the licensed trade (for instance pubs and clubs) and the retail trade (for instance supermarkets and off-licences) very differently; a manufacturer of wound dressings will market differently to the hospital sector and to the pharmacist; a car dealer will market differently to the family motorist and to a fleet buyer. The volume purchased by individual customers within the same segment might create differences that are reflected in the marketing effort. An fmcg manufacturer will create a different kind of marketing mix and customer relationship with the top six multiple supermarket chains than with the many thousands of small independent grocers.

The marketing manager for a particular segment or customer group will have a range of specialist support staff and will report to a senior marketing manager or director with overall responsibility for all segments.

Matrix organisation

A matrix approach allows the marketing department to get the best of more than one of the previous methods of organisation. It can be particularly useful in large diverse organisations or where specialists and project teams have to work on major cross-functional activities, for example PR, new product development or marketing research programmes.

eg

The Cendant (http://www.cedant.com) leisure and direct marketing holding company manages through a matrix structure, with each business unit supported by marketing specialists working across the company. This enables a wider cross-fertilisation of ideas into divisions, for example the direct marketing company can be used to promote discount travel services and hotel reservations.

No department

Of course, another option is not to have a department at all. Small organisations might not be able to afford specialist marketing staff and thus perhaps the owner finds himself or herself performing a multi-functional role as sales representative, promotional decision maker and strategist rolled into one. If a small organisation does decide to invest in marketing staff, the recruit might be put into an office-based administrative support role or into a sales role.

Sales-driven organisations

Some organisations are still driven by sales. They might have a few very large customers and be selling a complex technology. In such a case, the role of marketing is relegated to a support role that is largely concerned with PR and low-key promotional activity. Other organisations, particularly those currently or previously in the public sector, are still in the process of developing marketing departments. Universities, for example, are reappraising the role of marketing. Although they might have marketing departments, many of the key variables are beyond the control of their marketing managers. For example, academics, with or without the benefit of market research, develop and validate new courses; in another area, domestic full-time student fees and student numbers are agreed with the government. Often, universities see the marketing department's role as purely functional, handling student recruitment fairs, prospectuses, schools liaison and advertising. In short, there is no guarantee that having a department means that there will be a marketing orientation in the organisation.

Controlling marketing activities

Control is a vital aspect of implementing marketing plans, whether strategic or operational. It helps to ensure that activities happen as planned, with proper management. It also provides important feedback that enables managers to determine whether or not their decisions, actions and strategies are working appropriately in practice.

Strategic control takes a wide, long-term view, considering whether the overall marketing strategy is actually driving the organisation in the desired direction. This is normally assessed through the marketing audit process outlined at pp. 906 *et seq.* and is often conducted on an annual basis, either as a special *ad hoc* process or as part of the marketing planning cycle. *Operational control* takes a shorter-term view, checking whether detailed, functional marketing programmes are actually working in practice. These checks can take place on a daily basis if necessary, and certainly happen frequently enough to determine whether problem areas are developing. Operational control needs to pick up problems early, before too much damage is done, so that corrective action can be taken more easily. Designing an effective control system to suit the needs and characteristics of the organisation is a critical part of managing marketing effort.

The marketing control process

The marketing control phase, shown in Figure 21.7, is not an afterthought to be bolted on to the end of the planning process, but should be designed as an important part of that process. In setting marketing objectives, it is important to define them in terms of detailed time-specific goals against which performance can be measured. This makes the task of control more manageable, since those areas where serious deviation is occurring can then be easily diagnosed. Management effort can thus be focused on areas of greatest need rather than being spread too thinly.

When setting performance targets for marketing activities, however, it is important to ensure that they are realistic, that they can be measured and that the measurement criteria used are meaningful and relevant. This is especially important where managers' performance is partly judged by their achievement of the agreed targets. Typical measures might be sales volume or value, the number of new customers created, the number of enquiries generated, stock turnover, satisfaction surveys or relative market share. The MIS system considered in Chapter 6 should provide the essential flow of information that enables performance to be measured as well as highlighting emerging problem areas. This flow of data must, therefore, be timely and sufficiently detailed to allow deeper analysis.

Figure 21.7 Marketing control

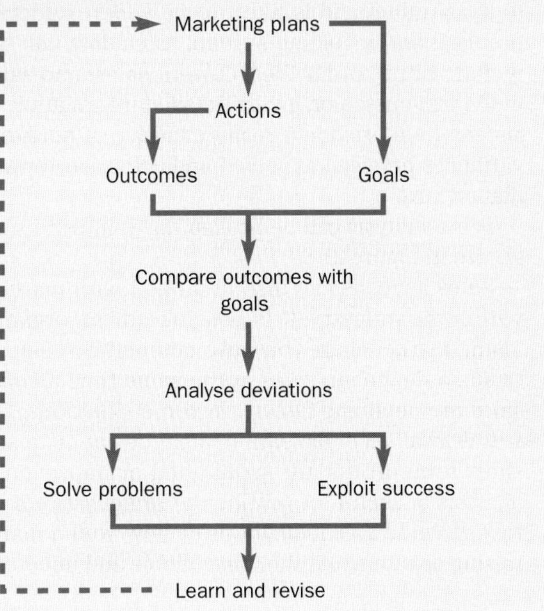

As soon as the control mechanism shows that a gap is opening between proposed targets and actual achievement, managers can start to look for reasons for this happening. Sometimes the reasons might be obvious, for example a stockout in a particular region or the loss of a major customer. In other situations, however, further research might have to be commissioned to support deeper analysis of the underlying causes. If, for example, a brand's market share continues to decline despite increased marketing effort, managers might start asking serious questions about customer responsiveness and the brand's competitive positioning.

Unless managers can be sure about why performance is off target, they cannot reliably define the right corrective actions. In some cases they might decide that no corrective action needs to be taken, in others they might devise a programme of major or minor changes to bring the marketing strategy back on track. Where a regional stockout occurs, the solution may be obvious, but if brand share is declining unexpectedly, a fairly radical revision of the brand's marketing strategy might be called for. Failure to achieve targets does not, however, mean automatic condemnation of the marketing plan and its manager. It could be that targets were hopelessly optimistic, in the light of the emerging market conditions. Alternatively, other departments within the organisation, for example production or logistics, may have failed to achieve their targets.

Managers should, however, be wary of overreaction. A certain amount of deviation is to be expected since no forward plan can be absolutely right. Part of the planning process is to agree what the threshold is between tolerable and intolerable deviation. Real customers buying real products in a real competitive market do not necessarily behave to order, and therefore some flexibility and patience should be exercised. There is also sometimes a lag effect between implementing marketing action and seeing the results of that action. Declaring a crisis and taking corrective action too soon might well be counterproductive. If, however, a major event happens that represents discontinuous change, corrective action might have to be taken long before its effects start to show in the computer printouts.

Methods of evaluating operational performance

There are several ways of evaluating marketing performance, two of which, sales analysis and costs and profitability analysis, are discussed here.

Sales analysis

Sales analysis is at the heart of any performance control system, as it most directly relates to the product and is likely to be widely understood across the organisation. Through the ordering and invoicing system, sales data can be accumulated within the MIS. These data include future order files, current sales, and sales history by product and perhaps even by individual customer, giving detailed information on location, price, quantity, etc. Sales analysis can thus provide a ready measure of performance to date, and through analysis of the variances between expected and actual performance, it can form a basis for planning remedial actions.

Sales analysis can be broken down into various subdivisions for more refined analysis, as shown in Figure 21.8.

Sales analysis can also be linked with market share analysis, reflecting general trends within the industry. It is possible for an organisation to have increasing sales, but to be losing market share (because competitors' sales are growing faster). Equally, it is possible to see a decline in sales at the same time as market share is rising (because competitors' sales are declining faster). In some situations, for example during harvesting and strategic withdrawal, an organisation might be happy to see both sales and share declining, as long as short-term profits are maintained or improved. Linking sales analysis with market share analysis is useful for putting the organisation's performance in its proper competitive context. It could give indications of how well a marketing mix has been formulated, as well as raising debate about the controllable and uncontrollable factors at work in the market.

Marketing costs and profitability analysis

Figure 21.9 shows the three controllable elements of marketing that contribute towards profit and those that create costs (Wilson *et al.*, 1992). Thus marketing profitability is created by what is sold, in what quantity and at what price, but reduced by the costs associated with achieving those results.

Although the categories of costs seem to be reasonably straightforward, it can be difficult in practice to identify and control some aspects of marketing costs. Wilson *et al.* (1992) suggest a number of characteristics of marketing costs that make them difficult to estimate, allocate or evaluate, a few of which are discussed below:

1 *Long-term or lagged effects*. An advertising campaign running now might only start to generate sales next year and the effects of that advertising might last much longer than the campaign itself. How should this be reflected in terms of profitability analysis?

Figure 21.8 Bases for sales analysis

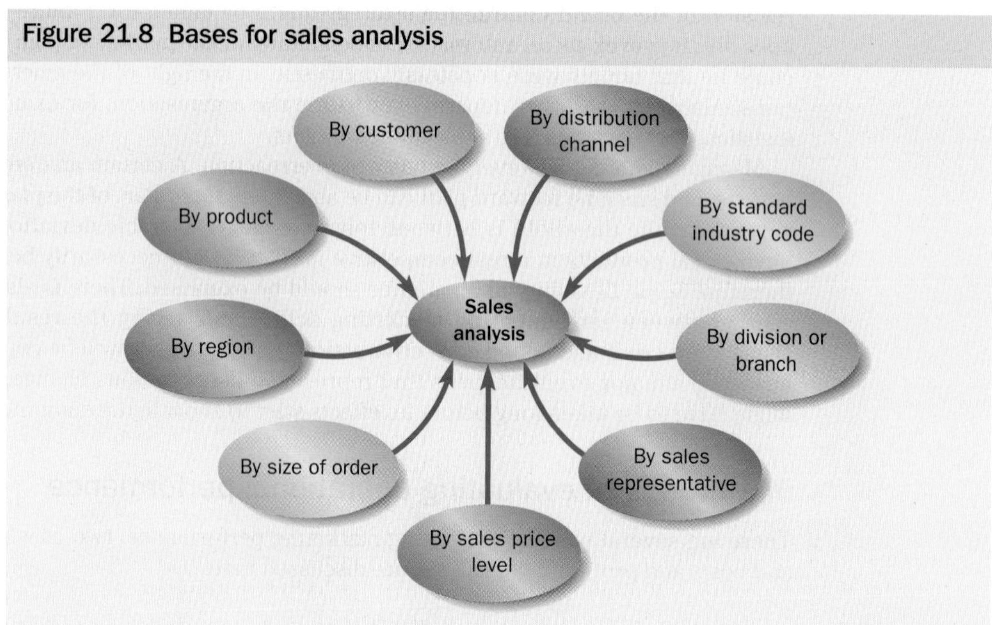

Figure 21.9 Marketing costs and profit

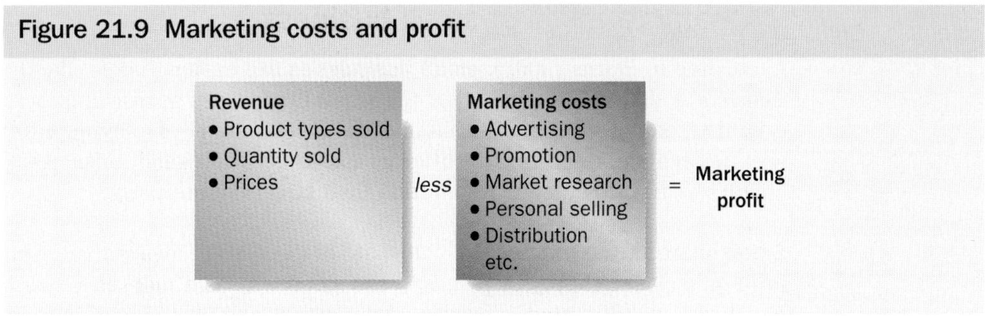

2 *Joint cost*. Some costs, for example corporate advertising or trade exhibition attendance, will be spread across different products, sales territories or segments, etc. Then there are the indirect central costs, such as general administration, some of which will be apportioned to the marketing department. What is the fairest way of allocating all these shared costs?
3 *Isolating effects*. Marketing results are achieved as a consequence of an integrated marketing mix and thus it can be difficult to isolate the influence of one activity and evaluate its financial efficiency. This is particularly true where there is close synergy between elements, for instance between advertising and sales promotion.

Despite such difficulties, it is important for strategic planning purposes to try to assess profitability by customer group, product, sales territory, etc., rather than just measuring sales. Conducting such assessments encourages managers to move away from the relentless pursuit of increasing sales volume as a means of increasing profit. Profitability analysis might highlight, for example, the fact that certain customer types, products, territories, segments, marketing activities, etc. are more lucrative than others. Certain combinations might be more attractive too. Customer A might purchase the same value of goods as customer B, but customer A might purchase more profitable goods from the range, demand fewer discounts, or be less expensive to service than customer B. It might, therefore, be worthwhile to invest more in developing a stronger relationship with customer A, or seeking more customers with a similar profile to A. Thus by focusing on the more profitable elements or combinations, the manager can increase the cost effectiveness and efficiency of the cash invested in marketing.

As an organisation becomes bigger and more complex, there is a greater need for analysis and control through formalised mechanisms. How costs are to be calculated and allocated should be clearly defined and the limitations of financial analysis in a marketing context should be understood. It is also important that there is close liaison between marketing and the accounts department to ensure that timely and appropriate information is gathered and disseminated.

Marketing planning for the smaller business

Although marketing principles, both strategic and operational, apply equally across all organisations regardless of their size, the application of marketing often varies greatly. A large business with a well-defined management structure and a strong resource base applies marketing principles very differently from a small firm with limited resources and managerial skills trying to establish itself or grow in the marketplace (Gilmore *et al.*, 2001). This is often reflected in the marketing planning process and the final marketing plans adopted.

This section examines the marketing planning issues facing the small business. After brief consideration of the definitions and nature of small business, the focus will shift to marketing in the various stages of a small firm's development from launch to maturity. Although there is some dispute over the actual stages of development and the criteria that should be used to describe them, small business marketing strategy will nevertheless be shown to evolve as the organisation changes and grows.

Characteristics of small business

According to Burns (2001), **small businesses** are easier to describe than define. Perhaps that is not surprising, given that the small businesses sector includes a large number of organisations at different stages in their development, displaying different strengths and weaknesses and operating in different markets. Often small businesses have a number of characteristics that identify them from their larger counterparts.

Small share of the market. A small share of the market means that a small business cannot influence either supply or prices in the same way as a market leader could. As previous chapters have suggested, however, a lot depends on how the market is defined. An organisation with a small share of a generally defined national or international market might nevertheless hold a dominant position in a specifically defined segment or niche.

Personal ownership. Many small businesses are characterised by the fact that it is not uncommon to find the owner at the heart of all the strategic decisions and in many operational issues. If the owner is not careful, however, this can lead to too much time spent on operational fire fighting, and not enough priority given to strategic marketing and external activities. The reality for many owners is that they are market analysts, strategists, sales representatives and service deliverers all rolled into one. Only as the business grows and a more formal organisational structure starts to form can the owner manager start to delegate and use specialists where appropriate.

Independence. This means that there is no external interference. A wholly owned subsidiary, for example, might have its decisions influenced by a remote management board. It might make its own promotional decisions, but have product range and pricing decisions imposed by the parent organisation. The small business thus has much more autonomy in its decision-making, but of course cannot benefit from the resources and expertise of a parent company.

Other differentiating factors. There are other approaches to describing the difference between large and small firms. Wynarczyk *et al.* (1993), for example, suggest that the level of uncertainty, the approach to innovation and organisational evolution are important factors that help to distinguish between large and small businesses. The degree of *external uncertainty* facing the small firm is thought to be greater than that facing the larger organisation. Without a diversified base of activity, any organisation can be vulnerable to sudden and unexpected changes in the business environment. There are also issues associated with *internal uncertainty*. In a smaller firm, the motivation and aspirations of the owner are key influences on the organisation's strategy and performance.

It has traditionally been thought that small firms are at the cutting edge of *innovation*. A greater degree of flexibility, a higher tolerance of risk and a willingness to enter non-standard niches are all held to be supportive of small firms' innovative approaches. By providing specialisation in product or service terms the smaller firm can exist alongside the larger operator. The smaller firm might be highly successful in bringing non-standard technology to a market, but unless the venture is carefully planned and resourced, it might lack the resources to exploit the opportunity effectively. The truly innovative small firm is the exception rather than the rule, however. Finally, a small firm can be distinguished from a large one by its tendency to evolve more quickly and change, often with step-like growth as particular projects achieve success. Each might require fundamental change within the business if it is to exploit the opportunity.

From a quantitative perspective a consensus is emerging across the EU for defining different types of enterprise, based on the number of employees (Storey, 1994):

- micro enterprises: 0–9 employees;
- small enterprises: 10–99 employees;
- medium enterprises: 100–499 employees;
- large enterprises: over 500 employees.

These definitions are not sector specific, where wide variations are likely and the 99 employees top limit means that the definition of small business encompasses both very small new starters and more established enterprises. For comparative purposes, this EU definition is probably the best available at a general level. Across Europe, small businesses, at least in terms of the sheer number of them, are the dominant organisational format. A recent European Commision report found that 99 per cent of all EU companies, some 20 million enterprises, have fewer than 50 employees. Although that does not reflect actual market structure, some will grow and eventually challenge the market leaders. Some will form the backbone of a competitive and knowledge-based European economy over the next ten years (Gribben, 2002).

Despite this level of economic and political significance, many of the special marketing problems faced by the small firm as it starts and grows are often ignored, compared with those of the larger organisation. The next section, therefore, turns to marketing planning during an enterprise's evolution.

Marketing planning during small business development

The business launch and development process can be generalised as a model, as shown in Figure 21.10. This model reflects the same basic concept as the product lifecycle (plc) model considered in Chapter 8. As with the plc, different businesses might exhibit very different profiles. Some might not even get as far as the start-up stage, if the initial business assessment appears to be too problematic. Others might never get beyond the survival stage as a result of a combination of marketing, financial or operational problems. Eventually, the owners might decide that the returns are not sufficient to justify all the risks and hours expended. The lucky and well-managed businesses, however, might continue to grow into ever larger organisations, becoming significant players in their industries. The rate of development of a small business might also vary depending on the nature of the industry, its stage of maturity and the degree of innovativeness of the new product or service idea. In the high-tech and innovative service sectors, growth can be very rapid indeed because of the faster rates of product adoption and acceptance. However, given that most businesses in Europe are small rather than large, the achievement of growth and significant size is the exception rather than the rule. The majority of micro enterprises start small and stay small

Figure 21.10 Business launch and development stages

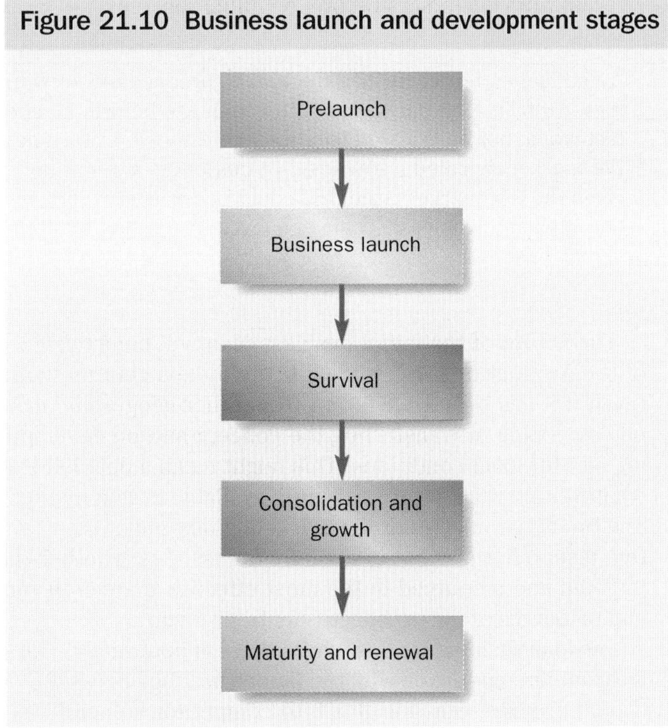

throughout their existence. They either do not want to grow or lack the marketing and management impact to manage the transition (Gallagher and Miller, 1991).

Each of the five stages in the development will now be considered in turn.

Marketing and planning in the prelaunch stage

The prelaunch stage covers the period up to the start of trading. There might be a few months or several years between a person first having the idea for a business venture and the launch of the business itself. People start their own businesses for many different reasons. Some are driven by a desire to succeed, and to experience independence and wealth through self-enterprise (McClelland, 1961). For others, however, it is not 'pull' factors but 'push' created by unemployment, frustration from being in a dead-end job, or other unexpected shocks to career or life development patterns (Birley, 1989). This latter group is less likely to be opportunity or wealth driven and more intent on making a living and surviving. Consequently, they might be far less market orientated. Many even lack any idea about which might be the best product or market area to enter. To this group, the idea of the entrepreneur as an innovator is rather a remote concept. Others may have acquired sector experience while in employment so may bring some market understanding and even contacts to a new start situation.

For example in the USA, 1 in 12 adults is trying to start a business compared with 1 in 67 in Finland (Campbell, 1999). In joint research undertaken by London Business School, Babson College and the Kauffman Centre for Entrepreneurship (http://www.entreworld.org), the conclusion was drawn that there is a link between economic growth rates and the number of start-ups, although it is of course more problematic to assess whether those start-ups are a cause or an effect of growth. Factors such as perception of opportunity, demographic profile, culture, education and the small business support infrastructure were all found to play a role in encouraging more start-ups.

Once the decision to start in business has been made, it is important to find an idea and then assess the chances of success carefully. This concerns far more than marketing issues and includes, for instance, staffing, finance, operations, premises, etc. Sometimes, these things are formally described in a business plan, but unfortunately many new businesses fail to give them serious consideration, and many assumptions and poorly researched decisions are used as a substitute. It is, however, often the marketing decisions that will determine the success of the business launch. The battle in any start-up situation is to generate sufficient revenue from customers before the initial reserves are exhausted.

eg

A budding entrepreneur had the idea to produce a boot warmer for those cold winter mornings. Switching on the warmer a few minutes before the boots were required meant that the feet would not be exposed to a nasty cold shock. Unfortunately, a preliminary assessment of the market revealed a low level of customer interest and questionable business viability given the low market price that could be realised. There was also general indifference from the retail and wholesale trade and direct marketing was not considered an option for a one-person business.

The nature of the initial business plan will be determined, in part, by the innovativeness of the product or service idea. If the idea is genuinely innovative in the planned market (even if it has been transferred from other geographic markets), the main focus should be on developing or transferring the concept and on developing the most appropriate marketing mix for local conditions. This might mean a detailed examination of current demand for whatever alternatives are currently available in that market, and their usage (*see* Chapter 5). The broad parameters of the marketing mix might then become evident from this comparative research, but what is actually the issue is whether that marketing mix is sufficiently targeted and resourced in the most effective manner. It must be compatible with the skills and resources of the prospective entrepreneur.

Particularly in situations where there is potentially a lot of competition, there has to be a clear understanding of why the launch will be successful. Market assessment and research should provide some insights into competitor vulnerability and weaknesses, and the sensitivity of potential customers to alternative marketing mix offerings. The entrepreneur should understand whether the focus should be on niching, service differentiation, pricing, branding, heavy promotional spending or whatever. For the inexperienced marketer, none of these decision areas is easy (*see* Chapter 20).

An important part of this process is the testing of the product or service idea. With a tangible product, it might be possible to undertake trials to iron out any problems before the full launch. In some cases, these might take the form of bench tests to minimise the risks of outright failure on specification/performance grounds. This might be followed or replaced by trials involving a sample of customers. The main risk, however, is of another organisation stealing the idea, if it is truly innovative. Many new starters do not have the resources to defend against such acts from larger, better-resourced competitors. Testing the product on real customers at the launch can prove to be even more costly and risky for the entrepreneur.

Marketing and planning for survival

After the initial launch, the emphasis in the new business is on ensuring survival. This means creating the niche in the market and using marketing tools to become competitive. The speed with which a market can be penetrated can often be over-estimated, however. Customer loyalty to existing suppliers or even risk aversion to changing suppliers can slow down the rate at which new products or suppliers will be tried. The time taken to locate potential customers, agree specifications, negotiate contracts, manufacture and deliver the goods, and of course to be paid can put a lot of pressure on cash flow. This is particularly acute for a manufacturing business where lead times can be prolonged. Service and retail businesses can generate positive cash flows relatively quickly, as long as sufficient attention is paid to creating customer awareness and willingness to try. It took nine months for an Irish manufacturer of diamond cutting heads to receive its first significant revenue from a customer. In contrast, a small bakery or takeaway business could generate customer revenue on day one. A number of factors will influence the ability to achieve a successful launch as shown in the following example.

eg

Andrew Barber and Robin Hall, both graduates in their 30s, both believed that the best rewards are gained from working for oneself and that they could design a better sports car than most, and so they decided to cut loose to design, produce and sell their own car. They spent many weekends and evenings building prototypes, but lacked the capital to take them into production. After seeking external advice, they decided to create a niche product and came up with a £26,000 V6 sports car concept, 'Census'. In 2000, this enabled them to attract £240,000 from two business angels, despite having no orders, to set up a factory in Brackley under the name FBS Engineering. The individual design and high performance made a big impact in motor shows and motoring trials and the Census was described by *Top Gear's* Tiff Needell as 'a real driver's car'.

The Census is positioned at a relatively moderate price against the BMW Z3, Alfa Spider V6 and Honda S2000 as a roadster that can achieve 0–60 mph in 5.8 seconds. To make acceptable profit levels, around 50 cars per year would have to be made, but by 2002 output was just one per month, with an expectation that this would increase during the year. The first sales boosted confidence, even though it had taken eight years from the initial idea to the first revenues being generated. Because of the company's size, the aim was to sell direct, either online or through motor shows and events. One of the advantages of being a niche player in the motor industry is that journalists tend to be interested in writing about something different, and in the case of the Census a steady flow of praise was received from the specialist press. This also avoided the need to spend heavily on advertising and to create a dealer network, although the owners recognise that dealers might become necessary as sales build up. Spares are supplied direct from Brackley and Ford dealers can be used for servicing as the Census has a Ford engine.

It is still early days for the business, and by mid-2002, breakeven had not yet been reached. There is, however, a waiting list for at least three cars and the first delivery took place in mid-2002. The emphasis must now turn to efficient production, a complex task for a product with 1,000 components, and to converting interest into sales at a rate that compensates for the steady outflows of cash. Around £6,000 gross profit is predicted when production reaches at least 50 cars per year. These are fundamental survival issues for many new small businesses, and time will tell whether FBS Engineering manages to achieve breakeven or becomes a casualty within the thriving low volume sports car industry. The early signs are encouraging, even if slow, and a left-hand drive version is under consideration to help open up the US and continental European markets in 2004. The company would develop a left-hand drive model earlier if a licensing agreement could be reached (Derrick, 2001; O'Donnell, 2001; *Warwickshire Choice*, 2001; http://www.fbs-eng.co.uk).

The Census: 'A real driver's car'.

Source: FBS Cars/Matt 1 600

Perceived, valued product differences. It is relatively easy for the entrepreneur to think that what is being offered is clearly differentiated from the competition and will be of value to the customer, but often the difference is either not perceived by the customer, or does not matter to them. Even where there is a technological lead, it may still take time for the product to be tested and evaluated.

Size of market niche. Even when some customers do find the product of interest, the size of the niche may be too small to generate a sufficient volume of initial or repeat business. Sometimes, the opposite might be true, and the market potential can prove to be too large. Full exploitation of the opportunity is beyond the resources of the individual operator. Better-capitalised and more experienced operators might quickly move in and start to dominate the market.

Market entry strategy. A well-thought-out entry plan in which all aspects of the mix are coordinated increases the chances of success. Areas of particular focus should include ensuring that product quality is maintained on a consistent basis and that there is a match between the product positioning and its price. Too low a price might mean that the business is not generating enough revenue to support marketing effort, and too high a price might not attract enough customers. Rarely, however, do the owners of small firms have a sufficient grasp of all the marketing tools and how they interact.

Ability to attract key customers. In manufacturing situations, the business launch is often based on promises of orders from one or two key customers. Attracting firm orders from these key customers could be crucial to the successful launch of the business. If the entrepreneur is completely unknown, it could take some time for potential customers to overcome the risks of dealing with an unproven supplier. The key requirements for winning orders are likely to be a combination of the product package offered and the way it is presented to the potential customer. Often, this latter point is overlooked.

Competitive reaction. It is surprising how often a small business start-up plan fails to take into account the likely reaction of competitors to a new entrant. Although clear market leaders might not be that bothered, other recent entrants and smaller operators might well increase their own marketing effort to combat the new threat. This could mean pressure on margins from price competition and the need for increased promotional effort from the new business. These two forces might not be compatible for the vulnerable and stretched new business, and result in stunted growth.

Distribution coverage. The best-laid launch plans can be thrown off course if the entrepreneur cannot gain distribution coverage. If the range is new, unproven and not supported with advertising and sales promotion, there might be little chance of getting shelf space in retail or wholesale outlets. Even if intermediaries choose to stock the product, they might not actively promote it. Direct distribution options are often not viable because of the cost efficiency reasons discussed in Chapter 12. However, the growth of internet usage is making online ordering an attractive option for some new-start businesses.

Awareness and interest generation. This is often a major challenge for the new business, as with a limited communications budget it could be very difficult to make any impact in the market. In B2B markets, the priority is likely to be to develop a campaign of personal sales visits, with sales letters and publicity material supporting direct sales. In consumer markets, the priority is often to create a basic level of awareness. Local media are often used, with the business graduating from the classified small advertisements to the display columns as resources grow.

Flexibility and responsiveness. During the start-up period, the entrepreneur has to learn very quickly from experience and try new ways of doing things. The business plan should have provided a general match between customer needs and the small business offering, but the start-up period enables the fine tuning to take place. Sometimes the changes can be very radical indeed as new opportunities are perceived. Those entrepreneurs who cannot learn, face failure.

eg

The Imray shop is located in the beautiful Fort Augustus area of the Scottish Highlands. It offers a range of gifts designed around Scottish culture such as history books, photos and art, music and so on. Loch Ness monster videos are, of course, a must. It also carries a speciality line in cross-stitch needlecraft kits as this could enable it to extend its reach beyond the typical English, American and German tourists. The owners, Cameron and Christine Donnelly, have tried to diversify their interests from an early stage to avoid the dangers of over-dependency on the tourist market. The UK foot-and-mouth disease crisis and September 11th, 2001 both hit the international tourist trade very badly. The Donnellys also have a B&B, operate self-catering accommodation and have another shop in Glasgow that has been rented out to a florist. Although revenue flows may be modest by the standards of many organisations featured in this book, the owners are being responsive and flexible to exploit new opportunities in areas in which they feel competent (Woodward, 2002).

Marketing factors are, of course, not the only consideration during this stage of development. All the business functions have to be well managed and mistakes can easily be made. Those businesses that cannot overcome the barriers might survive a year or two and then perhaps give up the struggle, if cash reserves do not build because of either poor inflows or poor expenditure management. Others move into the consolidation and growth stage.

Marketing and planning for consolidation and growth

The next stage occurs after the small business starter has survived the first year or so and has reached a position of having built a customer base and adjusted to the unexpected aspects of the launch. The character of the business might have already changed by this stage as a result of either new market opportunities, redefinition of target segments, or changes in the product or service concept emerging from practical experience. The first priority after survival is to consolidate any progress made. This might mean encouraging repeat purchases and expanding the customer base sufficiently to provide some security. Unfortunately, it is very easy for a smaller business at this stage to drift into a significant trading relationship with a major customer, as a result of which dependency starts to develop. The attractions of regular cash flow from a major customer are very tempting, but if the customer base is not diversified, the small business is extremely vulnerable to sudden changes in policy and buying patterns.

eg

Barefoot Books has successfully developed a niche in the children's publishing market. Its books are targeted at children up to 12 years old and are well produced to reflect themes such as folk tales and legends from across the world, as well as multi-layered early learning books, all with lots of illustrations. The two female owners started with very little, other than a talent for spotting a good story when they started in 1993. Gaining a market proved challenging at a time when education authorities were cutting back on book expenditure and large publishers were often reluctant to experiment with untried new books. Perseverance paid, however. Barefoot went for direct sales to the general public as well as targeting traditional book distributors and larger retail stores. The business now employs 28 staff out of offices in the UK and USA. The owners work closely with teachers, librarians, performing storytellers and children's theatre directors when formulating new themes and they are not averse to testing ideas on their own children.

The strength of the business has derived from careful selection of what is published and ensuring that the books have lots of child appeal in both text and illustrations. Since its launch in 1993, it has won a number of awards including the Books for Children Mother Goose Award in 1999 with *Tales of Wisdom and Wonder* and *The Gigantic Turnip* and the Oppenheim Gold Toy Award in 2000 with *The Animal Boogie* and *Mother Goose Remembers*. As business developed, the company made greater use of marketing activities, especially through bookshops. This has included in-store promotions, author and artist events, Barefoot newsletters, improved discounts and free listings, all in addition to corporate branding campaigns and online display and ordering (http://www.barefootbooks.com).

Consolidation assumes some kind of ongoing balance between cash inflows and outflows. Many small business owners are happy to stay at that level because they do not want to have to tackle the problems of growth or they feel that they do not have the capability to manage growth. The price for not moving far beyond survival might, however, be fairly low personal returns and a degree of vulnerability to external forces.

Only a small percentage of small businesses plan and achieve rapid growth. Storey (1994) argues that there are three key influences on the growth rate of a small firm. The first is the entrepreneur's background and access to resources. Factors such as previously acquired skills, education and experience might all play a part, but the central factor is often the motivation of the entrepreneur. Those who were 'pushed' into self-employment through redundancy tend to be less growth-orientated than those starting a small business for the attractions of independence and wealth (Kinsella *et al.*, 1993). The size of the company could also be a factor, as evidence suggests that the smallest firms are least likely to grow compared with larger businesses of between 25 and 49 employees (Hakim, 1989).

The quality of the strategic decisions taken once the business has been launched and has survived the difficult early period is of particular importance. The marketing areas that can be significant to the growth business include product and range development and refinement to better meet changing customer needs, regulations and competitive offerings; market development, perhaps reconsidering whether the original market niche pursued is still large enough to sustain the growth; professionalising the approach to marketing, perhaps taking the first steps towards developing a marketing plan to support planned expansion and to sustain business growth; and the strength of positioning because, as the business starts to grow, serious competitor reaction could emerge.

eg

The Iron Bed Company was formed by Simon and Ann Notley in 1994, survived the first critical years of business life, and has now grown to a £12 mn turnover selling traditional and contemporary style beds, most of which are made by the company itself, at above-average prices. It has grown from having two employees working out of a disused chicken shed to having 150 spread across 17 retail outlets in the UK and 4 in Germany. An important part of that success has been an ability to understand the market, to spot gaps and to pick winning designs. There have been cheaper imitations, but the focus on direct online and mail-order business enables selling prices to be kept down. The ability to sell direct and through directly owned retail showrooms, backed up by a prompt and reliable service, has also been critical. A deliberate decision was made not to sell through the trade as the owners did not want to lose marketing control nor to have to wait extended periods for payment. Using the shops and catalogues, the product range has been extended over the years to include linen, duvets, pillows and other accessories too (*Start and Run Your Business*, 2002; *The Sunday Times*, 1999; http://www.ironbed.com).

If there are real product or service advantages, a close match between customer specifications and the product offering, or a clear added value position, it can be harder for competitors to retaliate and the entrepreneur could have a slightly easier context in which to create and sustain planned growth. In order to do this, the entrepreneur will also have to learn how to use the marketing mix to good effect. If the organisation operates in a consumer market, very careful scheduling of media is required. Mass media are usually well beyond the limited resources available. Instead, targeted media such as specialist magazines can provide more effective communication, and direct marketing might also offer attractive and cost effective options. In B2B markets with clearly defined customers, there will be a need to ensure that regular contact is maintained and that suitable promotional material and exhibitions are used to support the selling effort. Where intermediaries are used, gaining their support will be crucial at this stage. This might mean gaining distribution or encouraging intermediaries to promote the product more heavily. Only by developing trade promotion policies can growth be maintained.

All these factors interact to encourage or restrict the development of the small firm. To cope with these forces, the entrepreneur must change and respond to emerging opportunities. The whole process will be highly demanding in terms of time and expertise. There are likely to be considerable demands on working capital for the growth business as the pursuit and achievement of new business drives up marketing and operational costs. This can lead to under-capitalisation that could restrict the pace of growth. Some businesses become high growth companies, star performers, that may become attractive to larger firms, as for example in the biotechnology and pharmaceutical sectors where innovative solutions have been found. Others may plateau and move into a steady state stage. Those who are better able to adapt and manage the market threats and opportunities will be better able to continue with high growth, reinvesting capital into further innovation.

Marketing and planning for maturity and renewal

This marks the end of the transition from start-up to established enterprise. The size and profile of the micro enterprise may have evolved to a small business or even to a medium enterprise with a management structure. At this stage, many of the marketing principles described in this book can become practical possibilities (Brooksbank, 1999). As the organisation grows, specialist staff in sales and marketing might be recruited, although the entrepreneur might still keep a close watch on key customers. The critical decision at this

eg

A packaging company specialising in shoe boxes decided not to seek further growth but to maintain sales to its established customer base. This was possible for a number of years because there was no significant market change. But there are risks in this approach. The company dealt with customers primarily by telephone and only visited them once every 18 months or two years. The company had little information about new opportunities or specification changes even within its core market, let alone the threat of new competition.

stage is whether to move forward with growth or whether to consolidate and primarily seek to retain market share. However, even then, no growth does not mean that there can be no change in the marketing and operation of the business (Gibb and Scott, 1985).

Even to stand still, because of turbulence and market forces, the entrepreneur might have to respond to new competitive threats, customer need changes and market dynamics. This could mean new products, product development and finding new customers to compensate for any losses. If there is no change and stagnation sets in, a decline may soon follow.

eg

Stuttgart-based Ejay was founded in 1994 by a former sound engineer, Helmut Schmitz, to develop music creation software. Although it took two years of research and development, in 1997 computer enthusiasts in the 15 to 35 age range were offered a software tool to create their own electronic music. It enabled those with only a limited knowledge of music to create reasonably good tunes. To generate cash during the development and start-up period, Ejay sold jingles and music tracks to local radio stations.

The basic product has remained unchanged since then but sales have expanded to new markets. It is claimed that Ejay has a 91 per cent share in Scandinavia; is a market leader in the UK and France; and even has a 12 per cent share of the large US market. Marketing has played an important part in that development. Ejay formed a partnership with MTV to broadcast tunes made by its software and negotiated deals with PC and computer hardware manufacturers to bundle its products with their equipment. It recently released an MP3 management software tool and is diversifying into PlayStation titles and mobile services for music fans. Nevertheless, the music software business still provides 90 per cent of its turnover (Benoit, 2001).

marketing *in action*

Driving a family business

Morgan is one of the smallest car makers in Britain, yet has an enviable reputation and a full order book for the next two years. Its two-seater, convertible sports car attracts an almost cult following across Europe which has been built up over many years through its handcrafted engineering, traditional workshop values and individuality. The company became especially famous in 1990 when John Harvey-Jones, the management guru, visited the company as part of a documentary series and concluded that it would go out of business if it did not change and reform its outdated and costly working practices. The company disagreed, perhaps not surprisingly, given that there was an 11-year waiting list for Morgans at that time, a situation that the MD thought was a sign of strength. John Harvey-Jones was pleasantly and politely told that he obviously did not understand Morgan.

Fortunately for the company, his son, Charles Morgan did understand the need to change, and when he took over as MD, modernisation started to take place within the context of the long-established values of craftsmanship and quality. Of greatest significance was the launch of the Aero 8 with a Morgan retro exterior but with state-of-the-art technology under the bonnet. The claim that it offers the comfort of a 7-series BMW and the performance of a McLaren F1 may be an exaggeration, but it does get from 0–60 mph in just 4.7 seconds due to its BMW engine and aluminium body. Despite the fact that it costs €80,000, the order book is full and extends for 18 months. The maximum a customer really wants to wait is two years, and after that they are prepared to surrender the €300 deposit and buy something else rather than wait any longer. Upgrading has also taken place on other models to bring them into line with EU emission regulations, drawing heavily on BMW which has also provided technical assistance. Lifecycles for Morgan models can extend over many years with only marginal upgrades.

In some ways, Morgan has thrown many conventional marketing techniques out of the window. The company rarely advertises, allows anybody to walk in off the street to wander around the factory at their leisure, and is planning a webcast so the prospective owner can watch his/her car being built day-by-day. The lack of conventional marketing does, however, cloud an astute appreciation of the meaning of brand heritage, values and appeal coupled with using scarcity-value to raise desire. There is a story of BMW engineers turning up at the plant in Malvern and being bemused as to how such a small company with tiny resources could generate the same sort of brand appeal as BMW with its 6,000 engineers. In some ways, even the limited production facilities are turned to advantage. Each car is valued and is going to be unique on the road. The German dealers are content with getting just 80 Aero 8 cars a year and even in the US, it is only planned to sell the Aero 8 through two dealers! And despite all the claims and counterclaims made about Morgan, it has been profitable for over 90 years and has been able to fund its new model without outside finance. The mix of family business values with the confidence to instigate change where it counts is clearly a powerful recipe for Morgan.

Sources: Hales (2000); Hutton (2000); Lofthouse (2002).

The stages presented in this section are by no means universal. High growth companies can move very quickly through the stages, often by large incremental steps as new projects are introduced. Others might stabilise very early and change very little, in line with the owner's wishes. This could mean that marketing is always treated as *ad hoc*, is poorly informed and is not integrated into the organisation. The attitudes, expertise and objectives of the owner or ownership team will be paramount.

Many small businesses have to run very hard just to survive. Many do not make it. As a generalisation, younger rather than older businesses are more likely to fail, very small micro enterprises are more vulnerable than larger ones and, most interestingly, those that grow soon after starting have a better chance of survival. It is interesting to consider some of the managerial deficiencies that can cause failure. The small business might fail (adapted from Burns, 2001) if:

- it cannot identify the target market or target customers;
- it cannot delineate its trading area;
- it cannot delegate;
- it considers advertising as an expense not an investment;
- it has poor knowledge of pricing and strategy;
- it has an immature understanding of distribution channels;
- it does not plan.

Marketing is indeed at the heart of small business development.

Chapter summary

- Marketing planning is about developing the objectives, strategies and marketing mixes that best exploit the opportunities available to the organisation. Planning should itself be a planned and managed process. This process helps organisations to analyse themselves and their marketing environments more systematically and honestly. It also helps organisations to coordinate and control their marketing activities more effectively. Planning should be a flexible, dynamic activity that is fed with accurate, reliable and timely information, and is not divorced from the managers who have the day-to-day responsibility for implementing the plans. Marketing plans can be strategic or operational. The plans help to integrate activities, schedule resources, specify responsibilities and provide benchmarks for measuring progress.
- There are eight main stages in the planning process: corporate objectives, the marketing audit, marketing analysis, setting marketing objectives, marketing strategies, marketing programmes, controls and evaluation and budgeting.
- In order to construct realistic plans, the whole area of forecasting is important for marketers. The more accurate the view of the future, the more appropriate the plans are likely to be. Forecasts can be general or specific, qualitative or quantitative. There are a number of forecasting techniques. The qualitative group includes management judgement, sales

force surveys, expert opinion and scenario techniques. Quantitative techniques include time series analysis, multiple regression, leading indicators and market tests.

- In order to fulfil its function properly, the marketing department should have a central role within the organisation, with senior management of equal status to those in other functional areas. It is also important, however, that the marketing philosophy pervades the whole enterprise, regardless of the size or formality of the marketing department. There are several approaches to structuring the marketing department itself. These are the functional, product based, regional, segmental or matrix approaches.
- As marketing plans are being implemented, they have to be monitored and controlled. Strategic control concerns the longer-term direction of marketing strategy, whereas operational control assesses the day-to-day success of marketing activities. Using information gathered in the monitoring process, the actual achievements of marketing strategies can be compared with planned or expected outcomes. Managers can then analyse gaps and decide whether they are significant enough to warrant corrective action. Although this can be a quantitative analysis, it should still be looked at in the context of more qualitative issues concerning customer needs and synergies between customers, markets or products.
- Small businesses tend to have certain characteristics in common: they have relatively small market shares, their owners tend to be closely involved in all aspects of both strategic and operational management, and they are often fully independent. Small businesses also face a high degree of uncertainty in their environment and can find innovation difficult because of shortage of resources. The four-stage model of small business development suggests that marketing plays an important part in the process of starting and developing a business. In the prelaunch stage, the entrepreneur must assess the feasibility and viability of the business idea. During the launch period, it is a fight for survival, ensuring that sufficient sales volume is generated to sustain the business. Many small businesses do not grow, but start small and stay small either because they do not want to grow or because there is no growth in the market. A small percentage of small firms do grow, some very rapidly indeed. This requires a more professional strategic marketing approach to maintain differentiation. The final stage, maturity and renewal, determines whether the business will grow even further to become a medium or large enterprise or stabilise. Stability does not, however, mean that strategic marketing can be neglected. Innovation in products and marketing might still be necessary to maintain the status quo. At any one of these four stages, failure can occur. Many of the factors contributing to failure are based on poor marketing.

key words and phrases

Control and evaluation	Market potential	Sales potential
Corporate objectives	Marketing audit	Small businesses
External audit	Marketing objectives	Strategic marketing plan
Forecasts	Operational marketing plan	SWOT analysis
Internal audit	Planning process	

questions for review

21.1 Define the stages in the *marketing planning process*.

21.2 What is a *SWOT analysis*?

21.3 What is the difference between *marketing strategies* and *marketing programmes*?

21.4 What are the four main choices for structuring the marketing department?

21.5 How can *operational performance* be evaluated?

questions for discussion

21.1 What is the mission statement of the university or college at which you are studying? From your general knowledge of the organisation and your experience as a customer, discuss the extent to which you feel it is fulfilling its mission.

21.2 Using whatever information you can find, develop a SWOT analysis for the organisation of your choice. What are the implications of your analysis for the organisation's short- and long-term priorities?

21.3 Discuss the importance of market and sales forecasting in the marketing planning process and outline the relative advantages and disadvantages of three different forecasting methods.

21.4 What kind of marketing organisational structure would be appropriate for each of the following situations and why?

(a) a small single product engineering company;
(b) a large fmcg manufacturer selling a wide range of products into several different European markets;
(c) a pharmaceutical company manufacturing both prescription and 'over the counter' medicines.

21.5 Discuss the role played by control and evaluation in both the planning and implementation of marketing strategies and programmes.

case study 21.1

Prudential (B): Moving from strategy to action

As mentioned in Case Study 20.1, The Pru's *Concerto* strategic review reorganised the UK business into seven or eight discrete strategic business units (SBUs). *Concerto* was run by a steering group consisting of the CEO, the financial director and four or five executive directors and senior executives. Each SBU team was effectively creating a new business and had to report back on its blueprint for organising and structuring that business unit. Once those new business units were set up they were run in two ways:

- developing their own internal SBU plans and managing their budgets etc.; and
- monthly meetings of all the SBU directors reviewing each SBU's plans and progress compared with its blueprint.

Each SBU has to add value if The Pru is to achieve its total shareholder return targets. Each SBU has to ask 'what do we need to achieve in terms of net profits etc. if we are to achieve our target total shareholder return?' This then filters down to divisional level targets. Every six months or so – sometimes more frequently – an SBU or several SBUs will come to HQ for a strategic dialogue. This reviews the management agenda, a series of issues that the SBU is trying to progress, for example trying to get unit costs down; trying to get economies of distribution lower; or testing ideas for increasing productivity. Within these dialogues, the team will make a presentation and offer analyses and plans for feedback and discussion.

The planning timescales are three- to five-year rolling plans with detailed targets and action plans spelt out. Each SBU is required to produce an annual marketing plan that guides the main activities for the forthcoming year. This is costed, agreed with the Executive Board and monitored through the year. Given the recent fundamental change in distribution strategy, marketing planning is especially important to ensure that changing customer needs are being met in a cost efficient manner. For the period 2001–2004, The Pru announced its commitment to take a further £175 mn out of the annual cost base to drive down expenses to just 1 per cent of funds being managed.

Within the marketing plans, there are a number of issues shaping marketing mix decisions as follows:

Place

There are four major channels of distribution, each of which has its own detailed plan:

- *Independent Financial Advisers.* Losing the direct sales force has made The Pru very dependent on IFAs. The Pru is also awaiting the outcome of the polarisation debate – there is some uncertainty as to whether IFAs will be permitted to become multi-tied. Currently, IFAs MUST be independent and broker the whole market. At the other end of the scale are tied agents (effectively a direct sales force) that can only sell one company's products. Multi-tied agents, i.e. representing two or three companies only, are not allowed. Depending on the outcome of the debate, the support strategy will have to be planned very carefully.

- *B2B*. This is potentially a very large channel and represents a good opportunity, especially since Equitable Life, which as The Pru's biggest rival in the corporate pensions market in this channel used to outsell it, has become a less potent force because of its own internal problems (*see* p. 729). There are 22 million employees in occupational pension schemes in the UK and 4.7 million have defined benefits. In B2B situations where The Pru and Equitable Life jointly provide products, the business has tended to shift towards The Pru. Another issue is uncertainty about what the government will do about stakeholder pensions. People are not taking them up so there is a possibility that the government will make them compulsory. B2B is thus a big channel with lots of potential. The Pru currently sells corporate pensions using sales teams of advisers who sell via tender to trustees. Having thus sold the corporate pension to the employer, The Pru then has to shift its focus to selling it to individual members of the workforce as participation in a corporate or occupational pension scheme is not compulsory. The employer and The Pru work together to distribute information and then a worksite marketing team does presentations. In some cases, contracts do not permit The Pru to cross-sell other products to those individuals – for example The Pru runs the teachers', but it cannot use the information it holds from that scheme to contact teachers and market other products to them directly.
- *Direct to consumer (D2C)*. The Pru uses a mix of internet, telephone, off the page direct response advertising, outbound telemarketing, and service mailings to existing customers. The Pru itself (disregarding its Egg internet banking subsidiary which is a separate entity) has a rather product-orientated website. Interested potential customers are faced with a 'key features' area and can download PDF files, but it is all organised around type of product rather than consumer lifestage or any more meaningful segmentation variables. The Pru increasingly has the ability to transact online, but its customers do not want to do this. The Pru's customers say that they want to speak to real people more often, depending on the product type. They want explanations and to be talked through the products on offer. They could, therefore, telephone through to a call centre, get the information and answers they want, then ask for a brochure and application form to be sent to them. There is also a lot of outbound call activity. The Pru called its top 500,000 customers and asked them what they wanted. They said they wanted The Pru to call them from time to time, so The Pru started doing just that.
- *Affinities*. In the wake of new market circumstances, there could be more scope for affinities, or strategic alliances between companies. A parallel is the supermarkets' arrangements with banks to market banking products.

Product

Some products, such as Prudence Bond, are designed specifically for the IFA market. The Pru has tried to simplify its products and the explanations of products to help the customer and better suit their needs. The B2B market is being driven by what is happening in stakeholder pensions. To serve the stakeholder pensions market, large investments in computer systems etc. are required which in turn means that high sales volumes are needed to generate any kind of return. Thus some sort of shakeout is likely to happen in this market, reducing the number of providers.

This part of the plan also incorporates new product launches. The Pru has prioritised high growth medium- to long-term savings products, including annuities, pensions, with-profits bonds and ISAs. Under the overall Pru brand name, new product variants are introduced. With a leading brand awareness position in the 45+ age group which accounts for 70 per cent of the savings market, some products are highly targeted to particular groups, e.g. pre/post retirement etc.

Price

This mix element is driven by regulation and competition. Some insurance companies offer a cheap headline rate, but cannot offer the quality of service to go with it when a claim is made. The Pru, it is claimed, does not offer the cheapest products, but it offers good value for money and good levels of service. Price is not the only consideration when selling direct but it does count up to a point: although some life insurance and some annuities are sold mainly on price, The Pru seeks to ensure that security and branding issues count too.

Pricing can be complex. Some annuities are priced daily. For planning purposes, an assumed margin and an assumed level of charges are fed into the equation to calculate probable profitability. Virtually everything is assumption-driven as things like stock market returns, mortality rates and morbidity can be unpredictable. The only certain thing is expenses! Anything with life content is changeable on pricing. For example, at the height of the AIDS scare in the late

1980s/early 1990s, life insurance prices shot up, then slowly came down as it became clear that the impact of AIDS was less than had been feared.

There is a great need to understand the sensitivity of the customer to price and what kind and level of incentives, financial or otherwise, will make products more attractive.

Promotion

In B2C markets, The Pru had not been involved in above-the-line advertising. This was seen as wasteful and unnecessary given the then presence of the DSF. The emphasis since DSF closure has been on direct marketing service mailings and on the IFA market. Each campaign is carefully planned and fully integrated. Some promotions, are run through IFAs. B2B communications take place through the workplace via seminars and the client company's intranet.

Of course, not all customers can be spoken to directly. Some have opted out via MPS and TPS, others cannot be contacted because of the ban on cross-selling to corporate pension scheme members. Nevertheless, since the closure of the direct sales force, the amount of D2C communication has gone up massively. Even smaller campaigns can be very effective if they are properly targeted. The Pru mailed a one-sided A4 letter to pension holders at the tax year-end. The letter invited them to contact The Pru if they wanted to put a lump sum into their pension fund. That letter generated business very cost effectively. Telemarketing is also considered to be effective. The conversion rate over the telephone is about 20 per cent of inbound callers.

Managing the database is a challenge to The Pru as although it has about 6 million customers, that figure represents the number of lives insured or assured and they are not all separate customers (for example a husband and wife taking out a joint policy are not separate customers even though both are counted as part of the 6 million). Also, a lot of those customers have policies that are not being paid any more, for example if you left a job and stopped paying into its associated pension scheme 10 years ago, you remain on The Pru's books as a customer until you retire. This means that the database has to be carefully managed and categorised to ensure that customers can be grouped according to likely response to different approaches.

The Pru will have to learn quickly to master D2C marketing techniques. The major strength of the DSF was that it helped create high brand awareness levels among those who are currently over 45 years old. By definition that group will decrease in numbers. The 25–34 age group will have a lot less exposure to The Pru unless the D2C campaigns help build the same sort of awareness that the DSF achieved with the older groups.

The Pru is new to the D2C market and is up against a number of other companies that have had a head start in online marketing operations. Market research and analysis has been extensive to understand better what the consumer wants, how the market is segmented and structured, and what competitors are doing, especially in key segments. Focus groups were held, for example, to find out what customers wanted from ISAs (although a subsequent test market of a product developed from this overturned those focus group findings!). In designing products, a lot of thought is given to competitors' positioning and ensuring that The Pru product has a clear differential advantage. Innovation is also being driven by the existing customer base with maturing policies, in terms of investigating what those customers are planning for that money. Nevertheless, it is still a challenge to ensure that the direct marketing plan can create the same pre-eminence that the DSF used to provide just ten years ago.

Source: With grateful thanks to Neil Bradley, Business Development Director – Direct Distribution, Prudential.

Questions

1 Why is a formal approach to marketing management and planning so important for a company like The Pru? How important is the role of the *Concerto* steering group in helping SBUs to develop and implement plans?

2 How might The Pru go about assessing market and sales potential for corporate pensions?

3 Using the information in Case Study 20.1 as well as in this one, outline a rough SWOT analysis for The Pru.

4 What do you think are the biggest issues that would have to be addressed in developing marketing plans for the D2C SBU?

case study 21.2

Chuft Toys and Gifts

Chuft Toys and Gifts, launched in 1992, is a small business manufacturing a range of specialist wooden toys. After graduating, both partners in the business became quickly disillusioned with working in large companies and met each other by chance while backpacking in Australia. Although their degrees were in production engineering and product design technology, their first business venture was developing a backpacker's travel guide based on their first-hand experiences. This guide still survives today. However Chuft, the young entrepreneurs' second venture, was the real basis for developing a full-time business. Sales grew from £150,000 in the first year to £500,000 by year four.

The initial product was a wooden steam train whistle, which they designed. The prototype and first production run were produced in a draughty garage at the home of one of the partners. They both enjoyed the fun of designing and establishing the most appropriate way of manufacturing the early batches. They approached the heritage line, the North Yorkshire Moors Railway, which agreed to place a pilot order in its station shops to see how well the whistles sold. To everyone's surprise, 30 whistles were sold in one weekend. Chuft thus made the transition from being a possible enterprise to being a trading concern. The partners managed to raise capital for production machinery and found premises in an Enterprise Centre. Although resources were tight, they had just sufficient to build a basic business infrastructure.

The company now sees itself as primarily being in the gift market. The steam train whistle, with a few variants, is still the company's core line, although other products have also been developed, including low-priced wooden novelties and puzzles and 'equilibria', balancing wooden clowns. Another range is 'Toys With Noise', a tractor, a traction engine, a steam engine, a fire engine and a police car, each of which makes a suitably characteristic noise when pushed or blown. Chuft also markets a whistling train, comprising a wooden locomotive, caboose and carriage as a boxed set. The locomotive whistles when you blow into the cab.

A common characteristic of all the toys and gifts is the high quality of the materials and finish, and the attention paid to packaging, which follows a strong, unified and coherent design and image. Considerable thought has gone into the colours, materials, information provided and not least the shape of the packaging, so that it stands out in display areas and communicates the product's quality. Wooden toys and gifts tend to be bought on impulse rather than as planned purchases. Although cheaper alternatives are available, the quality positioning commands an above average price and this is supported by a selective distribution strategy.

Finding the best price and trade margin took some time, a few mistakes, and considerable trial and error. Initially, the toys were exhibited at national and regional toy and trade fairs. The partners decided to expand further, however, by carefully selecting outlets that valued premium quality rather than cheap products. These included preserved railways, Harrods, Jenners (Edinburgh), the National Trust and other heritage sites. One of the partners was responsible for selling while the other managed production. They did not meet very much sales resistance, as they allowed retailers to try small pilot orders to assess whether larger-volume sales could be realised.

While they expanded steadily in the home market, the first export enquiries were received. This was a source of surprise to the partners. Attendance at exhibitions generated the enquiries that soon led to further trial orders. There was no plan to move into exports or to modify their activities to suit export markets. Orders from these buyers were taken on a reactive basis, with the view 'Why refuse an order?' This exposed the partners to some of the problems of exporting, including documentation and procedures. From these initial export orders, a number of buyers suggested that they themselves should become agents for Chuft in their own markets. Chuft did not feel that it had the resources to become directly involved in developing new markets, so any arrangement with foreign intermediaries was considered appropriate.

Although no major changes in the marketing mix took place for export customers, a number of new decisions had to be made. First, changes were made to the product packaging to emphasise 'Heritage' and 'Britishness' as the selling points, thus taking into account comments from the foreign buyers. New languages such as French, Japanese and German were introduced to the packaging. Price setting was never very sophisticated, but the partners decided to apply a standard discount, with little variation for the volume of orders. Agents were selected mainly on the strength of trust and a feeling that they were reliable, rather than on any kind of objective criteria. Regardless of trust, however, Chuft always insisted on cash in advance for export orders.

Chuft Toys and Gifts expanded and diversified its product range as the business grew.

Source: Chuft.

Exports have grown to 30 per cent of output, although profit margins are tighter than in the domestic market. This volume is considered useful for spreading the load of the factory and in reducing the effects of concentrating on just one market. The main markets are Japan, America and Germany, although other European markets also provide some sales. The partners do not want to sell to developing countries and are determined not to be swamped by US demand.

The future challenge for the business is in keeping the product range fresh. Lifecycles are tending to become shorter as the range increasingly moves into novelty products. Despite the success, there are still many other problems to overcome. Deciding on whether to manufacture or subcontract, obtaining suitable premises as production expands, achieving production efficiency and assembling the resources to hit a market harder than has been possible in the past have all become priorities. Although the business now employs 20 people, sales are still handled by the partners. There appear to be many opportunities for further expansion, but the need to develop a sound strategy to enable further growth to be properly managed is starting to occupy the partners' minds. They think that they have reached a crossroads. Should they continue to expand, should they consolidate, or should they seek radically new options?

The increased contact in mainland Europe led to a French distributor approaching Chuft recently with the prospect of a significant order, provided it could deliver in time for the Christmas season. This would require an immediate start in production and raw material planning so that the first deliveries could begin soon after the initial contract was placed. The partners were delighted at the prospect of an order that could provide the funds for further expansion, but were nervous over the scale of the order as it would require both additional machinery and staff. They were not yet strong enough financially to absorb the risk or loss if the sales volume did not materialise, yet they knew risks would have to be taken if they were to grow. The distributor was, however, confident of success and had already given a verbal go ahead to start production.

Note: Some case details have been modified to protect the partners' interests.

Source: Adapted from a case prepared by Gerry Kirkwood.

Questions

1. What do you think are the problems facing two young graduates wanting to start a new business?
2. To what would you attribute Chuft's initial success?
3. Where does Chuft go from here? What do you think might be the main dangers facing this firm?
4. Should Chuft accept the big French order?

References for chapter 21

Abell, D. F. (1982), 'Metamorphosis in Market Planning,' in K. K. Cox and V. J. McGinnis (eds), *Strategic Market Decisions*, Prentice Hall.

Andersen, T. (2000), 'Strategic Planning, Autonomous Actions and Corporate Performance', *Long Range Planning*, 33 (2), pp. 184–200.

Batchelor, C. (2001), 'Cendant May Sell NCP Arm for £1bn', *Financial Times*, 7 December, p. 27.

Benoit, B. (2001), 'Easing Over Bumps in the Road', *Financial Times*, 28 May, p. 2.

Birley, S. (1989), 'The Start Up', in P. Burns and J. Dewhurst (eds), *Small Business and Entrepreneurship*, Macmillan.

Brooksbank, R. (1999), 'The Theory and Practice of Marketing Planning in the Smaller Business', *Marketing Intelligence and Planning*, 17 (2).

Bunn, D. and Taylor, J. (2001), 'Setting Accuracy Targets for Short-term Judgemental Sales Forecasting', *International Journal of Forecasting*, 17 (2), pp. 159–69.

Burns, P. (2001), 'Introduction', in P. Burns (ed.), *Small Business and Entrepreneurship*, 3rd edn Macmillan.

Campbell, K. (1999), 'Varying Stakes of Start Up', *Financial Times*, 22 June, p. 16.

Cox, W. E. (1979), *Industrial Market Research*, Wiley.

Day, G. (1990), *Market Driven Strategy*, Free Press.

Derrick, S. (2001), 'Fast Company', *Growing Business*, December.

Done, K. (2001), 'Ryanair Plans Big Expansion at Frankfurt-Hahn', *Financial Times*, 23 November, p. 25.

Doran, A-J. (2001), 'WH Smith – A Year of Change Ahead', *Publishers Weekly*, 14 May, p. 22.

Douglas, T. (2002), 'BBC3 – Are Many of Us Really Going to Watch it?', *Marketing Week*, 21 March, p. 17.

Drucker, P. (1955), *The Practice of Management*, Heinemann.

The Economist (2002), 'Towards the Wild Blue Yonder: Special Report', *The Economist*, 27 April, pp. 75–7.

Edwards, O. (2001), 'Flying High on the World Stage', *EuroBusiness*, November, pp. 62–3.

Firn, D. (2001), 'African Cactus Could Help Fight Obesity', *Financial Times*, 11 April, p. 2.

Foley, S. (2002), 'Pilkington's Glass Markets Losing Shine', *The Independent*, 11 April, p. 25.

Foster, M. (1996), 'NCP Fights for its Space', *Management Today*, February, pp. 54–8.

Gallagher, C. and Miller, P. (1991), 'New Fast Growing Companies Create Jobs', *Long Range Planning*, 24(1), 96–101.

Gamble, J. (2001), 'The Struggle to Get Nappies Off the Ground', *Financial Times*, 31 May, p. 14.

Genna, A. (1997), 'What's Wrong With Sales Forecasts?', *Purchasing*, 5 June, pp. 20–1.

Gibb, A. and Scott, M. (1985), 'Strategic Awareness, Personal Commitment and the Process of Planning in the Small Business', *Journal of Management Studies*, 22(6), 596–631.

Gilmore, A., Carson, D. and Grant, K. (2001), 'SME Marketing in Practice', *Marketing Intelligence and Planning*, 19 (1), pp. 6–11.

Gribben, R. (2002), 'UK Leads Europe in Start-up Zone', *The Daily Telegraph*, 18 February, p. 29.

The Grocer (2002), 'Smarties Go into a Resealable Ringpull', *The Grocer*, 23 March, p. 65.

Grosvenor, A. (2001), 'Miracle Drugs, Mega Profits', *Investors Chronicle*, 7 December, pp. 34–7.

Guiltinan, J. and Paul, G. (1988), *Marketing Management: Strategies and Programs*, McGraw-Hill.

Hakim, C. (1989), 'Identifying Fast Growth Firms', *Employment Gazette*, January, pp. 29–41.

Hales, M. (2000), 'Classic Style with Space Age Extras', *The Daily Telegraph*, 30 December, p. 4.

Hardcastle, S. (2001), 'Pasta and Pasta Sauces', *The Grocer*, 10 November, pp. 41–4.

Harnischfeger, U (2002), 'Lufthansa Threatens to Start Budget Airline', *Financial Times*, 23 January, p. 29.

Harper, K. (2000), 'Labour's Transport Plan: Buses', *The Guardian*, 21 July, p. 1.4.

Hirst, C. (2001), 'New Chapter at WH Smith', *The Independent*, 28 January, p. 7.

Hoare, S. (2002), 'The Man Who Went into Overdrive', *The Times*, 19 February, p. 9.

Hollinger, P. and Rawsthorn, A. (1999), 'WH Smith Books a Place in New Retailing Era', *Financial Times*, 25 May, p. 21.

Hutton, R. (2000), 'The Ugly Duckling', *The Sunday Times*, 26 November, p. 30.

Jameson, A. (2002), 'Venture Capitalists Set to Bet on Parking', *The Times*, 7 May, p. 37.

Kerstetter, J. (2001), 'Silicon Seer', *Business Week*, 27 August, p. 112.

Kingsley-Jones, M. and Duffy, P. (2001), 'Over the Precipice', *Flight International*, 16–22 October, pp. 40–69.

Kinsella, R. *et al.* (1993), *Fast Growth Firms and Selectivity*, Irish Management Institute.

Kleinman, M. (2002), 'WH Smith Selects B&Q Marketer for Customer Drive', *Marketing*, 7 March, p. 3.

Kleinman, M. (2001), 'WH Smith Plans High-tech Leisure Store', *Marketing*, 1 November, p. 3.

Lofthouse, R. (2002), 'Morgan Meets Munich', *EuroBusiness*, January, pp. 80–2.

McClelland, D. (1961), *The Achieving Society*, Van Nostrand.

McDonald, M. (1989), *Marketing Plans*, Butterworth-Heinemann.

Mentzer, J. and Bienstock, C. (1998), *Sales Forecasting Management*, Sage.

Mowbray, S. (2002), 'A New Bite at the Bar', *The Grocer*, 16 March, pp. 40–1.

Murphy, C. (1999), 'Cadbury's Quiet Revolution', *Marketing*, 11 February, pp. 24–5.

O'Brien, C. (2001), 'Batteries', *The Grocer*, 15 September, pp. 49–53.

O'Donnell, J. (2001), 'Insiders Show How to Raise Venture Capital', *The Sunday Times*, 18 February, p. 3.16.

Peachey, P. (2002), 'Ryanair "Misled" Public Over Flight Destinations', *The Independent*; 13 March, p. 4.

Smith, P. and Chaffey, D. (2001), *eMarketing eXcellence: At the Heart of e-Business*, Butterworth-Heinemann.

Sonko, K. (2002), "Bumsters" to Get the Bum Rush', *African Business*, April, pp. 46–7.

Start and Run Your Business (2002), 'How They Did It: Iron Bed Co.', *Start and Run Your Business*, May, pp. 70–1.

Storey, D. (1994), *Understanding the Small Business Sector*, Routledge.

The Sunday Times (1999), 'Virgin Atlantic Fast Track 100' supplement to *The Sunday Times*, 5 December.

Turner, M. (2002), 'Cadbury's Clean Conscience', *Financial Times*, 18 February, p. 18.

Wall, M. (2001), 'www.holidayautos.com', *Sunday Times*, 8 July, p. 4.

Warwickshire Choice (2001), 'They Made it in Britain', *Warwickshire Choice*, July/August.

Weinberg, R. (1969), 'Developing Marketing Strategies for Short Term Profits and Long Term Growth', paper presented at Advanced Management Research Inc. Seminar, New York.

Wensley, J. (1987), 'Marketing Strategy', in M. J. Baker (ed.), *The Marketing Book*, Heinemann.

Wheelwright, S. and Makridakis, S. (1977), *Forecasting Methods for Management* (2nd edn), Wiley.

Wilson, R. *et al.* (1992), *Strategic Marketing Management*, Butterworth-Heinemann.

Wolfe, H. (1966), *Business Forecasting Methods*, Holt, Rinehart and Winston.

Woodward, R. (2002), 'Gift Shops: All Wrapped Up', *Start and Run Your Business*, May, pp. 32–3.

Wynarczyk, P. *et al.* (1993), *The Managerial Labour Market in Small and Medium Sized Enterprises*, Routledge.

chapter 22

Services and non-profit marketing

Introduction

LEARNING OBJECTIVES

This chapter will help you to:

1 define the characteristics that differentiate services from other products and outline their impact on marketing;

2 develop an extended marketing mix of 7Ps that takes the characteristics of services into account and allows comprehensive marketing strategies to be developed for services;

3 understand the importance and impact of service quality and productivity issues;

4 appreciate the impact of franchising and its role in service markets;

5 understand the special characteristics of non-profit organisations within the service sector, and the implications for their marketing activities.

The focus of this chapter is on the marketing of services, whether sold for profit or not. Service products cover a wide range of applications. In the profit making sector, services marketing includes travel and tourism, banking and insurance, and personal and professional services ranging from accountancy, legal services and business consultancy through to hairdressing and garden planning and design. In the non-profit-making sector, services marketing applications include education, medicine and charities through to various aspects of government activity that need to be 'sold' to the public.

Marketing these kinds of services is somewhat different from marketing physical products. The major marketing principles discussed in this book, segmenting the market, the need for research, sensible design of the marketing mix and the need for creativity, strategic thinking and innovation, are, of course, universally applicable, regardless of the type of product involved. Where the difference arises is in the detailed design and implementation of the marketing mix. There are several special factors that provide additional challenges for the services marketer.

This chapter will, therefore, examine in detail the special aspects of services that differentiate them from physical products. It will then look at the issues involved in designing the services marketing mix and the marketing management challenges arising from its implementation. The chapter also provides a detailed consideration of franchising. For many franchisees the franchise route is an attractive way of getting into business, and for franchisors it is an attractive way of expanding an easily replicated service idea. The decision to enter such a relationship, however, has major implications for the marketing strategies of both parties. Finally, the whole area of marketing services in the non-profit sector will be considered.

eg

Hoteliers want every visitor to thoroughly enjoy an overnight stay with them. If there is a mismatch between customers' expectations and their experiences, if they are unhappy with the room, service or choice in the hotel, they may not make a return visit. As discussed throughout this book, most businesses rely on repeat business. This requires a considerable attention to detail on the part of the hotelier, for example communicating the location of the hotel, providing car park security, levels of service in the front office, and not least creating the ambience and ensuring the functionality of the room itself. Increasingly, the type of services offered are being targeted at specific customer groups. The Marriott chain is testing a facility where business travellers can use a central hotel printer from their room (Bray, 2002). The next major phase of development will include broadband and wireless connectivity to the bedroom, videoconferencing units, high-definition television, wireless smart-card keys, full corporate office systems, and two-way video devices (Moore, 2001). Others are investing in enhancing keep fit facilities, not just with a fitness suite, but with a fitness delivery service which allows a personal trainer to be delivered to your room along with any equipment for accompanied workouts. Others are offering 20 minute yoga sessions with leading instructors through cable television in their rooms. Yoga is said to be an especially effective treatment for jet lag (Lewis, 2002). Although there is a trade-off between price and the value offered, the experience must be up to scratch. Again, with the impact of IT and its ability to create and update a guest database, the accommodation experience will soon become far more personalised. Your preferred room temperature, a television that lists your favourite programmes and videos, a menu displayed on the television tailored to your tastes, a mini bar with your choice of drinks, a room with your preferred style and location (type of bed, floor covering, smoking etc.) are just some of the variables that a database could flag up to make your experience that bit more special. Oh yes, and all this would be in your native language (Warren, 1999)!

Perspectives on service markets

Services are not a homogeneous group of products. There is wide variety within the services category, in terms of both the degree of service involved and the type of service product offered. Nevertheless, there are some general characteristics, common to many service products, that differentiate them as a genre from physical goods. It is often especially important, for example, to adopt an integrative approach to linking customers, employees and operations within service situations (Looy *et al.*, 1998). This section, therefore, explores the criteria by which service products can be classified, and then goes on to look at the special characteristics of services and their implications for marketing.

Classifying services

There are few pure services. In reality, many product 'packages' involve a greater or lesser level of service. Products can be placed along a spectrum, with virtually pure personal service involving few, if any, props at one end, and pure product that involves little or no service at the other. Most products do have some combination of physical good and service, as shown in Figure 22.1. The purchase of a chocolate bar, for example, involves little or no service other than the involvement of a checkout or till operator. The purchase of a gas appliance will involve professional fitting, and thus is a combination of physical and service product. A new office computer system could similarly involve installation and initial training. A visit to a theme park or theatre could involve some limited support products, such as guides and gifts, while the main product purchased is the experience itself. Finally, a visit to a psychiatrist or a hairdresser may involve a couch, a chair and some minor allied props such as an interview checklist or a hair-dryer. The real product purchased here, however, is the personal service manufactured by the service deliverer, the psychiatrist or the hairdresser.

Figure 22.1 The product spectrum

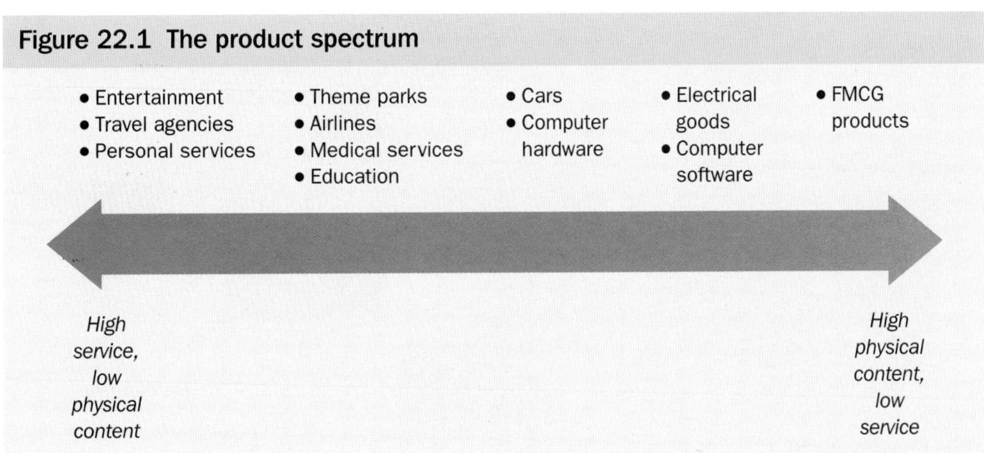

Tangibility is not the only way of classifying service products. Lovelock *et al.* (1999) suggest several other ways of grouping services along dimensions that might have implications for the marketing mix employed in designing and delivering the service. These include how the service is delivered, the extent to which supply is constrained or demand fluctuates, the degree of involvement of people and facilities in the service, the level of customisation, the relationship between the service organisation and its customers, the duration of the benefits of the service and the duration of the service delivery.

Special characteristics of service markets

Five main characteristics, as shown in Figure 22.2, have been identified as being unique to service markets (*see*, e.g., Sasser *et al.*, 1978; Cowell, 1984).

Lack of ownership

Perhaps the most obvious aspect of a service product is that no goods change hands, as such, and therefore there is no transfer of ownership of anything. A legal transaction does still take place; an insurance company agrees to provide certain benefits as long as the premiums are paid and the terms and conditions of the policy are met. A car rental company allows the customer full use of a vehicle for an agreed length of time, subject to some restraints on named drivers and type of usage, but the ownership of the vehicle remains with the rental company. A train seat can be reserved for a journey, but it is not owned. A subscription to the National Trust provides rights of access free of charge but no actual share in the ownership of its properties. The access, use or experience of the service is, therefore, often time specific, usage specific and subject to contractual terms and conditions.

The lack of ownership raises the issue of the transient nature of the purchase. Most service products involve some kind of 'experience' for the customer. This might be surrounded by props, for example a stage, lighting and sound systems, a lecture theatre, an insurance policy, a vehicle or a room, but these only serve to enhance or degrade the experience of the service. The faulty fuel gauge which means that the car hirer runs out of petrol in the most remote location, the hotel room next to the building site, the ineffective microphone at a concert all spoil the memory of the service consumed. Most service products are about the expectation of 'temporary use' and the memories arising therefrom, for example the stories of the annual holiday in Marbella or trekking through the Himalayas.

The growth of timeshare provides an interesting case where the service package includes partial ownership of something. The customer does purchase a share in a holiday property, but is also purchasing the timeshare operator's services in administering and maintaining the property. The operator might also provide an exchange service, whereby the customer can join a network of owners to swap timeshares. With services that do not involve ownership, frequent flyer programmes, membership clubs and loyalty schemes can encourage customers to feel a sense of ownership and belonging to the service product.

Figure 22.2 Characteristics of service markets

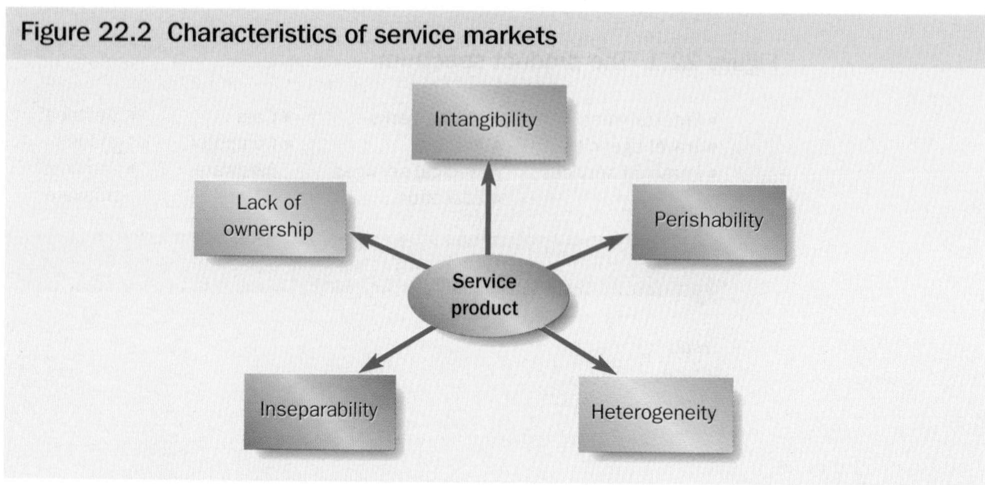

Intangibility

A visit to a retail store reveals an inviting display of products to purchase. These products can be examined, touched, tried on, sampled, smelt or listened to. All this can help the customer to examine what is on offer and to make choices between competing brands. The consumer regularly uses the whole range of senses to assist decision-making (see Chapter 3). Touch, sight, sound, smell and taste are powerful influences on consumer purchasing, enabling them to assess what is being offered, to weigh up value, and to develop the confidence to act. This is especially important before the purchase is made, but even after the sale the product can be assessed in terms of its use, its durability and whether it lives up to general expectations. If there is a fault with a physical product, it can be returned or exchanged.

With service products, it is far more difficult to use the senses in the same way as a means of making a purchase decision because the actual service experience can only take place after that decision has been made. The heart of a service is the experience created for the customer, whether individually as with a personal service such as dentistry or hairdressing, or as a group experience, such as a lecture, a show or a flight. In many cases, once the purchase decision has been made, all the customer will receive is a ticket, a confirmation of booking or some promise of future benefit. The service experience itself is intangible, and is only delivered after the customer is committed to the purchase.

eg

The Scottish Tourist Board ran a 'reawaken your senses' campaign to promote spring breaks. The campaign attempted to capture the intangible nature of the tourist experience by concentrating on visual imagery, such as fish, sea spray and scenery. The problem for this type of promotion is that it is difficult to distinguish the Scottish product offering from the many others available in equally scenic locations (http://www.visitscotland.com).

Despite the problem of **intangibility**, the potential customer can make some kind of prior assessment of the service product. Using available tangible cues, the customer can assess whether a particular service provider is likely to deliver what is wanted. The actual cues used and the priority given to them will vary according to the customer's particular needs at the time. In choosing a hotel, for example, a customer might look at the following:

1 *Location.* If the customer is on holiday, then perhaps a hotel near to the beach or other tourist attraction would be preferred, or one in a very peaceful scenic setting. A business traveller, in contrast, might look for one that is convenient for the airport or close to the client being visited.
2 *Appearance.* A customer's expectations about a hotel are likely to be affected by its appearance. Does it look shabby or well kept? Is it too big or too small? Does it look welcoming? What is the decor like, both internally and externally? Do the rooms seem spacious enough and well appointed? Those who are familiar with the Parador hotel chain in Spain will realise what an impact can be made by building a hotel around the conversion of historic buildings such as castles and stately homes.
3 *Additional services.* The customer might be concerned about the peripheral aspects of the service on offer. The tourist who will be spending two weeks in a hotel might be interested in the variety of bars and restaurants provided; hairdressing, laundry or creche facilities; shopping and postal services; or the nightlife. The business traveller might be more concerned about car parking, shuttle buses to the airport, or fax and telephone provision.
4 *Customer handling.* If the potential customer contacts the hotel for further information or to make a reservation, the quality of the handling they receive might affect the purchase decision. Courtesy and friendliness will make a good impression, as will a prompt and accurate response to the query. This kind of efficiency implies a commitment to staff training and good operating systems to assist easy access to relevant information and the speedy processing of bookings.

marketing in action

The multiplex: Oscar winner or turkey?

A visit to the cinema has been revolutionised over recent years, and further changes are still expected as efforts continue to be made to upgrade the customer experience. It is not very long ago that going to the cinema meant a choice of one main feature and a 'B' film and that was all. Stern-faced usherettes guided you with their torches towards a seat (usually the one you did not want), then they doubled up as ice-cream sellers during the interval (until they ran out of stock). Parking was usually non-existent, as cinemas were located in town centres, and queuing was the norm for more popular shows as no advance booking was possible. The seating was not particularly comfortable, and the whole episode was not very customer friendly. It is perhaps not surprising that cinema audiences declined over many years as people switched to new leisure pursuits. In the late 1940s, around 1.6 billion tickets were sold each year, but this had shrunk to 54 million by 1984 (Rushe, 2001). Television and video were thought to be the culprits behind the dramatic decline.

Multiscreen cinemas offer a variety of films for all age ranges along with opportunities to buy food, confectionery and drinks. Trailers and posters will encourage the customer to come back soon to see the next blockbuster.

Source: Odeon Cinemas/Red Consultancy.

Since the opening of the first multiplex in Milton Keynes in 1985, the decline has stopped as marketing strategies have become far more orientated towards the modern consumer's needs. Cinema entered a second golden age that is still with us. This is very evident from a visit to a multiplex cinema, a format which has been a major influence in the rise in cinema attendances in the UK. A multiplex is a large building containing a number of small, individual cinemas around a central circulation area. A multiplex can thus show 12 or more different films at any one time and can seat up to 3,500 customers in total. The size of the individual cinemas varies, so that, for example, blockbusting new releases can be put into bigger ones or even be shown in two cinemas at once, reflecting the expected popularity of the film. The seating in all the cinemas is invariably of a high standard.

Despite the undoubted success of the multiplex format in offering choice and an experience that cannot be replicated on a small screen, there is growing concern over how long the rapid development of new sites can continue. Between 1988 and 1991 around 14 sites per year were added, stopped by the recession in the early 1990s. The period 1992–1995 saw growth again, but at a rate of six sites per year. Since 1996, however, the number of new multiplexes has risen to 25 per year (Dodona, 2001). Warner Village, UGC (formerly Virgin) and Cine UK have added the most, followed by Odeon, UCI and Showcase. There are now ten UK cities with more than 50 multiplex screens within a 15–20 minute drive of the city centres although some smaller towns still have no provision (Cox, 2002).

The impact of multiplex cinemas might not yet have been fully played out, as they have become part of the property development business. The concept has expanded into Multi-leisure parks (MLPs) that are now taking prime edge-of-town sites with plenty of parking, with the multiplex as the anchor tenant, a bowling alley and a choice of restaurants making the sites 'one-stop shop entertainment experiences'. Following the US lead, there are 170 sites already in the UK and more are planned. Star City outside Birmingham, for example, has a 36-screen cinema, 12 restaurants and shops. These sites are attracting leisure trade that previously used the city centre. Town centres can attract between 15 and 20 per cent of their income from the night time economy, so a competitive response is likely, probably through efforts to create a café, pub and club culture to draw people back (McCarthy, 2002).

There is an alternative view, however, that suggests that significant growth in demand for multiplex cinemas is over, and in 2001 four actually closed (in Dundee, Romford and two in Manchester). The cinema market is not in decline, but it may be oversupplied thus affecting individual site viability. This is parallelled in the United States where an oversupply led to rationalisation (Rushe, 2001). Estimates vary about how many seats are needed to make a profit, some suggesting that a seat must be sold between three and four hundred times a year to make money. Some multiplexes are struggling to reach 200 times. As most of the costs are fixed, an empty seat is lost revenue for ever but with the same cost of providing it. Dodona (2001) estimates that by 2005 there will be nearly 3,400 screens, a growth of 1,400 on current levels so it is critical for the multiplex operators that audiences should continue to rise. The real victims could, however, be the remaining traditional cinemas and those multiplexes that either are poorly sited or not modernising further. Warner Village is building five new multiplexes across London and is giving priority to wider seats, better views and special effects in an effort to build brand loyalty (Rogers, 2001). Others are improving booking systems including online reservations and pre-booking seat allocations. The aim now is not just to attract customers, but also to build loyalty.

Sources: Cox (2002); Dodona (2001); McCarthy (2002); Rogers (2001); Rushe (2001).

In a wider sense, marketing and brand building are also important, of course. These help to raise awareness of a hotel chain's existence and positioning, and differentiate it from the competition. These communicate the key benefits on offer and thus help the customer to decide whether this is the kind of hotel they are looking for, developing their expectations. Advertising, glossy brochures and other marketing communications techniques can help to create and reinforce the potential customer's perception of location, appearance, additional services and customer handling, as well as the brand imagery. Strong marketing and branding also help to link a chain of hotels that might be spread worldwide, giving the customer some reassurance of consistency and familiarity. A business traveller in a strange city can seek out a known hotel name, such as Novotel, Holiday Inn, Sheraton, Campanile or Formula 1, and be fairly certain about what they are purchasing.

The more intangible the product, the greater the pressure on marketers to create what tangibility they can. This makes it easier for the consumer to do some pre-purchase evaluation and gives them the confidence to buy. The secret of franchising's success is to make a service offering tangible so that the customers know what to expect before purchase, regardless of the geographic location of the outlet.

eg

Pizza Hut's menu, decor, servers, order processing, equipment, cooking procedures, etc. are all standardised (or allow minor variations and adaptations for local conditions), creating a consistent and familiar experience for the customer all over the world. Customers thus have a strong tangible impression of the character of Pizza Hut, what to expect of it, and what it delivers.

One of the greatest problems of intangibility is that it is difficult to assess quality both during and after the service has been experienced. Customers will use a combination of criteria, both objective and subjective, to judge their level of satisfaction, although it is often based on impressions, memories and expectations. Different customers attach significance to different things. The frequent business traveller might be extremely annoyed by check-in delays or the noise from the Friday night jazz cabaret, while the holidaymaker might grumble about the beach being 20 minutes' walk away rather than the 5 minutes promised in the brochure. Memories fade over time, but some bad ones, such as a major service breakdown or a confrontation with service staff, will remain. In a restaurant, assessing the quality of the food or the cleanliness of the cutlery might well be straightforward and consistent between different customers, but atmosphere, music and interaction with the serving staff are much more individual and subjective.

Perishability

Services are manufactured at the same time as they are consumed. A lecturer paces the lecture theatre creating a service experience that is immediately either consumed or slept through by the students. Manchester United, Ajax or AC Milan manufacture sporting entertainment that either thrills, bores or frustrates their fans as they watch the match live. Similarly, audiences at Covent Garden or La Scala absorb live opera as it unfolds before them. With both sport and entertainment, it is likely that the customer's enjoyment of the 'product' is heightened by the unpredictability of live performance and the audience's own emotional involvement in what is going on. This highlights another peculiarity of service products: customers are often directly involved in the production process and the synergy between them and the service provider affects the quality of the experience. A friend might tell you, 'Yes, it was a brilliant concert. The band were on top form and the atmosphere was great!' To create such a complete experience, the band and their equipment do have to perform to the expected standard, the lighting and sound crews have to get it right on the night, and the venue has to have adequate facilities and efficient customer handling processes. The atmosphere, however, is created by the interaction between performer and audience and can inspire the performer to deliver a better experience. The customer therefore has to be prepared to give as well as take, and make their own contribution to the quality of the service product.

Perishability thus means that a service cannot be manufactured and stored either before or after the experience. Manufacture and consumption are simultaneous. A hotel is, of course, a permanent structure with full-time staff, and exists regardless of whether it has customers or not on a particular night. The hotel's service product, however, is only being delivered when there is a customer present to purchase and receive it. The product is perishable in the sense that if a room is not taken on a particular night, then it is a completely lost opportunity. Room 101 for the night of Wednesday, 3 September 2003 is a unique, time-dependent service product. The same is true of most service products, such as airline seats, theatre tickets, management consultancy or dental appointments. If a dentist cannot fill the appointment book for a particular day, then that revenue-earning opportunity is lost for ever. In situations where demand is reasonably steady, it is relatively easy to plan capacity and adapt the organisation to meet the expected demand pattern.

eg

The Tussauds group owns the Alton Towers theme park in Staffordshire. Predicting capacity and occupancy were essential elements of the analysis justifying a £40 mn investment in a new hotel and water theme complex. The new 216-room hotel, Calypso Springs, and the first covered water amusement park in the UK will provide many new features to attract customers. The current 175-room hotel, however, finds that its occupancy fluctuates from 100 per cent in the high season to just 19 per cent in the low season. It is expected that an all-year-round facility will enable occupancy levels to be raised in the shoulder months and in the low season when the outdoor climate is less predictable (Reece, 2002).

Even where demand does fluctuate, as long as it is fairly predictable managers can plan to raise or reduce service capacity accordingly. A larger plane or an additional performance might be provided to cater for short-term demand increases. It can be more difficult, however, if there are very marked fluctuations in demand that might result in facilities lying idle for a long time or in severe overcapacity. The profitability of companies servicing peak-hour transport demands can be severely affected because vehicles and rolling stock are unused for the rest of the day. Airlines too face seasonal fluctuations in demand.

eg

Balkanair mothballs a number of its holiday jets over the winter, as the Black Sea resorts in Bulgaria virtually close down and there is little demand from foreign tourists. Sports and entertainment can be hit by unpredictable demand fluctuations. A football team that hits a run of bad luck can see its crowd fall to 5,000 but still have to maintain a 50,000-seater stadium. More drastically, a West End show that gets universally bad reviews might have to end its run early because it cannot fill the theatre on a regular enough basis.

Sometimes, of course, changes in demand or events within the marketing environment mean a flood of extra customers. This can put severe strain on the service delivery system and on capacity, if the service provider cannot respond in sufficient time.

In happier circumstances, success might lead to increased demand. A non-league football team experiencing a good cup run might 'borrow' a bigger and better-equipped ground for a fixture against a high-profile opponent, or a show that gets good reviews and good word-of-mouth recommendations might extend its run or insert extra performances.

eg

The main rail freight operator through the channel tunnel, SNCF, suffered major disruption due to having to restrict services because of the efforts of asylum seekers held in the French Sangatte refugee camp to reach the UK. The UK government fined SNCF £2,000 per stowaway caught on its trains and so SNCF cancelled dozens of freight services rather than run the risk. That revenue was not only lost for the duration of the crisis, but some users of freight services switched to ferry transport and thus the revenue earning capability could be lost for ever (Bennett *et al.*, 2002).

The concept of perishability means that a range of marketing strategies is needed to try to even out demand and bring capacity handling into line with it. These strategies might include pricing or product development to increase demand during quieter periods or to divert it from busier ones, or better scheduling and forecasting through the booking and reservation system.

eg

The attractive and discounted deals offered by top hotels in the aftermath of September 11th 2001 (*see* p. 440) did not last through to the following summer. Prices that fell by around 30 per cent to chase a suddenly much smaller market, started to climb again as travel confidence returned and the demand for bed nights improved. The hoteliers also switched focus. Some sought long-term deals with corporate clients, while others in London switched attention to the domestic market to achieve an 80 per cent occupancy level by the spring of 2002. Some hotels expected the market to have fully recovered by 2003, assuming that there were no further terrorist attacks (Rice and Upton, 2002).

Similarly, the capacity and service delivery system can be adapted to meet peaks or troughs in demand through such strategies as part-time workers, increased mechanisation or cooperation with other service providers. These will be considered in more detail later (*see* pp. 974 *et seq.*).

Inseparability

Many physical products are produced well in advance of purchase and consumption, and production staff rarely come into direct contact with the customer. Often, production and consumption are distanced in both space and time, connected only by the physical distribution system considered in Chapter 12. Sales forecasts based on reasonable expectations of changes in demand provide important guidelines for production schedules. If demand rises unexpectedly, opportunities might well exist to increase production or to reduce stockholding to meet customer needs.

As has already been said, with service products, however, the involvement of the customer in the service experience means that there can be no prior production, no storage and that consumption takes place simultaneously with production. The service delivery, therefore, cannot be separated from the service providers and thus the fourth characteristic of service products is **inseparability**. The terminology used to order a service product might vary: booking, making an appointment, reserving a seat or prepaying an entrance fee. All of these terms, however, imply that the customer is being granted legitimate access to consume a service experience at an agreed time and place in the future, with the cooperation and participation of the provider.

Inseparability means that the customer often comes into direct contact with the service provider(s), either individually, as with a doctor, or as part of a team of providers, as with air travel. The team includes reservations clerks, check-in staff, aircrew and perhaps transfer staff. In an airline, the staff team has a dual purpose. Clearly, they have to deliver their aspect of the service efficiently, but they also have to interact with the customer in the delivery of the service. An uncooperative check-in clerk might not provide the customer's desired seat, but in contrast, a friendly and empathic air hostess can alleviate the fear of a first-time flyer. The service provider can thus affect the quality of the service delivered and the manner in which it is delivered.

eg

British Airways (BA) is training all of its 13,500 cabin staff to be more aware of other cultures. The airline carries people from many different nationalities (over 60 per cent of its passengers are not from the UK) and it feels that it is important for cabin crew to think about different cultures and how they might behave when on board. Handling sensitive issues around food and drink can be especially important for cabin crew, for instance. How different cultures handle conflict situations with other passengers or crew can also vary. In addition to training, BA is looking to employ more staff from ethnic minority backgrounds. The recruitment drive improved numbers by 14 per cent from an average of just 85 UK-based flight attendants and 3,000 extra staff worldwide from a diverse range of ethnic backgrounds (http://www.ba.com).

While the delivery of a personal service can be controlled, since there are fewer opportunities for outside interference, the situation becomes more complex when other customers are experiencing service at the same time. The 'mass service experience' means that other customers can potentially affect the perceived quality of that experience, positively or negatively. As mentioned earlier, the enjoyment of the atmosphere at a sporting event or a concert, for example, depends on the emotional charge generated by a large number of like-minded individuals. In other situations, however, the presence of many other customers can negatively affect aspects of the service experience. If the facility or the staff do not have the capacity or the ability to handle larger numbers than forecast, queues, overcrowding and dissatisfaction can soon result. Although reservation or prebooking can reduce the risk, service providers can still be caught out. Airlines routinely overbook flights deliberately, on the basis that not all booked passengers will actually turn up. Sometimes, however, they miscalculate and end up with more passengers than the flight can actually accommodate and have to offer free air miles, cash or other benefits to encourage some passengers to switch to a later flight. At theme parks, much more time can be spent waiting to get on to a ride than on the ride itself during times of peak demand. Although attempts are made to manage that situation by providing information about waiting times, planning the queuing procedure to give the impression of constant forward movement, and providing entertainment while people wait, customers would still prefer shorter queues and less competition for the park's facilities.

What the other customers are like also affects the quality of the experience. This reflects the segmentation policy of the service provider. If a relatively undifferentiated approach is offered, there are all sorts of potential conflicts (or benefits) from mixing customers who are perhaps looking for different benefits. A hotel, for example, might have problems if families with young children are mixed with guests on an over-50s holiday. Where possible, therefore, the marketer should carefully target segments to match the service product being offered. By attracting like-minded individuals, not only will the service experience be enhanced for all customers, but there will also be less opportunity for those seeking a peaceful retreat at a hotel being disturbed by a Club 18–30 all-night rave!

Finally, the behaviour of other customers can be positive, leading to new friends, comradeship and enjoyable social interaction, or it can be negative if it is rowdy, disruptive or

eg

Following on from the cabin crew example earlier, anyone who has experienced rowdy behaviour on an aircraft or at a sports match will know how distressing the experience can be and how it can detract from the overall willingness to repeat purchase. With airlines, cabin crew are in the front line of handling abuse, yet it is surprising that over two-thirds of airlines do not train their crew in how to handle such behaviour (Fox, 2001). Hearts football club in Scotland wants to be regarded as a family club, so it takes a strong line on hooligans and on drunk and disorderly behaviour. Six so-called fans were banned for life for their misdemeanours. One shouted out Republican chants during a minute's silence and five were thrown out for abusive and drunken behaviour (Cameron, 2002). The lesson from these examples is clear. The selling organisation must take responsibility for countering disruptive customers through its policy and deeds, and staff must be trained to deal with the incidents that occur all too frequently.

even threatening. Marketers prefer, of course, to try to develop the positive aspects. Social evenings for new package holiday arrivals, name badges on coach tours, and warm-up acts to build atmosphere at live shows all help to break the ice. To prevent disruptive behaviour, the service package might have to include security measures and clearly defined and enforced 'house rules' such as those found at soccer matches. Of course, there can be real problems for marketers in keeping some segments apart, for example in soccer grounds.

The implications of inseparability for marketing strategy will be considered at pp. 970 *et seq.*

Heterogeneity

With simultaneous production and consumption and the involvement of service staff and other customers, it can be difficult to standardise the service experience as planned. **Heterogeneity** means that each service experience is likely to be different, depending on the interaction between the customer and other customers, service staff, and other factors such as time, location and the operating procedures. The problems of standardising the desired service experience are greater when there is finite capacity and the service provided is especially labour intensive. The maxim 'when the heat is on the service is gone' reflects the risk of service breakdown when demand puts the system under pressure, especially if it is unexpected. This might mean no seats available on the train, delays in serving meals on a short-haul flight, or a queue in the bank on a Friday afternoon.

Katz *et al.* (1996) found that people significantly overestimate the amount of time they spend in queues and quickly become very impatient, especially when their time is unoccupied. For that reason, clever service operators make sure that there is some entertainment while customers are waiting and plan the queuing area layout to encourage a number of short, moving lines, rather than the appearance of one long line stretching all the way to eternity!

eg

Virgin Trains has been struggling to make a success of its rail service. It is a tough challenge, with one in five trains running late or cancelled, and yet 75 per cent of the problems are out of Virgin's control, resting with the railway infrastructure. If the track or signalling is not up to scratch, or the non-Virgin locomotive in front breaks down, then it is difficult to offer a reliable service. With 28 million passenger journeys a year, there is plenty of scope for the complaining passenger and ironically, although many other train operators are also failing in service reliability, the high profile of Virgin often means that it is subject to more complaints.

An internal report on a typical day on Connex South Central in 2001 was alleged to contain details of 49 cancelled trains, 276 missed stations, and only 30 per cent of trains running on time (Syal, 2001). Most of the problems were due to driver shortages but broken signals, technical difficulties with the rolling stock, and even a fatality at Clapham Junction all played their part. Such is the nature of heterogeneity for the rail operators.

The new Virgin Trains are a pleasure to travel in and offer routes that other train operators do not.

Source: Virgin Trains.

Sometimes the differences are more subtle, but they can still affect the perception of service performance. On one day a lecturer might deliver an entertaining and informative lecture, but on the next day, perhaps suffering from the effects of a late night, the performance might be well below average. Following an inconsistent soccer team can be a rollercoaster; a great match and a convincing win one week, but an eminently forgettable performance the next. A multi-location service provider might regularly provide excellent service in one branch, but very poor service in another. There can also, of course, be inconsistencies between different service providers. Within a single branch of a bank, some clerks can be bright, friendly and helpful, while others will be surly and offer service grudgingly. Some travellers assess the check-in staff at an airport to decide which one looks more likely to turn a blind eye to excess luggage or to allocate the best seats!

Some of the heterogeneity in the service cannot be planned for or avoided, but quality assurance procedures can minimise the worst excesses of service breakdown. This can be done by designing in 'failsafes', creating mechanisms to spot problems quickly and to resolve them early before they cause a major service breakdown. Universities, for example, have numerous quality assurance procedures to cover academic programmes, staffing and support procedures that involve self-assessment, student evaluation and external subject and quality assessment.

Not all service breakdowns are caused by the service provider, but, whatever their cause, they can still fundamentally affect the quality of the service experience. Technical problems with a plane are the responsibility of an airline, but not the fog, air traffic delays or problems with the baggage handlers. A state agency might have responsibility for promoting regional tourism, but is dependent on the hotels, guest houses, tourist attractions, taxi drivers and other service providers to deliver the required service to a proper standard for the region's tourism to develop.

eg

Mystery shoppers are widely used to monitor service levels and the service experience provided. They eat at restaurants to check food, service and facilities, stay in hotels, drink in pubs, travel on planes, and visit cinemas, health clubs and garages. The lucky ones even get to go on expensive foreign holidays. The feedback provides front-line commentary and however revealing, often shows companies the difference between the service promise and the reality of what is delivered. Most of the time, the focus is on the overall experience rather than individual performance, although at times staff are also the focus of attention. Normally, the mystery shopper is given a checklist of points to watch out for and they have to be skilled in classifying and memorising elements of the delivered service. To be effective, the mystery shopper must be believable and natural and thus cannot go round with a checklist on a clipboard (McLuhan, 2002). So next time you are in Burger King or Pret à Manger, to name but two, you could be next to a shopper on a mission.

Management therefore has to develop ways of reducing the impact of heterogeneity. To help in that process, they need to focus on operating systems, procedures and staff training in order to ensure consistency. New lecturers, for example, might be required to undertake a special induction programme to help them learn teaching skills, preparing materials and handling some of the difficulties associated with disruptive students. Managers have to indicate clearly what they expect of staff in terms of the desired level of service. This must cover not only compliance with procedures in accordance with training, but also staff attitudes and the manner in which they deal with customers. Many franchising chains

eg

The Welsh Tourist Board (http://www.visitwales.com) operates a quality assurance scheme that establishes the minimum standards that a tourist might expect when visiting or holidaying in Wales. Inspectors examine all aspects of the accommodation before awarding a star category. These range from five stars for exceptional quality and exemplary service to one star for a fair to good standard of furnishings and adequate service and guest care. The scheme extends to activity holidays and self-catering accommodation, and is designed to provide some standardisation in an inherently non-standard holiday experience for tourists.

have successfully managed growth, yet maintained service consistency and control through the careful design of the operating manual, extensive staff training, and regular monitoring and feedback.

Lovelock *et al.* (1999), however, feel that these characteristics are somewhat overgeneralised and are not necessarily applicable to all service products. An alternative list of eight generic differences between physical products and services, summarised in Table 22.1, is therefore suggested as a more practical approach. This list does, nevertheless, include many of the concepts discussed above, albeit under different labels.

Table 22.1 Generic differences between services and physical goods

1	The nature of the product
2	Customers' involvement in the production process
3	People as part of the product
4	Greater problems in maintaining quality
5	Harder for customers to evaluate
6	Absence of inventories
7	Relative importance of time factors
8	Structure and nature of distribution channels

Source: Lovelock *et al*. (1999).

The characteristics of service products, regardless of how they are defined, create problems for marketers. They have to build and maintain competitive advantage through service design, delivery, differentiation and efficiency, while regularly providing consistent service. The next section, therefore, looks in more detail at the impact of the particular characteristics of service products on the design and implementation of the marketing programme.

Services marketing management

So far, this chapter has looked at the characteristics of service products in a very general way. This section looks further at the implications of those characteristics for marketers in terms of formulating strategy, developing and measuring quality in the service product and issues of training and productivity.

Services marketing strategy

The traditional marketing mix, consisting of the 4Ps, forms the basis of the structure of this book. For service products, however, additional elements of the marketing mix are necessary to reflect the special characteristics of services marketing. Shown in Figure 22.3, these are:

- *people*: whether service providers or customers who participate in the production and delivery of the service experience;
- *physical evidence*: the tangible cues that support the main service product. These will include facilities, the infrastructure and the products used to deliver the service;
- *processes*: the operating processes that take the customer through from ordering to the manufacture and delivery of the service.

Any of these extra marketing mix elements can enhance or detract from the customer's overall experience when consuming the service. However, despite the special considerations, the purpose of designing an effective marketing mix remains the same whether for services or physical products. The marketer is still trying to create a differentiated, attractive proposition for customers, ensuring that whatever is offered meets their needs and expectations.

Figure 22.3 The services marketing mix

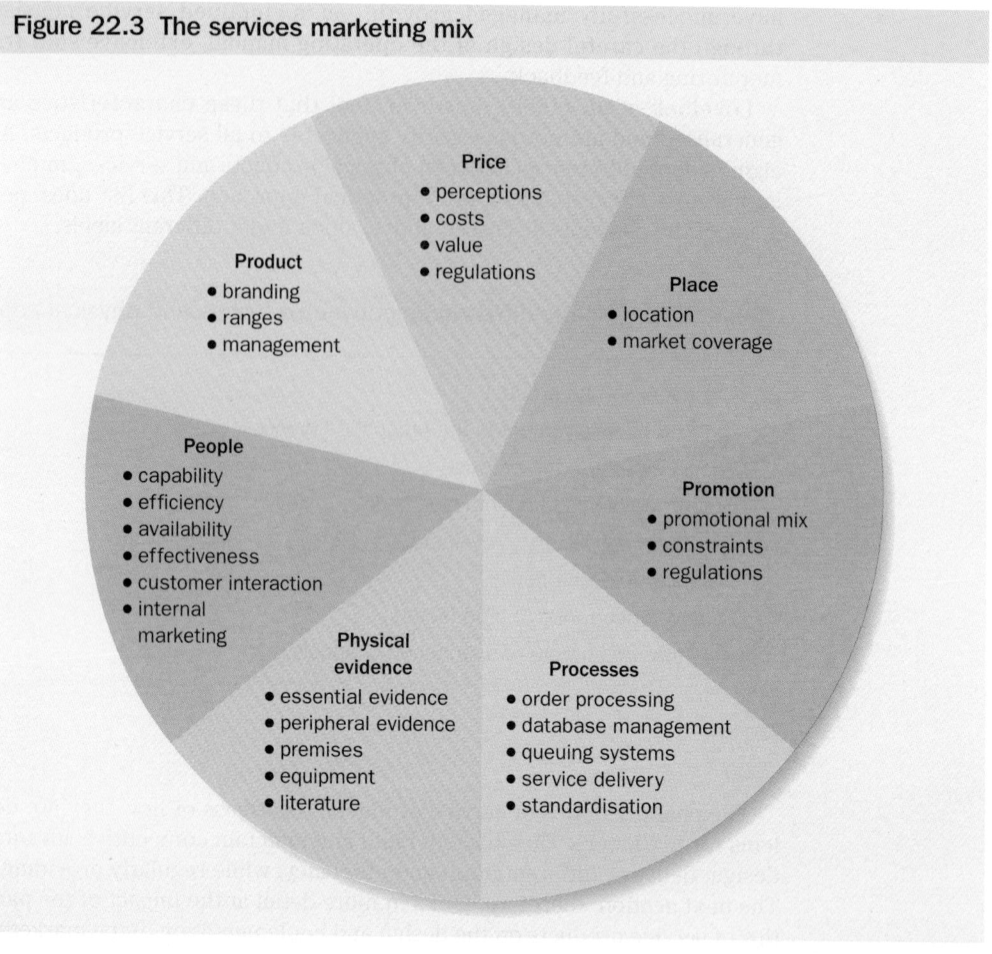

corporate social responsibility *in action*

A bloody theme park!

Taking measures to protect the environment is increasingly an area in which government and industry are expected to assume leadership and responsibility. From a government perspective, the needs of wider society, for employment, social stability and welfare, along with national prosperity have to be balanced against the preservation of a cultural and natural heritage and sustainable land use. Somehow it appears to be going wrong in Romania, where the government is actually promoting the destruction of an area of Transylvania renowned for its beauty, ancient oak forests and cultural heritage. And for what? A Dracula theme park experience in a country that has hardly been touched by the Hollywood legend.

Better-informed readers will know, of course, that Dracula never existed as such, but the character created by Bram Stoker was based on Vlad Tepes, a fifteenth-century ruler who shot to fame for impaling over 1,000 Turks after a particularly nasty battle. His real name was Vlad Dracul, Dracul meaning Devil in Romanian. The 'Tepes' (impaler) was added later for obvious reasons. Hollywood added the fangs, blood drinking and associated niceties. Vlad was born in the mediæval fortress city of Sighisoara, a UNESCO world heritage site which the Romanian government has undertaken to protect.

The project itself will initially develop 40 hectares of land, expanding to 60 in phase 2. It will cost around £30 mn and should be ready for tourists by 2004. Castle Dracula will be the centrepiece, housing a judgement chamber, vampire den and alchemy laboratory. Included will be a mock torture room with stakes and knives, folk workshops for vampire protecting armour, a vampire fashion house and the rides will have vampire themes, bringing a whole new meaning to 'The House of Horror'. The restaurants will have such delicacies as 'blood pudding' and 'dish of brains' and for those who are brave enough, there are on-site motels. Linked to the park will be a golf course, campsite, 700-bed hotel, souvenir shops, beer halls and a ballroom for 2,000 dancers. Something for everybody, but not eco-tourism (Moore Ede, 2002).

The park is expected to create around 3,000 jobs and is planned to generate $21 mn per year from 1 million visitors. It is a poor region in a poor country with a quality of life that has been likened to Namibia and Libya (Douglas-Home, 2001). The theme park offers jobs in an area with 17 per cent unemployment, and the chance to buy shares in the venture, with 100 shares costing about £20, one-third the average monthly wage. The company created to develop the park, Fondul Pentru Dezvoltare Turistica Sighisoara (FPDTS), will be 99 per cent owned by the Sighisoara municipality but it is intended as a profit-making enterprise. It is also argued that the city will be restored after many years of neglect.

From a government perspective, what better way for the Ministry of Tourism to start to rebuild the brand image of Romania, which for many Europeans is off the tourism scale? Although the Transylvania region has much to offer with fortified churches, castles, painted monasteries and unspoiled beauty, it is difficult to reach, about five hours by road from the capital Bucharest, it has little high standard tourism infrastructure such as hotels and restaurants, no effective waste disposal system and no service tradition as a result of the Communist era. Dracula could change all that, however, even though Dracula films were not legal until 1989 and the Stoker book was not published in Romanian until 1992. A 1973 'Dracula: Truth and legend' tour disappointed many foreigners as most of the time was spent tracing the life of Vlad, rather than the fangs and cape experience (George, 2002). The planned theme park would address many of the issues of infrastructure over the next few years and give the tourists what they really want.

The more of an outcry there is in western Europe, the less likely it is that the project will, at least in the short term, succeed. At least Walt Disney built on the outskirts of Los Angeles, not on the site of a rare mediæval city that would all but be destroyed by the development under the banner of 'modernisation'. The oak forest is protected by Romanian law and the city by its international obligations. For western investors and developers it will be a dilemma. Should they pursue the development contracts and be associated with the park, or should they indicate that it is a park too many? Some may even question whether they want to be associated with a park that glorifies blood, death and the macabre. The Romanian view is clear, 'This is a government project. No one can tell us what to do in our own country' (as quoted by George, 2002).

Ultimately, economics could doom the park, and perhaps that is another reason why western developers have been coy about investing. To succeed in any theme park a developer needs access to a constant flow of tourists, good infrastructure, an all-year-round congenial climate and proximity to a major city. Sighisoara meets none of these requirements. It also needs around 1 million tourists per year, and according to the business plan, 75 per cent will be living within 80 km. The local potential visitors are old, rurally-based and few have a car or the money to pay the expected $25 entrance fee. Will international tourists flock in? It would have to be a very sophisticated package to draw people in, given the plethora of other theme park holidays available across Europe and beyond. The danger is that the low development budget will mean that it is tacky and cheap. Even allowing for the low cost of building in Romania, Castle Dracula has a budget of around $2 mn compared with $200 mn for some similar experiences in the US. Perhaps Dracula should be left where he belongs after all – in Hollywood.

Sources: Douglas-Home (2001); George (2002); Moore Ede (2002).

All seven of the services marketing mix elements will now be considered in turn.

Product

From a supplier's perspective, many services can be treated like any other physical product in a number of ways. The supplier develops a range of products, each of which represents profit earning opportunities. A hotel company might treat each of its hotels as a separate product with its own unique product management requirements arising from its location, the state of the building and its facilities, local competition, and its strengths and weaknesses compared with others in the area. These products might, of course, be grouped into product lines and SBUs based on similarities and differences between them, just as physical products can be.

Similarly, an insurance company might have many different policies on offer, including pension plans, endowments, life insurance, house buildings and contents insurance, and motor or holiday insurance. Each one again might be considered as a product or as part of a range.

Many of the product concepts and the decisions concerning them that were discussed in Chapters 7 to 9 apply equally to services and physical products. Positioning, branding, developing a mix, designing new services and managing the product lifecycle are all relevant.

Product development. Product development in some service situations can be complex as it involves 'packaging' otherwise separate elements into a service product. Therefore a holiday company may need to work with airlines, hotels and local tour companies to blend a

eg

British Airways seeks to brand itself as a friendly, reliable and professional airline; Formula 1 positions itself as a no-frills, low-cost motel chain; BSkyB offers a range of satellite channels to cover sport, news, movies and other entertainment. Services can be repositioned too. Spain, for example, is trying to reposition itself and change its appeal because of too many new competitors in the sea, sun, sand and cheap alcohol segment of the market. It now wants to be regarded as a destination that still offers good value, but a wider range of tourist attractions and cultural activities.

package for the target segment. From a consumer perspective, any failure in any part of the system will be regarded as a criticism of the holiday company, even though air traffic delays or faulty plumbing may not be directly under the company's control. At a regional and national level, government and private companies may work together to develop new attractions and infrastructure for tourists.

eg

China is emerging as an international tourist destination, although there is still a need for considerable product development and many tourists' degree of prior knowledge is very limited. Many tourists' images are drawn from the media, from films such as *The Last Emperor* as well as the popular press, but beyond the Great Wall, the terracotta army, the Forbidden City and Tiananman Square the level of knowledge is poor and the general impression is not favourable (Richards, 2001). Thus product development is needed to ensure that new visitor attractions are made accessible, that the transport infrastructure improves and that the hotels outside the main centres reach international standards. This will especially be a challenge in Tibet which is about to open its doors to an expected 5.6 million tourists over the next five years, attracted by the mountainous scenery and its 'spiritual' connotations (Barton, 2001).

Price

Because services are intangible, their pricing can be very difficult to set and to justify. The customer is not receiving anything that can be touched or otherwise physically experienced, so it can be hard for them to appreciate the benefits they have gained in return for their expenditure.

eg

A solicitor's bill or the labour charges added to a repair bill can seem to be incredibly high to customers, because they do not stop to think about the training that has gone into developing professional skills nor of the peace of mind gained by having the job done 'properly'. As with any product, therefore, the customer's perception is central to assessing value for money.

The prices of some services are controlled by bodies other than the service provider. The amount that dentists charge for work under the National Health Service or that pharmacists charge to dispense a prescription is imposed by central government. Similarly, the BBC is funded by licence fees determined by government and charged to television owners. Other services price on a commission basis. An estate agent, for example, might charge the vendor a fee of 2 per cent of the selling price of the house, plus any expenses such as advertising. Some solicitors in the UK who specialise in pursuing compensation claims would like to be able to charge their clients a fee based on a percentage of the compensation achieved, but currently that is not allowed by their regulatory body, the Law Society.

Other service providers are completely free to decide their own prices, with due respect to competition and the needs, wants and perceptions of customers. In setting prices, however, service providers can find it very difficult to determine the true cost of provision, perhaps because of the difficulty of costing professional or specialist skills, or because the time and effort required to deliver a service vary widely between different customers, yet a standard price is needed. Perishability might also affect the pricing of professional services. A training provider, for example, who has little work on at the moment might agree to charge less than the normal daily rate, just to generate some income rather than none.

In service situations, price can play an important role in managing demand. By varying the price, depending on the time at which the service is delivered, service providers can try to discourage customers from purchasing at the busiest periods. Customers can also use price as a weapon. Passengers purchasing airline tickets shortly before the flight or visitors looking for a hotel room for the night might be able to negotiate a much lower price than that advertised. This is a result of the perishability of services: the airline would rather have a seat occupied and get something for it than let the flight take off with an empty one and, similarly, the hotel would rather have a room occupied than not.

eg

The rail pricing system has changed considerably in the UK in recent years. Traditionally, the passenger bought a ticket, walked on to the train and found a seat. Few bothered to pay the additional charge for a seat reservation. The emphasis is now on encouraging advance booking so that capacity can be better planned. The price mechanism is used to achieve a spread of customers. Suitably indexed to give equivalents in today's prices, an 'ordinary return' from London to Manchester was £51 in 1949. In 1969, period returns, usually for return travel within a month, could bring the price down to £41. By 1989, 'savers' again gave a price of £41, and a low of £32 could be found in 1994 with advance booking. Virgin Rail now has three main Value fares depending upon whether the ticket is purchased 3, 7 or 14 days in advance. Generally the longer the period before travel, the lower the fare. Thus some tickets can be as cheap as £20 return for the V14, but £40 for the V3. Other walk-on fares and special offers are used from time to time. The customer needs to be highly aware of the different pricing schemes yet, contrary to popular opinion, rail travel really can be as cheap as it was 50 years ago (Doe, 1999; http://www.virgintrainfares.co.uk).

Place

According to Cowell (1984), services are often supplied direct from the provider to the customer because production and consumption are simultaneous. Direct supply allows the provider to control what is going on; to differentiate through personal service; and to get direct feedback and interaction with the customer. Direct supply can take place from business premises, such as a hairdresser's salon, a solicitor's office or a university campus. Some services can also be supplied by telephone, such as insurance and banking services. Others are supplied by the service provider visiting the customer's home or premises, such as cleaning, repair of large appliances, equipment installation and servicing, or home hairdressing services.

Whatever the mode of direct supply, it can cause problems for the service provider. It limits the number of customers that can be dealt with and the geographic coverage of the service. For sole traders or small businesses who particularly value the rapport and personal relationships built up with regular clients, this might be perfectly acceptable. Businesses that want to expand might find that direct supply involving the original proprietor of the business is no longer feasible. Professional service businesses, such as accountants or solicitors, might employ additional qualified staff to expand the customer base or to expand geographic coverage.

eg

A fitness-oriented society coupled with rising levels of obesity has been a major factor behind the rapid growth of the health and fitness sector since the mid-1990s. Participation among the adult population grew from 3.8 per cent in 1996 to 7 per cent in 2001, with an expected peak of around 17 per cent, while membership has grown by 88 per cent over the same period. As the supply of clubs has grown, however, membership numbers have tended to remain static at individual clubs and the challenge has been to find new members to compensate for those leaving. Holmes Place, an operator of 56 premium clubs with a membership overall of 228,000 has a retention rate of 60 per cent which is high compared with the rest of the industry (Mesure, 2001). In the UK alone there are over 2,500 clubs, a growth of 25 per cent in five years. The premium clubs are especially vulnerable as they need to invest in more and varied facilities such as swimming pools and indoor tennis courts. The main means of growth for most clubs has been to open branches designed to a standard package in more towns and cities. Fitness First has grown to 225 clubs in 14 countries, with 112 in the UK alone (Daneskhu, 2002). The question is whether the growth can continue as the market becomes saturated, with operators turning to increasingly smaller towns to attract new interest. Other marketing activities also involve extending the reach with, for example, tie-ins with local sports associations, corporate membership drives and joint initiatives such as LA Fitness' 'Wellness Centres' operated in conjunction with BUPA.

Other service businesses such as fast food outlets, domestic cleaners or debt collection agencies might opt to expand by franchising, an area which will be covered later in this chapter. Some services will decide to move towards indirect supply through intermediaries paid on a commission basis. Thus the local pharmacist might act as an agent for a company that develops photographic film; a village shop might collect dry cleaning; insurance brokers distribute policies; travel agencies distribute holidays and business travel; and tourist information offices deal with hotel and guest house bookings. In some of these cases, the main benefit of using an intermediary is convenience for the customer and spreading the coverage of the service. In others, such as the travel agency and the insurance broker, the service provider gains the added benefit of having its product sold by a specialist alongside the competition.

Place is not just important for delivering the service; it also covers access to reservation and information systems. Travel agents, for example, have direct computer links with tour operators and other central reservation systems that are not available to the consumer. The tour operator benefits from being able to distribute information cost effectively and having its holidays sold by trained agents. The growth of Teletext, interactive shopping and the internet might revolutionise this aspect of the services marketing mix still further.

Promotion

Marketing communication objectives, implementation and management for services are largely the same as for any other product. There are a few specific issues to point out, however. As with pricing, some professional services are ethically constrained in what marketing communication they are allowed to do. Solicitors in the UK, for example, are allowed to use print advertising, but only if it is restrained and factual. An advertisement can tell the reader what areas of the law the practice specialises in, but it cannot make emotive promises about winning vast amounts of compensation for you, for example.

Service products face a particularly difficult communications task because of the intangibility of the product. They cannot show you pretty pack shots, they cannot whet your appetite with promises of strawberry and chocolate-flavoured variants, they cannot show you how much of this amazing product you are getting for your money. They can, however, show the physical evidence, they can show people like you apparently enjoying the service, they can emphasise the benefits of purchasing this service. Testimonials from satisfied customers can be an extremely effective tool, because they reassure the potential customer that the service works and that the outcomes will be positive. Linked with this, word-of-mouth communication is incredibly important, especially for the smaller business working in a limited geographic area. Overall, if the service provider can use communication to build a reputation for quality, reliability and trustworthiness, then it is well on the way to overcoming potential customers' doubts and overcoming intangibility.

Finally, it must be remembered that many service providers are small businesses, who could not afford to invest in glossy advertising campaigns even if they could see the point of it. Many can generate enough work to keep them going through word-of-mouth recommendation, websites and advertisements in the *Yellow Pages*. Much depends on the level of

eg

Jarvis Hotels (http://www.jarvis.co.uk) uses direct marketing to promote conference business in its 62 hotels in the UK. The information pack, which is targeted at potential business customers, includes a complete directory of locations, room configurations and prices along with a lot of visual imagery to show the standard of meeting rooms, food service and the range of staff who are employed to make the conference or meeting a success. The messages throughout stress quality and reliability.

competition and demand in the local market for the kind of service being offered. If the town's High Street supports four different restaurants, then perhaps a more concerted effort might be justified, including, for example, advertising in local newspapers, door-to-door leaflet drops and price promotions. Local service outlets that are franchises are likely to benefit from large-scale national corporate promotion, designed to create a consistent image for all branches. Nevertheless, franchisees might also have some discretion and flexibility to do their own communication tailored specifically to local conditions.

It is important to remember, however, that customers are likely to use marketing communication messages to build their expectations of what the service is likely to deliver. This is true of any product but, as will be discussed at pp. 970–3 *et seq.*, because of intangibility, the judgement of service quality is much more subjective. It is based on a comparison of prior expectations with actual perceived outcomes. The wilder or more unrealistic the communication claims, therefore, the greater the chances of a mismatch that will lead to a dissatisfied customer in the end. The service provider does, of course, need to create a sufficiently alluring image to entice the customer, but not to the point where the customer undergoing the service experience begins to wonder if this is actually the same establishment as that advertised.

eg

The Australian Tourist Commission also makes heavy use of imagery to portray the natural and cultural delights of Australia to European audiences. Whether it is kangaroos, Ayers Rock, the Great Barrier Reef or Sydney Opera House, the visual message is the same: vibrant, exciting and surprising. The media advertisements and PR usually reinforce these themes, making full use of holiday programmes and travel shows as well as supporting Australia-themed national supplements in some of the daily newspapers. 'Brand Australia' campaigns are, however, targeted to attract different audiences and a number of campaigns are run simultaneously in different geographical markets. In the UK, for example, the primary targets are younger travellers aged between 18 and 36 and older travellers, over 45, reflecting the reality that a 'full nest' family is more likely to stay nearer home. In Germany, three segments are targeted: Explorers (aged between 25 and 54), Third Age Independents (45–65) and Young Independents (18–29). There are unifying themes, however, such as overcoming the view that Australia is a remote, vast and 'once in a lifetime' destination to position it more as a 'liberating, civilised adventure' destination. A 'visiting journalist' programme, funded by the ATC is especially important for stimulating more and better PR coverage, and around 1,000 print and broadcast journalists are invited each year. It also helps to show Australia as being more than scenery and sun, with coverage of urban culture, food, wine, arts and cultural themes (http://www.atc.australia.com; http://www.australia).

The Australian Tourist Commission is keen to encourage visitors to see a different Australia from the one people expect. Here you see The Devil's Marbles which is a much less well-known place than Ayers Rock (Uhluru).

Source: Australian Tourist Commission.

People

Services depend on people and interaction between people, including the service provider's staff, the customer and other customers. As the customer is often a participant in the creation and delivery of the service product, there are implications for service product quality, productivity and staff training. The ability of staff to cope with customers, to deliver the service reliably to the required standard and to present an image consistent with what the organisation would want is of vital concern to the service provider. This is known as *internal marketing*, and will be discussed later at pp. 974 *et seq.* The role of the customer in the service is known as *interactive marketing*, and will be discussed at pp. 970 *et seq.*

Physical evidence

Physical evidence comprises the tangible elements that support the service delivery, and offer clues about the positioning of the service product or give the customer something solid to take away with them to symbolise the intangible benefits they have received. Shostack (1977) differentiates between *essential evidence* and *peripheral evidence*. Essential evidence is central to the service and is an important contributor to the customer's purchase decision. Examples of this might be the type and newness of aircraft operated by an airline or of the car fleet belonging to a car hire firm, the layout and facilities offered by a supermarket (*see* pp. 545 *et seq.* for more on this), or a university's lecture theatres and their equipment as well as IT and library provision. Peripheral evidence is less central to the service delivery and is likely to consist of items that the customer can have to keep or use.

eg

Aillwee Cave is situated in the remote Burren region of Ireland, famous for its limestone scenery, cultural heritage and spring flowers. Although lacking the size of the cave systems in the Dordogne in France or the accessibility of Cheddar caves in the UK, it has nevertheless become a major day visitor attraction. The cave owners have worked hard at creating an atmosphere for its visitors. The cave experience itself is similar to many others, with effective use of lighting on natural rock formations and fascinating tales of bears and mysteries. The staff are, however, well trained and are called 'actors', reflecting the role they are meant to play in raising the excitement during the visit. The guiding principle is an impeccable tour experience every time. However, surrounding the cave a number of other facilities have been opened, making full use of the local limestone and sympathetically designed to blend with the natural environment. Therefore, although cheese making and craft shops may not fit exactly with a cave experience, they do enhance the overall day-visitor attraction and, of course, generate further on-site expenditure. The longer the visitors stay, the more they tend to spend (http://www.aillweecave.com).

Processes

Because the creation and consumption of a service are usually simultaneous, the production of the service is an important part of its marketing as the customer either witnesses it or is directly involved in it. The service provider needs smooth, efficient customer-friendly procedures. Some processes work behind the scenes, for example administrative and data processing systems, processing paperwork and information relating to the service delivery and keeping track of customers.

eg

United Parcel Service (UPS) regards itself as a leading global commerce facilitator. Best known for its parcel and freight service, it has to gear its operating processes and infrastructure to handle 13.6 million packages every day in 200 countries. To achieve the service levels promised, including time-definite, guaranteed delivery, it operates a large fleet of vans, has over 350,000 employees, operates over 600 aircraft and has spent over $12 bn on technology to provide information processing, tracking and fulfilment. UPS uses a tracking number service not just for logistics but also as a selling point to customers. By having a tracking number assigned to the package the customer is able to track and verify arrival of any package (http://www.ups.com).

Systems that allow the service provider to send a postcard to remind customers that the next dental check-up or car service is due certainly help to generate repeat business, but also help in a small way to strengthen the relationship with the customer. Other processes are also 'invisible' to the customer, but form an essential part of the service package. The organisation of the kitchens in a fast food outlet, for example, ensures a steady supply of freshly cooked burgers available for counter staff to draw on as customers order. Well-designed processes are also needed as the service is delivered to ensure that the customer gets through with minimum fuss and delay and that all elements of the service are properly delivered. This might involve, for example, the design of forms and the information requested, payment procedures, queuing systems or even task allocation. At a hairdressing salon, for instance, a junior might wash your hair while the stylist finishes off the previous customer, and the receptionist will handle the payment at the end.

Banks have thought seriously about ways of making their services more accessible to their customers. Telephone banking, for example, with processes designed to protect customer security and to provide 24-hour coverage, allows customers easy access to their accounts from their own homes whenever they want it. In addition to this, there is an expectation that full use of online banking with the major banks is not far away. Already in Scandinavia, electronic banking services have made a big impact. The regional banks are encouraging customers to use online services for retail transactions as well as share trading and foreign currency transactions. Loans usually still require face-to-face meetings. SEB now has 260,000 customers using online banking, 20 per cent of its retail base. Svenska Handelsbanken has 140,000 internet customers, including 15,000 small businesses in which the service flexibility has been especially well received. The banks are offering incentives for customers to use the internet, including lower commission charges, and they believe that the next phase of competition between banks will be on customer service rather than price (Burt, 1999). If internet banking takes off across Europe, it could revolutionise the whole banking scene and remove many of the barriers associated with geography. The bank processing system could as easily be in Amsterdam or Bilbao as in Tokyo or New York. This could lead to new forms of alliances and mergers between the major banks (Graham, 1999).

e-marketing *in action*

Customer contact strategies for e-marketing

Smith and Chaffey (2001) review some of the ways in which customer service can be automated in the online environment. These are some of the service automation techniques used by e-tail sites such as Jungle (http://www.jungle.com), Blackstar (http://www.blackstar.co.uk), and Land's End (http://www.landsend.com):

- *Autoresponders*. These automatically generate an e-mail response when an individual or company e-mails an organisation, or submits an online form.
- *E-mail notification*. Automatically generated by a company's systems to update customers on the status of their order, for example, order received, item now in stock, order dispatched.
- *Call-back facility*. Customers fill in their telephone number on a form and specify a convenient time to be contacted. Dialling from a representative in the call centre occurs automatically at the appointed time and the company pays, which is popular.
- *Frequently asked questions (FAQ)*. For these, the art is in compiling and categorising the questions so customers that can easily find (a) the right question and (b) a helpful answer.
- *On-site search engines*. These help customers find what they're looking for quickly, and are popular when they are available.
- *Virtual assistants* come in varying degrees of sophistication and usually help to guide the customer through a maze of choices. These are sometimes referred to as 'avatars' when they take a human-like form.

The concept of 'customer self-service' is prevalent in e-marketing. Customer self-service enables the customer to obtain the information they need faster and saves the business money. However, marketers need to ask whether all customers want to conduct all their interactions online. Think of buying an airline ticket via the web. This is fine if you have a particular flight in mind, and it is available. If it is not, then it is usually quicker to talk to a customer service representative who is knowledgeable about the alternatives available.

As a consequence, many companies such as the Nationwide building society (http://www.nationwide.co.uk) use an inbound contact strategy of customer choice or 'customer preferred channel'. But others such as easyJet (http;//www.easyjet.com) show that you can give customers a choice, but steer them towards using the internet as a contact tool by directing them to carefully prepared FAQ.

A further issue in creating an inbound contact strategy is the average number of contacts to resolve an issue. Remember that many questions will not be answered by the first e-mail. Companies need to decide whether the best strategy is to switch the customer to the telephone or online chat to resolve the issue rather than bouncing multiple e-mails between the customer and the contact centre. Two-way interactions such as voice and online chat will be more effective in resolving an issue immediately.

Staff need to be trained and motivated whether they man the website, the telephones, the field sales, or the reception. What happens if a web transaction fails and the customer calls the centre – can call centre staff access the web database to complete the transaction, or do they have to collect all the details again? A seamless, integrated contact database is required.

A key resourcing issue is whether to identify specific staff to handle contacts from different channels or empower staff to answer questions from a variety of channels. Current thinking suggests the latter approach is best since this increases variety of work and results in more knowledgeable staff who can answer customer queries better.

Source: Smith and Chaffey (2001).

Interactive marketing: service quality

Central to the delivery of any service product is the *service encounter* between the provider and the customer. This is also known as **interactive marketing**. This aspect of services is an important determinant of quality because it brings together all the elements of the services marketing mix and is the point at which the product itself is created and delivered. The challenge for the service marketer is to bring quality, customer service and marketing together to build and maintain customer satisfaction (Christopher *et al.*, 1994). Quality issues are just as important for service products as they are for a physical product, but service quality is much more difficult to define and to control. These difficulties arise from the essential intangibility of the service, the fact that it is produced 'live' and the involvement of the customer in the production process. Because there is no physical product to look at and measure, service quality assessment is largely dependent on the customers' perceptions of what they have received and the extent to which that has fulfilled or exceeded their expectations. Authors such as Lovelock *et al.* (1999), Devlin and Dong (1994) and Zeithaml *et al.* (1990), for example, stress the importance of customer perceptions and use them as the basis for frameworks for measuring service quality.

eg

Home delivery of pizzas is usually associated with supplier guarantees of free pizzas if delivered outside a certain period. This helps emphasise the speed of delivery and reinforces the convenience of home ordering services. A number of chains such as Domino's have added online ordering, with a central call centre directing orders to the nearest retail stores. The customer is then free to browse the menu at leisure and the site can be frequently updated with offers etc. It has also gone further in ensuring improved service through the introduction of the Domino's Heat Wave hot bags with a patented electrically warmed heating mechanism. Once unplugged, it keeps the pizza hot during normal delivery times (http://www.dominos.co.uk).

Measuring service quality

Some aspects of the service product can, of course, be measured more objectively than others. Where tangible elements are involved, such as physical evidence and processes, quality can be defined and assessed more easily. In a fast food restaurant, for example, the cleanliness of the premises, the length of the queues, the consistency of the size of portions and their cooking, and the implementation and effectiveness of stock control systems can all be 'seen' and measured. Whether the customer actually *enjoyed* the burger, whether they *felt* that they had had to wait too long, or whether they *felt* that the premises were too busy, crowded or noisy are much more personal matters and thus far more difficult for managers to assess.

A particular group of researchers, Berry, Parasuraman and Zeithaml, have developed criteria for assessing service quality and a survey mechanism called SERVQUAL for collecting data relating to customer perceptions (*see*, e.g., Parasuraman *et al.*, 1985; Zeithaml *et al.*, 1988; Zeithaml *et al.*, 1990). They cite 10 main criteria that, between them, cover the whole service experience from the customer's point of view:

1 *Access*. How easy is it for the customer to gain access to the service? Is there an outlet for the service close to the customer? Is there 24-hour access by telephone to a helpline?
2 *Reliability*. Are all the elements of the service performed and are they delivered to the expected standard? Does the repair engineer clean up after himself after mending the washing machine and does the machine then work properly? Does the supermarket that promises to open another checkout when the queues get too long actually do so?
3 *Credibility*. Is the service provider trustworthy and believable? Is the service provider a member of a reputable trade association? Does it give guarantees with its work? Does it seem to treat the customer fairly?
4 *Security*. Is the customer protected from risk or doubt? Is the customer safe while visiting and using a theme park? Does an insurance policy cover all eventualities? Will the bank respect the customer's confidentiality? Can the cellular telephone network provider prevent hackers from hijacking a customer's mobile phone number?
5 *Understanding the customer*. Does the service provider make an effort to understand and adapt to the customer's needs and wants? Will a repair engineer give a definite time of arrival? Will a financial adviser take the time to understand the customer's financial situation and needs and then plan a complete package? Do front-line service staff develop good relationships with regular customers?

Those first five criteria influence the quality of the *outcome* of the service experience. The next five influence the quality of the *inputs* to the process to provide a solid foundation for the outputs.

6 *Responsiveness*. Is the service provider quick to respond to the customer and willing to help? Can a repair engineer visit within 24 hours? Will a bank manager explain in detail what the small print in a loan agreement means? Are customer problems dealt with quickly and efficiently?
7 *Courtesy*. Are service staff polite, friendly and considerate? Do they smile and greet customers? Are they pleasant? Do they show good manners? Do service staff who have to visit a customer's home treat it with proper respect and minimise the sense of intrusion?
8 *Competence*. Are service staff suitably trained and able to deliver the service properly? Does a financial adviser have extensive knowledge of available financial products and their appropriateness for the customer? Does a librarian know how to access and use information databases? Do theme park staff know where the nearest toilets are, what to do in a medical emergency or what to do about a lost child?
9 *Communication*. Do service staff listen to customers and take time to explain things to them understandably? Do staff seem sympathetic to customer problems and try to suggest appropriate solutions? Do medical, legal, financial or other professional staff explain things in plain language?
10 *Tangibles*. Are the tangible and visible aspects of the service suitably impressive or otherwise appropriate to the situation? Does the appearance of staff inspire confidence in the customer? Are hotel rooms clean, tidy and well appointed? Do lecture theatres have good acoustics and lighting, a full range of audiovisual equipment and good visibility from every seat? Does the repair engineer have all the appropriate equipment available to do the job quickly and properly? Are contracts and invoices easy to read and understand?

It is easy to appreciate just how difficult it is to create and maintain quality in all 10 of these areas, integrating them into a coherent service package. Parasuraman *et al.* (1985) suggest that there are four barriers to service quality, all of which are the fault of the service provider, and all of which will affect the customer's perception of the service experience. These barriers thus mean that there is a mismatch between what customers expected and what they perceived to be actually delivered.

1 *Misconceptions*. Management misunderstands what the customer wants and thus delivers an inappropriate or incomplete service product.
2 *Inadequate resources*. If a service provider is trying to cut costs, for example, the customer might suffer. There could be long queues because there are too few staff available, premises might be ill-equipped or shabby, or administrative support systems might start to break down. Students are often all too familiar with the effect of large classes and increasing staff–student ratios in many universities.
3 *Inadequate delivery*. Lack of training or poor recruitment might lead to staff with poor knowledge or with no real interest in the customer. This might mean that elements of the service package are not delivered at all or delivered in a very cursory and inadequate way.
4 *Exaggerated promises*. A service provider desperate to gain customers in a highly competitive environment might be tempted to be somewhat economical with the truth. In some cases, when choosing a hotel in a foreign holiday resort from a brochure, for example, customers can only really test the validity of the promises made after they have committed themselves to the purchase. The true picture emerges as the service is being consumed. Thus a hotel brochure might boast that it is within five minutes' walk of the beach and that all rooms have a sea view. Unless customers have been to the resort before, or can get word-of-mouth verification from friends, relatives or travel agents who have stayed there, the fact that they would have to be Olympic sprinters to get to the beach in five minutes and that they would need to stand on a chair with binoculars to see the sea might emerge too late. In this case, expectations are being raised that simply cannot be fulfilled. The customer's perception of service quality is therefore bound to suffer.

marketing **in action**

Smartcards keep queues moving smartish

The smartcard revolution is starting to impact upon European service provision, changing how we reserve, buy and use services and how we interact with service providers. Smartcards are a similar size to a credit card with an embedded microprocessor and a memory. Some cards are activated by physical contact with a reader, while others are 'contactless', activated by a signal-emitting device within the chip.

London Transport is planning to introduce an electronic fee collection system with contactless smartcards that can be used throughout the tube system and by the independent bus operators, thus overcoming the need for queues at ticket offices and platform barriers. Any reader who has waited ten or fifteen minutes in a ticket queue knows exactly how that impacts on perceptions of the service experience. Smartcards can be topped up via the internet or through devices linked to a bank account, so finding change will become a thing of the past. Some technology can even read the card when it is firmly locked away in a case or wallet. The costs of introducing the system are, however, considerable with around 16,500 pieces of equipment to install or modify, including gates, ticket machines and passenger ticket offices (Hibbert, 2000).

The cards are also very flexible in that they are not bounded by travel zones or time restrictions as are normal season tickets or travel cards. The card reader at the station will take account of the time of day and the distance travelled when calculating the fare to be deducted from the card. Discounts for frequent travellers, promotions or other concessions can also be implemented easily.

The good news is that smartcards can help to speed passenger flows and reduce the frustration factor. Operationally, they also mean that there is less cash handling to be done at stations because most passengers will pay for and top up their smartcards using credit cards. The cards also should reduce fraud, in that the card reader can check that the right fare is paid for any specific journey. Mutual authentication techniques will be used between cards and readers to undertake integrity checks and to ensure that no tampering has taken place. From a strategic planning perspective, the new system will also collect accurate information about who is travelling, between what destinations and when, as well as helping to monitor the effects of promotions, discounts and differential pricing initiatives. The only potential disadvantage, however, is that smartcards do also reduce contact with staff and some of the personal touch of services marketing.

Other transport operators are also at different stages of development. In the US, the Washington metro system claims 60 per cent usage of smartcards. Massachusetts rapid transit system is introducing a $120 mn scheme to improve both customer service and efficiency in 2003. Currently the system operators have to produce and distribute, every month, 240,000 system-wide passes, plus 40,000 commuter rail, 100,000 subway, 35,000 bus, 50,000 bus–subway combination, and 15,000 extended travel range bus–subway combination passes. Inevitably, that all incurs costs that ultimately impact upon fares (RePass, 2002). Smartcards can be updated from simple vending machines in the station areas. Research has indicated, however, that not all of its customers have credit cards or bank accounts, so it still needs to sell cards with fixed values, rather like 'pay-as-you-go' mobile phone cards.

There are other applications of smartcards beyond transport. In banking, for instance, the UK, Finland and France are leading the way in chip-based credit cards to reduce fraud and to lower the cost of banking (Bansal, 2002). In Sweden, camping is now easier due to *Camping Card Scandinavia*. The credit-card-style £6 pre-purchased card makes registration and check out much easier and in addition provides family accident insurance (Bryan-Brown, 2001). Hotels have been slow to adopt smartcards. As in banking, they are mainly used as an extra security device rather than a means of enhancing service and capturing valuable information on buyer behaviour. Nevertheless, they are beginning to be used by hotels to extend services to particular groups and to act as a charge card for additional in-hotel services and even for some services at nearby attractions.

The smartcard revolution is only just beginning. As technology and systems improve and there is more supplier and user confidence, the applications will grow. Along with the credit card and indeed as part of one integrated card, a significant step is being taken towards a cashless society and one in which service is enhanced in the process. There is always a downside, however. Under some transport plans, congestion charging, peak rate charging and zonal charging are all possible via smartcards fitted to cars (Winnett, 2002). Even children may not be immune from the 'big brother' effect as in Queensland, primary schools are piloting a smartcard that can be controlled by parents to prevent certain foods being purchased (chips!) and to prevent children making purchases in certain stores (*Retail World*, 2002).

Sources: Adams (2000); Bansal (2002); Bryan-Brown (2001); Glover (1999); Hibbert (2000); RePass (2002); *Retail World* (2002); Winnett (2002).

In summary, Figure 22.4 shows the service experience and the factors that affect consumers' expectations of what they will receive. The criteria that influence their perception of what they actually did receive are also shown, as well as the reasons why there might be a mismatch between expectations and perceptions. This can have an important impact on the customer's perception of value and willingness to repeat purchase (Caruana *et al.*, 2000).

Figure 22.4 Service quality: expectations, perceptions and gaps

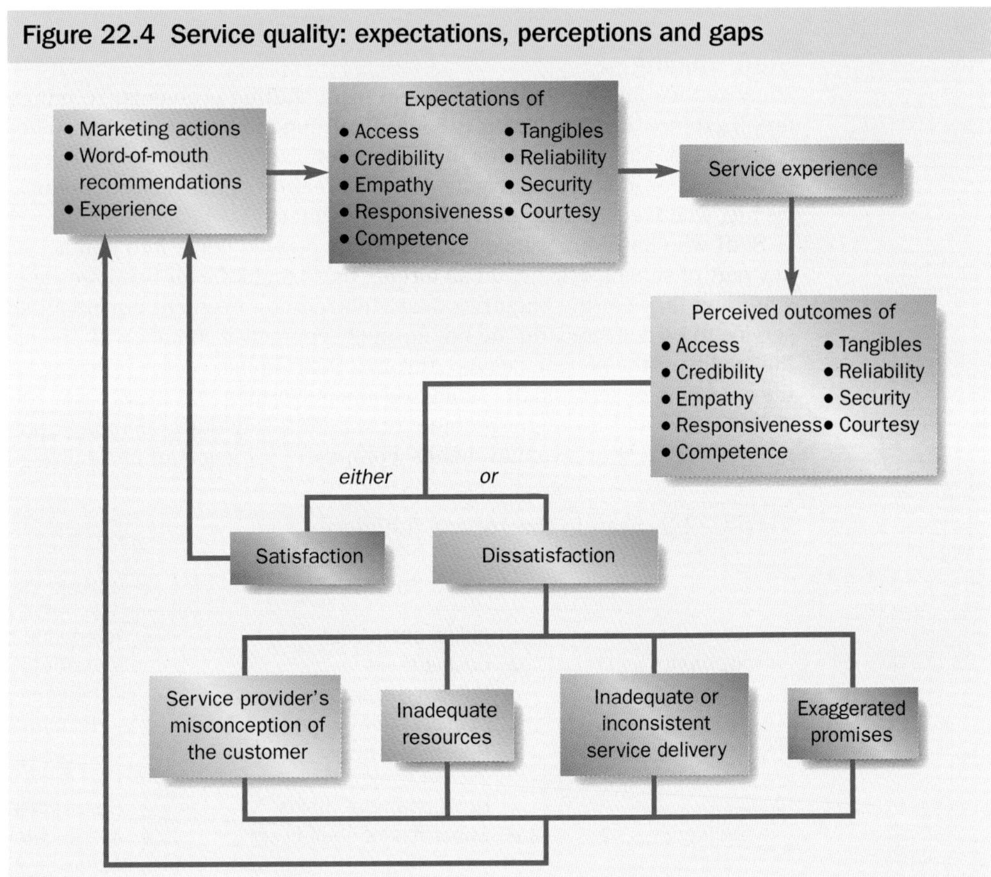

Internal marketing: training and productivity

Because of the interaction between customers and staff in the creation and delivery of a service, it is particularly important to focus on developing staff to deliver high levels of functional and service quality. This does not mean a takeover of personnel and operational management functions by marketing, but marketers must work closely with these line managers to ensure that the right staff are recruited, inducted and trained and that they then perform to the service standards set. The pay and rewards system employed can also help to boost staff morale and encourage them to take a positive approach to service delivery. Heskett *et al.* (1997) highlighted the connection between employee and customer satisfaction within services. The 'satisfaction mirror' can actually enhance the customer's experience if the service personnel are approaching service delivery in a positive way. They suggested that employees feeling enthusiastic about their job communicate this to customers both verbally and non-verbally and are also more eager to serve the customer. Similarly, employees who remain in the job longer reach higher capability levels and often a better understanding of customers, which again can enhance customers' feelings of satisfaction. Defining the ideal profile and right remuneration package for staff is not easy.

eg

Recent research from MORI suggested that staff attitude was more important than quality or price in influencing consumer choice when buying a service. It would appear that the young (aged between 15 and 34) and the more affluent are especially sensitive. Whether it is poor advice, indifferent attitudes, a failure to keep promises or just poor attention to detail, the message is clear to service providers. Many readers will almost certainly recall situations where poor staff attitude has had a bearing on the quality of the experience. This creates pressure to ensure that staff are well trained, not just about the products but also in how to deal sensitively with customers. Faced with increased difficulty in attracting the right calibre of younger staff, retailers such as Sainsbury's and B&Q have scrapped the upper age limit for their workers and actively seek older staff. Carphone Warehouse and Eagle Star are also employing older sales staff to attract the grey market (Buckley, 2002).

Staff training

Many service failures actually do stem from staffing problems. To minimise the risk of failure, therefore, it is important to identify all functions that involve customer contact and to train and remunerate staff for these functions accordingly. As Table 22.2 shows, some staff have direct or indirect involvement in the creation of the service product, and some staff are visible, whereas others are invisible to customers.

Staff who have direct involvement are those who come into contact with a customer as a key part of service delivery. In an airline, these might be air hostesses and stewards, check-in staff, and those at the enquiries desk. Indirect involvement covers all staff who enable the service to be delivered, but do not normally come into contact with the customer. They affect the quality of the service delivery through their impact on the efficiency and effectiveness of the operating system and the standards and performance possible from the facilities and infrastructure. Examples might include aircraft catering staff, cleaning and maintenance staff, ground staff at sports venues, banks' computer systems staff and railway signalmen.

Table 22.2 Staff in the service function

	Visible to the customer	*Invisible to the customer*
Direct involvement	■ Airline cabin crew ■ Cashiers ■ Sales assistants ■ Medical staff ■ Receptionists	■ Telephone based services – order takers – customer helplines – telephone banking
Indirect involvement	■ Hotel chamber maids ■ Supermarket shelf fillers	■ Office cleaners ■ Airline caterers ■ Administrative staff

eg

Jarvis Hotels (mentioned earlier on p. 966), places special emphasis on its staff training in its promotional material. Entitled 'Summit Quality Signature', its brochure outlines the various dimensions of training and the phased approach to awarding the quality signature to all members of staff. The first stage concentrates on core values and considers such issues as service delivery, clear merchandising, first impressions, introductions, cleanliness, freshness and how to encourage extra sales. The second stage is concerned with consistency. Quality standards are set for each core value and both self-checking and regular external 'flight tests' are organised to ensure that standards are being maintained and that, where necessary, corrective action is being taken (Jarvis Hotels corporate literature).

Jarvis Hotels are designed to give customers quality and reliability wherever they are.

Source: Jarvis Hotels EPC.

Visible staff (both those with direct involvement and those with indirect involvement with the customer) are in the front line of service delivery. Not only are they concerned with the practical aspects of service delivery to the required standards, but their appearance, interpersonal behaviour and mannerisms will also make an impression on the customer. Airlines, for example, will pay particular attention to a cabin attendant's personal grooming and dress standardisation to ensure a consistent visual impact. Dress is often used to help the customer identify visible staff, both those directly involved in the service, such as aircraft cabin crew, and those who are indirectly involved, such as stewards at soccer matches or security staff.

Indirect visible staff also include people such as the cleaners at McDonald's, chamber maids in hotels, or staff supporting the cashiers in banks. Invisible staff might or might not have direct contact with customers. Staff who take telephone bookings or those who deal with customer queries on the telephone are heard, but not seen. In some cases, these staff might be the only major point of contact for the customer, and thus although their visibility is limited, their ability to interact well with customers is still extremely important.

The organisation's strategy for **internal marketing** will vary, depending on the different categories of staff employed. Staff who are in the front line of service delivery, with a high level of customer contact, will have to be trained to deliver the standards expected. Staff who do not have direct contact still have to be motivated to perform their tasks effectively and efficiently. They have to understand that what they do affects the quality of the service delivered and the ability of the front-line staff to perform to expected standards. All of this strongly implies, however, that the different groups of staff have to work closely and efficiently together, and deliver a quality service to each other, which in turn will affect the quality of service delivered to the end customer (Mathews and Clark, 1996).

Lee (1997) argues that although internal marketing will not reverse a company's fortunes, it could strengthen the overall marketing effort if staff are committed to the company, brand(s) and mission. This is especially true in service situations where the employee often comes into direct contact with customers and may be part of the service delivery process. This means listening to staff and their ideas as well as involving them in shaping strategy and plans. An Institute of Employment Studies survey of staff and customer attitudes in a major retailer found a direct and strong link between employee commitment and customer satisfaction. The importance of creating a positive organisational culture and good-quality line management all contribute to enhancing the service experience (Bevan and Barber, 1999).

Staff productivity

Staff productivity within services is also a difficult issue for managers. According to Cowell (1984), there are several reasons for **service productivity** being difficult to measure. The main reason is that services are 'performed' not 'produced' and there are too many external factors influencing this live creation of a product. The service production process simply cannot be controlled and replicated as reliably and consistently as a mechanised factory line. Service productivity particularly suffers from the involvement of the customer. If customers do not fill forms in properly, if they are not familiar with procedures or they do not really know what they want, if they turn up late for appointments, if they want to spend time in idle chatter rather than getting on with the business in hand, then it will take service staff much longer to deliver the product. Where productivity is measured in terms of the number of transactions handled, the amount of revenue generated, or the number of customers processed, such delays essentially caused by the customer can reflect unfairly on service staff. This raises the whole question, however, of what constitutes appropriate and fair measures of service productivity. A customer who is given a great deal of individual help or who feels that service staff have taken time for a friendly chat with them might well feel that they have received a much better-quality service and appreciate not being treated with cold, bureaucratic efficiency. It might be worth tolerating a slightly longer queue if you feel that you will be treated with care, respect and humanity when you get to the front of it. Definitions and measures of productivity therefore need to be flexible and sympathetic, striking a fine balance between the customer's needs and the business's need to work efficiently.

None of this absolves managers from looking at ways in which service productivity can be improved. There are several possibilities for delivering services more efficiently without necessarily detracting too much from their quality.

Staff. Through improved recruitment and training, staff can be given better skills and knowledge for dealing with customers. A clerk in a travel agency, for example, can develop a better knowledge of which tour operators offer which resorts so that the key brochures can be immediately pulled out in response to a customer query. Library staff can be fully trained in the use and potential of databases and online search mechanisms so that customers can have their problems solved immediately without having to wait for a 'specialist' to return from a lunchbreak. Improving the staff profile might also allow more delegation or empowerment of front-line service staff. A customer does not want to be told 'I can't do that without checking with my supervisor' and then have to wait while this happens. Staff should be given the responsibility and flexibility to deal with the real needs of customers as they arise.

Systems and technology. The design of the service process and the introduction of more advanced technology can both help to improve service productivity and the service experience for the customer (Bitner *et al.*, 2000).

Technology combined with well-designed systems can be very powerful in creating market transactions where no interpersonal contact is required between buyer and seller (Rayport and Sviokla, 1994). Libraries, for example, have used technology to improve their

eg

Onboard catering on trains has always posed an operational nightmare for operators, yet in airlines the problem has been largely solved through a combination of systems and technology. Whereas most airline food is standardised, precooked, paid for in advance and delivered to a programmed schedule to passengers in pre-determined seats, on some rail services it was not unusual to find a cook frying eggs or cooking vegetables at 80 mph in a confined space and waiters taking orders from an albeit limited menu. Meals were not part of the ticket price, so likely demand per journey had to be forecast. On some occasions, the restaurant on wheels would even break down or supplies would not be forthcoming. Train catering became the butt of many jokes, even though the quality of food, when available, probably exceeded airline levels.

Some of the problem rested in the ambience of on-train facilities. For many years the layout was fixed: a 20-seat dining area, a kitchen in the middle and a take-away bar at the other end of the carriage. There was little space for passengers to mingle and socialise and the counters were far too small so that produce could not be displayed, an essential part of any food operation. Queues became excessive and often extended back into the adjacent carriage. Eating was functional and rarely pleasurable.

The new generation of operators are trying to change things. In France on the Atlantique TGV, a whole coach is allocated to catering with a small bar at one end and a large social area for eating and drinking at the other, all separate from the restaurant facilities. On German trains (DBAG), a bistro facility has been incorporated to offer light meals, snacks and drinks, again in a social environment. The focus has been on enhancing the experience for the traveller. In the UK, efforts have been made by operators such as Virgin and GNER to improve restaurant service to enhance the overall service experience. On the seven former inter-city routes, five provide classic restaurant cars with meals cooked on board by a trained chef. In some cases, such as Virgin and Midland Mainline, the meals and drinks are included in the First Class ticket price. The buffet bar service experience is still variable, however. The ambience is often poor, the trolleys unreliable and the food choice limited. Microwaved burgers still remain the most popular food. Virgin's new trains will, however, feature shops offering food, drinks, newspapers, CDs and some stationery to a potentially captive audience. Nevertheless, to some train operators, catering remains a cost and a necessary evil (and perhaps to some customers too!), rather than a means of adding value (Perren, 1999a, 1999b; Perren and Pyke, 2000).

productivity. Laser scanning barcodes in books make it far quicker to issue or receive returned items than with the old manual ticketing systems. This has also allowed them to improve the quality of their service. The librarian can immediately tell you, for instance, which books you have on loan, whether or not another reader has reserved a book you have, and which other reader has borrowed the book you want. Some technology means that the service provider need not provide human interaction at all. In the financial sector, 'hole in the wall' cash machines, for instance, give customers 24-hour, 7-day-a-week access to their bank accounts, usually without long queues, and because of the way these machines are networked they provide hundreds of convenient access points.

Within service premises, post offices, banks and supermarkets all use express tills or checkouts, for instance, to process customers with small or straightforward transactions faster. Supermarkets also use laser scanning of barcodes not only to help in stock control but also to move goods through the checkout more quickly. The problem with this, however, is that the customer still intrudes. Customers pack their shopping bags at their own pace, and then have to fumble in purses or wallets for enough cash or for a credit card to pay for it all.

Reduce service levels. Reducing service levels to increase productivity can be dangerous if it leads to a perception of reduced quality in the customer's mind, especially if customers have become used to high levels of service. Reducing the number of staff available to deliver the service might lead to longer queues or undue pressure on the customer to move through the system more quickly.

Reducing service levels also opens up opportunities for competitors to create a new differential advantage. As discussed in Chapter 13, discount supermarkets such as Aldi, Netto

eg

If a busy doctor's surgery introduces a system that schedules appointments at five-minute intervals, one of two things might happen. A doctor who wants to maintain the schedule might hurry patients through consultations without listening to them properly or allowing them time to relax enough to be able to say what is really worrying them. Patients might then feel that they have not got what they came for and that the doctor does not actually care about them. Alternatively, the doctor may put the patient first, and regardless of the five-minute rule take as long as is needed to sort out the individual patient. The patient emerges satisfied, but those still in the waiting room whose appointments are up to half-an-hour late might not feel quite so happy.

and Lidl keep their prices low partly through minimising service. Thus there are few check-out operators, no enquiries desk, and nobody to help customers pack their bags. The more mainstream supermarkets have been able to use this as a way of emphasising the quality of their service, and have deliberately invested in higher levels of service to differentiate themselves further. Thus Tesco, for example, promised its customers that if there were more than three people in a checkout queue, another checkout would be opened if possible. Tesco also announced that it was taking on extra staff in most of its branches, simply to help customers. These staff might help to unload your trolley on to the conveyor belt or pack your bags, or if you get to the checkout and realise that you have forgotten the milk, they will go and get it for you.

Customer interaction. Productivity might be improved by changing the way the customer interacts with the service provider and its staff. It might also mean developing or changing the role of the customer in the service delivery itself. The role of technology in assisting self-service through cash machines has already been mentioned. The whole philosophy of the supermarket is based on the idea of increasing the customer's involvement in the shopping process through self-service.

Customers might also have to get used to dealing with a range of different staff members, depending on their needs or the pressures on the service provider. Medical practices now commonly operate on a group basis, for example, and a patient might be asked to see any one of three or four doctors. If the patient only wants a repeat prescription then the receptionist might be able to handle it, or if a routine procedure is necessary, such as a blood test or a cervical smear, then the practice nurse might do it. The role of students in the delivery of educational services has also evolved, partly as a means of improving academic staff productivity. Student-centred learning, for example, means that students are encouraged to take more responsibility for their own education, with academic staff providing the broad structure, ongoing guidance and assessment rather than handing out the whole learning experience to a passive audience on a plate. This has led to a greater degree of partnership between staff and students, and in many ways has actually improved the quality of the service delivered.

If any measures are taken that relate to the nature of customer involvement and interaction, the service provider might have a problem convincing customers that these are for their benefit and that they should cooperate. Careful use of marketing communications is needed, through both personal and non-personal media, to inform customers of the benefits, to persuade them of the value of what is being done and to reassure them that their cooperation will not make too many heavy demands on them.

Reduce mismatch between supply and demand. Sometimes demand exceeds supply. Productivity might well then be high, but it could be higher still if the excess demand could be accommodated. Some customers will not want to wait and might decide either to take their business to an alternative service provider or not to purchase at all. At other times, supply will exceed demand and productivity will be low because resources are lying idle. If the service provider can even out some of these fluctuations, then perhaps overall productivity can be improved.

The service provider might be able to control aspects of supply and demand through fairly simple measures. Pricing, for example, might help to divert demand away from busy periods or to create extra demand at quiet times. Off-peak or off-season tariffs, prices or fares or time-specific promotions ('10 per cent off the price of a haircut on Wednesday afternoons between now and Christmas', for example) might help to achieve this. An appointment booking system might also help to ensure a steady trickle of customers at intervals that suit the service provider. The danger is, though, that if the customer cannot get the appointment slot that they want, they might not bother at all. Finding alternative uses for staff and facilities during quiet times can also create more demand and increase productivity. Universities, for instance, have long had the problem of facilities lying idle at weekends and during vacations. They have solved this by turning halls of residence into conference accommodation or cheap and cheerful holiday lets in the vacations, or hiring out their more attractive and historic buildings for weddings and other functions at weekends, with catering provided.

If the service provider cannot or does not wish to divert demand away from busy times, then the ability to supply the service to the maximum number of customers will have to be examined. If the peaks in demand are fairly predictable, then many service providers will bring in part-time staff to increase available supply. There might be limits to their ability to do so, however, which are imposed by constraints of physical space and facilities. A supermarket has only so many checkouts, a bank has only so many tills, a barber's shop has only so many chairs, a restaurant has only so many tables. Nevertheless, part-time staff can still be useful behind the scenes, easing the burden on front-line staff and speeding up the throughput of customers.

In other situations, physical constraints are less important.

eg

A business school operating a modular scheme might find that there are substantial numbers of students wanting to take marketing options. This might not put too much pressure on the weekly lecture programme, since as long as a large enough lecture theatre is available, a lecturer can talk to 200 students as easily as to 50. The problems arise with the number of seminar groups to be serviced and part-time staff might be brought in to take some of the burden off full-time staff. Physical facilities are not likely to pose too many problems in this case, especially if staff and students are prepared to tolerate less popular timetable slots such as 4 p.m. on a Friday!

Internal marketing is an extremely important element of service creation and delivery. As Heskett *et al.* (1994) suggest, there is a direct link between employee satisfaction and productivity, customer satisfaction and loyalty, and profit. If service creation and consumption are inseparable, then it is logical to assume that staff attitudes, efficiency and competence are also inseparable from the customer's judgement of quality, and thus satisfaction.

Franchising

As mentioned in Chapter 12, a **franchise** is a kind of vertical marketing system with a contractual relationship between the **franchisor** and the **franchisee**. Generally, it means that the owner of a product, trade mark, process or service licenses another person or organisation to use, buy, sell or operate it in exchange for some form of payment. This might be in the form of a royalty, a licence fee or a commitment to purchase products at supplier-dominated prices. Franchising is therefore both a distribution method through which market coverage can be extended and a business system through which enterprises can launch or grow.

eg

Marco Leer from Rotterdam in the Netherlands specialises in leather upholstery refinishing. After several years of R&D, the owner found an innovative way of mixing and applying paint to leather upholstery. This significantly reduced labour costs and created an opportunity to standardise prices. Soon after the launch in the Netherlands, the owner decided that franchising was the best method of expansion. He first appointed franchisees in other parts of the Netherlands, then in Europe, where there soon were 20 franchises across Belgium, Germany, the UK and Switzerland. The key ingredients of the package for franchisees are detailed business and technical training, field support and advice over finding a suitable business location. Location is important for the collection and delivery of furniture and premises adjacent to highways are preferred. It is the product concept, however, that lies at the heart of a franchise system that has led to business success. The ability to refurbish leather products to high standards, to train franchisees to achieve that standard, and the creation of a business system that can be replicated are central to growth. Although the sector is not as glamorous and as high profile as fast food or retailing, the franchising method has enabled an otherwise limited site operation to expand on a European scale (http://www.marcoleer.com).

Although franchising is primarily a method of marketing goods and services, it can also offer a small business a route for achieving more rapid growth, as seen in the Marco Leer case. From a slightly different perspective, it can also provide a prospective entrepreneur with a *quasi*-independent entry into a market with a tried-and-tested concept. Such an entrepreneur might be new to franchising or even new to business, but can nevertheless bring a bundle of skills and competencies acquired in a previous career.

There are five different types of franchise relationship, covering distributorships, licences to manufacture, celebrity endorsements, trade marks and the most popular form in recent years, business format franchising. The latter has emerged as the most potent and dynamic growth area in the retail and service sector throughout the developed world and will now be discussed in detail.

Business format franchise

A business format franchise provides opportunities for small, independent entrepreneurs, without a novel idea, to enter business and is an attractive route for an existing business with a proven concept to expand.

The **business format franchise** implies access not only to a product concept, but also to a comprehensive package that enables the product or service to be delivered in a standardised way, regardless of location. The package or format might include a wide range of different requirements and supports.

The business format therefore includes such issues as intellectual property rights relating to trade marks, trade names, shop signs, designs, copyrights, know-how or patents. All of these can be used to market more effectively, thus facilitating the resale of goods or the provision of services to end users.

eg

McDonald's (http://www.mcdonalds.com) is probably the most famous franchisor in the world. With over 30,000 outlets in 121 countries, the influence of the golden arches continues to spread at a rapid rate. Between 1,300 and 1,400 new restaurants are expected to be opened in 2002, although there are also closures of under-performing international restaurants, some 163 in 2001. Around 57 per cent of all outlets are franchised and the rest are either company operated (28 per cent) or affiliated (15 per cent). The typical cost to the franchisor is a start-up investment of between $455,000 and $768,000, a franchise fee payable to McDonald's of $45,000, and an ongoing royalty on sales of 12.5 per cent. The benefits in return can be very significant: access to one of the biggest global brands, a highly experienced and professional support team, proven procedures in food quality preparation, exceptional brand consistency, support with site development and launch, and ongoing national advertising and sales promotion to retain an interest in the brand. In the UK alone, the 1,200 restaurants are visited by more than 2.5 million customers every day, over 2,000 in each store. Some of these stores are in unique locations, such as Anfield, home of Liverpool FC, Guy's Hospital, and in listed buildings in places such as Stratford-upon-Avon and Windsor. Worldwide, over 46 million people per day visit McDonald's. Why? The brand power, the ability to select the best sites and the best franchisees, and the well-defined retail business model are all critical to its success. The menu may change a little depending on where you are in the world, but the basic propositions and the burger are ever present. Staff training is central to the franchise. Regardless of who they are and what experience they have had, the franchisee must attend a five-day restaurant assignment as a crew member, with no special treatment, and undergo any subsequent training as suggested by McDonald's.

Types of business format franchise. There are four main types of business format franchise:

1 *Executive.* This involves white-collar-orientated businesses, such as consultancy, estate agencies and personnel recruitment, where the franchisee usually visits the client to perform the service.
2 *Retail.* The franchisee operates from premises either in prime locations or from carefully selected sites. Examples of this type of franchise are fast food, picture framing and wine stores. Many of the issues considered in Chapter 13 apply to this group. Investment can be high, but so too can the returns.
3 *Distribution.* These franchisees often operate from vans delivering to retailers or direct to the public. Products include greeting cards, tools and pet accessories. The sales territory is normally firmly specified.
4 *Job.* These tend to be service franchises where the franchisee performs a service on the customer's premises. They often operate from a home base with a van. Cleaning, repairs and security services are all good examples.

The business format contract. A number of elements are incorporated into the business format franchise, providing the basis for the content of the contractual agreement and the mutual responsibilities created (Mendelsohn, 1999):

1 The contract should specify the nature and terms of the relationship. This should cover its duration, the geographic extent of any exclusive sales territory and the franchisee's and franchisor's mutual expectations and responsibilities.
2 The franchisor must have developed a successful, proven business format system with an identified brand name before offering it to franchisees. This is normally a requirement of the various national bodies that register and regulate bona fide franchises. It protects potential franchisees from the small minority of unethical franchisors who would take money from franchisees and leave them with an unproven concept that will quickly fail.
3 The franchisor should train the franchisee in the system before opening and fully assist in the planning and implementation of the opening.
4 The franchisor should maintain a business relationship with the franchisee through ongoing support in marketing and management. Such a relationship is important in the early stages of the franchise when the franchisee is still learning the business.
5 The franchisee is permitted, under the control of the franchisor, to use the brand name and to operate the business system in a defined geographic area. The franchisee is allowed to benefit from the goodwill created.
6 The franchisee should make a capital investment to launch the business.
7 The franchisee should legally own the business. This means that the consequences of business failure will fall primarily on the franchisee rather than on the franchisor.
8 The franchisee must pay the franchisor for the rights acquired and the ongoing services provided. This is normally by a combination of licence fee, royalty or mark-up on supplies purchased.

marketing *in action*

La Compagnie des Petits

The first shop belonging to La Compagnie des Petits opened in March 1992. Founded by three partners who all had experience in the textile industry, the purpose of the store was to offer children's clothing that was of good quality, well designed and fashionable, but not too expensive. The owners selected the franchise route as a means of expansion. By 2002, the network had grown to 97 stores, including stores in 70 French towns, with others in Belgium, Portugal, Asia and New Zealand. Total sales are around €30mn per year.

In its advertisement, the company offers potential franchisees premises, fixtures and fittings, as well as professional advice and support. It also claims to offer attractive gross margins on goods sold. Because it manufactures its goods in countries with low labour costs, and supplies its franchisees at cost price, gross margins of around 52 per cent are possible. The company's research suggests that the average spend in one of its stores is around €60, on goods priced between €5 and €60.

▶

As one might expect, the company, as a franchisor, says that it is looking for motivated people who want to take the welfare of an enterprise into their own hands. The franchisor claims too that because of their stake in the business, franchised stores in the chain perform a lot better than the wholly owned branches. The company thus wants to establish a real partnership with its franchisees, developing an extensive network without losing sight of the interests of the individual franchisee.

Franchisees, however, have to be able to raise sufficient finance to set themselves up in business. The franchisor will find and equip the premises to ensure that the right locations are selected. The 'entry fee' to buy into a franchise is €10,671 but the cost of investment in opening stock means that the franchisee should have around €80,000 to put into the business with at least 60 per cent of it from personal equity. There is also an annual royalty of 4.1 per cent of sales and an advertising contribution of 2.4 per cent to cover the ongoing involvement of the franchisor in the franchisee's business and the costs of developing the brand image and awareness of the franchise system as a whole.

Source: http://www.lacompagniedespetits.com.

Business format franchising can help the aspiring entrepreneur to start a new business in a new area. By providing the innovative idea and a potentially successful formula, franchisors are active in encouraging this route into self-employment. Typical advantages for the franchisee are the independence of ownership, control over one's own working environment and the freedom to guide one's own destiny. In the view of Felstead (1991), however, the degree of independence is highly variable depending on the design of the system, varying from high to low discretion franchising, as shown in Table 22.3.

The scope and growth of franchising

Although franchising is often regarded as a relatively recent phenomenon, its origins can actually be traced back to the tied house system in British brewing in the eighteenth century. Although such arrangements did not demonstrate the characteristics of a business format system, their roots lay in exclusive purchasing arrangements. The modern genesis of franchising, especially of the business format type, can be traced back to the USA with the Howard Johnson restaurant chain in the 1930s, which was followed by many other well-known franchises. Some of the early franchises centred on product and trade names in such areas as petrol retailing and soft drinks bottling. Most of the major growth in the USA, however, has been through business format franchising. It has been estimated that in the USA

Table 22.3 Variations in franchise independence

	High discretion/ 'Soft' franchising	*Low discretion/ 'Hard' franchising*
Controls on and nature of the productive process	High service content/low product content High level of expertise at the point of consumption Exclusive territory served by mobile operation High levels of local advertising/low levels of national advertising	Low service content/ high product content Low level of expertise at the point of consumption Single fixed store location Low levels of local advertising/high levels of national advertising
Revenue payments	Low royalties	High royalties
Ownership of the means of production	Absence of trade secret/special equipment/special products Weak 'ties' on physical means of production	Trade secret/special equipment/special products Strong 'ties' on physical means of production

Source: Felstead (1991).

there are something like 500,000 franchise operating units and over 2,500 franchisors, accounting for nearly half of US retail sales, turning over $1 trillion. Not all these franchisors offer international systems, but even this grew at a fast rate in the 1990s.

Europe has also experienced the franchise revolution. Many of the trends that fuelled growth in the USA have also been seen in Europe. Growing disposable incomes, urbanisation and home-centred families have all played their part in creating more service-orientated operations. Franchising is particularly well suited to services and people-intensive activities, especially where geographic proximity is needed. In Europe, it has been estimated that there are over 170,000 franchised outlets belonging to around 4,000 franchise systems, with a total turnover of around £70 bn, employing 1.5 million people.

The impact of franchising in Europe has been greatest in France, Netherlands and the UK, although Germany and Spain are also experiencing a growth in new systems. In the UK, around 30 per cent of retail sales are generated in franchised situations, deriving from 35,600 franchisees and 665 franchisors. The combined turnover is £9.3 bn and the industry employs 316,000 people. Interestingly, over 95 per cent of franchisees are thought to be operating at a profit, indicating the strength of proven franchised systems compared with new independent business start-ups in which failure rates can be high (NatWest/British Franchise Association, 2001). In the UK, the average annual gross sales varies according to the franchise type, as shown in Table 22.4.

Table 22.4 UK annual average gross sales by franchise type

Type	*Average gross sales (£)*
Retail premises	£500,000
Office or business premises	£331,000
Home-based franchise	£76,000
Mobile franchise	£53,000

Source: NatWest/British Franchise Association annual survey conducted by BDRC, (2001).

Although these figures conceal wide variations, the level of sales appear to have been sufficient for 72 per cent of franchisees who were facing contract renewal in the following three years and who confirmed that they would renew their contracts (NatWest/British Franchise Association, 2001).

The franchisor's perspective

Benefits

Both small and large companies can expand through franchising. The two main benefits are financial and managerial. From a financial point of view, rapid growth in market coverage and penetration can be achieved using the resources provided by the franchisees. To open a new directly owned outlet would involve an investment both in capital assets (shop fittings, equipment, property, etc.) and in working capital for stock and other operating costs. There would also be the risk of failing to achieve sales targets and financial projections. Many of these risks are effectively borne and financed by the franchisees through their start-up capital investment, licence fees and any other royalty payments.

eg

The key strengths of McDonald's (see p. 980) are powerful contributors to the success of the franchise system. It actually selects the site before it selects the franchisee. By undertaking all the site evaluation and planning, using many years of experience and sophisticated models, it is able to predict with some accuracy the likely sales performance of the outlet. It also constructs the building or converts it where necessary, and potential franchisees are offered the site only after they have completed their training and are approved to become owner-operators. They still have to pay, however, for the fitting-out and initial set up of the outlet (http://www.mcdonalds.com).

The franchisee also represents a committed management resource. The franchisee becomes the legal owner of the business and will therefore suffer from failure or benefit from success. By applying entrepreneurial skills within the framework of the franchise agreement, the franchisee will have to manage the local operation, promote sales and control resources. It would be very hard for the franchisor to motivate salaried staff to make the same effort, because they would not be running the same personal risks as a franchisee (Barrow, 2001).

There are other benefits from franchising. Of particular importance is the ability to develop economies of scale in purchasing, marketing and corporate image and branding without having a large organisation. Indeed, a small enterprise seeking to expand quickly can gain these benefits on the basis of the franchisees' capital. The important benefit of a business format franchise system, however, is that it can divorce service design and planning from service delivery and operations. The skill for a successful franchisor might therefore lie in opportunity assessment, system design and franchisee recruitment rather than in the technical area of production.

eg

The Subway restaurant chain provides an excellent example of the pace of network development possible through a franchised system. The chain was started in 1965 in the USA by a 17-year-old high school graduate wanting to pay his way through college. The franchise concept is simple: the provision of high-quality hot and cold sandwiches, deli style, with salad and hot and cold drinks, offering value and speed of service. The average store is between 50 and 150 m^2, with a take away and small eating-in area. Since starting to use franchising in the 1970s, the chain has opened over 16,000 units in 75 countries. Sales are in excess of $5 bn and although Subway is still primarily a US operation with over 13,000 outlets there, there are also 377 in Australia, 103 in Japan, 69 in the UK, but just 2 in France. Penetration has been more difficult in Europe given the different traditions of sandwich making. As with McDonald's, the menu stays the same around the world other than catering for minor cultural and religious variations (http://www.subway.com).

Disadvantages

There are, nevertheless, also problems associated with franchising a business. Some of them relate to handling difficult, ineffective or remote franchisees, especially as they become highly experienced in trading in the system area. This could lead to some questioning of the franchise relationship, if poor or ineffective support is being provided by the franchisor (Pettitt, 1988). Furthermore, if the franchisor is felt to be abusing its power, franchisees might start to group together to negotiate on more equal terms with the franchisor. Reputable and better-established franchisors often welcome the formation of formal franchisee groups, as a means of generating feedback and working together to develop a more effective franchise system.

The franchisee's perspective

In some respects, for the franchisee, the decision to start a franchised business is similar to the decision to start a fully independent one. The main difference is the need to select the most appropriate business sector from the franchise opportunities available. Some of the benefits of entering a franchise agreement are generic, in that they are related to the growth prospects in that particular product or service sector. Other benefits might only be realised if a 'good' franchisor is selected, one that offers a first-class support package and meets their commitments over time.

Ultimately, the decision is based on the individual's preparedness to accept a lower return for a lower risk. As indicated in the previous chapter, many new small businesses fail. This often reflects a lack of preparedness, experience or real and reasonably permanent market potential. Through careful site selection, concept packaging and training, the franchisee entrepreneur does not have to go through the same learning experience and trial-and-error process. While the returns may be lower, given the need for royalties and other means of remunerating the franchisor, because the concept is entirely proven, the risk in the launch phase might be much lower. The failure rate for franchised systems is often between one-eighth and one-tenth of failure rates of independent ventures.

Advantages of franchising

The main advantages in adopting a franchise are:

1 Participation in a system with an established image, name and reputation, often on a regional or national scale. As shown in Chapter 14, it can take a considerable time to get a company or brand name established in the consumer's mind. The franchisee can cut out much of this building process and, where a reputation already exists, it can be traded on.

eg

Domino's Pizza has a well-respected reputation in fast food franchising. With over 7,000 stores generating $3.8 bn of sales and operations in 64 countries with over 2,000 outlets outside the USA, Domino's needs a flow of new franchisees to continue its expansion programme. It offers a comprehensive initial and ongoing training and support programme for its franchisees. Before starting the franchise outlet, the franchisees participate in a franchise development programme focusing on operations, production, planning, food presentation, local marketing and business development. A preference is given to franchisees who have worked in a pizza retail environment, as this is found to speed up the induction process (http://www.dominos.com).

2 In well-organised systems, the franchisee receives a number of services as part of the start-up package. With the Prontoprint system these include site selection, planning and launch assistance, training for the franchisee and key staff in all aspects of the business, support in raising finance and, where necessary, the best combination of opening stock or supplies, marketing information and launch publicity. Often franchisors can provide special finance facilities for new franchisees.

3 National or regional advertising in addition to any undertaken by the franchisee can play an important role in building a stronger system (brand) identity. Prontaprint (http://www.prontaprint.com) can claim sales of $55 mn through 200 business communication centres in the UK and Ireland. It operates a central support function for marketing, advertising campaigns and PR and at a local level it will assist with launch events, organise sales promotion and local point-of-sale materials. However, it does expect the franchisee and local teams to be very active in direct customer contact, from prospecting to over-the-counter service and repeat business calling. Sales and telesales training is provided and in the franchisee selection process selling skills are considered to be crucial.

4 Where supplies or equipment have to be purchased, the franchisee will at least receive considerable guidance to avoid shortages or surpluses. At best, preferential terms might be passed on.

5 Ongoing advice and support might be available for management problem solving, whether in marketing, finance or any other aspect of business development. Amtrack Express Parcels goes further by covering all invoicing, cash flow and debt collection services for its franchisees.

6 New product development can also be important if a stream of product or service improvements would help the franchisee to keep the product portfolio fresh. From its origins in the full print design and copy service for smaller business, Prontaprint has had to reinvent the business with the changing impact of technology. Although it retains the core service of designing and printing letterheads and forms etc., new business areas have also been launched such as the web design service that enables franchisees to design sites, advise on online ordering and analyse visitor traffic. This has meant new manuals and training for all Prontaprint staff.

7 Some territorial protection will be offered if franchisees are given defined licence areas in which to trade. Of course, that is no protection from competitors operating within other franchise systems or independent operators. A Domino's Pizza franchise does not mean protection from Pizza Hut, Pizza Express or indeed non-pizza fast food outlets.

Problems in franchising

Despite the advantages of franchising that might contribute to an increased likelihood of success, there are potential problems that also need to be considered by the prospective entrepreneur before signing the franchise agreement. Perhaps the greatest problem arises from the contract itself.

1 The contract has to ensure systems compliance. This means rigorous control over the product range offered, its quality and specification, its delivery and the way in which it is marketed. Much of the freedom to experiment and adjust to the local environment might well be denied to a franchisee. In more mature franchise chains, such as Prontaprint, some local flexibility might be allowed, but in most franchise chains close control is exercised.
2 The option always exists for the independent operator to expand, sell out or cease trading according to personal objectives. Most franchisors, however, require that any franchise transfer can only be made with their approval, and that they must approve any new franchisee. Similarly, restrictions on market development might limit growth. Although EU competition law prohibits franchisors from delineating where franchisees can draw customers from, it does not affect their ability to restrict the number of new licences or to define broad sales territories.
3 A fundamental tension can creep into the franchise relationship. The franchisor might seek to increase volume in the system to achieve greater market presence and to raise royalties based on turnover. The franchisee might be more interested in return on investment than in chasing extra turnover for lower margins.
4 Any loss of reputation or poor decision-making by the franchisor might have negative effects on the franchisee. Some franchisors have been criticised for failing to fully develop their national promotional campaign in support of franchisees. Some franchise systems have failed.

eg

Franchise systems can fail, even though the majority succeed. Notable failures include Athena poster shops, the Pierre Victoire restaurant chain, and The Tanning Shop, which went into receivership owing £6 mn (Gwyther, 1998). The failure of the franchisor leaves many angry franchisees who have often invested personal savings and perhaps have built an effective local business.

When The Tanning Shop chain folded, franchisees lost between £7,000 and £50,000 each. They claimed that the locations selected were poor and that the financial forecasts used to encourage them to sign up were over-inflated, as were the prices of the supplies they were required to purchase from the franchisor. The network for the vertical tanning booth outlets grew quickly from one store in London in 1992 to 150 stores by 1996. However, the sales and thus the cash flow forecasts were not realistic. Regardless of location, the sales and business plans were based on inner London performance, levels that could not be sustained in market towns and small cities. Many of the prospective franchisees were not business wise and did not challenge the figures before joining. It really was a case of franchisee beware (Murray, 1998).

On balance, the advantages and disadvantages of the franchised route are a trade-off between the benefits of being associated with a franchised chain and the costs associated with the loss of complete independence and the ongoing franchisor involvement. Given the worldwide growth of franchising and the fact that many franchisees do renew their agreements when the original contract period expires, it would appear that many entrepreneurs are prepared to sacrifice their independence for lower start-up risk and that they do feel that operating a franchise is worthwhile.

Franchise blueprints and contracts

The keys to success in any franchise system are the development and testing of an unusual or attractive market concept, patented equipment and/or a readily identifiable trade mark and image. In the view of Mendelsohn (1999), any business that is capable of being run under remote management is also capable of being franchised. Table 22.5 indicates the wide

Table 22.5 Business areas franchised in Europe

Business area	*Specific products/services franchised*
Food and drink	sandwiches; pizzas; burgers; petfood; Chinese take-aways; Mexican restaurants; off-licences; sweet shops
Clothing and consumer goods	leisure wear; children's wear; bridal/formal wear; accessories; sports goods and clothing; greeting cards; toiletries
Domestic services	home cleaning; double glazing repair/maintenance; upholstery/carpet cleaning; interior decoration; drain clearance
Car services	windscreen replacement; scratch/dent repairs; car cleaning/valeting; servicing
Personal services	dating agencies; hairdressing; sunbeds; nursing care; party planning
Legal/business services	courier services; stock auditing; utility auditing; office training; computer training; workwear; office cleaning; printing; will writing; property sales.

range of areas that are currently being franchised across Europe. From a marketing perspective, there is really no difference between developing a successful independent business and developing a successful franchise system. The product or service must be valued, differentiated from its competitors by real or imaginary criteria and sustainable over time. There are, however, some other considerations that are relevant when an entrepreneur is deciding on the appropriateness of the franchising route. The system must be capable of replication according to the franchisor's design. This could include product, service and marketing effectiveness. It must also be capable of generating margins that can sustain the continued interest of both franchisor and franchisee.

The decision to build a franchise chain can stem from an existing business seeking to expand or from a new business start-up, where the investment may be large, as is typically found in the fast food business, or quite small, as in such areas as domestic services.

eg

A Prontaprint franchise blueprint provides a clear statement of the likely returns at different levels of turnover. Operating profits are quoted as around 17 per cent of turnover in the first year, rising to 25 per cent by year three. It also claims that its top twenty centres grew by 15 per cent per year in the period 1999–2000. Against that potential return, the investment options are presented. The total investment required to open a centre is between £100,000 and £200,000, including the start-up franchise fee, with the franchisee needing to provide a minimum of £40,000 from their own funds. Prontaprint has contacts that can then help the prospective franchisee to raise the balance from external finance. Although ultimately it is the franchisee's ability to sell the digital design, print and copy services that will determine the level of success, the experience offered by Prontaprint can help them to avoid a lot of mistakes in the early period (http://www.prontaprint.com).

In the case of a new start rather than an outgrowth such as the Marco Leer example (*see* pp. 979–80 above), it is normally expected that the franchise package will have been piloted before being offered to potential franchisees. This enables the concept to be fully tried and tested in field conditions.

Launching a new franchising system

There are seven stages in launching a new franchised system, as shown in Figure 22.5.

Developing the franchised business system concept. As indicated above, a franchised business system should offer many of the characteristics of any successful business plus the ability to replicate without the direct intervention of the concept owner. The more complex

Figure 22.5 Stages in launching a new franchised business system

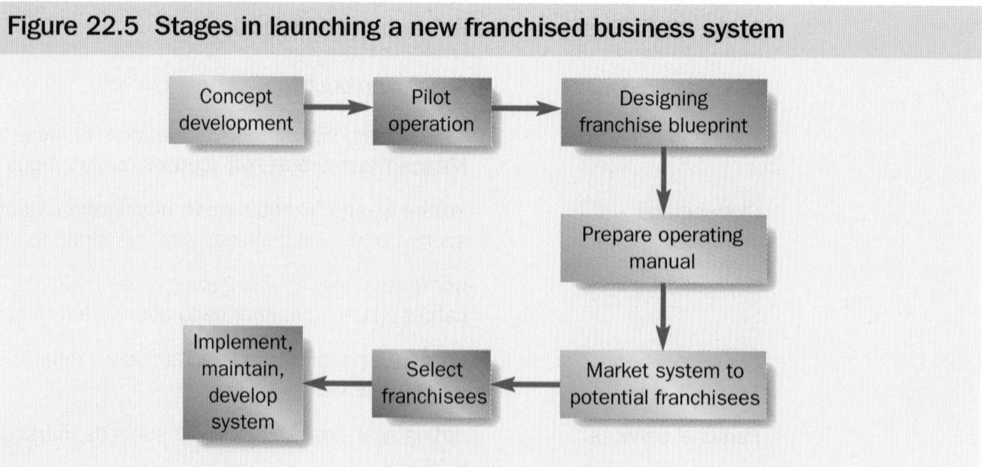

and technically orientated the business, the greater the difficulty of franchising, because of problems in replicating. The impact of franchising in industrial markets is, therefore, marginal, being reserved mainly for industrial services rather than manufacturing. In contrast, a fast food system can be standardised through the use of similar equipment, kitchen design, premises, raw materials, cooking instructions, food presentation, menu, seating configuration, etc.

As with any business launch, it is very important to have a clear idea of the target market and to assess the potential business likely to be generated across a geographic area. In some cases, the availability of suitable premises might be an important consideration. Often a franchisor agrees a town or city and even a site before advertising for franchisees. This might be especially crucial where impulse or passing trade is required.

Undertaking a pilot operation. Before the franchise is offered to a wider audience, it should be piloted in at least one location for at least one year. This enables a full market test to take place and the package to be fully developed and refined. If the franchisor is new to the trading concept, the experience gained will be invaluable later when advising others on managerial and operational problems. Many national franchise associations insist on a pilot period as a precondition of membership. Without such a pilot the franchisees, if they are prepared to take a chance, are effectively working on a trial-and-error basis and might not receive the same benefits as they would if they were entering a proven system.

Designing the franchise blueprint. The proven franchise package should be the output of the pilot period. The package represents the **franchise blueprint** for a successful operation, the key factors that are likely to maximise the chances of success. Obviously, these factors will vary from one system to another, depending on innovativeness, positioning and competitiveness.

As mentioned above, an important part of the blueprint will be the site selection, both specifically and in a general trading area. The way in which the area and site decisions are made will be similar to that of any other retail location decision, as discussed at pp. 545 *et seq*. Issues of market potential, customers' preparedness to travel and competition might all play a part in the decision to locate in a particular area. Proximity to other attractions might be important, for example siting a multiplex cinema in an edge-of-town retail park close to a

eg

It is not just global franchise systems that have been successful. In Vietnam, a country emerging from a very difficult economic period, the Trung Nguyen franchised café system has grown to over 400 outlets in just three years. The café lifestyle has caught on and made the franchisor a very wealthy business person. The franchisees also benefit, recouping their initial investment in one year. The key to the blueprint is supplying the coffee beans, ensuring consistency in menu choice, décor and operating systems, and growing rapidly to make it more difficult for other competitors to spring up. The next stop may be Singapore, Tokyo or New York (Johnson, 2001).

Burger King and a Pizza Hut. The selection of specific sites might also consider such factors as traffic flow analysis, space requirements, access, parking and, of course, rental or freehold costs. Perfect Pizza, for example, advertises for franchisees both for new territories yet to be developed and to take over existing stores.

Other areas for consideration in the blueprint will be the equipment, layout, service specification, interior design, product range, etc. These issues should all be detailed in the development of the operating manual. Similarly, work systems, material requirements, staffing, marketing literature and management systems such as stock control and accounting will have to be tested and included in a refined state in the package. A final part will be the development of a finance package that can help potential franchisees to raise capital. This must allow franchisees to generate a start-up proposal that will survive the close scrutiny of financiers and analysts. A franchisee might have a better chance of obtaining start-up capital from banks and leasing companies with the franchisor's support than if it was a completely independent business.

Some operators decide to adopt a mixed system in which some outlets are franchised and others are company owned. This enables the franchisor to maintain control and contact with the market, and allows for continuing updating of the concept and blueprint.

eg

It was a long way for John Dys to go to escape from serving in the Dutch army, but a move to Canada with the concept of the popular pannekoek house eventually gave rise to the De Dutch (http://www.dutchpannkoekhouse.com) franchise chain. The attraction is that the restaurants, in addition to being themed around Holland with menu items such as De Snack and Eggs Hollandict, also only serve breakfast and lunch, and allow both a lifestyle change for franchisees and a specialisation not possible in full-range restaurants. The choice of menu has been extensively tested to position the chain apart from the many other fast food restaurant facilities and considerable effort goes into selecting the best ingredients. The blueprint covers the menu, ideal site location and the food preparation and operating methods. The equipment and fittings are specified and are included in the c. C$250,000 investment. The franchise fee is C$37,000 and a royalty charge of 5 per cent, plus a 3 per cent advertising charge is levied. Although the franchise chain is still regional to British Columbia and Alberta, perhaps one day the first outlet will be exported back to the Netherlands.

Preparing the operating manual. The operating manual is an important document that specifies exactly how the franchisee should conduct the business. It formalises the blueprint that has been developed, and is usually copyrighted to provide extra protection for the concept. Usually, any induction training is built around the **franchise operating manual**, which is designed to guide the franchisee in all aspects of the operation.

The manual will vary according to the type of franchise. Operating instructions can be quite specific, down to such details as opening hours, staff schedules, pricing policies, staff duties, service standards, accounting procedures and point-of-sale promotion. Any standard forms that have to be regularly submitted to the franchisor are provided, along with associated instructions. In situations where the service is more technical and requires careful delivery, a technical supplement might explain in some detail the equipment used and how it must be maintained to ensure high standards.

Manuals not only serve as a practical guide to operations and as a constant source of reference, they can also be used to ascertain the maturity of the franchisor for a would-be franchisee. However, the more detailed the manual, the more control the franchisor has over the franchisee in terms of inspecting premises and assessing local systems, creating additional pressure to comply with quality standards (Chaplin, 1999).

All franchisees receive the manual and are expected to inform their staff of the relevant parts. In a restaurant franchise, for instance, the level of detail can even include how the food should be arranged on the plate!

Marketing to franchisees. Once the system has been designed and the necessary support made available, the franchisor needs to find and select suitable franchisees. There is little point in recruiting 'unsuitable' candidates, as they are more likely to fail or to demand

eg

Elite Introductions (http://www.eliteintroductions.com) has the clear mission of bringing people together. It achieves that by matching potential partners on its register in a tasteful and confidential manner. From a one-office beginning in 1994, it has grown to over 100 outlets and each franchisee needs £25,000 to start an office in an otherwise highly people-orientated business. Often working from home, the attraction to potential franchisees is the relatively low cost of entry and no need for extensive working capital, as stock and rent are not required in what is an essentially cash-based business. It advertises for new franchisees using franchise magazines and through its own website.

excessive franchisor time. Poor franchisees might also reflect badly on the reputation of the franchisor. Often the expansion of the network proceeds slowly in the first year or two in order to fine tune the system and franchisee recruitment.

Franchisors use a variety of methods to reach prospective franchisees. Magazines such as the *Franchise Magazine* are an obvious source, as are franchise exhibitions such as the European Franchise Exhibition, and advertising in general media. Once potential franchisees have made an initial approach, there should be a preliminary screening before a detailed analysis of the suitability of a potential candidate.

Selecting franchisees. The level of detail and formality in the selection phase will often depend on the care taken by the franchisor, the range of alternatives, and the scale of the investment required. In reality, this phase is actually about mutual selection, since the franchisee must also be convinced that the relationship is worth the investment and commitment.

A number of issues might be explored by the franchisor, including the candidate's motivation, commitment, transferable skills, financial resources, career history and ability to adopt a multi-functional entrepreneurial role. Many franchisors develop a franchisee profile to guide their selection. Over time, this can reflect the franchisor's actual experiences of franchisees rather than an idealised profile. Certain skills might emerge ahead of others. Sometimes, these skills are marketing and sales related, reflecting an ability to adopt a planned, proactive approach to market development.

eg

JaniKing is a global commercial cleaning franchise company with over 9,000 franchisees working through 100 regional offices worldwide. Training is an important part of the support package. It covers all aspects of providing a professional cleaning service as well as sales, marketing and management techniques. A range of training methods are employed including classroom sessions, demonstrations, video presentations, and hands-on practical training, all backed up by the manual and printed training support guide. Refresher training is also offered to ensure that new methods are passed on to the franchisees. JaniKing prefers its franchisees to have local knowledge and to be prepared to become engaged in the networks in which they operate (http://www.jani-king.com).

The franchisor does have a responsibility to avoid selecting unsuitable applicants, despite the temptation of more licence fees. Often, a potential franchisee is investing a significant sum of money, perhaps from savings or redundancy. The loss of this through business failure could be devastating. Ultimately, any franchise system will only sustain itself if all its parts are strong. Rumours of high failure rates among franchisees will soon spread and deter potential candidates.

From the franchisee's perspective, the decision to take out a franchise should be treated just like any other investment decision. The franchisee should thoroughly investigate the character and track record of the franchisor, as well as thinking through the feasibility of the franchise itself under different market conditions. The franchisee should be particularly concerned about the level of initial and ongoing support offered by the franchisor in site selection, opening, training and marketing. Often the best source of information is existing franchisees. Any franchisor who is reluctant to provide such contacts might be regarded as dubious. If the system appears to be working well, the real question is whether it will transfer to the area being considered and whether the applicant has the necessary skills and interest to make it work.

The franchise contract specifies, usually very precisely, the obligations of both parties and the basis on which the agreement may be terminated. It is a legal document, is rarely negotiable and always needs careful scrutiny before signing. Once the agreement is signed it is legally binding for the contract period. The agreement normally specifies (based on Barrow and Golzen, 1990):

- the nature and name of the activity being franchised;
- the franchise territory;
- the terms of the franchise;
- the franchise fee and royalty;
- franchisor responsibilities;
- franchisee obligations;
- the conditions under which the franchisee may sell or assign the business;
- the conditions under which the franchisee may terminate the franchise;
- the terms and obligations of the franchisor in similar circumstances.

It is often considered that once the contract has to be quoted, normal working relationships have either become very strained or broken down. Most franchise systems have less confrontational ways of resolving difficulties as they emerge. These include regular meetings and associations of franchisees to represent the collective interest.

Maintaining and developing the franchised system. After the contract has been signed, an initial franchise fee will be payable. This normally reflects a payment for the initial service in establishing a new unit, including site selection and acquisition, training and an element of goodwill in entering an established network. To the franchisor much of this payment represents a direct contribution. Other capital for specified equipment, leases, etc. will have to be paid directly or to specified suppliers. In some cases, a turnkey package might be offered in which the whole operation, including equipment, is prepared by the franchisor, leaving the new franchisee to concentrate on staffing, learning new systems and launch marketing. To the franchisor, especially in the early stages, this return for the systems investment can be an important source of income.

Continuing fees are also normally paid in order to cover the provision of ongoing services, especially in advertising, product development and management advice. This is based on a direct fee for management services, a royalty on sales, or a mark-up on goods that have to be purchased from the franchisor.

eg

Following on from the JaniKing example above, each franchisee is offered advice, business development support and technical support on an ongoing basis from the regional offices. Customer invoicing and administration is also handled at the offices to enable the franchisees to concentrate on service delivery and sales. Each office also has back–up professional sales and marketing staff to create new business opportunities for individual franchisees. A royalty on sales is charged to cover the costs associated with providing this support and involvement (http://www.jani-king.com).

In some cases, a special levy may also be imposed solely for advertising, on the basis that national advertising and promotion benefits all members of the system. Central coordination also enables the franchisor to control the form and content of the advertisements for the whole system.

As with any business, the inflow of fees from the franchisees must not only meet the franchisor's profit requirements, but also be able to support the renewal of the franchise system. This can be achieved by new product lines, fresh advertising campaigns, more effective training or any other means of maintaining competitive edge. As it becomes harder to find really innovative service ideas, competition between similar franchise systems and fully independent operators is increasing.

Non-profit marketing

The marketing concerns of **non-profit organisations**, including those in the public sector, became increasingly important over the 1980s and 1990s for a number of reasons. In the UK, the government pursued a deliberate policy of exposing public sector services to commercial market forces and of increasing their autonomy and accountability. The main focus of this section, however, is the charities aspect of non-profit marketing, reflecting the growth of cause related marketing (CRM) and the radical changes in the ways in which charities generate revenue, their attitudes to their 'businesses' and their increasingly professional approaches to marketing. Cause-related organisations form an important part of the non-proft sector. According to the Charities Association, in 2000 in the UK, over £28 bn was generated by over 161,000 charities. Many are very small and just 393 of them generate over 43 per cent of all income. Two-thirds of charities raise less than £10,000 in income (http://www.fundraising.co.uk). Increasingly, charities are becoming brands with attributes, emotive appeals and value statements that are designed to appeal to the population of interest. Research by BRMB, for example, indicates that 20 per cent of the population intends to leave money to charities in their wills, 39 per cent support children's charities and 29 per cent will support illness/research charities (Singh, 2001).

Like many other organisations, charities have found that the environment within which they operate has changed. There are many more charities competing for attention and donations, and the attitudes of both individual and corporate donors have changed. The case of the corporate donor was discussed earlier at pp. 825 *et seq*. Thus all sorts of organisations that have not traditionally seen themselves as 'being in business' have had to become more

eg

The National Missing Persons Helpline (NMPH) was registered as a charity in the UK in 1993. It was set up because at any one time there are up to 250,000 people 'missing' in the UK, yet there was no central body to offer advice and support to missing persons' families, to coordinate information on missing people, or for missing people to contact for help. Although many people do 'go missing' on purpose and do not wish to be found, others disappear because they are distressed, ill or confused and need help and reassurance to solve their problems. A few are the victims of abduction.

The NMPH therefore offers a number of services, including:

- a national 24-hour telephone helpline for families of missing people;
- a confidential 'Free Call Message Home' 24-hour freefone telephone helpline so that missing people who do not want to be 'found' can at least leave a message to reassure their families that they are all right;
- a national computerised database of missing people;
- searching for missing people, using contacts among the homeless population, and advertising and publicity;
- an image-enhancing 'age progression' computer that can create a photograph of what someone who has been missing for several years might look like now.

The charity's 'customers' are not just missing people and their families. The police find the NMPH and its database invaluable in assisting with identifying corpses and helping with missing persons cases generally.

In marketing terms, the NMPH's main problem is generating a steady and reliable flow of income. NMPH does not charge commercial rates for its services, even to the police. It hopes, of course, that those who have benefited from the service will make a donation, but this is unlikely to cover the full cost. It thus relies heavily on cash donations, corporate donations of goods and services, fundraising and promotional events. The higher the profile of the event, the greater the opportunity to raise cash. In 2002 a sponsored Glasgow to London walk was organised and various celebrities and families of missing people joined the core walkers. It also runs a celebrity memorabilia web auction where celebrity items such as a signed photo of Michael Owen would fetch over £30. It is particularly dependent on some of the 'donations in kind', for example television airtime or print advertising space, in order to carry on its work effectively.

Sources: NMPH literature; briefing given by Elaine Quigley at Buckinghamshire Chilterns University College; http://www.missingpersons.org.uk.

businesslike, fighting for and justifying resources and funding.

This section, therefore, discusses the characteristics that differentiate non-profit from profit-making organisations. Then, the implications for marketing will be explored.

Classifying non-profit organisations

As suggested above, non-profit organisations can exist in either the public or private sector, although the distinction between them is rather blurred in some cases. A hospital that treats both National Health patients and private patients, for example, is involved in both sectors. Table 22.6 gives examples of organisations in both sectors.

Table 22.6 Non-profit organisations

Public sector	*Private sector*
Public hospital	Private hospital
University	Private school
Public library	Charity
State railway	Franchised rail service operator

Characteristics of non-profit organisations

Clearly, all non-profit organisations operate in different types of market and face different challenges, but they do have a number of characteristics in common that differentiate them from ordinary commercial businesses (Lovelock and Weinberg, 1984; Kotler, 1982). These are as follows.

Multiple publics. Most profit-making organisations focus their attention on their target market. Although they do depend on shareholders to provide capital, most day-to-day cash flow is generated from sales revenue. Effectively, therefore, the recipient of the product or service and the source of income are one and the same. Non-profit organisations, however, have to divide their attention much more equally between two important groups, as shown in Figure 22.6. First, there are the customers or clients who receive the product or service. They do not necessarily pay the full cost of it. A charity, for example, might offer advice or

Figure 22.6 Non-profit organisations: multiple publics

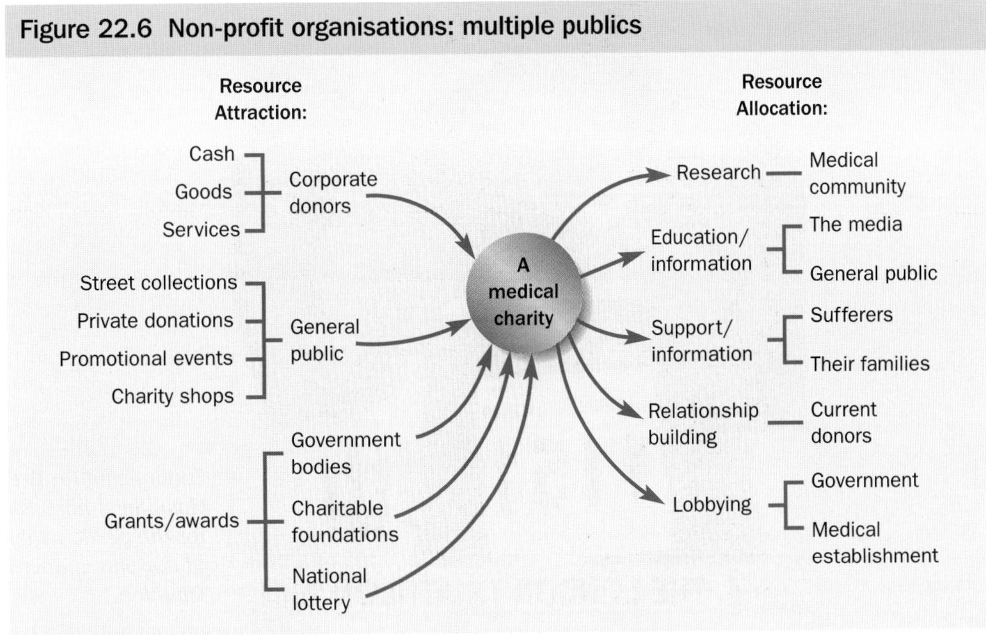

help free to those in need, whereas a museum might charge a nominal entry fee that is heavily subsidised from other sources. Thus clients or customers concern the non-profit organisation largely from a *resource allocation* point of view. The second important group is the funders, those who provide the income to allow the organisation to do its work. A charity, for example, might depend mainly on individuals making donations and corporate sponsors, a medical practice on government funding and a museum on government grants, lottery cash, individual donations and corporate sponsorship as well as entrance fees. Thus funders concern the organisation from a *resource attraction* point of view.

eg

Great Ormond Street Children's Hospital (http://www.gosh.org.uk) has the widest range of pediatric specialists in the UK, and welcomes over 22,000 inpatients and 78,000 outpatients every year, 50 per cent of whom are aged under two years. In order to provide care, to maintain its position at the frontier of medical research and to enhance its reputation for pioneering surgery, it needs to supplement the income it gets from the government via the National Health Service. Each year, the Great Ormond Street Hospital Children's Charity (GOSHCC) aims to raise £12 mn from individuals and organisations to fund pioneering research into childhood diseases, buy vital new medical equipment and offer improved support services to families.

The hospital must therefore interact with a number of publics if it is to achieve its targets. Its core activities mean that it is working with patients, parents, local hospital consultants and doctors. Each has an interest in the pediatric care work of the hospital. The government and the National Health Service also have an interest in the hospital, given its role, profile and of course its prime funding source. However, the donor publics are critical to the future of GOSH and thus the hospital has an active fund raising programme through GOSHCC. Schemes include sponsorship, advertisements on the website, private donations, payroll covenants and legacies, company giving and joint sales promotions such as one undertaken with Baby Bio, which raised £20,000. Zoom.com supported GOSHCC by contributing 5p per card for the first 50,000 e-cards sent from its site. That was good for Zoom in terms of viral marketing as well as being good for GOSHCC. Employee fund raising through adopting GOSHCC for a month, a year or for a special event provides a further source of funds as well as raising the profile.

Fundraising for Great Ormond Street Hospital is both challenging and fun for the participants. Here we see one of the partcipants for the London Triathlon.

Source: Great Ormond Street Hospital Children's Charity.

Employees at Ford went on a two-year fund raising programme to raise £100,000. Activities included a team of 12 cyclists undertaking a GOSHCC Anglo-Italian cycle challenge; 18 employees taking part in the London Marathon; and a further team undertaking the Three Peaks Challenge in Yorkshire. Perhaps the most exotic campaign was the Inca Challenge 2002, a ten-day expedition in the Peruvian mountains in search of a lost city. It attracted 44 people and raised over £60,000 for the charity through individual sponsorship. All of these events and programmes mean that GOSHCC has to plan its activities carefully to maintain good relations with individuals and organisations to attract resources and in return to ensure that the gratitude and goodwill from the well-being of its patients is fed back to the supporters.

Multiple objectives. One definition of marketing offered earlier in this book is to create and hold a customer at a profit. As we have seen, there are many different ways of achieving this and many possible subobjectives on the way, but in the end for most organisations it is all about profit. As a result, success criteria can be fairly easily defined and measured. In the non-profit sector, however, there might be multiple objectives, some of which could be difficult to define and quantify. They might concern fund raising, publicity generation, contacting customers or clients (or getting them to visit you), dispensing advice, increasing geographic coverage or giving grants to needy clients.

eg

The Swanage Railway is a heritage line owned by its members in southern England and concentrates on running preserved locomotives, often steam, on a short stretch of track from Swanage to Norden, near Corfe Castle. It is primarily a line run by enthusiasts and supported by volunteers all intent on recreating scenes from bygone days. Members donate as much as they can afford and 'premier life membership' costs £350, which allows as much free travel as is wanted. General fund raising and special appeals to members are also operated from time to time, such as appeals to raise money to restore rolling stock or to help towards the cost of extending the line a few extra miles to Wareham. The main objective is to finish the complete reopening of the line and to run as wide a range of heritage stock on the line as possible. However, in order to achieve this objective a number of other objectives have to be realised first. Realistically, the line needs to become a tourist attraction, bringing in customers who may not be railway enthusiasts as such. This could mean some compromise of purist ideals, especially with the two Thomas the Tank Engine weekends in the shoulder months when Thomas himself and all the other working locos are adorned with faces, anathema to a real enthusiast. Nevertheless, even they would have to admit that Thomas weekends provide a significant source of additional revenues by attracting families with young children. The line runs 19 services per day in the summer season and the more passengers are on board, the higher the revenue and the sooner the main objectives can be realised. Grants and loans also have to be won, such as £500,000 funding from the Rural Development Commission for a 130-space car park at one of the stations. Similarly, the local authority has supported the line as it regards it as a valuable tourist feature. Therefore fund raising, membership and revenue earning operations have to be undertaken successfully, even though they may conflict at times, if the core enthusiasts want to catch a whiff of steam and nostalgia (http://www.swanagerailway.co.uk).

Service rather than physical goods orientation. Most non-profit organisations are delivering a service product of some sort rather than manufacturing and selling a physical product. Many of the services marketing concepts already covered in this chapter therefore apply to them. In some non-profit bodies, the emphasis is on generating awareness about a cause, perhaps to generate funds, and giving information to allow people to help themselves solve a problem. Particularly where charities are concerned in generating funds, donors as a target audience are not directly benefiting from their participation in the production of this service, other than from the warm glow of satisfying their social conscience. This contrasts with the more commercial sector, where the customer who pays gets a specific service performed for their benefit (a haircut, a washing machine repaired, a bank account managed for them, etc.).

eg

Oxfam International is not only delivering a service product, but one that is often directed at beneficiaries many thousands of kilometres away. Its many programmes vary from very high profile activities such as dealing with humanitarian crises in Kosovo, Rwanda or Jenin, or helping in the aftermath of hurricanes, or participation in longer-term projects lasting many years. The River Basin Programme is one of Oxfam's largest projects aimed at helping poor people along the Ganges and Brahmaputra rivers and their hundreds of tributaries in Bangladesh and India. Areas more than 1,000 km wide are prone to severe flooding and Oxfam works on social and environmental aspects to help alleviate the worst effects.

Oxfam needs high profile media coverage to make the suffering of people and the effective impact even of small donations more tangible. With natural disasters, much of the media coverage is done for Oxfam and the focus is on directing goodwill and sympathy to make donating easy. In other cases, more subtle lobbying and influence are required to achieve the mission of 'saving lives and restoring hope'. Reports highlighting, for example, that in the world there are 870 million illiterate people, that 70 per cent of them are women, that 125 million children do not start school and that another 150 million drop out after four years are designed to stimulate debate. Reports and briefing papers are published and sent to politicians alongside lobbying for change. One campaign is concentrated on fair trade by seeking to help poor producers to access international export markets and offering a protected, fair trade market during transition while they acquire new skills and competencies. Over the last twenty years, although international trade has tripled, the 48 least-developed countries containing 10 per cent of the world's population, have seen their share of world exports decline to just 0.4 per cent over the period. Central to Oxfam's campaign are informing consumers about trade-related causes of poverty, promoting a consumer movement in favour of fair and ethical trade and lobbying for change in world trading systems where these cause poverty. The greater the publicity, the more tangible the problems and the more powerful the call for help (http://www.oxfam.org).

Public scrutiny and accountability. Where public money is concerned or where organisations rely on donations, there is greater public interest in the activities and efficiency of the organisation. To maintain the flow of donations, a charity has to be seen to be transparently honest, trustworthy and to be producing 'results'. The public wants to know how much money is going into administrative costs and how much into furthering the real work of the charity.

eg

Greenpeace (http://www.greenpeace.org) relies exclusively on support from individuals and foundations. It makes a deliberate point in its publicity of stating that it does not seek funds from governments, corporations or political parties and will not take individual donations if they compromise its independence of action. It is proud to state that it has no permanent allies or enemies. Such a principled stand means that Greenpeace must be entirely transparent if it is to avoid criticism from parties who have suffered from its direct action, or even the wider publics that support its cause.

To achieve a policy of openness, Greenpeace must make public its campaigns, its governance arrangements and its financial affairs. The annual reports reveal detailed information in all areas. The campaigns in climate, toxins, nuclear, oceans, forests, ocean dumping and genetic engineering are all specified and details provided of the main achievements in each area. A number of the campaigns have already been considered in this book, such as the Amazon rain forest, Sellafield and the whaling industry. An important part of retaining public support is highlighting successes. In 2001, for example, it highlighted its success in lobbying the European Parliament to ban PVC containing toxic substances. The substances, widely used in children's toys had resulted in damage to the kidneys, liver and testicles in animal experiments.

The financial breakdown of income and expenditure revealed a net income of €103.1 mn, after €43 mn of fund-raising expenditure was deducted. Around 47 per cent of expenditure went on direct campaigns, 33 per cent on overhead support for those campaigns, and 20 per cent on organisational support. This indicates that around half of any donation is ploughed back into the campaigning for which it was intended. Finally, details of the 40 offices and the various boards of trustees are presented along with the respective roles of Greenpeace International in the Netherlands, the overall strategy group, and each local board is specified. With many powerful detractors and 2.4 million supporters on a global scale, Greenpeace must show the results and the methods used to reach them.

Marketing implications

In general terms, the same principles of marketing apply equally to non-profit organisation as to any purely commercial concern (Sargeant, 1999). There are, however, a few specific points to note. A non-profit organisation might have quite a wide-ranging **product portfolio**, if the needs of both funders and customers or clients are taken into account. Their products might, for instance, vary from information, reassurance and advice to medical research and other practical help such as cash grants or equipment. Donors might be 'purchasing' association with a high profile good cause or the knowledge that they have done a good deed by giving. Because the products vary so much, from the extremely intangible to the extremely tangible, and because there are so many different publics to serve, a strong corporate image and good marketing communication are particularly important to pull the whole organisation together.

eg

The National Meningitis Trust (http://www.meningitis-trust.org.uk) has a specialised, highly focused portfolio concerned with meningitis. It aims to create awareness of the disease, to fund research and provide support to patients via grants and online support. A particular success was in its participation in the campaign to get students better informed of the dangers of meningitis within university halls of residence.

Compare this with the National Trust (http://www.nationaltrust.org.uk), which has a large portfolio of activity and interests. It owns 248,000 hectares of countryside, 600 miles of coastline and 200 buildings and gardens of outstanding interest, including 19 castles and 49 churches and chapels. It cares for nearly 3,000 listed buildings of which 300 are open at a charge. The National Trust must manage its portfolio to generate sufficient revenue to support the acquisition, maintenance and development of its property and land. The portfolio includes entrance fees, memberships, individual and corporate donations, fund raising, including special appeals, renting out 300 holiday cottages, and the sale of branded merchandise such as gifts, china, glass and over 60 book titles. It must manage its resources from 38,000 volunteers, 2.7 million members and 12 million visitors annually. Although the objectives are not commercial, a businesslike approach is needed for portfolio management to ensure adequate returns on activities and that any cross-subsidisation is appropriate.

If dispensing information and advice or increasing the profile of a cause are central objectives of the non-profit organisation, then **marketing communication** is an essential tool. This might mean using conventional advertising media, although that can be expensive for organisations such as smaller charities unless advertising agencies and media owners can be persuaded to offer their services cheap or free as a donation in kind. The National Trust defines its marketing tasks for all its activities as:

- marketing the properties to attract visitors;
- marketing its membership scheme to attract and retain supporters;
- fund raising for appeals aimed at generating financial support for projects;
- marketing to encourage potential legators to name the Trust in their wills; and
- a national retail and catering operation that helps attract visitors as well as raising income for the National Trust.
  (http://www.nationaltrust.org.uk).

Publicity can also be an invaluable tool for the non-profit organisation, not only because of its cost effectiveness, but also because of its ability to reach a wide range of audiences. Publicity might encourage fund raising, help to educate people or generate clients or customers. Association with high-profile commercial sponsors can similarly help to spread the message, through publicity, sponsored fund-raising events or joint or sponsored promotions.

In sectors where a non-profit organisation offers a more clearly defined product to a specific target segment within a competitive market, then a more standard approach to marketing communication might be used. A university, for example, is offering degree courses to potential students. As discussed elsewhere in this book, it might use advertising media to tell potential students why this is the best place to study; printed material such as

eg

The RSPCA is the UK's best known animal welfare charity. It not only monitors animal welfare and rehomes animals, but also campaigns and lobbies on relevant issues, such as battery farming (see Case Study 19.2). Fund raising is vital to the RSPCA – its annual running costs are around £71 mn per year and it gets no government or lottery funding. Marketing communication is clearly important in creating and retaining donors. Direct marketing is under strain with response rates dropping and thus it needs to be better targeted than ever and more creative than ever in finding mechanisms for asking for money. The charity has done a lot of work on its databases and their management in tracking the frequency of response, type of appeal responded to, size of donations, spontaneous donation rates, preferred ways of giving, etc. to help it plan its marketing better. The RSPCA makes five appeals per year through direct mail and appeals are tailored to suit different donor groups. One such group is people who give regularly via the 'payroll giving' scheme. Mailings to them are less focused on 'more money please' than on 'do you know about these other ways you can help us?'. The RSPCA is looking to develop the most integrated marketing strategy it can in terms of creating donors and then maximising their value through getting them involved in as many other areas as possible. Thus a donor might sign up for an affinity card, for example, and then be persuaded to buy Christmas cards or set up a standing order for a regular direct donation.

the prospectus, brochures and leaflets to give more detail about the institution, its location and the courses on offer; visits to schools and education fairs to meet potential recruits face to face, and publicity to increase awareness and improve its corporate image.

Pricing is applied somewhat differently in the non-profit sector than in the commercial world. As mentioned earlier, those providing income might be totally different from those receiving the product. It is accepted in most areas of the non-profit sector that the recipient might not have to bear the full cost of the service or product provided. In other words, the recipient's need comes first rather than the ability to pay. In the profit-making sector it is more likely to be the other way around: if you can pay for it, you can have it. Non-profit pricing, therefore, might be very flexible and varied. Some customers will not be asked to pay at all, others will be asked to make whatever donation they can afford for the service they have received, others will be charged a full market price.

eg

The National Trust, mentioned earlier, has to apply many pricing principles to generate sufficient revenue to meet the preservation objectives. In addition to pricing merchandise and in some cases charging entrance fees, a comprehensive range of membership options are available. For example, individual members pay £32.50 per year, families £60 and a child £15.00. Life membership options are also available starting at £770, but with lower prices for pensioners. Educational group memberships allow benefits to groups of up to 60 students and pupils. The 2.7 million members in return are granted free access to sites, can participate in local clubs and associations, and receive newsletters and magazines. The management of the Trust do not seek to charge premium pricing for sometimes exclusive and unique sites; instead a more moderate approach is adopted that rewards loyalty and frequent users, but still generates enough revenue from all sources to meet the planned development needs.

Issues of distribution, process and physical evidence, where applicable, are similar for non-profit organisations to those of other types of organisation. The organisation has to ensure that the product or service is available when and where the customer or client can conveniently access it. This might or might not involve physical premises. Clearly, non-profit institutions such as universities, hospitals, museums and the like do operate from premises. They face the same issues as any other service provider of making sure that those premises are sufficiently well equipped to allow a service to be delivered and to deal with likely demand. They also have to realise that the premises are part of the marketing effort and contribute to the customer's or client's perception of quality. Prospective students visiting a university on an open day might not be able to judge the quality of the courses very well, but they can certainly tell whether the campus would be a good place for them to live and work, whether the teaching rooms are pleasant and well equipped, and how well resourced the library and IT facilities seem to be.

Some non-profit organisations that focus mainly on giving information and advice by mail or by telephone do not, of course, need to invest in smart premises. Their priority is to ensure that customers or clients are aware of how to access the service and that enquiries are dealt with quickly, sympathetically and effectively.

eg

The Samaritans (http://www.samaritans.org.uk) exists to provide a confidential counselling service to those in a desperate emotional state who are contemplating suicide. The service is offered 24 hours a day from 154 branches staffed by volunteers who answer the telephones and raise local donations. There is no move towards developing a central call centre as it would undermine the whole structure of the service. Volunteers are carefully selected and trained locally, and give of their time for no charge. In 2001, there were 12,800 volunteers across England on various shifts, normally giving no more than 180 hours per year each. Although the caller may not care where the Samaritan is located, the organisation insists that its volunteers should not have to travel more than 60 miles to an office. There were 3.8 million calls in 2000 in England and the operation had to be able to cope with that demand, especially during the recognised peaks between 10 p.m. and 2 a.m. Each volunteer takes over 250 calls per year, and some calls can last for a long time, depending on the needs of the caller. Each branch runs as an autonomous operation, generating its own funds to cover the c. £17,000 cost per phone line and office expenses.

Marketing in non-profit-making areas is rapidly evolving and the techniques used in commercial situations are being transferred, tested and evolved to cope better with the complexity of causes, ideas and attitude change in a wide range of situations. Marketing thinking is being applied to encouraging more 'users' and 'customers' to come forward to benefit from supportive contact for people or children at risk, such as that provided by the Samaritans and the NSPCC. It is also being applied backwards to attract resources into charitable organisations that often rely on voluntary staff and generous donations from individuals and corporations.

In addition, corporate sponsorship and affiliated programmes have been fast developing, as association with a number of the causes listed above does little harm to a corporate reputation. For example Tesco, Green Flag and Lindt all work with the RSPCA for their mutual benefit. Whether they take the form of joint promotions, supported advertising, or sponsored programmes and campaigns, the opportunities for cooperation are considerable.

Chapter summary

- Although the variety of service products is very wide, all of them share some common characteristics that differentiate them from other types of product. With service products, for instance, there is often no transfer of ownership of anything, because a service is intangible. Services are also perishable, because they are generally performed at a particular time and are consumed as they are produced. This means that they cannot be stored in advance of demand, nor can they be kept in stock until a customer comes along. The customer is often directly involved in the production of the service product and thus the manufacture and delivery of the product cannot be separated. It also means that there is extensive interaction between the customer and the service provider's staff. Finally, because of the 'live' nature of the service experience and the central role of human interaction, it is very difficult to standardise the service experience.
- The normal model of a marketing mix consisting of the 4Ps is useful but insufficient for describing services, and an additional 3Ps, people, processes and physical evidence, have been added to deal with the extra dimensions peculiar to services. *People* takes account of the human interactions involved in the service product; *physical evidence* looks at the tangible elements that contribute either directly or indirectly to the creation, delivery, quality or positioning of the service; and *processes* defines the systems that allow the service to be created and delivered efficiently, reliably and cost effectively.

- Service quality is is hard to define and measure. Judgement of quality arises largely from customers' comparisons of what they expected from various facets of the service with what they think they actually received. Management can ensure that the service product is designed with the customer's real needs and wants in mind; that it is adequately resourced; that it is delivered properly; and they can try not to raise unrealistic expectations in the mind of the customer, but in the end, quality is a subjective issue. Staff are an important element of service and its delivery and must be fully qualified and trained to deal with customers and their needs, and to deliver the service reliably and consistently. The emphasis that is put on this will vary depending on whether staff have direct or indirect involvement with customers, and whether they are visible to customers or not. Like quality, productivity is a difficult management issue because of the live nature of services and the involvement of the customer in the process. Managers have to think and plan carefully in terms of staff recruitment and training, systems and technology, the service levels offered and the way in which customers interact with the service, to try to maintain control and efficiency in the service delivery system. Trying to manage supply and demand can also help to streamline productivity.
- Franchising represents a way for established businesses with a good idea to grow rapidly and achieve wider geographic coverage, and also a way for individuals to get into business with a relatively low risk. Most franchised systems are governed by a contract that formally lays out both parties' obligations and rights. There is also likely to be a blueprint or manual that can specify a wide range of operating procedures and systems that allow each individual franchise to be operated effectively and to the same standards as others. Failure in franchise situations is lower than for independent small businesses. Although the franchisee must sacrifice a certain amount of independence, the risks are greatly reduced and the franchisee can benefit from the franchisor's experience and managerial support.
- Non-profit organisations, which might be in the public or private sector, form a specialist area of services marketing. They differ because they are likely to serve multiple publics; they have multiple objectives that can often be difficult to quantify; they offer services, but the funder of the service is likely to be different from the recipient of it; and finally, they are subject to closer scrutiny and tighter accountability than many other organisations. It is also possible that where non-profit organisations are in receipt of government funding or where their existence or operation is subject to regulation, there will be limits placed on their freedom to use the marketing mix as they wish. Pricing or promotion, for example, might be prescribed or set within narrow constraints.

key words and phrases

Business format franchise
Franchise
Franchise blueprint
Franchisee
Franchise operating manual
Franchisor
Heterogeneity
Inseparability
Intangibility
Interactive marketing
Internal marketing
Marketing communication
Non-profit organisations
Perishability
Product portfolio
Service productivity
Services
Visible staff

questions for review

22.1 What are the main characteristics that distinguish *services* from physical products?

22.2 Define *inseparability* and its implications for the service product.

22.3 What are the 10 criteria that affect customers' perceptions of service quality?

22.4 In what ways do *non-profit organisations* differ from other types of business?

22.5 What benefits does *franchising* offer

(a) the franchisor; and
(b) the franchisee?

questions for discussion

22.1 Discuss the impact of perishability on the management and marketing of a service business.

22.2 Design a short questionnaire for assessing the quality of service offered by a local dental practice.

22.3 In what ways might the following service organisations define and improve their productivity:

(a) a theme park;
(b) a university;
(c) a fast food outlet?

22.4 What do you think might be the main sources of revenue for the following types of non-profit organisation and what revenue generation problems do you think each faces:

(a) a small local charity;
(b) a National Health Service hospital;
(c) a public museum?

22.5 Find out about a potential franchise opportunity. How much is the licence fee and what does it include? What benefits would the franchisee derive and what risks would they run if they decided to take up this opportunity?

case study 22.1

Developing a new franchise proposal: budget-priced hostels

(The name of the company featured in this case has been changed.)

Western Hostels is based in a picturesque part of Ireland, overlooking the Atlantic Ocean. The area is popular with tourists, although the season tends to be short. The business idea for a budget tourist hostel developed from the owners' experience in running a small hotel. They saw two backpackers having breakfast by the side of the road early one morning and after some investigation they realised that there was a gap in the market for accommodation located somewhere between a tent and a bed-and-breakfast guesthouse on the luxury scale. This gap was not just based on price but also on the customer's preferred accommodation experience. Independent backpackers are not just young people, but come from all age ranges. What they have in common is the desire for a different type of more informal holiday experience.

The entrepreneurs, having done some careful analysis, developed a business plan and opened a hostel for all age ranges. They were surprised with the scale of the response. It was especially attractive to the French and Germans who were visiting Ireland on walking or cycling holidays. In the main season, the hostel was often fully booked and was turning customers away. Demand was even steady in the shoulder months of March–April and October–November at the beginning and end of the main season. There was little demand in the winter months, so they decided to close for refurbishment and a rest. The owners did not live on the premises, but they did live nearby so that they could keep a watch on the hostel. The cost of the hostel was around €200,000, which had been covered by a secured business loan.

The hostel concept was simple: communal, single-sex sleeping, a community kitchen and lounge, all of which allowed plenty of opportunity for guests to mingle and share experiences. The range of facilities was basic, but of high quality, and prices were a little lower than typical bed-and-breakfast rates. No food was served, although guests could cook their own. Most of the marketing that was undertaken was through travel guides and some specialist hiking magazines. Organised groups such as walking clubs, universities, schools and churches were direct mailed. A few add-on services were offered, for example a rent-a-bike scheme, a *bureau de change*, a limited selection of groceries, stationery, etc., along with musical instruments that could be hired for the evening.

After two seasons the owners contemplated the next stage in development. They became interested in the franchise option after attending a business seminar. Although there were other hostels in Ireland, they were independent and of variable standard. By franchising the product concept to a specified standard and then developing and implementing a brand identity and group marketing, the basis of a successful franchise system seemed possible. The direct experience they had gained would enable them to produce an operating manual, especially covering start-up, maintenance, pricing, promotion and service standards. If a number of franchisees could be found, an advertising royalty could be used to develop a centralised reservation system and to produce a central brochure for key markets. The initial capital would be around €100,000 to cover equipping premises with 30 or more beds, and a levy on sales would also be made. In addition, the property could be acquired by the franchisee on a mortgage basis, so the capital and interest charges could be extended over a longer period.

They thought they knew the main ingredients for a franchise package, but they were still not entirely convinced that it was the best way to expand. Their plan would be for five franchises in Ireland and at least 10 in the UK within five years. Each franchisee could expect to generate around £3,000 per week in the high season, based on a price of £12 to £15 per person per night and at least 30 beds. Ancillary sales would add to those revenues. After an advertisement in a franchise magazine, the owners arranged to meet with three serious franchisee enquiries. They started to prepare for the meeting.

Questions

1. Is franchising the best way forward for this business? What are its alternatives?
2. Is the product concept, as outlined in this case, a good candidate for franchising?
3. If you were one of the potential franchisees at the meeting, what questions would you be asking?
4. What are the next stages the owners will have to go through to create and implement a franchised system?

case study 22.2

Full Stop

The NSPCC has one simple aim: to ensure that cruelty to children stops. However, it has to decide between many different, and sometimes conflicting, objectives to achieve its aim. The challenge is to ensure that the public is aware of the extent of the problem, when sometimes it is uncomfortable to think that such cruelty goes on in a modern society. The message has to be got across that, for example, every week in the UK one child dies at the hands of parents or carers and 600 children are added to the child protection registers.

The main objective of the charity is to end cruelty to children altogether, but as the figures above demonstrate, it is unfortunately a long way from that goal. It runs a series of programmes and campaigns to tackle child abuse, in the home, at work, at school, and in the community and in society. Since the campaign began, the NSPCC has been able to handle more calls on its National Child Protection Helpline, expand its schools service, produce parenting packs and work directly with over 10,000 children. To achieve its main objective, it must raise donations directly through fundraising and from individuals, corporate contributions. These sources provide 86 per cent of its income. It needs volunteers to raise funds, to campaigns and to help with some of the core services. All of these contributors must believe they are doing a worthwhile thing in supporting the NSPCC rather than another charity. The NSPCC is therefore a prime lobbying and pressure group on child welfare issues. Campaigns have been run to influence government to raise such issues on the political agenda, government spending priorities and in law and policy making.

The NSPCC actually ran into trouble for being too hard hitting with some advertisements as part of its Full Stop campaign. Overall, the campaign aimed to shake the reader out of complacency and to change public attitudes to enlist more support. The campaign's first stage was targeted at raising awareness of the brutality and types of child abuse that go on through a series of advertisements following a high-profile launch supported by Ewan McGregor and Madonna. The Prime Minister said at the launch, 'The private passion we feel for our own children should become a public passion we feel for all our children. I believe that ending cruelty is the right idea at the right time' (as quoted by Gray, 2001). The advertisements' imagery was very powerful and disturbing: 'Stop it, Daddy, stop it'. It featured well-known personalities such as pop group the Spice Girls, cartoon character Rupert Bear and footballer Alan Shearer covering their eyes as background voices focused on adults either physically abusing or just about to molest a child. Such an approach was considered necessary to shock readers and to bring home the reality of what sadly does go on for a small percentage of children. The first phase of the campaign was a great success, with independent research in 2001 confirming that the NSPCC generated the highest spontaneous awareness of any UK charity with a 12 per cent increase pre- and post-campaign. It also helped to raise over £90 mn from donations.

This was followed by equally powerful imagery in the 'Real Children Don't Bounce Back' campaign. It featured a cartoon boy being beaten up by a human father against a background of canned laughter. It ends with the cartoon boy falling down the stairs and then transforming into a real, but unconscious – possibly lifeless – child lying at the foot of the stairs. The television advertisements generated over 100 complaints to the ITC, but the NSPCC's intention was to bring home the reality of abuse, a reality that we are sometimes keen to ignore. The advertising made its point: it doubled the number of calls to the child protection helpline and enabled public awareness to be raised further as well as carrying the message that whatever the emotional stresses on parents, it should never turn to violence and child abuse. The television campaign, only shown after the 9 p.m. watershed, was designed to leave the viewer in no doubt that 'together we can stop abuse', and that the helpline could be used by anyone who suspects child cruelty.

The NSPCC has also entered into partnerships with companies to provide corporate support and assistance with fund raising. Microsoft is a major supporter of the Full Stop Campaign, directly sponsoring school fund-raising activities to provide £10 mn for the NSPCC and also championing the cause within the IT industry to raise awareness and a further £5 mn. Meanwhile, retailer The Early Learning Centre gave out 50,000 leaflets on protecting babies and 25,000 'Have Fun and Be Safe' leaflets in-store. There is close synergy between the customer base targeted by ELC and child welfare. Finally, Mars agreed some joint on-pack promotions to raise donations for the charity.

A number of other more targeted campaigns are run by the NSPCC. The 2002 Annual Children's Day was themed around 'Hitting Children Must Stop. Full Stop. It's Simple Enough for a Child to Understand', highlighting the dangers of smacking and was supported by 2,000 billboard posters. One poster indicates again the power of the imagery used. Called 'She was hit because she wet herself. She wet herself because she was hit' highlighted the emotional scars left by physical punishment and how it can damage the child–parent relationship. Supported by Microsoft, a website, there4me, has been launched and targeted at 12–16 year olds who may be suffering from abuse and who can access the internet. Private 'in box' facilities, confidential passwords and a chat line with a real counsellor supplement considerable information to enable young people to take matters further if appropriate. It also supports a team of educational advisors who work with teachers, schools and local education authorities to promote child protection.

Managing the media and PR is an important part of the marketing effort. The NSPCC actively lobbies Westminster, such as for the 'Tighten the Net' campaign which persuaded the Home Office to invest £1.5 mn in a public awareness campaign to show the dangers to children from chatlines and the internet. It also succeeded in arguing for the first Child Commissioner appointed in the UK, approved by the Welsh Assembly. Things do not always go to plan, however. Victoria Climbie was murdered by her great aunt and boyfriend in February 2000. It emerged that she had been referred to an NSPCC-run family centre seven months prior to her death. If someone had acted on this referral, they should have found out about and put a stop to the appalling abuse Victoria was being subjected to. The Director of the NSPCC at the inquiry did not seek to avoid responsibility, stating that 'It is clear that we had an opportunity to help Victoria. It is profoundly to my regret that we did not act in a timely, adequate and appropriate way and this opportunity was lost. We have taken the issues raised by this tragic case for all the agencies involved very seriously. At every stage crucial lessons that have come out of our review of Victoria's case have been acted upon' (as quoted by Chandiramani, 2002). By adopting an honest approach and accepting a degree of responsibility, the NSPCC was able to avoid the worst aspects of a media backlash that could have been harmful to the wider cause.

As the NSPCC relies on donations for 86 per cent of its income, it is essential that it gets its message across. With a plan to raise £250 mn over five years in support of its revitalised action programmes, the NSPCC believes that it must use sometimes shocking promotional techniques to stir people out of complacency. Funds are also needed for the distribution of 1 million publications, to maintain the child protection helpline. The latter received 125,000 calls from people concerned about children's welfare. Faced with the reality, it is perhaps not surprising that it is prepared to push the frontiers of shock campaigning.

Sources: Chandiramani (2002); Gray (2001), http://www.nspcc.org.

Questions

1. In what ways do the special characteristics of services and the 7Ps of the services marketing mix apply to a charity?
2. List the multiple publics for both resource attraction and resource allocation that an organisation like the NSPCC might be targeting. What kind of problems do you think might arise from having such diverse target audiences?
3. What benefits does a charity get from a promotional tie-in, such as the one between the NSPCC and The ELC?
4. To what extent can 'shock' campaigns such as those produced by the NSPCC be justified? What are the potential advantages and disadvantages of such a campaign?

References for chapter 22

Adams, B. (2000), 'A Few Hotels are Reaping Benefits from Smartcards', *Hotel and Motel Management*, 3 July, pp. 62–3.

Bansal, P. (2002), 'Smart Cards Spread Across Europe', *The Banker, March*, pp. 122–3.

Barrow, C. (2001), 'Franchising', in P. Burns (ed.), *Small Business and Entrepreneurship*, Macmillan.

Barrow, C. and Golzen, G. (1990), *Taking Up a Franchise*, Kogan Page.

Barton, R. (2001), 'Tibet Smells a Rat in China's Decision to Embrace Tourism', *The Independent*, 27 May, p. 2.

Bennett, R., Eaglesham, J. and Jowit, J. (2002), 'Tunnel Rail Operator Acts Against Paris', *Financial Times*, 17 May, p. 2.

Bevan, S. and Barber, L. (1999), 'The Benefits of Service with a Smile', *Financial Times*, 24 June, p. 15.

Bitner, M., Brown, S. and Meuter, M. (2000), 'Technology Infusion in Service Encounters', *Journal of the Academy of Marketing Science*, 28 (1), pp. 138–49.

Bray, R. (2002), 'Marriott Yests Central Punters', *Financial Times*, 26 March, p.17.

Bryan-Brown, C. (2001), 'Sweden on Wheels', *The Times*, 15 December, p. 19.

Buckley, C. (2002), 'Will Retirement Become a Thing of the Past?', *The Times*, 18 January, p. 26.

Burt, T. (1999), 'The Northern Lights of Electronic Banking', *Financial Times*, 19 July, p. 17.

Cameron, N. (2002), 'Hearts Ban Rowdy Fans', *Daily Record*, 13 February, pp. 47, 52.

Caruana, A., Money, A. and Berthon, P. (2000), 'Service Quality and Satisfaction – The Moderating Role of Value', *European Journal of Marketing*, 34 (11/12), pp. 1338–53.

Chandiramani, R. (2002), 'Call to Action', *Marketing*, 28 March, p. 18.

Chaplin, D. (1999), 'Do You Know What You Want to Know?', *Franchise International*, March/April, pp. 124–7.

Christopher, M. *et al.* (1994), *Relationship Marketing: Bringing Quality, Customer Service and Marketing Together* (2nd edn), Butterworth-Heinemann.

Cowell, D. (1984), *The Marketing of Services*, Butterworth-Heinemann.

Cox, J. (2002), 'Leisure Property Trends: Is it the End for Multiplex Anchors?', *Journal of Leisure Property*, 2 (1), pp. 83–93.

Daneskhu, S. (2002), 'Competition Puts Pressure on Once Healthy Bottom-lines', *Financial Times*, 15 March, p. 2.

Devlin, S. and Dong, H. (1994), 'Service Quality From the Customers' Perspective', *Marketing Research*, 6(1), pp. 5–13.

Dodona (2001), Cinemagoing 9, *Dodona Research*, Leicester.

Doe, B. (1999), 'Service Please', *Modern Railways*, August, p. 597.

Douglas-Home, J. (2001), 'Dracula Goes Disney', *The Times*, 6 November, p. 2.5.

Felstead, A. (1991), 'Facing up to the Fragility of "Minding Your Own Business" as a Franchise', in J. Curran and R. Blackburn (eds), *Paths of Enterprise: the Future of the Small Business*, Routledge.

Fox, A. (2001), 'Unfriendly Skies', *HR Magazine*, September, p. 12.

George, R. (2002), 'Mickey Mouse With Fangs', *The Independent*, 27 January, pp. 18–21.

Glover, J. (1999), 'London Joins the Smartcard Set', *Modern Railways*, August, p. 585.

Graham, G. (1999), 'Alternatives to Mergers', *Financial Times*, 19 July, p. 17.

Gray, R. (2001), 'Partnerships for a Wider Awareness', *Marketing*, 3 May, pp. 31–2.

Gwyther, M. (1998) 'Franchise Nation', *Management Today*, December, pp. 40–46.

Heskett, J. *et al.* (1994), 'Putting the Service–Profit Chain to Work', *Harvard Business Review*, March/April, pp. 164–74.

Heskett, J. *et al.* (1997), *The Service Profit Chain*, Free Press.

Hibbert, L. (2000), 'It's Easier by Card', *Professional Engineering*, 6 September, pp. 38–9.

Johnson, K. (2001), 'The Cafe King', *Asian Business*, July, p. 63.

Katz, K. *et al.* (1996), 'Managing Perceptions of Waiting Times and Service Queues', *International Journal of Service Industry Management*, 7(5), pp. 44–61.

Kotler, P. (1982), *Marketing for Non-Profit Organisations* (2nd edn), Prentice Hall.

Lee, J. (1997), 'Customising Staff to Win Hearts and Minds', *The Times*, 9 December, p. 31.

Lewis, K. (2002), 'Fitness on Delivery', *Sunday Times*, 28 April, p. 44.

Looy, B. *et al.* (1998), *Services Management: An Integrated Approach*, Financial Times Pitman Publishing.

Lovelock, C., Vandermerwe, S. and Lewis, B. (1999), *Services Marketing*, Financial Times Prentice Hall.

Lovelock, C. and Weinberg, C. (1984), *Marketing for Public and Non-Profit Managers*, John Wiley and Sons.

Mathews, B. and Clark, M. (1996), 'Comparability of Quality Determinants in Internal and External Service Encounters', in *Proceedings: Workshop on Quality Management in Services VI*, Universidad Carlos III de Madrid: 15–16 April.

McCarthy, M. (2002), 'Multiplex Cinemas Pose Threat to Town Centres', *The Independent*, 5 January, p. 8.

McLuhan, R. (2002), 'Brands Put Service Under the Spotlight', *Marketing*, 21 February, p. 33.

Mendelsohn, M. (1999), *Guide to Franchising*, Cassell (6 edn).

Mesure, S. (2001), 'As Economic Downturn Bites, Can Britain's Health Clubs Keep in Shape?', *The Independent*, 12 September, p. 19.

Moore Ede, P. (2002), 'Bloody Hell', *The Ecologist*, March, p. 47.

Moore, C. (2001), 'Hotels Open Doors to Wireless, Broadband', *InfoWorld*, 26 March, p. 34.

Murphy, C. (1999), 'How McDonald's Conquered the UK', *Marketing*, 18 February, pp. 30–31.

Murray, I. (1998), 'Franchisees Furious over Tanning Loss', *The Express*, 12 January, pp. 31–2.

NatWest/British Franchise Association (2001), *NatWest/British Franchise Association Survey of Franchising in the UK 2001*.

Parasuraman, A. *et al.* (1985), 'A Conceptual Model of Service Quality and Its Implications For Future Research', *Journal of Marketing*, 49 (Fall), pp. 41–50.

Perren, B. and Pyke, N. (2000), 'Passenger Power: Joke Railway Sandwich Refuses to Die', *The Independent*, 27 August, p. 7.

Perren, B. (1999a), 'Service on Board', *Modern Railways*, May, p. 352.

Perren, B. (1999b), 'Service on Board', *Modern Railways*, August, p. 595.

Pettitt, S. (1988), 'Marketing Decision Making within Franchised Systems', *Proceedings of the Society of Franchising*, San Francisco, USA.

Rayport, J. and Sviokla, J. (1994), 'Managing in the Marketspace', *Harvard Business Review*, 72 (November/December), pp. 2–11.

Reece, D. (2002), 'Tussauds Splashes Out', *The Sunday Telegraph*, 17 March, p. 2.

RePass, J. (2002), 'Smart and Smarter at the MBTA', *Railway Age*, February, pp. 20–1.

Retail World (2002), 'Smart Card Trial Pressures Ranging', *Retail World*, 15–26 April, p. 10.

Rice, K. and Upton, G. (2002), 'Not Quite So Much Room at the Inn', *Financial Times*, 7 May, p. 17.

Richards, G. (2001), 'Marketing China Overseas: The Role of Theme Parks and Tourist Attractions', *Journal of Vacation Marketing*, December, pp. 28–38.

Rogers, D. (2001), 'Cinema Bucks the Media Trend', *Marketing*, 29 November, p. 7.

Rushe, D. (2001), 'Multiplex Cinemas Close Their Doors', *Sunday Times*, 25 March, p. 6.

Sargeant, A. (1999), *Marketing Management for Nonprofit Organizations*, Oxford University Press.

Sasser, W. *et al.* (1978), *Management of Service Operations: Text, Cases and Readings*, Allyn & Bacon.

Shostack, L. (1977), 'Breaking Free From Product Marketing', *Journal of Marketing*, 41 (April), pp. 73–80.

Singh, S. (2001), 'Charity Begins in Your Pocket', *Marketing Week*, 1 November, pp. 36–7.

Smith, P. and Chaffey, D. (2001), *eMarketing eXcellence: At the Heart of eBusiness*, Butterworth-Heinemann.

Syal, R. (2001), 'Secret Rail Dossier of Commuter Chaos', *The Sunday Telegraph*, 12 August, p. 8.

Warren, P. (1999), 'Welcome to the Hotel Room that Knows You Better than Your Mother', *The Express*, 17 January, p. 24.

Winnett, R. (2002), 'Road Tolls at Rush Hour Could Replace Car Tax', *Sunday Times*, 24 February, p. 28.

Zeithaml, V. *et al.* (1988). 'SERVQUAL: A Multiple Item Scale for Measuring Consumer Perceptions of Service Quality', *Journal of Retailing*, 64(1), pp. 13–37.

Zeithaml, V. *et al.* (1990), *Delivering Quality Service: Balancing Customer Perceptions and Expectations*, The Free Press.

chapter 23

international marketing

Introduction

LEARNING OBJECTIVES

This chapter will help you to:

1 understand what international marketing is, and why it is so important to many organisations;

2 appreciate the problems of analysing international marketing environments and selecting markets to enter;

3 define the various available methods of international market entry, outlining their advantages and disadvantages within the context of the broad factors influencing the choice of market entry method;

4 develop an overview of the factors that encourage organisations to adapt their marketing offerings to suit specific international markets, and those that push them towards standardisation; and

5 appreciate the reasons that individual elements of the marketing mix might have to be treated differently in different international markets.

Although international trade has been a feature of civilisation for thousands of years, the last century saw an enormous growth in the scale and complexity of trade across national frontiers. Now, most large organisations and many smaller ones assume that they will have to trade across national boundaries, and indeed for many such organisations, international trade is essential for their survival. For some organisations, an international orientation is so deeply ingrained into their strategy and operations that the domestic market in which the corporate headquarters are located is regarded as a relatively minor part of the total trading picture. Others, however, take a much more ad hoc approach, simply responding to any export enquiries that might drift in but with no special commitment to developing new markets. In between are those who proactively want to develop an international strand to their businesses. Many smaller firms in Europe have learned and benefited from the potential offered by the SEM and are now actively pursuing marketing opportunities wherever they occur in the world.

Organisations that are looking to expand their customer base internationally, however, face challenges that might be very different from those encountered in domestic markets. Decisions have to be made about the most attractive markets to pursue and develop, the best methods of entering new markets, and how much adaptation of the marketing package is necessary to achieve the desired positioning in the context of local needs and buyer expectations. These decisions are not, of course, too different from those required for domestic markets, and many of the key concepts presented in this book are just as applicable when dealing with Americans, Japanese or Danes. What are different, however, are the practice and implementation of marketing in order to take into account local customs, trading contexts, competition and other special factors that might inhibit or encourage free trade. Some organisations, such as McDonald's and Coca-Cola, choose to ignore any differences and market in the same way internationally, but the majority have to modify their marketing carefully to suit local conditions.

This chapter starts with an examination of the rationale for international marketing and the philosophy behind it in different types of organisation. This will help to explain better the motivation and direction that organisations take as they plan their marketing strategies. The next part of the chapter, building on the concepts introduced in Chapter 2, will consider the special environmental forces that affect international markets. Sometimes these forces can be so great that it becomes undesirable, difficult or extremely risky to enter a market. The analysis of environmental forces can help to identify which countries (for example Peru, Ukraine or Vietnam) or regions (for example South America, eastern Europe or South-East Asia) should be given priority in the organisation's international development

eg

London-based graphic design company Rude was delighted when soon after start up it received enquiries from some leading overseas retail stores such as Barney's in New York and Peek and Cloppenburg in Germany. Rude's original intention was primarily to supply the UK market with its designer T-shirts, but the unexpected enquiries started to draw the business into exporting at a time when there was no strategy or plan. There was no distribution strategy, no market selection, no appreciation of market rules and regulations on labelling etc. and no organisation to cope with the special demands of some foreign retailers. In Portugal, for instance, individual items are bagged and tagged as a matter of course, and a German retail store demanded that products be tested to destruction for fabric safety. Understanding letters of credit, dealing with freight forwarders and overseas distributors all required rapid learning. Rude survived, however, overcame its early problems and now sees exporting as an important part of its business development. The appointment of overseas distributors and agents was a big step in allowing Rude to concentrate on what it was good at, design and manufacture, rather than proactive overseas marketing. It has a turnover of £600,000 and has stumbled by chance on the opportunities that can arise from adopting an international perspective. The next phase is to design graphic prints on fabrics, wallpapers, ceramics and glassware as well as clothes, with both the export and UK market in mind (Arnold, 2002).

plans. Having decided on which market(s) to target, the organisation then has to decide on a market entry method. Each method carries its own risks and benefits and is appropriate for different kinds of organisations and situations. We look at this decision area later in this chapter (*see* pp. 1024 *et seq.*). Finally, the more practical issues of designing the international marketing mix are introduced, applying the concepts outlined elsewhere in this book. In this section, the most important issue is balancing the pressure to adapt and modify the marketing mix to suit local needs against the benefits of adopting a standardised approach across a whole range of different international markets to achieve economies of scale and a greater sense of consistency.

The meaning of international marketing

International marketing is, of course, concerned with marketing across national boundaries. At its simplest, the small business, such as Rude (see earlier example) that receives an order to supply its product to a buyer in another country is involved in international marketing. Even in such a straightforward situation, however, practical problems such as those encountered by Rude will have to be solved. Decisions will have to be made, for example, about what currency the price is quoted in and whether it has to cover shipping costs, import duties or other taxes. Special documentation will probably be necessary to enable the product to be shipped and transferred across national boundaries, and then the specific transportation and insurance arrangements will have to be made. The mechanism through which payment for the goods is to be transferred from country to country will have to be agreed between the buyer and the seller and might have to involve their bankers. In some cases, the seller might also have to consider installation and after-sales service arrangements. All these activities differ from normal domestic arrangements in complexity and design.

As soon as the organisation decides to seek markets proactively beyond its own national boundaries, the complexity increases still further. Promotional material and methods will have to be fine tuned to suit the local market environment in terms of language, culture, business practice, etc. Successful trading on a longer-term basis might require a physical presence in the market through a sales office or distribution point from which customers can be serviced. Regardless of how committed or long term the presence, however, the principle of simple international marketing still holds: the organisation operates from its home base and supplies customers in a country other than its own. This is *exporting*.

The difficulty with such a simple principle of international marketing, however, is that it can become less applicable as the organisation intensifies its international activity. An organisation might, for example, acquire or set up a manufacturing company to serve the

eg

Europe receives imports from some surprising sources. Eritrea is one of the poorest nations in Africa, yet the Intraocular Lens Laboratory has won acclaim for its quality and innovation. Intraocular lenses help patients with cataract problems which particularly affect the elderly living in tropical regions. Set up by a New Zealander, the company's lens production has grown from 15,000 in 1995 to an expected 250,000 in 2003, most of which are made to ISO 9002 standards. The local market is very small, so the company was forced to export early on. Its main markets are in South and South-East Asia, the Middle East, South Africa, and Sudan, as well as other parts of Africa. The next phase of development is the European market. It means some changes, as in Europe soft lenses rather than hard ones are in most demand, but the attraction is that it is a high price market, with lenses typically sold at $100. One of the problems that will have to be overcome, however, is prejudice against products from developing countries (Biemnet, 2002).

market in a foreign country. That company is part of an international group, but at a local level it does not market across national boundaries but concentrates on its own domestic market. The parent organisation might get involved to a greater or lesser extent in critical issues such as strategic direction, resource allocation or product strategies, but otherwise the manufacturer is largely autonomous. Truly global organisations such as Shell, Rank Xerox and McDonald's, therefore, are likely to have production, distribution and/or marketing organisations to serve different nations or regions. International marketing is, therefore, far more complex and less easy to define than the simple principle suggests. Its complexity arises not only from operational considerations, but also from the attitude of organisations towards it. International marketing could be an integral part of the corporate culture or it could be viewed as an add-on extra of less importance than domestic marketing.

Lynch (1994) proposed five broad categories of European organisation that will differ in their attitude and approach towards international marketing:

1 *Local scale organisations* operate within national or even local boundaries and have little opportunity or desire to trade internationally. This group might include the local garage, a television repair shop or a small metal fabricator, for example. There might be little competitive advantage to be gained in transferring existing skills and experience to new markets. In some cases, 'exporting' could mean trading in another part of the same country rather than going abroad.
2 *National scale organisations* focus mainly on their own domestic market, but might find a number of opportunities emerging from a more integrated Europe as well as *ad hoc* enquiries from around the world. Fullers, based in London, is a long established beer company with interests in 116 managed pubs and bars, a number of hotels collectively providing 546 bedrooms and, of course, on- and off-trade beer sales. Its most popular beer, *London Pride* is the third largest premium cask ale in the UK. The business concentrates on the UK market, and focuses on expanding its brands and service facilities without adding the complexity of international operations (http://www.fullers.co.uk).
3 *Regional scale organisations* might experience some growth with the economic changes in Europe. Rather than operating throughout Europe, their first stage of development may be to operate on a regional scale, for example in Scandinavia or

eg

KarstadtQuelle, Europe's largest department store and mail order organisation, is still primarily focused on the German market which generates around 90 per cent of its sales. It has 189 department stores and a 36 per cent share of department store sales in Germany. It is, however, becoming more internationally focused, primarily through its mail order business which has operations in the Netherlands, France and Belgium as well as Germany, and this trend is expected to continue (http://www.karstadtquelle.com).

Hiestand, the Swiss fresh and frozen bread and bakery producer is also in transition from a national to a regional orientation. Famous for its Swiss Butter Croissants, its first step to internationalisation was expanding into Germany with its ready-made croissants and it is now the market leader in both countries. Around 78 per cent of sales still derive from these two countries; however, Poland is now being targeted, generating 7 per cent of sales, with the rest coming from other countries around the world including the United States (http://www.hiestand.ch).

Benelux/Northern Germany. Irish companies have a long tradition of exporting to the UK as a first experience of operating beyond national boundaries. UK companies often used to focus on Commonwealth countries as export markets, although there is now more emphasis on Europe.

By operating on a regional scale, a firm gains early experience of operating beyond the domestic market, and is exposed to such issues as cultural differences, administration and logistics within a less hostile setting. Often organisations in this category are in transition as they seek similar niches beyond their domestic markets.

4 *European scale organisations*. It is perhaps in this area that there will be considerable growth over the next 10 years as organisations with a strong national presence expand to take advantage of the single market. Hennes & Mauritz from Sweden is moving from being a regional scale to being a European scale organisation with parallel moves into the North American market. Siemens AG, with 52 per cent of its sales generated in Europe in 2001 and 30 per cent from the Americas is already at an advanced stage of transition from being purely European to being a world scale company (http://www.siemens.com). Others are now seeking to strengthen their European presence from a traditionally strong domestic base.

eg

Hennes & Mauritz, the leading Swedish clothing retailer and Sweden's third biggest company, is now looking to become a world scale organisation. Expansion has already been successful in Europe, with 653 of its 771 stores located in 13 countries (12 of which are in the EU) other than Sweden. The first steps to internationalisation were taken in 1976 when a UK store was opened, followed by entry to Germany in 1980. Germany has been an especially successful market, becoming H&M's most important market in 1995. Although H&M's share of that market is small, the low-priced, well designed, value for money fashion lines are nevertheless popular and a store expansion programme is still under way. Sales outside Sweden generate 88 per cent of turnover and that figure is likely to rise as more stores are added. In 2002, around 90 new stores are planned, mainly in Germany, France, Spain, UK and the USA, all following the same retail format. H&M normally opens its first store in a country in the largest population centre and then expands out to smaller centres. The moves into the United States have been more problematic. Despite being a highly efficient and effective organisation, H&M has found in the UK, and in the US, that making progress is far more difficult against equally effective competitors (http://www.hm.com).

The new H&M store in Stockholm offers the customers a bright, modern environment in which they can choose the latest fashions.

Source: H&M.

5 *World scale organisations* have a strong European base, but now operate in a range of different world markets on a direct investment, joint venture or exporting basis. Companies such as Shell, Unilever, Pilkington and GlaxoSmithKline derive a significant proportion of their sales from outside Europe. Often Europe is seen as one geographic market containing segments that transcend national boundaries, and the priority is to compete against powerful international competitors, especially from the Far East and the USA. A successful European base provides a good foundation from which to compete internationally.

eg

Alstom has become a world scale organisation even though it still generates 75 per cent of its sales in Europe. Alstom is a global specialist in energy and transport infrastructure (see Case Study 4.1). Through a process of direct manufacturing, joint ventures, mergers and acquisitions, it has extended from its French base to elsewhere in Europe and beyond. It employs 118,000 people in over 70 countries. It has to regard the world as its market if it wishes to develop its multimillion euro contract business and it plans its strategy accordingly. When it competes for contracts, it is usually up against other world scale organisations along with some more local operators. Despite Alstom's growth, France still generates 30 per cent of its sales and sets the values and style of the organisation. Nestlé is further advanced in its transition to world scale, with products distributed in virtually every country, 479 factories worldwide, but European sales still comprising 32 per cent of its total turnover (http://www.alstom.com).

The distinction drawn between different types of organisations is important, as it highlights a Europe in transition. It could be argued that within the SEM there is no such thing as exporting, but just one large domestic market. Some organisations might adopt a European niching strategy as a matter of course, and see that as their 'home' market. For others with a national or local bias, moves to expand within Europe would be regarded as significant strategic developments that require major learning and adjustment. To these organisations, the decision to trade elsewhere within Europe differs little from a decision to trade in the USA, which is seen as just as risky and difficult. Although some of the risks and barriers to trade have been eliminated within Europe, others such as language or different distribution and communication channels require a different marketing approach.

Thus international marketing means different things to different organisations. To small organisations and companies still primarily operating from one main manufacturing base, most marketing involves product movement across national boundaries and the design of a marketing mix for each market. For other organisations, the scale of international operation has become so great that product movement across national boundaries is minimal or part of a carefully planned strategy. To such multinational or transnational organisations, the distinction between international and domestic marketing becomes very artificial from a strategic marketing perspective.

The rationale for international marketing

Nations encourage their businesses to export their goods and services as a means of earning the foreign currency to pay for necessary imports, whether oil or oranges. The smaller and less well-endowed a nation, the greater the need for foreign trade. But even the more powerful economies in the world still need exports and positively encourage their business communities to generate them. A number of small firms in the USA, for example, have been accused of not giving exporting sufficient priority because of the size and potential of the domestic market.

Apart from the warm glow arising from the sense of having done one's duty as a good corporate citizen in contributing towards the nation's balance of payments, there are other reasons, both positive and negative, that organisations consider international development as an option. For many, there is in fact no choice, unless the objective is to remain a local or national operator. This might be possible where careful positioning or regulation provides a shelter from which the organisation can ignore most of what is happening in the international marketplace. In reality, however, few businesses are immune from the impact of

e-marketing *in action*

The internet: encouraging small businesses to export

The internet is often described as providing great potential for market development for small and medium-sized enterprises (SMEs). Cookson's Tools, a builders' merchant in Cheshire, north-west England provides a good example of the international sales available through the internet. 'We were battling hard just to hold our own, rather than being able to grow the business,' says Stuart Armstrong, managing director. 'To stay in business, we had to change the way we operated'. Then the company decided to try selling via the internet and since then it has gone from serving customers in a seven-mile radius of its depot in Stockport, to serving customers worldwide. Cooksons.com has even sold Korean tools back to customers in Korea.

Turnover from the traditional business, established more than 40 years ago, now stands at £1 mn per year. The website, which went live in March 1999, rapidly attracted orders worth £1,600 a day. Turnover doubled every two and a half months in the first year of operation. Cookson's managed to do this without cannibalising its existing business – less than 1 per cent of orders on the website come from existing customers. Mr Armstrong says that the margin on internet sales is lower, but because sales volume is higher and the costs of selling are lower, the company can afford to sell goods 15 per cent cheaper.

Despite similar success stories many SMEs have not embarked on using the internet to drive international revenue. Hamill and Gregory (1997) suggest that there are many barriers to SMEs wishing to export overseas. What role can the internet play in reducing these barriers? Table 23.1 below summarises the barriers to SME internationalisation and suggests how the internet can help.

Sources: Chaffey (2002); Hamill and Gregory (1997); Moran (2000).

Table 23.1 The role of the internet in overcoming SME resistance to exporting

Barrier	*How the internet can help*
1. Psychological	Can help increase knowledge of overseas markets. Success stories of companies who have become exporters. International enquiries to prototype websites can highlight demand.
2. Operational	E-commerce facilities can simplify the handling of international transactions. Can supply information on export issues.
3. Organisational	Overcomes lack of financial and staff resources to sell abroad. Knowledge of international markets and cultures. Creation of networks of partners.
4. Product/market	Feedback from customers or market research facilitated by internet may indicate the suitability of products for the overseas market.

Source: Chaffey (2002); Based on Hamill and Gregory (1997); www.ft.com/ftit.

international trade. As trade become more liberalised and domestic markets consequently become less well protected, tough and sometimes powerful competitors can enter the market with a sufficiently attractive product and the resources to make a significant impact.

Whole industries have been effectively wiped out by the inability of domestic producers to withstand the impact of international competition.

eg

In the 1990s, many traditional industries in Central Europe found life difficult. The Hungarian glass industry suffered very badly from exposure to European competition and most of the local companies disappeared after takeovers by companies such as Owens-Illinois, a US glass bottle maker or had little choice but to get involved in joint ventures with foreign companies (Wright, 1999). Despite the changes, the industry is still struggling to find international competitiveness. The Hungarian electronics industry has a similar story to tell, but has emerged stronger with electronics accounting for 25 per cent of exports. Philips, IBM, Samsung and Flextronics all established plants in Hungary, initially attracted by a skilled, low-cost workforce and government incentives to invest. At first, Philips worked with local firm Videoton to produce VCRs, but it has now established its own facilities. Videoton survives as a supplier on contract to other international manufacturers, having gained from the association with Philips. Since the end of Communism the infrastructure has improved, the workforce is highly educated, and productivity and quality are both high. Philips and Flextronics have now established low skilled manufacturing operations in Ukraine and Romania where wage costs are well below even Hungarian rates (Kester, 2001b).

To ignore or underestimate international competitors and to position poorly against them can have serious consequences. Waiting until the competitor has entered and gained a foothold in the market could be too late.

Defending the organisation against the worst effects of foreign competition might involve rather more than just creating a strong positioning strategy for products, however.

eg

In the 1970s and 1980s, many companies found themselves trying to withstand competitive pressure from a resurgent Japan, seeking world domination in various sectors. Some companies, for example those manufacturing cameras, photocopiers or motorcycles, succumbed, but other European and American producers survived. Organisations such as Ford, GM and SKF all undertook major manufacturing rationalisation programmes to ensure that their respective cost bases were low enough to compete on price, while Bosch and Alstom relied on technical superiority and building strong customer relations, even to the point of forming joint ventures in local markets. Although the threat of Japanese market domination has now been largely contained through counter-strategies, China's entry into the WTO and the resurgence of the Asian tiger economies could spark a further round of major global competition in the future. In China, however, western organisations have sought to be proactive by forming significant joint ventures and setting up local operations by which the Chinese gain access to state-of-the-art technology and know-how and the western organisations gain access to a large and developing market.

There are also positive reasons for organisations actively pursuing international opportunities. Each of these, shown in Figure 23.1, is considered in turn.

Small or saturated domestic markets

If the domestic market is limited in size or has become saturated (in that there are too many suppliers chasing too few customers), the organisation might look towards international markets sooner rather than later. An Irish producer of specialist furniture, for example, might soon find that with a domestic population of around 3.5 million there are too few potential customers to maintain a viable level of business activity. In this case, the feasibility of exporting and willingness to try it might have been an important part of the business start-up process, as considered in Chapter 21. A similar manufacturer in Germany or Italy might, however, have a much larger domestic market to target before reasonable opportunities are exhausted.

The more an organisation decides to niche, the smaller the segment and the greater the chance of reaching saturation.

Figure 23.1 Reasons for internationalisation

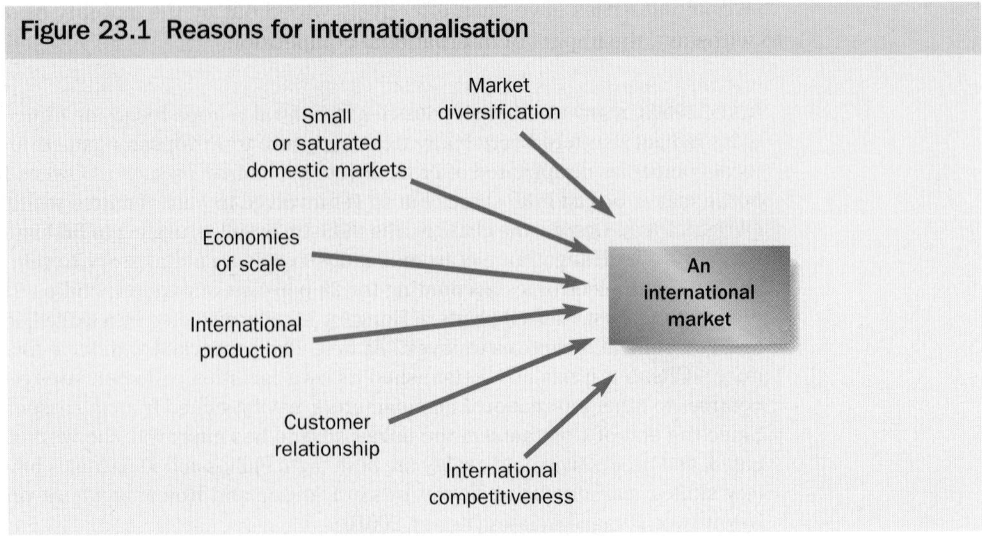

eg

Bulgarian rose oil production suffered with the collapse of communism as quality control, productivity and supply consistency became a problem to western perfume manufacturers. The 'Valley of Roses' in the Balkan mountain range has been a centre of growing and processing for many years and rose oil became a major export earner. The competitive advantage is based on the local rose having a strong and lasting aroma. The home market was very small, so it was essential to persuade such companies as Chanel of France to use Bulgarian rose oil. However, Bulgarian rose oil production is now returning to its former levels, and in 2001 over 1,200 kg of rose oil was exported, 60 per cent to EU countries and 35 per cent to the USA. The challenge will be winning back lost international market share at the premium prices it used to attract. During the 1990s, Bulgaria's share of the world rose oil market dropped from 50 per cent to 35 per cent and other suppliers, especially from Turkey, gained market share at its expense (Hope and Troev, 2002).

Ultimately, the judgement as to whether a market is too small or too saturated lies with the organisation. What might be a comfortable niche for a small business might appear to be not worth the effort for a large organisation. In a mainstream market, if two or three very large organisations hold most of the market share between them, other companies might decide that there is no room for them to develop as they would wish, and thus they might look to foreign markets for opportunities.

eg

Schindler, a Swiss company, is the world's largest producer of escalators and moving walks, and the second-largest manufacturer of elevators. It could not have achieved that status by concentrating on Europe alone and has grown to compete globally with competitors such as Otis and TKI. By operating in many countries, it is able to minimise its risk as it is heavily dependent upon the fortunes of the construction industry for new orders. In the US for example, the knock-on effects of September 11th 2001 may be to dampen down the growth of new airport terminals, thus having an impact on market demand. The construction market in China and Japan, where public investment in infrastructure and residential building is attractive to lift and elevator companies, is growing, however. Although it is a Swiss company, most of Schindler's $4.1 bn sales derives from other countries. It has joint ventures and operations in most major markets. It acquired a 51 per cent share in a Moscow elevator company Liftremont, for instance, and in the Moscow region alone, the number of new installations and maintenance contracts is greater than in the whole of Switzerland (http://www.schindler.com).

Economies of scale

The Schindler example above also demonstrates the importance of developing internationally to achieve economies of scale. Serving a large market with high volumes from one plant enables cost competitiveness to be maintained. Ford believes that there will only be six major car makers within a decade. This is inevitable when operating margins are very tight, heavy R&D costs have to be recouped, and marketing becomes more global. To achieve low unit costs in production and to spread marketing costs, Ford has to ensure a high degree of standardisation in critical parts such as the chassis and engines, allowing more superficial styling changes for local markets, for example air conditioning. To achieve such economics of scale a consolidation of factories is likely to be inevitable and some smaller manufacturers, such as Volvo, have already been acquired. In the latter case, although the marque will be maintained for its market appeal, opportunities are also created for savings in adopting common components in some areas (Pitcher, 1999).

While the prospect of economies of scale is not necessarily enough in itself to push an organisation into international markets and does not guarantee success, it can provide a flexible foundation for developing the international marketing package.

International production

Differential labour costs around the world have been an incentive for some organisations to shift production abroad. Not only do they save on labour and possibly operating costs, but they also save on transport and import costs as well as benefiting from government incentives to encourage inward investment. Furthermore, the organisation might want to develop a regional presence for marketing purposes.

Customer relationships

As customers become more international in orientation, suppliers have to follow suit. Those supplying components to the automotive industry might have to be able to supply standard parts to any one of several manufacturing plants around the world. They might even be expected to expand their own manufacturing operations so that they themselves have plants close to the car manufacturer's locations.

In service industries in particular, it might be necessary to locate closer to customers, wherever they might be. Engineering consulting and testing service providers or advertising agencies, for example, might also feel that they can develop better customer relationships and better service by having branch offices or subsidiaries in a number of foreign markets where potential customers are concentrated.

Market diversification

The broader the range of markets served, the less likely it is that failure in any one market will cause terminal corporate decline. As discussed in Chapter 20, different markets are at different stages of development and competitive intensity, and make different resource demands. If, therefore, the organisation has a well-spread portfolio, resources can be shifted for further development, for combating short-term difficulties, or even to allow withdrawal. Central and eastern Europe and the Far East are currently regarded as markets that need investment if a long-term presence is to be built, whereas many western European markets are generally regarded as mature, with any growth arising from aggressive techniques for stealing share from competitors.

eg

Netherlands based United Pan-Europe Communications is a leading broadband communications company. It has built markets in 17 European countries and has more than 7 million subscribers to its 'Triple Play' service, featuring video, internet and telephone services to residential users. It is also at the cutting-edge by installing fibre optics and cable upgrading to allow interactive TV. By developing a cross-section of markets it is able to spread its risk for as long as its technology is leading-edge (http://www.upc.corp.com).

Using the cutting-edge technology including digital satellite dishes, UPC keeps at the forefront as a broadband communications company.

Source: United Pan-Europe Communications.

International competitiveness

Finally, it should not be forgotten that one of the main reasons for international development is the pursuit of market opportunities, with a view to either beating the competition or strengthening one's position against them.

SKF is a global supplier of products, solutions and services in the rolling bearing and seals business. It has achieved its world leadership position by continuous investment in technology, technical support, efficient logistics and the cost benefit from worldwide bearing standardisation. Despite having thousands of alternative bearing and seal sizes around a range of product types, being based on metric measurements, many can be used in applications around the world. It also operates its well tried system of appointing distributors (7,000 worldwide in 70 countries) to handle all but the largest OEM and technically advanced customer applications.

Part of the competitiveness also comes from having 83 production sites across 24 countries so that it can better integrate into local economies. Currently, it is pursuing a programme of rationalising the degree of vertical integration in its manufacturing through divestment and acquiring new capacity in growing technical areas such as its 75 per cent share of NSK Aerospace Europe in Stonehouse, Gloucestershire. That purchase will give it a stronger presence in the design and manufacture of bearings for main shafts and gearboxes in jet engines, such as those produced by Rolls Royce, the main customer of NSK. At the same time, SKF sold its Italian-based sheet metal component manufacturing business to a local company, CMSP, and its machine tool manufacturing facility in Lindkoping in Sweden. The many purchases and divestments of companies within the SKF group is part of an ongoing process to retain global competitiveness through efficient manufacturing and effective marketing (http://www.skf.com).

Whatever the motivation for entering and developing international markets, a planned approach considerably increases the chances of success. The main stages in that process include identifying opportunities, assessing markets, planning entry and allocating resources to ensure a match between opportunities, objectives and capabilities.

Understanding international markets

Once the decision has been made to pursue international development, the organisation has to choose which foreign markets to target. It might already have a shortlist of two or three areas that clearly show potential, but further, more detailed analysis is necessary in order to choose between them or to set priorities. Understanding the marketing environments involved can form the basis of detailed market assessment and selection.

International marketing environment

The STEP factors making up the marketing environment have already been covered in detail in Chapter 2. Much of that discussion is as relevant to international markets as it is to the domestic situation. This section, therefore, will simply highlight briefly a few issues under each factor that might influence international marketing decisions and strategies specifically.

Sociocultural factors

As well as the normal consideration of market structure in terms of demographics, the international marketer needs to pay special attention to sociocultural factors, issues of cultural difference. These could affect not only the way in which a product is marketed to consumers, but also the way in which business negotiations are handled. Cultural differences might be seen in terms of language, social structures and mores (including class structure, gender roles and the effect of religion) and prevalent values and attitudes. As Ricks (1993) points out, a failure to take cultural differences between countries into account has been behind many international business failures.

marketing *in action*

Broadcasting products around the world

Continental Microwave Ltd (CML) is a medium-sized manufacturer of communications equipment, for both fixed and mobile links, for broadcasting, telecommunications, PTT and other communications applications worldwide. Its customers range from the BBC, CNN and other national broadcasters, to UK and US defence departments. The company is selling what is effectively capital equipment in a technologically dynamic global market with relatively few potential customers. Nevertheless, it is still an overall growth market that is not yet mature. Digital television, for instance, means more channels, more choices and more broadcasting, especially in sport which requires outside broadcasting equipment, of course.

The ultimate in mobile communications equipment.

Source: Continental Microwave Ltd.

In the mid-1990s, the company had found that there was a lot of nationalism in purchasing decisions, for instance German customers tended to prefer to buy from German suppliers and French customers from French suppliers. This is still true to an extent. To overcome this, in France, for instance, CML developed an alliance with French electronics giant Thomson. Thomson purchases exclusive CML satellite systems, puts its own branding on them and then resells them in France or beyond if it wishes. Through Thomson's patronage, CML is actually achieving significant additional sales. 'We do not deal direct into France any more, yet sales, thanks to Thomson, have gone from zero to millions in France, and through into the rest of the world.'

Non-aligned and Commonwealth countries provide the major export focus for CML. The EU is significant but business is hard to get. The cost per result is high but CML has cracked most of the EU and gets what it regards as its fair share of business. CML has also looked at eastern Europe as a whole, but it is a fragmented market and with the collapse of the state infrastructure, there is a new business philosophy. CML has taken on a front-line salesman who knows the markets and can open doors, generate leads and gather information. This is helping CML to make a much better market impact.

One market that is orthodox and traditional and thus suits an orthodox and traditional supplier is China, and CML broke into this market with a £1 mn order. The Chinese are risk averse. If Chinese managers buy the wrong thing, it stays with them long-term because they do not have the job mobility and are held responsible. The buying decision is thus not just about specification but also longer-term relationships and this is in the Chinese manager's own self-interest in a long-term job. In buying, the Chinese therefore probe a supplier's commitment as well as its product and CML's commitment was demonstrated with a competent first-line agent who knows the product and visits customers regularly whether they have problems or not to do some 'positive stroking'. This initial order was extremely important: in China, the regional operators are looking at what systems have been bought in Beijing and tend to buy the same, and therefore CML has also gained further regional orders too.

In other markets, the buying imperative is somewhat different and the world as a whole is becoming tougher. The telecoms industry, for example, now has a high management staff turnover so purchasers do not really care about the long-term implications of their decisions because they will be long gone by the time it is realised that they made bad choices. It is a similar situation in the broadcasting industry. While long-term loyalties do still exist, they are the exception rather than the rule. Thus the market is now more price-driven and customers cannot justify paying a premium for what they see as 'over specification'. A customer, especially one in the third world, now has to justify not buying the cheapest, although over time when problems begin to arise with cheap systems, this could reverse.

CML is effectively selling development projects and works closely with its customers to make sure everything goes as it should. The managing director has a major role in the early stages of a relationship, providing a senior presence and getting involved in introductions. For instance in developing business in Nigeria or Algeria, he would visit ministers and other influencers as well as customer companies. Once the contract is won, regional managers take over.

Source: Interviews with Ian Aizlewood, former Managing Director of Continental Microwave Ltd.

Language. Language is a minefield for the international marketer. Many British and Irish exporting companies assume (and indeed expect) all foreigners to speak and to negotiate in English (Clarke, 2000; Davies, 1995). Unfortunately, this arrogance is often misplaced. In much of continental Europe, small and medium-sized companies cannot operate in English, and others resent being expected to do so. It is not unreasonable to expect a marketing-orientated organisation to make the effort to deal with customers in the customer's own language. A survey in the UK, however, revealed that only around one-third of executives had a foreign language and the number is falling (Kelly, 2002). This compares poorly with many European organisations that regularly operate in at least two main languages and the survey of 5,000 companies indicated that in countries such as Denmark, Finland and Poland over 80 per cent of executives operate in at least one foreign language. More generally, only one-third of British people can cope with a major second language compared to over one-half across Europe (Berliner, 2001). DSM, the Dutch chemical manufacturer based in Limburg, is typical of many larger businesses in the Netherlands. It regards itself as an international organisation, despite the fact that it considers nearby Germany and some other EU countries to be part of the domestic market. Dutch, German and English, along with some other languages are widely spoken in the company.

eg

There are two broad approaches to the handling of international languages. First, staff can be trained to the required level. When Peebles Transformers from Edinburgh won a contract to supply the Tianhuangping pumped storage site, it used a multimedia training package in Mandarin as well as hiring a local translator for support. In contrast, Simpson Photo Imaging, a small ceramics decorating business, employed a linguist who spoke nine languages for customer contact, especially at exhibitions, although again it also encouraged other staff to learn a second language consistent with its export priorities (Bloom, 1998). DSM, the Netherlands' largest chemical manufacturer based in Limberg, is a European organisation that trades internationally rather than a domestically orientated company that happens to export. It now considers Germany as much of a domestic market as the Netherlands, and German, along with the other main European languages, is widely spoken (Cramb, 1999).

Language can also be a problem within the marketing mix. As seen at p. 288, brand names do not necessarily transfer easily across borders. Not only might the name itself have an unfortunate meaning or be difficult to pronounce in other languages, but the subtle associative elements of some names might be lost in translation or when used by people ignorant of the original language. Some of the classics include KFC's 'finger lickin good' becoming 'bite your fingers off' in Chinese and another claim of 'turn it loose' translating into Spanish as 'drink [our beer] and get diarrhoea'! Sales brochures and literature, manuals and instruction leaflets have to be carefully translated. Most of us have come across instruction books for Japanese electronic goods that have been translated by someone with a less than perfect grasp of English idiom. At best this is amusing, but it can irritate and frustrate the customer, and it does not give the best impression of the organisation that has produced it.

Social structures, customs and mores. Social factors can affect what is or is not acceptable in terms of the product itself, its marketing mix, or the business negotiation process. In any consumer market, the marketer needs to understand as much as possible about the individual and the influences of various groups on them (*see* pp. 109 *et seq.* and 118 *et seq.* to revise these concepts). The role of women in society or the structure and centrality of the family might affect product positioning and what is portrayed in advertising, for example.

Any exporter to South Africa has to be aware of the changing social structure in the post-apartheid period. In a society in which 73 per cent of the population is black and the middle-class/middle-income black consumer is a fast growing segment, traditional racial segmentation approaches are no longer appropriate. Marketers have to be aware of changing values and attitudes within a group that has been suppressed for so long, such as its aspirational orientation, symbols of personal achievement and group belonging, which are especially powerful within the emergent black middle class. Race is no longer a sufficient segmentation base and it is even risky to treat the middle-class black group as homogeneous. Instead, lifestyle variables cutting across race and gender are now more appropriate for an international marketer (Ives, 1999).

Business culture also needs to be understood in detail. Negotiating styles and etiquette can differ widely. Figure 23.2, based on Mead (1990), summarises some of the considerations that the international marketer has to take into account.

In international markets, there is a strong chance that ethical problems will have to be faced sooner or later. The ethical standards exhibited in the conduct of business in one environment might not be the same in another. This poses a moral dilemma as to whether to participate in practices that would be considered offensive or illegal in the home environment. If the marketer does not participate, however, it could jeopardise sales and the employment of staff back home. In short, what price morality?

Shell had to face such a dilemma through allegations of guilt by association. By opposing the environmental protection views of Ken Saro-Wiwa in Nigeria, the company was seen as being linked with the political regime that eventually ordered his execution as part of the human rights oppression of the Ogoni people. In the West, scandals and corruption have affected organisations, with even the Olympic games bidding process being questioned. Some companies have been heavily criticised for buying from firms using child labour in Asia and the Far East. With the growth of the internet, it is becoming increasingly difficult for organisations to turn a blind eye to questionable practices in far-away places.

The EU has just drawn up a voluntary code of conduct to guide multinationals operating in the developing countries. It covers best practice on the environment, employment issues, corruption and human rights. The OECD anti-bribery convention could end the common practice of treating bribes as deductible operating expenses. The full impact of these measures is yet to be realised, however, as this is a large-scale problem.

Figure 23.2 Behavioural factors influencing business conduct

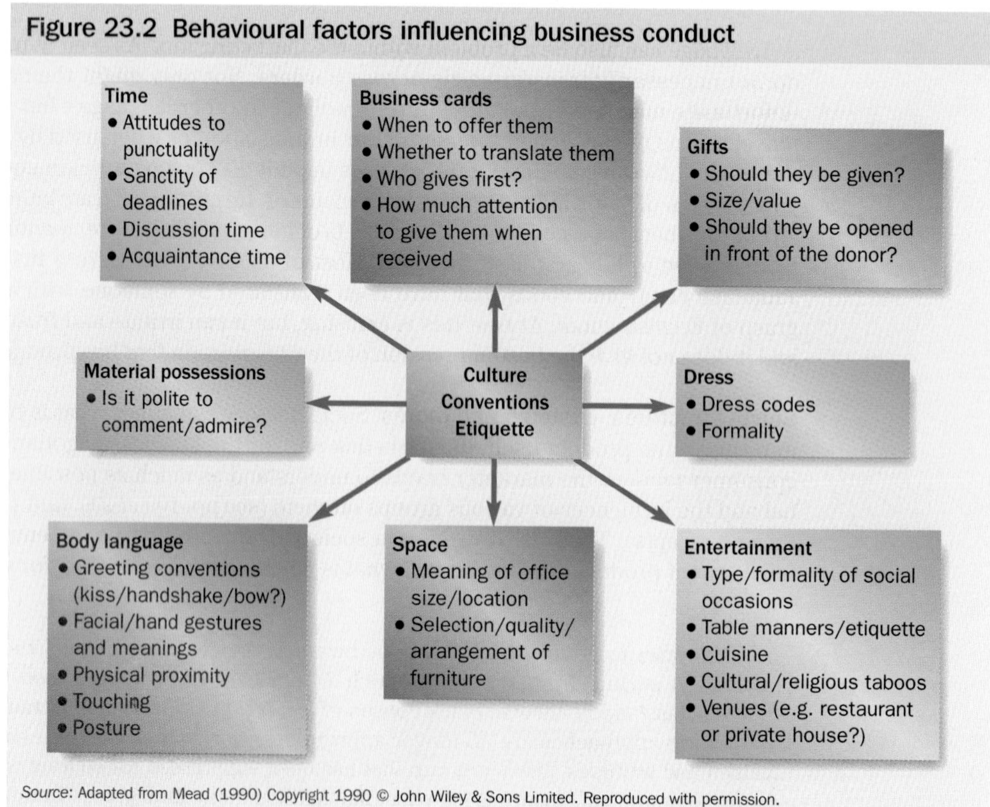

Source: Adapted from Mead (1990) Copyright 1990 © John Wiley & Sons Limited. Reproduced with permission.

ICI believes that compromising core values and common standards, ranging from 'commission', 'expediting payments' to fundamental breaches of human rights, should not be allowed and it makes a point of telling customers of the standards within its ethical code, turning a potential problem into a competitive strength. Perhaps there is some business that is simply not worth the price of winning (Maitland, 1999).

Values and attitudes. Values and attitudes can affect reaction to a product or to its origins. In Chapter 13, the media and lobby pressure to boycott companies with Burmese supply chains was considered, and the British beef industry is having to work hard to convince foreign consumers that its beef is safe and BSE free. Similarly, during the days of apartheid, consumer pressure and trade sanctions imposed by governments meant that South African products were not imported, while consumer boycotts affected those European companies that invested in South Africa. Quite apart from such specific political issues, some cultures are more resistant to foreign goods than others. As seen at pp. 191 *et seq.* (Paitra, 1993), even within Europe there are different attitudes to the origin of goods. Germans tend to be traditionalists, orientated more towards long-established home-produced products, whereas France and Italy are much more open to new foreign ideas.

eg

Sara Lee and its Kiwi Shoe Polish (http://www.kiwicare.com) brand found interesting differences between the South African and some European markets in terms of attitudes to shoe care. It is important for Kiwi to understand these differences if it is to maintain its 72 per cent share of the South African market. South Africa is a nation with one of the highest levels of shoe polish penetration. Interestingly, consumers take a keen interest in the preservation and presentation of their shoes, unlike in some other markets where cleaning is often an act of last resort. In part, the consumer involvement is driven by climatic differences given the relatively high dust levels in South Africa, and also reflects a desire to extend the life of a shoe. Sara Lee does not only need to understand differences between nations, it also needs to track whether there are significant differences in attitudes and values within the country (Dorrian, 1998).

Nevertheless, some companies do trade successfully using their country of origin as a major international selling point. IKEA, for example, emphasises its Swedishness because in most countries Scandinavian design is much admired. Both Burberry and Laura Ashley trade on their Englishness, with an image of quality and quaint heritage. Meanwhile, McDonald's and Coca-Cola carry the American dream around the world. This can backfire, of course, if customers in a foreign market do not hold or believe the 'right' stereotypical images of Englishness or Swedishness. National images can also be damaged by international political events. The Spanish tourist industry is having to work hard to convince Europeans that Spain is a safe travel destination after the actions of Basque separatists in planting car bombs in prime destinations. The summer is the main period of their activity with the objective of disrupting the $43 bn tourism industry.

When candles went out of fashion after the Second World War, the industry virtually died. In the 1980s, however, the atmospheric impact of ambient light led to a resurgence in demand for candles from bars and restaurants and for home use. Candles became a lifestyle product, even offering scents such as lavender and chocolate. For UK producer Colony, around 15 per cent of production is exported, especially to the USA, Japan and mainland Europe, reflecting the style, fragrance and gift potential of candles that are now anything but white. It would appear that the lifestyle appeal and a trend towards multi-sensory experiences through such items as aromatherapy and scented candles is driving demand disregardless of national borders (Jones, 1999; Gardyn, 2000).

It is important when studying international markets to see things in the context of the value systems and attitudes in the buying country. These may be fair or grossly inaccurate but they are real to the customer and can influence behaviour. A report in *African Business*, for example, suggested that the alleged intervention of the US embassy on behalf of a US company in a $7 mn tender for upgrading Kenya's telecommunications system was an undue exercise of political muscle designed to usurp the open tendering process and an example of 'Amercia's bullying tactics' (Vesely, 2002). Any intervention can be open to interpretation:

approaches to a Minister, promises of aid without mentioning any link with trade, and offering the favour with the US administration have all been cited as tactics used in the US's strategy for influencing the procurement board in Kenya. All this goes to show that some individuals and some nations are quick to judge and talk about 'American big sticks' or 'British colonialism' as stereotypes to promote their own counter-values and attitidues (Vesely, 2002).

Not surprisingly, many organisations prefer to gain international experience initially by choosing countries that are culturally as similar as possible to their own. Thus smaller Irish companies might begin by exporting to the UK, while Swedish companies might begin by trading in other Scandinavian markets. This reduces the risks and barriers to market entry and allows the organisation to learn a little about what international marketing means before it launches itself into more far-flung territories.

Technological factors

The stage of technological development that a market has reached can have many implications. A manufacturer of 'ready-to-microwave' meals might not have much success selling into markets where the penetration of microwave ovens is very low! Similarly, sophisticated computer peripherals or software need markets with an established IT base. Technology available within a market might also affect goods handling, stock control or the preservation of perishable goods. This raises questions as to whether the exporter can work within the existing technological infrastructure or whether investment will have to be made in developing it or finding alternative solutions.

eg

The technological infrastructure also limits the potential for internet use, with its benefit of online trading and building stronger customer relationships regardless of geographic location. Internet use reveals big differences between nations for technological, economic and attitudinal reasons. In France, penetration is just 30 per cent, but in Scandinavia it is between 60 and 70 per cent. Germany has the largest number of users with 30 million, followed by the UK with 20 million. Across Europe, the overall average for internet use is 39 per cent, totalling 116 million users, but the profile of users largely remains well educated young people. Asia is likely to be a major growth market over the next five to ten years, especially in China and India as more people acquire PCs. The compound annual rate of growth is predicted at 45 per cent across Asia and by 2005 it will comprise 25 per cent of the world's online population. With internet penetration currently less than 2 per cent in China, but with a population of 1.3 billion and major infrastructure projects for cabling in progress, China may well eventually overtake the West in terms of e-commerce (Fisher, 2000). The implications of these differences concern not just what is possible when developing a foreign market, but also that any e-commerce lead that the West has, especially the US, may disappear over the next decade (*Marketing Week*, 2002).

Economic and competitive factors

As might be expected, the international marketer is interested in the size of the foreign market and its market potential. Basic information about per capita disposable income, consumption patterns and unemployment trends can help to paint a background picture of how that market is developing in the longer term. The international marketer will also be interested in inflation, the stability of exchange rates and any exchange control regulations. An exporter wanting payment in hard currencies such as sterling or dollars rather than in the importer's local currency might face problems if the importer's government tightly controls their access to hard currency. The existence and levels of import tariffs, duties and local taxes can also add to the costs and problems of entering foreign markets. We discussed the impact of VERs on the car market at p. 71 *et seq*. Chapter 2 also discussed the problems of varying VAT rates and excise duties on cross-border trade within the EU.

In terms of competitive analysis, the procedure is the same as for any domestic market, and organisations need to look at the number of competitors, the structure of the market and the sophistication of market positioning and marketing mixes. Of particular interest in foreign markets is the extent to which other exporters have managed to penetrate that market and the problems they have faced in doing so.

Political and legal factors

Some countries are more politically stable than others. In some a change in government makes little difference to commercial life, but in others the changes can be dramatic. The last thing an organisation needs is to invest in setting up a manufacturing plant in a country with a liberal regime, only to have it 'confiscated' by a subsequent hardline government with a hostile attitude to foreign ownership of assets. This is an extreme case, although it must be said that some governments do restrict foreign ownership. This might mean, for example, that the foreign manufacturer has to enter into a joint venture with a local company, with the local company retaining 51 per cent ownership of the joint enterprise.

Organisations thinking about setting up a manufacturing plant in a foreign country are going to have to look not only at ownership restrictions, but also, for example, at employment law, health and safety regulations, financial law and patent protection relevant to that market. Any organisation wanting to sell or market a product will also need to know about advertising, sales promotion and direct marketing constraints, pricing regulations, contract law and consumer protection legislation.

eg

An organisation trading in the EU has to exercise care when providing distributors with extra incentives if it already has a market share above 40 per cent. The EU is investigating large EU and US companies such as Coca-Cola and Microsoft to ensure that their dominant positions have not led to what might be considered anti-competitive practices (Hargreaves, 2001). The Commission has the power to fine companies up to 10 per cent of their global sales revenue if they are found guilty of abusing such a position. Coca-Cola dominates the European market for carbonated drinks to the degree that it believes that its nearest competitor is tap water! It thus has to be careful about using marketing practices that might be regarded as normal and legitimate in other markets. Prime space in supermarkets, exclusive deals, dedicated chilled cabinets, loyalty bonuses and additional rewards to better performing distributors could all be misinterpreted by the European Commission. Coca-Cola goes to great lengths to argue down any 'dominant position abuse' claims, for example by stating that it is not the share of the carbonated drinks market that counts but share of all drinks. Pepsi-Cola thinks otherwise, however, and has complained about Coca-Cola's loyalty bonuses and rebates. The EU regulatory bodies are obliged to investigate. Lawyers are often needed to find routes through the regulations. For example, the theoretical position is that dominant operators can give discounts to distributors as long as they relate directly to costs and as long as the price differentials do not exclude others from the market. That is clearly open to interpretation and challenge.

Action taken by trading blocs and governments can also have a profound influence. Trade relations between the United States and the Europe Commission are often delicate, for example, and from time to time tariffs and quotas are imposed despite both parties' supposed belief in world trade liberalisation. The US imposed 30 per cent tariffs on imported steel to protect its own industry, but it also has a direct effect on the fragile European steel industry (Harrison, 2002). Any gains were short-lived, as the EU immediately instigated actions to curb US steel imports through quotas and tariffs. Other threatened action includes the imposition of export subsidies for some food products as a response to the US Farm Bill which effectively subsidises US farmers and distorts the market (Mortishead and Watson, 2002). Retaliation can also be directed at other 'innocent' sectors, thus the European Commission notified the WTO of a long list of goods that were to be hit with higher tariffs, including ink jet printers, fruit juices and textiles, as well as steel products (Thornton, 2002).

Market selection

Once the marketing environment is understood, the organisation needs to look at it in its own context. This means matching the opportunities and threats emerging from the marketing environment with the organisation's own strengths, weaknesses, assets, skills and aspirations. The quality of this assessment will have a big impact on international marketing success or failure for a company (Andersen and Strandskov, 1998).

eg

Aston Martin produce some of the world's most prestigious sports cars, such as the DB7, based on traditional values of craftsmanship, attention to detail and exclusivity. Over 70 per cent of its sales are generated by exports and it naturally seeks markets in which a reasonably-sized segment exists capable of spending up to $100,000 for a car. It is perhaps not surprising that the USA, Canada, Germany, Japan, Italy and Switzerland have been selected as prime markets in which a dealer and service support infrastructure should be established. Changes are planned, however, with production expected to treble over the next few years, the introduction of a new entry-level car priced at just $65,000 and the dealer network doubled to create a presence in 35 countries, all designed to improve the international market position (Burt, 2002).

Some of the issues associated with market selection that might be considered are shown in Figure 23.3 and discussed below.

Product fit factors

Is there a gap in the market for our product? Is there demand for our sort of product? Would we have to adapt the product to suit local conditions and, if so, how much?

Market factors

Is it a completely undeveloped market, is it still in its growth stage, or has it reached maturity? Is there sufficient potential future demand to warrant our long-term commitment to this market? Are there established distribution channels we can use or would we have to invest in creating them? How long are the distribution channels and how sophisticated is their infrastructure?

Competitive factors

Who are the existing competitors in this market and how well established are they? How intense and how aggressive is the competition? To what extent have existing competitors obtained control over distribution channels? How likely are competitors to react aggressively to our entry into the market and what barriers to entry can they raise?

Entry factors

What market entry methods are feasible for this market, and how much would each cost us? Do we have any established contacts in this market who could help us? What marketing costs are going to be incurred in getting established in this market and developing a market share? How similar is the culture in this market to our own, and how well do we understand any differences? Is this going to cause us problems in entering the market?

Figure 23.3 Factors influencing international market selection

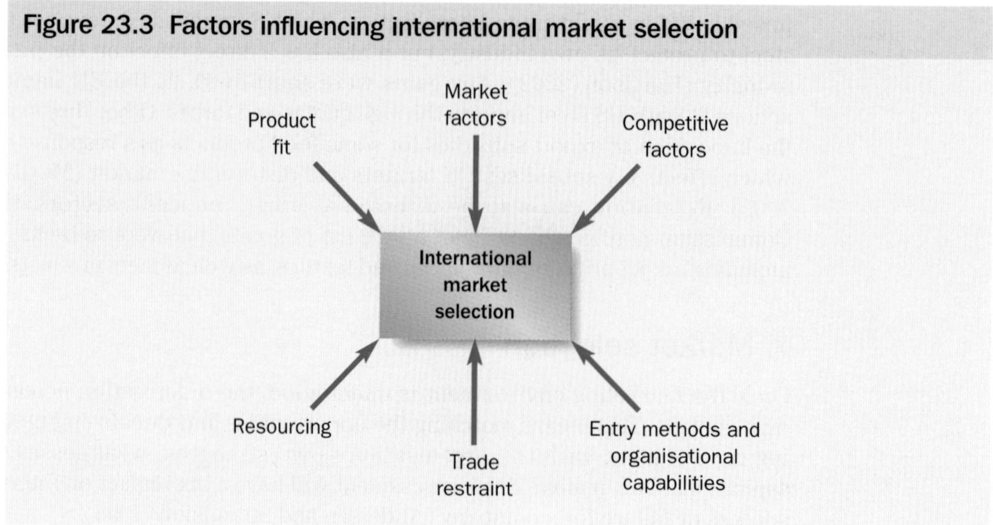

Resourcing factors

What are we going to have to invest in entering this market? Are we going to have to recruit local staff and/or relocate our own staff? Are we going to have to train staff in languages, export procedures, business culture, etc.?

Trade restraint factors

What legal and regulatory factors will influence our operation in this market? Do we have to manufacture to different quality or safety standards? Can we use advertising and sales promotion as we would wish? Are there import tariffs or quotas that apply to us? Will we be allowed to repatriate any/all our profits (i.e. take money out of the country)? Are there any constraints on foreign companies operating in this market, for example a ban on foreign ownership of companies? Young (2001) argues that international marketers pay too little attention to the potential impact that global economic, legal/institutional and political/social developments could have on their ability to trade.

Throughout the whole process, there is a need for sound market intelligence and information. It is very difficult to undertake detailed research on 180 sovereign states, hence the need for a scan to reduce the shortlist to two or three serious contenders. The screening process will become more detailed as options are eliminated. Early screening will soon reveal the options that are unattractive because of clearly unfavourable environmental forces. Desk research alone can show up markets with low potential, leaving a much smaller number for more detailed investigation. In reality, however, market screening can be random, driven as much by enquiries or knowledge gained through media and personal networks as by systematic research. At some point, however, it is likely that a visit will have to be made to a potential market to see at first hand how it operates and to make preliminary contacts.

marketing *in action*

Tesco and the art of selling an octopus

Tesco has been expanding into Asia, but has deliberately sought to adapt to local culture, traditions and tastes. To succeed in South Korea, it had to recreate an environment in which shoppers felt at home and it had to ensure that the assortment of products and services was based not on the UK experience, but on Korean customer demand. After all, buying a live octopus, a pet iguana, fish chopped up alive sushi-style, or dental services are not normal UK supermarket shopping experiences, but they do form part of Tesco's local adaptation strategy in South Korea (Ward, 2002).

Tesco was helped in developing this approach by entering the market through a joint venture with Samsung, a powerful brand name in its own right and one of the leading conglomerates in South Korea. The localised approach means a lot more fresh food than in the UK to recreate a market atmosphere, as well as fast food outlets, coffee shops, toddlers' play areas and even car servicing. The Tesco Home Stores in South Korea have been positioned as 'culture centres' where mothers and customers can take classes, learn new skills, or use an internet café all because Tesco realised that many Korean mothers prefer to look after their children rather than work (Taplin, 2002). Serving a million customers a week, Tesco's aim is the same as in the UK: to create value to build and retain store loyalty. It is the methods employed that are different.

Part of the localisation strategy has been to ensure that local suppliers and own-brand goods that have been produced in Korea form a prominent part of the range offered. Tesco brings considerable expertise in buying, logistics and merchandising, and adapting that to local circumstances has been critical to its strategy. In some areas such as internal design, service bundling, merchandising techniques and layout, local ideas have been so successful that they are now being transferred back to the UK (Warman, 2001). Although larger supermarkets are a relatively new phenomenon, the market is expected to grow significantly over the next few years and Tesco plans to open 55 stores and capture 29 per cent of the market based on a combination of local knowledge and adaptability implemented with Western professionalism.

Sources: Taplin (2002); Ward (2002); Warman (2001).

Market entry methods

Once an organisation has decided which are the best markets to enter, it must then decide how to enter. The choice of **market entry method** depends on a number of factors. Paliwoda (1993) cites six main factors, as summarised in Figure 23.4. They are briefly outlined here, but will be further considered as each entry method is discussed later in this section.

1 *Speed.* How quickly does the organisation want to get into the market? Some market entry methods might take many months or even years to plan and implement, whereas others can be put into action almost immediately.
2 *Costs.* How much is it going to cost to enter the market by each method? Do the benefits derived from using one method rather than another justify its higher cost?
3 *Flexibility.* How much flexibility does the organisation want to retain? Some entry methods allow the organisation to leave the market or expand further relatively easily. Others require long-term contractual agreements or long-term financial commitments that could restrict the organisation's future options.
4 *Risk factors.* These are wide ranging, covering all aspects of the marketing environment, but particularly competitive and political risks. Again, some entry methods can help to reduce certain types of risk. Long-term investment in a manufacturing plant in a foreign country, for example, not only helps to overcome import quotas and duties, but also might be viewed more kindly by the government.
5 *Payback period.* There might be pressure from within the organisation to produce a quick return on any investment in a foreign market. If this is the case, acquiring an established manufacturer might be a more appealing option than building a new factory from nothing, if it means that revenues can be generated within one year rather than five years.
6 *Long-term profit objectives.* The organisation has to look ahead to what it wants to achieve in the future and how it can best exploit the opportunities available in the foreign market. The choice of market entry strategy is just the first stage in a longer-term strategic plan for that market.

Of course, much also depends on the nature of the product itself and its market. Some services lend themselves naturally to international franchising, while mass production can make it cost effective to manufacture abroad. As discussed in Chapter 2, Japanese car manufacturers have established manufacturing plants within the EU to overcome import quotas and to delete the costs of shipping finished goods half-way across the world.

The range of market entry methods from which the organisation can choose is wide and varied, as can be seen in Figure 23.5. When looking at this figure, remember that the definition of *customer* needs to be flexible. In some cases, it might mean an individual consumer or end user, in others it might be a wholesaler or retailer within a longer distribution channel, but in others it might be a manufacturer who is buying in components or raw materials.

Figure 23.4 Factors influencing the choice of market entry method

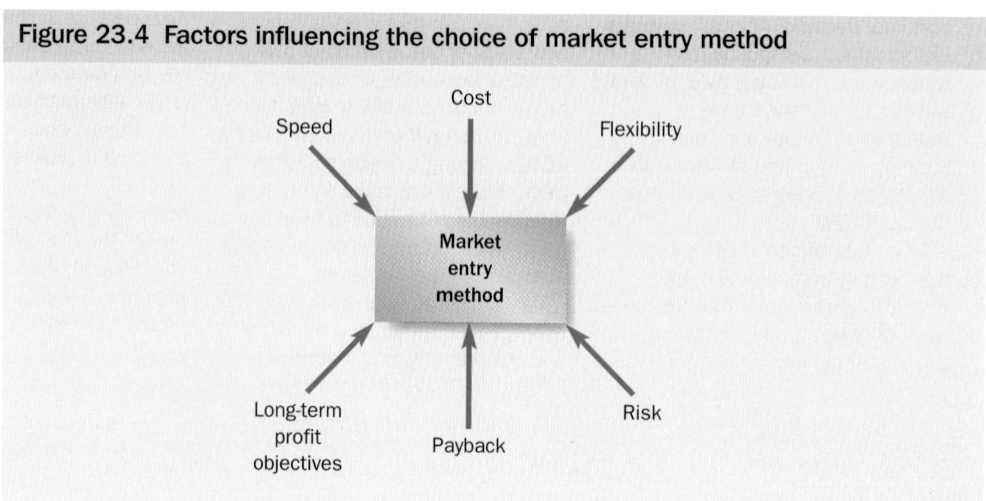

Figure 23.5 Market entry methods

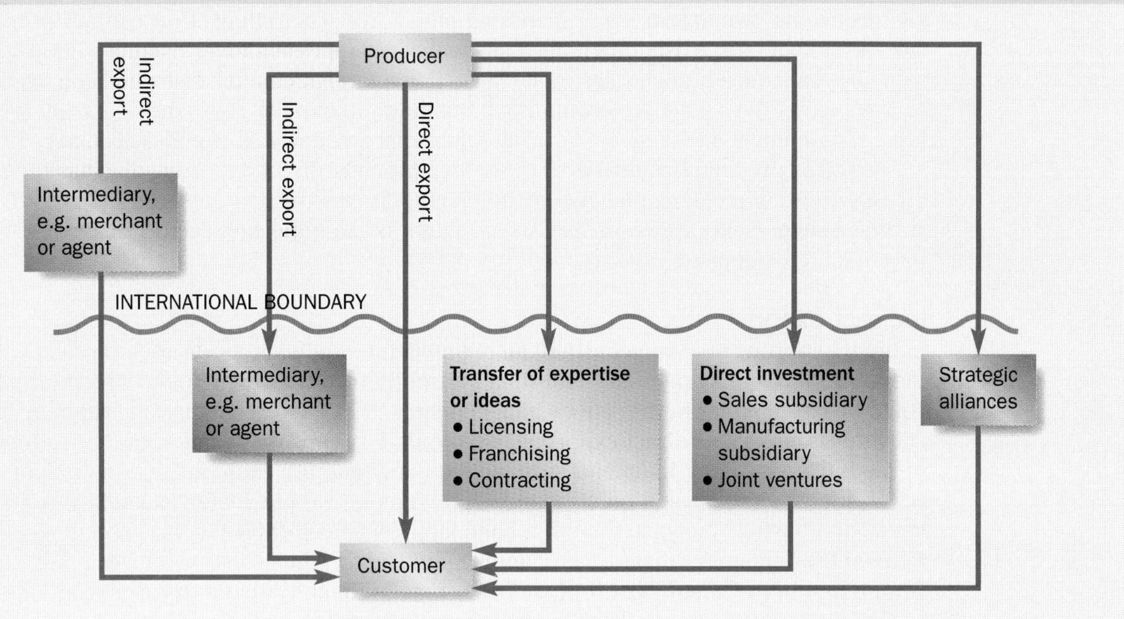

Burgel and Murray (2000) in a study of international market entry strategies for start-up companies found that it is the support needs of the customer that must be balanced with the resources available.

The classification of market entry methods is not easy, as there are many relevant criteria, such as the level and type of investment involved and whether it is indirect or direct; whether the goods or services are manufactured or produced at home or abroad; whether the exporter deals directly or indirectly with the buyer, or whether the transaction involves exporting goods and services, knowledge and expertise or investment. For further exploration of these issues see, for example, Brooke (1992), Young *et al.* (1989), or Paliwoda (1993). The groupings presented in Figure 23.5 are largely based on Brooke (1992) and will now be discussed in turn.

Trade in goods and services

There are two main methods of trading in goods and services: **direct export** and **indirect export**.

Direct export

Direct exporting means that the organisation produces the product at home and then sells to the foreign customer without the use of an intermediary. The seller thus has to take responsibility for finding customers, negotiating with them, processing their orders and arranging shipment and after-sales service.

eg

Although the priority for many US and European companies is creating joint ventures or direct export to China, the shape of things to come was vividly demonstrated when the first Chinese manufactured cars were exported to the United States. Although just 252 cars were produced by the Tianjin Auto Group, to some it was reminiscent of the first Japanese and Korean car exports in the 1960s and 1970s. The first cars were exported on a trial basis to ensure that they met safety and emission standards, and with a retail price of $10,000, the Xiali could represent a historic first step towards a new influx of cheap vehicles from Asia similar to that experienced nearly thirty years ago. In the 1980s, Chinese white goods and consumer electronics were considered a poor buy, but now the Chinese can compete in the international arena through exports strengthened by the transfer of technology from foreign partners (Ibison and McGregor, 2002; Kynge, 2002).

Clearly, this involves some investment and can represent a big step, especially for the smaller firm. The costs can be high, but at least the seller maintains complete control by selling through its own export department and sales force. The selling effort can be coordinated and run from the organisation's home base with sales representatives making trips abroad, or it can be run from a branch sales office located in a foreign country. It depends on the organisation's objectives and the volume of business it expects to handle. Ultimately, the organisation might decide to set up a sales subsidiary, which will be considered at p. 1030.

As well as providing control over the selling process, direct exporting also has the advantage of building a clear presence in the market. It creates contacts and helps to develop stronger buyer–seller relationships, which might be an important factor for buyers looking for committed suppliers.

Indirect export

Indirect exporting takes place where an organisation produces goods at home and then sells them through an intermediary and thus indirectly to the foreign buyer. The intermediary could be based either in the seller's home country or in the foreign market (although technically this is classed as direct exporting) and could be acting on behalf of the seller, on behalf of the buyer or totally independently. An export agent, for example, acts on behalf of the seller, undertaking to sell on a commission basis into a particular market. A confirming house or a buying house, on the other hand, acts on behalf of foreign buyers and earns commission from them. An export merchant is effectively a wholesaler who buys goods outright from a number of manufacturers and then resells them, perhaps to foreign retailers at a profit. Whether the intermediary is a merchant or an agent, the exporting manufacturer benefits from the intermediary's knowledge of the foreign market concerned, their contacts within the distribution channel, and their experience of how business is done in that country. Similarly, the foreign buyer using a buying agent is also benefiting from the intermediary's knowledge and contacts in the export market.

eg

Cambridge-based John Lusty is an intermediary company that provides a major channel through which foreign exporters can sell in the UK. With divisions selling to supermarkets and caterers (Trustin Unimerchants), wholesalers and the impulse sector, the company provides a service that the direct exporter would find difficult to set up: it has customers, contacts, ordering and delivery facilities in the UK. Some of its success stories include San Pellegrino sparkling water, now one of the top 20 fastest growing soft drinks in the UK; Belgian chocolate brand Duc d'Or, Spanish olive oil producer Camacho, and Gaea of Greece's biscuit brand. John Lusty has also helped to turn Bonne Maman jam into a £10 mn brand in the UK. What attracts all these foreign organisations is John Lusty's experience and market knowledge which includes consumer and market research before a marketing programme is agreed with the exporter. The advice it gives indirect exporters is to think internationally but plan locally for the specifics of a market (*The Grocer*, 2001c).

Because of the reliance on the expertise of an intermediary, indirect exporting is an ideal starting point for a small business entering the international arena. It also carries little risk and little commitment because there is no investment in market development. It can, therefore, be a useful method if the organisation is dealing in small volumes or is somewhat uncertain, either about its own future or whether the product is appropriate for an international market.

Trade in knowledge and expertise

So far, the methods discussed have involved the transfer of goods or services from a domestic producer to a foreign customer. Here, however, we look at the transfer of ideas, concepts and processes, a transfer that is usually carried out so that goods and services can be produced abroad by foreign producers. This gives the originating organisation the benefit of selling a product with a 'made in …' label that shows that it was produced in the country in which it is being sold rather than being overtly a 'foreign' product.

The main methods to be covered here are licensing, franchising and contracting.

Licensing

Licensing can be an attractive option for entering international markets. The licensor grants a licensee the right to manufacture a product, use patents, use particular processes or exploit trade marks in a defined market in return for a royalty payment. Franchising applications of licence agreements are considered separately.

In manufacturing, **licensing** is useful for markets that are very remote or not worth the costs of direct involvement. The domestic manufacturer might be producing up to full capacity in its own plants and might not want to invest in new facilities or to divert capacity for a particular foreign market. Licensing helps to overcome high import tariffs, but also avoids the costs and commitment of direct investment. The licensor does, however, need to be sure that the licensee can handle the necessary production and marketing, otherwise a gap might be left for competition.

Licensing can be a particularly effective way of achieving technology transfer, that is, the movement of technological advance to new nations.

eg

Love it or hate it, the SPAM® Family of Products are big business, with sales in over 56 countries and a museum dedicated to it in the US. Tulip International, the Danish food company, gained the licence to manufacture SPAM® for sale in the UK. The licensor Hormel Foods Corporation in the USA, wanted to work with a licensee that would seek to move the brand away from a speciality, almost nostalgic position, more into the mainstream. Tulip decided to commit £150,000 supporting the brand showing how versatile the product actually is to a nation reared on SPAM® fritters rather than Spicy SPAM® kebabs and stuffed peppers. Changing perceptions will not be easy in some target segments, however, given the school dinner associations with SPAM®, despite it being Monty Python's favourite canned meat, according to a sketch in 1970. (Carmichael, 2001; http://www.hormel.com).

SPAM® (spiced ham) has grown as product since its launch in 1937. For some people it deserves to be set on a pedestal.

Source: Hormel Foods Corporation. Copyright Hormel Foods Corporation. Reprinted with permission.

Licensing can thus be viewed favourably by foreign governments, as it brings in new technology and helps in the training and skilling of the local workforce. Licensing can also be useful in some specific industrial sectors, such as defence, as a means of winning government contracts.

The financial risk of licensing could be relatively low, as the licensee is the one who will be investing in plant, machinery and marketing. There could, however, be risks to the licensor's reputation if the licensee degrades or abuses the licensor's name or intellectual property. There is also a risk that the licensee, having gained experience, might then decide to go it alone at the end of the contract period and turn into a competitor.

A major strength of licensing is that it combines the skills and knowledge of the licensor with the local contacts and experience of the licensee. Its success, however, is very dependent on whether production quality and marketing effectiveness can be created and sustained. Like any distribution decision, the choice of licensing as an entry strategy is based on a trade-off between the increased coverage and lower risk gained, and the potentially reduced financial returns because of the high level of involvement of the licensee.

Franchising

The previous chapter looked at the impact of franchising across Europe and the development of some large international franchisors such as KFC, Subway and Domino's Pizza. Some franchisors, such as McDonald's in the UK, have grown through direct involvement between the franchisor and its franchisees. Sometimes, however, indirect methods are adopted that involve a sharing of know-how, resources and marketing effort. McDonald's, for example, preferred to use a joint venture to enter the Russian market because of the alien and relatively unknown nature of the marketing and operating environment. By far the most popular indirect method, however, is the **master franchising** system.

Master franchising. Master franchising means that an individual or organisation in a country is given an exclusive right to develop the franchising system. The master franchisee can then develop a network of sub-franchises on a regional, multiple or individual unit basis. The master franchisee might receive extensive training from the franchisor, not only in operating a unit, but also in franchisee recruitment, staff training and managing a franchised system. It is then the master franchisee's responsibility to use local knowledge and contacts to develop the network in a manner that is satisfactory to the franchisor. The master franchisee earns a percentage of the fees or royalties paid by individual franchisees.

eg

Oil and Vinegar is a franchise chain concentrated in Benelux countries with around twenty stores. The theme is Southern European food and non-food items, including olive oils, vinegars, mustards, pestos, herbs and spices, as well as books, ceramics, olive dishes, etc. Having been tested through the initial twenty stores, the concept is being expanded into Germany, the UK and Norway. Master franchisees were sought to develop each national market, to appoint individual franchisees, and to provide field support and expertise on the most appropriate sites to select. This enables the franchisor to concentrate on refining the business concept and ensuring that the product assortment evolves to meet the overall expansion plans, without becoming embroiled in detailed operations (Oil and Vinegar, 2002; http://www.oilvinegar.nl).

Area development agreement. The franchisor might not want to appoint a single master franchisee to cover a whole country. After all, this does put a great deal of power into the master franchisee's hands, and if the master franchisee fails to fulfil their part of the agreement or to maintain high standards among the sub-franchisees, the franchisor stands to lose both reputation and the competitive initiative in that country. The franchisor might, therefore, prefer to enter into *area development agreements* in which several master franchisees are appointed, each with responsibility for a clearly defined regional territory. The agreement might also specify that a certain number of outlets are expected to be opened over a defined period of time in return for the exclusive territory. This approach has all the benefits of the master franchisee system, in terms of reducing the network development costs, the time taken to develop a new market and exploiting the local knowledge of the master franchisees, while reducing the potential losses from a poor master franchisee.

Subway (*see* p. 984) uses development agents in new countries to open up the market. These agents are contracted to find an agreed number of franchisees, either through master franchise arrangements or direct to individual franchisees. They use their local knowledge to assist with site selection, site negotiation, setting up the operation, training and ongoing operations. In return, they receive a percentage of the start-up franchise fee and a percentage of the company royalty from that area.

Contracting

A manufacturing contract means that the manufacturer contracts with a company in the foreign market to produce or assemble the product on their behalf. This saves the time and costs involved in physically transporting the finished product from abroad. This allows a more flexible approach for entering markets where international logistics costs might otherwise reduce effectiveness and margins. Like licensing, **contracting** also avoids the problems of currency fluctuations and import barriers, but potentially creates a new competitor. Nevertheless, contracting can be particularly useful if the volume of business in the foreign market is too much for direct importation of goods, but not sufficient to warrant direct investment in production facilities. As Gilligan and Hird (1986) make clear, contracting also allows the contractor to retain control over marketing and distribution, unlike licensing.

Management contracts are widely used in service markets, such as hotels. An independent enterprise contracts to operate all the management functions in return for a fee, and occasionally for a share in the profits. The company awarded the contract has responsibility for operational matters such as human resource management, financial control, marketing and service delivery, but does not normally get involved in strategic or policy issues, nor does it have any share in the ownership of the business.

Hilton Hotels operates over 230 full-service hotels and resorts throughout the US and a further 380 hotels run by Hilton International in nearly 70 countries. It has a combination of directly owned, franchised, joint venture and management contract-run hotels. In the latter case, it has no equity stake, but uses its management expertise and knowledge at a local level. For example, it entered into a contract with London and Regional properties to manage the 163-bed luxury Hilton London Green Park Hotel. The various arrangements enable the Hilton to do what it does best, operating and marketing hotels, without the risks and problems associated with building and capital investment. However, franchise operations are the most popular operating method, with 74 per cent of the US sites but Hilton International is increasingly taking on management contracts to acquire access to prime sites in city centres, at or near international airports and in prime resorts where other methods may not be available (http://www. hilton.com).

The careful use of management contracts can help the 'exporter' to increase market coverage and to develop international segments more quickly.

Investment

This group of entry methods involves a major commitment for the organisation because it involves some level of investment in the foreign market. As mentioned earlier, this might mean simply setting up a sales subsidiary to market and distribute goods imported from the home country, or it might mean acquiring a local company or setting up a new manufacturing facility to produce goods closer to the market, thus avoiding international logistics costs and import barriers. Whatever the type of investment, it certainly helps the organisation to create a presence in the market and to build much closer relationships with customers.

Foreign companies have pumped $40 bn of investment into Poland since the end of the communist era in the form of joint ventures, manufacturing investments and acquisitions. This has given rise to some concern because with so many assets being foreign owned, during any global slowdown, some of the operations hit hard times, such as Warsaw's Daewoo FSO car plant. A downturn in the local market and Daewoo's bankruptcy mean that prospects for the plant currently look bleak, a far cry from the optimism when the venture was founded in 1996. Foreign hypermarkets have taken a keen interest in Poland, but the result has been the rapid decimation of local retailers unable to undertake the niching and service innovation necessary for survival. In the technology sector, although local joint ventures have upgraded quality and technical capability, most of the R&D is kept outside Poland so there is little additional capacity for spin-offs and innovation. This goes to show that inbound investment can have both positive and negative impacts on a local economy (Reed, 2002).

Because investment is such a big decision, there are a number of specific issues to be taken into account. These are summarised in Figure 23.6, based on Walsh (1993), and cover the whole range of operational and marketing environmental factors.

Within this section, three particular forms of investment are considered: **sales subsidiaries, manufacturing subsidiaries** and **joint ventures**.

Sales subsidiaries

Sales subsidiaries play no part in manufacturing the product, but do take responsibility for marketing, selling and distributing it. They might also get involved in after-sales service. Sales subsidiaries can be specially created or they can be developed from an existing acquired company. Staff, therefore, can either be transferred from the parent organisation or recruited locally. With local staff, the organisation acquires local contacts and knowledge, but might have to give product and management training. With transferred staff, the product and management knowledge might well be in place, but local knowledge will have to be developed.

The advantage of selling through sales subsidiaries rather than through the domestic sales force lies in the dedicated local knowledge and expertise that builds up and the closeness to the customer. Also, in the event of failure in that market, any losses can be confined to the subsidiary rather than having an extensive impact on the parent company.

Manufacturing subsidiaries

The establishment of manufacturing subsidiaries involves assembling or manufacturing the product in local markets. Again, such an operation can be set up from scratch or developed from an acquisition. It becomes an integral part of the manufacturing base of the host country, and can thus become a significant contributor to the local economy.

Figure 23.6 Factors influencing the investment decision

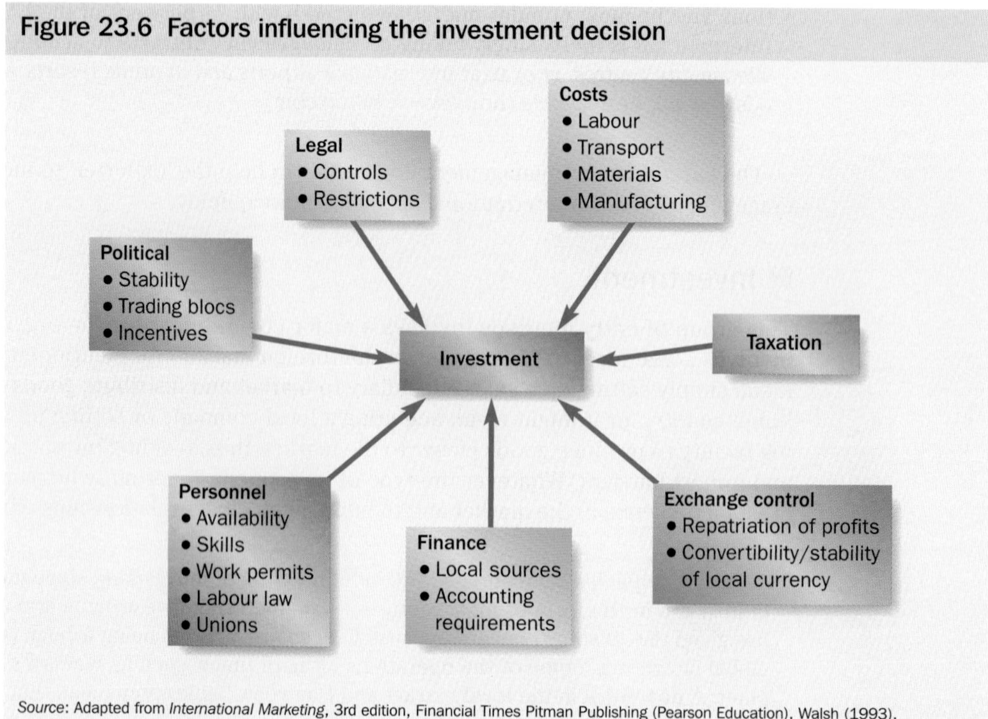

Source: Adapted from *International Marketing*, 3rd edition, Financial Times Pitman Publishing (Pearson Education), Walsh (1993).

eg

JCB, a UK-based construction equipment company, has traditionally operated through either direct sales, sales offices or subsidiaries, with the majority of manufacturing concentrated at its Staffordshire plant and then exported. Over 60 per cent of its machines are exported, although it now has manufacturing bases in the USA, India and South America (Marsh, 2001). Its first major non-UK plant is at Savannah, Georgia, built at a cost of $62 mn. Although not in full production, it enables 'Made in America' labels to be attached to the machines and as a result enables JCB to compete better with large US competitors such as Caterpillar and Case (Marsh, 2000). While the EU market can be adequately supplied from the UK, the Savannah plant will provide 24 per cent of JCB's global output and provide a bridgehead to penetrate the large US market further (http://www.jcb.com).

The Belgian steel wire maker Bekaert is much further down the road in creating manufacturing subsidiaries, some of which are run on a joint venture basis. It operates 96 production centres in 29 countries and has an extensive network of sales offices and agencies in the other countries. It has established a global presence in a series of specialist niches such as making the wire for champagne corks, in which it has 80 per cent of the global market. Other product lines include wire for fencing, bridges and filters. It has been developing the South American market for over 40 years through taking a stake in existing or new steel wire producers in most of the countries. As a result of creating over 20 of these manufacturing subsidiaries, Bekaert has now gained a 48 per cent share of the South American steel wire market. New ideas are transferred from the European and other markets so that local businesses can keep up with industry standards and continue to outperform other local competitors (Marsh, 1999). As a result of this strategy it now has become a truly diversified company in terms of geographic markets and for wire products, the EU in total only accounts for 20 per cent of its sales (http://www.bekaert.com).

As discussed in Chapter 2, because of the employment and wealth creation potential involved, many governments are keen to attract this sort of inward investment, offering incentives and grants to manufacturers to set up plants in key regions. Many of these manufacturing subsidiaries themselves export their goods to nearby markets. Japanese cars, for example Nissan and Toyota, manufactured in the UK are exported to other European countries.

Joint ventures

A joint venture is set up when two organisations come together to create a jointly owned third company. The two parents share the ownership, control and profits, as well as the risks. There are many reasons for taking this route. The partners might feel that separately they do not have the necessary resources (whether financial, physical or managerial) to develop or make an impact on a market. This motivation could be especially important if they are up against larger, more powerful competitors. The partners are likely to have complementary assets or skills. One might have cash, the other know-how; one might have technical expertise, the other might be an ailing manufacturing plant at the geographic heart of the market; one might have marketing and distribution skills, the other an unexploited product idea. A joint venture might be the only choice if an organisation wants to enter a country whose government is hostile to foreign companies having 100 per cent ownership of any aspect of production (whether physical assets or know-how).

eg

Scottish & Newcastle brewery received an extra advantage when it took over Hartwell, the Finnish brewer, as it gained a stake in a 50:50 joint venture with Carlsberg in the Russian and eastern European markets. Hartwell has a 45 per cent share of the Finnish beer, water and soft drinks market with its Lapin Kulta and the association with S&N will enable that position to be strengthened at a time when Hartwell needed cash to retain its market leadership in the Baltic States and to service the growing Russian market.

The prime interest for S&N was the stake in faster growing emerging markets such as Russia (George and Jones, 2002a). Unlike a number of other joint brewing ventures, Hartwell's formation of BBH with Carlsberg in the early 1990s was successful. It has gained a 30 per cent share of the large Russian market and is also popular in the Baltic states and the Ukraine. The combination of acquired local breweries and organic growth, coupled with investment in brewing technology and quality has enabled a leading position to be established. BBH's main brand, Baltika, has become the third largest beer brand in Europe by volume and thus the acquisition of Hartwell has given S&N a prime platform for further exploiting the marketing opportunities (George and Jones, 2002b).

Joint ventures have been an important force in the privatisation and regeneration of the industries of central and eastern European countries. Western companies have been encouraged to invest cash and managerial skills in joint ventures with local companies that provide production facilities that can be updated, labour that can be retrained and access to the market. The partners work together to develop products and markets and share the benefits. Not all joint ventures run smoothly, however.

eg

China was a tough market for Unilever to crack through its 14 joint venture arrangements. Its relatively poor showing in the 1990s, despite early market entry, has been attributed to poor distribution and inefficient joint ventures. Many of the joint venture companies are partly state owned and they also require considerable investment. Often management, marketing and distribution functions overlap, resulting in cost inefficiencies and slow decision-making (Jacob, 2000). The situation was not helped by a retailing system that did not allow Unilever brands the same prominence as in Western markets, and a buying public that still tended to buy on price. The problems that Unilever faced were typical of many early pioneers in China who were forced by the government into inappropriate joint ventures to ensure that they did not compete head-on with local firms. As the legal system has developed, however, and with China's entry into the WTO, more options are becoming available such as establishing a joint stock company under Chinese law. Now, Unilever has merged its four joint ventures into a joint stock company with Unilever holding the majority share. This has enabled it to regain management control and to treat each original joint venture as part of the larger corporation (McGregor, 2002). Although this will help Unilever with marketing and distribution, it still must overcome some of the market barriers to branding.

This example shows just how exposed to risk the organisation is when entering a market with such a level of commitment. Political, legal and economic issues all add to the normal commercial and marketing problems of operating in relatively unknown environments. Opportunities that seem attractive on the surface could prove to be far more difficult to exploit in practice. Commitments made by local partners or even governments have to be honoured. Although access to an otherwise difficult or prohibited market may be gained, distribution and competitive structures could militate against rapid change. Benefits are rarely realisable in the short term and those organisations looking for quick success are often frustrated and can become disillusioned.

Nevertheless, joint ventures can be very successful, as long as both partners plan the venture carefully and are clear about their objectives. They also need good communication and mutual understanding of what each party is bringing to the venture, what each one's responsibilities are within it and what each expects to get out of it. Figure 23.7 suggests a number of factors that might contribute towards a more successful joint venture partnership.

Figure 23.7 Factors contributing to a successful joint venture partnership

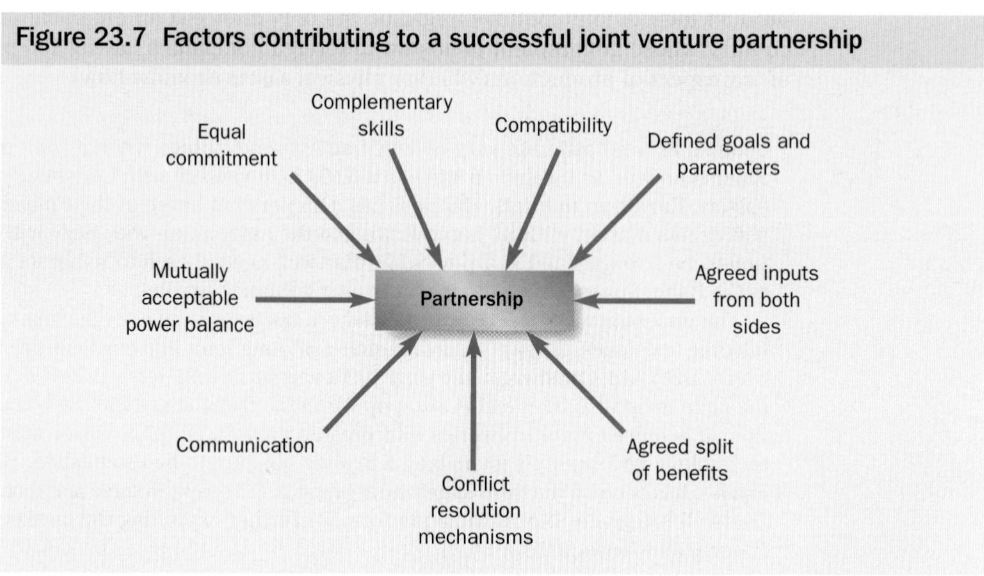

Strategic alliances

The term **strategic alliance** is wide ranging, covering any kind of collaborative agreement or activity between two or more organisations. It can include joint ventures, but not all strategic alliances have to be joint ventures. Whereas a joint venture specifically means creating a separate, jointly owned entity, a strategic alliance can be much looser and informal. It could be two companies joining R&D forces to develop a specific product for a specific market, or agreeing to share a distribution channel, or agreeing to sell each other's products. The benefits from a strategic alliance are similar in principle to those derived from a joint venture, in that it brings together complementary assets and skills creating synergy. Strategic alliances do not, however, necessarily carry the same degree of long-term commitment and risk, as there is no equity stake, just commitment to a specific project or activity.

eg

Despite the difficulties of establishing strategic alliances, powerful international combinations have the potential to make a significant impact on domestic markets. The alliance between Goodyear and Sumitomo Rubber Industries in Japan is bound to affect EU manufacturers such as Continental in Germany, Pirelli in Italy and Michelin in France. A large, efficient competitor with reduced costs, strong distribution and powerful brands could stimulate further alliances within Europe as a defensive measure. The Goodyear–Sumitomo alliance provides for joint ventures in Europe, Japan and the US, with Goodyear controlling four of the six joint ventures and Sumitomo having the lead role in Japan. The alliance enables combined distribution, marketing, global purchasing, and production, and for joint R&D on tyre technology, enabling both parties to achieve some rationalisation (Griffiths, 1999). Sumitomo, for example, was able to end truck tyre manufacturing in the UK and Goodyear was able to shut a plant in Italy as part of a pooled joint venture in Europe (Griffiths, 2000). Although the alliance cost considerable time, resources and effort to set up in 1999, it is already delivering benefits. Goodyear has moved from holding 2 per cent of the replacement market and zero per cent for the OEM market to gaining 6 per cent of each by 2001. From that market position, it is better able to expand in an otherwise difficult market to penetrate (Griffiths, 2001).

Goodyear Wrangler light truck tyres move along automated conveyors in its Napanee, Ontario, Canada plant.

Source: Goodyear.

The number of strategic alliances of all kinds has increased rapidly over the last 10 years or so. As competition has become more aggressive, markets have become more global and technology has increased its rate of change. Alliances are particularly prevalent in fast moving, high technology industries such as defence, communications, pharmaceuticals (all requiring heavy investment in R&D to keep up with the pace of technological change and to deliver necessary innovation) and airlines (under pressure from competition and national protectionism). As Houlder (1995) points out, a strategic alliance can help an organisation to enter new markets, obtain access to expertise and technology and achieve economies of scale much more quickly. She does, however, sound a note of caution, quoting a survey that suggested that only 17 per cent of US managers thought that alliances were effective while 31 per cent thought they were downright dangerous. The risks arise from ill-matched partnerships, poor definition of the alliance's purpose and the mutual responsibilities involved, or poor implementation of the alliance. Figure 23.7 suggested ways of creating more successful joint ventures, but imagine how much damage can be done when one or more of the factors considered there goes wrong, as they often do in practice. Houlder (1995) sums up the real-world problems neatly:

> *There is a dilemma at the heart of alliance-making. Trust, flexibility and commitment are widely seen as the keys to success. But companies dare not blind themselves to the risks involved. Today's ally may be tomorrow's competitor; a joint venture may turn out to be a takeover by the back door. For the growing number of companies engaged in alliances, ambiguity is a fact of life.*

International marketing strategy

Once an organisation has analysed the characteristics of the target foreign market and has decided how to enter it, the next stage is to design the marketing programme. In principle, this is no different from designing a marketing mix in a domestic market. The organisation has to define and select target segments, position the product and decide whether to modify the marketing mix to suit conditions in the foreign market, whether it is close to home in Europe or elsewhere in the world. Just because a particular marketing mix is successful in the domestic market, however, it cannot necessarily be successfully transferred elsewhere. A whole range of factors within the marketing environment, for example culture, customs or competition, might point to the wisdom of adapting some or all of the marketing mix elements.

marketing *in action*

The alliance that never got off the ground

The announcement in the mid-1990s of a proposed strategic alliance between British Airways (BA) and American Airlines (AA) was a further move in the changing face of competition in the transatlantic passenger market. International alliances are increasingly being used as a means of controlling routes and for developing new business. To competitors, however, the proposed BA–AA alliance was seen as dangerous, as they thought it would create a very powerful airline partnership that could distort fair trade. Ironically, BA had used a similar argument to criticise the Lufthansa–United Airlines alliance that was designed to seek antitrust immunity in the USA.

The BA–AA proposal, at first glance, appeared to be straightforward. All BA and AA flights between the UK and the USA would have had coordinated schedules that would have enabled smoother transfers for passengers between the two airlines. By placing joint flight codes on their UK–USA flights, they would also have shared the revenues generated. It would also have meant, however, that around 40 per cent of weekly take-off and landing slots at Heathrow, 60 per cent of the total transatlantic market, and 70 per cent of flights between London and New York would have been covered by the agreement. They would also have been able to access parts of each other's databases for mailing and promotion purposes. This could seriously have affected the competitive position of a number of smaller airlines who are excluded from similar deals. Richard Branson, speaking for Virgin Atlantic, claimed at the time that the BA–AA alliance would be bad for the market, because it could lead to reduced competition and higher fares. Even in 2002, some Virgin planes still carry 'No way BA' messages as a reminder of its views. Ironically, some analysts believe that Virgin's concern was less to do with the BA–AA alliance than the prospect of new competitors landing at Heathrow.

Not surprisingly, regulatory bodies on both sides of the Atlantic were very interested in the proposal. What should have been an April 1997 launch for the alliance was postponed as the EU Competition Commissioner deliberated over the implications of the deal and considered what conditions should be imposed if it was to go ahead. BA–AA had always known that they would be required to give up some slots as part of the deal, but the question was how many. They had offered 196 per week, whereas the EU initially demanded 350. The EU ruling eventually came in July 1998: 267 slots had to be given away free. BA–AA said that this was too many and that they wanted to sell slots for around £2 mn each. Some argued that this should be allowed as the slots are a legitimate valuable asset of the airlines, others argued that the slots were given free to the airlines in the first place and if a sale was allowed at all, the proceeds should go to the taxpayer.

The issue then became more complicated because the BA–AA deal became entangled in the wider debate between the US and UK governments on 'open skies' policies, i.e. allowing each other's airlines to fly freely to each other's airports without restriction. Under the agreement prevailing at that time, only BA and Virgin Atlantic from the UK and AA and United Airlines from the USA were allowed to fly to the USA from Heathrow. US approval for the BA–AA alliance hinged on the two governments resolving the 'open skies' issue, but by July 1999 there was still no agreement about opening Heathrow Airport to more competition. Yet US approval for the BA–AA alliance hinged on the opening of Heathrow to more competition. The US regulators eventually demanded that 224 take-off and landing slots at Heathrow had to be surrendered to other transatlantic operators, but this was considered too many by both parties as it would have undermined both their competitive positions. Effectively, BA decided that the closer links with AA were not as strategically valuable as retaining slots on transatlantic routes. The deal started to collapse. The UK government would not open its skies at Heathrow without the BA–AA deal and the open skies deal was required by Washington to agree the deal. BA could not afford to risk losing £400 mn operating profit if it gave up slots. In 2002, BA and AA therefore withdrew the application to the US Department of Transportation for the alliance and considered other cooperation options that were less high profile but subject to the same degree of scrutiny. The opportunity for both airlines to act as a merged airline, setting fares, determining schedules, sharing revenues and dominating the important US–London market option has now receded. Some believe that it may have been only delayed, pending wider progress on deregulating international airline traffic. Other options do exist on a less high profile basis: code sharing for example would allow BA to sell seats on AA's American domestic flights as if they were its own. This all goes to show that international strategic alliances between large organisations must be carefully planned and that the role of governments and regulatory authorities in the approval process cannot be underestimated, whatever the economic logic.

Sources: Ashworth (1998); Bond (2002) Done (2002); O'Connell (2002); Odell and Spiegel (2002); Parsley (1998); Skapinker (1999a, 1999b).

We now look more closely at the pressures affecting the debate on the merits of the standardisation as compared with adaptation, and later we take a more general view of the implementation of the marketing mix in international contexts.

Standardisation or adaptation

The decision on whether to standardise or to adapt is a major one for any organisation operating in more than one environment. There could be conflicting pressures, perhaps arising from the marketing environment and/or the culture, objectives and marketing operations focus of the organisation, some of which push the organisation towards adapting the marketing mix to suit local conditions, and some of which push the organisation towards standardisation of the marketing approach, regardless of local market conditions (Dittschar, 2000).

There are risks in either approach. If there is too much adaptation, the organisation could fail to exploit the synergies possible from operating in many different markets. Global branding and the transfer of new product ideas across boundaries are all possible with standardisation. In the extreme case of adaptation, each domestic market is treated differently and that can create vulnerability if the product is up against powerful internationally branded competitors (Shay, 1998). If, however, a multinational loses touch with local markets, it can also cause difficulties. Wind (1998) argues that a serious global company should have representatives of different parts of the world in key management positions, be sensitive to different cultures and employ managers that are capable of operating anywhere in the world. We look first at pressures leading towards **adaptation**, which are summarised in Figure 23.8.

Figure 23.8 Factors influencing the adaptation or standardisation decision

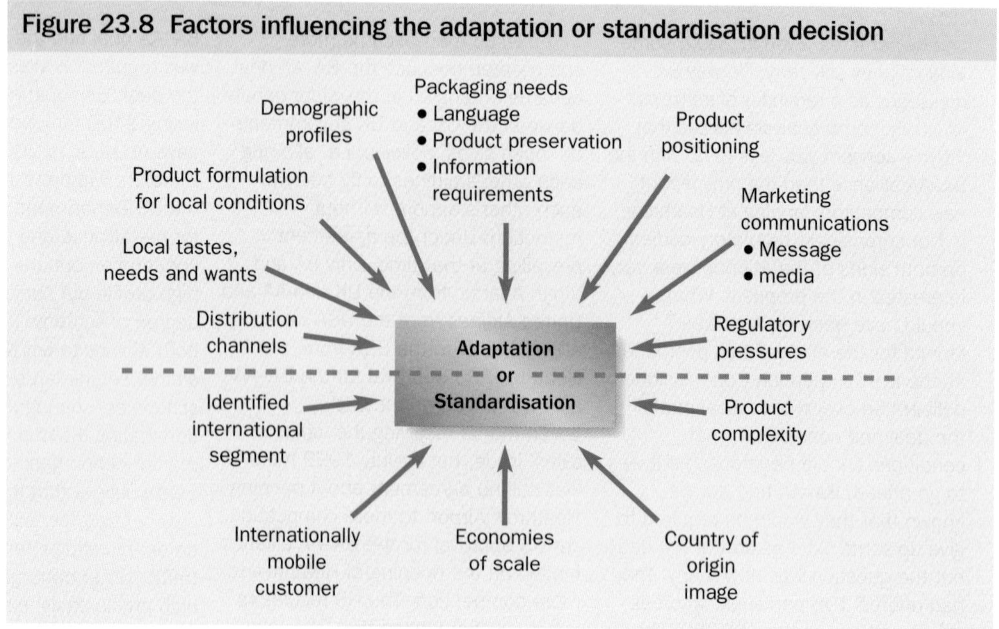

Pressures towards adaptation

Customer needs. Any organisation has to think carefully about customer needs and wants and the extent to which the marketing mix satisfies them. If those needs and wants are different in an international market, then some adaptation might be necessary. A food product, for example, might have to be flavoured differently, be more or less sweet, be more or less salty, be more or less fizzy, contain less fat, have a different smell or be a different colour to meet the preferences and expectations of the local market. Clothing too might have to be adapted for the local market and use different fabrics, different colours, and be produced in different size ranges. In an earlier chapter (*see* p. 185), for example, it was shown how Gossard, the lingerie company, had to vary its product mixes across Europe to cater for different average sizes, different attitudes towards the purpose of lingerie, and different fabric preferences. Benetton produces garments centrally to the same designs for all its worldwide markets in undyed yarns and fabrics. Batches of garments are then dyed on demand to meet the colour requirements of different markets.

Parker (1995) argues that customer needs in markets cannot fully converge because of the physioeconomic framework. Climate, natural resources and other environmental influences all help to shape society and the individual, creating different attitudes and physiological needs. There is an inverse relationship, for example, between the number of calories people eat and the ambient temperature. In colder climates, for example, more alcoholic drink is consumed, which generates a lot of calories to retain body heat (that's our excuse, anyway). These fundamental influences all help to create cultural diversity, but of course may be less important in explaining differences within a climatic zone. Other influences, however, such as natural minerals, proximity to oceans or major rivers, could all then play a part in shaping customer preferences and behaviour.

Practical considerations. It is not just customers' aesthetic preferences that prompt adaptation, but practical considerations as well. The paper used for printing postage stamps has to be adapted depending on the climate of the destination country. This is because the gum used in a temperate climate could not withstand the humidity of some Far Eastern countries. The stamps would simply go gooey and be unusable. Similarly, the paper used to wrap soap in hot climates has to be treated with a mould inhibitor.

Packaging and communication. It might not, of course, be necessary to go as far as redesigning or reformulating the product itself. The focus of adaptation could be brand imagery, packaging or marketing communication, for instance. Brand image might have to

eg

Wine cartons are cheaper, lighter, easier to handle and can keep wine more fresh, yet they are not popular in the UK and they are perceived to contain downmarket wine. What may have been acceptable to take to a party in the 1980s was definite not so by the end of the century. Some retailers are now trying to sell better wines in cartons, capitalising on improvements in the lining technology which can keep the wine fresher. However Tetra Pak, a leading supplier of carton wine boxes has captured far bigger market shares in continental Europe, especially in Germany, Italy and Spain, in the table wine sector and in Argentina 66 per cent of all table wine is sold in cartons. In the UK, however, the consumer is as yet unconvinced that quality can come in a carton (Lawrence, 2001).

be adapted to avoid embarrassing connotations in foreign languages or to create a clearer and stronger positioning statement within the local marketing environment.

Packaging design can help to reinforce image, but might also have to be adapted in practical terms for the local language or to give instructions relevant to local usage of the product. Nevertheless, some consumer products do manage to standardise their packaging for a number of international markets, regardless of language. Provided that the same brand name is used, it is possible to print lists of ingredients and basic instructions in several languages.

Marketing communication. All of this is likely to follow through into the adaptation of advertising and other marketing communication activities, again to create something to which the local target audience can better relate, and to differentiate the product more clearly.

eg

HSBC Holdings (http://www.hsbc.com) purchased the Midland Bank in the UK in 1992, but retained the familiar High Street brand name for a period to reassure customers. Although mention was always made to 'Member of the HSBC Group' and the distinctive HSBC logo was featured, the separate names survived. This applied to other familiar names around the world such as the Hong Kong Bank and Marine Midland Bank. However, HSBC eventually decided to abandon its policy of retaining local names in its global empire, arguing that in a global market with rapid international communication, retaining separate names could reduce the impact of the overall brand. Thus a global campaign was launched to establish an HSBC umbrella brand, featuring the red and white symbols. This meant rebranding 19 different banking brands in 79 countries. By 2002, HSBC operated 7,000 offices in 81 countries and the use of the umbrella brand name had given it the opportunity to build a powerful global brand that transcended national boundaries. To reinforce this, in 2002 a global campaign using a single agency, Lowe Lintas, was developed. The campaign aimed to brand HSBC as a bank that understands different cultures around the world and is, therefore, the world's 'local bank'. The advertising campaign demonstrated the 'importance of local knowledge by exploring distinctive national customs and practices. Carrying the strapline "the world's local bank" the advertising showed that anyone who banks with HSBC can benefit from services and advice from a company with international experience, delivered by people sensitive to the customs and needs of their community' (http://www/hsbc.co.uk). By adopting this approach, HSBC aims to combine the benefits of globalisation with its local presence in many local markets (*Marketing*, 2002; http://www.hsbc.co.uk).

Marketing communication might also have to be adapted to take account of the different buyer readiness stages of different markets. A product that is mature in the domestic market, and only needs reminder advertising and low key promotional activity, might be unknown in a foreign market and need a promotional mix that is much more geared towards awareness, generating trial and attitude building. Communication might also have to be adapted to the effects of local media availability and consumption habits.

eg

When Swedish company Target Games wanted to develop US sales of its refillable candy dispensers, it decided that originality was everything. It developed three brand names with appropriately designed dispensers. The names were Snot!, Fart! and Burpp! and the dispensers were designed with orifices that gave off appropriate sounds (*The Grocer*, 1999).

Distribution channels. Another practical consideration is the sophistication and structure of distribution channels. An fmcg producer selling into eastern Europe, for example, will not find the same concentration of retailing in hypermarkets and superstores owned by large chains as in Western Europe. This means that the producer has to find ways of achieving geographic coverage through thousands of small independent grocers, which could prove to be difficult and expensive, particularly if the wholesale sector is similarly underdeveloped. Logistics might also have to be adapted, if deliveries are being made direct to small stores rather than to a big retailer's regional depots. Also, if it takes longer to get the product into the shops, perhaps because of poor transport infrastructure to outlying areas, then the producer might have to address issues of product freshness. This problem could be compounded if retailers cannot provide appropriate and reliable storage conditions. Shops might not have the capacity to keep food chilled at a safe temperature or might not have sufficient freezer or chiller space to store any significant quantity of goods.

eg

When logistics operators moved into Poland in the 1990s, they had to build distribution systems that fitted local conditions. The population to be served is large (39 million), but the road infrastructure was not adequate to meet demands for improved customer service and 24-hour delivery. One operator, McLane, chose a hub and spoke design that enabled products to be quickly handled in local centres close to markets. From three hubs, near Warsaw, Gdynia and Katowice, eleven cross-docking stations, or spokes, were established in the metropolitan areas to enable fast bulk-breaking from 44-foot trailers and then onward transportation in smaller vans to individual retail outlets (Coia, 2002).

Product positioning. Some products might require a high degree of customisation, regardless of where they are sold. In some B2B markets, the supply of engineering components for example, the product and its associated marketing and service mix are designed and tailored for the specific customer. Similarly, large capital projects for bridges, tunnels or major public buildings are unique and have to be designed, managed and implemented according to local conditions and customer requirements. Clearly, in such circumstances, there is little room for standardisation. Linked with the practical need for adaptation, the organisation could develop a deliberate strategy to seek special niches in the market and to position itself as a specialist in tailor-made packages to suit individual customer requirements.

eg

As discussed in Case Study 2.2 Fisherman's Friend's positioning varies in different markets. In the UK, is it perceived as a semi-medicinal cough sweet by both retailers and consumers. It is therefore displayed in stores alongside other cough remedies and tends to be given more prominent shelf space in the winter. In overseas markets, however, there are no such prejudices and Fisherman's Friend is positioned as 'adult confectionery'. In these markets, there is much less seasonality and the product retains its normal shelf position throughout the year.

Mode of entry to market. It is also possible that the organisation's mode of entry to the market might influence its willingness to adapt. If the product is being manufactured locally, either under licence or through a subsidiary, then it might be easier to design adaptations into the product or the manufacturing process and to allow local marketing managers to adapt the marketing approach to suit local conditions. In an organisation that is more centrally controlled and where more functions, such as R&D and manufacture, are undertaken by the parent organisation, the more likely it is that there would be a standard marketing approach.

eg

A Hungarian company has become a success in selling buses to city transport networks across the USA. In order to penetrate the US market, it was necessary to have a manufacturing facility in the USA. The company, North American Bus Industries (NABI), has a plant in Hungary from which bus bodies are shipped to a plant acquired in Anniston, Alabama, for final assembly (http://www.nabisua.com). By having a US base it is better able to service the market, can become closer to customers and can also overcome some of the regulations and tariff barriers that could otherwise restrict growth. The move was successful as it enabled some very large contracts to be won. A deal for 1,070 buses from the Los Angeles Metropolitan Transit Authority, worth over $225 mn was the largest ever order for transit buses in the USA by a single authority (Kester, 2000). By 2001, the order book was for over 3,000 buses (Kester, 2001a).

Regulations. Finally, the organisation might be forced towards adaptation by technical or commercial regulations. Toys imported into the EU, for example, have to conform to certain safety standards. Some Far Eastern manufacturers, therefore, have had to adapt their product designs and improve their quality standards or face exclusion from European markets. Regulations might also cover product labelling (relating to weight, country of origin or declaration of ingredients, for example) and product claims (relating to the extent to which it can be recycled, health warnings, nutritional or other alleged benefits).

eg

The world's first cholesterol-cutting food ingredient, Benecol, had to overcome extensive regulatory barriers before it could be sold in the North American market. Raisio (http://www.raisio.com), the Finnish company behind the product, and Johnson & Johnson, which has the international marketing and production rights, were in a race against time to beat an alternative offering from Unilever. Although the USA is considered the prime market for health-conscious low fat margarine and spread buyers, Europe proved an easier bet for regulatory acceptance of the product's health claims. The subsequent battle with Unilever's Flora Pro-Activ took place on the worldwide stage, however, and by using a different ingredient as a cholesterol lowering agent, Unilever was able to gain a competitive price advantage as soon as the product was approved. Even in its home market of Finland, Raisio only has a 60 per cent share compared with Unilever's 40 per cent, and it is believed that original targets for the product have not been met, despite its being the first to market (*Chemical Market Reporter*, 2002).

As discussed in Chapter 2, other elements of the marketing mix, such as pricing, sales promotion, advertising and direct marketing, are likely to be subject to widely differing regulation in different international markets, and therefore might have to be adapted in order to conform.

Pressures towards standardisation

If an organisation is operating in a market where customer needs and preferences are largely universal, then there might be little enthusiasm for adaptation and **standardisation** might be considered to be preferable. Unfortunately, such markets are not very easy to find. Coca-Cola has virtually created such a market, but even it occasionally adapts the sweetness or fizziness of the product to suit local market preferences.

Identified international segment. What is more likely to happen is that the organisation will define an international lifestyle or usage segment (*see*, for example, the discussion of Euro-segments at pp. 191 *et seq.*) which cuts across geographic borders and allows a standardised marketing mix to be developed.

eg

Finding an international segment is not necessarily easy, but is attempted by brands such as Cadbury, Wash & Go, American Express, Nescafé and Carte Noir. Car manufacturers also try to standardise their marketing approaches as much as possible, across Europe at least. Some retailers, particularly the franchised ones, including companies like Benetton, The Body Shop, Toys 'Я' Us, and IKEA, also aim for standardisation.

As mentioned earlier, some retailers and product manufacturers use their country of origin as a key element of the product's appeal, and that is clearly going to imply a degree of standardisation.

eg

The Scottish salmon farming industry has a fine reputation around the world. Rather than individual farmers seeking markets, the Scottish Quality Salmon (SQS) organisation represents many of them. They work collectively through SQS, accounting for 65 per cent of the tonnage produced, and SQS is at the forefront of plans to increase the sales value from £300 mn to £500 mn and to double export value to £150 mn by 2007. In order to use SQS's quality brand name, all members must participate in an independent product certification scheme to ensure quality consistency and must give full regard to the environment and sustainability. All of this helps to reinforce the overall brand reputation of Scottish salmon, regardless of the individual enterprise producing it (*The Grocer*, 2001b; *Sunday Times*, 2001; http://www.scottishsalmon.co.uk).

Working collectively to represent individual farmers, Scottish Quality Salmon guarantees the customer a consistently good product.

Source: Scottish Quality Salmon.

Economies of scale. Such standardisation does not stem just from the existence of international lifestyle or usage segments, but also from a practical desire to achieve economies of scale, where possible. If aspects of the marketing mix can be standardised, then costs will be lower. A standardised product with standardised packaging can be produced in larger, more economic quantities and then distributed to a number of different markets. If a product is particularly complex to manufacture or involves sophisticated technology, then the pressure towards standardising it in all markets might be considerable. The costs and implications of trying to adapt could be just too high.

eg

Whirlpool, the large US white goods company, designs its products on 'platforms' that enable small adaptations for local markets to be incorporated into an otherwise standardised product that can be produced in large quantities to achieve low unit costs of production and faster development times. One of the problems faced is that while Europeans favour front-loader washing machines, the US prefers the less energy efficient top loaders, often designed to cope with large loads. From a plant in Stuttgart, 'a new world washer', a front loader, is now manufactured for the US market with adaptations for the demands of larger loads, and a similar model, slightly different in size and styling is to be launched in Europe. From the common platform, it is planned to sell the basic machine into Asia, again with minor modifications to suit the local market. Although the higher price, about €1,500, means that it will not become market leader, it is expected that a significant niche for a larger, environmentally friendly front-loader will be created. The use of basic platforms can still, therefore, allow some customisation to take place for worldwide demand differences, yet still keep product within sensible price ranges. This philosophy has been applied in other diverse sectors such as cars, fork-lift trucks, tractors and locomotives too (Marsh, 2002).

Mobile customers. International service industries aim to standardise their offerings as far as possible, as discussed in Chapter 22. A hotel chain serving business travellers, for example, will want to create a strong international brand image so that experiencing a stay at a Sheraton hotel in Sofia is as similar as possible to a stay at a Sheraton hotel in London. In this case, although the hotels are located in different countries, the market segment served is not geographically tied and thus the product has to be standardised for consistent positioning in the customer's mind. Other products, also targeted at international customers, implement a deliberate standardisation strategy. Kodak or Fuji films, for example, have to be immediately recognisable by tourists wherever they are.

Degree of adaptation or standardisation

As this discussion has implied, the degree of adaptation can be total or partial, or there can be no adaptation at all. If the marketing environment warrants it, adaptation could mean a complete overhaul of all elements of the marketing mix. At the other extreme, it could just mean a standardised product with slight alteration to the labelling on the package to make it conform to local regulations. Keegan (1969), looking at adaptation in terms of product and promotion in particular, came up with five alternative strategies, reflecting differing levels of adaptation. These are summarised, with examples, in Figure 23.9. The important point, however, is that any adaptation, however great or small, should be justified by the market or its environment, although its cost effectiveness should also be taken into account. It is equally important that a decision to standardise should be based on an appreciation of different market needs rather than on cultural arrogance. That was a message that Disney had to learn the hard way when it first opened its Paris theme park. There are now greater pressures to standardise using global media and global agencies, and there are opportunities to promote a product anywhere in the world using the same message, the same media and the same creative execution. Even then, however, there is often a need to allow the local business to vary the detailed content while leaving the core creative theme essentially untouched. Sometimes this is achieved by pick-and-mix images so that local companies can select appropriately to suit local conditions best (Clegg, 2002). Wind (1998) argues that

Figure 23.9 Five product adaptation strategies

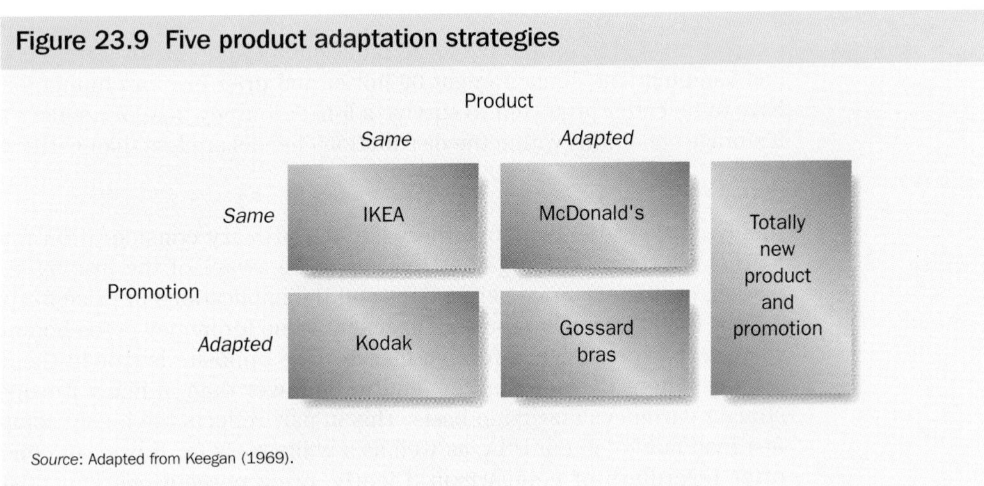

Source: Adapted from Keegan (1969).

there will always be a tension between global strategy and local interest. What is needed is a blend of standardisation and differentiation that can allow local adaptation to suit local market needs, yet still enable cross-country coordination, integration and synergy. The challenge, according to him, is to 'think and act globally, regionally and locally'. The organisational structure and the degree of local autonomy will be important determinants of an organisation's ability to standardise and adapt (Dittschar, 2000; Solberg, 2000).

International marketing mixes

The principles of designing a marketing mix for international markets are the same as those employed in domestic markets. Sound market analysis and understanding should precede any detailed decision-making in the selection and scheduling of the marketing tools. As discussed above, the marketing strategy and programme might have to be tailored to exploit strengths and opportunities and minimise weaknesses and threats in the context of the local marketing environment. This includes the need to appreciate the social and cultural influences on consumer decision-making, the state of technological capability and the sophistication of distribution channels. Also, as considered at pp. 1007 *et seq.*, the segmentation and positioning strategy will be an important determinant of the shape of the marketing mix.

As a way of summarising many of the points made throughout this chapter, each element of the marketing mix will now be considered briefly.

Product

The specification of the whole product package must be driven by customer needs and wants rather than pure convenience. It might be possible to define a standard product that can be sold across a number of international markets, for example consumer electronic goods, kitchen appliances or some toiletries. Otherwise, the product might have to be adapted for local needs in major or minor ways. Part of the success of many Australian wines within the traditional markets of the EU has been due to their careful positioning as premium wines, attracting higher price points. This has been supported by technological advances such as pioneering 'bag-in-a-box wines' and using computers for maintaining product quality and consistency (Smith and Robinson, 1999). Packaging and brand imagery are likely to have to be adapted to reflect local culture or to help create a market position that is compatible with the local marketing environment.

eg

Some national products are difficult to transfer across boundaries. Kellogg, for example, could have a problem if it tried to move its cereal Hoshi No Yasaibatake (The Vegetable Garden of Star) into European markets. Although popular with Japanese children, a mix of dehydrated carrot, spinach and pumpkin in brown sugar and honey might not be to British or German tastes. However, there may be no reason why the product could not be exported to some other Asian countries where tastes could be similar.

Packaging might also have to be redesigned to cope with different physical conditions and handling. The climate might be hotter and drier or more humid, or the product might have to be better protected to survive a longer journey time or a longer shelf life, especially if storage conditions within the distribution channel are less than perfect.

Price

In any market, domestic or otherwise, the primary consideration for price is what the market will bear. The organisation has to be aware of the pricing structure within the market, customers' price perceptions and the implications of price for product positioning. A price level that might represent excellent value for money in the home market could seem to be very expensive in a foreign market. The opposite is true in the case of McDonald's pricing, where US menu prices tend to be lower than in many European countries on a straight currency conversion basis. This in part reflects the highly competitive state of the fast food market in the USA, as well as a willingness for European consumers to value the offer regardless of comparison. Clearly, price perceptions and positioning are partly

eg

The growth of online trading is removing some of the opportunities for companies to offer different prices in different markets. Amazon (http://www.amazon.com) can take orders from the same customer on its European websites and on its US main site (see pp. 563 *et seq.*). It is possible, therefore, for the consumer to compare prices allowing for exchange rates and any additional delivery costs. Below cost selling is banned in Ireland as it is claimed that it would lead to the closure of many smaller retailers which would not be in the public interest. German discounters such as Aldi and Lidl operating in Ireland have, therefore, to watch their pricing in Ireland carefully for fear of infringement. In an effort to keep prices low, however, they tend to source away from Irish suppliers and that in turn is causing concern within the Irish Farmers' Association (Garvey, 2002).

affected by competitors' approaches to pricing. The organisation thus has strategic decisions to make about whether to match the competitors' prices or to price significantly higher or lower.

The cost structure associated with a product might also change in international markets. If an organisation is exporting goods, it potentially faces higher logistics costs, for example in terms of insurance and transportation, especially if the goods are being sent to quite remote markets. There could also be additional administration and banking costs in arranging shipping and payment. If, for example, a buyer wants to pay for the goods through a letter of credit, then banks have to act as intermediaries, checking documentation and arranging the international transfer of funds. Banks charge for this service, as well as charging for foreign currency exchange. Price might also have to reflect a 'cushion' against fluctuations in exchange rates, to avoid losses.

Selling costs can also be higher, for example if sales representatives are being sent abroad on sales trips or the organisation is attending international trade fairs and exhibitions. In addition to these costs, there is the cost of preparing sales materials, brochures and other sales aids. A great deal of cash might have to be invested in market development before any significant level of orders is generated. This cost will have to be recouped somehow.

Longer-term capital investment in a country can also affect cost structures. Building a manufacturing plant, for example, might lead to a lower unit cost and reduce distribution costs, but nevertheless a return will be expected on the capital. Alternatively, if there is major adaptation and market development activity, there might be pressure to get a faster payback. Where goods are traded between the home organisation and a foreign subsidiary, issues of transfer pricing (as discussed at pp. 459 *et seq.*) arise. If transfer prices are set too low, and cannot be defended in commercial terms, then the organisation might be open to accusations of 'dumping', that is, exporting goods at unfairly low prices in order to get rid of them outside the home market. Different countries regulate transfer pricing to different extents and in different ways, and thus the organisation should investigate carefully how much flexibility there actually is with transfer prices.

Place

The organisation should develop an appreciation of what is 'normal' in the local market for distributing products similar to its own. This includes an understanding of how customers purchase, where they expect to find the goods and what support services they expect from intermediaries. Unless the organisation is prepared to invest heavily, its distribution strategy needs to be built around available intermediaries and their capabilities, including their stock control systems, online ordering capacity, goods handling capacity and storage conditions.

eg

Hertz would like to be able to open up the Chinese car rental market but faces many difficulties in the short term. Firstly, only Chinese nationals may drive, so the potentially lucrative international segment is not available. Secondly, driving on Chinese roads can be quite an experience for the unsuspecting traveller. Whether it's the unreadable road signs, the standard of driving and (lack of!) attitude to road safety, the condition of some of the roads, or the trials of congestion in the larger cities, there is much to deter the unwary and indeed to deter a rental company wanting to safeguard its cars. Herz has nevertheless opened up three offices in Beijing, Shanghai and Guangzhou where customers who give 48 hours' notice can rent or lease chauffeur-driven vehicles (Bray, 2002).

Delivery size and frequency will have to be tailored to suit the channel. Logistics thus have to be planned around intermediaries' needs and available modes of transport. They also have to be timed to take into account problems such as crossing borders.

The safety of Alpine road tunnels following fires in the Gotthard, Mont Blanc and Tauern tunnels is leading to reconsideration of how dangerous some products are when transported through confined spaces. Rail operator DB in Germany started a marketing campaign highlighting the view that dangerous goods should be moved by rail, and legislation could be stiffened to restrict dangerous and hazardous materials from using the network of tunnels through the Alps.

Promotion

Promotional mixes are highly likely to have to be tailored to suit the local environment. Advertising has to conform to local regulations, in terms of both media choice and content. Furthermore, a campaign has to take into account available media and their costs, as well as the target market's media consumption patterns. Sales promotion, as seen in Chapter 16, is also subject to different degrees of regulation. The choice of sales promotion techniques therefore has to respect local regulations and reflect the target market's preferences. In some markets, for example, coupons distributed through print advertisements might stimulate more response than those printed on packs.

Multinational organisations are increasingly adapting from essentially global campaigns. Ahold has moved to global sales promotion with centralised procurement covering 50 suppliers, 25 countries and 8,000 stores for just one campaign. It found that using scale and coverage gave rise to significant short-term sales boosts. One promotional theme, 'Festival of Food and Fun', covered 14 languages and was adapted to local tastes, store formats and culture (*The Grocer*, 2002).

Public relations activities, particularly publicity, might call for the services of a local PR agency that knows the media scene and has established contacts. Public relations can be particularly useful if the organisation wants to be seen to be integrating into the local community. Some kind of sponsorship, for example, gives an opportunity to demonstrate a willingness to give something back to the community, and to participate in its life. Finally, personal selling in a foreign market might mean training sales staff in language and culture, including negotiation styles, business etiquette and social interaction. If the organisation does not have an established name in the international market, the sales force could face a great deal of cold calling and rejection. The sales manager, therefore, should take particular care to ensure that the sales force is properly motivated and supported, and that their morale is kept up, especially if they are working a long way from home.

corporate social responsibility *in action*

Genetically modifying the message

Care must be taken in designing the messages and promotional mix so that they avoid causing offence and alienating consumers through approaches that do not transfer easily across international markets. The US company Monsanto seriously misjudged the European attitude to genetically modified food and as a result faced some difficult PR problems that it did not originally envisage. In 1998, Monsanto ran a £1 mn campaign to prepare the consumer for accepting more genetically modified foods with what was effectively a consumer education campaign that even invited people to consider the alternative views of Greenpeace and Friends of the Earth. The informed debate that Monsanto sought revolved around the promise of biotechnology and the risks associated with it.

The outcome was perhaps predictable; the scientific debate was lost in an aggressive counter-campaign to discredit GM food and eventually Monsanto accepted that it had lost the PR battle and that it had 'irritated and antagonised more people than it had persuaded' by trying to tell and argue rather than listen. Although it still retained its confidence in GM products, it accepted that public concerns were valid, and thus a more subtle, less confrontational approach was to be adopted in markets outside the US (Wrong, 1999).

While GM arguments and products had been pretty well received in the US, many Europeans showed markedly different reactions to the claims that GM crops were here to stay and were essential for feeding the world. Monsanto's new commitment stated that it would respect the religious, cultural and ethical concerns of people, would not sell GM grain products until they had been fully tested, and would operate under strict controls in the use of genes taken from animal or human sources. Monsanto had tried to transfer arguments that had been convincing in the US, but found that they had to be adapted and changed elsewhere in the world.

Monsanto still has not gone far enough for some campaigners, however, who claim that its focus has now turned to less developed nations. India recently lifted a ban on growing GM crops to allow bio-engineered cotton to be produced, and the consideration of permitting GM soya and corn is thought to be at an advanced stage. Similar progress is being made in Brazil, which along with the US and Argentina accounts for 80 per cent of the world's soya production. This would mean that GM crops could still find their way back into Europe, whatever the local agreements. Thus although the aggressive selling of GM may now have ended, the softer sell, along with scientific support appears to have led to advances in the developing world, regardless of a sceptical Europe.

Sources: Blackledge (1999); Bowe (2002); Lean and Branford (2002); Tomkins (1999); Vidal (2000); Wrong (1999); http://www.monsanto.com.

Chapter summary

- International marketing is of concern to organisations of all types and sizes, but it is complex, not only because it potentially involves greater administrative and operational marketing effort, but also because it involves an understanding of marketing environments that might be very different from the domestic market. There are many reasons why organisations seek international marketing opportunities. The limitations of the domestic market might encourage organisations to look further afield for growth opportunities, or the domestic market could be under threat from foreign competition. International marketing might open up an opportunity to manufacture more cheaply abroad or to develop economies of scale in the home manufacturing operation. Customers who operate internationally might also expect their suppliers to follow and do the same.
- Whatever the reason, the choice of foreign market has to be made carefully and a full analysis of the STEP factors should provide a foundation for an informed decision. By comparing a number of possible markets on criteria such as product fit, market factors, competitive factors, market entry issues, resource constraints and trading constraints, an organisation can decide which one presents the best opportunity.
- There are many possible market entry methods, and the choice depends on how quickly the organisation wants to get into the market, what it is prepared to invest in terms of time, money and long-term commitment to do so, its willingness to take risks and its financial objectives. Some organisations begin their international careers by direct exporting, selling to a foreign customer or through a foreign-based intermediary, or by indirect exporting, selling through an intermediary based in the domestic market. If an organisation is selling expertise or knowledge rather than goods and services, then available options include licensing, franchising and contracting. Where an organisation wishes to make a long-term commitment to a market or region, then investment might be appropriate, acquiring or setting up manufacturing or sales subsidiaries, or entering into joint ventures or strategic alliances. By having such a strong local presence in the market, an organisation might be able to overcome any political hostility to importers and might gain a better understanding of how best to adapt the product and its marketing package to suit local needs.
- A major concern for any organisation is whether to standardise or adapt its marketing offering for an international market. If it decides to adapt, it needs to think about which elements of the marketing mix should be adapted and to what extent. Standardisation is attractive, in that it can lead to economies of scale and easier marketing administration, but it can be dangerous unless there are clear indications that it is appropriate within the international marketing environment.

- In any market, even if the product can be standardised, it is likely that the price will have to be adapted. Different markets face different cost structures and are subject to different taxes and import duties. Customers might have different price perceptions and expectations. Advertising and other marketing communication activities will face different regulatory environments and might well have to be adapted to conform, quite apart from any cultural differences.

key words and phrases

Adaptation	Joint ventures	Sales subsidiaries
Contracting	Licensing	Standardisation
Direct export	Manufacturing subsidiaries	Strategic alliance
Indirect export	Market entry methods	
International marketing	Master franchising	

questions *for review*

23.1 Define Lynch's five categories of international European organisation.

23.2 Why do organisations internationalise?

23.3 What six broad groups of factors should be taken into account when selecting a foreign market?

23.4 What factors influence the choice of *market entry method*?

23.5 Summarise the factors that might create pressure towards *adapting* the marketing mix for a foreign market.

questions *for discussion*

23.1 To what extent do you think that internationalisation is essential for today's organisations?

23.2 Choose an fmcg product from your home market that has not yet become an international product. Decide which foreign market you would like to launch this product in and find out as much relevant information as you can about the marketing environment in that country. What recommendations would you make to the manufacturer of your chosen product about the launch?

23.3 Discuss the problems that small businesses might face in internationalising and the feasibility of the various market entry methods for them.

23.4 Find an example of a successful joint venture in an international market. What benefits have the parties to the venture derived from it?

23.5 Citing examples that you have found, discuss whether standardisation is possible or desirable in international markets.

case study 23.1

Going international in banking: standardisation or adaptation?

Broder Dittschar

Since the fall of communism in 1989, the Polish banking sector has seen huge changes. Before 1989, the sector was very tightly regulated and all the major banks were state-owned, serving different geographic and other niches with little or no overt competition between them. The levels of service offered were low and customers did not expect much more than basic products such as current accounts or savings accounts. Many individuals did not even have bank accounts because they made and received payments in cash and opportunities to invest money were very limited. After 1989, that began to change. Under economic reform programmes, the sector was deregulated and opened up to both domestic competition, mergers and foreign investment. Many foreign banks saw Poland as an attractive market with a lot of potential and began to invest.

Thus by the end of 2000, Western banks had taken over seven out of the ten major Polish banks or, at least had major shareholdings in them, and had come to dominate approximately 70 per cent of all bank assets on the Polish market. Internationalising banks need to make crucial decisions about their marketing strategies. They have to decide whether it is better to adapt their strategies to the Polish market environment; whether a standardised strategy appears more likely to succeed; or whether elements of their strategies require a certain degree of adaptation, while others could be standardised. Banks come to contrary conclusions, but operate, nevertheless, very successfully. This case study, therefore, looks at two specific foreign banks and the rationale behind their initial entry to the Polish market in terms of marketing decisions.

The American bank, St Lawrence Bank started from scratch but opted for a two-step entry strategy when it first entered the Polish market. The first step was to offer services for corporate clients and the second step was to target private clients. The first step was undertaken in 1991 when the first multinational companies came to Poland and St Lawrence Bank felt that it would have to follow its customers. At that time, St Lawrence Bank saw no potential for establishing a retail banking business. By 1997, the situation had changed due to Poland's rapid economic growth and the emergence of more affluent and increasingly demanding private customer segments. In 1997, St Lawrence Bank thus launched its first retail product, namely the credit card, and has expanded its product range gradually since then.

St Lawrence Bank has a notable sense of standardisation and strives to utilise its experiences drawn from other markets. With the help of a dedicated product portfolio for different world regions, the American bank offers fairly standardised products around the world. St Lawrence Bank is also striving for a consistent image across markets. For this purpose, the bank uses the same brand name, the same font and the same logo across the world. The overall promotion concepts are designed centrally before they are adapted to the local markets, acknowledging, for example, local sociocultural peculiarities such as the importance of the Catholic church in Poland. St Lawrence Bank employs the national branches of the same advertising agency worldwide. This enables it to benefit from the parent agency's familiarity with St Lawrence Bank's promotion strategy and the national branch's expertise on the national markets. The relatively small size of St Lawrence Bank's Polish operation forced the bank to adapt its distribution strategy, however. In addition to very standardised traditional branches, which can be found in all markets, St Lawrence Bank employs agents who distribute its products in Poland. The reason for this is that Poland is a comparatively under-banked and geographically large and diverse market which is difficult and expensive to cover with a comprehensive branch network. Worldwide, St Lawrence Bank does not compete on price but on service. Prices are calculated using very similar models in all markets, although the price decisions are made locally since inflation, competition, interest rates and other macroeconomic factors differ across countries. Standardised profit margins only apply to multinational corporate clients.

Standardisation is considered a part of the corporate culture. This clearly impacts on the way of thinking and is even reflected by slightly minor aspects, such as the use of the English language for written communication. However, St Lawrence Bank acknowledges the need for some degree of adaptation. Different approaches for different world regions have, therefore, been developed. For example, St Lawrence Bank leaves it to local management to decide which retail products to introduce at what time. St Lawrence Bank seeks economies of scale by means of standardisation, but cost reductions are not considered a main objective of the bank's standardisation strategy.

The Portuguese bank Tagus Bank acquired its initial stake in the Polish Wisla Bank in 1998. Two years later, Tagus Bank became, jointly with affiliated financial services providers, the dominant strategic investor in Wisla Bank. In contrast to St Lawrence Bank, the Portuguese Tagus Bank pursues a strategy which emphasises adaptation to local market conditions. Wisla Bank's relationship with its parent bank Tagus Bank is characterised by both a high degree of independence from the parent bank and a high degree of adaptation to the Polish market. Based on Tagus Bank's strategy to treat members of the Tagus Bank Group as partners and based on the concept of knowledge sharing, Wisla Bank formulates its marketing mix strategy (product, price, promotion and place) independently from Tagus Bank. However, Wisla Bank's retail chain New Century, in particular, benefits greatly from Tagus Bank's expertise in modern retail banking. It is considered helpful regarding strategy development that both Poland's economy and Poland's society are going through the same kind of rapid development process that Portugal went through after it became a member of the EU. Therefore, the Portuguese bank can build its strategy on the experience drawn from its home market.

Tagus Bank wants its units abroad to adapt to local market conditions as much as possible in order to serve markets in the most focused way. Standardisation is considered an obstacle rather than a tool for meeting this objective. Tagus Bank does not consider standardisation a means of cost reduction. Costs that could be saved through the application of standardised concepts would not outweigh the losses that would derive from a less focused customer orientation. The concept of Wisla Bank's retail arm 'New Century Bank' was the starting point of the cooperation between the Polish and the Portuguese banks and is clearly an area where Wisla Bank has benefited greatly from Tagus Bank's know-how. Although the New Century Bank concept is not an outcome of standardisation efforts, it is evident that the concept is very similar to Tagus Bank's retail chain in Portugal. There seem to be no negative connotations about Portugal in Poland, and this clearly eases the partnership between the two banks. Cooperation which is based on knowledge sharing and mutual learning is a further bonus. Tagus Bank's expertise in modern retail banking, in conjunction with its flexibility to adapt to both the Polish environment and Wisla Bank's organisational characteristics (e.g. openness to change), make the cooperation rewarding for both partners.

Source: Dittschar (2001).

Note: the names of the banks involved have been disguised.

Questions

1. In assessing the Polish market as a potential new target, what factors would St Lawrance Bank and Tagus Bank probably have taken into account and why?
2. Why do you think Tagus Bank decided to enter the Polish market via the stakeholding in a local company while St Lawrance Bank set up its own operations from scratch?
3. Summarise the views of the St Lawrance Bank and Tagus Bank on the advantages and disadvantages of standardisation and adaptation. To what extent do you think it is possible or wise for a foreign bank to standardise in a new market?
4. How do you think generally that the international marketing of financial services products might differ from the international marketing of fmgc products such as toiletries or confectionery?

case study 23.2

Wine wars

French wine could soon lose its dominant position in global markets, overtaken by so called 'New World' wines from Australia, America, Chile and South Africa. The French decline in competitive position is not a result of any changes to its wines, but has arisen because aggressive new competitors have deliberately targeted mass markets in Europe, Asia and America with a high degree of success. What traditionally was an international market largely dominated by the French has now become a battle for long-term market share.

The root of the problem goes back to the industry in France. It is primarily made up of a lot of small family-owned vineyards operating independently or communes, each proud of its own label. That may be fine for the wine experts searching for the right vintage from the right vineyard, but it does little for mass marketing and branding. As wine drinking has grown in popularity (although ironically in France per head wine consumption has nearly halved since 1960), new consumers have been attracted into the market without the detailed interest or knowledge of wines, and most are used to associating heavy branding with quality and consistency in drinks. With such a proliferation of small brands, the French producers were vulnerable in the growing mass market to new entrants using a full range of marketing techniques to create awareness and preference. French wine is still characterised by a myriad of labels that many consumers find confusing and difficult to assess before purchase. The expert and wealthy may still seek refuge in 'good French wines' and will pay €400 a bottle for the privilege, but the mass market is more interested in price points between €5 and €10 per bottle.

The scale of the wine industry in France is impressive, and any loss of market share has a direct impact on the economy. It accounts for 15 per cent of all French agricultural production, supports over 200,000 people and is worth $6.2 bn in sales. Domestic consumption of wine, however, has been falling in France while it has been rising elsewhere. In the face of the threat posed by new competitors in the 1980s and 1990s, the French reaction was to seek regulation and to subsidise. An €81 mn subsidy from the French government to enable table wine to be converted to industrial uses was introduced. The producers' union of Beaujolais, faced with 13 million unsold bottles of wine agreed that it should be turned into vinegar, distilled into road fuel, or just poured away rather than creating a 'wine lake'.

To make matters worse, prices have declined in world markets, and that, coupled with declining French share in many export markets, has intensified the problems the French industry faces due to international competition. French pleas for Europeans to stop drinking Coca-Cola and to drink more good French wine have had little impact. In the US, France's market share has dropped from 7 per cent to 5 per cent in just three years, while Australian wines have trebled in volume. It is a similar picture in the UK. Exports from Bordeaux, the largest wine exporting region of France, to the EU fell by 6 per cent in 2000–2001 and in the UK, sales of Bordeaux fell by 15 per cent despite growth in the overall wine market. At the time of writing, Australian wine sales in the UK were expected to overtake French wine sales for the first time. The best-selling European wine brand in the UK is Le Piat D'Or, a name that makes the connoisseur shudder due to its mass market appeal. Nevertheless, it was still lagging behind seven Australian and two Californian imports in the top ten of European sales.

In contrast, the Australian industry, typical of New World producers, is controlled by four large operators and the formula is to keep it simple, create a small number of strong brands such as Rosemount, Jacob's Creek and Banrock Station, and market them aggressively. To the Australians, the grape becomes the brand rather than the chateau (as in France), and there is little concern for where it is grown. It is thus far easier to gather together grapes from a large area, unlike the tight regional approach in France. The same aggressive approach is adopted in the United States, where just one New World operator spends more on marketing than the entire Bordeaux wine industry. By investing more in branding, selling and promotion, many of the New World producers, such as E&J Gallo (USA) and Foster Group (Australia) have successfully transferred fmcg practices to the wine industry. In the UK, the wine category grew by 5 per cent in 2001, but the top brands grew by 25 per cent. Only slowly have the French reacted, for example, a new campaign for Bordeaux shows a sexy model in lingerie with a muscular man, with the caption 'Let the mood take you to Bordeaux'.

New World success has not just been about promotional strategies. Product development and management have been vital in providing an innovative edge over traditional French wines. In France, the quality assurance system (appellation contrôlée) provides specific guidelines on what types of grapes can be grown in what region, and how they should be planted, picked and bottled. There are around 450 such appellations. This is a strength in that consumers know exactly what they are getting if they buy a Bordeaux or Côte du Rhône for example, but it has also inhibited innovation. To meet new tastes, fruit-flavoured wines such as Chardonnay with peach flavour have been introduced by New World producers and more generally, the wines are younger and easier to drink than more acidic French wines. 'Oaked' Chardonnays have been launched that use artificial methods of providing an oak taste without waiting for years for the wine to mature in the barrel. Product innovation along with modern production methods have enabled New World wines to erode the market share held by the French who regarded many of these innovations as detracting from quality. Some have argued that a way of fighting back would be to use some of the better known upmarket French labels and develop lower priced but good quality mass market wines.

Australian wine sellers have also taken care over the price positioning of popular brands. Although they rarely sell for less than £3.50 a bottle, the average price is between £4 and £5 per bottle, the typical spend of the UK consumer. There is some evidence that as the price increases, consumers will switch to French wines. However at £3–£4 with labels in English, Australian wine has been successful in drawing many new consumers into the wine market. The French have reacted by emphasising vin de pays (country wine) brands which do not have the status of a chateau label or the appellation contrôlée seal of approval, but do offer a cut-price alternative for the table wine segment. As the wine lake grows, however, French producers are anxious not to divert production into this segment in order to avoid creating further instability.

The supermarkets have played a role in the changes in the wine industry. In the UK about 70 per cent of all wine sales are made through the larger supermarkets and 50 per cent in the USA. Big producers offering large volumes, not dependent upon whether it was a 'good year' or not, along with brand and marketing support, find it far easier to deal with big supermarkets and vice versa, where reliability and scale appear to work together. Many of these large producers are still seeking to buy up vineyards, even in France. The chairman of the world's ninth largest producer of wine, Mondavi, is quoted as saying that the industry is being converted from a cottage industry to a competitive consumer goods industry. The trouble is that many French producers are being left behind. Although there is still a market for the small producers through smaller independent retailers, they do not generate the same sales volumes. There may be even more polarisation in future if retailers move, as expected, to cut down on the 1,000 wine varieties typically displayed.

It remains to be seen whether marketing can offer a recovery route to prevent further share erosion. Some think that it is too late and that share has been lost forever. There is a possibility of ripping up some of the vineyards to avoid over production, while some are calling for an end to regulation through the appellation system and learning more from New World production and marketing methods.

Sources: Andrews (2001); Echikson *et al.* (2001); Fletcher (2002); *The Grocer* (2001a); Johnson (2001); Millward (2001); Mortishead (2002).

Questions

1. Summarise the reasons why France is losing share in its export markets for wine.
2. Why and how have the New World producers sought to enter foreign markets? How successful do you think they have been?
3. What risks and problems might the French wine industry face if it tries to replicate the kind of marketing strategies that the New World producers have used?
4. What is the best way forward for French producers such as Bordeaux now?

References for chapter 23

Andersen, P. and Strandskov, J. (1998), 'International Market Selection: A Cognitive Mapping Perspective', *Journal of Global Marketing*, 11 (3), pp. 65–84.

Andrews, J. (2001), 'In Vino Europa', *Europe*, June, pp. 34–5.

Arnold, H. (2002), 'One Rude Awakening', *Financial Times*, 9 May, p. 14.

Ashworth, J. (1998), 'Brussels Ready to Set Terms for BA's Tie-up', *The Times*, 6 July, p. 48.

Berliner, W. (2001), 'The High Cost of Not Speaking the Lingo', *The Independent*, 14 June, p. 9.

Biemnet, E. (2002), 'Local Lenses Head for Europe', *African Business*, March, pp. 45–6.

Blackledge, C. (1999), 'Benefits that Go Against the Grain', *Life Sciences* supplement to *Financial Times*, 15 March, p. IV.

Bloom, J. (1998), 'Mind Your Language', *Management Today*, August, pp. 72–3.

Bond, D. (2002), 'US–UK Open Skies Stymied as AA, BA Balk', *Aviation Week and Space Technology*, 4 February, pp. 42–4.

Bowe, C. (2002), 'Monsanto Set to Save $124m from Revamp', *Financial Times*, 5 April, p. 24.

Bray, R. (2002), 'Hertz Drives into China', *Financial Times*, 2 April, p. 10.

Brook, M. (1992), *International Management* (2nd edn), Stanley Thornes (Publishers) Ltd.

Burgel, O. and Murray, G. (2000), 'The International Market Entry Choices of Start-up Companies in High-technology Industries', *Journal of International Marketing*, 8 (2), pp. 33–62.

Burt, T. (2002), 'Aston Martin Gets Serious about Luxury', *Financial Times*, 25 February, p. 23.

Carmichael, M. (2001), 'Old Campaigner's New Guns', *The Grocer*, 6 October, p. 51.

Chaffey, D. (2002), *E-business and E-commerce Management: Strategy, Implementation and Practice*, Financial Times Prentice Hall.

Chemical Market Reporter (2002), 'Raisio Earnings Impacted by Unilever Push', *Chemical Market Reporter*, 25 February, p. 6.

Clarke, W. (2000), 'The Use of Foreign Languages by Irish Exporters', *European Journal of Marketing*, 34 (1/2), pp. 80–90.

Clegg, A. (2002), 'One Ad One World', *Marketing Week*, 20 June, pp. 51–2.

Coia, A. (2002), 'A New Market Emerges for Europe', *Logistics Management and Distribution Report*, February, pp. E3–E6.

Cramb, C. (1999), 'Dutch Group Holds its Own', *Rhine-Maas* supplement to *Financial Times*, 11 May, p. III.

Davies, W. (1995), 'Second Language Skills are Vital to Business', *Marketing Business*, November, p. 7.

Dittschar, B. (2001), 'The Adaptation vs Standardisation Paradigm in International Financial Services Marketing: A Qualitative Analysis Focusing on Western Banks and their Polish Partners', unpublished PhD thesis, Brunel University.

Dittschar, B. (2000), 'Toward a Model of Adaptation vs Standardisation in Financial Services: A Summary Literature Review', *Proceedings of the 13th UK Services Marketing Workshop*, UK Academy of Marketing, Nottingham.

Done, K. (2002), 'American and BA Withdraw Request', *Financial Times*, 15 February, p. 10.

Dorrian, P. (1998), *Marketing Magic*, Zebra Press, South Africa.

Eddy, K. (1999), 'Bus Group on Road to Success', *Financial Times*, 26 May, p. 28.

Echikson, W., Balfour, F., Capell, K., Himelstein, L. and Khermouch, G. (2001), 'Wine War', *Business Week*, 3 September, pp. 36–42.

Fisher, A. (2000), 'Gap Widens Between the "Haves" and "Have-nots"', *Financial Times*, 6 December, p. 5.

Fletcher, I. (2002), 'Australia's Wines Poised to Nose Ahead of French', *Mail on Sunday*, 17 February, p. 44.

Franchise Magazine (1999), 'BMS Technologies', *Franchise Magazine*, March–April, p. 186.

Gardyn, B. (2000), 'The Perfect Present', *American Demographics*, October, pp. 18–9.

Garvey, A. (2002), 'Lidl By Lidl', *The Grocer*, 23 February, p. 36.

George, N. and Jones, A. (2002a), 'Scottish & Newcastle Looks to Expansion in Russia', *Financial Times*, 15 February, p. 19.

George, N. and Jones, A. (2002b), 'S&N Travels to Russia with Love', *Financial Times*, 15 February, p. 20.

Gilligan, C. and Hird, M. (1986), *International Marketing: Strategy and Management*, Croom Helm.

Griffiths, J. (2001), 'Goodyear Strives to Ride Out Perfect Storm', *Financial Times*, 28 November, p. 36.

Griffiths, J. (2000), 'Sumitomo, Goodyear Cut Jobs in Shake-up', *Financial Times*, 7 January, p. 24.

Griffiths, J. (1999), 'Europe Stands by for a Rolling Tide', *Financial Times*, 4 February, p. 34.

The Grocer (2002), 'Global Promotions Bring Record Sales', *The Grocer*, 9 February, p. 16.

The Grocer (2001a), 'Picking From a Global Vineyard', *The Grocer*, 18 August, pp. 4–5.

The Grocer (2001b), 'Scottish Aquaculture: "Quality Key to Future"', *The Grocer*, 8 December, p. 20.

The Grocer (2001c), 'Educating Your Partners', *The Grocer*, 8 December, p. 41.

The Grocer (1999), 'International', *The Grocer*, 16 January, p. 54.

Hamill, J. and Gregory, K. (1997), 'Internet Marketing in the Internationalisation of UK SMEs', *Journal of Marketing Management*, 13 (Jan–Apr), pp. 9–28.

Hargreaves, D. (2001), 'Jumping Through EU Hoops', *Financial Times*, 1 February, p. 12.

Harrison, M. (2002), 'EU to Escalate Steel Dispute by Imposing Strict Import Quotas', *The Independent*, 19 March, p. 19.

Hope, K. and Troev, T. (2002), 'Bulgaria's "Valley of Roses" Blooms Again', *Financial Times*, 23 April, p. 30.

Houlder, V. (1995), 'Today's Friend, Tomorrow's Foe', *Financial Times*, 2 October.

Ibison, D. and McGregor, R. (2002), 'China Exports First Cars to US', *Financial Times*, 12 June, p. 7.

Ives, V. (1999), 'Black Magic', *Marketing Mix*, July, pp. 26–32.

Jacob, R. (2000), 'A Chinese Clean-up Operation', *Financial Times*, 19 May, p. 18.

Johnson, J. (2001), 'French Wine All at Sea', *Financial Times*, 10 November, p. 1.

Jones, S. (1999), 'Candle Makers Get a Flicker of Hope as US Lifts Threat of Trade Sanctions', *Financial Times*, 17 April, p. 5.

Keegan, W. (1969), 'Multinational Product Planning: Strategic Alternatives', *Journal of Marketing*, 33 (January).

Kelly, J. (2002), 'Executives Fail the Business Language Test', *Financial Times*, 16 February, p. 4.

Kester, E. (2000), 'Nabi Announces $333m Order for 1,070 Buses', *Financial Times*, 30 May, p. 12.

Kester, E. (2001a), 'Bus Builder Caught in Budapest Traffic Jam', *Financial Times*, 15 February, p. 33.

Kester, E. (2001b), 'Manufacturing Momentum Comes Under Pressure', *Financial Times*, 20 November, p. 4.

Kynge, J. (2002), 'China's Reverse Shock', *Financial Times*, 7 June, p. 18.

Lawrence, F. (2001), 'Chablis Deployed to Burnish Wine Box Image', *The Guardian*, 10 May, p. 1.11.

Lean, G. and Branford, S. (2002), 'GM-free Nations Fall to Monsanto', *The Independent*, 31 March, p. 8.

Lynch, R. (1994), *European Business Strategies: The European and Global Strategies of Europe's Top Companies*, Kogan Page.

Maitland, A. (1999), 'A Code to Export Better Practice', *Financial Times*, 26 January, p. 14.

Marketing (2002), 'Company CV: HSBC', *Marketing*, 30 May, p. 42.

Marketing Week (2002), 'Europe Continues to Embrace the Web', *Marketing Week*, 25 April, p. 40.

Marsh, P. (2002), 'The World's Wash Day', *Financial Times*, 29 April, p. 8.

Marsh, P. (2001), 'Tough Times for JCB as Trade Softens', *Financial Times*, 3 July, p. 27.

Marsh, P. (2000), 'Getting Closer to the Marketplace', *Financial Times*, 14 July, p. 2.

Marsh, P. (1999), 'Bekaert Ties up the Wire Market', *Financial Times*, 10 February, p. 21.

McGregor, R. (2002), 'Global Giants Strike Out on their Own', *Financial Times*, 15 March, p. 2.

Mead, R. (1990), *Cross-cultural Management Communication*, John Wiley & Sons.

Millward, D. (2001), 'New World Wines Put French in Shade', *The Daily Telegraph*, 11 August, p. 5.

Moran, N. (2000), 'SMEs Can Punch Above Their Weight', *Information Technology* supplement to *Financial Times*, 3 May.

Mortishead, C. (2001), 'Beaujolais Swallows Hard and Turns Wine to Vinegar', *The Times*, 25 June, p. 23.

Mortishead, C. and Watson, R. (2002), 'Europe Fears Looming Trade War', *The Times*, 21 May, p. 15.

O'Connell, D. (2002), 'British Airways to Seek New Alliance with American Airlines', *Sunday Times*, 17 February, p. 1.

Odell, M. and Speigel, P. (2002), 'BA Refuses to Pay Price for Approval', *Financial Times*, 26 January, p. 18.

Oil and Vinegar (2002), Advertisement in *Franchise Magazine*, May, p. 122.

Paitra, J. (1993), 'The Euro-consumer: Myth or Reality?', in C. Halliburton and R. Hunerberg (eds), *European Marketing: Readings and Cases*, Addison-Wesley.

Paliwoda, S. (1993), *International Marketing* (2nd edn), Butterworth-Heinemann.

Parker, P (1995), *Climatic Effects on Individual, Social and Economic Behaviour: a Physioeconomic Review of Research across Disciplines*, Greenwood Press.

Parsley, D. (1998), 'BA Fights for Right to Sell Airport Slots', *Sunday Times*, 13 September, p. 3.4.

Pitcher, G. (1999), 'Ford Takes Pole Position in the Battle for Worldwide Domination', *Marketing Week*, 4 February, p. 25.

Reed, J. (2002), 'Protecting Poland', *Financial Times*, 24 April, p. 13.

Ricks, D. (1993), *Blunders in International Business*, Blackwell.

Shay, A. (1998), 'Finding the Right International Mix', *Mastering Marketing* supplement to *Financial Times*, 16 November, pp. 2–3.

Skapinker, M. (1999a), 'US and Britain Plan Open Sky Deal this Year', *Financial Times*, 20 May, p. 9.

Skapinker, M. (1999b), 'UK Calls off Open Sky Talks with US', *Financial Times*, 1 July, p. 6.

Smith, M. and Robinson, G. (1999), 'Australia's Confident Winemakers Ready to Pit Themselves against World's Best', *Financial Times*, 18 May, p. 8.

Solberg, C. (2000), 'Standardization or Adaptation of the International Marketing Mix: The Role of the Local Subsidiary/representative', *Journal of International Marketing*, 8 (1), pp. 78–98.

Sunday Times (2001), 'Scottish Fish Farms', *Sunday Times*, 21 October, p. 18.

Taplin, R. (2002), 'Tesco Racks up a Local Success', *The Times*, 18 April, p. 53.

Thornton, P. (2002), 'Trade Wars Set to Dominate OECD Talks as EU Prepares Retaliatory Measures', *The Independent*, 15 May, p. 19.

Tomkins, T. (1999), 'Monsanto Scores an Own Goal', *Financial Times*, 23 February, p. 16.

Vesely, M. (2002), 'Return of the Ugly American?', *African Business*, May, pp. 31–32.

Vidal, J. (2000), 'Contrite GM Firm Pledges to Turn Over a New Leaf', *The Guardian*, 1 December, p. 1.7.

Walsh, L. S. (1993), *International Marketing* (3rd edn), Pitman publishing.

Ward, A. (2002), 'An Octopus in the Shopping Trolley', *Financial Times*, 11 January, p. 12.

Warman, C. (2001), 'A Foreign Working Climate', *The Times*, 5 April, p. 13.

Wind, J. (1998), 'Strategic Thinking in the Global Era', *Mastering Marketing* supplement to *Financial Times*, 16 November, pp. 8–9.

Wright, R. (1999), 'Shattering Blow for Hungary's Glass Industry', *Financial Times*, 14 May, p. 33.

Wrong, M. (1999), 'Monsanto Chief Admits Public Relations Disaster', *Financial Times*, 7 October, p. 2.

Young, S. (2001), 'What Do Researchers Know About the Global Business Environment?', *International Marketing Review*, 18 (2), pp. 120–9.

Young, S. *et al.* (1989), *International Market Entry and Development: Strategies and Management*, Harvester Wheatsheaf.

chapter 24

e-marketing and new media

Introduction

LEARNING OBJECTIVES

This chapter will help you to:

1 understand the nature of internet marketing;

2 appreciate the major trends in internet penetration and usage in both consumer and B2B markets;

3 gain insight into the marketing uses of the internet and its future development;

4 appreciate the nature and usage of the three main elements of new media: e-mail marketing, wireless marketing and interactive television marketing.

> *With the net, a new way of conducting business is available, but it doesn't change the laws of business or most of what really creates a competitive advantage. The fundamentals of competition remain unchanged.*
>
> Professor Michael Porter (quoted by Newing, 2002)

Porter is absolutely right: the internet does not change any of the fundamentals of doing 'good business' or 'good marketing'. Understanding the target customer's needs and wants and designing an integrated marketing package that delivers them remains critically important regardless of whether a company is a **dotcom** or a 'traditional' organisation. Porter goes on to say that the companies that will succeeded and benefit from the internet will be those that keep their core strategic objectives in view and then work out how to integrate, use and mould the internet to help achieve those objectives and to create and sustain competitive advantage. Those that fail will be those that adopt a 'me too' attitude, jumping on the internet bandwagon because 'our competitors are doing it' or that view internet applications as a diversification, parallel and almost completely separate from their core traditional business.

To a lesser extent, the same can be said of the new marketing communications media, such as viral marketing, SMS, and interactive television, that are emerging from technological innovation. Some companies are adopting them because they can see how they complement the use of traditional media within the context of the wider integrated communications strategy, and have defined a distinct 'fit' between the medium, the message and the target market (see, for instance, the 'Hey, Sexy!' Kiss 100 Marketing in Action vignette on pp. 1087–8). Others, however, seem to be adopting them because they are the latest sexy thing that everyone else seems to be doing. No prizes for guessing which are likely to be the most successful campaigns!

eg

Friends Reunited is a dotcom company with a difference. It is unashamedly in the nostalgia business and the number of users is growing at such a rapid rate that it is a challenge just to keep up with the necessary computer capacity to run it all. The site aims to link old school friends and work colleagues and has been responsible, if the press is to be believed, not just for reunions galore, but also marriages, divorces and even litigation from allegedly libelled teachers. Based on a similar idea in America (http://www.classmates.com), since its launch in October 2000 Friends Reunited has registered 7 million members, 45,500 schools and recorded 220 million page impressions in one month alone (http://www. friendsreunited.co.uk). It is one of the UK's most popular websites. On average, a user spends over 30 minutes per month on the site, 40 per cent of the users are female and 72 per cent are aged between 25 and 49 (Snoddy, 2001).

In the light of its high traffic levels and its phenomenal growth, the owners are very proud to admit that they have spent no money on advertising and promotion. That said, the human interest angle means that a steady stream of reunion stories keeps the press coverage high and it may, in time, come to be regarded as one of the best word-of-mouth campaigns in promotional history. Although accessing the site is free, it costs £5 to become a registered member so that you can use the e-mail service. The other main source of revenue is banner advertising on the site. With such high traffic levels, it is not surprising that profits are already starting to flow (*Financial Times*, 2001). Further expansion has already taken place in Australia, South Africa and New Zealand, as first mover advantage is crucial for this type of operation.

Bass Brewers prefers to stick to traditional ways of selling beer rather than dabbling in dotcoms, but it does make creative use of new media opportunities. The 'Have You Seen My Sister?' campaign was a big hit, impressive in its simplicity but very effective. It involved an actor drinking bottles of Worthingtons in selected bars. Just before leaving a bar, he asks other consumers to call him on his mobile if his sister arrives. Not long after, the sister appears and when the consumers call the mobile number they receive a text message entitling them to two free bottles of Worthingtons, and of course the sister starts to hand out the samples on the spot. It created a lot of interest and proved to be an effective sales promotion (http://www.spca.org.uk).

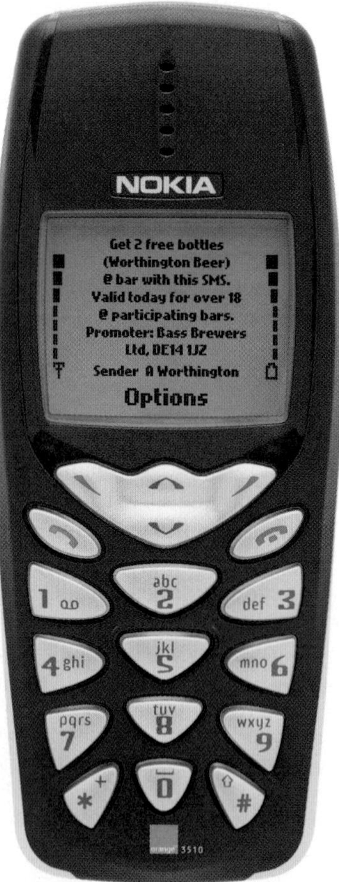

Although generally using traditional marketing strategies to sell beer? Bass Brewers had a hit recently with the 'Have you seen my sister?' campaign. A text message followed by immediate free samples made sure drinkers remembered their beer.

Source: Bass Brewers/BD. BD originated the idea and implemented the sampling activity for Bass.

The purpose of this chapter is to examine the ways in which the internet and new media are providing new opportunities for marketers to get to know their customers better and to serve their needs and wants more effectively, and in some cases, a lot more engagingly. Throughout, we will be presenting examples and vignettes of organisations that are successfully using the internet and new media with clear strategic purposes relating to the creation of competitive advantage in mind.

Many relevant themes have already been explored in this book: every chapter features examples of organisations using the internet and/or new media in pursuit of competitive advantage. Those themes will be brought together here, however, in the specific context of a fast-moving technological environment peopled by marketers and customers who are both trying to get to grips with adopting and exploiting the technology to its full potential. The first part of the chapter looks at that relatively well established tool: the internet. We examine its increasing penetration of both consumer and B2B markets and the ways in which markets are using and might use it in the future. The chapter then turns to the less familiar world of new media, focusing particularly on e-mail marketing (including viral marketing), wireless marketing and interactive television. Again, we consider how these techniques are being used and their potential for the future.

Internet marketing

The nature of internet marketing

As more and more homes and businesses either get connected or develop their own websites, the internet has become an increasingly important tool of marketing. The potential for **internet marketing** emerged in a significant and dynamic way in the 1990s and has since had a dramatic effect on approaches to marketing and communications strategies. The website has become a marketing tool of varying purposes and importance in most 'traditional' commercial companies. Some use it largely for PR purposes, to reinforce the company image and disseminate information (see for instance the Shell example at p. 1072); some use it as 'brochureware' to complement or as a substitute for brochures, catalogues and sales literature, using it to present and explain product ranges and generate sales leads that can then followed up by more traditional means (*see* Case Study 24.1); some use it as a sales promotion tool, offering freebies or competitions (*see* the Jaffa Cakes and Lunchables example at pp. 1069–71); some use it as a means of direct selling (*see* for instance http://www.calypso.co.uk); some use it as a means of cultivating and managing relationships with suppliers more effectively and efficiently. All of these uses will be explored further within this chapter.

Smith and Chaffey (2001) (*see* pp. 910–11 and Smith and Taylor (2002) summarise the main benefits of investing in **e-marketing** as the 5Ss:

- *Sell*. Selling goods and services online, potentially to a global market.
- *Serve*. Using the website as a way of providing additional customer service or of streamlining service delivery.
- *Save*. Saving money in terms of the overheads associated with more traditional forms of doing business.
- *Speak*. Websites offer companies a chance to enter into one-to-one dialogue with customers more easily than ever before. As well as providing valuable feedback, with good database management, that dialogue can be the basis for fruitful customer relationship management.
- *Sizzle*. A website that is well designed, both in terms of its content and its visual impact, can add an extra 'something' to a brand or corporate image through engaging, educating and/or entertaining the visitor to the site. Increasingly, organisations are introducing an element of fun into their websites to grab and retain attention. Interactive games, webcam and video feeds, cartoons, free downloads and relaxed informality have all been introduced to keep the viewer's attention and to make company and product information more interesting.

Whatever its purpose, and however much is spent on it, a website should provide a powerful supplementary marketing tool. It should have all the creative flair of an advertisement, the style and information of a company brochure, the personal touch and tailored presentation of face-to-face interaction and, not least, always leave the visitor clear as to what action should be taken next.

eg

Within a traditional business, the acceptance and integration of internet technology might not be entirely welcomed. Mols (2000) undertook an interesting survey of Danish bank managers to see how they felt about internet banking, and a number of discrete groups emerged. 'The Nervous' group recognises the potential opportunities that the internet has opened up, but worries that the self-service aspects of it will damage a bank's close relationship with its customers. In contrast, 'The Positive' group do not discern any serious threat from the internet, and see it positively as a means of delivering even more products and services. Both these groups take a proactive attitude, that internet banking should be developed because customers want it and because it provides an important complementary distribution channel, although cannibalisation is a concern.

'The Sceptics' have a similar view to the Positive group but are a little more sceptical about just how far the banks will eventually embrace the opportunities. Their view is that internet banking should be developed because competitors are doing it, i.e. a reactive approach. The final group, 'The Reluctant' think that the development of internet banking will be slow and do not expect it to be used extensively for direct marketing or product/service delivery.

It would seem, therefore, that those who are developing banks' internet strategies need to pay serious attention to internal marketing as well as educating customers.

For some small businesses, the internet can become a valuable means of communicating with a potentially global audience easily and cost effectively, freeing them from the constraints of geographic catchment areas. We saw in Chapter 23, for example, how Cookson's, a builder's merchant, successfully extended its horizons (and its turnover) from serving a customer base largely restricted to a 7-mile radius of Stockport to a global reach through the internet (*see* p. 1011).

eg

Bluewave is a company that designs websites, describing itself as 'a global online solutions company, serving clients in the visualisation, development and ongoing enhancement of their online business' (http://www.bluewave.com). In conjunction with the Royal National Institute of the Blind (RNIB), Bluewave developed the first viral fund raising application using Macromedia Flash MX that is fully accessible to blind and partially sighted internet users. One objective was to encourage voluntary donations for RNIB's work with blind and partially sighted children, and another was to raise awareness of the RNIB's Campaign for Good Web Design, particularly among website designers.

The site (http://www.lookloud.bluewave.com) was linked with the RNIB's 'Look Loud Day' on 14 June 2002 when people all over the UK were asked to dress in their most garish and outrageous clothes and raise money for blind and partially sighted children. Julie Howell of the RNIB said, 'RNIB is really pleased that Bluewave has been able to use Macromedia Flash MX to produce a viral application that is fully usable by blind and partially sighted people. While we hope "Look Louder" will be an effective fund raising tool, we are also encouraging web designers to think about the needs of all potential users when designing viral applications. With the sophisticated web-design tools available today there really are no excuses for designing applications that people with disabilities can't use'. The site makes use of audio and visual techniques that guide the user experience and uses Flash MX's new accessibility features so that the application to be read by Windoweyes, a screenreading tool used by many blind internet users.

Visitors to the Look Loud website can choose a head, items of 'loud' clothing and accessories for a screen-based cartoon character which can then be sent on to friends and colleagues. The hope is that they too will visit the site and create their own badly dressed characters. The website also offers the visitor the chance to make an online donation to the RNIB Look Loud campaign (http://www.bluewave.com; http://www.rnib.org.uk; http://www.lookloud.bluewave.com).

Commercial companies are not the only types of organisation benefiting from an internet presence. As the RNIB example shows, the internet can also be an effective tool for charities, allowing them to explain their work, encourage people to make donations and even provide a mechanism for making an online donation on the spot. A charity's website is also an important forum for pursuing its campaigns, such as the RNIB's campaign for better website accessibility for the disabled. Other sites are concerned with promoting a particular political, social or environmental viewpoint, which may have to be countered by any organisations targeted (*see* pp. 1072 *et seq.*, for example).

The dotcom boom and bust

While traditional companies have largely sought to integrate and use the internet and the 5Ss within the context of their existing businesses, the late 1990s also saw the rapid rise and equally rapid fall of many so-called dotcom businesses. These were businesses that came into being specifically to use the internet as a platform for delivering goods and/or services in an innovative way. Many potential investors were carried away by the enthusiasm of the dotcom entrepreneurs and promises of mega-profits, pouring money into these businesses. It soon became clear, however, that many dotcoms were running into problems. Some ran into technical problems that made it difficult to deliver on their promises and others simply found that paying customers were a lot thinner on the ground than forecast.

eg

Sports website Sportal was set up in July 1998 with about £4.8 mn to offer action, information and links with sports clubs and events with a mission to 'create the first major sport brand of the 21st century'. It signed up for the internet rights of the top European football clubs, allowing it to show any action involving those clubs on the internet. Sportal earned revenue from showing football action and earned advertising revenue from running club websites. By the end of 1999, it had a number of offices in Europe and further afield, and was sufficiently well established to raise another £50 mn in investment capital. This helped it to expand its services, for example supplying football content to Yahoo! and launching a WAP mobile phone service. The highlight of 2000 was winning the contract to design and produce the Euro 2000 website. While the website was very successful and helped to improve Sportal's brand image, it actually cost the company £5 mn. Overall, insufficient revenue was flowing in, but the deals were still being done. It is reported that Sportal spent a seven-figure sum to sponsor the shirts for Juventus' Champions League matches. In the last three months of 2000, Sportal made losses of more than £13 mn.

Part of the problem was that Sportal was not the only sports site on the internet, and once Euro 2000 had finished, Sportal had nothing particularly distinctive to offer. Furthermore, people were not willing to pay for what it did offer, nor were the advertising revenues flowing. As one expert on online business said, 'Sport is about killer data – scores, tips and rumours. People will only visit a site regularly if they think they will find killer data' (as quoted by Barr, 2002).

In May 2001, redundancies were made, and Sportal, a company worth £270 mn at its peak and employing 360 staff in 11 countries, limped on until November 2001 when it was sold for £1 (yes, that's £1 for the company itself, although its hardware was sold for £190,000) to UKBetting.com. The intention is that Sportal should be dedicated to the more light-hearted side of sport, featuring competitions, chat rooms and online games, complementing sister sites SportingLife.com (with a focus on news and information), bettingzone.co.uk (focus on independent betting news and statistics) and totalbet.com (focus on placing bets) which are also owned by UKBetting.com. Thus although the mission might have changed, at least the Sportal brand name has managed to survive.

Sources: Barr, 2002; Doward, 2002; *Marketing*, 2002; Nichols, 2001.

The dotcom boom was followed by the dotcom bust as businesses collapsed or were taken over by their more astute competitors. Those that have survived and established themselves as leaders in their marketplaces, such as lastminute.co.uk (*see* Case Study 1.2), eBay, and Amazon (*see* Case Study 13.2) have done so not only by astute marketing and offering goods and services that people want and are prepared to pay for, but also by careful attention to defining and nurturing their competitive advantage along with some sober financial management. Investors have had to be patient, however: it took Amazon 8 years before it was able to report its first small profits in January 2002.

The website

A US survey of 300 daily internet users found that two-thirds of people said that if a website did not meet their expectations, they would never return to it again. According to the survey, the four essential characteristics of a 'good' website are that it must be continually updated, easy to navigate, have in-depth information on its subject and offer quick loading and response times (Gaudin, 2002).

The need for fast loading and response times is still a difficulty for marketers because of the technology driving website use. Speeds can still be relatively slow when traffic levels are high. As the number of people logging on to the internet increases, the problem will become more severe unless bandwidth and capacity problems are resolved. Once online, the quality of viewing can be reduced and the irritation level increased if graphics take a long time to load and in some cases crash the computer if they overload it. Better video plug-ins and ever more sophisticated browsers have enhanced quality and reduced loading times, but as yet for the average internet user the experience can still be frustrating.

eg

A well designed website with user-friendly pages is very important for capturing the user's attention. The user is not very patient, however. Nielsen//NetRatings' review of internet usage statistics for June 2002 (http://www.netratings.com) showed that people spend on average only 48 seconds on any single page. For e-tailers of high involvement goods this means that there is very little time in which to engage the user and lead them into a selling process. Even then, the potential customer can be lost. If images or pages are slow to download or if the checkout procedure is lengthy and complicated, there is always a risk that the customer will abandon their virtual shopping cart and run away before the transaction is complete.

Apparel Industry Magazine (2000) set up a focus group to explore and assess four fashion e-tail sites. The results give an interesting insight into what people are looking for in terms of website design and facilities/services offered. Complexity of navigation was raised as a problem. On one site, users found they had to do a tutorial to learn how to use the site and make purchases. Even then it was easy to make mistakes. The user could have up to ten windows open at a time and closing the wrong one would mean exiting the site altogether and having to start again. As Kolesar and Galbraith (2000) said, the customer is an integral part of the e-tail service experience and the role they play has to be in keeping with their knowledge and abilities as well as their self-image.

Users did like having the facility to dress a virtual mannequin and get her to 'do a twirl' so that they could see the effect of putting different garments together as an outfit. They also liked being able to ask for recommendations, for example to find some shoes to match a garment already chosen. Detailed product descriptions, including fabric care, and the ability to zoom in on garments to see fabric and styling detail were also appreciated, but the quality of photographs and colour reproduction was generally thought to be poor and inconsistent. Uncluttered pages were preferred rather than those trying to show nine or more garments per page. Users were frustrated by missing product photographs and messages such as 'unavailable in the size/colour requested'. When sites offer a very large assortment of goods, users liked being able to use menus or search facilities to specify product types, size ranges or price bands that they were interested in to narrow down the number of products shown.

All the sites examined were e-tail stores bringing together a number of brand names and designer labels on the one site. The focus group best liked the sites that gave them an 'aggregated shopping cart' so that they could select goods from lots of different labels and pay for them in one transaction. The group was less impressed with the fashion e-tailers that simply acted as portals, so that clicking on a label name took them through to that label's own site. This means that the shopper cannot have the facility to see what one label's sweater would look like with another label's jeans, for example. It also means the inconvenience of having to undertake individual transactions with individual sites. Also on the processing side, users wanted clear information about shipping costs and times and returns policies.

Interestingly, researchers have also found that the industries that tend to deliver the good websites are the ones that have faced the fiercest dotcom competition. Thus Amazon, for instance, has set the benchmark for any online bookseller in terms of the quality of the website that customers expect to see (Gaudin, 2002). Cap Gemini Ernst & Young (CGE&Y) interviewed 6,000 consumers across nine European countries to find out what online shoppers felt to be important about the e-tailers they dealt with. Honesty, respect and reliability were all rated a lot more highly than having the highest quality merchandise or the lowest prices. These are not necessarily easy virtues to communicate or 'prove' and if another survey of 1,500 US internet users is anything to go by, companies face a difficult task in winning the trust of a fundamentally suspicious public. Only 29 per cent of respondents said that they trust e-commerce sites either 'just about always' or 'most of the time'. Sixty-four per cent trust them 'only some of the time' or 'never'. The survey also found, however, that a respondent's propensity to trust websites depended on whether they were novice internet users; how comfortable they felt using a credit card online; and whether they tended to trust people in general or not (Greenspan, 2002a). Prabhaker (2000) summarises the issues of trust as covering three areas: the future use of personal information that has been gathered in the course of a consumer's interaction with a website, the potential transfer of that information to third parties, and companies' access to private information about individuals' finances or health. Companies that are seen to be acting responsibly in using customer data and preserving customers' privacy are the ones that are most likely to gain the consumer's repect and custom.

McKinsey has also found a marked degree of mistrust among internet users. Only about 4 per cent of online users routinely register at websites, and two-thirds of those who do not register say that it is because of lack of trust or protection of their privacy. If, therefore, companies want consumers to register, then they will have to make sure they are offering products, services, information and/or promotions that consumers really want and that will encourage them to overcome their misgivings about registering. McKinsey's research also suggsts that companies that do get the consumer past this initial barrier and start to build relationships through well-targeted constant and interactive communication benefit from it. Amazon, for instance, generates 50 per cent of its sales from repeat customers against an average of 25 per cent for e-tailers generally (Saunders, 2001).

In the light of this debate on trust, it is interesting to note that a survey conducted by MORI on behalf of internet bank Egg showed that 31 per cent of all UK adults would be interested in being able to make payments to individuals or pay bills to businesses via e-mail rather than using cheques. This figure grew to 54 per cent among e-mail users. Furthermore, half of all UK internet users said they have either arranged or serviced a financial product over the internet (Pastore, 2002). Clearly it is possible for marketers to overcome the trust barrier, particularly those offering a distinct service that is perceived to make the consumer's life a lot easier.

Consumer internet penetration and spending

Clearly, the opportunities for internet marketing are closely linked with a target market's ability to access the internet. The internet's penetration is still evolving and growing. As Table 24.1 shows, in many EU countries, the percentage of households connected to the internet is set to double between 2000 and 2006, and in the currently less technologically advanced countries, such as Greece and Portugal, Euromonitor is predicting an increase of over four times the current penetration.

Table 24.1 Online household penetration 2000–2006 (% of households)

	2000	*2001*	*2002*	*2003*	*2004*	*2005*	*2006*
Austria	28	34	39	42	45	47	48
Belgium	20	25	30	35	38	42	45
Denmark	47	52	56	59	61	63	64
Finland	34	39	44	48	51	54	56
France	18	25	31	35	38	41	44
Germany	31	37	42	46	50	52	53
Greece	7	11	16	21	25	29	32
Ireland	18	25	32	37	42	45	48
Italy	19	25	31	36	40	43	44
Luxembourg	26	31	36	41	45	48	51
Netherlands	44	51	54	57	59	60	62
Portugal	8	12	17	22	27	31	35
Spain	12	17	22	27	31	35	38
Sweden	55	59	63	66	68	69	71
UK	28	35	41	45	49	51	53

Source: Euromonitor (2002), extracted from Table 12.7, p. 286.

The figures and predictions for online penetration among individuals are very similar, according to Euromonitor. Table 24.2 again shows a rapid rise in the percentage of online individuals between 2000 and 2006. A UK survey found in 2002 that 45 per cent of UK adults use the internet for personal use and another 10 per cent intend to go online within the next two years (Pastore, 2002). These figures are very similar to Euromonitor's forecasts reported in Table 24.2. With many more people having access to the internet at home, at school, college or University, at work, and at public libraries and cybercafés, its attraction to the marketer as a medium for communication, selling and other transactions is obvious.

Table 24.2 Online penetration (individuals) 2000–2006 (%)

	2000	*2001*	*2002*	*2003*	*2004*	*2005*	*2006*
Austria	30	35	39	42	45	47	48
Belgium	23	27	31	35	39	43	45
Denmark	48	53	56	59	62	63	65
Finland	37	42	45	49	52	55	57
France	17	23	27	32	37	41	44
Germany	28	35	41	46	49	52	54
Greece	6	10	15	20	24	29	32
Ireland	27	32	36	40	44	47	49
Italy	19	27	34	36	40	43	44
Luxembourg	30	34	39	43	46	49	52
Netherlands	41	47	51	55	58	60	62
Portugal	9	13	18	22	27	31	35
Spain	14	19	23	28	32	36	39
Sweden	58	62	65	67	69	70	72
UK	32	38	43	47	50	52	54

Source: Euromonitor (2002), extracted from Table 12.9, p. 288.

Nevertheless, marketers need to exercise some caution. As Table 24.3 shows, as at 2002, in all EU countries, less than half of online users were actually using the internet to buy things. In Belgium it was less than 20 per cent, while the best figures come from the UK with 41.6 per cent. While this is a significant improvement on the 2000 figures, marketers still have a long way to go in fully realising the internet's potential as a retail channel. Even by 2006, only a few countries are expected to have more than 60 per cent of users actually buying online. Of course, the internet is not solely about e-tailing, but for many consumer

Table 24.3 Percentage of online users that buy online 2000–2006

	2000	*2001*	*2002*	*2003*	*2004*	*2005*	*2006*
Austria	20.1	31.3	38.6	47.5	54.2	58.8	61.9
Belgium	11.3	15.5	18.9	21.9	24.6	26.4	27.7
Denmark	21.8	31.1	39.0	44.8	50.4	54.1	56.3
Finland	22.5	31.1	38.5	44.1	49.7	53.4	55.6
France	21.5	29.6	37.5	43.6	49.9	54.2	57.0
Germany	25.0	34.6	41.5	49.1	55.7	60.4	63.4
Greece	11.0	17.0	22.0	26.7	31.7	35.3	37.9
Ireland	16.1	25.1	31.7	38.7	44.3	48.1	50.4
Italy	14.8	21.6	26.6	32.0	37.2	40.9	43.4
Luxembourg	16.2	21.9	26.7	30.4	34.0	36.5	38.1
Netherlands	18.8	27.7	34.9	42.5	48.4	52.4	54.6
Portugal	13.6	20.0	25.1	30.0	34.7	38.3	40.6
Spain	17.1	23.3	28.4	33.2	38.1	41.5	43.7
Sweden	23.6	31.8	37.6	42.7	46.8	49.5	51.1
UK	27.4	34.7	41.6	47.7	53.3	57.1	59.4

Source: Euromonitor (2002), extracted from Table 12.12, p. 291.

goods companies it is a natural extension of their business, and it is important to them to see consumers becoming confident and accustomed to buying online to give them an opportunity to extend their customer base and generate extra revenues and economies of scale.

The good news for marketers is that the average spend per online buyer is rising. According to BMRB in 2002, 56 per cent of UK internet users were shopping online. In May 2002, the average total online spend per shopper over the previous six months was £560. Extrapolating from these figures, BMRB estimated that the annual total value of consumer e-commerce in the UK is £11.9 bn (Milsom, 2002). Euromonitor forecasts suggest that average spend will continue to rise. Table 24.4 shows the average spend per online buyer across the EU and it is interesting to see that the UK buyer is spending much more on average than anyone else. Table 24.5 perhaps offers some clues about why this is. UK consumers are spending far more than anyone else in Europe on online grocery shopping; more than twice as much as the Germans who themselves are spending more than twice as much as their nearest rivals, the French. The UK spend reflects the proactive and very competitive approaches taken to online grocery shopping by the dominant supermarket chains who have invested a lot of money in setting up and refining the infrastructure to allow online shopping and home deliveries, as well as investing in marketing efforts to develop an online customer base.

eg

Tesco.com, offering over 40,000 product lines, has around 75 per cent share of the UK e-grocery market. It makes over 80,000 deliveries a week in its fleet of 800 vans, covering 96.6 per cent of the UK. Its customer base consists of well over 1 million households, mainly consisting of better-off families with both parents working. Nearly 94 per cent of its users are loyal to it and 30 per cent shop nowhere else online. The average spend per order is £85 (compared with £21 in-store) leading to sales in 2001 of £356 mn, up 50 per cent on the previous year. The potential for e-grocery shopping is huge: few people enjoy tramping round a busy store and lugging their shopping home afterwards. A survey by Barclays Bank has calculated that internet users could save over 63 hours a year by using the internet to buy what they need, the equivalent of seven Saturdays or 25 evenings of late-night shopping.

While Tesco's success might make it look like an easy way to make money, other retailers have not fared so well with their online operations. Sainsbury's online business, Sainsbury's to You, is not performing as well as Tesco.com. Analysts estimate that it is generating less than £100 mn in revenue and will make a loss of £50 mn in 2002 and £35 mn in 2003. ASDA is struggling to find an operating model that works, and in November 2001, Safeway analysed the results of a trial scheme and decided not to introduce a home-shopping operation at all because of the high level of investment required.

Sources: *Birmingham Post*, 2002; Bruce, 2002; Goodley, 2002; Gregory, 2002.

Table 24.4 Online spending per buyer 2000–2006 (US$)

	2000	*2001*	*2002*	*2003*	*2004*	*2005*	*2006*
Austria	214.9	237.2	277.6	302.4	340.9	395.7	472.7
Belgium	270.8	328.6	375.2	434.7	498.8	578.0	689.1
Denmark	359.4	412.5	460.7	519.9	574.0	649.5	745.5
Finland	372.1	430.0	474.4	525.6	566.1	625.6	703.7
France	354.3	427.4	456.7	488.7	509.9	553.1	615.9
Germany	298.5	344.0	388.3	424.9	473.3	545.4	646.0
Greece	131.8	181.5	197.0	200.6	206.9	218.5	244.9
Ireland	174.0	214.1	251.8	278.3	311.6	358.1	422.1
Italy	192.3	252.4	283.1	298.6	316.2	352.1	403.9
Luxembourg	319.4	372.1	414.6	479.2	546.1	629.3	745.0
Netherlands	296.5	351.0	396.6	428.9	469.9	529.7	606.5
Portugal	176.6	227.3	241.1	257.1	274.0	298.1	339.0
Spain	249.0	298.5	326.9	356.5	383.3	423.8	484.6
Sweden	355.7	387.4	438.5	493.4	556.1	639.8	742.5
UK	517.6	601.2	659.2	725.6	792.0	882.5	1007.1

Source: Euromonitor (2002), extracted from Table 12.13, p. 292.

Table 24.5 Online expenditure by type 2001 (US$ million)

	Apparel	*Books*	*Consumer electronics*	*Groceries*	*Music*	*PCs*	*Peripherals*	*Software*	*Toys*	*Travel and tourism*	*Videos*	*Other*
Austria	13.01	13.2	11.95	20.10	10.64	18.21	7.09	8.03	2.02	7.09	2.48	45.01
Belgium	11.00	7.22	3.87	14.85	10.96	17.96	11.89	6.46	2.30	11.89	0.99	27.60
Denmark	32.59	30.19	8.56	41.42	16.93	55.85	18.14	16.48	1.99	18.14	2.27	45.49
Finland	18.27	17.56	8.29	28.88	9.29	63.71	20.26	11.76	1.53	20.26	1.65	49.12
France	129.96	53.97	42.57	186.68	38.24	89.06	37.50	38.59	5.70	37.50	6.36	271.59
Germany	250.44	215.85	143.73	490.84	193.80	314.46	120.63	115.59	18.13	120.63	29.83	572.36
Greece	4.35	1.50	2.54	2.27	0.55	2.14	1.44	2.14	0.22	1.44	0.57	8.42
Ireland	4.22	4.77	1.82	7.95	3.58	3.19	0.84	3.78	0.69	0.84	0.82	14.92
Italy	28.46	54.08	56.06	25.54	11.15	88.46	27.87	52.05	8.81	27.87	5.11	211.17
Luxembourg	0.67	0.97	0.46	0.95	0.68	2.09	0.58	0.36	0.12	0.58	0.12	2.25
Netherlands	45.66	50.95	27.98	71.38	31.66	98.84	38.63	28.11	2.75	38.63	6.66	138.95
Portugal	2.11	6.25	2.51	10.85	1.04	3.36	1.91	1.71	0.41	1.91	0.55	12.18
Spain	31.51	93.39	14.92	50.95	10.58	33.21	20.66	17.96	2.67	20.66	3.00	44.92
Sweden	44.76	62.93	17.31	93.57	36.47	92.61	33.18	37.79	2.88	33.18	4.45	103.77
UK	196.57	255.23	106.00	1017.73	205.71	300.89	96.78	174.15	36.57	96.78	37.42	627.47

Source: Euromonitor (2002), extracted from Table 12.14, p. 293.

Another notable category in which UK and German consumers were spending much more freely than other Europeans in 2001 is books. Here, the influence of Amazon cannot be ignored. Amazon.co.uk and amazon.de have done a lot to encourage online book (and video and music) buying in the UK and Germany respectively, again, through proactive market-building strategies. The birth of amazon.fr will perhaps start to stimulate French spend on books, videos/DVDs and music similarly.

B2B internet spending

According to eMarketer's 'E-Commerce Trade and B2B Exchanges' report (CyberAtlas, 2002a), worldwide B2B e-commerce for 2002 was estimated to be worth $823.4 bn, but by 2004, it is forecast that it will be worth nearly $2.4 trillion. The International Data Corp. is even more optimistic, quoting an estimate of $4.3 trillion by 2005 (http://www.idc.com). Much of this growth is being driven by companies recognising the advantages of moving to B2B e-commerce solutions, such as convenience, cost saving (up to 22 per cent in some supply chains), customer and competitor pressure as well as opportunities to generate new revenue.

Online procurement, pioneered by large, global organisations represents a large part of B2B online commerce. A US survey showed that 73 per cent of organisations use the internet for indirect purchases and 54 per cent for purchases of direct material, with organisations with big purchasing budgets reporting the greatest involvement (Faloon, 2001). Nearly 43 per cent of large-volume purchasers said that the internet was likely to be 'critical' or 'very important' in their future purchasing plans and a further 47 per cent said that it would be somewhat important. This could mean a lot of business. IBM, for example, spent over $43 billion via e-procurement during 2000, and Boeing processes more than 20,000 daily transactions via its website (Pastore, 2001).

Some B2B online trading is being encouraged by the emergence of both independent and consortium-owned online 'marketplaces' or 'exchanges' that bring buyers and sellers together, facilitating transactions. They offer buyers access to a global network of suppliers and information on all aspects of their processes, practices, facilities and their marketing focus. Acting as an intermediary, the marketplace helps would-be buyers to prepare their 'request for quotation' which advertises their needs to potential suppliers, and helps would-be suppliers to prepare their bids. FreeMarkets is one of the leading online exchanges, and any bids that are made through it include a cost breakdown so that the buyer can assess how realistic it is. The Royal Bank Group in London uses FreeMarkets and while up to £70 mn of its purchasing went through Freemarkets in 2001, the company can envisage an increasing proportion of its total annual spend of £2 bn being spent through that channel in the future. This is perhaps not surprising, given that FreeMarkets estimates that its clients save between 2 and 25 per cent on their purchases (Anderson and Patel, 2001). As Johnson (2000) emphasises, however, simply bringing buyers and sellers together is not enough.

Operators of B2B exchanges must ensure that they add value to the exchange, by facilitating the whole flow of goods through the supply chain, for example by incorporating logistics services to help move the goods quickly and efficiently from the seller to the buyer and to track their progress.

While online reverse auctions might be seen as a return to the bad old days of adversarial buyer–seller relationships, some companies and industries have thought in terms of 'e-collaboration' pooling information, data and resources online, often with direct competitors, and streamlining and integrating people, data and processes (Hewson, 2000). In October

corporate social responsibility *in action*

The buyer–supplier relationship under the hammer (or under the cosh?)

Through sites such as e-Bay, the idea of an internet auction has become well established in consumer markets. The seller advertises the goods and the would-be buyer makes a bid. The highest bid made by the time the auction deadline passes gets to buy the goods. In B2B markets, the online reverse auction has started to become more common. The buyer advertises the specifications of what they want to buy and a starting price and then would-be suppliers make bids undercutting that price. All the bidders can see what others are bidding and can thus design their bids appropriately. Often, but by no means always, the lowest bid made by the close of the auction 'wins'.

Understandably, buyers and suppliers have very different views on the benefits and usefulness of reverse auctions, as well as on the ethics underlying them. Some see it as a cynical way of frightening existing suppliers into reducing their prices. They find themselves pitched into an auction against both obvious well-known competitors and a few unknown companies and although they don't make the lowest bid in the auction they still get to retain the business – but at a lower price than before. One existing supplier found that it did lose the business to an unknown competitor but later got a call asking it to continue to supply temporarily (at the new price, of course) because the auction winner had no experience of manufacturing that product and could not meet the delivery quantities required. Suppliers argue that if buyers were satisfied that all bidders could actually supply the quantities required to the specifications stated then the lowest price would always win – but it doesn't. 'Auctions are not about getting the lowest price *per se* but getting the lowest price per supplier' as one manufacturer (as quoted by Watson, 2002b) put it.

Suppliers also feel that it is too impersonal a process with no room for old fashioned face-to-face negotiation. There is too much emphasis on price and not enough on issues of collaboration and longer-term business development for the benefit of both parties. Suppliers feel that buyers are damaging relationships built up over years for the sake of short-term cost savings that are often not reflected in retail prices to the end consumer. Some buyers, such as Cisco and Dell agree, and have said that they will not subject their suppliers to this kind of process.

Most buyers who use auctions do not see it like this, however. They see it as a much more transparent process that can work in the supplier's favour as they can see exactly what rival bidders are offering and decide whether to undercut it (or not) and by how much, rather than going all-out for the lowest possible bid they can manage. Some suppliers are, however, cynical about just how genuine some of the bids are. One supplier, claiming to be number one in its field, said that the opening price on a relevant auction was 25 per cent lower than its best price. But as one buyer (quoted by Watson, 2002b) said, 'At the end of the day, it's a pain in the arse to change a supplier. We're not going to hold an auction unless there is a chance of a significant price reduction. And if we set a ridiculous price to open, we just shoot ourselves in the foot. After all, no one has to bid'. That may well be true, but it would be a brave supplier that would boycott an auction or would gamble on which rival bids should be taken seriously and which ignored.

Buyers also claim that they do not use auctions in product areas where they have strategic relationships with suppliers as they do not wish to damage those relationships, but suppliers are claiming that buyers work on the principle that 'As long as you can define the product and more than one supplier can make it, you can auction it' (as quoted by Watson, 2002a).

Overall, the appropriateness of online reverse auctions and their impact on the long-term quality of buyer–supplier relationships is debatable. What seems clear is that their use in an industry seems to depend on the relative power balance between the parties and the nature of the goods and services being traded. High-tech companies such as Cisco and Dell operating in industries where there are few alternative suppliers, where suppliers hold the bargaining power, and where long-term innovation and collaboration are paramount may well see little point in risking relationships for the sake of short-term cost savings. Where the buyers are few and powerful, where switching costs are relatively low, and where there are many alternative suppliers, then it seems that the reverse auction is here to stay. Rosenthal (2002) suggests that by 2006, it will account for 15 per cent of worldwide B2B e-commerce. It might not sound a lot, but in value terms it represents a significant amount of trade. What, however, does it contribute to the ethical treatment of suppliers?

Sources: Anderson and Patel (2001); Rosenthal (2002); Watson (2002a, 2002b).

2000, Covisint, an 'e-marketplace' or 'B2B exchange' serving the motor industry started trading. Covisint was set up collaboratively by General Motors, Ford, DaimlerChrysler, Renault and Nissan at a cost of $270 mn with the intention of becoming the internet focal point for the global motor industry, a portal to which every buyer and supplier goes in order to find and place business. Covisint would conduct auctions and also be used to help run collaborative product development projects, taking products through from the drawing board to development and testing and into production.

Sadly, it seems that this particular e-collaboration was a Utopian dream and that the motor manufacturers had underestimated the level of mistrust and cynicism among the 7,000 participating suppliers. The kind of objections outlined in the *CSR in Action* vignette in this section began to be voiced. Suppliers felt that it was all just a mechanism to squeeze their prices down and did not like the idea of sensitive pricing information about their businesses being so readily available to competitors (Grant, 2002).

B2B e-procurement is thus not all plain sailing. One survey found that nearly half of respondents said that exchanges had 'mostly' or 'absolutely' failed to meet their expectations; only 10 per cent felt that exchanges had actually met their expectations (CyberAtlas, 2002a). Nevertheless, most repondents expected to use them for a greater proportion of their future B2B spending as they do appreciate their potential to make B2B transactions and collaboration easier and more effective.

The marketing uses of a website

There are many reasons for an organisation considering using the internet, but they tend to group into three broad categories: as a research and planning tool; as a distribution channel; and for communication and promotion, as seen in Table 24.6.

Table 24.6 Marketing uses of the internet

Research and planning tool

- Obtain market information
- Conduct primary research
- Analyse customer feedback and response

Distribution and customer service

- Take orders
- Update product offerings frequently
- Help the customer buy online
- Process payments securely
- Raise customer service levels
- Reduce marketing and distribution costs
- Distribute digital products

Communication and promotion

- Generate enquiries
- Enable low cost direct communication
- Reinforce corporate identity
- Produce and display product catalogues
- Entertain, amuse and build goodwill
- Inform investors
- Detail current and old press releases
- Provide basic product and location information
- Present company in a favourable light – history, mission, achievements, views, etc.
- Educate customers on the products, processes, etc.
- Inform suppliers of developments
- Communicate with employees
- Attract new job recruits
- Answer questions about the company and its products

Research and planning tool

The internet provides direct access to a considerable amount of secondary marketing information. Some sources are free, but many can only be accessed through subscription. Increasingly, the need to visit the library or purchase bulky directories and reports is decreasing as the power, convenience and flexibility of online searching become better known. Most organisations offering subscription services, such as Mintel, *Financial Times*, and International Data Corp. will update their sites frequently by adding new and updated information and reports. Many of the secondary data sources considered in Chapter 6 can also be accessed online.

As internet usage increases, the possibilities for primary research are also growing. Through online visitor books, feedback using structured questionnaires or via e-mail, web discussion groups and analysing visitor and online ordering traffic, useful information can be gathered for marketing planning purposes.

eg

Market researchers undertook a survey of 50,000 people in the US to see how effective banner advertising is in terms of affecting brand awareness, advertising recall and purchase intent. The research, on behalf of Nestlé Purina PetCare Co., showed that consumers exposed to Purina banner advertisements were nearly 50 per cent more likely to cite it as the first dog food brand that came to mind. The more times consumers were exposed to the advertising, the higher the awareness levels, thus among the group of respondents who had received 1–5 impressions, brand awareness rose from 22.3 per cent to 28.2 per cent while among those who had received 6–20 impressions, it rose to 35.4 per cent. The number of impressions received also had an effect on purchase intent. Looking at one particular product in the range, Purina ONE, purchase intent rose from 23.6 per cent to 34.7 per cent among those receiving 1–5 impressions, and to 38.4 per cent among those receiving 6–20.

The banner advertising performed well in advertising unaided recall tests too although it is interesting to see that the number of impressions is less relevant here. Of those who had been exposed to 1–5 impressions, 5.5 per cent later recalled having seen a Purina advertisement, while only 5.1 per cent of those receiving 6–20 impressions did so. Among dog owners, the results were 6.3 per cent (1–5 impressions) and 6.4 percent (6–20 impressions).

This research not only shows the important role that internet advertising generally can play in brand building, but also the importance of the corporate or brand website itself in reinforcing brand loyalty, as existing Purina dog food buyers were far more likely to visit Purina.com than other internet users (Saunders, 2002).

Distribution channel

Many examples have been given throughout this book of the impact of the internet on distribution channels. Chapter 13 specifically examined online retailing and the growth of Amazon shows just how the power of the internet can have an impact on a conventional distribution channel. The impact will grow in the future as consumers gain more confidence in online purchasing. There are several advantages of online distribution:

- The viewer is actively searching for products and services, and so every site hit could gain a potential customer if interest can be maintained. Regular and loyal customers can take short cuts and skip all the general background information. 'Shopping baskets' help the customer to keep track of what they have bought on this visit and help give the impression of a store just like any other. In the late 1990s, four main sectors were considered to be at the forefront of online direct distribution: travel, books, music and software. As seen in Table 24.5 earlier, however, groceries, clothing, and electrical goods, including PCs, have all become significant contributors to the e-tail economy. This is perhaps a sign that consumers are gaining enough confidence in online shopping to start making riskier purchases either in terms of financial risk (e.g. buying a high-priced PC or even a car and having sufficient faith that the online seller will deliver the goods in the first place and then be there to sort out any after-sales problems) or psychological risk (e.g. buying clothing on the basis of verbal descriptions and 2-dimensional pictures).

- Print and mailing costs are eliminated because no catalogue has to be produced and distributed each season. Although costs will be incurred in developing and maintaining an interesting website, they still represent a saving, especially because a website increases the seller's flexibility as it can be changed far more easily than the printed page with instant updates on prices, product availability and special offers. Amazon has well over 8 million users, yet the cost of communicating with them is a fraction of the cost that would have been incurred through direct mail or media advertising.

eg

Companies selling goods over the internet need to be careful that the constant need to update information and the sheer volume of changes that are made do not lead to costly carelessness, however. Despite the fact that errors can be put right almost as soon as they are spotted, the fast-moving nature of the internet means that a lot of damage can still be done in a very short space of time.

Kodak probably didn't feel like smiling for the camera in January 2002 after it made a slight mistake on its UK website. A digital camera was advertised for sale via the website for £100 for just 12 hours before Kodak realised that an error had been made and revised the price to £329. It was too late, however. Word-of-mouth had spread news of the bargain and thousands of orders had been placed before the error was rectified. Kodak's immediate response was to e-mail the 10,000 hopeful buyers and tell them that the orders would not be fulfilled at the £100 price. Its view was that when a potential customer places an order (s)he is simply making an offer to buy which the seller can then accept or reject. There is no binding contract until the offer to buy is accepted by the seller. Kodak intended to exercise its right to refuse the kind offers that its would-be customers were making.

Customers were not prepared to accept this, however, and threatened legal proceedings on the basis that Kodak had acknowledged receipt of the orders which legally is tantamount to accepting the customer's offer and creating a contract. Rather than pursue the matter through the courts, Kodak decided to honour the orders at a cost of £2 mn (*The Daily Telegraph*, 2002; Eaglesham, 2002).

- Order processing and handling costs are reduced with online ordering as everything is already in electronic form and the customer is handling all the order entry without assistance. McNutt (1998), however, has argued that it is important for organisations to realise that opening the front door to customers with a website providing ordering capability means that they have to ensure that all the 'behind the scenes' logistics operations can cope with changes in ordering patterns. Linking back into the organisational systems for stock control and order fulfilment is essential if customer service levels are to be maintained.

marketing *in action*

Fulfilling the customer's desires

Given the potential scale of online grocery shopping (*see* earlier example of Tesco.com), e-grocery services need to be sure that they have the right technological infrastructure and order processing and fulfilment design to ensure that they can deliver as promised. One ongoing debate is about the relative merits of warehouse versus store-based picking models, i.e. is it better to assemble and deliver a customer's order from a local store or to have dedicated regional warehouses that deal solely with e-shoppers?

Ocado is purely an e-grocer. Although it is 40 per cent owned by retailer Waitrose, it has no retail stores of its own. It thus uses the warehouse model. It has built a huge dedicated warehouse, the size of 20 normal supermarkets, in Hatfield and is confident that it can serve London and the whole of the South East of England from that one site. Ocado's view is that it is a lot more cost-effective to operate like this than from individual stores. Other companies with dedicated warehouse facilities for e-grocery shopping are not so sure about the benefits. Sainsbury's has struggled with its dedicated warehouses and is running with a mixed model, using two dedicated facilities in Manchester and London supplemented from 41 stores in large cities. ASDA completely abandoned its attempt to operate from two dedicated warehouses. Tesco.com, however, Europe's biggest online grocer, does not use dedicated warehouses and manages to service over 80,000 deliveries a week from its store network profitably.

Whatever the models used, the infrastructure has to be able to tackle certain key issues that affect the service quality that the customer experiences. The biggest problems from the customer's perspective are lack of availability of products, substitution of products and mistimed deliveries (i.e. outside the specified time window). Ocado claims that its IT systems have solved the availability/substitution problems, with sophisticated software that integrates the orders that are in the system with stock levels in the warehouse so that stock-outs are less likely to happen. If a product is not available, then the customer can be told at the time they place the order and can choose a substitute if they want. This is a lot more difficult under a store-based operating model because product availability depends on what is in stock in a particular store at the time when the order is assembled and that can be unpredictable because 'real' shoppers are continuously buying things and emptying the shelves! This means that substitution decisions are made by the member of staff who is assembling the order. Ocado claims that Tesco.com has to substitute about 15 per cent of items in any one order because of lack of availability in the local store, but Tesco claims that the substitution rate is a lot lower than that.

In terms of delivery times, Tesco.com may have the edge with local deliveries being made from local stores. With vans travelling relatively short distances, there is less scope for getting stuck in traffic and it is less likely that local van drivers will get lost! Ocado is serving a huge geographic area from one location and that involves negotiating the nightmare that passes for a road system in and around London and the South East with the potentially long delays frequently caused by the sheer volume of traffic or accidents. While Ocado uses sophisticated route planning and navigation software, the long distances involved still make it difficult to predict exact delivery times.

Many improvements are being made to the service all the time, but there is still much to be done. *The Grocer* magazine regularly monitors online grocery services through mystery shopping. Sites are becoming easier to access and navigate but *The Grocer* has found that stock-outs on very basic items, delivery errors (e.g. delivering someone else's order) and inconvenient delivery times are still major problems.

Sources: Birmingham Post (2002); Goodley (2002); *The Grocer* (2001, 2002); Patten (2002).

- The IT systems have to be able to offer real time information flows between the customer, customer support, distribution and the supply chain. Only then can realistic claims be made for cost efficient and effective customer service, whether a small parcel is delivered to Milan or Middlesbrough. Federal Express made a virtue of its integrated system by allowing customers to track the exact whereabouts of a particular parcel on the internet as a means of reassurance. It also turned this service into an effective selling tool to differentiate itself from competitors.
- Better after-sales service can be provided online, not only because of cheaper and easier communication, but also through feedback links, usage information, news flashes on any product changes and mechanisms for fault reporting.
- Digital products, in the form of magazines, music and video, are capable of being distributed via the internet, without the need even to send a parcel through the post. The distribution of music products that can be downloaded on to a computer is causing concern to CD manufacturers for copyright and piracy reasons.

eg

Online file-sharing services act as an intermediary, allowing people to contribute music or MP3 files or to download them. US research has indicated that 19 per cent of Americans aged 12 or over have downloaded files from such sites. Among 18- to 24-year-olds, the figures are even higher: 45 per cent. It is not an alien activity to older age groups, either. Fourteen per cent of US 35- to 54-year-olds have downloaded files from these sites. The interest in file-sharing has been driven to a large extent by technology, with PC manufacturers promoting music-focused packages including CD-R drives and appropriate software for downloading and recording music. This might look like bad news for the record companies, but in the research, 81 per cent of downloaders said that their CD purchases had stayed the same or increased since they began downloading music from the internet. Furthermore, 84 per cent said that they did not just use the internet for downloading music, they also used it to research bands and tour information, to listen to song clips and find out more about lyrics before actually buying a CD. Nearly half of them go on to say that they have purchased a particular band's or artist's CD purely because of something they first found on the internet. Other global studies have reported similar findings, with about 41 per cent of teenage/young adult internet users admitting to having downloaded music files in some format or another (Greenspan, 2002b).

- Manufacturers can get closer to the customer and potentially reduce costs through **disintermediation**, which simply means cutting one or more intermediaries out of the distribution channel (Rowley, 2002). Thus the package holiday company that sells online direct to the consumer rather than through a travel agent is bypassing an intermediary, as is the designer-label clothing manufacturer that sells direct rather than through a trendy Oxford Street retailer. There is a risk attached to this (quite apart from alienating the traditional intermediaries who are losing business), however. As discussed in Chapter 12, one of the roles of the intermediary is to bring assortments of products together and make them visible to the target market in one place. Online direct selling by a manufacturer loses this advantage and depends heavily on the consumer's ability to find the manufacturer's website. To overcome this, a new kind of intermediary, the **cybermediary** (Sarkar *et al.*, 1996) has developed including not only e-tail stores such as Amazon, but also virtual shopping malls (*see* Case Study 24.2), online directories and search engines, among others, to help guide the consumer to relevant sites or to sell goods to them as a retailer would.
- In time, however, the growth of powerful ISPs and the emergence of customers in full control of what they will and will not search for and purchase could mean that the most powerful intermediaries in the twenty-first century will be the ISPs and search engine providers who build a wealth of information on individual customer preferences and requirements (Mitchell, 1999).

marketing ***in action***

Engineering search results

In the vastness of cyberspace, no-one can hear you scream. It can be very difficult for the average internet user to find what they are looking for, and thus search engines such as Google, Lycos and Ask Jeeves have become an integral part of their internet usage patterns. It has been estimated that 9 out of 10 internet users use a search engine every month and that more than 85 per cent of internet users rely on search engines. Thus if marketers want to bring their websites to internet users' attention, it is in their interests to make sure that those sites come up in any relevant search that an internet user may do.

Because of this, a whole new field of search engine management (SEM) has emerged in recent years, accounting for a growing proportion of companies' online marketing budgets. SEM means making sure that a search engine features your website in relevant search results lists and preferably includes it near the top of the results list. SEM specialist agencies offering SEO (search engine optimisation) services undertake research to help marketers to decide which search engines they should be targeting and then will liaise and negotiate with the search engine provider about inclusion and then monitor performance. It is a similar role to that of the advertising agency in more traditional media. Annual fees for SEM specialist agencies are between £5,000 and £15,000, although for more complex contracts involving extra services or a wide range of brand names, it can be a lot more. One agency suggests that a company wanting a properly professional service should not be spending less than £1,500 per month.

The role of the SEM specialist agency is important. Each search engine provides a different audience profile, although the differences can be subtle, and the agency will find the right one(s) to match the client's marketing objectives. It is also important to understand how people search. Consumers are not necessarily very adept at using search engines, and will use very general terms or make spelling errors. The agency can thus help with selecting appropriate keywords to ensure that a site does come up in a search and that internet users are directed to the most relevant pages within a site. SEM specialist agencies can track search engine performance, not only monitoring how much traffic a site receives from a search engine and what search keywords and phrases led it there, but even how much of that traffic actually goes on to make an online purchase, helping to justify the client's investment in SEM.

As well as the agency's services, the marketer may well have to make payments to the search engine owner. Search engines make their money less by selling banner advertising space and more through 'pay per click' and 'paid inclusion' revenues from website owners. Pay per click means that every time a user clicks on a website link from a search engine, the website owner pays 'commission' to the search engine. Paid inclusion guarantees that a site will be monitored by a search engine and included in the results of relevant searches, but it does not guarantee where in the results list it will appear. That is critical, because 75 per cent of internet users do not look beyond page two of the search results, yet if the user has input a very general keyword, they could be faced with hundreds of pages of results. To guarantee placement on the first couple of pages, therefore, means investing in a 'pay for placement' scheme, i.e. for a price, a search engine will place your website at the top or close to the top of the results list. The drawback, however, is that it works on a 'highest bidder' basis, so that if your competitor pays more, it will appear higher up the list than your site. This can be linked with a pay per click mechanism so that if you have agreed to pay the search engine $1 every time someone clicks through from the search engine, you will feature higher up the results list than a competitor which is only willing to pay 80 cents, for example.

Sources: Dwek (2002b); Smallpiece (2002); Thelwall (2001); http://www.makemetop.com.

Communication and promotion

The internet is now as good as any other tool for communicating with customers and target audiences. Many of the principles discussed in Chapters 14 and 15 apply equally to the internet. As well as operating a dedicated website, companies are also taking advertising space on other companies' websites as joint or paid promotions. As can be seen from Table 24.6, extensive use is made of the internet for communications purposes. Many of the entries are self-explanatory. The main uses are as follows.

As an advertising medium. Table 24.7 shows the advantages and disadvantages of using the internet as an advertising medium (Pickton and Broderick, 2001).

Table 24.7 The principal characteristics of the internet as an advertising medium

Advantages	*Disadvantages*
■ Message can be changed quickly and easily	■ Limited visual presentation
■ Interactivity possible	■ Audience not guaranteed
■ Can create own pages cheaply	■ 'Hits' may not represent interest – casual browsers
■ Can advertise on others' web pages	■ Relies on browsers finding page
■ Very low cost possible	■ Can create irritation
■ Very large audience potential	■ Large numbers of target groups may not use internet yet
■ Direct sales possible	■ Creative limitations
■ High information content possible on own web pages	

Source: Adapted from *Integrated Marketing Communications*, Financial Times Prentice-Hall, (Pickton, D and Broderick, A. 2001), Copyright © 2001 David Pickton and Amanda Broderick, reprinted by permission of Pearson Education Limited. Extracted from Exhibit 11.3, p. 210.

Table 24.7 demonstrates the internet is not a perfect advertising medium by any means. Its limitations and disadvantages are no more 'fatal' than those of any other medium, however, and simply emphasise the importance of incorporating internet activities fully into the wider marketing plan and using the medium within a coherent integrated communications strategy. It is also important, as we shall see with several examples within this section, to understand the target market and its internet usage patterns in order to identify the most appropriate use of the internet.

Advertising on the internet is thus similar to advertising through any other medium. The message should be communicated simply, clearly and by creating interest that will move the viewer through to further action, whether that is an enquiry, an order or just getting better informed about what is available. Many of the free internet access providers exploit this area to the full with comprehensive and sometimes intrusive display and banner advertising messages. Most of these messages are linked to the advertiser's website for further information and action. As the quality of information on web users improves, many of the ISPs have started to target advertising to their users, so for example a user with an interest in sport may receive banner advertisements on sports events and equipment. Amazon has gone further by creating a link with some search facilities, so if you want to know more about an organisation or market, you will be invited to allow Amazon to search for titles on that theme.

eg

Choosing the right website upon which to advertise is obviously an important decision and there needs to be a close match between the brand's target audience and the profile of the audience delivered by the website. A number of brands targeting the 5- to 16-year-old age group have found the CiTV website (http://www.citv.co.uk) to be a successful medium for advertising and linked promotional activity. This website is connected with children's ITV and offers a fun, interactive environment with games, competitions, jokes, message boards, audio interviews, etc. Children are drawn to it not only because of its magazine-type content, but also because of its on-screen exposure during children's programming on the ITV channels and their desire to follow up links with specific programmes. The website regularly attracts over 170,000 page impressions a day.

McVities wanted to promote its Jaffa Cakes brand interactively online to children and to create a database. This was done successfully through a link up between McVities, Manchester United and the CiTV website. A competition was run over six weeks on the website offering a main prize of a week's training at the Manchester United youth academy and runners-up prizes of signed footballs and photos every two weeks. Similarly, Kraft Foods wanted to raise awareness of its Lunchables brand among children. For a month, a Lunchables sponsorship campaign ran across the website, including a competition to win a Gameboy and Pokémon Yellow Cartridge. The competition was promoted in the CiTV newsletter and in banner advertising running across the website (24/7 Europe, 2002b, 2002c).

Kraft Dairylea Lunchables were highlighted to children by appearing on the CITV website.

Source: Kraft Europe.

Banner advertisements are still the main form of internet advertising, and normally appear either on an ISP's pages while the customer is logging on to the internet, alongside a search engine, or as part of a joint promotion on another organisation's website. Overall, internet advertising in the UK was worth just $210 mn in 2000, but is expected to grow to $1,098 mn by 2006 (Euromonitor, 2002).

Most banner and other display advertisements enable the viewer to access the main information or booking page for the product or company with one click. Despite their power and convenience, there is some evidence from the US that banner advertisements are being ignored by viewers as wallpaper or background clutter, so their effect is wearing off, despite their intrusive capability. However, BMRB's Internet Monitor found that in spite of the fact that over half of internet users agreed that 'all web advertising annoys me', 40 per cent had clicked a banner in the previous month. Only 20 per cent of internet users agreed with positive statements such as 'I find web advertising interesting' and 'I find web advertising entertaining'. While internet advertising does still seem to be driving people towards advertised websites, BMRB also found that television advertising was playing a role too.

Internet users are noting website addresses from advertisements that interest them and then visiting the sites later (BMRB, 2000).

Table 24.8 gives the top ten online advertisers in the UK for June 2002. Although Amazon is not at the top of the league in terms of impressions (i.e. the number of times an advertising banner is downloaded and presumably seen by visitors) it has the best performance in terms of reach (i.e. the proportion of active internet users who saw the advertisement). TRUSTe (http://www.truste.com), which heads the table, is a US-based site representing an organisation which provides a code of practice for companies in terms of online privacy policies and principles, and procedures and practices for dealing with oversights and complaints. Companies signing up to the scheme display the TRUSTe 'trustmark' which presumably explains the very high number of impressions. Its UK reach is, however, still quite low.

Table 24.8 Top 10 UK web advertisers for the month of June 2002

Advertiser	*Impressions*	*Reach (%)*
TRUSTe	281,070,385	17.37
e-Bay	125,047,637	26.82
MSN	89,136,721	31.07
Amazon	71,443,915	37.67
02	67,133,252	13.88
Freeserve	64,800,688	21.26
MNBA Europe Bank	63,607,644	33.62
Dell	54,246,003	30.49
Casino On Net	51,895,393	35.76
British Telecom	49,372,797	29.92

Source: Nielsen//NetRatings, accessed via http://www.netratings.com.

Loyalty reinforcement. The organisational website itself is also a powerful tool for increasing the level of interaction between the customer and the brand to reinforce loyalty. If the viewer can be entertained and informed, and enjoys coming back to the site, the brand values and image are enhanced.

eg

Imperial Leather is long-established as a leading soap and bath/shower products brand in the UK. Cussons UK Ltd, the brand's owner, wanted to use online marketing communications to help increase brand awareness, educate the target market about the product range and the variants within the range, and to complement an advertising campaign running in more traditional media, such as television and posters. Since the target market mainly consisted of women from the ABC1 socioeconomic groups, it was decided to use a banner advertisement on http://www.handbag.com, the leading UK women's portal. The banner, featuring the Cussons' duck logo, ran at the top of the health and beauty channel within handbag.com and allowed users to click through to Cussons' website. There was also a button on Handbag's make-up and skincare sub-channel taking users to an advertorial page. The banner advertisement achieved a click through rate of 3.4 per cent, and the button 1.92 per cent (24/7 Europe, 2002a).

Loyalty is clearly a big issue for e-tail sites too, trying to generate repeat business. As in any other form of marketing, it is cheaper and easier to sell to an existing online customer than to create a new one. Researchers tracked visitors to e-tail websites in six European countries in November 2001 and then followed them for three months from December 2001 to February 2002 to see how many of them returned to those sites (CyberAtlas, 2002b). Amazon performed very well in most geographic markets, which is not surprising given that we mentioned earlier that Amazon generates some 50 per cent of its business from returning customers. This study showed that Amazon's highest retention rate (40 per cent) was in the UK while its lowest was in Switzerland (28 per cent).

Engendering loyalty through providing a trusted, quality product and service package is also important for e-tailers because it helps to deflect the consumer's attention away from pricing issues. One of the problems caused by the dotcom boom is that many e-tailers emphasised low price rather than service, product assortment or convenience as prime reasons to buy. This set up an unrealistic expectation in the minds of consumers that prices should be between 10 and 15 per cent lower on the internet than elsewhere. As seen in Chapters 10 and 11, this is a dangerous strategy because if the e-tailer cannot deliver lower prices, then the consumer will not buy from them, and if the e-tailer does deliver low prices, it is vulnerable to making losses or to losing business to leaner, meaner competitors who can undercut. Many dotcoms were not sufficiently tightly managed financially to control costs and allow them to cut margins and many also underestimated the marketing costs involved in attracting shoppers to an unknown site in the first place (Franklin, 2002). Thus in the wake of the dotcom shakeout, companies are perhaps taking a more sensible approach to pricing and trying to develop and emphasise less tangible and less vulnerable sources of competitive advantage and customer loyalty.

Corporate communications. The internet has been widely used by organisations to create goodwill, better understanding and provide important information to shareholders and the community alike. Many organisations detail their financial reports on the web and often provide considerable coverage of their community relations programmes.

Often press releases are automatically placed on the web and so regular updating is necessary. Not only does this service help the media, but it also enables the organisation to get its message across to a wider audience in a more direct manner. Often press release archives can be accessed, going back several years. Even when full text is not available, contact details are provided to the press office for further enquiry.

eg

Some web pages are designed to counter negative stories and views expressed by unofficial or even anti-lobbying group sites. Shell had to contend with a host of highly critical sites over its environmental record, particularly over its disposal of the Brent Spar oil rig, and its involvement in Nigeria. It now uses both special web-based discussion lines and campaigns, along with a free flow of information, to counter some of the wilder allegations that are not actionable.

From its home page on http://www.shell.com, the visitor can click onto Tell Shell, a series of open discussion forums that are uncensored, other than for legal necessity. At the time of writing, the featured topics were 'How much freedom should we trade for our security?', 'The environment: issues and comments', 'Society and multinationals', and 'Energy and technology: now and in the future'. Anyone can contribute anything, whether it is critical of Shell or not. Shell will also put its own point of view, entering into the debate as it evolves. As Bowen (2002) describes it, it is 'a clever way of being transparent while getting its own views across'.

Sometimes, though, such openness can be abused. Monbiot (2002) discusses a PR firm that specialises in internet lobbying and claims that one of its methods is to create phantom individuals, apparently unconnected with any commercial interest, who infiltrate chat rooms and discussion forums to propagate or denigrate a particular point of view or organisation. While Monbiot focuses on a specific incident in the biotech industry, it is easy to see how Shell's hospitality could be similarly abused by a competitor or pressure group.

Sales promotion. Because of the relative ease of updating a web page and the flexibility it provides, it is possible to target offers on various products or over a defined period. Offers can be changed by the hour and the response of customers assessed (Wilson, 1999). Using price promotions, gifts and bonuses can all help increase short-term sales.

Personal selling. By its very nature, the web is impersonal and the internet is designed more for sales support and generating enquiries rather than for making direct sales. The cost per potential customer hit can be very low, and because people who do visit a site are likely to be interested in what it has to offer, the potential for increasing the level of enquiries is very

eg

Games-related competitions seem to be a popular promotional feature of websites. Drinks brand T&T, for example, offered prizes to visitors who became adept at its Quencha game (similar to Pac Man), accessed via http://ttbeverages.com. The five people who were top of the highest scores list every week won two cases (48 cans) of T&T drinks. A competition like this not only keeps people making repeat visits to the site to try to better their performance but also encourages them to leave personal details that could be added (via an opt-in mechanism) to a database for future marketing purposes. Kellogg's similarly uses games-related prizes on its child-oriented Kellogg's World site (http://www.kelloggs.co.uk). The site offers a wide range of games, and over a certain period, everyone who made it onto a leader board for any of the games offered was put into a monthly prize draw. Kellogg's website is also used to draw the consumer's attention to its current on-pack offers across all its brands. Presumable, the consumer can then make a positive decision to participate in a promotion and consciously seek out the relevant brand in-store.

great as net usage expands. Even in highly routine order-taking roles (*see* Chapter 17), the internet can be made more interactive if the customer database is able to personalise communication and relate it to offers that could appeal, based on a customer's previous enquiries and sales history.

Overall, the organisation should plan its use of the internet carefully and be sure that it is integrated into the rest of the marketing mix. Sumner (1999) argues that as much consideration should be given to the offline use of the website as to its online use. By featuring a web address in other advertising and promotional media, the overall site visibility is increased and additional site traffic could be generated. A glance at much poster, print and television advertising will often show a mention of an internet address for contact. It is important too that all of the internet budget should not be spent on highly interactive, fun websites at the expense of the more mundane, but critical, job of responding to e-mail enquiries.

Broadband

The wider adoption of broadband links, as opposed to the current dominance of narrow band, is likely to revolutionise the potential for internet usage. In the UK, in 2002 around 500,000 users had already switched to broadband and a further 20,000 a week were being connected according to Oftel (McLuhan, 2002) and BT alone was claiming 12,000 per week (Budden, 2002). A US consultancy firm, ARC suggested that by 2007 one-third of all internet users will have broadband and that broadband business applications will grow significantly. Europe will account for one-third of the 300 million broadband users worldwide (Greenspan, 2002c; ARC Group, 2002).

Broadband not only means faster internet connection, but because the bandwidth is greater it enables video and audio streaming rather than have the 'jerky' buffering and slower connections from normal line use. This means that live news and entertainment becomes a real possibility as a supplement, if not an alternative to television. There is, however, still some way to go before there is widespread adoption of broadband across Europe. Sweden has a high level of adoption, but the five major European economies (France, Spain, the UK, Italy and Germany) are still some way off a 10 per cent broadband penetration figure and some argue that it will not be reached until 2005 (Wheelwright, 2002). The rate of progress will depend upon the interaction of supply and demand. At present, there are not that many streaming applications that merit the extra investment, after all why watch a film on a PC when there is top quality, high definition digital television available? Until revenues and penetration pick up, it is not worth the broadcasters' while to consider producing dedicated content for broadband. It soon becomes a vicious circle, slowing the rate of growth.

What is needed is new applications that can compete with television. Watching sports or business highlights from work or on the move, accessing specialist material such as DIY or gardening information, or holiday brochures could all be enhanced by broadband. Such programmes are less likely to be mainstream broadcasting, even for the specialist satellite and cable television companies. The challenge for marketers, therefore, is to think through the applications where virtually real-time audio or visual would enhance the proposition or support to the customer. According to ARC Group (2002) again, the top uses are likley to be:

- communication and entertainment;
- information services;
- commerce; and
- home finance and management.

It goes on to predict that the first two will be far ahead of the others in terms of usage, reflecting the benefits of high speed connectivity. Although Tanner (2002) has suggested that people spend three times longer online each week (25 hours per week) when using broadband than narrowband, this may simply reflect the profile of heavier users and early adopters who would gain more from speed and flexibility. Just because using the internet can be faster does not mean that the average user will spend more time online.

The range of applications for marketers using broadband as part of an integrated marketing communications programme or for e-commerce is still in its infancy. The ability to video stream is the major additional benefit. Applications in corporate information distribution, sales demonstrations, video conferencing, product promotion, sales information provision and remote learning and product support are all feasible (Wheelwright, 2002).

eg

Would you like the experience of the car chase movie? BMWfilms' (http://www.bmwfilms.com) service 'The Hire' shows four films of car chases and claims to bring 'the power and quality of feature-length movies to a format designed for the internet'. Pure entertainment, but the idea is that you inform your friends about it and then of course there is a link to 'The Machines' featuring the BMW range. If all of that is too much for you, the Prudential's website shows its Chief Executive discussing various aspects of his company's performance, currently suited to narrow band using Real Player and Windows Media Players, but with broadband the interviews would be far more powerful if the picture fuzziness and delay could be avoided (http://www.prudential.co.uk).

Once broadband becomes more widely adopted, it will place the marketer in the role of broadcaster and empower the consumer to interact in real time. Suppliers, distributors, customers, and field staff could all be contacted with news updates or other important imformation. In time, it would be possible to conduct some sales presentations in real time, especially for follow-up calls. Consumers can be empowered to choose what they want to see. A replay of a favourite advertisement, a virtual sightseeing tour or anything on demand would be possible. Already with the latter, video on demand technology is already possible allowing the consumer to select the movie and replay, stop and search just like the real thing. This could be extended into virtual VCR, so that if a particular sports event or episode of a soap were missed, it would be possible to catch up on demand.

For broadband to achieve its full potential, technology, marketing and content need to be in line. A failure in any one can lead to delays and disappointment. As more material is compressed from video format, as new marketing applications are found and as broadband is installed, the power of the internet will be demonstrated to an even greater degree than in the first wave revolution.

The future of internet marketing?

So what of the future of the internet in marketing? There are almost as many answers as there are pundits. What is certain is that more and more users will be attracted to the internet; bandwidth increases will enable more powerful applications and real-time communication (Karakaya and Charlton, 2002); and finally the technologies will become more integrated, whether they are television-, PC-, or mobile-based and might even integrate some other home management systems such as hi-fi, security and climate control. To some, the internet will become part of television entertainment (Duboff and Spaeth, 2000), and others argue for more mobile media through 3G and even 4G, but most consider the future role of the PC for internet access to be limited in comparison (Feather, 2002).

For marketers this not only means greater opportuinities for service provison, but also a more powerful medium for reaching consumers. it means more online research using chat-based focus groups, e-mail and internet-based surveys, more secure online buying, more of a role for intermediaries to search, select and recommend buying options, as most organisations offer some form of electronic transaction facility (Tapp, 2002).

Tapp (2002) goes on to argue that **infomediaries** will act on behalf of consumers, not sellers in taking the pain out of the buying process and they in part will replace traditional intermediaries. These infomediaries will gather information on preferences, record information on purchases, and build, in time, a holistic view of consumer purchases and preferences. One request will produce a range of alternatives with preferences by geography, brand, specifications, price points and other recorded learned critieria taken into account.

Finally, in a mobile, last-minute society, wireless internet access will provide significant opportunities for attracting transient trade. Feather (2002) believes that there will be a move from 'www' to 'mmm' (mobile media mode), reflecting the increased use of access via mobiles. This will be considered later in this chapter. To Feather, the range of applications from mmm is very large indeed:

> *Appliances will sense when food stocks need replenishing and order replacements to be delivered automatically to the home. Cars will call home, turning on appliances, setting room temperatures, filling the jacuzzi, and starting dinner. Even physical health will be automatically monitored and appropriate steps taken on your behalf.*
>
> Feather (2002)

He then goes on to argue that by 2010, the internet will account for 31 per cent of all retail spending and most bricks and mortar retailers will be in trouble if they have not embraced e-tailing, largely due to the fully integrated nature of internet usage in individuals' lifestyles.

All of these exciting developments will depend less on technology, however; indeed in a number of cases the technology already exists. They will depend upon customer willingness to trust and participate with e-anything along with the suppliers of information and commerce services. With the service comes the loss of privacy when it is fully realised that virtually every click on the internet can be recorded and analysed. So the power will shift to the consumer for as long the consumer is willing to use the low costs of switching and searching to full advantage. In part, that runs counter to many of the points mentioned earlier in this book about brand and company loyalty, buying inertia and risk aversion with some purchases.

Marketing and new media

As we have already seen in this chapter, technology is having a big impact on marketing. Two previously parallel technologies are now merging to create new opportunities that could revolutionise some aspects of marketing as we currently know it.

First, digital technology has enabled marketing to become increasingly driven by databases that can be constantly updated, refined and accessed to identify ever-smaller target groups of customers. Data capture, as we saw in Chapter 6, can record geodemographic data such as age, gender, income, and postcode along with some lifestyle data. The additional dimension is now, however, the ability to track previous transactions and all interactions between the business and the customer. Every click, every portal used and every search can be and often is recorded for customer profiling. This means that mass segmentation can be replaced with smaller segments and closer and closer targeting to ensure that the marketing mix can be increasingly tailored subtly for different groups.

Second, digitalisation has created new media opportunities to target messages better and to enable a far more effective personalised approach to acquiring and retaining customers. The advent of e-mail, wireless marketing and interactive television (iTV) has added a new dimension to integrated marketing communication and fragmented media usage to a degree not considered possible until a few years ago (Barwise, 2002). These new media opportunities have not replaced more traditional print and broadcast media, but are supplementing them as resources are reallocated to allow mass advertising and brand building *and* the more direct customer contact that is possible using new media. The success of most new media, however, relies on the consumer responding to them, but increasingly consumers have to give permission to be approached through these media – they have to **opt-in**. Sending unwanted 'junk' e-mails or text messages can actually detract from a brand's reputation and the trust that consumers place in it.

Digital technology and new media are, therefore, important change agents in marketing in general and customer interaction in particular. At a time when more and more data on individual consumers are being gathered and held by marketers, and when media are increasingly becoming fragmented by targeted approaches, better integration is needed to ensure that all of the marketing elements considered in this book are reconsidered in the light of the bricks, clicks and interactive world. This section therefore examines the impact of three main elements of new media: **e-mail marketing**, **wireless marketing** and **interactive television** marketing.

E-mail marketing

More and more people use e-mail on a regular basis. A survey by Net Value estimated that in any one month we each send on average 12.3 e-mails and receive 39.1 from 13 million home computers. Overall, in January 2002 in the UK around 550 million e-mails were sent, over twice the number of letters sent over the same period and one-third more e-mails than in Germany or France (Dwek, 2002a). E-mail has thus emerged as a powerful means of communication that marketers are increasingly adopting as part of their promotional activity. The trouble is, as with any medium, there are risks arising from bad practice and over-crowding. We primarily use e-mails to keep in touch with friends, colleagues and contacts, and occasionally we use them to search for information or to place an online order. We may even welcome an incoming e-mail from a company that we have done business with previously or where we have declared an interest in what they are offering. What we do not want is to be bombarded with offers of cheap financing deals, special travel discounts, get rich quick schemes, herbal viagra or pornography. Unsurprisingly, most recipients scan the list of incoming e-mails and a first selection is quickly made according to the subject or the sender. Many recipients are also wary of receiving viruses via e-mails from unrecognised sources and therefore tend to delete 'cold calling' e-mails without opening them, just to be safe.

Marketers are attracted to the potential of e-mail marketing as a communication tool that can target individuals rather than using mass media approaches. Carefully designed e-mail marketing can help to create initial contact as well as helping to develop an online relation-

eg

Love it or hate it, Chelsea FC has a loyal following of fans, including 30,000 who are more than happy to be contacted by the soccer club. When Chelsea decided to launch a television channel with Sky, it used those fans as targets for an e-mail campaign. Research indicated that 56 per cent of the fans accessed the club's website on a daily basis and most would be highly receptive to a direct offer. The campaign, part of a wider promotional exercise, featured three e-mails highlighting Chelsea TV, giving details of a subscription hotline, and offering the incentive of a competition, along with further information. The campaign was a great success. The Chelsea TV call centre experienced three times the volume of calls in the period just after the e-mails were sent out and 91 per cent of subscribers were familiar with the campaign before the TV channel launch (http://www.edesigns.co.uk).

ship once transactions have taken place. The aim from a marketing perspective is primarily to encourage the reader to look at a website and to obtain permission to send more information to the recipient or to a third party. Typical uses of an e-mail marketing campaign are shown in Figure 24.1.

A survey by the Direct Marketing Association (DMA) with Experian revealed that although a significant number of companies were using e-mail marketing, only 8.5 per cent of respondents said that it accounted for more than 20 per cent of their marketing budget. Thus e-mail campaigns are still in their infancy, but are expected to increase significantly in the coming years. The most mentioned benefits were low cost, speed and ease of delivery, with the greatest concerns being the intrusiveness of e-mail and the association with junk mail. Surprisingly, only a small percentage mentioned driving prospects or customers to a website, yet for some this is the most powerful role for e-mail in an integrated campaign (Murphy, 2002).

Rizzi (2001) argues that e-mail marketing has gone through three distinct phases since the first messages were sent through cyberspace in 1971, as shown in Figure 24.2. First there was the 'Broadcast/Spam Era' when e-mails were sent out indiscriminately, often with little attempt to target and tailor messages to the recipient. Consider sending out an e-mail message about Chelsea TV to an Arsenal supporter. Not only would response rates be very

Figure 24.1 Typical uses of e-mail marketing

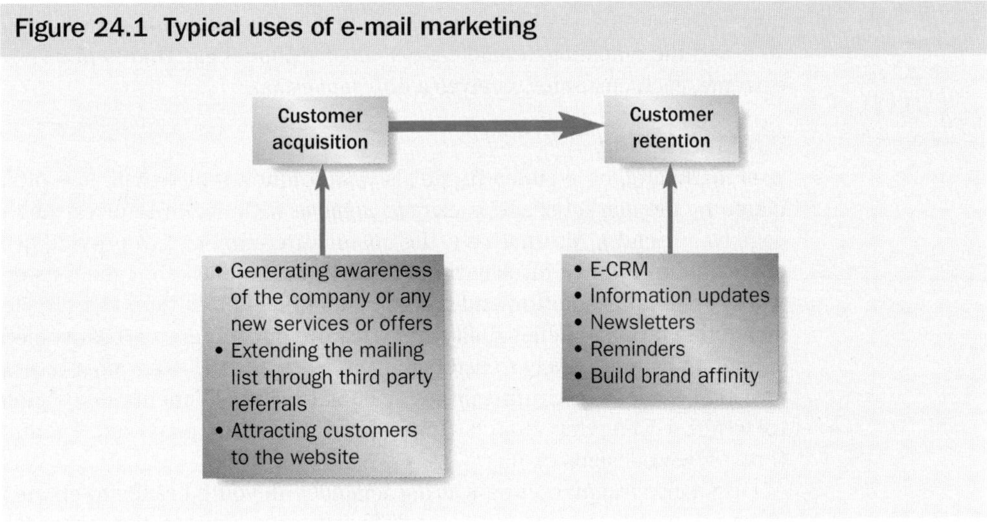

Figure 24.2 E-mail marketing evolution

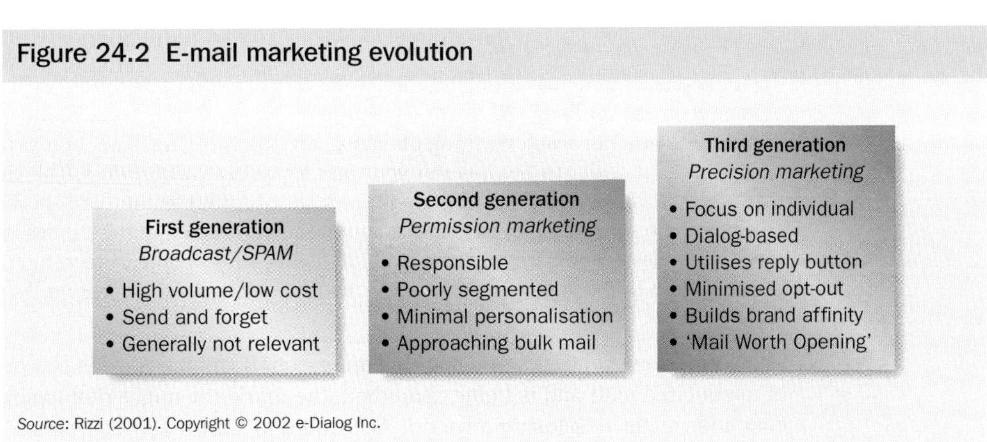

Source: Rizzi (2001). Copyright © 2002 e-Dialog Inc.

low, but it might actually generate (even more!) hostility to the sender. Some companies still operate this way, although European regulation is threatening to restrict spamming by moving from '**opt-out**' to '**opt-in**' schemes, thus assuming that people do not want to get e-mails unless they specifically request them. This has been prompted by the intrusive nature and sometimes dubious content of some spam e-mails.

The second generation represents the majority of e-mail marketers at present. **Permission marketing** offers the consumer the opportunity to volunteer to receive regular messages on special offers or new products (Dawe, A. 2002). Effectively it is an opt-in system but has been liable to some abuse as the low cost and higher response rates from e-mail have been interpreted by some senders as permission to bulk e-mail rather than to select messages relevant to recognised customer needs and interests (Rizzi, 2001). Permission is the starting point, not the objective of an e-mail campaign so it is not, therefore, surprising that e-mail marketing is moving into a third phase, 'Precision Marketing'. This combines the power of e-mail with the power of IT to record and analyse responses to ensure even greater targeting and almost individual CRM. In theory, each customer could receive slightly different mail.

An example of precision marketing can be drawn from specialist bookselling. A bookseller could have e-mail contact details of 2,000 quality customers. By tracking enquiries, orders, areas visited on the website and so on, those who are primarily interested in French history could receive one list of special offers by e-mail and those with a passion for aeroplanes another. By focusing down even further, the French history list could be divided into those interested specifically in the Napoleonic era and those interested in the First World War, and the e-mailings could reflect those differences. That is precision marketing. At the extreme, each customer receives a different e-mail.

Viral marketing

Viral marketing, or 'e-mail a friend', is word-of-mouth by e-mail. It is often deliberately stimulated by the marketer and is easy to achieve with use of a forwarding facility ('e-mail this page to a friend'). Alternatively, the customer could elect to provide details of friends who might like to receive information direct from the marketer. As considered in Chapter 15, word-of-mouth promotion and recommendation is often the most effective form of communication in terms of believability and trust. If your friend says that something is a good deal, you might be more likely to listen and act. Normally the offer must be good and an incentive provided, such as discounts, prizes or gifts. Chelsea TV mentioned earlier ran a competition to win a UEFA Cup match ticket for those who provided e-mail details of friends (http://www.edesigns.co.uk).

Originally viral marketing was associated with youth brands to create a bit of excitement. If the material or the attachment is different and enjoyable, then there is more chance that it will be passed on. Lastminute.com (*see* Case Study 1.2), Budweiser and Levi's have all used viral marketing.

eg

Sara Lee used viral marketing for Brylcreem as part of an integrated campaign. Press advertising featured an Easy Wash Wax hair product for men. The creative message was of a man in middle of a car wash washing his hair, carrying the strap line 'Use your Head', implying that it is a lot easier to get wax out your hair if you use this product. The viral campaign gave access to a 15-second video clip along the lines of a TV commercial, showing the man in the car with the sunroof open so that his hair could be washed in the car wash. This was sent to people on an e-mail database and to 2,500 highly viral people. Interested readers can download it from http://www.punchbaby.com, a viral factory site (*Marketing Week*, 2001b).

There are, however, risks in using this approach. If the message is too promotional, smacks of unsolicited mail and is being spammed, the marketer might risk losing a customer or the customer might risk losing a friend. According to Carter (2002a), this is causing marketers to seek to add more value to their viral campaigns on the premise that it is becoming harder to get customers to listen, let alone act. This can be achieved through an interactive web facility, for example as used by men's toiletry brand Lynx and its 'zerogravity' campaign targeted at 18- to 24-year-old men,. The www.lynxwhitelabel.com site enables the user to mix a dance track and create a personalised DJ name before sending it on to a third party. Response rates were high, with 45 per cent arriving at the site via an 'e-mail a friend' facility, and 20 per cent of them subsequently registered on the site (Ray, 2001).

Customer acquisition

Viral marketing is one way of building an e-mailing list. For many of the reasons considered in Chapter 18, the marketer must add to and refine the list from a combination of off- and online sources. *Offline lists* can be purchased from specialist brokers, or be derived from surveys, customer lists, guarantee forms, old enquiries and competitions. Many of the criteria considered on p. 749 still apply.

Lists, whether they are purchased or rented, must be based on permission, a willingness to receive e-mails acknowledged by an opt-in mechanism. It is risky to use large, cheap lists of people to whom your communication may be most unwelcome. Some list owners are taking particular care about how their lists are used to avoid inappropriate or over-use. Lifestyle data gatherers such as Claritas and Consodata often record e-mail addresses as do online list builders such as Bananalotto and My Offers which sell permission-based lists. Some website operators now offer lists as a sideline, gathered from the users of their sites. TheMutual.net and Another.com, for example, have developed lists of relatively affluent young users who may be an attractive target for an e-mailing. Despite the attraction of these lists, the click through rate may however be low, and rarely does it exceed 10 per cent for cold mailings (http://www.emailvision.com).

Online lists depend heavily on the sender's ability to track contacts from within its website. Sources can include online surveys, website registrations and responses to competitions and offers over the website. Web forms vary in the degree of information required beyond the e-mail details. Some seek data to enable customer profiling to take place and better targeted messages to be sent before gathering the more specific information generated when/if clicks or orders are made. It is often advisable to seek only limited information at any one go, perhaps with three or four questions, rather than making the site visitor feel that they are being interrogated and delayed unnecessarily. If that happens, the visitor might lose patience or become uncomfortable about giving personal information away and fail to complete the registration process.

eg

When Vodafone decided to adopt an e-mail marketing campaign to promote m-commerce in B2B markets, it established a list of existing and potential customers and then assessed them against pre-determined qualifying criteria to ensure that they were appropriate decision makers. At that stage Vodafone gathered the appropriate opt-in permission to enable it to e-mail only willing recipients confidently.

Customer retention

One of the greatest benefits for e-mail marketing is its ability to create and build a relationship with a customer on an individual basis. It can, therefore, play an important part in any customer relationship (CRM) programme. This requires a 'permission centre' (http://www.emailvision.com) comprising a list of opt-in respondents. Once the list has been developed, the response mechanism tracking can develop usable and powerful customer profiles. E-mails can be tracked for opening, clicks and purchases, so quite a detailed history, far superior to anything direct mail can achieve, can soon be built up.

Much depends on the quality of the lists used. According to Hendricks (2002), e-mail lists can be segmented into:

- openers;
- clickers;
- repeat clickers;
- buyers;
- repeat buyers.

All of that can be tracked and recorded in a database. When it is subsequently linked with behavioural and lifestyle data, a highly targeted e-mailing or e-CRM campaign can emerge that achieves Rizzi's (2001) three golden rules for e-mail marketing: precision, precision, precision. Repeat clickers living in Scotland with an interest in gardening would receive very different messages from openers who also live in Scotland and like gardening. The more powerful and carefully designed the database, the easier it is to define small, well-focused subsegments for targeting. The trend now is towards smaller and smaller segments, *micro segments*, perhaps comprising a list of just 100 people (Trollinger, 2002).

Although recording customer use of websites is a valuable tool for targeting offers and messages, some organisations now use e-mail newsletters to keep in touch with current and previous customers. These newsletters can play an important part of a more general CRM programme.

eg

The British Museum runs an e-mail newsletter for its opt-in subscribers. The content varies but focuses primarily on featured books such as *Ming Ceramics in The British Museum* and *A Pocket Dictionary of Egyptian Gods and Goddesses*, along with information on new products in the store and up-to-date information on exhibitions and events. This enables it to maintain contact with customers who are sympathetic to the mission of the museum and who may be prepared to support it with online or store purchases of its specialised book and ancillary product collections (http://www.digivate.com).

Personalisation is the aim of most marketers when building customer relationships. When successful, it combines all the benefits of personal selling with the cost effectiveness of technology-driven marketing. Personalisation can take many forms including:

- content;
- offer proposition;
- prefered frequency of contact;
- transmission format (text, flash, etc.);
- subjects of interest;
- personalisation by spend, product or interest.

The challenge for the e-mail marketer is to ensure that the database can facilitate data gathering and extraction to suit the particular purposes of a campaign.

Creative message design

Targeted, permission-based customer lists win every time, especially for e-CRM campaigns. Evidence from Forrester Research (*Marketing Week*, 2001a) highlighted that consumers were willing and ready to receive e-mails as long as they were relevant, quality messages and definitely not spammed. In some sectors, especially sport affiliations, hobby-related and travel areas, unsubscription rates can be very low. E-mail is becoming part of our lives, with 56 per cent of consumers in the 16–34 age group spending around nine hours a week online.

Many of the principles of creative direct mail copy apply to e-mail messages. There is a need to make the right offer with a strong response-orientated copy (Friesen, 2002). This means careful targeting, a sound knowledge of customer clicking behaviour, personalisation wherever possible and tailored rather than bland messages for mass e-mailing. The type of message will depend on the e-mail format, plain text, graphical html or rich media. Given the speed of response to campaigns, with 90 per cent of responses within a 48-hour period, adjustment can be made after piloting (Rizzi, 2001).

eg

Viewlondon.co.uk is a web-based guide to 11,500 restaurants, bars, pubs and clubs in London. In order to attract a greater number of hits on the site, given that its ultimate success lies in its effectiveness as an advertising medium, it ran a competition entitled 'Are you Cockney or Mockney?' testing the visitor's knowledge of London. Although anyone could play, to have a chance of a prize, such as CDs, free drinks and free tickets, full registration was required. During the campaign, there were over 500,000 page clicks, the game was played 98,000 times and most importantly for Viewlondon, 2,500 new registrations were made. To keep people interested, there are new games and quizzes each month (Murphy, 2002). So if you know whether it's the Taj Mahal, Eiffel Tower or Statue of Liberty that is in Paris, your name, postcode and e-mail address are all you need to enter. All these traffic builders support its aim to become the first point of reference for Londoners searching for entertainment in London.

There are some simple rules for creative e-mail messages that can act as a checklist as shown in Table 24.9.

Table 24.9 Guidelines for effective e-mail creative design

- Target messages to hit market micro segments
- Respect those who ask for their names to be removed from the list
- Capture usage at all stages: opening, clicks, response
- Have time-limited offers
- Have final reminders with 24 or 48 hours to go
- Get to the point early with the offer
- Make it worthwhile to visit the site: offer free access, gift, voucher or discount
- Personalise the message to 'I' and 'we'
- Remember past events: holidays, birthdays, etc.
- Make response clear and easy
- Integrate the e-mail campaign into the broader promotional strategy
- Always measure and analyse performance

Source: adapted from Friesen (2002) based on excerpts from 'How to develop an effective e-mail creative strategy', in *Target Marketing Magazine*, Feb. 2002.

Even smaller organisations can, with creative design, use e-mail marketing effectively. For them it can be a very powerful promotional tool, given the often low level of resources available for promotion.

eg

The Fabulous Bakin' Boys from Witney near Oxford uses e-mail marketing. It created a database of jokes which could be downloaded from its website by registered users. The registration process asks basic questions such as gender, age, where you have seen the company's muffins for sale, and when you eat muffins. The prospect of some free samples is mentioned. It then introduced online games and cheeky advertisements are regularly mailed out to previous website respondents (http://www.bakinboys.co.uk). The games, such as Muffin Munchin' and Cake Invaders are designed to attract repeat traffic and each can be 'mailed to a mate' as part of a viral campaign. Online ordering is possible and look out for the fly past (visit the site to see what we mean)! The theme 'Live fast, play hard and eat muffins' enabled the new company, which is growing at a rapid rate, to be less conventional than a larger company to stimulate interest in the site (Hunt, 2001).

As more organisations become familiar with using the internet as more than just a brochure supplement, the use of e-mail linked website activity will also grow for smaller businesses. The fragmentation of high cost, national media and the availability of targeted media that are within the reach of small business marketing budgets mean that there is likely to be a lot greater use of e-mail marketing in the next few years.

Response and review

One of the major advantages of e-mail campaigns is the speed of response. Ray (2001) described the situation at a holiday auction company where a newsletter issued between 4 p.m. and 5.50 p.m. will generate a significant number of responses by 6.30 p.m. and the bulk of the responses are in within two days. This means that considerable care must be taken to have a system in place to handle the response traffic generated. In part, the technology infra-

marketing **in action**

Stay out of jail

Centennial, a leading supplier of technology inventory management solutions, wants to keep you out of jail. The problem of software piracy is well known, but less well known is the growing pressure for better software auditing to ensure that licences have been obtained and are being complied with. Software manufacturers want guilty companies to be fined heavily and in extreme cases, the Directors responsible jailed for up to two years. Inspections from Microsoft, The Federation Against Software Theft or The Business Software Alliance could reveal unauthorised software and then lead to prosecution and a lot of negative publicity. Desktop PCs often have many different specifications and different software packages with different licensing requirements, especially when users are free to download directly from the internet, which can be very confusing. The issue then for Centennial is how to get the message about the seriousness of piracy across to people who either don't know or don't think it is a real problem and are therefore likely to screen out any weak or subtle warning messages.

Centennial decided to run an integrated personalised e-mail and telemarketing campaign to warn IT Directors about their personal responsibility and liability if they allow non-licensed software to be used, whether or not they know it is happening. The challenge was to get across to a busy, highly selective audience the urgency of asking certain questions about licensing within their own organisations so that they could be assured of compliance.

Inbox Media designed a campaign that was hard-hitting, memorable and clearly linked to the need for a response. The target audience of IT Directors and decision makers was identified and highly personalised e-mails were sent direct to their inboxes. A further click enabled a movie to be played in an e-mail window with full animation and audio, like a personal television advertisement. A series of questions were flashed in the advertisement, such as 'Are you using unlicensed software?', 'Not sure?', 'Not enough time to check?', ending with a dramatic 'You've got TIME now', accompanied by the sound of a prison door slamming shut along with a visual of prison bars. By adopting such powerful imagery, Inbox was seeking to override complacency and to use visuals and sound to end the ad with a stark finality suggesting that the game would be up if no action was taken. Recipients were then invited to use a viral facility to forward the message to a colleague, and/or to visit the Centennial website to find out more. An opt-out was also provided.

Inbox used its own technology to track the e-mails in real time according to the response generated. The target was a significant increase in response rates and then to link them either to direct sales visits or a telemarketing follow-up. The campaign generated a good response rate and led to many more enquiries to Centennial about its software licensing services.

Sources: http://www.centennial.co.uk; http://www.inbox.co.uk, and with grateful thanks to Nik Margolis, Inbox Media.

structure can help to handle 'bounced' e-mails, undeliverable e-mails and routine enquiries, but in some cases, it may be necessary to have an inbound e-mail answering service.

eg

In the Vodafone example mentioned earlier, a real-time reporting and tracking engine was employed that could list how many e-mails were sent, how many opened and how many clicked through. Normally, only 50 e-mails at a time were sent to allow for tracking, primarily over a six-hour period. Of the e-mails sent, over 50 per cent were opened and read and 21 per cent clicked through to the appropriate section of the website. Many of the latter were then converted into leads by the telemarketing team (http://www.inbox.co.uk).

Overall, targeted permission-based mailing campaigns generate an average response rate of 10–15 per cent, but this can drop to 2 per cent for bought-in prospect e-mail addresses (Murphy, 2002). After all responses are in, the analysis of campaign effectiveness can begin. This often requires careful pre-planning to cross-check unsubscribers, assign codes to different target segments or different message types and to record the type of response generated, including where clicking has taken place but no formal response has followed. Data measured by campaign, customer or product on the number of openings and clicks, unsubscription rates, and bouncing, as well as responses, can be collected. This is an invaluable aid to updating records and further campaign planning.

Wireless marketing

If you are a Cahoot customer and about to go overdrawn you may receive a text message to warn you, and if you are on the Blue Arrow temps register you may be texted with information about vacancies as they become available (Middleton, 2002). Text messaging is becoming an ever popular form of wireless marketing. Wireless marketing, sometimes called **m-marketing** or **mobile marketing**, has emerged as another major opportunity to target customers more closely, and as with e-mail marketing, its application is expected to grow significantly over the next few years. With over 1 billion mobiles in the world and 8 billion text messages exchanged in Europe every month, it is not surprising that marketers are attracted to the possibility of being able to reach consumers when and where they want (http://www.flytxt.com). Wireless marketing can also include messages direct to PC via the internet.

M-marketing provides the means to carry voice messages, but is primarily used for sending text messages to targeted individuals at any time. Because of its intrusiveness and because different customers will be more receptive at different times of day, however, the m-marketer must fully appreciate consumer lifestyles and be careful in setting the right tone of the communication to avoid damaging any trust in the sender's brand (Carter, 2002b). Consider, for example, your receptivity to a text message received as you dash for an important meeting compared with one received over a relaxing lunchtime meal.

As in e-marketing, compiling target lists and profiles is an essential staring point. Consumers must be able to choose whether they want to receive information and there is a responsibility to ensure that any information is relevant. Irritation will soon grow if a torrent of mortgage deal messages are sent to students struggling to find next week's rent. It also follows that it must be easy to opt-out from receiving messages. Again, therefore, as with e-mail marketing, content selection should derive from customer profiling, but because of the medium, most text messages need to be short, alerting the individual to a special offer or promotion or engaging them with an interactive game that could direct them to a website.

eg

When Dunkin' Donuts opened its Rome franchise outlet it made heavy use of mobile technology. A press and poster campaign featured a telephone number that invited consumers to call to receive a text message voucher by return. The voucher could be presented at the new store when ordering donuts. Further questions were then asked of the voucher-holder at the point of purchase to build a database of mobile contact numbers and lifestyle information that could all be used for future promotions. The campaign, although difficult to administer proved a successful traffic builder for store visits and has enabled an ongoing series of promotions to be considered (*Marketing Week*, 2002a).

Most text messaging, such as the one in the Dunkin' Donuts example above, is currently SMS (short messaging service), which, as the name implies, usually means short, sharp messages to remind or inform. Marks & Spencer, for example, used e-mail and text messaging vouchers to encourage shoppers to visit a new branch in London with the offer of a free lunch, while Diageo ran trials targeting 16- to 24-year-olds with SMS text information and money-off vouchers if they provided their mobile numbers on entering some shopping centres (Carter, 2002b). Organisations such as Cadbury, Nike, Pepsi and the Ministry of Sound have all used text messaging campaigns successfully as part of their promotional activity. Many campaigns, however, tend to be one-way communication, and fail to inspire or encourage interactivity. The next phase of development is likely to witness integration between voice and text, games, images and sounds to better entertain and engage the receiver (http://www.wirelessmarketing.org.uk).

eg

Warner Brothers and Eurosport formed a marketing partnership to create the first multinational mobile marketing campaign as the film company sought to promote its then forthcoming film *Ocean's Eleven*. The campaign ran for six weeks simultaneously in the UK, Germany, Italy, Spain and Netherlands on television trailers on Eurosport. At the end of the commercial, viewers were invited to enter a text message competition that offered as one of the prizes a visit to Warner Bros Movie World. The real aim was to generate awareness for the film but also to help build long-term relationships with Euro consumers via their mobile phones. Respondents were able to opt-in to receive information on all future film releases (Chandiramani, 2001).

A survey of cost per response from different promotional media, shown in Table 24.10, demonstrates the effectiveness of SMS compared with some other media.

Table 24.10 Average cost per response from promotional media

SMS	£1.42
Classified ad in the local newspaper	£2.50
Flyer distribution	£2.67
Local radio advertising	£66.00
Local door drop	£20.00
Local paper insert with a circulation of 95,000	£24.51

Source: Middleton (2002).

The very strength of SMS could soon become its weakness, as more and more marketers are attracted to this new medium. One of the potential barriers to the development of text messaging is the continued bad practice of sending unsolicited text messages, along the lines of the earlier comments on e-mail spamming. One example that will surely become a classic was when an individual became alarmed at receiving a text message asking him to report to his local army recruitment centre after September 11th, 2001 only to find that it was an advertisement for a computer war game. Some other activities are scams designed to encourage premium rate telephone calls. There are computer programs that will generate random mobile numbers and send out SMS messages to all of them, whether there has been an opt-in or not, thus constant vigilance is needed from the service providers.

All of that must be measured, however, against those who would welcome reminders or updates on something of relevance. How many garages contact their customers to remind them that their car is due for its annual service? Text messaging would enable low cost reminders to be sent out along with a call for instant action to make a booking.

eg

Harper Collins targeted the readers of the teenage girls magazine *Sugar* as part of a promotion for two new book series under the Mary Kate and Ashley brand. The target was girls aged from 7 to 16 and the main objective of the campaign was to encourage them to seek the titles out in-store. An opt-in system was used and an important consideration was not to destroy the trust in the Sugar brand by association with inappropriate advertising. With such campaigns, response rates can be as high as 30 per cent, compared with the 1 to 2 per cent from unsolicited, poorly targeted text messaging campaigns (Head, 2002; http://www.aerodeon.co.uk). Harper Collins has to be mindful, however, of the wider implications of text messaging to under-age children and that some parents may not appreciate such approaches.

To counter many of the concerns over unsolicited text messaging, the UK, along with a number of other European countries, will be introducing tighter controls under the European E-commerce Directive. This will require service providers to make information about themselves easily and permanently available and SMS advertisements will have to have a clearly specified sponsor. The legislation and guidelines will only affect European countries, however, although an increasing number of spammed messages originate from outside the EU (Dawe, T., 2002).

The alternative to SMS is interactive voice response (IVR), regarded by some as a lower cost alternative to SMS that in addition can generate revenue from call charges. Virgin Mobile has introduced a 4321 service that enables diallers to access a voice activated portal to gain information on sport, entertainment, and news; to enter a virtual shopping mall; to buy CDs and DVDs; and even get a horoscope. Charged at 10p per minute, callers can, for example, find information on a good pub or restaurant in their vicinity, effectively making the service another media outlet for advertising (Jolley, 2002).

The main additional benefit of IVR is that by the inclusion of a voice, a human element is introduced and a less virtual experience is created. However, its continued progress will be determined by its effectiveness in generating traffic. Consumers are aware that calls cost money and there is a perception that text messaging is cheaper. In addition, the marketing organisation has to react to calls rather than being proactive (as with SMS) so the hit rates are a lot less certain.

Users

The target market for wireless marketing campaigns tends to be younger and more willing to try new ways of communicating (Barwise and Strong, 2002). Mobile usage has become an important part of our lifestyles; witness the scenes in any High Street or, more annoyingly, in a crowded commuter train. It has moved from being a status symbol to an essential communication device, and fits well with the rushed, high pressure, and last-minute lifestyles of many younger people who leave decisions to the last minute and often make them 'on the run' (again, *see* Case Study 1.2 on Lastminute.com). That plays into the hands of the m-marketers.

Happy Dog, a wireless marketing consultancy, proposed three broad categories of prime customers for targeting in its Moby Study (reported in Carter 2002b):

- *Nomads*. Usually in the 18–24 age range, have few responsibilities, mainly live at home and tend towards last-minute decision-making rather than forward planning.
- *Gatherers*. Usually in the 25–40+ age range with the normal range of family responsibilities and career expectations. The mobile is used as an extension of the domestic phone as a matter of routine.
- *Hunters*. May be in the 20–35 age range, with few family responsibilities but enjoying to the full the stability and lifestyle that a career can bring.

These three groups may not represent all mobile users, but the profiles do suggest that the propensity to respond and the information sought will vary considerably between groups. This again highlights the importance of considering lifestyles as well as actual product usage behaviour when deciding on a particular campaign.

Systems and processes

Any successful wireless marketing campaign needs to be underpinned by an enabling technological infrastructure either established in-house or through the use of a specialist agency. Such a system is shown in Figure 24.3 which highlights how applications can be supported by databases, systems, network providers, and handling logistics.

Figure 24.3 Wireless marketing system

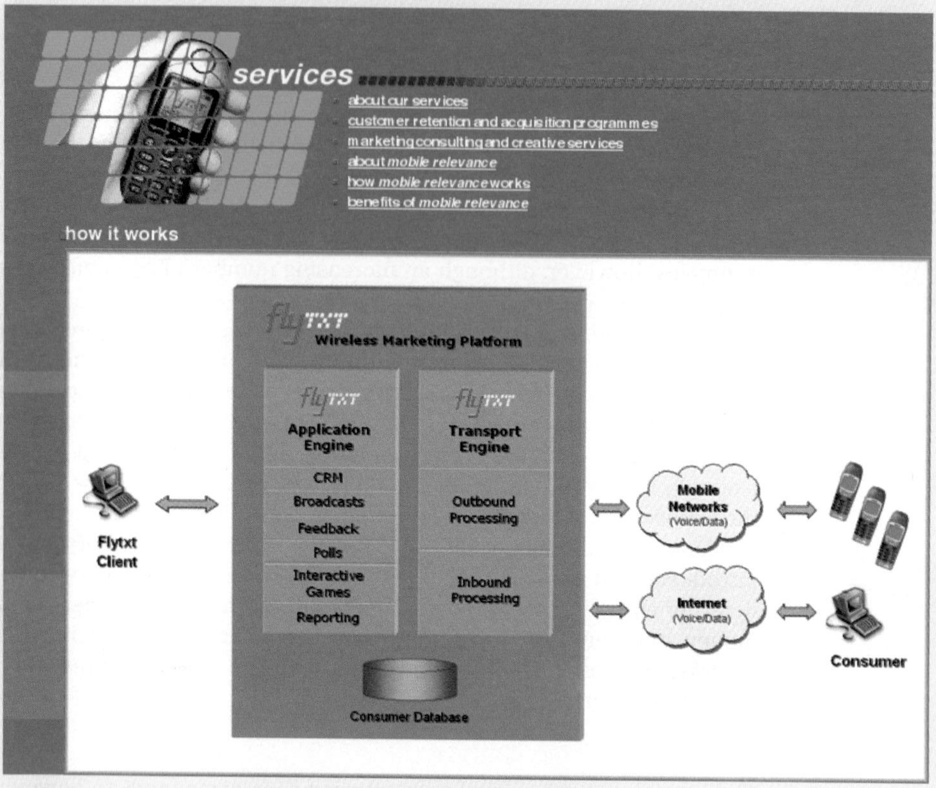

Source: http://www.flytext.com/how.html; Flytxt (2002).

The technological infrastructure enables reporting and tracking, personalisation, and the interactivity interface, and it must be capable of handling large numbers of outbound and inbound messages without crashing the system. Many organisations prefer to use established technology available from specialist agencies. Inbox (http://www.inbox.co.uk), for example, has a response management system that on receipt of an inbound message, sends a text message to the salesperson, orders a brochure to be sent to the sender by a fulfilment house, and e-mails an agent in a call centre. The priority then is to integrate the sophisticated technology that the specialist agency provides with the systems that individual marketers operate. MindMatics, for example, offers a 'Wireless Interactive Toolkit' that allows companies to start mobile marketing through standard applications without the need for any additional infrastructure. It uses a Windows-based application that connects directly with MindMatics' SMS gateway for sending and receiving.

The integration of these systems emphasises that it is dangerous to give too much attention to the creative and marketing application at the expense of the infrastructure that enables it to be adopted in the first place and to proceed effectively.

Next generation

SMS has limitations, in that only relatively simple text messages can be sent and it has been suggested that the number of text messages will soon start to plateau until the next generation of text services starts to become more widely available (Wray, 2002). The next innovation may incorporate wider use of EMS (enhanced messaging service) allowing small logos and icons to be sent over the air. A number of operators are, however, delaying major investment until MMS (multimedia messaging service) is introduced. MMS allows full colour pictures to be sent over the air and in conjunction with video has the power to bring a handset to life. This will enable pictures, melodies, animation and styled text to be fully exploited in message design. Currently, however, the mass launch of the necessary 3G technology has been delayed and only pilot schemes are in operation (*see* Case Study 9.1).

There are also issues about consumer acceptance of the new technology and their willingness to spend significantly more for the enhanced services because of the higher than expected cost of the handsets. Most text messaging takes place between friends and although it might be convenient for marketers if enhanced MMS is adopted, the added value to the consumer is small unless there are significant changes in the desire for accessing information and entertainment on the move. It could be that the latest score from Wimbledon or the World Cup, or stock market prices could be relevant to some, but that has to be related to increased rental or service charges. Others have argued that the best services have not yet been dreamed up, but the hard reality is that there will have to be clear evidence that financial rewards will flow from any investment, given the early stage of the technology lifecycle (Shillingford, 2002).

Despite uncertainty over the timing and scale of impact of MMS, Forrester Research concluded that by 2006, 37 per cent of all message traffic will be sent by MMS as long as the operators' focus shifts from the technology to customer usage (Forrester Research, 2002). Some companies are raring to go with MMS. Hasbro, which owns the board game Monopoly, tested a customised version using 2.5G rather than the 3G technology associated with MMS. By offering colour images, moving pictures and sound, it wanted to establish how effective mobile phones could be in drawing custom to its £95 MyMonopoly offer on http://www.mymonopoly.com (*Marketing Week*, 2002d).

Making an offer of a monopoly game priced at £95 to phone owners is a gamble that Hasbro has taken. Just what the uptake will be has yet to be seen.

Source: MindMatics.

marketing *in action*

Hey, sexy!

Kiss 100 is London's youth radio station. It started life as a pirate station but was legalised in 1990. Its success has come from the central role it has played in popularising dance music and pioneering the growth of genres such as House, Garage, Hip Hop Jungle, Ambient and Breakbeat. It is recognised as being at the cutting edge of dance music and therefore attracts a loyal band of listeners. It seeks to generate ratings by day, and a reputation for being 'hot and sexy' by night through its associated clubs. Every week, it reaches around 50 per cent of London's 15 to 24-year-olds who are among its 1.5 million listeners per week. It attracts a further 2 million viewers on its non-stop music channel on Sky Digital TV and the brand has been extended to holidays, clubs and network dance shows. Its Kiss CDs have sold 2 million.

Kiss is an experience brand that appeals to young people who enjoy fun and being sexy and has attracted an almost cult following. Kiss, therefore, wanted to use new media to create a strong customer relationship management programme (CRM) for a generation that is unlikely to be responsive to direct mail and general mass media advertising. Kiss 100, with help from its retained creative agency, Angel Uplifting Marketing and Flytxt, the wireless marketing expert, has thus used SMS effectively to promote greater listening and brand loyalty among its most loyal, committed listeners.

As part of a previous promotion, a database of 56,000 mobile phone numbers was created, called 'HeySexy' Club. This database of listeners who had opted-in to receive more information created a valuable marketing tool for maintaining regular contact with a willing audience, but it needed creativity and worthwhile ideas to keep them on the list and involved. Listeners initially registered by text message, via the website, or through a 0700HEYSEXY telephone line. Data captured included the registration medium, birth date and gender, as well as the obvious personal details. Two agencies, Flytxt, a mobile marketing specialist, and Angel Uplifting Marketing were then able to design a campaign to improve loyalty through games, competitions and promotions targeted primarily at the HeySexy members.

In all, over 20 different campaigns were designed to retain customer interest. These included:

- *The free 'Bamster' voicemail offer*, whereby listeners could phone an IVR line and download a free Bamster voicemail for their mobiles.
- The *'text to win'* competition that invited listeners to text in to the station while a particular track was being played, the track being repeated several times a day. Winners received a £100 prize, and there was evidence that listeners actually tuned in for longer periods to have a go at the competition.
- *'The Birthday Greeting'*. Every HeySexy member received a greeting from a Kiss DJ on their birthday, usually by the time the member woke up in the morning. The message is clear to the initiated 'HeySexy! Bam Bam here. Happy damn birthday from me and every1else here@Kiss100-have a blinder & keep listening! TXT STP2 unsub.'
- *'The Anonymous Valentine Service'*. Listeners could send anonymous Valentine's messages by texting a message along with the mobile number of loved ones to Kiss 100 for resending.
- *'The Peach Party promotion'* enabled listeners to sign up via text message for a £7 discount at the Peach Party guest list, a Kiss club at the Camden Palais.

The whole series of SMS promotions has been highly successful. Not only has the number of people on the HeySexy list grown, but an average of 13 per cent response rate for campaigns is normally achieved, which is well above what was expected. The response rate for the free Bamster voicemail was over 18 per cent. The Peach Party guest list contained over 16 per cent of all database members.

This example highlights the value of SMS in maintaining loyalty and developing a CRM campaign using a medium that this particular age group is very familiar with and with content that is relevant to its lifestyle and language. Creating and retaining customer loyalty like this is very important to Kiss 100 as it seeks to attack Capital FM's dominant position among London's 15 to 24-year-olds (*Marketing*, 2001).

Sources: *Marketing* (2001); http://www.kiss100.com; and with grateful thanks to Lars Becker and Annabel Knight, Flytxt.

Kiss 100 used its SMS database to send 'Hey Sexy' messages to 15–24-year-olds to encourage them to register their phones and possibly win prizes.

Source: http://www.flytxt.com.

iTV marketing

Interactive television (iTV) marketing is still in its infancy, but does have the potential to revolutionise marketing communications by allowing the user, rather than the advertiser to tailor information content and actions to individual needs. iTV is two-way communication between the consumer and the service provider who is responsible for delivering the communication to a television set-top box via satellite, cable or aerial and then creating the technology for a 'back service' to allow the user to interact. Normally the back service is provided via a normal telephone line, wireless or, as in the case of NTL/Telewest, by special cable.

The problem with the development of iTV marketing relates to the overall take up of digital television, a situation made worse by the demise of ITV Digital in the UK. According to Forrester Research (http://www.forrester.com), there are 7.9 million homes in the UK with iTV, well ahead of France, Spain and Germany combined. However, the majority of applications tend to be linked with live television formats, such as quiz shows, voting, sports action (for example the player cam on Sky Sports), and only to a much lesser extent with interactive advertising. According to Two Way TV (http://www.twowaytv.com), gaming still dominates use. It found that:

- 10 per cent of households play Two Way TV games each month.
- 30 per cent of households play at least one game per month.
- 1.5 million games are played each month.
- Each player spends over £7.50 per month, with heavy users spending £30 per month.

The challenge is to convince advertising agencies and marketers that iTV offers a valuable addition to the media mix.

eg

When Rimmel launched a new range of lipsticks, Exaggerate Hydracolour, it wanted to encourage product sampling among women aged between 16 and 44. It decided to experiment with iTV as part of a TV campaign, so that viewers of Sky could go interactive to request a free sample and have the opportunity to win one of thirty Rimmel cosmetic sets. The creative execution featured a traditional advertisement with a link to go interactive to a supporting advertisement, consistent in its use of voice-over, music and imagery. A single response page was used where viewers could answer a few questions, claim their lipstick, answer a simple question about Rimmel's competitors and then to opt-in or -out of future contact. The maximum on-time expected on the screen was 30 seconds. The campaign generated 52,000 responses, in line with the original objectives and double the normal interactive response rate, at 3.2 per cent. The resulting data were then analysed by lifestyle groups and with 68 per cent opting in, a list of over 30,000 new names was generated, useful for other promotions and offers (NetImperative, 2002).

For iTV to become an important part of the media mix it will have to be accepted by users and valued by advertisers and marketers. As many as 72 per cent of television viewers do not associate the TV with interactivity or commerce (Macklin, 2002). That means a consumer education task for service providers at a time when they are financially stretched building networks and customer bases. Just because the consumer can interact with the television, does not mean that they will. The growth of interactive programme guides (IPG) which help viewers to navigate the multitude of channels by genre, time and other criteria is an important first step in making the bewildering range of screen choices digestible, acting like an internet portal on television. Given the early stage of consumer adoption of interactivity, there is a real risk that marketing initiatives will run ahead of consumer ability to understand how to work the system.

eg

Egg, the Prudential's internet bank, ran an iTV campaign 'Daisy goes to Russia to buy herself a husband (with her credit card)'. The main action point was to encourage credit card registration which could be achieved by pressing the red button on a television handset remote control to go interactive and then blue for registration. However, many consumers became confused, as there were then so many options that it was easy to get lost (http://www.broadbandbananas.com).

From the marketer's perspective the main benefits of iTV advertising and marketing are perceived to be (in order of importance) targeting niche audiences; personalisation and one-to-one dialogue; providing a new channel to market; deepening the brand; and revenue generation (http://www.emarketer.com).

Targeting and personalisation are well ahead of the other perceived benefits. The set-top box is a source of considerable information to the service provider and enables it to build up a user profile just like any other media publisher. For on-screen interactivity, the growing number of specialist television channels covering everything from holidays to music and sport to motoring, allows careful targeting and the profiling of subsequent replies by the box. There is some concern that the power of tracking that is possible from the set-top box raises issues of privacy. Once this is addressed, it may curtail some monitoring (http://www.broadbandbananas.com). In an era of greater personalisation rather than mass media advertising, iTV offers the potential to bring back some of the power of television advertising while also being able to follow through on a more tailored basis. Nissan used iTV to generate leads for its Primera. Viewers can link with full-screen video, explore the features of the car and request a brochure through the service. Such integration makes iTV a powerful complement to the mainstream advertising campaign.

Some organisations have also used iTV as a distribution channel to enable them to take orders on a similar basis to the internet. The ability to respond to an instantaneous desire has been especially beneficial to Domino's Pizza. It uses iTV as a marketing channel to make it easier to order after its on-screen advertisements are broadcast. Although still only generating a small percentage of its total orders, interactive advertising, along with the website, has helped to drive up pizza orders, and this is expected to fuel further growth supported by wider strategies to ensure hot, fast and fresh home delivery (Macklin, 2002; *Marketing Week*, 2002c).

Despite some successes in the use of iTV, it is still early days for more widespread adoption. Even existing digital users regard the television as being for entertainment and the internet for information searching, so with current adopters, the full range of interactive services are rarely activated. The service providers will have to promote the wider service benefits more positively, rather than focusing on the services at present that generate direct revenues. An advertising system that can show a standard car advertisement, for example, and with a press of the 'i button' can provide a menu of further information, show more footage, show the car in a selected colour and even allow a test drive to be organised, all from the comfort of an armchair, has many advantages over more conventional media that require telephone and mail responses. Its role for higher involvement, high priced, infrequently purchased items appears to be stronger than for more routine fmcg purchases.

Currently, around 90 per cent of homes in the Western world have television, but the cost of creating the digital network and providing the boxes and return facility means an initial set up cost of around £320 and £170 per year service cost per household to be recouped from the service providers. Only when the costs are bundled, such as combining telephone, broadband connection and pay-television services, do the costs per unit fall significantly (NetImperative, 2002). Nevertheless, service providers will still only recoup their costs if they can attract advertising revenue. Worldwide, it has been estimated that there are 38 million iTV users, but this is expected to grow to 200 million by 2006 (http://www.emarketer.com). Such growth in usage, as long as consumer confusion is resolved, will mean that iTV marketing can then play its full part in new media development.

All three forms of new media are still evolving, reflecting technological advances such as broadband, MMS messaging and two-way television. The opportunity to send personalised messages or to allow consumers opportunities to tailor the information they receive has been well received by marketers at a time of media fragmentation and greater difficulty in getting the message across. Coca-Cola, for example, has shifted some of its spend from television advertising into new media where it can target younger people with live music, sport and viral marketing (Day, 2002). As the technology improves, there will be more opportunities to create more complex campaigns to attract and retain attention, but only by encouraging interactivity will the real power of new media become evident.

Detica (reported by *Marketing Week*, 2002b), found that consumers feel frustrated with some self-service new media technology largely because of a lack of confidence or skill in using the technology and a feeling that such technology is there to benefit the organisation, not the consumer. Coupled with concern that as the volume of messages grows it will lead to a negative impact on whole industry (Gander, 2001), the future of some of the new media platforms is far from certain. Marketers must not be blinded by technology ahead of customer adoption, understanding and acceptance, especially as the adoption process spreads away from more innovative age groups into the mainstream population, as text messaging has done. Mazur (2002) reminds us that viral marketing from the customer's perspective is not something that is done to them, but something they think they do, as happy or unhappy customers. Similarly with all interactive media, the majority of users believe that they control their own access to cyberspace and networks, rather than seeing themselves as the target of a marketer's strategy (Ellis, 2002). It is perhaps time to put the customer experience and usage back at the centre of new media strategies.

There are still important issues to overcome in all areas, especially concerning privacy and data protection. Although privacy does not always appear to be a major topic for consumers, that may reflect the low level of understanding of just how companies collect and manage data about individuals (Barwise, 2002). With legislative trends and industry standards being imposed, the question remains whether the impact of controls on spamming and poor targeting can come quickly enough to avoid consumer resentment at being bombarded with a series of unwanted messages. The last thing genuine marketers want is to have their brands devalued by being regarded as 'pushy', or by association with spammers.

Chapter summary

- Internet marketing has a wide variety of uses within an organisation, including information dissemination, PR, selling, CRM and market research, and is centred around the organisation's website which must be well designed to offer the user what they want in a form that is appealing and user-friendly. Internet marketing can be useful in any size and type of organisation, and can be very cost-effective in achieving marketing objectives when integrated with more traditional marketing tools and methods. The dotcom bust demonstrated that the 'traditional marketing values' of customer orientation, clear differential advantage and tightly controlled marketing planning and management and controls are still essential even for companies trading wholly on the internet. Generating and maintaining consumer trust are also seen as major factors in Internet marketing success.
- Internet marketing is increasing in importance as internet penetration among the general population rises. As individuals gain experience of using the internet and as their trust in it grows, they are likely to start spending more money via this channel on a much wider range of goods and services. The number of people buying via the internet and their average spend is already increasing rapidly. Businesses too are spending more on e-procurement. B2B exchanges or e-marketplaces run by independent organisations have emerged to help match buyers and sellers quickly and cost-effectively. Industry-specific exchanges, such as Covisint, dominated by large buyers have also arisen to streamline distribution chains and make them more cost-effective. E-collaboration on major projects is being experimented with, but so far has been disappointing.
- The three main categories of internet use for organisations are for research and planning, as a distribution channel, and as a communiucations medium. The internet has opened up a vast wealth of information sources, both free and paid-for, and has provided a new way of undertaking various types of market research. It has also become an additional cost-effective distribution channel with the emergence of e-tailers and cybermediaries alongside traditional companies using it in parallel with 'normal' retail channels.The internet has also become an advertising medium in its own right to complement other media and is also a means of delivering imaginative sales promotions and other incentives. It can add a lot of value to customer service and customer relationship programmes. In the future as the technology underpinning the internet improves (e.g. with the advent of broadband), its marketing uses are likely to become more sophisticated and consumers and businesses alike will come to regard it very much as a mainstream marketing tool.

- The three main elements of the so-called 'new media' are e-mail marketing, wireless marketing and interactive television (iTV). E-mail marketing is primarily used as a means of CRM, to create and nurture relationships with customers through regular, targeted, relevant contact. Imaginative and well designed messages can be used in viral marketing campaigns, encouraging the recipient to pass the message on to a friend to exploit word-of-mouth advantages. Wireless marketing (m-marketing or mobile marketing) harnesses the power of the mobile telephone and mainly involves text messaging as a form of marketing communication. This allows the marketer to send immediate short, sharp messages to remind or inform the recipient. The benefits must be traded off against the risk of irritating the recipient with an overload of what is perceived as 'junk' messages, however. As with the internet advances in technology are likely to open up new applications for wireless marketing. iTV marketing provides the opportunity for two-way communication between the marketer and an individual via the television set. The consumer can use the interactive facility on the remote control to request further information about a product, or to interact in many ways as they would on the internet. The main problems, however, are the costs of creating the necessary digital networks to deliver the iTV service, and consumer acceptance and adoption of the full range of iTV capabilities.

key words and phrases

Cybermediary	Infomediaries	Opt-in
Disintermediation	Interactive television (iTV)	Opt-out
Dotcom	Internet marketing	Permission marketing
E-mail marketing	M-marketing	Viral marketing
E-marketing	Mobile marketing	Wireless marketing

questions for review

24.1 What are the 5Ss of internet marketing?

24.2 What are the major advantages and disadvantages of reverse auctions from the B2B supplier's point of view?

24.3 Outline the three main categories of website usage for businesses.

24.4 For what do marketers use e-mail marketing?

24.5 What is viral marketing and why is it so useful to the marketer?

questions for discussion

24.1 Compile a checklist of criteria against which a fashion e-tail website might be assessed. Visit three websites e-tailing clothing to a similar target audience. Compare and contrast those sites in terms of their performance on those criteria. How could each of them improve its offering?

24.2 Your campus-based university bookshop is worried that it might be losing business to online booksellers. Design and conduct a programme of primary research among students to establish the extent of the problem, analyse your findings and make appropriate recommendations to the bookshop.

24.3 'New media have nothing more to offer the marketer than the more traditional forms of marketing communications'. Discuss.

24.4 Draw up a table listing the advantages and disadvantages of e-mail marketing compared with more traditional approaches to direct marketing. In what kind of situations do you think e-mail marketing might work best?

24.5 Find out about a recent m-marketing campaign. Analyse its impact and its contribution to the wider marketing communications strategy.

case study 24.1

'Here's a bit of marketing for you, son'

Noel Dennis and Alan Smith, University of Teesside Business School

A recent visit to a Reg Vardy dealership led to an interesting quote from a sales executive which provided an example of how people in the motor trade sometimes view marketing. 'Dave' explained the intricate workings and short-term benefits of purchasing pre-registered cars, which he prefaced with the words 'here's a bit of marketing for you son'. This case examines some of the marketing issues currently surrounding Reg Vardy plc.

Reg Vardy plc is one of the leading motor retail groups in the UK, with a total of 81 dealerships. The company's origins date back to the 1920s, when the company's founder, Reg Vardy, began a haulage business at Houghton-le-Spring near Durham. It was in 1946 that Reg Vardy began to sell cars, and four years later the company was appointed as a retail dealer with Ford Motor Company at Stoneygate, Houghton-le-Spring.

Today, the organisation has a turnover in excess of £1.3 million, employs over 4,700 people and is the third largest motor retailer in the UK. With dealerships from Aberdeen to Bromley, Reg Vardy turns over more than 150,000 cars per annum.

In 1982 Reg Vardy expanded into the volume car market and by 1988 had a total of 12 dealerships, with a turnover of almost £100 million. In 1989 Reg Vardy Ltd became Reg Vardy plc as the business was floated on the stock exchange. The flotation raised £6 million, which allowed Reg Vardy to pursue its growth strategy and grow the business in other regions of the UK as well as the North East.

The 1990s saw further expansion for Reg Vardy with the addition of both prestige marques and volume marques including Mercedes, BMW, Nissan, Renault and Fiat. In 1998 there was a rights issue which raised £26 mn. This capital was used to acquire the Trust Motor Group and also allowed two further strategic business units to be developed: Vardy Contract Motoring and Vardy Marketing.

Vardy Contract Motoring is the group's contract hire and leasing division and has a fleet of over 5,000 units that is set to grow over the next few years. Vardy Marketing is the company's own in-house marketing agency, which has been established to handle the group's £17 mn annual advertising and marketing spend.

Currently the automotive industry is a massive investor in IT, including systems for sales and marketing. In particular, dealerships like Reg Vardy are using the available technology to develop customer databases in order to develop relationships with customers. Typical sources of information for these databases include:

- New vehicle registrations
- Used car sales
- New car-buyer studies
- Customer satisfaction studies
- Customer complaints
- Dealer attitudes.

Despite this investment in customer database development there appears to be a feeling in the motor industry that customer relationship marketing has much more potential than is currently being recognised. The way Reg Vardy collects customer information is mainly via customer profiling, which is completed when a customer enters the dealership and engages with a member of the sales team. Recently this has been done using the internet, whereby a potential customer enters their details along with the type of car they are interested in. This information is then forwarded to their nearest dealership where follow-up takes place.

Reg Vardy has a major internet presence (http://www.regvardy.com) and uses the medium to:

- Build customer relationships on the web
- Act as an online product catalogue
- Offer product/price information on a 24/7 basis
- Customise the product and the deal, i.e. choose the car and finance package
- Offer online incentives and promotions, i.e. low deposits and low-rate finance
- Communicate online with customers on a regular basis (e-mail marketing).

For Reg Vardy the main value of the internet is as an information tool rather than an alternative channel of distribution. According to Reg Vardy's internet manager, the overall effect of the website has been to stop customers travelling from branch to branch to look at cars, as they can now make a shortlist from the internet. The website has also enabled the sale of cars in geographic areas that Vardy's does not target with traditional media such as newspapers, radio and television. The internet presence continues to build brand awareness through links on other commercial sites such as Lycos and Alliance & Leicester.

Currently Reg Vardy does not offer online discounts or process orders online. As yet, it does not appear to follow the 'bricks and clicks' concept, i.e.

acquiring customers offline (via local newpapers, radio and television), and retaining them online through a relationship marketing strategy aimed at customer retention. It does, however, use its database to cluster customers into groups which allows for precise targeting with relevant offers. A frequently used method is the 'cost-price evening'. The database identifies customers at the appropriate point in their buying cycle and invites them to a special evening at their local dealership where they can save up to 10 per cent off the price of a new car.

One potential threat to Reg Vardy is disintermediation. Companies such as Jamjar.com, for example, offer vehicles for sale online at lower prices thus reducing the traditional role of the car dealer. At a time when a lot of customers are unhappy with the traditional car dealer as the main channel of access, this presents an opportunity for new forms of disintermediation to take place. Reg Vardy could, for example, use its internet site to its maximum potential to drive traffic to its dealerships and to develop interactive online communication with customers through personalised communications. After all, the more companies know about their customers the more successful they will be at satisfying their needs. Good use of e-technology and a well-managed customer database enables this to take place.

For Reg Vardy, and indeed the motor trade as a whole, customer relationship marketing offers a great deal of potential. Traditionally, car dealerships initiate marketing campaigns. However, there is now a move towards groups of customers using the internet to package themselves together in order to negotiate discounts with dealers. This represents a paradigm shift in the standard buyer–seller relationship whereby suppliers seek customers, to customers now seeking suppliers. The role of the traditional, short-term, transaction-orientated car salesperson is diminishing. The future seems to lie with developing long-term customer relationships. Now there's a bit of marketing for you, son.

Source: http://www.regvardy.com

Questions

1 How could Reg Vardy further use the internet to build customer relationships?

2 Discuss the concept of disintermediation using examples from other industries.

3 As a marketing executive you have been asked to develop Reg Vardy's customer database. Compile a list of information sources that would make up the database. These should include both internal and external sources.

4 In what way do you think the role of the car salesperson should change to adapt to the new kind of buyer–seller relationship?

case study 3.2

From dotcom to dotbomb to dotboom?

One of the most high-profile, not to mention stylish dotcom failures was boo.com. It started trading in November 1999, and collapsed in May 2000, yet in principle, the idea seemed like a good one: Boo wanted to tap into the boom in online shopping and the popularity of branded sportswear to offer labels such as DKNY, Puma, and Fubu to a global audience. Investors thought it was a good idea too. In 1998, Boo's two founders, Ernst Malmsten and Kajsa Leander, raised $135 mn in venture capital to fund the start-up of the business. High profile advertising began in May 1999, anticipating a June launch, but because of technical problems, the launch had to be postponed. A Boo employee said, 'There was an incredible buzz in the offices about establishing the brand, the technology came second. We thought we'd sort the gizmos later' (as quoted by Barr, 2002).

In truth, the brand was indeed the focal point. A crew of fashion consultants was even hired for $5,000 per day to perfect the look of Miss Boo, the virtual personal shopper. The company became famous (notorious?) for its PR activities. As one employee said, '[The founders'] secret was to overwhelm employees, investors and journalists with wild evenings at glamorous locations, providing them with a passport to outrageous people and places. There wasn't a newspaper or magazine they wouldn't pose for, spinning journalists a crazy tale of how a poetry critic and a model came to be running a multimillion-dollar business' (as quoted by Kanarek, 2001). Initially, the media fell for it, and Boo claimed that the positive coverage and its appearance on the front page of *Fortune* magazine persuaded its largest investor (worth $50 mn) to make contact.

Meanwhile, the initial staff base of 30 people had expanded to 500, working in seven offices across the world, and money was flowing freely out of the business, but as yet no revenues were coming in. The launch plan was ambitious, but was backed by little in the way of sound planning, effective decision-making or attention to detail. Everything had to be built from scratch: financial systems, a pool of suppliers, warehousing, distribution and customer service, etc. Boo was to launch in 17 countries simultaneously, a complex and costly undertaking, and yet nobody was overseeing the detail to make it work in practical terms. The database of clothing sizes did not reflect variations between countries, and nobody had worked out how customers were to return goods from different countries or how credit card refunds were to be managed, for instance.

All the hype and the triumph of style over substance really came home to roost when boo.com started trading in October 1999. People were visiting the site, although less than 25 per cent of those who tried to access it actually succeeded. The number of visitors to the site on the first day of trading was 25,000 rather than the one million predicted. Of those who did get through to the site, few were buying anything. The site was technologically so complex that it was running very slowly and people were losing patience with it. In addition, consumers found that Boo's prices were no lower than those of more traditional retailers, so why bother buying from Boo? Sales were less than one-tenth of what had been promised.

An overhaul in early 2000 led to restructuring to cut costs and improvements in the technology. The business began to be managed more effectively and sensibly, and revenues began to flow. But it was too little too late. Boo had failed to 'get big fast' which was the only way it was ever going to succeed and survive. In April, the Nasdaq, the US technology stockmarket, suffered a huge drop and investors started to get jittery and more realistic in their expectations of dotcom companies. Boo began to lose its supporters and backers and the media coverage started to become hostile. One journalist who attempted to order a pair of trainers from boo.com wrote incredulously, 'Eighty-one minutes to pay too much money for a pair of shoes I'm still going to have to wait a week to get?' (as quoted by Woodward, 2002).

By May 2000, it was all over. Boo went bust and its investors and unsecured creditors, who were owed around $150 mn, got nothing back. The brand, the logo and the right to use the domain were bought for a mere $250,000 (estimated) by fashionmall.com, a US company that acts as a portal to other e-tail sites selling designer clothes, accessories, footwear and beauty products. Fashionmall generates its revenue by earning transaction fees on sales made on those sites and by selling advertising space on its own site to e-tailers.

By the end of October 2000, Boo was thus relaunched as a youth fashion portal. Miss Boo was back and she told website visitors, 'I've been off on holiday jetting the world and I've squandered a fortune! But I'm back with some yummy things for you to wear and do this season – not to mention a glorious sun-tan ...' (as quoted by *The Independent*, 2000).

Fashionmall hoped to benefit from the enormous brand awareness that Boo had built up through its huge marketing budget, making it one of the top ten most recognised brands on the internet, and felt that although 'the business model of Boo has been discredited, the brand has not. Boo still stands for leading-edge fashion and style' (as quoted by Barker, 2000). Under Fashionmall's ownership, however, Boo was no longer selling goods directly from its own stock but introducing customers to relevant sites where they could buy what they want. 'The old Boo would have sold you a pair of Nike trainers from its warehouses ... Now the shopper will go straight to Nike. Our job is not to send you products. Our job is to introduce you to the person [who] has the product [and] can send it to you' (as quoted by Heavens and Kirchgaessner, 2000). As with Fashionmall's existing operation, revenue came from transactions fees and advertising. The plan was that on the basis of a $1 mn marketing spend (compared with the $40 mn the original Boo spent), the site would become profitable within two years.

Just over a year later, however, in December 2001, the headlines started to have a horribly familiar look with Boo reported as being 'poised to crash into oblivion for a second time' (Beaton, 2001). Fashionmall itself was said to be in difficulties with falling revenues and was also said to be considering abandoning online retailing because it could not make any money. While the Boo brand could be put up for sale, the reality was that very little business was being channelled through it.

As at July 2002, however, Fashionmall was still in business. The boo.com website was still operational, transferring the internet user through to the Boo page on fashionmall.com. Other than the visibility of the Boo branding on the page, there does not appear to be anything particularly distinctive on offer: the page just offers a series of hyperlinks to various companies' websites. It seems that Miss Boo's heart just isn't in her job any more.

Sources: Barker (2000); Barr (2002); Barrow (2000); Beaton (2001); Heavens and Kirchgaessner (2000); *The Independent* (2000); Kanarek (2001); Mathieson (2000); Sliwa (2000); Snoddy (2000); Stockport *et al*. (2001); Woodward (2002).

Questions

1 Summarise the reasons why Boo originally failed.

2 If Fashionmall were to decide to sell the Boo brand, to what extent is it still likely to be attractive to a prospective purchaser?

3 Is clothing e-tailing ever likely to succeed in the same way that other product sectors such as books and CDs have? Why or why not?

References for chapter 24

24/7 Europe (2002a), 'Cussons Imperial Leather Advertorial and DHTML Banner', accessed via http://www.247europe.com.

24/7 Europe (2002b), 'Kraft Foods "Lunchables" Integrated Online Promotion', accessed via http://www.247europe.com.

24/7 Europe (2002c), 'Jaffa Cakes/Manchester United Campaign', accessed via http://www.247europe.com.

Anderson, J. and Patel, P. (2001), 'B2B Makes Seller Suffer', *The Times*, 12 July, p. 2.9.

Apparel Industry Magazine (2000), 'Who Will e-tail Your Products Best?', *Apparel Industry Magazine*, February, pp. 40–41.

ARC Group (2002), 'Content and Applications for Broadband and Digital TV', *ARC Group Stratgeic Reports.2002*, accessed via http://www.arcgroup.com.

Barker, T. (2000), 'Miss Boo Makes Virtual Return at Fashionmall', *Financial Times*, 7 October, p. 16.

Barr, D. (2002), 'Whatever Happened to these Likely Fads?', *Evening Standard*, 11 June, p. 14.

Barrow, B. (2000), 'Boo Back in Business, This Time on a Budget', *The Daily Telegraph*, 30 October, p. 25.

Barwise, P. (2002), 'Great Ideas. Now Make Them Work', *Financial Times*, 28 May, p. 4.

Barwise, P. and Strong, C. (2002), 'Permission-based Mobile Advertising', *Journal of Interactive Marketing*, 16 (1), pp. 14–24.

Beaton, G. (2001), 'Boo On the Brink (Part 2)', *Mail on Sunday*, 2 December, p. 5.

Birmingham Post (2002), 'E-business: Tesco in Grocery Delivery Switch', *Birmingham Post*, 30 April, p. 20.

BMRB (2000), 'Users Ignore Banners, But Off-line Makes Up the Difference', accessed via http://www.bmrb.co.uk.

Bowen, D. (2002), 'Handling the Bad News', *Financial Times*, 25 January, p. 11.

Bruce, A. (2002), 'Clubcard Takes to the Internet as Tesco.com Strives for Perfection', *The Grocer*, 4 May, p. 8.

Budden, R. (2002), 'Broadband Boost for BT', *Financial Times*, 18 July.

Carter, M. (2002a), 'Branded "Viruses" Mutate to Entice Consumers', *Financial Times*, 7 January, p. 14.

Carter, M. (2002b), 'How to Hit a Moving Target', *The Guardian*, 27 May, p. 42.

Chandiramani, R. (2001), 'Warner Bros in Eurosport Mobile Tie-up', *Marketing*, 20 December, p. 9.

CyberAtlas (2002a), 'B2B E-commerce Headed for Trillions', 6 March, accessed via http://cyberatlas.internet.com.

CyberAtlas (2002b), 'European Brands Have Room to Improve Loyalty', 14 March, accessed via http://cyberatlas.internet.com.

The Daily Telegraph (2002), '£2m Bill Over Camera Error', *The Daily Telegraph*, 2 February, p. 12.

Dawe, A. (2002), 'Hitting the Target', *Director*, February, p. 17.

Dawe, T. (2002), 'The Birth of a New Cold Caller', *The Times*, 28 March.

Day, J. (2001), 'Hard Sell in Your Hand', *The Guardian*, 19 March, p. 50.

Doward, B. (2002), 'Sportal Bounces Back', *The Observer*, 3 March, p. 2.

Duboff, R. and Spaeth, J. (2000), 'Researching the Future Internet', *Direct Marketing*, 63 (3), pp. 42–54.

Dwek, R. (2002a), 'E-mail in the UK Overtakes Snail', *Marketing Week*, 21 March, p. 44.

Dwek, R. (2002b), 'Helping the Needle out of the Haystack', *Marketing Week*, 23 May, pp. 46-9.

Eaglesham, J. (2002), 'A Troubled Deal on the Internet', *Financial Times*, 11 February, p. 18.

Ellis, J. (2002), 'Yahoo Kisses it All Good-bye', *Fast Company*, July, pp. 114–6.

Euromonitor (2002), *European Marketing Data and Statistics 2002*, Euromonitor (37th edn).

Faloon, K. (2001), 'B2B Adoption of Online Activities Expanding', *Supply House Times*, September, p. 30.

Feather, F. (2002), *FutureConsumer.Com: The Webolution of Shopping to 2010*, Warwick Publications.

Financial Times (2001), 'Friends Reunited', *Financial Times*, 9 October, p. 8.

Forrester Research (2002), 'Mobile Messaging's Next Generation', accessed via http://www.forrester.com.

Franklin, C. (2002), 'The Price Isn't Right!', *The Guardian*, 31 January, p. 6.

Friesen, P. (2002), 'How to Develop an Effective E-mail Creative Strategy', *Target Marketing*, February, pp. 46–50.

Gander, P. (2001), 'Mobile Options', *Marketing Week*, 6 September, p. 41.

Gaudin, S. (2002), 'The Site of No Return', 28 May, accessed via http://cyberatlas.internet.com.

Goodley, S. (2002), 'Yes, We Have No Bananas', *The Daily Telegraph*, 15 January, p. 27.

Grant, J. (2002), 'Covisint Fails to Move Up into the Fast Lane', *Financial Times*, 4 July, p. 23.

Greenspan, R. (2002a), 'Consumers Rank Trust Above Low Prices', 23 April, accessed via http://cyberatlas.internet.com.

Greenspan, R. (2002b), 'Making Money on Free Music', 12 June, accessed via http://cyberatlas.internet.com.

Greenspan, R. (2002c), 'Broadband Appeal', accessed via http://www.cyberatlas.internet.com.

Gregory, H. (2002), 'Dotcom Driver', *The Grocer*, 16 February, pp. 36-8.

The Grocer (2001), 'Online Orders Grow at "Fantastic Rate"', *The Grocer*, 20 October, p. 8.

The Grocer (2002), 'Online Order Fulfilment Still Dogged by Delivery Glitches', *The Grocer*, 6 April, p. 5.

Head, J. (2002), 'Pandora's Inbox', *The Guardian*, 25 March, p. 40.

Heavens, A. and Kirchgaessner, S. (2000), 'US Portal Breathes Life into Boo.com', *Financial Times*, 2 June, p. 23.

Hendricks, D. (2002), 'E-mail Marketing: Not Just a Shot in the Dark', *Target Marketing*, March, pp. 44–7.

Hewson, D. (2000), 'Firms Reap Net Profits by Learning to Work Together', *e-business* supplement to *Sunday Times*, 26 November, p. 2.

Hunt, J. (2001), 'Marketing's a Piece of Cake', *The Guardian*, 4 October, p. 7.

The Independent (2000), 'No Catcalls for the New Boo', *The Independent*, 22 October, p. 8.

Johnson, M. (2000), 'Money for Nothing', *CIO*, 15 September, pp. 58–60.

Jolley, R. (2002), 'Marketers Warm to Voice Services', *Marketing*, 7 February, p. 23.

Kanarek, P. (2001), 'How We Went from Boo to Bust', *The Daily Telegraph*, 5 October, p. 23.

Karakaya, F. and Charlton, E. (2001), 'Electronic Commerce: Current and Future Practices', *Managerial Finance*, 27 (7), pp. 42–53.

Kolesar, M. and Galbraith, W. (2000), 'A Services Marketing Perspective on E-retailing: Implications for E-retailers and Directions for Further Research', *Internet Research*, 10 (5), pp. 424–38.

Macklin, B. (2002), 'What Every Marketer Needs to Know About iTV', accessed via http://www.emarketer.com.

Marketing (2002), 'Sportal Prepares to Relaunch with Agenda for "Fun"', *Marketing*, 17 January, p. 4.

Marketing (2001), 'Best Use of Technology: Customer Loyalty', *The Marketing Awards: Connections 2001 supplement to Marketing*, November 2001.

Marketing Week (2002a), 'When in Rome, Eat as the Americans Do', *Marketing Week*, 28 February, p. 55.

Marketing Week (2002b), 'Self Service Fails to Impress Consumers', *Marketing Week*, 23 May, p. 39.

Marketing Week (2002c), 'Grabbing a Bigger Pizza the Online Action', *Marketing Week*, 23 May, p. 40.

Marketing Week (2002d), 'MyMonopoly', *Marketing Week*, 18 July, p. 12.

Marketing Week (2001a), 'Content and Consent Boost E-mail Marketing', *Marketing Week*, 25 October, p. 52.

Marketing Week (2001b), 'First Brylcreem Viral Push Develops Press Ad Theme', *Marketing Week*, 6 December, p. 15.

Mathieson, C. (2000), 'Investors Face Total Loss, Says Boo.com Liquidator', *The Times*, 3 June, p. 26.

Mazur, L. (2002), 'Firms Can't "Do" Viral Marketing: It is Done to You', *Marketing*, 27 June, p. 16.

McLuhan, R. (2002), 'Using Streaming to Boost Brands', *Marketing*, 30 May, p. 25.

McNutt, B. (1998), 'A Matter of Priority', *Precision Marketing*, 21 December, p. 16.

Middleton, T. (2002), 'Sending Out the Winning Messages', *Marketing Week*, 16 May, pp. 43-5.

Milsom, P. (2002), 'Online Shoppers Exceed 10 Million for First Time in GB', *Revolution*, 2 July, accessed via http://www.bmrb.co.uk.

Mitchell, A. (1999), 'Online Markets Could See Brands Lose Control', *Marketing Week*, 15 April, pp. 24–5.

Mols, N. (2000), 'The Internet and Services Marketing – The Case of Danish Retail Banking', *Internet Research*, 10 (1), pp. 7–18.

Monbiot, G. (2002), 'The Fake Persuaders', *The Guardian*, 14 May, p. 1.15.

Murphy, D. (2002), 'Marketers Put E-mail to the Test', *Marketing*, 6 June, pp. 19–20.

NetImperative (2002), 'Interactive TV Sector Report', June, accessed via http://www.broadbandbananas.com.

Newing, R. (2002), 'Crucial Importance of Clear Business Goals', *Financial Times*, 5 June, p. 4.

Nichols, P. (2001), 'Sport's Dot.com Meltdown', *The Guardian*, 10 November, p. 16.

Pastore, M. (2001), 'Global Companies Lead B2B Charge', 14 August, accessed via http://cyberatlas.internet.com.

Pastore, M. (2002), 'Britons Increase Use of Interactive Technologies', 15 March, accessed via http://cyberatlas.internet.com.

Patten, S. (2002), 'E-grocers Step up Battle of the Van Man', *The Times*, 26 March, p. 31.

Pickton, D. and Broderick, A. (2001), *Integrated Marketing Communications*, Financial Times Prentice Hall.

Prabhaker, P. (2000), 'Who Owns the Online Consumer?', *Journal of Consumer Marketing*, 17 (2), pp. 158–71.

Ray, A. (2001), 'Profiting From the E-mail Grapevine', *Marketing*, 11 October, p. 27.

Rizzi, D. (2001), 'Precision E-mail Marketing', *Direct Marketing*, November, pp. 56–60

Rosenthal, R. (2002), *Worldwide B2B Dynamic Pricing Forecast, 2002–2006: 'What Am I Bid for This…'*, March, Doc #26801 accessed via http://www.idc.com.

Rowley, J. (2002), *E-business: Principles and Practice*, Palgrave.

Sarkar, M., Butler, B. and Steinfield, C. (1996), 'Intermediaries and Cybermediaries: A Continuing Role for Mediating Players in the Electronic Marketplace', *Journal of Computer Mediated Communication*, 1 (3).

Saunders, C. (2002), 'Branding Benefited by Banners', 17 April, accessed via http://www.cyberatlas.internet.com.

Saunders, C. (2001), 'Trust Central to E-commerce, Online Marketing', 20 November, accessed via http://cyberatlas.internet.com.

Shillingford, J. (2002), 'The Quest for "Must Have" Mobile Services', *Financial Times*, 15 May, p. 5.

Sliwa, C. (2000), 'Boo.com To Rise Again, Run by Fashionmall', *Computerworld*, 21 August, p. 35.

Smallpiece, T. (2002), 'Finding the Way Forward with SEM', *Marketing Week*, 23 May, p. 46.

Smith, P. and Chaffey, D. (2001), *eMarketing eXcellence: At the Heart of e-Business*, Butterworth Heinemann.

Smith, P. and Taylor, J. (2002), *Marketing Communications: An Integrated Approach*, (3rd edn), Kogan Page.

Snoddy, J. (2001), 'Fallen for an Old Flame? Just Log on for Counselling', *The Independent*, 9 September, p. 8.

Snoddy, J. (2000), 'Boo is Reborn in Confident Fashion', *The Guardian*, 27 October, p. 1.30.

Stockport, G., Kunnath, G. and Sedick, R. (2001), 'Boo.com: The Path to Failure', *Journal of Interactive Marketing*, 15 (4), pp. 56–70.

Sumner, I. (1999), 'Web Site Novelties Can Bring PR Opportunities', *Marketing*, 17 June, p. 31.

Tanner, J. (2002), 'Broadband Vision', *America's Network*, 1 May.

Tapp, A. (2002), 'Proactive or Reactive Marketing? The Influence of the Internet on Direct Marketing, Part 3', *Journal of Database Marketing*, 9 (3), pp. 238–47.

Thelwall, M. (2001), 'Commercial Website Links', *Internet Research: Electronic Networking Applications and Policy*, 11 (2), pp. 114–24.

Trollinger, S. (2002), 'The Role of E-mail in Micro-segmentation', *Target Marketing*, May, pp. 28–30.

Watson, E. (2002a), 'Online Auctions Come Under Fire', *The Grocer*, 29 July, p. 4.

Watson, E. (2002b), 'Hitting the Floor', *The Grocer*, 6 July, pp. 34–5.

Wheelwright, G. (2002), 'Video Streaming Over Networks', *Financial Times*, 19 June, p. 5.

Wilson, R. (1999), 'Discerning Habits', *Marketing Week*, 1 July, pp. 45–7.

Woodward, D. (2002), 'Making a Drama Out of a Crisis', *Director*, May, pp. 58-62.

Wray, R. (2002), 'Mobile Chiefs Get the Message', *The Guardian*, 14 May, p. 20.

glossary

(Words which are set in *italics* have their own entries in the glossary, where they are further defined.)

4Ps: otherwise known as the *marketing mix*, these are the basic tools of marketing: product, place, price and promotion.

7Ps: an extended *marketing mix* that takes account of the particular characteristics of services markets: product, price, place, promotion, physical evidence, people and processes.

Adaptation: (a) tailoring a product or other aspects of the *marketing mix* to suit the different needs and demands of other markets, usually international; (b) changing production methods or product specifications in a *B2B* market in order to better meet an individual customer's requirements.

Advertising: a paid form of non-personal communication transmitted through a mass medium.

Advertising media: the means through which advertisements are delivered to the target audience. Media include broadcast media, print media, cinema, hoardings and outdoor media.

Advertorial: a form of print *advertising* that is designed to mimic the editorial content, style and *layout* of the publication in which it appears.

Agents and brokers: *intermediaries* who have legal authority to act on behalf of a seller in negotiating sales, but who do not take title to goods themselves.

Alternative currencies: trading stamps, tokens or loyalty scheme points awarded on the basis of the amount spent by the customer that can be accumulated and then exchanged for gifts or discounts.

Ansoff matrix: a framework for considering the relationship between general strategic direction and *marketing strategies*. The four-cell matrix looks at permutations of new/existing products and new/existing markets.

Atmosphere: (a) the elements that come together to make an impact on retail customers' senses as they enter and browse in a store; (b) creating a feeling appropriate to the character of the store and the desired mood of the customers.

Attitude: the stance that individuals take on a subject that predisposes them to act and react in certain ways.

Augmented product: add-on extras that do not form an integral part of the product but which might be used, particularly by retailers, to increase the product's benefits or attractiveness. Includes guarantees, installation, after-sales service, etc.

Awareness: the consciousness that a product or organisation exists.

B2B goods: goods that are sold to organisations for: (a) incorporation into producing other products; or (b) supporting the production of other products directly or indirectly; or (c) resale.

B2B marketing: (also known as industrial marketing or organisational marketing) activities directed towards the *marketing* of goods and services by one organisation to another.

Banner advertising: advertising that appears on a website, usually as a banner across the top of a page that clicks the user through to the advertiser's website.

Behaviour segmentation: grouping consumers in terms of their relationship with the product, for instance their usage rate, the purpose of use, their willingness and readiness to buy, etc.

BIGIF: a form of *product based sales promotion* – buy one get one free also known as BOGOFF.

Boston Box: (also known as the BCG matrix) a tool for analysing a *product portfolio*, plotting relative market share against market growth rate for each product. The resultant matrix classifies products as cash cows, dogs, question marks and stars.

Brand loyalty: occurs when a consumer consistently buys the same brand over a long period.

Branding: the creation of a three-dimensional character for a product, defined in terms of name, packaging, colours, symbols, etc., that helps to differentiate it from its competitors, and helps the customer to develop a relationship with the product.

Breadth of range: the variety of different *product lines* either (a) produced by a manufacturer; or (b) stocked by a retailer.

Breakeven analysis: shows the relationship between total costs and total revenue in order to assess the profitability of different levels of sales volume.

Bulk breaking: buying large quantities of goods and then reselling them in smaller lots, reflecting some of the cost savings made through bulk buying in the resale price. A prime function of *intermediaries*.

Business format franchise: allows a *franchisee* access not only to a product concept, but also to a comprehensive package that allows the product or service to be delivered in a standardised way regardless of the location.

Business to business marketing: see *B2B marketing*.

Buyer readiness stages: categorise consumers in terms of how close they are to making a purchase or a decision. Stages range from initial awareness, through to interest, desire and, finally, action.

Buyer–seller relationship: the nature and quality of the social and economic interaction between two parties.

Buying centre: a group of individuals, potentially from any level within an organisation or from any functional area, either contributing towards or taking direct responsibility for organisational purchasing decisions. The buying centre might be formally constituted, or be a loose informal grouping.

CAPI: computer aided personal interviewing.

Cash rebate: a form of *sales promotion* usually involving the collection of a specified number of proofs of purchase in order to qualify for a cash sum or for a *coupon*.

Catalogue showrooms: a High Street store selling goods through catalogues displayed in the outlet, with the customer collecting goods immediately from a pick-up point on the premises.

CATI: computer aided telephone interviewing.

Cause related marketing: linkages between commercial organisations and charities that can be used by both parties to enhance their profiles and to help achieve their marketing objectives.

Channel of distribution: the structure linking a group of organisations or individuals through which a product or service is made available to potential buyers.

Channel strategy: decision taken about the allocation of roles within a *channel of distribution*, and the way in which the channel is formally or informally managed and administered.

Closed questions: market research questions which offer the respondent a limited list of alternative answers to choose from.

Closing the sale: the stage of the *personal selling* process in which the customer agrees to purchase.

Cognitive dissonance: a state of psychological discomfort arising when a consumer tries to reconcile two conflicting states of mind, for example, the positive feeling of having chosen to buy a product and the negative feeling of being disappointed with it afterwards.

Cold calling: unsolicited visits or calls made by sales representatives to potential customers.

Collaborative R&D: pooling resources and expertise with one or more other organisations to undertake a research and development project jointly.

Commission: a percentage of the value of goods sold paid as total or partial remuneration to a sales representative or agent.

Comparative advertising: a type of *advertising* that seeks to make direct comparison between a product and one or more of its competitors on features or benefits that are important to the target market.

Competitive advertising: a commonly used type of *advertising* that communicates the unique benefits of a product, differentiating it from the competition.

Competitive edge: having a clear advantage over the competition in terms of one or more elements of the *marketing mix* that is valued by potential customers.

Competitive position: the organisation's strategic position in a market compared with its competitors: leader, challenger, follower or nicher.

Competitive posture: an organisation's means of dealing with competitors' actions in a market, proactively or reactively. Postures can be aggressive, defensive, cooperative or independent.

Competitive strategy: how an organisation chooses to compete within a market, with particular regard to the relative positioning and strategies of competitors.

Concept testing: the presentation of a new product concept, in terms of its function, benefits, design, branding, etc., to a sample of potential customers to assess their reactions, *attitudes* and purchasing intentions towards it.

Concessions: (also known as stores within stores) trading areas usually within *department stores*, sold, licensed or rented out to manufacturers or other retail names so that they can create their own distinctive trading image.

Consumer decision-making: the process that consumers go through in deciding what to purchase, including *problem recognition*, information searching, evaluation of alternatives, making the decision, and *post-purchase evaluation*.

Consumer goods: goods that are sold to individuals for their own or their families' use.

Contracting: a type of *market entry method* whereby a manufacturer contracts with a company in a foreign market to produce or assemble goods on its behalf.

Contests and sweepstakes: a form of *sales promotion* in which customers are invited to compete for a specified number of prizes. Contests must involve a degree of skill or knowledge, whereas sweepstakes are effectively open lotteries.

Continuous innovation: products are upgraded and updated regularly in relatively small ways that make no great changes to the customer's buying behaviour.

Continuous research: research undertaken, usually by commercial market research organisations, on a long-term, ongoing basis, to track changing patterns in markets.

Control and evaluation: mechanisms for ensuring that *marketing plans* are properly implemented, that their progress is regularly measured and assessed and that any deviations are picked up early enough to allow corrective action to be taken.

Convenience goods: relatively inexpensive frequently purchased consumer goods; related to *routine problem solving* buying behaviour.

Convenience stores: usually small neighbourhood grocery stores that differentiate themselves from the *supermarkets* through longer opening hours and easy accessibility.

Conversion rate: the number of enquiries from potential customers or sales visits made by sales representatives that actually turn into orders or sales.

Co-operative advertising: a form of *sales promotion* targeted at *intermediaries* through which manufacturers agree to fund a percentage of the *intermediary's* local advertising costs as long as the manufacturer's product appears in the *advertising* material.

Copywriting: writing the verbal (written or spoken) elements of an advertisement.

Core product: the prime purpose of a product's existence which might be expressed in terms of functional or psychological benefits.

Corporate chain: multiple retail outlets under common ownership, usually with national coverage.

Corporate identity: the character and image of an organisation, reflecting its culture, that is presented to its various *publics*, including the organisation's name and logo.

Corporate objectives: the overall objectives of the organisation that influence the direction of *marketing strategy*.

Corporate PR: *public relations* activities focused on enhancing or protecting the overall corporate image of an organisation.

Corporate social responsibility (CSR): the need for organisations to consider the good of the wider communities, local and global, within which they exist in terms of the economic, legal, ethical and philanthropic impact of their way of conducting business and the activities they undertake. 'The CSR firm should strive to make a profit, obey the law, be ethical, and be a good corporate citizen' (Carroll, 1991 *see* Chapter 1 references).

Count and recount: a form of *sales promotion* targeted at *intermediaries* through which rebates are given for all stock sold during a specified promotional period.

Coupons: a form of *sales promotion* consisting of printed vouchers, distributed in a variety of ways, that allow a customer to claim a price reduction on a particular product or at a particular retailer's stores.

Creative appeal: the way in which an *advertising* message is formulated in order to provoke the desired response from the target audience. Types of appeal include rational, emotional, product-orientated or consumer-orientated appeal.

CSR: see *corporate social responsibility*.

Culture: the personality of the society in which an individual lives, manifest in terms of the built environment, literature, the arts, beliefs and value systems.

Cybermediary: an *e-tailer* that sells direct to the customer; also any online *intermediary* that helps the individual to locate a specific website or guides them towards sites of interest. Search engines, online shopping malls and online directories are all cybermediaries.

Data-based budget setting: setting *advertising* or marketing budgets using methods that do not involve guesswork or arbitrary figures. The two main methods are competitive parity, and objective and task.

Database marketing: compiling, analysing and using data held about customers in order to create better tailored, better timed offers that will maximise customer value and loyalty.

Decision-making unit (DMU): see *buying centre*.

Demographic segmentation: grouping consumers on the basis of one or more *demographic* factors.

Demographics: the measurable aspects of population structure, such as birth rates, age profiles, family structures, education levels, occupation, income and expenditure patterns.

Department stores: large stores, usually located in town centres, which are divided into discrete departments selling a very wide range of diverse goods, from clothing to travel, from cosmetics to washing machines.

Depth of range: the amount of choice or assortment within a *product line*.

Derived demand: where demand for products or components in *B2B* markets depends on consumer demand further down the chain; for example demand for washing machine motors is derived from consumer demand for washing machines.

Differential advantage: see *competitive edge*.

Diffusion of innovation: a concept suggesting that customers first enter a market at different times, depending on their attitude to innovation and new products, and their willingness to take risks. Customers can thus be classified as innovators, early adopters, early majority, late majority and laggards.

Direct export: selling goods to foreign buyers without the intervention of an *intermediary*.

Direct mail: a *direct marketing* technique involving the delivery of promotional material to named individuals at their homes or organisational premises.

Direct marketing: an interactive system of marketing that uses one or more *advertising media* to effect a measurable response at any location, forming a basis for further developing an ongoing relationship between an organisation and its customers.

Direct response advertising: *advertising* through mainstream *advertising media* that encourages direct action from the audience, for example, requests for more information, requests for a sales visit, or orders for goods.

Direct supply: a distribution channel in which the producer deals directly with the end customer without the involvement of *intermediaries*.

Discontinuous innovation: represents a completely new product concept unlike anything the customer has yet experienced, and thus involves a major learning experience for the customer with much information searching and evaluation.

Discount clubs: similar to *wholesalers*, but re-selling in bulk to consumers who are members of the club rather than small retailers.

Disintermediation: cutting one or more *intermediaries* out of the distribution channel.

Distributors and dealers: *intermediaries* who add value through the provision of special services associated with the selling of a product and the after-sales care of the customer.

Diversification: developing new products for new markets.

Dotcom: a company set up specifically to sell or deliver goods and/or services via the internet.

DSS: decision support system; an extension of the *MIS* that allows the marketing decision maker to manipulate data to explore scenarios and 'what if …' questions as an aid to decision-making.

Durable products: products that last for many years and are thus likely to be infrequently purchased, such as electrical goods and capital equipment.

Dynamically continuous innovation: the introduction of new products with an element of significant innovation that could require major reassessment of the product within customers' buying behaviour.

E-mail marketing: the use of e-mail as a *direct marketing* channel.

E-marketing: the use of electronic media such as the internet, *wireless* marketing and *iTV* for any marketing purpose.

E-tailer: an online *retailer*, including *dotcom* companies that sell goods/services, online 'branches' of High Street stores, and manufacturers' online direct selling sites.

Economic and competitive environment: trends and developments in terms of the economic well-being and condition of individuals, nations or trading blocs, including taxation and interest rates, etc.; the structure of markets in terms of the number of competitors and their ability to influence the market.

Environmental scanning: the collection and evaluation of data and information from the marketing environment that can influence the organisation's *marketing strategies*.

EPOS: electronic point of sale systems which streamline stock control and ordering systems through barcode scanning and allow the automatic processing of credit card payments for goods.

Eurobrand: (also known as a pan-European brand) a brand which is marketed and sold with a standardised offering across a number of different European countries.

Evoked set: the shortlist of potential products that the consumer has to choose from within the purchasing decision-making process.

Exchange process: the interaction between buyer and seller in which each party gives the other something of value. Usually, the seller offers goods and services, and the buyer offers money.

Extended problem solving: a *purchasing situation* usually involving a great deal of time and conscious information searching and analysis, as it involves high-priced goods which are purchased very infrequently; the consequences of making a 'wrong' decision are severe and thus the customer is prepared to invest time and effort in the process.

Extending the product line: adding further *product items* into a *product line* to extend coverage of the market, for instance introducing a bottom of the range cut-price version of a product, or developing a premium quality product to extend the top end of the range.

Family lifecycle: a model representing the way in which a family's structure changes naturally over time.

Field marketing agencies: agencies which undertake in-store *sales promotions*, *sampling*, and/or the setting up and maintenance of POS material.

Filling the product range: adding further *product items* into a *product line* to fill gaps within the range, for instance introducing additional flavours, pack sizes or packaging formats.

Fmcg products: fast moving consumer goods; relatively low-priced, frequently purchased items, such as groceries and toiletries.

Focus group: a small group of people, considered to be representative of the target segment, invited to discuss openly products or issues at their leisure in a relaxed environment.

Forecasts: estimates of future demand, sales or other trends, calculated using quantitative and/or qualitative techniques.

Franchise: a contractual *vertical marketing system* in which a *franchisor* licenses a *franchisee* to produce and market goods or services to criteria laid down by the *franchisor* in return for fees and/or royalties.

Franchisee: an *intermediary* who holds a contract to supply and market a product or service to operating standards and criteria set by the *franchisor*.

Franchisor: the individual or organisation offering *franchise* opportunities.

Frequency: the average number of times that a member of the target audience will have been exposed to an advertisement during a specified period.

Full service agencies: *advertising* agencies that provide a full range of services, including research, planning, creative work, advertising production, media buying, etc. Such agencies might also offer other marketing communications services such as *direct mail*, *sales promotion*, and *PR*.

GE matrix: a tool for analysing a *product portfolio*, plotting industry attractiveness against business position for each product, resulting in a nine-cell matrix.

Generic strategies: three broad strategic options that set the direction for more detailed strategic planning: cost leadership, differentiation and focus.

Geodemographics: a combination of *geographic* and *demographic segmentation* that can either give the demographic characteristics of particular regions, neighbourhoods and even streets, or show the geographic spread of any demographic characteristics.

Geographic segmentation: grouping customers in either *B2B* or consumer markets in terms of their geographic location.

Heterogeneity: a characteristic of *services*, describing how difficult it is to ensure consistency in a service product because of its 'live' production and the interaction between different customers and service providers.

House journal: an internal publication produced by an organisation in order to inform and entertain its employees and to generate better internal communication and relationships.

Hypermarkets: very large self-service *out-of-town* outlets, 5,000 m^2 or more, stocking not only a wide range of grocery and *fmcg products*, but also other consumer goods such as clothing, electrical goods, home maintenance products, etc.

Independent retail outlet: a single retail outlet, or a chain of two or three stores, managed by either a sole trader or a family firm.

Indirect export: selling goods to foreign buyers through *intermediaries* such as export agents, export merchants or buying houses.

Industrial marketing: see *B2B marketing*.

Infomediaries: information brokers that gather information about online consumers, their preferences and shopping habits and then sell it on to other organisations and/or use it to act as a *cybermediary* on behalf of consumers to help them locate appropriate sites.

Information overload: having so much information available that the consumer either cannot assimilate it all or feels too overwhelmed to take any of it in.

Inseparability: a characteristic of *services*, describing how service products tend to be produced at the same time as they are consumed.

Institutional advertising: a type of *advertising* that does not focus on a specific product, but on the corporate image of the advertiser.

Intangibility: a characteristic of *services*, describing their non-physical nature.

Interactive marketing: (a) in *services* markets, the encounter and interaction between the service provider and the customer. (b) see *Internet marketing*.

Interactive television: (iTV) a means of providing two-way communication between the consumer and the service provider using a television set-top box sending and receiving signals via satellite, cable or aerial.

Intermediary: an organisation or individual through whom products pass on their way from the manufacturer to the end buyer.

Internal marketing: the development and training of staff to ensure high levels of quality and consistency in service delivery and support. Internal marketing includes recruitment, training, motivation and productivity.

International marketing: a particular application of *marketing* concerned with developing and managing trade across international boundaries.

Internet marketing: (also known as online marketing) the use of the internet to disseminate information, communicate with the marketplace, advertise, promote, sell and/or distribute products or services.

Inventory management: controlling stock levels within the *physical distribution* function to balance the need for product availability against the need for minimising stock holding and handling costs.

iTV: see *Interactive television*.

Joint demand: where demand for one product or component in a *B2B* market is dependent on the supply or availability of another, for example a computer assembler's demand for casings might depend on the supply or availability of disk drives.

Joint promotion: *sales promotion* activity undertaken by two or more brands or manufacturers jointly, for example collecting tokens from Virgin Cola in order to get two Eurostar tickets for the price of one.

Joint ventures: a jointly owned company set up by two or more other organisations: (a) as a means of *market entry method*; or (b) as a means of pooling complementary resources and exploiting synergy.

Judgemental budget setting: setting advertising or marketing budgets using methods that involve some degree of guesswork or arbitrary figures. Methods include: arbitrary, affordable, percentage of past sales, and percentage of future sales.

Layout: (a) in retailing, the arrangement of fixtures, fittings and goods in the store; (b) in *advertising*, the arrangement of the various elements of a print or poster advertisement.

Leads: names, addresses and/or other details of individuals or organisations which could be potential customers.

Learning: the change in behaviour that results from experience and practice.

Licensing: an arrangement under which an organisation (the licensor) grants another organisation (the licensee) the right to manufacture goods, use patents, use processes, or exploit trade marks within a defined market. Often used as an international *market entry method*.

Lifestyle segmentation: grouping consumers on the basis of *psychographic* characteristics.

Limited problem solving: a *purchasing situation* usually involving some degree of conscious information searching and analysis, as it involves moderately high priced goods which are not purchased too frequently, and thus the customer might be prepared to shop around to a limited extent.

Limited service agencies: advertising agencies that specialise in one or just a few parts of the whole *advertising* process; for example they might specialise in creative work, or media buying or advertising research.

Loading up: an objective of *sales promotion*, encouraging customers to advance their buying cycles, i.e. to buy greater quantities of a product in the short term than normal.

Logistics: the handling and movement of inbound raw materials and other supplies as well as outbound *physical distribution*.

M-marketing: (also known as mobile marketing) see *wireless marketing*.

Macro segments: segments in *B2B* markets defined in terms of broad organisational characteristics such as size, location and usage rates, or in terms of product applications.

Mail order: a form of non-store retailing usually involving a catalogue from which customers select goods, then mail or telephone their orders to the supplier. Goods are delivered to the customer's home.

Mailing list: a list of names and addresses, which can be compiled from organisational records or purchased, used as the basis for *direct marketing* activities.

Manufacturer brands: *branding* applied to goods that are produced and sold by a manufacturer who owns the rights to the brand.

Manufacturing subsidiary: a subsidiary company set up in a foreign market to manufacture or assemble a product.

Mark-up: the sum added to the trade price paid for a product to cover the *intermediary's* costs and profit. Mark-up can be measured as a percentage of the trade price or as a percentage of the resale price.

Market coverage: ensuring that the product is made available through appropriate *intermediaries* so that: (a) the potential customer can access it as easily as possible; and (b) the product is properly displayed, sold and supported within the *channel of distribution*. Market coverage might involve intensive distribution, selective distribution or exclusive distribution.

Market development: selling existing products into new segments or geographic markets.

Market entry methods: ways of getting into international markets, including *direct exporting*, *indirect exporting*, *licensing*, *franchising*, *sales* or *manufacturing subsidiaries*, *joint ventures*, or *strategic alliances*.

Market penetration: increasing sales volume in current markets.

Market potential: the total level of sales achievable in a market assuming that every potential customer in that market is buying, that they are using the product on every possible occasion, and that they are using the full amount of product on each occasion.

Market segmentation: breaking a total market down into groups of customers and/or potential customers who have something significant in common in terms of their needs and wants or characteristics.

Marketing: creating and holding customers by producing goods or services that they need and want, communicating product benefits to customers, ensuring that goods and services are accessible, and that they are available at a price that customers are prepared to pay.

Marketing audit: the systematic collection, analysis and evaluation of information relating to the internal and external environments that answers the question 'Where are we now?' for the organisation.

Marketing concept: a philosophy of business, permeating the whole organisation, that holds that the key to organisational success is meeting customers' needs and wants more effectively and more closely than competitors.

Marketing environment: the external world in which the organisation and its potential customers have to exist, and within the context of which *marketing* decisions have to be made.

Marketing mix: the combination of the *4Ps* that creates an integrated and consistent offering to potential customers that satisfies their needs and wants.

Marketing objectives: what the organisation is trying to achieve through its *marketing* activities during a specified period. Closely linked with *corporate objectives*.

Marketing orientation: an approach to business that centres its activities on satisfying the needs and wants of its customers.

Marketing plan: a detailed written statement specifying target markets, *marketing programmes*, responsibilities, time-scales, controls and resources. Plans may be short term or long term, strategic or operational in focus.

Marketing PR: *public relations* activities focused on particular products or aspects of their marketing campaigns.

Marketing programmes: specific marketing actions, specified within the marketing plan, involving the use of the *marketing mix* elements in order to achieve marketing objectives.

Marketing research: the process of collecting and analysing information in order to solve marketing problems.

Marketing strategy: the broad marketing thinking that will enable an organisation to develop its products and *marketing mixes* in the right direction, consistent with overall *corporate objectives*.

Master franchising: a *franchisor* grants an individual or organisation in a particular country or other trading region the exclusive right to develop a *franchise* network by sub-franchising within that territory.

Micro segments: segments in *B2B* markets defined in terms of detailed organisational characteristics such as management philosophy, decision-making structures, *purchasing policies*, etc.

MIS: marketing information system; the formalised collection, sorting, analysis, evaluation, storage and distribution of marketing data.

Mobile marketing: (also known as m-marketing) see *wireless marketing*.

Modified re-buy: goods and services purchased relatively infrequently by organisations which might want to update their information on available products and suppliers before making a repeat purchase decision.

Money-based sales promotions: *sales promotions* that centre around some kind of financial incentive: money-off packs, *cash rebate* offers, or *coupons*.

Motivation: the driving forces that make people act as they do.

Multiple sourcing: the sourcing of a particular *B2B good* or service from more than one supplier simultaneously.

Multivariable segmentation: using a number of different variables to develop a rich profile of a target group of customers.

Negotiation: a give and take process between a buyer and a seller in which precise terms of supply, specification, delivery, price, and after-sales service, etc. are agreed.

New product development (NPD): the process of seeking and screening new product ideas, analysing their commercial feasibility, developing and *test marketing* the product and its associated *marketing mix*, launching the product fully, then monitoring and evaluating its initial progress.

New task purchasing: goods and services that are purchased extremely infrequently by organisations, and involve a high level of formalised information collection and analysis before a purchasing decision is made.

Non-durable products: products that can only be used once or a few times before replacement, such as groceries or office stationery.

Non-profit marketing: marketing activities undertaken by organisations which do not have profit generation as a prime corporate objective, such as charities, public sector health care, and educational establishments.

Online marketing: see *Internet marketing*.

Open-ended questions: market research questions which do not offer a respondent a list of alternative answers. The respondents are encouraged to answer spontaneously and to enter into explanation of their answers.

Opt-in: a mechanism by which an individual can signify agreement or specifically request to be included on a *telemarketing*, *direct mail* or *e-mail marketing* list.

Opt-out: a mechanism by which an individual can specifically request to be excluded from or deleted from a *telemarketing*, *direct mail* or *e-mail marketing* list.

Order maker: a sales representatives with responsibility for: (a) finding new customers and making sales to them; and (b) actively increasing the volume or variety of sales to existing customers.

Order taker: a sales representative who either has a set pattern of customer contact or waits for customers to contact him/her when they want to buy.

Organisational marketing: (also known as industrial marketing or business-to-business (*B2B*) marketing) activities directed towards the *marketing* of goods and services by one organisation to another.

Out of town: describes large retail sites located away from the town centres so that they are easily accessible to large numbers of car-borne shoppers.

Outsourcing R&D: commissioning other organisations or research bodies to undertake specific research and development projects, rather than handling them in-house.

Own-label brands: *branding* applied to goods that are produced by a manufacturer on behalf of a retailer or wholesaler who owns the rights to the brand.

Penetration pricing: setting prices low in order to gain as much market share as possible as quickly as possible.

Perception: the way in which individuals analyse and interpret incoming information and make sense of it.

Perishability: a characteristic of *services*, describing how service products cannot be stored because they are produced and offered at particular moments in time.

Permission marketing: developing a marketing campaign on the basis that an individual or organisation has explicitly consented to being targeted, for example through the use of *opt-in* and *opt-out* mechanisms.

Personal selling: interpersonal communication, often face to face, between a sales representative and an individual or group, usually with the objective of making a sale.

Personality: features, traits, behaviours and experiences that make each person a unique individual.

Physical distribution: the handling and movement of outbound goods from an organisation to its customers.

Pioneer advertising: *advertising* used in the early stages of a *product lifecycle* to explain what a product is, what it can do and what benefits it offers.

Political and legal environment: the governmental influences, at local, national and European levels, that inhibit or encourage business; the legal and regulatory frameworks within which organisations have to operate, including national and European law, local by-laws, regulations imposed by statutory bodies and voluntary codes of practice.

POS: point of sale; marketing communication activity, for example *sales promotions*, displays, videos, leaflets, posters, etc., which appears in retail outlets at the place where the product is displayed and sold.

Post-purchase evaluation: the stage after a product or *service* has been purchased and used in which the consumer reflects on whether the product met expectations, exceeded them or was disappointing.

Post-testing: evaluation undertaken during or after an *advertising* campaign to assess its impact and effects.

Potential product: what the product could and should be in the future to maintain its *differentiation*.

PR: see *Public relations*.

Premium price: a price which is distinctly higher than average to reflect better product quality, exclusivity or status.

Pre-testing: showing an advertisement to a sample of the target audience during its development to check whether it is conveying the desired message in the desired way with the desired effect.

Press relations: cultivating good relationships between an organisation and the media as an aid to *public relations* activities.

Price: a medium of exchange; what is offered in return for something else; usually measured in terms of money.

Price comparison: using price as a means of comparing two or more products in order to judge: (a) their likely quality in the absence of other information; (b) which offers the best value for money.

Price differential: any difference in the prices charged for the same product to different *market segments* or in different geographic regions.

Price elasticity of demand: the responsiveness of demand to changes in prices. Elastic products are very responsive, so that a price increase leads to a fall in demand, while inelastic products are very unresponsive and thus a rise in price leads to little or no change in demand.

Price negotiation: bargaining between a buyer and a seller to agree a mutually acceptable price.

Price objectives: what the organisation is trying to achieve through its pricing, measured in financial or market share terms, and closely linked with overall *corporate* and *marketing objectives*.

Price perception: a customer's judgement of a price in terms of whether it is thought to be too high, about right or extremely good value for money; this judgement might vary with different circumstances and is often formed in the light of what other alternative products are available.

Price sensitivity: the extent to which price is an important criterion in the customer's decision-making process; thus a price sensitive customer is likely to notice a price rise and switch to a cheaper brand or supplier.

Pricing method: the means by which prices are calculated. Methods can be cost-orientated, demand orientated, or competition-orientated.

Pricing policies and strategies: the overall strategic guidelines for the pricing decision, specifying pricing's role within an integrated *marketing mix*.

Pricing tactics: short-term manipulation of price to achieve specific goals, as for example in *money-based sales promotions*.

Primary research: *marketing research* specially commissioned and undertaken for a specific purpose.

Problem recognition: the realisation, triggered by either internal or external factors, that the consumer or the organisation has a problem that can be solved through purchasing goods or services.

Product-based sales promotions: *sales promotions* that centre around some kind incentive connected with the product: extra product free, *BIGIF*, or *samples*.

Product development: selling new or improved products into existing markets.

Product items: the individual products or brands that make up a *product line*.

Product lifecycle (PLC): a concept suggesting that a product goes through various stages in the course of its life: introduction, growth, maturity and decline. At each stage, a product's *marketing mix* might change, as will its revenue and profit profile.

Product lines: a group of products, closely related by production or marketing considerations, that exists within the overall *product mix*.

Product manager: the individual within an organisation responsible for the day-to-day management and welfare of a product or family of products at all stages of their *product lifecycle*, including their initial development.

Product mix: the total sum of all the *product items* and their variants offered by an organisation.

Product orientation: an approach to business that centres its activities on continually improving and refining its products, assuming that customers simply want the best possible quality for their money.

Product portfolio: the set of different products that an organisation produces, ideally balanced so that some products are mature, some are still in their growth stage while others are waiting to be introduced.

Product positioning: developing a product and associated *marketing mix* that: (a) is 'placed' as close as possible in the minds of target customers to their ideal in terms of important features and attributes; and (b) clearly differentiates it from the competition.

Product repositioning: refining the product and/or its associated *marketing mix* in order to change its *positioning* either: (a) to bring it closer to the customer's ideal; or (b) to move it further away from the competition.

Product specification: the criteria to which an organisational purchase must conform in terms of quality, design, compatibility, performance, price, etc.

Production orientation: an approach to business that centres its activities on producing goods more efficiently and cost effectively, assuming that price is the only factor important to customers.

Promotional mix: the elements that combine to make an organisation's marketing communications strategy: *advertising*, *sales promotion*, *personal selling*, *direct marketing* and *public relations*.

Prospecting: in *personal selling*, finding new potential customers who have the ability, authority and willingness to purchase.

Psychographics: (also known as lifestyle segmentation) defining consumers in terms of their *attitudes*, interests and opinions.

Psychological pricing: using price as a means of influencing a consumer's behaviour or perceptions, for example using high prices to reinforce a quality image, or selling at £2.99 instead of £3.00 to make the product appear much cheaper.

Pull strategy: a communications strategy that focuses on the end consumer rather than other members of the *channel of distribution*. Thus a manufacturer might focus on communication to consumers, rather than to *wholesalers* or *retailers*, thus helping to pull the product down the channel.

Public relations (PR): a deliberate, planned and sustained effort to institute and maintain mutual understanding between an organisation and its *publics* (Institute of Public Relations definition).

Publicity: a tool of *public relations* focused on generating editorial media coverage for an organisation and/or its products.

Publics: any group, with some common characteristic with which an organisation needs to communicate, including the media, government bodies, financial institutions, pressure groups, etc. as well as customers and suppliers.

Purchasing policy: an organisation's preferences, systems and procedures for purchasing including, for example, attitude towards favoured or approved suppliers, *single* or *multiple sourcing*, and rules and guidelines.

Purchasing situation: the context in which a consumer purchasing decision is made, defined by the frequency of purchase, the risks involved, and the level of information searching undertaken: *routine problem solving*, *limited problem solving*, and *extended problem solving*.

Push strategy: a communications strategy that focuses on the next member of the *channel of distribution* rather than on the end consumer. Thus a manufacturer might focus on communication to wholesalers or retailers rather than to consumers, thus helping to push the product down the channel.

Qualified prospects: potential customers who have been screened to check that they meet relevant criteria as potential purchasers, for example checking their financial status or that they do actually need the product.

Qualitative research: the collection of data that are open to interpretation, for instance on *attitudes* and opinions, and that might not be validated statistically.

Quantitative research: the collection of quantified data, for example sales figures, *demographic* data, purchase frequency, etc., that can be subjected to statistical analysis.

Rating scales: a form of multiple choice market research questionnaire question in which respondents are asked to indicate their answer on a scale, for example ranging from 1 to 5 where 5 = 'strongly agree' and 1 = 'strongly disagree' with a given statement.

Reach: the percentage of the target market exposed to an advertisement at least once during a specified period.

Reference groups: groups to which an individual belongs or to which the individual aspires to belong, and which influence the individual's *motivation*, *attitudes* and behaviour.

Relationship lifecycle: the evolution of *buyer–seller* relationships in *B2B* markets, through stages including awareness, exploration, expansion, commitment and dissolution.

Relationship marketing: a form of *marketing* that puts particular emphasis on building a longer-term, more intimate bond between an organisation and its individual customers.

Reminder and reinforcement advertising: a type of *advertising*, targeted at consumers who have already tried and used the product before, that reminds consumers of a product's continued existence and of its unique benefits.

Repeat purchase: the purchase and use of a product on more than one occasion by a particular customer.

Retailer: an *intermediary* which buys products either from manufacturers or from *wholesalers* and resells them to consumers.

Rolling launch: the gradual launch of a new product, region by region.

Routine problem solving: a *purchasing situation* usually involving low-risk, low-priced, regularly purchased goods, which does not involve much, if any, information searching or analysis on the part of the buyer.

Routine re-buy: goods and services purchased frequently by organisations from established suppliers, with little, if any, formal decision-making involved in the *repeat purchase*.

Sales orientation: an approach to business that centres its activities on selling whatever it can produce, assuming that customers are inherently reluctant to purchase.

Sales potential: the share of a total market that the organisation can reasonably expect to capture.

Sales presentation: the stage of the *personal selling* process in which the sales representative outlines the product's features and benefits.

Sales promotion: usually short-term tactical incentives offering something over and above the normal product offering to encourage customers to act in particular ways.

Sales quotas: the sales targets that a sales representative has to achieve, broken down into individual product areas and specified as sales value or volume.

Sales subsidiaries: a subsidiary company set up in a foreign market to handle marketing, sales, distribution and customer care in that market.

Sampling: (a) a form of *product-based sales promotion* involving the distribution of samples of products in a variety of ways, so that consumers can try them and judge them for themselves; and (b) in market research, the process of setting criteria and then selecting the required number of respondents for a research study.

Sampling process: defining the target population for a market research study; finding a means of access to that population, and selecting the individuals to be surveyed within that population.

Secondary research: data which already exist in some form, having been collected for a different purpose, perhaps even by a different organisation, and which might be useful in solving a current problem.

Self-liquidating offers: a form of merchandise-based *sales promotion* that invites the consumer to send cash, and often proofs of purchase, in return for merchandise. The price charged covers the cost of the merchandise and a contribution to handling and postage.

SEM: single European market; since 1992, completely free trade has been possible between member states of the EU, although the process of harmonising marketing regulations, product standards, tax rates, etc. is an ongoing process that has not yet been fully achieved.

Semi-structured interview: a form of market research that involves some *closed questions* for collecting straightforward data and some *open-ended questions* to allow the respondent to explain more complex feelings and *attitudes*, for example.

Services: goods that are largely or mainly non-physical in character, such as personal services, travel and tourism, medical care or management consultancy.

Shell directional policy matrix: a tool for analysing a *product portfolio*, plotting competitive capability against prospects for sector profitability for each product, resulting in a nine-cell matrix.

Shopping goods: consumer goods purchased less frequently than *convenience goods*, and thus requiring some information search and evaluation; related to *limited problem solving* buying behaviour.

SIC code: standard industrial classification; a means of categorising organisations in terms of the nature of their business.

Single sourcing: the sourcing of a particular *B2B* good or service from only one supplier.

Skimming: setting *prices* high in order to attract the least price-sensitive customers and to generate profit quickly before competitors enter the market and start to force prices down.

Slice of life: a style of *advertising* that shows how the product fits into a lifestyle that is similar to that of the target audience, or represents a lifestyle that they can identify with or aspire to.

Small business: small businesses are usually defined as those with fewer than 100 employees.

Social class: a form of stratification that structures and divides a society, often on the basis of income and occupation, for marketing purposes.

Sociocultural environment: trends and developments within society as a whole, affecting the *demographic* structure of the population, lifestyles, *attitudes*, *culture*, issues of public and private concern, tastes and demands.

Source credibility: the trustworthiness, likeability, respect or expertise of the perceived source of a marketing message in the minds of the target audience. Source credibility might be transferable to the actual subject of the message, or might at least ensure that the message is listened to.

Speciality goods: expensive, infrequently purchased consumer goods; related to *extended problem solving* buying behaviour.

Speciality stores: stores which tend to concentrate on one clearly defined product area, focusing on *depth of range*.

Sponsorship: the provision of financial or material support to individuals, teams, events or organisations, outside the sponsor's normal sphere of operations. This might involve sport, the arts, community or charity work.

Standardisation: a deliberate strategy to maintain the same *product* and *marketing mix* across all international markets without adapting it for local conditions.

STEP factors: the four broad categories of influences that create the *marketing environment*: sociocultural, technological, economic and competitive, and political and legal.

Store image: the *positioning* of a store in terms of its *branding*, product selection, interior and exterior design, fixtures and fittings, lighting, etc.

Storyboard: part of the process of developing a television or cinema advertisement, a storyboard shows sketches of the main scenes in the advertisement, describes what is happening at that point, and what sound effects should be used.

Strategic alliance: a collaborative agreement entered into by two or more organisations with a specific purpose in mind. It might include *joint ventures* or looser arrangements that do not involve any equity stakes.

Strategic business unit (SBU): a group of products, markets or operating divisions with common strategic characteristics, that is a profit centre in its own right. An individual product, market or operating division could also be defined as an SBU if appropriate.

Strong theory of communication: a theory that assumes that marketing communication takes the potential buyer through the *buyer readiness stages* in sequence, thus forming attitudes and opinions before a purchase has taken place.

Supermarkets: self-service stores carrying a wide range of grocery and *fmcg products*, with smaller branches located in town centres and larger stores located on *out-of-town* sites.

Sustainable marketing: the establishment, maintenance and enhancement of customer relationships so that the objectives of the parties involved are met without compromising the ability of future generations to achieve their own objectives.

Switchers: consumers who are not loyal to any one brand of a particular product and switch between two or more brands within the category.

SWOT analysis: a technique that takes the findings of the *marketing audit* and categorises key points as strengths, weaknesses, opportunities or threats.

Tangible product: the way in which the concept of the *core product* is turned into something 'real' that the customer can interact with, including design, quality, *branding*, and product features.

Targeting: deciding how many *market segments* to aim for and how to do it. There are three broad targeting strategies: concentrated, differentiated and undifferentiated.

Technological environment: trends and developments in the technological field that might: (a) improve production; (b) create new product opportunities; (c) render existing products obsolete; (d) change the ways in which goods and services are marketed; or (e) change the profile of customers' needs and wants.

Telemarketing: using the telephone: (a) to make sales directly; or (b) to develop customer relationships and customer care programmes further. Calls might be: (a) outbound, instigated by the organisation; or (b) inbound, instigated by the customer.

Teleshopping: a form of non-store retailing including shopping by telephone and shopping via computer networks.

Tendering: where potential suppliers bid competitively for a contract, quoting a price to the buyer.

Test marketing: the stage within the *new product development process* in which a product and its associated *marketing mix* are launched within a confined geographic area to get as realistic a picture as possible of how that product is likely to perform when fully commercialised.

Trade shows and exhibitions: centralised events, large or small, local or international, focused on an industry or a product area, that bring together a wide range of relevant suppliers and interested customers under one roof.

Trading up: an objective of *sales promotion*, encouraging customers either to buy bigger sized packs of products, or to buy the more expensive products in a range.

Transfer pricing: prices charged for the exchange of goods and services between different departments or operating divisions within the same organisation.

Trial: the purchase and use of a product for the first time by a particular customer.

Trial price: a very low or minimal temporary price often used for new products to encourage consumers to try them.

Trial sizes: a form of *product-based sales promotion* involving the sale of products in smaller than normal packs, so that consumers can buy and try them with minimal risk.

Unsought goods: goods that consumers did not even know they needed until either (a) an emergency arose that needed an immediate purchasing decision to help resolve it; or (b) an aggressive sales representative pressurised them into a purchase.

Value: a customer's assessment of the worth of what they are getting in terms of a product's functional or psychological benefits.

Value management: the analysis of products and processes to see where the greatest costs are being incurred and where the greatest value is added. This can lead to cost savings and better value for money to the customer.

Variety stores: smaller than *department stores*, variety stores stock a relatively limited number of different product categories, but in greater depth.

Vertical marketing systems: a *channel of distribution* which is viewed as a coordinated whole and is effectively managed or led by one channel member. The leadership might be contractual, or derived from the power or dominance of one member, or arise from the ownership of other channel members by one organisation.

Viral marketing: the marketer uses electronic media to stimulate and encourage word-of-mouth or electronic message dissemination between individuals.

Weak theory of communication: a theory that assumes that marketing communication creates awareness of products, but that *attitudes* and opinions are only created after purchase and *trial*.

Wholesaler: an *intermediary* which buys products in bulk, usually from manufacturers, and resells them to trade customers, usually small retailers.

Wireless marketing: (also known as m-marketing or mobile marketing) the use of text messaging via a mobile telephone as a means of marketing communication.

index

3G technology 382–4, 1087
4Ps 25–7, 72, 907, 961, 1042–4
5Ss 910–11, 1055
7Ps 27–8, 963–9
11Ps of loyalty marketing 674
360 degree reporting 18

acceptability of brand names 289
accessibility
  advertising agencies 632
  market segments 205
  services 971
accessory goods 275
accommodative decision-making 128
account management 718–20
accountability, non-profit organisations 996
accuracy, invoicing 513
achievers 190–91
ACORN 188, 776
Action on Smoking and Health (ASH) 58
activities, market segmentation 190
adaptation
  facilitating 720
  international marketing strategies 1035–9, 1041–2
added value 137, 481–4, 653
adjustments, prices 453–5
administered vertical marketing systems 493
administration 66, 507
adversarial approach to supplier handling 168–9
advertising 11
  advocacy 604, 607
  agencies 631–4, 866–7
  broadcast presentation 619–21, 623–5, 641
  campaigns 634–43
  celebrities 591–2
  cinema 626
  comparative 605–6, 613
  competitive 604, 605–6
  cooperative 681–2
  customer-oriented appeals 615–18
  creative appeals 612–18
  definition 604
  development 638–9
  direct response 753–7
  evaluation 642–3
  frequency 622, 623
  green issues and 587–9
  image building 604
  institutional 607
  internet marketing 1069–71
  magazines 626–8
  in marketing mix 607–9
  media 66, 621–30, 636–8, 641–2
  messages 610–21, 641
  newspapers 628
  outdoor 629–30
  opportunity to see (OTS) 622–3, 641
  pioneering 604–5
  posters 629
  print presentation 618–19, 641
  product-oriented 604–7, 613–15
  promotional mix 569, 582–3, 603–49
  public relations and 793, 803
  publicity compared 802–3
  radio 619–21, 625, 757
  ratings 622
  reach 622, 623
  regulation 80, 81–4
  reminder and reinforcement 604, 606–7
  role 604–10
  source credibility 591–2
  television 619–21, 623–4, 637
  testing 638–9
Advertising Standards Authority (ASA) 81–2, 588–9, 748–9
advertorials 614–15
advice 524–5
advocacy advertising 604, 607
affective attitudes 115
affective communications objectives 580, 590
affinities 944
affordable budgets 593–4
after-sales, direct marketing 773
age 48–50
agencies
  advertising 631–4, 866–7
  field marketing 678
  mail orde r 765–6
  new product idea s 362
  sales promotion 686
agents 474, 477, 478, 479–80
aggressive strategies 880–82
agree and counter technique 714
agriculture 44–5
  battery farming 833–4
  Common Agricultural Policy (CAP) 77
  farm produce 76
  intensive food production 55
AIDA response hierarchy model 196, 322, 580, 747
aided recall, advertising campaigns 642
aircraft 156, 332, 361, 457, 488, 616, 869, 919
airlines 70, 398, 449–50
  advertising 645–7
  B2B buying 137
  bumping 46
  business travellers 179
  catering 977
  comfort 60–61, 63
  inseparability 957–8
  privatisation 72
  strategic alliances 1034–5
  telemarketing 760
  visible staff 975
alcohol 68, 73, 83, 589, 647–9
  see also beer; wine
alliances *see* strategic alliances
allowances 455, 678–81, 682
alternative closes of sales 717
alternative currencies 674
aluminium 143
AMA (American Marketing Association) 4–7, 9
ambient advertising 629–30
American Marketing Association (AMA) 4–7, 9
analysis
  breakeven 446
  business 365–6
  competitive 453
  competitors 865–70
  data 254–5
  financial, new products 366
  marginal 444–5
  marketing 908
  marketing costs 930–31
  morphological 362
  profitability 930–31
  sales 930
  statistical series 917–18
  strategic marketing 849–57
  SWOT 908–10
  time series 922
animals 53, 55–6, 325
animation, advertising appeals 617, 620
annual reports 804
Ansoff matrix 858–61, 864
anti-competitive practices 410, 1021
appraisal of suppliers 155–6
appropriate prices 163–4
arbitrary budgets 593
area development agreements 1028–9
area sampling 245
arts 816, 823–5, 827–8
ASA *see* Advertising Standards Authority
ASH (Action on Smoking and Health) 58
aspirant groups 123
assessment, facilitating 719
assets, brands 285–6
associative brand names 288
assortment 482, 510–11, 550–51
assumptive closes of sales 717
atmosphere 499–500, 552–4
attack strategies 880–82
attention
  seeking, direct mail 749
  selective 111

attitudes
  benefit segmentation 195
  international marketing 1019–20
  psychological influences 115–18
  public relations evaluation 807
  to risks 846–7
  staff 974
  tests, advertising campaigns 642
attractiveness 855
attribute listing 362
attrition rates, advertising campaigns 641
auctions, internet 401, 883, 1063
audits 219, 221, 687, 906–7
augmented products 268, 269, 270
Austria 296
authority publics 795
Autobus 220
autoresponders 969
availability of brand names 289
avatars 969
awareness 98, 105, 169, 289, 806, 937

B1G1F 666–9
B2B
  advertising 613
    cost savings 615
    target audience 635
    testimonials 614
  buyer–seller contact models 158
  buyer–seller relationships 150, 370
  buying
    behaviour 135–6
    centres 160–62
    criteria 163–6
    decision-making process 151–6
    roles in process 157–60
  customers 138–41
  customisation 370
  goods 33
    channel structures 477–80
    user-based product classifications 274–6
  internet spending 1062–4
  marketing 136–8
  marketing planning 944
  marketing research 215
    mail surveys 238
    sampling 245–6
    unstructured interviews 235
  markets 141–50
    branding 290
    customer specified products 337–9
    discounts 454
    Eurobrands 341
    geographic adjustments 455
    innovators 322
    new product development 361
    packaging 294
    price sensitivity 407
    pricing 399–401, 452–5
    products 583–4
    purchases as investments 393
    quality 301
    sales promotion 683
    segmentation 181–3, 205
    structure 370
    target markets 577–8
    tendering 458–9
  online marketplaces 154
  personal selling
    account management 718–19
    need satisfaction 712–13
    prospecting 709–10
    sales representatives 711
  products
    life span and purchase frequency 370
    test marketing 370–71
  purchasing policy 146–8
  services
    user-based product classifications 274–6
  supply chains 167–71
B2G3F 667
backward integration 492, 862
bad publicity 803
bananas 71
banks and banking 73–4, 181, 689–91, 969, 1037, 1046–8, 1056
banner advertising 637–8, 1070–71
barbecues 195–6
bargain hunters 98
battery farming 833–4
BCG matrix 851–4, 899, 900
beer 68, 78, 604, 605, 1031, 1054
behaviour
  B2B buying 135–6
  buyer readiness stage 580, 583
  buying 488
  communications objectives 590
  consumers *see* consumers
  distribution channel aspects 494–500
  organisational decision-making 151–6
  personal selling roles, influences on 699
  segmentation 193–6
belongingness needs 113, 114
benefit segments 193–4
benefits
  branding *see* brands and branding
  financing 483
  marketing planning 899–900
  products 392–4, 773
  segmentation 193–4, 203
  usage, advertising appeals 616
bidding 458–9
biotech sector 847
birth 223–4
birth rate 48
blueprints, franchising 986–91
BMRA (British Market Research Association) 258
BOGOFF 666–9
books 68, 563–4, 1062
boomerang demand curves 403–4
boomerang technique 714–15
Boston Box 850–55
bots 442
boutique store layouts 555
BPMA (British Promotional Merchandising Association) 686
brainstorming 362
brand managers 379
brands and branding 11
  assets 285–6
  associations 289
  attitudes to 116
  awareness 289
  benefits of branding
    consumer perspective 282–3
    manufacturer perspective 283–5
    retailer perspective 285–6
  consumer market beliefs 101
  definition of brand 279
  discreet branding 290–91
  Eurobrands 340–42, 416
  extension 291–3
  generic brands 290
  international marketing 1036–7
  lifecycles 320–21
  loyalty 195, 289
  manufacturer brands 286–7
  manufacturers, power 499
  meaning of branding 280–2
  names 281, 288–9
  own-label brands *see* own-label brands
  policy 290–91
  positioning 417
  quality 289, 302
  retailer bands 287–8
  strategy 288–93
  values 285–6
  wholesaler brands 287–8
bras 185
Brazil 54
breadth of range 530–32
breakdown methods 917–18
breakeven analysis 446
breast implants 587
bribery 166–7, 1018
briefings 806
British Heart Foundation 58
British Market Research Association (BMRA) 258
British Promotional Merchandising Association (BPMA) 686
broadband 1073–4
broadcasting
  advertising 619–21, 623–5, 641, 757
  sponsorship 816, 821–3
  see also television
brokers 474, 478
budgets and budgeting 593–5
  advertising campaigns 636, 638
  marketing 913–15
  public relations 806
build up methods 918
Bulgaria 1013
bulk breaking 483
bulk discounts 454
bundle pricing 451
burst advertising 639–40
buses 1038–9
business ability, advertising agencies 633
business analysis 365–6
business ethics *see* ethics
business format franchises 980–83

business orientations 10–20
business promotions 659
business retention 98
business services 276
Business Software Alliance 1082
business strengths 855
business-to-business *see* B2B
business travel 179
busy periods, evening out 657
'buyer beware' 701–2, 711
buyer readiness 195–6, 580–83
buyer–seller contact models 158
buyer–seller relationships 150, 370
buyer–supplier relationships 8–9, 1063
buyers 161–2
buying
  B2B *see* B2B
  behaviour 488
  complexity 146–50, 488
  locally 497
  groups 559
  situations 104–7
  see also purchasing
bypass attacks 882

cable television 624
CAD (computer aided design) 64–5
call-back facilities 969
call centres 761, 762–3
CAM (computer aided manufacturing) 65
CAMEO 186
cameras 394
campaigns
  advertising 634–43
  direct mail 749–53
  direct marketing 770–75
  plans 897
  sales promotion 685
camping holidays 786–8
candles 1019
CAP (Common Agricultural Policy) 77
capabilities, organisational 487
capacity utilisation 440
CAPI (computer aided personal interviewing) 220, 253
Capibus 220
capital goods 274–5
capital investment 400
car rental 896
career security 165
cargo, insurance, freight (CIF) prices 455
cartels 886
cartoons 617, 620
case bonuses, promotions to retailers 678–9
cash and carry 559
cash cows 851, 853–4, 857, 864
cash discounts 455
cash flows 430–31
cash rebates 664–5
catalogue showrooms 532, 543
catalogues, mail order 765–8
catchment 546, 547
category killers 539
category management (CM) 234–5, 511, 552
CATI (computer aided telephone interviewing) 220, 237, 253–4
causal research 217
cause-related marketing (CRM) 608, 905, 825–6, 992
CE marking 79
censuses 918
Central and Eastern Europe 12
CFC (chlorofluorocarbons) 84
challengers 878
chambers of commerce 231
changing environment 488–9
channels
  communication 571–2, 574
  distribution *see* distribution: channels
charities
  cause related marketing 825–6
  donations to 816
  non-profit marketing 992–9
Chartered Institute of Marketing (CIM) 4–7, 9
children 199–200
  advertising 127–8, 1069–70
  cruelty to 1002–3
  marketing research 257
  mobile phones 367–8
China 13, 137, 145, 167, 172–5, 472–3, 964, 1012, 1025, 1032, 1043
china clay 856
chips 194
chlorofluorocarbons (CFC) 84
chocolate 57, 80
churning 729
CIF prices 455
cigarettes 434–5
CIM (Chartered Institute of Marketing) 4–7, 9
cinemas 626, 954
city centre retail sites 548
claims procedures 513
class 118
classification
  dominance displays 556–7
  international market entry 1025
  non-profit organisations 993–6
  products 270–76
  services 951–2
classified advertisements 628
cleaning materials 854
client–agency relationships, advertising 633–4
closed-loop verification 240
closed questions 248, 249–51
closing sales 717–18
clothing
  design 333
  ethical issues 57–8
  fashions 53
  manufacturers and suppliers 139
  stores, own-label brands 287
  supermarkets 462–3
  synthetics in 64
cluster analysis 254
clusters, competitive 866–7
CM *see* category management
cocoa 57
coding, questionnaires 251–2
coercive power 498
coffee 57, 175–7, 408–9
cognitive attitudes 115
cognitive communications objectives 580, 590
cognitive dissonance 102
cold calling 80, 543, 710, 711, 764
  see also outbound telemarketing
collaborative approach to supplier handling 168–9
collaborative R&D 378, 380
collection of data 228–30
collusion 886
combination selling 770
commercial enterprises 138–9
commercial publications 231
commercial publics 795
commercialisation, new products 371–2
commission, sales representatives 729–31
commitment
  in relationships 170
  suppliers 155–6
commodity positioning matrix 158–9
Common Agricultural Policy (CAP) 77
communicability 324
communication 570
  channel systems 495
  channels 571–2, 574
  costs 685
  e-communication 765
  internal 805–6
  international marketing 1036–7
  internet marketing 1064, 1069–73
  models 571–3, 575, 577–96
  new technology impacts 743–4
  non-profit organisations 997
  promotional mix 569–71, 577–96
  sales promotion 660, 661
  services 971
  sponsorship, assessing results 829
  theories 571–6, 580–83
  tone of, direct marketing 773
  see also advertising; information; integrated marketing communication
communications equipment 1016
company histories 804
comparative advertising 605–6, 613
comparison of products, advertising 613
compatibility 324, 633
compensation, sales representatives 728–31
competence, services 971
competition 72
  in channels 491–2
  countering by sales promotions 655, 659
  direct marketing opportunities 742
  euro effects 418
  monopolistic 75, 409
  perfect 75–6, 409
  price, indirect 662
  segmentation benefits 203
  see also competitors

competition-based pricing 452–3
Competition Commission 73–4, 77, 80–81
competitive activity levels 916
competitive advantage 284, 871
competitive advertising 604, 605–6
competitive analysis 453
competitive clusters 866–7
competitive edge 28, 30
competitive environment 45–6, 67–76
competitive factors
 advertising campaigns 638
 international marketing 1020, 1022
competitive information systems 870
competitive negotiation 457, 716
competitive parity 594
competitive positions 552, 876–80
competitive postures 876, 880–84
competitive reaction 870, 937
competitive response to new products 366, 369
competitive strategies 844, 865–76
competitive strengths and weaknesses 869
competitiveness, international 1015
competitors 20, 407–8
 analysis 865–70
 communications planning and 588
 entry timing 326–7
 identification 866
 new products 360
 objective s 869–70
 price cuts 440–41
 price increases 443
 reactions to new businesses 937
 sales representatives monitoring 703
 strategic marketing 865–76
complaints 513
completeness, product assortment 551
complexity 324, 488
components 62–5, 275
computer aided design (CAD) 64–5
computer aided manufacturing (CAM) 65
computer aided personal interviewing (CAPI) 220, 253
computer aided telephone interviewing (CATI) 220, 237, 253–4
computer games 598–9
computerised kiosks 541–2
computers
 deep computing 62
 pervasive computing 62
 schools 827
 in vehicles 48
conative attitudes 115
concentrated targeting 198
concentration
 geographic 145–6
 industrial 144–5
concentric diversification 861–2
concept testing 364–5
concessions 533–4
condition of goods on arrival 513
condoms 261–2
confectionery 199–200
conflict 495–7
conglomerate diversification 862
consensual decision-making 126–8
consistency
 corporate reputation 810
 delivery 512
consolidation 938–9
consultants, new product ideas 362
consumer audits 687
consumer electronics 357
consumer forces 57–9
consumer goods 32
 channel structures 475–7
 user-based product classifications 271–4
 see also fast moving consumer goods
consumer marketing 137–8
consumer markets
 customer specified products 339
 innovators 322
 marketing research 214–15
 pricing 396–7
 products 583–4
 sales force support 682
 target markets 577–8
consumer panels 219–20
consumer services
 user-based product classifications 271–4
consumerism 57–9
consumers
 behaviour 93–5
  buying situations 104–7
  decision-making process 95–103, 126–8
  diffusion of innovation 322–4
  environmental influences 107–9
  psychological influences 109–18
  real-time recording 242
  sociocultural influences 118–28
 branding benefits perspective 282–3
 internet penetration and spending 1059–62
 market beliefs 101
 market segmentation 183–97
 pricing, influences on 402
 sales promotion
  gift-, prize- or merchandise-based methods 671–7
  manufacturer promotions 657–9
  money-based methods 661–5
  product-based methods 665–71
  retailer promotions 655–7
  store-based methods 677–8
 satisfaction 11
 spending 50–51
 see also customers
Consumers' Association 57–8, 84
contact lenses 411
contacts 711–12, 743
contests 675–7, 682
contingency plan s 897
continuous innovation 355
continuous replenishment 511
continuous research 219–21
contracting, international market entry 1029
contracting out 318
contraction defences 883–4
contracts, franchising 981–2, 986–91
contractual systems 529
contractual vertical marketing systems 492–3
controlled distribution minimarkets 370
controls, marketing 915, 928–31
convenience goods 271–2, 546
convenience stores 271, 541–2
cooperation 494–5, 884–6
cooperative advertising 681–2
cooperative negotiation 716
cooperatives, retail 493
coordinated displays 556
coordination
 sales representatives, within own organisations 701
copywriting 618–19, 752
core products 268–9
corporate boosts 781
corporate chains 529
corporate communications 590, 1072
corporate governance 905
corporate identity 810–16, 831–2
corporate intelligence 867–8
corporate internet communications 1072
corporate objectives 901–4
corporate plans 898
corporate PR 798
corporate rationalisation 534
corporate reputation 808–10
corporate social responsibility (CSR) 16–18, 57, 904–5
corporate strategies 842–4
corporate values 901–4
corporate vertical marketing systems 492
correlation analysis 254
correlation methods 922–3
cosmetics 384–5
cost-based pricing 447–9
cost-based transfer pricing 460
cost leadership 871–3
cost-plus pricing 448
costs 394–6, 415
 cost–volume–profit relationship 444–6
 definitions 444
 distribution 500
 international market entry 1024
 joint 931
 marginal 445
 marketing 930–31
 media 742
 personal selling 698
 physical distribution management 502–3
 pressures 443
 sales 742
 sales promotion 685
 savings, B2B advertising 615
 total logistics concept 505–9
count and recount, promotions to retailers 679
counter-offensive defences 884
coupons 656, 663–4, 754–5, 756
courtesy, services 971
creative appeals, advertising 612–18
creative development 773–4

creative implementation 752
creative message design, e-mail marketing 1080–82
creativity, organised 362
credibility 802, 971
credit cards 557
cricket 819–20
crisis insurance 720
critical success factors 869
CRM *see* cause-related marketing; customer relationship management
cross-docking 511
cross-functional teams 381
cross-selling 534, 743, 777
CSR *see* corporate social responsibility
Cuba 150
cultivation, personal selling 697
cultural aspects of environment 587
culture 120–23, 810
cumulative discounts 454
current customers 20
customer-based structure, sales forces 723–4
customer importance structure, sales forces 724
customer-oriented appeals, advertising 615–18
customer relationship management (CRM) 223, 1080, 1087–8
customer specified products 337–9
customers
  acquisition, e-mail marketing 1079
  attracting 937
  B2B 138–41
  confidence 742
  contact strategies, e-marketing 969–70
  current 20
  information, databases 775–6
  interaction 978
  lapsed 777
  loyalty schemes *see* loyalty
  marketing and 66–7
  mix, changing 913
  needs 5
    identifying 24–5
    international marketing 1036
    satisfying 25–8
  new, attracting 658
  new products and 354–6, 360–61
  perspectives on prices 392–4
  potential 20, 101–2
  pricing, influences on 402
  profiling 1076
  relationships, international marketing 1014
  reselling to 776–7
  retention 776–7, 1079
  segmentation benefits 203
  service 164, 509–14
    centres 761
    internet uses 1064
  turnover, advertising campaigns 640
  understanding, services 971
  see also consumers
customs 1017–19
cuts in prices 439–41
cybermediaries 1068
cycles 922

D2C (direct to customer) 944
damp proofing 701–2
data
  analysis 254–5
  capture 1075
  coding 252
  collection 228–30
  geodemographic 772
  interpretation 254–5
  origins 218–19
  primary 229–30, 232–56
  protection 80, 240, 748–9
  qualitative 254–5
  quantitative 254
  sales 687
  secondary 229–32, 918, 924
data-based budget setting 594–5
databases 66, 225
  creation and management 775–7
  online 232
  technology 107, 743
datedness 811
dealers 473
debit cards 557
debt 56
deciders 161
decision domain conflict 496
decision-making
  B2B buying process 151–6
  group 149
  locations, retailers 546–7
  organisational behaviour 151–6
  process 95–103, 126–8
  units (DMU) 160, 161
decision problems 156
decision support systems (DSS) 225–6
decline of products 315–21, 586
decoding 572, 574–5
deep computing 62
deep vein thrombosis (DVT) 63
defence 877, 882–4
defendability, market segments 205
deflecting price cuts 441
deforestation 54
deletion of products 336–7
delivery 155–6
  consistency 512
  flexibility 512–13
  inadequacies, services 972
  reliability 512
  times 512–13
  see also distribution
Delphi method 922
demand
  curbing 443
  curves 403–5, 450–51
  derived 142–3
  determinants 402–3
  elastic 405
  elasticity of 143
  inelastic 143–4, 405
  joint 143
  maximum 916
  price elasticity 404–7
  pricing 449–52
  services 978–9
  structure of 144–6
  unitary 406
demographics 48–52, 184–6, 190, 742
demonstrations 678, 701, 779
denial technique 715
Denmark 78
department stores 533–5
departmental marketers 14
dependency 150, 499
depth of range 530–32
deregulation 78
derived demand 142–3
descriptive research 217
design, products 298–9, 301, 333
desk research *see* secondary research
destination management systems 789
detergents 74–5, 336
developing countries 1018
development
  advertising 638–9
  agreements 1028–9
  joint 168
  markets 860
  see also new products; research and development
diamonds 346
dichotomous questions 249
diet products 83
diets 58–9
differential advantage 28
differentiated targeting 199
differentiation 451–2, 812, 873–4
diffusion of innovation 322–4
digital innovation 325–6
digital technology 1075
digital television 437
direct exports 1025–6
direct mail 670, 745–53
direct marketing 9, 80, 739
  campaign management 770–75
  definition 740–41
  objectives 769–70, 771, 773
  promotional mix 569, 769–70
  rise of 741–4
  techniques 744–69
Direct Marketing Association (DMA) 84, 588, 1077
direct response advertising 753–7
Direct Selling Association (DSA) 711
direct supply 475, 965
direct taxation 67
direct to customer (D2C) 944
directed buyers 98
directed information seekers 98
directional policy matrix 855–6
discontinuous innovation 355–6
discount clubs 542
discount grocery retailers 536–7
discount overriders, promotions to retailers 679
discounts 454–5, 678–81
discreet branding 290–91
disintermediation 1068

dispersion 487
display advertising 628
displays 555–7
dissociative groups 124
dissolution of relationships 170
distance selling *see* direct marketing
distinctiveness 204, 289, 810
distribution 7–8, 66
  chains 407
  channels 11, 407, 472–3, 943–4
    behavioural aspects 494–500
    channel strategies 484–90
    channel structures 474–80, 484–5, 490–93
    intermediaries 473–4, 480–84
    international marketing 1038
    internet uses 1064, 1065–8
    management 501
    new 742–3
    non-store catalogues 767
  coverage 937
  exclusive 485, 486
  franchises 981
  infrastructure 471
  intensive 485
  non-profit organisations 998
  physical 500–3
    customer service 509–14
  selective 485, 486
  see also delivery; logistics
distributors 473, 559–60, 562–3
  channel structures 478, 479–80
  sales representatives 683
  see also wholesalers
diversification 861–2, 863, 864, 1014
divisibility 324
DMA *see* Direct Marketing Association
DMU (decision-making units) 160, 161
dodos 854–5, 857
dogs 851, 852
dolphins 58
domestic markets 1012–13
dominance, supermarkets 535–7
dominant positions 1021
door-to-door samples 670–71
door-to-door selling 543
dotcoms 1053, 1057, 1094–5
double glazing 583–4, 708–9
drinking and driving 648–10
drip advertising 639–40
'drive thru' grocery shopping 525
driving, drinking and 648–10
drop errors 373
dropping products 337
DRTV (direct response advertising on television) 754, 756–7
DSA (Direct Selling Association) 711
DSS (decision support systems) 225–6
durability 167–8, 270, 300
duration of test marketing 369–70
duties 67–8
DVD recorders 314
DVT (deep vein thrombosis) 63
dynamically continuous innovation 355

e-business 62
e-commerce 61, 68, 527, 748, 908
e-communication 765
e-mail
  focus groups 240
  marketing 1076–8
    creative message design 1080–82
    customer acquisition 1079
    customer retention 1080
    response and review 1082–3
    viral 1078–9, 1090–91
  notification 969
  surveys by 240
  unsolicited 772
e-marketing 32–3, 969–70
  e-mail marketing 1076–83
  internet marketing 1055–76
e-tailing 563
early adopters 323
early differentiators 326
early imitators 326
early majority 323
early nichers 326
Earth Island Institute 58
EAS (electronic article surveillance) 155
Eastern Europe 12
ecolabelling 297
economic and competitive environment 45–6, 67–76, 109
economic dimension 168
economic factors, international marketing 1020
economic influences 109, 163–4
economic policy 67–70
economies of scale 872, 1013, 1040–41
ECR (efficient consumer response) 510–11
EDI (electronic data interchange) 480
EEA (European Economic Area) 71
efficient consumer response (ECR) 510–11
EFTA (European Free Trade Association) 71
EFTPOS (electronic funds transfer at point of sale) 557
elastic demand 405
elasticity of demand *see* demand
elderly people 615–16
electoral roll 751
electricity industry 81, 152, 701
electronic article surveillance (EAS) 155
electronic data interchange (EDI) 480
electronic funds transfer at point of sale (EFTPOS) 557
electronic marketplaces 154
electronic point-of-sale (EPOS) 224, 488, 557
electronics 146
emergent marketing philosophies 16–20
emotional appeals, advertising 612–13
empathy, advertising agencies 633
employees, new product ideas 360
EMS (enhanced messaging service) 1086–7
encirclement attacks 881
encoding 571, 573–4, 575
end use 193
engineering 22, 159
enhanced messaging service (EMS) 1086–7
enquiry tests, advertising campaigns 642
entertainment seekers 98
entertainment software 344–5
entrenchment 865
entry *see* market entry
envelopes, direct mail 752
environment 53–6, 77, 526–7
  consumer behaviour 107–9
  external 20–21, 45–6
  internal 21–2
  situation analysis 587–9
  see also marketing environment
environmental scanning 47–8, 225
EPMA (European Promotional Marketing Alliance) 686
EPOS *see* Electronic Point of Sale
ESOMAR (European Society for Opinion and Marketing Research) 256, 258
essential evidence 968
esteem needs 113, 114
ethics
  business 53, 57
  corporate reputation 808
  global sourcing 549–50
  international marketing 1018
  marketing 16–18
  marketing research 256–8
  personal 53, 56–7
  see also corporate social responsibility
ethnic communities 121–2
euro 416–19, 595
Eurobrands 340–42, 416
Europe
  market segmentation 191–2
  marketing environment 44–5
    economic and competitive environment 67–76
    nature 45–8
    political and regulatory environment 76–85
    sociocultural environment 48–59
    technological environment 59–67
  retail sector structure 527–32
  see also European Union
European Brands Association 284
European Direct Marketing Association 771
European Economic Area (EEA) 71
European Free Trade Association (EFTA) 71
European Parliament 76
European Promotional Marketing Alliance (EPMA) 686
European scale organisations 1009
European Society for Opinion and Marketing Research (ESOMAR) 256, 258
European Union
  anti-competitive practices 1021
  battery farming 833
  Common Agricultural Policy (CAP) 77
  comparative advertising 606
  developing countries 1018
  Distance Selling Directive 764, 769

distribution by intermediaries 488–9
duty-free access to markets 70
e-commerce 1085
e-mail spam 772
ecolabelling 297
enlargement 70–71
harmonisation 79–80, 686
marketing environment *see* European marketing environment
membership candidates 70–71
monopolies 73
political and regulatory environment 79–80
product guarantees 302–3
public procurement 140–41, 458
sales promotion harmonisation 686
secondary data sources 231
Single European Market (SEM) 70, 71, 79, 140, 183, 191, 415–19
small businesses 932–3
trade marks 281–2, 289
United States trade relations 1021
Europeanisation 558, 611
EVA (Exhibition Venues Association) 782–3
evaluation
advertising 642–3
corporate identity changes 815
information 99–100, 103
integrated marketing communication 595–6
marketing 915
marketing research 256
new product development 372–3
operational performance 929–31
performance, sales representatives 731–2
post-purchase 102–4
public relations 806–8
sales promotion 687
sponsorship 829–30
evening out fluctuating sales 655
events 803–4
evidence, physical 28, 968
evoked sets 99
ex-works prices 455
exaggerated promises, services 972
exchange processes 5
exchange rates 69–70
exchange transactions 7
exchanges 154
excitement 802
exclusive distribution 485, 486
executive franchises 981
Exhibition Venues Association (EVA) 782–3
exhibitions 740, 777–84
exit evaluation, advertising campaigns 642
expanding usage 658
expansion 169–70, 877
expectations 496–8
experience curves 448–9, 872
experimentation 243
expert power 498–9
expertise, international trade in 1026–9
experts, panels of 921
exploration of relationships 169
exploratory research 216–17
exports 1025–6
extended problem solving 106–7
external environment 45–6
external influences on pricing decisions 401–12
external marketing audits 906–7
external marketing information sources 222, 224
external order takers 703–4
external organisational environment 20–21
external uncertainty 932
extra product promotions 665–6

FAB (flavoured alcoholic beverages) 604, 853
face-to-face omnibus surveys 220
facilitating agents 166
facilitating factors, direct marketing 741, 743–4
facilitating values 483–4
facilitators 501–3
facility support services 845
factor analysis 254
factory farming 833–4
facts, advertising 614
fads 53, 320
failure 320, 374–6, 846–7
families 125–8
FAQ (frequently asked questions) 969
farming *see* agriculture
fashion products 320
fashions 53
FAST (Federation Against Software Theft) 1082
fast moving consumer goods (fmcg) 26, 102, 290
fear 612–13, 615
Federation Against Software Theft (FAST) 1082
feedback 484, 572, 575, 595–6, 687, 702–3, 829
feelings 612–13
fempro 86–7
field marketing 678, 706–7, 784
field research *see* primary research
Fiji 202
file sharing services 1067
filling product ranges 335–6
finance function 22, 160
financial analysis, new products 366
financial benefits of products 393
financial characteristics, product lifecycles 327
financial objectives 430–35
financial publics 795
financial services 600–1, 702, 888–90, 943–5
Financial Services Authority (FSA) 729
financial targets 902
financing benefits 483
fine fragrances 404, 486
fire products 736–7
Five Forces Model 865–6
fixed costs 444
fixed endorsed approach to branding 291
fixed position defences 882
flank attacks 880–81
flanking defences 883
flavoured alcoholic beverages (FAB) 604, 853
flexibility 512–13, 749, 937, 1024
flexible endorsed approach to branding 291
flowers 6, 70
fmcg *see* fast moving consumer goods
FOB prices 455
focus 874–5, 898
focus groups 236–7, 240, 1058
followers 879
food 44–5, 52, 55, 71, 335, 850–51
see also genetic modification
football 333, 422–3, 818–19, 820, 821–2
forced relationships 362
forecasts 918–24
foreign exchange rates 69–70
Forest Stewardship Council (FSC) 54
forests 54
formula selling 712
forward integration 492, 862–3
France 119, 518–19
franchising 529, 979–80, 1001–2
blueprints 986–91
business format franchises 980–83
contracts 981–2, 986–91
franchisees 473–4
marketing to 989–90
perspectives of 984–6
franchisors' perspectives 983–4
international 1028–9
operating manuals 989
systems 493
free flow store layouts 555
free gifts 80, 673
free mail-ins 672
free merchandise, promotions to retailers 680
free on board (FOB) prices 455
free products 665–6
free-range farming 833–4
freephone numbers 743–4, 754–5, 756, 757, 763
freepost addresses 743–4, 754–6
frequency, advertising 622, 623
frequently asked questions (FAQ) 969
friendship 165
frontal attacks 880
FSA (Financial Services Authority) 729
FSC (Forest Stewardship Council) 54
fulfilment costs 685
full service advertising agencies 631
full service retailing 530
full service wholesalers 559
functional benefits of products 392
functional discounts 454
functional organisation 925
functional packaging 294
functional plans 898

gas industry 81, 701
gatekeepers 161, 162
gatherers 1085
GATT (General Agreement on Tariffs and Trade) 72
gay market 208–10
GE matrix 855, 899
General Agreement on Tariffs and Trade (GATT) 72
general intelligence 362
general public 797
generational marketing 48
generic brands 290
generic strategies 871–6
genetic modification 82, 795, 1044–5
geodemographics 186–9, 197, 772
geographic adjustments to prices 455
geographic concentration 145–6
geographic focus, advertising campaigns 638
geographic information systems (GIS) 547
geographic segmentation 183–4
geographic structure, sales forces 722
Germany 80, 119, 296
gifts 80, 166, 671–7, 816
  see also sponsorship
GIS (geographic information systems) 547
glass 901
global sourcing 162
GM (genetic modification) 82, 795, 1044–5
Go-betweens, European segmentation 191–2
go errors 373
goals
  incompatible 495
  see also objectives
golden zones 655
good publicity 800–2
goods 5, 7–8
  condition on arrival 513
  consumer *see* consumer goods
  international trade 1025–6
  merchandise lines, retailing 530–32
  see also products
goodwill 285–6
governments
  bodies as purchasers 140–41
  economic policy 67–70
  political and regulatory environment 76–8
  spending 69
  see also local governments
grading 483
green issues 16–18, 587–9
  see also corporate social responsibility
grey market 48–9, 191, 462–3
grid pattern store layouts 554–5
groceries 476, 525, 529, 536–7, 1066–7
group decision-making 149
group interviews 236–7
groups, sociocultural influences 118–28
growth 938–9
  products 313–14, 323, 584–5
  strategies 858–64
guarantees 302–3, 513
guerilla attacks 882
guidelines, sales promotion 685–6

harmonisation 79–80, 686
harvesting 317, 864
head-to-head confrontations 884
health and fitness sector 965–6
health and safety 53
health concerns 56
hens 833–4
heterogeneity, services 959–61
hi-fi equipment 843
hierarchy of needs 113–15
high-tech products 64
higher education 713
  see also universities
hoardings 629–30
holidays 49, 202, 273–4, 438, 493, 705, 786–90
  see also tourism
home audits 219
home deliveries 525
home shopping 524, 766
  see also mail order
horizontal competition 491
horizontal integration 863
hospitals 78
hostels 1001–2
hot-air dryers 395
hotels 260–61, 398, 440, 950–51, 953–5, 957, 973, 975
house journals 806
hubs 154
human rights 905
humour, advertising appeals 616
Hungary 1011
hunters 1085
hypermarkets 518–19, 537–8

ideas 5, 7–8, 359–65
identification
  competitors 866
  customer needs 24–5
identity, corporate 810–16, 831–2
IFA (independent financial advisers) 943–4
image 604, 607, 616, 813
  see also corporate identity
imitative products 320
impact
  personal selling 696
  sponsorship 828
implementation
  advertising campaigns 639–42
  corporate identity changes 814
  integrated marketing communication 595–6
  sales promotion 685
imposition, distribution channels 484
impulse purchases 551
in-home selling 543
in-pack promotions 673
inbound telemarketing 758, 760–61
incentives 72, 660–61
income 50
incompatible goals 495
increases in prices 442–3
increasing frequency and amount of purchases 656
independence 884–6, 932
independent financial advisers (IFA) 943–4
independent retail outlets 528–9
Independent Television Commission (ITC) 77, 83, 822
India 317
indirect exports 1026
indirect taxation 67–9
individuals, psychological influences 109–18
industrial concentration 144–5
industrial goods *see* B2B: goods
industrial marketing *see* B2B: marketing
industry attractiveness 855
inelastic demand 143–4, 405
influencers 161
infomediaries 1075
information 212
  customer databases 775–6
  direct marketing 769, 773
  dissemination 658
  evaluation 99–100, 103
  exchange facilitating 719
  flow 524–5
  overload 97
  sales representatives gathering 702–3
  searches 96–9
  services 705
  value added services 484
  see also communication; data; marketing information systems
informing, sales representatives 700
infrastructure, distribution 471
initiation, direct marketing 770
innovation 350, 353–5, 932
  diffusion of 322–4
  digital 325–6
innovative products 319
innovators 322–3
inseparability, services 957–9
inside order takers 704
installation support 513
installing, sales representatives 701
instant-win promotions 675
Institute of Practitioners in Advertising (IPA) 84
Institute of Public Relations (IPR) 84, 793
Institute of Sales Promotion (ISP) 84, 588, 685–6
institutional advertising 607
institutions as purchasers 141
intangibility, services 953–5
integrated marketing communication
  budgeting 593–5
  definition 570
  environment 587–9
  evaluation 595–6
  implementation 595–6
  objectives 589–90

products 583–7
strategies 590–3
target markets 577–83
integrated online sales promotions 666
integration 492, 862–3
integrative business function, marketing as 22–4
intelligence 225, 867–8
intensive distribution 485
intensive growth 859–61, 863
interactive marketing 970
interactive programme guides (IPG) 1089
interactive television (iTV) 576, 1089–91
interactive voice response (IVR) 1085
interest generation 937
interest rates 69
interests, market segmentation 190
interface, marketing as 23
interim evaluation, advertising campaigns 642
intermediaries 20–21
distribution channels 473–4, 480–84
sales promotions to 654–5, 661
internal communication 804–6
internal influences on pricing decisions 412–15
internal marketing
audits 907
information sources 222, 224–5
services 974–9
internal organisational environment 21–2
internal publics 795
internal uncertainty 932
international exhibitions 778
international marketing 35, 1006–7
environment 1015–21
market entry methods 1024–34
meaning 1007–10
understanding markets 1015–23
rationale for 1010–15
strategies 1034–45
international production 1013
international trading blocs 70–72
internationalisation 558, 848
internet
airline bookings 760
auctions 400, 883, 1063
B2B spending 1062–4
banner advertising 637–8, 1070–71
brands online 289–90
channel structures and 480
consumer penetration and spending 1059–62
corporate communications 1072
databases 232
direct response advertising 756
file sharing services 1067
international marketing 1011
lists 1079
marketing 9
advertising 1069–71
broadband 1074–5
communication 1069–73
direct marketing links 744
future 1074–5
loyalty reinforcement 1071–2
nature 1055–7
promotion 1069–73
website uses 1064–73
marketing research 239–40
marketplaces 154
new product development 373–4
omnibus surveys 220
ordering 66–7
price comparisons 442
public relations online 801
retailing 563–4
reverse auctions 1063
sales promotions 666
searching behaviour 98
secondary data sources 231, 233
service providers (ISP) 452
shopping 303, 544
small and medium-sized enterprises (SME) growth strategies 864
sponsorship online 801
technologies 62
websites 66, 1057–9
marketing uses 1064–73
suppliers 148
women, use by 108
interpretation of data 254–5
intertype competition 491–2
interviewers 252–3
interviews 232–8, 240
introduction of products 313, 584
invention 350
inventory 502, 507, 512, 655
investment, international market entry 1029–32
invitations, sales promotions 661
invoicing 513
IPA (Institute of Practitioners in Advertising) 84
IPG (interactive programme guides) 1089
IPR (Institute of Public Relations) 84, 793
Iraq 150
ISP (Institute of Sales Promotion) *see* Institute of Sales Promotion
ISP (internet service providers) 452
IT sector 869
ITC *see* Independent Television Commission
iTV (interactive television) 576, 1089–91
IVR (interactive voice response) 1085

Japan 31, 71, 1012
jeans 891
JIT *see* just-in-time
job franchises 981
joint costs 931
joint demand 143
joint development 168
joint sales promotion 687–9
Joint Strike Fighter programme 338
joint ventures 885–6, 1031–2
journalism 796
judgemental budget setting 593–4
judgemental sampling 245–6
junk mail 739
just-in-time (JIT) 65, 164, 508, 512–13

Kenya 6, 1019–20
kiosks, computerised 541–2
knowledge, international trade in 1026–9

labelling 297
laggards 323
language 288, 1017
lapsed customers 777
large enterprises 932–3
late adopters 323
late entrants 327
late imitators 327
late majority 323
launch of identity changes 814
launch of new products 371–2
layouts
advertising 619
stores 554–5
leading indicators 923
leading questions 250
leads 710, 779
learning 112
learning experiences, exhibitions 779
leather 734–5
legal environment 45–6, 588
buying process 150
international marketing 1021
pricing 410–12
legitimate power 498
Lesotho 166
less developed countries 70
licensing 361–2, 885, 1027–8
lifecycles
families 125–6
products *see* products
relationships 169–71
lifestyles 58–9, 742
displays 556
segmentation 188, 189–93
slice-of-life advertising 614, 620
Likert summated ratings 250, 251
limited problem solving 105–6
limited service advertising agencies 631
limited service retailing 530
limited service wholesalers 559–60
lines *see* products
linkage effectiveness 872–3
lists 748, 1079
see also mailing lists
loading up 659
lobbying 84–5, 795, 804, 833–4
local buying 497
local governments
political and legal environment 78
as purchasers 140
local procurement 162
local scale organisations 1008
local transportation 508
location 182
advertising agencies 632
organisational, of marketing 924
retailers 545–8
see also place

logging 54
logistical values 481–3
logistics 500, 1038, 1044
  customer service 509–14
  management 503–5
  total logistics cost concept 505–9
  see also distribution
logos 810
London Marathon 817, 828
long channels 475–7
long-term plans 897
long-term profit objectives, international market entry 1024
love needs 113, 114
low calorie sweeteners 63
loyalty 194–5
  brand 195, 289
  cards 9, 197, 224, 657, 674–5, 691–2
  reinforcement, internet marketing 1071–2
  schemes 653, 656–7, 660, 674–5, 691
luxuries 52

m-marketing 1083–8
mackerel 403
macro segments 181–3
macroeconomic environment 67–72
magazines 186, 626–8
maggots 78
mail-ins 672
mail order 544, 765–8
mail questionnaires 238
mailing lists 746, 747–8, 750–52
maintenance
  products 300–1
  services 276
Malawi 6
management
  judgement 920–21
  marketing *see* marketing management
  process, marketing as 5
  products *see* products: management
managerial influences on personal selling roles 699
manifest conflict 495
manufacturers
  branding benefits perspective 283–5
  brands 286–7
  channel structures 477–80
  concessions in department stores 534
  consumer promotions 657–9
  intermediary sales promotions 654–5
  manufacturer promotions 659
manufacturing subsidiaries 1030–31
mapping, perceptual 330
marginal analysis 444–5
marginal costs 445
marginal revenue 445
margins 473
mark-downs 451
mark-up 447–8
market attractiveness model 855
market beliefs 101
market challengers 878
market characteristics, product lifecycles 327
market coverage 484, 485–6
market defence 440
market development 860, 864
market dominance 440
market entry
  international marketing 1022, 1024–34, 1038–9
  small businesses 936–7
market evolution 322–8
market factors 1022
market followers 879
market forecasting 918–24
market leadership 876–7
market managers 379–80
market nichers 879–80
market niches 936
market opportunities 847–9
market penetration 859, 864
market potential 915–16, 917–18
market presence 781
market prices 460
market research 66, 212
Market Research Quality Standards Association 258
Market Research Society (MRS) 257, 258
market segments *see* segmentation
market selection, international marketing 1021–3
market share 431, 850–55, 877, 932
market size 487
market structures 847–9
market tests 923
marketing
  concept 10, 20–4
  definitions 3, 4–10
  development of 10
marketing alliances 885–6
marketing analysis 908
marketing audits 906–7
marketing budgets 913–15
marketing channels *see* distribution: channels
marketing communication *see* communication
marketing controls 915, 928–31
marketing costs analysis 930–31
marketing dynamics 3–43
marketing environment 21
  elements 45–6
  international 1015–21
  trends 916
marketing evaluation 915
marketing factors, advertising campaigns 640
marketing functions 160
marketing information systems (MIS) 213, 221–5, 870, 928
marketing management 24–30, 895, 961–79
marketing mix 25–8, 47
  advertising in 607–9
  international 1042–5
  language 1017
  packaging in 295–6
  pricing and 395
  product lifecycles 327
  segmentation benefits 203
  services 961–9
marketing myopia 30
marketing myths 11
marketing objectives 327, 413–14, 431, 910–12
marketing orientation 10, 12, 14–15
marketing philosophers 14
marketing planning 895–6
  benefits 899–900
  internet uses 1064, 1065
  market forecasting 918–24
  market potential 915–16, 917–18
  organising marketing activities 924–8
  problems 899–900
  process 900–15
  purpose 901
  sales forecasting 918–24
  sales potential 916–18
  smaller businesses 931–41
  strategic marketing plans and planning 896–900
marketing plans 844, 900–1
marketing PR 797–8
marketing programmes 844, 913
marketing research
  briefs 228
  causal research 217
  conducting 252–4
  continuous research 219–21
  decision support systems 225–6
  definition 213–14
  descriptive research 217
  ethics 256–8
  evaluation 256
  exploratory research 216–17
  marketing information systems *see* marketing information systems
  objectives 227
  planning 227–8
  predictive research 217–18
  primary research 229–30, 232–56
  process 226–30
  qualitative research 218
  quantitative research 218–19
  reports 255
  role 214–16
  secondary research 229, 230–32
  selling and, conflicts of interest 256–8
marketing scope 32–5
marketing strategies 53, 365–6, 844, 846–9, 912–13
  international 1034–45
  services 961–70
  see also strategic marketing
markets, street and indoor 542
Maslow's hierarchy of needs 113–15
mass production 148
master franchising 1028
materials
  handling 65, 509
  technological environment 62–5
matrix organisation 925, 927
maturity 314–15, 585–6, 939–41
maximisation of profits 430, 445

media
  advertising 621–30, 636–8, 641–2
  direct marketing 773
  ethnic communities 121
  fragmentation 742
  involving 802
  new 765
  pressure groups, use by 59
  public relations 807
  relationships 795–7, 800–3
  sponsorship exposure measurement 829
medicines 106, 420
medium enterprises 932–3
medium-term plans 897
MEG (moderated e-mail groups) 240
membership groups 123
merchandise *see* goods; products
merchandise-based sales promotion methods 671–7
merchandising allowances 682
merchandising strategies, retailers 554–7
messages 571–6
  advertising 610–21, 641
  creative design 1080–82
  precision 697
MFA (multi fibre arrangement) 71–2
micro enterprises 932–3
micro factors 547
micro segments 182–3, 1080
microchips 64
microeconomic environment 72–6
middle class 119
milk 59, 368, 423–4
milking strategy 317
MIS *see* marketing information systems
mis-selling 729
misconceptions, services 972
mission statements 903
missionary sales representatives 707
MLP (multi-leisure parks) 954
MMC (Monopolies and Mergers Commission) 410
MMS (multimedia messaging service) 1087
mobile commerce 383
mobile customers 1041
mobile defences 882–3
mobile exhibitions 784
mobile home holidays 786–8
mobile marketing 1083–8
mobile phones
  health risks 367–8
  marketing research 240
  product lifecycle 314–15
  sponsorship by operators 816
  third generation 382–4
moderated e-mail groups (MEG) 240
Moderns, European segmentation 191
modifications to products 331–4
modified re-buys 149–50
money-based sales promotion methods 661–5
money-off coupons *see* coupons
money saving or making, advertising appeals 615
monitoring 595
  corporate identity changes 815
  new product development 372–3
  see also evaluation
monolithic approach to branding 291
monopolies 72–4, 346, 408
Monopolies and Mergers Commission (MMC) 410
monopolistic competition 75, 409
morphological analysis 362
MOSAIC 186–9, 776
motivation 112–13, 728–31, 813
motor industry
  advertising 616, 621
  channel system competition 492
  dealership marketing 1093–4
  distribution 471–2, 486
  marketing environment 47–8, 55
  marketing planning 940–41
  pricing 438, 463–5
  products 305–6, 317, 320, 332, 336
  public relations 803–4
MRS (Market Research Society) 257, 258
multi fibre arrangement (MFA) 71–2
multi-leisure parks (MLP) 954
multimedia messaging service (MMS) 1087
multiple-choice questions 249–50
multiple objectives, non-profit organisations 995
multiple publics 993–5
multiple sourcing 138, 146–7
multivariable segmentation 196–7
multivariate analysis 254
music 523, 617–18
mutual understanding 793
mystery shopping 241, 960

names
  brands 281, 288–9
  changes 810–11, 831–2
nanotechnology 379
nappies 316
national scale organisations 1008
Natural Resources Institute (NRI) 57
Ncompass 220
necessities 52
needs 5
  identifying 24–5
  Maslow's hierarchy 113–15
  satisfaction 25–8, 712–13
  social 165
negotiated prices 460
negotiation
  distribution channels 484
  personal selling 715–17, 720
  prices 456–8
Netherlands 80, 119
new media 1075–91
new products
  committees 380
  demonstrations 779
  development (NPD) 350–51, 861, 864
    failure 374–6
    importance 356–8
    organisation for 379–81
    process 358–74, 376–81
    services 963–4
  introduction 511, 584
  launch 655, 779
  managers 380
  meanings 351–6
  pricing strategies 436–8
new task purchasing 150
New Zealand 788
news
  advertising 614
  conferences 801
newsletters 806
newspaper advertising 628
nichers 879–80
niches 936
'no growth' options 864–5
noise 573, 575, 576
nomads 1085
non-durable products 270
non-economic influences 164–6
non-profit marketing 34, 992–9
non-profit markets 398–9
non-random sampling 245–6
non-store catalogues 767
non-store retailing 543–5
novels 823
NPD *see* new products: development
NRI (Natural Resources Institute) 57
nuclear industry 116, 804–5
nursing relationships 799

objections, handling 714–15
objective budgeting 594–5
objectives
  advertising campaigns 635–6, 637
  competitors 869–70
  corporate 901–4
  corporate identity changes 813
  direct marketing 769–70, 771, 773
  financial 430–35
  integrated marketing communication 589–90
  marketing 413–14, 431, 910–12
  marketing research 227
  multiple, non-profit organisations 995
  organisational 413, 487, 845–6
  pricing 428–35
  quality, interaction with 431
  questionnaires 247–8
  sales 431, 721
  sales promotion 659–61, 684
observational research 240–43
odd-even pricing 450
OECD 1018
OEM (original equipment manufacturers) 139
offer promises 773
Office of Fair Trading (OFT) 77, 80–81, 410
office supplies 584
offline lists 1079
Ofgem 81, 701
Oflot 410
OFT *see* Office of Fair Trading
Oftel 81, 1074

Ofwat 81
older people *see* grey market
oligopolies 74–5, 408
olives 77
omnibus surveys 220
on-pack promotions 673
on-pack reduced prices 663–4
on-pack samples 669
one-price selling 438
online *see* internet
open displays 555
open-ended questions 248
operating manuals, franchising 989
operating methods, retailers 532
operating supplies 276
operating targets 902
operational benefits of products 393
operational control 928
operational issues, telemarketing 763–4
operational marketing plans 900–1
operational performance evaluation 929–31
operational plans 898
operations 159
opinions, market segmentation 190
opportunities 908
opportunity to see (OTS) 622–3, 641
opt-in schemes 1076, 1078
opt-out schemes 1078
oranges 479
orders
  convenience of ordering 512
  cycle time 512
  direct ordering 769
  makers 705–6
  online ordering 66–7
  processing and administration 507
  size constraints 512
  status information 513
  takers 703–6
Organisation for Economic Co-operation and Development (OECD) 1018
organisation for new product development 379–81
organisational alternatives 924–8
organisational behaviour, decision-making 151–6
organisational capabilities 487
organisational characteristics of macro segmentation 181–2
organisational focus 898
organisational level plans 897
organisational location of marketing 924
organisational marketing *see* B2B
organisational objectives 413, 487, 845–6
organisational resources 487, 845–6
organised creativity 362
organising marketing activities 924–8
original equipment manufacturers (OEM) 139
origins of data 218–19
OTS (opportunity to see) 622–3, 641
out-of-town retail parks 537–8, 548–9
out-of-town speciality stores 539
outbound telemarketing 758, 759, 761–3, 764
outdoor advertising 629–30
outflanking and attacking 884
outlets 508–9
outsourcing R&D 377–8, 380
over the counter medicines 106
own-label brands 87, 287–8, 518, 557–9, 657
ownership
  retailing 528–9
  services and 952

packaging 64, 293–4, 912
  consumer market beliefs 101
  direct mail 752
  functional 294
  international marketing 1036–7
  labelling 297
  in marketing mix 295–6
  promotional 294–5
  waste 296–7
panels of experts 921
parallel demand curves 404
parallel trading 420
Pareto effect 724
park and ride transport 399
partnerships, channel systems 494–5
parts 275
party plans 543
patronage 816–17
payback periods, international market entry 1024
PCB (printed circuit boards) 338
PDM (physical distribution management) 500–3, 504
penetration pricing 437–8
penknives 320
pensions mis-selling 729
people 28, 968
  see also consumers; customers
perceived demand curves 403
perceived product differences 936
perceived risk 324
percentage of sales budgeting methods 594
perception 111–12
perceptions of reality 496
perceptual mapping 329
perfect competition 75–6, 409
performance
  evaluation
    operational performance 929–31
    sales representatives 731–2
  new products 372
  products 300, 333–4
peripheral evidence 968
perishability, services 955–7, 964
permission 1076
permission-based e-mailing 1083
permission marketing 748, 1078
personal benefits of products 393–4
personal chemistry, advertising agencies 633
personal ethics 53, 56–7
personal factors 166
personal interviews 234–6
personal ownership 932
personal selling 13, 694–5
  definition 695
  exhibitions and, comparison of benefits 779–80
  forms of 703–8
  internet 1072–3
  process 708–20
  promotional mix 569
  role 695–9
  sales management 720–32
  see also sales representatives
personalisation 749, 1080, 1090
personalised registration plates 391
personality 110
persuading, sales representatives 700–1
Peru 175–6
pervasive computing 62
pet food 321
petrol 64, 75, 201
petrol station forecourt retailing 271, 541
pharmaceuticals 56, 83, 579, 707, 761, 847, 898–9
phased withdrawal 317–18
phasing out products 337
philosophical targets 902–3
PhoneBus 220
phones *see* mobile phones; telephones
physical distribution management (PDM) 500–3, 504
physical evidence 28, 968
physiological needs 113
pianos 873
piloting 252
pioneering advertising 604–5
pioneers 326
pizzas 429
place
  marketing mix 27, 1043–4
  services 965–6
  utility 524
  see also distribution; location; logistics; retailers; wholesalers
planned economies 13
planning
  definition 896
  exhibitions 783–4
  marketing plans 844
  marketing research 227–8
  personal selling 710–11
  sales 721–5
  see also marketing planning
planning permission 78–9
plans 896–8
PLC *see* products: lifecycles
pneumatic conveying 207–8
PNS (Pre- and Post-Natal Survey) 219
point-of-purchase (POP) materials 611
point-of-sale (POS) displays 677
points, loyalty cards 674–5
Poland 120, 181, 1029–30, 1038, 1046–8
police 812
policies
  brands and branding 290–91
  pricing 435–43
political and legal environment 45–6, 76–85, 109, 588, 1021

POP (point-of-purchase) materials 611
population definition 244
Porter's five forces 865–6
portfolios, products 328
POS (point-of-sale) displays 677
positioning 98, 328–34, 463–4
 direct marketing 774
 brands 417
 international marketing 1038
 prices and 431
 public relations evaluation 808
 repositioning 331–3, 912
 retailers 552
post-purchase evaluation 102–4
post-tests, advertising campaigns 642
post-transactional variables 513–14
postcodes 747
posters, advertising 84, 629
potatoes 193
potential customers 20, 101–2
potential products 268, 269
power 497–9, 716
PPS (pre-packaged spirits) 132–3
PR *see* public relations
Pre- and Post-Natal Survey (PNS) 219
pre-emptive defences 884
pre-packaged spirits (PPS) 132–3
pre-testing, advertising 638–9
pre-transactional variables 510
precipitation 152–3, 156
precision
 marketing 1078
 personal selling 696–7
 targeting 696–7, 743
predictive research 217–18
pregnancy 223–4
prelaunch of small businesses 934–5
premium money 682
premium prices 394
prescription medicines 420
press briefings 802
press conferences 801–2
press receptions 802
press relations 800
press releases 801, 1072
pressure groups 57–9, 84–5
prestige 165
prestige pricing 450
price elasticity of demand 404–7
prices 7–8, 391–2, 427–8
 adjustments 453–5
 appropriate 163–4
 banding 396
 changes 439–43
 comparison 397
 competition, indirect 662
 competition-based pricing 452–3
 consumer market beliefs 101
 contexts of pricing 396–7
 cost-based pricing 447–9, 460
 customers' perspectives 392–4
 cuts 439–41
 demand-based pricing 449–52
 differentials 419–20
 differentiation 451–2
 discipline 397
 discounts 454–5
 European influences on pricing 415–20
 external influences 47, 401–12
 fixing 410
 geographic adjustments 455
 increases 442–3
 internal influences on pricing decisions 412–15
 leadership 413
 legal and regulatory framework 410–12
 lining 450–51
 market 460
 marketing mix 26–7, 395, 1042–3
 marketing strategies 913
 negotiated 460
 negotiations 456–8
 non-profit organisations 998
 objectives 428–35
 online comparisons 442
 penetration pricing 437–8
 perceptions 392–6
 policies 435–43
 premium prices 394
 product mix pricing strategies 438
 psychological pricing 450–52
 range setting 443–53
 reduced, offers 662–4
 role 392–6
 sellers' perspectives 394–6
 sensitivity 272, 397, 399, 406–7
 service markets 397–401
 services 964–5
 skimming 437
 special adjustments 453–5
 strategies 435–43
 structures 453
 tactics 453–5
 transfer pricing 459–61
 transparency 416
pricing *see* prices
primary data 229–30, 232–56
primary research 229–30, 232–56, 923
print media, sample distribution 670
print presentation, advertising 618–19, 641
printed circuit boards (PCB) 338
privacy 1091
privatisation 72–3, 812
prize-based sales promotion methods 671–7
PRiZM 188
proactive approach to new product development 357–8
probability sampling 245
problems
 decision 156
 definition, marketing research 226–7
 marketing planning 899–900
 recognition 95–6
 solving 104–7
processes 28
 services 968–9
 wireless marketing 1086
producers 475–7
product-based sales promotion methods 665–71
product-based structure, sales forces 722–3
product champions 340
product fit factors 1022
product managers 339–40, 379
product–market matrix 858–61
product mix
 pricing strategies 438
product organisation 925, 926
product-oriented advertising 604–7, 613–15
production 22
 functions 159
 international 1013
 new products 366
 orientation 10, 12
 processes 64
productivity 872, 913, 976–9
products 267–8
 accumulation 482
 application, macro segmentation 182
 assortment 550–51
 augmented 268, 269, 270
 B2B markets 583–4
 benefits 392–4, 773
 characteristics 488
 classification 270–76
 comparison 613
 consumer markets 101, 583–4
 core 268–9
 current needs 24
 customer needs 25–6
 definition 268
 deletion 336–7
 design 298–9, 301, 333
 durability 270, 300
 failure 320
 future needs 24
 guarantees 302–3, 513
 integrated marketing communication 583–7
 items 278
 lifecycles (PLC) 312
  characteristics 327
  communication 584–7
  decline 315–21, 586
  growth 313–14, 323, 584–5
  introduction 313
  maturity 314–15, 585–6
  pricing 414
  product levels, classes, forms and brands 320–21
  shape 319–20
  strategies 327
  targeting 201–2
 lines 277
  length and depth 278, 334–5
 maintenance 300–1
 management 311–12
  customer specified products 337–9
  European strategy 340–42
  market evolution 322–8
  organisation 339–40
  product lifecycles *see* lifecycles *above*

product mix 328–37
marketing mix 25–6, 1042–4
meaning 268–70
mix 277
management 328–37
width 278
modifications 331–4
non-durable 270
orientation 12
perceived differences 936
performance 300, 333–4
portfolios 328, 849
analysis 850–57
non-profit organisations 997
positioning 328–34, 463–4, 1038
potential 268, 269
quality 299–302, 331–3
ranges 276–9, 290–1, 334–6, 523–4, 530–32, 549–52
reliability 300–1
repositioning 331–3
services 270, 963–4
situation analysis 583–7
specification 152–3, 156, 164
storage 482
style 301
tangible 268, 269, 270
technological environment 62–5
types 551
see also brands and branding; goods; new products; packaging; services
professional purchasing 148
profitability analysis 930–31
profits 394–6
cost–volume–profit relationship 444–6
long-term objectives, international marketing 1024
maximisation 430, 445
return on investment 430
project plans 897
promotion 7–8
consumer market beliefs 101
efficient 510
internet marketing 1064, 1069–73
marketing mix 27, 1044
services 966–7
see also advertising; direct marketing; exhibitions; integrated marketing communication; personal selling; public relations; sales promotion; sponsorship
promotional allowances 455
promotional mix
advertising 569, 582–3, 603–49
communication 569–71, 577–96
direct marketing 569, 769–70
international 1044
personal selling 569, 694–737
public relations 569, 792–816
sales promotion 569, 652–92
promotional packaging 294–5
promotional pricing 451
prompted recall, advertising campaigns 642
prospecting 700, 708–10
prospects 710, 771–2
protectionism 71
psychographics 189–93
psychological discomfort 102
psychological influences, consumer behaviour 109–18
psychological pricing 450–52
public procurement 140–41, 458
public relations 792–3
advertising and 793, 803
corporate identity 810–16, 831–2
corporate reputation 808–10
definition 793–4
direct mail 746
evaluation 806–8
exhibition spin-offs 781
international marketing 1044
online 801
promotional mix 569
role 797–9
techniques 799–806
public scrutiny, non-profit organisations 996
public utilities 410
publications 231, 804
publicity 800–3
international marketing 1044
non-profit organisations 997–8
publics 794–7, 993–5
pull factors, direct marketing 741, 742–3
pull strategies 579, 707
purchase decisions 98
purchase frequency and volatility, advertising campaigns 640
purchase significance 149–50
purchasing
B2B policy 146–8
facilitating 98
function 22, 157–9
situations 93
see also buying
purpose, product assortment 550
push factors, direct marketing 741–2
push strategies 578–9

QA (quality assurance) 65
QC (quality control) 65
qualified prospects 710
qualitative data 254–5
qualitative forecasting methods 920–22
qualitative research 218
qualitative targets 903–4
quality 155–6
assurance (QA) 65
B2B markets 301
brands and branding 289, 302
consistency 164
control (QC) 65
Eurobrands 340
objectives 431
products 299–302, 331–3, 392–3
services 970–73
quangos 81, 410
quantitative data 254
quantitative forecasting methods 922–4
quantitative research 218–19
quantitative targets 901–2
quantity discounts 454
question marks 851, 852–3
questionnaires 238, 247–52
quota sampling 246

R&D *see* research and development
RA (Radio Authority) 83
radar detection equipment 299
radiation, mobile phones and 367–8
radio advertising 619–21, 625, 757
Radio Authority (RA) 83
rail transport 364, 367, 957, 959, 965, 977, 995, 1044
railway rolling stock 153–4
random factors 922
random sampling 245
range management 334–6
range setting, prices 443–53
ranges
products *see* products
services 523–4
rating scales 250, 251
ratings, advertising 622
rational appeals, advertising 612
rationalisation, corporate 534
raw materials 275
re-buys 149–50
reach 622, 623, 802, 1071
reactive approach to new product development 356–7
reality, perceptions of 496
rebates 664–5
recall 642
receivers of messages 573
recruitment, sales representatives 725–6
recycling 19–20, 64, 777
redemptions 687
reduced prices 662–4
reduction on service levels 977–8
reference groups 123–4
referent power 498
regional organisation 925, 926–7
regional scale organisations 1008–9
registration plates, personalised 391
regression analysis 254
regularity of planning 897
regulatory environment 76–85
buying process 150
communication 588
consumer behaviour 109
distribution 488–9
international marketing 1039
pricing 410–12
telemarketing 764
reinforcement advertising 604, 606–7
relationship managers 702
relationship marketing 8–9, 66, 167
relationship portfolios 169
relationships
building 743, 770
buyer–seller 150, 370
buyer–supplier 8–9, 1063
competitive strategies 876
customers, international marketing 1014
durability 167–8

forced 362
lifecycles 169–71
management 138
media 795–7, 800–3
sales representatives maintaining 702
supplier portfolios 169
relative advantage 324
relative power balance 716
relevance, sponsorship 827
reliability
delivery 512
products 300–1
services 971
supply 164
reminder and reinforcement advertising 604, 606–7
remoteness 487
renewal 777, 939–41
repair, services 276
repeat purchases 105
repertoire of significance tests 254
replacement parts 513
replenishment 510–11
reports, marketing research 255
repositioning 331–3, 912
reputation, corporate 808–10
resale price maintenance 410
research
corporate identity changes 813
internet uses 1064, 1065
see also marketing research
research and development (R&D) 22–4, 59–64, 160, 359, 376–9, 380
resellers 137, 139
reselling 776–7
resources 190
allocation, non-profit organisations 994
attraction, non-profit organisations 994
competitive strategies 876
Eurobrands 340
inadequacies, services 972
organisational 487, 845–6
resourcing factors, international marketing 1023
response
generation, public relations evaluation 808
hierarchy 196, 322, 580–83
initiation 773
management 774–5
mechanisms, direct mail 753
rates, direct mail 749
responsiveness 937, 971
retail audits 221, 687
retail cooperatives 493
retail franchises 981
retail markets, pricing 397
retail parks 537–8, 548–9
retail warehouses 509
retailers 473, 522–3
atmosphere 552–4
branding benefits perspective 285–6
brands 287–8
channel structures 475–7
competitive positioning 552
European retail sector structure 527–32
Europeanisation 558
location 545–8
merchandising strategies 554–7
nature of retailing 523–7
non-store retailing 543–5
own-brands 557–8
product range 549–52
sales force support for 682
sales promotions by 655–7
sales promotions to 678–82
selling and marketing assistance to 681–2
store image 552–4
strategic alliances 558
strategies 545–58
technology 557
types 533–43
retention 111, 641, 776–7
return on investment (ROI) 430, 854–5
'return to sender' mail 752
revenue 394–6, 445
reverse auctions 400, 1063
reverse selection of channel members 490
reviewing databases 777
revitalisation products 320
reward power 498
rewards 72, 660–61
rising damp 701–2
risks 481
attitudes to 846–7
factors, international market entry 1024
mobile phones, health 367–8
perceived 324
road haulage 79
ROI (return on investment) 430, 854–5
role conflict 495–6
roll-cage sequencing 511
roller towels 395
Romania 962–3
Rothschild's communications planning process model 577, 596
routine problem solving 104–5
routine re-buys 149
rules, questionnaires 251–2
running out 337

safety 53, 113–14
salaries, sales representatives 730–31
sale or return promotions 655
sales 11
analysis 930
fluctuating, evening out 659
forecasting 918–24
mix, changing 913
potentia l 916–18
objectives 431
public relations evaluation 808
sponsorship results measuring 829
volume 431–3
sales branches 478
sales contests 682
sales-driven organisations 928
sales engineers 708
sales forces *see* sales representatives
sales management 720–32
sales offices 478
sales orientation 10, 12, 13
sales presentations 710, 712–13
sales promotion 80, 652–3
agencies 686
B2B markets 683
definition 653–4
evaluation 687
gift-, prize- or merchandise-based methods 671–7
internet 666, 1072
joint 687–9
management process 683–8
money-based methods 661–5
objectives 659–61, 684
product-based methods 665–71
programmes 685–6
promotional mix 569
to retail trade 678–82
role 653–61
store-based methods 677–8
sales quotas 721
sales representatives 696
automation of sales forces 718
B2B markets 711
feedback 687
sales management 720–32
support 67, 682
surveys 921
tasks 699–703
types of 703–8
sales subsidiaries 1030
sales support 706–8
sales supporters 14
sales tests, advertising campaigns 642
salt 201
samples 102, 244–7, 667–71
sanpro (sanitary protection) 86–7
satellite television 624
satisfaction
consumers 11
of customer needs 24–5
saturated domestic markets 1012–13
sausages 432
SBU (strategic business units) 844, 943
scenario techniques 921–2
scent 553
scheduling, advertising campaigns 639–42
schools 826–7
Schramm communications model 575–6
screening ideas 363–5
search engine management (SEM) 1068
search engines 969, 1068
seasonal discounts 454
seasonality 922
secondary data 229–32, 918, 924
secondary research 229, 230–32
security 615–16, 971
segmental organisation 925, 927
segmentation 179–80
B2B markets 181–3, 205
benefits 203

concept of 180
consumer markets 183–97
dangers 203–4
implementation 197–202
international marketing 1039
micro segments 1080
sales promotion and 685
success criteria 204–5
selection
channel members 489–90
international markets 1021–3
sales representatives 725–6
suppliers 154–5, 156
selective attention 111
selective distribution 485, 486
selective perception 111
selective retention 111
self-actualisation needs 113, 114–15
self-esteem, advertising appeals 616
self-fulfilling prophecies 318–19
self-liquidating offers 671–2
self-medication 106
self-orientation 190
self-service retailing 530
sellers
buyer–seller contact models 158
buyer–seller relationships 150
perspectives on prices 394–6
resellers 137, 139
selling
assistance to retailers 681–2
brands 318
combination 770
cross selling 534, 743, 777
declining products 337
marketing research and, conflicts of interest 256–8
orientation 10, 12, 13
up 777
see also personal selling; retailers; wholesalers
SEM (search engine management) 1068
SEM (single European market) *see* European Union
semantic differential scales 250, 251
semi-finished goods 275
semi-structured interviews 234–6
senders of messages 573
senior market *see* grey market
sensitivity
people 251
prices 272, 397, 399, 406–7
sensory experiences 552–3
Serbia 150
service goods 33
service industries 65
service orientation, non-profit organisations 995–6
services 5, 7–8, 950–51
application, macro segmentation 182
characteristics 952–61
classifying 951–2
consumer 271–4
internal marketing 974–9
international trade 1025–6
levels 530, 977–8
marketing management 961–79
markets, prices 397–401
people 968
perspectives on markets 951–61
physical evidence 968
place 965–6
price 964–5
processes 968–9
productivity 976–9
products 270, 963–4
promotion 966–7
quality 970–73
ranges 523–4
test marketing 370
training 974–6
servicing 513
SERVQUAL 971
sex, advertising appeals 616–17
SFA (sales force automation) 718
shape of product lifecycles 319–20
share prices 808
shared meanings 573–6
shelf reduced prices 662
shelf space 655
Shell's directional policy matrix 855–6
shipbuilding industry 69
shopping *see* home shopping; retailers
shopping goods 272–3, 546
short channels 475
short messaging service (SMS) 1084–5, 1086
short-term plans 897
SIC (standard industrial classification) 182
sight 552–3
significance tests 254
silicone breast implants 587
simulated test markets 369
Singapore 167
single European market (SEM) *see* European Union
single sourcing 138, 146–7
situation analysis 577–89
size
markets 487
orders, constraints 512
organisations 181
people 184
skills 876
skimming 437
slice-of-life advertising 614, 620
slogans 610
small and medium-sized enterprises (SME) 518
internet growth strategies 864
small businesses
marketing 34
marketing planning 931–41
characteristics 932–3
small domestic markets 1012–13
smartcards 972–3
SME *see* small and medium-sized enterprises
smells 553
SMS (short messaging service) 1084–5, 1086
soccer *see* football
social class 118
social dimension 168
social interaction, personal selling 720
social needs 165
social structures 1017–19
societal attitudes on marketing strategy 53
societal marketing 16–18
Society of Competitive Intelligence Professionals 867
sociocultural environment 45–6, 48–59, 587
consumer behaviour 107, 118–28
international marketing 1015–20
socioeconomic groupings 118
software piracy 1082
sorting 483
sound 553
soups 193
source credibility 591–2
South Africa 70, 479, 1017–18, 1019
space, shortages 534
Spain 77, 120, 295–6, 772
spam 772
spatial marketing 547
special adjustments, prices 453–5
specialisms, advertising agencies 632–3
speciality goods 273
speciality stores 539–41
'specialogues' 544
speed, international market entry 1 024
speeding motorists 299
spending patterns 50
spin-off promotion 828–9
sponsorship
arts 816, 823–5, 827–8
broadcasting 816, 821–3
cause related marketing 825–6
definition 816
evaluation 829–30
online 801
role 826–9
sport 212–13, 816, 817–21, 827, 828
spontaneous recall, advertising campaigns 642
sport
sponsorship 212–13, 816, 817–21, 827, 828
see also cricket; football
sports drinks 331–2
Sports Marketing Surveys 246
spreadsheets 225
sprinkler strategy 371
stability seeking 877
standard industrial classification (SIC) 182
standardisation 913, 1035, 1039–42
stars 851, 853, 857
state-owned monopolies 73
statistical series analysis 917–18
status 190–91, 550–51
status quo 433–4
STEP 45–6, 47, 109, 906, 1015
stepped demand curves 450–51
stereotypes 588, 612

stimulus–response approach 712
stock *see* inventory
storage 482, 524
store-based sales promotion methods 677–8
store catalogues 768
stores
  assortment, efficient 510–11
  consumer market beliefs 101
  image 552–4
  layouts 554–5
  traffic 656
  types 533–41
storyboards 619
strategic alliances 558, 885–6, 1033–5
strategic business units (SBU) 844, 943
strategic control 928
strategic marketing 840–41
  analysis 849–57
  competitive positions and postures 876–86
  competitor s 865–76
  definitions and perspectives 841–9
  frameworks 842–4
  growth strategies 858–65
  influences on 845–9
  'no growth' options 864–5
  plans and planning 896–901
  see also marketing strategies
strategic vision 29–30
strategies
  branding 288–93
  channels 484–90
  competitive 844, 865–76
  competitors 849, 869–70
  corporate 842–4
  integrated marketing communication 590–3
  international marketing 1034–45
  marketing *see* marketing strategies; strategic marketing
  pricing 435–43
  product lifecycles 327
  retailers 545–58
  sales 721–5
  services marketing 961–70
stratified sampling 245
strengths 908
strivers 191
Strong theory of communication 580–83
structured interviews 234–6
structures
  channel *see* distribution: channels
  market 847–9
  prices 453
  social 1017–19
strugglers 1 91
students 214–15, 689–91, 978
style, products 301
subcultures 121–2
subsidiaries, international 1030–31
substitute effect 197
suburban retail sites 548
success factors 869
sugging 256
suncare 853
supermarkets 79
  animal welfare 325
  clothing 462–3
  distribution costs 500
  dominance 535–7
  guarantees 303
  local buying 497
  loyalty cards 197, 691–2
  own brands 87, 287–8
  power 499
  sales promotion 662, 691–2
  store layouts 554–5
  wine 1049
suppliers 21
  appraisal of 155–6
  B2B buying decision-making process 151–6
  buyer–supplier relationships 8–9, 1063
  buying centres and 162–3
  choice 708
  commitment 155–6
  handling approaches 168–9
  multiple sourcing 146–7
  potential customers, attitudes to 101–2
  relationship portfolios 169
  selection 154–5, 156
  single sourcing 146–7
  third-world 175–7
supply
  chains 167–71
  direct 475, 965
  reliability and continuity 164
  services 978–9
supportive brand names 289
surveys 220, 232–8, 918
survival 435, 935–8
sustainability 19
sustainable competitive advantage 871
sustainable development 18
sustainable marketing 19–20
sweepstakes 675, 676–7
sweeteners, low calorie 63
sweets 199–200
switchers 194
Switzerland 121, 296
SWOT analysis 908–10
synectics 362
synthetics in clothing 64
systems, services 976–7

Taiwan 174
tangibility, market segments 204
tangible products 268, 269, 270
tangibles, services 971
Tanzania 176
Target Group Index (TGI) 219
targets
  advertising campaigns 636
  audiences
    advertising 635, 636, 637
    direct marketing 773
  direct mail 747–9
  direct marketing 771–2
  financial 902
  iTV marketing 1090
  markets
    integrated marketing communication 577–83
    sales promotion 685
  operating 902
  philosophical 902–3
  precision, targeting 696–7, 743
  qualitative 903–4
  quantitative 901–2
  segmentation 198–202
task budgeting 594–5
taxation 67–9
technological environment 45–6, 59–67
  consumer behaviour 107–9
  international marketing 1020
  personal selling roles 699
technological impact 325–6
technology 488
  advances, databases 743
  communication impacts 743–4
  retailers 557
  services 976–7
teenagers *see* young people
telecommunications 65, 66, 72
telemarketing 709–10, 758–64
telephone banking 969
telephone preference service (TPS) 764
telephones
  industry 81
  interviews 237
  omnibus surveys 220
  selling 543
  unsolicited calls 764
  see also freephone numbers; mobile phones
teleshopping 544, 768–9
television
  advertising 619–21, 623–4, 637
  digital 437
  direct response advertising (DRTV) 754, 756–7
  interactive (iTV) 576, 1089–91
  sponsorship 821–3
  sports sponsorship 817
  viewership panels 219
tendering 140–41, 458–9
test marketing 368–71
testimonials, advertising 614
testing
  advertising 638–9
  concept 364–5
text messaging 1083–8
textile industry 71–2
TGI (Target Group Index) 219
theme displays 556
theme parks 956, 962–3
third-world suppliers 175–7
threats 908
time pressure closes of sales 717
time series analysis 922
time-specific mark-downs 451
time utility 524
time values 427
timeshares 952
timing
  advertising campaigns 638

Eurobrands 340
test marketing 369–70
title 481, 525–6
toasters 272
tobacco 68, 83, 434–5
toilet tissue 329–30
tokens 674–5
total costs 444
total logistics cost concept 505–9
total market 877, 916, 917
total quality management (TQM) 299
tourism 440, 788–90, 953, 960, 962–3, 964, 967, 968
see also holidays; hotels
town centre speciality stores 540–41
toys 946–7, 1039
TPS (telephone preference service) 764
TQM (total quality management) 299
traceability 57
trade agreements 70
trade associations 84–5, 231
trade discounts 454
trade marks 281–2, 289
trade names 281
trade promotions 654–5, 680
trade restraint, international marketing 1022
trade shows 740, 777
trading blocs 70–72
trading stamps 674
trading standards officers 78
trading up 658–9
Traditionals, European segmentation 192
training
retailers' sales forces 682
sales representatives 726–8
services staff 974–6
value added services 484
trains *see* rail transport
transactional values 481
transactional variables 510–13
transfer pricing 459–61
transparency, corporate reputation 810
transport-oriented media 630
transportation 483, 508, 524
see also delivery; distribution; logistics
travel
agents 883
business 179
see also holidays; tourism
trends 916, 922
trial 105, 657, 669, 770
trunk transportation 508
trust 166, 168
tuna fishing 58
turkeys 324–5
tyres 55

Uganda 176
UK *see* United Kingdom
unaided recall, advertising campaigns 642
uncertainty 932
uncontrollability of publicity 802–3
undercutting 441
underlying conflict 495
undifferentiated targeting 200–1
undirected information seekers 98
unifying diverse activities 812–13
uniqueness, sponsorship 828
unitary demand 406
United Kingdom
government sources of secondary data 231
monopolies 73
sales promotion 80
waste recycling 296
United States 106, 190, 271, 306–7, 1021
universities 702, 794, 800, 925, 928, 979
unleaded petrol 64
unsolicited e-mails 772
unsolicited mail 746
unsolicited telephone calls 764
unsolicited text messaging 1085
unsought goods 274
unstructured interviews 234–6
unsures 14–15
USA *see* United States
usage
benefits, advertising appeals 616
expanding 658
rates 182, 194
user-based product classifications
B2B goods and services 274–6
consumer goods and services 271–4
users 138–9, 161, 477–80, 1085
utilities 410
utility, place and time 524

vacuum cleaners 353
VALS-2 (Values and Life Style) 190
value added 137, 653
value added services 481–4
value added tax (VAT) 67–9, 417
value management 401
value pricing 438
values
brands 285–6
corporate 901–4
facilitating 483–4
international marketing 1019–20
logistical 481–3
statements 902–3
transactional 481
Values and Life Style (VALS-2) 190
variable costs 444
variety stores 535
VAT (value added tax) 67–9, 417
vending machines 102, 545
venture teams 380
VER (voluntary export restraint) 71
vertical competition 491, 492
vertical marketing systems (VMS) 491, 492–3
viability 547
video catalogues 544
video games 326, 344–5, 598–9
videos 314, 804
Vietnam 150
village grocery shops 529
viral marketing 1078–9, 1090–91
virtual assistants 969
VisCAP model 592
visible staff 975
vision
statements 902–3
strategic 29–30
visit generation 770
visual atmosphere, advertising appeals 617–18
VMS (vertical marketing systems) 491, 492–3
volumes
allowances, promotions to retailers 679
cost–volume–profit relationship 444–6
sales 431–3
voluntary chains 493, 662
voluntary export restraint (VER) 71
voting 580

Wales 788–90
WAP interviews 240
war horses 854, 857
warehousing 508–9
waste 65
packaging 296–7
recycling *see* recycling
watches 635
water industry 71
waterfall strategy 371–2
weak theory of communication 580, 582
weaknesses 908
websites 66
websites *see* internet
welcome calls 764, 776
whales 31
whisky 315
wholesale markets 397
wholesalers 473, 523
brands 287–8
channel structures 475–7
full service 559
limited service 559–60
nature of wholesaling 523–7
voluntary chains 493
wind power 78, 860
wine 1037, 1048–9
win–win negotiation 716
wireless marketing 1083–8
withdrawal 865
women
internet use 108
sanpro (sanitary protection) 86–7
working patterns 488
world scale organisations 1010

yo-yos 321
yogurt 93
young people 48–50
youth markets 122–3, 130–31, 823
see also students

Zimbabwe 6
zoned pricing 455

Index of Company Names

Note: Names are indexed under the first part of the name, eg John Lewis

3M 319, 612
20th Century Fox 862

A C Nielsen 219, 220, 242
AA 94–5, 743
AB Konstruktions-Bakelit 478
Abbey National 73–4, 81, 152, 214–15, 442, 759
Abbots Labs 377
Abbott Laboratories 307
Aberdeen Asset Management 671
Accantia Health and Beauty 285
Access Omnibus Surveys 220
Accountancy Age 627
Acuvue 613
Adidas 123, 288, 819, 821
ADtranz 613
Aer Lingus 911
Aeroflot 116
Age Concern 617
Ahold 493, 517, 522, 528, 536, 558, 1044
Aico 7 04
Airbus 60–61, 137, 145, 457, 488, 869, 919
Albert Heijn 287, 296, 511, 522
ALC 458
Aldi 124, 413, 528, 536, 557, 977, 1043
Alfa Laval 478
Alfa Romeo 616, 784, 935
Alitalia 70
Alliance & Leicester 600–1, 1093
Allison Transmissions 778
Allsports 5 34
Alstom 153–4, 172–5, 1010, 1012
Amazon 15, 412, 563–4, 570, 599, 878, 908, 1043, 1057, 1058, 1062, 1071
Ambassador 317
Ambre Solaire 853
American Airlines 1034
American Express 752, 777, 819, 862, 1039
Amoco 207
Amora Maille 337, 858
AMR Research 154
Amtrak Express Parcels 985
Andersen Consulting 564
Andrex 329, 441–2
Angel Uplifting 1088
Ann Summers 543
Another.com 1079
AOL 314
Apparel Industry Magazine 1058
Apple 282, 311, 504
ARC 1074
Arcadia Group 540
Argos 272, 532, 543, 544, 768, 864
Ariel 613
Ariston 272
Arjo Wiggins 290
Arriva 811
Arsenal FC 282, 422, 818
Artis LLC 361
ASDA 79, 106, 262, 288, 410, 429, 462, 525, 533, 536, 537, 692, 848, 1066
Ask Jeeves 1068
ASK McGowan 863
Askey's 879
Aston Martin 781, 843, 1022
AT&T 383
Athena 986
Auchan 419, 518, 528, 535, 538
Audi 282, 305, 336, 420, 781
Audiostreet.com 290
Australian Tourist Commission 967
Austrian Airlines 70
Autan 196
Automobile Association 94–5, 743
Avantis 279
Aventis 885
Avis 896, 903
Avon 695–6, 730, 824
Axa 817

B&Q 427, 527, 540, 558, 974
Babcock and Wilcox 792
Babcock Rosyth Defence 69
Babson College 934
Bacardi 132, 853
BAe 149, 338, 377
Bailey's 216
Baldessarini 36–8
Balfour Beatty 166
Balkanair 956
Bananalotto 1079
Barbie 280, 373, 823
Barclaycard 212–13, 817, 819, 883
Barclays Bank 544, 690–91, 801, 1061
Barefoot Books 938
Barilla 474
Barker's 713
barnesandnoble.com 564
Barney's 1007
BASF 19, 410–11
Bass 209, 361, 1054
Batchelor's 193
Baxters 193, 885
Bayer 307, 377, 420, 798, 885
Bayern Munich 333, 422
BBC 819, 921, 964, 1016
BBH 1031
Bechstein 873
Beiersdorf UK 285
Bekaert 1031
Belam 876
Ben & Jerry's 858
Bendicks 680
Benetton 10, 505, 506, 529, 558, 611, 612, 1036, 1039
Bentley 269
Berlin Philharmonic Orchestra 823
Bestfoods 858–9, 913
Bestway 496, 559–60
bettingzone.co.uk 1057
BhS 535
Bic 441, 881
Bicks 196
Bijenkorf 533
Bird's Eye 123, 207, 288
Bird's Eye Walls 678
Black & Decker 300, 301, 359
Blackstar 969
Blackwells 544
Bloomsbury Publishing 861
Blue Arrow 1083
Bluewater 535, 548–9
Bluewave 1056
Bluthner 873
BMG 243
bmi media 630
BMRB 1061, 1070–71
BMW 269, 302, 305–6, 336, 373, 393, 420, 504, 707, 812, 878, 935, 1074, 1093
Boddingtons 605
The Body Shop 55, 57, 148, 285, 1039
Boeing 60–61, 137, 145, 457, 488, 614, 869, 903, 919
BOL.com 564
Bombardier 153, 364
Bonatrans 153
Bonne Maman 1026
Bonusprint 755–6
boo.com 1094–5
Book Club Associates 757
Booker-Iceland 559
Boots 108, 224, 262, 285, 411, 534, 540, 668, 670, 748–9, 761, 769, 848
Borders 15–16
borders.com 564
Bosch 278, 300, 301, 302, 1012
Boss 36–8
Boston Consulting Group 564, 850, 872
Botton Village 581
Boulanger 535
Bounty 223–4, 588, 670
Bourne 316
BP 75, 207, 271, 886
Bristol Myers Squibb 799
British Aerospace 149, 338, 377
British Airways 70, 179, 449, 606, 617, 627, 776, 801, 803, 821, 866, 868, 879, 911, 958, 964, 1034
British Army 609
British Central Electrical 482
British Gas 761
British Library 823
british midland 645–7, 879, 880, 884

British Museum 1080
British Nuclear Fuels 804–5
British Steel 33, 813
British Telecommunications *see* BT
Britvic 508, 672, 848
Brown and Root 812
Bryant and May 196
BSkyB 821, 964
BT 121, 413, 615, 727, 744, 757, 763, 1071, 1074
BT Cellnet 227
Budget 896
Budweiser 1078
Buena Vista 862
Bulgari 823
BUPA 757, 966
Burberry 1019
Bureau Veritas 154
Burger King 271, 593, 960, 989
Burmah Castrol 286
Burton 540
Burton-Marsteller 793
Business Life 627
Butlins 316
Buzz 645
BW 153
Byte 861

C&A 529
Cadbury Schweppes 286, 904–5, 914, 926
Cadbury Trebor Bassett 199, 752
Cadbury's 57, 207, 281, 291, 302, 393, 590, 616, 822, 1039, 1084
Cafedirect 176–7
Cahoot 1083
Caledonian MacBrayne 456
Calypso Soft Drinks 680–81
Camacho 1026
Campaign for Real Ale (CAMRA) 217
Campanile 955
Campbell 193, 859
Camphill Village Trust 581
Camping Card Scandinavia 973
Canon 341
Cap Gemini Ernst & Young 1058
Cape Reefers 479
Capespan International 479
Capital Gold 820
Carillion 811
Carling 818, 819, 824
Carlsberg 816, 823, 1031
Carphone Warehouse 564, 666, 974
Carrefour 419, 472–3, 517, 518, 528, 535, 536, 537, 538, 557
Carte Noir 1039
Case 1031
Casino 6, 528, 536
Casino on Net 1071
Castorama 540
Castrol 804
Caterpillar 1031
CBB Research 231
CCN 772
Cemex 846
Cendant 927
Census 935–6
Centennial 1082
Centrica 95
CGU Life 820
Champion 756
Chanel 1013
Channel 4: 819
Channel Tunnel 865
Chelsea TV 1076, 1078
Cheltenham & Gloucester 96–7
Chematch 154
Chemistry in Britain 627
Chiquita 509
Chiquita Brands 71
Chivers Hartley 480, 877
Christie's 883, 886
Chronos Publishing 209
Chrysalis 618
Chubb 736
Chuft 946–7
Cimpor 863
Cipem 518
Circular Distributors 667
Cisco 1063
Citibank 286
CitroÎn 48, 818
CiTV 1069–70
Claridges 440
Clarins 613
Claritas 223, 1079
Clark's 495
Classic CD 670
Classic FM 625, 828
Clearlybusiness 801
Clover 687
Club 18–30: 82, 268–9, 958
CMSP 1015
CNN 1016
Co-op 294
Co-operative Bank 177, 864
Cobblewood Mushrooms 497
Coca-Cola 75, 122, 267, 281, 286, 311, 312, 332, 352, 586–7, 591, 611, 612, 674, 678, 807, 816, 817, 819, 821–2, 827, 885, 1006, 1019, 1021, 1039, 1048, 1090
Cockerill Sambre 863
Codepar/SPCD 858
Coffee Republic 408
Colgate 128, 877
Colgate-Palmolive 285, 341, 342, 702
Colman 337
Colomer 734–5
Colony 1019
Comet 272, 540
Comic Relief 608
Commercial Union 822
Compass 330
Compassion in World Farming 325, 833–4
Concourse Initiatives 668
Condomania 262
Condomi 262
Connex South Central 959
Conquest Fitted Furniture 756
Consignia 810, 831–2
Consodata 1079
Contender 862
Continent 518
Continental Microwave 1016
Continental Tyres 55, 1033
ConvaTec 799
Cookson's Tools 1011
Cornhill 819
Corus 813
Costa Coffee 408
Costco 295, 496, 498, 542
Covent Garden Soups 193
Covinor 474
Covisint 154, 1064
Cowie 811
Crédit Agricole 817
Credit Suisse 729
Cressida 858
Cross & Blackwell 193
Culture Lab 242
Cummins 876
Curry's 272, 540, 557, 574
Cussons 285, 669, 1071

Daewoo 311, 677, 1029
Daimler-Chrysler 804, 1064
Dairy Crest 368, 424
The Dalesman 627
Danone 82, 509
Danzas 154
Darty 540
Data Exchange 751
Datamonitor 759
David Lloyd 784
David Wilson Homes 756
DB 1044
De Beers 346–7
De Dutch 989
Debenham's 533
Decathlon 535
Delhaize de Lion 528, 536, 558
Dell 885, 1063, 1071
Deloitte Touche Tohmatsu 154
DeLonghi 701
Denso 377
Deutsche Grammophon 670
Deutsche Telekom 383
Dexion 482
DHL 290
Diageo 831, 1084
Diesel 84
Digital Paper Corp. 614
Dikema & Chabot 863
Direct Line 890
Disney 286, 290, 672, 673, 707, 757, 885, 963
Disney World 302
Disneyland Paris 122
Disteel 863
Dixon's 314, 540
Dollond & Aitcheson 411
Dolphin Telecommunications 700
Domino's Pizza 821, 970, 985, 1028, 1090
Dorothy Perkins 540

Dr Oetker 857
Dreamworks Studio 298
Dresdner Kleinwort Benson 525
Drilcon 489
DSM 1017
Dualit 272
Duarig 518
Duc d'Or 1026
Dun & Bradstreet 231, 244, 751
Dunkin' Donuts 271, 1083
Dunlop 33
Dunne's 287
DuPont 142
Duracell 302, 359, 701, 913
Durex 262
Dwr y Cwm 879
Dyson 353

E&J Gallo 1049
Eagle Star 974
Early Learning Centre 229, 774, 1003
East India Company 823
Eastman Kodak 377
Easy Cottages 100
easyJet 292, 449, 645, 760, 801, 879, 880, 910–11, 970
eBay 400, 883, 1057, 1063, 1071
The Economist 626
Edeka 528
Eden Project 177
Eden Vale 859
Egg 284, 290, 888, 944, 1059, 1089
EGL Homecare 854
Eidos 344–5
Ejay 940
ELC International 231
Electrolux 353
Electronic Arts 344, 377
Electronics Boutique 598
Elementis 831
Eli Lilly 307
Elior 105
Elite Introductions 990
Elo Pak 13
Emap 615
eMarketer 1062
EMI 670
Energizer 913
English China Clays 856
English National Ballet 823
Ennis Foods 870
Enron 730
Entertainer Group 321
Equitable Life 944
Ericsson 823
Ernst and Young 824
Esso 75, 271
Euro Food Brands 474
Eurocamp 786–8
Euromonitor 231, 232, 924, 1059–62
European Central Bank 595
Euroquest 130–31
Eurosport 1084
Eurostar 866
Evans 184, 540
Executive Airlines 616
Experian 186–9, 1077
Express by Holiday Inn 398
Express Dairies 424
Exxon Corporation 792–3

Fabulous Bakin' Boys 1082
Fairtrade Foundation 175–7
The Farmer 627
Fashionmall 1095
Fastex 458
Faulding Consumer 853
FBS Engineering 935–6
FCUK 82, 122–3
Federal Express 1067
Ferrar 816
Fiat 350, 420, 459, 1093
Fidelity Investments 757
Filippo Berio 841
Financial Times 1065
Findus 288, 863
Firestone 33, 492
First Milk 423–4
Fisher-Price 886, 302
Fisherman's Friend 88–9, 516, 1038
Fitness First 966
Fleetdrive 820
Fleischmann 779
Flextronics 1011
Flora 817, 819, 828
Flytxt 1088
FogDog 878
Fondul Pentru Dezvoltare Turistica Sighisoara 963
Ford 152, 199, 285, 290, 291, 305, 350, 377, 438, 486, 613, 819, 995, 1012, 1013, 1064, 1093
Formula 1: 398, 955
Forrester Research 525, 1080, 1087, 1089
Forte 757
Foster Group 1049
Fox 850
Foyles 15–16
France Telecom 383, 603
Franklin Mint 754–5, 765
FreeMarkets 400, 1062
Freeserve 290, 314, 801, 1071
French Connection 122–3, 269
Fresh Produce Terminals 479
Freundin 627
Friends of the Earth 5, 58, 84, 1044
Friends United 1053–4
Fuji 853, 1041
Fullers 1008
Future Brand 311
Future Foundation 214, 239
Fyffes 479

Gaea of Greece 1026
Galeries Lafayette 533
Gallaher 434–5
Gallup 253
Gambia Tourist Authority 917
Game 345
Gap 558, 848, 891
Gartner Dataquest 383
Gateshead Metro Centre 542, 548
GeneData 847
General Electric 173, 855
General Motors 350, 360, 377, 438, 463, 464, 614, 778, 1012, 1064
Georgia Pacific 354
Gesellschaft für Diamantprodukte 379
Gethal 54
GetThere 883
Gibb 166
Gillette 341, 881
Glaxo Wellcome 207, 825
GlaxoSmithKline 277, 307, 401, 442, 508, 573, 1010
GNER 977
GNX 154
Go 645, 761, 801, 884
Golden Wonder 592, 883
Goodyear 33, 55, 1033
Google 1068
Gossard 185, 532, 1036, 1041
Graham and Trotmans 231
Granada 330, 822
Great Ormond Street Children's Hospital 750, 752, 994–5
Green Flag 999
Greenpeace 5, 54, 58, 84, 793, 795, 805, 996, 1044
Grey Europe 606
Grolsch 361
The Guardian 817
Guardian Direct 757
Guidant 377
Guinness 618, 623, 668
Gulfstream 616

H Samuel 692
Häagen Dazs 25, 559, 668, 866
Haberman 301
Haburi.com 221
Hachette 105
Halfords 380, 540
Hamlin Electronics 29
handbag.com 108, 772, 1071
Happy Dog 1085
Haribo 680
Harley-Davidson 124, 739, 745–6
Harper Collins 1085
Harris Research Centr e 235
Harrods 328, 530, 823, 946
Hartwell 1031
Hasbro 1087
Heidelberger Druckmaschinen 377
Heinz 66, 183, 184, 193, 207, 278, 287, 291, 293, 311, 335, 341, 393
Hellman's 658, 859, 877
Hema 533
Henkel 612
Henley Centre 758
Hennes & Mauritz 531, 540, 848, 1009
Herbert Smith 823
Hermelin Research 237
Hershey 57

Hertz 896, 1043
Hertz Lease 758
Hewlett Packard 378
Hiestand 1008
High and Mighty 184
High Life 627
Higswa Junior 848
Hilton 440, 885–6, 1029
Hino Motors 885
HLB 751
HMV 345, 523–4, 540, 872
Hodder Headline 908
Holcim 846, 863, 871
Holiday Autos 896
Holiday Break 786–8
Holiday Inn 955
Holmes Place 965
Holsten 604, 853
Homebase 535
Honda 71, 707, 935
Hong Kong Bank 1037
Hoogovens 813
Hoover 269, 284, 675
Hormel Foods 1027
Hotpoint 269, 272
House of Fraser 533, 549
Howard Johnson 982
HP Foods 706
HSBC 819, 1037
HSM 758
Hugo 36–8
Huntingdon Life Sciences 56
Hyperion 670

I-Flex 869
i2iexchangeitaly 154
Iberia 70, 72
Ibis 398
IBM 61, 136, 145, 377, 471–2, 484, 612, 698, 728, 1011
Iceland 82
Icelandair 433
ICI 142, 207, 286, 1019
Icos Corporation 307
IKEA 453, 509, 526, 556, 558, 768, 808, 1019, 1039, 1041
illy Caffe 474
Imerys 856
Impex 89, 516
Imray 937
Inbox 1086
Inbox Media 1082
Incyte 719
Indesit 269
Industrial Equipment News 627
Industry to Industry 154
Ingersoll-Rand 276, 489
Inner Medical 587
Institute of Grocery Distribution 552
Intel 145, 378, 823, 849
Interbrand Newell & Sorrell 285–6
Interbrew 74, 196
Intermarchè 537
International Data Corp. 1065
International Fund for Animal Welfare (IFAW) 31
Intraocular Lens Laboratory 1008
Invensys 831
Ipsos UK 213
Irish Farmers' Association 1043
Irish Fire Products 736–7
Irish Tourist Board 788
Iron Bed Company 939
ISS 845
ITM Enterprises 528
ITV 819, 821–2
ITV Digital 1089
iVillage.co.uk 108

J-17 627
J&B Rare Scotch Whisky 825
Jaboneria 858
Jaeger 333, 533
Jaguar 177, 285, 332, 781
James Meade 768
Jamjar 442, 1094
Jane's 751
JaniKing 990, 991
Jarvis Hotels 966, 975
JCB 683, 1031
Jenks 196
Jenners 946
Jet 541
Jeyes 170, 719
JJB Sports 423
JMC 273
John Lewis 177, 272, 533, 535, 549
John Lusty 1026
John Smith 611
Johnson & Johnson 160, 207, 341, 614, 724, 1039
Johnson Wax 859
Jordan 870
Jungheinrich 913
Jungle 969
Jupiter MMXI 108
Jury's Kensington 440
JVC 816, 818

KarstadtQuelle 528, 533, 1008
Kauffman Centre for Entrepreneurship 934
Kaufhalle 535
KEF 414
Kelda Group 18
Kelkoo 441
Kellogg 3–4, 128, 136, 207–8, 269, 284, 288, 291, 302, 331, 397, 607, 617, 623, 673, 819, 821, 870, 1042, 1073
Kettle Chips 841
Keynote Reports 231
KFC 593, 1017, 1028
Kids 'R' Us 539
Kier International 166
Kimberly-Clark 441
Kinder 666
Kingfisher 528, 540, 818
Kings Hotel, Kraków 260–61
Kiss 100: 1087–8
Kitchen Devils 672
Kiwi Shoe Polish 1019
Kleenex 317, 329
Klemm 489, 490
KLM 70, 215, 449
Kodak 288, 302, 360, 614, 829, 853, 1041, 1066
Kodak-Eastman 826
Kompass 244
Kookaï 630
Kooshies Baby Products 916
KPN Mobile 382, 383
Kraft 44, 409, 1070
Kruidvat 155
Kudos Group 209
Kwik Fit 237, 380
Kwik Save 287, 413

La Compagnie des Petits 981–2
LA Fitness 966
Laboratoires Garnier 384
Lada 116, 269, 301
Lafarge 846, 863
Lambourghini 301
Land's End 303, 767, 969
Landmark 496, 559
Landor 645
Lapin Kulta 1031
lastminute.com 39–41, 1057, 1078
Laura Ashley 768, 1019
Lawson Mardon Group 170
Lazenby's 432
Le Piat D'Or 1048–9
Leclerc 528
Lee 891
Lego 288, 302, 687, 822
Leroy Merlin 535
LetsBuyit 442
Lever Brothers 74, 75, 281
Lever Fabergè 278, 285, 508, 593, 608
Levi Strauss 269, 284, 462–3, 532, 618, 891–2, 1078
Lewinger 518
Lexus 878
Lidl 413, 528, 536, 557, 978, 1043
Life Search 757
Liftremont 1013
Lindt 999
The Link 540
Linn 843
Lion Biosciences 847
Lipton 852
Littlewood's 503, 508
Lloyds TSB 73–4, 81, 816, 821, 824
Lockheed Martin 338
Lofthouse of Fleetwood 88–9, 516–17
Londis 541, 559
London Book Fair 778
London Business School 934
London Transport 18, 972
L'Orèal 384–5, 613
L'Orèal Elvive 188
Los Angeles Metropolitan Transit Authority 1039

LOT 260
Lowe Digital 108
Lowe Lintas 1037
Lucozade 331–2, 352, 611, 620, 848
Lufthansa 911, 1034
Lurpak 413
LVMH 347
Lycos 1068, 1093
Lynx 278–9, 1079

M&G 888
Mace 541, 559
Macintosh 808
Macmillan Cancer Trust 825
Madonna 267, 268
Madrange 52
Makro 559, 560
Malibu 853
Malmaison 398
Manchester United 283, 333, 422–3, 534, 816, 818, 1070
Manor 533
Manor Bakeries 608
Manor House Press 231
Manto Group 209
Marco Leer 979–80, 987
Marine Midland Bank 1037
Marketing Week 749
marketplaceitaly.com 154
Marklin 779
Marks & Spencer 6, 184, 284, 287, 302, 311, 493, 498, 513, 528, 535, 547, 549–50, 821, 834, 862, 1084
Marmite 666
Marriott 950–51
Mars 199, 288, 340, 356, 375, 508, 706, 707, 912, 1003
Martini 611, 612
Mastercard 817, 819
Mates Healthcare 262
Mattel 280, 823
Maxell 617
McCain 194, 857
McDonald's 57, 128, 144, 271, 282, 285, 341, 474, 593, 712, 713, 902, 975, 980, 983, 984, 1006, 1008, 1019, 1028, 1041, 1042
McEwan's 816
McGhan 587
McLane 1038
McQuillan Engineering Industries 488
McVities 293, 1070
MD Foods 424
Meadowhall 548
Mediae Trust 905
Mercedes-Benz 302, 305, 336, 420, 781, 812, 819, 878, 1093
Merck 30
Merlin Timber Products 713
Meto 155
Metro 528, 536, 560
Metronic 519
MFI 808
MG 613
MG Rover 781
Michelin 361, 1033
Microgen 705
Microsoft 255, 298, 311, 313, 326, 344, 377, 598–9, 615, 808, 884, 1003, 1021, 1082
Midland Bank 1037
Midland Mainline 977
Miele 409
Migros 6, 528, 549
Milk Marque 423
Mill Film 298
Millennium Pharmaceuticals 377
Miller 618
Millivres-Prowler Group 209
MindMatics 1086
Minerva 820
Mini 305–6
Ministry of Sound 1084
Minolta 277
Mintel 231, 1065
Miss Selfridge 540
Mitsubishi 173, 377, 471–2, 761
Mizz 87, 627
MNBA Europe Bank 1071
Mobil 271
Modern Originals 774
Momentum 707
Mondavi 1049
Moneybox 542
moneysupermarket.com 442
Monoprix 535
Monsanto 795, 797, 1044–5
Morgan 940–41
MORI 220
Morpheos 299
Morrisons 536, 692
Moser GmbH 478
Mothercare 501, 847–8
Motorcycle News 745
Motorola 145
Mountfield 756
Mr Lucky Bags 199–200
MRB 219
MRSL 229
MSN 1071
MTV Network Europe 823
M¸ller 93, 859
Must Win Club 675
Mustang 486
MVC 540
My Offers 1079

National Canine Defence League 754
National Car Parks 906–7
National Geographic 826
National Health Service 964
National Lottery 410, 541
National Meningitis Trust 997
National Missing Persons Helpline 992
National Trust 946, 997, 998
Nationwide 241, 816, 817, 825, 969–70
NatWest 828
NEC 359
Nedan Zoetwaren BV 516–17
Nederman 29
Nekermann 544
Nestlé 20, 44, 57, 199, 207, 277, 278, 285, 311, 340, 341, 371, 408–9, 508, 652–3, 668, 673, 849, 850–51, 857, 863, 870, 900, 912, 1039, 1065
NetGenics 847
Netto 124, 413, 536, 977
NetValue 220, 1076
Neu Engineering 207–8
Neville Johnson 755, 756
New Era 117
Newman Books 231
Next 529, 530, 540, 558, 768, 848
Next Directory 744, 764, 767, 776
NFU Mutual 615
Nike 123, 180, 279, 282, 284, 423, 613, 812, 818, 819, 878, 1084, 1095
Nintendo 326, 598–9, 866, 884
Nippon Suisan 859
Nisa Today 559
Nissan 71, 420, 576, 770, 1031, 1064, 1090, 1093
Nivea 759, 769, 853
Nokia 145, 162–3, 761
NOP 108
Nordtank Energy Systems 860
Norsk Hydro 825
North American Bus Industries 1038–9
North Yorkshire Moors Railway 946
Northrup Grumman Space Systems 300
Norwich Union 763, 817
Novellus Systems 377
Novotel 955
Npower 817, 819
NSK Aerospace Europe 1015
NSPCC 157, 999, 1002–3
NTC Publications 231
NTL 817
NTT DoCoMo 383
Nu-Swift 736
Nucare 694–5
Nurdin and Peacock 560
Nycomed 207

O2 1071
Oasis 316
Ocado 1066–7
Office World 477
O'Hagan 432
Oil and Vinegar 1028
Olay 670
The Oldie 627
Olympic 70
Olympic Games 821, 828–9, 1018
Olympus 395
One2One 383
Opel 463, 816
Orange 279, 284, 285, 290, 603, 817, 824–5
Otis 1013
OTRA NV 482
Otto Versand 528, 544, 877
Our Price 262
Owens-Illinois 1011
Oxfam 34, 409, 996
Oxford University 702
Oxley 879–80
Oxo 673

P. J. Holloway 802
P&O 8
Pact 704
Palatin Technologies 307
Palladium 518
Palm Computing 756
Pampers 316, 574, 576, 670, 886
Parcelforce 831–2
Partners Andrews Aldridge 745
Partners BDDH 645–7, 745
PC World 540
Pearl Assurance 726
Pearlfisher 269
Pear's Soap 823
Pedigree 878
Peebles Transformers 1017
Peek and Cloppenburg 1007
Pellegrino 1026
Pennine Telecom 700
Pepe Jeans 122
Pepsi 5, 75, 122, 352, 591, 1021, 1084
Perfect Pizza 989
Performance Group 846
Perrier 850
Peugeot 618, 621
Pfizer 306–7, 377, 846, 898
Pharmacia 750
PhD 645
Philips 146, 613, 667, 670, 671, 723, 803, 885, 1011
PhoneSites 630
Phytopharm 898–9, 918
Pierre Victoire 986
Pilkington Glass 901, 903, 1010
Pirelli 55, 1033
Pizza Express 985
Pizza Hut 271, 339, 813, 814, 955, 985, 989
Playboy 627
PMC Sierra 377
PMU Group 863
Polaroid 317
Porsche 273, 781
Post Office 529, 744, 810, 831–2
Postoptics 412
Pot Noodles 375
Powerwatch 367
PPP 761, 769, 822
Pratt and Whitney 338
Precious Woods Amazon 54
Pret à Manger 960
Preussag 284, 493
Priceline 442
PricewaterhouseCoopers 154, 231, 813
Princes 56
Princess Yachts 755
Principles 540
Pringle 335
Printemps 533
Procter & Gamble 11, 74, 75, 86–7, 112, 281, 285, 288, 341, 377, 384, 576, 586, 593, 667, 668, 692, 706, 720–21, 829, 848, 854, 867–8, 885, 886, 927
Prolog 758–9
PromodËs 6
Prontaprint 985, 987
Prudential 290, 888–90, 943–5, 1074

Quaker 318, 327, 823, 870, 878
Quelle 544
QVC 768–9

Racing Green 767
Radion 96, 99
Railtrack 792, 809, 832
Raisio 1039
Rank 316
Rank Hovis McDougall 281, 286
Rank Xerox 1008
Raytheon 332
RCA 670
ReaD Group 746–7
Reader's Digest 626, 676
Real Madrid 333
Reckitt and Benckiser 291–2
Red 670
Red Bull 269, 332, 352
Red Cat 774
Red Cross 886
Reebok 123, 180, 282, 532, 638, 722, 724, 878
Reg Vardy 1093–4
Renault 305, 336, 376, 378, 380, 420, 618, 757, 761, 763, 1064, 1093
Rennie 637
Rentokil Initial 728
Rentokil Tropical Plants 700
Respect for Animals 591
Reuters 377
Rewe 528
Rey & Co 84
RHM 281, 286
Ribena 573–4, 848–9
Richmond Events Ltd 633
Ricola 612
Ride and Bike 745
Rider's Edge 746
Rimmel 1089
Rivarossi 779
Robert Humm 768
Robert Wiseman 424
Robinsons 672, 848
Roche 410–11
Rockwater 812
Rodier 819
Rolls Royce 1015
Rosenberg Ventilation 802
Rothman 347
Routin 518
Rover 828
Royal Bank Group 1062
Royal Mail 751–2, 831–2
Royal National Institute for the Blind 1056
Royal Vendex KBB 533
RS Components 562–3, 864
RSGB Omnibus 220
RSPCA 834, 998, 999
Rude 1007
Rural Shops Alliance 529
Rutland Gilts 298
Ryanair 449, 606, 645, 760, 879, 880, 911
Rymans 477

Saab 478, 488, 707, 739–40, 803
Sabena 70, 72, 449
Sabre 820
Safeway 176, 463, 497, 522, 536, 547, 656, 692, 824, 834
Saga 49, 191, 574, 885–6
Sainsbury's 75, 196, 287, 497, 525, 528, 533, 534, 535, 536, 545, 553, 591, 614, 657, 692, 974, 1061, 1066
Salveson Masters Fresh Foods 509
Samaritans 999
Samsung 207, 1011
Sandals 83
Sandoz 30
Sara Lee 1019, 1078
SAS 660
SCA 87
Scania 885
Schindler 1013
Schwan 857
Scoot 763–4
Scott Worldwide 340
Scottish & Newcastle 209, 286, 1031
Scottish Courage 248
Scottish Quality Salmon 1040
Scottish Telecom 811
Scottish Tourist Board 953
Scottish Widows 754
Screenshop 758–9
Sears 823
Seat 781, 808
SEB 969
Security Backup Systems 152
Seeboard 762–3
Sega 818, 866
Seiko 881
Sellotape 913
Senta 281
Severn Trent 18, 19
SGS 154
Sharwoods 779
Shaw's 525
Shell 75, 541, 611, 792, 806, 1008, 1010, 1018, 1072
Sheraton 955, 1041
Siebel Systems 921
Siemens 145, 153, 173, 377, 378, 903, 926, 1009
Siemens Computer Systems 756
Sierex BV 6
Sight Savers International 757
Simpson Photo Imaging 1017
Sinbad 627
Singapore Airlines 60, 457
Sitel 761
Skelair 489, 490
SKF 145, 459, 701, 1012, 1015
Skoda 116–17, 781, 802
Sky 819, 823, 1076, 1089
Sleep Inn 398
Slendertone UK 753–4

Slim Fast 858
Smile 864
Smirnoff 132, 589, 853
Smit 812
SmithKline Beecham 30
Smiths Crisps 883
SNCF 74, 957
Snecma 377
Soleco 482–3
Somerfield 536
Sonera 383
Sony 284, 302, 311, 319, 326, 344, 357, 598–9, 670, 884
Sotheby's 883, 886
Spar 528, 541, 559, 662
Specialist Computer Holdings 861
Sportal 1057
SportingLife.com 1057
Sports Marketing Surveys 229, 246
SSL International 262
St Ivel 859
St James Palace 729
St Lawrence Bank 1047
Staples 477
Star City 954
Starbucks 408
Steinway 873
Stella Artois 828
Stergene 865
Stewart Grand Prix 164
Streetsonline 801
Strongbow 132, 853
Subway 903, 984, 1028, 1029
Sugro UK 476
Sumitomo Rubber Industries 1033
Sun Microsystems 108
Superbreaks 440
Superdrug 106, 262, 486, 540, 670
Svenska Handelsbanken 969
Swanage Railway 995
Swissair 449
Systembolaget 73
Systême U 518

T-Mobile 383
T&T 585, 674, 1073
Tagus Bank 1047–8
talkSPORT 625
Tambrands 86–7
Tango 320
Tanning Shop 986
TAP 72
Target Games 1037
Tarmac Construction Services 811
Tate and Lyle 207
Taxi Media 630
Taylor Nelson Sofres 219–20
TDI 630
Teadirect 176
Teijo Pesukoneet 478
Telder 237
Telegen 762–3
Teletext 966
Telia 72
Tengelmann 528, 537
Tennents Caledonian Breweries 241
Tesco 9, 79, 108, 152, 196, 224, 290, 462–3, 497, 511, 517, 525, 528, 533, 535, 536, 545, 557–8, 607, 657, 667, 674, 691–2, 825, 827, 848, 891, 978, 999, 1023, 1061, 1066–7
Tetra Pak 13, 1037
Teuscher 873–4
Texaco 271, 675–6
TheMutual.net 1079
Thomas Cook 83, 677
Thomson 174, 1016
Thomson Holidays 273, 274
Thorntons 540, 541
Thus 811
Tianjin Auto Group 1025
Tibbet & Britten 501, 502
Tie Rack 530, 549
Time magazine 626
Tiscali 341
TKP 1013
Today's 541
Tom and Daisy 848
Topman 262, 540
Topshop 540
Total Research 301
totalbet.com 1057
Tottenham Hotspur 422
Tourism Ireland 757, 763
Toyota 71, 360, 377, 630, 829, 878, 1031
Toys 'Я' Us 539, 544, 1039
Transparency International 167
Travel Inn 398, 811–12, 814
Travelman 545
Triumph International 550
Trung Nguyen 988
Trust Motor Group 1093
TRUSTe 1071
TUI 284
Tulip International 1027
Tupolev 137
Tupperware 543
Turtle Island 202
Tussauds 956
Twinings 670, 673
Two Way TV 1089

UBS 902
UKBetting.com 1057
Umbro 423
Unigate 859
Unilever 20, 337, 356, 384, 706, 829, 841, 857, 858–9, 865, 867–8, 881, 900, 913, 1010, 1032, 1039
Unimills 859
Union Carbide 792–3
United Airlines 1034
United Pan-Europe Communications 1014
United Parcel Services 968
Universal 862
Upper Crust 271

Valdunes Holding 153
Valio 413
Van den Bergh 235, 614
Van Dyck 277
Vauxhall Motors 463–5, 547
Velden Engineering (UK) 164
Vendex 533
Verizon Wireless 368
Vestas Wind Systems 860
Vestech Japan Corporation 860
Viagra 306–7
Victoria Wine 544
Video Net 298
Videoton 1011
viewlondon.co.uk 1081
Virgin 284, 286, 292, 345, 868
Virgin Atlantic 1034–5
Virgin Cars 420, 442
Virgin Megastores 177, 262, 598–9
Virgin Mobile 1085
Virgin Money 749–50
Virgin Radio 625
Virgin Trains 364, 367, 959, 965, 977
Virgin Wines 564
Vision Direct 411–12
Vivendi 816, 902
Vizzavi 816
VK Vodka 823
Vodafone 285, 368, 383, 816, 817, 818, 1079, 1083
Vogue 627
Volvo 9, 47, 478, 504, 614, 707, 808, 1013
Vroom & Dressman 533
VW 117, 305, 350, 781

Waitrose 525, 614, 834, 1066
Wal-Mart 106, 692, 872
Wales Tourist Board 788–90
Walker's Crisps 591–2, 841
Wallis 540
Wall's 866
Wanadoo 314
Warner Brothers 862, 1084
Wash & Go 1039
webpackaging.com 148
Weetabix 870
Wegert 540
Welcome Holidays 100
Wella 829
Welsh Tourist Board 960
Werther's 680
West Coast Fish Products 909–10, 912, 913
WH Smith 209, 513, 540, 588, 908–9
Whirlpool 1040–41
Whitbread 811
Whitworths 436
Wilkinson Sword 881
Wincanton 503, 508
Winterthur Life 729
Wisla Bank 1047
Wolfking 875
Wolverhampton University 800
World Books 643
World Duty Free 668
Wrangler 891, 892
Wrigley 877
Wyvern Direct Response 751

Xbox 598–9
Xerox 728

Yahoo! 290, 1057
Yell 756
Yellow Pages 97, 99, 966
Yomega 322
yorg.com 257
Yorkshire Water 378
Yves St Laurent 295

Zanussi 269, 272
Zeneca 207
Zenith International 352
Zurich 817, 828